The Researchers Library of Ancient Texts
VOLUME 4

The Reformers

Select Sermons from Martin Luther,
Desiderius Erasmus, John Calvin,
William Tyndale, and John Wesley

DEFENSE
CRANE, MO 65633

The Researcher's Library of Ancient Texts
Volume 4
The Reformers: Select Works of Martin Luther, Desiderius Erasmus, John Calvin, William Tyndale, and John Wesley

Defender
Crane, MO 65633
©2014 by Thomas Horn
All rights reserved. Published 2014.
Printed in the United States of America.

ISBN 13: 978-0-9856045-8-5

A CIP catalog record of this book is available from the Library of Congress.

Cover illustration and design by Daniel Wright.

Contents

A Commentary on St. Paul's Epistle to the Galatians 1

St. Paul's Epistle to the Galatians 3

The Manual of a Christian Knight 94

Institutes of the Christian Religion 188

   Book First:
   Of the Knowledge of God the Creator 205

   Book Second:
   Of the Knowledge of God the Redeemer, in Christ, as First Manifested to the Fathers,
   Under the Law, and Thereafter to Us Under the Gospel 297

   Book Third:
   The Mode of Obtaining the Grace of Christ. The Benefits it Confers,
   and the Effects Resulting from It 435

   Book Fourth:
   Of the Holy Catholic Church 655

   One Hundred Aphorisms 879

The Obedience of a Christian Man and
How Christian Rulers Ought to Govern 887

Sermons on Several Occasions 965

A Commentary on St. Paul's Epistle to the Galatians

by
Martin Luther
A New Abridged Translation by
THEODORE GRAEBNER, D.D.
Professor of Philosophy and New Testament Interpretation
Concordia Seminary, St. Louis, Missouri

PREFACE

The preparation of this edition of Luther's Commentary on Galatians was first suggested to me by Mr. P. J. Zondervan, of the firm of publishers, in March, 1937. The consultation had the twofold merit of definiteness and brevity.

"Luther is still the greatest name in Protestantism. We want you to help us publish some leading work of Luther's for the general American market. Will you do it?"

"I will, on one condition."

"And what is that?"

"The condition is that I will be permitted to make Luther talk American, 'streamline' him, so to speak—because you will never get people, whether in or outside the Lutheran Church, actually to read Luther unless we make him talk as he would talk today to Americans."

I illustrated the point by reading to Mr. Zondervan a few sentences from an English translation lately reprinted by an American publisher, of one of Luther's outstanding reformatory essays.

The demonstration seemed to prove convincing for it was agreed that one may as well offer Luther in the original German or Latin as expect the American church-member to read any translations that would adhere to Luther's German or Latin constructions and employ the Mid-Victorian type of English characteristic of the translations now on the market.

"And what book would be your choice?"

"There is one book that Luther himself liked better than any other. Let us begin with that: his *Commentary on Galatians*..."

The undertaking, which seemed so attractive when viewed as a literary task, proved a most difficult one, and at times became oppressive. The Letter to the Galatians consists of six short chapters. Luther's commentary fills seven hundred and thirty-three octavo pages in the Weidman Edition of his works. It was written in Latin. We were resolved not to present this entire mass of exegesis. It would have run to more than fifteen hundred pages, ordinary octavo (like this), since it is impossible to use the compressed structure of sentences which is characteristic of Latin, and particularly of Luther's Latin. The work had to be condensed. German and English translations are available, but the most acceptable English version, besides laboring under the handicaps of an archaic style, had to be condensed into half its volume in order to accomplish the "streamlining" of the book. Whatever merit the translation now presented to the reader may possess should be written to the credit of Rev. Gerhardt Mahler of Geneva, N.Y., who came to my assistance in a very busy season by making a rough draft of the translation and later preparing a revision of it, which forms the basis of the final draft submitted to the printer.

A word should now be said about the origin of Luther's *Commentary on Galatians*.

The Reformer had lectured on this Epistle of St. Paul's in 1519 and again in 1523. It was his favorite among all the Biblical books. In his table talks the saying is recorded: "The Epistle to the Galatians is my epistle. To it I am as it were in wedlock. It is my Katherine." Much later when a friend of his was preparing an edition of all his Latin works, he remarked to his home circle: "If I had my way about it they would republish only those of my books which have doctrine. My Galatians, for instance." The lectures which are preserved in the works herewith submitted to the American public were delivered in 1531. They were taken down by George Roerer, who held something of a deanship at Wittenberg University and who was one of Luther's aids in the translation of the Bible. Roerer took down Luther's lectures and this manuscript has been preserved to the present day, in a copy which contains also additions by Veit Dietrich and by Cruciger, friends of Roerer's, who with him attended Luther's lectures. In other words, these three men took down the lectures which Luther addressed to his students in the course of Galatians, and Roerer prepared the manuscript for the printer. A German translation by Justus Menius appeared in the Wittenberg Edition of Luther's writings, published in 1539.

One cannot discuss this famous document of the Reformation Age without adverting of the experience of John Bunyan. Greatly afflicted on account of his "original and inward pollution" and wretched in the knowledge of his transgressions, Bunyan looked around for some ancient work that might satisfy him. He had found that the writers of his own day had not gone "down themselves into the deep." Rummaging around he found an old copy, ready to fall to pieces, of Martin Luther's Commentary on Galatians. He says "When I had but a little way perused, I found my condition in his experience so largely and profoundly handled, as if his book had been written out of my heart. I prefer this book of Martin Luther on the Galatians (excepting the Holy Bible) before all the books that ever I have seen, as most fit for a wounded conscience."

The importance of this Commentary on Galatians for the history of Protestantism is very great. It presents like no other of Luther's writings the central thought of Christianity, the justification of the sinner for the sake of Christ's merits alone. We have permitted in the final revision of the manuscript many a passage to stand which seemed weak and ineffectual when compared with the trumpet tones of the Latin original. But the essence of Luther's lectures is there. May the reader accept with indulgence where in this translation we have gone too far in modernizing Luther's expression—making him "talk American." And may the divine blessing rest upon this, we trust, even in its new dress, eloquent disquisition of Martin Luther on those central doctrines upon which the Christian church depends for its inner life and for success in its evangelical mission.

At the end of his lectures in 1531, Luther uttered a brief prayer and then dictated two Scriptural texts, which we shall inscribe at the end of these introductory remarks:

"The Lord who has given us power to teach and to hear, let Him also give us the power to serve and to do."

LUKE 2
Glory to God in the highest,
And on earth peace,
Good will to men.

ISAIAH 40
The Word of our God
shall stand forever.
  Theodore Graebner
St. Louis, Missouri

FROM LUTHER'S INTRODUCTION, 1538

In my heart reigns this one article, faith in my dear Lord Christ, the beginning, middle and end of whatever spiritual and divine thoughts I may have, whether by day or by night.

St. Paul's Epistle to the Galatians

GALATIONS 1

Verse 1. Paul, an apostle, (not of men, neither by man, but by Jesus Christ, and God the Father, who raised him from the dead).

St. Paul wrote this epistle because, after his departure from the Galatian churches, Jewish-Christian fanatics moved in, who perverted Paul's Gospel of man's free justification by faith in Christ Jesus.

The world bears the Gospel a grudge because the Gospel condemns the religious wisdom of the world. Jealous for its own religious views, the world in turn charges the Gospel with being a subversive and licentious doctrine, offensive to God and man, a doctrine to be persecuted as the worst plague on earth.

As a result we have this paradoxical situation: The Gospel supplies the world with the salvation of Jesus Christ, peace of conscience, and every blessing. Just for that the world abhors the Gospel.

These Jewish-Christian fanatics who pushed themselves into the Galatian churches after Paul's departure, boasted that they were the descendants of Abraham, true ministers of Christ, having been trained by the apostles themselves, that they were able to perform miracles.

In every way they sought to undermine the authority of St. Paul. They said to the Galatians: "You have no right to think highly of Paul. He was the last to turn to Christ. But we have seen Christ. We heard Him preach. Paul came later and is beneath us. Is it possible for us to be in error—we who have received the Holy Ghost? Paul stands alone. He has not seen Christ, nor has he had much contact with the other apostles. Indeed, he persecuted the Church of Christ for a long time."

When men claiming such credentials come along, they deceive not only the naive, but also those who seemingly are well-established in the faith. This same argument is used by the papacy. "Do you suppose that God for the sake of a few Lutheran heretics would disown His entire Church? Or do you suppose that God would have left His Church floundering in error all these centuries?" The Galatians were taken in by such arguments with the result that Paul's authority and doctrine were drawn in question.

Against these boasting, false apostles, Paul boldly defends his apostolic authority and ministry. Humble man that he was, he will not now take a back seat. He reminds them of the time when he opposed Peter to his face and reproved the chief of the apostles.

Paul devotes the first two chapters to a defense of his office and his Gospel, affirming that he received it, not from men, but from the Lord Jesus Christ by special revelation, and that if he or an angel from heaven preach any other gospel than the one he had preached, he shall be accursed.

The Certainty of Our Calling

Every minister should make much of his calling and impress upon others the fact that he has been delegated by God to preach the Gospel. As the ambassador of a government is honored for his office and not for his private person, so the minister of Christ should exalt his office in order to gain authority among men. This is not vain glory, but needful glorying.

Paul takes pride in his ministry, not to his own praise

but to the praise of God. Writing to the Romans, he declares, "Inasmuch as I am the apostle of the Gentiles, I magnify mine office," i.e., I want to be received not as Paul of Tarsus, but as Paul the apostle and ambassador of Jesus Christ, in order that people might be more eager to hear. Paul exalts his ministry out of the desire to make known the name, the grace, and the mercy of God.

Verse 1. *Paul, an apostle, (not of men, etc.)*

Paul loses no time in defending himself against the charge that he had thrust himself into the ministry. He says to the Galatians: "My call may seem inferior to you. But those who have come to you are either called of men or by man. My call is the highest possible, for it is by Jesus Christ, and God the Father."

When Paul speaks of those called "by men," I take it he means those whom neither God nor man sent, but who go wherever they like and speak for themselves.

When Paul speaks of those called "by man" I take it he means those who have a divine call extended to them through other persons. God calls in two ways. Either He calls ministers through the agency of men, or He calls them directly as He called the prophets and apostles. Paul declares that the false apostles were called or sent neither by men, nor by man. The most they could claim is that they were sent by others. "But as for me I was called neither of men, nor by man, but directly by Jesus Christ. My call is in every respect like the call of the apostles. In fact I am an apostle."

Elsewhere Paul draws a sharp distinction between an apostleship and lesser functions, as in I Corinthians 12:28: "And God hath set some in the church; first, apostles; secondarily, prophets; thirdly, teachers." He mentions the apostles first because they were appointed directly by God.

Matthias was called in this manner. The apostles chose two candidates and then cast lots, praying that God would indicate which one He would have. To be an apostle he had to have his appointment from God. In the same manner Paul was called as the apostle of the Gentiles.

The call is not to be taken lightly. For a person to possess knowledge is not enough. He must be sure that he is properly called. Those who operate without a proper call seek no good purpose. God does not bless their labors. They may be good preachers, but they do not edify. Many of the fanatics of our day pronounce words of faith, but they bear no good fruit, because their purpose is to turn men to their perverse opinions. On the other hand, those who have a divine call must suffer a good deal of opposition in order that they may become fortified against the running attacks of the devil and the world.

This is our comfort in the ministry, that ours is a divine office to which we have been divinely called. Reversely, what an awful thing it must be for the conscience if one is not properly called. It spoils one's best work. When I was a young man I thought Paul was making too much of his call. I did not understand his purpose. I did not then realize the importance of the ministry. I knew nothing of the doctrine of faith because we were taught sophistry instead of certainty, and nobody understood spiritual boasting. We exalt our calling, not to gain glory among men, or money, or satisfaction, or favor, but because people need to be assured that the words we speak are the words of God. This is no sinful pride. It is holy pride.

Verse 1. *And God the Father, who raised him from the dead.*

Paul is so eager to come to the subject matter of his epistle, the righteousness of faith in opposition to the righteousness of works, that already in the title he must speak his mind. He did not think it quite enough to say that he was an apostle "by Jesus Christ"; he adds, "and God the Father, who raised him from the dead."

The clause seems superfluous on first sight. Yet Paul had a good reason for adding it. He had to deal with Satan and his agents who endeavored to deprive him of the righteousness of Christ, who was raised by God the Father from the dead. These perverters of the righteousness of Christ resist the Father and the Son, and the works of them both.

In this whole epistle Paul treats of the resurrection of Christ. By His resurrection Christ won the victory over law, sin, flesh, world, devil, death, hell, and every evil. And this His victory He donated unto us. These many tyrants and enemies of ours may accuse and frighten us, but they dare not condemn us, for Christ, whom God the Father has raised from the dead is our righteousness and our victory.

Do you notice how well suited to his purpose Paul writes? He does not say, "By God who made heaven and earth, who is Lord of the angels," but Paul has in mind the righteousness of Christ, and speaks to the point, saying, "I am an apostle, not of men, neither by man, but by Jesus Christ, and God the Father, who raised him from the dead."

Verse 2. *And all the brethren which are with me.*

This should go far in shutting the mouths of the false

apostles. Paul's intention is to exalt his own ministry while discrediting theirs. He adds for good measure the argument that he does not stand alone, but that all the brethren with him attest to the fact that his doctrine is divinely true. "Although the brethren with me are not apostles like myself, yet they are all of one mind with me, think, write, and teach as I do."

Verse 2. *Unto the churches of Galatia.*

Paul had preached the Gospel throughout Galatia, founding many churches which after his departure were invaded by the false apostles. The Anabaptists in our time imitate the false apostles. They do not go where the enemies of the Gospel predominate. They go where the Christians are. Why do they not invade the Catholic provinces and preach their doctrine to godless princes, bishops, and doctors, as we have done by the help of God? These soft martyrs take no chances. They go where the Gospel has a hold, so that they may not endanger their lives. The false apostles would not go to Jerusalem of Caiaphas, or to the Rome of the Emperor, or to any other place where no man had preached before as Paul and the other apostles did. But they came to the churches of Galatia, knowing that where men profess the name of Christ they may feel secure.

It is the lot of God's ministers not only to suffer opposition at the hand of a wicked world, but also to see the patient indoctrination of many years quickly undone by such religious fanatics. This hurts more than the persecution of tyrants. We are treated shabbily on the outside by tyrants, on the inside by those whom we have restored to the liberty of the Gospel, and also by false brethren. But this is our comfort and our glory, that being called of God we have the promise of everlasting life. We look for that reward which "eye hath not seen, nor ear heard, neither hath entered into the heart of man."

Jerome raises the question why Paul called them churches that were no churches, inasmuch as the Galatians had forsaken the grace of Christ for the law of Moses. The proper answer is: Although the Galatians had fallen away from the doctrine of Paul, baptism, the Gospel, and the name of Christ continued among them. Not all the Galatians had become perverted. There were some who clung to the right view of the Word and the Sacraments. These means cannot be contaminated. They remain divine regardless of men's opinion. Wherever the means of grace are found, there is the Holy Church, even though Antichrist reigns there. So much for the title of the epistle. Now follows the greeting of the apostle.

Verse 3. *Grace be to you, and peace, from God the Father, and from our Lord Jesus Christ.*

The terms of grace and peace are common terms with Paul and are now pretty well understood. But since we are explaining this epistle, you will not mind if we repeat what we have so often explained elsewhere. The article of justification must be sounded in our ears incessantly because the frailty of our flesh will not permit us to take hold of it perfectly and to believe it with all our heart.

The greeting of the Apostle is refreshing. Grace remits sin, and peace quiets the conscience. Sin and conscience torment us, but Christ has overcome these fiends now and forever. Only Christians possess this victorious knowledge given from above. These two terms, grace and peace, constitute Christianity. Grace involves the remission of sins, peace, and a happy conscience. Sin is not canceled by lawful living, for no person is able to live up to the Law. The Law reveals guilt, fills the conscience with terror, and drives men to despair. Much less is sin taken away by man-invented endeavors. The fact is, the more a person seeks credit for himself by his own efforts, the deeper he goes into debt. Nothing can take away sin except the grace of God. In actual living, however, it is not so easy to persuade oneself that by grace alone, in opposition to every other means, we obtain the forgiveness of our sins and peace with God.

The world brands this a pernicious doctrine. The world advances free will, the rational and natural approach of good works, as the means of obtaining the forgiveness of sin. But it is impossible to gain peace of conscience by the methods and means of the world. Experience proves this. Various holy orders have been launched for the purpose of securing peace of conscience through religious exercises, but they proved failures because such devices only increase doubt and despair. We find no rest for our weary bones unless we cling to the word of grace.

The Apostle does not wish the Galatians grace and peace from the emperor, or from kings, or from governors, but from God the Father. He wishes them heavenly peace, the kind of which Jesus spoke when He said, "Peace I leave unto you: my peace I give unto you." Worldly peace provides quiet enjoyment of life and possessions. But in affliction, particularly in the hour of death, the grace and peace of the world will not deliver us. However, the grace and peace of God will. They make a person strong and courageous to bear and to overcome all difficulties, even death itself, because we have the victory of Christ's death and the assurance of the forgiveness of our sins.

Men Should Not Speculate About the Nature of God

The Apostle adds to the salutation the words, "and from our Lord Jesus Christ." Was it not enough to say, "from God the Father"?

It is a principle of the Bible that we are not to inquire curiously into the nature of God. "There shall no man see me, and live," Exodus 33:20. All who trust in their own merits to save them disregard this principle and lose sight of the Mediator, Jesus Christ.

True Christian theology does not inquire into the nature of God, but into God's purpose and will in Christ, whom God incorporated in our flesh to live and to die for our sins. There is nothing more dangerous than to speculate about the incomprehensible power, wisdom, and majesty of God when the conscience is in turmoil over sin. To do so is to lose God altogether because God becomes intolerable when we seek to measure and to comprehend His infinite majesty.

We are to seek God as Paul tells us in I Corinthians 1:23, 24: "We preach Christ crucified, unto the Jews a stumbling block, and unto the Greeks foolishness; but unto them which are called, both Jews and Greeks, Christ the power of God, and the wisdom of God." Begin with Christ. He came down to earth, lived among men, suffered, was crucified, and then He died, standing clearly before us, so that our hearts and eyes may fasten upon Him. Thus we shall be kept from climbing into heaven in a curious and futile search after the nature of God.

If you ask how God may be found, who justifies sinners, know that there is no other God besides this man Christ Jesus. Embrace Him, and forget about the nature of God. But these fanatics who exclude our Mediator in their dealings with God, do not believe me. Did not Christ Himself say: "I am the way, and the truth, and the life: no man cometh unto the Father, but by me"? Without Christ there is no access to the Father, but futile rambling; no truth, but hypocrisy; no life, but eternal death.

When you argue about the nature of God apart from the question of justification, you may be as profound as you like. But when you deal with conscience and with righteousness over against the law, sin, death, and the devil, you must close your mind to all inquiries into the nature of God, and concentrate upon Jesus Christ, who says, "Come unto me, all ye that labor and are heavy laden, and I will give you rest." Doing this, you will recognize the power, and majesty condescending to your condition according to Paul's statement to the Colossians, "In Christ are hid all the treasures of wisdom and knowledge," and, "In him dwelleth all the fulness of the Godhead bodily." Paul in wishing grace and peace not alone from God the Father, but also from Jesus Christ, wants to warn us against the curious incursions into the nature of God. We are to hear Christ, who has been appointed by the Father as our divine Teacher.

Christ is God by Nature

At the same time, Paul confirms our creed, "that Christ is very God." We need such frequent confirmation of our faith, for Satan will not fail to attack it. He hates our faith. He knows that it is the victory which overcometh him and the world. That Christ is very God is apparent in that Paul ascribes to Him divine powers equally with the Father, as for instance, the power to dispense grace and peace. This Jesus could not do unless He were God.

To bestow peace and grace lies in the province of God, who alone can create these blessings. The angels cannot. The apostles could only distribute these blessings by the preaching of the Gospel. In attributing to Christ the divine power of creating and giving grace, peace, everlasting life, righteousness, and forgiveness of sins, the conclusion is inevitable that Christ is truly God.

Similarly, St. John concludes from the works attributed to the Father and the Son that they are divinely One. Hence, the gifts which we receive from the Father and from the Son are one and the same. Otherwise Paul should have written: "Grace from God the Father, and peace from our Lord Jesus Christ." In combining them he ascribes them equally to the Father and the Son. I stress this on account of the many errors emanating from the sects.

The Arians were sharp fellows. Admitting that Christ had two natures, and that He is called "very God of very God," they were yet able to deny His divinity. The Arians took Christ for a noble and perfect creature, superior even to the angels, because by Him God created heaven and earth. Mohammed also speaks highly of Christ. But all their praise is mere palaver to deceive men. Paul's language is different. To paraphrase him: "You are established in this belief that Christ is very God because He gives grace and peace, gifts which only God can create and bestow."

Verse 4. *Who gave himself for our sins.*

Paul sticks to his theme. He never loses sight of the purpose of his epistle. He does not say, "Who received our works," but "who gave." Gave what? Not gold, or silver, or paschal lambs, or an angel, but Himself. What for? Not for a crown, or a kingdom, or our goodness, but for our sins. These words are like so many thunderclaps of protest from heaven against every kind and type of self-merit. Underscore these words, for they are full of comfort for sore consciences.

How may we obtain remission of our sins? Paul answers: "The man who is named Jesus Christ and the Son of God gave himself for our sins." The heavy artillery of these words explodes papacy, works, merits, superstitions. For if our sins could be removed by our own efforts, what need was there for the Son of God to be given for them? Since Christ was given for our sins it stands to reason that they cannot be put away by our own efforts.

This sentence also defines our sins as great, so great, in fact, that the whole world could not make amends for a single sin. The greatness of the ransom, Christ, the Son of God, indicates this. The vicious character of sin is brought out by the words "who gave himself for our sins." So vicious is sin that only the sacrifice of Christ could atone for sin. When we reflect that the one little word "sin" embraces the whole kingdom of Satan, and that it includes everything that is horrible, we have reason to tremble. But we are careless. We make light of sin. We think that by some little work or merit we can dismiss sin.

This passage, then, bears out the fact that all men are sold under sin. Sin is an exacting despot who can be vanquished by no created power, but by the sovereign power of Jesus Christ alone.

All this is of wonderful comfort to a conscience troubled by the enormity of sin. Sin cannot harm those who believe in Christ, because He has overcome sin by His death. Armed with this conviction, we are enlightened and may pass judgment upon the papists, monks, nuns, priests, Mohammedans, Anabaptists, and all who trust in their own merits, as wicked and destructive sects that rob God and Christ of the honor that belongs to them alone.

Note especially the pronoun "our" and its significance. You will readily grant that Christ gave Himself for the sins of Peter, Paul, and others who were worthy of such grace. But feeling low, you find it hard to believe that Christ gave Himself for your sins. Our feelings shy at a personal application of the pronoun "our," and we refuse to have anything to do with God until we have made ourselves worthy by good deeds.

This attitude springs from a false conception of sin, the conception that sin is a small matter, easily taken care of by good works; that we must present ourselves unto God with a good conscience; that we must feel no sin before we may feel that Christ was given for our sins.

This attitude is universal and particularly developed in those who consider themselves better than others. Such readily confess that they are frequent sinners, but they regard their sins as of no such importance that they cannot easily be dissolved by some good action, or that they may not appear before the tribunal of Christ and demand the reward of eternal life for their righteousness. Meantime they pretend great humility and acknowledge a certain degree of sinfulness for which they soulfully join in the publican's prayer, "God be merciful to me a sinner." But the real significance and comfort of the words "for our sins" is lost upon them.

The genius of Christianity takes the words of Paul "who gave himself for our sins" as true and efficacious. We are not to look upon our sins as insignificant trifles. On the other hand, we are not to regard them as so terrible that we must despair. Learn to believe that Christ was given, not for picayune and imaginary transgressions, but for mountainous sins; not for one or two, but for all; not for sins that can be discarded, but for sins that are stubbornly ingrained.

Practice this knowledge and fortify yourself against despair, particularly in the last hour, when the memory of past sins assails the conscience. Say with confidence: "Christ, the Son of God, was given not for the righteous, but for sinners. If I had no sin I should not need Christ. No, Satan, you cannot delude me into thinking I am holy. The truth is, I am all sin. My sins are not imaginary transgressions, but sins against the first table, unbelief, doubt, despair, contempt, hatred, ignorance of God, ingratitude towards Him, misuse of His name, neglect of His Word, etc.; and sins against the second table, dishonor of parents, disobedience of government, coveting of another's possessions, etc. Granted that I have not committed murder, adultery, theft, and similar sins in deed, nevertheless I have committed them in the heart, and therefore I am a transgressor of all the commandments of God.

"Because my transgressions are multiplied and my own efforts at self-justification rather a hindrance than a furtherance, therefore Christ the Son of God gave Himself into death for my sins." To believe this is to have eternal life.

Let us equip ourselves against the accusations of Satan with this and similar passages of Holy Scripture. If he says, "Thou shalt be damned," you tell him: "No, for I fly to Christ who gave Himself for my sins. In accusing me of being a damnable sinner, you are cutting your own throat, Satan. You are reminding me of God's fatherly goodness toward me, that He so loved the world that He gave His only-begotten Son that whosoever believeth in Him should not perish, but have everlasting life. In calling me a sinner, Satan, you really comfort me above measure." With such heavenly cunning we are to meet the devil's craft and put from us the memory of sin.

St. Paul also presents a true picture of Christ as the virgin-born Son of God, delivered into death for our sins. To entertain a true conception of Christ is important, for the devil describes Christ as an exacting and cruel judge who condemns and punishes men. Tell him that his definition of Christ is wrong, that Christ has given Himself for our sins, that by His sacrifice He has taken away the sins of the whole world.

Make ample use of this pronoun "our." Be assured that Christ has canceled the sins, not of certain persons only, but your sins. Do not permit yourself to be robbed of this lovely conception of Christ. Christ is no Moses, no law-giver, no tyrant, but the Mediator for sins, the Giver of grace and life.

We know this. Yet in the actual conflict with the devil, when he scares us with the Law, when he frightens us with the very person of the Mediator, when he misquotes the words of Christ, and distorts for us our Savior, we so easily lose sight of our sweet High-Priest.

For this reason I am so anxious for you to gain a true picture of Christ out of the words of Paul "who gave himself for our sins." Obviously, Christ is no judge to condemn us, for He gave Himself for our sins. He does not trample the fallen but raises them. He comforts the broken-hearted. Otherwise Paul should lie when he writes "who gave himself for our sins."

I do not bother my head with speculations about the nature of God. I simply attach myself to the human Christ, and I find joy and peace, and the wisdom of God in Him. These are not new truths. I am repeating what the apostles and all teachers of God have taught long ago. Would to God we could impregnate our hearts with these truths.

Verse 4. *That he might deliver us from this present evil world.*

Paul calls this present world evil because everything in it is subject to the malice of the devil, who reigns over the whole world as his domain and fills the air with ignorance, contempt, hatred, and disobedience of God. In this devils's kingdom we live.

As long as a person is in the world he cannot by his own efforts rid himself of sin, because the world is bent upon evil. The people of the world are the slaves of the devil. If we are not in the Kingdom of Christ, it is certain we belong to the kingdom of Satan and we are pressed into his service with every talent we possess.

Take the talents of wisdom and integrity. Without Christ, wisdom is double foolishness and integrity double sin, because they not only fail to perceive the wisdom and righteousness of Christ, but hinder and blaspheme the salvation of Christ. Paul justly calls it the evil or wicked world, for when the world is at its best the world is at its worst. The grossest vices are small faults in comparison with the wisdom and righteousness of the world. These prevent men from accepting the Gospel of the righteousness of Christ. The white devil of spiritual sin is far more dangerous than the black devil of carnal sin because the wiser, the better men are without Christ, the more they are likely to ignore and oppose the Gospel.

With the words, "that he might deliver us," Paul argues that we stand in need of Christ. No other being can possibly deliver us from this present evil world. Do not let the fact disturb you that a great many people enjoy excellent reputations without Christ. Remember what Paul says, that the world with all its wisdom, might, and righteousness is the devil's own. God alone is able to deliver us from the world.

Let us praise and thank God for His mercy in delivering us from the captivity of Satan, when we were unable to do so by our own strength. Let us confess with Paul that all our work-righteousness is loss and dung. Let us condemn as filthy rags all talk about free will, all religious orders, masses, ceremonies, vows, fastings, and the like.

In branding the world the devil's kingdom of iniquity, ignorance, error, sin, death, and everlasting despair, Paul at the same time declares the Kingdom of Christ to be a kingdom of equity, light, grace, remission of sin, peace, saving health, and everlasting life into which we are translated by our Lord Jesus Christ, to whom be glory forever.

In this passage Paul contends against the false apostles for the article of Justification. Christ, says Paul, has delivered us from this wicked kingdom of the devil and the world according to the good will, the pleasure and commandment of the Father. Hence we are not delivered by our own will, or shrewdness, or wisdom, but by the mercy and love of God, as it is written, I John 4:10, "Herein is love, not that we loved God, but that he loved us, and sent his Son to be the propitiation for our sins."

Another reason why Paul, like John, emphasizes the Father's will is Christ's habit of directing attention to the Father. For Christ came into the world to reconcile God with us and to draw us to the Father.

Not by curious inquiries into the nature of God shall

we know God and His purpose for our salvation, but by taking hold of Christ, who according to the will of the Father has given Himself into death for our sins. When we understand this to be the will of the Father in Christ, then shall we know God to be merciful, and not angry. We shall realize that He loved us wretched sinners so much indeed that He gave us His only-begotten Son into death for us.

The pronoun "our" refers to both God and Father. He is our God and our Father. Christ's Father and our Father are one and the same. Hence Christ said to Mary Magdalene: "Go to my brethren, and say unto them, I ascend unto my Father, and your Father; and to my God, and your God." God is our Father and our God, but only in Christ Jesus.

Verse 5. *To whom be glory for ever and ever. Amen.*

Hebrew writing is interspersed with expressions of praise and gratitude. This peculiarity can be traced in the apostolic writings, particularly in those of Paul. The name of the Lord is to be mentioned with great reverence and thanksgiving.

Verse 6. *I marvel.*

How patiently Paul deals with his seduced Galatians! He does not pounce on them but, like a father, he fairly excuses their error. With motherly affection he talks to them yet he does it in a way that at the same time he also reproves them. On the other hand, he is highly indignant at the seducers whom he blames for the apostasy of the Galatians. His anger bursts forth in elemental fury at the beginning of his epistle. "If any man," he cries, "preach any other gospel unto you than that ye have received, let him be accursed." Later on, in the fifth chapter, he threatens the false apostles with damnation. "He that troubleth you shall bear his judgment, whosoever he be." He pronounces a curse upon them. "I would they were even cut off which trouble you."

He might have addressed the Galatians after this fashion: "I am ashamed of you. Your ingratitude grieves me. I am angry with you." But his purpose was to call them back to the Gospel. With this purpose in his mind he speaks very gently to them. He could not have chosen a milder expression than this, "I marvel." It indicates his sorrow and his displeasure.

Paul minds the rule which he himself lays down in a later chapter where he says: "Brethren, if a man be overtaken in a fault, ye which are spiritual, restore such an one in the spirit of meekness; considering thyself, lest thou also be tempted." Toward those who have been misled we are to show ourselves parentally affectionate, so that they may perceive that we seek not their destruction but their salvation. Over against the devil and his missionaries, the authors of false doctrines and sects, we ought to be like the Apostle, impatient, and rigorously condemnatory, as parents are with the dog that bites their little one, but the weeping child itself they soothe.

The right spirit in Paul supplies him with an extraordinary facility in handling the afflicted consciences of the fallen. The Pope and his bishops, inspired by the desire to lord it over men's souls, crack out thunders and curses upon miserable consciences. They have no care for the saving of men's souls. They are interested only in maintaining their position.

Verse 6. That ye are so soon.

Paul deplores the fact that it is difficult for the mind to retain a sound and steadfast faith. A man labors for a decade before he succeeds in training his little church into orderly religion, and then some ignorant and vicious poltroon comes along to overthrow in a minute the patient labor of years. By the grace of God we have effected here in Wittenberg the form of a Christian church. The Word of God is taught as it should be, the Sacraments are administered, and everything is prosperous. This happy condition, secured by many years of arduous labors, some lunatic might spoil in a moment. This happened in the churches of Galatia which Paul had brought into life in spiritual travail. Soon after his departure, however, these Galatian churches were thrown into confusion by the false apostles.

The church is a tender plant. It must be watched. People hear a couple of sermons, scan a few pages of Holy Writ, and think they know it all. They are bold because they have never gone through any trials of faith. Void of the Holy Spirit, they teach what they please as long as it sounds good to the common people who are ever ready to join something new.

We have to watch out for the devil lest he sow tares among the wheat while we sleep. No sooner had Paul turned his back on the churches of Galatia, than the false apostles went to work. Therefore, let us watch over ourselves and over the whole church.

Verse 6. *I marvel that ye are so soon removed.*

Again the Apostle puts in a gentle word. He does not berate the Galatians, "I marvel that ye are so unsteady, unfaithful." He says, "I marvel that ye are so soon removed." He does not address them as evildoers. He speaks to them as people who have suffered great loss. He condemns those who removed them rather than the Galatians. At the same time he gently reproves them for permitting themselves to be removed. The criticism is implied that they should have been a little more settled in their beliefs. If they had taken better hold of the Word they could not have been removed so easily.

Jerome thinks that Paul is playing upon the name Galatians, deriving it from the Hebrew word *Galath*, which means fallen or carried away, as though Paul wanted to say, "You are true Galatians, i.e., fallen away in name and in fact." Some believe that the Germans are descended from the Galatians. There may be something to that. For the Germans are not unlike the Galatians in their lack of constancy. At first we Germans are very enthusiastic, but presently our emotions cool and we become slack. When the light of the Gospel first came to us many were zealous, heard sermons greedily, and held the ministry of God's Word in high esteem. But now that religion has been reformed, many who formerly were such earnest disciples have discarded the Word of God, have become sow-bellies like the foolish and inconsistent Galatians.

Verse 6. *From him that called you into the grace of Christ.*

The reading is a little doubtful. The sentence may be construed to read: "From that Christ that called you into grace"; or it may be construed to read: "From God that called you into the grace of Christ." I prefer the former for it seems to me that Paul's purpose is to impress upon us the benefits of Christ. This reading also preserves the implied criticism that the Galatians withdrew themselves from that Christ who had called them not unto the law, but unto grace. With Paul we decry the blindness and perverseness of men in that they will not receive the message of grace and salvation, or having received it they quickly let go of it, in spite of the fact that the Gospel bestows all good things spiritual: forgiveness of sins, true righteousness, peace of conscience, everlasting life; and all good things temporal: good judgment, good government, and peace.

Why does the world abhor the glad tidings of the Gospel and the blessings that go with it? Because the world is the devil's. Under his direction the world persecutes the Gospel and would if it could nail again Christ, the Son of God, to the Cross although He gave Himself into death for the sins of the world. The world dwells in darkness. The world is darkness.

Paul accentuates the point that the Galatians had been called by Christ unto grace. "I taught you the doctrine of grace and of liberty from the Law, from sin and wrath, that you should be free in Christ, and not slaves to the hard laws of Moses. Will you allow yourselves to be carried away so easily from the living fountain of grace and life?"

Verse 6. *Unto another gospel.*

Note the resourcefulness of the devil. Heretics do not advertise their errors. Murderers, adulterers, thieves disguise themselves. So the devil masquerades all his devices and activities. He puts on white to make himself look like an angel of light. He is astoundingly clever to sell his patent poison for the Gospel of Christ. Knowing Satan's guile, Paul sardonically calls the doctrine of the false apostles "another gospel," as if he would say, "You Galatians have now another gospel, while my Gospel is no longer esteemed by you."

We infer from this that the false apostles had depreciated the Gospel of Paul among the Galatians on the plea that it was incomplete. Their objection to Paul's Gospel is identical to that recorded in the fifteenth chapter of the Book of Acts to the effect that it was not enough for the Galatians to believe in Christ, or to be baptized, but that it was needful to circumcise them, and to command them to keep the law of Moses, for "except ye be circumcised after the manner of Moses, ye cannot be saved." As though Christ were a workman who had begun a building and left it for Moses to finish.

Today the Anabaptists and others, finding it difficult to condemn us, accuse us Lutherans of timidity in professing the whole truth. They grant that we have laid the foundation in Christ, but claim that we have failed to go through with the building. In this way these perverse fanatics parade their cursed doctrine as the Word of God, and, flying the flag of God's name, they deceive many. The devil knows better than to appear ugly and black. He prefers to carry on his nefarious activities in the name of God. Hence the German proverb: "All mischief begins in the name of God."

When the devil sees that he cannot hurt the cause of the Gospel by destructive methods, he does it under the guise of correcting and advancing the cause of the Gospel. He would like best of all to persecute us with fire and sword, but this method has availed him little because through the blood of martyrs the church has been watered. Unable to prevail by force, he engages wicked and ungodly teachers who at first make common cause with us, then claim that they are particularly called to teach the hidden mysteries of the Scriptures to superimpose upon the first principles of Christian doctrine that we teach. This sort of thing brings the Gospel into trouble. May we all cling to the Word of Christ against the wiles of the devil, "for we wrestle not against flesh and blood, but against principalities, against powers, against the rulers of the darkness of this world, against spiritual wickedness in high places."

Verse 7. *Which is not another; but there be some that trouble you.*

Here again the apostle excuses the Galatians, while he blames the false apostles for disturbing their consciences and for stealing them out of his hand. How angry he gets at these deceivers! He calls them troublemakers, seducers of poor consciences.

This passage adduces further evidence that the false apostles defamed Paul as an imperfect apostle and a weak and erroneous preacher. They condemn Paul, Paul condemns them. Such warfare of condemnation is always going on in the church. The papists and the fanatics hate us, condemn our doctrine, and want to kill us. We in turn hate and condemn their cursed doctrine. In the meanwhile the people are uncertain whom to follow and which way to turn, for it is not given to everybody to judge these matters. But the truth will win out. So much is certain, we persecute no man, neither does our doctrine trouble men. On the contrary, we have the testimony of many good men who thank God on their knees for the consolation that our doctrine has brought them. Like Paul, we are not to blame that the churches have trouble. The fault lies with the Anabaptists and other fanatics.

Every teacher of work-righteousness is a troublemaker. Has it never occurred to you that the pope, cardinals, bishops, monks, and that the whole synagogue of Satan are trouble-makers? The truth is, they are worse than false apostles. The false apostles taught that in addition to faith in Christ the works of the Law of God were necessary unto salvation. But the papists omit faith altogether and teach self-devised traditions and works that are not commanded of God, indeed are contrary to the Word of God, and for these traditions they demand preferred attention and obedience.

Paul calls the false apostles troublers of the church because they taught circumcision and the keeping of the Law as needful unto salvation. They insisted that the Law must be observed in every detail. They were supporters in this contention by the Jews, with the result that those who were not firmly established in faith were easily persuaded that Paul was not a sincere teacher of God because he ignored the Law. The Jews were offended at the idea that the Law of God should be entirely ignored by Paul and that the Gentiles, former idol-worshippers, should gratuitously attain to the station of God's people without circumcision, without the penitentiary performance of the law, by grace alone through faith in Christ Jesus.

These criticisms were amplified by the false apostles. They accused Paul of designs to abolish the law of God and the Jewish dispensation, contrary to the law of God, contrary to their Jewish heritage, contrary to apostolic example, contrary to Paul's own example. They demanded that Paul be shunned as a blasphemer and a rebel, while they were to be heard as true teachers of the Gospel and authentic disciples of the apostles. Thus Paul stood defamed among the Galatians. He was forced to attack the false apostles. He did so without hesitation.

Verse 7. *And would pervert the gospel of Christ.*

To paraphrase this sentence: "These false apostles do not merely trouble you, they abolish Christ's Gospel. They act as if they were the only true Gospel-preachers. For all that they muddle Law and Gospel. As a result they pervert the Gospel. Either Christ must live and the Law perish, or the Law remains and Christ must perish; Christ and the Law cannot dwell side by side in the conscience. It is either grace or law. To muddle the two is to eliminate the Gospel of Christ entirely."

It seems a small matter to mingle the Law and Gospel, faith and works, but it creates more mischief than man's brain can conceive. To mix Law and Gospel not only clouds the knowledge of grace, it cuts out Christ altogether.

The words of Paul, "and would pervert the gospel of Christ," also indicate how arrogant these false apostles were. They were shameless boasters. Paul simply had to exalt his own ministry and Gospel.

Verse 8. *But though we, or an angel from heaven, preach any other gospel unto you than that which we have preached unto you, let him be accursed.*

Paul's zeal for the Gospel becomes so fervent that it almost leads him to curse angels. "I would rather that I, my brethren, yes, the angels of heaven be anathematized than that my gospel be overthrown."

The Greek word *anathema*, Hebrew *herem*, means to accurse, execrate, to damn. Paul first (hypothetically) curses himself. Knowing persons first find fault with themselves in order that they may all the more earnestly reprove others.

Paul maintains that there is no other gospel besides the one he had preached to the Galatians. He preached, not a gospel of his own invention, but the very same Gospel God had long ago prescribed in the Sacred Scriptures.

No wonder Paul pronounces curses upon himself and upon others, upon the angels of heaven, if anyone should dare to preach any other gospel than Christ's own.

Verse 9. *As we said before, so say I now again. If any man preach any other gospel unto you than that ye have received, let him be accursed.*

Paul repeats the curse, directing it now upon other persons. Before, he cursed himself, his brethren, and an angel from heaven. "Now," he says, "if there are any others who preach a gospel different from that you have received from us, let them also be accursed." Paul herewith curses and excommunicates all false teachers including his opponents. He is so worked up that he dares to curse all who pervert his Gospel. Would to God that this terrible pronouncement of the Apostle might strike fear into the hearts of all who pervert the Gospel of Paul.

The Galatians might say: "Paul, we do not pervert the Gospel you have brought unto us. We did not quite understand it. That is all. Now these teachers who came after you have explained everything so beautifully."

This explanation the Apostle refuses to accept. They must add nothing; they must correct nothing. "What you received from me is the genuine Gospel of God. Let it stand. If any man brings any other gospel than the one I brought you, or promises to deliver better things than you have received from me, let him be accursed."

In spite of this emphatic denunciation so many accept the pope as the supreme judge of the Scriptures. "The Church," they say, "chose only four gospels. The Church might have chosen more. Ergo the Church is above the Gospel." With equal force one might argue: "I approve the Scriptures. Ergo I am above the Scriptures. John the Baptist confessed Christ. Hence he is above Christ." Paul subordinates himself, all preachers, all the angels of heaven, everybody to the Sacred Scriptures. We are not the masters, judges, or arbiters, but witnesses, disciples, and confessors of the Scriptures, whether we be pope, Luther, Augustine, Paul, or an angel from heaven.

Verse 10. *For do I now persuade men, or God?*

With the same vehemence Paul continues: "You Galatians ought to be able to tell from my preaching and from the many afflictions which I have endured, whether I serve men or God. Everybody can see that my preaching has stirred up persecution against me everywhere, and has earned for me the cruel hatred of my own people, in fact the hatred of all men. This should convince you that by my preaching I do not seek the favor and praise of men, but the glory of God."

No man can say that we are seeking the favor and praise of men with our doctrine. We teach that all men are naturally depraved. We condemn man's free will, his strength, wisdom, and righteousness. We say that we obtain grace by the free mercy of God alone for Christ's sake. This is no preaching to please men. This sort of preaching procures for us the hatred and disfavor of the world, persecutions, excommunications, murders, and curses.

"Can't you see that I seek no man's favor by my doctrine?" asks Paul. "If I were anxious for the favor of men I would flatter them. But what do I do? I condemn their works. I teach things only that I have been commanded to teach from above. For that I bring down upon my head the wrath of Jews and Gentiles. My doctrine must be right. It must be divine. Any other doctrine cannot be better than mine. Any other doctrine must be false and wicked."

With Paul we boldly pronounce a curse upon every doctrine that does not agree with ours. We do not preach for the praise of men, or the favor of princes. We preach for the favor of God alone whose grace and mercy we proclaim. Whosoever teaches a gospel contrary to ours, or different from ours, let us be bold to say that he is sent of the devil.

Verse 10. *Or do I seek to please men?*

"Do I serve men or God?" Paul keeps an eye on the false apostles, those flatterers of men. They taught circumcision to avoid the hatred and persecution of men.

To this day you will find many who seek to please men in order that they may live in peace and security. They teach whatever is agreeable to men, no matter whether it is contrary to God's Word or their own conscience. But we who endeavor to please God and not men, stir up hell itself. We must suffer reproach, slanders, death.

For those who go about to please men we have a word from Christ recorded in the fifth chapter of St. John: "How can ye believe, which receive honor one of another, and seek not the honor that cometh from God alone?"

Verse 10. *For if I yet pleased men, I should not be the servant of Christ.*

Observe the consummate cleverness with which the false apostles went about to bring Paul into disrepute. They combed Paul's writings for contradictions (our opponents do the same) to accuse him of teaching contradictory things. They found that Paul had circumcised Timothy according to the Law, that Paul had purified himself with four other men in the Temple at Jerusalem, that Paul had shaven his head at Cenchrea. The false apostles slyly suggested that Paul had been constrained by the other apostles to observe these ceremonial laws. We know that Paul observed these decora out of charitable regard for the weak brethren. He did not want to offend them. But the false apostles turned Paul's charitable regard to his disadvantage. If Paul had preached the Law and circumcision, if he had commended the strength and free will of man, he would not have been so obnoxious to the Jews. On the contrary they would have praised his every action.

Verses 11, 12. *But I certify you, brethren, that the gospel which was preached of me is not after man. For I neither received it of man, neither was I taught it, but by the revelation of Jesus Christ.*

This passage constitutes Paul's chief defense against the accusations of his opponents. He maintains under oath that he received his Gospel not from men, but by the revelation of Jesus Christ.

In declaring that his Gospel is not after man, Paul does not merely wish to state that his Gospel is not mundane. The false apostles made the same claim for their gospel. Paul means to say that he learned his Gospel not in the usual and accepted manner through the agency of men by hearing, reading, or writing. He received the Gospel by special revelation directly from Jesus Christ.

Paul received his Gospel on the way to Damascus when Christ appeared to him. St. Luke furnishes an account of the incident in the ninth chapter of the Book of Acts. "Arise," said Christ to Paul, "and go into the city, and it shall be told thee what thou must do." Christ did not send Paul into the city to learn the Gospel from Ananias. Ananias was only to baptize Paul, to lay his hands on Paul, to commit the ministry of the Word unto Paul, and to recommend him to the Church. Ananias recognized his limited assignment when he said to Paul: "Brother Saul, the Lord, even Jesus, that appeared unto thee in the way as thou camest, hath sent me, that thou mightest receive thy sight, and be filled with the Holy Ghost." Paul did not receive instruction from Ananias. Paul had already been called, enlightened, and taught by Christ in the road. His contact with Ananias was merely a testimonial to the fact that Paul had been called by Christ to preach the Gospel.

Paul was forced to speak of his conversion to combat the slanderous contention of the false apostles to the effect that this apostleship was inferior to that of the other apostles.

If it were not for the example of the Galatian churches I would never have thought it possible that anybody who had received the Word of God with such eagerness as they had, could so quickly let go of it. Good Lord, what terrible mischief one single false statement can create.

The article of justification is fragile. Not in itself, of course, but in us. I know how quickly a person can forfeit the joy of the Gospel. I know in what slippery places even those stand who seem to have a good footing in the matters of faith. In the midst of the conflict when we should be consoling ourselves with the Gospel, the Law rears up and begins to rage all over our conscience. I say the Gospel is frail because we are frail.

What makes matters worse is that one-half of ourselves, our own reason, stands against us. The flesh resists the spirit, or as Paul puts it, "The flesh lusteth against the Spirit." Therefore we teach that to know Christ and to believe in Him is no achievement of man, but the gift of God. God alone can create and preserve faith in us. God creates faith in us through the Word. He increases, strengthens and confirms faith in us through His Word. Hence the best service that anybody can render God is diligently to hear and read God's Word. On the other hand, nothing is more perilous than to be weary of the Word of God. Thinking he knows enough, a person begins little by little to despise the Word until he has lost Christ and the Gospel altogether.

Let every believer carefully learn the Gospel. Let him continue in humble prayer. We are molested not by puny foes, but by mighty ones, foes who never grow tired of warring against us. These, our enemies, are many: Our own flesh, the world, the Law, sin, death, the wrath and judgment of God, and the devil himself.

The arguments which the false apostles advanced impress people to this day. "Who are you to dissent from the fathers and the entire Church, and to bring a contradictory doctrine? Are you wiser than so many holy men, wiser than the whole Church?" When Satan, abetted by our own reason, advances these arguments against us, we lose heart, unless we keep on saying to ourselves: "I don't care if Cyprian, Ambrose, Augustine, Peter, Paul, John, or an angel from heaven, teaches so and so. I know that I teach the truth of God in Christ Jesus."

When I first took over the defense of the Gospel, I remembered what Doctor Staupitz said to me. "I like it well," he said, "that the doctrine which you proclaim gives glory to God alone and none to man. For never can too much glory, goodness, and mercy be ascribed unto God." These words of the worthy Doctor comforted and confirmed me. The Gospel is true because it deprives men of all glory, wisdom, and righteousness and turns over all honor to the Creator alone. It is safer to attribute too much glory unto God than unto man.

You may argue that the Church and the fathers are holy. Yet the Church is compelled to pray: "Forgive us our trespasses." I am not to be believed, nor is the Church to be believed, or the fathers, or the apostles, or an angel from heaven, if they teach anything contrary to the Word of God. Let the Word of God abide forever.

Peter erred in life and in doctrine. Paul might have dismissed Peter's error as a matter of no consequence. But Paul saw that Peter's error would lead to the damage of the whole Church unless it were corrected. Therefore he withstood Peter to his face. The Church, Peter, the apostles, angels from heaven, are not to be heard unless they teach the genuine Word of God.

This argument is not always to our advantage. People ask: "Whom then shall we believe?" Our opponents maintain that they teach the pure Word of God. We do not believe them. They in turn hate and persecute us for vile heretics. What can we do about it? With Paul we glory in the Gospel of Jesus Christ. What do we gain? We are told that our glorying is idle vanity and unadulterated blasphemy. The moment we abase ourselves and give in to the rage of our opponents, Papists and Anabaptists grow arrogant. The Anabaptists hatch out some new monstrosity. The Papists revive their old abominations. What to do? Let everybody become sure of his calling and doctrine, that he may boldly say with Paul: "But though we, or an angel from heaven, preach any other gospel unto you than ye have received, let him be accursed."

Verses 13, 14. *For ye have heard of my conversation in time past in the Jews' religion, how that beyond measure I persecuted the church of God, and wasted it: And profited in the Jews' religion above many my equals in mine own nation.*

This passage does not contain doctrine. Paul adduces his own case for an example. "I have," he says, "at one time defended the traditions of the Pharisees more fiercely than any of your false apostles. Now, if the righteousness of the Law had been worth anything I would never have forsaken it. So carefully did I live up to the Law that I excelled many of my companions. So zealous was I in defense of the Law that I wasted the church of God."

Verse 14. *Being more exceedingly zealous of the traditions of my fathers.*

Speaking now of the Mosaic Law, Paul declares that he was wrapped up in it. To the Philippians he wrote: "As touching the law, a Pharisee; concerning zeal, persecuting the church; touching the righteousness which is in the law, blameless." He means to say, "I can compare myself with the best and holiest of all those who are of the circumcision. Let them show me if they can, a more earnest defender of the Mosaic Law than I was at one time. This fact, O Galatians, should have put you on your guard against these deceivers who make so much of the Law. If anybody ever had reason to glory in the righteousness of the Law, it was I."

I too may say that before I was enlightened by the Gospel, I was as zealous for the papistical laws and traditions of the fathers as ever a man was. I tried hard to live up to every law as best I could. I punished myself with fasting, watching, praying, and other exercises more than all those who today hate and persecute me. I was so much in earnest that I imposed upon my body more than it could stand. I honored the pope as a matter of conscience. Whatever I did, I did with a single heart to the glory of God. But our opponents, well-fed idlers that they are, will not believe what I and many others have endured.

Verses 15, 16, 17. *But when it pleased God, who separated me from my mother's womb, and called me by his grace, To reveal his Son in me, that I might preach him among the heathen; immediately I conferred not with flesh and blood: Neither went I up to Jerusalem to them which were apostles before me; but I went into Arabia, and returned again unto Damascus.*

Here Paul relates that immediately upon being called by God to preach the Gospel to the Gentiles, he went into Arabia without consulting a single person. "When it had pleased God," he writes, "I did not deserve it. I had been an enemy of Christ. I had blasphemed His Gospel. I had shed innocent blood. In the midst of my frenzy I was called. Why? On account of my outrageous cruelty? Indeed not. My gracious God who shows mercy unto whom He will, pardoned all mine iniquities. He bestowed His grace upon me, and called me for an apostle."

We also have come to the knowledge of the truth by the same kindness of God. I crucified Christ daily in my cloistered life, and blasphemed God by my wrong faith. Outwardly I kept myself chaste, poor, and obedient. I was much given to fasting, watching, praying, saying of masses, and the like. Yet under the cloak of my outward respectability I continually mistrusted, doubted, feared, hated, and blasphemed God. My righteousness was a filthy puddle. Satan loves such saints. They are his darlings, for they quickly destroy their body and soul by depriving them of the blessings of God's generous gifts.

I tell you I stood in awe of the pope's authority. To

dissent from him I considered a crime worthy of eternal death. I thought of John Hussas a cursed heretic. I counted it a sin even to think of him. I would gladly have furnished the wood to burn him. I would have felt I had done God a real service.

In comparison with these sanctimonious hypocrites of the papacy, publicans and harlots are not bad. They at least feel remorse. They at least do not try to justify their wicked deeds. But these pretended saints, so far from acknowledging their errors, justify them and regard them as acceptable sacrifices unto God.

Verse 15. *When it pleased God.*

"By the favor of God I, a wicked and cursed wretch, a blasphemer, persecutor, and rebel, was spared. Not content to spare me, God granted unto me the knowledge of His salvation, His Spirit, His Son, the office of an apostle, everlasting life." Paul speaking.

God not only pardoned our iniquities, but in addition overwhelmed us with blessings and spiritual gifts. Many, however, are ungrateful. Worse, by opening again a window to the devil many begin to loathe God's Word, and end by perverting the Gospel.

Verse 15. *Who separated me from my mother's womb.*

This is a Hebrew expression, meaning to sanctify, ordain, prepare. Paul is saying, "When I was not yet born God ordained me to be an apostle, and in due time confirmed my apostleship before the world. Every gift, be it small or great, spiritual or temporal, and every good thing I should ever do, God has ordained while I was yet in my mother's womb where I could neither think nor perform any good thing. After I was born God supported me. Heaping mercy upon mercy, He freely forgave my sins, replenishing me with His grace to enable me to learn what great things are ours in Christ. To crown it all, He called me to preach the Gospel to others."

Verse 15. *And called me by his grace.*

"Did God call me on account of my holy life? Or on account of my pharisaical religion? Or on account of my prayers, fastings, and works? Never. Well, then, it is certain God did not call me on account of my blasphemies, persecutions, oppressions. What prompted Him to call me? His grace alone."

Verse 16. *To reveal his Son to me.*

We now hear what kind of doctrine was committed to Paul: The doctrine of the Gospel, the doctrine of the revelation of the Son of God. This doctrine differs greatly from the Law. The Law terrorizes the conscience. The Law reveals the wrath and judgment of God. The Gospel does not threaten. The Gospel announces that Christ is come to forgive the sins of the world. The Gospel conveys to us the inestimable treasures of God.

Verse 16. *That I might preach him among the heathen.*

"It pleased God," says the Apostle, "to reveal himself in me. Why? For a twofold purpose. That I personally should believe in the Son of God, and that I should reveal Him to the Gentiles."

Paul does not mention the Jews, for the simple reason that he was the called and acknowledged apostle of the Gentiles, although he preached Christ also to the Jews.

We can hear the Apostle saying to himself: "I will not burden the Gentiles with the Law, because I am their apostle and not their lawgiver. Not once did you Galatians hear me speak of the righteousness of the Law or of works. My job was to bring you the Gospel. Therefore you ought to listen to no teachers of the Law, but the Gospel; not Moses, but the Son of God; not the righteousness of works, but the righteousness of faith must be proclaimed to the Gentiles. That is the right kind of preaching for Gentiles."

Verse 16. *Immediately I conferred not with flesh and blood.*

Once Paul had received the Gospel from Christ, he conferred with nobody in Damascus. He asked no man to teach him. He did not go up to Jerusalem to sit at the feet of Peter and the other apostles. At once he preached Jesus Christ in Damascus.

Verse 17. *Neither went I up to Jerusalem to them which were apostles before me; but I went into Arabia, and returned again unto Damascus.*

"I went to Arabia before I saw any of the apostles. I took it upon myself to preach the Gospel to the Gentiles without delay, because Christ had called me for that purpose." This statement refutes the assertion of the false apostles that Paul had been a pupil of the apostles, from which the false apostles inferred that Paul had been instructed in the obedience of the Law, that therefore the Gentiles also ought to keep the Law and submit to circumcision.

Verses 18, 19. *Then after three years I went up to Jerusalem to see Peter, and abode with him fifteen days. But other of the apostles saw I none, save James the Lord's brother.*

Paul minutely recounts his personal history to stop the cavil of the false apostles. Paul does not deny that he had been with some of the apostles. He went to Jerusalem uninvited, not to be instructed, but to visit with Peter. Luke reports the occasion in the ninth chapter of the Book of Acts. Barnabas introduced Paul to the apostles and related to them how Paul had met the Lord Jesus on the way to Damascus, also how Paul had preached boldly at Damascus in the name of Jesus. Paul says that he saw Peter and James, but he denies that he learned anything from them.

Why does Paul harp on this seemingly unimportant fact? To convince the churches of Galatia that his Gospel was the true Word of Christ which he learned from Christ Himself and from no man. Paul was forced to affirm and re-affirm this fact. His usefulness to all the churches that had used him as their pastor and teacher was at stake.

Verse 20. *Now the things which I write unto you, behold, before God, I lie not.*

Was it necessary for Paul to go under oath? Yes. Paul is reporting personal history. How else would the churches believe him? The false apostles might say, "Who knows whether Paul is telling the truth?" Paul, the elect vessel of God, was held in so little esteem by his own Galatians to whom he had preached Christ that it was necessary for him to swear an oath that he spoke the truth. If this happened to Paul, what business have we to complain when people doubt our words, or hold us in little regard, we who cannot begin to compare ourselves with the Apostle?

Verse 21. *Afterwards I came into the regions of Syria and Cilicia.*

Syria and Cilicia are adjacent countries. Paul traces his movements carefully in order to convince the Galatians that he had never been the disciple of any apostle.

Verses 22, 23, 24. *And was unknown by face unto the churches of Judaea which were in Christ: But they had heard only, that he which persecuted us in times past now preacheth the faith which once he destroyed. And they glorified God in me.*

In Syria and Cilicia Paul won the indorsement of all the churches of Judea, by his preaching. All the churches everywhere, even those of Judea, could testify that he had preached the same faith everywhere. "And," Paul adds, "these churches glorified God in me, not because I taught that circumcision and the law of Moses should be observed, but because I urged upon all faith in the Lord Jesus Christ."

GALATIONS 2

Verse 1. Then fourteen years after I went up again to Jerusalem.

Paul taught justification by faith in Christ Jesus, without the deeds of the Law. He reported this to the disciples at Antioch. Among the disciples were some that had been brought up in the ancient customs of the Jews. These rose against Paul in quick indignation, accusing him of propagating a gospel of lawlessness.

Great dissension followed. Paul and Barnabas stood up for the truth. They testified: "Wherever we preached to the Gentiles, the Holy Ghost came upon those who received the Word. This happened everywhere. We preached not circumcision, we did not require observance of the Law. We preached faith in Jesus Christ. At our preaching of faith, God gave to the hearers the Holy Ghost." From this fact Paul and Barnabas inferred that the Holy Ghost approved the faith of the Gentiles without the Law and circumcision. If the faith of the Gentiles had not pleased the Holy Ghost, He would not have manifested His presence in the uncircumcised hearers of the Word.

Unconvinced, the Jews fiercely opposed Paul, asserting that the Law ought to be kept and that the Gentiles ought to be circumcised, or else they could not be saved.

When we consider the obstinacy with which Romanists cling to their traditions, we can very well understand the zealous devotion of the Jews for the Law. After all, they had received the Law from God. We can understand how impossible it was for recent converts from Judaism suddenly to break with the Law. For that matter, God did bear with them, as He bore with the infirmity of Israel when the people halted between two religions. Was not God patient with us also while we were blindfolded by the papacy? God is longsuffering and full of mercy. But we dare not abuse the patience of the Lord. We dare no longer continue in error now that the truth has been revealed in the Gospel.

The opponents of Paul had his own example to prefer against him. Paul had circumcised Timothy. Paul defended his action on the ground that he had circumcised Timothy, not from compulsion, but from Christian love, lest the weak in faith should be offended. His opponents would not accept Paul's explanation.

When Paul saw that the quarrel was getting out of hand he obeyed the direction of God and left for Jerusalem, there to confer with the other apostles. He did this not for his own sake, but for the sake of the people.

Verse 1. With Barnabas, and took Titus with me also.

Paul chose two witnesses, Barnabas and Titus. Barnabas had been Paul's preaching companion to the Gentiles. Barnabas was an eye-witness of the fact that the Holy Ghost had come upon the Gentiles in response to the simple preaching of faith in Jesus Christ. Barnabas stuck to Paul on this point, that it was not necessary for the Gentiles to be bothered with the Law as long as they believed in Christ.

Titus was superintendent of the churches in Crete, having been placed in charge of the churches by Paul. Titus was a former Gentile.

Verse 2. And I went up by revelation.

If God had not ordered Paul to Jerusalem, Paul would never have gone there.

Verse 2. And communicated unto them that gospel.

After an absence of fourteen years, respectively eighteen years, Paul returned to Jerusalem to confer with the other apostles.

Verse 2. Which I preach among the Gentiles.

Among the Jews Paul allowed Law and circumcision to stand for the time being. So did all the apostles. Nevertheless Paul held fast to the liberty of the Gospel. On one occasion he said to the Jews: "Through this man (Christ) is preached unto you forgiveness of sins; and by him all that believe are justified from all things, from which ye could not be justified by the law of Moses" (Acts 13:39). Always remembering the weak, Paul did not insist that they break at once with the Law.

Paul admits that he conferred with the apostles concerning his Gospel. But he denies that the conference benefited or taught him anything. The fact is he resisted those who wanted to force the practice of the Law upon the Gentiles. They did not overcome him, he overcame them. "Your false apostles lie, when they say that I circumcised Timothy, shaved my head in Cenchrea, and went up to Jerusalem, at the request of the apostles. I went to Jerusalem at the request of God. What is more, I won the indorsement of the apostles. My opponents lost out."

The matter upon which the apostles deliberated in conference was this: Is the observance of the Law requisite unto justification? Paul answered: "I have preached faith in Christ to the Gentiles, and not the Law. If the Jews want to keep the Law and be circumcised, very well, as long as they do so from a right motive."

Verse 2. But privately to them which were of reputation.

This is to say, "I conferred not only with the brethren, but with the leaders among them."

Verse 2. Lest by any means I should run, or had run, in vain.

Not that Paul himself ever thought he had run in vain. However, many did think that Paul had preached the Gospel in vain, because he kept the Gentiles free from the yoke of the Law. The opinion that obedience to the Law was mandatory unto salvation was gaining ground. Paul meant to remedy this evil. By this conference he hoped to establish the identity of his Gospel with that of the other apostles, to stop the talk of his opponents that he had been running around in vain.

Verse 3. But neither Titus, who was with me, being a Greek, was compelled to be circumcised.

The word "compelled" acquaints us with the outcome of the conference. It was resolved that the Gentiles should not be compelled to be circumcised.

Paul did not condemn circumcision in itself. Neither by word nor deed did he ever inveigh against circumcision. But he did protest against circumcision being made a condition for salvation. He cited the case of the Fathers. "The fathers were not justified by circumcision. It was to them a sign and seal of righteousness. They looked upon circumcision as a confession of their faith."

The believing Jews, however, could not get it through their heads that circumcision was not necessary for salvation. They were encouraged in their wrong attitude by the false apostles. The result was that the people were up in arms against Paul and his doctrine.

Paul did not condemn circumcision as if it were a sin to receive it. But he insisted, and the conference upheld him, that circumcision had no bearing upon salvation and was therefore not to be forced upon the Gentiles. The conference agreed that the Jews should be permitted to keep their ancient customs for the time being, so long as they did not regard those customs as conveying God's justification of the sinner.

The false apostles were dissatisfied with the verdict of the conference. They did not want to rest circumcision and the practice of the Law in Christian liberty. They insisted that circumcision was obligatory unto salvation.

As the opponents of Paul, so our own adversaries [Luther's, the enemies of the Reformation] contend that the traditions of the Fathers dare not be neglected without loss of salvation. Our opponents will not agree with us on anything. They defend their blasphemies. They go as far to enforce them with the sword.

Paul's victory was complete. Titus, who was with Paul, was not compelled to be circumcised, although he stood in the midst of the apostles when this question of circumcision was debated. This was a blow to the false apostles. With the living fact that Titus was not compelled to be circumcised Paul was able to squelch his adversaries.

Verses 4, 5. And that because of false brethren unawares brought in, who came in privily to spy out our liberty which we have in Christ Jesus, that they might bring us into bondage: To whom we gave place by subjection, no, not for an hour; that the truth of the gospel might continue with you.

Paul here explains his motive for going up to Jerusalem. He did not go to Jerusalem to be instructed or confirmed in his Gospel by the other apostles. He went to Jerusalem in order to preserve the true Gospel for the Galatian churches and for all the churches of the Gentiles.

When Paul speaks of the truth of the Gospel he implies by contrast a false gospel. The false apostles also had a gospel, but it was an untrue gospel. "In holding out against them," says Paul, "I conserved the truth of the pure Gospel."

Now the true Gospel has it that we are justified by faith alone, without the deeds of the Law. The false gospel has it that we are justified by faith, but not without the deeds of the Law. The false apostles preached a conditional gospel.

So do the papists. They admit that faith is the foundation of salvation. But they add the conditional clause that faith can save only when it is furnished with good works. This is wrong. The true Gospel declares that good works are the embellishment of faith, but that faith itself is the gift and work of God in our hearts. Faith is able to justify, because it apprehends Christ, the Redeemer.

Human reason can think only in terms of the Law. It mumbles: "This I have done, this I have not done." But faith looks to Jesus Christ, the Son of God, given into death for the sins of the whole world. To turn one's eyes away from Jesus means to turn them to the Law.

True faith lays hold of Christ and leans on Him alone. Our opponents cannot understand this. In their blindness they cast away the precious pearl, Christ, and hang onto their stubborn works. They have no idea what faith is. How can they teach faith to others?

Not satisfied with teaching an untrue gospel, the false apostles tried to entangle Paul. "They went about," says Paul, "to spy out our liberty which we have in Christ Jesus, that they might bring us into bondage."

When Paul saw through their scheme, he attacked the false apostles. He says, "We did not let go of the liberty which we have in Christ Jesus. We routed them by the judgment of the apostles, and we would not give in to them, no, not an inch."

We too were willing to make all kinds of concessions to the papists. Yes, we are willing to offer them more than we should. But we will not give up the liberty of conscience which we have in Christ Jesus. We refuse to have our conscience bound by any work or law, so that by doing this or that we should be righteous, or leaving this or that undone we should be damned.

Since our opponents will not let it stand that only faith in Christ justifies, we will not yield to them. On the question of justification we must remain adamant, or else we shall lose the truth of the Gospel. It is a matter of life and death. It involves the death of the Son of God, who died for the sins of the world. If we surrender faith in Christ, as the only thing that can justify us, the death and resurrection of Jesus are without meaning; that Christ is the Savior of the world would be a myth. God would be a liar, because He would not have fulfilled His promises. Our stubbornness is right, because we want to preserve the liberty which we have in Christ. Only by preserving our liberty shall we be able to retain the truth of the Gospel inviolate.

Some will object that the Law is divine and holy. Let it be divine and holy. The Law has no right to tell me that I must be justified by it. The Law has the right to tell me that I should love God and my neighbor, that I should live in chastity, temperance, patience, etc. The Law has no right to tell me how I may be delivered from sin, death, and hell. It is the Gospel's business to tell me that. I must listen to the Gospel. It tells me, not what I must do, but what Jesus Christ, the Son of God, has done for me.

To conclude, Paul refused to circumcise Titus for the reason that the false apostles wanted to compel him to circumcise Titus. Paul refused to accede to their demands. If they had asked it on the plea of brotherly love, Paul would not have denied them. But because they demanded it on the ground that it was necessary for salvation, Paul defied them, and prevailed. Titus was not circumcised.

Verse 6. *But of those who seemed to be somewhat, whatsoever they were, it maketh no matter to me.*

This is a good point in Paul's refutation. Paul disparages the authority and dignity of the true apostles. He says of them, "Which seemed to be somewhat." The authority of the apostles was indeed great in all the churches. Paul did not want to detract from their authority, but he had to speak disparagingly of their authority in order to conserve the truth of the Gospel, and the liberty of conscience.

The false apostles used this argument against Paul: "The apostles lived with Christ for three years. They heard His sermons. They witnessed His miracles. They themselves preached and performed miracles while Christ was on earth. Paul never saw Jesus in the flesh. Now, whom ought you to believe: Paul, who stands alone, a mere disciple of the apostles, one of the last and least; or will you believe those grand apostles who were sent and confirmed by Christ Himself long before Paul?"

What could Paul say to that? He answered: "What they

say has no bearing on the argument. If the apostles were angels from heaven, that would not impress me. We are not now discussing the excellency of the apostles. We are talking about the Word of God now, and the truth of the Gospel. That Gospel is more excellent than all apostles."

Verse 6. God accepteth no man's person.

Paul is quoting Moses: "Thou shalt not respect the person of the poor, nor honor the person of the mighty" (Lev. 19:15). This quotation from Moses ought to shut the mouths of the false apostles. "Don't you know that God is no respecter of persons?" cries Paul. The dignity or authority of men means nothing to God. The fact is that God often rejects just such who stand in the odor of sanctity and in the aura of importance. In doing so God seems unjust and harsh. But men need deterring examples. For it is a vice with us to esteem personality more highly than the Word of God. God wants us to exalt His Word and not men.

There must be people in high office, of course. But we are not to deify them. The governor, the mayor, the preacher, the teacher, the scholar, father, mother, are persons whom we are to love and revere, but not to the extent that we forget God. Lest we attach too much importance to the person, God leaves with important persons offenses and sins, sometimes astounding shortcomings, to show us that there is a lot of difference between any person and God. David was a good king. But when the people began to think too well of him, down he fell into horrible sins, adultery and murder. Peter, excellent apostle that he was, denied Christ. Such examples of which the Scriptures are full, ought to warn us not to repose our trust in men. In the papacy appearance counts for everything. Indeed, the whole papacy amounts to nothing more than a mere kowtowing of persons and outward mummery. But God alone is to be feared and honored.

I would honor the Pope, I would love his person, if he would leave my conscience alone, and not compel me to sin against God. But the Pope wants to be adored himself, and that cannot be done without offending God. Since we must choose between one or the other, let us choose God. The truth is we are commissioned by God to resist the Pope, for it is written, "We ought to obey God rather than men" (Acts 5:29).

We have seen how Paul refutes the argument of the false apostles concerning the authority of the apostles. In order that the truth of the Gospel may continue; in order that the Word of God and the righteousness of faith may be kept pure and undefiled, let the apostles, let an angel from heaven, let Peter, let Paul, let them all perish.

Verse 6. For they who seemed to be somewhat in conference added nothing to me.

The Apostle repeats: "I did not so confer with the apostles that they taught me anything. What could they possibly teach me since Christ by His revelation had taught me all things? It was but a conference, and no disputation. I learned nothing, neither did I defend my cause. I only stated what I had done, that I had preached to the Gentiles faith in Christ, without the Law, and that in response to my preaching the Holy Ghost came down upon the Gentiles. When the apostles heard this, they were glad that I had taught the truth."

If Paul would not give in to the false apostles, much less ought we to give in to our opponents. I know that a Christian should be humble, but against the Pope I am going to be proud and say to him: "You, Pope, I will not have you for my boss, for I am sure that my doctrine is divine." Such pride against the Pope is imperative, for if we are not stout and proud we shall never succeed in defending the article of the righteousness of faith.

If the Pope would concede that God alone by His grace through Christ justifies sinners, we would carry him in our arms, we would kiss his feet. But since we cannot obtain this concession, we will give in to nobody, not to all the angels in heaven, not to Peter, not to Paul, not to a hundred emperors, not to a thousand popes, not to the whole world. If in this matter we were to humble ourselves, they would take from us the God who created us, and Jesus Christ who has redeemed us by His blood. Let this be our resolution, that we will suffer the loss of all things, the loss of our good name, of life itself, but the Gospel and our faith in Jesus Christ—we will not stand for it that anybody take them from us.

Verses 7, 8. But contrariwise, when they saw that the gospel of the uncircumcision was committed unto me, as the gospel of the circumcision was unto Peter; [For he that wrought effectually in Peter to the apostleship of the circumcision, the same was mighty in me toward the Gentiles.]

Here the Apostle claims for himself the same authority which the false apostles attributed to the true apostles. Paul simply inverts their argument. "to bolster their evil cause," says he, "the false apostles quote the authority of the great apostles against me. I can quote the same authority against them, for the apostles are on my side. They gave me the right hand of fellowship. They approved my ministry. O my Galatians, do not believe the counterfeit apostles!"

What does Paul mean by saying that the gospel of the

uncircumcision was committed unto him, and that of the circumcision to Peter? Did not Paul preach to the Jews, while Peter preached to the Gentiles also? Peter converted the Centurion. Paul's custom was to enter into the synagogues of the Jews, there to preach the Gospel. Why then should he call himself the apostle of the Gentiles, while he calls Peter the apostle of the circumcision?

Paul refers to the fact that the other apostles remained in Jerusalem until the destruction of the city became imminent. But Paul was especially called the apostle of the Gentiles. Even before the destruction of Jerusalem Jews dwelt here and there in the cities of the Gentiles. Coming to a city, Paul customarily entered the synagogues of the Jews and first brought to them as the children of the kingdom, the glad tidings that the promises made unto the fathers were fulfilled in Jesus Christ. When the Jews refused to hear these glad tidings, Paul turned to the Gentiles. He was the apostle of the Gentiles in a special sense, as Peter was the apostle of the Jews.

Paul reiterates that Peter, James, and John, the accepted pillars of the Church, taught him nothing, nor did they commit unto him the office of preaching the Gospel unto the Gentiles. Both the knowledge of the Gospel and the commandment to preach it to the Gentiles, Paul received directly from God. His case was parallel to that of Peter's, who was particularly commissioned to preach the Gospel to the Jews.

The apostles had the same charge, the identical Gospel. Peter did not proclaim a different Gospel, nor had he appointed his fellow apostles. They were equals. They were all taught of God. None was greater than the other, none could point to prerogatives above the other. To justify his usurped primacy in the Church the Pope claims that Peter was the chief of the apostles. This is an impudent falsehood.

Verse 8. For he that wrought effectually in Peter.

With these words Paul refutes another argument of the false apostles. "What reason have the false apostles to boast that the Gospel of Peter was mighty, that he converted many, that he wrought great miracles, and that his very shadow healed the sick? These reports are true enough. But where did Peter acquire this power? God gave him the power. I have the same power. I received my power, not from Peter, but from the same God. The same Spirit who was mighty in Peter was mighty in me also." Luke corroborates Paul's statement in the words: "And God wrought special miracles by the hands of Paul, so that from his body were brought unto the sick handkerchiefs or aprons, and the diseases departed from them, and the evil spirits went out of them" (Acts 19:11, 12).

To conclude, Paul is not going to be inferior to the rest of the apostles. Some secular writers put Paul's boasting down as carnal pride. But Paul had no personal interest in his boasting. It was with him a matter of faith and doctrine. The controversy was not about the glory of Paul, but the glory of God, the Word of God, the true worship of God, true religion, and the righteousness of faith.

Verse 9. And when James, Cephas and John, who seemed to be pillars, perceived the grace that was given unto me, they gave to me and Barnabas the right hands of fellowship; that we should go unto the heathen, and they unto the circumcision.

"The fact is, when the apostles heard that I had received the charge to preach the Gospel to the Gentiles from Christ; when they heard that God had wrought many miracles through me; that great numbers of the Gentiles had come to the knowledge of Christ through my ministry; when they heard that the Gentiles had received the Holy Ghost without Law and circumcision, by the simple preaching of faith; when they heard all this they glorified God for His grace in me." Hence, Paul was justified in concluding that the apostles were for him, and not against him.

Verse 9. The right hands of fellowship.

As if the apostles had said to him: "We, Paul, do agree with you in all things. We are companions in doctrine. We have the same Gospel with this difference, that to you is committed the Gospel for the uncircumcised, while the Gospel for the circumcision is committed unto us. But this difference ought not to hinder our friendship, since we preach one and the same Gospel."

Verse 10. Only they would that we should remember the poor; the same which I also was forward to do.

Next to the preaching of the Gospel, a true and faithful pastor will take care of the poor. Where the Church is, there must be the poor, for the world and the devil persecute the Church and impoverish many faithful Christians.

Speaking of money, nobody wants to contribute nowadays to the maintenance of the ministry, and the erection of schools. When it comes to establishing false worship and idolatry, no cost is spared. True religion is ever in need of money, while false religions are backed by wealth.

Verse 11. But when Peter was come to Antioch, I withstood him to the face, because he was to be blamed.

Paul goes on in his refutation of the false apostles by saying that in Antioch he withstood Peter in the presence of the whole congregation. As he stated before, Paul had no small matter in hand, but the chief article of the

Christian religion. When this article is endangered, we must not hesitate to resist Peter, or an angel from heaven. Paul paid no regard to the dignity and position of Peter, when he saw this article in danger. It is written: "He that loveth father or mother or his own life, more than me, is not worthy of me" (Matt. 10:37).

For defending the truth in our day, we are called proud and obstinate hypocrites. We are not ashamed of these titles. The cause we are called to defend, is not Peter's cause, or the cause of our parents, or that of the government, or that of the world, but the cause of God. In defense of that cause we must be firm and unyielding.

When he says, "to his face," Paul accuses the false apostles of slandering him behind his back. In his presence they dared not to open their mouths. He tells them, "I did not speak evil of Peter behind his back, but I withstood him frankly and openly."

Others may debate here whether an apostle might sin. I claim that we ought not to make Peter out as faultless. Prophets have erred. Nathan told David that he should go ahead and build the Temple of the Lord. But his prophecy was afterwards corrected by the Lord. The apostles erred in thinking of the Kingdom of Christ as a worldly state. Peter had heard the command of Christ, "Go ye into all the world, and preach the Gospel to every creature." But if it had not been for the heavenly vision and the special command of Christ, Peter would never have gone to the home of Cornelius. Peter also erred in this matter of circumcision. If Paul had not publicly censured him, all the believing Gentiles would have been compelled to receive circumcision and accept the Jewish law. We are not to attribute perfection to any man.

Luke reports "that the contention between Paul and Barnabas was so sharp that they departed asunder one from the other." The cause of their disagreement could hardly have been small since it separated these two, who had been joined together for years in a holy partnership. Such incidents are recorded for our consolation. After all, it is a comfort to know that even saints might and do sin.

Samson, David, and many other excellent men fell into grievous sins. Job and Jeremiah cursed the day of their birth. Elijah and Jonah became weary of life and prayed for death. Such offenses on the part of the saints, the Scriptures record for the comfort of those who are near despair. No person has ever sunk so low that he cannot rise again. On the other hand, no man's standing is so secure that he may not fall. If Peter fell, I may fall. If he rose again, I may rise again. We have the same gifts that they had, the same Christ, the same baptism and the same Gospel, the same forgiveness of sins. They needed these saving ordinances just as much as we do.

Verse 12. For before that certain came from James, he did eat with the Gentiles.

The Gentiles who had been converted to faith in Christ, ate meats forbidden by the Law. Peter, visiting some of these Gentiles, ate meat and drank wine with them, although he knew that these things were forbidden in the Law. Paul declared that he did likewise, that he became as a Jew to the Jews, and to them that were without law, as without law. He ate and drank with the Gentiles unconcerned about the Jewish Law. When he was with the Jews, however, he abstained from all things forbidden in the Law, for he labored to serve all men, that he "might by all means save some." Paul does not reprove Peter for transgressing the Law, but for disguising his attitude to the Law.

Verse 12. But when they were come, he withdrew and separated himself, fearing them which were of the circumcision.

Paul does not accuse Peter of malice or ignorance, but of lack of principle, in that he abstained from meats, because he feared the Jews that came from James. Peter's weak attitude endangered the principle of Christian liberty. It is the deduction rather than the fact which Paul reproves. To eat and to drink, or not to eat and drink, is immaterial. But to make the deduction "If you eat, you sin; if you abstain you are righteous"—this is wrong.

Meats may be refused for two reasons. First, they may be refused for the sake of Christian love. There is no danger connected with a refusal of meats for the sake of charity. To bear with the infirmity of a brother is a good thing. Paul himself taught and exemplified such thoughtfulness. Secondly, meats may be refused in the mistaken hope of thereby obtaining righteousness. When this is the purpose of abstaining from meats, we say, let charity go. To refrain from meats for this latter reason amounts to a denial of Christ. If we must lose one or the other, let us lose a friend and brother, rather than God, our Father.

Jerome, who understood not this passage, nor the whole epistle for that matter, excuses Peter's action on the ground "that it was done in ignorance." But Peter offended by giving the impression that he was indorsing the Law. By his example he encouraged Gentiles and Jews to forsake the truth of the Gospel. If Paul had not reproved him, there would have been a sliding back of Christians into the Jewish religion, and a return to the burdens of the Law.

It is surprising that Peter, excellent apostle that he was,

should have been guilty of such vacillation. In a former council at Jerusalem he practically stood alone in defense of the truth that salvation is by faith, without the Law. Peter at that time valiantly defended the liberty of the Gospel. But now by abstaining from meats forbidden in the Law, he went against his better judgment. You have no idea what danger there is in customs and ceremonies. They so easily tend to error in works.

Verse 13. *And the other Jews dissembled likewise with him; insomuch that Barnabas also was carried away with their dissimulation.*

It is marvelous how God preserved the Church by one single person. Paul alone stood up for the truth, for Barnabas, his companion, was lost to him, and Peter was against him. Sometimes one lone person can do more in a conference than the whole assembly.

I mention this to urge all to learn how properly to differentiate between the Law and the Gospel, in order to avoid dissembling. When it come to the article of justification we must not yield, if we want to retain the truth of the Gospel.

When the conscience is disturbed, do not seek advice from reason or from the Law, but rest your conscience in the grace of God and in His Word, and proceed as if you had never heard of the Law. The Law has its place and its own good time. While Moses was in the mountain where he talked with God face to face, he had no law, he made no law, he administered no law. But when he came down from the mountain, he was a lawgiver. The conscience must be kept above the Law, the body under the Law.

Paul reproved Peter for no trifle, but for the chief article of Christian doctrine, which Peter's hypocrisy had endangered. For Barnabas and other Jews followed Peter's example. It is surprising that such good men as Peter, Barnabas, and others should fall into unexpected error, especially in a matter which they knew so well. To trust in our own strength, our own goodness, our own wisdom, is a perilous thing. Let us search the Scriptures with humility, praying that we may never lose the light of the Gospel. "Lord, increase our faith."

Verse 14. *But when I saw that they walked not uprightly according to the truth of the gospel.*

No one except Paul had his eyes open. Consequently it was his duty to reprove Peter and his followers for swerving from the truth of the Gospel. It was no easy task for Paul to reprimand Peter. To the honor of Peter it must be said that he took the correction. No doubt, he freely acknowledged his fault.

The person who can rightly divide Law and Gospel has reason to thank God. He is a true theologian. I must confess that in times of temptation I do not always know how to do it. To divide Law and Gospel means to place the Gospel in heaven, and to keep the Law on earth; to call the righteousness of the Gospel heavenly, and the righteousness of the Law earthly; to put as much difference between the righteousness of the Gospel and that of the Law, as there is difference between day and night. If it is a question of faith or conscience, ignore the Law entirely. If it is a question of works, then lift high the lantern of works and the righteousness of the Law. If your conscience is oppressed with a sense of sin, talk to your conscience. Say: "You are now groveling in the dirt. You are now a laboring ass. Go ahead, and carry your burden. But why don't you mount up to heaven? There the Law cannot follow you!" Leave the ass burdened with laws behind in the valley. But your conscience, let it ascend with Isaac into the mountain.

In civil life obedience to the law is severely required. In civil life Gospel, conscience, grace, remission of sins, Christ Himself, do not count, but only Moses with the lawbooks. If we bear in mind this distinction, neither Gospel nor Law shall trespass upon each other. The moment Law and sin cross into heaven, i.e., your conscience, kick them out. On the other hand, when grace wanders unto the earth, i.e., into the body, tell grace: "You have no business to be around the dreg and dung of this bodily life. You belong in heaven."

By his compromising attitude Peter confused the separation of Law and Gospel. Paul had to do something about it. He reproved Peter, not to embarrass him, but to conserve the difference between the Gospel which justifies in heaven, and the Law which justifies on earth.

The right separation between Law and Gospel is very important to know. Christian doctrine is impossible without it. Let all who love and fear God, diligently learn the difference, not only in theory but also in practice.

When your conscience gets into trouble, say to yourself: "There is a time to die and a time to live; a time to learn the Law, and a time to unlearn the Law; a time to hear the Gospel, and a time to ignore the Gospel. Let the Law now depart, and let the Gospel enter, for now is the right time to hear the Gospel, and not the Law." However, when the conflict of conscience is over and external duties must be performed, close your ears to the Gospel, and open them wide to the Law.

Verse 14. *I said unto Peter before them all, If thou*

being a Jew, livest after the manner of Gentiles, and not as do the Jews, why compellest thou the Gentiles to live as do the Jews?

To live as a Jew is nothing bad. To eat or not to eat pork, what difference does it make? But to play the Jew, and for conscience' sake to abstain from certain meats, is a denial of Christ. When Paul saw that Peter's attitude tended to this, he withstood Peter and said to him: "You know that the observance of the law is not needed unto righteousness. You know that we are justified by faith in Christ. You know that we may eat all kinds of meats. Yet by your example you obligate the Gentiles to forsake Christ, and to return to the Law. You give them reason to think that faith is not sufficient unto salvation."

Peter did not say so, but his example said quite plainly that the observance of the Law must be added to faith in Christ, if men are to be saved. From Peter's example the Gentiles could not help but draw the conclusion that the Law was necessary unto salvation. If this error had been permitted to pass unchallenged, Christ would have lost out altogether.

The controversy involved the preservation of pure doctrine. In such a controversy Paul did not mind if anybody took offense.

Verse 15. *We who are Jews by nature, and not sinners of the Gentiles.*

"When we Jews compare ourselves with the Gentiles, we look pretty good. We have the Law, we have good works. Our rectitude dates from our birth, because the Jewish religion is natural to us. But all this does not make us righteous before God."

Peter and the others lived up to the requirements of the Law. They had circumcision, the covenant, the promises, the apostleship. But because of these advantages they were not to think themselves righteous before God. None of these prerogatives spell faith in Christ, which alone can justify a person. We do not mean to imply that the Law is bad. We do not condemn the Law, circumcision, etc., for their failure to justify us. Paul spoke disparagingly of these ordinances, because the false apostles asserted that mankind is saved by them without faith. Paul could not let this assertion stand, for without faith all things are deadly.

Verse 16. *Knowing that a man is not justified by the works of the law, but by the faith of Jesus Christ.*

For the sake of argument let us suppose that you could fulfill the Law in the spirit of the first commandment of God: "Thou shalt love the Lord, thy God, with all thy heart." It would do you no good. A person simply is not justified by the works of the Law.

The works of the Law, according to Paul, include the whole Law, judicial, ceremonial, moral. Now, if the performance of the moral law cannot justify, how can circumcision justify, when circumcision is part of the ceremonial law?

The demands of the Law may be fulfilled before and after justification. There were many excellent men among the pagans of old, men who never heard of justification. They lived moral lives. But that fact did not justify them. Peter, Paul, all Christians, live up to the Law. But that fact does not justify them. "For I know nothing by myself," says Paul, "yet am I not hereby justified" (I Cor. 4:4).

The nefarious opinion of the papists, which attributes the merit of grace and the remission of sins to works, must here be emphatically rejected. The papists say that a good work performed before grace has been obtained, is able to secure grace for a person, because it is no more than right that God should reward a good deed. When grace has already been obtained, any good work deserves everlasting life as a due payment and reward for merit. For the first, God is no debtor, they say; but because God is good and just, it is no more than right (they say) that He should reward a good work by granting grace for the service. But when grace has already been obtained, they continue, God is in the position of a debtor, and is in duty bound to reward a good work with the gift of eternal life. This is the wicked teaching of the papacy.

Now, if I could perform any work acceptable to God and deserving of grace, and once having obtained grace my good works would continue to earn for me the right and reward of eternal life, why should I stand in need of the grace of God and the suffering and death of Christ? Christ would be of no benefit to me. Christ's mercy would be of no use to me.

This shows how little insight the pope and the whole of his religious coterie have into spiritual matters, and how little they concern themselves with the spiritual health of their forlorn flocks. They cannot believe that the flesh is unable to think, speak, or do anything except against God. If they could see evil rooted in the nature of man, they would never entertain such silly dreams about man's merit or worthiness.

With Paul we absolutely deny the possibility of self-merit. God never yet gave to any person grace and everlasting life as a reward for merit. The opinions of the papists are the intellectual pipe-dreams of idle pates, that serve no other purpose but to draw men away from the true worship of God. The papacy is founded upon hallucinations.

The true way of salvation is this. First, a person must realize that he is a sinner, the kind of a sinner who is congenitally unable to do any good thing. "Whatsoever is not of faith, is sin." Those who seek to earn the grace of God by their own efforts are trying to please God with sins. They mock God, and provoke His anger. The first step on the way to salvation is to repent.

The second part is this. God sent His only-begotten Son into the world that we may live through His merit. He was crucified and killed for us. By sacrificing His Son for us God revealed Himself to us as a merciful Father who donates remission of sins, righteousness, and life everlasting for Christ's sake. God hands out His gifts freely unto all men. That is the praise and glory of His mercy.

The scholastics explain the way of salvation in this manner. When a person happens to perform a good deed, God accepts it and as a reward for the good deed God pours charity into that person. They call it "charity infused." This charity is supposed to remain in the heart. They get wild when they are told that this quality of the heart cannot justify a person.

They also claim that we are able to love God by our own natural strength, to love God above all things, at least to the extent that we deserve grace. And, say the scholastics, because God is not satisfied with a literal performance of the Law, but expects us to fulfill the Law according to the mind of the Lawgiver, therefore we must obtain from above a quality above nature, a quality which they call "formal righteousness."

We say, faith apprehends Jesus Christ. Christian faith is not an inactive quality in the heart. If it is true faith it will surely take Christ for its object. Christ, apprehended by faith and dwelling in the heart, constitutes Christian righteousness, for which God gives eternal life.

In contrast to the doting dreams of the scholastics, we teach this: First a person must learn to know himself from the Law. With the prophet he will then confess: "All have sinned, and come short of the glory of God." And, "there is none that doeth good, no, not one." And, "against thee, thee only, have I sinned."

Having been humbled by the Law, and having been brought to a right estimate of himself, a man will repent. He finds out that he is so depraved, that no strength, no works, no merits of his own will ever deliver him from his guilt. He will then understand the meaning of Paul's words: "I am sold under sin"; and "they are all under sin."

At this state a person begins to lament: "Who is going to help me?" In due time comes the Word of the Gospel, and says: "Son, thy sins are forgiven thee. Believe in Jesus Christ who was crucified for your sins. Remember, your sins have been imposed upon Christ."

In this way are we delivered from sin. In this way are we justified and made heirs of everlasting life.

In order to have faith you must paint a true portrait of Christ. The scholastics caricature Christ into a judge and tormentor. But Christ is no law giver. He is the Lifegiver. He is the Forgiver of sins. You must believe that Christ might have atoned for the sins of the world with one single drop of His blood. Instead, He shed His blood abundantly in order that He might give abundant satisfaction for our sins.

Here let me say, that these three things, faith, Christ, and imputation of righteousness, are to be joined together. Faith takes hold of Christ. God accounts this faith for righteousness.

This imputation of righteousness we need very much, because we are far from perfect. As long as we have this body, sin will dwell in our flesh. Then, too, we sometimes drive away the Holy Spirit; we fall into sin, like Peter, David, and other holy men. Nevertheless we may always take recourse to this fact, "that our sins are covered," and that "God will not lay them to our charge." Sin is not held against us for Christ's sake. Where Christ and faith are lacking, there is no remission or covering of sins, but only condemnation.

After we have taught faith in Christ, we teach good works. "Since you have found Christ by faith," we say, "begin now to work and do well. Love God and your neighbor. Call upon God, give thanks unto Him, praise Him, confess Him. These are good works. Let them flow from a cheerful heart, because you have remission of sin in Christ."

When crosses and afflictions come our way, we bear them patiently. "For Christ's yoke is easy, and His burden is light." When sin has been pardoned, and the conscience has been eased of its dreadful load, a Christian can endure all things in Christ.

To give a short definition of a Christian: A Christian is not somebody who has no sin, but somebody against whom God no longer chalks sin, because of his faith in Christ. This doctrine brings comfort to consciences in serious trouble. When a person is a Christian he is above law and sin. When the Law accuses him, and sin wants to drive the wits out of him, a Christian looks to Christ. A Christian is free. He has no master except Christ. A Christian is greater than the whole world.

Verse 16. *Even we have believed in Jesus Christ, that we might be justified.*

The true way of becoming a Christian is to be justified by faith in Jesus Christ, and not by the works of the Law.

We know that we must also teach good works, but they must be taught in their proper turn, when the discussion is concerning works and not the article of justification.

Here the question arises, by what means are we justified? We answer with Paul, "By faith only in Christ are we pronounced righteous, and not by works." Not that we reject good works. Far from it. But we will not allow ourselves to be removed from the anchorage of our salvation.

The Law is a good thing. But when the discussion is about justification, then is no time to drag in the Law. When we discuss justification we ought to speak of Christ and the benefits He has brought us.

Christ is no sheriff. He is "the Lamb of God, which taketh away the sin of the world" (John 1:29).

Verse 16. *That we might be justified by the faith of Christ, and not by the works of the Law.*

We do not mean to say that the Law is bad. Only it is not able to justify us. To be at peace with God, we have need of a far better mediator than Moses or the Law. We must know that we are nothing. We must understand that we are merely beneficiaries and recipients of the treasures of Christ.

So far, the words of Paul were addressed to Peter. Now Paul turns to the Galatians and makes this summary statement:

Verse 16. *For by the works of the law shall no flesh be justified.*

By the term "flesh" Paul does not understand manifest vices. Such sins he usually calls by their proper names, as adultery, fornication, etc. By "flesh" Paul understands what Jesus meant in the third chapter of John, "That which is born of the flesh is flesh" (John 3:6). "Flesh" here means the whole nature of man, inclusive of reason and instincts. "This flesh," says Paul, "is not justified by the works of the law."

The papists do not believe this. They say, "A person who performs this good deed or that, deserves the forgiveness of his sins. A person who joins this or that holy order, has the promise of everlasting life."

To me it is a miracle that the Church, so long surrounded by vicious sects, has been able to survive at all. God must have been able to call a few who in their failure to discover any good in themselves to cite against the wrath and judgment of God, simply took to the suffering and death of Christ, and were saved by this simple faith.

Nevertheless God has punished the contempt of the Gospel and of Christ on the part of the papists, by turning them over to a reprobate state of mind in which they reject the Gospel, and receive with gusto the abominable rules, ordinances, and traditions of men in preference to the Word of God, until they went so far as to forbid marriage. God punished them justly, because they blasphemed the only Son of God.

This is, then, our general conclusion: "By the works of the law shall no flesh be justified."

Verse 17. *But if, while we seek to be justified by Christ, we ourselves also are found sinners, is therefore Christ the minister of sin? God forbid.*

Either we are not justified by Christ, or we are not justified by the Law. The fact is, we are justified by Christ. Hence, we are not justified by the Law. If we observe the Law in order to be justified, or after having been justified by Christ, we think we must further be justified by the Law, we convert Christ into a legislator and a minister of sin.

"What are these false apostles doing?" Paul cries. "They are turning Law into grace, and grace into Law. They are changing Moses into Christ, and Christ into Moses. By teaching that besides Christ and His righteousness the performance of the Law is necessary unto salvation, they put the Law in the place of Christ, they attribute to the Law the power to save, a power that belongs to Christ only."

The papists quote the words of Christ: "If thou wilt enter into life, keep the commandments" (Matt. 19:17). With His own words they deny Christ and abolish faith in Him. Christ is made to lose His good name, His office, and His glory, and is demoted to the status of a law enforcer, reproving, terrifying, and chasing poor sinners around.

The proper office of Christ is to raise the sinner, and extricate him from his sins.

Papists and Anabaptists deride us because we so earnestly require faith. "Faith," they say, "makes men reckless." What do these law-workers know about faith, when they are so busy calling people back from baptism, from faith, from the promises of Christ to the Law?

With their doctrine these lying sects of perdition deface the benefits of Christ to this day. They rob Christ of His glory as the Justifier of mankind and cast Him into the role of a minister of sin. They are like the false apostles. There is not a single one among them who knows the difference between law and grace.

We can tell the difference. We do not here and now argue whether we ought to do good works, or whether the Law is any good, or whether the Law ought to be kept at all. We will discuss these questions some other time. We are now concerned with justification. Our opponents refuse to make this distinction. All they can do is to bellow that good works ought to be done. We know that. We know that good works ought to be done, but we will talk about that when the proper time comes. Now we are dealing with justification, and here good works should not be so much as mentioned.

Paul's argument has often comforted me. He argues: "If we who have been justified by Christ are counted unrighteous, why seek justification in Christ at all? If we are justified by the Law, tell me, what has Christ achieved by His death, by His preaching, by His victory over sin and death? Either we are justified by Christ, or we are made worse sinners by Him."

The Sacred Scriptures, particularly those of the New Testament, make frequent mention of faith in Christ. "Whosoever believeth in him is saved, shall not perish, shall have everlasting life, is not judged," etc. In open contradiction to the Scriptures, our opponents misquote, "He that believeth in Christ is condemned, because he has faith without works." Our opponents turn everything topsy-turvy. They make Christ over into a murderer, and Moses into a savior. Is not this horrible blasphemy?

Verse 17. Is therefore Christ the minister of sin?

This is Hebrew phraseology, also used by Paul in II Corinthians, chapter 3. There Paul speaks of two ministers: The minister of the letter, and the minister of the spirit; the minister of the Law, and the minister of grace; the minister of death, and the minister of life. "Moses," says Paul, "is the minister of the Law, of sin, wrath, death, and condemnation."

Whoever teaches that good works are indispensable unto salvation, that to gain heaven a person must suffer afflictions and follow the example of Christ and of the saints, is a minister of the Law, of sin, wrath, and of death, for the conscience knows how impossible it is for a person to fulfill the Law. Why, the Law makes trouble even for those who have the Holy Spirit. What will not the Law do in the case of the wicked who do not even have the Holy Spirit?

The Law requires perfect obedience. It condemns all do not accomplish the will of God. But show me a person who is able to render perfect obedience. The Law cannot justify. It can only condemn according to the passage: "Cursed is every one that continueth not in all things which are written in the book of the law to do them."

Paul has good reason for calling the minister of the Law the minister of sin, for the Law reveals our sinfulness. The realization of sin in turn frightens the heart and drives it to despair. Therefore all exponents of the Law and of works deserve to be called tyrants and oppressors.

The purpose of the Law is to reveal sin. That this is the purpose of the Law can be seen from the account of the giving of the Law as reported in the nineteenth and twentieth chapters of Exodus. Moses brought the people out of their tents to have God speak to them personally from a cloud. But the people trembled with fear, fled, and standing aloof they begged Moses: "Speak thou with us, and we will hear: but let not God speak with us, lest we die." The proper office of the Law is to lead us out of our tents, in other words, out of the security of our self-trust, into the presence of God, that we may perceive His anger at our sinfulness.

All who say that faith alone in Christ does not justify a person, convert Christ into a minister of sin, a teacher of the Law, and a cruel tyrant who requires the impossible. All merit-seekers take Christ for a new lawgiver.

In conclusion, if the Law is the minister of sin, it is at the same time the minister of wrath and death. As the Law reveals sin it fills a person with the fear of death and condemnation. Eventually the conscience wakes up to the fact that God is angry. If God is angry with you, He will destroy and condemn you forever. Unable to stand the thought of the wrath and judgment of God, many a person commits suicide.

Verse 17. God forbid.

Christ is not the minister of sin, but the Dispenser of righteousness and the Giver of life. Christ is Lord over law, sin and death. All who believe in Him are delivered from law, sin and death.

The Law drives us away from God, but Christ reconciles God unto us, for "He is the Lamb of God, that taketh away the sins of the world." Now if the sin of the world is taken away, it is taken away from me. If sin is taken away, the wrath of God and His condemnation are also taken away. Let us practice this blessed conviction.

Verse 18. For if I build again the things which I destroyed, I make myself a transgressor.

"I have not preached to the end that I build again the

things which I destroyed. If I should do so, I would not only be laboring in vain, but I would make myself guilty of a great wrong. By the ministry of the Gospel I have destroyed sin, heaviness of heart, wrath, and death. I have abolished the Law, so that it should not bother your conscience any more. Should I now once again establish the Law, and set up the rule of Moses? This is exactly what I should be doing, if I would urge circumcision and the performance of the Law as necessary unto salvation. Instead of righteousness and life, I would restore sin and death."

By the grace of God we know that we are justified through faith in Christ alone. We do not mingle law and grace, faith and works. We keep them far apart. Let every true Christian mark the distinction between law and grace, and mark it well.

We must not drag good works into the article of justification as the monks do who maintain that not only good works, but also the punishment which evildoers suffer for their wicked deeds, deserve everlasting life. When a criminal is brought to the place of execution, the monks try to comfort him in this manner: "You want to die willingly and patiently, and then you will merit remission of your sins and eternal life." What cruelty is this, that a wretched thief, murderer, robber should be so miserably misguided in his extreme distress, that at the very point of death he should be denied the sweet promises of Christ, and directed to hope for pardon of his sins in the willingness and patience with which he is about to suffer death for his crimes? The monks are showing him the paved way to hell.

These hypocrites do not know the first thing about grace, the Gospel, or Christ. They retain the appearance and the name of the Gospel and of Christ for a decoy only. In their confessional writings faith or the merit of Christ are never mentioned. In their writings they play up the merits of man, as can readily be seen from the following form of absolution used among the monks.

"God forgive thee, brother. The merit of the passion of our Lord Jesus Christ, and of the blessed Saint Mary, always a virgin, and of all the saints; the merit of thy order, the strictness of thy religion, the humility of thy profession, the contrition of thy heart, the good works thou hast done and shalt do for the love of our Lord Jesus Christ, be available unto thee for the remission of thy sins, the increase of thy worth and grace, and the reward of everlasting life. Amen."

True, the merit of Christ is mentioned in this formula of absolution. But if you look closer you will notice that Christ's merit is belittled, while monkish merits are aggrandized. They confess Christ with their lips, and at the same time deny His power to save. I myself was at one time entangled in this error. I thought Christ was a judge and had to be pacified by a strict adherence to the rules of my order. But now I give thanks unto God, the Father of all mercies, who has called me out of darkness into the light of His glorious Gospel, and has granted unto me the saving knowledge of Christ Jesus, my Lord.

We conclude with Paul, that we are justified by faith in Christ, without the Law. Once a person has been justified by Christ, he will not be unproductive of good, but as a good tree he will bring forth good fruit. A believer has the Holy Spirit, and the Holy Spirit will not permit a person to remain idle, but will put him to work and stir him up to the love of God, to patient suffering in affliction, to prayer, thanksgiving, to the habit of charity towards all men.

Verse 19. *For I through the law am dead to the law, that I might live unto God.*

This cheering form of speech is frequently met with in the Scriptures, particularly in the writings of St. Paul, when the Law is set against the Law, and sin is made to oppose sin, and death is arrayed against death, and hell is turned loose against hell, as in the following quotations: "Thou hast led captivity captive," Psalm 68:18. "O death, I will be thy plagues; O grave, I will be thy destruction," Hosea 13:14. "And for sin, condemned sin in the flesh," Romans 8:3.

Here Paul plays the Law against the Law, as if to say: "The Law of Moses condemns me; but I have another law, the law of grace and liberty which condemns the accusing Law of Moses."

On first sight Paul seems to be advancing a strange and ugly heresy. He says, "I am dead to the law, that I might live unto God." The false apostles said the very opposite. They said, "If you do not live to the law, you are dead unto God."

The doctrine of our opponents is similar to that of the false apostles in Paul's day. Our opponents teach, "If you want to live unto God, you must live after the Law, for it is written, Do this and thou shalt live." Paul, on the other hand, teaches, "We cannot live unto God unless we are dead unto the Law." If we are dead unto the Law, the Law can have no power over us.

Paul does not only refer to the Ceremonial Law, but to the whole Law. We are not to think that the Law is wiped out. It stays. It continues to operate in the wicked. But a Christian is dead to the Law. For example, Christ by His resurrection became free from the grave, and yet the grave remains. Peter was delivered from prison, yet the prison remains. The Law is abolished as far as I am concerned, when it has driven me into the arms of Christ. Yet the Law continues to exist and to function. But it no longer exists for me.

"I have nothing to do with the Law," cries Paul. He could not have uttered anything more devastating to the prestige of the Law. He declares that he does not care for the Law, that he does not intend ever to be justified by the Law.

To be dead to the Law means to be free of the Law. What right, then, has the Law to accuse me, or to hold anything against me? When you see a person squirming in the clutches of the Law, say to him: "Brother, get things straight. You let the Law talk to your conscience. Make it talk to your flesh. Wake up, and believe in Jesus Christ, the Conqueror of Law and sin. Faith in Christ will lift you high above the Law into the heaven of grace. Though Law and sin remain, they no longer concern you, because you are dead to the Law and dead to sin."

Blessed is the person who knows how to use this truth in times of distress. He can talk. He can say: "Mr. Law, go ahead and accuse me as much as you like. I know I have committed many sins, and I continue to sin daily. But that does not bother me. You have got to shout louder, Mr. Law. I am deaf, you know. Talk as much as you like, I am dead to you. If you want to talk to me about my sins, go and talk to my flesh. Belabor that, but don't talk to my conscience. My conscience is a lady and a queen, and has nothing to do with the likes of you, because my conscience lives to Christ under another law, a new and better law, the law of grace."

We have two propositions: To live unto the Law, is to die unto God. To die unto the Law, is to live unto God. These two propositions go against reason. No law-worker can ever understand them. But see to it that you understand them. The Law can never justify and save a sinner. The Law can only accuse, terrify, and kill him. Therefore to live unto the Law is to die unto God. Vice versa, to die unto the Law is to live unto God. If you want to live unto God, bury the Law, and find life through faith in Christ Jesus.

We have enough arguments right here to conclude that justification is by faith alone. How can the Law effect our justification, when Paul so plainly states that we must be dead to the Law if we want to live unto God? If we are dead to the Law and the Law is dead to us, how can it possibly contribute anything to our justification? There is nothing left for us but to be justified by faith alone.

This nineteenth verse is loaded with consolation. It fortifies a person against every danger. It allows you to argue like this:

"I confess I have sinned."
"Then God will punish you."
"No, He will not do that."
"Why not? Does not the Law say so?"
"I have nothing to do with the Law."
"How so?"
"I have another law, the law of liberty."
"What do you mean—'liberty'?"
"The liberty of Christ, for Christ has made me free from the Law that held me down. That Law is now in prison itself, held captive by grace and liberty."

By faith in Christ a person may gain such sure and sound comfort, that he need not fear the devil, sin, death, or any evil. "Sir Devil," he may say, "I am not afraid of you. I have a Friend whose name is Jesus Christ, in whom I believe. He has abolished the Law, condemned sin, vanquished death, and destroyed hell for me. He is bigger than you, Satan. He has licked you, and holds you down. You cannot hurt me." This is the faith that overcomes the devil.

Paul manhandles the Law. He treats the Law as if it were a thief and a robber. He treats the Law as contemptible to the conscience, in order that those who believe in Christ may take courage to defy the Law, and say: "Mr. Law, I am a sinner. What are you going to do about it?"

Or take death. Christ is risen from death. Why should we now fear the grave? Against my death I set another death, or rather life, my life in Christ.

Oh, the sweet names of Jesus! He is called my law against the Law, my sin against sin, my death against death. Translated, it means that He is my righteousness, my life, my everlasting salvation. For this reason was He made the law of the Law, the sin of sin, the death of death, that He might redeem me from the curse of the Law. He permitted the Law to accuse Him, sin to condemn Him, and death to take Him, to abolish the Law, to condemn sin, and to destroy death for me.

This peculiar form of speech sounds much sweeter than if Paul had said: "I through liberty am dead to the law." By putting it in this way, "I through the law am dead to the law," he opposes one law with another law, and has them fight it out.

In this masterly fashion Paul draws our attention away from the Law, sin, death, and every evil, and centers it upon Christ.

Verse 20. I am crucified with Christ.

Christ is Lord over the Law, because He was crucified unto the Law. I also am lord over the Law, because by faith I am crucified with Christ.

Paul does not here speak of crucifying the flesh, but he speaks of that higher crucifying wherein sin, devil, and death are crucified in Christ and in me. By my faith in Christ I am crucified with Christ. Hence these evils are crucified and dead unto me.

Verse 20. Nevertheless I live.

"I do not mean to create the impression as though I did not live before this. But in reality I first live now, now that I have been delivered from the Law, from sin, and death. Being crucified with Christ and dead unto the Law, I may now rise unto a new and better life."

We must pay close attention to Paul's way of speaking. He says that we are crucified and dead unto the Law. The fact is, the Law is crucified and dead unto us. Paul purposely speaks that way in order to increase the portion of our comfort.

Verse 20. Yet not I.

Paul explains what constitutes true Christian righteousness. True Christian righteousness is the righteousness of Christ who lives in us. We must look away from our own person. Christ and my conscience must become one, so that I can see nothing else but Christ crucified and raised from the dead for me. If I keep on looking at myself, I am gone.

If we lose sight of Christ and begin to consider our past, we simply go to pieces. We must turn our eyes to the brazen serpent, Christ crucified, and believe with all our heart that He is our righteousness and our life. For Christ, on whom our eyes are fixed, in whom we live, who lives in us, is Lord over Law, sin, death, and all evil.

Verse 20. But Christ liveth in me.

"Thus I live," the Apostle starts out. But presently he corrects himself, saying, "Yet not I, but Christ liveth in me." He is the form of my perfection. He embellishes my faith.

Since Christ is now living in me, He abolishes the Law, condemns sin, and destroys death in me. These foes vanish in His presence. Christ abiding in me drives out every evil. This union with Christ delivers me from the demands of the Law, and separates me from my sinful self. As long as I abide in Christ, nothing can hurt me.

Christ domiciling in me, the old Adam has to stay outside and remain subject to the Law. Think what grace, righteousness, life, peace, and salvation there is in me, thanks to that inseparable conjunction between Christ and me through faith!

Paul has a peculiar style, a celestial way of speaking. "I live," he says, "I live not; I am dead, I am not dead; I am a sinner, I am not a sinner; I have the Law, I have no Law." When we look at ourselves we find plenty of sin. But when we look at Christ, we have no sin. Whenever we separate the person of Christ from our own person, we live under the Law and not in Christ; we are condemned by the Law, dead before God.

Faith connects you so intimately with Christ, that He and you become as it were one person. As such you may boldly say: "I am now one with Christ. Therefore Christ's righteousness, victory, and life are mine." On the other hand, Christ may say: "I am that big sinner. His sins and his death are mine, because he is joined to me, and I to him."

Whenever remission of sins is freely proclaimed, people misinterpret it according to Romans 3:8, "Let us do evil, that good may come." As soon as people hear that we are not justified by the Law, they reason maliciously: "Why, then let us reject the Law. If grace abounds, where sin abounds, let us abound in sin, that grace may all the more abound." People who reason thus are reckless. They make sport of the Scriptures and slander the sayings of the Holy Ghost.

However, there are others who are not malicious, only weak, who may take offense when told that Law and good works are unnecessary for salvation. These must be instructed as to why good works do not justify, and from what motives good works must be done. Good works are not the cause, but the fruit of righteousness. When we have become righteous, then first are we able and willing to do good. The tree makes the apple; the apple does not make the tree.

Verse 20. And the life which I now live in the flesh I live by the faith of the Son of God.

Paul does not deny the fact that he is living in the flesh. He performs the natural functions of the flesh. But he says that this is not his real life. His life in the flesh is not a life after the flesh.

"I live by the faith of the Son of God," he says. "My speech is no longer directed by the flesh, but by the Holy Ghost. My sight is no longer governed by the flesh, but by the Holy Ghost. My hearing is no longer determined by the flesh, but by the Holy Ghost. I cannot teach, write, pray, or give thanks without the instrumentality of the flesh; yet these activities do not proceed from the flesh, but from God."

A Christian uses earthly means like any unbeliever. Outwardly they look alike. Nevertheless there is a great difference between them. I may live in the flesh, but I do not live after the flesh. I do my living now "by the faith of the Son of God." Paul had the same voice, the same tongue, before and after his conversion. Before his conversion his tongue uttered blasphemies. But after his conversion his tongue spoke a spiritual, heavenly language.

We may now understand how spiritual life originates. It enters the heart by faith. Christ reigns in the heart with His Holy Spirit, who sees, hears, speaks, works, suffers, and does all things in and through us over the protest and the resistance of the flesh.

Verse 20. Who loved me, and gave himself for me.

The sophistical papists assert that a person is able by natural strength to love God long before grace has entered his heart, and to perform works of real merit. They believe they are able to fulfill the commandments of God. They believe they are able to do more than God expects of them, so that they are in a position to sell their superfluous merits to laymen, thereby saving themselves and others. They are saving nobody. On the contrary, they abolish the Gospel, they deride, deny, and blaspheme Christ, and call upon themselves the wrath of God. This is what they get for living in their own righteousness, and not in the faith of the Son of God.

The papists will tell you to do the best you can, and God will give you His grace. They have a rhyme for it:

"God will no more require of man,
Than of himself perform he can."

This may hold true in ordinary civic life. But the papists apply it to the spiritual realm where a person can perform nothing but sin, because he is sold under sin.

Our opponents go even further than that. They say, nature is depraved, but the qualities of nature are untainted. Again we say: This may hold true in everyday life, but not in the spiritual life. In spiritual matters a person is by nature full of darkness, error, ignorance, malice, and perverseness in will and in mind.

In view of this, Paul declares that Christ began and not we. "He loved me, and gave Himself for me. He found in me no right mind and no good will. But the good Lord had mercy upon me. Out of pure kindness He loved me, loved me so that He gave Himself for me, that I should be free from the Law, from sin, devil, and death."

The words, "The Son of God who loved me, and gave Himself for me," are so many thunderclaps and lightning bolts of protest from heaven against the righteousness of the Law. The wickedness, error, darkness, ignorance in my mind and my will were so great, that it was quite impossible for me to be saved by any other means than by the inestimable price of Christ's death.

Let us count the price. When you hear that such an enormous price was paid for you, will you still come along with your cowl, your shaven pate, your chastity, your obedience, your poverty, your works, your merits? What do you want with all these trappings? What good are the works of all men, and all the pains of the martyrs, in comparison with the pains of the Son of God dying on the Cross, so that there was not a drop of His precious blood, but it was all shed for your sins. If you could properly evaluate this incomparable price, you would throw all your ceremonies, vows, works, and merits into the ash can. What awful presumption to imagine that there is any work good enough to pacify God, when to pacify God required the invaluable price of the death and blood of His own and only Son?

Verse 20. *For me.*

Who is this "me"? I, wretched and damnable sinner, dearly beloved of the Son of God. If I could by work or merit love the Son of God and come to Him, why should He have sacrificed Himself for me? This shows how the papists ignore the Scriptures, particularly the doctrine of faith. If they had paid any attention at all to these words, that it was absolutely necessary for the Son of God to be given into death for me, they would never have invented so many hideous heresies.

I always say, there is no remedy against the sects, no power to resist them, except this article of Christian righteousness. If we lose this article we shall never be able to combat errors or sects. What business have they to make such a fuss about works or merits? If I, a condemned sinner, could have been purchased and redeemed by any other price, why should the Son of God have given Himself for me? Just because there was no other price in heaven and on earth big and good enough, was it necessary for the Son of God to be delivered for me. This He did out of His great love for me, for the Apostle says, "Who loved me."

Did the Law ever love me? Did the Law ever sacrifice itself for me? Did the Law ever die for me? On the contrary, it accuses me, it frightens me, it drives me crazy. Somebody else saved me from the Law, from sin and death unto eternal life. That Somebody is the Son of God, to whom be praise and glory forever.

Hence, Christ is no Moses, no tyrant, no lawgiver, but the Giver of grace, the Savior, full of mercy. In short, He is no less than infinite mercy and ineffable goodness, bountifully giving Himself for us. Visualize Christ in these His true colors. I do not say that it is easy. Even in the present diffusion of the Gospel light, I have much trouble to see Christ as Paul portrays Him. So deeply has the diseased opinion that Christ is a lawgiver sunk into my bones. You younger men are a good deal better off than we who are old. You have never become infected with the nefarious errors on which I suckled all my youth, until at the mention of the name of Christ I shivered with fear. You, I say, who are young may learn to know Christ in all His sweetness.

For Christ is Joy and Sweetness to a broken heart. Christ is a Lover of poor sinners, and such a Lover that He gave Himself for us. Now if this is true, and it is true, then are we never justified by our own righteousness.

Read the words "me" and "for me" with great emphasis. Print this "me" with capital letters in your heart, and do not ever doubt that you belong to the number of those who are meant by this "me." Christ did not only love Peter and Paul. The same love He felt for them He feels for us. If we cannot deny that we are sinners, we cannot deny that Christ died for our sins.

Verse 21. *I do not frustrate the grace of God.*

Paul is now getting ready for the second argument of his Epistle, to the effect that to seek justification by works of the Law, is to reject the grace of God. I ask you, what sin can be more horrible than to reject the grace of God, and to refuse the righteousness of Christ? It is bad enough that we are wicked sinners and transgressors of all the commandments of God; on top of that to refuse the grace of God and the remission of sins offered unto us by Christ, is the worst sin of all, the sin of sins. That is the limit. There is no sin which Paul and the other apostles detested more than when a person despises the grace of God in Christ Jesus. Still there is no sin more common. That is why Paul can get so angry at the Antichrist, because he snubs Christ, rebuffs the grace of God, and refuses the merit of Christ. What else would you call it but spitting in Christ's face, pushing Christ to the side, usurping Christ's throne, and to say: "I am going to justify you people; I am going to save you." By what means? By masses, pilgrimages, pardons, merits, etc. For this is Antichrist's doctrine: Faith is no good, unless it is reinforced by works. By this abominable doctrine Antichrist has spoiled, darkened, and buried the benefit of Christ, and in place of the grace of Christ and His Kingdom, he has established the doctrine of works and the kingdom of ceremonies.

We despise the grace of God when we observe the Law for the purpose of being justified. The Law is good, holy, and profitable, but it does not justify. To keep the Law in order to be justified means to reject grace, to deny Christ, to despise His sacrifice, and to be lost.

Verse 21. *For if righteousness come by the law, then Christ is dead in vain.*

Did Christ die, or did He not die? Was His death worthwhile, or was it not? If His death was worthwhile, it follows that righteousness does not come by the Law. Why was Christ born anyway? Why was He crucified? Why did He suffer? Why did He love me and give Himself for me? It was all done to no purpose if righteousness is to be had by the Law.

Or do you think that God spared not His Son, but delivered Him for us all, for the fun of it? Before I would admit anything like that, I would consign the holiness of the saints and of the angels to hell.

To reject the grace of God is a common sin, of which everybody is guilty who sees any righteousness in himself or in his deeds. And the Pope is the sole author of this iniquity. Not content to spoil the Gospel of Christ, he has filled the world with his cursed traditions, e.g., his bulls and indulgences.

We will always affirm with Paul that either Christ died in vain, or else the Law cannot justify us. But Christ did not suffer and die in vain. Hence, the Law does not justify.

If my salvation was so difficult to accomplish that it necessitated the death of Christ, then all my works, all the righteousness of the Law, are good for nothing. How can I buy for a penny what cost a million dollars? The Law is a penny's worth when you compare it with Christ. Should I be so stupid as to reject the righteousness of Christ which cost me nothing, and slave like a fool to achieve the righteousness of the Law which God disdains?

Man's own righteousness is in the last analysis a despising and rejecting of the grace of God. No combination of words can do justice to such an outrage. It is an insult to say that any man died in vain. But to say that Christ died in vain is a deadly insult. To say that Christ died in vain is to make His resurrection, His victory, His glory, His kingdom, heaven, earth, God Himself, of no purpose and benefit whatever.

That is enough to set any person against the righteousness of the Law and all the trimmings of men's own righteousness, the orders of monks and friars, and their superstitions.

Who would not detest his own vows, his cowls, his shaven crown, his bearded traditions, yes, the very Law of Moses, when he hears that for such things he rejected the grace of God and the death of Christ. It seems that such a horrible wickedness could not enter a man's heart, that he should reject the grace of God, and despise the death of Christ. And yet this atrocity is all too common. Let us be warned. Everyone who seeks righteousness without Christ, either by works, merits, satisfactions, actions, or by the Law, rejects the grace of God, and despises the death of Christ.

GALATIONS 3

Verse 1. O foolish Galatians.

The Apostle Paul manifests his apostolic care for the Galatians. Sometimes he entreats them, then again he reproaches them, in accordance with his own advice to Timothy: "Preach the word; be instant in season, out of season; reprove, rebuke, exhort."

In the midst of his discourse on Christian righteousness Paul breaks off, and turns to address the Galatians. "O foolish Galatians," he cries. "I have brought you the true Gospel, and you received it with eagerness and gratitude. Now all of a sudden you drop the Gospel. What has got into you?"

Paul reproves the Galatians rather sharply when he calls them "fools, bewitched, and disobedient." Whether he is indignant or sorry, I cannot say. He may be both. It is the duty of a Christian pastor to reprove the people committed to his charge. Of course, his anger must not flow from malice, but from affection and a real zeal for Christ.

There is no question that Paul is disappointed. It hurts him to think that his Galatians showed so little stability. We can hear him say: "I am sorry to hear of your troubles, and disappointed in you for the disgraceful part you played." I say rather much on this point to save Paul from the charge that he railed upon the churches, contrary to the spirit of the Gospel.

A certain distance and coolness can be noted in the title with which the Apostle addresses the Galatians. He does not now address them as his brethren, as he usually does. He addresses them as Galatians in order to remind them of their national trait to be foolish.

We have here an example of bad traits that often cling to individual Christians and entire congregations. Grace does not suddenly transform a Christian into a new and perfect creature. Dregs of the old and natural corruption remain. The Spirit of God cannot at once overcome human deficiency. Sanctification takes time.

Although the Galatians had been enlightened by the Holy Spirit through the preaching of faith, something of their national trait of foolishness plus their original depravity clung to them. Let no man think that once he has received faith, he can presently be converted into a faultless creature. The leavings of old vices will stick to him, be he ever so good a Christian.

Verse 1. *Who hath bewitched you, that ye should not obey the truth?*

Paul calls the Galatians foolish and bewitched. In the fifth chapter he mentions sorcery among the works of the flesh, declaring that witchcraft and sorcery are real manifestations and legitimate activities of the devil. We are all exposed to the influence of the devil, because he is the prince and god of the world in which we live.

Satan is clever. He does not only bewitch men in a crude manner, but also in a more artful fashion. He bedevils the minds of men with hideous fallacies. Not only is he able to deceive the self-assured, but even those who profess the true Christian faith. There is not one among us who is not at times seduced by Satan into false beliefs.

This accounts for the many new battles we have to wage nowadays. But the attacks of the old Serpent are not without profit to us, for they confirm our doctrine and strengthen our faith in Christ. Many a time we were wrestled down in these conflicts with Satan, but Christ has always triumphed and always will triumph. Do not think that the Galatians were the only ones to be bewitched by the devil. Let us realize that we too may be seduced by Satan.

Verse 1. *Who hath bewitched you?*

In this sentence Paul excuses the Galatians, while he blames the false apostles for the apostasy of the Galatians. As if he were saying: "I know your defection was not willful. The devil sent the false apostles to you, and they talked you into believing that you are justified by the Law. With this our epistle we endeavor to undo the damage which the false apostles have inflicted upon you."

Like Paul, we struggle with the Word of God against the fanatical Anabaptists of our day; and our efforts are not entirely in vain. The trouble is there are many who refuse to be instructed. They will not listen to reason; they will not listen to the Scriptures, because they are bewitched by the tricky devil who can make a lie look like the truth.

Since the devil has this uncanny ability to make us believe a lie until we would swear a thousand times it were the truth, we must not be proud, but walk in fear and humility, and call upon the Lord Jesus to save us from temptation.

Although I am a doctor of divinity, and have preached Christ and fought His battles for a long time, I know from personal experience how difficult it is to hold fast to the truth. I cannot always shake off Satan. I cannot always apprehend Christ as the Scriptures portray Him. Sometimes the devil distorts Christ to my vision. But thanks be to God, who keeps us in His Word, in faith, and in prayer.

The spiritual witchery of the devil creates in the heart a wrong idea of Christ. Those who share the opinion that a person is justified by the works of the Law, are simply bewitched. Their belief goes against faith and Christ.

Verse 1. *That ye should not obey the truth.*

Paul incriminates the Galatians in worse failure. "You are so bewitched that you no longer obey the truth. I fear many of you have strayed so far that you will never return to the truth."

The apostasy of the Galatians is a fine indorsement of the Law, all right. You may preach the Law ever so fervently; if the preaching of the Gospel does not accompany it, the Law will never produce true conversion and heartfelt repentance. We do not mean to say that the preaching of the Law is without value, but it only serves to bring home to us the wrath of God. The Law bows a person down. It takes the Gospel and the preaching of faith in Christ to raise and save a person.

Verse 1. *Before whose eyes Jesus Christ hath been evidently set forth.*

Paul's increasing severity becomes apparent as he reminds the Galatians that they disobeyed the truth in defiance of the vivid description he had given them of Christ. So vividly had he described Christ to them that they could almost see and handle Him. As if Paul were to say: "No artist with all his colors could have pictured Christ to you as vividly as I have pictured Him to you by my preaching. Yet you permitted yourselves to be seduced to the extent that you disobeyed the truth of Christ."

Verse 1. *Crucifed among you.*

"You have not only rejected the grace of God, you have shamefully crucified Christ among you." Paul employs the same phraseology in Hebrews 6:6: "Seeing they crucify to themselves the Son of God afresh, and put him to an open shame."

It should make any person afraid to hear Paul say that those who seek to be justified by the Law, not only deny Christ, but also crucify Him anew. If those who seek to be justified by the Law and its works are crucifiers of Christ, what are they, I like to know, who seek salvation by the filthy rags of their own work-righteousness?

Can there be anything more horrible than the papacy, an alliance of people who crucify Christ in themselves, in the Church, and in the hearts of the believers?

Of all the diseased and vicious doctrines of the papacy the worst is this: "If you want to serve God you must earn your own remission of sins and everlasting life, and in addition help others to obtain salvation by giving them the benefit of your extra work-holiness." Monks, friars, and all the rest of them brag that besides the ordinary requirements common to all Christians, they do the works of supererogation, i.e., the performance of more than is required. This is certainly a fiendish illusion.

No wonder Paul employs such sharp language in his effort to recall the Galatians from the doctrine of the false apostles. He says to them: "Don't you realize what you have done? You have crucified Christ anew because you seek salvation by the Law."

True, Christ can no longer be crucified in person, but He is crucified in us when we reject grace, faith, free remission of sins and endeavor to be justified by our own works, or by the works of the Law.

The Apostle is incensed at the presumptuousness of any person who thinks he can perform the Law of God to his own salvation. He charges that person with the atrocity of crucifying anew the Son of God.

Verse 2. *This only would I learn of you, Received ye the Spirit by the works of the law, or by the hearing of faith?*

There is a touch of irony in these words of the Apostle. "Come on now, my smart Galatians, you who all of a sudden have become doctors, while I seem to be your pupil: Received ye the Holy Ghost by the works of the Law, or by the preaching of the Gospel?" This question gave them something to think about, because their own experience contradicted them.

"You cannot say that you received the Holy Spirit by the Law. As long as you were servants of the Law, you never received the Holy Ghost. Nobody ever heard of the Holy Ghost being given to anybody, be he doctor or dunce, as a result of the preaching of the Law. In your own case, you have not only learned the Law by heart, you have labored with all your might to perform it. You most of all should have received the Holy Ghost by the Law, if that were possible. You cannot show me that this ever happened. But as soon as the Gospel came your way, you received the Holy Ghost by the simple hearing of faith, before you ever had a chance to do a single good deed." Luke verifies this statement of Paul in the Book of Acts: "While Peter yet spake these words, the Holy Ghost fell on all them which heard the word" (Acts 10:44). "And as I began to speak, the Holy Ghost fell on them, as on us at the beginning" (Acts 11:15).

Try to appreciate the force of Paul's argument which

is so often repeated in the Book of Acts. That Book was written for the express purpose of verifying Paul's assertion, that the Holy Ghost comes upon men, not in response to the preaching of the Law, but in response to the preaching of the Gospel. When Peter preached Christ at the first Pentecost, the Holy Ghost fell upon the hearers, "and the same day there were added unto them about three thousand souls." Cornelius received the Holy Ghost while Peter was speaking of Christ. "The Holy Ghost fell on all of them which heard the word." These are actual experiences that cannot very well be denied. When Paul and Barnabas returned to Jerusalem and reported what they had been able to accomplish among the Gentiles, the whole Church was astonished, particularly when it heard that the uncircumcised Gentiles had received the Holy Ghost by the preaching of faith in Christ.

Now as God gave the Holy Ghost to the Gentiles without the Law by the simple preaching of the Gospel, so He gave the Holy Ghost also to the Jews, without the Law, through faith alone. If the righteousness of the Law were necessary unto salvation, the Holy Ghost would never have come to the Gentiles, because they did not bother about the Law. Hence the Law does not justify, but faith in Christ justifies.

How was it with Cornelius? Cornelius and his friends whom he had invited over to his house, do nothing but sit and listen. Peter is doing the talking. They just sit and do nothing. The Law is far removed from their thoughts. They burn no sacrifices. They are not at all interested in circumcision. All they do is to sit and listen to Peter. Suddenly the Holy Ghost enters their hearts. His presence is unmistakable, "for they spoke with tongues and magnified God."

Right here we have one more difference between the Law and the Gospel. The Law does not bring on the Holy Ghost. The Gospel, however, brings on the gift of the Holy Ghost, because it is the nature of the Gospel to convey good gifts. The Law and the Gospel are contrary ideas. They have contrary functions and purposes. To endow the Law with any capacity to produce righteousness is to plagiarize the Gospel. The Gospel brings donations. It pleads for open hands to take what is being offered. The Law has nothing to give. It demands, and its demands are impossible.

Our opponents come back at us with Cornelius. Cornelius, they point out, was "a devout man, and one that feared God with all his house, which gave much alms to the people and prayed God always." Because of these qualifications, he merited the forgiveness of sins, and the gift of the Holy Ghost. So reason our opponents.

I answer: Cornelius was a Gentile. You cannot deny it. As a Gentile he was uncircumcised. As a Gentile he did not observe the Law. He never gave the Law any thought. For all that, he was justified and received the Holy Ghost. How can the Law avail anything unto righteousness?

Our opponents are not satisfied. They reply: "Granted that Cornelius was a Gentile and did not receive the Holy Ghost by the Law, yet the text plainly states that he was a devout man who feared God, gave alms, and prayed. Don't you think he deserved the gift of the Holy Ghost?"

I answer: Cornelius had the faith of the fathers who were saved by faith in the Christ to come. If Cornelius had died before Christ, he would have been saved because he believed in the Christ to come. But because the Messiah had already come, Cornelius had to be apprized of the fact. Since Christ has come we cannot be saved by faith in the Christ to come, but we must believe that he has come. The object of Peter's visit was to acquaint Cornelius with the fact that Christ was no longer to be looked for, because He is here.

As to the contention of our opponents that Cornelius deserved grace and the gift of the Holy Ghost, because he was devout and just, we say that these attributes are the characteristics of a spiritual person who already has faith in Christ, and not the characteristics of a Gentile or of natural man. Luke first praises Cornelius for being a devout and God-fearing man, and then Luke mentions the good works, the alms and prayers of Cornelius. Our opponents ignore the sequence of Luke's words. They pounce on this one sentence, "which gave much alms to the people," because it serves their assertion that merit precedes grace. The fact is that Cornelius gave alms and prayed to God because he had faith. And because of his faith in the Christ to come, Peter was delegated to preach unto Cornelius faith in the Christ who had already come. This argument is convincing enough. Cornelius was justified without the Law, therefore the Law cannot justify.

Take the case of Naaman, the Syrian, who was a Gentile and did not belong to the race of Moses. Yet his flesh was cleansed, the God of Israel was revealed unto him, and he received the Holy Ghost. Naaman confessed his faith: "Behold, now I know that there is no God in all the earth, but in Israel" (II Kings 5:15). Naaman does not do a thing. He does not busy himself with the Law. He was never circumcised. That does not mean that his faith was inactive. He said to the Prophet Elisha: "Thy servant will henceforth offer neither burnt offering nor sacrifice unto other gods, but unto the Lord. In this thing the Lord pardon thy servant, that when my master goeth into the house of Rimmon to worship there, and he leaneth on my hand, and I bow myself in the house of Rimmon: when I bow down myself in the house of Rimmon, the Lord pardon thy servant in this thing." What did the Prophet tell him?" "Go in peace." The Jews do not like to hear the prophet say this. "What," they exclaim, "should this heathen be justified without the Law? Should he be made equal to us who are circumcised?"

Long before the time of Moses, God justified men without the Law. He justified many kings of Egypt and Babylonia. He justified Job. Nineveh, that great city, was justified and received the promise of God that He would not destroy the city. Why was Nineveh spared? Not because it fulfilled the Law, but because Nineveh believed the word of God. The Prophet Jonah writes: "So the people of Nineveh believed God, and proclaimed a fast, and put on sackcloth." They repented. Nowhere in the Book of Jonah do you read that the Ninevites received the Law of Moses, or that they were circumcised, or that they offered sacrifices.

All this happened long before Christ was born. If the Gentiles were justified without the Law and quietly received the Holy Spirit at a time when the Law was in full force, why should the Law count unto righteousness now, now that Christ has fulfilled the Law?

And yet many devote much time and labor to the Law, to the decrees of the fathers, and to the traditions of the Pope. Many of these specialists have incapacitated themselves for any kind of work, good or bad, by their rigorous attention to rules and laws. All the same, they could not obtain a quiet conscience and peace in Christ. But the moment the Gospel of Christ touches them, certainty comes to them, and joy, and a right judgment.

I have good reason for enlarging upon this point. The heart of man finds it difficult to believe that so great a treasure as the Holy Ghost is gotten by the mere hearing of faith. The hearer likes to reason like this: Forgiveness of sins, deliverance from death, the gift of the Holy Ghost, everlasting life are grand things. If you want to obtain these priceless benefits, you must engage in correspondingly great efforts. And the devil says, "Amen."

We must learn that forgiveness of sins, Christ, and the Holy Ghost, are freely granted unto us at the preaching of faith, in spite of our sinfulness. We are not to waste time thinking how unworthy we are of the blessings of God. We are to know that it pleased God freely to give us His unspeakable gifts. If He offers His gifts free of charge, why not take them? Why worry about our lack of worthiness? Why not accept gifts with joy and thanksgiving?

Right away foolish reason is once more offended. It scolds us. "When you say that a person can do nothing to obtain the grace of God, you foster carnal security. People become shiftless and will do no good at all. Better not preach this doctrine of faith. Rather urge the people to exert and to exercise themselves in good works, so that the Holy Ghost will feel like coming to them."

What did Jesus say to Martha when she was very "careful and troubled about many things" and could hardly stand to see her sister Mary sitting at the feet of Jesus, just listening? "Martha, Martha," Jesus said, "thou art careful and troubled about many things: but one thing is needful; and Mary hath chosen that good part, which shall not be taken away from her." A person becomes a Christian not by working, but by hearing. The first step to being a Christian is to hear the Gospel. When a person has accepted the Gospel, let him first give thanks unto God with a glad heart, and then let him get busy on the good works to strive for, works that really please God, and not man-made and self-chosen works.

Our opponents regard faith as an easy thing, but I know from personal experience how hard it is to believe. That the Holy Ghost is received by faith, is quickly said, but not so quickly done.

All believers experience this difficulty. They would gladly embrace the Word with a full faith, but the flesh deters them. You see, our reason always thinks it is too easy and cheap to have righteousness, the Holy Spirit, and life everlasting by the mere hearing of the Gospel.

Verse 3. *Are ye so foolish? having begun in the Spirit, are ye now made perfect by the flesh?*

Paul now begins to warn the Galatians against a twofold danger. The first danger is: "Are ye so foolish, that after ye have begun in the Spirit, ye would now end in the flesh?"

"Flesh" stands for the righteousness of reason which seeks justification by the accomplishment of the Law. I am told that I began in the spirit under the papacy, but am ending up in the flesh because I got married. As though single life were a spiritual life, and married life a carnal life. They are silly. All the duties of a Christian husband, e.g., to love his wife, to bring up his children, to govern his family, etc., are the very fruits of the Spirit.

The righteousness of the Law which Paul also terms the righteousness of the flesh is so far from justifying a person that those who once had the Holy Spirit and lost Him, end up in the Law to their complete destruction.

Verse 4. *Have ye suffered so many things in vain?*

The other danger against which the Apostle warns the

Galatians is this: "Have ye suffered so many things in vain?" Paul wants to say: "Consider not only the good start you had and lost, but consider also the many things you have suffered for the sake of the Gospel and for the name of Christ. You have suffered the loss of your possessions, you have borne reproaches, you have passed through many dangers of body and life. You endured much for the name of Christ and you endured it faithfully. But now you have lost everything, the Gospel, faith, and the spiritual benefit of your sufferings for Christ's sake. What a miserable thing to endure so many afflictions for nothing."

Verse 4. *If it be yet in vain.*

The Apostle adds the afterthought: "If it be yet in vain. I do not despair of all hope for you. But if you continue to look to the Law for righteousness, I think you should be told that all your past true worship of God and all the afflictions that you have endured for Christ's sake are going to help you not at all. I do not mean to discourage you altogether. I do hope you will repent and amend."

Verse 5. *He therefore that ministereth to you the Spirit, and worketh miracles among you, doeth he it by the works of the law, or by the hearing of faith?*

This argument based on the experience of the Galatians, pleased the Apostle so well that he returns to it after he had warned them against their twofold danger. "You have not only received the Spirit by the preaching of the Gospel, but by the same Gospel you were enabled to do things." "What things?" we ask. Miracles. At least the Galatians had manifested the striking fruits of faith which true disciples of the Gospel manifested in those days. On one occasion the Apostle wrote: "The kingdom of God is not in word, but in power." This "power" revealed itself not only in readiness of speech, but in demonstrations of the supernatural ability of the Holy Spirit.

When the Gospel is preached unto faith, hope, love, and patience, God gives His wonder-working Spirit. Paul reminds the Galatians of this. "God had not only brought you to faith by my preaching. He had also sanctified you to bring forth the fruits of faith. And one of the fruits of your faith was that you loved me so devotedly that you were willing to pluck out your eyes for me." To love a fellow-man so devotedly as to be ready to bestow upon him money, goods, eyes in order to secure his salvation, such love is the fruit of the Holy Spirit.

"These products of the Spirit you enjoyed before the false apostles misled you," the Apostle reminds the Galatians. "But you haven't manifested any of these fruits under the regime of the Law. How does it come that you do not grow the same fruits now? You no longer teach truly; you do not believe boldly; you do not live well; you do not work hard; you do not bear things patiently. Who has spoiled you that you no longer love me; that you are not now ready to pluck out your eyes for me? What has happened to cool your personal interest in me?"

The same thing happened to me. When I began to proclaim the Gospel, there were many, very many who were delighted with our doctrine and had a good opinion of us. And now? Now they have succeeded in making us so odious to those who formerly loved us that they now hate us like poison.

Paul argues: "Your experience ought to teach you that the fruits of love do not grow on the stump of the Law. You had not virtue prior to the preaching of the Gospel and you have no virtues now under the regime of the false apostles."

We, too, may say to those who misname themselves "evangelical" and flout their new-found liberty: Have you put down the tyranny of the Pope and obtained liberty in Christ through the Anabaptists and other fanatics? Or have you obtained your freedom from us who preach faith in Christ Jesus? If there is any honesty left in them they will have to confess that their freedom dates from the preaching of the Gospel.

Verse 6. *Even as Abraham believed God, and it was accounted to him for righteousness.*

The Apostle next adduces the example of Abraham and reviews the testimony of the Scriptures concerning faith. The first passage is taken from Genesis 15:6: "And he believed in the Lord; and he counted it to him for righteousness." The Apostle makes the most of this passage. Abraham may have enjoyed a good standing with men for his upright life, but not with God. In the sight of God, Abraham was a condemned sinner. That he was justified before God was not due to his own exertions, but due to his faith. The Scriptures expressly state: "Abraham believed in the Lord; and he counted it to him for righteousness."

Paul places the emphasis upon the two words: Abraham believed. Faith in God constitutes the highest worship, the prime duty, the first obedience, and the foremost sacrifice. Without faith God forfeits His glory, wisdom, truth, and mercy in us. The first duty of man is to believe in God and to honor Him with his faith. Faith is truly the height of wisdom, the right kind of righteousness, the only real religion. This will give us an idea of the excellence of faith.

To believe in God as Abraham did is to be right with God because faith honors God. Faith says to God: "I believe what you say."

When we pay attention to reason, God seems to propose impossible matters in the Christian Creed. To reason it seems absurd that Christ should offer His body and blood in the Lord's Supper; that Baptism should be the washing of regeneration; that the dead shall rise; that Christ the Son of God was conceived in the womb of the Virgin Mary, etc. Reason shouts that all this is preposterous. Are you surprised that reason thinks little of faith? Reason thinks it ludicrous that faith should be the foremost service any person can render unto God.

Let your faith supplant reason. Abraham mastered reason by faith in the Word of God. Not as though reason ever yields meekly. It put up a fight against the faith of Abraham. Reason protested that it was absurd to think that Sarah who was ninety years old and barren by nature, should give birth to a son. But faith won the victory and routed reason, that ugly beast and enemy of God. Everyone who by faith slays reason, the world's biggest monster, renders God a real service, a better service than the religions of all races and all the drudgery of meritorious monks can render.

Men fast, pray, watch, suffer. They intend to appease the wrath of God and to deserve God's grace by their exertions. But there is no glory in it for God, because by their exertions these workers pronounce God an unmerciful slave driver, an unfaithful and angry Judge. They despise God, make a liar out of Him, snub Christ and all His benefits; in short they pull God from His throne and perch themselves on it.

Faith truly honors God. And because faith honors God, God counts faith for righteousness.

Christian righteousness is the confidence of the heart in God through Christ Jesus. Such confidence is accounted righteousness for Christ's sake. Two things make for Christian righteousness: Faith in Christ, which is a gift of God; and God's acceptance of this imperfect faith of ours for perfect righteousness. Because of my faith in Christ, God overlooks my distrust, the unwillingness of my spirit, my many other sins. Because the shadow of Christ's wing covers me I have no fear that God will cover all my sins and take my imperfections for perfect righteousness.

God "winks" at my sins and covers them up. God says: "Because you believe in My Son I will forgive your sins until death shall deliver you from the body of sin."

Learn to understand the constitution of your Christian righteousness. Faith is weak, but it means enough to God that He will not lay sin to our charge. He will not punish nor condemn us for it. He will forgive our sins as though they amount to nothing at all. He will do it not because we are worthy of such mercy. He will do it for Jesus' sake in whom we believe.

Paradoxically, a Christian is both right and wrong, holy and profane, an enemy of God and a child of God. These contradictions no person can harmonize who does not understand the true way of salvation. Under the papacy we were told to toil until the feeling of guilt had left us. But the authors of this deranged idea were frequently driven to despair in the hour of death. It would have happened to me, if Christ had not mercifully delivered me from this error.

We comfort the afflicted sinner in this manner: Brother, you can never be perfect in this life, but you can be holy. He will say: "How can I be holy when I feel my sins?" I answer: You feel sin? That is a good sign. To realize that one is ill is a step, and a very necessary step, toward recovery. "But how will I get rid of my sin?" he will ask. I answer: See the heavenly Physician, Christ, who heals the broken-hearted. Do not consult that Quackdoctor, Reason. Believe in Christ and your sins will be pardoned. His righteousness will become your righteousness, and your sins will become His sins.

On one occasion Jesus said to His disciples: "The Father loveth you." Why? Not because the disciples were Pharisees, or circumcised, or particularly attentive to the Law. Jesus said: "The Father loveth you, because ye have loved me, and have believed that I came out from God. It pleased you to know that the Father sent me into the world. And because you believed it the Father loves you." On another occasion Jesus called His disciples evil and commanded them to ask for forgiveness.

A Christian is beloved of God and a sinner. How can these two contradictions be harmonized: I am a sinner and deserve God's wrath and punishment, and yet the Father loves me? Christ alone can harmonize these contradictions. He is the Mediator.

Do you now see how faith justifies without works? Sin lingers in us, and God hates sin. A transfusion of righteousness therefore becomes vitally necessary. This transfusion of righteousness we obtain from Christ because we believe in Him.

Verse 7. *Know ye therefore that they which are of faith, the same are the children of Abraham.*

This is the main point of Paul's argument against the Jews: The children of Abraham are those who believe and not those who are born of Abraham's flesh and blood. This point Paul drives home with all his might because the Jews attached saving value to the genealogical fact: "We are the seed and children of Abraham."

Let us begin with Abraham and learn how this friend of God was justified and saved. Not because he left his country, his relatives, his father's house; not because he was circumcised; not because he stood ready to sacrifice his own son Isaac in whom he had the promise of posterity. Abraham was justified because he believed. Paul's argumentation runs like this: "Since this is the unmistakable testimony of Holy Writ, why do you take your stand upon circumcision and the Law? Was not Abraham, your father, of whom you make so much, justified and saved without circumcision and the Law by faith alone?" Paul therefore concludes: "They which are of faith, the same are the children of Abraham."

Abraham was the father of the faithful. In order to be a child of the believing Abraham you must believe as he did. Otherwise you are merely the physical offspring of the procreating Abraham, i.e., you were conceived and born in sin unto wrath and condemnation.

Ishmael and Isaac were both the natural children of Abraham. By rights Ishmael should have enjoyed the prerogatives of the firstborn, if physical generation had any special value. Nevertheless he was left out in the cold while Isaac was called. This goes to prove that the children of faith are the real children of Abraham.

Some find fault with Paul for applying the term "faith" in Genesis 15:6 to Christ. They think Paul's use of the term too wide and general. They think its meaning should be restricted to the context. They claim Abraham's faith had no more in it than a belief in the promise of God that he should have seed.

We reply: Faith presupposes the assurance of God's mercy. This assurance takes in the confidence that our sins are forgiven for Christ's sake. Never will the conscience trust in God unless it can be sure of God's mercy and promises in Christ. Now all the promises of God lead back to the first promise concerning Christ: "And I will put enmity between thee and the woman, and between thy seed and her seed; it shall bruise thy head, and thou shalt bruise his heel." The faith of the fathers in the Old Testament era, and our faith in the New Testament are one and the same faith in Christ Jesus, although times and conditions may differ. Peter acknowledged this in the words: "Which neither our fathers nor we were able to bear? But we believe that through the grace of the Lord Jesus Christ we shall be saved, even as they" (Acts 15: 10, 11). And Paul writes: "And did all drink the spiritual drink; for they drank of that spiritual Rock that followed them: and that Rock was Christ" (I Cor. 10:4). And Christ Himself declared: "Your father Abraham rejoiced to see my day: and he saw it and was glad" (John 8:56). The faith of the fathers was directed at the Christ who was to come, while ours rests in the Christ who has come. Time does not change the object of true faith, or the Holy Spirit. There has always been and always will be one mind, one impression, one faith concerning Christ among true believers whether they live in times past, now, or in times to come. We too believe in the Christ to come as the fathers did in the Old Testament, for we look for Christ to come again on the last day to judge the quick and the dead.

Verse 7. *Know ye therefore that they which are of faith, the same are the children of Abraham.*

Paul is saying: "You know from the example of Abraham and from the plain testimony of the Scriptures that they are the children of Abraham, who have faith in Christ, regardless of their nationality, regardless of the Law, regardless of works, regardless of their parentage. The promise was made unto Abraham, 'Thou shalt be a father of many nations'; again, 'And in thee shall all families of the earth be blessed.'" To prevent the Jews from misinterpreting the word "nations," the Scriptures are careful to say "many nations." The true children of Abraham are the believers in Christ from all nations.

Verse 8. *And the Scripture, foreseeing that God would justify the heathen through faith.*

"Your boasting does not get you anywhere," says Paul to the Galatians, "because the Sacred Scriptures foresaw and foretold long before the Law was ever given, that the heathen should be justified by the blessed 'seed' of Abraham and not by the Law. This promise was made four hundred and thirty years before the Law was given. Because the Law was given so many years after Abraham, it could not abolish the promised blessing." This argument is strong because it is based on the exact factor of time. "Why should you boast of the Law, my Galatians, when the Law came four hundred and thirty years after the promise?"

The false apostles glorified the Law and despised the promise made unto Abraham, although it antedated the Law by many years. It was after Abraham was accounted righteous because of his faith that the Scriptures first make mention of circumcision. "The Scriptures," says Paul, "meant to forestall your infatuation for the righteousness of the Law by installing the righteousness of faith before circumcision and the Law ever were ordained."

Verse 8. *Preached before the gospel unto Abraham, saying, In thee shall all nations be blessed.*

The Jews misconstrue this passage. They want the

term "to bless" to mean "to praise." They want the passage to read: In thee shall all the nations of the earth be praised. But this is a perversion of the words of Holy Writ. With the words "Abraham believed" Paul describes a spiritual Abraham, renewed by faith and regenerated by the Holy Ghost, that he should be the spiritual father of many nations. In that way all the Gentiles could be given to him for an inheritance.

The Scriptures ascribe no righteousness to Abraham except through faith. The Scriptures speak of Abraham as he stands before God, a man justified by faith. Because of his faith God extends to him the promise: "In thee shall all nations be blessed."

Verse 9. *So then they which be of faith are blessed with faithful Abraham.*

The emphasis lies on the words "with faithful Abraham." Paul distinguishes between Abraham and Abraham. There is a working and there is a believing Abraham. With the working Abraham we have nothing to do. Let the Jews glory in the generating Abraham; we glory in the believing Abraham of whom the Scriptures say that he received the blessing of righteousness by faith, not only for himself but for all who believe as he did. The world was promised to Abraham because he believed. The whole world is blessed if it believes as Abraham believed.

The blessing is the promise of the Gospel. That all nations are to be blessed means that all nations are to hear the Gospel. All nations are to be declared righteous before God through faith in Christ Jesus. To bless simply means to spread abroad the knowledge of Christ's salvation. This is the office of the New Testament Church which distributes the promised blessing by preaching the Gospel, by administering the sacraments, by comforting the broken-hearted, in short, by dispensing the benefits of Christ.

The Jews exhibited a working Abraham. The Pope exhibits a working Christ, or an exemplary Christ. The Pope quotes Christ's saying recorded in John 13:15, "I have given you an example, that ye should do as I have done to you." We do not deny that Christians ought to imitate the example of Christ; but mere imitation will not satisfy God. And bear in mind that Paul is not now discussing the example of Christ, but the salvation of Christ.

That Abraham submitted to circumcision at the command of God, that he was endowed with excellent virtues, that he obeyed God in all things, was certainly admirable of him. To follow the example of Christ, to love one's neighbor, to do good to them that persecute you, to pray for one's enemies, patiently to bear the ingratitude of those who return evil for good, is certainly praiseworthy. But praiseworthy or not, such virtues do not acquit us before God. It takes more than that to make us righteous before God. We need Christ Himself, not His example, to save us. We need a redeeming, not an exemplary Christ, to save us. Paul is here speaking of the redeeming Christ and the believing Abraham, not of the model Christ or the sweating Abraham.

The believing Abraham is not to lie buried in the grave. He is to be dusted off and brought out before the world. He is to be praised to the sky for his faith. Heaven and earth ought to know about him and about his faith in Christ. The working Abraham ought to look pretty small next to the believing Abraham.

Paul's words contain the implication of contrast. When he quotes Scripture to the effect that all nations that share the faith of faithful Abraham are to be blessed, Paul means to imply the contrast that all nations are accursed without faith in Christ.

Verse 10. *For as many as are of the works of the law are under the curse.*

The curse of God is like a flood that swallows everything that is not of faith. To avoid the curse we must hold on to the promise of the blessing in Christ.

The reader is reminded that all this has no bearing upon civil laws, customs, or political matters. Civil laws and ordinances have their place and purpose. Let every government enact the best possible laws. But civil righteousness will never deliver a person from the condemnation of God's Law.

I have good reason for calling your attention to this. People easily mistake civil righteousness for spiritual righteousness. In civil life we must, of course, pay attention to laws and deeds, but in the spiritual life we must not think to be justified by laws and works, but always keep in mind the promise and blessing of Christ, our only Savior.

According to Paul everything that is not of faith is sin. When our opponents hear us repeat this statement of Paul, they make it appear as if we taught that governments should not be honored, as if we favored rebellion against the constituted authorities, as if we condemned all laws. Our opponents do us a great wrong, for we make a clear-cut distinction between civil and spiritual affairs.

Governmental laws and ordinances are blessings of God for this life only. As for everlasting life, temporal blessings are not good enough. Unbelievers enjoy more temporal blessings than the Christians. Civil or legal righteousness may be good enough for this life but not for the life hereafter. Otherwise the infidels would be nearer heaven than the Christians, for infidels often excel in civil righteousness.

Verse 10. *For it is written, Cursed is every one that continueth not in all things which are written in the book of the law to do them.*

Paul goes on to prove from this quotation out of the Book of Deuteronomy that all men who are under the Law are under the sentence of sin, of the wrath of God, and of everlasting death. Paul produces his proof in a roundabout way. He turns the negative statement, "Cursed is every one that continueth not in all things which are written in the book of the law to do them," into a positive statement, "As many as are of the works of the law are under the curse." These two statements, one by Paul and the other by Moses, appear to conflict. Paul declares, "Whosoever shall do the works of the Law, is accursed." Moses declares, "Whosoever shall not do the works of the Law, is accursed." How can these two contradictory statements be reconciled? How can the one statement prove the other? No person can hope to understand Paul unless he understands the article of justification. These two statements are not at all inconsistent.

We must bear in mind that to do the works of the Law does not mean only to live up to the superficial requirements of the Law, but to obey the spirit of the Law to perfection. But where will you find the person who can do that? Let him step forward and we will praise him.

Our opponents have their answer ready-made. They quote Paul's own statement in Romans 2:13, "The doers of the law shall be justified." Very well. But let us first find out who the doers of the law are. They call a "doer" of the Law one who performs the Law in its literal sense. This is not to "do" the Law. This is to sin. When our opponents go about to perform the Law, they sin against the first, the second, and the third commandments; in fact they sin against the whole Law. For God requires above all that we worship Him in spirit and in faith. In observing the Law for the purpose of obtaining righteousness without faith in Christ these law-workers go smack against the Law and against God. They deny the righteousness of God, His mercy, and His promises. They deny Christ and all His benefits.

In their ignorance of the true purpose of the Law the exponents of the Law abuse the Law, as Paul says, Romans 10:3, "For they, being ignorant of God's righteousness, and going about to establish their own righteousness, have not submitted themselves unto the righteousness of God."

In their folly our opponents rush into the Scriptures, pick out a sentence here and a sentence there about the Law and imagine they know all about it. Their work-righteousness is plain idolatry and blasphemy against God. No wonder they abide under the curse of God.

Because God saw that we could not fulfill the Law, He provided a way of salvation long before the Law was ever given, a salvation that He promised to Abraham, saying, "In thee shall all nations be blessed."

The very first thing for us to do is to believe in Christ. First, we must receive the Holy Spirit, who enlightens and sanctifies us so that we can begin to do the Law, i.e., to love God and our neighbor. Now, the Holy Ghost is not obtained by the Law, but by faith in Christ. In the last analysis, to do the Law means to believe in Jesus Christ. The tree comes first, and then come the fruits.

The scholastics admit that a mere external and superficial performance of the Law without sincerity and good will is plain hypocrisy. Judas acted like the other disciples. What was wrong with Judas? Mark what Rome answers, "Judas was a reprobate. His motives were perverse, therefore his works were hypocritical and no good." Well, well. Rome does admit, after all, that works in themselves do not justify unless they issue from a sincere heart. Why do our opponents not profess the same truth in spiritual matters? There, above all, faith must precede everything. The heart must be purified by faith before a person can lift a finger to please God.

There are two classes of doers of the Law, true doers and hypocritical doers. The true doers of the Law are those who are moved by faith in Christ to do the Law. The hypocritical doers of the Law are those who seek to obtain righteousness by a mechanical performance of good works while their hearts are far removed from God. They act like the foolish carpenter who starts with the roof when he builds a house. Instead of doing the Law, these law-conscious hypocrites break the Law. They break the very first commandment of God by denying His promise in Christ. They do not worship God in faith. They worship themselves.

No wonder Paul was able to foretell the abominations that Antichrist would bring into the Church. That Antichrists would come, Christ Himself prophesied, Matthew 24:5, "For many shall come in my name, saying, I am Christ; and shall deceive many." Whoever seeks righteousness by works denies God and makes himself God. He is an Antichrist because he ascribes to his own works the omnipotent capability of conquering sin, death, devil, hell, and the wrath of God. An Antichrist lays claim to the honor of Christ. He is an idolater of himself. The law-righteous person is the worst kind of infidel.

Those who intend to obtain righteousness by their own efforts do not say in so many words: "I am God; I am Christ." But it amounts to that. They usurp the divinity and office of Christ. The effect is the same as if they said, "I am Christ; I am a Savior. I save myself and others." This is the impression the monks give out.

The Pope is the Antichrist, because he is against Christ, because he takes liberties with the things of God, because he lords it over the temple of God.

I cannot tell you in words how criminal it is to seek righteousness before God without faith in Christ, by the works of the Law. It is the abomination standing in the holy place. It deposes the Creator and deifies the creature.

The real doers of the Law are the true believers. The Holy Spirit enables them to love God and their neighbor. But because we have only the first-fruits of the Spirit and not the tenth-fruits, we do not observe the Law perfectly. This imperfection of ours, however, is not imputed to us, for Christ's sake.

Hence, the statement of Moses, "Cursed is every one that continueth not in all things which are written in the book of the law to do them," is not contrary to Paul. Moses requires perfect doers of the Law. But where will you find them? Nowhere. Moses himself confessed that he was not a perfect doer of the Law. He said to the Lord: "Pardon our iniquity and our sin." Christ alone can make us innocent of any transgression. How so? First, by the forgiveness of our sins and the imputation of His righteousness. Secondly, by the gift of the Holy Ghost, who engenders new life and activity in us.

Objections to the Doctrine of Faith Disproved

Here we shall take the time to enter upon the objections which our opponents raise against the doctrine of faith. There are many passages in the Bible that deal with works and the reward of works which our opponents cite against us in the belief that these will disprove the doctrine of faith which we teach.

The scholastics grant that according to the reasonable order of nature being precedes doing. They grant that any act is faulty unless it proceeds from a right motive. They grant that a person must be right before he can do right. Why don't they grant that the right inclination of the heart toward God through faith in Christ must precede works?

In the eleventh chapter of the Epistle to the Hebrews we find a catalogue of various works and deeds of the saints of the Bible. David, who killed a lion and a bear, and defeated Goliath, is mentioned. In the heroic deeds of David the scholastic can discover nothing more than outward achievement. But the deeds of David must be evaluated according to the personality of David. When we understand that David was a man of faith, whose heart trusted in the Lord, we shall understand why he could do such heroic deeds. David said: "The Lord that delivered me out of the paw of the lion, and out of the paw of the bear, he will deliver me out of the hand of this Philistine." Again: "Thou comest to me with a sword, and with a spear, and with a shield: but I come to thee in the name of the Lord of hosts, the God of the armies of Israel, whom thou hast defied. This day will the Lord deliver thee into mine hand; and I will smite thee, and take thine head from thee" (I Samuel 17:37, 45, 46). Before David could achieve a single heroic deed he was already a man beloved of God, strong and constant in faith.

Of Abel it is said in the same Epistle: "By faith Abel offered unto God a more excellent sacrifice than Cain." When the scholastics come upon the parallel passage in Genesis 4:4, they get no further than the words: "And the Lord had respect unto Abel and to his offering." "Aha!" they cry. "See, God has respect to offerings. Works do justify." With mud in their eyes they cannot see that the text says in Genesis that the Lord had respect to the person of Abel first. Abel pleased the Lord because of his faith. Because the person of Abel pleased the Lord, the offering of Abel pleased the Lord also. The Epistle to the Hebrews expressly states: "By faith Abel offered unto God a more excellent sacrifice."

In our dealings with God the work is worth nothing without faith, for "without faith it is impossible to please him" (Hebrews 11:6). The sacrifice of Abel was better than the sacrifice of Cain, because Abel had faith. As to Cain he had no faith or trust in God's grace, but strutted about in his own fancied worth. When God refused to recognize Cain's worth, Cain got angry at God and at Abel.

The Holy Spirit speaks of faith in different ways in the Sacred Scriptures. Sometimes He speaks of faith independently of other matters. When the Scriptures speak of faith in the absolute or abstract, faith refers to justification directly. But when the Scripture speaks of rewards and works it speaks of compound or relative faith. We will furnish some examples. Galatians 5:6, "Faith which worketh by love." Leviticus 18:5, "Which if a man do, he shall live in them." Matthew 19:17, "If thou wilt enter into life, keep the commandments." Psalm 37:27, "Depart from evil, and do good." In these and other passages where mention is made of doing, the Scriptures always speak of a faith-ful doing, a doing inspired by faith. "Do this and thou shalt live,," means: First have faith in Christ, and Christ will enable you to do and to live.

In the Word of God all things that are attributed to works are attributable to faith. Faith is the divinity of works. Faith permeates all the deeds of the believer, as Christ's divinity permeated His humanity. Abraham was accounted righteous because faith pervaded his whole personality and his every action.

When you read how the fathers, prophets, and kings accomplished great deeds, remember to explain them as the Epistle to the Hebrews accounts for them: "Who through faith subdued kingdoms, wrought righteousness, obtained promises, stopped the mouths of lions" (Hebrews 11:33). In this way will we correctly interpret all those passages that seem to support the righteousness of works. The Law is truly observed only through faith. Hence, every "holy," "moral" law-worker is accursed.

Supposing that this explanation will not satisfy the scholastics, supposing that they should completely wrap me up in their arguments (they cannot do it), I would rather be wrong and give all credit to Christ alone. Here is Christ. Paul, Christ's apostle, declares that "Christ hath redeemed us from the curse of the law, being made a curse for us" (Gal. 3:13). I hear with my own ears that I cannot be saved except by the blood and death of Christ. I conclude, therefore, that it is up to Christ to overcome my sins, and not up to the Law, or my own efforts. If He is the price of my redemption, if He was made sin for my justification, I don't give a care if you quote me a thousand Scripture passages for the righteousness of works against the righteousness of faith. I have the Author and Lord of the Scriptures on my side. I would rather believe Him than all that riffraff of "pious" law-workers.

Verse 11. *But that no man is justified by the law in the sight of God, it is evident: for, The just shall live by faith.*

The Apostle draws into his argument the testimony of the Prophet Habakkuk: "The just shall live by his faith." This passage carries much weight because it eliminates the Law and the deeds of the Law as factors in the process of our justification.

The scholastics misconstrue this passage by saying: "The just shall live by faith, if it is a working faith, or a faith formed and performed by charitable works." Their annotation is a forgery. To speak of formed or unformed faith, a sort of double faith, is contrary to the Scriptures. If charitable works can form and perfect faith I am forced to say eventually that charitable deeds constitute the essential factor in the Christian religion. Christ and His benefits would be lost to us.

Verse 12. *And the law is not of faith.*

In direct opposition to the scholastics Paul declares: "The law is not of faith." What is this charity the scholastics talk so much about? Does not the Law command charity? The fact is the Law commands nothing but charity, as we may gather from the following Scripture passages: "Thou shalt love the Lord thy God with all thine heart, and with all thy soul, and with all thy might" (Deut. 6:5). "Shewing mercy unto thousands of them that love me, and keep my commandments" (Exodus 20:6). "On these two commandments hang all the law and the prophets" (Matt. 22:40). If the law requires charity, charity is part of the Law and not of faith. Since Christ has displaced the Law which commands charity, it follows that charity has been abrogated with the Law as a factor in our justification, and only faith is left.

Verse 12. *But, The man that doeth them shall live in them.*

Paul undertakes to explain the difference between the righteousness of the Law and the righteousness of faith. The righteousness of the Law is the fulfillment of the Law according to the passage: "The man that doeth them shall live in them." The righteousness of faith is to believe the Gospel according to the passage: "The just shall live by faith." The Law is a statement of debit, the Gospel a statement of credit. By this distinction Paul explains why charity which is the commandment of the Law cannot justify, because the Law contributes nothing to our justification.

Indeed, works do follow after faith, but faith is not therefore a meritorious work. Faith is a gift. The character and limitations of the Law must be rigidly maintained.

When we believe in Christ we live by faith. When we believe in the Law we may be active enough but we have no life. The function of the Law is not to give life; the function of the Law is to kill. True, the Law says: "The man that doeth them shall live in them." But where is the person who can do "them," i.e., love God with all his heart, soul, and mind, and his neighbor as himself?

Paul has nothing against those who are justified by faith and therefore are true doers of the Law. He opposes those who think they can fulfill the Law when in reality they can only sin against the Law by trying to obtain righteousness by the Law. The Law demands that we fear, love, and worship God with a true faith. The law-workers fail to do this. Instead, they invent new modes of worship and new kinds of works which God never commanded. They provoke His anger according to the passage: "But in vain they do worship me, teaching for doctrines the commandments of men" (Matthew 15:9). Hence, the law-righteous workers are downright rebels against God, and idolaters who constantly sin against the first commandment. In short, they are no good at all though outwardly they seem to be extremely solicitous of the honor of God.

We who are justified by faith as the saints of old, may be under the Law, but we are not under the curse of the Law because sin is not imputed to us for Christ's sake. If the Law cannot be fulfilled by the believers, if sin continues to cling to them despite their love for God, what can you expect of people who are not yet justified by faith, who are still enemies of God and His Word, like the unbelieving law-workers? It goes to show how impossible it is for those who have not been justified by faith to fulfill the Law.

Verse 13. *Christ hath redeemed us from the curse of the law, being made a curse for us: for it is written, Cursed is every one that hangeth on a tree.*

Jerome and his present-day followers rack their miserable brains over this comforting passage in an effort to save Christ from the fancied insult of being called a curse. They say: "This quotation from Moses does not apply to Christ. Paul is taking liberties with Moses by generalizing the statements in Deuteronomy 21:23. Moses has 'he that is hanged.' Paul puts it 'every one that hangeth.' On the other hand, Paul omits the words 'of God' in his quotation from Moses: 'For he that is hanged is accursed of God.' Moses speaks of a criminal who is worthy of death." "How," our opponents ask, "can this passage be applied to the holy Christ as if He were accursed of God and worthy to be hanged?" This piece of exegesis may impress the naive as a zealous attempt to defend the honor and glory of Christ. Let us see what Paul has in mind.

Paul does not say that Christ was made a curse for Himself. The accent is on the two words "for us." Christ is personally innocent. Personally, He did not deserve to be hanged for any crime of His own doing. But because Christ took the place of others who were sinners, He was hanged like any other transgressor. The Law of Moses leaves no loopholes. It says that a transgressor should be hanged. Who are the other sinners? We are. The sentence of death and everlasting damnation had long been pronounced over us. But Christ took all our sins and died for them on the Cross. "He was numbered with the transgressors; and he bare the sin of many, and made intercession for the transgressors" (Isaiah 53:12).

All the prophets of old said that Christ should be the greatest transgressor, murderer, adulterer, thief, blasphemer that ever was or ever could be on earth. When He took the sins of the whole world upon Himself, Christ was no longer an innocent person. He was a sinner burdened with the sins of a Paul who was a blasphemer; burdened with the sins of a Peter who denied Christ; burdened with the sins of a David who committed adultery and murder, and gave the heathen occasion to laugh at the Lord. In short, Christ was charged with the sins of all men, that He should pay for them with His own blood. The curse struck Him. The Law found Him among sinners. He was not only in the company of sinners. He had gone so far as to invest Himself with the flesh and blood of sinners. So the Law judged and hanged Him for a sinner.

In separating Christ from us sinners and holding Him up as a holy exemplar, errorists rob us of our best comfort. They misrepresent Him as a threatening tyrant who is ready to slaughter us at the slightest provocation.

I am told that it is preposterous and wicked to call the Son of God a cursed sinner. I answer: If you deny that He is a condemned sinner, you are forced to deny that Christ died. It is not less preposterous to say, the Son of God died, than to say, the Son of God was a sinner.

John the Baptist called Him "the lamb of God, which taketh away the sin of the world." Being the unspotted Lamb of God, Christ was personally innocent. But because He took the sins of the world, His sinlessness was defiled with the sinfulness of the world. Whatever sins I, you, all of us have committed or shall commit, they are Christ's sins as if He had committed them Himself. Our sins have to be Christ's sins or we shall perish forever.

Isaiah declares of Christ: "The Lord hath laid on him the iniquity of us all." We have no right to minimize the force of this declaration. God does not amuse Himself with words. What a relief for a Christian to know that Christ is covered all over with my sins, your sins, and the sins of the whole world.

The papists invented their own doctrine of faith. They say charity creates and adorns their faith. By stripping Christ of our sins, by making Him sinless, they cast our sins back at us, and make Christ absolutely worthless to us. What sort of charity is this? If that is a sample of their vaunted charity, we want none of it.

Our merciful Father in heaven saw how the Law oppressed us and how impossible it was for us to get out from under the curse of the Law. He therefore sent His only Son into the world and said to Him: "You are now Peter, the liar; Paul, the persecutor; David, the adulterer; Adam, the disobedient; the thief on the cross. You, My Son, must pay the world's iniquity." The Law growls: "All right. If Your Son is taking the sin of the world, I see no sins anywhere else but in Him. He shall die on the Cross." And the Law kills Christ. But we go free.

The argument of the Apostle against the righteousness of the Law is impregnable. If Christ bears our sins, we do not bear them. But if Christ is innocent of our sins and does not bear them, we must bear them, and we shall die in our sins. "But thanks be to God, which giveth us the victory through our Lord Jesus Christ."

Let us see how Christ was able to gain the victory over our enemies. The sins of the whole world, past, present, and future, fastened themselves upon Christ and condemned Him. But because Christ is God, He had an everlasting and unconquerable righteousness. These two, the sin of the world and the righteousness of God, met in a death struggle. Furiously the sin of the world assailed the righteousness of God. Righteousness is immortal and invincible. On the other hand, sin is a mighty tyrant who subdues all men. This tyrant pounces on Christ. But Christ's righteousness is unconquerable. The result is inevitable. Sin is defeated and righteousness triumphs and reigns forever.

In the same manner was death defeated. Death is emperor of the world. He strikes down kings, princes, all men. He has an idea to destroy all life. But Christ has immortal life, and life immortal gained the victory over death. Through Christ death has lost her sting. Christ is the Death of death.

The curse of God waged a similar battle with the eternal mercy of God in Christ. The curse meant to condemn God's mercy. But it could not do it because the mercy of God is everlasting. The curse had to give way. If the mercy of God in Christ had lost out, God Himself would have lost out, which, of course, is impossible.

"Christ," says Paul, "spoiled principalities and powers, He made a show of them openly, triumphing over them in it" (Col. 2:15). They cannot harm those who hide in Christ. Sin, death, the wrath of God, hell, and the devil are mortified in Christ. Where Christ is near the powers of evil must keep their distance. St. John says: "And this is the victory that overcometh the world, even our faith" (I John 5:4).

You may now perceive why it is imperative to believe and confess the divinity of Christ. To overcome the sin of a whole world, and death, and the wrath of God was no work for any creature. The power of sin and death could be broken only by a greater power. God alone could abolish sin, destroy death, and take away the curse of the Law. God alone could bring righteousness, life, and mercy to light. In attributing these achievements to Christ the Scriptures pronounce Christ to be God forever. The article of justification is indeed fundamental. If we remain sound in this one article, we remain sound in all the other articles of the Christian faith. When we teach justification by faith in Christ we confess at the same time that Christ is God.

I cannot get over the blindness of the Pope's theologians. To imagine that the mighty forces of sin, death, and the curse can be vanquished by the righteousness of man's paltry works, by fasting, pilgrimages, masses, vows, and such gewgaws. These blind leaders of the blind turn the poor people over to the mercy of sin, death, and the devil. What chance has a defenseless human creature against these powers of darkness? They train sinners who are ten times worse than any thief, whore, murderer. The divine power of God alone can destroy sin and death, and create righteousness and life.

When we hear that Christ was made a curse for us, let us believe it with joy and assurance. By faith Christ changes places with us. He gets our sins, we get His holiness.

By faith alone can we become righteous, for faith invests us with the sinlessness of Christ. The more fully we believe this, the fuller will be our joy. If you believe that sin, death, and the curse are void, why, they are null, zero. Whenever sin and death make you nervous, write it down as an illusion of the devil. There is no sin now, no curse, no death, no devil because Christ has done away with them. This fact is sure. There is nothing wrong with the fact. The defect lies in our lack of faith.

In the Apostolic Creed we confess: "I believe in the holy Christian Church." That means, I believe that there is no sin, no curse, no evil in the Church of God. Faith says: "I believe that." But if you want to believe your eyes, you will find many shortcomings and offenses in the members of the holy Church. You see them succumb to temptation, you see them weak in faith, you see them giving way to anger, envy, and other evil dispositions. "How can the Church be holy?" you ask. It is with the Christian Church as it is with the individual Christian. If I examine myself, I find enough unholiness to shock me. But when I look at Christ in me, I find that I am altogether holy. And so it is with the Church.

Holy Writ does not say that Christ was under the curse. It says directly that Christ was made a curse. In II Corinthians 5:21 Paul writes: "For he (God) hath made him (Christ) to be sin for us, who knew no sin; that we might be made the righteousness of God in him." Although this and similar passages may be properly explained by saying that Christ was made a sacrifice for the curse and for sin, yet in my judgment it is better to leave these passages stand as they read: Christ was made sin itself; Christ was made the curse itself. When a sinner gets wise to himself, he does not only feel miserable, he feels like misery personified; he does not only feel like a sinner, he feels like sin itself.

To finish with this verse: All evils would have overwhelmed us, as they shall overwhelm the unbelievers forever, if Christ had not become the great transgressor and guilty bearer of all our sins. The sins of the world got Him down for a moment. They came around Him like water. Of Christ, the Old Testament Prophet complained: "Thy fierce wrath goeth over me; thy terrors have cut me off" (Psalm 88:16). By Christ's salvation we have been delivered from the terrors of God to a life of eternal felicity.

Verse 14. *That the blessing of Abraham might come on the Gentiles through Jesus Christ.*

Paul always keeps this text before him: "In thy seed shall all the nations of the earth be blessed." The blessing promised unto Abraham could come upon the Gentiles only by Christ, the seed of Abraham. To become a blessing unto all nations Christ had to be made a curse to take away the curse from the nations of the earth. The merit that we plead, and the work that we proffer is Christ who was made a curse for us.

Let us become expert in the art of transferring our sins, our death, and every evil from ourselves to Christ; and Christ's righteousness and blessing from Christ to ourselves.

Verse 14. *That we might receive the promise of the Spirit through faith.*

"The promise of the Spirit" is Hebrew for "the promised Spirit." The Spirit spells freedom from the Law, sin, death, the curse, hell, and the judgment of God. No merits are mentioned in connection with this promise of the Spirit and all the blessings that go with Him. This Spirit of many blessings is received by faith alone. Faith alone builds on the promises of God, as Paul says in this verse.

Long ago the prophets visualized the happy changes Christ would effect in all things. Despite the fact that the Jews had the Law of God they never ceased to look longingly for Christ. After Moses no prophet or king added a single law to the Book. Any changes or additions were deferred to the time of Christ's coming. Moses told the people: "The Lord thy God will raise up unto thee a Prophet from the midst of thee, of thy brethren, like unto me; unto him ye shall hearken" (Deut. 18:15).

God's people of old felt that the Law of Moses could not be improved upon until the Messiah would bring better things than the Law, i.e., grace and remission of sins.

Verse 15. *Brethren, I speak after the manner of men; Though it be but a man's covenant, yet if it be confirmed, no man disannulleth, or addeth thereto.*

After the preceding, well-taken argument, Paul offers another based on the similarity between a man's testament and God's testament. A man's testament seems too weak a premise for the Apostle to argue from in confirmation of so important a matter as justification. We ought to prove earthly things by heavenly things, and not heavenly things by earthly things. But where the earthly thing is an ordinance of God, we may use it to prove divine matters. In Matthew 7:11 Christ Himself argued from earthly to heavenly things when He said: "If ye then, being evil, know how to give good gifts to your children, how much more shall your Father which is in heaven give good things to them that ask him?"

To come to Paul's argument. Civil law, which is God's ordinance, prohibits tampering with any testament of man. Any person's last will and testament must be respected. Paul asks: "Why is it that man's last will is scrupulously respected and not God's testament? You would not think of breaking faith with a man's testament. Why do you not keep faith with God's testament?"

The Apostle says that he is speaking after the manner of men. He means to say: "I will give you an illustration from the customs of men. If a man's last will is respected, and it is, how much more ought the testament of God be honored: 'In thy seed shall all the nations of the earth be blessed.' When Christ died, this testament was sealed by His blood. After His death the testament was opened, it was published to the nations. No man ought to alter God's testament as the false apostles do who substitute the Law and traditions of men for the testament of God."

As the false prophets tampered with God's testament in the days of Paul, so many do in our day. They will observe human laws punctiliously, but the laws of God they transgress without the flicker of an eyelid. But the time will come when they will find out that it is no joke to pervert the testament of God.

Verse 16. *Now to Abraham and his seed were the promises made. He saith not, And to seeds, as of many; but as of one, And to thy seed, which is Christ.*

The word testament is another name for the promise that God made unto Abraham concerning Christ. A testament is not a law, but an inheritance. Heirs do not look for laws and assessments when they open a last will; they look for grants and favors. The testament which God made out to Abraham did not contain laws. It contained promises of great spiritual blessings.

The promises were made in view of Christ, in one seed, not in many seeds. The Jews will not accept this interpretation. They insist that the singular "seed" is put for the plural "seeds." We prefer the interpretation of Paul, who makes a fine case for Christ and for us out of the singular "seed," and is after all inspired to do so by the Holy Ghost.

Verse 17. *And this I say, that the covenant, that was confirmed before of God in Christ, the law which was four hundred and thirty years after, cannot disannul, that it should make the promise of none effect.*

The Jews assert that God was not satisfied with His promises, but after four hundred and thirty years He gave the Law. "God," they say, "must have mistrusted His own promises, and considered them inadequate for salvation. Therefore He added to His promises something better, the Law. The Law," they say, "canceled the promises."

Paul answers: "The Law was given four hundred and thirty years after the promise was made to Abraham. The Law could not cancel the promise because the promise was the testament of God, confirmed by God in Christ many years before the Law. What God has once promised He does not take back. Every promise of God is a ratified promise."

Why was the Law added to the promise? Not to serve as a medium by which the promise might be obtained. The Law was added for these reasons: That there might be in the world a special people, rigidly controlled by the Law, a people out of which Christ should be born in due time; and that men burdened by many laws might sigh and long for Him, their Redeemer, the seed of Abraham. Even the ceremonies prescribed by the Law foreshadowed Christ. Therefore the Law was never meant to cancel the promise of God. The Law was meant to confirm the promise until the time should come when God would open His testament in the Gospel of Jesus Christ.

God did well in giving the promise so many years before the Law, that it may never be said that righteousness is granted through the Law and not through the promise. If God had meant for us to be justified by the Law, He would have given the Law four hundred and thirty years before the promise, at least He would have given the Law at the same time He gave the promise. But He never breathed a word about the Law until four hundred years after. The promise is therefore better than the Law. The Law does not cancel the promise, but faith in the promised Christ cancels the Law.

The Apostle is careful to mention the exact number of four hundred and thirty years. The wide divergence in the time between the promise and the Law helps to clinch Paul's argument that righteousness is not obtained by the Law.

Let me illustrate. A man of great wealth adopts a strange lad for his son. Remember, he does not owe the lad anything. In due time he appoints the lad heir to his entire fortune. Several years later the old man asks the lad to do something for him. And the young lad does it. Can the lad then go around and say that he deserved the inheritance by his obedience to the old man's request? How can anybody say that righteousness is obtained by obedience to the Law when the Law was given four hundred and thirty years after God's promise of the blessing?

One thing is certain, Abraham was never justified by the Law, for the simple reason that the Law was not in his day. If the Law was non-existent how could Abraham obtain righteousness by the Law? Abraham had nothing else to go by but the promise. This promise he believed and that was counted unto him for righteousness. If the father obtained righteousness through faith, the children get it the same way.

We use the argument of time also. We say our sins were taken away by the death of Christ fifteen hundred years ago, long before there were any religious orders, canons, or rules of penance, merits, etc. What did people do about their sins before these new inventions were hatched up?

Paul finds his arguments for the righteousness of faith everywhere. Even the element of time serves to build his case against the false apostles. Let us fortify our conscience with similar arguments. They help us in the trials of our faith. They turn our attention from the Law to the promises, from sin to righteousness; from death to life.

It is not for nothing that Paul bears down on this argument. He foresaw this confusion of the promise and the Law creeping into the Church. Accustom yourself to separate Law and Gospel even in regard to time. When the Law comes to pay your conscience a visit, say: "Mister Law, you come too soon. The four hundred and thirty years aren't up yet. When they are up, you come again. Won't you?"

Verse 18. *For if the inheritance be of the law, it is no more of promise.*

In Romans 4:14, the Apostle writes: "For if they which

are made of the law be heirs, faith is made void, and the promise made of none effect." It cannot be otherwise. That the Law is something entirely different from the promise is plain. The Law thunders: "Thou shalt, thou shalt not." The promise of the "seed" pleads: "Take this gift of God." If the inheritance of the gifts of God were obtained by the Law, God would be a liar. We would have the right to ask Him: "Why did you make this promise in the first place: 'In thy seed shall all the nations of the earth be blessed'? Why did you not say: 'In thy works thou shalt be blessed'?"

Verse 18. *But God gave it to Abraham by promise.*

So much is certain, before the Law ever existed, God gave Abraham the inheritance or blessing by the promise. In other words, God granted unto Abraham remission of sins, righteousness, salvation, and everlasting life. And not only to Abraham but to all believers, because God said: "In thy seed shall all the nations of the earth be blessed." The blessing was given unconditionally. The Law had no chance to butt in because Moses was not yet born. "How then can you say that righteousness is obtained by the Law?"

The Apostle now goes to work to explain the province and purpose of the Law.

Verse 19. *Wherefore then serveth the law?*

The question naturally arises: If the Law was not given for righteousness or salvation, why was it given? Why did God give the Law in the first place if it cannot justify a person?

The Jews believed if they kept the Law they would be saved. When they heard that the Gospel proclaimed a Christ who had come into the world to save sinners and not the righteous; when they heard that sinners were to enter the kingdom of heaven before the righteous, the Jews were very much put out. They murmured: "These last have wrought but one hour, and thou hast made them equal unto us, which have borne the burden and heat of the day" (Matthew 20:12). They complained that the heathen who at one time had been worshipers of idols obtained grace without the drudgery of the Law that was theirs.

Today we hear the same complaints. "What was the use of our having lived in a cloister, twenty, thirty, forty years; what was the sense of having vowed chastity, poverty, obedience; what good are all the masses and canonical hours that we read; what profit is there in fasting, praying, etc., if any man or woman, any beggar or scour woman is to be made equal to us, or even be considered more acceptable unto God than we?"

Reason takes offense at the statement of Paul: "The law was added because of transgressions." People say that Paul abrogated the Law, that he is a radical, that he blasphemed God when he said that. People say: "We might as well live like wild people if the Law does not count. Let us abound in sin that grace may abound. Let us do evil that good may come of it."

What are we to do? Such scoffing distresses us, but we cannot stop it. Christ Himself was accused of being a blasphemer and rebel. Paul and all the other apostles were told the same things. Let the scoffers slander us, let them spare us not. But we must not on their own account keep silent. We must speak frankly in order that afflicted consciences may find surcease. Neither are we to pay any attention to the foolish and ungodly people for abusing our doctrine. They are the kind that would scoff, Law or no Law. Our first consideration must be the comfort of troubled consciences, that they may not perish with the multitudes.

When he saw that some were offended at his doctrine, while others found in it encouragement to live after the flesh, Paul comforted himself with the thought that it was his duty to preach the Gospel to the elect of God, and that for their sake he must endure all things. Like Paul we also do all these things for the sake of God's elect. As for the scoffers and skeptics, I am so disgusted with them that in all my life I would not open my mouth for them once. I wish that they were back there where they belong under the iron heel of the Pope.

People foolish but wise in their conceits jump to the conclusion: If the Law does not justify, it is good for nothing. How about that? Because money does not justify, would you say that money is good for nothing? Because the eyes do not justify, would you have them taken out? Because the Law does not justify it does not follow that the Law is without value. We must find and define the proper purpose of the Law. We do not offhand condemn the Law because we say it does not justify.

We say with Paul that the Law is good if it is used properly. Within its proper sphere the Law is an excellent thing. But if we ascribe to the Law functions for which it was never intended, we pervert not only the Law but also the Gospel.

It is the universal impression that righteousness is obtained through the deeds of the Law. This impression is instinctive and therefore doubly dangerous. Gross sins and vices may be recognized or else repressed by the threat of punishment. But this sin, this opinion of man's own righteousness refuses to be classified as sin. It wants to be esteemed as high-class religion. Hence, it constitutes the mighty influence of the devil over the entire world. In order to point out the true office of the Law, and thus to stamp out that false impression of the righteousness of the Law, Paul answers the question: "Wherefore then serveth the Law?" with the words:

Verse 19. *It was added because of transgressions.*

All things differ. Let everything serve its unique purpose. Let the sun shine by day, the moon and the stars by night. Let the sea furnish fish, the earth grain, the woods trees, etc. Let the Law also serve its unique purpose. It must not step out of character and take the place of anything else. What is the function of the Law? "Transgression," answers the Apostle.

The Twofold Purpose of the Law

The Law has a twofold purpose. One purpose is civil. God has ordained civil laws to punish crime. Every law is given to restrain sin. Does it not then make men righteous? No. In refraining from murder, adultery, theft, or other sins, I do so under compulsion because I fear the jail, the noose, the electric chair. These restrain me as iron bars restrain a lion and a bear. Otherwise they would tear everything to pieces. Such forceful restraint cannot be regarded as righteousness, rather as an indication of unrighteousness. As a wild beast is tied to keep it from running amuck, so the Law bridles mad and furious man to keep him from running wild. The need for restraint shows plainly enough that those who need the Law are not righteous, but wicked men who are fit to be tied. No, the Law does not justify.

The first purpose of the Law, accordingly, is to restrain the wicked. The devil gets people into all kinds of scrapes. Therefore God instituted governments, parents, laws, restrictions, and civil ordinances. At least they help to tie the devil's hands so that he does not rage up and down the earth. This civil restraint by the Law is intended by God for the preservation of all things, particularly for the good of the Gospel that it should not be hindered too much by the tumult of the wicked. But Paul is not now treating of this civil use and function of the Law.

The second purpose of the Law is spiritual and divine. Paul describes this spiritual purpose of the Law in the words, "Because of transgressions," i.e., to reveal to a person his sin, blindness, misery, his ignorance, hatred, and contempt of God, his death, hell, and condemnation.

This is the principal purpose of the Law and its most valuable contribution. As long as a person is not a murderer, adulterer, thief, he would swear that he is righteous.

How is God going to humble such a person except by the Law? The Law is the hammer of death, the thunder of hell, and the lightning of God's wrath to bring down the proud and shameless hypocrites. When the Law was instituted on Mount Sinai it was accompanied by lightning, by storms, by the sound of trumpets, to tear to pieces that monster called self-righteousness. As long as a person thinks he is right he is going to be incomprehensibly proud and presumptuous. He is going to hate God, despise His grace and mercy, and ignore the promises in Christ. The Gospel of the free forgiveness of sins through Christ will never appeal to the self-righteous.

This monster of self-righteousness, this stiff-necked beast, needs a big axe. And that is what the Law is, a big axe. Accordingly, the proper use and function of the Law is to threaten until the conscience is scared stiff.

The awful spectacle at Mount Sinai portrayed the proper use of the Law. When the children of Israel came out of Egypt a feeling of singular holiness possessed them. They boasted: "We are the people of God. All that the Lord hath spoken we will do" (Ex. 19:8). This feeling of holiness was heightened when Moses ordered them to wash their clothes, to refrain from their wives, and to prepare themselves all around. The third day came and Moses led the people out of their tents to the foot of the mountain into the presence of the Lord. What happened? When the children of Israel saw the whole mountain burning and smoking, the black clouds rent by fierce lightning flashing up and down in the inky darkness, when they heard the sound of the trumpet blowing louder and longer, shattered by the roll of thunder, they were so frightened that they begged Moses: "Speak thou with us, and we will hear: but let not God speak with us, lest we die" (Ex. 20:19). I ask you, what good did their scrubbing, their snow-white clothes, and their continence do them? No good at all. Not a single one could stand in the presence of the glorious Lord. Stricken by the terror of God, they fled back into their tents, as if the devil were after them.

The Law is meant to produce the same effect today which it produced at Mount Sinai long ago. I want to encourage all who fear God, especially those who intend to become ministers of the Gospel, to learn from the Apostle the proper use of the Law. I fear that after our time the right handling of the Law will become a lost art. Even now, although we continually explain the separate functions of the Law and the Gospel, we have those among us who do not understand how the Law should be used. What will it be like when we are dead and gone?

We want it understood that we do not reject the Law as our opponents claim. On the contrary, we uphold the Law. We say the Law is good if it is used for the purposes for which it was designed, to check civil transgression, and to magnify spiritual transgressions. The Law is also a light like the Gospel. But instead of revealing the grace of God, righteousness, and life, the Law brings sin, death, and the wrath of God to light. This is the business of the Law, and here the business of the Law ends, and should go no further.

The business of the Gospel, on the other hand, is to quicken, to comfort, to raise the fallen. The Gospel carries the news that God for Christ's sake is merciful to the most unworthy sinners, if they will only believe that Christ by His death has delivered them from sin and everlasting death unto grace, forgiveness, and everlasting life. By keeping in mind the difference between the Law and the Gospel we let each perform its special task. Of this difference between the Law and the Gospel nothing can be discovered in the writings of the monks or scholastics, nor for that matter in the writings of the ancient fathers. Augustine understood the difference somewhat. Jerome and others knew nothing of it. The silence in the Church concerning the difference between the Law and the Gospel has resulted in untold harm. Unless a sharp distinction is maintained between the purpose and function of the Law and the Gospel, the Christian doctrine cannot be kept free from error.

Verse 19. *It was added because of transgressions.*

In other words, that transgressions might be recognized as such and thus increased. When sin, death, and the wrath of God are revealed to a person by the Law, he grows impatient, complains against God, and rebels. Before that he was a very holy man; he worshipped and praised God; he bowed his knees before God and gave thanks, like the Pharisee. But now that sin and death are revealed to him by the Law he wishes there were no God. The Law inspires hatred of God. Thus sin is not only revealed by the Law; sin is actually increased and magnified by the Law.

The Law is a mirror to show a person what he is like, a sinner who is guilty of death, and worthy of everlasting punishment. What is this bruising and beating by the hand of the Law to accomplish? This, that we may find the way to grace. The Law is an usher to lead the way to grace. God is the God of the humble, the miserable, the afflicted. It is His nature to exalt the humble, to comfort the sorrowing, to heal the broken-hearted, to justify the sinners, and to save the condemned. The fatuous idea that a person can be holy by himself denies God the pleasure of saving sinners. God must therefore first take the sledge-hammer of the Law in His fists and smash the beast of self-righteousness and its brood of self-confidence, self-wisdom, self-righteousness, and self-help. When the conscience has been thoroughly frightened by the Law it welcomes the Gospel of grace with its message of a Savior who came into the world, not to break the bruised reed, nor to quench the smoking flax, but to preach glad tidings to the poor, to heal the broken-hearted, and to grant forgiveness of sins to all the captives.

Man's folly, however, is so prodigious that instead of embracing the message of grace with its guarantee of the forgiveness of sin for Christ's sake, man finds himself more laws to satisfy his conscience. "If I live," says he, "I will mend my life. I will do this, I will do that." Man, if you don't do the very opposite, if you don't send Moses with the Law back to Mount Sinai and take the hand of Christ, pierced for your sins, you will never be saved.

When the Law drives you to the point of despair, let it drive you a little farther, let it drive you straight into the arms of Jesus who says: "Come unto me, all ye that labour and are heavy laden, and I will give you rest."

Verse 19. *Till the seed should come to whom the promise was made.*

The Law is not to have its say indefinitely. We must know how long the Law is to put in its licks. If it hammers away too long, no person would and could be saved. The Law has a boundary beyond which it must not go. How long ought the Law to hold sway? "Till the seed should come to whom the promise was made."

That may be taken literally to mean until the time of the Gospel. "From the days of John the Baptist," says Jesus, "until now the kingdom of heaven suffereth violence, and the violent take it by force. For all the prophets and the law prophesied until John" (Matthew 11:12, 13). When Christ came the Law and the ceremonies of Moses ceased.

Spiritually, it means that the Law is not to operate on a person after he has been humbled and frightened by the exposure of his sins and the wrath of God. We must then say to the Law: "Mister Law, lay off him. He has had enough. You scared him good and proper." Now it is the Gospel's turn. Now let Christ with His gracious lips talk to him of better things, grace, peace, forgiveness of sins, and eternal life.

Verse 19. *And it was ordained by angels in the hand of a mediator.*

The Apostle digresses a little from his immediate

theme. Something occurred to him and he throws it in by the way. It occurred to him that the Law differs from the Gospel in another respect, in respect to authorship. The Law was delivered by the angels, but the Gospel by the Lord Himself. Hence, the Gospel is superior to the Law, as the word of a lord is superior to the word of his servant.

The Law was handed down by a being even inferior to the angels, by a middleman named Moses. Paul wants us to understand that Christ is the mediator of a better testament than mediator Moses of the Law. Moses led the people out of their tents to meet God. But they ran away. That is how good a mediator Moses was.

Paul says: "How can the Law justify when that whole sanctified people of Israel and even mediator Moses trembled at the voice of God? What kind of righteousness do you call that when people run away from it and hate it the worst way? If the Law could justify, people would love the Law. But look at the children of Israel running away from it."

The flight of the children of Israel from Mount Sinai indicates how people feel about the Law. They don't like it. If this were the only argument to prove that salvation is not by the Law, this one Bible history would do the work. What kind of righteousness is this law-righteousness when at the commencement exercises of the Law Moses and the scrubbed people run away from it so fast that an iron mountain, the Red Sea even, could not have stopped them until they were back in Egypt once again? If they could not hear the Law, how could they ever hope to perform the Law?

If all the world had stood at the mountain, all the world would have hated the Law and fled from it as the children of Israel did. The whole world is an enemy of the Law. How, then, can anyone be justified by the Law when everybody hates the Law and its divine author?

All this goes to show how little the scholastics know about the Law. They do not consider its spiritual effect and purpose, which is not to justify or to pacify afflicted consciences, but to increase sin, to terrify the conscience, and to produce wrath. In their ignorance the papists spout about man's good will and right judgment, and man's capacity to perform the Law of God. Ask the people of Israel who were present at the presentation of the Law on Mount Sinai whether what the scholastics say is true. Ask David, who often complains in the Psalms that he was cast away from God and in hell, that he was frantic about his sin, and sick at the thought of the wrath and judgment of God. No, the Law does not justify

Verse 20. *Now a mediator is not a mediator of one.*

Here the Apostle briefly compares the two mediators: Moses and Christ. "A mediator," says Paul, "is not a mediator of one." He is necessarily a mediator of two: The offender and the offended. Moses was such a mediator between the Law and the people who were offended at the Law. They were offended at the Law because they did not understand its purpose. That was the veil which Moses put over his face. The people were also offended at the Law because they could not look at the bare face of Moses. It shone with the glory of God. When Moses addressed the people he had to cover his face with that veil of his. They could not listen to their mediator Moses without another mediator, the veil. The Law had to change its face and voice. In other words, the Law had to be made tolerable to the people.

Thus covered, the Law no longer spoke to the people in its undisguised majesty. It became more tolerable to the conscience. This explains why men fail to understand the Law properly, with the result that they become secure and presumptuous hypocrites. One of two things has to be done: Either the Law must be covered with a veil and then it loses its full effectiveness, or it must be unveiled and then the full blast of its force kills. Man cannot stand the Law without a veil over it. Hence, we are forced either to look beyond the Law to Christ, or we go through life as shameless hypocrites and secure sinners.

Paul says: "A mediator is not a mediator of one." Moses could not be a mediator of God only, for God needs no mediator. Again, Moses could not be a mediator of the people only. He was a mediator between God and the people. It is the office of a mediator to conciliate the party that is offended and to placate the party that is the offender. However, Moses' mediation consisted only in changing the tone of the Law to make it more tolerable to the people. Moses was merely a mediator of the veil. He could not supply the ability to perform the Law.

What do you suppose would have happened if the Law had been given without a mediator and the people had been denied the services of a go-between? The people would have perished, or in case they had escaped they would have required the services of another mediator to preserve them alive and to keep the Law in force. Moses came along and he was made the mediator. He covered his face with a veil. But that is as much as he could do. He could not deliver men's consciences from the terror of the Law. The sinner needs a better mediator.

That better mediator is Jesus Christ. He does not change the voice of the Law, nor does He hide the Law with a veil. He takes the full blast of the wrath of the Law and fulfills its demands most meticulously.

Of this better Mediator Paul says: "A mediator is not a mediator of one." We are the offending party; God is the party offended. The offense is of such a nature that God cannot pardon it. Neither can we render adequate satisfaction for our offenses. There is discord between God and us. Could not God revoke His Law? No. How about running away from God? It cannot be done. It took Christ to come between us and God and to reconcile God to us. How did Christ do it? "Blotting out the handwriting of ordinances that was against us, which was contrary to us, and took it out of the way, nailing it to his cross" (Col. 2:14).

This one word, "mediator," is proof enough that the Law cannot justify. Otherwise we should not need a mediator.

In Christian theology the Law does not justify. In fact it has the contrary effect. The Law alarms us, it magnifies our sins until we begin to hate the Law and its divine Author. Would you call this being justified by the Law?

Can you imagine a more arrant outrage than to hate God and to abhor His Law? What an excellent Law it is. Listen: "I am the Lord thy God, which have brought thee out of the land of Egypt, out of the house of bondage. Thou shalt have no other gods... showing mercy unto thousands... honor thy father and thy mother: that thy days may be long upon the land... " (Ex. 20:2, 3, 6, 12). Are these not excellent laws, perfect wisdom? "Let not God speak with us, lest we die," cried the children of Israel. Is it not amazing that a person should refuse to hear things that are good for him? Any person would be glad to hear, I should think, that he has a gracious God who shows mercy unto thousands. Is it not amazing that people hate the Law that promotes their safety and welfare, e.g., "Thou shalt not kill; thou shalt not commit adultery; thou shalt not steal"?

The Law can do nothing for us except to arouse the conscience. Before the Law comes to me I feel no sin. But when the Law comes, sin, death, and hell are revealed to me. You would not call this being made righteous. You would call it being condemned to death and hell-fire.

Verse 20. *But God is one.*

God does not offend anybody, therefore He needs no mediator. But we offend God, therefore we need a mediator. And we need a better mediator than Moses. We need Christ.

Verse 21. *Is the law then against the promises of God?*

Before he digressed Paul stated that the Law does not justify. Shall we then discard the Law? No, no. It supplies a certain need. It supplies men with a needed realization of their sinfulness. Now arises another question: If the Law does no more than to reveal sin, does it not oppose the promises of God? The Jews believed that by the restraint and discipline of the Law the promises of God would be hastened, in fact earned by them.

Paul answers: "Not so. On the contrary, if we pay too much attention to the Law the promises of God will be slowed up. How can God fulfill His promises to a people that hates the Law?"

Verse 21. *God forbid.*

God never said to Abraham: "In thee shall all the nations of the earth be blessed because thou hast kept the Law." When Abraham was still uncircumcised and without the Law or any law, indeed, when he was still an idol worshiper, God said to him: "Get thee out of thy country, etc.; I am thy shield, etc.; In thy seed shall all the nations of the earth be blessed." These are unconditional promises which God freely made to Abraham without respect to works.

This is aimed especially at the Jews who think that the promises of God are impeded by their sins. Paul says: "The Lord is not slack concerning His promises because of our sins, or hastens His promises because of any merit on our part." God's promises are not influenced by our attitudes. They rest in His goodness and mercy.

Just because the Law increases sin, it does not therefore obstruct the promises of God. The Law confirms the promises, in that it prepares a person to look for the fulfillment of the promises of God in Christ.

The proverb has it that Hunger is the best cook. The Law makes afflicted consciences hungry for Christ. Christ tastes good to them. Hungry hearts appreciate Christ. Thirsty souls are what Christ wants. He invites them: "Come unto me, all ye that labour and are heavy laden, and I will give you rest." Christ's benefits are so precious that He will dispense them only to those who need them and really desire them.

Verse 21. *For if there had been a law given which could have given life, verily righteousness should have been by the law.*

The Law cannot give life. It kills. The Law does not justify a person before God; it increases sin. The Law does not secure righteousness; it hinders righteousness. The Apostle declares emphatically that the Law of itself cannot save.

Despite the intelligibility of Paul's statement, our enemies fail to grasp it. Otherwise they would not emphasize free will, natural strength, the works of supererogation, etc. To escape the charge of forgery they always have their convenient annotation handy, that Paul is referring only to the ceremonial and not to the moral law. But Paul includes all laws. He expressly says: "If there had been a law given."

There is no law by which righteousness may be obtained, not a single one. Why not?

Verse 22. *But the Scripture hath concluded all under sin.*

Where? First in the promises concerning Christ in Genesis 3:15 and in Genesis 22:18, which speak of the seed of the woman and the seed of Abraham. The fact that these promises were made unto the fathers concerning Christ implies that the fathers were subject to the curse of sin and eternal death. Otherwise why the need of promises?

Next, Holy Writ "concludes" all under sin in this passage from Paul: "For as many as are of the works of the law are under the curse." Again, in the passage which the Apostle quotes from Deuteronomy 27:26, "Cursed is every one that continueth not in all things which are written in the book of the law to do them." This passage clearly submits all men to the curse, not only those who sin openly against the Law, but also those who sincerely endeavor to perform the Law, inclusive of monks, friars, hermits, etc.

The conclusion is inevitable: Faith alone justified without works. If the Law itself cannot justify, much less can imperfect performance of the Law or the works of the Law, justify.

Verse 22. *That the promise by faith of Jesus Christ might be given to them that believe.*

The Apostle stated before that "the Scripture hath concluded all under sin." Forever? No, only until the promise should be fulfilled. The promise, you will recall, is the inheritance itself or the blessing promised to Abraham, deliverance from the Law, sin, death, and the devil, and the free gift of grace, righteousness, salvation, and eternal life. This promise, says Paul, is not obtained by any merit, by any law, or by any work. This promise is given. To whom? To those who believe. In whom? In Jesus Christ.

Verse 23. *But before faith came.*

The Apostle proceeds to explain the service which the Law is to render. Previously Paul had said that the Law was given to reveal the wrath and death of God upon all sinners. Although the Law kills, God brings good out of evil. He uses the Law to bring life. God saw that the universal illusion of self-righteousness could not be put down in any other way but by the Law. The Law dispels all self-illusions. It puts the fear of God in a man. Without this fear there can be no thirst for God's mercy. God accordingly uses the Law for a hammer to break up the illusion of self-righteousness, that we should despair of our own strength and efforts at self-justification.

Verse 23. *But before faith came, we were kept under the law, shut up unto the faith which should afterwards be revealed.*

The Law is a prison to those who have not as yet obtained grace. No prisoner enjoys the confinement. He hates it. If he could he would smash the prison and find his freedom at all cost. As long as he stays in prison he refrains from evil deeds. Not because he wants to, but because he has to. The bars and the chains restrain him. He does not regret the crime that put him in jail. On the contrary, he is mighty sore that he cannot rob and kill as before. If he could escape he would go right back to robbing and killing.

The Law enforces good behavior, at least outwardly. We obey the Law because if we don't we will be punished. Our obedience is inspired by fear. We obey under duress and we do it resentfully. Now what kind of righteousness is this when we refrain from evil out of fear of punishment? Hence, the righteousness of the Law is at bottom nothing but love of sin and hatred of righteousness.

All the same, the Law accomplishes this much, that it will outwardly at least and to a certain extent repress vice and crime.

But the Law is also a spiritual prison, a veritable hell. When the Law begins to threaten a person with death and the eternal wrath of God, a man just cannot find any comfort at all. He cannot shake off at will the nightmare of terror which the Law stirs up in his conscience. Of this terror of the Law the Psalms furnish many glimpses.

The Law is a civil and a spiritual prison. And such it should be. For that the Law is intended. Only the confinement in the prison of the Law must not be unduly prolonged. It must come to an end. The freedom of faith must succeed the imprisonment of the Law.

Happy the person who knows how to utilize the Law so that it serves the purposes of grace and of faith. Unbelievers are ignorant of this happy knowledge. When Cain was first shut up in the prison of the Law he felt no pang at the fratricide he had committed. He thought he could pass it off as an incident with a shrug of the shoulder. "Am I my brother's keeper?" he answered God flippantly. But when he heard the ominous words, "What hast thou done? the voice of thy brother's blood crieth unto me from the ground," Cain began to feel his imprisonment.

Did he know how to get out of prison? No. He failed to call the Gospel to his aid. He said: "My punishment is greater than I can bear." He could only think of the prison. He forgot that he was brought face to face with his crime so that he should hurry to God for mercy and for pardon. Cain remained in the prison of the Law and despaired.

As a stone prison proves a physical handicap, so the spiritual prison of the Law proves a chamber of torture. But this it should only be until faith be revealed. The silly conscience must be educated to this. Talk to your conscience. Say: "Sister, you are now in jail all right. But you don't have to stay there forever. It is written that we are 'shut up unto faith which should afterwards be revealed.' Christ will lead you to freedom. Do not despair like Cain, Saul, or Judas. They might have gone free if they had called Christ to their aid. Just take it easy, Sister Conscience. It's good for you to be locked up for a while. It will teach you to appreciate Christ."

How anybody can say that he by nature loves the Law is beyond me. The Law is a prison to be feared and hated. Any unconverted person who says he loves the Law is a liar. He does not know what he is talking about. We love the Law about as well as a murderer loves his gloomy cell, his straight-jacket, and the iron bars in front of him. How then can the Law justify us?

Verse 23. *Shut up unto the faith which should afterwards be revealed.*

We know that Paul has reference to the time of Christ's coming. It was then that faith and the object of faith were fully revealed. But we may apply the historical fact to our inner life. When Christ came He abolished the Law and brought liberty and life to light. This He continues to do in the hearts of the believers. The Christian has a body in whose members, as Paul says, sin dwells and wars. I take sin to mean not only the deed but root, tree, fruit, and all. A Christian may perhaps not fall into the gross sins of murder, adultery, theft, but he is not free from impatience, complaints, hatreds, and blasphemy of God. As carnal lust is strong in a young man, in a man of full age the desire for glory, and in an old man covetousness, so impatience, doubt, and hatred of God often prevail in the hearts of sincere Christians. Examples of these sins may be garnered from the Psalms, Job, Jeremiah, and all the Sacred Scriptures.

Accordingly each Christian continues to experience in his heart times of the Law and times of the Gospel. The times of the Law are discernible by heaviness of heart, by a lively sense of sin, and a feeling of despair brought on by the Law. These periods of the Law will come again and again as long as we live. To mention my own case. There are many times when I find fault with God and am impatient with Him. The wrath and the judgment of God displease me, my wrath and impatience displease Him. Then is the season of the Law, when "the flesh lusteth against the Spirit, and the Spirit against the flesh."

The time of grace returns when the heart is enlivened by the promise of God's mercy. It soliloquizes: "Why art thou cast down, O my soul? and why art thou disquieted within me? Can you see nothing but law, sin, death, and hell? Is there no grace, no forgiveness, no joy, peace, life, heaven, no Christ and God? Trouble me no more, my soul. Hope in God who has not spared His own dear Son but has given Him into death for thy sins." When the Law carries things too far, say: "Mister Law, you are not the whole show. There are other and better things than you. They tell me to trust in the Lord."

There is a time for the Law and a time for grace. Let us study to be good timekeepers. It is not easy. Law and grace may be miles apart in essence, but in the heart, they are pretty close together. In the heart fear and trust, sin and grace, Law and Gospel cross paths continually.

When reason hears that justification before God is obtained by grace alone, it draws the inference that the Law is without value. The doctrine of the Law must therefore be studied carefully lest we either reject the Law altogether, or are tempted to attribute to the Law a capacity to save.

There are three ways in which the Law may be abused. First, by the self-righteous hypocrites who fancy that they can be justified by the Law. Secondly, by those who claim that Christian liberty exempts a Christian from the observance of the Law. "These," says Peter, "use their liberty for a cloak of maliciousness," and bring the name and the Gospel of Christ into ill repute. Thirdly, the Law is abused by those who do not understand that the Law is meant to drive us to Christ. When the Law is properly used its value cannot be too highly appraised. It will take me to Christ every time.

Verse 24. *Wherefore the law was our schoolmaster to bring us unto Christ.*

This simile of the schoolmaster is striking. Schoolmasters are indispensable. But show me a pupil who loves his schoolmaster. How little love is lost upon them the Jews showed by their attitude toward Moses. They would have been glad to stone Moses to death (Ex. 17:4). You cannot expect anything else. How can a pupil love a teacher who frustrates his desires? And if the pupil disobeys, the schoolmaster whips him, and the pupil has to like it and even kiss the rod with which he was beaten. Do you think the schoolboy feels good about it? As soon as the teacher turns his back, the pupil breaks the rod and throws it into the fire. And if he were stronger than the teacher he would not take the beatings, but beat up the teacher. All the same, teachers are indispensable, otherwise the children would grow up without discipline, instruction, and training.

But how long are the scolding and the whippings of the schoolmaster to continue? Only for a time, until the boy has been trained to be a worthy heir of his father. No father wants his son to be whipped all the time. The discipline is to last until the boy has been trained to be his father's worthy successor.

The Law is such a schoolmaster. Not for always, but until we have been brought to Christ. The Law is not just another schoolmaster. The Law is a specialist to bring us to Christ. What would you think of a schoolmaster who could only torment and beat a child? Yet of such schoolmasters there were plenty in former times, regular bruisers. The Law is not that kind of a schoolmaster. It is not to torment us always. With its lashings it is only too anxious to drive us to Christ. The Law is like the good schoolmaster who trains his children to find pleasure in doing things they formerly detested.

Verse 24. *That we might be justified by faith.*

The Law is not to teach us another Law. When a person feels the full force of the Law he is likely to think: I have transgressed all the commandments of God; I am guilty of eternal death. If God will spare me I will change and live right from now on. This natural but entirely wrong reaction to the Law has bred the many ceremonies and works devised to earn grace and remission of sins.

The Law means to enlarge my sins, to make me small, so that I may be justified by faith in Christ. Faith is neither law nor word; but confidence in Christ "who is the end of the law." How so is Christ the end of the Law? Not in this way that He replaced the old Law with new laws. Nor is Christ the end of the Law in a way that makes Him a hard judge who has to be bribed by works as the papists teach. Christ is the end or finish of the Law to all who believe in Him. The Law can no longer accuse or condemn them.

But what does the Law accomplish for those who have been justified by Christ? Paul answers this question next.

Verse 25. *But after that faith is come, we are no longer under a schoolmaster.*

The Apostle declares that we are free from the Law. Christ fulfilled the Law for us. We may live in joy and safety under Christ. The trouble is, our flesh will not let us believe in Christ with all our heart. The fault lies not with Christ, but with us. Sin clings to us as long as we live and spoils our happiness in Christ. Hence, we are only partly free from the Law. "With the mind I myself serve the law of God; but with the flesh the law of sin" (Romans 7:25).

As far as the conscience is concerned it may cheerfully ignore the Law. But because sin continues to dwell in the flesh, the Law waits around to molest our conscience. More and more, however, Christ increases our faith and in the measure in which our faith is increased, sin, Law, and flesh subside.

If anybody objects to the Gospel and the sacraments on the ground that Christ has taken away our sins once and for always, you will know what to answer. You will answer: Indeed, Christ has taken away my sins. But my flesh, the world, and the devil interfere with my faith. The little light of faith in my heart does not shine all over me at once. It is a gradual diffusion. In the meanwhile I console myself with the thought that eventually my flesh will be made perfect in the resurrection.

Verse 26. *For we are all the children of God by faith in Christ Jesus.*

Paul as a true apostle of faith always has the word "faith" on the tip of his tongue. By faith, says he, we are the children of God. The Law cannot beget children of God. It cannot regenerate us. It can only remind us of the old birth by which we were born into the kingdom of the devil. The best the Law can do for us is to prepare us for a new birth through faith in Christ Jesus. Faith in Christ regenerates us into the children of God. St. John bears witness to this in his Gospel: "As many as received him, to them gave he power to become the sons of God, even to them that believe on his name" (John 1:12). What tongue of man or angel can adequately extol the mercy of God toward us miserable sinners in that He adopted us for His own children and fellow-heirs with His Son by the simple means of faith in Christ Jesus!

Verse 27. *For as many of you as have been baptized into Christ have put on Christ.*

To "put on Christ" may be understood in two ways, according to the Law and according to the Gospel. According to the Law as in Romans 13:14, "Put ye on the Lord Jesus Christ," which means to follow the example of Christ.

To put on Christ according to the Gospel means to clothe oneself with the righteousness, wisdom, power, life, and Spirit of Christ. By nature we are clad in the garb of Adam. This garb Paul likes to call "the old man." Before we can become the children of God this old man must be put off, as Paul says, Ephesians 4:29. The garment of Adam must come off like soiled clothes. Of course, it is not as simple as changing one's clothes. But God makes it simple. He clothes us with the righteousness of Christ by means of Baptism, as the Apostle says in this verse: "As many of you as have been baptized into Christ have put on Christ." With this change of garments a new birth, a new life stirs in us. New affections toward God spring up in the heart. New determinations affect our will. All this is to put on Christ according to the Gospel. Needless to say, when we have put on the robe of the righteousness of Christ we must not forget to put on also the mantle of the imitation of Christ.

Verse 28. *There is neither Jew nor Greek, there is neither bond nor free, there is neither male nor female; for ye are all one in Christ Jesus.*

The list might be extended indefinitely: There is neither preacher nor hearer, neither teacher nor scholar, neither master nor servant, etc. In the matter of salvation, rank, learning, righteousness, influence count for nothing.

With this statement Paul deals a death blow to the Law. When a person has put on Christ nothing else matters. Whether a person is a Jew, a punctilious and circumcised observer of the Law of Moses, or whether a person is a noble and wise Greek does not matter. Circumstances, personal worth, character, achievements have no bearing upon justification. Before God they count for nothing. What counts is that we put on Christ.

Whether a servant performs his duties well; whether those who are in authority govern wisely; whether a man marries, provides for his family, and is an honest citizen; whether a woman is chaste, obedient to her husband, and a good mother: all these advantages do not qualify a person for salvation. These virtues are commendable, of course; but they do not count points for justification. All the best laws, ceremonies, religions, and deeds of the world cannot take away sin guilt, cannot dispatch death, cannot purchase life.

There is much disparity among men in the world, but there is no such disparity before God. "For all have sinned, and come short of the glory of God" (Romans 3:23). Let the Jews, let the Greeks, let the whole world keep silent in the presence of God. Those who are justified are justified by Christ. Without faith in Christ the Jew with his laws, the monk with his holy orders, the Greek with his wisdom, the servant with his obedience, shall perish forever.

Verse 28. *For ye are all one in Christ Jesus.*

There is much imparity among men in the world. And it is a good thing. If the woman would change places with the man, if the son would change places with the father, the servant with the master, nothing but confusion would result. In Christ, however, all are equal. We all have one and the same Gospel, "one faith, one baptism, one God and Father of all," one Christ and Savior of all. The Christ of Peter, Paul, and all the saints is our Christ. Paul can always be depended on to add the conditional clause, "In Christ Jesus." If we lose sight of Christ, we lose out.

Verse 29. *And if ye be Christ's, then are ye Abraham's seed, and heirs according to the promise.*

"If ye be Christ's" means, if you believe in Christ. If you believe in Christ, then are you the children of Abraham indeed. Through our faith in Christ Abraham gains paternity over us and over the nations of the earth according to the promise: "In thy seed shall all the nations of the earth be blessed." Through faith we belong to Christ and Christ to us.

GALATIONS 4

Verse 1. Now I say, That the heir, as long as he is a child, differeth nothing from a servant, though he be Lord of all;

Verse 2. But is under tutors and governors until the time appointed of the father.

The Apostle had apparently finished his discourse on justification when this illustration of the youthful heir occurred to him. He throws it in for good measure. He knows that plain people are sooner impressed by an apt illustration than by learned discussion.

"I want to give you another illustration from everyday life," he writes to the Galatians. "As long as an heir is under age he is treated very much like a servant. He is not permitted to order his own affairs. He is kept under constant surveillance. Such discipline is good for him, otherwise he would waste his inheritance in no time. This discipline, however, is not to last forever. It is to last only until 'the time appointed of the father.'"

Verse 3. *Even so we, when we were children, were in bondage under the elements of the world.*

As children of the Law we were treated like servants and prisoners. We were oppressed and condemned by the Law. But the tyranny of the Law is not to last forever. It is to last only until "the time appointed of the father," until Christ came and redeemed us.

Verse 3. *Under the elements of the world.*

By the elements of the world the Apostle does not understand the physical elements, as some have thought. In calling the Law "the elements of the world" Paul means to say that the Law is something material, mundane, earthly. It may restrain evil, but it does not deliver from sin. The Law does not justify; it does not bring a person to heaven. I do not obtain eternal life because I do not kill, commit adultery, steal, etc. Such mere outward decency does not constitute Christianity. The heathen observe the same restraints to avoid punishment or to secure the advantages of a good reputation. In the last analysis such restraint is simple hypocrisy. When the Law exercises its higher function it accuses and condemns the conscience. All these effects of the Law cannot be called divine or heavenly. These effects are elements of the world.

In calling the Law the elements of the world Paul refers to the whole Law, principally to the ceremonial law which dealt with external matters, as meat, drink, dress, places, times, feasts, cleansings, sacrifices, etc. These are mundane matters which cannot save the sinner. Ceremonial laws are like the statutes of governments dealing with purely civil matters, as commerce, inheritance, etc. As for the pope's church laws forbidding marriage and meats, Paul calls them elsewhere the doctrines of devils. You would not call such laws elements of heaven.

The Law of Moses deals with mundane matters. It holds the mirror to the evil which is in the world. By revealing the evil that is in us it creates a longing in the heart for the better things of God. The Law forces us into the arms of Christ, "who is the end of the law for righteousness to every one that believeth" (Romans 1:4). Christ relieves the conscience of the Law. In so far as the Law impels us to Christ it renders excellent service.

I do not mean to give the impression that the Law should be despised. Neither does Paul intend to leave that impression. The Law ought to be honored. But when it is a matter of justification before God, Paul had to speak disparagingly of the Law, because the Law has nothing to do with justification. If it thrusts its nose into the business of justification we must talk harshly to the Law to keep it in its place. The conscience ought not to be on speaking terms with the Law. The conscience ought to know only Christ. To say this is easy, but in times of trial, when the conscience writhes in the presence of God, it is not so easy to do. As such times we are to believe in Christ as if there were no Law or sin anywhere, but only Christ. We ought to say to the Law: "Mister Law, I do not get you. You stutter so much. I don't think that you have anything to say to me."

When it is not a question of salvation or justification with us, we are to think highly of the Law and call it "holy, just, and good" (Romans 7:12). The Law is of no comfort to a stricken conscience. Therefore it should not be allowed to rule in our conscience, particularly in view of the fact that Christ paid so great a price to deliver the conscience from the tyranny of the Law. Let us understand that the Law and Christ are impossible bedfellows. The Law must leave the bed of the conscience, which is so narrow that it cannot hold two, as Isaiah says, chapter 28, verse 20.

Only Paul among the apostles calls the Law "the elements of the world, weak and beggarly elements, the strength of sin, the letter that killeth," etc. The other apostles do not speak so slightingly of the Law. Those who want to be first-class scholars in the school of Christ want to pick up the language of Paul. Christ called him a chosen vessel and equipped with a facility of expression far above that of the other apostles, that he as the chosen vessel should establish the doctrine of justification in clear-cut words.

Verses 4, 5. *But when the fullness of the time was come, God sent forth his Son, made of a woman, made under the law, to redeem them that were under the law.*

"The fullness of the time" means when the time of the Law was fulfilled and Christ was revealed. Note how Paul explains Christ. "Christ," says he, "is the Son of God and the son of a woman. He submitted Himself under the Law to redeem us who were under the Law." In these words the Apostle explains the person and office of Christ. His person is divine and human. "God sent forth His Son, made of a woman." Christ therefore is true God and true man. Christ's office the Apostle describes in the words: "Made under the law, to redeem them that were under the law."

Paul calls the Virgin Mary a woman. This has been frequently deplored even by some of the ancient fathers who felt that Paul should have written "virgin" instead of woman. But Paul is now treating of faith and Christian righteousness, of the person and office of Christ, not of the virginity of Mary. The inestimable mercy of God is sufficiently set forth by the fact that His Son was born of a woman. The more general term "woman" indicates that Christ was born a true man. Paul does not say that Christ was born of man and woman, but only of woman. That he has a virgin in mind is obvious.

This passage furthermore declares that Christ's purpose in coming was the abolition of the Law, not with the intention of laying down new laws, but "to redeem them that were under the law." Christ himself declared: "I judge no man" (John 8:15). Again, "I came not to judge the world, but to save the world" (John 12:47). In other words: "I came not to bring more laws, or to judge men according to the existing Law. I have a higher and better office. I came to judge and to condemn the Law, so that it may no more judge and condemn the world."

How did Christ manage to redeem us? "He was made under the law." When Christ came He found us all in prison. What did He do about it? Although He was the Lord of the Law, He voluntarily placed Himself under the Law and permitted it to exercise dominion over Him, indeed to accuse and to condemn Him. When the Law takes us into judgment it has a perfect right to do so. "For we are by nature the children of wrath, even as others" (Eph. 2:3). Christ, however, "did no sin, neither was guile found in his mouth" (I Pet. 2:22). Hence the Law had no jurisdiction over Him. Yet the Law treated this innocent, just, and blessed Lamb of God as cruelly as it treated us. It accused Him of blasphemy and treason. It made Him guilty of the sins of the whole world. It overwhelmed him with such anguish of soul that His sweat was as blood. The Law condemned Him to the shameful death on the Cross.

It is truly amazing that the Law had the effrontery to turn upon its divine Author, and that without a show of right. For its insolence the Law in turn was arraigned before the judgment seat of God and condemned. Christ might have overcome the Law by an exercise of His omnipotent authority over the Law. Instead, He humbled Himself under the Law for and together with them that were under the Law. He gave the Law license to accuse and condemn Him. His present mastery over the Law was obtained by virtue of His Sonship and His substitutionary victory.

Thus Christ banished the Law from the conscience. It dare no longer banish us from God. For that matter,— the Law continues to reveal sin. It still raises its voice in condemnation. But the conscience finds quick relief in the words of the Apostle: "Christ has redeemed us from the law." The conscience can now hold its head high and say to the Law: "You are not so holy yourself. You crucified the Son of God. That was an awful thing for you to do. You have lost your influence forever."

The words, "Christ was made under the law," are worth all the attention we can bestow on them. They declare that the Son of God did not only fulfill one or two easy requirements of the Law, but that He endured all the tortures of the Law. The Law brought all its fright to bear upon Christ until He experienced anguish and terror such as nobody else ever experienced. His bloody sweat. His need of angelic comfort, His tremulous prayer in the garden, His lamentation on the Cross, "My God, my God, why hast thou forsaken me?" bear eloquent witness to the sting of the Law. He suffered "to redeem them that were under the law."

The Roman conception of Christ as a mere lawgiver more stringent than Moses, is quite contrary to Paul's teaching. Christ, according to Paul, was not an agent of the Law but a patient of the Law. He was not a law-giver, but a law-taker.

True enough, Christ also taught and expounded the Law. But it was incidental. It was a sideline with Him. He did not come into the world for the purpose of teaching the Law, as little as it was the purpose of His coming to perform miracles. Teaching the Law and performing miracles did not constitute His unique mission to the world. The prophets also taught the Law and performed miracles. In fact, according to the promise of Christ, the apostles performed greater miracles than Christ Himself (John 14:12). The true purpose of Christ's coming was the abolition of the Law, of sin, and of death.

If we think of Christ as Paul here depicts Him, we shall never go wrong. We shall never be in danger of misconstruing the meaning of the Law. We shall understand that the Law does not justify. We shall understand why a Christian observes laws: For the peace of the world, out of gratitude to God, and for a good example that others may be attracted to the Gospel.

Verse 5. *That we might receive the adoption of sons.*

Paul still has for his text Genesis 22:18, "In thy seed shall all the nations of the earth be blessed." In the course of his Epistle he calls this promise of the blessing righteousness, life, deliverance from the Law, the testament, etc. Now he also calls the promise of blessing "the adoption of sons," the inheritance of everlasting life.

Whatever induced God to adopt us for His children and heirs? What claim can men who are subservient to sin, subject to the curse of the Law, and worthy of everlasting death, have on God and eternal life? That God adopted us is due to the merit of Jesus Christ, the Son of God, who humbled Himself under the Law and redeemed us law-ridden sinners.

Verse 6. *And because ye are sons, God hath sent forth the Spirit of his Son into your hearts.*

In the early Church the Holy Spirit was sent forth in

visible form. He descended upon Christ in the form of a dove (Matt. 3:16), and in the likeness of fire upon the apostles and other believers (Acts 2:3). This visible outpouring of the Holy Spirit was necessary to the establishment of the early Church, as were also the miracles that accompanied the gift of the Holy Ghost. Paul explained the purpose of these miraculous gifts of the Spirit in I Corinthians 14:22, "Tongues are for a sign, not to them that believe, but to them that believe not." Once the Church had been established and properly advertised by these miracles, the visible appearance of the Holy Ghost ceased.

Next, the Holy Ghost is sent forth into the hearts of the believers, as here stated, "God sent the Spirit of his Son into your hearts." This sending is accomplished by the preaching of the Gospel through which the Holy Spirit inspires us with fervor and light, with new judgment, new desires, and new motives. This happy innovation is not a derivative of reason or personal development, but solely the gift and operation of the Holy Ghost.

This renewal by the Holy Spirit may not be conspicuous to the world, but it is patent to us by our better judgment, our improved speech, and our unashamed confession of Christ. Formerly we did not confess Christ to be our only merit, as we do now in the light of the Gospel. Why, then, should we feel bad if the world looks upon us as ravagers of religion and insurgents against constituted authority? We confess Christ and our conscience approves of it.

Then, too, we live in the fear of God. If we sin, we sin not on purpose, but unwittingly, and we are sorry for it. Sin sticks in our flesh, and the flesh gets us into sin even after we have been imbued by the Holy Ghost. Outwardly there is no great difference between a Christian and any honest man. The activities of a Christian are not sensational. He performs his duty according to his vocation. He takes good care of his family, and is kind and helpful to others. Such homely, everyday performances are not much admired. But the setting-up exercises of the monks draw great applause. Holy works, you know. Only the acts of a Christian are truly good and acceptable to God, because they are done in faith, with a cheerful heart, out of gratitude to Christ.

We ought to have no misgivings about whether the Holy Ghost dwells in us. We are "the temple of the Holy Ghost" (I Cor. 3:16). When we have a love for the Word of God, and gladly hear, talk, write, and think of Christ, we are to know that this inclination toward Christ is the gift and work of the Holy Ghost. Where you come across contempt for the Word of God, there is the devil. We meet with such contempt for the Word of God mostly among the common people. They act as though the Word of God does not concern them. Wherever you find a love for the Word, thank God for the Holy Spirit who infuses this love into the hearts of men. We never come by this love naturally, neither can it be enforced by laws. It is the gift of the Holy Spirit.

The Roman theologians teach that no man can know for a certainty whether he stands in the favor of God or not. This teaching forms one of the chief articles of their faith. With this teaching they tormented men's consciences, excommunicated Christ from the Church, and limited the operations of the Holy Ghost.

St. Augustine observed that "every man is certain of his faith, if he has faith." This the Romanists deny. "God forbid," they exclaim piously, "that I should ever be so arrogant as to think that I stand in grace, that I am holy, or that I have the Holy Ghost." We ought to feel sure that we stand in the grace of God, not in view of our own worthiness, but through the good services of Christ. As certain as we are that Christ pleases God, so sure ought we to be that we also please God, because Christ is in us. And although we daily offend God by our sins, yet as often as we sin, God's mercy bends over us. Therefore sin cannot get us to doubt the grace of God. Our certainty is of Christ, that mighty Hero who overcame the Law, sin, death, and all evils. So long as He sits at the right hand of God to intercede for us, we have nothing to fear from the anger of God.

This inner assurance of the grace of God is accompanied by outward indications such as gladly to hear, preach, praise, and to confess Christ, to do one's duty in the station in which God has placed us, to aid the needy, and to comfort the sorrowing. These are the affidavits of the Holy Spirit testifying to our favorable standing with God.

If we could be fully persuaded that we are in the good grace of God, that our sins are forgiven, that we have the Spirit of Christ, that we are the beloved children of God, we would be ever so happy and grateful to God. But because we often feel fear and doubt we cannot come to that happy certainty.

Train your conscience to believe that God approves of you. Fight it out with doubt. Gain assurance through the Word of God. Say: "I am all right with God. I have the Holy Ghost. Christ, in whom I do believe, makes me worthy. I gladly hear, read, sing, and write of Him. I would like nothing better than that Christ's Gospel be known throughout the world and that many, many be brought to faith in Him."

Verse 6. *Crying, Abba, Father.*

Paul might have written, "God sent forth the Spirit of his Son into your hearts, calling Abba, Father." Instead, he wrote, "Crying, Abba, Father." In the eighth chapter of the Epistle to the Romans the Apostle describes this crying of the Spirit as "groanings which cannot be uttered." He writes in the 26th verse: "Likewise the Spirit also helpeth our infirmities: for we know not what we should pray for as we ought: but the Spirit itself maketh intercession for us with groanings which cannot be uttered."

The fact that the Spirit of Christ in our hearts cries unto God and makes intercession for us with groanings should reassure us greatly. However, there are many factors that prevent such full reassurance on our part. We are born in sin. To doubt the good will of God is an inborn suspicion of God with all of us. Besides, the devil, our adversary, goeth about seeking to devour us by roaring: "God is angry at you and is going to destroy you forever." In all these difficulties we have only one support, the Gospel of Christ. To hold on to it, that is the trick. Christ cannot be perceived with the senses. We cannot see Him. The heart does not feel His helpful presence. Especially in times of trials a Christian feels the power of sin, the infirmity of his flesh, the goading darts of the devil, the agues of death, the scowl and judgment of God. All these things cry out against us. The Law scolds us, sin screams at us, death thunders at us, the devil roars at us. In the midst of the clamor the Spirit of Christ cries in our hearts: "Abba, Father." And this little cry of the Spirit transcends the hullabaloo of the Law, sin, death, and the devil, and finds a hearing with God.

The Spirit cries in us because of our weakness. Because of our infirmity the Holy Ghost is sent forth into our hearts to pray for us according to the will of God and to assure us of the grace of God.

Let the Law, sin, and the devil cry out against us until their outcry fills heaven and earth. The Spirit of God outcries them all. Our feeble groans, "Abba, Father," will be heard of God sooner than the combined racket of hell, sin, and the Law.

We do not think of our groanings as a crying. It is so faint we do not know we are groaning. "But he," says Paul, "that searcheth the hearts knoweth what is the mind of the Spirit" (Romans 8:27). To this Searcher of hearts our feeble groaning, as it seems to us, is a loud shout for help in comparison with which the howls of hell, the din of the devil, the yells of the Law, the shouts of sin are like so many whispers.

In the fourteenth chapter of Exodus the Lord addresses Moses at the Red Sea: "Wherefore criest thou unto me?" Moses had not cried unto the Lord. He trembled so he could hardly talk. His faith was at low ebb. He saw the people of Israel wedged between the Sea and the approaching armies of Pharaoh. How were they to escape? Moses did not know what to say. How then could God say that Moses was crying to Him? God heard the groaning heart of Moses and the groans to Him sounded like loud shouts for help. God is quick to catch the sigh of the heart.

Some have claimed that the saints are without infirmities. But Paul says: "The Spirit helpeth our infirmities, and maketh intercession for us with groanings which cannot be uttered." We need the help of the Holy Spirit because we are weak and infirm. And the Holy Spirit never disappoints us. Confronted by the armies of Pharaoh, retreat cut off by the waters of the Red Sea, Moses was in a bad spot. He felt himself to blame. The devil accused him: "These people will all perish, for they cannot escape. And you are to blame because you led the people out of Egypt. You started all this." And then the people started in on Moses. "Because there were no graves in Egypt, hast thou taken us away to die in the wilderness? For it had been better for us to serve the Egyptians, than that we should die in the wilderness" (Ex. 14:11, 12). But the Holy Ghost was in Moses and made intercession for him with unutterable groanings, sighings unto the Lord: "O Lord, at Thy commandment have I led forth this people. So help me now."

The Spirit intercedes for us not in many words or long prayers, but with groanings, with little sounds like "Abba." Small as this word is, it says ever so much. It says: "My Father, I am in great trouble and you seem so far away. But I know I am your child, because you are my Father for Christ's sake. I am loved by you because of the Beloved." This one little word "Abba" surpasses the eloquence of a Demosthenes and a Cicero.

I have spent much time on this verse in order to combat the cruel teaching of the Roman church, that a person ought to be kept in a state of uncertainty concerning his status with God. The monasteries recruit the youth on the plea that their "holy" orders will assuredly recruit them for heaven. But once inside the monastery the recruits are told to doubt the promises of God.

In support of their error the papists quote the saying of Solomon: "The righteous, and the wise, and their works, are in the hand of God: no man knoweth either love or hatred by all that is before them" (Eccles. 9:1). They take this hatred to mean the wrath of God to come. Others take it to mean God's present anger. None of them seem to understand this passage from Solomon. On every page the Scriptures urge us to believe that God is merciful, loving, and patient; that He is faithful and true, and that He keeps His promises. All the promises of God were fulfilled in the gift of His only-begotten Son, that "whosoever believeth in him should not perish, but have everlasting life." The Gospel is reassurance for sinners. Yet this one saying from Solomon, misinterpreted at that, is made to count for more than all the many promises of all the Scriptures.

If our opponents are so uncertain about their status with God, and even go so far as to say that the conscience ought to be kept in a state of doubt, why is it that they persecute us as vile heretics? When it comes to persecuting us they do not seem to be in doubt and uncertainty one minute.

Let us not fail to thank God for delivering us from the doctrine of doubt. The Gospel commands us to look away from our own good works to the promises of God in Christ, the Mediator. The pope commands us to look away from the promises of God in Christ to our own merit. No wonder they are the eternal prey of doubt and despair. We depend upon God for salvation. No wonder that our doctrine is certified, because it does not rest in our own strength, our own conscience, our own feelings, our own person, our own works. It is built on a better foundation. It is built on the promises and truth of God.

Besides, the passage from Solomon does not treat of the hatred and love of God towards men. It merely rebukes the ingratitude of men. The more deserving a person is, the less he is appreciated. Often those who should be his best friends, are his worst enemies. Those who least deserve the praise of the world, get most. David was a holy man and a good king. Nevertheless he was chased from his own country. The prophets, Christ, the apostles, were slain. Solomon in this passage does not speak of the love and hatred of God, but of love and hatred among men. As though Solomon wanted to say: "There are many good and wise men whom God uses for the advancement of mankind. Seldom, if ever, are their efforts crowned with gratitude. They are usually repaid with hatred and ingratitude."

We are being treated that way. We thought we would find favor with men for bringing them the Gospel of peace, life, and eternal salvation. Instead of favor, we found fury. At first, yes, many were delighted with our doctrine and received it gladly. We counted them as our friends and brethren, and were happy to think that they would help us in sowing the seed of the Gospel. But they revealed themselves as false brethren and deadly enemies of the Gospel. If you experience the ingratitude of men, don't let it get you down. Say with Christ: "They hated me without cause." And, "For my love they are my adversaries; but I give myself unto prayer" (Ps. 109:4).

Let us never doubt the mercy of God in Christ Jesus, but make up our minds that God is pleased with us, that He looks after us, and that we have the Holy Spirit who prays for us.

Verse 7. *Wherefore thou art no more a servant, but a son.*

This sentence clinches Paul's argument. He says: "With the Holy Spirit in our hearts crying, 'Abba, Father,' there can be no doubt that God has adopted us for His children and that our subjection to the Law has come to an end." We are now the free children of God. We may now say to the Law: "Mister Law, you have lost your throne to Christ. I am free now and a son of God. You cannot curse me any more." Do not permit the Law to lie in your conscience. Your conscience belongs to Christ. Let Christ be in it and not the Law.

As the children of God we are the heirs of His eternal heaven. What a wonderful gift heaven is, man's heart cannot conceive, much less describe. Until we enter upon our heavenly inheritance we are only to have our little faith to go by. To man's reason our faith looks rather forlorn. But because our faith rests on the promises of the infinite God, His promises are also infinite, so much so that nothing can accuse or condemn us.

Verse 7. *And if a son, then an heir of God through Christ.*

A son is an heir, not by virtue of high accomplishments, but by virtue of his birth. He is a mere recipient. His birth makes him an heir, not his labors. In exactly the same way we obtain the eternal gifts of righteousness, resurrection, and everlasting life. We obtain them not as agents, but as beneficiaries. We are the children and heirs of God through faith in Christ. We have Christ to thank for everything.

We are not the heirs of some rich and mighty man, but heirs of God, the almighty Creator of all things. If a person could fully appreciate what it means to be a son and heir of God, he would rate the might and wealth of nations small change in comparison with his heavenly inheritance. What is the world to him who has heaven? No wonder Paul greatly desired to depart and to be with Christ. Nothing would be more welcome to us than early death, knowing that it would spell the end of all our miseries and the beginning of all our happiness. Yes, if a person could perfectly believe this he would not long remain alive. The anticipation of his joy would kill him.

But the law of the members strives against the law of the mind, and makes perfect joy and faith impossible. We need the continued help and comfort of the Holy Spirit. We need His prayers. Paul himself cried out: "O wretched man that I am! Who shall deliver me from the body of this death?" The body of this death spoiled the joy of his spirit. He did not always entertain the sweet and glad expectation of his heavenly inheritance. He often felt miserable.

This goes to show how hard it is to believe. Faith is feeble, because the flesh wars against the spirit. If we could have perfect faith, our loathing for this life in the world would be complete. We would not be so careful about this life. We would not be so attached to the world and the things of the world. We would not feel so good when we have them; we would not feel so bad when we lose them. We would be far more humble and patient and kind. But our faith is weak, because our spirit is weak. In this life we can have only the first-fruits of the Spirit, as Paul says.

Verse 7. *Through Christ.*

The Apostle always has Christ on the tip of his tongue. He foresaw that nothing would be less known in the world some day than the Gospel of Christ. Therefore he talks of Christ continually. As often as he speaks of righteousness, grace, the promise, the adoption, and the inheritance of heaven, he adds the words, "In Christ," or "Through Christ," to show that these blessings are not to be had by the Law, or the deeds of the Law, much less by our own exertions, or by the observance of human traditions, but only by and through and in Christ.

Verses 8, 9. *Howbeit then, when ye knew not God, ye did service unto them which by nature are no gods. But now, after that ye have known God, or rather are known of God, how turn ye again to the weak and beggarly elements, whereunto ye desire again to be in bondage?*

This concludes Paul's discourse on justification. From now to the end of the Epistle the Apostle writes mostly of Christian conduct. But before he follows up his doctrinal discourse with practical precepts he once more reproves the Galatians. He is deeply displeased with them for relinquishing their divine doctrine. He tells them: "You have taken on teachers who intend to recommit you to the Law. By my doctrine I called you out of the darkness of ignorance into the wonderful light of the knowledge of God. I led you out of bondage into the freedom of the sons of God, not by the prescription of laws, but by the gift of heavenly and eternal blessings through Christ Jesus. How could you so soon forsake the light and return to darkness? How could you so quickly stray from grace into the Law, from freedom into bondage?"

The example of the Galatians, of Anabaptists, and other sectarians in our day bears testimony to the ease with which faith may be lost. We take great pains in setting forth the doctrine of faith by preaching and by writing. We are careful to apply the Gospel and the Law in their proper turn. Yet we make little headway because the devil seduces people into misbelief by taking Christ out of their sight and focusing their eyes upon the Law.

But why does Paul accuse the Galatians of reverting to the weak and beggarly elements of the Law when they never had the Law? Why does he not say to them: "At one time you Galatians did not know God. You then served idols that were no gods. But now that you have come to know the true God, why do you go back to the worship of idols?" Paul seems to identify their defection from the Gospel to the Law with their former idolatry. Indeed he does. Whoever gives up the article of justification does not know the true God. It is one and the same thing whether a person reverts to the Law or to the worship of idols. When the article of justification is lost, nothing remains except error, hypocrisy, godlessness, and idolatry.

God will and can be known in no other way than in and through Christ according to the statement of John 1:18, "The only begotten Son, which is in the bosom of the Father, he hath declared him." Christ is the only means whereby we can know God and His will. In Christ we perceive that God is not a cruel judge, but a most loving and merciful Father who to bless and to save us "spared not his own Son, but gave him up for us all." This is truly to know God.

Those who do not know God in Christ arrive at this erroneous conclusion: "I will serve God in such and such a way. I will join this or that order. I will be active in this or that charitable endeavor. God will sanction my good intentions and reward me with everlasting life. For is He not a merciful and generous Father who gives good things even to the unworthy and ungrateful? How much more will He grant unto me everlasting life as a due payment in return for my many good deeds and merits." This is the religion of reason. This is the natural religion of the world. "The natural man receiveth not the things of the Spirit of God" (I Cor. 2:14). "There is none that understandeth, there is none that seeketh after God" (Romans 3:11). Hence, there is really no difference between a

Jew, a Mohammedan, and any other old or new heretic. There may be a difference of persons, places, rites, religions, ceremonies, but as far as their fundamental beliefs are concerned they are all alike.

Is it therefore not extreme folly for Rome and the Mohammedans to fight each other about religion? How about the monks? Why should one monk want to be accounted more holy than another monk because of some silly ceremony, when all the time their basic beliefs are as much alike as one egg is like the other? They all imagine, if we do this or that work, God will have mercy on us; if not, God will be angry.

God never promised to save anybody for his religious observance of ceremonies and ordinances. Those who rely upon such things do serve a god, but it is their own invention of a god, and not the true God. The true God has this to say: No religion pleases Me whereby the Father is not glorified through His Son Jesus. All who give their faith to this Son of Mine, to them I am God and Father. I accept, justify, and save them. All others abide under My curse because they worship creatures instead of Me.

Without the doctrine of justification there can be only ignorance of God. Those who refuse to be justified by Christ are idolaters. They remain under the Law, sin, death, and the power of the devil. Everything they do is wrong.

Nowadays there are many such idolaters who want to be counted among the true confessors of the Gospel. They may even teach that men are delivered from their sins by the death of Christ. But because they attach more importance to charity than to faith in Christ they dishonor Him and pervert His Word. They do not serve the true God, but an idol of their own invention. The true God has never yet smiled upon a person for his charity or virtues, but only for the sake of Christ's merits.

The objection is frequently raised that the Bible commands that we should love God with all our heart. True enough. But because God commands it, it does not follow that we do it. If we could love God with all our heart we should undoubtedly be justified by our obedience, for it is written, "Which if a man do, he shall live in them" (Lev. 18:5). But now comes the Gospel and says: "Because you do not do these things, you cannot live in them." The words, "Thou shalt love the Lord, thy God," require perfect obedience, perfect fear, perfect trust, and perfect love. But where are the people who can render perfection? Hence, this commandment, instead of justifying men, only accuses and condemns them. "Christ is the end of the law for righteousness to every one that believeth" (Romans 10:4).

How may these two contradictory statements of the Apostle, "Ye knew not God," and "Ye worshipped God," be reconciled? I answer: By nature all men know that there is a God, "because that which may be known of God is manifest in them, for God hath showed it unto them. For the invisible things of him from the creation of the world are clearly seen" (Romans 1:19, 20). Furthermore, the different religions to be found among all nations at all times bear witness to the fact that all men have a certain intuitive knowledge of God.

If all men know God how can Paul say that the Galatians did not know God prior to the hearing of the Gospel? I answer: There is a twofold knowledge of God, general and particular. All men have the general and instinctive recognition that there is a God who created heaven and earth, who is just and holy, and who punishes the wicked. How God feels about us, what His intentions are, what He will do for us, or how He will save us, that men cannot know instinctively. It must be revealed to them. I may know a person by sight, and still not know him, because I do not know how he feels about me. Men know instinctively that there is a God. But what His will is toward them, they do not know. It is written: "There is none that understandeth God" (Romans 3:11). Again, "No man hath seen God" (John 1:18). Now, what good does it do you if you know that there is a God, if you do not know how He feels about you, or what He wants of you? People have done a good deal of guessing. The Jew imagines he is doing the will of God if he concentrates on the Law of Moses. The Mohammedan thinks his Koran is the will of God. The monk fancies he is doing the will of God if he performs his vows. But they deceive themselves and become "vain in their imaginations," as Paul says, Romans 1:21. Instead of worshipping the true God, they worship the vain imaginations of their foolish hearts.

What Paul means by saying to the Galatians, "When ye knew not God," is simply this: "There was a time when you did not know the will of God in Christ, but you worshipped gods of your own invention, thinking that you had to perform this or that labor."

Whether you understand the "elements of the world" to mean the Law of Moses, or the religions of the heathen nations, it makes no difference. Those who lapse from the Gospel to the Law are no better off than those who lapse from grace into idolatry. Without Christ all religion is idolatry. Without Christ men will entertain false ideas about God, call their ideas what you like, the laws of Moses, the ordinances of the Pope, the Koran of the Mohammedans, or what have you.

Verse 9. *But now, after that ye have known God.*

"Is it not amazing," cries Paul, "that you Galatians who knew God intimately by the hearing of the Gospel, should all of a sudden revert from the true knowledge of His will in which I thought you were confirmed, to the weak and beggarly elements of the Law which can only enslave you again?"

Verse 9. *Or rather are known of God.*

The Apostle turns the foregoing sentence around. He fears the Galatians have lost God altogether. "Alas," he cries, "have you come to this, that you no longer know God? What else am I to think? Nevertheless, God knows you." Our knowledge of God is rather passive than active. God knows us better than we know God. "Ye are known of God" means that God brings His Gospel to our attention, and endows us with faith and the Holy Spirit. Even in these words the Apostle denies the possibility of our knowing God by the performance of the Law. "No man knoweth who the Father is, but the Son, and he to whom the Son will reveal him" (Luke 10:22). "By his knowledge shall my righteous servant justify many; for he shall bear their iniquities" (Isaiah 53:11).

The Apostle frankly expresses his surprise to the Galatians that they who had known God intimately through the Gospel, should so easily be persuaded by the false apostles to return to the weak and beggarly elements of the Law. I would not be surprised to see my church perverted by some fanatic through one or two sermons. We are no better than the apostles who had to witness the subversion of the churches which they had planted with their own hands. Nevertheless, Christ will reign to the end of the world, and that miraculously, as He did during the Dark Ages.

Paul seems to think rather ill of the Law. He calls it the elements of the world, the weak and beggarly elements of the world. Was it not irreverent for him to speak that way about the holy Law of God? The Law ought to prepare the way of Christ into the hearts of men. That is the true purpose and function of the Law. But if the Law presumes to usurp the place and function of the Gospel, it is no longer the holy Law of God, but a pseudo-Gospel.

If you care to amplify this matter you may add the observation that the Law is a weak and beggarly element because it makes people weak and beggarly. The Law has no power and affluence to make men strong and rich before God. To seek to be justified by the Law amounts to the same thing as if a person who is already weak and feeble should try to find strength in weakness, or as if a person with the dropsy should seek a cure by exposing himself to the pestilence, or as if a leper should go to a leper, and a beggar to a beggar to find health and wealth.

Those who seek to be justified by the Law grow weaker and more destitute right along. They are weak and bankrupt to begin with. They are by nature the children of wrath. Yet for salvation they grasp at the straw of the Law. The Law can only aggravate their weakness and poverty. The Law makes them ten times weaker and poorer than they were before.

I and many others have experienced the truth of this. I have known monks who zealously labored to please God for salvation, but the more they labored the more impatient, miserable, uncertain, and fearful they became. What else can you expect? You cannot grow strong through weakness and rich through poverty. People who prefer the Law to the Gospel are like Aesop's dog who let go of the meat to snatch at the shadow of the water. There is no satisfaction in the Law. What satisfaction can there be in collecting laws with which to torment oneself and others? One law breeds ten more until their number is legion.

Who would have thought it possible that the Galatians, taught as they were by that efficient apostle and teacher, Paul, could so quickly be led astray by the false apostles? To fall away from the Gospel is an easy matter because few people appreciate what an excellent treasure the knowledge of Christ really is. People are not sufficiently exercised in their faith by afflictions. They do not wrestle against sin. They live in security without conflict. Because they have never been tried in the furnace of affliction they are not properly equipped with the armor of God and know not how to use the sword of the Spirit. As long as they are being shepherded by faithful pastors, all is well. But when their faithful shepherds are gone and wolves disguised as sheep break into the fold, back they go to the weak and beggarly elements of the Law.

Whoever goes back to the Law loses the knowledge of the truth, fails in the recognition of his sinfulness, does not know God, nor the devil, nor himself, and does not understand the meaning and purpose of the Law. Without the knowledge of Christ a man will always argue that the Law is necessary for salvation, that it will strengthen the weak and enrich the poor. Wherever this opinion holds sway the promises of God are denied, Christ is demoted, hypocrisy and idolatry are established.

Verse 9. *Whereunto ye desire again to be in bondage.*

The Apostle pointedly asks the Galatians whether they desire to be in bondage again to the Law. The Law is weak and poor, the sinner is weak and poor—two feeble beggars trying to help each other. They cannot do it. They only wear each other out. But through Christ a weak and poor sinner is revived and enriched unto eternal life.

Verse 10. Ye observe days, and months, and times, and years.

The Apostle Paul knew what the false apostles were teaching the Galatians: The observance of days, and months, and times, and years. The Jews had been obliged to keep holy the Sabbath Day, the new moons, the feast of the passover, the feast of tabernacles, and other feasts. The false apostles constrained the Galatians to observe these Jewish feasts under threat of damnation. Paul hastens to tell the Galatians that they were exchanging their Christian liberty for the weak and beggarly elements of the world.

Verse 11. I am afraid of you, lest I have bestowed upon you labor in vain.

It grieves the Apostle to think that he might have preached the Gospel to the Galatians in vain. But this statement expresses more than grief. Behind his apparent disappointment at their failure lurks the sharp reprimand that they had forsaken Christ and that they were proving themselves to be obstinate unbelievers. But he does not openly condemn them for fear that oversharp criticism might alienate them altogether. He therefore changes the tone of his voice and speaks kindly to them.

Verse 12. Be as I am; for I am as ye are.

Up to this point Paul has been occupied with the doctrinal aspect of the apostasy of the Galatians. He did not conceal his disappointment at their lack of stability. He had rebuked them. He had called them fools, crucifiers of Christ, etc. Now that the more important part of his Epistle has been finished, he realizes that he has handled the Galatians too roughly. Anxious lest he should do more harm than good, he is careful to let them see that his criticism proceeds from affection and a true apostolic concern for their welfare. He is eager to mitigate his sharp words with gentle sentiments in order to win them again.

Like Paul, all pastors and ministers ought to have much sympathy for their poor straying sheep, and instruct them in the spirit of meekness. They cannot be straightened out in any other way. Oversharp criticism provokes anger and despair, but no repentance. And here let us note, by the way, that true doctrine always produces concord. When men embrace errors, the tie of Christian love is broken.

At the beginning of the Reformation we were honored as the true ministers of Christ. Suddenly certain false brethren began to hate us. We had given them no offense, no occasion to hate us. They knew then as they know now that ours is the singular desire to publish the Gospel of Christ everywhere. What changed their attitude toward us? False doctrine. Seduced into error by the false apostles, the Galatians refused to acknowledge St. Paul as their pastor. The name and doctrine of Paul became obnoxious to them. I fear this Epistle recalled very few from their error.

Paul knew that the false apostles would misconstrue his censure of the Galatians to their own advantage and say: "So this is your Paul whom you praise so much. What sweet names he is calling you in his letter. When he was with you he acted like a father, but now he acts like a dictator." Paul knew what to expect of the false apostles and therefore he is worried. He does not know what to say. It is hard for a man to defend his cause at a distance, especially when he has reason to think that he personally has fallen into disfavor.

Verse 12. Be as I am; for I am as ye are.

In beseeching the Galatians to be as he is, Paul expresses the hope that they might hold the same affection for him that he holds for them. "Perhaps I have been a little hard with you. Forgive it. Do not judge my heart according to my words."

We request the same consideration for ourselves. Our way of writing is incisive and straightforward. But there is no bitterness in our heart. We seek the honor of Christ and the welfare of men. We do not hate the Pope as to wish him ill. We do not desire the death of our false brethren. We desire that they may turn from their evil ways to Christ and be saved with us. A teacher chastises the pupil to reform him. The rod hurts, but correction is necessary. A father punishes his son because he loves his son. If he did not love the lad he would not punish him but let him have his own way in everything until he comes to harm. Paul beseeches the Galatians to look upon his correction as a sign that he really cared for them. "Now no chastening for the present seemeth to be joyous, but grievous; nevertheless, afterward it yieldeth the peaceable fruit of righteousness unto them which are exercised thereby" (Heb. 12:11).

Although Paul seeks to soften the effect of his reproachful words, he does not take them back. When a physician administers a bitter potion to a patient, he does it to cure the patient. The fact that the medicine is bitter is no fault of the physician. The malady calls for a bitter medicine. Paul wants the Galatians to judge his words according to the situation that made them necessary.

Verse 12. Brethren, I beseech you... Ye have not injured me at all.

Would you call it beseeching the Galatians to call them "bewitched," "disobedient," "crucifiers of Christ"? The Apostle calls it an earnest beseeching. And so it is. When a father corrects his son it means as if he were saying: "My son, I beseech you, be a good boy."

Verse 12. Ye have not injured me at all.

"I am not angry with you," says Paul. "Why should I be angry with you, since you have done me no injury at all?"

To this the Galatians reply: "Why, then, do you say that we are perverted, that we have forsaken the true doctrine, that we are foolish, bewitched, etc., if you are not angry? We must have offended you somehow."

Paul answers: "You Galatians have not injured me. You have injured yourselves. I chide you not because I wish you ill. I have no reason to wish you ill. God is my witness, you have done me no wrong. On the contrary, you have been very good to me. The reason I write to you is because I love you."

The bitter potion must be sweetened with honey and sugar to make it palatable. When parents have punished their children they give them apples, pears, and other good things to show them that they mean well.

Verses 13, 14. Ye know how through infirmity of the flesh I preached the gospel unto you at the first. And my temptation which was in my flesh ye despised not, nor rejected; but received me as an angel of God, even as Christ Jesus.

"You Galatians were very good to me. When I began to preach the Gospel to you in the infirmity of my flesh and in great temptation you were not at all offended. On the contrary, you were so loving, so kind, so friendly towards me, you received me like an angel, like Jesus Himself."

Indeed, the Galatians are to be commended for receiving the Gospel from a man as unimposing and afflicted all around as Paul was. Wherever he preached the Gospel, Jews and Gentiles raved against him. All the influential and religious people of his day denounced him. But the Galatians did not mind it. That was greatly to their honor. And Paul does not neglect to praise them for it. This praise Paul bestows on none of the other churches to which he wrote.

St. Jerome and others of the ancient fathers allege this infirmity of Paul's to have been some physical defect, or concupiscence. Jerome and the other diagnosticians lived at a time when the Church enjoyed peace and prosperity, when the bishops increased in wealth and standing, when pastors and bishops no longer sat over the Word of God. No wonder they failed to understand Paul.

When Paul speaks of the infirmity of his flesh he does not mean some physical defect or carnal lust, but the sufferings and afflictions which he endured in his body. What these infirmities were he himself explains in II Corinthians 12:9, 10: "Most gladly therefore will I rather glory in my infirmities, that the power of Christ may rest upon me. Therefore I take pleasure in infirmities, in reproaches, in necessities, in persecutions, in distresses for Christ's sake: for when I am weak, then am I strong." And in the eleventh chapter of the same Epistle the Apostle writes: "In labors more abundant, in stripes above measure, in prisons more frequent, in deaths oft. Of the Jews five times received I forty stripes save one. Thrice was I beaten with rods, once was I stoned, thrice I suffered shipwreck," etc. (II Cor. 11:23–25.) By the infirmity of his flesh Paul meant these afflictions and not some chronic disease. He reminds the Galatians how he was always in peril at the hands of the Jews, Gentiles, and false brethren, how he suffered hunger and want.

Now, the afflictions of the believers always offend people. Paul knew it and therefore has high praise for the Galatians because they over looked his afflictions and received him like an angel. Christ forewarned the faithful against the offense of the Cross, saying: "Blessed is he, whosoever shall not be offended in me" (Matt. 11:6). Surely it is no easy thing to confess Him Lord of all and Savior of the world who was a reproach of men, and despised of the people, and the laughing stock of the world (Ps. 22:7). I say, to value this poor Christ, so spitefully scorned, spit upon, scourged, and crucified, more than the riches of the richest, the strength of the strongest, the wisdom of the wisest, is something. It is worth being called blessed.

Paul not only had outward afflictions but also inner, spiritual afflictions. He refers to these in II Corinthians 7:6, "Without were fightings, within were fears." In his letter to the Philippians Paul makes mention of the restoration of Epaphroditus as a special act of mercy on the part of God, "lest I should have sorrow upon sorrow."

Considering the many afflictions of Paul, we are not surprised to hear him loudly praising the Galatians for not being offended at him as others were. The world thinks us mad because we go about to comfort, to help, to save others while we ourselves are in distress. People tell us: "Physician, heal thyself" (Luke 4:23).

The Apostle tells the Galatians that he will keep their kindness in perpetual remembrance. Indirectly, he also reminds them how much they had loved him before the invasion of the false apostles, and gives them a hint that they should return to their first love for him.

Verse 15. Where is then the blessedness ye spake of?

"How much happier you used to be. And how you Galatians used to tell me that you were blessed. And how much did I not praise and commend you formerly." Paul reminds them of former and better times in an effort to mitigate his sharp reproaches, lest the false apostles should slander him and misconstrue his letter to his disadvantage and to their own advantage. Such snakes in the grass are equal to anything. They will pervert words spoken from a sincere heart and twist them to mean just the opposite of what they were intended to convey. They are like spiders that suck venom out of sweet and fragrant flowers. The poison is not in the flowers, but it is the nature of the spider to turn what is good and wholesome into poison.

Verse 15. For I bear you record, that, if it had been possible, ye would have plucked out your own eyes, and have given them to me.

The Apostle continues his praise of the Galatians. "You did not only treat me very courteously. If it had been necessary you would have plucked out your eyes and sacrificed your lives for me." And in very fact the Galatians sacrificed their lives for Paul. By receiving and maintaining Paul they called upon their own heads the hatred and malice of all the Jews and Gentiles.

Nowadays the name of Luther carries the same stigma. Whoever praises Luther is a worse sinner than an idolater, perjurer, or thief.

Verse 16. Am I therefore become your enemy, because I tell you the truth?

Paul's reason for praising the Galatians is to avoid giving them the impression as if he were their enemy because he had reprimanded them.

A true friend will admonish his erring brother, and if the erring brother has any sense at all he will thank his friend. In the world truth produces hatred. Whoever speaks the truth is counted an enemy. But among friends it is not so, much less among Christians. The Apostle wants his Galatians to know that just because he had told them the truth they are not to think that he dislikes them. "I told you the truth because I love you."

Verse 17. They zealously affect you, but not well.

Paul takes the false apostles to task for their flattery. Satan's satellites softsoap the people. Paul calls it "by good words and fair speeches to deceive the hearts of the simple" (Romans 16:18).

The false apostles manifested a zeal for the Galatians that did them no good. At any rate, they succeeded in making the Galatians believe that they were very much concerned about them. Paul warns them to discriminate between a good zeal and a wrong zeal. "I am as zealous for you," says Paul, "as they are. Judge which zeal is better, mine or theirs. Do not be so easily taken in by their zeal."

Verse 17. Yea, they would exclude you, that ye might affect them.

"Do you Galatians know why the false apostles are so zealous about you? They expect you to reciprocate. And that would leave me out. If their zeal were right they would not mind your loving me. But they hate my doctrine and want to stamp it out. In order to bring this to pass they go about to alienate your hearts from me and to make me obnoxious to you." In this way Paul brings the false apostles into suspicion. He questions their motives. He maintains that their zeal is mere pretense to deceive the Galatians. Our Savior Christ also warned us, saying: "Beware of false prophets, which come to you in sheep's clothing" (Matt. 7:15).

Paul was considerably disturbed by the commotions and changes that followed in the wake of his preaching. He was accused of being "a pestilent fellow, a mover of sedition among all the Jews throughout the world" (Acts 24:5). In Philippi the townspeople cried that he troubled their city and taught customs which were not lawful for them to receive (Acts 16:20, 21).

All troubles, calamities, famines, wars were laid to the charge of the Gospel of the apostles. However, the apostles were not deterred by such calumnies from preaching the Gospel. They knew that they "ought to obey God rather than men," and that it was better for the world to be upset than to be ignorant of Christ.

Do you think for a moment that these reactions did not worry the apostles? They were not made of iron. They foresaw the revolutionary character of the Gospel. They also foresaw the dissensions that would creep into the Church. It was bad news for Paul when he heard that the Corinthians were denying the resurrection of the dead, that the churches he had planted were experiencing all kinds of difficulties, and that the Gospel was being supplanted by false doctrines.

But Paul also knew that the Gospel was not to blame. He did not resign his office because he knew that the Gospel he preached was the power of God unto salvation to every one that believes.

The same criticism which was leveled at the apostles is leveled at us. The doctrine of the Gospel, we are told, is the cause of all the present unrest in the world. There is no wrong that is not laid to our charge. But why? We do not spread wicked lies. We preach the glad tidings of Christ. Our opponents will bear us out when we say that we never fail to urge respect for the constituted authorities, because that is the will of God.

All of these vilifications cannot discourage us. We know that there is nothing the devil hates worse than the Gospel. It is one of his little tricks to blame the Gospel for every evil in the world. Formerly, when the traditions of the fathers were taught in the Church, the devil was not excited as he is now. It goes to show that our doctrine is of God, else "behemoth would lie under shady trees, in the covert of the reed, and fens." The fact that he is again walking about as a roaring lion to stir up riots and disorders is a sure sign that he has begun to feel the effect of our preaching.

Verse 18. *But it is good to be zealously affected always in a good thing, and not only when I am present with you.*

"When I was present with you, you loved me, although I preached the Gospel to you in the infirmity of my flesh. The fact that I am now absent from you ought not to change your attitude towards me. Although I am absent in the flesh, I am with you in spirit and in my doctrine which you ought to retain by all means because through it you received the Holy Spirit."

Verse 19. *My little children, of whom I travail in birth again until Christ be formed in you.*

With every single word the Apostle seeks to regain the confidence of the Galatians. He now calls them lovingly his little children. He adds the simile: "Of whom I travail in birth again." As parents reproduce their physical characteristics in their children, so the apostles reproduced their faith in the hearts of the hearers, until Christ was formed in them. A person has the form of Christ when he believes in Christ to the exclusion of everything else. This faith in Christ is engendered by the Gospel as the Apostle declares in I Corinthians 4:15: "In Christ Jesus I have begotten you through the Gospel"; and in II Corinthians 3:3, "Ye are the epistle of Christ ministered by us, written not with ink, but with the Spirit of the living God." The Word of God falling from the lips of the apostle or minister enters into the heart of the hearer. The Holy Ghost impregnates the Word so that it brings forth the fruit of faith. In this manner every Christian pastor is a spiritual father who forms Christ in the hearts of his hearers.

At the same time Paul indicts the false apostles. He says: "I have begotten you Galatians through the Gospel, giving you the form of Christ. But these false apostles are giving you a new form, the form of Moses." Note the Apostle does not say, "Of whom I travail in birth again until I be formed in you," but "until Christ be formed in you." The false apostles had torn the form of Christ out of the hearts of the Galatians and substituted their own form. Paul endeavors to reform them, or rather reform Christ in them.

Verse 20. *I desire to be present with you now, and to change my voice.*

A common saying has it that a letter is a dead messenger. Something is lacking in all writing. You can never be sure how the written page will affect the reader, because his mood, his circumstances, his affections are so changeable. It is different with the spoken word. If it is harsh and ill-timed it can always be remodeled. No wonder the Apostle expresses the wish that he could speak to the Galatians in person. He could change his voice according to their attitude. If he saw that they were repentant he could soften the tone of his voice. If he saw that they were stubborn he could speak to them more earnestly. This way he did not know how to deal with them by letter. If his Epistle is too severe it will do more damage than good. If it is too gentle, it will not correct conditions. But if he could be with them in person he could change his voice as the occasion demanded.

Verse 20. *For I stand in doubt of you.*

"I do not know how to take you. I do not know how to approach you by letter." In order to make sure that he leaves no stone unturned in his effort to recall them to the Gospel of Christ, he chides, entreats, praises, and blames the Galatians, trying every way to hit the right note and tone of voice.

Verse 21. *Tell me, ye that desire to be under the law, do ye not hear the law?*

Here Paul would have closed his Epistle because he did not know what else to say. He wishes he could see the Galatians in person and straighten out their difficulties. But he is not sure whether the Galatians have fully understood the difference between the Gospel and the Law. To make sure, he introduces another illustration. He knows people like illustrations and stories. He knows that Christ Himself made ample use of parables.

Paul is an expert at allegories. They are dangerous things. Unless a person has a thorough knowledge of Christian doctrine he had better leave allegories alone.

The allegory which Paul is about to bring is taken from the Book of Genesis which he calls the Law. True, that book contains no mention of the Law. Paul simply follows the custom of the Jews who included the first book of Moses in the collective term, "Law." Jesus even included the Psalms.

Verses 22, 23. *For it is written, that Abraham had two sons, the one by a bondmaid, the other by a freewoman. But he who was of the bondwoman was born after the flesh; but he of the freewoman was by promise.*

This is Paul's allegory. Abraham had two sons: Ishmael by Hagar, and Isaac by Sarah. They were both the true sons of Abraham, with this difference, that Ishmael was born after the flesh, i.e., without the commandment and promise of God, while Isaac was born according to the promise.

With the permission of Sarah, Abraham took Hagar, Sarah's bondwoman, to wife. Sarah knew that God had promised to make her husband Abraham the father of a nation, and she hoped that she would be the mother of this promised nation. But with the passage of the years her hope died out. In order that the promise of God should not be annulled by her barrenness this holy woman resigned her right and honor to her maid. This was no easy thing for her to do. She abased herself. She thought: "God is no liar. What He has promised He will perform. But perhaps God does not want me to be the mother of Abraham's posterity. Perhaps He prefers Hagar for the honor."

Ishmael was thus born without a special word or promise of God, at the mere request of Sarah. God did not command Abraham to take Hagar, nor did God promise to bless the coalition. It is evident that Ishmael was the son of Abraham after the flesh, and not after the promise.

In the ninth chapter of the Epistle to the Romans St. Paul advances the same argument which he amplifies into an allegory in writing to the Galatians. There he argues that all the children of Abraham are not the children of God. For Abraham had two kinds of children, children born of the promise, like Isaac, and other children born without the promise, as Ishmael. With this argument Paul squelched the proud Jews who gloried that they were the children of God because they were the seed and the children of Abraham. Paul makes it clear enough that it takes more than an Abrahamic pedigree to be a child of God. To be a child of God requires faith in Christ.

Verse 24. *Which things are an allegory.*

Allegories are not very convincing, but like pictures they visualize a matter. If Paul had not brought in advance indisputable arguments for the righteousness of faith over against the righteousness of works this allegory would do little good. Having first fortified his case with invincible arguments, he can afford to inject this allegory to add impressiveness and beauty to his presentation.

Verses 24, 25. *For these are the two covenants; the one from the mount Sinai, which gendereth to bondage, which is Agar. For this Agar is mount Sinai in Arabia.*

In this allegory Abraham represents God. Abraham had two sons, born respectively of Hagar and Sarah. The two women represent the two Testaments. The Old Testament is Mount Sinai, the bondwoman, Hagar. The Arabians call Mount Sinai Agar. It may be that the similarity of these two names gave Paul his idea for this allegory. As Hagar bore Abraham a son who was not an heir but a servant, so Sinai, the Law, the allegorical Hagar, bore God a carnal and servile people of the Law without promise. The Law has a promise but it is a conditional promise, depending upon whether people fulfill the Law.

The Jews regarded the conditional promises of the Law as if they were unconditional. When the prophets foretold the destruction of Jerusalem, the Jews stoned them as blasphemers of God. They never gave it any thought that there was a condition attached to the Law which reads: "If you keep the commandments it shall be well with thee."

Verse 25. *And answereth to Jerusalem which now is, and is in bondage with her children.*

A little while ago Paul called Mount Sinai, Hagar. He would now gladly make Jerusalem the Sarah of the New Testament, but he cannot. The earthly Jerusalem is not Sarah, but a part of Hagar. Hagar lives there in the home of the Law, the Temple, the priesthood, the ceremonies, and whatever else was ordained in the Law at Mount Sinai.

I would have been tempted to call Jerusalem, Sarah, or the New Testament. I would have been pleased with this turn of the allegory. It goes to show that not everybody has the gift of allegory. Would you not think it perfectly proper to call Sinai Hagar and Jerusalem Sarah? True, Paul does call Sarah Jerusalem. But he has the spiritual and heavenly Jerusalem in mind, not the earthly Jerusalem. Sarah represents that spiritual Jerusalem where there is no Law but only the promise, and where the inhabitants are free.

To show that the Law has been quite abolished, the earthly Jerusalem was completely destroyed with all her ornaments, temples, and ceremonies.

Verse 26. *But Jerusalem which is above is free, which is the mother of us all.*

The earthly Jerusalem with its ordinances and laws represents Hagar and her offspring. They are slaves to the

Law, sin and death. But the heavenly Jerusalem is Sarah, the free woman. This heavenly Jerusalem is the Church, that is to say the number of all believers throughout the world, having one and the same Gospel, one and the same faith in Christ, one and the same Holy Ghost, and the same sacraments.

Do not mistake this one word "above" to refer to the triumphant Church in heaven, but to the militant Church on earth. In Philippians 3:20, the Apostle uses the phrase: "Our conversation is in heaven," not locally in heaven, but in spirit. When a believer accepts the heavenly gifts of the Gospel he is in heaven. So also in Ephesians 1:3, "Who hath blessed us with all spiritual blessings in heavenly places in Christ." Jerusalem here means the universal Christian Church on earth.

Sarah, the Church, as the bride of Christ bears free children who are not subject to the Law.

Verse 27. *For it is written, Rejoice, thou barren that bearest not; break forth and cry, thou that travailest not: for the desolate hath many more children than she which hath an husband.*

Paul quotes the allegorical prophecy of Isaiah to the effect that the mother of many children must die desolately, while the barren woman shall have an abundance of children (Isaiah 54:1). He applies this prophecy to Hagar and Sarah, to the Law and the Gospel. The Law as the husband of the fruitful woman procreates many children. For men of all ages have had the idea that they are right when they follow after the Law and outwardly perform its requirements.

Although the Law has many children, they are not free. They are slaves. As servants they cannot have a share in the inheritance, but are driven from the house as Ishmael was cast out of the house of Abraham. In fact the servants of the Law are even now barred from the kingdom of light and liberty, for "he that believeth not, is condemned already" (John 3:18). As the servants of the Law they remain under the curse of the Law, under sin and death, under the power of the devil, and under the wrath and judgment of God.

On the other hand, Sarah, the free Church, seems barren. The Gospel of the Cross which the Church proclaims does not have the appeal that the Law has for men, and therefore it does not find many adherents. The Church does not look prosperous. Unbelievers have always predicted the death of the Church. The Jews were quite certain that the Church would not long endure. They said to Paul: "As concerning this sect, we know that everywhere it is spoken against" (Acts 28:22). No matter how barren and forsaken, how weak and desolate the Church may seem, she alone is really fruitful before God. By the Gospel she procreates an infinite number of children that are free heirs of everlasting life.

The Law, "the old husband," is really dead. But not all people know it, or want to know it. They labor and bear the burden and the heat of the day, and bring forth many children, children that are bastards like themselves, children born to be put out of the house like Ishmael to perish forever. Accursed be that doctrine, life, and religion which endeavors to obtain righteousness before God by the Law and its creeds.

The scholastics think that the judicial and ceremonial laws of Moses were abolished by the coming of Christ, but not the moral law. They are blind. When Paul declares that we are delivered from the curse of the Law he means the whole Law, particularly the moral law which more than the other laws accuses, curses, and condemns the conscience. The Ten Commandments have no right to condemn that conscience in which Jesus dwells, for Jesus has taken from the Ten Commandments the right and power to curse us.

Not as if the conscience is now insensitive to the terrors of the Law, but the Law cannot drive the conscience to despair. "There is now no condemnation to them which are in Christ Jesus" (Romans 8:1). "If the Son shall make you free, ye shall be free indeed" (John 8:36).

You will complain: "But I am not doing anything." That is right. You cannot do a thing to be delivered from the tyranny of the Law. But listen to the glad tidings which the Holy Ghost brings to you in the words of the prophet: "Rejoice, thou barren." As Christ is greater than the Law, so much more excellent is the righteousness of Christ than the righteousness of the Law.

In one more respect the Law has been abolished. The civil laws of Moses do not concern us, and should not be put back in force. That does not mean that we are exempt from obedience to the civil laws under which we live. On the contrary, the Gospel commands Christians to obey government "not only for wrath, but also for conscience sake" (Romans 13:5).

Neither do the ordinances of Moses or those of the Pope concern us. But because life cannot go on without some ordinances, the Gospel permits regulations to be made in the Church in regard to special days, times, places, etc., in order that the people may know upon what day, at what hour, and in what place to assemble for the Word of God. Such directions are desirable that "all things be done decently and in order" (I Cor. 14:40).

These directions may be changed or omitted altogether, as long as no offense is given to the weak.

Paul, however, refers particularly to the abolition of the moral law. If faith alone in Christ justifies, then the whole Law is abolished without exception. And this the Apostle proves by the testimony of Isaiah, who bids the barren to rejoice because she will have many children, whereas she that has a husband and many children will be forsaken.

Isaiah calls the Church barren because her children are born without effort by the Word of faith through the Spirit of God. It is a matter of birth, not of exertion. The believer too works, but not in an effort to become a son and an heir of God. He is that before he goes to work. He is born a son and an heir. He works for the glory of God and the welfare of his fellowmen.

Verse 28. *Now we, brethren, as Isaac was, are the children of promise.*

The Jews claimed to be the children of God because they were the children of Abraham. Jesus answered them, John 8:39, 40, "If ye were Abraham's children, ye would do the works of Abraham. But now ye seek to kill me, a man that hath told you the truth." And in verse 42: "If God were your Father, ye would love me." In other words: "You are not the children of God. If you were, you would know and love me. Brothers born and living together in the same house recognize each other. You do not recognize me. You are of your father, the devil."

We are not like these Jews, the children of the bondwoman, the Law, who were cast out of the house by Jesus. We are children of the promise like Isaac, born of grace and faith unto an everlasting inheritance.

Verse 29. *But as that he that was born after the flesh persecuted him that was born after the Spirit, even so it is now.*

This is a cheering thought. We who are born of the Gospel, and live in Christ, and rejoice in our inheritance, have Ishmael for our enemy. The children of the Law will always persecute the children of the Gospel. This is our daily experience. Our opponents tell us that everything was at peace before the Gospel was revived by us. Since then the whole world has been upset. People blame us and the Gospel for everything, for the disobedience of subjects to their rulers, for wars, plagues, and famines, for revolutions, and every other evil that can be imagined. No wonder our opponents think they are doing God a favor by hating and persecuting us. Ishmael will persecute Isaac.

We invite our opponents to tell us what good things attended the preaching of the Gospel by the apostles. Did not the destruction of Jerusalem follow on the heels of the Gospel? And how about the overthrow of the Roman Empire? Did not the whole world seethe with unrest as the Gospel was preached in the whole world? We do not say that the Gospel instigated these upheavals. The iniquity of man did it.

Our opponents blame our doctrine for the present turmoil. But ours is a doctrine of grace and peace. It does not stir up trouble. Trouble starts when the people, the nations and their rulers of the earth rage and take counsel together against the Lord, and against His anointed (Psalm 2). But all their counsels shall be brought to naught. "He that sitteth in the heavens shall laugh: the Lord shall have them in derision" (Psalm 2:4). Let them cry out against us as much as they like. We know that they are the cause of all their own troubles.

As long as we preach Christ and confess Him to be our Savior, we must be content to be called vicious trouble makers. "These that have turned the world upside down are come hither also; and these all do contrary to the decrees of Caesar," so said the Jews of Paul and Silas (Acts 17:6, 7). Of Paul they said: "We have found this man a pestilent fellow, and a mover of sedition among all the Jews throughout the world, and a ringleader of the sect of the Nazarenes." The Gentiles uttered similar complaints: "These men do exceedingly trouble our city."

This man Luther is also accused of being a pestilent fellow who troubles the papacy and the Roman empire. If I would keep silent, all would be well, and the Pope would no more persecute me. The moment I open my mouth the Pope begins to fume and to rage. It seems we must choose between Christ and the Pope. Let the Pope perish.

Christ foresaw the reaction of the world to the Gospel. He said: "I am come to send fire on the earth, and what will I, if it be already kindled?" (Luke 12:49.)

Do not take the statement of our opponents seriously, that no good can come of the preaching of the Gospel. What do they know? They would not recognize the fruits of the Gospel if they saw them.

At any rate, our opponents cannot accuse us of adultery, murder, theft, and such crimes. The worst they can say about us is that we have the Gospel. What is wrong with the Gospel? We teach that Christ, the Son of God, has redeemed us from sin and everlasting death. This is not our doctrine. It belongs to Christ. If there is anything wrong with it, it is not our fault. If they want to condemn Christ for being our Savior and Redeemer, that is their lookout. We are mere onlookers, watching to see who will win the victory, Christ or His opponents.

On one occasion Jesus remarked: "If ye were of the

world, the world would love his own, but because ye are not of the world, but I have chosen you out of the world, therefore the world hateth you" (John 15:19). In other words: "I am the cause of all your troubles. I am the one for whose sake you are killed. If you did not confess my name, the world would not hate you. The servant is not greater than his lord. If they have persecuted me, they will also persecute you."

Christ takes all the blame. He says: "You have not incurred the hatred and persecutions of the world. I have. But be of good cheer; I have overcome the world."

Verse 30. *Nevertheless what saith the Scripture? Cast out the bondwoman and her son: for the son of the bondwoman shall not be heir with the son of the free woman.*

Sarah's demand that the bondwoman and her son be cast out of the house was undoubtedly a blow to Abraham. He felt sorry for his son Ishmael. The Scripture explicitly states Abraham's grief in the words: "And the thing was very grievous in Abraham's sight, because of his son" (Gen. 21:11). But God approved Sarah's action and said to Abraham: "Let it not be grievous in thy sight because of the lad, and because of thy bondwoman; in all that Sarah hath said unto thee, hearken unto her voice; for in Isaac shall thy seed be called" (Gen. 21:12).

The Holy Ghost contemptuously calls the admirers of the Law the children of the bondwoman. "If you do not know your mother, I will tell you what kind of a woman she is. She is a slave. And you are slaves. You are slaves of the Law and therefore slaves of sin, death, and everlasting damnation. You are not fit to be heirs. You are put out of the house."

This is the sentence which God pronounces upon the Ishmaelites, the papists, and all others who trust in their own merits, and persecute the Church of Christ. Because they are slaves and persecutors of the children of the free woman, they shall be cast out of the house of God forever. They shall have no inheritance with the children of the promise. This sentence stands forever.

This sentence affects not only those popes, cardinals bishops, and monks who were notoriously wicked and made their bellies their Gods. It strikes, also, those who lived in all sincerity to please God and to merit the forgiveness of their sins through a life of self-denial. Even these will be cast out, because they are children of the bondwoman.

Our opponents do not defend their own moral delinquency. The better ones deplore and abhor it. But they defend and uphold their doctrine of works which is of the devil. Our quarrel is not with those who live in manifest sins. Our quarrel is with those among them who think they live like angels, claiming that they do not only perform the Ten Commandments of God, but also the sayings of Christ, and many good works that God does not expect of them. We quarrel with them because they refuse to have Jesus' merit count alone for righteousness.

St. Bernard was one of the best of the medieval saints. He lived a chaste and holy life. But when it came to dying he did not trust in his chaste life for salvation. He prayed: "I have lived a wicked life. But Thou, Lord Jesus, hast a heaven to give unto me. First, because Thou art the Son of God. Secondly, because Thou hast purchased heaven for me by Thy suffering and death. Thou givest heaven to me, not because I earned it, but because Thou hast earned it for me." If any of the Romanists are saved it is because they forget their good deeds and merits and feel like Paul: "Not having mine own righteousness which is of the law, but that which is through the faith of Christ" (Phil. 3:9).

Verse 31. *So then, brethren, we are not children of the bondwoman, but of the free.*

With this sentence the Apostle Paul concludes his allegory of the barren Church. This sentence forms a clear rejection of the righteousness of the Law and a confirmation of the doctrine of justification. In the next chapter Paul lays special stress upon the freedom which the children of the free woman enjoy. He treats of Christian liberty, the knowledge of which is very necessary. The liberty which Christ purchased for us is a bulwark to us in our battle against spiritual tyranny. Therefore we must carefully study this doctrine of Christian liberty, not only for the confirmation of the doctrine of justification, but also for the comfort and encouragement of those who are weak in faith.

GALATIONS 5

In this chapter the Apostle Paul presents the doctrine of Christian liberty in a final effort to persuade the Galatians to give up the nefarious doctrine of the false apostles. To accomplish his purpose he adduces threats and promises, trying in every way possible to keep them in the liberty which Christ purchased for them.

Verse 1. *Stand fast therefore in the liberty wherewith Christ hath made us free.*

"Be steadfast, not careless. Lie not down and sleep, but stand up. Be watchful. Hold fast the liberty wherewith Christ hath made you free." Those who loll cannot keep this liberty. Satan hates the light of the Gospel. When it begins to shine a little he fights against it with might and main.

What liberty does Paul mean? Not civil liberty (for which we have the government to thank), but the liberty which Christ has procured for us.

At one time the emperor was compelled to grant to the bishop of Rome certain immunities and privileges. This is civil liberty. That liberty exempts the clergy from certain public charges. Then there is also another kind of "liberty," when people obey neither the laws of God nor the laws of men, but do as they please. This carnal liberty the people want in our day. We are not now speaking of this liberty. Neither are we speaking of civil liberty.

Paul is speaking of a far better liberty, the liberty "wherewith Christ hath made us free," not from material bonds, not from the Babylonian captivity, not from the tyranny of the Turks, but from the eternal wrath of God.

Where is this liberty?

In the conscience.

Our conscience is free and quiet because it no longer has to fear the wrath of God. This is real liberty, compared with which every other kind of liberty is not worth mentioning. Who can adequately express the boon that comes to a person when he has the heart-assurance that God will nevermore be angry with him, but will forever be merciful to him for Christ's sake? This is indeed a marvelous liberty, to have the sovereign God for our Friend and Father who will defend, maintain, and save us in this life and in the life to come.

As an outgrowth of this liberty, we are at the same time free from the Law, sin, death, the power of the devil, hell, etc. Since the wrath of God has been assuaged by Christ no Law, sin, or death may now accuse and condemn us. These foes of ours will continue to frighten us, but not too much. The worth of our Christian liberty cannot be exaggerated.

Our conscience must he trained to fall back on the freedom purchased for us by Christ. Though the fears of the Law, the terrors of sin, the horror of death assail us occasionally, we know that these feelings shall not endure, because the prophet quotes God as saying: "In a little wrath I hid my face from thee for a moment: but with everlasting kindness will I have mercy on thee" (Isa. 54:8).

We shall appreciate this liberty all the more when we bear in mind that it was Jesus Christ, the Son of God, who purchased it with His own blood. Hence, Christ's liberty is given us not by the Law, or for our own righteousness, but freely for Christ's sake. In the eighth chapter of the Gospel of St. John, Jesus declares: "If the Son shall make you free, ye shall be free indeed." He only stands between us and the evils which trouble and afflict us and which He has overcome for us.

Reason cannot properly evaluate this gift. Who can fully appreciate the blessing of the forgiveness of sins and of everlasting life? Our opponents claim that they also possess this liberty. But they do not. When they are put to the test all their self-confidence slips from them. What else can they expect when they trust in works and not in the Word of God?

Our liberty is founded on Christ Himself, who sits at the right hand of God and intercedes for us. Therefore our liberty is sure and valid as long as we believe in Christ. As long as we cling to Him with a steadfast faith we possess His priceless gifts. But if we are careless and indifferent we shall lose them. It is not without good reason that Paul urges us to watch and to stand fast. He knew that the devil delights in taking this liberty away from us.

Verse 1. *And be not entangled again with the yoke of bondage.*

Because reason prefers the righteousness of the Law to the righteousness of faith, Paul calls the Law a yoke, a yoke of bondage. Peter also calls it a yoke. "Why tempt ye God, to put a yoke upon the neck of the disciples which neither our fathers nor we were able to bear?" (Acts 15:10.)

In this passage Paul again disparages the pernicious notion that the Law is able to make men righteous before God, a notion deeply rooted in man's reason. All mankind is so wrapped up in this idea that it is hard to drag it out of people. Paul compares those who seek to be justified by the Law to oxen that are hitched to the yoke. Like oxen that toil in the yoke all day, and in the evening are turned out to graze along the dusty road, and at last are marked for slaughter when they no longer can draw the burden, so those who seek to be justified by the Law are "entangled with the yoke of bondage," and when they have grown old and broken-down in the service of the Law they have earned for their perpetual reward God's wrath and everlasting torment.

We are not now treating of an unimportant matter. It is a matter that involves everlasting liberty or everlasting slavery. For as a liberation from God's wrath through the kind office of Christ is not a passing boon, but a permanent blessing, so also the yoke of the Law is not a temporary but an everlasting affliction.

Rightly are the doers of the Law called devil's martyrs. They take more pains to earn hell than the martyrs of Christ to obtain heaven. Theirs is a double misfortune. First they torture themselves on earth with self-inflicted penances and finally when they die they gain the reward of eternal damnation.

Verse 2. *Behold, I Paul say unto you, that if ye be circumcised, Christ shall profit you nothing.*

Paul is incensed at the thought of the tyranny of the Law. His antagonism to the Law is a personal matter with him. "Behold, I, Paul," he says, "I who have received the Gospel not from men, but by the revelation of Jesus Christ: I who have been commissioned from above to preach the Gospel to you: I Paul say to you, If you submit to circumcision Christ will profit you nothing." Paul emphatically declares that for the Galatians to be circumcised would mean for them to lose the benefits of Christ's suffering and death. This passage may well serve as a criterion for all the religions. To teach that besides faith in Christ other devices like works, or the observance of rules, traditions, or ceremonies are necessary for the attainment of righteousness and everlasting life, is to make Christ and His salvation of no benefit to anybody.

This passage is an indictment of the whole papacy. All priests, monks, and nuns—and I am now speaking of the best of them—who repose their hope for salvation in their own works, and not in Christ, whom they imagine to be an angry judge, hear this sentence pronounced against them that Christ shall profit them nothing. If one can earn the forgiveness of sins and everlasting life through one's own efforts to what purpose was Christ born? What was the purpose of His suffering and death, His resurrection, His victory over sin, death, and the devil, if men may overcome these evils by their own endeavor? Tongue cannot express, nor heart conceive what a terrible thing it is to make Christ worthless.

The person who is not moved by these considerations to leave the Law and the confidence in his own righteousness for the liberty in Christ, has a heart that is harder than stone and iron.

Paul does not condemn circumcision in itself. Circumcision is not injurious to the person who does not ascribe any particular importance to it. Neither are works injurious provided a person does not attach any saving value to them. The Apostle does not say that works are objectionable, but to build one's hopes for righteousness on works is disastrous, for that makes Christ good for nothing.

Let us bear this in mind when the devil accuses our conscience. When that dragon accuses us of having done no good at all, but only evil, say to him: "You trouble me with the remembrance of my past sins; you remind me that I have done no good. But this does not bother me, because if I were to trust in my own good deeds, or despair because I have done no good deeds, Christ would profit me neither way. I am not going to make him unprofitable to me. This I would do, if I should presume to purchase for myself the favor of God and everlasting life by my good deeds, or if I should despair of my salvation because of my sins."

Verse 3. *For I testify again to every man that is circumcised, that he is a debtor to do the whole law.*

The first fault with circumcision is that it makes Christ unprofitable. The second fault is that it obligates those who are circumcised to observe the whole Law. Paul is so very much in earnest about this matter that he confirms it with an oath. "I testify," he says, "I swear by the living God." Paul's statement may be explained negatively to mean: "I testify to every man who is being circumcised that he cannot perform the Law in any point. In the very act of circumcision he is not being circumcised, and in the very act of fulfilling the Law he fulfills it not." This seems to be the simple meaning of Paul's statement. Later on in the sixth chapter he explicitly states, "They themselves which are circumcised keep not the law. The fact that you are circumcised does not mean you are righteous and free from the Law. The truth is that by circumcision you have become debtors and servants of the Law. The more you endeavor to perform the Law, the more you will become tangled up in the yoke of the Law."

The truth of this I have experienced in myself and in others. I have seen many work themselves down to the bones in their hungry effort to obtain peace of conscience. But the harder they tried the more they worried. Especially in the presence of death they were so uneasy that I have seen murderers die with better grace and courage.

This holds true also in regard to the church regulations. When I was a monk I tried ever so hard to live up to the strict rules of my order. I used to make a list of my sins, and I was always on the way to confession, and whatever penances were enjoined upon me I performed religiously. In spite of it all, my conscience was always in a fever of doubt. The more I sought to help my poor stricken conscience the worse it got. The more I paid attention to the regulations the more I transgressed them.

Hence those that seek to be justified by the Law are much further away from the righteousness of life than the publicans, sinners, and harlots. They know better than to trust in their own works. They know that they cannot ever hope to obtain forgiveness by their sins.

Paul's statement in this verse may be taken to mean

that those who submit to circumcision are thereby submitting to the whole Law. To obey Moses in one point requires obedience to him in all points. It does no good to say that only circumcision is necessary, and not the rest of Moses' laws. The same reasons that obligate a person to accept circumcision also obligate a person to accept the whole Law. Thus to acknowledge the Law is tantamount to declaring that Christ is not yet come. And if Christ is not yet come, then all the Jewish ceremonies and laws concerning meats, places, and times are still in force, and Christ must be awaited as one who is still to come. The whole Scripture, however, testifies that Christ has come, that by His death He has abolished the Law, and that He has fulfilled all things which the prophets have foretold about Him.

Some would like to subjugate us to certain parts of the Mosaic Law. But this is not to be permitted under any circumstances. If we permit Moses to rule over us in one thing, we must obey him in all things.

Verse 4. *Christ is become of no effect unto you, whosoever of you are justified by the law; ye are fallen from grace.*

Paul in this verse discloses that he is not speaking so much of circumcision as the trust which men repose in the outward act. We can hear him say: "I do not condemn the Law in itself; what I condemn is that men seek to be justified by the Law, as if Christ were still to come, or as if He alone were unable to justify sinners. It is this that I condemn, because it makes Christ of no effect. It makes you void of Christ so that Christ is not in you, nor can you be partakers of the knowledge, the spirit, the fellowship, the liberty, the life, or the achievements of Christ. You are completely separated from Him, so much so that He has nothing to do with you any more, or for that matter you with Him." Can anything worse be said against the Law? If you think Christ and the Law can dwell together in your heart, you may be sure that Christ dwells not in your heart. For if Christ is in your heart He neither condemns you, nor does He ever bid you to trust in your own good works. If you know Christ at all, you know that good works do not serve unto righteousness, nor evil works unto condemnation. I do not want to withhold from good works their due praise, nor do I wish to encourage evil works. But when it comes to justification, I say, we must concentrate upon Christ alone, or else we make Him non-effective. You must choose between Christ and the righteousness of the Law. If you choose Christ you are righteous before God. If you stick to the Law, Christ is of no use to you.

Verse 4. *Ye are fallen from grace.*

That means you are no longer in the kingdom or condition of grace. When a person on board ship falls into the sea and is drowned it makes no difference from which end or side of the ship he falls into the water. Those who fall from grace perish no matter how they go about it. Those who seek to be justified by the Law are fallen from grace and are in grave danger of eternal death. If this holds true in the case of those who seek to be justified by the moral Law, what will become of those, I should like to know, who endeavor to be justified by their own regulations and vows? They will fall to the very bottom of hell. "Oh, no," they say, "we will fly straight into heaven. If you live according to the rules of Saint Francis, Saint Dominick, Saint Benedict, you will obtain the peace and mercy of God. If you perform the vows of chastity, obedience, etc., you will be rewarded with everlasting life." Let these playthings of the devil go to the place where they came from and listen to what Paul has to say in this verse in accordance with Christ's own teaching: "He that believeth in the Son of God, hath everlasting life; but he that believeth not in the Son shall not see life, but the wrath of God abideth in him."

The words, "Ye are fallen from grace," must not be taken lightly. They are important. To fall from grace means to lose the atonement, the forgiveness of sins, the righteousness, liberty, and life which Jesus has merited for us by His death and resurrection. To lose the grace of God means to gain the wrath and judgment of God, death, the bondage of the devil, and everlasting condemnation.

Verse 5. *For we through the Spirit wait for the hope of righteousness by faith.*

Paul concludes the whole matter with the above statement. "You want to be justified by the Law, by circumcision, and by works. We cannot see it. To be justified by such means would make Christ of no value to us. We would be obliged to perform the whole law. We rather through the Spirit wait for the hope of righteousness." The Apostle is not satisfied to say "justified by faith." He adds hope to faith.

Holy Writ speaks of hope in two ways: as the object of the emotion, and hope as the emotion itself. In the first chapter of the Epistle to the Colossians we have an instance of its first use: "For the hope which is laid up for you in heaven," i.e., the thing hoped for. In the sense of emotion we quote the passage from the eighth chapter of the Epistle to the Romans: "For we are saved by hope." As Paul uses the term "hope" here in writing to the Galatians, we may take it in either of its two meanings. We may understand Paul to say, "We wait in spirit, through faith, for the righteousness that we hope for, which in due time will be revealed to us." Or we may understand Paul to say: "We wait in Spirit, by faith for righteousness with great hope and desire." True, we are righteous, but our righteousness is not yet revealed; as long as we live here sin stays with us, not to forget the law in our members striving against the law of our mind. When sin rages in our body and we through the Spirit wrestle against it, then we have cause for hope. We are not yet perfectly righteous. Perfect righteousness is still to be attained. Hence we hope for it.

This is sweet comfort for us. And we are to make use of it in comforting the afflicted. We are to say to them: "Brother, you would like to feel God's favor as you feel your sin. But you are asking too much. Your righteousness rests on something much better than feelings. Wait and hope until it will be revealed to you in the Lord's own time. Don't go by your feelings, but go by the doctrine of faith, which pledges Christ to you."

The question occurs to us, What difference is there between faith and hope? We find it difficult to see any difference. Faith and hope are so closely linked that they cannot be separated. Still there is a difference between them.

First, hope and faith differ in regard to their sources. Faith originates in the understanding, while hope rises in the will.

Secondly, they differ in regard to their functions. Faith says what is to be done. Faith teaches, describes, directs. Hope exhorts the mind to be strong and courageous.

Thirdly, they differ in regard to their objectives. Faith concentrates on the truth. Hope looks to the goodness of God.

Fourthly, they differ in sequence. Faith is the beginning of life before tribulation (Hebrews 11). Hope comes later and is born of tribulation (Romans 5).

Fifthly, they differ in regard to their effects. Faith is a judge. It judges errors. Hope is a soldier. It fights against tribulations, the Cross, despondency, despair, and waits for better things to come in the midst of evil.

Without hope faith cannot endure. On the other hand, hope without faith is blind rashness and arrogance because it lacks knowledge. Before anything else a Christian must have the insight of faith, so that the intellect may know its directions in the day of trouble and the heart may hope for better things. By faith we begin, by hope we continue.

This passage contains excellent doctrine and much comfort. It declares that we are justified not by works, sacrifices, or ceremonies, but by Christ alone. The world may judge certain things to be ever so good; without Christ they are all wrong. Circumcision and the law and good works are carnal. "We," says Paul, "are above such things. We possess Christ by faith and in the midst of our afflictions we hopefully wait for the consummation of our righteousness."

You may say, "The trouble is I don't feel as if I am righteous." You must not feel, but believe. Unless you believe that you are righteous, you do Christ a great wrong, for He has cleansed you by the washing of regeneration, He died for you so that through Him you may obtain righteousness and everlasting life.

Verse 6. *For in Jesus Christ neither circumcision availeth any thing, nor uncircumcision, but faith which worketh by love.*

Faith must of course be sincere. It must be a faith that performs good works through love. If faith lacks love it is not true faith. Thus the Apostle bars the way of hypocrites to the kingdom of Christ on all sides. He declares on the one hand, "In Christ Jesus circumcision availeth nothing," i.e., works avail nothing, but faith alone, and that without any merit whatever, avails before God. On the other hand, the Apostle declares that without fruits faith serves no purpose. To think, "If faith justifies without works, let us work nothing," is to despise the grace of God. Idle faith is not justifying faith. In this terse manner Paul presents the whole life of a Christian. Inwardly it consists in faith towards God, outwardly in love towards our fellow-men.

Verse 7. Ye did run well; who did hinder you that ye should not obey the truth?

This is plain speaking. Paul asserts that he teaches the same truth now which he has always taught, and that the Galatians ran well as long as they obeyed the truth. But now, misled by the false apostles, they no longer run. He compares the Christian life to a race. When everything runs along smoothly the Hebrews spoke of it as a race. "Ye did run well," means that everything went along smoothly and happily with the Galatians. They lived a Christian life and were on the right way to everlasting life. The words, "Ye did run well," are encouraging indeed. Often our lives seem to creep rather than to run. But if we abide in the true doctrine and walk in the spirit, we have nothing to worry about. God judges our lives differently. What may seem to us a life slow in Christian development may seem to God a life of rapid progression in grace.

Verse 7. Who did hinder you that ye should not obey the truth?

The Galatians were hindered in the Christian life when they turned from faith and grace to the Law. Covertly the Apostle blames the false apostles for impeding the Christian progress of the Galatians. The false apostles persuaded the Galatians to believe that they were in error and that they had made little or no progress under the influence of Paul. Under the baneful influence of the false apostles the Galatians thought they were well off and advancing rapidly in Christian knowledge and living.

Verse 8. This persuasion cometh not of him that calleth you.

Paul explains how those who had been deceived by false teachers may be restored to spiritual health. The false apostles were amiable fellows. Apparently they surpassed Paul in learning and godliness. The Galatians were easily deceived by outward appearances. They supposed they were being taught by Christ Himself. Paul proved to them that their new doctrine was not of Christ, but of the devil. In this way he succeeded in regaining many. We also are able to win back many from the errors into which they were seduced by showing that their beliefs are imaginary, wicked, and contrary to the Word of God.

The devil is a cunning persuader. He knows how to enlarge the smallest sin into a mountain until we think we have committed the worst crime ever committed on earth. Such stricken consciences must be comforted and set straight as Paul corrected the Galatians by showing them that their opinion is not of Christ because it runs counter to the Gospel, which describes Christ as a meek and merciful Savior.

Satan will circumvent the Gospel and explain Christ in this his own diabolical way: "Indeed Christ is meek, gentle, and merciful, but only to those who are holy and righteous. If you are a sinner you stand no chance. Did not Christ say that unbelievers are already damned? And did not Christ perform many good deeds, and suffer many evils patiently, bidding us to follow His example? You do not mean to say that your life is in accord with Christ's precepts or example? You are a sinner. You are no good at all."

Satan is to be answered in this way: The Scriptures present Christ in a twofold aspect. First, as a gift. "He of God is made unto us wisdom, and righteousness, and sanctification and redemption" (I Cor. 1:30). Hence my many and grievous sins are nullified if I believe in Him.

Secondly, the Scriptures present Christ for our example. As an exemplar He is to be placed before me only at certain times. In times of joy and gladness that I may have Him as a mirror to reflect upon my shortcomings. But in the day of trouble I will have Christ only as a gift. I will not listen to anything else, except that Christ died for my sins.

To those that are cast down on account of their sins Christ must be introduced as a Savior and Gift, and not as an example. But to sinners who live in a false assurance, Christ must be introduced as an example. The hard sayings of Scripture and the awful judgments of God upon sin must be impressed upon them. Defy Satan in times of despair. Say: "O cursed Satan, you choose a nice time to talk to me about doing and working when you know very well that I am in trouble over my sins. I will not listen to you. I will listen to Christ, who says that He came into the world to save sinners. This is the true Christ and there is none other. I can find plenty of examples for a holy life in Abraham, Isaiah, John the Baptist, Paul, and other saints. But they cannot forgive my sins. They cannot save me. They cannot procure for me everlasting life. Therefore I will not have you for my teacher, O Satan."

Verse 9. A little leaven leaveneth the whole lump.

Paul's concern for them meant nothing to some of the Galatians. Many had disowned him as their teacher and gone over to the false apostles. No doubt the false apostles took every occasion to defame Paul as a stubborn and contemptuous fellow who thought nothing of disrupting the unity of the churches for no other reason than his selfish pride and jealousy.

Others of the Galatians perhaps saw no harm in deviating a trifle from the doctrine of justification and faith. When they noticed that Paul made so much ado about a matter that seemed of no particular importance to them they raised their eyebrows and thought within themselves: "What if we did deviate a little from the doctrine of Paul? What if we are a little to blame? He ought to overlook the whole matter, and not make such an issue out of it, lest the unity of the churches be disturbed." To this Paul replies: "A little leaven leaveneth the whole lump."

Our opponents record the same complaints about us. They put us down as contentious, ill-tempered faultfinders. But these are the crafty passes of the devil, with which he seeks to overthrow our faith. We answer with Paul: "A little leaven leaveneth the whole lump."

Small faults grow into big faults. To tolerate a trifling error inevitably leads to crass heresy. The doctrine of the Bible is not ours to take or to allow liberties with. We have no right to change even a tittle of it. When it comes to life we are ready to do, to suffer, to forgive anything our opponents demand as long as faith and doctrine remain pure and uncorrupt. The Apostle James says, "For whosoever shall keep the whole law and yet offend in one point, he is guilty of all." This passage supports us over against our critics who claim that we disregard all charity to the great injury of the churches. We protest we desire nothing more than peace with all men. If they would only permit us to keep our doctrine of faith! The pure doctrine takes precedence before charity, apostles, or an angel from heaven.

Let others praise charity and concord to the skies; we magnify the authority of the Word and faith. Charity may be neglected at times without peril, but not the Word and faith. Charity suffers all things, it gives in. Faith suffers nothing; it never yields. Charity is often deceived but is never put out because it has nothing to lose; it continues to do well even to the ungrateful. When it comes to faith and salvation in the midst of lies and errors that parade as truth and deceive many, charity has no voice or vote. Let us not be influenced by the popular cry for charity and unity. If we do not love God and His Word what difference does it make if we love anything at all?

Paul, therefore, admonishes both teachers and hearers not to esteem lightly the doctrine of faith as if it were a toy with which to amuse oneself in idle hours.

Verse 10. I have confidence in you through the Lord.

"I have taught, admonished, and reproved you enough. I hope the best for you."

The question occurs to us whether Paul did well to trust the Galatians. Does not Holy Writ forbid us to trust in men? Faith trusts in God and is never wrong. Charity trusts in men and is often wrong. This charitable trust in man is necessary to life. Without it life would be impossible in the world. What kind of life would ours be if nobody could trust anybody else? True Christians are more ready to believe in men than the children of this world. Such charitable confidence is the fruit of the Spirit. Paul had such trust in the Galatians although they had forsaken his doctrine. He trusts them "through the Lord," insofar as they were in Christ and Christ in them. Once they had forsaken Christ altogether, the Apostle will trust the Galatians no longer.

Verse 10. That ye will be none otherwise minded.

"Not minded otherwise than I have taught you. In other words, I have confidence that you will accept no doctrine that is contrary to the one you have learned from me."

Verse 10. But he that troubleth you shall bear his judgment, whosoever he be.

Paul assumes the role of a judge and condemns the false apostles as troublers of the Galatians. He wants to frighten the Galatians with his severe judgments of the false apostles into avoiding false doctrine like a contagious disease. We can hear him say to the Galatians: "Why do you give these pestilent fellows a hearing in the first place? They only trouble you. The doctrine they bring causes your conscience only trouble."

The clause, "whosoever he be," seems to indicate that the false apostles in outward appearance at least were very good and devout men. It may be that among them was some outstanding disciple of the apostles, a man of fame and authority. The Apostle must have been faced by this very situation, otherwise his vehemence would have been uncalled for. No doubt many of the Galatians were taken back with the vehemency of the Apostle. They perhaps thought: why should he be so stubborn in such small matters? Why is he so quick to pronounce damnation upon his brethren in the ministry?

I cannot say it often enough, that we must carefully differentiate between doctrine and life. Doctrine is a piece of heaven, life is a piece of earth. Life is sin, error, uncleanness, misery, and charity must forbear, believe, hope, and suffer all things. Forgiveness of sins must be continuous so that sin and error may not be defended and sustained. But with doctrine there must be no error, no need of pardon. There can be no comparison between doctrine and life. The least little point of doctrine is of greater importance than heaven and earth. Therefore we cannot allow the least jot of doctrine to be corrupted. We may overlook the offenses and errors of life, for we daily sin much. Even the saints sin, as they themselves confess in the Lord's Prayer and in the Creed. But our doctrine, God be praised, is pure, because all the articles of our faith are grounded on the Holy Scriptures.

Verse 11. And I, brethren, if I yet preach circumcision, why do I yet suffer persecution? then is the offense of the cross ceased.

In his great desire to recall the Galatians, Paul draws himself into the argument. He says: "Because I refuse to recognize circumcision as a factor in our salvation, I have brought upon myself the hatred and persecution of my whole nation. If I were to acknowledge circumcision the Jews would cease to persecute me; in fact they would love and praise me. But because I preach the Gospel of Christ and the righteousness of faith I must suffer persecution. The false apostles know how to avoid the Cross and the deadly hatred of the Jewish nation. They preach circumcision and thus retain the favor of the Jews. If they had their way they would ignore all differences in doctrine and preserve unity at all cost. But their unionistic dreams cannot be realized without loss to the pure doctrine of the Cross. It would be too bad if the offense of the Cross were to cease." To the Corinthians he expressed the same conviction: "Christ sent me… to preach the gospel: not with wisdom of words, lest the cross of Christ should be made of none effect" (I Cor. 1:17).

Here someone may be tempted to call the Christians crazy. Deliberately to court danger by preaching and confessing the truth, and thus to bring upon ourselves the hatred and enmity of the whole world, is this not madness? But Paul does not mind the enmity of the world. It made him all the bolder to confess Christ. The enmity of the world in his estimation augurs well for the success and growth of the Church, which fares best in times of persecution. When the offense of the Cross ceases, when the rage of the enemies of the Cross abates, when everything is quiet, it is a sign that the devil is the door-keeper of the Church and that the pure doctrine of God's Word has been lost.

Saint Bernard observed that the Church is in best shape when Satan assaults it on every side by trickery and violence; and in worst shape when it is at peace. In support of his statement he quotes the passage from the song of Hezekiah: "Behold, for peace I had great bitterness." Paul looks with suspicion upon any doctrine that does not provoke antagonism.

Persecution always follows on the heels of the Word of God as the Psalmist experienced. "I believe, therefore have I spoken: I was greatly afflicted" (Ps. 116:10). The Christians are accused and slandered without mercy. Murderers and thieves receive better treatment than Christians. The world regards true Christians as the worst offenders, for whom no punishment can be too severe. The world hates the Christians with amazing brutality, and without compunction commits them to the most shameful death, congratulating itself that it has rendered God and the cause of peace a distinct service by ridding the world of the undesired presence of these Christians. We are not to let such treatment cause us to falter in our adherence to Christ. As long as we experience such persecutions we know all is well with the Gospel.

Jesus held out the same comfort to His disciples in the fifth chapter of St. Matthew. "Blessed are ye, when men shall revile you and persecute you, and shall say all manner of evil against you falsely, for my sake. Rejoice, and be exceeding glad; for great is your reward in heaven." The Church must not come short of this joy. I would not want to be at peace with the pope, the bishops, the princes, and the sectarians, unless they consent to our doctrine. Unity with them would be an unmistakable sign that we have lost the true doctrine. Briefly, as long as the Church proclaims the doctrine she must suffer persecution, because the Gospel declares the mercy and glory of God. This in turn stirs up the devil, because the Gospel shows him up for what he is, the devil, and not God. Therefore as long as the Gospel holds sway persecution plays the accompaniment, or else there is something the matter with the devil. When he is hit you will know it by the havoc he raises everywhere.

So do not be surprised or offended when hell breaks loose. Look upon it as a happy indication that all is well with the Gospel of the Cross. God forbid that the offense of the Cross should ever be removed. This would be the case if we were to preach what the prince of this world and his followers would be only too glad to hear, the righteousness of works. You would never know the devil could be so gentle, the world so sweet, the Pope so gracious, and the princes so charming. But because we seek the advantage and honor of Christ, they persecute us all around.

Verse 12. I would they were even cut off which trouble you.

It hardly seems befitting an apostle, not only to denounce the false apostles as troublers of the Church, and to consign them to the devil, but also to wish that they were utterly cut off—what else would you call it but plain cursing? Paul, I suppose, is alluding to the rite of circumcision. As if he were saying to the Galatians: "The false apostles compel you to cut off the foreskin of your flesh. Well, I wish they themselves were utterly cut off by the roots."

We had better answer at once the question, whether it is right for Christians to curse. Certainly not always, nor for every little cause. But when things have come to such a pass that God and His Word are openly blasphemed, then we must say: "Blessed be God and His Word, and cursed be everything that is contrary to God and His Word, even though it should be an apostle, or an angel from heaven."

This goes to show again how much importance Paul attached to the least points of Christian doctrine, that he dared to curse the false apostles, evidently men of great popularity and influence. What right, then, have we to make little of doctrine? No matter how nonessential a point of doctrine may seem, if slighted it may prove the gradual disintegration of the truths of our salvation.

Let us do everything to advance the glory and authority of God's Word. Every tittle of it is greater than heaven and earth. Christian charity and unity have nothing to do with the Word of God. We are bold to curse and condemn all men who in the least point corrupt the Word of God, "for a little leaven leaveneth the whole lump."

Paul does right to curse these troublers of the Galatians, wishing that they were cut off and rooted out of the Church of God and that their doctrine might perish forever. Such cursing is the gift of the Holy Ghost. Thus Peter cursed Simon the sorcerer, "Thy money perish with thee." Many instances of this holy cursing are recorded in the sacred Scriptures, especially in the Psalms, e.g., "Let death seize upon them, and let them go down quick into hell" (Ps. 55:15).

The Doctrine of Good Works

Now come all kinds of admonitions and precepts. It was the custom of the apostles that after they had taught faith and instructed the conscience they followed it up with admonitions unto good works, that the believers might manifest the duties of love toward each other. In order to avoid the appearance as if Christianity militated against good works or opposed civil government, the Apostle also urges us to give ourselves unto good works, to lead an honest life, and to keep faith and love with one another. This will give the lie to the accusations of the world that we Christians are the enemies of decency and of public peace. The fact is we Christians know better what constitutes a truly good work than all the philosophers and legislators of the world because we link believing with doing.

Verse 13. *For, brethren, ye have been called unto liberty; only use not liberty for an occasion to the flesh, but by love serve one another.*

In other words: "You have gained liberty through Christ, i.e., You are above all laws as far as conscience is concerned. You are saved. Christ is your liberty and life. Therefore law, sin, and death may not hurt you or drive you to despair. This is the constitution of your priceless liberty. Now take care that you do not use your wonderful liberty for an occasion of the flesh."

Satan likes to turn this liberty which Christ has gotten for us into licentiousness. Already the Apostle Jude complained in his day: "There are certain men crept in unawares... turning the grace of our God into lasciviousness" (Jude 4). The flesh reasons: "If we are without the law, we may as well indulge ourselves. Why do good, why give alms, why suffer evil when there is no law to force us to do so?"

This attitude is common enough. People talk about Christian liberty and then go and cater to the desires of covetousness, pleasure, pride, envy, and other vices. Nobody wants to fulfill his duties. Nobody wants to help out a brother in distress. This sort of thing makes me so impatient at times that I wish the swine who trampled precious pearls under foot were back once again under the tyranny of the Pope. You cannot wake up the people of Gomorrah with the gospel of peace.

Even we creatures of the world do not perform our duties as zealously in the light of the Gospel as we did before in the darkness of ignorance, because the surer we are of the liberty purchased for us by Christ, the more we neglect the Word, prayer, well-doing, and suffering. If Satan were not continually molesting us with trials, with the persecution of our enemies, and the ingratitude of our brethren, we would become so careless and indifferent to all good works that in time we would lose our faith in Christ, resign the ministry of the Word, and look for an easier life. Many of our ministers are beginning to do that very thing. They complain about the ministry, they maintain they cannot live on their salaries, they whimper about the miserable treatment they receive at the hand of those whom they delivered from the servitude of the law by the preaching of the Gospel. These ministers desert our poor and maligned Christ, involve themselves in the affairs of the world, seek advantages for themselves and not for Christ. With what results they shall presently find out.

Since the devil lies in ambush for those in particular who hate the world, and seeks to deprive us of our liberty of the spirit or to brutalize it into the liberty of the flesh, we plead with our brethren after the manner of Paul, that they may never use this liberty of the spirit purchased for us by Christ as an excuse for carnal living, or as Peter expresses it, I Peter 2:16, "for a cloak of maliciousness."

In order that Christians may not abuse their liberty the Apostle encumbers them with the rule of mutual love that they should serve each other in love. Let everybody perform the duties of his station and vocation diligently and help his neighbor to the limit of his capacity.

Christians are glad to hear and obey this teaching of love. When others hear about this Christian liberty of ours they at once infer, "If I am free, I may do what I like. If salvation is not a matter of doing why should we do anything for the poor?" In this crude manner they turn the liberty of the spirit into wantonness and licentiousness. We want them to know, however, that if they use their lives and possessions after their own pleasure, if they do not help the poor, if they cheat their fellow-men in business and snatch and scrape by hook and by crook everything they can lay their hands on, we want to tell them that they are not free, no matter how much they think they are, but they are the dirty slaves of the devil, and are seven times worse than they ever were as the slaves of the Pope.

As for us, we are obliged to preach the Gospel which offers to all men liberty from the Law, sin, death, and God's wrath. We have no right to conceal or revoke this liberty proclaimed by the Gospel. And so we cannot do anything with the swine who dive headlong into the filth of licentiousness. We do what we can, we diligently admonish them to love and to help their fellow-men. If our admonitions bear no fruit, we leave them to God, who will in His own good time take care of these disrespecters of His goodness. In the meanwhile we comfort ourselves with the thought that our labors are not lost upon the true believers. They appreciate this spiritual liberty and stand ready to serve others in love and, though their number is small, the satisfaction they give us far outweighs the discouragement which we receive at the hands of the large number of those who misuse this liberty.

Paul cannot possibly be misunderstood for he says: "Brethren, ye have been called unto liberty." In order that nobody might mistake the liberty of which he speaks for the liberty of the flesh, the Apostle adds the explanatory note, "only use not liberty for an occasion to the flesh, but by love serve one another." Paul now explains at the hand of the Ten Commandments what it means to serve one another in love.

Verse 14. *For all the law is fulfilled in one word, even in this, THOU SHALT LOVE THY NEIGHBOUR AS THYSELF.*

It is customary with Paul to lay the doctrinal foundation first and then to build on it the gold, silver, and gems of good deeds. Now there is no other foundation than Jesus Christ. Upon this foundation the Apostle erects the structure of good works which he defines in this one sentence: "Thou shalt love thy neighbour as thyself."

In adding such precepts of love the Apostle embarrasses the false apostles very much, as if he were saying to the Galatians: "I have described to you what spiritual life is. Now I will also teach you what truly good works are. I am doing this in order that you may understand that the silly ceremonies of which the false apostles make so much are far inferior to the works of Christian love." This is the hall-mark of all false teachers, that they not only pervert the pure doctrine but also fail in doing good. Their foundation vitiated, they can only build wood, hay, and stubble. Oddly enough, the false apostles who were such earnest champions of good works never required the work of charity, such as Christian love and the practical charity of a helpful tongue, hand, and heart. Their only requirement was that circumcision, days, months, years, and times should be observed. They could not think of any other good works.

The Apostle exhorts all Christians to practice good works after they have embraced the pure doctrine of faith, because even though they have been justified they still have the old flesh to refrain them from doing good. Therefore it becomes necessary that sincere preachers cultivate the doctrine of good works as diligently as the doctrine of faith, for Satan is a deadly enemy of both. Nevertheless faith must come first because without faith it is impossible to know what a God-pleasing deed is.

Let nobody think that he knows all about this commandment, "Thou shalt love thy neighbour as thyself." It sounds short and easy, but show me the man who can teach, learn, and do this commandment perfectly. None of us heed, or urge, or practice this commandment properly. Though the conscience hurts when we fail to fulfill this commandment in every respect we are not overwhelmed by our failure to bear our neighbor sincere and brotherly love.

The words, "for all the law is fulfilled in one word," entail a criticism of the Galatians. "You are so taken up by your superstitions and ceremonies that serve no good purpose, that you neglect the most important thing, love." St. Jerome says: "We wear our bodies out with watching, fasting, and labor and neglect charity, the queen of all good works." Look at the monks, who meticulously fast, watch, etc. To skip the least requirement of their order would be a crime of the first magnitude. At the same time they blithely ignored the duties of charity and hated each other to death. That is no sin, they think.

The Old Testament is replete with examples that indicate how much God prizes charity. When David and his companions had no food with which to still their hunger they ate the showbread which lay-people were forbidden to eat. Christ's disciples broke the Sabbath law when they plucked the ears of corn. Christ himself broke the Sabbath (as the Jews claimed) by healing the sick on the Sabbath. These incidents indicate that love ought to be given consideration above all laws and ceremonies.

Verse 14. For all the Law is fulfilled in one word.

We can imagine the Apostle saying to the Galatians: "Why do you get so worked up over ceremonies, meats, days, places, and such things? Leave off this foolishness and listen to me. The whole Law is comprehended in this one sentence, 'Thou shalt love thy neighbour as thyself.' God is not particularly interested in ceremonies, nor has He any use for them. The one thing He requires of you is that you believe in Christ whom He hath sent. If in addition to faith, which comes first as the most acceptable service unto God, you want to add laws, then you want to know that all laws are comprehended in this short commandment, 'Thou shalt love thy neighbour as thyself.'"

Paul knows how to explain the law of God. He condenses all the laws of Moses into one brief sentence. Reason takes offense at the brevity with which Paul treats the Law. Therefore reason looks down upon the doctrine of faith and its truly good works. To serve one another in love, i.e., to instruct the erring, to comfort the afflicted, to raise the fallen, to help one's neighbor in every possible way, to bear with his infirmities, to endure hardships, toil, ingratitude in the Church and in the world, and on the other hand to obey government, to honor one's parents, to be patient at home with a nagging wife and an unruly family, these things are not at all regarded as good works. The fact is, they are such excellent works that the world cannot possibly estimate them at their true value.

It is tersely spoken: "Love thy neighbour as thyself." But what more needs to be said? You cannot find a better or nearer example than your own. If you want to know how you ought to love your neighbor, ask yourself how much you love yourself. If you were to get into trouble or danger, you would be glad to have the love and help of all men. You do not need any book of instructions to teach you how to love your neighbor. All you have to do is to look into your own heart, and it will tell you how you ought to love your neighbor as yourself.

My neighbor is every person, especially those who need my help, as Christ explained in the tenth chapter of Luke. Even if a person has done me some wrong, or has hurt me in any way, he is still a human being with flesh and blood. As long as a person remains a human being, so long is he to be an object of our love.

Paul therefore urges his Galatians and, incidentally, all believers to serve each other in love. "You Galatians do not have to accept circumcision. If you are so anxious to do good works, I will tell you in one word how you can fulfill all laws. 'By love serve one another.' You will never lack people to whom you may do good. The world is full of people who need your help."

Verse 15. *But if ye bite and devour one another take heed that ye be not consumed one of another.*

When faith in Christ is overthrown peace and unity come to an end in the church. Diverse opinions and dissensions about doctrine and life spring up, and one member bites and devours the other, i.e., they condemn each other until they are consumed. To this the Scriptures and the experience of all times bear witness. The many sects at present have come into being because one sect condemns the other. When the unity of the spirit has been lost there can be no agreement in doctrine or life. New errors must appear without measure and without end.

For the avoidance of discord Paul lays down the principle: "Let every person do his duty in the station of life into which God has called him. No person is to vaunt himself above others or find fault with the efforts of others while lauding his own. Let everybody serve in love."

It is not an easy matter to teach faith without works, and still to require works. Unless the ministers of Christ are wise in handling the mysteries of God and rightly divide the word, faith and good works may easily be confused. Both the doctrine of faith and the doctrine of good works must be diligently taught, and yet in such a way that both the doctrines stay within their God-given sphere. If we only teach works, as our opponents do, we shall lose the faith. If we only teach faith people will come to think that good works are superfluous.

Verse 16. *This I say then, Walk in the Spirit, and ye shall not fulfill the lust of the flesh.*

"I have not forgotten what I told you about faith in the first part of my letter. Because I exhort you to mutual love you are not to think that I have gone back on my teaching of justification by faith alone. I am still of the same opinion. To remove every possibility for misunderstanding I have added this explanatory note: 'Walk in the Spirit, and ye shall not fulfill the lust of the flesh.'"

With this verse Paul explains how he wants this sentence to be understood: By love serve one another. When I bid you to love one another, this is what I mean and require, 'Walk in the Spirit.' I know very well you will not fulfill the Law, because you are sinners as long as you live. Nevertheless, you should endeavor to walk in the spirit, i.e., fight against the flesh and follow the leads of the Holy Ghost."

It is quite apparent that Paul had not forgotten the doctrine of justification, for in bidding the Galatians to walk in the Spirit he at the same time denies that good works can justify. "When I speak of the fulfilling of the Law I do not mean to say that you are justified by the Law. All I mean to say is that you should take the Spirit for your guide and resist the flesh. That is the most you shall ever be able to do. Obey the Spirit and fight against the flesh."

Verse 16. *And ye shall not fulfill the lust of the flesh.*

The lust of the flesh is not altogether extinct in us. It rises up again and again and wrestles with the Spirit. No flesh, not even that of the true believer, is so completely under the influence of the Spirit that it will not bite or devour, or at least neglect, the commandment of love. At the slightest provocation it flares up, demands to be revenged, and hates a neighbor like an enemy, or at least does not love him as much as he ought to be loved.

Therefore the Apostle establishes this rule of love for the believers. Serve one another in love. Bear the infirmities of your brother. Forgive one another. Without such bearing and forbearing, giving and forgiving, there can be no unity because to give and to take offense are unavoidably human.

Whenever you are angry with your brother for any cause, repress your violent emotions through the Spirit. Bear with his weakness and love him. He does not cease to be your neighbor or brother because he offended you. On the contrary, he now more than ever before requires your loving attention.

The scholastics take the lust of the flesh to mean carnal lust. True, believers too are tempted with carnal lust. Even the married are not immune to carnal lusts. Men set little value upon that which they have and covet what they have not, as the poet says:

*"The things most forbidden we always desire,
And things most denied we seek to acquire."*

I do not deny that the lust of the flesh includes carnal lust. But it takes in more. It takes in all the corrupt desires with which the believers are more or less infected, as pride, hatred, covetousness, impatience. Later on Paul enumerates among the works of the flesh even idolatry and heresy. The apostle's meaning is clear. "I want you to love one another. But you do not do it. In fact you cannot do it, because of your flesh. Hence we cannot be justified by deeds of love. Do not for a moment think that I am reversing myself on my stand concerning faith. Faith and hope must continue. By faith we are justified, by hope we endure to the end. In addition we serve each other in love because true faith is not idle. Our love, however, is faulty. In bidding you to walk in the Spirit I indicate to you that our love is not sufficient to justify us. Neither do I demand that you should get rid of the flesh, but that you should control and subdue it."

Verse 17. For the flesh lusteth against the Spirit and the Spirit against the flesh.

When Paul declares that "the flesh lusteth against the Spirit, and the Spirit against the flesh," he means to say that we are not to think, speak or do the things to which the flesh incites us. "I know," he says, "that the flesh courts sin. The thing for you to do is to resist the flesh by the Spirit. But if you abandon the leadership of the Spirit for that of the flesh, you are going to fulfill the lust of the flesh and die in your sins."

Verse 17. *And these are contrary the one to the other; so that ye cannot do the things that ye would.*

These two leaders, the flesh and the Spirit, are bitter opponents. Of this opposition the Apostle writes in the seventh chapter of the Epistle to the Romans: "I see another law in my members, warring against the law of my mind, and bringing me into the captivity to the law of sin which is in my members. O wretched man that I am! who shall deliver me from the body of this death?"

The scholastics are at a loss to understand this confession of Paul and feel obliged to save his honor. That the chosen vessel of Christ should have had the law of sin in his members seems to them incredible and absurd. They circumvent the plain-spoken statement of the Apostle by saying that he was speaking for the wicked. But the wicked never complain of inner conflicts, or of the captivity of sin. Sin has its unrestricted way with them. This is Paul's very own complaint and the identical complaint of all believers.

Paul never denied that he felt the lust of the flesh. It is likely that at times he felt even the stirrings of carnal lust, but there is no doubt that he quickly suppressed them. And if at any time he felt angry or impatient, he resisted these feelings by the Spirit. We are not going to stand by idly and see such a comforting statement as this explained away. The scholastics, monks, and others of their ilk fought only against carnal lust and were proud of a victory which they never obtained. In the meanwhile they harbored within their breasts pride, hatred, disdain, self-trust, contempt of the Word of God, disloyalty, blasphemy, and other lusts of the flesh. Against these sins they never fought because they never took them for sins.

Christ alone can supply us with perfect righteousness. Therefore we must always believe and always hope in Christ. "Whosoever believeth shall not be ashamed" (Rom. 9:33).

Do not despair if you feel the flesh battling against the

Spirit or if you cannot make it behave. For you to follow the guidance of the Spirit in all things without interference on the part of the flesh is impossible. You are doing all you can if you resist the flesh and do not fulfill its demands.

When I was a monk I thought I was lost forever whenever I felt an evil emotion, carnal lust, wrath, hatred, or envy. I tried to quiet my conscience in many ways, but it did not work, because lust would always come back and give me no rest. I told myself: "You have permitted this and that sin, envy, impatience, and the like. Your joining this holy order has been in vain, and all your good works are good for nothing." If at that time I had understood this passage, "The flesh lusteth against the Spirit, and the Spirit against the flesh," I could have spared myself many a day of self-torment. I would have said to myself: "Martin, you will never be without sin, for you have flesh. Despair not, but resist the flesh."

I remember how Doctor Staupitz used to say to me: "I have promised God a thousand times that I would become a better man, but I never kept my promise. From now on I am not going to make any more vows. Experience has taught me that I cannot keep them. Unless God is merciful to me for Christ's sake and grants unto me a blessed departure, I shall not be able to stand before Him." His was a God-pleasing despair. No true believer trusts in his own righteousness, but says with David, "Enter not into judgment with thy servant; for in thy sight shall no man living be justified" (Ps. 143:2). Again, "If thou, Lord, shouldest mark iniquities, O Lord, who shall stand?" (Ps. 130:3.)

No man is to despair of salvation just because he is aware of the lust of the flesh. Let him be aware of it so long as he does not yield to it. The passion of lust, wrath, and other vices may shake him, but they are not to get him down. Sin may assail him, but he is not to welcome it. Yes, the better Christian a man is, the more he will experience the heat of the conflict. This explains the many expressions of regret in the Psalms and in the entire Bible.

Everybody is to determine his peculiar weakness and guard against it. Watch and wrestle in spirit against your weakness. Even if you cannot completely overcome it, at least you ought to fight against it.

According to this description a saint is not one who is made of wood and never feels any lusts or desires of the flesh. A true saint confesses his righteousness and prays that his sins may be forgiven. The whole Church prays for the forgiveness of sins and confesses that it believes in the forgiveness of sins. If our antagonists would read the Scriptures they would soon discover that they cannot judge rightly of anything, either of sin or of holiness.

Verse 18. *But if ye be led of the Spirit, ye are not under the law.*

Here someone may object: "How come we are not under the law? You yourself say, Paul, that we have the flesh which wars against the Spirit, and brings us into subjection."

But Paul says not to let it trouble us. As long as we are led by the Spirit, and are willing to obey the Spirit who resists the flesh, we are not under the Law. True believers are not under the Law. The Law cannot condemn them although they feel sin and confess it.

Great then is the power of the Spirit. Led by the Spirit, the Law cannot condemn the believer though he commits real sin. For Christ in whom we believe is our righteousness. He is without sin, and the Law cannot accuse Him. As long as we cling to Him we are led by the Spirit and are free from the Law. Even as he teaches good works, the Apostle does not lose sight of the doctrine of justification, but shows at every turn that it is impossible for us to be justified by works.

The words, "If ye be led of the Spirit, ye are not under the law," are replete with comfort. It happens at times that anger, hatred, impatience, carnal desire, fear, sorrow, or some other lust of the flesh so overwhelms a man that he cannot shake them off, though he try ever so hard. What should he do? Should he despair? God forbid. Let him say to himself: "My flesh seems to be on a warpath against the Spirit again. Go to it, flesh, and rage all you want to. But you are not going to have your way. I follow the leading of the Spirit."

When the flesh begins to cut up the only remedy is to take the sword of the Spirit, the word of salvation, and fight against the flesh. If you set the Word out of sight, you are helpless against the flesh. I know this to be a fact. I have been assailed by many violent passions, but as soon as I took hold of some Scripture passage, my temptations left me. Without the Word I could not have helped myself against the flesh.

Verse 19. *Now the works of the flesh are manifest, which are these.*

Paul is saying: "That none of you may hide behind the plea of ignorance I will enumerate first the works of the flesh, and then also the works of the Spirit."

There were many hypocrites among the Galatians, as there are also among us, who pretend to be Christians and talk much about the Spirit, but they walk not according to the Spirit; rather according to the flesh. Paul is out to show them that they are not as holy as they like to have others think they are.

Every period of life has its own peculiar temptations. Not one true believer whom the flesh does not again and again incite to impatience, anger, pride. But it is one thing to be tempted by the flesh, and another thing to yield to the flesh, to do its bidding without fear or remorse, and to continue in sin.

Christians also fall and perform the lusts of the flesh. David fell horribly into adultery. Peter also fell grievously when he denied Christ. However great these sins were, they were not committed to spite God, but from weakness. When their sins were brought to their attention these men did not obstinately continue in their sin, but repented. Those who sin through weakness are not denied pardon as long as they rise again and cease to sin. There is nothing worse than to continue in sin. If they do not repent, but obstinately continue to fulfill the desires of the flesh, it is a sure sign that they are not sincere.

No person is free from temptations. Some are tempted in one way, others in another way. One person is more easily tempted to bitterness and sorrow of spirit, blasphemy, distrust, and despair. Another is more easily tempted to carnal lust, anger, envy, covetousness. But no matter to which sins we are disposed, we are to walk in the Spirit and resist the flesh. Those who are Christ's own crucify their flesh.

Some of the old saints labored so hard to attain perfection that they lost the capacity to feel anything. When I was a monk I often wished I could see a saint. I pictured him as living in the wilderness, abstaining from meat and drink and living on roots and herbs and cold water. This weird conception of those awesome saints I had gained out of the books of the scholastics and church fathers. But we know now from the Scriptures who the true saints are. Not those who live a single life, or make a fetish of days, meats, clothes, and such things. The true saints are those who believe that they are justified by the death of Christ. Whenever Paul writes to the Christians here and there he calls them the holy children and heirs of God. All who believe in Christ, whether male or female, bond or free, are saints; not in view of their own works, but in view of the merits of God which they appropriate by faith. Their holiness is a gift and not their own personal achievement.

Ministers of the Gospel, public officials, parents, children, masters, servants, etc., are true saints when they take Christ for their wisdom, righteousness, sanctification, and redemption, and when they fulfill the duties of their several vocations according to the standard of God's Word and repress the lust and desires of the flesh by the Spirit. Not everybody can resist temptations with equal facilities. Imperfections are bound to show up. But this does not prevent them from being holy. Their unintentional lapses are forgiven if they pull themselves together by faith in Christ. God forbid that we should sit in hasty judgment on those who are weak in faith and life, as long as they love the Word of God and make use of the supper of the Lord.

I thank God that He has permitted me to see (what as a monk I so earnestly desired to see) not one but many saints, whole multitudes of true saints. Not the kind of saints the papists admire, but the kind of saints Christ wants. I am sure I am one of Christ's true saints. I am baptized. I believe that Christ my Lord has redeemed me from all my sins, and invested me with His own eternal righteousness and holiness. To hide in caves and dens, to have a bony body, to wear the hair long in the mistaken idea that such departures from normalcy will obtain some special regard in heaven is not the holy life. A holy life is to be baptized and to believe in Christ, and to subdue the flesh with the Spirit.

To feel the lusts of the flesh is not without profit to us. It prevents us from being vain and from being puffed up with the wicked opinion of our own work-righteousness. The monks were so inflated with the opinion of their own righteousness, they thought they had so much holiness that they could afford to sell some of it to others, although their own hearts convinced them of unholiness. The Christian feels the unholy condition of his heart, and it makes him feel so low that he cannot trust in his good works. He therefore goes to Christ to find perfect righteousness. This keeps a Christian humble.

Verses 19, 20. *Now the works of the flesh are manifest, which are these: adultery, fornification, uncleanness, lasciviousness, idolatry, witchcraft…*

Paul does not enumerate all the works of the flesh, but only certain ones. First, he mentions various kinds of carnal lusts, as adultery, fornication, wantonness, etc. But carnal lust is not the only work of the flesh, and so he counts among the works of the flesh also idolatry, witchcraft, hatred, and the like. These terms are so familiar that they do not require lengthy explanations.

Idolatry

The best religion, the most fervent devotion without Christ is plain idolatry. It has been considered a holy act when the monks in their cells meditate upon God and

His works, and in a religious frenzy kneel down to pray and to weep for joy. Yet Paul calls it simply idolatry. Every religion which worships God in ignorance or neglect of His Word and will is idolatry.

They may think about God, Christ, and heavenly things, but they do it after their own fashion and not after the Word of God. They have an idea that their clothing, their mode of living, and their conduct are holy and pleasing to Christ. They not only expect to pacify Christ by the strictness of their life, but also expect to be rewarded by Him for their good deeds. Hence their best "spiritual" thoughts are wicked thoughts. Any worship of God, any religion without Christ is idolatry. In Christ alone is God well pleased.

I have said before that the works of the flesh are manifest. But idolatry puts on such a good front and acts so spiritual that the sham of it is recognized only by true believers.

Witchcraft

This sin was very common before the light of the Gospel appeared. When I was a child there were many witches and sorcerers around who "bewitched" cattle, and people, particularly children, and did much harm. But now that the Gospel is here you do not hear so much about it because the Gospel drives the devil away. Now he bewitches people in a worse way with spiritual sorcery.

Witchcraft is a brand of idolatry. As witches used to bewitch cattle and men, so idolaters, i.e., all the self-righteous, go around to bewitch God and to make Him out as one who justifies men not by grace through faith in Christ but by the works of men's own choosing. They bewitch and deceive themselves. If they continue in their wicked thoughts of God they will die in their idolatry.

Sects

Under sects Paul here understands heresies. Heresies have always been found in the church. What unity of faith can exist among all the different monks and the different orders? None whatever. There is no unity of spirit, no agreement of minds, but great dissension in the papacy. There is no conformity in doctrine, faith, and life. On the other hand, among evangelical Christians the Word, faith, religion, sacraments, service, Christ, God, heart, and mind are common to all. This unity is not disturbed by outward differences of station or of occupation.

Drunkenness, Gluttony

Paul does not say that eating and drinking are works of the flesh, but intemperance in eating and drinking, which is a common vice nowadays, is a work of the flesh. Those who are given to excess are to know that they are not spiritual but carnal. Sentence is pronounced upon them that they shall not inherit the kingdom of heaven. Paul desires that Christians avoid drunkenness and gluttony, that they live temperate and sober lives, in order that the body may not grow soft and sensual.

Verse 21. *Of the which I tell you before, as I have also told you in the past, that they which do such things shall not inherit the kingdom of God.*

This is a hard saying, but very necessary for those false Christians and hypocrites who speak much about the Gospel, about faith, and the Spirit, yet live after the flesh. But this hard sentence is directed chiefly at the heretics who are large with their own self-importance, that they may be frightened into taking up the fight of the Spirit against the flesh.

Verses 22, 23. *But the fruit of the Spirit is love, joy, peace, longsuffering, gentleness, goodness, faith, meekness, temperance.*

The Apostle does not speak of the works of the Spirit as he spoke of the works of the flesh, but he attaches to these Christian virtues a better name. He calls them the fruits of the Spirit.

Love

It would have been enough to mention only the single fruit of love, for love embraces all the fruits of the Spirit. In I Corinthians 13, Paul attributes to love all the fruits of the Spirit: "Charity suffereth long, and is kind," etc. Here he lets love stand by itself among other fruits of the Spirit to remind the Christians to love one another, "in honor preferring one another," to esteem others more than themselves because they have Christ and the Holy Ghost within them.

Joy

Joy means sweet thoughts of Christ, melodious hymns and psalms, praises and thanksgiving, with which Christians instruct, inspire, and refresh themselves. God does not like doubt and dejection. He hates dreary doctrine, gloomy and melancholy thought. God likes cheerful hearts. He did not send His Son to fill us with sadness, but to gladden our hearts. For this reason the prophets, apostles, and Christ Himself urge, yes, command us to rejoice and be glad. "Rejoice greatly, O daughter of Zion; shout, O daughter of Jerusalem; behold, thy king cometh unto thee" (Zech. 9:9). In the Psalms we are repeatedly told to be "joyful in the Lord." Paul says: "Rejoice in the

Lord always." Christ says: "Rejoice, for your names are written in heaven."

Peace

Peace towards God and men. Christians are to be peaceful and quiet. Not argumentative, not hateful, but thoughtful and patient. There can be no peace without longsuffering, and therefore Paul lists this virtue next.

Longsuffering

Longsuffering is that quality which enables a person to bear adversity, injury, reproach, and makes them patient to wait for the improvement of those who have done him wrong. When the devil finds that he cannot overcome certain persons by force he tries to overcome them in the long run. He knows that we are weak and cannot stand anything long. Therefore he repeats his temptation time and again until he succeeds. To withstand his continued assaults we must be longsuffering and patiently wait for the devil to get tired of his game.

Gentleness

Gentleness in conduct and life. True followers of the Gospel must not be sharp and bitter, but gentle, mild, courteous, and soft-spoken, which should encourage others to seek their company. Gentleness can overlook other people's faults and cover them up. Gentleness is always glad to give in to others. Gentleness can get along with forward and difficult persons, according to the old pagan saying: "You must know the manners of your friends, but you must not hate them." Such a gentle person was our Savior Jesus Christ, as the Gospel portrays Him. Of Peter it is recorded that he wept whenever he remembered the sweet gentleness of Christ in His daily contact with people. Gentleness is an excellent virtue and very useful in every walk of life.

Goodness

A person is good when he is willing to help others in their need.

Faith

In listing faith among the fruits of the Spirit, Paul obviously does not mean faith in Christ, but faith in men. Such faith is not suspicious of people but believes the best. Naturally the possessor of such faith will be deceived, but he lets it pass. He is ready to believe all men, but he will not trust all men. Where this virtue is lacking men are suspicious, forward, and wayward and will believe nothing nor yield to anybody. No matter how well a person says or does anything, they will find fault with it, and if you do not humor them you can never please them. It is quite impossible to get along with them. Such faith in people therefore, is quite necessary. What kind of life would this be if one person could not believe another person?

Meekness

A person is meek when he is not quick to get angry. Many things occur in daily life to provoke a person's anger, but the Christian gets over his anger by meekness.

Temperance

Christians are to lead sober and chaste lives. They should not be adulterers, fornicators, or sensualists. They should not be quarrelers or drunkards. In the first and second chapters of the Epistle to Titus, the Apostle admonishes bishops, young women, and married folks to be chaste and pure.

Verse 23. Against such there is no law.

There is a law, of course, but it does not apply to those who bear these fruits of the Spirit. The Law is not given for the righteous man. A true Christian conducts himself in such a way that he does not need any law to warn or to restrain him. He obeys the Law without compulsion. The Law does not concern him. As far as he is concerned there would not have to be any Law.

Verse 24. And they that are Christ's have crucified the flesh with the affections and lusts.

True believers are no hypocrites. They crucify the flesh with its evil desires and lusts. Inasmuch as they have not altogether put off the sinful flesh they are inclined to sin. They do not fear or love God as they should. They are likely to be provoked to anger, to envy, to impatience, to carnal lust, and other emotions. But they will not do the things to which the flesh incites them. They crucify the flesh with its evil desires and lusts by fasting and exercise and, above all, by a walk in the Spirit.

To resist the flesh in this manner is to nail it to the Cross. Although the flesh is still alive it cannot very well act upon its desires because it is bound and nailed to the Cross.

Verse 25. If we live in the Spirit, let us also walk in the Spirit.

A little while ago the Apostle had condemned those who are envious and start heresies and schisms. As if he had forgotten that he had already berated them, the Apostle once more reproves those who provoke and envy others. Was not one reference to them sufficient? He repeats his admonition in order to emphasize the viciousness of pride that had caused all the trouble in the churches of Galatia, and has always caused the Church of Christ no end of difficulties. In his Epistle to Titus the Apostle states that a vainglorious man should not be ordained as a minister, for pride, as St. Augustine points out, is the mother of all heresies.

Now vainglory has always been a common poison in the world. There is no village too small to contain someone who wants to be considered wiser or better than the rest. Those who have been bitten by pride usually stand upon the reputation for learning and wisdom. Vainglory is not nearly so bad in a private person or even in an official as it is in a minister.

When the poison of vainglory gets into the Church you have no idea what havoc it can cause. You may argue about knowledge, art, money, countries, and the like without doing particular harm. But you cannot quarrel about salvation or damnation, about eternal life and eternal death without grave damage to the Church. No wonder Paul exhorts all ministers of the Word to guard against this poison. He writes: "If we live in the Spirit." Where the Spirit is, men gain new attitudes. Where formerly they were vainglorious, spiteful and envious, they now become humble, gentle and patient. Such men seek not their own glory, but the glory of God. They do not provoke each other to wrath or envy, but prefer others to themselves.

As dangerous to the Church as this abominable pride is, yet there is nothing more common. The trouble with the ministers of Satan is that they look upon the ministry as a stepping-stone to fame and glory, and right there you have the seed for all sorts of dissensions.

Because Paul knew that the vainglory of the false Apostles had caused the churches of Galatia endless trouble, he makes it his business to suppress this abominable vice. In his absence the false apostles went to work in Galatia. They pretended that they had been on intimate terms with the apostles, while Paul had never seen Christ in person or had much contact with the rest of the apostles. Because of this they delivered him, rejected his doctrine, and boosted their own. In this way they troubled the Galatians and caused quarrels among them until they provoked and envied each other; which goes to show that neither the false apostles nor the Galatians walked after the Spirit, but after the flesh.

The Gospel is not there for us to aggrandize ourselves. The Gospel is to aggrandize Christ and the mercy of God. It holds out to men eternal gifts that are not gifts of our own manufacture. What right have we to receive praise and glory for gifts that are not of our own making?

No wonder that God in His special grace subjects the ministers of the Gospel to all kinds of afflictions, otherwise they could not cope with this ugly beast called vainglory. If no persecution, no cross, or reproach trailed the doctrine of the Gospel, but only praise and reputation, the ministers of the Gospel would choke with pride. Paul had the Spirit of Christ. Nevertheless there was given unto him the messenger of Satan to buffet him in order that he should not come to exalt himself, because of the grandeur of his revelations. St. Augustine's opinion is well taken: "If a minister of the Gospel is praised, he is in danger; if he is despised, he is also in danger."

The ministers of the Gospel should be men who are not too easily affected by praise or criticism, but simply speak out the benefit and the glory of Christ and seek the salvation of souls.

Whenever you are being praised, remember it is not you who is being praised but Christ, to whom all praise belongs. When you preach the Word of God in its purity and also live accordingly, it is not your own doing, but God's doing. And when people praise you, they really mean to praise God in you. When you understand this—and you should because "what hast thou that thou didst not receive?"—you will not flatter yourself on the one hand and on the other hand you will not carry yourself with the thought of resigning from the ministry when you are insulted, reproached, or persecuted.

It is really kind of God to send so much infamy, reproach, hatred, and cursing our way to keep us from getting proud of the gifts of God in us. We need a millstone around our neck to keep us humble. There are a few on our side who love and revere us for the ministry of the Word, but for every one of these there are a hundred on the other side who hate and persecute us.

The Lord is our glory. Such gifts as we possess we acknowledge to be the gifts of God, given to us for the good of the Church of Christ. Therefore we are not proud because of them. We know that more is required of them to whom much is given, than of such to whom little is given. We also know that God is no respecter of persons. A plain factory hand who does his work faithfully pleases God just as much as a minister of the Word.

Verse 26. Let us not be desirous of vain glory.

To desire vainglory is to desire lies, because when one person praises another he tells lies. What is there in anybody to praise? But it is different when the ministry is praised. We should not only desire people to praise the ministry of the Gospel but also do our utmost to make the ministry worthy of praise because this will make the ministry more effective. Paul warns the Romans not to bring Christianity into disrepute. "Let not then your good be evil spoken of" (Rom. 14:16). He also begged the Corinthians to "give no offense in anything, that the ministry be not blamed" (I Cor. 6:3). When people praise our ministry they are not praising our persons, but God.

Verse 26. Provoking one another, envying one another.

Such is the ill effect of vainglory. Those who teach errors provoke others. When others disapprove and reject the doctrine the teachers of errors get angry in turn, and then you have strife and trouble. The sectarians hate us furiously because we will not approve their errors. We did not attack them directly. We merely called attention to certain abuses in the Church. They did not like it and became sore at us, because it hurt their pride. They wish to be the lone rulers of the church.

GALATIONS 6

Verse 1. Brethren, if a man be overtaken in a fault ye which are spiritual, restore such an one in the spirit of meekness.

If we carefully weigh the words of the Apostle we perceive that he does not speak of doctrinal faults and errors, but of much lesser faults by which a person is overtaken through the weakness of his flesh. This explains why the Apostle chooses the softer term "fault." To minimize the offense still more, as if he meant to excuse it altogether and to take the whole blame away from the person who has committed the fault, he speaks of him as having been "overtaken," seduced by the devil and of the flesh. As if he meant to say, "What is more human than for a human being to fall, to be deceived and to err?" This comforting sentence at one time saved my life. Because Satan always assails both the purity of doctrine which he endeavors to take away by schisms and the purity of life which he spoils with his continual temptations to sin, Paul explains how the fallen should be treated. Those who are strong are to raise up the fallen in the spirit of meekness.

This ought to be borne in mind particularly by the ministers of the Word in order that they may not forget the parental attitude which Paul here requires of those who have the keeping of souls. Pastors and ministers must, of course, rebuke the fallen, but when they see that the fallen are sorry they are to comfort them by excusing the fault as well as they can. As unyielding as the Holy Spirit is in the matter of maintaining and defending the doctrine of faith, so mild and merciful is He toward men for their sins as long as sinners repent.

The Pope's synagogue teaches the exact opposite of what the Apostle commands. The clerics are tyrants and butchers of men's conscience. Every small offense is closely scrutinized. To justify the cruel inquisitiveness they quote the statement of Pope Gregory: "It is the property of good lives to be afraid of a fault where there is no fault." "Our censors must be feared, even if they are unjust and wrong." On these pronouncements the papists base their doctrine of excommunication. Rather than terrify and condemn men's consciences, they ought to raise them up and comfort them with the truth.

Let the ministers of the Gospel learn from Paul how to deal with those who have sinned. "Brethren," he says, "if any man be overtaken with a fault, do not aggravate his grief, do not scold him, do not condemn him, but lift him up and gently restore his faith. If you see a brother despondent over a sin he has committed, run up to him, reach out your hand to him, comfort him with the Gospel and embrace him like a mother. When you meet a willful sinner who does not care, go after him and rebuke him sharply." But this is not the treatment for one who has been overtaken by a sin and is sorry. He must be dealt with in the spirit of meekness and not in the spirit of severity. A repentant sinner is not to be given gall and vinegar to drink.

Verse 1. *Considering thyself, lest thou also be tempted.*

This consideration is very much needed to put a stop to the severity of some pastors who show the fallen no mercy. St. Augustine says: "There is no sin which one person has committed, that another person may not commit it also." We stand in slippery places. If we become overbearing and neglect our duty, it is easy enough to fall into sin. In the book entitled "The Lives of Our Fathers," one of the Fathers is reported to have said when informed that a brother had fallen into adultery: "He fell yesterday; I may fall today." Paul therefore warns the pastors not to be too rigorous and unmerciful towards offenders, but to show them every affection, always remembering: "This man fell into sin; I may fall into worse sin. If those who are always so eager to condemn others would investigate themselves they would find that the sins of others are motes in comparison to their own."

"Wherefore let him that thinketh he standeth take heed lest he fall" (I Cor. 10:12). If David who was a hero of faith and did so many great things for the Lord, could fall so badly that in spite of his advanced age he was overcome by youthful lust after he had withstood so many different temptations with which the Lord had tested his faith, who are we to think that we are more stable? These object lessons of God should convince us that of all things God hates pride.

Verse 2. *Bear ye one another's burdens, and so fulfill the law of Christ.*

The Law of Christ is the Law of love. Christ gave us no other law than this law of mutual love: "A new commandment I give unto you, That ye love one another." To love means to bear another's burdens. Christians must have strong shoulders to bear the burdens of their fellow Christians. Faithful pastors recognize many errors and offenses in the church, which they oversee. In civil affairs an official has to overlook much if he is fit to rule. If we can overlook our own shortcomings and wrongdoings, we ought to overlook the shortcomings of others in accordance with the words, "Bear ye one another's burdens."

Those who fail to do so expose their lack of understanding of the law of Christ. Love, according to Paul, "believeth all things, hopeth all things, endureth all things." This commandment is not meant for those who deny Christ; neither is it meant for those who continue to live in sin. Only those who are willing to hear the Word of God and then inadvertently fall into sin to their own great sorrow and regret, carry the burdens which the Apostle encourages us to bear. Let us not be hard on them. If Christ did not punish them, what right have we to do it?

Verse 3. *For if a man think himself to be something, when he is nothing, he deceiveth himself.*

Again the Apostle takes the authors of sects to task for being hard-hearted tyrants. They despise the weak and demand that everything be just so. Nothing suits them except what they do. Unless you eulogize whatever they say or do, unless you adapt yourself to their slightest whim, they become angry with you. They are that way because, as St. Paul says, they "think themselves to be something," they think they know all about the Scriptures.

Paul has their number when he calls them zeros. They deceive themselves with their self-suggested wisdom and holiness. They have no understanding of Christ or the law of Christ. By insisting that everything be perfect they not only fail to bear the burdens of the weak, they actually offend the weak by their severity. People begin to hate and shun them and refuse to accept counsel or comfort from them.

Paul describes these stiff and ungracious saints accurately when he says of them, "They think themselves to be something." Bloated by their own silly ideas and schemes they entertain a pretty fair opinion of themselves, when in reality they amount to nothing.

Verse 4. *But let every man prove his own work, and then shall he have rejoicing in himself alone, and not in another.*

In this verse the Apostle continues his attack upon the vainglorious sectarians. Although this passage may be applied to any work, the Apostle has in mind particularly the work of the ministry.

The trouble with these seekers after glory is that they never stop to consider whether their ministry is straightforward and faithful. All they think about is whether people will like and praise them. Theirs is a threefold sin. First, they are greedy of praise. Secondly, they are very sly and wily in suggesting that the ministry of other pastors is not what it should be. By way of contrast they hope to rise in the estimation of the people. Thirdly, once they have established a reputation for themselves they become so chesty that they stop short of nothing. When they have won the praise of men, pride leads them on to belittle the work of other men and to applaud their own. In this artful manner they hoodwink the people who rather enjoy to see their former pastors taken down a few notches by such upstarts.

"Let a minister be faithful in his office," is the apostolic injunction. "Let him not seek his own glory or look for praise. Let him desire to do good work and to preach the Gospel in all its purity. Whether an ungrateful world appreciates his efforts is to give him no concern because, after all, he is in the ministry not for his own glory but for the glory of Christ."

A faithful minister cares little what people think of him, as long as his conscience approves of him. The approval of his own good conscience is the best praise a minister can have. To know that we have taught the Word of God and administered the sacraments rightly is to have a glory that cannot be taken away.

The glory which the sectarians seek is quite unstable, because it rests in the whim of people. If Paul had had to depend on this kind of glory for his ministry he would have despaired when he saw the many offenses and evils following in the wake of his preaching.

If we had to feel that the success of our ministry depended upon our popularity with men we would die, because we are not popular. On the contrary, we are hated by the whole world with rare bitterness. Nobody praises us. Everybody finds fault with us. But we can glory in the Lord and attend to our work cheerfully. Who cares whether our efforts please or displease the devil? Who cares whether the world praises or hates us? We go ahead "by honour and dishonour, by evil report and good report" (II Cor. 6:8).

The Gospel entails persecution. The Gospel is that kind of a doctrine. Furthermore, the disciples of the Gospel are not all dependable. Many embrace the Gospel today and tomorrow discard it. To preach the Gospel for praise is bad business especially when people stop praising you. Find your praise in the testimony of a good conscience.

This passage may also be applied to other work besides the ministry. When an official, a servant, a teacher minds his business and performs his duty faithfully without concerning himself about matters that are not in his line he may rejoice in himself. The best commendation of any work is to know that one has done the work that God has given him well and that God is pleased with his effort.

Verse 5. *Every man shall bear his own burden.*

That means: For anybody to covet praise is foolish because the praise of men will be of no help to you in the hour of death. Before the judgment throne of Christ everybody will have to bear his own burden. As it is the praise of men stops when we die. Before the eternal Judge it is not praise that counts but your own conscience.

True, the consciousness of work well done cannot quiet the conscience. But it is well to have the testimony of a good conscience in the last judgment that we have performed our duty faithfully in accordance with God's will.

For the suppression of pride we need the strength of prayer. What man even if he is a Christian is not delighted with his own praise? Only the Holy Spirit can preserve us from the misfortune of pride.

Verse 6. *Let him that is taught in the word communicate unto him that teacheth in all good things.*

Now the Apostle also addresses the hearers of the Word requesting them to bestow "all good things" upon those who have taught them the Gospel. I have often wondered why all the apostles reiterated this request with such embarrassing frequency. In the papacy I saw the people give generously for the erection and maintenance of luxurious church buildings and for the sustenance of men appointed to the idolatrous service of Rome. I saw bishops and priests grow rich until they possessed the choicest real estate. I thought then that Paul's admonitions were overdone. I thought he should have requested the people to curtail their contributions. I saw how the generosity of the people of the Church was encouraging covetousness on the part of the clergy. I know better now.

As often as I read the admonitions of the Apostle to the effect that the churches should support their pastors and raise funds for the relief of impoverished Christians I am half ashamed to think that the great Apostle Paul had to touch upon this subject so frequently. In writing to the Corinthians he needed two chapters to impress this matter upon them. I would not want to discredit Wittenberg as Paul discredited the Corinthians by urging them at such length to contribute to the relief of the poor. It seems to be a by-product of the Gospel that nobody wants to contribute to the maintenance of the Gospel ministry. When the doctrine of the devil is preached people are prodigal in their willing support of those who deceive them.

We have come to understand why it is so necessary to repeat the admonition of this verse. When Satan cannot suppress the preaching of the Gospel by force he tries to accomplish his purpose by striking the ministers of the Gospel with poverty. He curtails their income to such an extent that they are forced out of the ministry because they cannot live by the Gospel. Without ministers to proclaim the Word of God the people go wild like savage beasts.

Paul's admonition that the hearers of the Gospel share all good things with their pastors and teachers is certainly in order. To the Corinthians he wrote: "If we have sown unto you spiritual things is it a great thing if we shall reap your carnal things?" (I Cor. 9:11.) In the old days when the Pope reigned supreme everybody paid plenty for masses. The begging friars brought in their share. Commercial priests counted the daily offerings. From these extortions our countrymen are now delivered by the Gospel. You would think they would be grateful for their emancipation and give generously for the support of the ministry of the Gospel and the relief of impoverished Christians. Instead, they rob Christ. When the members of a Christian congregation permit their pastor to struggle along in penury, they are worse than heathen.

Before very long they are going to suffer for their ingratitude. They will lose their temporal and spiritual possessions. This sin merits the severest punishment. The reason why the churches of Galatia, Corinth, and other places were troubled by false apostles was this, that they had so little regard for their faithful ministers. You cannot refuse to give God a penny who gives you all good things, even life eternal, and turn around and give the devil, the giver of all evil and death eternal, pieces of gold, and not be punished for it.

The words "in all good things" are not to be understood to mean that people are to give all they have to their ministers, but that they should support them liberally and give them enough to live well.

Verse 7. *Be not deceived; God is not mocked.*

The Apostle is so worked up over this matter that he is not content with a mere admonition. He utters the threatening words, "God is not mocked." Our countrymen think it good sport to despise the ministry. They like to treat the ministers like servants and slaves. "Be not deceived," warns the Apostle, "God is not mocked." God will not be mocked in His ministers. Christ said: "He that despiseth you, despiseth me" (Luke 10:16). To Samuel God said: "They have not rejected thee, but they have rejected me" (I Sam. 8:7). Be careful, you scoffers. God may postpone His punishment for a time, but He will find you out in time, and punish you for despising His servants. You cannot laugh at God. Maybe the people are little impressed by the threats of God, but in the hour of their death they shall know whom they have mocked. God is not ever going to let His ministers starve. When the rich suffer the pangs of hunger God will feed His own servants. "In the days of famine they shall be satisfied" (Ps. 37:19).

Verse 7. *For whatever a man soweth, that shall he also reap.*

These passages are all meant to benefit us ministers. I must say I do not find much pleasure in explaining these verses. I am made to appear as if I am speaking for my own benefit. If a minister preaches on money he is likely to be accused of covetousness. Still people must be told these things that they may know their duty over against their pastors. Our Savior says: "Eating and drinking such things as they give; for the laborer is worthy of his hire" (Luke 10:7). And Paul says elsewhere: "Do ye not know that they which minister about holy things live of the things of the temple? and they which wait at the altar are partakers with the altar? Even so hath the Lord ordained, that they which preach the gospel should live of the gospel" (I Cor. 9:13, 14).

Verse 8. *For he that soweth to his flesh shall of the flesh reap corruption; but he that soweth to the Spirit shall of the Spirit reap everlasting life.*

This simile of sowing and reaping also refers to the proper support of ministers. "He that soweth to the Spirit," i.e., he that honors the ministers of God is doing a spiritual thing and will reap everlasting life. "He that soweth to the flesh," i.e., he that has nothing left for the ministers of God, but only thinks of himself, that person will reap of the flesh corruption, not only in this life but also in the life to come. The Apostle wants to stir up his readers to be generous to their pastors.

That the ministers of the Church need support any man with common sense can see. Though this support is something physical the Apostle does not hesitate to call it sowing to the Spirit. When people scrape up everything they can lay their hands on and keep everything for themselves the Apostle calls it a sowing to the flesh. He pronounces those who sow to the Spirit blessed for this life and the life to come, while those who sow to the flesh are accursed now and forever.

Verse 9. *And let us not be weary in well doing: for in due season we shall reap, if we faint not.*

The Apostle intends soon to close his Epistle and therefore repeats once more the general exhortation unto good deeds. He means to say "Let us do good not only to the ministers of the Gospel, but to everybody, and let us do it without weariness." It is easy enough to do good once or twice, but to keep on doing good without getting disgusted with the ingratitude of those whom we have benefited, that is not so easy. Therefore the Apostle does not only admonish us to do good, but to do good untiringly. For our encouragement he adds the promise: "For in due season we shall reap, if we faint not." "Wait for the harvest and then you will reap the reward of your sowing to the Spirit. Think of that when you do good and the ingratitude of men will not stop you from doing good."

Verse 10. *As we have therefore opportunity, let us do good unto all men, especially unto them who are of the household of faith.*

In this verse the Apostle summarizes his instructions on the proper support of the ministers and of the poor. He paraphrases the words of Christ: "I must work the works of him that sent me, while it is day: the night cometh, when no man can work" (John 9:4). Our good deeds are to be directed primarily at those who share the Christian faith with us, "the household of faith," as Paul calls them, among whom the ministers rank first as objects of our well doing.

Verse 11. *Ye see how large a letter I have written unto you with mine own hand.*

With these words the Apostle intends to draw the Galatians on. "I never," he says, "wrote such a long letter with my own hand to any of the other churches." His other epistles he dictated, and only subscribed his greetings and his signature with his own hand.

Verse 12. *As many as desire to make a fair shew in the*

flesh, they constrain you to be circumcised; only lest they should suffer persecution for the cross of Christ.

Paul once more scores the false apostles in an effort to draw the Galatians away from their false doctrine. "The teachers you have now do not seek the glory of Christ and the salvation of your souls, but only their own glory. They avoid the Cross. They do not understand what they teach."

These three counts against the false apostles are of so serious a nature that no Christian could have fellowship with them. But not all the Galatians obeyed the warning of Paul.

The Apostle's attack upon the false apostles was not unjustified. Neither are our attacks upon the papacy. When we call the Pope the Antichrist and his minions an evil brood, we do not slander them. We merely judge them by the touchstone of God's Word recorded in the first chapter of this Epistle: "Though we, or an angel from heaven, preach any other gospel unto you than that which we have preached unto you, let him be accursed."

Verse 13. *For neither they themselves who are circumcised keep the law; but desire to have you circumcised, that they may glory in your flesh.*

In other words: "I shall tell you what kind of teachers you have now. They avoid the Cross, they teach no certain truths. They think they are performing the Law, but they are not. They have not the Holy Spirit and without Him nobody can keep the Law." Where the Holy Ghost does not dwell in men there dwells an unclean spirit, a spirit that despises God and turns every effort at keeping the Law into a double sin.

Mark what the Apostle is saying: Those who are circumcised do not fulfill the Law. No self-righteous person ever does. To work, pray, or suffer apart from Christ is to work, pray, and to suffer in vain, "for whatsoever is not of faith is sin." It does a person no good to be circumcised, to fast, to pray, or to do anything, if in his heart he despises Christ.

"Why do the false apostles insist that you should be circumcised? Not for the sake of your righteousness," although they give that impression, but "that they may glory in your flesh." Now what sort of an ambition is that? Worst of all, they force circumcision upon you for no other reason than the satisfaction they get out of your submission.

Verse 14. *But God forbid that I should glory, save in the cross of our Lord Jesus Christ.*

"God forbid," says the Apostle, "that I should glory in anything as dangerous as the false apostles glory in because what they glory in is a poison that destroys many souls, and I wish it were buried in hell. Let them glory in the flesh if they wish and let them perish in their glory. As for me I glory in the Cross of our Lord Jesus Christ." He expresses the same sentiment in the fifth chapter of the Epistle to the Romans, where he says: "We glory in tribulations"; and in the twelfth chapter of the Second Epistle to the Corinthians: "Most gladly, therefore, will I rather glory in my infirmities." According to these expressions the glory of a Christian consists in tribulations, reproaches, and infirmities.

And this is our glory today with the Pope and the whole world persecuting us and trying to kill us. We know that we suffer these things not because we are thieves and murderers, but for Christ's sake whose Gospel we proclaim. We have no reason to complain. The world, of course, looks upon us as unhappy and accursed creatures, but Christ for whose sake we suffer pronounces us blessed and bids us to rejoice. "Blessed are ye," says He, "when men shall revile you, and persecute you, and shall say all manner of evil against you falsely, for my sake. Rejoice, and be exceeding glad" (Matt. 5:11, 12).

By the Cross of Christ is not to be understood here the two pieces of wood to which He was nailed, but all the afflictions of the believers whose sufferings are Christ's sufferings. Elsewhere Paul writes: "Who now rejoice in my sufferings for you, and fill up that which is behind of the afflictions of Christ in my flesh for his body's sake, which is the church" (Col. 1:24).

It is good for us to know this lest we sink into despair when our opponents persecute us. Let us bear the cross for Christ's sake. It will ease our sufferings and make them light as Christ says, Matthew 11:30, "My yoke is easy, and my burden is light."

Verse 14. *By whom the world is crucified unto me, and I unto the world.*

"The world is crucified unto me," means that I condemn the world. "I am crucified unto the world," means that the world in turn condemns me. I detest the doctrine, the self-righteousness, and the works of the world. The world in turn detests my doctrine and condemns me as a revolutionary heretic. Thus the world is crucified unto us and we unto the world.

The monks imagined the world was crucified unto them when they entered the monastery. Not the world, but Christ, is crucified in the monasteries.

In this verse Paul expresses his hatred of the world. The hatred was mutual. As Paul, so we are to despise the world and the devil. With Christ on our side we can defy him and say: "Satan, the more you hurt me, the more I oppose you."

Verse 15. *For in Christ Jesus neither circumcision availeth anything, nor uncircumcision, but a new creature.*

Since circumcision and uncircumcision are contrary matters we would expect the Apostle to say that one or the other might accomplish some good. But he denies that either of them do any good. Both are of no value because in Christ Jesus neither circumcision nor uncircumcision avail anything.

Reason fails to understand this, "for the natural man receiveth not the things of the Spirit of God" (I Cor. 2:14). It therefore seeks righteousness in externals. However, we learn from the Word of God that there is nothing under the sun that can make us righteous before God and a new creature except Christ Jesus.

A new creature is one in whom the image of God has been renewed. Such a creature cannot be brought into life by good works, but by Christ alone. Good works may improve the outward appearance, but they cannot produce a new creature. A new creature is the work of the Holy Ghost, who imbues our hearts with faith, love, and other Christian virtues, grants us the strength to subdue the flesh and to reject the righteousness of the world.

Verse 16. *And as many as walk according to this rule, peace be on them, and mercy.*

This is the rule by which we ought to live, "that ye put on the new man, which after God is created in righteousness and true holiness" (Eph. 4:24). Those who walk after this rule enjoy the favor of God, the forgiveness of their sins, and peace of conscience. Should they ever be overtaken by any sin, the mercy of God supports them.

Verse 17. *From henceforth let no man trouble me.*

The Apostle speaks these words with a certain amount of indignation. "I have preached the Gospel to you in conformity with the revelation which I received from Jesus Christ. If you do not care for it, very well. Trouble me no more. Trouble me no more."

Verse 17. *For I bear in my body the marks of the Lord Jesus.*

"The marks on my body indicate whose servant I am. If I was anxious to please men, if I approved of circumcision and good works as factors in our salvation, if I would take delight in your flesh as the false apostles do, I would not have these marks on my body. But because I am the servant of Jesus Christ and publicly declare that no person can obtain the salvation of his soul outside of Christ, I must bear the badge of my Lord. These marks were given to me against my will as decorations from the devil and for no other merit but that I made known Jesus."

Of the marks of suffering which he bore in his body the Apostle makes frequent mention in his epistles. "I think," he says, "that God hath set forth us the apostles last, as it were appointed to death: for we are made a spectacle unto the world, and to angels, and to men" (I Cor. 4:9). Again, "Unto this present hour we both hunger, and thirst, and are naked, and are buffeted, and have no certain dwellingplace; And labour, working with our hands: being reviled, we bless; being persecuted, we suffer it; being defamed, we intreat: we are made as the filth of the world, and are the offscouring of all things unto this day" (I Cor. 4:11–13).

Verse 18. *Brethren, the grace of our Lord Jesus Christ be with your spirit. Amen.*

This is the Apostle's farewell. He ends his Epistle as he began it by wishing the Galatians the grace of God. We can hear him say: "I have presented Christ to you, I have pleaded with you, I have reproved you, I have overlooked nothing that I thought might be of benefit to you. All I can do now is to pray that our Lord Jesus Christ would bless my Epistle and grant you the guidance of the Holy Ghost."

The Lord Jesus Christ, our Savior, who gave me the strength and the grace to explain this Epistle and granted you the grace to hear it, preserve and strengthen us in faith unto the day of our redemption. To Him, the Father and the Son and the Holy Spirit, be glory, world without end. Amen.

The Manual of a Christian Knight

By Desiderius Erasmus (1501)
A Book called in Latin ENCHIRIDION MILITIS CHRISTIANI
and in English THE MANUAL OF THE CHRISTIAN KNIGHT
Replenished with most wholesome precepts
Made by the famous clerk ERASMUS OF ROTTERDAM
to the which is added a new and marvelous profitable preface
METHUEN CO. 36 ESSEX STREET W.C.
LONDON
This Edition was first Published in 1905

THE BOOK SPEAKETH

To please all sorts of men I do not pass,
    To please the good and learned is a fair thing,
    Yea, and these both were more than covenant was
And more than I look for. Whoso the learning
Of Christ doth favour, if he like well all thing
I seek no further, Christ is mine Apollo,
Only strengthening me to speak this that I do.

THE PRINTER TO THE FAITHFUL READER

The mortal world a field is of battle
    Which is the cause that strife doth never fail
    Against man, by warring of the flesh
    With the devil, that always fighteth fresh
    The spirit to oppress by false envy;
    The which conflict is continually
    During his life, and like to lose the field.
But he be armed with weapon and shield
Such as behoveth to a Christian knight,
Where God each one, by his Christ chooseth right
Sole captain, and his standard to bear.
Who knoweth it not, then this will teach him here
In his brevyer, poynarde, or manual
The love shewing of high Emanuell.
In giving us such harness of war
Erasmus is the only furbisher
Scouring the harness, cankered and adust
Which negligence had so sore fret with rust
Then champion receive as thine by right
The manual of the true Christian knight.

ENCHIRIDION THE EPISTLE

Erasmus of Roterdame sendeth greeting to the reverend father in Christ (and lord) the lord Paul Wolzius, the most religious abbot of the monastery the which is commonly called Hughes court.

Albeit, most virtuous father, that the little book, to the which I have given this name or title *Enchiridion militis Christiani*, which many a day ago I made for myself only, and for a certain friend of mine being utterly unlearned, hath begun to mislike and displease me the less, forasmuch as I do see that it is allowed of you and other virtuous and learned men such as you be, of whom (as ye are indeed endued with godly learning, and also with learned godliness) I know nothing to be approved, but that which is both holy and also clerkly: yet it hath begun well nigh also to please and like me now, when I see it (after that it hath been so oftentimes printed) yet still to be desired and greatly called for, as if it were a new work made of late: if so be the printers do not lie to flatter me withal. But again there is another thing which oftentimes grieveth me in my mind, that a certain well learned friend of mine long ago said, very properly and sharply checking me, that there was more holiness seen in the little book than in the whole author and maker thereof. Indeed he spake these words in his jesting bourdyngly, but would to God he had not spoken so truly as he bourded bitterly. And that grieveth me so much the more because the same thing hath chanced to come likewise to pass in him, for the changing of whose manners principally I took upon me this labour and travail, for he also not only hath not withdrawn himself from the court, but is daily much deeper drowned therein than he was aforetime, for what good purpose I cannot tell, but as he confesseth himself with much great misery. And yet for all that I do not greatly pity my friend, because that peradventure adversity of fortune may teach him once to repent himself, and to amend, seeing that he would not follow and do after my counsel and admonitions.

Trouble or adversity correcteth some.

And verily though I, enforcing me to the same thing and purpose, have been turned and tossed with so many chances and tempests, that Ulixes a man living ever in trouble (which Homer speaketh of) might be counted in comparison to me even Polycrates which ever lived in prosperity without any manner trouble.

Fortunate Polycrates.

I do not utterly repent me of my labour, seeing it hath moved and provoked so many unto the study of godly virtue: nor I myself am not utterly to be blamed and rebuked although my living be not in all points agreeing to mine own precepts and counsels. It is some part of godliness when one with all his heart desireth and is willing to be made good and virtuous: nor such a mind so well intending I suppose is not to be cast away, although his purpose be not ever luckily performed. To this we ought to endeavour ourselves all our life long, and no doubt but by the reason that we so oftentimes shall attempt it, once at the last we shall attain it. Also he hath dispatched a good piece of a doubtful journey which hath learned well of the journey the way. Therefore am I nothing moved with the mocks of certain persons which despise this little book, as nothing erudite and clerkly, saying that it might have been made of a child that learned his A, B, C, because it entreateth nothing of Duns's questions: as though nothing without those could be done with learning. I do not care if it be not so quick, so it be godly: let it not make them instruct and ready to disputations in schools, so that it make them apt to keep Christ's peace. Let it not be profitable or helping for the disputation in divinity, so it make for a divine life. For what good should it do to entreat of that thing that every man intermeddleth with? Who hath not in handling questions of divinity, or what else do all our swarms of schoolmen? There be almost as many commentaries upon the Master of the Sentence as be names of divines. There is neither measure nor number of summaries, which after the manner of apothecaries mingle oftentimes sundry things together, and make of old things new, of new things old, of one thing many, of many things one. How can it be that these great volumes instruct us to live well and after a Christian manner, which a man in all his life cannot have leisure once to look over. In like manner as if a physician should prescribe unto him that lieth sick in peril of death to read *Jacobus de partibus,* or such other huge volumes, saying that there he should find remedy for his disease: but in the meantime the patient dieth, wanting present remedy wherewith he might be holpen. In such a fugitive life it is necessary to have a ready medicine at the hand. How many volumes have they made of restitution, of confession, of slander, and other things innumerable? And though they boult and search out by piecemeal everything by itself, and so define every thing as if they mistrusted all other men's wits, yea as though they mistrusted the goodness and mercy of God, whiles they do prescribe how he ought to punish and reward every fact either good or bad: yet they agree not amongst themselves, nor yet sometimes do open the thing plainly, if a man would look near upon it, so much diversity both of wits and circumstances is there. Moreover although it were so that they had determined all things well and truly, yet besides this that they handle and treat of these things after a barbarous and unpleasant fashion, there is not one amongst a thousand that can have any leisure to read over these volumes: or who is able to bear about with him *Secundam secunde,* the work of St Thomas?

The great volumes.

And yet there is no man but he ought to use a good life, to the which Christ would that the way should be plain and open for every man, and that not by inexplicable crooks of disputations, not able to be resolved, but by a true and sincere faith and charity not feigned, whom hope doth follow which is never ashamed.

The theology appertaineth to few men, but the salvation appertaineth to all.

And finally let the great doctors, which must needs be but few in comparison to all other men, study and busy themselves in those great volumes. And yet nevertheless the unlearned and rude multitude which Christ died for ought to be provided for: and he hath taught a great portion of Christian virtue which hath inflamed men unto the love thereof.

Those be noted that of purpose make the faculty which they profess obscure and hard.

The wise king, when he did teach his son true wisdom, took much more pain in exhorting him thereunto than in teaching him, as who should say that to love wisdom were in a manner to have attained it. It is a great shame and rebuke both for lawyers and physicians that they have of a set purpose, and for the nonce, made their art and science full of difficulty, and hard to be attained or come by, to the intent that both their gains and advantage might be the more plentiful, and their glory and praise among the unlearned people the greater: but it is a much more shameful thing to do the same in the philosophy of Christ: but rather contrariwise we ought to endeavour ourselves with all our strengths to make it so easy as can be, and plain to every man. Nor let not this be our study to appear learned ourselves, but to allure very many to a Christian man's life.

The war against the Turks.

Preparation and ordinance is made now for war to be made against the Turks, which for whatsoever purpose it is begun, we ought to pray not that it may turn to the profit of a few certain persons, but that it may be to the common and general profit of all men. But what think you should come of it, if to such of them as shall be overcome (for I do not suppose that they shall all be killed with weapons) we shall lay the works of Occam, Durandus, Duns, Gabriell, Alvaros, or any such schoolmen, for the intent to bring them in mind to take Christ's profession upon them? What shall they imagine and think in their minds (for surely even they, though they be naught else, are men and have wit and reason) when they shall hear those thorny and cumbrous inextricable subtle imaginations of instances, of formalities, of quiddities, of relation: namely when they shall see these great doctors and teachers of religion and holiness so far disagreeing, and of so sundry opinions among themselves that oftentimes they dispute and reason so long one with another, until they change colour and be pale, and revile one another, spitting each at other and finally dealing buffets and blows each to other.

The discord among divines.

When they shall see the black friars fight and scold for their Thomas, and then the grey friars matched with them, defending one the other party their subtle and fervent hot doctors, which they call Seraphicos, some speaking as Reals, some as Nominals. When they shall also see the thing to be of so great difficulty that they can never discuss sufficiently with what words they may speak of Christ: as though one did deal or had to do with a wayward spirit which he had raised up unto his own destruction, if he did fail never so little in the prescribed words of conjuring, and not rather with our most merciful Saviour, which desireth nothing else of us but a pure life and a simple. I beseech thee for the love of God shew me what shall we bring about with all these reckonings, specially if our manners and our life be like to the proud doctrine and learning?

The life used amongst Christian people.

And if they shall see and well perceive our ambition and desirousness of honour by our gorgeousness, more than ever any tyrant did use: our avarice and covetousness by our bribing and pollyng, our lecherousness by the defiling of maidens and wives, our cruelty by the oppressions done of us? With what face or how for shame shall we offer to them the doctrine of Christ which is far away contrary to all these things.

With what artillery chiefly the Turks ought to be overcome.

The best way and most effectual to overcome and win the Turks, should be if they shall perceive that thing which Christ taught and expressed in his living to shine in us. If they shall perceive that we do not highly gape for their empires, do not desire their gold and good, do not covet their possessions, but that we seek nothing else but only their souls' health and the glory of God. This is that right true and effectuous divinity, the which in time past subdued unto Christ arrogant and proud philosophers, and also the mighty and invincible princes: and if we thus do, then shall Christ ever be present and help us.

The part of a Christian man is to save and not to destroy.

For truly it is not meet nor convenient to declare ourselves Christian men by this proof or token, if we kill very many, but rather if we save very many: not if we send thousands of heathen people to hell, but if we make many infidels faithful: not if we cruelly curse and excommunicate them, but if we with devout prayers and with all our hearts desire their health and pray unto God to send them better minds. If this be not our intent it shall sooner come to pass that we shall degenerate and turn into Turks ourselves, than that we shall cause them to become Christian men. And although the chance of war, which is ever doubtful and uncertain, should fall so luckily to us that we had gotten the victory, so should it be brought to pass that the Pope's dominion and his Cardinals' might be enlarged, but not the kingdom of Christ, which finally flourisheth and is in prosperity if faith, love, peace and chastity be quick and strong, which thing I trust shall be brought to pass by the good governance and provision of the Pope Leo the Tenth, unless the great trouble and rage of worldly business pluck him from his very good purpose another way.

The kingdom of Christ.

Christ doth profess to be primate and head himself in the heavenly kingdom, which never doth flourish but when celestial things be advanced. Nor Christ did not die for this purpose that goods of the world, that riches, that armour, and the rest of ruffling fashion of the world, be now in the hands and rule of certain priests, which things were wont to be in the hands of the gentiles, or at least amongst lay princes, not much differing from gentiles. But in my mind it were the best, before we should try with them in battle to attempt them with epistles and some little books: but with what manner of epistles? Not with threatening epistles, or with books full of tyranny, but with those which might shew fatherly charity, and resemble the very heart and mind of Peter and of Paul, and which should not only pretend and shew outwardly the title of the apostles, but which also should savour and taste of the efficacy and strength of the apostles.

The difficulty of holy scripture.

Not because I do not know that all the true fountain and vein of Christ's philosophy is hid in the gospel and the epistles of the apostles: but the strange manner of phrase, and oftentimes the troublous speaking of divers crooked figures and tropes be of so great difficulty, that oftentimes we ourselves also must labour right sore before we can perceive them. Therefore in mine opinion the best were that some both well learned men and good of living should have this office assigned and put unto them, to make a collection and to gather the sum of Christ's philosophy out of the pure fountain of the gospel and the epistles and most approved interpreters, and so plainly that yet it might be clerkly and erudite, and so briefly that it might also be plain.

The briefness of Christ's doctrine.

Those things which concern faith or belief, let them be contained in a few articles. Those also that appertain to the manner of living let them be shewed and taught in few words, and that after such fashion that they may perceive the yoke of Christ to be pleasant and easy, and not grievous and painful: so that they may perceive that they have gotten fathers and not tyrants, feeders and not robbers, pyllers nor pollers, and that they be called to their soul health and not compelled to servitude. Undoubted they also be men, neither their hearts be of so hard iron or adamant but that they may be mollified and won with benefits and kindness, wherewith even very wild beasts be waxen gentle and tame.

The Turks be men.

And the most effectuous thing is the true verity of Christ. But let the Pope also command them whom he appointeth to this business, that they never swerve nor go from the true pattern and example of Christ, nor in any place have any respect to the carnal affections and desires of men. And such a thing my mind was about to bring to pass as well as I could, when I made this book of *Enchiridion*.

The corruptness of the world.

I did see the common people of Christendom, not only in effect, but also in opinions to be corrupted. I considered the most part of those which profess themselves to be pastors and doctors to abuse the titles of Christ to their proper advantage. And yet will I make no mention of those men after whose will and pleasure the world is ruled and turned up and down, whose vices though they be never so manifest, a man may scarcely once wince. And in such great darkness, in such great troublous ruffling of the world, in so great diversity of men's opinions, whither should we rather fly for succour than to the very great and sure anchor of Christ's doctrine, which is the gospel.

The sure anchor.

Who being a good man in deed, doth not see and lament this marvellous corrupt world? When was there ever more tyranny? When did avarice reign more largely and less punished? When were ceremonies at any time more in estimation? When did our iniquity so largely flow with more liberty? When was ever charity so cold? What is brought, what is read, what is decreed or determined but it tasteth and savoureth of ambition and lucre? Oh how unfortunate were we if Christ had not left some sparks of his doctrine unto us, and as it were lively and everlasting veins of his godly mind.

In things confused we must have recourse to the Evangels.

Hereto therefore we must enforce ourselves to know these sparks, leaving the coals of men's phantasies: let us seek these veins until we find fresh water which springeth into everlasting life. We delve and dig the ground marvellously deep for to pluck out riches, which nourisheth vice: and shall we not labour then the rich earth of Christ to get out that thing which is our souls' health? There was never no storm of vices that did so overcome and quench the heat of charity, but it might be restored again at this flint stone.

1 Cor. x.
Gen. xvi.
Gen. xxvi.

Christ is a stone, but this stone hath sparks of celestial fire, and veins of lively water. In time past Abraham in every land did dig pits and holes, fetching in every place the veins of lively water: but those same being stopped up again by the Phylistyens with earth, Isaac and his servants did delve again, and not being only content to restore the old, did also make new.

The Phylistyans of our time.

But then the Philistyans did scold and chide, yet he did not cease from digging. And in this our time we have Phylistyans which do prefer the naughty earth to the lively fountains, even those which be worldly-wise, and have their respect to earthly things, and wring and wrest God's doctrine and his gospel to their carnal affections, making it serve to their ambition, bolstering up therewith their filthy lucre and tyranny. And if now any Isaac or any of his family should dig and find some true and pure vein, by and by they brable and cry against him, perceiving right well that that vein should hurt their advantage, should hurt their ambition, although it make never so much for the glory of Christ: straightway they cast in naughty earth, and with a corrupt interpretation they stop up the vein, and drive away the digger: or at the least they make it so muddy with clay and filthiness, that whosoever drinketh thereof shall draw unto him more slime and naughtiness than he shall good liquor.

Hiere. ij.

They will not that those that thirst and desire righteousness do drink of the pure liquor, but they bring them unto their old worn and all too trodden cisterns, which have broken stones and mortar, but water they have none. But yet for all this the very true children of Isaac that be the true worshippers of Christ, must not be wearied and driven away from this labour: for verily even they which thrust naughty earth into the fountain of the gospel, would be counted the very worshippers of Christ. So that indeed nothing nowadays is more perilous than to teach truly Christ's learning, so greatly have the Philistyens prevailed fighting for their earth, preaching earthly things for celestial, and men's inventions for God's commandments: that is to say, not teaching those things which make for the glory of Christ, but those things which be for their own advantage, which be pardons, compositions, and suchlike pilferings.

The merchants of pardons.

And these they do so much more perilously because they cloke their covetousness with the titles and names of great princes, of the Pope of Rome, yea of Christ also Himself. But there is no man that doth more for the Pope's profit or business, than he that teacheth Christ's learning purely and truly, whereof he is the chief teacher. There is no man that doth more good to princes or deserveth more of them, than he which endeavoureth himself that the people may be wealthy and in prosperity. But some of the flock of schoolmen will here speak against me, saying it is easy to any man to give general precepts what is to be desired and what is to be eschewed: but what shall be answered then to those that ask counsel for so many fortunes and chances? First I answer that there be more divers kinds of such worldly business than that any living person can give direct and sure answer to each one of them.

A man can make no certain answer to everything.

Secondarily there is such diversity of circumstances, which if a man do not know, it is not well possible to make an answer. In conclusion, I doubt greatly whether they themselves have any sure answer that they may make, seeing they differ in so many things amongst themselves. And those also which amongst them be more wise than other do not thus answer: This ye shall do, this ye shall not do; but of this manner: This in mine opinion were the better, this I suppose to be tolerable.

The light of faith.

But if we have that simple and bright eye which the gospel speaketh of, if the house of our mind have in it the candle of pure faith set upon a candlestick, all these trifles shall easily be put away and avoided as it were clouds or mists. If we have the rule and pattern of Christ's charity, to it we may apply and make meet all other things right easily. But what will ye do when this rule doth not agree with those things which hath been commonly used so many hundred years, and which be ordained and stablished by the laws of princes, for this thing chanceth very oft? Ye must not condemn that thing which princes do in executing their office, but again do not corrupt and defile the heavenly philosophy with men's deeds.

Christ is the centre.

Let Christ continue and abide, as he is indeed, a very centre or middle point unmoved, having certain circles going round about him: move not the mark out of his own place.

Three circles.
The first men of the Church.

Those which be in the first circle next to the centre (that is to say next to Christ) as priests, bishops, cardinals, popes, and such to whom it belongeth to follow the Lamb whithersoever he shall go, let them embrace and hold fast that most pure part, and so far forth as they may let them communicate and plenteously give the same unto their next neighbours.

The second of princes.

In the second circle all temporal and lay princes be, which in keeping war and making laws, after a certain manner do service to Christ, either when with rightful battle they drive away their enemies and defend and maintain the public peace and tranquillity of the commonwealth: or else when with punishment according to the laws, they punish malefactors and evil-doers. And yet because they cannot choose but of necessity be occupied and busied in such things as be joined with the most vile dregs and filth of the earth, and with the business of the world, it is jeopardous lest they do fall further from the centre and mark, as lest they should make sometimes war for their own pleasure, and not for the commonwealth: lest under the pretext of justice they should use cruelty upon those whom they might reform with mercy: lest under the title of lordship they should pyll and polle those people whose goods they ought to defend.

The office of sacerdotes.

And moreover as Christ like the fountain of everlasting fire, doth draw next unto him the order of priests, and maketh them of like nature, that is to say pure and clean from all corruption of worldly dregs and filthiness: so in like case it is the office of priests, and specially of the highest, so much as they can to call and draw unto them those that be princes and have power and authority. And if it fortune at any time that war do rise suddenly in any place, let the bishops endeavour themselves so much as in them is, either to end the strifes and variances without shedding of blood: or if that cannot be brought to pass, by reason of the great storms of worldly business, yet let them so do that as little blood as may be be shed, and that the war may shortly be brought to an end. In times past the bishops' authority had place even in just punishments, and hath gotten divers times (as Saint Augustyne plainly in his epistle doth testify) the malefactor from the hands of temporal judges.

Augustyne.

For some things there be so necessary unto the order of the commonwealth, that partly yet Christ did dissemble at them, and partly he put them from him, and partly neither approving nor disallowing them did in a manner wink and look beside them. He would not know the money of Cesar, nor the scripture upon it.

What things and how far forth they appertain to the heads of the Church.

The tribute he commanded to be paid if it were due and debt, as though it little pertained to him, so that God had his duty. The woman taken and found in adultery he neither condemned neither openly absolved, but only did bid her that she should no more do so. Of those which were condemned of Pylate, whose blood he intermingled amongst their sacrifices, he neither said it was well done nor evil, but only threatened every man that they should be punished with a like destruction if they did not amend. Moreover, when he was desired to divide the inheritance between the two brethren, he plainly refused it as an unworthy thing for him to give judgment of such gross matters, which did teach things heavenly.

What things Christ openly rebuked.

And also of the other part there be certain things which he openly abhorred, as the covetous Phariseys, the hypocrites, the proud rich folks, saying unto them Woe be unto you. He never rebuked the apostles more sharply than when they would have been avenged, or when they were ambitious. When they asked him whether they should command fire to be sent down from heaven to have burned up the city from whence they were shut forth, he answered and said to them, Ye know not of what spirit ye are. When Peter was about to have called him unto the world from his passion suffering, he called him an adversary. When they contended about preeminence which of them should be the best, how often and how many ways doth he call them back to a contrary mind?

What things Christ teacheth openly.

And other things there be which he teacheth and commandeth openly to be observed, as not to resist evil, to do good to thine enemies, to use meekness of mind, and other like. These must be departed in sunder, and every of them set in order in his own place.

Princes' laws are of the mean sort of things.

Let us not therefore straightway make Christ an author of all things which be done by princes and temporal officers, nor defend it (as we call it) to be done by God's law. They deal and meddle with many things which be low and gross, not altogether of the very pureness of a Christian man: yet they be not to be rebuked inasmuch as they be necessary to the maintenance of order to be observed. Nor we be not by the ministering of their office made good, albeit that by them it is caused that we be less evil, and that they which be evil do less hurt and annoyance to the commonwealth. And therefore they also ought to have their honour because they do somewhat serve the justice of God and the public and common tranquillity, without the which sometime those things be troubled and vexed which belong to godly holiness.

Evil rulers must be suffered.

They must be honoured when they do their office: and if sometimes they use their power for their own pleasure or profit, yet peradventure it were the best to suffer them, lest more hurt should spring thereof: for there appeareth an image or rather a shadow of the divine justice in them, which justice yet ought to shine more evidently and more purely in the living and laws of priests. An image doth of another manner shew in a mirror of glass, than it doth in iron.

The third circle.

And in the third circle must all the common people be, as the most gross part of all this world, but not yet so gross but that they pertain unto the mystical body of Christ: for the eyes be not only members of the body, but also the legs, the feet, and the privy parts. And those which be in the third circle we ought so to suffer in their infirmity, that as much as is possible we do call them unto those things which be more approved of Christ. For in the mystical body he that but late was the foot may be the eye. And like as the princes if they be not all the best, must not with chiding be exasperate, lest (as Saint Augustyne saith) when they be moved they stir up more perilous tragedies, so the weak people like as Christ suffered his apostles and nourished them, must be suffered, and after a fatherly manner cherished until they wax more aged and strong in Christ.

The weak must be forborne.

For godliness also hath his infancy, it hath mean age, it hath full strength and perfect age. Yet all men after their degree must endeavour themselves to attain and come unto Christ. The elements have every one his proper place, but the fire which hath the highest place by little and little draweth all the other unto him, and so much as he can turneth them into his nature. The clear water he turneth into the air, and the air clarified he transformeth into his own nature.

The change of one element into another.

The clear water he turneth into the air, and the air clarified he transformeth into his own nature. Saint Paul doth in many things suffer and pardon the Corynthyans, but in the mean season putting difference between those things which he did proffer in the name of his Lord unto them that were perfect, and those things which he did pardon that were written in his own name to them that were yet weak and young in Christ: but ever on this trust that they should profit and go forward to more strength and perfection. And also he travaileth again to bring forth the Galathyans, until Christ be fashioned in them. Now if any man will think this circle to be more convenient for princes, I will not strive greatly with him. But whatsoever is without the third circle is at all times and in all points to be hated and refused, as ambition and desire of money, lechery, ire, vengeance, envy, backbiting, and such other pestilences, which then only be made incurable, when they disguised with the visor and cloak of holiness and virtue do creep into the circle afore spoken: that is when under the pretext of executing the law and justice we use our tyranny. When by the occasion of religion we provide for great lucre. When under the title of defending the church we hunt for worldly power and authority: and whensoever those things be commanded as things pertaining unto Christ which be disagreeing much from his learning.

The mark may not be changed.

Therefore the mark must be set before every man which they ought to shoot at: and there is but one mark, which is Christ and his most pure learning. If thou set forth a worldly mark in the stead of a celestial mark, then shall there be nothing whereunto a man ought justly enforce himself, which laboureth to profit and go forward.

The mark may not be changed.

Every man ought to enforce himself to that which is best and most perfect, that at the least we may attain and come to the mean things. And there is no cause why we should put away any kind or manner of living from this mark.

All must labour to perfectness.

The perfection of Christ consisteth only in the affections, and not in the manner or kind of living: it consisteth in the minds and not in the garments or in meats and drinks. There be among the monks which be scarce able to be put in the third circle, and yet I speak of those which be good, but yet weak and not perfect. There be amongst these that have had two wives which Christ thinketh worthy for the first circle. Nor yet in the mean time I do no wrong to any manner of living or profession, though I propound and set forth afore every man that thing which is best and most perfect: unless ye would think Plato to have done injury against all cities because in his book of the governing of a city or a commonwealth, he feigned such example of a commonwealth as yet never any man could see. Or except ye do think that Quintilian hath hurt the whole order of orators, because he feigned such an example of an orator as yet never was. And though thou be far from the principal and chief patron Christ, thou art not yet therefore cast away, but stimulated and moved to go forward and profit. Art thou near the mark? Then art thou monished and counselled to approach more near: for there was never yet any man that went so far forward, but that he might have gone much more near the mark. There is no kind of living but it hath some perilous points annexed unto it, to cause men to degenerate from the truth: and whosoever sheweth those jeopardous and dangerous points, doth not derogate or minish the honour of the order, nor speak against it, but rather is for the profit thereof.

The common vices of princes.

As the felicity of princes is in danger to fall into tyranny, is in danger and jeopardy of foolishness and flattering, now whosoever sheweth those dangers to be eschewed, doth deserve thanks of the order of princes. Nor he doth not speak against their majesty, wherein they glory, which doth shew in what things their very majesty doth consist, which also doth put them in remembrance whereto they were sworn when they took their authority, what is their duty unto their people, and what they ought to do unto their officers.

Bishops and other.
1 Pet. v.

The heads and rulers of the church have in a manner affinity with pestilent vices, avarice and ambition, which well perceiving St Peter the chief pastor next unto Christ, doth monish the bishops to feed their flock, and not to pyll, poll, and flay them: nor that they should not feed them because of any filthy advantage, but of their free and ready will: nor that they should use themselves as lords upon them, but that by the example of life, they should provoke them to godliness rather than by threatening and power. Doth he then speak against the order of priests which doth shew by what means, and how the bishops may truly be great, mighty, and rich?

To which vices the common sort of monks be prone.

Moreover the kind of religious men is accompanied most commonly (besides other enormities) with superstition, pride, hypocrisy, and backbiting. He doth not straight condemn their manner of living which doth shew and admonish them in what things most true religion doth stand or rest, and how much the true godliness of a Christian man is away from pride, and how far true charity is from all feigning and deceit: how much backbiting and slandering and venemousness of tongue is contrary to pure and true holiness. And specially if he shew what is to be eschewed after such sober and discreet manner, that he do neither name any man nor touch any order. What thing is that in this mortal life so fortunate and prosperous, but hath some pestilent things annexed unto it? Therefore like as he doth not noye the health of the body but helpeth it, whosoever sheweth what things corrupteth health and what things preserveth it: so he doth not dissuade men from religion, but exhorteth them rather unto it, which sheweth the corrupt infections thereof and also the remedies.

The quarrel of some persons.

For I am informed that there be divers which so judgeth of this book, as though the precepts thereof did withdraw and turn away men's minds from the life of religious men, because they do not so much praise and allow ceremonies, neither yet man's constitutions as some would, which indeed overmuch regard them. And there can be nothing so circumspectly spoken, but that thereof lewd and evil persons do take occasion either of quarrelling or else of sinning: so that it is dangerous nowadays to any man to teach anything well. If a man should dissuade some such war and battle which now of long time hath been used, worse than was ever any amongst the gentiles, for things of no value, he should be noted by and by of the pick-quarrels to be one of those which thinketh that no war is lawful for a Christian man.

Nothing is free from the cavilling of lewd persons.

For these which were the bringers up and authors of this sentence we have made heretics, because a pope, I wot not who, doth seem to approve and allow war.

Battle.

And yet he is not suspected nor noted of heresy, which doth provoke and stir up men to battle, and bloweth the trumpet thereunto for every trifling matter, against the doctrine both of Christ and of his apostles. If a man admonish that this is a deed truly belonging to the successor of an apostle to bring the Turks unto religion with Christ's help, rather than with war: anon he is suspected as though he affirmed not to be lawful for Christian men to withstand the Turks, when they invade us.

Poverty.

If a man shew and praise the temperance that was in the apostles, and speak anything against the great superfluity that is used nowadays, he should be noted as a favourer of the Ebyonytes. And if a man did exhort diligently that these which be married should rather be joined together by the consents and agreeing of their minds, than by the embracings of their bodies, and so purely to use matrimony that as much as might be it were made like to virginity: he should be anon suspected to think that every act of matrimony were sin and unlawful, as the Marcionytes did. If a man do admonish that in exercise and disputations, specially of divinity, there should be no ambitious pertinacity to overcome his fellow in defending his own opinions, nor no ambition to shew what they can do in commonplaces: he is wrongfully accused as though he did condemn utterly all school learning. Nor Saint Augustyne when he giveth warning to the logicians that they should beware of lust to brawl and chide, doth not condemn logic, but sheweth the pestilence thereof that it might be eschewed.

The subverted judgments of virtues and vices.

Also he doth not dispraise virtue nor praise vice, which sheweth the preposterous and wrong judgment of the common people, which among virtues esteem those to be of most great value and chiefest which be of the lowest sort: and among vices most sore hateth and abhorreth those most small faults and trifles, and so contrariwise. Anon he is accused as though he should favour those vices which he sheweth to be more grievous than other, and as though he should condemn those good deeds and benefits to whom he preferreth other more holy and better. As if a man did admonish and give us warning, that it is more sure to trust unto good deeds than to trust to the pope's pardon, yet he doth not forsooth condemn the pope's pardons, but preferreth that which by Christ's learning and doctrine is of more certainty.

Pardons.

Also if a man do teach those for to do better which tarry at home and provide for their wife and children, than those which go to see Rome, Hierusalem or Saint James, and that money which they should spend in that long and perilous journey to be better and more devoutly spent upon poor folks, yet condemneth not he their good intent, but preferreth that which is more near to very godliness.

They which go to Hierusalem do no great thing.

And this is a thing not only used now in our time but also in times heretofore past, to abhor some vices as though there were none other, fawning upon the rest as they were no vices at all, when in very deed they be more detestable than those which we so hate and abhor.

Only voluptuousness is abhorred in sacerdotes.

Saint Augustyne doth complain in his epistles that lasciviousness of the flesh is only imputed unto the priests of Affryke as a vice, and that the vice of covetousness and drunkenness be taken well nigh for a praise. This specially we speak most against, and cry out upon and exaggerate for an exceeding abominable fact, if one touch the body of Christ with the same hands wherewith he hath touched the body of a harlot. And there be some over-raging bold that be not afraid openly to affirm that it is less sin for a woman to commit carnal act with a brute beast than to lie with a priest. Now he that something rebuketh their shamelessness, doth not therefore favour the naughtiness of priests, but sheweth that they regard not those offences which be a great deal more to be cried out upon.

A sacerdote being a dicer or fighter.

But if a priest be a dicer, a fighter, a brawler, all unlearned, drowned and wrapped in temporal business, all given to the evil service of evil princes, yet against him they cry nothing at all which altogether worldly and polluted doth handle and intermeddle with holy mysteries.

A sacerdote pick-quarrel.

When a priest is a flatterer or a pick-quarrel, which with his bitter tongue and false lies doth hurt the names of those which never offended him, but rather hath done him pleasures, why do we not now cry out? Oh what an horrible sin is this to receive the Lord God, which suffered his passion for sinners, with that tongue which is full of poison of hell, and with that mouth wherewith thou killest and flayest an innocent. But this evil and ungraciousness we set so little by that in a manner those men are even praised for it, which profess themselves to be the most religious amongst religious men. There is no man that denieth but they be to be reprehended and sore rebuked which nourish and keep at home concubines, to the evil example of all the common people; but yet these other evil vices be more hateful to God. Nor he doth therefore say that butter is naught which sayeth that honey is better and more to be preferred: nor yet doth not approve the fever that counselleth the frenzy more to be avoided. And it is hard to tell and express how great infection of manners and disposition doth spring of these perverse and wrong judgments.

Certain things have only an outward shew of godliness.

There be divers things nowadays received into the order of virtues, which rather have the visor and appearance of godliness than the nature and strength of it, insomuch that unless we look well into them and take good heed of them, they do quench and utterly destroy virtue. If it had been but a little pestilence of religion which in ceremonies do lie covert, Paul would never so sharply have spoken against them in all his epistles.

Ceremonies be of the mean sort.

And yet do not we condemn in any place ceremonies that be moderately observed, but that all holiness be ascribed unto them we cannot suffer.

A rule of Saint Augustyne.

Saint Augustyne did prohibit those of the clergy which were in house with him to use any notable vesture, but if they would be commended of the people, that they should rather bring that to pass by their manners and virtuous living than by any sundry fashion of raiment. But nowadays it is a world for to see what new and wonderful fashions of apparel and vesture there be.

The rules of men.

But yet I speak not against that, but this I marvel of, that those things are so overmuch regarded and set by, which peradventure might by right be reprehended. And again that those things be so little regarded which we should only behold and regard. I do not rail against the grey friars and black monks that they make much of their own rule, but because certain of them regard more their own rules than they do the Gospel: which thing would to God were not found in the most part of them. I do not speak against that, that some eat fish, some live with herbs, other with eggs: but I admonish those to err and to be far out of the way which will of those things justify themselves after the manner of the Jews, thinking themselves better, and preferring themselves to other for such trifles of men's invention, and take it for no default at all to hurt another man's good name with false lies.

Diversity of meats.

Of the diversity of meat and drink Christ never commanded anything, nor the apostles: but Paul oftentimes did dissuade us from it. Christ curseth bitter slandering, which also all the apostles doth detest and abhor: and yet that notwithstanding we will appear religious in such using of meats, and in hurting men's fame we be bold and hardy. I pray you think you that he which doth admonish these both in general not touching any man, and also lovingly, doth hurt religion? Who is so mad that he would be accounted eloquent for shewing and bringing to light the vices that belong to monks? But these peradventure fear lest their convents and brethren would be less obedient, and lest also there do not so many desire to be shaven into their order: yet verily, no man is more obedient to his head than he which inspired with the Holy Ghost is free and at liberty. True and very charity taketh all things well in worth, and suffereth all things, refuseth nothing, is obedient unto rulers, not only to those that be sober and gentle, but also to those that be sharp and rough.

The inferiors' obedience may not be abused.

But yet rulers must be wise of this that they do not turn the obedience of other men into their own tyranny, and that they had liefer therefore to have them superstitious than holy and virtuous, whereby they might be more obedient at every beck. They have pleasure to be called fathers: but what carnal father is there that would have his children ever infants and young because he might use his power upon them at his own pleasure? And of the other part all those that purpose to profit in the liberty of Christ, this they must be ware of, lest as Saint Paul doth admonish they make their liberty a cloke or covert to their carnal living: or as Saint Peter teacheth, with their liberty they make a cover and a cloke to their maliciousness. And if that one or two do abuse this liberty, yet it is not right forthwith that all other therefore be ever kept in superstitiousness and bondage of ceremonies like unto the Jews. And whosoever will mark it shall perceive that amongst these religious men, no man causeth the ceremonies to be more straitly observed than they which under the precepts thereof doth bear rule and serve their bellies rather than Christ.

The more religious a man is, the less he yieldeth to ceremonies.

Moreover they need not be afraid lest such kind of Essenes be not enough spread abroad in so great diversity of men's natures, whereby it is caused that nothing is so unreasonable but divers and many will love and desire it, although theirselves ought more to desire that they had true professors of religion rather than many. But would to God that it were provided and ordained by a law that no man should be taken in such snares afore he were thirty years of age, before he something knew himself, or knew what the nature and virtue of true religion is.

Matt. xxiii.

But these which like unto the Phariseys, doing their own business and providing for their own profit, wander about to make novices both by sea and land, shall never fail of young men lacking experience whom they may allure into their veils and nets, and also deceive. There be a great number of fools and simple souls in every place. But I desire even with all my heart, and I doubt not but so do all that be very good men, that the religion of the Gospel should be so pleasant to every man that they being contented therewith, should not desire the religion of black monks or grey friars.

All things give place to the glory of Christ.

And I doubt not but so would Saint Benedicte and Fraunces themselves. Moses did rejoice that his own honour was defaced and dimmed with the glory of Christ: and so should those other be glad if for the love of Christ's law we set nothing by man's constitutions. I would that all Christian men should so live that these which now be called only religious, should appear little religious, which thing even at this day is of truth and that in many: for why should I dissemble that thing that is so manifest?

The first beginning of monks in old time.

And yet in the old time the beginning of the monastical life was nothing else but a going aside into a secret place from the cruelness of idolaters. And anon after the manner of living of religious men which followed them was nothing else but a reformation and calling again to Christ: for the courts of princes in the old time shewed them christened in their titles rather than in their living. The bishops anon after were corrupt with ambition and covetousness, and the common people also fainted and waxed cold from that charity which was in the primitive church: and for this purpose did Saint Benet seek a solitary life, and then after him Barnarde, and after that divers other did associate themselves together, for this intent only that they might use the pure and simple life of Christian men.

From whence ceremonies came.

Then after in process of time when their riches and ceremonies did increase, their true godliness and simpleness did abate and decrease. And now although we see men of religion to be overmuch out of good order, and to use manners like unto gentiles, yet is the world filled with new institutions and kinds of religion as though they should not fall to the same point hereafter that other have done afore them. In times past, as I said, a religious life was nothing but a solitary life.

Monks most worldly.

And now these be called religious which be altogether drowned in worldly business, using plainly certain tyranny in worldly matters, and yet these for their apparel and title I cannot tell what, doth challenge such holiness to their selves that they do account all other in comparison of themselves no Christian men at all. Why do we make so strait and narrow Christ's religion which he would have so large? If we be moved with magnifical and high terms, I pray you what thing else is a city but a great monastery?

A city is a great monastery.

Monks be obedient to their abbot and governour, the citizens obey the bishops and curates, whom Christ himself made rulers, and not the authority of man.

Obedience, poverty, chastity.

The monks live in idleness, and be fed of other men's liberality, possessing that amongst them in common, which they never laboured or sweat for (yet speak I nothing of them that be vicious). The citizens bestow that which they have gotten with their labour and great travail, to them that have need, every man as he is of ability and power. Now as concerning the vow of chastity I dare not be bold to express what difference is betwixt the religious man unmarried and the chaste matrimony of the other. And to be short he shall not very greatly lack those three vows of man's invention, that doth keep and observe purely and sincerely that first only vow which we all solemnly make unto Christ, and not unto man, when we receive our baptism. And if we compare those that be evil of one kind, with those that be evil of the other, without doubt the temporal men be much better. But if we compare those which be good of the one sort with those that be good of the other there is little difference, if there be any at all, saving that those appear to be more religious that keep their religion and duty with less coercion.

No kind of life ought to be reproved.

The rest is therefore that no man foolishly stand in his own conceit, neither for his diversity of living from other men, nor despise or condemn the rule or order of other men's living. But in every kind of living let this be our common study, that every man according to his power endeavour himself to attain unto the mark of Christ, which is set open to all men, and that every man do exhort other to it, and also help other, neither envying them that over run us in this course, nor disdaining them that be weak and cannot yet overtake us.

The confidence in ourselves is most pernicious.

In conclusion when every man hath done that he can, let him not be like unto the Pharisey whom the Gospel maketh mention of, which doth boast his good deeds unto God saying: I fast twice in the week, I pay all my tithes and so forth. But after Christ's counsel let him speak from the heart and to himself, and not to other, saying I am an unprofitable servant, for I have done no more than I ought to do. There is no man that better trusteth than he that so distrusteth. There is no man further from true religion than he that thinketh himself to be very religious. Nor Christ's godliness is never at worse point, than when that thing which is worldly is writhen unto Christ, and the authority of man is preferred unto the authority of God. We must all hang of that head if we will be true Christian men. Moreover whosoever is obedient to a man which doth persuade and call him unto Christ, he is obedient unto Christ, and not unto man. And whosoever doth tolerate and suffer those men which be subtle, cruel and imperious, teaching that thing which maketh not for religion, but for their tyranny, he useth the patience meet for a Christian man, so that these things which they command be not utterly wicked and contrary to Christ's doctrine, for then it shall be convenient to have that answer of the apostles at hand: we must rather be obedient unto God than to any man.

How far prelates must be obeyed.

But we have long ago passed the measure and quantity of an epistle, so greatly the time deceiveth us, whiles we come and talk most pleasantly with our well-beloved friend. This book is sent unto you in Frobenius' print, as though it were new-born again, much more ornate and better corrected than it was before. I have put unto it certain fragments of mine old study in times past. Methought it most convenient to dedicate this edition (such as it is) unto you, that whosoever shall take any precepts to live well of Erasmus, should have an example ready at hand of our father Wolzius. Our Lord preserve you, good father, the honour and worship of all religion. I pray you counsel Sapidus that he be wise, that is, that he go forth as he hath begun: and to Wynphelyngus ye shall speak also, that he prepare all his armour to fight shortly with the Turks, forasmuch as he hath kept war long enough with keepers of concubines. And I have great hope and trust to see him once a bishop, and to ride upon a mule, and to be set high in honour with a mitre and cross. But in earnest I pray you commend me heartily both unto them and unto Ruferus and the rest of my friends, and in your devout prayers made to God I pray you remember Erasmus, and pray for his soul's health. At Basyle the even of the assumption of our Lady, in the year of our Lord God M. CCCCC. and xviii.

ENCHIRIDION

A compendious treatise of the soldier of Christ, called Enchiridion, which Erasmus of Roterdame wrote unto a certain courtier, a friend of his.

Thou hast desired me with fervent study, singular beloved brother in Christ, that I should describe for thee compendiously, a certain craft of virtuous living, by whose help thou mightest attain a virtuous mind, according to a true Christian man. For thou sayest that thou art and hast been a great while weary of the pastime of the court.

Egypt betokeneth sinful living.

And dost compass in thy mind by what means thou mightest escape Egypt with all her both vices and pleasures, and be prepared happily with the captain Moses unto the journey of virtue. The more I love thee, the gladder I am of this thine so holy purpose, which I trust (yea without our help) he that hath vouchsafed to stir it up in thee, shall make prosperous, and bring to good effect.

The land of promise signifieth pure life.

Notwithstanding yet have I very gladly and willingly accomplished thy desire, partly because thou art so great a friend of mine, partly also because thou requirest so charitable things. Now enforce thyself, and do thine endeavour, that neither thou mayst seem to have desired my service and duty in vain, or else I to have satisfied my mind without any fruit. Yea let us both indifferently beseech the benign spirit of Jesu, that he both put wholesome things in my mind while I write and make the same to thee of strength and efficacy.

CHAPTER 1

We must watch and look about us evermore while we be in this life.

The first point is, we must needs have in mind continually, that the life of mortal men is nothing but a certain perpetual exercise of war: as Job witnesseth, a warrior proved to the uttermost and never overcome.

The life of man is but a warfare, saith Job vii.

And that the most part of men be overmuch deceived, whose minds this world as a juggler holdeth occupied with delicious and flattering pleasures, which also as though they had conquered all their enemies, make holiday out of season, none otherwise verily than in a very assured peace.

The comparison of the world to a juggler.

It is a marvellous thing to behold how without care and circumspection we live, how idly we sleep, now upon the one side, and now upon the other, when without ceasing we are besieged with so great a number of armed vices, sought and hunted for with so great craft, invaded daily with so great lying await.

Peace, peace, and yet there is no peace at all.
Divers enemies from above.

Behold over thy head wicked devils that never sleep, but keep watch for our destruction, armed against us with a thousand deceits, with a thousand crafts of noysances, which enforce from on high to wound our minds with weapons burning and dipped in deadly poison, than the which weapons neither Hercules nor Cephalus had ever a surer dart, except they be received on the sure and impenetrable shield of faith.

Enemies at hand.

Then again, on the right hand and on the left hand, afore and behind, this world striveth against us, which after the saying of Saint John is set all on vice and mischief: and therefore to Christ both contrary and hated. Neither is it one manner of fight, for sometime with groans of adversity raging, as with open war he shaketh the walls of the soul. Sometime with great promises (but yet most vain) he provoketh to treason: and sometime by undermining he stealeth on us unaware to catch us among the idle and careless men.

Enemies of Hell.

Last of all underneath, the slippery serpent, the first breaker of peace, father of unquietness, otherwhiles hid in the green grass, lurking in his caves, wrapped together in a hundred round coils ceaseth not to watch and lie in wait beneath in the heel of woman, whom he once poisoned.

Eve signifieth affections.

By the woman is understood the carnal part of a man, otherwise called sensuality. This is our Eve by whom the most crafty serpent doth entice and draw our minds to mortal and deadly pleasures. And furthermore as though it were but a trifle that so great a company of enemies should assault us on every side, we bear about with us wheresoever we go in the very secret parts of the mind an enemy nearer than one of acquaintance, or one of household. And as nothing is more inward, so nothing is more perilous.

Old earthly Adam betokeneth appetites or affections.

This is the old and earthly Adam, which, by acquaintance and customary familiarity, is more near to us than a citizen, and is in all manner studies and pastimes to us more contrary than any mortal enemy, whom thou canst keep off with no bulwark, neither is it lawful to expel him out of thy pavilion. This fellow must be watched with an hundred eyes, lest peradventure he setteth open the castle or city of God for devils to enter in. Seeing therefore that we be vexed with so fearful and cruel war, and that we have to do or strive with so many enemies, which have conspired and sworn our death, which be so busy, so appointed, so false and expert: ought not we madmen on the other side to arm ourselves and take weapons in our hands to keep watch and have all things suspect? But we as though all things were at rest and peace, sleep so fast that we rowte again and give ourself to idleness, to pleasure, and as the common proverb is, give our minds to revelling and making good cheer, as though our life were a feasting or banqueting, such as the Greeks used, and not warfare. For in the stead of tents and pavilions we tumble and welter in our beds. And in the stead of sallettes and hard armour we be crowned with roses and fresh flowers, bathed in damask and rose waters, smoked in pomanders and with musk balls, changing points of war with riot and idleness. And in the stead of weapons belonging to the war, we handle and take unto us the unhardy harp, as this peace were not of all wars the most shameful.

There is no peace to wicked persons.

For whosoever is at one with vices, hath broken truce made between him and God in time of baptism. And thou, oh madman, criest peace, peace, when thou hast God thine enemy, which only is peace and the author of peace, and he himself with open mouth crieth the contrary by the mouth of his prophet, saying there is no peace to sinners or wicked persons which love not God. And there is none other condition of peace with him except that we (as long as we war in the fortress of this body) with deadly hate and with all our might hold fight against vices. For if we be at one with them, we shall have him twice our enemy, which only being our friend may make us blessed. And if he be our foe may destroy us, both because that we stand on their side which only can never agree with God, for how can light and darkness agree? and also that because we as men most unkind abide not by the promise that we made to him, but unjustly have broken the appointment made between him and us with protestation and holy ceremonies.

In time of baptism we profess with protestation to fight ever under the standard of Christ.

Oh thou Christian man, rememberest thou not when thou wert professed and consecrate with the holy mysteries of the fountain of life, how thou boundest thyself to be a faithful soldier unto thy captain Christ, to whom thou owest thy life twice, both because he gave it thee, and also because he restored it again to thee, to whom thou owest more than thou art able to pay? Cometh it not to thy mind how when thou were bound with his sacraments as with holy gifts, thou were sworn with words for the nonce to take the part of so courteous an emperoure, and that thou didst curse and ban thine own head, desiring vengeance to fall upon thine own self, if thou didst not abide by thy promise?

Badges and signs of baptism.

For what intent was the sign of the cross printed in thy forehead, but that as long as thou livest thou shouldst fight under his standard? For what intent wert thou anointed with his holy oil, but that thou for ever shouldst wrestle and fight against vices? What shame and how great abomination is it accounted with all men if a man forsake his king or chief lord? Why settest thou so light, then, by thy captain Christ? neither kept down with the fear of him, seeing he is God, nor refraining for love, seeing for thy sake he was made man yea and seeing thou usurpest his name thou ought to remember what thou hast promised him.

The name of Christ ought to put us in remembrance.

Why departest thou away from him like a false forsworn man, and goest unto thine enemy, from whence he once redeemed thee with the ransom of his precious blood? Why dost thou, so oft a renegate, war and fight under the standard of his adversary? With what face presumest thou to set up contrary banners against thy king which for thy sake bestowed his own life? Whosoever is not on his part, as he saith himself (Luke xi.) standeth against him. And he that gathereth not with him scattereth abroad. Thou warrest not only with filthy title or quarrel, but also for a miserable reward. Wilt thou hear whosoever thou be that art servant or soldier to the world, what shall be thy need?

The guerdon of sin.

Paul the standard-bearer in the war of Christ, answereth thee. The reward (saith he) of sin is death. And who would take upon him to fight in a just and an honest cause, if he were sure to die but bodily only, and thou fightest in a wrong and also a filthy quarrel to obtain for thy reward the death of thy soul. In these mad wars that man maketh against man, either through beastly fury or for miserable necessity: seest thou not if at any time the greatness of the prey promised or hoped for, or comfort of the captain, or the cruelness of the enemies, or shame of cowardice cast in their teeth, or in conclusion if desire of praise hath pricked and stirred up the soldiers' minds: with what courage and with what lusty stomachs finish they whatsoever labour remaineth, how little they regard their lives, with how great fierceness run they upon their enemies, well is him that may go foremost.

Comparison of rewards.

And, I beseech thee, how small is the reward which those wretched men go about to get with so great jeopardies and diligence? Verily but to have praise of a wretched man their captain, and that they might be praised with a rude and homely song, such as are used to be made in the time of war, to have haply their names written in a harper's beadroll, to get a garland of grass or oaken leaves, or at the most to bring home a little more vantage or winning with them. We, on the other side clean contrary, be kindled neither with shame nor with hope of reward, and yet he beholdeth us while we fight that shall quit our pain if we win the field. But what reward setteth forth the chief ruler of our game for them that win the mastery? not mules as Achilles did in Homer, not tripods, that is to say meat boards with three feet, as Eneas did in Virgil: but such as the eye never saw, nor the ear never heard, neither could sink into the heart of man. And these rewards he giveth in the mean season to his (whiles they be yet fighting) as solaces and things to comfort them in their labours and travails. And what hereafter? Certes, blessed immortality. But in games of sport, as running, wrestling, leaping, in which the chiefest part of reward is praise, they which be overcome have likewise their rewards assigned unto them. But our matter is tried with great and doubtful peril, neither we fight for praise, but for life, and as reward of most value is proffered to him that quitteth himself most manfully, so pain most terrible is appointed for him that giveth back. Heaven is promised to him that fighteth lustily. And why is not the quick courage of a gentle stomach enflamed with the hope of so blessed a reward, namely what He promiseth, which as he cannot die, even so he cannot deceive?

God beholdeth us.

All things be done in the sight of God which all things beholdeth. We have all the company of Heaven beholders of our conflict. And how are we not moved, at the least way, even for very shame? He shall praise our virtue and diligence, of whom to be lauded is very felicity. Why seek we not this praise, yea, with the loss of our lives? It is a cowardly mind that will be quickened with no manner of reward.

Achilles slew Hector.

The veriest heartless coward in the world for fear of perils ofttime taketh courage to him. And in worldly battles though thine adversary be never so cruel, yet rageth he but on thy goods and body only. What more than that could cruel Achilles do to Hector? But here the immortal part of thee is assaulted and thy carcass is not drawn about the sepulchre as Hector's, but thy body and soul is cast down into hell: there the greatest calamity or hurt is, that a sword shall separate the soul from the body: here is taken from thy soul the life, which is God himself. It is natural for the body to die, which if no man kill, yet must it needs die. But thy soul to die, is extreme misery.

The death of the body seemeth terrible, the death of the soul is not perceived.

With how great cawtell avoid we the wounds of the body, with how great diligence cure we them, and set we so little of the wounds of the soul. Our hearts ariseth and grudgeth at the remembrance of death of the body as a terrible or outrageous thing, because it is seen with bodily eyes. The soul to die, because no man seeth and few believeth, therefore very few fear it. And is this death more cruel yet than the other? Even as much as the soul doth pass the body, and God excelleth the soul. Wilt thou that I show thee certain conjectures, examples or tokens whereby thou mayest perceive the sickness and death of the soul?

The token of a sick soul.

Thy stomach digesteth ill, it keepeth no meat, thou perceivest by and by thy body to be out of temper. And bread is not so natural meat to the body as the word of God is meat for thy soul. If that seem bitter, if thy mind rise against it, why doubtest thou yet but that the mouth of the soul is out of taste, and infected with some disease? If thy memory the stomach of the soul, keep not the learning of God, if by continual meditation thou digestest not, if when it is digested, thou sendest it not to all parts by operation, thou hast an evident token that thy soul is acrased. When thy knees for weakness bow under thee, and it be much work to draw thy limbs after thee, thou perceivest plainly thy body to be evil at ease. And dost thou not perceive the sickness of thy soul, when he grudgeth and is weak and faint to all deeds of piety, when he hath no strength to suffer patiently the least rebuke in the world, and is troubled and angry with the loss of a halfpenny? after that the sight is departed from the eyes, and the ears cease to hear, after that all the body hath lost his feeling: no man doubteth then but the soul is departed. When the eyes of the heart be waxen dim, insomuch that thou canst not see the most clearest light, which is virtue or truth: when thou hearest not with thy inward ears the voice of God: when thou lackest all thy inward feeling and perceiving of the knowledge of God, thinkest thou that thy soul is alive? Thou seest thy brother ungoodly entreated, thy mind is nothing moved, so thy matter be in good case. Why feeleth thy soul nothing here? Certainly because he is dead. Why dead? Because her life is away, that is God.

God is life of the soul.

For, verily, where God is, there is charity, love and compassion of thy neighbours, for God is that charity. For if thou were a quick member, how could any part of thy body ache, thou not sorrowing, no not once feeling or perceiving it? Take a more evident token.

Feeling is a token of life.

Thou hast deceived thy friend, thou hast committed adultery, thy soul hath caught a deadly wound, and yet it grieveth thee not, insomuch as thou joyest as it were of great winning, and boastest thyself of that thou shamefully hast committed. Believe surely that thy soul lieth dead. Thy body is not alive if it feel not the pricking of a pin. And is thy soul alive which lacketh the feeling of so great a wound? Thou hearest some man use lewd and presumptuous communication, words of backbiting, unchaste and filthy, raging furiously against his neighbour: think not the soul of that man to be alive. There lieth a rotten carcase in the sepulchre of that stomach from whence such stench ariseth and infecteth every man that cometh nigh. Christ called the Pharisees painted sepulchres. Why so? Because they bear dead souls about with them. And king David the prophet saith, their throat is a sepulchre wide open, they spake deceitfully with their tongues.

The bodies of good men be the temples of the Holy Ghost.

The bodies of holy people be the temples of the Holy Ghost.

The body is the burial, or grave.

And lewd men's bodies be the sepulchre of dead corpses, that the interpretations of the grammarians to them might well be applied, *Soma quasi Sima*. It is called a body because it is the burial, that is to say, the grave of the soul. The breast is the sepulchre, the mouth and the throat is the gaping of the sepulchre, and the body destitute of the soul is not so dead as is the soul when she is forsaken of Almighty God, neither any corpse stinketh in the nose of man so sore as the stench of a soul buried four days offendeth the nose of God and all saints. Therefore conclude, whensoever dead words proceed out of thy heart, it must needs be that a dead corpse lieth buried within. For when (according to the Gospel) the mouth speaketh of the abundance of the heart, no doubt he would speak the lively words of God, if there were life present, that is to wit, God. In another place of the Gospel the disciples say to Christ, Master, whither shall we go, thou hast the words of life? Why so, I pray thee, the words of life? Certainly for because they sprung out of the soul from whom the Godhead, which restored us again to life immortal, never departed not yet one moment. The physician easeth the body sometimes when thou art diseased. Good and holy men sometimes have called the body dead to life again. But a dead soul nothing but God only of his free and singular power restoreth to life again, yea, and he restoreth her not again if she being dead have once forsaken the body. Moreover of the bodily death is the feeling little or none at all. But of the soul, is the feeling eternal. And though also the soul in that case be more than dead, yet as touching the feeling of eternal death, she is ever immortal. Therefore seeing we must needs fight with so strange and marvellous jeopardy, what dulness, what negligence, what foolishness is that of our mind, whom fear of so great mischief sharpeneth not.

Many causes why a Christian man ought to be of good comfort, and to have confidence.

And again on the contrary part there is no cause wherefore either the greatness of peril, or else the multitude, the violence, the subtlety of thine adversaries should abate the courage of thy mind. It cometh to thy mind how grievous an adversary thou hast. Remember also on the other side how present how ready at hand thou hast help and succour. Against thee be innumerable, yea but he that taketh thy part, himself alone is more of power than all they. If God be on our side, what matter is it who be against us? If he stay thee, who shall cast thee down? But thou must be inflamed in all thy heart and brain in fervent desire of victory.

Our enemy was overcome many years agone.

Let it come to thy remembrance that thou strivest not, nor hast not to do with a fresh soldier and a new adversary, but with him that was many years ago discomforted, overthrown, spoiled and led captive in triumph of us, but then in Christ our head, by whose might no doubt he shall be subdued again in us also. Take heed therefore that thou be a member of the body and thou shalt be able to do all things in the power of the head.

No man is strong in his own strength.

In thyself thou art very weak, in him thou art valiant, and nothing is there that thou art not able to do. Wherefore the end of our war is not doubtful, because the victory dependeth not of fortune, but is put wholly in the hands of God, and by him in our hands. No man is here that hath not overcome, but he that would not. The benignity of our protector never failed man. If thou take heed to answer and to do thy part again, thou art sure of the victory, for he shall fight for thee, and his liberality shall be imputed to thee for merit. Thou must thank him altogether for the victory, which first of all himself alone being immaculate, pure and clean from sin, oppressed the tyranny of sin. But this victory shall not come without thine own diligence also, for he that said, Have confidence, I have overcome the world, would have thee to be of a good comfort, but not careless and negligent. On this manner in conclusion is his strength, and by him we shall overcome.

Scilla is a jeopardous place in the sea of Cecyle. Charibdis is a swallow or whirlpool in the same sea.

Profiting by his example, we shall fight as he fought, wherefore thou must so keep a mean course, as it were between Scylla and Charibdis, that neither trusting too much and bearing thee overbold upon the grace of God thou be careless and reckless, neither yet so mistrusting in thyself, feared with the difficulties of the war, do cast from thee courage, boldness, or confidence of mind together with harness and weapons also.

CHAPTER 2

Of the weapons to be used in the war of a Christian man.

And I suppose that nothing pertaineth so much to the discipline of this war than that thou surely know, and presently have recorded and exercised in thy mind alway with what kind of armour or weapons thou oughtest to fight, and against what enemies thou must encounter and joust. Moreover that thy weapons be always ready at hand, lest thine so subtle an enemy should take thee sleeping and unarmed. In these worldly wars a man may be oftentimes at rest, as in the deep of the winter, or in time of truce: but we as long as we keep war in this body, may depart from our harness and weapons no season, no not as the saying is one finger breadth.

A Christian man should never cease from war.

We must ever stand afore the tents and make watch, for our adversary is never idle: but when he is most calm and still, when he feigneth to flee or to make truce, even then most of all he imagineth guile: and thou hast never more heed to keep watch than when he maketh countenance or semblance of peace. Thou hast never less need to fear than when he assaulteth thee with open war. Therefore let thy first care be that thy mind be not unarmed. We arm our body, because we would have no need to fear the dagger or privy murderer of the thief. Shall we not arm our mind likewise, that he might be in safeguard? Our enemies be armed to destroy us, doth it grieve us to take our weapons of defence, that we perish not? They watch to kill, shall not we watch to be out of danger? But of the armour and weapons of a Christian man we shall make special mention when we come to the places convenient.

The seven nations inhabited the land of behest or promission promised to Abraham and his offspring.

In the mean season to speak briefly, whosoever will assail with battle the seven nations that be called Cananei, Cethei, Amorrei, Pherezei, Gergezei, Evei, and Jebuzei, that is to say, whosoever will take upon him to fight against the whole host of vices, of the which seven be counted as chief captains, must provide him of two special weapons.

Prayer and knowledge be the chief armour of a Christian man.

Prayer and knowledge, otherwise called learning. Paul would we should be ever armed, which biddeth us pray continually without stop. Prayer pure and perfect lifteth up thine affection to heaven, a tower beyond thine enemies' reach. Learning or knowledge fenceth or armeth the mind with wholesome precepts and honest opinions, and putteth thee ever in remembrance of virtue, so that neither can be lacking to the other. These twain cleaveth so together like friends, the one ever requiring the other's help. The one maketh intercession and prayeth. The other sheweth what is to be desired and what thou oughtest to pray. To pray fervently, and (as James exhorteth us) without doubting or mistrusting, faith and hope bringeth to pass. To pray in the name of Jesu, which is nothing else but to desire things wholesome for thy soul's health only, learning or doctrine teacheth thee.

The sons of Zebedei be James the more, and John the evangelist.

Said not Christ to the sons of Zebedei, Ye know not what ye ask? But prayer verily is the more excellent, as she that cometh and talketh familiarly with Almighty God. Yet for all that is doctrine no less necessary. And I cannot tell whether that thou, fled from Egypt, mightest without great jeopardy commit thyself to so long a journey, so hard and full of difficulty, without the captains Aaron and Moses.

Aaron signifieth prayer, Moses betokeneth knowledge.

Aaron which was charged with things dedicate to the service of God's temple, betokeneth prayer. By Moses is figured the knowledge of the law of God. And as knowledge of God ought not to be unprofitable, so prayer should not be faint, slack, without courage or quickness. Moses with the weapons of prayer fought against his enemies, but had his hands lifted up to Heaven, which when he let down, the Israelites had the worse. Thou, haply, when thou prayest, considerest only how much of thy psalms thou hast mumbled up, and thinkest much babbling to be the strength and virtue of prayer: which is chiefly the vice of them which (as infants) cleave to the literal sense, and are not yet grown up to the ripeness of the spirit. But hear what Christ teacheth us in Matthew, saying, When ye pray speak not much, as the ethnics and gentiles do, for they think their prayers to be accepted because of much babbling. Counterfeit them not therefore, for your Father knoweth whereof ye have need before ye desire it of Him. And Paul to the Corynthes despiseth ten thousand words babbled with mouth in comparison of five spoken in knowledge. Moses opened not his lips, and yet God said to him, Why criest thou so to me? It is not the noise of thy lips, but the fervent desire of thy mind, which (as it were a very shrill voice) beateth the ears of God. Let this, therefore, be a customable thing with thee that as soon as thine enemy ariseth against thee, and the vices which thou hast forsaken trouble thee, thou then without tarrying with sure confidence and trust lift up thy mind to heaven, from whence help shall come to thee, and thither also lift up thy hands.

Pity is not taken for compassion, but for the honouring and worshipping of God with charity or love ordained, as Christ taught us to love.

The surest thing of all is to be occupied in deeds of piety, that thy deeds may be referred and applied, not to worldly business but unto Christ. Yet lest thou shouldst despise the help of knowledge, consider one thing. Beforetime it was enough for the Israelytes to flee and escape from their enemies, but they were never so bold as to provoke the Amalachytes, and to try with them hand for hand before they were refreshed with manna from heaven and water running out of the hard rock.

Manna is a honeydew wherewith the children of Israel were fed forty years, and it is signified knowledge, and also by water likewise.

The noble warrior David refreshed and made strong with these cates, set nought by the whole host of his adversaries, saying, Oh good Lord thou hast set a table of meat before me to defend me against all men that trouble me. Believe me well, brother singularly beloved in my heart, there is none so great violence of thy foes, that is to say, none so great temptation which fervent study or meditation of holy scripture is not able to put aback, nor any so grievous adversity which it maketh not easy. And lest I should seem to be somewhat too bold an interpreter (though I could defend myself with great authority) what thing, I pray thee, could more properly have signified the knowledge of the secret law of God than did manna? For first in that it sprang not out of the earth, but rained down from heaven. By this property thou perceivest the difference between the doctrine of God and the doctrine of man. For all holy scripture came by divine inspiration and from God the author. In that it is small or little in quantity, is signified the humility, lowliness or homeliness of the style under rude words including great mystery. That it is white, by this property is signified the purity and cleanness of God's law. For there is no doctrine of man which is not defiled with some black spot of error, only the doctrine of Christ everywhere bright, everywhere pure and clean. That it is somewhat hard and some deal rough and sharp, betokeneth secret mysteries hid in the literal sense. If thou handle the outer side and if I may so call it the cod, what is more hard or unsavoury? They tasted but the outer rind of manna which said to Christ, This is a hard saying, and who may abide the hearing thereof. But get out the spiritual sense, and nothing is more sweeter nor more full of pleasure and sweet juice. Moreover manna is in the Hebrew tongue as much to say as What is this? Which question agreeth well to holy scripture, which hath nothing in it idle or in vain, no not one tittle or prick, unworthy to be searched, unworthy to be pondered, unworthy of this saying, What is this? It is a common use unto the Holy Ghost to signify by water the knowledge of the law of God. Thou readest of the water of comfort by whose banks David rejoiceth to have been nourished up: thou readest of the waters which wisdom conveyeth into the tops of every way: thou readest of the mystical river into the which Ezechiel entered, and could not wade over: thou readest of the wells that Abraham digged, which when they were stopped of the Philistiens Isaac repaired again. Thou readest of twelve fountains in which the Israelytes after they had walked through forty mansions, and began then to be weary and faint, rested and refreshed themselves and made them strong to the long journey of desert. Thou also readest in the Gospel of the well whereupon Christ sat wearied in his journey.

Siloe is a pool within Jerusalem at the foot of the mount Syon.

Thou readest of the water of Siloe, whither he sendeth the blind to recover his sight. Thou readest of the water poured into the basin to wash the apostles' feet. And because it needeth not to rehearse all places in this signification, often mention is made in scripture of wells, fountains and rivers, by which is signified nothing else but that we ought to enquire and search diligently for the mysteries hid in scripture. What signifieth water hid in the veins of the earth but mystery covered or hid in the literal sense? What meaneth the same conveyed abroad but mystery opened and expounded? Which being spread and dilated both wide and broad to the edifying of the hearers, what cause is there why it might not be called a river? Wherefore if thou dedicate thyself wholly to the study of scripture and exercise thy mind day and night in the law of God, no fear shall trouble thee, neither by day nor night: but thou shalt against all assaults of thine enemies be armed and exercised also. And I disallow it not utterly if a man for a season (to begin withal) do exercise and sport himself in works of poets and philosophers which were gentiles, as in his A B C or introductory to a more perfect thing, so that he taste of them measurably, and whiles youth shall give him leave, and even as though a man took them in his way, but not abide and tarry upon them still, and to wax old and die in them, as he were bound to the rocks of Sirenes, that is to put his whole delectation in them and never go farther.

Sirenes were three ladies dwelling in an island, which with sweetness of song drew unto them whosoever sailed by, and after killed them. But Ulixes returning from the siege of Troy having that way a necessary journey stopped his mariners' ears with wax, and bound himself to the mast, so heard he their songs avoiding all jeopardy.

For holy Basilius to such pastime exhorteth young men, whom he himself had induced to the conversation of Christian men. And our Augustyn calleth back again his friend Licentius to pass the time with the Muses, neither Jerom repenteth himself that he hath loved a woman taken prisoner in war. Cyprian is commended because he garnished the temple of God with the spoils of the Egyptians. But in no case would I that thou with the gentiles' learning shouldest also suck the gentiles' vices and conversation. For if thou do not, thou shalt find many things helping to honest living, neither is it to be refused whatsoever an author (yea though he be a gentile) teacheth well. For Moses verily though he were never so familiar with God, yet despised he not the counsels of his father-in-law Jetro. Those sciences fashion and quicken a child's wit, and maketh him apt aforehand marvellously to the understanding of holy scripture. Whereunto suddenly and irreverently to presume with hands and feet unwashed, is in manner a certain kind of sacrilege. And Jerom checketh the shameless pertness of them which straightway from secular or worldly science dare take in hand to meddle or interpret holy scripture. But how much shamefuller do they which never tasted other science, and yet at the first dare do the same thing. But as the scripture is not much fruitful if thou stand and stick still in the letter: in like manner the poetry of Homer and Virgil shall not profit a little, if thou remember that it must be understood in the sense allegory, which thing no man will deny that hath assayed or tasted of the learning of old antiquities never so little, yea with the tip of his tongue, or uttermost part of his lips. As for the poets which write uncleanly, I would counsel thee not once to touch them, or at the least way not to look far in them: except thou can the better abhor vices when they be described to thee, and in comparisons of filthy things the more fervently love things honest. Of the philosophers my mind is that thou follow them that were of Plato's sect, because both in very many sentences, and much more in their style and manner of speaking, they come very nigh to the figure and property of speech used of the prophets and in the Gospels. And to make an end shortly, it shall be profitable to taste of all manner of learning of the gentiles, if it so be done as I shewed before, both in years according and measurably, moreover with caution and judgment discreetly, furthermore with speed and after the manner of a man that intendeth but to pass over the country only and not to dwell or inhabit, in conclusion (which thing is chiefest of all) if everything be applied and referred to Christ.

As Salomon had sixty queens, eighty concubines and damsels innumerable, yet one chief queen, whom all the rest honoured, so may we of all sciences have authors innumerable, if holy scripture be chief of all other for the honouring of her.

For so all shall be clean to them that be clean when on the other side to them that be unclean nothing is clean. And it shall be no rebuke to thee, if after the example of Salomon thou nourish up at home in thy house sixty queens, eighty sovereign ladies and damsels innumerable of secular wisdom: so that the wisdom of God be above all other, thy best beloved, thy dove, thy sweetheart, which only seemeth beautiful. And an Israelyte loveth a stranger and a barbarous damsel, overcome with her beauty: but first he shaveth off her hair and pareth her nails, and maketh her of an alien an Israelyte. And the prophet Ozee married an harlot, and of her had children not for himself, but for the Lord of Sabaoth and the holy fornication of the prophet augmented the household of God. The Hebrews after they had forsaken Egypt lived with light and pure white bread for a season, but it was not sufficient to so great a journey.

The Israelyte might take to wife a stranger taken in war so that her nails were first pared and her hair shaven: so may Christian men honour God with gentiles' learning, if we cut off that is superfluous.

Therefore that bread loathed at once, thou must make as good speed as can be unto manna of celestial wisdom the which shall nourish thee abundantly and strengthen thee until thou obtain thy purpose, and win by victory the reward that never shall cease: but thou must ever remember in the mean season that holy scripture may not be touched but with clean and washen hands, that is to understand, but with high pureness of mind, lest that which of itself is a preservative or treacle, by thine own fault turn to thee into poison, and lest manna to thee begin to putrify, except that thou convey or send it into the inward parts of thy mind and affection, and lest haply it should fortune to thee as it did to Oza, which feared not to set his profane and unclean hands to the ark of God inclining on the one side and with sudden death was punished for his lewd service.

The light and pure white bread betokeneth the gentiles' living. Manna betokeneth the wisdom of God. David intended to translate the Ark of God out of the house of Amynadab, which was in Gaboa, they put the ark upon a cart, Oza with his brethren waited on it on either side, as the ark inclined and bowed Oza set his hand to stay it and was smitten with sudden death for his presumption.

The first point is that thou have good opinion of the holy scriptures, and that thou esteem them of no less value and dignity than they are worthy to be esteemed, and that they came out of the secret closet of the mind of God. Thou shalt perceive that thou art inspired of God moved inwardly, rapt and in an unspeakable manner altered and changed to another manner, figure or shape, if thou shalt come religiously, if with reverence and meekly thou shalt see the pleasures, delicacies, or dainties of the blessed spouse. Thou shalt see the precious jewels of rich Salomon, thou shalt see the secret treasure of eternal wisdom: but beware that thou break not malapertly into the secret closet, the door is low, beware lest thou strike the door with thy head, and be fain to leap back again.

Scripture must be had in great reverence.

Think on this wise, nothing that thou seest with thine eyes, nothing that thou handlest with thy fingers to be indeed the same thing which it appeareth, so surely as these things be true in holy scripture: for that if heaven and earth should perish, yet of the words of God not one jot or tittle shall perish, but all shall be fulfilled.

Faith must be given to holy scripture.

Though men lie, though men err, yet the verity of God neither deceiveth nor is deceived.

The chief interpreters of holy scripture.

Of the interpreters of scripture, choose them above all other that go farthest from the letter, which chiefly next after Paul be Origene, Ambrose, Jerom and Augustyne. For I see the divines of later time stick very much in the letter, and with good will give more study to subtle and deceitful arguments, than to search out the mysteries, as though Paul had not said truly our law to be spiritual.

Master Doctor Dunce.

I have heard some men myself which stood so greatly in their own conceit with the fantastical traditions, imaginations and inventions of man, that they despised the interpretation of old doctors that were nigh to Christ and his apostles both in time and living also, and account them as dreams, yea and Master Dunce gave them such confidence that notwithstanding they never once read the holy scripture, yet thought they themselves to be perfect divines, which persons though they speak things never so crafty and subtle, yet whether they speak things worthy of the Holy Ghost and the meek spirit of Christ or not, let other men judge. But if thou haddest liefer to be somewhat lusty and quick of spirit, than to be armed to contention, that is to say to brawling or scolding: if thou seek rather to have thy soul made fat, than thy wit to be vainly delighted: study and read over chiefly the old doctors and expositors, whose godliness and holy life is more proved and known, whose religion to God is more to be pondered and looked upon, whose learning is more plenteous and sage also, whose style is neither bare nor rude and interpretation more agreeable to the holy mysteries. And I say not this because I despise these new divines, but because I set more by things more profitable and more apt for the purpose.

The speaking of scripture.

And also the Spirit of God hath a certain tongue or speech appropriate to himself, he hath his figures similitudes, parables, comparisons, proverbs and riddles which thou must observe and mark diligently, if thou wouldest understand them. The wisdom of God stuttereth and lispeth as it were a diligent mother fashioneth her words according to our infancy and feebleness. She giveth milk to them that be infants in Christ, weak meat to feeble stomachs. Thou therefore make speed thou were a man, make haste to perfect and strong meat, and prepare a man's stomach. She stoopeth down and boweth herself to thy humility and lowness. Arise then upon the other side and ascend to her height and excellency. It is like a monster and unnatural to be ever a child. He is too heartless that never ceaseth to be feeble and weak.

Reading without understanding.

The recording of one verse shall be more savoury in thy mouth, and shall nourish thee better if thou break the cod and taste of the sweetness which is within, than if thou shouldest sing the whole psalter, understood only after the literal sense, whereof verily I give admonition a great deal the rather, because I know by experience that this error hath not infected the lay people only, but also the minds of them which profess and shew outward in their habit and name or title, perfect religion, insomuch that they think the very service of God to be put chiefly in this one thing, if they shall say over every day as much as they can of the psalms scarce understood, yea, in the literal sense.

The charitable living of monks.

Neither I think any other thing to be the cause why we see the charitable living of our monks and cloisterers to fail everywhere, to be so cold, so slacked, so faint and so to vanish away, but that they continue all their life and wax old in the letter and never enforce to come to the spiritual knowledge of scripture, neither hear they Christ crying in the Gospel, the flesh, that is to say, the letter, or that ye see outward profiteth not at all.

The flesh is called in scripture whatsoever is visible or perceived outward with any sensible power.

It is the Spirit within that quickeneth or giveth life. They hear not Paul affirming with his master, that the letter killeth, and it is the spirit giveth life. And again we know (saith he) that the law is spiritual, and not carnal. Spiritual things must be compared with spiritual things.

The spirit is called whatsoever is perceived inwardly with the eye of the soul.

In time past the Father of all spiritual gifts would be honoured in the mountain, but now he will be honoured in the spirit.

A similitude of meekness of them which lack capacity.

Howbeit I despise not the feebleness of them, which for lack of knowledge and understanding doth that they only be able to do, pronouncing the mystical psalms with pure faith without dissimulation or hypocrisy, but rather as in charms and enchantments of magic certain words not understood, no not of them which pronounce them, yet be believed to be of virtue and strength. Even so the words of God, though they be not perfectly understood, nevertheless we must trust that they be profitable to them that either say them or hear them with perfect faith, with pure affection and mind, and that the angels which are present and doth understand be provoked to help them. And Paul despiseth not them which say psalms with their mouth which speaketh with tongues that thing they understand not: but he exhorteth them to leave their infancy, and to follow more perfect gifts, unto which if a man cannot attain, not through the default of a corrupt mind, but for lack of capacity, let him not bark against them which enforce better things. And after the precept of Paul let not him which eateth despise him which eateth not, neither he that eateth not judge him that eateth. Nevertheless I will not have thee which art endowed with so happy a wit to be slow and to tarry long in the barren letter, but to make speed unto more secret mysteries, and to help the continual endeavour and enforcement of thine industry and will with often prayers until he open to thee the book clasped with seven clasps, which hath the key of David, the which also shutteth and no man openeth the privities of the Father, which never man knew but his Son, and he to whom his Son hath vouchsafed to disclose them. But whither goeth our style aside? Mine intent was to describe the form of living not of learning: but I turned out of the way thus far while I laboured to shew thee a meet shop from whence thou oughtest to fetch thy new armour and weapons belonging to the new war. Therefore to come to our purpose again, if thou shalt pick and choose out of the books of the gentiles of every thing the best: and also if thou by the example of the bee, flying round about by the gardens of old authors shalt suck out only the wholesome and sweet juice (the poison refused and left behind) thy mind shall be better apparelled a great deal, and armed unto the common life or conversation, in which we live one with another in honest manner. For the philosophers and learned men of the gentiles in their war use certain weapons and armour not to be despised. Nevertheless whatsoever thing of honesty or truth thou findest anywhere, think that to be Christ's.

The artillery of Vulcanus.

But that divine armour and (to speak as the poets do) that harness of Vulcanus' making, which with no weapons can be pierced, is fetched only out of the armoury of holy scripture, where our noble captain David laid up all his ordinance of war for his soldiers with which they should fight afar and at hand against the uncircumcised Philistiens.

Achilles overcome with ire, Eneas overcome with love.

With this harness was clothed neither Achilles, of whom Homer writeth, neither Eneas, of whom Virgil speaketh, though they be so feigned. Of which the one with ire, the other with love was overcome shamefully.

Poets the feigners of gods.

And it is not spoken without reason that those weapons be not forged in the workhouse of man, but in the workhouse or forge that is common to Vulcan and Pallas, otherwise called Mynerva. For poets the feigners of gods maketh Vulcan lord of fire, and Mynerva lady of wit, faculties, sciences and crafts, which thing I judge to be done in very deed (as thou mayest easily perceive) when the fire of love of God hath armed thy wit, endued with honest faculties so strongly, that if all the world should fall on thy head yet should not the stroke put thee to fear.

King Saul armed David to fight against Golyas with heavy and cumbrous harness putting on him a salet of brass and a coat of mail but David put it off and gathered five stones out of a brook, and with a sling hit Golyas in the forehead with a stone and slew him.

But first thou must cast away the harness of proud Saul, which rather loadeth a man than be anything necessary or profitable, and cumbered David ready to fight with Golyas and holpe him not at all. Moreover from the bank of the brook of holy scripture thou must gather five stones, which peradventure be the five words of Paul, which he speaketh in knowledge. Then take a sling in thy right hand; with these weapons is overthrown our only enemy, the father of pride, Satan, whom at the last with what weapons did our head Christ Jesu overcome?

When Sathan would have had Christ to turn stones into bread Christ answered with scripture saying Man liveth not only by bread, but by every word that proceedeth of the mouth of God. Then he would have had Christ to fall from the pinnacle. Christ answered with scripture saying A man should not tempt his Lord God. Then the devil bade Christ honour him. Christ answered A man must honour his Lord God and serve him only.

Did not he smite the forehead of our adversary as it had been with stones fetched out of the brook when he answered him in time of temptation with words of scripture. Wilt thou hear the instruments or artillery of Christian men's war? And the zeal of him (saith scripture) shall take harness and shall harness his creature to avenge his enemies, he will put on justice for his breastplate, and take for his helmet sure and true judgment. He will take a shield of equity impenetrable or that cannot be pierced, yea, and he will sharpen or fashion cruel wrath into a spear. Thou readest also in Isai he is armed with justice, as with an habergeon and a salet of health upon his head, he is clothed with the vestures of vengeance and covered as it were with a cloak of zeal. Now if thou list to go to the storehouse of Paul, that valiant captain, certainly thou shalt also find there the armour of war, not carnal things, but valiant in God to destroy fortresses and counsels, and every high thing that exalteth himself against the doctrine of God. Thou shalt find there the armour of God, by the which thou mayest resist in a woeful day. Thou shalt find the harness of justice on the right hand, and on the left thou shalt find the defence of thy sides' verity, and the habergeon of justice the buckler of faith, wherewith thou mayest quench all the hot and fiery weapons of thy cruel adversary.

If zeal be in knowledge, it is good, if not, it is evil. As the Pharysees for zeal of their traditions persecuted Christ and the apostles.

Thou shalt find also the helmet of health and the sword of the Spirit, which is the word of God, with the which all if a man shall be diligently covered and fenced, he may boldly without fear bring forth the bold saying of Paul. Who shall separate us from the love of God? shall tribulation? shall straitness or difficulty? shall hunger? shall nakedness? shall peril? shall persecution? shall a sword? Behold how mighty enemies and how much feared of all men he setteth at nought. But hear also a certain greater thing, for it followeth. But in all things we have overcome by his help which loved us. And I am assured (saith he) that neither death, nor life, nor angels, neither principalities, neither virtues, neither present things, neither things to come, neither strength, neither height, neither lowness, nor none other creature shall or may separate us from the love of God which is in Christ Jesu. Oh happy trust and confidence which the weapons or armour of light giveth to Paul, that is by interpretation a little man, which calleth himself the refuse or outcast of the world! Of such armour therefore abundantly shall holy scripture minister to thee, if thou wilt occupy thy time in it with all thy might: so that thou shalt not need our counsel or admonitions. Nevertheless seeing it is thy mind, lest I should seem not to have obeyed thy request, I have forged for thee this little treatise called *Enchiridion*, that is to say, a certain little dagger, whom never lay out of thy hand, no not when thou art at meat or in thy chamber. Insomuch that if at any time thou shalt be compelled to make a pilgrimage in these worldly occupations, and shalt be too cumbered to bear about with thee the whole and complete armour and harness of holy scripture, yet commit not that the subtle lier in wait at any season should come upon thee and find thee utterly unarmed, but at the least let it not grieve thee to have with thee this little hanger, which shall not be heavy to bear, nor unprofitable for thy defence, for it is very little, yet if thou use it wisely, and couple with it the buckler of faith, thou shalt be able to withstand the fierce and raging assault of thine enemy: so that thou shalt have no deadly wound. But now it is time that I begin to give thee a certain rule of the use of these weapons which if thou shalt put in execution or practice, I trust it will come to pass that our captain Jesus Christ shall translate thee a conqueror out of this little castle or garrison into his great city Jerusalem with triumph, where is no rage at all of any battle, but eternal quietness, perfect peace, assured tranquillity: whereas in the mean season all hope and confidence of safeguard is put in armour and weapon.

CHAPTER 3

That the first point of wisdom is to know thyself, and of two manner wisdoms, the true wisdom, and the apparent.

That excellent good thing desired and sought for of all men, is peace or quietness: unto which the lovers of this world also refer all their study, but they seek a false peace, and shoot at a wrong mark. The same peace the philosophers also promised unto the followers of their conclusions, but yet falsely, for Christ only giveth it, the world giveth it not.

A man must fight against himself.

To come to this quietness the only way or means is (if we make war) against ourself, if we fight strongly against our own vices, for with these enemies God, which is our peace, is at variance with deadly hate, seeing he is naturally virtue itself and father and lord of all virtue.

God is our peace and felicity.

And whereas a filthy puddle or a sink gathered together of all kind of vices, is named of the stoics, which are the most fervent defenders of virtue, foolishness, and in our scripture the same is called malice, in like manner virtue or goodness lacking in no point of both parts, is called wisdom.

Stoics were philosophers as Socrates and Plato, with their followers, which put felicity in true pleasure in virtue only and within the conscience, without any outward pleasure or riches. Foolishness is misery. Wisdom is felicity. Fools also be wretches and unhappy. Wise men also be happy and fortunate. Filthiness is foolishness, virtue is wisdom.

But after the saying of the wise man—doth not wisdom overcome malice? The father and head of malice is the ruler of darkness, Belial: whose steps whosoever followeth walketh in the night and shall come to eternal night. On the other side the ground of wisdom and indeed wisdom itself is Christ Jesus, which is very light and the brightness of the glory of his Father, putting away by himself only the night of the foolishness of the world. The which (witnessing Paul) as he was made redemption and justification to us that be born again in him: even likewise was made also our wisdom. We (saith Paul) preach Christ crucified, which to the Jews is an occasion of unity, and to the gentiles foolishness. But to the elected both of the Jews and also of the gentiles we preach Christ the virtue or strength of God, and the wisdom of God, by whose wisdom through his example we may beat away the victory of our enemy malice, if we shall be wise in him in whom also we shall be conquerors.

Worldly wisdom is very foolishness.

Make much of this wisdom and take her in thine arms. Worldly wisdom set at nought, which with false title and under a feigned colour of honesty boasteth and showeth herself gay to fools, when after Paul there is no greater foolishness with God than worldly wisdom, a thing that must be forgotten indeed again of him that will be wise indeed.

He must be a fool in this world that will be wise in God.

If any man (saith Paul) among you seemeth to be wise in this world, let him be a fool that he may be wise, for the wisdom of this world is foolishness with God.

The searchers were the philosophers which searched for worldly wisdom yet could they attain no wisdom to save the soul of man until Christ came.

And a little afore Paul saith, It is written, I will destroy the wisdom of wise men, and the prudence of prudent men I will reprove. Where is the wise man, where is the subtle lawyer, where is the searcher of this world? Hath not God made the wisdom of this world foolishness? And I doubt not but even now with great hate these foolish wise men bark against thee, and these blind captains or guides of blind men cry out and roar against thee, saying that thou art deceived, that thou dotest and art mad as a bedlam man, because thou intendest to depart unto Christward.

Many be Christian men but in name only but the very Christian men be they which keep and observe inwardly Christ's precepts. A true Christian man must despise the foolishness of worldly men. He is good for nothing, saith Hesiodus which neither hath wisdom, nor yet will learn it. To have knowledge is best of all. To be willing to learn and obedient to the truth is also a good thing. To lack knowledge is a very evil thing. To disdain to learn is worse but to with-stand and repugne against the truth to them which teach the truth is worst of all and farthest from grace.

These be in name only Christian men, but in very deed they are both mockers and also enemies of Christ's doctrine. Take heed and beware that their foolish babbling move thee not, whose miserable blindness ought rather to be wept, sorrowed and mourned than to be counterfeited or followed. Oh what foolish kind of wisdom and clean out of order is this in trifles and things of no value, yea to filthiness only to be clear witted, ware and expert: but in those things which only make for our safe-guard or health, not to have much more understanding than a brute beast! Paul would we should be wise but in goodness, and children in evil. These men be wise to all iniquity: but they have no learning to do good. And for as much as that fecund and Greek poet Hesiodus counteth him good for nothing which neither is wise of himself, neither yet will follow and do after him that giveth him good counsel: of what degree then shall they be counted which when they themselves be most shamefully deceived, yet never cease to trouble, to laugh to scorn and put in fear them which already be come to their wits again? But shall not the mocker be mocked? He that dwelleth in heaven shall mock them again, and our Lord shall laugh them to scorn. Thou readest in the Book of Sapience, They shall see verily and shall despise him, but God shall mock them. To be mocked of lewd men, is as it were a praise. And no doubt it is a blessed thing to follow our head, Christ and his apostles, and a fearful thing truly to be mocked of God.

Evil men say, ye good men, as ye live now, so lived such and such pope holy fools, and this came of them and so we trust to see happen of you.

I also (saith the Wisdom) will laugh when ye perish, and mock you when that thing hath happened to you which ye feared, that is to say, when they awaked out of their dream and come again to themselves, when it is too late, shall say, These be they whom we have had in derision and reproof, we for lack of understanding have counted their lives to be madness, and their end to be without honour. This wisdom is beastly, and as James saith, diabolic and of the devil, and is an enemy to God, whose end is destruction.

Note how one vice bringeth in another.

For always after this wisdom followeth as a waiting-servant or hand-maid mischievous presumption, after presumption followeth blindness of mind, after blindness of mind followeth fervent rage and tyranny of affections and appetites, after the tyranny of affections followeth the whole heap of all vices and liberty to do what he listeth. Then followeth custom, after followeth most wretched dulness or insensibility of mind, a dazing of the wits for lack of capacity. By which it is caused that evil men perceive not themselves to sin. And whiles they be in such insensibility without any feeling or perceiving of themselves, bodily death cometh suddenly on them, and after it followeth the second death, which is death everlasting.

The wisdom of Christ.

Thou seest how the mother of the extreme mischief is worldly wisdom, but of the wisdom of Christ which the world thinketh foolishness, this wise thou readest. All good things came to men by heaps with her, and inestimable honesty by the hands of her. And I rejoiced in all things because this wisdom went before me, and I was not aware that she was mother of all good things. This wisdom bringeth with her as companions soberness and meekness. Meekness disposeth and maketh us apt to receive the spirit of God. For in the lowly, humble and meek person he rejoiceth to rest. And when the spirit hath replenished our minds with his sevenfold grace, then forth withal springeth that plenteous herbage of all virtue, with those blessed fruits of which the chief is the secret joy of a clear conscience, which joy is known of none but only of such to whom it hath chanced to taste of it. Joy that never vanisheth away, nor fadeth with the joys of this world, but increaseth and groweth to eternal gladness and mirth. This wisdom my brother (after the counsel of James) must thou require of God with fervent and burning desire. And after the counsel of the wise man dig her out of the veins of holy scripture, as it were treasure hid in the earth. The chief part of this wisdom is that thou shouldest know thyself, which word to have descended from heaven the antiquity believed, and so much hath that saying pleased great authors, that they judged all plenty of wisdom to be shortly comprehended in this little sentence, that is to wit, if a man know himself. But let the weight or authority of this conclusion and doctrine be of no value with us, except it agree with our learning. The mystical lover in Canticles threateneth his spouse, and biddeth her to get herself out of the doors, except she know herself, saying, O thou beautiful among all women, if thou know not thyself, go out of the doors and walk after the steps of thy flock and sort. Therefore let no man presumptuously take upon him this so great a thing, to think that he knoweth himself well enough. I am not sure whether any man knoweth his body unto the uttermost, and then how can a man know the state of his mind surely enough? Paul, whom God so loved that he saw the mysteries of the third heaven, yet durst he not judge himself which thing doubtless he would have been bold to do, if he had known himself surely enough. If so spiritual a man which discerneth all things, and is himself to be judged of no man, was not surely enough known to himself, how should we carnal men presume? In conclusion let him seem to be a very unprofitable soldier, which surely enough neither knew his own company, neither his enemies' host.

Thou mayst read of Jason and divers other how they sowed serpents' teeth and how of them sprang giants which fought among themselves and slew each other.

But so it is that one Christian man hath not war with another but with himself, and verily a great host of adversaries spring out of our own flesh, out of the very bowels and inward part of us. Likewise as it is read in certain poets' tales of the brethren gendered of the earth. And there is so little difference between our enemy and our friend, and so hard to know the one from the other, that there is great jeopardy lest we somewhat recklessly or negligently defend our enemy instead of our friend, or hurt our friend instead of our enemy. The noble captain Josue was in doubt of an angel of light, saying Art thou on our part, or of our enemies' part. Therefore seeing that thou hast taken upon thee war against thyself, and the chief hope and comfort of victory is if thou know thyself to the uttermost, I will paint a certain image of thyself, as it were in a table, and set it before thine eyes that thou mayst perfectly know what thou art inwardly and within thy skin.

CHAPTER 4

Of the outward and inward man.

A man is then a certain monstrous beast compact together of parts two or three of great diversity.

A man is a certain monstrous beast.

Of a soul as of a certain goodly thing, and of a body as it were a brute or dumb beast. For certainly we so greatly excel not all other kinds of brute beasts in perfectness of body, but that we in all his natural gifts are found to them inferiors. In our minds verily we be so celestial and of godly capacity that we may surmount above the nature of angels, and be unite, knit and made one with God.

God is the author of peace.

If thy body had not been added to thee, thou hadst been a celestial or godly thing. If this mind had not been grafted in thee, plainly thou hadst been a brute beast.

The serpent is the maker of debate.

These two natures between themselves so diverse, that excellent workman had coupled together with blessed concord: but the serpent the enemy of peace put them asunder again with unhappy discord: so that now they neither can be separate without very great torment and pain, neither live joined together without continual war.

He holdeth the wolf by the ears, this proverb we use on them which be in such cumbrance from whence they can in no wise rid themselves. The proverb this wise sprang. A certain man walked in a forest upon whom came a wolf and he could make no other shift but took him by the ears, which were so short that it was hard to hold them: yet durst he not let them go, nor lay hand on his weapons for fear of biting, but held fast and cried for help.

And plainly, after the common saying, each in the other holdeth the wolf by the ears, and either may say very well and accordingly to the other that proper and pleasant verse of Catullus, I neither can live with thee nor without thee. Such ruffling, wrangling and trouble they make between themselves with cumberous debate as things diverse, which indeed are but one. The body verily as he himself is visible, so delighteth he in things visible. As he is mortal, so followeth he things temporal. As he is heavy, so sinketh he downward. On the other part, the soul mindful of her celestial nature enforceth upward with great violence and with a terrible haste striveth and wrestleth with the heavy burden of the earthly body. She despiseth these things that are seen, for she knoweth them to be transitory, she seeketh true things of substance which be permanent and ever abiding, and because she is immortal and also celestial she loveth things immortal and celestial, and rejoiceth with things of like nature, except she be utterly drowned in the filth of the body and by contagiousness of him hath gone out of kind from her native gentleness.

Poets feign Prometheus to have made men of clay and through help of Pallas to put life in them and portion of everybeast as the fierceness of the lion, the wiliness of the fox, the fearfulness of the hare and so of other beasts.

And verily neither Prometheus, so much spoken of among poets, sowed this discord in us a portion of every beast mixed to our mind, neither our primitive and first making gave it, that is to say, it sprang not in us naturally, or nature gave it not to us in our first creation or nativity: but sin hath evil-corrupted and decayed that which was well created, sowing the poison of dissension between them that were honestly agreed, for before that time both the mind ruled the body without business, and the body obeyed without grudging. Now is it clean contrary. The order between them is so troubled, the affections or appetites of the body strive to go before reason, and reason is in a manner compelled to incline and follow the judgment of the body.

Man is compared to a commonwealth or realm, where is king, lords and the common people.

Thou mayst compare therefore a man properly to a commonalty, where is debate and part taking among themselves. Which commonalty for as much as it is made of sundry kinds of men gathered together, which be of diverse and contrary appetites: it cannot be avoided but that much strife shall arise therein, and parts taken often times, unless the chief rule and authority be in one. And he himself be such a fellow that will command nothing but that which shall be wholesome and profitable for the commonwealth. And for that cause it must needs be that he which is most wise should most bear rule. And he needs must obey that least perceiveth or understandeth. Now there is nothing more foolish than the rascal or vile commonalty. And therefore ought they to obey the officers and rulers, and bear no rule nor office themselves. The noble estates or such men which be most ancient of age, ought to be heard: but so that it lie only in the king's arbitrament to make statutes and laws, whom it is meet to be advertised to be put in remembrance or counselled now and then.

The king obeyeth the law only.

But it is not meet that he should be compelled, or that any man should be master or rule him. And finally the king obeyeth no man but the law only. The law must be correspondent to the original decree of nature or the first example of honesty. Wherefore if this order subverted, the unruly commons, and that raging dregs of the city shall strive to go before the seniors: or if the chief lords shall despise the commandment of the king, then ariseth perilous sedition or division in our commonwealth, yea and except the provision, decree or authority of God succour, all the matter weigheth and inclineth to extreme mischief and to utter destruction.

Reason is king in a man.

In man reason beareth the room of a king. Thou mayest account for the chief lords certain affections and them of the body: but yet not all things so beastly.

The lords be certain gentle affections.

Of the which kind is natural reverence toward the father and mother, love to thy brethren, a benevolent mind toward thy friends and lovers, compassion upon them that be vexed with adversity or cumbered with sickness, fear of infamy, slander or loss of thy good name, desire of honest reputation, and such other like.

The commoners be vile appetites.

But such affections or passions which be very greatly disagreeing from the decrees of reason, and which be cast down and must bow even to the vileness of brute beasts: think and reckon those to be as it were the most rascal and vile sort of the common people. Of which kind and sort be lechery, riot, envy, and such like diseases, which all without exception must be kept under in prison and with punishment as vile and bond servants, that they render to their master their task and work appointed to them if they can: but if not at the least they do no harm. Which things Plato perceiving by inspiration of God, wrote in his book called *Timeus* how the sons of gods had forged in man to their own likeness two kinds of souls, the one kind spiritual and immortal, the other as it were mortal, in danger to divers perturbations or motions of unquietness. Of which the first is voluptuousness (as he saith) the bait whereby men are allured and brought to ungraciousness or mischief.

Four affections of the mind: joy, sorrow, hope and fear.

The next is sorrow or grief which letteth men, and driveth them from virtue or goodness. After that fear and presumptuous boldness, two mad counsellors: whom accompanieth indurate wrath, the desire of vengeance. Moreover flattering hope with beastly imagination and knowledge not governed of reason, and worldly love that layeth hands violently on all things. These be almost the words of Plato, and it was not unknown to him the felicity of this life to be put in refraining of such perturbations, for he writeth in the same work them for to live justly and blessedly, which should have overcome these appetites, and them for to live unjustly and miserably that should be overcome of the same.

Reason dwelleth in the brain as in the palace.

And to that soul which is like unto the nature of God, that is to say, unto reason, as unto a king, he appointed a place in the brain, as in the chief tower of our city: and as thou mayest see the highest part of our body, and next to heaven, and most far from the nature of a beast, as a thing verily which is both of a very thin bone, and neither laid with gross sinews nor flesh, but surely furnished and appointed within and also without, with powers of knowledge, that through the showing of them no debate should rise in our commonwealth, which he should not immediately perceive: but as touching the parts of the mortal soul, that is, to wit, the affections and appetites as every one of them is, either obedient, or else grudgeth against reason: so he removed them from him, for between the neck and the midriff he set that part of the soul, wherein is contained boldness, wrath or anger, a seditious affection verily and full of debate, which needs must be refrained: but he is not very brutish or beastly, and therefore he separates him in a mean space from the highest and lowest, lest if he had been too nigh to either of them, he would either have troubled the king's quietness, or else corrupted with the contagiousness of them of the lowest sorts should with them also conspire against him.

The power wherein is contained wrath and hate.

Last of all that power which desireth the voluptuous pleasure of meat and drink, whereby also we be moved to bodily lust, he banished utterly away far from the king's palace down alow beneath the midriff in to the liver and the paunch, that as it were a certain wild beast untamed he should there stable and dwell at the rack, for because that power is accustomed to raise up motions most violent, and to be disobedient to the commandments of the king.

The power wherein is contained desire.

What beastliness yea and what rebellion is in the lowest portion of this power, at the leastway the privy parts of thy body may teach thee, in which part chiefly this power of concupiscence rageth and tyranny reigneth, which also of all members only ever among maketh rebellion with uncleanly motions, the king crying the contrary, and that in vain. Thou seest then evidently how that this noble beast man, so goodly a thing above plainly and without any exception endeth in an unreasonable or brute beast.

The ornaments of a king.

But that noble counsellor which sitteth like a king or a ruler in his high tower, having alway in remembrance his own beginning thinketh no filthy nor low thing. And he hath whereby he may be known from other a sceptre of ivory, because he doth command nothing but that which is right and good, in whose top writeth Homer to set an eagle, because that reason, mounting up to celestial things, beholdeth from above those things that be on the ground disdainfully, as it were with eagles' eyes. In conclusion he is crowned with a crown of gold, for gold in the mystical letters most commonly betokeneth wisdom. And the circle betokeneth that the wisdom of the king should be perfect and pure in every part. These be the very gifts or virtues properly belonging to kings. First that they be very wise that they do not amiss by reason of error and lack of true knowledge. And that such things as they know to be good and right, those only to will and purpose to do, that they do nothing against the decree or judgment of reason inordinately, forwardly and corruptly. And whosoever lacketh any of these two points, count him to be not a king, that is to say a ruler, but a robber.

CHAPTER 5
Of the diversity of affections.

We ought to live after reason and not after affections.

Our king Reason may be oppressed verily, yet because of the eternal law which God hath graven in him he cannot be corrupted but that he shall grudge and call back.

Peripateticy will that affections should be refrained, only thinking them necessary to provoke and to stir a man to virtue.

To whom, if the residue of the commonalty will obey, he shall never commit anything at all either to be repented or of any jeopardy: but all things shall be administered with great moderation discreetly, with much quietness and tranquillity. But as touching affections, verily stoics and peripatetics vary somewhat, though both agree in this that we ought to live after reason, and not after affections.

Stoics be the followers of Plato which put felicity and blessedness in the inward constancy of the mind only. If a man were so armed with all virtues that he might be wounded with no dart of adversity or fortune, saying also no outward goods of fortune nor outward gifts of nature be required necessarily unto felicity but the testimony of conscience inward to be sufficient.

But stoics will when we have used for a season (as it were a schoolmaster to teach us our first principles) the affections which immediately are stirred up of the sensual powers, and now become to judgment and true examination what is to be ensured or chosen, and what to be eschewed or forsaken, that then we utterly damn and forsake them. For then are they (as they say) not only no profit to very wisdom, but also hurtful and noxious, and therefore they will that a perfect wise man should lack all such motions, as diseases or sicknesses of the mind, yea and scarcely they grant to a wise man those first motions, more gentle preventing reason which they call fantasies or imaginations. Peripatetics teach the affections not to be destroyed utterly, but to be refrained, and that the use of them is not utterly to be refused, for because they think them to be given of nature, as a prick or a spur to stir a man to virtue: as wrath maketh a man bold and hardy, and is a matter of fortitude. Envy is a great cause of policy, and in likewise of the other.

Peripatetics be Arystotel's followers which say a man apparelled with all kind of virtue and with a pure conscience to be a good man, yet not happy or blessed, for then will beatitude to rest in the act or outward practice of virtue in profiting the commonwealth. Therefore, say they, riches, friends, strength of body, health, eloquence and such like to be required necessarily without which a man cannot profit another, yet would they not such things to be desired for love of the things themselves, but to profit the commonwealth and for the conversion of mankind.

Socrates in a certain book that Plato made called *Phedo* seemeth to agree with stoics, where he thinketh philosophy to be nothing else but a meditation or practising of death, that is to say that the mind withdraw herself as much as she can from corporal and sensible things, and convey herself to those things which be perceived with reason only, and not of the sensible powers. First of all therefore thou must behold and consider diligently all the motions, movings or stirring of thy mind and have them surely known. Furthermore thou must understand no motions to be so violent but they may be either refrained of reason, or else turned to virtue. Notwithstanding I hear everywhere this contagious opinion, that some should say they be constrained to vices: and on the other side many for lack of knowledge of themselves follow such motions as the sayings or decrees of reason: in so much that whatsoever wrath or envy doth counsel or move them to do, that they call the zeal of God: and as thou seest one commonwealth to be more unquiet than another: so is one man more inclined or prone to virtue than another, which difference cometh not of the diversity of minds, but either of the influence of celestial bodies, or else of our progenitors, or else of the bringing up in youth, or of the complexion of the body.

Some man is more prone to virtue than some.

The fable of Socrates of carters and horses good and bad is none old wives' tale: for thou mayst see some to be born of so moderate, soft, quiet and gentle disposition, so easy to be handled, to be turned and winded, that without business they may be induced to virtue, and runneth forward by their own courage without any spurring.

The rebellion of nature is to be imputed to no man.

To some clean contrary thou mayst perceive to have happened: a body rebellious as a wild and kicking horse: in so much that he which tameth him shall have enough to do and sweat apace, and yet scarce with a very rough bit, scarce with a waster and with sharp spurs can subdue his fierceness. If any such one hath happened to them, let never that, rather thy heart fail thee, but so much the more fervently set upon it, thinking on this wise: not that the way of virtue is stopped or shut up from thee: but a larger matter of virtue to be offered unto thee. But and if so be that nature hath endued thee with a gentle mind, thou art not therefore straightway better than another man, but happier, and yet again on that manner wise art thou more happy, so that thou art also more bound. How be it what is he that is endued with so happy gifts of nature, which hath not abundantly things enough to wrestle withal.

Some vices follow the countries.

Therefore in what part shall be perceived most rage or rebellion to be, in that part reason our king must watch diligently. There be certain vices appropriate to every country, as to break promise is familiar to some: to some riot or prodigality: to some bodily lust or pleasure of the flesh, and this happeneth to them by the disposition of their countries.

Some vices follow the complexion of the body.

Some vices accompany the complexion of the body, as appetite and lust for the company of women and the desire of pleasures and wanton sports accompany the sanguine men. Wrath, fierceness, cursed speaking followeth the choleric men. Grossness of mind, lack of activity, sluggishness of body, and to be given to much sleep, followeth the phlegmatic man. Envy, inward heaviness, bitterness, to be solitary, self-minded, sullen and churlish followeth the melancholic person.

Vices following the age.

Some vices abate and increase after the age of man, as in youth lust of the body, wasteful expenses and rashness, or foolish-hardiness. In old age niggardliness or too much saving, waywardness and avarice.

Vices appropriate to kind.

Some vices there be which should seem appropriate to kind as fierceness to the man, vanity to the woman and desire of wreak, or to be revenged. It fortuneth now and then that nature, as it were to make amends, recompenseth one disease or sickness of the mind, with another certain contrary good gift or property. One man is somewhat prone or inclined to pleasure of worldly pastimes, but nothing angry, nothing envious at all.

An ill disease of the mind is sometimes recompensed with another good gift in property.

Another is chaste, but somewhat proud or high-minded, somewhat hasty, somewhat too greedy upon the world. And there be which be vexed with certain wonderful and fatal vices, with theft, sacrilege and homicide: which truly thou must withstand with all thy might, against whose assault must be cast a certain brazen wall of sure purpose. On the other side some affections be so nigh neighbours to virtue, that it is jeopardous lest we should be deceived, the diversity is so dangerous and doubtful.

Let the vices which draw near unto virtues be corrected.

These affections are to be corrected and amended, and may be turned very well to that virtue which they most nigh resemble. There is some man (because of example) which is soon set a-fire, is hot, at once provoked to anger with the least thing in the world, let him refrain and sober his mind, and he shall be bold and courageous, nothing faint-hearted or fearful, he shall be free of speech without dissimulation. There is another man somewhat holding, or too much saving, let him put to reason, and he shall be called thrifty and a good husband. He that is somewhat flattering shall be with moderation courtesy and pleasantness. He that is obstinate may be constant. Solemness may be turned to gravity. And that hath too much of foolish toys, may be a good companion.

Put not the name of virtue to any manner of vice.

And after the same manner of other somewhat easier diseases of the mind, we must beware of this only that we cloak not the vice of nature with the name of virtue, calling heaviness of mind gravity, cruelty justice, envy zeal, filthy niggardliness thrift, flattering good fellowship, knavery or ribaldry urbanity or merry speaking.

Know thyself.

The only way therefore to felicity is first that thou

know thyself: moreover that thou do nothing after affections, but in all things after the judgment of reason: let reason be sound and pure and without corruption: let not his mouth be out of taste, that is to say, let him behold honest things.

Do all things after the judgment of reason.

But thou wilt say: it is an hard thing that thou commandest: who sayeth nay? And verily the saying of Plato is true: whatsoever things be fair and honest, the same be hard and travailful to obtain. Nothing is more hard than that a man should overcome himself.

The saying of Saint Jerome.

But then is there no greater reward than is felicity? Jheronymus spake that thing excellently as he doth all other things: nothing is more happy than a Christian man, to whom is promised the kingdom of heaven: nothing is in greater peril than he which every hour is in jeopardy of his life: nothing is more strong than he that overcometh the devil: nothing is more weak than he that is overcome of the flesh. If thou ponder thine own strength only, nothing is harder than to subdue the flesh unto the spirit. If thou shalt look on God thy helper, nothing is more easy. Then now therefore conceive with all thy might and with a fervent mind the purpose and profession of the perfect life.

To be willing to be a Christian man is a great part of christendom.

And when thou hast grounded thyself upon a sure purpose, set upon it and go to it lustily: man's mind never purposed anything fervently that he was not able to bring to pass. It is a great part of a Christian life to desire with full purpose and with all his heart to be a Christian man, that thing which at the first sight or meeting, at the first acquaintance or coming to shall seem impossible to be conquered or won, in process of time shall be gentle enough and with use easy: in conclusion with custom it shall be very pleasant.

The way of virtue in process waxeth easy.

It is a very proper saying of Hesiodus: the way of virtue is hard at the beginning, but after thou hast crept up to the top there remaineth for thee very sure quietness. No beast is so wild which waxeth not tame by the craft of man. And is there no craft to tame the mind of him that is the tamer of all things? That thou might be whole in thy body, thou canst steadfastly purpose and command thyself for certain years to abstain from drinking of wine, to forbear the flesh and company of women: which things the physician being a man prescribed to thee. And to live quietly all thy life canst thou not rule thine affections, no not a few months? Which thing God, that is thy creator and maker, commandeth thee to do? To save thy body from sickness there is nothing which thou doeth not: to deliver thy body and thy soul also from eternal death dost thou not these things which infidels, ethnics and gentiles have done.

CHAPTER 6

Of the inward and outward man and of the two parts of man, proved by holy scripture.

Christ in Matthew saith he came to make not peace but dissension, to set the father against the son, the son against his father, the wife against her husband, the husband against his wife and so forth. The history meaneth that at some time and in some places the husband should accept the faith of Christ only, and follow his wholesome doctrine and the wife should persecute him. Some times the wife should follow Christ and the husband persecute her, and in likewise the son his father and the father the son.

Certainly I am ashamed in Christian men's behalf, of whom the most part follow as they were brute beasts, their affections and sensual appetites, and in this kind of war are so rude and unexercised, that they do not as much as know the diversity between reason and affections or passions. They suppose the thing only to be the man which they see and feel and they think nothing to be beside the things which offer themselves to the sensible wits when it is nothing less than so. What so ever they greatly covet, that they think to be right: they call peace, certain and assured bondage, while reason oppressed and blinded followeth whither so ever the appetite or affection calleth, without resistance. This is that miserable peace which Christ, the author of very peace that knit two in one, came to break, stirring up a wholesome war between the father and the son, between the husband and the wife, between those things which filthy concord had evil-coupled together. Now then let the authority of the philosophers be of little weight, except those same things be all taught in holy scripture, though not with the same words. That the philosophers call reason, that calleth Paul, sometime the spirit, sometime the inner man, other while the law of the mind. That they call affection, he calleth sometime the flesh: sometime the body: another time the outer man, and the law of the members.

Reason, the spirit, the inner man, the law of the mind, be one thing with Paul.

Walk (saith Paul) in the spirit, and ye shall not accomplish the desires and lusts of the flesh, for the flesh desireth contrary to the spirit, and the spirit contrary to the flesh, that ye cannot do whatsoever things ye would.

Affection, the flesh, the body, the outer man, the law of the members, be one thing with Paul.

And in another place: If ye shall live after the flesh, ye shall die. If ye shall, walking in the spirit, mortify the deeds of the flesh, ye shall live. Certainly this is a new change of things, that peace should be sought in war, and war in peace: in death life, and in life death: in bondage liberty, in liberty bondage.

Peace, life, liberty of soul, is the war, death, bondage of the body.

For Paul writeth in another place: I chastise my body and bring him into servitude. Hear also the liberty. If ye be led with the spirit, ye be not subject to the law. And we have not (saith he) received again the spirit of bondage in fear, but the spirit which hath elected us to be the children of God. He saith in another place: I see another law in my members repugnynge against the law of my mind, subduing me to the law of sin which law is in my members. Thou readest with him also of the outer man which is corrupt, and of the inner man which is renewed day by day. Plato put two souls to be in one man.

A double man.

Paul in one man maketh two men so coupled together, that neither without other can be either in heaven or hell: and again so separate that the death of the one should be life of the other. To the same (as I suppose) pertain those things which he wrote to the Chorintes. The first man was made into a living soul.

The last Adam is Christ.

The last Adam was made into a spirit quickening: but that is not first which is spiritual, but that which is living: then followeth that which is spiritual. The first man came of the earth himself terrestrial. The second came from heaven and he himself celestial. And because it should more evidently appear these things to pertain not only to Christ and Adam, but to us all, he added saying: As was the man of the earth, such are terrestrial and earthly persons. As is the celestial man, such are the celestial persons. Therefore as we have borne the image of the earthly man: even so now let us bear the image of the celestial man.

Jacob figureth the spirit. Esau the flesh. Jacob and Esau the sons of Isaac and Rebecca fought in their mother's belly: she counselled with God, and He answered: Of them shall spring two contrary people which should ever be at war but the elder should serve the younger. Esau was first born and Jacob followed holding Esau fast by the foot. Afterward Esau being a-hungered sold to Jacob his inheritance for a mess of pottage, when Isaac was old he bad Esau to kill some venison: that I might eat of it and bless thee or I die. But by the device and meanness of the mother Jacob stole away his father's blessing and was made lord of his brother. Then came Esau wailing to have a blessing, then answered the father: I have made him thy lord. After that Jacob saw our Lord face to face.

For this I say, brethren, that flesh and blood shall not possess the kingdom of heaven, nor corruption shall possess incorruption. Thou perceivest plainly how in this place he calleth Adam made of earth that thing which in another place he calleth the flesh and the outer man which is corrupt. And this same thing certainly is also the body of death, wherewith Paul aggrieved cried out: Oh wretch that I am, who shall deliver me from this body of death? In conclusion Paul declaring the most diverse fruit of the flesh and of the spirit writeth in another place, saying: He that followeth in his flesh shall reap or mow of his flesh corruption: but he that soweth in the spirit shall reap or mow of the spirit life eternal. This is the old debate of two twins Jacob and Esau, which before they were brought forth into light wrestled within the cloisters of the mother's belly, and Esau verily caught from Jacob the preeminence of birth and was first-born: but Jacob prevented him again of his father's blessing. That which is carnal cometh first, but the spiritual thing is ever best. The one was red, high coloured and rough with hair: the other smooth. The one unquiet and a hunter: the other rejoiced in domestical quietness. And the one also for hunger sold the right that pertained to him by inheritance, in that he was the elder brother, while he, enticed with a vile price and reward of voluptuousness, fell from his native liberty into the bondage of sin. The other procured by craft of grace that which belonged not to him by right of law. Between these two brethren though both were born of one belly, and at one time, yet was there never joined perfect concord. For Esau hateth Jacob, Jacob for his part, though he quitteth not hate for hate, yet he fleeth and hath ever Esau suspected, neither dare come within his danger. To thee likewise what so ever thing affection counselleth or persuadeth: let it be suspected, for the doubtful credence of the counsellor. Jacob only saw the Lord: Esau as one delighting in blood liveth by the sword. To conclude, when the mother asked counsel of the Lord he answered: the elder shall be servant to the younger: but the father Isaac added: thou Esau shalt do service to thy brother: and the time shall come when thou shalt shake off and loose his yoke from thy neck.

In good men the spirit which is figured by Jacob ruleth and the body obeyeth. In evil men the flesh which is signified by Esau ruleth of him the empire or dominion of the spirit.

The Lord prophesieth of good and obedient persons, the father of evil and disobedient persons. The one declareth what ought to be done of all men: the other told aforehand what the most part would do. Paul willeth that the wife be obedient to her husband: for better is (saith scripture) the iniquity of the man than the goodness of the woman.

The woman here signifieth a carnal person which, changed by grace of faith, followeth the bidding of the spirit in everything.

Our Eve is carnal affection, whose eyes the subtle and crafty serpent daily troubleth and vexeth with temptation, and she once corrupted goeth forth and ceaseth not to provoke and entice the man also through consent to be partaker of the iniquity or mischievous deed. But what readest thou of the new woman, of her I mean that is obedient to her husband?

The woman figureth affection, the man reason.

I will put hatred between thee (meaning the serpent and the woman) and between her generation and thine, she shall tread down thy head and thou shalt lay await to her heel. The serpent was cast down on his breast, the death of Christ weakened his violence, he now only lieth await to her heel privily.

Abraham had a son by his servant Agar whose name was Ismael, and another by his wife Sara whom he called Isaac. Ismael was much older than Isaac and in playing together misentreated Isaac. Wherewith, Sara, displeased, bade Abraham: put away thy servant Agar with her son also; which Abraham was loth to do but God commanded him to obey his wife's request.

But the woman through grace of faith changed as it were into a man boldly treadeth down his venomous head. Grace is increased and the tyranny of the flesh is diminished. When Sara was minished and decayed, then did Abraham (God being the author) grow and increase. And then she calleth him not husband but lord, neither yet could she obtain to have a child before she was dried up and barren. What I pray thee brought she forth at the last to her lord Abraham now in her old days, yea, and past child bearing? Verily Isaac, that is to say joy, for as soon as affections have waxed old and are weakened in a man, then at the last springeth up the blessed tranquillity of an innocent mind, with sure quietness of the spirit, as it were a continual feast. And as the father let not his wife have her pleasure without advisement: even so hath the sporting of the children together suspect, I mean of Isaac with Ismael. Sara would not the child of a bondwoman and the child of a free woman should have conversation together at that age: but that Ismael (while as yet youth is fervent) should be banished out of presence, lest under a colour of pastime he might entice and draw into his own manners Isaac yet young and tender of age.

Let youth flee the occasion of sin.

Now was Sara an old wife and now had brought forth Isaac, yet mistrusteth Abraham except the answer of God had approved his wife's counsel, he is not sure of the woman until he heard of God: In all things that Sara hath said to thee, hear her voice. O happy old age of them in whom so mortified is the carnal man made of the earth, that he in nothing defieth the spirit, which agreement whether in all things perfect may happen to any man in this life or no, verily I dare not affirm, peradventure it were not expedient, for even unto Paul was given unquietness and trouble of the flesh, the messenger of Satan, to vex him withal.

Trouble of the flesh is expedient to the exercise of virtue and custody of humility.

And at the third time he refused to have the messenger taken from him. Then had he none other answer of God but only this: Paul, my grace is sufficient for thee. For strength is wrought and made perfect in weakness. Indeed this is a new kind of remedy. Paul, lest he should be proud, is tempted with pride, that he might be strong in Christ: he is compelled to be weak in himself: he bare the treasure of celestial revelations in a vessel of earth, that the excellency should depend on the might of God, and not on himself, which one example of the apostle putteth us in remembrance and warneth us of many things.

When thou art tempted fall to prayer.

First of all that when we be assaulted of vices, immediately we must give ourselves to prayer again, and desire help of God.

Hydra was a serpent with many heads, of which one was immortal. With her fought Hercules and when he smote one head, seven sprang for it. At the last he fought with a burning sword, and so severed he their necks that they could no more spring.

Moreover that temptations to perfect men are not perilous: but also are very expedient to the continuance and preserving of virtue. Last of all when all other things are full tamed then the vice of vainglory even in the chief time of virtues layeth await: and this vice to be as it were Hydra, whom Hercules fought withal, a quick monster long of life and fruitful, by reason of her own wounds, which at the last end, when all labours be overcome, can scarce be destroyed. Nevertheless continual and importunate labour overcometh all thing. In the meantime while thy mind rageth and is vexed with vehement perturbations, by all manner of means thrust together, draw down, hold and bind this Protheus with tough bands while he goeth about to change himself into all manner monsters and affections of things, into fire, into the shape of some terrible wild beast and into a running river, until he come again into his own natural likeness and shape.

Protheus, that is to say, affection, must be held down. Protheus is a god which changes him to all manner of fashions. He is a great prophesier, but he will tell nothing without compulsion. Virgil rehearseth of Aristæus which had lost his beasts, and consulted with his mother Cyrene, a goddess, how he might restore them again. She sent him to Protheus, and taught a craft to bind him until he had told the truth. Then taught Protheus, how, of a dead and putrified ox they might be restored again.

What is so like Protheus as is the affections and appetites of fools, which draw them sometime into beastly and bodily lust, sometime into mad ire or wrath, otherwhiles into poison, envy and strange fashions of vices? Agreeth it not well that the excellent cunning poet Virgil said: There shall diverse similitudes and fashions of wild beasts delude and mock, for suddenly he will be a fearful swine and foul tiger, and a dragon full of scales, and a lioness with a red mane, or shall counterfeit the quick sound of the flame of fire. But here have in remembrance what followeth. The more he changeth himself into all manner of similitudes, the more, my son (saith Virgil), strain thy tough bands. And also because we shall not need to return again to fables of poets, thou shalt by the example of the holy patriarch Jacob learn to endure and to wrestle lustily all night until the morning, by the help of God, begin to give light. And thou shalt say, I will not let thee depart except thou shalt have given me thy blessing first. But what reward of his victory and great virtue that mighty and excellent strong wrestler obtained, it is certainly very profitable to hear. First of all God blessed him in that same place.

Jacob wrestled with an angel all night, whom in the morning he would not let go until he had blessed him in the same place. The angel smote his thigh and the sinews shrank so that Jacob halted on the one leg after that.

For evermore after that the temptation is overcome, a certain singular increase of divine grace is added unto a man, whereby he should be another time much more surely armed than he was before against the assault of his enemy. Furthermore through touching of the thigh the sinew of the conqueror waxed withered and shrunk, and he began to halt on the one foot. God curseth them by the mouth of his prophet which halt on both their feet, that is to say, them which will both live carnally, and please God also. But they be happy in whom carnal affections be so mortified, that they bear and lean most of all to the right foot, that is, to the spirit. Finally, his name was changed: of Jacob he was made Israel, and of a busy wrestler a quiet person.

God appeareth after a great tempest. He hath walked xl. days and xl. nights unto the mount of Oreb where he prayed in a cave. A voice bade him come forth and stand afore God. And then came a great wind, then a quaking, then fire, and God not in the fire. Then followed the hissing of a thin air and then appeared God to Elyas.

After that thou hast chastised thy flesh or thy body, and crucified him with vices and concupiscences, then shall tranquillity and quietness without all trouble come unto thee, that thou mayst be at leisure to behold the Lord, that thou mayst taste and feel that the Lord is pleasant and sweet, for that thing is signified by Israel. God is not seen in fire, neither in the whirlwind and troublous rage of temptation, but after the tempest of the devil (if so be that thou shalt endure perseveringly) followeth the hissing of a thin air or wind of spiritual consolation. After that air hath breathed quietly upon thee, then apply thine inward eyes, and thou shalt be Israel, and shalt say with him, I have seen my Lord, and my soul is made whole. Thou shalt see him that said: No flesh shall see me, that is to say, no carnal man. Consider thyself diligently, if thou be flesh, thou shalt not see God: if you see him not, thy soul shall not be made whole. Take heed therefore that thou be a spirit.

CHAPTER 7

Of three parts of man, the spirit, the soul, and the flesh.

These things afore written had been and that a great deal more than sufficient: nevertheless that thou mayst be somewhat more sensibly known unto thyself, I will rehearse compendiously the division of a man, after the description of Origene, for he followeth Paul making three parts, the spirit, the soul and the flesh, which three parts Paul joined together, writing to the Thessalonieences.

Origene in his first book upon the epistle of Paul to the Romans maketh this division.

That your spirit (saith he) your soul and your body may be kept clean and uncorrupt, that ye be not blamed or accused at the coming of our Lord Jesu Christ. And Esaias (leaving out the lowest part) maketh mention of two, saying, My soul shall desire and long for thee in the night, yea, and in my spirit and my heart strings I will wake in the mornings for to please thee. Also Daniel saith, Let the spirits and souls of good men laud God.

The flesh.

Out of the which places of scripture Origene gathereth not against reason the three partitions of man, that is to wit, the body, otherwise called the flesh, the most vile part of us, wherein the malicious serpent through original trespass hath written the law of sin, wherewithal we be provoked to filthiness. And also if we be overcome, we be coupled and made one with the devil.

The spirit.

Then the spirit wherein we represent the similitude of the nature of God, in which also our most blessed maker after the original pattern and example of his own mind hath graven the eternal law of honesty with his finger, that is, with his spirit the Holy Ghost. By this part we be knit to God, and made one with him. In the third place, and in the midst between these two he putteth the soul, which is partaker of the sensible wits and natural motions.

Thou must remember the soul and the spirit to be one substance, but in the soul be many powers, as wit, will, memory: but the spirit is the most pure and farthest from corruption, the most high and divine portion of our soul. Capax of God immediately wherein God hath graven the law of honesty, that is to say, the law natural, after the similitude of the eternal law of his own mind.

She is in a seditious and wrangling commonwealth and must needs join herself to the one part or the other, she is troubled of both parts, she is at her liberty to whether part she will incline. If she forsake the flesh and convey herself to the parts of the spirit, she herself shall be spiritual also. But if she cast herself down to the appetites of the body she shall grow out of kind into the manner of the body. This is it that Paul meant writing to the Chorintes. Remember ye not that he that joineth himself to an harlot is made one body with her: but he that cleaveth to the Lord, is one spirit with him. He calleth the harlot the frail and weak part of the man. This is that pleasant and flattering woman of whom thou readest in the second chapter of Proverbs on this wise. That thou mayst be delivered from a strange woman and from a woman of another country, which maketh her words sweet and pleasant, and forsaketh her husband to whom she was married in her youth, and hath forgot the promise she made to her Lord God: her house boweth down to death and her path is to hell. Whosoever goeth into hell, shall never return: nor shall attain the path of life. And in the vi. chapter. That thou mayst keep thee from an evil woman, and from the flattering tongue of a strange woman, let not thy heart melt on her beauty, be not thou deceived with her beckonings, for the price of an harlot is scarce worth a piece of bread: but the woman taketh away the precious soul of the man. Did he not when he made mention of the harlot, the heart and the soul express by name three parts of the man? Again, in the ix. chapter: A foolish woman ever babbling and full of words, swimming in pleasures, and hath no learning at all, sitteth in the doors of her house upon a stool in a high place of the city to call them that pass by the way and be going in their journey, Whosoever is a child, let him turn in to me: and she said unto a fool and an heartless person, Water that is stolen is pleasanter, and bread that is hid privily is sweeter. And he was not aware that there be giants, and their jests be in the bottom of hell. For whosoever shall be coupled to her, he shall descend into hell. And whosoever shall depart from her, shall be saved. I beseech thee with what colours could more workmanly have been painted and set out either the venomous enticements and wanton pleasures of the poisoned flesh, provoking and tempting the soul to filthiness of sin, or else the importunity of the same crying and striving against the spirit, or the wretched end that followeth when she doth overcome the spirit. To conclude therefore, the spirit maketh us gods, the flesh maketh us beasts: the soul maketh us men: the spirit maketh us religious, obedient to God, kind and merciful. The flesh maketh us despisers of God, disobedient to God, unkind and cruel. The soul maketh us indifferent, that is to say, neither good nor bad. The spirit desireth celestial things: the flesh desireth delicate and pleasant things: the soul desireth necessary things: the spirit carryeth us up to heaven: the flesh thrusteth us down to hell. To the soul nothing is imputed, that is to say, it doth neither good nor harm: whatsoever is carnal or springeth of the flesh that is filthy: whatsoever is spiritual proceeding of the spirit, that is pure, perfect and godly: whatsoever is natural and proceedeth of the soul, is a medium and indifferent thing, neither good nor bad. Wilt thou more plainly have the diversity of these three parts shewed unto thee as it were with a man's finger? Certainly I will essay.

That which is natural deserveth no reward.

Thou doest reverence to thy father and mother: thou lovest thy brother, thy children and thy friend: it is not of so great virtue to do these things, as it is abominable not to do them. For why shouldest thou not being a Christian man do that thing which the gentiles by the teaching of nature do, yea which brute beasts do? That thing that is natural shall not be imputed unto merit. But thou art come in to such a strait case that either the reverence toward thy father must be despised, the inward love towards thy children must be subdued, the benevolence to thy friend set at nought, or God must be offended. What wilt thou now do? The soul standeth in the midst between two ways: the flesh crieth upon her on the one side, the spirit on the other side. The spirit saith, God is above thy father: thou art bound to thy father but for thy body only. To God thou art bound for all thing that thou hast. The flesh putteth thee in remembrance, saying: Except thou obey thy father, he will disinherit thee, thou shalt be called of every man an unkind and unnatural child, look to thy profit, have respect to thy good name and fame. God either doth not see, or else dissimuleth and wittingly looketh beside it, or at the least, will be soon pacified again.

The soul doubteth.

Now thy soul doubteth, now she wavereth hither and thither, to whether of either part she turn herself. That same shall she be, that that thing is she went unto. If she obey the harlot, that is to say the flesh (the spirit despised) she shall be one body with the flesh. But if she lift up herself and ascend to the spirit (the flesh set at nought) she shall be transposed and changed to the nature of the spirit. After this manner accustom to examine thyself prudently. The error of those men is exceeding great which oftentimes weeneth that thing to be perfect virtue and goodness which is but of nature and no virtue at all.

Some affections be disguised with visors of virtue. An example of the judge.

Certain affections somewhat honest in appearance, and as they were disguised with visors of virtue, deceiveth negligent persons. The judge is hasty and cruel against the felon, or him that hath trespassed the law, he seemeth to himself constant and of gravity uncorrupt and a man of good conscience, wilt thou have this man discussed? If he favour his own mind too much and follow a certain natural rigorousness without any grief of mind, peradventure with some pleasure or delectation: yet not leaning from the office and duty of a judge, let him not forthwith stand too much in his own conceit: it is an indifferent thing that he doth. But if he abuse the law for private hate or lucre, now it is carnal that he doth, and he committeth murder. But and if he feel great sorrow in his mind because he is compelled to destroy and kill him, whom he had liefer amended and saved: also if he enjoin punishment according to the trespass with such a mind, with such sorrow of heart, as the father commandeth his singularly beloved son to be cut, lanced or seared: of this manner shall it be spiritual that he doth.

Some men rejoice naturally with some certain things.

The most part of men through proneness of nature and some special property, either rejoice in, or abhor certain things. Some there be whom bodily lust tickleth not at all: let not them by and by ascribe that unto virtue which is an indifferent thing, for not to lack bodily lust, but to overcome bodily lust is the office of virtue.

The rule of true piety.

Another man hath a pleasure to fast, a pleasure to be at mass, a pleasure to be much at church and to say a great deal of psalmody: examine after this rule that thing which he doeth: if he regard the common fame or advantage, it smelleth of the flesh and not of the spirit: if he do follow but his own inclination (for he doth that which pleaseth his own mind) then he hath not whereof he so ought greatly to rejoice, but rather whereof he ought to fear.

Let a Christian man mark this well.

Behold a jeopardous thing unto thyself. Thou prayest, and judgest him that prayeth not. Thou fasteth, and condemneth him that fasteth not. Whosoever doeth not that thou doest, thou thinkest thyself better than he: beware lest thy fast pertain to thy flesh. Thy brother hath need of thy help, thou in the mean space mumblest in thy prayers unto God, and wilt not be known of thy brother's necessity. God shall abhor these prayers: for how shall God hear thee while thou prayest, when thou which art a man canst not find in thy heart to hear another man. Perceive also another thing. Thou lovest thy wife for this cause only, that she is thy wife. Thou doest no great thing, for this thing is common as well to infidels as to thee: or else thou lovest her for none other thing but because she is to thee pleasant and delectable. Thy love now draweth to thee fleshward.

The chaste love towards thy wife.

But thou lovest her for this thing chiefly, because thou hast perceived in her the image of Christ, which is godly reverence, modesty, soberness, chastity: and now lovest not her in her self but in Christ: yea rather Christ in her. After this manner lovest spiritually. Notwithstanding we shall say more of these things in their places.

CHAPTER 8

Certain general rules of true Christian living.

Enchiridion.

Now for because we have opened as me seemeth the way (howsoever we have done it), and have prepared as it were certain stuff and matter unto the thing which was purposed, we must haste to that which remaineth, lest it should not be an *Enchiridion*, that is to say, a little treatise handsome to be carried in a man's hand, but rather a great volume; we will enforce to give certain rules, as they were certain points of wrestling, by whose guiding and conveyance, as it were by the guiding of the thread of Dedalus, men may easily plunge up out of the blind errors of this world, as out of Labirinthus, which is a certain cumbrous maze, and come into the pure and clear light of spiritual living. None other science is there which hath not her rules. And shall the craft of blessed living only be without the help of all manner of precepts?

Learn the craft of virtue.

There is without fail a certain craft of virtuous living and a discipline, in which whosoever exercise themselves manfully, them shall favour that Holy Spirit, which is the promoter and bringer forward of all holy enforcement and godly purposes. But whosoever saith, Depart from us we will not have the knowledge of thy ways: these men the mercy of God refuseth, because they first have refused knowledge. These rules shall be taken partly of the person of God, of the person of the devil, and of our person, partly of things, that is to say, of virtues and vices, and of things to them annexed, partly of the matter or stuff whereof virtues or vices be wrought. They shall profit singularly against the evil things remaining of original sin. For though baptism hath wiped away the spot, yet there cleaveth still in us a certain thing of the old disease left behind, both partly for the custody of humility, and also for the matter and increase of virtue. These be blindness, the flesh and infirmity or weakness. Blindness with the mist of ignorance dimmeth the judgment of reason. For partly the sin of our first progenitors hath not a little dusked that so pure a light of the countenance, resemblance, or similitude of God, which our creator hath shewed upon us. And much more corrupt bringing up, lewd company, froward affections, darkness of vices, custom of sin hath so cankered it, that of the law graven in us of God scarce any signs or tokens doth appear.

Nota.

Then as I began, blindness causeth that we in the election of things be as good as half blinded and deceived with error, in the stead of the best, following the worst, preferring things of less value before things of greater price. The flesh troubleth the affection so much, that even though we know what is best, yet love we the contrary. Infirmity and weakness maketh us that we being overcome either with tediousness or with temptation, forsake the virtue which we had once gotten and attained. Blindness hurteth the judgment, the flesh corrupteth the will, infirmity weakeneth constancy.

Evil must be known and had in hate.

The first point therefore is that thou can discern things to be refused from things to be accepted: and therefore blindness must be taken away lest we stumble or stagger in the election of things. The next is, that thou hate the evil as soon as it is once known, and love that which is honest and good: and in this thing the flesh must be overcome, lest contrary to the judgment of the mind we should love sweet and delectable things in the stead of wholesome things.

Perseverance must be had.

The third is, that we continue in these things which we began well: and therefore the weakness must be underset, lest we forsake the way of virtue with greater shame than if we had been never about to walk or enter therein. Ignorance must be remedied, that thou mayst see which way to go. The flesh must be tamed, lest she lead thee aside out of the highway, once known, into bypaths. Weakness must be comforted, lest when thou hast entered into the strait way thou shouldst either faint or stop or turn back again, or lest after thou hast once set thy hand to the plough shouldst look backward, but shouldst rejoice as a strong giant to haste the way, ever stretching forth thyself to those things which be afore thee, without remembrance of those things which be behind thee, until thou mayst lay hand on the reward appointed and on the crown promised to them that continue unto these three things: therefore we shall apply certain rules according to our little power.

CHAPTER 9

Against the evil of ignorance. The first rule.

We must judge well of scripture.

But inasmuch as faith is the only gate unto Christ, the first rule must be that thou judge very well both of him and also of scripture given by his spirit, and that thou believe not with mouth only, not faintly, not negligently, not doubtfully, as the common rascal of Christian men do: but let it be set fast and immovable throughout all thy breast, not one jot to be contained in them that appertaineth not greatly unto thy health.

Counterfeit not evil persons.

Let it move thee nothing at all that thou seest a great part of men so live, as though heaven and hell were but some manner of tales of old wives, to fear or flatter young children withal: but believe thou surely and make no haste, though the whole world should be mad at once, though the elements should be changed, though the angels should rebel: yet verity cannot lie, it cannot but come which God told before should come.

Probations of Christian faith.

If thou believe he is God, thou must needs believe that he is true also, and on this wise think without wavering, nothing to be so true, nothing to be so sure, and without doubt of the things which thou hearest with thine ears, which thou presently beholdest with thine eyes, which thou handlest with thy hands, as those things be true which thou readest in the scriptures, that God of heaven, that is to say verity, gave by inspiration, which the holy prophets brought forth, and the blood of so many martyrs hath approved: unto which now so many hundred years the consent of all good men hath agreed and set their seals: which Christ here being in flesh, both taught in his doctrine and expressly represented or counterfeited in his manners and living. Unto which also miracles bear witness, the devils confess and so much believe, that they quake and tremble for fear. Last of all which be so agreeable unto the equity of nature, which so agree between themselves, and be everywhere like themselves, which so ravisheth the minds of them that attend, so moveth and changeth them. If these so great tokens agree unto them alone, what devil's madness is it to doubt in the faith? Yea of those things past thou mayst easily conjecture what shall follow: how many and great things also, how incredible to be spoken did the prophets tell before of Christ: which of these things came not to pass? Shall he in other things deceive which in them deceived not? In conclusion, the prophets lied not, and shall Christ the Lord of prophets lie? If with this and such other like cogitations thou often stir up the flame of faith, and then fervently desire of God to increase thy faith, I shall marvel if thou canst be any long time an evil man. For who is all together so unhappy and full of mischief that would not depart from vices, if so be he utterly believed, that with these momentary pleasures, beside the unhappy vexation of conscience and mind, is purchased also eternal punishments: on the other side, if he surely believed for this temporal and little worldly vexation to be rewarded or recompensed to good men an hundred fold joy of pure conscience presently: and at the last life immortal.

CHAPTER 10

The second rule.

Let the first point be therefore that thou doubt in no wise of the promises of God.

We must enter into the way of health or salvation boldly and with a jocund courage.

The next that thou go unto the way of life, not slothfully, not fearfully: but with sure purpose, with all thy heart, with a confident mind, and (if I may so say) with such mind as he hath that would rather fight than drink: so that thou be ready at all hours for Christ's sake to lose both life and goods. A slothful man will and will not. The kingdom of heaven is not gotten of negligent and reckless persons, but plainly rejoiceth to suffer violence: and violent persons violently obtain it.

Egypt signifieth bondage, affliction, vices, and blindness.

Suffer not the affection of them whom thou lovest singularly to hold thee back hasting thither ward: let not the pleasures of this world call thee back again: let not the care of thy household be any hindrance to thee. The chain of worldly business must be cut asunder, for surely it cannot otherwise be loosed.

The Israelytes being a-hungered in desert wished to go back again to Egypt, saying to Moses, How happy were we when we sat there by the pots of flesh.

Egypt must be forsaken in such a manner that thou turn not again in thy mind at any time unto the pots of the flesh. Sodoma must be forsaken utterly hastily, yea, and at once: it is not lawful to look back. The woman looked back and she was turned into the image of a stone. The man had no leisure anywhere to abide in any region, but was commanded to haste into the mountain, unless that he had liefer to have perished.

Lot was commanded to depart hastily out of Sodoma and not to look back. His wife looked back and was turned into a salt stone. So we may neither with the Israelytes desire to go back again to the pleasures of Egypt, of vices and sin: neither with the wife of Lot may look back again to our old conversation.

The prophet crieth out that we should flee out of the midst of Babylon. The departing of the Israelytes from Egypt is called flight or running away. We be commanded to flee out of Babylon hastily, and not to remove a little and a little slowly. Thou mayst see the most part of men prolong the time, and with very slow purpose go about to flee from vices. When I have once rid myself out of such and such matters, say they, yea when I have brought that and that business to pass. Oh fool, what and if God this same day take again thy soul from thee? Perceivest thou not one business to rise of another, and one vice to call in another? Why rather doest thou not to-day that thing which the sooner thou doest, the easier shall it be done? Be diligent some other where. In this matter to do rashly, to run headlong and suddenly, is chiefest of all and most profitable.

There may be no prolonging time in fleeing vices.

Regard not nor ponder how much thou forsakest, but be sure Christ only shall be sufficient for all things: only be bold to commit thyself to him with all thine heart: set thou mistrust in thine own self, adventure to put unto him all the governance of thyself: trust to thyself no longer, but with full confidence cast thyself from thyself to him, and he shall receive thee: commit thy care and thought to the Lord, and he shall nourish thee up, that thou mayst sing the song of the same prophet.

Confidence in God.
Serve Christ altogether and no man else.

The Lord is my governor, and I shall lack nothing. In a place of pasture he hath set me, by the water side of comfort he hath brought up me: he hath converted my soul. Be not minded to part thyself into two, to the world and to Christ: thou canst not serve two masters: there is no fellowship between God and Belial. God cannot away with them which halt on both their legs: his stomach abhorreth them which be neither hot nor cold, but lukewarm. God is a very jealous lover of souls: he will possess only and altogether that thing which he redeemed with his blood: he cannot suffer the fellowship of the devil, whom he once overcame with death.

Two ways only. The one of salvation the other of perdition.

There be but two ways only, the one which by obedience of the affections leadeth to perdition: the other which through mortifying of the flesh, leadeth to life. Why doubtest thou in thyself, there is no third way, into one of these two thou must needs enter, wilt thou or wilt thou not, whatsoever thou art, or of what degree, thou must needs enter into this strait way, in which few mortal men walk? But this way Christ himself hath trod, and have trodden since the world began whosoever pleased God.

Adrastia, Nemesis, or Rhamnusia is a goddess which punisheth insolence. She forbiddeth that any man look too high. If any so do he escapeth not unpunished though it be never so late. If any be too full of insolence we say: Take heed, Rhamnusia seeth thee well enough.

This is doubtless the inevitable necessity of the goddess Adrastia, otherwise called Nemesis or Rhamnusia, that is to say, it cannot be chosen but that thou be crucified with Christ as touching the world, if thou purpose to live with Christ. Why like fools flatter we ourselves, why in so weighty a matter deceive we ourselves? One saith, I am not of the clergy or a spiritual man, I am of the world, I cannot but use the world. Another thinketh, though I be a priest yet am I no monk, let him look upon it. And the monk also hath found a thing to flatter himself withal, though I be a monk yet am I not of so strait an order as such and such. Another saith, I am a young man, I am a gentleman, I am rich, I am a courtier, and to be short, a prince, those things pertain not to me which were spoken to the apostles.

Every man putteth to another the life of Christ and sayings of his apostles.

Oh wretch, then appertaineth it nothing to thee that thou shouldst live in Christ? If thou be in the world, in Christ thou art not: if thou call the sky, the earth, the sea and this common air the world: so is there no man which is not in the world: but and if thou call the world ambition, that is to say, desire of honour, promotion, or authority: if thou call the world pleasures, covetousness, bodily lust: certainly if thou be worldly, thou art not a Christian man.

The world.

Christ spake indifferently to all men: whosoever would not take his cross and follow him, could be no meet man for him, or be his disciple: to die with Christ as touching the flesh is nothing to thee, if to live by his spirit pertaineth nothing to thee: to be crucified as touching the world pertaineth nothing to thee, if to live godly or in God, pertain nothing to thee: to be buried together with Christ belongeth nothing to thee, if to arise again to eternal glory belong nothing to thee: the humility, poverty, tribulation, vile reputation, the laborious agonies and sorrows of Christ, pertain nothing at all unto thee, if the kingdom of him pertain nothing unto thee.

The reward is given to him that laboureth.

What can be more lewd than to think the reward to be common as well to thee as to other: and yet nevertheless to put the labours whereby the reward is obtained, from thee, to a certain few persons? What can be more a wanton thing than to desire to reign with the Head, and yet wilt thou take no pain with him? Therefore, my brother, look not so greatly what other men do, and in comparison of them flatter or please thyself.

Monks.

To die as touching sin: to die as touching carnal desires: to die as touching the world is a certain hard thing and known to very few, yea though they be monks, and yet this is the common or general profession of all Christian men. This thing a great while agone thou hast sworn and holily promised in the time of baptism: than which vow what other thing can there be either more holy or religious? Either we must perish, or else without exception we must go this way to health, whether we be knights or ploughmen. Notwithstanding though it fortune not to all men to attain the perfect counterfeiting or following of the Head, yet all must enforce with feet and hands to come thereto. He hath a great part of a Christian man's living, which with all his heart, with a sure and steadfast purpose, hath determined to be a Christian man.

CHAPTER 11

The third rule.

But lest that thing fear thee from the way of virtue because it seemeth sharp and grievous, partly because thou must forsake worldly commodities, partly because thou must fight continually against three very cruel enemies, the flesh, the devil, and the world, set this third rule before thee alway, bear thyself in hand that all the fearful things and fantasies which appear forthwith unto thee as it were in the first entering of hell ought to be counted for a thing of nought, by the example of Virgilius' *Eneas*.

Eneas in the vi. book of Virgil went down into hell accompanied with the prophetess Sibyl. In the first entry appeared many fantasies and wonderful monsters, not so perilous indeed as they appeared.

For certainly, if thou shalt consider the very thing somewhat groundly and steadfastly (setting at nought these apparent things which beguiled thine eyes) thou shalt perceive that none other way is more commodious than the way of Christ: though thou account this thing not at all, that this way only leadeth to eternal life, yea and though thou have no respect unto the reward. For I beseech thee what kind of living after the common course of the world is there that thou canst choose in which thou shall not bear and suffer things enough abundantly both careful and grievous? Who is he that knoweth not the life of courtiers to be full of grievous labour and wretched misery, except it be either he that never proved it or certainly a very natural fool? Oh immortal God, what bondage, how long and how ungoodly must there be suffered even unto the life's end! What a cumbrous business is there in seeking in purchasing the prince's love and grace! A man must flatter to obtain the favour of all such as may either hinder or further one. The countenances must now and then be feigned and new fashioned. The injuries of the greater men must be whispered or muttered with silence secretly.

The life of warriors.

Consequently, what kind of evil life can be imagined whereof the life of warriors is not full? Of either life then mayst thou be a very good witness, which hast learned both at thine own peril.

The life of merchants.

And as touching the merchant man what is that he either doth not or suffereth not fleeing poverty by sea, by land, through fire and water?

The misery of matrimony.

In matrimony what a mountain of household cares be there?

In bearing of offices.

What misery feel not they there which proveth and hath experience of it! In bearing of offices how much vexation, how much labour, and how much peril is there! which way so ever thou turn thyself an huge company of incommodities meeteth thee. The very life of mortal men of itself without addition of any other thing is cumbered and tangled with a thousand miseries which be common and indifferent as well to good as bad.

A Christian man obtaineth merit in everything.

They all shall grow into a great heap of merits unto thee if they shall find thee in the way of Christ: if not they shall be the more grievous, moreover fruitless, and yet must nevertheless be suffered. Whosoever be soldiers of this world, first how many years do they pant, blow, sweat, and canvass the world, tormenting themselves with thought and care, moreover for how transitory and things of naught? Last of all, in how doubtful hope? Add to this that there is no rest or easement of miseries, in so much that the more they have laboured, the more grievous is the pain. And when all is past, what shall the end be of so tedious and laborious a life? verily eternal punishment. So now and with this life compare the way of virtue, which at the first ceaseth to be tedious, in process is made easier, is made pleasant and delectable, by which way also we go with very sure hope to eternal felicity. Were it not the uttermost madness to have liefer with equal labour to purchase eternal death rather than life immortal?

Ticius, because he would have joined with Apollo's mother, was cast of Apollo down to hell, where vultures gnaw his heart ever increasing again. The meaning of the fable is this. He was a great man and could not be contented but would have more, and advanced himself to more honour, and would have put Apollo out of his country, which was signified by his mother. But Apollo subdued him and spoiled him of his possessions so that afterward he lived in care and misery among the lowest sort and could not obtain any further honour. Ixion was cast of Juno, lady of honour, into hell, where he runneth round and continually compasseth for honour, but he could not obtain. Sisiphus rolleth a stone from the hill foot to the top, then slideth the stone, and he descendeth to fetch him up again. Ambition is ever at the hill foot. He is never so high but that he hath one hill more to climb, he seeth one thing more which he coveteth. Tantalus standeth still in hell in a river of wine ever athirst, and all manner of fruits about him, and yet he is ever hungry neither is suffered to drink oreat.

Yet are these worldly men much madder than so, that they choose with extreme labour to go to labour everlasting, rather than with less labours to go to immortal quietness. Moreover if the way of piety, or obedience to God were so much more laborious than the way of the world, yet here the grievousness of the labour is assuaged with hope of reward, and the comfort of God is not lacking which turneth the bitterness of the gall into the sweetness of honey. There one care calleth in another, of one sorrow springeth another, no quietness is there at all. The labour and affliction withoutforth, the grievous cares and thoughts withinforth cause the very easements to be sharp and bitter. These things so to be was not unknown to the poets of the gentiles which, by the punishment of Ticius, Ixion, Tantalus, Sisiphus, and of Pentheus, painted and described the miserable and grievous life of lewd and wretched persons: of whom is also the late confession in the book of Sapyence. We be wearied in the way of iniquity and perdition, we have walked hard ways, but the way of God we know not. What could be either filthier or more laborious than the servitude of Egypt? What could be more grievous than the captivity of Babylon? What more intolerable than the yoke of Pharao and of Nabugodonosor? But what saith Christ? Take my yoke upon your necks and ye shall find rest unto your souls: my yoke, saith he, is pleasant and my burden light. To speak briefly, no pleasure is lacking where is not lacking a quiet conscience. No misery is there lacking where an unhappy conscience crucifieth the mind. These things must be taken as of most certainty, but and if thou yet doubt go ask of them which in time past have been converted out of the middle of Babylon, unto the Lord: and by experience of them at the least way believe nothing to be more troublous and grievous than vices, nothing to be more easy or of quicker speed than not to be drowned in business, nothing more cheerful and more comfortable than is virtue. Nevertheless go to let it be that the wages be like, and that the labours be like also, yet for all that how greatly ought a man to desire to war under the standard of Christ, rather than under the banners of the devil. Yea, how much liefer were it to be vexed or to suffer affliction with Christ, than to swim in pleasures with the devil. Moreover, ought not a man with wind and weather, with ship sail and swiftness of horses, to fly from a lord not very filthy only, but very cruel and deceitful, which requireth so cruel service and so strait a task, which promiseth again things so uncertain, so caduke, so transitory, which so soon fade and vanish away, of the which very same things yet deceiveth he the wretches, and that not seldom.

Covetous men dare not use their goods but be hungry and thirsty for more.

Or though he perform his promise once, yet another time when it pleaseth him he taketh them away again, so that the sorrow and thought for the loss of things once possessed is much more than was the grievous labour in purchasing them.

Pentheus was turned into an hart and eaten of his own dogs, and he did none other thing all his life but hunt and follow dogs, so he consumed himself and his substance like a fool wretchedly and beastly.

After that the merchant man hath mingled together both right and wrong for the intent of increasing his goods, after he hath put his honest reputation of good report that is sprung of him, his life, his soul in a thousand jeopardies, if it so be then that the chance of fortune hap aright at the latter end with all his travail, what other thing hath he prepared for himself more than the matter of miserable care if he keep his goods, if he lose them a perpetual torment?

The troublous care of a merchant.

If fortune chance amiss what remaineth but that he should be made twice a wretch wrapped in double misery, partly because he is disappointed of the thing whereon his hope hanged, beside that because he cannot remember so great labour spent in waste without much both sorrow of heart and grief of mind? No man enforceth with sure purpose to come to good living or conversation which hath not attained it. Christ as he is not mocked, so neither he mocketh any man. Remember another thing, when thou fliest out of the world unto Christ, if the world have any commodities or pleasures that thou forsakest them not, but changest trifles with things of more value. Who will not be very glad to change silver for gold, flint for precious stone? Thy friends be displeased? What then? thou shalt find more pleasant and better companions. Thou shalt lack outward pleasures of thy body, but thou shalt enjoy the inward pleasures of the mind, which be better, purer, and more certain. Thy goods must be diminished, nevertheless these riches increase which neither the moths destroy nor thieves take away. Thou ceasest to be of price in the world, but thou for all that art well beloved of Christ: thou pleasest the fewer, but yet the better. Thy body waxeth lean, but thy mind waxeth fat. The beauty of thy skin vanisheth away, but the beauty of thy mind appeareth bright. And in like manner if thou shalt reckon all other things thou shalt perceive nothing not of all these apparent good things to be forsaken in this world, that is not recompensed largely with greater advantage and more excellent a great way.

Many things may be received and possessed but not desired.

But if there be any things which though they cannot be desired without vice, yet without vice may be possessed: of which kind of things is the good estimation of the people, favour of the commonalty, love or to be in conceit, authority, friends, honour due to virtue: for the most part it chanceth that all these things be given without searching for, to them that above all things seek the kingdom of heaven, which selfsame thing Christ promised and God performed to Salomon. Fortune for the most part followeth them that flieth from her, and flieth from them that follow her. Certainly whatsoever shall happen to them that love, nothing can be but prosperous unto whom loss is turned to advantage, torment, vexation or adversity to solace, rebukes to laud, punishment to pleasure, bitter things to sweetness, evil things to good. Doubtest thou then to enter in to this way and forsake that other way, seeing there is so unequal comparison, yea none at all, of God unto the devil, of hope to hope, of reward to reward, of labour to labour, of solace to solace.

CHAPTER 12

The fourth rule.

Let Christ be thy mark and example of living.

But that thou mayst haste and make speed unto felicity with a more sure course, let this be unto thee the fourth rule, that thou have Christ alway in thy sight as the only mark of all thy living and conversation, unto whom only thou shouldst direct all thine enforcements, all thy pastimes and purposes, all thy rest and quietness, and also thy business.

What Christ is.

And think thou not Christ to be a voice or sound without signification, but think him to be nothing else save charity, simplicity, or innocency, patience, cleanness, and shortly whatsoever Christ taught.

What the devil is.

Understand well also that the devil is none other thing but whatsoever calleth away from such things as Christ taught. He directeth his journey to Christ which is carried to virtue only. And he becometh bond to the devil which giveth himself to vices. Let thine eye therefore be pure, and all thy body shall be bright and full of light. Let thine eye look unto Christ alone as unto only and very felicity, so that thou love nothing, marvel at nothing, desire nothing but either Christ or else for Christ. Also that thou hate nothing, abhor nothing, fly nothing, nothing avoid but only sin or else for sin's sake. By this means it will come to pass that whatsoever thou shalt do, whether thou sleep, whether thou wake, whether thou eat, whether thou drink, and to conclude that thy very sports and pastimes, yea (I will speak more boldly) that some vices of the lighter sort into which we fall now and then while we haste to virtue, all the whole shall grow and turn in thee unto a great heap of rewards. But and if thine eye shall not be pure, but look any otherward than unto Christ, yea though thou do certain things which be good or honest of themselves, yet shall they be unfruitful or peradventure very perilous and hurtful.

How far forth things preferred unsought for ought to be refused.

For it is a great fault to do a good thing not well. And therefore that man that hasteth the strait way unto the mark of very felicity, whatsoever things shall come and meet him by the way, so far forth ought he either refuse or receive them, as they either further or hinder his journey: of which things there be three orders or three degrees. Certain things verily be of such manner filthy that they cannot be honest, as to avenge wrong, to wish evil to another.

Three orders of things.

These things ought alway to be had in hate, yea though thou shouldest have never so great advantage to commit them, or never so great punishment if thou didst them not, for nothing can hurt a good man but filthiness only.

Things honest.

Certain things on the other side be in such manner honest that they cannot be filthy, of which kind be to will or wish all men good, to help thy friends with honest means, to hate vices, to rejoice with virtuous communication. Certain things verily be indifferent or between both, of their own nature neither good nor bad, honest nor filthy: as health, beauty, strength, fecundity, cunning, and such other. Of this last kind of things therefore nothing ought to be desired for itself, neither ought to be usurped more or less, but as far forth as they make and be necessary to the chief mark, I mean, to follow Christ's living. The very philosophers have certain marks also imperfect and indifferent, in which a man ought not to stand still nor tarry, which also a man may conveniently use, referring them to a better purpose, and not to enjoy them and tarry upon them, putting his whole felicity in them: notwithstanding those mean and indifferent things do not all after one manner and equally either further or hinder them that be going unto Christ, therefore they must be received or refused, after as each of them is more or less of value unto thy purpose.

Piety signifieth service, honour, reverence, obedience, due to God.

Knowledge helpeth more unto piety than beauty or strength of body or riches: and though all learning may be applied to Christ, yet some helpeth more compendiously than some.

Science must be loved for Christ's sake.

Of this end and purpose, see thou measure the profitableness or unprofitableness of all mean things. Thou lovest learning, it is very well if thou do it for Christ's sake: but if thou love it therefore only because thou wouldst know it, then makest thou a stop and tarrying therefrom whence thou oughtest to have made a step to climb further. But if thou desire sciences that thou by their help mightest more clearly behold Christ hid in the secrets of scripture, and when thou knowest him love him, when thou knowest and lovest him teach, declare, and open him to other men, and in thyself enjoy him: then prepare thyself unto study of sciences, but no further than thou mayst think them profitable to good living.

How far forth the letters of the gentiles be to be read. Look in the second chapter what this meaneth.

If thou have confidence in thyself and trust to have great advantage in Christ, go forth boldly as an adventurous merchant to walk as a stranger somewhat further, yea in the learning of gentiles, and apply the riches or treasure of the Egyptians unto the honesting of the temple of God. But if thou fear greater loss than thou hopest of advantage, then return again to our first rule: know thyself and pass not thy bounds, keep thee within thy lists. It is better to have less knowledge and more of love, than to have more of knowledge and not to love. Knowledge therefore hath the mastery or chief room amongst mean things. After that is health, the gifts of nature, eloquence, beauty, strength, dignity, favour, authority, prosperity, good reputation, kin, friends, stuff of household. Every one of these things as it helpeth most and nighest way unto virtue, so shall it most chiefly be applied in case they be offered unto us hasting in our way, if not then may we not for cause of them turn aside from our journey purposed.

Money should this wise be loved.

Money chanced unto thee, if it let nothing to good living, minister it, make friends with the wicked mammon: but if thou fear loss of virtue and good mind, despise that advantage full of damage and loss, and follow thou even Crates of Thebes flinging thy grievous and cumbrous pack into the sea, rather than it should hold thee back from Christ.

Crates of the city of Thebes cast a great sum of gold into the sea, saying, Hence ye mischievous riches: better it is that I drown you than you me. He supposed that he could not possess riches and virtue both together.

That thing mayst thou do the easier, if, as I have said, thou shalt custom thyself to marvel at none of those things which be without thee, that is to say, which pertain not unto the inner man, for by that means it will come to pass that thou canst neither wax proud or forget thyself. If these things fortune unto thee, neither thou shalt be vexed in thy mind if they should either be denied thee or taken from thee, forasmuch as thou puttest thy whole felicity in Christ only. But and if it chance they come unto thee besides thine own labour, be more diligent and circumspect, having no less care than thou hadst before: have in mind that a matter to exercise thyself virtuously on, is given to thee of God, but yet not without jeopardy and danger.

Because Prometheus had made a man of clay and with fire stolen from heaven put life into him, Jupyter sent Pandora a woman with a box full of all kinds of diseases to him, but Prometheus was provided and refused it, but his brother Epymetheus received it and opened it and then all manner of sicknesses flew abroad. Prometheus taught rude men civil and honest manner, yet would he bear no rule amongst them but fled to solitariness, thinking all kinds of misery to be in bearing rule, but his brother Epymetheus took the misery upon him.

But if thou have the benignity of fortune suspected, counterfeit Prometheus, do not receive the deceitful box, and go light and naked unto that which is only very felicity. Certainly whosoever with great thought and care desire money as a precious thing, and count the chief succour of life to be therein, thinking themselves happy as long as it is safe, calling themselves wretches when it is lost: those men no doubt have made or feigned unto themselves many gods. Thou hast set up thy money and made it equal unto Christ, if it can make thee happy or unhappy. That I have spoken of money understand the same likewise of honours, voluptuousness, health, yea and of the very life of the body. We must enforce to come to our only mark, which is Christ, so fervently that we should have no leisure to care for any of these things, either when they be given us, or else when they be taken from us, for the time is short as saith Paul: Henceforward, saith he, they that use the world, must be as they used it not. This mind I know well the world laugheth to scorn as foolish and mad: nevertheless it pleaseth God by this foolishness to save them that believe. And the foolishness of God is wiser than man. After this rule thou shalt examine, yea whatsoever thou doest. Thou exercisest a craft? It is very well done if thou do it without fraud: but whereunto lookest thou to find thy household? But for what intent to find thy household, to win thy household to Christ?

When labour is profitable.

Thou runnest well.

When fasting is superstitious.

Thou fastest, verily a good work as it appeareth outward: but unto what end referrest thou thyself, to spare thy victuals or that thou mayst be counted the more holy? Thine eye is wanton, corrupt, and not pure. Peradventure thou fastest lest thou should fall into some disease or sickness. Why fearest thou sickness? Lest it would take thee from the use of voluptuous pleasures: thine eye is corrupt. But thou desireth health because thou mayst be able to study. To what purpose I beseech thee referrest thou thy study, to get thee a benefice withal? With what mind desirest thou a benefice? Verily to live at thine own pleasure, not at Christ's. Thou hast missed the mark which a Christian man ought to have everywhere prefixed before his eyes. Thou takest meat that thou mightest be strong in thy body, and thou wilt have thy body strong that thou mightest be sufficient unto holy exercises and watch. Thou hast hit the mark. But thou providest for health and good living lest thou shouldest be more evil favoured or deformed, lest thou shouldst not be strong enough unto bodily lust, thou hast fallen from Christ making unto thee another God.

The superstitious honouring of saints.
Christofer.
Rochus.
Barbara.
George.
Apolyne.
Job.
Jherom.

There be which honour certain saints with certain ceremonies. One saluteth Christofer every day, but not except he behold his image. Whither looketh he? Verily to this point, he hath borne himself in hand that he shall be all that day sure from evil death. Another worshippeth one Rochus, but why? Because he believeth that he will keep away the pestilence from his body. Another mumbleth certain prayers to Barbara or George, lest he should fall into his enemy's hands. This man fasteth to Saint Apolyne lest his teeth should ache. That man visiteth the image of holy Job, because he should be without scabs. Some assign and name certain portion of their winning to poor men, lest their merchandise should perish by shipwreck. A taper is light before Saint Hierom to the intent that thing which is lost may be had again.

A cock to Esculapius.

In conclusion after this same manner look how many things be which we either favour or else love, so many saints have we made governors of the same things, which same saints be divers in divers natures: so that Paul doth the same thing among the Frenchmen that Hieron doth with our countrymen the Almayns, and neither James nor John can do that thing in everywhere which they do in this or that place: which honouring of saints truly, except it be referred from the respect of corporal commodities or incommodities unto Christ, is not for a Christian man, insomuch that it is not far from the superstitiousness of them which in time past vowed the tenth part of their goods to Hercules, to the intent they might wax rich or a cock to Esculapius that they might be recovered of their diseases: or which sacrificed a bull to Neptunus that they might have good passage by sea and prosperous sailing.

A bull to Neptunus.

The names be changed, but verily they have both one end and intent.

Thou prayest for long life.

Thou prayest God that thou mayst not die too soon, or while thou art young, and prayest not rather that he would give to thee a good mind that in whatsoever place death should come upon thee he should not find thee unprepared. Thou thinkest not of changing thy life, and prayest God thou mightest not die. What prayest thou for then? Certainly that thou mightest sin as long as is possible. Thou desireth riches and cannot use riches, doest not thou then desire thine own confusion? Thou desirest health and canst not use health, is not now thy honouring of God dishonouring of God? In this place I am sure some of our holy men will cry out against me with open mouths, which think lucre to be to the honouring of God, and as the same Paul saith, with certain sweet benedictions deceive the minds of innocent persons while they obey and serve their belly and not Jesu Christ. Then will they say, forbiddest thou worship of saints in whom God is honoured?

They account the honouring of saints for absolute piety.

I verily dispraise not them so greatly which do those things with certain simple and childish superstition for lack of instruction or capacity of wit, as I do them which seeking their own advantage prayeth and magnifieth those things for most great and perfect holiness, which things peradventure be tolerable and may be suffered, and for their own profit and advantage cherish and maintain the ignorance of the people, which neither I myself do despise, but I cannot suffer that they should account things to be highest and most chief, which of themselves be neither good nor bad, and those things to be greatest and of most value which be smallest and of least value. I will praise it and be content that they desire health of Rochus whom they so greatly honour, if they consecrate it unto Christ. But I will praise it more if they would pray for nothing else but that with the hate of vices the love of virtues might be increased: and as touching to live or to die let them put it into the hands of God, and let them say with Paul, whether we live, whether we die, to God and at God's pleasure we live or die. It shall be a perfect thing if they desire to be dissolved from the body and to be with Christ: if they put their glory and joy in diseases or sickness, in loss or other damages of fortune, that they might be accounted worthy, which even in this world should be like or conformable unto their head. To do therefore such manner of things is not so much to be rebuked as it is perilous to abide still and cleave to them. I suffer infirmity and weakness, but with Paul I show a more excellent way. If thou shalt examine thy studies and all thy acts by this rule, and shalt not stand anywhere in mean things till thou come even unto Christ, thou shalt neither go out of thy way at any time, neither shalt do or suffer any thing in all thy life which shall not turn and be unto thee a matter of serving and honouring God.

CHAPTER 13

The fifth rule.

Perfect piety.

Let us add also the fifth rule as an aider unto this foresaid fourth rule, thou put perfect piety, that is to say the honouring of God, in this thing only, if thou shalt enforce alway from things visible, which almost every one be imperfect or else indifferent to ascend to things invisible after the division of a man above rehearsed. This precept is appertaining to the matter so necessarily, that whether it be through negligence or for lack of knowledge of it, the most part of Christian men instead of true honourers of God are but plain superstitious, and in all other things save in the name of Christian men only, vary not greatly from the superstition of the gentiles.

Two worlds.

Let us imagine therefore two worlds, the one intelligible the other visible. The intelligible which also we may call the angelical world, wherein God is with blessed minds. The visible world, the circle of heaven, the planets, and stars, with all that included is in them as the four elements. Then let us imagine man as a certain third world, partaker of both the other: of the visible world if thou behold his body, of the invisible world if thou consider his soul. In the visible world because we be but strangers we ought never rest, but what thing soever offereth itself to the sensible powers, that is to say to the five wits, that must we under a certain apt comparison or similitude apply to the angelical world, or else (which is most profitable) unto manners and to that part of man which is correspondent to the angelic world, that is to say to the soul of man.

The sun is the divine mind of God.

What this visible sun is in the visible world that is the divine mind, that is to say God, in the intelligible world, and in that part of thee which is of that same nature, that is to say in the spirit. Look what the moon is in the visible world, that in the invisible world is the congregation of angels and of blessed souls called the triumphant church, and that in thee is the spirit. Whatsoever heavens above worketh in the earth under them, that same doth God in the soul. The sun goeth down, ariseth, rageth in heat, is temperate, quickeneth, bringeth forth, maketh ripe, draweth to him, maketh subtle and thin, purgeth, hardeneth, mollifieth, illumineth, cleareth, cherisheth and comforteth. Therefore whatsoever thou beholdest in him, yea whatsoever thou seest in the gross part of this world of the elements which many have separated from the heavens above and circles of the firmament, in conclusion whatsoever thou considerest in the grosser part of thyself, accustom to apply it to God and to the invisible portion of thyself. So shall it come to pass that whatsoever thing shall anywhere offer itself to any of the sensible wits, that same thing shall be to thee an occasion of piety, to honour God.

The occasion of piety.

When it delighteth thy corporal eyes as oft as this visible sun spreadeth himself on the earth with new light, by and by call to remembrance how great the pleasure is of the inhabitants of heaven, unto whom the eternal sun ever springeth and ariseth, but never goeth down.

The glory of God appeared in the face of Moses, but we behold the glory of God in the face of Jesus Christ. The grace of God is called light, and night is compared to sin.

How great are the joys of that pure mind whereupon the light of God always shineth and casteth his beams. Thus by occasion of the visible creature pray with the words of Paul, that he which commanded light to shine out of darkness may shine in thy heart, to give light and knowledge of the glory of God in the face of Jesu Christ. Repeat such like places of holy scripture in which here and there the grace of the spirit of God is compared to light. The night seemeth tedious to thee and dark, think on a soul destitute of the light of God and dark with vices: yea and if thou canst perceive any darkness of night in thee, pray that the sun of justice may arise unto thee. This wise think and surely believe that things invisible which thou seest not are so excellent, so pure, so perfect, that things which be seen in comparison of them are scarce very shadows representing to the eyes a small and a thin similitude of them. Therefore in this outward corporal things whatsoever thy sensible wits either desire or abhor, it shall be a great deal meeter that the spirit love or hate the same thing in inward and incorporal things.

Whatsoever is perceived in the body that same is to be understood in the mind.

The goodly beauty of thy body pleaseth thine eyes, think then how honest a thing is the beauty of the soul. A deformed visage seemeth an unpleasant thing, remember how odious a thing is a mind defiled with vices: and of all other thine do likewise. For as the soul hath certain beauty wherewith one while she pleaseth God, and a deformity wherewith another while she pleaseth the devil, as like unto like: so hath she also her youth, her age, sickness, health, death, life, poverty, riches, joy, sorrow, war, peace, cold, heat, thirst, drink, hunger, meat. To conclude shortly, whatsoever is filthy in the body, that same is to be understood in the soul.

The nature of filthy pleasure.

Therefore in this thing resteth the journey to the spiritual and pure life, if by a little and little we shall accustom to withdraw ourself from these things which be not truly in very deed, but partly appear to be that they be not: as filthy and voluptuous pleasure, honour of this world, partly vanish away and haste to return to naught, and shall be ravished and carried to these things which indeed are eternal, immutable and pure: which thing Socrates saw full well, a philosopher not so much in tongue and words as in living and deeds, for he saith that so only shall the soul depart happily from her body at the last end, if aforehand she have diligently through true knowledge recorded and practised death, and also have long time before by the despising of things corporal, and by the contemplation and loving of things spiritual, used herself to be as it were in a manner absent from the body.

What is the cross of Christ.

Neither the cross unto which Christ calleth and exhorteth us, neither that death in which Paul willeth us to die with our head, as also the prophet saith: for thy sake we be slain all the day long, we be accounted as sheep appointed to be killed: neither that which the apostle writeth in other terms saying, seek those things that be above, not which be on the earth. Taste and have perceivance of things above, meaneth it any other thing than that we unto things corporal should be dull and made as though we were insensible and utterly without capacity? So that the less feeling we have in things of the body, so much the more sweetness we might find in things pertaining to the spirit, and might begin to live so much the trulier inwardly in the spirit, the less we lived outwardly in the body. In conclusion to speak more plainly, so much the less should move us things caduke and transitory, the more acquainted we were with things eternal. So much the less should we regard the shadows of things, the more we have begun to look up upon the very true things. This rule therefore must be had ever ready at hand, that we in no wise stand still anywhere in temporal things, but that we rise thence making as it were a step unto the love of spiritual things by matching the one with the other, or else in comparison of things which are invisible that we begin to despise that which is visible. The disease of thy body will be the easier if thou wouldest think it to be a remedy for thy soul. Thou shouldest care the less for the health of thy body if thou wouldest turn all thy care to defend and maintain the health of the mind. The death of the body putteth thee in fear, the death of the soul is much more to be feared. Thou abhorrest the poison which thou seest with thine eyes, because it bringeth mischief to the body: much more is the poison to be abhorred which slayeth the soul.

Cicuta is a poison herb.

Cicuta is poison of the body, but voluptuousness is much more and ready poison to the soul. Thou quakest and tremblest for fear, thy hair standeth upright, thou art speechless, thy spirits forsake thee and thou waxest pale, fearing lest the lightning which appeareth out of the clouds should smite thee, but how much more is it to be feared lest there should come on thee the invisible lightning of the wrath of God, which saith: Go ye cursed persons into eternal fire? The beauty of the body ravisheth thee, why rather lovest thou not fervently that fairness that is not seen? Translate thy love into that beauty that is perpetual, that is celestial, that is without corruption, and the discreetlier shalt thou love the caduke and transitory shape of the body.

The mystery in all things must be looked upon. Holy scripture is Silenus of Alcibiades. Silenus be images made with joints so that they may be opened, containing outward the similitude of a fool or an ape or such like trifles: and when they are opened suddenly appeareth some excellent or marvellous thing, unto such things Alcibiades, a noble man of Athens, compared the philosopher Socrates, for Socrates was so simple outward, and so excellent inward.

Thou prayest that thy field may be watered with rain lest it dry up, pray rather that God will vouchsafe to water thy mind lest it was barren from the fruit of virtues. Thou restorest and increasest again with great care the waste of thy money: the greatest care of all oughtest thou have to restore again the loss of the mind. Thou hast a respect long aforehand to age, lest anything should be lacking to thy body: and shouldest thou not provide that nothing be lacking to the mind? And this verily ought to be done in those things which daily meeteth our sensible wits, and as everything is of a diverse kind, even so diversely doth move us with hope, fear, love, hate, sorrow and joy. The same thing must be observed and kept in all manner of learning which include in themselves a plain sense and a mystery, even as they were made of a body and a soul, that the literal sense little regarded thou shouldest look chiefly to the mystery. Of which manner are the letters of all poets and philosophers, chiefly the followers of Plato. But most of all, holy scripture, which being in a manner like to Silenus of Alcibiades, under a rude and foolish covering include pure divine and godly things: for else if thou shalt read without the allegory the image of Adam formed of moist clay and the soul breathed into him, and Eve plucked out of the rib, how they were forbid the tree of knowledge of good and evil, the serpent enticing to eat, God walking at the air: when they knew they had sinned, how they hid themselves, the angel set at the doors with a turning sword lest after they were ejected, the way to them should be open to come again shortly: if thou shouldest read the whole history of the making of the world, if thou read (I say) superficially these things, seeking no further than appeareth outwardly, I cannot perceive what other great thing thou shalt do than if thou shouldest sing of the image of clay made by Prometheus, or of fire stolen from heaven by subtlety and put into the image to give life to the clay.

The fable of the giants. A great number of giants builded mountain upon mountain to pluck Jupiter out of heaven, but Jupiter undermined their mountains and slew them with lightning.

Yea peradventure a poet's fable in the allegory shall be read with somewhat more fruit than a narration of holy books, if thou rest in the rind or outer part. If when thou readest the fable of the giants, it warneth and putteth thee in remembrance that thou strive not with God and things more mighty than thou, or that thou oughtest to abstain from such studies as nature abhorreth, and that thou shouldest set thy mind unto these things (if so be they be honest) whereunto thou art most apt naturally. That thou tangle not thyself with matrimony, if chastity be more agreeable to thy manners.

Circe was a woman which by enchantment turned men to divers fashions of beasts with poisons or drenches.

Again that thou bind not thyself to chastity if thou seem more apt to marriage: for most commonly those things come evil to pass which thou provest against nature. If the cup of Circe teach that men with voluptuousness as with witchcraft fall out of their mind and be changed utterly from men unto beasts.

Tantalus.

If thirsty Tantalus teach thee that it is a very miserable thing for a man to sit gaping upon his riches heaped together and dare not use them.

Sisyphus.

The stone of Sisyphus, that ambition is laborious and miserable.

The labours of Hercules.

If the labours of Hercules putteth thee in remembrance that heaven must be obtained with honest labours and enforcements indefatigable: learnest thou not that thing in the fable which the philosophers teach and also divines, masters of good living?

Without allegory scripture is barren.

But if (without allegory) thou shalt read the infants wrestling in their mother's belly, the inheritance of the elder brother sold for a mess of pottage, the blessing of the father prevented and taken away by fraud, Goly smitten with the sling of David, and the hair of Sampson shaven: it is not of so great value as if thou shouldest read the feigning of some poet.

Many ungoodly things in scripture as they appear outward.

What difference is there whether thou read the book of Kings or of the Judges in the Old Testament, or else the history of Titus Livyus, so thou have respect to the allegory nere nother?

David committed adultery with Barsabe, and caused Urye her husband to be slain.

For in the one, that is to say Titus Livyus, be many things which would amend the common manners: in the other be some things, yea, ungoodly as they seem at the first looking on, which also if they be understood superficially should hurt good manners: as the theft of David, and adultery bought with homicide, how the daughters of Lot lay with their father by stealth, and conceived, and a thousand other like matters. Therefore the flesh of the scripture despised chiefly of the Old Testament, it shall be meet and convenient to search out the mystery of the spirit. Manna to thee shall have such taste as thou bringest with thee in thy mouth.

The mysteries must be handled with craft.

But in opening of mysteries thou mayst not follow the conjectures of thine own mind, but the rule must be known and a certain craft, which one Dionisius teacheth in a book entitled *De divinis nominibus,* that is to say, of the names of God: and Saint Augustyne in a certain work called *Doctrina Christiana,* that is to say, the doctrine of a Christian man.

Allegory.

The apostle Paul after Christ opened certain fountains of allegory, whom Origene followed, and in that part of divinity obtained doubtless the chief room and mastery.

Our divines.

But our divines either set naught by the allegory or handle it very dreamingly and unfruitfully: yet are they in subtlety of disputation equal or rather superiors to old divines. But in treating of this craft that is to say in pure, apt, and fruitful handling, the allegory not once to be compared with them, and that specially as I guess for two causes. The one, that the mystery can be but weak and barren that is not fortified with strength of eloquence, and tempered with certain sweetness of speaking, in which our elders were passing excellent, and we not once taste of it.

Arystotle only is read now-a-days.

Another cause is, for they content with Arystotle only, expel from schools the sect of Plato and Pictagoras, and yet Saint Augustyn preferreth these latter, not only because they have many sentences much agreeable to our religion, but also because the very manner of open and clear speech, which they use (as I have said before) full of allegories, draweth very nigh to the style of holy scripture.

Old divines with help of eloquence handled the allegories well favouredly.

No marvel therefore though they have more commodiously handled the allegories of the word of God, which with plenteous oration were able to increase and dilate to colour and garnish any manner thing never so barren, simple, or homely, which men also being most expert and cunning of all antiquity had practised and exercised long before in poets and books of Plato, that thing which they should do after in divine mysteries. I had liefer that thou shouldest read the commentaries of those men, for I would instruct and induce thee not unto contention of arguments, but rather unto a pure mind. But and if thou cannot attain the mystery, remember yet that some thing lieth hid which though it be not known, yet verily to have trust to obtain it shall be better than to rest in the letter which killeth. And that see thou do not only in the Old Testament, but also in the New.

The gospel hath her flesh and spirit.

The gospel hath her flesh, she hath also her spirit: for though the veil be pulled from the face of Moses, nevertheless yet unto this day Paul saith *per speculum in enigmate,* not the thing itself and clearly, but the image or similitude of the very thing as it were in a glass imperfectly and obscurely: and as Christ himself sayeth in his gospel of John, The flesh profiteth nothing at all, it is the spirit that giveth life. I verily would have been afraid to have said it profiteth not at all, it should have been enough to say the flesh profiteth somewhat, but much more the spirit: but now verity himself hath said it profiteth not at all. And so greatly it profiteth not, that after the mind of Paul it is but death, except it be referred to the spirit: yet at the least way in this thing is the flesh profitable for that she leadeth our infirmity as it were with certain graces or steps unto the spirit. The body without the spirit can have no being: the spirit of the body hath no need. Wherefore if after the doctrine of Christ the spirit be so great and excellent a thing, that he only giveth life: hither to this point must our journey be, that in all manner letters, in all our acts, we have respect to the spirit, and not to the flesh. And if a man would take heed, he should soon perceive that this thing only is it whereunto exhorteth us among the prophets specially Esaias, among the apostles Paul, which almost in every epistle playeth this part and crieth that we should have no confidence in the flesh, and that in the spirit is life, liberty, light, adoption: and those noble fruits so greatly to be desired which he numbereth.

Adoption is inheritance not by birth but by election.

The flesh everywhere he despiseth, condemneth, and counselleth from her. Take heed and thou shalt perceive that our master Christ doth the same thing here and there, whiles in pulling the ass out of the pit, in restoring the sight to the blind, in rubbing the ears of corn, in unwashen hands, in the feasts of sinners, in the parable of the pharisee and the publican, in fastings, in the carnal brethren, in the rejoicing of the Jews that they were the children of Abraham, in offering of gifts in the temple, in praying, in dilating of their phylacteries, and in many like places he despiseth the flesh of the law, and superstition of them which had liefer be Jews openly in the sight of man than privily in the sight of God.

Phylacteries were papers which the pharisees wore on high in their foreheads, having the ten commandments written in them.

And when he said to the woman of Samary, believe me that the hour shall come when ye shall honour the father neither in this mountain, neither in Jerusalem: but the hour shall be and now is when the very true worshippers shall worship the father in spirit and verity: for surely the father requireth such to honour him: the father is a spirit, and they which honour him must honour in spirit and verity. He signified the same thing indeed when at the marriage he turned the water of the cold and unsavoury letter into wine of the spirit, making drunk the spiritual souls, even unto the contempt and despising of their life. And lest thou shouldest think it a great thing that Christ despised these things which now I have rehearsed, yea he despised the eating of his own flesh and drinking of his own blood, except it were done spiritually. To whom thinkest thou spake he these things: The flesh profiteth nothing at all, it is the spirit that quickeneth and giveth life?

Saint John's gospel hanging at their necks.

Verily not to them which with Saint John's gospel or an *agnus dei* hanging about their necks think themselves sure from all manner of harm, and suppose that thing to be the very perfect religion of a Christian man: but to them to whom he opened the high mystery of eating his own body. If so great a thing be of no value, yea if it be pernicious or perilous: what cause is there wherefore we should have confidence in any other carnal things except the spirit be present? Thou peradventure sayest mass daily and livest at thine own pleasure, and art not once moved with thy neighbour's hurts, no, no more than if they pertained nothing at all to thee: thou art yet in the flesh of the sacrament: but and if while thou sayest, thou enforcest to be the very same thing which is signified by receiving that sacrament, that is to say, to be one spirit with the spirit of Christ, to be one body with the body of Christ, to be a quick member of the church: if thou love nothing but in Christ, if thou think all thy goods to be common to all men, if the incommodities of all men grieve thee even as thine own: then no doubt thou sayest mass with great fruit, and that because thou doest it spiritually. If thou perceive that thou art in a manner transfigured and changed into Christ, and that thou livest now less and less in thine own self, give thanks to the spirit which only quickeneth and giveth life. Many been wont to number how many masses they have been at every day, and having confidence in this thing as of most value (as though now they were no farther bound to Christ) as soon as they be departed out of the church return to their old manners again: that they embrace the flesh of piety, that is to say of pure life or service of God I dispraise not: that they there stop I praise not: let that be performed in thee which is there represented to thine eyes.

Let it be performed in thee that is represented in the mass.

There is represented to thee, the death of thy head: discuss thyself withinforth, and (as the saying is) in thy bosom, how nigh thou art dead to the world. For if thou be possessed wholly with wrath, ambition, covetousness, envy, yea though thou touch the altar, yet art thou far from mass. Christ was slain for thee, flee thou therefore these beasts, sacrifice thyself to him which for thy sake sacrificed himself to his father: if thou once think not on these things, and hast confidence in the other, God hateth thy carnal and gross religion. Thou art baptised, think not forthwith that thou art a Christian man, thy mind altogether favoureth nothing but this world: thou art in the sight of the world a Christian man, but secret and before God thou art more heathen than any heathen man. Why so? For thou hast the body of the sacrament and art without the spirit which only profiteth. Thy body is washed, what matter maketh that while thy mind remaineth still defiled and inquinate? Thy body is touched with salt, what then when thy mind is yet unsavoury? Thy body is anointed, but thy mind unanointed. But if thou be buried with Christ withinforth, and studiest to walk with him in the new life I then know thee for a Christian man.

Sprinkling of holy water.

Thou art sprinkled with holy water, what good doth that, if so be thou wipe not away the inward filth from thy mind?

Touching of relics.

Thou honourest saints and art joyous and glad to touch their relics, but thou despiseth the chief relics which they left behind them, that is to be understood the examples of pure living.

The true honouring of saints.

There is no honour more pleasant to Mary than if thou shouldest counterfeit her humility. No religion is more acceptable to saints or more appropriate than if thou wouldest labour to represent and follow their virtues. Wilt thou deserve the love and favour of Peter or of Paul, counterfeit the one's faith, and the other's charity, and thou shalt do a greater thing than if thou shouldest run to Rome x. times. Wilt thou worship Saint Fraunces singularly? Thou art high minded, thou art a great lover of money, thou art stubborn and self-willed, full of contention, wise in thine own opinion, give this to the saint, assuage thy mind, and by the example of Saint Fraunces be more sober, humble or meek, despise filthy lucre, and be desirous of riches of the mind, put away striving and debates with thy neighbours and with goodness overcome evil. The saint setteth more by this honour than if thou shouldest set before him a thousand burning tapers. Thou thinkest it a special thing to be put in thy grave wrapped in the cowl or habit of Saint Fraunces? Trust me, like vesture shall profit thee nothing at all when thou art dead, if thy living and manners be found unlike when thou were alive. And though the sure example of all true virtue and pure life, shewing how thou shouldest honour God in everything, is set of Christ most commodiously in such manner, that in no wise thou canst be deceived.

Let us counterfeit Christ in his saints.

Nevertheless if the worshipping of Christ in his saints delight thee so greatly, see that thou counterfeit Christ in his saints, and for the honour of every saint look thou put away all vices, vice by vice, so that thou sacrifice to every saint singularly some one vice singularly, or else study to embrace and counterfeit some one singular virtue in every saint, such as thou perceivest to have reigned most chiefly in every saint, singularly of them which thou worshippest so specially. If this shall come to pass, then will I not reprove those things which be done outwardly. Thou hast in great reverence the ashes of Paul, I damn it not, if thy religion be perfect in every point, but if thou have in reverence the dead ashes or powder of his body, and settest no store by his quick image yet speaking, and as it were breathing, which remaineth in his doctrine: is not thy religion preposterous and out of order and according to the common proverb, the cart set before the horse?

Let us honour the quick image of Paul.

Honourest thou the bones of Paul hid in the shrine, and honourest thou not the mind of Paul hid in his writings? Magnifiest thou a piece of his carcase shining through a glass, and regardest not thou the whole mind of Paul shining through his letters? Thou worshippest the ashes in whose presence now and then the deformities and diseases of bodies be taken away, why rather honourest thou not his doctrine, wherewith the deformities and diseases of souls are cured and remedied? Let the unfaithful marvel at these miracles and signs for whom they be wrought: but thou that art a faithful man embrace his books, that as thou doubtest not, but that God can do all things, even so thou mightest learn to love him above all things.

The very image of Christ is expressly painted in the gospel.

Thou honourest the image of the bodily countenance of Christ formed in stone or tree, or else portrayed with colours: with much greater reverence is to be honoured the image of his mind, which by workmanship of the Holy Ghost is figured and expressed in the gospels.

Apelles was the most cunning painter that ever was.

Never any Apelles so expressly fashioned with pencil the proportions and figure of the body as in the oration and doctrine of every man appeareth the image of the mind, namely in Christ, which when he was very simplicity and pure verity, no discord, no unlike thing at all could be between the spirit and chief pattern of his divine mind and the image of his doctrine and learning from thence deduct and derivate, as nothing is more like the father of heaven than his son, which is the word, the wisdom and knowledge of the father, springing forth of his most secret heart: so is nothing more like unto Christ than the word, the doctrine and teaching of Christ, given forth out of the privy parts of his most holy breast: and ponderest thou not this image? Honourest it not? Lookest thou not substantially with devout eyes upon it? Embracest it not in thy heart? Hast thou of thy lord and master relics so holy, so full of virtue and strength, and setting them at nought, seekest thou things much more alienate, stranger and farther off? Thou beholdest a coat or a sudorye, that is said to have been Christ's, astonied thereat as though thy wits were rapt: and art thou in a dream or a slumber when thou readest the divine oracles or answers of Christ?

The honouring of the cross.

Thou believest it to be a great thing, yea a greater than the greatest that thou possessest at home a little piece of the cross: but that is nothing to be compared to this, if thou bear shrined in thy heart the mystery of the cross. Or else if such things make a man religious and devout, what can be more religious than the Jews, of which very many (though they were never so wicked) yet with their eyes saw Jesus Christ living bodily, heard him with their ears, with their hands handled him. What is more happy than Judas, which with his mouth kissed the divine mouth of Christ? So much doth the flesh without the spirit profit nothing at all, that it should not once have profited the holy virgin his mother that she of her own flesh begat him, except she in her spirit had conceived his spirit also: this is a very great thing, but hear a greater.

The very apostles as long as Christ was present wavered in the faith.

The apostles enjoyed the corporal presence and fellowship of Christ (readest thou not) how weak, how childish they were, how gross and without capacity. Who would desire any other thing unto the most perfect health of his soul, than so long familiarity and conversation together with him that was both God and man? Yet after so many miracles shewed, after the doctrine of his own mouth taught and declared to them, after sure and evident tokens that he was risen again, did he not at the last hour when he should be received up into heaven cast in their teeth their unstability in the faith? What was then the cause? Verily the flesh of Christ did let: and thence it is that he saith: Except I go away, the Holy Ghost will not come, it is expedient for you that I depart. The corporal presence of Christ is unprofitable unto health. And dare we in any corporal thing beside that put perfect piety, that is to say, the love and honour of God? Paul saw Christ in his humanity, what supposest thou to be a greater thing than that? Yet setteth he nought by it, saying, though (saith he) we have known Christ carnally, now we do not so. Why knew he him not carnally? For he had profited and ascended unto more perfect gifts of the spirit. I use peradventure more words in disputing these things than should be meet for him which giveth rules: nevertheless I do it the more diligently (and not without a great cause) for that in very deed I do perceive this error to be the common pestilence of all christendom: which bringeth and occasioneth, yea for this causeth, the greater mischief: forasmuch as in semblance and appearance it is next unto godly love or holiness. For there are no vices more perilous than they which counterfeit virtue: for besides this that good men may lightly fall into them: none are with more difficulty cured, because the common people unlearned thinketh our religion to be violate when such things are rebuked: let incontinent all the world cry out against me, let certain preachers, such as are wont to cry out in their pulpits, bark which with right good will sing these things inwardly in their own stomachs looking verily not unto Christ, but unto their own advantage, through whose either superstition without learning, or feigned holiness, I am compelled oftentimes to shew and declare that I in no wise rebuke or check the corporal ceremonies of Christian men and devout minds of simple persons: namely in such things that are approved by authority of the church. For they are now and then partly signs of piety and partly helpers thereunto.

The use of ceremonies.

And because they are somewhat necessary to young infants in Christ, till they wax older and grow up unto a perfect man: therefore it is not meet they should be disdained of them which are perfect, lest by their example the weak person should take harm. That thou doest I approve, so the end be not amiss. Moreover if thou stop not there whence thou oughtest to ascend to things more near to health: but to worship Christ with visible things instead of invisible and in them to put the highest point of religion, and for them to stand in thine own conceit, to condemn other men, to set thy whole mind upon them, and also to die in them, and to speak shortly that thou be withdrawn from Christ with the very same things which be ordained for the intent only that they should help unto Christ: this is verily to depart from the law of the gospel which is spiritual, and fall into certain superstition of ceremonies like unto the Jews: which thing peradventure is of no less jeopardy than if without such superstition thou shouldest be infect with great and manifest vices of the mind: this is forsooth the more deadly disease.

The commonality is turned to the confidence of ceremonies.

Be it, but the other is worse to be cured. How much everywhere sweateth the chief defender of the spirit Paul to call away the Jews from the confidence of deeds and ceremonies, and to promote them unto those things which are spiritual: and now I see the commonality of Christian men to be returned hither again. But what said I the commonality? That might be yet suffered had not this error invaded and caught a great part both of priests and doctors: and to be short, the flocks of them almost throughout which profess in title and habit a spiritual life. If they which should be the very salt be unsavoury: wherewithal shall other be seasoned?

Superstitious persons are touched.

I am ashamed to rehearse with what superstition the most part of them observe certain ceremonies of men's inventions, yet not institute for such purpose. How odiously they require them of other men: what confidence without mistrust they have in them: how indifferently they judge other men: how earnestly they defend them. To these their deeds they think heaven to be due, in which if they be once rooted at once they think themselves Pauls and Antonys.

Paul and Antony were hermits of passing holy conversation.

They begin, O good Lord, with what gravity, with how great authority, to correct other men's lives, after the rule of fools and indiscreet persons (as saith Terence), so that they think nothing well done but that they do themselves.

The defenders of ceremonies.

But for all that when they be waxen old sires in their manner of living thou shalt see that as yet they savour or taste of Christ nothing at all: but to be beastly swimming in certain churlish vices in their living and pastime froward, and scarce can suffer and forbear their own self: in charity cold: in wrath fervent: in hate as tough as white leather: in their tongues venemous and full of poison: in exercising and putting forth of their malice conquerors and not able to be overcome: ready to strive for every little trifle: and so far from the perfection of Christ, that they be not once endued with these common virtues, which the very ethnics or heathen men have learned, either by reason given to them of nature, or by use of living, or by the precepts of philosophers. Thou shalt also see them in spiritual things clean without capacity, fierce that no man shall know how to entreat or handle them, full of strife and contention, greedy upon voluptuous pleasure, at the word of God ready to spue, kind to no man, misdeeming other men, flattering their own selves. It is come to this point now at last with the labours of so many years, that thou shouldest be of all men the worst, and yet think thyself the best: that instead of a Christian man thou shouldest be but a plain Jew, observing only unfruitful traditions and ceremonies of the inventions of man, that thou shouldest have thy glory and joy, not in secret before God, but openly afore the world. But and if thou hast walked in the spirit and not in the flesh: where be the fruits of the spirit? Where is charity? Where is that cheerfulness or joyous mirth of a pure mind? Where is tranquillity and peace towards all men? Where is patience? Where is perseverance of soft mind, wherewith thou lookest day by day continually for the amendment even of thine enemies? where is courtesy or gentleness, where is freeness of heart, where is meekness, fidelity, discretion, measure or soberness, temperance and chastity? where is the image of Christ in thy manners? I am, sayst thou, no keeper of whores, no thief, no violator of holy things, I keep my profession.

The hypocrisy of religious persons.

But what other thing is this to say than I am not like other men, extortioners, adulterers, yea and I fast twice in a week? I had liefer have a publican humble and lowly asking mercy than this kind of pharisees rehearsing their good deeds. But what is thy profession? is it I pray thee that thou shouldest not perform that thing thou promised long ago when thou wert baptised, which was that thou wouldest be a Christian man, that is to say, a spiritual person, and not a carnal Jew, which for the traditions of man shouldest transgress the commandments of God? Is not the life of a Christian man spiritual? Hear Paul speaking to the Romans. No damnation is to them that are grafted in Christ Jesu, which walk not carnally or after the flesh: for the law of the spirit of life in Christ Jesu hath delivered me from the law of sin and death: for that which the law weakened by reason of the flesh could not perform or make good, that same, God made good, sending his Son in the similitude of flesh prone to sin, and of sin condemned sin in the flesh, that the justifying of the law might be fulfilled in us which walk not after the flesh but after the spirit: for they that be in the flesh, be wise in things pertaining to the flesh: but they which be in the spirit perceive those things that pertain to the spirit: for wisdom of the flesh is death, and wisdom of the spirit is life and peace: for the wisdom of the flesh is an enemy to God because she is not obedient to the law of God, nor yet can be.

The exposition and mind of some clerks.

They that be in the flesh, they cannot please God: what could be spoken more largely? What more plainly? nevertheless many men subtle and crafty to flatter or favour their own vices: but prone and ready without advisement to check other men's, think these things to pertain to themselves nothing at all: and that Paul spake of walking carnally or after the flesh, they refer to adulterers only and keepers of queans: that he spake of wisdom of the flesh which is enemy to God, they turned it to them which have learned humanity, or that they call secular sciences: in either other they set up their crests, and clap their hands for joy, both that they neither be adulterers, and in all sciences stark fools.

The flesh and the spirit after Paul.

Moreover to live in the spirit they dream to be none other thing than to do as they themselves do: which persons if they would as diligently observe the tongue of Paul as they maliciously despise Tully's, they should soon perceive that the apostle calleth the flesh that thing that is visible and the spirit that thing that is invisible: for he teacheth everywhere that things visible ought to serve to things invisible: and not contrarywise invisible things to serve things visible. Thou of a preposterous order appliest Christ to those things which were meet to be applied unto Christ: requirest thou of me record that this word flesh pertaineth not only to filthy and superstitious lust of the body? Hold and understand that thing which the said apostle (doing that same which he in all places doth) writeth to the Colocenses. Let no man mislead you for the nonce in the humility and religion of angels which things he never saw, walking in vain, inflate with the imagination of the flesh, and not holding the head, that is to say Christ, of whom all the body by couples and joints ministered up and compact, groweth into the increase of God. And lest thou shouldest doubt any thing that he spake of them which having confidence in certain corporal ceremonies bark against the spiritual purposes of other men: take heed what followeth: If ye be dead with Christ, *ab elementis hujus mundi*, from traditions, ceremonies and inventions of men: why have ye yet such decrees among you, as though ye lived unto the world? And anon after calling us from the same things, saith: If ye be risen up again with Christ, seek those things that are above where Christ sitteth on the right hand of God. Be expert and wise in those things that be above, and not on the earth. Moreover giving precepts of the spiritual life, what exhorteth he us to do at last? whether that we should use such or such ceremonies: whether that we should be this or that wise arrayed, that we should live with this or that meats, that we should say customably any certain number of psalms? he made mention of no such things. What then?

Mortify the members on the earth.

Mortify (said he) your members which be on the earth, fornication, uncleanness, bodily lust, evil concupiscence, and avarice which is the service of idols: and a little after, that now put from you all such things, wrath, indignation, malice: and again, spoiling yourself of the old man with all his acts putting on you the new man which is renewed in knowledge of God after the image of him which made him. But who is the old man?

The old man.

Verily Adam, he that was made of the earth, whose conversation is in earth, not in heaven. By the earth understand whatsoever is visible, and therefore temporal and transitory. Who is that new man? Verily the celestial man that descended from heaven, Christ. And by heaven understand whatsoever is invisible, and therefore eternal and everlasting. At the last, lest we should be minded to purchase the favour of God after the manner of the Jews with certain observances, as ceremonies magical, he teacheth that our deeds are pleasant and allowed of God, so long as they are referred unto charity, and also spring thereof, saying: Above all these things keep charity the bond of perfection, and let the peace of God rejoice as a victor in your hearts, in which also ye be called in one body. I will give thee a more plain token and evident probation that this word flesh signifieth not the lust of the body only. Paul nameth often the flesh, often the spirit, writing to a certain people named Galatas, which he called not only from lust of the body to chaste living but enforceth to withdraw them from the sect of the Jews and confidence of work into which they were induced by false apostles. In this place therefore numbering the deeds of the flesh, mark what vices he rehearseth. The deeds of the flesh (saith he) be manifest, which are fornication, uncleanness, to be shameless, lechery, worshipping of idols, witchcraft, privy hate, discord, otherwise called contention or strife, emulation that may be called indignation or disdain, ire otherwise called wrath, scolding dissension, that is to say, diversity in maintaining of opinions, sects, or maintaining of quarrels, envy, homicide, drunkenness, excess in eating, and such like. And not long after he saith: If we live in the spirit, let us walk in the spirit.

Vainglory is a pestilence contrary to the spirit.

After that as declaring and uttering a pestilence contrary to the spirit, he addeth: Let us not be made desirous of vainglory, provoking one the other, and envying one another. The tree is known by the fruit. That thou omittest not watch, fasting, silence, orisons, and such other like observances, I pass not thereon, I will not believe that thou art in the spirit except I may see the fruits of the spirit. Why may I not affirm thee to be in the flesh when after almost a hundred years exercise of these things, yet in thee I find the deeds of the flesh, enviousness more than is in any woman, continual wrath and fierceness as in a man of war, scolding, lust and pleasure insatiable, malicious cursing, backbiting with tongue more venomous than the poison of a serpent, an high mind, stubbornness, light of thy promise, vanity, feigning, flattering? Thou judgest thy brother in his meat, drink or raiment, but Paul judgeth thee of thy deeds. Doth that separate thee from worldly and carnal men, that thou art in lighter causes verily but yet with the same vices infected? is he more filthy, which, for his inheritance taken from him or it came to his hands, for his daughter defiled, for hurt done to his father, for some office, for his prince's favour: conceiveth wrath, hatred, emulation (which may be called indignation or disdain), than thou which (I am ashamed to tell) for how little a trifle, yea for nothing, doest all the same things much more maliciously, the lighter occasion to sin lighteneth not, but aggravateth the sin, neither it maketh matter in how little or great a thing thou sin, so it be done with like affection: and yet is there difference verily: for so much the grievouser doth every man trespass, the less the occasion is wherewith he is pulled away from honesty.

Monks.

I speak not now of those monks or religious persons whose manners even the whole world abhorreth, but of them whom the common people honoureth not as men, but as angels, which selfsame notwithstanding ought not to be displeased with these words, which rebuketh the vices and noteth not the persons: but and if they be good men, let them also be glad to be warned of whatsoever man it be, in those things which pertaineth to health: neither it is unknown to me that amongst them are very many which holpen with learning and wit have tasted the mysteries of the spirit, (but as Livius saith) it fortuneth almost every where, that the greater part overcometh the better. Notwithstanding (if it be lawful to confess the truth) see we not all the most strait kind of monks to put the chief point of religion either in ceremonies or in a certain manner or form of saying, that they call their divine service, or in a labour of the body, which monks if a man should examine and appose of spiritual things, he should scarce find any at all that walked not in the flesh.

Preposterous is setting behind that that should be before.

And hereof cometh this so great infirmity of minds, trembling for fear where is no fear, and therein surety and careless where is most peril of all: hereof cometh the perpetual infancy in Christ (to speak no more grievously) that the preposterous esteemers of things make most of such things which by themselves are of no value: those set at nought which only are sufficient, ever living under tutors or schoolmasters, ever in bondage, never advancing ourselves up to the liberty of the spirit, never growing up to the large stature of charity: when Paul crieth to a certain people called Galathas, Stand fast, be not ye locked again under the yoke of bondage. And in another place the law was our tutor or schoolmaster in Christ, that of faith we should be justified. But seeing that faith is come, now we be no more under a tutor or schoolmaster: for every one of you (saith he) is the very son of God through faith which he hath in Christ Jesu. And not much after he saith, And we also when we were little ones were in service and bondage under the ceremonies and law of this world. But when the time was fully expired, God sent his Son made of a woman, made under the law, to redeem them which were under the law, that we by adoption should be his sons. And for because ye be the sons of God, God hath sent the spirit of his Son into your hearts, crying, *Abba, pater* (as a man would say, Dada, father). And so is he not now a servant but a son to God. And again in another place: Brethren ye be called into liberty, let not your liberty be an occasion unto you to live in the flesh, but in charity of the spirit serve one another: for all the law is fulfilled in one saying: Love thy neighbour as thyself, but and if ye bite and eat one the other, take heed lest ye be consumed one of another. And again, to the Romans: Ye have not received the spirit of bondage again in fear, but the spirit that maketh you the sons of God by adoption, in whom we cry, Dada, father. Unto the same also pertaineth that he writeth to Timothy, saying: Exercise thyself under the deeds of piety: for bodily exercise is good but for a small thing, piety is good unto all manner things. And to the Corynthes: God is a spirit, and where the spirit is, there is liberty. But why rehearse I one or two places, when Paul is altogether at this point, that the flesh which is full of contention should be despised, and that he might settle us in the spirit which is the author of charity and liberty. For these companions be ever inseparable, on the one side, the flesh, bondage, unquietness, contention or strife: and on the other side, the spirit, peace, love, liberty. These things everywhere Paul mingleth with other sayings. And seek we a better master of our religion, namely when all divine scripture agreeth to him? This was the greatest commandment in the law of Moses. This Christ iterateth and finisheth in the gospel: and for this cause chiefly was he born: for this cause died he, to teach us not to counterfeit the Jews, but to love.

To love is the greatest commandment.

After the last supper made the even before his passion, how diligently, how tenderly, and how affectionately gave he charge to his disciples, not of meat, not of drink, but of charity to be kept one towards another: what other thing teacheth he, what other thing desireth his disciple John, than that we love one another?

Christ last of all warneth us of charity.

Paul everywhere (as I have said) commendeth charity, but specially writing unto the Corynthes he preferreth charity both before miracles and prophecies, and also before the tongues of angels. And say not thou by and by that charity is, to be oft at the church, to crouch down before the images of saints, to light tapers or wax candles, to say many lady psalters or Saint Katheryne's knots. God hath no need of these things.

What is true charity.

Paul calleth charity to edify thy neighbor, to count that we all be members of one body, to think that we all are but one in Christ, to rejoice in God of thy neighbour's wealth even as thou doest of thine own, to remedy his incommodities or losses as thine own. If any brother err or go out of the right way, to warn him, to admonish him, to tell him his fault meekly, soberly and courteously: to teach the ignorant: to lift up him that is fallen: to comfort and courage him that is in heaviness: to help him that laboureth: to succour the needy. In conclusion to refer all riches and substance, all thy study, all thy cares to this point, that thou in Christ shouldest help as much as thy power extendeth to.

The life of religious men is grievous and tedious.

That as he neither was born for himself, nor lived to his own pleasure, neither died for himself but dedicate himself wholly to our profits: even so should we apply ourselves, and await upon the commodities of our brethren, and not our own: which thing if it were used, nothing should be either more pleasant or else easy than the life of religious persons, which we see now clean contrary, grievous almost everywhere and laborious, and also full of superstition, like unto the Jews, neither pure from any vices of the lay people, and in many sundry things much more defiled, which kind of men Saint Augustyne (of whom many glory and rejoice as of the author and founder of their living) if he now might live again, certainly would not once know, and would cry out, saying that he would approve nothing less than this kind of life, and that he had instituted an order and manner of living, not after the superstition of the Jews, but after the rule of the apostles.

Saint Augustyne would not know monks and canons of his own religion if he were now alive.

But I hear even now what certain men (which are somewhat well advised) will answer unto me.

How far forth we ought to cleave to the small things.

A man must take heed in little and small things, lest a little and a little he should fall into greater vices, I hear it right well, and I allow the saying, nevertheless thou oughtest to take heed a great deal more that thou so cleave not to these little and small things that thou shouldest fall clean from the most chief and greatest things. There is the jeopardy more evident, but here more grievous. So flee Scylla that thou fall not into Charybdis.

Scylla and Charybdis. Look what they mean at the end of the first chapter.

To observe these little things is wholesome verily: but to cleave utterly unto them is very jeopardous. Paul forbiddeth not thee to use the law and ceremonies, but he will not him to be bound to the law and ceremonies which is free in Christ: he condemneth not the law of deeds, if a man use it lawfully: without these things peradventure thou shalt not be a Christian man, but they make thee not a Christian man, they will help unto piety and godliness, even so yet if thou use them for that purpose.

Corporal things help to piety.

But and if thou shalt begin to enjoy them, to put thy trust and confidence in them, at once they utterly destroy all the living of a Christian man.

Vyctyma was the sacrifice of a beast whereof he that offered did eat part, and part went to the use of the priests. The caul, the kidneys and the fat about them was burned to God; that same sacrifice for certain considerations is also called hostia.

The apostle setteth nought by the deeds of Abraham, which to have been very perfect no man doubteth: and hast thou confidence in thine? God disdaineth certain sacrifices called victim, the sabbotes and certain holy days called Neomenye of his people the Jews, of which things he himself was author and commander, and darest thou compare thine own observances with the precepts of the law of God? yet hear God ready to spue at them and aggrieved with them. For what intent (saith he) offer ye to me the multitude of victims, I am full. As for holocausts of wethers, tallow or inward suet and fat of beasts, blood of calves, of lambs and goats, I would not have, when ye come before my presence, who hath required these things of your hands that ye might walk in my houses?

Holocausts, that is the whole beast sacrificed to God, no man having part thereof.

Offer ye no more sacrifice in vain, your incense is abomination to me, I will not suffer any more the feast of the Neomenye and sabbath day, with other feast days.

Sabbot day was every seventh day as our Sunday. Neomenye were holidays at the new of the moon. Kalendas that same that neomenyes be.

The companies of you are infected with iniquity, my soul hath hated your kalendas and your solemn feasts. These things be grievous unto me, I was even sick to abide them. And when ye put forth your hands, I will turn mine eyes from you, when ye rehearse the observances and manners of holy feasts and sacrifice: moreover the multiplying of prayers, noteth he not them as though he pointed them with his finger, which measure their religion with a certain number of psalms and prayers, which they call daily service.

Esayas.

Mark also another thing, how marvellously the facundyous prophet expresseth heaping together the disdain or indignation of God: so that he now could suffer neither with ears, neither eyes. What things (I beseech thee)? verily those things which he himself had ordained to be kept so religiously, which also were observed so reverently so many years of holy kings and prophets. And these things abhorreth he as yet in the carnal law. And trustest thou in ceremonies made at home in thine own house, now in the law of the spirit? God in another place biddeth the same prophet to cry incessantly and to put out his breast after the manner of a trump, as in an earnest matter and worthy to be rebuked sharply, and such a matter as unneth could be obtained of these men but with much ado. Me (saith he) they seek from day to day, and know they well my ways, as a people that hath done justice, and hath not forsaken the judgment of their God. They ask me for the judgments of justice, and desire to draw nigh to God: why have we fasted (say they) and thou hast not looked upon us and meeked our souls, and thou wouldest not know it: lo, in the day of your fast (answereth the prophet) your own will is found in you, and ye seek out all your debtors, lo, unto strife and contention ye fast, and ye smite with your fist cruelly, fast ye not as ye have fasted unto this day, that your cry might be heard on high. Is this the fast that I have chosen, that a man should vex and trouble himself for one day, either that a man should bow down his head as a hook or circle, and to straw underneath him sackcloth and ashes? wilt thou call this a fast or a day acceptable unto God? But what shall we say this to be? doth God condemn that thing, which he himself commanded? Nay, forsooth. What then? but to cleave and stick fast in the flesh of the law, and to have confidence of a thing of nothing, that is it verily which he hateth deadly. Therefore he sheweth that he would have added in either place. Be ye washed (said he) and made clean, take away your evil cogitations and thoughts out of my sight. When thou hearest the evil thoughts rehearsed, toucheth he not evidently the spirit and the inward man? The eyes of God seeth not outward, but in secret, neither he judgeth after the sight of the eyes, neither rebuketh after the hearing of the ears. God knoweth not the foolish virgins, smooth and gay outward, empty of good works inward: he knoweth not them which say with lips, Master, master.

The use of spiritual life.

Moreover he putteth us in remembrance that the use of the spiritual life standeth not so greatly in ceremonies as in the charity of thy neighbour. Seek (saith he) judgment or justice, succour him that is oppressed, give true judgment and right to him that is fatherless and motherless or friendless, defend the widow. Such like things did he knit to the other place, where he speaketh of fasting.

Esayas.

Is not this rather (saith he) that fast I have chosen: loose or cancel cruel obligations, unbind the burdens which make them stoop to the ground that bear them: let them that be bruised go free and break asunder all burden: break thy bread to hungry. The needy and them which hath no place of habitation, lead in to thy house. When thou seest a naked man clothe him, and despise not thine own flesh. What shall a Christian man do then? Shall he despise the commandments of the church? Shall he set at naught the honest traditions of forefathers?

The traditions of our elders.

Shall he condemn godly and holy customs? Nay, if he be weak and as a beginner he shall observe them as things necessary, but and if he be strong and perfect so much the rather shall he observe them, lest with his knowledge he should hurt his brother which is yet weak, lest he also should kill him for whom Christ died: we may not omit these things, but of necessity we must do other things. Corporal deeds be not condemned, but spiritual are preferred. This visible honouring of God is not condemned, but God is not pleased saving with invisible piety and service. God is a spirit and is moved and stirred with invisible sacrifice. It is a great shame for Christian men not to know that thing which a certain poet being a gentile knew right well, which giving a precept of due serving God, saith: If God be a mind as scripture sheweth us, see that thou honour him chiefly with a pure mind. Let us not despise the author being either an heathen man or without degree of school, the sentence becometh yea a right great divine: and (as I very well have perceived) is likewise understood of few as it is read of many. The intellection of the sentence verily is this, like rejoysen with like. Thou thinkest God to be moved greatly with an ox killed and sacrificed, or with the vapour or smoke of frankincense, as though he were a body. God is a mind, and verily mind most pure, most subtle and perfect, therefore ought he to be honoured most chiefly with a pure mind. Thou thinkest that a taper lighted is sacrifice, but a sacrifice to God (saith David) is a woeful or sorrowful spirit.

Inward things be represented by inward things.

And though he hath despised the blood of goats and calves, yet will he not despise a heart contrite and humble. If thou do that thing which is given to the eyes of men, much rather take heed that thing not to be away which the eyes of God require. Thy body is covered with a cowl or habit: what is that to the purpose if thy mind bear a secular vesture? If thy outer man be cloaked in a cloak white as snow, let the vestments of thy inner man be white as snow also, agreeable to the same. Thou keepest silence outward, much more procure that thy mind be quiet within. In the visible temple thou bowest down the knees of thy body: that is nothing worthy if in the temple of thy breast thou stand upright against God. Thou honourest the tree of the cross, much more follow the mystery of the cross. Thou keepest the fasting day and abstainest from those things which defile not a man: and why abstainest thou not from filthy talking, which polluteth thine own conscience and other men's also? Meat is withdrawn from the body, but why glutteth thy soul herself with cods of beans, pease, and such like which are meat meet for swine? Thou makest the church of stone gay with goodly ornaments, thou honourest holy places: what is it to the purpose if the temple of thy heart, whose walls the prophet Ezechyell bored through, be profaned or polluted with the abominations of Egypt?

The sabbath day the day of rest.

Thou keepest the sabbath day outward, and within all things be unquiet through the rage and tumbling of vices together. Thy body committeth no adultery, but thou art covetous: now is thy mind a fornicator. Thou singest or prayest with thy bodily tongue, but take heed within what thy mind saith. With thy mouth thou blessest, and with thy heart thou cursest. In thy body thou art closed within a strait cell, and in thy cogitation thou wanderest throughout all the world. Thou hearest the word of God with thy corporal ears, rather hear it within. What saith the prophet? Except ye hear within, your soul shall mourn and weep. Yea, and what readest thou in the gospel? that when they see they should not see, and when they hear they should not hear. And again the prophet saith, with your ear ye shall hear and ye shall not perceive. Blessed be they therefore which hear the word of God within. Happy are they to whom God speaketh within, and their souls shall be saved. This ear to incline is commanded, that noble daughter of the king, whose beauty and goodliness is altogether within in golden hems. Finally what availeth it if thou do not those evil things outward, which with affection thou desirest and covetest inward? What availeth it to do good deeds outward, unto which within are committed things clean contrary? Is it so great a thing if thou go to Hierusalem in thy body, when within thine own self is both Sodome, Egypt, and Babylon?

Pilgrimages unto holy places.

It is no great thing to have trodden the steps of Christ with thy bodily heels, but it is a great thing to follow the steps of Christ in affection. If it be a very great thing to have touched the sepulchre of Christ, shall it not be also a very great thing to have expressed the mystery of his burying?

Confession.

Thou accusest and utterest thy sins to a priest, which is a man: take heed how thou accusest and utterest them before God, for to accuse them afore him is to hate them inwardly. Thou believest perchance all thy sins and offences to be washed away at once with a little paper or parchment sealed with wax, with a little money or images of wax offered, with a little pilgrimage going. Thou art utterly deceived and clean out of the way. The wound is received inwardly, the medicine therefore must needs be laid to within: thine affection is corrupt, thou hast loved that which was worthy of hate, and hated that which ought to have been beloved. Sweet was to thee sour, and bitter was sweet. I regard not what thou show outward: but and if clean contrary thou shalt begin to hate, to fly, to abhor that which thou lately lovedst, if that wax sweet to thine appetite which lately had the taste of gall: of this wise at the last I perceive and take a token of health. Magdalayne loved much, and many sins were forgiven her. The more thou lovest Christ, the more thou shalt hate vices: for the hate of sin followeth the love of piety as the shadow followeth the body. I had liefer have thee hate once thy vicious manners within and in deed, than to defy them before a priest ten times in word.

In all business the spirit is within.

Therefore (as I have rehearsed certain things for love of example) in the whole spectacle and sight of this visible world, in the old law, in the new law, in all the commandments of the church, finally in thyself and in all business appertaining to man, withoutforth is there a certain flesh, and within a spirit.

What things follow charity.

In which things if we shall not make a preposterous order, neither in things which are seen shall put very great confidence, but even as they do help to better things, and shall always have respect to the spirit and to things of charity: then shall we wax not heavy as men in sorrow and pain (as those men be) not feeble, ever children (as it is a proverb) not beastly and dry bones (as saith the prophet) without life, drowsy and forgetful as men diseased of the lethargy, not dull having no quickness, not brawlers and scolders, not envious and whisperers or backbiters, but excellent in Christ, large in charity, strong and stable both in prosperity and adversity, looking beside small things and enforcing up to things of most profit, full of mirth, full also of knowledge: which knowledge whosoever refuseth them doth that noble lord of all knowledge refuse.

Prosperity and adversity.

For verily ignorance or lack of experience, whom for the most part accompanieth dulness of learning, and that gentlewoman whom the Greeks call Philancia, that is to say, love of thyself, only bringeth to pass (as Esayas saith) that we put confidence in things of nothing, and speak vanities, that we conceive labour and bring forth iniquity, and that we always be fearful and vile bond servants unto the ceremonies of the Jews. Of which manner persons Paul speaking saith, I bear them record that the zeal of God they have, but not after knowledge. But what knew they not?

Christ is the end of the law.

Verily that the end of the law is Christ, and Christ verily is a spirit, he is also charity. But Esayas more plainly describeth the miserable and unprofitable bondage of these men in the flesh: Therefore, saith he, my people be led in captivity because they had no knowledge, and the nobles of them perished for hunger, and the multitude of them dried away for thirst. It is no marvel that the common people be servants to the law and principles of this world, as they which are unlearned, neither have wisdom more than they borrow of other men's heads: it is more to be marvelled that they which are as chief of Christ's religion, in the same captivity perish for hunger, and wither away for thirst. Why perish they for hunger? Because they have not learned of Christ to break barley loaves, they only lick round about the rough and sharp cod or husk, they suck out no marrow or sweet liquor. And why wither they so away for thirst? For because they have not learned of Moses to fetch water out of the spiritual rock of stone, neither have drunk of the rivers of the water of life which floweth, issueth, or springeth out of the belly of Christ: and that was spoken verily of the spirit, not of the flesh.

By the wings of love we must fly up to the spirit.

Thou therefore my brother, lest with sorrowful labours thou shouldest not much prevail, but that with mean exercise mightest shortly wax big in Christ and lusty, diligently embrace this rule, and creep not always on the ground with the unclean beasts, but always sustained with those wings which Plato believeth to spring ever afresh, through the heat of love in the mind of men. Lift up thyself as it were with certain steps of the ladder of Jacob, from the body to the spirit, from the visible world unto the invisible, from the letter to the mystery, from things sensible to things intelligible, from things gross and compound unto things single and pure.

Inaccessible is to understand that no man can attain. Incogitable that cannot be comprehended with man's reason.

Whosoever after this manner shall approach and draw near to the Lord, the Lord of his part shall again approach and draw nigh to him. And if thou for thy part shalt endeavour to arise out of the darkness and troubles of the sensual powers, he will come against thee pleasantly and for thy profit, out of his light inaccessible, and out of that noble silence incogitable: in which not only all rage of sensual powers, but also similitudes or imaginations of all the intelligible powers doth cease and keep silence.

CHAPTER 14

The sixth rule.

And forasmuch as in sudden writing, one thing calleth another to remembrance, I will now add the sixth rule, which is in a manner of kindred to them that go before: a rule for all men as necessary unto health as it is of few regarded.

Thou must vary from the common people.
The example of piety.

That rule is thus, that the mind of him which enforceth and laboureth to Christward, vary as much as is possible both from the deeds and also opinions of the common lay people, and that the example of piety be not set of any other save of Christ only: for he is the only chief patron, the only and chief example or form of living, from whom whosoever wrieth one inch or nail breadth, goeth besides the right path and roameth out of the way. Wherefore Plato with gravity, verily as he doth many things in his books of the governance of a city or commonwealth, denieth any man to be able to defend virtue constantly which hath not instructed his mind with sure and undoubted opinions of filthiness and of honesty. But how much more perilous is it if false opinions of the things which pertain to health should sink into the deep bottom of the mind. For that consideration therefore he thinketh that this thing should be cared for and looked upon chiefly, that the governors themselves whom it behoveth to lack all manner of uncleanliness, grave in their own minds very good opinions of things to be ensued and eschewed, that is to say of good and evil, of vices and of virtues, and that they have them very assured, all doubt laid apart as certain laws very holy and goodly: for whatsoever thing cleaveth in the mind surely rooted with steadfast belief, that, every man declareth in his manners and conversation.

The bringing up of Christian men's children.

Therefore the chief care of Christian men ought to be applied to this point, that their children straightway from the cradle, amongst the very flatterings of the nurses, whiles the father and mother kiss them, may receive and suck under the hands of them which are learned opinions and persuasions meet and worthy of Christ: because that nothing either sinketh deeper or cleaveth faster in the mind than that which (as Fabyus saith) in the young and tender years is poured in. Let be afar off from the ears of little bodies wanton songs of love, which Christian men sing at home and wheresoever they ride or go, much more filthy than ever the common people of the heathen men would suffer to be had in use. Let them not hear their mother wail and wring her hands for a little loss of worldly goods, nor for the loss of her sister let them hear her cry out, alas that ever she was born, saying that she is but a wretch, a woman lost or cast away, left alone, desolate and destitute. Let them not hear their father rebuking and upbraiding him of cowardice which hath not recompensed injury or wrong with double: neither yet lauding them which have gathered together great abundance of worldly substance, by whatsoever manner it were. The disposition of man is frail and prone to vices, he catcheth mischievous example at once: none otherwise than tow catcheth fire if it be put to.

Virtue is the knowledge of things to be avoided and of things to be desired and loved.

How be it this selfsame thing is to be done in every age, that all the errors of the lay people might be plucked out again from the mind by the hard roots, and in their places might be planted wholesome opinions, and so might be roborate that with no violence they could be shaken or plucked asunder: which thing whosoever hath done shall easily and without business by his own accord follow virtue, and shall account them that do otherwise worthy to be lamented and pitied, and not to be counterfeited or followed. Unto this thing pertaineth that not indiscreet saying of Socrates (though it were rebuked of Aristotle), that virtue was nothing else but the knowledge of things to be ensued and followed, and of things to be eschewed or fled: not but that Socrates saw the difference between knowledge of honesty and the love of the same. But as Demosthenes answered, pronunciation to be the first, the second, and also the third point of eloquence, signifying that to be the chief part, in so much that he thought eloquence to rest altogether in that thing only: in likewise Socrates, disputing with Prothagoras, proveth by arguments, knowledge in all virtue to bear such room, that vices can no other whence proceed than of false opinions.

Sin springeth of false opinions.

For certainly, brother, both he that loveth Christ, and he also that loveth voluptuousness, money, false honour, doth follow that thing which is to either of them sweet, good, and beautiful, but the one slideth through ignorance, instead of a sweet thing embracing a thing out of measure sour, fleeing as a sour thing that which is sweetest of all: also following that thing for good and for lucre which is naught else but damage and loss, and fearing that thing for loss, which is chief gains or advantage: and judging that thing to be fair which is foul, and weening or trowing that to be shameful which only is glorious and praiseful. In conclusion, if a man were surely and inwardly brought in belief, and if also it were digested in to the substance of his mind as meat in to the substance of the body, that only virtue were best, most sweet, most fair, most honest, most profitable. And on the other side filthiness only to be an evil thing, a painful torment or punishment, a foul thing, shameful, full of damage or loss: and did measure these things not by the opinion of the common people, but by the very nature of the things, it could not be (such persuasion or belief enduring) that he should stick fast and cleave long time in evil things.

The common people is the worst author or institutor of living.

For now long ago the common people is found to be the most mischievous author or captain both of living and also of judgment: neither was the world ever in so good state and condition, but that the worst hath pleased the most part. Beware lest thou this wise think: no man is there that doth not this, mine elders before me have walked in these steps, of this opinion is such a man, so great a philosopher, so great a divine: this is the custom and manner of living of kings, this wise live great men, this do both bishops and popes, these verily are no common people. Let not these great names move thee one inch. I measure or judge not the common or rascal sort by the room, estate, or degree, but by the mind and stomach.

Plato willeth that we should imagine a certain number of men to be bound with their heads upright so that they could not once stir, before them a wall, a cave at their backs higher than their heads, without that a fire and that all things should come to and fro between the fire and the cave's mouth, that the shadows of all things might appear upon the wall before them, so should they see nothing but shadows, so be the ignorant and unlearned people bound with the bounds of affections that they never see the truth with eyes of reason.

Whosoever in the famous cave of Plato bound with the bonds of their own affections wonder at the vain images and shadows of things instead of very true things, they be the common people. Should he not do preposterously or out of order if a man would go about to try not the stone by the ruler or square, but the ruler by the stone? And were it not much more unreasonable if a man would go about to bow and turn, not the manners of men to Christ, but Christ to the living of men? Think it not therefore well or aright because that great men or because that the most men do it, but this wise only shall it be well and right whatsoever is done, if it agree to the rule of Christ: yea and therefore ought a thing to be suspected because it pleaseth the most part. It is a small flock and ever shall be, to whom is pleasant the simplicity or plainness, the poverty, the verity of Christ. It is a small flock verily but a blessed, as unto whom doubtless is due only the kingdom of heaven. Strait is the way of virtue and of very few trodden on, but none other leadeth to life. To conclude, whether doth a wise builder fetch his example of the most common and used or of the best work? Painters set afore them none but the best tables or patrons of imagery. Our example is Christ, in whom only be all rules of blessed living, him may we counterfeit without exception. But in good and virtuous men it shall be meet that thou call to example everything, so far forth as it shall agree with the first example of Christ.

The flock of good men is but small.

As touching the common sort of Christian men think thus, that they were never more corrupt, no not amongst the gentiles, as appertaining to the opinions of their manners.

The common people of Christian men be most corrupt.

Moreover as touching their faith what opinions they have advise them. This surely is doubtless and to be abidden by, faith without manners worthy of faith prevaileth nothing, insomuch also that it groweth to a heap of damnation. Search the histories of antiquity, to them compare the manners that be now-a-days.

The manner of the world now-a-days.

When was virtue and true honesty more despised? When was so had in price riches gotten not regarded whence? In what world at any time was truer that saying of Horacius: verily that lady money giveth a wife with dowry, credence, friendship, nobleness, noble kin and also beauty.

Horace the poet.

And again this saying of the same Horace, nobleness and virtue, except a man have good withal, is viler than a rush or a straw. Who readeth not in good earnest that biting mock of the same poet: Oh citizens, citizens, first seek money, after seek virtue. When was riot or excess more immoderate than now? When was adultery and all other kinds of unchaste living either more appert in the sight of every man, or more unpunished, or else less had in shame, rebuke or abomination? While princes favour their own vices, in other men suffering them unpunished, and every man accounteth that most comely and beautiful to be done whatsoever is used and taken up among courtiers. To whom seemeth not poverty extreme evil, and uttermost shame and rebuke?

The liberty of old time.

In time past against keepers of queans, filthy nigards, glorious or gorgeous persons, lovers and regarders of money, were cast in the teeth with rebukeful and slanderous scoffings and jestings, yea with authority. And also in comedies, tragedies, and other common plays of the gentiles a great clapping of hands and a shout was made for joy of the lay people, when vices were craftily and properly rebuked and checked: at the which same vices now-a-days being evil praised there is made a shout and clapping of hands for joy even of the nobles and estates of Christian men.

When the ambassadors of king Philip had offered to Phosyon great gifts and had exhorted him to receive them saying, though you may spare them well enough yet shall they be necessary for your children to whom it shall be hard to obtain to come to such honour as you are in, Phosyon answered, if my children shall be like me this same possession shall find them which hath brought me to see great honour, if they should be unlike me, I will not that their riot be nourished and augmented at my cost.

The Athenes in their common house appointed for disguisings and interludes could not forbear nor suffer a jester in playing a certain tragedy of Euripides, to sing the words of a certain covetous man which preferred money only before all other commodities and pleasure of man's life: and they would plainly have clapped out of the play, yea and violently cast out of the house the player with all the fable, except the poet by and by arising up had desired them to tarry a little and behold to what point that so great a wonderer at money should come. How many examples be there in the histories of gentiles, of them which of the commonwealth well governed and ministered brought nothing in to their poor household but an honest opinion or reputation: which set more by fidelity than money, by chastity than by life, whom neither prosperity could make proud, wild and wanton, neither adversity could overcome and make heavy hearted, which regarded honest jeopardies and dangers before voluptuousness and pleasures, which contented only with the conscience of pure life, desired neither honours, neither riches, nor any other commodities of fortune.

Fabricius was a nobleman of Rome whom no man could make to possess riches or receive gifts or to use craft or fraud against his enemies in time of mortal war. Camyllus was so constant of mind that no fortune could move him nor no injury could make him unkind to the commonwealth. Brute slew his own sons because they conspired against the commonwealth. Pyctagoras was the author of chaste living. Socrates said that he knew well himself to be unlearned and he never laughed and yet was he merry. The continence of Saint Augustyne.

And to overhyp and make no rehearsal of the holiness of Phocion, of poverty of Fabricius more excellent than riches, of the strong and courageous mind of Camyllus, of the strait and indifferent justice of Brutus, of the chastity of Pithagoras, of the temperance of Socrates, of the sound and constant virtue of Cato: and a thousand most goodly beams of all sorts of virtues which are read everywhere in the histories of the Lacedemones, of the Perces, of the Athenes, and of the Romanes, to our great shame verily. Holy Aurelius Augustyne, as he of himself witnesseth in the commentaries of his own confessions, long time before he put Christ on him despised money, counted honours for naught, was not moved with glory, praise, or fame, and to voluptuousness kept the bridle so strait that he then a young man was content with one little wench, to whom he kept also promise and faith of marriage. Such examples among courtiers, among men of the church: I will also say amongst religious persons, shall not a man lightly find; or else if any such shall be, by and by he shall be pointed, wondered, or mocked at as it were an ass among apes: he shall be called with one voice of all men a doting fool, a gross head, an hypocrite in nothing expert, melancholy mad, and shall not be judged to be a man. So we Christian men honour the doctrine of Christ: so counterfeit we it that every where now-a-days nothing is accounted more foolish, more vile, more to be ashamed of, than to be a Christian man indeed, with all the mind and heart: as though that either Christ in vain had been conversant in earth, or that christendom were some other thing now than in time past, or as it indifferently pertained not to all men. I will therefore that thou from these men vary with all thy mind, and esteem the value of everything by the communion or fellowship of Christ only.

To be a very Christian man is accounted everywhere a very vile thing.

Who thinketh it not everywhere to be an excellent thing, and to be numbered among the chief of all good things, if a man descend of a worshipful stock and of honourable ancestors, which thing they call nobleness?

The vanity of noblemen.

Let it not move thee one whit when thou hearest the wise men of this world, men of sadness endued with great authority, so earnestly disputing of the degrees of their genealogies or lineage, having their forehead and upper brows drawn together with very great gravity, as it were a matter of marvellous difficulty, yea and with great enforcement bringing forth plain trifles.

Democrytus laughed at whatsoever thing was done in the life of mortal men: it seemed to him so foolish a thing.

Nor let it move thee when thou seest other so high minded for the noble acts of their grandfathers or great grandfathers, that think other in comparison of themselves scarce to be men: but thou laughing at the error of these men after the manner of Democrytus shalt count (as true it is indeed) that the only and most perfect nobleness is to be regenerate in Christ, and to be grafted and planted in the body of him, to be one body and one spirit with God. Let other men be kings' sons: to thee let it be greatest honour that can be, that thou art called, and art so indeed, the son of God.

The chiefest nobleness is to be the son of God.

Let them stand in their own conceits, because they are daily conversant in great princes' courts: choose thou rather to be with David, vile abject in the house of God. Take heed what manner fellows Christ chooseth, feeble persons, fools, vile as touching this world. In Adam we are all born of low degree. In Christ we are all one thing, neither high nor low of degree one more than another. Very nobleness is to despise this vain nobleness: very nobleness is to be servant to Christ. Think them to be thine ancestors whose virtues thou both lovest and counterfeitest. Also hark what the true esteemer of nobleness said in the gospel against the Jews which boasted themselves to be of the generation of Abraham: a man verily not excellent only, not rich only, not the conqueror of kings only, but also for his divine virtues lauded of God himself. Who would not think this to be a noble thing and worthy whereof a man might rejoice? Hark yet what they heard: ye are (said Christ) of your father the devil, and the deeds of your father ye do.

You may see here how Paul esteemeth noble blood.

And hear also Paul, how he esteemeth gentle blood, according to his master's rule: Not all they (saith he) which be of circumcision of Israel be Israelites, neither all they that be of the seed of Abraham be the sons of Abraham. It is a low degree and shameful to serve filthiness, and to have no kindred with Christ which acknowledgeth kindred with no man but with such as fulfilleth the will of his Father in heaven. He is with much shame a bastard which hath the devil to his father, and verily whosoever doth the deeds of the devil hath the devil to his father, except Christ lied: but the truth cannot lie.

The highest degree that can be is to be the son and heir of God, the brother and co-heir with Christ: what their badges and cognisances mean let them take heed.

The badges of true nobleness.

The badges of Christ be common to all men, and the most honourable, which be the cross, the crown of thorn, the nails, the spear, the signs or tokens which Paul rejoiceth to bear in his body. Of nobleness therefore thou seest how much otherwise I would have thee to judge and think than the lay people imagine. Who calleth not him blessed, rich, and happy among the common people which hath heaped together at home a great deal of gold?

Rich men be not blessed.

But judge thou him to be blessed enough, yea that he only is blessed which possesseth Christ, very felicity, and of all things the best. Judge him happy which hath bought the noble and precious margaryte of pure mind with the loss either of all his goods or his body also, which hath found the treasure of wisdom preciouser than all riches, which to be made rich hath bought of Christ, that is most rich, gold purified and proved with fire. What things then be these which the common people wondereth at, as gold, precious stones, livelihood? in a wrong name they be riches, in the true name they be very thorns, which choke the seed of the word of God, according to the parable of the Gospel.

What is riches?

They be packs or fardels with which whosoever be laden neither can follow poor Christ by strait way, neither enter by the low door into the kingdom of heaven.

Mydas and Cresus were two rich kings.

Think not thyself better by one hair if thou shouldest pass in riches either Mydas or Cresus, but think thyself more bound, more tangled, more laden. He hath abundantly enough that can utterly despise such things. He is provided for sufficiently to whom Christ promised nothing should be lacking. He shall not be an hungered to whose mouth manna of the word of God seemeth pleasant. He shall not be naked which hath put Christ upon him.

There is no damage in the loss of riches.

Think this only to be a loss, as oft as any thing of godliness is minished, and anything of vices is increased. Think it a great lucre or advantage when thy mind through increase of virtue is waxed better. Think thou lackest nothing as long as thou possessest him in whom is all things. But what is this which wretches call pleasure? Surely it is nothing less than that it is called. What is it then?

Ayax in his madness hanged up two great swine supposing the one to have been Agamenon the other Ulyxes his two mortal enemies, then with much laughter he raged against them casting many injuries in their teeth, but when he was come to his wits again he killed himself for shame and sorrow, so because of voluptuous pleasure followeth mischief, it may be well called the laughter of Ayax. Melosii Siberte were people which lived delicately. Epycure put felicity in voluptuousness. That is sweet which savoureth to a whole man.

Pure madness it is, and plainly (as Greeks be wont to say) the laughter of Ayax, sweet poison, pleasant mischief. True and only pleasure is the inward joy of a pure conscience. The most noble and daintiest dish that can be is the study of holy scripture. The most delectable songs be the psalms indited of the Holy Ghost. The most pleasant fellowship is the communion of all saints. The highest dainties of all is the fruition and enjoying of the very truth. Purge now thy eyes, purge thy ears, purge thy mouth, and Christ shall begin to wax sweet and pleasant to thee which tasted once sourly: yea, if Milesii Sibarite, if all incontinent rioters and epicureans, shortly if the university of imaginers and devisers of pleasures should heap together all their flattering subtleties and dainty dishes, in comparison of him only they shall seem to provoke ye to spue. That is not by and by sweet which is savoury, but that which is savoury to a whole man: if water have the taste of wine to him which burneth in a hot fever, no man will call that a pleasure but a disease. Thou art deceived if thou believe not that the very tears be much more pleasant to devout and holy men than be to wicked men laughings, mockings, jestings or scoffings: if thou also believe not fasting to be sweeter to the one than to the other plovers, quails, pheasants, partridges, pike, trout, porpoise, or the fresh sturgeon. And the moderate boards of the one appointed with herbs and fruits to be much more delicate than the costly and disdainful feasts of the other. Finally the true pleasure is, for the love of Christ not to be once moved with false apparent pleasures. Behold now how much the world abuseth the names of love and hate.

Foolish love.

When a foolish young man is clear out of his wit and mad for a wench's sake, that the common people calleth love, and yet is there no verier hate in the world. True love even with his own loss desireth to see unto another man's profit. Whereunto looketh he save unto his own pleasure, therefore he loveth not her but himself: yet loveth he not himself verily, for no man can love another except he love himself first, yea and except he love himself aright. No man can hate any man at all except he first hate himself. Nevertheless sometime to love well is to hate well, and to hate well is to love well. Whosoever therefore for his little pleasure (as he supposeth it) layeth await and goeth about to beguile a maiden with flattering and gifts, with fair promises to pluck from her the best thing she hath, that is to wit her perfectness, her chastity, her simplicity, her innocency, her good mind, and her good name, whether seemeth this man to hate or to love? Certainly there is no hate more cruel than is this hate, when the foolish father and mother favour the vices of their children: the common saying is, how tenderly love they their children.

Tenderness towards their children.

But I pray thee how cruelly hate they their children which (while they follow their own affections) regard not at all the wealth of their children. What other wisheth to us our most hateful enemy the devil, than that we here sinning unpunished should fall into eternal punishment? They call him an easy master and a merciful prince, which at certain grievous offences either wink or favour them, that the more unpunished men sin, the more boldly and at large they might sin. But what other thing threateneth God by his prophet to them whom he judgeth unworthy of his mercy? I will not (saith he) visit their daughters when they commit fornication, nor their daughters-in-law when they commit adultery. Unto David what promised he? I will (saith he) with a rod look upon their iniquities, and with whips their sins, but I will not take my mercy from them. Thou seest how all things are renewed in Christ, and how the names of things are changed. Whosoever love himself otherwise than well, hateth himself deadly. Whosoever be evil merciful toward himself is a tyrant most cruel. To care well is not to regard. To hurt well is to do good. To destroy well is to save. Thou shalt care well for thyself if thou shalt despise the desires of the flesh, if in good manner thou shalt rage against vices, thou shalt do to the man a good turn. If thou shalt kill the sinner thou shalt save the man. If thou shalt destroy that man hath made, thou shalt restore that God hath made. Come off now and let us go further: What thinketh the error of the people, power, wickedness, manhood, and cowardness to be? Call they not him mighty which can lightly hurt whom him list? though it be a very odious power to be able to hurt, for in that are they resembled to noisome worms and scorpions, and to the devil himself, that is to wit in doing harm. Only God is mighty indeed, which neither can hurt if he would, neither yet would if he could, for his nature is to do good. But this mighty fellow, how doth he I beseech thee hurt a man? He shall take away thy money? He shall beat thy body? He shall rob thee of thy life? If he do it to him that feareth God well, he hath done a good deed instead of an evil: but and if he have done it to an evil man, the one hath ministered an occasion verily, but the other hath hurt himself: for no man is hurt but of himself. No man goeth about to hurt another except the same man hath much more grievously hurt himself aforehand. Thou enforcest to hurt me in my money or goods. Now hast thou through the loss of charity hurt thyself most grievously. Thou canst not fasten a wound in me, but if thou have received a wound much more grievous. Thou canst not take from me the life of my body, unless thou have slain thine own soul before. But Paul, which to do wrong was a man very weak and feeble, to suffer wrong most valiant and strong, rejoiceth that he could do all thing in Christ. They call him everywhere manly and bold which being fierce and of impotent mind, for the least displeasure that can be rageth, seetheth, or boileth in wrath, and acquitteth a shrewd word with a shrewd word, a check with a check, one evil turn with another. On the other side whosoever when he hath received wrong maketh nothing ado, but dissimuleth as no such thing were done, him they call a coward, a bastard, heartless, meet for nothing: yea but what is more contrary to the greatness of the mind than with a little word to be put aside from the quiet and constancy of the spirit, and to be so unable to set at naught another man's foolishness, that thou shouldest think thyself to be no man except thou shouldest overcome one shrewd turn with another. But how much more manful is it with an excellent and large mind to be able to despise all manner injuries, and moreover for an evil deed to recompense a good?

A bold man and a strong indeed.

I would not call him a bold man which durst jeopard on his enemy, which scale castle or town walls, which (his life not regarded) putteth himself in all manner jeopardies, a thing common almost to all warriors, but whosoever could overcome his own mind, whosoever could will them good which doth him harm, pray for them which curse him.

A bold man and a strong indeed.

To this man is due the proper name of a bold and strong man and of excellent mind. Let us also discuss another thing, what the world calleth praise, rebuke, and shame.

True praise.

Thou art praised, for what cause and of whom? If for filthy things and of filthy persons, this verily is a false praise and a true rebuke. Thou art dispraised, thou art mocked or laughed at, for what cause and of whom? For godliness and innocency, and that of evil men: this is not a rebuke, no, there is no truer praise. Be it that all the world reprove, refuse, and disallow it, yet can it not be but glorious and of great praise that Christ approveth. And though whatsoever is in the world agree, consent, and allow, crying with a shout that is a noble deed, yet can it not be but shameful that displeaseth God.

Wisdom of the world.

They call wisdom everywhere, to get good stoutly, when it is gotten to maintain it lustily, and to provide long before for the time to come: for so we hear them say everywhere and in good earnest of them which in short time get substance somewhat abundantly, he is a thrifty man, ware and wise, circumspect and provident. Thus saith the world which is both a liar himself and also his father. But what saith verity: Fool, saith he, I will set again this night thy soul from thee. He had filled his barns with corn, he had stuffed his store-houses with provision of all victuals, and had laid up at home abundantly of money enough: he thought nothing was to be done more. Thus had he done, not because he intended as a needy keeper to sit abroad on his riches heaped together, as the poets feign the dragon to have kept the golden fleece (which thing men do almost everywhere), but he intended to have spent joyously, and yet doth the gospel call this man a fool.

While we gape at shadows we lose the very things, as the dog of Ysope which while he gaped at the shadow lost his bone in the water.

For what is more foolish, what is more gross imagination or more fondness than to gape at the shadows, and lose the very things, a thing which we be wont to laugh at in the famous dog of Ysope: and in the manners of Christian men is it not more to be laughed at, or rather to be wept at? He may be counted a rude and unexpert merchant that knew not this saying of Terence: To refuse money at a season is sometime a great advantage, or whosoever would receive a little advantage in hand when he knew great loss should follow. How much more foolishness and unadvisedness is it to make provision with so great care for this present life which is but a shadow, every hour ready to fail: namely when God (if we believe the gospel) will minister all thing necessary for this life, if we have confidence in him, and for the life to come to make no provision at all, which we must lead alway full of misery and wretchedness, if provision be not made now aforehand with great diligence.

To hearken for tidings out of all countries is rebuked.

Hear another error: they call him peerless, politic and in all things expert, which hearkening for all manner tidings knoweth what is done throughout all the world, what is the chance of merchandise, what the king of England intendeth, what new thing is done at Rome, what is chanced in France, how the Danes and the Sytes live, what matters great princes have in council: to make an end shortly, whoever can babble with all kinds of men of all manner business, him they say to be wise. But what can be farther from the thought of a wise man, or near to the nature of a fool, than to search for those things which be done afar off and pertain to thee nothing at all, and not so much as once verily to think on those things which are done in thine own breast and pertain to thee only. Thou tellest me of the trouble and business of England, tell me rather what trouble maketh in thy breast, wrath, envy, bodily lust, ambition, how nigh these be brought into subjection, what hope is of victory, how much of this host is put to flight, how reason is decked or appointed. In these things if thou shalt be watching and have a quick ear and also an eye, if thou shalt smell, if thou shalt be circumspect, I will call thee politic and peerless: and that thing which the world is wont to cast against us, I will hurl again at him: he is not wise at all, which is not wise for his own profit. After this manner if thou shalt examine all the cares of mortal men, their joys, hopes, fears, studies, their minds or judgments, thou shalt find all thing full of error while they call good evil, and evil good, while they make sweet sour and sour sweet, make light darkness and darkness light. And this sort of men is the most part by a great deal. Notwithstanding thou must even at once both defy them and set no store of them, lest thou shouldest be minded to be like them: and also pity them so that thou wouldest fain have them like unto thee. And to use the words of Saint Augustyn: then is it meet both to weep for them which are worthy to be laughed at, and to laugh at them which are worthy to be wept for. Be not in evil things conformable to this world but be reformed in the new wit, that thou mayst approve not those things which men wonder at, but what is the will of God, which is good, well pleasing and perfect. Thou art very nigh jeopardy and no doubt fallest suddenly from the true way if thou shalt begin to look about thee what the most part of men do, and to hearken what they think or imagine: but suffer thou, which art the child of life and of light also, that dead men bury their dead bodies: and let the blind captains of blind men go away together into the ditch: see thou once move not the eyes of thy heart any whither from the first patron and chief example of Christ.

Eurypus is a certain place in the sea where the flood changeth seven times in a day and as oft a night so that no ship can sail against the stream.

Thou shalt not go out of the way, if thou follow the guiding of verity.

Bragmanyes were people of a certain isle in India with whom all things were common and they lived perfectly despising riches, possessions and all worldly things.

Thou shalt not stumble in darkness, if thou walk after light, the light shining before thee: if thou shalt separate coloured good things, from good things indeed: and evil things indeed from apparent evil things: thou shalt abhor and not counterfeit the blindness of the common people, raging and chafing themselves after the manner of the ebbing and flowing of the sea at the most vain illusions and worldly things, with certain caresses of affections of wrath, envy, love, hate, hope, fear, joy, sorrow, raging more unquietly than any Eurypus.

Cinikes be the followers of Dyogenes the philosopher which churlishly checketh the vices of men.

The Bragmanyes, Cynikes, Stoikes be wont to defend their principles stiffly with tooth and nail: and even the whole world repugning, all men crying and darkening against them, yet hold they stiffly that thing whereunto they once have given sure credence. Be thou bold likewise to fasten surely in thy mind the decrees of thy sect. Be bold without mistrust, and with all that thou canst, make to follow the mind of thine author, departing from all contrary opinions and sects.

CHAPTER 15

Here follow opinions meet for a Christian man.

Let this excellent learning and paradoxes of the true Christian faith be sure and stedfast with thee, that no Christian man may think that he is born for himself: neither ought to have the mind to live to himself: but whatsoever he hath, whatsoever he is, that altogether let him ascribe not to himself, but unto God the author thereof, and of whom it came, all his goods let him think to be common to all men.

A Christian man is not born for himself either to follow his own pleasure.

The charity of a Christian man knoweth no property: let him love good men in Christ, evil men for Christ's sake, which so loved us first when we were yet his enemies, that he bestowed himself on us altogether for our redemption: let him embrace the one because they be good: the other nevertheless to make them good: he shall hate no man at all, no more verily than a faithful physician hateth a sick man: let him be an enemy only unto vices: the greater the disease is, the greater cure will pure charity put thereto: he is an adulterer, he hath committed sacrilege, he is a Turk: let a Christian man defy the adulterer, not the man: let him despise the committer of sacrilege, not the man: let him kill the Turk, not the man: let him find the means that the evil man perish such as he hath made himself to be, but let the man be saved whom God made: let him will well, wish well, and do well, to all men unfeignedly: neither hurt them which have deserved it, but do good to them which have not deserved it; let him be glad of all men's commodities as well as of his own, and also be sorry for all men's harms none otherwise than for his own.

He must defy and abhor the vices, but not the man.

For verily this is that which the apostle commandeth: to weep with them that weep, to joy with them that joy, yea let him rather take another man's harm grievouser than his own: and of his brother's wealth be gladder than of his own. It is not a Christian man's part to think on this wise: what have I to do with this fellow, I know not whether he be black or white, he is unknown to me, he is a stranger to me, he never did aught for me, he hath hurt me sometime, but did me never good. Think none of these things: remember only for what deserving can those things which Christ hath done for thee, which would his kindness done to thee, should be recompensed, not in himself, but in thy neighbour. Only see of what things he hath need, and what thou art able to do for him. Think this thing only, he is my brother in our Lord, co-heir in Christ, a member of the same body, redeemed with one blood, a fellow in the common faith, called unto the very same grace and felicity of the life to come, even as the apostle said, one body and one spirit as ye be called in one hope of your calling, one lord and one faith, one baptism, one God, and father of all which is above all and everywhere, and in all us. How can he be a stranger to whom thou art coupled with so manifold bonds of unity? Among the gentiles let those circumstances of rhetoricians be of no little value and weight, either unto benevolence or unto malevolence, he is a citizen of the same city, he is of alliance, he is my cousin, he is my familiar friend, he is my father's friend, he hath well deserved, he is kind, born of an honest stock, rich or otherwise. In Christ all these things either be nothing, or after the mind of Paul be all one, and the very selfsame thing: let this be ever present before thine eyes and let this suffice thee, he is my flesh, he is my brother in Christ. Whatsoever is bestowed upon any member reboundeth it not to all the body, and from thence into the head? We all be members each one of another, members cleaving together make a body. The head of the body is Jesu Christ, the head of Christ is God. It is done to thee it is done to everyone, it is done to Christ it is done to God: whatsoever is done to any one member whichsoever it be, whether it be well done or evil: All these things are one, God, Christ, the body, and the members. That saying hath no place conveniently among Christian men, like with like. And the other saying, diversity is mother of hate: for unto what purpose pertain words of dissension where so great unity is, it savoureth not of Christian faith that commonly a courtier to a town dweller: one of the country to an inhabiter of the city: a man of high degree, to another of low degree: an officer, to him that is officeless: the rich to the poor: a man of honour, to a vile person: the mighty to the weak: the Italyen to the Germayne: the Frenssheman to the Englysshman: the Englysshe to the Scotte: the grammarian to the divine: the logician to the grammarian: the physician to the man of law: the learned to the unlearned: the eloquent to him that is not facounde and lacketh utterance: the single to the married: the young to the old; the clerk to the layman: the priest to the monk:

the Carmelytes to the Jacobytes: and that (lest I rehearse all diversities) in a very trifle unlike to unlike, is somewhat partial and unkind: where is charity which loveth even his enemy: when the surname changed, when the colour of the vesture a little altered, when the girdle or the shoe and like fantasies of men make me hated unto thee?

Charity is not in them which hate another man because his vesture or garment is a little altered and changed.

Why rather leave we not these childish trifles, and accustom to have before our eyes that which pertaineth to the very thing: whereof Paul warneth us in many places, that all we in Christ our head be members of one body, endued with life by one spirit (if so be we live in him) so that we should neither envy the happier members, and should gladly succour and aid the weak members: that we might perceive that we ourselves have received a good turn, when we have done any benefit to our neighbour: and that we ourselves be hurt, when hurt is done to our brother: and that we might understand how no man ought to study privately for himself, but every man for his own part should bestow in common that thing which he hath received of God, that all things might redound and rebound thither again, from whence they sprung, that is to wit, from the head.

Let every man bestow in common whatsoever he received of God.

This verily is the thing which Paul writeth to the Corynthes, saying, As the body is one and hath many members, and all the members of the body though they be many, yet be they but one body: even so likewise is Christ, for in one spirit we be all baptised to make one body, whether we be Jews or gentiles, whether we be bond or free, and all we have drunk of one spirit, for the body (saith Paul) is not one member but many: if the foot shall say, I am not the hand, I am not of the body: is he therefore not of the body? If the ear shall say, I am not the eye, I am not of the body: is he therefore not of the body? If all the body should be the eye, where is then the hearing: if all the body were the hearing, where then should be the smelling? But now God hath put the members every one of them in the body, as it pleased him: for if all were but one member, where were the body? but now verily be there many members, yet but one body. The eye cannot say to the hand I have no need of thy help, or again the head to the feet, ye be not to me necessary: but those members of the body which seem to be the weaker are much more necessary: and to those which we think to be the viler members of the body we give more abundant honour: and those which be our unhonest members have more abundant honesty, for our honest members have need of nothing. But God hath tempered and ordered the body, giving plenteous honour to that part which lacked, because there should be no division, debate or strife in the body, but that the members should care one for another indifferently. But it is ye which are the body of Christ and members one depending of another. He writeth like things to the Romans, saying, in one body we have many members, and all members have not one office.

Every member hath his occupation necessary to the profit of the soul.

Even so we being many are but one body in Christ: but singularly we be members each one of another, having gifts divers after the grace which is given to us. And again to the Epheses. Working verity (saith he) in charity, let us in all manner things grow in him which is the head, that is to wit Christ, in whom all the body compact and knit by every joint, whereby one part ministereth to another according to the operation and virtue which springeth of the head and capacity of every member, in receiving maketh the increase of the body for the edifying of himself in charity. And in another place he biddeth every man to bear one another's burden, because we be members one of another. Look then whether they pertain unto this body whom thou hearest speaking everywhere after this manner, it is my good, it came to me by inheritance, I possess it by right and not by fraud, why shall not I use it and abuse it after mine own mind, why should I give them of it any deal at all to whom I owe nothing? I spill, I waste, I destroy, that which perisheth is mine own, it maketh no matter to other men. Thy member complaineth and grinneth for hunger and thou spuest up partridges. Thy naked brother shivereth for cold, and with thee so great plenty of raiment is corrupt with moths and long lying. One night's dicing hath lost thee a thousand pieces of gold, while in the mean season some wretched wench (need compelling her) hath set forth her chastity to sell, and is become a common harlot, and thus perisheth the soul for whom Christ hath bestowed his life. Thou sayest again: what is that to me? I entreat that which is mine own after mine own fashion: and after all this with this so corrupt mind thinkest thou thyself to be a Christian man, which art not once a man verily? Thou hearest in the presence of a great multitude the good name or fame of this or that man to be hurt, thou holdest thy peace, or peradventure rejoicest and art well content with the backbiter. Thou sayest, I would have reproved him if those things which were spoken had pertained to me, but I have nothing ado with him which was there slandered. Then to conclude, thou hast nothing ado with the body, if thou have nothing ado with the member, neither hast thou aught ado with the head, verily, if the body nothing appertain to thee. A man (say they now-a-days) with violence may defend and put aback violence: what the Emperour's laws permit I pass not thereon. This I marvel, how these voices came in to the manners of Christian men. I hurt him, but I was provoked, I had liefer hurt than be hurt. Be it man's laws punish not that which they have permitted. But what will the Emperour Christ do, if thou beguile his law which is written in Matthew?

Desire not vengeance.

I command you (saith Christ there) not once to withstand harm: but if a man shall give thee a blow on the right cheek, offer to him also the other. And whosoever will strive with thee in the law, and take from thee thy coat, yield up to him also thy cloak or mantle. And whosoever shall compel thee to go with him one mile, go with him two more other. Love your enemies, and do good to them which hate you, and pray for them which persecute you and pick matters against you, that ye may be the sons of your father which is in heaven, which maketh the sun to rise upon good and evil, and sendeth rain upon just and unjust. Thou answerest, he spake not this to me, he spake it to his apostles, he spake it to perfect persons. Heardest thou not how he said that ye may be the sons of your father? if thou care not to be the son of God, that law pertaineth not to thee.

This is spoken to all Christian men.

Nevertheless he is not good verily which would not be perfect. Hark also another thing: if thou desire no reward, the commandment belongeth not to thee: for it followeth. If ye love them which love you, what reward shall ye have? as who should say, none: for verily, to do these things (that is to say, to love them that loveth thee) is not virtue: but not to do it, is an evil thing: there is debt of neither side where is just recompense made of both sides. Hear Paul, both a great wise man and cunning and an interpreter also of Christ's law. Bless (saith he) them that persecute you, bless them, and curse them in no wise, rendering to no man evil for evil, if it may be as much as in you is, having rest and peace with all men, not defending yourself, my best beloved brethren, but give place and withstand ye not wrath: for it is written, Vengeance shall be reserved to me and I will requite them saith our Lord. But if thine enemy shall be hungry, give to him meat: if he be athirst, give to him drink: for if thou do this, thou shalt heap coals of fire upon his head, that is to say, thou shalt make him to love fervently. Be not overcome of evil, but overcome evil in goodness. What shall then follow, sayest thou, if I shall with my softness nourish up the knappyshnes or malice and froward audacity of another man, and in suffering an old injury provoke a new?

To a Christian man, it is better to suffer than to do.

If thou can without thine own evil either avoid or put by evil, no man forbiddeth thee to do it: but if not, look thou say not, it is better to do than to suffer. Amend thine enemy if thou can, either lading him with benefits, or overcoming him with meekness: if that help not, it is better that the one perish than both: it is better that thou wax rich with the lucre and advantage of patience than that while either to other rendereth evil both be made evil.

The decree of Christian men.

Let this therefore be a decree among Christian men, to compare with all men in love, in meekness, and in benefits, or doing good: but in striving, hate or backbiting, in rebukes and injury, to give place ever to them that be of lowest degree, and that with good will. But he is unworthy to whom a good turn should be done, or an evil forgiven, yet is it meet for thee to do it, and Christ is worthy for whose sake it is done. I will neither (say they) hurt any man, neither suffer myself to be hurt: yet when thou art hurt, see thou forgive the trespass with all thy heart, providing always that nothing be which any man should remit or forgive unto thee. Be as ware and diligent in avoiding that none offence or trespass proceed from thee, as thou art easy and ready to remit another man's.

Offences must be forgiven.

The greater man thou art, so much the more submit thyself, that thou in charity apply thyself to all men.

A gentleman.

If thou come of a noble stock, manners worthy of Christ shall not dishonour, but honour the nobleness of thy birth.

A cunning man.

If thou be cunning and well learned, so much the more soberly suffer and amend the ignorance of the unlearned.

A rich man.

The more is committed and lent to thee, the more art thou bound to thy brother. Thou art rich, remember thou art the dispenser, not the lord: take heed circumspectly how thou entreatest the common good.

Poverty is not enjoined to monks only.

Believest thou that property or impropriation was prohibit and voluntary poverty enjoined to monks only? Thou art deceived, both pertain indifferently to all Christian men. The law punisheth thee if thou take away anything of another man's: it punisheth not if thou withdraw thine own from thy needy brother: but Christ will punish both. If thou be an officer, let not the honour make thee more fierce, but let the charge make thee more diligent and fuller of care. I bear not (sayest thou) no office of the church, I am not a shepherd or a bishop. Let us grant you that, but also art thou not a Christian man, consider thou of whence thou art, if thou be not of the church. So greatly Christ is coming into contempt to the world, that they think it a goodly and excellent thing to have nothing to do with him: and that so much the more every man should be despised, the more coupled he were to him.

Incest is to meddle with their own kin. Sacrilege is to violate persons sacred to God, or to rob churches.

Hearest thou not daily of the lay persons in their fury, the names of a clerk, of a priest, of a monk, to be cast in our teeth, instead of a sharp and cruel rebuke, saying, thou clerk, thou priest, thou monk, that thou art: and it is done, utterly with none other mind, with none other voice or pronouncing, than if they should cast in our teeth incest or sacrilege. I verily marvel why they also cast not in our teeth baptism, why also object they not against us with the Sarazyns the name of Christ as an opprobrious thing. If they said, an evil clerk, an unworthy priest, or an unreligious monk, in that they might be suffered as men which note the manners of the persons, and not despise the profession of virtue. But whosoever counteth praise in themselves the deflowering of virgins, good taken away in war, money either won or lost at dice or other chance, and have nothing to lay against another man more spiteful or opprobrious or more to be ashamed of, than the names of a monk or a priest. Certainly it is easy to conjecture what these, in name only Christian men, judge of Christ.

Symonyake.

There is not one Lord of the bishops and another of the temporal officers, but both be under one, and to the same both must give accounts: If thou look any other where save unto him only, either when thou receivest the office or when thou ministerest it, it maketh no matter though the world call thee not a symonyake, he surely will punish thee as a symonyake. If thou labour and make means to obtain a common office, not to profit in common, but to provide for thine own wealth privately, and to avenge thyself of them to whom thou owest a grudge, thy office is bribery or robbery afore God. Thou huntest after thieves not that he should receive his own that is robbed, but lest it should not be with thee which is with the thieves. How much difference I pray thee is there between the thieves and thee, except peradventure that they be the robbers of merchants, and thou the robber of robbers.

A pretty note for shrieves and other officers.

In conclusion, except thou bear thine office with this mind, that thou be ready, and that with the loss, I will not say of thy goods but, of thy life to defend that which is right, Christ will not approve thy administration. I will add also another thing of the mind or judgment of Plato: no man is worthy of an office which is gladly in an office.

He is worthy to be an officer which is in office against his will.

If thou be a prince, beware lest these perilous witches, the voices of flatterers, do enchant or bewitch thee. Thou art a lord, over the laws thou art free, whatsoever thou doest is honest, to thee is lawful whatsoever thou list.

Christ is Lord both of laymen and also of priests.

Those things pertain not to thee which are preached daily of priests to the common people: yea, but think thou rather which is true, that there is one master over all men, and he is Christ Jesus, to whom thou oughtest to be as like as is possible, to whom thou oughtest to conform thyself in all things, as unto him certainly whose authority or room thou bearest. No man ought to follow his doctrine more straitly than thou, of whom he will ask accounts more straitly than of other. Think not straightway that to be right that thou wilt, but only will thou which is right.

Desire but that which is right.

Whatsoever may be filthy to any man in the world, see that thou think not that an honest thing to thee, but see thou in no wise permit to thyself any thing which is used to be forgiven and pardoned among the common sort. That which in other men is but a small trespass, think in thyself to be a great outrage or excess. Let not thy riches greater than the common people bring unto thee honour, reverence, and dignity, favour, and authority: but let thy manners better than the common people's utterly deserve them.

The honesty of good manners.

Suffer not the common people to wonder at those things in thee, wherewith are provoked and enticed the very same mischievous deeds which thou punishest daily. Take away this wondering and praise of riches, and where be thieves, where be oppressors of the commonwealth, where be committers of sacrilege, where be errant thieves and robbers or rievers: take away wondering at voluptuousness, and where be ravishers of women, where be adulterers? As often as thou wilt appear somewhat according after thy degree among thy friends and subjects or them over whom thou bearest office, room or authority, set not open thy riches and treasure to the eyes of foolish persons. When thou wilt seem somewhat wealthy, shew not in boast the riotous example of expense and voluptuousness. First of all let them learn in thee to despise such things, let them learn to honour virtue, to have measure in price, to rejoice in temperance, to give honour to sober lowliness or meekness. Let none of those things be seen in thy manners and conversation, which thine authority punisheth in the manners and conversation of the people. Thou shalt banish evil deeds in the best wise, if men shall not see riches and voluptuousness, the matter and ground of evil deeds to be magnified in thee. Thou shalt not despise in comparison of thyself any man, no not the vilest of the lowest degree, for common and indifferent is the price wherewith ye both were redeemed. Let not the noise of ambition, neither fierceness, neither weapons, nor men of the guard, defend thee from contempt, but pureness of living, gravity, manners uncorrupt and sound from all manner vices of the common people.

The rule of Christian princes.

Nothing forbiddeth (in bearing rule) to keep the chief room, and yet in charity to discern no room. Think bearing of room or rule to be this, not to excel and go before other men in abundance of riches, but to profit all men as much as is possible. Turn not to thine own profit things which are common, but bestow those things which be thine own, and thine own self, altogether upon the commonwealth. The common people oweth very many things to thee, but thou owest all things to them. Though thine ears be compelled to suffer names of ambition, as most mighty, most christened, holiness, and majesty, yet let thy mind not be a-knowen of them, but refer all these things unto Christ, to whom only they agree. Let the crime of treason against thine own person (which other with great words make an heinous offence) be counted of thee a very trifle.

The majesty of a prince.

He violateth the majesty of a prince indeed, which in the prince's name doth any thing cruelly, violently, mischievously, contrary to right. Let no man's injury move thee less than that which pertaineth to thee privately: remember thou art a public person, and that thou oughtest not to think but of common matters.

The manner and form of bearing rule must be set of Christ.

If thou have any courage with thee and readiness of wit, consider with thyself not how great a man thou art, but how great a charge thou bearest on thy back: and the more in jeopardy thou art so much the less favour thyself, fetching example of ministering thine office not of thy predecessors or else of flatterers, but of Christ: for what is more unreasonable than that a Christian prince should set before him for an example Hanyball, great Alexandre, Cesar or Pompey, in the which same persons when he cannot attain some certain virtues, he shall counterfeit those things most chiefly which only were to be refused and avoided. Let it not forth withal be taken for an example if Cesar have done anything lauded in histories, but if he have done anything which varyeth not from the doctrine of our Lord Jesu Christ, or be such that though it be not worthy to be counterfeited yet may it be applied to the study or exercise of virtue. Let not an whole empire be of so great value to thee that thou wouldest wittingly once bow from the right: put off that rather than thou shouldest put off Christ. Doubt not Christ hath to make thee amends for the empire refused, far better than the empire.

What is comely for princes.

Nothing is so comely, so excellent, so glorious unto kings as to draw as nigh as is possible unto the similitude of the highest king Jesu, which as he was the greatest so was he also the best.

Christ is the greatest, he is also the best.

But that he was the greatest, that dissimuled he, and hid secret here in earth: that he was the best, that he had liefer we should perceive and feel, because he had liefer we should counterfeit that. He denied his kingdom to be of this world, when he was Lord of heaven and earth also. But the princes of the gentiles use dominion upon them. A Christian man exerciseth no power over his but charity, and he which is the chiefest thinketh himself to be minister unto all men, not master or lord.

The clergy is touched of ambition and vain titles of names.

Wherefore I marvel the more a great deal how these ambitious names of power and dominion were brought in, even unto the very popes and bishops, and that our divines be not ashamed no less indiscreetly than ambitiously to be called everywhere our masters, when Christ forbade his disciples that they should not suffer to be called either lords, or masters: for we must remember that one is in heaven both lord and master Christ Jesus, which is also head unto us all.

The names of office.

Apostle, a shepherd, a bishop, be names of office or service, not of dominion and rule: A pope, an abbot, be names of love, not of power. But why enter I into that great sea of the common errors? Unto whatsoever kind of men he shall turn himself, a very spiritual man shall see many things which he may laugh at, and more which he ought to weep at, he shall see very many opinions so far corrupt and varying from the doctrine of Christ both far and wide: of the which a great part springeth there hence, that we have brought even into christendom a certain world, and that which is read of the world among the old divines, men of small learning now-a-days refer to them which be not monks. The world in the gospel, with the apostles, with Saint Augustyne, Ambrose, and Hierome, be called infidels, strangers from the faith, the enemies of the cross of Christ. Blasphemers of God, they that are such care for to-morrow and for the time to come, for whosoever mistrusteth Christ neither believe on him, they be they which fight and strive for riches, for rule, for worldly pleasure, as men which, blinded with delyces of sensible things, set their minds and whole affections upon apparent good things, instead of very good things. This world hath not known Christ the very and true light. This world is altogether set on mischief, loveth himself, liveth to himself, studyeth for himself and for his own pleasure, and all for lack he hath not put upon him Christ which is very and true charity. From this world separated Christ not his apostles only, but all men whosoever and as many as he judged worthy of him. After what manner then and fashion I pray you do we mingle with christendom this world, everywhere in holy scripture condemned? And with the vain name of the world favour, flatter, and maintain our own vices. Many doctors and teachers augment this pestilence, which corrupting the word of God (as Paul saith) wrest and fashion his holy scripture according to the manners of every time, when it were more convenient that the manners should be addressed and amended by the rule of his scripture. And no mischievouser kind of flattering verily is there, than when with the words of the gospel and of the prophets we flatter the diseases of the mind and cure them not.

All power is of God.

A prince heareth all power is of God: forthwith (as the proverb saith) his comb riseth. Why hath the scripture made thee high or swelling in mind rather than circumspect and careful? Thinkest thou that God hath committed to thee an empire to be governed, and thinkest thou not that the same will require of thee a strait reckoning of the ordering thereof? The covetous man heareth it to be forbid unto Christian men to have two coats at once.

Thou shalt not have two coats.

The divine interpreteth the second coat to be whatsoever should be superfluous and more than enough for the necessity of nature, and should appertain to the disease of covetousness: that is very well (saith the gross fellow) for I yet lack very many things.

A new order of charity.

The natural wise man and cold from charity heareth this to be the order of charity, that thou shouldest regard and set more of thine own money than of another man's, of thine own life than of another man's, of thine own fame than of another man's. I will therefore, saith he, give nothing lest peradventure I should lack myself. I will not defend another man's good fame or good name, lest mine own be spotted thereby. I will forsake my brother in jeopardy, lest I myself should fall in peril also. To speak shortly

I will live altogether to myself that no incommodity come to me for any other man's cause. We have also learned if holy men have done anything not to be counterfeited or followed, that only to take of them and draw in to the example of living. Adulterers and murderers flatter and clawen themselves with the example of David. Such as gapeth after worldly riches lay against us for their excuse rich Abraham. Princes which count it but a sport or pastime everywhere to corrupt and defile virgins, number and reckon up to cloke their vice the queens concubines of Salomon. They whose belly is their god, layeth for their excuse the drunkenness of Noe. Incests which pollute their own kinswomen, cloke and cover their filthiness with the example of Loth, which lay with his own daughters. Why turn we our eyes from Christ to these men?

Nothing ought to be counterfeited which varies from Christ.

I dare be bold to say that it ought not to be counterfeited and followed, no not so much as in the prophets or Christ's apostles verily, if anything swerve or wry from the doctrine of Christ. But if it delight men so greatly to counterfeit holy sinners, I do not gainsay them, so that they counterfeit them whole and altogether. Thou hast followed David in adultery, much more follow him in repentance. Thou hast counterfeited Mary Magdalayne a sinner, counterfeit her also loving much, counterfeit her weeping, counterfeit her casting herself down at the feet of Jesu. Thou hast persecuted the church of God as Paul did, thou hast forsworn thyself as Peter did: see likewise that thou stretch forth thy neck for the faith and religion of Christ after the example of Paul, and that thou fear not the cross no more than Peter. For this cause God suffereth even great and right excellent men also to fall into certain vices, that we when we have fallen should not despair, but with this condition, if that we, as we have been their fellows in sinning and doing amiss, even so will be their companions and partners in the amending of our sins and misdeeds.

We turn good things to evil.

Now do we greatly praise and magnify that same thing which was not to be counterfeited and followed, and certain things which were well done of them, we do deprave and corrupt, after the manner of spiders sucking out the poison only, if any be therein, or else turning even the wholesome juice also into poison to ourselves.

A covetous man followeth not Abraham.

What doth Abraham's example belong to thee, which makest of thy money thy God?

Cresus.

Because he was enriched with increase of cattle (God making his substance and goods prosperously to multiply) and that in the old law which was but carnal: shall it therefore be lawful to thee which art a Christian man, by right or wrong, by hook or crook, from whencesoever it be, to heap together riches as much as ever king Cresus had (whose exceeding great riches is come into a common proverb), which riches once gotten thou mightest either evil spend and lewdly waste, or else (which is a great deal worse) hide and bury most covetously deep in the ground? How little Abraham did set his mind upon his goods and riches, which came to him abundantly by their own accord, even this thing may be an evident token and proof, that without delay at the voice of God commanding him, he brought forth his only son to be slain. How much thinkest thou despised he his droves of oxen which despised even his own son?

Ready to deceive thy brother for money.

And thinkest thou which dreamest nothing else but of filthy lucre and advantage, which praisest and settest by nothing but only money, which art ready as soon as there chance any hope of lucre, be it never so little, either to deceive thy brother, or to set Christ at naught, that there is any similitude or like thing between thee and Abraham? The simple and innocent wenches, the daughters of Loth, when they beheld all the region round about on every part burning and flaming with fire, and supposed that it, which was then in sight afore their eyes, had been all the whole world, and that no man was preserved from that so large and wasteful fire but only themselves, lay privily and by stealth with their own father, not of a filthy but virtuous and holy purpose, that is to wit, lest none issue of mankind should have remained after them, and that, when this precept of God (grow and multiply) was as yet in full vigour and strength. And darest thou compare thy filthy and prodigious voluptuousness and lechery with the deed of these wenches?

The wedlock of some men is worse than the incest of Loth's daughters.

Nay I would not doubt to count thy matrimony not so good as their incest committed with their father, if in matrimony thou dost not study for issue, but to satisfy thine own voluptuous appetite or lust.

The misdeeds or sins of holy men we pass far now-a-days, and that many ways.

David, after so many excellent and noble examples of virtue and good living shewed, fell once into adultery by occasion and opportunity given him: and shall it be lawful therefore to thee straightway at thy liberty, to roll, welter, and tumble from house to house in other men's beds all thy life long? Peter once for fear of death denied his master Christ, for whose sake afterward he died with good will: Shall it be lawful thinkest thou then to thee for that cause, to forswear thyself for every trifle? Paul sinned not purposely and for the nonce, but fell through ignorance: when he was warned and taught, he repented forthwith and came into the right way. Thou both ware and wise, and seeing what thou doest, wittingly and willingly continuest from youth to age in vices and sins, and yet by the example of Paul strokest thou thine own head. Matthew being commanded but with one word, without any tarrying, at once utterly forsook all his office of receiving custom or tollage: but thou art so sworn and married to thy money that neither so many examples of holy men, neither the gospels of often heard, nor so many preachings can divorce or pluck thee from it.

Saint Austen is excused he had but one at once.

The bishops say unto me, Saint Augustyne (as it is read) had two sovereign ladies or concubines: yea but he then was an heathen man, and we be nourished up in christendom: he was young, and our heads be hoar for age. A worshipful comparison, because that he being young, and also an heathen man, to avoid the snares of matrimony, had a little wench instead of a wife, and yet to her which was not his wife kept he the promise of wedlock. Shall it be therefore the less shame for us Christian men being old, being priests, yea being bishops, to be altogether spotted and defiled in every puddle one after another of bodily lusts? Farewell good manners when we have given to vices the names of virtues, and have begun to be more wily and subtle in defending our vices than diligent to amend them, most specially when we have learned to nourish, to underset, and to strengthen our froward opinions, with the help and aid of holy scripture. Thou therefore my most sweet brother (the common people altogether set at naught with their both opinions and deeds) purely and wholly hasten thee unto the Christian sect. Whatsoever in this life appeareth to thy sensible powers either to be hated or loved, all that for the love of piety and virtuous life indifferently despised, let Christ only to thee be sufficient, the only author both of true judging and also of blessed living. And this verily the world thinketh to be pure foolishness and madness: nevertheless by this foolishness it pleaseth God to save them which on him believe. And he is happily a fool that is wise in Christ: and he is wofully wise that is foolish in Christ.

A man may not bark everywhere against the deeds of other men.

But hearest thou, as I would have thee to vary strongly from the common people, so I would not that thou shewing a point of currishness, shouldst everywhere bark against the opinions and deeds of other men, and with authority condemn them, prattle odiously against all men, furiously preach against the living of every person, lest thou purchase to thyself two evils together. The one that thou shouldest fall into hate of all men: the other that when thou art hated thou shouldest do good to no man. But be thou all things to all men, to win all men to Christ; as much as may be (piety not offended) so shape and fashion thyself to all men outwardly, that within thy purpose remain sure, stedfast and unmoved, withoutforth let gentleness, courteous language, softness, profitableness allure and entice thy brother, whom it is meet with fair means to be induced to Christ, and not to be feared with cruelness. In conclusion that which is in thy breast is not so greatly to be roared forth with cruel words, as to be declared and uttered with honest manners. And again thou oughtest not so to favour the infirmity of the common people that thou durst not at a time strongly defend the verity: with humanity men must be amended, and not deceived.

CHAPTER 16

The seventh rule.

Moreover if through infancy and feebleness of mind we cannot as yet attain to these spiritual things, we ought nevertheless to study not the sluggisher one deal, that at the least we draw as nigh as is possible.

We must still be climbing yea though we despair to attain to the top.

How be it the very and compendious way to felicity is, if at once we shall turn our whole mind to the contemplation and beholding of celestial things so fervently, that as the body bringeth with him his shadow, even so the love of Christ, the love of eternal things and honest, bringeth with him naturally the loathsomeness of caduke and transitory things and the hate of filthy things. For either other necessarily followeth the other: and the one with the other either augmenteth or minisheth. As much as thou shalt profit in the love of Christ, so much shalt thou hate the world. The more thou shalt love and set by things invisible, the more vile shall wax things vain and momentary. We must therefore do even that same in the discipline of virtue which Fabius counselleth to be done in sciences or faculties of learning, that we at once press up to the best, which thing yet if through our own fault will not come to pass, the next of all is that we at the least may by certain natural prudence abstain from great vices, and keep ourselves (as much as may be) whole and sound to the beneficence of God.

Capax apt to receive.

For as that body is near unto health, which (though it be wasted) is free yet and out of the danger of noisome humours, even so is that mind more capax of the benefit of God, which is not yet inquynate or defiled with grievous offences, though she lack yet true and perfect virtue.

If thou cannot counterfeit holy saints, be not yet inferior to heathen men.

If we be too weak to follow the apostles, to follow the martyrs, to follow the virgins, at the least way let us not commit that the Ethnykes or heathen men should seem to over-run us in this plain or lists. Of the which very many when they neither knew God whom they should dread, neither believed any hell whom they should fear: yet determined they that a man ought by all crafts to avoid and eschew filthiness for the thing itself. In so much that many of them chose rather to suffer the loss of fame, loss of goods, in conclusion to suffer loss of life, than to depart from honesty. If sin itself be such a manner thing, that for no commodities or incommodities proffered to man it ought to be committed, certainly if neither the justice of God fear us, neither his beneficence discourage us and move us to the contrary, if no hope of immortality or fear of eternal pain call us aback, or else if the very natural filthiness of sin withdraw us not, which could withdraw the minds of the very gentiles, at the least way let a thousand incommodities which accompany the sinner in this life put a Christian man in fear: as infamy, loss or waste of goods, poverty, the contempt and hate of good men, grief of mind, unquietness and torment of conscience most miserable of all, which though many

feel not now presently, either because they be blinded with dulness of youth, or made drunk with the voluptuousness and pleasure of sin, yet shall they feel it hereafter: and plainly the later it happeneth, so much the more unhappily shall they feel it: wherefore young men most specially should be warned and exhorted that they would rather believe so many authors that the very nature and property of sin were thus indeed than with miserable and woful experience learn it in themselves, and that they would not contaminate nor defile their life before they knew surely what life meant.

Ponder in thy mind the incommodities of sin.
Hear that is in civil or moral virtues.

If Christ be to thee vile, to whom thou art so costly, at the leastway for thine own sake refrain thyself from filthy things. And though it be very perilous to tarry anywhere in this state, as between the ways (as it is in the proverb), nevertheless unto them which cannot as yet climb up to the pure, perfect and excellent virtue, it shall not be a little profitable to be in the civil or moral virtues rather than to run headlong in to all kind of vices and uncleanliness. Here is not the resting place and quiet haven of felicity, but from hence is a shorter journey and an easier stair up to felicity. In the mean season for all that, we must pray God that he will vouchsafe to pluck us up to better things.

CHAPTER 17

The eighth rule.

If the storm of temptation shall rise against thee somewhat thick and grievously, begin not forthwithal to be discontent with thyself, as though for that cause God either cared not for thee, or favoured thee not, or that thou shouldest be but an easy Christian man, or else the less perfect: but rather give thanks to God because he instructeth thee as one which shall be his heir in time to come, because he beateth or scourgeth thee as his most singular beloved son and proveth thee as his assured friend. It is a very great token a man to be reject from the mercy of God when he is vexed with no temptations. Let come to thy mind the apostle Paul which obtained to be admitted or let in even in to the mysteries of the third heaven, yet was he beaten of the angel of Satan.

Temptation is a sign that God loveth us.

Let come to remembrance the friend of God, Job:

remember Jerom, Benedict, Frauncys, and with these innumerable other holy fathers, vexed and troubled of very great vices: if that which thou sufferest be common to so great men, be common to so many men as well as to thee, what cause is there wherefore thou shouldest be smit out of countenance, shouldest be abashed or fall into despair? Enforce rather and strive that thou mayst overcome as they did, God shall not forsake thee, but with temptation shall make increase, that thou mayst be able to endure.

CHAPTER 18

The ninth rule.

We must ever keep watch.
Let temptation be held down at the beginning while it is fresh.

As expert captains are wont to cause, when all things are quiet, at rest and at peace, that the watch nevertheless be duly kept: likewise see thou that thou have alway thy mind watching and circumspect against the sudden assault of thine enemy (for he ever compasseth round about seeking whom he might devour) that thou mayst be the more ready as soon as he assaulteth thee to put him back manfully, to confound him and forthwith to tread underfoot the head of the pestiferous and poison serpent: for he is never overcome either more easily or more surely and perfectly, than by that means.

The children of Babylon signifieth subjection or temptation or the first motions to sin.

Therefore it is a very wise point to dash the young children of Babylon (as soon as they be born) against the stone which is Christ, or they grow strong and great.

CHAPTER 19

The tenth rule.

Remedies against temptation.

But the tempter is put back most of all by this means, if thou shalt either vehemently hate, abhor and defy, and in a manner spit at him straightway whensoever he enticeth and moveth thee with any temptation, or else if thou pray fervently or get thyself to some holy occupation, setting thine whole mind thereunto: or if thou make answer to the tempter with words set out of holy scripture, as I have warned thee before. In which thing verily it shall not profit meanly against all kind of temptation to have some certain sentences prepared and ready, specially those with which thou hast felt thy mind to be moved and stirred vehemently.

CHAPTER 20

The eleventh rule.

The night fear is fear lest we should be overcome.

Two dangers chiefly follow good men, one lest in temptation they give up their hold. Another lest after the victory in their consolation and spiritual joy they wax wanton and stand in their own conceit, or else please themselves.

The devil of mid-day is pride.

Therefore that thou mayst be sure not only from the night fear, but also from the devil of mid-day: look when thine enemy stirreth thee unto filthy things that thou behold not thine own feebleness or weakness, but remember only that thou canst do all things in Christ, which said not to his apostles only, but to thee also and to all his members, even unto the very lowest: Have confidence for I have overcome the world.

Remember thou art able to do all things in Christ.

Again whensoever either after thine enemy is overcome, or in doing some holy work, thou shalt feel thy mind inwardly to be comforted with certain privy delectations: then beware diligently that thou ascribe nothing thereof unto thine own merits but thank only the free beneficence of God for altogether, and hold down and refrain thyself with the words of Paul, saying: What hast thou, that thou hast not received? If thou have received it, why rejoicest thou as though thou haddest not received it? And so against this double mischief shall there be a double remedy, if thou in the conflict mistrusting thine own strength dost flee for succour unto thy head Christ, putting the whole trust of conquering in the benevolence of him only. And if also in the spiritual comfort and consolation, thou immediately give thanks to him for his benefit, humbly knowing and confessing thine unworthiness.

CHAPTER 21

The twelfth rule.

When thou fightest with thine enemies, think it not enough for thee to avoid his stroke, or put it back, except thou also take the weapon from him manfully, and lay therewith again at the owner, killing him with his own sword. That shall come to pass on this wise.

Of temptation take ever an occasion of virtue.

If when thou art provoked unto evil thou do not only abstain from sin, but thereof dost take unto thee an occasion of virtue: and as poets elegantly feign that Hercules did grow and was also hardened in courage through the dangers that Juno put unto him of displeasure: thou likewise give also attendance that by the instigations of thine enemy not only thou be not the worse but rather be made much better. Thou art stirred unto bodily lust, know thy weakness, and also lay apart somewhat the more of lawful pleasures, and add some increase unto chaste and holy occupations. Thou art pricked unto covetousness and nyggysshe keeping: increase alms deeds. Thou art moved unto vain glory: so much the more humble thyself in all things.

Let temptations be ever the renewing of thy holy purpose.

And thus shall it be brought about that every temptation may be a certain renewing of thy holy purpose, and an increase of piety and virtuous living. And verily other means is there none at all of so great virtue and strength to vanquish and overthrow our enemy: for he shall be afraid to provoke thee afresh, lest he which rejoiceth to be the beginner and chief captain of wickedness should minister an occasion of piety, virtue and godliness.

CHAPTER 22

The thirteenth rule.

But alway take heed that thou fight with this mind and hope, as though that should be the last fight that ever thou shalt have, if thou get the over hand: for it may be verily that the benignity of God will give and grant this reward unto thy virtue and noble act: that thine enemy once overcome to his shame, shall never afterward come upon thee again. A thing which we read to have happened to divers holy men: neither believeth Origene against reason, that when Christian men overcome, then is the power of their enemies minished, whiles the adversary once put back manfully is never suffered to return again to make a fresh battle. Be bold therefore in the conflict, to hope for perpetual peace.

After one battle we must look for another.

But again after thou hast overcome, so behave thyself as though thou shouldest go again to fight straightway, for after one temptation, we must look ever for another: we may never depart from our harness and weapons: we may never forsake our standing: we may never leave off watch as long as we war in the garrison of this body. Every man must have alway that saying of the prophet in his heart, I will keep my standing.

CHAPTER 23

The fourteenth rule.

We must take very good heed that we despise not any vice as light, for no enemy overcometh oftener than he which is not set off: in which thing I perceive not a few men to be greatly deceived: for they deceive themselves while they favour themselves in one or two vices, which every man after his own appetite thinketh to be venial, and all other grievously abhor.

Some men fancy their own vices.

A great part of them which the common people call perfect and uncorrupt, greatly defieth theft, extortion, murder, adultery, incest: but single fornication and moderate use of voluptuous pleasures as a small trespass, they refuse not all. Some one man being unto all other things uncorrupt enough is somewhat a good drinker, is in riot and expenses somewhat wasteful. Another is somewhat liberal of his tongue. Another is cumbered with vanity, vainglory and boasting. At the last, what vice shall we lack if every man after this manner shall favour his own vice?

The images of virtue.

It is an evident token that those men which favour any vice at all should not truly possess the other virtues but rather some images of virtues which either nature or bringing up, finally very custom, hath grafted in the minds of the very gentiles. But he, which with Christian hatred abhorreth any one vice, must needs abhor all: for he whose mind true charity hath once possessed hateth indifferently the whole host of evil things, and flattereth not himself so much as in venial sins, lest he might fall a little and a little from the smallest to the greatest: and while he is negligent in light things might fall from the chiefest things of all.

Daily must somewhat of our evils be taken away, and of good things be added.

And though thou as yet canst not pluck up by the roots the whole generation of vices: nevertheless somewhat of our evil properties must be plucked away day by day, and something added to good manners: after that manner diminisheth or augmenteth the great heap of Hesiodus.

CHAPTER 24

The fifteenth rule.

If the labour which thou must take in the conflict of temptation shall fear thee, this shall be a remedy. See thou compare not the grief of the fight with the pleasure of the sin: but match me the present bitterness of the fight with the bitterness of the sin hereafter which followeth him that is overthrown: and then set the present sweetness of the sin which enticeth thee, with the pleasure of the victory hereafter, and with the tranquillity of mind which followeth him that fighteth lustily: and anon thou shalt perceive how unequal a comparison there shall be.

The bitterness of the fight must be compared with the pain which followeth the sin.

But in this thing they which be but little circumspect are deceived, because they compare the displeasure of the fight with the pleasure of the sin, and consider not what followeth the one and the other. For there followeth him which is overcome, grief both more painful a great deal and also of longer continuance than he should have had in time of fight, if he had won the victory. And likewise there followeth the conquerors more pleasure by a great deal and of longer endurance than was the pleasure which carried him into sin that was overcome: which thing he shall lightly judge, that hath had the proof of both.

Prove sometime what it shall be to overcome.

But no man that is christened ought to be so outright a coward though he were daily subdued of temptation, but that he should once at the least do his endeavour to prove what thing it is to overcome temptation, which thing the oftener he shall do, the pleasanter shall the victory be made unto him.

CHAPTER 25

The sixteenth rule.

But if at any time it shall fortune thee to receive a deadly wound, beware lest by and by (thy shield cast away and weapons forsaken) thou yield thyself to thine enemies' hands, which thing I have perceived to happen unto many, whose minds naturally are somewhat feeble and soft without resistance, that after they were once overthrown, they ceased to wrestle any more, but permitted and gave themselves altogether unto affections, never thinking any more to recover their liberty again.

Despair not though thou be overcome.

Too too much perilous is this weakness of spirit, which now and then though it be not coupled with the most wits in the world, yet is it wont to bring to that point which is worst of all, to desperation verily.

A fall sometimes courageth a man to wrestle more strongly.

Against this weakness therefore thy mind must be aforehand armed with this rule, that after we have fallen into sin not only we should not despair, but counterfeit bold men of war, whom not seldom shame of rebuke and grief of the wound received not only putteth not to flight but sharpeneth and refresheth again to fight more fiercely than they did before. In like case also after that we have been brought in to deadly sin, let us haste anon to come again to ourselves and to take a good heart to us, and to repair again the rebuke and shame of the fall with new courage and lustiness of strength. Thou shalt heal one wound sooner than many: thou shalt easier cure a fresh wound than that which is now old and putrefied. Comfort thyself with that famous verse which Demostenes is said to have used: A man that fleeth will yet fight again. Call to remembrance David the prophet, Salomon the king, Peter a captain of the church, Paul the apostle, so great lights of holiness: into what great sins for all that fell they? Which all peradventure even for this cause God suffered to fall, lest thou when thou haddest fallen shouldest despair: rise up again therefore upon thy feet but that quickly and with a lusty courage, and go to it afresh, both fiercer and also more circumspect. It happeneth sometime that deadly offences grow to good men into a heap of virtuous living, while they love more fervently which erred most shamefully.

CHAPTER 26

The seventeenth rule.

But against sundry and diverse assaults of the tempter thine enemy, sundry and diverse remedies are very meet and convenient.

The cross of Christ.

Nevertheless the only and chief remedy which of all remedies is of most efficacy and strength against all kinds either of adversity or else temptation is the cross of Christ. The which selfsame is both an example to them that go out of the way, and a refreshing to them that labour, and also armour or harness to them that fight. This is a thing to be cast against all manner weapons and darts of our most wicked enemy. And therefore it is necessary to be exercised diligently therein, not after the common manner, as some men repeat daily the history of the passion of Christ, or honour the image of the cross, or with a thousand signs of it arm all their body round on every side, or keep some piece of that holy tree laid up at home in their house, or at certain hours so call to remembrance Christ's punishment, that they may have compassion and weep for him with natural affection, as they would for a man that is very just and suffereth great wrong unworthily.

The very fruit of the cross is mortifying of our members that is to say of our passions and affections bodily.

This is not the true fruit of that tree: nevertheless let it in the mean season be the milk of the souls which be younglings and weak in Christ. But climb thou up into the date tree, that is to say the tree of victory, that thou mayest take hold of the true fruits thereof. These be the chief if we, which be members, shall endeavour ourselves to be semblable unto our head in mortifying our affections, which be our members upon the earth, which thing unto us ought only to be nothing bitter, but also very pleasant and fervently to be desired, if so be the spirit of Christ live in us. For who loveth truly and heartily that person to whom he rejoiceth to be as unlike as may be, and in living and conversation clean contrary? Notwithstanding that thou mayest the more profit, in thy mind record the mystery of the cross. It shall behoveful that every man prepare unto himself a certain way and godly craft of fighting and therein diligently exercise, that as soon as need shall require it may be ready at hand. Such may the craft be, that in certifying of every thine affections thou mayest apply that part of the cross which most specially thereto agreeth: for there is not at all any either temptation, either adversity, which hath not his proper remedy in the cross.

Affections are this wise crucified.

As when thou art tickled with ambition of this world, when thou art ashamed to be had in derision and to be set at naught: consider thou then, most vile member, how great Christ thy head is, and unto what vileness he humbled himself for thy sake.

Nota.

When the evil of envy invadeth thy mind, remember how kindly, how lovingly he bestowed himself every whit unto our use and profit, how good he is even unto the worst. When thou art moved with gluttony, have in mind how he drank gall with eysell. When thou art tempted with filthy pleasure, call to remembrance how far from all manner of pleasure the whole life of thy head was, and how full of incommodities, vexation, and grief. When ire provoketh thee, let him come immediately to thy mind, which like a lamb before the shearer held his peace and opened not his mouth. If poverty wring thee evil, or covetousness disquiet thee, anon let him be rolled in thy mind that is the Lord of all things, and yet was made so poor and needy for thy sake that he had not whereupon to rest his head. And after the same manner if thou shalt do in all other temptations also, not only it shall not be grievous to have oppressed thine affections, but surely pleasant and delectable, for because thou shalt perceive that thou by this means art conformed and shapen like unto thy head, and that thou dost as it were recompense him for his infinite sorrows, which for thy sake he suffered unto the uttermost.

CHAPTER 27

The eighteenth rule.

And verily this manner of remedy, though it alone of all remedies be most present and ready, most sure and quick in working to them which be meanly entered in the way of living, nevertheless to the weaker sort these things also shall somewhat profit: if when affection moveth unto iniquity, then at once they call before the eyes of the mind how filthy, how abominable, how mischievous a thing sin is: on the other side how great is the dignity of man.

Consider the filthiness of sin and the dignity of man.

In trifles and matters such as skilleth not if all the world knew, we take some deliberation and advisement with ourselves. In this matter of all matters most weighty and worthy to be pondered, before that with consent as with our own hand writing we bind ourselves to the fiend, shall we not reckon and account with our mind of how noble a craftsman we were made, in how excellent estate we are set, with how exceeding great price we are bought, unto how great felicity we are called, and that man is that gentle and noble creature for whose sake only God hath forged the marvellous building of this world, that he is of the company of angels, the son of God, the heir of immortality, a member of Christ, a member of the church, that our bodies be the temple of the Holy Ghost, our minds the images and also the secret habitations of the deity. And on the other side that sin is the most filthy pestilence and consumption both of the mind and of the body also, for both of them through innocency springeth anew into their own natural kind, and through contagion of sin both putrefy and rot even in this world. Sin is that deadly poison of the most filthy serpent, the prest wages of the devil, and of that service which is not most filthy only, but also most miserable. After thou hast considered this and such like with thyself, ponder wisely and take sure advisement and deliberation whether it should be wisely done or no, for an apparent momentary and poisoned little short pleasure of sin, to fall from so great dignity into so vile and wretched estate, from whence thou canst not rid and deliver thyself by thine own power and help.

CHAPTER 28

The nineteenth rule.

Furthermore compare together those two captains by themselves most contrary and unlike, God and the devil, of which the one thou makest thine enemy when thou sinnest, and the other thy lord and master. Through innocency and grace thou art called in to the number of the friends of God, art elect unto the right title and inheritance of the sons of God. By sin verily thou art made both the bond servant and son of the devil.

We must have in mind the beneficence of God, and the maleficence or noysaunce of the devil.

The one of them is that eternal fountain and original patron and true example of very and sure beauty, of very true pleasure, of most perfect goodness, ministering himself to all things. The other is father of all mischief, of extreme filthiness, of uttermost infelicity. Remember the benefits and goodness of the one done to thee, and the evil deeds of the other. With what goodness hath the one made thee? With what mercy redeemed thee? With what liberty and freedom endued thee? With what tenderness daily suffereth he and sustaineth thee, a wretched sinner, patiently abiding and looking for amendment? With what joy and gladness doth he receive thee amended, and when thou art come again to thyself? Contrary to all these things with how natural hate and envy long ago did the devil lay wait to thy health? Into what grievous and cumbrous vexation hath he cast thee, and also what other thing imagineth he daily but to draw all mankind with him into eternal mischief? All these things on this side and that side, well and substantially weighed and pondered, thus think with thyself: shall I unmindful of mine original beginning from whence I came, unmindful of so great and manifold benefits, for so small a morsel of feigned and false pleasure, unkindly depart from so noble, from so loving, from so beneficial a father, and shall mancipate and make myself bond willingly unto a most filthy and a most cruel master? Shall I not at the least way make good to the one that thing which I would perform to a vile man, which had shewed kindness, or done me any good? Shall I not fly from the other, which would fly from a man that coveted or were about to do me hurt?

CHAPTER 29

The twentieth rule.

And verily the rewards be no less unequal than the captains and givers of them be contrary and unlike.

The reward of virtue is heaven.

For what is more unequal than eternal death and immortal life? Than without end to enjoy everlasting felicity and blessedness, in the company and fellowship of the heavenly citizens, and without end to be tormented and punished with extreme vengeance, in the most unhappy and wretched company of damned souls? And whosoever doubteth of this thing, he is not so much as a man verily, and therefore he is no Christian man. And whosoever thinketh not on this, nor hath it in remembrance, is even madder than madness itself.

The fruits of piety in this world.

Moreover and besides all this, virtue and wickedness hath in the mean season even in this life their fruits very much unlike, for of the one is reaped assured tranquillity and quietness of mind, and that blessed joy of pure and clean conscience, which joy, whosoever shall once have tasted, there is nothing in all this world so precious nor nothing so pleasant, wherewith he would be glad or desirous to change it. Contrariwise there followeth the other, that is to say wickedness, a thousand other evils, but most specially that most wretched torment and vexation of unclean conscience. That is that hundredfold reward of spiritual joy which Christ promised in the gospel, as a certain earnest or taste of eternal felicity.

The fruit of sin in this world.

These be those marvellous rewards that the apostle speaketh of which eye neither saw nor ear hath heard, neither hath sunk into the heart of any man, which God hath prepared for them that love him, and verily in this life, when in the mean season the worm of wicked men dieth not, and they suffer their hell pains here even in this world. Neither any other thing is that flame in which is tormented the rich glutton of whom is made mention in the gospel: neither any other things be those punishments of them in hell of whom the poets write so many things, save a perpetual grief, unquietness or gnawing of the mind which accompanieth the custom of sin. He that will therefore, let him set aside the reward of the life to come, which be so diverse and unlike: yet in this life virtue hath annexed to her wherefore she abundantly ought to be desired, and vice hath coupled unto him for whose sake he ought to be abhorred.

CHAPTER 30

The twenty-first rule.

Moreover consider how full of grief and misery, how short and transitory is this present life, how on every side death lieth in await against us, how everywhere he catcheth us suddenly and unaware. And when no man is sure, no not of one moment of life, how great peril it is to prolong and continue that kind of life in which (as it often fortuneth) if sudden death should take thee thou were but lost and undone for ever.

CHAPTER 31

The twenty-second rule.

Besides all this impenitency or obduration of mind is to be feared of all mischiefs the extreme and worst: namely if a man would ponder this one thing of so many, how few there be which truly and with all their hearts come to themselves again, and be clean converted from sin, and with due repentance reconciled to God again: specially of them which have drawn along the lives of iniquity even unto the last end of their life.

The fox and the goat descended both into a pit to drink: when they had drunk they could not get out again, therefore had the goat to stand up against the wall, and the fox leapt upon his back and so up, promising afore to pull up the goat after; the goat desired the fox to fulfill his promise and to help him up, the fox answered, oh goat, goat, if thou haddest had as much wit in thy head as thou has hair in thy beard thou wouldest not have entered in except thou haddest known how to come out.

Slippery verily and easy is the fall or descent into filthiness, but to return back again therehence, and to scape up unto spiritual light, this is a work, this is a labour. Therefore at the leastway thou being monished and warned by the chance of Esope's goat, before thou descend into the pit of sin, remember that there is not so easy coming back again.

CHAPTER 32

Remedies against certain sins and special vices, and first against bodily lust.

Hitherto have we verily opened and declared (howsoever it be done) common remedies against all kind of vices. Now we shall assay to give also certain special and particular remedies, how and by what means thou oughtest withstand every vice and sin, and first of all how thou mayst resist the lust of the body. Than the which evil there is none other that sooner invadeth us, neither sharper assaileth or vexeth us, nor extendeth larger nor draweth more unto their utter destruction. If at any time therefore filthy lust shall stir thy mind, with these weapons and armour remember forthwith to meet him: first think how uncleanly, how filthy, how unworthy for any man whatsoever he be that pleasure is which assimuleth and maketh us, that be a divine work, equal not to beasts only, but also unto filthy swine, to goats, to dogs, and of all brute beasts, unto the most brute, yea which farther forth casteth down far under the condition and state of beasts, us which be appointed unto the company of angels and fellowship of the deity.

Weapons against bodily lust.

Let come to thy mind also how momentary the same is, how impure, how ever having more aloes than of honey.

Aloes is a bitter thing and is put for bitterness.

And on the contrary side how noble a thing the soul is, how worshipful a thing the body of a man is, as I have rehearsed in the rules above. What the devil's peevishness is it that for so little, so uncleanly tickling of momentary pleasures to defile at one time both soul and body with ungodly manners? To profane and pollute that temple which Christ hath consecrate to himself with his blood?

The incommodities of bodily lust.

Consider that also what an heap of mischievous incommodities that flattering pleasant pestilence bringeth with him. First of all it pulleth from thee thy good fame, a possession far-away most precious, for the rumour of no vice stinketh more carenly than the name of lechery: it consumeth thy patrimony, it killeth at once both the strength and also the beauty of the body, it decayeth and greatly hurteth health, it engendereth diseases innumerable and them filthy, it disfigureth the flower of youth long before the day, it hasteth or accelerateth reviled and evil favoured age, it taketh away the quickness and strength of the wit, it dulleth the sight of the mind, and grafteth in a man as it were a beastly mind, it withdraweth at once from all honest studies and pastimes, and plungeth and souseth a man everywhit in the puddle and mire be he never so excellent, that now he hath lust to think on nothing but that which is sluttish, vile, and filthy: and it taketh away the use of reason which was the native property of man, it maketh youth mad, peevish, and slanderous, and age odious, filthy, and wretched. Be wise therefore and on this wise reckon with thyself name by name, this and that pleasure came so evil to pass, brought with her so much loss, so much disworship, dishonour and dishonesty, so much tediousness, labour and disease: and shall I now, a fool most natural, devour that hook wittingly? Shall I again commit that thing whereof I should repent of fresh?

Refrain thyself by the example of other men.

And likewise refrain thyself by the example of other men, which thou hast known to have followed voluptuous pleasures filthily and unfortunately. On the other side courage and bold thyself unto chastity by the examples of so many young men, of so many young and tender virgins nourished up delicately and in pleasures: And (the circumstances compared together) lay against thyself thy sluggishness, why thou at the last should not be able to do that thing which such and such, of that kind or sex, of that age, so born, so brought up were and yet be able to do? Love as much as they did, and thou shalt be able to do no less than they did. Think how honest, how pleasant, how lusty and flourishing a thing is pureness of body and of mind, the most of all maketh us acquainted and familiar with angels, and apt to receive the Holy Ghost: for verily that noble spirit, the lover of pureness, so greatly fleeth back from no vice at all as from uncleanliness, he resteth and sporteth him nowhere so much as in pure virgins' minds.

The ungoodly office of lovers.

Set before thine eyes how ungoodly it is, how altogether a mad thing to love, to wax pale, to be made lean, to weep, to flatter, and shamefully to submit thyself unto a stinking harlot most filthy and rotten, to gape and sing all night at her chamber window, to be made to the lure and be obedient at a beck, nor dare do anything except she nod or wag her head, to suffer a foolish woman to reign over thee, to chide thee: to lay unkindness one against the other, to fall out, to be made at one again, to give thyself willing unto a quean, that she might mock, kocke, mangle and spoil thee. Where is, I beseech thee, among all these things the name of a man? Where is thy beard? Where is that noble mind created unto most beautiful and noble things? Consider also another thing with thyself, how great a flock of mischiefs voluptuousness (if she be let in) is wont to bring with her. Other vices peradventure have some acquaintance with certain virtues, filthy lust hath none at all, but is annexed and alway coupled with those sins that be greatest and most in number. Let it be but a trifle or a light matter to follow queans, yet is it a grievous thing not to regard thy father and mother, to set at naught thy friends, to consume thy father's good in waste, to pluck away from other men, to forswear thyself, to drink all night, to rob, to use witchcraft, to fight, to commit murder, to blaspheme. Into which all and grievouser than these, the lady pleasure will draw thee headlong, after thou once hast ceased to be thine own man, and hast put thy wretched head under her girdle. Ponder moreover how this life vanisheth away faster than smoke, less of substance than a shadow, and how many snares death pitcheth for us, laying await in every place and at all seasons.

Sudden death.

Here and at this point it shall profit singularly, to call to remembrance and that name by name, if that sudden death hath taken away any sometime of thine acquaintance, of thy familiar friends, of thy companions, or else of them which were younger than thou: and most specially of them which in time passed thou hast had fellows of filthy pastime. And learn of another man's peril to be more ware and circumspect. Remember how deliciously they lived, but how bitterly they departed: how late they waxed wise, how late they began to hate their mortiferous and deadly pleasures.

The straitness of the extreme judgment.

Let come to remembrance the sharpness of the extreme judgment, and the terrible lightning of that fearful sentence never to be revoked, sending wicked men into eternal fire, and that this pleasure of an hour, short and little, must be punished with eternal torments.

The joys of pure mind is much sweeter than is the pleasure of sin.

In this place weigh diligently in a pair of balances, how unequal a change it is for the most filthy and very short delectation of lust, both to lose in this life the joy of the mind, being much sweeter and more excellent, and in the life to come to be spoiled of joys everlasting. Moreover with so shadow-like and little vain pleasure to purchase sorrows never to be ended. Finally if it seem a hard thing to despise that so small delectation for Christ's sake, remember what pains he took upon him for the tender love he bare to thee. And beside the common injuries of man's life, how much of his holy blood shed he, how shameful, how bitter death suffered he, and all for thee. And thou of all those things unmindful crucifiest again the son of God, iterating afresh those mad pleasures which caused and compelled thy head and lord unto so cruel torments.

The benefits of God.

Then according to the rule above rehearsed, call to mind how much of benefits he heaped on thee, when as yet thou haddest deserved nothing at all: for the which although no sufficient or like recompense can be made of thy part for the least, yet desireth he again none other thank but that thou, after his example, shouldest refrain thy mind from deadly and mortal pleasures, and turn thee unto the love of infinite goodness and of infinite pleasures and beauty.

Venus is the goddess of love and she is put for love. Cupydo is the god of love, and is also put for love.

Compare together these two, Venus and two Cupydes of Plato, that is to say honest love and filthy love, holy pleasure and uncleanly pastime, compare together the unlike matter of either other.

Here is a good note for every Christian man.

Compare the natures, compare the rewards: and in all temptations, but namely when thou art stirred to filthy lust, set to thee before thine eyes thy good angel, which is thy keeper and continual beholder and witness of all things thou doest or thinkest, and God ever looking on, unto whose eyes all things are open, which sitteth above the heavens and beholdeth the secret places of the earth: and wilt not thou be afraid before the angel present and even hard by thee, before God, and all the company of heaven looking on and abhorring, to commit a thing so abominable and filthy that it would shame thee to do the same thing in the presence of one vile man? This thing I wouldest thou shouldest think as it is indeed.

Lynx is a beast of most purest sight among all beasts.

And if it were so that thou haddest eyes much sharper of sight than hath a beast called lynx, or much clearer than hath the eagle, yet with these eyes in the most clearest light that could be, couldest thou not behold more surely that thing which a man doeth before thee, than all the privy and secret parts of thy mind be open unto the sight of God and of his angels.

Obstinacy of a froward mind springeth of bodily lust.

This also count in thy mind when thou art overcome of bodily lust, of two things the one must follow, either that voluptuousness, once tasted, so shall enchant and darken thy mind, that thou must go from filthiness to filthiness, until thou clean blinded shall be brought in *sensum reprobum*, that is to say, into a lewd and reproved judgment: and so, made obstinate and sturdy in evil, canst not, no truly not then, yield up filthy pleasure when she hath forsaken thee, which thing we see to have happened to very many, that when the body is wasted, when beauty is withered and vanished, when the blood is cold, when strength faileth, and the eyes wax dim, yet still continually they itch without ceasing. And with greater mischief are now filthy speakers than before time, they have been unshameful livers, than which thing what can be more abominable and monstrous? The other is, if peradventure it shall happen thee by the special favour of God to come again to thyself. Then must that short and fugitive pleasure be purged with very great sorrow of mind, with mighty and strong labour, with continual streams of tears: how much more wisdom therefore is it not to receive at all the poison of carnal pleasure, than either to be brought into so uncurable blindness, or else to recompense so little, and that also false pleasure, with so great grievance and dolorous pain. Moreover thou mayst take many things of the circumstance of thine own person, which might call thee back from voluptuous pleasure.

A priest.

Thou art a priest, remember that thou art altogether consecrate to things pertaining unto God: what a mischievous deed, how ungoodly, how unmeet, and how unworthy it should be to touch the rotten and stinking flesh of an whore with that mouth wherewith thou receivest that precious body so greatly to be honoured, and to handle loathsome and abominable filth with the same hands wherewithal (even the angels ministering to thee and assisting thee) thou executest that ineffable and incomprehensible mystery. Now these things agree not, to be made one body and one spirit with God, and to be made one body with an whore.

If thou be learned.

If thou be learned, so much the nobler and liker unto God is thy mind, and so much the more unworthy of this shame and rebuke.

A gentleman.

If thou be a gentleman, if thou be a prince, the more aperte and open the abomination is: the grievouser occasion giveth it unto other inferiors to follow the same.

A married man.

If thou be married, remember what an honest thing is a bed undefiled. And give diligence (as much as infirmity shall suffer) that thy wedlock may counterfeit the most holy marriage of Christ and his church, whose image it beareth: that is to wit, that thy marriage may be clean barren in uncleanliness, and plenteous in procreation: for in no kind of living can it be but very filthy to serve and be bound to uncleanly lusts.

A young man.

If thou be a young man, take good heed busily that thou pollute not unadvisedly the flower of thy youth, which shall never spring again: and that thou cast not away upon a thing most filthy thy best and very golden years, which flee away most swiftly, and never return again: beware also lest now through the ignorance and negligence of youth, thou commit that thing which should grudge thee hereafter by all thy whole life, the conscience of thy misdeeds ever persecuting thee with those his most bitter, most grievous and sharp stings, which when pleasure departeth she leaveth behind her in our minds.

Filthy pleasure leaveth behind her sting in our minds.
A woman.

If thou be a woman, this kind nothing more becometh than chastity, than shame, and fear of dishonesty.

A man.

If thou be a man, so much the more art thou meet and worthy of greater things, and unmeet and unworthy of these so lewd things.

An old man.

If thou be old, wish thou haddest some other man's eyes to behold thyself withal, that thou mightest see how evil voluptuousness should become thee, which in youth verily is miserable and to be bridled, but in an old fool verily wonderful and monstrous, and also even unto the very followers of pleasure, a jesting and mocking stock. Among all monsters none is more wonderful than filthy lust in age.

Against the lechery of old men and women.

Oh dotypol, oh too much forgetful of thyself: at the least way behold at a glass the hoar hairs and white snow of thy head, thy forehead furrowed with wrinkles, and thy carrion face most like unto a dead corpse: and now at the last end when thou art come even unto the pit's brink care for other things more agreeable unto thy years: at the leastway that which became thee to have done before time (reason moving thee) do now, thy years putting thee in remembrance or rather compelling thee.

David was so old that he could get no heat in his limbs; then brought the Israelites unto David Abisac a fair young maid which lay with him and kept him warm: he knew her not, she remained a pure maid. By her is signified wisdom, a thing most meet for age: all filthiness and uncleanness laid apart.

Even now pleasure herself casteth thee off, saying, neither I now am comely unto thee, neither yet thou meet or apt unto me. Thou hast played enough, thou hast eaten enough, thou hast drunk enough, it is time for thee to depart, why holdest thou yet so fast and art so greedy on pleasures of this life, when very life herself forsaketh thee. Now it is time for that mystical concubine Abysac that once she may begin to rest in thy bosom, let her with holy rage of love heat thy mind, and with the embracings of her keep thee warm and comfort thy cold members.

CHAPTER 33

A short recapitulation of remedies against the flame of lust.

Avoiding occasions.

Finally to make a short and compendious conclusion, these be the most special things which will make thee sure from pleasures and enticings of the flesh, first of all, circumspect and diligent avoiding of all occasions, which precept though it be meet to be observed also in other things, because that he which loveth perils is worthy to perish therein, yet these be most chiefly those Syrenes which almost never man at all hath escaped, save he which hath kept far off.

Syrenes be mere maidens.

Secondly, moderation of eating and drinking and of sleep, temperance and abstinence from pleasures, yea from such as be lawful and permitted: the regard of thine own death, and the contemplation of the death of Christ, and those things also will help if thou shalt live with such as be chaste and uncorrupted: if thou shalt eschew as a certain pestilence the communication of corrupt and wanton persons: if thou shalt flee idle solitariness and sluggish idleness: if thou shalt exercise thy mind strongly in the meditation of celestial things, and in honest studies. But specially if thou shalt consecrate thyself with all thy might unto the investigation or searching of mysteries of holy scripture: if thou shalt pray both oft and purely, most of all when temptation invadeth and assaulteth thee.

CHAPTER 34

Against the enticings and provokings unto avarice.

Avarice.

If thou shalt perceive that thou art either by nature anything inclined to the vice of avarice, or stirred by the devil: call to remembrance (according to the rules above rehearsed) the dignity of thy condition or state, which for this thing only wast created, for this redeemed, that thou ever shouldest enjoy that infinite good thing God, for God hath forged all the whole building of this world that all things should obey unto thy use and necessity. How filthy then and of how strait and narrow a mind is it, not to use but so greatly to wonder at things dumb and most vile: take away the error of men, what shall gold and silver be but red earth and white? Shalt thou be the disciple of poor Christ and, called to a better possession, wonder at that as a certain great and excellent thing which no philosopher of the gentiles did not set at naught?

To despise riches is a noble thing.

Not to possess riches, but to despise riches, is a noble thing. But the commonalty of Christian men by name only cry out against me, and be glad to deceive themselves most craftily: very necessity (say they) compelleth us to gather good together, whereof if there should be none at all, then could we not once live verily: if it should be thin and poor, then should we live in much misery without pleasure. But and if it be somewhat clean and honest, and somewhat plenteous withal, it bringeth many commodities to man. The good liking of body is well seen unto, provision is made for our children, we lend and profit our friends, we are delivered from contempt and be the more set by: in conclusion also a man shall have the better name when he is somewhat wealthy. Of a great many thousands of Christian men thou canst scarce find one or two that doth not both say and think the same. Nevertheless to answer these men unto both parts.

Christ, in the gospel of Matthew, lest his disciples should care for meat drink or clothes, bade them to behold the lilies how they were clothed and the birds how they were fed saying, if your father of heaven make provision for so vile things much more ye cannot lack whom he loveth so singularly.

First of all because they cloak their covetousness with the name of necessity, I will lay against them the parable rehearsed in the gospel of the lilies and of the birds living from day to day without farther provision, whose example Christ exhorteth us to counterfeit. I will lay against them that the same Christ would not once suffer so much as a scrip to be carried about of his disciples. I will lay against them, that he commandeth us (all other things laid apart) before all things to seek the kingdom of heaven, and promiseth that all things shall be cast and given to us. When at any time had not they things necessary to maintain life withal sufficiently, which with all their hearts have given themselves to virtue and to the true life of a Christian man? And how small a thing is that which nature requireth of us? But thou measurest necessity not by the needs of nature, but by the bounds of covetousness. But unto good men even that is enough that scarcely contenteth nature.

Friars.

How-be-it verily I do not so greatly set of these which forsake at one chop their whole substance every whit that they might the more shamefully beg of other. It is none offence to possess money, but to love and set store by money that is a vice and cousin to sin. If riches flow unto thee, use the office of a good dispenser: but and if it ebb and go away, be not consumed with thought, as though thou were robbed of a greater thing, but rather rejoice that thou art delivered of a perilous fardel.

Nestor lived three hundred years.

Notwithstanding he which consumeth the chief study and pastime of his life in heaping up riches together, which gapeth at them as a certain excellent or noble thing, and highly to be desired, and layeth them up in store, that he may have enough to serve him for long time, yea though he should live even to the age of Nestor: this man peradventure may well be called a good merchant, but verily I would not say that he were a very good Christian man, that hangeth all together of himself, and hath distrust of the promises of Christ, whose goodness, it is easy to wit, shall not fail a good man putting his trust in him, seeing that he so liberally both feedeth and clotheth the poor sparrows. But let us now cast accounts of the commodities, which riches is believed to bring with him. First of all even by the common consent of the gentile philosophers: among the good things which are called *bona utilia,* that is to say, good profitable things, riches hath the lowest place.

Riches among profitable things obtain the lowest room.

And when all other things (after the division of Epictetus) are without man, except only virtue of the mind: yet nothing is so much without us as money is, nothing bringeth so little commodity.

Riches helpeth nothing to virtue.

For whatsoever there is anywhere of gold, whatsoever there is of precious stones, if thou alone hadst it every deal in thy possession, shall thy mind be therefore the better by the value of one hair? Shalt thou be the wiser? Shalt thou be the cunninger? Shalt thou be any whit the more in good health of body? Shall it make thee more strong and lusty? More fair and beauteous? More young? No, truly. But you will say that it purchaseth pleasures, truth it is: but they be deadly pleasures; it getteth a man honour: but what honour I pray you?

To false pleasures and vain honours they help somewhat.

Verily false honour, which they give, that prayeth nothing, setteth by nothing but only foolish things, and of whom to be praised, is well near to be dispraised. True honour is to be lauded of them which are commendable and praiseworthy themselves.

Honour is the reward of virtue, and not of riches.

The highest honour that can be is to have pleased Christ. True honour is the reward, not of riches, but of virtue. The foolish people giveth thee room and place, gazeth upon thee, and giveth thee honour and reverence. Oh fool, they wonder at thine apparel, and honoureth it, and not thee: Why dost thou not descend into thine own conscience, and consider the miserable poverty of thy mind? Which if the common people saw, then would they judge thee as miserable and wretched, as they now call thee happy and blessed. But good getteth friends. I grant, but yet feigned and false friends: neither getteth it friends to thee but to itself. And certainly the rich man is in this point of all men most unfortunate and wretched, because he cannot so much as discern or know his true friends and lovers from other.

Riches getteth friends but those false and feigned.

One hateth him privily and secretly in heart and mind as an hard niggard. Another hath envy at him, because he passeth him in riches. Another looking to his own profit and advantage flattereth him, and holdeth up his yea and his nay, and smileth upon him, to the end that he may scrape and get something from him. He that before his face is most loving and kind wisheth and prayeth for his quick and hasty death. There is none that loveth him so heartily and entirely, but that he had liefer have him dead than alive. No man is so familiar with him, that he will tell him the truth. But be it in case there were one special friend among a thousand that loved a rich man heartily without any manner of feigning, yet cannot the rich man but have in suspicion and mistrust every man. He judgeth all men to be vultures and ravenous birds gaping for carrion: he thinketh all men to be flies flying to him, to suck out some profit of him for themselves. Whatsoever commodity therefore riches seemeth to bring, it for the most part, or else altogether is but coloured and deceitful, it is shadow-like and full of delusion, appearing otherwise than it is in very deed. But they bring very many things which are evil indeed, and taketh away very many of these things which are good in very deed. Therefore if thou wilt lay accounts well and perfectly of that which is won, and that which is lost: doubtless thou shalt find that they never do bring so much of commodities, but that they draw with them too, too much more of incommodities and displeasures. With how painful and sore labours are they gotten, and with how great jeopardies? With how great thought and care be they kept? With how great heaviness and sorrow are they lost?

Wherefore Christ compareth riches to thorns.

For which causes Christ calleth them, yea, thorns, because they rend, tear and pluck in sunder all the tranquillity and quietness of the mind, with a thousand cares, than the which tranquillity of mind, nothing is to man more sweet and pleasant, and they never quench thirst and desire of themselves, but kindleth and increaseth it more and more. They drive a man headlong into all mischief. Neither flatter thyself in vain, saying nothing forbiddeth but that a man at one time may be both rich and good.

It is hard for a rich man to be a good man.

Remember what verity saith, that it is more easy for a camel to creep through the eye of a needle than a rich man to enter into the kingdom of heaven. And plainly without exception true is that saying of Saint Jerome. A rich man to be either unjust himself or the heir of an unjust man: great riches can never be either gotten or else kept without sin.

Avarice is called idolatry.

Remember of how much better riches they rob thee, for he hateth the very taste and smell of virtue, he hateth all honest crafts, whosoever setteth his heart upon gold. Moreover the vice of avarice only is called idolatry of Paul.

Mammon is the devil which tempteth and stirreth to covetousness.

Neither with any other vice at all Christ hath less acquaintance, neither the selfsame person can please God and mammon also.

CHAPTER 35

The recapitulation of the remedies against the vice of avarice.

Thou shalt lightly therefore cease to wonder at money if thou wilt ponder and weigh diligently very good things with those that be false and apparent good, of painted and coloured commodities with those that be very commodities indeed.

The mind of man is of great capacity, God only filleth it.

If thou wilt learn with thine inner eyes to behold and to love that noble good thing which is infinite, which only when it is present, yea though all other things should be lacking, abundantly doth satisfy the mind of man, which is wider and larger of capacity than that it can be sufficed with all the good things of this world.

Naked we came and naked we shall go.

If thou shalt oft call again before thine eyes in what condition and state thou were when the earth first received thee when thou were first born: likewise in what state that same shall receive thee again when thou diest. If ever shall be present in thy memory that famous fool of whom is made mention in the gospel. To whom it is said: This night I will fet again thy soul from thee: and these things which thou hast gathered together, whose shall they then be? If thou shalt turn thy mind from the corrupt manners of the common sort unto the poverty of Mary, Christ's mother, unto the poverty of the apostles, of the martyrs, and most of all of Christ thy head. And set before thee that fearful word Vae, that is interpreted, woe be to you: which Christ so menaceth and threateneth unto the rich men of this world.

CHAPTER 36

Against ambition or desire of honour and authority.

If at any time ambition shall cumber and vex thy mind through her enchantments, with these remedies thou shalt arm thyself beforehand without tarrying (according to the rules which I gave before), take and hold this with tooth and nail, that to be honour only which springeth of true virtue, which selfsame nevertheless a man must sometime refuse, even as taught us both with doctrine and example our master Jesus Christ.

Honour springeth of virtue only.

And this to be the chief honour and only honour which a Christian man should desire and wish for, to be praised not of men, but of God, for whom he commendeth (as saith the apostle) that man is perfect and worthy of honour indeed.

It is an honest thing to be lauded of God.

But if honour be given of man for an ungoodly and unhonest thing, and so of ungoodly persons: This is not honour but great dishonesty, shame and rebuke. If for any mean and indifferent thing, as for beauty, strength, riches, kin: yet verily shall it not be called truly honour, for no man deserveth honour with that thing whereof he deserveth not to be praised.

Honour given of unhonest persons.

If for an honest thing indeed it shall be honour: yet he which deserveth it shall not desire it, but verily shall be content with the very virtue and conscience of his good deed. Behold therefore how foolish and how worthy to be laughed at these honours be, for whose desire the common people so greatly burn and rage.

Honour given of common people.

First of all of whom are they given? Truly of them with whom is no difference between honesty and dishonesty. Wherefore are they given? Very oft for mean things, now and then for filthy things. To whom? To him which is unworthy. Whosoever therefore giveth honour, either he doth it for fear, and then is he to be feared again, or because thou wouldest do him a good turn, and then he mocketh thee: or because he is astonished at things of naught and worthy of no honour, and then he is to be pitied: or because he supposed thee to be endued with such things as honour is given of duty, wherein if he be deceived, give diligence that thou mayest be that he supposeth thee to be. But and if he hit aright, refer all the honour that is offered thee unto to whom thou art bound, yea for all those things whereunto the honour is given. As thou oughtest not ascribe to thine own self the virtue, so is it unfitting to take upon thee the honour thereof.

To whom honour chanceth most commonly.

Besides this, what is greater madness than to esteem the value of thyself by the opinions of foolish men, in whose hands it lieth to take away again whensoever they list the very same honour which they give, and dishonest thee which was even now honested. Therefore nothing can be more foolish than either to rejoice for such honours when they happen, or to be sorry or mourn when they be taken away, which not to be true honours thou shalt perceive at the least way by this probation and argument, for so much as they be common to the worst and lewdest persons of all: yea they chance almost to none more plenteously than to them which of true honours be most unworthy.

The quietness of a private life.

Remember how blessed is the quietness of a mean life, both private, that is to say, charged with no common business, and separate and removed out of the way from all noise, haunt, or press. On the other side consider how full of pricks, how full of cares, of perils, of sorrows, is the life of great men, and what difficulty it is not to forget thyself in prosperity, how hard it is for a man standing in a slippery place not to fall, how grievous the fall is from an high. And remember that all honour is coupled with great charge, and how strait the judgment of the high judge shall be against them which here in usurping of honours, prefer themselves afore other men. For surely whosoever shall humble and submit himself, him as an innocent or harmless person mercy shall succour: but whosoever exalteth himself as a perfect man, the same person excludeth from himself the help and succour of grace.

Let it not exalt thy mind because thou bearest rule over other men.

Let ever the example of Christ thy head stick fast in thy mind. What thing as touching to the world was more vile, more despised or less honoured than he? How forsook he honours when they were proffered him, which was greater than any honour? How set he no store of honours when he rode upon an ass? How condemned he them when he was clothed in pall and crowned with thorn? How unglorious or vile a death chose he? But whom the world despised him the father glorified. Let thy glory be in the cross of Christ, in whom also is thy health, wealth, saving, defence and protection. What good shall worldly honours do to thee if God cast thee away and depise thee, and the angels loathe, abhor, and defy thee?

CHAPTER 37

Against elation otherwise called pride or swelling of the mind

Know thyself.

Thou shalt not swell in thy mind if, (according to the common proverb used of every man) thou wouldest know thyself: that is whatsoever great thing, whatsoever goodly or beautiful thing, whatsoever excellent thing is in thee, thou account that to be the gift of God, and not thy good. On the other side, if whatsoever is low or vile, whatsoever is foul or filthy, whatsoever is shrewd or evil thou ascribe that altogether unto thine own self: if thou remember in how much filth thou were conceived, in how much born, how naked, how needy, how brutish, how wretched, how miserably thou creepest into this light. If thou remember into how many diseases or sickness on every side, unto how many chances, unto how many encumbrances, griefs, and troubles this wretched body is dangered. And again how little a thing were able shortly to consume and bring to naught this cruel and unruly giant, swelling with so mighty a spirit.

Perceive whereof thou stoodest so greatly in thine own conceit.

Ponder also this, what manner thing that is whereof thou takest upon thee: if it be a mean or an indifferent thing, it is foolishness: if a filthy thing, it is madness: if an unhonest thing, it is unkindness. Remember also nothing to be a more sure document or proof of stark foolishness and lack of understanding, than if a man stand greatly in his own conceit. And again that no kind of folly is more uncurable, if thy mind begin to arise and wax great because a vile man submitteth himself to thee. Think how much greater and mightier God hangeth over thine head, which crusheth down every proud neck erect straight up, and bringeth every hill unto a plain, which spared not, no verily not so much as the angel when he was fallen into pride. And these things also shall be good though they seem somewhat as they were trifles, if thou wouldest compare thyself alway with excellent persons. Thou likest thyself because of a little beauty of thy body: compare thyself to them which in beauty be far before thee. A little cunning maketh thee to set up thy feathers, turn thine eyes unto them in comparison of whom thou mayst seem to have learned nothing at all. Moreover if thou wilt account not how much of good things thou hast, but how much thou lackest: And with Paul, forgetful of those things which be behind thee, wouldest stretch forth thyself to those things which remain afore thee. Furthermore that also shall not be an unwise thing, if when the wind of pride doth blow, by and by we turn our very evil things into a remedy, as it were expelling one poison with another.

Consider thine own vices and deformities.

That thing shall this wise come to pass, if when any great vice or deformity of body, when any notable damage either fortune hath given, or folly hath brought to us which might gnaw us vehemently by the stomach, we set that before our eyes, and by the example of the peacock we behold ourselves chiefly in that part of us in which we be most deformed, and so shall thy feathers fall forthwith and thy pride abate.

Arrogancy, presumption or pertinacy, is a hated vice.

Beyond all these (besides that none other vice is more hated unto God) remember also that arrogancy, pride, and presumption is notably hated and had in derision everywhere among men: when contrariwise lowliness and meekness, both purchaseth the favour of God, and knitteth on to the benevolence of man. Therefore to speak compendiously, two things chiefly shall refrain thee from pride, if thou consider what thou art in thyself, filthy in thy birth, a bubble (such as riseth in the water) throughout all thy life, worms' meat in thy death, and what Christ was made for thee.

CHAPTER 38

Against wrath and desire of vengeance.

Wrath is a childish thing.

When fervent sorrow of the mind stirreth thee up unto vengeance, remember wrath to be nothing less than that which it falsely counterfeiteth, that is to wit fortitude or manfulness: for nothing is so childish, so weak, nothing so feeble and of so vile a mind as to rejoice in vengeance. Thou wouldest be counted a man of great stomach, and therefore thou sufferest not injury to be unavenged: but in conclusion by this means thou utterest thy childishness, seeing thou canst not rule thine own mind, which is the very property and office of a man.

Regard little another man's folly.

How much manlier, how much excellenter it is to set another man's folly at naught than to counterfeit it? But he hath hurt thee, he is proud and fierce, he scorneth thee. The filthier he is, so much the more beware lest thou be made like him. What the devil's madness is it that thou to avenge another man's lewdness wouldest be made the lewder thyself? If thou despise the rebuke, all men shall perceive that it was done to one unworthy thereof: but and if thou be moved, thou shalt make his quarrel which did the wrong much the better. Furthermore take the thing as it is, if any wrong be received, that is not eased one whit with vengeance but augmented. For in conclusion what end shall there be of injuries on both sides if every man go forth and proceed to revenge his own grief? Enemies increase on both parts, the sorrow waxeth fresh and raw again, and the longer it endureth the more uncurable it is: but with softness and with sufferance is healed now and then, yea even he which did the wrong, and after he is come to himself again, of an enemy is made a very trusty and faithful friend. But the very same hurt which by vengeance thou covetest to put from thee reboundeth back again upon thee, and not without increase of harm. And that also shall be a sovereign remedy against wrath if, according to the division of things above rehearsed, thou shouldest consider that one man cannot hurt another unless he will himself, save in those things only which be outward goods, which so greatly pertain not unto man: for the very good things of the mind God only is able to take away, which he is not wont to do but unto unkind persons, and only he can give them, which he hath not used to do unto cruel and furious persons. No Christian man therefore is hurt but of himself. Injury hurteth no man but the worker thereof. These things also help (though they be not weighty) that thou shalt not follow the sorrow of thy mind: If, the circumstances of rhetoricians well gathered together, thou both make light of thine own harms, and also minish the wrong done of another man commonly after this manner: He hurt me, but it will be soon amended. Moreover he is a child, he is of things unexpert, he is a young man, it is a woman, he did it through another man's motion or counsel, he did it unaware, or when he had well drunk, it is meet that I forgive him. And on the other side he hath hurt me grievously. Certain, but he is my father, my brother, my master, my friend, my wife, it is according that this grief should be forgiven, either for the love, or else for the authority of the person. Or else thou shalt set one thing against another, and recompense the injury with other good benefits done of him unto thee. Or with thine offences done to him afore season shalt account it even, and so make quit. This man hath hurt me verily, but other times how oft hath he done me good. It cometh of an unliberal mind to forget the good benefits and only to remember a little wrong or displeasure. Now he hath offended me, but how oft offended of me. I will forgive him, that he in likewise by mine example may pardon me, if I another time trespass against him. Finally it shall be a remedy of much greater virtue and of strong operation, if in the misdoing of another man against thee thou didest think in thyself, what things, how grievous, and how oft thou hast sinned against God, how many manner of ways thou art in debt to him: as much as thou shalt remit unto thy brother which is in thy debt, so much shall God forgive unto thee.

Forgive thy debtor.

This way of forgiving other men's debts hath he taught us which is himself a creditor, he will not refuse the law which he himself made. To be absolved or loosed from thy sins thou runnest to Rome, sailest to Saint James, buyest pardons most large. I dispraise not verily that thing which thou doest: but when all is done, there is no readier way, no surer means whereby (if thou have offended) thou mightest come to favour again and be reconciled to God, than if thou, when thou art offended, be reconciled again unto thy brother, forgive a little trespass unto thy neighbour (for it is but small whatsoever one man trespasseth against another) that Christ may forgive thee so many thousand offences. But it is hard (thou sayest) to subdue the mind when he beginneth to wax hot.

By the example of Christ suage thy mind.

Rememberest thou not, how much harder things Christ suffered for thee? what were thou when he for thy sake bestowed his precious life? Were thou not his enemy? With what softness suffereth he the daily repeating thine old sins? Last of all how meekly suffered he the uttermost rebukes, bonds, stripes, finally death most shameful? Why? Why? Boastest thou thyself of the head, if thou care not to be in the body? Thou shalt not be a member of Christ except thou follow the steps of Christ. But he is unworthy to be forgiven.

We must pardon the unworthy.

Even so were not thou unworthy whom God should forgive? In thine own self thou wilt have mercy exercised, and against thy brother wilt thou use extreme and cruel justice? Is it so great a thing if thou being a sinner thyself shouldest forgive a sinner, when Christ prayed his father for them which crucified him? Is it an hard thing not to strike thy brother whom thou art also commanded to love? Is it an hard thing not to pay again an evil deed, for which except thou wouldest recompense a good, thou shalt not be that toward thy fellow that Christ was toward his servant? Finally if this man be unworthy to whom for an evil turn a good should be recompensed, yet art thou worthy to do it, Christ is worthy, for whose sake it is done. But in suffering an old displeasure I call in a new, he will do injury again if he should escape unpunished for this: if without offence thou canst avoid, avoid it: if thou canst ease or remedy it, ease it: if thou canst heal a mad man, heal him, if not let him perish himself alone rather than with thee. This man which thinketh himself to have done harm, think thou worthy to be pitied, and not to be punished. Wilt thou be angry to thy commendation and laud?

Be angry and aggrieved with the vice.

Be angry with the vice, not with the man. But the more thou art inclined by nature to this kind of vice, so much the more diligently arm thyself long beforehand, and once for altogether print sure in thy mind this decree or purpose: that thou neither say nor do anything at any time while thou art angry: believe not thyself when thou art moved: have suspected whatsoever that sudden motion or rage of the mind designeth or judgeth, yea though it be honest.

Say nor do anything if thou be angry.

Remember none other difference to be between a frantic person and him that rageth in ire than is between a short madness that dureth but a season and a continual perseverant madness. Call to mind how many things in anger thou hast said or done worthy to be repeated, which now though in vain thou wouldest fain were changed. Therefore when that wrath waxeth hot and boileth: if thou cannot straightway save and deliver thyself altogether from anger, at the least way come thus far forth to thyself and soberness that thou remember thyself not to be well advised or in thy right mind: To remember this is a great part of health. On this wise reason with thyself, now verily so am I minded, but anon hereafter I shall be of another mind much contrary, why should I in the mean season say against my friend (while I am moved) that thing which hereafter when I am appeased and my malice ceased I could not change: why should I now do in my malice or anger that thing which when I am sobered and come to myself again I should greatly sorrow and repent. Why rather should not reason, why should not pity, at the last why should not Christ obtain that of me now, which a little pause of time shall shortly hereafter obtain. To no man (I suppose) hath nature given so much of black colour but at the least way he might so far forth rule himself.

The mind must be hardened against wrath.

But it shall be a very good thing for thee thus instructed to harden thy mind with reason, with continuance and custom that thou couldest not be moved at all: it shall be a perfect thing, if thou, having indignation only at the vice, for a displeasure or rebuke done to thee, shalt render again a deed of charity. To conclude, even natural temperance, which ought to be in every man, requireth that thou shouldst not suffer affections to rule thee utterly. Not to be wroth at all is a thing most like unto God, and therefore most comely and beautiful. To overcome evil with goodness, malice with kindness, is to counterfeit the perfect charity of Christ Jesu. To hold wrath under and keep him back with a bridle is the property of a wise man. To follow the appetite of wrath is not a point of a man verily, but plainly of beasts, and that of wild beasts. But if thou wouldest know how much uncomely it were to a man to be overcome with wrath, look when thou art sober that thou mark the countenance of an angry person, or else when thou thyself art angry, go unto a glass.

Behold thine own countenance when thou art angry.

When thine eyes so burn flaming in fire, when thy cheeks be pale, when thy mouth is drawn awry, thy lips foam, all thy members quake, when thy voice soundeth so maliciously, neither thy gestures be of one fashion, who would judge thee to be a man? Thou perceivest now my most sweetest friend how large a sea is open all abroad to dispute of other vices after this same manner. But we in the midst of our course will strike sail leaving the rest to thy discretion. Neither certain was it my mind, purpose, or intention (for that should be an infinite work) as I began, even so to dissuade thee from every vice, vice by vice, as it were with sundry declamations, and to bold and courage thee to the contrary virtues.

Declamations. Sermons. Orations. Preachings.

This only was my desire (which I thought sufficient for thee) to shew a certain manner and craft of a new kind of war, how thou mightest arm thyself against the evils of the old life burgeoning forth again and springing afresh.

Certain decrees must be written in our minds.

Therefore as we have done in one or two things (because of example) so must thou thyself do partly in everything, one by one: but most of all in the things whereunto thou shalt perceive thyself to be stirred or instigate peculiarly, whether it be through vice of nature, custom, or evil bringing up, against these things some certain decrees must be written in the table of thy mind, and they must be renewed now and then, lest they should fail or be forgotten through disuse, as against the vices of backbiting, filthy speaking, envy, guile, and other like: these be the only enemies of Christ's soldiers, against whose assault the mind must be armed long aforehand with prayer, with noble sayings of wise men, with the doctrine of holy scripture, with example of devout and holy men, and specially of Christ.

Why he wrote this book somewhat quicklier and with more speed.

Though I doubt not but that the reading of holy scripture shall minister all these things to thee abundantly, nevertheless charity which one brother oweth to another hath moved and exhorted me that at the least way with this sudden and hasty writings, I should further and help thy holy purpose as much as lieth in me: a thing which I have done somewhat the rather because I somewhat feared lest thou shouldest fall into that superstitious kind of religious men, which partly awaiting on their own advantage, partly with great zeal, but not according to knowledge, walk round about both by sea and land, and if anywhere they get a man recovering from vices unto virtue, him straightway with most importune and lewd exhortations, threatenings, and flatterings they enforce to thrust into the order of monks, even as though without a cowl there were no christendom.

Religious men.

Furthermore when they have filled his breast with pure scrupulosity and doubts insoluble, then they bind him to certain traditions found by man, and plainly thrust the wretched person headlong into a certain bondage of ceremonies like unto the manner of the Jews, and teach him to tremble and fear, but not to love.

The order of monks.

The order of monkship is not piety, but a kind of living to every man after the disposition of his body and his mind, also either profitable or unprofitable, whereunto verily as I do not courage thee, so likewise I counsel not from it. This thing only I warn thee of, that thou put piety neither in meat nor in raiment or habit, nor in any visible thing, but in those things which have been declared and shewed thee afore: and in whatsoever persons thou shalt find or perceive the true image of Christ, with them couple thyself. Moreover when such men be lacking whose conversation should make thee better, withdraw thyself as much as thou mayst from the company of man, and call the holy prophet, Christ and the apostles unto communication, but specially make Paul of familiar acquaintance with thee.

What companions a man should choose to live withal.

This fellow must be had ever in thy bosom to be read and studied both night and day: finally and to be learned without the book word by word, upon whom we have now a good while enforced with great diligence to make a comment or a narration, a bold deed truly. But notwithstanding we, trusting in the help of God, will endeavour ourself busily, lest after Origene, Ambrose, and Augustyne, lest after so many new interpreters we should seem to have taken this labour upon us utterly either without a cause or without fruit: and also that certain busy and unquiet pick-quarrels, which think it perfect religion to know nothing at all of good learning, may understand and well perceive that whereas we in youth have embraced and made much of the pure learning of old authors, and also have gotten, and that not without great sweat and watch, a mean understanding of both the tongues Greke and Latyn.

Good learning profiteth unto piety.

We have not in so doing looked unto a vain and foolish fame, or unto the childish pastime and pleasure of our mind, but that we were minded long before to adorn and garnish the Lord's temple with the riches of other strange nations and countries to the uttermost of our power. Which temple some men with their ignorance and barbarousness hath overmuch dishonested, that by the reason of such riches excellent wits might also be inflamed unto the love of holy scripture. But this so great a thing a few days laid apart, we have taken upon us this labour for thy sake, that unto thee (as it were with a finger) we might shew the way which leadeth straight unto Christ. And I beseech Jesu the father of this holy purpose (as I hope) that he would vouchsafe benignly to favour thy wholesome enforcements, yea that he would in changing of thee increase his grace, and make thee perfect, that thou mightest quickly wax big and strong in him, and spring up unto a perfect man. In whom also fare thou well, brother and friend, always verily beloved in my heart, but now much more than before both dear and plesant. At the town of Saint Andomers, the year of Christ's birth 1501.

Here endeth this book called Enchiridion or the manual of the Christian knight, made by Erasmus of Roterdame, in the which book is contained many goodly lessons very necessary and profitable for the soul's health of all true Christian people: Imprinted at London by Wynkyn de Worde, for Johan Byddell, otherwise Salisbury, the xv. day of Novembre. And be for to sell at the sign of our Lady of pytie next to Flete Bridge. 1533.

INSTITUTES OF THE CHRISTIAN RELIGION

*By
John Calvin
Translated by Henry Beveridge
A New Translation by Henry Beveridge, Esq
The Institution of the Christian Religion, written in Latin, by master John Calvin,
and translated into English according to the author's last edition.
Seen and allowed according to the order appointed in the Queries maiesties injunctions.*

INTRODUCTION

By the Rev. John Murray, M.A., Th.M.

The publication in English of another edition of the *opus magnum* of Christian theology is an event fraught with much encouragement. Notwithstanding the decadence so patent in our present-day world and particularly in the realm of Christian thought and life, the publishers have confidence that there is sufficient interest to warrant such an undertaking. If this faith is justified we have reason for thanksgiving to God. For what would be a better harbinger of another Reformation than widespread recourse to the earnest and sober study of the Word of God which would be evinced by the readiness carefully to peruse *The Institutes of the Christian Religion*.

Dr. B. B. Warfield in his admirable article, "On the Literary History of the *Institutes*," has condensed for us the appraisal accorded Calvin's work by the critics who have been most competent to judge. Among these tributes none expresses more adequately, and none with comparable terseness, the appraisal which is Calvin's due than that of the learned Joseph Scaliger, "Solus inter theologos Calvinus."

It would be a presumptuous undertaking to try to set forth all the reasons why Calvin holds that position of eminence in the history of Christian theology. By the grace and in the overruling providence of God there was the convergence of multiple factors, and all of these it would be impossible to trace in their various interrelations and interactions. One of these, however, calls for special mention. Calvin was an exegete and biblical theologian of the first rank. No other one factor comparably served to equip Calvin for the successful prosecution of his greatest work which in 1559 received its definitive edition.

The attitude to Scripture entertained by Calvin and the principles which guided him in its exposition are nowhere stated with more simplicity and fervor than in the Epistle Dedicatory to his first commentary, the commentary on the epistle to the Romans. "Such veneration," he says, "we ought indeed to entertain for the Word of God, that we ought not to pervert it in the least degree by varying expositions; for its majesty is diminished, I know not how much, especially when not expounded with great discretion and with great sobriety. And if it be deemed a great wickedness to contaminate any thing that is dedicated to God, he surely cannot be endured, who, with impure, or even with unprepared hands, will handle that very thing, which of all things is the most sacred on earth. It is therefore an audacity, closely allied to a sacrilege, rashly to turn Scripture in any way we please, and to indulge our fancies as in sport; which has been done by many in former times" (English Translation, Grand Rapids, 1947, p. 27).

It was Calvin preeminently who set the pattern for the exercise of that sobriety which guards the science of exegesis against those distortions and perversions to which allegorizing methods are ever prone to subject the interpretation and application of Scripture. The debt we owe to Calvin in establishing sound canons of interpretation and in thus directing the future course of exegetical study is incalculable. It is only to be lamented that too frequently the preaching of Protestant and even Reformed communions has not been sufficiently grounded in the hermeneutical principles which Calvin so nobly exemplified.

One feature of Calvin's exegetical work is his concern for the analogy of Scripture. He is always careful to take account of the unity and harmony of Scripture teaching. His expositions are not therefore afflicted with the vice of expounding particular passages without respect to the teaching of Scripture elsewhere and without respect to the system of truth set forth in the Word of God. His exegesis, in a word, is theologically oriented. It is this quality that lies close to that which was *par excellence* his genius.

However highly we assess Calvin's exegetical talent and product, his eminence as an exegete must not be allowed to overshadow what was, after all, his greatest gift. He was *par excellence* a theologian. It was his systematizing genius preeminently that equipped him for the prosecution and completion of his masterpiece.

When we say that he was *par excellence* a theologian we must dissociate from our use of this word every notion that is suggestive of the purely speculative. No one has ever fulminated with more passion and eloquence against "vacuous and meteoric speculation" than has Calvin. And no one has ever been more keenly conscious that the theologian's task was the humble and, at the same time, truly noble one of being a disciple of the Scripture. "No man," he declares, "can have the least knowledge of true and sound doctrine without having been a disciple of the Scripture. Hence originates all true wisdom, when we embrace with reverence the testimony which God hath been pleased therein to deliver concerning himself. For obedience is the source, not only of an absolutely perfect and complete faith, but of all right knowledge of God" (*Inst.* 1, 6, 2). In the words of William Cunningham: "In theology there is, of course, no room for originality properly so called, for its whole materials are contained in the actual statements of God's word; and he is the greatest and best theologian who has most accurately apprehended the meaning of the statements of Scripture—who, by comparing and combining them, has most fully and correctly brought out the whole mind of God on all the topics on which the Scriptures give us information—who classifies and digests the truths of Scripture in the way best fitted to commend them to the apprehension and acceptance of men—and who can most clearly and forcibly bring out their scriptural evidence, and most skillfully and effectively defend them against the assaults of adversaries . . . Calvin was far above the weakness of aiming at the invention of novelties in theology, or of wishing to be regarded as the discoverer of new opinions" (*The Reformers and the Theology of the Reformation*, Edinburgh, 1866, p. 296). As we bring even elementary understanding to bear upon our reading of the *Institutes* we shall immediately discover the profound sense of the majesty of God, veneration for the Word of God, and the jealous care for faithful exposition and systematization which were marked features of the author. And because of this we shall find the *Institutes* to be suffused with the warmth of godly fear. The *Institutes* is not only the classic of Christian theology; it is also a model of Christian devotion. For what Calvin sought to foster was that "pure and genuine religion" which consists in "faith united with the serious fear of God, such fear as may embrace voluntary reverence and draw along with it legitimate worship such as is prescribed in the law" (*Inst.* 1, 2, 2).

The present edition is from the translation made by Henry Beveridge in 1845 for the Calvin Translation Society. The reader may be assured that the translation faithfully reflects the teaching of Calvin but must also bear in mind that no translation can perfectly convey the thought of the original. It may also be added that a more adequate translation of Calvin's *Institutes* into English is a real *desideratum*. In fulfilling this need the translator or translators would perform the greatest service if the work of translation were supplemented by footnotes in which at crucial points, where translation is difficult or most accurate translation impossible, the Latin text would be reproduced and comment made on its more exact import. Furthermore, footnotes which would supply the reader with references to other places in Calvin's writings where he deals with the same subject would be an invaluable help to students of Calvin and to the cause of truth. Admittedly such work requires linguistic skill of the highest order, thorough knowledge of Calvin's writings, and deep sympathy with his theology. It would also involve prodigious labour. We may hope that the seed being sown by the present venture may bear fruit some day in such a harvest.

John Murray,
Professor of Systematic Theology,
Westminster Theological Seminary.
Philadelphia, Penna.

THE PRINTERS TO THE READERS.

Whereas some men have thought and reported it to be [very great negligence in us for that we have so long kept back from you this,] being so profitable a work for you, namely before the master J[ohnne] Dawes had translated it and delivered it into our hands more than a twelvemonth past: you shall understand for our excuse in that behalf, that we could not well imprint it sooner. For we have been by diverse necessary causes constrained with our earnest entreatance to procure an other frede or oures to translate it whole again. This translation, we trust, you shall well allow. For it hath not only been faithfully done by the translator himself, but also hath been wholly perused by such men, whose ingement and credit all the godly learned in England well know I estheme. But since it is now come forth, we pray you accept it, and see it. If any faults have passed us by oversight, we beseech you let us have your patience, as you have had our diligence.

The Institution of Christian Religion, written in Latin by M. John Calvin, and translated into English according to the Authors last edition, with sundry Tables to find the principal matters entreated of in this book, and also the declaration of places of Scripture therein expounded, by Thomas Norton. Whereunto there are newly added in the margen of the book, notes containing in briefs the substance of the matter handled in each Section.

Printed at London by Arnold Hatfield, for Bonham Norton. 1599

THE ORIGINAL TRANSLATOR'S PREFACE.

Prefixed to the fourth edition 1581 and reprinted verbatim in all the subsequent editions. T[homas] N[orton], the translator to the reader.

Good reader, here is now offered you, the fourth time printed in English, M. Calvin's book of the Institution of Christian Religion; a book of great labour to the author, and of great profit to the Church of God. M. Calvin first wrote it when he was a young man, a book of small volume, and since that season he has at sundry times published it with new increases, still protesting at every edition himself to be one of those *qui scribendo proficiunt, et proficiendo scribunt*, which with their writing do grow in profiting, and with their profiting do proceed in writing. At length having, in many [of] his other works, traveled about exposition of sundry books of the Scriptures, and in the same finding occasion to discourse of sundry common-places and matters of doctrine, which being handled according to the occasions of the text that were offered him, and not in any other method, were not so ready for the reader's use, he therefore entered into this purpose to enlarge this book of Institutions, and therein to treat of all those titles and commonplaces largely, with this intent, that whensoever any occasion fell in his other books to treat of any such cause, he would not newly amplify his books of commentaries and expositions therewith, but refer his reader wholly to this storehouse and treasure of that sort of divine learning. As age and weakness grew upon him, so he hastened his labour; and, according to his petition to God, he in manner ended his life with his work, for he lived not long after.

So great a jewel was meet to be made most beneficial, that is to say, applied to most common use. Therefore, in the very beginning of the Queen's Majesty's most blessed reign, I translated it out of Latin into English for the commodity of the Church of Christ, at the special request of my dear friends of worthy memory, Reginald Wolfe and Edward Whitchurch, the one her Majesty's printer for the Hebrew, Greek, and Latin tongues, the other her Highness' printer of the books of Common Prayer. I performed my work in the house of my said friend, Edward Whitchurch, a man well known of upright heart and dealing, an ancient zealous gospeller, as plain and true a friend as ever I knew living, and as desirous to do anything to common good, especially by the advancement of true religion.

At my said first edition of this book, I considered how the author thereof had of long time purposely laboured to write the same most exactly, and to pack great plenty of matter in small room of words; yea, and those so circumspectly and precisely ordered, to avoid the cavillations of such as for enmity to the truth therein contained would gladly seek and abuse all advantages which might be found by any oversight in penning of it, that the sentences were thereby become so full as nothing might well be added without idle superfluity, and again so highly pared, that nothing could be diminished without taking away some necessary substance of matter therein expressed. This manner of writing, beside the peculiar terms of arts and figures, and the difficulty of the matters themselves, being throughout interlaced with the school men's controversies, made a great hardness in the author's own book, in that tongue wherein otherwise he is both plentiful and easy, insomuch that it sufficeth not to read him once, unless you can be content to read in vain.

This consideration encumbered me with great doubtfulness for the whole order and frame of my translation. If I should follow the words, I saw that of necessity the hardness in the translation must needs be greater than was in the tongue wherein it was originally written. If I should leave the course of words, and grant myself liberty after the natural manner of my own tongue, to say that in English which I conceived to be his meaning in Latin, I plainly perceived how hardly I might escape error, and on the other side, in this matter of faith and religion, how perilous it was to err. For I durst not presume to warrant myself to have his meaning without his words. And they that wet what it is to translate well and faithfully, especially in matters of religion, do know that not the only grammatical construction of words sufficeth, but the very building and order to observe all advantages of vehemence or grace, by placing or accent of words, maketh much to the true setting forth of a writer's mind.

In the end, I rested upon this determination, to follow the words so near as the phrase of the English tongue would suffer me. Which purpose I so performed, that if the English book were printed in such paper and letter as the Latin is, it should not exceed the Latin in quantity. Whereby, beside all other commodities that a faithful translation of so good a work may bring, this one benefit is moreover provided for such as are desirous to attain some knowledge of the Latin tongue (which is, at this time, to be wished in many of those men for whose profession this book most fitly serveth), that they shall not find any more English than shall suffice to construe the Latin withal, except in such few places where the great difference of the phrases of the languages enforced me: so that, comparing the one with the other, they shall both profit in good matter, and furnish themselves with understanding of that speech, wherein the greatest treasures of knowledge are disclosed.

In the doing hereof, I did not only trust mine own wit or ability, but examined my whole doing from sentence to sentence throughout the whole book with conference and overlooking of such learned men, as my translation being allowed by their Judgment, I did both satisfy mine own conscience that I had done truly, and their approving of it might be a good warrant to the reader that nothing should herein be delivered him but sound, unmingled, and uncorrupted doctrine, even in such sort as the author himself had first framed it. All that I wrote, the grave, learned, and virtuous man, M. David Whitehead (whom I name with honourable remembrance), did, among others, compare with the Latin, examining every sentence throughout the whole book. Beside all this, I privately required many, and generally all men with whom I ever had any talk of this matter, that if they found anything either not truly translated, or not plainly Englished, they would inform me thereof, promising either to satisfy them or to amend it. Since which time, I have not been advertised by any man of anything which they would require to be altered. Neither had I myself, by reason of my profession, being otherwise occupied, any leisure to peruse it. And that is the cause, why not only at the second and third time, but also at this impression, you have no change at all in the work, but altogether as it was before.

Indeed, I perceived many men well-minded and studious of this book, to require a table for their ease and furtherance. Their honest desire I have fulfilled in the second edition, and have added thereto a plentiful table, which is also here inserted, which I have translated out of the Latin, wherein the principal matters discoursed in this book are named by their due titles in order of alphabet, and under every title is set forth a brief sum of the whole doctrine taught in this book concerning the matter belonging to that title or common-place; and therewith is added the book, chapter, and section or division of the chapter, where the same doctrine is more largely expressed and proved. And for the readier finding thereof, I have caused the number of the chapters to be set upon every leaf in the book, and quoted the sections also by their due numbers with the usual figures of algorism. And now at this last publishing, my friends, by whose charge it is now newly imprinted in a Roman letter and smaller volume, with divers other Tables which, since my second edition, were gathered by M. Marlorate, to be translated and here added for your benefit.

Moreover, whereas in the first edition the evil manner of my scribbling hand, the interlining of my copy, and some other causes well known among workmen of that faculty, made very many faults to pass the printer, I have, in the second impression, caused the book to be composed by the printed copy, and corrected by the written; whereby it must needs be that it was much more truly done than the other was, as I myself do know above three hundred faults amended. And now at this last printing, the composing after a printed copy bringeth some ease, and the diligence used about the correction having been right faithfully looked unto, it cannot be but much more truly set forth. This also is performed, that the volume being smaller, with a letter fair and legible, it is of more easy price, that it may be of more common use, and so to more large communicating of so great a treasure to those that desire Christian knowledge for instruction of their faith, and guiding of their duties. Thus, on the printer's behalf and mine, your ease and commodity (good readers) provided for. Now resteth your own diligence, for your own profit, in studying it.

To spend many words in commending the work itself were needless; yet thus much I think, I may both not unruly and not vainly say, that though many great learned men have written books of common-places of our religion, as Melancthon, Sarcerius, and others, whose works are very good and profitable to the Church of God, yet by the consenting Judgment of those that understand the same, there is none to be compared to this work of Calvin, both for his substantial sufficiency of doctrine, the sound declaration of truth in articles of our religion, the large and learned confirmation of the same, and the most deep and strong confutation of all old and new heresies; so that (the Holy Scriptures excepted) this is one of the most profitable books for all students of Christian divinity. Wherein (good readers), as I am glad for the glory of God, and for your benefit, that you may have this profit of my travel, so I beseech you let me have this use of your gentleness, that my doings may be construed to such good end as I have meant them; and that if any thing mislike you by reason of hardness, or any other cause that may seem to be my default, you will not forthwith condemn the work, but read it after; in which doing you will find (as many have confessed to me that they have found by experience) that those things which at the first reading shall displease you for hardness, shall be found so easy as so hard matter would suffer, and, for the most part, more easy than some other phrase which should with greater looseness and smoother sliding away deceive your understanding. I confess, indeed, it is not finely and pleasantly written, nor carrieth with it such delightful grace of speech as some great wise men have bestowed upon some foolisher things, yet it containeth sound truth set forth with faithful plainness, without wrong done to the author's meaning; and so, if you accept and use it, you shall not fail to have great profit thereby, and I shall think my labour very well employed.

Thomas Norton.

PREFATORY ADDRESS

To His Most Christian Majesty, the most Mighty and Illustrious Monarch, Francis, King of the French, HIS SOVEREIGN; JOHN CALVIN PRAYS PEACE AND SALVATION IN CHRIST.

Sire,—When I first engaged in this work, nothing was farther from my thoughts than to write what should afterwards be presented to your Majesty. My intention was only to furnish a kind of rudiments, by which those who feel some interest in religion might be trained to true godliness. And I toiled at the task chiefly for the sake of my countrymen the French, multitudes of whom I perceived to be hungering and thirsting after Christ, while very few seemed to have been duly imbued with even a slender knowledge of him. That this was the object which I had in view is apparent from the work itself, which is written in a simple and elementary form adapted for instruction.

But when I perceived that the fury of certain bad men had risen to such a height in your realm, that there was no place in it for sound doctrine, I thought it might be of service if I were in the same work both to give instruction to my countrymen, and also lay before your Majesty a Confession, from which you may learn what the doctrine is that so inflames the rage of those madmen who are this day, with fire and sword, troubling your kingdom. For I fear not to declare, that what I have here given may be regarded as a summary of the very doctrine which, they vociferate, ought to be punished with confiscation, exile, imprisonment, and flames, as well as exterminated by land and sea.

I am aware, indeed, how, in order to render our cause as hateful to your Majesty as possible, they have filled your ears and mind with atrocious insinuations; but you will be pleased, of your clemency, to reflect, that neither in word nor deed could there be any innocence, were it sufficient merely to accuse. When any one, with the view of exciting prejudice, observes that this doctrine, of which I am endeavouring to give your Majesty an account, has been condemned by the suffrages of all the estates, and was long ago stabbed again and again by partial sentences of courts of law, he undoubtedly says nothing more than that it has sometimes been violently oppressed by the power and faction of adversaries, and sometimes fraudulently and insidiously overwhelmed by lies, cavils, and calumny. While a cause is unheard, it is violence to pass sanguinary sentences against it; it is fraud to charge it, contrary to its deserts, with sedition and mischief.

That no one may suppose we are unjust in thus complaining, you yourself, most illustrious Sovereign, can bear us witness with what lying calumnies it is daily traduced in your presence, as aiming at nothing else than to wrest the sceptres of kings out of their hands, to overturn all tribunals and seats of justice, to subvert all order and government, to disturb the peace and quiet of society, to abolish all laws, destroy the distinctions of rank and property, and, in short, turn all things upside down. And yet, that which you hear is but the smallest portion of what is said; for among the common people are disseminated certain horrible insinuations—insinuations which, if well founded, would justify the whole world in condemning the doctrine with its authors to a thousand fires and gibbets. Who can wonder that the popular hatred is inflamed against it, when credit is given to those most iniquitous accusations? See, why all ranks unite with one accord in condemning our persons and our doctrine!

Carried away by this feeling, those who sit in judgment merely give utterance to the prejudices which they have imbibed at home, and think they have duly performed their part if they do not order punishment to be inflicted on any one until convicted, either on his own confession, or on legal evidence. But of what crime convicted? "Of that condemned doctrine," is the answer. But with what justice condemned? The very essence of the defence was, not to abjure the doctrine itself, but to maintain its truth. On this subject, however, not a whisper is allowed!

Justice, then, most invincible Sovereign, entitles me to demand that you will undertake a thorough investigation of this cause, which has hitherto been tossed about in any kind of way, and handled in the most irregular manner, without any order of law, and with passionate heat rather than judicial gravity.

Let it not be imagined that I am here framing my own private defence, with the view of obtaining a safe return to my native land. Though I cherish towards it the feelings which become me as a man, still, as matters now are, I can be absent from it without regret. The cause which I plead is the common cause of all the godly, and therefore the very cause of Christ—a cause which, throughout your realm, now lies, as it were, in despair, torn and trampled upon in all kinds of ways, and that more through the tyranny of certain Pharisees than any sanction from yourself. But it matters not to inquire how the thing is done; the fact that it is done cannot be denied. For so far have the wicked prevailed, that the truth of Christ, if not utterly routed and dispersed, lurks as if it were ignobly buried; while the poor Church, either wasted by cruel slaughter or driven into exile, or intimidated and terror—struck, scarcely ventures to breathe. Still her enemies press on with their wonted rage and fury over the ruins which they have made, strenuously assaulting the wall, which is already giving way. Meanwhile, no man comes forth to offer his protection against such furies. Any who would be thought most favourable to the truth, merely talk of pardoning the error and imprudence of ignorant men For so those modest personages speak; giving the name of *error and imprudence* to that which they know to be the infallible truth of God, and of *ignorant men* to those whose intellect they see that Christ has not despised, seeing he has deigned to intrust them with the mysteries of his heavenly wisdom. Thus all are ashamed of the Gospel.

Your duty, most serene Prince, is, not to shut either your ears or mind against a cause involving such mighty interests as these: how the glory of God is to be maintained on the earth inviolate, how the truth of God is to preserve its dignity, how the kingdom of Christ is to continue amongst us compact and secure. The cause is worthy of your ear, worthy of your investigation, worthy of your throne.

The characteristic of a true sovereign is, to acknowledge that, in the administration of his kingdom, he is a minister of God. He who does not make his reign subservient to the divine glory, acts the part not of a king, but a robber. He, moreover, deceives himself who anticipates long prosperity to any kingdom which is not ruled by the sceptre of God, that is, by his divine word. For the heavenly oracle is infallible which has declared, that "where there is no vision the people perish" (Prov. 29:18).

Let not a contemptuous idea of our insignificance dissuade you from the investigation of this cause. We, indeed, are perfectly conscious how poor and abject we are: in the presence of God we are miserable sinners, and in the sight of men most despised—we are (if you will) the mere dregs and off—scourings of the world, or worse, if worse can be named: so that before God there remains nothing of which we can glory save only his mercy, by which, without any merit of our own, we are admitted to the hope of eternal salvation: and before men not even this much remains, since we can glory only in our infirmity, a thing which, in the estimation of men, it is the greatest ignominy even tacitly to confess. But our doctrine must stand sublime above all the glory of the world, and invincible by all its power, because it is not ours, but that of the living God and his Anointed, whom the Father has appointed King, that he may rule from sea to sea, and from the rivers even to the ends of the earth; and so rule as to smite the whole earth and its strength of iron and brass, its splendour of gold and silver, with the mere rod of his mouth, and break them in pieces like a potter's vessel; according to the magnificent predictions of the prophets respecting his kingdom (Dan. 2:34; Isaiah 11:4; Psalm 2:9).

Our adversaries, indeed, clamorously maintain that our appeal to the word of God is a mere pretext,—that we are, in fact, its worst corrupters. How far this is not only malicious calumny, but also shameless effrontery, you will be able to decide, of your own knowledge, by reading our Confession. Here, however, it may be necessary to make some observations which may dispose, or at least assist, you to read and study it with attention.

When Paul declared that all prophecy ought to be according to the analogy of faith (Rom. 12:6), he laid down the surest rule for determining the meaning of Scripture. Let our doctrine be tested by this rule and our victory is secure. For what accords better and more aptly with faith than to acknowledge ourselves divested of all virtue that we may be clothed by God, devoid of all goodness that we may be filled by Him, the slaves of sin that he may give us freedom, blind that he may enlighten, lame that he may cure, and feeble that he may sustain us; to strip ourselves of all ground of glorying that he alone may shine forth glorious, and we be glorified in him? When these things, and others to the same effect, are said by us, they interpose, and querulously complain, that in this way we overturn some blind light of nature, fancied preparatives, free will, and works meritorious of eternal salvation, with their own supererogations also; because they cannot bear that the entire praise and glory of all goodness, virtue, justice, and wisdom, should remain with God. But we read not of any having been blamed for drinking too much of the fountain of living water; on the contrary, those are severely reprimanded who "have hewed them out cisterns, broken cisterns, that can hold no water" (Jer. 2:13). Again, what more agreeable to faith than to feel assured that God is a propitious Father when Christ is acknowledged as a brother and propitiator, than confidently to expect all prosperity and gladness from Him, whose ineffable love towards us was such that He "spared not his own Son, but delivered him up for us all" (Rom. 8:32), than to rest in the sure hope of salvation and eternal life whenever Christ, in whom such treasures are hid, is conceived to have been given by the Father? Here they attack us, and loudly maintain that this sure confidence is not free from arrogance and presumption. But as nothing is to be presumed of ourselves, so all things are to be presumed of God; nor are we stript of vainglory for any other reason than that we may learn to glory in the Lord. Why go farther? Take but a cursory view, most valiant King, of all the parts of our cause, and count us of all wicked men the most iniquitous, if you do not discover plainly, that "therefore we both labour and suffer reproach because we trust in the living God" (1 Tim. 4:10); because we believe it to be "life eternal" to know "the only true God, and Jesus Christ," whom he has sent (John 17:3). For this hope some of us are in bonds, some beaten with rods, some made a gazing—stock, some proscribed, some most cruelly tortured, some obliged to flee; we are all pressed with straits, loaded with dire execrations, lacerated by slanders, and treated with the greatest indignity.

Look now to our adversaries (I mean the priesthood, at whose beck and pleasure others ply their enmity against us), and consider with me for a little by what zeal they are actuated. The true religion which is delivered in the Scriptures, and which all ought to hold, they readily permit both themselves and others to be ignorant of, to neglect and despise; and they deem it of little moment what each man believes concerning God and Christ, or disbelieves, provided he submits to the judgment of the Church with what they call implicit faith; nor are they greatly concerned though they should see the glow of God dishonoured by open blasphemies, provided not a finger is raised against the primacy of the Apostolic See and the authority of holy mother Church. Why, then, do they war for the mass, purgatory, pilgrimage, and similar follies, with such fierceness and acerbity, that though they cannot prove one of them from the word of God, they deny godliness can be safe without faith in these things—faith drawn out, if I may so express it, to its utmost stretch? Why? just because their belly is their God, and their kitchen their religion; and they believe, that if these were away they would not only not be Christians, but not even men. For although some wallow in luxury, and others feed on slender crusts, still they all live by the same pot, which without that fuel might not only cool, but altogether freeze. He, accordingly, who is most anxious about his stomach, proves the fiercest champion of his faith. In short, the object on which all to a man are bent, is to keep their kingdom safe or their belly filled; not one gives even the smallest sign of sincere zeal.

Nevertheless, they cease not to assail our doctrine, and to accuse and defame it in what terms they may, in order to render it either hated or suspected. They call it new, and of recent birth; they carp at it as doubtful and uncertain; they bid us tell by what miracles it has been confirmed; they ask if it be fair to receive it against the consent of so many holy Fathers and the most ancient custom; they urge us to confess either that it is schismatical in giving battle to the Church, or that the Church must have been without life during the many centuries in which nothing of the kind was heard. Lastly, they say there is little need of argument, for its quality may be known by its fruits, namely, the large number of sects, the many seditious disturbances, and the great licentiousness which it has produced. No doubt, it is a very easy matter for them, in presence of an ignorant and credulous multitude, to insult over an undefended cause; but were an opportunity of mutual discussion afforded, that acrimony which they now pour out upon us in frothy torrents, with as much license as impunity, would assuredly boil dry.

1. First, in calling it new, they are exceedingly injurious to God, whose sacred word deserved not to be charged with novelty. To them, indeed, I very little doubt it is new, as Christ is new, and the Gospel new; but those who are acquainted with the old saying of Paul, that Christ Jesus "died for our sins, and rose again for our justification" (Rom. 4:25), will not detect any novelty in us. That it long lay buried and unknown is the guilty consequence of man's impiety; but now when, by the kindness of God, it is restored to us, it ought to resume its antiquity just as the returning citizen resumes his rights.

2. It is owing to the same ignorance that they hold it to be doubtful and uncertain; for this is the very thing of which the Lord complains by his prophet, "The ox knoweth his owner, and the ass his master's crib; but Israel doth not know, my people doth not consider" (Isaiah 1:3). But however they may sport with its uncertainty, had they to seal their own doctrine with their blood, and at the expense of life, it would be seen what value they put upon it. Very different is our confidence—a confidence which is not appalled by the terrors of death, and therefore not even by the judgment—seat of God.

3. In demanding miracles from us, they act dishonestly; for we have not coined some new gospel, but retain the very one the truth of which is confirmed by all the miracles which Christ and the apostles ever wrought. But they have a peculiarity which we have not—they can confirm their faith by constant miracles down to the present day! Way rather, they allege miracles which might produce wavering in minds otherwise well disposed; they are so frivolous and ridiculous, so vain and false. But were they even exceedingly wonderful, they could have no effect against the truth of God, whose name ought to be hallowed always, and everywhere, whether by miracles, or by the natural course of events. The deception would perhaps be more specious if Scripture did not admonish us of the legitimate end and use of miracles. Mark tells us (Mark 16:20) that the signs which followed the preaching of the apostles were wrought in confirmation of it; so Luke also relates that the Lord "gave testimony to the word of his grace, and granted signs and wonders to be done" by the hands of the apostles (Acts 14:3). Very much to the same effect are those words of the apostle, that salvation by a preached gospel was confirmed, "The Lord bearing witness with signs and wonders, and with divers miracles" (Heb. 2:4). Those things which we are told are seals of the gospel, shall we pervert to the subversion of the gospel? What was destined only to confirm the truth, shall we misapply to the confirmation of lies? The proper course, therefore, is, in the first instance, to ascertain and examine the doctrine which is said by the Evangelist to precede; then after it has been proved, but not till then, it may receive confirmation from miracles. But the mark of sound doctrine given by our Saviour himself is its tendency to promote the glory not of men, but of God (John 7:18; 8:50). Our Saviour having declared this to be test of doctrine, we are in error if we regard as miraculous, works which are used for any other purpose than to magnify the name of God. And it becomes us to remember that Satan has his miracles, which, although they are tricks rather than true wonders, are still such as to delude the ignorant and unwary. Magicians and enchanters have always been famous for miracles, and miracles of an astonishing description have given support to idolatry: these, however, do not make us converts to the superstitions either of magicians or idolaters. In old times, too, the Donatists used their power of working miracles as a battering-ram, with which they shook the simplicity of the common people. We now give to our opponents the answer which Augustine then gave to the Donatists (in Joan. Tract. 23), "The Lord put us on our guard against those wonder—workers, when he foretold that false prophets would arise, who, by lying signs and divers wonders, would, if it were possible, deceive the very elect" (Mt. 24:24). Paul, too, gave warning that the reign of antichrist would be "withall power, and signs, and lying wonders" (2 Thess. 2:9).

But our opponents tell us that their miracles are wrought not by idols, not by sorcerers, not by false prophets, but by saints: as if we did not know it to be one of Satan's wiles to transform himself "into an angel of light" (2 Cor. 11:14). The Egyptians, in whose neighbourhood Jeremiah was buried, anciently sacrificed and paid other divine honours to him (Hieron. in Praef. Jerem). Did they not make an idolatrous abuse of the holy prophet of God? and yet, in recompense for so venerating his tomb, they thought that they were cured of the bite of serpents. What, then, shall we say but that it has been, and always will be, a most just punishment of God, to send on those who do not receive the truth in the love of it, "strong delusion, that they should believe a lie"? (2 Thess. 2:11). We, then, have no lack of miracles, sure miracles, that cannot be gainsaid; but those to which our opponents lay claim are mere delusions of Satan, inasmuch as they draw off the people from the true worship of God to vanity.

4. It is a calumny to represent us as opposed to the Fathers (I mean the ancient writers of a purer age), as if the Fathers were supporters of their impiety. Were the contest to be decided by such authority (to speak in the most moderate terms), the better part of the victory would be ours. While there is much that is admirable and wise in the writings of those Fathers, and while in some things it has fared with them as with ordinary men; these pious sons, forsooth, with the peculiar acuteness of intellect, and judgment, and soul, which belongs to them, adore only their slips and errors, while those things which are well said they either overlook, or disguise, or corrupt; so that it may be truly said their only care has been to gather dross among gold. Then, with dishonest clamour, they assail us as enemies and despisers of the Fathers. So far are we from despising them, that if this were the proper place, it would give us no trouble to support the greater part of the doctrines which we now hold by their suffrages. Still, in studying their writings, we have endeavoured to remember (1 Cor. 3:21–23; see also Augustin. Ep. 28), that all things are ours, to serve, not lord it over us, but that we axe Christ's only, and must obey him in all things without exception. He who does not draw this distinction will not have any fixed principles in religion; for those holy men were ignorant of many things, are often opposed to each other, and are sometimes at variance with themselves.

It is not without cause (remark our opponents) we are thus warned by Solomon, "Remove not the ancient landmarks which thy fathers have set" (Prov. 22:28). But the same rule applies not to the measuring of fields and the obedience of faith. The rule applicable to the latter is, "Forget also thine own people, and thy father's house" (Ps. 45:10). But if they are so fond of allegory, why do they not understand the apostles, rather than any other class of Fathers, to be meant by those whose landmarks it is unlawful to remove? This is the interpretation of Jerome, whose words they have quoted in their canons. But as regards those to whom they apply the passage, if they wish the landmarks to be fixed, why do they, whenever it suits their purpose, so freely overleap them?

Among the Fathers there were two, the one of whom said, "Our God neither eats nor drinks, and therefore has no need of chalices and salvers;" and the other "Sacred rites do not require gold, and things which are not bought with gold, please not by gold." They step beyond the boundary, therefore, when in sacred matters they are so much delighted with gold, driver, ivory, marble, gems, and silks, that unless everything is overlaid with costly show, or rather insane luxury, they think God is not duly worshipped.

It was a Father who said, "He ate flesh freely on the day on which others abstained from it, because he was a Christian." They overleap the boundaries, therefore, when they doom to perdition every soul that, during Lent, shall have tasted flesh.

There were two Fathers, the one of whom said, "A monk not labouring with his own hands is no better than a violent man and a robber;" and the other, "Monks, however assiduous they may be in study, meditation, and prayer, must not live by others." This boundary, too, they transgressed, when they placed lazy gormandising monks in dens and stews, to gorge themselves on other men's substance.

It was a Father who said, "It is a horrid abomination to see in Christian temples a painted image either of Christ or of any saint." Nor was this pronounced by the voice era single individual; but an Ecclesiastical Council also decreed, "Let nought that is worshipped be depicted on walls." Very far are they from keeping within these boundaries when they leave not a corner without images.

Another Father counselled, "That after performing the office of humanity to the dead in their burial, we should leave them at rest." These limits they burst through when they keep up a perpetual anxiety about the dead.

It is a Father who testifies, "That the substance of bread and wine in the Eucharist does not cease but remains, just as the nature and substance of man remains united to the Godhead in the Lord Jesus Christ." This boundary they pass in pretending that, as soon as the words of our

Lord are pronounced, the substance of bread and wine ceases, and is transubstantiated into body and blood.

They were Fathers, who, as they exhibited only one Eucharist to the whole Church, and kept back from it the profane and flagitious; so they, in the severest terms, censured all those who, being present, did not communicate How far have they removed these landmarks, in filling not churches only, but also private houses, with their masses, admitting all and sundry to be present, each the more willingly the more largely he pays, however wicked and impure he may be,—not inviting any one to faith in Christ and faithful communion in the sacraments, but rather vending their own work for the grace and merits of Christ!

There were two Fathers, the one of whom decided that those were to be excluded altogether from partaking of Christ's sacred supper, who, contented with communion in one kind, abstained from the other; while the other Father strongly contends that the blood of the Lord ought not to be denied to the Christian people, who, in confessing him, are enjoined to shed their own blood. These landmarks, also, they removed, when, by an unalterable law, they ordered the very thing which the former Father punished with excommunication, and the latter condemned for a valid reason.

It was a Father who pronounced it rashness, in an obscure question, to decide in either way without clear and evident authority from Scripture. They forgot this landmark when they enacted so many constitutions, so many canons, and so many dogmatical decisions, without sanction from the word of God.

It was a Father who reproved Montanus, among other heresies, for being the first who imposed laws of fasting. They have gone far beyond this landmark also in enjoining fasting under the strictest laws.

It was a Father who denied that the ministers of the Church should be interdicted from marrying, and pronounced married life to be a state of chastity; and there were other Fathers who assented to his decision. These boundaries they overstepped in rigidly binding their priests to celibacy.

It was a Father who thought that Christ only should be listened to, from its being said, "hear him;" and that regard is due not to what others before us have said or done, but only to what Christ, the head of all, has commanded. This landmark they neither observe themselves nor allow to be observed by others, while they subject themselves and others to any master whatever, rather than Christ.

There is a Father who contends that the Church ought not to prefer herself to Christ, who always judges truly, whereas ecclesiastical judges, who are but men, are generally deceived. Having burst through this barrier also, they hesitate not to suspend the whole authority of Scripture on the judgment of the Church.

All the Fathers with one heart execrated, and with one mouth protested against, contaminating the word of God with the subtleties sophists, and involving it in the brawls of dialecticians. Do they keep within these limits when the sole occupation of their lives is to entwine and entangle the simplicity of Scripture with endless disputes, and worse than sophistical jargon? So much so, that were the Fathers to rise from their graves, and listen to the brawling art which bears the name of speculative theology, there is nothing they would suppose it less to be than a discussion of a religious nature.

But my discourse would far exceed its just limits were I to show, in detail, how petulantly those men shake off the yoke of the Fathers, while they wish to be thought their most obedient sons. Months, nay, years would fail me; and yet so deplorable and desperate is their effrontery, that they presume to chastise us for overstepping the ancient landmarks!

5. Then, again, it is to no purpose they call us to the bar of custom. To make everything yield to custom would be to do the greatest injustice. Were the judgments of mankind correct, custom would be regulated by the good. But it is often far otherwise in point of fact; for, whatever the many are seen to do, forthwith obtains the force of custom. But human affairs have scarcely ever been so happily constituted as that the better course pleased the greater number. Hence the private vices of the multitude have generally resulted in public error, or rather that common consent in vice which these worthy men would have to be law. Any one with eyes may perceive that it is not one flood of evils which has deluged us; that many fatal plagues have invaded the globe; that all things rush headlong; so that either the affairs of men must be altogether despaired of, or we must not only resist, but boldly attack prevailing evils. The cure is prevented by no other cause than the length of time during which we have been accustomed to the disease. But be it so that public error must have a place in human society, still, in the kingdom of God, we must look and listen only to his eternal truth, against which no series of years, no custom, no conspiracy, can plead prescription. Thus Isaiah formerly taught the people of God, "Say ye not, A confederacy, to all to whom this people shall say, A confederacy;"

i.e. do not unite with the people in an impious consent; "neither fear ye their fear, nor be afraid. Sanctify the Lord of hosts himself; and let him be your fear, and let him be your dread" (Is. 8:12). Now, therefore, let them, if they will, object to us both past ages and present examples; if we sanctify the Lord of hosts, we shall not be greatly afraid. Though many ages should have consented to like ungodliness, He is strong who taketh vengeance to the third and fourth generation; or the whole world should league together in the same iniquity. He taught experimentally what the end is of those who sin with the multitude, when He destroyed the whole human race with a flood, saving Noah with his little family, who, by putting his faith in Him alone, "condemned the world" (Heb. 11:7). In short, depraved custom is just a kind of general pestilence in which men perish not the less that they fall in a crowd. It were well, moreover, to ponder the observation of Cyprian, that those who sin in ignorance, though they cannot be entirely exculpated, seem, however, to be, in some sense, excusable; whereas those who obstinately reject the truth, when presented to them by the kindness of God, have no defence to offer.

6. Their dilemma does not push us so violently as to oblige us to confess, either that the Church was a considerable time without life, or that we have now a quarrel with the Church. The Church of Christ assuredly has lived, and will live, as long as Christ shall reign at the right hand of the Father. By his hand it is sustained, by his protection defended, by his mighty power preserved in safety. For what he once undertook he will undoubtedly perform, he will be with his people always, "even to the end of the world" (Mt. 28:20). With the Church we wage no war, since, with one consent, in common with the whole body of the faithful, we worship and adore one God, and Christ Jesus the Lord, as all the pious have always adored him. But they themselves err not a little from the truth in not recognising any church but that which they behold with the bodily eye, and in endeavouring to circumscribe it by limits, within which it cannot be confined.

The hinges on which the controversy turns are these: first, in their contending that the form of the Church is always visible and apparent; and, secondly, in their placing this form in the see of the Church of Rome and its hierarchy. We, on the contrary, maintain, both that the Church may exist without any apparent form, and, moreover, that the form is not ascertained by that external splendour which they foolishly admire, but by a very different mark, namely, by the pure preaching of the word of God, and the due administration of the sacraments. They make an outcry whenever the Church cannot be pointed to with the finger. But how oft was it the fate of the Church among the Jews to be so defaced that no comeliness appeared? What do we suppose to have been the splendid form when Elijah complained that he was left alone? (1 Kings 19:14). How long after the advent of Christ did it lie hid without form? How often since has it been so oppressed by wars, seditions, and heresies, that it was nowhere seen in splendour? Had they lived at that time, would they have believed there was any Church? But Elijah learned that there remained seven thousand men who had not bowed the knee to Baal; nor ought we to doubt that Christ has always reigned on earth ever since he ascended to heaven. Had the faithful at that time required some discernible form, must they not have forthwith given way to despondency? And, indeed, Hilary accounted it a very great fault in his day, that men were so possessed with a foolish admiration of Episcopal dignity as not to perceive the deadly hydra lurking under that mask. His words are (Cont. Auxentium), "One advice I give: Beware of Antichrist; for, unhappily, a love of walls has seized you; unhappily, the Church of God which you venerate exists in houses and buildings; unhappily, under these you find the name of peace. Is it doubtful that in these Antichrist will have his seat? Safer to me are mountains, and woods, and lakes, and dungeons, and whirlpools; since in these prophets, dwelling or immersed, did prophesy."

And what is it at the present day that the world venerates in its horned bishops, unless that it imagines those who are seen presiding over celebrated cities to be holy prelates of religion? Away, then, with this absurd mode of judging! Let us rather reverently admit, that as God alone knows who are his, so he may sometimes withdraw the external manifestation of his Church from the view of men. This, I allow, is a fearful punishment which God sends on the earth; but if the wickedness of men so deserves, why do we strive to oppose the just vengeance of God? It was thus that God, in past ages, punished the ingratitude of men; for after they had refused to obey his truth, and had extinguished his light, he allowed them, when blinded by sense, both to be deluded by lying vanities and plunged in thick darkness, so that no face of a true Church appeared. Meanwhile, however, though his own people were dispersed and concealed amidst errors and darkness, he saved them from destruction. No wonder; for he knew how to preserve them even in the confusion of Babylon and the flame of the fiery furnace.

But as to the wish that the form of the Church should be ascertained by some kind of vain pomp, how perilous it is I will briefly indicate, rather than explain, that I may not exceed all bounds. What they say is, that the Pontiff, who holds the apostolic see, and the priests who are anointed and consecrated by him, provided they have the insignia of fillets and mitres, represent the Church, and ought to be considered as in the place of the Church, and therefore cannot err. Why so? because they are pastors of the Church, and consecrated to the Lord. And were not Aaron and other prefects of Israel pastors? But Aaron and his sons, though already set apart to the priesthood, erred notwithstanding when they made the calf (Exod. 32:4). Why, according to this view, should not the four hundred prophets who lied to Ahab represent the Church? (1 Kings 22:11, &c.). The Church, however, stood on the side of Micaiah. He was alone, indeed, and despised, but from his mouth the truth proceeded. Did not the prophets also exhibit both the name and face of the Church, when, with one accord, they rose up against Jeremiah, and with menaces boasted of it as a thing impossible that the law should perish from the priest, or counsel from the wise, or the word from the prophet? (Jer. 18:18). In opposition to the whole body of the prophets, Jeremiah is sent alone to declare from the Lord (Jer. 4:9), that a time would come when the law would perish from the priest, counsel from the wise, and the word from the prophet. Was not like splendour displayed in that council when the chief priests, scribes, and Pharisees assembled to consult how they might put Jesus to death? Let them go, then, and cling to the external mask, while they make Christ and all the prophets of God schismatics, and, on the other hand, make Satan's ministers the organs of the Holy Spirit!

But if they are sincere, let them answer me in good faith,—in what place, and among whom, do they think the Church resided, after the Council of Basle degraded and deposed Eugenius from the popedom, and substituted Amadeus in his place? Do their utmost, they cannot deny that that Council was legitimate as far as regards external forms, and was summoned not only by one Pontiff, but by two. Eugenius, with the whole herd of cardinals and bishops who had joined him in plotting the dissolution of the Council, was there condemned of contumacy, rebellion, and schism. Afterwards, however, aided by the favour of princes, he got back his popedom safe. The election of Amadeus, duly made by the authority of a general holy synod, went to smoke; only he himself was appeased with a cardinal's cap, like a piece of offal thrown to a barking dog. Out of the lap of these rebellious and contumacious schismatics proceeded all future popes, cardinals, bishops, abbots, and presbyters. Here they are caught, and cannot escape. For, on which party will they bestow the name of Church? Will they deny it to have been a general Council, though it lacked nothing as regards external majesty, having been solemnly called by two bulls, consecrated by the legate of the Roman See as its president, constituted regularly in all respects, and continuing in possession of all its honours to the last? Will they admit that Eugenius, and his whole train, through whom they have all been consecrated, were schismatical? Let them, then, either define the form of the Church differently, or, however numerous they are, we will hold them all to be schismatics in having knowingly and willingly received ordination from heretics. But had it never been discovered before that the Church is not tied to external pomp, we are furnished with a lengthened proof in their own conduct, in proudly vending themselves to the world under the specious title of Church, notwithstanding that they are the deadly pests of the Church. I speak not of their manners and of those tragical atrocities with which their whole life teems, since it is said that they are Pharisees who should be heard, not imitated. By devoting some portion of your leisure to our writings, you will see, not obscurely, that their doctrine—the very doctrine to which they say it is owing that they are the Church—is a deadly murderer of souls, the firebrand, ruin, and destruction of the Church.

7. Lastly, they are far from candid when they invidiously number up the disturbances, tumults, and disputes, which the preaching of our doctrine has brought in its train, and the fruits which, in many instances, it now produces; for the doctrine itself is undeservedly charged with evils which ought to be ascribed to the malice of Satan. It is one of the characteristics of the divine word, that whenever it appears, Satan ceases to slumber and sleep. This is the surest and most unerring test for distinguishing it from false doctrines which readily betray themselves, while they are received by all with willing ears, and welcomed by an applauding world. Accordingly, for several ages, during which all things were immersed in profound darkness, almost all mankind were mere jest and sport to the god of this world, who, like any Sardanapalus, idled and luxuriated undisturbed. For what else could he do but laugh and sport while in tranquil and undisputed possession of his kingdom? But when light beaming from above somewhat dissipated the darkness—when the strong man arose and aimed a blow at

his kingdom—then, indeed, he began to shake off his wonted torpor, and rush to arms. And first he stirred up the hands of men, that by them he might violently suppress the dawning truth; but when this availed him not, he turned to snares, exciting dissensions and disputes about doctrine by means of his Catabaptists, and other portentous miscreants, that he might thus obscure, and, at length, extinguish the truth. And now he persists in assailing it with both engines, endeavouring to pluck up the true seed by the violent hand of man, and striving, as much as in him lies, to choke it with his tares, that it may not grow and bear knit. But it will be in vain, if we listen to the admonition of the Lord, who long ago disclosed his wiles, that we might not be taken unawares, and armed us with full protection against all his machinations. But how malignant to throw upon the word of God itself the blame either of the seditions which wicked men and rebels, or of the sects which impostors stir up against it! The example, however, is not new. Elijah was interrogated whether it were not he that troubled Israel. Christ was seditious, according to the Jews; and the apostles were charged with the crime of popular commotion. What else do those who, in the present day, impute to us all the disturbances, tumults, and contentions which break out against us? Elijah, however, has taught us our answer (1 Kings 18:17, 18). It is not we who disseminate errors or stir up tumults, but they who resist the mighty power of God.

But while this single answer is sufficient to rebut the rash charges of these men, it is necessary, on the other hand, to consult for the weakness of those who take the alarm at such scandals, and not unfrequently waver in perplexity. But that they may not fall away in this perplexity, and forfeit their good degree, let them know that the apostles in their day experienced the very things which now befall us. There were then unlearned and unstable men who, as Peter tells us (2 Pet. 3:16), wrested the inspired writings of Paul to their own destruction. There were despisers of God, who, when they heard that sin abounded in order that grace might more abound, immediately inferred, "We will continue in sin that grace may abound" (Rom. 6:1); when they heard that believers were not under the law, but under grace, forthwith sung out, "We will sin because we are not under the law, but under grace" (Rom. 6:15). There were some who charged the apostle with being the minister of sin. Many false prophets entered in privily to pull down the churches which he had reared. Some preached the gospel through envy and strife, not sincerely (Phil. 1:15)—maliciously even—thinking to add affliction to his bonds. Elsewhere the gospel made little progress. All sought their own, not the things which were Jesus Christ's. Others went back like the dog to his vomit, or the sow that was washed to her wallowing in the mire. Great numbers perverted their spiritual freedom to carnal licentiousness. False brethren crept in to the imminent danger of the faithful. Among the brethren themselves various quarrels arose. What, then, were the apostles to do? Were they either to dissemble for the time, or rather lay aside and abandon that gospel which they saw to be the seed—bed of so many strifes, the source of so many perils, the occasion of so many scandals? In straits of this kind, they remembered that "Christ was a stone of stumbling, and a rock of offence," "set up for the fall and rising again of many," and "for a sign to be spoken against" (Luke 2:34); and, armed with this assurance, they proceeded boldly through all perils from tumults and scandals. It becomes us to be supported by the same consideration, since Paul declares that it is a neverfailing characteristic of the gospel to be a "savour of death unto death in them that perish" (2 Cor. 2:16), although rather destined to us for the purpose of being a savour of life unto life, and the power of God for the salvation of believers. This we should certainly experience it to be, did we not by our ingratitude corrupt this unspeakable gift of God, and turn to our destruction what ought to be our only saving defence.

But to return, Sire. Be not moved by the absurd insinuations with which our adversaries are striving to frighten you into the belief that nothing else is wished and aimed at by this new gospel (for so they term it), than opportunity for sedition and impunity for all kinds of vice. Our God is not the author of division, but of peace; and the Son of God, who came to destroy the works of the devil, is not the minister of sin. We, too, are undeservedly charged with desires of a kind for which we have never given even the smallest suspicion. We, forsooth, meditate the subversion of kingdoms; we, whose voice was never heard in faction, and whose life, while passed under you, is known to have been always quiet and simple; even now, when exiled from our home, we nevertheless cease not to pray for all prosperity to your person and your kingdom. We, forsooth, are aiming after an unchecked indulgence in vice, in whose manners, though there is much to be blamed, there is nothing which deserves such an imputation; nor (thank God) have we profited so little in the gospel that our life may not be to these slanderers an example of chastity, kindness, pity, temperance, patience, moderation, or any other virtue. It is plain, indeed, that we fear God sincerely, and worship him in truth, since, whether by life or by death, we desire his name to be hallowed; and hatred herself has been forced to bear testimony to the innocence and civil integrity of some of our people on whom death was inflicted for the very thing which deserved the highest praise. But if any, under pretext of the gospel, excite tumults (none such have as yet been detected in your realm), if any use the liberty of the grace of God as a cloak for licentiousness (I know of numbers who do), there are laws and legal punishments by which they may be punished up to the measure of their deserts—only, in the mean time, let not the gospel of God be evil spoken of because of the iniquities of evil men.

Sire, That you may not lend too credulous an ear to the accusations of our enemies, their virulent injustice has been set before you at sufficient length; I fear even more than sufficient, since this preface has grown almost to the bulk of a full apology. My object, however, was not to frame a defence, but only with a view to the hearing of our cause, to mollify your mind, now indeed turned away and estranged from us—I add, even inflamed against us—but whose good will, we are confident, we should regain, would you but once, with calmness and composure, read this our Confession, which we desire your Majesty to accept instead of a defence. But if the whispers of the malevolent so possess your ear, that the accused are to have no opportunity of pleading their cause; if those vindictive furies, with your connivance, are always to rage with bonds, scourgings, tortures, maimings, and burnings, we, indeed, like sheep doomed to slaughter, shall be reduced to every extremity; yet so that, in our patience, we will possess our souls, and wait for the strong hand of the Lord, which, doubtless, will appear in its own time, and show itself armed, both to rescue the poor from affliction, and also take vengeance on the despisers, who are now exulting so securely.

Most illustrious King, may the Lord, the King of kings, establish your throne in righteousness, and your sceptre in equity.

Basle, 1st *August* 1536.

THE EPISTLE TO THE READER

[PREFIXED TO THE SECOND EDITION, PUBLISHED AT STRASBURG IN 1539.]

In the First Edition of this work, having no expectation of the success which God has, in his goodness, been pleased to give it, I had, for the greater part, performed my office perfunctorily, as is usual in trivial undertakings. But when I perceived that almost all the godly had received it with a favour which I had never dared to wish, far less to hope for, being sincerely conscious that I had received much more than I deserved, I thought I should be very ungrateful if I did not endeavour, at least according to my humble ability, to respond to the great kindness which had been expressed towards me, and which spontaneously urged me to diligence. I therefore ask no other favour from the studious for my new work than that which they have already bestowed upon me beyond my merits. I feel so much obliged, that I shall be satisfied if I am thought not to have made a bad return for the gratitude I owe. This return I would have made much earlier, had not the Lord, for almost two whole years, exercised me in an extraordinary manner. But it is soon enough if well enough. I shall think it has appeared in good season when I perceive that it produces some fruit to the Church of God. I may add, that my object in this work was to prepare and train students of theology for the study of the Sacred Volume, so that they might both have an easy introduction to it, and be able to proceed in it, with unfaltering step, seeing I have endeavoured to give such a summary of religion in all its parts, and have digested it into such an order as may make it not difficult for any one, who is rightly acquainted with it, to ascertain both what he ought principally to look for in Scripture, and also to what head he ought to refer whatever is contained in it. Having thus, as it were, paved the way, I shall not feel it necessary, in any Commentaries on Scripture which I may afterwards publish, to enter into long discussions of doctrines or dilate on common places, and will, therefore, always compress them. In this way the pious reader will be saved much trouble and weariness, provided he comes furnished with a knowledge of the present work as an essential prerequisite. As my Commentary on the Epistle to the Romans will give a specimen of this plan, I would much rather let it speak for itself than declare it in words. Farewell, dear reader, and if you derive any fruit from my labours, give me the benefit of your prayers to the Lord.

Strasbourg, 1*st August* 1539.

SUBJECT OF THE PRESENT WORK.

[PREFIXED TO THE FRENCH EDITION, PUBLISHED AT GENEVA IN 1545.]

In order that my Readers may be the better able to profit by the present work, I am desirous briefly to point out the advantage which they may derive from it. For by so doing I will show them the end at which they ought to aim, and to which they ought to give their attention in reading it.

Although the Holy Scriptures contain a perfect doctrine, to which nothing can be added—our Lord having been pleased therein to unfold the infinite treasures of his wisdom—still every person, not intimately acquainted with them, stands in need of some guidance and direction, as to what he ought to look for in them, that he may not wander up and down, but pursue a certain path, and so attain the end to which the Holy Spirit invites him.

Hence it is the duty of those who have received from God more light than others to assist the simple in this matter, and, as it were, lend them their hand to guide and assist them in finding the sum of what God has been pleased to teach us in his word. Now, this cannot be better done in writing than by treating in succession of the principal matters which are comprised in Christian philosophy. For he who understands these will be prepared to make more progress in the school of God in one day than any other person in three months, inasmuch as he, in a great measure, knows to what he should refer each sentence, and has a rule by which to test whatever is presented to him.

Seeing, then, how necessary it was in this manner to aid those who desire to be instructed in the doctrine of salvation, I have endeavoured, according to the ability which God has given me, to employ myself in so doing, and with this view have composed the present book. And first I wrote it in Latin, that it might be serviceable to all studious persons, of what nation soever they might be; afterwards, desiring to communicate any fruit which might be in it to my French countrymen, I translated it into our own tongue. I dare not bear too strong a testimony in its favour, and declare how profitable the reading of it will be, lest I should seem to prize my own work too highly. However I may promise this much, that it will be a kind of key opening up to all the children of God a right and ready access to the understanding of the sacred volume. Wherefore, should our Lord give me henceforth means and opportunity of composing some Commentaries, I will use the greatest possible brevity, as there will be no occasion to make long digressions, seeing that I have in a manner deduced at length all the articles which pertain to Christianity.

And since we are bound to acknowledge that all truth and sound doctrine proceed from God, I will venture boldly to declare what I think of this work, acknowledging it to be God's work rather than mine. To him, indeed, the praise due to it must be ascribed. My opinion of the work then is this: I exhort all, who reverence the word of the Lord, to read it, and diligently imprint it on their memory, if they would, in the first place, have a summary of Christian doctrine, and, in the second place, an introduction to the profitable reading both of the Old and New Testament. When they shall have done so, they will know by experience that I have not wished to impose upon them with words. Should any one be unable to comprehend all that is contained in it, he must not, however, give it up in despair; but continue always to read on, hoping that one passage will give him a more familiar exposition of another. Above all things, I would recommend that recourse be had to Scripture in considering the proofs which I adduce from it.

EPISTLE TO THE READER.

[PREFIXED TO THE LAST EDITION, REVISED BY THE AUTHOR.]

In the first edition of this work, having not the least expectation of the success which God, in his boundless goodness, has been pleased to give it, I had, for the greater part, performed my task in a perfunctory manner (as is usual in trivial undertakings); but when I understood that it had been received, by almost all the pious with a favour which I had never dared to ask, far less to hope for, the more I was sincerely conscious that the reception was beyond my deserts, the greater I thought my ingratitude would be, if, to the very kind wishes which had been expressed towards me, and which seemed of their own accord to invite me to diligence, I did not endeavour to respond, at least according to my humble ability. This I attempted not only in the Second Edition, but in every subsequent one the work has received some improvement. But though I do not regret the labour previously expended, I never felt satisfied until the work was arranged in the order in which it now appears. Now I trust it will approve itself to the Judgment of all my readers. As a clear proof of the diligence with which I have laboured to perform this service to the Church of God, I may be permitted to mention, that last winter, when I thought I was dying of quartan ague, the more the disorder increased, the less I spared myself, in order that I might leave this book behind me, and thus make some return to the pious for their kind urgency. I could have wished to give it sooner, but it is soon enough if good enough. I shall think it has appeared in good time when I see it more productive of benefit than formerly to the Church of God. This is my only wish.

And truly it would fare ill with me if, not contented with the approbation of God alone, I were unable to despise the foolish and perverse censures of ignorant as well as the malicious and unjust censures of ungodly men. For although, by the blessing of God, my most ardent desire has been to advance his kingdoms and promote the public good,—although I feel perfectly conscious, and take God and his angels to witness, that ever since I began to discharge the office of teacher in the Church, my only object has been to do good to the Church, by maintaining the pure doctrine of godliness, yet I believe there never was a man more assailed, stung, and torn by calumny [as well by the declared enemies of the truth of God, as by many worthless persons who have crept into his Church—as well by monks who have brought forth their frocks from their cloisters to spread infection wherever they come, as by other miscreants not better than they]. After this letter to the reader was in the press, I had undoubted information that, at Augsburg, where the Imperial Diet was held, a rumour of my defection to the papacy was circulated, and entertained in the courts of the princes more readily than might have been expected. This, forsooth, is the return made me by those who certainly are not unaware of numerous proofs of my constancy—proofs which, while they rebut the foul charge, ought to have defended me against it, with all humane and impartial judges. But the devil, with all his crew, is mistaken if he imagines that, by assailing me with vile falsehoods, he can either cool my zeal, or diminish my exertions. I trust that God, in his infinite goodness, will enable me to persevere with unruffled patience in the course of his holy vocation. Of this I give the pious reader a new proof in the present edition.

I may further observe, that my object in this work has been, so to prepare and train candidates for the sacred office, for the study of the sacred volume, that they may both have an easy introduction to it, and be able to prosecute it with unfaltering step; for, if I mistake not, I have given a summary of religion in all its parts, and digested it in an order which will make it easy for any one, who rightly comprehends it, to ascertain both what he ought chiefly to look for in Scripture, and also to what head he ought to refer whatever is contained in it. Having thus, as it were, paved the way, as it will be unnecessary, in any Commentaries on Scripture which I may afterwards publish, to enter into long discussions of doctrinal points, and enlarge on commonplaces, I will compress them into narrow compass. In this way much trouble and fatigue will be spared to the pious reader, provided he comes prepared with a knowledge of the present work as an indispensable prerequisite. The system here followed being set forth as in a mirror in all my Commentaries, I think it better to let it speak for itself than to give any verbal explanation of it.

Farewell, kind reader: if you derive any benefit from my labours, aid me with your prayers to our heavenly Father.

GENEVA, 1*st August* 1559.

The zeal of those whose cause I undertook,
Has swelled a short defence into a book.

"I profess to be one of those who, by profiting, write, and by writing profit."—*Augustine*, Epist. 7.

METHOD AND ARRANGEMENT, OR SUBJECT OF THE WHOLE WORK.

[FROM AN EPITOME OF THE INSTITUTIONS, BY GASPAR OLEVIAN.]

The subject handled by the author of these Christian Institutes is twofold: the former, the knowledge of God, which leads to a blessed immortality; and the latter (which is subordinate to the former), the knowledge of ourselves. With this view the author simply adopts the arrangement of the Apostles' Creed, as that with which all Christians are most familiar. For as the Creed consists of four parts, the first relating to God the Father, the second to the Son, the third to the Holy Spirit, and the fourth to the Church, so the author, in fulfilment of his task, divides his Institutes into four parts, corresponding to those of the Creed. Each of these parts it will now be proper to explain separately.

I. The first article of the Apostles' Creed is concerning *God the Father*, the creation, preservation, and government of the universe, as implied in his omnipotence. Accordingly, the First Book of the Institutes treats of the knowledge of God, considered as the Creator, Preserver, and Governor of the world, and of every thing contained in it. It shows both wherein the true knowledge of the Creator consists, and what the end of this knowledge is, chap. 1 and 2; that it is not learned at school, but that every one is self-taught it from the womb, chap. 3. Such, however, is man's depravity, that he stifles and corrupts this knowledge, partly by ignorance, partly by wicked design; and hence does not by means of it either glorify God as he ought, or attain to happiness, chap. 4. This inward knowledge is aided from without, namely by the creatures in which, as in a mirror, the perfections of God may be contemplated. But man does not properly avail himself of this assistance, and hence to those to whom God is pleased to make himself more intimately known for salvation, he communicates his written word. This leads to a consideration of the Holy Scriptures, in which God has revealed that not the Father only, but along with the Father, the Son, and Holy Spirit, is that Creator of heaven and earth, whom, in consequence of our innate depravity we were unable, either from innate natural knowledge, or the beautiful mirror of the world, to know so as to glorify. Here the author treats of the manifestation of God in Scripture; and in connection with it, of the one divine essence in three persons. But, lest man should lay the blame of his voluntary blindness on God, the author shows in what state man was created at first, introducing dissertations on the image of God, free will, and original righteousness. The subject of Creation being thus disposed of, the preservation and government of the world is considered in the three last chapters, which contain a very full discussion of the doctrine of Divine Providence.

II. As man, by sinning, forfeited the privileges conferred on him at his creation, recourse must be had to Christ. Accordingly, the next article in the Creed is, *And in Jesus Christ his only Son, &c.* In like manner, the Second Book of the Institutes treats of the knowledge of God considered as a Redeemer in Christ, And showing man his falls conducts him to Christ the Mediator. Here the subject of original sin is considered, and it is shown that man has no means within himself, by which he can escape from guilt, and the impending curse: that, on the contrary, until he is reconciled and renewed, every thing that proceeds from him is of the nature of sin. This subject is considered as far as the 6th chapter. Man being thus utterly undone in himself, and incapable of working out his own cure by thinking a good thought, or doing what is acceptable to God, must seek redemption without himself—viz. in Christ. The end for which the Law was given, was not to secure worshipers for itself, but to conduct them unto Christ. This leads to an exposition of the Moral Law. Christ was known to the Jews under the Law as the author of salvation, but is more fully revealed under the Gospel in which he was manifested to the world. Hence arises the doctrine concerning the similarity and difference of the two Testaments, the Old and the New, the Law and the Gospel. These topics occupy as far as the 12th chapter. It is next shown that, in order to secure a complete salvation, it was necessary that the eternal Son of God should become man, and assume a true human nature. It is also shown in what way these two natures constitute one person. In order to purchase a full salvation by his own merits, and effectually apply it, Christ was appointed to the offices of Prophet, Priest, and King. The mode in which Christ performs these offices is considered, and also whether in point of fact he did accomplish the work of redemption. Here an exposition is given of the articles relating to Christ's death, resurrection, and ascension into heaven. In conclusion, it is proved that Christ is rightly and properly said to have merited divine grace and salvation for us.

III. So long as Christ is separated from us we have no benefit from him. We must be ingrafted in him like branches in the vine. Hence the Creed, after treating of Christ, proceeds in its third article, *I believe in the Holy Spirit,*—the Holy Spirit being the bond of union between us and Christ. In like manner, the Third Book of the Institutes treats of the Holy Spirit which unites us to Christ, and, in connection with it, of faith, by which we embrace Christ with a double benefit—viz. that of gratuitous righteousness which he imputes to us, and regeneration, which he begins in us by giving us repentance. In order to show the worthlessness of a faith which is not accompanied with a desire of repentance, the author, before proceeding to a full discussion of justification, treats at length from chapter 3–10 of repentance, and the constant study of it—repentance, which Christ, when apprehended by faith, begets in us by his Spirit. Chapter 11 treats of the primary and peculiar benefit of Christ when united to us by the Holy Spirit—viz. justification. This subject is continued to the 20th chapter, which treats of prayer, the hand, as it were, to receive the blessings which faith knows to be treasured up for it with God, according to the word of promise. But, as the Holy Spirit, who creates and preserves our faith, does not unite all men to Christ, who is the sole author of salvation, chapter 21 treats of the eternal election of God, to which it is owing that we, in whom he foresaw no good which he had not previously bestowed, are given to Christ, and united to him by the effectual calling of the Gospel. This subject is continued to the 25th chapter, which treats of complete regeneration and felicity, namely, the final resurrection to which we must raise our eyes, seeing that, in regard to fruition, the happiness of the godly is only begun in this world.

IV. Since the Holy Spirit does not ingraft all men into Christ, or endue them with faith, and those whom he does so endue he does not ordinarily endue without means, but uses for that purpose the preaching of the Gospel and the dispensation of the Sacraments, together with the administration of all kinds of discipline, the Creed contains the following article, *I believe in the Holy Catholic Church*, namely, that Church which, when lying in eternal death, the Father, by gratuitous election, freely reconciled to himself in Christ, and endued with the Holy Spirit, that, being ingrafted into Christ, it might have communion with him as its proper head; whence flow perpetual remission of sins, and full restoration to eternal life. Accordingly the Church is treated of in the first fourteen chapters of the Fourth Book, which thereafter treats of the means which the Holy Spirit employs in calling us effectually from spiritual death, and preserving the Church, in other words, Baptism and the Lord's Supper. These means are, as it were, the royal sceptre of Christ, by which, through the efficacy of his Spirit, he commences his spiritual reign in the Church, advances it from day to day, and after this life, without the use of means, finally perfects it. This subject is continued to the 20th chapter.

And because civil governments are, in this life, the hospitable entertainers (*hospitia*) of the Church (though civil government is distinct from the spiritual kingdom of Christ), the author shows how great blessings they are, blessings which the Church is bound gratefully to acknowledge, until we are called away from this tabernacle to the heavenly inheritance, where God will be all in all.

Such is the arrangement of the Institutes which may be thus summed up: Man being at first created upright, but afterwards being not partially but totally ruined, finds his entire salvation out of himself in Christ, to whom being united by the Holy Spirit freely given without any foresight of future works, he thereby obtains a double blessing—viz. full imputation of righteousness, which goes along with us even to the grave, and the commencement of sanctification, which daily advances till at length it is perfected in the day of regeneration or resurrection of the body, and this, in order that the great mercy of God may be celebrated in the heavenly mansions, throughout eternity.

BOOK FIRST: OF THE KNOWLEDGE OF GOD THE CREATOR

ARGUMENT.

The First Book treats of the knowledge of God the Creator. But as it is in the creation of man that the divine perfections are best displayed, so man also is made the subject of discourse. Thus the whole book divides itself into two principal heads—the former relating to the knowledge of God, and the latter to the knowledge of man. In the first chapter, these are considered jointly; and in each of the following chapters, separately: occasionally, however, intermingled with other matters which refer to one or other of the heads; *e.g.*, the discussions concerning Scripture and images, falling under the former head, and the other three concerning the creation of the world, the holy angels and devils, falling under the latter. The last point discussed—viz. the method of the divine government, relates to both.

With regard to the former head—viz. the knowledge of God, it is shown, in the first place, what the kind of knowledge is which God requires, Chap. 2. And, in the second place (Chap. 3–9), where this knowledge must be sought, namely, not in man; because, although naturally implanted in the human mind, it is stifled, partly by ignorance, partly by evil intent, Chap. 3 and 4; not in the frame of the world: because, although it shines most clearly there, we are so stupid that these manifestations, however perspicuous, pass away without any beneficial result, Chap. 5; but in Scripture (Chap. 6), which is treated of, Chap. 7–9. In the third place, it is shown what the character of God is, Chap. 10. In the fourth place, how impious it is to give a visible form to God (here images, the worship of them, and its origin, are considered), Chap. 11. In the fifth place, it is shown that God is to be solely and wholly worshipped, Chap. 12. Lastly, Chap. 13 treats of the unity of the divine essence, and the distinction of three persons.

With regard to the latter head—viz. the knowledge of man, first, Chap. 14 treats of the creation of the world, and of good and bad angels (these all having reference to man). And then Chap. 15, taking up the subject of man himself, examines his nature and his powers.

The better to illustrate the nature both of God and man, the three remaining Chapters—viz. 16–18, proceed to treat of the general government of the world, and particularly of human actions, in opposition to fortune and fate, explaining both the doctrine and its use. In conclusion, it is shown, that though God employs the instrumentality of the wicked, he is pure from sin and from taint of every kind.

CHAPTER 1

THE KNOWLEDGE OF GOD AND OF OURSELVES MUTUALLY CONNECTED. — NATURE OF THE CONNECTION.

Sections:

1. The sum of true wisdom—viz. the knowledge of God and of ourselves. Effects of the latter.

2. Effects of the knowledge of God, in humbling our pride, unveiling our hypocrisy, demonstrating the absolute perfections of God, and our own utter helplessness.

3. Effects of the knowledge of God illustrated by the examples, 1. of holy patriarchs; 2. of holy angels; 3. of the sun and moon.

1. Our wisdom, in so far as it ought to be deemed true and solid Wisdom, consists almost entirely of two parts: the knowledge of God and of ourselves. But as these are connected together by many ties, it is not easy to determine which of the two precedes and gives birth to the other. For, in the first place, no man can survey himself without forthwith turning his thoughts towards the God in whom he lives and moves; because it is perfectly obvious, that the endowments which we possess cannot possibly be from ourselves; nay, that our very being is nothing else than subsistence in God alone. In the second place, those blessings which unceasingly distil to us from heaven, are like streams conducting us to the fountain. Here, again, the infinitude of good which resides in God becomes more apparent from our poverty. In particular, the miserable ruin into which the revolt of the first man has plunged us, compels us to turn our eyes upwards; not only that while hungry and famishing we may thence ask what we want, but being aroused by fear may learn humility. For as there exists in man something like a world of misery, and ever since we were stript of the divine attire our naked shame discloses an immense series of disgraceful properties every man, being stung by the consciousness of his own unhappiness, in this way necessarily obtains at least some knowledge of God. Thus, our feeling of ignorance, vanity, want, weakness, in short, depravity and corruption, reminds us (see Calvin on John 4:10), that in the Lord, and none but He, dwell the true light of wisdom, solid virtue, exuberant goodness. We are accordingly urged by our own evil things to consider the good things of God; and, indeed, we cannot aspire to Him in earnest until we have begun to be displeased with ourselves. For what man is not disposed to rest in himself? Who, in fact, does not thus rest, so long as he is unknown to himself; that is, so long as he is contented with his own endowments, and unconscious or unmindful of his misery? Every person, therefore, on coming to the knowledge of himself, is not only urged to seek God, but is also led as by the hand to find him.

2. On the other hand, it is evident that man never attains to a true self-knowledge until he has previously contemplated the face of God, and come down after such contemplation to look into himself. For (such is our innate pride) we always seem to ourselves just, and upright, and wise, and holy, until we are convinced, by clear evidence, of our injustice, vileness, folly, and impurity. Convinced, however, we are not, if we look to ourselves only, and not to the Lord also —He being the only standard by the application of which this conviction can be produced. For, since we are all naturally prone to hypocrisy, any empty semblance of righteousness is quite enough to satisfy us instead of righteousness itself. And since nothing appears within us or around us that is not tainted with very great impurity, so long as we keep our mind within the confines of human pollution, anything which is in some small degree less defiled delights us as if it were most pure just as an eye, to which nothing but black had been previously presented, deems an object of a whitish, or even of a brownish hue, to be perfectly white. Nay, the bodily sense may furnish a still stronger illustration of the extent to which we are deluded in estimating the powers of the mind. If, at mid-day, we either look down to the ground, or on the surrounding objects which lie open to our view, we think ourselves endued with a very strong and piercing eyesight; but when we look up to the sun, and gaze at it unveiled, the sight which did excellently well for the earth is instantly so dazzled and confounded by the refulgence, as to oblige us to confess that our acuteness in discerning terrestrial objects is mere dimness when applied to the sun. Thus too, it happens in estimating our spiritual qualities. So long as we do not look beyond the earth, we are quite pleased with our own righteousness, wisdom, and vir-

tue; we address ourselves in the most flattering terms, and seem only less than demigods. But should we once begin to raise our thoughts to God, and reflect what kind of Being he is, and how absolute the perfection of that righteousness, and wisdom, and virtue, to which, as a standard, we are bound to be conformed, what formerly delighted us by its false show of righteousness will become polluted with the greatest iniquity; what strangely imposed upon us under the name of wisdom will disgust by its extreme folly; and what presented the appearance of virtuous energy will be condemned as the most miserable impotence. So far are those qualities in us, which seem most perfect, from corresponding to the divine purity.

3. Hence that dread and amazement with which as Scripture uniformly relates, holy men were struck and overwhelmed whenever they beheld the presence of God. When we see those who previously stood firm and secure so quaking with terror, that the fear of death takes hold of them, nay, they are, in a manner, swallowed up and annihilated, the inference to be drawn is that men are never duly touched and impressed with a conviction of their insignificance, until they have contrasted themselves with the majesty of God. Frequent examples of this consternation occur both in the Book of Judges and the Prophetical Writings; so much so, that it was a common expression among the people of God, "We shall die, for we have seen the Lord." Hence the Book of Job, also, in humbling men under a conviction of their folly, feebleness, and pollution, always derives its chief argument from descriptions of the Divine wisdom, virtue, and purity. Nor without cause: for we see Abraham the readier to acknowledge himself but dust and ashes the nearer he approaches to behold the glory of the Lord, and Elijah unable to wait with unveiled face for His approach; so dreadful is the sight. And what can man do, man who is but rottenness and a worm, when even the Cherubim themselves must veil their faces in very terror? To this, undoubtedly, the Prophet Isaiah refers, when he says (Isaiah 24:23), "The moon shall be confounded, and the sun ashamed, when the Lord of Hosts shall reign;" *i.e.*, when he shall exhibit his refulgence, and give a nearer view of it, the brightest objects will, in comparison, be covered with darkness.

But though the knowledge of God and the knowledge of ourselves are bound together by a mutual tie, due arrangement requires that we treat of the former in the first place, and then descend to the latter.

CHAPTER 2

WHAT IT IS TO KNOW GOD,— TENDENCY OF THIS KNOWLEDGE.

Sections:

1. The knowledge of God the Creator defined. The substance of this knowledge, and the use to be made of it.

2. Further illustration of the use, together with a necessary reproof of vain curiosity, and refutation of the Epicureans. The character of God as it appears to the pious mind, contrasted with the absurd views of the Epicureans. Religion defined.

1. By the knowledge of God, I understand that by which we not only conceive that there is some God, but also apprehend what it is for our interest, and conducive to his glory, what, in short, it is befitting to know concerning him. For, properly speaking, we cannot say that God is known where there is no religion or piety. I am not now referring to that species of knowledge by which men, in themselves lost and under curse, apprehend God as a Redeemer in Christ the Mediator. I speak only of that simple and primitive knowledge, to which the mere course of nature would have conducted us, had Adam stood upright. For although no man will now, in the present ruin of the human race, perceive God to be either a father, or the author of salvation, or propitious in any respect, until Christ interpose to make our peace; still it is one thing to perceive that God our Maker supports us by his power, rules us by his providence, fosters us by his goodness, and visits us with all kinds of blessings, and another thing to embrace the grace of reconciliation offered to us in Christ. Since, then, the Lord first appears, as well in the creation of the world as in the general doctrine of Scripture, simply as a Creator, and afterwards as a Redeemer in Christ,—a twofold knowledge of him hence arises: of these the former is now to be considered, the latter will afterwards follow in its order. But although our mind cannot conceive of God, without rendering some worship to him, it will not, however, be sufficient simply to hold that he is the only being whom all ought to worship and adore, unless we are also persuaded that he is the fountain of all goodness, and that we must seek everything in him, and in none but him. My meaning is: we must be persuaded not only that as he once formed the world, so he sustains it by his boundless power,

governs it by his wisdom, preserves it by his goodness, in particular, rules the human race with justice and Judgment, bears with them in mercy, shields them by his protection; but also that not a particle of light, or wisdom, or justice, or power, or rectitude, or genuine truth, will anywhere be found, which does not flow from him, and of which he is not the cause; in this way we must learn to expect and ask all things from him, and thankfully ascribe to him whatever we receive. For this sense of the divine perfections is the proper master to teach us piety, out of which religion springs. By piety I mean that union of reverence and love to God which the knowledge of his benefits inspires. For, until men feel that they owe everything to God, that they are cherished by his paternal care, and that he is the author of all their blessings, so that nought is to be looked for away from him, they will never submit to him in voluntary obedience; nay, unless they place their entire happiness in him, they will never yield up their whole selves to him in truth and sincerity.

2. Those, therefore, who, in considering this question, propose to inquire what the essence of God is, only delude us with frigid speculations,—it being much more our interest to know what kind of being God is, and what things are agreeable to his nature. For, of what use is it to join Epicures in acknowledging some God who has cast off the care of the world, and only delights himself in ease? What avails it, in short, to know a God with whom we have nothing to do? The effect of our knowledge rather ought to be, *first*, to teach us reverence and fear; and, *secondly*, to induce us, under its guidance and teaching, to ask every good thing from him, and, when it is received, ascribe it to him. For how can the idea of God enter your mind without instantly giving rise to the thought, that since you are his workmanship, you are bound, by the very law of creation, to submit to his authority?—that your life is due to him?—that whatever you do ought to have reference to him? If so, it undoubtedly follows that your life is sadly corrupted, if it is not framed in obedience to him, since his will ought to be the law of our lives. On the other hand, your idea of his nature is not clear unless you acknowledge him to be the origin and fountain of all goodness. Hence would arise both confidence in him, and a desire of cleaving to him, did not the depravity of the human mind lead it away from the proper course of investigation.

For, first of all, the pious mind does not devise for itself any kind of God, but looks alone to the one true God; nor does it feign for him any character it pleases, but is contented to have him in the character in which he manifests himself always guarding, with the utmost diligences against transgressing his will, and wandering, with daring presumptions from the right path. He by whom God is thus known perceiving how he governs all things, confides in him as his guardian and protector, and casts himself entirely upon his faithfulness,—perceiving him to be the source of every blessing, if he is in any strait or feels any want, he instantly recurs to his protection and trusts to his aid,—persuaded that he is good and merciful, he reclines upon him with sure confidence, and doubts not that, in the divine clemency, a remedy will be provided for his every time of need,—acknowledging him as his Father and his Lord he considers himself bound to have respect to his authority in all things, to reverence his majesty aim at the advancement of his glory, and obey his commands,—regarding him as a just judge, armed with severity to punish crimes, he keeps the Judgment-seat always in his view. Standing in awe of it, he curbs himself, and fears to provoke his anger. Nevertheless, he is not so terrified by an apprehension of Judgment as to wish he could withdraw himself, even if the means of escape lay before him; nay, he embraces him not less as the avenger of wickedness than as the rewarder of the righteous; because he perceives that it equally appertains to his glory to store up punishment for the one, and eternal life for the other. Besides, it is not the mere fear of punishment that restrains him from sin. Loving and revering God as his father, honouring and obeying him as his master, although there were no hell, he would revolt at the very idea of offending him.

Such is pure and genuine religion, namely, confidence in God coupled with serious fear—fear, which both includes in it willing reverence, and brings along with it such legitimate worship as is prescribed by the law. And it ought to be more carefully considered that all men promiscuously do homage to God, but very few truly reverence him. On all hands there is abundance of ostentatious ceremonies, but sincerity of heart is rare.

CHAPTER 3

THE KNOWLEDGE OF GOD NATURALLY IMPLANTED IN THE HUMAN MIND.

Sections:
1. The knowledge of God being manifested to all makes the reprobate without excuse. Universal belief and acknowledgement of the existence of God.
2. Objection—that religion and the belief of a Deity

are the inventions of crafty politicians. **Refutation of the objection. This universal belief confirmed by the examples of wicked men and Atheists.**

3. Confirmed also by the vain endeavours of the wicked to banish all fear of God from their minds. Conclusion, that the knowledge of God is naturally implanted in the human mind.

1. That there exists in the human minds and indeed by natural instinct, some sense of Deity, we hold to be beyond dispute, since God himself, to prevent any man from pretending ignorance, has endued all men with some idea of his Godhead, the memory of which he constantly renews and occasionally enlarges, that all to a man being aware that there is a God, and that he is their Maker, may be condemned by their own conscience when they neither worship him nor consecrate their lives to his service. Certainly, if there is any quarter where it may be supposed that God is unknown, the most likely for such an instance to exist is among the dullest tribes farthest removed from civilisation. But, as a heathen tells us, there is no nation so barbarous, no race so brutish, as not to be imbued with the conviction that there is a God. Even those who, in other respects, seem to differ least from the lower animals, constantly retain some sense of religion; so thoroughly has this common conviction possessed the mind, so firmly is it stamped on the breasts of all men. Since, then, there never has been, from the very first, any quarter of the globe, any city, any household even, without religion, this amounts to a tacit confession, that a sense of Deity is inscribed on every heart. Nay, even idolatry is ample evidence of this fact. For we know how reluctant man is to lower himself, in order to set other creatures above him. Therefore, when he chooses to worship wood and stone rather than be thought to have no God, it is evident how very strong this impression of a Deity must be; since it is more difficult to obliterate it from the mind of man, than to break down the feelings of his nature,—these certainly being broken down, when, in opposition to his natural haughtiness, he spontaneously humbles himself before the meanest object as an act of reverence to God.

2. It is most absurd, therefore, to maintain, as some do, that religion was devised by the cunning and craft of a few individuals, as a means of keeping the body of the people in due subjection, while there was nothing which those very individuals, while teaching others to worship God, less believed than the existence of a God. I readily acknowledge, that designing men have introduced a vast number of fictions into religion, with the view of inspiring the populace with reverence or striking them with terror, and thereby rendering them more obsequious; but they never could have succeeded in this, had the minds of men not been previously imbued with that uniform belief in God, from which, as from its seed, the religious propensity springs. And it is altogether incredible that those who, in the matter of religion, cunningly imposed on their ruder neighbours, were altogether devoid of a knowledge of God. For though in old times there were some, and in the present day not a few are found who deny the being of a God, yet, whether they will or not, they occasionally feel the truth which they are desirous not to know. We do not read of any man who broke out into more unbridled and audacious contempt of the Deity than C. Caligula, and yet none showed greater dread when any indication of divine wrath was manifested. Thus, however unwilling, he shook with terror before the God whom he professedly studied to condemn. You may every day see the same thing happening to his modern imitators. The most audacious despiser of God is most easily disturbed, trembling at the sound of a falling leaf. How so, unless in vindication of the divine majesty, which smites their consciences the more strongly the more they endeavour to flee from it. They all, indeed, look out for hiding-places where they may conceal themselves from the presence of the Lord, and again efface it from their mind; but after all their efforts they remain caught within the net. Though the conviction may occasionally seem to vanish for a moment, it immediately returns, and rushes in with new impetuosity, so that any interval of relief from the gnawing of conscience is not unlike the slumber of the intoxicated or the insane, who have no quiet rest in sleep, but are continually haunted with dire horrific dreams. Even the wicked themselves, therefore, are an example of the fact that some idea of God always exists in every human mind.

3. All men of sound Judgment will therefore hold, that a sense of Deity is indelibly engraven on the human heart. And that this belief is naturally engendered in all, and thoroughly fixed as it were in our very bones, is strikingly attested by the contumacy of the wicked, who, though they struggle furiously, are unable to extricate themselves from the fear of God. Though Diagoras, and others of like stamps make themselves merry with whatever has been believed in all ages concerning religion, and Dionysus scoffs at the Judgment of heaven, it is but a Sardonian grin; for the worm of conscience, keener than burning steel, is gnawing them within. I do

not say with Cicero, that errors wear out by age, and that religion increases and grows better day by day. For the world (as will be shortly seen) labours as much as it can to shake off all knowledge of God, and corrupts his worship in innumerable ways. I only say, that, when the stupid hardness of heart, which the wicked eagerly court as a means of despising God, becomes enfeebled, the sense of Deity, which of all things they wished most to be extinguished, is still in vigour, and now and then breaks forth. Whence we infer, that this is not a doctrine which is first learned at school, but one as to which every man is, from the womb, his own master; one which nature herself allows no individual to forget, though many, with all their might, strive to do so. Moreover, if all are born and live for the express purpose of learning to know God, and if the knowledge of God, in so far as it fails to produce this effect, is fleeting and vain, it is clear that all those who do not direct the whole thoughts and actions of their lives to this end fail to fulfil the law of their being. This did not escape the observation even of philosophers. For it is the very thing which Plato meant (in *Phæd. et Theact.*) when he taught, as he often does, that the chief good of the soul consists in resemblance to God; *i.e.*, when, by means of knowing him, she is wholly transformed into him. Thus Gryllus, also, in Plutarch (*lib. guod bruta anim. ratione utantur*), reasons most skilfully, when he affirms that, if once religion is banished from the lives of men, they not only in no respect excel, but are, in many respects, much more wretched than the brutes, since, being exposed to so many forms of evil, they continually drag on a troubled and restless existence: that the only thing, therefore, which makes them superior is the worship of God, through which alone they aspire to immortality.

CHAPTER 4

THE KNOWLEDGE OF GOD STIFLED OR CORRUPTED, IGNORANTLY OR MALICIOUSLY.

Sections:

1. The knowledge of God suppressed by ignorance, many falling away into superstition. Such persons, however, inexcusable, because their error is accompanied with pride and stubbornness.

2. Stubbornness the companion of impiety.

3. No pretext can justify superstition. This proved, first, from reason; and, secondly, from Scripture.

4. **The wicked never willingly come into the presence of God. Hence their hypocrisy. Hence, too, their sense of Deity leads to no good result.**

1. But though experience testifies that a seed of religion is divinely sown in all, scarcely one in a hundred is found who cherishes it in his heart, and not one in whom it grows to maturity so far is it from yielding fruit in its season. Moreover, while some lose themselves in superstitious observances, and others, of set purpose, wickedly revolt from God, the result is that, in regard to the true knowledge of him, all are so degenerate, that in no part of the world can genuine godliness be found. In saying that some fall away into superstition, I mean not to insinuate that their excessive absurdity frees them from guilt; for the blindness under which they labour is almost invariably accompanied with vain pride and stubbornness. Mingled vanity and pride appear in this, that when miserable men do seek after God, instead of ascending higher than themselves as they ought to do, they measure him by their own carnal stupidity, and, neglecting solid inquiry, fly off to indulge their curiosity in vain speculation. Hence, they do not conceive of him in the character in which he is manifested, but imagine him to be whatever their own rashness has devised. This abyss standing open, they cannot move one footstep without rushing headlong to destruction. With such an idea of God, nothing which they may attempt to offer in the way of worship or obedience can have any value in his sight, because it is not him they worship, but, instead of him, the dream and figment of their own heart. This corrupt procedure is admirably described by Paul, when he says, that "thinking to be wise, they became fools" (Rom. 1:22). He had previously said that "they became vain in their imaginations," but lest any should suppose them blameless, he afterwards adds that they were deservedly blinded, because, not contented with sober inquiry, because, arrogating to themselves more than they have any title to do, they of their own accord court darkness, nay, bewitch themselves with perverse, empty show. Hence it is that their folly, the result not only of vain curiosity, but of licentious desire and overweening confidence in the pursuit of forbidden knowledge, cannot be excused.

2. The expression of David (Psalm 14:1, 53:1), "The fool hath said in his heart, There is no God," is primarily applied to those who, as will shortly farther appear, stifle the light of nature, and intentionally stupefy themselves. We see many, after they have become hardened

in a daring course of sin, madly banishing all remembrance of God, though spontaneously suggested to them from within, by natural sense. To show how detestable this madness is, the Psalmist introduces them as distinctly denying that there is a God, because although they do not disown his essence, they rob him of his justice and providence, and represent him as sitting idly in heaven. Nothing being less accordant with the nature of God than to cast off the government of the world, leaving it to chance, and so to wink at the crimes of men that they may wanton with impunity in evil courses; it follows, that every man who indulges in security, after extinguishing all fear of divine Judgment, virtually denies that there is a God. As a just punishment of the wicked, after they have closed their own eyes, God makes their hearts dull and heavy, and hence, seeing, they see not. David, indeed, is the best interpreter of his own meaning, when he says elsewhere, the wicked has "no fear of God before his eyes" (Psalm 36:1); and, again, "He has said in his heart, God has forgotten; he hideth his face; he will never see it." Thus although they are forced to acknowledge that there is some God, they, however, rob him of his glory by denying his power. For, as Paul declares, "If we believe not, he abideth faithful, he cannot deny himself" (2 Tim. 2:13); so those who feign to themselves a dead and dumb idol, are truly said to deny God. It is, moreover, to be observed, that though they struggle with their own convictions, and would fain not only banish God from their minds, but from heaven also, their stupefaction is never so complete as to secure them from being occasionally dragged before the divine tribunal. Still, as no fear restrains them from rushing violently in the face of God, so long as they are hurried on by that blind impulse, it cannot be denied that their prevailing state of mind in regard to him is brutish oblivion.

3. In this way, the vain pretext which many employ to clothe their superstition is overthrown. They deem it enough that they have some kind of zeal for religion, how preposterous soever it may be, not observing that true religion must be conformable to the will of God as its unerring standard; that he can never deny himself, and is no spectra or phantom, to be metamorphosed at each individual's caprice. It is easy to see how superstition, with its false glosses, mocks God, while it tries to please him. Usually fastening merely on things on which he has declared he sets no value, it either contemptuously overlooks, or even undisguisedly rejects, the things which he expressly enjoins, or in which we are assured that he takes pleasure. Those, therefore, who set up a fictitious worship, merely worship and adore their own delirious fancies; indeed, they would never dare so to trifle with God, had they not previously fashioned him after their own childish conceits. Hence that vague and wandering opinion of Deity is declared by an apostle to be ignorance of God: "Howbeit, then, when ye knew not God, ye did service unto them which by nature are no gods." And he elsewhere declares, that the Ephesians were "without God" (Eph. 2:12) at the time when they wandered without any correct knowledge of him. It makes little difference, at least in this respect, whether you hold the existence of one God, or a plurality of gods, since, in both cases alike, by departing from the true God, you have nothing left but an execrable idol. It remains, therefore, to conclude with Lactantius (*Instit. Div.* lib 1:2, 6), "No religion is genuine that is not in accordance with truth."

4. To this fault they add a second—viz. that when they do think of God it is against their will; never approaching him without being dragged into his presence, and when there, instead of the voluntary fear flowing from reverence of the divine majesty, feeling only that forced and servile fear which divine Judgment extorts Judgment which, from the impossibility of escape, they are compelled to dread, but which, while they dread, they at the same time also hate. To impiety, and to it alone, the saying of Statius properly applies: "Fear first brought gods into the world" (*Theb.* lib. 1). Those whose inclinations are at variance with the justice of God, knowing that his tribunal has been erected for the punishment of transgression, earnestly wish that that tribunal were overthrown. Under the influence of this feeling they are actually warring against God, justice being one of his essential attributes. Perceiving that they are always within reach of his power, that resistance and evasion are alike impossible, they fear and tremble. Accordingly, to avoid the appearance of condemning a majesty by which all are overawed, they have recourse to some species of religious observance, never ceasing meanwhile to defile themselves with every kind of vice, and add crime to crime, until they have broken the holy law of the Lord in every one of its requirements, and set his whole righteousness at nought; at all events, they are not so restrained by their semblance of fear as not to luxuriate and take pleasure in iniquity, choosing rather to indulge their carnal propensities than to curb them with the bridle of the Holy Spirit. But since this shadow of religion (it scarcely even deserves to be called a shadow) is false and vain, it is easy to infer how much this confused knowledge of God differs from that piety which is instilled into the breasts of believers, and from which alone true religion springs. And yet hypo-

crites would fain, by means of tortuous windings, make a show of being near to God at the very time they are fleeing from him. For while the whole life ought to be one perpetual course of obedience, they rebel without fear in almost all their actions, and seek to appease him with a few paltry sacrifices; while they ought to serve him with integrity of heart and holiness of life, they endeavour to procure his favour by means of frivolous devices and punctilios of no value. Nay, they take greater license in their grovelling indulgences, because they imagine that they can fulfil their duty to him by preposterous expiations; in short, while their confidence ought to have been fixed upon him, they put him aside, and rest in themselves or the creatures. At length they bewilder themselves in such a maze of error, that the darkness of ignorance obscures, and ultimately extinguishes, those sparks which were designed to show them the glory of God. Still, however, the conviction that there is some Deity continues to exist, like a plant which can never be completely eradicated, though so corrupt, that it is only capable of producing the worst of fruit. Nay, we have still stronger evidence of the proposition for which I now contend—viz. that a sense of Deity is naturally engraven on the human heart, in the fact, that the very reprobate are forced to acknowledge it. When at their ease, they can jest about God, and talk pertly and loquaciously in disparagement of his power; but should despair, from any cause, overtake them, it will stimulate them to seek him, and dictate ejaculatory prayers, proving that they were not entirely ignorant of God, but had perversely suppressed feelings which ought to have been earlier manifested.

CHAPTER 5

THE KNOWLEDGE OF GOD CONSPICUOUS IN THE CREATION, AND CONTINUAL GOVERNMENT OF THE WORLD.

This chapter consists of two parts: 1. The former, which occupies the first ten sections, divides all the works of God into two great classes, and elucidates the knowledge of God as displayed in each class. The one class is treated of in the first six, and the other in the four following sections: 2. The latter part of the chapter shows, that, in consequence of the extreme stupidity of men, those manifestations of God, however perspicuous, lead to no useful result. This latter part, which commences at the eleventh section, is continued to the end of the chapter.

Sections:

1. The invisible and incomprehensible essence of God, to a certain extent, made visible in his works.

2. This declared by the first class of works—viz. the admirable motions of the heavens and the earth, the symmetry of the human body, and the connection of its parts; in short, the various objects which are presented to every eye.

3. This more especially manifested in the structure of the human body.

4. The shameful ingratitude of disregarding God, who, in such a variety of ways, is manifested within us. The still more shameful ingratitude of contemplating the endowments of the soul, without ascending to Him who gave them. No objection can be founded on any supposed organism in the soul.

5. The powers and actions of the soul, a proof of its separate existence from the body. Proofs of the soul's immortality. Objection that the whole world is quickened by one soul. Reply to the objection. Its impiety.

6. Conclusion from what has been said—viz. that the omnipotence, eternity, and goodness of God, may be learned from the first class of works, i.e., those which are in accordance with the ordinary course of nature.

7. The second class of works—viz. those above the ordinary course of nature, afford clear evidence of the perfections of God, especially his goodness, justice, and mercy.

8. Also his providence, power, and wisdom.

9. Proofs and illustrations of the divine Majesty. The use of them—viz. the acquisition of divine knowledge in combination with true piety.

10. The tendency of the knowledge of God to inspire the righteous with the hope of future life, and remind the wicked of the punishments reserved for them. Its tendency, moreover, to keep alive in the hearts of the righteous a sense of the divine goodness.

11. The second part of the chapter, which describes the stupidity both of learned and unlearned, in ascribing the whole order of things, and the admirable arrangements of divine Providence, to fortune.

12. Hence Polytheism, with all its abominations, and the endless and irreconcilable opinions of the philosophers concerning God.

13. All guilty of revolt from God, corrupting pure religion, either by following general custom, or the impious consent of antiquity.

14. Though irradiated by the wondrous glories of creation, we cease not to follow our own ways.

15. Our conduct altogether inexcusable, the dullness of perception being attributable to ourselves, while we are fully reminded of the true path, both by the structure and the government of the world.

1. Since the perfection of blessedness consists in the knowledge of God, he has been pleased, in order that none might be excluded from the means of obtaining felicity, not only to deposit in our minds that seed of religion of which we have already spoken, but so to manifest his perfections in the whole structure of the universe, and daily place himself in our view, that we cannot open our eyes without being compelled to behold him. His essence, indeed, is incomprehensible, utterly transcending all human thought; but on each of his works his glory is engraven in characters so bright, so distinct, and so illustrious, that none, however dull and illiterate, can plead ignorance as their excuse. Hence, with perfect truth, the Psalmist exclaims, "He covereth himself with light as with a garment" (Psalm 104:2); as if he had said, that God for the first time was arrayed in visible attire when, in the creation of the world, he displayed those glorious banners, on which, to whatever side we turn, we behold his perfections visibly portrayed. In the same place, the Psalmist aptly compares the expanded heavens to his royal tent, and says, "He layeth the beams of his chambers in the waters, maketh the clouds his chariot, and walketh upon the wings of the wind," sending forth the winds and lightnings as his swift messengers. And because the glory of his power and wisdom is more refulgent in the firmament, it is frequently designated as his palace. And, first, wherever you turn your eyes, there is no portion of the world, however minute, that does not exhibit at least some sparks of beauty; while it is impossible to contemplate the vast and beautiful fabric as it extends around, without being overwhelmed by the immense weight of glory. Hence, the author of the Epistle to the Hebrews elegantly describes the visible worlds as images of the invisible (Heb. 11:3), the elegant structure of the world serving us as a kind of mirror, in which we may behold God, though otherwise invisible. For the same reason, the Psalmist attributes language to celestial objects, a language which all nations understand (Psalm 19:1), the manifestation of the Godhead being too clear to escape the notice of any people, however obtuse. The apostle Paul, stating this still more clearly, says, "That which may be known of God is manifest in them, for God has showed it unto them. For the invisible things of him from the creation of the world are clearly seen, being understood by the things that are made, even his eternal power and Godhead" (Rom. 1:20).

2. In attestation of his wondrous wisdom, both the heavens and the earth present us with innumerable proofs not only those more recondite proofs which astronomy, medicine, and all the natural sciences, are designed to illustrate, but proofs which force themselves on the notice of the most illiterate peasant, who cannot open his eyes without beholding them. It is true, indeed, that those who are more or less intimately acquainted with those liberal studies are thereby assisted and enabled to obtain a deeper insight into the secret workings of divine wisdom. No man, however, though he be ignorant of these, is incapacitated for discerning such proofs of creative wisdom as may well cause him to break forth in admiration of the Creator. To investigate the motions of the heavenly bodies, to determine their positions, measure their distances, and ascertain their properties, demands skill, and a more careful examination; and where these are so employed, as the Providence of God is thereby more fully unfolded, so it is reasonable to suppose that the mind takes a loftier flight, and obtains brighter views of his glory. Still, none who have the use of their eyes can be ignorant of the divine skill manifested so conspicuously in the endless variety, yet distinct and well ordered array, of the heavenly host; and, therefore, it is plain that the Lord has furnished every man with abundant proofs of his wisdom. The same is true in regard to the structure of the human frame. To determine the connection of its parts, its symmetry and beauty, with the skill of a Galen (Lib. *De Usu Partium*), requires singular acuteness; and yet all men acknowledge that the human body bears on its face such proofs of ingenious contrivance as are sufficient to proclaim the admirable wisdom of its Maker.

3. Hence certain of the philosophers have not improperly called man a *microcosm* (*miniature world*), as being a rare specimen of divine power, wisdom, and goodness, and containing within himself wonders sufficient to occupy our minds, if we are willing so to employ them. Paul, accordingly, after reminding the Athenians that they "might feel after God and find him," immediately adds, that "he is not far from every one of us" (Acts 17:27); every man having within himself undoubted evidence of the heavenly grace by which he lives, and moves, and has his being. But if, in order to apprehend God, it is unnecessary to go farther than ourselves, what excuse can there be for the sloth of any man who will not take the trouble of descending into himself that he may find Him? For the same reason, too, David, after briefly celebrating the

wonderful name and glory of God, as everywhere displayed, immediately exclaims, "What is man, that thou art mindful of him?" and again, "Out of the mouths of babes and sucklings thou hast ordained strength" (Psalm 8:2, 4). Thus he declares not only that the human race are a bright mirror of the Creator's works, but that infants hanging on their mothers' breasts have tongues eloquent enough to proclaim his glory without the aid of other orators. Accordingly, he hesitates not to bring them forward as fully instructed to refute the madness of those who, from devilish pride, would fain extinguish the name of God. Hence, too, the passage which Paul quotes from Aratus, "We are his offspring" (Acts 17:28), the excellent gifts with which he has endued us attesting that he is our Father. In the same way also, from natural instinct, and, as it were, at the dictation of experience, heathen poets call him the father of men. No one, indeed, will voluntarily and willingly devote himself to the service of God unless he has previously tasted his paternal love, and been thereby allured to love and reverence Him.

4. But herein appears the shameful ingratitude of men. Though they have in their own persons a factory where innumerable operations of God are carried on, and a magazine stored with treasures of inestimable value—instead of bursting forth in his praise, as they are bound to do, they, on the contrary, are the more inflated and swelled with pride. They feel how wonderfully God is working in them, and their own experience tells them of the vast variety of gifts which they owe to his liberality. Whether they will or not, they cannot but know that these are proofs of his Godhead, and yet they inwardly suppress them. They have no occasion to go farther than themselves, provided they do not, by appropriating as their own that which has been given them from heaven, put out the light intended to exhibit God clearly to their minds. At this day, however, the earth sustains on her bosom many monster minds—minds which are not afraid to employ the seed of Deity deposited in human nature as a means of suppressing the name of God. Can any thing be more detestable than this madness in man, who, finding God a hundred times both in his body and his soul, makes his excellence in this respect a pretext for denying that there is a God? He will not say that chance has made him differ from the brutes that perish; but, substituting nature as the architect of the universe, he suppresses the name of God. The swift motions of the soul, its noble faculties and rare endowments, bespeak the agency of God in a manner which would make the suppression of it impossible, did not the Epicureans, like so many Cyclops, use it as a vantage-ground, from which to wage more audacious war with God. Are so many treasures of heavenly wisdom employed in the guidance of such a worm as man, and shall the whole universe be denied the same privilege? To hold that there are organs in the soul corresponding to each of its faculties, is so far from obscuring the glory of God, that it rather illustrates it. Let Epicurus tell what concourse of atoms, cooking meat and drink, can form one portion into refuse and another portion into blood, and make all the members separately perform their office as carefully as if they were so many souls acting with common consent in the superintendence of one body.

5. But my business at present is not with that stye: I wish rather to deal with those who, led away by absurd subtleties, are inclined, by giving an indirect turn to the frigid doctrine of Aristotle, to employ it for the purpose both of disproving the immortality of the soul, and robbing God of his rights. Under the pretext that the faculties of the soul are organised, they chain it to the body as if it were incapable of a separate existence, while they endeavour as much as in them lies, by pronouncing eulogiums on nature, to suppress the name of God. But there is no ground for maintaining that the powers of the soul are confined to the performance of bodily functions. What has the body to do with your measuring the heavens, counting the number of the stars, ascertaining their magnitudes, their relative distances, the rate at which they move, and the orbits which they describe? I deny not that Astronomy has its use; all I mean to show is, that these lofty investigations are not conducted by organised symmetry, but by the faculties of the soul itself apart altogether from the body. The single example I have given will suggest many others to the reader. The swift and versatile movements of the soul in glancing from heaven to earth, connecting the future with the past, retaining the remembrance of former years, nay, forming creations of its own—its skill, moreover, in making astonishing discoveries, and inventing so many wonderful arts, are sure indications of the agency of God in man. What shall we say of its activity when the body is asleep, its many revolving thoughts, its many useful suggestions, its many solid arguments, nay, its presentiment of things yet to come? What shall we say but that man bears about with him a stamp of immortality which can never be effaced? But how is it possible for man to be divine, and yet not acknowledge his Creator? Shall we, by means of a power of judging implanted in our breast, distinguish between justice and injustice, and yet there be no judge in heaven?

Shall some remains of intelligence continue with us in sleep, and yet no God keep watch in heaven? Shall we be deemed the inventors of so many arts and useful properties that God may be defrauded of his praise, though experience tells us plainly enough, that whatever we possess is dispensed to us in unequal measures by another hand? The talk of certain persons concerning a secret inspiration quickening the whole world, is not only silly, but altogether profane. Such persons are delighted with the following celebrated passage of Virgil:—

> Know, first, that heaven, and earth's compacted frame,
>   And flowing waters, and the starry flame,
>   And both the radiant lights, one common soul
>   Inspires and feeds—and animates the whole.
>   This active mind, infused through all the space,
>   Unites and mingles with the mighty mass:
>   Hence, men and beasts the breath of life obtain,
>   And birds of air, and monsters of the main.
>   Th' ethereal vigour is in all the same,
>   And every soul is filled with equal flame.

The meaning of all this is, that the world, which was made to display the glory of God, is its own creator. For the same poet has, in another place, adopted a view common to both Greeks and Latins:—

> Hence to the bee some sages have assigned
>   A portion of the God, and heavenly mind;
>   For God goes forth, and spreads throughout the whole,
>   Heaven, earth, and sea, the universal soul;
>   Each, at its birth, from him all beings share,
>   Both man and brute, the breath of vital air;
>   To him return, and, loosed from earthly chain,
>   Fly whence they sprung, and rest in God again;
>   Spurn at the grave, and, fearless of decay,
>   Dwell in high heaven, art star th' ethereal way.

Here we see how far that jejune speculation, of a universal mind animating and invigorating the world, is fitted to beget and foster piety in our minds. We have a still clearer proof of this in the profane verses which the licentious Lucretius has written as a deduction from the same principle. The plain object is to form an unsubstantial deity, and thereby banish the true God whom we ought to fear and worship. I admit, indeed that the expressions "Nature is God," may be piously used, if dictated by a pious mind; but as it is inaccurate and harsh (Nature being more properly the order which has been established by God), in matters which are so very important, and in regard to which special reverence is due, it does harm to confound the Deity with the inferior operations of his hands.

6. Let each of us, therefore, in contemplating his own nature, remember that there is one God who governs all natures, and, in governing, wishes us to have respect to himself, to make him the object of our faith, worship, and adoration. Nothing, indeed, can be more preposterous than to enjoy those noble endowments which bespeak the divine presence within us, and to neglect him who, of his own good pleasure, bestows them upon us. In regard to his power, how glorious the manifestations by which he urges us to the contemplation of himself; unless, indeed, we pretend not to know whose energy it is that by a word sustains the boundless fabric of the universe—at one time making heaven reverberate with thunder, sending forth the scorching lightning, and setting the whole atmosphere in a blaze; at another, causing the raging tempests to blow, and forthwith, in one moment, when it so pleases him, making a perfect calm; keeping the sea, which seems constantly threatening the earth with devastation, suspended as it were in air; at one time, lashing it into fury by the impetuosity of the winds; at another, appeasing its rage, and stilling all its waves. Here we might refer to those glowing descriptions of divine power, as illustrated by natural events, which occur throughout Scripture; but more especially in the book of Job, and the prophecies of Isaiah. These, however, I purposely omit, because a better opportunity of introducing them will be found when I come to treat of the Scriptural account of the creation. (*Infra*, chap. 14 s. 1, 2, 20, *sq*). I only wish to observe here, that this method of investigating the divine perfections, by tracing the lineaments of his countenance as shadowed forth in the firmament and on the earth, is common both to those within and to those without the pale of the Church. From the power of God we are naturally led to consider his eternity since that from which all other things derive their origin must necessarily be selfexistent and eternal. Moreover, if it be asked what cause induced him to create all things at first, and now inclines him to preserve them, we shall find that there could be no other cause than his own goodness. But if this is the only cause, nothing more should be required to draw forth our love towards him; every creature, as the Psalmist reminds us, participating in his mercy. "His tender mercies are over all his works" (Ps. 145:9).

7. In the second class of God's works, namely those which are above the ordinary course of nature, the

evidence of his perfections are in every respect equally clear. For in conducting the affairs of men, he so arranges the course of his providence, as daily to declare, by the clearest manifestations, that though all are in innumerable ways the partakers of his bounty, the righteous are the special objects of his favour, the wicked and profane the special objects of his severity. It is impossible to doubt his punishment of crimes; while at the same time he, in no unequivocal manner, declares that he is the protector, and even the avenger of innocence, by shedding blessings on the good, helping their necessities, soothing and solacing their griefs, relieving their sufferings, and in all ways providing for their safety. And though he often permits the guilty to exult for a time with impunity, and the innocent to be driven to and fro in adversity, nay, even to be wickedly and iniquitously oppressed, this ought not to produce any uncertainty as to the uniform justice of all his procedure. Nay, an opposite inference should be drawn. When any one crime calls forth visible manifestations of his anger, it must be because he hates all crimes; and, on the other hand, his leaving many crimes unpunished, only proves that there is a Judgment in reserve, when the punishment now delayed shall be inflicted. In like manner, how richly does he supply us with the means of contemplating his mercy when, as frequently happens, he continues to visit miserable sinners with unwearied kindness, until he subdues their depravity, and woos them back with more than a parent's fondness?

8. To this purpose the Psalmist (Ps. 107) mentioning how God, in a wondrous manner, often brings sudden and unexpected succour to the miserable when almost on the brink of despair, whether in protecting them when they stray in deserts, and at length leading them back into the right path, or supplying them with food when famishing for want, or delivering them when captive from iron fetters and foul dungeons, or conducting them safe into harbour after shipwreck, or bringing them back from the gates of death by curing their diseases, or, after burning up the fields with heat and drought, fertilising them with the river of his grace, or exalting the meanest of the people, and casting down the mighty from their lofty seats:—the Psalmist, after bringing forward examples of this description, infers that those things which men call fortuitous events, are so many proofs of divine providence, and more especially of paternal clemency, furnishing ground of joy to the righteous, and at the same time stopping the mouths of the ungodly. But as the greater part of mankind, enslaved by error, walk blindfold in this glorious theatre, he exclaims that it is a rare and singular wisdom to meditate carefully on these works of God, which many, who seem most sharp-sighted in other respects, behold without profit. It is indeed true, that the brightest manifestation of divine glory finds not one genuine spectator among a hundred. Still, neither his power nor his wisdom is shrouded in darkness. His power is strikingly displayed when the rage of the wicked, to all appearance irresistible, is crushed in a single moment; their arrogance subdued, their strongest bulwarks overthrown, their armour dashed to pieces, their strength broken, their schemes defeated without an effort, and audacity which set itself above the heavens is precipitated to the lowest depths of the earth. On the other hand, the poor are raised up out of the dust, and the needy lifted out of the dung hill (Ps. 113:7), the oppressed and afflicted are rescued in extremity, the despairing animated with hope, the unarmed defeat the armed, the few the many, the weak the strong. The excellence of the divine wisdom is manifested in distributing everything in due season, confounding the wisdom of the world, and taking the wise in their own craftiness (1 Cor. 3:19); in short, conducting all things in perfect accordance with reason.

9. We see there is no need of a long and laborious train of argument in order to obtain proofs which illustrate and assert the Divine Majesty. The few which we have merely touched, show them to be so immediately within our reach in every quarter, that we can trace them with the eye, or point to them with the finger. And here we must observe again (see chap. 2 s. 2), that the knowledge of God which we are invited to cultivate is not that which, resting satisfied with empty speculation, only flutters in the brain, but a knowledge which will prove substantial and fruitful wherever it is duly perceived, and rooted in the heart. The Lord is manifested by his perfections. When we feel their power within us, and are conscious of their benefits, the knowledge must impress us much more vividly than if we merely imagined a God whose presence we never felt. Hence it is obvious, that in seeking God, the most direct path and the fittest method is, not to attempt with presumptuous curiosity to pry into his essence, which is rather to be adored than minutely discussed, but to contemplate him in his works, by which he draws near, becomes familiar, and in a manner communicates himself to us. To this the Apostle referred when he said, that we need not go far in search of him (Acts 17:27), because, by the continual working of his power, he dwells in every one of us. Accordingly, David (Psalm 145), after acknowledging that his greatness is

unsearchable, proceeds to enumerate his works, declaring that his greatness will thereby be unfolded. It therefore becomes us also diligently to prosecute that investigation of God which so enraptures the soul with admiration as, at the same time, to make an efficacious impression on it. And, as Augustine expresses it (in Psalm 144), since we are unable to comprehend Him, and are, as it were, overpowered by his greatness, our proper course is to contemplate his works, and so refresh ourselves with his goodness.

10. By the knowledge thus acquired, we ought not only to be stimulated to worship God, but also aroused and elevated to the hope of future life. For, observing that the manifestations which the Lord gives both of his mercy and severity are only begun and incomplete, we ought to infer that these are doubtless only a prelude to higher manifestations, of which the full display is reserved for another state. Conversely, when we see the righteous brought into affliction by the ungodly, assailed with injuries, overwhelmed with calumnies, and lacerated by insult and contumely, while, on the contrary, the wicked flourish, prosper, acquire ease and honour, and all these with impunity, we ought forthwith to infer, that there will be a future life in which iniquity shall receive its punishment, and righteousness its reward. Moreover, when we observe that the Lord often lays his chastening rod on the righteous, we may the more surely conclude, that far less will the unrighteous ultimately escape the scourges of his anger. There is a well-known passage in Augustine (De Civitat. Dei, lib. 1 c. 8), "Were all sin now visited with open punishment, it might be thought that nothing was reserved for the final Judgment; and, on the other hand, were no sin now openly punished, it might be supposed there was no divine providence." It must be acknowledged, therefore, that in each of the works of God, and more especially in the whole of them taken together, the divine perfections are delineated as in a picture, and the whole human race thereby invited and allured to acquire the knowledge of God, and, in consequence of this knowledge, true and complete felicity. Moreover, while his perfections are thus most vividly displayed, the only means of ascertaining their practical operation and tendency is to descend into ourselves, and consider how it is that the Lord there manifests his wisdom, power, and energy,—how he there displays his justice, goodness, and mercy. For although David (Psalm 92:6) justly complains of the extreme infatuation of the ungodly in not pondering the deep counsels of God, as exhibited in the government of the human race, what he elsewhere says (Psalm 40) is most true, that the wonders of the divine wisdom in this respect are more in number than the hairs of our head. But I leave this topic at present, as it will be more fully considered afterwards in its own place (Book I. c. 16, see. 6–9).

11. Bright, however, as is the manifestation which God gives both of himself and his immortal kingdom in the mirror of his works, so great is our stupidity, so dull are we in regard to these bright manifestations, that we derive no benefit from them. For in regard to the fabric and admirable arrangement of the universe, how few of us are there who, in lifting our eyes to the heavens, or looking abroad on the various regions of the earth, ever think of the Creator? Do we not rather overlook Him, and sluggishly content ourselves with a view of his works? And then in regard to supernatural events, though these are occurring every day, how few are there who ascribe them to the ruling providence of God—how many who imagine that they are casual results produced by the blind evolutions of the wheel of chance? Even when under the guidance and direction of these events, we are in a manner forced to the contemplation of God (a circumstance which all must occasionally experience), and are thus led to form some impressions of Deity, we immediately fly off to carnal dreams and depraved fictions, and so by our vanity corrupt heavenly truth. This far, indeed, we differ from each other, in that every one appropriates to himself some peculiar error; but we are all alike in this, that we substitute monstrous fictions for the one living and true God—a disease not confined to obtuse and vulgar minds, but affecting the noblest, and those who, in other respects, are singularly acute. How lavishly in this respect have the whole body of philosophers betrayed their stupidity and want of sense? To say nothing of the others whose absurdities are of a still grosser description, how completely does Plato, the soberest and most religious of them all, lose himself in his round globe? What must be the case with the rest, when the leaders, who ought to have set them an example, commit such blunders, and labour under such hallucinations? In like manner, while the government of the world places the doctrine of providence beyond dispute, the practical result is the same as if it were believed that all things were carried hither and thither at the caprice of chance; so prone are we to vanity and error. I am still referring to the most distinguished of the philosophers, and not to the common herd, whose madness in profaning the truth of God exceeds all bounds.

12. Hence that immense flood of error with which the

whole world is overflowed. Every individual mind being a kind of labyrinth, it is not wonderful, not only that each nation has adopted a variety of fictions, but that almost every man has had his own god. To the darkness of ignorance have been added presumption and wantonness, and hence there is scarcely an individual to be found without some idol or phantom as a substitute for Deity. Like water gushing forth from a large and copious spring, immense crowds of gods have issued from the human mind, every man giving himself full license, and devising some peculiar form of divinity, to meet his own views. It is unnecessary here to attempt a catalogue of the superstitions with which the world was overspread. The thing were endless; and the corruptions themselves, though not a word should be said, furnish abundant evidence of the blindness of the human mind. I say nothing of the rude and illiterate vulgar; but among the philosophers who attempted, by reason and learning, to pierce the heavens, what shameful disagreement! The higher any one was endued with genius, and the more he was polished by science and art, the more specious was the colouring which he gave to his opinions. All these, however, if examined more closely, will be found to be vain show. The Stoics plumed themselves on their acuteness, when they said that the various names of God might be extracted from all the parts of nature, and yet that his unity was not thereby divided: as if we were not already too prone to vanity, and had no need of being presented with an endless multiplicity of gods, to lead us further and more grossly into error. The mystic theology of the Egyptians shows how sedulously they laboured to be thought rational on this subject. And, perhaps, at the first glance, some show of probability might deceive the simple and unwary; but never did any mortal devise a scheme by which religion was not foully corrupted. This endless variety and confusion emboldened the Epicureans, and other gross despisers of piety, to cut off all sense of God. For when they saw that the wisest contradicted each others they hesitated not to infer from their dissensions, and from the frivolous and absurd doctrines of each, that men foolishly, and to no purpose, brought torment upon themselves by searching for a God, there being none: and they thought this inference safe, because it was better at once to deny God altogether, than to feign uncertain gods, and thereafter engage in quarrels without end. They, indeed, argue absurdly, or rather weave a cloak for their impiety out of human ignorance; though ignorance surely cannot derogate from the prerogatives of God. But since all confess that there is no topic on which such difference exists, both among learned and unlearned, the proper inference is, that the human mind, which thus errs in inquiring after God, is dull and blind in heavenly mysteries. Some praise the answer of Simonides, who being asked by King Hero what God was, asked a day to consider. When the king next day repeated the question, he asked two days; and after repeatedly doubling the number of days, at length replied, "The longer I consider, the darker the subject appears." He, no doubt, wisely suspended his opinion, when he did not see clearly: still his answer shows, that if men are only naturally taught, instead of having any distinct, solid, or certain knowledge, they fasten only on contradictory principles, and, in consequence, worship an unknown God.

13. Hence we must hold, that whosoever adulterates pure religion (and this must be the case with all who cling to their own views), make a departure from the one God. No doubt, they will allege that they have a different intention; but it is of little consequence what they intend or persuade themselves to believe, since the Holy Spirit pronounces all to be apostates, who, in the blindness of their minds, substitute demons in the place of God. For this reason Paul declares that the Ephesians were "without God" (Eph. 2:12), until they had learned from the Gospel what it is to worship the true God. Nor must this be restricted to one people only, since, in another place, he declares in general, that all men "became vain in their imaginations," after the majesty of the Creator was manifested to them in the structure of the world. Accordingly, in order to make way for the only true God, he condemns all the gods celebrated among the Gentiles as lying and false, leaving no Deity anywhere but in Mount Zion where the special knowledge of God was professed (Hab. 2:18, 20). Among the Gentiles in the time of Christ, the Samaritans undoubtedly made the nearest approach to true piety; yet we hear from his own mouth that they worshipped they knew not what (John 4:22); whence it follows that they were deluded by vain errors. In short, though all did not give way to gross vice, or rush headlong into open idolatry, there was no pure and authentic religion founded merely on common belief. A few individuals may not have gone all insane lengths with the vulgar; still Paul's declaration remains true, that the wisdom of God was not apprehended by the princes of this world (1 Cor. 2:8). But if the most distinguished wandered in darkness, what shall we say of the refuse? No wonder, therefore, that all worship of man's device is repudiated by the Holy Spirit as degenerate. Any opinion which man can form in heavenly mysteries, though

it may not beget a long train of errors, is still the parent of error. And though nothing worse should happen, even this is no light sin—to worship an unknown God at random. Of this sin, however, we hear from our Saviour's own mouth (John 4:22), that all are guilty who have not been taught out of the law who the God is whom they ought to worship. Nay, even Socrates in Xenophon (lib. 1 Memorabilia), lauds the response of Apollo enjoining every man to worship the gods according to the rites of his country, and the particular practice of his own city. But what right have mortals thus to decide of their own authority in a matter which is far above the world; or who can so acquiesce in the will of his forefathers, or the decrees of the people, as unhesitatingly to receive a god at their hands? Every one will adhere to his own Judgment, sooner than submit to the dictation of others. Since, therefore, in regulating the worship of God, the custom of a city, or the consent of antiquity, is a too feeble and fragile bond of piety; it remains that God himself must bear witness to himself from heaven.

14. In vain for us, therefore, does Creation exhibit so many bright lamps lighted up to show forth the glory of its Author. Though they beam upon us from every quarter, they are altogether insufficient of themselves to lead us into the right path. Some sparks, undoubtedly, they do throw out; but these are quenched before they can give forth a brighter effulgence. Wherefore, the apostle, in the very place where he says that the worlds are images of invisible things, adds that it is *by faith* we understand that they were framed by the word of God (Heb. 11:3); thereby intimating that the invisible Godhead is indeed represented by such displays, but that we have no eyes to perceive it until they are enlightened through faith by internal revelation from God. When Paul says that that which may be known of God is manifested by the creation of the world, he does not mean such a manifestation as may be comprehended by the wit of man (Rom. 1:19); on the contrary, he shows that it has no further effect than to render us inexcusable (Acts 17:27). And though he says, elsewhere, that we have not far to seek for God, inasmuch as he dwells within us, he shows, in another passage, to what extent this nearness to God is availing. God, says he, "in times past, suffered all nations to walk in their own ways. Nevertheless, he left not himself without witness, in that he did good, and gave us rain from heaven, and fruitful seasons, filling our hearts with food and gladness" (Acts 14:16, 17). But though God is not left without a witness, while, with numberless varied acts of kindness, he woos men to the knowledge of himself, yet they cease not to follow their own ways, in other words, deadly errors.

15. But though we are deficient in natural powers which might enable us to rise to a pure and clear knowledge of God, still, as the dullness which prevents us is within, there is no room for excuse. We cannot plead ignorance, without being at the same time convicted by our own consciences both of sloth and ingratitude. It were, indeed, a strange defence for man to pretend that he has no ears to hear the truth, while dumb creatures have voices loud enough to declare it; to allege that he is unable to see that which creatures without eyes demonstrate, to excuse himself on the ground of weakness of mind, while all creatures without reason are able to teach. Wherefore, when we wander and go astray, we are justly shut out from every species of excuse, because all things point to the right path. But while man must bear the guilt of corrupting the seed of divine knowledge so wondrously deposited in his mind, and preventing it from bearing good and genuine fruit, it is still most true that we are not sufficiently instructed by that bare and simple, but magnificent testimony which the creatures bear to the glory of their Creator. For no sooner do we, from a survey of the world, obtain some slight knowledge of Deity, than we pass by the true God, and set up in his stead the dream and phantom of our own brain, drawing away the praise of justice, wisdom, and goodness, from the fountain-head, and transferring it to some other quarter. Moreover, by the erroneous estimate we form, we either so obscure or pervert his daily works, as at once to rob them of their glory and the author of them of his just praise.

CHAPTER 6

THE NEED OF SCRIPTURE, AS A GUIDE AND TEACHER, IN COMING TO GOD AS A CREATOR.

Sections:

1. God gives his elect a better help to the knowledge of himself—viz. the Holy Scriptures. This he did from the very first.

2. First, By oracles and visions, and the ministry of the Patriarchs. Secondly, By the promulgation of the Law, and the preaching of the Prophets. Why the doctrines of religion are committed to writing.

3. This view confirmed, 1. By the depravity of our nature making it necessary in every one who would

know God to have recourse to the word; 2. From those passages of the Psalms in which God is introduced as reigning.

4. Another confirmation from certain direct statements in the Psalms. Lastly, From the words of our Saviour.

1. Therefore, though the effulgence which is presented to every eye, both in the heavens and on the earth, leaves the ingratitude of man without excuse, since God, in order to bring the whole human race under the same condemnation, holds forth to all, without exception, a mirror of his Deity in his works, another and better help must be given to guide us properly to God as a Creator. Not in vain, therefore, has he added the light of his Word in order that he might make himself known unto salvation, and bestowed the privilege on those whom he was pleased to bring into nearer and more familiar relation to himself. For, seeing how the minds of men were carried to and fro, and found no certain resting-place, he chose the Jews for a peculiar people, and then hedged them in that they might not, like others, go astray. And not in vain does he, by the same means, retain us in his knowledge, since but for this, even those who, in comparison of others, seem to stand strong, would quickly fall away. For as the aged, or those whose sight is defective, when any books however fair, is set before them, though they perceive that there is something written are scarcely able to make out two consecutive words, but, when aided by glasses, begin to read distinctly, so Scripture, gathering together the impressions of Deity, which, till then, lay confused in our minds, dissipates the darkness, and shows us the true God clearly. God therefore bestows a gift of singular value, when, for the instruction of the Church, he employs not dumb teachers merely, but opens his own sacred mouth; when he not only proclaims that some God must be worshipped, but at the same time declares that He is the God to whom worship is due; when he not only teaches his elect to have respect to God, but manifests himself as the God to whom this respect should be paid.

The course which God followed towards his Church from the very first, was to supplement these common proofs by the addition of his Word, as a surer and more direct means of discovering himself. And there can be no doubt that it was by this help, Adam, Noah, Abraham, and the other patriarchs, attained to that familiar knowledge which, in a manner, distinguished them from unbelievers. I am not now speaking of the peculiar doctrines of faith by which they were elevated to the hope of eternal blessedness. It was necessary, in passing from death unto life, that they should know God, not only as a Creator, but as a Redeemer also; and both kinds of knowledge they certainly did obtain from the Word. In point of order, however, the knowledge first given was that which made them acquainted with the God by whom the world was made and is governed. To this first knowledge was afterwards added the more intimate knowledge which alone quickens dead souls, and by which God is known not only as the Creator of the worlds and the sole author and disposer of all events, but also as a Redeemer, in the person of the Mediator. But as the fall and the corruption of nature have not yet been considered, I now postpone the consideration of the remedy (for which, see Book 2 c. 6 &c). Let the reader then remember, that I am not now treating of the covenant by which God adopted the children of Abraham, or of that branch of doctrine by which, as founded in Christ, believers have, properly speaking, been in all ages separated from the profane heathen. I am only showing that it is necessary to apply to Scripture, in order to learn the sure marks which distinguish God, as the Creator of the world, from the whole herd of fictitious gods. We shall afterward, in due course, consider the work of Redemption. In the meantime, though we shall adduce many passages from the New Testament, and some also from the Law and the Prophets, in which express mention is made of Christ, the only object will be to show that God, the Maker of the world, is manifested to us in Scripture, and his true character expounded, so as to save us from wandering up and down, as in a labyrinth, in search of some doubtful deity.

2. Whether God revealed himself to the fathers by oracles and visions, or, by the instrumentality and ministry of men, suggested what they were to hand down to posterity, there cannot be a doubt that the certainty of what he taught them was firmly engraven on their hearts, so that they felt assured and knew that the things which they learnt came forth from God, who invariably accompanied his word with a sure testimony, infinitely superior to mere opinion. At length, in order that, while doctrine was continually enlarged, its truth might subsist in the world during all ages, it was his pleasure that the same oracles which he had deposited with the fathers should be consigned, as it were, to public records. With this view the law was promulgated, and prophets were afterwards added to be its interpreters. For though the uses of the law were manifold (Book 2 c. 7 and 8), and the special office assigned to Moses and all the prophets

was to teach the method of reconciliation between God and man (whence Paul calls Christ "the end of the law," Rom. 10:4); still I repeat that, in addition to the proper doctrine of faith and repentance in which Christ is set forth as a Mediator, the Scriptures employ certain marks and tokens to distinguish the only wise and true God, considered as the Creator and Governor of the world, and thereby guard against his being confounded with the herd of false deities. Therefore, while it becomes man seriously to employ his eyes in considering the works of God, since a place has been assigned him in this most glorious theatre that he may be a spectator of them, his special duty is to give ear to the Word, that he may the better profit. Hence it is not strange that those who are born in darkness become more and more hardened in their stupidity; because the vast majority instead of confining themselves within due bounds by listening with docility to the Word, exult in their own vanity. If true religion is to beam upon us, our principle must be, that it is necessary to begin with heavenly teaching, and that it is impossible for any man to obtain even the minutest portion of right and sound doctrine without being a disciple of Scripture. Hence, the first step in true knowledge is taken, when we reverently embrace the testimony which God has been pleased therein to give of himself. For not only does faith, full and perfect faith, but all correct knowledge of God, originate in obedience. And surely in this respect God has with singular Providence provided for mankind in all ages.

3. For if we reflect how prone the human mind is to lapse into forgetfulness of God, how readily inclined to every kind of error, how bent every now and then on devising new and fictitious religions, it will be easy to understand how necessary it was to make such a depository of doctrine as would secure it from either perishing by the neglect, vanishing away amid the errors, or being corrupted by the presumptuous audacity of men. It being thus manifest that God, foreseeing the inefficiency of his image imprinted on the fair form of the universe, has given the assistance of his Word to all whom he has ever been pleased to instruct effectually, we, too, must pursue this straight path, if we aspire in earnest to a genuine contemplation of God;—we must go, I say, to the Word, where the character of God, drawn from his works is described accurately and to the life; these works being estimated, not by our depraved Judgment, but by the standard of eternal truth. If, as I lately said, we turn aside from it, how great soever the speed with which we move, we shall never reach the goal, because we are off the course. We should consider that the brightness of the Divine countenance, which even an apostle declares to be inaccessible (1 Tim. 6:16), is a kind of labyrinth,—a labyrinth to us inextricable, if the Word do not serve us as a thread to guide our path; and that it is better to limp in the way, than run with the greatest swiftness out of it. Hence the Psalmist, after repeatedly declaring (Psalm 93, 96, 97, 99, &c). that superstition should be banished from the world in order that pure religion may flourish, introduces God as *reigning*; meaning by the term, not the power which he possesses and which he exerts in the government of universal nature, but the doctrine by which he maintains his due supremacy: because error never can be eradicated from the heart of man until the true knowledge of God has been implanted in it.

4. Accordingly, the same prophet, after mentioning that the heavens declare the glory of God, that the firmament sheweth forth the works of his hands, that the regular succession of day and night proclaim his Majesty, proceeds to make mention of the Word:—"The law of the Lord," says he, "is perfect, converting the soul; the testimony of the Lord is sure, making wise the simple. The statutes of the Lord are right, rejoicing the heart; the commandment of the Lord is pure, enlightening the eyes" (Psalm 19:1–9). For though the law has other uses besides (as to which, see Book 2 c. 7, sec. 6, 10, 12), the general meaning is, that it is the proper school for training the children of God; the invitation given to all nations, to behold him in the heavens and earth, proving of no avail. The same view is taken in the 29th Psalm, where the Psalmist, after discoursing on the dreadful voice of God, which, in thunder, wind, rain, whirlwind, and tempest, shakes the earth, makes the mountains tremble, and breaks the cedars, concludes by saying, "that in his temple does every one speak of his glory," unbelievers being deaf to all God's words when they echo in the air. In like manner another Psalm, after describing the raging billows of the sea, thus concludes, "Thy testimonies are very sure; holiness becometh thine house for ever" (Psalm 93:5). To the same effect are the words of our Saviour to the Samaritan woman, when he told her that her nation and all other nations worshipped they knew not what; and that the Jews alone gave worship to the true God (John 4:22). Since the human mind, through its weakness, was altogether unable to come to God if not aided and upheld by his sacred word, it necessarily followed that all mankind, the Jews excepted, inasmuch as they sought God without the Word, were labouring under vanity and error.

CHAPTER 7

THE TESTIMONY OF THE SPIRIT NECESSARY TO GIVE FULL AUTHORITY TO SCRIPTURE. THE IMPIETY OF PRETENDING THAT THE CREDIBILITY OF SCRIPTURE DEPENDS ON THE JUDGMENT OF THE CHURCH.

Section:

1. The authority of Scripture derived not from men, but from the Spirit of God. Objection, That Scripture depends on the decision of the Church. Refutation, I. The truth of God would thus be subjected to the will of man. II. It is insulting to the Holy Spirit. III. It establishes a tyranny in the Church. IV. It forms a mass of errors. V. It subverts conscience. VI. It exposes our faith to the scoffs of the profane.

2. Another reply to the objection drawn from the words of the Apostle Paul. Solution of the difficulties started by opponents. A second objection refuted.

3. A third objection founded on a sentiment of Augustine considered.

4. Conclusion, That the authority of Scripture is founded on its being spoken by God. This confirmed by the conscience of the godly, and the consent of all men of the least candour. A fourth objection common in the mouths of the profane. Refutation.

5. Last and necessary conclusion, That the authority of Scripture is sealed on the hearts of believers by the testimony of the Holy Spirit. The certainty of this testimony. Confirmation of it from a passage of Isaiah, and the experience of believers. Also, from another passage of Isaiah.

1. Before proceeding farther, it seems proper to make some observations on the authority of Scripture, in order that our minds may not only be prepared to receive it with reverence, but be divested of all doubt.

When that which professes to be the Word of God is acknowledged to be so, no person, unless devoid of common sense and the feelings of a man, will have the desperate hardihood to refuse credit to the speaker. But since no daily responses are given from heaven, and the Scriptures are the only records in which God has been pleased to consign his truth to perpetual remembrance, the full authority which they ought to possess with the faithful is not recognised, unless they are believed to have come from heaven, as directly as if God had been heard giving utterance to them. This subject well deserves to be treated more at large, and pondered more accurately. But my readers will pardon me for having more regard to what my plan admits than to what the extent of this topic requires.

A most pernicious error has very generally prevailed—viz. that Scripture is of importance only in so far as conceded to it by the suffrage of the Church; as if the eternal and inviolable truth of God could depend on the will of men. With great insult to the Holy Spirit, it is asked, who can assure us that the Scriptures proceeded from God; who guarantee that they have come down safe and unimpaired to our times; who persuade us that *this* book is to be received with reverence, and *that one* expunged from the list, did not the Church regulate all these things with certainty? On the determination of the Church, therefore, it is said, depend both the reverence which is due to Scripture, and the books which are to be admitted into the canon. Thus profane men, seeking, under the pretext of the Church, to introduce unbridled tyranny, care not in what absurdities they entangle themselves and others, provided they extort from the simple this one acknowledgement—viz. that there is nothing which the Church cannot do. But what is to become of miserable consciences in quest of some solid assurance of eternal life, if all the promises with regard to it have no better support than man's Judgment? On being told so, will they cease to doubt and tremble? On the other hand, to what jeers of the wicked is our faith subjected—into how great suspicion is it brought with all, if believed to have only a precarious authority lent to it by the good will of men?

2. These ravings are admirably refuted by a single expression of an apostle. Paul testifies that the Church is "built on the foundation of the apostles and prophets" (Eph. 2:20). If the doctrine of the apostles and prophets is the foundation of the Church, the former must have had its certainty before the latter began to exist. Nor is there any room for the cavil, that though the Church derives her first beginning from thence, it still remains doubtful what writings are to be attributed to the apostles and prophets, until her Judgment is interposed. For if the Christian Church was founded at first on the writings of the prophets, and the preaching of the apostles, that doctrine, wheresoever it may be found, was certainly ascertained and sanctioned antecedently to the Church, since, but for this, the Church herself never could have existed. Nothings therefore can be more absurd than the fiction, that the power of judging Scripture is in the Church, and that on her nod its certainty depends. When the Church

receives it, and gives it the stamp of her authority, she does not make that authentic which was otherwise doubtful or controverted but, acknowledging it as the truth of God, she, as in duty bounds shows her reverence by an unhesitating assent. As to the question, How shall we be persuaded that it came from God without recurring to a decree of the Church? it is just the same as if it were asked, How shall we learn to distinguish light from darkness, white from black, sweet from bitter? Scripture bears upon the face of it as clear evidence of its truth, as white and black do of their colour, sweet and bitter of their taste.

3. I am aware it is usual to quote a sentence of Augustine in which he says that he would not believe the gospel, were he not moved by the authority of the Church (Aug. Cont. Epist. Fundament. c. 5). But it is easy to discover from the context, how inaccurate and unfair it is to give it such a meaning. He was reasoning against the Manichees, who insisted on being implicitly believed, alleging that they had the truth, though they did not show they had. But as they pretended to appeal to the gospel in support of Manes, he asks what they would do if they fell in with a man who did not even believe the gospel—what kind of argument they would use to bring him over to their opinion. He afterwards adds, "But I would not believe the gospel," &c.; meaning, that were he a stranger to the faith, the only thing which could induce him to embrace the gospel would be the authority of the Church. And is it any thing wonderful, that one who does not know Christ should pay respect to men?

Augustine, therefore, does not here say that the faith of the godly is founded on the authority of the Church; nor does he mean that the certainty of the gospel depends upon it; he merely says that unbelievers would have no certainty of the gospel, so as thereby to win Christ, were they not influenced by the consent of the Church. And he clearly shows this to be his meaning, by thus expressing himself a little before: "When I have praised my own creed, and ridiculed yours, who do you suppose is to judge between us; or what more is to be done than to quit those who, inviting us to certainty, afterwards command us to believe uncertainty, and follow those who invite us, in the first instance, to believe what we are not yet able to comprehend, that waxing stronger through faith itself, we may become able to understand what we believe— no longer men, but God himself internally strengthening and illuminating our minds? These unquestionably are the words of Augustine (August. Cont. Epist. Fundament. cap. 4); and the obvious inference from them is, that this holy man had no intention to suspend our faith in Scripture on the nod or decision of the Church, but only to intimate (what we too admit to be true) that those who are not yet enlightened by the Spirit of God, become teachable by reverence for the Church, and thus submit to learn the faith of Christ from the gospel. In this way, though the authority of the Church leads us on, and prepares us to believe in the gospel, it is plain that Augustine would have the certainty of the godly to rest on a very different foundation.

At the same time, I deny not that he often presses the Manichees with the consent of the whole Church, while arguing in support of the Scriptures, which they rejected. Hence he upbraids Faustus (lib. 32) for not submitting to evangelical truth—truth so well founded, so firmly established, so gloriously renowned, and handed down by sure succession from the days of the apostles. But he nowhere insinuates that the authority which we give to the Scriptures depends on the definitions or devices of men. He only brings forward the universal Judgment of the Church, as a point most pertinent to the cause, and one, moreover, in which he had the advantage of his opponents. Any one who desires to see this more fully proved may read his short treatises, *De Utilitate Credendi* (The Advantages of Believing), where it will be found that the only facility of believing which he recommends is that which affords an introduction, and forms a fit commencement to inquiry; while he declares that we ought not to be satisfied with opinion, but to strive after substantial truth.

4. It is necessary to attend to what I lately said, that our faith in doctrine is not established until we have a perfect conviction that God is its author. Hence, the highest proof of Scripture is uniformly taken from the character of him whose Word it is. The prophets and apostles boast not their own acuteness or any qualities which win credit to speakers, nor do they dwell on reasons; but they appeal to the sacred name of God, in order that the whole world may be compelled to submission. The next thing to be considered is, how it appears not probable merely, but certain, that the name of God is neither rashly nor cunningly pretended. If, then, we would consult most effectually for our consciences, and save them from being driven about in a whirl of uncertainty, from wavering, and even stumbling at the smallest obstacle, our conviction of the truth of Scripture must be derived from a higher source than human conjectures, Judgments, or reasons; namely, the secret testimony of the Spirit. It is true, indeed, that if we choose to proceed in the way of arguments it is easy

to establish, by evidence of various kinds, that if there is a God in heaven, the Law, the Prophecies, and the Gospel, proceeded from him. Nay, although learned men, and men of the greatest talent, should take the opposite side, summoning and ostentatiously displaying all the powers of their genius in the discussion; if they are not possessed of shameless effrontery, they will be compelled to confess that the Scripture exhibits clear evidence of its being spoken by God, and, consequently, of its containing his heavenly doctrine. We shall see a little farther on, that the volume of sacred Scripture very far surpasses all other writings. Nay, if we look at it with clear eyes, and unblessed Judgment, it will forthwith present itself with a divine majesty which will subdue our presumptuous opposition, and force us to do it homage.

Still, however, it is preposterous to attempt, by discussion, to rear up a full faith in Scripture. True, were I called to contend with the craftiest despisers of God, I trust, though I am not possessed of the highest ability or eloquence, I should not find it difficult to stop their obstreperous mouths; I could, without much ado, put down the boastings which they mutter in corners, were anything to be gained by refuting their cavils. But although we may maintain the sacred Word of God against gainsayers, it does not follow that we shall forthwith implant the certainty which faith requires in their hearts. Profane men think that religion rests only on opinion, and, therefore, that they may not believe foolishly, or on slight grounds, desire and insist to have it proved by reason that Moses and the prophets were divinely inspired. But I answer, that the testimony of the Spirit is superior to reason. For as God alone can properly bear witness to his own words, so these words will not obtain full credit in the hearts of men, until they are sealed by the inward testimony of the Spirit. The same Spirit, therefore, who spoke by the mouth of the prophets, must penetrate our hearts, in order to convince us that they faithfully delivered the message with which they were divinely entrusted. This connection is most aptly expressed by Isaiah in these words, "My Spirit that is upon thee, and my words which I have put in thy mouth, shall not depart out of thy mouth, nor out of the mouth of thy seed, nor out of the mouth of thy seed's seed, saith the Lord, from henceforth and for ever" (Isa. 59:21). Some worthy persons feel disconcerted, because, while the wicked murmur with impunity at the Word of God, they have not a clear proof at hand to silence them, forgetting that the Spirit is called an earnest and seal to confirm the faith of the godly, for this very reason, that, until he enlightens their minds, they are tossed to and fro in a sea of doubts.

5. Let it therefore be held as fixed, that those who are inwardly taught by the Holy Spirit acquiesce implicitly in Scripture; that Scripture, carrying its own evidence along with it, deigns not to submit to proofs and arguments, but owes the full conviction with which we ought to receive it to the testimony of the Spirit. Enlightened by him, we no longer believe, either on our own Judgment or that of others, that the Scriptures are from God; but, in a way superior to human Judgment, feel perfectly assured—as much so as if we beheld the divine image visibly impressed on it—that it came to us, by the instrumentality of men, from the very mouth of God. We ask not for proofs or probabilities on which to rest our Judgment, but we subject our intellect and Judgment to it as too transcendent for us to estimate. This, however, we do, not in the manner in which some are wont to fasten on an unknown object, which, as soon as known, displeases, but because we have a thorough conviction that, in holding it, we hold unassailable truth; not like miserable men, whose minds are enslaved by superstition, but because we feel a divine energy living and breathing in it—an energy by which we are drawn and animated to obey it, willingly indeed, and knowingly, but more vividly and effectually than could be done by human will or knowledge. Hence, God most justly exclaims by the mouth of Isaiah, "Ye are my witnesses, saith the Lord, and my servant whom I have chosen, that ye may know and believe me, and understand that I am he" (Isa. 43:10).

Such, then, is a conviction which asks not for reasons; such, a knowledge which accords with the highest reason, namely knowledge in which the mind rests more firmly and securely than in any reasons; such in fine, the conviction which revelation from heaven alone can produce. I say nothing more than every believer experiences in himself, though my words fall far short of the reality. I do not dwell on this subject at present, because we will return to it again: only let us now understand that the only true faith is that which the Spirit of God seals on our hearts. Nay, the modest and teachable reader will find a sufficient reason in the promise contained in Isaiah, that all the children of the renovated Church "shall be taught of the Lord" (Isaiah 54:13). This singular privilege God bestows on his elect only, whom he separates from the rest of mankind. For what is the beginning of true doctrine but prompt alacrity to hear the Word of God? And God, by the mouth of Moses, thus demands to be heard: "It is not in heavens that thou shouldest say, Who shall go up for us to heaven, and bring it unto us, that we may hear and do it? But the word is very nigh unto thee, in thy mouth and in thy heart" (Deut. 30:12, 14). God having been pleased to reserve the treasure of intelligence for his children, no wonder that so much ignorance and stupidity is seen in the *generality* of mankind. In the generality, I include even those specially chosen, until they are ingrafted into the body of the Church. Isaiah, moreover, while reminding us that the prophetical doctrine would prove incredible not only to strangers, but also to the Jews, who were desirous to be thought of the household of God, subjoins the reason, when he asks, "To whom has the arm of the Lord been revealed?" (Isaiah 53:1). If at any time, then we are troubled at the small number of those who believe, let us, on the other hand, call to mind, that none comprehend the mysteries of God save those to whom it is given.

CHAPTER 8

THE CREDIBILITY OF SCRIPTURE SUFFICIENTLY PROVED IN SO FAR AS NATURAL REASON ADMITS.

This chapter consists of four parts. The first contains certain general proofs which may be easily gathered out of the writings both of the Old and New Testament—viz. the arrangement of the sacred volume, its dignity, truth, simplicity, efficacy, and majesty, sec. 1, 2. The second part contains special proofs taken from the Old Testament—viz. the antiquity of the books of Moses, their authority, his miracles and prophecies, sec. 3–7; also, the predictions of the other prophets and their wondrous harmony, sec. 8. There is subjoined a refutation of two objections to the books of Moses and the Prophets, sec. 9, 10. The third part exhibits proofs gathered out of the New Testament, e.g., the harmony of the Evangelists in their account of heavenly mysteries, the majesty of the writings of John, Peter, and Paul, the remarkable calling of the Apostles and conversion of Paul, sec. 11. The last part exhibits the proofs drawn from ecclesiastical history, the perpetual consent of the Church in receiving and preserving divine truth, the invincible force of the truth in defending itself, the agreement of the godly (though otherwise differing so much from one another), the pious profession of the same doctrine by many illustrious men; in fine, the more than human constancy of the martyrs, sec. 12, 13. This is followed by a conclusion of the particular topic discussed.

Sections:

1. Secondary helps to establish the credibility of Scripture. I. The arrangement of the sacred volume. II. Its dignity. III. Its truth. IV. Its simplicity. V. Its efficacy.

2. The majesty conspicuous in the writings of the Prophets.

3. Special proofs from the Old Testament. I. The antiquity of the Books of Moses.

4. This antiquity contrasted with the dreams of the Egyptians. II. The majesty of the Books of Moses.

5. The miracles and prophecies of Moses. A profane objection refuted.

6. Another profane objection refuted.

7. The prophecies of Moses as to the sceptre not departing from Judah, and the calling of the Gentiles.

8. The predictions of other prophets. The destruction of Jerusalem; and the return from the Babylonish captivity. Harmony of the Prophets. The celebrated prophecy of Daniel.

9. Objection against Moses and the Prophets. Answer to it.

10. Another objection and answer. Of the wondrous Providence of God in the preservation of the sacred books. The Greek Translation. The carefulness of the Jews.

11. Special proofs from the New Testament. I. The harmony of the Evangelists, and the sublime simplicity of their writings. II. The majesty of John, Paul, and Peter. III. The calling of the Apostles. IV. The conversion of Paul.

12. Proofs from Church history. I. Perpetual consent of the Church in receiving and preserving the truth. II. The invincible power of the truth itself. III. Agreement among the godly, not withstanding of their many differences in other respects.

13. The constancy of the martyrs. Conclusion. Proofs of this description only of use after the certainty of Scripture has been established in the heart by the Holy Spirit.

1. In vain were the authority of Scripture fortified by argument, or supported by the consent of the Church, or confirmed by any other helps, if unaccompanied by an assurance higher and stronger than human Judgment can give. Till this better foundation has been laid, the authority of Scripture remains in suspense. On the other hand, when recognising its exemption from the common rule, we receive it reverently, and according to its dignity, those proofs which were not so strong as to produce and rivet

a full conviction in our minds, become most appropriate helps. For it is wonderful how much we are confirmed in our belief, when we more attentively consider how admirably the system of divine wisdom contained in it is arranged—how perfectly free the doctrine is from every thing that savours of earth—how beautifully it harmonises in all its parts—and how rich it is in all the other qualities which give an air of majesty to composition. Our hearts are still more firmly assured when we reflect that our admiration is elicited more by the dignity of the matter than by the graces of style. For it was not without an admirable arrangement of Providence, that the sublime mysteries of the kingdom of heaven have for the greater part been delivered with a contemptible meanness of words. Had they been adorned with a more splendid eloquence, the wicked might have cavilled, and alleged that this constituted all their force. But now, when an unpolished simplicity, almost bordering on rudeness, makes a deeper impression than the loftiest flights of oratory, what does it indicate if not that the Holy Scriptures are too mighty in the power of truth to need the rhetorician's art?

Hence there was good ground for the Apostle's declaration, that the faith of the Corinthians was founded not on "the wisdom of men," but on "the power of God" (1 Cor. 2:5), this speech and preaching among them having been "not with enticing words of man's wisdom, but in demonstration of the Spirit and of power" (1 Cor. 2:5). For the truth is vindicated in opposition to every doubt, when, unsupported by foreign aid, it has its sole sufficiency in itself. How peculiarly this property belongs to Scripture appears from this, that no human writings, however skilfully composed, are at all capable of affecting us in a similar way. Read Demosthenes or Cicero, read Plato, Aristotle, or any other of that class: you will, I admit, feel wonderfully allured, pleased, moved, enchanted; but turn from them to the reading of the Sacred Volume, and whether you will or not, it will so affect you, so pierce your heart, so work its way into your very marrow, that, in comparison of the impression so produced, that of orators and philosophers will almost disappear; making it manifest that in the Sacred Volume there is a truth divine, a something which makes it immeasurably superior to all the gifts and graces attainable by man.

2. I confess, however, that in elegance and beauty, nay, splendour, the style of some of the prophets is not surpassed by the eloquence of heathen writers. By examples of this description, the Holy Spirit was pleased to show that it was not from want of eloquence he in other instances used a rude and homely style. But whether you read David, Isaiah, and others of the same class, whose discourse flows sweet and pleasant; or Amos the herdsman, Jeremiah, and Zechariah, whose rougher idiom savours of rusticity; that majesty of the Spirit to which I adverted appears conspicuous in all. I am not unaware, that as Satan often apes God, that he may by a fallacious resemblance the better insinuate himself into the minds of the simple, so he craftily disseminated the impious errors with which he deceived miserable men in an uncouth and semi-barbarous style, and frequently employed obsolete forms of expression in order to cloak his impostures. None possessed of any moderate share of sense need be told how vain and vile such affectation is. But in regard to the Holy Scriptures, however petulant men may attempt to carp at them, they are replete with sentiments which it is clear that man never could have conceived. Let each of the prophets be examined, and not one will be found who does not rise far higher than human reach. Those who feel their works insipid must be absolutely devoid of taste.

3. As this subject has been treated at large by others, it will be sufficient here merely to touch on its leading points. In addition to the qualities already mentioned, great weight is due to the antiquity of Scripture (Euseb. Prepar. Evang. lib. 2 c. 1). Whatever fables Greek writers may retail concerning the Egyptian Theology, no monument of any religion exists which is not long posterior to the age of Moses. But Moses does not introduce a new Deity. He only sets forth that doctrine concerning the eternal God which the Israelites had received by tradition from their fathers, by whom it had been transmitted, as it were, from hand to hand, during a long series of ages. For what else does he do than lead them back to the covenant which had been made with Abraham? Had he referred to matters of which they had never heard, he never could have succeeded; but their deliverance from the bondage in which they were held must have been a fact of familiar and universal notoriety, the very mention of which must have immediately aroused the attention of all. It is, moreover, probable, that they were intimately acquainted with the whole period of four hundred years. Now, if Moses (who is so much earlier than all other writers) traces the tradition of his doctrine from so remote a period, it is obvious how far the Holy Scriptures must in point of antiquity surpass all other writings.

4. Some perhaps may choose to credit the Egyptians in carrying back their antiquity to a period of six thousand

years before the world was created. But their garrulity, which even some profane authors have held up to derision, it cannot be necessary for me to refute. Josephus, however, in his work against Appion, produces important passages from very ancient writers, implying that the doctrine delivered in the law was celebrated among all nations from the remotest ages, though it was neither read nor accurately known. And then, in order that the malignant might have no ground for suspicion, and the ungodly no handle for cavil, God has provided, in the most effectual manner, against both dangers. When Moses relates the words which Jacob, under Divine inspiration, uttered concerning his posterity almost three hundred years before, how does he ennoble his own tribe? He stigmatises it with eternal infamy in the person of Levi. "Simon and Levi," says he, "are brethren; instruments of cruelty are in their habitations. O my soul, come not thou into their secret; unto their assembly mine honour be not thou united" (Gen. 49:5, 6). This stigma he certainly might have passed in silence, not only that he might spare his own ancestor, but also save both himself and his whole family from a portion of the disgrace. How can any suspicion attach to him, who, by voluntarily proclaiming that the first founder of his family was declared detestable by a Divine oracle, neither consults for his own private interest, nor declines to incur obloquy among his tribe, who must have been offended by his statement of the fact? Again, when he relates the wicked murmuring of his brother Aaron, and his sister Miriam (Numb. 12:1), shall we say that he spoke his own natural feelings, or that he obeyed the command of the Holy Spirit? Moreover, when invested with supreme authority, why does he not bestow the office of High Priest on his sons, instead of consigning them to the lowest place? I only touch on a few points out of many; but the Law itself contains throughout numerous proofs, which fully vindicate the credibility of Moses, and place it beyond dispute, that he was in truth a messenger sent forth from God.

5. The many striking miracles which Moses relates are so many sanctions of the law delivered, and the doctrine propounded, by him. His being carried up into the mount in a cloud; his remaining there forty days separated from human society; his countenance glistening during the promulgation of the law, as with meridian effulgence; the lightnings which flashed on every side; the voices and thunderings which echoed in the air; the clang of the trumpet blown by no human mouth; his entrance into the tabernacle, while a cloud hid him from the view of the people; the miraculous vindication of his authority, by the fearful destruction of Korah, Nathan, and Abiram, and all their impious faction; the stream instantly gushing forth from the rock when struck with his rod; the manna which rained from heaven at his prayer;—did not God by all these proclaim aloud that he was an undoubted prophet? If any one object that I am taking debatable points for granted, the cavil is easily answered. Moses published all these things in the assembly of the people. How, then, could he possibly impose on the very eye-witnesses of what was done? Is it conceivable that he would have come forward, and, while accusing the people of unbelief, obstinacy, ingratitude, and other crimes, have boasted that his doctrine had been confirmed in their own presence by miracles which they never saw?

6. For it is also worthy of remark, that the miracles which he relates are combined with disagreeable circumstances, which must have provoked opposition from the whole body of the people, if there had been the smallest ground for it. Hence it is obvious that they were induced to assent, merely because they had been previously convinced by their own experience. But because the fact was too ascribed them to magic (Exod. 9:11). But with what probability is a charge of magic brought against him, who held it in such abhorrence, that he ordered every one who should consult soothsayers and magicians to be stoned? (Lev. 20:27). Assuredly, no impostor deals in tricks, without studying to raise his reputation by amazing the common people. But what does Moses do? By crying out, that he and Aaron his brother are nothing (Exod. 16:7), that they merely execute what God has commanded, he clears himself from every approach to suspicion. Again, if the facts are considered in themselves, what kind of incantation could cause manna to rain from heaven every day, and in sufficient quantity to maintain a people, while any one, who gathered more than the appointed measure, saw his incredulity divinely punished by its turning to worms? To this we may add, that God then suffered his servant to be subjected to so many serious trials, that the ungodly cannot now gain anything by their glamour. When (as often happened) the people proudly and petulantly rose up against him, when individuals conspired, and attempted to overthrow him, how could any impostures have enabled clear to leave it free for heathen writers to deny that Moses did perform miracles, the father of lies suggested a calumny, and him to elude their rage? The event plainly shows that by these means his doctrine was attested to all succeeding ages.

7. Moreover, it is impossible to deny that he was guided by a prophetic spirit in assigning the first place to

the tribe of Judah in the person of Jacob, especially if we take into view the fact itself, as explained by the event. Suppose that Moses was the inventor of the prophecy, still, after he committed it to writing, four hundred years pass away, during which no mention is made of a sceptre in the tribe of Judah. After Saul is anointed, the kingly office seems fixed in the tribe of Benjamin (1 Sam. 11:15; 16:13). When David is anointed by Samuel, what apparent ground is there for the transference? Who could have looked for a king out of the plebeian family of a herdsman? And out of seven brothers, who could have thought that the honour was destined for the youngest? And then by what means did he afterwards come within reach of the throne? Who dare say that his anointing was regulated by human art, or skill, or prudence, and was not rather the fulfilment of a divine prophecy? In like manner, do not the predictions, though obscure, of the admission of the Gentiles into the divine covenant, seeing they were not fulfilled till almost two thousand years after, make it palpable that Moses spoke under divine inspiration? I omit other predictions which so plainly betoken divine revelation, that all men of sound mind must see they were spoken by God. In short, his Song itself (Deut. 32) is a bright mirror in which God is manifestly seen.

8. In the case of the other prophets the evidence is even clearer. I will only select a few examples, for it were too tedious to enumerate the whole. Isaiah, in his own day, when the kingdom of Judah was at peace, and had even some ground to confide in the protection of the Chaldeans, spoke of the destruction of the city and the captivity of the people (Isaiah 55:1). Supposing it not to be sufficient evidence of divine inspiration to foretell, many years before, events which, at the time, seemed fabulous, but which ultimately turned out to be true, whence shall it be said that the prophecies which he uttered concerning their return proceeded, if it was not from God? He names Cyrus, by whom the Chaldeans were to be subdued and the people restored to freedom. After the prophet thus spoke, more than a hundred years elapsed before Cyrus was born, that being nearly the period which elapsed between the death of the one and the birth of the other. It was impossible at that time to guess that some Cyrus would arise to make war on the Babylonians, and after subduing their powerful monarchy, put an end to the captivity of the children of Israel. Does not this simple, unadorned narrative plainly demonstrate that what Isaiah spoke was not the conjecture of man, but the undoubted oracle of God? Again, when Jeremiah, a considerable time before the people were led away, assigned seventy years as the period of captivity, and fixed their liberation and return, must not his tongue have been guided by the Spirit of God? What effrontery were it to deny that, by these evidences, the authority of the prophets is established, the very thing being fulfilled to which they appeal in support of their credibility! "Behold, the former things are come to pass, and new things do I declare; before they spring forth I tell you of them" (Isaiah 42:9). I say nothing of the agreement between Jeremiah and Ezekiel, who, living so far apart, and yet prophesying at the same time, harmonise as completely in all they say as if they had mutually dictated the words to one another. What shall I say of Daniel? Did not he deliver prophecies embracing a future period of almost six hundred years, as if he had been writing of past events generally known? (Dan. 9, &c). If the pious will duly meditate on these things, they will be sufficiently instructed to silence the cavils of the ungodly. The demonstration is too clear to be gainsaid.

9. I am aware of what is muttered in corners by certain miscreants, when they would display their acuteness in assailing divine truth. They ask, how do we know that Moses and the prophets wrote the books which now bear their names? Nay, they even dare to question whether there ever was a Moses. Were any one to question whether there ever was a Plato, or an Aristotle, or a Cicero, would not the rod or the whip be deemed the fit chastisement of such folly? The law of Moses has been wonderfully preserved, more by divine providence than by human care; and though, owing to the negligence of the priests, it lay for a short time buried,—from the time when it was found by good King Josiah (2 Kings 22:8; 2 Chron. 34:15),—it has continued in the hands of men, and been transmitted in unbroken succession from generation to generation. Nor, indeed, when Josiah brought it forth, was it as a book unknown or new, but one which had always been matter of notoriety, and was then in full remembrance. The original writing had been deposited in the temple, and a copy taken from it had been deposited in the royal archives (Deut. 17:18, 19); the only thing which had occurred was, that the priests had ceased to publish the law itself in due form, and the people also had neglected the wonted reading of it. I may add, that scarcely an age passed during which its authority was not confirmed and renewed. Were the books of Moses unknown to those who had the Psalms of David in their hands? To sum up the whole in one word, it is certain beyond dispute, that these writings passed down, if I may so express it, from hand to hand, being transmitted in an unbroken series from the fathers, who either

with their own ears heard them spoken, or learned them from those who had, while the remembrance of them was fresh.

10. An objection taken from the history of the Maccabees (1 Macc. 1:57, 58) to impugn the credibility of Scripture, is, on the contrary, fitted the best possible to confirm it. First, however, let us clear away the gloss which is put upon it: having done so, we shall turn the engine which they erect against us upon themselves. As Antiochus ordered all the books of Scripture to be burnt, it is asked, where did the copies we now have come from? I, in my turn, ask, In what workshop could they have been so quickly fabricated? It is certain that they were in existence the moment the persecution ceased, and that they were acknowledged without dispute by all the pious who had been educated in their doctrine, and were familiarly acquainted with them. Nay, while all the wicked so wantonly insulted the Jews as if they had leagued together for the purpose, not one ever dared to charge them with having introduced spurious books. Whatever, in their opinion, the Jewish religion might be, they acknowledged that Moses was the founder of it. What, then, do those babblers, but betray their snarling petulance in falsely alleging the spuriousness of books whose sacred antiquity is proved by the consent of all history? But not to spend labour in vain in refuting these vile calumnies, let us rather attend to the care which the Lord took to preserve his Word, when against all hope he rescued it from the truculence of a most cruel tyrant as from the midst of the flames—inspiring pious priests and others with such constancy that they hesitated not, though it should have been purchased at the expense of their lives, to transmit this treasure to posterity, and defeating the keenest search of prefects and their satellites.

Who does not recognise it as a signal and miraculous work of God, that those sacred monuments which the ungodly persuaded themselves had utterly perished, immediately returned to resume their former rights, and, indeed, in greater honour? For the Greek translation appeared to disseminate them over the whole world. Nor does it seem so wonderful that God rescued the tables of his covenant from the sanguinary edicts of Antiochus, as that they remained safe and entire amid the manifold disasters by which the Jewish nation was occasionally crushed, devastated, and almost exterminated. The Hebrew language was in no estimation, and almost unknown; and assuredly, had not God provided for religion, it must have utterly perished. For it is obvious from the prophetical writings of that age, how much the Jews, after their return from the captivity, had lost the genuine use of their native tongue. It is of importance to attend to this, because the comparison more clearly establishes the antiquity of the Law and the Prophets. And whom did God employ to preserve the doctrine of salvation contained in the Law and the Prophets, that Christ might manifest it in its own time? The Jews, the bitterest enemies of Christ; and hence Augustine justly calls them the librarians of the Christian Church, because they supplied us with books of which they themselves had not the use.

11. When we proceed to the New Testament, how solid are the pillars by which its truth is supported! Three evangelists give a narrative in a mean and humble style. The proud often eye this simplicity with disdain, because they attend not to the principal heads of doctrine; for from these they might easily infer that these evangelists treat of heavenly mysteries beyond the capacity of man. Those who have the least particle of candour must be ashamed of their fastidiousness when they read the first chapter of Luke. Even our Saviour's discourses, of which a summary is given by these three evangelists, ought to prevent every one from treating their writings with contempt. John, again, fulminating in majesty, strikes down more powerfully than any thunderbolt the petulance of those who refuse to submit to the obedience of faith. Let all those acute censors, whose highest pleasure it is to banish a reverential regard of Scripture from their own and other men's hearts, come forward; let them read the Gospel of John, and, willing or unwilling, they will find a thousand sentences which will at least arouse them from their sloth; nay, which will burn into their consciences as with a hot iron, and check their derision. The same thing may be said of Peter and Paul, whose writings, though the greater part read them blindfold, exhibit a heavenly majesty, which in a manner binds and rivets every reader. But one circumstance, sufficient of itself to exalt their doctrine above the world, is, that Matthew, who was formerly fixed down to his money-table, Peter and John, who were employed with their little boats, being all rude and illiterate, had never learned in any human school that which they delivered to others. Paul, moreover, who had not only been an avowed but a cruel and bloody foe, being changed into a new man, shows, by the sudden and unhoped-for change, that a heavenly power had compelled him to preach the doctrine which once he destroyed. Let those dogs deny that the Holy Spirit descended upon the apostles, or, if not, let them refuse credit to the history, still the very circumstances proclaim that the Holy Spirit must have been the teacher of those

who, formerly contemptible among the people, all of a sudden began to discourse so magnificently of heavenly mysteries.

12. Add, moreover, that, for the best of reasons, the consent of the Church is not without its weight. For it is not to be accounted of no consequence, that, from the first publication of Scripture, so many ages have uniformly concurred in yielding obedience to it, and that, notwithstanding of the many extraordinary attempts which Satan and the whole world have made to oppress and overthrow it, or completely efface it from the memory of men, it has flourished like the palm tree and continued invincible. Though in old times there was scarcely a sophist or orator of any note who did not exert his powers against it, their efforts proved unavailing. The powers of the earth armed themselves for its destruction, but all their attempts vanished into smoke. When thus powerfully assailed on every side, how could it have resisted if it had trusted only to human aid? Nay, its divine origin is more completely established by the fact, that when all human wishes were against it, it advanced by its own energy. Add that it was not a single city or a single nation that concurred in receiving and embracing it. Its authority was recognised as far and as wide as the world extends—various nations who had nothing else in common entering for this purpose into a holy league. Moreover, while we ought to attach the greatest weight to the agreement of minds so diversified, and in all other things so much at variance with each other—an agreement which a Divine Providence alone could have produced—it adds no small weight to the whole when we attend to the piety of those who thus agree; not of all of them indeed, but of those in whom as lights God was pleased that his Church should shine.

13. Again, with what confidence does it become us to subscribe to a doctrine attested and confirmed by the blood of so many saints? They, when once they had embraced it, hesitated not boldly and intrepidly, and even with great alacrity, to meet death in its defence. Being transmitted to us with such an earnest, who of us shall not receive it with firm and unshaken conviction? It is therefore no small proof of the authority of Scripture, that it was sealed with the blood of so many witnesses, especially when it is considered that in bearing testimony to the faith, they met death not with fanatical enthusiasm (as erring spirits are sometimes wont to do), but with a firm and constant, yet sober godly zeal. There are other reasons, neither few nor feeble, by which the dignity and majesty of the Scriptures may be not only proved to the pious, but also completely vindicated against the cavils of slanderers. These, however, cannot of themselves produce a firm faith in Scripture until our heavenly Father manifest his presence in it, and thereby secure implicit reverence for it. Then only, therefore, does Scripture suffice to give a saving knowledge of God when its certainty is founded on the inward persuasion of the Holy Spirit. Still the human testimonies which go to confirm it will not be without effect, if they are used in subordination to that chief and highest proof, as secondary helps to our weakness. But it is foolish to attempt to prove to infidels that the Scripture is the Word of God. This it cannot be known to be, except by faith. Justly, therefore, does Augustine remind us, that every man who would have any understanding in such high matters must previously possess piety and mental peace.

CHAPTER 9

ALL THE PRINCIPLES OF PIETY SUBVERTED BY FANATICS, WHO SUBSTITUTE REVELATIONS FOR SCRIPTURE.

Sections:

1. The temper and error of the Libertines, who take to themselves the name of spiritual, briefly described. Their refutation. 1. The Apostles and all true Christians have embraced the written Word. This confirmed by a passage in Isaiah; also by the example and words of Paul. 2. The Spirit of Christ seals the doctrine of the written Word on the minds of the godly.

2. Refutation continued. 3. The impositions of Satan cannot be detected without the aid of the written Word. First Objection. The Answer to it.

3. Second Objection from the words of Paul as to the letter and spirit. The Answer, with an explanation of Paul's meaning. How the Spirit and the written Word are indissolubly connected.

1. Those who, rejecting Scripture, imagine that they have some peculiar way of penetrating to God, are to be deemed not so much under the influence of error as madness. For certain giddy men have lately appeared, who, while they make a great display of the superiority of the Spirit, reject all reading of the Scriptures themselves, and deride the simplicity of those who only delight in what they call the dead and deadly letter. But I wish they would tell me what spirit it is whose inspiration raises them to such a sublime height that they dare despise the

doctrine of Scripture as mean and childish. If they answer that it is the Spirit of Christ, their confidence is exceedingly ridiculous; since they will, I presume, admit that the apostles and other believers in the primitive Church were not illuminated by any other Spirit. None of these thereby learned to despise the word of God, but every one was imbued with greater reverence for it, as their writings most clearly testify. And, indeed, it had been so foretold by the mouth of Isaiah. For when he says, "My Spirit that is upon thee, and my words which I have put in thy mouth, shall not depart out of thy mouth, nor out of the mouth of thy seed, nor out of the mouth of thy seed's seed, saith the Lord, from henceforth and for ever," he does not tie down the ancient Church to external doctrine, as he were a mere teacher of elements; he rather shows that, under the reign of Christ, the true and full felicity of the new Church will consist in their being ruled not less by the Word than by the Spirit of God. Hence we infer that these miscreants are guilty of fearful sacrilege in tearing asunder what the prophet joins in indissoluble union. Add to this, that Paul, though carried up even to the third heaven, ceased not to profit by the doctrine of the law and the prophets, while, in like manner, he exhorts Timothy, a teacher of singular excellence, to give attention to reading (1 Tim. 4:13). And the eulogium which he pronounces on Scripture well deserves to be remembered—viz. that "it is profitable for doctrine, for reproof, for correction, and for instruction in righteousness, that the man of God may be perfect" (2 Tim. 3:16). What an infatuation of the devil, therefore, to fancy that Scripture, which conducts the sons of God to the final goal, is of transient and temporary use? Again, I should like those people to tell me whether they have imbibed any other Spirit than that which Christ promised to his disciples. Though their madness is extreme, it will scarcely carry them the length of making this their boast. But what kind of Spirit did our Saviour promise to send? One who should not speak of himself (John 16:13), but suggest and instil the truths which he himself had delivered through the word. Hence the office of the Spirit promised to us, is not to form new and unheard-of revelations, or to coin a new form of doctrine, by which we may be led away from the received doctrine of the gospel, but to seal on our minds the very doctrine which the gospel recommends.

2. Hence it is easy to understand that we must give diligent heed both to the reading and hearing of Scripture, if we would obtain any benefit from the Spirit of God (just as Peter praises those who attentively study the doctrine of the prophets (2 Pet. 1:19), though it might have been thought to be superseded after the gospel light arose), and, on the contrary, that any spirit which passes by the wisdom of God's Word, and suggests any other doctrine, is deservedly suspected of vanity and falsehood. Since Satan transforms himself into an angel of light, what authority can the Spirit have with us if he be not ascertained by an infallible mark? And assuredly he is pointed out to us by the Lord with sufficient clearness; but these miserable men err as if bent on their own destruction, while they seek the Spirit from themselves rather than from Him. But they say that it is insulting to subject the Spirit, to whom all things are to be subject, to the Scripture: as if it were disgraceful to the Holy Spirit to maintain a perfect resemblance throughout, and be in all respects without variation consistent with himself. True, if he were subjected to a human, an angelical, or to any foreign standard, it might be thought that he was rendered subordinate, or, if you will, brought into bondage, but so long as he is compared with himself, and considered in himself, how can it be said that he is thereby injured? I admit that he is brought to a test, but the very test by which it has pleased him that his majesty should be confirmed. It ought to be enough for us when once we hear his voice; but lest Satan should insinuate himself under his name, he wishes us to recognise him by the image which he has stamped on the Scriptures. The author of the Scriptures cannot vary, and change his likeness. Such as he there appeared at first, such he will perpetually remain. There is nothing contumelious to him in this, unless we are to think it would be honourable for him to degenerate, and revolt against himself.

3. Their cavil about our cleaving to the dead letter carries with it the punishment which they deserve for despising Scripture. It is clear that Paul is there arguing against false apostles (2 Cor. 3:6), who, by recommending the law without Christ, deprived the people of the benefit of the New Covenant, by which the Lord engages that he will write his law on the hearts of believers, and engrave it on their inward parts. The letter therefore is dead, and the law of the Lord kills its readers when it is dissevered from the grace of Christ, and only sounds in the ear without touching the heart. But if it is effectually impressed on the heart by the Spirit; if it exhibits Christ, it is the word of life converting the soul, and making wise the simple. Nay, in the very same passage, the apostle calls his own preaching the ministration of the Spirit (2 Cor. 3:8), intimating that the Holy Spirit so cleaves to his own truth, as he has expressed it in Scripture, that he then

only exerts and puts forth his strength when the word is received with due honour and respect.

There is nothing repugnant here to what was lately said (chap. 7) that we have no great certainty of the word itself, until it be confirmed by the testimony of the Spirit. For the Lord has so knit together the certainty of his word and his Spirit, that our minds are duly imbued with reverence for the word when the Spirit shining upon it enables us there to behold the face of God; and, on the other hand, we embrace the Spirit with no danger of delusion when we recognise him in his image, that is, in his word. Thus, indeed, it is. God did not produce his word before men for the sake of sudden display, intending to abolish it the moment the Spirit should arrive; but he employed the same Spirit, by whose agency he had administered the word, to complete his work by the efficacious confirmation of the word. In this way Christ explained to the two disciples (Luke 24:27), not that they were to reject the Scriptures and trust to their own wisdom, but that they were to understand the Scriptures. In like manner, when Paul says to the Thessalonians, "Quench not the Spirit," he does not carry them aloft to empty speculation apart from the word; he immediately adds, "Despise not prophesying" (1 Thess. 5:19, 20). By this, doubtless, he intimates that the light of the Spirit is quenched the moment prophesying fall into contempt. How is this answered by those swelling enthusiasts, in whose idea the only true illumination consists, in carelessly laying aside, and bidding adieu to the Word of God, while, with no less confidence than folly, they fasten upon any dreaming notion which may have casually sprung up in their minds? Surely a very different sobriety becomes the children of God. As they feel that without the Spirit of God they are utterly devoid of the light of truth, so they are not ignorant that the word is the instrument by which the illumination of the Spirit is dispensed. They know of no other Spirit than the one who dwelt and spake in the apostles—the Spirit by whose oracles they are daily invited to the hearing of the word.

CHAPTER 10

IN SCRIPTURE, THE TRUE GOD OPPOSED, EXCLUSIVELY, TO ALL THE GODS OF THE HEATHEN.

Sections:

1. Explanation of the knowledge of God resumed. God as manifested in Scripture, the same as delineated in his works.

2. The attributes of God as described by Moses, David, and Jeremiah. Explanation of the attributes. Summary. Uses of this knowledge.

3. Scripture, in directing us to the true God, excludes the gods of the heathen, who, however, in some sense, held the unity of God.

1. We formerly observed that the knowledge of God, which, in other respects, is not obscurely exhibited in the frame of the world, and in all the creatures, is more clearly and familiarly explained by the word. It may now be proper to show, that in Scripture the Lord represents himself in the same character in which we have already seen that he is delineated in his works. A full discussion of this subject would occupy a large space. But it will here be sufficient to furnish a kind of index, by attending to which the pious reader may be enabled to understand what knowledge of God he ought chiefly to search for in Scripture, and be directed as to the mode of conducting the search. I am not now adverting to the peculiar covenant by which God distinguished the race of Abraham from the rest of the nations. For when by gratuitous adoption he admitted those who were enemies to the rank of sons, he even then acted in the character of a Redeemer. At present, however, we are employed in considering that knowledge which stops short at the creation of the world, without ascending to Christ the Mediator. But though it will soon be necessary to quote certain passages from the New Testament (proofs being there given both of the power of God the Creator, and of his providence in the preservation of what he originally created), I wish the reader to remember what my present purpose is, that he may not wander from the proper subject. Briefly, then, it will be sufficient for him at present to understand how God, the Creator of heaven and earth, governs the world which was made by him. In every part of Scripture we meet with descriptions of his paternal kindness and readiness to do good, and we also meet with examples of severity which show that he is the just punisher of the wicked, especially when they continue obstinate notwithstanding of all his forbearance.

2. There are certain passages which contain more vivid descriptions of the divine character, setting it before us as if his genuine countenance were visibly portrayed. Moses, indeed, seems to have intended briefly to comprehend whatever may be known of God by man, when he said, "The Lord, The Lord God, merciful and gracious, long-suffering, and abundant in goodness and truth, keeping mercy for thousands, forgiving iniquity and transgression

and sin, and that will by no means clear the guilty; visiting the iniquity of the fathers upon the children, and upon the children's children, unto the third and to the fourth generation" (Ex. 34:6, 7). Here we may observe, *first*, that his eternity and selfexistence are declared by his magnificent name twice repeated; and, *secondly*, that in the enumeration of his perfections, he is described not as he is in himself, but in relation to us, in order that our acknowledgement of him may be more a vivid actual impression than empty visionary speculation. Moreover, the perfections thus enumerated are just those which we saw shining in the heavens, and on the earth—compassion, goodness, mercy, justice, Judgment, and truth. For power and energy are comprehended under the name Jehovah. Similar epithets are employed by the prophets when they would fully declare his sacred name. Not to collect a great number of passages, it may suffice at present to refer to one Psalm (145) in which a summary of the divine perfections is so carefully given that not one seems to have been omitted. Still, however, every perfection there set down may be contemplated in creation; and, hence, such as we feel him to be when experience is our guide, such he declares himself to be by his word. In Jeremiah, where God proclaims the character in which he would have us to acknowledge him, though the description is not so full, it is substantially the same. "Let him that glorieth," says he, "glory in this, that he understandeth and knoweth me, that I am the Lord which exercise loving-kindness, Judgment, and righteousness, in the earth" (Jer. 9:24). Assuredly, the attributes which it is most necessary for us to know are these three: Loving-kindness, on which alone our entire safety depends: Judgment, which is daily exercised on the wicked, and awaits them in a severer form, even for eternal destruction: Righteousness, by which the faithful are preserved, and most benignly cherished. The prophet declares, that when you understand these, you are amply furnished with the means of glorying in God. Nor is there here any omission of his truth, or power, or holiness, or goodness. For how could this knowledge of his loving-kindness, Judgment, and righteousness, exist, if it were not founded on his inviolable truth? How, again, could it be believed that he governs the earth with Judgment and righteousness, without presupposing his mighty power? Whence, too, his loving-kindness, but from his goodness? In fine, if all his ways are loving-kindness, Judgment, and righteousness, his holiness also is thereby conspicuous. Moreover, the knowledge of God, which is set before us in the Scriptures, is designed for the same purpose as that which shines in creation—viz. that we may thereby learn to worship him with perfect integrity of heart and unfeigned obedience, and also to depend entirely on his goodness.

3. Here it may be proper to give a summary of the general doctrine. First, then, let the reader observe that the Scripture, in order to direct us to the true God, distinctly excludes and rejects all the gods of the heathen, because religion was universally adulterated in almost every age. It is true, indeed, that the name of one God was everywhere known and celebrated. For those who worshipped a multitude of gods, whenever they spoke the genuine language of nature, simply used the name god, as if they had thought one god sufficient. And this is shrewdly noticed by Justin Martyr, who, to the same effect, wrote a treatise, entitled, On the Monarchy of God, in which he shows, by a great variety of evidence, that the unity of God is engraven on the hearts of all. Tertullian also proves the same thing from the common forms of speech. But as all, without exception, have in the vanity of their minds rushed or been dragged into lying fictions, these impressions, as to the unity of God, whatever they may have naturally been, have had no further effect than to render men inexcusable. The wisest plainly discover the vague wanderings of their minds when they express a wish for any kind of Deity, and thus offer up their prayers to unknown gods. And then, in imagining a manifold nature in God, though their ideas concerning Jupiter, Mercury, Venus, Minerva, and others, were not so absurd as those of the rude vulgar, they were by no means free from the delusions of the devil. We have elsewhere observed, that however subtle the evasions devised by philosophers, they cannot do away with the charge of rebellion, in that all of them have corrupted the truth of God. For this reason, Habakkuk (2:20), after condemning all idols, orders men to seek God in his temple, that the faithful may acknowledge none but Him, who has manifested himself in his word.

CHAPTER II

IMPIETY OF ATTRIBUTING A VISIBLE FORM TO GOD.—THE SETTING UP OF IDOLS A DEFECTION FROM THE TRUE GOD.

There are three leading divisions in this chapter. The first contains a refutation of those who ascribe a visible form to God (s. 1 and 2), with an answer to the objection of those who, because it is said that God manifested his presence by certain symbols, use it as a

defence of their error (s. 3 and 4). Various arguments are afterwards adduced, disposing of the trite objection from Gregory's expression, that images are the books of the unlearned (s. 5–7). The second division of the chapter relates to the origin of idols or images, and the adoration of them, as approved by the Papists (s. 8–10). Their evasion refuted (s. 11). The third division treats of the use and abuse of images (s. 12). Whether it is expedient to have them in Christian Churches (s. 13). The concluding part contains a refutation of the second Council of Nice, which very absurdly contends for images in opposition to divine truth, and even to the disparagement of the Christian name.

Sections:

1. God is opposed to idols, that all may know he is the only fit witness to himself. He expressly forbids any attempt to represent him by a bodily shape.

2. Reasons for this prohibition from Moses, Isaiah, and Paul. The complaint of a heathen. It should put the worshipers of idols to shame.

3. Consideration of an objection taken from various passages in Moses. The Cherubim and Seraphim show that images are not fit to represent divine mysteries. The Cherubim belonged to the tutelage of the Law.

4. The materials of which idols are made, abundantly refute the fiction of idolaters. Confirmation from Isaiah and others. Absurd precaution of the Greeks.

5. Objection,—That images are the books of the unlearned. Objection answered, 1. Scripture declares images to be teachers of vanity and lies.

6. Answer continued, 2. Ancient Theologians condemn the formation and worship of idols.

7. Answer continued, 3. The use of images condemned by the luxury and meretricious ornaments given to them in Popish Churches. 4. The Church must be trained in true piety by another method.

8. The second division of the chapter. Origin of idols or images. Its rise shortly after the flood. Its continual progress.

9. Of the worship of images. Its nature. A pretext of idolaters refuted. Pretexts of the heathen. Genius of idolaters.

10. Evasion of the Papists. Their agreement with ancient idolaters.

11. Refutation of another evasion or sophism—viz. the distinction of δυλια and λατρια.

12. Third division of the chapter—viz. the use and abuse of images.

13. Whether it is expedient to have images in Christian temples.

14. Absurd defence of the worship of images by the second so-called Council of Nice. Sophisms or perversions of Scripture in defence of images in churches.

15. Passages adduced in support of the worship of images.

16. The blasphemous expressions of some ancient idolaters approved by not a few of the more modern, both in word and deed.

1. As Scripture, in accommodation to the rude and gross intellect of man, usually speaks in popular terms, so whenever its object is to discriminate between the true God and false deities, it opposes him in particular to idols; not that it approves of what is taught more elegantly and subtilely by philosophers, but that it may the better expose the folly, nay, madness of the world in its inquiries after God, so long as every one clings to his own speculations. This exclusive definition, which we uniformly meet with in Scripture, annihilates every deity which men frame for themselves of their own accord—God himself being the only fit witness to himself. Meanwhile, seeing that this brutish stupidity has overspread the globe, men longing after visible forms of God, and so forming deities of wood and stone, silver and gold, or of any other dead and corruptible matter, we must hold it as a first principle, that as often as any form is assigned to God, his glory is corrupted by an impious lie. In the Law, accordingly, after God had claimed the glory of divinity for himself alone, when he comes to show what kind of worship he approves and rejects, he immediately adds, "Thou shalt not make unto thee any graven image, or any likeness of any thing that is in heaven above, or in the earth beneath, or in the water under the earth" (Exod. 20:4). By these words he curbs any licentious attempt we might make to represent him by a visible shape, and briefly enumerates all the forms by which superstition had begun, even long before, to turn his truth into a lie. For we know that the Sun was worshipped by the Persian. As many stars as the foolish nations saw in the sky, so many gods they imagined them to be. Then to the Egyptians, every animal was a figure of God. The Greeks, again, plumed themselves on their superior wisdom in worshipping God under the human form (Maximum Tyrius Platonic. Serm. 38). But God makes no comparison between images, as if one were more, and another less befitting; he rejects, without exception, all shapes and pictures, and other symbols by which the superstitious imagine they can bring him near to them.

2. This may easily be inferred from the reasons which

he annexes to his prohibition. First, it is said in the books of Moses (Deut. 4:15), "Take ye therefore good heed unto yourselves; for ye saw no manner of similitude in the day that the Lord spake unto you in Horeb, out of the midst of the fire, lest ye corrupt yourselves, and make you a graven image, the similitude of any figure," &c. We see how plainly God declares against all figures, to make us aware that all longing after such visible shapes is rebellion against him. Of the prophets, it will be sufficient to mention Isaiah, who is the most copious on this subject; (Isaiah 40:18; 41:7, 29; 45:9; 46:5), in order to show how the majesty of God is defiled by an absurd and indecorous fiction, when he who is incorporeal is assimilated to corporeal matter; he who is invisible to a visible image; he who is a spirit to an inanimate object; and he who fills all space to a bit of paltry wood, or stone, or gold. Paul, too, reasons in the same way, "Forasmuch, then, as we are the offspring of God, we ought not to think that the Godhead is like unto gold, or silver, or stone, graven by art and man's device" (Acts 17:29). Hence it is manifest, that whatever statues are set up or pictures painted to represent God, are utterly displeasing to him, as a kind of insults to his majesty. And is it strange that the Holy Spirit thunders such responses from heaven, when he compels even blind and miserable idolaters to make a similar confession on the earth? Seneca's complaint, as given by Augustine De Civit. Dei, c. 10, is well known. He says "The sacred immortal, and invisible gods they exhibit in the meanest and most ignoble materials, and dress them in the clothing of men and beasts; some confound the sexes, and form a compound out of different bodies, giving the name of deities to objects, which, if they were met alive, would be deemed monsters." Hence, again, it is obvious, that the defenders of images resort to a paltry quibbling evasion, when they pretend that the Jews were forbidden to use them on account of their proneness to superstition; as if a prohibition which the Lord founds on his own eternal essences and the uniform course of nature, could be restricted to a single nation. Besides, when Paul refuted the error of giving a bodily shape to God, he was addressing not Jews, but Athenians.

3. It is true that the Lord occasionally manifested his presence by certain signs, so that he was said to be seen face to face; but all the signs he ever employed were in apt accordance with the scheme of doctrine, and, at the same time, gave plain intimation of his incomprehensible essence. For the cloud, and smoke, and flame, though they were symbols of heavenly glory (Deut. 4:11), curbed men's minds as with a bridle, that they might not attempt to penetrate farther. Therefore, even Moses (to whom, of all men, God manifested himself most familiarly) was not permitted though he prayed for it, to behold that face, but received for answer, that the refulgence was too great for man (Exod. 33:20). The Holy Spirit appeared under the form of a dove, but as it instantly vanished, who does not see that in this symbol of a moment, the faithful were admonished to regard the Spirit as invisible, to be contented with his power and grace, and not call for any external figure? God sometimes appeared in the form of a man, but this was in anticipation of the future revelation in Christ, and, therefore, did not give the Jews the least pretext for setting up a symbol of Deity under the human form. The mercy-seat, also (Exod. 25:17, 18, 21), where, under the Law, God exhibited the presence of his power, was so framed, as to intimate that God is best seen when the mind rises in admiration above itself: the Cherubim with outstretched wings shaded, and the veil covered it, while the remoteness of the place was in itself a sufficient concealment. It is therefore mere infatuation to attempt to defend images of God and the saints by the example of the Cherubim. For what, pray, did these figures mean, if not that images are unfit to represent the mysteries of God, since they were so formed as to cover the mercy-seat with their wings, thereby concealing the view of God, not only from the eye, but from every human sense, and curbing presumption? To this we may add, that the prophets depict the Seraphim, who are exhibited to us in vision, as having their faces veiled; thus intimating, that the refulgence of the divine glory is so great, that even the angels cannot gaze upon it directly, while the minute beams which sparkle in the face of angels are shrouded from our view. Moreover, all men of sound Judgment acknowledge that the Cherubim in question belonged to the old tutelage of the law. It is absurd, therefore, to bring them forward as an example for our age. For that period of puerility, if I may so express it, to which such rudiments were adapted, has passed away. And surely it is disgraceful, that heathen writers should be more skilful interpreters of Scripture than the Papists. Juvenal (Sat. 14) holds up the Jews to derision for worshipping the thin clouds and firmament. This he does perversely and impiously; still, in denying that any visible shape of Deity existed among them, he speaks more accurately than the Papists, who prate about there having been some visible image. In the fact that the people every now and then rushed forth with boiling haste in pursuit of idols, just like water gushing forth with violence from a copious spring, let us learn how prone our nature is to idolatry,

that we may not, by throwing the whole blame of a common vice upon the Jews, be led away by vain and sinful enticements to sleep the sleep of death.

4. To the same effect are the words of the Psalmist (Psalms 115:4, 135:15), "Their idols are silver and gold, the works of men's hands." From the materials of which they are made, he infers that they are not gods, taking it for granted that every human device concerning God is a dull fiction. He mentions silver and gold rather than clay or stone, that neither splendour nor cost may procure reverence to idols. He then draws a general conclusion, that nothing is more unlikely than that gods should be formed of any kind of inanimate matter. Man is forced to confess that he is but the creature of a day (see Book 3 c. 9 s. 2), and yet would have the metal which he has deified to be regarded as God. Whence had idols their origin, but from the will of man? There was ground, therefore, for the sarcasm of the heathen poet (Hor. Sat. I. 8), "I was once the trunk of a fig-tree, a useless log, when the tradesman, uncertain whether he should make me a stool, &c., chose rather that I should be a god." In other words, an earth-born creature, who breathes out his life almost every moment, is able by his own device to confer the name and honour of deity on a lifeless trunk. But as that Epicurean poet, in indulging his wit, had no regard for religion, without attending to his jeers or those of his fellows, let the rebuke of the prophet sting, nay, cut us to the heart, when he speaks of the extreme infatuation of those who take a piece of wood to kindle a fire to warm themselves, bake bread, roast or boil flesh, and out of the residue make a god, before which they prostrate themselves as suppliants (Isaiah 44:16). Hence, the same prophet, in another place, not only charges idolaters as guilty in the eye of the law, but upbraids them for not learning from the foundations of the earth, nothing being more incongruous than to reduce the immense and incomprehensible Deity to the stature of a few feet. And yet experience shows that this monstrous proceeding, though palpably repugnant to the order of nature, is natural to man. It is, moreover, to be observed, that by the mode of expression which is employed, every form of superstition is denounced. Being works of men, they have no authority from God (Isa. 2:8, 31:7; Hos. 14:3; Mic. 5:13); and, therefore, it must be regarded as a fixed principle, that all modes of worship devised by man are detestable. The infatuation is placed in a still stronger light by the Psalmist (Psalm 115:8), when he shows how aid is implored from dead and senseless objects, by beings who have been endued with intelligence for the very purpose of enabling them to know that the whole universe is governed by Divine energy alone. But as the corruption of nature hurries away all mankind collectively and individually into this madness, the Spirit at length thunders forth a dreadful imprecation, "They that make them are like unto them, so is every one that trusteth in them." And it is to be observed, that the thing forbidden is likeness, whether sculptured or otherwise. This disposes of the frivolous precaution taken by the Greek Church. They think they do admirably, because they have no sculptured shape of Deity, while none go greater lengths in the licentious use of pictures. The Lord, however, not only forbids any image of himself to be erected by a statuary, but to be formed by any artist whatever, because every such image is sinful and insulting to his majesty.

5. I am not ignorant, indeed, of the assertion, which is now more than threadbare, "that images are the books of the unlearned." So said Gregory: but the Holy Spirit goes a very different decision; and had Gregory got his lesson in this matter in the Spirit's school, he never would have spoken as he did. For when Jeremiah declares that "the stock is a doctrine of vanities" (Jer. 10:8), and Habakkuk, "that the molten image" is "a teacher of lies," the general doctrine to be inferred certainly is, that every thing respecting God which is learned from images is futile and false. If it is objected that the censure of the prophets is directed against those who perverted images to purposes of impious superstition, I admit it to be so; but I add (what must be obvious to all), that the prophets utterly condemn what the Papists hold to be an undoubted axiom—viz. that images are substitutes for books. For they contrast images with the true God, as if the two were of an opposite nature, and never could be made to agree. In the passages which I lately quoted, the conclusion drawn is, that seeing there is one true God whom the Jews worshipped, visible shapes made for the purpose of representing him are false and wicked fictions; and all, therefore, who have recourse to them for knowledge are miserably deceived. In short, were it not true that all such knowledge is fallacious and spurious, the prophets would not condemn it in such general terms. This at least I maintain, that when we teach that all human attempts to give a visible shape to God are vanity and lies, we do nothing more than state *verbatim* what the prophets taught.

6. Moreover, let Lactantius and Eusebius be read on this subject. These writers assume it as an indisputable fact, that all the beings whose images were erected were originally men. In like manner, Augustine distinctly declares,

that it is unlawful not only to worship images, but to dedicate them. And in this he says no more than had been long before decreed by the Libertine Council, the thirty-sixth Canon of which is, "There must be no pictures used in churches: Let nothing which is adored or worshipped be painted on walls." But the most memorable passage of all is that which Augustine quotes in another place from Varro, and in which he expressly concurs:—"Those who first introduced images of the gods both took away fear and brought in error." Were this merely the saying of Varro, it might perhaps be of little weight, though it might well make us ashamed, that a heathen, groping as it were in darkness, should have attained to such a degree of light, as to see that corporeal images are unworthy of the majesty of God, and that, because they diminish reverential fear and encourage error. The sentiment itself bears witness that it was uttered with no less truth than shrewdness. But Augustine, while he borrows it from Varro, adduces it as conveying his own opinion. At the outset, indeed, he declares that the first errors into which men fell concerning God did not originate with images, but increased with them, as if new fuel had been added. Afterwards, he explains how the fear of God was thereby extinguished or impaired, his presence being brought into contempt by foolish, and childish, and absurd representations. The truth of this latter remark I wish we did not so thoroughly experience. Whosoever, therefore, is desirous of being instructed in the true knowledge of God must apply to some other teacher than images.

7. Let Papists, then, if they have any sense of shame, henceforth desist from the futile plea, that images are the books of the unlearned—a plea so plainly refuted by innumerable passages of Scripture. And yet were I to admit the plea, it would not be a valid defence of their peculiar idols. It is well known what kind of monsters they obtrude upon us as divine. For what are the pictures or statues to which they append the names of saints, but exhibitions of the most shameless luxury or obscenity? Were any one to dress himself after their model, he would deserve the pillory. Indeed, brothels exhibit their inmates more chastely and modestly dressed than churches do images intended to represent virgins. The dress of the martyrs is in no respect more becoming. Let Papists then have some little regard to decency in decking their idols, if they would give the least plausibility to the false allegation, that they are books of some kind of sanctity. But even then we shall answer, that this is not the method in which the Christian people should be taught in sacred places. Very different from these follies is the doctrine in which God would have them to be there instructed. His injunction is, that the doctrine common to all should there be set forth by the preaching of the Word, and the administration of the sacraments,—a doctrine to which little heed can be given by those whose eyes are carried too and fro gazing at idols. And who are the unlearned, whose rudeness admits of being taught by images only? Just those whom the Lord acknowledges for his disciples; those whom he honours with a revelation of his celestial philosophy, and desires to be trained in the saving mysteries of his kingdom. I confess, indeed, as matters now are, there are not a few in the present day who cannot want such books. But, I ask, whence this stupidity, but just because they are defrauded of the only doctrine which was fit to instruct them? The simple reason why those who had the charge of churches resigned the office of teaching to idols was, because they themselves were dumb. Paul declares, that by the true preaching of the gospel Christ is portrayed and in a manner crucified before our eyes (Gal. 3:1). Of what use, then, were the erection in churches of so many crosses of wood and stone, silver and gold, if this doctrine were faithfully and honestly preached—viz. Christ died that he might bear our curse upon the tree, that he might expiate our sins by the sacrifice of his body, wash them in his blood, and, in short, reconcile us to God the Father? From this one doctrine the people would learn more than from a thousand crosses of wood and stone. As for crosses of gold and silver, it may be true that the avaricious give their eyes and minds to them more eagerly than to any heavenly instructor.

8. In regard to the origin of idols, the statement contained in the Book of Wisdom has been received with almost universal consent—viz. that they originated with those who bestowed this honour on the dead, from a superstitious regard to their memory. I admit that this perverse practice is of very high antiquity, and I deny not that it was a kind of torch by which the infatuated proneness of mankind to idolatry was kindled into a greater blaze. I do not, however, admit that it was the first origin of the practice. That idols were in use before the prevalence of that ambitious consecration of the images of the dead, frequently adverted to by profane writers, is evident from the words of Moses (Gen. 31:19). When he relates that Rachel stole her father's images, he speaks of the use of idols as a common vice. Hence we may infer, that the human mind is, so to speak, a perpetual forge of idols. There was a kind of renewal of the world at the deluge, but before many years elapse, men are forging gods at

will. There is reason to believe, that in the holy Patriarch's lifetime his grandchildren were given to idolatry: so that he must with his own eyes, not without the deepest grief, have seen the earth polluted with idols—that earth whose iniquities God had lately purged with so fearful a Judgment. For Joshua testifies (Josh. 24:2), that Torah and Nachor, even before the birth of Abraham, were the worshipers of false gods. The progeny of Shem having so speedily revolted, what are we to think of the posterity of Ham, who had been cursed long before in their father? Thus, indeed, it is. The human mind, stuffed as it is with presumptuous rashness, dares to imagine a god suited to its own capacity; as it labours under dullness, nay, is sunk in the grossest ignorance, it substitutes vanity and an empty phantom in the place of God. To these evils another is added. The god whom man has thus conceived inwardly he attempts to embody outwardly. The mind, in this way, conceives the idol, and the hand gives it birth. That idolatry has its origin in the idea which men have, that God is not present with them unless his presence is carnally exhibited, appears from the example of the Israelites: "Up," said they, "make us gods, which shall go before us; for as for this Moses, the man that brought us up out of the land of Egypt, we wet not what is become of him" (Exod. 22:1). They knew, indeed, that there was a God whose mighty power they had experienced in so many miracles, but they had no confidence of his being near to them, if they did not with their eyes behold a corporeal symbol of his presence, as an attestation to his actual government. They desired, therefore, to be assured by the image which went before them, that they were journeying under Divine guidance. And daily experience shows, that the flesh is always restless until it has obtained some figment like itself, with which it may vainly solace itself as a representation of God. In consequence of this blind passion men have, almost in all ages since the world began, set up signs on which they imagined that God was visibly depicted to their eyes.

9. After such a figment is formed, adoration forthwith ensues: for when once men imagined that they beheld God in images, they also worshipped him as being there. At length their eyes and minds becoming wholly engrossed by them, they began to grow more and more brutish, gazing and wondering as if some divinity were actually before them. It hence appears that men do not fall away to the worship of images until they have imbibed some idea of a grosser description: not that they actually believe them to be gods, but that the power of divinity somehow or other resides in them. Therefore, whether it be God or a creature that is imaged, the moment you fall prostrate before it in veneration, you are so far fascinated by superstition. For this reason, the Lord not only forbade the erection of statues to himself, but also the consecration of titles and stones which might be set up for adoration. For the same reason, also, the second commandment has an additional part concerning adoration. For as soon as a visible form is given to God, his power also is supposed to be annexed to it. So stupid are men, that wherever they figure God, there they fix him, and by necessary consequence proceed to adore him. It makes no difference whether they worship the idol simply, or God in the idol; it is always idolatry when divine honours are paid to an idol, be the colour what it may. And because God wills not to be worshipped superstitiously whatever is bestowed upon idols is so much robbed from him.

Let those attend to this who set about hunting for miserable pretexts in defence of the execrable idolatry in which for many past ages true religion has been buried and sunk. It is said that the images are not accounted gods. Nor were the Jews so utterly thoughtless as not to remember that there was a God whose hand led them out of Egypt before they made the calf. Indeed, Aaron saying, that these were the gods which had brought them out of Egypt, they intimated, in no ambiguous terms, that they wished to retain God, their deliverer, provided they saw him going before them in the calf. Nor are the heathen to be deemed to have been so stupid as not to understand that God was something else than wood and stone. For they changed the images at pleasure, but always retained the same gods in their minds; besides, they daily consecrated new images without thinking they were making new gods. Read the excuses which Augustine tells us were employed by the idolaters of his time (*August. in Ps.* 113). The vulgar, when accused, replied that they did not worship the visible object, but the Deity which dwelt in it invisibly. Those, again, who had what he calls a more refined religion, said, that they neither worshipped the image, nor any inhabiting Deity, but by means of the corporeal image beheld a symbol of that which it was their duty to worship. What then? All idolaters whether Jewish or Gentile, were actuated in the very way which has been described. Not contented with spiritual understanding, they thought that images would give them a surer and nearer impression. When once this preposterous representation of God was adopted, there was no limit until, deluded every now and then by new impostures, they came to think that God exerted his power in images. Still the Jews were persuaded, that under such images they worshipped the eternal God, the one true Lord of heaven and earth; and the Gentiles, also, in worshipping their own false gods, supposed them to dwell in heaven.

10. It is an impudent falsehood to deny that the thing which was thus anciently done is also done in our day. For why do men prostrate themselves before images? Why, when in the act of praying, do they turn towards them as to the ears of God? It is indeed true, as Augustine says (in Ps. 113), that no person thus prays or worships, looking at an image, without being impressed with the idea that he is heard by it, or without hoping that what he wishes will be performed by it. Why are such distinctions made between different images of the same God, that while one is passed by, or receives only common honour, another is worshipped with the highest solemnities? Why do they fatigue themselves with votive pilgrimages to images while they have many similar ones at home? Why at the present time do they fight for them to blood and slaughter, as for their altars and hearths, showing more willingness to part with the one God than with their idols? And yet I am not now detailing the gross errors of the vulgar—errors almost infinite in number, and in possession of almost all hearts. I am only referring to what those profess who are most desirous to clear themselves of idolatry. They say, we do not call them our gods. Nor did either the Jews or Gentiles of old so call them; and yet the prophets never ceased to charge them with their adulteries with wood and stone for the very acts which are daily done by those who would be deemed Christians, namely, for worshipping God carnally in wood and stone.

11. I am not ignorant, however, and I have no wish to disguise the fact, that they endeavour to evade the charge by means of a more subtle distinction, which shall afterwards be fully considered (see *infra*, s. 16, and chap. 12 s. 2). The worship which they pay to their images they cloak with the name of εἰδωλοδυλεία (ιδολοδυλια), and deny to be εἰδωλολατρεία (ιδολατρια). So they speaks holding that the worship which they call δυλια may, without insult to God, be paid to statues and pictures. Hence, they think themselves blameless if they are only the *servants*, and not the *worshippers*, of idols; as if it were not a lighter matter to *worship* than *to serve*. And yet, while they take refuge in a Greek term, they very childishly contradict themselves. For the Greek word λατρεύειν having no other meaning than *to worship*, what they say is just the same as if they were to confess that they worship their images without worshipping them. They cannot object that I am quibbling upon words. The fact is, that they only betray their ignorance while they attempt to throw dust in the eyes of the simple. But how eloquent soever they may be, they will never prove by their eloquence that one and the same thing makes two. Let them show how the things differ if they would be thought different from ancient idolaters. For as a murderer or an adulterer will not escape conviction by giving some adventitious name to his crime, so it is absurd for them to expect that the subtle device of a name will exculpate them, if they, in fact, differ in nothing from idolaters whom they themselves are forced to condemn. But so far are they from proving that their case is different, that the source of the whole evil consists in a preposterous rivalship with them, while they with their minds devise, and with their hands execute, symbolical shapes of God.

12. I am not, however, so superstitious as to think that all visible representations of every kind are unlawful. But as sculpture and painting are gifts of God, what I insist for is, that both shall be used purely and lawfully,—that gifts which the Lord has bestowed upon us, for his glory and our good, shall not be preposterously abused, nay, shall not be perverted to our destruction. We think it unlawful to give a visible shape to God, because God himself has forbidden it, and because it cannot be done without, in some degree, tarnishing his glory. And lest any should think that we are singular in this opinion, those acquainted with the productions of sound divines will find that they have always disapproved of it. If it be unlawful to make any corporeal representation of God, still more unlawful must it be to worship such a representation instead of God, or to worship God in it. The only things, therefore, which ought to be painted or sculptured, are things which can be presented to the eye; the majesty of God, which is far beyond the reach of any eye, must not be dishonored by unbecoming representations. Visible representations are of two classes—viz. historical, which give a representation of events, and pictorial, which merely exhibit bodily shapes and figures. The former are of some use for instruction or admonition. The latter, so far as I can see, are only fitted for amusement. And yet it is certain, that the latter are almost the only kind which have hitherto been exhibited in churches. Hence we may infer, that the exhibition was not the result of judicious selection, but of a foolish and inconsiderate longing. I say nothing as to the improper and unbecoming form in which they are presented, or the wanton license in which sculptors and painters have here indulged (a point to which I alluded a little ago, *supra*, s. 7). I only say, that though they were otherwise faultless, they could not be of any utility in teaching.

13. But, without reference to the above distinction, let us here consider, whether it is expedient that churches should contain representations of any kind, whether of events or human forms. First, then, if we attach any weight to the authority of the ancient Church, let us remember, that for five hundred years, during which religion was in a more prosperous condition, and a purer doctrine flourished, Christian churches were completely free from visible representations (see Preface, and Book 4, c. 9 s. 9). Hence their first admission as an ornament to churches took place after the purity of the ministry had somewhat degenerated. I will not dispute as to the rationality of the grounds on which the first introduction of them proceeded, but if you compare the two periods, you will find that the latter had greatly declined from the purity of the times when images were unknown. What then? Are we to suppose that those holy fathers, if they had judged the thing to be useful and salutary, would have allowed the Church to be so long without it? Undoubtedly, because they saw very little or no advantage, and the greatest danger in it, they rather rejected it intentionally and on rational grounds, than omitted it through ignorance or carelessness. This is clearly attested by Augustine in these words (Ep. 49. See also De Civit. Dei, lib 4 c. 31) "When images are thus placed aloft in seats of honour, to be beheld by those who are praying or sacrificing, though they have neither sense nor life, yet from appearing as if they had both, they affect weak minds just as if they lived and breathed," &c. And again, in another passage (in Ps. 112) he says, "The effect produced, and in a manner extorted, by the bodily shape, is, that the mind, being itself in a body, imagines that a body which is so like its oven must be similarly affected," &c. A little farther on he says, "Images are more capable of giving a wrong bent to an unhappy soul, from having mouth, eyes, ears, and feet, than of correcting it, as they neither speak, nor see, nor hear, nor walk." This undoubtedly is the reason why John (1 John 5:21) enjoins us to beware, not only of the worship of idols, but also of idols themselves. And from the fearful infatuation under which the world has hitherto laboured, almost to the entire destruction of piety, we know too well from experience that the moment images appear in churches, idolatry has as it were raised its banner; because the folly of manhood cannot moderate itself, but forthwith falls away to superstitious worship. Even were the danger less imminent, still, when I consider the proper end for which churches are erected, it appears to me more unbecoming their sacredness than I well can tell, to admit any other images than those living symbols which the Lord has consecrated by his own word: I mean Baptism and the Lord's Supper, with the other ceremonies. By these our eyes ought to be more steadily fixed, and more vividly impressed, than to require the aid of any images which the wit of man may devise. Such, then, is the incomparable blessing of images—a blessing, the want of which, if we believe the Papists, cannot possibly be compensated!

14. Enough, I believe, would have been said on this subject, were I not in a manner arrested by the Council of Nice; not the celebrated Council which Constantine the Great assembled, but one which was held eight hundred years ago by the orders and under the auspices of the Empress Irene. This Council decreed not only that images were to be used in churches, but also that they were to be worshipped. Every thing, therefore, that I have said, is in danger of suffering great prejudice from the authority of this Synod. To confess the truth, however, I am not so much moved by this consideration, as by a wish to make my readers aware of the lengths to which the infatuation has been carried by those who had a greater fondness for images than became Christians. But let us first dispose of this matter. Those who defend the use of images appeal to that Synod for support. But there is a refutation extant which bears the name of Charlemagne, and which is proved by its style to be a production of that period. It gives the opinions delivered by the bishops who were present, and the arguments by which they supported them. John, deputy of the Eastern Churches, said, "God created man in his own image," and thence inferred that images ought to be used. He also thought there was a recommendation of images in the following passage, "Show me thy face, for it is beautiful." Another, in order to prove that images ought to be placed on altars, quoted the passage, "No man, when he has lighted a candle, putteth it under a bushel." Another, to show the utility of looking at images, quoted a verse of the Psalms "The light of thy countenance, O Lord, has shone upon us." Another laid hold of this similitude: As the Patriarchs used the sacrifices of the Gentiles, so ought Christians to use the images of saints instead of the idols of the Gentiles. They also twisted to the same effect the words, "Lord, I have loved the beauty of thy house." But the most ingenious interpretation was the following, "As we have heard, so also have we seen;" therefore, God is known not merely by the hearing of the word, but also by the seeing of images. Bishop Theodore was equally acute: "God," says he, "is to be admired in his saints;" and it is elsewhere said, "To the saints who are on earth;" there-

fore this must refer to images. In short, their absurdities are so extreme that it is painful even to quote them.

15. When they treat of adoration, great stress is laid on the worship of Pharaoh, the staff of Joseph, and the inscription which Jacob set up. In this last case they not only pervert the meaning of Scripture, but quote what is nowhere to be found. Then the passages, "Worship at his footstool"—"Worship in his holy mountain"—"The rulers of the people will worship before thy face," seem to them very solid and apposite proofs. Were one, with the view of turning the defenders of images into ridicule, to put words into their mouths, could they be made to utter greater and grosser absurdities? But to put an end to all doubt on the subject of images, Theodosius Bishop of Mira confirms the propriety of worshipping them by the dreams of his archdeacon, which he adduces with as much gravity as if he were in possession of a response from heaven. Let the patrons of images now go and urge us with the decree of this Synod, as if the venerable Fathers did not bring themselves into utter discredit by handling Scripture so childishly, or wresting it so shamefully and profanely.

16. I come now to monstrous impieties, which it is strange they ventured to utter, and twice strange that all men did not protest against with the utmost detestation. It is right to expose this frantic and flagitious extravagance, and thereby deprive the worship of images of that gloss of antiquity in which Papists seek to deck it. Theodosius Bishop of Amora fires oft an anathema at all who object to the worship of images. Another attributes all the calamities of Greece and the East to the crime of not having worshipped them. Of what punishment then are the Prophets, Apostles, and Martyrs worthy, in whose day no images existed? They afterwards add, that if the statue of the Emperor is met with odours and incense, much more are the images of saints entitled to the honour. Constantius, Bishop of Constantia in Cyprus, professes to embrace images with reverence, and declares that he will pay them the respect which is due to the ever blessed Trinity: every person refusing to do the same thing he anathematises and classes with Marcionites and Manichees. Lest you should think this the private opinion of an individual, they all assent. Nay, John the Eastern legate, carried still farther by his zeal, declares it would be better to allow a city to be filled with brothels than be denied the worship of images. At last it is resolved with one consent that the Samaritans are the worst of all heretics, and that the enemies of images are worse than the Samaritans. But that the play may not pass off without the accustomed *Plaudite*, the whole thus concludes, "Rejoice and exult, ye who, having the image of Christ, offer sacrifice to it." Where is now the distinction of λατρια and δυλια with which they would throw dust in all eyes, human and divine? The Council unreservedly relies as much on images as on the living God.

CHAPTER 12

GOD DISTINGUISHED FROM IDOLS, THAT HE MAY BE THE EXCLUSIVE OBJECT OF WORSHIP.

Sections:

1. **Scripture, in teaching that there is but one God, does not make a dispute about words, but attributes all honour and religious worship to him alone. This proved, 1st, By the etymology of the term. 2d, By the testimony of God himself, when he declares that he is a jealous God, and will not allow himself to be confounded with any fictitious Deity.**

2. **The Papists in opposing this pure doctrine, gain nothing by their distinction of δυλια and λατρια.**

3. **Passages of Scripture subversive of the Papistical distinction, and proving that religious worship is due to God alone. Perversions of Divine worship.**

1. We said at the commencement of our work (chap. 2), that the knowledge of God consists not in frigid speculation, but carries worship along with it; and we touched by the way (chap. 5 s. 6, 9, 10) on what will be more copiously treated in other places (Book 2, chap. 8)—viz. how God is duly worshipped. Now I only briefly repeat, that whenever Scripture asserts the unity of God, it does not contend for a mere name, but also enjoins that nothing which belongs to Divinity be applied to any other; thus making it obvious in what respect pure religion differs from superstition. The Greek word εὐσέβεια means "right worship;" for the Greeks, though groping in darkness, were always aware that a certain rule was to be observed, in order that God might not be worshipped absurdly. Cicero truly and shrewdly derives the name *religion* from *relego*, and yet the reason which he assigns is forced and farfetched—viz. that honest worshipers *read* and *read again*, and ponder what is true. I rather think the name is used in opposition to *vagrant license*—the greater part of mankind rashly taking up whatever first comes in their way, whereas piety, that it may stand with a firm step, confines itself within due bounds. In

the same way superstition seems to take its name from its not being contented with the measure which reason prescribes, but accumulating a superfluous mass of vanities. But to say nothing more of words, it has been universally admitted in all ages, that religion is vitiated and perverted whenever false opinions are introduced into it, and hence it is inferred, that whatever is allowed to be done from inconsiderate zeal, cannot be defended by any pretext with which the superstitious may choose to cloak it. But although this confession is in every man's mouth, a shameful stupidity is forthwith manifested, inasmuch as men neither cleave to the one God, nor use any selection in their worship, as we have already observed.

But God, in vindicating his own right, first proclaims that he is a jealous God, and will be a stern avenger if he is confounded with any false god; and thereafter defines what due worship is, in order that the human race may be kept in obedience. Both of these he embraces in his Law when he first binds the faithful in allegiance to him as their only Lawgiver, and then prescribes a rule for worshipping him in accordance with his will. The Law, with its manifold uses and objects, I will consider in its own place; at present I only advert to this one, that it is designed as a bridle to curb men, and prevent them from turning aside to spurious worship. But it is necessary to attend to the observation with which I set out—viz. that unless everything peculiar to divinity is confined to God alone, he is robbed of his honour, and his worship is violated.

It may be proper here more particularly to attend to the subtleties which superstition employs. In revolting to strange gods, it avoids the appearance of abandoning the Supreme God, or reducing him to the same rank with others. It gives him the highest place, but at the same time surrounds him with a tribe of minor deities, among whom it portions out his peculiar offices. In this way, though in a dissembling and crafty manner, the glory of the Godhead is dissected, and not allowed to remain entire. In the same way the people of old, both Jews and Gentiles, placed an immense crowd in subordination to the father and ruler of the gods, and gave them, according to their rank, to share with the supreme God in the government of heaven and earth. In the same way, too, for some ages past, departed saints have been exalted to partnership with God, to be worshipped, invoked, and lauded in his stead. And yet we do not even think that the majesty of God is obscured by this abomination, whereas it is in a great measure suppressed and extinguished—all that we retain being a frigid opinion of his supreme power. At the same time, being deluded by these entanglements, we go astray after divers gods.

2. The distinction of what is called δυλια and λατρια was invented for the very purpose of permitting divine honours to be paid to angels and dead men with apparent impunity. For it is plain that the worship which Papists pay to saints differs in no respect from the worship of God: for this worship is paid without distinction; only when they are pressed they have recourse to the evasion, that what belongs to God is kept unimpaired, because they leave him λατρια. But since the question relates not to the word, but the thing, how can they be allowed to sport at will with a matter of the highest moment? But not to insist on this, the utmost they will obtain by their distinction is, that they give worship to God, and service to the others. For λατρεὶα in Greek has the same meaning as *worship* in Latin; whereas δουλεὶα properly means service, though the words are sometimes used in Scripture indiscriminately. But granting that the distinction is invariably preserved, the thing to be inquired into is the meaning of each. Δουλεὶα unquestionably means service, and λατρεὶα worship. But no man doubts that to *serve* is something higher than to *worship*. For it were often a hard thing to serve him whom you would not refuse to reverence. It is, therefore, an unjust division to assign the greater to the saints and leave the less to God. But several of the ancient fathers observed this distinction. What if they did, when all men see that it is not only improper, but utterly frivolous?

3. Laying aside subtleties, let us examine the thing. When Paul reminds the Galatians of what they were before they came to the knowledge of Gods he says that they "did service unto them which by nature are no gods" (Gal. 4:8). Because he does not say λατρια, was their superstition excusable? This superstition, to which he gives the name of δυλια, he condemns as much as if he had given it the name of λατρια. When Christ repels Satan's insulting proposal with the words, "It is written, Thou shalt worship the Lord thy God, and him only shalt thou serve" (Mt. 4:10), there was no question of λατρια. For all that Satan asked was προσκὐνεσις (obeisance). In like manners when John is rebuked by the angel for falling on his knees before him (Rev. 19:10; 22:8, 9), we ought not to suppose that John had so far forgotten himself as to have intended to transfer the honour due to God alone to an angel. But because it was impossible that a worship connected with religion should not savour somewhat of divine worship, he could not προσκυνεῖν (do obeisance to) the angel without derogating from the glory of God.

True, we often read that men were worshipped; but that was, if I may so speak, civil honour. The case is different with religious honour, which, the moment it is conjoined with worship, carries profanation of the divine honour along with it. The same thing may be seen in the case of Cornelius (Acts 10:25). He had not made so little progress in piety as not to confine supreme worship to God alone. Therefore, when he prostrates himself before Peter, he certainly does it not with the intention of adoring him instead of God. Yet Peter sternly forbids him. And why, but just because men never distinguish so accurately between the worship of God and the creatures as not to transfer promiscuously to the creature that which belongs only to God. Therefore, if we would have one God, let us remember that we can never appropriate the minutest portion of his glory without retaining what is his due. Accordingly, when Zechariah discourses concerning the repairing of the Church, he distinctly says not only that there would be one God, but also that he would have only one name—the reason being, that he might have nothing in common with idols. The nature of the worship which God requires will be seen in its own place (Book 2, c. 7 and 8). He has been pleased to prescribe in his Law what is lawful and right, and thus restrict men to a certain rule, lest any should allow themselves to devise a worship of their own. But as it is inexpedient to burden the reader by mixing up a variety of topics, I do not now dwell on this one. Let it suffice to remember, that whatever offices of piety are bestowed anywhere else than on God alone, are of the nature of sacrilege. First, superstition attached divine honours to the sun and stars, or to idols: afterwards ambition followed—ambition which, decking man in the spoils of God, dared to profane all that was sacred. And though the principle of worshipping a supreme Deity continued to be held, still the practice was to sacrifice promiscuously to genii and minor gods, or departed heroes: so prone is the descent to this vice of communicating to a crowd that which God strictly claims as his own peculiar right!

CHAPTER 13

THE UNITY OF THE DIVINE ESSENCE IN THREE PERSONS TAUGHT, IN SCRIPTURE, FROM THE FOUNDATION OF THE WORLD.

This chapter consists of two parts. The former delivers the orthodox doctrine concerning the Holy Trinity. This occupies from sec. 1–21, and may be divided into four heads; the first, treating of the meaning of Person, including both the term and the thing meant by it, sec. 2–6; the second, proving the deity of the Son, sec. 7–13; the third, the deity of the Holy Spirit, sec. 14 and 15; and the fourth, explaining what is to be held concerning the Holy Trinity. The second part of the chapter refutes certain heresies which have arisen, particularly in our age, in opposition to this orthodox doctrine. This occupies from sec. 21 to the end.

Sections:

1. Scripture, in teaching that the essence of God is immense and spiritual, refutes not only idolaters and the foolish wisdom of the world, but also the Manichees and Anthropomorphites. These latter briefly refuted.

2. In this one essence are three persons, yet so that neither is there a triple God, nor is the simple essence of God divided. Meaning of the word Person in this discussion. Three hypostases in God, or the essence of God.

3. Objection of those who, in this discussion, reject the use of the word Person. Answer 1. That it is not a foreign term, but is employed for the explanation of sacred mysteries.

4. Answer continued, 2. The orthodox compelled to use the terms, Trinity, Subsistence, and Person. Examples from the case of the Arians and Sabellians.

5. Answer continued, 3. The ancient Church, though differing somewhat in the explanation of these terms, agree in substance. Proofs from Hilary, Jerome, Augustine, in their use of the words Essence, Substance, Hypostasis. 4. Provided the orthodox meaning is retained, there should be no dispute about mere terms. But those who object to the terms usually favour the Arian and Sabellian heresy.

6. After the definition of the term follows a definition and explanation of the thing meant by it. The distinction of Persons.

7. Proofs of the eternal Deity of the Son. The Son the λόγος of the Eternal Father, and, therefore, the Son Eternal God. Objection. Reply.

8. Objection, that the Λόγος began to be when the creating God spoke. Answer confirmed by Scripture and argument.

9. The Son called God and Jehovah. Other names of the Eternal Father applied to him in the Old Testament. He is, therefore, the Eternal God. Another objection refuted. Case of the Jews explained.

10. The angel who appeared to the fathers under

the Law asserts that he is Jehovah. That angel was the Λόγος of the Eternal Father. The Son being that Λόγος is Eternal God. Impiety of Servetus refuted. Why the Son appeared in the form of an angel.

11. Passages from the New Testament in which the Son is acknowledged to be the Lord of Hosts, the Judge of the world, the God of glory, the Creator of the world, the Lord of angels, the King of the Church, the eternal Λόγος, God blessed for ever, God manifest in the flesh, the equal of God, the true God and eternal life, the Lord and God of all believers. Therefore, the Eternal God.

12. Christ the Creator, Preserver, Redeemer, and Searcher of hearts. Therefore, the Eternal God.

13. Christ, by his own inherent power, wrought miracles, and bestowed the power of working them on others. Out of the Eternal God there is no salvation, no righteousness, no life. All these are in Christ. Christ, consequently, is the Eternal God. He in whom we believe and hope, to whom we pray, whom the Church acknowledges as the Saviour of the faithful, whom to know is life eternal, in whom the pious glory, and through whom eternal blessings are communicated, is the Eternal God. All these Christ is, and, therefore, he is God.

14. The Divinity of the Spirit proved. I. He is the Creator and Preserver of the world. II. He sent the Prophets. III. He quickeneth all things. IV. He is everywhere present. V. He renews the saints, and fits them for eternal life. VI. All the offices of Deity belong to him.

15. The Divinity of the Spirit continued. VII. He is called God. VIII. Blasphemy against him is not forgiven.

16. What view to be taken of the Trinity. The form of Christian baptism proves that there are in one essence. The Arian and Macedonian heresies.

17. Of the distinction of Persons. They are distinct, but not divided. This proved.

18. Analogies taken from human affairs to be cautiously used. Due regard to be paid to those mentioned by Scripture.

19. How the Three Persons not only do not destroy, but constitute the most perfect unity

20. Conclusion of this part of the chapter, and summary of the true doctrine concerning the unity of Essence and the Three Persons.

21. Refutation of Arian, Macedonian, and Anti Trinitarian heresies. Caution to be observed.

22. The more modern Anti Trinitarians, and especially Servetus, refuted.

23. Other Anti Trinitarians refuted. No good objection that Christ is called the Son of God, since he is also called God. Impious absurdities of some heretics.

24. The name of God sometimes given to the Son absolutely as to the Father. Same as to other attributes. Objections refuted.

25. Objections further refuted. Caution to be used.

26. Previous refutations further explained.

27. Reply to certain passages produced from Irenaeus. The meaning of Irenaeus.

28. Reply to certain passages produced from Tertullian. The meaning of Tertullian.

29. Anti Trinitarians refuted by ancient Christian writers; e.g., Justin, Hilary. Objections drawn from writings improperly attributed to Ignatius. Conclusion of the whole discussion concerning the Trinity.

1. The doctrine of Scripture concerning the immensity and the spirituality of the essence of God, should have the effect not only of dissipating the wild dreams of the vulgar, but also of refuting the subtleties of a profane philosophy. One of the ancients thought he spake shrewdly when he said that everything we see and everything we do not see is God (Senec. Praef. lib. 1 Quaest. Nat.) In this way he fancied that the Divinity was transfused into every separate portion of the world. But although God, in order to keep us within the bounds of soberness, treats sparingly of his essence, still, by the two attributes which I have mentioned, he at once suppresses all gross imaginations, and checks the audacity of the human mind. His immensity surely ought to deter us from measuring him by our sense, while his spiritual nature forbids us to indulge in carnal or earthly speculation concerning him. With the same view he frequently represents heaven as his dwelling-place. It is true, indeed, that as he is incomprehensible, he fills the earth also, but knowing that our minds are heavy and grovel on the earth, he raises us above the worlds that he may shake off our sluggishness and inactivity. And here we have a refutation of the error of the Manichees, who, by adopting two first principles, made the devil almost the equal of God. This, assuredly, was both to destroy his unity and restrict his immensity. Their attempt to pervert certain passages of Scripture proved their shameful ignorance, as the very nature of the error did their monstrous infatuation. The Anthropomorphites also, who dreamed of a corporeal God, because mouth, ears, eyes, hands, and feet, are often ascribed to him in Scripture, are easily refuted. For who is so devoid of intellect as not to understand that God, in so speaking, lisps with us as nurses are wont to do with little

children? Such modes of expression, therefore, do not so much express what kind of a being God is, as accommodate the knowledge of him to our feebleness. In doing so, he must, of course, stoop far below his proper height.

2. But there is another special mark by which he designates himself, for the purpose of giving a more intimate knowledge of his nature. While he proclaims his unity, he distinctly sets it before us as existing in three persons. These we must hold, unless the bare and empty name of Deity merely is to flutter in our brain without any genuine knowledge. Moreover, lest any one should dream of a threefold God, or think that the simple essence is divided by the three Persons, we must here seek a brief and easy definition which may effectually guard us from error. But as some strongly inveigh against the term Person as being merely of human inventions let us first consider how far they have any ground for doing so.

When the Apostle calls the Son of God "the express image of his person" (Heb. 1:3), he undoubtedly does assign to the Father some subsistence in which he differs from the Son. For to hold with some interpreters that the term is equivalent to essence (as if Christ represented the substance of the Father like the impression of a seal upon wax), were not only harsh but absurd. For the essence of God being simple and undivided, and contained in himself entire, in full perfection, without partition or diminution, it is improper, nay, ridiculous, to call it his express image (χαρακτερ). But because the Father, though distinguished by his own peculiar properties, has expressed himself wholly in the Son, he is said with perfect reason to have rendered his person (hypostasis) manifest in him. And this aptly accords with what is immediately added—viz. that he is "the brightness of his glory." The fair inference from the Apostle's words is, that there is a proper subsistence (hypostasis) of the Father, which shines refulgent in the Son. From this, again it is easy to infer that there is a subsistence (hypostasis) of the Son which distinguishes him from the Father. The same holds in the case of the Holy Spirit; for we will immediately prove both that he is God, and that he has a separate subsistence from the Father. This, moreover, is not a distinction of essence, which it were impious to multiply. If credit, then, is given to the Apostle's testimony, it follows that there are three persons (hypostases) in God. The Latins having used the word *Persona* to express the same thing as the Greek ὑπόστατις, it betrays excessive fastidiousness and even perverseness to quarrel with the term. The most literal translation would be *subsistence*. Many have used *substance* in the same sense. Nor, indeed, was the use of the term Person confined to the Latin Church. For the Greek Church in like manner, perhaps, for the purpose of testifying their consent, have taught that there are three πρόσωπα (*aspects*) in God. All these, however, whether Greeks or Latins, though differing as to the word, are perfectly agreed in substance.

3. Now, then, though heretics may snarl and the excessively fastidious carp at the word Person as inadmissible, in consequence of its human origin, since they cannot displace us from our position that three are named, each of whom is perfect God, and yet that there is no plurality of gods, it is most uncandid to attack the terms which do nothing more than explain what the Scriptures declare and sanction. "It were better," they say, "to confine not only our meanings but our words within the bounds of Scripture, and not scatter about foreign terms to become the future seedbeds of brawls and dissensions. In this way, men grow tired of quarrels about words; the truth is lost in altercation, and charity melts away amid hateful strife." If they call it a *foreign* term, because it cannot be pointed out in Scripture in so many syllables, they certainly impose an unjust law—a law which would condemn every interpretation of Scripture that is not composed of other words of Scripture. But if by *foreign* they mean that which, after being idly devised, is superstitiously defended,—which tends more to strife than edification,—which is used either out of place, or with no benefit which offends pious ears by its harshness, and leads them away from the simplicity of God's Word, I embrace their soberness with all my heart. For I think we are bound to speak of God as reverently as we are bound to think of him. As our own thoughts respecting him are foolish, so our own language respecting him is absurd. Still, however, some medium must be observed. The unerring standard both of thinking and speaking must be derived from the Scriptures: by it all the thoughts of ours minds, and the words of our mouths, should he tested. But in regard to those parts of Scripture which, to our capacities, are dark and intricate, what forbids us to explain them in clearer terms—terms, however, kept in reverent and faithful subordination to Scripture truth, used sparingly and modestly, and not without occasion? Of this we are not without many examples. When it has been proved that the Church was impelled, by the strongest necessity, to use the words Trinity and Person, will not he who still inveighs against novelty of terms be deservedly suspected of taking offence at the light of truth, and of

having no other ground for his invective, than that the truth is made plain and transparent?

4. Such novelty (if novelty it should be called) becomes most requisite, when the truth is to be maintained against calumniators who evade it by quibbling. Of this, we of the present day have too much experience in being constantly called upon to attack the enemies of pure and sound doctrine. These slippery snakes escape by their swift and tortuous windings, if not strenuously pursued, and when caught, firmly held. Thus the early Christians, when harassed with the disputes which heresies produced, were forced to declare their sentiments in terms most scrupulously exact in order that no indirect subterfuges might remain to ungodly men, to whom ambiguity of expression was a kind of hiding-place. Arius confessed that Christ was God, and the Son of God; because the passages of Scripture to this effect were too clear to be resisted, and then, as if he had done well, pretended to concur with others. But, meanwhile, he ceased not to give out that Christ was created, and had a beginning like other creatures. To drag this man of wiles out of his lurking-places, the ancient Church took a further step, and declared that Christ is the eternal Son of the Father, and consubstantial with the Father. The impiety was fully disclosed when the Arians began to declare their hatred and utter detestation of the term ὁμοούσιος. Had their first confession—viz. that Christ was God, been sincere and from the heart, they would not have denied that he was consubstantial with the Father. Who dare charge those ancient writers as men of strife and contention, for having debated so warmly, and disturbed the quiet of the Church for a single word? That little word distinguished between Christians of pure faith and the blasphemous Arians. Next Sabellius arose, who counted the names of Father, Son, and Holy Spirit, as almost nonentities; maintaining that they were not used to mark out some distinction, but that they were different attributes of God, like many others of a similar kind. When the matter was debated, he acknowledged his belief that the Father was God, the Son God, the Spirit God; but then he had the evasion ready, that he had said nothing more than if he had called God powerful, and just, and wise. Accordingly, he sung another note—viz. that the Father was the Son, and the Holy Spirit the Father, without order or distinction. The worthy doctors who then had the interests of piety at heart, in order to defeat it is man's dishonesty, proclaimed that three subsistence were to be truly acknowledged in the one God. That they might protect themselves against tortuous craftiness by the simple open truth, they affirmed that a Trinity of Persons subsisted in the one God, or (which is the same thing) in the unity of God.

5. Where names have not been invented rashly, we must beware lest we become chargeable with arrogance and rashness in rejecting them. I wish, indeed, that such names were buried, provided all would concur in the belief that the Father, Son, and Spirit, are one God, and yet that the Son is not the Father, nor the Spirit the Son, but that each has his peculiar subsistence. I am not so minutely precise as to fight furiously for mere words. For I observe, that the writers of the ancient Church, while they uniformly spoke with great reverence on these matters, neither agreed with each other, nor were always consistent with themselves. How strange the formula used by Councils, and defended by Hilary! How extravagant the view which Augustine sometimes takes! How unlike the Greeks are to the Latins! But let one example of variance suffice. The Latins, in translating ὁμοούσιος used consubstantialis (consubstantial), intimating that there was one substance of the Father and the Son, and thus using the word Substance for Essence. Hence Jerome, in his Letter to Damasus, says it is profane to affirm that there are three substances in God. But in Hilary you will find it said more than a hundred times that there are three substances in God. Then how greatly is Jerome perplexed with the word Hypostasis! He suspects some lurking poison, when it is said that there are three Hypostases in God. And he does not disguise his belief that the expression, though used in a pious sense, is improper; if, indeed, he was sincere in saying this, and did not rather designedly endeavour, by an unfounded calumny, to throw odium on the Eastern bishops whom he hated. He certainly shows little candour in asserting, that in all heathen schools οὐσία is equivalent to Hypostasis—an assertion completely refuted by trite and common use.

More courtesy and moderation is shown by Augustine (De Trinit. lib. 5 c. 8 and 9), who, although he says that Hypostasis in this sense is new to Latin ears, is still so far from objecting to the ordinary use of the term by the Greeks, that he is even tolerant of the Latins, who had imitated the Greek phraseology. The purport of what Socrates says of the term, in the Sixth Book of the Tripartite History, is, that it had been improperly applied to this purpose by the unskilful. Hilary (De Trinitat. lib. 2) charges it upon the heretics as a great crime, that their misconduct had rendered it necessary to subject to the peril of human utterance things which ought to have been reverently confined within the mind, not disguising his opinion that those who do so, do what is unlawful, speak what is ineffable, and pry into what is forbidden. Shortly after, he apologises at great length for presuming to introduce new terms. For, after putting down the natural names of Father, Son, and Spirit, he adds, that all further inquiry transcends the significance of words, the discernment of sense, and the apprehension of intellect. And in another place (De Conciliis), he congratulates the Bishops of France in not having framed any other confession, but received, without alteration, the ancient and most simple confession received by all Churches from the days of the Apostles. Not unlike this is the apology of Augustine, that the term had been wrung from him by necessity from the poverty of human language in so high a matter: not that the reality could be thereby expressed, but that he might not pass on in silence without attempting to show how the Father, Son, and Spirit, are three.

The modesty of these holy men should be an admonition to us not instantly to dip our pen in gall, and sternly denounce those who may be unwilling to swear to the terms which we have devised, provided they do not in this betray pride, or petulance, or unbecoming heat, but are willing to ponder the necessity which compels us so to speak, and may thus become gradually accustomed to a useful form of expression. Let men also studiously beware, that in opposing the Arians on the one hand, and the Sabellians on the other, and eagerly endeavouring to deprive both of any handle for cavil, they do not bring themselves under some suspicion of being the disciples of either Arius or Sabellius. Arius says that *Christ is God*, and then mutters that *he was made and had a beginning*. He says, that *he is one with the Father*, but secretly whispers in the ears of his party, *made one*, like other believers, though with special privilege. Say, *he is consubstantial*, and you immediately pluck the mask from this chameleon, though you add nothing to Scripture. Sabellius says that *the Father, Son, and Spirit, indicate some distinction in God*. Say, *they are three*, and he will bawl out that you are making three Gods. Say, that *there is a Trinity of Persons in one Divine essence*, you will only express in one word what the Scriptures say, and stop his empty prattle. Should any be so superstitiously precise as not to tolerate these terms, still do their worst, they will not be able to deny that when *one* is spoken of, a unity of substance must be understood, and when *three* in one essence, the persons in this Trinity are denoted. When this is confessed without equivocations we dwell not on words. But I was long ago made aware, and, indeed, on more than one occasion, that those who contend pertinaciously about words are tainted with some hidden poison; and, therefore, that it is more expedient to provoke them purposely, than to court their favour by speaking obscurely.

6. But to say nothing more of words, let us now attend to the thing signified. By *person*, then, I mean a subsistence in the Divine essence,—a subsistence which, while related to the other two, is distinguished from them by incommunicable properties. By *subsistence* we wish something else to be understood than *essence*. For if the Word were God simply and had not some property peculiar to himself, John could not have said correctly that he had always been with God. When he adds immediately after, that the Word was God, he calls us back to the one essence. But because he could not be with God without dwelling in the Father, hence arises that subsistence, which, though connected with the essence by an indissoluble tie, being incapable of separation, yet has a special mark by which it is distinguished from it. Now, I say that each of the three subsistences while related to the others is distinguished by its own properties. Here relation is distinctly expressed, because, when God is mentioned simply and indefinitely the name belongs not less to the Son and Spirit than to the Father. But whenever the Father is compared with the Son, the peculiar property of each distinguishes the one from the other. Again, whatever is proper to each I affirm to be incommunicable, because nothing can apply or be transferred to the Son which is attributed to the Father as a mark of distinction. I have no objections to adopt the definition of Tertullian, provided it is properly understood, "that there is in God a certain arrangement or economy, which makes no change on the unity of essence."—Tertull. Lib. contra Praxeam.

7. Before proceeding farther, it will be necessary to prove the divinity of the Son and the Holy Spirit. Thereafter, we shall see how they differ from each other. When the Word of God is set before us in the Scriptures, it were certainly most absurd to imagine that it is only a fleeting and evanescent voice, which is sent out into the air, and comes forth beyond God himself, as was the case with the communications made to the patriarchs, and all the prophecies. The reference is rather to the wisdom ever dwelling with God, and by which all oracles and prophecies were inspired. For, as Peter testifies (1 Pet. 1:11), the ancient prophets spake by the Spirit of Christ just as did the apostles, and all who after them were ministers of the heavenly doctrine. But as Christ was not yet manifested, we necessarily understand that the Word was begotten of the Father before all ages. But if that Spirit, whose organs the prophets were, belonged to the Word, the inference

is irresistible, that the Word was truly God. And this is clearly enough shown by Moses in his account of the creation, where he places the Word as intermediate. For why does he distinctly narrate that God, in creating each of his works, said, Let there be this—let there be that, unless that the unsearchable glory of God might shine forth in his image? I know prattlers would easily evade this, by saying that *Word* is used for *order* or *command*; but the apostles are better expositors, when they tell us that the worlds were created by the Son, and that he sustains all things by his mighty word (Heb. 1:2). For we here see that *word* is used for the nod or command of the Son, who is himself the eternal and essential Word of the Father. And no man of sane mind can have any doubt as to Solomon's meaning, when he introduces Wisdom as begotten by God, and presiding at the creation of the world, and all other divine operations (Prov. 8:22). For it were trifling and foolish to imagine any temporary command at a time when God was pleased to execute his fixed and eternal counsel, and something more still mysterious. To this our Saviour's words refer, "My Father worketh hitherto, and I work" (John 5:17). In thus affirming, that from the foundation of the world he constantly worked with the Father, he gives a clearer explanation of what Moses simply touched. The meaning therefore is, that God spoke in such a manner as left the Word his peculiar part in the work, and thus made the operation common to both. But the clearest explanation is given by John, when he states that the Word—which was from the beginning, God and with God, was, together with God the Father, the maker of all things. For he both attributes a substantial and permanent essence to the Word, assigning to it a certain peculiarity, and distinctly showing how God spoke the world into being. Therefore, as all revelations from heaven are duly designated by the title of the Word of God, so the highest place must be assigned to that substantial Word, the source of all inspiration, which, as being liable to no variation, remains for ever one and the same with God, and is God.

8. Here an outcry is made by certain men, who, while they dare not openly deny his divinity, secretly rob him of his eternity. For they contend that the Word only began to be when God opened his sacred mouth in the creation of the world. Thus, with excessive temerity, they imagine some change in the essence of God. For as the names of God, which have respect to external work, began to be ascribed to him from the existence of the work (as when he is called the Creator of heaven and earth), so piety does not recognise or admit any name which might indicate that a change had taken place in God himself. For if any thing adventitious took place, the saying of James would cease to be true, that "every good gift, and every perfect gift, is from above, and cometh down from the Father of lights, with whom is no variableness, neither shadow of turning" (James 1:17). Nothing, therefore, is more intolerable than to fancy a beginning to that Word which was always God, and afterwards was the Creator of the world. But they think they argue acutely, in maintaining that Moses, when he says that God then spoke for the first time, must be held to intimate that till then no Word existed in him. This is the merest trifling. It does not surely follow, that because a thing begins to be manifested at a certain time, it never existed previously. I draw a very different conclusion. Since at the very moment when God said, "Let there be light," the energy of the Word was immediately exerted, it must have existed long before. If any inquire how long, he will find it was without beginning. No certain period of time is defined, when he himself says, "Now O Father, glorify thou me with thine own self with the glory which I had with thee before the world was" (John 17:5). Nor is this omitted by John: for before he descends to the creation of the world, he says, that "in the beginning was the Word, and the Word was with God." We, therefore, again conclude, that the Word was eternally begotten by God, and dwelt with him from everlasting. In this way, his true essence, his eternity, and divinity, are established.

9. But though I am not now treating of the office of the Mediator, having deferred it till the subject of redemption is considered, yet because it ought to be clear and incontrovertible to all, that Christ is that Word become incarnate, this seems the most appropriate place to introduce those passages which assert the Divinity of Christ. When it is said in the forty-fifth Psalm, "Thy throne, O God, is for ever and ever," the Jews quibble that the name Elohim is applied to angels and sovereign powers. But no passage is to be found in Scripture, where an eternal throne is set up for a creature. For he is not called God simply, but also the eternal Ruler. Besides, the title is not conferred on any man, without some addition, as when it is said that Moses would be a God to Pharaoh (Exod. 7:1). Some read as if it were in the genitive case, but this is too insipid. I admit, that anything possessed of singular excellence is often called divine, but it is clear from the context, that this meaning here were harsh and forced, and totally inapplicable. But if their perverseness still refuses to yield, surely there is no obscurity in Isaiah, where Christ is introduced both us God, and as pos-

sessed of supreme powers one of the peculiar attributes of God, "His name shall be called the Mighty God, the Everlasting Father, the Prince of Peace" (Isa. 9:6). Here, too, the Jews object, and invert the passage thus, This is the name by which the mighty God, the Everlasting Father, will call him; so that all which they leave to the Son is, " Prince of Peace." But why should so many epithets be here accumulated on God the Father, seeing the prophet's design is to present the Messiah with certain distinguished properties which may induce us to put our faith in him? There can be no doubt, therefore, that he who a little before was called Emmanuel, is here called the Mighty God. Moreover, there can be nothing clearer than the words of Jeremiah, "This is the name whereby he shall be called, THE LORD OUR RIGHTEOUSNESS" (Jer. 23:6). For as the Jews themselves teach that the other names of God are mere epithets, whereas this, which they call the ineffable name, is substantive, and expresses his essence, we infer, that the only begotten Son is the eternal God, who elsewhere declares, "My glory will I not give to another" (Isa. 42:8). An attempt is made to evade this from the fact, that this name is given by Moses to the altar which he built, and by Ezekiel to the New Jerusalem. But who sees not that the altar was erected as a memorial to show that God was the exalter of Moses, and that the name of God was applied to Jerusalem, merely to testify the Divine presence? For thus the prophet speaks, "The name of the city from that day shall be, The Lord is there" (Ezek. 48:35). In the same way, "Moses built an altar, and called the name of it JEHOVAH-nissi" (Jehovah my exaltation). But it would seem the point is still more keenly disputed as to another passage in Jeremiah, where the same title is applied to Jerusalem in these words, "In those days shall Judah be saved, and Jerusalem shall dwell safely; and this is the name wherewith she shall be called, The Lord our Righteousness." But so far is this passage from being adverse to the truth which we defend, that it rather supports it. The prophet having formerly declared that Christ is the true Jehovah from whom righteousness flows, now declares that the Church would be made so sensible of this as to be able to glory in assuming his very name. In the former passage, therefore, the fountain and cause of righteousness is set down, in the latter, the effect is described.

10. But if this does not satisfy the Jews, I know not what cavils will enable them to evade the numerous passages in which Jehovah is said to have appeared in the form of an Angel (Judges 6:7; 13:16–23, &c). This Angel claims for himself the name of the Eternal God. Should it be alleged that this is done in respect of the office which he bears, the difficulty is by no means solved. No servant would rob God of his honour, by allowing sacrifice to be offered to himself. But the Angel, by refusing to eat bread, orders the sacrifice due to Jehovah to be offered to him. Thus the fact itself proves that he was truly Jehovah. Accordingly, Manoah and his wife infer from the sign, that they had seen not only an angel, but God. Hence Manoah's exclamation, "We shall die; for we have seen the Lord." When the woman replies, "If Jehovah had wished to slay us, he would not have received the sacrifice at our hand," she acknowledges that he who is previously called an angel was certainly God. We may add, that the angel's own reply removes all doubt, "Why do ye ask my name, which is wonderful?" Hence the impiety of Servetus was the more detestable, when he maintained that God was never manifested to Abraham and the Patriarchs, but that an angel was worshipped in his stead. The orthodox doctors of the Church have correctly and wisely expounded, that the Word of God was the supreme angel, who then began, as it were by anticipation, to perform the office of Mediator. For though he were not clothed with flesh, yet he descended as in an intermediate form, that he might have more familiar access to the faithful. This closer intercourse procured for him the name of the Angel; still, however, he retained the character which justly belonged to him—that of the God of ineffable glory. The same thing is intimated by Hosea, who, after mentioning the wrestling of Jacob with the angel, says, "Even the Lord God of hosts; the Lord is his memorial" (Hosea 12:5). Servetus again insinuates that God personated an angel; as if the prophet did not confirm what had been said by Moses, "Wherefore is it that thou dost ask after my name?" (Gen. 32:29, 30). And the confession of the holy Patriarch sufficiently declares that he was not a created angel, but one in whom the fulness of the Godhead dwelt, when he says, "I have seen God face to face." Hence also Paul's statement, that Christ led the people in the wilderness (1 Cor. 10:4. See also Calvin on Acts 7:30, and *infra*, chap. 14, s. 9). Although the time of humiliation had not yet arrived, the eternal Word exhibited a type of the office which he was to fulfil. Again, if the first chapter of Zechariah (ver. 9, &c). and the second (ver. 3, &c). be candidly considered, it will be seen that the angel who sends the other angel is immediately after declared to be the Lord of hosts, and that supreme power is ascribed to him. I omit numberless passages in which our faith rests secure, though they may not have much weight with the Jews. For when it is said in Isaiah, "Lo, this is our

God; we have waited for him, and he will save us; this is the Lord: we have waited for him, we will be glad and rejoice in his salvation" (Isa. 25:9), even the blind may see that the God referred to is he who again rises up for the deliverance of his people. And the emphatic description, twice repeated, precludes the idea that reference is made to any other than to Christ. Still clearer and stronger is the passage of Malachi, in which a promise is made that the messenger who was then expected would come to his own temple (Mal. 3:1). The temple certainly was dedicated to Almighty God only, and yet the prophet claims it for Christ. Hence it follows, that he is the God who was always worshipped by the Jews.

11. The New Testament teems with innumerable passages, and our object must therefore be, the selection of a few, rather than an accumulation of the whole. But though the Apostles spoke of him after his appearance in the flesh as Mediator, every passage which I adduce will be sufficient to prove his eternal Godhead. And the first thing deserving of special observation is that predictions concerning the eternal God are applied to Christ, as either already fulfilled in him, or to be fulfilled at some future period. Isaiah prophesies, that "the Lord of Hosts" shall be "for a stone of stumbling, and for a rock of offence" (Isa. 8:14). Paul asserts that this prophecy was fulfilled in Christ (Rom. 9:33), and, therefore, declares that Christ is that Lord of Hosts. In like manner, he says in another passage, "We shall all stand before the Judgment-seat of Christ. For it is written, As I live, saith the Lord, every knee shall bow to me, and every tongue shall confess to God." Since in Isaiah God predicts this of himself (Isa. 45:23), and Christ exhibits the reality fulfilled in himself, it follows that he is the very God, whose glory cannot be given to another. It is clear also, that the passage from the Psalms (Ps. 68:19) which he quotes in the Epistle to the Ephesians, is applicable only to God, "When he ascended up on high, he led captivity captive" (Eph. 4:8). Understanding that such an ascension was shadowed forth when the Lord exerted his power, and gained a glorious victory over heathen nations, he intimates that what was thus shadowed was more fully manifested in Christ. So John testifies that it was the glory of the Son which was revealed to Isaiah in a vision (John 12:41; Isa. 6:4), though Isaiah himself expressly says that what he saw was the Majesty of God. Again, there can be no doubt that those qualities which, in the Epistle to the Hebrews, are applied to the Son, are the brightest attributes of God, "Thou, Lord, in the beginning hast laid the foundation of the earth," &c., and, "Let all the angels of God worship him" (Heb. 1:10, 6). And yet he does not pervert the passages in thus applying them to Christ, since Christ alone performed the things which these passages celebrate. It was he who arose and pitied Zion—he who claimed for himself dominion over all nations and islands. And why should John have hesitated to ascribe the Majesty of God to Christ, after saying in his preface that the Word was God? (John 1:14). Why should Paul have feared to place Christ on the Judgment-seat of God (2 Cor. 5:10), after he had so openly proclaimed his divinity, when he said that he was God over all, blessed for ever? And to show how consistent he is in this respect, he elsewhere says that "God was manifest in the flesh" (1 Tim. 3:16). If he is God blessed for ever, he therefore it is to whom alone, as Paul affirms in another place, all glory and honour is due. Paul does not disguise this, but openly exclaims, that "being in the form of God (he) thought it not robbery to be equal with God, but made himself of no reputation" (Phil. 2:6). And lest the wicked should glamour and say that he was a kind of spurious God, John goes farther, and affirms, "This is the true God, and eternal life." Though it ought to be enough for us that he is called God, especially by a witness who distinctly testifies that we have no more gods than one, Paul says, "Though there be that are called gods, whether in heaven or in earth (as there be gods many, and lords many), but to us there is but one God" (1 Cor. 8:5, 6). When we hear from the same lips that God was manifest in the flesh, that God purchased the Church with his own blood, why do we dream of any second God, to whom he makes not the least allusion? And there is no room to doubt that all the godly entertained the same view. Thomas, by addressing him as his Lord and God, certainly professes that he was the only God whom he had ever adored (John 20:28).

12. The divinity of Christ, if judged by the works which are ascribed to him in Scripture, becomes still more evident. When he said of himself, "My Father worketh hitherto, and I work," the Jews, though most dull in regard to his other sayings, perceived that he was laying claim to divine power. And, therefore, as John relates (John 5:17), they sought the more to kill him, because he not only broke the Sabbath, but also said that God was his Father, making himself equal with God. What, then, will be our stupidity if we do not perceive from the same passage that his divinity is plainly instructed? To govern the world by his power and providence, and regulate all things by an energy inherent in himself (this an Apostle ascribes to him, Heb. 1:3), surely belongs

to none but the Creator. Nor does he merely share the government of the world with the Father, but also each of the other offices, which cannot be communicated to creatures. The Lord proclaims by his prophets "I, even I, am he that blotteth out thy transgressions for mine own sake" (Is. 43:25). When, in accordance with this declaration, the Jews thought that injustice was done to God when Christ forgave sins, he not only asserted, in distinct terms, that this power belonged to him, but also proved it by a miracle (Mt. 9:6). We thus see that he possessed in himself not the ministry of forgiving sins, but the inherent power which the Lord declares he will not give to another. What! Is it not the province of God alone to penetrate and interrogate the secret thoughts of the heart? But Christ also had this power, and therefore we infer that Christ is God.

13. How clearly and transparently does this appear in his miracles? I admit that similar and equal miracles were performed by the prophets and apostles; but there is this very essential difference, that they dispensed the gifts of God as his ministers, whereas he exerted his own inherent might. Sometimes, indeed, he used prayer, that he might ascribe glory to the Father, but we see that for the most part his own proper power is displayed. And how should not he be the true author of miracles, who, of his own authority, commissions others to perform them? For the Evangelist relates that he gave power to the apostles to cast out devils, cure the lepers, raise the dead, &c. And they, by the mode in which they performed this ministry, showed plainly that their whole power was derived from Christ. "In the name of Jesus Christ of Nazareth," says Peter (Acts 3:6), "rise up and walk." It is not surprising, then, that Christ appealed to his miracles in order to subdue the unbelief of the Jews, inasmuch as these were performed by his own energy, and therefore bore the most ample testimony to his divinity.

Again, if out of God there is no salvation, no righteousness, no life, Christ, having all these in himself, is certainly God. Let no one object that life or salvation is transfused into him by God. For it is said not that he received, but that he himself is salvation. And if there is none good but God, how could a mere man be pure, how could he be, I say not good and just, but goodness and justice? Then what shall we say to the testimony of the Evangelist, that from the very beginning of the creation "in him was life, and this life was the light of men?" Trusting to such proofs, we can boldly put our hope and faith in him, though we know it is blasphemous impiety to confide in any creature. "Ye believe in God," says he, "believe also in me" (John 14:1). And so Paul (Rom. 10:11, and 15:12) interprets two passages of Isaiah "Whose believeth in him shall not be confounded" (Isa. 28:16); and, "In that day there shall be a root of Jesse, which shall stand for an ensign of the people; to it shall the Gentiles seek" (Isa. 11:10). But why adduce more passages of Scripture on this head, when we so often meet with the expression, "He that believeth in me has eternal life?"

Again, the prayer of faith is addressed to him—prayer, which specially belongs to the divine majesty, if anything so belongs. For the Prophet Joel says, "And it shall come to pass, that whosoever shall call on the name of the Lord (Jehovah) shall be delivered" (Joel 2:32). And another says, "The name of the Lord (Jehovah) is a strong tower; the righteous runneth into it and is safe" (Prov. 18:10). But the name of Christ is invoked for salvation, and therefore it follows that he is Jehovah. Moreover, we have an example of invocation in Stephen, when he said, "Lord Jesus, receive my spirit;" and thereafter in the whole Church, when Ananias says in the same book, "Lord, I have heard by many of this man, how much evil he has done to thy saints at Jerusalem; and here he has authority from the chief priests to bind all that call on thy name" (Acts 9:13, 14). And to make it more clearly understood that in Christ dwelt the whole fulness of the Godhead bodily, the Apostle declares that the only doctrine which he professed to the Corinthians, the only doctrine which he taught, was the knowledge of Christ (1 Cor. 2:2). Consider what kind of thing it is, and how great, that the name of the Son alone is preached to us, though God command us to glory only in the knowledge of himself (Jer. 9:24). Who will dare to maintain that he, whom to know forms our only ground of glorying, is a mere creature? To this we may add, that the salutations prefixed to the Epistles of Paul pray for the same blessings from the Son as from the Father. By this we are taught, not only that the blessings which our heavenly Father bestows come to us through his intercession, but that by a partnership in power, the Son himself is their author. This practical knowledge is doubtless surer and more solid than any idle speculation. For the pious soul has the best view of God, and may almost be said to handle him, when it feels that it is quickened, enlightened, saved, justified, and sanctified by him.

14. In asserting the divinity of the Spirit, the proof must be derived from the same sources. And it is by no means an obscure testimony which Moses bears in the history of the creation, when he says that the Spirit of God was expanded over the abyss or shapeless matter;

for it shows not only that the beauty which the world displays is maintained by the invigorating power of the Spirit, but that even before this beauty existed the Spirit was at work cherishing the confused mass. Again, no cavils can explain away the force of what Isaiah says, "And now the Lord God, and his Spirit, has sent me" (Isa. 48:16), thus ascribing a share in the sovereign power of sending the prophets to the Holy Spirit. (Calvin in Acts 20:28). In this his divine majesty is clear.

But, as I observed, the best proof to us is our familiar experience. For nothing can be more alien from a creature, than the office which the Scriptures ascribe to him, and which the pious actually feel him discharging,—his being diffused over all space, sustaining, invigorating, and quickening all things, both in heaven and on the earth. The mere fact of his not being circumscribed by any limits raises him above the rank of creatures, while his transfusing vigour into all things, breathing into them being, life, and motion, is plainly divine. Again, if regeneration to incorruptible life is higher, and much more excellent than any present quickening, what must be thought of him by whose energy it is produced? Now, many passages of Scripture show that he is the author of regeneration, not by a borrowed, but by an intrinsic energy; and not only so, but that he is also the author of future immortality. In short, all the peculiar attributes of the Godhead are ascribed to him in the same way as to the Son. He searches the deep things of Gods and has no counsellor among the creatures; he bestows wisdom and the faculty of speech, though God declares to Moses (Exod. 4:11) that this is his own peculiar province. In like manner, by means of him we become partakers of the divine nature, so as in a manner to feel his quickening energy within us. Our justification is his work; from him is power, sanctification, truth, grace, and every good thought, since it is from the Spirit alone that all good gifts proceed. Particular attention is due to Paul's expression, that though there are diversities of gifts, "all these worketh that one and the self-same Spirit" (1 Cor. 12:11), he being not only the beginning or origin, but also the author; as is even more clearly expressed immediately after in these words "dividing to every man severally as he will." For were he not something subsisting in God, will and arbitrary disposal would never be ascribed to him. Most clearly, therefore does Paul ascribe divine power to the Spirit, and demonstrate that he dwells hypostatically in God.

15. Nor does the Scripture, in speaking of him, withhold the name of God. Paul infers that we are the temple of God, from the fact that "the Spirit of God dwelleth in us" (1 Cor. 3:16; 6:19; and 2 Cor. 6:16). Now it ought not to be slightly overlooked, that all the promises which God makes of choosing us to himself as a temple, receive their only fulfilment by his Spirit dwelling in us. Surely, as it is admirably expressed by Augustine (Ad Maximinum, Ep. 66), "were we ordered to make a temple of wood and stone to the Spirit, inasmuch as such worship is due to God alone, it would be a clear proof of the Spirit's divinity; how much clearer a proof in that we are not to make a temple to him, but to be ourselves that temple." And the Apostle says at one time that we are the temple of God, and at another time, in the same sense, that we are the temple of the Holy Spirit. Peter, when he rebuked Ananias for having lied to the Holy Spirit, said, that he had not lied unto men, but unto God. And when Isaiah had introduced the Lord of Hosts as speaking, Paul says, it was the Holy Spirit that spoke (Acts 28:25, 26). Nay, words uniformly said by the prophets to have been spoken by the Lord of Hosts, are by Christ and his apostles ascribed to the Holy Spirit. Hence it follows that the Spirit is the true Jehovah who dictated the prophecies. Again, when God complains that he was provoked to anger by the stubbornness of the people, in place of Him, Isaiah says that his Holy Spirit was grieved (Isa. 63:10). Lastly, while blasphemy against the Spirit is not forgiven, either in the present life or that which is to come, whereas he who has blasphemed against the Son may obtain pardon, that majesty must certainly be divine which it is an inexpiable crime to offend or impair. I designedly omit several passages which the ancient fathers adduced. They thought it plausible to quote from David, "By the word of the Lord were the heavens made, and all the host of them by the breath (Spirit) of his mouth" (Ps. 33:6), in order to prove that the world was not less the work of the Holy Spirit than of the Son. But seeing it is usual in the Psalms to repeat the same thing twice, and in Isaiah the *spirit* (breath) of the mouth is equivalent to *word*, that proof was weak; and, accordingly, my wish has been to advert briefly to those proofs on which pious minds may securely rest.

16. But as God has manifested himself more clearly by the advent of Christ, so he has made himself more familiarly known in three persons. Of many proofs let this one suffice. Paul connects together these three, God, Faith, and Baptism, and reasons from the one to the other—viz. because there is one faith he infers that there is one God; and because there is one baptism he infers that there is one faith. Therefore, if by baptism we are initiated into the faith and worship of one God, we must

of necessity believe that he into whose name we are baptised is the true God. And there cannot be a doubt that our Saviour wished to testify, by a solemn rehearsal, that the perfect light of faith is now exhibited, when he said, "Go and teach all nations, baptising them in the name of the Father, and of the Son, and of the Holy Spirit" (Mt. 28:19), since this is the same thing as to be baptised into the name of the one God, who has been fully manifested in the Father, the Son, and the Spirit. Hence it plainly appears, that the three persons, in whom alone God is known, subsist in the Divine essence. And since faith certainly ought not to look hither and thither, or run up and down after various objects, but to look, refer, and cleave to God alone, it is obvious that were there various kinds of faith, there behaved also to be various gods. Then, as the baptism of faith is a sacrament, its unity assures us of the unity of God. Hence also it is proved that it is lawful only to be baptised into one God, because we make a profession of faith in him in whose name we are baptised. What, then, is our Saviour's meaning in commanding baptism to be administered in the name of the Father, and the Son, and the Holy Spirit, if it be not that we are to believe with one faith in the name of the Father, and the Son, and the Holy Spirit? But is this any thing else than to declare that the Father, Son, and Spirit, are one God? Wherefore, since it must be held certain that there is one God, not more than one, we conclude that the Word and Spirit are of the very essence of God. Nothing could be more stupid than the trifling of the Arians, who, while acknowledging the divinity of the Son, denied his divine essence. Equally extravagant were the ravings of the Macedonians, who insisted that by the Spirit were only meant the gifts of grace poured out upon men. For as wisdom understanding, prudence, fortitude, and the fear of the Lord, proceed from the Spirit, so he is the one Spirit of wisdom, prudence, fortitude, and piety. He is not divided according to the distribution of his gifts, but, as the Apostle assures us (1 Cor. 12:11), however they be divided, he remains one and the same.

17. On the other hand, the Scriptures demonstrate that there is some distinction between the Father and the Word, the Word and the Spirit; but the magnitude of the mystery reminds us of the great reverence and soberness which ought to he employed in discussing it. It seems to me, that nothing can be more admirable than the words of Gregory Nanzianzen: "Οὐ φθάνω τὸ ἓν νοῆσαι, καὶ τοῖς τρισὶ περιλάμπομαι οὐ φθάνω τὰ τρία διελεῖν καὶ εἰς τὸ ἓν ἀναφέρομαι" (Greg. Nanzian. in Serm. de Sacro Baptis.). "I cannot think of the unity without being irradiated by the Trinity: I cannot distinguish between the Trinity without being carried up to the unity." Therefore, let us beware of imagining such a Trinity of persons as will distract our thoughts, instead of bringing them instantly back to the unity. The words Father, Son, and Holy Spirit, certainly indicate a real distinction, not allowing us to suppose that they are merely epithets by which God is variously designated from his works. Still they indicate distinction only, not division. The passages we have already quoted show that the Son has a distinct subsistence from the Father, because the Word could not have been with God unless he were distinct from the Father; nor but for this could he have had his glory with the Father. In like manner, Christ distinguishes the Father from himself when he says that there is another who bears witness of him (John 5:32; 8:16). To the same effect is it elsewhere said, that the Father made all things by the Word. This could not be, if he were not in some respect distinct from him. Besides, it was not the Father that descended to the earth, but he who came forth from the Father; nor was it the Father that died and rose again, but he whom the Father had sent. This distinction did not take its beginning at the incarnation: for it is clear that the only begotten Son previously existed in the bosom of the Father (John 1:18). For who will dare to affirm that the Son entered his Father's bosom for the first time, when he came down from heaven to assume human nature? Therefore, he was previously in the bosom of the Father, and had his glory with the Father. Christ intimates the distinction between the Holy Spirit and the Father, when he says that the Spirit proceedeth from the Father, and between the Holy Spirit and himself, when he speaks of him as another as he does when he declares that he will send another Comforter; and in many other passages besides (John 14:6; 15:26; 14:16).

18. I am not sure whether it is expedient to borrow analogies from human affairs to express the nature of this distinction. The ancient fathers sometimes do so, but they at the same time admits that what they bring forward as analogous is very widely different. And hence it is that I have a great dread of any thing like presumption here, lest some rash saying may furnish an occasion of calumny to the malicious, or of delusion to the unlearned. It were unbecoming, however, to say nothing of a distinction which we observe that the Scriptures have pointed out. This distinction is, that to the Father is attributed the beginning of action, the fountain and source of all things; to the Son, wisdom, counsel, and arrangement in action, while the energy and efficacy of action is assigned to the

Spirit. Moreover, though the eternity of the Father is also the eternity of the Son and Spirit, since God never could be without his own wisdom and energy; and though in eternity there can be no room for first or last, still the distinction of order is not unmeaning or superfluous, the Father being considered first, next the Son from him, and then the Spirit from both. For the mind of every man naturally inclines to consider, first, God, secondly, the wisdom emerging from him, and, lastly, the energy by which he executes the purposes of his counsel. For this reason, the Son is said to be of the Father only; the Spirit of both the Father and the Son. This is done in many passages, but in none more clearly than in the eighth chapter to the Romans, where the same Spirit is called indiscriminately the Spirit of Christ, and the Spirit of him who raised up Christ from the dead. And not improperly. For Peter also testifies (1 Pet. 1:21), that it was the Spirit of Christ which inspired the prophets, though the Scriptures so often say that it was the Spirit of God the Father.

19. Moreover, this distinction is so far from interfering with the most perfect unity of God, that the Son may thereby be proved to be one God with the Father, inasmuch as he constitutes one Spirit with him, and that the Spirit is not different from the Father and the Son, inasmuch as he is the Spirit of the Father and the Son. In each hypostasis the whole nature is understood the only difference being that each has his own peculiar subsistence. The whole Father is in the Son, and the whole Son in the Father, as the Son himself also declares (John 14:10), "I am in the Father, and the Father in me;" nor do ecclesiastical writers admit that the one is separated from the other by any difference of essence. "By those names which denote distinctions" says Augustine "is meant the relation which they mutually bear to each other, not the very substance by which they are one." In this way, the sentiments of the Fathers, which might sometimes appear to be at variance with each other, are to be reconciled. At one time they teach that the Father is the beginning of the Son, at another they assert that the Son has both divinity and essence from himself, and therefore is one beginning with the Father. The cause of this discrepancy is well and clearly explained by Augustine, when he says, "Christ, as to himself, is called God, as to the Father he is called Son." And again, "The Father, as to himself, is called God, as to the Son he is called Father. He who, as to the Son, is called Father, is not Son; and he who, as to himself, is called Father, and he who, as to himself, is called Son, is the same God." Therefore, when we speak of the Son simply, without reference to the Father, we truly and properly affirm that he is of himself, and, accordingly, call him the only beginning; but when we denote the relation which he bears to the Father, we correctly make the Father the beginning of the Son. Augustine's fifth book on the Trinity is wholly devoted to the explanation of this subject. But it is far safer to rest contented with the relation as taught by him, than get bewildered in vain speculation by subtle prying into a sublime mystery.

20. Let those, then, who love soberness, and are contented with the measure of faith, briefly receive what is useful to be known. It is as follows:—When we profess to believe in one God, by the name God is understood the one simple essence, comprehending three persons or hypostases; and, accordingly, whenever the name of God is used indefinitely, the Son and Spirit, not less than the Father, is meant. But when the Son is joined with the Father, relation comes into view, and so we distinguish between the Persons. But as the Personal subsistence carry an order with them, the principle and origin being in the Father, whenever mention is made of the Father and Son, or of the Father and Spirit together, the name of God is specially given to the Father. In this way the unity of essence is retained, and respect is had to the order, which, however derogates in no respect from the divinity of the Son and Spirit. And surely since we have already seen how the apostles declare the Son of God to have been He whom Moses and the prophets declared to be Jehovah, we must always arrive at a unity of essence. We, therefore, hold it detestable blasphemy to call the Son a different God from the Father, because the simple name God admits not of relation, nor can God, considered in himself, be said to be this or that. Then, that the name Jehovah, taken indefinitely, may be applied to Christ, is clear from the words of Paul, "For this thing I besought the Lord thrice." After giving the answer, "My grace is sufficient for thee," he subjoins, "that the power of Christ may rest upon me" (2 Cor. 12:8, 9). For it is certain that the name of Lord (Κυρίος) is there put for Jehovah, and, therefore, to restrict it to the person of the Mediator were puerile and frivolous, the words being used absolutely, and not with the view of comparing the Father and the Son. And we know that, in accordance with the received usage of the Greeks, the apostles uniformly substitute the word Κυρίος for Jehovah. Not to go far for an example, Paul besought the Lord in the same sense in which Peter quotes the passage of Joel, "Whosoever shall call upon the name of the Lord shall be saved" (Acts 2:21; Joel 2:28). Where this name is specially applied to the Son, there is a

different ground for it, as will be seen in its own place; at present it is sufficient to remember, that Paul, after praying to God absolutely, immediately subjoins the name of Christ. Thus, too, the Spirit is called God absolutely by Christ himself. For nothing prevents us from holding that he is the entire spiritual essence of God, in which are comprehended Father, Son, and Spirit. This is plain from Scripture. For as God is there called a Spirit, so the Holy Spirit also, in so far as he is a hypostasis of the whole essence, is said to be both of God and from God.

21. But since Satan, in order to pluck up our faith by the roots, has always provoked fierce disputes, partly concerning the divine essence of the Son and Spirit, and partly concerning the distinction of persons; since in almost every age he has stirred up impious spirits to vex the orthodox doctors on this head, and is attempting in the present day to kindle a new flame out of the old embers, it will be proper here to dispose of some of these perverse dreams. Hitherto our chief object has been to stretch out our hand for the guidance of such as are disposed to learn, not to war with the stubborn and contentious; but now the truth which was calmly demonstrated must be vindicated from the calumnies of the ungodly. Still, however it will be our principal study to provide a sure footing for those whose ears are open to the word of God. Here, if any where, in considering the hidden mysteries of Scripture, we should speculate soberly and with great moderation, cautiously guarding against allowing either our mind or our tongue to go a step beyond the confines of God's word. For how can the human minds which has not yet been able to ascertain of what the body of the sun consists, though it is daily presented to the eye, bring down the boundless essence of God to its little measure? Nay, how can it, under its own guidance, penetrate to a knowledge of the substance of God while unable to understand its own? Wherefore, let us willingly leave to God the knowledge of himself. In the words of Hilary (De Trinit. lib. 1), "He alone is a fit witness to himself who is known only by himself." This knowledge, then, if we would leave to God, we must conceive of him as he has made himself known, and in our inquiries make application to no other quarter than his word. On this subject we have five homilies of Chrysostom against the Anomoei (De Incomprehensit. Dei Natura), in which he endeavoured, but in vain, to check the presumption of the sophists, and curb their garrulity. They showed no more modesty here than they are wont to do in everything else. The very unhappy results of their temerity should be a warning to us to bring more docility than acumen to the discussion of this question, never to attempt to search after God anywhere but in his sacred word, and never to speak or think of him farther than we have it for our guide. But if the distinction of Father, Son, and Spirit, subsisting in the one Godhead (certainly a subject of great difficulty), gives more trouble and annoyance to some intellects than is meet, let us remember that the human mind enters a labyrinth whenever it indulges its curiosity, and thus submit to be guided by the divine oracles, how much soever the mystery may be beyond our reach.

22. It were tedious, and to no purpose toilsome, to form a catalogue of the errors by which, in regard to this branch of doctrine, the purity of the faith has been assailed. The greater part of heretics have with their gross deliriums made a general attack on the glory of God, deeming it enough if they could disturb and shake the unwary. From a few individuals numerous sects have sprung up, some of them rending the divine essence, and others confounding the distinction of Persons. But if we hold, what has already been demonstrated from Scripture, that the essence of the one God, pertaining to the Father, Son, and Spirit, is simple and indivisible, and again, that the Father differs in some special property from the Son, and the Son from the Spirit, the door will be shut against Arius and Sabellius, as well as the other ancient authors of error. But as in our day have arisen certain frantic men, such as Servetus and others, who, by new devices, have thrown every thing into confusion, it may be worthwhile briefly to discuss their fallacies.

The name of Trinity was so much disliked, nay detested, by Servetus, that he charged all whom he called Trinitarians with being Atheists. I say nothing of the insulting terms in which he thought proper to make his charges. The sum of his speculations was, that a threefold Deity is introduced wherever three Persons are said to exist in his essence, and that this Triad was imaginary, inasmuch as it was inconsistent with the unity of God. At the same time, he would have it that the Persons are certain external ideas which do not truly subsist in the Divine essence, but only figure God to us under this or that form: that at first, indeed, there was no distinction in God, because originally the Word was the same as the Spirit, but ever since Christ came forth God of God, another Spirit, also a God, had proceeded from him. But although he sometimes cloaks his absurdities in allegory, as when he says that the eternal Word of God was the Spirit of Christ with God, and the reflection of the idea, likewise that the Spirit was a shadow of Deity, he at last reduces the divinity of both to nothing; maintaining that, according to the mode of distribution, there is a part of God as well in the Son as in the Spirit, just as the same Spirit substantially is a portion of God in us, and also in wood and stone. His absurd babbling concerning the person of the Mediator will be seen in its own place.

The monstrous fiction that a Person is nothing else than a visible appearance of the glory of God, needs not a long refutation. For when John declares that before the world was created the Logos was God (John 1:1), he shows that he was something very different from an idea. But if even then, and from the remotest eternity, that Logos, who was God, was with the Father, and had his own distinct and peculiar glory with the Father (John 17:5), he certainly could not be an external or figurative splendour, but must necessarily have been a hypostasis which dwelt inherently in God himself. But although there is no mention made of the Spirit antecedent to the account of the creation, he is not there introduced as a shadow, but as the essential power of God, where Moses relates that the shapeless mass was unborn by him (Gen. 1:2). It is obvious that the eternal Spirit always existed in God, seeing he cherished and sustained the confused materials of heaven and earth before they possessed order or beauty. Assuredly he could not then be an image or representation of God, as Servetus dreams. But he is elsewhere forced to make a more open disclosure of his impiety when he says, that God by his eternal reason decreeing a Son to himself, in this way assumed a visible appearance. For if this be true, no other Divinity is left to Christ than is implied in his having been ordained a Son by God's eternal decree. Moreover, those phantoms which Servetus substitutes for the hypostases he so transforms as to make new changes in God. But the most execrable heresy of all is his confounding both the Son and Spirit promiscuously with all the creatures. For he distinctly asserts, that there are parts and partitions in the essence of God, and that every such portion is God. This he does especially when he says, that the spirits of the faithful are co-eternal and consubstantial with God, although he elsewhere assigns a substantial divinity, not only to the soul of man, but to all created things.

23. This pool has bred another monster not unlike the former. For certain restless spirits, unwilling to share the disgrace and obloquy of the impiety of Servetus, have confessed that there were indeed three Persons, but added, as a reason, that the Father, who alone is truly and properly God, transfused his Divinity into the Son and Spirit when he formed them. Nor do they refrain from expressing themselves in such shocking terms as these: that the Father is essentially distinguished from the Son and Spirit by this; that he is the only *essentiator*. Their first pretext for this is, that Christ is uniformly called the Son of God. From this they infer, that there is no proper God but the Father. But they forget, that although the name of God is common also to the Son, yet it is sometimes, by way of excellence, ascribed to the Father, as being the source and principle of Divinity; and this is done in order to mark the simple unity of essence. They object, that if the Son is truly God, he must be deemed the Son of a person: which is absurd. I answer, that both are true; namely, that he is the Son of God, because he is the Word, begotten of the Father before all ages; (for we are not now speaking of the Person of the Mediator), and yet, that for the purpose of explanation, regard must be had to the Person, so that the name God may not be understood in its absolute sense, but as equivalent to Father. For if we hold that there is no other God than the Fathers this rank is clearly denied to the Son.

In every case where the Godhead is mentioned, we are by no means to admit that there is an antithesis between the Father and the Son, as if to the former only the name of God could competently be applied. For assuredly, the God who appeared to Isaiah was the one true God, and yet John declares that he was Christ (Isa. 6; John 12:41). He who declared, by the mouth of Isaiah, that he was to be "for a stone of stumbling" to the Jews, was the one God; and yet Paul declares that he was Christ (Isa. 8:14; Rom. 9:33). He who proclaims by Isaiah, "Unto me every knee shall bow," is the one God; yet Paul again explains that he is Christ (Isa. 45:23; Rom. 14:11). To this we may add the passages quoted by an Apostle, "Thou, Lord, hast laid the foundations of the earth;" "Let all the angels of God worship him" (Heb. 1:10; 10:6; Ps. 102:26; 97:7). All these apply to the one God; and yet the Apostle contends that they are the proper attributes of Christ. There is nothing in the cavil, that what properly applies to God is transferred to Christ, because he is the brightness of his glory. Since the name of Jehovah is everywhere applied to Christ, it follows that, in regard to Deity, he is of himself. For if he is Jehovah, it is impossible to deny that he is the same God who elsewhere proclaims by Isaiah, "I am the first, and I am the last; and beside me there is no God" (Is. 44:6). We would also do well to ponder the words of Jeremiah, "The gods that have not made the heavens and the earth, even they shall perish from the earth and from under these heavens" (Jer. 10:11); whence it follows conversely, that He whose divinity Isaiah repeatedly proves from the creation of the world, is none other than the Son of God. And how is it possible that the Creator, who gives to all should not be of himself, but should borrow his essence from another? Whosoever says that the Son was *essentiated* by the Father, denies his selfexistence. Against this, however, the Holy Spirit protests, when he calls him Jehovah. On the supposition, then, that the whole essence is in the Father only, the essence becomes divisible, or is denied to the Son, who, being thus robbed of his essences will be only a titular God. If we are to believe these triflers, divine essence belongs to the Father only, on the ground that he is sole God, and *essentiator* of the Son. In this way, the divinity of the Son will be something abstracte from the essence of God, or the derivation of a part from the whole. On the same principle it must also be conceded, that the Spirit belongs to the Father only. For if the derivation is from the primary essence which is proper to none but the Father, the Spirit cannot justly be deemed the Spirit of the Son. This view, however, is refuted by the testimony of Paul, when he makes the Spirit common both to Christ and the Father. Moreover, if the Person of the Father is expunged from the Trinity, in what will he differ from the Son and Spirit, except in being the only God? They confess that Christ is God, and that he differs from the Father. If he differs, there must be some mark of distinction between them. Those who place it in the essence, manifestly reduce the true divinity of Christ to nothing, since divinity cannot exist without essence, and indeed without entire essence. The Father certainly cannot differ from the Son, unless he have something peculiar to himself, and not common to him with the Son. What, then, do these men show as the mark of distinction? If it is in the essence, let them tell whether or not he communicated essence to the Son. This he could not do in part merely, for it were impious to think of a divided God. And besides, on this supposition, there would be a rending of the Divine essence. The whole entire essence must therefore be common to the Father and the Son; and if so, in respect of essence there is no distinction between them. If they reply that the Father, while essentiating, still remains the only God, being the possessor of the essence, then Christ will be a figurative God, one in name or semblance only, and not in reality, because no property can be more peculiar to God than essence, according to the words, "I Am hath sent me unto you" (Ex. 3:4).

24. The assumption, that whenever God is mentioned absolutely, the Father only is meant, may be proved erroneous by many passages. Even in those which they quote in support of their views they betray a lamentable inconsistency because the name of Son occurs there by way of contrast, showing that the other name God is used relatively, and in that way confined to the person of the Father. Their objection may be disposed of in a single word. Were not the Father alone the true God, he would, say they, be his own Father. But there is nothing absurd in the name of God being specially applied, in respect of order and degree, to him who not only of himself begat his own wisdom, but is the God of the Mediator, as I will more fully show in its own place. For ever since Christ was manifested in the flesh he is called the Son of God, not only because begotten of the Father before all worlds he was the Eternal Word, but because he undertook the person and office of the Mediator that he might unite us to God. Seeing they are so bold in excluding the Son from the honour of God, I would fain know whether, when he declares that there is "none good but one, that is, God," he deprives himself of goodness. I speak not of his human nature, lest perhaps they should object, that whatever goodness was in it was derived by gratuitous gift: I ask whether the Eternal Word of God is good, yes or no? If they say no, their impiety is manifest; if yes, they refute themselves. Christ's seeming at the first glance to disclaim the name of good (Mt. 19:17), rather confirms our view. Goodness being the special property of God alone, and yet being at the time applied to him in the ordinary way of salutation, his rejection of false honour intimates that the goodness in which he excels is Divine. Again, I ask whether, when Paul affirms that God alone is "immortal," "wise, and true" (1 Tim. 1:17), he reduces Christ to the rank of beings mortal, foolish, and false. Is not he immortal, who, from the beginning, had life so as to bestow immortality on angels? Is not he wise who is the eternal wisdom of God? Is not he true who is truth itself?

I ask, moreover, whether they think Christ should be worshipped. If he claims justly, that every knee shall bow to him, it follows that he is the God who, in the law, forbade worship to be offered to any but himself. If they insist on applying to the Father only the words of Isaiah, "I am, and besides me there is none else" (Is. 44:6), I turn the passage against themselves, since we see that every property of God is attributed to Christ. There is no room for the cavil that Christ was exalted in the flesh in which he humbled himself, and in respect of which all power is given to him in heaven and on earth. For although the majesty of King and Judge extends to the whole person of the Mediator, yet had he not been God manifested in the flesh, he could not have been exalted to such a height without coming into collision with God. And the dispute is admirably settled by Paul, when he declares that he was equal with God before he humbled himself, and assumed the form of a servants (Phil. 2:6, 7). Moreover, how could such equality exist, if he were not that God whose name is Jah and Jehovah, who rides upon the cherubim, is King of all the earth, and King of ages? Let them glamour as they may, Christ cannot be robbed of the honour described by Isaiah, "Lo, this is our God; we have waited for him" (Is. 25:9); for these words describe the advent of God the Redeemer, who was not only to bring back the people from Babylonish captivity, but restore the Church, and make her completely perfect.

Nor does another cavil avail them, that Christ was God in his Father. For though we admit that, in respect of order and gradation, the beginning of divinity is in the Father, we hold it a detestable fiction to maintain that essence is proper to the Father alone, as if he were the deifier of the Son. On this view either the essence is manifold, or Christ is God only in name and imagination. If they grant that the Son is God, but only in subordination to the Father, the essence which in the Father is unformed and unbegotten will in him be formed and begotten. I know that many who would be thought wise deride us for extracting the distinction of persons from the words of Moses when he introduces God as saying, "Let us make man in our own image" (Gen. 1:26). Pious readers, however, see how frigidly and absurdly the colloquy were introduced by Moses, if there were not several persons in the Godhead. It is certain that those whom the Father addresses must have been untreated. But nothing is untreated except the one God. Now then, unless they concede that the power of creating was common to the Father, Son, and Spirit, and the power of commanding common, it will follow that God did not speak thus inwardly with himself, but addressed other extraneous architects. In fine, there is a single passage which will at once dispose of these two objections. The declaration of Christ that "God is a Spirit" (John 4:24), cannot be confined to the Father only, as if the Word were not of a spiritual nature. But if the name Spirit applies equally to the Son as to the Father, I infer that under the indefinite name of God the Son is included. He adds immediately after, that the only worshipers approved by the Father are those who worship him in spirit and in truth; and hence I also infer, that because Christ performs the office of teacher under a head, he applies the name God to the Father, not for the purpose of destroying his own Divinity, but for the purpose of raising us up to it as it were step by step.

25. The hallucination consists in dreaming of individuals, each of whom possesses a part of the essence. The Scriptures teach that there is essentially but one God, and, therefore, that the essence both of the Son and Spirit is unbegotten; but inasmuch as the Father is first in order, and of himself begat his own Wisdom, he, as we lately observed, is justly regarded as the principle and fountain of all the Godhead. Thus God, taken indefinitely, is unbegotten, and the Father, in respect of his person, is unbegotten. For it is absurd to imagine that our doctrine gives any ground for alleging that we establish a quaternion of gods. They falsely and calumniously ascribe to us the figment of their own brain, as if we virtually held that three persons emanate from one essence, whereas it is plain, from our writings, that we do not disjoin the persons from the essence, but interpose a distinction between the persons residing in it. If the persons were separated from the essence, there might be some plausibility in their argument; as in this way there would be a trinity of Gods, not of persons comprehended in one God. This affords an answer to their futile question—whether or not the essence concurs in forming the Trinity; as if we imagined that three Gods were derived from it. Their objection, that there would thus be a Trinity without a God, originates in the same absurdity. Although the essence does not contribute to the distinction, as if it were a part or member, the persons are not without it, or external to it; for the Father, if he were not God, could not be the Father; nor could the Son possibly be Son unless he were God. We say, then, that the Godhead is absolutely of itself. And hence also we hold that the Son, regarded as God, and without reference to person, is also of himself; though we also say that, regarded as Son, he is of the Father. Thus his essence is without beginning, while his person has its beginning in God. And, indeed, the orthodox writers who in former times spoke of the Trinity, used this term only with reference to the Persons. To have included the essence in the distinction, would not only have been an absurd error, but gross impiety. For those who class the three thus—Essence, Son, and Spirit—plainly do away with the essence of the Son and Spirit; otherwise the parts being intermingled would merge into each other—a circumstance which would vitiate any distinction. In short, if God and Father were synonymous terms, the Father would be deifier in a sense which would leave the Son nothing but a shadow;

and the Trinity would be nothing more than the union of one God with two creatures.

26. To the objection, that if Christ be properly God, he is improperly called the Son of God, it has been already answered, that when one person is compared with another, the name God is not used indefinitely, but is restricted to the Father, regarded as the beginning of the Godhead, not by *essentiating*, as fanatics absurdly express it, but in respect of order. In this sense are to be understood the words which Christ addressed to the Father, "This is life eternal, that they might know thee the only true God, and Jesus Christ whom thou hast sent" (John 17:3). For speaking in the person of the Mediator, he holds a middle place between God and man; yet so that his majesty is not diminished thereby. For though he humbled (emptied) himself, he did not lose the glory which he had with the Father, though it was concealed from the world. So in the Epistle to the Hebrews (Heb. 1:10; 2:9), though the apostle confesses that Christ was made a little lower than the angels, he at the same time hesitates not to assert that he is the eternal God who founded the earth. We must hold, therefore, that as often as Christ, in the character of Mediator, addresses the Father, he, under the term God, includes his own divinity also. Thus, when he says to the apostles, "It is expedient for you that I go away," "My Father is greater than I," he does not attribute to himself a secondary divinity merely, as if in regard to eternal essence he were inferior to the Father; but having obtained celestial glory, he gathers together the faithful to share it with him. He places the Father in the higher degree, inasmuch as the full perfection of brightness conspicuous in heaven, differs from that measure of glory which he himself displayed when clothed in flesh. For the same reason Paul says, that Christ will restore "the kingdom to God, even the Father," "that God may be all in all" (1 Cor. 15:24, 28). Nothing can be more absurd than to deny the perpetuity of Christ's divinity. But if he will never cease to be the Son of God, but will ever remain the same that he was from the beginning, it follows that under the name of Father the one divine essence common to both is comprehended. And assuredly Christ descended to us for the very purpose of raising us to the Father, and thereby, at the same time, raising us to himself, inasmuch as he is one with the Father. It is therefore erroneous and impious to confine the name of God to the Father, so as to deny it to the Son. Accordingly, John, declaring that he is the true God, has no idea of placing him beneath the Father in a subordinate rank of divinity. I wonder what these fabricators of new gods mean, when they confess that Christ is truly God, and yet exclude him from the godhead of the Father, as if there could be any true God but the one God, or as if transfused divinity were not a mere modern fiction.

27. In the many passages which they collect from Irenæus, in which he maintains that the Father of Christ is the only eternal God of Israel, they betray shameful ignorance, or very great dishonesty. For they ought to have observed, that that holy man was contending against certain frantic persons, who, denying that the Father of Christ was that God who had in old times spoken by Moses and the prophets, held that he was some phantom or other produced from the pollution of the world. His whole object, therefore, is to make it plain, that in the Scriptures no other God is announced but the Father of Christ; that it is wicked to imagine any other. Accordingly, there is nothing strange in his so often concluding that the God of Israel was no other than he who is celebrated by Christ and the apostles. Now, when a different heresy is to be resisted, we also say with truth, that the God who in old times appeared to the fathers, was no other than Christ. Moreover, if it is objected that he was the Father, we have the answer ready, that while we contend for the divinity of the Son, we by no means exclude the Father. When the reader attends to the purpose of Irenæus, the dispute is at an end. Indeed, we have only to look to lib. 3 c. 6, where the pious writer insists on this one point, "that he who in Scripture is called God absolutely and indefinitely, is truly the only God; and that Christ is called God absolutely." Let us remember (as appears from the whole work, and especially from lib. 2 c. 46), that the point under discussion was, that the name of Father is not applied enigmatically and parabolically to one who was not truly God. We may adds that in lib. 3 c. 9, he contends that the Son as well as the Father united was the God proclaimed by the prophets and apostles. He afterwards explains (lib. 3 c. 12) how Christ, who is Lord of all, and King and Judge, received power from him who is God of all, namely, in respect of the humiliation by which he humbled himself, even to the death of the cross. At the same time he shortly after affirms (lib. 3 c. 16), that the Son is the maker of heaven and earth, who delivered the law by the hand of Moses, and appeared to the fathers. Should any babbler now insist that, according to Irenaeus, the Father alone is the God of Israel, I will refer him to a passage in which Irenaeus distinctly says (lib. 3 c. 18, 23), that Christ is ever one and the same, and also applies to Christ the words of the prophecy of Habakkuk, "God cometh from the south." To the same

effect he says (lib. 4 c. 9), "Therefore, Christ himself, with the Father, is the God of the living." And in the 12th chapter of the same book he explains that Abraham believed God, because Christ is the maker of heaven and earth, and very God.

28. With no more truth do they claim Tertullian as a patron. Though his style is sometimes rugged and obscure, he delivers the doctrine which we maintain in no ambiguous manner, namely, that while there is one God, his Word, however, is with dispensation or economy; that there is only one God in unity of substance; but that, nevertheless, by the mystery of dispensation, the unity is arranged into Trinity; that there are three, not in state, but in degree—not in substance, but in form—not in power, but in order. He says indeed that he holds the Son to be second to the Father; but he means that the only difference is by distinction. In one place he says the Son is visible; but after he has discoursed on both views, he declares that he is invisible regarded as the Word. In fine, by affirming that the Father is characterised by his own Person, he shows that he is very far from countenancing the fiction which we refute. And although he does not acknowledge any other God than the Father, yet, explaining himself in the immediate context, he shows that he does not speak exclusively in respect of the Son, because he denies that he is a different God from the Father; and, accordingly, that the one supremacy is not violated by the distinction of Person. And it is easy to collect his meaning from the whole tenor of his discourse. For he contends against Praxeas, that although God has three distinct Persons, yet there are not several gods, nor is unity divided. According to the fiction of Praxeas, Christ could not be God without being the Father also; and this is the reason why Tertullian dwells so much on the distinction. When he calls the Word and Spirit a portion of the whole, the expression, though harsh, may be allowed, since it does not refer to the substance, but only (as Tertullian himself testifies) denotes arrangement and economy which applies to the persons only. Accordingly, he asks, "How many persons, Praxeas, do you think there are, but just as many as there are names for?" In the same way, he shortly after says, "That they may believe the Father and the Son, each in his own name and person." These things, I think, sufficiently refute the effrontery of those who endeavour to blind the simple by pretending the authority of Tertullian.

29. Assuredly, whosoever will compare the writings of the ancient fathers with each other, will not find any thing in Irenaeus different from what is taught by those who come after him. Justin is one of the most ancient, and he agrees with us out and out. Let them object that, by him and others, the Father of Christ is called the one God. The same thing is taught by Hilary, who uses the still harsher expression, that Eternity is in the Father. Is it that he may withhold divine essence from the Son? His whole work is a defence of the doctrine which we maintain; and yet these men are not ashamed to produce some kind of mutilated excerpts for the purpose of persuading us that Hilary is a patron of their heresy. With regard to what they pretend as to Ignatius, if they would have it to be of the least importance, let them prove that the apostles enacted laws concerning Lent, and other corruptions. Nothing can be more nauseating, than the absurdities which have been published under the name of Ignatius; and therefore, the conduct of those who provide themselves with such masks for deception is the less entitled to toleration.

Moreover, the consent of the ancient fathers clearly appears from this, that in the Council of Nice, no attempt was made by Arius to cloak his heresy by the authority of any approved author; and no Greek or Latin writer apologises as dissenting from his predecessors. It cannot be necessary to observe how carefully Augustine, to whom all these miscreants are most violently opposed, examined all ancient writings, and how reverently he embraced the doctrine taught by them (August. lib. de Trinit. &c). He is most scrupulous in stating the grounds on which he is forced to differ from them, even in the minutest point. On this subject, too, if he finds any thing ambiguous or obscure in other writers, he does not disguise it. And he assumes it as an acknowledged fact, that the doctrine opposed by the Arians was received without dispute from the earliest antiquity. At the same time, he was not ignorant of what some others had previously taught. This is obvious from a single expression. When he says (De Doct. Christ. lib. 1). that "unity is in the Father," will they pretend that he then forgot himself? In another passage, he clears away every such charge, when he calls the Father the beginning of the Godhead, as being from none—thus wisely inferring that the name of God is specially ascribed to the Father, because, unless the beginning were from him, the simple unity of essence could not be maintained. I hope the pious reader will admit that I have now disposed of all the calumnies by which Satan has hitherto attempted to pervert or obscure the pure doctrine of faith. The whole substance of the doctrine has, I trust, been faithfully expounded, if my readers will set bounds to their curiosity, and not long more eagerly than they ought for perplexing disputation. I did not undertake to satisfy those who delight in speculate views, but I have not designedly omitted any thing which I thought adverse to me. At the same time, studying the edification of the Church, I have thought it better not to touch on various topics, which could have yielded little profit, while they must have needlessly burdened and fatigued the reader. For instance, what avails it to discuss, as Lombard does at length (lib. 1 dist. 9), Whether or not the Father always generates? This idea of continual generation becomes an absurd fiction from the moment it is seen, that from eternity there were three persons in one God.

CHAPTER 14

IN THE CREATION OF THE WORLD, AND ALL THINGS IN IT, THE TRUE GOD DISTINGUISHED BY CERTAIN MARKS FROM FICTITIOUS GODS.

In this chapter commences the second part of Book First—viz. the knowledge of man. Certain things premised. I. The creation of the world generally (s. 1 and 2). II. The subject of angels considered (s. 3–13). III. Of bad angels or devils (s. 13–20); and, IV. The practical use to be made of the history of the creation (s. 20–22).

Sections:

1. The mere fact of creation should lead us to acknowledge God, but to prevent our falling away to Gentile fictions, God has been pleased to furnish a history of the creation. An impious objection, Why the world was not created sooner? Answer to it. Shrewd saying of an old man.

2. For the same reason, the world was created, not in an instant, but in six days. The order of creation described, showing that Adam was not created until God had, with infinite goodness made ample provision for him.

3. The doctrine concerning angels expounded. 1. That we may learn from them also to acknowledge God. 2. That we may be put on our guard against the errors of the worshippers of angels and the Manichees. Manicheeism refuted. Rule of piety.

4. The angels created by God. At what time and in what order it is inexpedient to inquire. The garrulity of the Pseudo-Dionysius.

5. The nature, offices, and various names of angels.

6. Angels the dispensers of the divine beneficence to us.

7. A kind of prefects over kingdoms and provinces, but specially the guardians of the elect. Not certain that every believer is under the charge of a single angel. Enough, that all angels watch over the safety of the Church.

8. The number and orders of angels not defined. Why angels said to be winged.

9. Angels are ministering spirits and spiritual essences.

10. The heathen error of placing angels on the throne of God refuted. 1. By passages of Scripture.

11. Refutation continued. 2. By inferences from other passages. Why God employs the ministry of angels.

12. Use of the doctrine of Scripture concerning the holy angels.

13. The doctrine concerning bad angels or devils reduced to four heads. 1. That we may guard against their wiles and assaults.

14. That we may be stimulated to exercises of piety. Why one angel in the singular number often spoken of.

15. The devil being described as the enemy of man, we should perpetually war against him.

16. The wickedness of the devil not by creation but by corruption. Vain and useless to inquire into the mode, time, and character of the fall of angels.

17. Though the devil is always opposed in will and endeavour to the will of God, he can do nothing without his permission and consent.

18. God so overrules wicked spirits as to permit them to try the faithful, and rule over the wicked.

19. The nature of bad angels. They are spiritual essences endued with sense and intelligence.

20. The latter part of the chapter briefly embracing the history of creation, and showing what it is of importance for us to know concerning God.

21. The special object of this knowledge is to prevent us, through ingratitude or thoughtlessness, from overlooking the perfections of God. Example of this primary knowledge.

22. Another object of this knowledge—viz. that perceiving how these things were created for our use, we may be excited to trust in God, pray to him, and love him.

1. Although Isaiah justly charges the worshipers of false gods with stupidity, in not learning from the foundations of the earth, and the circle of the heavens, who the true God is (Isa. 40:21); yet so sluggish and grovelling

is our intellect, that it was necessary he should be more clearly depicted, in order that the faithful might not fall away to Gentile fictions. the idea that God is the soul of the world, though the most tolerable that philosophers have suggested, is absurd; and, therefore, it was of importance to furnish us with a more intimate knowledge in order that we might not wander to and fro in uncertainty. Hence God was pleased that a history of the creation should exist—a history on which the faith of the Church might lean without seeking any other God than Him whom Moses sets forth as the Creator and Architect of the world. First, in that history, the period of time is marked so as to enable the faithful to ascend by an unbroken succession of years to the first origin of their race and of all things. This knowledge is of the highest use not only as an antidote to the monstrous fables which anciently prevailed both in Egypt and the other regions of the world, but also as a means of giving a clearer manifestation of the eternity of God as contrasted with the birth of creation, and thereby inspiring us with higher admiration. We must not be moved by the profane jeer, that it is strange how it did not sooner occur to the Deity to create the heavens and the earth, instead of idly allowing an infinite period to pass away, during which thousands of generations might have existed, while the present world is drawing to a close before it has completed its six thousandth year. Why God delayed so long it is neither fit nor lawful to inquire. Should the human mind presume to do it, it could only fail in the attempt, nor would it be useful for us to know what God, as a trial of the modesty of our faith, has been pleased purposely to conceal. It was a shrewd saying of a good old man, who when some one pertly asked in derision what God did before the world was created, answered he made a hell for the inquisitive (August. Confess., lib. 11 c. 12). This reproof, not less weighty than severe, should repress the tickling wantonness which urges many to indulge in vicious and hurtful speculation.

In fine, let us remember that that invisible God, whose wisdom, power, and justice, are incomprehensible, is set before us in the history of Moses as in a mirror, in which his living image is reflected. For as an eye, either dimmed by age or weakened by any other cause, sees nothing distinctly without the aid of glasses, so (such is our imbecility) if Scripture does not direct us in our inquiries after God, we immediately turn vain in our imaginations. Those who now indulge their petulance, and refuse to take warning, will learn, when too late, how much better it had been reverently to regard the secret counsels of God, than to belch forth blasphemies which pollute the face of heaven. Justly does Augustine complain that God is insulted whenever any higher reason than his will is demanded. (Lib. de Gent.). He also in another place wisely reminds us that it is just as improper to raise questions about infinite periods of time as about infinite space. (De Civit. Dei.). However wide the circuit of the heavens may be, it is of some definite extent. But should any one expostulate with God that vacant space remains exceeding creation by a hundred-fold, must not every pious mind detest the presumption? Similar is the madness of those who charge God with idleness in not having pleased them by creating the world countless ages sooner than he did create it. In their cupidity they affect to go beyond the world, as if the ample circumference of heaven and earth did not contain objects numerous and resplendent enough to absorb all our senses; as if, in the period of six thousand years, God had not furnished facts enough to exercise our minds in ceaseless meditation. Therefore, let us willingly remain hedged in by those boundaries within which God has been pleased to confine our persons, and, as it were, enclose our minds, so as to prevent them from losing themselves by wandering unrestrained.

2. With the same view Moses relates that the work of creation was accomplished not in one moment, but in six days. By this statement we are drawn away from fiction to the one God who thus divided his work into six days, that we may have no reluctance to devote our whole lives to the contemplation of it. For though our eyes, in what direction soever they turn, are forced to behold the works of God, we see how fleeting our attention is, and holy quickly pious thoughts, if any arise, vanish away. Here, too, objection is taken to these progressive steps as inconsistent with the power of God, until human reason is subdued to the obedience of faith, and learns to welcome the calm quiescence to which the sanctification of the seventh day invited us. In the very order of events, we ought diligently to ponder on the paternal goodness of God toward the human race, in not creating Adam until he had liberally enriched the earth with all good things. Had he placed him on an earth barren and unfurnished; had he given life before light, he might have seemed to pay little regard to his interest. But now that he has arranged the motions of the sun and stars for man's use, has replenished the air, earth, and water, with living creatures, and produced all kinds of fruit in abundance for the supply of food, by performing the office of a provident and industrious head of a family, he has

shown his wondrous goodness toward us. These subjects, which I only briefly touch, if more attentively pondered, will make it manifest that Moses was a sure witness and herald of the one only Creator. I do not repeat what I have already explained—viz. that mention is here made not of the bare essence of God, but that his eternal Wisdom and Spirit are also set before us, in order that we may not dream of any other God than Him who desires to be recognised in that express image.

3. But before I begin to treat more fully of the nature of man (chap. 15 and B. 2 c. 1), it will be proper to say something of angels. For although Moses, in accommodation to the ignorance of the generality of men, does not in the history of the creation make mention of any other works of God than those which meet our eye, yet, seeing he afterwards introduces angels as the ministers of God, we easily infer that he for whom they do service is their Creator. Hence, though Moses, speaking in popular language, did not at the very commencement enumerate the angels among the creatures of God, nothing prevents us from treating distinctly and explicitly of what is delivered by Scripture concerning them in other places. For if we desire to know God by his works, we surely cannot overlook this noble and illustrious specimen. We may add that this branch of doctrine is very necessary for the refutation of numerous errors. The minds of many are so struck with the excellence of angelic natures, that they would think them insulted in being subjected to the authority of God, and so made subordinate. Hence a fancied divinity has been assigned them. Manes, too, has arisen with his sect, fabricating to himself two principles—God and the devil, attributing the origin of good things to God, but assigning all bad natures to the devil as their author. Were this delirium to take possession of our minds, God would be denied his glory in the creation of the world. For, seeing there is nothing more peculiar to God than eternity and αὐτουσία, *i.e.* self-existence, or existence of himself, if I may so speak, do not those who attribute it to the devil in some degree invest him with the honour of divinity? And where is the omnipotence of God, if the devil has the power of executing whatever he pleases against the will, and notwithstanding of the opposition of God? But the only good ground which the Manichees have—viz. that it were impious to ascribe the creation of any thing bad to a good God, militates in no degree against the orthodox faith, since it is not admitted that there is any thing naturally bad throughout the universe; the depravity and wickedness whether of man or of the devil, and the sins thence resulting, being not from nature, but from the corruption of nature; nor, at first, did anything whatever exist that did not exhibit some manifestation of the divine wisdom and justice. To obviate such perverse imaginations, we must raise our minds higher than our eyes can penetrate. It was probably with this view that the Nicene Creed, in calling God the creator of all things, makes express mention of things invisible. My care, however, must be to keep within the bounds which piety prescribes, lest by indulging in speculations beyond my reach, I bewilder the reader, and lead him away from the simplicity of the faith. And since the Holy Spirit always instructs us in what is useful, but altogether omits, or only touches cursorily on matters which tend little to edification, of all such matters, it certainly is our duty to remain in willing ignorance.

4. Angels being the ministers appointed to execute the commands of God, must, of course, be admitted to be his creatures, but to stir up questions concerning the time or order in which they were created (see Lombard, lib. 2 dist. 2, sqq.), bespeaks more perverseness than industry. Moses relates that the heavens and the earth were finished, with all their host; what avails it anxiously to inquire at what time other more hidden celestial hosts than the stars and planets also began to be? Not to dwell on this, let us here remember that on the whole subject of religion one rule of modesty and soberness is to be observed, and it is this, in obscure matters not to speak or think, or even long to know, more than the Word of God has delivered. A second rule is, that in reading the Scriptures we should constantly direct our inquiries and meditations to those things which tend to edification, not indulge in curiosity, or in studying things of no use. And since the Lord has been pleased to instruct us, not in frivolous questions, but in solid piety, in the fear of his name, in true faith, and the duties of holiness, let us rest satisfied with such knowledge. Wherefore, if we would be duly wise, we must renounce those vain babblings of idle men, concerning the nature, ranks, and number of angels, without any authority from the Word of God. I know that many fasten on these topics more eagerly, and take greater pleasure in them than in those relating to daily practice. But if we decline not to be the disciples of Christ, let us not decline to follow the method which he has prescribed. In this way, being contented with him for our master, we will not only refrain from, but even feel averse to, superfluous speculations which he discourages. None can deny that Dionysus (whoever he may have been) has many shrewd and subtle disquisitions in his Celestial Hierarchy, but on looking at them more closely,

every one must see that they are merely idle talk. The duty of a Theologian, however, is not to tickle the ear, but confirm the conscience, by teaching what is true, certain, and useful. When you read the work of Dionysus, you would think that the man had come down from heaven, and was relating, not what he had learned, but what he had actually seen. Paul, however, though he was carried to the third heaven, so far from delivering any thing of the kind, positively declares, that it was not lawful for man to speak the secrets which he had seen. Bidding adieu, therefore, to that nugatory wisdom, let us endeavour to ascertain from the simple doctrine of Scripture what it is the Lord's pleasure that we should know concerning angels.

5. In Scripture, then, we uniformly read that angels are heavenly spirits, whose obedience and ministry God employs to execute all the purposes which he has decreed, and hence their name as being a kind of intermediate messengers to manifest his will to men. The names by which several of them are distinguished have reference to the same office. They are called hosts, because they surround their Prince as his court,—adorn and display his majesty,—like soldiers, have their eyes always turned to their leader's standard, and are so ready and prompt to execute his orders, that the moment he gives the nod, they prepare for, or rather are actually at work. In declaring the magnificence of the divine throne, similar representations are given by the prophets, and especially by Daniel, when he says, that when God stood up to Judgment, "thousand thousands ministered unto him, and ten thousand times ten thousand stood before him" (Dan. 7:10). As by these means the Lord wonderfully exerts and declares the power and might of his hand, they are called virtues. Again, as his government of the world is exercised and administered by them, they are called at one time Principalities, at another Powers, at another Dominions (Col. 1:16; Eph. 1:21). Lastly, as the glory of God in some measure dwells in them, they are also termed Thrones; though as to this last designation I am unwilling to speak positively, as a different interpretation is equally, if not more congruous. To say nothing, therefore, of the name of Thrones, the former names are often employed by the Holy Spirit in commendation of the dignity of angelic service. Nor is it right to pass by unhonoured those instruments by whom God specially manifests the presence of his power. Nay, they are more than once called Gods, because the Deity is in some measure represented to us in their service, as in a mirror. I am rather inclined, however, to agree with ancient writers, that in those passages wherein it is stated that the angel of the Lord appeared to Abraham, Jacob, and Moses, Christ was that angel. Still it is true, that when mention is made of all the angels, they are frequently so designated. Nor ought this to seem strange. For if princes and rulers have this honour given them, because in their office they are vicegerents of God, the supreme King and Judge, with far greater reason may it be given to angels, in whom the brightness of the divine glory is much more conspicuously displayed.

6. But the point on which the Scriptures specially insist is that which tends most to our comfort, and to the confirmation of our faith, namely, that angels are the ministers and dispensers of the divine bounty towards us. Accordingly, we are told how they watch for our safety, how they undertake our defence, direct our path, and take heed that no evil befall us. There are whole passages which relate, in the first instance, to Christ, the Head of the Church, and after him to all believers. "He shall give his angels charge over thee, to keep thee in all thy ways. They shall bear thee up in their hands, lest thou dash thy foot against a stone." Again, "The angel of the Lord encampeth round about them that fear him, and delivereth them." By these passages the Lord shows that the protection of those whom he has undertaken to defend he has delegated to his angels. Accordingly, an angel of the Lord consoles Hagar in her flight, and bids her be reconciled to her mistress. Abraham promises to his servant that an angel will be the guide of his journey. Jacob, in blessing Ephraim and Manasseh, prays "The angel which redeemed me from all evil bless the lads." So an angel was appointed to guard the camp of the Israelites; and as often as God was pleased to deliver Israel from the hands of his enemies, he stirred up avengers by the ministry of angels. Thus, in fine (not to mention more), angels ministered to Christ, and were present with him in all straits. To the women they announced his resurrection; to the disciples they foretold his glorious advent. In discharging the office of our protectors, they war against the devil and all our enemies, and execute vengeance upon those who afflict us. Thus we read that an angel of the Lord, to deliver Jerusalem from siege, slew one hundred and eighty-five thousand men in the camp of the king of Assyria in a single night.

7. Whether or not each believer has a single angel assigned to him for his defence, I dare not positively affirm. When Daniel introduces the angel of the Persian and the angel of the Greeks, he undoubtedly intimates that certain angels are appointed as a kind of presidents over kingdoms and provinces. Again, when Christ says

that the angels of children always behold the face of his Father, he insinuates that there are certain angels to whom their safety has been entrusted. But I know not if it can be inferred from this, that each believer has his own angel. This, indeed, I hold for certain, that each of us is cared for, not by one angel merely, but that all with one consent watch for our safety. For it is said of all the angels collectively, that they rejoice "over one sinner that repenteth, more than over ninety and nine just persons which need no repentance." It is also said, that the angels (meaning more than one) carried the soul of Lazarus into Abraham's bosom. Nor was it to no purpose that Elisha showed his servant the many chariots of fire which were specially allotted him.

There is one passage which seems to intimate somewhat more clearly that each individual has a separate angel. When Peter, after his deliverance from prison, knocked at the door of the house where the brethren were assembled, being unable to think it could be himself, they said that it was his angel. This idea seems to have been suggested to them by a common belief that every believer has a single angel assigned to him. Here, however, it may be alleged, that there is nothing to prevent us from understanding it of any one of the angels to whom the Lord might have given the charge of Peter at that particular time, without implying that he was to be his, perpetual guardian, according to the vulgar imagination (see Calvin on Mark 5:9), that two angels a good and a bad, as a kind of genii, are assigned to each individual. After all, it is not worth-while anxiously to investigate a point which does not greatly concern us. If any one does not think it enough to know that all the orders of the heavenly host are perpetually watching for his safety, I do not see what he could gain by knowing that he has one angel as a special guardian. Those, again, who limit the care which God takes of each of us to a single angel, do great injury to themselves and to all the members of the Church, as if there were no value in those promises of auxiliary troops, who on every side encircling and defending us, embolden us to fight more manfully.

8. Those who presume to dogmatize on the ranks and numbers of angels, would do well to consider on what foundation they rest. As to their rank, I admit that Michael is described by David as a mighty Prince, and by Jude as an Archangel. Paul also tells us, that an archangel will blow the trumpet which is to summon the world to Judgment. But how is it possible from such passages to ascertain the gradations of honour among the angels to determine the insignia, and assign the place and station of each? Even the two names, Michael and Gabriel, mentioned in Scripture, or a third, if you choose to add it from the history of Tobit, seem to intimate by their meaning that they are given to angels in accommodation to the weakness of our capacity, though I rather choose not to speak positively on the point. As to the number of angels, we learn from the mouth of our Saviour that there are many legions, and from Daniel that there are many myriads. Elisha's servant saw a multitude of chariots, and their vast number is declared by the fact, that they encamp round about those that fear the Lord. It is certain that spirits have no bodily shape, and yet Scripture, in accommodation to us, describes them under the form of winged Cherubim and Seraphim; not without cause, to assure us that when occasion requires, they will hasten to our aid with incredible swiftness, winging their way to us with the speed of lightning. Farther than this, in regard both to the ranks and numbers of angels, let us class them among those mysterious subjects, the full revelation of which is deferred to the last day, and accordingly refrain from inquiring too curiously, or talking presumptuously.

9. There is one point, however, which though called into doubt by certain restless individuals, we ought to hold for certain—viz. that angels are ministering spirits (Heb. 1:14); whose service God employs for the protection of his people, and by whose means he distributes his favours among men, and also executes other works. The Sadducees of old maintained, that by angels nothing more was meant than the movements which God impresses on men, or manifestations which he gives of his own power (Acts 23:8). But this dream is contradicted by so many passages of Scriptures that it seems strange how such gross ignorance could have had any countenance among the Jews. To say nothing of the passages I have already quoted, passages which refer to thousands and legions of angels, speak of them as rejoicing, as bearing up the faithful in their hands, carrying their souls to rest, beholding the face of their Father, and so forth: there are other passages which most clearly prove that they are real beings possessed of spiritual essence. Stephen and Paul say that the Law was enacted in the hands of angels. Our Saviour, moreover says that at the resurrection the elect will be like angels; that the day of Judgment is known not even to the angels; that at that time he himself will come with the holy angels. However much such passages may be twisted, their meaning is plain. In like manner, when Paul beseeches Timothy to keep his precepts as before Christ and his elect angels, it is not qualities or inspirations without substance that he speaks of, but true

spirits. And when it is said, in the Epistle to the Hebrews, that Christ was made more excellent than the angels, that the world was not made subject to them, that Christ assumed not their nature, but that of man, it is impossible to give a meaning to the passages without understanding that angels are blessed spirits, as to whom such comparisons may competently be made. The author of that Epistle declares the same thing when he places the souls of believers and the holy angels together in the kingdom of heaven. Moreover, in the passages we have already quoted, the angels of children are said to behold the face of God, to defend us by their protection, to rejoice in our salvation, to admire the manifold grace of God in the Church, to be under Christ their head. To the same effect is their frequent appearance to the holy patriarchs in human form, their speaking, and consenting to be hospitably entertained. Christ, too, in consequence of the supremacy which he obtains as Mediator, is called the Angel (Mal. 3:1). It was thought proper to touch on this subject in passing, with the view of putting the simple upon their guard against the foolish and absurd imaginations which, suggested by Satan many centuries ago, are ever and anon starting up anew

10. It remains to give warning against the superstition which usually begins to creep in, when it is said that all blessings are ministered and dispensed to us by angels. For the human mind is apt immediately to think that there is no honour which they ought not to receive, and hence the peculiar offices of Christ and God are bestowed upon them. In this ways the glory of Christ was for several former ages greatly obscured, extravagant eulogiums being pronounced on angels without any authority from Scripture. Among the corruptions which we now oppose, there is scarcely any one of greater antiquity. Even Paul appears to have had a severe contest with some who so exalted angels as to make them almost the superiors of Christ. Hence he so anxiously urges in his Epistle to the Colossians (Col. 1:16, 20), that Christ is not only superior to all angels, but that all the endowments which they possess are derived from him; thus warning us against forsaking him, by turning to those who are not sufficient for themselves, but must draw with us at a common fountain. As the refulgence of the Divine glory is manifested in them, there is nothing to which we are more prone than to prostrate ourselves before them in stupid adoration, and then ascribe to them the blessings which we owe to God alone. Even John confesses in the Apocalypse (Rev. 19:10; 22:8, 9), that this was his own case, but he immediately adds the answer which was given to him, "See thou do it not; I am thy fellow servant: worship God."

11. This danger we will happily avoid, if we consider why it is that Gods instead of acting directly without their agency, is wont to employ it in manifesting his power, providing for the safety of his people, and imparting the gifts of his beneficence. This he certainly does not from necessity, as if he were unable to dispense with them. Whenever he pleases, he passes them by, and performs his own work by a single nod: so far are they from relieving him of any difficulty. Therefore, when he employs them it is as a help to our weakness, that nothing may be wanting to elevate our hopes or strengthen our confidence. It ought, indeed, to be sufficient for us that the Lord declares himself to be our protector. But when we see ourselves beset by so many perils, so many injuries, so many kinds of enemies, such is our frailty and effeminacy, that we might at times be filled with alarm, or driven to despair, did not the Lord proclaim his gracious presence by some means in accordance with our feeble capacities. For this reason, he not only promises to take care of us, but assures us that he has numberless attendants, to whom he has committed the charge of our safety, that whatever dangers may impend, so long as we are encircled by their protection and guardianship, we are placed beyond all hazard of evil. I admit that after we have a simple assurance of the divine protection, it is improper in us still to look round for help. But since for this our weakness the Lord is pleased, in his infinite goodness and indulgence, to provide, it would ill become us to overlook the favour. Of this we have an example in the servant of Elisha (2 Kings 6:17), who, seeing the mountain encompassed by the army of the Assyrians, and no means of escape, was completely overcome with terror, and thought it all over with himself and his master. Then Elisha prayed to God to open the eyes of the servant, who forthwith beheld the mountain filled with horses and chariots of fire; in other words, with a multitude of angels, to whom he and the prophet had been given in charge. Confirmed by the vision he received courage, and could boldly defy the enemy, whose appearance previously filled him with dismay.

12. Whatever, therefore, is said as to the ministry of angels, let us employ for the purpose of removing all distrust, and strengthening our confidence in God. Since the Lord has provided us with such protection, let us not be terrified at the multitude of our enemies as if they could prevail notwithstanding of his aid, but let us adopt the sentiment of Elisha, that more are for us than against us.

How preposterous, therefore, is it to allow ourselves to be led away from God by angels who have been appointed for the very purpose of assuring us of his more immediate presence to help us? But we are so led away, if angels do not conduct us directly to him—making us look to him, invoke and celebrate him as our only defender—if they are not regarded merely as hands moving to our assistance just as he directs—if they do not direct us to Christ as the only Mediator on whom we must wholly depend and recline, looking towards him, and resting in him. Our minds ought to give thorough heed to what Jacob saw in his vision (Gen. 28:12),—angels descending to the earth to men, and again mounting up from men to heaven, by means of a ladder, at the head of which the Lord of Hosts was seated, intimating that it is solely by the intercession of Christ that the ministry of angels extends to us, as he himself declares, "Hereafter ye shall see heaven open, and the angels of God ascending and descending upon the Son of man" (John 1:51). Accordingly, the servant of Abraham, though he had been commended to the guardianship of an angel (Gen. 24:7), does not therefore invoke that angel to be present with him, but trusting to the commendation, pours out his prayers before the Lord, and entreats him to show mercy to Abraham. As God does not make angels the ministers of his power and goodness, that he may share his glory with them, so he does not promise his assistance by their instrumentality, that we may divide our confidence between him and them. Away, then, with that Platonic philosophy of seeking access to God by means of angels and courting them with the view of making God more propitious (*Plat. in Epinomide et Cratylo*),—a philosophy which presumptuous and superstitious men attempted at first to introduce into our religion, and which they persist in even to this day.

13. The tendency of all that Scripture teaches concerning devils is to put us on our guard against their wiles and machinations, that we may provide ourselves with weapons strong enough to drive away the most formidable foes. For when Satan is called the god and ruler of this world, the strong man armed, the prince of the power of the air, the roaring lion, the object of all these descriptions is to make us more cautious and vigilant, and more prepared for the contest. This is sometimes stated in distinct terms. For Peter, after describing the devil as a roaring lion going about seeking whom he may devour, immediately adds the exhortation, "whom resist steadfast in the faith" (1 Pet. 5:9). And Paul, after reminding us that we wrestle not against flesh and blood, but against principalities, against powers, against the rulers of the darkness of this world, against spiritual wickedness in high places, immediately enjoins us to put on armour equal to so great and perilous a contest (Ephes. 6:12). Wherefore, let this be the use to which we turn all these statements. Being forewarned of the constant presence of an enemy the most daring, the most powerful, the most crafty, the most indefatigable, the most completely equipped with all the engines and the most expert in the science of war, let us not allow ourselves to be overtaken by sloth or cowardice, but, on the contrary, with minds aroused and ever on the alert, let us stand ready to resist; and, knowing that this warfare is terminated only by death, let us study to persevere. Above all, fully conscious of our weakness and want of skill, let us invoke the help of God, and attempt nothing without trusting in him, since it is his alone to supply counsel, and strength, and courage, and arms.

14. That we may feel the more strongly urged to do so, the Scripture declares that the enemies who war against us are not one or two, or few in number, but a great host. Mary Magdalene is said to have been delivered from seven devils by which she was possessed; and our Saviour assures us that it is an ordinary circumstance, when a devil has been expelled, if access is again given to it, to take seven other spirits, more wicked than itself, and resume the vacant possession. Nay, one man is said to have been possessed by a whole legion. By this, then, we are taught that the number of enemies with whom we have to war is almost infinite, that we may not, from a contemptuous idea of the fewness of their numbers, be more remiss in the contest, or from imagining that an occasional truce is given us, indulge in sloth. In one Satan or devil being often mentioned in the singular number, the thing denoted is that domination of iniquity which is opposed to the reign of righteousness. For, as the Church and the communion of saints has Christ for its head, so the faction of the wicked and wickedness itself, is portrayed with its prince exercising supremacy. Hence the expression, "Depart, ye cursed, into everlasting fire, prepared for the devil and his angels" (Mt. 25:41).

15. One thing which ought to animate us to perpetual contest with the devil is, that he is everywhere called both our adversary and the adversary of God. For, if the glory of God is dear to us, as it ought to be, we ought to struggle with all our might against him who aims at the extinction of that glory. If we are animated with proper zeal to maintain the Kingdom of Christ, we must wage irreconcilable war with him who conspires its ruin. Again, if we have any anxiety about our own salvation, we ought

to make no peace nor truce with him who is continually laying schemes for its destruction. But such is the character given to Satan in the third chapter of Genesis, where he is seen seducing man from his allegiance to God, that he may both deprive God of his due honour, and plunge man headlong in destruction. Such, too, is the description given of him in the Gospels (Mt. 13:28), where he is called the enemy, and is said to sow tares in order to corrupt the seed of eternal life. In one word, in all his actions we experience the truth of our Saviour's description, that he was "a murderer from the beginning, and abode not in the truth" (John 8:44). Truth he assails with lies, light he obscures with darkness. The minds of men he involves in error; he stirs up hatred, inflames strife and war, and all in order that he may overthrow the kingdom of God, and drown men in eternal perdition with himself. Hence it is evident that his whole nature is depraved, mischievous, and malignant. There must be extreme depravity in a mind bent on assailing the glory of God and the salvation of man. This is intimated by John in his Epistle, when he says that he "sinneth from the beginning" (1 John 3:8), implying that he is the author, leader, and contriver of all malice and wickedness.

16. But as the devil was created by God, we must remember that this malice which we attribute to his nature is not from creation, but from depravation. Every thing damnable in him he brought upon himself, by his revolt and fall. Of this Scripture reminds us, lest, by believing that he was so created at first, we should ascribe to God what is most foreign to his nature. For this reason, Christ declares (John 8:44), that Satan, when he lies, "speaketh of his own," and states the reason, "because he abode not in the truth." By saying that he abode not in the truth, he certainly intimates that he once was in the truth, and by calling him the father of lies, he puts it out of his power to charge God with the depravity of which he was himself the cause. But although the expressions are brief and not very explicit, they are amply sufficient to vindicate the majesty of God from every calumny. And what more does it concern us to know of devils? Some murmur because the Scripture does not in various passages give a distinct and regular exposition of Satan's fall, its cause, mode, date, and nature. But as these things are of no consequence to us, it was better, if not entirely to pass them in silence, at least only to touch lightly upon them. The Holy Spirit could not deign to feed curiosity with idle, unprofitable histories. We see it was the Lord's purpose to deliver nothing in his sacred oracles which we might not learn for edification. Therefore, instead of dwelling on superfluous matters, let it be sufficient for us briefly to hold, with regard to the nature of devils, that at their first creation they were the angels of God, but by revolting they both ruined themselves, and became the instruments of perdition to others. As it was useful to know this much, it is clearly taught by Peter and Jude; "God," they say, "spared not the angels that sinned, but cast them down to hell, and delivered them into chains of darkness to be reserved unto Judgment" (2 Pet. 2:4; Jude ver. 6). And Paul, by speaking of the elect angels, obviously draws a tacit contrast between them and reprobate angels.

17. With regard to the strife and war which Satan is said to wage with God, it must be understood with this qualification, that Satan cannot possibly do anything against the will and consent of God. For we read in the history of Job, that Satan appears in the presence of God to receive his commands, and dares not proceed to execute any enterprise until he is authorised. In the same way, when Ahab was to be deceived, he undertook to be a lying spirit in the mouth of all the prophets; and on being commissioned by the Lord, proceeds to do so. For this reason, also, the spirit which tormented Saul is said to be an evil spirit from the Lord, because he was, as it were, the scourge by which the misdeeds of the wicked king were punished. In another place it is said that the plagues of Egypt were inflicted by God through the instrumentality of wicked angels. In conformity with these particular examples, Paul declares generally that unbelievers are blinded by God, though he had previously described it as the doing of Satan. It is evident, therefore, that Satan is under the power of God, and is so ruled by his authority, that he must yield obedience to it. Moreover, though we say that Satan resists God, and does works at variance with His works, we at the same time maintain that this contrariety and opposition depend on the permission of God. I now speak not of Satan's will and endeavour, but only of the result. For the disposition of the devil being wicked, he has no inclination whatever to obey the divine will, but, on the contrary, is wholly bent on contumacy and rebellion. This much, therefore, he has of himself, and his own iniquity, that he eagerly, and of set purpose, opposes God, aiming at those things which he deems most contrary to the will of God. But as God holds him bound and fettered by the curb of his power, he executes those things only for which permission has been given him, and thus, however unwilling, obeys his Creator, being forced, whenever he is required, to do Him service.

18. God thus turning the unclean spirits hither and

thither at his pleasure, employs them in exercising believers by warring against them, assailing them with wiles, urging them with solicitations, pressing close upon them, disturbing, alarming, and occasionally wounding, but never conquering or oppressing them; whereas they hold the wicked in thraldom, exercise dominion over their minds and bodies, and employ them as bond-slaves in all kinds of iniquity. Because believers are disturbed by such enemies, they are addressed in such exhortations as these: "Neither give place to the devil;" "Your adversary the devil, as a roaring lion, walketh about seeking whom he may devour; whom resist steadfast in the faith" (Eph. 4:27; 1 Pet. 5:8). Paul acknowledges that he was not exempt from this species of contest when he says, that for the purpose of subduing his pride, a messenger of Satan was sent to buffet him (2 Cor. 12:7). This trial, therefore, is common to all the children of God. But as the promise of bruising Satan's head (Gen. 3:15) applies alike to Christ and to all his members, I deny that believers can ever be oppressed or vanquished by him. They are often, indeed, thrown into alarm, but never so thoroughly as not to recover themselves. They fall by the violence of the blows, but they get up again; they are wounded, but not mortally. In fine, they labour on through the whole course of their lives, so as ultimately to gain the victory, though they meet with occasional defeats. We know how David, through the just anger of God, was left for a time to Satan, and by his instigation numbered the people (2 Sam. 24:1); nor without cause does Paul hold out a hope of pardon in case any should have become ensnared by the wiles of the devil (2 Tim. 2:26). Accordingly, he elsewhere shows that the promise above quoted commences in this life where the struggle is carried on, and that it is completed after the struggle is ended. His words are, "The God of peace shall bruise Satan under your feet shortly" (Rom. 16:20). In our Head, indeed, this victory was always perfect, because the prince of the world "had nothing" in him (John 14:30); but in us, who are his members, it is now partially obtained, and will be perfected when we shall have put off our mortal flesh, through which we are liable to infirmity, and shall have been filled with the energy of the Holy Spirit. In this way, when the kingdom of Christ is raised up and established, that of Satan falls, as our Lord himself expresses it, "I beheld Satan as lightning fall from heaven" (Luke 10:18). By these words, he confirmed the report which the apostles gave of the efficacy of their preaching. In like manner he says, "When a strong man armed keepeth his palace, his goods are in peace. But when a stronger than he shall come upon him, and overcome him, he taketh from him all his armour wherein he trusted, and divideth his spoils" (Luke 11:21, 22). And to this end, Christ, by dying, overcame Satan, who had the power of death (Heb. 2:14), and triumphed over all his hosts that they might not injure the Church, which otherwise would suffer from them every moment. For (such being our weakness, and such his raging fury), how could we withstand his manifold and unintermitted assaults for any period, however short, if we did not trust to the victory of our leader? God, therefore, does not allow Satan to have dominion over the souls of believers, but only gives over to his sway the impious and unbelieving, whom he deigns not to number among his flock. For the devil is said to have undisputed possession of this world until he is dispossessed by Christ. In like manner, he is said to blind all who do not believe the Gospel, and to do his own work in the children of disobedience. And justly; for all the wicked are vessels of wrath, and, accordingly, to whom should they be subjected but to the minister of the divine vengeance? In fine, they are said to be of their father the devil. For as believers are recognised to be the sons of God by bearing his image, so the wicked are properly regarded as the children of Satan, from having degenerated into his image.

19. Having above refuted that nugatory philosophy concerning the holy angels, which teaches that they are nothing but good motions or inspirations which God excites in the minds of men, we must here likewise refute those who foolishly allege that devils are nothing but bad affections or perturbations suggested by our carnal nature. The brief refutation is to be found in passages of Scripture on this subject, passages neither few nor obscure. First, when they are called unclean spirits and apostate angels (Mt. 12:43; Jude, verse 6), who have degenerated from their original, the very terms sufficiently declare that they are not motions or affections of the mind, but truly, as they are called, minds or spirits endued with sense and intellect. In like manner, when the children of God are contrasted by John, and also by our Saviour, with the children of the devil, would not the contrast be absurd if the term devil meant nothing more than evil inspirations? And John adds still more emphatically, that the devil sinneth from the beginning (1 John 3:8). In like manner, when Jude introduces the archangel Michael contending with the devil (Jude, verse 9), he certainly contrasts a wicked and rebellious with a good angel. To this corresponds the account given in the Book of Job, that Satan appeared in the presence of God with

the holy angels. But the clearest passages of all are those which make mention of the punishment which, from the Judgment of God, they already begin to feel, and are to feel more especially at the resurrection, "What have we to do with thee, Jesus, thou Son of God? art thou come hither to torment us before the time?" (Mt. 8:29); and again, "Depart, ye cursed, into everlasting fire, prepared for the devil and his angels" (Mt. 25:41). Again, "If God spared not the angels that sinned, but cast them down to hell, and delivered them into chains of darkness to be reserved unto Judgment," &c. (2 Pet. 2:4). How absurd the expressions, that devils are doomed to eternal punishment, that fire is prepared for them, that they are even now excruciated and tormented by the glory of Christ, if there were truly no devils at all? But as all discussion on this subject is superfluous for those who give credit to the Word of God, while little is gained by quoting Scripture to those empty speculators whom nothing but novelty can please, I believe I have already done enough for my purpose, which was to put the pious on their guard against the delirious dreams with which restless men harass themselves and the simple. The subject, however, deserved to be touched upon, lest any, by embracing that errors should imagine they have no enemy and thereby be more remiss or less cautious in resisting.

20. Meanwhile, being placed in this most beautiful theatre, let us not decline to take a pious delight in the clear and manifest works of God. For, as we have elsewhere observed, though not the chief, it is, in point of order, the first evidence of faith, to remember to which side soever we turn, that all which meets the eye is the work of God, and at the same time to meditate with pious care on the end which God had in view in creating it. Wherefore, in order that we may apprehend with true faith what it is necessary to know concerning God, it is of importance to attend to the history of the creation, as briefly recorded by Moses and afterwards more copiously illustrated by pious writers, more especially by Basil and Ambrose. From this history we learn that God, by the power of his Word and his Spirit, created the heavens and the earth out of nothing; that thereafter he produced things inanimate and animate of every kind, arranging an innumerable variety of objects in admirable order, giving each kind its proper nature, office, place, and station; at the same time, as all things were liable to corruption, providing for the perpetuation of each single species, cherishing some by secret methods, and, as it were, from time to time instilling new vigour into them, and bestowing on others a power of continuing their race, so preventing it from perishing at their own death. Heaven and earth being thus most richly adorned, and copiously supplied with all things, like a large and splendid mansion gorgeously constructed and exquisitely furnished, at length man was made—man, by the beauty of his person and his many noble endowments, the most glorious specimen of the works of God. But, as I have no intention to give the history of creation in detail, it is sufficient to have again thus briefly touched on it in passing. I have already reminded my reader, that the best course for him is to derive his knowledge of the subject from Moses and others who have carefully and faithfully transmitted an account of the creation.

21. It is unnecessary to dwell at length on the end that should be aimed at in considering the works of God. The subject has been in a great measure explained elsewhere, and in so far as required by our present work, may now be disposed of in a few words. Undoubtedly were one to attempt to speak in due terms of the inestimable wisdom, power, justice, and goodness of God, in the formation of the world, no grace or splendour of diction could equal the greatness of the subject. Still there can be no doubt that the Lord would have us constantly occupied with such holy meditation, in order that, while we contemplate the immense treasures of wisdom and goodness exhibited in the creatures as in so many mirrors, we may not only run our eye over them with a hasty, and, as it were, evanescent glance, but dwell long upon them, seriously and faithfully turn them in our minds, and every now and then bring them to recollection. But as the present work is of a didactic nature, we cannot fittingly enter on topics which require lengthened discourse. Therefore, in order to be compendious, let the reader understand that he has a genuine apprehension of the character of God as the Creator of the world; first, if he attends to the general rule, never thoughtlessly or obliviously to overlook the glorious perfections which God displays in his creatures; and, secondly, if he makes a self application of what he sees, so as to fix it deeply on his heart. The former is exemplified when we consider how great the Architect must be who framed and ordered the multitude of the starry host so admirably, that it is impossible to imagine a more glorious sight, so stationing some, and fixing them to particular spots that they cannot move; giving a freer course to others yet setting limits to their wanderings; so tempering the movement of the whole as to measure out day and night, months, years, and seasons, and at the same time so regu-

lating the inequality of days as to prevent every thing like confusion. The former course is, moreover, exemplified when we attend to his power in sustaining the vast mass, and guiding the swift revolutions of the heavenly bodies, &c. These few examples sufficiently explain what is meant by recognising the divine perfections in the creation of the world. Were we to attempt to go over the whole subject we should never come to a conclusion, there being as many miracles of divine power, as many striking evidences of wisdom and goodness, as there are classes of objects, nay, as there are individual objects, great or small, throughout the universe.

22. The other course which has a closer relation to faith remains to be considered—viz. that while we observe how God has destined all things for our good and salvation, we at the same time feel his power and grace, both in ourselves and in the great blessings which he has bestowed upon us; thence stirring up ourselves to confidence in him, to invocation, praise, and love. Moreover, as I lately observed, the Lord himself, by the very order of creation, has demonstrated that he created all things for the sake of man. Nor is it unimportant to observe, that he divided the formation of the world into six days, though it had been in no respect more difficult to complete the whole work, in all its parts, in one moment than by a gradual progression. But he was pleased to display his providence and paternal care towards us in this, that before he formed man, he provided whatever he foresaw would be useful and salutary to him. How ungrateful, then, were it to doubt whether we are cared for by this most excellent Parent, who we see cared for us even before we were born! How impious were it to tremble in distrust, lest we should one day be abandoned in our necessity by that kindness which, antecedent to our existence, displayed itself in a complete supply of all good things! Moreover, Moses tells us that everything which the world contains is liberally placed at our disposal. This God certainly did not that he might delude us with an empty form of donation. Nothing, therefore, which concerns our safety will ever be wanting. To conclude, in one word; as often as we call God the Creator of heaven and earth, let us remember that the distribution of all the things which he created are in his hand and power, but that we are his sons, whom he has undertaken to nourish and bring up in allegiance to him, that we may expect the substance of all good from him alone, and have full hope that he will never suffer us to be in want of things necessary to salvation, so as to leave us dependent on some other source; that in everything we desire we may address our prayers to him, and, in every benefit we receive, acknowledge his hand, and give him thanks; that thus allured by his great goodness and beneficence, we may study with our whole heart to love and serve him.

CHAPTER 15

STATE IN WHICH MAN WAS CREATED. THE FACULTIES OF THE SOUL— THE IMAGE OF GOD—FREE WILL— ORIGINAL RIGHTEOUSNESS.

This chapter is thus divided:—I. The necessary rules to be observed in considering the state of man before the fall being laid down, the point first considered is the creation of the body, and the lesson taught by its being formed out of the earth, and made alive, sec. 1. II. The immortality of the human soul is proved by various solid arguments, sec. 2. III. The image of God (the strongest proof of the soul's immortality) is considered, and various absurd fancies are refuted, sec. 3. IV. Several errors which obscure the light of truth being dissipated, follows a philosophical and theological consideration of the faculties of the soul before the fall.

Sections:

1. A twofold knowledge of God—viz. before the fall and after it. The former here considered. Particular rules or precautions to be observed in this discussion. What we are taught by a body formed ant of the dust, and tenanted by a spirit.

2. The immortality of the soul proved from, 1. The testimony of conscience. 2. The knowledge of God. 3. The noble faculties with which it is endued. 4. Its activity and wondrous fancies in sleep. 5. Innumerable passages of Scripture.

3. The image of God one of the strongest proofs of the immortality of the soul. What meant by this image. The dreams of Osiander concerning the image of God refuted. Whether any difference between "image" and "likeness." Another objection of Osiander refuted. The image of God conspicuous in the whole Adam.

4. The image of God is in the soul. Its nature may be learnt from its renewal by Christ. What comprehended under this renewal. What the image of God in man before the fall. In what things it now appears. When and where it will be seen in perfection.

5. The dreams of the Manichees and of Servetus, as

to the origin of the soul, refuted. Also of Osiander, who denies that there is any image of God in man without essential righteousness.

6. The doctrine of philosophers as to the faculties of the soul generally discordant, doubtful, and obscure. The excellence of the soul described. Only one soul in each man. A brief review of the opinion of philosophers as to the faculties of the soul. What to be thought of this opinion.

7. The division of the faculties of the soul into intellect and will, more agreeable to Christian doctrine.

8. The power and office of the intellect and will in man before the fall. Man's free will. This freedom lost by the fall—a fact unknown to philosophers. The delusion of Pelagians and Papists. Objection as to the fall of man when free, refuted.

1. We have now to speak of the creation of man, not only because of all the works of God it is the noblest, and most admirable specimen of his justice, wisdom, and goodness, but, as we observed at the outset, we cannot clearly and properly know God unless the knowledge of ourselves be added. This knowledge is twofold,—relating, first, to the condition in which we were at first created; and, secondly to our condition such as it began to be immediately after Adam's fall. For it would little avail us to know how we were created if we remained ignorant of the corruption and degradation of our nature in consequence of the fall. At present, however, we confine ourselves to a consideration of our nature in its original integrity. And, certainly, before we descend to the miserable condition into which man has fallen, it is of importance to consider what he was at first. For there is need of caution, lest we attend only to the natural ills of man, and thereby seem to ascribe them to the Author of nature; impiety deeming it a sufficient defence if it can pretend that everything vicious in it proceeded in some sense from God, and not hesitating, when accused, to plead against God, and throw the blame of its guilt upon Him. Those who would be thought to speak more reverently of the Deity catch at an excuse for their depravity from nature, not considering that they also, though more obscurely, bring a charge against God, on whom the dishonour would fall if anything vicious were proved to exist in nature. Seeing, therefore, that the flesh is continually on the alert for subterfuges, by which it imagines it can remove the blame of its own wickedness from itself to some other quarter, we must diligently guard against this depraved procedure, and accordingly treat of the calamity of the human race in such a way as may cut off every evasion, and vindicate the justice of God against all who would impugn it. We shall afterwards see, in its own place (Book 2 chap. 1 sec. 3), how far mankind now are from the purity originally conferred on Adam. And, first, it is to be observed, that when he was formed out of the dust of the ground a curb was laid on his pride—nothing being more absurd than that those should glory in their excellence who not only dwell in tabernacles of clay, but are themselves in part dust and ashes. But God having not only deigned to animate a vessel of clay, but to make it the habitation of an immortal spirit, Adam might well glory in the great liberality of his Maker.

2. Moreover, there can be no question that man consists of a body and a soul; meaning by soul, an immortal though created essence, which is his nobler part. Sometimes he is called a spirit. But though the two terms, while they are used together differ in their meaning, still, when spirit is used by itself it is equivalent to soul, as when Solomon speaking of death says, that the spirit returns to God who gave it (Eccles. 12:7). And Christ, in commending his spirit to the Father, and Stephen his to Christ, simply mean, that when the soul is freed from the prison-house of the body, God becomes its perpetual keeper. Those who imagine that the soul is called a spirit because it is a breath or energy divinely infused into bodies, but devoid of essence, err too grossly, as is shown both by the nature of the thing, and the whole tenor of Scripture. It is true, indeed, that men cleaving too much to the earth are dull of apprehension, nay, being alienated from the Father of Lights, are so immersed in darkness as to imagine that they will not survive the grave; still the light is not so completely quenched in darkness that all sense of immortality is lost. Conscience, which, distinguishing, between good and evil, responds to the Judgment of God, is an undoubted sign of an immortal spirit. How could motion devoid of essence penetrate to the Judgment-seat of God, and under a sense of guilt strike itself with terror? The body cannot be affected by any fear of spiritual punishment. This is competent only to the soul, which must therefore be endued with essence. Then the mere knowledge of a God sufficiently proves that souls which rise higher than the world must be immortal, it being impossible that any evanescent vigour could reach the very fountain of life. In fine, while the many noble faculties with which the human mind is endued proclaim that something divine is engraven on it, they are so many evidences of an immortal essence. For such sense as the lower animals possess goes not beyond the body,

or at least not beyond the objects actually presented to it. But the swiftness with which the human mind glances from heaven to earth, scans the secrets of nature, and, after it has embraced all ages, with intellect and memory digests each in its proper order, and reads the future in the past, clearly demonstrates that there lurks in man a something separated from the body. We have intellect by which we are able to conceive of the invisible God and angels—a thing of which body is altogether incapable. We have ideas of rectitude, justice, and honesty—ideas which the bodily senses cannot reach. The seat of these ideas must therefore be a spirit. Nay, sleep itself, which stupefying the man, seems even to deprive him of life, is no obscure evidence of immortality; not only suggesting thoughts of things which never existed, but foreboding future events. I briefly touch on topics which even profane writers describe with a more splendid eloquence. For pious readers, a simple reference is sufficient. Were not the soul some kind of essence separated from the body, Scripture would not teach that we dwell in houses of clay, and at death remove from a tabernacle of flesh; that we put off that which is corruptible, in order that, at the last day, we may finally receive according to the deeds done in the body. These, and similar passages which everywhere occur, not only clearly distinguish the soul from the body, but by giving it the name of man, intimate that it is his principal part. Again, when Paul exhorts believers to cleanse themselves from all filthiness of the flesh and the spirit, he shows that there are two parts in which the taint of sin resides. Peter, also, in calling Christ the Shepherd and Bishop of souls, would have spoken absurdly if there were no souls towards which he might discharge such an office. Nor would there be any ground for what he says concerning the eternal salvation of souls, or for his injunction to purify our souls, or for his assertion that fleshly lusts war against the soul; neither could the author of the Epistle to the Hebrews say, that pastors watch as those who must give an account for our souls, if souls were devoid of essence. To the same effect Paul calls God to witness upon his soul, which could not be brought to trial before God if incapable of suffering punishment. This is still more clearly expressed by our Saviour, when he bids us fear him who, after he has killed the body, is able also to cast into hell fire. Again when the author of the Epistle to the Hebrews distinguishes the fathers of our flesh from God, who alone is the Father of our spirits, he could not have asserted the essence of the soul in clearer terms. Moreover, did not the soul, when freed from the fetters of the body, continue to exist, our Saviour would not have represented the soul of Lazarus as enjoying blessedness in Abraham's bosom, while, on the contrary, that of Dives was suffering dreadful torments. Paul assures us of the same thing when he says, that so long as we are present in the body, we are absent from the Lord. Not to dwell on a matter as to which there is little obscurity, I will only add, that Luke mentions among the errors of the Sadducees that they believed neither angel nor spirit.

3. A strong proof of this point may be gathered from its being said, that man was created in the image of God. For though the divine glory is displayed in man's outward appearance, it cannot be doubted that the proper seat of the image is in the soul. I deny not, indeed, that external shape, in so far as it distinguishes and separates us from the lower animals, brings us nearer to God; nor will I vehemently oppose any who may choose to include under the image of God that

While the mute creation downward bend
   Their sight, and to their earthly mother tend,
   Man looks aloft, and with erected eyes,
   Beholds his own hereditary skies.

Only let it be understood, that the image of God which is beheld or made conspicuous by these external marks, is spiritual. For Osiander (whose writings exhibit a perverse ingenuity in futile devices), extending the image of God indiscriminately as well to the body as to the soul, confounds heaven with earth. He says, that the Father, the Son, and the Holy Spirit, placed their image in man, because, even though Adam had stood entire, Christ would still have become man. Thus, according to him, the body which was destined for Christ was a model and type of that corporeal figure which was then formed. But where does he find that Christ is an image of the Spirit? I admit, indeed, that in the person of the Mediator, the glory of the whole Godhead is displayed: but how can the eternal Word, who in order precedes the Spirit, be called his image? In short, the distinction between the Son and the Spirit is destroyed when the former is represented as the image of the latter. Moreover, I should like to know in what respect Christ in the flesh in which he was clothed resembles the Holy Spirit, and by what marks, or lineaments, the likeness is expressed. And since the expression, "Let us make man in our own image," is used in the person of the Son also, it follows that he is the image of himself—a thing utterly absurd. Add that, according to the figment of Osiander, Adam was formed after the model or type of the man Christ. Hence Christ, in as much as he was to be clothed with flesh, was the idea according to which Adam was formed, whereas the Scriptures teach very differently—viz. that he was formed in the image of God. There is more plausibility in the imagination of those who interpret that Adam was created in the image of God, because it was conformable to Christ, who is the only image of God; but not even for this is there any solid foundation. The "image" and "likeness" has given rise to no small discussion; interpreters searching without cause for a difference between the two terms, since "likeness" is merely added by way of exposition. First, we know that repetitions are common in Hebrew, which often gives two words for one thing; And, secondly, there is no ambiguity in the thing itself, man being called the image of God because of his likeness to God. Hence there is an obvious absurdity in those who indulge in philosophical speculation as to these names, placing the *Zelem*, that is the image, in the substance of the soul, and the *Demuth*, that is the likeness, in its qualities, and so forth. God having determined to create man in his own image, to remove the obscurity which was in this terms adds, by way of explanation, in *his likeness*, as if he had said, that he would make man, in whom he would, as it were, image himself by means of the marks of resemblance impressed upon him. Accordingly, Moses, shortly after repeating the account, puts down the image of God twice, and makes no mention of the likeness. Osiander frivolously objects that it is not a part of the man, or the soul with its faculties, which is called the image of God, but the whole Adam, who received his name from the dust out of which he was taken. I call the objection frivolous, as all sound readers will judge. For though the whole man is called mortal, the soul is not therefore liable to death, nor when he is called a rational animal is reason or intelligence thereby attributed to the body. Hence, although the soul is not the man, there is no absurdity in holding that he is called the image of God in respect of the soul; though I retain the principle which I lately laid down, that the image of God extends to everything in which the nature of man surpasses that of all other species of animals. Accordingly, by this term is denoted the integrity with which Adam was endued when his intellect was clear, his affections subordinated to reason, all his senses duly regulated, and when he truly ascribed all his excellence to the admirable gifts of his Maker. And though the primary seat of the divine image was in the mind and the heart, or in the soul and its powers, there was no part even of the body in which some rays of glory did not shine. It is certain that in every part of the world some lineaments of divine glory are beheld and hence we may infer, that when his image is placed in man, there is a kind of tacit antithesis, as it were, setting man apart from the crowd, and exalting him above all the other creatures. But it cannot be denied that the angels also were created in the likeness of God, since, as Christ declares (Mt. 22:30), our highest perfection will consist in being like them. But it is not without good cause that Moses commends the favour of God towards us by giving us this peculiar title, the more especially that he was only comparing man with the visible creation.

4. But our definition of the image seems not to be complete until it appears more clearly what the faculties are in which man excels, and in which he is to be regarded as a mirror of the divine glory. This, however, cannot be better known than from the remedy provided for the corruption of nature. It cannot be doubted that when Adam lost his first estate he became alienated from God. Wherefore, although we grant that the image of God was not utterly effaced and destroyed in him, it was, however, so corrupted, that any thing which remains is fearful deformity; and, therefore, our deliverance begins with that renovation which we obtain from Christ, who is, therefore, called the second Adam, because he restores us to true and substantial integrity. For although Paul, contrasting the quickening Spirit which believers receive from Christ, with the living soul which Adam was created (1 Cor. 15:45), commends the richer measure of grace bestowed in regeneration, he does not, however, contradict the statement, that the end of regeneration is to form us anew in the image of God. Accordingly, he elsewhere shows that the new man is renewed after the image of him that created him (Col. 3:19). To this corresponds another passage, "Put ye on the new man, who after God is created" (Eph. 4:24). We must now see what particulars Paul comprehends under this renovation. In the first place, he mentions knowledge, and in the second, true righteousness and holiness. Hence we infer, that at the beginning the image of God was manifested by light of intellect, rectitude of heart, and the soundness of every part. For though I admit that the forms of expression are elliptical, this principle cannot be overthrown—viz. that the leading feature in the renovation of the divine image must also have held the highest place in its creation. To the same effect Paul elsewhere says, that beholding the glory of Christ with unveiled face, we are transformed into the same image. We now see how Christ is the most perfect image of God, into which we

are so renewed as to bear the image of God in knowledge, purity, righteousness, and true holiness. This being established, the imagination of Osiander, as to bodily form, vanishes of its own accord. As to that passage of St Paul (1 Cor. 11:7), in which the man alone to the express exclusion of the woman, is called the image and glory of God, it is evident from the context, that it merely refers to civil order. I presume it has already been sufficiently proved, that the image comprehends everything which has any relation to the spiritual and eternal life. The same thing, in different terms, is declared by St John when he says, that the light which was from the beginning, in the eternal Word of God, was the light of man (John 1:4). His object being to extol the singular grace of God in making man excel the other animals, he at the same time shows how he was formed in the image of God, that he may separate him from the common herd, as possessing not ordinary animal existence, but one which combines with it the light of intelligence. Therefore, as the image of God constitutes the entire excellence of human nature, as it shone in Adam before his fall, but was afterwards vitiated and almost destroyed, nothing remaining but a ruin, confused, mutilated, and tainted with impurity, so it is now partly seen in the elect, in so far as they are regenerated by the Spirit. Its full lustre, however, will be displayed in heaven. But in order to know the particular properties in which it consists, it will be proper to treat of the faculties of the soul. For there is no solidity in Augustine's speculation, that the soul is a mirror of the Trinity, inasmuch as it comprehends within itself, intellect, will, and memory. Nor is there probability in the opinion of those who place likeness to God in the dominion bestowed upon man, as if he only resembled God in this, that he is appointed lord and master of all things. The likeness must be within, in himself. It must be something which is not external to him but is properly the internal good of the soul.

5. But before I proceed further, it is necessary to advert to the dream of the Manichees, which Servetus has attempted in our day to revive. Because it is said that God breathed into man's nostrils the breath of life (Gen. 2:7), they thought that the soul was a transmission of the substance of God; as if some portion of the boundless divinity had passed into man. It cannot take long time to show how many gross and foul absurdities this devilish error carries in its train. For if the soul of man is a portion transmitted from the essence of God, the divine nature must not only be liable to passion and change, but also to ignorance, evil desires, infirmity, and all kinds of vice.

There is nothing more inconstant than man, contrary movements agitating and distracting his soul. He is ever and anon deluded by want of skill, and overcome by the slightest temptations; while every one feels that the soul itself is a receptacle for all kinds of pollution. All these things must be attributed to the divine nature, if we hold that the soul is of the essence of God, or a secret influx of divinity. Who does not shudder at a thing so monstrous? Paul, indeed, quoting from Aratus, tells us we are his offspring (Acts 17:28); not in substance, however, but in quality, in as much as he has adorned us with divine endowments. Meanwhile, to lacerate the essence of the Creator, in order to assign a portion to each individual, is the height of madness. It must, therefore, be held as certain, that souls, notwithstanding of their having the divine image engraven on them, are created just as angels are. Creation, however, is not a transfusion of essence, but a commencement of it out of nothing. Nor, though the spirit is given by God, and when it quits the flesh again returns to him, does it follow that it is a portion withdrawn from his essence. Here, too, Osiander, carried away by his illusions entangled himself in an impious error, by denying that the image of God could be in man without his essential righteousness; as if God were unable, by the mighty power of his Spirit, to render us conformable to himself, unless Christ were substantially transfused into us. Under whatever colour some attempt to gloss these delusions, they can never so blind the eyes of intelligent readers as to prevent them from discerning in them a revival of Manicheism. But from the words of Paul, when treating of the renewal of the image (2 Cor. 3:18), the inference is obvious, that man was conformable to God, not by an influx of substance, but by the grace and virtue of the Spirit. He says, that by beholding the glory of Christ, we are transformed into the same image as by the Spirit of the Lord; and certainly the Spirit does not work in us so as to make us of the same substance with God.

6. It were vain to seek a definition of the soul from philosophers, not one of whom, with the exception of Plato, distinctly maintained its immortality. Others of the school of Socrates, indeed, lean the same way, but still without teaching distinctly a doctrine of which they were not fully persuaded. Plato, however, advanced still further, and regarded the soul as an image of God. Others so attach its powers and faculties to the present life, that they leave nothing external to the body. Moreover, having already shown from Scripture that the substance of the soul is incorporeal, we must now add, that though

it is not properly enclosed by space, it however occupies the body as a kind of habitation, not only animating all its parts, and rendering the organs fit and useful for their actions, but also holding the first place in regulating the conduct. This it does not merely in regard to the offices of a terrestrial life, but also in regard to the service of God. This, though not clearly seen in our corrupt state, yet the impress of its remains is seen in our very vices. For whence have men such a thirst for glory but from a sense of shame? And whence this sense of shame but from a respect for what is honourable? Of this, the first principle and source is a consciousness that they were born to cultivate righteousness,—a consciousness akin to religion. But as man was undoubtedly created to meditate on the heavenly life, so it is certain that the knowledge of it was engraven on the soul. And, indeed, man would want the principal use of his understanding if he were unable to discern his felicity, the perfection of which consists in being united to God. Hence, the principal action of the soul is to aspire thither, and, accordingly, the more a man studies to approach to God, the more he proves himself to be endued with reason.

Though there is some plausibility in the opinion of those who maintain that man has more than one soul, namely, a sentient and a rational, yet as there is no soundness in their arguments, we must reject it, unless we would torment ourselves with things frivolous and useless. They tell us (see chap. 5 sec. 4), there is a great repugnance between organic movements and the rational part of the soul. As if reason also were not at variance with herself, and her counsels sometimes conflicting with each other like hostile armies. But since this disorder results from the depravation of nature, it is erroneous to infer that there are two souls, because the faculties do not accord so harmoniously as they ought. But I leave it to philosophers to discourse more subtilely of these faculties. For the edification of the pious, a simple definition will be sufficient. I admit, indeed, that what they ingeniously teach on the subject is true, and not only pleasant, but also useful to be known; nor do I forbid any who are inclined to prosecute the study. First, I admit that there are five senses, which Plato (in Theæteto) prefers calling organs, by which all objects are brought into a common sensorium, as into a kind of receptacle: Next comes the imagination (*phantasia*), which distinguishes between the objects brought into the sensorium: Next, reason, to which the general power of Judgment belongs: And, lastly, intellect, which contemplates with fixed and quiet look whatever reason discursively revolves. In like manner, to intellect, fancy, and reason, the three cognitive faculties of the soul, correspond three appetite faculties—viz. will—whose office is to choose whatever reason and intellect propound; irascibility, which seizes on what is set before it by reason and fancy; and concupiscence, which lays hold of the objects presented by sense and fancy.

Though these things are true, or at least plausible, still, as I fear they are more fitted to entangle, by their obscurity, than to assist us, I think it best to omit them. If any one chooses to distribute the powers of the mind in a different manner, calling one appetive, which, though devoid of reason, yet obeys reason, if directed from a different quarter, and another intellectual, as being by itself participant of reason, I have no great objection. Nor am I disposed to quarrel with the view, that there are three principles of action—viz. sense, intellect, and appetite. But let us rather adopt a division adapted to all capacities—a thing which certainly is not to be obtained from philosophers. For they, when they would speak most plainly, divide the soul into appetite and intellect, but make both double. To the latter they sometimes give the name of *contemplative*, as being contented with mere knowledge and having no active powers (which circumstance makes Cicero designate it by the name of intellect, *ingenii*) (De Fin. lib. 5). At other times they give it the name of *practical*, because it variously moves the will by the apprehension of good or evil. Under this class is included the art of living well and justly. The former—viz. appetite—they divide into will and concupiscence, calling it βούλεσις, so whenever the appetite, which they call ὁρμή, obeys the reason. But when appetite, casting off the yoke of reason, runs to intemperance, they call it πάτηος. Thus they always presuppose in man a reason by which he is able to guide himself aright.

7. From this method of teaching we are forced somewhat to dissent. For philosophers, being unacquainted with the corruption of nature, which is the punishment of revolt, erroneously confound two states of man which are very different from each other. Let us therefore hold, for the purpose of the present work, that the soul consists of two parts, the intellect and the will (Book 2 chap. 2 sec. 2, 12),—the office of the intellect being to distinguish between objects, according as they seem deserving of being approved or disapproved; and the office of the will, to choose and follow what the intellect declares to be good, to reject and shun what it declares to be bad (Plato, in Phædro). We dwell not on the subtlety of Aristotle, that the mind has no motion of itself; but that the moving power is choice, which he also terms the appetite intellect. Not to lose ourselves in superfluous questions,

let it be enough to know that the intellect is to us, as it were, the guide and ruler of the soul; that the will always follows its beck, and waits for its decision, in matters of desire. For which reason Aristotle truly taught, that in the appetite there is a pursuit and rejection corresponding in some degree to affirmation and negation in the intellect (Aristot. Ethic. lib. 6 sec. 2). Moreover, it will be seen in another place (Book 2 c. 2 see. 12–26), how surely the intellect governs the will. Here we only wish to observe, that the soul does not possess any faculty which may not be duly referred to one or other of these members. And in this way we comprehend sense under intellect. Others distinguish thus: They say that sense inclines to pleasure in the same way as the intellect to good; that hence the appetite of sense becomes concupiscence and lust, while the affection of the intellect becomes will. For the term appetite, which they prefer, I use that of will, as being more common.

8. Therefore, God has provided the soul of man with intellect, by which he might discern good from evil, just from unjust, and might know what to follow or to shun, reason going before with her lamp; whence philosophers, in reference to her directing power, have called her τὸ ἐγεμονικὸν. To this he has joined will, to which choice belongs. Man excelled in these noble endowments in his primitive condition, when reason, intelligence, prudence, and Judgment, not only sufficed for the government of his earthly life, but also enabled him to rise up to God and eternal happiness. Thereafter choice was added to direct the appetites, and temper all the organic motions; the will being thus perfectly submissive to the authority of reason. In this upright state, man possessed freedom of will, by which, if he chose, he was able to obtain eternal life. It were here unseasonable to introduce the question concerning the secret predestination of God, because we are not considering what might or might not happen, but what the nature of man truly was. Adam, therefore, might have stood if he chose, since it was only by his own will that he fell; but it was because his will was pliable in either directions and he had not received constancy to persevere, that he so easily fell. Still he had a free choice of good and evil; and not only so, but in the mind and will there was the highest rectitude, and all the organic parts were duly framed to obedience, until man corrupted its good properties, and destroyed himself. Hence the great darkness of philosophers who have looked for a complete building in a ruin, and fit arrangement in disorder. The principle they set out with was, that man could not be a rational animal unless he had a free choice of good and evil. They also imagined that the distinction between virtue and vice was destroyed, if man did not of his own counsel arrange his life. So far well, had there been no change in man. This being unknown to them, it is not surprising that they throw every thing into confusion. But those who, while they profess to be the disciples of Christ, still seek for free-will in man, notwithstanding of his being lost and drowned in spiritual destruction, labour under manifold delusion, making a heterogeneous mixture of inspired doctrine and philosophical opinions, and so erring as to both. But it will be better to leave these things to their own place (see Book 2 chap. 2) At present it is necessary only to remember, that man, at his first creation, was very different from all his posterity; who, deriving their origin from him after he was corrupted, received a hereditary taint. At first every part of the soul was formed to rectitude. There was soundness of mind and freedom of will to choose the good. If any one objects that it was placed, as it were, in a slippery position, because its power was weak, I answer, that the degree conferred was sufficient to take away every excuse. For surely the Deity could not be tied down to this condition,—to make man such, that he either could not or would not sin. Such a nature might have been more excellent; but to expostulate with God as if he had been bound to confer this nature on man, is more than unjust, seeing he had full right to determine how much or how little He would give. Why He did not sustain him by the virtue of perseverance is hidden in his counsel; it is ours to keep within the bounds of soberness. Man had received the power, if he had the will, but he had not the will which would have given the power; for this will would have been followed by perseverance. Still, after he had received so much, there is no excuse for his having spontaneously brought death upon himself. No necessity was laid upon God to give him more than that intermediate and even transient will, that out of man's fall he might extract materials for his own glory.

CHAPTER 16

THE WORLD, CREATED BY GOD, STILL CHERISHED AND PROTECTED BY HIM. EACH AND ALL OF ITS PARTS GOVERNED BY HIS PROVIDENCE.

The divisions of this chapter are, I. The doctrine of the special providence of God over all the creatures,

singly and collectively, as opposed to the dreams of the Epicureans about fortune and fortuitous causes. II. The fiction of the Sophists concerning the omnipotence of God, and the error of philosophers, as to a confused and equivocal government of the world, sec. 1–5. All animals, but especially mankind, from the peculiar superintendence exercised over them, are proofs, evidences, and examples of the providence of God, sec. 6, 7. III. A consideration of fate, fortune, chance, contingence, and uncertain events (on which the matter here under discussion turns).

Sections:

1. Even the wicked, under the guidance of carnal sense, acknowledge that God is the Creator. The godly acknowledge not this only, but that he is a most wise and powerful governor and preserver of all created objects. In so doing, they lean on the Word of God, some passages from which are produced.

2. Refutation of the Epicureans, who oppose fortune and fortuitous causes to Divine Providence, as taught in Scripture. The sun, a bright manifestation of Divine Providence.

3. Figment of the Sophists as to an indolent Providence refuted. Consideration of the Omnipotence as combined with the Providence of God. Double benefit resulting from a proper acknowledgement of the Divine Omnipotence. Cavils of Infidelity.

4. A definition of Providence refuting the erroneous dogmas of Philosophers. Dreams of the Epicureans and Peripatetics.

5. Special Providence of God asserted and proved by arguments founded on a consideration of the Divine Justice and Mercy. Proved also by passages of Scripture, relating to the sky, the earth, and animals.

6. Special Providence proved by passages relating to the human race, and the more especially that for its sake the world was created.

7. Special Providence proved, lastly, from examples taken from the history of the Israelites, of Jonah, Jacob, and from daily experience.

8. Erroneous views as to Providence refuted:—I. The sect of the Stoics. II. The fortune and chance of the Heathen.

9. How things are said to be fortuitous to us, though done by the determinate counsel of God. Example. Error of separating contingency and event from the secret, but just, and most wise counsel of God. Two examples.

1. It were cold and lifeless to represent God as a momentary Creator, who completed his work once for all, and then left it. Here, especially, we must dissent from the profane, and maintain that the presence of the divine power is conspicuous, not less in the perpetual condition of the world then in its first creation. For, although even wicked men are forced, by the mere view of the earth and sky, to rise to the Creator, yet faith has a method of its own in assigning the whole praise of creation to God. To this effect is the passage of the Apostle already quoted that by faith we understand that the worlds were framed by the Word of God (Heb. 11:3); because, without proceeding to his Providence, we cannot understand the full force of what is meant by God being the Creator, how much soever we may seem to comprehend it with our mind, and confess it with our tongue. The carnal mind, when once it has perceived the power of God in the creation, stops there, and, at the farthest, thinks and ponders on nothing else than the wisdom, power, and goodness displayed by the Author of such a work (matters which rise spontaneously, and force themselves on the notice even of the unwilling), or on some general agency on which the power of motion depends, exercised in preserving and governing it. In short, it imagines that all things are sufficiently sustained by the energy divinely infused into them at first. But faith must penetrate deeper. After learning that there is a Creator, it must forthwith infer that he is also a Governor and Preserver, and that, not by producing a kind of general motion in the machine of the globe as well as in each of its parts, but by a special providence sustaining, cherishing, superintending, all the things which he has made, to the very minutest, even to a sparrow. Thus David, after briefly premising that the world was created by God, immediately descends to the continual course of Providence, "By the word of the Lord were the heavens framed, and all the host of them by the breath of his mouth;" immediately adding, "The Lord looketh from heaven, he beholdeth the children of men" (Ps. 33:6, 13, &c). He subjoins other things to the same effect. For although all do not reason so accurately, yet because it would not be credible that human affairs were superintended by God, unless he were the maker of the world, and no one could seriously believe that he is its Creator without feeling convinced that he takes care of his works; David with good reason, and in admirable order, leads us from the one to the other. In general, indeed, philosophers teach, and the human mind conceives, that all the parts of the world are invigorated by the secret inspiration of God. They do not, however

reach the height to which David rises taking all the pious along with him, when he says, "These wait all upon thee, that thou mayest give them their meat in due season. That thou givest them they gather: thou openest thine hand, they are filled with good. Thou hidest thy face, they are troubled: thou takest away their breath, they die, and return to their dust. Thou sendest forth thy Spirit, they are created, and thou renewest the face of the earth" (Ps. 104:27–30). Nay, though they subscribe to the sentiment of Paul, that in God "we live, and move, and have our being" (Acts 17:28), yet they are far from having a serious apprehension of the grace which he commends, because they have not the least relish for that special care in which alone the paternal favour of God is discerned.

2. That this distinction may be the more manifest, we must consider that the Providence of God, as taught in Scripture, is opposed to fortune and fortuitous causes. By an erroneous opinion prevailing in all ages, an opinion almost universally prevailing in our own day—viz. that all things happen fortuitously, the true doctrine of Providence has not only been obscured, but almost buried. If one falls among robbers, or ravenous beasts; if a sudden gust of wind at sea causes shipwreck; if one is struck down by the fall of a house or a tree; if another, when wandering through desert paths, meets with deliverance; or, after being tossed by the waves, arrives in port, and makes some wondrous hair-breadth escape from death—all these occurrences, prosperous as well as adverse, carnal sense will attribute to fortune. But whose has learned from the mouth of Christ that all the hairs of his head are numbered (Mt. 10:30), will look farther for the cause, and hold that all events whatsoever are governed by the secret counsel of God. With regard to inanimate objects again we must hold that though each is possessed of its peculiar properties, yet all of them exert their force only in so far as directed by the immediate hand of God. Hence they are merely instruments, into which God constantly infuses what energy he sees meet, and turns and converts to any purpose at his pleasure. No created object makes a more wonderful or glorious display than the sun. For, besides illuminating the whole world with its brightness, how admirably does it foster and invigorate all animals by its heat, and fertilise the earth by its rays, warming the seeds of grain in its lap, and thereby calling forth the verdant blade! This it supports, increases, and strengthens with additional nurture, till it rises into the stalk; and still feeds it with perpetual moisture, till it comes into flower; and from flower to fruit, which it continues to ripen till it attains maturity. In like manner, by its warmth trees and vines bud, and put forth first their leaves, then their blossom, then their fruit. And the Lord, that he might claim the entire glory of these things as his own, was pleased that light should exist, and that the earth should be replenished with all kinds of herbs and fruits before he made the sun. No pious man, therefore, will make the sun either the necessary or principal cause of those things which existed before the creation of the sun, but only the instrument which God employs, because he so pleases; though he can lay it aside, and act equally well by himself: Again, when we read, that at the prayer of Joshua the sun was stayed in its course (Josh. 10:13); that as a favour to Hezekiah, its shadow receded ten degrees (2 Kings 20:11); by these miracles God declared that the sun does not daily rise and set by a blind instinct of nature, but is governed by Him in its course, that he may renew the remembrance of his paternal favour toward us. Nothing is more natural than for spring, in its turns to succeed winter, summer spring, and autumn summer; but in this series the variations are so great and so unequal as to make it very apparent that every single year, month, and day, is regulated by a new and special providence of God.

3. And truly God claims omnipotence to himself, and would have us to acknowledge it,—not the vain, indolent, slumbering omnipotence which sophists feign, but vigilant, efficacious, energetic, and ever active,—not an omnipotence which may only act as a general principle of confused motion, as in ordering a stream to keep within the channel once prescribed to it, but one which is intent on individual and special movements. God is deemed omnipotent, not because he can act though he may cease or be idle, or because by a general instinct he continues the order of nature previously appointed; but because, governing heaven and earth by his providence, he so overrules all things that nothing happens without his counsel. For when it is said in the Psalms, "He has done whatsoever he has pleased" (Ps. 115:3), the thing meant is his sure and deliberate purpose. It were insipid to interpret the Psalmist's words in philosophic fashion, to mean that God is the primary agent, because the beginning and cause of all motion. This rather is the solace of the faithful, in their adversity, that every thing which they endure is by the ordination and command of God, that they are under his hand. But if the government of God thus extends to all his works, it is a childish cavil to confine it to natural influx. Those moreover who confine the providence of God within narrow limits, as if he allowed all things to be borne along freely according to a perpetual law of nature, do not more defraud God of his glory than

themselves of a most useful doctrine; for nothing were more wretched than man if he were exposed to all possible movements of the sky, the air, the earth, and the water. We may add, that by this view the singular goodness of God towards each individual is unbecomingly impaired. David exclaims (Ps. 8:3), that infants hanging at their mothers breasts are eloquent enough to celebrate the glory of God, because, from the very moment of their births they find an aliment prepared for them by heavenly care. Indeed, if we do not shut our eyes and senses to the fact, we must see that some mothers have full provision for their infants, and others almost none, according as it is the pleasure of God to nourish one child more liberally, and another more sparingly. Those who attribute due praise to the omnipotence of God thereby derive a double benefit. He to whom heaven and earth belong, and whose nod all creatures must obey, is fully able to reward the homage which they pay to him, and they can rest secure in the protection of Him to whose control everything that could do them harm is subject, by whose authority, Satan, with all his furies and engines, is curbed as with a bridle, and on whose will everything adverse to our safety depends. In this way, and in no other, can the immoderate and superstitious fears, excited by the dangers to which we are exposed, be calmed or subdued. I say superstitious fears. For such they are, as often as the dangers threatened by any created objects inspire us with such terror, that we tremble as if they had in themselves a power to hurt us, or could hurt at random or by chance; or as if we had not in God a sufficient protection against them. For example, Jeremiah forbids the children of God " to be dismayed at the signs of heaven, as the heathen are dismayed at them" (Jer. 10:2). He does not, indeed, condemn every kind of fear. But as unbelievers transfer the government of the world from God to the stars, imagining that happiness or misery depends on their decrees or presages, and not on the Divine will, the consequence is, that their fear, which ought to have reference to him only, is diverted to stars and comets. Let him, therefore, who would beware of such unbelief, always bear in mind, that there is no random power, or agency, or motion in the creatures, who are so governed by the secret counsel of God, that nothing happens but what he has knowingly and willingly decreed.

4. First, then, let the reader remember that the providence we mean is not one by which the Deity, sitting idly in heaven, looks on at what is taking place in the world, but one by which he, as it were, holds the helms and overrules all events. Hence his providence extends not less to the hand than to the eye. When Abraham said to his son, *God will provide* (Gen. 22:8), he meant not merely to assert that the future event was foreknown to Gods but to resign the management of an unknown business to the will of Him whose province it is to bring perplexed and dubious matters to a happy result. Hence it appears that providence consists in action. What many talk of bare prescience is the merest trifling. Those do not err quite so grossly who attribute government to God, but still, as I have observed, a confused and promiscuous government which consists in giving an impulse and general movement to the machine of the globe and each of its parts, but does not specially direct the action of every creature. It is impossible, however, to tolerate this error. For, according to its abettors, there is nothing in this providence, which they call universal, to prevent all the creatures from being moved contingently, or to prevent man from turning himself in this direction or in that, according to the mere freedom of his own will. In this ways they make man a partner with God,—God, by his energy, impressing man with the movement by which he can act, agreeably to the nature conferred upon him while man voluntarily regulates his own actions. In short, their doctrine is, that the world, the affairs of men, and men themselves, are governed by the power, but not by the decree of God. I say nothing of the Epicureans (a pest with which the world has always been plagued), who dream of an inert and idle God, and others, not a whit sounder, who of old feigned that God rules the upper regions of the air, but leaves the inferior to Fortune. Against such evident madness even dumb creatures lift their voice.

My intention now is, to refute an opinion which has very generally obtained—an opinion which, while it concedes to God some blind and equivocal movement, withholds what is of principal moment—viz. the disposing and directing of every thing to its proper end by incomprehensible wisdom. By withholding government, it makes God the ruler of the world in name only, not in reality. For what, I ask, is meant by government, if it be not to preside so as to regulate the destiny of that over which you preside? I do not, however, totally repudiate what is said of an universal providence, provided, on the other hand, it is conceded to me that the world is governed by God, not only because he maintains the order of nature appointed by him, but because he takes a special charge of every one of his works. It is true, indeed, that each species of created objects is moved by a secret instinct of nature, as if they obeyed the eternal command of God, and spontaneously followed the course which

God at first appointed. And to this we may refer our Saviour's words, that he and his Father have always been at work from the beginning (John 5:17); also the words of Paul, that "in him we live, and move, and have our being" (Acts 17:28); also the words of the author of the Epistle to the Hebrews, who, when wishing to prove the divinity of Christ, says, that he upholdeth "all things by the word of his power" (Heb. 1:3). But some, under pretext of the general, hide and obscure the special providence, which is so surely and clearly taught in Scripture, that it is strange how any one can bring himself to doubt of it. And, indeed, those who interpose that disguise are themselves forced to modify their doctrine, by adding that many things are done by the special care of God. This, however, they erroneously confine to particular acts. The thing to be proved, therefore, is, that single events are so regulated by God, and all events so proceed from his determinate counsel, that nothing happens fortuitously.

5. Assuming that the beginning of motion belongs to God, but that all things move spontaneously or casually, according to the impulse which nature gives, the vicissitudes of day and nights summer and winter, will be the work of God; inasmuch as he, in assigning the office of each, appointed a certain law, namely, that they should always with uniform tenor observe the same course, day succeeding night, month succeeding month, and year succeeding year. But, as at one time, excessive heat, combined with drought, burns up the fields; at another time excessive rains rot the crops, while sudden devastation is produced by tempests and storms of hail, these will not be the works of God, unless in so far as rainy or fair weather, heat or cold, are produced by the concourse of the stars, and other natural causes. According to this view, there is no place left either for the paternal favour, or the Judgments of God. If it is said that God fully manifests his beneficence to the human race, by furnishing heaven and earth with the ordinary power of producing food, the explanation is meagre and heathenish: as if the fertility of one year were not a special blessing, the penury and dearth of another a special punishment and curse from God. But as it would occupy too much time to enumerate all the arguments, let the authority of God himself suffice. In the Law and the Prophets he repeatedly declares, that as often as he waters the earth with dew and rain, he manifests his favour, that by his command the heaven becomes hard as iron, the crops are destroyed by mildew and other evils, that storms and hail, in devastating the fields, are signs of sure and special vengeance. This being admitted, it is certain that not a drop of rain falls without the express command of God. David, indeed (Ps. 146:9), extols the general providence of God in supplying food to the young ravens that cry to him but when God himself threatens living creatures with famine, does he not plainly declare that they are all nourished by him, at one time with scanty, at another with more ample measure? It is childish, as I have already said, to confine this to particular acts, when Christ says, without reservation, that not a sparrow falls to the ground without the will of his Father (Mt. 10:29). Surely, if the flight of birds is regulated by the counsel of God, we must acknowledge with the prophet, that while he "dwelleth on high," he "humbleth himself to behold the things that are in heaven and in the earth" (Ps. 113:5, 6).

6. But as we know that it was chiefly for the sake of mankind that the world was made, we must look to this as the end which God has in view in the government of it. The prophet Jeremiah exclaims, "O Lord, I know that the way of man is not in himself: it is not in man that walketh to direct his steps" (Jer. 10:23). Solomon again says, "Man's goings are of the Lord: how can a man then understand his own way?" (Prov. 20:24). Will it now be said that man is moved by God according to the bent of his nature, but that man himself gives the movement any direction he pleases? Were it truly so, man would have the full disposal of his own ways. To this it will perhaps be answered, that man can do nothing without the power of God. But the answer will not avail, since both Jeremiah and Solomon attribute to God not power only, but also election and decree. And Solomon, in another place, elegantly rebukes the rashness of men in fixing their plans without reference to God, as if they were not led by his hand. "The preparations of the heart in man, and the answer of the tongue, is from the Lord" (Prov. 16:1). It is a strange infatuation, surely for miserable men, who cannot even give utterance except in so far as God pleases, to begin to act without him! Scriptures moreover, the better to show that every thing done in the world is according to his decree, declares that the things which seem most fortuitous are subject to him. For what seems more attributable to chance than the branch which falls from a tree, and kills the passing traveller? But the Lord sees very differently, and declares that He delivered him into the hand of the slayer (Exod. 21:13). In like manners who does not attribute the lot to the blindness of Fortune? Not so the Lord, who claims the decision for himself (Prov. 16:33). He says not, that by his power the lot is thrown into the lap, and taken out, but declares that the only thing which could be attributed to chance is

from him. To the same effect are the words of Solomon, "The poor and the deceitful man meet together; the Lord lighteneth both their eyes" (Prov. 29:13). For although rich and poor are mingled together in the world, in saying that the condition of each is divinely appointed, he reminds us that God, Who enlightens all, has his own eye always open, and thus exhorts the poor to patient endurance, seeing that those who are discontented with their lot endeavour to shake off a burden which God has imposed upon them. Thus, too, another prophet upbraids the profane, who ascribe it to human industry, or to fortune, that some grovel in the mire while others rise to honour. "Promotion cometh neither from the east, nor from the west, nor from the south. But God is the judge: he putteth down ones and setteth up another" (Ps. 75:6, 7). Because God cannot divest himself of the office of judge, he infers that to his secret counsel it is owing that some are elevated, while others remain without honour.

7. Nay, I affirm in general, that particular events are evidences of the special providence of God. In the wilderness God caused a south wind to blow, and brought the people a plentiful supply of birds (Exod. 19:13). When he desired that Jonah should be thrown into the sea, he sent forth a whirlwind. Those who deny that God holds the reins of government will say that this was contrary to ordinary practice, whereas I infer from it that no wind ever rises or rages without his special command. In no way could it be true that "he maketh the winds his messengers, and the flames of fire his ministers;" that "he maketh the clouds his chariot, and walketh upon the wings of the wind" (Ps. 104:3, 4), did he not at pleasure drive the clouds and winds and therein manifest the special presence of his power. In like manner, we are elsewhere taught, that whenever the sea is raised into a storm, its billows attest the special presence of God. "He commandeth and raiseth the stormy wind, which lifteth up the waves." "He maketh the storm a calm, so that the waves thereof are still" (Ps. 107:25, 29). He also elsewhere declares, that he had smitten the people with blasting and mildew (Amos 4:9). Again while man naturally possesses the power of continuing his species, God describes it as a mark of his special favour, that while some continue childless, others are blessed with offspring: for the fruit of the womb is his gift. Hence the words of Jacob to Rachel, "Am I in God's stead, who has withheld from thee the fruit of the womb?" (Gen. 30:2). To conclude in one word. Nothing in nature is more ordinary than that we should be nourished with bread. But the Spirit declares not only that the produce of the earth is God's special gift, but "that man does not live by bread only" (Deut. 8:3), because it is not mere fulness that nourishes him but the secret blessing of God. And hence, on the other hand, he threatens to take away "the stay and the staff, the whole stay of bread, and the whole stay of water" (Is. 3:1). Indeed, there could be no serious meaning in our prayer for daily bread, if God did not with paternal hand supply us with food. Accordingly, to convince the faithful that God, in feeding them, fulfils the office of the best of parents, the prophet reminds them that he "giveth food to all flesh" (Ps. 136:25). In fine, when we hear on the one hand, that "the eyes of the Lord are upon the righteous, and his ears are open unto their cry," and, on the other hand, that "the face of the Lord is against them that do evil, to cut off the remembrance of them from the earth" (Ps. 34:15, 16), let us be assured that all creatures above and below are ready at his service, that he may employ them in whatever way he pleases. Hence we infer, not only that the general providence of God, continuing the order of nature, extends over the creatures, but that by his wonderful counsel they are adapted to a certain and special purpose.

8. Those who would cast obloquy on this doctrine, calumniate it as the dogma of the Stoics concerning fate. The same charge was formerly brought against Augustine (lib. ad Bonifac. 2, c. 6 et alibi). We are unwilling to dispute about words; but we do not admit the term Fate, both because it is of the class which Paul teaches us to shun, as profane novelties (1 Tim. 6:20), and also because it is attempted, by means of an odious term, to fix a stigma on the truth of God. But the dogma itself is falsely and maliciously imputed to us. For we do not with the Stoics imagine a necessity consisting of a perpetual chain of causes, and a kind of involved series contained in nature, but we hold that God is the disposer and ruler of all things,—that from the remotest eternity, according to his own wisdom, he decreed what he was to do, and now by his power executes what he decreed. Hence we maintain, that by his providence, not heaven and earth and inanimate creatures only, but also the counsels and wills of men are so governed as to move exactly in the course which he has destined. What, then, you will say, does nothing happen fortuitously, nothing contingently? I answer, it was a true saying of Basil the Great, that Fortune and Chance are heathen terms; the meaning of which ought not to occupy pious minds. For if all success is blessing from God, and calamity and adversity are his curse, there is no place left in human affairs for fortune

and chance. We ought also to be moved by the words of Augustine (Retract. lib. 1 cap. 1), "In my writings against the Academics," says he, "I regret having so often used the term Fortune; although I intended to denote by it not some goddess, but the fortuitous issue of events in external matters, whether good or evil. Hence, too, those words, Perhaps, Perchance, Fortuitously, which no religion forbids us to use, though everything must be referred to Divine Providence. Nor did I omit to observe this when I said, Although, perhaps, that which is vulgarly called Fortune, is also regulated by a hidden order, and what we call Chance is nothing else than that the reason and cause of which is secret. It is true, I so spoke, but I repent of having mentioned Fortune there as I did, when I see the very bad custom which men have of saying, not as they ought to do, 'So God pleased,' but, 'So Fortune pleased.' " In short, Augustine everywhere teaches, that if anything is left to fortune, the world moves at random. And although he elsewhere declares (Quæstionum, lib. 83). that all things are carried on, partly by the free will of man, and partly by the Providence of God, he shortly after shows clearly enough that his meaning was, that men also are ruled by Providence, when he assumes it as a principle, that there cannot be a greater absurdity than to hold that anything is done without the ordination of God; because it would happen at random. For which reason, he also excludes the contingency which depends on human will, maintaining a little further on, in clearer terms, that no cause must be sought for but the will of God. When he uses the term permission, the meaning which he attaches to it will best appear from a single passage (De Trinity. lib. 3 cap. 4), where he proves that the will of God is the supreme and primary cause of all things, because nothing happens without his order or permission. He certainly does not figure God sitting idly in a watch-tower, when he chooses to permit anything. The will which he represents as interposing is, if I may so express it, active (*actualis*), and but for this could not be regarded as a cause.

9. But since our sluggish minds rest far beneath the height of Divine Providence, we must have recourse to a distinction which may assist them in rising. I say then, that though all things are ordered by the counsel and certain arrangement of God, to us, however, they are fortuitous,—not because we imagine that Fortune rules the world and mankind, and turns all things upside down at random (far be such a heartless thought from every Christian breast); but as the order, method, end, and necessity of events, are, for the most part, hidden in the counsel of God, though it is certain that they are produced by the will of God, they have the appearance of being fortuitous, such being the form under which they present themselves to us, whether considered in their own nature, or estimated according to our knowledge and Judgment. Let us suppose, for example, that a merchant, after entering a forest in company with trust-worthy individuals, imprudently strays from his companions and wanders bewildered till he falls into a den of robbers and is murdered. His death was not only foreseen by the eye of God, but had been fixed by his decree. For it is said, not that he foresaw how far the life of each individual should extend, but that he determined and fixed the bounds which could not be passed (Job 14:5). Still, in relation to our capacity of discernment, all these things appear fortuitous. How will the Christian feel? Though he will consider that every circumstance which occurred in that person's death was indeed in its nature fortuitous, he will have no doubt that the Providence of God overruled it and guided fortune to his own end. The same thing holds in the case of future contingencies. All future events being uncertain to us, seem in suspense as if ready to take either direction. Still, however, the impression remains seated in our hearts, that nothing will happen which the Lord has not provided. In this sense the term event is repeatedly used in Ecclesiastes, because, at the first glance, men do not penetrate to the primary cause which lies concealed. And yet, what is taught in Scripture of the secret providence of God was never so completely effaced from the human heart, as that some sparks did not always shine in the darkness. Thus the soothsayers of the Philistine, though they waver in uncertainty, attribute the adverse event partly to God and partly to chance. If the ark, say they, "Goes up by the way of his own coast to Bethshemish, then he has done us this great evil; but if not, then we shall know that it is not his hand that smote us, it was a chance that happened to us." (1 Sam. 6:9). Foolishly, indeed, when divination fails them they flee to fortune. Still we see them constrained, so as not to venture to regard their disaster as fortuitous. But the mode in which God, by the curb of his Providence, turns events in whatever direction he pleases, will appear from a remarkable example. At the very same moment when David was discovered in the wilderness of Maon, the Philistines make an inroad into the country, and Saul is forced to depart (1 Sam. 23:26, 27). If God, in order to provide for the safety of his servant, threw this obstacle in the way of Saul, we surely cannot say, that though the Philistine took up arms contrary to human expectation, they

did it by chance. What seems to us contingence, faith will recognise as the secret impulse of God. The reason is not always equally apparent, but we ought undoubtedly to hold that all the changes which take place in the world are produced by the secret agency of the hand of God. At the same time, that which God has determined, though it must come to pass, is not, however, precisely, or in its own nature, necessary. We have a familiar example in the case of our Saviour's bones. As he assumed a body similar to ours, no sane man will deny that his bones were capable of being broken and yet it was impossible that they should be broken (John 19:33, 36). Hence, again, we see that there was good ground for the distinction which the Schoolmen made between necessity, *secundum quid*, and necessity absolute, also between the necessity of *consequent* and of *consequence*. God made the bones of his Son frangible, though he exempted them from actual fracture; and thus, in reference to the necessity of his counsel, made that impossible which might have naturally taken place.

CHAPTER 17

USE TO BE MADE OF THE DOCTRINE OF PROVIDENCE.

This chapter may be conveniently divided into two parts:—I. A general explanation is given of the doctrine of Divine Providence, in so far as conducive to the solid instruction and consolation of the godly, sect. 1, and specially sect. 2–12. First, however, those are refuted who deny that the world is governed by the secret and incomprehensible counsel of God; those also who throw the blame of all wickedness upon God, and absurdly pretend that exercises of piety are useless, sect. 2–5. Thereafter is added a holy meditation on Divine Providence, which, in the case of prosperity, is painted to the life, sect. 6–11.

II. A solution of two objections from passages of Scripture, which attribute repentance to God, and speak of something like an abrogation of his decrees.

Sections:

1. Summary of the doctrine of Divine Providence. 1. It embraces the future and the past. 2. It works by means, without means, and against means. 3. Mankind, and particularly the Church, the object of special care. 4. The mode of administration usually secret, but always just. This last point more fully considered.

2. The profane denial that the world is governed by the secret counsel of God, refuted by passages of Scripture. Salutary counsel.

3. This doctrine, as to the secret counsel of God in the government of the world, gives no countenance either to the impiety of those who throw the blame of their wickedness upon God, the petulance of those who reject means, or the error of those who neglect the duties of religion.

4. As regards future events, the doctrine of Divine Providence not inconsistent with deliberation on the part of man.

5. In regard to past events, it is absurd to argue that crimes ought not to be punished, because they are in accordance with the divine decrees. 1. The wicked resist the declared will of God. 2. They are condemned by conscience. 3. The essence and guilt of the crime is in themselves, though God uses them as instruments.

6. A holy meditation on Divine Providence. 1. All events happen by the ordination of God. 2. All things contribute to the advantage of the godly. 3. The hearts of men and all their endeavours are in the hand of God. 4. Providence watches for the safety of the righteous. 5. God has a special care of his elect.

7. Meditation on Providence continued. 6. God in various ways curbs and defeats the enemies of the Church. 7. He overrules all creatures, even Satan himself, for the good of his people.

8. Meditation on Providence continued. 8. He trains the godly to patience and moderation. Examples. Joseph, Job, and David. 9. He shakes off their lethargy, and urges them to repentance.

9. Meditation continued. 10. The right use of inferior causes explained. 11. When the godly become negligent or imprudent in the discharge of duty, Providence reminds them of their fault. 12. It condemns the iniquities of the wicked. 13. It produces a right consideration of the future, rendering the servants of God prudent, diligent, and active. 14. It causes them to resign themselves to the wisdom and omnipotence of God, and, at the same time, makes them diligent in their calling.

10. Meditation continued. 15. Though human life is beset with innumerable evils, the righteous, trusting to Divine Providence, feel perfectly secure.

11. The use of the foregoing meditation.

12. The second part of the chapter, disposing of two objections. 1. That Scripture represents God as changing his purpose, or repenting, and that, therefore, his Providence is not fixed. Answer to this first objection. Proof from Scripture that God cannot repent.

13. Why repentance attributed to God.

14. Second objection, that Scripture speaks of an annulment of the divine decrees. Objection answered. Answer confirmed by an example.

1. Moreover, such is the proneness of the human mind to indulge in vain subtleties, that it becomes almost impossible for those who do not see the sound and proper use of this doctrine, to avoid entangling themselves in perplexing difficulties. It will, therefore, be proper here to advert to the end which Scripture has in view in teaching that all things are divinely ordained. And it is to be observed, first, that the Providence of God is to be considered with reference both to the past and the future; and, secondly, that in overruling all things, it works at one time with means, at another without means, and at another against means. Lastly, the design of God is to show that He takes care of the whole human race, but is especially vigilant in governing the Church, which he favours with a closer inspection. Moreover, we must add, that although the paternal favour and beneficence, as well as the judicial severity of God, is often conspicuous in the whole course of his Providence, yet occasionally as the causes of events are concealed, the thought is apt to rise, that human affairs are whirled about by the blind impulse of Fortune, or our carnal nature inclines us to speak as if God were amusing himself by tossing men up and down like balls. It is true, indeed, that if with sedate and quiet minds we were disposed to learn, the issue would at length make it manifest, that the counsel of God was in accordance with the highest reason, that his purpose was either to train his people to patience, correct their depraved affections, tame their wantonness, inure them to self-denial, and arouse them from torpor; or, on the other hand, to cast down the proud, defeat the craftiness of the ungodly, and frustrate all their schemes. How much soever causes may escape our notice, we must feel assured that they are deposited with him, and accordingly exclaim with David, "Many, O Lord my God, are thy wonderful works which thou hast done, and thy thoughts which are to us-ward: if I would declare and speak of them, they are more than can be numbered" (Ps. 40:5). For while our adversities ought always to remind us of our sins, that the punishment may incline us to repentance, we see, moreover, how Christ declares there is something more in the secret counsel of his Father than to chastise every one as he deserves. For he says of the man who was born blind, "Neither has this man sinned, nor his parents: but that the works of God should be made manifest in him" (John 9:3). Here, where calamity takes precedence even of birth, our carnal sense murmurs as if God were unmerciful in thus afflicting those who have not offended. But Christ declares that, provided we had eyes clear enough, we should perceive that in this spectacle the glory of his Father is brightly displayed. We must use modesty, not as it were compelling God to render an account, but so revering his hidden Judgments as to account his will the best of all reasons. When the sky is overcast with dense clouds, and a violent tempest arises, the darkness which is presented to our eye, and the thunder which strikes our ears, and stupefies all our senses with terror, make us imagine that every thing is thrown into confusion, though in the firmament itself all continues quiet and serene. In the same way, when the tumultuous aspect of human affairs unfits us for judging, we should still hold, that God, in the pure light of his justice and wisdom, keeps all these commotions in due subordination, and conducts them to their proper end. And certainly in this matter many display monstrous infatuation, presuming to subject the works of God to their calculation, and discuss his secret counsels, as well as to pass a precipitate Judgment on things unknown, and that with greater license than on the doings of mortal men. What can be more preposterous than to show modesty toward our equals, and choose rather to suspend our Judgment than incur the blame of rashness, while we petulantly insult the hidden Judgments of God, Judgments which it becomes us to look up to and revere.

2. No man, therefore, will duly and usefully ponder on the providence of God save he who recollects that he has to do with his own Maker, and the Maker of the world, and in the exercise of the humility which becomes him, manifests both fear and reverence. Hence it is, that in the present day so many dogs tear this doctrine with envenomed teeth, or, at least, assail it with their bark, refusing to give more license to God than their own reason dictates to themselves. With what petulance, too, are we assailed for not being contented with the precepts of the Law, in which the will of God is comprehended, and for maintaining that the world is governed by his secret counsels? As if our doctrine were the figment of our own brain, and were not distinctly declared by the Spirit, and repeated in innumerable forms of expression! Since some feeling of shame restrains them from daring to belch forth their blasphemies against heaven, that they may give the freer vent to their rage, they pretend to pick a quarrel with us. But if they refuse to admit that every event which happens in the world is governed by the incomprehensible

counsel of God, let them explain to what effect Scripture declares, that "his Judgments are a great deep" (Ps. 36:7). For when Moses exclaims that the will of God "is not in heaven that thou shouldest say, Who shall go up for us to heaven, and bring it unto us? Neither is it beyond the sea that thou shouldest say, Who shall go over the sea and bring it unto us?" (Deut. 30:12, 13), because it was familiarly expounded in the law, it follows that there must be another hidden will which is compared to " a great deep." It is of this will Paul exclaims, "O! the depths of the riches of the wisdom and knowledge of God! How unsearchable are his Judgments, and his ways past finding out! For who has known the mind of the Lord, or who has been his counsellor?" (Rom. 11:33, 34). It is true, indeed, that in the law and the gospel are comprehended mysteries which far transcend the measure of our sense; but since God, to enable his people to understand those mysteries which he has deigned to reveal in his word, enlightens their minds with a spirit of understanding, they are now no longer a deep, but a path in which they can walk safely—a lamp to guide their feet—a light of life—a school of clear and certain truth. But the admirable method of governing the world is justly called a deep, because, while it lies hid from us, it is to be reverently adored. Both views Moses has beautifully expressed in a few words. "Secret things," saith he, "belong unto the Lord our God, but those things which are revealed belong unto us and to our children for ever" (Deut. 29:29). We see how he enjoins us not only studiously to meditate on the law, but to look up with reverence to the secret Providence of God. The Book of Job also, in order to keep our minds humble, contains a description of this lofty theme. The author of the Book, after taking an ample survey of the universe, and discoursing magnificently on the works of God, at length adds, "Lo, these are parts of his ways: but how little a portion is heard of him?" (Job 26:14). For which reason he, in another passage, distinguishes between the wisdom which dwells in God, and the measure of wisdom which he has assigned to man (Job 28:21, 28). After discoursing of the secrets of nature, he says that wisdom "is hid from the eyes of all living;" that "God understandeth the way thereof." Shortly after he adds, that it has been divulged that it might be investigated; for "unto man he said, Behold the fear of the Lord, that is wisdom." To this the words of Augustine refer, "As we do not know all the things which God does respecting us in the best order, we ought, with good intention, to act according to the Law, and in some things be acted upon according to the Law, his Providence being a Law immutable" (August. Quest. lib. 83 c. 27). Therefore, since God claims to himself the right of governing the world, a right unknown to us, let it be our law of modesty and soberness to acquiesce in his supreme authority regarding his will as our only rule of justice, and the most perfect cause of all things,—not that absolute will, indeed, of which sophists prate, when by a profane and impious divorce, they separate his justice from his power, but that universal overruling Providence from which nothing flows that is not right, though the reasons thereof may be concealed.

3. Those who have learned this modesty will neither murmur against God for adversity in time past, nor charge him with the blame of their own wickedness, as Homer's Agamemnon does.— Ἐγὼ δ' οὐκ αἴτιός εἰμι, ἀλλὰ Ζεὺς καὶ μοῖρα. "*Blame not me, but Jupiter and fate.*" On the other hand, they will note like the youth in Plautus, destroy themselves in despairs as if hurried away by the Fates. "Unstable is the condition of affairs; instead of doing as they list, men only fulfil their fate: I will hie me to a rock, and there end my fortune with my life." Nor will they, after the example of another, use the name of God as a cloak for their crimes. For in another comedy Lyconides thus expresses himself:—"God was the impeller: I believe the gods wished it. Did they not wish it, it would not be done, I know." They will rather inquire and learn from Scripture what is pleasing to God, and then, under the guidance of the Spirit, endeavour to attain it. Prepared to follow whithersoever God may call, they will show by their example that nothing is more useful than the knowledge of this doctrine, which perverse men undeservedly assail, because it is sometimes wickedly abused. The profane make such a bluster with their foolish puerilities, that they almost, according to the expression, confound heaven and earth. If the Lord has marked the moment of our death, it cannot be escaped,—it is vain to toil and use precaution. Therefore, when one ventures not to travel on a road which he hears is infested by robbers; when another calls in the physician, and annoys himself with drugs, for the sake of his health; a third abstains from coarser food, that he may not injure a sickly constitution; and a fourth fears to dwell in a ruinous house; when all, in short, devise, and, with great eagerness of mind, strike out paths by which they may attain the objects of their desire; either these are all vain remedies, laid hold of to correct the will of God, or his certain decree does not fix the limits of life and death, health and sickness, peace and war, and other matters which men, according as they desire and hate,

study by their own industry to secure or avoid. Nay, these trifles even infer, that the prayers of the faithful must be perverse, not to say superfluous, since they entreat the Lord to make a provision for things which he has decreed from eternity. And then, imputing whatever happens to the providence of God, they connive at the man who is known to have expressly designed it. Has an assassin slain an honest citizen? He has, say they, executed the counsel of God. Has some one committed theft or adultery? The deed having been provided and ordained by the Lord, he is the minister of his providence. Has a son waited with indifference for the death of his parent, without trying any remedy? He could not oppose God, who had so predetermined from eternity. Thus all crimes receive the name of virtues, as being in accordance with divine ordination.

4. As regards future events, Solomon easily reconciles human deliberation with divine providence. For while he derides the stupidity of those who presume to undertake anything without God, as if they were not ruled by his hand, he elsewhere thus expresses himself: "A man's heart deviseth his ways but the Lord directeth his steps" (Prov. 16:9); intimating, that the eternal decrees of God by no means prevent us from proceeding, under his will, to provide for ourselves, and arrange all our affairs. And the reason for this is clear. For he who has fixed the boundaries of our life, has at the same time entrusted us with the care of it, provided us with the means of preserving it, forewarned us of the dangers to which we are exposed, and supplied cautions and remedies, that we may not be overwhelmed unawares. Now, our duty is clear, namely, since the Lord has committed to us the defence of our life,—to defend it; since he offers assistance,—to use it; since he forewarns us of danger,—not to rush on heedless; since he supplies remedies,—not to neglect them. But it is said, a danger that is not fatal will not hurt us, and one that is fatal cannot be resisted by any precaution. But what if dangers are not fatal, merely because the Lord has furnished you with the means of warding them off, and surmounting them? See how far your reasoning accords with the order of divine procedure: You infer that danger is not to be guarded against, because, if it is not fatal, you shall escape without precaution; whereas the Lord enjoins you to guard against its just because he wills it not to be fatal. These insane cavillers overlook what is plainly before their eyes—viz. that the Lord has furnished men with the artful of deliberation and caution, that they may employ them in subservience to his providence, in the preservation of their life; while, on the contrary, by neglect and sloth, they bring upon themselves the evils which he has annexed to them. How comes it that a provident man, while he consults for his safety, disentangles himself from impending evils; while a foolish man, through unadvised temerity, perishes, unless it be that prudence and folly are, in either case, instruments of divine dispensation? God has been pleased to conceal from us all future events that we may prepare for them as doubtful, and cease not to apply the provided remedies until they have either been overcome, or have proved too much for all our care. Hence, I formerly observed, that the Providence of God does not interpose simply; but, by employing means, assumes, as it were, a visible form.

5. By the same class of persons, past events are referred improperly and inconsiderately to simple providence. As all contingencies whatsoever depend on it, therefore, neither thefts nor adulteries, nor murders, are perpetrated without an interposition of the divine will. Why, then, they ask, should the thief be punished for robbing him whom the Lord chose to chastise with poverty? Why should the murderer be punished for slaying him whose life the Lord had terminated? If all such persons serve the will of God, why should they be punished? I deny that they serve the will of God. For we cannot say that he who is carried away by a wicked mind performs service on the order of God, when he is only following his own malignant desires. He obeys God, who, being instructed in his will, hastens in the direction in which God calls him. But how are we so instructed unless by his word? The will declared by his word is, therefore, that which we must keep in view in acting, God requires of us nothing but what he enjoins. If we design anything contrary to his precept, it is not obedience, but contumacy and transgression. But if he did not will it, we could not do it. I admit this. But do we act wickedly for the purpose of yielding obedience to him? This, assuredly, he does not command. Nay, rather we rush on, not thinking of what he wishes, but so inflamed by our own passionate lust, that, with destined purpose, we strive against him. And in this way, while acting wickedly, we serve his righteous ordination, since in his boundless wisdom he well knows how to use bad instruments for good purposes. And see how absurd this mode of arguing is. They will have it that crimes ought not to be punished in their authors, because they are not committed without the dispensation of God. I concede more—that thieves and murderers, and other evil-doers, are instruments of Divine Providence, being employed by the Lord himself to execute the Judgments which he has resolved to inflict. But I deny that this

forms any excuse for their misdeeds. For how? Will they implicate God in the same iniquity with themselves, or will they cloak their depravity by his righteousness? They cannot exculpate themselves, for their own conscience condemns them: they cannot charge God, since they perceive the whole wickedness in themselves, and nothing in Him save the legitimate use of their wickedness. But it is said he works by their means. And whence, I pray, the foetid odour of a dead body, which has been unconfined and putrefied by the sun's heat? All see that it is excited by the rays of the sun, but no man therefore says that the fetid odour is in them. In the same way, while the matter and guilt of wickedness belongs to the wicked man, why should it be thought that God contracts any impurity in using it at pleasure as his instrument? Have done, then, with that dog-like petulance which may, indeed, bay from a distance at the justice of God, but cannot reach it!

6. These calumnies, or rather frenzied dreams, will easily be dispelled by a pure and holy meditation on Divine Providence, meditation such as piety enjoins, that we may thence derive the best and sweetest fruit. The Christian, then, being most fully persuaded, that all things come to pass by the dispensation of God, and that nothing happens fortuitously, will always direct his eye to him as the principal cause of events, at the same time paying due regard to inferior causes in their own place. Next, he will have no doubt that a special providence is awake for his preservation, and will not suffer anything to happen that will not turn to his good and safety. But as its business is first with men and then with the other creatures, he will feel assured that the providence of God reigns over both. In regard to men, good as well as bad, he will acknowledge that their counsels, wishes, aims and faculties are so under his hand, that he has full power to turn them in whatever direction, and constrain them as often as he pleases. The fact that a special providence watches over the safety of believers, is attested by a vast number of the clearest promises. "Cast thy burden upon the Lord, and he shall sustain thee: he shall never suffer the righteous to be moved." "Casting all your care upon him: for he careth for you." "He that dwelleth in the secret place of the Most High, shall abide under the shadow of the Almighty." "He that toucheth you, toucheth the apple of mine eye." "We have a strong city: salvation will God appoint for walls and bulwarks." "Can a woman forget her sucking child, that she should not have compassion on the son of her womb? yea, they may forget, yet will I not forget thee." Nay, the chief aim of the historical books of Scripture is to show that the ways of his saints are so carefully guarded by the Lord, as to prevent them even from dashing their foot against a stone. Therefore, as we a little ago justly exploded the opinion of those who feign a universal providence, which does not condescend to take special care of every creature, so it is of the highest moment that we should specially recognise this care towards ourselves. Hence, our Saviour, after declaring that even a sparrow falls not to the ground without the will of his Father, immediately makes the application, that being more valuable than many sparrows, we ought to consider that God provides more carefully for us. He even extends this so far, as to assure us that the hairs of our head are all numbered. What more can we wish, if not even a hair of our head can fall, save in accordance with his will? I speak not merely of the human race in general. God having chosen the Church for his abode, there cannot be a doubt, that in governing it, he gives singular manifestations of his paternal care.

7. The servant of God being confirmed by these promises and examples, will add the passages which teach that all men are under his power, whether to conciliate their minds, or to curb their wickedness, and prevent it from doing harm. For it is the Lord who gives us favour, not only with those who wish us well, but also in the eyes of the Egyptians (Exod. 3:21), in various ways defeating the malice of our enemies. Sometimes he deprives them of all presence of mind, so that they cannot undertake anything soundly or soberly. In this ways he sends Satan to be a lie in the mouths of all the prophets in order to deceive Ahab (1 Kings 22:22), by the counsel of the young men he so infatuates Rehoboam, that his folly deprives him of his kingdom (1 Kings 12:10, 15). Sometimes when he leaves them in possession of intellect, he so fills them with terror and dismays that they can neither will nor plan the execution of what they had designed. Sometimes, too, after permitting them to attempt what lust and rage suggested, he opportunely interrupts them in their career, and allows them not to conclude what they had begun. Thus the counsel of Ahithophel, which would have been fatal to David, was defeated before its time (2 Sam. 17:7, 14). Thus, for the good and safety of his people, he overrules all the creatures, even the devil himself who, we see, durst not attempt any thing against Job without his permission and command. This knowledge is necessarily followed by gratitude in prosperity, patience in adversity, and incredible security for the time to come. Every thing, therefore, which turns out prosperous and according to his wish, the Christian will ascribe entirely to God, whether he has experienced his beneficence through the

instrumentality of men, or been aided by inanimate creatures. For he will thus consider with himself: Certainly it was the Lord that disposed the minds of these people in my favour, attaching them to me so as to make them the instruments of his kindness. In an abundant harvest he will think that it is the Lord who listens to the heaven, that the heaven may listen to the earth, and the earth herself to her own offspring; in other cases, he will have no doubt that he owes all his prosperity to the divine blessing, and, admonished by so many circumstances, will feel it impossible to be ungrateful.

8. If any thing adverse befalls him, he will forthwith raise his mind to God, whose hand is most effectual in impressing us with patience and placid moderation of mind. Had Joseph kept his thoughts fixed on the treachery of his brethren, he never could have resumed fraternal affection for them. But turning toward the Lord, he forgot the injury, and was so inclined to mildness and mercy, that he even voluntarily comforts his brethren, telling them, "Be not grieved nor angry with yourselves that ye sold me hither; for God did send me before you to preserve life." "As for you, ye thought evil against me; but God meant it unto good" (Gen. 45:5; 50:20). Had Job turned to the Chaldees, by whom he was plundered, he should instantly have been fired with revenge, but recognising the work of the Lord, he solaces himself with this most beautiful sentiment: "The Lord gave, and the Lord has taken away; blessed be the name of the Lord" (Job 1:21). So when David was assailed by Shimei with stones and curses, had he immediately fixed his eyes on the man, he would have urged his people to retaliate the injury; but perceiving that he acts not without an impulse from the Lord, he rather calms them. "So let him curse," says he, "because the Lord has said unto him, Curse David." With the same bridle he elsewhere curbs the excess of his grief, "I was dumb, I opened not my mouth, because thou didst it" (Ps. 39:9). If there is no more effectual remedy for anger and impatience, he assuredly has not made little progress who has learned so to meditate on Divine Providence, as to be able always to bring his mind to this, The Lord willed it, it must therefore be borne; not only because it is unlawful to strive with him, but because he wills nothing that is not just and befitting. The whole comes to this. When unjustly assailed by men, overlooking their malice (which could only aggravate our grief, and whet our minds for vengeance), let us remember to ascend to God, and learn to hold it for certain, that whatever an enemy wickedly committed against us was permitted, and sent by his righteous dispensation. Paul, in order to suppress our desire to retaliate injuries, wisely reminds us that we wrestle not with flesh and blood, but with our spiritual enemy the devil, that we may prepare for the contest (Eph. 6:12). But to calm all the impulses of passion, the most useful consideration is, that God arms the devil, as well as all the wicked, for conflict, and sits as umpire, that he may exercise our patience. But if the disasters and miseries which press us happen without the agency of men, let us call to mind the doctrine of the Law (Deut. 28:1), that all prosperity has its source in the blessing of God, that all adversity is his curse. And let us tremble at the dreadful denunciation, "And if ye will not be reformed by these things, but will walk contrary unto me; then will I also walk contrary unto you" (Lev. 26:23, 24). These words condemn our torpor, when, according to our carnal sense, deeming that whatever happens in any way is fortuitous, we are neither animated by the kindness of God to worship him, nor by his scourge stimulated to repentance. And it is for this reason that Jeremiah (Lament. 3:38), and Amos (Amos 3:6), expostulated bitterly with the Jews, for not believing that good as well as evil was produced by the command of God. To the same effect are the words in Isaiah, "I form the light and create darkness: I make peace and create evil. I the Lord do all these things" (Is. 45:7).

9. At the same time, the Christian will not overlook inferior causes. For, while he regards those by whom he is benefited as ministers of the divine goodness, he will not, therefore, pass them by, as if their kindness deserved no gratitude, but feeling sincerely obliged to them, will willingly confess the obligation, and endeavour, according to his ability, to return it. In fine, in the blessings which he receives, he will revere and extol God as the principal author, but will also honour men as his ministers, and perceive, as is the truth, that by the will of God he is under obligation to those, by whose hand God has been pleased to show him kindness. If he sustains any loss through negligence or imprudence, he will, indeed, believe that it was the Lord's will it should so be, but, at the same time, he will impute it to himself. If one for whom it was his duty to care, but whom he has treated with neglect, is carried off by disease, although aware that the person had reached a limit beyond which it was impossible to pass, he will not, therefore, extenuate his fault, but, as he had neglected to do his duty faithfully towards him, will feel as if he had perished by his guilty negligence. Far less where, in the case of theft or murder, fraud and preconceived malice have existed, will he palliate it under the pretext of Divine Providence, but in the

same crime will distinctly recognise the justice of God, and the iniquity of man, as each is separately manifested. But in future events, especially, will he take account of such inferior causes. If he is not left destitute of human aid, which he can employ for his safety, he will set it down as a divine blessing; but he will not, therefore, be remiss in taking measures, or slow in employing the help of those whom he sees possessed of the means of assisting him. Regarding all the aids which the creatures can lend him, as hands offered him by the Lord, he will avail himself of them as the legitimate instruments of Divine Providence. And as he is uncertain what the result of any business in which he engages is to be (save that he knows, that in all things the Lord will provide for his good), he will zealously aim at what he deems for the best, so far as his abilities enable him. In adopting his measures, he will not be carried away by his own impressions, but will commit and resign himself to the wisdom of God, that under his guidance he may be led into the right path. However, his confidence in external aid will not be such that the presence of it will make him feel secure, the absence of it fill him with dismay, as if he were destitute. His mind will always be fixed on the Providence of God alone, and no consideration of present circumstances will be allowed to withdraw him from the steady contemplation of it. Thus Joab, while he acknowledges that the issue of the battle is entirely in the hand of God, does not therefore become inactive, but strenuously proceeds with what belongs to his proper calling, "Be of good courage," says he, "and let us play the men for our people, and for the cities of our God; and the Lord do that which seemeth him good" (2 Sam. 10:12). The same conviction keeping us free from rashness and false confidence, will stimulate us to constant prayer, while at the same time filling our minds with good hope, it will enable us to feel secure, and bid defiance to all the dangers by which we are surrounded.

10. Here we are forcibly reminded of the inestimable felicity of a pious mind. Innumerable are the ills which beset human life, and present death in as many different forms. Not to go beyond ourselves, since the body is a receptacle, nay the nurse, of a thousand diseases, a man cannot move without carrying along with him many forms of destruction. His life is in a manner interwoven with death. For what else can be said where heat and cold bring equal danger? Then, in what direction soever you turn, all surrounding objects not only may do harm, but almost openly threaten and seem to present immediate death. Go on board a ship, you are but a plank's breadth from death. Mount a horse, the stumbling of a foot endangers your life. Walk along the streets, every tile upon the roofs is a source of danger. If a sharp instrument is in your own hand, or that of a friend, the possible harm is manifest. All the savage beasts you see are so many beings armed for your destruction. Even within a high walled garden, where everything ministers to delight, a serpent will sometimes lurk. Your house, constantly exposed to fire, threatens you with poverty by day, with destruction by night. Your fields, subject to hail, mildew, drought, and other injuries, denounce barrenness, and thereby famine. I say nothing of poison, treachery, robbery, some of which beset us at home, others follow us abroad. Amid these perils, must not man be very miserable, as one who, more dead than alive, with difficulty draws an anxious and feeble breath, just as if a drawn sword were constantly suspended over his neck? It may be said that these things happen seldom, at least not always, or to all, certainly never all at once. I admit it; but since we are reminded by the example of others, that they may also happen to us, and that our life is not an exception any more than theirs, it is impossible not to fear and dread as if they were to befall us. What can you imagine more grievous than such trepidation? Add that there is something like an insult to God when it is said, that man, the noblest of the creatures, stands exposed to every blind and random stroke of fortune. Here, however, we were only referring to the misery which man should feel, were he placed under the dominion of chance.

11. But when once the light of Divine Providence has illumined the believer's soul, he is relieved and set free, not only from the extreme fear and anxiety which formerly oppressed him, but from all care. For as he justly shudders at the idea of chance, so he can confidently commit himself to God. This, I say, is his comfort, that his heavenly Father so embraces all things under his power—so governs them at will by his nod—so regulates them by his wisdom, that nothing takes place save according to his appointment; that received into his favour, and entrusted to the care of his angels neither fire, nor water, nor sword, can do him harm, except in so far as God their master is pleased to permit. For thus sings the Psalm, "Surely he shall deliver thee from the snare of the fowler, and from the noisome pestilence. He shall cover thee with his feathers, and under his wings shalt thou trust; his truth shall be thy shield and buckler. Thou shalt not be afraid for the terror by night; nor for the arrow that flieth by day; nor for the pestilence that walketh in darkness; nor for the destruction that wasteth at noonday" &c. (Ps. 91:2–6). Hence the exulting confidence of the saints, "The Lord is on my

side; I will not fear: what can man do unto me? The Lord taketh my part with them that help me." "Though an host should encamp against me, my heart shall not fear." "Yea, though I walk through the valley of the shadow of death, I will fear no evil." (Ps. 118:6; 27:3; 23:4).

How comes it, I ask, that their confidence never fails, but just that while the world apparently revolves at random, they know that God is every where at work, and feel assured that his work will be their safety? When assailed by the devil and wicked men, were they not confirmed by remembering and meditating on Providence, they should, of necessity, forthwith despond. But when they call to mind that the devil, and the whole train of the ungodly, are, in all directions, held in by the hand of God as with a bridle, so that they can neither conceive any mischief, nor plan what they have conceived, nor how much soever they may have planned, move a single finger to perpetrate, unless in so far as he permits, nay, unless in so far as he commands; that they are not only bound by his fetters, but are even forced to do him service,—when the godly think of all these things they have ample sources of consolation. For, as it belongs to the lord to arm the fury of such foes and turn and destine it at pleasure, so it is his also to determine the measure and the end, so as to prevent them from breaking loose and wantoning as they list. Supported by this conviction, Paul, who had said in one place that his journey was hindered by Satan (1 Thess. 2:18), in another resolves, with the permission of God, to undertake it (1 Cor. 16:7). If he had only said that Satan was the obstacle, he might have seemed to give him too much power, as if he were able even to overturn the counsels of God; but now, when he makes God the disposer, on whose permission all journeys depend, he shows, that however Satan may contrive, he can accomplish nothing except in so far as He pleases to give the word. For the same reason, David, considering the various turns which human life undergoes as it rolls, and in a manner whirls around, retakes himself to this asylum, "My times are in thy hand" (Ps. 31:15). He might have said the course of life or *time* in the singular number, but by *times* he meant to express, that how unstable soever the condition of man may be, the vicissitudes which are ever and anon taking place are under divine regulation. Hence Rezin and the king of Israel, after they had joined their forces for the destruction of Israel, and seemed torches which had been kindled to destroy and consume the land, are termed by the prophet "smoking fire brands." They could only emit a little smoke (Is. 7:4). So Pharaoh, when he was an object of dread to all by his wealth and strength, and the multitude of his troops, is compared to the largest of beasts, while his troops are compared to fishes; and God declares that he will take both leader and army with his hooks, and drag them whither he pleases (Ezek. 29:4). In one word, not to dwell longer on this, give heed, and you will at once perceive that ignorance of Providence is the greatest of all miseries, and the knowledge of it the highest happiness.

12. On the Providence of God, in so far as conducive to the solid instruction and consolation of believers (for, as to satisfying the curiosity of foolish men, it is a thing which cannot be done, and ought not to be attempted), enough would have been said, did not a few passages remain which seem to insinuate, contrary to the view which we have expounded, that the counsel of God is not firm and stable, but varies with the changes of sublunary affairs. First, in reference to the Providence of God, it is said that he repented of having made man (Gen. 6:6), and of having raised Saul to the kingdom (1 Sam. 15:11), and that he will repent of the evil which he had resolved to inflict on his people as soon as he shall have perceived some amendment in them (Jer. 18:8). Secondly, his decrees are sometimes said to be annulled. He had by Jonah proclaimed to the Ninevites, "Yet forty days and Nineveh shall be overthrown," but, immediately on their repentance, he inclined to a more merciful sentence (Jonah 3:4–10). After he had, by the mouth of Isaiah, given Hezekiah intimation of his death, he was moved by his tears and prayers to defer it (Is. 38:15; 2 Kings 20:15). Hence many argue that God has not fixed human affairs by an eternal decree, but according to the merits of each individual, and as he deems right and just, disposes of each single year, and day, and hour. As to repentance, we must hold that it can no more exist in God than ignorance, or error, or impotence. If no man knowingly or willingly reduces himself to the necessity of repentance, we cannot attribute repentance to God without saying either that he knows not what is to happen, or that he cannot evade it, or that he rushes precipitately and inconsiderately into a resolution, and then forthwith regrets it. But so far is this from the meaning of the Holy Spirit, that in the very mention of repentance he declares that God is not influenced by any feeling of regret, that he is not a man that he should repent. And it is to be observed, that, in the same chapter, both things are so conjoined, that a comparison of the passages admirably removes the appearance of contradiction. When it is said that God repented of having made Saul king, the term *change* is used figuratively. Shortly after, it is added, "The

Strength of Israel will not lie nor repent; for he is not a man, that he should repent" (1 Sam. 15:29). In these words, his immutability is plainly asserted without figure. Wherefore it is certain that, in administering human affairs, the ordination of God is perpetual and superior to every thing like repentance. That there might be no doubt of his constancy, even his enemies are forced to bear testimony to it. For, Balaam, even against his will, behaved to break forth into this exclamation, "God is not a man, that he should lie; neither the son of man, that he should repent: has he said, and shall he not do it? or has he spoken, and shall he not make it good?" (Num. 23:19).

13. What then is meant by the term repentance? The very same that is meant by the other forms of expression, by which God is described to us humanly. Because our weakness cannot reach his height, any description which we receive of him must be lowered to our capacity in order to be intelligible. And the mode of lowering is to represent him not as he really is, but as we conceive of him. Though he is incapable of every feeling of perturbation, he declares that he is angry with the wicked. Wherefore, as when we hear that God is angry, we ought not to imagine that there is any emotion in him, but ought rather to consider the mode of speech accommodated to our sense, God appearing to us like one inflamed and irritated whenever he exercises Judgment, so we ought not to imagine any thing more under the term repentance than a change of action, men being wont to testify their dissatisfaction by such a change. Hence, because every change whatever among men is intended as a correction of what displeases, and the correction proceeds from repentance, the same term applied to God simply means that his procedure is changed. In the meantime, there is no inversion of his counsel or will, no change of his affection. What from eternity he had foreseen, approved, decreed, he prosecutes with unvarying uniformity, how sudden soever to the eye of man the variation may seem to be.

14. Nor does the Sacred History, while it relates that the destruction which had been proclaimed to the Ninevites was remitted, and the life of Hezekiah, after an intimation of death, prolonged, imply that the decrees of God were annulled. Those who think so labour under delusion as to the meaning of *threatenings*, which, though they affirm simply, nevertheless contain in them a tacit condition dependent on the result. Why did the Lord send Jonah to the Ninevites to predict the overthrow of their city? Why did he by Isaiah give Hezekiah intimation of his death? He might have destroyed both them and him without a message to announce the disaster. He had something else in view than to give them a warning of death, which might let them see it at a distance before it came. It was because he did not wish them destroyed but reformed, and thereby saved from destruction. When Jonah prophesies that in forty days Nineveh will be overthrown, he does it in order to prevent the overthrow. When Hezekiah is forbidden to hope for longer life, it is that he may obtain longer life. Who does not now see that, by threatening of this kind, God wished to arouse those to repentance whom he terrified, that they might escape the Judgment which their sins deserved? If this is so, the very nature of the case obliges us to supply a tacit condition in a simple denunciation. This is even confirmed by analogous cases. The Lord rebuking King Abimelech for having carried off the wife of Abraham, uses these words: "Behold, thou art but a dead man, for the woman which thou hast taken; for she is a man's wife." But, after Abimelech's excuse, he thus speaks: "Restore the man his wife, for he is a prophet, and he shall pray for thee, and thou shalt live; and if thou restore her not, know thou that thou shalt surely die, thou and all that art thine" (Gen. 20:3, 7). You see that, by the first announcement, he makes a deep impression on his mind, that he may render him eager to give satisfaction, and that by the second he clearly explains his will. Since the other passages may be similarly explained, you must not infer from them that the Lord derogated in any respect from his former counsel, because he recalled what he had promulgated. When, by denouncing punishment, he admonishes to repentance those whom he wishes to spare, he paves the way for his eternal decree, instead of varying it one whit either in will or in language. The only difference is, that he does not express, in so many syllables, what is easily understood. The words of Isaiah must remain true, "The Lord of hosts has purposed, and who shall disannul it? And his hand is stretched out, and who shall turn it back?" (Isaiah 14:27).

CHAPTER 18

THE INSTRUMENTALITY OF THE WICKED EMPLOYED BY GOD, WHILE HE CONTINUES FREE FROM EVERY TAINT.

This last chapter of the First Book consists of three parts: I. It having been said above that God bends all the reprobate, and even Satan himself, at his will,

three objections are started. First, that this happens by the permission, not by the will of God. To this objection there is a twofold reply, the one, that angels and men, good and bad, do nothing but what is appointed by God; the second, that all movements are secretly directed to their end by the hidden inspiration of God, sec. 1, 2. II. A second objection is, that there are two contrary wills in God, if by a secret counsel he decrees what he openly prohibits by his law. This objection refuted, sec. 3. III. The third objection is, that God is made the author of all wickedness, when he is said not only to use the agency of the wicked, but also to govern their counsels and affections, and that therefore the wicked are unjustly punished. This objection refuted in the last section.

Sections:

1. The carnal mind the source of the objections which are raised against the Providence of God. A primary objection, making a distinction between the permission and the will of God, refuted. Angels and men, good and bad, do nought but what has been decreed by God. This proved by examples.

2. All hidden movements directed to their end by the unseen but righteous instigation of God. Examples, with answers to objections.

3. These objections originate in a spirit of pride and blasphemy. Objection, that there must be two contrary wills in God, refuted. Why the one simple will of God seems to us as if it were manifold.

4. Objection, that God is the author of sin, refuted by examples. Augustine's answer and admonition.

1. From other passages, in which God is said to draw or bend Satan himself, and all the reprobate, to his will, a more difficult question arises. For the carnal mind can scarcely comprehend how, when acting by their means, he contracts no taint from their impurity, nay, how, in a common operation, he is exempt from all guilt, and can justly condemn his own ministers. Hence a distinction has been invented between *doing* and *permitting* because to many it seemed altogether inexplicable how Satan and all the wicked are so under the hand and authority of God, that he directs their malice to whatever end he pleases, and employs their iniquities to execute his Judgments. The modesty of those who are thus alarmed at the appearance of absurdity might perhaps be excused, did they not endeavour to vindicate the justice of God from every semblance of stigma by defending an untruth. It seems absurd that man should be blinded by the will and command of God, and yet be forthwith punished for his blindness. Hence, recourse is had to the evasion that this is done only by the permission, and not also by the will of God. He himself, however, openly declaring that he *does* this, repudiates the evasion. That men do nothing save at the secret instigation of God, and do not discuss and deliberate on any thing but what he has previously decreed with himself and brings to pass by his secret direction, is proved by numberless clear passages of Scripture. What we formerly quoted from the Psalms, to the effect that he does whatever pleases him, certainly extends to all the actions of men. If God is the arbiter of peace and war, as is there said, and that without any exception, who will venture to say that men are borne along at random with a blind impulse, while He is unconscious or quiescent? But the matter will be made clearer by special examples. From the first chapter of Job we learn that Satan appears in the presence of God to receive his orders, just as do the angels who obey spontaneously. The manner and the end are different, but still the fact is, that he cannot attempt anything without the will of God. But though afterwards his power to afflict the saint seems to be only a bare permission, yet as the sentiment is true, "The Lord gave, and the Lord has taken away; as it pleased the Lord, so it has been done," we infer that God was the author of that trial of which Satan and wicked robbers were merely the instruments. Satan's aim is to drive the saint to madness by despair. The Sabeans cruelly and wickedly make a sudden incursion to rob another of his goods. Job acknowledges that he was deprived of all his property, and brought to poverty, because such was the pleasure of God. Therefore, whatever men or Satan himself devise, God holds the helm, and makes all their efforts contribute to the execution of his Judgments. God wills that the perfidious Ahab should be deceived; the devil offers his agency for that purpose, and is sent with a definite command to be a lying spirit in the mouth of all the prophets (2 Kings 22:20). If the blinding and infatuation of Ahab is a Judgment from God, the fiction of bare permission is at an end; for it would be ridiculous for a judge only to permit, and not also to decree, what he wishes to be done at the very time that he commits the execution of it to his ministers. The Jews purposed to destroy Christ. Pilate and the soldiers indulged them in their fury; yet the disciples confess in solemn prayer that all the wicked did nothing but what the hand and counsel of God had decreed (Acts 4:28), just as Peter had previously said in his discourse, that Christ was delivered to death by the

determinate counsel and foreknowledge of God (Acts 2:23); in other words, that God, to whom all things are known from the beginning, had determined what the Jews had executed. He repeats the same thing elsewhere, "Those things, which God before had showed by the mouth of all his prophets, that Christ should suffer, he has so fulfilled" (Acts 4:18). Absalom incestuously defiling his father's bed, perpetrates a detestable crime. God, however, declares that it was his work; for the words are, "Thou midst it secretly, but I will do this thing before all Israel, and before the sun." The cruelties of the Chaldeans in Judea are declared by Jeremiah to be the work of God. For which reason, Nebuchadnezzar is called the servant of God. God frequently exclaims, that by his hiss, by the clang of his trumpet, by his authority and command, the wicked are excited to war. He calls the Assyrian the rod of his anger, and the axe which he wields in his hand. The overthrow of the city and downfall of the temple, he calls his own work. David, not murmuring against God, but acknowledging him to be a just judge, confesses that the curses of Shimei are uttered by his orders. "The Lord," says he, "has bidden him curse." Often in sacred history whatever happens is said to proceed from the Lord, as the revolt of the ten tribes, the death of Eli's sons, and very many others of a similar description. Those who have a tolerable acquaintance with the Scriptures see that, with a view to brevity, I am only producing a few out of many passages, from which it is perfectly clear that it is the merest trifling to substitute a bare permission for the providence of God, as if he sat in a watch-tower waiting for fortuitous events, his Judgments meanwhile depending on the will of man.

2. With regard to secret movements, what Solomon says of the heart of a king, that it is turned hither and thither, as God sees meet, certainly applies to the whole human race, and has the same force as if he had said, that whatever we conceive in our minds is directed to its end by the secret inspiration of God. And certainly, did he not work internally in the minds of men, it could not have been properly said, that he takes away the lip from the true, and prudence from the aged—takes away the heart from the princes of the earth, that they wander through devious paths. To the same effect, we often read that men are intimidated when He fills their hearts with terror. Thus David left the camp of Saul while none knew of its because a sleep from God had fallen upon all. But nothing can be clearer than the many passages which declare, that he blinds the minds of men, and smites them with giddiness, intoxicates them with a spirit of stupor, renders them infatuated, and hardens their hearts. Even these expressions many would confine to permissions as if, by deserting the reprobate, he allowed them to be blinded by Satan. But since the Holy Spirit distinctly says, that the blindness and infatuation are inflicted by the just Judgment of God, the solution is altogether inadmissible. He is said to have hardened the heart of Pharaoh, to have hardened it yet more, and confirmed it. Some evade these forms of expression by a silly cavil, because Pharaoh is elsewhere said to have hardened his own heart, thus making his will the cause of hardening it; as if the two things did not perfectly agree with each other, though in different senses—viz. that man, though acted upon by God, at the same time also acts. But I retort the objection on those who make it. If to harden means only bare permission, the contumacy will not properly belong to Pharaoh. Now, could any thing be more feeble and insipid than to interpret as if Pharaoh had only allowed himself to be hardened? We may add, that Scripture cuts off all handle for such cavils: "I," saith the Lord, "will harden his heart" (Exod. 4:21). So also, Moses says of the inhabitants of the land of Canaan, that they went forth to battle because the Lord had hardened their hearts (Josh. 11:20). The same thing is repeated by another prophet, "He turned their hearts to hate his people" (Psalm 105:25). In like manner, in Isaiah, he says of the Assyrian, "I will send him against a hypocritical nation, and against the people of my wrath will I give him a charge to take the spoil, and to take the prey" (Isaiah 10:6); not that he intends to teach wicked and obstinate man to obey spontaneously, but because he bends them to execute his Judgments, just as if they carried their orders engraven on their minds. And hence it appears that they are impelled by the sure appointment of God. I admit, indeed, that God often acts in the reprobate by interposing the agency of Satan; but in such a manner, that Satan himself performs his part, just as he is impelled, and succeeds only in so far as he is permitted. The evil spirit that troubled Saul is said to be from the Lord (1 Sam. 16:14), to intimate that Saul's madness was a just punishment from God. Satan is also said to blind the minds of those who believe not (2 Cor. 4:4). But how so, unless that a spirit of error is sent from God himself, making those who refuse to obey the truth to believe a lie? According to the former view, it is said, "If the prophet be deceived when he has spoken a thing, I the Lord have deceived that prophet" (Ezek. 14:9). According to the latter view, he is said to have given men over to a reprobate mind (Rom. 1:28), because he is the special author of his own just vengeance; whereas Satan is only his min-

ister (see Calv. in Ps. 141:4). But as in the Second Book (Chap. 4 sec. 3, 4), in discussing the question of man's freedom, this subject will again be considered, the little that has now been said seems to be all that the occasion requires. The sum of the whole is this,—since the will of God is said to be the cause of all things, all the counsels and actions of men must be held to be governed by his providence; so that he not only exerts his power in the elect, who are guided by the Holy Spirit, but also forces the reprobate to do him service.

3. As I have hitherto stated only what is plainly and unambiguously taught in Scripture, those who hesitate not to stigmatise what is thus taught by the sacred oracles, had better beware what kind of censure they employ. If, under a pretence of ignorance, they seek the praise of modesty, what greater arrogance can be imagined than to utter one word in opposition to the authority of God—to say, for instance, "I think otherwise,"—"I would not have this subject touched?" But if they openly blaspheme, what will they gain by assaulting heaven? Such petulance, indeed, is not new. In all ages there have been wicked and profane men, who rabidly assailed this branch of doctrine. But what the Spirit declared of old by the mouth of David (Ps. 51:6), they will feel by experience to be true—God will overcome when he is judged. David indirectly rebukes the infatuation of those whose license is so unbridled, that from their grovelling spot of earth they not only plead against God, but arrogate to themselves the right of censuring him. At the same time, he briefly intimates that the blasphemies which they belch forth against heaven, instead of reaching God, only illustrate his justice, when the mists of their calumnies are dispersed. Even our faith, because founded on the sacred word of God, is superior to the whole world, and is able from its height to look down upon such mists.

Their first objection—that if nothing happens without the will of God, he must have two contrary wills, decreeing by a secret counsel what he has openly forbidden in his law—is easily disposed of. But before I reply to it, I would again remind my readers, that this cavil is directed not against me, but against the Holy Spirit, who certainly dictated this confession to that holy man Job, "The Lord gave, and the Lord has taken away," when, after being plundered by robbers, he acknowledges that their injustice and mischief was a just chastisement from God. And what says the Scripture elsewhere? The sons of Eli "hearkened not unto the voice of their father, because the Lord would slay them" (1 Sam. 2:25). Another prophet also exclaims, "Our God is in the heavens: he has done whatsoever he has pleased" (Ps. 115:3). I have already shown clearly enough that God is the author of all those things which, according to these objectors, happen only by his inactive permission. He testifies that he creates light and darkness, forms good and evil (Is. 45:7); that no evil happens which he has not done (Amos 3:6). Let them tell me whether God exercises his Judgments willingly or unwillingly. As Moses teaches that he who is accidentally killed by the blow of an axe, is delivered by God into the hand of him who smites him (Deut. 19:5), so the Gospel, by the mouth of Luke, declares, that Herod and Pontius Pilate conspired "to do whatsoever thy hand and thy counsel determined before to be done" (Acts 4:28). And, in truth, if Christ was not crucified by the will of God, where is our redemption? Still, however, the will of God is not at variance with itself. It undergoes no change. He makes no pretence of not willing what he wills, but while in himself the will is one and undivided, to us it appears manifold, because, from the feebleness of our intellect, we cannot comprehend how, though after a different manner, he wills and wills not the very same thing. Paul terms the calling of the Gentiles a hidden mystery, and shortly after adds, that therein was manifested the manifold wisdom of God (Eph. 3:10). Since, on account of the dullness of our sense, the wisdom of God seems manifold (or, as an old interpreter rendered it, multiform), are we, therefore, to dream of some variation in God, as if he either changed his counsel, or disagreed with himself? Nay, when we cannot comprehend how God can will that to be done which he forbids us to do, let us call to mind our imbecility, and remember that the light in which he dwells is not without cause termed inaccessible (1 Tim. 6:16), because shrouded in darkness. Hence, all pious and modest men will readily acquiesce in the sentiment of Augustine: "Man sometimes with a good will wishes something which God does not will, as when a good son wishes his father to live, while God wills him to die. Again, it may happen that man with a bad will wishes what God wills righteously, as when a bad son wishes his father to die, and God also wills it. The former wishes what God wills not, the latter wishes what God also wills. And yet the filial affection of the former is more consonant to the good will of God, though willing differently, than the unnatural affection of the latter, though willing the same thing; so much does approbation or condemnation depend on what it is befitting in man, and what in God to will, and to what end the will of each has respect. For the things which God rightly wills, he accomplishes by the evil wills of bad men,"—

(*August. Enchirid. ad Laurent. cap.* 101). He had said a little before (cap. 100), that the apostate angels, by their revolt, and all the reprobate, as far as they themselves were concerned, did what God willed not; but, in regard to his omnipotence, it was impossible for them to do so: for, while they act against the will of God, his will is accomplished in them. Hence he exclaims, "Great is the work of God, exquisite in all he wills! so that, in a manner wondrous and ineffable, that is not done without his will which is done contrary to it, because it could not be done if he did not permit; nor does he permit it unwillingly, but willingly; nor would He who is good permit evil to be done, were he not omnipotent to bring good out of evil" (*Augustin. in* Ps. 111:2).

4. In the same way is solved, or rather spontaneously vanishes, another objection—viz. If God not only uses the agency of the wicked, but also governs their counsels and affections, he is the author of all their sins; and, therefore, men, in executing what God has decreed, are unjustly condemned, because they are obeying his will. Here *will* is improperly confounded with *precept*, though it is obvious, from innumerable examples, that there is the greatest difference between them. When Absalom defiled his father's bed, though God was pleased thus to avenge the adultery of David, he did not therefore enjoin an abandoned son to commit incest, unless, perhaps, in respect of David, as David himself says of Shimei's curses. For, while he confesses that Shimei acts by the order of God, he by no means commends the obedience, as if that petulant dog had been yielding obedience to a divine command; but, recognising in his tongue the scourge of God, he submits patiently to be chastised. Thus we must hold, that while by means of the wicked God performs what he had secretly decreed, they are not excusable as if they were obeying his precept, which of set purpose they violate according to their lust.

How these things, which men do perversely, are of God, and are ruled by his secret providence, is strikingly shown in the election of King Jeroboam (1 Kings 12:20), in which the rashness and infatuation of the people are severely condemned for perverting the order sanctioned by God, and perfidiously revolting from the family of David. And yet we know it was God's will that Jeroboam should be anointed. Hence the apparent contradiction in the words of Hosea (Hosea 8:4; 13:11), because, while God complained that that kingdom was erected without his knowledge, and against his will, he elsewhere declares, that he had given King Jeroboam in his anger. How shall we reconcile the two things,—that Jeroboam's reign was not of God, and yet God appointed him king? In this way: The people could not revolt from the family of David without shaking off a yoke divinely imposed on them, and yet God himself was not deprived of the power of thus punishing the ingratitude of Solomon. We, therefore, see how God, while not willing treachery, with another view justly wills the revolt; and hence Jeroboam, by unexpectedly receiving the sacred unction, is urged to aspire to the kingdom. For this reason, the sacred history says, that God stirred up an enemy to deprive the son of Solomon of part of the kingdom (1 Kings 11:23). Let the reader diligently ponder both points: how, as it was the will of God that the people should be ruled by the hand of one king, their being rent into two parties was contrary to his will; and yet how this same will originated the revolt. For certainly, when Jeroboam, who had no such thought, is urged by the prophet verbally, and by the oil of unction, to hope for the kingdom, the thing was not done without the knowledge or against the will of God, who had expressly commanded it; and yet the rebellion of the people is justly condemned, because it was against the will of God that they revolted from the posterity of David. For this reason, it is afterwards added, that when Rehoboam haughtily spurned the prayers of the people, "the cause was from the Lord, that he might perform his saying, which the Lord spake by Ahijah" (I Kings 12:15). See how sacred unity was violated against the will of God, while, at the same time, with his will the ten tribes were alienated from the son of Solomon. To this might be added another similar example—viz. the murder of the sons of Ahab, and the extermination of his whole progeny by the consent, or rather the active agency, of the people. Jehu says truly "There shall fall unto the earth nothing of the word of the Lord, which the Lord spake concerning the house of Ahab: for the Lord has done that which he spake by his servant Elijah" (2 Kings 10:10). And yet, with good reason, he upbraids the citizens of Samaria for having lent their assistance. "Ye be righteous: behold, I conspired against my master, and slew him, but who slew all these?"

If I mistake not, I have already shown clearly how the same act at once betrays the guilt of man, and manifests the righteousness of God. Modest minds will always be satisfied with Augustine's answer, "Since the Father delivered up the Son, Christ his own body, and Judas his Master, how in such a case is God just, and man guilty, but just because in the one act which they did, the reasons for which they did it are different?" (*August. Ep. 48, ad Vincentium*). If any are not perfectly satisfied with this explanation—viz. that there is no concurrence between God and man, when by His righteous impulse man does what he ought not to do, let them give heed to what Augustine elsewhere observes: "Who can refrain from trembling at those Judgments when God does according to his pleasure even in the hearts of the wicked, at the same time rendering to them according to their deeds?" (*De Grat. et lib. Arbit. ad Valent.* c. 20). And certainly, in regard to the treachery of Judas, there is just as little ground to throw the blame of the crime upon God, because He was both pleased that his Son should be delivered up to death, and did deliver him, as to ascribe to Judas the praise of our redemption. Hence Augustine, in another place, truly observes, that when God makes his scrutiny, he looks not to what men could do, or to what they did, but to what they wished to do, thus taking account of their will and purpose. Those to whom this seems harsh had better consider how far their captiousness is entitled to any toleration, while, on the ground of its exceeding their capacity, they reject a matter which is clearly taught by Scripture, and complain of the enunciation of truths, which, if they were not useful to be known, God never would have ordered his prophets and apostles to teach. Our true wisdom is to embrace with meek docility, and without reservation, whatever the Holy Scriptures, have delivered. Those who indulge their petulance, a petulance manifestly directed against God, are undeserving of a longer refutation.

END OF THE FIRST BOOK.

BOOK SECOND: OF THE KNOWLEDGE OF GOD THE REDEEMER, IN CHRIST, AS FIRST MANIFESTED TO THE FATHERS, UNDER THE LAW, AND THEREAFTER TO US UNDER THE GOSPEL

ARGUMENT.

The First Part of the Apostles' Creed—viz. the knowledge of God the Creator, being disposed of, we now come to the Second Part, which relates to the knowledge of God as a Redeemer in Christ. The subjects treated of accordingly are, *first*, the Occasion of Redemption—viz. Adam's fall; and, *secondly*, Redemption itself. The first five chapters are devoted to the former subject, and the remainder to the latter.

Under the Occasion of Redemption, the Fall is considered not only in a general way, but also specially in its effects. Hence the first four chapters treat of original sin, free will, the corruption of human nature, and the operation of God in the heart. The fifth chapter contains a refutation of the arguments usually urged in support of free will.

The subject of redemption may be reduced to five particular heads:

I. The character of him in whom salvation for lost man must be sought, Chap. 6.

II. How he was manifested to the world, namely, in a twofold manner. First, under the Law. Here the Decalogue is expounded, and some other points relating to the law discussed, Chap. 7 and 8. Secondly, under the Gospel. Here the resemblance and difference of the two dispensations are considered, Chap. 9, 10, 11.

III. What kind of person Christ was, and behaved to be, in order to perform the office of Mediator—viz. God and man in one person, Chap. 12, 13, 14.

IV. For what end he was sent into the world by the Father. Here Christ's prophetical, kingly, and priestly offices are considered, Chap. 15.

V. In what way, or by what successive steps, Christ fulfilled the office of our Redeemer, Chap. 16. Here are considered his crucifixion, death, burial, descent to hell, resurrection, ascension to heaven, and seat at the right hand of the Father, together with the practical use of the whole doctrine. Chapter 17 contains an answer to the question, Whether Christ is properly said to have merited the grace of God for us.

CHAPTER I

THROUGH THE FALL AND REVOLT OF ADAM, THE WHOLE HUMAN RACE MADE ACCURSED AND DEGENERATE. OF ORIGINAL SIN.

I. How necessary the knowledge of ourselves is, its nature, the danger of mistake, its leading parts, sect. 1, 2, 3. II. The causes of Adam's fearful fall, sect. 4. III. The effects of the fall extending to Adam's posterity, and all the creatures, sect. 5, to the end of the Chapter, where the nature, propagation, and effect of original sin are considered.

Sections:

1. The knowledge of ourselves most necessary. To use it properly we must be divested of pride, and

clothed with true humility, which will dispose us to consider our fall, and embrace the mercy of God in Christ.

2. Though there is plausibility in the sentiment which stimulates us to self-admiration, the only sound sentiment is that which inclines us to true humbleness of mind. Pretexts for pride. The miserable vanity of sinful man.

3. Different views taken by carnal wisdom and by conscience, which appeals to divine justice as its standard. The knowledge of ourselves, consisting of two parts, the former of which having already been discussed, the latter is here considered.

4. In considering this latter part, two points to be considered; 1. How it happened that Adam involved himself and the whole human race in this dreadful calamity. This the result not of sensual intemperance, but of infidelity (the source of other heinous sins), which led to revolt from God, from whom all true happiness must be derived. An enumeration of the other sins produced by the infidelity of the first man.

5. The second point to be considered is, the extent to which the contagious influence of the fall extends. It extends, 1. To all the creatures, though unoffending; and, 2. To the whole posterity of Adam. Hence hereditary corruption, or original sin, and the depravation of a nature which was previously pure and good. This depravation communicated to the whole posterity of Adam, but not in the way supposed by the Pelagians and Celestians.

6. Depravation communicated not merely by imitation, but by propagation. This proved, 1. From the contrast drawn between Adam and Christ. Confirmation from passages of Scripture; 2 From the general declaration that we are the children of wrath.

7. Objection, that if Adam's sin is propagated to his posterity, the soul must be derived by transmission. Answer. Another objection—viz. that children cannot derive corruption from pious parents. Answer.

8. Definition of original sin. Two parts in the definition. Exposition of the latter part. Original sin exposes us to the wrath of God. It also produces in us the works of the flesh. Other definitions considered.

9. Exposition of the former part of the definition—viz. that hereditary depravity extends to all the faculties of the soul.

10. From the exposition of both parts of the definition it follows that God is not the author of sin, the whole human race being corrupted by an inherent viciousness.

11. This, however, is not from nature, but is an adventitious quality. Accordingly, the dream of the Manichees as to two principles vanishes.

1. It was not without reason that the ancient proverb so strongly recommended to man the knowledge of himself. For if it is deemed disgraceful to be ignorant of things pertaining to the business of life, much more disgraceful is self-ignorance, in consequence of which we miserably deceive ourselves in matters of the highest moment, and so walk blindfold. But the more useful the precept is, the more careful we must be not to use it preposterously, as we see certain philosophers have done. For they, when exhorting man to know himself, state the motive to be, that he may not be ignorant of his own excellence and dignity. They wish him to see nothing in himself but what will fill him with vain confidence, and inflate him with pride. But self-knowledge consists in this, *first*, When reflecting on what God gave us at our creation, and still continues graciously to give, we perceive how great the excellence of our nature would have been had its integrity remained, and, at the same time, remember that we have nothing of our own, but depend entirely on God, from whom we hold at pleasure whatever he has seen it meet to bestow; *secondly*, When viewing our miserable condition since Adam's fall, all confidence and boasting are overthrown, we blush for shame, and feel truly humble. For as God at first formed us in his own image, that he might elevate our minds to the pursuit of virtue, and the contemplation of eternal life, so to prevent us from heartlessly burying those noble qualities which distinguish us from the lower animals, it is of importance to know that we were endued with reason and intelligence, in order that we might cultivate a holy and honourable life, and regard a blessed immortality as our destined aim. At the same time, it is impossible to think of our primeval dignity without being immediately reminded of the sad spectacle of our ignominy and corruption, ever since we fell from our original in the person of our first parent. In this way, we feel dissatisfied with ourselves, and become truly humble, while we are inflamed with new desires to seek after God, in whom each may regain those good qualities of which all are found to be utterly destitute.

2. In examining ourselves, the search which divine truth enjoins, and the knowledge which it demands, are such as may indispose us to every thing like confidence in our own powers, leave us devoid of all means of boasting, and so incline us to submission. This is the course which we must follow, if we would attain to the true goal,

both in speculation and practice. I am not unaware how much more plausible the view is, which invites us rather to ponder on our good qualities, than to contemplate what must overwhelm us with shame—our miserable destitution and ignominy. There is nothing more acceptable to the human mind than flattery, and, accordingly, when told that its endowments are of a high order, it is apt to be excessively credulous. Hence it is not strange that the greater part of mankind have erred so egregiously in this matter. Owing to the innate self-love by which all are blinded, we most willingly persuade ourselves that we do not possess a single quality which is deserving of hatred; and hence, independent of any countenance from without, general credit is given to the very foolish idea, that man is perfectly sufficient of himself for all the purposes of a good and happy life. If any are disposed to think more modestly, and concede somewhat to God, that they may not seem to arrogate every thing as their own, still, in making the division, they apportion matters so, that the chief ground of confidence and boasting always remains with themselves. Then, if a discourse is pronounced which flatters the pride spontaneously springing up in man's inmost heart, nothing seems more delightful. Accordingly, in every age, he who is most forward in extolling the excellence of human nature, is received with the loudest applause. But be this heralding of human excellence what it may, by teaching man to rest in himself, it does nothing more than fascinate by its sweetness, and, at the same time, so delude as to drown in perdition all who assent to it. For what avails it to proceed in vain confidence, to deliberate, resolve, plan, and attempt what we deem pertinent to the purpose, and, at the very outset, prove deficient and destitute both of sound intelligence and true virtue, though we still confidently persist till we rush headlong on destruction? But this is the best that can happen to those who put confidence in their own powers. Whosoever, therefore, gives heed to those teachers, who merely employ us in contemplating our good qualities, so far from making progress in self-knowledge, will be plunged into the most pernicious ignorance.

3. While revealed truth concurs with the general consent of mankind in teaching that the second part of wisdom consists in self-knowledge, they differ greatly as to the method by which this knowledge is to be acquired. In the judgment of the flesh man deems his self-knowledge complete, when, with overweening confidence in his own intelligence and integrity, he takes courage, and spurs himself on to virtuous deeds, and when, declaring war upon vice, he uses his utmost endeavour to attain to the honourable and the fair. But he who tries himself by the standard of divine justice, finds nothing to inspire him with confidence; and hence, the more thorough his self-examination, the greater his despondency. Abandoning all dependence on himself, he feels that he is utterly incapable of duly regulating his conduct. It is not the will of God, however, that we should forget the primeval dignity which he bestowed on our first parents—a dignity which may well stimulate us to the pursuit of goodness and justice. It is impossible for us to think of our first original, or the end for which we were created, without being urged to meditate on immortality, and to seek the kingdom of God. But such meditation, so far from raising our spirits, rather casts them down, and makes us humble. For what is our original? One from which we have fallen. What the end of our creation? One from which we have altogether strayed, so that, weary of our miserable lot, we groan, and groaning sigh for a dignity now lost. When we say that man should see nothing in himself which can raise his spirits, our meaning is, that he possesses nothing on which he can proudly plume himself. Hence, in considering the knowledge which man ought to have of himself, it seems proper to divide it thus, *first*, to consider the end for which he was created, and the qualities—by no means contemptible qualities—with which he was endued, thus urging him to meditate on divine worship and the future life; and, *secondly*, to consider his faculties, or rather want of faculties—a want which, when perceived, will annihilate all his confidence, and cover him with confusion. The tendency of the former view is to teach him what his duty is, of the latter, to make him aware how far he is able to perform it. We shall treat of both in their proper order.

4. As the act which God punished so severely must have been not a trivial fault, but a heinous crime, it will be necessary to attend to the peculiar nature of the sin which produced Adam's fall, and provoked God to inflict such fearful vengeance on the whole human race. The common idea of sensual intemperance is childish. The sum and substance of all virtues could not consist in abstinence from a single fruit amid a general abundance of every delicacy that could be desired, the earth, with happy fertility, yielding not only abundance, but also endless variety. We must, therefore, look deeper than sensual intemperance. The prohibition to touch the tree of the knowledge of good and evil was a trial of obedience, that Adam, by observing it, might prove his willing submission to the command of God. For the very term shows the end of

the precept to have been to keep him contented with his lot, and not allow him arrogantly to aspire beyond it. The promise, which gave him hope of eternal life as long as he should eat of the tree of life, and, on the other hand, the fearful denunciation of death the moment he should taste of the tree of the knowledge of good and evil, were meant to prove and exercise his faith. Hence it is not difficult to infer in what way Adam provoked the wrath of God. Augustine, indeed, is not far from the mark, when he says (in Psal. 19), that pride was the beginning of all evil, because, had not man's ambition carried him higher than he was permitted, he might have continued in his first estate. A further definition, however, must be derived from the kind of temptation which Moses describes. When, by the subtlety of the devil, the woman faithlessly abandoned the command of God, her fall obviously had its origin in disobedience. This Paul confirms, when he says, that, by the disobedience of one man, all were destroyed. At the same time, it is to be observed, that the first man revolted against the authority of God, not only in allowing himself to be ensnared by the wiles of the devil, but also by despising the truth, and turning aside to lies. Assuredly, when the word of God is despised, all reverence for Him is gone. His majesty cannot be duly honoured among us, nor his worship maintained in its integrity, unless we hang as it were upon his lips. Hence infidelity was at the root of the revolt. From infidelity, again, sprang ambition and pride, together with ingratitude; because Adam, by longing for more than was allotted him, manifested contempt for the great liberality with which God had enriched him. It was surely monstrous impiety that a son of earth should deem it little to have been made in the likeness, unless he were also made the equal of God. If the apostasy by which man withdraws from the authority of his Maker, nay, petulantly shakes off his allegiance to him, is a foul and execrable crime, it is in vain to extenuate the sin of Adam. Nor was it simple apostasy. It was accompanied with foul insult to God, the guilty pair assenting to Satan's calumnies when he charged God with malice, envy, and falsehood. In fine, infidelity opened the door to ambition, and ambition was the parent of rebellion, man casting off the fear of God, and giving free vent to his lust. Hence, Bernard truly says, that, in the present day, a door of salvation is opened to us when we receive the gospel with our ears, just as by the same entrance, when thrown open to Satan, death was admitted. Never would Adam have dared to show any repugnance to the command of God if he had not been incredulous as to his word. The strongest curb to keep all his affections under due restraint, would have been the belief that nothing was better than to cultivate righteousness by obeying the commands of God, and that the highest possible felicity was to be loved by him. Man, therefore, when carried away by the blasphemies of Satan, did his very utmost to annihilate the whole glory of God.

5. As Adam's spiritual life would have consisted in remaining united and bound to his Maker, so estrangement from him was the death of his soul. Nor is it strange that he who perverted the whole order of nature in heaven and earth deteriorated his race by his revolt. "The whole creation groaneth," saith St Paul, "being made subject to vanity, not willingly" (Rom. 8:20, 22). If the reason is asked, there cannot be a doubt that creation bears part of the punishment deserved by man, for whose use all other creatures were made. Therefore, since through man's fault a curse has extended above and below, over all the regions of the world, there is nothing unreasonable in its extending to all his offspring. After the heavenly image in man was effaced, he not only was himself punished by a withdrawal of the ornaments in which he had been arrayed—viz. wisdom, virtue, justice, truth, and holiness, and by the substitution in their place of those dire pests, blindness, impotence, vanity, impurity, and unrighteousness, but he involved his posterity also, and plunged them in the same wretchedness. This is the hereditary corruption to which early Christian writers gave the name of Original Sin, meaning by the term the depravation of a nature formerly good and pure. The subject gave rise to much discussion, there being nothing more remote from common apprehension, than that the fault of one should render all guilty, and so become a common sin. This seems to be the reason why the oldest doctors of the church only glance obscurely at the point, or, at least, do not explain it so clearly as it required. This timidity, however, could not prevent the rise of a Pelagius with his profane fiction—that Adam sinned only to his own hurt, but did no hurt to his posterity. Satan, by thus craftily hiding the disease, tried to render it incurable. But when it was clearly proved from Scripture that the sin of the first man passed to all his posterity, recourse was had to the cavil, that it passed by imitation, and not by propagation. The orthodoxy, therefore, and more especially Augustine, laboured to show, that we are not corrupted by acquired wickedness, but bring an innate corruption from the very womb. It was the greatest impudence to deny this. But no man will wonder at the presumption of the Pelagians and Celestians, who has learned from the writings of that holy man how extreme the effrontery of these heretics

was. Surely there is no ambiguity in David's confession, "I was shapen in iniquity; and in sin did my mother conceive me" (Ps. 51:5). His object in the passage is not to throw blame on his parents; but the better to commend the goodness of God towards him, he properly reiterates the confession of impurity from his very birth. As it is clear, that there was no peculiarity in David's case, it follows that it is only an instance of the common lot of the whole human race. All of us, therefore, descending from an impure seed, come into the world tainted with the contagion of sin. Nay, before we behold the light of the sun we are in God's sight defiled and polluted. "Who can bring a clean thing out of an unclean? Not one," says the Book of Job (Job 14:4).

6. We thus see that the impurity of parents is transmitted to their children, so that all, without exception, are originally depraved. The commencement of this depravity will not be found until we ascend to the first parent of all as the fountain head. We must, therefore, hold it for certain, that, in regard to human nature, Adam was not merely a progenitor, but, as it were, a root, and that, accordingly, by his corruption, the whole human race was deservedly vitiated. This is plain from the contrast which the Apostle draws between Adam and Christ, "Wherefore, as by one man sin entered into the world, and death by sin; and so death passed upon all men, for that all have sinned; even so might grace reign through righteousness unto eternal life by Jesus Christ our Lord" (Rom. 5:19–21). To what quibble will the Pelagians here recur? That the sin of Adam was propagated by imitation! Is the righteousness of Christ then available to us only in so far as it is an example held forth for our imitation? Can any man tolerate such blasphemy? But if, out of all controversy, the righteousness of Christ, and thereby life, is ours by communication, it follows that both of these were lost in Adam that they might be recovered in Christ, whereas sin and death were brought in by Adam, that they might be abolished in Christ. There is no obscurity in the words, "As by one man's disobedience many were made sinners, so by the obedience of one shall many be made righteous." Accordingly, the relation subsisting between the two is this, As Adam, by his ruin, involved and ruined us, so Christ, by his grace, restored us to salvation. In this clear light of truth I cannot see any need of a longer or more laborious proof. Thus, too, in the First Epistle to the Corinthians, when Paul would confirm believers in the confident hope of the resurrection, he shows that the life is recovered in Christ which was lost in Adam (1 Cor. 15:22). Having already declared that all died in Adam, he now also openly testifies, that all are imbued with the taint of sin. Condemnation, indeed, could not reach those who are altogether free from blame. But his meaning cannot be made clearer than from the other member of the sentence, in which he shows that the hope of life is restored in Christ. Every one knows that the only mode in which this is done is, when by a wondrous communication Christ transfuses into us the power of his own righteousness, as it is elsewhere said, "The Spirit is life because of righteousness" (1 Cor. 15:22). Therefore, the only explanation which can be given of the expression, "in Adam all died," is, that he by sinning not only brought disaster and ruin upon himself, but also plunged our nature into like destruction; and that not only in one fault, in a matter not pertaining to us, but by the corruption into which he himself fell, he infected his whole seed. Paul never could have said that all are "by nature the children of wrath" (Eph. 2:3), if they had not been cursed from the womb. And it is obvious that the nature there referred to is not nature such as God created, but as vitiated in Adam; for it would have been most incongruous to make God the author of death. Adam, therefore, when he corrupted himself, transmitted the contagion to all his posterity. For a heavenly Judge, even our Saviour himself, declares that all are by birth vicious and depraved, when he says that "that which is born of the flesh is fleshy" (John 3:6), and that therefore the gate of life is closed against all until they have been regenerated.

7. To the understanding of this subject, there is no necessity for an anxious discussion (which in no small degree perplexed the ancient doctors), as to whether the soul of the child comes by transmission from the soul of the parent. It should be enough for us to know that Adam was made the depository of the endowments which God was pleased to bestow on human nature, and that, therefore, when he lost what he had received, he lost not only for himself but for us all. Why feel any anxiety about the transmission of the soul, when we know that the qualities which Adam lost he received for us not less than for himself, that they were not gifts to a single man, but attributes of the whole human race? There is nothing absurd, therefore, in the view, that when he was divested, his nature was left naked and destitute that he having been defiled by sin, the pollution extends to all his seed. Thus, from a corrupt root corrupt branches proceeding, transmit their corruption to the saplings which spring from them. The children being vitiated in their parent, conveyed the taint to the grandchildren; in other words, corruption commencing in Adam, is, by perpetual descent, conveyed

from those preceding to those coming after them. The cause of the contagion is neither in the substance of the flesh nor the soul, but God was pleased to ordain that those gifts which he had bestowed on the first man, that man should lose as well for his descendants as for himself. The Pelagian cavil, as to the improbability of children deriving corruption from pious parents, whereas, they ought rather to be sanctified by their purity, is easily refuted. Children come not by spiritual regeneration but carnal descent. Accordingly, as Augustine says, "Both the condemned unbeliever and the acquitted believer beget offspring not acquitted but condemned, because the nature which begets is corrupt." Moreover, though godly parents do in some measure contribute to the holiness of their offspring, this is by the blessing of God; a blessing, however, which does not prevent the primary and universal curse of the whole race from previously taking effect. Guilt is from nature, whereas sanctification is from supernatural grace.

8. But lest the thing itself of which we speak be unknown or doubtful, it will be proper to define original sin. (Calvin, in Conc. Trident. 1, Dec. Sess. 5). I have no intention, however, to discuss all the definitions which different writers have adopted, but only to adduce the one which seems to me most accordant with truth. Original sin, then, may be defined a hereditary corruption and depravity of our nature, extending to all the parts of the soul, which first makes us obnoxious to the wrath of God, and then produces in us works which in Scripture are termed works of the flesh. This corruption is repeatedly designated by Paul by the term sin (Gal. 5:19); while the works which proceed from it, such as adultery, fornication, theft, hatred, murder, revellings, he terms, in the same way, the fruits of sin, though in various passages of Scripture, and even by Paul himself, they are also termed sins. The two things, therefore, are to be distinctly observed—viz. that being thus perverted and corrupted in all the parts of our nature, we are, merely on account of such corruption, deservedly condemned by God, to whom nothing is acceptable but righteousness, innocence, and purity. This is not liability for another's fault. For when it is said, that the sin of Adam has made us obnoxious to the justice of God, the meaning is not, that we, who are in ourselves innocent and blameless, are bearing his guilt, but that since by his transgression we are all placed under the curse, he is said to have brought us under obligation. Through him, however, not only has punishment been derived, but pollution instilled, for which punishment is justly due. Hence Augustine, though he often terms it another's sin (that he may more clearly show how it comes to us by descent), at the same time asserts that it is each individual's own sin. And the Apostle most distinctly testifies, that "death passed upon all men, for that all have sinned" (Rom. 5:12); that is, are involved in original sin, and polluted by its stain. Hence, even infants bringing their condemnation with them from their mother's womb, suffer not for another's, but for their own defect. For although they have not yet produced the fruits of their own unrighteousness, they have the seed implanted in them. Nay, their whole nature is, as it were, a seed-bed of sin, and therefore cannot but be odious and abominable to God. Hence it follows, that it is properly deemed sinful in the sight of God; for there could be no condemnation without guilt. Next comes the other point—viz. that this perversity in us never ceases, but constantly produces new fruits, in other words, those works of the flesh which we formerly described; just as a lighted furnace sends forth sparks and flames, or a fountain without ceasing pours out water. Hence, those who have defined original sin as the want of the original righteousness which we ought to have had, though they substantially comprehend the whole case, do not significantly enough express its power and energy. For our nature is not only utterly devoid of goodness, but so prolific in all kinds of evil, that it can never be idle. Those who term it *concupiscence* use a word not very inappropriate, provided it were added (this, however, many will by no means concede), that everything which is in man, from the intellect to the will, from the soul even to the flesh, is defiled and pervaded with this concupiscence; or, to express it more briefly, that the whole man is in himself nothing else than concupiscence.

9. I have said, therefore, that all the parts of the soul were possessed by sin, ever since Adam revolted from the fountain of righteousness. For not only did the inferior appetites entice him, but abominable impiety seized upon the very citadel of the mind, and pride penetrated to his inmost heart (Rom. 7:12; Book 4, chap. 15, sec. 10–12), so that it is foolish and unmeaning to confine the corruption thence proceeding to what are called sensual motions, or to call it an excitement, which allures, excites, and drags the single part which they call sensuality into sin. Here Peter Lombard has displayed gross ignorance (Lomb., lib. 2 Dist. 31). When investigating the seat of corruption, he says it is in the flesh (as Paul declares), not properly, indeed, but as being more apparent in the flesh. As if Paul had meant that only a part of the soul, and not the whole nature, was opposed to supernatural grace. Paul

himself leaves no room for doubt, when he says, that corruption does not dwell in one part only, but that no part is free from its deadly taint. For, speaking of corrupt nature, he not only condemns the inordinate nature of the appetites, but, in particular, declares that the understanding is subjected to blindness, and the heart to depravity (Eph. 4:17, 18). The third chapter of the Epistle to the Romans is nothing but a description of original sin; The same thing appears more clearly from the mode of renovation. For the spirit, which is contrasted with the old man, and the flesh, denotes not only the grace by which the sensual or inferior part of the soul is corrected, but includes a complete reformation of all its parts (Eph. 4:23). And, accordingly, Paul enjoins not only that gross appetites be suppressed, but that we be renewed in the spirit of our mind (Eph. 4:23), as he elsewhere tells us to be transformed by the renewing of our mind (Rom. 12:2). Hence it follows, that that part in which the dignity and excellence of the soul are most conspicuous, has not only been wounded, but so corrupted, that mere cure is not sufficient. There must be a new nature. How far sin has seized both on the mind and heart, we shall shortly see. Here I only wished briefly to observe, that the whole man, from the crown of the head to the sole of the foot, is so deluged, as it were, that no part remains exempt from sin, and, therefore, everything which proceeds from him is imputed as sin. Thus Paul says, that all carnal thoughts and affections are enmity against God, and consequently death (Rom. 8:7).

10. Let us have done, then, with those who dare to inscribe the name of God on their vices, because we say that men are born vicious. The divine workmanship, which they ought to look for in the nature of Adam, when still entire and uncorrupted, they absurdly expect to find in their depravity. The blame of our ruin rests with our own carnality, not with God, its only cause being our degeneracy from our original condition. And let no one here glamour that God might have provided better for our safety by preventing Adam's fall. This objection, which, from the daring presumption implied in it, is odious to every pious mind, relates to the mystery of predestination, which will afterwards be considered in its own place (Tertull. de Præscript., Calvin, Lib. de Predest). Meanwhile let us remember that our ruin is attributable to our own depravity, that we may not insinuate a charge against God himself, the Author of nature. It is true that nature has received a mortal wound, but there is a great difference between a wound inflicted from without, and one inherent in our first condition. It is plain that this wound was inflicted by sin; and, therefore, we have no ground of complaint except against ourselves. This is carefully taught in Scripture. For the Preacher says, "Lo, this only have I found, that God made man upright; but they have sought out many inventions" (Eccl. 7:29). Since man, by the kindness of God, was made upright, but by his own infatuation fell away unto vanity, his destruction is obviously attributable only to himself (Athanas. in Orat. Cont. Idola).

11. We say, then, that man is corrupted by a natural viciousness, but not by one which proceeded from nature. In saying that it proceeded not from nature, we mean that it was rather an adventitious event which befell man, than a substantial property assigned to him from the beginning. We, however call it *natural* to prevent any one from supposing that each individual contracts it by depraved habit, whereas all receive it by a hereditary law. And we have authority for so calling it. For, on the same grounds the apostle says, that we are "by nature the children of wrath" (Eph. 2:3). How could God, who takes pleasure in the meanest of his works be offended with the noblest of them all? The offence is not with the work itself, but the corruption of the work. Wherefore, if it is not improper to say, that, in consequence of the corruption of human nature, man is naturally hateful to God, it is not improper to say, that he is naturally vicious and depraved. Hence, in the view of our corrupt nature, Augustine hesitates not to call those sins natural which necessarily reign in the flesh wherever the grace of God is wanting. This disposes of the absurd notion of the Manichees, who, imagining that man was essentially wicked, went the length of assigning him a different Creator, that they might thus avoid the appearance of attributing the cause and origin of evil to a righteous God.

CHAPTER 2

MAN NOW DEPRIVED OF FREEDOM OF WILL, AND MISERABLY ENSLAVED.

Having in the first chapter treated of the fall of man, and the corruption of the human race, it becomes necessary to inquire, Whether the sons of Adam are deprived of all liberty; and if any particle of liberty remains, how far its power extends? The four next chapters are devoted to this question. This second chapter may be reduced to three general heads: I. The foundation of the whole discussion. II. The opinions of others on the subject of human freedom, see. 2–9. III. The true doctrine on the subject, see. 10–27.

Sections:

1. Connection of the previous with the four following chapters. In order to lay a proper foundation for the discussion of free will, two obstacles in the way to be removed—viz. sloth and pride. The basis and sum of the whole discussion. The solid structure of this basis, and a clear demonstration of it by the argument a majori ad minus. Also from the inconveniences and absurdities arising from the obstacle of pride.

2. The second part of the chapter containing the opinions of others. 1. The opinions of philosophers.

3. The labyrinths of philosophers. A summary of the opinion common to all the philosophers.

4. The opinions of others continued—viz. The opinions of the ancient theologians on the subject of free will. These composed partly of Philosophy and partly of Theology. Hence their falsehood, extravagance, perplexity, variety, and contradiction. Too great fondness for philosophy in the Church has obscured the knowledge of God and of ourselves. The better to explain the opinions of philosophers, a definition of Free Will given. Wide difference between this definition and these opinions.

5. Certain things annexed to Free Will by the ancient theologians, especially the Schoolmen. Many kinds of Free Will according to them.

6. Puzzles of scholastic divines in the explanation of this question.

7. The conclusion that so trivial a matter ought not to be so much magnified. Objection of those who have a fondness for new terms in the Church. Objection answered.

8. Another answer. The Fathers, and especially Augustine, while retaining the term Free Will, yet condemned the doctrine of the heretics on the subject, as destroying the grace of God.

9. The language of the ancient writers on the subject of Free Will is, with the exception of that of Augustine, almost unintelligible. Still they set little or no value on human virtue, and ascribe the praise of all goodness to the Holy Spirit.

10. The last part of the chapter, containing a simple statement of the true doctrine. The fundamental principle is, that man first begins to profit in the knowledge of himself when he becomes sensible of his ruined condition. This confirmed, 1. by passages of Scripture.

11. Confirmed, 2. by the testimony of ancient theologians.

12. The foundation being laid, to show how far the power both of the intellect and will now extends, it is maintained in general, and in conformity with the views of Augustine and the Schoolmen, that the natural endowments of man are corrupted, and the supernatural almost entirely lost. A separate consideration of the powers of the Intellect and the Will. Some general considerations, 1. The intellect possesses some powers of perception. Still it labours under a twofold defect.

13. Man's intelligence extends both to things terrestrial and celestial. The power of the intellect in regard to the knowledge of things terrestrial. First, with regard to matters of civil polity.

14. The power of the intellect, secondly, with regard to the arts. Particular gifts in this respect conferred on individuals, and attesting the grace of God.

15. The rise of this knowledge of things terrestrial, first, that we may see how human nature, notwithstanding of its fall, is still adorned by God with excellent endowments.

16. Use of this knowledge continued. Secondly, that we may see that these endowments bestowed on individuals are intended for the common benefit of mankind. They are sometimes conferred even on the wicked.

17. Some portion of human nature still left. This, whatever be the amount of it, should be ascribed entirely to the divine indulgence. Reason of this. Examples.

18. Second part of the discussion, namely, that which relates to the power of the human intellect in regard to things celestial. These reducible to three heads, namely, divine knowledge, adoption, and will. The blindness of man in regard to these proved and thus tested by a simile.

19. Proved, moreover, by passages of Scripture, showing, 1. That the sons of Adam are endued with some light, but not enough to enable them to comprehend God. Reasons.

20. Adoption not from nature, but from our heavenly Father, being sealed in the elect by the Spirit of regeneration. Obvious from many passages of Scripture, that, previous to regeneration, the human intellect is altogether unable to comprehend the things relating to regeneration. This fully proved. First argument. Second argument. Third argument.

21. Fourth argument. Scripture ascribes the glory of our adoption and salvation to God only. The human intellect blind as to heavenly things until it is illuminated. Disposal of a heretical objection.

22. Human intellect ignorant of the true knowledge

of the divine law. This proved by the testimony of an Apostle, by an inference from the same testimony, and from a consideration of the end and definition of the Law of Nature. Plato obviously mistaken in attributing all sins to ignorance.

23. Themistius nearer the truth in maintaining, that the delusion of the intellect is manifested not so much in generals as in particulars. Exception to this rule.

24. Themistius, however, mistaken in thinking that the intellect is so very seldom deceived as to generals. Blindness of the human intellect when tested by the standard of the Divine Law, in regard both to the first and second tables. Examples.

25. A middle view to be taken—viz. that all sins are not imputable to ignorance, and, at the same time, that all sins do not imply intentional malice. All the human mind conceives and plans in this matter is evil in the sight of God. Need of divine direction every moment.

26. The will examined. The natural desire of good, which is universally felt, no proof of the freedom of the human will. Two fallacies as to the use of terms, appetite and good.

27. The doctrine of the Schoolmen on this subject opposed to and refuted by Scripture. The whole man being subject to the power of sin, it follows that the will, which is the chief seat of sin, requires to be most strictly curbed. Nothing ours but sin.

1. Having seen that the dominion of sin, ever since the first man was brought under it, not only extends to the whole race, but has complete possession of every soul, it now remains to consider more closely, whether from the period of being thus enslaved, we have been deprived of all liberty; and if any portion still remains, how far its power extends. In order to facilitate the answer to this question it may be proper in passing to point out the course which our inquiry ought to take. The best method of avoiding error is to consider the dangers which beset us on either side. Man being devoid of all uprightness, immediately takes occasion from the fact to indulge in sloth, and having no ability in himself for the study of righteousness, treats the whole subject as if he had no concern in it. On the other hand, man cannot arrogate any thing, however minute, to himself, without robbing God of his honour, and through rash confidence subjecting himself to a fall. To keep free of both these rocks, our proper course will be, first, to show that man has no remaining good in himself, and is beset on every side by the most miserable destitution; and then teach him to aspire to the goodness of which he is devoid, and the liberty of which he has been deprived: thus giving him a stronger stimulus to exertion than he could have if he imagined himself possessed of the highest virtue. How necessary the latter point is, everybody sees. As to the former, several seem to entertain more doubt than they ought. For it being admitted as incontrovertible that man is not to be denied any thing that is truly his own, it ought also to be admitted, that he is to be deprived of every thing like false boasting. If man had no title to glory in himself, when, by the kindness of his Maker, he was distinguished by the noblest ornaments, how much ought he to be humbled now, when his ingratitude has thrust him down from the highest glory to extreme ignominy? At the time when he was raised to the highest pinnacle of honour, all which Scripture attributes to him is, that he was created in the image of God, thereby intimating that the blessings in which his happiness consisted were not his own, but derived by divine communication. What remains, therefore, now that man is stript of all his glory, than to acknowledge the God for whose kindness he failed to be grateful, when he was loaded with the riches of his grace? Not having glorified him by the acknowledgment of his blessings, now, at least, he ought to glorify him by the confession of his poverty. In truth, it is no less useful for us to renounce all the praise of wisdom and virtue, than to aim at the glory of God. Those who invest us with more than we possess only add sacrilege to our ruin. For when we are taught to contend in our own strength, what more is done than to lift us up, and then leave us to lean on a reed which immediately gives way? Indeed, our strength is exaggerated when it is compared to a reed. All that foolish men invent and prattle on this subject is mere smoke. Wherefore, it is not without reason that Augustine so often repeats the well-known saying, that free will is more destroyed than established by its defenders (August. in Evang. Joann. Tract. 81). It was necessary to premise this much for the sake of some who, when they hear that human virtue is totally overthrown, in order that the power of God in man may be exalted, conceive an utter dislike to the whole subject, as if it were perilous, not to say superfluous, whereas it is manifestly both most necessary and most useful.

2. Having lately observed, that the faculties of the soul are seated in the mind and the heart, let us now consider how far the power of each extends. Philosophers generally maintain, that reason dwells in the mind like a lamp, throwing light on all its counsels, and like a queen, governing the will—that it is so pervaded with divine light as to

be able to consult for the best, and so endued with vigour as to be able perfectly to command; that, on the contrary, sense is dull and short-sighted, always creeping on the ground, grovelling among inferior objects, and never rising to true vision; that the appetite, when it obeys reason, and does not allow itself to be subjugated by sense, is borne to the study of virtue, holds a straight course, and becomes transformed into will; but that when enslaved by sense, it is corrupted and depraved so as to degenerate into lust. In a word, since, according to their opinion, the faculties which I have mentioned above, namely, intellect, sense, and appetite, or will (the latter being the term in ordinary use), are seated in the soul, they maintain that the intellect is endued with reason, the best guide to a virtuous and happy life, provided it duly avails itself of its excellence, and exerts the power with which it is naturally endued; that, at the same time, the inferior movement, which is termed sense, and by which the mind is led away to error and delusion, is of such a nature, that it can be tamed and gradually subdued by the power of reason. To the will, moreover, they give an intermediate place between reason and sense, regarding it as possessed of full power and freedom, whether to obey the former, or yield itself up to be hurried away by the latter.

3. Sometimes, indeed, convinced by their own experience, they do not deny how difficult it is for man to establish the supremacy of reason in himself, inasmuch as he is at one time enticed by the allurements of pleasure; at another, deluded by a false semblance of good; and, at another, impelled by unruly passions, and pulled away (to use Plato's expression) as by ropes or sinews (Plato, De Legibus, lib. 1). For this reason, Cicero says, that the sparks given forth by nature are immediately extinguished by false opinions and depraved manners (Cicero, Tusc, Quæst. lib. 3). They confess that when once diseases of this description have seized upon the mind, their course is too impetuous to be easily checked, and they hesitate not to compare them to fiery steeds, which, having thrown off the charioteer, scamper away without restraint. At the same time, they set it down as beyond dispute, that virtue and vice are in our own power. For (say they), If it is in our choice to do this thing or that, it must also be in our choice not to do it: Again, If it is in our choice not to act, it must also be in our choice to act: But both in doing and abstaining we seem to act from free choice; and, therefore, if we do good when we please, we can also refrain from doing it; if we commit evil, we can also shun the commission of it (Aristot. Ethic. lib. 3 c. 5). Nay, some have gone the length of boasting (Seneca, *passim*), that it is the gift of the gods that we live, but our own that we live well and purely. Hence Cicero says, in the person of Cotta, that as every one acquires virtue for himself, no wise man ever thanked the gods for it. "We are praised," says he, "for virtue, and glory in virtue, but this could not be, if virtue were the gift of God, and not from ourselves" (Cicero, De Nat. Deorum). A little after, he adds, "The opinion of all mankind is, that fortune must be sought from God, wisdom from ourselves." Thus, in short, all philosophers maintain, that human reason is sufficient for right government; that the will, which is inferior to it, may indeed be solicited to evil by sense, but having a free choice, there is nothing to prevent it from following reason as its guide in all things.

4. Among ecclesiastical writers, although there is none who did not acknowledge that sound reason in man was seriously injured by sin, and the will greatly entangled by vicious desires, yet many of them made too near an approach to the philosophers. Some of the most ancient writers appear to me to have exalted human strengths from a fear that a distinct acknowledgment of its impotence might expose them to the jeers of the philosophers with whom they were disputing, and also furnish the flesh, already too much disinclined to good, with a new pretext for sloth. Therefore, to avoid teaching anything which the majority of mankind might deem absurd, they made it their study, in some measure, to reconcile the doctrine of Scripture with the dogmas of philosophy, at the same time making it their special care not to furnish any occasion to sloth. This is obvious from their words. Chrysostom says, "God having placed good and evil in our power, has given us full freedom of choice; he does not keep back the unwilling, but embraces the willing" (Homil. de Prodit. Judae). Again, "He who is wicked is often, when he so chooses, changed into good, and he who is good falls through sluggishness, and becomes wicked. For the Lord has made our nature free. He does not lay us under necessity, but furnishing apposite remedies, allows the whole to depend on the views of the patient" (Homily. 18, in Genesis). Again, "As we can do nothing rightly until aided by the grace of God, so, until we bring forward what is our own, we cannot obtain favour from above" (Homily. 52). He had previously said, "As the whole is not done by divine assistance, we ourselves must of necessity bring somewhat." Accordingly, one of his common expressions is, "Let us bring what is our own, God will supply the rest." In unison with this, Jerome says, "It is ours to begin, God's to finish: it is ours to offer what we can, his to supply what we cannot" (Dialog. 3 Cont. Pelag).

From these sentences, you see that they have bestowed on man more than he possesses for the study of virtue, because they thought that they could not shake off our innate sluggishness unless they argued that we sin by ourselves alone. With what skill they have thus argued we shall afterwards see. Assuredly we shall soon be able to show that the sentiments just quoted are most inaccurate. Moreover although the Greek Fathers, above others, and especially Chrysostom, have exceeded due bounds in extolling the powers of the human will, yet all ancient theologians, with the exception of Augustine, are so confused, vacillating, and contradictory on this subject, that no certainty can be obtained from their writings. It is needless, therefore, to be more particular in enumerating every separate opinion. It will be sufficient to extract from each as much as the exposition of the subject seems to require. Succeeding writers (every one courting applause for his acuteness in the defence of human nature) have uniformly, one after the other, gone more widely astray, until the common dogma came to be, that man was corrupted only in the sensual part of his nature, that reason remained entire, and will was scarcely impaired. Still the expression was often on their lips, that man's natural gifts were corrupted, and his supernatural taken away. Of the thing implied by these words, however, scarcely one in a hundred had any distinct idea. Certainly, were I desirous clearly to express what the corruption of nature is, I would not seek for any other expression. But it is of great importance attentively to consider what the power of man now is when vitiated in all the parts of his nature, and deprived of supernatural gifts. Persons professing to be the disciples of Christ have spoken too much like the philosophers on this subject. As if human nature were still in its integrity, the term free will has always been in use among the Latins, while the Greeks were not ashamed to use a still more presumptuous term—viz. aujtexouvsion, as if man had still full power in himself.

But since the principle entertained by all, even the vulgar, is, that man is endued with free will, while some, who would be thought more skilful, know not how far its power extends; it will be necessary, first to consider the meaning of the term, and afterwards ascertain, by a simple appeal to Scripture, what man's natural power for good or evil is. The thing meant by free will, though constantly occurring in all writers, few have defined. Origen, however, seems to have stated the common opinion when he said, It is a power of reason to discern between good and evil; of will, to choose the one or other. Nor does Augustine differ from him when he says, It is a power of reason and will to choose the good, grace assisting,—to choose the bad, grace desisting. Bernard, while aiming at greater acuteness, speaks more obscurely, when he describes it as consent, in regard to the indestructible liberty of the wills and the inalienable judgment of reason. Anselm's definition is not very intelligible to ordinary understandings. He calls it a power of preserving rectitude on its own account. Peter Lombard, and the Schoolmen, preferred the definition of Augustine, both because it was clearer, and did not exclude divine grace, without which they saw that the will was not sufficient of itself. They however add something of their own, because they deemed it either better or necessary for clearer explanation. First, they agree that the term *will* (arbitrium) has reference to reason, whose office it is to distinguish between good and evil, and that the epithet *free* properly belongs to the will, which may incline either way. Wherefore, since liberty properly belongs to the will, Thomas Aquinas says (Part 1 Quast. 83, Art. 3), that the most congruous definition is to call free will an elective power, combining intelligence and appetite, but inclining more to appetite. We now perceive in what it is they suppose the faculty of free will to consist—viz. in reason and will. It remains to see how much they attribute to each.

5. In general, they are wont to place under the free will of man only intermediate things—viz. those which pertain not to the kingdom of God, while they refer true righteousness to the special grace of God and spiritual regeneration. The author of the work, "De Vocatione Gentium" (On the Calling of the Gentiles), wishing to show this, describes the will as threefold—viz. sensitive, animal, and spiritual. The two former, he says, are free to man, but the last is the work of the Holy Spirit. What truth there is in this will be considered in its own place. Our intention at present is only to mention the opinions of others, not to refute them. When writers treat of free will, their inquiry is chiefly directed not to what its power is in relation to civil or external actions, but to the obedience required by the divine law. The latter I admit to be the great question, but I cannot think the former should be altogether neglected; and I hope to be able to give the best reason for so thinking (sec. 12 to 18). The schools, however, have adopted a distinction which enumerates three kinds of freedom (see Lombard, lib. 2 Dist. 25); the first, a freedom from necessity; the second, a freedom from sin; and the third, a freedom from misery: the first naturally so inherent in man, that he cannot possibly be deprived of it; while through sin the other two have been lost. I willingly admit this distinction, except in so far as

it confounds *necessity* with *compulsion*. How widely the things differ, and how important it is to attend to the difference, will appear elsewhere.

6. All this being admitted, it will be beyond dispute, that free will does not enable any man to perform good works, unless he is assisted by grace; indeed, the special grace which the elect alone receive through regeneration. For I stay not to consider the extravagance of those who say that grace is offered equally and promiscuously to all (Lomb. lib. 2 Dist. 26). But it has not yet been shown whether man is entirely deprived of the power of well-doing, or whether he still possesses it in some, though in a very feeble and limited degree—a degree so feeble and limited, that it can do nothing of itself, but when assisted by grace, is able also to perform its part. The Master of the Sentences (Lombard, ibid). wishing to explain this, teaches that a twofold grace is necessary to fit for any good work. The one he calls Operating. To it, it is owing that we effectually will what is good. The other, which succeeds this good will, and aids it, he calls Co-operating. My objection to this division (see *infra*, chap. 3 sec. 10, and chap. 7 sec. 9) is, that while it attributes the effectual desire of good to divine grace, it insinuates that man, by his own nature, desires good in some degree, though ineffectually. Thus Bernard, while maintaining that a good will is the work of God, concedes this much to man—viz. that of his own nature he longs for such a good will. This differs widely from the view of Augustine, though Lombard pretends to have taken the division from him. Besides, there is an ambiguity in the second division, which has led to an erroneous interpretation. For it has been thought that we co-operate with subsequent grace, inasmuch as it pertains to us either to nullify the first grace, by rejecting its or to confirm it, by obediently yielding to it. The author of the work De Vocatione Gentium expresses it thus: It is free to those who enjoy the faculty of reason to depart from grace, so that the not departing is a reward, and that which cannot be done without the co-operation of the Spirit is imputed as merit to those whose will might have made it otherwise (lib. 2 cap. 4). It seemed proper to make these two observations in passing, that the reader may see how far I differ from the sounder of the Schoolmen. Still further do I differ from more modern sophists, who have departed even more widely than the Schoolmen from the ancient doctrine. The division, however, shows in what respect free will is attributed to man. For Lombard ultimately declares (lib. 2 Dist. 25), that our freedom is not to the extent of leaving us equally inclined to good and evil in act or in thought, but only to the extent of freeing us from compulsion. This liberty is compatible with our being depraved, the servants of sin, able to do nothing but sin.

7. In this way, then, man is said to have free will, not because he has a free choice of good and evil, but because he acts voluntarily, and not by compulsion. This is perfectly true: but why should so small a matter have been dignified with so proud a title? An admirable freedom! that man is not forced to be the servant of sin, while he is, however, ejthelodou'lo" (a voluntary slave); his will being bound by the fetters of sin. I abominate mere verbal disputes, by which the Church is harassed to no purpose; but I think we ought religiously to eschew terms which imply some absurdity, especially in subjects where error is of pernicious consequence. How few are there who, when they hear free will attributed to man, do not immediately imagine that he is the master of his mind and will in such a sense, that he can of himself incline himself either to good or evil? It may be said that such dangers are removed by carefully expounding the meaning to the people. But such is the proneness of the human mind to go astray, that it will more quickly draw error from one little word, than truth from a lengthened discourse. Of this, the very term in question furnishes too strong a proof. For the explanation given by ancient Christian writers having been lost sight of, almost all who have come after them, by attending only to the etymology of the term, have been led to indulge a fatal confidence.

8. As to the Fathers (if their authority weighs with us), they have the term constantly in their mouths; but they, at the same time, declare what extent of meaning they attach to it. In particular, Augustine hesitates not to call the will *a slave*. In another passages he is offended with those who deny free will; but his chief reason for this is explained when he says, "Only lest any one should presume so to deny freedom of will, from a desire to excuse sin." It is certain, he elsewhere admits, that without the Spirit the will of man is not free, inasmuch as it is subject to lusts which chain and master it. And again, that nature began to want liberty the moment the will was vanquished by the revolt into which it fell. Again, that man, by making a bad use of free will, lost both himself and his will. Again, that free will having been made a captive, can do nothing in the way of righteousness. Again, that no will is free which has not been made so by divine grace. Again, that the righteousness of God is not fulfilled when the law orders, and man acts, as it were, by his own strength, but when the Spirit assists, and the

will (not the free will of man, but the will freed by God) obeys. He briefly states the ground of all these observations, when he says, that man at his creation received a great degree of free will, but lost it by sinning. In another place, after showing that free will is established by grace, he strongly inveighs against those who arrogate any thing to themselves without grace. His words are, "How much soever miserable men presume to plume themselves on free will before they are made free, or on their strength after they are made free, they do not consider that, in the very expression *free will*, liberty is implied. 'Where the Spirit of the Lord is, there is liberty,' (2 Cor. 3:17). If, therefore, they are the servants of sin, why do they boast of free will? He who has been vanquished is the servant of him who vanquished him. But if men have been made free, why do they boast of it as of their own work? Are they so free that they are unwilling to be the servants of Him who has said, 'Without me ye can do nothing'?" (John 15:5). In another passage he even seems to ridicule the word, when he says, "That the will is indeed free, but not freed—free of righteousness, but enslaved to sin." The same idea he elsewhere repeats and explains, when he says, "That man is not free from righteousness save by the choice of his will, and is not made free from sin save by the grace of the Saviour." Declaring that the freedom of man is nothing else than emancipation or manumission from righteousness, he seems to jest at the emptiness of the name. If any one, then, chooses to make use of this term, without attaching any bad meaning to it, he shall not be troubled by me on that account; but as it cannot be retained without very great danger, I think the abolition of it would be of great advantage to the Church. I am unwilling to use it myself; and others if they will take my advice, will do well to abstain from it.

9. It may, perhaps, seem that I have greatly prejudiced my own view by confessing that all the ecclesiastical writers, with the exception of Augustine, have spoken so ambiguously or inconsistently on this subject, that no certainty is attainable from their writings. Some will interpret this to mean, that I wish to deprive them of their right of suffrage, because they are opposed to me. Truly, however, I have had no other end in view than to consult, simply and in good faith, for the advantage of pious minds, which, if they trust to those writers for their opinion, will always fluctuate in uncertainty. At one time they teach, that man having been deprived of the power of free will must flee to grace alone; at another, they equip or seem to equip him in armour of his own. It is not difficult, however, to show, that notwithstanding of the ambiguous manner in which those writers express themselves, they hold human virtue in little or no account, and ascribe the whole merit of all that is good to the Holy Spirit. To make this more manifest, I may here quote some passages from them. What, then, is meant by Cyprian in the passage so often lauded by Augustine, "Let us glory in nothing, because nothing is ours," unless it be, that man being utterly destitute, considered in himself, should entirely depend on God? What is meant by Augustine and Eucherius, when they expound that Christ is the tree of life, and that whoso puts forth his hand to it shall live; that the choice of the will is the tree of the knowledge of good and evil, and that he who, forsaking the grace of God, tastes of it shall die? What is meant by Chrysostom, when he says, "That every man is not only naturally a sinner, but is wholly sin?" If there is nothing good in us; if man, from the crown of the head to the sole of the foot, is wholly sin; if it is not even lawful to try how far the power of the will extends,—how can it be lawful to share the merit of a good work between God and man? I might quote many passages to the same effect from other writers; but lest any caviller should say, that I select those only which serve my purpose, and cunningly pass by those which are against me, I desist. This much, however, I dare affirm, that though they sometimes go too far in extolling free will, the main object which they had in view was to teach man entirely to renounce all self-confidence, and place his strength in God alone. I now proceed to a simple exposition of the truth in regard to the nature of man.

10. Here however, I must again repeat what I premised at the outset of this chapter, that he who is most deeply abased and alarmed, by the consciousness of his disgrace, nakedness, want, and misery, has made the greatest progress in the knowledge of himself. Man is in no danger of taking too much from himself, provided he learns that whatever he wants is to be recovered in God. But he cannot arrogate to himself one particle beyond his due, without losing himself in vain confidence, and, by transferring divine honour to himself, becoming guilty of the greatest impiety. And, assuredly, whenever our minds are seized with a longing to possess a somewhat of our own, which may reside in us rather than in God, we may rest assured that the thought is suggested by no other counsellor than he who enticed our first parents to aspire to be like gods, knowing good and evil. It is sweet, indeed, to have so much virtue of our own as to be able to rest in ourselves; but let the many solemn passages by which our pride is sternly humbled, deter us from indulging

this vain confidence: "Cursed be the man that trusteth in man, and maketh flesh his arm." (Jer. 17:5). "He delighteth not in the strength of the horse; he taketh not pleasure in the legs of a man. The Lord taketh pleasure in those that fear him, in those that hope in his mercy" (Ps. 147:10, 11). "He giveth power to the faint; and to them that have no might he increaseth strength. Even the youths shall faint and be weary, and the young men shall utterly fall: But they that wait upon the Lord shall renew their strength" (Is. 40:29–31). The scope of all these passages is that we must not entertain any opinion whatever of our own strength, if we would enjoy the favour of God, who "resisteth the proud, but giveth grace unto the humble" (James 4:6). Then let us call to mind such promises as these, "I will pour water upon him that is thirsty, and floods upon the dry ground" (Is. 44:3); "Ho, every one that thirsteth, come ye to the waters" (Is. 55:1). These passages declare, that none are admitted to enjoy the blessings of God save those who are pining under a sense of their own poverty. Nor ought such passages as the following to be omitted: "The sun shall no more be thy light by day; neither for brightness shall the moon give light unto thee: but the Lord shall be unto thee an everlasting light, and thy God thy glory" (Is. 60:19). The Lord certainly does not deprive his servants of the light of the sun or moon, but as he would alone appear glorious in them, he dissuades them from confidence even in those objects which they deem most excellent.

11. I have always been exceedingly delighted with the words of Chrysostom, "The foundation of our philosophy is humility;" and still more with those of Augustine, "As the orator, when asked, What is the first precept in eloquence? answered, Delivery: What is the second? Delivery: What the third? Delivery: so, if you ask me in regard to the precepts of the Christian Religion, I will answer, first, second, and third, Humility." By humility he means not when a man, with a consciousness of some virtue, refrains from pride, but when he truly feels that he has no refuge but in humility. This is clear from another passage, "Let no man," says he, "flatter himself: of himself he is a devil: his happiness he owes entirely to God. What have you of your own but sin? Take your sin which is your own; for righteousness is of God." Again, "Why presume so much on the capability of nature? It is wounded, maimed, vexed, lost. The thing wanted is genuine confession, not false defence." "When any one knows that he is nothing in himself, and has no help from himself, the weapons within himself are broken, and the war is ended." All the weapons of impiety must be bruised, and broken, and burnt in the fire; you must remain unarmed, having no help in yourself. The more infirm you are, the more the Lord will sustain you. So, in expounding the seventieth Psalm, he forbids us to remember our own righteousness, in order that we may recognise the righteousness of God, and shows that God bestows his grace upon us, that we may know that we are nothing; that we stand only by the mercy of God, seeing that in ourselves eve are altogether wicked. Let us not contend with God for our right, as if anything attributed to him were lost to our salvation. As our insignificance is his exaltation, so the confession of our insignificance has its remedy provided in his mercy. I do not ask, however, that man should voluntarily yield without being convinced, or that, if he has any powers, he should shut his eyes to them, that he may thus be subdued to true humility; but that getting quit of the disease of self-love and ambition, *filautiva kai; filoneikiva*, under the blinding of which he thinks of himself more highly than he ought to think, he may see himself as he really is, by looking into the faithful mirror of Scripture.

12. I feel pleased with the well-known saying which has been borrowed from the writings of Augustine, that man's natural gifts were corrupted by sin, and his supernatural gifts withdrawn; meaning by supernatural gifts the light of faith and righteousness, which would have been sufficient for the attainment of heavenly life and everlasting felicity. Man, when he withdrew his allegiance to God, was deprived of the spiritual gifts by which he had been raised to the hope of eternal salvation. Hence it follows, that he is now an exile from the kingdom of God, so that all things which pertain to the blessed life of the soul are extinguished in him until he recover them by the grace of regeneration. Among these are faith, love to God, charity towards our neighbour, the study of righteousness and holiness. All these, when restored to us by Christ, are to be regarded as adventitious and above nature. If so, we infer that they were previously abolished. On the other hand, soundness of mind and integrity of heart were, at the same time, withdrawn, and it is this which constitutes the corruption of natural gifts. For although there is still some residue of intelligence and judgment as well as will, we cannot call a mind sound and entire which is both weak and immersed in darkness. As to the will, its depravity is but too well known. Therefore, since reason, by which man discerns between good and evil, and by which he understands and judges, is a natural gift, it could not be entirely destroyed; but being partly weakened and partly corrupted, a shape-

less ruin is all that remains. In this sense it is said (John 1:5), that "the light shineth in darkness, and the darkness comprehended it not;" these words clearly expressing both points—viz. that in the perverted and degenerate nature of man there are still some sparks which show that he is a rational animal, and differs from the brutes, inasmuch as he is endued with intelligence, and yet, that this light is so smothered by clouds of darkness that it cannot shine forth to any good effect. In like manner, the will, because inseparable from the nature of man, did not perish, but was so enslaved by depraved lusts as to be incapable of one righteous desire. The definition now given is complete, but there are several points which require to be explained. Therefore, proceeding agreeably to that primary distinction (Book 1 c. 15 sec. 7 and 8), by which we divided the soul into intellect and will, we will now inquire into the power of the intellect.

To charge the intellect with perpetual blindness, so as to leave it no intelligence of any description whatever, is repugnant not only to the Word of God, but to common experience. We see that there has been implanted in the human mind a certain desire of investigating truth, to which it never would aspire unless some relish for truth antecedently existed. There is, therefore, now, in the human mind, discernment to this extent, that it is naturally influenced by the love of truth, the neglect of which in the lower animals is a proof of their gross and irrational nature. Still it is true that this love of truth fails before it reaches the goal, forthwith falling away into vanity. As the human mind is unable, from dullness, to pursue the right path of investigation, and, after various wanderings, stumbling every now and then like one groping in darkness, at length gets completely bewildered, so its whole procedure proves how unfit it is to search the truth and find it. Then it labours under another grievous defect, in that it frequently fails to discern what the knowledge is which it should study to acquire. Hence, under the influence of a vain curiosity, it torments itself with superfluous and useless discussions, either not adverting at all to the things necessary to be known, or casting only a cursory and contemptuous glance at them. At all events, it scarcely ever studies them in sober earnest. Profane writers are constantly complaining of this perverse procedure, and yet almost all of them are found pursuing it. Hence Solomon, throughout the Book of Ecclesiastes, after enumerating all the studies in which men think they attain the highest wisdom, pronounces them vain and frivolous.

13. Still, however, man's efforts are not always so utterly fruitless as not to lead to some result, especially when his attention is directed to inferior objects. Nay, even with regard to superior objects, though he is more careless in investigating them, he makes some little progress. Here, however, his ability is more limited, and he is never made more sensible of his weakness than when he attempts to soar above the sphere of the present life. It may therefore be proper, in order to make it more manifest how far our ability extends in regard to these two classes of objects, to draw a distinction between them. The distinction is, that we have one kind of intelligence of earthly things, and another of heavenly things. By earthly things, I mean those which relate not to God and his kingdom, to true righteousness and future blessedness, but have some connection with the present life, and are in a manner confined within its boundaries. By heavenly things, I mean the pure knowledge of God, the method of true righteousness, and the mysteries of the heavenly kingdom. To the former belong matters of policy and economy, all mechanical arts and liberal studies. To the latter (as to which, see the eighteenth and following sections) belong the knowledge of God and of his will, and the means of framing the life in accordance with them. As to the former, the view to be taken is this: Since man is by nature a social animal, he is disposed, from natural instinct, to cherish and preserve society; and accordingly we see that the minds of all men have impressions of civil order and honesty. Hence it is that every individual understands how human societies must he regulated by laws, and also is able to comprehend the principles of those laws. Hence the universal agreement in regard to such subjects, both among nations and individuals, the seeds of them being implanted in the breasts of all without a teacher or lawgiver. The truth of this fact is not affected by the wars and dissensions which immediately arise, while some, such as thieves and robbers, would invert the rules of justice, loosen the bonds of law, and give free scope to their lust; and while others (a vice of most frequent occurrence) deem that to be unjust which is elsewhere regarded as just, and, on the contrary, hold that to be praiseworthy which is elsewhere forbidden. For such persons do not hate the laws from not knowing that they are good and sacred, but, inflamed with headlong passion, quarrel with what is clearly reasonable, and licentiously hate what their mind and understanding approve. Quarrels of this latter kind do not destroy the primary idea of justice. For while men dispute with each other as to particular enactments, their ideas of equity agree in substance. This, no doubt, proves the weakness of the human mind, which, even when it seems on the right path, halts and hesitates. Still,

however, it is true, that some principle of civil order is impressed on all. And this is ample proof, that, in regard to the constitution of the present life, no man is devoid of the light of reason.

14. Next come manual and liberal arts, in learning which, as all have some degree of aptitude, the full force of human acuteness is displayed. But though all are not equally able to learn all the arts, we have sufficient evidence of a common capacity in the fact, that there is scarcely an individual who does not display intelligence in some particular art. And this capacity extends not merely to the learning of the art, but to the devising of something new, or the improving of what had been previously learned. This led Plato to adopt the erroneous idea, that such knowledge was nothing but recollection. So cogently does it oblige us to acknowledge that its principle is naturally implanted in the human mind. But while these proofs openly attest the fact of a universal reason and intelligence naturally implanted, this universality is of a kind which should lead every individual for himself to recognise it as a special gift of God. To this gratitude we have a sufficient call from the Creator himself, when, in the case of idiots, he shows what the endowments of the soul would be were it not pervaded with his light. Though natural to all, it is so in such a sense that it ought to be regarded as a gratuitous gift of his beneficence to each. Moreover, the invention, the methodical arrangement, and the more thorough and superior knowledge of the arts, being confined to a few individuals cannot be regarded as a solid proof of common shrewdness. Still, however, as they are bestowed indiscriminately on the good and the bad, they are justly classed among natural endowments.

15. Therefore, in reading profane authors, the admirable light of truth displayed in them should remind us, that the human mind, however much fallen and perverted from its original integrity, is still adorned and invested with admirable gifts from its Creator. If we reflect that the Spirit of God is the only fountain of truth, we will be careful, as we would avoid offering insult to him, not to reject or condemn truth wherever it appears. In despising the gifts, we insult the Giver. How, then, can we deny that truth must have beamed on those ancient lawgivers who arranged civil order and discipline with so much equity? Shall we say that the philosophers, in their exquisite researches and skilful description of nature, were blind? Shall we deny the possession of intellect to those who drew up rules for discourse, and taught us to speak in accordance with reason? Shall we say that those who, by the cultivation of the medical art, expended their industry in our behalf were only raving? What shall we say of the mathematical sciences? Shall we deem them to be the dreams of madmen? Nay, we cannot read the writings of the ancients on these subjects without the highest admiration; an admiration which their excellence will not allow us to withhold. But shall we deem anything to be noble and praiseworthy, without tracing it to the hand of God? Far from us be such ingratitude; an ingratitude not chargeable even on heathen poets, who acknowledged that philosophy and laws, and all useful arts were the inventions of the gods. Therefore, since it is manifest that men whom the Scriptures term carnal, are so acute and clear-sighted in the investigation of inferior things, their example should teach us how many gifts the Lord has left in possession of human nature, notwithstanding of its having been despoiled of the true good.

16. Moreover, let us not forget that there are most excellent blessings which the Divine Spirit dispenses to whom he will for the common benefit of mankind. For if the skill and knowledge required for the construction of the Tabernacle behaved to be imparted to Bezaleel and Aholiab, by the Spirit of God (Exod. 31:2; 35:30), it is not strange that the knowledge of those things which are of the highest excellence in human life is said to be communicated to us by the Spirit. Nor is there any ground for asking what concourse the Spirit can have with the ungodly, who are altogether alienated from God? For what is said as to the Spirit dwelling in believers only, is to be understood of the Spirit of holiness by which we are consecrated to God as temples. Notwithstanding of this, He fills, moves, and invigorates all things by the virtue of the Spirit, and that according to the peculiar nature which each class of beings has received by the Law of Creation. But if the Lord has been pleased to assist us by the work and ministry of the ungodly in physics, dialectics, mathematics, and other similar sciences, let us avail ourselves of it, lest, by neglecting the gifts of God spontaneously offered to us, we be justly punished for our sloth. Lest any one, however, should imagine a man to be very happy merely because, with reference to the elements of this world, he has been endued with great talents for the investigation of truth, we ought to add, that the whole power of intellect thus bestowed is, in the sight of God, fleeting and vain whenever it is not based on a solid foundation of truth. Augustine (*supra*, sec. 4 and 12), to whom, as we have observed, the Master of Sentences (lib. 2 Dist. 25), and the Schoolmen, are forced to subscribe, says most correctly that as the gratuitous gifts bestowed on man were withdrawn, so

the natural gifts which remained were corrupted after the fall. Not that they can be polluted in themselves in so far as they proceed from God, but that they have ceased to be pure to polluted man, lest he should by their means obtain any praise.

17. The sum of the whole is this: From a general survey of the human race, it appears that one of the essential properties of our nature is reason, which distinguishes us from the lower animals, just as these by means of sense are distinguished from inanimate objects. For although some individuals are born without reason, that defect does not impair the general kindness of God, but rather serves to remind us, that whatever we retain ought justly to be ascribed to the Divine indulgence. Had God not so spared us, our revolt would have carried along with it the entire destruction of nature. In that some excel in acuteness, and some in judgment, while others have greater readiness in learning some peculiar art, God, by this variety commends his favour toward us, lest any one should presume to arrogate to himself that which flows from His mere liberality. For whence is it that one is more excellent than another, but that in a common nature the grace of God is specially displayed in passing by many and thus proclaiming that it is under obligation to none. We may add, that each individual is brought under particular influences according to his calling. Many examples of this occur in the Book of Judges, in which the Spirit of the Lord is said to have come upon those whom he called to govern his people (Judges 6:34). In short, in every distinguished act there is a special inspiration. Thus it is said of Saul, that "there went with him a band of men whose hearts the Lord had touched" (1 Sam. 10:26). And when his inauguration to the kingdom is foretold, Samuel thus addresses him, "The Spirit of the Lord will come upon thee, and thou shalt prophesy with them, and shalt be turned into another man" (1 Sam. 10:6). This extends to the whole course of government, as it is afterwards said of David, "The Spirit of the Lord came upon David from that day forward" (1 Sam. 16:13). The same thing is elsewhere said with reference to particular movements. Nay, even in Homer, men are said to excel in genius, not only according as Jupiter has distributed to each, but according as he leads them day by day. And certainly experience shows when those who were most skilful and ingenious stand stupefied, that the minds of men are entirely under the control of God, who rules them every moment. Hence it is said, that "He poureth contempt upon princes, and causeth them to wander in the wilderness where there is no way" (Ps. 107:40). Still, in this diversity we can trace some remains of the divine image distinguishing the whole human race from other creatures.

18. We must now explain what the power of human reason is, in regard to the kingdom of God, and spiritual discernments which consists chiefly of three things— the knowledge of God, the knowledge of his paternal favour towards us, which constitutes our salvation, and the method of regulating of our conduct in accordance with the Divine Law. With regard to the former two, but more properly the second, men otherwise the most ingenious are blinder than moles. I deny not, indeed, that in the writings of philosophers we meet occasionally with shrewd and apposite remarks on the nature of God, though they invariably savour somewhat of giddy imagination. As observed above, the Lord has bestowed on them some slight perception of his Godhead that they might not plead ignorance as an excuse for their impiety, and has, at times, instigated them to deliver some truths, the confession of which should be their own condemnation. Still, though seeing, they saw not. Their discernment was not such as to direct them to the truth, far less to enable them to attain it, but resembled that of the bewildered traveller, who sees the flash of lightning glance far and wide for a moment, and then vanish into the darkness of the night, before he can advance a single step. So far is such assistance from enabling him to find the right path. Besides, how many monstrous falsehoods intermingle with those minute particles of truth scattered up and down in their writings as if by chance. In short, not one of them even made the least approach to that assurance of the divine favour, without which the mind of man must ever remain a mere chaos of confusion. To the great truths, What God is in himself, and what he is in relation to us, human reason makes not the least approach. (See Book 3 c. 2 sec. 14, 15, 16).

19. But since we are intoxicated with a false opinion of our own discernment, and can scarcely be persuaded that in divine things it is altogether stupid and blind, I believe the best course will be to establish the fact, not by argument, but by Scripture. Most admirable to this effect is the passage which I lately quoted from John, when he says, "In him was life; and the life was the light of men. And the light shineth in darkness; and the darkness comprehended it not" (John 1:4, 5). He intimates that the human soul is indeed irradiated with a beam of divine light, so that it is never left utterly devoid of some small flame, or rather spark, though not such as to enable it to comprehend God. And why so? Because its acuteness is, in reference to

the knowledge of God, mere blindness. When the Spirit describes men under the term darkness, he declares them void of all power of spiritual intelligence. For this reason, it is said that believers, in embracing Christ, are "born, not of blood, nor of the will of the flesh, nor of the will of man, but of God" (John 1:13); in other words, that the flesh has no capacity for such sublime wisdom as to apprehend God, and the things of God, unless illumined by His Spirit. In like manner our Saviour, when he was acknowledged by Peter, declared that it was by special revelation from the Father (Mt. 16:17).

20. If we were persuaded of a truth which ought to be beyond dispute—viz. that human nature possesses none of the gifts which the elect receive from their heavenly Father through the Spirit of regeneration, there would be no room here for hesitation. For thus speaks the congregation of the faithful, by the mouth of the prophet: "With thee is the fountain of life: in thy light shall we see light" (Ps. 36:9). To the same effect is the testimony of the Apostle Paul, when he declares, that "no man can say that Jesus is the Lord, but by the Holy Ghost" (1 Cor. 12:3). And John Baptist, on seeing the dullness of his disciples, exclaims, "A man can receive nothing, unless it be given him from heaven" (John 3:27). That the gift to which he here refers must be understood not of ordinary natural gifts, but of special illumination, appears from this—that he was complaining how little his disciples had profited by all that he had said to them in commendation of Christ. "I see," says he, "that my words are of no effect in imbuing the minds of men with divine things, unless the Lord enlighten their understandings by His Spirit." Nay, Moses also, while upbraiding the people for their forgetfulness, at the same time observes, that they could not become wise in the mysteries of God without his assistance. "Ye have seen all that the Lord did before your eyes in the land of Egypt, unto Pharaoh, and unto all his servants, and unto all his land; the great temptations which thine eyes have seen, the signs, and these great miracles: yet the Lord has not given you an heart to perceive, and eyes to see, and ears to hear, unto this, day" (Deut. 29:2, 3, 4). Would the expression have been stronger had he called us mere blocks in regard to the contemplation of divine things? Hence the Lord, by the mouth of the Prophet, promises to the Israelites as a singular favour, "I will give them an heart to know me" (Jer. 24:7); intimating, that in spiritual things the human mind is wise only in so far as he enlightens it. This was also clearly confirmed by our Saviour when he said, "No man can come to me, except the Father which has sent me draw him" (John 6:44). Nay, is not he himself the living image of his Father, in which the full brightness of his glory is manifested to us? Therefore, how far our faculty of knowing God extends could not be better shown than when it is declared, that though his image is so plainly exhibited, we have not eyes to perceive it. What? Did not Christ descend into the world that he might make the will of his Father manifest to men, and did he not faithfully perform the office? True! He did; but nothing is accomplished by his preaching unless the inner teacher, the Spirit, open the way into our minds. Only those, therefore, come to him who have heard and learned of the Father. And in what is the method of this hearing and learning? It is when the Spirit, with a wondrous and special energy, forms the ear to hear and the mind to understand. Lest this should seem new, our Saviour refers to the prophecy of Isaiah, which contains a promise of the renovation of the Church. "For a small moment have I forsaken thee; but with great mercies will I gather thee" (Is. 54:7). If the Lord here predicts some special blessing to his elect, it is plain that the teaching to which he refers is not that which is common to them with the ungodly and profane.

It thus appears that none can enter the kingdom of God save those whose minds have been renewed by the enlightening of the Holy Spirit. On this subject the clearest exposition is given by Paul, who, when expressly handling it, after condemning the whole wisdom of the world as foolishness and vanity, and thereby declaring man's utter destitution, thus concludes, "The natural man receiveth not the things of the Spirit of God: for they are foolishness unto him: neither can he know them, for they are spiritually discerned" (1 Cor. 2:14). Whom does he mean by the "natural man"? The man who trusts to the light of nature. Such a man has no understanding in the spiritual mysteries of God. Why so? Is it because through sloth he neglects them? Nay, though he exert himself, it is of no avail; they are "spiritually discerned." And what does this mean? That altogether hidden from human discernment, they are made known only by the revelation of the Spirit; so that they are accounted foolishness wherever the Spirit does not give light. The Apostle had previously declared, that "Eye has not seen, nor ear heard, neither have entered into the heart of man, the things which God has prepared for them that love him;" nay, that the wisdom of the world is a kind of veil by which the mind is prevented from beholding God (1 Cor. 2:9). What would we more? The Apostle declares that God has "made foolish the wisdom of this world" (1 Cor. 1:20); and shall we attribute to it an acuteness capable of penetrating to God, and the hidden mysteries of his kingdom? Far from us be such presumption!

21. What the Apostle here denies to man, he, in another place, ascribes to God alone, when he prays, "that the God of our Lord Jesus Christ, the Father of glory, may give unto you the spirit of wisdom and revelation" (Eph. 1:17). You now hear that all wisdom and revelation is the gift of God. What follows? "The eyes of your understanding being enlightened." Surely, if they require a new enlightening, they must in themselves be blind. The next words are, "that ye may know what is the hope of his calling" (Eph. 1:18). In other words, the minds of men have not capacity enough to know their calling. Let no prating Pelagian here allege that God obviates this rudeness or stupidity, when, by the doctrine of his word, he directs us to a path which we could not have found without a guide. David had the law, comprehending in it all the wisdom that could be desired, and yet not contented with this, he prays, "Open thou mine eyes, that I may behold wondrous things out of thy law" (Ps. 119:18). By this expression, he certainly intimates, that it is like sunrise to the earth when the word of God shines forth; but that men do not derive much benefit from it until he himself, who is for this reason called the Father of lights (James 1:17), either gives eyes or opens them; because, whatever is not illuminated by his Spirit is wholly darkness. The Apostles had been duly and amply instructed by the best of teachers. Still, as they wanted the Spirit of truth to complete their education in the very doctrine which they had previously heard, they were ordered to wait for him (John 14:26). If we confess that what we ask of God is lacking to us, and He by the very thing promised intimates our want, no man can hesitate to acknowledge that he is able to understand the mysteries of God, only in so far as illuminated by his grace. He who ascribes to himself more understanding than this, is the blinder for not acknowledging his blindness.

22. It remains to consider the third branch of the knowledge of spiritual things—viz. the method of properly regulating the conduct. This is correctly termed the knowledge of the works of righteousness, a branch in which the human mind seems to have somewhat more discernment than in the former two, since an Apostle declares, "When the Gentiles, which have not the law, do by nature the things contained in the law, these, having not the law, are a law unto themselves: which show the work of the law written in their hearts, their conscience also bearing witness, and their thoughts the meantime accusing or else excusing one another" (Rom. 2:14, 15).

If the Gentiles have the righteousness of the law naturally engraven on their minds, we certainly cannot say that they are altogether blind as to the rule of life. Nothing, indeed is more common, than for man to be sufficiently instructed in a right course of conduct by natural law, of which the Apostle here speaks. Let us consider, however for what end this knowledge of the law was given to men. For from this it will forthwith appear how far it can conduct them in the way of reason and truth. This is even plain from the words of Paul, if we attend to their arrangement. He had said a little before, that those who had sinned in the law will be judged by the law; and those who have sinned without the law will perish without the law. As it might seem unaccountable that the Gentiles should perish without any previous judgment, he immediately subjoins, that conscience served them instead of the law, and was therefore sufficient for their righteous condemnation. The end of the natural law, therefore, is to render man inexcusable, and may be not improperly defined—the judgment of conscience distinguishing sufficiently between just and unjust, and by convicting men on their own testimony depriving them of all pretext for ignorance. So indulgent is man towards himself, that, while doing evil, he always endeavours as much as he can to suppress the idea of sin. It was this, apparently, which induced Plato (in his Protagoras) to suppose that sins were committed only through ignorance. There might be some ground for this, if hypocrisy were so successful in hiding vice as to keep the conscience clear in the sight of God. But since the sinner, when trying to evade the judgment of good and evil implanted in him, is ever and anon dragged forward, and not permitted to wink so effectually as not to be compelled at times, whether he will or not, to open his eyes, it is false to say that he sins only through ignorance.

23. Themistius is more accurate in teaching (Paraphr. in Lib. 3 de Anima, cap. 46), that the intellect is very seldom mistaken in the general definition or essence of the matter; but that deception begins as it advances farther, namely, when it descends to particulars. That homicide, putting the case in the abstract, is an evil, no man will deny; and yet one who is conspiring the death of his enemy deliberates on it as if the thing was good. The adulterer will condemn adultery in the abstract, and yet flatter himself while privately committing it. The ignorance lies here: that man, when he comes to the particular, forgets the rule which he had laid down in the general case. Augustine treats most admirably on this subject in his exposition of the first verse of the fifty-seventh

Psalm. The doctrine of Themistius, however, does not always hold true: for the turpitude of the crime sometimes presses so on the conscience, that the sinner does not impose upon himself by a false semblance of good, but rushes into sin knowingly and willingly. Hence the expression,—I see the better course, and approve it: I follow the worse (Medea of Ovid). For this reason, Aristotle seems to me to have made a very shrewd distinction between incontinence and intemperance (Ethic. lib. 7 cap. 3) Where incontinence (*ajkrasiva*) reigns, he says, that through the passion (*pavtho"*) particular knowledge is suppressed: so that the individual sees not in his own misdeed the evil which he sees generally in similar cases; but when the passion is over, repentance immediately succeeds. Intemperance (*ajkolasiva*), again, is not extinguished or diminished by a sense of sin, but, on the contrary, persists in the evil choice which it has once made.

24. Moreover, when you hear of a universal judgment in man distinguishing between good and evil, you must not suppose that this judgment is, in every respect, sound and entire. For if the hearts of men are imbued with a sense of justice and injustice, in order that they may have no pretext to allege ignorance, it is by no means necessary for this purpose that they should discern the truth in particular cases. It is even more than sufficient if they understand so far as to be unable to practice evasion without being convicted by their own conscience, and beginning even now to tremble at the judgment-seat of God. Indeed, if we would test our reason by the Divine Law, which is a perfect standard of righteousness, we should find how blind it is in many respects. It certainly attains not to the principal heads in the First Table, such as, trust in God, the ascription to him of all praise in virtue and righteousness, the invocation of his name, and the true observance of his day of rest. Did ever any soul, under the guidance of natural sense, imagine that these and the like constitute the legitimate worship of God? When profane men would worship God, how often soever they may be drawn off from their vain trifling, they constantly relapse into it. They admit, indeed, that sacrifices are not pleasing, to God, unless accompanied with sincerity of mind; and by this they testify that they have some conception of spiritual worship, though they immediately pervert it by false devices: for it is impossible to persuade them that every thing which the law enjoins on the subject is true. Shall I then extol the discernment of a mind which can neither acquire wisdom by itself, nor listen to advice? As to the precepts of the Second Table, there is considerably more knowledge of them, inasmuch as they are more closely connected with the preservation of civil society. Even here, however, there is something defective. Every man of understanding deems it most absurd to submit to unjust and tyrannical domination, provided it can by any means be thrown off, and there is but one opinion among men, that it is the part of an abject and servile mind to bear it patiently, the part of an honourable and high-spirited mind to rise up against it. Indeed, the revenge of injuries is not regarded by philosophers as a vice. But the Lord condemning this too lofty spirit, prescribes to his people that patience which mankind deem infamous. In regard to the general observance of the law, concupiscence altogether escapes our animadversion. For the natural man cannot bear to recognise diseases in his lusts. The light of nature is stifled sooner than take the first step into this profound abyss. For, when philosophers class immoderate movements of the mind among vices, they mean those which break forth and manifest themselves in grosser forms. Depraved desires, in which the mind can quietly indulge, they regard as nothing (see *infra*, chap. 8 sect. 49).

25. As we have above animadverted on Plato's error, in ascribing all sins to ignorance, so we must repudiate the opinion of those who hold that all sins proceed from preconceived gravity and malice. We know too well from experience how often we fall, even when our intention is good. Our reason is exposed to so many forms of delusion, is liable to so many errors, stumbles on so many obstacles, is entangled by so many snares, that it is ever wandering from the right direction. Of how little value it is in the sight of God, in regard to all the parts of life, Paul shows, when he says, that we are not "sufficient of ourselves to think any thing as of ourselves" (2 Cor. 3:5). He is not speaking of the will or affection; he denies us the power of thinking aright how any thing cam be duly performed. Is it, indeed, true, that all thought, intelligence, discernment, and industry, are so defective, that, in the sight of the Lord, we cannot think or aim at any thing that is right? To us, who can scarcely bear to part with acuteness of intellect (in our estimation a most precious endowment), it seems hard to admit this, whereas it is regarded as most just by the Holy Spirit, who "knoweth the thoughts of man, that they are vanity" (Ps. 94:11), and distinctly declares, that "every imagination of the thoughts of his heart was only evil continually" (Gen. 6:5; 8:21). If every thing which our mind conceives, meditates plans, and resolves, is always evil, how can it ever think of doing what is pleasing to God, to whom righteousness and holiness alone are acceptable? It is thus plain, that our mind, in what direction soever it turns, is

miserably exposed to vanity. David was conscious of its weakness when he prayed, "Give me understanding, and I shall keep thy law" (Ps. 119:34). By desiring to obtain a new understanding, he intimates that his own was by no means sufficient. This he does not once only, but in one psalm repeats the same prayer almost ten times, the repetition intimating how strong the necessity which urged him to pray. What he thus asked for himself alone, Paul prays for the churches in general. "For this cause," says he, "we also, since the day we heard it, do not cease to pray for you, and to desire that ye might be filled with the knowledge of his will, in all wisdom and spiritual understanding; that you might walk worthy of the Lord," &c. (Col. 1:9, 10). Whenever he represents this as a blessing from God, we should remember that he at the same time testifies that it is not in the power of man. Accordingly, Augustine, in speaking of this inability of human reason to understand the things of God, says, that he deems the grace of illumination not less necessary to the mind than the light of the sun to the eye (*August. de Peccat. Merit. et Remiss.* lib. 2 cap. 5). And, not content with this, he modifies his expression, adding, that we open our eyes to behold the light, whereas the mental eye remains shut, until it is opened by the Lord. Nor does Scripture say that our minds are illuminated in a single day, so as afterwards to see of themselves. The passage, which I lately quoted from the Apostle Paul, refers to continual progress and increase. David, too, expresses this distinctly in these words: "With my whole heart have I sought thee: O let me not wander from thy commandments" (Ps. 119:10). Though he had been regenerated, and so had made no ordinary progress in true piety, he confesses that he stood in need of direction every moment, in order that he might not decline from the knowledge with which he had been endued. Hence, he elsewhere prays for a renewal of a right spirit, which he had lost by his sin, (Ps. 51:12). For that which God gave at first, while temporarily withdrawn, it is equally his province to restore.

26. We must now examine the will, on which the question of freedom principally turns, the power of choice belonging to it rather than the intellect, as we have already seen (*supra*, sect. 4). And at the outset, to guard against its being thought that the doctrine taught by philosophers, and generally received—viz. that all things by natural instinct have a desire of good, is any proof of the rectitude of the human will,—let us observe, that the power of free will is not to be considered in any of those desires which proceed more from instinct than mental deliberation. Even the schoolmen admit (*Thomas*, Part 1, *Quæst.* 83, art. 3), that there is no act of free will, unless when reason looks at opposites. By this they mean, that the things desired must be such as may be made the object of choice, and that to pave the way for choice, deliberation must precede. And, undoubtedly, if you attend to what this natural desire of good in man is, you will find that it is common to him with the brutes. They, too, desire what is good; and when any semblance of good capable of moving the sense appears, they follow after it. Here, however, man does not, in accordance with the excellence of his immortal nature, rationally choose, and studiously pursue, what is truly for his good. He does not admit reason to his counsel, nor exert his intellect; but without reason, without counsel, follows the bent of his nature like the lower animals. The question of freedom, therefore, has nothing to do with the fact of man's being led by natural instinct to desire good. The question is, Does man, after determining by right reason what is good, choose what he thus knows, and pursue what he thus chooses? Lest any doubt should be entertained as to this, we must attend to the double misnomer. For this *appetite* is not properly a movement of the will, but natural inclination; and this *good* is not one of virtue or righteousness, but of condition—viz. that the individual may feel comfortable. In fine, how much soever man may desire to obtain what is good, he does not follow it. There is no man who would not be pleased with eternal blessedness; and yet, without the impulse of the Spirit, no man aspires to it. Since, then, the natural desire of happiness in man no more proves the freedom of the will, than the tendency in metals and stones to attain the perfection of their nature, let us consider, in other respects, whether the will is so utterly vitiated and corrupted in every part as to produce nothing but evil, or whether it retains some portion uninjured, and productive of good desires.

27. Those who ascribe our willing effectually, to the primary grace of Gods (*supra*, sect. 6), seem conversely to insinuate that the soul has in itself a power of aspiring to good, though a power too feeble to rise to solid affection or active endeavour. There is no doubt that this opinion, adopted from Origin and certain of the ancient Fathers, has been generally embraced by the schoolmen, who are wont to apply to man in his natural state (*in puris naturalibus*, as they express it) the following description of the apostle:—"For that which I do I allow not: for what I would, that do I not; but what I hate, that do I." "To will is present with me; but how to perform that which is good I find not" (Rom. 7:15, 18). But, in this way, the whole scope of Paul's discourse is inverted. He is speaking of the Chris-

tian struggle (touched on more briefly in the Epistle to the Galatians), which believers constantly experience from the conflict between the flesh and the Spirit. But the Spirit is not from nature, but from regeneration. That the apostle is speaking of the regenerate is apparent from this, that after saying, "in me dwells no good thing," he immediately adds the explanation, "in my flesh." Accordingly, he declares, "It is no more I that do it, but sin that dwelleth in me." What is the meaning of the correction, "in me (that is, in my flesh?)" It is just as if he had spoken in this way, No good thing dwells in me, of myself, for in my flesh nothing good can be found. Hence follows the species of excuse, It is not I myself that do evil, but sin that dwelleth in me. This applies to none but the regenerate, who, with the leading powers of the soul, tend towards what is good. The whole is made plain by the conclusion, "I delight in the law of God after the inward man: but I see another law in my members, warring against the law of my mind" (Rom. 7:22, 23). Who has this struggle in himself, save those who, regenerated by the Spirit of God, bear about with them the remains of the flesh? Accordingly, Augustine, who had at one time thought that the discourse related to the natural man (August. ad Bonifac. lib. 1 c. 10), afterwards retracted his exposition as unsound and inconsistent. And, indeed if we admit that men, without grace, have any motions to good, however feeble, what answer shall we give to the apostles who declares that "we are incapable of thinking a good thought?" (2 Cor. 3:6). What answer shall we give to the Lord, who declares, by Moses, that "every imagination of man's heart is only evil continually?" (Gen. 8:21). Since the blunder has thus arisen from an erroneous view of a single passage, it seems unnecessary to dwell upon it. Let us rather give due weight to our Saviour's words, "Whosoever committeth sin is the servant of sin" (John 8:34). We are all sinners by nature, therefore we are held under the yoke of sin. But if the whole man is subject to the dominion of sin, surely the will, which is its principal seat, must be bound with the closest chains. And, indeed, if divine grace were preceded by any will of ours, Paul could not have said that "it is God which worketh in us both to will and to do" (Phil. 2:13). Away, then, with all the absurd trifling which many have indulged in with regard to preparation. Although believers sometimes ask to have their heart trained to the obedience of the divine law, as David does in several passages (Ps. 51:12), it is to be observed, that even this longing in prayer is from God. This is apparent from the language used. When he prays, "Create in me a clean heart," he certainly does not attribute the beginning of the creation to himself. Let us therefore rather adopt the sentiment of Augustine, "God will prevent you in all things, but do you sometimes prevent his anger. How? Confess that you have all these things from God, that all the good you have is from him, all the evil from yourself" (August. De Verbis Apost. Serm. 10). Shortly after he says "Of our own we have nothing but sin."

CHAPTER 3

EVERY THING PROCEEDING FROM THE CORRUPT NATURE OF MAN DAMNABLE.

The principal matters in this chapter are—I. A recapitulation of the former chapter, proving, from passages of Scriptures that the intellect and will of man are so corrupted, that no integrity, no knowledge or fear of God, can now be found in him, sect. 1 and 2. II. Objections to this doctrine, from the virtues which shone in some of the heathen, refuted, sect. 3 and 4. III. What kind of will remains in man, the slave of sin, sect. 5. The remedy and cure, sect. 6. IV. The opinion of Neo-Pelagian sophists concerning the preparation and efficacy of the will, and also concerning perseverance and co-operating grace, refuted, both by reason and Scripture, sect. 7–12. V. Some passages from Augustine confirming the truth of this doctrine, sect. 13 and 14.

Sections:

1. The intellect and will of the whole man corrupt. The term flesh applies not only to the sensual, but also to the higher part of the soul. This demonstrated from Scripture.

2. The heart also involved in corruption, and hence in no part of man can integrity, or knowledge or the fear of God, be found.

3. Objection, that some of the heathen were possessed of admirable endowments, and, therefore, that the nature of man is not entirely corrupt. Answer, Corruption is not entirely removed, but only inwardly restrained. Explanation of this answer.

4. Objection still urged, that the virtuous and vicious among the heathen must be put upon the same level, or the virtuous prove that human nature, properly cultivated, is not devoid of virtue. Answer, That these are not ordinary properties of human nature, but special gifts of God. These gifts defiled by ambition, and hence the actions proceeding from them, however esteemed by man, have no merit with God.

5. Though man has still the faculty of willing there

is no soundness in it. He falls under the bondage of sin necessarily, and yet voluntarily. Necessity must be distinguished from compulsion. The ancient Theologians acquainted with this necessity. Some passages condemning the vacillation of Lombard.

6. Conversion to God constitutes the remedy or soundness of the human will. This not only begun, but continued and completed; the beginning, continuance, and completion, being ascribed entirely to God. This proved by Ezekiel's description of the stony heart, and from other passages of Scripture.

7. Various Objections.—1. The will is converted by God, but, when once prepared, does its part in the work of conversion. Answer from Augustine. 2. Grace can do nothing without will, nor the will without grace. Answer. Grace itself produces will. God prevents the unwilling, making him willing, and follows up this preventing grace that he may not will in vain. Another answer gathered from various passages of Augustine.

8. Answer to the second Objection continued. No will inclining to good except in the elect. The cause of election out of man. Hence right will, as well as election, are from the good pleasure of God. The beginning of willing and doing well is of faith; faith again is the gift of God; and hence mere grace is the cause of our beginning to will well. This proved by Scripture.

9. Answer to second Objection continued. That good will is merely of grace proved by the prayers of saints. Three axioms 1. God does not prepare man's heart, so that he can afterwards do some good of himself, but every desire of rectitude, every inclination to study, and every effort to pursue it, is from Him. 2. This desire, study, and effort, do not stop short, but continue to effect. 3. This progress is constant. The believer perseveres to the end. A third Objection, and three answers to it.

10. A fourth Objection. Answer. Fifth Objection. Answer. Answer confirmed by many passages of Scripture, and supported by a passage from Augustine.

11. Perseverance not of ourselves, but of God. Objection. Two errors in the objection. Refutation of both.

12. An objection founded on the distinction of co-operating grace. Answer. Answer confirmed by the testimony of Augustine and Bernard.

13. Last part of the chapter, in which it is proved by many passages of Augustine, that he held the doctrine here taught.

14. An objection, representing Augustine at variance with himself and other Theologians, removed. A summary of Augustine's doctrine on free will.

1. The nature of man, in both parts of his soul—viz. intellect and will—cannot be better ascertained than by attending to the epithets applied to him in Scripture. If he is fully depicted (and it may easily be proved that he is) by the words of our Saviour, "that which is born of the flesh is flesh" (John 3:6), he must be a very miserable creature. For, as an apostle declares, "to be carnally minded is death" (Rom. 8:8), "It is enmity against God, and is not subject to the law of God, neither indeed can be." Is it true that the flesh is so perverse, that it is perpetually striving with all its might against God? that it cannot accord with the righteousness of the divine law? that, in short, it can beget nothing but the materials of death? Grant that there is nothing in human nature but flesh, and then extract something good out of it if you can. But it will be said, that the word *flesh* applies only to the sensual, and not to the higher part of the soul. This, however, is completely refuted by the words both of Christ and his apostle. The statement of our Lord is, that a man must be born again, because he is flesh. He requires not to be born again, with reference to the body. But a mind is not born again merely by having some portion of it reformed. It must be totally renewed. This is confirmed by the antithesis used in both passages. In the contrast between the Spirit and the flesh, there is nothing left of an intermediate nature. In this way, everything in man, which is not spiritual, falls under the denomination of carnal. But we have nothing of the Spirit except through regeneration. Everything, therefore, which we have from nature is flesh. Any possible doubt which might exist on the subject is removed by the words of Paul (Eph. 4:23), where, after a description of the old man, who, he says, "is corrupt according to the deceitful lusts," he bids us "be renewed in the spirit" of our mind. You see that he places unlawful and depraved desires not in the sensual part merely, but in the mind itself, and therefore requires that it should be renewed. Indeed, he had a little before drawn a picture of human nature, which shows that there is no part in which it is not perverted and corrupted. For when he says that the "Gentiles walk in the vanity of their mind, having the understanding darkened being alienated from the life of God through the ignorance that is in them, because of the blindness of their heart" (Eph. 4:17, 18), there can be no doubt that his words apply to all whom the Lord has not yet formed anew both to wisdom and righteousness. This is rendered more clear by the comparison which immediately follows, and by which he reminds believers that they "have not so learned Christ" these words implying that

the grace of Christ is the only remedy for that blindness and its evil consequences. Thus, too, had Isaiah prophesied of the kingdom of Christ, when the Lord promised to the Church, that though darkness should "cover the earth, and gross darkness the people," yet that he should "arise" upon it, and "his glory" should be seen upon it (Isaiah 40:2). When it is thus declared that divine light is to arise on the Church alone, all without the Church is left in blindness and darkness. I will not enumerate all that occurs throughout Scripture, and particularly in the Psalms and Prophetical writings, as to the vanity of man. There is much in what David says, "Surely men of low degree are vanity, and men of high degree are a lie: to be laid in the balance, they are altogether lighter than vanity" (Ps. 62:10). The human mind receives a humbling blow when all the thoughts which proceed from it are derided as foolish, frivolous, perverse, and insane.

2. In no degree more lenient is the condemnation of the heart, when it is described as "deceitful above all things, and desperately wicked" (Jer. 17:9). But as I study brevity, I will be satisfied with a single passage, one, however, in which as in a bright mirror, we may behold a complete image of our nature. The Apostle, when he would humble man's pride, uses these words: "There is none righteous no, not one: there is none that understandeth, there is none that seeketh after God. They are all gone out of the way, they are together become unprofitable; there is none that does good, no, not one. Their throat is an open sepulchre; with their tongues they have used deceit; the poison of asps is under their lips: Whose mouth is full of cursing and bitterness: their feet are swift to shed blood: destruction and misery are in their ways: and the way of peace have they not known: there is no fear of God before their eyes" (Rom. 3:10–18). Thus he thunders not against certain individuals, but against the whole posterity of Adam—not against the depraved manners of any single age, but the perpetual corruption of nature. His object in the passage is not merely to upbraid men in order that they may repent, but to teach that all are overwhelmed with inevitable calamity, and can be delivered from it only by the mercy of God. As this could not be proved without previously proving the overthrow and destruction of nature, he produced those passages to show that its ruin is complete.

Let it be a fixed point, then, that men are such as is here described, not by vicious custom, but by depravity of nature. The reasoning of the Apostle, that there is no salvation for man, save in the mercy of God, because in himself he is desperate and undone, could not otherwise stand. I will not here labour to prove that the passages apply, with the view of removing the doubts of any who might think them quoted out of place. I will take them as if they had been used by Paul for the first time, and not taken from the Prophets. First, then, he strips man of righteousness, that is, integrity and purity; and, secondly, he strips him of sound intelligence. He argues, that defect of intelligence is proved by apostasy from God. To seek Him is the beginning of wisdom, and, therefore, such defect must exist in all who have revolted from Him. He subjoins, that all have gone astray, and become as it were mere corruption; that there is none that does good. He then enumerates the crimes by which those who have once given loose to their wickedness pollute every member of their bodies. Lastly, he declares that they have no fear of God, according to whose rule all our steps should be directed. If these are the hereditary properties of the human race, it is vain to look for anything good in our nature. I confess indeed, that all these iniquities do not break out in every individual. Still it cannot be denied that the hydra lurks in every breast. For as a body, while it contains and fosters the cause and matter of disease, cannot be called healthy, although pain is not actually felt; so a soul, while teeming with such seeds of vice, cannot be called sound. This similitude, however, does not apply throughout. In a body however morbid the functions of life are performed; but the soul, when plunged into that deadly abyss, not only labours under vice, but is altogether devoid of good.

3. Here, again we are met with a question very much the same as that which was previously solved. In every age there have been some who, under the guidance of nature, were all their lives devoted to virtue. It is of no consequence, that many blots may be detected in their conduct; by the mere study of virtue, they evinced that there was somewhat of purity in their nature. The value which virtues of this kind have in the sight of God will be considered more fully when we treat of the merit of works. Meanwhile however, it will be proper to consider it in this place also, in so far as necessary for the exposition of the subject in hand. Such examples, then, seem to warn us against supposing that the nature of man is utterly vicious, since, under its guidance, some have not only excelled in illustrious deeds, but conducted themselves most honourably through the whole course of their lives. But we ought to consider, that, notwithstanding of the corruption of our nature, there is some room for divine grace, such grace as, without purifying it, may lay it under internal restraint. For, did the Lord let every

mind loose to wanton in its lusts, doubtless there is not a man who would not show that his nature is capable of all the crimes with which Paul charges it (Rom. 3 compared with Ps. 14:3, &c). What? Can you exempt yourself from the number of those whose feet are swift to shed blood; whose hands are foul with rapine and murder; whose throats are like open sepulchres; whose tongues are deceitful; whose lips are venomous; whose actions are useless, unjust, rotten, deadly; whose soul is without God; whose inward parts are full of wickedness; whose eyes are on the watch for deception; whose minds are prepared for insult; whose every part, in short, is framed for endless deeds of wickedness? If every soul is capable of such abominations (and the Apostle declares this boldly), it is surely easy to see what the result would be, if the Lord were to permit human passion to follow its bent. No ravenous beast would rush so furiously, no stream, however rapid and violent, so impetuously burst its banks. In the elect, God cures these diseases in the mode which will shortly be explained; in others, he only lays them under such restraint as may prevent them from breaking forth to a degree incompatible with the preservation of the established order of things. Hence, how much soever men may disguise their impurity, some are restrained only by shame, others by a fear of the laws, from breaking out into many kinds of wickedness. Some aspire to an honest life, as deeming it most conducive to their interest, while others are raised above the vulgar lot, that, by the dignity of their station, they may keep inferiors to their duty. Thus God, by his providence, curbs the perverseness of nature, preventing it from breaking forth into action, yet without rendering it inwardly pure.

4. The objection, however, is not yet solved. For we must either put Cataline on the same footing with Camillus, or hold Camillus to be an example that nature, when carefully cultivated, is not wholly void of goodness. I admit that the specious qualities which Camillus possessed were divine gifts, and appear entitled to commendation when viewed in themselves. But in what way will they be proofs of a virtuous nature? Must we not go back to the mind, and from it begin to reason thus? If a natural man possesses such integrity of manners, nature is not without the faculty of studying virtue. But what if his mind was depraved and perverted, and followed anything rather than rectitude? Such it undoubtedly was, if you grant that he was only a natural man. How then will you laud the power of human nature for good, if, even where there is the highest semblance of integrity, a corrupt bias is always detected? Therefore, as you would not commend a man for virtue whose vices impose upon you by a show of virtue, so you will not attribute a power of choosing rectitude to the human will while rooted in depravity (see August. lib. 4, Cont. Julian). Still, the surest and easiest answer to the objection is, that those are not common endowments of nature, but special gifts of God, which he distributes in divers forms, and, in a definite measure, to men otherwise profane. For which reason, we hesitate not, in common language, to say, that one is of a good, another of a vicious nature; though we cease not to hold that both are placed under the universal condition of human depravity. All we mean is that God has conferred on the one a special grace which he has not seen it meet to confer on the other. When he was pleased to set Saul over the kingdom, he made him as it were a new man. This is the thing meant by Plato, when, alluding to a passage in the Iliad, he says, that the children of kings are distinguished at their birth by some special qualities—God, in kindness to the human race, often giving a spirit of heroism to those whom he destines for empire. In this way, the great leaders celebrated in history were formed. The same judgment must be given in the case of private individuals. But as those endued with the greatest talents were always impelled by the greatest ambitions (a stain which defiles all virtues and makes them lose all favour in the sight of God), so we cannot set any value on anything that seems praiseworthy in ungodly men. We may add, that the principal part of rectitude is wanting, when there is no zeal for the glory of God, and there is no such zeal in those whom he has not regenerated by his Spirit. Nor is it without good cause said in Isaiah, that on Christ should rest "the spirit of knowledge, and of the fear of the Lord" (Isa. 11:2); for by this we are taught that all who are strangers to Christ are destitute of that fear of God which is the beginning of wisdom (Ps. 111:10). The virtues which deceive us by an empty show may have their praise in civil society and the common intercourse of life, but before the judgment-seat of God they will be of no value to establish a claim of righteousness.

5. When the will is enchained as the slave of sin, it cannot make a movement towards goodness, far less steadily pursue it. Every such movement is the first step in that conversion to God, which in Scripture is entirely ascribed to divine grace. Thus Jeremiah prays, "Turn thou me, and I shall be turned" (Jer. 31:18). Hence, too, in the same chapter, describing the spiritual redemption of believers, the Prophet says, "The Lord has redeemed Jacob, and ransomed him from the hand of him that was stronger than he" (Jer. 31:11); intimating how close the fetters are with

which the sinner is bound, so long as he is abandoned by the Lord, and acts under the yoke of the devil. Nevertheless, there remains a will which both inclines and hastens on with the strongest affection towards sin; man, when placed under this bondage, being deprived not of will, but of soundness of will. Bernard says not improperly, that all of us have a will; but to will well is proficiency, to will ill is defect. Thus simply to will is the part of man, to will ill the part of corrupt nature, to will well the part of grace. Moreover, when I say that the will, deprived of liberty, is led or dragged by necessity to evil, it is strange that any should deem the expression harsh, seeing there is no absurdity in it, and it is not at variance with pious use. It does, however, offend those who know not how to distinguish between necessity and compulsion. Were any one to ask them, Is not God necessarily good, is not the devil necessarily wicked, what answer would they give? The goodness of God is so connected with his Godhead, that it is not more necessary to be God than to be good; whereas the devil, by his fall, was so estranged from goodness, that he can do nothing but evil. Should any one give utterance to the profane jeer (see Calvin Adv. Pighium), that little praise is due to God for a goodness to which he is forced, is it not obvious to every man to reply, It is owing not to violent impulse, but to his boundless goodness, that he cannot do evil? Therefore, if the free will of God in doing good is not impeded, because he necessarily must do good; if the devil, who can do nothing but evil, nevertheless sins voluntarily; can it be said that man sins less voluntarily because he is under a necessity of sinning? This necessity is uniformly proclaimed by Augustine, who, even when pressed by the invidious cavil of Celestius, hesitated not to assert it in the following terms: "Man through liberty became a sinner, but corruption, ensuing as the penalty, has converted liberty into necessity" (August. lib. de Perf. Justin). Whenever mention is made of the subject, he hesitates not to speak in this way of the necessary bondage of sin (August. de Nature et Gratia, et alibi). Let this, then, be regarded as the sum of the distinction. Man, since he was corrupted by the fall, sins not forced or unwilling, but voluntarily, by a most forward bias of the mind; not by violent compulsion, or external force, but by the movement of his own passion; and yet such is the depravity of his nature, that he cannot move and act except in the direction of evil. If this is true, the thing not obscurely expressed is, that he is under a necessity of sinning. Bernard, assenting to Augustine, thus writes: "Among animals, man alone is free, and yet sin intervening, he suffers a kind of violence, but a violence proceeding from his will, not from nature, so that it does not even deprive him of innate liberty" (Bernard, Sermo. super Cantica, 81). For that which is voluntary is also free. A little after he adds, "Thus, by some means strange and wicked, the will itself, being deteriorated by sin, makes a necessity; but so that the necessity, in as much as it is voluntary, cannot excuse the will, and the will, in as much as it is enticed, cannot exclude the necessity." For this necessity is in a manner voluntary. He afterwards says that "we are under a yoke, but no other yoke than that of voluntary servitude; therefore, in respect of servitude, we are miserable, and in respect of will, inexcusable; because the will, when it was free, made itself the slave of sin." At length he concludes, "Thus the soul, in some strange and evil way, is held under this kind of voluntary, yet sadly free necessity, both bond and free; bond in respect of necessity, free in respect of will: and what is still more strange, and still more miserable, it is guilty because free, and enslaved because guilty, and therefore enslaved because free." My readers hence perceive that the doctrine which I deliver is not new, but the doctrine which of old Augustine delivered with the consent of all the godly, and which was afterwards shut up in the cloisters of monks for almost a thousand years. Lombard, by not knowing how to distinguish between necessity and compulsion, gave occasion to a pernicious error.

6. On the other hand, it may be proper to consider what the remedy is which divine grace provides for the correction and cure of natural corruption. Since the Lord, in bringing assistance, supplies us with what is lacking, the nature of that assistance will immediately make manifest its converse—viz. our penury. When the Apostle says to the Philippians, "Being confident of this very thing, that he which has begun a good work in you, will perform it until the day of Jesus Christ" (Phil. 1:6), there cannot be a doubt, that by the good work thus begun, he means the very commencement of conversion in the will. God, therefore, begins the good work in us by exciting in our hearts a desire, a love, and a study of righteousness, or (to speak more correctly) by turning, training, and guiding our hearts unto righteousness; and he completes this good work by confirming us unto perseverance. But lest any one should cavil that the good work thus begun by the Lord consists in aiding the will, which is in itself weak, the Spirit elsewhere declares what the will, when left to itself, is able to do. His words are, "A new heart also will I give you, and a new spirit will I put within you: and I will take away the stony heart out of your flesh, and I will give you an heart of flesh. And I will put my Spirit

within you, and cause you to walk in my statutes, and ye shall keep my judgments, and do them" (Ezek. 36:26, 27). How can it be said that the weakness of the human will is aided so as to enable it to aspire effectually to the choice of good, when the fact is, that it must be wholly transformed and renovated? If there is any softness in a stone; if you can make it tender, and flexible into any shape, then it may be said, that the human heart may be shaped for rectitude, provided that which is imperfect in it is supplemented by divine grace. But if the Spirit, by the above similitude, meant to show that no good can ever be extracted from our heart until it is made altogether new, let us not attempt to share with Him what He claims for himself alone. If it is like turning a stone into flesh when God turns us to the study of rectitude, everything proper to our own will is abolished, and that which succeeds in its place is wholly of God. I say the will is abolished, but not in so far as it is will, for in conversion everything essential to our original nature remains: I also say, that it is created anew, not because the will then begins to exist, but because it is turned from evil to good. This, I maintains is wholly the work of God, because, as the Apostle testifies, we are not "sufficient of ourselves to think any thing as of ourselves" (2 Cor. 3:5). Accordingly, he elsewhere says, not merely that God assists the weak or corrects the depraved will, but that he worketh in us to will (Phil. 2:13). From this it is easily inferred, as I have said, that everything good in the will is entirely the result of grace. In the same sense, the Apostle elsewhere says, "It is the same God which worketh all in all" (I Cor. 12:6). For he is not there treating of universal government, but declaring that all the good qualities which believers possess are due to God. In using the term "all," he certainly makes God the author of spiritual life from its beginning to its end. This he had previously taught in different terms, when he said that there is "one Lord Jesus Christ, by whom are all things, and we by him" (1 Cor. 8:6); thus plainly extolling the new creation, by which everything of our common nature is destroyed. There is here a tacit antithesis between Adam and Christ, which he elsewhere explains more clearly when he says, "We are his workmanship, created in Christ Jesus unto good works, which God has before ordained that we should walk in them" (Eph. 2:10). His meaning is to show in this way that our salvation is gratuitous because the beginning of goodness is from the second creation which is obtained in Christ. If any, even the minutest, ability were in ourselves, there would also be some merit. But to show our utter destitution, he argues that we merit nothing, because we are created in Christ Jesus unto good works, which God has prepared; again intimating by these words, that all the fruits of good works are originally and immediately from God. Hence the Psalmist, after saying that the Lord "has made us," to deprive us of all share in the work, immediately adds, "not we ourselves." That he is speaking of regeneration, which is the commencement of the spiritual life, is obvious from the context, in which the next words are, "we are his people, and the sheep of his pasture" (Psalm 100:3). Not contented with simply giving God the praise of our salvation, he distinctly excludes us from all share in it, just as if he had said that not one particle remains to man as a ground of boasting. The whole is of God.

7. But perhaps there will be some who, while they admit that the will is in its own nature averse to righteousness, and is converted solely by the power of God, will yet hold that, when once it is prepared, it performs a part in acting. This they found upon the words of Augustine, that grace precedes every good work; the will accompanying, not leading; a handmaid, and not a guide (August. ad Bonifac. Ep. 106). The words thus not improperly used by this holy writer, Lombard preposterously wrests to the above effect (Lombard, lib. 2, Dist. 25). But I maintain, that as well in the words of the Psalmist which I have quoted, as in other passages of Scripture, two things are clearly taught—viz. that the Lord both corrects, or rather destroys, our depraved will, and also substitutes a good will from himself. In as much as it is prevented by grace, I have no objection to your calling it a handmaid; but in as much as when formed again, it is the work of the Lord, it is erroneous to say, that it accompanies preventing grace as a voluntary attendant. Therefore, Chrysostom is inaccurate in saying, that grace cannot do any thing without will, nor will any thing without grace (Serm. de Invent. Sanct. Crucis); as if grace did not, in terms of the passage lately quoted from Paul, produce the very will itself. The intention of Augustine, in calling the human will the handmaid of grace, was not to assign it a kind of second place to grace in the performance of good works. His object merely was to refute the pestilential dogma of Pelagius, who made human merit the first cause of salvation. As was sufficient for his purpose at the time, he contends that grace is prior to all merit, while, in the meantime, he says nothing of the other question as to the perpetual effect of grace, which, however, he handles admirably in other places. For in saying, as he often does, that the Lord prevents the unwilling in order to make him willing, and follows after the willing that he may not will in vain,

he makes Him the sole author of good works. Indeed, his sentiments on this subject are too clear to need any lengthened illustration. "Men," says he, "labour to find in our will something that is our own, and not God's; how they can find it, I wot not" (August. de Remiss. Peccat., lib. 2 c. 18). In his First Book against Pelagius and Celestius, expounding the saying of Christ, "Every man therefore that has heard, and has learned of the Father, cometh unto me" (John 6:45), he says, "The will is aided not only so as to know what is to be done, but also to do what it knows." And thus, when God teaches not by the letter of the Law, but by the grace of the Spirit, he so teaches, that every one who has learned, not only knowing, sees, but also willing, desires, and acting, performs.

8. Since we are now occupied with the chief point on which the controversy turns, let us give the reader the sum of the matter in a few, and those most unambiguous, passages of Scripture; thereafter, lest any one should charge us with distorting Scripture, let us show that the truth, which we maintain to be derived from Scripture, is not unsupported by the testimony of this holy man (I mean Augustine). I deem it unnecessary to bring forward every separate passage of Scripture in confirmation of my doctrine. A selection of the most choice passages will pave the way for the understanding of all those which lie scattered up and down in the sacred volume. On the other hand, I thought it not out of place to show my accordance with a man whose authority is justly of so much weight in the Christian world. It is certainly easy to prove that the commencement of good is only with God, and that none but the elect have a will inclined to good. But the cause of election must be sought out of man; and hence it follows that a right will is derived not from man himself, but from the same good pleasure by which we were chosen before the creation of the world. Another argument much akin to this may be added. The beginning of right will and action being of faith, we must see whence faith itself is. But since Scripture proclaims throughout that it is the free gift of God, it follows, that when men, who are with their whole soul naturally prone to evil, begin to have a good will, it is owing to mere grace. Therefore, when the Lord, in the conversion of his people, sets down these two things as requisite to be done—viz. to take away the heart of stone, and give a heart of flesh, he openly declares, that, in order to our conversion to righteousness, what is ours must be taken away, and that what is substituted in its place is of himself. Nor does he declare this in one passage only. For he says in Jeremiah "I will give them one heart, and one way, that they may fear me for ever;" and a little after he says, "I will put my fear in their hearts, that they shall not depart from me" (Jer. 32:39, 40). Again, in Ezekiel, "I will give them one heart, and I will put a new spirit within you; and I will take the stony heart out of their flesh, and will give them an heart of flesh" (Ezek. 11:19). He could not more clearly claim to himself, and deny to us, everything good and right in our will, than by declaring, that in our conversion there is the creation of a new spirit and a new heart. It always follows, both that nothing good can proceed from our will until it be formed again, and that after it is formed again in so far as it is good, it is of God, and not of us.

9. With this view, likewise the prayers of the saints correspond. Thus Solomon prays that the Lord may "incline our hearts unto him, to walk in his ways, and keep his commandments" (1 Kings 8:58); intimating that our heart is perverse, and naturally indulges in rebellion against the Divine law, until it be turned. Again, it is said in the Psalms, "Incline my heart unto thy testimonies" (Ps. 119:36). For we should always note the antithesis between the rebellious movement of the heart, and the correction by which it is subdued to obedience. David feeling for the time that he was deprived of directing grace, prays, "Create in me a clean heart, O God; and renew a right spirit within me" (Ps. 51:10). Is not this an acknowledgment that all the parts of the heart are full of impurity, and that the soul has received a twist, which has turned it from straight to crooked? And then, in describing the cleansing, which he earnestly demands as a thing to be created by God, does he not ascribe the work entirely to Him? If it is objected, that the prayer itself is a symptom of a pious and holy affection, it is easy to reply, that although David had already in some measure repented, he was here contrasting the sad fall which he had experienced with his former state. Therefore, speaking in the person of a man alienated from God, he properly prays for the blessings which God bestows upon his elect in regeneration. Accordingly, like one dead, he desires to be created anew, so as to become, instead of a slave of Satan, an instrument of the Holy Spirit. Strange and monstrous are the longings of our pride. There is nothing which the Lord enjoins more strictly than the religious observance of his Sabbath, in other words resting from our works; but in nothing do we show greater reluctance than to renounce our own works, and give due place to the works of God. Did not arrogance stand in the way, we could not overlook the clear testimony which Christ has borne to the efficacy of his grace. "I," said he,

"am the true vine, and my Father is the husband man." "As the branch cannot bear fruit of itself, except it abide in the vine; no more can ye, except ye abide in me" (John 15:1, 4). If we can no more bear fruit of ourselves than a vine can bud when rooted up and deprived of moisture, there is no longer any room to ask what the aptitude of our nature is for good. There is no ambiguity in the conclusion, "For without me ye can do nothing." He says not that we are too weak to suffice for ourselves; but, by reducing us to nothing, he excludes the idea of our possessing any, even the least ability. If, when engrafted into Christ, we bear fruit like the vine, which draws its vegetative power from the moisture of the ground, and the dew of heaven, and the fostering warmth of the sun, I see nothing in a good work, which we can call our own, without trenching upon what is due to God. It is vain to have recourse to the frivolous cavil, that the sap and the power of producing are already contained in the vine, and that, therefore, instead of deriving everything from the earth or the original root, it contributes something of its own. Our Saviour's words simply mean, that when separated from him, we are nothing but dry, useless wood, because, when so separated, we have no power to do good, as he elsewhere says, "Every plant which my heavenly Father has not planted, shall be rooted up" (Mt. 15:13). Accordingly, in the passage already quoted from the Apostle Paul, he attributes the whole operation to God, "It is God which worketh in you both to will and to do of his good pleasure" (Phil. 2:13). The first part of a good work is the will, the second is vigorous effort in the doing of it. God is the author of both. It is, therefore, robbery from God to arrogate anything to ourselves, either in the will or the act. Were it said that God gives assistance to a weak will, something might be left us; but when it is said that he makes the will, every thing good in it is placed without us. Moreover, since even a good will is still weighed down by the burden of the flesh, and prevented from rising, it is added, that, to meet the difficulties of the contest, God supplies the persevering effort until the effect is obtained. Indeed, the Apostle could not otherwise have said, as he elsewhere does, that "it is the same God which worketh all in all" (1 Cor. 12:6); words comprehending, as we have already observed (sec. 6), the whole course of the spiritual life. For which reason, David, after praying, "Teach me thy way, O Lord, I will walk in thy truths" adds, "unite my heart to fear thy name" (Ps. 86:11); by these words intimating, that even those who are well-affected are liable to so many distractions that they easily become vain, and fall away, if not strengthened to persevere. And hence, in another passage, after praying, "Order my steps in thy word," he requests that strength also may be given him to carry on the war, "Let not any iniquity have dominion over me" (Ps. 119:133). In this way, the Lord both begins and perfects the good work in us, so that it is due to Him, first, that the will conceives a love of rectitude, is inclined to desire, is moved and stimulated to pursue it; secondly, that this choice, desire, and endeavour fail not, but are carried forward to effect; and, lastly, that we go on without interruption, and persevere even to the end.

10. This movement of the will is not of that description which was for many ages taught and believed—viz. a movement which thereafter leaves us the choice to obey or resist it, but one which affects us efficaciously. We must, therefore, repudiate the oft-repeated sentiment of Chrysostom, "Whom he draws, he draws willingly;" insinuating that the Lord only stretches out his hand, and waits to see whether we will be pleased to take his aid. We grant that, as man was originally constituted, he could incline to either side, but since he has taught us by his example how miserable a thing free will is if God works not in us to will and to do, of what use to us were grace imparted in such scanty measure? Nay, by our own ingratitude, we obscure and impair divine grace. The Apostle's doctrine is not, that the grace of a good will is offered to us if we will accept of it, but that God himself is pleased so to work in us as to guide, turn, and govern our heart by his Spirit, and reign in it as his own possession. Ezekiel promises that a new spirit will be given to the elect, not merely that they may be able to walk in his precepts, but that they may really walk in them (Ezek. 11:19; 36:27). And the only meaning which can be given to our Saviour's words, "Every man, therefore, that has heard and learned of the Father, cometh unto me" (John 6:45), is, that the grace of God is effectual in itself. This Augustine maintains in his book De Prædestinatione Sancta. This grace is not bestowed on all promiscuously, according to the common brocard (of Occam, if I mistake not), that it is not denied to any one who does what in him lies. Men are indeed to be taught that the favour of God is offered, without exception, to all who ask it; but since those only begin to ask whom heaven by grace inspires, even this minute portion of praise must not be withheld from him. It is the privilege of the elect to be regenerated by the Spirit of God, and then placed under his guidance and government. Wherefore Augustine justly derides some who arrogate to themselves a certain power of willing, as well as censures others who

imagine that that which is a special evidence of gratuitous election is given to all (August. de Verbis Apost. Serm. 21). He says, "Nature is common to all, but not grace;" and he calls it a showy acuteness "which shines by mere vanity, when that which God bestows, on whom he will is attributed generally to all." Elsewhere he says, "How came you? By believing. Fear, lest by arrogating to yourself the merit of finding the right way, you perish from the right way. I came, you say, by free choice, came by my own will. Why do you boast? Would you know that even this was given you? Hear Christ exclaiming, 'No man comets unto me, except the Father which has sent me draw him.'" And from the words of John (6:44), he infers it to be an incontrovertible fact, that the hearts of believers are so effectually governed from above, that they follow with undeviating affection. "Whosoever is born of God does not commit sin; for his seed remaineth in him" (I John 3:9). That intermediate movement which the sophists imagine, a movement which every one is free to obey or to reject, is obviously excluded by the doctrine of effectual perseverance.

11. As to perseverance, it would undoubtedly have been regarded as the gratuitous gift of God, had not the very pernicious error prevailed, that it is bestowed in proportion to human merit, according to the reception which each individual gives to the first grace. This having given rise to the idea that it was entirely in our own power to receive or reject the offered grace of God, that idea is no sooner exploded than the error founded on it must fall. The error, indeed, is twofold. For, besides teaching that our gratitude for the first grace and our legitimate use of it is rewarded by subsequent supplies of grace, its abettors add that, after this, grace does not operate alone, but only co-operates with ourselves. As to the former, we must hold that the Lord, while he daily enriches his servants, and loads them with new gifts of his grace, because he approves of and takes pleasure in the work which he has begun, finds that in them which he may follow up with larger measures of grace. To this effect are the sentences, "To him that has shall be given." "Well done, good and faithful servant: thou hast been faithful over a few things, I will make thee ruler over many things" (Mt. 25:21, 23, 29; Luke 19:17, 26). But here two precautions are necessary. It must not be said that the legitimate use of the first grace is rewarded by subsequent measures of grace, as if man rendered the grace of God effectual by his own industry, nor must it be thought that there is any such remuneration as to make it cease to be the gratuitous grace of God. I admit, then, that believers may expect as a blessing from God, that the better the use they make of previous, the larger the supplies they will receive of future grace; but I say that even this use is of the Lord, and that this remuneration is bestowed freely of mere good will. The trite distinction of operating and co-operating grace is employed no less sinistrously than unhappily. Augustine, indeed, used it, but softened it by a suitable definition—viz. that God, by co-operating, perfects what he begins by operating,—that both graces are the same, but obtain different names from the different manner in which they produce their effects. Whence it follows, that he does not make an apportionment between God and man, as if a proper movement on the part of each produced a mutual concurrence. All he does is to mark a multiplication of grace. To this effect, accordingly, he elsewhere says, that in man good will precedes many gifts from God; but among these gifts is this good will itself. (*August. Enchiridion ad Laurent.* cap. 32). Whence it follows, that nothing is left for the will to arrogate as its own. This Paul has expressly stated. For, after saying, "It is God which worketh in you both to will and to do," he immediately adds, "of his good pleasure" (Phil. 2:13); indicating by this expression, that the blessing is gratuitous. As to the common saying, that after we have given admission to the first grace, our efforts co-operate with subsequent grace, this is my answer:—If it is meant that after we are once subdued by the power of the Lord to the obedience of righteousness, we proceed voluntarily, and are inclined to follow the movement of grace, I have nothing to object. For it is most certain, that where the grace of God reigns, there is also this readiness to obey. And whence this readiness, but just that the Spirit of God being everywhere consistent with himself, after first begetting a principle of obedience, cherishes and strengthens it for perseverance? If, again, it is meant that man is able of himself to be a fellow-labourer with the grace of God, I hold it to be a most pestilential delusion.

12. In support of this view, some make an ignorant and false application of the Apostle's words: "I laboured more abundantly than they all: yet not I, but the grace of God which was with me" (1 Cor. 15:10). The meaning they give them is, that as Paul might have seemed to speak somewhat presumptuously in preferring himself to all the other apostles, he corrects the expression so far by referring the praise to the grace of God, but he, at the same time, calls himself a co-operator with grace. It is strange that this should have proved a stumbling-block to so many writers, otherwise respectable. The Apostle says not that the grace of God laboured with him so as

to make him a co-partner in the labour. He rather transfers the whole merit of the labour to grace alone, by thus modifying his first expression, "It was not I," says he, "that laboured, but the grace of God that was present with me." Those who have adopted the erroneous interpretation have been misled by an ambiguity in the expression, or rather by a preposterous translation, in which the force of the Greek article is overlooked. For to take the words literally, the Apostle does not say that grace was a fellow-worker with him, but that the grace which was with him was sole worker. And this is taught not obscurely, though briefly, by Augustine when he says, "Good will in man precedes many gifts from God, but not all gifts, seeing that the will which precedes is itself among the number." He adds the reason, "for it is written, 'the God of my mercy shall prevent me,' (Ps. 59:10), and 'Surely goodness and mercy shall follow me,' (Ps. 23:6); it prevents him that is unwilling, and makes him willing; it follows him that is willing, that he may not will in vain." To this Bernard assents, introducing the Church as praying thus, "Draw me, who am in some measure unwilling, and make me willing; draw me, who am sluggishly lagging, and make me run" (Serm. 2 in Cantic).

13. Let us now hear Augustine in his own words, lest the Pelagians of our age, I mean the sophists of the Sorbonne, charge us after their wont with being opposed to all antiquity. In this indeed they imitate their father Pelagius, by whom of old a similar charge was brought against Augustine. In the second chapter of his Treatise De Correptione et Gratis, addressed to Valentinus, Augustine explains at length what I will state briefly, but in his own words, that to Adam was given the grace of persevering in goodness if he had the will; to us it is given to will, and by will overcome concupiscence: that Adam, therefore, had the power if he had the will, but did not will to have the power, whereas to us is given both the will and the power; that the original freedom of man was to be able not to sin, but that we have a much greater freedom—viz. not to be able to sin. And lest it should be supposed, as Lombard erroneously does (lib. 2 Dist. 25), that he is speaking of the perfection of the future state, he shortly after removes all doubt when he says, "For so much is the will of the saints inflamed by the Holy Spirit, that they are able, because they are willing; and willing, because God worketh in them so to will." For if, in such weakness (in which, however, to suppress pride, "strength" must be made "perfect,") their own will is left to them, in such sense that, by the help of God, they are able, if they will, while at the same time God does not work in them so as to make them will; among so many temptations and infirmities the will itself would give way, and, consequently, they would not be able to persevere. Therefore, to meet the infirmity of the human will, and prevent it from failing, how weak soever it might be, divine grace was made to act on it inseparably and uninterruptedly. Augustine (ibid. cap. 14). next entering fully into the question, how our hearts follow the movement when God affects them, necessarily says, indeed, that the Lord draws men by their own wills; wills, however, which he himself has produced. We have now an attestation by Augustine to the truth which we are specially desirous to maintain—viz. that the grace offered by the Lord is not merely one which every individual has full liberty of choosing to receive or reject, but a grace which produces in the heart both choice and will: so that all the good works which follow after are its fruit and effect; the only will which yields obedience being the will which grace itself has made. In another place, Augustine uses these words, "Every good work in us is performed only by grace" (August. Ep. 105).

14. In saying elsewhere that the will is not taken away by grace, but out of bad is changed into good, and after it is good is assisted,—he only means, that man is not drawn as if by an extraneous impulse without the movement of the heart, but is inwardly affected so as to obey from the heart. Declaring that grace is given specially and gratuitously to the elect, he writes in this way to Boniface: "We know that Divine grace is not given to all men, and that to those to whom it is given, it is not given either according to the merit of works, or according to the merit of the will, but by free grace: in regard to those to whom it is not given, we know that the not giving of it is a just judgment from God" (August. ad Bonifac. Ep. 106). In the same epistle, he argues strongly against the opinion of those who hold that subsequent grace is given to human merit as a reward for not rejecting the first grace. For he presses Pelagius to confess that gratuitous grace is necessary to us for every action, and that merely from the fact of its being truly grace, it cannot be the recompense of works. But the matter cannot be more briefly summed up than in the eighth chapter of his Treatise De Correptione et Gratia, where he shows, *First*, that human will does not by liberty obtain grace, but by grace obtains liberty. *Secondly*, that by means of the same grace, the heart being impressed with a feeling of delight, is trained to persevere, and strengthened with invincible fortitude. *Thirdly*, that while grace governs the will, it never falls; but when grace abandons it, it falls forthwith. *Fourthly*, that by the

free mercy of God, the will is turned to good, and when turned, perseveres. *Fifthly*, that the direction of the will to good, and its constancy after being so directed, depend entirely on the will of God, and not on any human merit. Thus the will (free will, if you choose to call it so), which is left to man, is, as he in another place (Ep. 46) describes it, a will which can neither be turned to God, nor continue in God, unless by grace; a will which, whatever its ability may be, derives all that ability from grace.

CHAPTER 4

HOW GOD WORKS IN THE HEARTS OF MEN.

The leading points discussed in this chapter are, I. Whether in bad actions anything is to be attributed to God; if anything, how much. Also, what is to be attributed to the devil and to man, sec. 1–5. II. In indifferent matters, how much is to be attributed to God, and how much is left to man, sec. 6. III. Two objections refuted, sec. 7, 8.

Sections:

1. Connection of this chapter with the preceding. Augustine's similitude of a good and bad rider. Question answered in respect to the devil.

2. Question answered in respect to God and man. Example from the history of Job. The works of God distinguished from the works of Satan and wicked men. 1. By the design or end of acting. How Satan acts in the reprobate. 2. How God acts in them.

3. Old Objection, that the agency of God in such cases is referable to prescience or permission, not actual operation. Answer, showing that God blinds and hardens the reprobate, and this in two ways; 1. By deserting them; 2. By delivering them over to Satan.

4. Striking passages of Scripture, proving that God acts in both ways, and disposing of the objection with regard to prescience. Confirmation from Augustine.

5. A modification of the former answer, proving that God employs Satan to instigate the reprobate, but, at the same time, is free from all taint.

6. How God works in the hearts of men in indifferent matters. Our will in such matters not so free as to be exempt from the overruling providence of God. This confirmed by various examples.

7. Objection, that these examples do not form the rule. An answer, fortified by the testimony of universal experience, by Scripture, and a passage of Augustine.

8. Some, in arguing against the error of free will, draw an argument from the event. How this is to be understood.

1. That man is so enslaved by the yoke of sin, that he cannot of his own nature aim at good either in wish or actual pursuit, has, I think, been sufficiently proved. Moreover, a distinction has been drawn between compulsion and necessity, making it clear that man, though he sins necessarily, nevertheless sins voluntarily. But since, from his being brought into bondage to the devil, it would seem that he is actuated more by the devil's will than his own, it is necessary, first, to explain what the agency of each is, and then solve the question, Whether in bad actions anything is to be attributed to God, Scripture intimating that there is some way in which he interferes? Augustine (in Psalm 31 and 33) compares the human will to a horse preparing to start, and God and the devil to riders. "If God mounts, he, like a temperate and skilful rider, guides it calmly, urges it when too slow, reins it in when too fast, curbs its forwardness and over-action, checks its bad temper, and keeps it on the proper course; but if the devil has seized the saddle, like an ignorant and rash rider, he hurries it over broken ground, drives it into ditches, dashes it over precipices, spurs it into obstinacy or fury." With this simile, since a better does not occur, we shall for the present be contented. When it is said, then, that the will of the natural man is subject to the power of the devil, and is actuated by him, the meaning is not that the wills while reluctant and resisting, is forced to submit (as masters oblige unwilling slaves to execute their orders), but that, fascinated by the impostures of Satan, it necessarily yields to his guidance, and does him homage. Those whom the Lord favours not with the direction of his Spirit, he, by a righteous judgment, consigns to the agency of Satan. Wherefore, the Apostle says, that "the god of this world has blinded the minds of them which believe not, lest the light of the glorious gospel of Christ, who is the image of God, should shine into them." And, in another passage, he describes the devil as "the spirit that now worketh in the children of disobedience" (Eph. 2:2). The blinding of the wicked, and all the iniquities consequent upon it, are called the works of Satan; works the cause of which is not to be Sought in anything external to the will of man, in which the root of the evil lies, and in which the foundation of Satan's kingdom, in other words, sin, is fixed.

2. The nature of the divine agency in such cases is very different. For the purpose of illustration, let us refer to the calamities brought upon holy Job by the Chaldeans.

They having slain his shepherds, carry off his flocks. The wickedness of their deed is manifest, as is also the hand of Satan, who, as the history informs us, was the instigator of the whole. Job, however, recognises it as the work of God, saying, that what the Chaldeans had plundered, "the Lord" had "taken away." How can we attribute the same work to God, to Satan, and to man, without either excusing Satan by the interference of God, or making God the author of the crime? This is easily done, if we look first to the end, and then to the mode of acting. The Lord designs to exercise the patience of his servant by adversity; Satan's plan is to drive him to despair; while the Chaldeans are bent on making unlawful gain by plunder. Such diversity of purpose makes a wide distinction in the act. In the mode there is not less difference. The Lord permits Satan to afflict his servant; and the Chaldeans, who had been chosen as the ministers to execute the deed, he hands over to the impulses of Satan, who, pricking on the already depraved Chaldeans with his poisoned darts, instigates them to commit the crime. They rush furiously on to the unrighteous deed, and become its guilty perpetrators. Here Satan is properly said to act in the reprobate, over whom he exercises his sway, which is that of wickedness. God also is said to act in his own way; because even Satan when he is the instrument of divine wrath, is completely under the command of God, who turns him as he will in the execution of his just judgments. I say nothing here of the universal agency of God, which, as it sustains all the creatures, also gives them all their power of acting. I am now speaking only of that special agency which is apparent in every act. We thus see that there is no inconsistency in attributing the same act to God, to Satan, and to man, while, from the difference in the end and mode of action, the spotless righteousness of God shines forth at the same time that the iniquity of Satan and of man is manifested in all its deformity.

3. Ancient writers sometimes manifest a superstitious dread of making a simple confession of the truth in this matter, from a fear of furnishing impiety with a handle for speaking irreverently of the works of God. While I embrace such soberness with all my heart, I cannot see the least danger in simply holding what Scripture delivers. when Augustine was not always free from this superstition, as when he says, that blinding and hardening have respect not to the operation of God, but to prescience (Lib. de Predestina. et Gratia). But this subtilty is repudiated by many passages of Scriptures which clearly show that the divine interference amounts to something more than prescience. And Augustine himself, in his book against Julian, contends at length that sins are manifestations not merely of divine permission or patience, but also of divine power, that thus former sins may be punished. In like manner, what is said of permission is too weak to stand. God is very often said to blind and harden the reprobate, to turn their hearts, to incline and impel them, as I have elsewhere fully explained (Book 1 c. 18). The extent of this agency can never be explained by having recourse to prescience or permission. We, therefore, hold that there are two methods in which God may so act. When his light is taken away, nothing remains but blindness and darkness: when his Spirit is taken away, our hearts become hard as stones: when his guidance is withdrawn, we immediately turn from the right path: and hence he is properly said to incline, harden, and blind those whom he deprives of the faculty of seeing, obeying, and rightly executing. The second method, which comes much nearer to the exact meaning of the words, is when executing his judgments by Satan as the minister of his anger, God both directs men's counsels, and excites their wills, and regulates their efforts as he pleases. Thus when Moses relates that Simon, king of the Amorites, did not give the Israelites a passage, because the Lord "had hardened his spirit, and made his heart obstinate," he immediately adds the purpose which God had in view—viz. that he might deliver him into their hand (Deut. 2:30). As God had resolved to destroy him, the hardening of his heart was the divine preparation for his ruin.

4. In accordance with the former methods it seems to be said, "The law shall perish from the priests and counsel from the ancients." "He poureth contempt upon princes, and causeth them to wander in the wilderness, where there is no way." Again "O Lord, why hast thou made us to err from thy ways, and hardened our heart from thy fear?" These passages rather indicate what men become when God deserts them, than what the nature of his agency is when he works in them. But there are other passages which go farther, such as those concerning the hardening of Pharaoh: "I will harden his heart, that he shall not let the people go." The same thing is afterwards repeated in stronger terms. Did he harden his heart by not softening it? This is, indeed, true; but he did something more: he gave it in charge to Satan to confirm him in his obstinacy. Hence he had previously said, "I am sure he will not let you go." The people come out of Egypt, and the inhabitants of a hostile region come forth against them. How were they instigated? Moses certainly declares of Sihon, that it was the Lord who "had hardened his spirit, and made his heart obstinate" (Deut. 2:30). The

Psalmists relating the same history says, "He turned their hearts to hate his people" (Psalm 105:25). You cannot now say that they stumbled merely because they were deprived of divine counsel. For if they are *hardened* and *turned*, they are purposely bent to the very end in view. Moreover, whenever God saw it meet to punish the people for their transgression, in what way did he accomplish his purpose by the reprobate? In such a way as shows that the efficacy of the action was in him, and that they were only ministers. At one time he declares, "that he will lift an ensign to the nations from far, and will hiss unto them from the end of the earth;" at another, that he will take a net to ensnare them; and at another, that he will be like a hammer to strike them. But he specially declared that he was not inactive among theme when he called Sennacherib an axe, which was formed and destined to be wielded by his own hand. Augustine is not far from the mark when he states the matter thus, That men sin, is attributable to themselves: that in sinning they produce this or that result, is owing to the mighty power of God, who divides the darkness as he pleases (August. de Prædest. Sanct).

5. Moreover, that the ministry of Satan is employed to instigate the reprobate, whenever the Lord, in the course of his providence, has any purpose to accomplish in them, will sufficiently appear from a single passage. It is repeatedly said in the First Book of Samuel, that an evil spirit from the Lord came upon Saul, and troubled him (1 Sam. 16:14; 18:10; 19:9). It were impious to apply this to the Holy Spirit. An impure spirit must therefore be called a spirit from the Lord, because completely subservient to his purpose, being more an instrument in acting than a proper agent. We should also add what Paul says, "God shall send them strong delusion, that they should believe a lie: that they all might be damned who believed not the truth" (2 Thess. 2:11, 12). But in the same transaction there is always a wide difference between what the Lord does, and what Satan and the ungodly design to do. The wicked instruments which he has under his hand and can turn as he pleases, he makes subservient to his own justice. They, as they are wicked, give effect to the iniquity conceived in their wicked minds. Every thing necessary to vindicate the majesty of God from calumny, and cut off any subterfuge on the part of the ungodly, has already been expounded in the Chapters on Providence (Book 1 Chapter 16–18). Here I only meant to show, in a few words, how Satan reigns in the reprobate, and how God works in both.

6. In those actions, which in themselves are neither good nor bad, and concern the corporeal rather than the spiritual life, the liberty which man possesses, although we have above touched upon it (*supra*, Chap. 2 sect. 13–17), has not yet been explained. Some have conceded a free choice to man in such actions; more, I suppose, because they were unwilling to debate a matter of no great moment, than because they wished positively to assert what they were prepared to concede. While I admit that those who hold that man has no ability in himself to do righteousness, hold what is most necessary to be known for salvation, I think it ought not to be overlooked that we owe it to the special grace of God, whenever, on the one hand, we choose what is for our advantage, and whenever our will inclines in that direction; and on the other, whenever with heart and soul we shun what would otherwise do us harm. And the interference of Divine Providence goes to the extent not only of making events turn out as was foreseen to be expedient, but of giving the wills of men the same direction. If we look at the administration of human affairs with the eye of sense, we will have no doubt that, so far, they are placed at man's disposal; but if we lend an ear to the many passages of Scripture which proclaim that even in these matters the minds of men are ruled by God, they will compel us to place human choice in subordination to his special influence. Who gave the Israelites such favour in the eyes of the Egyptians, that they lent them all their most valuable commodities? (Exod. 11:3). They never would have been so inclined of their own accord. Their inclinations, therefore, were more overruled by God than regulated by themselves. And surely, had not Jacob been persuaded that God inspires men with divers affections as seemeth to him good, he would not have said of his son Joseph (whom he thought to be some heathen Egyptian), "God Almighty give you mercy before the man" (Gen. 43:14). In like manner, the whole Church confesses that when the Lord was pleased to pity his people, he made them also to be pitied of all them that carried them captives (Ps. 106:46). In like manner, when his anger was kindled against Saul, so that he prepared himself for battle, the cause is stated to have been, that a spirit from God fell upon him (1 Sam. 11:6). who dissuaded Absalom from adopting the counsel of Ahithophel, which was wont to be regarded as an oracle? (2 Sam. 17:14). Who disposed Rehoboam to adopt the counsel of the young men? (1 Kings 12:10). Who caused the approach of the Israelites to strike terror into nations formerly distinguished for valour? Even the harlot Rahab recognised the hand of the Lord. Who, on the other hand, filled the hearts

of the Israelites with fear and dread (Lev. 26:36), but He who threatened in the Law that he would give them a nn "trembling heart"? (Deut. 28:65).

7. It may be objected, that these are special examples which cannot be regarded as a general rule. They are sufficient, at all events, to prove the point for which I contend—viz. that whenever God is pleased to make way for his providence, he even in external matters so turns and bends the wills of men, that whatever the freedom of their choice may be, it is still subject to the disposal of God. That your mind depends more on the agency of God than the freedom of your own choice, daily experience teaches. Your judgment often fails, and in matters of no great difficulty, your courage flags; at other times, in matters of the greatest obscurity, the mode of explicating them at once suggests itself, while in matters of moment and danger, your mind rises superior to every difficulty. In this way, I interpret the words of Solomon, "The hearing ear, and the seeing eye, the Lord hath made even both of them" (Prov. 20:12). For they seem to me to refer not to their creation, but to peculiar grace in the use of them, when he says, "The king's heart is in the hand of the Lord as the rivers of water; he turneth it whithersoever he will" (Prov. 21:1), he comprehends the whole race under one particular class. If any will is free from subjection, it must be that of one possessed of regal power, and in a manner exercising dominion over other wills. But if it is under the hand of God, ours surely cannot be exempt from it. On this subject there is an admirable sentiment of Augustine, "Scripture, if it be carefully examined, will show not only that the good wills of men are made good by God out of evil, and when so made, are directed to good acts, even to eternal life, but those which retain the elements of the world are in the power of God, to turn them whither he pleases, and when he pleases, either to perform acts of kindness, or by a hidden, indeed, but, at the same time, most just judgment to inflict punishment" (August. De Gratia et Lib. Arb. ad Valent. cap. 20).

8. Let the reader here remember, that the power of the human will is not to be estimated by the event, as some unskilful persons are absurdly wont to do. They think it an elegant and ingenious proof of the bondage of the human will, that even the greatest monarchs are sometimes thwarted in their wishes. But the ability of which we speak must be considered as within the man, not measured by outward success. In discussing the subject of free will, the question is not, whether external obstacles will permit a man to execute what he has internally resolved, but whether, in any matter whatever, he has a free power of judging and of willing. If men possess both of these, Attilius Regulus, shut up in a barrel studded with sharp nails, will have a will no less free than Augustus Caesar ruling with imperial sway over a large portion of the globe.

CHAPTER 5

THE ARGUMENTS USUALLY ALLEGED IN SUPPORT OF FREE WILL REFUTED.

Objections reduced to three principal heads:—I. Four absurdities advanced by the opponents of the orthodox doctrine concerning the slavery of the will, stated and refuted, sec. 1–5. II. The passages of Scripture which they pervert in favour of their error, reduced to five heads, and explained, sec. 6–15. III. Five other passages quoted in defence of free will expounded, sec. 16–19.

Sections:

1. Absurd fictions of opponents first refuted, and then certain passages of Scripture explained. Answer by a negative. Confirmation of the answer.

2. Another absurdity of Aristotle and Pelagius. Answer by a distinction. Answer fortified by passages from Augustine, and supported by the authority of an Apostle.

3. Third absurdity borrowed from the words of Chrysostom. Answer by a negative.

4. Fourth absurdity urged of old by the Pelagians. Answer from the works of Augustine. Illustrated by the testimony of our Saviour. Another answer, which explains the use of exhortations.

5. A third answer, which contains a fuller explanation of the second. Objection to the previous answers. Objection refuted. Summary of the previous answers.

6. First class of arguments which the Neo-Pelagians draw from Scripture in defence of free will. 1. The Law demands perfect obedience and therefore God either mocks us, or requires things which are not in our power. Answer by distinguishing precepts into three sorts. The first of these considered in this and the following section.

7. This general argument from the Law of no avail to the patrons of free will. Promises conjoined with precepts, prove that our salvation is to be found in the grace of God. Objection, that the Law was given to the persons living at the time. Answer, confirmed by passages from Augustine.

8. A special consideration of the three classes of precepts of no avail to the defenders of free will. 1. Precepts enjoining us to turn to God. 2. Precepts which simply speak of the observance of the Law. 3. Precepts which enjoin us to persevere in the grace of God.

9. Objection. Answer. Confirmation of the answer from Jeremiah. Another objection refuted.

10. A second class of arguments in defence of free will drawn from the promises of God—viz. that the promises which God makes to those who seek him are vain if it is not in our power to do, or not do, the thing required. Answer, which explains the use of promises, and removes the supposed inconsistency.

11. Third class of arguments drawn from the divine upbraidings,—that it is in vain to upbraid us for evils which it is not in our power to avoid. Answer. Sinners are condemned by their own consciences, and, therefore, the divine upbraidings are just. Moreover, there is a twofold use in these upbraidings. Various passages of Scripture explained by means of the foregoing answers.

12. Objection founded on the words of Moses. Refutation by the words of an Apostle. Confirmation by argument.

13. Fourth class of arguments by the defenders of free will. God waits to see whether or not sinners will repent; therefore they can repent. Answer by a dilemma. Passage in Hosea explained.

14. Fifth class of arguments in defence of free will. God and bad works described as our own, and therefore we are capable of both. Answer by an exposition, which shows that this argument is unavailing. Objection drawn from analogy. Answer. The nature and mode of divine agency in the elect.

15. Conclusion of the answer to the last class of arguments.

16. Third and last division of the chapter discussing certain passages of Scripture. 1. A passage from Genesis. Its true meaning explained.

17. 2. Passage from the Epistle to the Romans. Explanation. Refutation of an objection. Another refutation. A third refutation from Augustine. 3. A passage from First Corinthians. Answer to it.

18. 4. A passage from Ecclesiastes. Explanation. Another explanation.

19. 5. A passage from Luke. Explanation. Allegorical arguments weak. Another explanation. A third explanation. A fourth from Augustine. Conclusion and summary of the whole discussion concerning free will.

1. Enough would seem to have been said on the subject of man's will, were there not some who endeavour to urge him to his ruin by a false opinion of liberty, and at the same time, in order to support their own opinion, assail ours. First, they gather together some absurd inferences, by which they endeavour to bring odium upon our doctrine, as if it were abhorrent to common sense, and then they oppose it with certain passages of Scripture (*infra*, sec. 6). Both devices we shall dispose of in their order. If sin, say they, is necessary, it ceases to be sin; if it is voluntary, it may be avoided. Such, too, were the weapons with which Pelagius assailed Augustine. But we are unwilling to crush them by the weight of his name, until we have satisfactorily disposed of the objections themselves. I deny, therefore, that sin ought to be the less imputed because it is necessary; and, on the other hand, I deny the inference, that sin may be avoided because it is voluntary. If any one will dispute with God, and endeavour to evade his judgment, by pretending that he could not have done otherwise, the answer already given is sufficient, that it is owing not to creation, but the corruption of nature, that man has become the slave of sin, and can will nothing but evil. For whence that impotence of which the wicked so readily avail themselves as an excuse, but just because Adam voluntarily subjected himself to the tyranny of the devil? Hence the corruption by which we are held bound as with chains, originated in the first man's revolt from his Maker. If all men are justly held guilty of this revolt, let them not think themselves excused by a necessity in which they see the clearest cause of their condemnation. But this I have fully explained above; and in the case of the devil himself, have given an example of one who sins not less voluntarily that he sins necessarily. I have also shown, in the case of the elect angels, that though their will cannot decline from good, it does not therefore cease to be will. This Bernard shrewdly explains when he says (Serm. 81, in Cantica), that we are the more miserable in this, that the necessity is voluntary; and yet this necessity so binds us who are subject to it, that we are the slaves of sin, as we have already observed. The second step in the reasoning is vicious, because it leaps from *voluntary* to *free*; whereas we have proved above, that a thing may be done voluntarily, though not subject to free choice.

2. They add, that unless virtue and vice proceed from free choice, it is absurd either to punish man or reward him. Although this argument is taken from Aristotle, I admit that it is also used by Chrysostom and Jerome. Jerome, however, does not disguise that it was familiar to the Pelagians. He even quotes their words, "If grace

acts in us, grace, and not we who do the work, will be crowned" (*Hieron. in Ep. ad Ctesiphont. et Dialog. 1*) With regard to punishment, I answer, that it is properly inflicted on those by whom the guilt is contracted. What matters it whether you sin with a free or an enslaved judgment, so long as you sin voluntarily, especially when man is proved to be a sinner because he is under the bondage of sin? In regard to the rewards of righteousness, is there any great absurdity in acknowledging that they depend on the kindness of God rather than our own merits? How often do we meet in Augustine with this expression,—"God crowns not our merits but his own gifts; and the name of reward is given not to what is due to our merits, but to the recompense of grace previously bestowed?" Some seem to think there is acuteness in the remark, that there is no place at all for the mind, if good works do not spring from free will as their proper source; but in thinking this so very unreasonable they are widely mistaken. Augustine does not hesitate uniformly to describe as necessary the very thing which they count it impious to acknowledge. Thus he asks, "What is human merit? He who came to bestow not due recompense but free grace, though himself free from sin, and the giver of freedom, found all men sinners" (*Augustin. in Psal. 31*). Again, "If you are to receive your due, you must be punished. What then is done? God has not rendered you due punishment, but bestows upon you unmerited grace. If you wish to be an alien from grace, boast your merits" (*in Psal. 70*). Again, "You are nothing in yourself, sin is yours, merit God's. Punishment is your due; and when the reward shall come, God shall crown his own gifts, not your merits" (*Ep. 52*). To the same effect he elsewhere says (*De Verb. Apostol. Serm. 15*), that grace is not of merit, but merit of grace. And shortly after he concludes, that God by his gifts anticipates all our merit, that he may thereby manifest his own merit, and give what is absolutely free, because he sees nothing in us that can be a ground of salvation. But why extend the list of quotations, when similar sentiments are ever and anon recurring in his works? The abettors of this error would see a still better refutation of it, if they would attend to the source from which the apostle derives the glory of the saints,—"Moreover, whom he did predestinate, them he also called; and whom he called, them he also justified; and whom he justified, them he also glorified" (Rom. 8:30). On what ground, then, the apostle being judge (2 Tim. 4:8), are believers crowned? Because by the mercy of God, not their own exertions, they are predestinated, called, and justified. Away, then, with the vain fear, that unless free will stand, there will no longer be any merit! It is most foolish to take alarm, and recoil from that which Scripture inculcates. "If thou didst receive it, why dost thou glory as if thou hadst not received it?" (1 Cor. 4:7). You see how every thing is denied to free will, for the very purpose of leaving no room for merit. And yet, as the beneficence and liberality of God are manifold and inexhaustible, the grace which he bestows upon us, inasmuch as he makes it our own, he recompenses as if the virtuous acts were our own.

3. But it is added, in terms which seem to be borrowed from Chrysostom (*Homil. 22, in Genes.*), that if our will possesses not the power of choosing good or evil, all who are partakers of the same nature must be alike good or alike bad. A sentiment akin to this occurs in the work De Vocatione Gentium (lib. 4 c. 4), usually attributed to Ambrose, in which it is argued, that no one would ever decline from faith, did not the grace of God leave us in a mutable state. It is strange that such men should have so blundered. How did it fail to occur to Chrysostom, that it is divine election which distinguishes among men? We have not the least hesitation to admit what Paul strenuously maintains, that all, without exception, are depraved and given over to wickedness; but at the same time we add, that through the mercy of God all do not continue in wickedness. Therefore, while we all labour naturally under the same disease, those only recover health to whom the Lord is pleased to put forth his healing hand. The others whom, in just judgment, he passes over, pine and rot away till they are consumed. And this is the only reason why some persevere to the end, and others, after beginning their course, fall away. Perseverance is the gift of God, which he does not lavish promiscuously on all, but imparts to whom he pleases. If it is asked how the difference arises—why some steadily persevere, and others prove deficient in steadfastness, we can give no other reason than that the Lord, by his mighty power, strengthens and sustains the former, so that they perish not, while he does not furnish the same assistance to the latter, but leaves them to be monuments of instability.

4. Still it is insisted, that exhortations are vain, warnings superfluous, and rebukes absurd, if the sinner possesses not the power to obey. When similar objections were urged against Augustine, he was obliged to write his book, De Correptione et Gratia, where he has fully disposed of them. The substance of his answer to his opponents is this: "O, man! learn from the precept what you ought to do; learn from correction, that it is your own fault you have not the power; and learn in prayer,

whence it is that you may receive the power." Very similar is the argument of his book, De Spiritu et Litera, in which he shows that God does not measure the precepts of his law by human strength, but, after ordering what is right, freely bestows on his elect the power of fulfilling it. The subject, indeed, does not require a long discussion. For we are not singular in our doctrine, but have Christ and all his apostles with us. Let our opponents, then, consider how they are to come off victorious in a contest which they wage with such antagonists. Christ declares, "without me ye can do nothing" (John 15:5). Does he the less censure and chastise those who, without him, did wickedly? Does he the less exhort every man to be intent on good works? How severely does Paul inveigh against the Corinthians for want of charity (1 Cor. 3:3); and yet at the same time, he prays that charity may be given them by the Lord. In the Epistle to the Romans, he declares that "it is not of him that willeth, nor of him that runneth, but of God that showeth mercy" (Rom. 9:16). Still he ceases not to warn, exhort, and rebuke them. Why then do they not expostulate with God for making sport with men, by demanding of them things which he alone can give, and chastising them for faults committed through want of his grace? Why do they not admonish Paul to spare those who have it not in their power to will or to run, unless the mercy of God, which has forsaken them, precede? As if the doctrine were not founded on the strongest reason—reason which no serious inquirer can fail to perceive. The extent to which doctrine, and exhortation, and rebuke, are in themselves able to change the mind, is indicated by Paul when he says, "Neither is he that planteth any thing, neither he that watereth; but God that giveth the increase" (1 Cor 3:7) in like manner, we see that Moses delivers the precepts of the Law under a heavy sanction, and that the prophets strongly urge and threaten transgressors though they at the same time confess, that men are wise only when an understanding heart is given them; that it is the proper work of God to circumcise the heart, and to change it from stone into flesh; to write his law on their inward parts; in short, to renew souls so as to give efficacy to doctrine.

5. What purpose, then, is served by exhortations? It is this: As the wicked, with obstinate heart, despise them, they will be a testimony against them when they stand at the judgment-seat of God; nay, they even now strike and lash their consciences. For, however they may petulantly deride, they cannot disapprove them. But what, you will ask, can a miserable mortal do, when softness of heart, which is necessary to obedience, is denied him? I ask, in reply, Why have recourse to evasion, since hardness of heart cannot be imputed to any but the sinner himself? The ungodly, though they would gladly evade the divine admonitions, are forced, whether they will or not, to feel their power. But their chief use is to be seen in the case of believers, in whom the Lord, while he always acts by his Spirit, also omits not the instrumentality of his word, but employs it, and not without effect. Let this, then, be a standing truth, that the whole strength of the godly consists in the grace of God, according to the words of the prophet, "I will give them one heart, and I will put a new spirit within you; and I will take the stony heart out of their flesh, and will give them an heart of flesh, that they may walk in my statutes" (Ezek. 11:19, 20). But it will be asked, why are they now admonished of their duty, and not rather left to the guidance of the Spirit? Why are they urged with exhortations when they cannot hasten any faster than the Spirit impels them? and why are they chastised, if at any time they go astray, seeing that this is caused by the necessary infirmity of the flesh? "O, man! who art thou that replies against God?" If, in order to prepare us for the grace which enables us to obey exhortation, God sees meet to employ exhortation, what is there in such an arrangement for you to carp and scoff at? Had exhortations and reprimands no other profit with the godly than to convince them of sin, they could not be deemed altogether useless. Now, when, by the Spirit of God acting within, they have the effect of inflaming their desire of good, of arousing them from lethargy, of destroying the pleasure and honeyed sweetness of sin, making it hateful and loathsome, who will presume to cavil at them as superfluous?

Should any one wish a clearer reply, let him take the following:—God works in his elect in two ways: inwardly, by his Spirit; outwardly, by his Word. By his Spirit illuminating their minds, and training their hearts to the practice of righteousness, he makes them new creatures, while, by his Word, he stimulates them to long and seek for this renovation. In both, he exerts the might of his hand in proportion to the measure in which he dispenses them. The Word, when addressed to the reprobate, though not effectual for their amendment, has another use. It urges their consciences now, and will render them more inexcusable on the day of judgment. Thus, our Saviour, while declaring that none can come to him but those whom the Father draws, and that the elect come after they have heard and learned of the Father (John 6:44, 45), does not lay aside the office of teacher, but carefully invites those who must be taught inwardly by the Spirit before they can make any profit. The reprobate, again, are admonished by Paul, that the doctrine is not in vain; because, while it is in them a savour of death unto death, it is still a sweet savour unto God (2 Cor. 2:16).

6. The enemies of this doctrine are at great pains in collecting passages of Scripture, as if, unable to accomplish any thing by their weight, they were to overwhelm us by their number. But as in battle, when it is come to close quarters, an unwarlike multitude, how great soever the pomp and show they make, give way after a few blows, and take to flight, so we shall have little difficulty here in disposing of our opponents and their host. All the passages which they pervert in opposing us are very similar in their import; and hence, when they are arranged under their proper heads, one answer will suffice for several; it is not necessary to give a separate consideration to each. Precepts seem to be regarded as their stronghold. These they think so accommodated to our abilities, as to make it follow as a matter of course, that whatever they enjoin we are able to perform. Accordingly, they run over all the precepts, and by them fix the measure of our power. For, say they, when God enjoins meekness, submission, love, chastity, piety, and holiness, and when he forbids anger, pride, theft, uncleanness, idolatry, and the like, he either mocks us, or only requires things which are in our power.

All the precepts which they thus heap together may be divided into three classes. Some enjoin a first conversion unto God, others speak simply of the observance of the law, and others inculcate perseverance in the grace which has been received. We shall first treat of precepts in general, and then proceed to consider each separate class. That the abilities of man are equal to the precepts of the divine law, has long been a common idea, and has some show of plausibility. It is founded, however, on the grossest ignorance of the law. Those who deem it a kind of sacrilege to say, that the observance of the law is impossible, insist, as their strongest argument, that, if it is so, the Law has been given in vain (*infra*, Chap. 7 sec. 5). For they speak just as if Paul had never said anything about the Law. But what, pray, is meant by saying, that the Law "was added because of transgressions;" "by the law is the knowledge of sin;" "I had not known sin but by the law;" "the law entered that the offence might abound?" (Gal. 3:19; Rom. 3:20; 7:7; 5:20). Is it meant that the Law was to be limited to our strength, lest it should be given in vain? Is it not rather meant that it was placed far above us, in order to convince us of our utter feebleness? Paul indeed declares, that charity is the end and fulfilling of the Law (1 Tim. 1:5). But when he prays that the minds of the Thessalonians may be filled with it, he clearly enough acknowledges that the Law sounds in our ears without profit, if God do not implant it thoroughly in our hearts (1 Thess. 3:12).

7. I admit, indeed, that if the Scripture taught nothing else on the subject than that the Law is a rule of life by which we ought to regulate our pursuits, I should at once assent to their opinion; but since it carefully and clearly explains that the use of the Law is manifold, the proper course is to learn from that explanation what the power of the Law is in man. In regard to the present question, while it explains what our duty is it teaches that the power of obeying it is derived from the goodness of God, and it accordingly urges us to pray that this power may be given us. If there were merely a command and no promise, it would be necessary to try whether our strength were sufficient to fulfil the command; but since promises are annexed, which proclaim not only that aid, but that our whole power is derived from divine grace, they at the same time abundantly testify that we are not only unequal to the observance of the Law, but mere fools in regard to it. Therefore, let us hear no more of a proportion between our ability and the divine precepts, as if the Lord had accommodated the standard of justice which he was to give in the Law to our feeble capacities. We should rather gather from the promises how ill provided we are, having in everything so much need of grace. But say they, Who will believe that the Lord designed his Law for blocks and stones? There is no wish to make any one believe this. The ungodly are neither blocks nor stones, when, taught by the Law that their lusts are offensive to God, they are proved guilty by their own confession; nor are the godly blocks or stones, when admonished of their powerlessness, they take refuge in grace. To this effect are the pithy sayings of Augustine, "God orders what we cannot do, that we may know what we ought to ask of him. There is a great utility in precepts, if all that is given to free will is to do greater honour to divine grace. Faith acquires what the Law requires; nay, the Law requires, in order that faith may acquire what is thus required; nay, more, God demands of us faith itself, and finds not what he thus demands, until by giving he makes it possible to find it." Again, he says, "Let God give what he orders, and order what he wills."

8. This will be more clearly seen by again attending to the three classes of precepts to which we above referred. Both in the Law and in the Prophets, God repeatedly calls upon us to turn to him. But, on the other hand, a

prophet exclaims, "Turn thou me, and I shall be turned; for thou art the Lord my God. Surely after that I was turned, I repented." He orders us to circumcise the foreskins of our hearts; but Moses declares, that that circumcision is made by his own hand. In many passages he demands a new heart, but in others he declares that he gives it. As Augustine says, "What God promises, we ourselves do not through choice or nature, but he himself does by grace." The same observation is made, when, in enumerating the rules of Tichonius, he states the third in effect to be—that we distinguish carefully between the Law and the promises, or between the commands and grace (Augustin. de Doctrine Christiana, lib. 3). Let them now go and gather from precepts what man's power of obedience is, when they would destroy the divine grace by which the precepts themselves are accomplished. The precepts of the second class are simply those which enjoin us to worship God, to obey and adhere to his will, to do his pleasure, and follow his teaching. But innumerable passages testify that every degree of purity, piety, holiness, and justices which we possess, is his gift. Of the third class of precepts is the exhortation of Paul and Barnabas to the proselytes, as recorded by Luke; they "persuaded them to continue in the grace of God" (Acts 13:43). But the source from which this power of continuance must be sought is elsewhere explained by Paul, when he says, "Finally, my brethren, be strong in the Lord" (Eph. 6:10). In another passage he says, "Grieve not the Holy Spirit of God, whereby ye are sealed unto the day of redemption" (Eph. 4:30). But as the thing here enjoined could not be performed by man, he prays in behalf of the Thessalonians, that God would count them "worthy of this calling, and fulfil all the good pleasure of his goodness, and the work of faith with power" (2 Thess. 1:11). In the same way, in the Second Epistle to the Corinthians, when treating of alms, he repeatedly commends their good and pious inclination. A little farther on, however, he exclaims, "Thanks be to God, which put the same earnest care into the heart of Titus for you. For indeed he accepted the exhortation" (2 Cor. 8:16, 17). If Titus could not even perform the office of being a mouth to exhort others, except in so far as God suggested, how could the others have been voluntary agents in acting, if the Lord Jesus had not directed their hearts?

9. Some, who would be thought more acute, endeavour to evade all these passages, by the quibble, that there is nothing to hinder us from contributing our part, while God, at the same time, supplies our deficiencies. They, moreover, adduce passages from the Prophets, in which the work of our conversion seems to be shared between God and ourselves; "Turn ye unto me, saith the Lord of hosts, and I will turn unto you, saith the Lord of hosts" (Zech. 1:3). The kind of assistance which God gives us has been shown above (sect. 7, 8), and need not now be repeated. One thing only I ask to be conceded to me, that it is vain to think we have a power of fulfilling the Law, merely because we are enjoined to obey it. Since, in order to our fulfilling the divine precepts, the grace of the Lawgiver is both necessary, and has been promised to us, this much at least is clear, that more is demanded of us than we are able to pay. Nor can any cavil evade the declaration in Jeremiah, that the covenant which God made with his ancient people was broken, because it was only of the letter—that to make it effectual, it was necessary for the Spirit to interpose and train the heart to obedience (Jer. 31:32). The opinion we now combat is not aided by the words, "Turn unto me, and I will turn unto you." The turning there spoken of is not that by which God renews the heart unto repentance; but that in which, by bestowing prosperity, he manifests his kindness and favour, just in the same way as he sometimes expresses his displeasure by sending adversity. The people complaining under the many calamities which befell them, that they were forsaken by God, he answers, that his kindness would not fail them, if they would return to a right course, and to himself, the standard of righteousness. The passage, therefore, is wrested from its proper meaning when it is made to countenance the idea that the work of conversion is divided between God and man (*supra*, Chap. 2 sec. 27). We have only glanced briefly at this subject, as the proper place for it will occur when we come to treat of the Law (Chap. 7 sec. 2 and 3).

10. The second class of objections is akin to the former. They allege the promises in which the Lord makes a paction with our will. Such are the following: "Seek good, and not evil, that ye may live" (Amos 5:14). "If ye be willing and obedient, ye shall eat the good of the land: but if ye refuse and rebel, ye shall be devoured with the sword; for the mouth of the Lord has spoken it" (Isaiah 1:19, 20). "If thou wilt put away thine abominations out of my sight, then thou shalt not remove" (Jer. 4:1). "It shall come to pass, if thou shalt hearken diligently unto the voice of the Lord thy God, to observe and do all the commandments which I command thee this days that the Lord thy God will set thee on high above all nations of the earth" (Deut. 28:1). There are other similar passages (Lev. 26:3, &c). They think that the blessings contained in these promises are offered to our will absurdly

and in mockery, if it is not in our power to secure or reject them. It is, indeed, an easy matter to indulge in declamatory complaint on this subject, to say that we are cruelly mocked by the Lord, when he declares that his kindness depends on our wills if we are not masters of our wills—that it would be a strange liberality on the part of God to set his blessings before us, while we have no power of enjoying them,—a strange certainty of promises, which, to prevent their ever being fulfilled, are made to depend on an impossibility. Of promises of this description, which have a condition annexed to them, we shall elsewhere speak, and make it plain that there is nothing absurd in the impossible fulfilment of them. In regard to the matter in hand, I deny that God cruelly mocks us when he invites us to merit blessings which he knows we are altogether unable to merit. The promises being offered alike to believers and to the ungodly, have their use in regard to both. As God by his precepts stings the consciences of the ungodly, so as to prevent them from enjoying their sins while they have no remembrance of his judgments, so, in his promises, he in a manner takes them to witness how unworthy they are of his kindness. Who can deny that it is most just and most becoming in God to do good to those who worship him, and to punish with due severity those who despise his majesty? God, therefore, proceeds in due order, when, though the wicked are bound by the fetters of sin, he lays down the law in his promises, that he will do them good only if they depart from their wickedness. This would be right, though His only object were to let them understand that they are deservedly excluded from the favour due to his true worshipers. On the other hand, as he desires by all means to stir up believers to supplicate his grace, it surely should not seem strange that he attempts to accomplish by promises the same thing which, as we have shown, he to their great benefit accomplishes by means of precepts. Being taught by precepts what the will of God is, we are reminded of our wretchedness in being so completely at variance with that will, and, at the same time, are stimulated to invoke the aid of the Spirit to guide us into the right path. But as our indolence is not sufficiently aroused by precepts, promises are added, that they may attract us by their sweetness, and produce a feeling of love for the precept. The greater our desire of righteousness, the greater will be our earnestness to obtain the grace of God. And thus it is, that in the protestations, *if we be willing, if thou shalt hearken*, the Lord neither attributes to us a full power of willing and hearkening, nor yet mocks us for our impotence.

11. The third class of objections is not unlike the other two. For they produce passages in which God upbraids his people for their ingratitude, intimating that it was not his fault that they did not obtain all kinds of favour from his indulgence. Of such passages, the following are examples: "The Amalekites and the Canaanites are before you, and ye shall fall by the sword: because ye are turned away from the Lord, therefore the Lord will not be with you" (Num. 14:43). "Because ye have done all these works, saith the Lord, and I spake unto you, rising up early and speaking, but ye heard not; and I called you, but ye answered not; therefore will I do unto this house, which is called by my name, wherein ye trust, and unto the place which I gave to you and to your fathers, as I have done to Shiloh" (Jer. 7:13, 14). "They obeyed not thy voice, neither walked in thy law; they have done nothing of all that thou commandedst them to do: therefore thou hast caused all this evil to come upon them" (Jer. 32:23). How, they ask, can such upbraiding be directed against those who have it in their power immediately to reply,—Prosperity was dear to us: we feared adversity; that we did not, in order to obtain the one and avoid the other, obey the Lord, and listen to his voice, is owing to its not being free for us to do so in consequence of our subjection to the dominion of sin; in vain, therefore, are we upbraided with evils which it was not in our power to escape. But to say nothing of the pretext of necessity, which is but a feeble and flimsy defence of their conduct, can they, I ask, deny their guilt? If they are held convicted of any fault, the Lord is not unjust in upbraiding them for having, by their own perverseness, deprived themselves of the advantages of his kindness. Let them say, then, whether they can deny that their own will is the depraved cause of their rebellion. If they find within themselves a fountain of wickedness, why do they stand declaiming about extraneous causes, with the view of making it appear that they are not the authors of their own destruction? If it be true that it is not for another's faults that sinners are both deprived of the divine favour, and visited with punishment, there is good reason why they should hear these rebukes from the mouth of God. If they obstinately persist in their vices, let them learn in their calamities to accuse and detest their own wickedness, instead of charging God with cruelty and injustice. If they have not manifested docility, let them, under a feeling of disgust at the sins which they see to be the cause of their misery and ruin, return to the right path, and, with serious contrition, confess the very thing of which the Lord by his rebuke reminds them. Of what use those upbraidings of the prophets above quoted

are to believers, appears from the solemn prayer of Daniel, as given in his ninth chapter. Of their use in regard to the ungodly, we see an example in the Jews, to whom Jeremiah was ordered to explain the cause of their miseries, though the event could not be otherwise than the Lord had foretold. "Therefore thou shalt speak these words unto them; but they will not hearken unto thee: thou shalt also call unto them; but they will not answer thee" (Jer. 7:27). Of what use, then, was it to talk to the deaf? It was, that even against their will they might understand that what they heard was true, and that it was impious blasphemy to transfer the blame of their wickedness to God, when it resided in themselves.

These few explanations will make it very easy for the reader to disentangle himself from the immense heap of passages (containing both precepts and reprimands) which the enemies of divine grace are in the habit of piling up, that they may thereon erect their statue of free will. The Psalmist upbraids the Jews as "a stubborn and rebellious generation; a generation that set not their heart aright" (Psalm 78:8); and in another passage, he exhorts the men of his time, "Harden not your heart" (Psalm 95:8). This implies that the whole blame of the rebellion lies in human depravity. But it is foolish thence to infer, that the heart, the preparation of which is from the Lord, may be equally bent in either direction. The Psalmist says, "I have inclined my heart to perform thy statutes alway" (Psalm 119:112); meaning, that with willing and cheerful readiness of mind he had devoted himself to God. He does not boast, however, that he was the author of that disposition, for in the same psalm he acknowledges it to be the gift of God. We must, therefore, attend to the admonition of Paul, when he thus addresses believers, "Work out your own salvation with fear and trembling. For it is God which worketh in you both to will and to do of his good pleasure" (Phil. 2:12, 13). He ascribes to them a part in acting that they may not indulge in carnal sloth, but by enjoining fear and trembling, he humbles them so as to keep them in remembrance, that the very thing which they are ordered to do is the proper work of God—distinctly intimating, that believers act (if I may so speak) *passively* in as much as the power is given them from heaven, and cannot in any way be arrogated to themselves. Accordingly, when Peter exhorts us to "add to faith virtue" (2 Pet. 1:5), he does not concede to us the possession of a second place, as if we could do anything separately. He only arouses the sluggishness of our flesh, by which faith itself is frequently stifled. To the same effect are the words of Paul. He says, "Quench not the Spirit" (1 Thess. 5:19); because a spirit of sloth, if not guarded against, is ever and anon creeping in upon believers. But should any thence infer that it is entirely in their own power to foster the offered light, his ignorance will easily be refuted by the fact, that the very diligence which Paul enjoins is derived only from God (2 Cor. 7:1). We are often commanded to purge ourselves of all impurity, though the Spirit claims this as his peculiar office. In fine, that what properly belongs to God is transferred to us only by way of concession, is plain from the words of John, "He that is begotten of God keepeth himself" (1 John 5:18). The advocates of free will fasten upon the expression as if it implied, that we are kept partly by the power of God, partly by our own, whereas the very keeping of which the Apostle speaks is itself from heaven. Hence, Christ prays his Father to keep us from evil (John 17:15), and we know that believers, in their warfare against Satan, owe their victory to the armour of God. Accordingly, Peter, after saying, "Ye have purified your souls in obeying the truth," immediately adds by way of correction, "through the Spirit" (1 Pet. 1:22). In fine, the nothingness of human strength in the spiritual contest is briefly shown by John, when he says, that "Whosoever is born of God does not commit sin; for his seed remaineth in him" (1 John 3:9). He elsewhere gives the reasons "This is the victory that overcometh the world, even our faith" (1 John 5:4).

12. But a passage is produced from the Law of Moses, which seems very adverse to the view now given. After promulgating the Law, he takes the people to witness in these terms: "This commandment which I command thee this day, it is not hidden from thee, neither is it far off. It is not in heaven, that thou shouldest say, Who shall go up for us to heaven, and bring it unto us, that we may hear it, and do it? But the word is very nigh unto thee, in thy mouth, and in thy heart, that thou mayest do it" (Deut. 30:11, 12, 14). Certainly, if this is to be understood of mere precepts, I admit that it is of no little importance to the matter in hand. For, though it were easy to evade the difficulty by saying, that the thing here treated of is not the observance of the law, but the facility and readiness of becoming acquainted with it, some scruple, perhaps, would still remain. The Apostle Paul, however, no mean interpreter, removes all doubt when he affirms, that Moses here spoke of the doctrine of the Gospel (Rom. 10:8). If any one is so refractory as to contend that Paul violently wrested the words in applying them to the Gospel, though his hardihood is chargeable with impiety, we are still able, independently of the author-

ity of the Apostle, to repel the objection. For, if Moses spoke of precepts merely, he was only inflating the people with vain confidence. Had they attempted the observance of the law in their own strength, as a matter in which they should find no difficulty, what else could have been the result than to throw them headlong? Where, then, was that easy means of observing the law, when the only access to it was over a fatal precipice? Accordingly, nothing is more certain than that under these words is comprehended the covenant of mercy, which had been promulgated along with the demands of the law. A few verses before, he had said, "The Lord thy God will circumcise thine heart, and the heart of thy seed, to love the Lord thy God with all thine heart, and with all thy soul, that thou mayest live" (Deut. 30:6). Therefore, the readiness of which he immediately after speaks was placed not in the power of man, but in the protection and help of the Holy Spirit, who mightily performs his own work in our weakness. The passage, however, is not to be understood of precepts simply, but rather of the Gospel promises, which, so far from proving any power in us to fulfil righteousness, utterly disprove it. This is confirmed by the testimony of Paul, when he observes that the Gospel holds forth salvation to us, not under the harsh arduous, and impossible terms on which the law treats with us (namely, that those shall obtain it who fulfil all its demands), but on terms easy, expeditious, and readily obtained. This passage, therefore, tends in no degree to establish the freedom of the human will.

13. They are wont also to adduce certain passages in which God is said occasionally to try men, by withdrawing the assistance of his grace, and to wait until they turn to him, as in Hosea, "I will go and return to my place, till they acknowledge their offence, and seek my face" (Hosea 5:15). It were absurd (say they), that the Lord should wait till Israel should seek his face, if their minds were not flexible, so as to turn in either direction of their own accord. As if anything were more common in the prophetical writings than for God to put on the semblance of rejecting and casting off his people until they reform their lives. But what can our opponents extract from such threats? If they mean to maintain that a people, when abandoned by God, are able of themselves to think of turning unto him, they will do it in the very face of Scripture. On the other hand, if they admit that divine grace is necessary to conversion, why do they dispute with us? But while they admit that grace is so far necessary, they insist on reserving some ability for man. How do they prove it? Certainly not from this nor any similar passage; for it is one thing to withdraw from man, and look to what he will do when thus abandoned and left to himself, and another thing to assist his powers (whatever they may be), in proportion to their weakness. What, then, it will be asked, is meant by such expressions? I answer, just the same as if God were to say, Since nothing is gained by admonishing, exhorting, rebuking this stubborn people, I will withdraw for a little, and silently leave them to be afflicted; I shall see whether, after long calamity, any remembrance of me will return, and induce them to seek my face. But by the departure of the Lord to a distance is meant the withdrawal of prophecy. By his waiting to see what men will do is meant that he, while silent, and in a manner hiding himself, tries them for a season with various afflictions. Both he does that he may humble us the more; for we shall sooner be broken than corrected by the strokes of adversity, unless his Spirit train us to docility. Moreover, when the Lord, offended and, as it were, fatigued with our obstinate perverseness, leaves us for a while (by withdrawing his word, in which he is wont in some degree to manifest his presence), and makes trial of what we will do in his absence, from this it is erroneously inferred, that there is some power of free will, the extent of which is to be considered and tried, whereas the only end which he has in view is to bring us to an acknowledgment of our utter nothingness.

14. Another objection is founded on a mode of speaking which is constantly observed both in Scripture and in common discourse. God works are said to be ours, and we are said to do what is holy and acceptable to God, just as we are said to commit sin. But if sins are justly imputed to us, as proceeding from ourselves, for the same reason (say they) some share must certainly be attributed to us in works of righteousness. It could not be accordant with reason to say, that we do those things which we are incapable of doing of our own motion, God moving us, as if we were stones. These expressions, therefore, it is said, indicate that while, in the matter of grace, we give the first place to God, a secondary place must be assigned to our agency. If the only thing here insisted on were, that good works are termed *ours*, I, in my turn, would reply, that the bread which we ask God to give us is also termed *ours*. What, then, can be inferred from the title of possession, but simply that, by the kindness and free gift of Gods that becomes ours which in other respects is by no means due to us? Therefore let them either ridicule the same absurdity in the Lord's Prayer, or let them cease to regard it as absurd, that good works should be called ours, though our only property in them is derived from the

liberality of God. But there is something stronger in the fact, that we are often said in Scripture to worship God, do justice, obey the law, and follow good works. These being proper offices of the mind and will, how can they be consistently referred to the Spirit, and, at the same time, attributed to us, unless there be some concurrence on our part with the divine agency? This difficulty will be easily disposed of if we attend to the manner in which the Holy Spirit acts in the righteous. The similitude with which they invidiously assail us is foreign to the purpose; for who is so absurd as to imagine that movement in man differs in nothing from the impulse given to a stone? Nor can anything of the kind be inferred from our doctrine. To the natural powers of man we ascribe approving and rejecting, willing and not willing, striving and resisting— viz. approving vanity, rejecting solid good, willing evil and not willing good, striving for wickedness and resisting righteousness. What then does the Lord do? If he sees meet to employ depravity of this description as an instrument of his anger, he gives it whatever aim and direction he pleases, that, by a guilty hand, he may accomplish his own good work. A wicked man thus serving the power of God, while he is bent only on following his own lust, can we compare to a stone, which, driven by an external impulse, is borne along without motion, or sense, or will of its own? We see how wide the difference is. But how stands the case with the godly, as to whom chiefly the question is raised? When God erects his kingdom in them, he, by means of his Spirit, curbs their will, that it may not follow its natural bent, and be carried hither and thither by vagrant lusts; bends, frames trains, and guides it according to the rule of his justice, so as to incline it to righteousness and holiness, and establishes and strengthens it by the energy of his Spirit, that it may not stumble or fall. For which reason Augustine thus expresses himself (De Corrept. et Gratia, cap. 2), "It will be said we are therefore acted upon, and do not act. Nay, you act and are acted upon, and you then act well when you are acted upon by one that is good. The Spirit of God who actuates you is your helper in acting, and bears the name of helper, because you, too, do something." In the former member of this sentence, he reminds us that the agency of man is not destroyed by the motion of the Holy Spirit, because nature furnishes the will which is guided so as to aspire to good. As to the second member of the sentence, in which he says that the very idea of help implies that we also do something, we must not understand it as if he were attributing to us some independent power of action; but not to foster a feeling of sloth, he reconciles the agency of God with our own agency, by saying, that to wish is from nature, to wish well is from grace. Accordingly, he had said a little before, "Did not God assist us, we should not only not be able to conquer, but not able even to fight."

15. Hence it appears that the grace of God (as this name is used when regeneration is spoken of) is the rule of the Spirit, in directing and governing the human will. Govern he cannot, without correcting, reforming, renovating (hence we say that the beginning of regeneration consists in the abolition of what is ours); in like manner, he cannot govern without moving, impelling, urging, and restraining. Accordingly, all the actions which are afterwards done are truly said to be wholly his. Meanwhile, we deny not the truth of Augustine's doctrine, that the will is not destroyed, but rather repaired, by grace— the two things being perfectly consistent—viz. that the human will may be said to be renewed when its vitiosity and perverseness being corrected, it is conformed to the true standard of righteousness and that, at the same time, the will may be said to be made new, being so vitiated and corrupted that its nature must be entirely changed. There is nothing then to prevent us from saying, that our will does what the Spirit does in us, although the will contributes nothing of itself apart from grace. We must, therefore, remember what we quoted from Augustine, that some men labour in vain to find in the human will some good quality properly belonging to it. Any intermixture which men attempt to make by conjoining the effort of their own will with divine grace is corruption, just as when unwholesome and muddy water is used to dilute wine. But though every thing good in the will is entirely derived from the influence of the Spirit, yet, because we have naturally an innate power of willing, we are not improperly said to do the things of which God claims for himself all the praise; first, because every thing which his kindness produces in us is our own (only we must understand that it is not of ourselves); and, secondly, because it is our mind, our will, our study which are guided by him to what is good.

16. The other passages which they gather together from different quarters will not give much trouble to any person of tolerable understanding, who pays due attention to the explanations already given. They adduce the passage of Genesis, "Unto thee shall be his desire, and thou shalt rule over him" (Gen. 4:7). This they interpret of sin, as if the Lord were promising Cain that the dominion of sin should not prevail over his mind, if he would labour in subduing it. We, however, maintain that it is much more agreeable to the context to understand the words

as referring to Abel, it being there the purpose of God to point out the injustice of the envy which Cain had conceived against his brother. And this He does in two ways, by showing, first, that it was vain to think he could, by means of wickedness, surpass his brother in the favour of God, by whom nothing is esteemed but righteousness; and, secondly, how ungrateful he was for the kindness he had already received, in not being able to bear with a brother who had been subjected to his authority. But lest it should be thought that we embrace this interpretation because the other is contrary to our view, let us grant that God does here speak of sin. If so, his words contain either an order or a promise. If an order, we have already demonstrated that this is no proof of man's ability; if a promise, where is the fulfilment of the promise when Cain yielded to the sin over which he ought to have prevailed? They will allege a tacit condition in the promise, as if it were said that he would gain the victory if he contended. This subterfuge is altogether unavailing. For, if the dominion spoken of refers to sin, no man can have any doubt that the form of expression is imperative, declaring not what we are able, but what it is our duty to do, even if beyond our ability. Although both the nature of the case, and the rule of grammatical construction, require that it be regarded as a comparison between Cain and Abel, we think the only preference given to the younger brother was, that the elder made himself inferior by his own wickedness.

17. They appeal, moreover, to the testimony of the Apostle Paul, because he says, "It is not of him that willeth, nor of him that runneth, but of God that showeth mercy" (Rom. 9:15). From this they infer, that there is something in will and endeavour, which, though weak in themselves, still, being mercifully aided by God, are not without some measure of success. But if they would attend in sober earnest to the subject there handled by Paul, they would not so rashly pervert his meaning. I am aware they can quote Origin and Jerome in support of this exposition. To these I might, in my turn, oppose Augustine. But it is of no consequence what they thought, if it is clear what Paul meant. He teaches that salvation is prepared for those only on whom the Lord is pleased to bestow his mercy—that ruin and death await all whom he has not chosen. He had proved the condition of the reprobate by the example of Pharaoh, and confirmed the certainty of gratuitous election by the passage in Moses, "I will have mercy on whom I will have mercy." Thereafter he concludes, that it is not of him that willeth, nor of him that runneth, but of God that showeth mercy.

If these words are understood to mean that the will or endeavour are not sufficient, because unequal to such a task, the Apostle has not used them very appropriately. We must therefore abandon this absurd mode of arguing, "It is not of him that willeth, nor of him that runneth;" therefore, there is some will, some running. Paul's meaning is more simple—there is no will nor running by which we can prepare the way for our salvation—it is wholly of the divine mercy. He indeed says nothing more than he says to Titus, when he writes, "After that the kindness and love of God our Saviour toward man appeared, not by works of righteousness which we have done, but according to his mercy he saved us" (Titus 3:4, 5). Those who argue that Paul insinuated there was some will and some running when he said, "It is not of him that willeth, nor of him that runneth," would not allow me to argue after the same fashion, that we have done some righteous works, because Paul says that we have attained the divine favour, "not by works of righteousness which we have done." But if they see a flaw in this mode of arguing, let them open their eyes, and they will see that their own mode is not free from a similar fallacy. The argument which Augustine uses is well founded, "If it is said, 'It is not of him that willeth, nor of him that runneth,' because neither will nor running are sufficient; it may, on the other hand, be retorted, it is not 'of God that showeth mercy,' because mercy does not act alone" (August. Ep. 170, ad Vital. See also Enchirid. ad Laurent. cap. 32). This second proposition being absurd, Augustine justly concludes the meaning of the words to be, that there is no good will in man until it is prepared by the Lord; not that we ought not to will and run, but that both are produced in us by God. Some, with equal unskilfulness, wrest the saying of Paul, "We are labourers together with God" (1 Cor. 3:9). There cannot be a doubt that these words apply to ministers only, who are called "labourers with God," not from bringing any thing of their own, but because God makes use of their instrumentality after he has rendered them fit, and provided them with the necessary endowments.

18. They appeal also to Ecclesiasticus, who is well known to be a writer of doubtful authority. But, though we might justly decline his testimony, let us see what he says in support of free will. His words are, "He himself made man from the beginning, and left him in the hand of his counsel; If thou wilt, to keep the commandments, and perform acceptable faithfulness. He has set fire and water before thee: stretch forth thy hand unto whether thou wilt. Before man is life and death; and whether

him liketh shall be given him" (Ecclesiasticus 15:14–17). Grant that man received at his creation a power of acquiring life or death; what, then, if we, on the other hand, can reply that he has lost it? Assuredly I have no intention to contradict Solomon, who asserts that "God has made man upright;" that "they have sought out many inventions" (Eccl. 7:29). But since man, by degenerating, has made shipwreck of himself and all his blessings, it certainly does not follow, that every thing attributed to his nature, as originally constituted, applies to it now when vitiated and degenerate. Therefore, not only to my opponents, but to the author of Ecclesiasticus himself (whoever he may have been), this is my answer: If you mean to tell man that in himself there is a power of acquiring salvation, your authority with us is not so great as, in the least degree, to prejudice the undoubted word of God; but if only wishing to curb the malignity of the fleshy which by transferring the blame of its own wickedness to God, is wont to catch at a vain defence, you say that rectitude was given to man, in order to make it apparent he was the cause of his own destruction, I willingly assent. Only agree with me in this, that it is by his own fault he is stript of the ornaments in which the Lord at first attired him, and then let us unite in acknowledging that what he now wants is a physician, and not a defender.

19. There is nothing more frequent in their mouths than the parable of the traveller who fell among thieves, and was left half dead (Luke 10:32). I am aware that it is a common idea with almost all writers, that under the figure of the traveller is represented the calamity of the human race. Hence our opponents argue that man was not so mutilated by the robbery of sin and the devil as not to preserve some remains of his former endowments; because it is said he was left half dead. For where is the half living, unless some portion of right will and reason remain? First, were I to deny that there is any room for their allegory, what could they say? There can be no doubt that the Fathers invented it contrary to the genuine sense of the parable. Allegories ought to be carried no further than Scripture expressly sanctions: so far are they from forming a sufficient basis to found doctrines upon. And were I so disposed I might easily find the means of tearing up this fiction by the roots. The Word of God leaves no half life to man, but teaches, that, in regard to life and happiness, he has utterly perished. Paul, when he speaks of our redemption, says not that the half dead are cured (Eph. 2:5, 6; 5:14) but that those who were dead are raised up. He does not call upon the half dead to receive the illumination of Christ, but upon those who are asleep and buried. In the same way our Lord himself says, "The hour is coming, and now is, when the dead shall hear the voice of the Son of God" (John 5:25). How can they presume to set up a flimsy allegory in opposition to so many clear statements? But be it that this allegory is good evidence, what can they extort out of it? Man is half dead, therefore there is some soundness in him. True! he has a mind capable of understanding, though incapable of attaining to heavenly and spiritual wisdom; he has some discernment of what is honourable; he has some sense of the Divinity, though he cannot reach the true knowledge of God. But to what do these amount? They certainly do not refute the doctrine of Augustine— a doctrine confirmed by the common suffrages even of the Schoolmen, that after the fall, the free gifts on which salvation depends were withdrawn, and natural gifts corrupted and defiled (*supra*, chap. 2 sec. 2). Let it stand, therefore, as an indubitable truth, which no engines can shake, that the mind of man is so entirely alienated from the righteousness of God that he cannot conceive, desire, or design any thing but what is wicked, distorted, foul, impure, and iniquitous; that his heart is so thoroughly envenomed by sin that it can breathe out nothing but corruption and rottenness; that if some men occasionally make a show of goodness, their mind is ever interwoven with hypocrisy and deceit, their soul inwardly bound with the fetters of wickedness.

CHAPTER 6

REDEMPTION FOR MAN LOST TO BE SOUGHT IN CHRIST.

The parts of this chapter are, I. The excellence of the doctrine of Christ the Redeemer—a doctrine always entertained by the Church, sec. 1. II. Christ, the Mediator in both dispensations, was offered to the faith of the pious Israelites and people of old, as is plain from the institution of sacrifice, the calling of Abraham's family, and the elevation of David and his posterity, sec. 2. III. Hence the consolation, strength, hope, and confidence of the godly under the Law, Christ being offered to them in various ways by their heavenly Father.

Sections:

1. **The knowledge of God the Creator of no avail without faith in Christ the Redeemer. First reason. Second reason strengthened by the testimony of an Apostle. Conclusion. This doctrine entertained by the**

children of God in all ages from the beginning of the world. Error of throwing open heaven to the heathen, who know nothing of Christ. The pretexts for this refuted by passages of Scripture.

2. God never was propitious to the ancient Israelites without Christ the Mediator. First reason founded on the institution of sacrifice. Second reason founded on the calling of Abraham. Third reason founded on the elevation of David's family to regal dignity, and confirmed by striking passages of Scripture.

3. Christ the solace ever promised to the afflicted; the banner of faith and hope always erected. This confirmed by various passages of Scripture.

4. The Jews taught to have respect to Christ. This teaching sanctioned by our Saviour himself. The common saying, that God is the object of faith, requires to be explained and modified. Conclusion of this discussion concerning Christ. No saving knowledge of God in the heathen.

1. The whole human race having been undone in the person of Adam, the excellence and dignity of our origin, as already described, is so far from availing us, that it rather turns to our greater disgrace, until God, who does not acknowledge man when defiled and corrupted by sin as his own work, appear as a Redeemer in the person of his only begotten Son. Since our fall from life unto death, all that knowledge of God the Creator, of which we have discoursed, would be useless, were it not followed up by faith, holding forth God to us as a Father in Christ. The natural course undoubtedly was, that the fabric of the world should be a school in which we might learn piety, and from it pass to eternal life and perfect felicity. But after looking at the perfection beheld wherever we turn our eye, above and below, we are met by the divine malediction, which, while it involves innocent creatures in our fault, of necessity fills our own souls with despair. For although God is still pleased in many ways to manifest his paternal favour towards us, we cannot, from a mere survey of the world, infer that he is a Father. Conscience urging us within, and showing that sin is a just ground for our being forsaken, will not allow us to think that God accounts or treats us as sons. In addition to this are our sloth and ingratitude. Our minds are so blinded that they cannot perceive the truth, and all our senses are so corrupt that we wickedly rob God of his glory. Wherefore, we must conclude with Paul, "After that in the wisdom of God the world by wisdom knew not God, it pleased God by the foolishness of preaching to save them that believe" (1 Cor. 1:21). By the "wisdom of God," he designates this magnificent theatre of heaven and earth replenished with numberless wonders, the wise contemplation of which should have enabled us to know God. But this we do with little profit; and, therefore, he invites us to faith in Christ,—faith which, by a semblance of foolishness, disgusts the unbeliever. Therefore, although the preaching of the cross is not in accordance with human wisdom, we must, however, humbly embrace it if we would return to God our Maker, from whom we are estranged, that he may again become our Father. It is certain that after the fall of our first parent, no knowledge of God without a Mediator was effectual to salvation. Christ speaks not of his own age merely, but embraces all ages, when he says "This is life eternal that they might know thee the only true God, and Jesus Christ, whom thou hast sent" (John 17:3). The more shameful therefore is the presumption of those who throw heaven open to the unbelieving and profane, in the absence of that grace which Scripture uniformly describes as the only door by which we enter into life. Should any confine our Saviour's words to the period subsequent to the promulgation of the Gospel, the refutation is at hand; since on a ground common to all ages and nations, it is declared, that those who are estranged from God, and as such, are under the curse, the children of wrath, cannot be pleasing to God until they are reconciled. To this we may add the answer which our Saviour gave to the Samaritan woman "Ye worship ye know not what; we know what we worship: for salvation is of the Jews" (John 4:22). By these words, he both charges every Gentile religion with falsehood, and assigns the reason— viz. that under the Law the Redeemer was promised to the chosen people only, and that, consequently, no worship was ever pleasing to God in which respect was not had to Christ. Hence also Paul affirms, that all the Gentiles were "without God," and deprived of the hope of life. Now, since John teaches that there was life in Christ from the beginning, and that the whole world had lost it (John 1:4), it is necessary to return to that fountain; And, accordingly, Christ declares that inasmuch as he is a propitiator, he is life. And, indeed, the inheritance of heaven belongs to none but the sons of God (John 15:6). Now, it were most incongruous to give the place and rank of sons to any who have not been engrafted into the body of the only begotten Son. And John distinctly testifies that those become the sons of God who believe in his name. But as it is not my intention at present formally to discuss the subject of faith in Christ, it is enough to have thus touched on it in passing.

2. Hence it is that God never showed himself propitious to his ancient people, nor gave them any hope of grace without a Mediator. I say nothing of the sacrifices of the Law, by which believers were plainly and openly taught that salvation was not to be found anywhere but in the expiation which Christ alone completed. All I maintain is that the prosperous and happy state of the Church was always founded in the person of Christ. For although God embraced the whole posterity of Abraham in his covenant, yet Paul properly argues (Gal. 3:16), that Christ was truly the seed in which all the nations of the earth were to be blessed, since we know that all who were born of Abraham, according to the flesh, were not accounted the seed. To omit Ishmael and others, how came it that of the two sons of Isaac, the twin brothers, Esau and Jacob, while yet in the womb, the one was chosen and the other rejected? Nay, how came it that the first-born was rejected, and the younger alone admitted? Moreover, how happens it that the majority are rejected? It is plain, therefore, that the seed of Abraham is considered chiefly in one head, and that the promised salvation is not attained without coming to Christ, whose office it is to gather together those which were scattered abroad. Thus the primary adoption of the chosen people depended on the grace of the Mediator. Although it is not expressed in very distinct terms in Moses, it, however, appears to have been commonly known to all the godly. For before a king was appointed over the Israelites, Hannah, the mother of Samuel, describing the happiness of the righteous, speaks thus in her song, "He shall give strength unto his king, and exalt the horn of his anointed;" meaning by these words, that God would bless his Church. To this corresponds the prediction, which is afterwards added, "I will raise me up a faithful priest, and he shall walk before mine anointed for ever" (1 Sam. 2:10, 35). And there can be no doubt that our heavenly Father intended that a living image of Christ should be seen in David and his posterity. Accordingly, exhorting the righteous to fear Him, he bids them "Kiss the Son" (Psalm 2:12). Corresponding to this is the passage in the Gospel, "He that honoureth not the Son, honoureth not the Father" (John 5:23). Therefore, though the kingdom was broken up by the revolt of the ten tribes, yet the covenant which God had made in David and his successors behaved to stand, as is also declared by his Prophets, "Howbeit I will not take the whole kingdom out of his hand: but I will make him prince all the days of his life for David my servant's sake" (1 Kings 11:34). The same thing is repeated a second and third time. It is also expressly said, "I will for this afflict the seed of David, but not for ever" (1 Kings 11:39). Some time afterwards it was said, "Nevertheless, for David's sake did the Lord his God give him a lamp in Jerusalem, to set up his son after him, and to establish Jerusalem" (1 Kings 15:4). And when matters were bordering on destruction, it was again said, "Yet the Lord would not destroy Judah for David his servant's sake, as he had promised to give him alway a light, and to his children" (2 Kings 8:19).

The sum of the whole comes to this—David, all others being excluded, was chosen to be the person in whom the good pleasure of the Lord should dwell; as it is said elsewhere, "He forsook the tabernacle of Shiloh;" "Moreover, he refused the tabernacle of Joseph, and chose not the tribe of Ephraim;" "But chose the tribe of Judah, the mount Zion which he loved;" "He chose David also his servant, and took him from the sheep folds: from following the ewes great with young he brought him to feed Jacob his people, and Israel his inheritance" (Ps. 78:60, 67, 70, 71). In fine, God, in thus preserving his Church, intended that its security and salvation should depend on Christ as its head. Accordingly, David exclaims, "The Lord is their strength, and he is the saving strength of his anointed;" and then prays "Save thy people, and bless thine inheritance;" intimating, that the safety of the Church was indissolubly connected with the government of Christ. In the same sense he elsewhere says, "Save, Lord: let the king hear us when we call" (Ps. 20:9). These words plainly teach that believers, in applying for the help of God, had their sole confidence in this—that they were under the unseen government of the King. This may be inferred from another psalm, "Save now, I beseech thee O Lord: Blessed be he that cometh in the name of the Lord" (Ps. 118:25, 26). Here it is obvious that believers are invited to Christ, in the assurance that they will be safe when entirely in his hand. To the same effect is another prayer, in which the whole Church implores the divine mercy "Let thy hand be upon the Man of thy right hand, upon the Son of man, whom thou madest strong (or best fitted) for thyself" (Ps. 80:17). For though the author of the psalm laments the dispersion of the whole nations he prays for its revival in him who is sole Head. After the people were led away into captivity, the land laid waste, and matters to appearance desperate, Jeremiah, lamenting the calamity of the Church, especially complains, that by the destruction of the kingdom the hope of believers was cut off; "The breath of our nostrils, the anointed of the Lord, was taken in their pits, of whom we said, Under his shadow we shall live among the heathen"

(Lam. 4:20). From all this it is abundantly plain, that as the Lord cannot be propitious to the human race without a Mediator, Christ was always held forth to the holy Fathers under the Law as the object of their faith.

3. Moreover when comfort is promised in affliction, especially when the deliverance of the Church is described, the banner of faith and hope in Christ is unfurled. "Thou wentest forth for the salvation of thy people, even for salvation with thine anointed," says Habakkuk (3:13). And whenever mention is made in the Prophets of the renovation of the Church, the people are directed to the promise made to David, that his kingdom would be for ever. And there is nothing strange in this, since otherwise there would have been no stability in the covenant. To this purpose is the remarkable prophecy in Isaiah 7:14. After seeing that the unbelieving king Ahab repudiated what he had testified regarding the deliverance of Jerusalem from siege and its immediate safety, he passes as it were abruptly to the Messiah, "Behold, a virgin shall conceive and bear a son, and shall call his name Emmanuel;" intimating indirectly, that though the king and his people wickedly rejected the promise offered to them, as if they were bent on causing the faith of God to fail, the covenant would not be defeated—the Redeemer would come in his own time. In fine, all the prophets, to show that God was placable, were always careful to bring forward that kingdom of David, on which redemption and eternal salvation depended. Thus in Isaiah it is said, "I will make an everlasting covenant with you, even the sure mercies of David. Behold, I have given him for a witness to the people" (Isa. 55:3, 4); intimating, that believers, in calamitous circumstances, could have no hope, had they not this testimony that God would be ready to hear them. In the same way, to revive their drooping spirits, Jeremiah says, "Behold, the days come, saith the Lord, that I will raise unto David a righteous Branch, and a King shall reign and prosper, and shall execute judgment and justice in the earth. In his days Judah shall be saved, and Israel shall dwell safely" (Jer. 23:5, 6). In Ezekiel also it is said, "I will set up one Shepherd over them, and he shall feed them, even my servant David; he shall feed them, and he shall be their shepherd. And I the Lord will be their God, and my servant David a prince among them: I the Lord have spoken it. And I will make with them a covenant of peace" (Ezek. 34:23, 24, 25). And again, after discoursing of this wondrous renovation, he says, "David my servant shall be king over them: and they all shall have one shepherd." "Moreover, I will make a covenant of peace with them; it shall be an everlasting covenant with them" (Ezek. 37:24–26). I select a few passages out of many, because I merely wish to impress my readers with the fact, that the hope of believers was ever treasured up in Christ alone. All the other prophets concur in this. Thus Hosea, "Then shall the children of Judah and the children of Israel be gathered together, and appoint themselves one head" (Hosea 1:11). This he afterwards explains in clearer terms, "Afterward shall the children of Israel return, and seek the Lord their God, and David their king" (Hosea 3:5). Micah, also speaking of the return of the people, says expressly, "Their king shall pass before them, and the Lord on the head of them" (Micah 2:13). So Amos, in predicting the renovation of the people, says "In that day will I raise up the tabernacle of David that is fallen, and close up the breaches thereof; and I will raise up the ruins, and I will build it as in the days of old" (Amos 9:11); in other words, the only banner of salvation was, the exaltation of the family of David to regal splendour, as fulfilled in Christ. Hence, too, Zechariah, as nearer in time to the manifestation of Christ, speaks more plainly, "Rejoice greatly, O daughter of Zion; shout, O daughter of Jerusalem: behold, thy King cometh unto thee: he is just, and having salvation" (Zech. 9:9). This corresponds to the passage already quoted from the Psalms, "The Lord is their strength, and he is the saving health of their anointed." Here salvation is extended from the head to the whole body.

4. By familiarising the Jews with these prophecies, God intended to teach them, that in seeking for deliverance, they should turn their eyes directly towards Christ. And though they had sadly degenerated, they never entirely lost the knowledge of this general principle, that God, by the hand of Christ, would be the deliverer of the Church, as he had promised to David; and that in this way only the free covenant by which God had adopted his chosen people would be fulfilled. Hence it was, that on our Saviour's entry into Jerusalem, shortly before his death, the children shouted, "Hosannah to the son of David" (Mt. 21:9). For there seems to have been a hymn known to all, and in general use, in which they sung that the only remaining pledge which they had of the divine mercy was the promised advent of a Redeemer. For this reason, Christ tells his disciples to believe in him, in order that they might have a distinct and complete belief in God, "Ye believe in God, believe also in me" (John 14:1). For although, properly speaking, faith rises from Christ to the Father, he intimates, that even when it leans on God, it gradually vanishes away, unless he himself interpose to give it solid strength. The majesty of God is too high to be scaled

up to by mortals, who creep like worms on the earth. Therefore, the common saying that God is the object of faith (Lactantius, lib. 4 c. 16), requires to be received with some modification. When Christ is called the image of the invisible God (Col. 1:15), the expression is not used without cause, but is designed to remind us that we can have no knowledge of our salvation, until we behold God in Christ. For although the Jewish scribes had by their false glosses darkened what the Prophets had taught concerning the Redeemer, yet Christ assumed it to be a fact, received, as it were, with public consent, that there was no other remedy in desperate circumstances, no other mode of delivering the Church than the manifestation of the Mediator. It is true, that the fact adverted to by Paul was not so generally known as it ought to have been—viz. that Christ is the end of the Law (Rom. 10:4), though this is both true, and clearly appears both from the Law and the Prophets. I am not now, however, treating of faith, as we shall elsewhere have a fitter place (Book 3 Chap. 2), but what I wish to impress upon my readers in this way is, that the first step in piety is, to acknowledge that God is a Father, to defend, govern, and cherish us, until he brings us to the eternal inheritance of his kingdom; that hence it is plain, as we lately observed, there is no having knowledge of God without Christ, and that, consequently, from the beginning of the world Christ was held forth to all the elect as the object of their faith and confidence. In this sense, Irenæus says, that the Father, who is boundless in himself, is bounded in the Son, because he has accommodated himself to our capacity, lest our minds should be swallowed up by the immensity of his glory (Irenaeus, lib. 4 cap. 8). Fanatics, not attending to this, distort a useful sentiment into an impious dream, as if Christ had only a share of the Godhead, as a part taken from a whole; whereas the meaning merely is, that God is comprehended in Christ alone. The saying of John was always true, "whosoever denieth the Son, the same has not the Father" (1 John 2:23). For though in old time there were many who boasted that they worshipped the Supreme Deity, the Maker of heaven and earth, yet as they had no Mediator, it was impossible for them truly to enjoy the mercy of God, so as to feel persuaded that he was their Father. Not holding the head, that is, Christ, their knowledge of God was evanescent; and hence they at length fell away to gross and foul superstitions betraying their ignorance, just as the Turks in the present day, who, though proclaiming, with full throat, that the Creator of heaven and earth is their God, yet by their rejection of Christ, substitute an idol in his place.

CHAPTER 7

THE LAW GIVEN, NOT TO RETAIN A PEOPLE FOR ITSELF, BUT TO KEEP ALIVE THE HOPE OF SALVATION IN CHRIST UNTIL HIS ADVENT.

The divisions of this chapter are, I. The Moral and Ceremonial Law a schoolmaster to bring us to Christ, sec. 1, 2. II. This true of the Moral Law, especially its conditional promises. These given for the best reasons. In what respect the observance of the Moral Law is said to be impossible, sec. 3–5. III. Of the threefold office and use of the Moral Law, sec. 6–12. Antinomians refuted, sec. 13. IV. What the abrogation of the Law, Moral and Ceremonial, sec. 14–17.

Sections:

1. The whole system of religion delivered by the hand of Moses, in many ways pointed to Christ. This exemplified in the case of sacrifices, ablutions, and an endless series of ceremonies. This proved, 1. By the declared purpose of God; 2. By the nature of the ceremonies themselves; 3. From the nature of God; 4. From the grace offered to the Jews; 5. From the consecration of the priests.

2. Proof continued. 6. From a consideration of the kingdom erected in the family of David. 7. From the end of the ceremonies. 8. From the end of the Moral Law.

3. A more ample exposition of the last proof. The Moral Law leads believers to Christ. Showing the perfect righteousness required by God, it convinces us of our inability to fulfil it. It thus denies us life, adjudges us to death, and so urges us to seek deliverance in Christ.

4. The promises of the Law, though conditional, founded on the best reason. This reason explained.

5. No inconsistency in giving a law, the observance of which is impossible. This proved from reason, and confirmed by Scripture. Another confirmation from Augustine.

6. A consideration of the office and use of the Moral Law shows that it leads to Christ. The Law, while it describes the righteousness which is acceptable to God, proves that every man is unrighteous.

7. The Law fitly compared to a mirror, which shows us our wretchedness. This derogates not in any degree from its excellence.

8. When the Law discloses our guilt, we should not

despond, but flee to the mercy of God. How this may be done.

9. Confirmation of the first use of the Moral Law from various passages in Augustine.

10. A second use of the Law is to curb sinners. This most necessary for the good of the community at large; and this in respect not only of the reprobate, but also of the elect, previous to regeneration. This confirmed by the authority of an Apostle.

11. The Law showing our wretchedness, disposes us to admit the remedy. It also tends to keep us in our duty. Confirmation from general experience.

12. The third and most appropriate use of the Law respects the elect. 1. It instructs and teaches them to make daily progress in doing the will of God. 2. Urges them by exhortation to obedience. Testimony of David. How he is to be reconciled with the Apostle.

13. The profane heresy of the Antinomians must be exploded. Argument founded on a passage in David, and another in Moses.

14. Last part of the chapter treating of the abrogation of the Law. In what respect any part of the Moral Law abrogated.

15. The curse of the Law how abrogated.

16. Of the abrogation of the Ceremonial Law in regard to the observance only.

17. The reason assigned by the Apostle applicable not to the Moral Law, but to ceremonial observances only. These abrogated, not only because they separated the Jews from the Gentiles, but still more because they were a kind of formal instruments to attest our guilt and impunity. Christ, by destroying these, is justly said to have taken away the handwriting that was against us, and nailed it to his cross.

1. From the whole course of the observations now made, we may infer, that the Law was not superadded about four hundred years after the death of Abraham in order that it might lead the chosen people away from Christ, but, on the contrary, to keep them in suspense until his advent; to inflame their desire, and confirm their expectation, that they might not become dispirited by the long delay. By the Law, I understand not only the Ten Commandments, which contain a complete rule of life, but the whole system of religion delivered by the hand of Moses. Moses was not appointed as a Lawgiver, to do away with the blessing promised to the race of Abraham; nay, we see that he is constantly reminding the Jews of the free covenant which had been made with their fathers, and of which they were heirs; as if he had been sent for the purpose of renewing it. This is most clearly manifested by the ceremonies. For what could be more vain or frivolous than for men to reconcile themselves to God, by offering him the foul odour produced by burning the fat of beasts? or to wipe away their own impurities by be sprinkling themselves with water or blood? In short, the whole legal worship (if considered by itself apart from the types and shadows of corresponding truth) is a mere mockery. Wherefore, both in Stephen's address (Acts 7:44), and in the Epistle to the Hebrews, great weight is justly given to the passage in which God says to Moses, "Look that thou make them after the pattern which was showed thee in the mount" (Exod. 25:40). Had there not been some spiritual end to which they were directed, the Jews, in the observance of them, would have deluded themselves as much as the Gentiles in their vanities. Profane men, who have never made religion their serious study, cannot bear without disgust to hear of such a multiplicity of rites. They not merely wonder why God fatigued his ancient people with such a mass of ceremonies, but they despise and ridicule them as childish toys. This they do, because they attend not to the end; from which, if the legal figures are separated, they cannot escape the charge of vanity. But the type shows that God did not enjoin sacrifice, in order that he might occupy his worshippers with earthly exercises, but rather that he might raise their minds to something higher. This is clear even from His own nature. Being a spirit, he is delighted only with spiritual worship. The same thing is testified by the many passages in which the Prophets accuse the Jews of stupidity, for imagining that mere sacrifices have any value in the sight of God. Did they by this mean to derogate in any respect from the Law? By no means; but as interpreters of its true meaning, they wished in this way to turn the attention of the people to the end which they ought to have had in view, but from which they generally wandered. From the grace offered to the Jews we may certainly infer, that the law was not a stranger to Christ. Moses declared the end of the adoption of the Israelites to be, that they should be "a kingdom of priests, and an holy nation" (Exod. 19:6). This they could not attain, without a greater and more excellent atonement than the blood of beasts. For what could be less in accordance with reason, than that the sons of Adams who, from hereditary taint, are all born the slaves of sin, should be raised to royal dignity, and in this way made partakers of the glory of God, if the noble distinction were not derived from some other source? How, moreover, could the priestly

office exist in vigour among those whose vices rendered them abominable in the sight of God, if they were not consecrated in a holy head? Wherefore, Peter elegantly transposes the words of Moses, teaching that the fulness of grace, of which the Jews had a foretaste under the Law, is exhibited in Christ, "Ye are a chosen generation, a royal priesthood" (1 Pet. 2:9). The transposition of the words intimates that those to whom Christ has appeared in the Gospel, have obtained more than their fathers, inasmuch as they are all endued with priestly and royal honour, and can, therefore, trusting to their Mediator, appear with boldness in the presence of God.

2. And it is to be observed, by the way, that the kingdom, which was at length erected in the family of David, is part of the Law, and is comprehended under the dispensation of Moses; whence it follows, that, as well in the whole tribe of Levi as in the posterity of David, Christ was exhibited to the eyes of the Israelites as in a double mirror. For, as I lately observed (sec. 1), in no other way could those who were the slaves of sin and death, and defiled with corruption, be either kings or priests. Hence appears the perfect truth of Paul's statement, "The law was our schoolmaster to bring us unto Christ," "till the seed should come to whom the promise was made" (Gal. 3:24, 19). For Christ not yet having been made familiarly known to the Jews, they were like children whose weakness could not bear a full knowledge of heavenly things. How they were led to Christ by the ceremonial law has already been adverted to, and may be made more intelligible by several passages in the Prophets. Although they were required, in order to appease God, to approach him daily with new sacrifices, yet Isaiah promises, that all their sins would be expiated by one single sacrifice, and with this Daniel concurs (Isa. 53:5; Dan. 9:26, 27). The priests appointed from the tribe of Levi entered the sanctuary, but it was once said of a single priest, "The Lord has sworn, and will not repent, Thou art a priest for ever, after the order of Melchizedek" (Ps. 110:4). The unction of oil was then visible, but Daniel in vision declares that there will be another unction. Not to dwell on this, the author of the Epistle to the Hebrews proves clearly, and at length, from the fourth to the eleventh chapter, that ceremonies were vain, and of no value, unless as bringing us to Christ. In regard to the Ten Commandments, we must, in like manner, attend to the statement of Paul, that "Christ is the end of the law for righteousness to every one that believeth" (Rom. 10:4); and, again, that ministers of the new testament were "not of the letter, but of the spirit: for the letter killeth, but the split giveth life" (2 Cor. 3:6). The former passage intimates, that it is in vain to teach righteousness by precept, until Christ bestow it by free imputation, and the regeneration of the Spirit. Hence he properly calls Christ the end or fulfilling of the Law, because it would avail us nothing to know what God demands did not Christ come to the succour of those who are labouring, and oppressed under an intolerable yoke and burden. In another place, he says that the Law "was added because of transgressions" (Gal. 3:19), that it might humble men under a sense of their condemnation. Moreover, inasmuch as this is the only true preparation for Christ, the statements, though made in different words, perfectly agree with each other. But because he had to dispute with perverse teachers, who pretended that men merited justification by the works of the Law, he was sometimes obliged, in refuting their error, to speak of the Law in a more restricted sense, merely as law, though, in other respects, the covenant of free adoption is comprehended under it.

3. But in order that a sense of guilt may urge us to seek for pardon, it is of importance to know how our being instructed in the Moral Law renders us more inexcusable. If it is true, that a perfect righteousness is set before us in the Law, it follows, that the complete observance of it is perfect righteousness in the sight of God; that is, a righteousness by which a man may be deemed and pronounced righteous at the divine tribunal. Wherefore Moses, after promulgating the Law, hesitates not to call heaven and earth to witness, that he had set life and death, good and evil, before the people. Nor can it be denied, that the reward of eternal salvation, as promised by the Lord, awaits the perfect obedience of the Law (Deut. 30:19). Again, however, it is of importance to understand in what way we perform that obedience for which we justly entertain the hope of that reward. For of what use is it to see that the reward of eternal life depends on the observance of the Law, unless it moreover appears whether it be in our power in that way to attain to eternal life? Herein, then, the weakness of the Law is manifested; for, in none of us is that righteousness of the Law manifested, and, therefore, being excluded from the promises of life, we again fall under the curse. I state not only what happens, but what must necessarily happen. The doctrine of the Law transcending our capacity, a man may indeed look from a distance at the promises held forth, but he cannot derive any benefit from them. The only thing, therefore, remaining for him is, from their excellence to form a better estimate of his own misery, while he considers that the hope of salvation is cut off, and he is

threatened with certain death. On the other hand, those fearful denunciations which strike not at a few individuals, but at every individual without exceptions rise up; rise up, I say, and, with inexorable severity, pursue us; so that nothing but instant death is presented by the Law.

4. Therefore, if we look merely to the Law, the result must be despondency, confusion, and despair, seeing that by it we are all cursed and condemned, while we are kept far away from the blessedness which it holds forth to its observers. Is the Lord, then, you will ask, only sporting with us? Is it not the next thing to mockery, to hold out the hope of happiness, to invite and exhort us to it, to declare that it is set before us, while all the while the entrance to it is precluded and quite shut up? I answer, Although the promises, in so far as they are conditional, depend on a perfect obedience of the Law, which is nowhere to be found, they have not, however, been given in vain. For when we have learned, that the promises would be fruitless and unavailing, did not God accept us of his free goodness, without any view to our works, and when, having so learned, we, by faith, embrace the goodness thus offered in the gospel, the promises, with all their annexed conditions, are fully accomplished. For God, while bestowing all things upon us freely, crowns his goodness by not disdaining our imperfect obedience; forgiving its deficiencies, accepting it as if it were complete, and so bestowing upon us the full amount of what the Law has promised. But as this point will be more fully discussed in treating of justification by faith, we shall not follow it further at present.

5. What has been said as to the impossible observance of the Law, it will be proper briefly to explain and confirm, the general opinion being, that nothing can be more absurd. Hence Jerome has not hesitated to denounce anathema against it. What Jerome thought, I care not; let us inquire what is the truth. I will not here enter into a long and intricate discussion on the various kinds of possibility. By impossible, I mean, that which never was, and, being prevented by the ordination and decree of God, never will be. I say, that if we go back to the remotest period, we shall not find a single saint who, clothed with a mortal body, ever attained to such perfection as to love the Lord with all his heart, and soul, and mind, and strength; and, on the other hand, not one who has not felt the power of concupiscence. Who can deny this? I am aware, indeed of a kind of saints whom a foolish superstition imagines, and whose purity the angels of heaven scarcely equal. This, however, is repugnant both to Scripture and experience. But I say further, that no saint ever will attain to perfection, so long as he is in the body. Scripture bears clear testimony to this effect: "There is no man that sinneth not," saith Solomon (1 Kings 8:46). David says, "In thy sight shall no man living be justified" (Psalm 143:2). Job also, in numerous passages, affirms the same thing. But the clearest of all is Paul, who declares that "the flesh lusteth against the Spirit, and the Spirit against the flesh" (Gal. 5:17). And he proves, that "as many as are of the works of the law are under the curse," for the simple reason, that it is written, "Cursed is every one that continueth not in all things which are written in the book of the law to do them" (Gal. 3:10; Deut. 27:26); intimating, or rather assuming it as confessed, that none can so continue. But whatever has been declared by Scripture must be regarded as perpetual, and hence necessary. The Pelagians annoyed Augustine with the sophism, that it was insulting to God to hold, that he orders more than believers are able, by his grace, to perform; and he, in order to evade it, acknowledged that the Lord was able, if he chose, to raise a mortal man to angelic purity; but that he had never done, and never would do it, because so the Scripture had declared (Augustine, lib. de Nat. et Grat). This I deny not: but I add, that there is no use in absurdly disputing concerning the power of God in opposition to his truth; and therefore there is no ground for cavilling, when it is said that that thing cannot be, which the Scriptures declare will never be. But if it is the word that is objected to, I refer to the answer which our Saviour gave to his disciples when they asked, "Who then can be saved?" "With men," said he, "this is impossible; but with God all things are possible" (Mt. 19:25). Augustine argues in the most convincing manner, that while in the flesh, we never can give God the love which we owe him. "Love so follows knowledge, that no man can perfectly love God who has not previously a full comprehension of his goodness" (Augustin. de Spiritu et Litera, towards the end, and elsewhere). So long as we are pilgrims in the world, we see through a glass darkly, and therefore our love is imperfect. Let it therefore be held incontrovertible, that, in consequence of the feebleness of our nature, it is impossible for us, so long as we are in the flesh, to fulfil the law. This will also be proved elsewhere from the writings of Paul (Rom. 8:3).

6. That the whole matter may be made clearer, let us take a succinct view of the office and use of the Moral Law. Now this office and use seems to me to consist of three parts. First, by exhibiting the righteousness of God,—in other words, the righteousness which alone is acceptable to God,—it admonishes every one of his own unrigh-

teousness, certiorates, convicts, and finally condemns him. This is necessary, in order that man, who is blind and intoxicated with self-love, may be brought at once to know and to confess his weakness and impurity. For until his vanity is made perfectly manifest, he is puffed up with infatuated confidence in his own powers, and never can be brought to feel their feebleness so long as he measures them by a standard of his own choice. So soon, however, as he begins to compare them with the requirements of the Law, he has something to tame his presumption. How high soever his opinion of his own powers may be, he immediately feels that they pant under the heavy load, then totter and stumble, and finally fall and give way. He, then, who is schooled by the Law, lays aside the arrogance which formerly blinded him. In like manner must he be cured of pride, the other disease under which we have said that he labours. So long as he is permitted to appeal to his own judgment, he substitutes a hypocritical for a real righteousness, and, contented with this, sets up certain factitious observances in opposition to the grace of God. But after he is forced to weigh his conduct in the balance of the Law, renouncing all dependence on this fancied righteousness, he sees that he is at an infinite distance from holiness, and, on the other hand, that he teems with innumerable vices of which he formerly seemed free. The recesses in which concupiscence lies hid are so deep and tortuous that they easily elude our view; and hence the Apostle had good reason for saying, "I had not known lust, except the law had said, Thou shalt not covet." For, if it be not brought forth from its lurking-places, it miserably destroys in secret before its fatal sting is discerned.

7. Thus the Law is a kind of mirror. As in a mirror we discover any stains upon our face, so in the Law we behold, first, our impotence; then, in consequence of it, our iniquity; and, finally, the curse, as the consequence of both. He who has no power of following righteousness is necessarily plunged in the mire of iniquity, and this iniquity is immediately followed by the curse. Accordingly, the greater the transgression of which the Law convicts us, the severer the judgment to which we are exposed. To this effect is the Apostle's declaration, that "by the law is the knowledge of sin" (Rom. 3:20). By these words, he only points out the first office of the Law as experienced by sinners not yet regenerated. In conformity to this, it is said, "the law entered that the offence might abound;" and, accordingly, that it is "the ministration of death;" that it "worketh wrath" and kills (Rom. 5:20; 2 Cor. 3:7; Rom. 4:15). For there cannot be a doubt that the clearer the consciousness of guilt, the greater the increase of sin; because then to transgression a rebellious feeling against the Lawgiver is added. All that remains for the Law, is to arm the wrath of God for the destruction of the sinner; for by itself it can do nothing but accuse, condemn, and destroy him. Thus Augustine says, "If the Spirit of grace be absent, the law is present only to convict and slay us." But to say this neither insults the law, nor derogates in any degree from its excellence. Assuredly, if our whole will were formed and disposed to obedience, the mere knowledge of the law would be sufficient for salvation; but since our carnal and corrupt nature is at enmity with the Divine law, and is in no degree amended by its discipline, the consequence is, that the law which, if it had been properly attended to, would have given life, becomes the occasion of sin and death. When all are convicted of transgression, the more it declares the righteousness of God, the more, on the other hand, it discloses our iniquity; the more certainly it assures us that life and salvation are treasured up as the reward of righteousness, the more certainly it assures us that the unrighteous will perish. So far, however are these qualities from throwing disgrace on the Law, that their chief tendency is to give a brighter display of the divine goodness. For they show that it is only our weakness and depravity that prevents us from enjoying the blessedness which the law openly sets before us. Hence additional sweetness is given to divine grace, which comes to our aid without the law, and additional loveliness to the mercy which confers it, because they proclaim that God is never weary in doing good, and in loading us with new gifts.

8. But while the unrighteousness and condemnation of all are attested by the law, it does not follow (if we make the proper use of it) that we are immediately to give up all hope and rush headlong on despair. No doubt, it has some such effect upon the reprobate, but this is owing to their obstinacy. With the children of God the effect is different. The Apostle testifies that the law pronounces its sentence of condemnation in order "that every mouth may be stopped, and all the world may become guilty before God" (Rom. 3:19). In another place, however, the same Apostle declares, that "God has concluded them all in unbelief;" not that he might destroy all, or allow all to perish, but that "he might have mercy upon all" (Rom. 11:32); in other words, that divesting themselves of an absurd opinion of their own virtue, they may perceive how they are wholly dependent on the hand of God; that feeling how naked and destitute they are, they may take refuge in his mercy, rely upon it, and cover themselves up

entirely with it; renouncing all righteousness and merit, and clinging to mercy alone, as offered in Christ to all who long and look for it in true faith. In the precepts of the law, God is seen as the rewarder only of perfect righteousness (a righteousness of which all are destitute), and, on the other hand, as the stern avenger of wickedness. But in Christ his countenance beams forth full of grace and gentleness towards poor unworthy sinners.

9. There are many passages in Augustine, as to the utility of the law in leading us to implore Divine assistance. Thus he writes to Hilary, "The law orders, that we, after attempting to do what is ordered and so feeling our weakness under the law, may learn to implore the help of grace." In like manner, he writes to Asellius, "The utility of the law is, that it convinces man of his weakness, and compels him to apply for the medicine of grace, which is in Christ." In like manner, he says to Innocentius Romanus, "The law orders; grace supplies the power of acting." Again, to Valentinus, "God enjoins what we cannot do, in order that we may know what we have to ask of him." Again, "The law was given, that it might make you guilty—being made guilty might fear; fearing, might ask indulgence, not presume on your own strength." Again, "The law was given, in order to convert a great into a little man—to show that you have no power of your own for righteousness; and might thus, poor, needy, and destitute, flee to grace." He afterwards thus addresses the Almighty, "So do, O Lord, so do, O merciful Lord; command what cannot be fulfilled; nay, command what cannot be fulfilled, unless by thy own grace: so that when men feel they have no strength in themselves to fulfil it, every mouth may be stopped, and no man seem great in his own eyes. Let all be little ones; let the whole world become guilty before God." But I am forgetting myself in producing so many passages, since this holy man wrote a distinct treatise, which he entitled *De Spiritu et Litera*. The other branch of this first use he does not describe so distinctly, either because he knew that it depended on the former, or because he was not so well aware of it, or because he wanted words in which he might distinctly and clearly explain its proper meaning. But even in the reprobate themselves, this first office of the law is not altogether wanting. They do not, indeed, proceed so far with the children of God as, after the flesh is cast down, to be renewed in the inner man, and revive again, but stunned by the first terror, give way to despair. Still it tends to manifest the equity of the Divine judgment, when their consciences are thus heaved upon the waves. They would always willingly carp at the judgment of God; but now, though that judgment is not manifested, still the alarm produced by the testimony of the law and of their conscience bespeaks their deserts.

10. The second office of the Law is, by means of its fearful denunciations and the consequent dread of punishment, to curb those who, unless forced, have no regard for rectitude and justice. Such persons are curbed not because their mind is inwardly moved and affected, but because, as if a bridle were laid upon them, they refrain their hands from external acts, and internally check the depravity which would otherwise petulantly burst forth. It is true, they are not on this account either better or more righteous in the sight of God. For although restrained by terror or shame, they dare not proceed to what their mind has conceived, nor give full license to their raging lust, their heart is by no means trained to fear and obedience. Nay, the more they restrain themselves, the more they are inflamed, the more they rage and boil, prepared for any act or outbreak whatsoever were it not for the terror of the law. And not only so, but they thoroughly detest the law itself, and execrate the Lawgiver; so that if they could, they would most willingly annihilate him, because they cannot bear either his ordering what is right, or his avenging the despisers of his Majesty. The feeling of all who are not yet regenerate, though in some more, in others less lively, is, that in regard to the observance of the law, they are not led by voluntary submission, but dragged by the force of fear. Nevertheless, this forced and extorted righteousness is necessary for the good of society, its peace being secured by a provision but for which all things would be thrown into tumult and confusion. Nay, this tuition is not without its use, even to the children of God, who, previous to their effectual calling, being destitute of the Spirit of holiness, freely indulge the lusts of the flesh. When, by the fear of Divine vengeance, they are deterred from open outbreakings, though, from not being subdued in mind, they profit little at present, still they are in some measure trained to bear the yoke of righteousness, so that when they are called, they are not like mere novices, studying a discipline of which previously they had no knowledge. This office seems to be especially in the view of the Apostle, when he says, "That the law is not made for a righteous man, but for the lawless and disobedient, for the ungodly and for sinners, for unholy and profane, for murderers of fathers and murderers of mothers, for manslayers, for whoremongers, for them that defile themselves with mankind, for menstealers, for liars, for perjured persons, and if there be any other thing that is contrary to sound doctrine" (1 Tim.

1:9, 10). He thus indicates that it is a restraint on unruly lusts that would otherwise burst all bonds.

11. To both may be applied the declaration of the Apostle in another place, that "The law was our schoolmaster to bring us unto Christ" (Gal. 3:24); since there are two classes of persons, whom by its training it leads to Christ. Some (of whom we spoke in the first place), from excessive confidence in their own virtue or righteousness, are unfit to receive the grace of Christ, until they are completely humbled. This the law does by making them sensible of their misery, and so disposing them to long for what they previously imagined they did not want. Others have need of a bridle to restrain them from giving full scope to their passions, and thereby utterly losing all desire after righteousness. For where the Spirit of God rules not, the lusts sometimes so burst forth, as to threaten to drown the soul subjected to them in forgetfulness and contempt of God; and so they would, did not God interpose with this remedy. Those, therefore, whom he has destined to the inheritance of his kingdom, if he does not immediately regenerate, he, through the works of the law, preserves in fear, against the time of his visitation, not, indeed, that pure and chaste fear which his children ought to have, but a fear useful to the extent of instructing them in true piety according to their capacity. Of this we have so many proofs, that there is not the least need of an example. For all who have remained for some time in ignorance of God will confess, as the result of their own experience, that the law had the effect of keeping them in some degree in the fear and reverence of God, till, being regenerated by his Spirit, they began to love him from the heart.

12. The third use of the Law (being also the principal use, and more closely connected with its proper end) has respect to believers in whose hearts the Spirit of God already flourishes and reigns. For although the Law is written and engraven on their hearts by the finger of God, that is, although they are so influenced and actuated by the Spirit, that they desire to obey God, there are two ways in which they still profit in the Law. For it is the best instrument for enabling them daily to learn with greater truth and certainty what that will of the Lord is which they aspire to follow, and to confirm them in this knowledge; just as a servant who desires with all his soul to approve himself to his master, must still observe, and be careful to ascertain his master's dispositions, that he may comport himself in accommodation to them. Let none of us deem ourselves exempt from this necessity, for none have as yet attained to such a degree of wisdom, as that they may not, by the daily instruction of the Law, advance to a purer knowledge of the Divine will. Then, because we need not doctrine merely, but exhortation also, the servant of God will derive this further advantage from the Law: by frequently meditating upon it, he will be excited to obedience, and confirmed in it, and so drawn away from the slippery paths of sin. In this way must the saints press onward, since, however great the alacrity with which, under the Spirit, they hasten toward righteousness, they are retarded by the sluggishness of the flesh, and make less progress than they ought. The Law acts like a whip to the flesh, urging it on as men do a lazy sluggish ass. Even in the case of a spiritual man, inasmuch as he is still burdened with the weight of the flesh, the Law is a constant stimulus, pricking him forward when he would indulge in sloth. David had this use in view when he pronounced this high eulogium on the Law, "The law of the Lord is perfect, converting the soul: the testimony of the Lord is sure, making wise the simple. The statutes of the Lord are right, rejoicing the heart: the commandment of the Lord is pure, enlightening the eyes" (Ps. 19:7, 8). Again, "Thy word is a lamp unto my feet, and a light unto my path" (Ps. 119:105). The whole psalm abounds in passages to the same effect. Such passages are not inconsistent with those of Paul, which show not the utility of the law to the regenerate, but what it is able of itself to bestow. The object of the Psalmist is to celebrate the advantages which the Lord, by means of his law, bestows on those whom he inwardly inspires with a love of obedience. And he adverts not to the mere precepts, but also to the promise annexed to them, which alone makes that sweet which in itself is bitter. For what is less attractive than the law, when, by its demands and threatening, it overawes the soul, and fills it with terror? David specially shows that in the law he saw the Mediator, without whom it gives no pleasure or delight.

13. Some unskilful persons, from not attending to this, boldly discard the whole law of Moses, and do away with both its Tables, imagining it unchristian to adhere to a doctrine which contains the ministration of death. Far from our thoughts be this profane notion. Moses has admirably shown that the Law, which can produce nothing but death in sinners, ought to have a better and more excellent effect upon the righteous. When about to die, he thus addressed the people, "Set your hearts unto all the words which I testify among you this day, which ye shall command your children to observe to do, all the words of this law. For it is not a vain thing for you; because it is your life" (Deut. 32:46, 47). If it cannot be denied that

it contains a perfect pattern of righteousness, then, unless we ought not to have any proper rule of life, it must be impious to discard it. There are not various rules of life, but one perpetual and inflexible rule; and, therefore, when David describes the righteous as spending their whole lives in meditating on the Law (Psalm 1:2), we must not confine to a single age, an employment which is most appropriate to all ages, even to the end of the world. Nor are we to be deterred or to shun its instructions, because the holiness which it prescribes is stricter than we are able to render, so long as we bear about the prison of the body. It does not now perform toward us the part of a hard taskmaster, who will not be satisfied without full payment; but, in the perfection to which it exhorts us, points out the goal at which, during the whole course of our lives, it is not less our interest than our duty to aim. It is well if we thus press onward. Our whole life is a race, and after we have finished our course, the Lord will enable us to reach that goal to which, at present, we can only aspire in wish.

14. Since, in regard to believers, the law has the force of exhortation, not to bind their consciences with a curse, but by urging them, from time to time, to shake off sluggishness and chastise imperfection,—many, when they would express this exemption from the curse, say, that in regard to believers the Law (I still mean the Moral Law) is abrogated: not that the things which it enjoins are no longer right to be observed, but only that it is not to believers what it formerly was; in other words, that it does not, by terrifying and confounding their consciences, condemn and destroy. It is certainly true that Paul shows, in clear terms, that there is such an abrogation of the Law. And that the same was preached by our Lord appears from this, that he would not have refuted the opinion of his destroying the Law, if it had not been prevalent among the Jews. Since such an opinion could not have arisen at random without some pretext, there is reason to presume that it originated in a false interpretation of his doctrine, in the same way in which all errors generally arise from a perversion of the truth. But lest we should stumble against the same stone, let us distinguish accurately between what has been abrogated in the Law, and what still remains in force. When the Lord declares, that he came not to destroy the Law, but to fulfil (Mt. 5:17); that until heaven and earth pass away, not one jot or little shall remain unfulfilled; he shows that his advent was not to derogate, in any degree, from the observance of the Law. And justly, since the very end of his coming was to remedy the transgression of the Law. Therefore, the doctrine of the Law has not been infringed by Christ, but remains, that, by teaching, admonishing, rebuking, and correcting, it may fit and prepare us for every good work.

15. What Paul says, as to the abrogation of the Law, evidently applies not to the Law itself, but merely to its power of constraining the conscience. For the Law not only teaches, but also imperiously demands. If obedience is not yielded, nay, if it is omitted in any degree, it thunders forth its curse. For this reason, the Apostle says, that "as many as are of the works of the law are under the curse: for it is written, Cursed is every one that continueth not in all things which are written in the book of the law to do them" (Gal. 3:10; Deut. 27:26). Those he describes as under the works of the Law, who do not place righteousness in that forgiveness of sins by which we are freed from the rigour of the Law. He therefore shows, that we must be freed from the fetters of the Law, if we would not perish miserably under them. But what fetters? Those of rigid and austere exaction, which remits not one iota of the demand, and leaves no transgression unpunished. To redeem us from this curse, Christ was made a curse for us: for it is written, Cursed is every one that hangeth on a tree (Deut. 21:23, compared with Gal. 3:13, 4:4). In the following chapter, indeed, he says, that "Christ was made under the law, in order that he might redeem those who are under the law;" but the meaning is the same. For he immediately adds, "That we might receive the adoption of sons." What does this mean? That we might not be, all our lifetime, subject to bondage, having our consciences oppressed with the fear of death. Meanwhile, it must ever remain an indubitable truth, that the Law has lost none of its authority, but must always receive from us the same respect and obedience.

16. The case of ceremonies is different, these having been abrogated not in effect but in use only. Though Christ by his advent put an end to their use, so far is this from derogating from their sacredness, that it rather commends and illustrates it. For as these ceremonies would have given nothing to God's ancient people but empty show, if the power of Christ's death and resurrection had not been prefigured by them,—so, if the use of them had not ceased, it would, in the present day, be impossible to understand for what purpose they were instituted. Accordingly, Paul, in order to prove that the observance of them was not only superfluous, but pernicious also, says that they "are a shadow of things to come; but the body is of Christ" (Col. 2:17). We see, therefore, that the truth is made clearer by their abolition than if Christ, who has

been openly manifested, were still figured by them as at a distance, and as under a veil. By the death of Christ, the veil of the temple was rent in vain, the living and express image of heavenly things, which had begun to be dimly shadowed forth, being now brought fully into view, as is described by the author of the Epistle to the Hebrews (Heb. 10:1). To the same effect, our Saviour declares, that "the law and the prophets were until John: since that time the kingdom of God is preached, and every man presseth into it" (Luke 16:16); not that the holy fathers were left without the preaching of the hope of salvation and eternal life, but because they only saw at a distance, and under a shadow, what we now behold in full light. Why it behaved the Church to ascend higher than these elements, is explained by John the Baptist, when he says, "The law was given by Moses, but grace and truth came by Jesus Christ" (John 1:17). For though it is true that expiation was promised in the ancient sacrifices, and the ark of the covenant was a sure pledge of the paternal favour of God, the whole would have been delusory had it not been founded on the grace of Christ, wherein true and eternal stability is found. It must be held as a fixed point, that though legal rites ceased to be observed, their end serves to show more clearly how great their utility was before the advent of Christ, who, while he abolished the use, sealed their force and effect by his death.

17. There is a little more difficulty in the following passage of Paul: "You, being dead in your sins and the uncircumcision of your flesh, has he quickened together with him, having forgiven you all trespasses; blotting out the handwriting of ordinances that was against us, which was contrary to us, and took it out of the way, nailing it to his cross," &c. (Col. 2:13, 14). He seems to extend the abolition of the Law considerably farther, as if we had nothing to do with its injunctions. Some err in interpreting this simply of the Moral Law, as implying the abolition not of its injunctions, but of its inexorable rigour. Others examining Paul's words more carefully, see that they properly apply to the Ceremonial Law, and show that Paul repeatedly uses the term *ordinance* in this sense. He thus writes to the Ephesians: "He is our peace, who has made both one, and has broken down the middle wall of partition between us; having abolished in his flesh the enmity, even the law of commandments contained in ordinances; for to make in himself of twain one new man" (Eph. 2:14). There can be no doubt that he is there treating of ceremonies, as he speaks of "the middle wall of partition" which separated Jews and Gentiles. I therefore hold that the former view is erroneous; but, at the same time, it does not appear to me that the latter comes fully up to the Apostle's meaning. For I cannot admit that the two passages are perfectly parallel. As his object was to assure the Ephesians that they were admitted to fellowship with the Jews, he tells them that the obstacle which formerly stood in the way was removed. This obstacle was in the ceremonies. For the rites of ablution and sacrifice, by which the Jews were consecrated to the Lord, separated them from the Gentiles. But who sees not that, in the Epistle to the Colossians, a sublimer mystery is adverted to? No doubt, a question is raised there as to the Mosaic observances, to which false apostles were endeavouring to bind the Christian people. But as in the Epistle to the Galatians he takes a higher view of this controversy, and in a manner traces it to its fountain, so he does in this passage also. For if the only thing considered in rites is the necessity of observing them, of what use was it to call it a handwriting which was contrary to us? Besides, how could the bringing in of it be set down as almost the whole sum of redemption? Wherefore, the very nature of the case clearly shows that reference is here made to something more internal. I cannot doubt that I have ascertained the genuine interpretation, provided I am permitted to assume what Augustine has somewhere most truly affirmed, nay, derived from the very words of the Apostle—viz. that in the Jewish ceremonies there was more a confession than an expiation of sins. For what more was done in sacrifice by those who substituted purifications instead of themselves, than to confess that they were conscious of deserving death? What did these purifications testify but that they themselves were impure? By these means, therefore, the handwriting both of their guilt and impurity was ever and anon renewed. But the attestation of these things was not the removal of them. Wherefore, the Apostle says that Christ is "the mediator of the new testament,—by means of death, for the redemption of the transgressions that were under the first testament" (Heb. 9:15). Justly, therefore, does the Apostle describe these handwritings as against the worshipers, and contrary to them, since by means of them their impurity and condemnation were openly sealed. There is nothing contrary to this in the fact that they were partakers of the same grace with ourselves. This they obtained through Christ, and not through the ceremonies which the Apostle there contrasts with Christ, showing that by the continued use of them the glory of Christ was obscured. We perceive how ceremonies, considered in themselves, are elegantly and appositely termed handwritings, and contrary to the salvation of man, in as much as they were a kind of formal instruments which attested his

liability. On the other hand, when false apostles wished to bind them on the Christian Church, Paul, entering more deeply into their signification, with good reason warned the Colossians how seriously they would relapse if they allowed a yoke to be in that way imposed upon them. By so doing, they, at the same time, deprived themselves of all benefit from Christ, who, by his eternal sacrifice once offered, had abolished those daily sacrifices, which were indeed powerful to attest sin, but could do nothing to destroy it.

CHAPTER 8

EXPOSITION OF THE MORAL LAW.

This chapter consists of four parts. I. Some general observations necessary for the understanding of the subject are made by way of preface, sec. 1–5. II. Three things always to be attended to in ascertaining and expounding the meaning of the Moral Law, sec. 6–12. III. Exposition of the Moral Law, or the Ten Commandments, sec. 13–15. IV. The end for which the whole Law is intended—viz. to teach not only elementary principles, but perfection, sec. 51, to the end of the chapter.

Sections:

1. The Law was committed to writing, in order that it might teach more fully and perfectly that knowledge, both of God and of ourselves, which the law of nature teaches meagrely and obscurely. Proof of this, from an enumeration of the principal parts of the Moral Law; and also from the dictate of natural law, written on the hearts of all, and, in a manner, effaced by sin.

2. Certain general maxims. 1. From the knowledge of God, furnished by the Law, we learn that God is our Father and Ruler. Righteousness is pleasing, iniquity is an abomination in his sight. Hence, how weak soever we may be, our duty is to cultivate the one, and shun the other.

3. From the knowledge of ourselves, furnished by the Law, we learn to discern our own utter powerlessness, we are ashamed; and seeing it is in vain to seek for righteousness in ourselves, are induced to seek it elsewhere.

4. Hence, God has annexed promises and threatening to his promises. These not limited to the present life, but embrace things heavenly and eternal. They, moreover, attest the spotless purity of God, his love of righteousness, and also his kindness towards us.

5. The Law shows, moreover, that there is nothing more acceptable to God than obedience. Hence, all superstitious and hypocritical modes of worship are condemned. A remedy against superstitious worship and human presumption.

6. The second part of the chapter, containing three observations or rules. First rule, Our life must be formed by the Law, not only to external honesty, but to inward and spiritual righteousness. In this respect, the Law of God differs from civil laws, he being a spiritual Lawgiver, man not. This rule of great extent, and not sufficiently attended to.

7. This first rule confirmed by the authority of Christ, and vindicated from the false dogma of Sophists, who say that Christ is only another Moses.

8. Second observation or rule to be carefully attended to—viz. that the end of the command must be inquired into, until it is ascertained what the Lawgiver approves or disapproves. Example. Where the Law approves, its opposite is condemned, and vice versa.

9. Full explanation of this latter point. Example.

10. The Law states what is most impious in each transgression, in order to show how heinous the transgression is. Example.

11. Third observation or rule regards the division of the Law into Two Tables: the former comprehending our duty to God; the latter, our duty to our neighbour. The connection between these necessary and inseparable. Their invariable order. Sum of the Law.

12. Division of the Law into Ten Commandments. Various distinctions made with regard to them, but the best distinction that which divides them into Two Tables. Four commandments belong to the First, and six to the Second Table.

13. The third part of the chapter, containing an exposition of the Decalogue. The preface vindicates the authority of the Law. This it does in three ways. First, by a declaration of its majesty.

14. The preface to the Law vindicates its authority. Secondly, by calling to mind God's paternal kindness.

15. Thirdly, by calling to mind the deliverance out of the land of Egypt. Why God distinguishes himself by certain epithets. Why mention is made of the deliverance from Egypt. In what way, and how far, the remembrance of this deliverance should still affect us.

16. Exposition of the First Commandment. Its end. What it is to have God, and to have strange gods. Adoration due to God, trust, invocation, thanksgiving, and also true religion, required by the Commandment.

Superstition, Polytheism, and Atheism, forbidden. What meant by the words, "before me."

17. Exposition of the Second Commandment. The end and sum of it. Two parts. Short enumeration of forbidden shapes.

18. Why a threatening is added. Four titles applied to God, to make a deeper impression. He is called Mighty, Jealous, an Avenger, Merciful. Why said to be jealous. Reason drawn from analogy.

19. Exposition of the threatening which is added. First, as to visiting the iniquity of the fathers upon the children. A misinterpretation on this head refuted, and the genuine meaning of the threatening explained.

20. Whether this visiting of the sins of parents inconsistent with the divine justice. Apparently conflicting passages reconciled.

21. Exposition of the latter part—viz. the showing mercy to thousands. The use of this promise. Consideration of an exception of frequent occurrence. The extent of this blessing.

22. Exposition of the Third Commandment. The end and sum of it. Three parts. These considered. What it is to use the name of God in vain. Swearing. Distinction between this commandment and the Ninth.

23. An oath defined. It is a species of divine worship. This explained.

24. Many modes in which this commandment is violated. 1. By taking God to witness what we know is false. The insult thus offered.

25. Modes of violation continued. 2. Taking God to witness in trivial matters. Contempt thus shown. When and how an oath should be used. 3. Substituting the servants of God instead of himself when taking an oath.

26. The Anabaptists, who condemn all oaths, refuted. 1. By the authority of Christ, who cannot be opposed in anything to the Father. A passage perverted by the Anabaptists explained. The design of our Saviour in the passage. What meant by his there prohibiting oaths.

27. The lawfulness of oaths confirmed by Christ and the apostles. Some approve of public, but not of private oaths. The lawfulness of the latter proved both by reason and example. Instances from Scripture.

28. Exposition of the Fourth Commandment. Its end. Three purposes.

29. Explanation of the first purpose—viz. a shadowing forth of spiritual rest. This the primary object of the precept. God is therein set forth as our sanctifier; and hence we must abstain from work, that the work of God in us may not be hindered.

30. The number seven denoting perfection in Scripture, this commandment may, in that respect, denote the perpetuity of the Sabbath, and its completion at the last day.

31. Taking a simpler view of the commandment, the number is of no consequence, provided we maintain the doctrine of a perpetual rest from all our works, and, at the same time, avoid a superstitious observance of days. The ceremonial part of the commandment abolished by the advent of Christ.

32. The second and third purposes of the Commandment explained. These twofold and perpetual. This confirmed. Of religious assemblies.

33. Of the observance of the Lord's day, in answer to those who complain that the Christian people are thus trained to Judaism. Objection.

34. Ground of this institution. There is no kind of superstitious necessity. The sum of the Commandment.

35. The Fifth Commandment (the first of the Second Table), expounded. Its end and substance. How far honour due to parents. To whom the term father applies.

36. It makes no difference whether those to whom this honour is required are worthy or unworthy. The honour is claimed especially for parents. It consists of three parts. 1. Reverence.

37. Honour due to parents continued. 2. Obedience. 3. Gratitude. Why a promise added. In what sense it is to be taken. The present life a testimony of divine blessing. The reservation considered and explained.

38. Conversely a curse denounced on disobedient children. How far obedience due to parents, and those in the place of parents.

39. Sixth Commandment expounded. Its end and substance. God, as a spiritual Lawgiver, forbids the murder of the heart, and requires a sincere desire to preserve the life of our neighbour.

40. A twofold ground for this Commandment. 1. Man is the image of God. 2. He is our flesh.

41. Exposition of the Seventh Command. The end and substance of it. Remedy against fornication.

42. Continence an excellent gift, when under the control of God only. Altogether denied to some; granted only for a time to others. Argument in favour of celibacy refuted.

43. Each individual may refrain from marriage so long as he is fit to observe celibacy. True celibacy, and the proper use of it. Any man not gifted with continence wars with God and with nature, as constituted by him, in remaining unmarried. Chastity defined.

44. Precautions to be observed in married life. Everything repugnant to chastity here condemned.

45. Exposition of the Eighth Commandment. Its end and substance. Four kinds of theft. The bad acts condemned by this Commandment. Other peculiar kinds of theft.

46. Proper observance of this Commandment. Four heads. Application. 1. To the people and the magistrate. 2. To the pastors of the Church and their flocks. 3. To parents and children. 4. To the old and the young. 5. To servants and masters. 6. To individuals.

47. Exposition of the ninth Commandment. Its end and substance. The essence of the Commandment—detestation of falsehood, and the pursuit of truth. Two kinds of falsehood. Public and private testimony. The equity of this Commandment.

48. How numerous the violations of this Commandment. 1. By detraction. 2. By evil speaking—a thing contrary to the offices of Christian charity. 3. By scurrility or irony. 4. By prying curiosity, and proneness to harsh judgments.

49. Exposition of the Tenth Commandment. Its end and substance. What meant by the term Covetousness. Distinction between counsel and the covetousness here condemned.

50. Why God requires so much purity. Objection. Answer. Charity toward our neighbour here principally commended. Why house, wife, man-servant, maid-servant, ox, and ass, &c., are mentioned. Improper division of this Commandment into two.

51. The last part of the chapter. The end of the Law. Proof. A summary of the Ten Commandments. The Law delivers not merely rudiments and first principles, but a perfect standard of righteousness, modelled on the divine purity.

52. Why, in the Gospels and Epistles, the latter table only mentioned, and not the first. The same thing occurs in the Prophets.

53. An objection to what is said in the former section removed.

54. A conduct duly regulated by the divine Law, characterised by charity toward our neighbour. This subverted by those who give the first place to self-love. Refutation of their opinion.

55. Who our neighbour. Double error of the Schoolmen on this point.

56. This error consists, I. In converting precepts into counsels to be observed by monks.

57. Refutation of this error from Scripture and the ancient Theologians. Sophistical objection obviated.

58. Error of the Schoolmen consists, II. In calling hidden impiety and covetousness venial sins. Refutation drawn, 1. From a consideration of the whole Decalogue. 2. The testimony of an Apostle. 3. The authority of Christ. 4. The nature and majesty of God. 5. The sentence pronounced against sin. Conclusion.

59. Refutation drawn, 1. From a consideration of the whole Decalogue. 2. The testimony of an Apostle. 3. The authority of Christ. 4. The nature and majesty of God. 5. The sentence pronounced against sin. Conclusion.

1. I believe it will not be out of place here to introduce the Ten Commandments of the Law, and give a brief exposition of them. In this way it will be made more clear, that the worship which God originally prescribed is still in force (a point to which I have already adverted); and then a second point will be confirmed—viz. that the Jews not only learned from the law wherein true piety consisted, but from feeling their inability to observe it were overawed by the fear of judgments and so drawn, even against their will, towards the Mediator. In giving a summary of what constitutes the true knowledge of God, we showed that we cannot form any just conception of the character of God, without feeling overawed by his majesty, and bound to do him service. In regard to the knowledge of ourselves, we showed that it principally consists in renouncing all idea of our own strength, and divesting ourselves of all confidence in our own righteousness, while, on the other hand, under a full consciousness of our wants, we learn true humility and self-abasement. Both of these the Lord accomplishes by his Law, first, when, in assertion of the right which he has to our obedience, he calls us to reverence his majesty, and prescribes the conduct by which this reverence is manifested; and, secondly, when, by promulgating the rule of his justice (a rule, to the rectitude of which our nature, from being depraved and perverted, is continually opposed, and to the perfection of which our ability, from its infirmity and nervelessness for good, is far from being able to attain), he charges us both with impotence and unrighteousness. Moreover, the very things contained in the two tables are, in a manner, dictated to us by that internal law, which, as has been already said, is in a manner written and stamped on every heart. For conscience, instead of allowing us to stifle our perceptions, and sleep on without interruption, acts as an inward witness and monitor, reminds us of what we owe to God, points out the distinction between

good and evil, and thereby convicts us of departure from duty. But man, being immured in the darkness of error, is scarcely able, by means of that natural law, to form any tolerable idea of the worship which is acceptable to God. At all events, he is very far from forming any correct knowledge of it. In addition to this, he is so swollen with arrogance and ambition, and so blinded with self-love, that he is unable to survey, and, as it were, descend into himself, that he may so learn to humble and abase himself, and confess his misery. Therefore, as a necessary remedy, both for our dullness and our contumacy, the Lord has given us his written Law, which, by its sure attestations, removes the obscurity of the law of nature, and also, by shaking off our lethargy, makes a more lively and permanent impression on our minds.

2. It is now easy to understand the doctrine of the law—viz. that God, as our Creator, is entitled to be regarded by us as a Father and Master, and should, accordingly, receive from us fear, love, reverence, and glory; nay, that we are not our own, to follow whatever course passion dictates, but are bound to obey him implicitly, and to acquiesce entirely in his good pleasure. Again, the Law teaches, that justice and rectitude are a delight, injustice an abomination to him, and, therefore, as we would not with impious ingratitude revolt from our Maker, our whole life must be spent in the cultivation of righteousness. For if we manifest becoming reverence only when we prefer his will to our own, it follows, that the only legitimate service to him is the practice of justice, purity, and holiness. Nor can we plead as an excuse, that we want the power, and, like debtors, whose means are exhausted, are unable to pay. We cannot be permitted to measure the glory of God by our ability; whatever we may be, he ever remains like himself, the friend of righteousness, the enemy of unrighteousness, and whatever his demands from us may be, as he can only require what is right, we are necessarily under a natural obligation to obey. Our inability to do so is our own fault. If lust, in which sin has its dominion, so enthrals us, that we are not free to obey our Father, there is no ground for pleading necessity as a defence, since this evil necessity is within, and must be imputed to ourselves.

3. When, under the guidance of the Law, we have advanced thus far, we must, under the same guidance, proceed to descend into ourselves. In this way, we at length arrive at two results: First, contrasting our conduct with the righteousness of the Law, we see how very far it is from being in accordance with the will of God, and, therefore, how unworthy we are of holding our place among his creatures, far less of being accounted his sons; and, secondly, taking a survey of our powers, we see that they are not only unequal to fulfil the Law, but are altogether null. The necessary consequence must be, to produce distrust of our own ability, and also anxiety and trepidation of mind. Conscience cannot feel the burden of its guilt, without forthwith turning to the judgment of God, while the view of this judgment cannot fail to excite a dread of death. In like manner, the proofs of our utter powerlessness must instantly beget despair of our own strength. Both feelings are productive of humility and abasement, and hence the sinner, terrified at the prospect of eternal death (which he sees justly impending over him for his iniquities), turns to the mercy of God as the only haven of safety. Feeling his utter inability to pay what he owes to the Law, and thus despairing of himself, he rethinks him of applying and looking to some other quarter for help.

4. But the Lord does not count it enough to inspire a reverence for his justice. To imbue our hearts with love to himself, and, at the same time, with hatred to iniquity, he has added promises and threatening. The eye of our mind being too dim to be attracted by the mere beauty of goodness, our most merciful Father has been pleased, in his great indulgence, to allure us to love and long after it by the hope of reward. He accordingly declares that rewards for virtue are treasured up with him, that none who yield obedience to his commands will labour in vain. On the other hand, he proclaims not only that iniquity is hateful in his sight, but that it will not escape with impunity, because he will be the avenger of his insulted majesty. That he may encourage us in every way, he promises present blessings, as well as eternal felicity, to the obedience of those who shall have kept his commands, while he threatens transgressors with present suffering, as well as the punishment of eternal death. The promise, "Ye shall therefore keep my statutes, and my judgments; which if a man do, he shall live in them" (Lev. 18:5), and corresponding to this the threatening, "The souls that sinneth, it shall die" (Ezek. 18:4, 20); doubtless point to a future life and death, both without end. But though in every passage where the favour or anger of God is mentioned, the former comprehends eternity of life and the latter eternal destruction, the Law, at the same time, enumerates a long catalogue of present blessings and curses (Lev. 26:4; Deut. 28:1). The threatening attest the spotless purity of God, which cannot bear iniquity, while the promises attest at once his infinite love of righteousness (which he cannot leave unrewarded), and his wondrous

kindness. Being bound to do him homage with all that we have, he is perfectly entitled to demand everything which he requires of us as a debt; and as a debt, the payment is unworthy of reward. He therefore foregoes his right, when he holds forth reward for services which are not offered spontaneously, as if they were not due. The amount of these services, in themselves, has been partly described and will appear more clearly in its own place. For the present, it is enough to remember that the promises of the Law are no mean commendation of righteousness as they show how much God is pleased with the observance of them, while the threatening denounced are intended to produce a greater abhorrence of unrighteousness, lest the sinner should indulge in the blandishments of vice, and forget the judgment which the divine Lawgiver has prepared for him.

5. The Lord, in delivering a perfect rule of righteousness, has reduced it in all its parts to his mere will, and in this way has shown that there is nothing more acceptable to him than obedience. There is the more necessity for attending to this, because the human mind, in its wantonness, is ever and anon inventing different modes of worship as a means of gaining his favour. This irreligious affectation of religion being innate in the human mind, has betrayed itself in every age, and is still doing so, men always longing to devise some method of procuring righteousness without any sanction from the Word of God. Hence in those observances which are generally regarded as good works, the precepts of the Law occupy a narrow space, almost the whole being usurped by this endless host of human inventions. But was not this the very license which Moses meant to curb, when, after the promulgation of the Law, he thus addressed the people: "Observe and hear all these words which I command thee, that it may go well with thee, and with thy children after thee for ever, when thou does that which is good and right in the sight of the Lord thy God." "What thing soever I command you, observe to do it: thou shalt not add thereto, nor diminish from it" (Deut 12:28–32). Previously, after asking "what nation is there so great, that has statutes and judgments so righteous as all this law, which I set before you this day?" he had added, "Only take heed to thyself, and keep thy soul diligently, lest thou forget the things which thine eyes have seen, and lest they depart from thy heart all the days of thy life" (Deut. 4:8, 9). God foreseeing that the Israelites would not rest, but after receiving the Law, would, unless sternly prohibited give birth to new kinds of righteousness, declares that the Law comprehended a perfect righteousness. This ought to have been a most powerful restraint, and yet they desisted not from the presumptuous course so strongly prohibited. How do we act? We are certainly under the same obligation as they were; for there cannot be a doubt that the claim of absolute perfection which God made for his Law is perpetually in force. Not contented with it, however, we labour prodigiously in feigning and coining an endless variety of good works, one after another. The best cure for this vice would be a constant and deepseated conviction that the Law was given from heaven to teach us a perfect righteousness; that the only righteousness so taught is that which the divine will expressly enjoins; and that it is, therefore, vain to attempt, by new forms of worship, to gain the favour of God, whose true worship consists in obedience alone; or rather, that to go a wandering after good works which are not prescribed by the Law of God, is an intolerable violation of true and divine righteousness. Most truly does Augustine say in one place, that the obedience which is rendered to God is the parent and guardian; in another, that it is the source of all the virtues.

6. After we shall have expounded the Divine Law, what has been previously said of its office and use will be understood more easily, and with greater benefit. But before we proceed to the consideration of each separate commandment, it will be proper to take a general survey of the whole. At the outset, it was proved that in the Law human life is instructed not merely in outward decency but in inward spiritual righteousness. Though none can deny this, yet very few duly attend to it, because they do not consider the Lawgiver, by whose character that of the Law must also be determined. Should a king issue an edict prohibiting murder, adultery, and theft, the penalty, I admit, will not be incurred by the man who has only felt a longing in his mind after these vices, but has not actually committed them. The reason is, that a human lawgiver does not extend his care beyond outward order, and, therefore, his injunctions are not violated without outward acts. But God, whose eye nothing escapes, and who regards not the outward appearance so much as purity of heart, under the prohibition of murder, adultery, and thefts includes wrath, hatred, lust, covetousness, and all other things of a similar nature. Being a spiritual Lawgiver, he speaks to the soul not less than the body. The murder which the soul commits is wrath and hatred; the theft, covetousness and avarice; and the adultery, lust. It may be alleged that human laws have respect to intentions and wishes, and not fortuitous events. I admit this but then these must manifest themselves externally. They

consider the *animus* with which the act was done, but do not scrutinise the secret thoughts. Accordingly, their demand is satisfied when the hand merely refrains from transgression. On the contrary, the law of heaven being enacted for our minds, the first thing necessary to a due observance of the Law is to put them under restraint. But the generality of men, even while they are most anxious to conceal their disregard of the Law, only frame their hands and feet and other parts of their body to some kind of observance, but in the meanwhile keep the heart utterly estranged from everything like obedience. They think it enough to have carefully concealed from man what they are doing in the sight of God. Hearing the commandments, "Thou shalt not kill," "Thou shalt not commit adultery," "Thou shalt not steal," they do not unsheathe their sword for slaughter, nor defile their bodies with harlots, nor put forth their hands to other men's goods. So far well; but with their whole soul they breathe out slaughter, boil with lust, cast a greedy eye at their neighbour's property, and in wish devour it. Here the principal thing which the Law requires is wanting. Whence then, this gross stupidity, but just because they lose sight of the Lawgiver, and form an idea of righteousness in accordance with their own disposition? Against this Paul strenuously protests, when he declares that the "*law is spiritual*" (Rom. 7:14); intimating that it not only demands the homage of the soul, and mind, and will, but requires an angelic purity, which, purified from all filthiness of the flesh, savours only of the Spirit.

7. In saying that this is the meaning of the Law, we are not introducing a new interpretation of our own; we are following Christ, the best interpreter of the Law (Mt. 5:22, 28, 44). The Pharisees having instilled into the people the erroneous idea that the Law was fulfilled by every one who did not in external act do anything against the Law, he pronounces this a most dangerous delusion, and declares that an immodest look is adultery, and that hatred of a brother is murder. "Whosoever is angry with his brother without a cause, shall be in danger of the judgment;" whosoever by whispering or murmuring gives indication of being offended, "shall be in danger of the council;" whosoever by reproaches and evil-speaking gives way to open anger, "shall be in danger of hell-fire." Those who have not perceived this, have pretended that Christ was only a second Moses, the giver of an evangelical, to supply the deficiency of the Mosaic Law. Hence the common axiom as to the perfection of the Evangelical Law, and its great superiority to that of Moses. This idea is in many ways most pernicious. For it will appear from Moses himself, when we come to give a summary of his precepts, that great indignity is thus done to the Divine Law. It certainly insinuates, that the holiness of the fathers under the Law was little else than hypocrisy, and leads us away from that one unvarying rule of righteousness. It is very easy, however, to confute this error, which proceeds on the supposition that Christ added to the Law, whereas he only restored it to its integrity by maintaining and purifying it when obscured by the falsehood, and defiled by the leaven of the Pharisees.

8. The next observation we would make is, that there is always more in the requirements and prohibitions of the Law than is expressed in words. This, however, must be understood so as not to convert it into a kind of Lesbian code; and thus, by licentiously wresting the Scriptures, make them assume any meaning that we please. By taking this excessive liberty with Scripture, its authority is lowered with some, and all hope of understanding it abandoned by others. We must, therefore, if possible, discover some path which may conduct us with direct and firm step to the will of God. We must consider, I say, how far interpretation can be permitted to go beyond the literal meaning of the words, still making it apparent that no appending of human glosses is added to the Divine Law, but that the pure and genuine meaning of the Lawgiver is faithfully exhibited. It is true that, in almost all the commandments, there are elliptical expressions, and that, therefore, any man would make himself ridiculous by attempting to restrict the spirit of the Law to the strict letter of the words. It is plain that a sober interpretation of the Law must go beyond these, but how far is doubtful, unless some rule be adopted. The best rule, in my opinion, would be, to be guided by the principle of the commandment—viz. to consider in the case of each what the purpose is for which it was given. For example, every commandment either requires or prohibits; and the nature of each is instantly discerned when we look to the principle of the commandment as its end. Thus, the end of the Fifth Commandment is to render honour to those on whom God bestows it. The sum of the commandment, therefore, is, that it is right in itself, and pleasing to God, to honour those on whom he has conferred some distinction; that to despise and rebel against such persons is offensive to Him. The principle of the First Commandment is, that God only is to be worshipped. The sum of the commandment, therefore is that true piety, in other words, the worship of the Deity, is acceptable, and impiety is an abomination, to him. So in each of the commandments we must first look to the matter of

which it treats, and then consider its end, until we discover what it properly is that the Lawgiver declares to be pleasing or displeasing to him. Only, we must reason from the precept to its contrary in this way: If this pleases God, its opposite displeases; if that displeases, its opposite pleases: if God commands this, he forbids the opposite; if he forbids that, he commands the opposite.

9. What is now touched on somewhat obscurely will become perfectly clear as we proceed and get accustomed to the exposition of the Commandments. It is sufficient thus to have adverted to the subject; but perhaps our concluding statement will require to be briefly confirmed, as it might otherwise not be understood, or, though understood mighty perhaps, at the outset appear unsound. There is no need of proving, that when good is ordered the evil which is opposed to it is forbidden. This every one admits. It will also be admitted, without much difficulty, that when evil is forbidden, its opposite is enjoined. Indeed, it is a common saying, that censure of vice is commendation of virtue. We, however, demand somewhat more than is commonly understood by these expressions. When the particular virtue opposed to a particular vice is spoken of, all that is usually meant is abstinence from that vice. We maintain that it goes farther, and means opposite duties and positive acts. Hence the commandment, "Thou shalt not kill," the generality of men will merely consider as an injunction to abstain from all injury and all wish to inflict injury. I hold that it moreover means, that we are to aid our neighbour's life by every means in our power. And not to assert without giving my reasons I prove it thus: God forbids us to injure or hurt a brother, because he would have his life to be dear and precious to us; and, therefore, when he so forbids, he, at the same time, demands all the offices of charity which can contribute to his preservation.

10. But why did God thus deliver his commandments, as it were, by halves, using elliptical expressions with a larger meaning than that actually expressed? Other reasons are given, but the following seems to me the best:—As the flesh is always on the alert to extenuate the heinousness of sin (unless it is made, as it were, perceptible to the touch), and to cover it with specious pretexts, the Lord sets forth, by way of example, whatever is foulest and most iniquitous in each species of transgression, that the delivery of it might produce a shudder in the hearer, and impress his mind with a deeper abhorrence of sin. In forming an estimate of sins, we are often imposed upon by imagining that the more hidden the less heinous they are. This delusion the Lord dispels by accustoming us to refer the whole multitude of sins to particular heads, which admirably show how great a degree of heinousness there is in each. For example, wrath and hatred do not seem so very bad when they are designated by their own names; but when they are prohibited under the name of murder, we understand better how abominable they are in the sight of God, who puts them in the same class with that horrid crime. Influenced by his judgment, we accustom ourselves to judge more accurately of the heinousness of offences which previously seemed trivial.

11. It will now be proper to consider what is meant by the division of the divine Law into Two Tables. It will be judged by all men of sense from the formal manner in which these are sometimes mentioned, that it has not been done at random, or without reason. Indeed, the reason is so obvious as not to allow us to remain in doubt with regard to it. God thus divided his Law into two parts, containing a complete rule of righteousness, that he might assign the first place to the duties of religion which relate especially to His worship, and the second to the duties of charity which have respect to man. The first foundation of righteousness undoubtedly is the worship of God. When it is subverted, all the other parts of righteousness, like a building rent asunder, and in ruins, are racked and scattered. What kind of righteousness do you call it, not to commit theft and rapine, if you, in the meantime, with impious sacrilege, rob God of his glory? or not to defile your body with fornication, if you profane his holy name with blasphemy? or not to take away the life of man, if you strive to cut off and destroy the remembrance of God? It is vain, therefore, to talk of righteousness apart from religion. Such righteousness has no more beauty than the trunk of a body deprived of its head. Nor is religion the principal part merely: it is the very soul by which the whole lives and breathes. Without the fear of God, men do not even observe justice and charity among themselves. We say, then, that the worship of God is the beginning and foundation of righteousness; and that wherever it is wanting, any degree of equity, or continence, or temperance, existing among men themselves, is empty and frivolous in the sight of God. We call it the source and soul of righteousness, in as much as men learn to live together temperately, and without injury, when they revere God as the judge of right and wrong. In the First Table, accordingly, he teaches us how to cultivate piety, and the proper duties of religion in which his worship consists; in the second, he shows how, in the fear of his name, we are to conduct ourselves towards our fellow-men. Hence, as related by the Evangelists (Mt. 22:37;

Luke 10:27), our Saviour summed up the whole Law in two heads—viz. to love the Lord with all our heart, with all our soul, and with all our strength, and our neighbour as ourselves. You see how, of the two parts under which he comprehends the whole Law, he devotes the one to God, and assigns the other to mankind.

12. But although the whole Law is contained in two heads, yet, in order to remove every pretext for excuse, the Lord has been pleased to deliver more fully and explicitly in Ten Commandments, every thing relating to his own honour, fear, and love, as well as every thing relating to the charity which, for his sake, he enjoins us to have towards our fellowmen. Nor is it an unprofitable study to consider the division of the commandments, provided we remember that it is one of those matters in which every man should have full freedom of judgment, and on account of which, difference of opinion should not lead to contention. We are, indeed, under the necessity of making this observation, lest the division which we are to adopt should excite the surprise or derision of the reader, as novel or of recent invention.

There is no room for controversy as to the fact, that the Law is divided into ten heads since this is repeatedly sanctioned by divine authority. The question, therefore, is not as to the number of the parts, but the method of dividing them. Those who adopt a division which gives three commandments to the First Table, and throws the remaining seven into the Second Table, expunge the commandment concerning images from the list, or at least conceal it under the first, though there cannot be a doubt that it was distinctly set down by the Lord as a separate commandment; whereas the tenth, which prohibits the coveting of what belongs to our neighbour, they absurdly break down into two. Moreover, it will soon appear, that this method of dividing was unknown in a purer age. Others count four commandments in the First Table as we do, but for the first set down the introductory promise, without adding the precept. But because I must hold, unless I am convinced by clear evidence to the contrary, that the "ten words" mentioned by Moses are Ten Commandments and because I see that number arranged in most admirable order, I must, while I leave them to hold their own opinion, follow what appears to me better established—viz. that what they make to be the first commandment is of the nature of a preface to the whole Law, that thereafter follow four commandments in the First Table, and six in the Second, in the order in which they will here be reviewed. This division Origin adopts without discussion, as if it had been every where received in his day. It is also adopted by Augustine, in his book addressed to Boniface, where, in enumerating the commandments, he follows this order, Let one God be religiously obeyed, let no idol be worshipped, let the name of God be not used in vain; while previously he had made separate mention of the typical commandment of the Sabbath. Elsewhere, indeed, he expresses approbation of the first division, but on too slight grounds, because, by the number three (making the First Table consist of three commandments), the mystery of the Trinity would be better manifested. Even here, however, he does not disguise his opinion, that in other respects, our division is more to his mind. Besides these, we are supported by the author of an unfinished work on Matthew. Josephus, no doubt with the general consent of his age, assigns five commandments to each table. This, while repugnant to reason, inasmuch as it confounds the distinction between piety and charity, is also refuted by the authority of our Saviour, who in Matthew places the command to honour parents in the list of those belonging to the Second Table (Mt. 19:19). Let us now hear God speaking in his own words.

First Commandment.

I AM THE LORD THY GOD, WHICH BROUGHT THEE OUT OF THE LAND OF EGYPT, OUT OF THE HOUSE OF BONDAGE. THOU SHALT HAVE NO OTHER GODS BEFORE ME.

13. Whether you take the former sentence as a part of the commandment, or read it separately is to me a matter of indifference, provided you grant that it is a kind of preface to the whole Law. In enacting laws, the first thing to be guarded against is their being forthwith abrogated by contempt. The Lord, therefore, takes care, in the first place, that this shall not happen to the Law about to be delivered, by introducing it with a triple sanction. He claims to himself power and authority to command, that he may impress the chosen people with the necessity of obedience; he holds forth a promise of favour, as a means of alluring them to the study of holiness; and he reminds them of his kindness, that he may convict them of ingratitude, if they fail to make a suitable return. By the name, Lord, are denoted power and lawful dominion. If all things are from him, and by him consist, they ought in justice to bear reference to him, as Paul says (Rom. 11:36). This name, therefore, is in itself sufficient to bring us under the authority of the divine majesty: for

it were monstrous for us to wish to withdraw from the dominion of him, out of whom we cannot even exist.

14. After showing that he has a right to command, and to be obeyed, he next, in order not to seem to drag men by mere necessity, but to allure them, graciously declares, that he is the God of the Church. For the mode of expression implies, that there is a mutual relation included in the promise, "I will be their God, and they shall be my people" (Jer. 31:33). Hence Christ infers the immortality of Abraham, Isaac, and Jacob, from the fact that God had declared himself to be their God (Mt. 22:32). It is, therefore, the same as if he had said, I have chosen you to myself, as a people to whom I shall not only do good in the present life, but also bestow felicity in the life to come. The end contemplated in this is adverted to in the Law, in various passages. For when the Lord condescends in mercy to honour us so far as to admit us to partnership with his chosen people, he chooses us, as Moses says, "to be a holy people," "a peculiar people unto himself," to "keep all his commandments" (Deut. 7:6; 14:2; 26:18). Hence the exhortation, "Ye shall be holy; for I the Lord your God am holy" (Lev. 19:2). These two considerations form the ground of the remonstrance, "A son honoureth his father, and a servant his master; if then I be a father, where is mine honour? and if I be a master, where is my fear? saith the Lord of hosts" (Mal. 1:6).

15. Next follows a commemoration of his kindness, which ought to produce upon us an impression strong in proportion to the detestation in which ingratitude is held even among men. It is true, indeed, he was reminding Israel of a deliverance then recent, but one which, on account of its wondrous magnitude, was to be for ever memorable to the remotest posterity. Moreover, it is most appropriate to the matter in hand. For the Lord intimates that they were delivered from miserable bondage, that they might learn to yield prompt submission and obedience to him as the author of their freedom. In like manners to keep us to his true worship, he often describes himself by certain epithets which distinguish his sacred Deity from all idols and fictitious gods. For, as I formerly observed, such is our proneness to vanity and presumption, that as soon as God is named, our minds, unable to guard against error, immediately fly off to some empty delusion. In applying a remedy to this disease, God distinguishes his divinity by certain titles, and thus confines us, as it were, within distinct boundaries, that we may not wander hither and thither, and feign some new deity for ourselves, abandoning the living God, and setting up an idol. For this reason, whenever the Prophets would bring him properly before us, they invest, and, as it were, surround him with those characters under which he had manifested himself to the people of Israel. When he is called the God of Abraham, or the God of Israel, when he is stationed in the temple of Jerusalem, between the Cherubim, these, and similar modes of expression, do not confine him to one place or one people, but are used merely for the purpose of fixing our thoughts on that God who so manifested himself in the covenant which he made with Israel, as to make it unlawful on any account to deviate from the strict view there given of his character. Let it be understood, then, that mention is made of deliverance, in order to make the Jews submit with greater readiness to that God who justly claims them as his own. We again, instead of supposing that the matter has no reference to us, should reflect that the bondage of Israel in Egypt was a type of that spiritual bondage, in the fetters of which we are all bound, until the heavenly avenger delivers us by the power of his own arm, and transports us into his free kingdom. Therefore, as in old times, when he would gather together the scattered Israelites to the worship of his name, he rescued them from the intolerable tyranny of Pharaoh, so all who profess him now are delivered from the fatal tyranny of the devil, of which that of Egypt was only a type. There is no man, therefore, whose mind ought not to be aroused to give heed to the Law, which, as he is told, proceeded from the supreme King, from him who, as he gave all their being, justly destines and directs them to himself as their proper end. There is no man, I say, who should not hasten to embrace the Lawgiver, whose commands, he knows, he has been specially appointed to obey, from whose kindness he anticipates an abundance of all good, and even a blessed immortality, and to whose wondrous power and mercy he is indebted for deliverance from the jaws of death.

16. The authority of the Law being founded and established, God delivers his First Commandment—

THOU SHALT HAVE NO OTHER GODS BEFORE ME. The purport of this commandment is, that the Lord will have himself alone to be exalted in his people, and claims the entire possession of them as his own. That it may be so, he orders us to abstain from ungodliness and superstition of every kind, by which the glory of his divinity is diminished or obscured; and, for the same reason, he requires us to worship and adore him with truly pious zeal. The simple terms used obviously amount to this. For seeing we cannot have God without embracing everything which belongs to him, the prohibition against having strange gods means, that nothing which belongs to him is to be transferred to any other.

The duties which we owe to God are innumerable, but they seem to admit of being not improperly reduced to four heads: Adoration, with its accessory spiritual submission of conscience, Trust, Invocation, Thanksgiving. By Adoration, I mean the veneration and worship which we render to him when we do homage to his majesty; and hence I make part of it to consist in bringing our consciences into subjection to his Law. Trust, is secure resting in him under a recognition of his perfections, when, ascribing to him all power, wisdom, justice, goodness, and truth, we consider ourselves happy in having been brought into intercourse with him. Invocation, may be defined the retaking of ourselves to his promised aid as the only resource in every case of need. Thanksgiving, is the gratitude which ascribes to him the praise of all our blessings. As the Lord does not allow these to be derived from any other quarter, so he demands that they shall be referred entirely to himself. It is not enough to refrain from other gods. We must, at the same time, devote ourselves wholly to him, not acting like certain impious despisers, who regard it as the shortest method, to hold all religious observance in derision. But here precedence must be given to true religion, which will direct our minds to the living God. When duly imbued with the knowledge of him, the whole aim of our lives will be to revere, fear, and worship his majesty, to enjoy a share in his blessings, to have recourse to him in every difficulty, to acknowledge, laud, and celebrate the magnificence of his works, to make him, as it were, the sole aim of all our actions. Next, we must beware of superstition, by which our minds are turned aside from the true God, and carried to and fro after a multiplicity of gods. Therefore, if we are contented with one God, let us call to mind what was formerly observed, that all fictitious gods are to be driven far away, and that the worship which he claims for himself is not to be mutilated. Not a particle of his glory is to be withheld: everything belonging to him must be reserved to him entire. The words, "before me," go to increase the indignity, God being provoked to jealousy whenever we substitute our fictions in his stead; just as an unfaithful wife stings her husband's heart more deeply when her adultery is committed openly before his eyes. Therefore, God having by his present power and grace declared that he had respect to the people whom he had chosen, now, in order to deter them from the wickedness of revolt, warns them that they cannot adopt strange gods without his being witness and spectator of the sacrilege. To the audacity of so doing is added the very great impiety of supposing that they can mock the eye of God with their evasions. Far from this the Lord proclaims that everything which we design, plan, or execute, lies open to his sight. Our conscience must, therefore, keep aloof from the most distant thought of revolt, if we would have our worship approved by the Lord. The glory of his Godhead must be maintained entire and incorrupt, not merely by external profession, but as under his eye, which penetrates the inmost recesses of his heart.

Second Commandment.

THOU SHALT NOT MAKE UNTO THEE ANY GRAVEN IMAGE, OR ANY LIKENESS OF ANYTHING THAT IS IN HEAVEN ABOVE, OR THAT IS IN THE EARTH BENEATH, OR THAT IS IN THE WATER UNDER THE EARTH: THOU SHALT NOT BOW DOWN THYSELF TO THEM, NOR SERVE THEM.

17. As in the first commandment the Lord declares that he is one, and that besides him no gods must be either worshipped or imagined, so he here more plainly declares what his nature is, and what the kind of worship with which he is to be honoured, in order that we may not presume to form any carnal idea of him. The purport of the commandment, therefore, is, that he will not have his legitimate worship profaned by superstitious rites. Wherefore, in general, he calls us entirely away from the carnal frivolous observances which our stupid minds are wont to devise after forming some gross idea of the divine nature, while, at the same time, he instructs us in the worship which is legitimate, namely, spiritual worship of his own appointment. The grossest vice here prohibited is external idolatry. This commandment consists of two parts. The former curbs the licentious daring which would subject the incomprehensible God to our senses, or represent him under any visible shape. The latter forbids the worship of images on any religious ground. There is, moreover, a brief enumeration of all the forms by which the Deity was usually represented by heathen and superstitious nations. By "any thing which is in heaven above" is meant the sun, the moon, and the stars, perhaps also birds, as in Deuteronomy, where the meaning is explained, there is mention of birds as well as stars (Deut. 4:15). I would not have made this observation, had I not seen that some absurdly apply it to the angels. The other particulars I pass, as requiring no explanation. We have already shown clearly enough (Book 1. chap. 11, 12) that every visible shape of Deity which man

devises is diametrically opposed to the divine nature; and, therefore, that the moment idols appear, true religion is corrupted and adulterated.

18. The threatening subjoined ought to have no little effect in shaking off our lethargy. It is in the following terms:—

I THE LORD THY GOD AM A JEALOUS GOD, VISITING THE INIQUITY OF THE FATHERS UPON THE CHILDREN UNTO THE THIRD AND FOURTH GENERATION OF THEM THAT HATE ME; AND SHEWING MERCY UNTO THOUSANDS OF THEM THAT LOVE ME, AND KEEP MY COMMANDMENTS. The meaning here is the same as if he had said, that our duty is to cleave to him alone. To induce us to this, he proclaims his authority which he will not permit to be impaired or despised with impunity. It is true, the word used is *El*, which means God; but as it is derived from a word meaning *strength*, I have had no hesitations in order to express the sense more fully, so to render it as inserted on the margin. Secondly, he calls himself *jealous*, because he cannot bear a partner. Thirdly, he declares that he will vindicate his majesty and glory, if any transfer it either to the creatures or to graven images; and that not by a simple punishment of brief duration, but one extending to the third and fourth generation of such as imitate the impiety of their progenitors. In like manner, he declares his constant mercy and kindness to the remote posterity of those who love him, and keep his Law. The Lord very frequently addresses us in the character of a husband; the union by which he connects us with himself, when he receives us into the bosom of the Church, having some resemblance to that of holy wedlock, because founded on mutual faith. As he performs all the offices of a true and faithful husband, so he stipulates for love and conjugal chastity from us; that is, that we do not prostitute our souls to Satan, to be defiled with foul carnal lusts. Hence, when he rebukes the Jews for their apostasy, he complains that they have cast off chastity, and polluted themselves with adultery. Therefore, as the purer and chaster the husband is, the more grievously is he offended when he sees his wife inclining to a rival; so the Lord, who has betrothed us to himself in truth, declares that he burns with the hottest jealousy whenever, neglecting the purity of his holy marriage, we defile ourselves with abominable lusts, and especially when the worship of his Deity, which ought to have been most carefully kept unimpaired, is transferred to another, or adulterated with some superstition; since, in this way, we not only violate our plighted troth, but defile the nuptial couch, by giving access to adulterers.

19. In the threatening we must attend to what is meant when God declares that he will visit the iniquity of the fathers upon the children unto the third and fourth generation. It seems inconsistent with the equity of the divine procedure to punish the innocent for another's fault; and the Lord himself declares, that "the son shall not bear the iniquity of the father" (Ezek. 18:20). But still we meet more than once with a declaration as to the postponing of the punishment of the sins of fathers to future generations. Thus Moses repeatedly addresses the Lord as "visiting the iniquity of the fathers upon the children unto the third and fourth generation" (Num. 14:18). In like manner, Jeremiah, "Thou showest lovingkindness unto thousands, and recompenses the iniquity of the fathers into the bosom of their children after them" (Jer. 32:18). Some feeling sadly perplexed how to solve this difficulty, think it is to be understood of temporal punishments only, which it is said sons may properly bear for the sins of their parents, because they are often inflicted for their own safety. This is indeed true; for Isaiah declared to Hezekiah, that his children should be stript of the kingdom, and carried away into captivity, for a sin which he had committed (Isa. 39:7); and the households of Pharaoh and Abimelech were made to suffer for an injury done to Abraham (Gen. 12:17; 20:3–18). But the attempt to solve the question in this way is an evasion rather than a true interpretation. For the punishment denounced here and in similar passages is too great to be confined within the limits of the present life. We must therefore understand it to mean, that a curse from the Lord righteously falls not only on the head of the guilty individual, but also on all his lineage. When it has fallen, what can be anticipated but that the father, being deprived of the Spirit of God, will live most flagitiously; that the son, being in like manner forsaken of the Lord, because of his father's iniquity, will follow the same road to destruction; and be followed in his turn by succeeding generations, forming a seed of evil-doers?

20. First, let us examine whether such punishment is inconsistent with the divine justice. If human nature is universally condemned, those on whom the Lord does not bestow the communication of his grace must be doomed to destruction; nevertheless, they perish by their own iniquity, not by unjust hatred on the part of God. There is no room to expostulate, and ask why the grace of God does not forward their salvation as it does that of others. Therefore, when God punishes the wicked and flagitious for their crimes, by depriving their families of

his grace for many generations, who will dare to bring a charge against him for this most righteous vengeance? But it will be said, the Lord, on the contrary, declares, that the son shall not suffer for the father's sin (Ezek. 18:20). Observe the scope of that passage. The Israelites, after being subjected to a long period of uninterrupted calamities, had begun to say, as a proverb, that their fathers had eaten the sour grape, and thus set the children's teeth on edge; meaning that they, though in themselves righteous and innocent, were paying the penalty of sins committed by their parents, and this more from the implacable anger than the duly tempered severity of God. The prophet declares it was not so: that they were punished for their own wickedness; that it was not in accordance with the justice of God that a righteous son should suffer for the iniquity of a wicked father; and that nothing of the kind was exemplified in what they suffered. For, if the visitation of which we now speak is accomplished when God withdraws from the children of the wicked the light of his truth and the other helps to salvation, the only way in which they are accursed for their fathers' wickedness is in being blinded and abandoned by God, and so left to walk in their parents' steps. The misery which they suffer in time, and the destruction to which they are finally doomed, are thus punishments inflicted by divine justice, not for the sins of others, but for their own iniquity.

21. On the other hand, there is a promise of mercy to thousands—a promise which is frequently mentioned in Scripture, and forms an article in the solemn covenant made with the Church—I will be "a God unto thee, and to thy seed after thee" (Gen. 17:7). With reference to this, Solomon says, "The just man walketh in his integrity: his children are blessed after him" (Prov. 20:7); not only in consequence of a religious education (though this certainly is by no means unimportant), but in consequence of the blessing promised in the covenant—viz. that the divine favour will dwell for ever in the families of the righteous. Herein is excellent consolation to believers, and great ground of terror to the wicked; for if, after death, the mere remembrance of righteousness and iniquity have such an influence on the divine procedure, that his blessing rests on the posterity of the righteous, and his curse on the posterity of the wicked, much more must it rest on the heads of the individuals themselves. Notwithstanding of this, however, the offspring of the wicked sometimes amends, while that of believers degenerates; because the Almighty has not here laid down an inflexible rule which might derogate from his free election. For the consolation of the righteous, and the dismay of the sinner, it is enough that the threatening itself is not vain or nugatory, although it does not always take effect. For, as the temporal punishments inflicted on a few of the wicked are proofs of the divine wrath against sin, and of the future judgment that will ultimately overtake all sinners, though many escape with impunity even to the end of their lives, so, when the Lord gives one example of blessing a son for his father's sake, by visiting him in mercy and kindness, it is a proof of constant and unfailing favour to his worshipers. On the other hand, when, in any single instance, he visits the iniquity of the father on the son, he gives intimation of the judgment which awaits all the reprobate for their own iniquities. The certainty of this is the principal thing here taught. Moreover, the Lord, as it were by the way, commends the riches of his mercy by extending it to thousands, while he limits his vengeance to four generations.

Third Commandment.

THOU SHALT NOT TAKE THE NAME OF THE LORD THY GOD IN VAIN.

22. The purport of this Commandment is, that the majesty of the name of God is to be held sacred. In sum, therefore, it means, that we must not profane it by using it irreverently or contemptuously. This prohibition implies a corresponding precept—viz. that it be our study and care to treat his name with religious veneration. Wherefore it becomes us to regulate our minds and our tongues, so as never to think or speak of God and his mysteries without reverence and great soberness, and never, in estimating his works, to have any feeling towards him but one of deep veneration. We must, I say, steadily observe the three following things:—*First*, Whatever our mind conceives of him, whatever our tongue utters, must bespeak his excellence, and correspond to the sublimity of his sacred name; in short, must be fitted to extol its greatness. *Secondly*, We must not rashly and preposterously pervert his sacred word and adorable mysteries to purposes of ambition, or avarice, or amusement, but, according as they bear the impress of his dignity, must always maintain them in due honour and esteem. *Lastly*, We must not detract from or throw obloquy upon his works, as miserable men are wont insultingly to do, but must laud every action which we attribute to him as wise, and just, and good. This is to sanctify the name of God. When we act otherwise, his name is profaned with vain and wicked abuse, because it is applied to a purpose for-

eign to that to which it is consecrated. Were there nothing worse, in being deprived of its dignity it is gradually brought into contempt. But if there is so much evil in the rash and unseasonable employment of the divine name, there is still more evil in its being employed for nefarious purposes, as is done by those who use it in necromancy, cursing, illicit exorcisms, and other impious incantations. But the Commandment refers especially to the case of oaths, in which a perverse employment of the divine name is particularly detestable; and this it does the more effectually to deter us from every species of profanation. That the thing here commanded relates to the worship of God, and the reverence due to his name, and not to the equity which men are to cultivate towards each other, is apparent from this, that afterwards, in the Second Table, there is a condemnation of the perjury and false testimony by which human society is injured, and that the repetition would be superfluous, if, in this Commandment, the duty of charity were handled. Moreover, this is necessary even for distinction, because, as was observed, God has, for good reason, divided his Law into two tables. The inference then is, that God here vindicates his own right, and defends his sacred name, but does not teach the duties which men owe to men.

23. In the first place, we must consider what an oath is. An oath, then, is calling God to witness that what we say is true. Execrations being manifestly insulting to God, are unworthy of being classed among oaths. That an oath, when duly taken, is a species of divine worship, appears from many passages of Scripture, as when Isaiah prophesies of the admission of the Assyrians and Egyptians to a participation in the covenant, he says, "In that day shall five cities in the land of Egypt speak the language of Canaan, and swear to the Lord of hosts" (Isaiah 19:18). Swearing by the name of the Lord here means, that they will make a profession of religion. In like manner, speaking of the extension of the Redeemer's kingdom, it is said, "He who blesseth himself in the earth shall bless himself in the God of truth: and he that sweareth in the earth shall swear by the God of truth" (Isaiah 65:16). In Jeremiah it is said, "If they will diligently learn the ways of my people, to swear by my name, The Lord liveth; as they taught my people to swear by Baal; then shall they be built in the midst of my people" (Jer. 12:16). By appealing to the name of the Lord, and calling him to witness, we are justly said to declare our own religious veneration of him. For we thus acknowledge that he is eternal and unchangeable truth, inasmuch as we not only call upon him, in preference to others, as a fit witness to the truth, but as its only assertor, able to bring hidden things to light, a discerner of the hearts. When human testimony fails, we appeal to God as witness, especially when the matter to be proved lies hid in the conscience. For which reason, the Lord is grievously offended with those who swear by strange gods, and construes such swearing as a proof of open revolt, "Thy children have forsaken me, and sworn by them that are no gods" (Jer. 5:7). The heinousness of the offence is declared by the punishment denounced against it, "I will cut off them that swear by the Lord, and that swear by Malcham" (Zeph. 1:4, 5).

24. Understanding that the Lord would have our oaths to be a species of divine worship, we must be the more careful that they do not, instead of worship, contain insult, or contempt, and vilification. It is no slight insult to swear by him and do it falsely: hence in the Law this is termed profanation (Lev. 19:12). For if God is robbed of his truth, what is it that remains? Without truth he could not be God. But assuredly he is robbed of his truth, when he is made the approver and attester of what is false. Hence, when Joshua is endeavouring to make Achan confess the truth, he says, "My son, give, I pray thee, glory to the Lord God of Israel" (Joshua 7:19); intimating, that grievous dishonour is done to God when men swear by him falsely. And no wonder; for, as far as in them lies, his sacred name is in a manner branded with falsehood. That this mode of expression was common among the Jews whenever any one was called upon to take an oath, is evident from a similar obtestation used by the Pharisees, as given in John (John 9:24); Scripture reminds us of the caution which we ought to use by employing such expressions as the following:—"As the Lord liveth;" "God do so and more also;" "I call God for a record upon my soul." Such expressions intimate, that we cannot call God to witness our statement, without imprecating his vengeance for perjury if it is false.

25. The name of God is vulgarised and vilified when used in oaths, which, though true, are superfluous. This, too, is to take his name in vain. Wherefore, it is not sufficient to abstain from perjury, unless we, at the same time, remember that an oath is not appointed or allowed for passion or pleasure, but for necessity; and that, therefore, a licentious use is made of it by him who uses it on any other than necessary occasions. Moreover, no case of necessity can be pretended, unless where some purpose of religion or charity is to be served. In this matter, great sin is committed in the present day—sin the more intolerable in this, that its frequency has made it cease to be regarded as a fault, though it certainly is not

accounted trivial before the judgment-seat of God. The name of God is everywhere profaned by introducing it indiscriminately in frivolous discourse; and the evil is disregarded, because it has been long and audaciously persisted in with impunity. The commandment of the Lord, however, stands; the penalty also stands, and will one day receive effect. Special vengeance will be executed on those who have taken the name of God in vain. Another form of violation is exhibited, when, with manifest impiety, we, in our oaths, substitute the holy servants of God for God himself, thus conferring upon them the glory of his Godhead. It is not without cause the Lord has, by a special commandment, required us to swear by his name, and, by a special prohibition, forbidden us to swear by other gods. The Apostle gives a clear attestation to the same effect, when he says, that "men verily swear by the greater;" but that "when God made promise to Abraham, because he could swear by no greater, he sware by himself;" (Heb. 6:16, 13).

26. The Anabaptists, not content with this moderate use of oaths, condemn all, without exception, on the ground of our Saviour's general prohibition, "I say unto you, Swear not at all:" "Let your speech be Yea, yea; Nay, nay: for whatsoever is more than these cometh of evil" (Mt. 5:34; James 5:12). In this way, they inconsiderately make a stumbling-stone of Christ, setting him in opposition to the Father, as if he had descended into the world to annul his decrees. In the Law, the Almighty not only permits an oath as a thing that is lawful (this were amply sufficient), but, in a case of necessity, actually commands it (Exod. 22:11). Christ again declares, that he and his Father are one; that he only delivers what was commanded of his Father; that his doctrine is not his own, but his that sent him (John 10:18, 30; 7:16). What then? Will they make God contradict himself, by approving and commanding at one time, what he afterwards prohibits and condemns? But as there is some difficulty in what our Saviour says on the subject of swearing, it may be proper to consider it a little. Here, however, we shall never arrive at the true meaning, unless we attend to the design of Christ, and the subject of which he is treating. His purpose was, neither to relax nor to curtail the Law, but to restore the true and genuine meaning, which had been greatly corrupted by the false glosses of the Scribes and Pharisees. If we attend to this we shall not suppose that Christ condemned all oaths but those only which transgressed the rule of the Law. It is evident, from the oaths themselves, that the people were accustomed to think it enough if they avoided perjury, whereas the Law prohibits not perjury merely, but also vain and superfluous oaths. Therefore our Lord, who is the best interpreter of the Law, reminds them that there is a sin not only in perjury, but in swearing. How in swearing? Namely, by swearing vainly. Those oaths, however, which are authorised by the Law, he leaves safe and free. Those who condemn oaths think their argument invincible when they fasten on the expression, *not at all*. The expression applies not to the word *swear*, but to the subjoined forms of oaths. For part of the error consisted in their supposing, that when they swore by the heaven and the earth, they did not touch the name of God. The Lord, therefore, after cutting off the principal source of prevarication, deprives them of all subterfuges, warning them against supposing that they escape guilt by suppressing the name of God, and appealing to heaven and earth. For it ought here to be observed in passing, that although the name of God is not expressed, yet men swear by him in using indirect forms, as when they swear by the light of life, by the bread they eat, by their baptism, or any other pledges of the divine liberality towards them. Some erroneously suppose that our Saviour, in that passage, rebukes superstition, by forbidding men to swear by heaven and earth, and Jerusalem. He rather refutes the sophistical subtilty of those who thought it nothing vainly to utter indirect oaths, imagining that they thus spared the holy name of God, whereas that name is inscribed on each of his mercies. The case is different, when any mortal living or dead, or an angel, is substituted in the place of God, as in the vile form devised by flattery in heathen nations, "*By the life or genius of the king*"; for, in this case, the false apotheosis obscures and impairs the glory of the one God. But when nothing else is intended than to confirm what is said by an appeal to the holy name of God, although it is done indirectly, yet his majesty is insulted by all frivolous oaths. Christ strips this abuse of every vain pretext when he says "Swear not at all". To the same effect is the passage in which James uses the words of our Saviour above quoted (James 5:12). For this rash swearing has always prevailed in the world, notwithstanding that it is a profanation of the name of God. If you refer the words, "*not at all*", to the act itself, as if every oath, without exception, were unlawful, what will be the use of the explanation which immediately follows—Neither by heaven, neither by the earth, &c.? These words make it clear, that the object in view was to meet the cavils by which the Jews thought they could extenuate their fault.

27. Every person of sound judgment must now see that in that passage our Lord merely condemned those oaths

which were forbidden by the Law. For he who in his life exhibited a model of the perfection which he taught, did not object to oaths whenever the occasion required them; and the disciples, who doubtless in all things obeyed their Master, followed the same rule. Who will dare to say that Paul would have sworn (Rom. 1:9; 2 Cor. 1:23) if an oath had been altogether forbidden? But when the occasion calls for it, he adjures without any scruple, and sometimes even imprecates. The question, however, is not yet disposed of. For some think that the only oaths exempted from the prohibition are public oaths, such as those which are administered to us by the magistrate, or independent states employ in ratifying treaties, or the people take when they swear allegiance to their sovereign, or the soldier in the case of the military oath, and others of a similar description. To this class they refer (and justly) those protestations in the writings of Paul, which assert the dignity of the Gospel; since the Apostles, in discharging their office, were not private individuals, but the public servants of God. I certainly deny not that such oaths are the safest because they are most strongly supported by passages of Scripture. The magistrate is enjoined, in a doubtful matter, to put the witness upon oath; and he in his turn to answer upon oath; and an Apostle says, that in this way there is an end of all strife (Heb. 6:16). In this commandment, both parties are fully approved. Nay, we may observe, that among the ancient heathens a public and solemn oath was held in great reverence, while those common oaths which were indiscriminately used were in little or no estimation, as if they thought that, in regard to them, the Deity did not interpose. Private oaths used soberly, sacredly, and reverently, on necessary occasions, it were perilous to condemn, supported as they are by reason and example. For if private individuals are permitted, in a grave and serious matter, to appeal to God as a judge, much more may they appeal to him as a witness. Your brother charges you with perfidy. You, as bound by the duties of charity, labour to clear yourself from the charge. He will on no account be satisfied. If, through his obstinate malice, your good name is brought into jeopardy, you can appeal, without offence, to the judgment of God, that he may in time manifest your innocence. If the terms are weighed, it will be found that it is a less matter to call upon him to be witness; and I therefore see not how it can be called unlawful to do so. And there is no want of examples. If it is pretended that the oath which Abraham and Isaac made with Abimelech was of a public nature, that by which Jacob and Laban bound themselves in mutual league was private. Boaz, though a private man, confirmed his promise of marriage to Ruth in the same way. Obadiah, too, a just man, and one that feared God, though a private individual, in seeking to persuade Elijah, asseverates with an oath. I hold, therefore, that there is no better rule than so to regulate our oaths that they shall neither be rash, frivolous, promiscuous, nor passionate, but be made to serve a just necessity; in other words, to vindicate the glory of God, or promote the edification of a brother. This is the end of the Commandment.

Fourth Commandment.

REMEMBER THE SABBATH DAY TO KEEP IT HOLY. SIX DAYS SHALT THOU LABOUR AND DO ALL THY WORK: BUT THE SEVENTH DAY IS THE SABBATH OF THE LORD THY GOD. IN IT THOU SHALT NOT DO ANY WORK, &C.

28. The purport of the commandment is, that being dead to our own affections and works, we meditate on the kingdom of God, and in order to such meditation, have recourse to the means which he has appointed. But as this commandment stands in peculiar circumstances apart from the others, the mode of exposition must be somewhat different. Early Christian writers are wont to call it typical, as containing the external observance of a day which was abolished with the other types on the advent of Christ. This is indeed true; but it leaves the half of the matter untouched. Wherefore, we must look deeper for our exposition, and attend to three cases in which it appears to me that the observance of this commandment consists. First, under the rest of the seventh days the divine Lawgiver meant to furnish the people of Israel with a type of the spiritual rest by which believers were to cease from their own works, and allow God to work in them. Secondly he meant that there should be a stated day on which they should assemble to hear the Law, and perform religious rites, or which, at least, they should specially employ in meditating on his works, and be thereby trained to piety. Thirdly, he meant that servants, and those who lived under the authority of others, should be indulged with a day of rest, and thus have some intermission from labour.

29. We are taught in many passages that this adumbration of spiritual rest held a primary place in the Sabbath. Indeed, there is no commandment the observance of which the Almighty more strictly enforces. When he

would intimate by the Prophets that religion was entirely subverted, he complains that his sabbaths were polluted, violated, not kept, not hallowed; as if, after it was neglected, there remained nothing in which he could be honoured. The observance of it he eulogises in the highest terms, and hence, among other divine privileges, the faithful set an extraordinary value on the revelation of the Sabbath. In Nehemiah, the Levites, in the public assembly, thus speak: "Thou madest known unto them thy holy sabbath, and commandedst them precepts, statutes, and laws, by the hand of Moses thy servant." You see the singular honour which it holds among all the precepts of the Law. All this tends to celebrate the dignity of the mystery, which is most admirably expressed by Moses and Ezekiel. Thus in Exodus: "Verily my sabbaths shall ye keep: for it is a sign between me and you throughout your generations; that ye may know that I am the Lord that does sanctify you. Ye shall keep my sabbath therefore; for it is holy unto you: every one that defileth it shall surely be put to death: for whosoever does any work therein, that soul shall be cut off from among his people. Six days may work be done; but in the seventh is the sabbath of rest, holy to the Lord: whosoever does any work in the sabbath day, he shall surely be put to death. Wherefore the children of Israel shall keep the sabbath, to observe the sabbath throughout their generations, for a perpetual covenant. It is a sign between me and the children of Israel for ever" (Exodus 31:13–17). Ezekiel is still more full, but the sum of what he says amounts to this: that the sabbath is a sign by which Israel might know that God is their sanctifier. If our sanctification consists in the mortification of our own will, the analogy between the external sign and the thing signified is most appropriate. We must rest entirely, in order that God may work in us; we must resign our own will, yield up our heart, and abandon all the lusts of the flesh. In short, we must desist from all the acts of our own mind, that God working in us, we may rest in him, as the Apostle also teaches (Heb. 3:13; 4:3, 9).

30. This complete cessation was represented to the Jews by the observance of one day in seven, which, that it might be more religiously attended to, the Lord recommended by his own example. For it is no small incitement to the zeal of man to know that he is engaged in imitating his Creator. Should any one expect some secret meaning in the number seven, this being in Scripture the number for perfection, it may have been selected, not without cause, to denote perpetuity. In accordance with this, Moses concludes his description of the succession of day and night on the same day on which he relates that the Lord rested from his works. Another probable reason for the number may be, that the Lord intended that the Sabbath never should be completed before the arrival of the last day. We here begin our blessed rest in him, and daily make new progress in it; but because we must still wage an incessant warfare with the flesh, it shall not be consummated until the fulfilment of the prophecy of Isaiah: "From one new moon to another, and from one sabbath to another, shall all flesh come to worship before me, saith the Lord" (Isaiah 66:23); in other words, when God shall be "all in all" (I Cor. 15:28). It may seem, therefore, that by the seventh day the Lord delineated to his people the future perfection of his Sabbath on the last day, that by continual meditation on the sabbath, they might throughout their whole lives aspire to this perfection.

31. Should these remarks on the number seem to any somewhat far-fetched, I have no objection to their taking it more simply: that the Lord appointed a certain day on which his people might be trained, under the tutelage of the Law, to meditate constantly on the spiritual rest, and fixed upon the seventh, either because he foresaw it would be sufficient, or in order that his own example might operate as a stronger stimulus; or, at least to remind men that the Sabbath was appointed for no other purpose than to render them conformable to their Creator. It is of little consequence which of these be adopted, provided we lose not sight of the principal thing delineated—viz. the mystery of perpetual resting from our works. To the contemplation of this, the Jews were every now and then called by the prophets, lest they should think a carnal cessation from labour sufficient. Beside the passages already quoted, there is the following: "If thou turn away thy foot from the sabbath, from doing thy pleasure on my holy day; and call the sabbath a delight, the holy of the Lord, honourable; and shalt honour him, not doing thine own ways, nor finding thine own pleasure, nor speaking thine own words: then shalt thou delight thyself in the Lord" (Isaiah 58:13, 14). Still there can be no doubt, that, on the advent of our Lord Jesus Christ, the ceremonial part of the commandment was abolished. He is the truth, at whose presence all the emblems vanish; the body, at the sight of which the shadows disappear. He, I say, is the true completion of the sabbath: "We are buried with him by baptism unto death: that like as Christ was raised up from the dead by the glory of the Father, even so we should walk in newness of life" (Rom. 6:4). Hence, as the Apostle elsewhere says, "Let no man therefore judge you in meat, or in drink, or in respect of an holiday, or of the

new moon, or of the sabbath days; which are a shadow of things to come; but the body is of Christ" (Col. 2:16, 17); meaning by body the whole essence of the truth, as is well explained in that passage. This is not contented with one day, but requires the whole course of our lives, until being completely dead to ourselves, we are filled with the life of God. Christians, therefore, should have nothing to do with a superstitious observance of days.

32. The two other cases ought not to be classed with ancient shadows, but are adapted to every age. The sabbath being abrogated, there is still room among us, first, to assemble on stated days for the hearing of the Word, the breaking of the mystical bread, and public prayer; and, secondly, to give our servants and labourers relaxation from labour. It cannot be doubted that the Lord provided for both in the commandment of the Sabbath. The former is abundantly evinced by the mere practice of the Jews. The latter Moses has expressed in Deuteronomy in the following terms: "The seventh day is the sabbath of the Lord thy God: in it thou shalt not do any work, thou, nor thy son, nor thy daughter, nor thy man-servant, nor thy maid-servant;—that thy man-servant and thy maid-servant may rest as well as thou" (Deut. 5:14). Likewise in Exodus, "That thine ox and thine ass may rest, and the son of thy handmaid, and the stranger, may be refreshed" (Exod. 23:12). Who can deny that both are equally applicable to us as to the Jews? Religious meetings are enjoined us by the word of God; their necessity, experience itself sufficiently demonstrates. But unless these meetings are stated, and have fixed days allotted to them, how can they be held? We must, as the apostle expresses it, do all things decently and in orders (1 Cor. 14:40). So impossible, however, would it be to preserve decency and order without this politic arrangements that the dissolution of it would instantly lead to the disturbance and ruin of the Church. But if the reason for which the Lord appointed a sabbath to the Jews is equally applicable to us, no man can assert that it is a matter with which we have nothing to do. Our most provident and indulgent Parent has been pleased to provide for our wants not less than for the wants of the Jews. Why, it may be asked, do we not hold daily meetings, and thus avoid the distinction of days? Would that we were privileged to do so! Spiritual wisdom undoubtedly deserves to have some portion of every day devoted to it. But if, owing to the weakness of many, daily meetings cannot be held, and charity will not allow us to exact more of them, why should we not adopt the rule which the will of God has obviously imposed upon us?

33. I am obliged to dwell a little longer on this because some restless spirits are now making an outcry about the observance of the Lord's day. They complain that Christian people are trained in Judaism, because some observance of days is retained. My reply is, That those days are observed by us without Judaism, because in this matter we differ widely from the Jews. We do not celebrate it with most minute formality, as a ceremony by which we imagine that a spiritual mystery is typified, but we adopt it as a necessary remedy for preserving order in the Church. Paul informs us that Christians are not to be judged in respect of its observance, because it is a shadow of something to come (Col. 2:16); and, accordingly, he expresses a fear lest his labour among the Galatians should prove in vain, because they still observed days (Gal. 4:10, 11). And he tells the Romans that it is superstitious to make one day differ from another (Rom. 14:5). But who, except those restless men, does not see what the observance is to which the Apostle refers? Those persons had no regard to that politic and ecclesiastical arrangement, but by retaining the days as types of spiritual things, they in so far obscured the glory of Christ, and the light of the Gospel. They did not desist from manual labour on the ground of its interfering with sacred study and meditation, but as a kind of religious observance; because they dreamed that by their cessation from labour, they were cultivating the mysteries which had of old been committed to them. It was, I say, against this preposterous observance of days that the Apostle inveighs, and not against that legitimate selection which is subservient to the peace of Christian society. For in the churches established by him, this was the use for which the Sabbath was retained. He tells the Corinthians to set the first day apart for collecting contributions for the relief of their brethren at Jerusalem (1 Cor. 16:2). If superstition is dreaded, there was more danger in keeping the Jewish sabbath than the Lord's day as Christians now do. It being expedient to overthrow superstition, the Jewish holy day was abolished; and as a thing necessary to retain decency, orders and peace, in the Church, another day was appointed for that purpose.

34. It was not, however, without a reason that the early Christians substituted what we call the Lord's day for the Sabbath. The resurrection of our Lord being the end and accomplishment of that true rest which the ancient sabbath typified, this day, by which types were abolished serves to warn Christians against adhering to a shadowy ceremony. I do not cling so to the number seven as to bring the Church under bondage to it, nor do I condemn churches for holding their meetings on other solemn

days, provided they guard against superstition. This they will do if they employ those days merely for the observance of discipline and regular order. The whole may be thus summed up: As the truth was delivered typically to the Jews, so it is imparted to us without figure; first, that during our whole lives we may aim at a constant rest from our own works, in order that the Lord may work in us by his Spirit; secondly that every individual, as he has opportunity, may diligently exercise himself in private, in pious meditation on the works of God, and, at the same time, that all may observe the legitimate order appointed by the Church, for the hearing of the word, the administration of the sacraments, and public prayer: And, thirdly, that we may avoid oppressing those who are subject to us. In this way, we get quit of the trifling of the false prophets, who in later times instilled Jewish ideas into the people, alleging that nothing was abrogated but what was ceremonial in the commandment, (this they term in their language the taxation of the seventh day), while the moral part remains—viz. the observance of one day in seven. But this is nothing else than to insult the Jews, by changing the day, and yet mentally attributing to it the same sanctity; thus retaining the same typical distinction of days as had place among the Jews. And of a truth, we see what profit they have made by such a doctrine. Those who cling to their constitutions go thrice as far as the Jews in the gross and carnal superstition of sabbatism; so that the rebukes which we read in Isaiah (Isa. 1:13; 58:13) apply as much to those of the present day, as to those to whom the Prophet addressed them. We must be careful, however, to observe the general doctrine—viz. in order that religion may neither be lost nor languish among us, we must diligently attend on our religious assemblies, and duly avail ourselves of those external aids which tend to promote the worship of God.

Fifth Commandment.

HONOUR THY FATHER AND THY MOTHER: THAT THY DAYS MAY BE LONG UPON THE LAND WHICH THE LORD THY GOD GIVETH THEE.

35. The end of this commandment is, that since the Lord takes pleasure in the preservation of his own ordinance, the degrees of dignity appointed by him must be held inviolable. The sum of the commandment, therefore, will be, that we are to look up to those whom the Lord has set over us, yielding them honour, gratitude, and obedience. Hence it follows, that every thing in the way of contempt, ingratitude, or disobedience, is forbidden. For the term *honour* has this extent of meaning in Scripture. Thus when the Apostle says, "Let the elders that rule well be counted worthy of double honour" (1 Tim. 5:17), he refers not only to the reverence which is due to them, but to the recompense to which their services are entitled. But as this command to submit is very repugnant to the perversity of the human mind (which, puffed up with ambitious longings will scarcely allow itself to be subject), that superiority which is most attractive and least invidious is set forth as an example calculated to soften and bend our minds to habits of submission. From that subjection which is most easily endured, the Lord gradually accustoms us to every kind of legitimate subjection, the same principle regulating all. For to those whom he raises to eminences he communicates his authority, in so far as necessary to maintain their station. The titles of Father, God, and Lord, all meet in him alone and hence whenever any one of them is mentioned, our mind should be impressed with the same feeling of reverence. Those, therefore, to whom he imparts such titles, he distinguishes by some small spark of his refulgence, so as to entitle them to honour, each in his own place. In this way, we must consider that our earthly father possesses something of a divine nature in him, because there is some reason for his bearing a divine title, and that he who is our prince and ruler is admitted to some communion of honour with God.

36. Wherefore, we ought to have no doubt that the Lord here lays down this universal rule—viz. that knowing how every individual is set over us by his appointment, we should pay him reverence, gratitude, obedience, and every duty in our power. And it makes no difference whether those on whom the honour is conferred are deserving or not. Be they what they may, the Almighty, by conferring their station upon them, shows that he would have them honoured. The commandment specifies the reverence due to those to whom we owe our being. This Nature herself should in some measure teach us. For they are monsters, and not men, who petulantly and contumeliously violate the paternal authority. Hence, the Lord orders all who rebel against their parents to be put to death, they being, as it where, unworthy of the light in paying no deference to those to whom they are indebted for beholding it. And it is evident, from the various appendices to the Law, that we were correct in stating, that the honour here referred to consists of three

parts, reverence, obedience, and gratitude. The first of these the Lord enforces, when he commands that whose curseth his father or his mother shall be put to death. In this way he avenges insult and contempt. The second he enforces, when he denounces the punishment of death on disobedient and rebellious children. To the third belongs our Saviour's declaration, that God requires us to do good to our parents (Mt. 15). And whenever Paul mentions this commandment, he interprets it as enjoining obedience.

37. A promise is added by way of recommendation, the better to remind us how pleasing to God is the submission which is here required. Paul applies that stimulus to rouse us from our lethargy, when he calls this the first commandment with promise; the promise contained in the First Table not being specially appropriated to any one commandment, but extended to the whole law. Moreover, the sense in which the promise is to be taken is as follows:—The Lord spoke to the Israelites specially of the land which he had promised them for an inheritance. If, then, the possession of the land was an earnest of the divine favour, we cannot wonder if the Lord was pleased to testify his favour, by bestowing long life, as in this way they were able long to enjoy his kindness. The meaning therefore is: Honour thy father and thy mother, that thou may be able, during the course of a long life, to enjoy the possession of the land which is to be given thee in testimony of my favour. But, as the whole earth is blessed to believers, we justly class the present life among the number of divine blessings. Whence this promise has, in like manner, reference to us also, inasmuch as the duration of the present life is a proof of the divine benevolence toward us. It is not promised to us, nor was it promised to the Jews, as if in itself it constituted happiness, but because it is an ordinary symbol of the divine favour to the pious. Wherefore, if any one who is obedient to parents happens to be cut off before mature age (a thing which not infrequently happens), the Lord nevertheless adheres to his promise as steadily as when he bestows a hundred acres of land where he had promised only one. The whole lies in this: We must consider that long life is promised only in so far as it is a blessing from God, and that it is a blessing only in so far as it is a manifestation of divine favour. This, however, he testifies and truly manifests to his servants more richly and substantially by death.

38. Moreover, while the Lord promises the blessing of present life to children who show proper respect to their parents, he, at the same time, intimates that an inevitable curse is impending over the rebellious and disobedient; and, that it may not fail of execution, he, in his Law, pronounces sentence of death upon theme and orders it to be inflicted. If they escape the judgment, he, in some way or other, will execute vengeance. For we see how great a number of this description of individuals fall either in battle or in brawls; others of them are overtaken by unwonted disasters, and almost all are a proof that the threatening is not used in vain. But if any do escape till extreme old age, yet, because deprived of the blessing of God in this life, they only languish on in wickedness, and are reserved for severer punishment in the world to come, they are far from participating in the blessing promised to obedient children. It ought to be observed by the way, that we are ordered to obey parents only in the Lord. This is clear from the principle already laid down: for the place which they occupy is one to which the Lord has exalted them, by communicating to them a portion of his own honour. Therefore the submission yielded to them should be a step in our ascent to the Supreme Parent, and hence, if they instigate us to transgress the law, they deserve not to be regarded as parents, but as strangers attempting to seduce us from obedience to our true Father. The same holds in the case of rulers, masters, and superiors of every description. For it were unbecoming and absurd that the honour of God should be impaired by their exaltation—an exaltation which, being derived from him, ought to lead us up to him.

Sixth Commandment.

THOU SHALT NOT KILL.

39. The purport of this commandment is that since the Lord has bound the whole human race by a kind of unity, the safety of all ought to be considered as entrusted to each. In general, therefore, all violence and injustice, and every kind of harm from which our neighbour's body suffers, is prohibited. Accordingly, we are required faithfully to do what in us lies to defend the life of our neighbour; to promote whatever tends to his tranquillity, to be vigilant in warding off harm, and, when danger comes, to assist in removing it. Remembering that the Divine Lawgiver thus speaks, consider, moreover, that he requires you to apply the same rule in regulating your mind. It were ridiculous, that he, who sees the thoughts of the heart, and has special regard to them, should train the body only to rectitude. This commandment, therefore, prohibits the murder of the heart, and requires a sincere

desire to preserve our brother's life. The hand, indeed, commits the murder, but the mind, under the influence of wrath and hatred, conceives it. How can you be angry with your brother, without passionately longing to do him harm? If you must not be angry with him, neither must you hate him, hatred being nothing but inveterate anger. However you may disguise the fact, or endeavour to escape from it by vain pretexts. Where either wrath or hatred is, there is an inclination to do mischief. If you still persist in tergiversation, the mouth of the Spirit has declared, that "whosoever hateth his brother is a murderer" (1 John 3:15); and the mouth of our Saviour has declared, that "whosoever is angry with his brother without a cause shall be in danger of the judgment: and whosoever shall say to his brother, Raca, shall be in danger of the council: but whosoever shall say, Thou fool, shall be in danger of hell fire" (Mt. 5:22).

40. Scripture notes a twofold equity on which this commandment is founded. Man is both the image of God and our flesh. Wherefore, if we would not violate the image of God, we must hold the person of man sacred—if we would not divest ourselves of humanity we must cherish our own flesh. The practical inference to be drawn from the redemption and gift of Christ will be elsewhere considered. The Lord has been pleased to direct our attention to these two natural considerations as inducements to watch over our neighbour's preservation—viz. to revere the divine image impressed upon him, and embrace our own flesh. To be clear of the crime of murder, it is not enough to refrain from shedding man's blood. If in act you perpetrate, if in endeavour you plot, if in wish and design you conceive what is adverse to another's safety, you have the guilt of murder. On the other hand, if you do not according to your means and opportunity study to defend his safety, by that inhumanity you violate the law. But if the safety of the body is so carefully provided for, we may hence infer how much care and exertion is due to the safety of the soul, which is of immeasurably higher value in the sight of God.

Seventh Commandment.

THOU SHALT NOT COMMIT ADULTERY.

41. The purport of this commandment is, that as God loves chastity and purity, we ought to guard against all uncleanness. The substance of the commandment therefore is, that we must not defile ourselves with any impurity or libidinous excess. To this corresponds the affirmative, that we must regulate every part of our conduct chastely and continently. The thing expressly forbidden is adultery, to which lust naturally tends, that its filthiness (being of a grosser and more palpable form, in as much as it casts a stain even on the body) may dispose us to abominate every form of lust. As the law under which man was created was not to lead a life of solitude, but enjoy a help meet for him, and ever since he fell under the curse the necessity for this mode of life is increased; the Lord made the requisite provision for us in this respect by the institution of marriage, which, entered into under his authority, he has also sanctified with his blessing. Hence, it is evident, that any mode of cohabitation different from marriage is cursed in his sight, and that the conjugal relation was ordained as a necessary means of preventing us from giving way to unbridled lust. Let us beware, therefore, of yielding to indulgence, seeing we are assured that the curse of God lies on every man and woman cohabiting without marriage.

42. Now, since natural feeling and the passions unnamed by the fall make the marriage tie doubly necessary, save in the case of those whom God has by special grace exempted, let every individual consider how the case stands with himself. Virginity, I admit, is a virtue not to be despised; but since it is denied to some, and to others granted only for a season, those who are assailed by incontinence, and unable successfully to war against it, should retake themselves to the remedy of marriage, and thus cultivate chastity in the way of their calling. Those incapable of self-restraint, if they apply not to the remedy allowed and provided for intemperance, war with God and resist his ordinance. And let no man tell me (as many in the present day do) that he can do all things, God helping! The help of God is present with those only who walk in his ways (Ps. 91:14), that is, in his callings from which all withdraw themselves who, omitting the remedies provided by God, vainly and presumptuously strive to struggle with and surmount their natural feelings. That continence is a special gift from God, and of the class of those which are not bestowed indiscriminately on the whole body of the Church, but only on a few of its members, our Lord affirms (Mt. 19:12). He first describes a certain class of individuals who have made themselves eunuchs for the kingdom of heavenly sake; that is, in order that they may be able to devote themselves with more liberty and less restraint to the things of heaven. But lest any one should suppose that such a sacrifice was in every man's power, he had shown a little before that all are not capable, but those only to whom it

is specially given from above. Hence he concludes, "He that is able to receive it, let him receive it." Paul asserts the same thing still more plainly when he says, "Every man has his proper gift of God, one after this manner, and another after that" (1 Cor. 7:7).

43. Since we are reminded by an express declaration, that it is not in every man's power to live chaste in celibacy although it may be his most strenuous study and aim to do so—that it is a special grace which the Lord bestows only on certain individuals, in order that they may be less encumbered in his service, do we not oppose God, and nature as constituted by him, if we do not accommodate our mode of life to the measure of our ability? The Lord prohibits fornication, therefore he requires purity and chastity. The only method which each has of preserving it is to measure himself by his capacity. Let no man rashly despise matrimony as a thing useless or superfluous to him; let no man long for celibacy unless he is able to dispense with the married state. Nor even here let him consult the tranquillity or convenience of the flesh, save only that, freed from this tie, he may be the readier and more prepared for all the offices of piety. And since there are many on whom this blessing is conferred only for a time, let every one, in abstaining from marriage, do it so long as he is fit to endure celibacy. If he has not the power of subduing his passion, let him understand that the Lord has made it obligatory on him to marry. The Apostle shows this when he enjoins: "Nevertheless, to avoid fornication, let every man have his own wife and let every woman have her own husband." "If they cannot contain, let them marry." He first intimates that the greater part of men are liable to incontinence; and then of those so liable, he orders all, without exception, to have recourse to the only remedy by which unchastity may be obviated. The incontinent, therefore, neglecting to cure their infirmity by this means, sin by the very circumstance of disobeying the Apostle's command. And let not a man flatter himself, that because he abstains from the outward act he cannot be accused of unchastity. His mind may in the meantime be inwardly inflamed with lust. For Paul's definition of chastity is purity of mind, combined with purity of body. "The unmarried woman careth for the things of the Lord, that she may be holy both in body and spirit" (1 Cor. 7:34). Therefore when he gives a reason for the former precept, he not only says that it is better to marry than to live in fornication, but that it is better to marry than to burn.

44. Moreover, when spouses are made aware that their union is blessed by the Lord, they are thereby reminded that they must not give way to intemperate and unrestrained indulgence. For though honourable wedlock veils the turpitude of incontinence, it does not follow that it ought forthwith to become a stimulus to it. Wherefore, let spouses consider that all things are not lawful for them. Let there be sobriety in the behaviour of the husband toward the wife, and of the wife in her turn toward the husband; each so acting as not to do any thing unbecoming the dignity and temperance of married life. Marriage contracted in the Lord ought to exhibit measure and modesty—not run to the extreme of wantonness. This excess Ambrose censured gravely, but not undeservedly, when he described the man who shows no modesty or comeliness in conjugal intercourse, as committing adultery with his wife. Lastly let us consider who the Lawgiver is that thus condemns fornication: even He who, as he is entitled to possess us entirely, requires integrity of body, soul, and spirit. Therefore, while he forbids fornication, he at the same time forbids us to lay snares for our neighbour's chastity by lascivious attire, obscene gestures, and impure conversation. There was reason in the remark made by Archelaus to a youth clothed effeminately and over-luxuriously, that it mattered not in what part his wantonness appeared. We must have respect to God, who abhors all contaminations whatever be the part of soul or body in which it appears. And that there may be no doubt about it, let us remember, that what the Lord here commends is chastity. If he requires chastity, he condemns every thing which is opposed to it. Therefore, if you aspire to obedience, let not your mind burn within with evil concupiscence, your eyes wanton after corrupting objects, nor your body be decked for allurement; let neither your tongue by filthy speeches, nor your appetite by intemperance, entice the mind to corresponding thoughts. All vices of this description are a kind of stains which despoil chastity of its purity.

Eighth Commandment.

THOU SHALT NOT STEAL.

45. The purport is, that injustice being an abomination to God, we must render to every man his due. In substance, then, the commandment forbids us to long after other men's goods, and, accordingly, requires every man to exert himself honestly in preserving his own. For we must consider, that what each individual possesses has not fallen to him by chance, but by the distribution of the

sovereign Lord of all, that no one can pervert his means to bad purposes without committing a fraud on a divine dispensation. There are very many kinds of theft. One consists in violence, as when a man's goods are forcibly plundered and carried off; another in malicious imposture, as when they are fraudulently intercepted; a third in the more hidden craft which takes possession of them with a semblance of justice; and a fourth in sycophancy, which wiles them away under the pretence of donation. But not to dwell too long in enumerating the different classes, we know that all the arts by which we obtain possession of the goods and money of our neighbours, for sincere affection substituting an eagerness to deceive or injure them in any way, are to be regarded as thefts. Though they may be obtained by an action at law, a different decision is given by God. He sees the long train of deception by which the man of craft begins to lay nets for his more simple neighbour, until he entangles him in its meshes—sees the harsh and cruel laws by which the more powerful oppresses and crushes the feeble—sees the enticements by which the more wily baits the hook for the less wary, though all these escape the judgment of man, and no cognisance is taken of them. Nor is the violation of this commandment confined to money, or merchandise, or lands, but extends to every kind of right; for we defraud our neighbours to their hurt if we decline any of the duties which we are bound to perform towards them. If an agent or an indolent steward wastes the substance of his employer, or does not give due heed to the management of his property; if he unjustly squanders or luxuriously wastes the means entrusted to him; if a servant holds his master in derision, divulges his secrets, or in any way is treacherous to his life or his goods; if, on the other hand, a master cruelly torments his household, he is guilty of theft before God; since every one who, in the exercise of his calling, performs not what he owes to others, keeps back, or makes away with what does not belong to him.

46. This commandment, therefore, we shall duly obey, if, contented with our own lot, we study to acquire nothing but honest and lawful gain; if we long not to grow rich by injustice, nor to plunder our neighbour of his goods, that our own may thereby be increased; if we hasten not to heap up wealth cruelly wrung from the blood of others; if we do not, by means lawful and unlawful, with excessive eagerness scrape together whatever may glut our avarice or meet our prodigality. On the other hand, let it be our constant aim faithfully to lend our counsel and aid to all so as to assist them in retaining their property; or if we have to do with the perfidious or crafty, let us rather be prepared to yield somewhat of our right than to contend with them. And not only so, but let us contribute to the relief of those whom we see under the pressure of difficulties, assisting their want out of our abundance. Lastly, let each of us consider how far he is bound in duty to others, and in good faith pay what we owe. In the same way, let the people pay all due honour to their rulers, submit patiently to their authority, obey their laws and orders, and decline nothing which they can bear without sacrificing the favour of God. Let rulers, again, take due charge of their people, preserve the public peace, protect the good, curb the bad, and conduct themselves throughout as those who must render an account of their office to God, the Judge of all. Let the ministers of churches faithfully give heed to the ministry of the word, and not corrupt the doctrine of salvation, but deliver it purely and sincerely to the people of God. Let them teach not merely by doctrine, but by example; in short, let them act the part of good shepherds towards their flocks. Let the people, in their turn, receive them as the messengers and apostles of God, render them the honour which their Supreme Master has bestowed on them, and supply them with such things as are necessary for their livelihood. Let parents be careful to bring up, guide, and teach their children as a trust committed to them by God. Let them not exasperate or alienate them by cruelty, but cherish and embrace them with the levity and indulgence which becomes their character. The regard due to parents from their children has already been adverted to. Let the young respect those advanced in years as the Lord has been pleased to make that age honourable. Let the aged also, by their prudence and their experience (in which they are far superior), guide the feebleness of youth, not assailing them with harsh and clamorous invectives but tempering strictness with ease and affability. Let servants show themselves diligent and respectful in obeying their masters, and this not with eye-service, but from the heart, as the servants of God. Let masters also not be stern and disobliging to their servants, nor harass them with excessive asperity, nor treat them with insult, but rather let them acknowledge them as brethren and fellow-servants of our heavenly Master, whom, therefore, they are bound to treat with mutual love and kindness. Let every one, I say, thus consider what in his own place and order he owes to his neighbours, and pay what he owes. Moreover, we must always have a reference to the Lawgiver, and

so remember that the law requiring us to promote and defend the interest and convenience of our fellow-men, applies equally to our minds and our hands.

Ninth Commandment.

THOU SHALT NOT BEAR FALSE WITNESS AGAINST THY NEIGHBOUR.

47. The purport of the commandment is, since God, who is truth, abhors falsehood, we must cultivate unfeigned truth towards each other. The sum, therefore, will be, that we must not by calumnies and false accusations injure our neighbour's name, or by falsehood impair his fortunes; in fine, that we must not injure any one from petulance, or a love of evil-speaking. To this prohibition corresponds the command, that we must faithfully assist every one, as far as in us lies, in asserting the truth, for the maintenance of his good name and his estate. The Lord seems to have intended to explain the commandment in these words: "Thou shalt not raise a false report: put not thine hand with the wicked to be an unrighteous witness." "Keep thee far from a false matter" (Exod. 23:1, 7). In another passage, he not only prohibits that species of falsehood which consists in acting the part of tale-bearers among the people, but says, "Neither shalt thou stand against the blood of thy neighbour" (Lev. 19:16). Both transgressions are distinctly prohibited. Indeed, there can be no doubt, that as in the previous commandment he prohibited cruelty unchastity, and avarice, so here he prohibits falsehood, which consists of the two parts to which we have adverted. By malignant or vicious detraction, we sin against our neighbour's good name: by lying, sometimes even by casting a slur upon him, we injure him in his estate. It makes no difference whether you suppose that formal and judicial testimony is here intended, or the ordinary testimony which is given in private conversation. For we must always recur to the consideration, that for each kind of transgression one species is set forth by way of example, that to it the others may be referred, and that the species chiefly selected, is that in which the turpitude of the transgression is most apparent. It seems proper, however, to extend it more generally to calumny and sinister insinuations by which our neighbours are unjustly aggrieved. For falsehood in a court of justice is always accompanied with perjury. But against perjury, in so far as it profanes and violates the name of God, there is a sufficient provision in the third commandment. Hence the legitimate observance of this precept consists in employing the tongue in the maintenance of truth, so as to promote both the good name and the prosperity of our neighbour. The equity of this is perfectly clear. For if a good name is more precious than riches, a man, in being robbed of his good name, is no less injured than if he were robbed of his goods; while, in the latter case, false testimony is sometimes not less injurious than rapine committed by the hand.

48. And yet it is strange, with what supine security men everywhere sin in this respect. Indeed, very few are found who do not notoriously labour under this disease: such is the envenomed delight we take both in prying into and exposing our neighbour's faults. Let us not imagine it is a sufficient excuse to say that on many occasions our statements are not false. He who forbids us to defame our neighbour's reputation by falsehood, desires us to keep it untarnished in so far as truth will permit. Though the commandment is only directed against falsehood, it intimates that the preservation of our neighbour's good name is recommended. It ought to be a sufficient inducement to us to guard our neighbour's good name, that God takes an interest in it. Wherefore, evil-speaking in general is undoubtedly condemned. Moreover, by evil-speaking, we understand not the rebuke which is administered with a view of correcting; not accusation or judicial decision, by which evil is sought to be remedied; not public censure, which tends to strike terror into other offenders; not the disclosure made to those whose safety depends on being forewarned, lest unawares they should be brought into danger, but the odious crimination which springs from a malicious and petulant love of slander. Nay, the commandment extends so far as to include that scurrilous affected urbanity, instinct with invective, by which the failings of others, under an appearance of sportiveness, are bitterly assailed, as some are wont to do, who court the praise of wit, though it should call forth a blush, or inflict a bitter pang. By petulance of this description, our brethren are sometimes grievously wounded. But if we turn our eye to the Lawgiver, whose just authority extends over the ears and the mind, as well as the tongue, we cannot fail to perceive that eagerness to listen to slander, and an unbecoming proneness to censorious judgments are here forbidden. It were absurd to suppose that God hates the disease of evil-speaking in the tongue, and yet disapproves not of its malignity in the mind. Wherefore, if the true fear and love of God dwell in us, we must endeavour, as far as is lawful and expedient, and as far as charity admits, neither to listen nor give utterance to bitter and acrimonious charges, nor rashly entertain

sinister suspicions. As just interpreters of the words and the actions of other men, let us candidly maintain the honour due to them by our judgment, our ear, and our tongue.

Tenth Commandment.

THOU SHALT NOT COVET THY NEIGHBOUR'S HOUSE, THOU SHALT NOT COVET THY NEIGHBOUR'S WIFE NOR HIS MAN-SERVANT, NOR HIS MAID-SERVANT, NOR HIS OX NOR HIS ASS, NOR ANYTHING THAT IS THY NEIGHBOUR'S.

49. The purport is: Since the Lord would have the whole soul pervaded with love, any feeling of an adverse nature must be banished from our minds. The sum, therefore, will be, that no thought be permitted to insinuate itself into our minds, and inhale them with a noxious concupiscence tending to our neighbour's loss. To this corresponds the contrary precept, that every thing which we conceive, deliberate, will, or design, be conjoined with the good and advantage of our neighbour. But here it seems we are met with a great and perplexing difficulty. For if it was correctly said above, that under the words adultery and theft, lust and an intention to injure and deceive are prohibited, it may seem superfluous afterwards to employ a separate commandment to prohibit a covetous desire of our neighbour's goods. The difficulty will easily be removed by distinguishing between *design* and *covetousness*. Design, such as we have spoken of in the previous commandments, is a deliberate consent of the will, after passion has taken possession of the mind. Covetousness may exist without such deliberation and assent, when the mind is only stimulated and tickled by vain and perverse objects. As, therefore, the Lord previously ordered that charity should regulate our wishes, studies, and actions, so he now orders us to regulate the thoughts of the mind in the same way, that none of them may be depraved and distorted, so as to give the mind a contrary bent. Having forbidden us to turn and incline our mind to wrath, hatred, adultery, theft, and falsehood, he now forbids us to give our thoughts the same direction.

50. Nor is such rectitude demanded without reason. For who can deny the propriety of occupying all the powers of the mind with charity? If it ceases to have charity for its aim, who can question that it is diseased? How comes it that so many desires of a nature hurtful to your brother enter your mind, but just because, disregarding him, you think only of yourself? Were your mind wholly imbued with charity, no portion of it would remain for the entrance of such thoughts. In so far, therefore, as the mind is devoid of charity, it must be under the influence of concupiscence. Some one will object that those fancies which casually rise up in the mind, and forthwith vanish away, cannot properly be condemned as concupiscences, which have their seat in the heart. I answer, That the question here relates to a description of fancies which while they present themselves to our thoughts, at the same time impress and stimulate the mind with cupidity, since the mind never thinks of making some choice, but the heart is excited and tends towards it. God therefore commands a strong and ardent affection, an affection not to be impeded by any portion, however minute, of concupiscence. He requires a mind so admirably arranged as not to be prompted in the slightest degree contrary to the law of love. Lest you should imagine that this view is not supported by any grave authority, I may mention that it was first suggested to me by Augustine. But although it was the intention of God to prohibit every kind of perverse desire, he, by way of example, sets before us those objects which are generally regarded as most attractive: thus leaving no room for cupidity of any kind, by the interdiction of those things in which it especially delights and loves to revel.

Such, then, is the Second Table of the Law, in which we are sufficiently instructed in the duties which we owe to man for the sake of God, on a consideration of whose nature the whole system of love is founded. It were vain, therefore, to inculcate the various duties taught in this table, without placing your instructions on the fear and reverence to God as their proper foundation. I need not tell the considerate reader, that those who make two precepts out of the prohibition of covetousness, perversely split one thing into two. There is nothing in the repetition of the words, "Thou shalt not covet." The "house" being first put down, its different parts are afterwards enumerated, beginning with the "wife;" and hence it is clear, that the whole ought to be read consecutively, as is properly done by the Jews. The sum of the whole commandment, therefore, is, that whatever each individual possesses remain entire and secure, not only from injury, or the wish to injure, but also from the slightest feeling of covetousness which can spring up in the mind.

51. It will not now be difficult to ascertain the general end contemplated by the whole Law—viz. the fulfilment of righteousness, that man may form his life on the model of the divine purity. For therein God has so

delineated his own character, that any one exhibiting in action what is commanded, would in some measure exhibit a living image of God. Wherefore Moses, when he wished to fix a summary of the whole in the memory of the Israelites, thus addressed them, "And now, Israel, what does the Lord thy God require of thee, but to fear the Lord thy God, to walk in all his ways, and to love him, and to serve the Lord thy God with all thy heart, and with all thy soul, to keep the commandments of the Lord and his statutes which I command thee this day for thy good?" (Deut. 10:12, 13). And he ceased not to reiterate the same thing, whenever he had occasion to mention the end of the Law. To this the doctrine of the Law pays so much regard, that it connects man, by holiness of life, with his God; and, as Moses elsewhere expresses it (Deut. 6:5; 11:13), and makes him cleave to him. Moreover, this holiness of life is comprehended under the two heads above mentioned. "Thou shalt love the Lord thy God with all thy heart, and with all thy soul, and with all thy mind, and with all thy strength, and thy neighbour as thyself." First, our mind must be completely filled with love to God, and then this love must forthwith flow out toward our neighbour. This the Apostle shows when he says, "The end of the commandment is charity out of a pure heart, and a good conscience, and of faith unfeigned" (1 Tim. 1:5). You see that conscience and faith unfeigned are placed at the head, in other words, true piety; and that from this charity is derived. It is a mistake then to suppose, that merely the rudiments and first principles of righteousness are delivered in the Law, to form, as it were, a kind of introduction to good works, and not to guide to the perfect performance of them. For complete perfection, nothing more can be required than is expressed in these passages of Moses and Paul. How far, pray, would he wish to go, who is not satisfied with the instruction which directs man to the fear of God, to spiritual worship, practical obedience; in fine, purity of conscience, faith unfeigned, and charity? This confirms that interpretation of the Law which searches out, and finds in its precepts, all the duties of piety and charity. Those who merely search for dry and meagre elements, as if it taught the will of God only by halves, by no means understand its end, the Apostle being witness.

52. As, in giving a summary of the Law, Christ and the Apostles sometimes omit the First Table, very many fall into the mistake of supposing that their words apply to both tables. In Matthew, Christ calls "judgment, mercy, and faith," the "weightier matters of the Law." I think it clear, that by *faith* is here meant veracity towards men. But in order to extend the words to the whole Law, some take it for piety towards God. This is surely to no purpose. For Christ is speaking of those works by which a man ought to approve himself as just. If we attend to this, we will cease to wonder why, elsewhere, when asked by the young man, "What good thing shall I do, that I may have eternal life?" he simply answers, that he must keep the commandments, "Thou shalt do no murder, Thou shalt not commit adultery, Thou shalt not steal, Thou shalt not bear false witness, Honour thy father and thy mother: and, Thou shalt love thy neighbour as thyself" (Mt. 19:16, 18). For the obedience of the First Table consisted almost entirely either in the internal affection of the heart, or in ceremonies. The affection of the heart was not visible, and hypocrites were diligent in the observance of ceremonies; but the works of charity were of such a nature as to be a solid attestation of righteousness. The same thing occurs so frequently in the Prophets, that it must be familiar to every one who has any tolerable acquaintance with them. For, almost on every occasion, when they exhort men to repentance, omitting the First Table, they insist on faith, judgment, mercy, and equity. Nor do they, in this way, omit the fear of God. They only require a serious proof of it from its signs. It is well known, indeed, that when they treat of the Law, they generally insist on the Second Table, because therein the cultivation of righteousness and integrity is best manifested. There is no occasion to quote passages. Every one can easily for himself perceive the truth of my observation.

53. Is it then true, you will ask, that it is a more complete summary of righteousness to live innocently with men, than piously towards God? By no means; but because no man, as a matter of course, observes charity in all respects, unless he seriously fear God, such observance is a proof of piety also. To this we may add, that the Lord, well knowing that none of our good deeds can reach him (as the Psalmist declares, Psalm 16:2), does not demand from us duties towards himself, but exercises us in good works towards our neighbour. Hence the Apostle, not without cause, makes the whole perfection of the saints to consist in charity (Eph. 3:19; Col. 3:14). And in another passage, he not improperly calls it the "fulfilling of the law," adding, that "he that loveth another has fulfilled the law" (Rom. 13:8). And again, "All the law is fulfilled in this: Thou shalt love thy neighbour as thyself" (Gal. 5:14). For this is the very thing which Christ himself teaches when he says, "All things whatsoever ye would that men should do to you, do ye even so to them: for this is the

law and the prophets" (Mt. 7:12). It is certain that, in the law and the prophets, faith, and whatever pertains to the due worship of God, holds the first place, and that to this charity is made subordinate; but our Lord means, that in the Law the observance of justice and equity towards men is prescribed as the means which we are to employ in testifying a pious fear of God, if we truly possess it.

54. Let us therefore hold, that our life will be framed in best accordance with the will of God, and the requirements of his Law, when it is, in every respect, most advantageous to our brethren. But in the whole Law, there is not one syllable which lays down a rule as to what man is to do or avoid for the advantage of his own carnal nature. And, indeed, since men are naturally prone to excessive self-love, which they always retain, how great soever their departure from the truth may be, there was no need of a law to inflame a love already existing in excess. Hence it is perfectly plain, that the observance of the Commandments consists not in the love of ourselves, but in the love of God and our neighbour; and that he leads the best and holiest life who as little as may be studies and lives for himself; and that none lives worse and more unrighteously than he who studies and lives only for himself, and seeks and thinks only of his own. Nay, the better to express how strongly we should be inclined to love our neighbour, the Lord has made self-love as it were the standard, there being no feeling in our nature of greater strength and vehemence. The force of the expression ought to be carefully weighed. For he does not (as some sophists have stupidly dreamed) assign the first place to self-love, and the second to charity. He rather transfers to others the love which we naturally feel for ourselves. Hence the Apostle declares, that charity "seeketh not her own" (1 Cor. 13:5). Nor is the argument worth a straw, That the thing regulated must always be inferior to the rule. The Lord did not make self-love the rule, as if love towards others was subordinate to it; but whereas, through natural pravity, the feeling of love usually rests on ourselves, he shows that it ought to diffuse itself in another direction—that we should be prepared to do good to our neighbour with no less alacrity, ardour, and solicitude, than to ourselves.

55. Our Saviour having shown, in the parable of the Samaritan (Luke 10:36), that the term *neighbour* comprehends the most remote stranger, there is no reason for limiting the precept of love to our own connections. I deny not that the closer the relation the more frequent our offices of kindness should be. For the condition of humanity requires that there be more duties in common between those who are more nearly connected by the ties of relationship, or friendship, or neighbourhood. And this is done without any offence to God, by whose providence we are in a manner impelled to do it. But I say that the whole human race, without exception, are to be embraced with one feeling of charity: that here there is no distinction of Greek or Barbarian, worthy or unworthy, friend or foe, since all are to be viewed not in themselves, but in God. If we turn aside from this view, there is no wonder that we entangle ourselves in error. Wherefore, if we would hold the true course in love, our first step must be to turn our eyes not to man, the sight of whom might oftener produce hatred than love, but to God, who requires that the love which we bear to him be diffused among all mankind, so that our fundamental principle must ever be, Let a man be what he may, he is still to be loved, because God is loved.

56. Wherefore, nothing could be more pestilential than the ignorance or wickedness of the Schoolmen in converting the precepts respecting revenge and the love of enemies (precepts which had formerly been delivered to all the Jews, and were then delivered universally to all Christians) into counsels which it was free to obey or disobey, confining the necessary observance of them to the monks, who were made more righteous than ordinary Christians, by the simple circumstance of voluntarily binding themselves to obey counsels. The reason they assign for not receiving them as laws is, that they seem too heavy and burdensome, especially to Christians, who are under the law of grace. Have they, indeed, the hardihood to remodel the eternal law of God concerning the love of our neighbour? Is there a page of the Law in which any such distinction exists; or rather do we not meet in every page with commands which, in the strictest terms, require us to love our enemies? What is meant by commanding us to feed our enemy if he is hungry, to bring back his ox or his ass if we meet it going astray, or help it up if we see it lying under its burden? (Prov. 25:21; Exod. 23:4). Shall we show kindness to cattle for man's sake, and have no feeling of good will to himself? What? Is not the word of the Lord eternally true: "Vengeance is mine, I will repay?" (Deut. 32:35). This is elsewhere more explicitly stated: "Thou shalt not avenge, nor bear any grudge against the children of thy people" (Lev. 19:18). Let them either erase these passages from the Law, or let them acknowledge the Lord as a Lawgiver, not falsely feign him to be merely a counsellor.

57. And what, pray, is meant by the following passage, which they have dared to insult with this absurd gloss? "Love your enemies, bless them that curse you, do good to them that hate you, and pray for them which despitefully use you, and persecute you; that ye may be the children of your Father which is in heaven" (Mt. 5:44, 45). Who does not here concur in the reasoning of Chrysostom (lib. de Compunctione Cordis, et ad Rom. 7), that the nature of the motive makes it plain that these are not exhortations, but precepts? For what is left to us if we are excluded from the number of the children of God? According to the Schoolmen, monks alone will be the children of our Father in heaven—monks alone will dare to invoke God as their Father. And in the meantime, how will it fare with the Church? By the same rule, she will be confined to heathens and publicans. For our Saviour says, "If ye love them which love you, what reward have ye? do not even the publicans the same?" It will truly be well with us if we are left only the name of Christians, while we are deprived of the inheritance of the kingdom of heaven! Nor is the argument of Augustine less forcible: "When the Lord forbids adultery, he forbids it in regard to the wife of a foe not less than the wife of a friend; when he forbids theft, he does not allow stealing of any description, whether from a friend or an enemy" (August. Lib. de Doctr. Christ). Now, these two commandments, "Thou shalt not steal, Thou shalt not commit adultery," Paul brings under the rule of love; nay, he says that they are briefly comprehended in this saying, "Thou shalt love thy neighbour as thyself" (Rom. 13:9). Therefore, Paul must either be a false interpreter of the Law, or we must necessarily conclude, that under this precept we are bound to love our enemies just as our friends. Those, then, show themselves to be in truth the children of Satan who thus licentiously shake off a yoke common to the children of God. It may be doubted whether, in promulgating this dogma, they have displayed greater stupidity or impudence. There is no ancient writer who does not hold it as certain that these are pure precepts. It was not even doubted in the age of Gregory, as is plain from his decided assertion; for he holds it to be incontrovertible that they are precepts. And how stupidly they argue! The burden, say they, were too difficult for Christians to hear! As if any thing could be imagined more difficult than to love the Lord with all the heart, and soul, and strength. Compared with this Law, there is none which may not seem easy, whether it be to love our enemy, or to banish every feeling of revenge from our minds. To our weakness, indeed, every thing, even to the minutest tittle of the Law, is arduous and difficult. In the Lord we have strength. It is his to give what he orders, and to order what he wills. That Christians are under the law of grace, means not that they are to wander unrestrained without law, but that they are engrafted into Christ, by whose grace they are freed from the curse of the Law, and by whose Spirit they have the Law written in their hearts. This grace Paul has termed, but not in the proper sense of the term, a law, alluding to the Law of God, with which he was contrasting it. The Schoolmen, laying hold of the term *Law*, make it the ground-work of their vain speculations.

58. The same must be said of their application of the term, venial sin, both to the hidden impiety which violates the First Table, and the direct transgression of the last commandment of the Second Table. They define venial sin to be, desire unaccompanied with deliberate assent, and not remaining long in the heart. But I maintain that it cannot even enter the heart unless through a want of those things which are required in the Law. We are forbidden to have strange gods. When the mind, under the influence of distrust, looks elsewhere or is seized with some sudden desire to transfer its blessedness to some other quarter, whence are these movements, however evanescent, but just because there is some empty corner in the soul to receive such temptations? And, not to lengthen out the discussion, there is a precept to love God with the whole heart, and mind, and soul; and, therefore, if all the powers of the soul are not directed to the love of God, there is a departure from the obedience of the Law; because those internal enemies which rise up against the dominion of God, and countermand his edicts prove that his throne is not well established in our consciences. It has been shown that the last commandment goes to this extent. Has some undue longing sprung up in our mind? Then we are chargeable with covetousness, and stand convicted as transgressors of the Law. For the Law forbids us not only to meditate and plan our neighbour's loss, but to be stimulated and inflamed with covetousness. But every transgression of the Law lays us under the curse, and therefore even the slightest desires cannot be exempted from the fatal sentence. "In weighing our sins," says Augustine, "let us not use a deceitful balance, weighing at our own discretion what we will, and how we will, calling this heavy and that light: but let us use the divine balance of the Holy Scriptures, as taken from the treasury of the Lord, and by it

weigh every offence, nay, not weigh, but rather recognise what has been already weighed by the Lord" (August. De Bapt. cont. Donatist. Lib. 2 chap. 6). And what saith the Scripture? Certainly when Paul says, that "the wages of sin is death" (Rom. 6:23), he shows that he knew nothing of this vile distinction. As we are but too prone to hypocrisy, there was very little occasion for this sop to soothe our torpid consciences.

59. I wish they would consider what our Saviour meant when he said, "Whosoever shall break one of these least commandments, and shall teach men so, he shall be called the least in the kingdom of heaven" (Mt. 5:19). Are they not of this number when they presume to extenuate the transgression of the Law, as if it were unworthy of death? The proper course had been to consider not simply what is commanded, but who it is that commands, because every least transgression of his Law derogates from his authority. Do they count it a small matter to insult the majesty of God in any one respect? Again, since God has explained his will in the Law, every thing contrary to the Law is displeasing to him. Will they feign that the wrath of God is so disarmed that the punishment of death will not forthwith follow upon it? He has declared plainly (if they could be induced to listen to his voice, instead of darkening his clear truth by their insipid subtleties), "The soul that sinneth it shall die" (Ezek. 18:20). Again, in the passage lately quoted, "The wages of sin is death." What these men acknowledge to be sin, because they are unable to deny it, they contend is not mortal. Having already indulged this madness too long, let them learn to repent; or, if they persist in their infatuation, taking no further notice of them, let the children of God remember that all sin is mortal, because it is rebellion against the will of God, and necessarily provokes his anger; and because it is a violation of the Law, against every violation of which, without exception, the judgment of God has been pronounced. The faults of the saints are indeed venial, not, however, in their own nature, but because, through the mercy of God, they obtain pardon.

CHAPTER 9

CHRIST, THOUGH KNOWN TO THE JEWS UNDER THE LAW, YET ONLY MANIFESTED UNDER THE GOSPEL.

There are three principal heads in this chapter. I. Preparatory to a consideration of the knowledge of Christ, and the benefits procured by him; the 1st and 2nd sections are occupied with the dispensation of this knowledge, which, after the manifestation of Christ in the flesh, was more clearly revealed than under the Law. II. A refutation of the profane dream of Servetus, that the promises are entirely abrogated, sec. 3. Likewise, a refutation of those who do not properly compare the Law with the Gospel, sec. 4. III. A necessary and brief exposition of the ministry of John Baptist, which occupies an intermediate place between the law and the Gospel.

Sections:

1. The holy fathers under the Law saw the day of Christ, though obscurely. He is more fully revealed to us under the Gospel. A reason for this, confirmed by the testimony of Christ and his Apostles.

2. The term Gospel, used in its most extensive sense, comprehends the attestations of mercy which God gave to the fathers. Properly, however, it means the promulgation of grace exhibited in the God-man Jesus Christ.

3. The notion of Servetus, that the promises are entirely abolished, refuted. Why we must still trust to the promises of God. Another reason. Solution of a difficulty.

4. Refutation of those who do not properly compare the Law and the Gospel. Answer to certain questions here occurring. The Law and the Gospel briefly compared.

5. Third part of the chapter. Of the ministry of John the Baptist.

1. Since God was pleased (and not in vain) to testify in ancient times by means of expiations and sacrifices that he was a Father, and to set apart for himself a chosen people, he was doubtless known even then in the same character in which he is now fully revealed to us. Accordingly Malachi, having enjoined the Jews to attend to the Law of Moses (because after his death there was to be an interruption of the prophetical office), immediately after declares that the Sun of righteousness should arise (Mal. 4:2); thus intimating, that though the Law had the effect of keeping the pious in expectation of the coming Messiah, there was ground to hope for much greater light on his advent. For this reason, Peter, speaking of the ancient prophets, says, "Unto whom it was revealed, that not unto themselves, but unto us, they did minister the things which are now reported unto you by them that have preached the gospel unto you, with the Holy Ghost sent down from heaven" (1 Pet. 1:12). Not that the prophetical doctrine was useless to the ancient people,

or unavailing to the prophets themselves, but that they did not obtain possession of the treasure which God has transmitted to us by their hands. The grace of which they testified is now set familiarly before our eyes. They had only a slight foretaste; to us is given a fuller fruition. Our Saviour, accordingly, while he declares that Moses testified of him, extols the superior measure of grace bestowed upon us (John 5:46). Addressing his disciples, he says, "Blessed are your eyes, for they see, and your ears, for they hear. For verily I say unto you, That many prophets and righteous men have desired to see those things which ye see, and have not seen them, and to hear those things which ye hear, and have not heard them" (Mt. 13:16; Luke 10:23). It is no small commendation of the gospel revelation, that God has preferred us to holy men of old, so much distinguished for piety. There is nothing in this view inconsistent with another passage, in which our Saviour says, "Your father Abraham rejoiced to see my day, and he saw it and was glad" (John 8:56). For though the event being remote, his view of it was obscure, he had full assurance that it would one day be accomplished; and hence the joy which the holy patriarch experienced even to his death. Nor does John Baptist, when he says, "No man has seen God at any time; the only begotten Son, which is in the bosom of the Father, he has declared him" (John 1:18), exclude the pious who had previously died from a participation in the knowledge and light which are manifested in the person of Christ; but comparing their condition with ours, he intimates that the mysteries which they only beheld dimly under shadows are made clear to us; as is well explained by the author of the Epistle to the Hebrews, in these words, "God, who at sundry times and in divers manners spake in time past unto the fathers by the prophets, has in these last days spoken unto us by his Son" (Heb. 1:1, 2). Hence, although this only begotten Son, who is now to us the brightness of his Father's glory and the express image of his person, was formerly made known to the Jews, as we have elsewhere shown from Paul, that he was the Deliverer under the old dispensation; it is nevertheless true, as Paul himself elsewhere declares, that "God, who commanded the light to shine out of darkness, has shined in our hearts, to give the light of the knowledge of the glory of God in the face of Jesus Christ" (2 Cor. 4:6); because, when he appeared in this his image, he in a manner made himself visible, his previous appearance having been shadowy and obscure. More shameful and more detestable, therefore, is the ingratitude of those who walk blindfold in this meridian light. Accordingly, Paul says that "the god of this world has blinded their minds, lest the light of the glorious gospel of Christ should shine unto them" (2 Cor. 4:4).

2. By the Gospel, I understand the clear manifestation of the mystery of Christ. I confess, indeed, that inasmuch as the term Gospel is applied by Paul to the doctrine of faith (2 Tim. 4:10), it includes all the promises by which God reconciles men to himself, and which occur throughout the Law. For Paul there opposes faith to those terrors which vex and torment the conscience when salvation is sought by means of works. Hence it follows that *Gospel*, taken in a large sense, comprehends the evidences of mercy and paternal favour which God bestowed on the Patriarchs. Still, by way of excellence, it is applied to the promulgation of the grace manifested in Christ. This is not only founded on general use, but has the sanction of our Saviour and his Apostles. Hence it is described as one of his peculiar characteristics, that he preached the Gospel of the kingdom (Mt. 4:23; 9:35; Mark 1:14). Mark, in his preface to the Gospel, calls it "*The beginning of the Gospel of Jesus Christ.*" There is no use of collecting passages to prove what is already perfectly known. Christ at his advent "brought life and immortality to light through the Gospel" (2 Tim. 1:10). Paul does not mean by these words that the Fathers were plunged in the darkness of death before the Son of God became incarnate; but he claims for the Gospel the honourable distinction of being a new and extraordinary kind of embassy, by which God fulfilled what he had promised, these promises being realised in the person of the Son. For though believers have at all times experienced the truth of Paul's declaration, that "all the promises of God in him are yea and amen," inasmuch as these promises were sealed upon their hearts; yet because he has in his flesh completed all the parts of our salvation, this vivid manifestation of realities was justly entitled to this new and special distinction. Accordingly, Christ says, "Hereafter ye shall see heaven open, and the angels of God ascending and descending upon the Son of man." For though he seems to allude to the ladder which the Patriarch Jacob saw in vision, he commends the excellence of his advent in this, that it opened the gate of heaven, and gave us familiar access to it.

3. Here we must guard against the diabolical imagination of Servetus, who, from a wish, or at least the pretence of a wish, to extol the greatness of Christ, abolishes the promises entirely, as if they had come to an end at the same time with the Law. He pretends, that by the faith of the Gospel all the promises have been fulfilled; as if there was no distinction between us and Christ. I lately

observed that Christ had not left any part of our salvation incomplete; but from this it is erroneously inferred, that we are now put in possession of all the blessings purchased by him; thereby implying, that Paul was incorrect in saying, "We are saved by hope" (Rom. 3:24). I admit, indeed, that by believing in Christ we pass from death unto life; but we must at the same time remember the words of John, that though we know we are "the sons of God," "it does not yet appear what we shall be: but we know that, when he shall appear, we shall be like him; for we shall see him as he is" (1 John 3:2). Therefore, although Christ offers us in the Gospel a present fulness of spiritual blessings, fruition remains in the keeping of hope, until we are divested of corruptible flesh, and transformed into the glory of him who has gone before us. Meanwhile, in leaning on the promises, we obey the command of the Holy Spirit, whose authority ought to have weight enough with us to silence all the barkings of that impure dog. We have it on the testimony of Paul, that "Godliness is profitable unto all things, having promise of the life that now is, and of that which is to come" (1 Tim. 4:8); for which reason, he glories in being "an apostle of Jesus Christ, according to the promise of life which is in Christ Jesus" (2 Tim. 1:1). And he elsewhere reminds us, that we have the same promises which were given to the saints in ancient time (2 Cor. 7:1). In fine, he makes the sum of our felicity consist in being sealed with the Holy Spirit of promise. Indeed we have no enjoyment of Christ, unless by embracing him as clothed with his own promises. Hence it is that he indeed dwells in our hearts and yet we are as pilgrims in regard to him, because "we walk by faith, not by sight" (2 Cor. 5:6, 7). There is no inconsistency in the two things—viz. that in Christ we possess every thing pertaining to the perfection of the heavenly life, and yet that faith is only a vision "of things not seen" (Heb. 11:1). Only there is this difference to be observed in the nature or quality of the promises, that the Gospel points with the finger to what the Law shadowed under types.

4. Hence, also, we see the error of those who, in comparing the Law with the Gospel, represent it merely as a comparison between the merit of works, and the gratuitous imputation of righteousness. The contrast thus made is by no means to be rejected, because, by the term Law, Paul frequently understands that rule of holy living in which God exacts what is his due, giving no hope of life unless we obey in every respect; and, on the other hand, denouncing a curse for the slightest failure. This Paul does when showing that we are freely accepted of God, and accounted righteous by being pardoned, because that obedience of the Law to which the reward is promised is nowhere to be found. Hence he appropriately represents the righteousness of the Law and the Gospel as opposed to each other. But the Gospel has not succeeded the whole Law in such a sense as to introduce a different method of salvation. It rather confirms the Law, and proves that every thing which it promised is fulfilled. What was shadow, it has made substance. When Christ says that the Law and the Prophets were until John, he does not consign the fathers to the curse, which, as the slaves of the Law, they could not escape. He intimates that they were only imbued with the rudiments, and remained far beneath the height of the Gospel doctrine. Accordingly Paul, after calling the Gospel "the power of God unto salvation to every one that believeth," shortly after adds, that it was "witnessed by the Law and the Prophets" (Rom. 1:16; 3:21). And in the end of the same Epistle, though he describes "the preaching of Jesus Christ" as "the revelation of the mystery which was kept secret since the world began," he modifies the expression by adding, that it is "now made manifest" "by the scriptures of the prophets" (Rom. 16:25, 26). Hence we infer, that when the whole Law is spoken of, the Gospel differs from it only in respect of clearness of manifestation. Still, on account of the inestimable riches of grace set before us in Christ, there is good reason for saying, that by his advent the kingdom of heaven was erected on the earth (Mt. 12:28).

5. John stands between the Law and the Gospel, holding an intermediate office allied to both. For though he gave a summary of the Gospel when he pronounced Christ to be "the Lamb of God who taketh away the sin of the world," yet, inasmuch as he did not unfold the incomparable power and glory which shone forth in his resurrection, Christ says that he was not equal to the Apostles. For this is the meaning of the words: "Among them that are born of woman, there has not risen a greater than John the Baptist: notwithstanding, he that is least in the kingdom of heaven is greater than he" (Mt. 11:28). He is not there commending the persons of men, but after preferring John to all the Prophets, he gives the first place to the preaching of the Gospel, which is elsewhere designated by the kingdom of heaven. When John himself, in answer to the Jews, says that he is only "a voice" (John 1:23), as if he were inferior to the Prophets it is not in pretended humility but he means to teach that the proper embassy was not entrusted to him, that he only performed the office of a messenger, as had been

foretold by Malachi, "Behold, I will send you Elijah the prophets before the coming of the great and dreadful day of the Lord" (Mal. 4:5). And, indeed, during the whole course of his ministry, he did nothing more than prepare disciples for Christ. He even proves from Isaiah that this was the office to which he was divinely appointed. In this sense, he is said by Christ to have been "a burning and a shining light" (John 5:35), because full day had not yet appeared. And yet this does not prevent us from classing him among the preachers of the gospel, since he used the same baptism which was afterwards committed to the Apostles. Still, however, he only began that which had freer course under the Apostles, after Christ was taken up into the heavenly glory.

CHAPTER 10

THE RESEMBLANCE BETWEEN THE OLD TESTAMENT AND THE NEW.

This chapter consists of four parts. I. The sum, utility, and necessity of this discussion, sec. 1. II. A proof that, generally speaking, the old and new dispensations are in reality one, although differently administered. Three points in which the two dispensations entirely agree, sec. 2–4. III. The Old Testament, as well as the New, had regard to the hope of immortality and a future life, whence two other resemblances or points of agreement follow—viz. that both were established by the free mercy of God, and confirmed by the intercession of Christ. This proved by many arguments, passages of Scripture, and examples, see. 5–23. IV. Conclusion of the whole chapter, where, for fuller confirmation, certain passages of Scripture are produced. Refutation of the cavils of the Sadducees and other Jews.

Sections:

1. Introduction, showing the necessity of proving the similarity of both dispensations in opposition to Servetus and the Anabaptists.

2. This similarity in general. Both covenants truly one, though differently administered. Three things in which they entirely agree.

3. First general similarity, or agreement—viz. that the Old Testament, equally with the New, extended its promises beyond the present life, and held out a sure hope of immortality. Reason for this resemblance. Objection answered.

4. The other two points of resemblance—viz. that both covenants were established in the mercy of God, and confirmed by the mediation of Christ.

5. The first of these points of resemblance being the foundation of the other two, a lengthened proof is given of it. The first argument taken from a passage, in which Paul, showing that the sacraments of both dispensations had the same meaning, proves that the condition of the ancient church was similar to ours.

6. An objection from John 6:49—viz. that the Israelites ate manna in the wilderness, and are dead, whereas Christians eat the flesh of Christ, and die not. Answer reconciling this passage of the Evangelist with that of the Apostle.

7. Another proof from the Law and the Prophets—viz. the power of the divine word in quickening souls before Christ was manifested. Hence the believing Jews were raised to the hope of eternal life.

8. Third proof from the form of the covenant, which shows that it was in reality one both before and after the manifestation of Christ in the flesh.

9. Confirmation of the former proof from the clear terms in which the form is expressed. Another confirmation derived from the former and from the nature of God.

10. Fourth proof from examples. Adam, Abel, and Noah, when tried with various temptations, neglecting the present, aspired with living faith and invincible hope to a better life. They, therefore, had the same aim as believers under the Gospel.

11. Continuation of the fourth proof from the example of Abraham, whose call and whole course of life shows that he ardently aspired to eternal felicity. Objection disposed of.

12. Continuation of the fourth proof from the examples of Isaac and Jacob.

13. Conclusion of the fourth proof. Adam, Abel, Noah, Abraham, Isaac, Jacob, and others under the Law, looked for the fulfilment of the divine promises not on the earth, but in heaven. Hence they termed this life an earthly pilgrimage, and desired to be buried in the land of Canaan, which was a figure of eternal happiness.

14. A fifth proof from Jacob's earnestness to obtain the birth-right. This shows a prevailing desire of future life. This perceived in some degree by Balaam.

15. A sixth proof from David, who expects such great things from the Lord, and yet declares the present life to be mere vanity.

16. A seventh proof also from David. His descriptions of the happiness of believers could only be realised in a future state.

17. An eighth proof from the common feeling and confession of all the pious who sought by faith and hope to obtain in heaven what they did not see in the present shadowy life.

18. A continuation and confirmation of the former proof from the exultation of the righteous, even amid the destruction of the world.

19. A ninth proof from Job, who spoke most distinctly of this hope. Two objections disposed of.

20. A tenth proof from the later Prophets, who taught that the happiness of the righteous was placed beyond the limits of the present life.

21. This clearly established by Ezekiel's vision of the dry bones, and a passage in Isaiah.

22. Last proof from certain passages in the Prophets, which clearly show the future immortality of the righteous in the kingdom of heaven.

23. Conclusion of the whole discussion concerning the similarity of both dispensations. For fuller confirmation, four passages of Scripture produced. Refutation of the error of the Sadducees and other Jews, who denied eternal salvation and the sure hope of the Church.

1. From what has been said above, it must now be clear, that all whom, from the beginning of the world, God adopted as his peculiar people, were taken into covenant with him on the same conditions, and under the same bond of doctrine, as ourselves; but as it is of no small importance to establish this point, I will here add it by way of appendix, and show, since the Fathers were partakers with us in the same inheritance, and hoped for a common salvation through the grace of the same Mediator, how far their condition in this respect was different from our own. For although the passages which we have collected from the Law and the Prophets for the purpose of proof, make it plain that there never was any other rule of piety and religion among the people of God; yet as many things are written on the subject of the difference between the Old and New Testaments in a manner which may perplex ordinary readers, it will be proper here to devote a special place to the better and more exact discussion of this subject. This discussion, which would have been most useful at any rate, has been rendered necessary by that monstrous miscreant, Servetus, and some madmen of the sect of the Anabaptists, who think of the people of Israel just as they would do of some herd of swine, absurdly imagining that the Lord gorged them with temporal blessings here, and gave them no hope of a blessed immortality. Let us guard pious minds against this pestilential error, while we at the same time remove all the difficulties which are wont to start up when mention is made of the difference between the Old and the New Testaments. By the way also, let us consider what resemblance and what difference there is between the covenant which the Lord made with the Israelites before the advent of Christ, and that which he has made with us now that Christ is manifested.

2. It is possible, indeed, to explain both in one word. The covenant made with all the fathers is so far from differing from ours in reality and substance, that it is altogether one and the same: still the administration differs. But because this brief summary is insufficient to give any one a full understanding of the subject, our explanation to be useful must extend to greater length. It were superfluous, however, in showing the similarity, or rather identity, of the two dispensations, again to treat of the particulars which have already been discussed, as it were unseasonable to introduce those which are still to be considered elsewhere. What we propose to insist upon here may be reduced to three heads:—*First*, That temporal opulence and felicity was not the goal to which the Jews were invited to aspire, but that they were admitted to the hope of immortality, and that assurance of this adoption was given by immediate communications, by the Law and by the Prophets. *Secondly*, That the covenant by which they were reconciled to the Lord was founded on no merits of their own, but solely on the mercy of God, who called them; and, *thirdly*, That they both had and knew Christ the Mediator, by whom they were united to God, and made capable of receiving his promises. The second of these, as it is not yet perhaps sufficiently understood, will be fully considered in its own place (Book 3 chap. 15–18). For we will prove by many clear passages in the Prophets, that all which the Lord has ever given or promised to his people is of mere goodness and indulgence. The third also has, in various places, been not obscurely demonstrated. Even the first has not been left unnoticed.

3. As the first is most pertinent to the present subject, and is most controverted, we shall enter more fully into the consideration of it, taking care, at the same time, where any of the others requires explanations to supply it by the way, or afterwards add it in its proper place. The Apostle, indeed, removes all doubt when he says that the Gospel which God gave concerning his Son, Jesus Christ, "he had promised aforetime by his prophets in the holy Scriptures" (Rom. 1:2). And again, that "the righteousness of God without the law is manifested, being witnessed by the law and the prophets" (Rom. 3:21). For

the Gospel does not confine the hearts of men to the enjoyment of the present life, but raises them to the hope of immortality; does not fix them down to earthly delights, but announcing that there is a treasure laid up in heaven, carries the heart thither also. For in another place he thus explains, "After that ye believed [the Gospel,] ye were sealed with that Holy Spirit of promise, which is the earnest of our inheritance unto the redemption of the purchased possession" (Eph. 1:13, 14). Again, "Since we heard of your faith in Christ Jesus, and of the love which ye have to all the saints, for the hope which is laid up for you in heaven, whereof ye heard before in the word of the truth of the Gospel" (Col. 1:4). Again, "Whereunto he called you by our Gospel to the obtaining of the glory of our Lord Jesus Christ" (2 Thess. 2:14). Whence also it is called the word of salvation and the power of God, with salvation to every one that believes, and the kingdom of heaven. But if the doctrine of the Gospel is spiritual, and gives access to the possession of incorruptible life, let us not suppose that those to whom it was promised and declared altogether neglected the care of the soul, and lived stupidly like cattle in the enjoyment of bodily pleasures. Let no one here quibble and say, that the promises concerning the Gospel, which are contained in the Law and the Prophets, were designed for a new people. For Paul, shortly after making that statement concerning the Gospel promised in the Law, adds, that "whatsoever things the law saith, it saith to those who are under the law." I admit, indeed, he is there treating of a different subject, but when he said that every thing contained in the Law was directed to the Jews, he was not so oblivious as not to remember what he had said a few verses before of the Gospel promised in the Law. Most clearly, therefore, does the Apostle demonstrate that the Old Testament had special reference to the future life, when he says that the promises of the Gospel were comprehended under it.

4. In the same way we infer that the Old Testament was both established by the free mercy of God and confirmed by the intercession of Christ. For the preaching of the Gospel declares nothing more than that sinners, without any merit of their own, are justified by the paternal indulgence of God. It is wholly summed up in Christ. Who, then, will presume to represent the Jews as destitute of Christ, when we know that they were parties to the Gospel covenant, which has its only foundation in Christ? Who will presume to make them aliens to the benefit of gratuitous salvation, when we know that they were instructed in the doctrine of justification by faith?

And not to dwell on a point which is clear, we have the remarkable saying of our Lord, "Your father Abraham rejoiced to see my day, and he saw it and was glad" (John 8:56). What Christ here declares of Abraham, an apostle shows to be applicable to all believers, when he says that Jesus Christ is the "same yesterday, to-day, and for ever" (Heb. 13:8). For he is not there speaking merely of the eternal divinity of Christ, but of his power, of which believers had always full proof. Hence both the blessed Virgin and Zachariah, in their hymns, say that the salvation revealed in Christ was a fulfilment of the mercy promised "to our fathers, to Abraham, and to his seed for ever" (Luke 1:55, 72). If, by manifesting Christ, the Lord fulfilled his ancient oath, it cannot be denied that the subject of that oath must ever have been Christ and eternal life.

5. Nay, the Apostle makes the Israelites our equals, not only in the grace of the covenant, but also in the signification of the Sacraments. For employing the example of those punishments, which the Scripture states to have been of old inflicted on the Jews, in order to deter the Corinthians from falling into similar wickedness, he begins with premising that they have no ground to claim for themselves any privilege which can exempt them from the divine vengeance which overtook the Jews, since the Lord not only visited them with the same mercies, but also distinguished his grace among them by the same symbols: as if he had said, If you think you are out of danger, because the Baptism which you received, and the Supper of which you daily partake, have excellent promises, and if, in the meantime, despising the goodness of God, you indulge in licentiousness, know that the Jews, on whom the Lord inflicted his severest judgments, possessed similar symbols. They were baptised in passing through the sea, and in the cloud which protected them from the burning heat of the sun. It is said, that this passage was a carnal baptism, corresponding in some degree to our spiritual baptism. But if so, there would be a want of conclusiveness in the argument of the Apostle, whose object is to prevent Christians from imagining that they excelled the Jews in the matter of baptism. Besides, the cavil cannot apply to what immediately follows—viz. that they did "all eat the same spiritual meat; and did all drink the same spiritual drink: for they drank of that spiritual Rock that followed them: and that Rock was Christ" (1 Cor. 10:3, 4).

6. To take off the force of this passage of Paul, an objection is founded on the words of our Saviour, "Your fathers did eat manna in the wilderness, and are dead." "If any

man eat of this bread, he shall live for ever" (John 6:49, 51). There is no difficulty in reconciling the two passages. The Lord, as he was addressing hearers who only desired to be filled with earthly food, while they cared not for the true food of the soul, in some degree adapts his speech to their capacity, and, in particular, to meet their carnal view, draws a comparison between manna and his own body. They called upon him to prove his authority by performing some miracle, such as Moses performed in the wilderness when he obtained manna from heaven. In this manna they saw nothing but a relief of the bodily hunger from which the people were then suffering; they did not penetrate to the sublimer mystery to which Paul refers. Christ, therefore, to demonstrate that the blessing which they ought to expect from him was more excellent than the lauded one which Moses had bestowed upon their fathers, draws this comparison: If, in your opinion, it was a great and memorable miracle when the Lord, by Moses, supplied his people with heavenly food that they might be supported for a season, and not perish in the wilderness from famine; from this infer how much more excellent is the food which bestows immortality. We see why our Lord omitted to mention what was of principal virtue in the manna, and mentioned only its meanest use. Since the Jews had, as it were by way of upbraiding, cast up Moses to him as one who had relieved the necessity of the people by means of manna, he answers, that he was the minister of a much larger grace, one compared with which the bodily nourishment of the people, on which they set so high a value, ought to be held worthless. Paul, again, knowing that the Lords when he rained manna from heaven, had not merely supplied their bodies with food, but had also dispensed it as containing a spiritual mystery to typify the spiritual quickening which is obtained in Christ, does not overlook that quality which was most deserving of consideration. Wherefore it is surely and clearly proved, that the same promises of celestial and eternal life, which the Lord now gives to us, were not only communicated to the Jews, but also sealed by truly spiritual sacraments. This subject is copiously discussed by Augustine in his work against Faustus the Manichee.

7. But if my readers would rather have passages quoted from the Law and the Prophets, from which they may see, as we have already done from Christ and the Apostles, that the spiritual covenant was common also to the Fathers, I will yield to the wish, and the more willingly, because opponents will thus be more surely convinced, that henceforth there will be no room for evasion. And I will begin with a proof which, though I know it will seem futile and almost ridiculous to supercilious Anabaptists, will have very great weight with the docile and soberminded. I take it for granted that the word of God has such an inherent efficacy, that it quickens the souls of all whom he is pleased to favour with the communication of it. Peter's statement has ever been true, that it is an incorruptible seed, "which liveth and abideth for ever" (1 Peter 1:23), as he infers from the words of Isaiah (Is. 40:6). Now when God, in ancient times, bound the Jews to him by this sacred bond, there cannot be a doubt that he separated them unto the hope of eternal life. When I say that they embraced the word which brought them nearer to God, I refer not to that general method of communication which is diffused through heaven and earth, and all the creatures of the world, and which, though it quickens all things, each according to its nature, rescues none from the bondage of corruption. I refer to that special mode of communication by which the minds of the pious are both enlightened in the knowledge of God, and, in a manner, linked to him. Adam, Abel, Noah, Abraham, and the other patriarchs, having been united to God by this illumination of the word, I say there cannot be the least doubt that entrance was given them into the immortal kingdom of God. They had that solid participation in God which cannot exist without the blessing of everlasting life.

8. If the point still seems somewhat involved, let us pass to the form of the covenant, which will not only satisfy calm thinkers, but sufficiently establish the ignorance of gainsayers. The covenant which God always made with his servants was this, "I will walk among you, and will be your God, and ye shall be my people" (Lev. 26:12). These words, even as the prophets are wont to expound them, comprehend life and salvation, and the whole sum of blessedness. For David repeatedly declares, and with good reason, "Happy is that people whose God is the Lord." "Blessed is the nation whose God is the Lord; and the people whom he has chosen for his own inheritance" (Psalm 144:15; 33:12); and this not merely in respect of earthly happiness, but because he rescues from death, constantly preserves, and, with eternal mercy, visits those whom he has adopted for his people. As is said in other prophets, "Art not thou from everlasting, O Lord my God, mine Holy One? we shall not die." "The Lord is our judge, the Lord is our lawgiver, the Lord is our king; he will save us" "Happy art thou, O Israel: who is like unto thee, O people saved by the Lord?" (Hab. 1:12; Isaiah 33:22; Deut. 33:29). But not to labour superflu-

ously, the prophets are constantly reminding us that no good thing and, consequently, no assurance of salvation, is wanting, provided the Lord is our God. And justly. For if his face, the moment it hath shone upon us, is a perfect pledge of salvation, how can he manifest himself to any one as his God, without opening to him the treasures of salvation? The terms on which God makes himself ours is to dwell in the midst of us, as he declared by Moses (Lev. 26:11). But such presence cannot be enjoyed without life being, at the same time, possessed along with it. And though nothing more had been expressed, they had a sufficiently clear promise of spiritual life in these words, "I am your God" (Exod. 6:7). For he declared that he would be a God not to their bodies only, but specially to their souls. Souls, however, if not united to God by righteousness, remain estranged from him in death. On the other hand, that union, wherever it exists, will bring perpetual salvation with it.

9. To this we may add, that he not only declared he was, but also promised that he would be, their God. By this their hope was extended beyond present good, and stretched forward into eternity. Moreover, that this observance of the future had the effect, appears from the many passages in which the faithful console themselves not only in their present evils, but also for the future, by calling to mind that God was never to desert them. Moreover, in regard to the second part of the promise—viz. the blessing of God, its extending beyond the limits of the present life was still more clearly confirmed by the words, I will be the God of your seed after you (Gen. 17:7). If he was to manifest his favour to the dead by doing good to their posterity, much less would he deny his favour to themselves. God is not like men, who transfer their love to the children of their friends, because the opportunity of bestowing kind offices as they wished upon themselves is interrupted by death. But God, whose kindness is not impeded by death, does not deprive the dead of the benefit of his mercy, which, on their account, he continues to a thousand generations. God, therefore, was pleased to give a striking proof of the abundance and greatness of his goodness which they were to enjoy after death, when he described it as overflowing to all their posterity (Exod. 20:6). The truth of this promise was sealed, and in a manner completed, when, long after the death of Abraham, Isaac, and Jacob, he called himself their God (Exod. 20:6). And why? Was not the name absurd if they had perished? It would have been just the same as if he had said, I am the God of men who exist not. Accordingly, the Evangelists relate that, by this very argument, our Saviour refuted the Sadducees (Mt. 22:23; Luke 20:32), who were, therefore, unable to deny that the resurrection of the dead was attested by Moses, inasmuch as he had taught them that all the saints are in his hand (Deut. 33:3). Whence it is easy to infer that death is not the extinction of those who are taken under the tutelage, guardianship, and protection of him who is the disposer of life and death.

10. Let us now see (and on this the controversy principally turns) whether or not believers themselves were so instructed by the Lord, as to feel that they had elsewhere a better life, and to aspire to it while disregarding the present. First, the mode of life which heaven had imposed upon them made it a constant exercise, by which they were reminded, that if in this world only they had hope, they were of all men the most miserable. Adam, most unhappy even in the mere remembrance of his lost felicity, with difficulty supplies his wants by anxious labours; and that the divine curse might not be restricted to bodily labour, his only remaining solace becomes a source of the deepest grief: Of two sons, the one is torn from him by the parricidal hand of his brother; while the other, who survives, causes detestation and horror by his very look. Abel, cruelly murdered in the very flower of his days, is an example of the calamity which had come upon man. While the whole world are securely living in luxury, Noah, with much fatigue, spends a great part of his life in building an ark. He escapes death, but by greater troubles than a hundred deaths could have given. Besides his ten months' residence in the ark, as in a kind of sepulchre, nothing could have been more unpleasant than to have remained so long pent up among the filth of beasts. After escaping these difficulties he falls into a new cause of sorrow. He sees himself mocked by his own son, and is forced, with his own mouth, to curse one whom, by the great kindness of God, he had received safe from the deluge.

11. Abraham alone ought to be to us equal to tens of thousands if we consider his faith, which is set before us as the best model of believing, to whose race also we must be held to belong in order that we may be the children of God. What could be more absurd than that Abraham should be the father of all the faithful, and not even occupy the meanest corner among them? He cannot be denied a place in the list; nay, he cannot be denied one of the most honourable places in it, without the destruction of the whole Church. Now, as regards his experience in life, the moment he is called by the command of God, he is torn away from friends, parents, and country, objects

in which the chief happiness of life is deemed to consist, as if it had been the fixed purpose of the Lord to deprive him of all the sources of enjoyment. No sooner does he enter the land in which he was ordered to dwell, than he is driven from it by famine. In the country to which he retires to obtain relief, he is obliged, for his personal safety, to expose his wife to prostitution. This must have been more bitter than many deaths. After returning to the land of his habitation, he is again expelled by famine. What is the happiness of inhabiting a land where you must so often suffer from hunger, nay, perish from famine, unless you flee from it? Then, again, with Abimelech, he is reduced to the same necessity of saving his head by the loss of his wife (Gen. 12:12). While he wanders up and down uncertain for many years, he is compelled, by the constant quarrelling of servants to part with his nephew, who was to him as a son. This departure must doubtless have cost him a pang something like the cutting off of a limb. Shortly after, he learns that his nephew is carried off captive by the enemy. Wherever he goes, he meets with savage-hearted neighbours, who will not even allow him to drink of the wells which he has dug with great labour. For he would not have purchased the use from the king of Gerar if he had not been previously prohibited. After he had reached the verge of life, he sees himself childless (the bitterest and most unpleasant feeling to old age), until, beyond expectation, Ishmael is born; and yet he pays dearly for his birth in the reproaches of Sarah, as if he was the cause of domestic disturbance by encouraging the contumacy of a female slave. At length Isaac is born, but in return, the first-born Ishmael is displaced, and almost hostilely driven forth and abandoned. Isaac remains alone, and the good man, now worn out with age, has his heart upon him, when shortly after he is ordered to offer him up in sacrifice. What can the human mind conceive more dreadful than for the father to be the murderer of his son? Had he been carried off by disease, who would not have thought the old man much to be pitied in having a son given to him in mockery, and in having his grief for being childless doubled to him? Had he been slain by some stranger, this would, indeed, have been much worse than natural death. But all these calamities are little compared with the murder of him by his father's hand. Thus, in fine, during the whole course of his life, he was harassed and tossed in such a way, that any one desirous to give a picture of a calamitous life could not find one more appropriate. Let it not be said that he was not so very distressed, because he at length escaped from all these tempests. He is not said to lead a happy life who, after infinite difficulties during a long period, at last laboriously works out his escape, but he who calmly enjoys present blessings without any alloy of suffering.

12. Isaac is less afflicted, but he enjoys very few of the sweets of life. He also meets with those vexations which do not permit a man to be happy on the earth. Famine drives him from the land of Canaan; his wife is torn from his bosom; his neighbours are ever and anon annoying and vexing him in all kinds of ways, so that he is even obliged to fight for water. At home, he suffers great annoyance from his daughters-in-law; he is stung by the dissension of his sons, and has no other cure for this great evil than to send the son whom he had blessed into exile (Gen. 26:27); Jacob, again, is nothing but a striking example of the greatest wretchedness. His boyhood is passed most uncomfortably at home amidst the threats and alarms of his elder brother, and to these he is at length forced to give way (Gen. 27:28); A fugitive from his parents and his native soil, in addition to the hardships of exile, the treatment he receives from his uncle Laban is in no respect milder and more humane (Gen. 29). As if it had been little to spend seven years of hard and rigorous servitude, he is cheated in the matter of a wife. For the sake of another wife, he must undergo a new servitude, during which, as he himself complains, the heat of the sun scorches him by day, while in frost and cold he spends the sleepless night (Gen. 31:40, 41). For twenty years he spends this bitter life, and daily suffers new injuries from his father-in-law. Nor is he quiet at home, which he sees disturbed and almost broken up by the hatreds, quarrels, and jealousies of his wives. When he is ordered to return to his native land, he is obliged to take his departure in a manner resembling an ignominious flight. Even then he is unable to escape the injustice of his father-in-law, but in the midst of his journey is assailed by him with contumely and reproach (Gen. 31:20.) By and bye a much greater difficulty befalls him (Gen. 32, 33). For as he approaches his brother, he has as many forms of death in prospect as a cruel foe could invent. Hence, while waiting for his arrival, he is distracted and excruciated by direful terrors; and when he comes into his sight, he falls at his feet like one half dead, until he perceives him to be more placable than he had ventured to hope. Moreover, when he first enters the land, he is bereaved of Rachel his only beloved wife. Afterwards he hears that the son whom she had borne him, and whom he loved more than all his other children, is devoured by a wild beast (Gen. 37:33). How deep the sorrow caused by his death he himself evinces, when, after long tears, he obstinately

refuses to be comforted, declaring that he will go down to the grave to his son mourning. In the meantime, what vexation, anxiety, and grief, must he have received from the carrying off and dishonour of his daughter, and the cruel revenge of his sons, which not only brought him into bad odour with all the inhabitants of the country, but exposed him to the greatest danger of extermination? (Gen. 34) Then follows the horrid wickedness of Reuben his first-born, wickedness than which none could be committed more grievous (Gen. 36:22). The dishonour of a wife being one of the greatest of calamities, what must be said when the atrocity is perpetrated by a son? Some time after, the family is again polluted with incest (Gen. 38:18). All these disgraces might have crushed a mind otherwise the most firm and unbroken by misfortune. Towards the end of his life, when he seeks relief for himself and his family from famine, he is struck by the announcement of a new misfortune, that one of his sons is detained in prison, and that to recover him he must entrust to others his dearly beloved Benjamin (Gen. 42, 43). Who can think that in such a series of misfortunes, one moment was given him in which he could breathe secure? Accordingly, his own best witness, he declares to Pharaoh, "Few and evil have the days of the years of my life been" (Gen. 47:9). In declaring that he had spent his life in constant wretchedness, he denies that he had experienced the prosperity which had been promised him by the Lord. Jacob, therefore, either formed a malignant and ungrateful estimate of the Lord's favour, or he truly declared that he had lived miserable on the earth. If so, it follows that his hope could not have been fixed on earthly objects.

13. If these holy Patriarchs expected a happy life from the hand of God (and it is indubitable that they did), they viewed and contemplated a different happiness from that of a terrestrial life. This is admirably shown by an Apostle, "By faith he [Abraham] sojourned in the land of promise, as in a strange country, dwelling in tabernacles with Isaac and Jacob, the heirs with him of the same promise: for he looked for a city which has foundations, whose builder and maker is God." "These all died in faith, not having received the promises, but having seen them afar off, and were persuaded of them, and embraced them, and confessed that they were strangers and pilgrims on the earth. For they that say such things declare plainly that they seek a country. And truly, if they had been mindful of that country from whence they came out, they might have had opportunity to have returned. But now they desire a better country, that is, an heavenly: wherefore God is not ashamed to be called their God: for he has prepared for them a city" (Heb. 11:9, 10, 13–16). They had been duller than blocks in so pertinaciously pursuing promises, no hope of which appeared upon the earth, if they had not expected their completion elsewhere. The thing which the Apostle specially urges, and not without reason, is, that they called this world a pilgrimage, as Moses also relates (Gen. 47:9). If they were pilgrims and strangers in the land of Canaan, where is the promise of the Lord which appointed them heirs of it? It is clear, therefore, that the promise of possession which they had received looked farther. Hence, they did not acquire a foot breadth in the land of Canaan, except for sepulture; thus testifying that they hoped not to receive the benefit of the promise till after death. And this is the reason why Jacob set so much value on being buried there, that he took Joseph bound by oath to see it done; and why Joseph wished that his bones should some ages later, long after they had mouldered into dust, be carried thither (Gen. 47:29, 30; 50:25).

14. In short, it is manifest, that in the whole course of their lives, they had an eye to future blessedness. Why should Jacob have aspired so earnestly to primogeniture, and intrigued for it at so much risk, if it was to bring him only exile and destitution, and no good at all, unless he looked to some higher blessing? And that this was his feeling, he declared in one of the last sentences he uttered, "I have waited for thy salvation, O God" (Gen. 49:18). What salvation could he have waited for, when he felt himself breathing his last, if he did not see in death the beginning of a new life? And why talk of saints and the children of God, when even one, who otherwise strove to resist the truth, was not devoid of some similar impression? For what did Balaam mean when he said, "Let me die the death of the righteous, and let my last end be like his" (Num. 23:10), unless he felt convinced of what David afterward declares, "Precious in the sight of the Lord is the death of his saints?" (Ps. 116:15; 34:12). If death were the goal and ultimate limit, no distinction could be observed between the righteous and the wicked. The true distinction is the different lot which awaits them after death.

15. We have not yet come farther down than the books of Moses, whose only office, according to our opponents, was to induce the people to worship God, by setting before them the fertility of the land, and its general abundance; and yet to every one who does not voluntarily shun the light, there is clear evidence of a spiritual covenant. But if we come down to the Prophets,

the kingdom of Christ and eternal life are there exhibited in the fullest splendour. First, David, as earlier in time, in accordance with the order of the Divine procedure, spoke of heavenly mysteries more obscurely than they, and yet with what clearness and certainty does he point to it in all he says. The value he put upon his earthly habitation is attested by these words, "I am a stranger with thee, and a sojourner, as all my fathers were. Verily every man at his best estate is altogether vanity. Surely every man walketh in a vain show. And now, Lord, what wait I for? my hope is in thee" (Ps. 39:12, 5, 6, 7). He who confesses that there is nothing solid or stable on the earth, and yet firmly retains his hope in God, undoubtedly contemplates a happiness reserved for him elsewhere. To this contemplation he is wont to invite believers whenever he would have them to be truly comforted. For, in another passages after speaking of human life as a fleeting and evanescent show, he adds, "The mercy of the Lord is from everlasting to everlasting upon them that fear him" (Ps. 103:17). To this there is a corresponding passage in another psalm, "Of old thou hast laid the foundation of the earth; and the heavens are the work of thy hands. They shall perish, but thou shalt endure; yea, all of them shall wax old like a garment; as a vesture shalt thou change them, and they shall be changed; but thou art the same, and thy years shall have no end. The children of thy servants shall continue, and their seed shall be established before thee" (Ps. 102:25–28). If, notwithstanding of the destruction of the heavens and the earth, the godly cease not to be established before God, it follows, that their salvation is connected with his eternity. But this hope could have no existence, if it did not lean upon the promise as expounded by Isaiah, "The heavens shall vanish away like smoke, and the earth shall wax old like a garment, and they that dwell therein shall die in like manner; but my salvation shall be for ever, and my righteousness shall not be abolished" (Isa. 51:6). Perpetuity is here attributed to righteousness and salvation, not as they reside in God, but as they are experienced by men.

16. Nor can those things which are everywhere said as to the prosperous success of believers be understood in any other sense than as referring to the manifestation of celestial glory. Of this nature are the following passages: "He preserveth the souls of his saints; he delivereth them out of the hand of the wicked. Light is sown for the righteous, and gladness for the upright in heart." "His righteousness endureth for ever; his horn shall be exalted with honour—the desire of the wicked shall perish." "Surely the righteous shall give thanks unto thy name; the upright shall dwell in thy presence." "The righteous shall be in everlasting remembrance." "The Lord redeemeth the soul of his servants." But the Lord often leaves his servants, not only to be annoyed by the violence of the wicked, but to be lacerated and destroyed; allows the good to languish in obscurity and squalid poverty, while the ungodly shine forth, as it were, among the stars; and even by withdrawing the light of his countenance does not leave them lasting joy. Wherefore, David by no means disguises the fact, that if believers fix their eyes on the present condition of the world, they will be grievously tempted to believe that with God integrity has neither favour nor reward; so much does impiety prosper and flourish, while the godly are oppressed with ignominy, poverty, contempt, and every kind of cross. The Psalmist says, "But as for me, my feet were almost gone; my steps had well nigh slipped. For I was envious of the foolish, when I saw the prosperity of the wicked." At length, after a statement of the case, he concludes, "When I thought to know this, it was too painful for me: until I went into the sanctuary of God; then understood I their end" (Ps. 73:2, 3, 16, 17).

17. Therefore, even from this confession of David, let us learn that the holy fathers under the Old Testament were not ignorant that in this world God seldom or never gives his servants the fulfilment of what is promised them, and therefore has directed their minds to his sanctuary, where the blessings not exhibited in the present shadowy life are treasured up for them. This sanctuary was the final judgment of God, which, as they could not at all discern it by the eye, they were contented to apprehend by faith. Inspired with this confidence, they doubted not that whatever might happen in the world, a time would at length arrive when the divine promises would be fulfilled. This is attested by such expressions as these: "As for me, I will behold thy face in righteousness: I shall be satisfied, when I awake, with thy likeness" (Psalm 17:15). "I am like a green olive tree in the house of God" (Psalm 52:8). Again, "The righteous shall flourish like the palm tree: he shall grow like a cedar in Lebanon. Those that be planted in the house of the Lord shall flourish in the courts of our God. They shall still bring forth fruit in old age; they shall be fat and flourishing" (Psalm 92:12–14). He had exclaimed a little before "O Lord, how great are thy works! and thy thoughts are very deep." "When the wicked spring as the grass, and when all the workers of iniquity do flourish: it is that they shall be destroyed for ever." Where was this splendour and beauty of the righteous, unless when the appearance of

this world was changed by the manifestation of the heavenly kingdom? Lifting their eyes to the eternal world, they despised the momentary hardships and calamities of the present life, and confidently broke out into these exclamations: "He shall never suffer the righteous to be moved. But thou, O God, shalt bring them down into the pit of destruction: bloody and deceitful men shall not live out half their days" (Psalm 55:22, 23). Where in this world is there a pit of eternal destruction to swallow up the wicked, of whose happiness it is elsewhere said, "They spend their days in wealth, and in a moment go down to the grave?" (Job 21:13). Where, on the other hand, is the great stability of the saints, who, as David complains, are not only disturbed, but everywhere utterly bruised and oppressed? It is here. He set before his eyes not merely the unstable vicissitudes of the world, tossed like a troubled sea, but what the Lord is to do when he shall one day sit to fix the eternal constitution of heaven and earth, as he in another place elegantly describes: "They that trust in their wealth, and boast themselves in the multitude of their riches; none of them can by any means redeem his brother, nor give to God a ransom for him." "For he sees that wise men die, likewise the fool and the brutish person perish, and leave their wealth to others. Their inward thought is, that their houses shall continue for ever, and their dwelling-places to all generations; they call their lands after their own names. Nevertheless, man being in honour abideth not: he is like the beasts that perish. This their way is their folly: yet their posterity approve their sayings. Like sheep they are laid in the grave; death shall feed on them; and the upright shall have dominion over them in the morning; and their beauty shall consume in the grave from their dwelling" (Psalm 49:6, 7, 10–14). By this derision of the foolish for resting satisfied with the slippery and fickle pleasures, of the world, he shows that the wise must seek for a very different felicity. But he more clearly unfolds the hidden doctrine of the resurrection when he sets up a kingdom to the righteous after the wicked are cast down and destroyed. For what, pray, are we to understand by the "morning," unless it be the revelation of a new life, commencing when the present comes to an end?

18. Hence the consideration which believers employed as a solace for their sufferings, and a remedy for their patience: "His anger endureth but a moment: in his favour is life" (Psalm 30:5). How did their afflictions, which continued almost throughout the whole course of life, terminate in a moment? Where did they see the long duration of the divine benignity, of which they had only the slightest taste? Had they clung to earth, they could have found nothing of the kind; but looking to heaven, they saw that the period during which the Lord afflicted his saints was but a moment, and that the mercies with which he gathers them are everlasting: on the other hand, they foresaw that for the wicked, who only dreamed of happiness for a day, there was reserved an eternal and never-ending destruction. Hence those expressions: "The memory of the just is blessed, but the name of the wicked shall rot" (Prov. 10:7). "Precious in the sight of the Lord is the death of his saints" (Psalm 116:15). Again in Samuel: "The Lord will keep the feet of his saints, and the wicked shall be silent in darkness" (1 Sam. 2:9); showing they knew well, that however much the righteous might be tossed about, their latter end was life and peace; that how pleasant soever the delights of the wicked, they gradually lead down to the chambers of death. They accordingly designated the death of such persons as the death "of the uncircumcised," that is, persons cut off from the hope of resurrection (Ezek. 28:10; 31:18). Hence David could not imagine a greater curse than this: "Let them be blotted out of the book of the living, and not be written with the righteous" (Psalm 69:28).

19. The most remarkable passage of all is that of Job: "I know that my Redeemer liveth, and that he shall stand at the latter day upon the earth: and though after my skin worms destroy this body, yet in my flesh shall I see God: whom I shall see for myself, and mine eyes shall behold, and not another" (Job 19:25–27). Those who would make a display of their acuteness, pretend that these words are to be understood not of the last resurrection, but of the day when Job expected that God would deal more gently with him. Granting that this is partly meant, we shall, however, compel them, whether they will or not, to admit that Job never could have attained to such fulness of hope if his thoughts had risen no higher than the earth. It must, therefore, be confessed, that he who saw that the Redeemer would be present with him when lying in the grave, must have raised his eyes to a future immortality. To those who think only of the present life, death is the extremity of despair; but it could not destroy the hope of Job. "Though he slay me," said he, "yet will I trust in him" (Job 13:15). Let no trifler here burst in with the objection that these are the sayings of a few, and do not by any means prove that there was such a doctrine among the Jews. To this my instant answer is, that these few did not in such passages give utterance to some hidden wisdom, to which only distinguished individuals were admitted privately and apart from others,

but that having been appointed by the Holy Spirit to be the teachers of the people, they openly promulgated the mysteries of God, which all in common behaved to learn as the principles of public religion. When, therefore, we hear that those passages in which the Holy Spirit spoke so distinctly and clearly of the spiritual life were public oracles in the Jewish Church, it were intolerably perverse to confine them entirely to a carnal covenant relating merely to the earth and earthly riches.

20. When we descend to the later prophets, we have it in our power to expatiate freely as in our own field. If, when David, Job, and Samuel, were in question, the victory was not difficult, much easier is it here; for the method and economy which God observed in administering the covenant of his mercy was, that the nearer the period of its full exhibition approached, the greater the additions which were daily made to the light of revelation. Accordingly, at the beginning, when the first promise of salvation was given to Adam (Gen. 3:15), only a few slender sparks beamed forth: additions being afterwards made, a greater degree of light began to be displayed, and continued gradually to increase and shine with greater brightness, until at length all the clouds being dispersed, Christ the Sun of righteousness arose, and with full refulgence illumined all the earth (Mal. 4). In appealing to the Prophets, therefore, we can have no fear of any deficiency of proof; but as I see an immense mass of materials, which would occupy us much longer than compatible with the nature of our present work (the subject, indeed, would require a large volume), and as I trust, that by what has already been said, I have paved the way, so that every reader of the very least discernment may proceed without stumbling, I will avoid a prolixity, for which at present there is little necessity; only reminding my readers to facilitate the entrance by means of the key which was formerly put into their hands (*supra*, Chap. 4 sec. 3, 4); namely, that whenever the Prophets make mention of the happiness of believers (a happiness of which scarcely any vestiges are discernible in the present life), they must have recourse to this distinction: that the better to commend the Divine goodness to the people, they used temporal blessings as a kind of lineaments to shadow it forth, and yet gave such a portrait as might lift their minds above the earth, the elements of this world, and all that will perish, and compel them to think of the blessedness of a future and spiritual life.

21. One example will suffice. When the Israelites were carried away to Babylon, their dispersion seemed to be the next thing to death, and they could scarcely be dissuaded from thinking that Ezekiel's prophecy of their restoration (Ezek. 37:4) was a mere fable, because it seemed to them the same thing as if he had prophesied that putrid caresses would be raised to life. The Lord, in order to show that, even in that case, there was nothing to prevent him from making room for his kindness, set before the prophet in vision a field covered with dry bones, to which, by the mere power of his word, he in one moment restored life and strength. The vision served, indeed, to correct the unbelief of the Jews at the time, but it also reminded them how much farther the power of the Lord extended than to the bringing back of the people, since by a single nod it could so easily give life to dry scattered bones. Wherefore, the passage may be fitly compared with one in Isaiah, "Thy dead men shall live, together with my dead body shall they arise. Awake and sing, ye that dwell in dust: for thy dew is as the dew of herbs, and the earth shall cast out the dead. Come, my people, enter thou into thy chambers, and shut thy doors about thee: hide thyself as it were for a little moment, until the indignation be overpast. For, behold, the Lord cometh out of his place to punish the inhabitants of the earth for their iniquity: the earth also shall disclose her blood, and shall no more cover her slain" (Isa. 26:19–21).

22. It were absurd however to interpret all the passages on a similar principle; for there are several which point without any veil to the future immortality which awaits believers in the kingdom of heaven. Some of them we have already quoted, and there are many others, but especially the following two. The one is in Isaiah, "As the new heavens and the new earth, which I will make, shall remain before me, saith the Lord, so shall your seed and your name remain. And it shall come to pass, that from one new moon to another, and from one sabbath to another, shall all flesh come to worship before me, saith the Lord. And they shall go forth, and look upon the caresses of the men that have transgressed against me: for their worm shall not die, neither shall their fire be quenched; and they shall be an abhorring unto all flesh" (Isa. 66:22–24). The other passage is in Daniel. "At that time shall Michael stand up, the great prince which standeth for the children of thy people: and there shall be a time of trouble, such as there never was since there was a nation even to that same time: and at that time thy people shall be delivered, every one shall be found written in the book. And many of them that sleep in the dust of the earth shall awake, some to everlasting life, and some to shame and everlasting contempt" (Dan. 12:1, 2).

23. In proving the two remaining points—viz. that

the Patriarchs had Christ as the pledge of their covenant, and placed all their hope of blessing in him, as they are clearer, and not so much controverted, I will be less particular. Let us then lay it down confidently as a truth which no engines of the devil can destroy—that the Old Testament or covenant which the Lord made with the people of Israel was not confined to earthly objects, but contained a promise of spiritual and eternal life, the expectation of which behaved to be impressed on the minds of all who truly consented to the covenant. Let us put far from us the senseless and pernicious notion, that the Lord proposed nothing to the Jews, or that they sought nothing but full supplies of food, carnal delights, abundance of wealth, external influence, a numerous offspring, and all those things which our animal nature deems valuable. For, even now, the only kingdom of heaven which our Lord Jesus Christ promises to his followers, is one in which they may sit down with Abraham, and Isaac and Jacob (Mt. 8:11); and Peter declared of the Jews of his day, that they were heirs of gospel grace because they were the sons of the prophets, and comprehended in the covenant which the Lord of old made with his people (Acts 3:25). And that this might not be attested by words merely, our Lord also approved it by act (Mt. 27:52). At the moment when he rose again, he deigned to make many of the saints partakers of his resurrection, and allowed them to be seen in the city; thus giving a sure earnest, that every thing which he did and suffered in the purchase of eternal salvation belonged to believers under the Old Testament, just as much as to us. Indeed, as Peter testifies, they were endued with the same spirit of faith by which we are regenerated to life (Acts 15:8). When we hear that that spirit, which is, as it were, a kind of spark of immortality in us (whence it is called the "earnest" of our inheritance, Eph. 1:14), dwelt in like manner in them, how can we presume to deny them the inheritance? Hence, it is the more wonderful how the Sadducees of old fell into such a degree of sottishness as to deny both the resurrection and the substantive existence of spirits, both of which where attested to them by so many striking passages of Scripture. Nor would the stupidity of the whole nation in the present day, in expecting an earthly reign of the Messiah, be less wonderful, had not the Scriptures foretold this long before as the punishment which they were to suffer for rejecting the Gospel, God, by a just judgment, blinding minds which voluntarily invite darkness, by rejecting the offered light of heaven. They read, and are constantly turning over the pages of Moses, but a veil prevents them from seeing the light which beams forth in his countenance (2 Cor. 3:14); and thus to them he will remain covered and veiled until they are converted to Christ, between whom and Moses they now study, as much as in them lies, to maintain a separation.

CHAPTER 11

THE DIFFERENCE BETWEEN THE TWO TESTAMENTS.

This chapter consists principally of three parts. I. Five points of difference between the Old and the New Testament, sec. 1–11. II. The last of these points being, that the Old Testament belonged to the Jews only, whereas the New Testament belongs to all; the calling of the Gentiles is shortly considered, sec. 12. III. A reply to two objections usually taken to what is here taught concerning the difference between the Old and the New Testaments, sec. 13, 14.

Sections:

1. Five points of difference between the Old and the New Testaments. These belong to the mode of administration rather than the substance. First difference. In the Old Testament the heavenly inheritance is exhibited under temporal blessings; in the New, aids of this description are not employed.

2. Proof of this first difference from the simile of an heir in pupillarity, as in Gal. 4:1.

3. This the reason why the Patriarchs, under the Law, set a higher value on this life and the blessings of it, and dreaded the punishments, these being even more striking. Why severe and sudden punishments existed under the Law.

4. A second difference. The Old Testament typified Christ under ceremonies. The New exhibits the immediate truth and the whole body. The scope of the Epistle to the Hebrews in explaining this difference. Definition of the Old Testament.

5. Hence the Law our Schoolmaster to bring us unto Christ.

6. Notwithstanding, among those under the Law, some of the strongest examples of faith are exhibited, their equals being scarcely to be found in the Christian Church. The ordinary method of the divine dispensation to be here attended to. These excellent individuals placed under the Law, and aided by ceremonies, that they might behold and hail Christ afar off.

7. Third difference. The Old Testament is literal, the New spiritual. This difference considered first generally.

8. Next treated specially, on a careful examination of the Apostle's text. A threefold antithesis. The Old Testament is literal, deadly, temporary. The New is spiritual, quickening, eternal. Difference between the letter and the spirit.

9. Fourth difference. The Old Testament belongs to bondage, the New to liberty. This confirmed by three passages of Scripture. Two objections answered.

10. Distinction between the three last differences and the first. Confirmation of the above from Augustine. Condition of the patriarchs under the Old Testament.

11. Fifth difference. The Old Testament belonged to one people only, the New to all.

12. The second part of the chapter depending on the preceding section. Of the calling of the Gentiles. Why the calling of the Gentiles scented to the Apostles so strange and new.

13. The last part of the chapter. Two objections considered. 1. God being immutable, cannot consistently disapprove what he once ordered. Answer confirmed by a passage of Scripture.

14. Objections. 2. God could at first have transacted with the Jews as he now does with Christians. Answer, showing the absurdity of this objection. Another answer founded on a just consideration of the divine will and the dispensation of grace.

1. What, then? you will say, Is there no difference between the Old and the New Testaments? What is to become of the many passages of Scripture in which they are contrasted as things differing most widely from each other? I readily admit the differences which are pointed out in Scripture, but still hold that they derogate in no respect from their established unity, as will be seen after we have considered them in their order. These differences (so far as I have been able to observe them and can remember) seem to be chiefly four, or, if you choose to add a fifth, I have no objections. I hold and think I will be able to show, that they all belong to the mode of administration rather than to the substance. In this way, there is nothing in them to prevent the promises of the Old and New Testament from remaining the same, Christ being the foundation of both. The first difference then is, that though, in old time, the Lord was pleased to direct the thoughts of his people, and raise their minds to the heavenly inheritance, yet, that their hope of it might be the better maintained, he held it forth, and, in a manner, gave a foretaste of it under earthly blessings, whereas the gift of future life, now more clearly and lucidly revealed by the Gospel, leads our minds directly to meditate upon it, the inferior mode of exercise formerly employed in regard to the Jews being now laid aside. Those who attend not to the divine purpose in this respect, suppose that God's ancient people ascended no higher than the blessings which were promised to the body. They hear the land of Canaan so often named as the special, and as it were the only, reward of the Divine Law to its worshipers; they hear that the severest punishment which the Lord denounces against the transgressors of the Law is expulsion from the possession of that land and dispersion into other countries; they see that this forms almost the sum of the blessings and curses declared by Moses; and from these things they confidently conclude that the Jews were separated from other nations not on their own account, but for another reason—viz. that the Christian Church might have an emblem in whose outward shape might be seen an evidence of spiritual things. But since the Scripture sometimes demonstrates that the earthly blessings thus bestowed were intended by God himself to guide them to a heavenly hope, it shows great unskilfulness, not to say dullness, not to attend to this mode of dispensation. The ground of controversy is this: our opponents hold that the land of Canaan was considered by the Israelites as supreme and final happiness, and now, since Christ was manifested, typifies to us the heavenly inheritance; whereas we maintain that, in the earthly possession which the Israelites enjoyed, they beheld, as in a mirror, the future inheritance which they believed to be reserved for them in heaven.

2. This will better appear from the similitude which Paul uses in Galatians (Gal. 4:1). He compares the Jewish nation to an heir in pupillarity, who, as yet unfit to govern himself, follows the direction of a tutor or guide to whose charge he has been committed. Though this simile refers especially to ceremonies, there is nothing to prevent us from applying it most appropriately here also. The same inheritance was destined to them as to us, but from nonage they were incapable of entering to it, and managing it. They had the same Church, though it was still in puerility. The Lord, therefore kept them under this tutelage, giving them spiritual promises, not clear and simple, but typified by earthly objects. Hence, when he chose Abraham, Isaac, and Jacob, and their posterity, to the hope of immortality, he promised them the land of Canaan for an inheritance, not that it might be the limit of their hopes, but that the view of it might train and confirm them in

the hope of that true inheritance, which, as yet, appeared not. And, to guard against delusion, they received a better promise, which attested that this earth was not the highest measure of the divine kindness. Thus, Abraham is not allowed to keep down his thoughts to the promised land: by a greater promise his views are carried upward to the Lord. He is thus addressed, "Fear not, Abram: I am thy shield, and thy exceeding great reward" (Gen. 15:1). Here we see that the Lord is the final reward promised to Abraham that he might not seek a fleeting and evanescent reward in the elements of this world, but look to one which was incorruptible. A promise of the land is afterwards added for no other reason than that it might be a symbol of the divine benevolence, and a type of the heavenly inheritance, as the saints declare their understanding to have been. Thus David rises from temporal blessings to the last and highest of all, "My flesh and my heart faileth: but God is the strength of my heart, and my portion for ever." "My heart and my flesh crieth out for the living God" (Ps. 73:26; 84:2). Again, "The Lord is the portion of mine inheritance and of my cup: thou maintainest my lot" (Ps. 16:5). Again "I cried unto thee O Lord: I said Thou art my refuge and my portion in the land of the living" (Ps. 142:5). Those who can venture to speak thus, assuredly declare that their hope rises beyond the world and worldly blessings. This future blessedness, however, the prophets often describe under a type which the Lord had taught them. In this way are to be understood the many passages in Job (Job 18:17) and Isaiah, to the effect, That the righteous shall inherit the earth, that the wicked shall be driven out of it, that Jerusalem will abound in all kinds of riches, and Sion overflow with every species at abundance. In strict propriety, all these things obviously apply not to the land of our pilgrimage, nor to the earthly Jerusalem, but to the true country, the heavenly city of believers, in which the Lord has commanded blessing and life for evermore (Ps. 133:3).

3. Hence the reason why the saints under the Old Testament set a higher value on this mortal life and its blessings than would now be meet. For, though they well knew, that in their race they were not to halt at it as the goal, yet, perceiving that the Lord, in accommodation to their feebleness, had there imprinted the lineaments of his favour, it gave them greater delight than it could have done if considered only in itself. For, as the Lord, in testifying his good will towards believers by means of present blessings, then exhibited spiritual felicity under types and emblems, so, on the other hand, by temporal punishments he gave proofs of his judgment against the reprobate. Hence, by earthly objects, the favour of the Lord was displayed, as well as his punishment inflicted. The unskilful, not considering this analogy and correspondence (if I may so speak) between rewards and punishments, wonder that there is so much variance in God, that those who, in old time, were suddenly visited for their faults with severe and dreadful punishments, he now punishes much more rarely and less severely, as if he had laid aside his former anger, and, for this reason, they can scarcely help imagining, like the Manichees, that the God of the Old Testament was different from that of the New. But we shall easily disencumber ourselves of such doubts if we attend to that mode of divine administration to which I have adverted—that God was pleased to indicate and typify both the gift of future and eternal felicity by terrestrial blessings, as well as the dreadful nature of spiritual death by bodily punishments, at that time when he delivered his covenant to the Israelites as under a kind of veil.

4. Another distinction between the Old and New Testaments is in the types, the former exhibiting only the image of truth, while the reality was absent, the shadow instead of the substance, the latter exhibiting both the full truth and the entire body. Mention is usually made of this, whenever the New Testament is contrasted with the Old, but it is nowhere so fully treated as in the Epistle to the Hebrews (chap. 7–10). The Apostle is there arguing against those who thought that the observances of the Mosaic Law could not be abolished without producing the total ruin of religion. In order to refute this error, he adverts to what the Psalmist had foretold concerning the priesthood of Christ (Ps. 110:4). seeing that an eternal priesthood is assigned to him, it is clear that the priesthood in which there was a daily succession of priests is abolished. And he proves that the institution of this new Priest must prevail, because confirmed by an oath. He afterwards adds, that a change of the priest necessarily led to a change of the covenant. And the necessity of this he confirms by the reason, that the weakness of the law was such, that it could make nothing perfect. He then goes on to show in what this weakness consists, namely, that it had external carnal observances which could not render the worshipers perfect in respect of conscience, because its sacrifices of beasts could neither take away sins nor procure true holiness. He therefore concludes that it was a shadow of good things to come, and not the very image of the things, and accordingly had no other office than to be an introduction to the better hope which is exhibited in the Gospel.

Here we may see in what respect the legal is compared with the evangelical covenant, the ministry of Christ with that of Moses. If the comparison referred to the substance of the promises, there would be a great repugnance between the two covenants; but since the nature of the case leads to a different view, we must follow it in order to discover the truth. Let us, therefore bring forward the covenant which God once ratified as eternal and unending. Its completion, whereby it is fixed and ratified, is Christ. Till such completion takes place, the Lord, by Moses, prescribes ceremonies which are, as it were formal symbols of confirmation. The point brought under discussion was, Whether or not the ceremonies ordained in the Law behaved to give way to Christ. Although these were merely accidents of the covenant, or at least additions and appendages, and, as they are commonly called, accessories, yet because they were the means of administering it, the name of covenant is applied to them, just as is done in the case of other sacraments. Hence, in general, the Old Testament is the name given to the solemn method of confirming the covenant comprehended under ceremonies and sacrifices. Since there is nothing substantial in it, until we look beyond it, the Apostle contends that it behaved to be annulled and become antiquated (Heb. 7:22), to make room for Christ, the surety and mediator of a better covenant, by whom the eternal sanctification of the elect was once purchased, and the transgressions which remained under the Law wiped away. But if you prefer it, take it thus: the covenant of the Lord was old, because veiled by the shadowy and ineffectual observance of ceremonies; and it was therefore temporary, being, as it were in suspense until it received a firm and substantial confirmation. Then only did it become new and eternal when it was consecrated and established in the blood of Christ. Hence the Saviour, in giving the cup to his disciples in the last supper, calls it the cup of the new testament in his blood; intimating, that the covenant of God was truly realised, made new, and eternal, when it was sealed with his blood.

5. It is now clear in what sense the Apostle said (Gal. 3:24; 4:1), that by the tutelage of the Law the Jews were conducted to Christ, before he was exhibited in the flesh. He confesses that they were sons and heirs of God, though, on account of nonage, they were placed under the guardianship of a tutor. It was fit, the Sun of Righteousness not yet having risen, that there should neither be so much light of revelation nor such clear understanding. The Lord dispensed the light of his word, so that they could behold it at a distance, and obscurely. Accordingly, this slender measure of intelligence is designated by Paul by the term *childhood*, which the Lord was pleased to train by the elements of this world, and external observances, until Christ should appear. Through him the knowledge of believers was to be matured. This distinction was noted by our Saviour himself when he said that the Law and the Prophets were until John, that from that time the gospel of the kingdom was preached (Mt. 11:13). What did the Law and the Prophets deliver to the men of their time? They gave a foretaste of that wisdom which was one day to be clearly manifested, and showed it afar off. But where Christ can be pointed to with the finger, there the kingdom of God is manifested. In him are contained all the treasures of wisdom and understanding, and by these we penetrate almost to the very shrine of heaven.

6. There is nothing contrary to this in the fact, that in the Christian Church scarcely one is to be found who, in excellence of faith, can be compared to Abraham, and that the Prophets were so distinguished by the power of the Spirit, that even in the present day they give light to the whole world. For the question here is, not what grace the Lord conferred upon a few, but what was the ordinary method which he followed in teaching the people, and which even was employed in the case of those very prophets who were endued with special knowledge above others. For their preaching was both obscure as relating to distant objects, and was included in types. Moreover, however wonderful the knowledge displayed in them, as they were under the necessity of submitting to the tutelage common to all the people, they must also be ranked among children. Lastly, none of them ever had such a degree of discernment as not to savour somewhat of the obscurity of the age. Whence the words of our Saviour, "Many kings and prophets have desired to see the things which you see, and have not seen them, and to hear the things which ye hear, and have not heard them. Blessed are your eyes, for they see, and your ears, for they hear" (Mt. 13:17). And it was right that the presence of Christ should have this distinguishing feature, that by means of it the revelation of heavenly mysteries should be made more transparent. To the same effect is the passage which we formerly quoted from the First Epistle of Peter, that to them it was revealed that their labour should be useful not so much to themselves as to our age.

7. I proceed to the third distinction, which is thus expressed by Jeremiah: "Behold, the days come, saith the Lord, that I will make a new covenant with the house of Israel, and with the house of Judah; not according to the

covenant that I made with their fathers, in the day that I took them by the hand, to bring them out of the land of Egypt; (which my covenant they brake, although I was an husband unto them, saith the Lord); but this shall be the covenant that I will make with the house of Israel; After those days, saith the Lord, I will put my law in their inward parts, and write it in their hearts; and will be their God, and they shall be my people. And they shall teach no more every man his neighbour, and every man his brother, saying, know the Lord: for they shall all know me, from the least of them unto the greatest of them" (Jer. 31:31–34). From these words, the Apostle took occasion to institute a comparison between the Law and the Gospel, calling the one a doctrine of the letter, the other a doctrine of the spirit; describing the one as formed on tables of stone, the other on tables of the heart; the one the preaching of death, the other of life; the one of condemnation, the other of justification; the one made void, the other permanent (2 Cor. 3:5, 6). The object of the Apostle being to explain the meaning of the Prophet, the worlds of the one furnish us with the means of ascertaining what was understood by both. And yet there is some difference between them. For the Apostle speaks of the Law more disparagingly than the Prophet. This he does not simply in respect of the Law itself, but because there were some false zealots of the Law who, by a perverse zeal for ceremonies, obscured the clearness of the Gospel, he treats of the nature of the Law with reference to their error and foolish affection. It will, therefore, be proper to attend to this peculiarity in Paul. Both, however, as they are contrasting the Old and New Testament, consider nothing in the Law but what is peculiar to it. For example, the Law everywhere contains promises of mercy; but as these are adventitious to it, they do not enter into the account of the Law as considered only in its own nature. All which is attributed to it is, that it commands what is right, prohibits crimes, holds forth rewards to the cultivators of righteousness, and threatens transgressors with punishment, while at the same time it neither changes nor amends that depravity of heart which is naturally inherent in all.

8. Let us now explain the Apostle's contrast step by step. The Old Testament is literal, because promulgated without the efficacy of the Spirit: the New spiritual, because the Lord has engraven it on the heart. The second antithesis is a kind of exposition of the first. The Old is deadly, because it can do nothing but involve the whole human race in a curse; the New is the instrument of life, because those who are freed from the curse it restores to favour with God. The former is the ministry of condemnation, because it charges the whole sons of Adam with transgression; the latter the ministry of righteousness, because it unfolds the mercy of God, by which we are justified. The last antithesis must be referred to the Ceremonial Law. Being a shadow of things to come, it behaved in time to perish and vanish away; whereas the Gospel, inasmuch as it exhibits the very body, is firmly established for ever. Jeremiah indeed calls the Moral Law also a weak and fragile covenant; but for another reason—namely, because it was immediately broken by the sudden defection of an ungrateful people; but as the blame of such violation is in the people themselves, it is not properly alleged against the covenant. The ceremonies, again, inasmuch as through their very weakness they were dissolved by the advent of Christ, had the cause of weakness from within. Moreover, the difference between the spirit and the letter must not be understood as if the Lord had delivered his Law to the Jews without any good result; i.e. as if none had been converted to him. It is used comparatively to commend the riches of the grace with which the same Lawgivers assuming, as it were a new characters honoured the preaching of the Gospel. When we consider the multitude of those whom, by the preaching of the Gospel, he has regenerated by his, Spirit, and gathered out of all nations into the communion of his Church, we may say that those of ancient Israel who, with sincere and heartfelt affections embraced the covenant of the Lord, were few or none, though the number is great when they are considered in themselves without comparison.

9. Out of the third distinction a fourth arises. In Scripture, the term bondage is applied to the Old Testaments because it begets fear, and the term freedom to the New, because productive of confidence and security. Thus Paul says to the Romans, "Ye have not received the spirit of bondage again to fear; but ye have received the Spirit of adoption whereby we cry, Abba, Father" (Rom. 8:15). To the same effect is the passage in the Hebrews, "For ye are not come unto the mount that might be touched, and that burned with fire, nor unto blackness, and darkness, and tempest, and the sound of a trumpet, and the voice of words; which voice they that heard entreated that the word should not be spoken to them any more: (for they could not endure that which was commanded, And if so much as a beast touch the mountain, it shall be stoned, or thrust through with a dart: and so terrible was the sight, that Moses said, I exceedingly fear and quake); but ye are come unto mount Sion, and unto the city of the liv-

ing God, the heavenly Jerusalem," &c. (Heb. 12:18–22). What Paul briefly touches on in the passage which we have quoted from the Romans, he explains more fully in the Epistles to the Galatians, where he makes an allegory of the two sons of Abraham in this way: "Agar is mount Sinai in Arabia, and answereth to Jerusalem which now is, and is in bondage with her children. But Jerusalem which is above is free, which is the mother of us all" (Gal. 4:25, 26). As the offspring of Agar was born in slavery, and could never attain to the inheritances while that of Sara was free and entitled to the inheritance, so by the Law we are subjected to slavery, and by the Gospel alone regenerated into liberty. The sum of the matter comes to this: The Old Testament filled the conscience with fear and trembling—The New inspires it with gladness. By the former the conscience is held in bondage, by the latter it is manumitted and made free. If it be objected, that the holy fathers among the Israelites, as they were endued with the same spirit of faith, must also have been partakers of the same liberty and joy, we answer, that neither was derived from the Law; but feeling that by the Law they were oppressed like slaves, and vexed with a disquieted conscience, they fled for refuge to the gospel; and, accordingly, the peculiar advantage of the Gospel was, that, contrary to the common rule of the Old Testament, it exempted those who were under it from those evils. Then, again, we deny that they did possess the spirit of liberty and security in such a degree as not to experience some measure of fear and bondage. For however they might enjoy the privilege which they had obtained through the grace of the Gospel, they were under the same bonds and burdens of observances as the rest of their nation. Therefore, seeing they were obliged to the anxious observance of ceremonies (which were the symbols of a tutelage bordering on slavery, and handwritings by which they acknowledged their guilt, but did not escape from it), they are justly said to have been, comparatively, under a covenant of fear and bondage, in respect of that common dispensation under which the Jewish people were then placed.

10. The three last contrasts to which we have adverted (sec. 4, 7, 9), are between the Law and the Gospel, and hence in these the Law is designated by the name of the Old, and the Gospel by that of the New Testament. The first is of wider extent (sec. 1), comprehending under it the promises which were given even before the Law. When Augustine maintained that these were not to be included under the name of the Old Testament (August. ad Bonifac. lib. 3 c. 14), he took a most correct view, and meant nothing different from what we have now taught; for he had in view those passages of Jeremiah and Paul in which the Old Testament is distinguished from the word of grace and mercy. In the same passage, Augustine, with great shrewdness remarks, that from the beginning of the world the sons of promise, the divinely regenerated, who, through faith working by love, obeyed the commandments, belonged to the New Testament; entertaining the hope not of carnal, earthly, temporal, but spiritual, heavenly, and eternal blessings, believing especially in a Mediator, by whom they doubted not both that the Spirit was administered to them, enabling them to do good, and pardon imparted as often as they sinned. The thing which he thus intended to assert was, that all the saints mentioned in Scripture, from the beginning of the world, as having been specially selected by God, were equally with us partakers of the blessing of eternal salvation. The only difference between our division and that of Augustine is, that ours (in accordance with the words of our Saviour, "All the prophets and the law prophesied until John," Mt. 11:13) distinguishes between the gospel light and that more obscure dispensation of the word which preceded it, while the other division simply distinguishes between the weakness of the Law and the strength of the Gospel. And here also, with regard to the holy fathers, it is to be observed, that though they lived under the Old Testament, they did not stop there, but always aspired to the New, and so entered into sure fellowship with it. Those who, contented with existing shadows, did not carry their thoughts to Christ, the Apostle charges with blindness and malediction. To say nothing of other matters, what greater blindness can be imagined, than to hope for the expiation of sin from the sacrifice of a beast, or to seek mental purification in external washing with water, or to attempt to appease God with cold ceremonies, as if he were greatly delighted with them? Such are the absurdities into which those fall who cling to legal observances, without respect to Christ.

11. The fifth distinction which we have to add consists in this, that until the advent of Christ, the Lord set apart one nation, to which he confined the covenant of his grace. Moses says, "When the Most High divided to the nations their inheritance, when he separated the sons of Adam, he set the bounds of the people according to the number of the children of Israel. For the Lord's portion is his people; Jacob is the lot of his inheritance" (Deut. 32:8, 9). In another passage he thus addresses the people: "Behold, the heaven and the heaven of heavens is the Lord's thy God, the earth also, with all that therein is.

Only the Lord had a delight in thy fathers to love them, and he chose their seed, after them, even you, above all people, as it is this day" (Deut. 10:14, 15). That people, therefore, as if they had been the only part of mankind belonging to him he favoured exclusively with the knowledge of his name, depositing his covenant, as it were, in their bosom, manifesting to them the presence of his divinity and honouring them with all privileges. But to say nothing of other favours, the only one here considered is his binding them to him by the communion of his word, so that he was called and regarded as their God. Meanwhile, other nations, as if they had had no kind of intercourse with him, he allowed to wander in vanity not even supplying them with the only means of preventing their destructions—viz. the preaching of his word. Israel was thus the Lord's favourite child the others were aliens. Israel was known and admitted to trust and guardianship, the others left in darkness; Israel was made holy, the others were profane; Israel was honoured with the presence of God, the others kept far aloof from him. But on the fulness of the time destined to renew all things, when the Mediator between God and man was manifested the middle wall of partition, which had long kept the divine mercy within the confines of Israel, was broken down, peace was preached to them who were afar off, as well as to those who were nigh, that being, together reconciled to God, they might unite as one people. Wherefore, there is now no respect of Jew or Greek, of circumcision or uncircumcision, but Christ is all and in all. To him the heathen have been given for his inheritance, and the uttermost parts of the earth for his possession (Ps. 2:8), that he may rule without distinction "from sea to sea, and from the river unto the ends of the earth" (Ps. 72:8).

12. The calling of the Gentiles, therefore, is a distinguishing feature illustrative of the superiority of the New over the Old Testament. This, it is true, had been previously declared by the prophets, in passages both numerous and clear, but still the fulfilment of it was deferred to the reign of the Messiah. Even Christ did not acknowledge it at the very outset of his ministry, but delayed it until having completed the whole work of redemption in all its parts, and finished the period of his humiliation, he received from the Father "a name which is above every name, that at the name of Jesus every knee should bow" (Phil. 2:9, 10). Hence the period being not yet completed, he declared to the woman of Canaan, "I am not sent but unto the lost sheep of the house of Israel" (Mt. 15:24). Nor in his first commission to the Apostles does he permit them to pass the same limits, "Go not into the way of the Gentiles, and into any city of the Samaritans enter ye not: but go rather to the lost sheep of the house of Israel" (Mt. 10:5, 6). However plainly the thing may have been declared in numerous passages, when it was announced to the Apostles, it seemed to them so new and extraordinary, that they were horrified at it as something monstrous. At length, when they did act upon it, it was timorously, and not without reluctance. Nor is this strange; for it seemed by no means in accordance with reason, that the Lord, who for so many ages had selected Israel from the rest of the nations should suddenly, as it were, change his purpose, and abandon his choice. Prophecy, indeed, had foretold it, but they could not be so attentive to prophecies, as not to be somewhat startled by the novel spectacle thus presented to their eye. It was not enough that God had in old times given specimens of the future calling of the Gentiles. Those whom he had so called were very few in number, and, moreover, he in a manner adopted them into the family of Abraham, before allowing them to approach his people. But by this public call, the Gentiles were not only made equal to the Jews, but seemed to be substituted into their place, as if the Jews had been dead. We may add, that any strangers whom God had formerly admitted into the body of the Church, had never been put on the same footing with the Jews. Wherefore, it is not without cause that Paul describes it as the mystery which has been hid from ages and from generations, but now is made manifest to his saints (Col. 1:26).

13. The whole difference between the Old and New Testaments has, I think, been fully and faithfully explained, under these four or five heads in so far as requisite for ordinary instruction. But since this variety in governing the Church, this diversity in the mode of teaching, this great change in rites and ceremonies, is regarded by some as an absurdity, we must reply to them before passing to other matters. And this can be done briefly, because the objections are not so strong as to require a very careful refutation. It is unreasonable they say, to suppose that God who is always consistent With himself permitted such a change as afterwards to disapprove what he had once ordered and commended. I answer, that God ought not to be deemed mutable, because he adapts different forms to different ages, as he knows to be expedient for each. If the husband man prescribes one set of duties to his household in winter, and another in summer, we do not therefore charge him with fickleness or think he deviates from the rules of good husbandry which depends on the regular course

of nature. In like manner, if a father of a family, in educating, governing, and managing his children, pursues one course in boyhood another in adolescence and another in manhood we do not therefore say that he is fickle, or abandons his opinions. Why, then do we charge God with inconstancy when he makes fit and congruous arrangements for diversities of times? The latter similitude ought to be completely satisfactory. Paul likens the Jews to children, and Christians to grown men (Gal. 4:1). What irregularity is there in the Divine arrangement, which confined them to the rudiments which were suitable to their age, and trains us by a firmer and more manly discipline? The constancy of God is conspicuous in this, that he delivered the same doctrine to all ages, and persists in requiring that worship of his name which he commanded at the beginning. His changing the external form and manner does not show that he is liable to change. In so far he has only accommodated himself to the mutable and diversified capacities of man.

14. But it is said, Whence this diversity, save that God chose to make it? Would it not have been as easy for him from the first, as after the advent of Christ, to reveal eternal life in clear terms without any figures, to instruct his people by a few clear sacraments, to bestow his Holy Spirit, and diffuse his grace over the whole globe? This is very much the same as to bring a charge against God, because he created the world at so late a period, when he could have done it at the first, or because he appointed the alternate changes of summer and winter, of day and night. With the feeling common to every pious mind, let us not doubt that every thing which God has done has been done wisely and justly, although we may be ignorant of the cause which required that it should be so done. We should arrogate too much to ourselves were we not to concede to God that he may have reasons for his counsel, which we are unable to discern. It is strange, they say, that he now repudiates and abominates the sacrifices of beasts, and the whole apparatus of that Levitical priesthood in which he formerly delighted. As if those external and transient matters could delight God, or affect him in any way! It has already been observed, that he appointed none of these things on his own account, but instituted them all for the salvation of men. If a physician, adopting the best method, effects a cure upon a youth, and afterwards, when the same individual has grown old, and is again subject to the same disease, employs a different method of cure, can it be said that he repudiates the method which he formerly approved?

Nay, continuing to approve of it, he only adapts himself to the different periods of life. In like manner, it was necessary in representing Christ in his absence, and predicting his future advent, to employ a different set of signs from those which are employed, now that his actual manifestation is exhibited. It is true, that since the advent of Christ, the calling of God is more widely addressed to all nations, and the graces of the Spirit more liberally bestowed than they had previously been. But who, I ask, can deny the right of God to have the free and uncontrolled disposal of his gifts, to select the nations which he may be pleased to illuminate, the places which he may be pleased to illustrate by the preaching of his word, and the mode and measure of progress and success which he may be pleased to give to his doctrine,—to punish the world for its ingratitude by withdrawing the knowledge of his name for certain ages, and again, when he so pleases, to restore it in mercy? We see, then, that in the calumnies which the ungodly employ in this matter, to perplex the minds of the simple, there is nothing that ought to throw doubt either on the justice of God or the veracity of Scripture.

CHAPTER 12

CHRIST, TO PERFORM THE OFFICE OF MEDIATOR, BEHOVED TO BECOME MAN.

The two divisions of this chapter are, I. The reasons why our Mediator behoved to be very God, and to become man, sec. 1–3. II. Disposal of various objections by some fanatics, and especially by Osiander, to the orthodox doctrine concerning the Mediator, sec. 4–7.

Sections:

1. Necessary, not absolutely, but by divine decree, that the Mediator should be God, and become man. Neither man nor angel, though pure, could have sufficed. The Son of God behoved to come down. Man in innocence could not penetrate to God without a Mediator, much less could he after the fall.

2. A second reason why the Mediator behoved to be God and man—viz. that he had to convert those who were heirs of hell into children of God.

3. Third reason, that in our flesh he might yield a perfect obedience, satisfy the divine justice, and pay the penalty of sin. Fourth reason, regarding the consolation and confirmation of the whole Church.

4. First objection against the orthodox doctrine:

Answer to it. Conformation from the sacrifices of the Law, the testimony of the Prophets, Apostles, Evangelists, and even Christ himself.

5. Second objection: Answer: Answer confirmed. Third objection: Answer. Fourth objection by Osiander: Answer.

6. Fifth objection, forming the basis of Osiander's errors on this subject: Answer. Nature of the divine image in Adam. Christ the head of angels and men.

7. Sixth objection: Answer. Seventh objection: Answer. Eighth objection: Answer. Ninth objection: Answer. Tenth objection: Answer. Eleventh objection: Answer. Twelfth objection: Answer. The sum of the doctrine.

1. It deeply concerned us, that he who was to be our Mediator should be very God and very man. If the necessity be inquired into, it was not what is commonly termed simple or absolute, but flowed from the divine decree on which the salvation of man depended. What was best for us, our most merciful Father determined. Our iniquities, like a cloud intervening between Him and us, having utterly alienated us from the kingdom of heaven, none but a person reaching to him could be the medium of restoring peace. But who could thus reach to him? Could any of the sons of Adam? All of them, with their parents, shuddered at the sight of God. Could any of the angels? They had need of a head, by connection with which they might adhere to their God entirely and inseparably. What then? The case was certainly desperate, if the Godhead itself did not descend to us, it being impossible for us to ascend. Thus the Son of God behoved to become our Emmanuel, the God with us; and in such a way, that by mutual union his divinity and our nature might be combined; otherwise, neither was the proximity near enough, nor the affinity strong enough, to give us hope that God would dwell with us; so great was the repugnance between our pollution and the spotless purity of God. Had man remained free from all taint, he was of too humble a condition to penetrate to God without a Mediator. What, then, must it have been, when by fatal ruin he was plunged into death and hell, defiled by so many stains, made loathsome by corruption; in fine, overwhelmed with every curse? It is not without cause, therefore, that Paul, when he would set forth Christ as the Mediator, distinctly declares him to be man. There is, says he, "one Mediator between God and man, the man Christ Jesus" (1 Tim. 2:5). He might have called him God, or at least, omitting to call him God he might also have omitted to call him man; but because the Spirit, speaking by his mouth, knew our infirmity, he opportunely provides for it by the most appropriate remedy, setting the Son of God familiarly before us as one of ourselves. That no one, therefore, may feel perplexed where to seek the Mediator, or by what means to reach him, the Spirit, by calling him man, reminds us that he is near, nay, contiguous to us, inasmuch as he is our flesh. And, indeed, he intimates the same thing in another place, where he explains at greater length that he is not a high priest who "cannot be touched with the feeling of our infirmities; but was in all points tempted like as we are, yet without sin" (Heb. 4:15).

2. This will become still clearer if we reflect, that the work to be performed by the Mediator was of no common description: being to restore us to the divine favour, so as to make us, instead of sons of men, sons of God; instead of heirs of hell, heirs of a heavenly kingdom. Who could do this unless the Son of God should also become the Son of man, and so receive what is ours as to transfer to us what is his, making that which is his by nature to become ours by grace? Relying on this earnest, we trust that we are the sons of God, because the natural Son of God assumed to himself a body of our body, flesh of our flesh, bones of our bones, that he might be one with us; he declined not to take what was peculiar to us, that he might in his turn extend to us what was peculiarly his own, and thus might be in common with us both Son of God and Son of man. Hence that holy brotherhood which he commends with his own lips, when he says, "I ascend to my Father, and your Father, to my God, and your God" (John 20:17). In this way, we have a sure inheritance in the heavenly kingdom, because the only Son of God, to whom it entirely belonged, has adopted us as his brethren; and if brethren, then partners with him in the inheritance (Rom. 8:17). Moreover, it was especially necessary for this cause also that he who was to be our Redeemer should be truly God and man. It was his to swallow up death: who but Life could do so? It was his to conquer sin: who could do so save Righteousness itself? It was his to put to flight the powers of the air and the world: who could do so but the mighty power superior to both? But who possesses life and righteousness, and the dominion and government of heaven, but God alone? Therefore, God, in his infinite mercy, having determined to redeem us, became himself our Redeemer in the person of his only begotten Son.

3. Another principal part of our reconciliation with God was, that man, who had lost himself by his

disobedience, should, by way of remedy, oppose to it obedience, satisfy the justice of God, and pay the penalty of sin. Therefore, our Lord came forth very man, adopted the person of Adam, and assumed his name, that he might in his stead obey the Father; that he might present our flesh as the price of satisfaction to the just judgment of God, and in the same flesh pay the penalty which we had incurred. Finally, since as God only he could not suffer, and as man only could not overcome death, he united the human nature with the divine, that he might subject the weakness of the one to death as an expiation of sin, and by the power of the other, maintaining a struggle with death, might gain us the victory. Those, therefore, who rob Christ of divinity or humanity either detract from his majesty and glory, or obscure his goodness. On the other hand, they are no less injurious to men, undermining and subverting their faith, which, unless it rest on this foundation, cannot stand. Moreover, the expected Redeemer was that son of Abraham and David whom God had promised in the Law and in the Prophets. Here believers have another advantage. Tracing up his origin in regular series to David and Abraham, they more distinctly recognise him as the Messiah celebrated by so many oracles. But special attention must be paid to what I lately explained, namely, that a common nature is the pledge of our union with the Son of God; that, clothed with our flesh, he warred to death with sin that he might be our triumphant conqueror; that the flesh which he received of us he offered in sacrifice, in order that by making expiation he might wipe away our guilt, and appease the just anger of his Father.

4. He who considers these things with due attention, will easily disregard vague speculations, which attract giddy minds and lovers of novelty. One speculation of this class is, that Christ, even though there had been no need of his interposition to redeem the human race, would still have become man. I admit that in the first ordering of creation, while the state of nature was entire, he was appointed head of angels and men; for which reason Paul designates him "the first-born of every creature" (Col. 1:15). But since the whole Scripture proclaims that he was clothed with flesh in order to become a Redeemer, it is presumptuous to imagine any other cause or end. We know well why Christ was at first promised—viz. that he might renew a fallen world, and succour lost man. Hence under the Law he was typified by sacrifices, to inspire believers with the hope that God would be propitious to them after he was reconciled by the expiation of their sins. Since from the earliest age, even before the Law was promulgated, there was never any promise of a Mediator without blood, we justly infer that he was destined in the eternal counsel of God to purge the pollution of man, the shedding of blood being the symbol of expiation. Thus, too, the prophets, in discoursing of him, foretold that he would be the Mediator between God and man. It is sufficient to refer to the very remarkable prophecy of Isaiah (Is. 53:4, 5), in which he foretells that he was "smitten for our iniquities;" that "the chastisement of our peace was upon him;" that as a priest "he was made an offering for sin;" "that by his stripes we are healed;" that as all "like lost sheep have gone astray," "it pleased the Lord to bruise him, and put him to grief," that he might "bear our iniquities." After hearing that Christ was divinely appointed to bring relief to miserable sinners, whose overleaps these limits gives too much indulgence to a foolish curiosity.

Then when he actually appeared, he declared the cause of his advent to be, that by appeasing God he might bring us from death unto life. To the same effect was the testimony of the Apostles concerning him (John 1:9; 10:14). Thus John, before teaching that the Word was made flesh, narrates the fall of man. But above all, let us listen to our Saviour himself when discoursing of his office: "God so loved the world, that he gave his only begotten Son, that whosoever believeth in him should not perish, but have everlasting life." Again, "The hour is coming, and now is, when the dead shall hear the voice of the Son of God: and they that hear shall live." "I am the resurrection and the life: he that believeth in me, though he were dead, yet shall he live." "The Son of man is come to save that which was lost." Again, "They that be whole need not a physician." I should never have done were I to quote all the passages. Indeed, the Apostles, with one consent, lead us back to this fountain; and assuredly, if he had not come to reconcile God, the honour of his priesthood would fall, seeing it was his office as priest to stand between God and men, and "offer both gifts and sacrifices for sins" (Heb. 5:1); nor could he be our righteousness, as having been made a propitiation for us in order that God might not impute to us our sins (2 Cor. 5:19). In short, he would be stript of all the titles with which Scripture invests him. Nor could Paul's doctrine stand "What the law could not do, in that it was weak through the flesh, God sending his own Son in the likeness of sinful flesh, and for sin, condemned sin in the flesh" (Rom. 8:3). Nor what he states in another passage: "The grace of God that bringeth salvation has appeared to all men" (Tit. 2:11). In fine, the only end which the Scripture uniformly assigns for the Son of God voluntarily assuming our nature, and even receiving it as a command from the Father, is, that he might propitiate the Father to us by becoming a victim. "Thus it is written, and thus it behoved Christ to suffer;"—"and that repentance and remission of sins should be preached in his name." "Therefore does my Father love me, because I lay down my life, that I might take it again."—"This commandment have I received of my Father." "As Moses lifted up the serpent in the wilderness, even so must the Son of man be lifted up." "Father, save me from this hour: but for this cause came I unto this hour. Father, glorify thy name." Here he distinctly assigns as the reason for assuming our nature, that he might become a propitiatory victim to take away sin. For the same reason Zacharias declares (Luke 1:79), that he came "to perform the mercy promised to our fathers," "to give light to them that sit in darkness, and in the shadow of death." Let us remember that all these things are affirmed of the Son of God, in whom, as Paul elsewhere declares, were "hid all the treasures of wisdom and knowledge," and save whom it was his determination "not to know any thing" (Col. 2:3; 1 Cor. 2:2).

5. Should any one object, that in this there is nothing to prevent the same Christ who redeemed us when condemned from also testifying his love to us when safe by assuming our nature, we have the brief answer, that when the Spirit declares that by the eternal decree of God the two things were connected together—viz. that Christ should be our Redeemer, and, at the same time, a partaker of our nature, it is unlawful to inquire further. He who is tickled with a desire of knowing something more, not contented with the immutable ordination of God, shows also that he is not even contented with that Christ who has been given us as the price of redemption. And, indeed, Paul not only declares for what end he was sent, but rising to the sublime mystery of predestination, seasonably represses all the wantonness and prurience of the human mind. "He has chosen us in him before the foundation of the world, that we should be holy and without blame before him in love: having predestinated us unto the adoption of children by Jesus Christ to himself, according to the good pleasure of his will, to the praise of the glory of his grace, wherein he has made us accepted in the Beloved: In whom we have redemption through his blood" (Eph. 1:4–7). Here certainly the fall of Adam is not presupposed as anterior in point of time, but our attention is directed to what God predetermined before all ages, when he was pleased to provide a cure for the misery of the human race. If, again, it is objected that this counsel of God depended on the fall of man, which he foresaw, to me it is sufficient and more to reply, that those who propose to inquire, or desire to know more of Christ than God predestinated by his secret decree, are presuming with impious audacity to invent a new Christ. Paul, when discoursing of the proper office of Christ, justly prays for the Ephesians that God would strengthen them "by his Spirit in the inner man," that they might "be able to comprehend with all saints what is the breadth and length, and depth and height; and to know the love of Christ which passeth knowledge" (Eph. 3:16, 18); as if he intended of set purpose to set barriers around our minds, and prevent them from declining one iota from the gift of reconciliation whenever mention is made of Christ. Wherefore, seeing it is as Paul declares it to be, "a faithful saying, and worthy of all acceptation, that Christ Jesus came into the world to save sinners" (1 Tim. 1:15), in it I willingly acquiesce. And since the same Apostle elsewhere declares that the grace which is now manifested by the Gospel "was given us in Christ Jesus before the world began" (2 Tim. 1:9), I am resolved to adhere to it firmly even to the end. This moderation is unjustly vituperated by Osiander, who has unhappily, in the present day, again agitated this question, which a few had formerly raised. He brings a charge of overweening confidence against those who deny that the Son of God would have appeared in the flesh if Adam had not fallen, because this notion is not repudiated by any passage of Scripture. As if Paul did not lay a curb on perverse curiosity when after speaking of the redemption obtained by Christ, he bids us "avoid foolish questions" (Tit. 3:9). To such insanity have some proceeded in their preposterous eagerness to seem acute, that they have made it a question whether the Son of God might not have assumed the nature of an ass. This blasphemy, at which all pious minds justly shudder with detestation, Osiander excuses by the pretext that it is no where distinctly refuted in Scripture; as if Paul, when he counted nothing valuable or worth knowing "save Jesus Christ and him crucified" (I Cor. 2:2), were admitting, that the author of salvation is an ass. He who elsewhere declares that Christ was by the eternal counsel of the Father appointed "head over all things to the church," would never have acknowledged another to whom no office of redemption had been assigned.

6. The principle on which Osiander founds is altogether frivolous. He will have it that man was created in the image of God, inasmuch as he was formed on the model of the future Messiah, in order to resemble him whom the Father had already determined to clothe with

flesh. Hence he infers, that though Adam had never fallen from his first and pure original, Christ would still have been man. How silly and distorted this view is, all men of sound judgment at once discern; still he thinks he was the first to see what the image of God was, namely, that not only did the divine glory shine forth in the excellent endowments with which he was adorned, but God dwelt in him essentially. But while I grant that Adam bore the image of God, inasmuch as he was united to God (this being the true and highest perfection of dignity), yet I maintain, that the likeness of God is to be sought for only in those marks of superiority with which God has distinguished Adam above the other animals. And likewise, with one consent, acknowledge that Christ was even then the image of God, and, accordingly, whatever excellence was engraven on Adam had its origin in this, that by means of the only begotten Son he approximated to the glory of his Maker. Man, therefore, was created in the image of God (Gen. 1:27), and in him the Creator was pleased to behold, as in a mirror, his own glory. To this degree of honour he was exalted by the kindness of the only begotten Son. But I add, that as the Son was the common head both of men and angels, so the dignity which was conferred on man belonged to the angels also. For when we hear them called the sons of God (Ps. 82:6), it would be incongruous to deny that they were endued with some quality in which they resembled the Father. But if he was pleased that his glory should be represented in men and angels, and made manifest in both natures, it is ignorant trifling in Osiander to say, that angels were postponed to men, because they did not bear the image of Christ. They could not constantly enjoy the immediate presence of God if they were not like to him; nor does Paul teach (Col. 3:10) that men are renewed in the image of God in any other way than by being associated with angels, that they may be united together under one head. In fine, if we believe Christ, our felicity will be perfected when we shall have been received into the heavens, and made like the angels. But if Osiander is entitled to infer that the primary type of the image of God was in the man Christ, on the same ground may any one maintain that Christ behoved to partake of the angelic nature, seeing that angels also possess the image of God.

7. Osiander has no reason to fear that God would be found a liar, if the decree to incarnate the Son was not previously immutably fixed in his mind. Even had Adam not lost his integrity, he would, with the angels, have been like to God; and yet it would not therefore have been necessary that the Son of God should become either a man or an angel. In vain does he entertain the absurd fear, that unless it had been determined by the immutable counsel of God, before man was created, that Christ should be born, not as the Redeemer, but as the first man, he might lose his precedence, since he would not have been born, except for an accidental circumstance, namely, that he might restore the lost race of man; and in this way would have been created in the image of Adam. For why should he be alarmed at what the Scripture plainly teaches, that "he was in all points tempted like as we are, yet without sin?" (Heb. 4:15). Hence Luke, also, hesitates not to reckon him in his genealogy as a son of Adam (Luke 3:38). I should like to know why Christ is termed by Paul the second Adam (1 Cor. 15:47), unless it be that a human condition was decreed him, for the purpose of raising up the ruined posterity of Adam. For if in point of order, that condition was antecedent to creation, he ought to have been called the first Adam. Osiander confidently affirms, that because Christ was in the purpose of God foreknown as man, men were formed after him as their model. But Paul, by calling him the second Adam, gives that revolt which made it necessary to restore nature to its primitive condition an intermediate place between its original formation and the restitution which we obtain by Christ: hence it follows, that it was this restitution which made the Son of God be born, and thereby become man. Moreover, Osiander argues ill and absurdly, that as long as Adam maintained his integrity, he would have been the image of himself, and not of Christ. I maintain, on the contrary, that although the Son of God had never become incarnate, nevertheless the image of God was conspicuous in Adam, both in his body and his soul; in the rays of this image it always appeared that Christ was truly head, and had in all things the pre-eminence. In this way we dispose of the futile sophism put forth by Osiander, that the angels would have been without this head, had not God purposed to clothe his Son with flesh, even independent of the sin of Adam. He inconsiderately assumes what no rational person will grant, that Christ could have had no supremacy over the angels, so that they might enjoy him as their prince, unless in so far as he was man. But it is easy to infer from the words of Paul (Col. 1:15), that inasmuch as he is the eternal Word of God, he is the first-born of every creature, not because he is created, or is to be reckoned among the creatures, but because the entire structure of the world, such as it was from the beginning, when adorned with exquisite beauty had no other beginning; then, inasmuch as he was made man, he is the first-born from the dead. For in one short

passage (Col. 1:16–18), the Apostle calls our attention to both views: that by the Son all things were created, so that he has dominion over angels; and that he became man, in order that he might begin to be a Redeemer. Owing to the same ignorance, Osiander says that men would not have had Christ for their king unless he had been a man; as if the kingdom of God could not have been established by his eternal Son, though not clothed with human flesh, holding the supremacy while angels and men were gathered together to participate in his celestial life and glory. But he is always deluded, or imposes upon himself by this false principle, that the church would have been akefalon—without a head—had not Christ appeared in the flesh. In the same way as angels enjoyed him for their head, could he not by his divine energy preside over men, and by the secret virtue of his Spirit quicken and cherish them as his body, until they were gathered into heaven to enjoy the same life with the angels? The absurdities which I have been refuting, Osiander regards as infallible oracles. Taking an intoxicating delight in his own speculations, his wont is to extract ridiculous plans out of nothing. He afterwards says that he has a much stronger passage to produce, namely, the prophecy of Adam, who, when the woman was brought to him, said, "This is now bone of my bone, and flesh of my flesh" (Gen. 2:23). But how does he prove it to be a prophecy? Because in Matthew Christ attributes the same expression to God! as if every thing which God has spoken by man contained a prophecy. On the same principle, as the law proceeded from God, let Osiander in each precept find a prophecy. Add, that our Saviour's exposition would have been harsh and grovelling, had he confined himself to the literal meaning. He was not referring to the mystical union with which he has honoured the Church, but only to conjugal fidelity, and states, that the reason why God declared man and wife to be one flesh, was to prevent any one from violating that indissoluble tie by divorce. If this simple meaning is too low for Osiander, let him censure Christ for not leading his disciples to the hidden sense, by interpreting his Father's words with more subtlety. Paul gives no countenance to Osiander's dream, when, after saying that "we are members of his body, of his flesh, and of his bones," he immediately adds, "This is a great mystery" (Eph. 5:30–32). For he meant not to refer to the sense in which Adam used the words, but sets forth, under the figure and similitude of marriage, the sacred union which makes us one with Christ. His words have this meaning; for reminding us that he is speaking of Christ and the Church, he, by way of correction, distinguishes between the marriage tie and the spiritual union of Christ with his Church. Wherefore, this subtlety vanishes at once. I deem it unnecessary to discuss similar absurdities: for from this very brief refutation, the vanity of them all will be discovered. Abundantly sufficient for the solid nurture of the children of God is this sober truth, that "when the fulness of the time was come, God sent forth his Son, made of a woman, made under the law, to redeem them who were under the law" (Gal. 4:4, 5).

CHAPTER 13

CHRIST CLOTHED WITH THE TRUE SUBSTANCE OF HUMAN NATURE.

The heads of this chapter are, I. The orthodoxy doctrine as to the true humanity of our Saviour, proved from many passages of Scripture, sec. 1. II. Refutation of the impious objections of the Marcionites, Manichees, and similar heretics, sec. 2–4.

Sections:

1. Proof of the true humanity of Christ, against the Manichees and Marcionites.
2. Impious objections of heretics further discussed. Six objections answered.
3. Other eight objections answered.
4. Other three objections answered.

1. Of the divinity of Christ, which has elsewhere been established by clear and solid proofs, I presume it were superfluous again to treat. It remains, therefore, to see how, when clothed with our flesh, he fulfilled the office of Mediator. In ancient times, the reality of his human nature was impugned by the Manichees and Marcionites, the latter figuring to themselves a phantom instead of the body of Christ, and the former dreaming of his having been invested with celestial flesh. The passages of Scripture contradictory to both are numerous and strong. The blessing is not promised in a heavenly seed, or the mask of a man, but the seed of Abraham and Jacob; nor is the everlasting throne promised to an aerial man, but to the Son of David, and the fruit of his loins. Hence, when manifested in the flesh, he is called the Son of David and Abraham, not because he was born of a virgin, and yet created in the air, but because, as Paul explains, he was "made of the seed of David, according to the flesh" (Rom. 1:3), as the same apostle elsewhere says, that he came of the Jews (Rom. 9:5). Wherefore, our Lord himself not

contented with the name of man, frequently calls himself the Son of man, wishing to express more clearly that he was a man by true human descent. The Holy Spirit having so often, by so many organs, with so much care and plainness, declared a matter which in itself is not abstruse, who could have thought that mortals would have had the effrontery to darken it with their glosses? Many other passages are at hand, were it wished to produce more: for instance, that one of Paul, that "God sent forth his Son, made of a woman" (Gal. 4:4), and innumerable others, which show that he was subject to hunger, thirst, cold, and the other infirmities of our nature. But from the many we must chiefly select those which may conduce to build up our minds in true faith, as when it is said, "Verily, he took not on him the nature of angels, but he took on him the seed of Abraham," "that through death he might destroy him that had the power of death" (Heb. 2:16, 14). Again, "Both he that sanctifieth and they who are sanctified are all of one: for which cause he is not ashamed to call them brethren." "Wherefore in all things it behoved him to be made like unto his brethren, that he might be a merciful and faithful high priest." (Heb. 2:11, 17). Again "We have not an high priest which cannot be touched with the feeling of our infirmities" (Heb. 4:15), and the like. To the same effect is the passage to which we lately referred, in which Paul distinctly declares, that the sins of the world behoved to be expiated in our flesh (Rom. 8:3). And certainly every thing which the Father conferred on Christ pertains to us for this reason, that "he is the head," that from him the whole body is "fitly joined together, and compacted by that which every joint supplieth" (Eph. 4:16). Nay, in no other way could it hold true as is said, that the Spirit was given to him without measure (John 1:16), and that out of his fulness have all we received; since nothing could be more absurd than that God, in his own essence, should be enriched by an adventitious gift. For this reason also, Christ himself elsewhere says, "For their sakes I sanctify myself" (John 17:19).

2. The passages which they produce in confirmation of their error are absurdly wrested, nor do they gain any thing by their frivolous subtleties when they attempt to do away with what I have now adduced in opposition to them. Marcion imagines that Christ, instead of a body, assumed a phantom, because it is elsewhere said, that he was made in the likeness of man, and found in fashion as a man. Thus he altogether overlooks what Paul is then discussing (Phil. 2:7). His object is not to show what kind of body Christ assumed, but that, when he might have justly asserted his divinity he was pleased to exhibit nothing but the attributes of a mean and despised man. For, in order to exhort us to submission by his example, he shows, that when as God he might have displayed to the world the brightness of his glory, he gave up his right, and voluntarily emptied himself; that he assumed the form of a servant, and, contented with that humble condition, suffered his divinity to be concealed under a veil of flesh. Here, unquestionably, he explains not what Christ was, but in what way he acted. Nay, from the whole context it is easily gathered, that it was in the true nature of man that Christ humbled himself. For what is meant by the words, he was "found in fashion as a man," but that for a time, instead of being resplendent with divine glory, the human form only appeared in a mean and abject condition? Nor would the words of Peter, that he was "put to death in the flesh, but quickened by the Spirits" (1 Pet. 3:18), hold true, unless the Son of God had become weak in the nature of man. This is explained more clearly by Paul, when he declares that "he was crucified through weakness" (2 Cor. 13:4). And hence his exaltation; for it is distinctly said, that Christ acquired new glory after he humbled himself. This could fitly apply only to a man endued with a body and a soul. Manes dreams of an aerial body, because Christ is called the second Adam, the Lord from heaven. But the apostle does not there speak of the essence of his body as heavenly, but of the spiritual life which derived from Christ quickens us (I Cor. 15:47). This life Paul and Peter, as we have seen, separate from his flesh. Nay, that passage admirably confirms the doctrine of the orthodox, as to the human nature of Christ. If his body were not of the same nature with ours, there would be no soundness in the argument which Paul pursues with so much earnestness,—If Christ is risen we shall rise also; if we rise not, neither has Christ risen. Whatever be the cavils by which the ancient Manichees, or their modern disciples, endeavour to evade this, they cannot succeed. It is a frivolous and despicable evasion to say, that Christ is called the Son of man, because he was promised to men; it being obvious that, in the Hebrew idiom, the Son of man means a true man: and Christ, doubtless, retained the idiom of his own tongue. Moreover, there cannot be a doubt as to what is to be understood by the sons of Adam. Not to go farther, a passage in the eighth psalm, which the apostles apply to Christ, will abundantly suffice: "What is man, that thou art mindful of him? and the son of man, that thou visitest him?" (Ps 8:4). Under

this figure is expressed the true humanity of Christ. For although he was not immediately descended of an earthly father, yet he originally sprang from Adam. Nor could it otherwise be said in terms of the passage which we have already quoted, "Forasmuch, then, as the children are partakers of flesh and blood, he also himself likewise took part of the same;" these words plainly proving that he was an associate and partner in the same nature with ourselves. In this sense also it is said, that "both he that sanctifieth and they who are sanctified are all of one." The context proves that this refers to a community of nature; for it is immediately added, "For which cause he is not ashamed to call them brethren" (Heb. 2:11). Had he said at first that believers are of God, where could there have been any ground for being ashamed of persons possessing such dignity? But when Christ of his boundless grace associates himself with the mean and ignoble, we see why it was said that "he is not ashamed." It is vain to object, that in this way the wicked will be the brethren of Christ; for we know that the children of God are not born of flesh and blood, but of the Spirit through faith. Therefore, flesh alone does not constitute the union of brotherhood. But although the apostle assigns to believers only the honour of being one with Christ, it does not however follow, that unbelievers have not the same origin according to the flesh; just as when we say that Christ became man, that he might make us sons of God, the expression does not extend to all classes of persons; the intervention of faith being necessary to our being spiritually ingrafted into the body of Christ. A dispute is also ignorantly raised as to the term *first-born*. It is alleged that Christ ought to have been the first son of Adam, in order that he might be the first-born among the brethren (Rom. 8:29). But primogeniture refers not to age, but to degree of honour and pre-eminence of virtue. There is just as little colour for the frivolous assertion that Christ assumed the nature of man, and not that of angels (Heb. 2:16), because it was the human race that he restored to favour. The apostle, to magnify the honour which Christ has conferred upon us, contrasts us with the angels, to whom we are in this respect preferred. And if due weight is given to the testimony of Moses (Gen. 3:15), when he says that the seed of the woman would bruise the head of the serpent, the dispute is at an end. For the words there used refer not to Christ alone, but to the whole human race. Since the victory was to be obtained for us by Christ, God declares generally, that the posterity of the woman would overcome the devil. From this it follows, that Christ is a descendant of the human race, the purpose of God in thus addressing Eve being to raise her hopes, and prevent her from giving way to despair.

3. The passages in which Christ is called the seed of Abraham, and the fruit of the loins of David, those persons, with no less folly than wickedness, wrap up in allegory. Had the term *seed* been used allegorically, Paul surely would not have omitted to notice it, when he affirms clearly, and without figure, that the promise was not given "to seeds, as of many; but as of one, And to thy seed, which is Christ" (Gal. 3:16). With similar absurdity they pretend that he was called the Son of David for no other reason but because he had been promised, and was at length in due time manifested. For Paul, after he had called him the Son of David, by immediately subjoining "*according to the flesh*", certainly designates his nature. So also (Rom. 9:5), while declaring him to be "God blessed for ever," he mentions separately, that, "as concerning the flesh, he was descended from the Jews." Again if he had not been truly begotten of the seed of David, what is the meaning of the expression, that he is the "fruit of his loins;" or what the meaning of the promise, "Of the fruit of thy body will I set upon thy throne?" (Ps. 132:11). Moreover their mode of dealing with the genealogy of Christ, as given by Matthew, is mere sophistry; for though he reckons up the progenitors not of Mary, but of Joseph, yet as he was speaking of a matter then generally understood, he deems it enough to show that Joseph was descended from the seed of David, since it is certain that Mary was of the same family. Luke goes still farther, showing that the salvation brought by Christ is common to the whole human race, inasmuch as Christ, the author of salvation, is descended from Adam, the common father of us all. I confess, indeed, that the genealogy proves Christ to be the Son of David only as being descended of the Virgin; but the new Marcionites, for the purpose of giving a gloss to their heresy, namely to prove that the body which Christ assumed was unsubstantial, too confidently maintain that the expression as to seed is applicable only to males, thus subverting the elementary principles of nature. But as this discussion belongs not to theology, and the arguments which they adduce are too futile to require any laboured refutation, I will not touch on matters pertaining to philosophy and the medical art. It will be sufficient to dispose of the objection drawn from the statement of Scripture, that Aaron and Jehoiadah married wives out of the tribe of Judah, and that thus the distinction of

tribes was confounded, if proper descent could come through the female. It is well known, that in regard to civil order, descent is reckoned through the male; and yet the superiority on his part does not prevent the female from having her proper share in the descent. This solution applies to all the genealogies. When Scripture gives a list of individuals, it often mentions males only. Must we therefore say that females go for nothing? Nay, the very children know that they are classified with men. For this reasons wives are said to give children to their husbands, the name of the family always remaining with the males. Then, as the male sex has this privilege, that sons are deemed of noble or ignoble birth, according to the condition of their fathers, so, on the other hand, in slavery, the condition of the child is determined by that of the mother, as lawyers say, *partus sequitur ventrem*. Whence we may infer, that offspring is partly procreated by the seed of the mother. According to the common custom of nations, mothers are deemed progenitors, and with this the divine law agrees, which could have had no ground to forbid the marriage of the uncle with the niece, if there was no consanguinity between them. It would also be lawful for a brother and sister uterine to intermarry, when their fathers are different. But while I admit that the power assigned to the woman is passive, I hold that the same thing is affirmed indiscriminately of her and of the male. Christ is not said to have been made by a woman, but of a woman (Gal. 4:4). But some of this herd, laying aside all shame, publicly ask whether we mean to maintain that Christ was procreated of the proper seed of a Virgin. I, in my turn, asks whether they are not forced to admit that he was nourished to maturity in the Virgin's womb. Justly, therefore, we infer from the words of Matthew, that Christ, inasmuch as he was begotten of Mary, was procreated of her seed; as a similar generation is denoted when Boaz is said to have been begotten of Rachab (Mt. 1:5, 16). Matthew does not here describe the Virgin as the channel through which Christ flowed, but distinguishes his miraculous from an ordinary birth, in that Christ was begotten by her of the seed of David. For the same reason for which Isaac is said to be begotten of Abraham, Joseph of Jacob, Solomon of David, is Christ said to have been begotten of his mother. The Evangelist has arranged his discourse in this way. Wishing to prove that Christ derives his descent from David, he deems it enough to state, that he was begotten of Mary. Hence it follows, that he assumed it as an acknowledged fact, that Mary was of the same lineage as Joseph.

4. The absurdities which they wish to fasten upon us are mere puerile calumnies. They reckon it base and dishonouring to Christ to have derived his descent from men; because, in that case, he could not be exempted from the common law which includes the whole offspring of Adam, without exception, under sin. But this difficulty is easily solved by Paul's antithesis, "As by one man sin entered into the world, and death by sin"—"even so by the righteousness of one the free gift came upon all men unto justification of life" (Rom. 5:12, 18). Corresponding to this is another passage, "The first man is of the earth, earthy: the second man is the Lord from heaven" (1 Cor. 15:47). Accordingly, the same apostle, in another passage, teaching that Christ was sent "in the likeness of sinful flesh, that the righteousness of the law might be fulfilled in us," distinctly separates him from the common lot, as being true man, and yet without fault and corruption (Rom. 8:3). It is childish trifling to maintain, that if Christ is free from all taint, and was begotten of the seed of Mary, by the secret operation of the Spirit, it is not therefore the seed of the woman that is impure, but only that of the man. We do not hold Christ to be free from all taint, merely because he was born of a woman unconnected with a man, but because he was sanctified by the Spirit, so that the generation was pure and spotless, such as it would have been before Adam's fall. Let us always bear in mind, that wherever Scripture adverts to the purity of Christ, it refers to his true human nature, since it were superfluous to say that God is pure. Moreover, the sanctification of which John speaks in his seventeenth chapter is inapplicable to the divine nature. This does not suggest the idea of a twofold seed in Adam, although no contamination extended to Christ, the generation of man not being in itself vicious or impure, but an accidental circumstance of the fall. Hence, it is not strange that Christ, by whom our integrity was to be restored, was exempted from the common corruption. Another absurdity which they obtrude upon us—viz. that if the Word of God became incarnate, it must have been enclosed in the narrow tenement of an earthly body, is sheer petulance. For although the boundless essence of the Word was united with human nature into one person, we have no idea of any enclosing. The Son of God descended miraculously from heaven, yet without abandoning heaven; was pleased to be conceived miraculously in the Virgin's womb, to live on the earth, and hang upon the cross, and yet always filled the world as from the beginning.

CHAPTER 14

HOW TWO NATURES CONSTITUTE THE PERSON OF THE MEDIATOR.

This chapter contains two principal heads: I. A brief exposition of the doctrine of Christ's two natures in one person, sec. 1–4. II. A refutation of the heresies of Servetus, which destroy the distinction of natures in Christ, and the eternity of the divine nature of the Son.

Sections:

1. Proof of two natures in Christ—a human and a divine. Illustrated by analogy, from the union of body and soul. Illustration applied.

2. Proof from passages of Scripture which distinguish between the two natures. Proof from the communication of properties.

3. Proof from passages showing the union of both natures. A rule to be observed in this discussion.

4. Utility and use of the doctrine concerning the two natures. The Nestorians. The Eutychians. Both justly condemned by the Church.

5. The heresies of Servetus refuted. General answer or sum of the orthodox doctrine concerning Christ. What meant by the hypostatic union. Objections of Servetus to the deity of Christ. Answer.

6. Another objection and answer. A twofold filiation of Christ.

7. Other objections answered.

8. Conclusion of the former objections. Other pestilential heresies of Servetus.

1. When it is said that the Word was made flesh, we must not understand it as if he were either changed into flesh, or confusedly intermingled with flesh, but that he made choice of the Virgin's womb as a temple in which he might dwell. He who was the Son of God became the Son of man, not by confusion of substance, but by unity of person. For we maintain, that the divinity was so conjoined and united with the humanity, that the entire properties of each nature remain entire, and yet the two natures constitute only one Christ. If, in human affairs, any thing analogous to this great mystery can be found, the most apposite similitude seems to be that of man, who obviously consists of two substances, neither of which however is so intermingled with the other as that both do not retain their own properties. For neither is soul body, nor is body soul. Wherefore that is said separately of the soul which cannot in any way apply to the body; and that, on the other hand, of the body which is altogether inapplicable to the soul; and that, again, of the whole man, which cannot be affirmed without absurdity either of the body or of the soul separately. Lastly, the properties of the soul are transferred to the body, and the properties of the body to the soul, and yet these form only one man, not more than one. Such modes of expression intimate both that there is in man one person formed of two compounds, and that these two different natures constitute one person. Thus the Scriptures speak of Christ. They sometimes attribute to him qualities which should be referred specially to his humanity and sometimes qualities applicable peculiarly to his divinity, and sometimes qualities which embrace both natures, and do not apply specially to either. This combination of a twofold nature in Christ they express so carefully, that they sometimes communicate them with each other, a figure of speech which the ancients termed *ijdiwmavtwn koinoniva* (a communication of properties).

2. Little dependence could be placed on these statements, were it not proved by numerous passages throughout the sacred volume that none of them is of man's devising. What Christ said of himself, "Before Abraham was I am" (John 8:58), was very foreign to his humanity. I am not unaware of the cavil by which erroneous spirits distort this passage—viz. that he was before all ages, inasmuch as he was foreknown as the Redeemer, as well in the counsel of the Father as in the minds of believers. But seeing he plainly distinguishes the period of his manifestation from his eternal existence, and professedly founds on his ancient government, to prove his precedence to Abraham, he undoubtedly claims for himself the peculiar attributes of divinity. Paul's assertion that he is "the first-born of every creature," that "he is before all things, and by him all things consist" (Col. 1:15, 17); his own declaration, that he had glory with the Father before the world was, and that he worketh together with the Father, are equally inapplicable to man. These and similar properties must be specially assigned to his divinity. Again, his being called the servant of the Father, his being said to grow in stature, and wisdom, and favour with God and man, not to seek his own glory, not to know the last day, not to speak of himself, not to do his own will, his being seen and handled, apply entirely to his humanity; since, as God, he cannot be in any respect said to grow, works always for himself, knows every thing, does all things after the counsel of his own will, and is incapable of being seen or handled. And yet he not merely ascribes these things

separately to his human nature, but applies them to himself as suitable to his office of Mediator. There is a communication of *ijdiwvmata*, or properties, when Paul says, that God purchased the Church "with his own blood" (Acts 20:28), and that the Jews crucified the Lord of glory (1 Cor. 2:8). In like manner, John says, that the Word of God was "handled." God certainly has no blood, suffers not, cannot be touched with hands; but since that Christ, who was true God and true man, shed his blood on the cross for us, the acts which were performed in his human nature are transferred improperly, but not ceaselessly, to his divinity. We have a similar example in the passage where John says that God laid down his life for us (1 John 3:16). Here a property of his humanity is communicated with his other nature. On the other hand, when Christ, still living on the earth, said, "No man has ascended up to heaven but he that came down from heaven, even the Son of man, which is in heaven" (John 3:13), certainly regarded as man in the flesh which he had put on, he was not then in heaven, but inasmuch as he was both God and man, he, on account of the union of a twofold nature, attributed to the one what properly belonged to the other.

3. But, above all, the true substance of Christ is most clearly declared in those passages which comprehend both natures at once. Numbers of these exist in the Gospel of John. What we there read as to his having received power from the Father to forgive sins; as to his quickening whom he will; as to his bestowing righteousness, holiness, and salvation; as to his being appointed judge both of the quick and the dead; as to his being honoured even as the Father, are not peculiar either to his Godhead or his humanity, but applicable to both. In the same way he is called the Light of the world, the good Shepherd, the only Door, the true Vine. With such prerogatives the Son of God was invested on his manifestation in the flesh, and though he possessed the same with the Father before the world was created, still it was not in the same manner or respect; neither could they be attributed to one who was a man and nothing more. In the same sense we ought to understand the saying of Paul, that at the end Christ shall deliver up "the kingdom to God, even the Father" (1 Cor. 15:24). The kingdom of God assuredly had no beginning, and will have no end: but because he was hid under a humble clothing of flesh, and took upon himself the form of a servant, and humbled himself (Phil. 2:8), and, laying aside the insignia of majesty, became obedient to the Father; and after undergoing this subjection was at length crowned with glory and honour (Heb. 2:7), and exalted to supreme authority, that at his name every knee should bow (Phil. 2:10); so at the end he will subject to the Father both the name and the crown of glory, and whatever he received of the Father, that God may be all in all (1 Cor. 15:28). For what end were that power and authority given to him, save that the Father might govern us by his hand? In the same sense, also, he is said to sit at the right hand of the Father. But this is only for a time, until we enjoy the immediate presence of his Godhead. And here we cannot excuse the error of some ancient writers, who, by not attending to the office of Mediator, darken the genuine meaning of almost the whole doctrine which we read in the Gospel of John, and entangle themselves in many snares. Let us, therefore, regard it as the key of true interpretation, that those things which refer to the office of Mediator are not spoken of the divine or human nature simply. Christ, therefore, shall reign until he appear to judge the world, inasmuch as, according to the measure of our feeble capacity, he now connects us with the Father. But when, as partakers of the heavenly glory, we shall see God as he is, then Christ, having accomplished the office of Mediator, shall cease to be the vicegerent of the Father, and will be content with the glory which he possessed before the world was. Nor is the name of Lord specially applicable to the person of Christ in any other respect than in so far as he holds a middle place between God and us. To this effect are the words of Paul, "To us there is but one God, the Father, of whom are all things, and we in him; and one Lord Jesus Christ, by whom are all things, and we by him" (1 Cor. 8:6); that is, to the latter a temporary authority has been committed by the Father until his divine majesty shall be beheld face to face. His giving up of the kingdom to the Father, so far from impairing his majesty, will give a brighter manifestation of it. God will then cease to be the head of Christ, and Christ's own Godhead will then shine forth of itself, whereas it is now in a manner veiled.

4. This observation, if the readers apply it properly, will be of no small use in solving a vast number of difficulties. For it is strange how the ignorant, nay, some who are not altogether without learning, are perplexed by these modes of expression which they see applied to Christ, without being properly adapted either to his divinity or his humanity, not considering their accordance with the character in which he was manifested as God and man, and with his office of Mediator. It is very easy to see how beautifully they accord with each other, provided they have a sober interpreter, one who examines these great mysteries with the reverence which is meet. But there is

nothing which furious and frantic spirits cannot throw into confusion. They fasten on the attributes of humanity to destroy his divinity; and, on the other hand, on those of his divinity to destroy his humanity: while those which, spoken conjointly of the two natures, apply to neither, they employ to destroy both. But what else is this than to contend that Christ is not man because he is God, not God because he is man, and neither God nor man because he is both at once. Christ, therefore, as God and man, possessing natures which are united, but not confused, we conclude that he is our Lord and the true Son of God, even according to his humanity, though not by means of his humanity. For we must put far from us the heresy of Nestorius, who, presuming to dissect rather than distinguish between the two natures, devised a double Christ. But we see the Scripture loudly protesting against this, when the name of the Son of God is given to him who is born of a Virgin, and the Virgin herself is called the mother of our Lord (Luke 1:32, 43). We must beware also of the insane fancy of Eutyches, lest, when we would demonstrate the unity of person, we destroy the two natures. The many passages we have already quoted, in which the divinity is distinguished from the humanity, and the many other passages existing throughout Scripture, may well stop the mouth of the most contentious. I will shortly add a few observations, which will still better dispose of this fiction. For the present, one passage will suffice—Christ would not have called his body a temple (John 2:19), had not the Godhead distinctly dwelt in it. Wherefore, as Nestorius had been justly condemned in the Council of Ephesus, so afterwards was Eutyches in those of Constantinople and Chalcedony, it being not more lawful to confound the two natures of Christ than to divide them.

5. But in our age, also, has arisen a not less fatal monster, Michael Servetus, who for the Son of God has substituted a figment composed of the essence of God, spirit, flesh, and three uncreated elements. First, indeed, he denies that Christ is the Son of God, for any other reason than because he was begotten in the womb of the Virgin by the Holy Spirit. The tendency of this crafty device is to make out, by destroying the distinction of the two natures, that Christ is somewhat composed of God and man, and yet is not to be deemed God and man. His aim throughout is to establish, that before Christ was manifested in the flesh there were only shadowy figures in God, the truth or effect of which existed for the first time, when the Word who had been destined to that honour truly began to be the Son of God. We indeed acknowledge that the Mediator who was born of the Virgin is properly the Son of God. And how could the man Christ be a mirror of the inestimable grace of God, had not the dignity been conferred upon him both of being and of being called the only-begotten Son of God? Meanwhile, however, the definition of the Church stands unmoved, that he is accounted the Son of God, because the Word begotten by the Father before all ages assumed human nature by hypostatic union,—a term used by ancient writers to denote the union which of two natures constitutes one person, and invented to refute the dream of Nestorius, who pretended that the Son of God dwelt in the flesh in such a manner as not to be at the same time man. Servetus calumniously charges us with making the Son of God double, when we say that the eternal Word before he was clothed with flesh was already the Son of God: as if we said anything more than that he was manifested in the flesh. Although he was God before he became man, he did not therefore begin to be a new God. Nor is there any greater absurdity in holding that the Son of God, who by eternal generation ever had the property of being a Son, appeared in the flesh. This is intimated by the angel's word to Mary: "That holy thing which shall be born of thee shall be called the Son of God" (Luke 1:35); as if he had said that the name of Son, which was more obscure under the law, would become celebrated and universally known. Corresponding to this is the passage of Paul, that being now the sons of God by Christ, we "have received the Spirit of adoption, whereby we cry, Abba, Father" (Rom. 8:15). Were not also the holy patriarchs of old reckoned among the sons of God? Yea, trusting to this privilege, they invoked God as their Father. But because ever since the only-begotten Son of God came forth into the world, his celestial paternity has been more clearly manifested, Paul assigns this to the kingdom of Christ as its distinguishing feature. We must, however, constantly hold, that God never was a Father to angels and men save in respect of his only-begotten Son: that men, especially, who by their iniquity were rendered hateful to God, are sons by gratuitous adoption, because he is a Son by nature. Nor is there anything in the assertion of Servetus, that this depends on the filiation which God had decreed with himself. Here we deal not with figures, as expiation by the blood of beasts was shown to be; but since they could not be the sons of God in reality, unless their adoption was founded in the head, it is against all reason to deprive the head of that which is common to the members. I go farther: since the Scripture gives the name of sons of God to the angels, whose

great dignity in this respect depended not on the future redemption, Christ must in order take precedence of them that he may reconcile the Father to them. I will again briefly repeat and add the same thing concerning the human race. Since angels as well as men were at first created on the condition that God should be the common Father of both; if it is true, as Paul says, that Christ always was the head, "the first-born of every creature—that in all things he might have the pre-eminence" (Col. 1:15, 18), I think I may legitimately infer, that he existed as the Son of God before the creation of the world.

6. But if his filiation (if I may so express it) had a beginning at the time when he was manifested in the flesh, it follows that he was a Son in respect of human nature also. Servetus, and others similarly frenzied, hold that Christ who appeared in the flesh is the Son of God, inasmuch as but for his incarnation he could not have possessed this name. Let them now answer me, whether, according to both natures, and in respect of both, he is a Son? So indeed they prate; but Paul's doctrine is very different. We acknowledge, indeed, that Christ in human nature is called a Son, not like believers by gratuitous adoption merely, but the true, natural, and, therefore, only Son, this being the mark which distinguishes him from all others. Those of us who are regenerated to a new life God honours with the name of sons; the name of true and only-begotten Son he bestows on Christ alone. But how is he an only Son in so great a multitude of brethren, except that he possesses by nature what we acquire by gift? This honour we extend to his whole character of Mediator, so that He who was born of a Virgin, and on the cross offered himself in sacrifice to the Father, is truly and properly the Son of God; but still in respect of his Godhead: as Paul teaches when he says, that he was "separated unto the gospel of God (which he had promised afore by his prophets in the Holy Scriptures), concerning his Son Jesus Christ our Lord, which was made of the seed of David according to the flesh; and declared to be the Son of God with power" (Rom. 1:1–4). When distinctly calling him the Son of David according to the flesh, why should he also say that he was "declared to be the Son of God," if he meant not to intimate, that this depended on something else than his incarnation? For in the same sense in which he elsewhere says, that "though he was crucified through weakness, yet he liveth by the power of God" (2 Cor. 13:4), so he now draws a distinction between the two natures. They must certainly admit, that as on account of his mother he is called the Son of David, so, on account of his Father, he is the Son of God, and that in some respect differing from his human nature. The Scripture gives him both names, calling him at one time the Son of God, at another the Son of Man. As to the latter, there can be no question that he is called a Son in accordance with the phraseology of the Hebrew language, because he is of the offspring of Adam. On the other hand, I maintain that he is called a Son on account of his Godhead and eternal essence, because it is no less congruous to refer to his divine nature his being called the Son of God, than to refer to his human nature his being called the Son of Man. In fine, in the passage which I have quoted, Paul does not mean, that he who according to the flesh was begotten of the seed of David, was declared to be the Son of God in any other sense than he elsewhere teaches that Christ, who descended of the Jews according to the flesh, is "over all, God blessed for ever" (Rom. 9:5). But if in both passages the distinction of two natures is pointed out, how can it be denied, that he who according to the flesh is the Son of Man, is also in respect of his divine nature the Son of God?

7. They indeed find a blustering defence of their heresy in its being said, that "God spared not his own Son," and in the communication of the angel, that He who was to be born of the Virgin should be called the "Son of the Highest" (Rom. 8:32; Luke 1:32). But before pluming themselves on this futile objection, let them for a little consider with us what weight there is in their argument. If it is legitimately concluded, that at conception he began to be the Son of God, because he who has been conceived is called a Son, it will follow, that he began to be the Word after his manifestation in the flesh, because John declares, that the Word of life of which he spoke was that which "our hands have handled" (1 John 1:1). In like manner we read in the prophet, "Thou, Bethlehem Ephratah, though thou be little among the thousands of Israel, yet out of thee shall he come forth that is to be a ruler in Israel; whose goings forth have been from of old, from everlasting" (Mic. 5:2). How will they be forced to interpret if they will follow such a method of arguing? I have declared that we by no means assent to Nestorius, who imagined a twofold Christ, when we maintain that Christ, by means of brotherly union, made us sons of God with himself, because in the flesh, which he took from us, he is the only-begotten Son of God. And Augustine wisely reminds us, that he is a bright mirror of the wonderful and singular grace of God, because as man he obtained honour which he could not merit. With this distinction, therefore, according to the flesh, was Christ honoured even from the womb—viz. to be

the Son of God. Still, in the unity of person we are not to imagine any intermixture which takes away from the Godhead what is peculiar to it. Nor is it more absurd that the eternal Word of God and Christ, uniting the two natures in one person, should in different ways be called the Son of God, than that he should in various respects be called at one time the Son of God, at another the Son of Man. Nor are we more embarrassed by another cavil of Servetus—viz. that Christ, before he appeared in the flesh, is nowhere called the Son of God, except under a figure. For though the description of him was then more obscure, yet it has already been clearly proved, that he was not otherwise the eternal God, than as he was the Word begotten of the eternal Father. Nor is the name applicable to the office of Mediator which he undertook, except in that he was God manifest in the flesh. Nor would God have thus from the beginning been called a Father, had there not been even then a mutual relation to the Son, "of whom the whole family in heaven and earth is named" (Eph. 3:15). Hence it is easy to infer, that under the Law and the Prophets he was the Son of God before this name was celebrated in the Church. But if we are to dispute about the word merely, Solomon, speaking of the incomprehensibility of God, affirms that his Son is like himself, incomprehensible: "What is his name, and what is his Son's name, if thou canst tell?" (Prov. 30:4). I am well aware that with the contentious this passage will not have sufficient weight; nor do I found much upon it, except as showing the malignant cavils of those who affirm that Christ is the Son of God only in so far as he became man. We may add, that all the most ancient writers, with one mouth and consent, testified the same thing so plainly, that the effrontery is no less ridiculous than detestable, which dares to oppose us with Irenaeus and Tertullian, both of whom acknowledge that He who was afterwards visibly manifested was the invisible Son of God.

8. But although Servetus heaped together a number of horrid dogmas, to which, perhaps, others would not subscribe, you will find, that all who refuse to acknowledge the Son of God except in the flesh, are obliged, when urged more closely, to admit that he was a Son, for no other reason than because he was conceived in the womb of the Virgin by the Holy Spirit; just like the absurdity of the ancient Manichees, that the soul of man was derived by transfusion from God, from its being said, that he breathed into Adam's nostrils the breath of life (Gen. 2:7). For they lay such stress on the name of Son that they leave no distinction between the natures, but babblingly maintain that the man Christ is the Son of God, because, according to his human nature, he was begotten of God. Thus, the eternal generation of Wisdom, celebrated by Solomon (Prov. 8:22, seq). is destroyed, and no kind of Godhead exists in the Mediator: or a phantom is substituted instead of a man. The grosser delusions of Servetus, by which he imposed upon himself and some others, it were useful to refute, that pious readers might be warned by the example, to confine themselves within the bounds of soberness and modesty: however, I deem it superfluous here, as I have already done it in a special treatise. The whole comes to this, that the Son of God was from the beginning an idea, and was even then a preordained man, who was to be the essential image of God. nor does he acknowledge any other word of God except in external splendour. The generation he interprets to mean, that from the beginning a purpose of generating the Son was begotten in God, and that this purpose extended itself by act to creation. Meanwhile, he confounds the Spirit with the Word, saying that God arranged the invisible Word and Spirit into flesh and soul. In short, in his view the typifying of Christ occupies the place of generation; but he says, that he who was then in appearance a shadowy Son, was at length begotten by the Word, to which he attributes a generating power. From this it will follow, that dogs and swine are not less sons of God, because created of the original seed of the Divine Word. But although he compounds Christ of three untreated elements, that he may be begotten of the essence of God, he pretends that he is the first-born among the creatures, in such a sense that, according to their degree, stones have the same essential divinity. But lest he should seem to strip Christ of his Deity, he admits that his flesh is *ojmoouvsion*, of the same substance with God, and that the Word was made man, by the conversion of flesh into Deity. Thus, while he cannot comprehend that Christ was the Son of God, until his flesh came forth from the essence of God and was converted into Deity, he reduces the eternal personality (*hypostasis*) of the Word to nothing, and robs us of the Son of David, who was the promised Redeemer. It is true, he repeatedly declares that the Son was begotten of God by knowledge and predestination, but that he was at length made man out of that matter which, from the beginning, shone with God in the three elements, and afterwards appeared in the first light of the world, in the cloud and pillar of fire. How shamefully inconsistent with himself he ever and anon becomes, it were too tedious to relate. From this brief account sound readers will gather, that by the subtle ambiguities of this infatuated man, the hope of salvation was utterly extinguished. For if the flesh

were the Godhead itself, it would cease to be its temple. Now, the only Redeemer we can have is He who being begotten of the seed of Abraham and David according to the flesh, truly became man. But he erroneously insists on the expression of John, "The Word was made flesh." As these words refute the heresy of Nestorius, so they give no countenance to the impious fiction of which Eutyches was the inventor, since all that the Evangelist intended was to assert a unity of person in two natures.

CHAPTER 15

THREE THINGS BRIEFLY TO BE REGARDED IN CHRIST—VIZ. HIS OFFICES OF PROPHET, KING, AND PRIEST.

The principal parts of this chapter are—I. Of the Prophetical Office of Christ, its dignity and use, sec. 1, 2. II. The nature of the Kingly power of Christ, and the advantage we derive from it, sec. 3–5. III. Of the Priesthood of Christ, and the efficacy of it, sec. 6.

Sections:

1. Among heretics and false Christians, Christ is found in name only; but by those who are truly and effectually called of God, he is acknowledged as a Prophet, King, and Priest. In regard to the Prophetical Office, the Redeemer of the Church is the same from whom believers under the Law hoped for the full light of understanding.

2. The unction of Christ, though it has respect chiefly to the Kingly Office, refers also to the Prophetical and Priestly Offices. The dignity, necessity, and use of this unction.

3. From the spirituality of Christ's kingdom its eternity is inferred. This twofold, referring both to the whole body of the Church, and to its individual members.

4. Benefits from the spiritual kingdom of Christ. 1. It raises us to eternal life. 2. It enriches us with all things necessary to salvation. 3. It makes us invincible by spiritual foes. 4. It animates us to patient endurance. 5. It inspires confidence and triumph. 6. It supplies fortitude and love.

5. The unction of our Redeemer heavenly. Symbol of this unction. A passage in the apostle reconciled with others previously quoted, to prove the eternal kingdom of Christ.

6. What necessary to obtain the benefit of Christ's Priesthood. We must set out with the death of Christ. From it follows, 1. His intercession for us. 2. Confidence in prayer. 3. Peace of conscience. 4. Through Christ, Christians themselves become priests. Grievous sin of the Papists in pretending to sacrifice Christ.

1. Though heretics pretend the name of Christ, truly does Augustine affirm (Enchir. ad Laurent. cap. 5), that the foundation is not common to them with the godly, but belongs exclusively to the Church: for if those things which pertain to Christ be diligently considered, it will be found that Christ is with them in name only, not in reality. Thus in the present day, though the Papists have the words, Son of God, Redeemer of the world, sounding in their mouths, yet, because contented with an empty name, they deprive him of his virtue and dignity; what Paul says of "not holding the head," is truly applicable to them (Col. 2:19). Therefore, that faith may find in Christ a solid ground of salvation, and so rest in him, we must set out with this principle, that the office which he received from the Father consists of three parts. For he was appointed both Prophet, King, and Priest; though little were gained by holding the names unaccompanied by a knowledge of the end and use. These too are spoken of in the Papacy, but frigidly, and with no great benefit, the full meaning comprehended under each title not being understood. We formerly observed, that though God, by supplying an uninterrupted succession of prophets, never left his people destitute of useful doctrine, such as might suffice for salvation; yet the minds of believers were always impressed with the conviction that the full light of understanding was to be expected only on the advent of the Messiah. This expectation, accordingly, had reached even the Samaritans, to whom the true religion had never been made known. This is plain from the expression of the woman, "I know that Messiah cometh, which is called Christ: when he is come, he will tell us all things" (John 4:25). Nor was this a mere random presumption which had entered the minds of the Jews. They believed what sure oracles had taught them. One of the most remarkable passages is that of Isaiah, "Behold, I have given him for a witness to the people, a leader and commander to the people" (Is. 55:4); that is, in the same way in which he had previously in another place styled him "Wonderful, Counsellor" (Is. 9:6). For this reason, the apostle commending the perfection of gospel doctrine, first says that "God, at sundry times and in divers manners spake in times past unto the prophets," and then adds, that he "has in these last days spoken unto us by

his Son" (Heb. 1:1, 2). But as the common office of the prophets was to hold the Church in suspense, and at the same time support it until the advent of the Mediator; we read, that the faithful, during the dispersion, complained that they were deprived of that ordinary privilege. "We see not our signs: there is no more any prophet, neither is there among us any that knoweth how long" (Ps. 74:9). But when Christ was now not far distant, a period was assigned to Daniel "to seal up the vision and prophecy" (Daniel 9:24), not only that the authority of the prediction there spoken of might be established, but that believers might, for a time, patiently submit to the want of the prophets, the fulfilment and completion of all the prophecies being at hand.

2. Moreover, it is to be observed, that the name *Christ* refers to those three offices: for we know that under the law, prophets as well as priests and kings were anointed with holy oil. Whence, also, the celebrated name of Messiah was given to the promised Mediator. But although I admit (as, indeed, I have elsewhere shown) that he was so called from a view to the nature of the kingly office, still the prophetical and sacerdotal unctions have their proper place, and must not be overlooked. The former is expressly mentioned by Isaiah in these words: "The Spirit of the Lord God is upon me: because the Lord has anointed me to preach good tidings unto the meek; he has sent me to bind up the broken-hearted, to proclaim liberty to the captive, and the opening of the prison to them that are bound; to proclaim the acceptable year of the Lord" (Is. 60:1, 2). We see that he was anointed by the Spirit to be a herald and witness of his Father's grace, and not in the usual way; for he is distinguished from other teachers who had a similar office. And here, again, it is to be observed, that the unction which he received, in order to perform the office of teacher, was not for himself, but for his whole body, that a corresponding efficacy of the Spirit might always accompany the preaching of the Gospel. This, however, remains certain, that by the perfection of doctrine which he brought, an end was put to all the prophecies, so that those who, not contented with the Gospel, annex somewhat extraneous to it, derogate from its authority. The voice which thundered from heaven, "This is my beloved Son, hear him" gave him a special privilege above all other teachers. Then from him, as head, this unction is diffused through the members, as Joel has foretold, "Your sons and your daughters shall prophesy, your old men shall dream dreams, and your young men shall see visions" (Joel 2:28). Paul's expressions, that he was "made unto us wisdom" (1 Cor. 1:30), and elsewhere, that in him "are hid all the treasures of wisdom and knowledge" (Col. 2:3), have a somewhat different meaning, namely, that out of him there is nothing worth knowing, and that those who, by faith, apprehend his true character, possess the boundless immensity of heavenly blessings. For which reason, he elsewhere says, "I determined not to know any thing among you, save Jesus Christ and him crucified" (1 Cor. 2:2). And most justly: for it is unlawful to go beyond the simplicity of the Gospel. The purpose of this prophetical dignity in Christ is to teach us, that in the doctrine which he delivered is substantially included a wisdom which is perfect in all its parts.

3. I come to the Kingly office, of which it were in vain to speak, without previously reminding the reader that its nature is spiritual; because it is from thence we learn its efficacy, the benefits it confers, its whole power and eternity. Eternity, moreover, which in Daniel an angel attributes to the office of Christ (Dan. 2:44), in Luke an angel justly applies to the salvation of his people (Luke 1:33). But this is also twofold, and must be viewed in two ways; the one pertains to the whole body of the Church the other is proper to each member. To the former is to be referred what is said in the Psalms, "Once have I sworn by my holiness, that I will not lie unto David. His seed shall endure for ever, and his throne as the sun before me. It shall be established for ever, as the moon, and as a faithful witness in heaven" (Ps. 89:35,37). There can be no doubt that God here promises that he will be, by the hand of his Son, the eternal governor and defender of the Church. In none but Christ will the fulfilment of this prophecy be found; since immediately after Solomon's death the kingdom in n great measure lost its dignity, and, with ignominy to the family of David, was transferred to a private individual. Afterwards decaying by degrees, it at length came to a sad and dishonourable end. In the same sense are we to understand the exclamation of Isaiah, "Who shall declare his generation?" (Isaiah 53:8). For he asserts that Christ will so survive death as to be connected with his members. Therefore, as often as we hear that Christ is armed with eternal power, let us learn that the perpetuity of the Church is thus effectually secured; that amid the turbulent agitations by which it is constantly harassed, and the grievous and fearful commotions which threaten innumerable disasters, it still remains safe. Thus, when David derides the audacity of the enemy who attempt to throw off the yoke of God and his anointed, and says, that kings and nations rage "in vain" (Ps. 2:2–4), because he who sitteth in the

heaven is strong enough to repel their assaults, assuring believers of the perpetual preservation of the Church, he animates them to have good hope whenever it is occasionally oppressed. So, in another place, when speaking in the person of God, he says, "The Lord said unto my Lord, Sit thou at my right hand, until I make thine enemies thy footstool" (Ps. 110:1), he reminds us, that however numerous and powerful the enemies who conspire to assault the Church, they are not possessed of strength sufficient to prevail against the immortal decree by which he appointed his Son eternal King. Whence it follows that the devil, with the whole power of the world, can never possibly destroy the Church, which is founded on the eternal throne of Christ. Then in regard to the special use to be made by each believer, this same eternity ought to elevate us to the hope of a blessed immortality. For we see that every thing which is earthly, and of the world, is temporary, and soon fades away. Christ, therefore, to raise our hope to the heavens, declares that his kingdom is not of this world (John 18:36). In fine, let each of us, when he hears that the kingdom of Christ is spiritual, be roused by the thought to entertain the hope of a better life, and to expect that as it is now protected by the hand of Christ, so it will be fully realised in a future life.

4. That the strength and utility of the kingdom of Christ cannot, as we have said, be fully perceived without recognising it as spiritual, is sufficiently apparent, even from this, that having during the whole course of our lives to war under the cross, our condition here is bitter and wretched. What then would it avail us to be ranged under the government of a heavenly King, if its benefits were not realised beyond the present earthly life? We must, therefore, know that the happiness which is promised to us in Christ does not consist in external advantages—such as leading a joyful and tranquil life, abounding in wealth, being secure against all injury, and having an affluence of delights, such as the flesh is wont to long for—but properly belongs to the heavenly life. As in the world the prosperous and desirable condition of a people consists partly in the abundance of temporal good and domestic peace, and partly in the strong protection which gives security against external violence; so Christ also enriches his people with all things necessary to the eternal salvation of their souls and fortifies them with courage to stand unassailable by all the attacks of spiritual foes. Whence we infer, that he reigns more for us than for himself, and that both within us and without us; that being replenished, in so far as God knows to be expedient, with the gifts of the Spirit, of which we are naturally destitute, we may feel from their first fruits, that we are truly united to God for perfect blessedness; and then trusting to the power of the same Spirit, may not doubt that we shall always be victorious against the devil, the world, and every thing that can do us harm. To this effect was our Saviour's reply to the Pharisees, "The kingdom of God is within you." "The kingdom of God cometh not with observation" (Luke 17:21, 22). It is probable that on his declaring himself to be that King under whom the highest blessing of God was to be expected, they had in derision asked him to produce his insignia. But to prevent those who were already more than enough inclined to the earth from dwelling on its pomp, he bids them enter into their consciences, for "the kingdom of God" is "righteousness, and peace, and joy in the Holy Ghost" (Rom. 14:17). These words briefly teach what the kingdom of Christ bestows upon us. Not being earthly or carnal, and so subject to corruption, but spiritual, it raises us even to eternal life, so that we can patiently live at present under toil, hunger, cold, contempt, disgrace, and other annoyances; contented with this, that our King will never abandon us, but will supply our necessities until our warfare is ended, and we are called to triumph: such being the nature of his kingdom, that he communicates to us whatever he received of his Father. Since then he arms and equips us by his power, adorns us with splendour and magnificence, enriches us with wealth, we here find most abundant cause of glorying, and also are inspired with boldness, so that we can contend intrepidly with the devil, sin, and death. In fine, clothed with his righteousness, we can bravely surmount all the insults of the world: and as he replenishes us liberally with his gifts, so we can in our turn bring forth fruit unto his glory.

5. Accordingly, his royal unction is not set before us as composed of oil or aromatic perfumes; but he is called the Christ of God, because "the Spirit of the Lord" rested upon him; "the Spirit of wisdom and understanding, the Spirit of counsel and might, the Spirit of knowledge and of the fear of the Lord" (Isaiah 11:2). This is the oil of joy with which the Psalmist declares that he was anointed above his fellows (Ps. 45:7). For, as has been said, he was not enriched privately for himself, but that he might refresh the parched and hungry with his abundance. For as the Father is said to have given the Spirit to the Son without measure (John 3:34), so the reason is expressed, that we might all receive of his fulness, and grace for grace (John 1:16). From this fountain flows the copious supply (of which Paul makes mention, Eph. 4:7) by which grace is variously distributed to believers according to the mea-

sure of the gift of Christ. Here we have ample confirmation of what I said, that the kingdom of Christ consists in the Spirit, and not in earthly delights or pomp, and that hence, in order to be partakers with him, we must renounce the world. A visible symbol of this grace was exhibited at the baptism of Christ, when the Spirit rested upon him in the form of a dove. To designate the Spirit and his gifts by the term "*unction*" is not new, and ought not to seem absurd (see 1 John 2:20, 27), because this is the only quarter from which we derive life; but especially in what regards the heavenly life, there is not a drop of vigour in us save what the Holy Spirit instils, who has chosen his seat in Christ, that thence the heavenly riches, of which we are destitute, might flow to us in copious abundance. But because believers stand invincible in the strength of their King, and his spiritual riches abound towards them, they are not improperly called Christians. Moreover, from this eternity of which we have spoken, there is nothing derogatory in the expression of Paul, "Then cometh the end, when he shall have delivered up the kingdom to God, even the Father" (1 Cor. 15:24); and also, "Then shall the Son also himself be subject unto him that put all things under him, that God may be all in and" (1 Cor. 15:28); for the meaning merely is, that, in that perfect glory, the administration of the kingdom will not be such as it now is. For the Father has given all power to the Son, that by his hand he may govern, cherish, sustain us, keep us under his guardianship, and give assistance to us. Thus, while we wander far as pilgrims from God, Christ interposes, that he may gradually bring us to full communion with God. And, indeed, his sitting at the right hand of the Father has the same meaning as if he was called the vicegerent of the Father, entrusted with the whole power of government. For God is pleased, mediately (so to speak) in his person to rule and defend the Church. Thus also his being seated at the right hand of the Father is explained by Paul, in the Epistle to the Ephesians, to mean, that "he is the head over all things to the Church, which is his body" (Eph. 1:20, 22). Nor is this different in purport from what he elsewhere teaches, that God has "given him a name which is above every name; that at the name of Jesus every knee shall bow, of things in heaven, and things in earth, and things under the earth, and that every tongue should confess that Jesus Christ is Lord, to the glory of God the Father" (Phil. 2:9–11). For in these words, also, he commends an arrangement in the kingdom of Christ, which is necessary for our present infirmity. Thus Paul rightly infers that God will then be the only Head of the Church, because the office of Christ, in defending the Church, shall then have been completed. For the same reason, Scripture throughout calls him *Lord*, the Father having appointed him over us for the express purpose of exercising his government through him. For though many lordships are celebrated in the world, yet Paul says, "To us there is but one God, the Father, of whom are all things, and we in him; and one Lord Jesus Christ, by whom are all things, and we by him" (1 Cor. 8:6). Whence it is justly inferred that he is the same God, who, by the mouth of Isaiah, declared, "The Lord is our Judge, the Lord is our Lawgiver, the Lord is our King: he will save us" (Isaiah 33:22). For though he every where describes all the power which he possesses as the benefit and gift of the Father, the meaning simply is, that he reigns by divine authority, because his reason for assuming the office of Mediator was, that descending from the bosom and incomprehensible glory of the Father, he might draw near to us. Wherefore there is the greater reason that we all should with one consent prepare to obey, and with the greatest alacrity yield implicit obedience to his will. For as he unites the offices of King and Pastor towards believers, who voluntarily submit to him, so, on the other hand, we are told that he wields an iron sceptre to break and bruise all the rebellious like a potter's vessel (Ps. 2:9). We are also told that he will be the Judge of the Gentiles, that he will cover the earth with dead bodies, and level down every opposing height (Ps. 110:6). Of this examples are seen at present, but full proof will be given at the final judgment, which may be properly regarded as the last act of his reign.

6. With regard to his Priesthood, we must briefly hold its end and use to be, that as a Mediator, free from all taint, he may by his own holiness procure the favour of God for us. But because a deserved curse obstructs the entrance, and God in his character of Judge is hostile to us, expiation must necessarily intervene, that as a priest employed to appease the wrath of God, he may reinstate us in his favour. Wherefore, in order that Christ might fulfil this office, it behoved him to appear with a sacrifice. For even under the law of the priesthood it was forbidden to enter the sanctuary without blood, to teach the worshipper that however the priest might interpose to deprecate, God could not be propitiated without the expiation of sin. On this subject the Apostle discourses at length in the Epistle to the Hebrews, from the seventh almost to the end of the tenth chapter. The sum comes to this, that the honour of the priesthood was competent to none but Christ, because, by the sacrifice of his death, he wiped away our guilt, and made satisfaction for sin.

Of the great importance of this matter, we are reminded by that solemn oath which God uttered, and of which he declared he would not repent, "Thou art a priest for ever, after the order of Melchizedek" (Ps. 110:4). For, doubtless, his purpose was to ratify that point on which he knew that our salvation chiefly hinged. For, as has been said, there is no access to God for us or for our prayers until the priest, purging away our defilements, sanctify us, and obtain for us that favour of which the impurity of our lives and hearts deprives us. Thus we see, that if the benefit and efficacy of Christ's priesthood is to reach us, the commencement must be with his death. Whence it follows, that he by whose aid we obtain favour, must be a perpetual intercessor. From this again arises not only confidence in prayer, but also the tranquillity of pious minds, while they recline in safety on the paternal indulgence of God, and feel assured, that whatever has been consecrated by the Mediator is pleasing to him. But since God under the Law ordered sacrifices of beasts to be offered to him, there was a different and new arrangement in regard to Christ—viz. that he should be at once victim and priest, because no other fit satisfaction for sin could be found, nor was any one worthy of the honour of offering an only begotten son to God. Christ now bears the office of priest, not only that by the eternal law of reconciliation he may render the Father favourable and propitious to us, but also admit us into this most honourable alliance. For we though in ourselves polluted, in him being priests (Rev. 1:6), offer ourselves and our all to God, and freely enter the heavenly sanctuary, so that the sacrifices of prayer and praise which we present are grateful and of sweet odour before him. To this effect are the words of Christ, "For their sakes I sanctify myself" (John 17:19); for being clothed with his holiness, inasmuch as he has devoted us to the Father with himself (otherwise we were an abomination before him), we please him as if we were pure and clean, nay, even sacred. Hence that unction of the sanctuary of which mention is made in Daniel (Dan. 9:24). For we must attend to the contrast between this unction and the shadowy one which was then in use; as if the angel had said, that when the shadows were dispersed, there would be a clear priesthood in the person of Christ. The more detestable, therefore, is the fiction of those who, not content with the priesthood of Christ, have dared to take it upon themselves to sacrifice him, a thing daily attempted in the Papacy, where the mass is represented as an immolation of Christ.

CHAPTER 16

HOW CHRIST PERFORMED THE OFFICE OF REDEEMER IN PROCURING OUR SALVATION. THE DEATH, RESURRECTION, AND ASCENSION OF CHRIST.

This chapter contains four leading heads—I. A general consideration of the whole subject, including a discussion of a necessary question concerning the justice of God and his mercy in Christ, sec. 1–4. II. How Christ fulfilled the office of Redeemer in each of its parts, sec. 5–17. His death, burial, descent to hell, resurrection, ascension to heaven, seat at the right hand of the Father, and return to judgment. III. A great part of the Creed being here expounded, a statement is given of the view which ought to be taken of the Creed commonly ascribed to the Apostles, sec. 18. IV. Conclusion, setting forth the doctrine of Christ the Redeemer, and the use of the doctrine, sec. 19.

Sections:

1. Every thing needful for us exists in Christ. How it is to be obtained.

2. Question as to the mode of reconciling the justice with the mercy of God. Modes of expression used in Scripture to teach us how miserable our condition is without Christ.

3. Not used improperly; for God finds in us ground both of hatred and love.

4. This confirmed from passages of Scripture and from Augustine.

5. The second part of the chapter, treating of our redemption by Christ. First generally. Redemption extends to the whole course of our Saviour's obedience, but is specially ascribed to his death. The voluntary subjection of Christ. His agony. His condemnation before Pilate. Two things observable in his condemnation. 1. That he was numbered among transgressors. 2. That he was declared innocent by the judge. Use to be made of this.

6. Why Christ was crucified. This hidden doctrine typified in the Law, and completed by the Apostles and Prophets. In what sense Christ was made a curse for us. The cross of Christ connected with the shedding of his blood.

7. Of the death of Christ. Why he died. Advantages from his death. Of the burial of Christ. Advantages.

8. Of the descent into hell. This article gradually introduced into the Church. Must not be rejected, nor confounded with the previous article respecting burial.

9. Absurd exposition concerning the Limbus Patrum. This fable refuted.

10. The article of the descent to hell more accurately expounded. A great ground of comfort.

11. Confirmation of this exposition from passages of Scripture and the works of ancient Theologians. An objection refuted. Advantages of the doctrine.

12. Another objection that Christ is insulted, and despair ascribed to him in its being said that he feared. Answer, from the statements of the Evangelists, that he did fear, was troubled in spirit, amazed, and tempted in all respects as we are, yet without sin. Why Christ was pleased to become weak. His fear without sin. Refutation of another objection, with an answer to the question, Did Christ fear death, and why? When did Christ descend to hell, and how? What has been said refutes the heresy of Apollinaris and of the Monothelites.

13. Of the resurrection of Christ. The many advantages from it. 1. Our righteousness in the sight of God renewed and restored. 2. His life the basis of our life and hope, also the efficacious cause of new life in us. 3. The pledge of our future resurrection.

14. Of the ascension of Christ. Why he ascended. Advantages derived from it.

15. Of Christ's seat at the Father's right hand. What meant by it.

16. Many advantages from the ascension of Christ. 1. He gives access to the kingdom which Adam had shut up. 2. He intercedes for us with the Father. 3. His virtue being thence transfused into us, he works effectually in us for salvation.

17. Of the return of Christ to judgment. Its nature. The quick and dead who are to be judged. Passages apparently contradictory reconciled. Mode of judgment.

18. Advantages of the doctrine of Christ's return to judgment. Third part of the chapter, explaining the view to be taken of the Apostles' Creed. Summary of the Apostles' Creed.

19. Conclusion of the whole chapter, showing that in Christ the salvation of the elect in all its parts is comprehended.

1. All that we have hitherto said of Christ leads to this one result, that condemned, dead, and lost in ourselves, we must in him seek righteousness, deliverance, life and salvation, as we are taught by the celebrated words of Peter, "Neither is there salvation in any other: for there is none other name under heaven given among men whereby we must be saved" (Acts 4:12). The name of Jesus was not given him at random, or fortuitously, or by the will of man, but was brought from heaven by an angel, as the herald of the supreme decree; the reason also being added, "for he shall save his people from their sins" (Matt. 1:21). In these words attention should be paid to what we have elsewhere observed, that the office of Redeemer was assigned him in order that he might be our Saviour. Still, however, redemption would be defective if it did not conduct us by an uninterrupted progression to the final goal of safety. Therefore, the moment we turn aside from him in the minutest degree, salvation, which resides entirely in him, gradually disappears; so that all who do not rest in him voluntarily deprive themselves of all grace. The observation of Bernard well deserves to be remembered: The name of Jesus is not only light but food also, yea, oil, without which all the food of the soul is dry; salt, without which as a condiment whatever is set before us is insipid; in fine, honey in the mouth, melody in the ear, joy in the heart, and, at the same time, medicine; every discourse where this name is not heard is absurd (Bernard in Cantica., Serm. 15). But here it is necessary diligently to consider in what way we obtain salvation from him, that we may not only be persuaded that he is the author of it, but having embraced whatever is sufficient as a sure foundation of our faith, may eschew all that might make us waver. For seeing no man can descend into himself, and seriously consider what he is, without feeling that God is angry and at enmity with him, and therefore anxiously longing for the means of regaining his favour (this cannot be without satisfaction), the certainty here required is of no ordinary description,—sinners, until freed from guilt, being always liable to the wrath and curse of God, who, as he is a just judge, cannot permit his law to be violated with impunity, but is armed for vengeance.

2. But before we proceed farther, we must see in passing, how can it be said that God, who prevents us with his mercy, was our enemy until he was reconciled to us by Christ. For how could he have given us in his only-begotten Son a singular pledge of his love, if he had not previously embraced us with free favour? As there thus arises some appearance of contradiction, I will explain the difficulty. The mode in which the Spirit usually speaks in Scripture is, that God was the enemy of men until they were restored to favour by the death of Christ

(Rom. 5:10); that they were cursed until their iniquity was expiated by the sacrifice of Christ (Gal. 3:10, 13); that they were separated from God, until by means of Christ's body they were received into union (Col. 1:21, 22). Such modes of expression are accommodated to our capacity, that we may the better understand how miserable and calamitous our condition is without Christ. For were it not said in clear terms, that Divine wrath, and vengeance, and eternal death, lay upon us, we should be less sensible of our wretchedness without the mercy of God, and less disposed to value the blessing of deliverance. For example, let a person be told, Had God at the time you were a sinner hated you, and cast you off as you deserved, horrible destruction must have been your doom; but spontaneously and of free indulgence he retained you in his favour, not suffering you to be estranged from him, and in this way rescued you from danger,—the person will indeed be affected, and made sensible in some degree how much he owes to the mercy of God. But again, let him be told, as Scripture teaches, that he was estranged from God by sin, an heir of wrath, exposed to the curse of eternal death, excluded from all hope of salvation, a complete alien from the blessing of God, the slave of Satan, captive under the yoke of sin; in fine, doomed to horrible destruction, and already involved in it; that then Christ interposed, took the punishment upon himself and bore what by the just judgment of God was impending over sinners; with his own blood expiated the sins which rendered them hateful to God, by this expiation satisfied and duly propitiated God the Father, by this intercession appeased his anger, on this basis founded peace between God and men, and by this tie secured the Divine benevolence toward them; will not these considerations move him the more deeply, the more strikingly they represent the greatness of the calamity from which he was delivered? In short, since our mind cannot lay hold of life through the mercy of God with sufficient eagerness, or receive it with becoming gratitude, unless previously impressed with fear of the Divine anger, and dismayed at the thought of eternal death, we are so instructed by divine truth, as to perceive that without Christ God is in a manner hostile to us, and has his arm raised for our destruction. Thus taught, we look to Christ alone for divine favour and paternal love.

3. Though this is said in accommodation to the weakness of our capacity, it is not said falsely. For God, who is perfect righteousness, cannot love the iniquity which he sees in all. All of us, therefore, have that within which deserves the hatred of God. Hence, in respect, first, of our corrupt nature; and, secondly, of the depraved conduct following upon it, we are all offensive to God, guilty in his sight, and by nature the children of hell. But as the Lord wills not to destroy in us that which is his own, he still finds something in us which in kindness he can love. For though it is by our own fault that we are sinners, we are still his creatures; though we have brought death upon ourselves he had created us for life. Thus, mere gratuitous love prompts him to receive us into favour. But if there is a perpetual and irreconcilable repugnance between righteousness and iniquity, so long as we remain sinners we cannot be completely received. Therefore, in order that all ground of offence may be removed, and he may completely reconcile us to himself, he, by means of the expiation set forth in the death of Christ, abolishes all the evil that is in us, so that we, formerly impure and unclean, now appear in his sight just and holy. Accordingly, God the Father, by his love, prevents and anticipates our reconciliation in Christ. Nay, it is because he first loves us, that he afterwards reconciles us to himself. But because the iniquity, which deserves the indignation of God, remains in us until the death of Christ comes to our aid, and that iniquity is in his sight accursed and condemned, we are not admitted to full and sure communion with God, unless, in so far as Christ unites us. And, therefore, if we would indulge the hope of having God placable and propitious to us, we must fix our eyes and minds on Christ alone, as it is to him alone it is owing that our sins, which necessarily provoked the wrath of God, are not imputed to us.

4. For this reason Paul says, that God "has blessed us with all spiritual blessings in heavenly places in Christ: according as he has chosen us in him before the foundation of the world" (Eph. 1:3, 4). These things are clear and conformable to Scripture, and admirably reconcile the passages in which it is said, that "God so loved the world, that he gave his only begotten Son" (John 3:16); and yet that it was "when we were enemies we were reconciled to God by the death of his Son" (Rom. 5:10). But to give additional assurance to those who require the authority of the ancient Church, I will quote a passage of Augustine to the same effect: "Incomprehensible and immutable is the love of God. For it was not after we were reconciled to him by the blood of his Son that he began to love us, but he loved us before the foundation of the world, that with his only begotten Son we too might be sons of God before we were any thing at all. Our being reconciled by the death of Christ must not be understood as if the Son reconciled us, in order that the Father, then

hating, might begin to love us, but that we were reconciled to him already, loving, though at enmity with us because of sin. To the truth of both propositions we have the attestation of the Apostle, 'God commendeth his love toward us, in that while we were yet sinners, Christ died for us,' (Rom. 5:8). Therefore he had this love towards us even when, exercising enmity towards him, we were the workers of iniquity. Accordingly in a manner wondrous and divine, he loved even when he hated us. For he hated us when we were such as he had not made us, and yet because our iniquity had not destroyed his work in every respect, he knew in regard to each one of us, both to hate what we had made, and love what he had made." Such are the words of Augustine (Tract in Jo. 110).

5. When it is asked then how Christ, by abolishing sin, removed the enmity between God and us, and purchased a righteousness which made him favourable and kind to us, it may be answered generally, that he accomplished this by the whole course of his obedience. This id proved by the testimony of Paul, "As by one man's disobedience many were made sinners, so by the obedience of one shall many be made righteous" (Rom. 5:19). And indeed he elsewhere extends the ground of pardon which exempts from the curse of the law to the whole life of Christ, "When the fulness of the time was come, God sent forth his Son, made of a woman, made under the law, to redeem them that were under the law" (Gal. 4:4, 5). Thus even at his baptism he declared that a part of righteousness was fulfilled by his yielding obedience to the command of the Father. In short, from the moment when he assumed the form of a servant, he began, in order to redeem us, to pay the price of deliverance. Scripture, however, the more certainly to define the mode of salvation, ascribes it peculiarly and specially to the death of Christ. He himself declares that he gave his life a ransom for many (Mt. 20:28). Paul teaches that he died for our sins (Rom. 4:25). John Baptist exclaimed, "Behold the Lamb of God, which taketh away the sin of the world" (John 1:29). Paul in another passage declares, "that we are justified freely by his grace, through the redemption that is in Christ Jesus: whom God has set forth to be a propitiation through faith in his blood" (Rom. 3:25). "Again, being justified by his blood, we shall be saved from wrath through him" (Rom. 5:9). Again "He has made him to be sin for us, who knew no sin; that we might be made the righteousness of God in him" (2 Cor. 5:21). I will not search out all the passages, for the list would be endless, and many are afterwards to be quoted in their order. In the Confession of Faith, called the Apostles' Creed, the transition is admirably made from the birth of Christ to his death and resurrection, in which the completion of a perfect salvation consists. Still there is no exclusion of the other part of obedience which he performed in life. Thus Paul comprehends, from the beginning even to the end, his having assumed the form of a servant, humbled himself, and become obedient to death, even the death of the cross (Phil. 2:7). And, indeed, the first step in obedience was his voluntary subjection; for the sacrifice would have been unavailing to justification if not offered spontaneously. Hence our Lord, after testifying, "I lay down my life for the sheep," distinctly adds, "No man taketh it from me" (John 10:15, 18). In the same sense Isaiah says, " Like a sheep before her shearers is dumb, so he opened not his mouth" (Is. 53:7). The Gospel History relates that he came forth to meet the soldiers; and in presence of Pilate, instead of defending himself, stood to receive judgment. This, indeed, he did not without a struggle, for he had assumed our infirmities also, and in this way it behoved him to prove that he was yielding obedience to his Father. It was no ordinary example of incomparable love towards us to struggle with dire terrors, and amid fearful tortures to cast away all care of himself that he might provide for us. We must bear in minds that Christ could not duly propitiate God without renouncing his own feelings and subjecting himself entirely to his Father's will. To this effect the Apostle appositely quotes a passage from the Psalms, "Lo, I come (in the volume of the book it is written of me) to do thy will, O God" (Heb. 10:5; Ps. 40:7, 8). Thus, as trembling consciences find no rest without sacrifice and ablution by which sins are expiated, we are properly directed thither, the source of our life being placed in the death of Christ. Moreover, as the curse consequent upon guilt remained for the final judgment of God, one principal point in the narrative is his condemnation before Pontius Pilate, the governor of Judea, to teach us, that the punishment to which we were liable was inflicted on that Just One. We could not escape the fearful judgment of God; and Christ, that he might rescue us from it, submitted to be condemned by a mortal, nay, by a wicked and profane man. For the name of Governor is mentioned not only to support the credibility of the narrative, but to remind us of what Isaiah says, that "the chastisement of our peace was upon him;" and that "with his stripes we are healed" (Is. 53:5). For, in order to remove our condemnation, it was not sufficient to endure any kind of death. To satisfy our ransom, it was necessary to select a mode of death in which he might deliver us, both by giving himself up to condemnations

and undertaking our expiation. Had he been cut off by assassins, or slain in a seditious tumult, there could have been no kind of satisfaction in such a death. But when he is placed as a criminal at the bar, where witnesses are brought to give evidence against him, and the mouth of the judge condemns him to die, we see him sustaining the character of an offender and evil-doer. Here we must attend to two points which had both been foretold by the prophets, and tend admirably to comfort and confirm our faith. When we read that Christ was led away from the judgment-seat to execution, and was crucified between thieves, we have a fulfilment of the prophecy which is quoted by the Evangelist, "He was numbered with the transgressors" (Is. 53:12; Mark 15:28). Why was it so? That he might bear the character of a sinner, not of a just or innocent person, inasmuch as he met death on account not of innocence, but of sin. On the other hand, when we read that he was acquitted by the same lips that condemned him (for Pilate was forced once and again to bear public testimony to his innocence), let us call to mind what is said by another prophet, "I restored that which I took not away" (Ps. 69:4). Thus we perceive Christ representing the character of a sinner and a criminal, while, at the same time, his innocence shines forth, and it becomes manifest that he suffers for another's and not for his own crime. He therefore suffered under Pontius Pilate, being thus, by the formal sentence of the judge, ranked among criminals, and yet he is declared innocent by the same judge, when he affirms that he finds no cause of death in him. Our acquittal is in this that the guilt which made us liable to punishment was transferred to the head of the Son of God (Is. 53:12). We must specially remember this substitution in order that we may not be all our lives in trepidation and anxiety, as if the just vengeance which the Son of God transferred to himself, were still impending over us.

6. The very form of the death embodies a striking truth. The cross was cursed not only in the opinion of men, but by the enactment of the Divine Law. Hence Christ, while suspended on it, subjects himself to the curse. And thus it behoved to be done, in order that the whole curse, which on account of our iniquities awaited us, or rather lay upon us, might be taken from us by being transferred to him. This was also shadowed in the Law, since *twm`a*, the word by which sin itself is properly designated, was applied to the sacrifices and expiations offered for sin. By this application of the term, the Spirit intended to intimate, that they were a kind of *kaqarmavton* (purifications), bearing, by substitutions the curse due to sin. But that which was represented figuratively in the Mosaic sacrifices is exhibited in Christ the archetype. Wherefore, in order to accomplish a full expiation, he made his soul to `*ai.e.*, a propitiatory victim for sin (as the prophet says, Is. 53:5, 10), on which the guilt and penalty being in a manner laid, ceases to be imputed to us. The Apostle declares this more plainly when he says, that "he made him to be sin for us, who knew no sin; that we might be made the righteousness of God in him" (2 Cor. 5:21). For the Son of God, though spotlessly pure, took upon him the disgrace and ignominy of our iniquities, and in return clothed us with his purity. To the same thing he seems to refer, when he says, that he "condemned sin in the flesh" (Rom. 8:3), the Father having destroyed the power of sin when it was transferred to the flesh of Christ. This term, therefore, indicates that Christ, in his death, was offered to the Father as a propitiatory victim; that, expiation being made by his sacrifice, we might cease to tremble at the divine wrath. It is now clear what the prophet means when he says, that "the Lord has laid upon him the iniquity of us all" (Is. 53:6); namely, that as he was to wash away the pollution of sins, they were transferred to him by imputation. Of this the cross to which he was nailed was a symbol, as the Apostle declares, "Christ has redeemed us from the curse of the law, being made a curse for us: for it is written, Cursed is every one that hangeth on a tree: that the blessing of Abraham might come on the Gentiles through Jesus Christ" (Gal. 3:13, 14). In the same way Peter says, that he "bare our sins in his own body on the tree" (1 Peter 2:24), inasmuch as from the very symbol of the curse, we perceive more clearly that the burden with which we were oppressed was laid upon him. Nor are we to understand that by the curse which he endured he was himself overwhelmed, but rather that by enduring it he repressed broke, annihilated all its force. Accordingly, faith apprehends acquittal in the condemnation of Christ, and blessing in his curse. Hence it is not without cause that Paul magnificently celebrates the triumph which Christ obtained upon the cross, as if the cross, the symbol of ignominy, had been converted into a triumphal chariot. For he says, that he blotted out the handwriting of ordinances that was against us, which was contrary to us, and took it out of the way, nailing it to his cross: that "having spoiled principalities and powers he made a show of them openly, triumphing over them in it" (Col. 2:14, 15). Nor is this to be wondered at; for, as another Apostle declares, Christ, "through the eternal Spirit, offered himself without spot to God" (Heb. 9:14), and hence that transformation of the cross which were

otherwise against its nature. But that these things may take deep root and have their seat in our inmost hearts, we must never lose sight of sacrifice and ablution. For, were not Christ a victim, we could have no sure conviction of his being *ajpoluvtrwsi'*, *ajntivlutron, kai*; *ijlasthvrion*, our substitute-ransom and propitiation. And hence mention is always made of blood whenever scripture explains the mode of redemption: although the shedding of Christ's blood was available not only for propitiation, but also acted as a laver to purge our defilements.

7. The Creed next mentions that he "was dead and buried". Here again it is necessary to consider how he substituted himself in order to pay the price of our redemption. Death held us under its yoke, but he in our place delivered himself into its power, that he might exempt us from it. This the Apostle means when he says, "that he tasted death for every man" (Heb. 2:9). By dying he prevented us from dying; or (which is the same thing) he by his death purchased life for us (see Calvin in Psychopann). But in this he differed from us, that in permitting himself to be overcome of death, it was not so as to be engulfed in its abyss but rather to annihilate it, as it must otherwise have annihilated us; he did not allow himself to be so subdued by it as to be crushed by its power; he rather laid it prostrate, when it was impending over us, and exulting over us as already overcome. In fine, his object was, "that through death he might destroy him that had the power of death, that is, the devil, and deliver them who through fear of death were all their lifetime subject to bondage" (Heb. 2:14, 15). This is the first fruit which his death produced to us. Another is, that by fellowship with him he mortifies our earthly members that they may not afterwards exert themselves in action, and kill the old man, that he may not hereafter be in vigour and bring forth fruit. An effect of his burials moreover is that we as his fellows are buried to sin. For when the Apostle says, that we are ingrafted into the likeness of Christ's deaths and that we are buried with him unto sin, that by his cross the world is crucified unto us and we unto the world, and that we are dead with him, he not only exhorts us to manifest an example of his death, but declares that there is an efficacy in it which should appear in all Christians, if they would not render his death unfruitful and useless. Accordingly in the death and burial of Christ a twofold blessing is set before us—viz. deliverance from death, to which we were enslaved, and the mortification of our flesh (Rom. 6:5; Gal. 2:19, 6:14; Col. 3:3).

8. Here we must not omit the descent to hell, which was of no little importance to the accomplishment of redemption. For although it is apparent from the writings of the ancient Fathers, that the clause which now stands in the Creed was not formerly so much used in the churches, still, in giving a summary of doctrine, a place must be assigned to it, as containing a matter of great importance which ought not by any means to be disregarded. Indeed, some of the ancient Fathers do not omit it, and hence we may conjecture, that having been inserted in the Creed after a considerable lapse of time, it came into use in the Church not immediately but by degrees. This much is uncontroverted, that it was in accordance with the general sentiment of all believers, since there is none of the Fathers who does not mention Christ's descent into hell, though they have various modes of explaining it. But it is of little consequence by whom and at what time it was introduced. The chief thing to be attended to in the Creed is, that it furnishes us with a full and every way complete summary of faith, containing nothing but what has been derived from the infallible word of God. But should any still scruple to give it admission into the Creed, it will shortly be made plain, that the place which it holds in a summary of our redemption is so important, that the omission of it greatly detracts from the benefit of Christ's death. There are some again who think that the article contains nothing new, but is merely a repetition in different words of what was previously said respecting burial, the word Hell (Infernis) being often used in Scripture for sepulchre. I admit the truth of what they allege with regard to the not infrequent use of the term *infernos* for *sepulchre*; but I cannot adopt their opinion, for two obvious reasons. First, What folly would it have been, after explaining a matter attended with no difficulty in clear and unambiguous terms, afterwards to involve rather than illustrate it by clothing it in obscure phraseology? When two expressions having the same meaning are placed together, the latter ought to be explanatory of the former. But what kind of explanation would it be to say, the expression, "*Christ was buried*", means, that "*he descended into hell*"? My second reason is the improbability that a superfluous tautology of this description should have crept into this compendium, in which the principal articles of faith are set down summarily in the fewest possible number of words. I have no doubt that all who weigh the matter with some degree of care will here agree with me.

9. Others interpret differently—viz. That Christ descended to the souls of the Patriarchs who died under the law, to announce his accomplished redemption, and bring them out of the prison in which they were con-

fined. To this effect they wrest the passage in the Psalms "He hath broken the gates of brass, and cut the bars of iron in sunder." (Ps. 107:16); and also the passage in Zechariah, "I have sent forth thy prisoners out of the pit wherein is no water" (Zech. 9:11). But since the psalm foretells the deliverance of those who were held captive in distant lands, and Zechariah comparing the Babylonish disaster into which the people had been plunged to a deep dry well or abyss, at the same time declares, that the salvation of the whole Church was an escape from a profound pit, I know not how it comes to pass, that posterity imagined it to be a subterraneous cavern, to which they gave the name of *Limbus*. Though this fable has the countenance of great authors, and is now also seriously defended by many as truth, it is nothing but a fable. To conclude from it that the souls of the dead are in prison is childish. And what occasion was there that the soul of Christ should go down thither to set them at liberty? I readily admit that Christ illumined them by the power of his Spirit, enabling them to perceive that the grace of which they had only had a foretaste was then manifested to the world. And to this not improbably the passage of Peter may be applied, wherein he says, that Christ "went and preached to the spirits that were in prison" (or rather "a watch-tower") (I Pet. 3:19). The purport of the context is, that believers who had died before that time were partakers of the same grace with ourselves: for he celebrates the power of Christ's death, in that he penetrated even to the dead, pious souls obtaining an immediate view of that visitation for which they had anxiously waited; while, on the other hand, the reprobate were more clearly convinced that they were completely excluded from salvation. Although the passage in Peter is not perfectly definite, we must not interpret as if he made no distinction between the righteous and the wicked: he only means to intimate, that the death of Christ was made known to both.

10. But, apart from the Creed, we must seek for a surer exposition of Christ's descent to hell: and the word of God furnishes us with one not only pious and holy, but replete with excellent consolation. Nothing had been done if Christ had only endured corporeal death. In order to interpose between us and God's anger, and satisfy his righteous judgment, it was necessary that he should feel the weight of divine vengeance. Whence also it was necessary that he should engage, as it were, at close quarters with the powers of hell and the horrors of eternal death. We lately quoted from the Prophet, that the "chastisement of our peace was laid upon him" that he "was bruised for our iniquities" that he "bore our infirmities;" expressions which intimate, that, like a sponsor and surety for the guilty, and, as it were, subjected to condemnation, he undertook and paid all the penalties which must have been exacted from them, the only exception being, that the pains of death could not hold him. Hence there is nothing strange in its being said that he descended to hell, seeing he endured the death which is inflicted on the wicked by an angry God. It is frivolous and ridiculous to object that in this way the order is perverted, it being absurd that an event which preceded burial should be placed after it. But after explaining what Christ endured in the sight of man, the Creed appropriately adds the invisible and incomprehensible judgment which he endured before God, to teach us that not only was the body of Christ given up as the price of redemption, but that there was a greater and more excellent price—that he bore in his soul the tortures of condemned and ruined man.

11. In this sense, Peter says that God raised up Christ, "having loosed the pains of death: because it was not possible he should be holden of it" (Acts 2:24). He does not mention death simply, but says that the Son of God endured the pains produced by the curse and wrath of God, the source of death. How small a matter had it been to come forth securely, and as it were in sport to undergo death. Herein was a true proof of boundless mercy, that he shunned not the death he so greatly dreaded. And there can be no doubt that, in the Epistle to the Hebrews, the Apostle means to teach the same thing, when he says that he "was heard in that he feared" (Heb. 5:7). Some instead of "feared," use a term meaning reverence or piety, but how inappropriately, is apparent both from the nature of the thing and the form of expression. Christ then praying in a loud voice, and with tears, is heard in that he feared, not so as to be exempted from death, but so as not to be swallowed up of it like a sinner, though standing as our representative. And certainly no abyss can be imagined more dreadful than to feel that you are abandoned and forsaken of God, and not heard when you invoke him, just as if he had conspired your destruction. To such a degree was Christ dejected, that in the depth of his agony he was forced to exclaim, "My God, my God, why hast thou forsaken me?" The view taken by some, that he here expressed the opinion of others rather than his own conviction, is most improbable; for it is evident that the expression was wrung from the anguish of his inmost soul. We do not, however, insinuate that God was ever hostile to him or angry with him. How could he be

angry with the beloved Son, with whom his soul was well pleased? or how could he have appeased the Father by his intercession for others if He were hostile to himself? But this we say, that he bore the weight of the divine anger, that, smitten and afflicted, he experienced all the signs of an angry and avenging God. Hence Hilary argues, that to this descent we owe our exemption from death. Nor does he dissent from this view in other passages, as when he says, "The cross, death, hell, are our life." And again, "The Son of God is in hell, but man is brought back to heaven." And why do I quote the testimony of a private writer, when an Apostle asserts the same thing, stating it as one fruit of his victory that he delivered "them who through fear of death were all their lifetime subject to bondage?" (Heb. 2:15). He behoved therefore, to conquer the fear which incessantly vexes and agitates the breasts of all mortals; and this he could not do without a contest. Moreover it will shortly appear with greater clearness that his was no common sorrow, was not the result of a trivial cause. Thus by engaging with the power of the devil, the fear of death, and the pains of hell, he gained the victory, and achieved a triumph, so that we now fear not in death those things which our Prince has destroyed.

12. Here some miserable creatures, who, though unlearned, are however impelled more by malice than ignorance, cry out that I am offering an atrocious insult to Christ, because it were most incongruous to hold that he feared for the safety of his soul. And then in harsher terms they urge the calumnious charge that I attribute despair to the Son of God, a feeling the very opposite of faith. First, they wickedly raise a controversy as to the fear and dread which Christ felt, though these are openly affirmed by the Evangelists. For before the hour of his death arrived, he was troubled in spirit, and affected with grief; and at the very onset began to be exceedingly amazed. To speak of these feelings as merely assumed, is a shameful evasion. It becomes us, therefore (as Ambrose truly teaches), boldly to profess the agony of Christ, if we are not ashamed of the cross. And certainly had not his soul shared in the punishment, he would have been a Redeemer of bodies only. The object of his struggle was to raise up those who were lying prostrate; and so far is this from detracting from his heavenly glory, that his goodness, which can never be sufficiently extolled, becomes more conspicuous in this, that he declined not to bear our infirmities. Hence also that solace to our anxieties and griefs which the Apostle sets before us: "We have not an high priest who cannot be touched with the feeling of our infirmities; but was in all respects tempted like as we are, yet without sin" (Heb. 4:15). These men pretend that a thing in its nature vicious is improperly ascribed to Christ; as if they were wiser than the Spirit of God, who in the same passage reconciles the two things—viz. that he was tempted in all respects like as we are, and yet was without sin. There is no reason, therefore, to take alarm at infirmity in Christ, infirmity to which he submitted not under the constraint of violence and necessity, but merely because he loved and pitied us. Whatever he spontaneously suffered, detracts in no degree from his majesty. One thing which misleads these detractors is, that they do not recognise in Christ an infirmity which was pure and free from every species of taint, inasmuch as it was kept within the limits of obedience. As no moderation can be seen in the depravity of our nature, in which all affections with turbulent impetuosity exceed their due bounds, they improperly apply the same standard to the Son of God. But as he was upright, all his affections were under such restraint as prevented every thing like excess. Hence he could resemble us in grief, fear, and dread, but still with this mark of distinction. Thus refuted, they fly off to another cavil, that although Christ feared death, yet he feared not the curse and wrath of God, from which he knew that he was safe. But let the pious reader consider how far it is honourable to Christ to make him more effeminate and timid than the generality of men. Robbers and other malefactors contumaciously hasten to death, many men magnanimously despise it, others meet it calmly. If the Son of God was amazed and terror-struck at the prospect of it, where was his firmness or magnanimity? We are even told, what in a common death would have been deemed most extraordinary, that in the depth of his agony his sweat was like great drops of blood falling to the ground. Nor was this a spectacle exhibited to the eyes of others, since it was from a secluded spot that he uttered his groans to his Father. And that no doubt may remain, it was necessary that angels should come down from heaven to strengthen him with miraculous consolation. How shamefully effeminate would it have been (as I have observed) to be so excruciated by the fear of an ordinary death as to sweat drops of blood, and not even be revived by the presence of angels? What? Does not that prayer, thrice repeated, "Father, if it be possible, let this cup pass from me" (Mt. 26:39), a prayer dictated by incredible bitterness of soul, show that Christ had a fiercer and more arduous struggle than with ordinary death?

Hence it appears that these triflers, with whom I am

disputing, presume to talk of what they know not, never having seriously considered what is meant and implied by ransoming us from the justice of God. It is of consequence to understand aright how much our salvation cost the Son of God. If any one now ask, Did Christ descend to hell at the time when he deprecated death? I answer, that this was the commencement, and that from it we may infer how dire and dreadful were the tortures which he endured when he felt himself standing at the bar of God as a criminal in our stead. And although the divine power of the Spirit veiled itself for a moment, that it might give place to the infirmity of the flesh, we must understand that the trial arising from feelings of grief and fear was such as not to be at variance with faith. And in this was fulfilled what is said in Peter's sermon as to having been loosed from the pains of death, because "it was not possible he could be holden of it" (Acts 2:24). Though feeling, as it were, forsaken of God, he did not cease in the slightest degree to confide in his goodness. This appears from the celebrated prayer in which, in the depth of his agony, he exclaimed, "My God, my God, why hast thou forsaken me?" (Mt. 27:46). Amid all his agony he ceases not to call upon his God, while exclaiming that he is forsaken by him. This refutes the Apollinarian heresy as well as that of those who are called Monothelites. Apollinaris pretended, that in Christ the eternal Spirit supplied the place of a soul, so that he was only half a man; as if he could have expiated our sins in any other way than by obeying the Father. But where does the feeling or desire of obedience reside but in the soul? And we know that his soul was troubled in order that ours, being free from trepidation, might obtain peace and quiet. Moreover, in opposition to the Monothelites, we see that in his human he felt a repugnance to what he willed in his divine nature. I say nothing of his subduing the fear of which we have spoken by a contrary affection. This appearance of repugnance is obvious in the words, "Father, save me from this hour: but for this cause came I unto this hour. Father, glorify thy name" (John 12:27, 28). Still, in this perplexity, there was no violent emotion, such as we exhibit while making the strongest endeavours to subdue our own feelings.

13. Next follows the resurrection from the dead, without which all that has hitherto been said would be defective. For seeing that in the cross, death, and burial of Christ, nothing but weakness appears, faith must go beyond all these, in order that it may be provided with full strength. Hence, although in his death we have an effectual completion of salvation, because by it we are reconciled to God, satisfaction is given to his justice, the curse is removed, and the penalty paid; still it is not by his death, but by his resurrection, that we are said to be begotten again to a living hope (1 Pet. 1:3); because, as he, by rising again, became victorious over death, so the victory of our faith consists only in his resurrection. The nature of it is better expressed in the words of Paul, "Who (Christ) was delivered for our offences, and was raised again for our justification" (Rom. 4:25); as if he had said, By his death sin was taken away, by his resurrection righteousness was renewed and restored. For how could he by dying have freed us from death, if he had yielded to its power? how could he have obtained the victory for us, if he had fallen in the contest?

Our salvation may be thus divided between the death and the resurrection of Christ: by the former sin was abolished and death annihilated; by the latter righteousness was restored and life revived, the power and efficacy of the former being still bestowed upon us by means of the latter. Paul accordingly affirms, that he was declared to be the Son of God by his resurrection (Rom. 1:4), because he then fully displayed that heavenly power which is both a bright mirror of his divinity, and a sure support of our faith; as he also elsewhere teaches, that "though he was crucified through weakness, yet he liveth by the power of God" (2 Cor. 13:4). In the same sense, in another passage, treating of perfection, he says, "That I may know him and the power of his resurrection" (Phil. 3:10). Immediately after he adds, "being made conformable unto his death." In perfect accordance with this is the passage in Peter, that God "raised him up from the dead, and gave him glory, that your faith and hope might be in God" (1 Pet. 1:21). Not that faith founded merely on his death is vacillating, but that the divine power by which he maintains our faith is most conspicuous in his resurrection. Let us remember, therefore, that when death only is mentioned, everything peculiar to the resurrection is at the same time included, and that there is a like synecdoche in the term *resurrection*, as often as it is used apart from death, everything peculiar to death being included. But as, by rising again, he obtained the victory, and became the resurrection and the life, Paul justly argues, "If Christ be not raised, your faith is vain; ye are yet in your sins" (1 Cor. 15:17). Accordingly, in another passage, after exulting in the death of Christ in opposition to the terrors of condemnation, he thus enlarges, "Christ that died, yea rather, that is risen again, who is even at the right hand of God, who also maketh intercession for us" (Rom. 8:34). Then, as we have already explained that the mortification of our flesh depends on communion with the cross, so we must also understand, that a corresponding benefit is derived from his resurrection. For as the Apostle says, "Like as Christ was raised up from the dead by the glory of the Father, even so we also should walk in newness of life" (Rom. 6:4). Accordingly, as in another passage, from our being dead with Christ, he inculcates, "Mortify therefore your members which are upon the earth" (Col. 3:5); so from our being risen with Christ he infers, "seek those things which are above, where Christ sitteth at the right hand of God" (Col. 3:1). In these words we are not only urged by the example of a risen Saviour to follow newness of life, but are taught that by his power we are renewed unto righteousness. A third benefit derived from it is, that, like an earnest, it assures us of our own resurrection, of which it is certain that his is the surest representation. This subject is discussed at length (1 Cor. 15). But it is to be observed, in passing, that when he is said to have "risen from the dead," these terms express the reality both of his death and resurrection, as if it had been said, that he died the same death as other men naturally die, and received immortality in the same mortal flesh which he had assumed.

14. The resurrection is naturally followed by the ascension into heaven. For although Christ, by rising again, began fully to display his glory and virtue, having laid aside the abject and ignoble condition of a mortal life, and the ignominy of the cross, yet it was only by his ascension to heaven that his reign truly commenced. This the Apostle shows, when he says he ascended "that he might fill all things" (Eph. 4:10); thus reminding us, that under the appearance of contradiction, there is a beautiful harmony, inasmuch as though he departed from us, it was that his departure might be more useful to us than that presence which was confined in a humble tabernacle of flesh during his abode on the earth. Hence John, after repeating the celebrated invitation, "If any man thirst, let him come unto me and drink," immediately adds, "the Holy Ghost was not yet given; because that Jesus was not yet glorified" (John 7:37, 39). This our Lord himself also declared to his disciples, "It is expedient for you that I go away: for if I go not away the Comforter will not come unto you" (John 16:7). To console them for his bodily absence, he tells them that he will not leave them comfortless, but will come again to them in a manner invisible indeed, but more to be desired, because they were then taught by a surer experience that the government which he had obtained, and the power which he exercises would enable his faithful followers not only to live well, but also to die happily. And, indeed we see how much more abundantly his Spirit was poured out, how much more gloriously his kingdom was advanced, how much greater power was employed in aiding his followers and discomfiting his enemies. Being raised to heaven, he withdrew his bodily presence from our sight, not that he might cease to be with his followers, who are still pilgrims on the earth, but that he might rule both heaven and earth more immediately by his power; or rather, the promise which he made to be with us even to the end of the world, he fulfilled by this ascension, by which, as his body has been raised above all heavens, so his power and efficacy have been propagated and diffused beyond all the bounds of heaven and earth. This I prefer to explain in the words of Augustine rather than my own: "Through death Christ was to go to the right hand of the Father, whence he is to come to judge the quick and the dead, and that in corporal presence, according to the sound doctrine and rule of faith. For, in spiritual presence, he was to be with them after his ascension" (August. Tract. in Joann. 109). In another passage he is more full and explicit: "In regard to ineffable and invisible grace, is fulfilled what he said, Lo, I am with you alway, even to the end of the world (Mt. 28:20); but in regard to the flesh which the Word assumed in regard to his being born of a Virgin, in regard to his being apprehended by the Jews, nailed to the tree, taken down from the cross, wrapt in linen clothes, laid in the sepulchre, and manifested on his resurrection, it may be said, Me ye have not always with you. Why? because, in bodily presence, he conversed with his disciples forty days, and leading them out where they saw, but followed not, he ascended into heaven, and is not here: for there he sits at the right hand of the Father: and yet he is here, for the presence of his Godhead was not withdrawn. Therefore, as regards his divine presence, we have Christ always: as regards his bodily presence, it was truly said to the disciples, Me ye have not always. For a few days the Church had him bodily present. Now, she apprehends him by faith, but sees him not by the eye" (August. Tract. 51).

15. Hence it is immediately added, that he "sitteth at the right hand of God the Father;" a similitude borrowed from princes, who have their assessors to whom they commit the office of ruling and issuing commands. Thus Christ, in whom the Father is pleased to be exalted, and by whose hand he is pleased to reign, is said to have been received up, and seated on his right hand (Mark 16:19); as if it had been said, that he was installed in the government of heaven and earth, and formally admitted

to possession of the administration committed to him, and not only admitted for once, but to continue until he descend to judgment. For so the Apostle interprets, when he says, that the Father "set him at his own right hand in the heavenly places, far above all principality, and power, and might, and dominion, and every name that is named not only in this world, but also in that which is to come; and has put all things under his feet, and given him to be the head over all things to the Church." You see to what end he is so seated namely, that all creatures both in heaven and earth should reverence his majesty, be ruled by his hand, do him implicit homage, and submit to his power. All that the Apostles intends when they so often mention his seat at the Father's hand, is to teach, that every thing is placed at his disposal. Those, therefore, are in error, who suppose that his blessedness merely is indicated. We may observe, that there is nothing contrary to this doctrine in the testimony of Stephen, that he saw him standing (Acts 7:56), the subject here considered being not the position of his body, but the majesty of his empire, *sitting* meaning nothing more than presiding on the judgment-seat of heaven.

16. From this doctrine faith derives manifold advantages. First, it perceives that the Lord, by his ascension to heaven, has opened up the access to the heavenly kingdom, which Adam had shut. For having entered it in our flesh, as it were in our name, it follows, as the Apostle says, that we are in a manner now seated in heavenly places, not entertaining a mere hope of heaven, but possessing it in our head. Secondly, faith perceives that his seat beside the Father is not without great advantage to us. Having entered the temple not made with hands, he constantly appears as our advocate and intercessor in the presence of the Father; directs attention to his own righteousness, so as to turn it away from our sins; so reconciles him to us, as by his intercession to pave for us a way of access to his throne, presenting it to miserable sinners, to whom it would otherwise be an object of dread, as replete with grace and mercy. Thirdly, it discerns his power, on which depend our strength, might, resources, and triumph over hell, "When he ascended up on high, he led captivity captive" (Eph. 4:8). Spoiling his foes, he gave gifts to his people, and daily loads them with spiritual riches. He thus occupies his exalted seat, that thence transferring his virtue unto us, he may quicken us to spiritual life, sanctify us by his Spirit, and adorn his Church with various graces, by his protection preserve it safe from all harm, and by the strength of his hand curb the enemies raging against his cross and our salvation; in fine, that he may possess all power in heaven and earth, until he have utterly routed all his foes, who are also ours and completed the structure of his Church. Such is the true nature of the kingdom, such the power which the Father has conferred upon him, until he arrive to complete the last act by judging the quick and the dead.

17. Christ, indeed, gives his followers no dubious proofs of present power, but as his kingdom in the world is in a manner veiled by the humiliation of a carnal condition, faith is most properly invited to meditate on the visible presence which he will exhibit on the last day. For he will descend from heaven in visible form, in like manner as he was seen to ascend, and appear to all, with the ineffable majesty of his kingdom, the splendour of immortality, the boundless power of divinity, and an attending company of angels. Hence we are told to wait for the Redeemer against that day on which he will separate the sheep from the goats and the elect from the reprobate, and when not one individual either of the living or the dead shall escape his judgment. From the extremities of the universe shall be heard the clang of the trumpet summoning all to his tribunal; both those whom that day shall find alive, and those whom death shall previously have removed from the society of the living. There are some who take the words, quick and dead, in a different sense; and, indeed, some ancient writers appear to have hesitated as to the exposition of them; but our meaning being plain and clear, is much more accordant with the Creed which was certainly written for popular use. There is nothing contrary to it in the Apostle's declaration, that it is appointed unto all men once to die. For though those who are surviving at the last day shall not die after a natural manner, yet the change which they are to undergo, as it shall resemble, is not improperly called, death (Heb. 9:27). "We shall not all sleep, but we shall all be changed" (1 Cor. 15:51). What does this mean? Their mortal life shall perish and be swallowed up in one moment, and be transformed into an entirely new nature. Though no one can deny that that destruction of the flesh will be death, it still remains true that the quick and the dead shall be summoned to judgment (1 Thess. 4:16); for "the dead in Christ shall rise first; then we which are alive and remain shall be caught up together with them in the clouds to meet the lord in the air." Indeed, it is probable, that these words in the Creed were taken from Peter's sermon as related by Luke (Acts 10:42), and from the solemn charge of Paul to Timothy (2 Tim. 4:1).

18. It is most consolatory to think, that judgment is vested in him who has already destined us to share with

him in the honour of judgment (Mt. 19:28); so far is it from being true, that he will ascend the judgment-seat for our condemnation. How could a most merciful prince destroy his own people? how could the head disperse its own members? how could the advocate condemn his clients? For if the Apostle, when contemplating the interposition of Christ, is bold to exclaim, "Who is he that condemneth?" (Rom. 8:33), much more certain is it that Christ, the intercessor, will not condemn those whom he has admitted to his protection. It certainly gives no small security, that we shall be sisted at no other tribunal than that of our Redeemer, from whom salvation is to be expected; and that he who in the Gospel now promises eternal blessedness, will then as judge ratify his promise. The end for which the Father has honoured the Son by committing all judgment to him (John 5:22), was to pacify the consciences of his people when alarmed at the thought of judgment. Hitherto I have followed the order of the Apostles' Creed, because it states the leading articles of redemption in a few words, and may thus serve as a tablet in which the points of Christian doctrine, most deserving of attention, are brought separately and distinctly before us. I call it the Apostles' Creed, though I am by no means solicitous as to its authorship. The general consent of ancient writers certainly does ascribe it to the Apostles, either because they imagined it was written and published by them for common use, or because they thought it right to give the sanction of such authority to a compendium faithfully drawn up from the doctrine delivered by their hands. I have no doubt, that, from the very commencement of the Church, and, therefore, in the very days of the Apostles, it held the place of a public and universally received confession, whatever be the quarter from which it originally proceeded. It is not probable that it was written by some private individual, since it is certain that, from time immemorial, it was deemed of sacred authority by all Christians. The only point of consequence we hold to be incontrovertible—viz. that it gives, in clear and succinct order, a full statement of our faith, and in every thing which it contains is sanctioned by the sure testimony of Scripture. This being understood, it were to no purpose to labour anxiously, or quarrel with any one as to the authorship, unless, indeed, we think it not enough to possess the sure truth of the Holy Spirit, without, at the same time, knowing by whose mouth it was pronounced, or by whose hand it was written.

19. When we see that the whole sum of our salvation, and every single part of it, are comprehended in Christ, we must beware of deriving even the minutes portion of it from any other quarter. If we seek salvation, we are taught by the very name of Jesus that he possesses it; if we seek any other gifts of the Spirit, we shall find them in his unction; strength in his government; purity in his conception; indulgence in his nativity, in which he was made like us in all respects, in order that he might learn to sympathise with us: if we seek redemption, we shall find it in his passion; acquittal in his condemnation; remission of the curse in his cross; satisfaction in his sacrifice; purification in his blood; reconciliation in his descent to hell; mortification of the flesh in his sepulchre; newness of life in his resurrection; immortality also in his resurrection; the inheritance of a celestial kingdom in his entrance into heaven; protection, security, and the abundant supply of all blessings, in his kingdom; secure anticipation of judgment in the power of judging committed to him. In fine, since in him all kinds of blessings are treasured up, let us draw a full supply from him, and none from any other quarter. Those who, not satisfied with him alone, entertain various hopes from others, though they may continue to look to him chiefly, deviate from the right path by the simple fact, that some portion of their thought takes a different direction. No distrust of this description can arise when once the abundance of his blessings is properly known.

CHAPTER 17

CHRIST RIGHTLY AND PROPERLY SAID TO HAVE MERITED GRACE AND SALVATION FOR US.

The three leading divisions of this chapter are,—I. A proof from reason and from Scripture that the grace of God and the merit of Christ (the prince and author of our salvation) are perfectly compatible, sec. 1 and 2. II. Christ, by his obedience, even to the death of the cross (which was the price of our redemption), merited divine favour for us, sec. 3–5. III. The presumptuous rashness of the Schoolmen in treating this branch of doctrine.

Sections:

1. Christ not only the minister, but also the author and prince of salvation. Divine grace not obscured by this mode of expression. The merit of Christ not opposed to the mercy of God, but depends upon it.

2. The compatibility of the two proved by various passages of Scripture.

3. Christ by his obedience truly merited divine grace for us.

4. This grace obtained by the shedding of Christ's blood, and his obedience even unto death.

5. In this way he paid our ransom.

6. The presumptuous manner in which the Schoolmen handle this subject.

1. A question must here be considered by way of supplement. Some men too much given to subtilty, while they admit that we obtain salvation through Christ, will not hear of the name of merit, by which they imagine that the grace of God is obscured; and therefore insist that Christ was only the instrument or minister, not the author or leader, or prince of life, as he is designated by Peter (Acts 3:15). I admit that were Christ opposed simply, and by himself, to the justice of God, there could be no room for merit, because there cannot be found in man a worth which could make God a debtor; nay, as Augustine says most truly, "The Saviour, the man Christ Jesus, is himself the brightest illustration of predestination and grace: his character as such was not procured by any antecedent merit of works or faith in his human nature. Tell me, I pray, how that man, when assumed into unity of person by the Word, co-eternal with the Father, as the only begotten Son at God, could merit this."—"Let the very fountain of grace, therefore, appear in our head, whence, according to the measure of each, it is diffused through all his members. Every man, from the commencement of his faith, becomes a Christian, by the same grace by which that man from his formation became Christ." Again, in another passage, "There is not a more striking example of predestination than the mediator himself. He who made him (without any antecedent merit in his will) of the seed of David a righteous man never to be unrighteous, also converts those who are members of his head from unrighteous into righteous" and so forth. Therefore when we treat of the merit of Christ, we do not place the beginning in him, but we ascend to the ordination of God as the primary cause, because of his mere good pleasure he appointed a Mediator to purchase salvation for us. Hence the merit of Christ is inconsiderately opposed to the mercy of God. It is a well known rule, that principal and accessory are not incompatible, and therefore there is nothing to prevent the justification of man from being the gratuitous result of the mere mercy of God, and, at the same time, to prevent the merit of Christ from intervening in subordination to this mercy. The free favour of God is as fitly opposed to our works as is the obedience of Christ, both in their order: for Christ could not merit anything save by the good pleasure of God, but only inasmuch as he was destined to appease the wrath of God by his sacrifice, and wipe away our transgressions by his obedience: in one word, since the merit of Christ depends entirely on the grace of God (which provided this mode of salvation for us), the latter is no less appropriately opposed to all righteousness of men than is the former.

2. This distinction is found in numerous passages of Scripture: "God so loved the world, that he gave his only begotten Son, that whosoever believeth in him might not perish" (John 3:16). We see that the first place is assigned to the love of God as the chief cause or origin, and that faith in Christ follows as the second and more proximate cause. Should any one object that Christ is only the formal cause, he lessens his energy more than the words justify. For if we obtain justification by a faith which leans on him, the groundwork of our salvation must be sought in him. This is clearly proved by several passages: "Herein is love, not that we loved God, but that he loved us, and sent his Son to be the propitiation for our sins" (1 John 4:10). These words clearly demonstrate that God, in order to remove any obstacle to his love towards us, appointed the method of reconciliation in Christ. There is great force in this word "*propitiation*"; for in a manner which cannot be expressed, God, at the very time when he loved us, was hostile to us until reconciled in Christ. To this effect are all the following passages: "He is the propitiation for our sins;" "It pleased the Father that in him should all fulness dwell, and having made peace by the blood of his cross, by him to reconcile all things unto himself;" "God was in Christ reconciling the world unto himself, not imputing their trespasses unto them;" "He has made us accepted in the Beloved," "That he might reconcile both into one body by the cross." The nature of this mystery is to be learned from the first chapter to the Ephesians, where Paul, teaching that we were chosen in Christ, at the same time adds, that we obtained grace in him. How did God begin to embrace with his favour those whom he had loved before the foundation of the world, unless in displaying his love when he was reconciled by the blood of Christ? As God is the fountain of all righteousness, he must necessarily be the enemy and judge of man so long as he is a sinner. Wherefore, the commencement of love is the bestowing of righteousness, as described by Paul: "He has made him to be sin for us who knew no sin; that we might be made the righteousness of God in him" (2 Cor. 5:21). He intimates, that by the sacrifice of Christ we obtain free justification, and become pleasing to God, though we are by nature the

children of wrath, and by sin estranged from him. This distinction is also noted whenever the grace of Christ is connected with the love of God (2 Cor. 13:13); whence it follows, that he bestows upon us of his own which he acquired by purchase. For otherwise there would be no ground for the praise ascribed to him by the Father, that grace is his, and proceeds from him.

3. That Christ, by his obedience, truly purchased and merited grace for us with the Father, is accurately inferred from several passages of Scripture. I take it for granted, that if Christ satisfied for our sins, if he paid the penalty due by us, if he appeased God by his obedience; in fine, if he suffered the just for the unjust, salvation was obtained for us by his righteousness; which is just equivalent to meriting. Now, Paul's testimony is, that we were reconciled, and received reconciliation through his death (Rom. 5:11). But there is no room for reconciliation unless where offence has preceded. The meaning, therefore, is, that God, to whom we were hateful through sin, was appeased by the death of his Son, and made propitious to us. And the antithesis which immediately follows is carefully to be observed, "As by one man's disobedience many were made sinners, so by the obedience of one shall many be made righteous" (Rom. 5:19). For the meaning is—As by the sin of Adam we were alienated from God and doomed to destruction, so by the obedience of Christ we are restored to his favour as if we were righteous. The future tense of the verb does not exclude present righteousness, as is apparent from the context. For he had previously said, "the free gift *is* of many offences unto justification."

4. When we say, that grace was obtained for us by the merit of Christ, our meaning is, that we were cleansed by his blood, that his death was an expiation for sin, "His blood cleanses us from all sin." "This is my blood, which is shed for the remission of sins" (1 John 1:7; Luke 22:20). If the effect of his shed blood is, that our sins are not imputed to us, it follows, that by that price the justice of God was satisfied. To the same effect are the Baptist's words, "Behold the Lamb of God, which taketh away the sin of the world" (John 1:29). For he contrasts Christ with all the sacrifices of the Law, showing that in him alone was fulfilled what these figures typified. But we know the common expression in Moses—Iniquity shall be expiated, sin shall be wiped away and forgiven. In short, we are admirably taught by the ancient figures what power and efficacy there is in Christ's death. And the Apostle, skilfully proceeding from this principle, explains the whole matter in the Epistle to the Hebrews, showing that without shedding of blood there is no remission (Heb. 9:22). From this he infers, that Christ appeared once for all to take away sin by the sacrifice of himself. Again, that he was offered to bear the sins of many (Heb. 9:12). He had previously said, that not by the blood of goats or of heifers, but by his own blood, he had once entered into the holy of holies, having obtained eternal redemption for us. Now, when he reasons thus, "If the blood of bulls and of goats, and the ashes of an heifer sprinkling the unclean, sanctifieth to the purifying of the flesh: how much more shall the blood of Christ, who through the eternal Spirit offered himself to God, purge your consciences from dead works to serve the living God?" (Heb. 9:13, 14), it is obvious that too little effect is given to the grace of Christ, unless we concede to his sacrifice the power of expiating, appeasing, and satisfying: as he shortly after adds, "For this cause he is the mediator of the new testament, that by means of his death, for the redemption of the transgressions that were under the first testament, they which are called might receive the promise of eternal inheritance" (Heb. 9:15). But it is especially necessary to attend to the analogy which is drawn by Paul as to his having been made a curse for us (Gal. 3:13). It had been superfluous and therefore absurd, that Christ should have been burdened with a curse, had it not been in order that, by paying what others owed, he might acquire righteousness for them. There is no ambiguity in Isaiah's testimony, "He was wounded for our transgressions, he was bruised for our iniquities: the chastisement of our peace was laid upon him; and with his stripes we are healed" (Is. 53:5). For had not Christ satisfied for our sins, he could not be said to have appeased God by taking upon himself the penalty which we had incurred. To this corresponds what follows in the same place, "for the transgression of my people was he stricken" (Is. 53:8). We may add the interpretation of Peter, who unequivocally declares, that he "bare our sins in his own body on the tree" (1 Pet. 2:24), that the whole burden of condemnation, of which we were relieved, was laid upon him.

5. The Apostles also plainly declare that he paid a price to ransom us from death: "Being justified freely by his grace, through the redemption that is in Christ Jesus: whom God has set forth to be a propitiation through faith in his blood" (Rom. 3:24, 25). Paul commends the grace of God, in that he gave the price of redemption in the death of Christ; and he exhorts us to flee to his blood, that having obtained righteousness, we may appear boldly before the judgment-seat of God. To the same effect are the words of Peter: "Forasmuch as ye know that

ye were not redeemed with corruptible things, as silver and gold," "but with the precious blood of Christ, as of a lamb without blemish and without spot" (1 Pet. 1:18, 19). The antithesis would be incongruous if he had not by this price made satisfaction for sins. For which reason, Paul says, "Ye are bought with a price." Nor could it be elsewhere said, there is "one mediator between God and men, the man Christ Jesus; who gave himself a ransom for all" (1 Tim. 2:5, 6), had not the punishment which we deserved been laid upon him. Accordingly, the same Apostle declares, that "we have redemption through his blood, even the forgiveness of sins" (Col. 1:14); as if he had said, that we are justified or acquitted before God, because that blood serves the purpose of satisfaction. With this another passage agrees—viz. that he blotted out "the handwriting of ordinances which was against us, which was contrary to us" (Col. 2:14). These words denote the payment or compensation which acquits us from guilt. There is great weight also in these words of Paul: "If righteousness come by the law, then Christ is dead in vain" (Gal. 2:21). For we hence infer, that it is from Christ we must seek what the Law would confer on any one who fulfilled it; or, which is the same thing, that by the grace of Christ we obtain what God promised in the Law to our works: "If a man do, he shall live in them" (Lev. 18:5). This is no less clearly taught in the discourse at Antioch, when Paul declares, "That through this man is preached unto you the forgiveness of sins; and by him all that believe are justified from all things, from which ye could not be justified by the law of Moses" (Acts 13:38, 39). For if the observance of the Law is righteousness, who can deny that Christ, by taking this burden upon himself, and reconciling us to God, as if we were the observers of the Law, merited favour for us? Of the same nature is what he afterwards says to the Galatians: "God sent forth his Son, made of a woman, made under the law, to redeem them that were under the law" (Gal. 4:4, 5). For to what end that subjection, unless that he obtained justification for us by undertaking to perform what we were unable to pay? Hence that imputation of righteousness without works, of which Paul treats (Rom. 4:5), the righteousness found in Christ alone being accepted as if it were ours. And certainly the only reason why Christ is called our "meat" (John 6:55), is because we find in him the substance of life. And the source of this efficacy is just that the Son of God was crucified as the price of our justification; as Paul says, Christ "has given himself for us an offering and a sacrifice to God for a sweet-smelling savour" (Eph. 5:2); and elsewhere, he "was delivered for our offences, and was raised again for our justification" (Rom. 4:25). Hence it is proved not only that salvation was given us by Christ, but that on account of him the Father is now propitious to us. For it cannot be doubted that in him is completely fulfilled what God declares by Isaiah under a figure, "I will defend this city to save it for mine own sakes and for my servant David's sake" (Isaiah 37:35). Of this the Apostle is the best witness when he says "Your sins are forgiven you for his name's sake" (1 John 2:12). For although the name of Christ is not expressed, John, in his usual manner, designates him by the pronoun "He" (*aujtov*). In the same sense also our Lord declares, "As the living Father has sent me, and I live by the Father: so he that eateth me, even he shall live by me" (John 6:57). To this corresponds the passage of Paul, "Unto you it is given in the behalf of Christ, not only to believe in him, but also to suffer for his sake" (Phil. 1:29).

6. To inquire, as Lombard and the Schoolmen do (Sent. Lib. 3 Dist. 18), whether he merited for himself, is foolish curiosity. Equally rash is their decision when they answer in the affirmative. How could it be necessary for the only Son of God to come down in order to acquire some new quality for himself? The exposition which God gives of his own purpose removes all doubt. The Father is not said to have consulted the advantage of his Son in his services, but to have given him up to death, and not spared him, because he loved the world (Rom. 8). The prophetical expressions should be observed: "To us a Son is born;" "Rejoice greatly, O daughter of Zion: shout, O daughter of Jerusalem: behold, thy King cometh unto thee" (Isaiah 9:6; Zech. 9:9). It would otherwise be a cold commendation of love which Paul describes, when he says, "God commendeth his love toward us, in that, while we were yet sinners, Christ died for us" (Rom. 5:8). Hence, again, we infer that Christ had no regard to himself; and this he distinctly affirms, when he says, "For their sakes I sanctify myself" (John 17:19). He who transfers the benefit of his holiness to others, testifies that he acquires nothing for himself. And surely it is most worthy of remark, that Christ, in devoting himself entirely to our salvation, in a manner forgot himself. It is absurd to wrest the testimony of Paul to a different effect: "Wherefore God has highly exalted him, and given him a name which is above every name" (Phil. 2:9). By what services could a man merit to become the judge of the world, the head of angels, to obtain the supreme government of God, and become the residence of that majesty of which all the virtues of men and angels cannot attain one thousandth part? The solution is easy and complete. Paul is not speaking of the

cause of Christ's exaltation, but only pointing out a consequence of it by way of example to us. The meaning is not much different from that of another passage: "Ought not Christ to have suffered these things, and to enter into his glory?" (Luke 24:26).

END OF THE SECOND BOOK.

BOOK THIRD: THE MODE OF OBTAINING THE GRACE OF CHRIST. THE BENEFITS IT CONFERS, AND THE EFFECTS RESULTING FROM IT.

ARGUMENT.

The two former Books treated of God the Creator and Redeemer. This Book, which contains a full exposition of the Third Part of the Apostles' Creed, treats of the mode of procuring the grace of Christ, the benefits which we derive and the effects which follow from it, or of the operations of the Holy Spirit in regard to our salvation.

The subject is comprehended under seven principal heads, which almost all point to the same end, namely, the doctrine of faith.

I. As it is by the secret and special operation of the Holy Spirit that we enjoy Christ and all his benefits, the First Chapter treats of this operation, which is the foundation of faith, new life, and all holy exercises.

II. Faith being, as it were, the hand by which we embrace Christ the Redeemer, offered to us by the Holy Spirit, Faith is fully considered in the Second Chapter.

III. In further explanation of Saving Faith, and the benefits derived from it, it is mentioned that true repentance always flows from true faith. The doctrine of Repentance is considered generally in the Third Chapter, Popish Repentance in the Fourth Chapter, Indulgences and Purgatory in the Fifth Chapter. Chapters Sixth to Tenth are devoted to a special consideration of the different parts of true Repentance—viz. mortification of the flesh, and quickening of the Spirit.

IV. More clearly to show the utility of this Faith, and the effects resulting from it, the doctrine of Justification by Faith is explained in the Eleventh Chapter, and certain questions connected with it explained from the Twelfth to the Eighteenth Chapter. Christian liberty a kind of accessory to Justification, is considered in the Nineteenth Chapter.

V. The Twentieth Chapter is devoted to Prayer, the principal exercise of faith, and, as it were, the medium or instrument through which we daily procure blessings from God.

VI. As all do not indiscriminately embrace the fellowship of Christ offered in the Gospel, but those only whom the Lord favors with the effectual and special grace of his Spirit, lest any should impugn this arrangement, Chapters Twenty-First to Twenty-Fourth are occupied with a necessary and apposite discussion of the subject of Election.

VII. Lastly, As the hard warfare which the Christian is obliged constantly to wage may have the effect of disheartening him, it is shown how it may be alleviated by meditating on the final resurrection. Hence the subject of the Resurrection is considered in the Twenty-Fifth Chapter.

CHAPTER 1

THE BENEFITS OF CHRIST MADE AVAILABLE TO US BY THE SECRET OPERATION OF THE SPIRIT.

The three divisions of this chapter are,—I. The secret operation of the Holy Spirit, which seals our salvation, should be considered first in Christ the Mediator as our Head, sec. 1 and 2. II. The titles given to the Holy Spirit show that we become members of Christ by his grace and energy, sec. 3. III. As the special influence of the Holy Spirit is manifested in the gift of faith, the former is a proper introduction to the latter, and thus prepares for the second chapter, sec. 4.

Sections:

1. The Holy Spirit the bond which unites us with Christ. This the result of faith produced by the secret operation of the Holy Spirit. This obvious from Scripture.

2. In Christ the Mediator the gifts of the Holy Spirit are to be seen in all their fulness. To what end. Why the Holy Spirit is called the Spirit of the Father and the Son.

3. Titles of the Spirit,—1. The Spirit of adoption. 2. An earnest and seal. 3. Water. 4. Life. 5. Oil and unction. 6. Fire. 7. A fountain. 8. The word of God. Use of these titles. 4. Faith being the special work of the Holy Spirit, the power and efficacy of the Holy Spirit usually ascribed to it.

1. We must now see in what way we become possessed of the blessings which God has bestowed on his only-begotten Son, not for private use, but to enrich the poor and

needy. And the first thing to be attended to is, that so long as we are without Christ and separated from him, nothing which he suffered and did for the salvation of the human race is of the least benefit to us. To communicate to us the blessings which he received from the Father, he must become ours and dwell in us. Accordingly, he is called our Head, and the first-born among many brethren, while, on the other hand, we are said to be ingrafted into him and clothed with him, all which he possesses being, as I have said, nothing to us until we become one with him. And although it is true that we obtain this by faith, yet since we see that all do not indiscriminately embrace the offer of Christ which is made by the gospel, the very nature of the case teaches us to ascend higher, and inquire into the secret efficacy of the Spirit, to which it is owing that we enjoy Christ and all his blessings. I have already treated of the eternal essence and divinity of the Spirit (Book 1 chap. 13 sect. 14,15); let us at present attend to the special point, that Christ came by water and blood, as the Spirit testifies concerning him, that we might not lose the benefits of the salvation which he has purchased. For as there are said to be three witnesses in heaven, the Father, the Word, and the Spirit, so there are also three on the earth, namely, water, blood, and Spirit. It is not without cause that the testimony of the Spirit is twice mentioned, a testimony which is engraven on our hearts by way of seal, and thus seals the cleansing and sacrifice of Christ. For which reason, also, Peter says, that believers are "elect" "through sanctification of the Spirit, unto obedience and sprinkling of the blood of Jesus Christ" (1 Pet. 1:2). By these words he reminds us, that if the shedding of his sacred blood is not to be in vain, our souls must be washed in it by the secret cleansing of the Holy Spirit. For which reason, also, Paul, speaking of cleansing and purification, says, "but ye are washed, but ye are sanctified, but ye are justified in the name of the Lord Jesus and by the Spirit of our God" (1 Cor. 6:11). The whole comes to this that the Holy Spirit is the bond by which Christ effectually binds us to himself. Here we may refer to what was said in the last Book concerning his anointing.

2. But in order to have a clearer view of this most important subjects we must remember that Christ came provided with the Holy Spirit after a peculiar manner, namely, that he might separate us from the world, and unite us in the hope of an eternal inheritance. Hence the Spirit is called the Spirit of sanctification, because he quickens and cherishes us, not merely by the general energy which is seen in the human race, as well as other animals, but because he is the seed and root of heavenly life in us. Accordingly, one of the highest commendations which the prophets give to the kingdom of Christ is, that under it the Spirit would be poured out in richer abundance. One of the most remarkable passages is that of Joel, "It shall come to pass afterward, that I will pour out my Spirit upon all flesh" (Joel 2:28). For although the prophet seems to confine the gifts of the Spirit to the office of prophesying, he yet intimates under a figure, that God will, by the illumination of his Spirit, provide himself with disciples who had previously been altogether ignorant of heavenly doctrine. Moreover, as it is for the sake of his Son that God bestows the Holy Spirit upon us, and yet has deposited him in all his fulness with the Son, to be the minister and dispenser of his liberality, he is called at one time the Spirit of the Father, at another the Spirit of the Son: "Ye are not in the flesh but in the Spirit, if so be that the Spirit of God dwell in you. Now, if any man have not the Spirit of Christ, he is none of his" (Rom. 8:9); and hence he encourages us to hope for complete renovation: "If the Spirit of him that raised up Jesus from the dead dwell in you, he that raised up Christ from the dead shall also quicken your mortal bodies by his Spirit that dwelleth in you" (Rom. 8:11). There is no inconsistency in ascribing the glory of those gifts to the Father, inasmuch as he is the author of them, and, at the same time, ascribing them to Christ, with whom they have been deposited, that he may bestow them on his people. Hence he invites all the thirsty to come unto him and drink (John 7:37). And Paul teaches, that "unto every one of us is given grace, according to the measure of the gift of Christ" (Eph. 4:7). And we must remember, that the Spirit is called the Spirit of Christ, not only inasmuch as the eternal Word of God is with the Father united with the Spirit, but also in respect of his office of Mediator; because, had he not been endued with the energy of the Spirit, he had come to us in vain. In this sense he is called the "last Adam," and said to have been sent from heaven "a quickening Spirit" (1 Cor. 15:45), where Paul contrasts the special life which Christ breathes into his people, that they may be one with him with the animal life which is common even to the reprobate. In like manner, when he prays that believers may have "the grace of our Lord Jesus Christ, and the love of God," he at the same time adds, "the communion of the Holy Ghost," without which no man shall ever taste the paternal favor of God, or the benefits of Christ. Thus, also, in another passage he says, "The love of God is shed abroad in our hearts by the Holy Ghost, which is given unto us" (Rom. 5:5).

3. Here it will be proper to point out the titles which the Scripture bestows on the Spirit, when it treats of the commencement and entire renewal of our salvation. First, he is called the "Spirit of adoption," because he is witness to us of the free favor with which God the Father embraced us in his well-beloved and only-begotten Son, so as to become our Fathers and give us boldness of access to him; nays he dictates the very words, so that we can boldly cry, "Abba, Father." For the same reason, he is said to have "sealed us, and given the earnest of the Spirit in our hearts," because, as pilgrims in the world, and persons in a manner dead, he so quickens us from above as to assure us that our salvation is safe in the keeping of a faithful God. Hence, also, the Spirit is said to be "life because of righteousness." But since it is his secret irrigation that makes us bud forth and produce the fruits of righteousness, he is repeatedly described as *water*. Thus in Isaiah "Ho, every one that thirsteth, come ye to the waters." Again, "I will pour water upon him that is thirsty, and floods upon the dry ground." Corresponding to this are the words of our Savior, to which I lately referred, "If any man thirst, let him come unto me and drink." Sometimes, indeed, he receives this name from his energy in cleansing and purifying, as in Ezekiel, where the Lord promises, "Then will I sprinkle you with clean water, and ye shall be clean." As those sprinkled with the Spirit are restored to the full vigor of life, he hence obtains the names of "*Oil*" and "*Unction*." On the other hand, as he is constantly employed in subduing and destroying the vices of our concupiscence, and inflaming our hearts with the love of God and piety, he hence receives the name of *Fire*. In fine, he is described to us as a *Fountain*, whence all heavenly riches flow to us; or as the *Hand* by which God exerts his power, because by his divine inspiration he so breathes divine life into us, that we are no longer acted upon by ourselves, but ruled by his motion and agency, so that everything good in us is the fruit of his grace, while our own endowments without him are mere darkness of mind and perverseness of heart. Already, indeed, it has been clearly shown, that until our minds are intent on the Spirit, Christ is in a manner unemployed, because we view him coldly without us, and so at a distance from us. Now we know that he is of no avail save only to those to whom he is a head and the first-born among the brethren, to those, in fine, who are clothed with him. To this union alone it is owing that, in regard to us, the Savior has not come in vain. To this is to be referred that sacred marriage, by which we become bone of his bone, and flesh of his flesh, and so one with him (Eph. 5:30), for it is by the Spirit alone that he unites himself to us. By the same grace and energy of the Spirit we become his members, so that he keeps us under him, and we in our turn possess him.

4. But as faith is his principal work, all those passages which express his power and operations are, in a great measure, referred to it, as it is, only by faith that he brings us to the light of the Gospel, as John teaches, that to those who believe in Christ is given the privilege "to become the sons of God, even to them that believe in his name, which were born not of blood, nor of the will of the flesh, nor of the will of man, but of God" (John 1:12). Opposing *God* to *flesh and blood*, he declares it to be a supernatural gift, that those who would otherwise remain in unbelief, receive Christ by faith. Similar to this is our Savior's reply to Peter, "Flesh and blood has not revealed it unto thee, but my Father which is in heaven" (Matt. 16:17). These things I now briefly advert to, as I have fully considered them elsewhere. To the same effect Paul says to the Ephesians, "Ye were sealed with that Holy Spirit of promise" (Eph. 1:13); thus showing that he is the internal teacher, by whose agency the promise of salvation, which would otherwise only strike the air or our ears, penetrates into our minds. In like manner, he says to the Thessalonians, "God has from the beginning chosen you to salvation, through sanctification of the Spirit and belief of the truth" (2 Thess. 2:13); by this passage briefly reminding us, that faith itself is produced only by the Spirit. This John explains more distinctly, "We know that he abideth in us, by the Spirit which he has given us;" again, "Hereby know we that we dwell in him and he in us, because he has given us of his Spirit" (1 John 3:24; 4:13). Accordingly to make his disciples capable of heavenly wisdom, Christ promised them "the Spirit of truth, whom the world cannot receive" (John 14:17). And he assigns it to him, as his proper office, to bring to remembrance the things which he had verbally taught; for in vain were light offered to the blind, did not that Spirit of understanding open the intellectual eye; so that he himself may be properly termed the key by which the treasures of the heavenly kingdom are unlocked, and his illumination, the eye of the mind by which we are enabled to see: hence Paul so highly commends the ministry of the Spirit (2 Cor. 3:6), since teachers would cry aloud to no purpose, did not Christ, the internal teacher, by means of his Spirit, draw to himself those who are given him of the Father. Therefore, as we have said that salvation is perfected in the person of Christ, so, in order to make us partakers of it, he baptizes us "with the Holy

Spirit and with fire" (Luke 3:16), enlightening us into the faith of his Gospel, and so regenerating us to be new creatures. Thus cleansed from all pollution, he dedicates us as holy temples to the Lord.

CHAPTER 2

OF FAITH. THE DEFINITION OF IT. ITS PECULIAR PROPERTIES.

This chapter consists of three principal parts.—I. A brief explanation of certain matters pertaining to the doctrine of Faith, sec. 1–14. First, of the object of faith, sec. 1. Second, of Implicit Faith, sec. 2–6. Third, Definition of Faith, sec. 7. Fourth, the various meanings of the term Faith, sec. 8–13. II. A full exposition of the definition given in the seventh section, sec. 14–40. III. A brief confirmation of the definition by the authority of an Apostle. The mutual relation between faith, hope, and charity, sec. 41–43.

Sections:

1. A brief recapitulation of the leading points of the whole discussion. The scope of this chapter. The necessity of the doctrine of faith. This doctrine obscured by the Schoolmen, who make God the object of faith, without referring to Christ. The Schoolmen refuted by various passages.

2. The dogma of implicit faith refuted. It destroys faith, which consists in a knowledge of the divine will. What this will is, and how necessary the knowledge of it.

3. Many things are and will continue to be implicitly believed. Faith, however, consists in the knowledge of God and Christ, not in a reverence for the Church. Another refutation from the absurdities to which this dogma leads.

4. In what sense our faith may be said to be implicit. Examples in the Apostles, in the holy women, and in all believers.

5. In some, faith is implicit, as being a preparation for faith. This, however, widely different from the implicit faith of the Schoolmen.

6. The word of God has a similar relation to faith, the word being, as it were, the source and basis of faith, and the mirror in which it beholds God. Confirmation from various passages of Scripture. Without the knowledge of the word there can be no faith. Sum of the discussion of the Scholastic doctrine of implicit faith.

7. What faith properly has respect to in the word of God, namely, the promise of grace offered in Christ, provided it be embraced with faith. Proper definition of faith.

8. Scholastic distinction between faith formed and unformed, refuted by a consideration of the nature of faith, which, as the gift of the Spirit, cannot possibly be disjoined from pious affection.

9. Objection from a passage of Paul. Answer to it. Error of the Schoolmen in giving only one meaning to faith, whereas it has many meanings. The testimony of faith improperly ascribed to two classes of men.

10. View to be taken of this. Who those are that believe for a time. The faith of hypocrites. With whom they may be compared.

11. Why faith attributed to the reprobate. Objection. Answer. What perception of grace in the reprobate. How the elect are distinguished from the reprobate.

12. Why faith is temporary in the reprobate, firm and perpetual in the elect. Reason in the case of the reprobate. Example. Why God is angry with his children. In what sense many are said to fall from faith.

13. Various meanings of the term faith. 1. Taken for soundness in the faith. 2. Sometimes restricted to a particular object. 3. Signifies the ministry or testimony by which we are instructed in the faith.

14. Definition of faith explained under six principal heads. 1. What meant by Knowledge in the definition.

15. Why this knowledge must be sure and firm. Reason drawn from the consideration of our weakness. Another reason from the certainty of the promises of God.

16. The leading point in this certainty. Its fruits. A description of the true believer.

17. An objection to this certainty. Answer. Confirmation of the answer from the example of David. This enlarged upon from the opposite example of Ahab. Also from the uniform experience and the prayers of believers.

18. For this reason the conflict between the flesh and the Spirit in the soul of the believer described. The issue of this conflict, the victory of faith.

19. On the whole, the faith of the elect certain and indubitable. Conformation from analogy.

20. Another confirmation from the testimony of an Apostle, making it apparent, that, though the faith of the elect is as yet imperfect, it is nevertheless firm and sure.

21. A fuller explanation of the nature of faith. 1. When the believer is shaken with fear, he retakes himself to the bosom of a merciful God. 2. He does not

even shun God when angry, but hopes in him. 3. He does not suffer unbelief to reign in his heart. 4. He opposes unbelief, and is never finally lost. 5. Faith, however often assailed, at length comes off victorious.

22. Another species of fear, arising from a consideration of the judgment of God against the wicked. This also faith overcomes. Examples of this description, placed before the eyes of believers, repress presumption, and fix their faith in God.

23. Nothing contrary to this in the exhortation of the Apostle to work out our salvation with fear and trembling. Fear and faith mutually connected. Confirmation from the words of a Prophet.

24. This doctrine gives no countenance to the error of those who dream of a confidence mingled with incredulity. Refutation of this error, from a consideration of the dignity of Christ dwelling in us. The argument retorted. Refutation confirmed by the authority of an Apostle. What we ought to hold on this question.

25. Confirmation of the preceding conclusion by a passage from Bernard.

26. True fear caused in two ways—viz. when we are required to reverence God as a Father, and also to fear him as Lord.

27. Objection from a passage in the Apostle John. Answer founded on the distinction between filial and servile fear.

28. How faith is said to have respect to the divine benevolence. What comprehended under this benevolence. Confirmation from David and Paul.

29. Of the Free Promise which is the foundation of Faith. Reason. Confirmation.

30. Faith not divided in thus seeking a Free Promise in the Gospel. Reason. Conclusion confirmed by another reason.

31. The word of God the prop and root of faith. The word attests the divine goodness and mercy. In what sense faith has respect to the power of God. Various passages of Isaiah, inviting the godly to behold the power of God, explained. Other passages from David. We must beware of going beyond the limits prescribed by the word, lest false zeal lead us astray, as it did Sarah, Rebekah, and Isaac. In this way faith is obscured, though not extinguished. We must not depart one iota from the word of God.

32. All the promises included in Christ. Two objections answered. A third objection drawn from example. Answer explaining the faith of Naaman, Cornelius, and the Eunuch.

33. Faith revealed to our minds, and sealed on our hearts, by the Holy Spirit. 1. The mind is purified so as to have a relish for divine truth. 2. The mind is thus established in the truth by the agency of the Holy Spirit.

34. Proof of the former. 1. By reason. 2. By Scripture. 3. By example. 4. By analogy.

35. 5. By the excellent qualities of faith. 6. By a celebrated passage from Augustine.

36. Proof of the latter by the argument a minore ad majus. Why the Spirit is called a seal, an earnest, and the Spirit of promise.

37. Believers sometimes shaken, but not so as to perish finally. They ultimately overcome their trials, and remain steadfast. Proofs from Scripture.

38. Objection of the Schoolmen. Answer. Attempt to support the objection by a passage in Ecclesiastes. Answer, explaining the meaning of the passage.

39. Another objection, charging the elect in Christ with rashness and presumption. Answer. Answer confirmed by various passages from the Apostle Paul. Also from John and Isaiah.

40. A third objection, impugning the final perseverance of the elect. Answer by an Apostle. Summary of the refutation.

41. The definition of faith accords with that given by the Apostle in the Hebrews. Explanation of this definition. Refutation of the scholastic error, that charity is prior to faith and hope.

42. Hope the inseparable attendant of true faith. Reason. Connection between faith and hope. Mutually support each other. Obvious from the various forms of temptation, that the aid of hope necessary to establish faith.

43. The terms faith and hope sometimes confounded. Refutation of the Schoolmen, who attribute a twofold foundation to hope—viz. the grace of God and the merit of works.

1. All these things will be easily understood after we have given a clearer definition of faith, so as to enable the readers to apprehend its nature and power. Here it is of importance to call to mind what was formerly taught, first, That since God by his Law prescribes what we ought to do, failure in any one respect subjects us to the dreadful judgment of eternal death, which it denounces. Secondly, Because it is not only difficult, but altogether beyond our strength and ability, to fulfill the demands of the Law, if we look only to ourselves and consider what is due to our merits, no ground of hope remains, but we

lie forsaken of God under eternal death. Thirdly, That there is only one method of deliverance which can rescue us from this miserable calamity—viz. when Christ the Redeemer appears, by whose hand our heavenly Father, out of his infinite goodness and mercy, has been pleased to succor us, if we with true faith embrace this mercy, and with firm hope rest in it. It is now proper to consider the nature of this faith, by means of which, those who are adopted into the family of God obtain possession of the heavenly kingdom. For the accomplishment of so great an end, it is obvious that no mere opinion or persuasion is adequate. And the greater care and diligence is necessary in discussing the true nature of faith, from the pernicious delusions which many, in the present day, labour under with regard to it. Great numbers, on hearing the term, think that nothing more is meant than a certain common assent to the Gospel History; nay, when the subject of faith is discussed in the Schools, by simply representing God as its object, they by empty speculation, as we have elsewhere said (Book 2, chap. 6, sec. 4), hurry wretched souls away from the right mark instead of directing them to it. For seeing that God dwells in light that is inaccessible, Christ must intervene. Hence he calls himself "the light of the world;" and in another passage, "the way, the truth, and the life." None cometh to the Father (who is the fountain of life) except by him; for "no man knoweth who the Father is but the Son, and he to whom the Son will reveal him." For this reason, Paul declares, "I count all things as loss for the excellency of the knowledge of Christ Jesus my Lord." In the twentieth chapter of the Acts, he states that he preached "faith towards our Lord Jesus Christ;" and in another passage, he introduces Christ as thus addressing him: "I have appeared unto thee for this purpose, to make thee a minister and a witness;" "delivering thee from the people, and from the Gentiles, unto whom now I send thee,"—"that they may receive forgiveness of sins, and inheritance among them which are sanctified through faith which is in me." Paul further declares, that in the person of Christ the glory of God is visibly manifested to us, or, which is the same thing, we have "the light of the knowledge of the glory of God in the face of Jesus Christ." It is true, indeed, that faith has respect to God only; but to this we should add, that it acknowledges Jesus Christ whom he has sent. God would remain far off, concealed from us, were we not irradiated by the brightness of Christ. All that the Father had, he deposited with his only begotten Son, in order that he might manifest himself in him, and thus by the communication of blessings express the true image of his glory. Since, as has been said, we must be led by the Spirit, and thus stimulated to seek Christ, so must we also remember that the invisible Father is to be sought nowhere but in this image. For which reason Augustine treating of the object of faith (De Civitate Dei, lib. 11, ch. 2), elegantly says, "The thing to be known is, whither we are to go, and by what way;" and immediately after infers, that "the surest way to avoid all errors is to know him who is both God and man. It is to God we tend, and it is by man we go, and both of these are found only in Christ." Paul, when he preaches faith towards God, surely does not intend to overthrow what he so often inculcates—viz. that faith has all its stability in Christ. Peter most appropriately connects both, saying, that by him "we believe in God" (1 Pet. 1:21).

2. This evil, therefore, must, like innumerable others, be attributed to the Schoolmen, who have in a manner drawn a veil over Christ, to whom, if our eye is not directly turned, we must always wander through many labyrinths. But besides impairing, and almost annihilating, faith by their obscure definition, they have invented the fiction of implicit faith, with which name decking the grossest ignorance, they delude the wretched populace to their great destruction. Nay, to state the fact more truly and plainly, this fiction not only buries true faith, but entirely destroys it. Is it faith to understand nothing, and merely submit your convictions implicitly to the Church? Faith consists not in ignorance, but in knowledge—knowledge not of God merely, but of the divine will. We do not obtain salvation either because we are prepared to embrace every dictate of the Church as true, or leave to the Church the province of inquiring and determining; but when we recognize God as a propitious Father through the reconciliation made by Christ, and Christ as given to us for righteousness, sanctification, and life. By this knowledge, I say, not by the submission of our understanding, we obtain an entrance into the kingdom of heaven. For when the Apostle says, "With the heart man believeth unto righteousness; and with the mouth confession is made unto salvation" (Rom. 10:10); he intimates, that it is not enough to believe implicitly without understanding, or even inquiring. The thing requisite is an explicit recognition of the divine goodness, in which our righteousness consists.

3. I indeed deny not (so enveloped are we in ignorance), that to us very many things now are and will continue to be completely involved until we lay aside this weight of flesh, and approach nearer to the presence of God. In such cases the fittest course is to suspend our judgment,

and resolve to maintain unity with the Church. But under this pretext, to honor ignorance tempered with humility with the name of faith, is most absurd. Faith consists in the knowledge of God and Christ (John 17:3), not in reverence for the Church. And we see what a labyrinth they have formed out of this implicit faith—every thing, sometimes even the most monstrous errors, being received by the ignorant as oracles without any discrimination, provided they are prescribed to them under the name of the Church. This inconsiderate facility, though the surest precipice to destruction, is, however, excused on the ground that it believes nothing definitely, but only with the appended condition, if such is the faith of the Church. Thus they pretend to find truth in error, light in darkness, true knowledge in ignorance. Not to dwell longer in refuting these views, we simply advise the reader to compare them with ours. The clearness of truth will itself furnish a sufficient refutation. For the question they raise is not, whether there may be an implicit faith with many remains of ignorance, but they maintain, that persons living and even indulging in a stupid ignorance duly believe, provided, in regard to things unknown, they assent to the authority and judgment of the Church: as if Scripture did not uniformly teach, that with faith understanding is conjoined.

4. We grant, indeed, that so long as we are pilgrims in the world faith is implicit, not only because as yet many things are hidden from us, but because, involved in the mists of error, we attain not to all. The highest wisdom, even of him who has attained the greatest perfection, is to go forward, and endeavor in a calm and teachable spirit to make further progress. Hence Paul exhorts believers to wait for further illumination in any matter in which they differ from each other, Phil. 3:15). And certainly experience teaches, that so long as we are in the flesh, our attainments are less than is to be desired. In our daily reading we fall in with many obscure passages which convict us of ignorance. With this curb God keeps us modest, assigning to each a measure of faith, that every teacher, however excellent, may still be disposed to learn. Striking examples of this implicit faith may be observed in the disciples of Christ before they were fully illuminated. We see with what difficulty they take in the first rudiments, how they hesitate in the minutest matters, how, though hanging on the lips of their Master, they make no great progress; nay, even after running to the sepulchre on the report of the women, the resurrection of their Master appears to them a dream. As Christ previously bore testimony to their faith, we cannot say that they were altogether devoid of it; nay, had they not been persuaded that Christ would rise again, all their zeal would have been extinguished. Nor was it superstition that led the women to prepare spices to embalm a dead body of whose revival they had no expectation; but, although they gave credit to the words of one whom they knew to be true, yet the ignorance which still possessed their minds involved their faith in darkness, and left them in amazement. Hence they are said to have believed only when, by the reality, they perceive the truth of what Christ had spoken; not that they then began to believe, but the seed of a hidden faith, which lay as it were dead in their hearts, then burst forth in vigor. They had, therefore, a true but implicit faith, having reverently embraced Christ as the only teacher. Then, being taught by him, they felt assured that he was the author of salvation: in fine, believed that he had come from heaven to gather disciples, and take them thither through the grace of the Father. There cannot be a more familiar proof of this, than that in all men faith is always mingled with incredulity.

5. We may also call their faith implicit, as being properly nothing else than a preparation for faith. The Evangelists describe many as having believed, although they were only roused to admiration by the miracles, and went no farther than to believe that Christ was the promised Messiah, without being at all imbued with Evangelical doctrine. The reverence which subdued them, and made them willingly submit to Christ, is honored with the name of faith, though it was nothing but the commencement of it. Thus the nobleman who believed in the promised cure of his son, on returning home, is said by the Evangelist (John 4:53) to have again believed; that is, he had first received the words which fell from the lips of Christ as an oracular response, and thereafter submitted to his authority and received his doctrine. Although it is to be observed that he was docile and disposed to learn, yet the word "*believed*" in the former passage denotes a particular faith, and in the latter gives him a place among those disciples who had devoted themselves to Christ. Not unlike this is the example which John gives of the Samaritans who believed the women, and eagerly hastened to Christ; but, after they had heard him, thus express themselves, "Now we believe, not because of thy saying, for we have heard him ourselves, and know that this is indeed the Christ, the Savior of the world" (John 4:42). From these passages it is obvious, that even those who are not yet imbued with the first principles, provided they are disposed to obey, are called *believers*, not properly indeed, but inasmuch as God is pleased in

kindness so highly to honor their pious feeling. But this docility, with a desire of further progress, is widely different from the gross ignorance in which those sluggishly indulge who are contented with the implicit faith of the Papists. If Paul severely condemns those who are "ever learning, and never able to come to the knowledge of the truth," how much more sharply ought those to be rebuked who avowedly affect to know nothing?

6. The true knowledge of Christ consists in receiving him as he is offered by the Father, namely, as invested with his Gospel. For, as he is appointed as the end of our faith, so we cannot directly tend towards him except under the guidance of the Gospel. Therein are certainly unfolded to us treasures of grace. Did these continue shut, Christ would profit us little. Hence Paul makes faith the inseparable attendant of doctrine in these words, "Ye have not so learned Christ; if so be that ye have heard him, and have been taught by him, as the truth is in Jesus" (Eph. 4:20, 21). Still I do not confine faith to the Gospel in such a sense as not to admit that enough was delivered to Moses and the Prophets to form a foundation of faith; but as the Gospel exhibits a fuller manifestation of Christ, Paul justly terms it the doctrine of faith (1 Tim. 4:6). For which reason, also he elsewhere says, that, by the coming of faith, the Law was abolished (Rom. 10:4), including under the expression a new and unwonted mode of teaching, by which Christ, from the period of his appearance as the great Master, gave a fuller illustration of the Father's mercy, and testified more surely of our salvation. But an easier and more appropriate method will be to descend from the general to the particular. First, we must remember, that there is an inseparable relation between faith and the word, and that these can no more be disconnected from each other than rays of light from the sun. Hence in Isaiah the Lord exclaims, "Hear, and your soul shall live" (Is. 4:3). And John points to this same fountain of faith in the following words, "These are written that ye might believe" (John 20:31). The Psalmist also exhorting the people to faith says, "To-day, if ye will hear his voice" (Ps. 95:7), to hear being uniformly taken for to believe. In fine, in Isaiah the Lord distinguishes the members of the Church from strangers by this mark, "All thy children shall be taught of the Lord" (Is. 54:13); for if the benefit was indiscriminate, why should he address his words only to a few? Corresponding with this, the Evangelists uniformly employ the terms believers and disciples as synonymous. This is done especially by Luke in several passages of the Acts. He even applies the term disciple to a woman (Acts 9:36). Wherefore, if faith declines in the least degree from the mark at which it ought to aim, it does not retain its nature, but becomes uncertain credulity and vague wandering of mind. The same word is the basis on which it rests and is sustained. Declining from it, it falls. Take away the word, therefore, and no faith will remain. We are not here discussing, whether, in order to propagate the word of God by which faith is engendered, the ministry of man is necessary (this will be considered elsewhere); but we say that the word itself, whatever be the way in which it is conveyed to us, is a kind of mirror in which faith beholds God. In this, therefore, whether God uses the agency of man, or works immediately by his own power, it is always by his word that he manifests himself to those whom he designs to draw to himself. Hence Paul designates faith as the obedience which is given to the Gospel (Rom. 1:5); and writing to the Philippians, he commends them for the obedience of faith (Phil. 2:17). For faith includes not merely the knowledge that God is, but also, nay chiefly, a perception of his will toward us. It concerns us to know not only what he is in himself, but also in what character he is pleased to manifest himself to us. We now see, therefore, that faith is the knowledge of the divine will in regard to us, as ascertained from his word. And the foundation of it is a previous persuasion of the truth of God. So long as your mind entertains any misgivings as to the certainty of the word, its authority will be weak and dubious, or rather it will have no authority at all. Nor is it sufficient to believe that God is true, and cannot lie or deceive, unless you feel firmly persuaded that every word which him is sacred, inviolable truth.

7. But since the heart of man is not brought to faith by every word of God, we must still consider what it is that faith properly has respect to in the word. The declaration of God to Adam was, "Thou shalt surely die" (Gen. 2:17); and to Cain, "The voice of thy brother's blood crieth unto me from the ground" (Gen. 4:10); but these, so far from being fitted to establish faith, tend only to shake it. At the same time, we deny not that it is the office of faith to assent to the truth of God whenever, whatever, and in whatever way he speaks: we are only inquiring what faith can find in the word of God to lean and rest upon. When conscience sees only wrath and indignation, how can it but tremble and be afraid? and how can it avoid shunning the God whom it thus dreads? But faith ought to seek God, not shun him. It is evident, therefore, that we have not yet obtained a full definition of faith, it being impossible to give the name to every kind of knowledge of the divine will. Shall we, then, for "*will*", which is often the messenger of bad news and the herald of terror,

substitute the benevolence or mercy of God? In this way, doubtless, we make a nearer approach to the nature of faith. For we are allured to seek God when told that our safety is treasured up in him; and we are confirmed in this when he declares that he studies and takes an interest in our welfare. Hence there is need of the gracious promise, in which he testifies that he is a propitious Father; since there is no other way in which we can approach to him, the promise being the only thing on which the heart of man can recline. For this reason, the two things, mercy and truth, are uniformly conjoined in the Psalms as having a mutual connection with each other. For it were of no avail to us to know that God is true, did He not in mercy allure us to himself; nor could we of ourselves embrace his mercy did not He expressly offer it. "I have declared thy faithfulness and thy salvation: I have not concealed thy loving-kindness and thy truth. Withhold not thy tender mercies from me, O Lord: let thy loving-kindness and thy truth continually preserve me" (Ps. 40:10, 11). "Thy mercy, O Lord, is in the heavens; and thy faithfulness reacheth unto the clouds" (Ps. 36:5). "All the paths of the Lord are mercy and truth unto such as keep his covenant and his testimonies" (Ps. 25:10). "His merciful kindness is great toward us: and the truth of the Lord endureth for ever" (Ps. 117:2). "I will praise thy name for thy loving-kindness and thy truth" (Ps. 138:2). I need not quote what is said in the Prophets, to the effect that God is merciful and faithful in his promises. It were presumptuous in us to hold that God is propitious to us, had we not his own testimony, and did he not prevent us by his invitation, which leaves no doubt or uncertainty as to his will. It has already been seen that Christ is the only pledge of love, for without him all things, both above and below speak of hatred and wrath. We have also seen, that since the knowledge of the divine goodness cannot be of much importance unless it leads us to confide in it, we must exclude a knowledge mingled with doubt,—a knowledge which, so far from being firm, is continually wavering. But the human mind, when blinded and darkened, is very far from being able to rise to a proper knowledge of the divine will; nor can the heart, fluctuating with perpetual doubt, rest secure in such knowledge. Hence, in order that the word of God may gain full credit, the mind must be enlightened, and the heart confirmed, from some other quarter. We shall now have a full definition of faith if we say that it is a firm and sure knowledge of the divine favor toward us, founded on the truth of a free promise in Christ, and revealed to our minds, and sealed on our hearts, by the Holy Spirit.

8. But before I proceed farther, it will be necessary to make some preliminary observations for the purpose of removing difficulties which might otherwise obstruct the reader. And first, I must refute the nugatory distinction of the Schoolmen as to formed and unformed faith. For they imagine that persons who have no fear of God, and no sense of piety, may believe all that is necessary to be known for salvation; as if the Holy Spirit were not the witness of our adoption by enlightening our hearts unto faith. Still, however, though the whole Scripture is against them, they dogmatically give the name of faith to a persuasion devoid of the fear of God. It is unnecessary to go farther in refuting their definition, than simply to state the nature of faith as declared in the word of God. From this it will clearly appear how unskillfully and absurdly they babble, rather than discourse, on this subject. I have already done this in part, and will afterwards add the remainder in its proper place. At present, I say that nothing can be imagined more absurd than their fiction. They insist that faith is an assent with which any despiser of God may receive what is delivered by Scripture. But we must first see whether any one can by his own strength acquire faith, or whether the Holy Spirit, by means of it, becomes the witness of adoption. Hence it is childish trifling in them to inquire whether the faith formed by the supervening quality of love be the same, or a different and new faith. By talking in this style, they show plainly that they have never thought of the special gift of the Spirit; since one of the first elements of faith is reconciliation implied in man's drawing near to God. Did they duly ponder the saying of Paul, "With the heart man believeth unto righteousness" (Rom. 10:10), they would cease to dream of that frigid quality. There is one consideration which ought at once to put an end to the debate—viz. that assent itself (as I have already observed, and will afterwards more fully illustrate) is more a matter of the heart than the head, of the affection than the intellect. For this reason, it is termed "the obedience of faith" (Rom. 1:5), which the Lord prefers to all other service, and justly, since nothing is more precious to him than his truth, which, as John Baptist declares, is in a manner signed and sealed by believers (John 3:33). As there can be no doubt on the matter, we in one word conclude, that they talk absurdly when they maintain that faith is formed by the addition of pious affection as an accessory to assent, since assent itself, such at least as the Scriptures describe, consists in pious affection. But we are furnished with a still clearer argument. Since faith embraces Christ as he is offered by the Father, and he is offered not only

for justification, for forgiveness of sins and peace, but also for sanctification, as the fountain of living waters, it is certain that no man will ever know him aright without at the same time receiving the sanctification of the Spirit; or, to express the matter more plainly, faith consists in the knowledge of Christ; Christ cannot be known without the sanctification of his Spirit: therefore faith cannot possibly be disjoined from pious affection.

9. In their attempt to mar faith by divesting it of love, they are wont to insist on the words of Paul, "Though I have all faith, so that I could remove mountains, and have not charity, I am nothing" (1 Cor. 13:2). But they do not consider what the faith is of which the Apostle there speaks. Having, in the previous chapter, discoursed of the various gifts of the Spirit (1 Cor. 12:10), including diversity of tongues, miracles, and prophecy, and exhorted the Corinthians to follow the better gifts, in other words, those from which the whole body of the Church would derive greater benefit, he adds, "Yet show I unto you a more excellent way" (1 Cor. 12:30). All other gifts, how excellent soever they may be in themselves, are of no value unless they are subservient to charity. They were given for the edification of the Church, and fail of their purpose if not so applied. To prove this he adopts a division, repeating the same gifts which he had mentioned before, but under different names. Miracles and faith are used to denote the same thing—viz. the power of working miracles. Seeing, then, that this miraculous power or faith is the particular gift of God, which a wicked man may possess and abuse, as the gift of tongues, prophecy, or other gifts, it is not strange that he separates it from charity. Their whole error lies in this, that while the term faith has a variety of meanings, overlooking this variety, they argue as if its meaning were invariably one and the same. The passage of James, by which they endeavor to defend their error, will be elsewhere discussed (*infra*, chap. 17, sec. 11). Although, in discoursing of faith, we admit that it has a variety of forms; yet, when our object is to show what knowledge of God the wicked possess, we hold and maintain, in accordance with Scripture, that the pious only have faith. Multitudes undoubtedly believe that God is, and admit the truth of the Gospel History, and the other parts of Scripture, in the same way in which they believe the records of past events, or events which they have actually witnessed. There are some who go even farther: they regard the Word of God as an infallible oracle; they do not altogether disregard its precepts, but are moved to some degree by its threatening and promises. To such the testimony of faith is attributed, but by *catachresis*; because they do not with open impiety impugn, reject, or condemn, the Word of God, but rather exhibit some semblance of obedience.

10. But as this shadow or image of faith is of no moment, so it is unworthy of the name. How far it differs from true faith will shortly be explained at length. Here, however, we may just indicate it in passing. Simon Magus is said to have believed, though he soon after gave proof of his unbelief (Acts 8:13–18). In regard to the faith attributed to him, we do not understand with some, that he merely pretended a belief which had no existence in his heart: we rather think that, overcome by the majesty of the Gospel, he yielded some kind of assent, and so far acknowledged Christ to be the author of life and salvation, as willingly to assume his name. In like manner, in the Gospel of Luke, those in whom the seed of the word is choked before it brings forth fruit, or in whom, from having no depth of earth, it soon withereth away, are said to believe for a time. Such, we doubt not, eagerly receive the word with a kind of relish, and have some feeling of its divine power, so as not only to impose upon men by a false semblance of faith, but even to impose upon themselves. They imagine that the reverence which they give to the word is genuine piety, because they have no idea of any impiety but that which consists in open and avowed contempt. But whatever that assent may be, it by no means penetrates to the heart, so as to have a fixed seat there. Although it sometimes seems to have planted its roots, these have no life in them. The human heart has so many recesses for vanity, so many lurking places for falsehood, is so shrouded by fraud and hypocrisy, that it often deceives itself. Let those who glory in such semblances of faith know that, in this respect, they are not a whit superior to devils. The one class, indeed, is inferior to them, inasmuch as they are able without emotion to hear and understand things, the knowledge of which makes devils tremble (James 2:19). The other class equals them in this, that whatever be the impression made upon them, its only result is terror and consternation.

11. I am aware it seems unaccountable to some how faith is attributed to the reprobate, seeing that it is declared by Paul to be one of the fruits of election; and yet the difficulty is easily solved: for though none are enlightened into faith, and truly feel the efficacy of the Gospel, with the exception of those who are fore-ordained to salvation, yet experience shows that the reprobate are sometimes affected in a way so similar to the elect, that even in their own judgment there is no difference between them. Hence it is not strange, that by the Apostle a taste

of heavenly gifts, and by Christ himself a temporary faith, is ascribed to them. Not that they truly perceive the power of spiritual grace and the sure light of faith; but the Lord, the better to convict them, and leave them without excuse, instills into their minds such a sense of his goodness as can be felt without the Spirit of adoption. Should it be objected, that believers have no stronger testimony to assure them of their adoption, I answer, that though there is a great resemblance and affinity between the elect of God and those who are impressed for a time with a fading faith, yet the elect alone have that full assurance which is extolled by Paul, and by which they are enabled to cry, Abba, Father. Therefore, as God regenerates the elect only for ever by incorruptible seed, as the seed of life once sown in their hearts never perishes, so he effectually seals in them the grace of his adoption, that it may be sure and steadfast. But in this there is nothing to prevent an inferior operation of the Spirit from taking its course in the reprobate. Meanwhile, believers are taught to examine themselves carefully and humbly, lest carnal security creep in and take the place of assurance of faith. We may add, that the reprobate never have any other than a confused sense of grace, laying hold of the shadow rather than the substance, because the Spirit properly seals the forgiveness of sins in the elect only, applying it by special faith to their use. Still it is correctly said, that the reprobate believe God to be propitious to them, inasmuch as they accept the gift of reconciliation, though confusedly and without due discernment; not that they are partakers of the same faith or regeneration with the children of God; but because, under a covering of hypocrisy, they seem to have a principle of faith in common with them. Nor do I even deny that God illumines their minds to this extent, that they recognize his grace; but that conviction he distinguishes from the peculiar testimony which he gives to his elect in this respect, that the reprobate never attain to the full result or to fruition. When he shows himself propitious to them, it is not as if he had truly rescued them from death, and taken them under his protection. He only gives them a manifestation of his present mercy. In the elect alone he implants the living root of faith, so that they persevere even to the end. Thus we dispose of the objection, that if God truly displays his grace, it must endure for ever. There is nothing inconsistent in this with the fact of his enlightening some with a present sense of grace, which afterwards proves evanescent.

12. Although faith is a knowledge of the divine favor towards us, and a full persuasion of its truth, it is not strange that the sense of the divine love, which though akin to faith differs much from it, vanishes in those who are temporarily impressed. The will of God is, I confess, immutable, and his truth is always consistent with itself; but I deny that the reprobate ever advance so far as to penetrate to that secret revelation which Scripture reserves for the elect only. I therefore deny that they either understand his will considered as immutable, or steadily embrace his truth, inasmuch as they rest satisfied with an evanescent impression; just as a tree not planted deep enough may take root, but will in process of time wither away, though it may for several years not only put forth leaves and flowers, but produce fruit. In short, as by the revolt of the first man, the image of God could be effaced from his mind and soul, so there is nothing strange in His shedding some rays of grace on the reprobate, and afterwards allowing these to be extinguished. There is nothing to prevent His giving some a slight knowledge of his Gospel, and imbuing others thoroughly. Meanwhile, we must remember that however feeble and slender the faith of the elect may be, yet as the Spirit of God is to them a sure earnest and seal of their adoption, the impression once engraven can never be effaced from their hearts, whereas the light which glimmers in the reprobate is afterwards quenched. Nor can it be said that the Spirit therefore deceives, because he does not quicken the seed which lies in their hearts so as to make it ever remain incorruptible as in the elect. I go farther: seeing it is evident, from the doctrine of Scripture and from daily experience, that the reprobate are occasionally impressed with a sense of divine grace, some desire of mutual love must necessarily be excited in their hearts. Thus for a time a pious affection prevailed in Saul, disposing him to love God. Knowing that he was treated with paternal kindness, he was in some degree attracted by it. But as the reprobate have no rooted conviction of the paternal love of God, so they do not in return yield the love of sons, but are led by a kind of mercenary affection. The Spirit of love was given to Christ alone, for the express purpose of conferring this Spirit upon his members; and there can be no doubt that the following words of Paul apply to the elect only: "The love of God is shed abroad in our hearts, by the Holy Ghost which is given unto us" (Rom. 5:5); namely, the love which begets that confidence in prayer to which I have above adverted. On the other hand, we see that God is mysteriously offended with his children, though he ceases not to love them. He certainly hates them not, but he alarms them with a sense of his anger, that he may humble the pride of the flesh, arouse them from lethargy, and urge them to repentance. Hence they,

at the same instant, feel that he is angry with them or their sins, and also propitious to their persons. It is not from fictitious dread that they deprecate his anger, and yet they retake themselves to him with tranquil confidence. It hence appears that the faith of some, though not true faith, is not mere pretence. They are borne along by some sudden impulse of zeal, and erroneously impose upon themselves, sloth undoubtedly preventing them from examining their hearts with due care. Such probably was the case of those whom John describes as believing on Christ; but of whom he says, "Jesus did not commit himself unto them, because he knew all men, and needed not that any should testify of man: for he knew what was in man" (John 2:24, 25). Were it not true that many fall away from the common faith (I call it common, because there is a great resemblance between temporary and living, everduring faith), Christ would not have said to his disciples, "If ye continue in my word, then are ye my disciples indeed; and ye shall know the truth, and the truth shall make you free" (John 8:31, 32). He is addressing those who had embraced his doctrine, and urging them to progress in the faith, lest by their sluggishness they extinguish the light which they have received. Accordingly, Paul claims faith as the peculiar privilege of the elect, intimating that many, from not being properly rooted, fall away (Tit. 1:1). In the same way, in Matthew, our Savior says, "Every plant which my heavenly Father has not planted shall be rooted up" (Mt. 16:13). Some who are not ashamed to insult God and man are more grossly false. Against this class of men, who profane the faith by impious and lying pretence, James inveighs (James 2:14). Nor would Paul require the faith of believers to be unfeigned (1 Tim. 1:5), were there not many who presumptuously arrogate to themselves what they have not, deceiving others, and sometimes even themselves, with empty show. Hence he compares a good conscience to the ark in which faith is preserved, because many, by falling away, have in regard to it made shipwreck.

13. It is necessary to attend to the ambiguous meaning of the term: for *faith* is often equivalent in meaning to *sound doctrine*, as in the passage which we lately quoted, and in the same epistle where Paul enjoins the deacons to hold "the mystery of the faith in a pure conscience;" in like manner, when he denounces the defection of certain from the faith. The meaning again is the same, when he says that Timothy had been brought up in the faith; and in like manner, when he says that profane babblings and oppositions of science, falsely so called, lead many away from the faith. Such persons he elsewhere calls reprobate as to the faith. On the other hand, when he enjoins Titus, "Rebuke them sharply, that they may be sound in the faith;" by soundness he means purity of doctrine, which is easily corrupted, and degenerates through the fickleness of men. And indeed, since in Christ, as possessed by faith, are "hid all the treasures of wisdom and knowledge" (Col. 1:2, 3), the term faith is justly extended to the whole sum of heavenly doctrine, from which it cannot be separated. On the other hand, it is sometimes confined to a particular object, as when Matthew says of those who let down the paralytic through the roof, that Jesus saw their faith (Mt. 9:2); and Jesus himself exclaims in regard to the centurion, "I have not found so great faith, no, not in Israel" (Mt. 8:10). Now, it is probable that the centurion was thinking only of the cure of his son, by whom his whole soul was engrossed; but because he is satisfied with the simple answer and assurance of Christ, and does not request his bodily presence, this circumstance calls forth the eulogium on his faith. And we have lately shown how Paul uses the term faith for the gift of miracles—a gift possessed by persons who were neither regenerated by the Spirit of God, nor sincerely reverenced him. In another passage, he uses faith for the doctrine by which we are instructed in the faith. For when he says, that "that which is in part shall be done away" (1 Cor. 13:10), there can be no doubt that reference is made to the ministry of the Church, which is necessary in our present imperfect state; in these forms of expression the analogy is obvious. But when the name of faith is improperly transferred to a false profession or lying assumption, the *catachresis* ought not to seem harsher than when the fear of God is used for vicious and perverse worship; as when it is repeatedly said in sacred history, that the foreign nations which had been transported to Samaria and the neighbouring districts, feared false gods and the God of Israel: in other words, confounded heaven with earth. But we have now been inquiring what the faith is, which distinguishes the children of God from unbelievers, the faith by which we invoke God the Father, by which we pass from death unto life, and by which Christ our eternal salvation and life dwells in us. Its power and nature have, I trust, been briefly and clearly explained.

14. Let us now again go over the parts of the definition separately: I should think that, after a careful examination of them, no doubt will remain. By knowledge we do not mean comprehension, such as that which we have of things falling under human sense. For that knowledge is so much superior, that the human mind

must far surpass and go beyond itself in order to reach it. Nor even when it has reached it does it comprehend what it feels, but persuaded of what it comprehends not, it understands more from mere certainty of persuasion than it could discern of any human matter by its own capacity. Hence it is elegantly described by Paul as ability "to comprehend with all saints what is the breadth, and length, and depth, and height; and to know the love of Christ, which passeth knowledge" (Eph. 3:18, 19). His object was to intimate, that what our mind embraces by faith is every way infinite, that this kind of knowledge far surpasses all understanding. But because the "mystery which has been hid from ages and from generations" is now "made manifest to the saints" (Col. 1:26), faith is, for good reason, occasionally termed in Scripture understanding (Col. 2:2); and knowledge, as by John (1 John 3:2), when he declares that believers know themselves to be the sons of God. And certainly they do know, but rather as confirmed by a belief of the divine veracity than taught by any demonstration of reason. This is also indicated by Paul when he says, that "whilst we are at home in the body, we are absent from the Lord: (For we walk by faith, not by sight)" (2 Cor. 5:6, 7) thus showing, that what we understand by faith is yet distant from us and escapes our view. Hence we conclude that the knowledge of faith consists more of certainty than discernment.

15. We add, that it is sure and firm, the better to express strength and constancy of persuasion. For as faith is not contented with a dubious and fickle opinion, so neither is it contented with an obscure and ill-defined conception. The certainty which it requires must be full and decisive, as is usual in regard to matters ascertained and proved. So deeply rooted in our hearts is unbelief, so prone are we to it, that while all confess with the lips that God is faithful, no man ever believes it without an arduous struggle. Especially when brought to the test, we by our wavering betray the vice which lurked within. Nor is it without cause that the Holy Spirit bears such distinguished testimony to the authority of God, in order that it may cure the disease of which I have spoken, and induce us to give full credit to the divine promises: "The words of the Lord" (says David, Ps. 12:6) "are pure words, as silver tried in a furnace of earth purified seven times:" "The word of the Lord is tried: he is a buckler to all those that trust in him" (Ps. 18:30). And Solomon declares the same thing almost in the same words, "Every word of God is pure" (Prov. 30:5). But further quotation is superfluous, as the 119th Psalm is almost wholly occupied with this subject. Certainly, whenever God thus recommends his word, he indirectly rebukes our unbelief, the purport of all that is said being to eradicate perverse doubt from our hearts. There are very many also who form such an idea of the divine mercy as yields them very little comfort. For they are harassed by miserable anxiety while they doubt whether God will be merciful to them. They think, indeed, that they are most fully persuaded of the divine mercy, but they confine it within too narrow limits. The idea they entertain is, that this mercy is great and abundant, is shed upon many, is offered and ready to be bestowed upon all; but that it is uncertain whether it will reach to them individually, or rather whether they can reach to it. Thus their knowledge stopping short leaves them only mid-way; not so much confirming and tranquilizing the mind as harassing it with doubt and disquietude. Very different is that feeling of full assurance (πλεροφορία) which the Scriptures uniformly attribute to faith—an assurance which leaves no doubt that the goodness of God is clearly offered to us. This assurance we cannot have without truly perceiving its sweetness, and experiencing it in ourselves. Hence from faith the Apostle deduces confidence, and from confidence boldness. His words are, "In whom (Christ) we have boldness and access with confidence by the faith of him" (Eph. 3:12) thus undoubtedly showing that our faith is not true unless it enables us to appear calmly in the presence of God. Such boldness springs only from confidence in the divine favor and salvation. So true is this, that the term faith is often used as equivalent to confidence.

16. The principal hinge on which faith turns is this: We must not suppose that any promises of mercy which the Lord offers are only true out of us, and not at all in us: we should rather make them ours by inwardly embracing them. In this way only is engendered that confidence which he elsewhere terms peace (Rom. 5:1); though perhaps he rather means to make peace follow from it. This is the security which quiets and calms the conscience in the view of the judgment of God, and without which it is necessarily vexed and almost torn with tumultuous dread, unless when it happens to slumber for a moment, forgetful both of God and of itself. And verily it is but for a moment. It never long enjoys that miserable obliviousness, for the memory of the divine judgment, ever and anon recurring, stings it to the quick. In one word, he only is a true believer who, firmly persuaded that God is reconciled, and is a kind Father to him, hopes everything from his kindness, who, trusting to the promises of the divine favor, with undoubting confidence anticipates salvation; as the Apostle shows in these words, "We are

made partakers of Christ, if we hold the beginning of our confidence steadfast unto the end" (Heb. 3:14). He thus holds, that none hope well in the Lord save those who confidently glory in being the heirs of the heavenly kingdom. No man, I say, is a believer but he who, trusting to the security of his salvation, confidently triumphs over the devil and death, as we are taught by the noble exclamation of Paul, "I am persuaded, that neither death, nor life, nor angels, nor principalities, nor powers, nor things present, nor things to come, nor height, nor depth, nor any other creature, shall be able to separate us from the love of God, which is in Christ Jesus our Lord" (Rom. 8:38). In like manner, the same Apostle does not consider that the eyes of our understanding are enlightened unless we know what is the hope of the eternal inheritance to which we are called (Eph. 1:18). Thus he uniformly intimates throughout his writings, that the goodness of God is not properly comprehended when security does not follow as its fruit.

17. But it will be said that this differs widely from the experience of believers, who, in recognizing the grace of God toward them, not only feel disquietude (this often happens), but sometimes tremble, overcome with terror, so violent are the temptations which assail their minds. This scarcely seems consistent with certainty of faith. It is necessary to solve this difficulty, in order to maintain the doctrine above laid down. When we say that faith must be certain and secure, we certainly speak not of an assurance which is never affected by doubt, nor a security which anxiety never assails; we rather maintain that believers have a perpetual struggle with their own distrust, and are thus far from thinking that their consciences possess a placid quiet, uninterrupted by perturbation. On the other hand, whatever be the mode in which they are assailed, we deny that they fall off and abandon that sure confidence which they have formed in the mercy of God. Scripture does not set before us a brighter or more memorable example of faith than in David, especially if regard be had to the constant tenor of his life. And yet how far his mind was from being always at peace is declared by innumerable complaints, of which it will be sufficient to select a few. When he rebukes the turbulent movements of his soul, what else is it but a censure of his unbelief? "Why art thou cast down, my soul? and why art thou disquieted in me? hope thou in God" (Psalm 42:6). His alarm was undoubtedly a manifest sign of distrust, as if he thought that the Lord had forsaken him. In another passage we have a fuller confession: "I said in my haste, I am cut off from before thine eyes" (Psalm 31:22). In another passage, in anxious and wretched perplexity, he debates with himself, nay, raises a question as to the nature of God: "Has God forgotten to be gracious? has he in anger shut up his tender mercies?" (Psalm 77:9). What follows is still harsher: "I said this is my infirmity; but I will remember the years of the right hand of the Most High." As if desperate, he adjudges himself to destruction. He not only confesses that he is agitated by doubt, but as if he had fallen in the contest, leaves himself nothing in reserve,—God having deserted him, and made the hand which was wont to help him the instrument of his destruction. Wherefore, after having been tossed among tumultuous waves, it is not without reason he exhorts his soul to return to her quiet rest (Psalm 116:7). And yet (what is strange) amid those commotions, faith sustains the believer's heart, and truly acts the part of the palm tree, which supports any weights laid upon it, and rises above them; thus David, when he seemed to be overwhelmed, ceased not by urging himself forward to ascend to God. But he who anxiously contending with his own infirmity has recourse to faith, is already in a great measure victorious. This we may infer from the following passage, and others similar to it: "Wait on the Lord: be of good courage, and he shall strengthen thine heart: wait, I say, on the Lord" (Psalm 27:14). He accuses himself of timidity, and repeating the same thing twice, confesses that he is ever and anon exposed to agitation. Still he is not only dissatisfied with himself for so feeling, but earnestly labors to correct it. Were we to take a nearer view of his case, and compare it with that of Ahaz, we should find a great difference between them. Isaiah is sent to relieve the anxiety of an impious and hypocritical king, and addresses him in these terms: "Take heed, and be quiet; fear not," &c. (Isaiah 7:4). How did Ahab act? As has already been said, his heart was shaken as a tree is shaken by the wind: though he heard the promise, he ceased not to tremble. This, therefore, is the proper hire and punishment of unbelief, so to tremble as in the day of trial to turn away from God, who gives access to himself only by faith. On the other hand, believers, though weighed down and almost overwhelmed with the burden of temptation, constantly rise up, though not without toil and difficulty; hence, feeling conscious of their own weakness, they pray with the Prophet, "Take not the word of truth utterly out of my mouths" (Psalm 119:43). By these words, we are taught that they at times become dumb, as if their faith were overthrown, and yet that they do not withdraw or turn their backs, but persevere in the contest, and by prayer stimulate their sluggishness, so as

not to fall into stupor by giving way to it. (See Calv. in Psalm 88:16).

18. To make this intelligible, we must return to the distinction between flesh and spirit, to which we have already adverted, and which here becomes most apparent. The believer finds within himself two principles: the one filling him with delight in recognizing the divine goodness, the other filling him with bitterness under a sense of his fallen state; the one leading him to recline on the promise of the Gospel, the other alarming him by the conviction of his iniquity; the one making him exult with the anticipation of life, the other making him tremble with the fear of death. This diversity is owing to imperfection of faith, since we are never so well in the course of the present life as to be entirely cured of the disease of distrust, and completely replenished and engrossed by faith. Hence those conflicts: the distrust cleaving to the remains of the flesh rising up to assail the faith enlisting in our hearts. But if in the believer's mind certainty is mingled with doubt, must we not always be carried back to the conclusion, that faith consists not of a sure and clear, but only of an obscure and confused, understanding of the divine will in regard to us? By no means. Though we are distracted by various thoughts, it does not follow that we are immediately divested of faith. Though we are agitated and carried to and fro by distrust, we are not immediately plunged into the abyss; though we are shaken, we are not therefore driven from our place. The invariable issue of the contest is, that faith in the long run surmounts the difficulties by which it was beset and seemed to be endangered.

19. The whole, then, comes to this: As soon as the minutest particle of faith is instilled into our minds, we begin to behold the face of God placid, serene, and propitious; far off, indeed, but still so distinctly as to assure us that there is no delusion in it. In proportion to the progress we afterwards make (and the progress ought to be uninterrupted), we obtain a nearer and surer view, the very continuance making it more familiar to us. Thus we see that a mind illumined with the knowledge of God is at first involved in much ignorance,—ignorance, however, which is gradually removed. Still this partial ignorance or obscure discernment does not prevent that clear knowledge of the divine favor which holds the first and principal part in faith. For as one shut up in a prison, where from a narrow opening he receives the rays of the sun indirectly and in a manner divided, though deprived of a full view of the sun, has no doubt of the source from which the light comes, and is benefited by it; so believers, while bound with the fetters of an earthly body, though surrounded on all sides with much obscurity, are so far illumined by any slender light which beams upon them and displays the divine mercy as to feel secure.

20. The Apostle elegantly adverts to both in different passages. When he says, "We know in part, and we prophesy in part;" and "Now we see through a glass darkly" (1 Cor. 13:9, 12), he intimates how very minute a portion of divine wisdom is given to us in the present life. For although those expressions do not simply indicate that faith is imperfect so long as we groan under a height of flesh, but that the necessity of being constantly engaged in learning is owing to our imperfection, he at the same time reminds us, that a subject which is of boundless extent cannot be comprehended by our feeble and narrow capacities. This Paul affirms of the whole Church, each individual being retarded and impeded by his own ignorance from making so near an approach as were to be wished. But that the foretaste which we obtain from any minute portion of faith is certain, and by no means fallacious, he elsewhere shows, when he affirms that "We all, with open face beholding as in a glass the glory of the Lord, are changed into the same image, from glory to glory, even as by the Spirit of the Lord" (2 Cor. 3:18). In such degrees of ignorance much doubt and trembling is necessarily implied, especially seeing that our heart is by its own natural bias prone to unbelief. To this we must add the temptations which, various in kind and infinite in number, are ever and anon violently assailing us. In particular, conscience itself, burdened with an incumbent load of sins, at one time complains and groans, at another accuses itself; at one time murmurs in secret, at another openly rebels. Therefore, whether adverse circumstances betoken the wrath of God, or conscience finds the subject and matter within itself, unbelief thence draws weapons and engines to put faith to flight, the aim of all its efforts being to make us think that God is adverse and hostile to us, and thus, instead of hoping for any assistance from him, to make us dread him as a deadly foe.

21. To withstand these assaults, faith arms and fortifies itself with the word of God. When the temptation suggested is, that God is an enemy because he afflicts, faith replies, that while he afflicts he is merciful, his chastening proceeding more from love than anger. To the thought that God is the avenger of wickedness, it opposes the pardon ready to be bestowed on all offences whenever the sinner retakes himself to the divine mercy. Thus the pious mind, how much soever it may be agitated and torn, at length rises superior to all difficulties, and allows not its

confidence in the divine mercy to be destroyed. Nay, rather, the disputes which exercise and disturb it tend to establish this confidence. A proof of this is, that the saints, when the hand of God lies heaviest upon them, still lodge their complaints with him, and continue to invoke him, when to all appearance he is least disposed to hear. But of what use were it to lament before him if they had no hope of solace? They never would invoke him did they not believe that he is ready to assist them. Thus the disciples, while reprimanded by their Master for the weakness of their faith in crying out that they were perishing, still implored his aid (Mt. 8:25). And he, in rebuking them for their want of faith, does not disown them or class them with unbelievers, but urges them to shake off the vice. Therefore, as we have already said, we again maintain, that faith remaining fixed in the believer's breast never can be eradicated from it. However it may seem shaken and bent in this direction or in that, its flame is never so completely quenched as not at least to lurk under the embers. In this way, it appears that the word, which is an incorruptible seed, produces fruit similar to itself. Its germ never withers away utterly and perishes. The saints cannot have a stronger ground for despair than to feel, that, according to present appearances, the hand of God is armed for their destruction; and yet Job thus declares the strength of his confidence: "Though he slay me, yet will I trust in him." The truth is, that unbelief reigns not in the hearts of believers, but only assails them from without; does not wound them mortally with its darts, but annoys them, or, at the utmost, gives them a wound which can be healed. Faith, as Paul (declares (Eph. 6:16), is our shield, which receiving these darts, either wards them off entirely, or at least breaks their force, and prevents them from reaching the vitals. Hence when faith is shaken, it is just as when, by the violent blow of a javelin, a soldier standing firm is forced to step back and yield a little; and again when faith is wounded, it is as if the shield were pierced, but not perforated by the blow. The pious mind will always rise, and be able to say with David, "Yea, though I walk through the valley of the shadow of death, I will fear no evil: for thou art with me" (Psalm 23:4). Doubtless it is a terrific thing to walk in the darkness of death, and it is impossible for believers, however great their strength may be, not to shudder at it; but since the prevailing thought is that God is present and providing for their safety, the feeling of security overcomes that of fear. As Augustine says,—whatever be the engines which the devil erects against us, as he cannot gain the heart where faith dwells, he is cast out. Thus, if we may judge by the event, not only do believers come off safe from every contest so as to be ready, after a short repose, to descend again into the arena, but the saying of John, in his Epistle, is fulfilled, "This is the victory that overcometh the world, even our faith" (1 John 5:4). It is not said that it will be victorious in a single fight, or a few, or some one assault, but that it will be victorious over the whole world, though it should be a thousand times assailed.

22. There is another species of fear and trembling, which, so far from impairing the security of faith, tends rather to establish it; namely, when believers, reflecting that the examples of the divine vengeance on the ungodly are a kind of beacons warning them not to provoke the wrath of God by similar wickedness keep anxious watch, or, taking a view of their own inherent wretchedness, learn their entire dependence on God, without whom they feel themselves to be fleeting and evanescent as the wind. For when the Apostle sets before the Corinthians the scourges which the Lord in ancient times inflicted on the people of Israel, that they might be afraid of subjecting themselves to similar calamities, he does not in any degree destroy the ground of their confidence; he only shakes off their carnal torpor which suppresses faith, but does not strengthen it. Nor when he takes occasion from the case of the Israelites to exhort, "Let him that thinketh he standeth take heed lest he fall" (1 Cor. 10:12), he does not bid us waver, as if we had no security for our steadfastness: he only removes arrogance and rash confidence in our strength, telling the Gentiles not to presume because the Jews had been cast off, and they had been admitted to their place (Rom. 11:20). In that passage, indeed, he is not addressing believers only, but also comprehends hypocrites, who gloried merely in external appearance; nor is he addressing individuals, but contrasting the Jews and Gentiles, he first shows that the rejection of the former was a just punishment of their ingratitude and unbelief, and then exhorts the latter to beware lest pride and presumption deprive them of the grace of adoption which had lately been transferred to them. For as in that rejection of the Jews there still remained some who were not excluded from the covenant of adoptions so there might be some among the Gentiles who, possessing no true faith, were only puffed up with vain carnal confidence, and so abused the goodness of God to their own destruction. But though you should hold that the words were addressed to elect believers, no inconsistency will follow. It is one thing, in order to prevent believers from indulging vain confidence, to repress the temerity which,

from the remains of the flesh, sometimes gains upon them, and it is another thing to strike terror into their consciences, and prevent them from feeling secure in the mercy of God.

23. Then, when he bids us work out our salvation with fear and trembling, all he requires is, that we accustom ourselves to think very meanly of our own strength, and confide in the strength of the Lord. For nothing stimulates us so strongly to place all our confidence and assurance on the Lord as self diffidence, and the anxiety produced by a consciousness of our calamitous condition. In this sense are we to understand the words of the Psalmist: "I will come into thy house in the multitude of thy mercy: and in thy fear will I worship toward thy holy temples" (Ps. 5:7). Here he appropriately unites confident faith leaning on the divine mercy with religious fear, which of necessity we must feel whenever coming into the presence of the divine majesty we are made aware by its splendor of the extent of our own impurity. Truly also does Solomon declare: "Happy is the man that feareth alway; but he that hardeneth his heart falleth into mischief" (Prov. 28:14). The fear he speaks of is that which renders us more cautious, not that which produces despondency, the fear which is felt when the mind confounded in itself resumes its equanimity in God, downcast in itself, takes courage in God, distrusting itself, breathes confidence in God. Hence there is nothing inconsistent in believers being afraid, and at the same time possessing secure consolation as they alternately behold their own vanity, and direct their thoughts to the truth of God. How, it will be asked, can fear and faith dwell in the same mind? Just in the same way as sluggishness and anxiety can so dwell. The ungodly court a state of lethargy that the fear of God may not annoy them; and yet the judgment of God so urges that they cannot gain their desire. In the same way God can train his people to humility, and curb them by the bridle of modesty, while yet fighting bravely. And it is plain, from the context, that this was the Apostle's meaning, since he states, as the ground of fear and trembling, that it is God who worketh in us to will and to do of his good pleasure. In the same sense must we understand the words of the Prophet, "The children of Israel" "shall fear the Lord and his goodness in the latter days" (Hos. 3:5). For not only does piety beget reverence to God, but the sweet attractiveness of grace inspires a man, though desponding of himself, at once with fear and admiration, making him feel his dependence on God, and submit humbly to his power.

24. Here, however, we give no countenance to that most pestilential philosophy which some semi-papists are at present beginning to broach in corners. Unable to defend the gross doubt inculcated by the Schoolmen, they have recourse to another fiction, that they may compound a mixture of faith and unbelief. They admit, that whenever we look to Christ we are furnished with full ground for hope; but as we are ever unworthy of all the blessings which are offered us in Christ, they will have us to fluctuate and hesitate in the view of our unworthiness. In short, they give conscience a position between hope and fear, making it alternate, by successive turns, to the one and the other. Hope and fear, again, they place in complete contrast,—the one falling as the other rises, and rising as the other falls. Thus Satan, finding the devices by which he was wont to destroy the certainty of faith too manifest to be now of any avail, is endeavoring, by indirect methods, to undermine it. But what kind of confidence is that which is ever and anon supplanted by despair? They tell you, if you look to Christ salvation is certain; if you return to yourself damnation is certain. Therefore, your mind must be alternately ruled by diffidence and hope; as if we were to imagine Christ standing at a distance, and not rather dwelling in us. We expect salvation from him—not because he stands aloof from us, but because ingrafting us into his body he not only makes us partakers of all his benefits, but also of himself. Therefore, I thus retort the argument, If you look to yourself damnation is certain: but since Christ has been communicated to you with all his benefits, so that all which is his is made yours, you become a member of him, and hence one with him. His righteousness covers your sins—his salvation extinguishes your condemnation; he interposes with his worthiness, and so prevents your unworthiness from coming into the view of God. Thus it truly is. It will never do to separate Christ from us, nor us from him; but we must, with both hands, keep firm hold of that alliance by which he has riveted us to himself. This the Apostle teaches us: "The body is dead because of sin; but the spirit is life because of righteousness" (Rom. 8:10). According to the frivolous trifling of these objectors, he ought to have said, Christ indeed has life in himself, but you, as you are sinners, remain liable to death and condemnation. Very different is his language. He tells us that the condemnation which we of ourselves deserve is annihilated by the salvation of Christ; and to confirm this he employs the argument to which I have referred—viz. that Christ is not external to us, but dwells in us; and not only unites us to himself by an undivided bond of fellowship, but by a wondrous communion brings us daily into

closer connection, until he becomes altogether one with us. And yet I deny not, as I lately said, that faith occasionally suffers certain interruptions when, by violent assault, its weakness is made to bend in this direction or in that; and its light is buried in the thick darkness of temptation. Still happen what may, faith ceases not to long after God.

25. The same doctrine is taught by Bernard when he treats professedly on this subject in his Fifth Homily on the Dedication of the Temple: "By the blessing of God, sometimes meditating on the soul, methinks, I find in it as it were two contraries. When I look at it as it is in itself and of itself, the truest thing I can say of it is, that it has been reduced to nothing. What need is there to enumerate each of its miseries? how burdened with sin, obscured with darkness, ensnared by allurements, teeming with lusts, ruled by passion, filled with delusions, ever prone to evil, inclined to every vice; lastly, full of ignominy and confusion. If all its righteousnesses, when examined by the light of truth, are but as filthy rags (Is. 64:6), what must we suppose its unrighteousness to be? 'If, therefore, the light that is in thee be darkness, how great is that darkness?' (Mt. 6:23). What then? man doubtless has been made subject to vanity—man here been reduced to nothing—man is nothing. And yet how is he whom God exalts utterly nothing? How is he nothing to whom a divine heart has been given? Let us breathe again, brethren. Although we are nothing in our hearts, perhaps something of us may lurk in the heart of God. O Father of mercies! O Father of the miserable! how plantest thou thy heart in us? Where thy heart is, there is thy treasure also. But how are we thy treasure if we are nothing? All nations before thee are as nothing. Observe, *before* thee; not *within* thee. Such are they in the judgment of thy truth, but not such in regard to thy affection. Thou callest the things which be not as though they were; and they are not, because thou callest them 'things that be not:' and yet they are because thou callest them. For though they are not as to themselves, yet they are with thee according to the declaration of Paul: 'Not of works, but of him that calleth,' " (Rom. 9:11). He then goes on to say that the connection is wonderful in both points of view. Certainly things which are connected together do not mutually destroy each other. This he explains more clearly in his conclusion in the following terms: "If, in both views, we diligently consider what we are,—in the one view our nothingness, in the other our greatness,—I presume our glorying will seem restrained; but perhaps it is rather increased and confirmed, because we glory not in ourselves, but in the Lord. Our thought is, if he determined to save us we shall be delivered; and here we begin again to breathe. But, ascending to a loftier height, let us seek the city of God, let us seek the temple, let us seek our home, let us seek our spouse. I have not forgotten myself when, with fear and reverence, I say, We are,—are in the heart of God. We are, by his dignifying, not by our own dignity."

26. Moreover, the fear of the Lord, which is uniformly attributed to all the saints, and which, in one passage, is called "the beginning of wisdom," in another *wisdom* itself, although it is one, proceeds from a twofold cause. God is entitled to the reverence of a Father and a Lord. Hence he who desires duly to worship him, will study to act the part both of an obedient son and a faithful servant. The obedience paid to God as a Father he by his prophet terms *honor*; the service performed to him as a master he terms *fear*. "A son honoureth his father, and a servant his master. If then I be a father, where is mine honor? and if I be a master, where is my fear?" But while he thus distinguishes between the two, it is obvious that he at the same time confounds them. The fear of the Lord, therefore, may be defined reverence mingled with honor and fear. It is not strange that the same mind can entertain both feelings; for he who considers with himself what kind of a father God is to us, will see sufficient reason, even were there no hell, why the thought of offending him should seem more dreadful than any death. But so prone is our carnal nature to indulgence in sin, that, in order to curb it in every way, we must also give place to the thought that all iniquity is abomination to the Master under whom we live; that those who, by wicked lives, provoke his anger, will not escape his vengeance.

27. There is nothing repugnant to this in the observation of John: "There is no fear in love; but perfect love casteth out fear: because fear has torment" (1 John 4:18). For he is speaking of the fear of unbelief, between which and the fear of believers there is a wide difference. The wicked do not fear God from any unwillingness to offend him, provided they could do so with impunity; but knowing that he is armed with power for vengeance, they tremble in dismay on hearing of his anger. And they thus dread his anger, because they think it is impending over them, and they every moment expect it to fall upon their heads. But believers, as has been said, dread the offense even more than the punishment. They are not alarmed by the fear of punishment, as if it were impending over them, but are rendered the more cautious of doing anything to provoke it. Thus the Apostle addressing believers says, "Let no man deceive you with

vain words; for because of these things, the wrath of God cometh upon the children of disobedience" (Eph. 5:6; Col. 3:6). He does not threaten that wrath will descend upon them; but he admonishes them, while they think how the wrath of God is prepared for the wicked, on account of the crimes which he had enumerated, not to run the risk of provoking it. It seldom happens that mere threatening have the effect of arousing the reprobate; nay, becoming more callous and hardened when God thunders verbally from heaven, they obstinately persist in their rebellion. It is only when actually smitten by his hand that they are forced, whether they will or not, to fear. This fear the sacred writers term *servile*, and oppose to the free and voluntary fear which becomes sons. Some, by a subtle distinction, have introduced an intermediate species, holding that that forced and servile fear sometimes subdues the mind, and leads spontaneously to proper fear.

28. The divine favor to which faith is said to have respect, we understand to include in it the possession of salvation and eternal life. For if, when God is propitious, no good thing can be wanting to us, we have ample security for our salvation when assured of his love. "Turn us again, O God, and cause thy face to shine," says the Prophet, "and we shall be saved" (Ps. 80:3). Hence the Scriptures make the sum of our salvation to consist in the removal of all enmity, and our admission into favor; thus intimating, that when God is reconciled all danger is past, and every thing good will befall us. Wherefore, faith apprehending the love of God has the promise both of the present and the future life, and ample security for all blessings (Eph. 2:14). The nature of this must be ascertained from the word. Faith does not promise us length of days, riches and honors (the Lord not having been pleased that any of these should be appointed us); but is contented with the assurance, that however poor we may be in regard to present comforts, God will never fail us. The chief security lies in the expectation of future life, which is placed beyond doubt by the word of God. Whatever be the miseries and calamities which await the children of God in this world, they cannot make his favor cease to be complete happiness. Hence, when we were desirous to express the sum of blessedness, we designated it by the favor of God, from which, as their source, all kinds of blessings flow. And we may observe throughout the Scriptures, that they refer us to the love of God, not only when they treat of our eternal salvation, but of any blessing whatever. For which reason David sings, that the loving-kindness of God experienced by the pious heart is sweeter and more to be desired than life itself (Ps. 63:3).

In short, if we have every earthly comfort to a wish, but are uncertain whether we have the love or the hatred of God, our felicity will be cursed, and therefore miserable. But if God lift on us the light of his fatherly countenance, our very miseries will be blessed, inasmuch as they will become helps to our salvation. Thus Paul, after bringing together all kinds of adversity, boasts that they cannot separate us from the love of God: and in his prayers he uniformly begins with the grace of God as the source of all prosperity. In like manner, to all the terrors which assail us, David opposes merely the favor of God,—"Yea, though I walk through the valley of the shadow of death, I will fear no evil: for thou art with me" (Ps. 23:4). And we feel that our minds always waver until, contented with the grace of God, we in it seek peace, and feel thoroughly persuaded of what is said in the psalm, "Blessed is the nation whose God is the Lord, and the people whom he has chosen for his own inheritance" (Ps. 33:12).

29. Free promise we make the foundation of faith, because in it faith properly consists. For though it holds that God is always true, whether in ordering or forbidding, promising or threatening; though it obediently receive his commands, observe his prohibitions, and give heed to his threatening; yet it properly begins with promise, continues with it, and ends with it. It seeks life in God, life which is not found in commands or the denunciations of punishment, but in the promise of mercy. And this promise must be gratuitous; for a conditional promise, which throws us back upon our works, promises life only in so far as we find it existing in ourselves. Therefore, if we would not have faith to waver and tremble, we must support it with the promise of salvation, which is offered by the Lord spontaneously and freely, from a regard to our misery rather than our worth. Hence the Apostle bears this testimony to the Gospel, that it is the word of faith (Rom. 10:8). This he concedes not either to the precepts or the promises of the Law, since there is nothing which can establish our faith, but that free embassy by which God reconciles the world to himself. Hence he often uses faith and the Gospel as correlative terms, as when he says, that the ministry of the Gospel was committed to him for "obedience to the faith;" that "it is the power of God unto salvation to every one that believeth;" that "therein is the righteousness of God revealed from faith to faith" (Rom. 1:5, 16, 17). No wonder: for seeing that the Gospel is "the ministry of reconciliation" (2 Cor. 5:18), there is no other sufficient evidence of the divine favor, such as faith requires to know. Therefore, when we say, that faith must rest on a free promise, we deny not

that believers accept and embrace the word of God in all its parts, but we point to the promise of mercy as its special object. Believers, indeed, ought to recognize God as the judge and avenger of wickedness; and yet mercy is the object to which they properly look, since he is exhibited to their contemplation as "good and ready to forgive," "plenteous in mercy," "slow to anger," "good to all," and shedding "his tender mercies over all his works". Ps. 86:5; 103:8; 145:8, 9).

30. I stay not to consider the rabid objections of Pighius, and others like-minded, who inveigh against this restriction, as rending faith, and laying hold of one of its fragments. I admit, as I have already said, that the general object of faith (as they express it) is the truth of God, whether he threatens or gives hope of his favor. Accordingly, the Apostle attributes it to faith in Noah, that he feared the destruction of the world, when as yet it was not seen (Heb. 11:17). If fear of impending punishment was a work of faith, threatening ought not to be excluded in defining it. This is indeed true; but we are unjustly and calumniously charged with denying that faith has respect to the whole word of God. We only mean to maintain these two points,—that faith is never decided until it attain to a free promise; and that the only way in which faith reconciles us to God is by uniting us with Christ. Both are deserving of notice. We are inquiring after a faith which separates the children of God from the reprobate, believers from unbelievers. Shall every man, then, who believes that God is just in what he commands, and true in what he threatens, be on that account classed with believers? Very far from it. Faith, then, has no firm footing until it stand in the mercy of God. Then what end have we in view in discoursing of faith? Is it not that we may understand the way of salvation? But how can faith be saving, unless in so far as it in grafts us into the body of Christ? There is no absurdity, therefore, when, in defining it, we thus press its special object, and, by way of distinction, add to the generic character the particular mark which distinguishes the believer from the unbeliever. In short, the malicious have nothing to carp at in this doctrine, unless they are to bring the same censure against the Apostle Paul, who specially designates the Gospel as "the word of faith" (Rom. 10:8).

31. Hence again we infer, as has already been explained, that faith has no less need of the word than the fruit of a tree has of a living root; because, as David testifies, none can hope in God but those who know his name (Ps. 9:10). This knowledge, however, is not left to every man's imagination, but depends on the testimony which God himself gives to his goodness. This the same Psalmist confirms in another passage, "Thy salvation according to thy word" (Ps. 119:41). Again, "Save me," "I hoped in thy word" (Ps. 119:146, 147). Here we must attend to the relation of faith to the word, and to salvation as its consequence. Still, however, we exclude not the power of God. If faith cannot support itself in the view of this power, it never will give Him the honor which is due. Paul seems to relate a trivial or very ordinary circumstance with regard to Abraham, when he says, that he believed that God, who had given him the promise of a blessed seed, was able also to perform it (Rom. 4:21). And in like manner, in another passage, he says of himself, "I know whom I have believed, and am persuaded that he is able to keep that which I have committed unto him against that day" (2 Tim. 1:12). But let any one consider with himself, how he is ever and anon assailed with doubts in regard to the power of God, and he will readily perceive, that those who duly magnify it have made no small progress in faith. We all acknowledge that God can do whatsoever he pleases; but while every temptation, even the most trivial, fills us with fear and dread, it is plain that we derogate from the power of God, by attaching less importance to his promises than to Satan's threatenings against them.

This is the reason why Isaiah, when he would impress on the hearts of the people the certainty of faith, discourses so magnificently of the boundless power of God. He often seems, after beginning to speak of the hope of pardon and reconciliation, to digress, and unnecessarily take a long circuitous course, describing how wonderfully God rules the fabric of heaven and earth, with the whole course of nature; and yet he introduces nothing which is not appropriate to the occasion; because unless the power of God, to which all things are possible is presented to our eye, our ears malignantly refuse admission to the word, or set no just value upon it. We may add, that an effectual power is here meant; for piety, as it has elsewhere been seen, always makes a practical application of the power of God; in particular, keeps those works in view in which he has declared himself to be a Father. Hence the frequent mention in Scripture of redemption; from which the Israelites might learn, that he who had once been the author of salvation would be its perpetual guardian. By his own example, also, David reminds us, that the benefits which God has bestowed privately on any individual, tend to confirm his faith for the time to come; nay, that when God seems to have forsaken us, we ought to extend our view farther, and take courage from his former favors, as is said in another psalm, "I remember the days of old: I meditate on all thy works" (Ps. 143:5). Again "I will remember the works of the Lord; surely I will remember thy wonders of old" (Ps. 77:11). But because all our conceptions of the power and works of God are evanescent without the word, we are not rash in maintaining, that there is no faith until God present us with clear evidence of his grace.

Here, however, a question might be raised as to the view to be taken of Sarah and Rebekah, both of whom, impelled as it would seem by zeal for the faith, went beyond the limits of the word. Sarah, in her eager desire for the promised seed, gave her maid to her husband. That she sinned in many respects is not to be denied; but the only fault to which I now refer is her being carried away by zeal, and not confining herself within the limits prescribed by the word. It is certain, however, that her desire proceeded from faith. Rebekah, again, divinely informed of the election of her son Jacob, procures the blessing for him by a wicked stratagem; deceives her husband, who was a witness and minister of divine grace; forces her son to lie; by various frauds and impostures corrupts divine truth; in fine, by exposing his promise to scorn, does what in her lies to make it of no effect. And yet this conduct, however vicious and reprehensible, was not devoid of faith. She must have overcome many obstacles before she obtained so strong a desire of that which, without any hope of earthly advantage, was full of difficulty and danger. In the same way, we cannot say that the holy patriarch Isaac was altogether void of faith, in that, after he had been similarly informed of the honor transferred to the younger son, he still continues his predilection in favor of his first-born, Esau. These examples certainly show that error is often mingled with faith; and yet that when faith is real, it always obtains the preeminence. For as the particular error of Rebekah did not render the blessing of no effect, neither did it nullify the faith which generally ruled in her mind, and was the principle and cause of that action. In this, nevertheless, Rebekah showed how prone the human mind is to turn aside whenever it gives itself the least indulgence. But though defect and infirmity obscure faith, they do not extinguish it. Still they admonish us how carefully we ought to cling to the word of God, and at the same time confirm what we have taught—viz. that faith gives way when not supported by the word, just as the minds of Sarah, Isaac, and Rebekah, would have lost themselves in devious paths, had not the secret restraint of Providence kept them obedient to the word.

32. On the other hand, we have good ground for comprehending all the promises in Christ, since the Apostle comprehends the whole Gospel under the knowledge of Christ, and declares that all the promises of God are in him yea, and amen. The reason for this is obvious. Every promise which God makes is evidence of his good will. This is invariably true, and is not inconsistent with the fact, that the large benefits which the divine liberality is constantly bestowing on the wicked are preparing them for heavier judgment. As they neither think that these proceed from the hand of the Lord, nor acknowledge them as his, or if they do so acknowledge them, never regard them as proofs of his favor, they are in no respect more instructed thereby in his mercy than brute beasts, which, according to their condition, enjoy the same liberality, and yet never look beyond it. Still it is true, that by rejecting the promises generally offered to them, they subject themselves to severer punishment. For though it is only when the promises are received in faith that their efficacy is manifested, still their reality and power are never extinguished by our infidelity or ingratitude. Therefore, when the Lord by his promises invites us not only to enjoy the fruits of his kindness, but also to meditate upon them, he at the same time declares his love. Thus we are brought back to our statement, that every promise is a manifestation of the divine favor toward us. Now, without controversy, God loves no man out of Christ. He is the beloved Son, in whom the love of the Father dwells, and from whom it afterwards extends to us. Thus Paul says "In whom he has made us accepted in the Beloved" (Eph. 1:6). It is by his intervention, therefore, that love is diffused so as to reach us. Accordingly, in another passage, the Apostle calls Christ "our peace" (Eph. 2:14), and also represents him as the bond by which the Father is united to us in paternal affection (Rom. 8:3). It follows, that whenever any promise is made to us, we must turn our eyes toward Christ. Hence, with good reasons Paul declares that in him all the promises of God are confirmed and completed (Rom. 15:8). Some examples are brought forward as repugnant to this view. When Naaman the Syrian made inquiry at the prophet as to the true mode of worshipping God, we cannot (it is said) suppose that he was informed of the Mediator, and yet he is commended for his piety (2 Kings 5:17–19). Nor could Cornelius, a Roman heathen, be acquainted with what was not known to all the Jews, and at best known obscurely. And yet his alms and prayers were acceptable to God (Acts 10:31), while the prophet by his answer approved of the sacrifices of Naaman. In both, this must

have been the result of faith. In like manner, the eunuch to whom Philip was sent, had he not been endued with some degree of faith, never would have incurred the fatigue and expense of a long and difficult journey to obtain an opportunity of worship (Acts 8:27, 31); and yet we see how, when interrogated by Philip, he betrays his ignorance of the Mediator. I admit that, in some respect, their faith was not explicit either as to the person of Christ, or the power and office assigned him by the Father. Still it is certain that they were imbued with principles which might give some, though a slender, foretaste of Christ. This should not be thought strange; for the eunuch would not have hastened from a distant country to Jerusalem to an unknown God; nor could Cornelius, after having once embraced the Jewish religion, have lived so long in Judea without becoming acquainted with the rudiments of sound doctrine. In regard to Naaman, it is absurd to suppose that Elisha, while he gave him many minute precepts, said nothing of the principal matter. Therefore, although their knowledge of Christ may have been obscure, we cannot suppose that they had no such knowledge at all. They used the sacrifices of the Law, and must have distinguished them from the spurious sacrifices of the Gentiles, by the end to which they referred—viz. Christ.

33. A simple external manifestation of the word ought to be amply sufficient to produce faith, did not our blindness and perverseness prevent. But such is the proneness of our mind to vanity, that it can never adhere to the truth of God, and such its dullness, that it is always blind even in his light. Hence without the illumination of the Spirit the word has no effect; and hence also it is obvious that faith is something higher than human understanding. Nor were it sufficient for the mind to be illumined by the Spirit of God unless the heart also were strengthened and supported by his power. Here the Schoolmen go completely astray, dwelling entirely in their consideration of faith, on the bare simple assent of the understanding, and altogether overlooking confidence and security of heart. Faith is the special gift of God in both ways,—in purifying the mind so as to give it a relish for divine truth, and afterwards in establishing it therein. For the Spirit does not merely originate faith, but gradually increases it, until by its means he conducts us into the heavenly kingdom. "That good thing which was committed unto thee," says Paul, "keep by the Holy Ghost which dwelleth in us" (2 Tim. 1:14). In what sense Paul says (Gal. 3:2), that the Spirit is given by the hearing of faith, may be easily explained. If there were only a single gift of the Spirit, he who is the author and cause of faith could not without absurdity be said to be its effect; but after celebrating the gifts with which God adorns his church, and by successive additions of faith leads it to perfection, there is nothing strange in his ascribing to faith the very gifts which faith prepares us for receiving. It seems to some paradoxical, when it is said that none can believe Christ save those to whom it is given; but this is partly because they do not observe how recondite and sublime heavenly wisdom is, or how dull the mind of man in discerning divine mysteries, and partly because they pay no regard to that firm and stable constancy of heart which is the chief part of faith.

34. But as Paul argues, "What man knoweth the things of a man, save the spirit of man which is in him? even so the things of God knoweth no man but the Spirit of God" (1 Cor. 2:11). If in regard to divine truth we hesitate even as to those things which we see with the bodily eye, how can we be firm and steadfast in regard to those divine promises which neither the eye sees nor the mind comprehends? Here human discernment is so defective and lost, that the first step of advancement in the school of Christ is to renounce it (Mt. 11:25; Luke 10:21). Like a veil interposed, it prevents us from beholding divine masteries, which are revealed only to babes. "Flesh and blood" does not reveal them (Mt. 16:17). "The natural man receiveth not the things of the Spirit of God: for they are foolishness unto him; neither can he know them, for they are spiritually discerned" (I Cor. 2:14). The supplies of the Holy Spirit are therefore necessary, or rather his agency is here the only strength. "For who has known the mind of the Lord? or who has been his counselor?" (Rom. 11:34); but "The Spirit searcheth all things, yea, the deep things of God" (1 Cor. 2:10). Thus it is that we attain to the mind of Christ: "No man can come to me, except the Father which has sent me draw him: and I will raise him up at the last day." "Every man therefore that has heard, and learned of the Father, cometh unto me. Not that any man has seen the Father, save he which is of God, he has seen the Father" (John 6:44, 45, 46). Therefore, as we cannot possibly come to Christ unless drawn by the Spirit, so when we are drawn we are both in mind and spirit exalted far above our own understanding. For the soul, when illumined by him, receives as it were a new eye, enabling it to contemplate heavenly mysteries, by the splendor of which it was previously dazzled. And thus, indeed, it is only when the human intellect is irradiated by the light of the Holy Spirit that it begins to have a taste of those things which pertain to the kingdom of God;

previously it was too stupid and senseless to have any relish for them. Hence our Savior, when clearly declaring the mysteries of the kingdom to the two disciples, makes no impression till he opens their minds to understand the Scriptures (Luke 24:27, 45). Hence also, though he had taught the Apostles with his own divine lips, it was still necessary to send the Spirit of truth to instill into their minds the same doctrine which they had heard with their ears. The word is, in regard to those to whom it is preached, like the sun which shines upon all, but is of no use to the blind. In this matter we are all naturally blind; and hence the word cannot penetrate our mind unless the Spirit, that internal teacher, by his enlightening power make an entrance for it.

35. Having elsewhere shown more fully, when treating of the corruption of our nature, how little able men are to believe (Book 2, c. 2, 3), I will not fatigue the reader by again repeating it. Let it suffice to observe, that the spirit of faith is used by Paul as synonymous with the very faith which we receive from the Spirit, but which we have not naturally (2 Cor. 4:13). Accordingly, he prays for the Thessalonians, "that our God would count you worthy of this calling, and fulfill all the good pleasure of his goodness, and the work of faith with power" (2 Thess. 1:2). Here, by designating faith the work of God, and distinguishing it by way of epithet, appropriately calling it his *good pleasure*, he declares that it is not of man's own nature; and not contented with this, he adds, that it is an illustration of divine power. In addressing the Corinthians, when he tells them that faith stands not "in the wisdom of man, but in the power of God" (1 Cor. 2:4), he is no doubt speaking of external miracles; but as the reprobate are blinded when they behold them, he also includes that internal seal of which he elsewhere makes mention. And the better to display his liberality in this most excellent gift, God does not bestow it upon all promiscuously, but, by special privilege, imparts it to whom he will. To this effect we have already quoted passages of Scripture, as to which Augustine, their faithful expositor, exclaims (De Verbo Apost. Serm. 2) "Our Savior, to teach that faith in him is a gift, not a merit, says, 'No man can come to me, except the Father, which has sent me, draw him,' (John 6:44). It is strange when two persons hear, the one despises, the other ascends. Let him who despises impute it to himself; let him who ascends not arrogate it to himself." In another passage he asks, "Wherefore is it given to the one, and not to the other? I am not ashamed to say, This is one of the deep things of the cross. From some unknown depth of the judgments of God, which we cannot scrutinize, all our ability proceeds. I see that I am able; but how I am able I see not:—this far only I see, that it is of God. But why the one, and not the other? This is too great for me: it is an abyss a depth of the cross. I can cry out with wonder; not discuss and demonstrate." The whole comes to this, that Christ, when he produces faith in us by the agency of his Spirit, at the same time ingrafts us into his body, that we may become partakers of all blessings.

36. The next thing necessary is, that what the mind has imbibed be transferred into the heart. The word is not received in faith when it merely flutters in the brain, but when it has taken deep root in the heart, and become an invincible bulwark to withstand and repel all the assaults of temptation. But if the illumination of the Spirit is the true source of understanding in the intellect, much more manifest is his agency in the confirmation of the heart; inasmuch as there is more distrust in the heart than blindness in the mind; and it is more difficult to inspire the soul with security than to imbue it with knowledge. Hence the Spirit performs the part of a seal, sealing upon our hearts the very promises, the certainty of which was previously impressed upon our minds. It also serves as an earnest in establishing and confirming these promises. Thus the Apostle says, "In whom also, after that ye believed, ye were sealed with that holy Spirit of promise, which is the earnest of our inheritance" (Eph. 1:13, 14). You see how he teaches that the hearts of believers are stamped with the Spirit as with a seal, and calls it the Spirit of promise, because it ratifies the gospel to us. In like manner he says to the Corinthians, "God has also sealed us, and given the earnest of the Spirit in our hearts" (2 Cor. 1:22). And again, when speaking of a full and confident hope, he founds it on the "earnest of the Spirit" (2 Cor. 5:5).

37. I am not forgetting what I formerly said, and experience brings daily to remembrance—viz. that faith is subject to various doubts, so that the minds of believers are seldom at rest, or at least are not always tranquil. Still, whatever be the engines by which they are shaken, they either escape from the whirlpool of temptation, or remain steadfast in their place. Faith finds security and protection in the words of the Psalm, "God is our refuge and strength, a very present help in trouble; therefore will not we fear, though the earth be removed, and the mountains be carried into the midst of the sea" (Ps. 46:1, 2). This delightful tranquillity is elsewhere described: "I laid me down and slept; I awaked, for the Lord sustained me" (Ps. 3:5). Not that David was uniformly in this joyful frame; but in so far as the measure of his faith made

him sensible of the divine favor, he glories in intrepidly despising every thing that could disturb his peace of mind. Hence the Scripture, when it exhorts us to faith, bids us be at peace. In Isaiah it is said, "In quietness and in confidence shall be your strength" (Is. 30:15); and in the psalm, "Rest in the Lord, and wait patiently for him." Corresponding to this is the passage in the Hebrews, "Ye have need of patience," &c. (Heb. 10:36).

38. Hence we may judge how pernicious is the scholastic dogma, that we can have no stronger evidence of the divine favor toward us than moral conjecture, according as each individual deems himself not unworthy of it. Doubtless, if we are to determine by our works in what way the Lord stands affected towards us, I admit that we cannot even get the length of a feeble conjecture: but since faith should accord with the free and simple promise, there is no room left for ambiguity. With what kind of confidence, pray, shall we be armed if we reason in this way—God is propitious to us, provided we deserve it by the purity of our lives? But since we have reserved this subject for discussion in its proper place, we shall not prosecute it farther at present, especially seeing it is already plain that nothing is more adverse to faith than conjecture, or any other feeling akin to doubt. Nothing can be worse than their perversion of the passage of Ecclesiastes, which is ever in their mouths: "No man knoweth either love or hatred by all that is before them" (Eccl. 9:1). For without insisting that the passage is erroneously rendered in the common version—even a child cannot fail to perceive what Solomon's meaning is—viz. that any one who would ascertain, from the present state of things, who are in the favor or under the displeasure of God, labors in vain, and torments himself to no useful purpose, since "All things come alike to all;" "to him that sacrificeth, and to him that sacrificeth not:" and hence God does not always declare his love to those on whom he bestows uninterrupted prosperity, nor his hatred against those whom he afflicts. And it tends to prove the vanity of the human intellect, that it is so completely in the dark as to matters which it is of the highest importance to know. Thus Solomon had said a little before, "That which befalleth the sons of men befalleth beasts; even one thing befalleth them: as the one dieth, so dieth the other" (Eccl. 3:19). Were any one thence to infer that we hold the immortality of the soul by conjecture merely, would he not justly be deemed insane? Are those then sane who cannot obtain any certainty of the divine favor, because the carnal eye is now unable to discern it from the present appearance of the world?

39. But, they say, it is rash and presumptuous to pretend to an undoubted knowledge of the divine will. I would grant this, did we hold that we were able to subject the incomprehensible counsel of God to our feeble intellect. But when we simply say with Paul, "We have received not the spirit of the world, but the Spirit which is of God; that we might know the things that are freely given to us of God" (1 Cor. 2:12), what can they oppose to this, without offering insult to the Spirit of God? But if it is Sacrilege to charge the revelation which he has given us with falsehood, or uncertainty, or ambiguity, how can we be wrong in maintaining its certainty? But they still exclaim, that there is great temerity in our presuming to glory in possessing the Spirit of God. Who could believe that these men, who desire to be thought the masters of the world, could be so stupid as to err thus grossly in the very first principles of religion? To me, indeed, it would be incredible, did not their own writings make it manifest. Paul declares that those only are the sons of God who are led by his Spirit (Rom. 8:14); these men would have those who are the sons of God to be led by their own, and void of the divine Spirit. He tells us that we call God our Father in terms dictated by the Spirit, who alone bears witness with our spirit that we are the sons of God (Rom. 8:16); they, though they forbid us not to invoke God, withdraw the Spirit, by whose guidance he is duly invoked. He declares that those only are the servants of Christ who are led by the Spirit of Christ (Rom. 8:9); they imagine a Christianity which has no need of the Spirit of Christ. He holds out the hope of a blessed resurrection to those only who feel His Spirit dwelling in them (Rom. 8:11); they imagine hope when there is no such feeling. But perhaps they will say, that they deny not the necessity of being endued with the Spirit, but only hold it to be the part of modesty and humility not to recognize it. What, then, does Paul mean, when he says to the Corinthians, "Examine yourselves whether ye be in the faith: prove your own selves. Know ye not your own selves, that Jesus Christ is in you, except ye be reprobates?" (2 Cor. 13:5). John, moreover, says, "Hereby we know that he abideth in us by the Spirit which he has given us" (1 John 3:24). And what else is it than to bring the promises of Christ into doubt, when we would be deemed servants of Christ without having his Spirit, whom he declared that he would pour out on all his people? (Isa. 44:3). What! do we not insult the Holy Spirit, when we separate faith, which is his peculiar work, from himself? These being the first rudiments of religion, it is the most wretched blindness to charge Christians with

arrogance, for presuming to glory in the presence of the Holy Spirit; a glorying without which Christianity itself does not exist. The example of these men illustrates the truth of our Savior's declaration, that his Spirit "the world cannot receive, because it seeth him not, neither knoweth him; but ye know him, for he dwelleth with you, and shall be in you" (John 14:17).

40. That they may not attempt to undermine the certainty of faith in one direction only, they attack it in another—viz. that though it be lawful for the believer, from his actual state of righteousness, to form a judgment as to the favor of God, the knowledge of final perseverance still remains in suspense. An admirable security, indeed, is left us, if, for the present moment only, we can judge from moral conjecture that we are in grace, but know not how we are to be to-morrow! Very different is the language of the Apostle, "I am persuaded that neither death, nor life, nor angels, nor principalities, nor powers, nor things present, nor things to come, nor height, nor depth, nor any other creature, shall be able to separate us from the love of God, which is in Christ Jesus our Lord" (Rom. 8:38). They endeavor to evade the force of this by frivolously pretending that the Apostle had this assurance by special revelation. They are too well caught thus to escape; for in that passage he is treating not of his individual experience, but of the blessings which all believers in common derive from faith. But then Paul in another passage alarms us by the mention of our weakness and inconstancy, "Let him that thinketh he standeth take heed lest he fall" (1 Cor. 10:12). True; but this he says not to inspire us with terror, but that we may learn to humble ourselves under the mighty hand of God, as Peter explains (1 Pet. 5:6). Then how preposterous is it to limit the certainty of faith to a point of time; seeing it is the property of faith to pass beyond the whole course of this life, and stretch forward to a future immortality? Therefore since believers owe it to the favor of God, that, enlightened by his Spirit, they, through faith, enjoy the prospect of heavenly life; there is so far from an approach to arrogance in each glorying, that any one ashamed to confess it, instead of testifying modesty or submission, rather betrays extreme ingratitude, by maliciously suppressing the divine goodness.

41. Since the nature of faith could not be better or more clearly evinced than by the substance of the promise on which it leans as its proper foundation, and without which it immediately falls or rather vanishes away, we have derived our definition from it—a definition, however, not at all at variance with that definition, or rather description, which the Apostle accommodates to his discourse, when he says that faith is "the substance of things hoped for, the evidence of things not seen" (Heb. 11:1). For by the term substance (ὑπόστασις), he means a kind of prop on which the pious mind rests and leans. As if he had said, that faith is a kind of certain and secure possession of those things which are promised to us by God; unless we prefer taking ὑπόστασις for confidence. I have no objection to this, though I am more inclined to adopt the other interpretation, which is more generally received. Again, to intimate that until the last day, when the books will be opened (Dan. 7:10; Rev. 20:12), the things pertaining to our salvation are too lofty to be perceived by our sense, seen by our eyes, or handled by our hands, and that in the meantime there is no possible way in which these can be possessed by us, unless we can transcend the reach of our own intellect, and raise our eye above all worldly objects; in short, surpass ourselves, he adds that this certainty of possession relates to things which are only hoped for, and therefore not seen. For as Paul says (Rom. 8:24), "A hope that is seen is not hope," that we "hope for that we see not." When he calls it the evidence or proof, or, as Augustine repeatedly renders it (see *Hom. in Joann.* 79 and 95), the conviction of things not present, the Greek term being ἔλεγχος, it is the same as if he had called it the appearance of things not apparent, the sight of things not seen, the clearness of things obscure, the presence of things absent, the manifestation of things hid. For the mysteries of God (and to this class belong the things which pertain to our salvation) cannot be discerned in themselves, or, as it is expressed, in their own nature; but we behold them only in his word, of the truth of which we ought to be as firmly persuaded as if we held that every thing which it says were done and completed. But how can the mind rise to such a perception and foretaste of the divine goodness, without being at the same time wholly inflamed with love to God? The abundance of joy which God has treasured up for those who fear him cannot be truly known without making a most powerful impression. He who is thus once affected is raised and carried entirely towards him. Hence it is not strange that no sinister perverse heart ever experiences this feeling, by which, transported to heaven itself, we are admitted to the most hidden treasures of God, and the holiest recesses of his kingdom, which must not be profaned by the entrance of a heart that is impure. For what the Schoolmen say as to the priority of love to faith and hope is a mere dream (see Sent. Lib. 3 Dist. 25, &c.) since it is faith alone that first engenders love. How much

better is Bernard, "The testimony of conscience, which Paul calls 'the rejoicing' of believers, I believe to consist in three things. It is necessary, first of all, to believe that you cannot have remission of sins except by the indulgence of God; secondly, that you cannot have any good work at all unless he also give it; lastly, that you cannot by any works merit eternal life unless it also be freely given" (Bernard, Serm. 1 in Annuntiatione). Shortly after he adds, "These things are not sufficient, but are a kind of commencement of faith; for while believing that your sins can only be forgiven by God, you must also hold that they are not forgiven until persuaded by the testimony of the Holy Spirit that salvation is treasured up for us; that as God pardons sins, and gives merits, and after merits rewards, you cannot halt at that beginning." But these and other topics will be considered in their own place; let it suffice at present to understand what faith is.

42. Wherever this living faith exists, it must have the hope of eternal life as its inseparable companion, or rather must of itself beget and manifest it; where it is wanting, however clearly and elegantly we may discourse of faith, it is certain we have it not. For if faith is (as has been said) a firm persuasion of the truth of God—a persuasion that it can never be false, never deceive, never be in vain, those who have received this assurance must at the same time expect that God will perform his promises, which in their conviction are absolutely true; so that in one word hope is nothing more than the expectation of those things which faith previously believes to have been truly promised by God. Thus, faith believes that God is true; hope expects that in due season he will manifest his truth. Faith believes that he is our Father; hope expects that he will always act the part of a Father towards us. Faith believes that eternal life has been given to us; hope expects that it will one day be revealed. Faith is the foundation on which hope rests; hope nourishes and sustains faith. For as no man can expect any thing from God without previously believing his promises, so, on the other hand, the weakness of our faith, which might grow weary and fall away, must be supported and cherished by patient hope and expectation. For this reason Paul justly says, "We are saved by hope" (Rom. 8:24). For while hope silently waits for the Lord, it restrains faith from hastening on with too much precipitation, confirms it when it might waver in regard to the promises of God or begin to doubt of their truth, refreshes it when it might be fatigued, extends its view to the final goal, so as not to allow it to give up in the middle of the course, or at the very outset. In short, by constantly renovating and reviving, it is ever and anon furnishing more vigor for perseverance. On the whole, how necessary the reinforcements of hope are to establish faith will better appear if we reflect on the numerous forms of temptation by which those who have embraced the word of God are assailed and shaken. First, the Lord often keeps us in suspense, by delaying the fulfillment of his promises much longer than we could wish. Here the office of hope is to perform what the prophet enjoins, "Though it tarry, wait for it" (Hab. 2:3). Sometimes he not only permits faith to grow languid, but even openly manifests his displeasure. Here there is still greater necessity for the aid of hope, that we may be able to say with another prophet, "I will wait upon the Lord that hideth his face from the house of Jacob, and I will look for him" (Isaiah 8:17). Scoffers also rise up, as Peter tells us, and ask, "Where is the promise of his coming? for since the fathers fell asleep, all things continue as they were from the beginning of the creation" (2 Pet. 3:4). Nay, the world and the flesh insinuate the same thing. Here faith must be supported by the patience of hope, and fixed on the contemplation of eternity, consider that "one day is with the Lord as a thousand years, and a thousand years as one day" (2 Pet. 3:8; Ps. 90:4).

43. On account of this connection and affinity Scripture sometimes confounds the two terms faith and hope. For when Peter says that we are "kept by the power of God through faith until salvation, ready to be revealed in the last times" (1 Pet. 1:5), he attributes to faith what more properly belongs to hope. And not without cause, since we have already shown that hope is nothing else than the food and strength of faith. Sometimes the two are joined together, as in the same Epistles "That your faith and hope might be in God" (1 Pet. 1:21). Paul, again, in the Epistle to the Philippians, from hope deduces expectation (Phil. 1:20), because in hoping patiently we suspend our wishes until God manifest his own time. The whole of this subject may be better understood from the tenth chapter of the Epistle to the Hebrews, to which I have already adverted. Paul, in another passage, though not in strict propriety of speech, expresses the same thing in these words, "For we through the Spirit wait for the hope of righteousness by faith" (Gal. 5:5); that is, after embracing the testimony of the Gospel as to free love, we wait till God openly manifest what is now only an object of hope. It is now obvious how absurdly Peter Lombard lays down a double foundation of hope—viz. the grace of God and the merit of works (Sent. Lib. 3, Dist. 26). Hope cannot have any other object than faith has. But we have already shown clearly that the only object of faith is the mercy of

God, to which, to use the common expression, it must look with both eyes. But it is worth while to listen to the strange reason which he adduces. If you presume, says he, to hope for any thing without merit, it should be called not hope, but presumption. Who, dear reader, does not execrate the gross stupidity which calls it rashness, and presumption to confide in the truth of God? The Lord desires us to expect every thing from his goodness and yet these men tell us, it is presumption to rest in it. O teacher, worthy of the pupils, whom you found in these insane raving schools! Seeing that, by the oracles of God, sinners are enjoined to entertain the hope of salvation, let us willingly presume so far on his truth as to cast away all confidence in our works, and trusting in his mercy, venture to hope. He who has said, "According to your faith be it unto you" (Mt. 9:29), will never deceive.

CHAPTER 3

REGENERATION BY FAITH. OF REPENTANCE.

This chapter is divided into five parts. I. The title of the chapter seems to promise a treatise on Faith, but the only subject here considered is Repentance, the inseparable attendant of faith. And, first, various opinions on the subject of repentance are stated, sec. 1–4. II. An exposition of the orthodox doctrine of Repentance, sec. 5–9. III. Reasons why repentance must be prolonged to the last moment of life, sec. 10–14. IV. Of the fruits of repentance, or its object and tendency, sec. 15–20. V. The source whence repentance proceeds, sec. 21–24. Of the sin against the Holy Spirit, and the impenitence of the reprobate, sec. 25.

Sections:

1. Connection of this chapter with the previous one and the subsequent chapters. Repentance follows faith, and is produced by it. Reason. Error of those who take a contrary view.

2. Their First Objection. Answer. In what sense the origin of Repentance ascribed to Faith. Cause of the erroneous idea that faith is produced by repentance. Refutation of it. The hypocrisy of Monks and Anabaptists in assigning limits to repentance exposed.

3. A second opinion concerning repentance considered.

4. A third opinion, assigning two forms to repentance, a legal and an Evangelical. Examples of each.

5. The orthodox doctrine of Repentance. 1. Faith and Repentance to be distinguished, not confounded or separated. 2. A consideration of the name. 3. A definition of the thing, or what repentance is. Doctrine of the Prophets and Apostles.

6. Explanation of the definition. This consists of three parts. 1. Repentance is a turning of our life unto God. This described and enlarged upon.

7. 2. Repentance produced by fear of God. Hence the mention of divine judgment by the Prophets and Apostles. Example. Exposition of the second branch of the definition from a passage in Paul. Why the fear of God is the first part of Repentance.

8. 3. Repentance consists in the mortification of the flesh and the quickening of the Spirit. These required by the Prophets. They are explained separately.

9. How this mortification and quickening are produced. Repentance just a renewal of the divine image in us. Not completed in a moment, but extends to the last moment of life.

10. Reasons why repentance must so extend. Augustine's opinion as to concupiscence in the regenerate examined. A passage of Paul which seems to confirm that opinion.

11. Answer. Confirmation of the answer by the Apostle himself. Another confirmation from a precept of the law. Conclusion.

12. Exception, that those desires only are condemned which are repugnant to the order of God. Desires not condemned in so far as natural, but in so far as inordinate. This held by Augustine.

13. Passages from Augustine to show that this was his opinion. Objection from a passage in James.

14. Another objection of the Anabaptists and Libertines to the continuance of repentance throughout the present life. An answer disclosing its impiety. Another answer, founded on the absurdities to which it leads. A third answer, contrasting sincere Christian repentance with the erroneous view of the objectors. Conformation from the example and declaration of an Apostle.

15. Of the fruits of repentance. Carefulness. Excuse. Indignation. Fear. Desire. Zeal. Revenge. Moderation to be observed, as most sagely counseled by Bernard.

16. Internal fruits of Repentance. 1. Piety towards God. 2. Charity towards man. 3. Purity of life. How carefully these fruits are commended by the Prophets. External fruits of repentance. Bodily exercises too much commended by ancient writers. Twofold excess in regard to them.

17. Delusion of some who consider these external exercises as the chief part of Repentance. Why received in the Jewish Church. The legitimate use of these exercises in the Christian Church.

18. The principal part of repentance consists in turning to God. Confession and acknowledgment of sins. What their nature should be. Distinction between ordinary and special repentance. Use of this distinction.

19. End of Repentance. Its nature shown by the preaching of John Baptist, our Savior, and his Apostles. The sum of this preaching.

20. Christian repentance terminates with our life.

21. Repentance has its origin in the grace of God, as communicated to the elect, whom God is pleased to save from death. The hardening and final impenitence of the reprobate. A passage of an Apostle as to voluntary reprobates, gives no countenance to the Novatians.

22. Of the sin against the Holy Ghost. The true definition of this sin as proved and explained by Scripture. Who they are that sin against the Holy Spirit. Examples:—1. The Jews resisting Stephen. 2. The Pharisees. Definition confirmed by the example of Paul.

23. Why that sin unpardonable. The paralogism of the Novatians in wresting the words of the Apostle examined. Two passages from the same Apostle.

24. First objection to the above doctrine. Answer. Solution of a difficulty founded on the example of Esau and the threatening of a Prophet. Second objection.

25. Third objection, founded on the seeming approval of the feigned repentance of the ungodly, as Ahab. Answer. Confirmation from the example of Esau. Why God bears for a time with the ungodly, pretending repentance. Exception.

1. Although we have already in some measure shown how faith possesses Christ, and gives us the enjoyment of his benefits, the subject would still be obscure were we not to add an exposition of the effects resulting from it. The sum of the Gospel is, not without good reason, made to consist in repentance and forgiveness of sins; and, therefore, where these two heads are omitted, any discussion concerning faith will be meager and defective, and indeed almost useless. Now, since Christ confers upon us, and we obtain by faith, both free reconciliation and newness of life, reason and order require that I should here begin to treat of both. The shortest transition, however, will be from faith to repentance; for repentance being properly understood it will better appear how a man is justified freely by faith alone, and yet that holiness of life, *real* holiness, as it is called, is inseparable from the free imputation of righteousness. That repentance not only always follows faith, but is produced by it, ought to be without controversy (see Calvin in Joann. 1:13). For since pardon and forgiveness are offered by the preaching of the Gospel, in order that the sinner, delivered from the tyranny of Satan, the yoke of sin, and the miserable bondage of iniquity, may pass into the kingdom of God, it is certain that no man can embrace the grace of the Gospel without retaking himself from the errors of his former life into the right path, and making it his whole study to practice repentance. Those who think that repentance precedes faith instead of flowing from, or being produced by it, as the fruit by the tree, have never understood its nature, and are moved to adopt that view on very insufficient grounds.

2. Christ and John, it is said, in their discourses first exhort the people to repentance, and then add, that the kingdom of heaven is at hand (Mt. 3:2; 4:17). Such too, is the message which the Apostles received and such the course which Paul followed, as is narrated by Luke (Acts 20:21). But clinging superstitiously to the juxtaposition of the syllables, they attend not to the coherence of meaning in the words. For when our Lord and John begin their preaching thus "Repent, for the kingdom of heaven is at hand" (Mt. 3:2), do they not deduce repentance as a consequence of the offer of grace and promise of salvation? The force of the words, therefore, is the same as if it were said, As the kingdom of heaven is at hand, for that reason repent. For Matthew, after relating that John so preached, says that therein was fulfilled the prophecy concerning the voice of one crying in the desert, "Prepare ye the way of the Lord, make straight in the desert a highway for our God" (Isaiah 40:3). But in the Prophet that voice is ordered to commence with consolation and glad tidings. Still, when we attribute the origin of repentance to faith, we do not dream of some period of time in which faith is to give birth to it: we only wish to show that a man cannot seriously engage in repentance unless he know that he is of God. But no man is truly persuaded that he is of God until he have embraced his offered favor. These things will be more clearly explained as we proceed. Some are perhaps misled by this, that not a few are subdued by terror of conscience, or disposed to obedience before they have been imbued with a knowledge, nay, before they have had any taste of the divine favor (see Calvin in Acts 20:21). This is that initial fear which some writers class among the virtues, because they think it approximates to true and genuine obedience. But

we are not here considering the various modes in which Christ draws us to himself, or prepares us for the study of piety: All I say is, that no righteousness can be found where the Spirit, whom Christ received in order to communicate it to his members, reigns not. Then, according to the passage in the Psalms, "There is forgiveness with thee, that thou mayest be feared" (Psalm 130:4), no man will ever reverence God who does not trust that God is propitious to him, no man will ever willingly set himself to observe the Law who is not persuaded that his services are pleasing to God. The indulgence of God in tolerating and pardoning our iniquities is a sign of paternal favor. This is also clear from the exhortation in Hosea, "Come, and let us return unto the Lord: for he has torn, and he will heal us; he has smitten, and he will bind us up" (Hos. 6:1); the hope of pardon is employed as a stimulus to prevent us from becoming reckless in sin. But there is no semblance of reason in the absurd procedure of those who, that they may begin with repentance, prescribe to their neophytes certain days during which they are to exercise themselves in repentance, and after these are elapsed, admit them to communion in Gospel grace. I allude to great numbers of Anabaptists, those of them especially who plume themselves on being spiritual, and their associates the Jesuits, and others of the same stamp. Such are the fruits which their giddy spirit produces, that repentance, which in every Christian man lasts as long as life, is with them completed in a few short days.

3. Certain learned men, who lived long before the present days and were desirous to speak simply and sincerely according to the rule of Scripture, held that repentance consists of two parts, mortification and quickening. By mortification they mean, grief of soul and terror, produced by a conviction of sin and a sense of the divine judgment. For when a man is brought to a true knowledge of sin, he begins truly to hate and abominate sin. He also is sincerely dissatisfied with himself, confesses that he is lost and undone, and wishes he were different from what he is. Moreover, when he is touched with some sense of the divine justice (for the one conviction immediately follows the other), he lies terrorstruck and amazed, humbled and dejected, desponds and despairs. This, which they regarded as the first part of repentance, they usually termed *contrition*. By quickening they mean, the comfort which is produced by faith, as when a man prostrated by a consciousness of sin, and smitten with the fear of God, afterwards beholding his goodness, and the mercy, grace, and salvation obtained through Christ, looks up, begins to breathe, takes courage, and passes, as it were, from death unto life. I admit that these terms, when rightly interpreted, aptly enough express the power of repentance; only I cannot assent to their using the term *quickening*, for the joy which the soul feels after being calmed from perturbation and fear. It more properly means, that desire of pious and holy living which springs from the new birth; as if it were said, that the man dies to himself that he may begin to live unto God.

4. Others seeing that the term is used in Scripture in different senses, have set down two forms of repentance, and, in order to distinguish them, have called the one Legal repentance; or that by which the sinner, stung with a sense of his sin, and overwhelmed with fear of the divine anger, remains in that state of perturbation, unable to escape from it. The other they term Evangelical repentance; or that by which the sinner, though grievously downcast in himself, yet looks up and sees in Christ the cure of his wound, the solace of his terror; the haven of rest from his misery. They give Cain, Saul and Judas, as examples of legal repentance. Scripture, in describing what is called their repentance, means that they perceived the heinousness of their sins, and dreaded the divine anger; but, thinking only of God as a judge and avenger, were overwhelmed by the thought. Their repentance, therefore, was nothing better than a kind of threshold to hell, into which having entered even in the present life, they began to endure the punishment inflicted by the presence of an offended God. Examples of evangelical repentance we see in all those who, first stung with a sense of sin, but afterwards raised and revived by confidence in the divine mercy, turned unto the Lord. Hezekiah was frightened on receiving the message of his death, but praying with tears, and beholding the divine goodness, regained his confidence. The Ninevites were terrified at the fearful announcement of their destruction; but clothing themselves in sackcloth and ashes, they prayed, hoping that the Lord might relent and avert his anger from them. David confessed that he had sinned greatly in numbering the people, but added "Now, I beseech thee O Lord, take away the iniquity of thy servant." When rebuked by Nathan, he acknowledged the crime of adultery, and humbled himself before the Lord; but he, at the same time, looked for pardon. Similar was the repentance of those who, stung to the heart by the preaching of Peter, yet trusted in the divine goodness, and added, "Men and brethren, what shall we do?" Similar was the case of Peter himself, who indeed wept bitterly, but ceased not to hope.

5. Though all this is true, yet the term *repentance* (in so far as I can ascertain from Scripture) must be differ-

ently taken. For in comprehending faith under repentance, they are at variance with what Paul says in the Acts, as to his "testifying both to the Jews and also to the Greeks, repentance toward God, and faith toward our Lord Jesus Christ" (Acts 20:21). Here he mentions faith and repentance as two different things. What then? Can true repentance exist without faith? By no means. But although they cannot be separated, they ought to be distinguished. As there is no faith without hope, and yet faith and hope are different, so repentance and faith, though constantly linked together, are only to be united, not confounded. I am not unaware that under the term *repentance* is comprehended the whole work of turning to God, of which not the least important part is faith; but in what sense this is done will be perfectly obvious, when its nature and power shall have been explained. The term repentance is derived in the Hebrew from conversion, or turning again; and in the Greek from a change of mind and purpose; nor is the thing meant inappropriate to both derivations, for it is substantially this, that withdrawing from ourselves we turn to God, and laying aside the old, put on a new mind. Wherefore, it seems to me, that repentance may be not inappropriately defined thus: A real conversion of our life unto God, proceeding from sincere and serious fear of God; and consisting in the mortification of our flesh and the old man, and the quickening of the Spirit. In this sense are to be understood all those addresses in which the prophets first, and the apostles afterwards, exhorted the people of their time to repentance. The great object for which they labored was, to fill them with confusion for their sins and dread of the divine judgment, that they might fall down and humble themselves before him whom they had offended, and, with true repentance, retake themselves to the right path. Accordingly, they use indiscriminately in the same sense, the expressions turning, or returning to the Lord; repenting, doing repentance. Whence, also, the sacred history describes it as repentance towards God, when men who disregarded him and wantoned in their lusts begin to obey his word, and are prepared to go whithersoever he may call them. And John Baptist and Paul, under the expression, bringing forth fruits meet for repentance, described a course of life exhibiting and bearing testimony, in all its actions, to such a repentance.

6. But before proceeding farther, it will be proper to give a clearer exposition of the definition which we have adopted. There are three things, then, principally to be considered in it. First, in the conversion of the life to God, we require a transformation not only in external works, but in the soul itself, which is able only after it has put off its old habits to bring forth fruits conformable to its renovation. The prophet, intending to express this, enjoins those whom he calls to repentance to make them "a new heart and a new spirit" (Ezek. 18:31). Hence Moses, on several occasions, when he would show how the Israelites were to repent and turn to the Lord, tells them that it must be done with the whole heart, and the whole soul (a mode of expression of frequent recurrence in the prophets), and by terming it the circumcision of the heart, points to the internal affections. But there is no passage better fitted to teach us the genuine nature of repentance than the following: "If thou wilt return, O Israel, saith the Lord, return unto me." "Break up your fallow ground, and sow not among thorns. Circumcise yourselves to the Lord, and take away the foreskins of your heart" (Jer. 4:1–4). See how he declares to them that it will be of no avail to commence the study of righteousness unless impiety shall first have been eradicated from their inmost heart. And to malice the deeper impression, he reminds them that they have to do with God, and can gain nothing by deceit, because he hates a double heart. For this reason Isaiah derides the preposterous attempts of hypocrites, who zealously aimed at an external repentance by the observance of ceremonies, but in the meanwhile cared not "to loose the bands of wickedness, to undo the heavy burdens, and to let the oppressed go free" (Isaiah 58:6). In these words he admirably shows wherein the acts of unfeigned repentance consist.

7. The second part of our definition is, that repentance proceeds from a sincere fear of God. Before the mind of the sinner can be inclined to repentance, he must be aroused by the thought of divine judgment; but when once the thought that God will one day ascend his tribunal to take an account of all words and actions has taken possession of his mind, it will not allow him to rest, or have one moment's peace, but will perpetually urge him to adopt a different plan of life, that he may be able to stand securely at that judgment-seat. Hence the Scripture, when exhorting to repentance, often introduces the subject of judgment, as in Jeremiah, "Lest my fury come forth like fire, and burn that none can quench it, because of the evil of your doings" (Jer. 4:4). Paul, in his discourse to the Athenians says, "The times of this ignorance God winked at; but now commandeth all men every where to repent: because he has appointed a day in the which he will judge the world in righteousness" (Acts 17:30, 31). The same thing is repeated in several other passages. Sometimes God is declared to be a judge, from

the punishments already inflicted, thus leading sinners to reflect that worse awaits them if they do not quickly repent. There is an example of this in the 29th chapter of Deuteronomy. As repentance begins with dread and hatred of sin, the Apostle sets down godly sorrow as one of its causes (2 Cor. 7:10). By godly sorrow he means when we not only tremble at the punishment, but hate and abhor the sin, because we know it is displeasing to God. It is not strange that this should be, for unless we are stung to the quick, the sluggishness of our carnal nature cannot be corrected; nay, no degree of pungency would suffice for our stupor and sloth, did not God lift the rod and strike deeper. There is, moreover, a rebellious spirit which must be broken as with hammers. The stern threatening which God employs are extorted from him by our depraved dispositions. For while we are asleep it were in vain to allure us by soothing measures. Passages to this effect are everywhere to be met with, and I need not quote them. But there is another reason why the fear of God lies at the root of repentance—viz. that though the life of man were possessed of all kinds of virtue, still if they do not bear reference to God, how much soever they may be lauded in the world, they are mere abomination in heaven, inasmuch as it is the principal part of righteousness to render to God that service and honor of which he is impiously defrauded, whenever it is not our express purpose to submit to his authority.

8. We must now explain the third part of the definition, and show what is meant when we say that repentance consists of two parts—viz. the mortification of the flesh, and the quickening of the Spirit. The prophets, in accommodation to a carnal people, express this in simple and homely terms, but clearly, when they say, "Depart from evil, and do good" (Ps. 34:14). "Wash you, make you clean, put away the evil of your doings from before mine eyes; cease to do evil; learn to do well; seek judgment; relieve the oppressed," &c. (Isaiah 1:16, 17). In dissuading us from wickedness they demand the entire destruction of the flesh, which is full of perverseness and malice. It is a most difficult and arduous achievement to renounce ourselves, and lay aside our natural disposition. For the flesh must not be thought to be destroyed unless every thing that we have of our own is abolished. But seeing that all the desires of the flesh are enmity against God (Rom. 8:7), the first step to the obedience of his law is the renouncement of our own nature. Renovation is afterwards manifested by the fruits produced by it—viz. justice, judgment, and mercy. Since it were not sufficient duly to perform such acts, were not the mind and heart previously endued with sentiments of justice, judgment, and mercy this is done when the Holy Spirit, instilling his holiness into our souls, so inspired them with new thoughts and affections, that they may justly be regarded as new. And, indeed, as we are naturally averse to God, unless self-denial precede, we shall never tend to that which is right. Hence we are so often enjoined to put off the old man, to renounce the world and the flesh, to forsake our lusts, and be renewed in the spirit of our mind. Moreover, the very name *mortification* reminds us how difficult it is to forget our former nature, because we hence infer that we cannot be trained to the fear of God, and learn the first principles of piety, unless we are violently smitten with the sword of the Spirit and annihilated, as if God were declaring, that to be ranked among his sons there must be a destruction of our ordinary nature.

9. Both of these we obtain by union with Christ. For if we have true fellowship in his death, our old man is crucified by his power, and the body of sin becomes dead, so that the corruption of our original nature is never again in full vigor (Rom. 6:5, 6). If we are partakers in his resurrection, we are raised up by means of it to newness of life, which conforms us to the righteousness of God. In one word, then, by repentance I understand regeneration, the only aim of which is to form in us anew the image of God, which was sullied, and all but effaced by the transgression of Adam. So the Apostle teaches when he says, "We all with open face beholding as in a glass the glory of the Lord, are changed into the same image from glory to glory, as by the Spirit of the Lord." Again, "Be renewed in the spirit of your minds" and "put ye on the new man, which after God is created in righteousness and true holiness." Again, "Put ye on the new man, which is renewed in knowledge after the image of him that created him." Accordingly through the blessing of Christ we are renewed by that regeneration into the righteousness of God from which we had fallen through Adam, the Lord being pleased in this manner to restore the integrity of all whom he appoints to the inheritance of life. This renewal, indeed, is not accomplished in a moment, a day, or a year, but by uninterrupted, sometimes even by slow progress God abolishes the remains of carnal corruption in his elect, cleanses them from pollution, and consecrates them as his temples, restoring all their inclinations to real purity, so that during their whole lives they may practice repentance, and know that death is the only termination to this warfare. The greater is the effrontery of an impure raver and apostate, named Staphylus, who pretends that I

confound the condition of the present life with the celestial glory, when, after Paul, I make the image of God to consist in righteousness and true holiness; as if in every definition it were not necessary to take the thing defined in its integrity and perfection. It is not denied that there is room for improvement; but what I maintain is, that the nearer any one approaches in resemblance to God, the more does the image of God appear in him. That believers may attain to it, God assigns repentance as the goal towards which they must keep running during the whole course of their lives.

10. By regeneration the children of God are delivered from the bondage of sin, but not as if they had already obtained full possession of freedom, and no longer felt any annoyance from the flesh. Materials for an unremitting contest remain, that they may be exercised, and not only exercised, but may better understand their weakness. All writers of sound judgment agree in this, that, in the regenerate man, there is still a spring of evil which is perpetually sending forth desires that allure and stimulate him to sin. They also acknowledge that the saints are still so liable to the disease of concupiscence, that, though opposing it, they cannot avoid being ever and anon prompted and incited to lust, avarice, ambition, or other vices. It is unnecessary to spend much time in investigating the sentiments of ancient writers. Augustine alone may suffice, as he has collected all their opinions with great care and fidelity. Any reader who is desirous to know the sense of antiquity may obtain it from him. There is this difference apparently between him and us, that while he admits that believers, so long as they are in the body, are so liable to concupiscence that they cannot but feel it, he does not venture to give this disease the name of sin. He is contented with giving it the name of infirmity, and says, that it only becomes sin when either external act or consent is added to conception or apprehension; that is, when the will yields to the first desire. We again regard it as sin whenever man is influenced in any degree by any desire contrary to the law of God; nay, we maintain that the very gravity which begets in us such desires is sin. Accordingly, we hold that there is always sin in the saints until they are freed from their mortal frame, because depraved concupiscence resides in their flesh, and is at variance with rectitude. Augustine himself dose not always refrain from using the name of sin, as when he says, "Paul gives the name of sin to that carnal concupiscence from which all sins arise. This in regard to the saints loses its dominion in this world, and is destroyed in heaven." In these words he admits that believers, in so far as they are liable to carnal concupiscence, are chargeable with sin.

11. When it is said that God purifies his Church, so as to be "holy and without blemish" (Eph. 5:26, 27), that he promises this cleansing by means of baptism, and performs it in his elect, I understand that reference is made to the guilt rather than to the matter of sin. In regenerating his people God indeed accomplishes this much for them; he destroys the dominion of sin, by supplying the agency of the Spirit, which enables them to come off victorious from the contest. Sin, however, though it ceases to reign, ceases not to dwell in them. Accordingly, though we say that the old man is crucified, and the law of sin is abolished in the children of God (Rom. 6:6), the remains of sin survive, not to have dominion, but to humble them under a consciousness of their infirmity. We admit that these remains, just as if they had no existence, are not imputed, but we, at the same time, contend that it is owing to the mercy of God that the saints are not charged with the guilt which would otherwise make them sinners before God. It will not be difficult for us to confirm this view, seeing we can support it by clear passages of Scripture. How can we express our view more plainly than Paul does in Rom. 7:6? We have elsewhere shown and Augustine by solid reasons proves, that Paul is there speaking in the person of a regenerated man. I say nothing as to his use of the words evil and sin. However those who object to our view may quibble on these words, can any man deny that aversion to the law of God is an evil, and that hindrance to righteousness is sin? In short, who will not admit that there is guilt where there is spiritual misery? But all these things Paul affirms of this disease. Again, the law furnishes us with a clear demonstration by which the whole question may be quickly disposed of. We are enjoined to love God with all our heart, with all our soul, with all our strength. Since all the faculties of our soul ought thus to be engrossed with the love of God, it is certain that the commandment is not fulfilled by those who receive the smallest desire into their heart, or admit into their minds any thought whatever which may lead them away from the love of God to vanity. What then? Is it not through the faculties of mind that we are assailed with sudden motions, that we perceive sensual, or form conceptions of mental objects? Since these faculties give admission to vain and wicked thoughts, do they not show that to that extent they are devoid of the love of God? He, then, who admits not that all the desires of the flesh are sins, and that that disease of concupiscence, which they call a

stimulus, is a fountain of sin, must of necessity deny that the transgression of the law is sin.

12. If any one thinks it absurd thus to condemn all the desires by which man is naturally affected, seeing they have been implanted by God the author of nature, we answer, that we by no means condemn those appetites which God so implanted in the mind of man at his first creation, that they cannot be eradicated without destroying human nature itself, but only the violent lawless movements which war with the order of God. But as, in consequence of the corruption of nature, all our faculties are so vitiated and corrupted, that a perpetual disorder and excess is apparent in all our actions, and as the appetites cannot be separated from this excess, we maintain that therefore they are vicious; or, to give the substance in fewer words, we hold that all human desires are evil, and we charge them with sin not in as far as they are natural, but because they are inordinate, and inordinate because nothing pure and upright can proceed from a corrupt and polluted nature. Nor does Augustine depart from this doctrine in reality so much as in appearance. From an excessive dread of the invidious charge with which the Pelagians assailed him, he sometimes refrains from using the term sin in this sense; but when he says (ad Bonif). that *the law of sin remaining in the saints, the guilt only is taken away*, he shows clearly enough that his view is not very different from ours.

13. We will produce some other passages to make it more apparent what his sentiments were. In his second book against Julian, he says, "This law of sin is both remitted in spiritual regeneration and remains in the mortal flesh; remitted, because the guilt is forgiven in the sacrament by which believers are regenerated, and yet remains, inasmuch as it produces desires against which believers fight." Again, "Therefore the law of sin (which was in the members of this great Apostle also) is forgiven in baptism, not ended." Again, "The law of sin, the guilt of which, though remaining, is forgiven in baptism, Ambrose called iniquity, for it is iniquitous for the flesh to lust against the Spirit." Again, "Sin is dead in the guilt by which it bound us; and until it is cured by the perfection of burial, though dead it rebels." In the fifth book he says still more plainly, "As blindness of heart is the sin by which God is not believed; and the punishment of sin, by which a proud heart is justly punished; and the cause of sin, when through the error of a blinded heart any evil is committed: so the lust of the flesh, against which the good Spirit wars, is also sin, because disobedient to the authority of the mind; and the punishment of sin, because the recompense rendered for disobedience; and the cause of sin, consenting by revolt or springing up through contamination." He here without ambiguity calls it sin, because the Pelagian heresy being now refuted, and the sound doctrine confirmed, he was less afraid of calumny. Thus, also, in his forty-first Homily on John, where he speaks his own sentiments without controversy, he says, "If with the flesh you serve the law of sin, do what the Apostle himself says, 'Let not sin, therefore, reign in your mortal body, that ye should obey it in the lusts thereof,' (Rom. 6:12). He does not say, *Let it not be*, but *Let it not reign*. As long as you live there must be sin in your members; but at least let its dominion be destroyed; do not what it orders." Those who maintain that concupiscence is not sin, are wont to found on the passage of James, "Then, when lust has conceived, it bringeth forth sin" (James 1:15). But this is easily refuted: for unless we understand him as speaking only of wicked works or actual sins, even a wicked inclination will not be accounted sin. But from his calling crimes and wicked deeds the fruits of lust, and also giving them the name of sins, it does not follow that the lust itself is not an evil, and in the sight of God deserving of condemnation.

14. Some Anabaptists in the present age mistake some indescribable sort of frenzied excess for the regeneration of the Spirit, holding that the children of God are restored to a state of innocence, and, therefore, need give themselves no anxiety about curbing the lust of the flesh; that they have the Spirit for their guide, and under his agency never err. It would be incredible that the human mind could proceed to such insanity, did they not openly and exultingly give utterance to their dogma. It is indeed monstrous, and yet it is just, that those who have resolved to turn the word of God into a lie, should thus be punished for their blasphemous audacity. Is it indeed true, that all distinction between base and honorable, just and unjust, good and evil, virtue and vice, is abolished? The distinction, they say, is from the curse of the old Adam, and from this we are exempted by Christ. There will be no difference, then, between whoredom and chastity, sincerity and craft, truth and falsehood, justice and robbery. Away with vain fear! (they say), the Spirit will not bid you do any thing that is wrong, provided you sincerely and boldly leave yourself to his agency. Who is not amazed at such monstrous doctrines? And yet this philosophy is popular with those who, blinded by insane lusts, have thrown off common sense. But what kind of Christ, pray, do they fabricate? what kind of Spirit do they belch forth? We acknowledge one Christ, and his one Spirit,

whom the prophets foretold and the Gospel proclaims as actually manifested, but we hear nothing of this kind respecting him. That Spirit is not the patron of murder, adultery, drunkenness, pride, contention, avarice, and fraud, but the author of love, chastity, sobriety, modesty, peace, moderation, and truth. He is not a Spirit of giddiness, rushing rashly and precipitately, without regard to right and wrong, but full of wisdom and understanding, by which he can duly distinguish between justice and injustice. He instigates not to lawless and unrestrained licentiousness, but, discriminating between lawful and unlawful, teaches temperance and moderation. But why dwell longer in refuting that brutish frenzy? To Christians the Spirit of the Lord is not a turbulent phantom, which they themselves have produced by dreaming, or received ready-made by others; but they religiously seek the knowledge of him from Scripture, where two things are taught concerning him; *first*, that he is given to us for sanctification, that he may purge us from all iniquity and defilement, and bring us to the obedience of divine righteousness, an obedience which cannot exist unless the lusts to which these men would give loose reins are tamed and subdued; *secondly* that though purged by his sanctification, we are still beset by many vices and much weakness, so long as we are enclosed in the prison of the body. Thus it is, that placed at a great distance from perfection, we must always be endeavoring to make some progress, and daily struggling with the evil by which we are entangled. Hence, too, it follows, that, shaking off sloth and security, we must be intently vigilant, so as not to be taken unawares in the snares of our flesh; unless, indeed, we presume to think that we have made greater progress than the Apostle, who was buffeted by a messenger of Satan, in order that his strength might be perfected in weakness, and who gives in his own person a true, not a fictitious representation, of the strife between the Spirit and the flesh (2 Cor. 12:7, 9; Rom. 7:6).

15. The Apostle, in his description of repentance (2 Cor. 7:2), enumerates seven causes, effects, or parts belonging to it, and that on the best grounds. These are carefulness, excuse, indignation fear, desire, zeal, revenge. It should not excite surprise that I venture not to determine whether they ought to be regarded as causes or effects: both views may be maintained. They may also be called affections conjoined with repentance; but as Paul's meaning may be ascertained without entering into any of these questions, we shall be contented with a simple exposition. He says then that godly sorrow produces *carefulness*. He who is really dissatisfied with himself for sinning against his God, is, at the same time, stimulated to care and attention, that he may completely disentangle himself from the chains of the devil, and keep a better guard against his snares, so as not afterwards to lose the guidance of the Holy Spirit, or be overcome by security. Next comes excuse, which in this place means not defense, in which the sinner to escape the judgment of God either denies his fault or extenuates it, but apologizing, which trusts more to intercession than to the goodness of the cause; just as children not altogether abandoned, while they acknowledge and confess their errors, yet employ deprecation; and to make room for it, testify, by every means in their power, that they have by no means cast off the reverence which they owe to their parents; in short, endeavor by excuse not to prove themselves righteous and innocent, but only to obtain pardon. Next follows *indignation*, under which the sinner inwardly murmurs expostulates, and is offended with himself on recognizing his perverseness and ingratitude to God. By the term fear is meant that trepidation which takes possession of our minds whenever we consider both what we have deserved, and the fearful severity of the divine anger against sinners. Accordingly, the exceeding disquietude which we must necessarily feel, both trains us to humility and makes us more cautious for the future. But if the carefulness or anxiety which he first mentioned is the result of fear, the connection between the two becomes obvious. *Desire* seems to me to be used as equivalent to diligence in duty, and alacrity in doing service, to which the sense of our misdeeds ought to be a powerful stimulus. To this also pertains zeal, which immediately follows; for it signifies the ardor with which we are inflamed when such goads as these are applied to us. "What have I done? Into what abyss had I fallen had not the mercy of God prevented?" The last of all is *revenge*, for the stricter we are with ourselves, and the severer the censure we pass upon our sins, the more ground we have to hope for the divine favor and mercy. And certainly when the soul is overwhelmed with a dread of divine judgment, it cannot but act the part of an avenger in inflicting punishment upon itself. Pious men, doubtless, feel that there is punishment in the shame, confusion, groans, self-displeasure, and other feelings produced by a serious review of their sins. Let us remember, however, that moderation must be used, so that we may not be overwhelmed with sadness, there being nothing to which trembling consciences are more prone than to rush into despair. This, too, is one of Satan's artifices. Those whom he sees thus overwhelmed with fear he plunges deeper and deeper into the abyss

of sorrow, that they may never again rise. It is true that the fear which ends in humility without relinquishing the hope of pardon cannot be in excess. And yet we must always beware, according to the apostolic injunction, of giving way to extreme dread, as this tends to make us shun God while he is calling us to himself by repentance. Wherefore, the advice of Bernard is good, "Grief for sins is necessary, but must not be perpetual. My advice is to turn back at times from sorrow and the anxious remembrance of your ways, and escape to the plain, to a calm review of the divine mercies. Let us mingle honey with wormwood, that the salubrious bitter may give health when we drink it tempered with a mixture of sweetness: while you think humbly of yourselves, think also of the goodness of the Lord" (Bernard in Cant. Serm. 11).

16. We can now understand what are the fruits of repentance—viz. offices of piety towards God, and love towards men, general holiness and purity of life. In short, the more a man studies to conform his life to the standard of the divine law, the surer signs he gives of his repentance. Accordingly, the Spirit, in exhorting us to repentance, brings before us at one time each separate precept of the law; at another the duties of the second table; although there are also passages in which, after condemning impurity in its fountain in the heart, he afterwards descends to external marks, by which repentance is proved to be sincere. A portraiture of this I will shortly set before the eye of the reader when I come to describe the Christian life (*infra*, chapter 6) I will not here collect the passages from the prophets in which they deride the frivolous observances of those who labour to appease God with ceremonies, and show that they are mere mockery; or those in which they show that outward integrity of conduct is not the chief part of repentance, seeing that God looks at the heart. Any one moderately versant in Scripture will understand by himself, without being reminded by others, that when he has to do with God, nothing is gained without beginning with the internal affections of the heart. There is a passage of Joel which will avail not a little for the understanding of others: "Rend your heart, and not your garments" (Joel 2:13). Both are also briefly expressed by James in these words: "Cleanse your hands, ye sinners; and purify your hearts, ye double-minded" (James 4:8). Here, indeed, the accessory is set down first; but the source and principle is afterwards pointed out—viz. that hidden defilements must be wiped away, and an altar erected to God in the very heart. There are, moreover, certain external exercises which we employ in private as remedies to humble us and tame our flesh, and in public, to testify our repentance. These have their origin in that revenge of which Paul speaks (2 Cor. 7:2), for when the mind is distressed, it naturally expresses itself in sackcloth, groans, and tears, shuns ornament and every kind of show, and abandons all delights. Then he who feels how great an evil the rebellion of the flesh is, tries every means of curbing it. Besides, he who considers aright how grievous a thing it is to have offended the justice of God, cannot rest until, in his humility, he have given glory to God. Such exercises are often mentioned by ancient writers when they speak of the fruits of repentance. But although they by no means place the power of repentance in them, yet my readers must pardon me for saying what I think—they certainly seem to insist on them more than is right. Any one who judiciously considers the matter will, I trust, agree with me that they have exceeded in two ways; first, by so strongly urging and extravagantly commending that corporal discipline, they indeed succeeded in making the people embrace it with greater zeal; but they in a manner obscured what they should have regarded as of much more serious moment. Secondly, the inflictions which they enjoined were considerably more rigorous than ecclesiastical mildness demands, as will be elsewhere shown.

17. But as there are some who, from the frequent mention of sackcloth, fasting, and tears, especially in Joel (2:12), think that these constitute the principal part of repentance, we must dispel their delusion. In that passage the proper part of repentance is described by the words, "turn ye even to me with your whole heart;" "rend your heart, and not your garments." The "fastings", "weeping," and "mourning," are introduced not as invariable or necessary effects, but as special circumstances. Having foretold that most grievous disasters were impending over the Jews, he exhorts them to turn away the divine anger not only by repenting, but by giving public signs of sorrow. For as a criminal, to excite the commiseration of the judge, appears in a supplicating posture, with a long beard, uncombed hair, and coarse clothing, so should those who are charged at the judgment-seat of God deprecate his severity in a garb of wretchedness. But although sackcloth and ashes were perhaps more conformable to the customs of these times, yet it is plain that weeping and fasting are very appropriate in our case whenever the Lord threatens us with any defeat or calamity. In presenting the appearance of danger, he declares that he is preparing, and, in a manner, arming himself for vengeance. Rightly, therefore, does the Prophet exhort those, on whose crimes he had said a little before that vengeance

was to be executed, to weeping and fasting,—that is, to the mourning habit of criminals. Nor in the present day do ecclesiastical teachers act improperly when, seeing ruin hanging over the necks of their people, they call aloud on them to hasten with weeping and fasting: only they must always urge, with greater care and earnestness, "rend your hearts, and not your garments." It is beyond doubt that fasting is not always a concomitant of repentance, but is specially destined for seasons of calamity. Hence our Savior connects it with mourning (Mt. 9:15), and relieves the Apostles of the necessity of it until, by being deprived of his presence, they were filled with sorrow. I speak of formal fasting. For the life of Christians ought ever to be tempered with frugality and sobriety, so that the whole course of it should present some appearance of fasting. As this subject will be fully discussed when the discipline of the Church comes to be considered, I now dwell less upon it.

18. This much, however, I will add: when the name *repentance* is applied to the external profession, it is used improperly, and not in the genuine meaning as I have explained it. For that is not so much a turning unto God as the confession of a fault accompanied with deprecation of the sentence and punishment. Thus to repent in sackcloth and ashes (Mt. 11:21; Luke 10:13), is just to testify self dissatisfaction when God is angry with us for having grievously offended him. It is, indeed, a kind of public confession by which, condemning ourselves before angels and the world, we prevent the judgment of God. For Paul, rebuking the sluggishness of those who indulge in their sins, says, "If we would judge ourselves, we should not be judged" (1 Cor. 11:31). It is not always necessary, however, openly to inform others, and make them the witnesses of our repentance; but to confess privately to God is a part of true repentance which cannot be omitted. Nothing were more incongruous than that God should pardon the sins in which we are flattering ourselves, and hypocritically cloaking that he may not bring them to light. We must not only confess the sins which we daily commit, but more grievous lapses ought to carry us farther, and bring to our remembrance things which seemed to have been long ago buried. Of this David sets an example before us in his own person (Ps. 51). Filled with shame for a recent crime he examines himself, going back to the womb, and acknowledging that even then he was corrupted and defiled. This he does not to extenuate his fault, as many hide themselves in the crowd, and catch at impunity by involving others along with them. Very differently does David, who ingenuously makes it an aggravation of his sin, that being corrupted from his earliest infancy he ceased not to add iniquity to iniquity. In another passage, also, he takes a survey of his past life, and implores God to pardon the errors of his youth (Ps. 25:7). And, indeed, we shall not prove that we have thoroughly shaken off our stupor until, groaning under the burden, and lamenting our sad condition, we seek relief from God. It is, moreover to be observed, that the repentance which we are enjoined assiduously to cultivate, differs from that which raises, as it were, from death those who had fallen more shamefully, or given themselves up to sin without restraint, or by some kind of open revolt, had thrown off the authority of God. For Scripture, in exhorting to repentance, often speaks of it as a passage from death unto life, and when relating that a people had repented, means that they had abandoned idolatry, and other forms of gross wickedness. For which reason Paul denounces woe to sinners, "who have not repented of the uncleanness, and fornication, and lasciviousness which they have committed" (2 Cor. 12:21). This distinction ought to be carefully observed, lest when we hear of a few individuals having been summoned to repent we indulge in supine security, as if we had nothing to do with the mortification of the flesh; whereas, in consequence of the depraved desires which are always enticing us, and the iniquities which are ever and anon springing from them, it must engage our unremitting care. The special repentance enjoined upon those whom the devil has entangled in deadly snares, and withdrawn from the fear of God, does not abolish that ordinary repentance which the corruption of nature obliges us to cultivate during the whole course of our lives.

19. Moreover if it is true, and nothing can be more certain, than that a complete summary of the Gospel is included under these two heads—viz. repentance and the remission of sins, do we not see that the Lord justifies his people freely, and at the same time renews them to true holiness by the sanctification of his Spirit? John, the messenger sent before the face of Christ to prepare his ways, proclaimed, "repent, for the kingdom of heaven is at hand" (Mt. 11:10; 3:2). By inviting them to repentance, he urged them to acknowledge that they were sinners, and in all respects condemned before God, that thus they might be induced earnestly to seek the mortification of the flesh, and a new birth in the Spirit. By announcing the kingdom of God he called for faith, since by the kingdom of God which he declared to be at hand, he meant forgiveness of sins, salvation, life, and every other blessing which we obtain in Christ; wherefore we read in the

other Evangelists, "John did baptize in the wilderness, and preach the baptism of repentance for the remission of sins" (Mark 1:4; Luke 3:3). What does this mean, but that, weary and oppressed with the burden of sin, they should turn to the Lord, and entertain hopes of forgiveness and salvation? Thus, too, Christ began his preaching, "The kingdom of God is at hand: repent ye, and believe the Gospel" (Mark 1:10). First, he declares that the treasures of the divine mercy were opened in him; next, he enjoins repentance; and, lastly, he encourages confidence in the promises of God. Accordingly, when intending to give a brief summary of the whole Gospel, he said that he behaved "to suffer, and to rise from the dead the third day, and that repentance and remission of sins should be preached in his name among all nations" (Luke 24:26, 46). In like manner, after his resurrection the Apostles preached, "Him has God exalted with his right hand, to be a Prince and a Savior, for to give repentance to Israel and forgiveness of sins" (Acts 5:31). Repentance is preached in the name of Christ, when men learn, through the doctrines of the Gospel, that all their thoughts, affections, and pursuits, are corrupt and vicious; and that, therefore, if they would enter the kingdom of God they must be born again. Forgiveness of sins is preached when men are taught that Christ "is made unto us wisdom, and righteousness, and sanctification, and redemption" (1 Cor. 1:30), that on his account they are freely deemed righteous and innocent in the sight of God. Though both graces are obtained by faith (as has been shown elsewhere), yet as the goodness of God, by which sins are forgiven, is the proper object of faith, it was proper carefully to distinguish it from repentance.

20. Moreover, as hatred of sin, which is the beginning of repentance, first gives us access to the knowledge of Christ, who manifests himself to none but miserable and afflicted sinners, groaning, laboring, burdened, hungry, and thirsty, pining away with grief and wretchedness, so if we would stand in Christ, we must aim at repentance, cultivate it during our whole lives, and continue it to the last. Christ came to call sinners, but to call them to repentance. He was sent to bless the unworthy, but by "turning away every one" "from his iniquities." The Scripture is full of similar passages. Hence, when God offers forgiveness of sins, he in return usually stipulates for repentance, intimating that his mercy should induce men to repent. "Keep ye judgment," saith he, "and do justice: for my salvation is near to come." Again, "The Redeemer shall come to Zion, and unto them that turn from transgression in Jacob." Again, "Seek ye the Lord while he may be found, call ye upon him while he is near. Let the wicked forsake his way, and the unrighteous man his thoughts, and let him return unto the Lord, and he will have mercy upon him." "Repent ye, therefore, and be converted, that your sins may be blotted out." Here, however, it is to be observed, that repentance is not made a condition in such a sense as to be a foundation for meriting pardon; nay, it rather indicates the end at which they must aim if they would obtain favor, God having resolved to take pity on men for the express purpose of leading them to repent. Therefore, so long as we dwell in the prison of the body, we must constantly struggle with the vices of our corrupt nature, and so with our natural disposition. Plato sometimes says, that the life of the philosopher is to meditate on death. More truly may we say, that the life of a Christian man is constant study and exercise in mortifying the flesh, until it is certainly slain, and the Spirit of God obtains dominion in us. Wherefore, he seems to me to have made most progress who has learned to be most dissatisfied with himself. He does not, however, remain in the miry clay without going forward; but rather hastens and sighs after God, that, ingrafted both into the death and the life of Christ, he may constantly meditate on repentance. Unquestionably those who have a genuine hatred of sin cannot do otherwise: for no man ever hated sin without being previously enamored of righteousness. This view, as it is the simplest of all, seemed to me also to accord best with Scripture truth.

21. Moreover, that repentance is a special gift of God, I trust is too well understood from the above doctrine to require any lengthened discourse. Hence the Church extols the goodness of God, and looks on in wonder, saying, "Then has God also to the Gentiles granted repentance unto life" (Acts 11:18); and Paul enjoining Timothy to deal meekly and patiently with unbelievers, says, "If God per adventure will give them repentance to the acknowledging of the truth, and that they may recover themselves out of the snare of the devil" (2 Tim. 2:25, 26). God indeed declares, that he would have all men to repent, and addresses exhortations in common to all; their efficacy, however, depends on the Spirit of regeneration. It were easier to create us at first, than for us by our own strength to acquire a more excellent nature. Wherefore, in regard to the whole process of regeneration, it is not without cause we are called God's "workmanship, created in Christ Jesus unto good works, which God has before ordained that we should walk in them" (Eph. 2:10) Those whom God is pleased to rescue from death, he quickens by the Spirit of regeneration; not that

repentance is properly the cause of salvation, but because, as already seen, it is inseparable from the faith and mercy of God; for, as Isaiah declares, "The Redeemer shall come to Zion, and unto them that turn from transgression in Jacob." This, indeed, is a standing truth, that wherever the fear of God is in vigor, the Spirit has been carrying on his saving work. Hence, in Isaiah, while believers complain and lament that they have been forsaken of God, they set down the supernatural hardening of the heart as a sign of reprobation. The Apostle, also, intending to exclude apostates from the hope of salvation, states, as the reason, that it is impossible to renew them to repentance (Heb. 6:6); that is, God by renewing those whom he wills not to perish, gives them a sign of paternal favor, and in a manner attracts them to himself, by the beams of a calm and reconciled countenance; on the other hand, by hardening the reprobate, whose impiety is not to be forgiven, he thunders against them. This kind of vengeance the Apostle denounces against voluntary apostates (Heb. 10:29), who, in falling away from the faith of the gospel, mock God, insultingly reject his favor, profane and trample under foot the blood of Christ, nay, as far as in them lies, crucify him afresh. Still, he does not, as some austere persons preposterously insist, leave no hope of pardon to voluntary sins, but shows that apostasy being altogether without excuse, it is not strange that God is inexorably rigorous in punishing sacrilegious contempt thus shown to himself. For, in the same Epistle, he says, that "it is impossible for those who were once enlightened, and have tasted of the heavenly gift, and were made partakers of the Holy Ghost, and have tasted the good word of God, and the powers of the world to come, if they shall fall away to renew them again to repentance, seeing they crucify the Son of God afresh, and put him to an open shame" (Heb. 7:4–6). And in another passage, "If we sin willingly, after that we have received the knowledge of the truth, there remaineth no more sacrifice for sins, but a certain fearful looking for of judgment," &c. (Heb. 11:25, 26). There are other passages, from a misinterpretation of which the Novatians of old extracted materials for their heresy; so much so, that some good men taking offense at their harshness, have deemed the Epistle altogether spurious, though it truly savors in every part of it of the apostolic spirit. But as our dispute is only with those who receive the Epistle, it is easy to show that those passages give no support to their error. First, the Apostle must of necessity agree with his Master, who declares, that "all manner of sin and blasphemy shall be forgiven unto men, but the blasphemy against the Holy Ghost shall not be forgiven unto men," "neither in this world, neither in the world to come" (Mt. 12:31; Luke 12:10). We must hold that this was the only exception which the Apostle recognized, unless we would set him in opposition to the grace of God. Hence it follows, that to no sin is pardon denied save to one, which proceeding from desperate fury cannot be ascribed to infirmity, and plainly shows that the man guilty of it is possessed by the devil.

22. Here, however, it is proper to consider what the dreadful iniquity is which is not to be pardoned. The definition which Augustine somewhere gives—viz. that it is obstinate perverseness, with distrust of pardon, continued till death,—scarcely agrees with the words of Christ, that it shall not be forgiven in this world. For either this is said in vain, or it may be committed in this world. But if Augustine's definition is correct, the sin is not committed unless persisted in till death. Others say, that the sin against the Holy Spirit consists in envying the grace conferred upon a brother; but I know not on what it is founded. Here, however, let us give the true definition, which, when once it is established by sound evidence, will easily of itself overturn all the others. I say therefore that he sins against the Holy Spirit who, while so constrained by the power of divine truth that he cannot plead ignorance, yet deliberately resists, and that merely for the sake of resisting. For Christ, in explanation of what he had said, immediately adds, "Whosoever speaketh a word against the Son of man, it shall be forgiven him; but whosoever speaketh against the holy Ghost, it shall not be forgiven him" (Mt. 12:31). And Matthew uses the term spirit of blasphemy for blasphemy against the Spirit. How can any one insult the Son, without at the same time attacking the Spirit? In this way. Those who in ignorance assail the unknown truth of God, and yet are so disposed that they would be unwilling to extinguish the truth of God when manifested to them, or utter one word against him whom they knew to be the Lord's Anointed, sin against the Father and the Son. Thus there are many in the present day who have the greatest abhorrence to the doctrine of the Gospel, and yet, if they knew it to be the doctrine of the Gospel, would be prepared to venerate it with their whole heart. But those who are convinced in conscience that what they repudiate and impugn is the word of God, and yet cease not to impugn it, are said to blaspheme against the Spirit, inasmuch as they struggle against the illumination which is the work of the Spirit. Such were some of the Jews, who, when they could not resist the Spirit speaking by Stephen, yet were bent on resisting (Acts 6:10). There can be no doubt

that many of them were carried away by zeal for the law; but it appears that there were others who maliciously and impiously raged against God himself, that is, against the doctrine which they knew to be of God. Such, too, were the Pharisees, on whom our Lord denounced woe. To depreciate the power of the Holy Spirit, they defamed him by the name of Beelzebub (Mt. 9:3, 4; 12:24). The spirit of blasphemy, therefore, is, when a man audaciously, and of set purpose, rushes forth to insult his divine name. This Paul intimates when he says, "but I obtained mercy, because I did it ignorantly in unbelief;" otherwise he had deservedly been held unworthy of the grace of God. If ignorance joined with unbelief made him obtain pardon, it follows, that there is no room for pardon when knowledge is added to unbelief.

23. If you attend properly, you will perceive that the Apostle speaks not of one particular lapse or two, but of the universal revolt by which the reprobate renounce salvation. It is not strange that God should be implacable to those whom John, in his Epistle, declares not to have been of the elect, from whom they went out (1 John 2:19). For he is directing his discourse against those who imagined that they could return to the Christian religion though they had once revolted from it. To divest them of this false and pernicious opinion, he says, as is most true, that those who had once knowingly and willingly cast off fellowship with Christ, had no means of returning to it. It is not, however so cast off by those who merely, by the dissoluteness of their lives, transgress the word of the Lord, but by those who avowedly reject his whole doctrine. There is a paralogism in the expression *casting off* and *sinning*. *Casting off*, as interpreted by the Novatians, is when any one, notwithstanding of being taught by the Law of the Lord not to steal or commit adultery, refrains not from theft or adultery. On the contrary, I hold that there is a tacit antithesis, in which all the things, contrary to those which had been said, must be held to be repeated, so that the thing expressed is not some particular vice, but universal aversion to God, and (so to speak) the apostasy of the whole man. Therefore, when he speaks of those falling away "who were once enlightened, and have tasted of the heavenly gift, and were made partakers of the Holy Ghost, and have tasted of the good word of God, and the powers of the world to come," we must understand him as referring to those who, with deliberate impiety, have quenched the light of the Spirit, tasted of the heavenly word and spurned it, alienated themselves from the sanctification of the Spirit, and trampled under foot the word of God and the powers of a world to come. The better to show that this was the species of impiety intended, he afterwards expressly adds the term *willfully*. For when he says, "If we sin willfully, after that we have received the knowledge of the truth, there remaineth no more sacrifice for sins," he denies not that Christ is a perpetual victim to expiate the transgressions of saints (this the whole Epistle, in explaining the priesthood of Christ, distinctly proclaims), but he says that there remains no other sacrifice after this one is abandoned. And it is abandoned when the truth of the Gospel is professedly abjured.

24. To some it seems harsh, and at variance with the divine mercy, utterly to deny forgiveness to any who retake themselves to it. This is easily disposed of. It is not said that pardon will be refused if they turn to the Lord, but it is altogether denied that they can turn to repentance, inasmuch as for their ingratitude they are struck by the just judgment of God with eternal blindness. There is nothing contrary to this in the application which is afterwards made of the example of Esau, who tried in vain, by crying and tears, to recover his lost birthright; nor in the denunciation of the Prophet, "They cried, and I would not hear." Such modes of expression do not denote true conversion or calling upon God, but that anxiety with which the wicked, when in calamity, are compelled to see what they before securely disregarded—viz. that nothing can avail but the assistance of the Lord. This, however, they do not so much implore as lament the loss of. Hence all that the Prophet means by crying, and the apostle by tears, is the dreadful torment which stings and excruciates the wicked in despair. It is of consequence carefully to observe this: for otherwise God would be inconsistent with himself when he proclaims through the Prophet, that "If the wicked will turn from all his sins that he has committed,"—"he shall surely live, he shall not die" (Ezek. 18:21, 22). And (as I have already said) it is certain that the mind of man cannot be changed for the better unless by his preventing grace. The promise as to those who call upon him will never fail; but the names of conversion and prayer are improperly given to that blind torment by which the reprobate are distracted when they see that they must seek God if they would find a remedy for their calamities, and yet shun to approach him.

25. But as the Apostle declares that God is not appeased by feigned repentance, it is asked how Ahab obtained pardon, and averted the punishment denounced against him (1 Kings 21:28, 29), seeing, it appears, he was only amazed on the sudden, and afterwards continued

his former course of life. He, indeed, clothed himself in sackcloth, covered himself with ashes, lay on the ground, and (as the testimony given to him bears) humbled himself before God. It was a small matter to rend his garments while his heart continued obstinate and swollen with wickedness, and yet we see that God was inclined to mercy. I answer, that though hypocrites are thus occasionally spared for a time, the wrath of God still lies upon them, and that they are thus spared not so much on their own account as for a public example. For what did Ahab gain by the mitigation of his punishment except that he did not suffer it alive on the earth? The curse of God, though concealed, was fixed on his house, and he himself went to eternal destruction. We may see the same thing in Esau (Gen. 27:38, 39). For though he met with a refusal, a temporal blessing was granted to his tears. But as, according to the declaration of God, the spiritual inheritance could be possessed only by one of the brothers, when Jacob was selected instead of Esau, that event excluded him from the divine mercy; but still there was given to him, as a man of a groveling nature, this consolation, that he should be filled with the fulness of the earth and the dew of heaven. And this, as I lately said, should be regarded as done for the example of others, that we may learn to apply our minds, and exert ourselves with greater alacrity, in the way of sincere repentance, as there cannot be the least doubt that God will be ready to pardon those who turn to him truly and with the heart, seeing his mercy extends even to the unworthy though they bear marks of his displeasure. In this way also, we are taught how dreadful the judgment is which awaits all the rebellious who with audacious brow and iron heart make it their sport to despise and disregard the divine threatening. God in this way often stretched forth his hand to deliver the Israelites from their calamities, though their cries were pretended, and their minds double and perfidious, as he himself complains in the Psalms, that they immediately returned to their former course (Psalm 78:36, 37). But he designed thus by kindness and forbearance to bring them to true repentance, or leave them without excuse. And yet by remitting the punishment for a time, he does not lay himself under any perpetual obligation. He rather at times rises with greater severity against hypocrites, and doubles their punishment, that it may thereby appear how much hypocrisy displeases him. But, as I have observed, he gives some examples of his inclination to pardon, that the pious may thereby be stimulated to amend their lives, and the pride of those who petulantly kick against the pricks be more severely condemned.

CHAPTER 4

PENITENCE, AS EXPLAINED IN THE SOPHISTICAL JARGON OF THE SCHOOLMEN, WIDELY DIFFERENT FROM THE PURITY REQUIRED BY THE GOSPEL. OF CONFESSION AND SATISFACTION.

The divisions of this chapter are,—I. The orthodox doctrine of repentance being already expounded, the false doctrine is refuted in the present chapter; a general summary survey being at the same time taken of the doctrine of the Schoolmen, sec. 1, 2. II. Its separate parts are afterwards examined. Contrition, sec. 2 and 3. Confession, sec. 4–20. Sanctification, from sec. 20 to the end of the chapter.

Sections:

1. Errors of the Schoolmen in delivering the doctrine of repentance. 1. Errors in defining it. Four different definitions considered. 2. Absurd division. 3. Vain and puzzling questions. 4. Mode in which they entangle themselves.

2. The false doctrine of the Schoolmen necessary to be refuted. Of contrition. Their view of it examined.

3. True and genuine contrition.

4. Auricular confession. Whether or not of divine authority. Arguments of Canonists and Schoolmen. Allegorical argument founded on Judaism. Two answers. Reason why Christ sent the lepers to the priests.

5. Another allegorical argument. Answer.

6. A third argument from two passages of Scripture. These passages expounded.

7. Confession proved not to be of divine authority. The use of it free for almost twelve hundred years after Christ. Its nature. When enacted into a law. Confirmation from the history of the Church. A representation of the ancient auricular confession still existing among the Papists, to bear judgment against them. Confession abolished in the Church of Constantinople.

8. This mode of confession disapproved by Chrysostom, as shown by many passages.

9. False confession being thus refuted, the confession enjoined by the word of God is considered. Mistranslation in the old version. Proof from Scripture that confession should be directed to God alone.

10. Effect of secret confession thus made to God. Another kind of confession made to men.

11. Two forms of the latter confession—viz. pub-

lic and private. Public confession either ordinary or extraordinary. Use of each. Objection to confession and public prayer. Answer.

12. Private confession of two kinds. 1. On our own account. 2. On account of our neighbor. Use of the former. Great assistance to be obtained from faithful ministers of the Church. Mode of procedure. Caution to be used.

13. The use of the latter recommended by Christ. What comprehended under it. Scripture sanctions no other method of confession.

14. The power of the keys exercised in these three kinds of confession. The utility of this power in regard to public confession and absolution. Caution to be observed.

15. Popish errors respecting confession. 1. In enjoining on all the necessity of confessing every sin. 2. Fictitious keys. 3. Pretended mandate to loose and bind. 4. To whom the office of loosing and binding committed.

16. Refutation of the first error, from the impossibility of so confessing, as proved by the testimony of David.

17. Refuted farther from the testimony of conscience. Impossible to observe this most rigid obligation. Necessarily leads to despair or indifference. Confirmation of the preceding remarks by an appeal to conscience.

18. Another refutation of the first error from analogy. Sum of the whole refutation. Third refutation, laying down the surest rule of confession. Explanation of the rule. Three objections answered.

19. Fourth objection—viz. that auricular confession does no harm, and is even useful. Answer, unfolding the hypocrisy, falsehood, impiety, and monstrous abominations of the patrons of this error.

20. Refutation of the second error. 1. Priests not successors of the Apostles. 2. They have not the Holy Spirit, who alone is arbiter of the keys.

21. Refutation of the third error. 1. They are ignorant of the command and promise of Christ. By abandoning the word of God they run into innumerable absurdities.

22. Objection to the refutation of the third error. Answers, reducing the Papists to various absurdities.

23. Refutation of the fourth error. 1. Petitio principii. 2. Inversion of ecclesiastical discipline. Three objections answered.

24. Conclusion of the whole discussion against this fictitious confession.

25. Of satisfaction, to which the Sophists assign the third place in repentance. Errors and falsehoods. These views opposed by the terms,—1. Forgiveness. 2. Free forgiveness. 3. God destroying iniquities. 4. By and on account of Christ. No need of our satisfaction.

26. Objection, confining the grace and efficacy of Christ within narrow limits. Answers by both John the Evangelist and John the Baptist. Consequence of these answers.

27. Two points violated by the fiction of satisfaction. First, the honor of Christ impaired. Secondly, the conscience cannot find peace. Objection, confining the forgiveness of sins to Catechumens, refuted.

28. Objection, founded on the arbitrary distinction between venial and mortal sins. This distinction insulting to God and repugnant to Scripture. Answer, showing the true distinction in regard to venial sin.

29. Objection, founded on a distinction between guilt and the punishment of it. Answer, illustrated by various passages of Scripture. Admirable saying of Augustine.

30. Answer, founded on a consideration of the efficacy of Christ's death, and the sacrifices under the law. Our true satisfaction.

31. An objection, perverting six passages of Scripture. Preliminary observations concerning a twofold judgment on the part of God. 1. For punishment. 2. For correction.

32. Two distinctions hence arising. Objection, that God is often angry with his elect. Answer, God in afflicting his people does not take his mercy from them. This confirmed by his promise, by Scripture, and the uniform experience of the Church. Distinction between the reprobate and the elect in regard to punishment.

33. Second distinction. The punishment of the reprobate a commencement of the eternal punishment awaiting them; that of the elect designed to bring them to repentance. This confirmed by passages of Scripture and of the Fathers.

34. Two uses of this doctrine to the believer. In affliction he can believe that God, though angry, is still favourable to him. In the punishment of the reprobate, he sees a prelude to their final doom.

35. Objection, as to the punishment of David, answered. Why all men here subjected to chastisement.

36. Objections, founded on five other passages, answered.

37. Answer continued.

38. Objection, founded on passages in the Fathers. Answer, with passages from Chrysostom and Augustine.

39. These satisfactions had reference to the peace of the Church, and not to the throne of God. The School-

men have perverted the meaning of some absurd statements by obscure monks.

1. I come now to an examination of what the scholastic sophists teach concerning repentance. This I will do as briefly as possible; for I leave no intention to take up every point, lest this work, which I am desirous to frame as a compendium of doctrine, should exceed all bounds. They have managed to envelop a matter, otherwise not much involved, in so many perplexities, that it will be difficult to find an outlet if once you get plunged but a little way into their mire. And, first, in giving a definition, they plainly show they never understood what repentance means. For they fasten on some expressions in the writings of the Fathers which are very far from expressing the nature of repentance. For instance, that to *repent* is to deplore past sins and not commit what is to be deplored. Again that it is to bewail past evils and not to sin to do what is to be bewailed. Again, that it is a kind of grieving revenge, punishing in itself what it grieves to have committed. Again, that it is sorrow of heart and bitterness of soul for the evils which the individual has committed, or to which he has consented. Supposing we grant that these things were well said by Fathers (though, if one were inclined to dispute, it were not difficult to deny it), they were not, however said with the view of describing repentance but only of exhorting penitents not again to fall into the same faults from which they had been delivered. But if all descriptions of this kind are to be converted into definitions, there are others which have as good a title to be added. For instance, the following sentence of Chrysostom: "Repentance is a medicine for the cure of sin, a gift bestowed from above, an admirable virtue, a grace surpassing the power of laws." Moreover, the doctrine which they afterwards deliver is somewhat worse than their definition. For they are so keenly bent on external exercises, that all you can gather from immense volumes is, that repentance is a discipline, and austerity, which serves partly to subdue the flesh, partly to chasten and punish sins: of internal renovation of mind, bringing with it true amendment of life, there is a strange silence. No doubt, they talk much of contrition and attrition, torment the soul with many scruples, and involve it in great trouble and anxiety; but when they seem to have deeply wounded the heart, they cure all its bitterness by a slight sprinkling of ceremonies. Repentance thus shrewdly defined, they divide into contrition of the heart, confession of the mouth, and satisfaction of works. This is not more logical than the definition, though they would be thought to have spent their whole lives in framing syllogisms. But if any one argues from the definition (a mode of argument prevalent with dialecticians) that a man may weep over his past sins and not commit things that cause weeping; may bewail past evils, and not commit things that are to be bewailed; may punish what he is grieved for having committed, though he does not confess it with the mouth,—how will they defend their division? For if he may be a true penitent and not confess, repentance can exist without confession. If they answer, that this division refers to repentance regarded as a sacrament, or is to be understood of repentance in its most perfect form, which they do not comprehend in their definitions, the mistake does not rest with me: let them blame themselves for not defining more purely and clearly. When any matter is discussed, I certainly am dull enough to refer everything to the definition as the hinge and foundation of the whole discussion. But granting that this is a license which masters have, let us now survey the different parts in their order. In omitting as frivolous several things which they vend with solemn brow as mysteries, I do it not from ignorance. It were not very difficult to dispose of all those points which they plume themselves on their acuteness and subtilty in discussing; but I consider it a sacred duty not to trouble the reader to no purpose with such absurdities. It is certainly easy to see from the questions which they move and agitate, and in which they miserably entangle themselves, that they are pealing of things they know not. Of this nature are the following: Whether repentance of one sin is pleasing to God, while there is an obstinate adherence to other sins. Again, whether punishments divinely indicted are available for satisfaction. Again, whether repentance can be several times repeated for mortal sins, whereas they grossly and wickedly define that daily repentance has to do with none but venial sins. In like manner, with gross error, they greatly torment themselves with a saying of Jerome, that repentance is a second plank after shipwreck. Herein they show that they have never awoke from brutish stupor, so as to obtain a distant view of the thousandth part of their sins.

2. I would have my readers to observe, that the dispute here relates not to a matter of no consequence; but to one of the most important of all—viz. the forgiveness of sins. For while they require three things in repentance—viz. compunction of heart, confession of the mouth, and satisfaction of work—they at the same time teach that these are necessary to obtain the pardon of sins. If there is any thing in the whole compass of religion which it is of importance to us to know, this certainly is one of

the most important—viz. to perceive and rightly hold by what means, what rule, what terms, with what facility or difficulty, forgiveness of sins may be obtained. Unless our knowledge here is clear and certain, our conscience can have no rest at all, no peace with God, no confidence or security, but is continually trembling, fluctuating, boiling, and distracted; dreads, hates, and shuns the presence of God. But if forgiveness of sins depends on the conditions to which they bind it, nothing can be more wretched and deplorable than our situation. *Contrition* they represent as the first step in obtaining pardon; and they exact it as due, that is, full and complete: meanwhile, they decide not when one may feel secure of having performed this contrition in due measure. I admit that we are bound strongly and incessantly to urge every man bitterly to lament his sins, and thereby stimulate himself more and more to dislike and hate them. For this is the "repentance to salvation not to be repented of" (2 Cor. 7:10). But when such bitterness of sorrow is demanded as may correspond to the magnitude of the offense, and be weighed in the balance with confidence of pardon, miserable consciences are sadly perplexed and tormented when they see that the contrition due for sin is laid upon them, and yet that they have no measure of what is due, so as to enable them to determine that they have made full payment. If they say, we are to do what in us lies, we are always brought back to the same point; for when will any man venture to promise himself that he has done his utmost in bewailing sin? Therefore, when consciences, after a lengthened struggle and long contests with themselves, find no haven in which they may rest, as a means of alleviating their condition in some degree, they extort sorrow and wring out tears, in order to perfect their contrition.

3. If they say that this is calumny on my part, let them come forward and point out a single individual who, by this doctrine of contrition, has not either been driven to despair, or has not, instead of true, opposed pretended fear to the justice of God. We have elsewhere observed, that forgiveness of sins never can be obtained without repentance, because none but the afflicted, and those wounded by a consciousness of sins, can sincerely implore the mercy of God; but we, at the same time, added, that repentance cannot be the cause of the forgiveness of sins: and we also did away with that torment of souls—the dogma that it must be performed as due. Our doctrine was, that the soul looked not to its own compunction or its own tears, but fixed both eyes on the mercy of God alone. Only we observed, that those who labour and are heavy laden are called by Christ, seeing he was sent "to preach good tidings to the meek;" "to bind up the broken-hearted; to proclaim liberty to the captives, and the opening of the prison to them that are bound;" "to comfort all that mourn." Hence the Pharisees were excluded, because, full of their own righteousness, they acknowledged not their own poverty; and despisers, because, regardless of the divine anger, they sought no remedy for their wickedness. Such persons neither labour nor are heavy laden, are not broken-hearted, bound, nor in prison. But there is a great difference between teaching that forgiveness of sins is merited by a full and complete contrition (which the sinner never can give), and instructing him to hunger and thirst after the mercy of God, that recognizing his wretchedness, his turmoil, weariness, and captivity, you may show him where he should seek refreshment, rest, and liberty; in fine, teach him in his humility to give glory to God.

4. *Confession* has ever been a subject of keen contest between the Canonists and the Scholastic Theologians; the former contending that confession is of divine authority—the latter insisting, on the contrary, that it is merely enjoined by ecclesiastical constitution. In this contest great effrontery has been displayed by the Theologians, who have corrupted and violently wrested every passage of Scripture they have quoted in their favour. And when they saw that even thus they could not gain their object, those who wished to be thought particularly acute had recourse to the evasion that confession is of divine authority in regard to the substance, but that it afterwards received its form from positive enactment. Thus the silliest of these quibblers refer the citation to divine authority, from its being said, "Adam, where art thou?" (Gen. 3:9, 12); and also the exception from Adam having replied as if excepting, "The women whom thou gavest to be with me," &c.; but say that the form of both was appointed by civil law. Let us see by what arguments they prove that this confession, formed or unformed, is a divine commandment. The Lord, they say, sent the lepers to the priests (Mt. 8:4). What? did he send them to confession? Who ever heard tell that the Levitical priests were appointed to hear confession? Here they resort to allegory. The priests were appointed by the Mosaic law to discern between leper and leper: sin is spiritual leprosy; therefore it belongs to the priests to decide upon it. Before I answer, I would ask, in passing, why, if this passage makes them judges of spiritual leprosy, they claim the cognizance of natural and carnal leprosy? This, for sooth, is not to play upon Scripture! The law gives the cogni-

zance of leprosy to the Levitical priests: let us usurp this to ourselves. Sin is spiritual leprosy: let us also have cognizance of sin. I now give my answer: There being a change of the priesthood, there must of necessity be a change of the law. All the sacerdotal functions were transferred to Christ, and in him fulfilled and ended (Heb. 7:12). To him alone, therefore, all the rights and honors of the priesthood have been transferred. If they are so fond then of hunting out allegories, let them set Christ before them as the only priest, and place full and universal jurisdiction on his tribunal: this we will readily admit. Besides, there is an incongruity in their allegory: it classes a merely civil enactment among ceremonies. Why, then, does Christ send the lepers to the priests? Lest the priests should be charged with violating the law, which ordained that the person cured of leprosy should present himself before the priest, and be purified by the offering of a sacrifice, he orders the lepers who had been cleansed to do what the law required. "Go and show thyself to the priest, and offer for thy cleansing according as Moses commanded for a testimony unto them." (Luke 5:17). And assuredly this miracle would be a testimony to them: they had pronounced them lepers; they now pronounce them cured. Whether they would or not, they are forced to become witnesses to the miracles of Christ. Christ allows them to examine the miracle, and they cannot deny it: yet, as they still quibble, they have need of a testimony. So it is elsewhere said, "This gospel of the kingdom shall be preached in all the world, for a witness unto all nations" (Mt. 24:14). Again, "Ye shall be brought before governors and kings for my sake, for a testimony against them and the Gentiles" (Mt. 10:18); that is, in order that, in the judgment of Gods they might be more filly convicted. But if they prefer taking the view of Chrysostom (Hom. 12 de Muliere Cananæa), he shows that this was done by Christ for the sake of the Jews also, that he might not be regarded as a violator of the law. But we are ashamed to appeal to the authority of any man in a matter so clear, when Christ declares that he left the legal right of the priests entire, as professed enemies of the Gospel, who were always intent on making a clamour if their mouths were not stopped. Wherefore, let the Popish priests, in order to retain this privilege, openly make common cause with those whom it was necessary to restrain, by forcible means, from speaking evil of Christ. For there is here no reference to his true ministers.

5. They draw their second argument from the same fountain,—I mean allegory; as if allegories were of much avail in confirming any doctrine. But, indeed, let them avail, if those which I am able to produce are not more specious than theirs. They say, then, that the Lord, after raising Lazarus, commanded his disciples to "loose him and let him go" (John 11:44). Their first statement is untrue: we nowhere read that the Lord said this to the disciples; and it is much more probable that he spoke to the Jews who were standing by, that from there being no suspicion of fraud the miracle might be more manifest, and his power might be the more conspicuous from his raising the dead without touching him, by a mere word. In the same way, I understand that our Lord, to leave no ground of suspicion to the Jews, wished them to roll back the stone, feel the stench, perceive the sure signs of death, see him rise by the mere power of a word, and first handle hint when alive. And this is the view of Chrysostom (Serm. C. Jud. Gent. et Haeret). But granting that it was said to the disciples, what can they gain by it? That the Lord gave the apostles the power of loosing? How much more aptly and dexterously might we allegorize and say, that by this symbol the Lord designed to teach his followers to loose those whom he raises up; that is, not to bring to remembrance the sins which he himself had forgotten, not to condemn as sinners those whom he had acquitted, not still to upbraid those whom he had pardoned, not to be stern and severe in punishing, while he himself was merciful and ready to forgive. Certainly nothing should more incline us to pardon than the example of the Judge who threatens that he will be inexorable to the rigid and inhumane. Let them go now and vend their allegories.

6. They now come to closer quarters, while they support their view by passages of Scripture which they think clearly in their favour. Those who came to John's baptism confessed their sins, and James bids us confess our sins one to another (James 5:16). It is not strange that those who wished to be baptized confessed their sins. It has already been mentioned, that John preached the baptism of repentance, baptized with water unto repentance. Whom then could he baptize, but those who confessed that they were sinners? Baptism is a symbol of the forgiveness of sins; and who could be admitted to receive the symbol but sinners acknowledging themselves as such? They therefore confessed their sins that they might be baptized. Nor without good reason does James enjoin us to confess our sins one to another. But if they would attend to what immediately follows, they would perceive that this gives them little support. The words are, "Confess your sins one to another, and pray one for another." He joins together mutual confession and mutual prayer. If, then, we are to confess to priests only, we are also to

pray for them only. What? It would even follow from the words of James, that priests alone can confess. In saying that we are to confess mutually, he must be addressing those only who can hear the confession of others. He says, "*allelous*", *mutually, by turns*, or, if they prefer it, *reciprocally*. But those only can confess reciprocally who are fit to hear confession. This being a privilege which they bestow upon priests only, we also leave them the office of confessing to each other. Have done then with such frivolous absurdities, and let us receive the true meaning of the apostle, which is plain and simple; *first*, That we are to deposit our infirmities in the breasts of each other, with the view of receiving mutual counsel, sympathy, and comfort; and, *secondly*, That mutually conscious of the infirmities of our brethren we are to pray to the Lord for them. Why then quote James against us who so earnestly insist on acknowledgment of the divine mercy? No man can acknowledge the mercy of God without previously confessing his own misery. Nay, we pronounce every man to be anathema who does not confess himself a sinner before God, before his angels, before the Church; in short, before all men. "The Scripture has concluded all under sin," "that every mouth may be stopped, and all the world may become guilty before God," that God alone may be justified and exalted (Gal. 3:22; Rom. 3:9, 19).

7. I wonder at their effrontery in venturing to maintain that the confession of which they speak is of divine authority. We admit that the use of it is very ancient; but we can easily prove that at one time it was free. It certainly appears, from their own records, that no law or constitution respecting it was enacted before the days of Innocent III. Surely if there had been a more ancient law they would have fastened on it, instead of being satisfied with the decree of the Council of Lateral, and so making themselves ridiculous even to children. In other matters, they hesitate not to coin fictitious decrees, which they ascribe to the most ancient Councils, that they may blind the eyes of the simple by veneration for antiquity. In this instance it has not occurred to them to practice this deception, and hence, themselves being witnesses, three centuries have not yet elapsed since the bridle was put, and the necessity of confession imposed by Innocent III. And to say nothing of the time, the mere barbarism of the terms used destroys the authority of the law. For when these worthy fathers enjoin that every person of *both sexes* (*utriusque sexus*) must once a year confess his sins to his own priest, men of wit humorously object that the precept binds hermaphrodites only, and has no application to any one who is either a male or a female.

A still grosser absurdity has been displayed by their disciples, who are unable to explain what is meant by one's own priest (*proprius sacerdos*). Let all the hired ravers of the Pope babble as they may, we hold that Christ is not the author of this law, which compels men to enumerate their sins; nay, that twelve hundred years elapsed after the resurrection of Christ before any such law was made, and that, consequently, this tyranny was not introduced until piety and doctrine were extinct, and pretended pastors had usurped to themselves unbridled license. There is clear evidence in historians, and other ancient writers, to show that this was a politic discipline introduced by bishops, not a law enacted by Christ or the Apostles. Out of many I will produce only one passage, which will be no obscure proof. Sozomen relates, that this constitution of the bishops was carefully observed in the Western churches, but especially at Rome; thus intimating that it was not the universal custom of all churches. He also says, that one of the presbyters was specially appointed to take charge of this duty. This abundantly confutes their falsehood as to the keys being given to the whole priesthood indiscriminately for this purpose, since the function was not common to all the priests, but specially belonged to the one priest whom the bishop had appointed to it. He it was (the same who at present in each of the cathedral churches has the name of penitentiary) who had cognizance of offenses which were more heinous, and required to be rebuked for the sake of example. He afterwards adds, that the same custom existed at Constantinople, until a certain matron, while pretending to confess, was discovered to have used it as a cloak to cover her intercourse with a deacon. In consequence of that crime, Nectarius, the bishop of that church—a man famous for learning and sanctity—abolished the custom of confessing. Here, then, let these asses prick up their ears. If auricular confession was a divine law, how could Nectarius have dared to abolish or remodel it? Nectarius, a holy man of God, approved by the suffrage of all antiquity, will they charge with heresy and schism? With the same vote they will condemn the church of Constantinople, in which Sozomen affirms that the custom of confessing was not only disguised for a time, but even in his own memory abolished. Nay, let them charge with defections not only Constantinople but all the Eastern churches, which (if they say true) disregarded an inviolable law enjoined on all Christians.

8. This abrogation is clearly attested in so many passages by Chrysostom, who lived at Constantinople, and was himself prelate of the church, that it is strange they

can venture to maintain the contrary: "Tell your sins", says he, "that you may efface them: if you blush to tell another what sins you have committed, tell them daily in your soul. I say not, tell them to your fellow-servant who may upbraid you, but tell them to God who cures them. Confess your sins upon your bed, that your conscience may there daily recognize its iniquities." Again, "Now, however, it is not necessary to confess before witnesses; let the examination of your faults be made in your own thought: let the judgment be without a witness: let God alone see you confessing." Again, "I do not lead you publicly into the view of your fellow servants; I do not force you to disclose your sins to men; review and lay open your conscience before God. Show your wounds to the Lord, the best of physicians, and seek medicine from him. Show to him who upbraids not, but cures most kindly." Again, "Certainly tell it not to man lest he upbraid you. Nor must you confess to your fellow servant, who may make it public; but show your wounds to the Lord, who takes care of you, who is kind and can cure." He afterwards introduces God speaking thus: "I oblige you not to come into the midst of a theatre, and have many witnesses; tell your sins to me alone in private, that I may cure the ulcer." Shall we say that Chrysostom, in writing these and similar passages, carried his presumption so far as to free the consciences of men from those chains with which they are bound by the divine law? By no means; but knowing that it was not at all prescribed by the word of God, he dares not exact it as necessary.

9. But that the whole matter may be more plainly unfolded, we shall first honestly state the nature of confession as delivered in the word of God, and thereafter subjoin their inventions—not all of them indeed (who could drink up that boundless sea?) but those only which contain summary of their secret confession. Here I am grieved to mention how frequently the old interpreter has rendered the word *confess* instead of *praise*, a fact notorious to the most illiterate, were it not fitting to expose their effrontery in transferring to their tyrannical edict what was written concerning the praises of God. To prove that confession has the effect of exhilarating the mind, they obtrude the passage in the psalm, "with the voice of joy and praise" (Vulgate, *confessionis*) (Ps. 42:4). But if such a metamorphosis is valid, any thing may be made of any thing. But, as they have lost all shame, let pious readers reflect how, by the just vengeance of God, they have been given over to a reprobate mind, that their audacity may be the more detestable. If we are disposed to acquiesce in the simple doctrine of Scripture, there will be no danger of our being misled by such glosses. There one method of confessing is prescribed; since it is the Lord who forgives, forgets and wipes away sins, to him let us confess them, that we may obtain pardon. He is the physician, therefore let us show our wounds to him. He is hurt and offended, let us ask peace of him. He is the discerner of the heart, and knows all one thoughts; let us hasten to pour out our hearts before him. He it is, in fine, who invites sinners; let us delay not to draw near to him. "I acknowledge my sin unto thee," says David; "and mine iniquity have I not hid. I said, I will confess my transgressions unto the Lord; and thou forgavest the iniquity of my sin" (Ps. 32:5). Another specimen of David's confessions is as follows: "Have mercy upon me, O God, according to thy loving kindness" (Ps. 51:1). The following is Daniel's confession: "We have sinned, and have committed iniquity, and have done wickedly, and have rebelled, even by departing from thy precepts and thy judgments" (Dan. 9:5). Other examples every where occur in Scripture: the quotation of them would almost fill a volume. "If we confess our sins," says John, "he is faithful and just to forgive us our sins" (1 John 1:9). To whom are we to confess? to Him surely;—that is, we are to fall down before him with a grieved and humbled heart, and sincerely accusing and condemning ourselves, seek forgiveness of his goodness and mercy.

10. He who has adopted this confession from the heart and as in the presence of God, will doubtless have a tongue ready to confess whenever there is occasion among men to publish the mercy of God. He will not be satisfied to whisper the secret of his heart for once into the ear of one individual, but will often, and openly, and in the hearing of the whole world, ingenuously make mention both of his own ignominy, and of the greatness and glory of the Lord. In this way David, after he was accused by Nathan, being stung in his conscience, confesses his sin before God and men. "I have sinned unto the Lord," says he (2 Sam. 12:13); that is, I have now no excuse, no evasion; all must judge me a sinner; and that which I wished to be secret with the Lord must also be made manifest to men. Hence the secret confession which is made to God is followed by voluntary confession to men, whenever that is conducive to the divine glory or our humiliation. For this reason the Lord anciently enjoined the people of Israel that they should repeat the words after the priest, and make public confession of their iniquities in the temple; because he foresaw that this was a necessary help to enable each one to form a just idea of himself. And it is proper that by confession of our misery, we should manifest the

mercy of our God both among ourselves and before the whole world.

11. It is proper that this mode of confession should both be ordinary in the Church, and also be specially employed on extraordinary occasions, when the people in common happen to have fallen into any fault. Of this latter description we have an example in the solemn confession which the whole people made under the authority and guidance of Ezra and Nehemiah (Neh. 1:6, 7). For their long captivity, the destruction of the temple, and suppression of their religion, having been the common punishment of their defection, they could not make meet acknowledgment of the blessing of deliverance without previous confession of their guilt. And it matters not though in one assembly it may sometimes happen that a few are innocent, seeing that the members of a languid and sickly body cannot boast of soundness. Nay, it is scarcely possible that these few have not contracted some taint, and so bear part of the blame. Therefore, as often as we are afflicted with pestilence, or war, or famine, or any other calamity whatsoever, if it is our duty to retake ourselves to mourning, fasting, and other signs of guiltiness, confession also, on which all the others depend, is not to be neglected. That ordinary confession which the Lord has moreover expressly commended, no sober man, who has reflected on its usefulness, will venture to disapprove. Seeing that in every sacred assembly we stand in the view of God and angels, in what way should our service begin but in acknowledging our own unworthiness? But this you will say is done in every prayer; for as often as we pray for pardon, we confess our sins. I admit it. But if you consider how great is our carelessness, or drowsiness, or sloth, you will grant me that it would be a salutary ordinance if the Christian people were exercised in humiliation by some formal method of confession. For though the ceremony which the Lord enjoined on the Israelites belonged to the tutelage of the Law, yet the thing itself belongs in some respect to us also. And, indeed, in all well ordered churches, in observance of an useful custom, the minister, each Lord's day, frames a formula of confession in his own name and that of the people, in which he makes a common confession of iniquity, and supplicates pardon from the Lord. In short, by this key a door of prayer is opened privately for each, and publicly for all.

12. Two other forms of private confession are approved by Scripture. The one is made on our own account, and to it reference is made in the passage in James, "Confess your sins one to another" (James 5:16); for the meaning is, that by disclosing our infirmities to each other, we are to obtain the aid of mutual counsel and consolation. The other is to be made for the sake of our neighbor, to appease and reconcile him if by our fault he has been in any respect injured. In the former, although James, by not specifying any particular individual into whose bosom we are to disburden our feelings, leaves us the free choice of confessing to any member of the church who may seem fittest; yet as for the most part pastors are to be supposed better qualified than others, our choice ought chiefly to fall upon them. And the ground of preference is, that the Lord, by calling them to the ministry, points them out as the persons by whose lips we are to be taught to subdue and correct our sins, and derive consolation from the hope of pardon. For as the duty of mutual admonition and correction is committed to all Christians, but is specially enjoined on ministers, so while we ought all to console each other mutually and confirm each other in confidence in the divine mercy, we see that ministers, to assure our consciences of the forgiveness of fins, are appointed to be the witnesses and sponsors of it, so that they are themselves said to forgive sins and loose souls (Mt. 16:19; 18:18). When you hear this attributed to them, reflect that it is for your use. Let every believer, therefore, remember, that if in private he is so agonized and afflicted by a sense of his sins that he cannot obtain relief without the aid of others, it is his duty not to neglect the remedy which God provides for him—viz. to have recourse for relief to a private confession to his own pastor, and for consolation privately implore the assistance of him whose business it is, both in public and private, to solace the people of God with Gospel doctrine. But we are always to use moderation, lest in a matter as to which God prescribes no certain rule, our consciences be burdened with a certain yoke. Hence it follows first, that confession of this nature ought to be free so as not to be exacted of all, but only recommended to those who feel that they have need of it; and, secondly, even those who use it according to their necessity must neither be compelled by any precept, nor artfully induced to enumerate all their sins, but only in so far as they shall deem it for their interest, that they may obtain the full benefit of consolation. Faithful pastors, as they would both eschew tyranny in their ministry, and superstition in the people, must not only leave this liberty to churches, but defend and strenuously vindicate it.

13. Of the second form of confession, our Savior speaks in Matthew. "If thou bring thy gift to the altar, and there remember that thy brother has ought against thee; leave there thy gift before the altar; first be reconciled to

thy brother, and then come and offer thy gift" (Mt. 5:23, 24). Thus love, which has been interrupted by our fault, must be restored by acknowledging and asking pardon for the fault. Under this head is included the confession of those who by their sin have given offense to the whole Church (*supra*, sec. 10). For if Christ attaches so much importance to the offense of one individual, that he forbids the sacrifice of all who have sinned in any respect against their brethren, until by due satisfaction they have regained their favor, how much greater reason is there that he, who by some evil example has offended the Church should be reconciled to it by the acknowledgment of his fault? Thus the member of the Church of Corinth was restored to communion after he had humbly submitted to correction (2 Cor. 2:6). This form of confession existed in the ancient Christian Church, as Cyprian relates: "They practice repentance," says he, "for a proper time, then they come to confession, and by the laying on of the hands of the bishop and clergy, are admitted to communion." Scripture knows nothing of any other form or method of confessing, and it belongs not to us to bind new chains upon consciences which Christ most strictly prohibits from being brought into bondage. Meanwhile, that the flock present themselves before the pastor whenever they would partake of the Holy Supper, I am so far from disapproving, that I am most desirous it should be everywhere observed. For both those whose conscience is hindered may thence obtain singular benefit, and those who require admonition thus afford an opportunity for it; provided always no countenance is given to tyranny and superstition.

14. The *power of the keys* has place in the three following modes of confession,—either when the whole Church, in a formal acknowledgment of its defects, supplicates pardon; or when a private individual, who has given public offense by some notable delinquency, testifies his repentance; or when he who from disquiet of conscience needs the aid of his minister, acquaints him with his infirmity. With regard to the reparation of offense, the case is different. For though in this also provision is made for peace of conscience, yet the principal object is to suppress hatred, and reunite brethren in the bond of peace. But the benefit of which I have spoken is by no means to be despised, that we may the more willingly confess our sins. For when the whole Church stands as it were at the bar of God, confesses her guilt, and finds her only refuge in the divine mercy, it is no common or light solace to have an ambassador of Christ present, invested with the mandate of reconciliations by whom she may hear her absolution pronounced. Here the utility of the keys is justly commended when that embassy is duly discharged with becoming order and reverence. In like manner, when he who has as it were become an alien from the Church receives pardon, and is thus restored to brotherly unity, how great is the benefit of understanding that he is pardoned by those to whom Christ said, "Whose soever sins ye remit, they are remitted unto them" (John 20:23). Nor is private absolution of less benefit or efficacy when asked by those who stand in need of a special remedy for their infirmity. It not seldom happens, that he who hears general promises which are intended for the whole congregation of the faithful, nevertheless remains somewhat in doubts, and is still disquieted in mind, as if his own remission were not yet obtained. Should this individual lay open the secret wound of his soul to his pastor, and hear these words of the Gospel specially addressed to him, "Son, be of good cheer, thy sins be forgiven thee" (Mt. 9:2), his mind will feel secure, and escape from the trepidation with which it was previously agitated. But when we treat of the keys, us must always beware of dreaming of any power apart from the preaching of the Gospel. This subject will be more fully explained when we come to treat of the government of the Church (Book 4 chap. 11, 12). There we shall see, that whatever privilege of binding and loosing Christ has bestowed on his Church is annexed to the word. This is especially true with regard to the ministry of the keys, the whole power of which consists in this, that the grace of the Gospel is publicly and privately sealed on the minds of believers by means of those whom the Lord has appointed; and the only method in which this can be done is by preaching.

15. What say the Roman theologians? That all persons of both sexes, so soon as they shall have reached the years of discretion, must, once a year at least, confess all their sins to their own priest; that the sin is not discharged unless the resolution to confess has been firmly conceived; that if this resolution is not carried into effect when an opportunity offers, there is no entrance into Paradise; that the priest, moreover has the power of the keys, by which he can loose and bind the sinner; because the declaration of Christ is not in vain: "Whatsoever ye shall bind on earth shall be bound in heaven" (Mt. 18:18). Concerning this power, however they wage a fierce war among themselves. Some say there is only one key essentially—viz. the power of binding and loosing; that knowledge, indeed, is requisite for the proper use of it, but only as an accessory, not as essentially inherent in it. Others seeing that this gave too unrestrained license, have

imagined two keys—viz. discernment and power. Others, again, seeing that the license of priests was curbed by such restraint, have forged other keys (*infra*, sec. 21), the authority of discerning to be used in defining, and the power to carry their sentences into execution; and to these they add knowledge as a counselor. This binding and loosing, however, they do not venture to interpret simply, to forgive and wipe away sins, because they hear the Lord proclaiming by the prophet, "I, even I, am the Lord; and beside me there is no savior." "I, even I, am he that blotteth out thy transgressions" (Isaiah 43:11, 25). But they say it belongs to the priest to declare who are bound or loosed, and whose sins are remitted or retained; to declare, moreover, either by confession, when he absolves and retains sins, or by sentence, when he excommunicates or admits to communion in the Sacraments. Lastly, perceiving that the knot is not yet untied, because it may always be objected that persons are often undeservedly bound and loosed, and therefore not bound or loosed in heaven; as their ultimate resource, they answer, that the conferring of the keys must be taken with limitations because Christ has promised that the sentence of the priest, properly pronounced, will be approved at his judgment-seat according as the bound or loosed asked what they merited. They say, moreover, that those keys which are conferred by bishops at ordination were given by Christ to all priests but that the free use of them is with those only who discharge ecclesiastical functions; that with priests excommunicated or suspended the keys themselves indeed remain, but tied and rusty. Those who speak thus may justly be deemed modest and sober compared with others, who on a new anvil have forged new keys, by which they say that the treasury of heaven is locked up: these we shall afterwards consider in their own place (chap. 5 sec. 2).

16. To each of these views I will briefly reply. As to their binding the souls of believers by their laws, whether justly or unjustly, I say nothing at present, as it will be seen at the proper place; but their enacting it as a law, that all sins are to be enumerated; their denying that sin is discharged except under the condition that the resolution to confess has been firmly conceived; their pretence that there is no admission into Paradise if the opportunity of confession has been neglected, are things which it is impossible to bear. Are all sins to be enumerated? But David, who, I presume, had honestly pondered with himself as to the confession of his sins, exclaimed, "Who can understand his errors? Cleanse thou me from secret faults" (Ps. 19:12); and in another passage, "Mine iniquities are gone over my head: as a heavy burden they are too heavy for me" (Ps. 38:4). He knew how deep was the abyss of our sins, how numerous the forms of wickedness, how many heads the hydra carried, how long a tail it drew. Therefore, he did not sit down to make a catalogue, but from the depth of his distress cried unto the Lord, "I am overwhelmed, and buried, and sore vexed; the gates of hell have encircled me: let thy right hand deliver me from the abyss into which I am plunged, and from the death which I am ready to die." Who can now think of a computation of his sins when he sees David's inability to number his?

17. By this ruinous procedure, the souls of those who were affected with some sense of God have been most cruelly racked. First, they retook themselves to calculation, proceeding according to the formula given by the Schoolmen, and dividing their sins into boughs, branches, twigs, and leaves; then they weighed the qualities, quantities, and circumstances; and in this way, for some time, matters proceeded. But after they had advanced farther, when they looked around, nought was seen but sea and sky; no road, no harbor. The longer the space they ran over, a longer still met the eye; nay, lofty mountains began to rise, and there seemed no hope of escape; none at least till after long wanderings. They were thus brought to a dead halt, till at length the only issue was found in despair. Here these cruel murderers, to ease the wounds which they had made, applied certain fomentations. Every one was to do his best. But new cares again disturbed, nay, new torments excruciated their souls. "I have not spent enough of time; I have not exerted myself sufficiently: many things I have omitted through negligence: forgetfulness proceeding from want of care is not excusable." Then new drugs were supplied to alleviate their pains. "Repent of your negligence; and provided it is not done supinely, it will be pardoned." All these things, however, could not heal the wound, being not so much alleviations of the sore as poison besmeared with honey, that its bitterness might not at once offend the taste, but penetrate to the vitals before it could be detected. The dreadful voice, therefore, was always heard pealing in their ears, "Confess all your sins," and the dread thus occasioned could not be pacified without sure consolation. Here let my readers consider whether it be possible to take an account of the actions of a whole year, or even to collect the sins committed in a single day, seeing every man's experience convinces him that at evening, in examining the faults of that single day, memory gets confused, so great is the number and variety presented. I am not speaking of dull

and heartless hypocrites, who, after animadverting on three or four of their grosser offenses, think the work finished; but of the true worshipers of God, who, after they have performed their examination, feeling themselves overwhelmed, still add the words of John: "If our heart condemn us, God is greater than our heart, and knoweth all things" (1 John 3:20); and, therefore, tremble at the thought of that Judge whose knowledge far surpasses our comprehension.

18. Though a good part of the world rested in these soothing suggestions, by which this fatal poison was somewhat tempered, it was not because they thought that God was satisfied, or they had quite satisfied themselves; it was rather like an anchor cast out in the middle of the deep, which for a little interrupts the navigation, or a weary, worn-out traveler, who lies down by the way. I give myself no trouble in proving the truth of this fact. Every one can be his own witness. I will mention generally what the nature of this law is. First, The observance of it is simply impossible; and hence its only results to destroy, condemn, confound, to plunge into ruin and despair. Secondly, By withdrawing sinners from a true sense of their sins, it makes them hypocritical, and ignorant both of God and themselves. For, while they are wholly occupied with the enumeration of their sins, they lose sight of that lurking hydra, their secret iniquities and internal defilements, the knowledge of which would have made them sensible of their misery. But the surest rule of confession is, to acknowledge and confess our sins to be an abyss so great as to exceed our comprehension. On this rule we see the confession of the publican was formed, "God be merciful to me, a sinner" (Luke 18:13); as if he had said, How great, how very great a sinner, how utterly sinful I am! the extent of my sins I can neither conceive nor express. Let the depth of thy mercy engulf the depth of sin! What! you will say, are we not to confess every single sin? Is no confession acceptable to God but that which is contained in the words, "I am a sinner"? Nay, our endeavor must rather be, as much as in us lies, to pour out our whole heart before the Lord. Nor are we only in one word to confess ourselves sinners, but truly and sincerely acknowledge ourselves as such; to feel with our whole soul how great and various the pollutions of our sins are; confessing not only that we are impure, but what the nature of our impurity is, its magnitude and its extent; not only that we are debtors, but what the debts are which burden us, and how they were incurred; not only that we are wounded, but how numerous and deadly are the wounds. When thus recognizing himself, the sinner shall have poured out his whole heart before God, let him seriously and sincerely reflect that a greater number of sins still remains, and that their recesses are too deep for him thoroughly to penetrate. Accordingly, let him exclaim with David, "Who can understand his errors? cleanse thou me from secret faults" (Ps. 19:12). But when the Schoolmen affirm that sins are not forgiven, unless the resolution to confess has been firmly conceived, and that the gate of Paradise is closed on him who has neglected the opportunity of confessing when offered, far be it from us to concede this to them. The remission of sins is not different now from what it has ever been. In all the passages in which we read that sinners obtained forgiveness from God, we read not that they whispered into the ear of some priest. Indeed, they could not then confess, as priests were not then confessionaries, nor did the confessional itself exist. And for many ages afterwards, this mode of confession, by which sins were forgiven on this condition, was unheard of: But not to enter into a long discussion, as if the matter were doubtful, the word of God, which abideth for ever, is plain, "When the wicked shall turn away from all his sins that he has committed, and keep all my statutes, and do that which is lawful and right, he shall surely live, he shall not die" (Ezek. 18:21). He who presumes to add to this declaration binds not sins, but the mercy of God. When they contend that judgment cannot be given unless the case is known, the answer is easy, that they usurp the right of judging, being only self-created judges. And it is strange, how confidently they lay down principles, which no man of sound mind will admit. They give out, that the office of binding and loosing has been committed to them, as a kind of jurisdiction annexed to the right of inquiry. That the jurisdiction was unknown to the Apostles their whole doctrine proclaims. Nor does it belong to the priest to know for certainty whether or not a sinner is loosed, but to Him from whom acquittal is asked; since he who only hears can ever know whether or not the enumeration is full and complete. Thus there would be no absolution, without restricting it to the words of him who is to be judged. We may add, that the whole system of loosing depends on faith and repentance, two things which no man can know of another, so as to pronounce sentence. It follows, therefore, that the certainty of binding and loosing is not subjected to the will of an earthly judge, because the minister of the word, when he duly executes his office, can only acquit conditionally, when, for the sake of the sinner, he repeats the words, "Whose soever sins ye remit;" lest he should doubt of the pardon, which,

by the command and voice of God, is promised to be ratified in heaven.

19. It is not strange, therefore, that we condemn that auricular confession, as a thing pestilent in its nature, and in many ways injurious to the Church, and desire to see it abolished. But if the thing were in itself indifferent, yet, seeing it is of no use or benefit, and has given occasion to so much impiety, blasphemy, and error, who does not think that it ought to be immediately abolished? They enumerate some of its uses, and boast of them as very beneficial, but they are either fictitious or of no importance. One thing they specially commend, that the blush of shame in the penitent is a severe punishment, which makes him more cautious for the future, and anticipates divine punishment, by his punishing himself. As if a man was not sufficiently humbled with shame when brought under the cognizance of God at his supreme tribunal. Admirable proficiency—if we cease to sin because we are ashamed to make one man acquainted with it, and blush not at having God as the witness of our evil conscience! The assertion, however, as to the effect of shame, is most unfounded, for we may every where see, that there is nothing which gives men greater confidence and license in sinning than the idea, that after making confession to priests, they can *wipe their lip, and say, I have not done it.* And not only do they during the whole year become bolder in sin, but, secure against confession for the remainder of it, they never sigh after God, never examine themselves, but continue heaping sins upon sins, until, as they suppose, they get rid of them all at once. And when they have got rid of them, they think they are disburdened of their load, and imagine they have deprived God of the right of judging, by giving it to the priest; have made God forgetful, by making the priest conscious. Moreover, who is glad when he sees the day of confession approaching? Who goes with a cheerful mind to confess, and does not rather, as if he were dragged to prison with a rope about his neck, go unwillingly, and, as it were, struggling against it? with the exception, perhaps, of the priests themselves, who take a fond delight in the mutual narrative of their own misdeeds, as a kind of merry tales. I will not pollute my page by retailing the monstrous abominations with which auricular confession teems; I only say, that if that holy man (Nectarius, of whom supra sec. 7) did not act unadvisedly when for one rumour of whoredom he banished confession from his church, or rather from the memory of his people, the innumerable acts of prostitution, adultery, and incest, which it produces in the present day, warn us of the necessity of abolishing it.

20. As to the pretence of the confessionaries respecting the power of the keys, and their placing in it, so to speak, the sum and substance of their kingdom, we must see what force it ought to have. Were the keys then (they ask), given without a cause? Was it said without a cause, "Whatsoever ye shall bind on earth shall be bound in heaven, and whatsoever ye shall loose on earth shall be loosed in heaven?" (Mt. 18:18). Do we make void the word of Christ? I answer, that there was a weighty reason for giving the keys, as I lately explained, and will again show at greater length when I come to treat of Excommunication (Book 4, cap. 12). But what if I should cut off the handle for all such questions with one sword—viz. that priests are neither vicars nor successors of the Apostles? But that also will be elsewhere considered (Book 4, cap. 6). Now, at the very place where they are most desirous to fortify themselves, they erect a battering-ram, by which all their own machinations are overthrown. Christ did not give his Apostles the power of binding and loosing before he endued them with the Holy Spirit. I deny, therefore, that any man, who has not previously received the Holy Spirit, is competent to possess the power of the keys. I deny that any one can use the keys, unless the Holy Spirit precede, teaching and dictating what is to be done. They pretend, indeed, that they have the Holy Spirit, but by their works deny him; unless, indeed, we are to suppose that the Holy Spirit is some vain thing of no value, as they certainly do feign, but we will not believe them. With this engine they are completely overthrown; whatever be the door of which they boast of having the key, we must always ask, whether they have the Holy Spirit, who is arbiter and ruler of the keys? If they reply, that they have, we must again ask, whether the Holy Spirit can err? This they will not venture to say distinctly, although by their doctrine they indirectly insinuate it. Therefore, we must infer, that no priestlings have the power of the keys, because they every where and indiscriminately loose what the Lord was pleased should be bound, and bind what he has ordered to be loosed.

21. When they see themselves convicted on the clearest evidence, of loosing and binding worthy and unworthy without distinction, they lay claim to power without knowledge. And although they dare not deny that knowledge is requisite for the proper use, they still affirm that the power itself has been given to bad administrators. This, however, is the power, "Whatsoever ye shall bind on earth shall be bound in heaven, and whatsoever ye shall loose on earth shall be loosed in heaven." Either the promise of Christ must be false, or those who are

endued with this power bind and loose properly. There is no room for the evasion, that the words of Christ are limited, according to the merits of him who is loosed or bound. We admit, that none can be bound or loosed but those who are worthy of being bound or loosed. But the preachers of the Gospel and the Church have the word by which they can measure this worthiness. By this word preachers of the Gospel can promise forgiveness of sins to all who are in Christ by faith, and can declare a sentence of condemnation against all, and upon all, who do not embrace Christ. In this word the Church declares, that "neither fornicators, nor idolaters, nor adulterers," "nor thieves, nor covetous, nor drunkards, nor revilers, nor extortioners shall inherit the kingdom of God" (1 Cor. 6:9, 10). Such it binds in sure fetters. By the same word it looses and consoles the penitent. But what kind of power is it which knows not what is to be bound or loosed? You cannot bind or loose without knowledge. Why, then, do they say, that they absolve by authority given to them, when absolution is uncertain? As regards us, this power is merely imaginary, if it cannot be used. Now, I holds either that there is no use, or one so uncertain as to be virtually no use at all. For when they confess that a good part of the priests do not use the keys duly, and that power without the legitimate use is ineffectual, who is to assure me, that the one by whom I am loosed is a good dispenser of the keys? But if he is a bad one, what better has he given me than this nugatory dispensation,—What is to be bound or loosed in you I know not, since I have not the proper use of the keys; but if you deserve it, I absolve you? As much might be done, I say not by a laic (since they would scarcely listen to such a statement), but by the Turk or the devil. For it is just to say, I have not the word of God, the sure rule for loosing, but authority has been given me to absolve you, if you deserve it. We see, therefore, what their object was, when they defined (see sec. 16) the keys as authority to discern and power to execute; and said, that knowledge is added as a counselor, and counsels the proper use; their object was to reign libidinously and licentiously, without God and his word.

22. Should any one object, first, that the lawful ministers of Christ will be no less perplexed in the discharge of their duty, because the absolution, which depends on faith, will always be equivocal; and, secondly, that sinners will receive no comfort at all, or cold comfort, because the minister, who is not a fit judge of their faith, is not certain of their absolution, we are prepared with an answer. They say that no sins are remitted by the priest, but such sins as he is cognizant of; thus, according to them, remission depends on the judgment of the priest, and unless he accurately discriminate as to who are worthy of pardon, the whole procedure is null and void. In short, the power of which they speak is a jurisdiction annexed to examination, to which pardon and absolution are restricted. Here no firm footing can be found, nay, there is a profound abyss; because, where confession is not complete, the hope of pardon also is defective; next, the priest himself must necessarily remain in suspense, while he knows not whether the sinner gives a faithful enumeration of his sins; lastly, such is the rudeness and ignorance of priests, that the greater part of them are in no respect fitter to perform this office than a cobbler to cultivate the fields, while almost all the others have good reason to suspect their own fitness. Hence the perplexity and doubt as to the Popish absolution, from their choosing to found it on the person of the priest, and not on his person only, but on his knowledge, so that he can only judge of what is laid before him investigated, and ascertained. Now, if any should ask at these good doctors, whether the sinner is reconciled to God when some sins are remitted? I know not what answer they could give, unless that they should be forced to confess, that whatever the priest pronounces with regard to the remission of sins which have been enumerated to him will be unavailing, so long as others are not exempted from condemnation. On the part of the penitent, again, it is hence obvious in what a state of pernicious anxiety his conscience will be held; because, while he leans on what they call the discernment of the priest, he cannot come to any decision from the word of God. From all these absurdities the doctrine which we deliver is completely free. For absolution is conditional, allowing the sinner to trust that God is propitious to him, provided he sincerely seek expiation in the sacrifice of Christ, and accept of the grace offered to him. Thus, he cannot err who, in the capacity of a herald, promulgates what has been dictated to him from the word of God. The sinner, again, can receive a clear and sure absolution when, in regard to embracing the grace of Christ, the simple condition annexed is in terms of the general rule of our Master himself,—a rule impiously spurned by the Papacy,— "According to your faith be it unto you" (Mt. 9:29).

23. The absurd jargon which they make of the doctrine of Scripture concerning the power of the keys, I have promised to expose elsewhere; the proper place will be in treating of the Government of the Church

(Book 4, c. 12). Meanwhile, let the reader remember how absurdly they wrest to auricular and secret confession what was said by Christ partly of the preaching of the Gospel, and partly of excommunication. Wherefore, when they object that the power of loosing was given to the Apostles, and that this power priests exercise by remitting sins acknowledged to them, it is plain that the principle which they assume is false and frivolous: for the absolution which is subordinate to faith is nothing else than an evidence of pardon, derived from the free promise of the Gospel, while the other absolution, which depends on the discipline of the Church, has nothing to do with secret sins; but is more a matter of example for the purpose of removing the public offense given to the Church. As to their diligence in searching up and down for passages by which they may prove that it is not sufficient to confess sins to God alone, or to laymen, unless the priest take cognizance, it is vile and disgraceful. For when the ancient fathers advise sinners to disburden themselves to their pastor, we cannot understand them to refer to a recital which was not then in use. Then, so unfair are Lombard and others like-minded, that they seem intentionally to have devoted themselves to spurious books, that they might use them as a cloak to deceive the simple. They, indeed, acknowledge truly, that as forgiveness always accompanies repentance, no obstacle properly remains after the individual is truly penitent, though he may not have actually confessed; and, therefore, that the priest does not so much remit sins, as pronounce and declare that they are remitted; though in the term *declaring*, they insinuate a gross error, surrogating ceremony in place of doctrine. But in pretending that he who has already obtained pardon before God is acquitted in the face of the Church, they unseasonably apply to the special use of every individual, that which we have already said was designed for common discipline when the offense of a more heinous and notorious transgression was to be removed. Shortly after they pervert and destroy their previous moderation, by adding that there is another mode of remission, namely, by the infliction of penalty and satisfaction, in which they arrogate to their priests the right of dividing what God has every where promised to us entire. While He simply requires repentance and faith, their division or exception is altogether blasphemous. For it is just as if the priest, assuming the office of tribune, were to interfere with God, and try to prevent him from admitting to his favor by his mere liberality any one who had not previously lain prostrate at the tribunicial bench, and there been punished.

24. The whole comes to this, when they wish to make God the author of this fictitious confession their vanity is proved as I have shown their falsehood in expounding the few passages which they cite. But while it is plain, that the law was imposed by men, I say that it is both tyrannical and insulting to God, who, in binding consciences to his word, would have them free from human rule. Then when confession is prescribed as necessary to obtain pardon, which God wished to be free, I say that the sacrilege is altogether intolerable, because nothing belongs more peculiarly to God than the forgiveness of sins, in which our salvation consists. I have, moreover, shown that this tyranny was introduced when the world was sunk in shameful barbarism. Besides, I have proved that the law is pestiferous, inasmuch as when the fear of God exists, it plunges men into despair, and when there is security soothing itself with vain flattery, it blunts it the more. Lastly, I have explained that all the mitigations which they employ have no other tendency than to entangle, obscure, and corrupt the pure doctrine, and cloak their iniquities with deceitful colors.

25. In repentance they assign the third place to satisfaction, all their absurd talk as to which can be refuted in one word. They say, that it is not sufficient for the penitent to abstain from past sins, and change his conduct for the better, unless he satisfy God for what he has done; and that there are many helps by which we may redeem sins, such as tears, fastings oblations, and offices of charity; that by them the Lord is to be propitiated; by them the debts due to divine justice are to be paid; by them our faults are to be compensated; by them pardon is to be deserved: for though in the riches of his mercy he has forgiven the guilt, he yet, as a just discipline, retains the penalty, and that this penalty must be bought off by satisfaction. The sum of the whole comes to this: that we indeed obtain pardon of our sins from the mercy of God, but still by the intervention of the merit of works, by which the evil of our sins is compensated, and due satisfaction made to divine justice. To such false views I oppose the free forgiveness of sins, one of the doctrines most clearly taught in Scripture. First, what is forgiveness but a gift of mere liberality? A creditor is not said to forgive when he declares by granting a discharge, that the money has been paid to him; but when, without any payment, through voluntary kindness, he expunges the debt. And why is the term *gratis* (free) afterwards added, but to take away all idea of satisfaction? With what confidence, then, do they still set up their satisfactions, which are thus struck down as with a thunderbolt? What? When the

Lord proclaims by Isaiah, "I, even I, am he that blotteth out thy transgressions for mine own sake, and will not remember thy sins," does he not plainly declare, that the cause and foundation of forgiveness is to be sought from his goodness alone? Besides, when the whole of Scripture bears this testimony to Christ, that through his name the forgiveness of sins is to be obtained (Acts 10:43), does it not plainly exclude all other names? How then do they teach that it is obtained by the name of satisfaction? Let them not deny that they attribute this to satisfactions, though they bring them in as subsidiary aids. For when Scripture says, *by the name of Christ*, it means, that we are to bring nothing, pretend nothing of our own, but lean entirely on the recommendation of Christ. Thus Paul, after declaring that "God was in Christ reconciling the world unto himself, not imputing their trespasses unto them," immediately adds the reason and the method, "For he has made him to be sin for us who knew no sin" (2 Cor. 5:19, 20).

26. But with their usual perverseness, they maintain that both the forgiveness of sins and reconciliation take place at once when we are received into the favor of God through Christ in baptism; that in lapses after baptism we must rise again by means of satisfactions; that the blood of Christ is of no avail unless in so far as it is dispensed by the keys of the Church. I speak not of a matter as to which there can be any doubt; for this impious dogma is declared in the plainest terms, in the writings not of one or two, but of the whole Schoolmen. Their master (Sent. Lib. 3, Dist. 9), after acknowledging, according to the doctrine of Peter, that Christ "bare our sins in his own body on the tree" (1 Pet. 2:24), immediately modifies the doctrine by introducing the exception, that in baptism all the temporal penalties of sin are relaxed; but that after baptism they are lessened by means of repentance, the cross of Christ and our repentance thus co-operating together. St. John speaks very differently, "If any man sin, we have an advocate with the Father, Jesus Christ the righteous; and he is the propitiation for our sins." "I write unto you, little children, because your sins are forgiven you for his name's sake" (1 John 2:1, 2, 12). He certainly is addressing believers, and while setting forth Christ as the propitiation for sins, shows them that there is no other satisfaction by which an offended God can be propitiated or appeased. He says not: God was once reconciled to you by Christ; now, seek other methods; but he makes him a perpetual advocate, who always, by his intercession, reinstates us in his Fathered favour—a perpetual propitiation by which sins are expiated. For what was said by another John will ever hold true, "Behold the Lamb of God, which taketh away the sins of the world" (John 1:29). He, I say, took them away, and no other; that is, since he alone is the Lamb of God, he alone is the offering for our sins; he alone is expiation; he alone is satisfaction. For though the right and power of pardoning properly belongs to the Father, when he is distinguished from the Son, as has already been seen, Christ is here exhibited in another view, as transferring to himself the punishment due to us, and wiping away our guilt in the sight of God. Whence it follows that we could not be partakers of the expiation accomplished by Christ, were he not possessed of that honor of which those who try to appease God by their compensations seek to rob him.

27. Here it is necessary to keep two things in view: that the honor of Christ be preserved entire and unimpaired, and that the conscience, assured of the pardon of sin, may have peace with God. Isaiah says that the Farther "has laid on him the iniquity of us all;" that "with his stripes we are healed" (Isa. 53:5, 6). Peter repeating the same thing, in other words says, that he "bare our sins in his own body on the tree" (1 Pet. 2:24). Paul's words are, "God sending his own Son in the likeness of sinful flesh, and for sin condemned sin in the flesh," "being made a curse for us" (Rom. 8:3; Gal. 3:13); in other words, the power and curse of sin was destroyed in his flesh when he was offered as a sacrifice, on which the whole weight of our sins was laid, with their curse and execration, with the fearful judgment of God, and condemnation to death. Here there is no mention of the vain dogma, that after the initial cleansing no man experiences the efficacy of Christ's passion in any other way than by means of satisfying penance: we are directed to the satisfaction of Christ alone for every fall. Now call to mind their pestilential dogma: that the grace of God is effective only in the first forgiveness of sins; but if we afterwards fall, our works co-operate in obtaining the second pardon. If these things are so, do the properties above attributed to Christ remain entire? How immense the difference between the two propositions—that our iniquities were laid upon Christ, that in his own person he might expiate them, and that they are expiated by our works; that Christ is the propitiation for our sins, and that God is to be propitiated by works. Then, in regard to pacifying the conscience, what pacification will it be to be told that sins are redeemed by satisfactions? How will it be able to ascertain the measure of satisfaction? It will always doubt whether God is propitious; will always fluctuate, always tremble. Those who rest satisfied with petty satisfactions

form too contemptible an estimate of the justice of God, and little consider the grievous heinousness of sin, as shall afterwards be shown. Even were we to grant that they can buy off some sins by due satisfaction, still what will they do while they are overwhelmed with so many sins that not even a hundred lives, though wholly devoted to the purpose, could suffice to satisfy for them? We may add, that all the passages in which the forgiveness of sins is declared refer not only to catechumens, but to the regenerate children of God; to those who have long been nursed in the bosom of the Church. That embassy which Paul so highly extols, "we pray you in Christ's stead, be ye reconciled to God" (2 Cor. 5:20), is not directed to strangers, but to those who had been regenerated long before. Setting satisfactions altogether aside, he directs us to the cross of Christ. Thus when he writes to the Colossians that Christ had "made peace through the blood of his cross," "to reconcile all things unto himself," he does not restrict it to the moment at which we are received into the Church but extends it to our whole course. This is plain from the context, where he says that in him "we have redemption by his blood, even the forgiveness of sins" (Col. 1:14). It is needless to collect more passages, as they are ever occurring.

28. Here they take refuge in the absurd distinction that some sins are *venial* and others *mortal*; that for the latter a weighty satisfaction is due, but that the former are purged by easier remedies; by the Lord's Prayer, the sprinkling of holy water, and the absolution of the Mass. Thus they insult and trifle with God. And yet, though they have the terms venial and mortal sin continually in their mouth, they have not yet been able to distinguish the one from the other, except by making impiety and impurity of heart to be venial sin. We, on the contrary, taught by the Scripture standard of righteousness and unrighteousness, declare that "the wages of sin is death;" and that "the soul that sinneth, it shall die" (Rom. 6:23; Ezek. 18:20). The sins of believers are venial, not because they do not merit death, but because by the mercy of God there is "now no condemnation to those which are in Christ Jesus" their sin being not imputed, but effaced by pardon. I know how unjustly they calumniate this our doctrine; for they say it is the paradox of the Stoics concerning the equality of sins: but we shall easily convict them out of their own mouths. I ask them whether, among those sins which they hold to be mortal, they acknowledge a greater and a less? If so, it cannot follow, as a matter of course, that all sins which are mortal are equal. Since Scripture declares that the wages of sin is death,—that obedience to the law is the way to life,—the transgression of it the way to death,—they cannot evade this conclusion. In such a mass of sins, therefore, how will they find an end to their satisfactions? If the satisfaction for one sin requires one day, while preparing it they involve themselves in more sins; since no man, however righteous, passes one day without falling repeatedly. While they prepare themselves for their satisfactions, number, or rather numbers without number, will be added. Confidence in satisfaction being thus destroyed, what more would they have? How do they still dare to think of satisfying?

29. They endeavor, indeed, to disentangle themselves, but it is impossible. They pretend a distinction between penalty and guilt, holding that the guilt is forgiven by the mercy of God; but that though the guilt is remitted, the punishment which divine justice requires to be paid remains. Satisfactions then properly relate to the remission of the penalty. How ridiculous this levity! They now confess that the remission of guilt is gratuitous; and yet they are ever and anon telling as to merit it by prayers and tears, and other preparations of every kind. Still the whole doctrine of Scripture regarding the remission of sins is diametrically opposed to that distinction. But although I think I have already done more than enough to establish this, I will subjoin some other passages, by which these slippery snakes will be so caught as to be afterwards unable to writhe even the tip of their tail: "Behold, the days come, saith the Lord, that I will make a new covenant with the house of Israel, and with the house of Judah." "I will forgive their iniquity, and I will remember their sin no more" (Jer. 31:31, 34). What this means we learn from another Prophet, when the Lord says, "When the righteous turneth away from his righteousness" "all his righteousness that he has done shall not be mentioned." "Again, when the wicked man turneth away from his wickedness that he has committed, and does that which is lawful and right, he shall save his soul alive" (Ezek. 18:24, 27). When he declares that he will not remember righteousness, the meaning is, that he will take no account of it to reward it. In the same way, not to remember sins is not to bring them to punishment. The same thing is denoted in other passages, by casting them behind his back, blotting them out as a cloud, casting them into the depths of the sea, not imputing them, hiding them. By such forms of expression the Holy Spirit has explained his meaning not obscurely, if we would lend a willing ear. Certainly if God punishes sins, he imputes them; if he avenges, he remembers; if he brings them to judgment, he has not hid them; if he

examines, he has not cast them behind his back; if he investigates, he has not blotted them out like a cloud; if he exposes them, he has not thrown them into the depths of the sea. In this way Augustine clearly interprets: "If God has covered sins, he willed not to advert to them; if he willed not to advert, he willed not to animadvert; if he willed not to animadvert, he willed not to punish: he willed not to take knowledge of them, he rather willed to pardon them. Why then did he say that sins were hid? Just that they might not be seen. What is meant by God seeing sins but punishing them?" (August. in Ps. 32:1). But let us hear from another prophetical passage on what terms the Lord forgives sins: "Though your sins be as scarlet, they shall be white as snow; though they be red like crimson, they shall be as wool" (Isa. 1:18). In Jeremiah again we read: "In those days, and in that time, saith the Lord, the iniquity of Israel shall be sought for, and there shall be none; and the sins of Judah, they shall not be found: for I will pardon them whom I reserve" (Jer. 50:20). Would you briefly comprehend the meaning of these words? Consider what, on the contrary, is meant by these expressions, "that transgression is sealed up in a bag;" "that the iniquity of Ephraim is bound up; his sin is hid;" that "the sin of Judah is written with a pen of iron, and with the point of a diamond." If they mean, as they certainly do, that vengeance will be recompensed, there can be no doubt that, by the contrary passages, the Lord declares that he renounces all thought of vengeance. Here I must entreat the reader not to listen to any glosses of mine, but only to give some deference to the word of God.

30. What, pray, did Christ perform for us if the punishment of sin is still exacted? For when we say that he "bare our sins in his own body on the tree" (1 Pet. 2:24), all we mean is, that he endured the penalty and punishment which was due to our sins. This is more significantly declared by Isaiah, when he says that the "chastisement (or correction) of our peace was upon him" (Isaiah 53:5). But what is the correction of our peace, unless it be the punishment due to our sins, and to be paid by us before we could be reconciled to God, had he not become our substitute? Thus you clearly see that Christ bore the punishment of sin that he might thereby exempt his people from it. And whenever Paul makes mention of the redemption procured by him, he calls it ἀπολύτροσις, by which he does not simply mean *redemption*, as it is commonly understood, but the very *price* and satisfaction of redemption. For which reason, he also says, that Christ gave himself an ἀντίλυτρον (ransom) for us. "What is propitiation with the Lord (says Augustine) but sacrifice? And what is sacrifice but that which was offered for us in the death of Christ?" But we have our strongest argument in the injunctions of the Mosaic Law as to expiating the guilt of sin. The Lord does not there appoint this or that method of satisfying, but requires the whole compensation to be made by sacrifice, though he at the same time enumerates all the rites of expiation with the greatest care and exactness. How comes it that he does not at all enjoin works as the means of procuring pardon, but only requires sacrifices for expiation, unless it were his purpose thus to testify that this is the only kind of satisfaction by which his justice is appeased? For the sacrifices which the Israelites then offered were not regarded as human works, but were estimated by their anti type, that is, the sole sacrifice of Christ. The kind of compensation which the Lord receives from us is elegantly and briefly expressed by Hosea: "Take with you words, and turn to the Lord: say unto him, Take away all iniquity, and receive us graciously," here is remission: "so will we render the calves of our lips," here is satisfaction (Hos. 14:2). I know that they have still a more subtle evasion, by making a distinction between eternal and temporal punishment; but as they define temporal punishment to be any kind of infliction with which God visits either the body or the soul, eternal death only excepted, this restriction avails them little. The passages which we have quoted above say expressly that the terms on which God receives us into favor are these—viz. he remits all the punishment which we deserved by pardoning our guilt. And whenever David or the other prophets ask pardon for their sins, they deprecate punishment. Nay, a sense of the divine justice impels them to this. On the other hand, when they promise mercy from the Lord, they almost always discourse of punishments and the forgiveness of them. Assuredly, when the Lord declares in Ezekiel, that he will put an end to the Babylonish captivity, not "for your sakes, O house of Israel, but for mine holy name's sake" (Ezek. 36:22), he sufficiently demonstrates that both are gratuitous. In short, if we are freed from guilt by Christ, the punishment consequent upon guilt must cease with it.

31. But since they also arm themselves with passages of Scripture, let us see what the arguments are which they employ. David, they say, when upbraided by Nathan the Prophet for adultery and murder, receives pardon of the sin, and yet by the death of the son born of adultery is afterwards punished (2 Sam. 12:13, 14). Such punishments which were to be inflicted after the remission of

the guilt, we are taught to ransom by satisfactions. For Daniel exhorted Nebuchadnezzar: "Break off thy sins by righteousness, and thine iniquities by showing mercy to the poor" (Dan. 4:27). And Solomon says, "by mercy and truth iniquity is purged" (Prov. 16:6); and again, "love covereth all sins" (Prov. 10:12). This sentiment is confirmed by Peter (1 Pet. 4:8). Also in Luke, our Lord says of the woman that was a sinner, "Her sins, which are many, are forgiven; for she loved much" (Luke 7:47). How perverse and preposterous the judgment they ever form of the doings of God! Had they observed, what certainly they ought not to have overlooked, that there are two kinds of divine judgment, they would have seen in the correction of David a very different form of punishment from that which must be thought designed for vengeance. But since it in no slight degree concerns us to understand the purpose of God in the chastisements by which he animadverts upon our sins and how much they differ from the exemplary punishments which he indignantly inflicts on the wicked and reprobate, I think it will not be improper briefly to glance at it. For the sake of distinction, we may call the one kind of judgment *punishment*, the other *chastisement*. In judicial punishment, God is to be understood as taking vengeance on his enemies, by displaying his anger against them, confounding, scattering, and annihilating them. By divine punishment, properly so called, let us then understand punishment accompanied with indignation. In judicial chastisement, he is offended, but not in wrath; he does not punish by destroying or striking down as with a thunderbolt. Hence it is not properly punishment or vengeance, but correction and admonition. The one is the act of a judge, the other of a father. When the judge punishes a criminal, he animadverts upon the crime, and demands the penalty. When a father corrects his son sharply, it is not to mulct or avenge, but rather to teach him, and make him more cautious for the future. Chrysostom in his writings employs a simile which is somewhat different, but the same in purport. He says, "A son is whipt, and a slave is whipt, but the latter is punished as a slave for his offense: the former is chastised as a freeborn son, standing in need of correction." The correction of the latter is designed to prove and amend him; that of the former is scourging and punishment.

32. To have a short and clear view of the whole matter, we must make two distinctions. First, whenever the infliction is designed to avenge, then the curse and wrath of God displays itself. This is never the case with believers. On the contrary, the chastening of God carries his blessing with it, and is an evidence of love, as Scripture teaches. This distinction is plainly marked throughout the word of God. All the calamities which the wicked suffer in the present life are depicted to us as a kind of anticipation of the punishment of hell. In these they already see, as from a distance, their eternal condemnation; and so far are they from being thereby reformed, or deriving any benefit, that by such preludes they are rather prepared for the fearful doom which finally awaits them. The Lord chastens his servants sore, but does not give them over unto death (Ps. 118:18). When afflicted, they acknowledge it is good for them, that they may learn his statutes (Ps. 119:71). But as we everywhere read that the saints received their chastisements with placid mind, so inflictions of the latter kind they always most earnestly deprecated. "O Lord, correct me," says Jeremiah, "but with judgment; not in thine anger, lest thou bring me to nothing. Pour out thy fury upon the heathen that know thee not, and upon the families that call not on thy name" (Jer. 10:24–25). David says "O Lord, rebuke me not in thine anger, neither chasten me in thy hot displeasure" (Ps. 6:1). There is nothing inconsistent with this in its being repeatedly said, that the Lord is angry with his saints when he chastens them for their sins (Ps. 38:7). In like manner, in Isaiah, "And in that day thou shalt say, O Lord, I will praise thee: though thou west angry with me, thine anger is turned away, and thou comfortedst me" (Isa. 12:1). Likewise in Habakkuk, "In wrath remember mercy" (Hab. 3:2); and in Micah, "I will bear the indignation of the Lord, because I have sinned against him" (Mic. 7:9). Here we are reminded not only that those who are justly punished gain nothing by murmuring, but that believers obtain a mitigation of their pain by reflecting on the divine intention. For the same reason, he is said to profane his inheritance; and yet we know that he will never profane it. The expression refers not to the counsel or purpose of God in punishing, but to the keen sense of pain, endured by those who are visited with any measure of divine severity. For the Lord not only chastens his people with a slight degree of austerity, but sometimes so wounds them, that they seem to themselves on the very eve of perdition. He thus declares that they have deserved his anger, and it is fitting so to do, that they may be dissatisfied with themselves for their sins, may be more careful in their desires to appease God, and anxiously hasten to seek his pardon; still, at this very time, he gives clearer evidence of his mercy than of his anger. For He who cannot deceive has declared, that the covenant made with us in our true Solomon stands

fast and will never be broken, "If his children forsake my law, and walk not in my judgments; if they break my statutes, and keep not my commandments; then will I visit their transgressions with the rod, and their iniquity with stripes. Nevertheless, my loving-kindness will I not utterly take from him, nor suffer my faithfulness to fail" (Ps. 89:31–34). To assure us of this mercy, he says, that the rod with which he will chastise the posterity of Solomon will be the "rod of men," and "the stripes of the children of men" (2 Sam. 7:14). While by these terms he denotes moderation and levity, he, at the same time, intimates, that those who feel the hand of God opposed to them cannot but tremble and be confounded. How much regard he has to this levity in chastening his Israel he shows by the Prophet, "Behold, I have refined thee, but not with silver; I have chosen thee in the furnace of affliction" (Isa. 48:10). Although he tells them that they are chastisements with a view to purification, he adds, that even these are so tempered, that they are not to be too much crushed by them. And this is very necessary, for the more a man reveres God, and devotes himself to the cultivation of piety, the more tender he is in bearing his anger (Ps. 90:11; and ibid. Calv). The reprobate, though they groan under the lash, yet because they weigh not the true cause, but rather turn their back, as well upon their sins as upon the divine judgment, become hardened in their stupor; or, because they murmur and kick, and so rebel against their judge, their infatuated violence fills them with frenzy and madness. Believers, again, admonished by the rod of God, immediately begin to reflect on their sins, and, struck with fear and dread, retake themselves as suppliants to implore mercy. Did not God mitigate the pains by which wretched souls are excruciated, they would give way a hundred times, even at slight signs of his anger.

33. The second distinction is, that when the reprobate are brought under the lash of God, they begin in a manner to pay the punishment due to his justice; and though their refusal to listen to these proofs of the divine anger will not escape with impunity, still they are not punished with the view of bringing them to a better mind, but only to teach them by dire experience that God is a judge and avenger. The sons of God are beaten with rods, not that they may pay the punishment due to their faults, but that they may thereby be led to repent. Accordingly, we perceive that they have more respect to the future than to the past. I prefer giving this in the words of Chrysostom rather than my own: "His object in imposing a penalty upon us, is not to inflict punishment on our sins but to correct us for the future" (Chrysost. Serm. de Pœnit. et Confess). So also Augustine, "The suffering at which you cry, is medicine, not punishment; chastisement, not condemnation. Do not drive away the rod, if you would not be driven away from the inheritance. Know, brethren, that the whole of that misery of the human race, under which the world groans, is a medicinal pain, not a penal sentence" (August. in Psal. 102, circa finem). It seemed proper to quote these passages, lest any one should think the mode of expression which I have used to be novel or uncommon. To the same effect are the indignant terms in which the Lord expostulates with his people, for their ingratitude in obstinately despising all his inflictions. In Isaiah he says, "Why should ye be stricken any more? ye will revolt more and more. The whole head is sick and the whole heart faint" (Isa. 1:5, 6). But as such passages abound in the Prophets, it is sufficient briefly to have shown, that the only purpose of God in punishing his Church is to subdue her to repentance. Thus, when he rejected Saul from the kingdoms he punished in vengeance (1 Sam. 15:23); when he deprived David of his child, he chastised for amendment (2 Sam. 12:18). In this sense Paul is to be understood when he says, "When we are judged, we are chastened of the Lord, that we should not be condemned with the world" (1 Cor. 11:32); that is, while we as sons of God are afflicted by our heavenly Father's hand, it is not punishment to confound, but only chastisement to train us. On this subject Augustine is plainly with us (De Peccator. Meritis ac Remiss. Lib. 2 cap. 33, 34). For he shows that the punishments with which men are equally chastened by God are to be variously considered; because the saints after the forgiveness of their sins have struggles and exercises, the reprobate without forgiveness are punished for their iniquity. Enumerating the punishments inflicted on David and other saints, he says, it was designed, by thus humbling them, to prove and exercise their piety. The passage in Isaiah, in which it is said, "Speak ye comfortably to Jerusalem, and cry unto her, that her warfare is accomplished that her iniquity is pardoned; for she has received of the Lord's hands double for all her sins" (Isa. 40:2), proves not that the pardon of sin depends on freedom from punishment. It is just as if he had said, Sufficient punishment has now been exacted; as for their number and heinousness you have long been oppressed with sorrow and mourning, it is time to send you a message of complete mercy, that your minds may be filled with joy on feeling me to be a Father. For God there assumes the character of a father

who repents even of the just severity which he has been compelled to us, towards his son.

34. These are the thoughts with which the believer ought to be provided in the bitterness of affliction, "The time is come that judgment must begin at the house of God," "the city which is called by my name" (1 Pet. 4:17; Jer. 25:29). What could the sons of God do, if they thought that the severity which they feel was vengeance? He who, smitten by the hand of God, thinks that God is a judge inflicting punishment, cannot conceive of him except as angry and at enmity with him; cannot but detest the rod of God as curse and condemnation; in short, Can never persuade himself that he is loved by God, while he feels that he is still disposed to inflict punishment upon him. He only profits under the divine chastening who considers that God, though offended with his sins, is still propitious and favorable to him. Otherwise, the feeling must necessarily be what the Psalmist complains that he had experienced, "Thy wrath lieth hard upon me, and thou hast afflicted me with all thy waves." Also what Moses says, "For we are consumed by thine anger, and by thy wrath we are troubled. Thou hast set our iniquities before thee, our secret sins in the light of thy countenance. For all our days are passed away in thy wrath; we spend our years as a tale that is told" (Ps. 90:7–9). On the other hand, David speaking of fatherly chastisements, to show how believers are more assisted than oppressed by them, thus sings "Blessed is the man whom thou chastenest, O Lord, and teachest him out of thy law; that thou mayest give him rest from the days of adversity, until the pit be digged for the wicked" (Ps. 94:12, 13). It is certainly a sore temptation, when God, sparing unbelievers and overlooking their crimes, appears more rigid towards his own people. Hence, to solace them, he adds the admonition of the law which teaches them, that their salvation is consulted when they are brought back to the right path, whereas the wicked are borne headlong in their errors, which ultimately lead to the pit. It matters not whether the punishment is eternal or temporary. For disease, pestilence, famine, and war, are curses from God, as much as even the sentence of eternal death, whenever their tendency is to operate as instruments of divine wrath and vengeance against the reprobate.

35. All, if I mistake not, now see what view the Lord had in chastening David, namely, to prove that murder and adultery are most offensive to God, and to manifest this offensiveness in a beloved and faithful servant, that David himself might be taught never again to dare to commit such wickedness; still, however, it was not a punishment designed in payment of a kind of compensation to God. In the same way are we to judge of that other correction, in which the Lord subjects his people to a grievous pestilence, for the disobedience of David in forgetting himself so far as to number the people. He indeed freely forgave David the guilt of his sin; but because it was necessary, both as a public example to all ages and also to humble David himself, not to allow such an offense to go unpunished, he chastened him most sharply with his whip. We ought also to keep this in view in the universal curse of the human race. For since after obtaining grace we still continue to endure the miseries denounced to our first parent as the penalty of transgression, we ought thereby to be reminded, how offensive to God is the transgression of his law, that thus humbled and dejected by a consciousness of our wretched condition, we may aspire more ardently to true happiness. But it were most foolish in any one to imagine, that we are subjected to the calamities of the present life for the guilt of sin. This seems to me to have been Chrysostom's meaning when he said, "If the purpose of God in inflicting punishment is to bring those persisting in evil to repentance, when repentance is manifested punishment would be superfluous" (Chrysos. Homily. 3 de Provid.). Wherefore, as he knows what the disposition of each requires, he treats one with greater harshness and another with more indulgence. Accordingly, when he wishes to show that he is not excessive in exacting punishment, he upbraids a hard hearted and obstinate people, because, after being smitten, they still continued in sin (Jer. 5:3). In the same sense he complains, that "Ephraim is a cake not turned" (Hos. 7:8), because chastisement did not make a due impression on their minds, and, correcting their vices, make them fit to receive pardon. Surely he who thus speaks shows, that as soon as any one repents he will be ready to receive him, and that the rigor which he exercises in chastising faults is wrung from him by our perverseness, since we should prevent him by a voluntary correction. Such, however, being the hardness and rudeness of all hearts, that they stand universally in need of castigation, our infinitely wise Parent has seen it meet to exercise all without exception, during their whole lives, with chastisement. It is strange how they fix their eyes so intently on the one example of David, and are not moved by the many examples in which they might have beheld the free forgiveness of sins. The publican is said to have gone down from the temple justified (Luke 18:14); no punishment follows. Peter obtained the pardon of his sin (Luke 22:61). "We read of his tears," says Ambrose (Serm. 46,

De Poenit. Petri), "we read not of satisfaction." To the paralytic it is said, "Son, be of good cheer; thy sins be forgiven thee" (Mt. 9:2); no penance is enjoined. All the acts of forgiveness mentioned in Scripture are gratuitous. The rule ought to be drawn from these numerous examples, rather than from one example which contains a kind of specialty.

36. Daniel, in exhorting Nebuchadnezzar to break off his sins by righteousness, and his iniquities by showing mercy to the poor (Dan. 4:27), meant not to intimate, that righteousness and mercy are able to propitiate God and redeem from punishment (far be it from us to suppose that there ever was any other ἀπολύτρωσις (*ransom*) than the blood of Christ); but the breaking off referred to in that passage has reference to man rather than to God: as if he had said, O king, you have exercised an unjust and violent domination, you have oppressed the humble, spoiled the poor, treated your people harshly and unjustly; instead of unjust exaction, instead of violence and oppression, now practice mercy and justice. In like manner, Solomon says, that love covers a multitude of sins; not, however, with God, but among men. For the whole verse stands thus, "Hatred stirreth up strifes; but love covereth all sins" (Prov. 10:12). Here, after his manner, he contrasts the evils produced by hatred with the fruits of charity, in this sense, Those who hate are incessantly biting, carping at, upbraiding, lacerating each other, making every thing a fault; but those who love mutually conceal each other's faults, wink at many, forgive many: not that the one approves the vices of the other, but tolerates and cures by admonishing, rather than exasperates by assailing. That the passage is quoted by Peter (1 Pet. 4:8) in the same sense we cannot doubt, unless we would charge him with corrupting or craftily wresting Scripture. When it is said, that "by mercy and truth iniquity is purged" (Prov. 16:6), the meaning is, not that by them compensation is made to the Lord, so that he being thus satisfied remits the punishment which he would otherwise have exacted; but intimation is made after the familiar manner of Scripture, that those who, forsaking their vices and iniquities turn to the Lord in truth and piety, will find him propitious: as if he had said, that the wrath of God is calmed, and his judgment is at rest, whenever we rest from our wickedness. But, indeed, it is not the cause of pardon that is described, but rather the mode of true conversion; just as the Prophets frequently declare, that it is in vain for hypocrites to offer God fictitious rites instead of repentance, seeing his delight is in integrity and the duties of charity. In like manner, also, the author of the Epistle to the Hebrews, commending kindness and humanity, reminds us, that "with such sacrifices God is well pleased" (Heb. 13:16). And indeed when Christ, rebuking the Pharisees because, intent merely on the outside of the cup and platter, they neglected purity of heart, enjoins them, in order that they may be clean in all respects, to give alms, does he exhort them to give satisfaction thereby? He only tells them what the kind of purity is which God requires. Of this mode of expression we have treated elsewhere (Mt. 23:25; Luke 11:39–41; see Calv. In Harm. Evang).

37. In regard to the passage in Luke (Luke 7:36, sq). no man of sober judgment, who reads the parable there employed by our Lord, will raise any controversy with us. The Pharisee thought that the Lord did not know the character of the woman whom he had so easily admitted to his presence. For he presumed that he would not have admitted her if he had known what kind of a sinner she was; and from this he inferred, that one who could be deceived in this way was not a prophet. Our Lord, to show that she was not a sinner, inasmuch as she had already been forgiven, spake this parable: "There was a certain creditor which had two debtors; the one owed five hundred pence, and the other fifty. And when they had nothing to pay, he frankly forgave them both. Tell me, therefore, which of them will love him most?" The Pharisee answers: "I suppose that he to whom he forgave most." Then our Savior rejoins: "Her sins, which are many, are forgiven; for she loved much." By these words it is plain he does not make love the cause of forgiveness, but the proof of it. The similitude is borrowed from the case of a debtor, to whom a debt of five hundred pence had been forgiven. It is not said that the debt is forgiven because he loved much, but that he loved much because it was forgiven. The similitude ought to be applied in this way: You think this woman is a sinner; but you ought to have acknowledged her as not a sinner, in respect that her sins have been forgiven her. Her love ought to have been to you a proof of her having obtained forgiveness, that love being an expression of gratitude for the benefit received. It is an argument a*posteriori*, by which something is demonstrated by the results produced by it. Our Lord plainly attests the ground on which she had obtained forgiveness, when he says, "Thy faith has saved thee." By faith, therefore, we obtain forgiveness: by love we give thanks, and bear testimony to the loving-kindness of the Lord.

38. I am little moved by the numerous passages in the writings of the Fathers relating to satisfaction. I see indeed that some (I will frankly say almost all whose books are

extant) have either erred in this matter, or spoken too roughly and harshly; but I cannot admit that they were so rude and unskillful as to write these passages in the sense in which they are read by our new satisfactionaries. Chrysostom somewhere says, "When mercy is implored interrogation ceases; when mercy is asked, judgment rages not; when mercy is sought, there is no room for punishment; where there is mercy, no question is asked; where there is mercy, the answer gives pardon" (Chrysos. Hom. 2 in Psal. 50). How much soever these words may be twisted, they can never be reconciled with the dogmas of the Schoolmen. In the book *De Dogmatibus Ecclesiasticis*, which is attributed to Augustine, you read (cap. 54), "The satisfaction of repentance is to cut off the causes of sins, and not to indulge an entrance to their suggestions." From this it appears that the doctrine of satisfaction, said to be paid for sins committed, was every where derided in those ages; for here the only satisfaction referred to is caution, abstinence from sin for the future. I am unwilling to quote what Chrysostom says (Hom. 10 in Genes) that God requires nothing more of us than to confess our faults before him with tears, as similar sentiments abound both in his writings and those of others. Augustine indeed calls works of mercy remedies for obtaining forgiveness of sins (Enchir. ad Laur.); but lest any one should stumble at the expression, he himself, in another passage, obviates the difficulty. "The flesh of Christ," says he, "is the true and only sacrifice for sins—not only for those which are all effaced in baptism, but those into which we are afterwards betrayed through infirmity, and because of which the whole Church daily cries, 'Forgive us our debts,' (Mt. 6:12). And they are forgiven by that special sacrifice."

39. By satisfaction, however, they, for the most part, meant not compensation to be paid to God, but the public testimony, by which those who had been punished with excommunication, and wished again to be received into communion, assured the Church of their repentance. For those penitents were enjoined certain fasts and other things, by which they might prove that they were truly, and from the heart, weary of their former life, or rather might obliterate the remembrance of their past deeds: in this way they were said to give satisfaction, not to God, but to the Church. The same thing is expressed by Augustine in a passage in his Enchiridion ad Laurentium, cap. 65. From that ancient custom the satisfactions and confessions now in use took their rise. It is indeed a viperish progeny, not even a vestige of the better form now remaining. I know that ancient writers sometimes speak harshly; nor do I deny, as I lately said, that they have perhaps erred; but dogmas, which were tainted with a few blemishes now that they have fallen into the unwashed hands of those men, are altogether defiled. And if we were to decide the contest by authority of the Fathers, what kind of Fathers are those whom they obtrude upon us? A great part of those, from whom Lombard their Coryphaeus framed his centos, are extracted from the absurd dreams of certain monks passing under the names of Ambrose, Jerome, Augustine, and Chrysostom. On the present subject almost all his extracts are from the book of Augustine *De Paenitentia*, a book absurdly compiled by some rhapsodist, alike from good and bad authors—a book which indeed bears the name of Augustine, but which no person of the least learning would deign to acknowledge as his. Wishing to save my readers trouble, they will pardon me for not searching minutely into all their absurdities. For myself it were not very laborious, and might gain some applause, to give a complete exposure of dogmas which have hitherto been vaunted as mysteries; but as my object is to give useful instruction, I desist.

CHAPTER 5

OF THE MODES OF SUPPLEMENTING SATISFACTION—VIZ. INDULGENCES AND PURGATORY.

Divisions of the chapter,—I. A summary description and refutation of Popish indulgences, sec. 1, 2. II. Confutation by Leo and Augustine. Answer to two objections urged in support of them, sec. 3, 4. A profane love of filthy lucre on the part of the Pope. The origin of indulgences unfolded, sec. 5. III. An examination of Popish purgatory. Its horrible impiety, sec. 6. An explanation of five passages of Scripture by which Sophists endeavor to support that dream, sec. 7, 8. Sentiments of the ancient Theologians concerning purgatory, sec. 10.

Sections:

1. The dogma of satisfaction the parent of indulgences. Vanity of both. The reason of it. Evidence of the avarice of the Pope and the Romish clergy: also of the blindness with which the Christian world was smitten

2. View of indulgences given by the Sophists. Their true nature. Refutation of them. Refutation confirmed by seven passages of Scripture.

3. Confirmed also by the testimony of Leo, a Roman Bishop, and by Augustine. Attempts of the

Popish doctors to establish the monstrous doctrine of indulgences, and even support it by Apostolical authority. First answer.

4. Second answer to the passage of an Apostle adduced to support the dogma of indulgences. Answer confirmed by a comparison with other passages, and from a passage in Augustine, explaining the Apostle's meaning. Another passage from the same Apostle confirming this view.

5. The Pope's profane thirst for filthy lucre exposed. The origin of indulgences.

6. Examination of the fictitious purgatory of the Papists. 1. From the nature of the thing itself. 2. From the authority of God. 3. From the consideration of the merit of Christ, which is destroyed by this fiction. Purgatory, what it is. 4. From the impiety teeming from this fountain.

7. Exposition of the passages of Scripture quoted in support of purgatory. 1. Of the Impardonable sin, from which it is inferred that there are some sins afterwards to be forgiven. 2. Of the passage as to paying the last farthing.

8. 3. The passage concerning the bending of the knee to Christ by things under the earth. 4. The example of Judas Maccabaeus in sending an oblation for the dead to Jerusalem.

9. 5. Of the fire which shall try every man's work. The sentiment of the ancient theologians. Answer, containing a reductio ad absurdum. Confirmation by a passage of Augustine. The meaning of the Apostle. What to be understood by fire. A clear exposition of the metaphor. The day of the Lord. How those who suffer loss are saved by fire.

10. The doctrine of purgatory ancient, but refuted by a more ancient Apostle. Not supported by ancient writers, by Scripture, or solid argument. Introduced by custom and a zeal not duly regulated by the word of God. Ancient writers, as Augustine, speak doubtfully in commending prayer for the dead. At all events, we must hold by the word of God, which rejects this fiction. A vast difference between the more ancient and the more modern builders of purgatory. This shown by comparing them.

1. From this dogma of satisfaction that of indulgences takes its rise. For the pretence is, that what is wanting to our own ability is hereby supplied; and they go the insane length of defining them to be a dispensation of the merits of Christ, and the martyrs which the Pope makes by his bulls. Though they are fitter for hellebore than for argument,—and it is scarcely worth while to refute these frivolous errors, which, already battered down, begin of their own accord to grow antiquated, and totter to their fall;—yet, as a brief refutation may be useful to some of the unlearned, I will not omit it. Indeed, the fact that indulgences have so long stood safe and with impunity, and wantoned with so much fury and tyranny, may be regarded as a proof into how deep a night of ignorance mankind were for some ages plunged. They saw themselves insulted openly, and without disguise, by the Pope and his bull-bearers; they saw the salvation of the soul made the subject of a lucrative traffic, salvation taxed at a few pieces of money, nothing given gratuitously; they saw what was squeezed from them in the form of oblations basely consumed on strumpets, pimps and gluttony, the loudest trumpeters of indulgences being the greatest despisers; they saw the monster stalking abroad, and every day luxuriating with greater license, and that without end, new bulls being constantly issued, and new sums extracted. Still indulgences were received with the greatest reverence, worshipped, and bought. Even those who saw more clearly than others deemed them pious frauds, by which, even in deceiving, some good was gained. Now, at length, that a considerable portion of the world have begun to rethink themselves, indulgences grow cool, and gradually even begin to freeze, preparatory to their final extinction.

2. But since very many who see the vile imposture, theft, and rapine (with which the dealers in indulgences have hitherto deluded and sported with us), are not aware of the true source of the impiety, it may be proper to show not only what indulgences truly are, but also that they are polluted in every part. They give the name of *treasury of the Church* to the merits of Christ, the holy Apostles and Martyrs. They pretend, as I have said, that the radical custody of the granary has been delivered to the Roman bishop, to whom the dispensation of these great blessings belongs in such a sense, that he can both exercise it by himself, and delegate the power of exercising it to others. Hence we have from the Pope at one time plenary indulgences, at another for certain years; from the cardinals for a hundred days, and from the bishops for forty. These, to describe them truly, are a profanation of the blood of Christ, and a delusion of Satan, by which the Christian people are led away from the grace of God and the life which is in Christ, and turned aside from the true way of salvation. For how could the blood of Christ be more shamefully profaned than by denying its suf-

ficiency for the remission of sins, for reconciliation and satisfaction, unless its defects, as if it were dried up and exhausted, are supplemented from some other quarter? Peter's words are: "To him give all the prophets witness, that through his name whosoever believeth in him shall receive remission of sins" (Acts 10:43); but indulgences bestow the remission of sins through Peter, Paul, and the Martyrs. "The blood of Jesus Christ his Son cleanseth us from all sin," says John (1 John 1:7). Indulgences make the blood of the martyrs an ablution of sins. "He has made him to be sin (*i.e.* a satisfaction for sin) for us who knew no sin," says Paul (2 Cor. 5:21), "that we might be made the righteousness of God in him." Indulgences make the satisfaction of sin to depend on the blood of the martyrs. Paul exclaimed and testified to the Corinthians, that Christ alone was crucified, and died for them (1 Cor. 1:13). Indulgences declare that Paul and others died for us. Paul elsewhere says that Christ purchased the Church with his own blood (Acts 20:28). Indulgences assign another purchase to the blood of martyrs. "By one offering he has perfected for ever them that are sanctified," says the Apostle (Heb. 10:14). Indulgences, on the other hand, insist that sanctification, which would otherwise be insufficient, is perfected by martyrs. John says that all the saints "have washed their robes, and made them white in the blood of the Lamb" (Rev. 7:14). Indulgences tell us to wash our robes in the blood of saints.

3. There is an admirable passage in opposition to their blasphemies in Leo, a Roman Bishop (ad Palæstinos, Ep. 81). "Although the death of many saints was precious in the sight of the Lord (Ps. 116:15), yet no innocent man's slaughter was the propitiation of the world. The just received crowns did not give them; and the fortitude of believers produced examples of patience, not gifts of righteousness: for their deaths were for themselves; and none by his final end paid the debt of another, except Christ our Lord, in whom alone all are crucified—all dead, buried, and raised up." This sentiment, as it was of a memorable nature, he has elsewhere repeated (Epist. 95). Certainly one could not desire a clearer confutation of this impious dogma. Augustine introduces the same sentiment not less appositely: "Although brethren die for brethren, yet no martyr's blood is shed for the remission of sins: this Christ did for us, and in this conferred upon us not what we should imitate, but what should make us grateful" (August. Tract. in Joann. 84). Again, in another passage: "As he alone became the Son of God and the Son of man, that he might make us to be with himself sons of God, so he alone, without any ill desert, undertook the penalty for us, that through him we mighty without good desert, obtain undeserved favor" (ad Bonif. Lib. 4, cap. 4). Indeed, as their whole doctrine is a patchwork of sacrilege and blasphemy, this is the most blasphemous of the whole. Let them acknowledge whether or not they hold the following dogmas: That the martyrs, by their death, performed more to God, and merited more than was necessary for themselves, and that they have a large surplus of merits which may be applied to others; that in order that this great good may not prove superfluous, their blood is mingled with the blood of Christ, and out of both is formed the treasury of the Church, for the forgiveness and satisfaction of sins; and that in this sense we must understand the words of Paul: "Who now rejoice in my sufferings, and fill up that which is behind of the afflictions of Christ in my flesh for his body's sake, which is the Church" (Col. 1:24). What is this but merely to leave the name of Christ, and at the same time make him a vulgar saintling, who can scarcely be distinguished in the crowd? He alone ought to be preached, alone held forth, alone named, alone looked to, whenever the subject considered is the obtaining of the forgiveness of sins, expiation, and sanctification. But let us hear their propositions. That the blood of martyrs may not be shed without fruit, it must be employed for the common good of the Church. Is it so? Was there no fruit in glorifying God by death? in sealing his truth with their blood? in testifying, by contempt of the present life, that they looked for a better? in confirming the faith of the Church, and at the same time disabling the pertinacity of the enemy by their constancy? But thus it is. They acknowledge no fruit if Christ is the only propitiation, if he alone died for our sins, if he alone was offered for our redemption. Nevertheless, they say, Peter and Paul would have gained the crown of victory though they had died in their beds a natural death. But as they contended to blood, it would not accord with the justice of God to leave their doing so barren and unfruitful. As if God were unable to augment the glory of his servants in proportion to the measure of his gifts. The advantage derived in common by the Church is great enough, when, by their triumphs, she is inflamed with zeal to fight.

4. How maliciously they wrest the passage in which Paul says, that he supplies in his body that which was lacking in the sufferings of Christ! (Col. 1:24). That defect or supplement refers not to the work of redemption, satisfaction, or expiation, but to those afflictions with which the members of Christ, in other words, all believers, behave to be exercised, so long as they are in

the flesh. He says, therefore, that part of the sufferings of Christ still remains—viz. that what he suffered in himself he daily suffers in his members. Christ so honors us as to regard and count our afflictions as his own. By the additional words—for *the Church*, Paul means not for the redemptions or reconciliations or satisfaction of the Church, but for edification and progress. As he elsewhere says, "I endure all things for the elect's sakes, that they may also obtain the salvation which is in Christ Jesus with eternal glory" (2 Tim. 2:10). He also writes to the Corinthians: "Whether we be afflicted, it is for your consolation and salvation, which is effectual in the enduring of the same sufferings which we also suffer" (2 Cor. 1:6). In the same place he immediately explains his meaning by adding, that he was made a minister of the Church, not for redemption, but according to the dispensation which he received to preach the gospel of Christ. But if they still desire another interpreter, let them hear Augustine: "The sufferings of Christ are in Christ alone, as in the head; in Christ and the Church as in the whole body. Hence Paul, being one member says, 'I fill up in my body that which is behind of the sufferings of Christ.' Therefore O hearers whoever you be, if you are among the members of Christ, whatever you suffer from those who are not members of Christ, was lacking to the sufferings of Christ" (August. in Ps. 16). He elsewhere explains the end of the sufferings of the Apostles undertaken for Christ: "Christ is my door to you, because ye are the sheep of Christ purchased by his blood: acknowledge your price, which is not paid by me, but preached by me" (August. Tract. in Joann. 47). He afterwards adds, "As he laid down his life, so ought we to lay down our lives for the brethren, to build up peace and maintain faith." Thus far Augustine. Far be it from us to imagine that Paul thought any thing was wanting to the sufferings of Christ in regard to the complete fulness of righteousness, salvation, and life, or that he wished to make any addition to it, after showing so clearly and eloquently that the grace of Christ was poured out in such rich abundance as far to exceed all the power of sin (Rom. 5:15). All saints have been saved by it alone, not by the merit of their own life or death, as Peter distinctly testifies (Acts 15:11); so that it is an insult to God and his Anointed to place the worthiness of any saint in any thing save the mercy of God alone. But why dwell longer on this, as if the matter were obscure, when to mention these monstrous dogmas is to refute them?

5. Moreover, to say nothing of these abominations, who taught the Pope to enclose the grace of Jesus Christ in lead and parchment, grace which the Lord is pleased to dispense by the word of the Gospel? Undoubtedly either the Gospel of God or indulgences must be false. That Christ is offered to us in the Gospel with all the abundance of heavenly blessings, with all his merits, all his righteousness, wisdom, and grace, without exception, Paul bears witness when he says, "Now then we are ambassadors for Christ, as though God did beseech you by us: we pray you in Christ's stead, be ye reconciled to God. For he has made him to be sin for us, who knew no sin; that we might be made the righteousness of God in him" (2 Cor. 5:20, 21). And what is meant by the fellowship (κοινωνία) of Christ, which according to the same Apostle (1 Cor. 1:9) is offered to us in the Gospel, all believers know. On the contrary, indulgences, bringing forth some portion of the grace of God from the armory of the Pope, fix it to lead, parchment, and a particular place, but dissever it from the word of God. When we inquire into the origin of this abuse, it appears to have arisen from this, that when in old times the satisfactions imposed on penitents were too severe to be borne, those who felt themselves burdened beyond measure by the penance imposed, petitioned the Church for relaxation. The remission so given was called indulgence. But as they transferred satisfactions to God, and called them compensations by which men redeem themselves from the justice of God, they in the same way transferred indulgences, representing them as expiatory remedies which free us from merited punishment. The blasphemies to which we have referred have been feigned with so much effrontery that there is not the least pretext for them.

6. Their purgatory cannot now give us much trouble, since with this ax we have struck it, thrown it down, and overturned it from its very foundations. I cannot agree with some who think that we ought to dissemble in this matter, and make no mention of purgatory, from which (as they say) fierce contests arise, and very little edification can be obtained. I myself would think it right to disregard their follies did they not tend to serious consequences. But since purgatory has been reared on many, and is daily propped up by new blasphemies; since it produces many grievous offenses, assuredly it is not to be connived at, however it might have been disguised for a time, that without any authority from the word of God, it was devised by prying audacious rashness, that credit was procured for it by fictitious revelations, the wiles of Satan, and that certain passages of Scripture were ignorantly wrested to its support. Although the Lord bears not that human presumption should thus force its way to the hidden recesses of his judgments; although he has

issued a strict prohibition against neglecting his voice, and making inquiry at the dead (Deut. 18:11), and permits not his word to be so erroneously contaminated. Let us grant, however, that all this might have been tolerated for a time as a thing of no great moment; yet when the expiation of sins is sought elsewhere than in the blood of Christ, and satisfaction is transferred to others, silence were most perilous. We are bound, therefore, to raise our voice to its highest pitch, and cry aloud that purgatory is a deadly device of Satan; that it makes void the cross of Christ; that it offers intolerable insult to the divine mercy; that it undermines and overthrows our faith. For what is this purgatory but the satisfaction for sin paid after death by the souls of the dead? Hence when this idea of satisfaction is refuted, purgatory itself is forthwith completely overturned. But if it is perfectly clear, from what was lately said, that the blood of Christ is the only satisfaction, expiation, and cleansing for the sins of believers, what remains but to hold that purgatory is mere blasphemy, horrid blasphemy against Christ? I say nothing of the sacrilege by which it is daily defended, the offenses which it begets in religion, and the other innumerable evils which we see teeming forth from that fountain of impiety.

7. Those passages of Scripture on which it is their wont falsely and iniquitously to fasten, it may be worth while to wrench out of their hands. When the Lord declares that the sin against the Holy Ghost will not be forgiven either in this world or the world to come, he thereby intimates (they say) that there is a remission of certain sins hereafter. But who sees not that the Lord there speaks of the guilt of sin? But if this is so, what has it to do with their purgatory, seeing they deny not that the guilt of those sins, the punishment of which is there expiated, is forgiven in the present life? Lest, however, they should still object, we shall give a plainer solution. Since it was the Lord's intention to cut off all hope of pardon from this flagitous wickedness, he did not consider it enough to say, that it would never be forgiven, but in the way of amplification employed a division by which he included both the judgment which every man's conscience pronounces in the present life, and the final judgment which will be publicly pronounced at the resurrection; as if he had said, Beware of this malignant rebellion, as you would of instant destruction; for he who of set purpose endeavors to extinguish the offered light of the Spirit, shall not obtain pardon either in this life, which has been given to sinners for conversion, or on the last day when the angels of God shall separate the sheep from the goats, and the heavenly kingdom shall be purged of all that offends. The next passage they produce is the parable in Matthew: "Agree with thine adversary quickly, whiles thou art in the way with him; lest at any time the adversary deliver thee to the judge, and the judge deliver thee to the officer, and thou be cast into prison. Verily, I say unto thee, Thou shalt by no means come out thence, till thou hast paid the uttermost earthing" (Mt. 5:25, 26). If in this passage the judge means God, the adversary the devil, the officer an angel, and the prison purgatory, I give in at once. But if every man sees that Christ there intended to show to how many perils and evils those expose themselves who obstinately insist on their utmost right, instead of being satisfied with what is fair and equitable, that he might thereby the more strongly exhort his followers to concord, where, I ask, are we to find their purgatory?

8. They seek an argument in the passage in which Paul declares, that all things shall bow the knee to Christ, "things in heaven, and things in earth, and things under the earth" (Phil. 2:10). They take it for granted, that by "things under the earth," cannot be meant those who are doomed to eternal damnation, and that the only remaining conclusion is, that they must be souls suffering in purgatory. They would not reason very ill if, by the bending of the knee, the Apostle designated true worship; but since he simply says that Christ has received a dominion to which all creatures are subject, what prevents us from understanding those "under the earth" to mean the devils, who shall certainly be sisted before the judgment-seat of God, there to recognize their Judge with fear and trembling? In this way Paul himself elsewhere interprets the same prophecy: "We shall all stand before the judgment-seat of Christ. For it is written, As I live, saith the Lord, every knee shall bow to me, and every tongue shall confess to God" (Rom. 14:10, 11). But we cannot in this way interpret what is said in the Apocalypse: "Every creature which is in heaven, and on the earth, and under the earth, and such as are in the sea, heard I saying, Blessing, and honor, and glory, and power, be unto him that sitteth upon the throne, and unto the Lamb, for ever and ever" (Rev. 5:13). This I readily admit; but what kinds of creatures do they suppose are here enumerated? It is absolutely certain, that both irrational and inanimate creatures are comprehended. All, then, which is affirmed is, that every part of the universe, from the highest pinnacle of heaven to the very centre of the earth, each in its own way proclaims the glory of the Creator.

To the passage which they produce from the history of the Maccabees (1 Macc. 12:43), I will not deign to reply, lest I should seem to include that work among the canonical books. But Augustine holds it to be canonical. First, with what degree of confidence? "The Jews," says he, "do not hold the book of the Maccabees as they do the Law, the Prophets, and the Psalms, to which the Lord bears testimony as to his own witnesses, saying, Ought not all things which are written in the Law, and the Psalms, and the Prophets, concerning me be fulfilled? (Luke 24:44). But it has been received by the Church not uselessly, if it be read or heard with soberness." Jerome, however, unhesitatingly affirms, that it is of no authority in establishing doctrine; and from the ancient little book, *De Expositione Symboli*; which bears the name of Cyprian, it is plain that it was in no estimation in the ancient Church. And why do I here contend in vain? As if the author himself did not sufficiently show what degree of deference is to be paid him, when in the end he asks pardon for any thing less properly expressed (2 Macc. 15:38). He who confesses that his writings stand in need of pardon, certainly proclaims that they are not oracles of the Holy Spirit. We may add, that the piety of Judas is commended for no other reason than for having a firm hope of the final resurrection, in sending his oblation for the dead to Jerusalem. For the writer of the history does not represent what he did as furnishing the price of redemption, but merely that they might be partakers of eternal life, with the other saints who had fallen for their country and religion. The act, indeed, was not free from superstition and misguided zeal; but it is mere fatuity to extend the legal sacrifice to us, seeing we are assured that the sacrifices then in use ceased on the advent of Christ.

9. But, it seems, they find in Paul an invincible support, which cannot be so easily overthrown. His words are, "Now if any man build upon this foundation gold, silver, precious stones, wood, hay, stubble; every man's work shall be made manifest: for the day shall declare it, because it shall be revealed by fire; and the fire shall try every man's work of what sort it is. If any man's work shall be burnt, he shall suffer loss: but he himself shall be saved; yet so as by fire" (1 Cor. 3:12–15). What fire (they ask) can that be but the fire of purgatory, by which the defilements of sin are wiped away, in order that we may enter pure into the kingdom of God? But most of the Fathers give it a different meaning—viz. the tribulation or cross by which the Lord tries his people, that they may not rest satisfied with the defilements of the flesh. This is much more probable than the fiction of a purgatory. I do not, however, agree with them, for I think I see a much surer and clearer meaning to the passage. But, before I produce it, I wish they would answer me, whether they think the Apostle and all the saints have to pass through this purgatorial fire? I am aware they will say, no; for it were too absurd to hold that purification is required by those whose superfluous merits they dream of as applicable to all the members of the Church. But this the Apostle affirms; for he says, not that the works of certain persons, but the works of all will be tried. And this is not my argument, but that of Augustine, who thus impugns that interpretation. And (what makes the thing more absurd) he says, not that they will pass through fire for certain works, but that even if they should have edified the Church with the greatest fidelity, they will receive their reward after their works shall have been tried by fire. First, we see that the Apostle used a metaphor when he gave the names of wood, hay, and stubble, to doctrines of man's device. The ground of the metaphor is obvious—viz. that as wood when it is put into the fire is consumed and destroyed, so neither will those doctrines be able to endure when they come to be tried. Moreover, every one sees that the trial is made by the Spirit of God. Therefore, in following out the thread of the metaphor, and adapting its parts properly to each other, he gave the name of fire to the examination of the Holy Spirit. For, just as silver and gold, the nearer they are brought to the fire, give stronger proof of their genuineness and purity, so the Lord's truth, the more thoroughly it is submitted to spiritual examination, has its authority the better confirmed. As hay, wood, and stubble, when the fire is applied to them, are suddenly consumed, so the inventions of man, not founded on the word of God, cannot stand the trial of the Holy Spirit, but forthwith give way and perish. In fine, if spurious doctrines are compared to wood, hay, and stubble, because, like wood, hay, and stubble, they are burned by fire and fitted for destruction, though the actual destruction is only completed by the Spirit of the Lord, it follows that the Spirit is that fire by which they will be proved. This proof Paul calls the *day of the Lord*; using a term common in Scripture. For the day of the Lord is said to take place whenever he in some way manifests his presence to men, his face being specially said to shine when his truth is manifested. It has now been proved, that Paul has no idea of any other fire than the trial of the Holy Spirit. But how are those who suffer the loss of their works saved by fire? This it will not be difficult to understand, if we consider of what kind of persons he speaks. For he designates them builders of the Church, who, retaining the proper foundation, build

different materials upon it; that is, who, not abandoning the principal and necessary articles of faith, err in minor and less perilous matters, mingling their own fictions with the word of God. Such, I say, must suffer the loss of their work by the destruction of their fictions. They themselves, however, are saved, yet so as by fire; that is, not that their ignorance and delusions are approved by the Lord, but they are purified from them by the grace and power of the Holy Spirit. All those, accordingly, who have tainted the golden purity of the divine word with the pollution of purgatory must necessarily suffer the loss of their work.

10. But the observance of it in the Church is of the highest antiquity. This objection is disposed of by Paul, when, including even his own age in the sentence, he declares, that all who in building the Church have laid upon it something not conformable to the foundation, must suffer the loss of their work. When, therefore, my opponents object, that it has been the practice for thirteen hundred years to offer prayers for the dead, I, in return, ask them, by what word of God, by what revelation, by what example it was done? For here not only are passages of Scripture wanting, but in the examples of all the saints of whom we read, nothing of the kind is seen. We have numerous, and sometimes long narratives, of their mourning and sepulchral rites, but not one word is said of prayers. But the more important the matter was, the more they ought to have dwelt upon it. Even those who in ancient times offered prayers for the dead, saw that they were not supported by the command of God and legitimate example. Why then did they presume to do it? I hold that herein they suffered the common lot of man, and therefore maintain, that what they did is not to be imitated. Believers ought not to engage in any work without a firm conviction of its propriety, as Paul enjoins (Rom. 14:23); and this conviction is expressly requisite in prayer. It is to be presumed, however, that they were influenced by some reason; they sought a solace for their sorrow, and it seemed cruel not to give some attestation of their love to the dead, when in the presence of God. All know by experience how natural it is for the human mind thus to feel.

Received custom too was a kind of torch, by which the minds of many were inflamed. We know that among all the Gentiles, and in all ages, certain rites were paid to the dead, and that every year lustrations were performed for their manes. Although Satan deluded foolish mortals by these impostures, yet the means of deceiving were borrowed from a sound principle—viz. that death is not destruction, but a passages from this life to another. And there can be no doubt that superstition itself always left the Gentiles without excuse before the judgment-seat of God, because they neglected to prepare for that future life which they professed to believe. Thus, that Christians might not seem worse than heathens, they felt ashamed of paying no office to the dead, as if they had been utterly annihilated. Hence their ill advised assiduity; because they thought they would expose themselves to great disgrace, if they were slow in providing funeral feasts and oblations. What was thus introduced by perverse rivalship, ever and anon received new additions, until the highest holiness of the Papacy consisted in giving assistance to the suffering dead. But far better and more solid comfort is furnished by scripture when it declares, "Blessed are the dead that die in the Lord;" and adds the reason, "for they rest from their labors" (Rev. 14:13). We ought not to indulge our love so far as to set up a perverse mode of prayer in the Church. Surely every person possessed of the least prudence easily perceives, that whatever we meet with on this subject in ancient writers, was in deference to public custom and the ignorance of the vulgar. I admit they were themselves also carried away into error, the usual effect of rash credulity being to destroy the judgment. Meanwhile the passages themselves show, that when they recommended prayer for the dead it was with hesitation. Augustine relates in his Confessions, that his mother, Monica, earnestly entreated to be remembered when the solemn rites at the altar were performed; doubtless an old woman's wish, which her son did not bring to the test of Scripture, but from natural affection wished others to approve. His book, *De Cura pro Mortals Agenda, On showing Care for the Dead*, is so full of doubt, that its coldness may well extinguish the heat of a foolish zeal. Should any one, in pretending to be a patron of the dead, deal merely in probabilities, the only effect will be to make those indifferent who were formerly solicitous.

The only support of this dogma is, that as a custom of praying for the dead prevailed, the duty ought not to be despised. But granting that ancient ecclesiastical writers deemed it a pious thing to assist the dead, the rule which can never deceive is always to be observed—viz. that we must not introduce anything of our own into our prayers, but must keep all our wishes in subordination to the word of God, because it belongs to Him to prescribe what he wishes us to ask. Now, since the whole Law and Gospel do not contain one syllable which countenances the right of praying for the dead, it is a profanation of prayer to go one step farther than God enjoins. But, lest our opponents boast of sharing their error with the ancient Church, I say, that there is a wide difference between the two. The latter made a commemoration of the dead, that they might not seem to have cast off all concern for them; but they, at the same time, acknowledged that they were doubtful as to their state; assuredly they made no such assertion concerning purgatory as implied that they did not hold it to be uncertain. The former insist, that their dream of purgatory shall be received without question as an article of faith. The latter sparingly and in a perfunctory manner only commended their dead to the Lord, in the communion of the holy supper. The former are constantly urging the care of the dead, and by their importunate preaching of it, make out that it is to be preferred to all the offices of charity. But it would not be difficult for us to produce some passages from ancient writers, which clearly overturn all those prayers for the dead which were then in use. Such is the passage of Augustine, in which he shows that the resurrection of the flesh and eternal glory is expected by all, but that rest which follows death is received by every one who is worthy of it when he dies. Accordingly, he declares that all the righteous, not less than the Apostles, Prophets, and Martyrs, immediately after death enjoy blessed rest. If such is their condition, what, I ask, will our prayers contribute to them? I say nothing of those grosser superstitions by which they have fascinated the minds of the simple; and yet they are innumerable, and most of them so monstrous, that they cannot cover them with any cloak of decency. I say nothing, moreover, of those most shameful traffickings, which they plied as they listed while the world was stupefied. For I would never come to an end; and, without enumerating them, the pious reader will here find enough to establish his conscience.

CHAPTER 6

THE LIFE OF A CHRISTIAN MAN. SCRIPTURAL ARGUMENTS EXHORTING TO IT.

This and the four following chapters treat of the Life of the Christian, and are so arranged as to admit of being classed under two principal heads.

First, it must be held to be an universally acknowledged point, that no man is a Christian who does not feel some special love for righteousness, chap. 6. Secondly, in regard to the standard by which every man ought to regulate his life, although it seems to be considered in chap. 7 only, yet the three following chapters also refer to it. For it shows that the Christian has two duties to perform. First, the observance being so arduous, he needs the greatest patience. Hence chap. 8 treats professedly of the utility of the cross, and chap. 9 invites to meditation on the future life. Lastly, chap. 10 clearly shows, as in no small degree conducive to this end, how we are to use this life and its comforts without abusing them.

This sixth chapter consists of two parts,—I. Connection between this treatise on the Christian Life and the doctrine of Regeneration and Repentance. Arrangement of the treatise, sec. 1–3. II. Extremes to be avoided; 1. False Christians denying Christ by their works condemned, sec. 4. 2. Christians should not despair, though they have not attained perfection, provided they make daily progress in piety and righteousness.

Sections:

1. Connection between this chapter and the doctrine of Regeneration. Necessity of the doctrine concerning the Christian Life. The brevity of this treatise. The method of it. Plainness and unadorned simplicity of the Scripture system of morals.

2. Two divisions. First, Personal holiness. 1. Because God is holy. 2. Because of our communion with his saints.

3. Second division, relating to our Redemption. Admirable moral system of Scripture. Five special inducements or exhortations to a Christian Life.

4. False Christians who are opposed to this life censured 1. They have not truly learned Christ. 2. The Gospel not the guide of their words or actions. 3. They do not imitate Christ the Master. 4. They would separate the Spirit from his word.

5. Christians ought not to despond: Provided 1. They take the word of God for their guide. 2. Sincerely cultivate righteousness. 3. Walk, according to their capacity, in the ways of the Lord. 4. Make some progress. 5. Persevere.

1. We have said that the object of regeneration is to bring the life of believers into concord and harmony with the righteousness of God, and so confirm the adoption by which they have been received as sons. But although the law comprehends within it that new life by which the image of God is restored in us, yet, as our sluggishness stands greatly in need both of helps and incentives it will be useful to collect out of Scripture a true account

of this reformations lest any who have a heartfelt desire of repentance should in their zeal go astray. Moreover, I am not unaware that, in undertaking to describe the life of the Christian, I am entering on a large and extensive subject, one which, when fully considered in all its parts, is sufficient to fill a large volume. We see the length to which the Fathers in treating of individual virtues extend their exhortations. This they do, not from mere loquaciousness; for whatever be the virtue which you undertake to recommend, your pen is spontaneously led by the copiousness of the matter so to amplify, that you seem not to have discussed it properly if you have not done it at length. My intention, however, in the plan of life which I now propose to give, is not to extend it so far as to treat of each virtue specially, and expatiate in exhortation. This must be sought in the writings of others, and particularly in the Homilies of the Fathers. For me it will be sufficient to point out the method by which a pious man may be taught how to frame his life aright, and briefly lay down some universal rule by which he may not improperly regulate his conduct. I shall one day possibly find time for more ample discourse, [or leave others to perform an office for which I am not so fit. I have a natural love of brevity, and, perhaps, any attempt of mine at copiousness would not succeed. Even if I could gain the highest applause by being more prolix, I would scarcely be disposed to attempt it], while the nature of my present work requires me to glance at simple doctrine with as much brevity as possible. As philosophers have certain definitions of rectitude and honesty, from which they derive particular duties and the whole train of virtues; so in this respect Scripture is not without order, but presents a most beautiful arrangement, one too which is every way much more certain than that of philosophers. The only difference is, that they, under the influence of ambition, constantly affect an exquisite perspicuity of arrangement, which may serve to display their genius, whereas the Spirit of God, teaching without affectation, is not so perpetually observant of exact method, and yet by observing it at times sufficiently intimates that it is not to be neglected.

2. The Scripture system of which we speak aims chiefly at two objects. The former is, that the love of righteousness, to which we are by no means naturally inclined, may be instilled and implanted into our minds. The latter is (see chap. 7), to prescribe a rule which will prevent us while in the pursuit of righteousness from going astray. It has numerous admirable methods of recommending righteousness. Many have been already pointed out in different parts of this work; but we shall here also briefly advert to some of them. With what better foundation can it begin than by reminding us that we must be holy, because "God is holy?" (Lev. 19:1; 1 Pet. 1:16). For when we were scattered abroad like lost sheep, wandering through the labyrinth of this world, he brought us back again to his own fold. When mention is made of our union with God, let us remember that holiness must be the bond; not that by the merit of holiness we come into communion with him (we ought rather first to cleave to him, in order that, pervaded with his holiness, we may follow whither he calls), but because it greatly concerns his glory not to have any fellowship with wickedness and impurity. Wherefore he tells us that this is the end of our calling, the end to which we ought ever to have respect, if we would answer the call of God. For to what end were we rescued from the iniquity and pollution of the world into which we were plunged, if we allow ourselves, during our whole lives, to wallow in them? Besides, we are at the same time admonished, that if we would be regarded as the Lord's people, we must inhabit the holy city Jerusalem (Isaiah rev. 8, *et alibi*); which, as he hath consecrated it to himself, it were impious for its inhabitants to profane by impurity. Hence the expressions, "Who shall abide in thy tabernacle? who shall dwell in thy holy hill? He that walketh uprightly, and worketh righteousness" (Ps. 15:1, 2; 24:3, 4); for the sanctuary in which he dwells certainly ought not to be like an unclean stall.

3. The better to arouse us, it exhibits God the Father, who, as he hath reconciled us to himself in his Anointed, has impressed his image upon us, to which he would have us to be conformed (Rom. 5:4). Come, then, and let them show me a more excellent system among philosophers, who think that they only have a moral philosophy duly and orderly arranged. They, when they would give excellent exhortations to virtue, can only tell us to live agreeably to nature. Scripture derives its exhortations from the true source, when it not only enjoins us to regulate our lives with a view to God its author to whom it belongs; but after showing us that we have degenerated from our true origin—viz. the law of our Creator, adds, that Christ, through whom we have returned to favour with God, is set before us as a model, the image of which our lives should express. What do you require more effectual than this? Nay, what do you require beyond this? If the Lord adopts us for his sons on the condition that our life be a representation of Christ, the bond of our adoption,—then, unless we dedicate and devote ourselves to righteousness, we not only, with the utmost perfidy,

revolt from our Creator, but also abjure the Saviour himself. Then, from an enumeration of all the blessings of God, and each part of our salvation, it finds materials for exhortation. Ever since God exhibited himself to us as a Father, we must be convicted of extreme ingratitude if we do not in turn exhibit ourselves as his sons. Ever since Christ purified us by the laver of his blood, and communicated this purification by baptism, it would ill become us to be defiled with new pollution. Ever since he ingrafted us into his body, we, who are his members, should anxiously beware of contracting any stain or taint. Ever since he who is our head ascended to heaven, it is befitting in us to withdraw our affections from the earth, and with our whole soul aspire to heaven. Ever since the Holy Spirit dedicated us as temples to the Lord, we should make it our endeavour to show forth the glory of God, and guard against being profaned by the defilement of sin. Ever since our soul and body were destined to heavenly incorruptibility and an unfading crown, we should earnestly strive to keep them pure and uncorrupted against the day of the Lord. These, I say, are the surest foundations of a well-regulated life, and you will search in vain for any thing resembling them among philosophers, who, in their commendation of virtue, never rise higher than the natural dignity of man.

4. This is the place to address those who, having nothing of Christ but the name and sign, would yet be called Christians. How dare they boast of this sacred name? None have intercourse with Christ but those who have acquired the true knowledge of him from the Gospel. The Apostle denies that any man truly has learned Christ who has not learned to put off "the old man, which is corrupt according to the deceitful lusts, and put on Christ" (Eph. 4:22). They are convicted, therefore, of falsely and unjustly pretending a knowledge of Christ, whatever be the volubility and eloquence with which they can talk of the Gospel. Doctrine is not an affair of the tongue, but of the life; is not apprehended by the intellect and memory merely, like other branches of learning; but is received only when it possesses the whole soul, and finds its seat and habitation in the inmost recesses of the heart. Let them, therefore, either cease to insult God, by boasting that they are what they are not, or let them show themselves not unworthy disciples of their divine Master. To doctrine in which our religion is contained we have given the first place, since by it our salvation commences; but it must be transfused into the breast, and pass into the conduct, and so transform us into itself, as not to prove unfruitful. If philosophers are justly offended, and banish from their company with disgrace those who, while professing an art which ought to be the mistress of their conduct, convert it into mere loquacious sophistry, with how much better reason shall we detest those flimsy sophists who are contented to let the Gospel play upon their lips, when, from its efficacy, it ought to penetrate the inmost affections of the heart, fix its seat in the soul, and pervade the whole man a hundred times more than the frigid discourses of philosophers?

5. I insist not that the life of the Christian shall breathe nothing but the perfect Gospel, though this is to be desired, and ought to be attempted. I insist not so strictly on evangelical perfection, as to refuse to acknowledge as a Christian any man who has not attained it. In this way all would be excluded from the Church, since there is no man who is not far removed from this perfection, while many, who have made but little progress, would be undeservedly rejected. What then? Let us set this before our eye as the end at which we ought constantly to aim. Let it be regarded as the goal towards which we are to run. For you cannot divide the matter with God, undertaking part of what his word enjoins, and omitting part at pleasure. For, in the first place, God uniformly recommends integrity as the principal part of his worship, meaning by integrity real singleness of mind, devoid of gloss and fiction, and to this is opposed a double mind; as if it had been said, that the spiritual commencement of a good life is when the internal affections are sincerely devoted to God, in the cultivation of holiness and justice. But seeing that, in this earthly prison of the body, no man is supplied with strength sufficient to hasten in his course with due alacrity, while the greater number are so oppressed with weakness, that hesitating, and halting, and even crawling on the ground, they make little progress, let every one of us go as far as his humble ability enables him, and prosecute the journey once begun. No one will travel so badly as not daily to make some degree of progress. This, therefore, let us never cease to do, that we may daily advance in the way of the Lord; and let us not despair because of the slender measure of success. How little soever the success may correspond with our wish, our labour is not lost when to-day is better than yesterday, provided with true singleness of mind we keep our aim, and aspire to the goal, not speaking flattering things to ourselves, nor indulging our vices, but making it our constant endeavour to become better, until we attain to goodness itself. If during the whole course of our life we seek and follow, we shall at length attain it, when relieved from the infirmity of flesh we are admitted to full fellowship with God.

CHAPTER 7

A SUMMARY OF THE CHRISTIAN LIFE. OF SELF-DENIAL.

The divisions of the chapter are,—I. The rule which permits us not to go astray in the study of righteousness, requires two things—viz. that man, abandoning his own will, devote himself entirely to the service of God; whence it follows, that we must seek not our own things, but the things of God, sec. 1, 2. II. A description of this renovation or Christian life taken from the Epistle to Titus, and accurately explained under certain special heads, sec. 3 to end.

Sections:

1. Consideration of the second general division in regard to the Christian life. Its beginning and sum. A twofold respect. 1. We are not our own. Respect to both the fruit and the use. Unknown to philosophers, who have placed reason on the throne of the Holy Spirit.

2. Since we are not our own, we must seek the glory of God, and obey his will. Self-denial recommended to the disciples of Christ. He who neglects it, deceived either by pride or hypocrisy, rushes on destruction.

3. Three things to be followed, and two to be shunned in life. Impiety and worldly lusts to be shunned. Sobriety, justice, and piety, to be followed. An inducement to right conduct.

4. Self-denial the sum of Paul's doctrine. Its difficulty. Qualities in us which make it difficult. Cures for these qualities. 1. Ambition to be suppressed. 2. Humility to be embraced. 3. Candour to be esteemed. 4. Mutual charity to be preserved. 5. Modesty to be sincerely cultivated.

5. The advantage of our neighbour to be promoted. Here self-denial most necessary, and yet most difficult. Here a double remedy. 1. The benefits bestowed upon us are for the common benefit of the Church. 2. We ought to do all we can for our neighbour. This illustrated by analogy from the members of the human body. This duty of charity founded on the divine command.

6. Charity ought to have for its attendants patience and kindness. We should consider the image of God in our neighbours, and especially in those who are of the household of faith. Hence a fourfold consideration which refutes all objections. A common objection refuted.

7. Christian life cannot exist without charity. Remedies for the vices opposed to charity. 1. Mercy. 2. Humility. 3. Modesty. 4. Diligence. 5. Perseverance.

8. Self-denial, in respect of God, should lead to equanimity and tolerance. 1. We are always subject to God. 2. We should shun avarice and ambition. 3. We should expect all prosperity from the blessing of God, and entirely depend on him.

9. We ought not to desire wealth or honours without the divine blessing, nor follow the arts of the wicked. We ought to cast all our care upon God, and never envy the prosperity of others.

10. We ought to commit ourselves entirely to God. The necessity of this doctrine. Various uses of affliction. Heathen abuse and corruption.

1. Although the Law of God contains a perfect rule of conduct admirably arranged, it has seemed proper to our divine Master to train his people by a more accurate method, to the rule which is enjoined in the Law; and the leading principle in the method is, that it is the duty of believers to present their "bodies a living sacrifice, holy and acceptable unto God, which is their reasonable service" (Rom. 12:1). Hence he draws the exhortation: "Be not conformed to this world: but be ye transformed by the renewing of your mind, that ye may prove what is that good, and acceptable, and perfect will of God." The great point, then, is, that we are consecrated and dedicated to God, and, therefore, should not henceforth think, speak, design, or act, without a view to his glory. What he hath made sacred cannot, without signal insult to him, be applied to profane use. But if we are not our own, but the Lord's, it is plain both what error is to be shunned, and to what end the actions of our lives ought to be directed. We are not our own; therefore, neither is our own reason or will to rule our acts and counsels. We are not our own; therefore, let us not make it our end to seek what may be agreeable to our carnal nature. We are not our own; therefore, as far as possible, let us forget ourselves and the things that are ours. On the other hand, we are God's; let us, therefore, live and die to him (Rom. 14:8). We are God's; therefore, let his wisdom and will preside over all our actions. We are God's; to him, then, as the only legitimate end, let every part of our life be directed. O how great the proficiency of him who, taught that he is not his own, has withdrawn the dominion and government of himself from his own reason that he may give them to God! For as the surest source of destruction to men is to obey themselves, so the only haven of safety is to have no other will, no other wisdom, than to follow

the Lord wherever he leads. Let this, then be the first step, to abandon ourselves, and devote the whole energy of our minds to the service of God. By service, I mean not only that which consists in verbal obedience, but that by which the mind, divested of its own carnal feelings, implicitly obeys the call of the Spirit of God. This transformation (which Paul calls *the renewing of the mind*, Rom. 12:2; Eph. 4:23), though it is the first entrance to life, was unknown to all the philosophers. They give the government of man to reason alone, thinking that she alone is to be listened to; in short, they assign to her the sole direction of the conduct. But Christian philosophy bids her give place, and yield complete submission to the Holy Spirit, so that the man himself no longer lives, but Christ lives and reigns in him (Gal. 2:20).

2. Hence follows the other principle, that we are not to seek our own, but the Lord's will, and act with a view to promote his glory. Great is our proficiency, when, almost forgetting ourselves, certainly postponing our own reason, we faithfully make it our study to obey God and his commandments. For when Scripture enjoins us to lay aside private regard to ourselves, it not only divests our minds of an excessive longing for wealth, or power, or human favour, but eradicates all ambition and thirst for worldly glory, and other more secret pests. The Christian ought, indeed, to be so trained and disposed as to consider, that during his whole life he has to do with God. For this reason, as he will bring all things to the disposal and estimate of God, so he will religiously direct his whole mind to him. For he who has learned to look to God in everything he does, is at the same time diverted from all vain thoughts. This is that self-denial which Christ so strongly enforces on his disciples from the very outset (Mt. 16:24), which, as soon as it takes hold of the mind, leaves no place either, first, for pride, show, and ostentation; or, secondly, for avarice, lust, luxury, effeminacy, or other vices which are engendered by self love. On the contrary, wherever it reigns not, the foulest vices are indulged in without shame; or, if there is some appearance of virtue, it is vitiated by a depraved longing for applause. Show me, if you can, an individual who, unless he has renounced himself in obedience to the Lord's command, is disposed to do good for its own sake. Those who have not so renounced themselves have followed virtue at least for the sake of praise. The philosophers who have contended most strongly that virtue is to be desired on her own account, were so inflated with arrogance as to make it apparent that they sought virtue for no other reason than as a ground for indulging in pride. So far, therefore, is God from being delighted with these hunters after popular applause with their swollen breasts, that he declares they have received their reward in this world (Mt. 6:2), and that harlots and publicans are nearer the kingdom of heaven than they (Mt. 21:31). We have not yet sufficiently explained how great and numerous are the obstacles by which a man is impeded in the pursuit of rectitude, so long as he has not renounced himself. The old saying is true, There is a world of iniquity treasured up in the human soul. Nor can you find any other remedy for this than to deny yourself, renounce your own reason, and direct your whole mind to the pursuit of those things which the Lord requires of you, and which you are to seek only because they are pleasing to Him.

3. In another passage, Paul gives a brief, indeed, but more distinct account of each of the parts of a well-ordered life: "The grace of God that bringeth salvation hath appeared to all men, teaching us that, denying ungodliness and worldly lusts, we should live soberly, righteously, and godly, in this present world; looking for that blessed hope, and the glorious appearance of the great God and our Saviour Jesus Christ; who gave himself for us, that he might redeem us from all iniquity, and purify to himself a peculiar people, zealous of good works" (Tit. 2:11–14). After holding forth the grace of God to animate us, and pave the way for His true worship, he removes the two greatest obstacles which stand in the way—viz. ungodliness, to which we are by nature too prone, and worldly lusts, which are of still greater extent. Under *ungodliness*, he includes not merely superstition, but everything at variance with the true fear of God. *Worldly lusts* are equivalent to the lusts of the flesh. Thus he enjoins us, in regard to both tables of the Law, to lay aside our own mind, and renounce whatever our own reason and will dictate. Then he reduces all the actions of our lives to three branches, sobriety, righteousness, and godliness. *Sobriety* undoubtedly denotes as well chastity and temperance as the pure and frugal use of temporal goods, and patient endurance of want. *Righteousness* comprehends all the duties of equity, in every one his due. Next follows *godliness*, which separates us from the pollutions of the world, and connects us with God in true holiness. These, when connected together by an indissoluble chain, constitute complete perfection. But as nothing is more difficult than to bid adieu to the will of the flesh, subdue, nay, abjure our lusts, devote ourselves to God and our brethren, and lead an angelic life amid the pollutions of the world, Paul, to set our minds free from all entangle-

ments, recalls us to the hope of a blessed immortality, justly urging us to contend, because as Christ has once appeared as our Redeemer, so on his final advent he will give full effect to the salvation obtained by him. And in this way he dispels all the allurements which becloud our path, and prevent us from aspiring as we ought to heavenly glory; nay, he tells us that we must be pilgrims in the world, that we may not fail of obtaining the heavenly inheritance.

4. Moreover, we see by these words that self-denial has respect partly to men and partly (more especially) to God (sec. 8–10). For when Scripture enjoins us, in regard to our fellow men, to prefer them in honour to ourselves, and sincerely labour to promote their advantages (Rom. 12:10; Phil. 2:3), he gives us commands which our mind is utterly incapable of obeying until its natural feelings are suppressed. For so blindly do we all rush in the direction of self-love, that every one thinks he has a good reason for exalting himself and despising all others in comparison. If God has bestowed on us something not to be repented of, trusting to it, we immediately become elated, and not only swell, but almost burst with pride. The vices with which we abound we both carefully conceal from others, and flatteringly represent to ourselves as minute and trivial, nay, sometimes hug them as virtues. When the same qualities which we admire in ourselves are seen in others, even though they should be superior, we, in order that we may not be forced to yield to them, maliciously lower and carp at them; in like manner, in the case of vices, not contented with severe and keen animadversion, we studiously exaggerate them. Hence the insolence with which each, as if exempted from the common lot, seeks to exalt himself above his neighbour, confidently and proudly despising others, or at least looking down upon them as his inferiors. The poor man yields to the rich, the plebeian to the noble, the servant to the master, the unlearned to the learned, and yet every one inwardly cherishes some idea of his own superiority. Thus each flattering himself, sets up a kind of kingdom in his breast; the arrogant, to satisfy themselves, pass censure on the minds and manners of other men, and when contention arises, the full venom is displayed. Many bear about with them some measure of mildness so long as all things go smoothly and lovingly with them, but how few are there who, when stung and irritated, preserve the same tenor of moderation? For this there is no other remedy than to pluck up by the roots those most noxious pests, self-love and love of victory (φιλονεικία καὶ φιλαυτία). This the doctrine of Scripture does. For it teaches us to remember, that the endowments which God has bestowed upon us are not our own, but His free gifts, and that those who plume themselves upon them betray their ingratitude. "Who maketh thee to differ," saith Paul, "and what hast thou that thou didst not receive? now if thou didst receive it, why dost thou glory, as if thou hadst not received it?" (1 Cor. 4:7). Then by a diligent examination of our faults let us keep ourselves humble. Thus while nothing will remain to swell our pride, there will be much to subdue it. Again, we are enjoined, whenever we behold the gifts of God in others, so to reverence and respect the gifts, as also to honour those in whom they reside. God having been pleased to bestow honour upon them, it would ill become us to deprive them of it. Then we are told to overlook their faults, not, indeed, to encourage by flattering them, but not because of them to insult those whom we ought to regard with honour and good will. In this way, with regard to all with whom we have intercourse, our behaviour will be not only moderate and modest, but courteous and friendly. The only way by which you can ever attain to true meekness, is to have your heart imbued with a humble opinion of yourself and respect for others.

5. How difficult it is to perform the duty of seeking the good of our neighbour! Unless you leave off all thought of yourself and in a manner cease to be yourself, you will never accomplish it. How can you exhibit those works of charity which Paul describes unless you renounce yourself, and become wholly devoted to others? "Charity (says he, 1 Cor. 13:4) suffereth long, and is kind; charity envieth not; charity vaunteth not itself, is not puffed up, doth not behave itself unseemly, seeketh not her own, is not easily provoked," &c. Were it the only thing required of us to seek not our own, nature would not have the least power to comply: she so inclines us to love ourselves only, that she will not easily allow us carelessly to pass by ourselves and our own interests that we may watch over the interests of others, nay, spontaneously to yield our own rights and resign it to another. But Scripture, to conduct us to this, reminds us, that whatever we obtain from the Lord is granted on the condition of our employing it for the common good of the Church, and that, therefore, the legitimate use of all our gifts is a kind and liberal communication of them with others. There cannot be a surer rule, nor a stronger exhortation to the observance of it, than when we are taught that all the endowments which we possess are divine deposits entrusted to us for the very purpose of being distributed for the good of our neighbour. But Scripture proceeds still farther when it likens these endowments to the different members of the body

(1 Cor. 12:12). No member has its function for itself, or applies it for its own private use, but transfers it to its fellow-members; nor does it derive any other advantage from it than that which it receives in common with the whole body. Thus, whatever the pious man can do, he is bound to do for his brethren, not consulting his own interest in any other way than by striving earnestly for the common edification of the Church. Let this, then, be our method of showing good-will and kindness, considering that, in regard to everything which God has bestowed upon us, and by which we can aid our neighbour, we are his stewards, and are bound to give account of our stewardship; moreover, that the only right mode of administration is that which is regulated by love. In this way, we shall not only unite the study of our neighbour's advantage with a regard to our own, but make the latter subordinate to the former. And lest we should have omitted to perceive that this is the law for duly administering every gift which we receive from God, he of old applied that law to the minutest expressions of his own kindness. He commanded the first-fruits to be offered to him as an attestation by the people that it was impious to reap any advantage from goods not previously consecrated to him (Exod. 22:29; 23:19). But if the gifts of God are not sanctified to us until we have with our own hand dedicated them to the Giver, it must be a gross abuse that does not give signs of such dedication. It is in vain to contend that you cannot enrich the Lord by your offerings. Though, as the Psalmist says "Thou art my Lord: my goodness extendeth not unto thee," yet you can extend it "to the saints that are in the earth" (Ps. 16:2, 3); and therefore a comparison is drawn between sacred oblations and alms as now corresponding to the offerings under the Law.

6. Moreover, that we may not weary in well-doing (as would otherwise forthwith and infallibly be the case), we must add the other quality in the Apostle's enumeration, "Charity suffereth long, and is kind, is not easily provoked" (1 Cor. 13:4). The Lord enjoins us to do good to all without exception, though the greater part, if estimated by their own merit, are most unworthy of it. But Scripture subjoins a most excellent reason, when it tells us that we are not to look to what men in themselves deserve, but to attend to the image of God, which exists in all, and to which we owe all honour and love. But in those who are of the household of faith, the same rule is to be more carefully observed, inasmuch as that image is renewed and restored in them by the Spirit of Christ. Therefore, whoever be the man that is presented to you as needing your assistance, you have no ground for declining to give it to him. Say he is a stranger. The Lord has given him a mark which ought to be familiar to you: for which reason he forbids you to despise your own flesh (Gal. 6:10). Say he is mean and of no consideration. The Lord points him out as one whom he has distinguished by the lustre of his own image (Isaiah 58:7). Say that you are bound to him by no ties of duty. The Lord has substituted him as it were into his own place, that in him you may recognize the many great obligations under which the Lord has laid you to himself. Say that he is unworthy of your least exertion on his account; but the image of God, by which he is recommended to you, is worthy of yourself and all your exertions. But if he not only merits no good, but has provoked you by injury and mischief, still this is no good reason why you should not embrace him in love, and visit him with offices of love. He has deserved very differently from me, you will say. But what has the Lord deserved? Whatever injury he has done you, when he enjoins you to forgive him, he certainly means that it should be imputed to himself. In this way only we attain to what is not to say difficult but altogether against nature, to love those that hate us, render good for evil, and blessing for cursing, remembering that we are not to reflect on the wickedness of men, but look to the image of God in them, an image which, covering and obliterating their faults, should by its beauty and dignity allure us to love and embrace them.

7. We shall thus succeed in mortifying ourselves if we fulfil all the duties of charity. Those duties, however, are not fulfilled by the mere discharge of them, though none be omitted, unless it is done from a pure feeling of love. For it may happen that one may perform every one of these offices, in so far as the external act is concerned, and be far from performing them aright. For you see some who would be thought very liberal, and yet accompany every thing they give with insult, by the haughtiness of their looks, or the violence of their words. And to such a calamitous condition have we come in this unhappy age, that the greater part of men never almost give alms without contumely. Such conduct ought not to have been tolerated even among the heathen; but from Christians something more is required than to carry cheerfulness in their looks, and give attractiveness to the discharge of their duties by courteous language. First, they should put themselves in the place of him whom they see in need of their assistance, and pity his misfortune as if they felt and bore it, so that a feeling of pity and humanity should incline them to assist him just as they would themselves. He who is thus minded will go and give assistance to his

brethren, and not only not taint his acts with arrogance or upbraiding but will neither look down upon the brother to whom he does a kindness, as one who needed his help, or keep him in subjection as under obligation to him, just as we do not insult a diseased member when the rest of the body labours for its recovery, nor think it under special obligation to the other members, because it has required more exertion than it has returned. A communication of offices between members is not regarded as at all gratuitous, but rather as the payment of that which being due by the law of nature it were monstrous to deny. For this reason, he who has performed one kind of duty will not think himself thereby discharged, as is usually the case when a rich man, after contributing somewhat of his substance, delegates remaining burdens to others as if he had nothing to do with them. Every one should rather consider, that however great he is, he owes himself to his neighbours, and that the only limit to his beneficence is the failure of his means. The extent of these should regulate that of his charity.

8. The principal part of self-denial, that which as we have said has reference to God, let us again consider more fully. Many things have already been said with regard to it which it were superfluous to repeat; and, therefore, it will be sufficient to view it as forming us to equanimity and endurance. First, then, in seeking the convenience or tranquillity of the present life, Scripture calls us to resign ourselves, and all we have, to the disposal of the Lord, to give him up the affections of our heart, that he may tame and subdue them. We have a frenzied desire, an infinite eagerness, to pursue wealth and honour, intrigue for power, accumulate riches, and collect all those frivolities which seem conducive to luxury and splendour. On the other hand, we have a remarkable dread, a remarkable hatred of poverty, mean birth, and a humble condition, and feel the strongest desire to guard against them. Hence, in regard to those who frame their life after their own counsel, we see how restless they are in mind, how many plans they try, to what fatigues they submit, in order that they may gain what avarice or ambition desires, or, on the other hand, escape poverty and meanness. To avoid similar entanglements, the course which Christian men must follow is this: first, they must not long for, or hope for, or think of any kind of prosperity apart from the blessing of God; on it they must cast themselves, and there safely and confidently recline. For, however much the carnal mind may seem sufficient for itself when in the pursuit of honour or wealth, it depends on its own industry and zeal, or is aided by the favour of men, it is certain that all this is nothing, and that neither intellect nor labour will be of the least avail, except in so far as the Lord prospers both. On the contrary, his blessing alone makes a way through all obstacles, and brings every thing to a joyful and favourable issue. Secondly, though without this blessing we may be able to acquire some degree of fame and opulence (as we daily see wicked men loaded with honours and riches), yet since those on whom the curse of God lies do not enjoy the least particle of true happiness, whatever we obtain without his blessing must turn out ill. But surely men ought not to desire what adds to their misery.

9. Therefore, if we believe that all prosperous and desirable success depends entirely on the blessing of God, and that when it is wanting all kinds of misery and calamity await us, it follows that we should not eagerly contend for riches and honours, trusting to our own dexterity and assiduity, or leaning on the favour of men, or confiding in any empty imagination of fortune; but should always have respect to the Lord, that under his auspices we may be conducted to whatever lot he has provided for us. First, the result will be, that instead of rushing on regardless of right and wrong, by wiles and wicked arts, and with injury to our neighbours, to catch at wealth and seize upon honours, we will only follow such fortune as we may enjoy with innocence. Who can hope for the aid of the divine blessing amid fraud, rapine, and other iniquitous arts? As this blessing attends him only who thinks purely and acts uprightly, so it calls off all who long for it from sinister designs and evil actions. Secondly, a curb will be laid upon us, restraining a too eager desire of becoming rich, or an ambitious striving after honour. How can any one have the effrontery to expect that God will aid him in accomplishing desires at variance with his word? What God with his own lips pronounces cursed, never can be prosecuted with his blessing. Lastly, if our success is not equal to our wish and hope, we shall, however, be kept from impatience and detestation of our condition, whatever it be, knowing that so to feel were to murmur against God, at whose pleasure riches and poverty, contempt and honours, are dispensed. In shorts he who leans on the divine blessing in the way which has been described, will not, in the pursuit of those things which men are wont most eagerly to desire, employ wicked arts which he knows would avail him nothing; nor when any thing prosperous befalls him will he impute it to himself and his own diligence, or industry, or fortune, instead of ascribing it to God as its author. If, while the affairs of others flourish, his make

little progress, or even retrograde, he will bear his humble lot with greater equanimity and moderation than any irreligious man does the moderate success which only falls short of what he wished; for he has a solace in which he can rest more tranquilly than at the very summit of wealth or power, because he considers that his affairs are ordered by the Lord in the manner most conducive to his salvation. This, we see, is the way in which David was affected, who, while he follows God and gives up himself to his guidance, declares, "Neither do I exercise myself in great matters, or in things too high for me. Surely I have behaved and quieted myself as a child that is weaned of his mother" (Ps. 131:1, 2).

10. Nor is it in this respect only that pious minds ought to manifest this tranquillity and endurance; it must be extended to all the accidents to which this present life is liable. He alone, therefore, has properly denied himself, who has resigned himself entirely to the Lord, placing all the course of his life entirely at his disposal. Happen what may, he whose mind is thus composed will neither deem himself wretched nor murmur against God because of his lot. How necessary this disposition is will appear, if you consider the many accidents to which we are liable. Various diseases ever and anon attack us: at one time pestilence rages; at another we are involved in all the calamities of war. Frost and hail, destroying the promise of the year, cause sterility, which reduces us to penury; wife, parents, children, relatives, are carried off by death; our house is destroyed by fire. These are the events which make men curse their life, detest the day of their birth, execrate the light of heaven, even censure God, and (as they are eloquent in blasphemy) charge him with cruelty and injustice. The believer must in these things also contemplate the mercy and truly paternal indulgence of God. Accordingly, should he see his house by the removal of kindred reduced to solitude even then he will not cease to bless the Lord; his thought will be, Still the grace of the Lord, which dwells within my house, will not leave it desolate. If his crops are blasted, mildewed, or cut off by frost, or struck down by hail, and he sees famine before him, he will not however despond or murmur against God, but maintain his confidence in him; "We thy people, and sheep of thy pasture, will give thee thanks for ever" (Ps. 79:13); he will supply me with food, even in the extreme of sterility. If he is afflicted with disease, the sharpness of the pain will not so overcome him, as to make him break out with impatience, and expostulate with God; but, recognising justice and lenity in the rod, will patiently endure. In short, whatever happens, knowing that it is ordered by the Lord, he will receive it with a placid and grateful mind, and will not contumaciously resist the government of him, at whose disposal he has placed himself and all that he has. Especially let the Christian breast eschew that foolish and most miserable consolation of the heathen, who, to strengthen their mind against adversity, imputed it to fortune, at which they deemed it absurd to feel indignant, as she was ἄσκοπος (aimless) and rash, and blindly wounded the good equally with the bad. On the contrary, the rule of piety is, that the hand of God is the ruler and arbiter of the fortunes of all, and, instead of rushing on with thoughtless violence, dispenses good and evil with perfect regularity.

CHAPTER 8

OF BEARING THE CROSS— ONE BRANCH OF SELF-DENIAL.

The four divisions of this chapter are,—I. The nature of the cross, its necessity and dignity, sec. 1, 2. II. The manifold advantages of the cross described, sec. 3–6. III. The form of the cross the most excellent of all, and yet it by no means removes all sense of pain, sec. 7, 8. IV. A description of warfare under the cross, and of true patience (not that of philosophers), after the example of Christ, sec. 9–11.

Sections:

1. What the cross is. By whom, and on whom, and for what cause imposed. Its necessity and dignity.

2. The cross necessary. 1. To humble our pride. 2. To make us apply to God for aid. Example of David.

3. To give us experience of God's presence. 3. Manifold uses of the cross. 1. Produces patience, hope, and firm confidence in God, gives us victory and perseverance. Faith invincible.

4. 2. Frames us to obedience. Example of Abraham. This training how useful.

5. The cross necessary to subdue the wantonness of the flesh. This portrayed by an apposite simile. Various forms of the cross.

6. 3. God permits our infirmities, and corrects past faults, that he may keep us in obedience. This confirmed by a passage from Solomon and an Apostle.

7. Singular consolation under the cross, when we suffer persecution for righteousness. Some parts of this consolation.

8. This form of the cross most appropriate to believers, and should be borne willingly and cheerfully. This cheerfulness is not unfeeling hilarity, but, while groaning under the burden, waits patiently for the Lord.

9. A description of this conflict. Opposed to the vanity of the Stoics. Illustrated by the authority and example of Christ.

10. Proved by the testimony and uniform experience of the elect. Also by the special example of the Apostle Peter. The nature of the patience required of us.

11. Distinction between the patience of Christians and philosophers. The latter pretend a necessity which cannot be resisted. The former hold forth the justice of God and his care of our safety. A full exposition of this difference.

1. The pious mind must ascend still higher, namely, whither Christ calls his disciples when he says, that every one of them must "take up his cross" (Mt. 16:24). Those whom the Lord has chosen and honoured with his intercourse must prepare for a hard, laborious, troubled life, a life full of many and various kinds of evils; it being the will of our heavenly Father to exercise his people in this way while putting them to the proof. Having begun this course with Christ the first-born, he continues it towards all his children. For though that Son was dear to him above others, the Son in whom he was "well pleased," yet we see, that far from being treated gently and indulgently, we may say, that not only was he subjected to a perpetual cross while he dwelt on earth, but his whole life was nothing else than a kind of perpetual cross. The Apostle assigns the reason, "Though he was a Son, yet learned he obedience by the things which he suffered" (Heb. 5:8). Why then should we exempt ourselves from that condition to which Christ our Head behoved to submit; especially since he submitted on our account, that he might in his own person exhibit a model of patience? Wherefore, the Apostle declares, that all the children of God are destined to be conformed to him. Hence it affords us great consolation in hard and difficult circumstances, which men deem evil and adverse, to think that we are holding fellowship with the sufferings of Christ; that as he passed to celestial glory through a labyrinth of many woes, so we too are conducted thither through various tribulations. For, in another passage, Paul himself thus speaks, "we must through much tribulation enter the kingdom of God" (Acts 14:22); and again, "that I may know him, and the power of his resurrection, and the fellowship of his sufferings, being made conformable unto his death" (Rom 8:29). How powerfully should it soften the bitterness of the cross, to think that the more we are afflicted with adversity, the surer we are made of our fellowship with Christ; by communion with whom our sufferings are not only blessed to us, but tend greatly to the furtherance of our salvation.

2. We may add, that the only thing which made it necessary for our Lord to undertake to bear the cross, was to testify and prove his obedience to the Father; whereas there are many reasons which make it necessary for us to live constantly under the cross. Feeble as we are by nature, and prone to ascribe all perfection to our flesh, unless we receive as it were ocular demonstration of our weakness, we readily estimate our virtue above its proper worth, and doubt not that, whatever happens, it will stand unimpaired and invincible against all difficulties. Hence we indulge a stupid and empty confidence in the flesh, and then trusting to it wax proud against the Lord himself; as if our own faculties were sufficient without his grace. This arrogance cannot be better repressed than when He proves to us by experience, not only how great our weakness, but also our frailty is. Therefore, he visits us with disgrace, or poverty, or bereavement, or disease, or other afflictions. Feeling altogether unable to support them, we forthwith, in so far as regards ourselves, give way, and thus humbled learn to invoke his strength, which alone can enable us to bear up under a weight of affliction. Nay, even the holiest of men, however well aware that they stand not in their own strength, but by the grace of God, would feel too secure in their own fortitude and constancy, were they not brought to a more thorough knowledge of themselves by the trial of the cross. This feeling gained even upon David, "In my prosperity I Said, I shall never be moved. Lord, by thy favour thou hast made my mountain to stand strong: thou didst hide thy face, and I was troubled" (Ps. 30:6, 7). He confesses that in prosperity his feelings were dulled and blunted, so that, neglecting the grace of God, on which alone he ought to have depended, he leant to himself, and promised himself perpetuity. If it so happened to this great prophet, who of us should not fear and study caution? Though in tranquillity they flatter themselves with the idea of greater constancy and patience, yet, humbled by adversity, they learn the deception. Believers, I say, warned by such proofs of their diseases, make progress in humility, and, divesting themselves of a depraved confidence in the flesh, betake themselves to the grace of God, and, when they have so betaken themselves, experience the presence of the divine power, in which is ample protection.

3. This Paul teaches when he says that tribulation worketh patience, and patience experience. God having promised that he will be with believers in tribulation, they feel the truth of the promise; while supported by his hand, they endure patiently. This they could never do by their own strength. Patience, therefore, gives the saints an experimental proof that God in reality furnishes the aid which he has promised whenever there is need. Hence also their faith is confirmed, for it were very ungrateful not to expect that in future the truth of God will be, as they have already found it, firm and constant. We now see how many advantages are at once produced by the cross. Overturning the overweening opinion we form of our own virtue, and detecting the hypocrisy in which we delight, it removes our pernicious carnal confidence, teaching us, when thus humbled, to recline on God alone, so that we neither are oppressed nor despond. Then victory is followed by hope, inasmuch as the Lord, by performing what he has promised, establishes his truth in regard to the future. Were these the only reasons, it is surely plain how necessary it is for us to bear the cross. It is of no little importance to be rid of your self-love, and made fully conscious of your weakness; so impressed with a sense of your weakness as to learn to distrust yourself—to distrust yourself so as to transfer your confidence to God, reclining on him with such heartfelt confidence as to trust in his aid, and continue invincible to the end, standing by his grace so as to perceive that he is true to his promises, and so assured of the certainty of his promises as to be strong in hope.

4. Another end which the Lord has in afflicting his people is to try their patience, and train them to obedience—not that they can yield obedience to him except in so far as he enables them; but he is pleased thus to attest and display striking proofs of the graces which he has conferred upon his saints, lest they should remain within unseen and unemployed. Accordingly, by bringing forward openly the strength and constancy of endurance with which he has provided his servants, he is said to try their patience. Hence the expressions that God tempted Abraham (Gen. 21:1, 12), and made proof of his piety by not declining to sacrifice his only son. Hence, too, Peter tells us that our faith is proved by tribulation, just as gold is tried in a furnace of fire. But who will say it is not expedient that the most excellent gift of patience which the believer has received from his God should be applied to uses by being made sure and manifest? Otherwise men would never value it according to its worth. But if God himself, to prevent the virtues which he has conferred upon believers from lurking in obscurity, nay, lying useless and perishing, does aright in supplying materials for calling them forth, there is the best reason for the afflictions of the saints, since without them their patience could not exist. I say, that by the cross they are also trained to obedience, because they are thus taught to live not according to their own wish, but at the disposal of God. Indeed, did all things proceed as they wish, they would not know what it is to follow God. Seneca mentions (De Vit. Beata, cap. 15) that there was an old proverb when any one was exhorted to endure adversity, "*Follow God*;" thereby intimating, that men truly submitted to the yoke of God only when they gave their back and hand to his rod. But if it is most right that we should in all things prove our obedience to our heavenly Father, certainly we ought not to decline any method by which he trains us to obedience.

5. Still, however, we see not how necessary that obedience is, unless we at the same time consider how prone our carnal nature is to shake off the yoke of God whenever it has been treated with some degree of gentleness and indulgence. It just happens to it as with refractory horses, which, if kept idle for a few days at hack and manger, become ungovernable, and no longer recognize the rider, whose command before they implicitly obeyed. And we invariably become what God complains of in the people of Israel—waxing gross and fat, we kick against him who reared and nursed us (Deut. 32:15). The kindness of God should allure us to ponder and love his goodness; but since such is our malignity, that we are invariably corrupted by his indulgence, it is more than necessary for us to be restrained by discipline from breaking forth into such petulance. Thus, lest we become emboldened by an over-abundance of wealth; lest elated with honour, we grow proud; lest inflated with other advantages of body, or mind, or fortune, we grow insolent, the Lord himself interferes as he sees to be expedient by means of the cross, subduing and curbing the arrogance of our flesh, and that in various ways, as the advantage of each requires. For as we do not all equally labour under the same disease, so we do not all need the same difficult cure. Hence we see that all are not exercised with the same kind of cross. While the heavenly Physician treats some more gently, in the case of others he employs harsher remedies, his purpose being to provide a cure for all. Still none is left free and untouched, because he knows that all, without a single exception, are diseased.

6. We may add, that our most merciful Father requires not only to prevent our weakness, but often to correct

our past faults, that he may keep us in due obedience. Therefore, whenever we are afflicted we ought immediately to call to mind our past life. In this way we will find that the faults which we have committed are deserving of such castigation. And yet the exhortation to patience is not to be founded chiefly on the acknowledgment of sin. For Scripture supplies a far better consideration when it says, that in adversity "we are chastened of the Lord, that we should not be condemned with the world" (1 Cor. 11:32). Therefore, in the very bitterness of tribulation we ought to recognise the kindness and mercy of our Father, since even then he ceases not to further our salvation. For he afflicts, not that he may ruin or destroy but rather that he may deliver us from the condemnation of the world. Let this thought lead us to what Scripture elsewhere teaches: "My son, despise not the chastening of the Lord; neither be weary of his correction: For whom the Lord loveth he correcteth; even as a father the son in whom he delighteth" (Prov. 3:11, 12). When we perceive our Father's rod, is it not our part to behave as obedient docile sons rather than rebelliously imitate desperate men, who are hardened in wickedness? God dooms us to destruction, if he does not, by correction, call us back when we have fallen off from him, so that it is truly said, "If ye be without chastisement," "then are ye bastards, and not sons" (Heb. 12:8). We are most perverse then if we cannot bear him while he is manifesting his good-will to us, and the care which he takes of our salvation. Scripture states the difference between believers and unbelievers to be, that the latter, as the slaves of inveterate and deep-seated iniquity, only become worse and more obstinate under the lash; whereas the former, like free-born sons turn to repentance. Now, therefore, choose your class. But as I have already spoken of this subject, it is sufficient to have here briefly adverted to it.

7. There is singular consolation, moreover, when we are persecuted for righteousness' sake. For our thought should then be, How high the honour which God bestows upon us in distinguishing us by the special badge of his soldiers. By suffering persecution for righteousness' sake, I mean not only striving for the defence of the Gospel, but for the defence of righteousness in any way. Whether, therefore, in maintaining the truth of God against the lies of Satan, or defending the good and innocent against the injuries of the bad, we are obliged to incur the offence and hatred of the world, so as to endanger life, fortune, or honour, let us not grieve or decline so far to spend ourselves for God; let us not think ourselves wretched in those things in which he with his own lips has pronounced us blessed (Mt. 5:10). Poverty, indeed considered in itself, is misery; so are exile, contempt, imprisonment, ignominy: in fine, death itself is the last of all calamities. But when the favour of God breathes upon is, there is none of these things which may not turn out to our happiness. Let us then be contented with the testimony of Christ rather than with the false estimate of the flesh, and then, after the example of the Apostles, we will rejoice in being "counted worthy to suffer shame for his name" (Acts 5:41). For why? If, while conscious of our innocence, we are deprived of our substance by the wickedness of man, we are, no doubt, humanly speaking, reduced to poverty; but in truth our riches in heaven are increased: if driven from our homes we have a more welcome reception into the family of God; if vexed and despised, we are more firmly rooted in Christ; if stigmatised by disgrace and ignominy, we have a higher place in the kingdom of God; and if we are slain, entrance is thereby given us to eternal life. The Lord having set such a price upon us, let us be ashamed to estimate ourselves at less than the shadowy and evanescent allurements of the present life.

8. Since by these, and similar considerations, Scripture abundantly solaces us for the ignominy or calamities which we endure in defence of righteousness, we are very ungrateful if we do not willingly and cheerfully receive them at the hand of the Lord, especially since this form of the cross is the most appropriate to believers, being that by which Christ desires to be glorified in us, as Peter also declares (1 Pet. 4:11, 14). But as to ingenuous natures, it is more bitter to suffer disgrace than a hundred deaths, Paul expressly reminds us that not only persecution, but also disgrace awaits us, "because we trust in the living God" (1 Tim. 4:10). So in another passage he bids us, after his example, walk "by evil report and good report" (2 Cor. 6:8). The cheerfulness required, however, does not imply a total insensibility to pain. The saints could show no patience under the cross if they were not both tortured with pain and grievously molested. Were there no hardship in poverty, no pain in disease, no sting in ignominy, no fear in death, where would be the fortitude and moderation in enduring them? But while every one of these, by its inherent bitterness, naturally vexes the mind, the believer in this displays his fortitude, that though fully sensible of the bitterness and labouring grievously, he still withstands and struggles boldly; in this displays his patience, that though sharply stung, he is however curbed by the fear of God from breaking forth into any excess; in this displays his alacrity, that though

pressed with sorrow and sadness, he rests satisfied with spiritual consolation from God.

9. This conflict which believers maintain against the natural feeling of pain, while they study moderation and patience, Paul elegantly describes in these words: "We are troubled on every side, yet not distressed; we are perplexed, but not in despair; persecuted, but not forsaken; cast down, but not destroyed" (2 Cor. 4:8, 9). You see that to bear the cross patiently is not to have your feelings altogether blunted, and to be absolutely insensible to pain, according to the absurd description which the Stoics of old gave of their hero as one who, divested of humanity, was affected in the same way by adversity and prosperity, grief and joy; or rather, like a stone, was not affected by anything. And what did they gain by that sublime wisdom? they exhibited a shadow of patience, which never did, and never can, exist among men. Nay, rather by aiming at a too exact and rigid patience, they banished it altogether from human life. Now also we have among Christians a new kind of Stoics, who hold it vicious not only to groan and weep, but even to be sad and anxious. These paradoxes are usually started by indolent men who, employing themselves more in speculation than in action, can do nothing else for us than beget such paradoxes. But we have nothing to do with that iron philosophy which our Lord and Master condemned—not only in word, but also by his own example. For he both grieved and shed tears for his own and others' woes. Nor did he teach his disciples differently: "Ye shall weep and lament, but the world shall rejoice" (John 16:20). And lest any one should regard this as vicious, he expressly declares, "Blessed are they that mourn" (Mt. 5:4). And no wonder. If all tears are condemned, what shall we think of our Lord himself, whose "sweat was as it were great drops of blood falling down to the ground?" (Luke 22:44; Mt. 26:38). If every kind of fear is a mark of unbelief, what place shall we assign to the dread which, it is said, in no slight degree amazed him; if all sadness is condemned, how shall we justify him when he confesses, "My soul is exceeding sorrowful, even unto death?"

10. I wished to make these observations to keep pious minds from despair, lest, from feeling it impossible to divest themselves of the natural feeling of grief, they might altogether abandon the study of patience. This must necessarily be the result with those who convert patience into stupor, and a brave and firm man into a block. Scripture gives saints the praise of endurance when, though afflicted by the hardships they endure, they are not crushed; though they feel bitterly, they are at the same time filled with spiritual joy; though pressed with anxiety, breathe exhilarated by the consolation of God. Still there is a certain degree of repugnance in their hearts, because natural sense shuns and dreads what is adverse to it, while pious affection, even through these difficulties, tries to obey the divine will. This repugnance the Lord expressed when he thus addressed Peter: "Verily, verily, I say unto thee, When thou wast young, thou girdedst thyself and walkedst whither thou wouldst; but when thou shalt be old, thou shalt stretch forth thy hands, and another shall gird thee; and carry thee whither thou wouldest not" (John 21:18). It is not probable, indeed, that when it became necessary to glorify God by death he was driven to it unwilling and resisting; had it been so, little praise would have been due to his martyrdom. But though he obeyed the divine ordination with the greatest alacrity of heart, yet, as he had not divested himself of humanity, he was distracted by a double will. When he thought of the bloody death which he was to die, struck with horror, he would willingly have avoided it: on the other hand, when he considered that it was God who called him to it, his fear was vanquished and suppressed, and he met death cheerfully. It must therefore be our study, if we would be disciples of Christ, to imbue our minds with such reverence and obedience to God as may tame and subjugate all affections contrary to his appointment. In this way, whatever be the kind of cross to which we are subjected, we shall in the greatest straits firmly maintain our patience. Adversity will have its bitterness, and sting us. When afflicted with disease, we shall groan and be disquieted, and long for health; pressed with poverty, we shall feel the stings of anxiety and sadness, feel the pain of ignominy, contempt, and injury, and pay the tears due to nature at the death of our friends: but our conclusion will always be, The Lord so willed it, therefore let us follow his will. Nay, amid the pungency of grief, among groans and tears this thought will necessarily suggest itself and incline us cheerfully to endure the things for which we are so afflicted.

11. But since the chief reason for enduring the cross has been derived from a consideration of the divine will, we must in few words explain wherein lies the difference between philosophical and Christian patience. Indeed, very few of the philosophers advanced so far as to perceive that the hand of God tries us by means of affliction, and that we ought in this matter to obey God. The only reason which they adduce is, that *so it must be*. But is not this just to say, that we must yield to God, because it is in vain to contend against him? For if we

obey God only because it is necessary, provided we can escape, we shall cease to obey him. But what Scripture calls us to consider in the will of God is very different, namely, first justice and equity, and then a regard to our own salvation. Hence Christian exhortations to patience are of this nature, Whether poverty, or exile, or imprisonment, or contumely, or disease, or bereavement, or any such evil affects us, we must think that none of them happens except by the will and providence of God; moreover, that every thing he does is in the most perfect order. What! do not our numberless daily faults deserve to be chastised, more severely, and with a heavier rod than his mercy lays upon us? Is it not most right that our flesh should be subdued, and be, as it were, accustomed to the yoke, so as not to rage and wanton as it lists? Are not the justice and the truth of God worthy of our suffering on their account? But if the equity of God is undoubtedly displayed in affliction, we cannot murmur or struggle against them without iniquity. We no longer hear the frigid cant, Yield, because it is necessary; but a living and energetic precept, Obey, because it is unlawful to resist; bear patiently, because impatience is rebellion against the justice of God. Then as that only seems to us attractive which we perceive to be for our own safety and advantage, here also our heavenly Father consoles us, by the assurance, that in the very cross with which he afflicts us he provides for our salvation. But if it is clear that tribulations are salutary to us, why should we not receive them with calm and grateful minds? In bearing them patiently we are not submitting to necessity but resting satisfied with our own good. The effect of these thoughts is, that to whatever extent our minds are contracted by the bitterness which we naturally feel under the cross, to the same extent will they be expanded with spiritual joy. Hence arises thanksgiving, which cannot exist unless joy be felt. But if the praise of the Lord and thanksgiving can emanate only from a cheerful and gladdened breasts and there is nothing which ought to interrupt these feelings in us, it is clear how necessary it is to temper the bitterness of the cross with spiritual joy.

CHAPTER 9

OF MEDITATING ON THE FUTURE LIFE.

The three divisions of this chapter,—I. The principal use of the cross is, that it in various ways accustoms us to despise the present, and excites us to aspire to the future life, sec. 1, 2. II. In withdrawing from the present life we must neither shun it nor feel hatred for it; but desiring the future life, gladly quit the present at the command of our sovereign Master, sec. 3, 4. III. Our infirmity in dreading death described. The correction and safe remedy, sec. 6.

Sections:

1. The design of God in afflicting his people. 1. To accustom us to despise the present life. Our infatuated love of it. Afflictions employed as the cure. 2. To lead us to aspire to heaven.

2. Excessive love of the present life prevents us from duly aspiring to the other. Hence the disadvantages of prosperity. Blindness of the human judgment. Our philosophizing on the vanity of life only of momentary influence. The necessity of the cross.

3. The present life an evidence of the divine favour to his people; and therefore, not to be detested. On the contrary, should call forth thanksgiving. The crown of victory in heaven after the contest on earth.

4. Weariness of the present life how to be tempered. The believer's estimate of life. Comparison of the present and the future life. How far the present life should be hated.

5. Christians should not tremble at the fear of death. Two reasons. Objection. Answer. Other reasons.

6. Reasons continued. Conclusion.

1. Whatever be the kind of tribulation with which we are afflicted, we should always consider the end of it to be, that we may be trained to despise the present, and thereby stimulated to aspire to the future life. For since God well knows how strongly we are inclined by nature to a slavish love of this world, in order to prevent us from clinging too strongly to it, he employs the fittest reason for calling us back, and shaking off our lethargy. Every one of us, indeed, would be thought to aspire and aim at heavenly immortality during the whole course of his life. For we would be ashamed in no respect to excel the lower animals; whose condition would not be at all inferior to ours, had we not a hope of immortality beyond the grave. But when you attend to the plans, wishes, and actions of each, you see nothing in them but the earth. Hence our stupidity; our minds being dazzled with the glare of wealth, power, and honours, that they can see no farther. The heart also, engrossed with avarice, ambition, and lust, is weighed down and cannot rise above them. In short, the whole soul, ensnared by the allurements of the flesh, seeks its happiness on the earth. To meet this

disease, the Lord makes his people sensible of the vanity of the present life, by a constant proof of its miseries. Thus, that they may not promise themselves deep and lasting peace in it, he often allows them to be assailed by war, tumult, or rapine, or to be disturbed by other injuries. That they may not long with too much eagerness after fleeting and fading riches, or rest in those which they already possess, he reduces them to want, or, at least, restricts them to a moderate allowance, at one time by exile, at another by sterility, at another by fire, or by other means. That they may not indulge too complacently in the advantages of married life, he either vexes them by the misconduct of their partners, or humbles them by the wickedness of their children, or afflicts them by bereavement. But if in all these he is indulgent to them, lest they should either swell with vain-glory, or be elated with confidence, by diseases and dangers he sets palpably before them how unstable and evanescent are all the advantages competent to mortals. We duly profit by the discipline of the cross, when we learn that this life, estimated in itself, is restless, troubled, in numberless ways wretched, and plainly in no respect happy; that what are estimated its blessings are uncertain, fleeting, vain, and vitiated by a great admixture of evil. From this we conclude, that all we have to seek or hope for here is contest; that when we think of the crown we must raise our eyes to heaven. For we must hold, that our mind never rises seriously to desire and aspire after the future, until it has learned to despise the present life.

2. For there is no medium between the two things: the earth must either be worthless in our estimation, or keep us enslaved by an intemperate love of it. Therefore, if we have any regard to eternity, we must carefully strive to disencumber ourselves of these fetters. Moreover, since the present life has many enticements to allure us, and great semblance of delight, grace, and sweetness to soothe us, it is of great consequence to us to be now and then called off from its fascinations. For what, pray, would happen, if we here enjoyed an uninterrupted course of honour and felicity, when even the constant stimulus of affliction cannot arouse us to a due sense of our misery? That human life is like smoke or a shadow, is not only known to the learned; there is not a more trite proverb among the vulgar. Considering it a fact most useful to be known, they have recommended it in many well-known expressions. Still there is no fact which we ponder less carefully, or less frequently remember. For we form all our plans just as if we had fixed our immortality on the earth. If we see a funeral, or walk among graves, as the image of death is then present to the eye, I admit we philosophise admirably on the vanity of life. We do not indeed always do so, for those things often have no effect upon us at all. But, at the best, our philosophy is momentary. It vanishes as soon as we turn our back, and leaves not the vestige of remembrance behind; in short, it passes away, just like the applause of a theatre at some pleasant spectacle. Forgetful not only of death, but also of mortality itself, as if no rumour of it had ever reached us, we indulge in supine security as expecting a terrestrial immortality. Meanwhile, if any one breaks in with the proverb, that man is the creature of a day, we indeed acknowledge its truth, but, so far from giving heed to it, the thought of perpetuity still keeps hold of our minds. Who then can deny that it is of the highest importance to us all, I say not, to be admonished by words, but convinced by all possible experience of the miserable condition of our earthly life; since even when convinced we scarcely cease to gaze upon it with vicious, stupid admiration, as if it contained within itself the sum of all that is good? But if God finds it necessary so to train us, it must be our duty to listen to him when he calls, and shakes us from our torpor, that we may hasten to despise the world, and aspire with our whole heart to the future life.

3. Still the contempt which believers should train themselves to feel for the present life, must not be of a kind to beget hatred of it or ingratitude to God. This life, though abounding in all kinds of wretchedness, is justly classed among divine blessings which are not to be despised. Wherefore, if we do not recognize the kindness of God in it, we are chargeable with no little ingratitude towards him. To believers, especially, it ought to be a proof of divine benevolence, since it is wholly destined to promote their salvation. Before openly exhibiting the inheritance of eternal glory, God is pleased to manifest himself to us as a Father by minor proofs—viz. the blessings which he daily bestows upon us. Therefore, while this life serves to acquaint us with the goodness of God, shall we disdain it as if it did not contain one particle of good? We ought, therefore, to feel and be affected towards it in such a manner as to place it among those gifts of the divine benignity which are by no means to be despised. Were there no proofs in Scripture (they are most numerous and clear), yet nature herself exhorts us to return thanks to God for having brought us forth into light, granted us the use of it, and bestowed upon us all the means necessary for its preservation. And there is a much higher reason when we reflect that here we are in a manner prepared for the glory of the heavenly kingdom.

For the Lord hath ordained, that those who are ultimately to be crowned in heaven must maintain a previous warfare on the earth, that they may not triumph before they have overcome the difficulties of war, and obtained the victory. Another reason is, that we here begin to experience in various ways a foretaste of the divine benignity, in order that our hope and desire may be whetted for its full manifestation. When once we have concluded that our earthly life is a gift of the divine mercy, of which, agreeably to our obligation, it behoves us to have a grateful remembrance, we shall then properly descend to consider its most wretched condition, and thus escape from that excessive fondness for it, to which, as I have said, we are naturally prone.

4. In proportion as this improper love diminishes, our desire of a better life should increase. I confess, indeed, that a most accurate opinion was formed by those who thought, that the best thing was not to be born, the next best to die early. For, being destitute of the light of God and of true religion, what could they see in it that was not of dire and evil omen? Nor was it unreasonable for those who felt sorrow and shed tears at the birth of their kindred, to keep holiday at their deaths. But this they did without profit; because, devoid of the true doctrine of faith, they saw not how that which in itself is neither happy nor desirable turns to the advantage of the righteous: and hence their opinion issued in despair. Let believers, then, in forming an estimate of this mortal life, and perceiving that in itself it is nothing but misery, make it their aim to exert themselves with greater alacrity, and less hinderance, in aspiring to the future and eternal life. When we contrast the two, the former may not only be securely neglected, but, in comparison of the latter, be disdained and contemned. If heaven is our country, what can the earth be but a place of exile? If departure from the world is entrance into life, what is the world but a sepulchre, and what is residence in it but immersion in death? If to be freed from the body is to gain full possession of freedom, what is the body but a prison? If it is the very summit of happiness to enjoy the presence of God, is it not miserable to want it? But "whilst we are at home in the body, we are absent from the Lord" (2 Cor. 5:6). Thus when the earthly is compared with the heavenly life, it may undoubtedly be despised and trampled under foot. We ought never, indeed, to regard it with hatred, except in so far as it keeps us subject to sin; and even this hatred ought not to be directed against life itself. At all events, we must stand so affected towards it in regard to weariness or hatred as, while longing for its termination, to be ready at the Lord's will to continue in it, keeping far from everything like murmuring and impatience. For it is as if the Lord had assigned us a post, which we must maintain till he recalls us. Paul, indeed, laments his condition, in being still bound with the fetters of the body, and sighs earnestly for redemption (Rom. 7:24); nevertheless, he declared that, in obedience to the command of Gods he was prepared for both courses, because he acknowledges it as his duty to God to glorify his name whether by life or by death, while it belongs to God to determine what is most conducive to His glory (Phil. 1:20–24). Wherefore, if it becomes us to live and die to the Lord, let us leave the period of our life and death at his disposal. Still let us ardently long for death, and constantly meditate upon it, and in comparison with future immortality, let us despise life, and, on account of the bondage of sin, long to renounce it whenever it shall so please the Lord.

5. But, most strange to say, many who boast of being Christians, instead of thus longing for death, are so afraid of it that they tremble at the very mention of it as a thing ominous and dreadful. We cannot wonder, indeed, that our natural feelings should be somewhat shocked at the mention of our dissolution. But it is altogether intolerable that the light of piety should not be so powerful in a Christian breast as with greater consolation to overcome and suppress that fear. For if we reflect that this our tabernacle, unstable, defective, corruptible, fading, pining, and putrid, is dissolved, in order that it may forthwith be renewed in sure, perfect, incorruptible, in fine, in heavenly glory, will not faith compel us eagerly to desire what nature dreads? If we reflect that by death we are recalled from exile to inhabit our native country, a heavenly country, shall this give us no comfort? But everything longs for permanent existence. I admit this, and therefore contend that we ought to look to future immortality, where we may obtain that fixed condition which nowhere appears on the earth. For Paul admirably enjoins believers to hasten cheerfully to death, not because they "would be unclothed, but clothed upon" (2 Cor. 5:2). Shall the lower animals, and inanimate creatures themselves even wood and stone, as conscious of their present vanity, long for the final resurrection, that they may with the sons of God be delivered from vanity (Rom. 8:19); and shall we, endued with the light of intellect, and more than intellect, enlightened by the Spirit of God, when our essence is in question, rise no higher than the corruption of this earth? But it is not my purpose, nor is this the place, to plead against this great perverseness. At the outset, I declared that I had no wish to engage in a

diffuse discussion of common-places. My advice to those whose minds are thus timid is to read the short treatise of Cyprian De Mortalitate, unless it be more accordant with their deserts to send them to the philosophers, that by inspecting what they say on the contempt of death, they may begin to blush. This, however let us hold as fixed, that no man has made much progress in the school of Christ who does not look forward with joy to the day of death and final resurrection (2 Tim. 4:18; Tit. 2:13) for Paul distinguishes all believers by this mark; and the usual course of Scripture is to direct us thither whenever it would furnish us with an argument for substantial joy. "Look up," says our Lord, "and lift up your heads: for your redemption draweth nigh" (Luke 21:28). Is it reasonable, I ask, that what he intended to have a powerful effect in stirring us up to alacrity and exultation should produce nothing but sadness and consternation? If it is so, why do we still glory in him as our Master? Therefore, let us come to a sounder mind, and how repugnant so ever the blind and stupid longing of the flesh may be, let us doubt not to desire the advent of the Lord not in wish only, but with earnest sighs, as the most propitious of all events. He will come as a Redeemer to deliver us from an immense abyss of evil and misery, and lead us to the blessed inheritance of his life and glory.

6. Thus, indeed, it is; the whole body of the faithful, so long as they live on the earth, must be like sheep for the slaughter, in order that they may be conformed to Christ their head (Rom. 8:36). Most deplorable, therefore, would their situation be did they not, by raising their mind to heaven, become superior to all that is in the world, and rise above the present aspect of affairs (1 Cor. 15:19). On the other hand, when once they have raised their head above all earthly objects, though they see the wicked flourishing in wealth and honour, and enjoying profound peace, indulging in luxury and splendour, and revelling in all kinds of delights, though they should moreover be wickedly assailed by them, suffer insult from their pride, be robbed by their avarice, or assailed by any other passion, they will have no difficulty in bearing up under these evils. They will turn their eye to that day (Isaiah 25:8; Rev. 7:17), on which the Lord will receive his faithful servants, wipe away all tears from their eyes, clothe them in a robe of glory and joy, feed them with the ineffable sweetness of his pleasures, exalt them to share with him in his greatness; in fine, admit them to a participation in his happiness. But the wicked who may have flourished on the earth, he will cast forth in extreme ignominy, will change their delights into torments, their laughter and joy into wailing and gnashing of teeth, their peace into the gnawing of conscience, and punish their luxury with unquenchable fire. He will also place their necks under the feet of the godly, whose patience they abused. For, as Paul declares, "it is a righteous thing with God to recompense tribulation to them that trouble you; and to you who are troubled rest with us, when the Lord Jesus shall be revealed from heaven" (2 Thess. 1:6, 7). This, indeed, is our only consolation; deprived of it, we must either give way to despondency, or resort to our destruction to the vain solace of the world. The Psalmist confesses, "My feet were almost gone: my steps had well nigh slipt: for I was envious at the foolish when I saw the prosperity of the wicked" (Psalm 73:3, 4); and he found no resting-place until he entered the sanctuary, and considered the latter end of the righteous and the wicked. To conclude in one word, the cross of Christ then only triumphs in the breasts of believers over the devil and the flesh, sin and sinners, when their eyes are directed to the power of his resurrection.

CHAPTER 10

HOW TO USE THE PRESENT LIFE, AND THE COMFORTS OF IT.

The divisions of this chapter are, I. The necessity and usefulness of this doctrine. Extremes to be avoided, if we would rightly use the present life and its comforts, sec. 1, 2. II. One of these extremes—viz. the intemperance of the flesh—to be carefully avoided. Four methods of doing so described in order, sec. 3–6.

Sections:
1. Necessity of this doctrine. Use of the goods of the present life. Extremes to be avoided. 1. Excessive austerity. 2. Carnal intemperance and lasciviousness.

2. God, by creating so many mercies, consulted not only for our necessities, but also for our comfort and delight. Confirmation from a passage in the Psalms, and from experience.

3. Excessive austerity, therefore, to be avoided. So also must the wantonness of the flesh. 1. The creatures invite us to know, love, and honour the Creator. 2. This not done by the wicked, who only abuse these temporal mercies.

4. All earthly blessings to be despised in comparison of the heavenly life. Aspiration after this life destroyed by an excessive love of created objects. First, Intemperance.

5. Second, Impatience and immoderate desire. Remedy of these evils. The creatures assigned to our use. Man still accountable for the use he makes of them.

6. God requires us in all our actions to look to his calling. Use of this doctrine. It is full of comfort.

1. By such rudiments we are at the same time well instructed by Scripture in the proper use of earthly blessings, a subject which, in forming a scheme of life, is by no mean to be neglected. For if we are to live, we must use the necessary supports of life; nor can we even shun those things which seem more subservient to delight than to necessity. We must therefore observe a mean, that we may use them with a pure conscience, whether for necessity or for pleasure. This the Lord prescribes by his word, when he tells us that to his people the present life is a kind of pilgrimage by which they hasten to the heavenly kingdom. If we are only to pass through the earth, there can be no doubt that we are to use its blessings only in so far as they assist our progress, rather than retard it. Accordingly, Paul, not without cause, admonishes us to use this world without abusing it, and to buy possessions as if we were selling them (1 Cor. 7:30, 31). But as this is a slippery place, and there is great danger of falling on either side, let us fix our feet where we can stand safely. There have been some good and holy men who, when they saw intemperance and luxury perpetually carried to excess, if not strictly curbed, and were desirous to correct so pernicious an evil, imagined that there was no other method than to allow man to use corporeal goods only in so far as they were necessaries: a counsel pious indeed, but unnecessarily austere; for it does the very dangerous thing of binding consciences in closer fetters than those in which they are bound by the word of God. Moreover, necessity, according to them, was abstinence from every thing which could be wanted, so that they held it scarcely lawful to make any addition to bread and water. Others were still more austere, as is related of Cratetes the Theban, who threw his riches into the sea, because he thought, that unless he destroyed them they would destroy him. Many also in the present day, while they seek a pretext for carnal intemperance in the use of external things, and at the same time would pave the way for licentiousness, assume for granted, what I by no means concede, that this liberty is not to be restrained by any modification, but that it is to be left to every man's conscience to use them as far as he thinks lawful. I indeed confess that here consciences neither can nor ought to be bound by fixed and definite laws; but that Scripture having laid down general rules for the legitimate uses we should keep within the limits which they prescribe.

2. Let this be our principle, that we err not in the use of the gifts of Providence when we refer them to the end for which their author made and destined them, since he created them for our good, and not for our destruction. No man will keep the true path better than he who shall have this end carefully in view. Now then, if we consider for what end he created food, we shall find that he consulted not only for our necessity, but also for our enjoyment and delight. Thus, in clothing, the end was, in addition to necessity, comeliness and honour; and in herbs, fruits, and trees, besides their various uses, gracefulness of appearance and sweetness of smell. Were it not so, the Prophet would not enumerate among the mercies of God "wine that maketh glad the heart of man, and oil to make his face to shine" (Ps. 104:15). The Scriptures would not everywhere mention, in commendation of his benignity, that he had given such things to men. The natural qualities of things themselves demonstrate to what end, and how far, they may be lawfully enjoyed. Has the Lord adorned flowers with all the beauty which spontaneously presents itself to the eye, and the sweet odour which delights the sense of smell, and shall it be unlawful for us to enjoy that beauty and this odour? What? Has he not so distinguished colours as to make some more agreeable than others? Has he not given qualities to gold and silver, ivory and marble, thereby rendering them precious above other metals or stones? In short, has he not given many things a value without having any necessary use?

3. Have done, then, with that inhuman philosophy which, in allowing no use of the creatures but for necessity, not only maliciously deprives us of the lawful fruit of the divine beneficence, but cannot be realised without depriving man of all his senses, and reducing him to a block. But, on the other hand, let us with no less care guard against the lusts of the flesh, which, if not kept in order, break through all bounds, and are, as I have said, advocated by those who, under pretence of liberty, allow themselves every sort of license. First one restraint is imposed when we hold that the object of creating all things was to teach us to know their author, and feel grateful for his indulgence. Where is the gratitude if you so gorge or stupify yourself with feasting and wine as to be unfit for offices of piety, or the duties of your calling? Where the recognition of God, if the flesh, boiling forth in lust through excessive indulgences infects the mind with its impurity, so as to lose the discernment of honour and rectitude? Where thankfulness to God for clothing,

if on account of sumptuous raiment we both admire ourselves and disdain others? if, from a love of show and splendour, we pave the way for immodesty? Where our recognition of God, if the glare of these things captivates our minds? For many are so devoted to luxury in all their senses that their mind lies buried: many are so delighted with marble, gold, and pictures, that they become marble-hearted—are changed as it were into metal, and made like painted figures. The kitchen, with its savoury smells, so engrosses them that they have no spiritual savour. The same thing may be seen in other matters. Wherefore, it is plain that there is here great necessity for curbing licentious abuse, and conforming to the rule of Paul, "make not provision for the flesh to fulfil the lusts thereof" (Rom. 13:14). Where too much liberty is given to them, they break forth without measure or restraint.

4. There is no surer or quicker way of accomplishing this than by despising the present life and aspiring to celestial immortality. For hence two rules arise: First, "it remaineth, that both they that have wives be as though they had none;" "and they that use this world, as not abusing it" (1 Cor. 7:29, 31). Secondly, we must learn to be no less placid and patient in enduring penury, than moderate in enjoying abundance. He who makes it his rule to use this world as if he used it not, not only cuts off all gluttony in regard to meat and drink, and all effeminacy, ambition, pride, excessive shows and austerity, in regard to his table, his house, and his clothes, but removes every care and affection which might withdraw or hinder him from aspiring to the heavenly life, and cultivating the interest of his soul. It was well said by Cato: Luxury causes great care, and produces great carelessness as to virtue; and it is an old proverb,—Those who are much occupied with the care of the body, usually give little care to the soul. Therefore while the liberty of the Christian in external matters is not to be tied down to a strict rule, it is, however, subject to this law—he must indulge as little as possible; on the other hand, it must be his constant aims not only to curb luxury, but to cut off all show of superfluous abundance, and carefully beware of converting a help into an hinderance.

5. Another rule is, that those in narrow and slender circumstances should learn to bear their wants patiently, that they may not become immoderately desirous of things, the moderate use of which implies no small progress in the school of Christ. For in addition to the many other vices which accompany a longing for earthly good, he who is impatient under poverty almost always betrays the contrary disease in abundance. By this I mean, that he who is ashamed of a sordid garment will be vain-glorious of a splendid one; he who not contented with a slender, feels annoyed at the want of a more luxurious supper, will intemperately abuse his luxury if he obtains it; he who has a difficulty, and is dissatisfied in submitting to a private and humble condition, will be unable to refrain from pride if he attain to honour. Let it be the aim of all who have any unfeigned desire for piety to learn, after the example of the Apostle, "both to be full and to be hungry, both to abound and to suffer need" (Phil. 4:12). Scripture, moreover, has a third rule for modifying the use of earthly blessings. We have already adverted to it when considering the offices of charity. For it declares that they have all been given us by the kindness of God, and appointed for our use under the condition of being regarded as trusts, of which we must one day give account. We must, therefore, administer them as if we constantly heard the words sounding in our ears, "Give an account of your stewardship." At the same time, let us remember by whom the account is to be taken—viz. by him who, while he so highly commends abstinence, sobriety, frugality, and moderation, abominates luxury, pride, ostentation, and vanity; who approves of no administration but that which is combined with charity, who with his own lips has already condemned all those pleasures which withdraw the heart from chastity and purity, or darken the intellect.

6. The last thing to be observed is, that the Lord enjoins every one of us, in all the actions of life, to have respect to our own calling. He knows the boiling restlessness of the human mind, the fickleness with which it is borne hither and thither, its eagerness to hold opposites at one time in its grasp, its ambition. Therefore, lest all things should be thrown into confusion by our folly and rashness, he has assigned distinct duties to each in the different modes of life. And that no one may presume to overstep his proper limits, he has distinguished the different modes of life by the name of callings. Every man's mode of life, therefore, is a kind of station assigned him by the Lord, that he may not be always driven about at random. So necessary is this distinction, that all our actions are thereby estimated in his sight, and often in a very different way from that in which human reason or philosophy would estimate them. There is no more illustrious deed even among philosophers than to free one's country from tyranny, and yet the private individual who stabs the tyrant is openly condemned by the voice of the heavenly Judge. But I am unwilling to dwell on particular examples; it is enough to know that in every thing the call of the Lord is the

foundation and beginning of right action. He who does not act with reference to it will never, in the discharge of duty, keep the right path. He will sometimes be able, perhaps, to give the semblance of something laudable, but whatever it may be in the sight of man, it will be rejected before the throne of God; and besides, there will be no harmony in the different parts of his life. Hence, he only who directs his life to this end will have it properly framed; because free from the impulse of rashness, he will not attempt more than his calling justifies, knowing that it is unlawful to overleap the prescribed bounds. He who is obscure will not decline to cultivate a private life, that he may not desert the post at which God has placed him. Again, in all our cares, toils, annoyances, and other burdens, it will be no small alleviation to know that all these are under the superintendence of God. The magistrate will more willingly perform his office, and the father of a family confine himself to his proper sphere. Every one in his particular mode of life will, without repining, suffer its inconveniences, cares, uneasiness, and anxiety, persuaded that God has laid on the burden. This, too, will afford admirable consolation, that in following your proper calling, no work will be so mean and sordid as not to have a splendour and value in the eye of God.

CHAPTER 11

OF JUSTIFICATION BY FAITH. BOTH THE NAME AND THE REALITY DEFINED.

In this chapter and the seven which follow, the doctrine of Justification by Faith is expounded, and opposite errors refuted. The following may be regarded as the arrangement of these chapters:—Chapter 11 states the doctrine, and the four subsequent chapters, by destroying the righteousness of works, confirm the righteousness of faith, each in the order which appears in the respective titles of these chapters. In Chapter 12 the doctrine of Justification is confirmed by a description of perfect righteousness; in Chapter 13 by calling attention to two precautions; in Chapter 14 by a consideration of the commencement and progress of regeneration in the regenerate; and in Chapter 15 by two very pernicious effects which constantly accompany the righteousness of works. The three other chapters are devoted to refutation; Chapter 16 disposes of the objections of opponents; Chapter 17 replies to the arguments drawn from the promises of the Law or the Gospel; Chapter 18 refutes what is said in support of the righteousness of faith from the promise of reward.

There are three principal divisions in the Eleventh Chapter. I. The terms used in this discussion are explained, sec. 1–4. II. Osiander's dream as to essential righteousness impugned, sec. 5–13. III. The righteousness of faith established in opposition to the righteousness of works.

Sections:

1. Connection between the doctrine of Justification and that of Regeneration. The knowledge of this doctrine very necessary for two reasons.

2. For the purpose of facilitating the exposition of it, the terms are explained. 1. What it is to be justified in the sight of God. 2. To be justified by works. 3. To be justified by faith. Definition.

3. Various meanings of the term Justification. 1. To give praise to God and truth. 2. To make a vain display of righteousness. 3. To impute righteousness by faith, by and on account of Christ. Confirmation from an expression of Paul, and another of our Lord.

4. Another confirmation from a comparison with other expressions, in which justification means free righteousness before God through faith in Jesus Christ. 1. Acceptance. 2. Imputation of righteousness. 3. Remission of sins. 4. Blessedness. 5. Reconciliation with God. 6. Righteousness by the obedience of Christ.

5. The second part of the chapter. Osiander's dream as to essential righteousness refuted. 1. Osiander's argument: Answer. 2. Osiander's second argument: Answer. Third argument: Answer.

6. necessity of this refutation. Fourth argument: Answer. Confirmation: Another answer. Fifth and sixth arguments and answers.

7. Seventh and eighth arguments.

8. Ninth argument: Answer.

9. Tenth argument: Answer.

10. In what sense Christ is said to be our righteousness. Eleventh and twelfth arguments and answers.

11. Thirteenth and fourteenth arguments: Answers. An exception by Osiander. Imputed and begun righteousness to be distinguished. Osiander confounds them. Fifteenth argument: Answer.

12. Sixteenth argument, a dream of Osiander: Answer. Other four arguments and answers. Conclusion of the refutation of Osiander's errors.

13. Last part of the chapter. Refutation of the Sophists pretending a righteousness compounded partly of faith and partly of works.

14. Sophistical evasion by giving the same name to different things: Two answers.

15. Second evasion: Two answers. First answer. Pernicious consequences resulting from this evasion.

16. Second answer, showing wherein, according to Scripture, Justification consists.

17. In explanation of this doctrine of Justification, two passages of Scripture produced.

18. Another passage of Scripture.

19. Third evasion. Papistical objection to the doctrine of Justification by Faith alone: Three answers. Fourth evasion: Three answers.

20. Fifth evasion, founded on the application of the term Righteousness to good works, and also on their reward: Answer, confirmed by the invincible argument of Paul. Sixth evasion: Answer.

21. Osiander and the Sophists being thus refuted, the accuracy of the definition of Justification by Faith established.

22. Definition confirmed. 1. By passages of Scripture. 2. By the writings of the ancient Fathers.

23. Man justified by faith, not because by it he obtains the Spirit, and is thus made righteous, but because by faith he lays hold of the righteousness of Christ. An objection removed. An example of the doctrine of Justification by Faith from the works of Ambrose.

1. I trust I have now sufficiently shown how man's only resource for escaping from the curse of the law, and recovering salvation, lies in faith; and also what the nature of faith is, what the benefits which it confers, and the fruits which it produces. The whole may be thus summed up: Christ given to us by the kindness of God is apprehended and possessed by faith, by means of which we obtain in particular a twofold benefit; first, being reconciled by the righteousness of Christ, God becomes, instead of a judge, an indulgent Father; and, secondly, being sanctified by his Spirit, we aspire to integrity and purity of life. This second benefit—viz. regeneration, appears to have been already sufficiently discussed. On the other hand, the subject of justification was discussed more cursorily, because it seemed of more consequence first to explain that the faith by which alone, through the mercy of God, we obtain free justification, is not destitute of good works; and also to show the true nature of these good works on which this question partly turns. The doctrine of Justification is now to be fully discussed, and discussed under the conviction, that as it is the principal ground on which religion must be supported, so it requires greater care and attention. For unless you understand first of all what your position is before God, and what the judgment which he passes upon you, you have no foundation on which your salvation can be laid, or on which piety towards God can be reared. The necessity of thoroughly understanding this subject will become more apparent as we proceed with it.

2. Lest we should stumble at the very threshold (this we should do were we to begin the discussion without knowing what the subject is), let us first explain the meaning of the expressions, *To be justified in the sight of God, to be Justified by faith or by works.* A man is said to be justified in the sight of God when in the judgment of God he is deemed righteous, and is accepted on account of his righteousness; for as iniquity is abominable to God, so neither can the sinner find grace in his sight, so far as he is and so long as he is regarded as a sinner. Hence, wherever sin is, there also are the wrath and vengeance of God. He, on the other hand, is justified who is regarded not as a sinner, but as righteous, and as such stands acquitted at the judgment-seat of God, where all sinners are condemned. As an innocent man, when charged before an impartial judge, who decides according to his innocence, is said to be justified by the judge, as a man is said to be justified by God when, removed from the catalogue of sinners, he has God as the witness and assertor of his righteousness. In the same manner, a man will be said to be *justified by works*, if in his life there can be found a purity and holiness which merits an attestation of righteousness at the throne of God, or if by the perfection of his works he can answer and satisfy the divine justice. On the contrary, a man will be *justified by faith* when, excluded from the righteousness of works, he by faith lays hold of the righteousness of Christ, and clothed in it appears in the sight of God not as a sinner, but as righteous. Thus we simply interpret justification, as the acceptance with which God receives us into his favor as if we were righteous; and we say that this justification consists in the forgiveness of sins and the imputation of the righteousness of Christ (see sec. 21 and 23).

3. In confirmation of this there are many clear passages of Scripture. First, it cannot be denied that this is the proper and most usual signification of the term. But as it were too tedious to collect all the passages, and compare them with each other, let it suffice to have called the reader's attention to the fact: he will easily convince himself of its truth. I will only mention a few passages in which the justification of which we speak is expressly handled. First, when Luke relates that all the people that heard Christ "justified God" (Luke 7:29), and when Christ declares,

that "Wisdom is justified of all her children" (Luke 7:35), Luke means not that they conferred righteousness which always dwells in perfection with God, although the whole world should attempt to wrest it from him, nor does Christ mean that the doctrine of salvation is made just: this it is in its own nature; but both modes of expression are equivalent to attributing due praise to God and his doctrine. On the other hand, when Christ upbraids the Pharisees for justifying themselves (Luke 16:15), he means not that they acquired righteousness by acting properly, but that they ambitiously courted a reputation for righteousness of which they were destitute. Those acquainted with Hebrew understand the meaning better: for in that language the name of wicked is given not only to those who are conscious of wickedness, but to those who receive sentence of condemnation. Thus, when Bathsheba says, "I and my son Solomon shall be counted offenders," she does not acknowledge a crime, but complains that she and her son will be exposed to the disgrace of being numbered among reprobates and criminals (1 Kings 1:21). It is, indeed, plain from the context, that the term even in Latin must be thus understood—viz. relatively—and does not denote any quality. In regard to the use of the term with reference to the present subject, when Paul speaks of the Scripture, "foreseeing that God would justify the heathen through faith" (Gal. 3:8), what other meaning can you give it than that God imputes righteousness by faith? Again, when he says, "that he (God) might be just, and the justifier of him who believeth in Jesus" (Rom. 3:26), what can the meaning be, if not that God, in consideration of their faith, frees them from the condemnation which their wickedness deserves? This appears still more plainly at the conclusion, when he exclaims, "Who shall lay any thing to the charge of God's elect? It is God that justifieth. Who is he that condemneth? It is Christ that died, yea rather, that is risen again, who is even at the right hand of God, who also maketh intercession for us" (Rom. 8:33, 34). For it is just as if he had said, Who shall accuse those whom God has acquitted? Who shall condemn those for whom Christ pleads? To *justify*, therefore, is nothing else than to acquit from the charge of guilt, as if innocence were proved. Hence, when God justifies us through the intercession of Christ, he does not acquit us on a proof of our own innocence, but by an imputation of righteousness, so that though not righteous in ourselves, we are deemed righteous in Christ. Thus it is said, in Paul's discourse in the Acts, "Through this man is preached unto you the forgiveness of sins; and by him all that believe are justified from all things from which ye could not be justified by the law of Moses" (Acts 13:38, 39). You see that after remission of sins justification is set down by way of explanation; you see plainly that it is used for acquittal; you see how it cannot be obtained by the works of the law; you see that it is entirely through the interposition of Christ; you see that it is obtained by faith; you see, in fine, that satisfaction intervenes, since it is said that we are justified from our sins by Christ. Thus when the publican is said to have gone down to his house "justified" (Luke 18:14), it cannot be held that he obtained this justification by any merit of works. All that is said is, that after obtaining the pardon of sins he was regarded in the sight of God as righteous. He was justified, therefore, not by any approval of works, but by gratuitous acquittal on the part of God. Hence Ambrose elegantly terms confession of sins "legal justification" (Ambrose on Psalm 118 Serm. 10).

4. Without saying more about the term, we shall have no doubt as to the thing meant if we attend to the description which is given of it. For Paul certainly designates justification by the term *acceptance*, when he says to the Ephesians, "Having predestinated us unto the adoption of children by Jesus Christ to himself, according to the good pleasure of his will, to the praise of the glory of his grace, wherein he has made us accepted in the Beloved" (Eph. 1:5, 6). His meaning is the very same as where he elsewhere says, "being justified freely by his grace" (Rom. 3:24). In the fourth chapter of the Epistle to the Romans, he first terms it the imputation of righteousness, and hesitates not to place it in forgiveness of sins: "Even as David also describeth the blessedness of the man unto whom God imputeth righteousness without works, saying, Blessed are they whose iniquities are forgiven," &c. (Rom. 4:6–8). There, indeed, he is not speaking of a part of justification, but of the whole. He declares, moreover, that a definition of it was given by David, when he pronounced him *blessed* who has obtained the *free* pardon of his sins. Whence it appears that this righteousness of which he speaks is simply opposed to judicial guilt. But the most satisfactory passage on this subject is that in which he declares the sum of the Gospel message to be reconciliation to God, who is pleased, through Christ, to receive us into favor by not imputing our sins (2 Cor. 5:18–21). Let my readers carefully weigh the whole context. For Paul shortly after adding, by way of explanation, in order to designate the mode of reconciliation, that Christ who knew no sin was made sin for us, undoubtedly understands by reconciliation nothing else than justification. Nor, indeed, could it be said, as he elsewhere

does, that we are made righteous "by the obedience" of Christ (Rom. 5:19), were it not that we are deemed righteous in the sight of God in him and not in ourselves.

5. But as Osiander has introduced a kind of monstrosity termed *essential righteousness*, by which, although he designed not to abolish free righteousness, he involves it in darkness, and by that darkness deprives pious minds of a serious sense of divine grace; before I pass to other matters, it may be proper to refute this delirious dream. And, first, the whole speculation is mere empty curiosity. He indeed, heaps together many passages of scripture showing that Christ is one with us, and we likewise one with him, a point which needs no proof; but he entangles himself by not attending to the bond of this unity. The explanation of all difficulties is easy to us, who hold that we are united to Christ by the secret agency of his Spirit, but he had formed some idea akin to that of the Manichees, desiring to transfuse the divine essence into men. Hence his other notion, that Adam was formed in the image of God, because even before the fall Christ was destined to be the model of human nature. But as I study brevity, I will confine myself to the matter in hand. He says, that we are one with Christ. This we admit, but still we deny that the essence of Christ is confounded with ours. Then we say that he absurdly endeavors to support his delusions by means of this principle: that Christ is our righteousness, because he is the eternal God, the fountain of righteousness, the very righteousness of God. My readers will pardon me for now only touching on matters which method requires me to defer to another place. But although he pretends that, by the term essential righteousness, he merely means to oppose the sentiment that we are reputed righteous on account of Christ, he however clearly shows, that not contented with that righteousness, which was procured for us by the obedience and sacrificial death of Christ, he maintains that we are substantially righteous in God by an infused essence as well as quality. For this is the reason why he so vehemently contends that not only Christ but the Father and the Spirit dwell in us. The fact I admit to be true, but still I maintain it is wrested by him. He ought to have attended to the mode of dwelling—viz. that the Father and the Spirit are in Christ; and as in him the fulness of the Godhead dwells, so in him we possess God entire. Hence, whatever he says separately concerning the Father and the Spirit, has no other tendency than to lead away the simple from Christ. Then he introduces a substantial mixture, by which God, transfusing himself into us, makes us as it were a part of himself. Our being made one with Christ by the agency of the Spirit, he being the head and we the members, he regards as almost nothing unless his essence is mingled with us. But, as I have said, in the case of the Father and the Spirit, he more clearly betrays his views—namely, that we are not justified by the mere grace of the Mediator, and that righteousness is not simply or entirely offered to us in his person, but that we are made partakers of divine righteousness when God is essentially united to us.

6. Had he only said, that Christ by justifying us becomes ours by an essential union, and that he is our head not only in so far as he is man, but that as the essence of the divine nature is diffused into us, he might indulge his dreams with less harm, and, perhaps, it were less necessary to contest the matter with him; but since this principle is like a cuttle-fish, which, by the ejection of dark and inky blood, conceals its many tails, if we would not knowingly and willingly allow ourselves to be robbed of that righteousness which alone gives us full assurance of our salvation, we must strenuously resist. For, in the whole of this discussion, the noun *righteousness* and the verb to *justify*, are extended by Osiander to two parts; to be justified being not only to be reconciled to God by a free pardon, but also to be made just; and righteousness being not a free imputation, but the holiness and integrity which the divine essence dwelling in us inspires. And he vehemently asserts (see sec. 8) that Christ is himself our righteousness, not in so far as he, by expiating sins, appeased the Father, but because he is the eternal God and life. To prove the first point—viz. that God justifies not only by pardoning but by regenerating, he asks, whether he leaves those whom he justifies as they were by nature, making no change upon their vices? The answer is very easy: as Christ cannot be divided into parts, so the two things, justification and sanctification, which we perceive to be united together in him, are inseparable. Whomsoever, therefore, God receives into his favor, he presents with the Spirit of adoption, whose agency forms them anew into his image. But if the brightness of the sun cannot be separated from its heat, are we therefore to say, that the earth is warmed by light and illumined by heat? Nothing can be more apposite to the matter in hand than this simile. The sun by its heat quickens and fertilizes the earth; by its rays enlightens and illumines it. Here is a mutual and undivided connection, and yet reason itself prohibits us from transferring the peculiar properties of the one to the other. In the confusion of a twofold grace, which Osiander obtrudes upon us, there is a similar absurdity. Because those whom God freely regards as righteous, he in fact

renews to the cultivation of righteousness, Osiander confounds that free acceptance with this gift of regeneration, and contends that they are one and the same. But Scriptures while combining both, classes them separately, that it may the better display the manifold grace of God. Nor is Paul's statement superfluous, that Christ is made unto us "righteousness and sanctification" (1 Cor. 1:30). And whenever he argues from the salvation procured for us, from the paternal love of God and the grace of Christ, that we are called to purity and holiness, he plainly intimates, that to be justified is something else than to be made new creatures. Osiander on coming to Scripture corrupts every passage which he quotes. Thus when Paul says, "to him that worketh not, but believeth on him that justifieth the ungodly, his faith is counted for righteousness," he expounds *justifying* as *making just*. With the same rashness he perverts the whole of the fourth chapter to the Romans. He hesitates not to give a similar gloss to the passage which I lately quoted, "Who shall lay any thing to the charge of God's elect? It is God that justifieth." Here it is plain that guilt and acquittal simply are considered, and that the Apostle's meaning depends on the antithesis. Therefore his futility is detected both in his argument and his quotations for support from Scripture. He is not a whit sounder in discussing the term righteousness, when it is said, that faith was imputed to Abraham for righteousness after he had embraced Christ (who is the righteousness of Gad and God himself) and was distinguished by excellent virtues. Hence it appears that two things which are perfect are viciously converted by him into one which is corrupt. For the righteousness which is there mentioned pertains not to the whole course of life; or rather, the Spirit testifies, that though Abraham greatly excelled in virtue, and by long perseverance in it had made so much progress, the only way in which he pleased God was by receiving the grace which was offered by the promise, in faith. From this it follows, that, as Paul justly maintains, there is no room for works in justification.

7. When he objects that the power of justifying exists not in faith, considered in itself, but only as receiving Christ, I willingly admit it. For did faith justify of itself, or (as it is expressed) by its own intrinsic virtue, as it is always weak and imperfect, its efficacy would be partial, and thus our righteousness being maimed would give us only a portion of salvation. We indeed imagine nothing of the kind, but say, that, properly speaking, God alone justifies. The same thing we likewise transfer to Christ, because he was given to us for righteousness; while we compare faith to a kind of vessel, because we are incapable of receiving Christ, unless we are emptied and come with open mouth to receive his grace. Hence it follows, that we do not withdraw the power of justifying from Christ, when we hold that, previous to his righteousness, he himself is received by faith. Still, however, I admit not the tortuous figure of the sophist, that faith is Christ; as if a vessel of clay were a treasure, because gold is deposited in it. And yet this is no reason why faith, though in itself of no dignity or value, should not justify us by giving Christ; Just as such a vessel filled with coin may give wealth. I say, therefore, that faith, which is only the instrument for receiving justification, is ignorantly confounded with Christ, who is the material cause, as well as the author and minister of this great blessing. This disposes of the difficulty—viz. how the term *faith* is to be understood when treating of justification.

8. Osiander goes still farther in regard to the mode of receiving Christ, holding, that by the ministry of the external word the internal word is received; that he may thus lead us away from the priesthood of Christ, and his office of Mediator, to his eternal divinity. We, indeed, do not divide Christ, but hold that he who, reconciling us to God in his flesh, bestowed righteousness upon us, is the eternal Word of God; and that he could not perform the office of Mediator, nor acquire righteousness for us, if he were not the eternal God. Osiander will have it, that as Christ is God and man, he was made our righteousness in respect not of his human but of his divine nature. But if this is a peculiar property of the Godhead, it will not be peculiar to Christ, but common to him with the Father and the Spirit, since their righteousness is one and the same. Thus it would be incongruous to say, that that which existed naturally from eternity was made ours. But granting that God was made unto us righteousness, what are we to make of Paul's interposed statement, that he was so made by God? This certainly is peculiar to the office of mediator, for although he contains in himself the divine nature, yet he receives his own proper title, that he may be distinguished from the Father and the Spirit. But he makes a ridiculous boast of a single passage of Jeremiah, in which it is said, that Jehovah will be our righteousness (Jer. 23:6; 33:16). But all he can extract from this is, that Christ, who is our righteousness, was God manifest in the flesh. We have elsewhere quoted from Paul's discourse, that God purchased the Church with his own blood (Acts 20:28). Were any one to infer from this that the blood by which sins were expiated was divine, and of a divine nature, who could endure so foul a heresy? But Osiander, thinking that he has gained the

whole cause by this childish cavil, swells, exults, and stuffs whole pages with his bombast, whereas the solution is simple and obvious—viz. that Jehovah, when made of the seed of David, was indeed to be the righteousness of believers, but in what sense Isaiah declares, "By his knowledge shall my righteous servant justify many" (Isa. 53:11). Let us observe that it is the Father who speaks. He attributes the office of justifying to the Son, and adds the reason,—because he is "righteous." He places the method, or *medium* (as it is called), in the doctrine by which Christ is known. For the word () is more properly to be understood in a passive sense. Hence I infer, first, that Christ was made righteousness when he assumed the form of a servant; secondly, that he justified us by his obedience to the Father; and, accordingly that he does not perform this for us in respect of his divine nature, but according to the nature of the dispensation laid upon him. For though God alone is the fountain of righteousness, and the only way in which we are righteous is by participation with him, yet, as by our unhappy revolt we are alienated from his righteousness, it is necessary to descend to this lower remedy, that Christ may justify us by the power of his death and resurrection.

9. If he objects that this work by its excellence transcends human, and therefore can only be ascribed to the divine nature; I concede the former point, but maintain, that on the latter he is ignorantly deluded. For although Christ could neither purify our souls by his own blood, nor appease the Father by his sacrifice, nor acquit us from the charge of guilt, nor, in short, perform the office of priest, unless he had been very God, because no human ability was equal to such a burden, it is however certain, that he performed all these things in his human nature. If it is asked, in what way we are justified? Paul answers, *by the obedience of Christ*. Did he obey in any other way than by assuming the form of a servant? We infer, therefore, that righteousness was manifested to us in his flesh. In like manner, in another passage (which I greatly wonder that Osiander does not blush repeatedly to quote), he places the fountain of righteousness entirely in the incarnation of Christ, "He has made him to be sin for us who knew no sin, that we might be made the righteousness of God in him" (2 Cor. 5:21). Osiander in turgid sentences lays hold of the expression, *righteousness of God*, and shouts victory! as if he had proved it to be his own phantom of essential righteousness, though the words have a very different meaning—viz. that we are justified through the expiation made by Christ. That the righteousness of God is used for the righteousness which is approved by God, should be known to mere tyros, as in John, the praise of God is contrasted with the praise of men (John 12:43). I know that by the righteousness of God is sometimes meant that of which God is the author, and which he bestows upon us; but that here the only thing meant is, that being supported by the expiation of Christ, we are able to stand at the tribunal of God, sound readers perceive without any observation of mine. The word is not of so much importance, provided Osiander agrees with us in this, that we are justified by Christ in respect he was made an expiatory victim for us. This he could not be in his divine nature. For which reason also, when Christ would seal the righteousness and salvation which he brought to us, he holds forth the sure pledge of it in his flesh. He indeed calls himself "living bread," but, in explanation of the mode, adds, "my flesh is meat indeed, and my blood is drink indeed" (John 6:55). The same doctrine is clearly seen in the sacraments; which, though they direct our faith to the whole, not to a part of Christ, yet, at the same time, declare that the materials of righteousness and salvation reside in his flesh; not that the mere man of himself justifies or quickens, but that God was pleased, by means of a Mediator, to manifest his own hidden and incomprehensible nature. Hence I often repeat, that Christ has been in a manner set before us as a fountain, whence we may draw what would otherwise lie without use in that deep and hidden abyss which streams forth to us in the person of the Mediator. In this way, and in this meaning, I deny not that Christ, as he is God and man, justifies us; that this work is common also to the Father and the Holy Spirit; in fine, that the righteousness of which God makes us partakers is the eternal righteousness of the eternal God, provided effect is given to the clear and valid reasons to which I have adverted.

10. Moreover, lest by his cavils he deceive the unwary, I acknowledge that we are devoid of this incomparable gift until Christ become ours. Therefore, to that union of the head and members, the residence of Christ in our hearts, in fine, the mystical union, we assign the highest rank, Christ when he becomes ours making us partners with him in the gifts with which he was endued. Hence we do not view him as at a distance and without us, but as we have put him on, and been ingrafted into his body, he deigns to make us one with himself, and, therefore, we glory in having a fellowship of righteousness with him. This disposes of Osiander's calumny, that we regard faith as righteousness; as if we were robbing Christ of his rights when we say, that, destitute in ourselves, we draw near to him by faith, to make way for his grace, that he alone may

fill us. But Osiander, spurning this spiritual union, insists on a gross mixture of Christ with believers; and, accordingly, to excite prejudice, gives the name of Zuinglians to all who subscribe not to his fanatical heresy of essential righteousness, because they do not hold that, in the supper, Christ is eaten substantially. For my part, I count it the highest honor to be thus assailed by a haughty man, devoted to his own impostures; though he assails not me only, but writers of known reputation throughout the world, and whom it became him modestly to venerate. This, however, does not concern me, as I plead not my own cause, and plead the more sincerely that I am free from every sinister feeling. In insisting so vehemently on essential righteousness, and an essential inhabitation of Christ within us, his meaning is, first, that God by a gross mixture transfuses himself into us, as he pretends that there is a carnal eating in the supper; And, secondly that by instilling his own righteousness into us, he makes us really righteous with himself since, according to him, this righteousness is as well God himself as the probity, or holiness, or integrity of God. I will not spend much time in disposing of the passages of Scripture which he adduces, and which, though used in reference to the heavenly life, he wrests to our present state. Peter says, that through the knowledge of Christ "are given unto us exceeding great and precious promises, that by them ye might be partakers of the divine nature" (2 Pet. 1:4); as if we now were what the gospel promises we shall be at the final advent of Christ; nay, John reminds us, that "when he shall appear we shall be like him, for we shall see him as he is" (1 John 3:2). I only wished to give my readers a slender specimen of Osiander, it being my intention to decline the discussion of his frivolities, not because there is any difficulty in disposing of them, but because I am unwilling to annoy the reader with superfluous labour.

11. But more poison lurks in the second branch, when he says that we are righteous together with God. I think I have already sufficiently proved, that although the dogma were not so pestiferous, yet because it is frigid and jejune, and falls by its own vanity, it must justly be disrelished by all sound and pious readers. But it is impossible to tolerate the impiety which, under the pretence of a twofold righteousness, undermines our assurance of salvation, and hurrying us into the clouds, tries to prevent us from embracing the gift of expiation in faith, and invoking God with quiet minds. Osiander derides us for teaching, that to be *justified* is a forensic term, because it behaves us to be in reality just: there is nothing also to which he is more opposed than the idea of our being justified by a free imputation. Say, then, if God does not justify us by acquitting and pardoning, what does Paul mean when he says "God was in Christ reconciling the world unto himself, not imputing their trespasses unto them"? "He made him to be sin for us who knew no sin; that we might be made the righteousness of God in him" (2 Cor. 5:19, 21). Here I learn, first, that those who are reconciled to God are regarded as righteous: then the method is stated, God justifies by pardoning; and hence, in another place, justification is opposed to accusation (Rom. 8:33); this antithesis clearly demonstrating that the mode of expression is derived from forensic use. And, indeed, no man, moderately verdant in the Hebrew tongue (provided he is also of sedate brain), is ignorant that this phrase thus took its rise, and thereafter derived its tendency and force. Now, then, when Paul says that David "describeth the blessedness of the man unto whom God imputeth righteousness without works, saying, Blessed are they whose iniquities are forgiven" (Rom. 4:6, 7; Ps. 32:1), let Osiander say whether this is a complete or only a partial definition. He certainly does not adduce the Psalmist as a witness that pardon of sins is a part of righteousness, or concurs with something else in justifying, but he includes the whole of righteousness in gratuitous forgiveness, declaring those to be blessed "whose iniquities are forgiven, and whose sins are covered," and "to whom the Lord will not impute sin." He estimates and judges of his happiness from this that in this way he is righteous not in reality, but by imputation.

Osiander objects that it would be insulting to God, and contrary to his nature, to justify those who still remain wicked. But it ought to be remembered, as I already observed, that the gift of justification is not separated from regeneration, though the two things are distinct. But as it is too well known by experience, that the remains of sin always exist in the righteous, it is necessary that justification should be something very different from reformation to newness of life. This latter God begins in his elect, and carries on during the whole course of life, gradually and sometimes slowly, so that if placed at his judgment-seat they would always deserve sentence of death. He justifies not partially, but freely, so that they can appear in the heavens as if clothed with the purity of Christ. No portion of righteousness could pacify the conscience. It must be decided that we are pleasing to God, as being without exception righteous in his sight. Hence it follows that the doctrine of justification is perverted and completely overthrown whenever doubt is instilled into the mind, confidence in salvation is shaken, and free and intrepid prayer is retarded; yea, whenever rest and tranquillity with spiritual joy are not established. Hence Paul argues against objectors, that "if the inheritance be of the law, it is no more of promise" (Gal. 3:18). that in this way faith would be made vain; for if respect be had to works it fails, the holiest of men in that case finding nothing in which they can confide. This distinction between justification and regeneration (Osiander confounding the two, calls them a twofold righteousness) is admirably expressed by Paul. Speaking of his real righteousness, or the integrity bestowed upon him (which Osiander terms his essential righteousness), he mournfully exclaims, "O wretched man that I am! who shall deliver me from the body of this death?" (Rom. 7:24); but retaking himself to the righteousness which is founded solely on the mercy of God, he breaks forth thus magnificently into the language of triumph: "Who shall lay any thing to the charge of God's elect? It is God that justifieth." "Who shall separate us from the love of Christ? shall tribulation, or distress, or persecution, or famine, or nakedness, or peril, or sword?" (Rom. 8:33, 35). He clearly declares that the only righteousness for him is that which alone suffices for complete salvation in the presence of God, so that that miserable bondage, the consciousness of which made him a little before lament his lot, derogates not from his confidence, and is no obstacle in his way. This diversity is well known, and indeed is familiar to all the saints who groan under the burden of sin, and yet with victorious assurance rise above all fears. Osiander's objection as to its being inconsistent with the nature of God, falls back upon himself; for though he clothes the saints with a twofold righteousness as with a coat of skins, he is, however, forced to admit, that without forgiveness no man is pleasing to God. If this be so, let him at least admit, that with reference to what is called the proportion of imputation, those are regarded as righteous who are not so in reality. But how far shall the sinner extend this gratuitous acceptance, which is substituted in the room of righteousness? Will it amount to the whole pound, or will it be only an ounce? He will remain in doubt, vibrating to this side and to that, because he will be unable to assume to himself as much righteousness as will be necessary to give confidence. It is well that he who would prescribe a law to God is not the judge in this cause. But this saying will ever stand true, "That thou mightest be justified when thou speakest, and be clear when thou judges" (Ps. 51:4). What arrogance to condemn the Supreme Judge when he acquits freely, and try to prevent the response from taking affect: "I will have mercy on whom I will have mercy." And yet the intercession of Moses, which God calmed by this answer, was not for pardon to some individual, but to all alike, by wiping away the guilt to which all were liable. And we, indeed, say, that the lost are justified before God by the burial of their sins; for (as he hates sin) he can only love those whom he justifies. But herein is the wondrous method of justification, that, clothed with the righteousness of Christ, they dread not the judgment of which they are worthy, and while they justly condemn themselves, are yet deemed righteous out of themselves.

12. I must admonish the reader carefully to attend to the mystery which he boasts he is unwilling to conceal from them. For after contending with great prolixity that we do not obtain favor with God through the mere imputation of the righteousness of Christ, because (to use his own words) it were impossible for God to hold those as righteous who are not so, he at length concludes that Christ was given to us for righteousness, in respect not of his human, but of his divine nature; and though this can only be found in the person of the Mediator, it is, however, the righteousness not of man, but of God. He does not now twist his rope of two righteousnesses, but plainly deprives the human nature of Christ of the office of justifying. It is worth while to understand what the nature of his argument is. It is said in the same passage that Christ is made unto us *wisdom* (1 Cor. 1:30); but this is true only of the eternal Word, and, therefore, it is not the man Christ that is made *righteousness*. I answer, that the only begotten Son of God was indeed his eternal wisdom, but that this title is applied to him by Paul in a different way—viz. because "in him are hid all the treasures of wisdom and righteousness" (Col. 2:3). That, therefore, which he had with the Father he manifested to us; and thus Paul's expression refers not to the essence of the Son of God, but to our use, and is fitly applied to the human nature of Christ; for although the light shone in darkness before he was clothed with flesh, yet he was a hidden light until he appeared in human nature as the *Sun of Righteousness*, and hence he calls himself the *light of the world*. It is also foolishly objected by Osiander, that justifying far transcends the power both of men and angels, since it depends not on the dignity of any creature, but on the ordination of God. Were angels to attempt to give satisfaction to God, they could have no success, because they are not appointed for this purpose, it being the peculiar office of Christ, who "has redeemed us from the curse of the law, being made a curse for us" (Gal. 3:13). Those who deny that Christ is our righteous-

ness, in respect of his divine nature, are wickedly charged by Osiander with leaving only a part of Christ, and (what is worse) with making two Gods; because, while admitting that God dwells in us, they still insist that we are not justified by the righteousness of God. For though we call Christ the author of life, inasmuch as he endured death that he might destroy him who had the power of death (Heb. 2:14), we do not thereby rob him of this honor, in his whole character as God manifested in the flesh. We only make a distinction as to the manner in which the righteousness of God comes to us, and is enjoyed by us,—a matter as to which Osiander shamefully erred. We deny not that that which was openly exhibited to us in Christ flowed from the secret grace and power of God; nor do we dispute that the righteousness which Christ confers upon us is the righteousness of God, and proceeds from him. What we constantly maintain is, that our righteousness and life are in the death and resurrection of Christ. I say nothing of that absurd accumulation of passages with which without selection or common understanding, he has loaded his readers, in endeavoring to show, that whenever mention is made of righteousness, this essential righteousness of his should be understood; as when David implores help from the righteousness of God. This David does more than a hundred times, and as often Osiander hesitates not to pervert his meaning. Not a whit more solid is his objection, that the name of righteousness is rightly and properly applied to that by which we are moved to act aright, but that it is God only that worketh in us both to will and to do (Phil. 2:13). For we deny not that God by his Spirit forms us anew to holiness and righteousness of life; but we must first see whether he does this of himself, immediately, or by the hand of his Son, with whom he has deposited all the fulness of the Holy Spirit, that out of his own abundance he may supply the wants of his members. When, although righteousness comes to us from the secret fountain of the Godhead, it does not follow that Christ, who sanctified himself in the flesh on our account, is our righteousness in respect of his divine nature (John 17:19). Not less frivolous is his observation, that the righteousness with which Christ himself was righteous was divine; for had not the will of the Father impelled him, he could not have fulfilled the office assigned him. For although it has been elsewhere said that all the merits of Christ flow from the mere good pleasure of God, this gives no countenance to the phantom by which Osiander fascinates both his own eyes and those of the simple. For who will allow him to infer, that because God is the source and commencement of our righteousness, we are essentially righteous, and the essence of the divine righteousness dwells in us? In redeeming us, says Isaiah, "he (God) put on righteousness as a breastplate, and an helmet of salvation upon his head" (Isaiah 59:17), was this to deprive Christ of the armour which he had given him, and prevent him from being a perfect Redeemer? All that the Prophet meant was, that God borrowed nothing from an external quarter, that in redeeming us he received no external aid. The same thing is briefly expressed by Paul in different terms, when he says that God set him forth "to declare his righteousness for the remission of sins." This is not the least repugnant to his doctrine: in another place, that "by the obedience of one shall many be made righteous" (Rom. 5:19). In short, every one who, by the entanglement of a twofold righteousness, prevents miserable souls from resting entirely on the mere mercy of God, mocks Christ by putting on him a crown of plaited thorns.

13. But since a great part of mankind imagine a righteousness compounded of faith and works let us here show that there is so wide a difference between justification by faith and by works, that the establishment of the one necessarily overthrows the other. The Apostle says, "Yea doubtless, and I count all things but loss for the excellency of the knowledge of Christ Jesus my Lord: for whom I have suffered the loss of all things, and do count them but dung, that I may win Christ, and be found in him, not having mine own righteousness, which is of the law, but that which is through the faith of Christ, the righteousness which is of God by faith" (Phil. 3:8, 9). You here see a comparison of contraries, and an intimation that every one who would obtain the righteousness of Christ must renounce his own. Hence he elsewhere declares the cause of the rejection of the Jews to have been, that "they being ignorant of God's righteousness, and going about to establish their own righteousness, have not submitted themselves unto the righteousness of God" (Rom. 10:3). If we destroy the righteousness of God by establishing our own righteousness, then, in order to obtain his righteousness, our own must be entirely abandoned. This also he shows, when he declares that boasting is not excluded by the Law, but by faith (Rom. 3:27). Hence it follows, that so long as the minutes portion of our own righteousness remains, we have still some ground for boasting. Now if faith utterly excludes boasting, the righteousness of works cannot in any way be associated with the righteousness of faith. This meaning is so clearly expressed in the fourth chapter to the Romans as to leave no room for cavil or evasion. "If Abraham were justified by works he has

whereof to glory;" and then it is added, "but not before God" (Rom. 4:2). The conclusion, therefore, is, that he was not justified by works. He then employs another argument from contraries—viz. when *reward* is paid to works, it is done *of debt*, not *of grace*; but the righteousness of faith is of grace: therefore it is not of the merit of works. Away, then, with the dream of those who invent a righteousness compounded of faith and works (see Calvin. ad Concilium Tridentinum).

14. The Sophists, who delight in sporting with Scripture and in empty cavils, think they have a subtle evasion when they expound *works* to mean, such as unregenerated men do literally, and by the effect of free will, without the grace of Christ, and deny that these have any reference to spiritual works. Thus according to them, man is justified by faith as well as by works, provided these are not his own works, but gifts of Christ and fruits of regeneration; Paul's only object in so expressing himself being to convince the Jews, that in trusting to their own strength they foolishly arrogated righteousness to themselves, whereas it is bestowed upon us by the Spirit of Christ alone, and not by studied efforts of our own nature. But they observe not that in the antithesis between Legal and Gospel righteousness, which Paul elsewhere introduces, all kinds of works, with whatever name adorned, are excluded (Gal. 3:11, 12). For he says that the righteousness of the Law consists in obtaining salvation by doing what the Law requires, but that the righteousness of faith consists in believing that Christ died and rose again (Rom. 10:5–9). Moreover, we shall afterwards see, at the proper place, that the blessings of sanctification and justification, which we derive from Christ, are different. Hence it follows, that not even spiritual works are taken into account when the power of justifying is ascribed to faith. And, indeed, the passage above quoted, in which Paul declares that Abraham had no ground of glorying before God, because he was not justified by works, ought not to be confined to a literal and external form of virtue, or to the effort of free will. The meaning is, that though the life of the Patriarch had been spiritual and almost angelic, yet he could not by the merit of works have procured justification before God.

15. The Schoolmen treat the matter somewhat more grossly by mingling their preparations with it; and yet the others instill into the simple and unwary a no less pernicious dogma, when, under cover of the Spirit and grace, they hide the divine mercy, which alone can give peace to the trembling soul. We, indeed, hold with Paul, that those who fulfill the Law are justified by God, but because we are all far from observing the Law, we infer that the works which should be most effectual to justification are of no avail to us, because we are destitute of them. In regard to vulgar Papists or Schoolmen, they are here doubly wrong, both in calling faith assurance of conscience while waiting to receive from God the reward of merits, and in interpreting divine grace to mean not the imputation of gratuitous righteousness, but the assistance of the Spirit in the study of holiness. They quote from an Apostle: "He that comes to God must believe that he is, and that he is the rewarder of them that diligently seek him" (Heb. 11:6). But they observe not what the method of seeking is. Then in regard to the term *grace*, it is plain from their writings that they labour under a delusion. For Lombard holds that justification is given to us by Christ in two ways. "First," says he (Lombard, Sent. Lib. 3, Dist. 16, c. 11), "the death of Christ justifies us when by means of it the love by which we are made righteous is excited in our hearts; and, secondly, when by means of it sin is extinguished, sin by which the devil held us captive, but by which he cannot now procure our condemnation." You see here that the chief office of divine grace in our justification he considers to be its directing us to good works by the agency of the Holy Spirit. He intended, no doubt, to follow the opinion of Augustine, but he follows it at a distance, and even wanders far from a true imitation of him both obscuring what was clearly stated by Augustine, and making what in him was less pure more corrupt. The Schools have always gone from worse to worse, until at length, in their downward path, they have degenerated into a kind of Pelagianism. Even the sentiment of Augustine, or at least his mode of expressing it, cannot be entirely approved of. For although he is admirable in stripping man of all merit of righteousness, and transferring the whole praise of it to God, yet he classes the grace by which we are regenerated to newness of life under the head of sanctification.

16. Scripture, when it treats of justification by faith, leads us in a very different direction. Turning away our view from our own works, it bids us look only to the mercy of God and the perfection of Christ. The order of justification which it sets before us is this: first, God of his mere gratuitous goodness is pleased to embrace the sinner, in whom he sees nothing that can move him to mercy but wretchedness, because he sees him altogether naked and destitute of good works. He, therefore, seeks the cause of kindness in himself, that thus he may affect the sinner by a sense of his goodness, and induce him, in distrust of his own works, to cast himself entirely upon

his mercy for salvation. This is the meaning of faith by which the sinner comes into the possession of salvation, when, according to the doctrine of the Gospel, he perceives that he is reconciled by God; when, by the intercession of Christ, he obtains the pardon of his sins, and is justified; and, though renewed by the Spirit of God, considers that, instead of leaning on his own works, he must look solely to the righteousness which is treasured up for him in Christ. When these things are weighed separately, they will clearly explain our view, though they may be arranged in a better order than that in which they are here presented. But it is of little consequence, provided they are so connected with each other as to give us a full exposition and solid confirmation of the whole subject.

17. Here it is proper to remember the relation which we previously established between faith and the Gospel; faith being said to justify because it receives and embraces the righteousness offered in the Gospel. By the very fact of its being said to be offered by the Gospel, all consideration of works is excluded. This Paul repeatedly declares, and in two passages, in particular, most clearly demonstrates. In the Epistle to the Romans, comparing the Law and the Gospel, he says, "Moses describeth the righteousness which is of the law, That the man which does those things shall live by them. But the righteousness which is of faith speaketh on this wise,—If thou shalt confess with thy mouth the Lord Jesus, and shalt believe in thine heart that God has raised him from the dead, thou shalt be saved" (Rom. 10:5, 6:9). Do you see how he makes the distinction between the Law and the Gospel to be, that the former gives justification to works, whereas the latter bestows it freely without any help from works? This is a notable passage, and may free us from many difficulties if we understand that the justification which is given us by the Gospel is free from any terms of Law. It is for this reason he more than once places the promise in diametrical opposition to the Law. "If the inheritance be of the law, it is no more of promise" (Gal. 3:18). Expressions of similar import occur in the same chapter. Undoubtedly the Law also has its promises; and, therefore, between them and the Gospel promises there must be some distinction and difference, unless we are to hold that the comparison is inept. And in what can the difference consist unless in this that the promises of the Gospel are gratuitous, and founded on the mere mercy of God, whereas the promises of the Law depend on the condition of works? But let no pester here allege that only the righteousness which men would obtrude upon God of their own strength and free will is repudiated; since Paul declares, without exceptions that the Law gained nothing by its commands, being such as none, not only of mankind in general, but none even of the most perfect, are able to fulfill. Love assuredly is the chief commandment in the Law, and since the Spirit of God trains us to love, it cannot but be a cause of righteousness in us, though that righteousness even in the saints is defective, and therefore of no value as a ground of merit.

18. The second passage is, "That no man is justified by the law in the sight of God, it is evident: for, The just shall live by faith. And the law is not of faith: but, The man that does them shall live in them" (Gal. 3:11, 12; Hab. 2:4). How could the argument hold unless it be true that works are not to be taken into account, but are to be altogether separated? The Law, he says, is different from faith. Why? Because to obtain justification by it, works are required; and hence it follows, that to obtain justification by the Gospel they are not required. From this statement, it appears that those who are justified by faith are justified independent of, nay, in the absence of, the merit of works, because faith receives that righteousness which the Gospel bestows. But the Gospel differs from the Law in this, that it does not confine justification to works, but places it entirely in the mercy of God. In like manner, Paul contends, in the Epistle to the Romans, that Abraham had no ground of glorying, because faith was imputed to him for righteousness (Rom. 4:2); and he adds in confirmation, that the proper place for justification by faith is where there are no works to which reward is due. "To him that worketh is the reward not reckoned of grace, but of debt." What is given to faith is gratuitous, this being the force of the meaning of the words which he there employs. Shortly after he adds, "Therefore it is of faith, that it might be by grace" (Rom. 4:16); and hence infers that the inheritance is gratuitous because it is procured by faith. How so but just because faith, without the aid of works, leans entirely on the mercy of God? And in the same sense, doubtless, he elsewhere teaches, that the righteousness of God without the Law was manifested, being witnessed by the Law and the Prophets (Rom. 3:21); for excluding the Law, he declares that it is not aided by worlds, that we do not obtain it by working, but are destitute when we draw near to receive it.

19. The reader now perceives with what fairness the Sophists of the present day cavil at our doctrine, when we say that a man is justified by faith alone (Rom. 4:2). They dare not deny that *he is justified by faith*, seeing Scripture so often declares it; but as the word *alone* is nowhere expressly used they will not tolerate its being added. Is

it so? What answer, then will they give to the words of Paul, when he contends that righteousness is not of faith unless it be gratuitous? How can it be gratuitous, and yet by works? By what cavils, moreover, will they evade his declaration in another place, that in the Gospel the righteousness of God is manifested? (Rom. 1:17). If righteousness is manifested in the Gospel, it is certainly not a partial or mutilated, but a full and perfect righteousness. The Law, therefore, has no part in its and their objection to the exclusive word *alone* is not only unfounded, but is obviously absurd. Does he not plainly enough attribute everything to faith alone when he disconnects it with works? What I would ask, is meant by the expressions, "The righteousness of God without the law is manifested;" "Being justified freely by his grace;" "Justified by faith without the deeds of the law?" (Rom. 3:21, 24, 28). Here they have an ingenious subterfuge, one which, though not of their own devising but taken from Origin and some ancient writers, is most childish. They pretend that the works excluded are ceremonial, not moral works. Such profit do they make by their constant wrangling, that they possess not even the first elements of logic. Do they think the Apostle was raving when he produced, in proof of his doctrine, these passages? "The man that does them shall live in them" (Gal. 3:12). "Cursed is every one that continueth not in all things that are written in the book of the law to do them" (Gal. 3:10). Unless they are themselves raving, they will not say that life was promised to the observers of ceremonies, and the curse denounced only against the transgressors of them. If these passages are to be understood of the Moral Law, there cannot be a doubt that moral works also are excluded from the power of justifying. To the same effect are the arguments which he employs. "By the deeds of the law there shall no flesh be justified in his sight: for by the law is the knowledge of sin" (Rom. 3:20). "The law worketh wrath" (Rom. 4:15), and therefore not righteousness. "The law cannot pacify the conscience," and therefore cannot confer righteousness. "Faith is imputed for righteousness," and therefore righteousness is not the reward of works, but is given without being due. Because "we are justified by faith," boasting is excluded. "Had there been a law given which could have given life, verily righteousness should have been by the law. But the Scripture has concluded all under sin, that the promise by faith of Jesus Christ might be given to them that believe" (Gal. 3:21, 22). Let them maintain, if they dare, that these things apply to ceremonies, and not to morals, and the very children will laugh at their effrontery. The true conclusion, therefore, is, that the whole Law is spoken of when the power of justifying is denied to it.

20. Should any one wonder why the Apostle, not contented with having named works, employs this addition, the explanation is easy. However highly works may be estimated, they have their whole value more from the approbation of God than from their own dignity. For who will presume to plume himself before God on the righteousness of works, unless in so far as He approves of them? Who will presume to demand of Him a reward except in so far as He has promised it? It is owing entirely to the goodness of God that works are deemed worthy of the honor and reward of righteousness; and, therefore, their whole value consists in this, that by means of them we endeavor to manifest obedience to God. Wherefore, in another passage, the Apostle, to prove that Abraham could not be justified by works, declares, "that the covenant, that was confirmed before of God in Christ, the law, which was four hundred and thirty years after, cannot disannul, that it should make the promise of none effect" (Gal. 3:17). The unskillful would ridicule the argument that there could be righteous works before the promulgation of the Law, but the Apostle, knowing that works could derive this value solely from the testimony and honor conferred on them by God, takes it for granted that, previous to the Law, they had no power of justifying. We see why he expressly terms them works of Law when he would deny the power of justifying to theme—viz. because it was only with regard to such works that a question could be raised; although he sometimes, without addition, excepts all kinds of works whatever, as when on the testimony of David he speaks of the man to whom the Lord imputeth righteousness without works (Rom. 4:5, 6). No cavils, therefore, can enable them to prove that the exclusion of works is not general. In vain do they lay hold of the frivolous subtilty, that the *faith alone*, by which we are justified, "*worketh by love*," and that love, therefore, is the foundation of justification. We, indeed, acknowledge with Paul, that the only faith which justifies is that which works by love (Gal. 3:6); but love does not give it its justifying power. Nay, its only means of justifying consists in its bringing us into communication with the righteousness of Christ. Otherwise the whole argument, on which the Apostle insists with so much earnestness, would fall. "To him that worketh is the reward not reckoned of grace, but of debt. But to him that worketh not, but believeth on him that justifieth the ungodly, his faith is counted for righteousness." Could he express more clearly than in this word, that there is justification

in faith only where there are no works to which reward is due, and that faith is imputed for righteousness only when righteousness is conferred freely without merit?

21. Let us now consider the truth of what was said in the definition—viz. that justification by faith is reconciliation with God, and that this consists solely in the remission of sins. We must always return to the axioms that the wrath of God lies upon all men so long as they continue sinners. This is elegantly expressed by Isaiah in these words: "Behold, the Lord's hand is not shortened, that it cannot save; neither his ear heavy, that it cannot hear: but your iniquities have separated between you and your God, and your sins have hid his face from you, that he will not hear" (Isaiah 59:1, 2). We are here told that sin is a separation between God and man; that His countenance is turned away from the sinner; and that it cannot be otherwise, since, to have any intercourse with sin is repugnant to his righteousness. Hence the Apostle shows that man is at enmity with God until he is restored to favour by Christ (Rom. 5:8–10). When the Lord, therefore, admits him to union, he is said to justify him, because he can neither receive him into favor, nor unite him to himself, without changing his condition from that of a sinner into that of a righteous man. We add, that this is done by remission of sins. For if those whom the Lord has reconciled to himself are estimated by works, they will still prove to be in reality sinners, while they ought to be pure and free from sin. It is evident therefore, that the only way in which those whom God embraces are made righteous, is by having their pollutions wiped away by the remission of sins, so that this justification may be termed in one word the remission of sins.

22. Both of these become perfectly clear from the words of Paul: "God was in Christ reconciling the world unto himself, not imputing their trespasses unto them; and has committed unto us the word of reconciliation." He then subjoins the sum of his embassy: "He has made him to be sin for us who knew no sin; that we might be made the righteousness of God in him" (2 Cor. 5:19–21). He here uses righteousness and reconciliation indiscriminately, to make us understand that the one includes the other. The mode of obtaining this righteousness he explains to be, that our sins are not imputed to us. Wherefore, you cannot henceforth doubt how God justifies us when you hear that he reconciles us to himself by not imputing our faults. In the same manner, in the Epistle to the Romans, he proves, by the testimony of David, that righteousness is imputed without works, because he declares the man to be blessed "whose transgression is forgiven, whose sin is covered," and "unto whom the Lord imputeth not iniquity" (Rom. 4:6; Ps. 32:1, 2). There he undoubtedly uses blessedness for righteousness; and as he declares that it consists in forgiveness of sins, there is no reason why we should define it otherwise. Accordingly, Zacharias, the father of John the Baptist, sings that the knowledge of salvation consists in the forgiveness of sins (Luke 1:77). The same course was followed by Paul when, in addressing the people of Antioch, he gave them a summary of salvation. Luke states that he concluded in this way: "Through this man is preached unto you the forgiveness of sins, and by him all that believe are justified from all things from which ye could not be justified by the law of Moses" (Acts 13:38, 39). Thus the Apostle connects forgiveness of sins with justification in such a way as to show that they are altogether the same; and hence he properly argues that justification, which we owe to the indulgence of God, is gratuitous. Nor should it seem an unusual mode of expression to say that believers are justified before God not by works, but by gratuitous acceptance, seeing it is frequently used in Scripture, and sometimes also by ancient writers. Thus Augustine says: "The righteousness of the saints in this world consists more in the forgiveness of sins than the perfection of virtue" (August. de Civitate Dei, lib. 19, cap. 27). To this corresponds the well-known sentiment of Bernard: "Not to sin is the righteousness of God, but the righteousness of man is the indulgence of God" (Bernard, Serm. 22, 23 in Cant). He previously asserts that Christ is our righteousness in absolution, and, therefore, that those only are just who have obtained pardon through mercy.

23. Hence also it is proved, that it is entirely by the intervention of Christ's righteousness that we obtain justification before God. This is equivalent to saying that man is not just in himself, but that the righteousness of Christ is communicated to him by imputation, while he is strictly deserving of punishment. Thus vanishes the absurd dogma, that man is justified by faith, inasmuch as it brings him under the influence of the Spirit of God by whom he is rendered righteous. This is so repugnant to the above doctrine that it never can be reconciled with it. There can be no doubt that he who is taught to seek righteousness out of himself does not previously possess it in himself. This is most clearly declared by the Apostle, when he says, that he who knew no sin was made an expiatory victim for sin, that we might be made the righteousness of God in him (2 Cor. 5:21). You see that our righteousness is not in ourselves, but in Christ; that the only way in which we become possessed of it is by being

made partakers with Christ, since with him we possess all riches. There is nothing repugnant to this in what he elsewhere says: "God sending his own Son in the likeness of sinful flesh, and for sin condemned sin in the flesh: that the righteousness of the law might be fulfilled in us" (Rom. 8:3, 4). Here the only fulfillment to which he refers is that which we obtain by imputation. Our Lord Jesus Christ communicates his righteousness to us, and so by some wondrous ways in so far as pertains to the justice of Gods transfuses its power into us. That this was the Apostle's view is abundantly clear from another sentiment which he had expressed a little before: "As by one man's disobedience many were made sinners, so by the obedience of one shall many be made righteous" (Rom. 5:19). To declare that we are deemed righteous, solely because the obedience of Christ is imputed to us as if it where our own, is just to place our righteousness in the obedience of Christ. Wherefore, Ambrose appears to me to have most elegantly adverted to the blessing of Jacob as an illustration of this righteousness, when he says that as he who did not merit the birthright in himself personated his brother, put on his garments which gave forth a most pleasant odour, and thus introduced himself to his father that he might receive a blessing to his own advantage, though under the person of another, so we conceal ourselves under the precious purity of Christ, our first-born brother, that we may obtain an attestation of righteousness from the presence of God. The words of Ambrose are,—"Isaac's smelling the odour of his garments, perhaps means that we are justified not by works, but by faith, since carnal infirmity is an impediment to works, but errors of conduct are covered by the brightness of faith, which merits the pardon of faults" (Ambrose de Jacobo et Vita Beats, Lib. 2, c. 2). And so indeed it is; for in order to appear in the presence of God for salvation, we must send forth that fragrant odour, having our vices covered and buried by his perfection.

CHAPTER 12

NECESSITY OF CONTEMPLATING THE JUDGMENT-SEAT OF GOD, IN ORDER TO BE SERIOUSLY CONVINCED OF THE DOCTRINE OF GRATUITOUS JUSTIFICATION.

The divisions of this chapter are,—I. A consideration of the righteousness of God overturns the righteousness of works, as is plain from passages of Scripture, and the confession and example of the saints, sec. 1–3. II. The same effect produced by a serious examination of the conscience, and a constant citation to the divine tribunal, sec. 4 and 5. III. Hence arises, in the hearts of the godly, not hypocrisy, or a vain opinion of merit, but true humility. This illustrated by the authority of Scripture and the example of the Publican, sec. 6, 7. IV. Conclusion—arrogance and security must be discarded, every man throwing an impediment in the way of the divine goodness in proportion as he trusts to himself.

Sections:

1. Source of error on the subject of Justification. Sophists speak as if the question were to be discussed before some human tribunal. It relates to the majesty and justice of God. Hence nothing accepted without absolute perfection. Passages confirming this doctrine. If we descend to the righteousness of the Law, the curse immediately appears.

2. Source of hypocritical confidence. Illustrated by a simile. Exhortation. Testimony of Job, David, and Paul.

3. Confession of Augustine and Bernard.

4. Another engine overthrowing the righteousness of works—viz. A serious examination of the conscience, and a comparison between the perfection of God and the imperfection of man.

5. How it is that we so indulge this imaginary opinion of our own works. The proper remedy to be found in a consideration of the majesty of God and our own misery. A description of this misery.

6. Christian humility consists in laying aside the imaginary idea of our own righteousness, and trusting entirely to the mercy of God, apprehended by faith in Christ. This humility described. Proved by passages of Scripture.

7. The parable of the Publican explained.

8. Arrogance, security, and self-confidence, must be renounced. General rule, or summary of the above doctrine.

1. Although the perfect truth of the above doctrine is proved by clear passages of Scripture, yet we cannot clearly see how necessary it is, before we bring distinctly into view the foundations on which the whole discussion ought to rest. First, then, let us remember that the righteousness which we are considering is not that of a human, but of a heavenly tribunal; and so beware of employing our own little standard to measure the perfection which is to satisfy the justice of God. It is strange

with what rashness and presumption this is commonly defined. Nay, we see that none talk more confidently, or, so to speak, more blusteringly, of the righteousness of works than those whose diseases are most palpable, and blemishes most apparent. This they do because they reflect not on the righteousness of Christ, which, if they had the slightest perception of it, they would never treat with so much insult. It is certainly undervalued, if not recognized to be so perfect that nothing can be accepted that is not in every respect entire and absolute, and tainted by no impurity; such indeed as never has been, and never will be, found in man. It is easy for any man, within the precincts of the schools, to talk of the sufficiency of works for justification; but when we come into the presence of God there must be a truce to such talk. The matter is there discussed in earnest, and is no longer a theatrical logomachy. Hither must we turn our minds if we would inquire to any purpose concerning true righteousness; the question must be: How shall we answer the heavenly Judge when he calls us to account? Let us contemplate that Judge, not as our own unaided intellect conceives of him, but as he is portrayed to us in Scripture (see especially the Book of Job), with a brightness which obscures the stars, a strength which melts the mountains, an anger which shakes the earth, a wisdom which takes the wise in their own craftiness, a purity before which all things become impure, a righteousness to which not even angels are equal (so far is it from making the guilty innocent), a vengeance which once kindled burns to the lowest hell (Exod. 34:7; Nahum 1:3; Deut. 32:22). Let Him, I say, sit in judgment on the actions of men, and who will feel secure in sisting himself before his throne? "Who among us," says the prophets "shall dwell with the devouring fire? who among us shall dwell with everlasting burnings? He that walketh righteously, and speaketh uprightly," &c. (Isaiah 33:14, 15). Let whoso will come forth. Nay, the answer shows that no man can. For, on the other hand, we hear the dreadful voice: "If thou, Lord, shouldst mark our iniquities, O Lord, who shall stand?" (Ps. 130:3). All must immediately perish, as Job declares, "Shall mortal man be more just than God? shall a man be more pure than his Maker? Behold, he put no trust in his servants; and his angels he charged with folly: How much less in them that dwell in houses of clay, whose foundation is in the dust, which are crushed before the moth? They are destroyed from morning to evening" (Job 4:17–20). Again, "Behold, he putteth no trust in his saints; yea, the heavens are not clean in his sight. How much more abominable and filthy is man, which drinketh iniquity like water?" (Job 15:15, 16). I confess, indeed, that in the Book of Job reference is made to a righteousness of a more exalted description than the observance of the Law. It is of importance to attend to this distinction; for even could a man satisfy the Law, he could not stand the scrutiny of that righteousness which transcends all our thoughts. Hence, although Job was not conscious of offending, he is still dumb with astonishment, because he sees that God could not be appeased even by the sanctity of angels, were their works weighed in that supreme balance. But to advert no farther to this righteousness, which is incomprehensible, I only say, that if our life is brought to the standard of the written law, we are lethargic indeed if we are not filled with dread at the many maledictions which God has employed for the purpose of arousing us, and among others, the following general one: "Cursed be he that confirmeth not all the words of this law to do them" (Deut. 27:26). In short, the whole discussion of this subject will be insipid and frivolous, unless we sist ourselves before the heavenly Judge, and anxious for our acquittal, voluntarily humble ourselves, confessing our nothingness.

2. Thus then must we raise our eyes that we may learn to tremble instead of vainly exulting. It is easy, indeed, when the comparison is made among men, for every one to plume himself on some quality which others ought not to despise; but when we rise to God, that confidence instantly falls and dies away. The case of the soul with regard to God is very analogous to that of the body in regard to the visible firmament. The bodily eye, while employed in surveying adjacent objects, is pleased with its own perspicacity; but when directed to the sun, being dazzled and overwhelmed by the refulgence, it becomes no less convinced of its weakness than it formerly was of its power in viewing inferior objects. Therefore, lest we deceive ourselves by vain confidence, let us recollect that even though we deem ourselves equal or superior to other men, this is nothing to God, by whose judgment the decision must be given. But if our presumption cannot be tamed by these considerations, he will answer us as he did the Pharisees, "Ye are they which justify yourselves before men; but God knoweth your hearts: for that which is highly esteemed among men is abomination in the sight of God" (Luke 16:15). Go now and make a proud boast of your righteousness among men, while God in heaven abhors it. But what are the feelings of the servants of God, of those who are truly taught by his Spirit? "Enter not into judgment with thy servant; for in thy sight shall no man living be justified" (Ps. 143:2). Another, though in a sense

somewhat different, says, "How should man be just with God? If he will contend with him he cannot answer him one of a thousand" (Job 9:2, 3). Here we are plainly told what the righteousness of God is, namely, a righteousness which no human works can satisfy which charges us with a thousand sins, while not one sin can be excused. Of this righteousness Paul, that chosen vessel of God, had formed a just idea, when he declared, "I know nothing by myself, yet am I not hereby justified" (1 Cor. 4:4).

3. Such examples exist not in the sacred volume only; all pious writers show that their sentiment was the same. Thus Augustine says, "Of all pious men groaning under this burden of corruptible flesh, and the infirmities of this life, the only hope is, that we have one Mediator Jesus Christ the righteous, and that he intercedes for our sins" (August. ad Bonif. lib. 3, c. 5). What do we hear? If this is their only hope, where is their confidence in works? When he says *only*, he leaves no other. Bernard says, "And, indeed, where have the infirm firm security and safe rest, but in the wounds of the Savior? Hold it then the more securely, the more powerful he is to save. The world frowns, the body presses, the devil lays snares: I fall not, because I am founded on a firm rock. I have sinned a grievous sin: conscience is troubled, but it shall not be overwhelmed, for I will remember the wounds of the Lord." He afterwards concludes, "My merit, therefore, is the compassion of the Lord; plainly I am not devoid of merit so long as he is not devoid of commiseration. But if the mercies of the Lord are many, equally many are my merits. Shall I sing of my own righteousness? O Lord, I will make mention of thy righteousness alone. That righteousness is mine also, being made mine by God" (Bernard, Serm. 61, in Cantic). Again, in another passage, "Man's whole merit is to place his whole hope in him who makes the whole man safe" (in Psal. Qui Habitat. Serm. 15). In like manner, reserving peace to himself, he leaves the glory to God: "Let thy glory remain unimpaired: it is well with me if I have peace; I altogether abjure boasting, lest if I should usurp what is not mine, I lose also what is offered" (Serm. 13, in Cantic). He says still more plainly in another place: "Why is the Church solicitous about merits? God purposely supplies her with a firmer and more secure ground of boasting. There is no reason for asking by what merits may we hope for blessings, especially when you hear in the prophet, 'Thus saith the Lord God, I do not this for your sakes, O house of Israel, but for mine holy name's sake,' (Ezek. 36:22, 32). It is sufficient for merit to know that merits suffice not; but as it is sufficient for merit not to presume on merit, so to be without merits is sufficient for condemnation" (Bernard, Serm. 68). The free use of the term merits for good works must be pardoned to custom. Bernard's purpose was to alarm hypocrites, who turned the grace of God into licentiousness, as he shortly after explains: "Happy the church which neither wants merit without presumption, nor presumption without merit. It has ground to presume, but not merit. It has merit, merit to deserve, not presume. Is not the absence of presumption itself a merit? He, therefore, to whom the many mercies of the Lord furnish ample grounds of boasting, presumes the more securely that he presumes not" (Bernard, Serm. 68).

4. Thus, indeed, it is. Aroused consciences, when they have to do with God, feel this to be the only asylum in which they can breathe safely. For if the stars which shine most brightly by night lose their brightness on the appearance of the sun, what think we will be the case with the highest purity of man when contrasted with the purity of God? For the scrutiny will be most strict, penetrating to the most hidden thoughts of the heart. As Paul says, it "will bring to light the hidden things of darkness and will make manifest the counsels of the heart" (1 Cor. 4:5); will compel the reluctant and dissembling conscience to bring forward everything, even things which have now escaped our memory. The devil, aware of all the iniquities which he has induced us to perpetrate, will appear as accuser; the external show of good works, the only thing now considered, will then be of no avail; the only thing demanded will be the true intent of the will. Hence hypocrisy, not only that by which a man, though consciously guilty before God, affects to make an ostentatious display before man, but that by which each imposes upon himself before God (so prone are we to soothe and flatter ourselves), will fall confounded, how much soever it may now swell with pride and presumption. Those who do not turn their thoughts to this scene may be able for the moment calmly and complacently to rear up a righteousness for themselves; but this the judgment of God will immediately overthrow, just as great wealth amassed in a dream vanishes the moment we awake. Those who, as in the presence of God, inquire seriously into the true standard of righteousness, will certainly find that all the works of men, if estimated by their own worth, are nothing but vileness and pollution, that what is commonly deemed justice is with God mere iniquity; what is deemed integrity is pollution; what deemed glory is ignominy.

5. Let us not decline to descend from this contem-

plation of the divine perfection, to look into ourselves without flattery or blind self-love. It is not strange that we are so deluded in this matter, seeing none of us can avoid that pestilential self-indulgence, which, as Scripture proclaims, is naturally inherent in all: "Every way of a man is right in his own eyes," says Solomon (Prov. 21:2). And again, "All the ways of a man are clean in his own eyes" (Prov. 16:2). What then? does this hallucination excuse him? No, indeed, as Solomon immediately adds, "The Lord weigheth the spirits;" that is, while man flatters himself by wearing an external mask of righteousness, the Lord weighs the hidden impurity of the heart in his balance. Seeing, therefore, that nothing is gained by such flattery, let us not voluntarily delude ourselves to our own destruction. To examine ourselves properly, our conscience must be called to the judgment-seat of God. His light is necessary to disclose the secret recesses of wickedness which otherwise lie too deeply hid. Then only shall we clearly perceive what the value of our works is; that man, so far from being just before God, is but rottenness and a worm, abominable and vain, drinking in "iniquity like water." For "who can bring a clean thing out of an unclean? not one" (Job 14:5). Then we shall experience the truth of what Job said of himself: "If I justify myself, mine own mouth shall condemn me: if I say I am perfect, it shall prove me perverse" (Job 9:20). Nor does the complaint which the prophet made concerning Israel apply to one age only. It is true of every age, that "all we like sheep have gone astray; we have turned every one to his own way" (Isaiah 53:6). Indeed, he there comprehends all to whom the gift of redemption was to come. And the strictness of the examination ought to be continued until it have completely alarmed us, and in that way prepared us for receiving the grace of Christ. For he is deceived who thinks himself capable of enjoying it, until he have laid aside all loftiness of mind. There is a well-known declaration, "God resisteth the proud, but giveth grace to the humble" (1 Pet. 5:5).

6. But what means is there of humbling us if we do not make way for the mercy of God by our utter indigence and destitution? For I call it not humility, so long as we think there is any good remaining in us. Those who have joined together the two things, to think humbly of ourselves before God and yet hold our own righteousness in some estimation, have hitherto taught a pernicious hypocrisy. For if we confess to God contrary to what we feel, we wickedly lie to him; but we cannot feel as we ought without seeing that every thing like a ground of boasting is completely crushed. Therefore, when you hear from the prophets "thou wilt save the afflicted people; but wilt bring down high looks" (Ps. 18:27), consider, first, that there is no access to salvation unless all pride is laid aside and true humility embraced; secondly, that that humility is not a kind of moderation by which you yield to God some article of your right (thus men are called humble in regard to each other when they neither conduct themselves haughtily nor insult over other, though they may still entertain some consciousness of their own excellence), but that it is the unfeigned submission of a mind overwhelmed by a serious conviction of its want and misery. Such is the description every where given by the word of God. When in Zephaniah the Lord speaks thus, "I will take away out of the midst of thee them that rejoice in thy pride, and thou shalt no more be haughty because of my holy mountain. I will also leave in the midst of thee an afflicted and poor people, and they shall trust in the name of the Lord" (Zeph. 3:11, 12), does he not plainly show who are the humble—viz. those who lie afflicted by a knowledge of their poverty? On the contrary, he describes the proud as rejoicing (*exultantes*), such being the mode in which men usually express their delight in prosperity. To the humble, whom he designs to save, he leaves nothing but hope in the Lord. Thus, also, in Isaiah, "To this man will I look, even to him that is poor and of a contrite spirit, and trembleth at my word" (Isaiah 66:2). again, "Thus saith the high and lofty One that inhabiteth eternity, whose name is Holy; I dwell in the high and holy place, with him also that is of a contrite and humble spirit, to revive the spirit of the humble, and to revive the heart of the contrite ones" (Isaiah 57:15). By the term contrition which you so often hear, understand a wounded heart, which, humbling the individual to the earth, allows him not to rise. With such contrition must your heart be wounded, if you would, according to the declaration of God, be exalted with the humble. If this is not your case, you shall be humbled by the mighty hand of God to your shame and disgrace.

7. Our divine Master, not confining himself to words, has by a parable set before us, as in a picture, a representation of true humility. He brings forward a publican, who standing afar off, and not daring to lift up his eyes to heaven, smites upon his breast, laments aloud, and exclaims, " God be merciful to me a sinner" (Luke 18:13). Let us not suppose that he gives the signs of a fictitious modesty when he dares not come near or lift up his eyes to heaven, but, smiting upon his breast, confesses himself a sinner; let us know that these are the

evidences of his internal feeling. With him our Lord contrasts the Pharisee, who thanks God "I am not as other men are, extortioners, unjust, adulterers, or even as this publican. I fast twice in the week, I give tithes of all that I possess." In this public confession he admits that the righteousness which he possesses is the gift of God; but because of his confidence that he is righteous, he departs from the presence of God unaccepted and abominated. The publican acknowledging his iniquity is justified. Hence we may see how highly our humility is valued by the Lord: our breast cannot receive his mercy until deprived completely of all opinion of its own worth. When such an opinion is entertained, the door of mercy is shut. That there might be no doubt on this matter, the mission on which Christ was sent into the world by his Father was "to preach good tidings to the meek," "to bind up the broken-hearted, to proclaim liberty to the captives, and the opening of the prison to them that are bound; to proclaim the acceptable year of the Lord, and the day of vengeance of our God; to comfort all that mourn; to appoint unto them that mourn in Zion to give unto them beauty for ashes, the oil of joy for mourning, the garment of praise for the spirit of heaviness" (Isa. 61:1–3). In fulfillment of that mission, the only persons whom he invites to share in his beneficence are the "weary and heavy laden." In another passage he says, " I am not come to call the righteous, but sinners to repentance" (Mt. 11:28; 9:13).

8. Therefore if we would make way for the call of Christ, we must put far from us all arrogance and confidence. The former is produced by a foolish persuasion of self-righteousness, when a man thinks that he has something in himself which deservedly recommends him to God; the latter may exist without any confidence in works. For many sinners, intoxicated with the pleasures of vice, think not of the judgment of God. Lying stupefied, as it were, by a kind of lethargy, they aspire not to the offered mercy. It is not less necessary to shake off torpor of this description than every kind of confidence in ourselves, in order that we may haste to Christ unencumbered, and while hungry and empty be filled with his blessings. Never shall we have sufficient confidence in him unless utterly distrustful of ourselves; never shall we take courage in him until we first despond of ourselves; never shall we have full consolation in him until we cease to have any in ourselves. When we have entirely discarded all self-confidence, and trust solely in the certainty of his goodness, we are fit to apprehend and obtain the grace of God. "When" (as Augustine says), "forgetting our own merits, we embrace the gifts of Christ, because if he should seek for merits in us we should not obtain his gifts" (August. de Verb. Apost. 8). With this Bernard admirably accords, comparing the proud who presume in the least on their merits, to unfaithful servants, who wickedly take the merit of a favor merely passing through them, just as if a wall were to boast of producing the ray which it receives through the window (Bernard, Serm. 13, in Cant). Not to dwell longer here, let us lay down this short but sure and general rule, That he is prepared to reap the fruits of the divine mercy who has thoroughly emptied himself, I say not of righteousness (he has none), but of a vain and blustering show of righteousness; for to whatever extent any man rests in himself, to the same extent he impedes the beneficence of God.

CHAPTER 13

TWO THINGS TO BE OBSERVED IN GRATUITOUS JUSTIFICATION.

The divisions of this chapter are,—I. **The glory of God, and peace of conscience, both secured by gratuitous justification. An insult to the glory of God to glory in ourselves and seek justification out of Christ, whose righteousness, apprehended by faith, is imputed to all the elect for reconciliation and eternal salvation, sec. 1, 2. II. Peace of conscience cannot be obtained in any other way than by gratuitous justification. This fully proved, sec. 3–5.**

Sections:

1. The glory of God remains untarnished, when he alone is acknowledged to be just. This proved from Scripture.

2. Those who glory in themselves glory against God. Objection. Answer, confirmed by the authority of Paul and Peter.

3. Peace of conscience obtained by free justification only. Testimony of Solomon, of conscience itself, and the Apostle Paul, who contends that faith is made vain if righteousness come by the law.

4. The promise confirmed by faith in the mercy of Christ. This is confirmed by Augustine and Bernard, is in accordance with what has been above stated, and is illustrated by clear predictions of the prophets.

5. Farther demonstration by an Apostle. Refutation of a sophism.

1. Here two ends must be kept specially in view, namely, that the glory of God be maintained unimpaired, and that our consciences, in the view of his tribunal, be secured in peaceful rest and calm tranquillity. When the question relates to righteousness, we see how often and how anxiously Scripture exhorts us to give the whole praise of it to God. Accordingly, the Apostle testifies that the purpose of the Lord in conferring righteousness upon us in Christ, was to demonstrate his own righteousness. The nature of this demonstration he immediately subjoins—viz. "that he might be just, and the justifier of him which believeth in Jesus" (Rom. 3:25). Observe, that the righteousness of God is not sufficiently displayed, unless He alone is held to be righteous, and freely communicates righteousness to the undeserving. For this reason it is his will, that "every mouth may be stopped, and all the world may become guilty before God" (Rom. 3:19). For so long as a man has any thing, however small, to say in his own defense, so long he deducts somewhat from the glory of God. Thus we are taught in Ezekiel how much we glorify his name by acknowledging our iniquity: "Then shall ye remember your ways and all your doings, wherein ye have been defiled; and ye shall loathe yourselves in your own sight, for all your evils that ye have committed. And ye shall know that I am the Lord, when I have wrought with you for my name's sake, not according to your wicked ways, nor according to your corrupt doings" (Ezek. 20:43, 44). If part of the true knowledge of God consists in being oppressed by a consciousness of our own iniquity, and in recognizing him as doing good to those who are unworthy of it, why do we attempt, to our great injury, to steal from the Lord even one particle of the praise of unmerited kindness? In like manner, when Jeremiah exclaims, "Let not the wise man glory in his wisdom, neither let the mighty man glory in his might, let not the rich man glory in his riches: but let him that glorieth glory" in the Lord (Jer. 9:23, 24), does he not intimate, that the glory of the Lord is infringed when man glories in himself? To this purpose, indeed, Paul accommodates the words when he says, that all the parts of our salvation are treasured up with Christ, that we may glory only in the Lord (1 Cor. 1:29). For he intimates, that whosoever imagines he has any thing of his own, rebels against God, and obscures his glory.

2. Thus, indeed, it is: we never truly glory in him until we have utterly discarded our own glory. It must, therefore, be regarded as an universal proposition, that whoso glories in himself glories against God. Paul indeed considers, that the whole world is not made subject to God until every ground of glorying has been withdrawn from men (Rom. 3:19). Accordingly, Isaiah, when he declares that "in the Lord shall all the seed of Israel be justified" adds, "and shall glory" (Isa. 45:25), as if he had said that the elect are justified by the Lord, in order that they may glory in him, and in none else. The way in which we are to glory in the Lord he had explained in the preceding verse, "Unto me every knee shall bow, every tongue shall swear;" "Surely, shall one say, in the Lord have I righteousness and strength, even to him shall men come." Observe, that the thing required is not simple confession, but confession confirmed by an oath, that it might not be imagined that any kind of fictitious humility might suffice. And let no man here allege that he does not glory, when without arrogance he recognizes his own righteousness; such a recognition cannot take place without generating confidence, nor such confidence without begetting boasting. Let us remember, therefore, that in the whole discussion concerning justification the great thing to be attended to is, that God's glory be maintained entire and unimpaired; since as the Apostle declares, it was in demonstration of his own righteousness that he shed his favor upon us; it was "that he might be just, and the justifier of him which believeth in Jesus" (Rom. 3:26). Hence, in another passage, having said that the Lord conferred salvation upon us, in order that he might show forth the glory of his name (Eph. 1:6), he afterwards, as if repeating the same thing, adds, "By grace are ye saved through faith; and that not of yourselves: it is the gift of God: not of works, lest any man should boast" (Eph. 2:8). And Peter, when he reminds us that we are called to the hope of salvation, "that ye should show forth the praises of him who has called you out of darkness into his marvelous light" (1 Pet. 2:9), doubtless intends thus to proclaim in the ears of believers only the praises of God, that they may bury in profound silence all arrogance of the flesh. The sum is, that man cannot claim a single particle of righteousness to himself, without at the same time detracting from the glory of the divine righteousness.

3. If we now inquire in what way the conscience can be quieted as in the view of God, we shall find that the only way is by having righteousness bestowed upon us freely by the gift of God. Let us always remember the words of Solomon, "Who can say I have made my heart clean, I am free from my sin?" (Prov. 20:9). Undoubtedly there is not one man who is not covered with infinite pollutions. Let the most perfect man descend into his own conscience, and bring his actions to account, and what will the result be? Will he feel calm and quiescent,

as if all matters were well arranged between himself and God; or will he not rather be stung with dire torment, when he sees that the ground of condemnation is within him if he be estimated by his works? Conscience, when it beholds God, must either have sure peace with his justice, or be beset by the terrors of hell. We gain nothing, therefore, by discoursing of righteousness, unless we hold it to be a righteousness stable enough to support our souls before the tribunal of God. When the soul is able to appear intrepidly in the presence of God, and receive his sentence without dismay, then only let us know that we have found a righteousness that is not fictitious. It is not, therefore, without cause, that the Apostle insists on this matter. I prefer giving it in his words rather than my own: "If they which are of the law be heirs, faith is made void, and the promise made of no effect" (Rom. 4:14). He first infers that faith is made void if the promise of righteousness has respect to the merit of our works, or depends on the observance of the law. Never could any one rest securely in it, for never could he feel fully assured that he had fully satisfied the law; and it is certain that no man ever fully satisfied it by works. Not to go far for proof of this, every one who will use his eyes aright may be his own witness. Hence it appears how deep and dark the abyss is into which hypocrisy plunges the minds of men, when they indulge so securely as, without hesitations to oppose their flattery to the judgment of God, as if they were relieving him from his office as judge. Very different is the anxiety which fills the breasts of believers, who sincerely examine themselves. Every mind, therefore, would first begin to hesitate, and at length to despair, while each determined for itself with how great a load of debt it was still oppressed, and how far it was from coming up to the enjoined condition. Thus, then, faith would be oppressed and extinguished. To have faith is not to fluctuate, to vary, to be carried up and down, to hesitate, remain in suspense, vacillate, in fine, to despair; it is to possess sure certainty and complete security of mind, to have whereon to rest and fix your foot.

4. Paul, moreover, adds, that the promise itself would be rendered null and void. For if its fulfillment depends on our merits when pray, will we be able to come the length of meriting the favor of God? Nay, the second clause is a consequence of the former, since the promise will not be fulfilled unless to those who put faith in it. Faith therefore failing, no power will remain in the promise. "Therefore it is of faith, that it might be by grace, to the end the promise might be sure to all the seed" (Rom. 4:16). It was abundantly confirmed when made to rest on the mercy of God alone, for mercy and truth are united by an indissoluble tie; that is, whatever God has mercifully promised he faithfully performs. Thus David, before he asks salvation according to the word of God, first places the source of it in his mercy. "Let, I pray thee, thy merciful kindness be for my comfort, according to thy word unto thy servant" (Ps. 119:76). And justly, for nothing but mere mercy induces God to promise. Here, then, we must place, and, as it were, firmly fix our whole hope, paying no respect to our works, and asking no assistance from them. And lest you should suppose that there is any thing novel in what I say, Augustine also enjoins us so to act. "Christ," says he, "will reign forever among his servants. This God has promised, God has spoken; if this is not enough, God has sworn. Therefore, as the promise stands firm, not in respect of our merits, but in respect of his mercy, no one ought to tremble in announcing that of which he cannot doubt" (August. in Ps. 88, Tract. 50). Thus Bernard also, "Who can be saved? ask the disciples of Christ. He replies, With men it is impossible, but not with God. This is our whole confidence, this our only consolation; this the whole ground of our hope: but being assured of the possibility, what are we to say as to his willingness? Who knows whether he is deserving of love or hatred? (Eccles. 9:1). 'Who has known the mind of the Lord that he may instruct him?' (1 Cor. 2:16). Here it is plain, faith must come to our aid: here we must have the assistance of truth, in order that the secret purpose of the Father respecting us may be revealed by the Spirit, and the Spirit testifying may persuade our hearts that we are the sons of God. But let him persuade by calling and justifying freely by faith: in these there is a kind of transition from eternal predestination to future glory" (Bert. in Dedica. Templi, Serm. 5). Let us thus briefly conclude: Scripture indicates that the promises of God are not surer unless they are apprehended with full assurance of conscience; it declares that wherever there is doubt or uncertainty, the promises are made void; on the other hand, that they can only waver and fluctuate if they depend on our works. Therefore, either our righteousness must perish, or without any consideration of our works, place must be given to faith alone, whose nature it is to prick up the ear, and shut the eye; that is, to be intent on the promise only, to give up all idea of any dignity or merit in man. Thus is fulfilled the celebrated prophecy of Zechariah: "I will remove the iniquity of that land in one day. In that day, saith the Lord of hosts, shall ye call every man his neighbor under the vine, and under the fig-tree" (Zech. 3:9,

10). Here the prophet intimates that the only way in which believers can enjoy true peace, is by obtaining the remission of their sins. For we must attend to this peculiarity in the prophets, that when they discourse of the kingdom of Christ, they set forth the external mercies of God as types of spiritual blessings. Hence Christ is called *the Prince of Peace, and our peace*, Isaiah 9:6; Eph. 2:14), because he calms all the agitations of conscience. If the method is asked, we must come to the sacrifice by which God was appeased, for no man will ever cease to tremble, until he hold that God is propitiated solely by that expiation in which Christ endured his anger. In short, peace must be sought nowhere but in the agonies of Christ our Redeemer.

5. But why employ a more obscure testimony? Paul uniformly declares that the conscience can have no peace or quiet joy until it is held for certain that we are justified by faith. And he at the same time declares whence this certainty is derived—viz. when "the love of God is shed abroad in our hearts by the Holy Ghost" (Rom. 5:5); as if he had said that our Souls cannot have peace until we are fully assured that we are pleasing to God. Hence he elsewhere exclaims in the person of believers in general, "Who shall separate us from the love of Christ?" (Rom. 8:35). Until we have reached that haven, the slightest breeze will make us tremble, but so long as the Lord is our Shepherd, we shall walk without fear in the valley of the shadow of death (Ps. 23). Thus those who pretend that justification by faith consists in being regenerated and made just, by living spiritually, have never tasted the sweetness of grace in trusting that God will be propitious. Hence also, they know no more of praying aright than do the Turks or any other heathen people. For, as Paul declares, faith is not true, unless it suggest and dictate the delightful name of Father; nay, unless it open our mouths and enable us freely to cry, Abba, Father. This he expresses more clearly in another passage, "In whom we have boldness and access with confidence by the faith of him" (Eph. 3:12). This, certainly, is not obtained by the gift of regeneration, which, as it is always defective in the present state, contains within it many grounds of doubt. Wherefore, we must have recourse to this remedy; we must hold that the only hope which believers have of the heavenly inheritance is, that being in grafted into the body of Christ, they are justified freely. For, in regard to justification, faith is merely passives bringing nothing of our own to procure the favor of God, but receiving from Christ every thing that we want.

CHAPTER 14

THE BEGINNING OF JUSTIFICATION. IN WHAT SENSE PROGRESSIVE.

To illustrate what has been already said, and show what kind of righteousness man can have during the whole course of his life, mankind are divided into four classes. I. First class considered, sec. 1–6. II. Second and third classes considered together, sec. 7, 8. III. Fourth class considered, sec. 9 to end.

Sections:

1. Men either idolatrous, profane, hypocritical, or regenerate. 1. Idolaters void of righteousness, full of unrighteousness, and hence in the sight of God altogether wretched and undone.

2. Still a great difference in the characters of men. This difference manifested. 1. In the gifts of God. 2. In the distinction between honorable and base. 3. In the blessings of the present life.

3. All human virtue, how praiseworthy soever it may appear, is corrupted. 1. By impurity of heart. 2. By the absence of a proper nature.

4. By the want of Christ, without whom there is no life.

5. Natural condition of man as described by Scripture. All men dead in sins before regeneration.

6. Passages of Scripture to this effect. Vulgar error confounding the righteousness of works with the redemption purchased by Christ.

7. The second and third classes of men, comprehending hypocrites and Christians in name only. Every action of theirs deserves condemnation. Passage from Haggai. Objection. Answer.

8. Other passages. Quotations from Augustine and Gregory.

9. The fourth class—viz. the regenerate. Though guided by the Spirit, corruption adheres to all they do, especially when brought to the bar of God.

10. One fault sufficient to efface all former righteousness. Hence they cannot possibly be justified by works.

11. In addition to the two former arguments, a third adduced against the Sophists, to show that whatever be the works of the regenerate, they are justified solely by faith and the free imputation of Christ's righteousness.

12. Sophism of the Schoolmen in opposition to the above doctrine. Answer.

13. Answer explained. Refutation of the fiction of

partial righteousness, and compensation by works of supererogation. This fiction necessarily falls with that of satisfaction.

14. Statement of our Savior—viz. that after we have done all, we are still unprofitable servants.

15. Objection founded on Paul's boasting. Answer, showing the Apostle's meaning. Other answers, stating the general doctrine out of Chrysostom. Third answer, showing that supererogation is the merest vanity.

16. Fourth answer, showing how Scripture dissuades us from all confidence in works. Fifth answer, showing that we have no ground of boasting.

17. Sixth answer, showing, in regard to four different classes, that works have no part in procuring our salvation. 1. The efficient cause is the free love of the Father. 2. The material cause is Christ acquiring righteousness for us. 3. The instrumental cause is faith. 4. The final cause the display of the divine justice and praise of the divine goodness.

18. A second objection, founded on the glorying of saints. An answer, explaining these modes of expression. How the saints feel in regard to the certainty of salvation. The opinion they have of their own works as in the sight of God.

19. Another answer—viz. that the elect, by this kind of glorying, refer only to their adoption by the Father as proved by the fruits of their calling. The order of this glorying. Its foundation, structure, and parts.

20. Conclusion. The saints neither attribute anything to the merits of works, nor derogate in any degree from the righteousness which they obtain in Christ. Confirmation from a passage of Augustine, in which he gives two reasons why no believer will presume to boast before God of his works.

21. A third objection—viz. that the good works of believers are the causes of divine blessings. Answer. There are inferior causes, but these depend on free justification, which is the only true cause why God blesses us. These modes of expression designate the order of sequence rather than the cause.

1. In farther illustration of the subject, let us consider what kind of righteousness man can have, during the whole course of his life, and for this purpose let us make a fourfold division. Mankind, either endued with no knowledge of God, are sunk in idolatry; or, initiated in the sacraments, but by the impurity of their lives denying him whom they confess with their mouths, are Christians in name only; or they are hypocrites, who with empty glosses hide the iniquity of the heart; or they are regenerated by the Spirit of God, and aspire to true holiness. In the first place, when men are judged by their natural endowments, not a iota of good will be found from the crown of the head to the sole of the foot, unless we are to charge Scripture with falsehood, when it describes all the sons of Adam by such terms as these: "The heart is deceitful above all things, and desperately wicked." "The imagination of man's heart is evil from his youth." "The Lord knoweth the thoughts of man that they are vanity." "They are all gone aside: they are altogether become filthy; there is none that does good, no, not one." In short, that they are *flesh*, under which name are comprehended all those works which are enumerated by Paul; adultery, fornication, uncleanness, lasciviousness idolatry witchcraft, hatred, variance, emulation, wrath, strife, seditions, heresies, envyings, murders, drunkenness, revellings, and all kinds of pollution and abomination which it is possible to imagine. Such, then, is the worth on which men are to plume themselves. But if any among them possess an integrity of manners which presents some semblance of sanctity among men, yet because we know that God regards not the outward appearance, we must penetrate to the very source of action, if we would see how far works avail for righteousness. We must, I say, look within, and see from what affection of the heart these works proceed. This is a very wide field of discussion, but as the matter may be explained in few words, I will use as much brevity as I can.

2. First, then, I deny not, that whatever excellent endowments appear in unbelievers are divine gifts. Nor do I set myself so much in opposition to common sense, as to contend that there was no difference between the justice, moderation, and equity of Titus and Trojan, and the rage, intemperance, and cruelty of Caligula, Nero, and Domitian; between the continence of Vespasian, and the obscene lusts of Tiberius; and (not to dwell on single virtues and vices) between the observance of law and justice, and the contempt of them. So great is the difference between justice and injustice, that it may be seen even where the former is only a lifeless image. For what order would remain in the world if we were to confound them? Hence this distinction between honorable and base actions God has not only engraven on the minds of each, but also often confirms in the administration of his providence. For we see how he visits those who cultivate virtue with many temporal blessings. Not that that external image of virtue in the least degree merits his favor, but he is pleased thus to show how much he delights in true

righteousness, since he does not leave even the outward semblance of it to go unrewarded. Hence it follows, as we lately observed, that those virtues, or rather images of virtues, of whatever kind, are divine gifts, since there is nothing in any degree praiseworthy which proceeds not from him.

3. Still the observation of Augustine is true, that all who are strangers to the true God, however excellent they may be deemed on account of their virtues are more deserving of punishment than of reward, because, by the pollution of their heart, they contaminate the pure gifts of God (August. contra Julia. Lib. 4). For though they are instruments of God to preserve human society by justice, continence, friendship, temperance, fortitude, and prudence, yet they execute these good works of God in the worst manner, because they are kept from acting ill, not by a sincere love of goodness, but merely by ambition or self-love, or some other sinister affection. Seeing then that these actions are polluted as in their very source, by impurity of heart, they have no better title to be classed among virtues than vices, which impose upon us by their affinity or resemblance to virtue. In short, when we remember that the object at which righteousness always aims is the service of God, whatever is of a different tendency deservedly forfeits the name. Hence, as they have no regard to the end which the divine wisdom prescribes, although from the performance the act seems good, yet from the perverse motive it is sin. Augustine, therefore, concludes that all the Fabriciuses, the Scipios, and Catos, in their illustrious deeds, sinned in this, that, wanting the light of faith, they did not refer them to the proper end, and that, therefore, there was no true righteousness in them, because duties are estimated not by acts but by motives.

4. Besides, if it is true, as John says, that there is no life without the Son of God (1 John 5:12), those who have no part in Christ, whoever they be, whatever they do or devise, are hastening on, during their whole career, to destruction and the judgment of eternal death. For this reason, Augustine says, "Our religion distinguishes the righteous from the wicked, by the law, not of works but of faith, without which works which seem good are converted into sins" (August. ad Bonif. Lib. 3, c. 5). He finely expresses the same idea in another passage, when he compares the zeal of such men to those who in a race mistake the course (August. Præf in Ps. 31). He who is off the course, the more swiftly he runs is the more distant from the goal and, therefore, the more unhappy. It is better to limp in the way than run out of the way. Lastly, as there is no sanctification without union with Christ, it is evident that they are bad trees which are beautiful and fair to look upon, and may even produce fruit, sweet to the taste, but are still very far from good. Hence we easily perceive that every thing which man thinks, designs, and performs, before he is reconciled to God by faith, is cursed, and not only of no avail for justification, but merits certain damnation. And why do we talk of this as if it were doubtful, when it has already been proved by the testimony of an apostle, that "without faith it is impossible to please God?" (Heb. 11:6).

5. But the proof will be still clearer if divine grace is set in opposition to the natural condition of man. For Scripture everywhere proclaims that God finds nothing in man to induce him to show kindness, but that he prevents him by free liberality. What can a dead man do to obtain life? But when he enlightens us with the knowledge of himself, he is said to raise us from the dead, and make us new creatures (John 5:25). On this ground we see that the kindness of God toward us is often commended, especially by the apostle: "God," says he, "who is rich in mercy, for his great love wherewith he loved us, even when we were dead in sins, has quickened us together with Christ" (Eph. 2:4). In another passage, when treating of the general call of believers under the type of Abraham, he says, "God quickeneth the dead, and calleth those things which be not as though they were" (Rom. 4:17). If we are nothing, what, pray, can we do? Wherefore, in the Book of Job the Lord sternly represses all arrogance in these words, "Who has prevented me, that I should repay him? whatsoever is under the whole heaven is mine" (Job 41:11). Paul explaining this sentence applies it in this way,—Let us not imagine that we bring to the Lord any thing but the mere disgrace of want and destitution (Rom. 11:35). Wherefore, in the passage above quoted, to prove that we attain to the hope of salvation, not by works but only by grace, he affirms that "we are his workmanship, created in Christ Jesus unto good works, which God has before ordained that we should walk in them" (Eph. 2:10); as if he had said, Who of us can boast of having challenged God by his righteousness, seeing our first power to act aright is derived from regeneration? For, as we are formed by nature, sooner shall oil be extracted from stone than good works from us. It is truly strange how man, convicted of such ignominy, dares still to claim any thing as his own. Let us acknowledge, therefore, with that chosen vessel, that God "has called us with an holy calling, not according to our works, but according to his own purpose and

grace;" and "that the kindness and love of God our Savior toward men appeared not by works of righteousness which we have done, but according to his mercy he saved us;" that being justified by his grace, we might become the heirs of everlasting life (2 Tim. 1:9; Tit. 3:4, 5). By this confession we strip man of every particle of righteousness, until by mere mercy he is regenerated unto the hope of eternal life, since it is not true to say we are justified by grace, if works contribute in any degree to our justification. The apostle undoubtedly had not forgotten himself in declaring that justification is gratuitous, seeing he argues in another place, that if works are of any avail, "grace is no more grace" (Rom. 11:6). And what else does our Lord mean, when he declares, "I am not come to call the righteous, but sinners to repentance?" (Mt. 9:13). If sinners alone are admitted, why do we seek admission by means of fictitious righteousness?

6. The thought is ever and anon recurring to me, that I am in danger of insulting the mercy of God by laboring with so much anxiety to maintain it, as if it were doubtful or obscure. Such, however, is our malignity in refusing to concede to God what belongs to him until most strongly urged that I am obliged to insist at greater length. But as Scripture is clear enough on this subject, I shall contend in its words rather than my own. Isaiah, after describing the universal destruction of the human race, finely subjoins the method of restitution. "The Lord saw it, and it displeased him that there was no judgment. And he saw that there was no man, and wondered that there was no intercessor: therefore his arm brought salvation unto him; and his righteousness, it sustained him" (Isaiah 59:15, 16). Where is our righteousness, if the prophet says truly, that no man in recovering salvation gives any assistance to the Lord? Thus another prophet, introducing the Lord as treating concerning the reconciliation of sinners, says, "I will betroth thee unto me for ever; yea, I will betroth thee unto me in righteousness, and in judgment, and in loving-kindness, and in mercies." "I will have mercy upon her that had not obtained mercy" (Hosea 2:19, 23). If a covenant of this kind, evidently forming our first union with God, depends on mercy, there is no foundation left for our righteousness. And, indeed, I would fain know, from those who pretend that man meets God with some righteousness of works, whether they imagine there is any kind of righteousness save that which is acceptable to Him. If it were insane to think so, can any thing agreeable to God proceed from his enemies, whom he abominates with all their deeds? Truth declares that we are all the avowed and inveterate enemies of God until we are justified and admitted to his friendship (Rom. 5:6; Col. 1:21). If justification is the beginning of love, how can the righteousness of works precede it? Hence John, to put down the arrogant idea, carefully reminds us that God first loved us (1 John 4:10). The Lord had formerly taught the same thing by his Prophet: "I will love them freely: for mine anger is turned away from him" (Hosea 14:4). Assuredly he is not influenced by works if his love turns to us spontaneously. But the rude and vulgar idea entertained is, that we did not merit the interposition of Christ for our redemption, but that we are aided by our works in obtaining possession of it. On the contrary, though we may be redeemed by Christ, still, until we are ingrafted into union with him by the calling of the Father, we are darkness, the heirs of death, and the enemies of God. For Paul declares that we are not purged and washed from our impurities by the blood of Christ until the Spirit accomplishes that cleansing in us (1 Cor. 6:11). Peter, intending to say the same thing, declares that the sanctification of the Spirit avails "unto obedience and sprinkling of the blood of Jesus Christ" (1 Pet. 1:2). If the sprinkling of the blood of Christ by the Spirit gives us purification, let us not think that, previous to this sprinkling, we are anything but sinners without Christ. Let us, therefore, hold it as certain, that the beginning of our salvation is as it were a resurrection from death unto life, because, when it is given us on behalf of Christ to believe on him (Phil. 1:29), then only do we begin to pass from death unto life.

7. Under this head the second and third class of men noted in the above division is comprehended. Impurity of conscience proves that as yet neither of these classes is regenerated by the Spirit of God. And, again, their not being regenerated proves their want of faith. Whence it is clear that they are not yet reconciled, not yet justified, since it is only by faith that these blessings are obtained. What can sinners, alienated from God, produce save that which is abominable in his sight? Such, however, is the stupid confidence entertained by all the wicked, and especially by hypocrites, that however conscious that their whole heart teems with impurity, they yet deem any spurious works which they may perform as worthy of the approbation of God. Hence the pernicious consequence, that though convicted of a wicked and impious minds they cannot be induced to confess that they are devoid of righteousness. Even acknowledging themselves to be unrighteous, because they cannot deny it, they yet arrogate to themselves some degree of righteousness. This vanity the Lord admirably refutes by the prophet: "Ask

now the priests concerning the law, saying, If one bear holy flesh in the skirt of his garment, and with his skirt do touch bread, or pottage, or wine, or oil, or any meat, shall it be holy? And the priests answered and said, No. Then said Haggai, If one that is unclean by a dead body touch any of these, shall it be unclean? And the priests answered and said, It shall be unclean. Then answered Haggai, and said, So is this people, and so is this nation before me, saith the Lord; and so is every work of their hands; and that which they offer there is unclean" (Haggai 2:11–14). I wish these sentiments could obtain full credit with us, and be deeply fixed on our memories. For there is no man, however flagitous the whole tenor of his life may be, who will allow himself to be convinced of what the Lord here so clearly declares. As soon as any person, even the most wicked, has performed some one duty of the law, he hesitates not to impute it to himself for righteousness; but the Lord declares that no degree of holiness is thereby acquired, unless the heart has previously been made pure. And not contented with this, he declares that all the works performed by sinners are contaminated by impurity of heart. Let us cease then to give the name of righteousness to works which the mouth of the Lord condemns as polluted. How well is this shown by that elegant similitude? It might be objected, that what the Lord has commanded is inviolably holy. But he, on the contrary, replies, that it is not strange that those things which are sanctified in the law are contaminated by the impurity of the wicked, the unclean hand profaning that which is sacred by handling it.

8. The same argument is admirably followed out by Isaiah: "Bring no more vain oblations; incense is an abomination unto me; the new moons and sabbaths, the calling of assemblies, I cannot away with; it is iniquity, even the solemn meeting. Your new moons and your appointed feasts my foul hateth: they are a trouble unto me; I am weary to bear them. And when ye spread forth your hands I will hide mine eyes from you; yea, when ye make many prayers, I will not hear: your hands are full of blood. Wash you, make you clean; put away the evil of your doings from before mine eyes" (Isaiah 1:13–16, compared with ch. 58) What is meant by the Lord thus nauseating the observance of his law? Nay, indeed, he does not repudiate any thing relating to the genuine observance of the law, the beginning of which is as he uniformly declares the sincere fear of his name. When this is wanting, all the services which are offered to him are not only nugatory but vile and abominable. Let hypocrites now go, and while keeping depravity wrapt up in their heart, study to lay God under obligation by their works. In this way they will only offend him more and more. "The sacrifice of the wicked is an abomination to the Lord; but the prayer of the upright is his delight" (Prov. 15:8). We hold it, therefore, as indubitable, indeed it should be notorious to all tolerably verdant with Scriptures that the most splendid works performed by men, who are not yet truly sanctified, are so far from being righteousness in the sight of the Lord, that he regards them as sins. And, therefore it is taught with perfect truth, that no man procures favor with God by means of works, but that, on the contrary, works are not pleasing to God unless the person has previously found favor in his sight. Here we should carefully observe the order which scripture sets before us. Moses says that "the Lord had respect unto Abel and to his offering" (Gen. 4:4). Observe how he says that the Lord was propitious (had respect) to Abel, before he had respect to his works. Wherefore, purification of heart ought to precede, in order that the works performed by us may be graciously accepted by God: for the saying of Jeremiah is always true, "O Lord, are not thine eyes upon the truth?" (Jer. 5:3). Moreover the Holy Spirit declared by the mouth of Peter, that it is by faith alone the heart is purified (Acts 15:9). Hence it is evident, that the primary foundation is in true and living faith.

9. Let us now see what kind of righteousness belongs to those persons whom we have placed in the fourth class. We admits that when God reconciles us to himself by the intervention of the righteousness of Christ, and bestowing upon us the free pardon of sins regards us as righteous, his goodness is at the same time conjoined with mercy, so that he dwells in us by means of his Holy Spirit, by whose agency the lusts of our flesh are every day more and more mortified while that we ourselves are sanctified; that is consecrated to the Lord for true purity of life, our hearts being trained to the obedience of the law. It thus becomes our leading desire to obey his will, and in all things advance his glory only. Still, however while we walk in the ways of the Lord, under the guidance of the Holy Spirit, lest we should become unduly elated, and forget ourselves, we have still remains of imperfection which serve to keep us humble: "There is no man that sinneth not," saith Scripture (1 Kings 8:46). What righteousness then can men obtain by their works? First, I say, that the best thing which can be produced by them is always tainted and corrupted by the impurity of the flesh, and has, as it were, some mixture of dross in it. Let the holy servant of God, I say, select from the whole course of his life the action which he deems most excellent,

and let him ponder it in all its parts; he will doubtless find in it something that savors of the rottenness of the flesh, since our alacrity in well-doing is never what it ought to be, but our course is always retarded by much weakness. Although we see that the stains by which the works of the righteous are blemished, are by no means unapparent, still, granting that they are the minutest possible, will they give no offense to the eye of God, before which even the stars are not clean? We thus see, that even saints cannot perform one work which, if judged on its own merits, is not deserving of condemnation.

10. Even were it possible for us to perform works absolutely pure, yet one sin is sufficient to efface and extinguish all remembrance of former righteousness, as the prophet says (Ezek. 18:24). With this James agrees, "Whosoever shall keep the whole law, and yet offend in one point, is guilty of all" (James 2:10). And since this mortal life is never entirely free from the taint of sin, whatever righteousness we could acquire would ever and anon be corrupted, overwhelmed, and destroyed, by subsequent sins, so that it could not stand the scrutiny of God, or be imputed to us for righteousness. In short, whenever we treat of the righteousness of works, we must look not to the legal work but to the command. Therefore, when righteousness is sought by the Law, it is in vain to produce one or two single works; we must show an uninterrupted obedience. God does not (as many foolishly imagine) impute that forgiveness of sins once for all, as righteousness; so that having obtained the pardon of our past life we may afterwards seek righteousness in the Law. This were only to mock and delude us by the entertainment of false hopes. For since perfection is altogether unattainable by us, so long as we are clothed with flesh, and the Law denounces death and judgment against all who have not yielded a perfect righteousness, there will always be ground to accuse and convict us unless the mercy of God interpose, and ever and anon absolve us by the constant remission of sins. Wherefore the statement which we set out is always true, If we are estimated by our own worthiness, in every thing that we think or devise, with all our studies and endeavors we deserve death and destruction.

11. We must strongly insist on these two things: That no believer ever performed one work which, if tested by the strict judgment of God, could escape condemnation; and, moreover, that were this granted to be possible (though it is not), yet the act being vitiated and polluted by the sins of which it is certain that the author of it is guilty, it is deprived of its merit. This is the cardinal point of the present discussion. There is no controversy between us and the sounder Schoolmen as to the beginning of justification. They admit that the sinner, freely delivered from condemnation, obtains justification, and that by forgiveness of sins; but under the term justification they comprehend the renovation by which the Spirit forms us anew to the obedience of the Law; and in describing the righteousness of the regenerate man, maintain that being once reconciled to God by means of Christ, he is afterwards deemed righteous by his good works, and is accepted in consideration of them. The Lord, on the contrary, declares, that he imputed Abraham's faith for righteousness (Rom. 4:3), not at the time when he was still a worshipper of idols, but after he had been many years distinguished for holiness. Abraham had long served God with a pure heart, and performed that obedience of the Law which a mortal man is able to perform: yet his righteousness still consisted in faith. Hence we infer, according to the reasoning of Paul, that it was *not of works*. In like manners when the prophet says, "The just shall live by his faith" (Hab. 2:4), he is not speaking of the wicked and profane, whom the Lord justifies by converting them to the faith: his discourse is directed to believers, and life is promised to them by faith. Paul also removes every doubt, when in confirmation of this sentiment he quotes the words of David, "Blessed is he whose transgression is forgiven, whose sin is covered" (Ps. 32:1). It is certain that David is not speaking of the ungodly but of believers such as he himself was, because he was giving utterance to the feelings of his own mind. Therefore we must have this blessedness not once only, but must hold it fast during our whole lives. Moreover, the message of free reconciliation with God is not promulgated for one or two days, but is declared to be perpetual in the Church (2 Cor. 5:18, 19). Hence believers have not even to the end of life any other righteousness than that which is there described. Christ ever remains a Mediator to reconcile the Father to us, and there is a perpetual efficacy in his death—viz. ablution, satisfaction, expiation; in short, perfect obedience, by which all our iniquities are covered. In the Epistle to the Ephesians, Paul says not that the beginning of salvation is of grace, but "by grace are ye saved," "not of works, lest any man should boast" (Eph. 2:8, 9).

12. The subterfuges by which the Schoolmen here endeavor to escape will not disentangle them. They say that good works are not of such intrinsic worth as to be sufficient to procure justification, but it is owing to accepting grace that they have this effect. Then because they are forced to confess that here the righteousness of

works is always imperfect, they grant that so long as we are in this life we stand in need of the forgiveness of sin in order to supply the deficiency of works, but that the faults which are committed are compensated by works of supererogation. I answer, that the grace which they call accepting, is nothing else than the free goodness with which the Father embraces us in Christ when he clothes us with the innocence of Christ, and accepts it as ours, so that in consideration of it he regards us as holy, pure, and innocent. For the righteousness of Christ (as it alone is perfect, so it alone can stand the scrutiny of God) must be sisted for us, and as a surety represent us judicially. Provided with this righteousness, we constantly obtain the remission of sins through faith. Our imperfection and impurity, covered with this purity, are not imputed but are as it were buried, so as not to come under judgment until the hour arrive when the old man being destroyed, and plainly extinguished in us, the divine goodness shall receive us into beatific peace with the new Adam, there to await the day of the Lord, on which, being clothed with incorruptible bodies, we shall be translated to the glory of the heavenly kingdom.

13. If these things are so, it is certain that our works cannot in themselves make us agreeable and acceptable to God, and even cannot please God, except in so far as being covered with the righteousness of Christ we thereby please him and obtain forgiveness of sins. God has not promised life as the reward of certain works, but only declares, "which if a man do, he shall live in them" (Lev. 18:5), denouncing the well-known curse against all who do not continue in all things that are written in the book of the Law to do them. In this way is completely refuted the fiction of a partial righteousness, the only righteousness acknowledged in heaven being the perfect observance of the Law. There is nothing more solid in their dogma of compensation by means of works of supererogation. For must they not always return to the proposition which has already been disproved—viz. that he who observes the Law in part is so far justified by works? This, which no man of sound judgment will concede to them, they are not ashamed to take for granted. The Lord having so often declared that he recognizes no justification by works unless they be works by which the Law is perfectly fulfilled,—how perverse is it, while we are devoid of such works, to endeavor to secure some ground of glorying to ourselves; that is not to yield it entirely to God, by boasting of some kind of fragments of works, and trying to supply the deficiency by other satisfactions? Satisfactions have already been so completely disposed of,

that we ought never again even to dream of them. Here all I say is, that those who thus trifle with sin do not at all consider how execrable it is in the sight of God; if they did, they would assuredly understand, that all the righteousness of men collected into one heap would be inadequate to compensate for a single sin. For we see that by one sin man was so cast off and forsaken by God, that he at the same time lost all power of recovering salvation. He was, therefore, deprived of the power of giving satisfaction. Those who flatter themselves with this idea will never satisfy God, who cannot possibly accept or be pleased with anything that proceeds from his enemies. But all to whom he imputes sin are enemies, and, therefore, our sins must be covered and forgiven before the Lord has respect to any of our works. From this it follows, that the forgiveness of sins is gratuitous, and this forgiveness is wickedly insulted by those who introduce the idea of satisfaction. Let us, therefore, after the example of the Apostle, "forgetting those things which are behind, and reaching forth unto those things which are before," "press toward the mark for the prize of the high calling of God in Jesus Christ" (Phil. 3:13, 14).

14. How can boasting in works of supererogation agree with the command given to us: "When ye shall have done all those things which are commanded you, say, We are unprofitable servants: we have done that which was our duty to do?" (Luke 17:10). To say or speak in the presence of God is not to feign or lie, but to declare what we hold as certain. Our Lord, therefore, enjoins us sincerely to feel and consider with ourselves that we do not perform gratuitous duties, but pay him service which is due. And truly. For the obligations of service under which we lie are so numerous that we cannot discharge them though all our thoughts and members were devoted to the observance of the Law; and, therefore, when he says "When ye shall have done all those things which are commanded you," it is just as if he had said that all the righteousness of men would not amount to one of these things. Seeing, then, that every one is very far distant from that goal, how can we presume to boast of having accumulated more than is due? It cannot be objected that a person, though failing in some measure in what is necessary, may yet in intention go beyond what is necessary. For it must ever be held that in whatever pertains to the worship of God, or to charity, nothing can ever be thought of that is not comprehended under the Law. But if it is part of the Law, let us not boast of voluntary liberality in matters of necessary obligation.

15. On this subject, they ceaselessly allege the boast

of Paul, that among the Corinthians he spontaneously renounced a right which, if he had otherwise chosen, he might have exercised (1 Cor. 9:15); thus not only paying what he owed them in duty, but gratuitously bestowing upon them more than duty required. They ought to have attended to the reason there expressed, that his object was to avoid giving offense to the weak. For wicked and deceitful workmen employed this pretence of kindness that they might procure favor to their pernicious dogmas, and excite hatred against the Gospel, so that it was necessary for Paul either to peril the doctrine of Christ, or to thwart their schemes. Now, if it is a matter of indifference to a Christian man whether or not he cause a scandal when it is in his power to avoid it, then I admit that the Apostle performed a work of supererogation to his Master; but if the thing which he did was justly required in a prudent minister of the Gospel, then I say he did what he was bound to do. In short, even when no such reason appears, yet the saying of Chrysostom is always true, that everything which we have is held on the same condition as the private property of slaves; it is always due to our Master. Christ does not disguise this in the parable, for he asks in regard to the master who, on return from his labour, requires his servant to gird himself and serve him, "Does he thank that servant because he did the things that were commanded him? I trow not" (Luke 17:9). But possibly the servant was more industrious than the master would have ventured to exact. Be it so: still he did nothing to which his condition as a servant did not bind him, because his utmost ability is his master's. I say nothing as to the kind of supererogations on which these men would plume themselves before God. They are frivolities which he never commanded, which he approves not, and will not accept when they come to give in their account. The only sense in which we admit works of supererogation is that expressed by the prophet, when he says, "Who has required this at your hand?" (Isaiah 1:12). But let them remember what is elsewhere said of them: "Wherefore do ye spend money for that which is not bread? and your labour for that which satisfieth not?" (Isaiah 55:2). It is, indeed, an easy matter for these indolent Rabbis to carry on such discussions sitting in their soft chairs under the shade, but when the Supreme Judge shall sit on his tribunal, all these blustering dogmas will behave to disappear. This, this I say, was the true question: not what we can fable and talk in schools and corners, but what ground of defense we can produce at his judgment-seat.

16. In this matter the minds of men must be specially guarded against two pestiferous dogmas—viz. against putting any confidence in the righteousness of works, or ascribing any glory to them. From all such confidence the Scriptures uniformly dissuade us when they declare that our righteousness is offensive in the sight of God unless it derives a sweet odour from the purity of Christ: that it can have no other effect than to excite the divine vengeance unless sustained by his indulgent mercy. Accordingly, the only thing they leave to us is to deprecate our Judge with that confession of David: "Enter not into judgment with thy servant: for in thy sight shall no living be justified" (Psalm 143:2). And when Job says, "If I be wicked, woe unto me: and if I be righteous, yet will I not lift up my head" (Job 10:15). Although he refers to that spotless righteousness of God, before which even angels are not clean, he however shows, that when brought to the bar of Gods all that mortals can do is to stand dumb. He does not merely mean that he chooses rather to give way spontaneously than to risk a contest with the divine severity, but that he was not conscious of possessing any righteousness that would not fall the very first moment it was brought into the presence of God. Confidence being banished, all glorying must necessarily cease. For who can attribute any merit of righteousness to works, which instead of giving confidence, only make us tremble in the presence of God? We must, therefore, come to what Isaiah invites us: "In the Lord shall all the seed of Israel be justified, and shall glory" (Isaiah 45:25); for it is most true, as he elsewhere says, that we are "the planting of the Lord, that he might be glorified" (Isaiah 61:3). Our soul, therefore, will not be duly purified until it ceases to have any confidence, or feel any exultation in works. Foolish men are puffed up to this false and lying confidence by the erroneous idea that the cause of their salvation is in works.

17. But if we attend to the four kinds of causes which philosophers bring under our view in regard to effects, we shall find that not one of them is applicable to works as a cause of salvation. The efficient cause of our eternal salvation the Scripture uniformly proclaims to be the mercy and free love of the heavenly Father towards us; the material cause to be Christ, with the obedience by which he purchased righteousness for us; and what can the formal or instrumental cause be but faith? John includes the three in one sentence when he says, "God so loved the world, that he gave his only begotten Son, that whosoever believeth in him should not perish but have everlasting life" (John 3:16). The Apostle, moreover, declares that the final cause is the demonstration of the divine righteousness and the praise of his goodness. There also

he distinctly mentions the other three causes; for he thus speaks to the Romans: "All have sinned, and come short of the glory of God, being justified freely by his grace" (Rom. 3:23, 24). You have here the head and primary source—God has embraced us with free mercy. The next words are, "through the redemption that is in Christ Jesus;" this is as it were the material cause by which righteousness is procured for us. "Whom God has set forth to be a propitiation through faith." Faith is thus the instrumental cause by which righteousness is applied to us. He lastly subjoins the final cause when he says, "To declare at this time his righteousness; that he might be just, and the justifier of him that believeth in Jesus." And to show by the way that this righteousness consists in reconciliation, he says that Christ was "set forth to be a propitiation." Thus also, in the Epistle to the Ephesians, he tells us that we are received into the favor of God by mere mercy; that this is done by the intervention of Christ; that it is apprehended by faith; the end of all being that the glory of the divine goodness may be fully displayed. When we see that all the parts of our salvation thus exist without us, what ground can we have for glorying or confiding in our works? Neither as to the efficient nor the final cause can the most sworn enemies of divine grace raise any controversy with us unless they would abjure the whole of Scripture. In regard to the material or formal cause they make a gloss, as if they held that our works divide the merit with faith and the righteousness of Christ. But here also Scripture reclaims, simply affirming that Christ is both righteousness and life, and that the blessing of justification is possessed by faith alone.

18. When the saints repeatedly confirm and console themselves with the remembrance of their innocence and integrity, and sometimes even abstain not from proclaiming them, it is done in two ways: either because by comparing their good cause with the bad cause of the ungodly, they thence feel secure of victory, not so much from commendation of their own righteousness, as from the just and merited condemnation of their adversaries; or because, reviewing themselves before God, even without any comparison with others the purity of their conscience gives them some comfort and security. The former reason will afterwards be considered (chap. 17, sec. 14, and chap. 20, sec. 10); let us now briefly show, in regard to the latter, how it accords with what we have above said, that we can have no confidence in works before the bar of God, that we cannot glory in any opinion of their worth. The accordance lies here, that when the point considered is the constitution and foundation of salvation, believers, without paying any respect to works, direct their eyes to the goodness of God alone. Nor do they turn to it only in the first instance, as to the commencement of blessedness, but rest in it as the completion. Conscience being thus founded, built up, and established is farther established by the consideration of works, inasmuch as they are proofs of God dwelling and reigning in us. Since, then, this confidence in works has no place unless you have previously fixed your whole confidence on the mercy of God, it should not seem contrary to that on which it depends. Wherefore, when we exclude confidence in works, we merely mean, that the Christian mind must not turn back to the merit of works as an aid to salvation, but must dwell entirely on the free promise of justification. But we forbid no believer to confirm and support this faith by the signs of the divine favor towards him. For if when we call to mind the gifts which God has bestowed upon us, they are like rays of the divine countenance, by which we are enabled to behold the highest light of his goodness; much more is this the case with the gift of good works, which shows that we have received the Spirit of adoption.

19. When believers therefore feel their faith strengthened by a consciousness of integrity, and entertain sentiments of exultation, it is just because the fruits of their calling convince them that the Lord has admitted them to a place among his children. Accordingly, when Solomon says, "In the fear of the Lord is strong confidence" (Prov. 14:26), and when the saints sometimes beseech the Lord to hear them, because they walked before his face in simplicity and integrity (Gen. 24:10; 2 Kings 20:3), these expressions apply not to laying the foundation of a firm conscience, but are of force only when taken *a posteriori*. For there is no where such a fear of God as can give full security, and the saints are always conscious that any integrity which they may possess is mingled with many remains of the flesh. But as the fruits of regeneration furnish them with a proof of the Holy Spirit dwelling in them, experiencing God to be a Father in a matter of so much moment, they are strengthened in no slight degree to wait for his assistance in all their necessities. Even this they could not do, had they not previously perceived that the goodness of God is sealed to them by nothing but the certainty of the promise. Should they begin to estimate it by their good works, nothing will be weaker or more uncertain; works, when estimated by themselves, no less proving the divine displeasure by their imperfection, than his good-will by their incipient purity. In short, while proclaiming the mercies of the Lord, they never lose sight

of his free favor, with all its "breadth and length, and depth and height," testified by Paul (Eph. 3:18); as if he had said, Whithersoever the believer turns, however loftily he climbs, however far and wide his thoughts extend, he must not go farther than the love of Christ, but must be wholly occupied in meditating upon it, as including in itself all dimensions. Accordingly, he declares that it "passeth knowledge," that "to know the love of Christ" is to "be filled with all the fulness of God" (Eph. 3:19). In another passage, where he glories that believers are victorious in every contest, he adds the reason, "through him that loved us" (Rom. 8:37).

20. We now see that believers have no such confidence in works as to attribute any merit to them (since they regard them only as divine gifts, in which they recognize his goodness, and signs of calling, in which they discern their election); nor such confidence as to derogate in any respect from the free righteousness of Christ; since on this it depends, and without this cannot subsist. The same thing is briefly but elegantly expressed by Augustine when he says, "I do not say to the Lord, Despise not the works of my hands; I have sought the Lord with my hands, and have not been deceived. But I commend not the works of my hands, for I fear that when thou examinest them thou wilt find more faults than merits. This only I say, this asks this desire, Despise not the works of thy hands. See in me thy work, not mine. If thou sees mine, thou condemnest; if thou sees thine own, thou crownest. Whatever good works I have are of thee" (August. in Ps. 137). He gives two reasons for not venturing to boast of his works before God: first, that if he has any good works, he does not see in them any thing of his own; and, secondly, that these works are overwhelmed by a multitude of sins. Whence it is, that the conscience derives from them more fear and alarm than security. Therefore, the only way in which he desires God to look at any work which he may have done aright is, that he may therein see the grace of his calling, and perfect the work which he has begun.

21. Moreover, when Scripture intimates that the good works of believers are causes why the Lord does them good, we must still understand the meaning so as to hold unshaken what has previously been said—viz. that the efficient cause of our salvation is placed in the love of God the Father; the material cause in the obedience of the Son; the instrumental cause in the illumination of the Spirit, that is, in faith; and the final cause in the praise of the divine goodness. In this, however, there is nothing to prevent the Lord from embracing works as inferior causes. But how so? In this way: Those whom in mercy he has destined for the inheritance of eternal life, he, in his ordinary administration, introduces to the possession of it by means of good works. What precedes in the order of administration is called the cause of what follows. For this reason, he sometimes makes eternal life a consequent of works; not because it is to be ascribed to them, but because those whom he has elected he justifies, that he may at length glorify (Rom. 8:30); he makes the prior grace to be a kind of cause, because it is a kind of step to that which follows. But whenever the true cause is to be assigned, he enjoins us not to take refuge in works, but to keep our thoughts entirely fixed on the mercy of God; "The wages of sin is death; but the gift of God is eternal life" (Rom. 6:23). Why, as he contrasts life with death, does he not also contrast righteousness with sin? Why, when setting down sin as the cause of death, does he not also set down righteousness as the cause of life? The antithesis which would otherwise be complete is somewhat marred by this variation; but the Apostle employed the comparison to express the fact, that death is due to the deserts of men, but that life was treasured up solely in the mercy of God. In short, by these expressions, the order rather than the cause is noted. The Lord adding grace to grace, takes occasion from a former to add a subsequent, so that he may omit no means of enriching his servants. Still, in following out his liberality, he would have us always look to free election as its source and beginning. For although he loves the gifts which he daily bestows upon us, inasmuch as they proceed from that fountain, still our duty is to hold fast by that gratuitous acceptance, which alone can support our souls; and so to connect the gifts of the Spirit, which he afterwards bestows, with their primary cause, as in no degree to detract from it.

CHAPTER 15

THE BOASTED MERIT OF WORKS SUBVERSIVE BOTH OF THE GLORY OF GOD, IN BESTOWING RIGHTEOUSNESS, AND OF THE CERTAINTY OF SALVATION.

The divisions of this chapter are,—I. To the doctrine of free justification is opposed the question, Whether or not works merit favor with God, sec. 1. This question answered, sec. 2 and 3. II. An exposition of certain passages of Scripture produced in support of the erroneous doctrine of merit, sec. 4 and 5. III. Sophisms of Semipe-

lagian Schoolmen refuted, sec. 6 and 7. IV. Conclusion, proving the sufficiency of the orthodox doctrine, sec. 8. Sections:

1. After a brief recapitulation, the question, Whether or not good works merit favor with God, considered.

2. First answer, fixing the meaning of the term Merit. This term improperly applied to works, but used in a good sense, as by Augustine, Chrysostom, Bernard.

3. A second answer to the question. First by a negative, then by a concession. In the rewarding of works what to be attributed to God, and what to man. Why good works please God, and are advantageous to those who do them. The ingratitude of seeking righteousness by works. This shown by a double similitude.

4. First objection taken from Ecclesiasticus. Second objection from the Epistle to the Hebrews. Two answers to both objections. A weak distinction refuted.

5. A third and most complete answer, calling us back to Christ as the only foundation of salvation. How Christ is our righteousness. Whence it is manifest that we have all things in Christ and he nothing in us.

6. We must abhor the sophistry which destroys the merit of Christ, in order to establish that of man. This impiety refuted by clear passages of Scripture.

7. Errors, of the younger Sophists extracted from Lombard. Refuted by Augustine. Also by Scripture.

8. Conclusion, showing that the foundation which has been laid is sufficient for doctrine, exhortation, and comfort. Summery of the orthodox doctrine of Justification.

1. The principal point in this subject has been now explained: as justifications if dependent upon works, cannot possibly stand in the sight of God, it must depend solely on the mercy of God and communion with Christ, and therefore on faith alone. But let us carefully attend to the point on which the whole subject hinges, lest we get entangled in the common delusion, not only of the vulgar, but of the learned. For the moment the question is raised as to the justification by faith or works, they run off to those passages which seem to ascribe some merit to works in the sight of God, just as if justification by works were proved whenever it is proved that works have any value with God. Above we have clearly shown that justification by works consists only in a perfect and absolute fulfillment of the law, and that, therefore, no man is justified by works unless he has reached the summit of perfection, and cannot be convicted of even the smallest transgression. But there is another and a separate question, Though works by no means suffice to justify, do they not merit favor with God?

2. First, I must premise with regard to the term Merit, that he, whoever he was, that first applied it to human works, viewed in reference to the divine tribunal, consulted very ill for the purity of the faith. I willingly abstain from disputes about words, but I could wish that Christian writers had always observed this soberness—that when there was no occasion for it, they had never thought of using terms foreign to the Scriptures—terms which might produce much offense, but very little fruit. I ask, what need was there to introduce the word Merit, when the value of works might have been fully expressed by another term, and without offense? The quantity of offense contained in it the world shows to its great loss. It is certain that, being a high sounding term, it can only obscure the grace of God, and inspire men with pernicious pride. I admit it was used by ancient ecclesiastical writers, and I wish they had not by the abuse of one term furnished posterity with matter of heresy, although in some passages they themselves show that they had no wish to injure the truth. For Augustine says, "Let human merits, which perished by Adam, here be silent, and let the grace of God reign by Jesus Christ" (August. de Prædest. Sanct). Again, "The saints ascribe nothing to their merits; every thing will they ascribe solely to thy mercy, O God" (August. in Psal. 139). Again, "And when a man sees that whatever good he has he has not of himself, but of his God, he sees that every thing in him which is praised is not of his own merits, but of the divine mercy" (August. in Psal. 88). You see how he denies man the power of acting aright, and thus lays merit prostrate. Chrysostom says, "If any works of ours follow the free calling of God, they are return and debt; but the gifts of God are grace, and beneficence, and great liberality." But to say nothing more of the name, let us attend to the thing. I formerly quoted a passage from Bernard: "As it is sufficient for merit not to presume on merit, so to be without merit is sufficient for condemnation" (Bernard in Cantic. Serm. 98). He immediately adds an explanation which softens the harshness of the expression, when he says, "Hence be careful to have merits; when you have them, know that they were given; hope for fruit from the divine mercy, and you have escaped all the perils of poverty, ingratitude, and presumption. Happy the Church which neither wants merit without presumption, nor presumption without merit." A little before he had abundantly shown

that he used the words in a sound sense, saying, "Why is the Church anxious about merits? God has furnished her with a firmer and surer ground of boasting. God cannot deny himself; he will do what he has promised. Thus there is no reason for asking by what merits may we hope for blessings; especially when you hear, 'Thus saith the Lord God; I do not this for your sakes, O house of Israel, but for mine holy name's sake,' (Ezek. 36:22). It suffices for merit to know that merits suffice not."

3. What all our works can merit Scripture shows when it declares that they cannot stand the view of God, because they are full of impurity; it next shows what the perfect observance of the law (if it can any where be found) will merit when it enjoins, "So likewise ye, when ye shall have done all those things which are commanded you, say, We are unprofitable servants, we have done that which was our duty to do" (Luke 17:10); because we make no free-offering to God, but only perform due service by which no favor is deserved. And yet those good works which the Lord has bestowed upon us he counts ours also, and declares, that they are not only acceptable to him, but that he will recompense them. It is ours in return to be animated by this great promise, and to keep up our courage, that we may not weary in well-doing, but feel duly grateful for the great kindness of God. There cannot be a doubt, that every thing in our works which deserves praise is owing to divine grace, and that there is not a particle of it which we can properly ascribe to ourselves. If we truly and seriously acknowledge this, not only confidence, but every idea of merit vanishes. I say we do not, like the Sophists share the praise of works between God and man, but we keep it entire and unimpaired for the Lord. All we assign to man is that, by his impurity he pollutes and contaminates the very works which were good. The most perfect thing which proceeds from man is always polluted by some stain. Should the Lord, therefore, bring to judgment the best of human works, he would indeed behold his own righteousness in them; but he would also behold man's dishonor and disgrace. Thus good works please God, and are not without fruit to their authors, since, by way of recompense, they obtain more ample blessings from God, not because they so deserve, but because the divine benignity is pleased of itself to set this value upon them. Such, however is our malignity, that not contented with this liberality on the part of God, which bestows rewards on works that do not at all deserve them, we with profane ambition maintain that that which is entirely due to the divine munificence is paid to the merit of works. Here I appeal to every man's common sense. If one who by another's liberality possesses the usufruct of a field, rear up a claim to the property of it, does he not by his ingratitude deserve to lose the possession formerly granted? In like manner, if a slave, who has been manumitted, conceals his humble condition of freedman, and gives out that he was freeborn, does he not deserve to be reduced to his original slavery? A benefit can only be legitimately enjoyed when we neither arrogate more to our selves than has been given, nor defraud the author of it of his due praise; nay, rather when we so conduct ourselves as to make it appear that the benefit conferred still in a manner resides with him who conferred it. But if this is the moderation to be observed towards men, let every one reflect and consider for himself what is due to God.

4. I know that the Sophists abuse some passages in order to prove that the Scriptures use the term *merit* with reference to God. They quote a passage from Ecclesiasticus: "Mercy will give place to every man according to the merit of his works" (Ecclesiasticus 16:14); and from the Epistle to the Hebrews: "To do good and communicate forget not; for with such sacrifices God is well pleased" (Heb. 13:16). I now renounce my right to repudiate the authority of Ecclesiasticus; but I deny that the words of Ecclesiasticus, whoever the writer may have been, are faithfully quoted. The Greek is as follows: Πάση ἐλεημοσύνῃ ποιήσει τόπον ἕκαστος γὰρ κατὰ τὰ ἔργα αὐτοῦ εὑρήσει. "He will make room for all mercy: for each shall find according to his works." That this is the genuine reading, and has been corrupted in the Latin version, is plain, both from the very structure of the sentence, and from the previous context. In the Epistle to the Hebrews there is no room for their quibbling on one little word, for in the Greek the Apostle simply says, that *such sacrifices are pleasing* and acceptable to God. This alone should amply suffice to quell and beat down the insolence of our pride, and prevent us from attaching value to works beyond the rule of Scripture. It is the doctrine of Scripture, moreover, that our good works are constantly covered with numerous stains by which God is justly offended and made angry against us, so far are they from being able to conciliate him, and call forth his favor towards us; and yet because of his indulgence, he does not examine them with the utmost strictness, he accepts them just as if they were most pure; and therefore rewards them, though undeserving, with innumerable blessings, both present and future. For I admit not the distinction laid down by otherwise learned and pious men, that good works merit the favors which are

conferred upon us in this life, whereas eternal life is the reward of faith only. The recompense of our toils, and crown of our contest, our Lord almost uniformly places in heaven. On the other hand, to attribute to the merit of works, so as to deny it to grace, that we are loaded with other gifts from the Lord, is contrary to the doctrine of Scripture. For though Christ says, "Unto every one that has shall be given;" "thou hast been faithful over a few things, I will make thee ruler over many things" (Mt. 25:29, 21), he, at the same time, shows that all additional gifts to believers are of his free benignity: "Ho, every one that thirsteth, come ye to the waters, and he that has no money, come ye, buy, and eat: yea, come, buy wine and milk, without money and without price" (Isaiah 55:1). Therefore, every help to salvation bestowed upon believers, and blessedness itself, are entirely the gift of God, and yet in both the Lord testifies that he takes account of works, since to manifest the greatness of his love toward us, he thus highly honors not ourselves only, but the gifts, which he has bestowed upon us.

5. Had these points been duly handled and digested in past ages, never could so many tumults and dissensions have arisen. Paul says, that in the architecture of Christian doctrine, it is necessary to retain the foundation which he had laid with the Corinthians, "Other foundation can no man lay than that which is laid, which is Jesus Christ" (1 Cor. 3:11). What then is our foundation in Christ? Is it that he begins salvation and leaves us to complete it? Is it that he only opened up the way, and left us to follow it in our own strength? By no means, but as Paul had a little before declared, it is to acknowledge that he has been given us for righteousness. No man, therefore, is well founded in Christ who has not entire righteousness in him, since the Apostle says not that he was sent to assist us in procuring, but was himself to be our righteousness. Thus, it is said that God "has chosen us in him before the foundation of the world," not according to our merit, but "according to the good pleasure of his will;" that in him "we have redemption through his blood, even the forgiveness of sins;" that peace has been made "through the blood of his cross;" that we are reconciled by his blood; that, placed under his protection, we are delivered from the danger of finally perishing; that thus ingrafted into him we are made partakers of eternal life, and hope for admission into the kingdom of God. Nor is this all. Being admitted to participation in him, though we are still foolish, he is our wisdom; though we are still sinners he is our righteousness; though we are unclean, he is our purity; though we are weak, unarmed, and exposed to Satan, yet ours is the power which has been given him in heaven and in earth, to bruise Satan under our feet, and burst the gates of hell (Mt. 28:18); though we still bear about with us a body of death, he is our life; in short, all things of his are ours, we have all things in him, he nothing in us. On this foundation, I say, we must be built, if we would grow up into a holy temple in the Lord.

6. For a long time the world has been taught very differently. A kind of good works called *moral* has been found out, by which men are rendered agreeable to God before they are ingrafted into Christ; as if Scripture spoke falsely when it says, "He that has the Son has life, and he that has not the Son of God has not life" (1 John 5:12). How can they produce the materials of life if they are dead? Is there no meaning in its being said that "whatsoever is not of faith is sin?" (Rom. 14:23); or can good fruit be produced from a bad tree? What have these most pestilential Sophists left to Christ on which to exert his virtue? They say that he merited for us the first grace, that is, the occasion of meriting, and that it is our part not to let slip the occasion thus offered. O the daring effrontery of impiety! Who would have thought that men professing the name of Christ would thus strip him of his power, and all but trample him under foot? The testimony uniformly borne to him in Scripture is that whoso believeth in him is justified; the doctrine of these men is, that the only benefit which proceeds from him is to open up a way for each to justify himself. I wish they could get a taste of what is meant by these passages: "He that hath the Son hath life." "He that hearth my word, and believeth in him that sent me," "is passed from death unto life." Whose believeth in him "is passed from death unto life." "Being justified freely by his grace, through the redemption that is in Christ Jesus." "He that keepeth his commandments dwelleth in him, and he in him." God "has raised us up together, and made us sit together in heavenly places in Christ." "Who has delivered us from the power of darkness, and has translated us into the kingdom of his dear Son." There are similar passages without number. Their meaning is not, that by faith in Christ an opportunity is given us of procuring justifications or acquiring salvation, but that both are given us. Hence, so soon as you are ingrafted into Christ by faith, you are made a son of God, an heir of heaven, a partaker of righteousness, a possessor of life, and (the better to manifest the false tenets of these men) you have not obtained an opportunity of meriting, but all the merits of Christ, since they are communicated to you.

7. In this way the schools of Sorbonne, the parents of all heresies, have deprived us of justification by faith,

which lies at the root of all godliness. They confess, indeed, in word, that men are justified by a formed faith, but they afterwards explain this to mean that of faith they have good works which avail to justification, so that they almost seem to use the term faith in mockery, because they were unable, without incurring great obloquy, to pass it in silence, seeing it is so often repeated by Scripture. And yet not contented with this, they by the praise of good works transfer to man what they steal from God. And seeing that good works give little ground for exultation, and are not even properly called merits, if they are regarded as the fruits of divine grace, they derive them from the power of free-will; in other words extract oil out of stone. They deny not that the principal cause is in grace; but they contend that there is no exclusion of free-will through which all merit comes. This is the doctrine, not only of the later Sophists, but of Lombard their Pythagoras (Sent. Lib. 2, Dist. 28), who, in comparison of them, may be called sound and sober. It was surely strange blindness, while he had Augustine so often in his mouth, not to see how cautiously he guarded against ascribing a single particle of praise to man because of good works. Above, when treating of free-will, we quoted some passages from him to this effect, and similar passages frequently occur in his writings (see in Psal. 104; Ep. 105), as when he forbids us ever to boast of our merits, because they themselves also are the gifts of God, and when he says that all our merits are only of grace, are not provided by our sufficiency, but are entirely the production of grace, &c. It is less strange that Lombard was blind to the light of Scripture, in which it is obvious that he had not been a very successful student. Still there cannot be a stronger declaration against him and his disciples than the words of the Apostles who, after interdicting all Christians from glorying, subjoins the reason why glorying is unlawful: "For we are his workmanship, created in Christ Jesus unto good works, which God has before ordained that we should walk in them" (Eph. 2:10). Seeing, then, that no good proceeds from us unless in so far as we are regenerated—and our regeneration is without exception wholly of God—there is no ground for claiming to ourselves one iota in good works. Lastly, while these men constantly inculcate good works, they, at the same time, train the conscience in such a way as to prevent it from venturing to confide that works will render God favorable and propitious. We, on the contrary, without any mention of merit, give singular comfort to believers when we teach them that in their works they please, and doubtless are accepted of God. Nay, here we even insist that no man shall attempt or enter upon any work without faith, that is, unless he previously have a firm conviction that it will please God.

8. Wherefore, let us never on any account allow ourselves to be drawn away one nail's breadth from that only foundation. After it is laid, wise architects build upon it rightly and in order. For whether there is need of doctrine or exhortation, they remind us that "for this purpose the Son of God was manifested, that he might destroy the works of the devil;" that "whosoever is born of God does not commit sin;" that "the time past of our life may suffice us to have wrought the will of the Gentiles;" that the elect of God are vessels of mercy, appointed "to honor," purged, "sanctified, and meet for the Master's use, and prepared unto every good work." The whole is expressed at once, when Christ thus describes his disciples, "If any man will come after me, let him deny himself, and take up his cross daily, and follow me." He who has denied himself has cut off the root of all evils so as no longer to seek his own; he who has taken up his cross has prepared himself for all meekness and endurance. The example of Christ includes this and all offices of piety and holiness. He obeyed his Father even unto death; his whole life was spent in doing the works of God; his whole soul was intent on the glory of his Father; he laid down his life for the brethren; he did good to his enemies, and prayed for them. And when there is need of comfort, it is admirably afforded in these words: "We are troubled on every side, yet not distressed; we are perplexed, but not in despair; persecuted but not forsaken; cast down, but not destroyed; always bearing about in the body the dying of the Lord Jesus, that the life also of Jesus might be made manifest in our body." " For if we be dead with him we shall also live with him; if we suffer, we shall also reign with him;" by means of "the fellowship of his sufferings, being made conformable unto his death;" the Father having predestinated us "to be conformed to the image of his Son, that he might be the first-born among many brethren." Hence it is, that "neither death, nor life, nor angels, nor principalities, nor powers, nor things present, nor things to come, nor height, nor depth, nor any other creature, shall be able to separate us from the love of God which is in Christ Jesus our Lord;" nay, rather all things will work together for our good. See how it is that we do not justify men before God by works, but say, that all who are of God are regenerated and made new creatures, so that they pass from the kingdom of sin into the kingdom of righteousness. In this way they make their calling sure, and, like trees, are judged by their fruits.

CHAPTER 16

REFUTATION OF THE CALUMNIES BY WHICH IT IS ATTEMPTED TO THROW ODIUM ON THIS DOCTRINE.

The divisions of this chapter are,—I. The calumnies of the Papists against the orthodox doctrine of Justification by Faith are reduced to two classes. The first class, with its consequences, refuted, sec. 1–3. II. The second class, which is dependent on the first, refuted in the last section.

Sections:

1. Calumnies of the Papists. 1. That we destroy good works, and give encouragement to sin. Refutation of the first calumny. 1. Character of those who censure us. 2. Justification by faith establishes the necessity of good works.

2. Refutation of a consequent of the former calumny—viz. that men are dissuaded from well-doing when we destroy merit. Two modes of refutation. First mode confirmed by many invincible arguments.

3. The Apostles make no mention of merit, when they exhort us to good works. On the contrary, excluding merit, they refer us entirely to the mercy of God. Another mode of refutation.

4. Refutation of the second calumny and of an inference from it—viz. that the obtaining righteousness is made too easy, when it is made to consist in the free remission of sins.

1. Our last sentence may refute the impudent calumny of certain ungodly men, who charge us, first, with destroying good works and leading men away from the study of them, when we say, that men are not justified, and do not merit salvation by works; and, secondly, with making the means of justification too easy, when we say that it consists in the free remission of sins, and thus alluring men to sin to which they are already too much inclined. These calumnies, I say, are sufficiently refuted by that one sentence; however, I will briefly reply to both. The allegation is that justification by faith destroys good works. I will not describe what kind of zealots for good works the persons are who thus charge us. We leave them as much liberty to bring the charge, as they take license to taint the whole world with the pollution of their lives. They pretend to lament that when faith is so highly extolled, works are deprived of their proper place. But what if they are rather ennobled and established? We dream not of a faith which is devoid of good works, nor of a justification which can exist without them: the only difference is, that while we acknowledge that faith and works are necessarily connected, we, however, place justification in faith, not in works. How this is done is easily explained, if we turn to Christ only, to whom our faith is directed and from whom it derives all its power. Why, then, are we justified by faith? Because by faith we apprehend the righteousness of Christ, which alone reconciles us to God. This faith, however, you cannot apprehend without at the same time apprehending sanctification; for Christ "is made unto us wisdom, and righteousness, and sanctification, and redemption" (1 Cor. 1:30). Christ, therefore, justifies no man without also sanctifying him. These blessings are conjoined by a perpetual and inseparable tie. Those whom he enlightens by his wisdom he redeems; whom he redeems he justifies; whom he justifies he sanctifies. But as the question relates only to justification and sanctification, to them let us confine ourselves. Though we distinguish between them, they are both inseparably comprehended in Christ. Would ye then obtain justification in Christ? You must previously possess Christ. But you cannot possess him without being made a partaker of his sanctification: for Christ cannot be divided. Since the Lord, therefore, does not grant us the enjoyment of these blessings without bestowing himself, he bestows both at once but never the one without the other. Thus it appears how true it is that we are justified not without, and yet not by works, since in the participation of Christ, by which we are justified, is contained not less sanctification than justification.

2. It is also most untrue that men's minds are withdrawn from the desire of well-doing when we deprive them of the idea of merit. Here, by the way, the reader must be told that those men absurdly infer merit from reward, as I will afterwards more clearly explain. They thus infer, because ignorant of the principle that God gives no less a display of his liberality when he assigns reward to works, than when he bestows the faculty of well-doing. This topic it will be better to defer to its own place. At present, let it be sufficient merely to advert to the weakness of their objection. This may be done in two ways. For, *first*, they are altogether in error when they say that, unless a hope of reward is held forth, no regard will be had to the right conduct of life. For if all that men do when they serve God is to look to the reward, and hire out or sell their labour to him, little is gained: he desires to be freely worshipped, freely loved: I say he approves the worshipper who, even if all hope of reward were cut off, would cease not to worship him. Moreover, when men are to be urged, there cannot be a stronger stimulus than

that derived from the end of our redemption and calling, such as the word of God employs when it says, that it were the height of impiety and ingratitude not to "love him who first loved us;" that by "the blood of Christ" our conscience is purged "from dead works to serve the living God;" that it were impious sacrilege in any one to count "the blood of the covenant, wherewith he was sanctified, an unholy thing;" that we have been "delivered out of the hands of our enemies," that we "might serve him without fear, in holiness and righteousness before him, all the days of our life;" that being "made free from sin," we "become the servants of righteousness;" "that our old man is crucified with him," in order that we might rise to newness of life. Again, "if ye then be risen with Christ (as becomes his members), seek those things which are above," living as pilgrims in the world, and aspiring to heaven, where our treasure is. "The grace of God has appeared to all men, bringing salvation, teaching us that, denying ungodliness and worldly lusts, we should live soberly, righteously, and godly in this present world; looking for that blessed hope, and the glorious appearing of the great God and our Savior Jesus Christ." "For God has not appointed us to wrath, but to obtain salvation through our Lord Jesus Christ." "Know ye not that ye are the temples of the Holy Spirit," which it were impious to profane? "Ye were sometimes darkness, but now are ye light in the Lord: walk as the children of light." "God has not called us unto uncleanness, but unto holiness." "For this is the will of God, even your sanctification, that ye should abstain" from all illicit desires: ours is a "holy calling," and we respond not to it except by purity of life. "Being then made free from sin, ye became the servants of righteousness." Can there be a stronger argument in eliciting us to charity than that of John? "If God so loved us, we ought also to love one another." "In this the children of God are manifest, and the children of the devil: whosoever does not righteousness is not of God, neither he that loveth not his brother." Similar is the argument of Paul, "Know ye not that your bodies are the members of Christ?" "For as the body is one, and has many members, and all the members of that one body being many, are one body, so also is Christ." Can there be a stronger incentive to holiness than when we are told by John, "Every man that has this hope in him purifieth himself; even as he is pure?" and by Paul, "Having, therefore, these promises, dearly beloved, cleanse yourselves from all filthiness of the flesh and spirit;" or when we hear our Savior hold forth himself as an example to us that we should follow his steps?

3. I have given these few passages merely as a specimen; for were I to go over them all, I should form a large volume. All the Apostles abound in exhortations, admonitions and rebukes, for the purpose of training the man of God to every good work, and that without any mention of merit. Nay, rather their chief exhortations are founded on the fact, that without any merit of ours, our salvation depends entirely on the mercy of God. Thus Paul, who during a whole Epistle had maintained that there was no hope of life for us save in the righteousness of Christ, when he comes to exhortations beseeches us by the mercy which God has bestowed upon us (Rom. 12:1). Andy indeed this one reason ought to have been sufficient, that God may be glorified in us. But if any are not so ardently desirous to promote the glory of God, still the remembrance of his kindness is most sufficient to incite them to do good (see Chrysost. Homily. in Genes). But those men, because, by introducing the idea of merit, they perhaps extract some forced and servile obedience of the Law, falsely allege, that as we do not adopt the same course, we have no means of exhorting to good works. As if God were well pleased with such services when he declares that he loves a cheerful giver, and forbids any thing to be given him grudgingly or of necessity (2 Cor. 9:7). I say not that I would reject that or omit any kind of exhortation which Scripture employs, its object being not to leave any method of animating us untried. For it states, that the recompense which God will render to every one is *according to his deeds*; but, first, I deny that that is the only, or, in many instances, the principal motive; and, secondly, I admit not that it is the motive with which we are to begin. Moreover, I maintain that it gives not the least countenance to those merits which these men are always preaching. This will afterwards be seen. Lastly, there is no use in this recompense, unless we have previously embraced the doctrine that we are justified solely by the merits of Christ as apprehended by faith, and not by any merit of works; because the study of piety can be fitly prosecuted only by those by whom this doctrine has been previously imbibed. This is beautifully intimated by the Psalmist when he thus addresses God, "There is forgiveness with thee, that thou mayest be feared" (Ps. 130:4). For he shows that the worship of God cannot exist without acknowledging his mercy, on which it is founded and established. This is specially deserving of notice, as showing us not only that the beginning of the due worship of God is confidence in his mercy; but that the fear of God (which Papists will have to be meritorious) cannot be entitled to the name of merit, for this reason, that it is founded on the pardon and remission of sins.

4. But the most futile calumny of all is, that men are invited to sin when we affirm that the pardon in which we hold that justification consists is gratuitous. Our doctrine is, that justification is a thing of such value, that it cannot be put into the balance with any good quality of ours; and, therefore, could never be obtained unless it were gratuitous: moreover, that it is gratuitous to us, but not also to Christ, who paid so dearly for it; namely his own most sacred blood, out of which there was no price of sufficient value to pay what was due to the justice of God. When men are thus taught they are reminded that it is owing to no merit of theirs that the shedding of that most sacred blood is not repeated every time they sin. Moreover, we say that our pollution is so great, that it can never be washed away save in the fountain of his pure blood. Must not those who are thus addressed conceive a greater horror of sin than if it were said to be wiped off by a sprinkling of good works? If they have any reverence for God, how can they, after being once purified, avoid shuddering at the thought of again wallowing in the mire, and as much as in them lies troubling and polluting the purity of this fountain? "I have washed my feet" (says the believing soul in the Song of Solomon, 5:3), "how shall I defile them?" It is now plain which of the two makes the forgiveness of sins of less value, and derogates from the dignity of justification. They pretend that God is appeased by their frivolous satisfactions; in other words, by mere dross. We maintain that the guilt of sin is too heinous to be so frivolously expiated; that the offense is too grave to be forgiven to such valueless satisfactions; and, therefore, that forgiveness is the prerogative of Christ's blood alone. They say that righteousness, wherever it is defective, is renewed and repaired by works of satisfaction. We think it too precious to be balanced by any compensation of works, and, therefore, in order to restore it, recourse must be had solely to the mercy of God. For the other points relating to the forgiveness of sins, see the following chapter.

CHAPTER 17

THE PROMISES OF THE LAW AND THE GOSPEL RECONCILED.

In the following chapter, the arguments of Sophists, who would destroy or impair the doctrine of Justification by Faith, are reduced to two classes. The former is general, the latter special, and contains some arguments peculiar to itself. I. The first class, which is general, and in a manner contains the foundation of all the arguments, draws an argument from the promises of the law. This is considered from sec. 1–3. II. The second class following from the former, and containing special proofs. An argument drawn from the history of Cornelius explained, sec. 4, 5. III. A full exposition of those passages of Scripture which represent God as showing mercy and favor to the cultivators of righteousness, sec. 6. IV. A third argument from the passages which distinguish good works by the name of righteousness, and declare that men are justified by them, sec. 7, 8. V. The adversaries of justification by faith placed in a dilemma. Their partial righteousness refuted, sec. 9, 10. VI. A fourth argument, setting the Apostle James in opposition to Paul, considered, sec. 11, 12. VII. Answer to a fifth argument, that, according to Paul, not the hearers but the doors of the law are justified, sec. 13. VIII. Consideration of a sixth argument, drawn from those passages in which believers boldly submit their righteousness to the judgment of God, and ask him to decide according to it, sec. 14. IX. Examination of the last argument, drawn from passages which ascribe righteousness and life to the ways of believers, sec. 15.

Sections:

1. Brief summary of Chapters 15 and 16. Why justification is denied to works. Argument of opponents founded on the promises of the law. The substance of this argument. Answer. Those who would be justified before God must be exempted from the power of the law. How this is done.

2. Confirmation of the answer ab impossibili, and from the testimony of an Apostle and of David.

3. Answer to the objection, by showing why these promises were given. Refutation of the sophistical distinction between the intrinsic value of works, and their value er parts.

4. Argument from the history of Cornelius. Answer, by distinguishing between two kinds of acceptance. Former kind. Sophistical objection refuted.

5. Latter kind. Plain from this distinction that Cornelius was accepted freely before his good works could be accepted. Similar explanations to be given of the passage in which God is represented as merciful and propitious to the cultivators of righteousness.

6. Exposition of these passages. Necessary to observe whether the promise is legal or evangelical. The legal

promise always made under the condition that we "do," the evangelical under the condition that we "believe."

7. Argument from the passages which distinguish good works by the name of righteousness, and declare that man is justified by them. Answer to the former part of the argument respecting the name. Why the works of the saints called works of righteousness. Distinction to be observed.

8. Answer to the second part of the argument—viz. that man is justified by works. Works of no avail by themselves; we are justified by faith only. This kind of righteousness defined. Whence the value set on good works.

9. Answer confirmed and fortified by a dilemma.

10. In what sense the partial imperfect righteousness of believers accepted. Conclusion of the refutation.

11. Argument founded on the Epistle of James. First answer. One Apostle cannot be opposed to another. Second answer. Third answer, from the scope of James. A double paralogism in the term Faith. In James the faith said not to justify is a mere empty opinion; in Paul it is the instrument by which we apprehend Christ our righteousness.

12. Another paralogism on the word justify. Paul speaks of the cause, James of the effects, of justification. Sum of the discussion.

13. Argument founded on Rom. 2:13. Answer, explaining the Apostles meaning. Another argument, containing a reduction ad impossibili. Why Paul used the argument.

14. An argument founded on the passages in which believers confidently appeal to their righteousness. Answer, founded on a consideration of two circumstances. 1. They refer only to a special cause. 2. They claim righteousness in comparison with the wicked.

15. Last argument from those passages which ascribe righteousness and life to the ways of believers. Answer. This proceeds from the paternal kindness of God. What meant by the perfection of saints.

1. Let us now consider the other arguments which Satan by his satellites invents to destroy or impair the doctrine of Justification by Faith. I think we have already put it out of the power of our calumniators to treat us as if we were the enemies of good works—justification being denied to works not in order that no good works may be done or that those which are done may be denied to be good; but only that we may not trust or glory in them, or ascribe salvation to them. Our only confidence and boasting, our only anchor of salvation is, that Christ the Son of God is ours, and that we are in him sons of God and heirs of the heavenly kingdom, being called, not by our worth, but the kindness of God, to the hope of eternal blessedness. But since, as has been said, they assail us with other engines, let us now proceed to demolish them also. First, they recur to the legal promises which the Lord proclaimed to the observers of the law, and they ask us whether we hold them to be null or effectual. Since it were absurd and ridiculous to say they are null, they take it for granted that they have some efficacy. Hence they infer that we are not justified by faith only. For the Lord thus speaks: "Wherefore it shall come to pass, if ye hearken to these judgments, and keep and do them, that the Lord thy God shall keep unto thee the covenant and the mercy which he sware unto thy fathers; and he will love thee, and bless thee and multiply thee" (Deut. 7:12, 13). Again, "If ye thoroughly amend your ways and your doings; if ye thoroughly execute judgment between a man and his neighbor; if ye oppress not the stranger, the fatherless, and the widow, and shed not innocent blood in this place, neither walk after other gods to your hurt: then will I cause you to dwell in this place, in the land that I gave to your fathers, for ever and ever" (Jer. 7:5–7). It were to no purpose to quote a thousand similar passages, which, as they are not different in meaning, are to be explained on the same principle. In substance, Moses declares that in the law is set down "a blessing and a curse," life and death (Deut. 11:26); and hence they argue, either that that blessing is become inactive and unfruitful, or that justification is not by faith only. We have already shown, that if we cleave to the law we are devoid of every blessing, and have nothing but the curse denounced on all transgressors. The Lord does not promise any thing except to the perfect observers of the law; and none such are any where to be found. The results therefore is that the whole human race is convicted by the law, and exposed to the wrath and curse of God: to be saved from this they must escape from the power of the law, and be as it were brought out of bondage into freedom,—not that carnal freedom which indisposes us for the observance of the law, tends to licentiousness, and allows our passions to wanton unrestrained with loosened reins; but that spiritual freedom which consoles and raises up the alarmed and smitten conscience, proclaiming its freedom from the curse and condemnation under which it was formerly held bound. This freedom from subjection to the law, this manumission, if I may so express it, we obtain when by faith we apprehend the

mercy of God in Christ, and are thereby assured of the pardon of sins, with a consciousness of which the law stung and tortured us.

2. For this reason, the promises offered in the law would all be null and ineffectual, did not God in his goodness send the gospel to our aid, since the condition on which they depend, and under which only they are to be performed—viz. the fulfillment of the law, will never be accomplished. Still, however the aid which the Lord gives consists not in leaving part of justification to be obtained by works, and in supplying part out of his indulgence, but in giving us Christ as in himself alone the fulfillment of righteousness. For the Apostle, after premising that he and the other Jews, aware that "a man is not justified by the works of the law," had "believed in Jesus Christ," adds as the reason, not that they might be assisted to make up the sum of righteousness by faith in Christ, but that they "might be justified by the faith of Christ, and not by the works of the law" (Gal. 2:16). If believers withdraw from the law to faith, that in the latter they may find the justification which they see is not in the former, they certainly disclaim justification by the law. Therefore, whose will, let him amplify the rewards which are said to await the observer of the law, provided he at the same time understand, that owing to our depravity, we derive no benefit from them until we have obtained another righteousness by faith. Thus David after making mention of the reward which the Lord has prepared for his servants (Ps. 25 almost throughout), immediately descends to an acknowledgment of sins, by which the reward is made void. In Psalm 19, also, he loudly extols the benefits of the law; but immediately exclaims, "Who can understand his errors? cleanse thou me from secret faults" (Ps. 19:12). This passage perfectly accords with the former, when, after saying, "the paths of the Lord are mercy and truth unto such as keep his covenant and his testimonies," he adds, "For thy name's sake, O Lord, pardon mine iniquity: for it is great" (Ps. 25:10, 11). Thus, too, we ought to acknowledge that the favor of God is offered to us in the law, provided by our works we can deserve it; but that it never actually reaches us through any such desert.

3. What then? Were the promises given that they might vanish away without fruit? I lately declared that this is not my opinion. I say, indeed, that their efficacy does not extend to us so long as they have respect to the merit of works, and, therefore, that, considered in themselves, they are in some sense abolished. Hence the Apostle shows, that the celebrated promise, "Ye shall therefore keep my statutes and my judgments: which if a man do, he shall live in them" (Lev. 18:5; Ezek. 20:10), will, if we stop at it, be of no avail, and will profit us not a whit more than if it were not given, being inaccessible even to the holiest servants of God, who are all far from fulfilling the law, being encompassed with many infirmities. But when the gospel promises are substituted, promises which announce the free pardon of sins, the result is not only that our persons are accepted of God, but his favor also is shown to our works, and that not only in respect that the Lord is pleased with them, but also because he visits them with the blessings which were due by agreement to the observance of his law. I admit, therefore, that the works of the faithful are rewarded with the promises which God gave in his law to the cultivators of righteousness and holiness; but in this reward we should always attend to the cause which procures favor to works. This cause, then, appears to be threefold. First, God turning his eye away from the works of his servants which merit reproach more than praise, embraces them in Christ, and by the intervention of faith alone reconciles them to himself without the aid of works. Secondly the works not being estimated by their own worth, he, by his fatherly kindness and indulgence, honors so far as to give them some degree of value. Thirdly, he extends his pardon to them, not imputing the imperfection by which they are all polluted, and would deserve to be regarded as vices rather than virtues. Hence it appears how much Sophists were deluded in thinking they admirably escaped all absurdities when they said, that works are able to merit salvation, not from their intrinsic worth, but according to agreement, the Lord having, in his liberality, set this high value upon them. But, meanwhile, they observed not how far the works which they insisted on regarding as meritorious must be from fulfilling the condition of the promises, were they not preceded by a justification founded on faith alone, and on forgiveness of sins—a forgiveness necessary to cleanse even good works from their stains. Accordingly, of the three causes of divine liberality to which it is owing that good works are accepted, they attended only to one: the other two, though the principal causes, they suppressed.

4. They quote the saying of Peter as given by Luke in the Acts, "Of a truth I perceive that God is no respecter of persons: but in every nation he that feareth him, and worketh righteousness, is accepted with him" (Acts 10:34, 35). And hence they infer, as a thing which seems to them beyond a doubt, that if man by right conduct procures the favor of God, his obtaining salvation is not

entirely the gift of God. Nay, that when God in his mercy assists the sinner, he is inclined to mercy by works. There is no way of reconciling the passages of Scripture, unless you observe that man's acceptance with God is twofold. As man is by nature, God finds nothing in him which can incline him to mercy, except merely big wretchedness. If it is clear then that man, when God first interposes for him, is naked and destitute of all good, and, on the other hand, loaded and filled with all kinds of evil,—for what quality, pray, shall we say that he is worthy of the heavenly kingdom? Where God thus clearly displays free mercy, have done with that empty imagination of merit. Another passage in the same book—viz. where Cornelius hears from the lips of an angel, "Thy prayer and thine alms are come up for a memorial before God" (Acts 10:4), is miserably wrested to prove that man is prepared by the study of good works to receive the favor of God. Cornelius being endued with true wisdom, in other words, with the fear of God, must have been enlightened by the Spirit of wisdom, and being an observer of righteousness, must have been sanctified by the same Spirit; righteousness being, as the Apostle testifies, one of the most certain fruits of the Spirit (Gal. 5:5). Therefore, all those qualities by which he is said to have pleased God he owed to divine grace: so far was he from preparing himself by his own strength to receive it. Indeed, not a syllable of Scripture can be produced which does not accord with the doctrine, that the only reason why God receives man into his favor is, because he sees that he is in every respect lost when left to himself; lost, if he does not display his mercy in delivering him. We now see that in thus accepting, God looks not to the righteousness of the individual, but merely manifests the divine goodness towards miserable sinners, who are altogether undeserving of this great mercy.

5. But after the Lord has withdrawn the sinner from the abyss of perdition, and set him apart for himself by means of adoption, having begotten him again and formed him to newness of life, he embraces him as a new creature, and bestows the gifts of his Spirit. This is the acceptance to which Peter refers, and by which believers after their calling are approved by God even in respect of works; for the Lord cannot but love and delight in the good qualities which he produces in them by means of his Spirit. But we must always bear in mind, that the only way in which men are accepted of God in respect of works is, that whatever good works he has conferred upon those whom he admits to favor, he by an increase of liberality honors with his acceptance. For whence their good works, but just that the Lord having chosen them as vessels of honor, is pleased to adorn them with true purity? And how are their actions deemed good as if there was no deficiency in them, but just that their merciful Father indulgently pardons the spots and blemishes which adhere to them? In one word, the only meaning of acceptance in this passage is, that God accepts and takes pleasure in his children, in whom he sees the traces and lineaments of his own countenance. We have else here said, that regeneration is a renewal of the divine image in us. Since God, therefore, whenever he beholds his own face, justly loves it and holds it in honor, the life of believers, when formed to holiness and justice, is said, not without cause, to be pleasing to him. But because believers, while encompassed with mortal flesh, are still sinners, and their good works only begun savor of the corruption of the flesh, God cannot be propitious either to their persons or their works, unless he embraces them more in Christ than in themselves. In this way are we to understand the passages in which God declares that he is clement and merciful to the cultivators of righteousness. Moses said to the Israelites, "Know, therefore, that the Lord thy God, he is God, the faithful God, which keepeth covenant and mercy with them that love him and keep his commandments, to a thousand generations." These words afterwards became a common form of expression among the people. Thus Solomon in his prayer at the dedication says, "Lord God of Israel, there is no God like thee, in heaven above, or on earth beneath, who keepest covenant and mercy with thy servants that walk before thee with all their heart" (1 Kings 8:23). The same words are repeated by Nehemiah (Neh. 1:5). As the Lord in all covenants of mercy stipulates on his part for integrity and holiness of life in his servants (Deut. 29:18), lest his goodness might be held in derision, or any one, puffed up with exultation in it, might speak flatteringly to his soul while walking in the depravity of his heart, so he is pleased that in this way those whom he admits to communion in the covenant should be kept to their duty. Still, however, the covenant was gratuitous at first, and such it ever remains. Accordingly, while David declares, "according to the cleanness of my hands has he recompensed me," yet does he not omit the fountain to which I have referred; "he delivered me, because he delighted in me" (2 Sam. 22:20, 21). In commending the goodness of his cause, he derogates in no respect from the free mercy which takes precedence of all the gifts of which it is the origin.

6. Here, by the way, it is of importance to observe how those forms of expression differ from legal promises. By

legal promises, I mean not those which lie scattered in the books of Moses (for there many Evangelical promises occur), but those which properly belong to the legal dispensation. All such promises, by whatever name they may be called, are made under the condition that the reward is to be paid on the things commanded being done. But when it is said that the Lord keeps a covenant of mercy with those who love him, the words rather demonstrate what kind of servants those are who have sincerely entered into the covenant, than express the reason why the Lord blesses them. The nature of the demonstration is this: As the end for which God bestows upon us the gift of eternal life is, that he may be loved, feared, and worshipped by us, so the end of all the promises of mercy contained in Scripture justly is that we may reverence and serve their author. Therefore, whenever we hear that he does good to those that observe his law, let us remember that the sons of God are designated by the duty which they ought perpetually to observe, that his reason for adopting us is, that we may reverence him as a father. Hence, if we would not deprive ourselves of the privilege of adoption, we must always strive in the direction of our calling. On the other hand, however, let us remember, that the completion of the Divine mercy depends not on the works of believers, but that God himself fulfill the promise of salvation to those who by right conduct correspond to their calling, because he recognizes the true badges of sons in those only who are directed to good by his Spirit. To this we may refer what is said of the members of the Church, "Lord, who shall abide in thy tabernacle? who shall dwell in thy holy hill? He that walketh uprightly, and worketh righteousness, and speaketh the truth in his heart," &c. (Ps. 15:1, 2). Again, in Isaiah, "Who among us shall dwell with the devouring fire? who among us shall dwell with everlasting burnings? He that walketh righteously," &c. (Isa. 33:14, 15). For the thing described is not the strength with which believers can stand before the Lord, but the manner in which our most merciful Father introduces them into his fellowship, and defends and confirms them therein. For as he detests sin and loves righteousness, so those whom he unites to himself he purifies by his Spirit, that he may render them conformable to himself and to his kingdom. Therefore, if it be asked, What is the first cause which gives the saints free access to the kingdom of God, and a firm and permanent footing in it? the answer is easy. The Lord in his mercy once adopted and ever defends them. But if the question relates to the manner, we must descend to regeneration, and the fruits of it, as enumerated in the fifteenth Psalm.

7. There seems much more difficulty in those passages which distinguish good works by the name of righteousness, and declare that man is justified by them. The passages of the former class are very numerous, as when the observance of the commandments is termed justification or righteousness. Of the other classes we have a description in the words of Moses, "It shall be our righteousness, if we observe to do all these commandments" (Deut. 6:25). But if you object, that it is a legal promise, which, having an impossible condition annexed to it, proves nothing, there are other passages to which the same answer cannot be made; for instance, "If the man be poor," "thou shalt deliver him the pledge again when the sun goes down:" "and it shall be righteousness unto thee before the Lord thy God" (Deut. 24:13). Likewise the words of the prophet, "Then stood up Phinehas, and executed judgment: and so the plague was stayed. And that was counted unto him for righteousness unto all generations for evermore" (Psal. 106:30, 31). Accordingly the Pharisees of our day think they have here full scope for exultation. For, as we say, that when justification by faith is established, justification by works falls; they argue on the same principle, If there is a justification by works, it is false to say that we are justified by faith only. When I grant that the precepts of the law are termed righteousness, I do nothing strange: for they are so in reality. I must, however, inform the reader, that the Hebrew word *yqj* has been rendered by the Septuagint, not very appropriately, δικαιώματα, *justifications*, instead of *edicts*. But I readily give up any dispute as to the word. Nor do I deny that the Law of God contains a perfect righteousness. For although we are debtors to do all the things which it enjoins, and, therefore, even after a full obedience, are unprofitable servants; yet, as the Lord has deigned to give it the name of righteousness, it is not ours to take from it what he has given. We readily admit, therefore, that the perfect obedience of the law is righteousness, and the observance of any precept a part of righteousness, the whole substance of righteousness being contained in the remaining parts. But we deny that any such righteousness ever exists. Hence we discard the righteousness of the law, not as being in itself maimed and defective, but because of the weakness of our flesh it nowhere appears. But then Scripture does not merely call the precepts of the law righteousness, it also gives this name to the works of the saints: as when it states that Zacharias and his wife "were both righteous before God, walking in all the commandments and ordinances of the Lord blameless" (Luke 1:6). Surely when it thus speaks, it estimates works more

according to the nature of the law than their own proper character. And here, again, I must repeat the observation which I lately made, that the law is not to be ascertained from a careless translation of the Greek interpreter. Still, as Luke chose not to make any change on the received version, I will not contend for this. The things contained in the law God enjoined upon man for righteousness but that righteousness we attain not unless by observing the whole law: every transgression whatever destroys it. While, therefore, the law commands nothing but righteousness, if we look to itself, every one of its precepts is righteousness: if we look to the men by whom they are performed, being transgressors in many things, they by no means merit the praise of righteousness for one work, and that a work which, through the imperfection adhering to it, is always in some respect vicious.

8. I come to the second class (sec. 1, 7, ad init.), in which the chief difficulty lies. Paul finds nothing stronger to prove justification by faith than that which is written of Abraham, he "believed God, and it was counted unto him for righteousness" (Rom. 4:3; Gal. 3:6). Therefore, when it is said that the achievement of Phinehas "was counted unto him for righteousness" (Psal. 106:30, 31), we may argue that what Paul contends for respecting faith applies also to works. Our opponents, accordingly, as if the point were proved, set it down that though we are not justified without faith, it is not by faith only; that our justification is completed by works. Here I beseech believers, as they know that the true standard of righteousness must be derived from Scripture alone, to consider with me seriously and religiously, how Scripture can be fairly reconciled with that view. Paul, knowing that justification by faith was the refuge of those who wanted righteousness of their own, confidently infers, that all who are justified by faith are excluded from the righteousness of works. But as it is clear that this justification is common to all believers, he with equal confidence infers that no man is justified by works; nay, more, that justification is without any help from works. But it is one thing to determine what power works have in themselves, and another to determine what place they are to hold after justification by faith has been established. If a price is to be put upon works according to their own worth, we hold that they are unfit to appear in the presence of God: that man, accordingly, has no works in which he can glory before God, and that hence, deprived of all aid from works, he is justified by faith alone. Justification, moreover, we thus define: The sinner being admitted into communion with Christ is, for his sake, reconciled to God; when purged by his blood he obtains the remission of sins, and clothed with righteousness, just as if it were his own, stands secure before the judgment-seat of heaven. Forgiveness of sins being previously given, the good works which follow have a value different from their merit, because whatever is imperfect in them is covered by the perfection of Christ, and all their blemishes and pollutions are wiped away by his purity, so as never to come under the cognizance of the divine tribunal. The guilt of all transgressions, by which men are prevented from offering God an acceptable service, being thus effaced, and the imperfection which is wont to sully even good works being buried, the good works which are done by believers are deemed righteous, or; which is the same thing, are imputed for righteousness.

9. Now, should any one state this to me as an objection to justification by faith, I would first ask him, Whether a man is deemed righteous for one holy work or two, while in all the other acts of his life lie is a transgressor of the law? This were, indeed, more than absurd. I would next ask, Whether he is deemed righteous on account of many good works if he is guilty of transgression in some one part? Even this he will not venture to maintain in opposition to the authority of the law, which pronounces, "Cursed be he that confirmeth not all the words of this law to do them" (Deut. 27:26). I would go still farther and ask, Whether there be any work which may not justly be convicted of impurity or imperfection? How, then, will it appear to that eye before which even the heavens are not clean, and angels are chargeable with folly? (Job 4:18). Thus he will be forced to confess that no good work exists that is not defiled, both by contrary transgression and also by its own corruption, so that it cannot be honored as righteousness. But if it is certainly owing to justification by faith that works, otherwise impure, unclean, defective, unworthy of the sight, not to say of the love of God, are imputed for righteousness, why do they by boasting of this imputation aim at the destruction of that justification, but for which the boast were vain? Are they desirous of having a viper's birth? To this their ungodly language tends. They cannot deny that justification by faith is the beginning, the foundation, the cause, the subject, the substance, of works of righteousness, and yet they conclude that justification is not by faith, because good works are counted for righteousness. Let us have done then with this frivolity, and confess the fact as it stands; if any righteousness which works are supposed to possess depends on justification by faith, this doctrine is not only not impaired, but on the contrary confirmed, its power being thereby more brightly dis-

played. Nor let us suppose, that after free justification works are commended, as if they afterwards succeeded to the office of justifying, or shared the office with faith. For did not justification by faith always remain entire, the impurity of works would be disclosed. There is nothing absurd in the doctrine, that though man is justified by faith, he is himself not only not righteous, but the righteousness attributed to his works is beyond their own deserts.

10. In this way we can admit not only that there is a partial righteousness in works (as our adversaries maintain), but that they are approved by God as if they were absolutely perfect. If we remember on what foundation this is rested, every difficulty will be solved. The first time when a work begins to be acceptable is when it is received with pardon. And whence pardon, but just because God looks upon us and all that belongs to us as in Christ? Therefore, as we ourselves when ingrafted into Christ appear righteous before God, because our iniquities are covered with his innocence; so our works are, and are deemed righteous, because every thing otherwise defective in them being buried by the purity of Christ is not imputed. Thus we may justly say, that not only ourselves, but our works also, are justified by faith alone. Now, if that righteousness of works, whatever it be, depends on faith and free justification, and is produced by it, it ought to be included under it and, so to speak, made subordinate to it, as the effect to its cause; so far is it from being entitled to be set up to impair or destroy the doctrine of justification. Thus Paul, to prove that our blessedness depends not on our works, but on the mercy of God, makes special use of the words of David, "Blessed is he whose transgression is forgiven, whose sin is covered;" "Blessed is the man unto whom the Lord imputeth not iniquity." Should any one here obtrude the numberless passages in which blessedness seems to be attributed to works, as, "Blessed is the man that feareth the Lord;" "He that has mercy on the poor, happy is he;" "Blessed is the man that walketh not in the counsel of the ungodly," and "that endureth temptation;" "Blessed are they that keep judgment," that are "pure in heart," "meek," "merciful," &c., they cannot make out that Paul's doctrine is not true. For seeing that the qualities thus extolled never all so exist in man as to obtain for him the approbation of God, it follows, that man is always miserable until he is exempted from misery by the pardon of his sins. Since, then, all the kinds of blessedness extolled in the Scripture are vain so that man derives no benefit from them until he obtains blessedness by the forgiveness of sins, a for- giveness which makes way for them, it follows that this is not only the chief and highest, but the only blessedness, unless you are prepared to maintain that it is impaired by things which owe their entire existence to it. There is much less to trouble us in the name of *righteous* which is usually given to believers. I admit that they are so called from the holiness of their lives, but as they rather exert themselves in the study of righteousness than fulfill righteousness itself, any degree of it which they possess must yield to justification by faith, to which it is owing that it is what it is.

11. But they say that we have a still more serious business with James, who in express terms opposes us. For he asks, "Was not Abraham our father justified by works?" and adds "You see then how that by works a man is justified, and not by faith only" (James 2:21,24). What then? Will they engage Paul in a quarrel with James? If they hold James to be a servant of Christ, his sentiments must be understood as not dissenting from Christ speaking by the mouth of Paul. By the mouth of Paul the Spirit declares that Abraham obtained justification by faith, not by works; we also teach that all are justified by faith without the works of the law. By James the same Spirit declares that both Abraham's justification and ours consists of works, and not of faith only. It is certain that the Spirit cannot be at variance with himself. Where, then, will be the agreement? It is enough for our opponents, provided they can tear up that justification by faith which we regard as fixed by the deepest roots: to restore peace to the conscience is to them a matter of no great concern. Hence you may see, that though they indeed carp at the doctrine of justification by faith, they meanwhile point out no goal of righteousness at which the conscience may rest. Let them triumph then as they will, so long as the only victory they can boast of is, that they have deprived righteousness of all its certainty. This miserable victory they will indeed obtain when the light of truth is extinguished, and the Lord permits them to darken it with their lies. But wherever the truth of God stands they cannot prevail. I deny, then, that the passage of James which they are constantly holding up before us as if it were the shield of Achilles, gives them the slightest countenance. To make this plain, let us first attend to the scope of the Apostle, and then show wherein their hallucination consists. As at that time (and the evil has existed in the Church ever since) there were many who, while they gave manifest proof of their infidelity, by neglecting and omitting all the works peculiar to believers, ceased not falsely to glory in the name of faith, James here dis-

sipates their vain confidence. His intention therefore is, not to derogate in any degree from the power of true faith, but to show how absurdly these triflers laid claim only to the empty name, and resting satisfied with it, felt secure in unrestrained indulgence in vice. This state of matters being understood, it will be easy to see where the error of our opponents lies. They fall into a double paralogism, the one in the term *faith*, the other in the term *justifying*. The Apostle, in giving the name of *faith* to an empty opinion altogether differing from true faith, makes a concession which derogates in no respect from his case. This he demonstrates at the outset by the words, "What does it profit, my brethren, though a man say he has faith, and have not works?" (James 2:14). He says not, "If a man have faith without works," but "if he say that he has." This becomes still clearer when a little after he derides this faith as worse than that of devils, and at last when he calls it "dead." You may easily ascertain his meaning by the explanation, "Thou believest that there is one God." Surely if all which is contained in that faith is a belief in the existence of God, there is no wonder that it does not justify. The denial of such a power to it cannot be supposed to derogate in any degree from Christian faith, which is of a very different description. For how does true faith justify unless by uniting us to Christ, so that being made one with him, we may be admitted to a participation in his righteousness? It does not justify because it forms an idea of the divine existence, but because it reclines with confidence on the divine mercy.

12. We have not made good our point until we dispose of the other paralogism: since James places a part of justification in works. If you would make James consistent with the other Scriptures and with himself, you must give the word *justify*, as used by him, a different meaning from what it has with Paul. In the sense of Paul we are said to be justified when the remembrance of our unrighteousness is obliterated and we are counted righteous. Had James had the same meaning it would have been absurd for him to quote the words of Moses, "Abraham believed God," &c. The context runs thus: "Was not Abraham our father justified by works when he had offered Isaac his son upon the altar? Seest thou how faith wrought with his works, and by works was faith made perfect? And the Scripture was fulfilled which saith, Abraham believed God, and it was imputed unto him for righteousness." If it is absurd to say that the effect was prior to its cause, either Moses falsely declares in that passage that Abraham's faith was imputed for righteousness or Abraham, by his obedience in offering up Isaac, did not merit righteousness. Before the existence of Ishmael, who was a grown youth at the birth of Isaac, Abraham was justified by his faith. How thee can we say that he obtained justification by an obedience which followed long after? Wherefore, either James erroneously inverts the proper order (this it were impious to suppose), or he meant not to say that he was justified, as if he deserved to be deemed just. What then? It appears certain that he is speaking of the manifestation, not of the imputation of righteousness, as if he had said, Those who are justified by true faith prove their justification by obedience and good works, not by a bare and imaginary semblance of faith. In one word, he is not discussing the mode of justification, but requiring that the justification of believers shall be operative. And as Paul contends that men are justified without the aid of works, so James will not allow any to be regarded as justified who are destitute of good works. Due attention to the scope will thus disentangle every doubt; for the error of our opponents lies chiefly in this, that they think James is defining the mode of justification, whereas his only object is to destroy the depraved security of those who vainly pretended faith as an excuse for their contempt of good works. Therefore, let them twist the words of James as they may, they will never extract out of them more than the two propositions: That an empty phantom of faith does not justify, and that the believer, not contented with such an imagination, manifests his justification by good works.

13. They gain nothing by quoting from Paul to the same effect, that "not the hearers of the law are just before God, but the doers of the law shall be justified" (Rom. 2:13). I am unwilling to evade the difficulty by the solution of Ambrose, that Paul spoke thus because faith in Christ is the fulfillment of the law. This I regard as a mere subterfuge, and one too for which there is no occasion, as the explanation is perfectly obvious. The Apostle's object is to suppress the absurd confidence of the Jews who gave out that they alone had a knowledge of the law, though at the very time they where its greatest despisers. That they might not plume themselves so much on a bare acquaintance with the law, he reminds them that when justification is sought by the law, the thing required is not the knowledge but the observance of it. We certainly mean not to dispute that the righteousness of the law consists in works, and not only so, but that justification consists in the dignity and merits of works. But this proves not that we are justified by works unless they can produce some one who has fulfilled the law. That Paul had no other meaning is abundantly obvious from the context. After charging Jews and Gentiles in common with unrigh-

teousness, he descends to particulars and says, that "as many as have sinned without law shall also perish without law," referring to the Gentiles, and that "as many as have sinned in the law shall be judged by the law," referring to the Jews. Moreover, as they, winking at their transgressions, boasted merely of the law, he adds most appropriately, that the law was passed with the view of justifying not those who only heard it, but those only who obeyed it; as if he had said, Do you seek righteousness in the law? do not bring forward the mere hearing of it, which is in itself of little weight, but bring works by which you may show that the law has not been given to you in vain. Since in these they were all deficient, it followed that they had no ground of boasting in the law. Paul's meaning, therefore, rather leads to an opposite argument. The righteousness of the law consists in the perfection of works; but no man can boast of fulfilling the law by works, and, therefore, there is no righteousness by the law.

14. They now betake themselves to those passages in which believers boldly submit their righteousness to the judgment of God, and wish to be judged accordingly; as in the following passages: "Judge me, O Lord, according to my righteousness, and according to mine integrity that is in me." Again, "Hear the right, O Lord;" "Thou hast proved mine heart; thou hast visited me in the night; thou hast tried me, and shalt find nothing." Again "The Lord regarded me according to my righteousness; according to the cleanness of my hands has he recompensed me. For I have kept the ways of the Lord, and have not wickedly departed from my God." "I was also upright before him, and I kept myself from mine iniquity." Again, "Judge me, O Lord; for I have walked in mine integrity;" "I have not sat with vain persons; neither will I go in with dissemblers;" "Gather not my soul with sinners, nor my life with bloody men; in whose hands is mischief, and their right hand is full of bribes. But as for me, I will walk in mine integrity." I have already spoken of the confidence which the saints seem to derive simply from works. The passages now quoted will not occasion much difficulty, if we attend to their περίστασις, their connection, or (as it is commonly called) special circumstances. These are of two kinds; for those who use them have no wish that their whole life should be brought to trial, so that they may be acquitted or condemned according to its tenor; all they wish is, that a decision should be given on the particular case; and even here the righteousness which they claim is not with reference to the divine perfection, but only by comparison with the wicked and profane. When the question relates to justification, the thing required is not that the individual have a good ground of acquittal in regard to some particular matter, but that his whole life be in accordance with righteousness. But when the saints implore the divine justice in vindication of their innocence, they do not present themselves as free from fault, and in every respect blameless but while placing their confidence of salvation in the divine goodness only, and trusting that he will vindicate his poor when they are afflicted contrary to justice and equity, they truly commit to him the cause in which the innocent are oppressed. And when they sist themselves with their adversaries at the tribunal of God, they pretend not to an innocence corresponding to the divine purity were inquiry strictly made, but knowing that in comparison of the malice, dishonesty, craft, and iniquity of their enemies, their sincerity justice, simplicity, and purity, are ascertained and approved by God, they dread not to call upon him to judge between them. Thus when David said to Saul, "The Lord render to every man his righteousness and his faithfulness" (1 Sam. 26:23), he meant not that the Lord should examine and reward every one according to his deserts, but he took the Lord to witness how great his innocence was in comparison of Saul's injustice. Paul, too, when he indulges in the boast, "Our rejoicing is this, the testimony of our conscience, that in simplicity and godly sincerity, not with fleshly wisdom, but by the grace of God, we have had our conversation in the world, and more abundantly to you-ward" (2 Cor. 1:12), means not to call for the scrutiny of God, but compelled by the calumnies of the wicked he appeals, in contradiction of all their slanders, to his faith and probity, which he knew that God had indulgently accepted. For we see how he elsewhere says, "I know nothing by myself; yet am I not hereby justified" (1 Cor. 4:4); in other words, he was aware that the divine judgment far transcended the blind estimate of man. Therefore, however believers may, in defending their integrity against the hypocrisy of the ungodly, appeal to God as their witness and judge, still when the question is with God alone, they all with one mouth exclaim, "If thou, Lord, should mark iniquities, O Lord, who shall stand?" Again, "Enter not into judgment with thy servant; for in thy sight shall no man living be justified." Distrusting their own words, they gladly exclaim, "Thy loving-kindness is better than life" (Ps. 130:3; 143:2; 63:3).

15. There are other passages not unlike those quoted above, at which some may still demur. Solomon says, "The just man walketh in his integrity" (Prov. 20:7). Again, "In the way of righteousness is life; and in the

pathway thereof there is no death" (Prov. 12:28). For this reason Ezekiel says, He that "has walked in my statutes, and has kept my judgments, to deal truly; he is just, he shall surely live" (Ezek. 18:9, 21; 23:15). None of these declarations do we deny or obscure. But let one of the sons of Adam come forward with such integrity. If there is none, they must perish from the presence of God, or retake themselves to the asylum of mercy. Still we deny not that the integrity of believers, though partial and imperfect, is a step to immortality. How so, but just that the works of those whom the Lord has assumed into the covenant of grace, he tries not by their merit, but embraces with paternal indulgence. By this we understand not with the Schoolmen, that works derive their value from accepting grace. For their meaning is, that works otherwise unfit to obtain salvation in terms of law, are made fit for such a purpose by the divine acceptance. On the other hand, I maintain that these works being sullied both by other transgressions and by their own deficiencies, have no other value than this, that the Lord indulgently pardons them; in other words, that the righteousness which he bestows on man is gratuitous. Here they unseasonably obtrude those passages in which the Apostle prays for all perfection to believers, "To the end he may establish your hearts unblamable in holiness before God, even our Father" (1 Thess. 3:13, and elsewhere). These words were strongly urged by the Celestines of old, in maintaining the perfection of holiness in the present life. To this we deem it sufficient briefly to reply with Augustine, that the goal to which all the pious ought to aspire is, to appear in the presence of God without spot and blemish; but as the course of the present life is at best nothing more than progress, we shall never reach the goal until we have laid aside the body of sin, and been completely united to the Lord. If any one choose to give the name of perfection to the saints, I shall not obstinately quarrel with him, provided he defines this perfection in the words of Augustine, "When we speak of the perfect virtue of the saints, part of this perfection consists in the recognition of our imperfection both in truth and in humility" (August. ad Bonif. lib. 3, c. 7).

CHAPTER 18

THE RIGHTEOUSNESS OF WORKS IMPROPERLY INFERRED FROM REWARDS.

There are three divisions in this chapter,—I. A solution of two general objections which are urged in support of justification by works. First, That God will render to every one according to his works, sec. 1. Second, That the reward of works is called eternal, sec. 2–6. II. Answer to other special objections derived from the former, and a perversion of passages of Scripture, sec. 6–9. III. Refutation of the sophism that faith itself is called a work, and, therefore, justification by it is by works, sec. 10.

Sections:

1. Two general objections. The former solved and explained. What meant by the term working.

2. Solution of the second general objection. 1. Works not the cause of salvation. This shown from the name and nature of inheritance. 2. A striking example that the Lord rewards the works of believers with blessings which he had promised before the works were thought of.

3. First reason why eternal life said to be the reward of works. This confirmed by passages of Scripture. The concurrence of Ambrose. A rule to be observed. Declarations of Christ and an Apostle.

4. Other four reasons. Holiness the way to the kingdom, not the cause of obtaining it. Proposition of the Sophists.

5. Objection that God crowns the works of his people. Three answers from Augustine. A fourth from Scripture.

6. First special objection—viz. that we are ordered to lay up treasure in heaven. Answer, showing in what way this can be done.

7. Second objection—viz. that the righteous enduring affliction are said to be worthy of the kingdom of heaven. Answer. What meant by righteousness.

8. A third objection founded on three passages of Paul. Answer.

9. Fourth objection founded on our Savior's words, "If ye would enter into life, keep the commandments." Answer, giving an exposition of the passage.

10. Last objection—viz. that faith itself is called a work. Answer—it is not as a work that faith justifies.

1. Let us now proceed to those passages which affirm that God will render to every one according to his deeds. Of this description are the following: "We must all appear before the judgment-seat of Christ; that every one may receive the things done in his body, according to that he has done, whether it be good or bad;" "Who will render to every man according to his deeds: to them who

by patient continuance in well-doing seek for glory, and honor, and immortality, eternal life;" but "tribulation and anguish upon every soul of man that does evil;" "They that have done good, unto the resurrection of life; and they that have done evil, unto the resurrection of damnation;" "Come, ye blessed of my Father;" "For I was an hungered, and ye gave me meat; I was thirsty, and ye gave me drink," &c. To these we may add the passages which describe eternal life as the reward of works, such as the following: "The recompense of a man's hands shall be rendered unto him;" "He that feareth the commandment shall be rewarded;" "Rejoice and be exceeding glad, for great is your reward in heaven;" "Every man shall receive his own rewards according to his own labour." The passages in which it is said that God will reward every man according to his works are easily disposed of. For that mode of expression indicates not the cause but the order of sequence. Now, it is beyond a doubt that the steps by which the Lord in his mercy consummates our salvation are these, "Whom he did predestinate, them he also called; and whom he called, them he also justified; and whom he justified, them he also glorified" (Rom. 8:30). But though it is by mercy alone that God admits his people to life, yet as he leads them into possession of it by the course of good works, that he may complete his work in them in the order which he has destined, it is not strange that they are said to be crowned according to their works, since by these doubtless they are prepared for receiving the crown of immortality. Nay, for this reason they are aptly said to work out their own salvation (Phil. 2:12), while by exerting themselves in good works they aspire to eternal life, just as they are elsewhere told to labour for the meat which perisheth not (John 6:27), while they acquire life for themselves by believing in Christ; and yet it is immediately added, that this meat "the Son of man shall give unto you." Hence it appears, that *working* is not at all opposed to *grace*, but refers to pursuit, and, therefore, it follows not that believers are the authors of their own salvation, or that it is the result of their works. What then? The moment they are admitted to fellowship with Christ, by the knowledge of the gospel, and the illumination of the Holy Spirit, their eternal life is begun, and then He which has begun a good work in them "will perform it until the day of Jesus Christ" (Phil. 1:6). And it is performed when in righteousness and holiness they bear a resemblance to their heavenly Father, and prove that they are not degenerate sons.

2. There is nothing in the term *reward* to justify the inference that our works are the cause of salvation. First, let it be a fixed principle in our hearts, that the kingdom of heaven is not the hire of servants, but the inheritance of sons (Eph. 1:18); an inheritance obtained by those only whom the Lord has adopted as sons, and obtained for no other cause than this adoption, "The son of the bond-women shall not be heir with the son of the free-woman" (Gal. 4:30). And hence in those very passages in which the Holy Spirit promises eternal glory as the reward of works, by expressly calling it an inheritance, he demonstrates that it comes to us from some other quarter. Thus Christ enumerates the works for which he bestows heaven as a recompense, while he is calling his elect to the possession of it, but he at the same time adds, that it is to be possessed by right of inheritance (Mt. 25:34). Paul, too, encourages servants, while faithfully doing their duty, to hope for reward from the Lord, but adds, "of the inheritance" (Col. 3:24). You see how, as it were, in formal terms they carefully caution us to attribute eternal blessedness not to works, but to the adoption of God. Why, then, do they at the same time make mention of works? This question will be elucidated by an example from Scripture (Gen. 15:5; 17:1). Before the birth of Isaac, Abraham had received promise of a seed in whom all the families of the earth should be blessed; the propagation of a seed that for number should equal the stars of heaven, and the sand of the sea, &c. Many years after he prepares, in obedience to a divine message, to sacrifice his son. Having done this act of obedience, he receives the promise, "By myself have I sworn, saith the Lord, for because thou hast done this thing, and hast not withheld thy son, thine only son; that in blessing I will bless thee, and in multiplying I will multiply thy seed as the stars of the heaven, and as the sand which is upon the sea-shore, and thy seed shall possess the gate of his enemies; and in thy seed shall all the nations of the earth be blessed, because thou hast obeyed my voice" (Gen. 22:16–18). What is it we hear? Did Abraham by his obedience merit the blessing which had been promised him before the precept was given? Here assuredly we see without ambiguity that God rewards the works of believers with blessings which he had given them before the works were thought of, there still being no cause for the blessings which he bestows but his own mercy.

3. And yet the Lord does not act in vain, or delude us when he says, that he renders to works what he had freely given previous to works. As he would have us to be exercised in good works, while aspiring to the manifestation, or, if I may so speak, the fruition of the things which he has promised, and by means of them to hasten on to

the blessed hope set before us in heaven, the fruit of the promises is justly ascribed to those things by which it is brought to maturity. Both things were elegantly expressed by the Apostle, when he told the Colossians to study the offices of charity, "for the hope which is laid up for you in heaven, whereof ye heard before in the word of the truth of the gospel" (Col. 1:5). For when he says that the gospel informed them of the hope which was treasured up for them in heaven, he declares that it depends on Christ alone, and not at all upon works. With this accords the saying of Peter, that believers "are kept by the power of God through faith unto salvation, ready to be revealed in the last time" (1 Pet. 1:5). When he says that they strive on account of it, he intimates that believers must continue running during the whole course of their lives in order that they may attain it. But to prevent us from supposing that the reward which is promised becomes a kind of merit, our Lord introduced a parable, in which he represented himself as a householder, who sent all the laborers whom he met to work in his vineyard, some at the first hour of the day, others at the second, others at the third, some even at the eleventh; at evening he paid them all alike. The interpretation of this parable is briefly and truly given by that ancient writer (whoever he was) who wrote the book *De Vocatione Gentium*, which goes under the name of Ambrose. I will give it in his words rather than my own: "By means of this comparison, our Lord represented the many various modes of calling as pertaining to grace alone, where those who were introduced into the vineyard at the eleventh hour and made equal to those who had toiled the whole day, doubtless represent the case of those whom the indulgence of God, to commend the excellence of grace, has rewarded in the decline of the day and the conclusion of life; not paying the price of labor, but shedding the riches of his goodness on those whom he chose without works; in order that even those who bore the heat of the day, and yet received no more than those who came last, may understand that they received a gift of grace, not the hire of works" (Lib. 1, cap. 5). Lastly, it is also worthy of remark, that in those passages in which eternal life is called the reward of works, it is not taken simply for that communion which we have with God preparatory to a blessed immortality, when with paternal benevolence he embraces us in Christ, but for the possession, or, as it is called, the fruition of blessedness, as the very words of Christ express it, "in the world to come eternal life" (Mark 10:30), and elsewhere, "Come, ye blessed of my Father, inherit the kingdom," &c. (Mt. 25:34). For this reasons also, Paul gives the name of *adoption* to that revelation of adoption which shall be made at the resurrection; and which adoption he afterwards interprets to mean, the redemption of our body (Rom. 8:23). But, otherwise, as alienation from God is eternal death,—so when man is received into favor by God that he may enjoy communion with him and become one with him, he passes from death unto life. This is owing to adoption alone. Although after their manner they pertinaciously urge the term *reward*, we can always carry them back to the declaration of Peter, that eternal life is the reward of faith (1 Pet. 1:9).

4. Let us not suppose, then, that the Holy Spirit, by this promise, commends the dignity of our works, as if they were deserving of such a reward. For Scripture leaves us nothing of which we may glory in the sight of God. Nay, rather its whole object is to repress, humble, cast down, and completely crush our pride. But in this way help is given to our weakness, which would immediately give way were it not sustained by this expectation, and soothed by this comfort. First, let every man reflect for himself how hard it is not only to leave all things, but to leave and abjure one's self. And yet this is the training by which Christ initiates his disciples, that is, all the godly. Secondly, he thus keeps them all their lifetime under the discipline of the cross, lest they should allow their heart to long for or confide in present good. In short, his treatment is usually such, that wherever they turn their eyes, as far as this world extends, they see nothing before them but despair; and hence Paul says "If in this life only we have hope in Christ, we are of all men most miserable" (1 Cor. 15:19). That they may not fail in these great straits, the Lord is present reminding them to lift their head higher and extend their view farther, that in him they may find a happiness which they see not in the world: to this happiness he gives the name of reward, hire, recompense, not as estimating the merit of works, but intimating that it is a compensation for their straits, sufferings, and affronts, &c. Wherefore, there is nothing to prevent us from calling eternal life a recompense after the example of Scripture, because in it the Lord brings his people from labour to quiet, from affliction to a prosperous and desirable condition, from sorrow to joy, from poverty to affluence, from ignominy to glory; in short, exchanges all the evils which they endured for blessings. Thus there will be no impropriety in considering holiness of life as the way, not indeed the way which gives access to the glory of the heavenly kingdom; but a way by which God conducts his elect to the manifestation of that kingdom, since his good pleasure is to glorify those whom he

has sanctified (Rom. 8:30). Only let us not imagine that merit and hire are correlative terms, a point on which the Sophists absurdly insist, from not attending to the end to which we have adverted. How preposterous is it when the Lord calls us to one end to look to another? Nothing is clearer than that a reward is promised to good works, in order to support the weakness of our flesh by some degree of comfort; but not to inflate our minds with vain glory. He, therefore, who from merit infers reward, or weighs works and reward in the same balance, errs very widely from the end which God has in view.

5. Accordingly, when the Scripture speaks of "a crown of righteousness which God the righteous Judge shall give" "at that day" (2 Tim. 4:8), I not only say with Augustine, "To whom could the righteous Judge give the crown if the merciful Father had not given grace, and how could there have been righteousness but for the precedence of grace which justified the ungodly? how could these be paid as things due were not things not due previously given?" (August. ad Valent. de Grat. et Lib. Art.); but I also add, how could he impute righteousness to our works, did not his indulgence hide the unrighteousness that is in them? How could he deem them worthy of reward, did he not with boundless goodness destroy what is unworthy in them? Augustine is wont to give the name of grace to eternal life, because, while it is the recompense of works, it is bestowed by the gratuitous gifts of God. But Scripture humbles us more, and at the same time elevates us. For besides forbidding us to glory in works, because they are the gratuitous gifts of God, it tells us that they are always defiled by some degrees of impurity, so that they cannot satisfy God when they are tested by the standard of his justice; but that lest our activity should be destroyed, they please merely by pardon. But though Augustine speaks somewhat differently from us, it is plain from his words that the difference is more apparent than real. After drawing a contrast between two individuals the one with a life holy and perfect almost to a miracle; the other honest indeed, and of pure morals, yet not so perfect as not to leave much room for desiring better, he at length infers, "He who seems inferior in conduct, yet on account of the true faith in God by which he lives (Hab. 2:4), and in conformity to which he accuses himself in all his faults, praises God in all his good works, takes shame to himself, and ascribes glory to God, from whom he receives both forgiveness for his sins, and the love of well-doing, the moment he is set free from this life is translated into the society of Christ. Why, but just on account of his faith? For though it saves no man without works (such faith being reprobate and not working by love), yet by means of it sins are forgiven; for the just lives by faith: without it works which seem good are converted into sins" (August. ad Bonifac., Lib. 3, c. 5). Here he not obscurely acknowledges what we so strongly maintains that the righteousness of good works depends on their being approved by God in the way of pardon.

6. In a sense similar to the above passages our opponents quote the following: "Make to yourselves friends of the mammon of unrighteousness; that when ye fail, they may receive you into everlasting habitations" (Luke 16:9). "Charge them that are rich in this world, that they be not high-minded, nor trust in uncertain riches, but in the living God, who giveth us richly all things to enjoy: that they do good, that they be rich in good works, ready to distribute, willing to communicate; laying up in store for themselves a good foundation against the time to come, that they may lay hold on eternal life" (1 Tim. 6:17–19). For the good works which we enjoy in eternal blessedness are compared to riches. I answer, that we shall never attain to the true knowledge of these passages unless we attend to the scope of the Spirit in uttering them. If it is true, as Christ says, "Where your treasure is, there will your heart be also" (Mt. 6:21), then, as the children of the world are intent on providing those things which form the delight of the present life, so it is the duty of believers, after they have learned that this life will shortly pass away like a dream, to take care that those things which they would truly enjoy be transmitted thither where their entire life is to be spent. We must, therefore, do like those who begin to remove to any place where they mean to fix their abode. As they send forward their effects, and grudge not to want them for a season, because they think the more they have in their future residence, the happier they are; so, if we think that heaven is our country, we should send our wealth thither rather than retain it here, where on our sudden departure it will be lost to us. But how shall we transmit it? By contributing to the necessities of the poor, the Lord imputing to himself whatever is given to them. Hence that excellent promise, "He that has pity on the poor lendeth to the Lord" (Prov. 19:17; Mt. 25:40); and again, "He which soweth bountifully shall reap also bountifully" (2 Cor. 9:6). What we give to our brethren in the exercise of charity is a deposit with the Lord, who, as a faithful depositary, will ultimately restore it with abundant interest. Are our duties, then, of such value with God that they are as a kind of treasure placed in his hand? Who can hesitate to say so when Scripture so often and so plainly attests it? But if any one would leap

from the mere kindness of God to the merit of works, his error will receive no support from these passages. For all you can properly infer from them is the inclination on the part of God to treat us with indulgence. For, in order to animate us in well-doing, he allows no act of obedience, however unworthy of his eye, to pass unrewarded.

7. But they insist more strongly on the words of the apostle when, in consoling the Thessalonians under their tribulations, he tells them that these were sent, "that ye may be counted worthy of the kingdom of God, for which ye also suffer; seeing it is a righteous thing with God to recompense tribulation to them that trouble you; and to you who are troubled, rest with us, when the Lord Jesus shall be revealed from heaven with his mighty angels" (2 Thess. 1:6–7). The author of the Epistle to the Hebrews says, "God is not unrighteous to forget your work and labour of love, which ye have showed towards his name, in that ye have ministered to the saints, and do minister" (Heb. 6:10). To the former passage I answer, that the worthiness spoken of is not that of merit, but as God the Father would have those whom he has chosen for sons to be conformed to Christ the first born, and as it behaved him first to suffer, and then to enter into his glory, so we also, through much tribulation, enter the kingdom of heaven. Therefore, while we suffer tribulation for the name of Christ, we in a manner receive the marks with which God is wont to stamp the sheep of his flock (Gal. 6:17). Hence we are counted worthy of the kingdom of God, because we bear in our body the marks of our Lord and Master, these being the insignia of the children of God. In this sense are we to understand the passages: "Always bearing about in the body the dying of the Lord Jesus, that the life also of Jesus might be made manifest in our body" (2 Cor. 4:10). "That I may know him and the power of his resurrection, and the fellowship of his sufferings, being made conformable unto his death" (Phil. 3:10). The reason which is subjoined is intended not to prove any merit, but to confirm our hope of the kingdom of God; as if he had said, As it is befitting the just judgment of God to take vengeance on your enemies for the tribulation which they have brought upon you, so it is also befitting to give you release and rest from these tribulations. The other passage, which speaks as if it were becoming the justice of God not to overlook the services of his people, and almost insinuates that it were unjust to forget them, is to be thus explained: God, to arouse us from sloth, assures us that every labour which we undertake for the glory of his name shall not be in vain. Let us always remember that this promise, like all other promises, will be of no avail unless it is preceded by the free covenant of mercy, on which the whole certainty of our salvation depends. Trusting to it, however, we ought to feel secure that however unworthy our services, the liberality of God will not allow them to pass unrewarded. To confirm us in this expectation, the Apostle declares that God is not unrighteous; but will act consistently with the promise once given. Righteousness, therefore, refers rather to the truth of the divine promise than to the equity of paying what is due. In this sense there is a celebrated saying of Augustine, which, as containing a memorable sentiment, that holy man declined not repeatedly to employ, and which I think not unworthy of being constantly remembered: "Faithful is the Lord, who has made himself our debtor, not by receiving any thing from us, but by promising us all things" (August. in Ps. 32, 109, *et alibi*).

8. Our opponents also adduce the following passages from Paul: "Though I have all faith, so that I could remove mountains, and have not charity, I am nothing" (1 Cor. 13:2). Again, "Now abideth faith, hope, charity, these three; but the greatest of these is charity" (1 Cor. 13:13). "Above all these things put on charity, which is the bond of perfectness" (Col. 3:14). From the two first passages our Pharisees contend that we are justified by charity rather than by faith, charity being, as they say, the better virtue. This mode of arguing is easily disposed of I have elsewhere shown that what is said in the first passage refers not to true faith. In the second passage we admit that charity is said to be greater than true faith, but not because charity is more meritorious, but because it is more fruitful, because it is of wider extent, of more general service, and always flourishes, whereas the use of faith is only for a time. If we look to excellence, the love of God undoubtedly holds the first place. Of it, however, Paul does not here speak; for the only thing he insists on is, that we should by mutual charity edify one another in the Lord. But let us suppose that charity is in every respect superior to faith, what man of sound judgment, nay, what man with any soundness in his brain, would argue that it therefore does more to justify? The power of justifying which belongs to faith consists not in its worth as a work. Our justification depends entirely on the mercy of God and the merits of Christ: when faith apprehends these, it is said to justify. Now, if you ask our opponents in what sense they ascribe justification to charity, they will answer, Being a duty acceptable to God, righteousness is in respect of its merit imputed to us by the acceptance of the divine goodness. Here you see

how beautifully the argument proceeds. We say that faith justifies not because it merits justification for us by its own worth, but because it is an instrument by which we freely obtain the righteousness of Christ. They overlooking the mercy of God, and passing by Christ, the sum of righteousness, maintain that we are justified by charity as being superior to faith; just as if one were to maintain that a king is fitter to make a shoe than a shoemaker, because the king is infinitely the superior of the two. This one syllogism is ample proof that all the schools of Sorbonne have never had the slightest apprehension of what is meant by justification by faith. Should any disputant here interpose, and ask why we give different meanings to the term faith as used by Paul in passages so near each other, I can easily show that I have not slight grounds for so doing. For while those gifts which Paul enumerates are in some degree subordinate to faith and hope, because they relate to the knowledge of God, he by way of summary comprehends them all under the name of faith and hope; as if he had said, Prophecy and tongues, and the gift of interpreting, and knowledge, are all designed to lead us to the knowledge of God. But in this life it is only by faith and hope that we acknowledge God. Therefore, when I name faith and hope, I at the same time comprehend the whole. "Now abideth faith, hope, charity, these three;" that is, how great soever the number of the gifts, they are all to be referred to them; but "the greatest of these is charity." From the third passage they infer, If charity is the bond of perfection, it must be the bond of righteousness, which is nothing else than perfection. First, without objecting that the name of perfection is here given by Paul to proper union among the members of a rightly constituted church, and admitting that by charity we are perfected before God, what new result do they gain by it? I will always object in reply, that we never attain to that perfection unless we fulfill all the parts of charity; and will thence infer, that as all are most remote from such fulfillment, the hope of perfection is excluded.

9. I am unwilling to discuss all the things which the foolish Sorbonnists have rashly laid hold of in Scripture as it chanced to come in their way, and throw out against us. Some of them are so ridiculous, that I cannot mention them without laying myself open to a charge of trifling. I will, therefore, conclude with an exposition of one of our Savior's expressions with which they are wondrously pleased. When the lawyer asked him, "Good Master, what good thing shall I do, that I may have eternal life?" he answers, "If thou wilt enter into life, keep the commandments" (Mt. 19:16, 17). What more (they ask) would we have, when the very author of grace bids us acquire the kingdom of heaven by the observance of the commandments? As if it were not plain that Christ adapted his answers to the characters of those whom he addressed. Here he is questioned by a Doctor of the Law as to the means of obtaining eternal life; and the question is not put simply, but is, What can men do to attain it? Both the character of the speaker and his question induced our Lord to give this answer. Imbued with a persuasion of legal righteousness, the lawyer had a blind confidence in works. Then all he asked was, what are the works of righteousness by which salvation is obtained? Justly, therefore, is he referred to the law, in which there is a perfect mirror of righteousness. We also distinctly declare, that if life is sought in works, the commandments are to be observed. And the knowledge of this doctrine is necessary to Christians; for how should they retake themselves to Christ, unless they perceived that they had fallen from the path of life over the precipice of death? Or how could they understand how far they have wandered from the way of life unless they previously understand what that way is? Then only do they feel that the asylum of safety is in Christ when they see how much their conduct is at variance with the divine righteousness, which consists in the observance of the law. The sum of the whole is this, If salvation is sought in works, we must keep the commandments, by which we are instructed in perfect righteousness. But we cannot remain here unless we would stop short in the middle of our course; for none of us is able to keep the commandments. Being thus excluded from the righteousness of the law, we must retake ourselves to another remedy—viz. to the faith of Christ. Wherefore, as a teacher of the law, whom our Lord knew to be puffed up with a vain confidence in works, was here directed by him to the law, that he might learn he was a sinner exposed to the fearful sentence of eternal death; so others, who were already humbled with this knowledge, he elsewhere solaces with the promise of grace, without making any mention of the law. "Come unto me, all ye that labour and are heavy laden, and I will give you rest." "Take my yoke upon you, and learn of me; for I am meek and lowly in heart: and ye shall find rest unto your souls" (Mt. 11:28, 29).

10. At length, after they have wearied themselves with perverting Scripture, they have recourse to subtleties and sophisms. One cavil is, that faith is somewhere called a work (John 6:29); hence they infer that we are in error in opposing faith to works; as if faith, regarded as obedience to the divine will, could by its own merit procure our

justification, and did not rather, by embracing the mercy of God, thereby seal upon our hearts the righteousness of Christ, which is offered to us in the preaching of the gospel. My readers will pardon me if I stay not to dispose of such absurdities; their own weakness, without external assault, is sufficient to destroy them. One objection, however, which has some semblance of reason, it will be proper to dispose of in passing, lest it give any trouble to those less experienced. As common sense dictates that contraries must be tried by the same rule, and as each sin is charged against us as unrighteousness, so it is right (say our opponents) that each good work should receive the praise of righteousness. The answer which some give, that the condemnation of men proceeds on unbelief alone, and not on particular sins does not satisfy me. I agree with them, indeed, that infidelity is the fountain and root of all evil; for it is the first act of revolt from God, and is afterwards followed by particular transgressions of the law. But as they seem to hold, that in estimating righteousness and unrighteousness, the same rule is to be applied to good and bad works, in this I dissent from them. The righteousness of works consists in perfect obedience to the law. Hence you cannot be justified by works unless you follow this straight line (if I may so call it) during the whole course of your life. The moment you decline from it you have fallen into unrighteousness. Hence it appears, that righteousness is not obtained by a few works, but by an indefatigable and inflexible observance of the divine will. But the rule with regard to unrighteousness is very different. The adulterer or the thief is by one act guilty of death, because he offends against the majesty of God. The blunder of these arguers of ours lies here: they attend not to the words of James, "Whosoever shall keep the whole law, and yet offend in one point, he is guilty of all. For he that said, Do not commit adultery, said also, Do not kill," &c. (James 2:10, 11). Therefore, it should not seem absurd when we say that death is the just recompense of every sin, because each sin merits the just indignation and vengeance of God. But you reason absurdly if you infer the converse, that one good work will reconcile a man to God notwithstanding of his meriting wrath by many sins.

CHAPTER 19

OF CHRISTIAN LIBERTY.

The three divisions of this chapter are,—I. Necessity of the doctrine of Christian Liberty, sec. 1. The principal parts of this liberty explained, sec. 2–8. II. The nature and efficacy of this liberty against the Epicureans and others who take no account whatever of the weak, sec. 9 and 10. III. Of offense given and received. A lengthened and not unnecessary discussion of this subject, sec. 11–16.

Sections:

1. Connection of this chapter with the previous one on Justification. A true knowledge of Christian liberty useful and necessary. 1. It purifies the conscience. 2. It checks licentiousness. 3. It maintains the merits of Christ, the truth of the Gospel, and the peace of the soul.

2. This liberty consists of three parts. First, Believers renouncing the righteousness of the law, look only to Christ. Objection. Answer, distinguishing between Legal and Evangelical righteousness.

3. This first part clearly established by the whole Epistle to the Galatians.

4. The second part of Christian liberty—viz. that the conscience, freed from the yoke of the law, voluntarily obeys the will of God. This cannot be done so long as we are under the law. Reason.

5. When freed from the rigorous exactions of the law, we can cheerfully and with much alacrity answer the call of God.

6. Proof of this second part from an Apostle. The end of this liberty.

7. Third part of liberty—viz. the free rise of things indifferent. The knowledge of this part necessary to remove despair and superstition. Superstition described.

8. Proof of this third part from the Epistle to the Romans. Those who observe it not only use evasion. 1. Despisers of God. 2. The desperate. 3. The ungrateful. The end and scope of this third part.

9. Second part of the chapter, showing the nature and efficacy of Christian liberty, in opposition to the Epicureans. Their character described. Pretext and allegation. Use of things indifferent. Abuse detected. Mode of correcting it.

10. This liberty maintained in opposition to those who pay no regard to the weak. Error of this class of men refuted. A most pernicious error. Objection. Reply.

11. Application of the doctrine of Christian liberty to the subject of offenses. These of two kinds. Offense given. Offense received. Of offense given, a subject comprehended by few. Of Pharisaical offense, or offense received.

12. Who are to be regarded as weak and Pharisaical. Proved by examples and the doctrine of Paul. The just moderation of Christian liberty. necessity of vindicating it. No regard to be paid to hypocrites. Duty of edifying our weak neighbors.

13. Application of the doctrine to things indifferent. Things necessary not to be omitted from any fear of offense.

14. Refutation of errors in regard to Christian liberty. The consciences of the godly not to be fettered by human traditions in matters of indifference.

15. Distinction to be made between Spiritual and Civil government. These must not be confounded. How far conscience can be bound by human constitutions. Definition of conscience. Definition explained by passages from the Apostolic writings.

16. The relation which conscience bears to external obedience; first, in things good and evil; secondly, in things indifferent.

1. We are now to treat of Christian Liberty, the explanation of which certainly ought not to be omitted by any one proposing to give a compendious summary of Gospel doctrine. For it is a matter of primary necessity, one without the knowledge of which the conscience can scarcely attempt any thing without hesitation, in many must demur and fluctuate, and in all proceed with fickleness and trepidation. In particular, it forms a proper appendix to Justification, and is of no little service in understanding its force. Nay, those who seriously fear God will hence perceive the incomparable advantages of a doctrine which wicked scoffers are constantly assailing with their jibes; the intoxication of mind under which they labour leaving their petulance without restraint. This, therefore, seems the proper place for considering the subject. Moreover, though it has already been occasionally adverted to, there was an advantage in deferring the fuller consideration of it till now, for the moment any mention is made of Christian liberty lust begins to boil, or insane commotions arise, if a speedy restraint is not laid on those licentious spirits by whom the best things are perverted into the worst. For they either, under pretext of this liberty, shake off all obedience to God, and break out into unbridled licentiousness, or they feel indignant, thinking that all choice, order, and restraint, are abolished. What can we do when thus encompassed with straits? Are we to bid adieu to Christian liberty, in order that we may cut off all opportunity for such perilous consequences? But, as we have said, if the subject be not understood, neither Christ, nor the truth of the Gospel, nor the inward peace of the soul, is properly known. Our endeavor must rather be, while not suppressing this very necessary part of doctrine, to obviate the absurd objections to which it usually gives rise.

2. Christian liberty seems to me to consist of three parts. First, the consciences of believers, while seeking the assurance of their justification before God, must rise above the law, and think no more of obtaining justification by it. For while the law, as has already been demonstrated (*supra*, chap. 17, sec. 1), leaves not one man righteous, we are either excluded from all hope of justification, or we must be loosed from the law, and so loosed as that no account at all shall be taken of works. For he who imagines that in order to obtain justification he must bring any degree of works whatever, cannot fix any mode or limit, but makes himself debtor to the whole law. Therefore, laying aside all mention of the law, and all idea of works, we must in the matter of justification have recourse to the mercy of God only; turning away our regard from ourselves, we must look only to Christ. For the question is, not how we may be righteous, but how, though unworthy and unrighteous, we may be regarded as righteous. If consciences would obtain any assurance of this, they must give no place to the law. Still it cannot be rightly inferred from this that believers have no need of the law. It ceases not to teach, exhort, and urge them to good, although it is not recognized by their consciences before the judgment-seat of God. The two things are very different, and should be well and carefully distinguished. The whole lives of Christians ought to be a kind of aspiration after piety, seeing they are called unto holiness (Eph. 1:4;1 Thess. 4:5). The office of the law is to excite them to the study of purity and holiness, by reminding them of their duty. For when the conscience feels anxious as to how it may have the favor of God, as to the answer it could give, and the confidence it would feel, if brought to his judgment-seat, in such a case the requirements of the law are not to be brought forward, but Christ, who surpasses all the perfection of the law, is alone to be held forth for righteousness.

3. On this almost the whole subject of the Epistle to the Galatians hinges; for it can be proved from express passages that those are absurd interpreters who teach that Paul there contends only for freedom from ceremonies. Of such passages are the following: "Christ has redeemed us from the curse of the law, being made a curse for us." "Stand fast, therefore, in the liberty wherewith Christ has made us free, and be not entangled again with the

yoke of bondage. Behold, I Paul say unto you, that if ye be circumcised, Christ shall profit you nothing. For I testify again to every man that is circumcised, that he is a debtor to do the whole law. Christ is become of no effect unto you, whosoever of you are justified by the law; ye are fallen from grace" (Gal. 3:13; 5:1–4). These words certainly refer to something of a higher order than freedom from ceremonies. I confess, indeed, that Paul there treats of ceremonies, because he was contending with false apostles, who were plotting, to bring back into the Christian Church those ancient shadows of the law which were abolished by the advent of Christ. But, in discussing this question, it was necessary to introduce higher matters, on which the whole controversy turns. First, because the brightness of the Gospel was obscured by those Jewish shadows, he shows that in Christ we have a full manifestation of all those things which were typified by Mosaic ceremonies. Secondly, as those impostors instilled into the people the most pernicious opinion, that this obedience was sufficient to merit the grace of God, he insists very strongly that believers shall not imagine that they can obtain justification before God by any works, far less by those paltry observances. At the same time, he shows that by the cross of Christ they are free from the condemnation of the law, to which otherwise all men are exposed, so that in Christ alone they can rest in full security. This argument is pertinent to the present subject (Gal. 4:5, 21, &c). Lastly, he asserts the right of believers to liberty of conscience, a liberty which may not be restrained without necessity.

4. Another point which depends on the former is, that consciences obey the law, not as if compelled by legal necessity; but being free from the yoke of the law itself, voluntarily obey the will of God. Being constantly in terror so long as they are under the dominion of the law, they are never disposed promptly to obey God, unless they have previously obtained this liberty. Our meaning shall be explained more briefly and clearly by an example. The command of the law is, "Thou shalt love the Lord thy God with all thine heart, and with all thy soul, and with all thy might" (Deut. 6:5). To accomplish this, the soul must previously be divested of every other thought and feeling, the heart purified from all its desires, all its powers collected and united on this one object. Those who, in comparison of others, have made much progress in the way of the Lord, are still very far from this goal. For although they love God in their mind, and with a sincere affection of heart, yet both are still in a great measure occupied with the lusts of the flesh, by which they are retarded and prevented from proceeding with quickened pace towards God. They indeed make many efforts, but the flesh partly enfeebles their strength, and partly binds them to itself. What can they do while they thus feel that there is nothing of which they are less capable than to fulfill the law? They wish, aspire, endeavor; but do nothing with the requisite perfection. If they look to the law, they see that every work which they attempt or design is accursed. Nor can any one deceive himself by inferring that the work is not altogether bad, merely because it is imperfect, and, therefore, that any good which is in it is still accepted of God. For the law demanding perfect love condemns all imperfection, unless its rigor is mitigated. Let any man therefore consider his work which he wishes to be thought partly good, and he will find that it is a transgression of the law by the very circumstance of its being imperfect.

5. See how our works lie under the curse of the law if they are tested by the standard of the law. But how can unhappy souls set themselves with alacrity to a work from which they cannot hope to gain any thing in return but cursing? On the other hand, if freed from this severe exaction, or rather from the whole rigor of the law, they hear themselves invited by God with paternal levity, they will cheerfully and alertly obey the call, and follow his guidance. In one word, those who are bound by the yoke of the law are like servants who have certain tasks daily assigned them by their masters. Such servants think that nought has been done; and they dare not come into the presence of their masters until the exact amount of labour has been performed. But sons who are treated in a more candid and liberal manner by their parents, hesitate not to offer them works that are only begun or half finished, or even with something faulty in them, trusting that their obedience and readiness of mind will be accepted, although the performance be less exact than was wished. Such should be our feelings, as we certainly trust that our most indulgent Parent will approve our services, however small they may be, and however rude and imperfect. Thus He declares to us by the prophet, "I will spare them as a man spareth his own son that serveth him" (Mal. 3:17); where the word *spare* evidently means indulgence, or connivance at faults, while at the same time service is remembered. This confidence is necessary in no slight degree, since without it every thing should be attempted in vain; for God does not regard any sock of ours as done to himself, unless truly done from a desire to serve him. But how can this be amidst these terrors, while we doubt whether God is offended or served by our work?

6. This is the reason why the author of the Epistle to the Hebrews ascribes to faith all the good works which the holy patriarchs are said to have performed, and estimates them merely by faith (Heb. 11:2). In regard to this liberty there is a remarkable passage in the Epistle to the Romans, where Paul argues, "Sin shall not have dominion over you; for ye are not under the law, but under grace" (Rom. 6:14). For after he had exhorted believers, "Let not sin therefore reign in your mortal body, that ye should obey it in the lusts thereof: Neither yield ye your members as instruments of unrighteousness unto sin; but yield yourselves unto God, as those that are alive from the dead, and your members as instruments of righteousness unto God;" they might have objected that they still bore about with them a body full of lust, that sin still dwelt in them. He therefore comforts them by adding, that they are freed from the law; as if he had said, Although you feel that sin is not yet extinguished, and that righteousness does not plainly live in you, you have no cause for fear and dejection, as if God were always offended because of the remains of sin, since by grace you are freed from the law, and your works are not tried by its standard. Let those, however who infer that they may sin because they are not under the law, understand that they have no right to this liberty, the end of which is to encourage us in well-doing.

7. The third part of this liberty is that we are not bound before God to any observance of external things which are in themselves indifferent (ἀδιάφορα), but that we are now at full liberty either to use or omit them. The knowledge of this liberty is very necessary to us; where it is wanting our consciences will have no rest, there will be no end of superstition. In the present day many think us absurd in raising a question as to the free eating of flesh, the free use of dress and holidays, and similar frivolous trifles, as they think them; but they are of more importance than is commonly supposed. For when once the conscience is entangled in the net, it enters a long and inextricable labyrinth, from which it is afterwards most difficult to escape. When a man begins to doubt whether it is lawful for him to use linen for sheets, shirts, napkins, and handkerchiefs, he will not long be secure as to hemp, and will at last have doubts as to tow; for he will revolve in his mind whether he cannot sup without napkins, or dispense with handkerchiefs. Should he deem a daintier food unlawful, he will afterwards feel uneasy for using loafbread and common eatables, because he will think that his body might possibly be supported on a still meaner food. If he hesitates as to a more genial wine, he will scarcely drink the worst with a good conscience; at last he will not dare to touch water if more than usually sweet and pure. In fine, he will come to this, that he will deem it criminal to trample on a straw lying in his way. For it is no trivial dispute that is here commenced, the point in debate being, whether the use of this thing or that is in accordance with the divine will, which ought to take precedence of all our acts and counsels. Here some must by despair be hurried into an abyss, while others, despising God and casting off his fear, will not be able to make a way for themselves without ruin. When men are involved in such doubts whatever be the direction in which they turn, every thing they see must offend their conscience.

8. "I know," says Paul, "that there is nothing unclean of itself" (by unclean meaning unholy); "but to him that esteemeth any thing to be unclean, to him it is unclean" (Rom. 14:14). By these words he makes all external things subject to our liberty, provided the nature of that liberty approves itself to our minds as before God. But if any superstitious idea suggests scruples, those things which in their own nature were pure are to us contaminated. Wherefore the apostle adds, "Happy is he that condemneth not himself in that which he alloweth. And he that doubteth is damned if he eat, because he eateth not of faith: for whatsoever is not of faith is sin" (Rom. 14:22, 23). When men, amid such difficulties, proceed with greater confidence, securely doing whatever pleases them, do they not in so far revolt from God? Those who are thoroughly impressed with some fear of God, if forced to do many things repugnant to their consciences are discouraged and filled with dread. All such persons receive none of the gifts of God with thanksgiving, by which alone Paul declares that all things are sanctified for our use (1 Tim. 4:5). By thanksgiving I understand that which proceeds from a mind recognizing the kindness and goodness of God in his gifts. For many, indeed, understand that the blessings which they enjoy are the gifts of God, and praise God in their words; but not being persuaded shalt these have been given to them, how can they give thanks to God as the giver? In one word, we see whither this liberty tends—viz. that we are to use the gifts of God without any scruple of conscience, without any perturbation of mind, for the purpose for which he gave them: in this way our souls may both have peace with him, and recognize his liberality towards us. For here are comprehended all ceremonies of free observance, so that while our consciences are not to be laid under the necessity of observing them, we are also to remember that, by

the kindness of God, the use of them is made subservient to edification.

9. It is, however, to be carefully observed, that Christian liberty is in all its parts a spiritual matter, the whole force of which consists in giving peace to trembling consciences, whether they are anxious and disquieted as to the forgiveness of sins, or as to whether their imperfect works, polluted by the infirmities of the flesh, are pleasing to God, or are perplexed as to the use of things indifferent. It is, therefore, perversely interpreted by those who use it as a cloak for their lusts, that they may licentiously abuse the good gifts of God, or who think there is no liberty unless it is used in the presence of men, and, accordingly, in using it pay no regard to their weak brethren. Under this head, the sins of the present age are more numerous. For there is scarcely any one whose means allow him to live sumptuously, who does not delight in feasting, and dress, and the luxurious grandeur of his house, who wishes not to surpass his neighbor in every kind of delicacy, and does not plume himself amazingly on his splendor. And all these things are defended under the pretext of Christian liberty. They say they are things indifferent: I admit it, provided they are used indifferently. But when they are too eagerly longed for, when they are proudly boasted of, when they are indulged in luxurious profusion, things which otherwise were in themselves lawful are certainly defiled by these vices. Paul makes an admirable distinction in regard to things indifferent: "Unto the pure all things are pure: but unto them that are defiled and unbelieving is nothing pure; but even their mind and conscience is defiled" (Tit. 1:15). For why is a woe pronounced upon the rich who have received their consolation? (Luke 6:24), who are full, who laugh now, who "lie upon beds of ivory and stretch themselves upon their couches;" "join house to house," and "lay field to field;" "and the harp and the viol, the tablet and pipe, and wine, are in their feasts" (Amos 6:6; Isa. 5:8, 10). Certainly ivory and gold, and riches, are the good creatures of God, permitted, nay destined, by divine providence for the use of man; nor was it ever forbidden to laugh, or to be full, or to add new to old and hereditary possessions, or to be delighted with music, or to drink wine. This is true, but when the means are supplied to roll and wallow in luxury, to intoxicate the mind and soul with present and be always hunting after new pleasures, is very far from a legitimate use of the gifts of God. Let them, therefore, suppress immoderate desire, immoderate profusion, vanity, and arrogance, that they may use the gifts of God purely with a pure conscience.

When their mind is brought to this state of soberness, they will be able to regulate the legitimate use. On the other hand, when this moderation is wanting, even plebeian and ordinary delicacies are excessive. For it is a true saying, that a haughty mind often dwells in a coarse and homely garb, while true humility lurks under fine linen and purple. Let every one then live in his own station, poorly or moderately, or in splendor; but let all remember that the nourishment which God gives is for life, not luxury, and let them regard it as the law of Christian liberty, to learn with Paul in whatever state they are, "therewith to be content," to know "both how to be abased," and "how to abound," "to be full and to be hungry, both to abound and to suffer need" (Phil. 4:11).

10. Very many also err in this: as if their liberty were not safe and entire, without having men to witness it, they use it indiscriminately and imprudently, and in this way often give offense to weak brethren. You may see some in the present day who cannot think they possess their liberty unless they come into possession of it by eating flesh on Friday. Their eating I blame not, but this false notion must be driven from their minds: for they ought to think that their liberty gains nothing new by the sight of men, but is to be enjoyed before God, and consists as much in abstaining as in using. If they understand that it is of no consequence in the sight of God whether they eat flesh or eggs, whether they are clothed in red or in black, this is amply sufficient. The conscience to which the benefit of this liberty was due is loosed. Therefore, though they should afterwards, during their whole life, abstain from flesh, and constantly wear one color, they are not less free. Nay, just because they are free, they abstain with a free conscience. But they err most egregiously in paying no regard to the infirmity of their brethren, with which it becomes us to bear, so as not rashly to give them offense. But it is sometimes also of consequence that we should assert our liberty before men. This I admit: yet must we use great caution in the mode, lest we should cast off the care of the weak whom God has specially committed to us.

11. I will here make some observations on offenses, what distinctions are to be made between them, what kind are to be avoided and what disregarded. This will afterwards enable us to determine what scope there is for our liberty among men. We are pleased with the common division into *offense given* and *offense taken*, since it has the plain sanction of Scripture, and not improperly expresses what is meant. If from unseasonable levity or wantonness, or rashness, you do any thing out of order

or not in its own place, by which the weak or unskillful are offended, it may be said that offense has been *given* by you, since the ground of offense is owing to your fault. And in general, offense is said to be *given* in any matter where the person from whom it has proceeded is in fault. Offense is said to be taken when a thing otherwise done, not wickedly or unseasonably, is made an occasion of offense from malevolence or some sinister feeling. For here offense was not given, but sinister interpreters ceaselessly take offense. By the former kind, the weak only, by the latter, the ill-tempered and Pharisaical are offended. Wherefore, we shall call the one the offense of the weak, the other the offense of Pharisees, and we will so temper the use of our liberty as to make it yield to the ignorance of weak brethren, but not to the austerity of Pharisees. What is due to infirmity is fully shown by Paul in many passages. "Him that is weak in the faith receive ye." Again, "Let us not judge one another any more: but judge this rather, that no man put a stumbling-block, or an occasion to fall, in his brother's way;" and many others to the same effect in the same place, to which, instead of quoting them here, we refer the reader. The sum is, "We then that are strong ought to bear the infirmities of the weak, and not to please ourselves. Let every one of us please his neighbor for his good to edification." elsewhere he says, "Take heed lest by any means this liberty of yours become a stumbling-block to them that are weak." Again "Whatsoever is sold in the shambles, that eat, asking no question for conscience sake." "Conscience, I say, not thine own, but of the other." Finally, "Give none offense, neither to the Jews nor to the Gentiles nor to the Church of God." Also in another passage, "Brethren, ye have been called into liberty, only use not liberty for an occasion to the flesh, but by love serve one another." Thus, indeed, it is: our liberty was not given us against our weak neighbors, whom charity enjoins us to serve in all things, but rather that, having peace with God in our minds, we should live peaceably among men. What value is to be set upon the offense of the Pharisees we learn from the words of our Lord, in which he says, "Let them alone: they be blind leaders of the blind" (Mt. 15:14). The disciples had intimated that the Pharisees were offended at his words. He answers that they are to be let alone that their offense is not to be regarded.

12. The matter still remains uncertain, unless we understand who are the weak and who the Pharisees: for if this distinction is destroyed, I see not how, in regard to offenses, any liberty at all would remain without being constantly in the greatest danger. But Paul seems to me to have marked out most clearly, as well by example as by doctrine, how far our liberty, in the case of offense, is to be modified or maintained. When he adopts Timothy as his companion, he circumcises him: nothing can induce him to circumcise Titus (Acts 16:3; Gal. 2:3). The acts are different, but there is no difference in the purpose or intention; in circumcising Timothy, as he was free from all men, he made himself the servant of all: "Unto the Jews I became as a Jew, that I might gain the Jews; to them that are under the law, as under the law, that I might gain them that are under the law; to them that are without law, as without law (being not without law to God, but under the law to Christ), that I might gain them that are without law. To the weak became I as weak that I might gain the weak: I am made all things to all men, that I might by all means save some" (1 Cor. 9:20–22). We have here the proper modification of liberty, when in things indifferent it can be restrained with some advantage. What he had in view in firmly resisting the circumcision of Titus, he himself testifies when he thus writes: "But neither Titus, who was with me, being a Greek, was compelled to be circumcised: and that because of false brethren unawares brought in, who came in privily to spy out our liberty which we have in Christ Jesus, that they might bring us into bondage: to whom we gave place by subjection, no, not for an hour, that the truth of the gospel might continue with you" (Gal. 2:3–5). We here see the necessity of vindicating our liberty when, by the unjust exactions of false apostles, it is brought into danger with weak consciences. In all cases we must study charity, and look to the edification of our neighbor. "All things are lawful for me," says he, "but all things are not expedient; all things are lawful for me, but all things edify not. Let no man seek his own, but every man another's wealth" (1 Cor. 10:23, 24). There is nothing plainer than this rule, that we are to use our liberty if it tends to the edification of our neighbor, but if inexpedient for our neighbor, we are to abstain from it. There are some who pretend to imitate this prudence of Paul by abstinence from liberty, while there is nothing for which they less employ it than for purposes of charity. Consulting their own ease, they would have all mention of liberty buried, though it is not less for the interest of our neighbor to use liberty for their good and edification, than to modify it occasionally for their advantage. It is the part of a pious man to think, that the free power conceded to him in external things is to make him the readier in all offices of charity.

13. Whatever I have said about avoiding offenses, I wish to be referred to things indifferent. Things which

are necessary to be done cannot be omitted from any fear of offense. For as our liberty is to be made subservient to charity, so charity must in its turn be subordinate to purity of faith. Here, too, regard must be had to charity, but it must go as far as the altar; that is, we must not offend God for the sake of our neighbor. We approve not of the intemperance of those who do every thing tumultuously, and would rather burst through every restraint at once than proceed step by step. But neither are those to be listened to who, while they take the lead in a thousand forms of impiety, pretend that they act thus to avoid giving offense to their neighbor, as if in the meantime they did not train the consciences of their neighbors to evil, especially when they always stick in the same mire without any hope of escape. When a neighbor is to be instructed, whether by doctrine or by example, then smooth-tongued men say that he is to be fed with milk, while they are instilling into him the worst and most pernicious opinions. Paul says to the Corinthians, "I have fed you with milk, and not with meat" (1 Cor. 3:2); but had there then been a Popish mass among them, would he have sacrificed as one of the modes of giving them milk? By no means: milk is not poison. It is false then to say they nourish those whom, under a semblance of soothing they cruelly murder. But granting that such dissimulation may be used for a time, how long are they to make their pupils drink that kind of milk? If they never grow up so as to be able to bear at least some gentle food, it is certain that they have never been reared on milk. Two reasons prevent me from now entering farther into contest with these people, first, their follies are scarcely worthy of refutation, seeing all men of sense must nauseate them; and, secondly, having already amply refuted them in special treatises, I am unwilling to do it over again. Let my readers only bear in mind, first, that whatever be the offenses by which Satan and the world attempt to lead us away from the law of God, we must, nevertheless, strenuously proceed in the course which he prescribes; and, secondly, that whatever dangers impend, we are not at liberty to deviate one nail's breadth from the command of God, that on no pretext is it lawful to attempt any thing but what he permits.

14. Since by means of this privilege of liberty which we have described, believers have derived authority from Christ not to entangle themselves by the observance of things in which he wished them to be free, we conclude that their consciences are exempted from all human authority. For it were unbecoming that the gratitude due to Christ for his liberal gift should perish or that the consciences of believers should derive no benefit from it. We must not regard it as a trivial matter when we see how much it cost our Savior, being purchased not with silver or gold, but with his own blood (1 Pet. 1:18, 19); so that Paul hesitates not to say that Christ has died in vain, if we place our souls under subjection to men (Gal. 5:1, 4; 1 Cor. 7:23). Several chapters of the Epistle to the Galatians are wholly occupied with showing that Christ is obscured, or rather extinguished to us, unless our consciences maintain their liberty; from which they have certainly fallen, if they can be bound with the chains of laws and constitutions at the pleasure of men. But as the knowledge of this subject is of the greatest importance, so it demands a longer and clearer exposition. For the moment the abolition of human constitutions is mentioned, the greatest disturbances are excited, partly by the seditious, and partly by calumniators, as if obedience of every kind were at the same time abolished and overthrown.

15. Therefore, lest this prove a stumbling-block to any, let us observe that in man government is twofold: the one spiritual, by which the conscience is trained to piety and divine worship; the other civil, by which the individual is instructed in those duties which, as men and citizens, we are bold to performs (see Book 4, chap. 10, sec. 3–6). To these two forms are commonly given the not inappropriate names of spiritual and temporal jurisdiction, intimating that the former species has reference to the life of the soul, while the latter relates to matters of the present life, not only to food and clothing, but to the enacting of laws which require a man to live among his fellows purely honorably, and modestly. The former has its seat within the soul, the latter only regulates the external conduct. We may call the one the spiritual, the other the civil kingdom. Now, these two, as we have divided them, are always to be viewed apart from each other. When the one is considered, we should call off our minds, and not allow them to think of the other. For there exists in man a kind of two worlds, over which different kings and different laws can preside. By attending to this distinction, we will not erroneously transfer the doctrine of the gospel concerning spiritual liberty to civil order, as if in regard to external government Christians were less subject to human laws, because their consciences are unbound before God, as if they were exempted from all carnal service, because in regard to the Spirit they are free. Again because even in those constitutions which seem to relate to the spiritual kingdom, there may be some delusion, it is necessary to distinguish between those which are

to be held legitimate as being agreeable to the Word of God, and those, on the other hand, which ought to have no place among the pious. We shall elsewhere have an opportunity of speaking of civil government (see Book 4, chap. 20). For the present, also, I defer speaking of ecclesiastical laws, because that subject will be more fully discussed in the Fourth Book when we come to treat of the Power of the Church. We would thus conclude the present discussion. The question, as I have said, though not very obscure, or perplexing in itself, occasions difficulty to many, because they do not distinguish with sufficient accuracy between what is called the external *forum*, and the *forum* of conscience. What increases the difficulty is, that Paul commands us to obey the magistrate, "not only for wrath, but also for conscience sake" (Rom. 13:1, 5). Whence it follows that civil laws also bind the conscience. Were this so, then what we said a little ago, and are still to say of spiritual governments would fall. To solve this difficulty, the first thing of importance is to understand what is meant by *conscience*. The definition must be sought in the etymology of the word. For as men, when they apprehend the knowledge of things by the mind and intellects are said to know, and hence arises the term knowledge or *science*, so when they have a sense of the divine justice added as a witness which allows them not to conceal their sins, but drags them forward as culprits to the bar of God, that sense is called *conscience*. For it stands as it were between God and man, not suffering man to suppress what he knows in himself; but following him on even to conviction. It is this that Paul means when he says, "Their conscience also bearing witness, and their thoughts the meanwhile accusing, or else excusing one another" (Rom. 2:15). Simple knowledge may exist in man, as it were shut up; therefore this sense, which sists man before the bar of God, is set over him as a kind of sentinel to observe and spy out all his secrets, that nothing may remain buried in darkness. Hence the ancient proverb, Conscience is a thousand witnesses. For the same reason Peter also employs the expression, "the answer of a good conscience" (1 Pet. 3:21), for tranquillity of mind; when persuaded of the grace of Christ, we boldly present ourselves before God. And the author of the Epistle to the Hebrews says, that we have "no more conscience of sins" (Heb. 10:2), that we are held as freed or acquitted, so that sin no longer accuses us.

16. Wherefore, as works have respect to men, so conscience bears reference to God, a good conscience being nothing else than inward integrity of heart. In this sense Paul says that "the end of the commandment is charity, out of a pure heart, and of a good consciences and of faith unfeigned" (1 Tim. 1:5). He afterwards, in the same chapter, shows how much it differs from intellect when he speaks of "holding faith, and a good conscience; which some having put away, have made shipwreck" (1 Tim. 1:19). For by these words he intimates, that it is a lively inclination to serve God, a sincere desire to live in piety and holiness. Sometimes, indeed, it is even extended to men, as when Paul testifies, "Herein do I exercise myself, to have always a conscience void of offense toward God, and toward men" (Acts 24:16). He speaks thus, because the fruits of a good conscience go forth and reach even to men. But, as I have said, properly speaking, it refers to God only. Hence a law is said to bind the conscience, because it simply binds the individual, without looking at men, or taking any account of them. For example, God not only commands us to keep our mind chaste and pure from lust, but prohibits all external lasciviousness or obscenity of language. My conscience is subjected to the observance of this law, though there were not another man in the world, and he who violates it sins not only by setting a bad example to his brethren, but stands convicted in his conscience before God. The same rule does not hold in things indifferent. We ought to abstain from every thing that produces offense, but with a free conscience. Thus Paul, speaking of meat consecrated to idols, says, "If any man say unto you, This is offered in sacrifice unto idols, eat not for his sake that showed it, and for conscience sake:" "Conscience, I say, not thine own, but of the other" (1 Cor. 10:28, 29). A believer, after being previously admonished, would sin were he still to eat meat so offered. But though abstinence, on his part, is necessary, in respect of a brother, as it is prescribed by God, still he ceases not to retain liberty of conscience. We see how the law, while binding the external act, leaves the conscience unbound.

CHAPTER 20

OF PRAYER—
A PERPETUAL EXERCISE OF FAITH.
THE DAILY BENEFITS DERIVED FROM IT.

The principal divisions of this chapter are,—I. Connection of the subject of prayer with the previous chapters. The nature of prayer, and its necessity as a Christian exercise, sec. 1, 2. II. To whom prayer is to be offered. Refutation of an objection which is too apt to present itself to the mind, sec. 3. III. Rules to be observed in prayer, sec. 4–16. IV. Through whom prayer is to be made, sec. 17–19. V. Refutation of an error as to the doctrine of our Mediator and Intercessor, with answers to the leading arguments urged in support of the intercession of saints, sec. 20–27. VI. The nature of prayer, and some of its accidents, sec. 28–33. VII. A perfect form of invocation, or an exposition of the Lord's Prayer, sec. 34–50. VIII. Some rules to be observed with regard to prayer, as time, perseverance, the feeling of the mind, and the assurance of faith, sec. 50–52.

Sections:

1. A general summary of what is contained in the previous part of the work. A transition to the doctrine of prayer. Its connection with the subject of faith.

2. Prayer defined. Its necessity and use.

3. Objection, that prayer seems useless, because God already knows our wants. Answer, from the institution and end of prayer. Confirmation by example. Its necessity and propriety. Perpetually reminds us of our duty, and leads to meditation on divine providence. Conclusion. Prayer a most useful exercise. This proved by three passages of Scripture.

4. Rules to be observed in prayer. First, reverence to God. How the mind ought to be composed.

5. All giddiness of mind must be excluded, and all our feelings seriously engaged. This confirmed by the form of lifting the hand in prayer. We must ask only in so far as God permits. To help our weakness, God gives the Spirit to be our guide in prayer. What the office of the Spirit in this respect. We must still pray both with the heart and the lips.

6. Second rule of prayer, a sense of our want. This rule violated, 1. By perfunctory and formal prayer 2. By hypocrites who have no sense of their sins. 3. By giddiness in prayer. Remedies.

7. Objection, that we are not always under the same necessity of praying. Answer, we must pray always. This answer confirmed by an examination of the dangers by which both our life and our salvation are every moment threatened. Confirmed farther by the command and permission of God, by the nature of true repentance, and a consideration of impenitence. Conclusion.

8. Third rule, the suppression of all pride. Examples. Daniel, David, Isaiah, Jeremiah, Baruch.

9. Advantage of thus suppressing pride. It leads to earnest entreaty for pardon, accompanied with humble confession and sure confidence in the Divine mercy. This may not always be expressed in words. It is peculiar to pious penitents. A general introduction to procure favour to our prayers never to be omitted.

10. Objection to the third rule of prayer. Of the glorying of the saints. Answer. Confirmation of the answer.

11. Fourth rule of prayer,—a sure confidence of being heard animating us to prayer. The kind of confidence required—viz. a serious conviction of our misery, joined with sure hope. From these true prayer springs. How diffidence impairs prayer. In general, faith is required.

12. This faith and sure hope regarded by our opponents as most absurd. Their error described and refuted by various passages of Scripture, which show that acceptable prayer is accompanied with these qualities. No repugnance between this certainty and an acknowledgment of our destitution.

13. To our unworthiness we oppose, 1. The command of God. 2. The promise. Rebels and hypocrites completely condemned. Passages of Scripture confirming the command to pray.

14. Other passages respecting the promises which belong to the pious when they invoke God. These realized though we are not possessed of the same holiness as other distinguished servants of God, provided we indulge no vain confidence, and sincerely betake ourselves to the mercy of God. Those who do not invoke God under urgent necessity are no better than idolaters. This concurrence of fear and confidence reconciles the different passages of Scripture, as to humbling ourselves in prayer, and causing our prayers to ascend.

15. Objection founded on some examples—viz. that prayers have proved effectual, though not according to the form prescribed. Answer. Such examples, though not given for our imitation, are of the greatest use. Objection, the prayers of the faithful sometimes not effectual. Answer confirmed by a noble passage of Augustine. Rule for right prayer.

16. The above four rules of prayer not so rigidly exacted, as that every prayer deficient in them in any respect is rejected by God. This shown by examples. Conclusion, or summary of this section.

17. Through whom God is to be invoked—viz. Jesus Christ. This founded on a consideration of the divine majesty, and the precept and promise of God himself. God therefore to be invoked only in the name of Christ.

18. From the first all believers were heard through him only: yet this specially restricted to the period subsequent to his ascension. The ground of this restriction.

19. The wrath of God lies on those who reject Christ

as a Mediator. This excludes not the mutual intercession of saints on the earth.

20. Refutation of errors interfering with the intercession of Christ. 1. Christ the Mediator of redemption; the saints mediators of intercession. Answer confirmed by the clear testimony of Scripture, and by a passage from Augustine. The nature of Christ's intercession.

21. Of the intercession of saints living with Christ in heaven. Fiction of the Papists in regard to it. Refuted. 1. Its absurdity. 2. It is no where mentioned by Scripture. 3. Appeal to the conscience of the superstitious. 4. Its blasphemy. Exception. Answers.

22. Monstrous errors resulting from this fiction. Refutation. Exception by the advocates of this fiction. Answer.

23. Arguments of the Papists for the intercession of saints. 1. From the duty and office of angels. Answer. 2. From an expression of Jeremiah respecting Moses and Samuel. Answer, retorting the argument. 3. The meaning of the prophet confirmed by a similar passage in Ezekiel, and the testimony of an apostle.

24. 4. Fourth Papistical argument from the nature of charity, which is more perfect in the saints in glory. Answer.

25. Argument founded on a passage in Moses. Answer.

26. Argument from its being said that the prayers of saints are heard. Answer, confirmed by Scripture, and illustrated by examples.

27. Conclusion, that the saints cannot be invoked without impiety. 1. It robs God of his glory. 2. Destroys the intercession of Christ. 3. Is repugnant to the word of God. 4. Is opposed to the due method of prayer. 5. Is without approved example. 6. Springs from distrust. Last objection. Answer.

28. Kinds of prayer. Vows. Supplications. Petitions. Thanksgiving. Connection of these, their constant use and necessity. Particular explanation confirmed by reason, Scripture, and example. Rule as to supplication and thanksgiving.

29. The accidents of prayer—viz. private and public, constant, at stated seasons, &c. Exception in time of necessity. Prayer without ceasing. Its nature. Garrulity of Papists and hypocrites refuted. The scope and parts of prayer. Secret prayer. Prayer at all places. Private and public prayer.

30. Of public places or churches in which common prayers are offered up. Right use of churches. Abuse.

31. Of utterance and singing. These of no avail if not from the heart. The use of the voice refers more to public than private prayer.

32. Singing of the greatest antiquity, but not universal. How to be performed.

33. Public prayers should be in the vulgar, not in a foreign tongue. Reason, 1. The nature of the Church. 2. Authority of an apostle. Sincere affection always necessary. The tongue not always necessary. Bending of the knee, and uncovering of the head.

34. The form of prayer delivered by Christ displays the boundless goodness of our heavenly Father. The great comfort thereby afforded.

35. Lord's Prayer divided into six petitions. Subdivision into two principal parts, the former referring to the glory of God, the latter to our salvation.

36. The use of the term Father implies, 1. That we pray to God in the name of Christ alone. 2. That we lay aside all distrust. 3. That we expect every thing that is for our good.

37. Objection, that our sins exclude us from the presence of him whom we have made a Judge, not a Father. Answer, from the nature of God, as described by an apostle, the parable of the prodigal son, and from the expression, Our Father. Christ the earnest, the Holy Spirit the witness, of our adoption.

38. Why God is called generally, Our Father.

39. We may pray specially for ourselves and certain others, provided we have in our mind a general reference to all.

40. In what sense God is said to be in heaven. A threefold use of this doctrine for our consolation. Three cautions. Summary of the preface to the Lord's Prayer.

41. The necessity of the first petition a proof of our unrighteousness. What meant by the name of God. How it is hallowed. Parts of this hallowing. A deprecation of the sins by which the name of God is profaned.

42. Distinction between the first and second petitions. The kingdom of God, what. How said to come. Special exposition of this petition. It reminds us of three things. Advent of the kingdom of God in the world.

43. Distinction between the second and third petitions. The will here meant not the secret will or good pleasure of God, but that manifested in the word. Conclusion of the three first petitions.

44. A summary of the second part of the Lord's Prayer. Three petitions. What contained in the first. Declares the exceeding kindness of God, and our distrust. What meant by bread. Why the petition for bread precedes that for the forgiveness of sins. Why it is called

ours. Why to be sought this day, or daily. The doctrine resulting from this petition, illustrated by an example. Two classes of men sin in regard to this petition. In what sense it is called, our bread. Why we ask God to give it to us.

45. Close connection between this and the subsequent petition. Why our sins are called debts. This petition violated, 1. By those who think they can satisfy God by their own merits, or those of others. 2. By those who dream of a perfection which makes pardon unnecessary. Why the elect cannot attain perfection in this life. Refutation of the libertine dreamers of perfection. Objection refuted. In what sense we are said to forgive those who have sinned against us. How the condition is to be understood.

46. The sixth petition reduced to three heads. 1. The various forms of temptation. The depraved conceptions of our minds. The wiles of Satan, on the right hand and on the left. 2. What it is to be led into temptation. We do not ask not to be tempted of God. What meant by evil, or the evil one. Summary of this petition. How necessary it is. Condemns the pride of the superstitious. Includes many excellent properties. In what sense God may be said to lead us into temptation.

47. The three last petitions show that the prayers of Christians ought to be public. The conclusion of the Lord's Prayer. Why the word Amen is added.

48. The Lord's Prayer contains every thing that we can or ought to ask of God. Those who go beyond it sin in three ways.

49. We may, after the example of the saints, frame our prayers in different words, provided there is no difference in meaning.

50. Some circumstances to be observed. Of appointing special hours of prayer. What to be aimed at, what avoided. The will of God, the rule of our prayers.

51. Perseverance in prayer especially recommended, both by precept and example. Condemnatory of those who assign to God a time and mode of hearing.

52. Of the dignity of faith, through which we always obtain, in answer to prayer, whatever is most expedient for us. The knowledge of this most necessary.

1. From the previous part of the work we clearly see how completely destitute man is of all good, how devoid of every means of procuring his own salvation. Hence, if he would obtain succour in his necessity, he must go beyond himself, and procure it in some other quarter. It has farther been shown that the Lord kindly and spontaneously manifests himself in Christ, in whom he offers all happiness for our misery, all abundance for our want, opening up the treasures of heaven to us, so that we may turn with full faith to his beloved Son, depend upon him with full expectation, rest in him, and cleave to him with full hope. This, indeed, is that secret and hidden philosophy which cannot be learned by syllogisms: a philosophy thoroughly understood by those whose eyes God has so opened as to see light in his light (Ps. 36:9). But after we have learned by faith to know that whatever is necessary for us or defective in us is supplied in God and in our Lord Jesus Christ, in whom it hath pleased the Father that all fulness should dwell, that we may thence draw as from an inexhaustible fountain, it remains for us to seek and in prayer implore of him what we have learned to be in him. To know God as the sovereign disposer of all good, inviting us to present our requests, and yet not to approach or ask of him, were so far from availing us, that it were just as if one told of a treasure were to allow it to remain buried in the ground. Hence the Apostle, to show that a faith unaccompanied with prayer to God cannot be genuine, states this to be the order: As faith springs from the Gospel, so by faith our hearts are framed to call upon the name of God (Rom. 10:14). And this is the very thing which he had expressed some time before— viz. that the Spirit of adoption, which seals the testimony of the Gospel on our hearts, gives us courage to make our requests known unto God, calls forth groanings which cannot be uttered, and enables us to cry, Abba, Father (Rom. 8:26). This last point, as we have hitherto only touched upon it slightly in passing, must now be treated more fully.

2. To *prayer*, then, are we indebted for penetrating to those riches which are treasured up for us with our heavenly Father. For there is a kind of intercourse between God and men, by which, having entered the upper sanctuary, they appear before Him and appeal to his promises, that when necessity requires they may learn by experiences that what they believed merely on the authority of his word was not in vain. Accordingly, we see that nothing is set before us as an object of expectation from the Lord which we are not enjoined to ask of Him in prayer, so true it is that prayer digs up those treasures which the Gospel of our Lord discovers to the eye of faith. The necessity and utility of this exercise of prayer no words can sufficiently express. Assuredly it is not without cause our heavenly Father declares that our only safety is in calling upon his name, since by it we invoke the presence of his providence to watch over our interests, of his power

to sustain us when weak and almost fainting, of his goodness to receive us into favour, though miserably loaded with sin; in fine, call upon him to manifest himself to us in all his perfections. Hence, admirable peace and tranquillity are given to our consciences; for the straits by which we were pressed being laid before the Lord, we rest fully satisfied with the assurance that none of our evils are unknown to him, and that he is both able and willing to make the best provision for us.

3. But some one will say, Does he not know without a monitor both what our difficulties are, and what is meet for our interest, so that it seems in some measure superfluous to solicit him by our prayers, as if he were winking, or even sleeping, until aroused by the sound of our voice? Those who argue thus attend not to the end for which the Lord taught us to pray. It was not so much for his sake as for ours. He wills indeed, as is just, that due honour be paid him by acknowledging that all which men desire or feel to be useful, and pray to obtain, is derived from him. But even the benefit of the homage which we thus pay him redounds to ourselves. Hence the holy patriarchs, the more confidently they proclaimed the mercies of God to themselves and others felt the stronger incitement to prayer. It will be sufficient to refer to the example of Elijah, who being assured of the purpose of God had good ground for the promise of rain which he gives to Ahab, and yet prays anxiously upon his knees, and sends his servant seven times to inquire (1 Kings 18:42); not that he discredits the oracle, but because he knows it to be his duty to lay his desires before God, lest his faith should become drowsy or torpid. Wherefore, although it is true that while we are listless or insensible to our wretchedness, he wakes and watches for use and sometimes even assists us unasked; it is very much for our interest to be constantly supplicating him; first, that our heart may always be inflamed with a serious and ardent desire of seeking, loving and serving him, while we accustom ourselves to have recourse to him as a sacred anchor in every necessity; secondly, that no desires, no longing whatever, of which we are ashamed to make him the witness, may enter our minds, while we learn to place all our wishes in his sight, and thus pour out our heart before him; and, lastly, that we may be prepared to receive all his benefits with true gratitude and thanksgiving, while our prayers remind us that they proceed from his hand. Moreover, having obtained what we asked, being persuaded that he has answered our prayers, we are led to long more earnestly for his favour, and at the same time have greater pleasure in welcoming the blessings which we perceive to have been obtained by our prayers. Lastly, use and experience confirm the thought of his providence in our minds in a manner adapted to our weakness, when we understand that he not only promises that he will never fail us, and spontaneously gives us access to approach him in every time of need, but has his hand always stretched out to assist his people, not amusing them with words, but proving himself to be a present aid. For these reasons, though our most merciful Father never slumbers nor sleeps, he very often seems to do so, that thus he may exercise us, when we might otherwise be listless and slothful, in asking, entreating, and earnestly beseeching him to our great good. It is very absurd, therefore, to dissuade men from prayer, by pretending that Divine Providence, which is always watching over the government of the universes is in vain importuned by our supplications, when, on the contrary, the Lord himself declares, that he is "nigh unto all that call upon him, to all that call upon him in truth" (Ps. 145:18). No better is the frivolous allegation of others, that it is superfluous to pray for things which the Lord is ready of his own accord to bestow; since it is his pleasure that those very things which flow from his spontaneous liberality should be acknowledged as conceded to our prayers. This is testified by that memorable sentence in the psalms to which many others corresponds: "The eyes of the Lord are upon the righteous, and his ears are open unto their cry" (Ps. 34:15). This passage, while extolling the care which Divine Providence spontaneously exercises over the safety of believers, omits not the exercise of faith by which the mind is aroused from sloth. The eyes of God are awake to assist the blind in their necessity, but he is likewise pleased to listen to our groans, that he may give us the better proof of his love. And thus both things are true, "He that keepeth Israel shall neither slumber nor sleep" (Ps. 121:4); and yet whenever he sees us dumb and torpid, he withdraws as if he had forgotten us.

4. Let the first rule of right prayer then be, to have our heart and mind framed as becomes those who are entering into converse with God. This we shall accomplish in regard to the mind, if, laying aside carnal thoughts and cares which might interfere with the direct and pure contemplation of God, it not only be wholly intent on prayer, but also, as far as possible, be borne and raised above itself. I do not here insist on a mind so disengaged as to feel none of the gnawings of anxiety; on the contrary, it is by much anxiety that the fervor of prayer is inflamed. Thus we see that the holy servants of God betray great anguish, not to say solicitude, when they cause the voice of complaint to ascend to the Lord from the deep abyss and the

jaws of death. What I say is, that all foreign and extraneous cares must be dispelled by which the mind might be driven to and fro in vague suspense, be drawn down from heaven, and kept groveling on the earth. When I say it must be raised above itself, I mean that it must not bring into the presence of God any of those things which our blind and stupid reason is wont to devise, nor keep itself confined within the little measure of its own vanity, but rise to a purity worthy of God.

5. Both things are specially worthy of notice. First, let every one in professing to pray turn thither all his thoughts and feelings, and be not (as is usual) distracted by wandering thoughts; because nothing is more contrary to the reverence due to God than that levity which bespeaks a mind too much given to license and devoid of fear. In this matter we ought to labour the more earnestly the more difficult we experience it to be; for no man is so intent on prayer as not to feel many thoughts creeping in, and either breaking off the tenor of his prayer, or retarding it by some turning or digression. Here let us consider how unbecoming it is when God admits us to familiar intercourse to abuse his great condescension by mingling things sacred and profane, reverence for him not keeping our minds under restraint; but just as if in prayer we were conversing with one like ourselves forgetting him, and allowing our thoughts to run to and fro. Let us know, then, that none duly prepare themselves for prayer but those who are so impressed with the majesty of God that they engage in it free from all earthly cares and affections. The ceremony of lifting up our hands in prayer is designed to remind us that we are far removed from God, unless our thoughts rise upward: as it is said in the psalm, "Unto thee, O Lord, do I lift up my soul" (Psalm 25:1). And Scripture repeatedly uses the expression to *raise our prayer*, meaning that those who would be heard by God must not grovel in the mire. The sum is, that the more liberally God deals with us, condescendingly inviting us to disburden our cares into his bosom, the less excusable we are if this admirable and incomparable blessing does not in our estimation outweigh all other things, and win our affection, that prayer may seriously engage our every thought and feeling. This cannot be unless our mind, strenuously exerting itself against all impediments, rise upward. Our second proposition was, that we are to ask only in so far as God permits. For though he bids us pour out our hearts (Ps. 62:8) he does not indiscriminately give loose reins to foolish and depraved affections; and when he promises that he will grant believers their wish, his indulgence does not proceed so far as to submit to their caprice. In both matters grievous delinquencies are everywhere committed. For not only do many without modesty, without reverence, presume to invoke God concerning their frivolities, but impudently bring forward their dreams, whatever they may be, before the tribunal of God. Such is the folly or stupidity under which they labour, that they have the hardihood to obtrude upon God desires so vile, that they would blush exceedingly to impart them to their fellow men. Profane writers have derided and even expressed their detestation of this presumption, and yet the vice has always prevailed. Hence, as the ambitious adopted Jupiter as their patron; the avaricious, Mercury; the literary aspirants, Apollo and Minerva; the warlike, Mars; the licentious, Venus: so in the present day, as I lately observed, men in prayer give greater license to their unlawful desires than if they were telling jocular tales among their equals. God does not suffer his condescension to be thus mocked, but vindicating his own light, places our wishes under the restraint of his authority. We must, therefore, attend to the observation of John, "This is the confidence that we have in him, that if we ask any thing according to his will, he heareth us" (1 John 5:14). But as our faculties are far from being able to attain to such high perfection, we must seek for some means to assist them. As the eye of our mind should be intent upon God, so the affection of our heart ought to follow in the same course. But both fall far beneath this, or rather, they faint and fail, and are carried in a contrary direction. To assist this weakness, God gives us the guidance of the Spirit in our prayers to dictate what is right, and regulate our affections. For seeing "we know not what we should pray for as we ought," "the Spirit itself maketh intercession for us with groanings which cannot be uttered" (Rom. 8:26) not that he actually prays or groans, but he excites in us sighs, and wishes, and confidence, which our natural powers are not at all able to conceive. Nor is it without cause Paul gives the name of *groanings which cannot be uttered* to the prayers which believers send forth under the guidance of the Spirit. For those who are truly exercised in prayer are not unaware that blind anxieties so restrain and perplex them, that they can scarcely find what it becomes them to utter; nay, in attempting to lisp they halt and hesitate. Hence it appears that to pray aright is a special gift. We do not speak thus in indulgence to our sloth, as if we were to leave the office of prayer to the Holy Spirit, and give way to that carelessness to which we are too prone. Thus we sometimes hear the impious expression, that we are to wait in suspense until he take possession of our

minds while otherwise occupied. Our meaning is, that, weary of our own heartlessness and sloth, we are to long for the aid of the Spirit. Nor, indeed, does Paul, when he enjoins us to pray *in the Spirit* (1 Cor. 14:15), cease to exhort us to vigilance, intimating, that while the inspiration of the Spirit is effectual to the formation of prayer, it by no means impedes or retards our own endeavours; since in this matter God is pleased to try how efficiently faith influences our hearts.

6. Another rule of prayer is, that in asking we must always truly feel our wants, and seriously considering that we need all the things which we ask, accompany the prayer with a sincere, nay, ardent desire of obtaining them. Many repeat prayers in a perfunctory manner from a set form, as if they were performing a task to God, and though they confess that this is a necessary remedy for the evils of their condition, because it were fatal to be left without the divine aid which they implore, it still appears that they perform the duty from custom, because their minds are meanwhile cold, and they ponder not what they ask. A general and confused feeling of their necessity leads them to pray, but it does not make them solicitous as in a matter of present consequence, that they may obtain the supply of their need. Moreover, can we suppose anything more hateful or even more execrable to God than this fiction of asking the pardon of sins, while he who asks at the very time either thinks that he is not a sinner, or, at least, is not thinking that he is a sinner; in other words, a fiction by which God is plainly held in derision? But mankind, as I have lately said, are full of depravity, so that in the way of perfunctory service they often ask many things of God which they think come to them without his beneficence, or from some other quarter, or are already certainly in their possession. There is another fault which seems less heinous, but is not to be tolerated. Some murmur out prayers without meditation, their only principle being that God is to be propitiated by prayer. Believers ought to be specially on their guard never to appear in the presence of God with the intention of presenting a request unless they are under some serious impression, and are, at the same time, desirous to obtain it. Nay, although in these things which we ask only for the glory of God, we seem not at first sight to consult for our necessity, yet we ought not to ask with less fervor and vehemence of desire. For instance, when we pray that his name be hallowed—that hallowing must, so to speak, be earnestly hungered and thirsted after.

7. If it is objected, that the necessity which urges us to pray is not always equal, I admit it, and this distinction is profitably taught us by James: "Is any among you afflicted? let him pray. Is any merry? let him sing psalms" (James 5:13). Therefore, common sense itself dictates, that as we are too sluggish, we must be stimulated by God to pray earnestly whenever the occasion requires. This David calls a time when God "may be found" (a seasonable time); because, as he declares in several other passages, that the more hardly grievances, annoyances, fears, and other kinds of trial press us, the freer is our access to God, as if he were inviting us to himself. Still not less true is the injunction of Paul to pray "always" (Eph. 6:18); because, however prosperously according to our view, things proceed, and however we may be surrounded on all sides with grounds of joy, there is not an instant of time during which our want does not exhort us to prayer. A man abounds in wheat and wine; but as he cannot enjoy a morsel of bread, unless by the continual bounty of God, his granaries or cellars will not prevent him from asking for daily bread. Then, if we consider how many dangers impend every moment, fear itself will teach us that no time ought to be without prayer. This, however, may be better known in spiritual matters. For when will the many sins of which we are conscious allow us to sit secure without suppliantly entreating freedom from guilt and punishment? When will temptation give us a truce, making it unnecessary to hasten for help? Moreover, zeal for the kingdom and glory of God ought not to seize us by starts, but urge us without intermission, so that every time should appear seasonable. It is not without cause, therefore, that assiduity in prayer is so often enjoined. I am not now speaking of perseverance, which shall afterwards be considered; but Scripture, by reminding us of the necessity of constant prayer, charges us with sloth, because we feel not how much we stand in need of this care and assiduity. By this rule hypocrisy and the device of lying to God are restrained, nay, altogether banished from prayer. God promises that he will be near to those who call upon him in truth, and declares that those who seek him with their whole heart will find him: those, therefore, who delight in their own pollution cannot surely aspire to him. One of the requisites of legitimate prayer is repentance. Hence the common declaration of Scripture, that God does not listen to the wicked; that their prayers, as well as their sacrifices, are an abomination to him. For it is right that those who seal up their hearts should find the ears of God closed against them, that those who, by their hardheartedness, provoke his severity should find him inflexible. In Isaiah he thus threatens: "When ye make many prayers, I will not hear:

your hands are full of blood" (Isaiah 1:15). In like manner, in Jeremiah, "Though they shall cry unto me, I will not hearken unto them" (Jer. 11:7, 8, 11); because he regards it as the highest insult for the wicked to boast of his covenant while profaning his sacred name by their whole lives. Hence he complains in Isaiah: "This people draw near to me with their mouth, and with their lips do honour me; but have removed their heart far from men" (Isaiah 29:13). Indeed, he does not confine this to prayers alone, but declares that he abominates pretense in every part of his service. Hence the words of James, "Ye ask and receive note because ye ask amiss, that ye may consume it upon your lusts" (James 4:3). It is true, indeed (as we shall again see in a little), that the pious, in the prayers which they utter, trust not to their own worth; still the admonition of John is not superfluous: "Whatsoever we ask, we receive of him, because we keep his commandments" (1 John 3:22); an evil conscience shuts the door against us. Hence it follows, that none but the sincere worshippers of God pray aright, or are listened to. Let every one, therefore, who prepares to pray feel dissatisfied with what is wrong in his condition, and assume, which he cannot do without repentance, the character and feelings of a poor suppliant.

8. The third rule to be added is: that he who comes into the presence of God to pray must divest himself of all vainglorious thoughts, lay aside all idea of worth; in short, discard all self-confidence, humbly giving God the whole glory, lest by arrogating any thing, however little, to himself, vain pride cause him to turn away his face. Of this submission, which casts down all haughtiness, we have numerous examples in the servants of God. The holier they are, the more humbly they prostrate themselves when they come into the presence of the Lord. Thus Daniel, on whom the Lord himself bestowed such high commendation, says, "We do not present our supplications before thee for our righteousness but for thy great mercies. O Lord, hear; O Lord, forgive; O Lord, hearken and do; defer not, for thine own sake, O my God: for thy city and thy people are called by thy name." This he does not indirectly in the usual manner, as if he were one of the individuals in a crowd: he rather confesses his guilt apart, and as a suppliant betaking himself to the asylum of pardon, he distinctly declares that he was confessing his own sin, and the sin of his people Israel (Dan. 9:18–20). David also sets us an example of this humility: "Enter not into judgment with thy servant: for in thy sight shall no man living be justified" (Psalm 143:2). In like manner, Isaiah prays, "Behold, thou art wroth; for we have sinned: in those is continuance, and we shall be saved. But we are all as an unclean thing, and all our righteousnesses are as filthy rags; and we all do fade as a leaf; and our iniquities, like the wind, have taken us away. And there is none that calleth upon thy name, that stirreth up himself to take hold of thee: for thou hast hid thy face from us, and hast consumed us, because of our iniquities. But now, O Lord, thou art our Father; we are the clay, and thou our potter; and we all are the work of thy hand. Be not wroth very sore, O Lord, neither remember iniquity for ever: Behold, see, we beseech thee, we are all thy people." (Isa. 64:5–9). You see how they put no confidence in any thing but this: considering that they are the Lord's, they despair not of being the objects of his care. In the same way, Jeremiah says, "O Lord, though our iniquities testify against us, do thou it for thy name's sake" (Jer. 14:7). For it was most truly and piously written by the uncertain author (whoever he may have been) that wrote the book which is attributed to the prophet Baruch, "But the soul that is greatly vexed, which goeth stooping and feeble, and the eyes that fail, and the hungry soul, will give thee praise and righteousness, O Lord. Therefore, we do not make our humble supplication before thee, O Lord our God, for the righteousness of our fathers, and of our kings." "Hear, O Lord, and have mercy; for thou art merciful: and have pity upon us, because we have sinned before thee" (Baruch 2:18, 19; 3:2).

9. In fine, supplication for pardon, with humble and ingenuous confession of guilt, forms both the preparation and commencement of right prayer. For the holiest of men cannot hope to obtain any thing from God until he has been freely reconciled to him. God cannot be propitious to any but those whom he pardons. Hence it is not strange that this is the key by which believers open the door of prayer, as we learn from several passages in The Psalms. David, when presenting a request on a different subject, says, "Remember not the sins of my youth, nor my transgressions; according to thy mercy remember me, for thy goodness sake, O Lord" (Psalm 25:7). Again, "Look upon my affliction and my pain, and forgive my sins" (Psalm 25:18). Here also we see that it is not sufficient to call ourselves to account for the sins of each passing day; we must also call to mind those which might seem to have been long before buried in oblivion. For in another passage the same prophet, confessing one grievous crime, takes occasion to go back to his very birth, "I was shapen in iniquity, and in sin did my mother conceive me" (Psalm 51:5); not to extenuate the fault by the corruption of his nature, but as it

were to accumulate the sins of his whole life, that the stricter he was in condemning himself, the more placable God might be. But although the saints do not always in express terms ask forgiveness of sins, yet if we carefully ponder those prayers as given in Scripture, the truth of what I say will readily appear; namely, that their courage to pray was derived solely from the mercy of God, and that they always began with appeasing him. For when a man interrogates his conscience, so far is he from presuming to lay his cares familiarly before God, that if he did not trust to mercy and pardon, he would tremble at the very thought of approaching him. There is, indeed, another special confession. When believers long for deliverance from punishment, they at the same time pray that their sins may be pardoned; for it were absurd to wish that the effect should be taken away while the cause remains. For we must beware of imitating foolish patients who, anxious only about curing accidental symptoms, neglect the root of the disease. Nay, our endeavour must be to have God propitious even before he attests his favour by external signs, both because this is the order which he himself chooses, and it were of little avail to experience his kindness, did not conscience feel that he is appeased, and thus enable us to regard him as altogether lovely. Of this we are even reminded by our Savior's reply. Having determined to cure the paralytic, he says, "Thy sins are forgiven thee;" in other words, he raises our thoughts to the object which is especially to be desired—viz. admission into the favour of God, and then gives the fruit of reconciliation by bringing assistance to us. But besides that special confession of present guilt which believers employ, in supplicating for pardon of every fault and punishment, that general introduction which procures favour for our prayers must never be omitted, because prayers will never reach God unless they are founded on free mercy. To this we may refer the words of John, "If we confess our sins, he is faithful and just to forgive us our sins and to cleanse us from all unrighteousness" (1 John 1:9). Hence, under the law it was necessary to consecrate prayers by the expiation of blood, both that they might be accepted, and that the people might be warned that they were unworthy of the high privilege until, being purged from their defilements, they founded their confidence in prayer entirely on the mercy of God.

10. Sometimes, however, the saints in supplicating God, seem to appeal to their own righteousness, as when David says, "Preserve my soul; for I am holy" (Ps. 86:2). Also Hezekiah, "Remember now, O Lord, I beseech thee how I have walked before thee in truth, and with a perfect heart, and have done that which is good in thy sight" (Is. 38:2). All they mean by such expressions is, that regeneration declares them to be among the servants and children to whom God engages that he will show favour. We have already seen how he declares by the Psalmist that his eyes "are upon the righteous, and his ears are open unto their cry" (Ps. 34:16) and again by the apostle, that "whatsoever we ask of him we obtain, because we keep his commandments" (John 3:22). In these passages he does not fix a value on prayer as a meritorious work, but designs to establish the confidence of those who are conscious of an unfeigned integrity and innocence, such as all believers should possess. For the saying of the blind man who had received his sight is in perfect accordance with divine truth, And God heareth not sinners (John 9:31); provided we take the term sinners in the sense commonly used by Scripture to mean those who, without any desire for righteousness, are sleeping secure in their sins; since no heart will ever rise to genuine prayer that does not at the same time long for holiness. Those supplications in which the saints allude to their purity and integrity correspond to such promises, that they may thus have, in their own experience, a manifestation of that which all the servants of God are made to expect. Thus they almost always use this mode of prayer when before God they compare themselves with their enemies, from whose injustice they long to be delivered by his hand. When making such comparisons, there is no wonder that they bring forward their integrity and simplicity of heart, that thus, by the justice of their cause, the Lord may be the more disposed to give them succour. We rob not the pious breast of the privilege of enjoying a consciousness of purity before the Lord, and thus feeling assured of the promises with which he comforts and supports his true worshippers, but we would have them to lay aside all thought of their own merits and found their confidence of success in prayer solely on the divine mercy.

11. The fourth rule of prayer is, that notwithstanding of our being thus abased and truly humbled, we should be animated to pray with the sure hope of succeeding. There is, indeed, an appearance of contradiction between the two things, between a sense of the just vengeance of God and firm confidence in his favour, and yet they are perfectly accordant, if it is the mere goodness of God that raises up those who are overwhelmed by their own sins. For, as we have formerly shown (chap. 3, sec. 1, 2) that repentance and faith go hand in hand, being united by an indissoluble tie, the one causing terror, the other joy, so in prayer they must both be present. This concurrence

David expresses in a few words: "But as for me, I will come into thy house in the multitude of thy mercy, and in thy fear will I worship toward thy holy temple" (Ps. 5:7). Under the goodness of God he comprehends faith, at the same time not excluding fear; for not only does his majesty compel our reverence, but our own unworthiness also divests us of all pride and confidence, and keeps us in fear. The confidence of which I speak is not one which frees the mind from all anxiety, and soothes it with sweet and perfect rest; such rest is peculiar to those who, while all their affairs are flowing to a wish are annoyed by no care, stung with no regret, agitated by no fear. But the best stimulus which the saints have to prayer is when, in consequence of their own necessities, they feel the greatest disquietude, and are all but driven to despair, until faith seasonably comes to their aid; because in such straits the goodness of God so shines upon them, that while they groan, burdened by the weight of present calamities, and tormented with the fear of greater, they yet trust to this goodness, and in this way both lighten the difficulty of endurance, and take comfort in the hope of final deliverance. It is necessary therefore, that the prayer of the believer should be the result of both feelings, and exhibit the influence of both; namely, that while he groans under present and anxiously dreads new evils, he should, at the same times have recourse to God, not at all doubting that God is ready to stretch out a helping hand to him. For it is not easy to say how much God is irritated by our distrust, when we ask what we expect not of his goodness. Hence, nothing is more accordant to the nature of prayer than to lay it down as a fixed rule, that it is not to come forth at random, but is to follow in the footsteps of faith. To this principle Christ directs all of us in these words, "Therefore, I say unto you, What things soever ye desire, when ye pray, believe that ye receive them, and ye shall have them" (Mark 11:24). The same thing he declares in another passage, "All things, whatsoever ye shall ask in prayer, believing, ye shall receive" (Mt. 21:22). In accordance with this are the words of James, "If any of you lack wisdom, let him ask of God, that giveth to all men liberally, and upbraideth not, and it shall be given him. But let him ask in faith, nothing wavering" (James 1:5). He most aptly expresses the power of faith by opposing it to wavering. No less worthy of notice is his additional statement, that those who approach God with a doubting, hesitating mind, without feeling assured whether they are to be heard or not, gain nothing by their prayers. Such persons he compares to a wave of the sea, driven with the wind and tossed. Hence, in another passage he terms genuine prayer "the prayer of faith" (James 5:15). Again, since God so often declares that he will give to every man according to his faith he intimates that we cannot obtain any thing without faith. In short, it is faith which obtains every thing that is granted to prayer. This is the meaning of Paul in the well known passage to which dull men give too little heed, "How then shall they call upon him in whom they have not believed? and how shall they believe in him of whom they have not heard?" "So then faith cometh by hearing, and hearing by the word of God" (Rom. 10:14, 17). Gradually deducing the origin of prayer from faith, he distinctly maintains that God cannot be invoked sincerely except by those to whom, by the preaching of the Gospel, his mercy and willingness have been made known, nay, familiarly explained.

12. This necessity our opponents do not at all consider. Therefore, when we say that believers ought to feel firmly assured, they think we are saying the absurdest thing in the world. But if they had any experience in true prayer, they would assuredly understand that God cannot be duly invoked without this firm sense of the Divine benevolence. But as no man can well perceive the power of faith, without at the same time feeling it in his heart, what profit is there in disputing with men of this character, who plainly show that they have never had more than a vain imagination? The value and necessity of that assurance for which we contend is learned chiefly from prayer. Every one who does not see this gives proof of a very stupid conscience. Therefore, leaving those who are thus blinded, let us fix our thoughts on the words of Paul, that God can only be invoked by such as have obtained a knowledge of his mercy from the Gospel, and feel firmly assured that that mercy is ready to be bestowed upon them. What kind of prayer would this be? "O Lord, I am indeed doubtful whether or not thou art inclined to hear me; but being oppressed with anxiety I fly to thee that if I am worthy, thou mayest assist me." None of the saints whose prayers are given in Scripture thus supplicated. Nor are we thus taught by the Holy Spirit, who tells us to "come boldly unto the throne of grace, that we may obtain mercy, and find grace to help in time of need" (Heb. 4:16); and elsewhere teaches us to "have boldness and access with confidence by the faith of Christ" (Eph. 3:12). This confidence of obtaining what we ask, a confidence which the Lord commands, and all the saints teach by their example, we must therefore hold fast with both hands, if we would pray to any advantage. The only prayer acceptable to God is that which springs (if I may so express it) from this presumption of faith,

and is founded on the full assurance of hope. He might have been contented to use the simple name of faith, but he adds not only confidence, but liberty or boldness, that by this mark he might distinguish us from unbelievers, who indeed like us pray to God, but pray at random. Hence, the whole Church thus prays "Let thy mercy O Lord, be upon us, according as we hope in thee" (Ps. 33:22). The same condition is set down by the Psalmist in another passage, "When I cry unto thee, then shall mine enemies turn back: this I know, for God is for me" (Ps. 56:9). Again, "In the morning will I direct my prayer unto thee, and will look up" (Ps. 5:3). From these words we gather, that prayers are vainly poured out into the air unless accompanied with faith, in which, as from a watchtower, we may quietly wait for God. With this agrees the order of Paul's exhortation. For before urging believers to pray in the Spirit always, with vigilance and assiduity, he enjoins them to take "the shield of faith," "the helmet of salvation, and the sword of the Spirit, which is the word of God" (Eph. 6:16–18). Let the reader here call to mind what I formerly observed, that faith by no means fails though accompanied with a recognition of our wretchedness, poverty, and pollution. How much soever believers may feel that they are oppressed by a heavy load of iniquity, and are not only devoid of every thing which can procure the favour of God for them, but justly burdened with many sins which make him an object of dread, yet they cease not to present themselves, this feeling not deterring them from appearing in his presence, because there is no other access to him. Genuine prayer is not that by which we arrogantly extol ourselves before God, or set a great value on any thing of our own, but that by which, while confessing our guilt, we utter our sorrows before God, just as children familiarly lay their complaints before their parents. Nay, the immense accumulation of our sins should rather spur us on and incite us to prayer. Of this the Psalmist gives us an example, "Heal my soul: for I have sinned against thee" (Ps. 41:4). I confess, indeed, that these stings would prove mortal darts, did not God give succour; but our heavenly Father has, in ineffable kindness, added a remedy, by which, calming all perturbation, soothing our cares, and dispelling our fears he condescendingly allures us to himself; nay, removing all doubts, not to say obstacles, makes the way smooth before us.

13. And first, indeed in enjoining us to pray, he by the very injunction convicts us of impious contumacy if we obey not. He could not give a more precise command than that which is contained in the psalms: "Call upon me in the day of trouble" (Ps. 50:15). But as there is no office of piety more frequently enjoined by Scripture, there is no occasion for here dwelling longer upon it. "Ask," says our Divine Master, "and it shall be given you; seek, and ye shall find; knock, and it shall be opened unto you" (Mt. 7:7). Here, indeed, a promise is added to the precept, and this is necessary. For though all confess that we must obey the precept, yet the greater part would shun the invitation of God, did he not promise that he would listen and be ready to answer. These two positions being laid down, it is certain that all who cavillingly allege that they are not to come to God directly, are not only rebellious and disobedient but are also convicted of unbelief, inasmuch as they distrust the promises. There is the more occasion to attend to this, because hypocrites, under a pretense of humility and modesty, proudly contemn the precept, as well as deny all credit to the gracious invitation of God; nay, rob him of a principal part of his worship. For when he rejected sacrifices, in which all holiness seemed then to consist, he declared that the chief thing, that which above all others is precious in his sight, is to be invoked in the day of necessity. Therefore, when he demands that which is his own, and urges us to alacrity in obeying, no pretexts for doubt, how specious soever they may be, can excuse us. Hence, all the passages throughout Scripture in which we are commanded to pray, are set up before our eyes as so many banners, to inspire us with confidence. It were presumption to go forward into the presence of God, did he not anticipate us by his invitation. Accordingly, he opens up the way for us by his own voice, "I will say, It is my people: and they shall say, The Lord is my God" (Zech. 13:9). We see how he anticipates his worshippers, and desires them to follow, and therefore we cannot fear that the melody which he himself dictates will prove unpleasing. Especially let us call to mind that noble description of the divine character, by trusting to which we shall easily overcome every obstacle: "O thou that hearest prayer, unto thee shall all flesh come" (Ps. 65:2). What can be more lovely or soothing than to see God invested with a title which assures us that nothing is more proper to his nature than to listen to the prayers of suppliants? Hence the Psalmist infers, that free access is given not to a few individuals, but to all men, since God addresses all in these terms, "Call upon me in the day of trouble: I will deliver thee, and thou shalt glorify me" (Ps. 50:15). David, accordingly, appeals to the promise thus given in order to obtain what he asks: "Thou, O Lord of hosts, God of Israel, hast revealed to thy servant, saying, I will build thee an house: therefore hath thy servant

found in his heart to pray this prayer unto thee" (2 Sam. 7:27). Here we infer, that he would have been afraid but for the promise which emboldened him. So in another passage he fortifies himself with the general doctrine, "He will fulfill the desire of them that fear him" (Ps. 145:19). Nay, we may observe in The Psalms how the continuity of prayer is broken, and a transition is made at one time to the power of God, at another to his goodness, at another to the faithfulness of his promises. It might seem that David, by introducing these sentiments, unseasonably mutilates his prayers; but believers well know by experience, that their ardor grows languid unless new fuel be added, and, therefore, that meditation as well on the nature as on the word of God during prayer, is by no means superfluous. Let us not decline to imitate the example of David, and introduce thoughts which may reanimate our languid minds with new vigor.

14. It is strange that these delightful promises affect us coldly, or scarcely at all, so that the generality of men prefer to wander up and down, forsaking the fountain of living waters, and hewing out to themselves broken cisterns, rather than embrace the divine liberality voluntarily offered to them. "The name of the Lord," says Solomon, "is a strong tower; the righteous runneth into it, and is safe." Joel, after predicting the fearful disaster which was at hand, subjoins the following memorable sentence: "And it shall come to pass, that whosoever shall call on the name of the Lord shall be delivered." This we know properly refers to the course of the Gospel. Scarcely one in a hundred is moved to come into the presence of God, though he himself exclaims by Isaiah, "And it shall come to pass, that before they call, I will answer; and while they are yet speaking, I will hear." This honour he elsewhere bestows upon the whole Church in general, as belonging to all the members of Christ: "He shall call upon me, and I will answer him: I will be with him in trouble; I will deliver him, and honour him." My intention, however, as I already observed, is not to enumerate all, but only select some admirable passages as a specimen how kindly God allures us to himself, and how extreme our ingratitude must be when with such powerful motives our sluggishness still retards us. Wherefore, let these words always resound in our ears: "The Lord is nigh unto all them that call upon him, to all that call upon him in truth" (Ps. 145:18). Likewise those passages which we have quoted from Isaiah and Joel, in which God declares that his ear is open to our prayers, and that he is delighted as with a sacrifice of sweet savour when we cast our cares upon him. The special benefit of these promises we receive when we frame our prayer, not timorously or doubtingly, but when trusting to his word whose majesty might otherwise deter us, we are bold to call him Father, he himself deigning to suggest this most delightful name. Fortified by such invitations it remains for us to know that we have therein sufficient materials for prayer, since our prayers depend on no merit of our own, but all their worth and hope of success are founded and depend on the promises of God, so that they need no other support, and require not to look up and down on this hand and on that. It must therefore be fixed in our minds, that though we equal not the lauded sanctity of patriarchs, prophets, and apostles, yet as the command to pray is common to us as well as them, and faith is common, so if we lean on the word of God, we are in respect of this privilege their associates. For God declaring, as has already been seen, that he will listen and be favourable to all, encourages the most wretched to hope that they shall obtain what they ask; and, accordingly, we should attend to the general forms of expression, which, as it is commonly expressed, exclude none from first to last; only let there be sincerity of heart, self-dissatisfaction humility, and faith, that we may not, by the hypocrisy of a deceitful prayer, profane the name of God. Our most merciful Father will not reject those whom he not only encourages to come, but urges in every possible way. Hence David's method of prayer to which I lately referred: "And now, O Lord God, thou art that God, and thy words be true, and thou hast promised this goodness unto thy servant, that it may continue for ever before thee" (2 Sam. 7:28). So also, in another passage, "Let, I pray thee, thy merciful kindness be for my comfort, according to thy word unto thy servant" (Psalm 119:76). And the whole body of the Israelites, whenever they fortify themselves with the remembrance of the covenant, plainly declare, that since God thus prescribes they are not to pray timorously (Gen. 32:13). In this they imitated the example of the patriarchs, particularly Jacob, who, after confessing that he was unworthy of the many mercies which he had received of the Lord's hand, says, that he is encouraged to make still larger requests, because God had promised that he would grant them. But whatever be the pretexts which unbelievers employ, when they do not flee to God as often as necessity urges, nor seek after him, nor implore his aid, they defraud him of his due honour just as much as if they were fabricating to themselves new gods and idols, since in this way they deny that God is the author of all their blessings. On the contrary, nothing more effectually frees pious minds from every doubt, than to be

armed with the thought that no obstacle should impede them while they are obeying the command of God, who declares that nothing is more grateful to him than obedience. Hence, again, what I have previously said becomes still more clear, namely, that a bold spirit in prayer well accords with fear, reverence, and anxiety, and that there is no inconsistency when God raises up those who had fallen prostrate. In this way forms of expression apparently inconsistent admirably harmonize. Jeremiah and David speak of humbly laying their supplications before God. In another passage Jeremiah says "Let, we beseech thee, our supplication be accepted before thee, and pray for us unto the Lord thy God, even for all this remnant." On the other hand, believers are often said to *lift up prayer*. Thus Hezekiah speaks, when asking the prophet to undertake the office of interceding. And David says, "Let my prayer be set forth before thee as incense; and the lifting up of my hands as the evening sacrifice." The explanation is, that though believers, persuaded of the paternal love of God, cheerfully rely on his faithfulness, and have no hesitation in imploring the aid which he voluntarily offers, they are not elated with supine or presumptuous security; but climbing up by the ladder of the promises, still remain humble and abased suppliants.

15. Here, by way of objection, several questions are raised. Scripture relates that God sometimes complied with certain prayers which had been dictated by minds not duly calmed or regulated. It is true, that the cause for which Jotham imprecated on the inhabitants of Shechem the disaster which afterwards befell them was well founded; but still he was inflamed with anger and revenge (Judges 9:20); and hence God, by complying with the execration, seems to approve of passionate impulses. Similar fervor also seized Samson, when he prayed, "Strengthen me, I pray thee, only this once, O God, that I may be at once avenged of the Philistines for my two eyes" (Judges 16:28). For although there was some mixture of good zeal, yet his ruling feeling was a fervid, and therefore vicious longing for vengeance. God assents, and hence apparently it might be inferred that prayers are effectual, though not framed in conformity to the rule of the word. But I answer, *first*, that a perpetual law is not abrogated by singular examples; and, *secondly*, that special suggestions have sometimes been made to a few individuals, whose case thus becomes different from that of the generality of men. For we should attend to the answer which our Saviour gave to his disciples when they inconsiderately wished to imitate the example of Elias, "Ye know not what manner of spirit ye are of" (Luke 9:55). We must, however, go farther and say, that the wishes to which God assents are not always pleasing to him; but he assents, because it is necessary, by way of example, to give clear evidence of the doctrine of Scripture—viz. that he assists the miserable, and hears the groans of those who unjustly afflicted implore his aid: and, accordingly, he executes his judgments when the complaints of the needy, though in themselves unworthy of attention, ascend to him. For how often, in inflicting punishment on the ungodly for cruelty, rapine, violence, lust, and other crimes, in curbing audacity and fury, and also in overthrowing tyrannical power, has he declared that he gives assistance to those who are unworthily oppressed though they by addressing an unknown deity only beat the air? There is one psalm which clearly teaches that prayers are not without effect, though they do not penetrate to heaven by faith (Ps. 107:6, 13, 19). For it enumerates the prayers which, by natural instinct, necessity extorts from unbelievers not less than from believers, and to which it shows by the event, that God is, notwithstanding, propitious. Is it to testify by such readiness to hear that their prayers are agreeable to him? Nay; it is, first, to magnify or display his mercy by the circumstance, that even the wishes of unbelievers are not denied; and, secondly, to stimulate his true worshippers to more urgent prayer, when they see that sometimes even the wailings of the ungodly are not without avail. This, however, is no reason why believers should deviate from the law divinely imposed upon them, or envy unbelievers, as if they gained much in obtaining what they wished. We have observed (chap. 3, sec. 25), that in this way God yielded to the feigned repentance of Ahab, that he might show how ready he is to listen to his elect when, with true contrition, they seek his favour. Accordingly, he upbraids the Jews, that shortly after experiencing his readiness to listen to their prayers, they returned to their own perverse inclinations. It is also plain from the Book of Judges that, whenever they wept, though their tears were deceitful, they were delivered from the hands of their enemies. Therefore, as God sends his sun indiscriminately on the evil and on the good, so he despises not the tears of those who have a good cause, and whose sorrows are deserving of relief. Meanwhile, though he hears them, it has no more to do with salvation than the supply of food which he gives to other despisers of his goodness. There seems to be a more difficult question concerning Abraham and Samuel, the one of whom, without any instruction from the word of God, prayed in behalf of the people of Sodom, and the other, contrary to an express

prohibition, prayed in behalf of Saul (Gen. 18:23; 1 Sam. 15:11). Similar is the case of Jeremiah, who prayed that the city might not be destroyed (Jer. 32:16). It is true their prayers were refused, but it seems harsh to affirm that they prayed without faith. Modest readers will, I hope, be satisfied with this solution—viz. that leaning to the general principle on which God enjoins us to be merciful even to the unworthy, they were not altogether devoid of faith, though in this particular instance their wish was disappointed. Augustine shrewdly remarks, "How do the saints pray in faith when they ask from God contrary to what he has decreed? Namely, because they pray according to his will, not his hidden and immutable will, but that which he suggests to them, that he may hear them in another manner; as he wisely distinguishes" (August. de Civit. Dei, Lib. 22 c. 2). This is truly said: for, in his incomprehensible counsel, he so regulates events, that the prayers of the saints, though involving a mixture of faith and error, are not in vain. And yet this no more sanctions imitation than it excuses the saints themselves, who I deny not exceeded due bounds. Wherefore, whenever no certain promise exists, our request to God must have a condition annexed to it. Here we may refer to the prayer of David, "Awake for me to the judgment that thou hast commanded" (Ps. 7:6); for he reminds us that he had received special instruction to pray for a temporal blessing.

16. It is also of importance to observe, that the four laws of prayer of which I have treated are not so rigorously enforced, as that God rejects the prayers in which he does not find perfect faith or repentance, accompanied with fervent zeal and wishes duly framed. We have said (sec. 4), that though prayer is the familiar intercourse of believers with God, yet reverence and modesty must be observed: we must not give loose reins to our wishes, nor long for any thing farther than God permits; and, moreover, lest the majesty of God should be despised, our minds must be elevated to pure and chaste veneration. This no man ever performed with due perfection. For, not to speak of the generality of men, how often do David's complaints savour of intemperance? Not that he actually means to expostulate with God, or murmur at his judgments, but failing, through infirmity, he finds no better solace than to pour his griefs into the bosom of his heavenly Father. Nay, even our stammering is tolerated by God, and pardon is granted to our ignorance as often as any thing rashly escapes us: indeed, without this indulgence, we should have no freedom to pray. But although it was David's intention to submit himself entirely to the will of God, and he prayed with no less patience than fervor, yet irregular emotions appear, nay, sometimes burst forth,—emotions not a little at variance with the first law which we laid down. In particular, we may see in a clause of the thirty-ninth Psalm, how this saint was carried away by the vehemence of his grief, and unable to keep within bounds. "O spare me, that I may recover strength, before I go hence, and be no more" (Ps. 39:13). You would call this the language of a desperate man, who had no other desire than that God should withdraw and leave him to relish in his distresses. Not that his devout mind rushes into such intemperance, or that, as the reprobate are wont, he wishes to have done with God; he only complains that the divine anger is more than he can bear. During those trials, wishes often escape which are not in accordance with the rule of the word, and in which the saints do not duly consider what is lawful and expedient. Prayers contaminated by such faults, indeed, deserve to be rejected; yet provided the saints lament, administer self-correction and return to themselves, God pardons. Similar faults are committed in regard to the second law (as to which, see sec. 6), for the saints have often to struggle with their own coldness, their want and misery not urging them sufficiently to serious prayer. It often happens, also, that their minds wander, and are almost lost; hence in this matter also there is need of pardon, lest their prayers, from being languid or mutilated, or interrupted and wandering, should meet with a refusal. One of the natural feelings which God has imprinted on our mind is, that prayer is not genuine unless the thoughts are turned upward. Hence the ceremony of raising the hands, to which we have adverted, a ceremony known to all ages and nations, and still in common use. But who, in lifting up his hands, is not conscious of sluggishness, the heart cleaving to the earth? In regard to the petition for remission of sins (sec. 8), though no believer omits it, yet all who are truly exercised in prayer feel that they bring scarcely a tenth of the sacrifice of which David speaks, "The sacrifices of God are a broken spirit: a broken and a contrite heart, O God, thou wilt not despise" (Ps. 51:17). Thus a twofold pardon is always to be asked; first, because they are conscious of many faults the sense of which, however, does not touch them so as to make them feel dissatisfied with themselves as they ought; and, secondly, in so far as they have been enabled to profit in repentance and the fear of God, they are humbled with just sorrow for their offenses, and pray for the remission of punishment by the judge. The thing which most of all vitiates prayer, did not God indulgently interpose, is

weakness or imperfection of faith; but it is not wonderful that this defect is pardoned by God, who often exercises his people with severe trials, as if he actually wished to extinguish their faith. The hardest of such trials is when believers are forced to exclaim, "O Lord God of hosts, how long wilt thou be angry against the prayer of thy people?" (Ps. 80:4), as if their very prayers offended him. In like manner, when Jeremiah says "Also when I cry and shout, he shutteth out my prayers" (Lam. 3:8), there cannot be a doubt that he was in the greatest perturbation. Innumerable examples of the same kind occur in the Scriptures, from which it is manifest that the faith of the saints was often mingled with doubts and fears, so that while believing and hoping, they, however, betrayed some degree of unbelief, But because they do not come so far as were to be wished, that is only an additional reason for their exerting themselves to correct their faults, that they may daily approach nearer to the perfect law of prayer, and at the same time feel into what an abyss of evils those are plunged, who, in the very cures they use, bring new diseases upon themselves: since there is no prayer which God would not deservedly disdain, did he not overlook the blemishes with which all of them are polluted. I do not mention these things that believers may securely pardon themselves in any faults which they commit, but that they may call themselves to strict account, and thereby endeavour to surmount these obstacles; and though Satan endeavours to block up all the paths in order to prevent them from praying, they may, nevertheless, break through, being firmly persuaded that though not disencumbered of all hindrances, their attempts are pleasing to God, and their wishes are approved, provided they hasten on and keep their aim, though without immediately reaching it.

17. But since no man is worthy to come forward in his own name, and appear in the presence of God, our heavenly Father, to relieve us at once from fear and shame, with which all must feel oppressed, has given us his Son, Jesus Christ our Lord, to be our Advocate and Mediator, that under his guidance we may approach securely, confiding that with him for our Intercessor nothing which we ask in his name will be denied to us, as there is nothing which the Father can deny to him (1 Tim. 2:5; 1 John 2:1; see sec. 36, 37). To this it is necessary to refer all that we have previously taught concerning faith; because, as the promise gives us Christ as our Mediator, so, unless our hope of obtaining what we ask is founded on him, it deprives us of the privilege of prayer. For it is impossible to think of the dread majesty of God without being filled with alarm; and hence the sense of our own unworthiness must keep us far away, until Christ interpose, and convert a throne of dreadful glory into a throne of grace, as the Apostle teaches that thus we can "come boldly unto the throne of grace, that we may obtain mercy, and find grace to help in time of need" (Heb. 4:16). And as a rule has been laid down as to prayer, as a promise has been given that those who pray will be heard, so we are specially enjoined to pray in the name of Christ, the promise being that we shall obtain what we ask in his name. "Whatsoever ye shall ask in my name," says our Saviour, "that will I do; that the Father may be glorified in the Son;" "Hitherto ye have asked nothing in my name; ask, and ye shall receive, that your joy may be full" (John 14:13; 16:24). Hence it is incontrovertibly clear that those who pray to God in any other name than that of Christ contumaciously falsify his orders, and regard his will as nothing, while they have no promise that they shall obtain. For, as Paul says "All the promises of God in him are yea, and in him amen;" (2 Cor. 1:20), that is, are confirmed and fulfilled in him.

18. And we must carefully attend to the circumstance of time. Christ enjoins his disciples to have recourse to his intercession after he shall have ascended to heaven: "At that day ye shall ask in my name" (John 16:26). It is certain, indeed, that from the very first all who ever prayed were heard only for the sake of the Mediator. For this reason God had commanded in the Law, that the priest alone should enter the sanctuary, bearing the names of the twelve tribes of Israel on his shoulders, and as many precious stones on his breast, while the people were to stand at a distance in the outer court, and thereafter unite their prayers with the priest. Nay, the sacrifice had even the effect of ratifying and confirming their prayers. That shadowy ceremony of the Law therefore taught, first, that we are all excluded from the face of God, and, therefore, that there is need of a Mediator to appear in our name, and carry us on his shoulders and keep us bound upon his breast, that we may be heard in his person; And secondly, that our prayers, which, as has been said, would otherwise never be free from impurity, are cleansed by the sprinkling of his blood. And we see that the saints, when they desired to obtain any thing, founded their hopes on sacrifices, because they knew that by sacrifice all prayers were ratified: "Remember all thy offerings," says David, "and accept thy burnt sacrifice" (Ps. 20:3). Hence we infer, that in receiving the prayers of his people, God was from the very first appeased by the intercession of Christ. Why then does Christ speak of a new period ("at

that day") when the disciples were to begin to pray in his name, unless it be that this grace, being now more brightly displayed, ought also to be in higher estimation with us? In this sense he had said a little before, "Hitherto ye have asked nothing in my name; ask." Not that they were altogether ignorant of the office of Mediator (all the Jews were instructed in these first rudiments), but they did not clearly understand that Christ by his ascent to heaven would be more the advocate of the Church than before. Therefore, to solace their grief for his absence by some more than ordinary result, he asserts his office of advocate, and says, that hitherto they had been without the special benefit which it would be their privilege to enjoy, when aided by his intercession they should invoke God with greater freedom. In this sense the Apostle says that we have "boldness to enter into the holiest by the blood of Jesus, by a new and living way, which he hath consecrated for us" (Heb. 10:19, 20). Therefore, the more inexcusable we are, if we do not with both hands (as it is said) embrace the inestimable gift which is properly destined for us.

19. Moreover since he himself is the only way and the only access by which we can draw near to God, those who deviate from this way, and decline this access, have no other remaining; his throne presents nothing but wrath, judgment, and terror. In short, as the Father has consecrated him our guide and head, those who abandon or turn aside from him in any way endeavour, as much as in them lies, to sully and efface the stamp which God has impressed. Christ, therefore, is the only Mediator by whose intercession the Father is rendered propitious and exorable (1 Tim. 2:5). For though the saints are still permitted to use intercessions, by which they mutually beseech God in behalf of each others salvation, and of which the Apostle makes mention (Eph. 6:18, 19; 1 Tim. 2:1); yet these depend on that one intercession, so far are they from derogating from it. For as the intercessions which, as members of one body we offer up for each other, spring from the feeling of love, so they have reference to this one head. Being thus also made in the name of Christ, what more do they than declare that no man can derive the least benefit from any prayers without the intercession of Christ? As there is nothing in the intercession of Christ to prevent the different members of the Church from offering up prayers for each other, so let it be held as a fixed principle, that all the intercessions thus used in the Church must have reference to that one intercession. Nay, we must be specially careful to show our gratitude on this very account, that God pardoning our unworthiness, not only allows each individual to pray for himself, but allows all to intercede mutually for each other. God having given a place in his Church to intercessors who would deserve to be rejected when praying privately on their own account, how presumptuous were it to abuse this kindness by employing it to obscure the honour of Christ?

20. Moreover, the Sophists are guilty of the merest trifling when they allege that Christ is the Mediator of *redemption*, but that believers are mediators of *intercession*; as if Christ had only performed a temporary mediation, and left an eternal and imperishable mediation to his servants. Such, forsooth, is the treatment which he receives from those who pretend only to take from him a minute portion of honour. Very different is the language of Scripture, with whose simplicity every pious man will be satisfied, without paying any regard to those importers. For when John says, "If any man sin, we have an advocate with the Father, Jesus Christ the righteous" (1 John 2:1), does he mean merely that we once had an advocate; does he not rather ascribe to him a perpetual intercession? What does Paul mean when he declares that he "is even at the right hand of God, who also maketh intercession for us"? (Rom. 8:32). But when in another passage he declares that he is the only Mediator between God and man (1 Tim. 2:5), is he not referring to the supplications which he had mentioned a little before? Having previously said that prayers were to be offered up for all men, he immediately adds, in confirmation of that statement, that there is one God, and one Mediator between God and man. Nor does Augustine give a different interpretation when he says, "Christian men mutually recommend each other in their prayers. But he for whom none intercedes, while he himself intercedes for all, is the only true Mediator. Though the Apostle Paul was under the head a principal member, yet because he was a member of the body of Christ, and knew that the most true and High Priest of the Church had entered not by figure into the inner veil to the holy of holies, but by firm and express truth into the inner sanctuary of heaven to holiness, holiness not imaginary, but eternal, he also commends himself to the prayers of the faithful. He does not make himself a mediator between God and the people, but asks that all the members of the body of Christ should pray mutually for each other, since the members are mutually sympathetic: if one member suffers, the others suffer with it. And thus the mutual prayers of all the members still laboring on the earth ascend to the Head, who has gone before into heaven, and in whom there is propitiation

for our sins. For if Paul were a mediator, so would also the other apostles, and thus there would be many mediators, and Paul's statement could not stand, 'There is one God, and one Mediator between God and men, the man Christ Jesus;' in whom we also are one if we keep the unity of the faith in the bond of peace" (August. Contra Parmenian, Lib. 2 cap. 8). Likewise in another passage Augustine says, "If thou requirest a priest, he is above the heavens, where he intercedes for those who on earth died for thee" (August. in Ps. 94) imagine not that he throws himself before his Father's knees, and suppliantly intercedes for us; but we understand with the Apostle, that he appears in the presence of God, and that the power of his death has the effect of a perpetual intercession for us; that having entered into the upper sanctuary, he alone continues to the end of the world to present the prayers of his people, who are standing far off in the outer court.

21. In regard to the saints who having died in the body live in Christ, if we attribute prayer to them, let us not imagine that they have any other way of supplicating God than through Christ who alone is the way, or that their prayers are accepted by God in any other name. Wherefore, since the Scripture calls us away from all others to Christ alone, since our heavenly Father is pleased to gather together all things in him, it were the extreme of stupidity, not to say madness, to attempt to obtain access by means of others, so as to be drawn away from him without whom access cannot be obtained. But who can deny that this was the practice for several ages, and is still the practice, wherever Popery prevails? To procure the favour of God, human merits are ever and anon obtruded, and very frequently while Christ is passed by, God is supplicated in their name. I ask if this is not to transfer to them that office of sole intercession which we have above claimed for Christ? Then what angel or devil ever announced one syllable to any human being concerning that fancied intercession of theirs? There is not a word on the subject in Scripture. What ground then was there for the fiction? Certainly, while the human mind thus seeks help for itself in which it is not sanctioned by the word of God, it plainly manifests its distrust (see s. 27). But if we appeal to the consciences of all who take pleasure in the intercession of saints, we shall find that their only reason for it is, that they are filled with anxiety, as if they supposed that Christ were insufficient or too rigorous. By this anxiety they dishonour Christ, and rob him of his title of sole Mediator, a title which being given him by the Father as his special privilege, ought not to be transferred to any other. By so doing they obscure the glory of his nativity and make void his cross; in short, divest and defraud of due praise everything which he did or suffered, since all which he did and suffered goes to show that he is and ought to be deemed sole Mediator. At the same time, they reject the kindness of God in manifesting himself to them as a Father, for he is not their Father if they do not recognize Christ as their brother. This they plainly refuse to do if they think not that he feels for them a brother's affection; affection than which none can be more gentle or tender. Wherefore Scripture offers him alone, sends us to him, and establishes us in him. "He," says Ambrose, "is our mouth by which we speak to the Father; our eye by which we see the Father; our right hand by which we offer ourselves to the Father. Save by his intercession neither we nor any saints have any intercourse with God" (Ambros. Lib. de Isaac et Anima). If they object that the public prayers which are offered up in churches conclude with the words, *through Jesus Christ our Lord*, it is a frivolous evasion; because no less insult is offered to the intercession of Christ by confounding it with the prayers and merits of the dead, than by omitting it altogether, and making mention only of the dead. Then, in all their litanies, hymns, and proses where every kind of honour is paid to dead saints, there is no mention of Christ.

22. But here stupidity has proceeded to such a length as to give a manifestation of the genius of superstition, which, when once it has shaken off the rein, is wont to wanton without limit. After men began to look to the intercession of saints, a peculiar administration was gradually assigned to each, so that, according to diversity of business, now one, now another, intercessor was invoked. Then individuals adopted particular saints, and put their faith in them, just as if they had been tutelar deities. And thus not only were gods set up according to the number of the cities (the charge which the prophet brought against Israel of old, Jer. 2:28; 11:13), but according to the number of individuals. But while the saints in all their desires refer to the will of God alone, look to it, and acquiesce in it, yet to assign to them any other prayer than that of longing for the arrival of the kingdom of God, is to think of them stupidly, carnally, and even insultingly. Nothing can be farther from such a view than to imagine that each, under the influence of private feeling, is disposed to be most favourable to his own worshippers. At length vast numbers have fallen into the horrid blasphemy of invoking them not merely as helping but presiding over their salvation. See the depth to which miserable men fall when they forsake their proper station, that is, the word

of God. I say nothing of the more monstrous specimens of impiety in which, though detestable to God, angels, and men, they themselves feel no pain or shame. Prostrated at a statue or picture of Barbara or Catherine, and the like, they mutter a *Pater Noster*; and so far are their pastors from curing or curbing this frantic course, that, allured by the scent of gain, they approve and applaud it. But while seeking to relieve themselves of the odium of this vile and criminal procedure, with what pretext can they defend the practice of calling upon Eloy (Eligius) or Medard to look upon their servants, and send them help from heaven, or the Holy Virgin to order her Son to do what they ask? The Council of Carthage forbad direct prayer to be made at the altar to saints. It is probable that these holy men, unable entirely to suppress the force of depraved custom, had recourse to this check, that public prayers might not be vitiated with such forms of expression as *Sancte Petre, ora pro nobis* —*St Peter, pray for us*. But how much farther has this devilish extravagance proceeded when men hesitate not to transfer to the dead the peculiar attributes of Christ and God?

23. In endeavouring to prove that such intercession derives some support from Scripture they labour in vain. We frequently read (they say) of the prayers of angels, and not only so, but the prayers of believers are said to be carried into the presence of God by their hands. But if they would compare saints who have departed this life with angels, it will be necessary to prove that saints are ministering spirits, to whom has been delegated the office of superintending our salvation, to whom has been assigned the province of guiding us in all our ways, of encompassing, admonishing, and comforting us, of keeping watch over us. All these are assigned to angels, but none of them to saints. How preposterously they confound departed saints with angels is sufficiently apparent from the many different offices by which Scripture distinguishes the one from the other. No one unless admitted will presume to perform the office of pleader before an earthly judge; whence then have worms such license as to obtrude themselves on God as intercessors, while no such office has been assigned them? God has been pleased to give angels the charge of our safety. Hence they attend our sacred meetings, and the Church is to them a theatre in which they behold the manifold wisdom of God (Eph. 3:10). Those who transfer to others this office which is peculiar to them, certainly pervert and confound the order which has been established by God and ought to be inviolable. With similar dexterity they proceed to quote other passages. God said to Jeremiah, "Though Moses and Samuel stood before me, yet my mind could not be toward this people" (Jer. 15:1). How (they ask) could he have spoken thus of the dead but because he knew that they interceded for the living? My inference, on the contrary, is this: since it thus appears that neither Moses nor Samuel interceded for the people of Israel, there was then no intercession for the dead. For who of the saints can be supposed to labour for the salvation of the peoples while Moses who, when in life, far surpassed all others in this matter, does nothing? Therefore, if they persist in the paltry quibble, that the dead intercede for the living, because the Lord said, "*If they stood before me*" (*intercesserint*), I will argue far more speciously in this way: Moses, of whom it is said, "*if he interceded*," did not intercede for the people in their extreme necessity: it is probable, therefore, that no other saint intercedes, all being far behind Moses in humanity, goodness, and paternal solicitude. Thus all they gain by their caviling is to be wounded by the very arms with which they deem themselves admirably protected. But it is very ridiculous to wrest this simple sentence in this manner; for the Lord only declares that he would not spare the iniquities of the people, though some Moses or Samuel, to whose prayers he had shown himself so indulgent, should intercede for them. This meaning is most clearly elicited from a similar passage in Ezekiel: "Though these three men, Noah, Daniel, and Job, were in it, they should deliver but their own souls by their righteousness, saith the Lord God" (Ezek. 14:14). Here there can be no doubt that we are to understand the words as if it had been said, If two of the persons named were again to come alive; for the third was still living, namely, Daniel, who it is well known had then in the bloom of youth given an incomparable display of piety. Let us therefore leave out those whom Scripture declares to have completed their course. Accordingly, when Paul speaks of David, he says not that by his prayers he assisted posterity, but only that he "served his own generation" (Acts 13:36).

24. They again object, Are those, then, to be deprived of every pious wish, who, during the whole course of their lives, breathed nothing but piety and mercy? I have no wish curiously to pry into what they do or meditate; but the probability is, that instead of being subject to the impulse of various and particular desires, they, with one fixed and immovable will, long for the kingdom of God, which consists not less in the destruction of the ungodly than in the salvation of believers. If this be so, there cannot be a doubt that their charity is confined to the communion of Christ's body, and extends no farther than is compatible with the nature of that communion. But

though I grant that in this way they pray for us, they do not, however, lose their quiescence so as to be distracted with earthly cares: far less are they, therefore, to be invoked by us. Nor does it follow that such invocation is to be used because, while men are alive upon the earth, they can mutually commend themselves to each other's prayers. It serves to keep alive a feeling of charity when they, as it were, share each other's wants, and bear each other's burdens. This they do by the command of the Lord, and not without a promise, the two things of primary importance in prayer. But all such reasons are inapplicable to the dead, with whom the Lord, in withdrawing them from our society, has left us no means of intercourse (Eccles. 9:5, 6), and to whom, so far as we can conjecture, he has left no means of intercourse with us. But if any one allege that they certainly must retain the same charity for us, as they are united with us in one faith, who has revealed to us that they have ears capable of listening to the sounds of our voice, or eyes clear enough to discern our necessities? Our opponents, indeed, talk in the shade of their schools of some kind of light which beams upon departed saints from the divine countenance, and in which, as in a mirror, they, from their lofty abode, behold the affairs of men; but to affirm this with the confidence which these men presume to use, is just to desire, by means of the extravagant dreams of our own brain, and without any authority, to pry and penetrate into the hidden judgments of God, and trample upon Scripture, which so often declares that the wisdom of our flesh is at enmity with the wisdom of God, utterly condemns the vanity of our mind, and humbling our reason, bids us look only to the will of God.

25. The other passages of Scripture which they employ to defend their error are miserably wrested. Jacob (they say) asks for the sons of Joseph, "Let my name be named on them, and the name of my fathers, Abraham and Isaac" (Gen. 48:16). First, let us see what the nature of this invocation was among the Israelites. They do not implore their fathers to bring succour to them, but they beseech God to remember his servants, Abraham, Isaac, and Jacob. Their example, therefore, gives no countenance to those who use addresses to the saints themselves. But such being the dullness of these blocks, that they comprehend not what it is to invoke the name of Jacob, nor why it is to be invoked, it is not strange that they blunder thus childishly as to the mode of doing it. The expression repeatedly occurs in Scripture. Isaiah speaks of women being called by the name of men, when they have them for husbands and live under their protection (Isa. 4:1). The calling of the name of Abraham over the Israelites consists in referring the origin of their race to him, and holding him in distinguished remembrance as their author and parent. Jacob does not do so from any anxiety to extend the celebrity of his name, but because he knows that all the happiness of his posterity consisted in the inheritance of the covenant which God had made with them. Seeing that this would give them the sum of all blessings, he prays that they may be regarded as of his race, this being nothing else than to transmit the succession of the covenant to them. They again, when they make mention of this subject in their prayers, do not betake themselves to the intercession of the dead, but call to remembrance that covenant in which their most merciful Father undertakes to be kind and propitious to them for the sake of Abraham, Isaac, and Jacob. How little, in other respects, the saints trusted to the merits of their fathers, the public voice of the Church declares in the prophets "Doubtless thou art our Father, though Abraham be ignorant of us, and Israel acknowledge us not; thou, O Lord, art our Father, our Redeemer" (Isa. 63:16). And while the Church thus speaks, she at the same time adds, "Return for thy servants' sake," not thinking of any thing like intercession, but adverting only to the benefit of the covenant. Now, indeed, when we have the Lord Jesus, in whose hand the eternal covenant of mercy was not only made but confirmed, what better name can we bear before us in our prayers? And since those good Doctors would make out by these words that the Patriarchs are intercessors, I should like them to tell me why, in so great a multitude, no place whatever is given to Abraham, the father of the Church? We know well from what a crew they select their intercessors. Let them then tell me what consistency there is in neglecting and rejecting Abraham, whom God preferred to all others, and raised to the highest degree of honour. The only reason is, that as it was plain there was no such practice in the ancient Church, they thought proper to conceal the novelty of the practice by saying nothing of the Patriarchs: as if by a mere diversity of names they could excuse a practice at once novel and impure. They sometimes, also, object that God is entreated to have mercy on his people "for David's sake" (Ps. 132:10; see Calv. Com). This is so far from supporting their error, that it is the strongest refutation of it. We must consider the character which David bore. He is set apart from the whole body of the faithful to establish the covenant which God made in his hand. Thus regard is had to the covenant rather than to the individual. Under him as a type the sole intercession of

Christ is asserted. But what was peculiar to David as a type of Christ is certainly inapplicable to others.

26. But some seem to be moved by the fact, that the prayers of saints are often said to have been heard. Why? Because they prayed. "They cried unto thee" (says the Psalmist), "and were delivered: they trusted in thee, and were not confounded" (Ps. 22:5). Let us also pray after their example, that like them we too may be heard. Those men, on the contrary, absurdly argue that none will be heard but those who have been heard already. How much better does James argue, "Elias was a man subject to like passions as we are, and he prayed earnestly that it might not rain: and it rained not on the earth by the space of three years and six months. And he prayed again and the heaven gave rain, and the earth brought forth her fruit." (James 5:17, 18). What? Does he infer that Elias possessed some peculiar privilege, and that we must have recourse to him for the use of it? By no means. He shows the perpetual efficacy of a pure and pious prayer, that we may be induced in like manner to pray. For the kindness and readiness of God to hear others is malignantly interpreted, if their example does not inspire us with stronger confidence in his promise, since his declaration is not that he will incline his ear to one or two, or a few individuals, but to all who call upon his name. In this ignorance they are the less excusable, because they seem as it were avowedly to contemn the many admonitions of Scripture. David was repeatedly delivered by the power of God. Was this to give that power to him that we might be delivered on his application? Very different is his affirmation: "The righteous shall compass me about; for thou shalt deal bountifully with me" (Ps. 142:7). Again, "The righteous also shall see, and fear, and shall laugh at him" (Ps. 52:6). "This poor man cried, and the Lord heard him, and saved him out of all his troubles" (Ps. 34:6). In The Psalms are many similar prayers, in which David calls upon God to give him what he asks, for this reason—viz. that the righteous may not be put to shame, but by his example encouraged to hope. Here let one passage suffice, "For this shall every one that is godly pray unto thee in a time when thou mayest be found" (Ps. 32:6, Calv. Com). This passage I have quoted the more readily, because those ravers who employ their hireling tongues in defense of the Papacy, are not ashamed to adduce it in proof of the intercession of the dead. As if David intended any thing more than to show the benefit which he shall obtain from the divine clemency and condescension when he shall have been heard. In general, we must hold that the experience of the grace of God, as well towards ourselves as towards others, tends in no slight degree to confirm our faith in his promises. I do not quote the many passages in which David sets forth the loving-kindness of God to him as a ground of confidence, as they will readily occur to every reader of The Psalms. Jacob had previously taught the same thing by his own example, "I am not worthy of the least of all thy mercies, and of all the truth which thou hast showed unto thy servant: for with my staff I passed over this Jordan; and now I am become two bands" (Gen. 32:10). He indeed alleges the promise, but not the promise only; for he at the same time adds the effect, to animate him with greater confidence in the future kindness of God. God is not like men who grow weary of their liberality, or whose means of exercising it become exhausted; but he is to be estimated by his own nature, as David properly does when he says, "Thou hast redeemed me, O Lord God of truth" (Ps 31:5). After ascribing the praise of his salvation to God, he adds that he is true: for were he not ever like himself, his past favour would not be an infallible ground for confidence and prayer. But when we know that as often as he assists us, he gives us a specimen and proof of his goodness and faithfulness, there is no reason to fear that our hope will be ashamed or frustrated.

27. On the whole, since Scripture places the principal part of worship in the invocation of God (this being the office of piety which he requires of us in preference to all sacrifices), it is manifest sacrilege to offer prayer to others. Hence it is said in the psalm: "If we have forgotten the name of our God, or stretched out our hands to a strange god, shall not God search this out?" (Ps. 44:20, 21). Again, since it is only in faith that God desires to be invoked, and he distinctly enjoins us to frame our prayers according to the rule of his word: in fine, since faith is founded on the word, and is the parent of right prayer, the moment we decline from the word, our prayers are impure. But we have already shown, that if we consult the whole volume of Scripture, we shall find that God claims this honour to himself alone. In regard to the office of intercession, we have also seen that it is peculiar to Christ, and that no prayer is agreeable to God which he as Mediator does not sanctify. And though believers mutually offer up prayers to God in behalf of their brethren, we have shown that this derogates in no respect from the sole intercession of Christ, because all trust to that intercession in commending themselves as well as others to God. Moreover, we have shown that this is ignorantly transferred to the dead, of whom we nowhere read that they were commanded to pray for us. The Scripture often

exhorts us to offer up mutual prayers; but says not one syllable concerning the dead; nay, James tacitly excludes the dead when he combines the two things, to "confess our sins one to another, and to pray one for another" (James 5:16). Hence it is sufficient to condemn this error, that the beginning of right prayer springs from faith, and that faith comes by the hearing of the word of God, in which there is no mention of fictitious intercession, superstition having rashly adopted intercessors who have not been divinely appointed. While the Scripture abounds in various forms of prayer, we find no example of this intercession, without which Papists think there is no prayer. Moreover, it is evident that this superstition is the result of distrust, because they are either not contented with Christ as an intercessor, or have altogether robbed him of this honour. This last is easily proved by their effrontery in maintaining, as the strongest of all their arguments for the intercession of the saints, that we are unworthy of familiar access to God. This, indeed, we acknowledge to be most true, but we thence infer that they leave nothing to Christ, because they consider his intercession as nothing, unless it is supplemented by that of George and Hypolyte, and similar phantoms.

28. But though prayer is properly confined to vows and supplications, yet so strong is the affinity between petition and thanksgiving, that both may be conveniently comprehended under one name. For the forms which Paul enumerates (1 Tim. 2:1) fall under the first member of this division. By prayer and supplication we pour out our desires before God, asking as well those things which tend to promote his glory and display his name, as the benefits which contribute to our advantage. By thanksgiving we duly celebrate his kindnesses toward us, ascribing to his liberality every blessing which enters into our lot. David accordingly includes both in one sentence, "Call upon me in the day of trouble: I will deliver thee, and thou shalt glorify me" (Ps. 50:15). Scripture, not without reason, commands us to use both continually. We have already described the greatness of our want, while experience itself proclaims the straits which press us on every side to be so numerous and so great, that all have sufficient ground to send forth sighs and groans to God without intermission, and suppliantly implore him. For even should they be exempt from adversity, still the holiest ought to be stimulated first by their sins, and, secondly, by the innumerable assaults of temptation, to long for a remedy. The sacrifice of praise and thanksgiving can never be interrupted without guilt, since God never ceases to load us with favour upon favour, so as to force us to gratitude, however slow and sluggish we may be. In short, so great and widely diffused are the riches of his liberality towards us, so marvellous and wondrous the miracles which we behold on every side, that we never can want a subject and materials for praise and thanksgiving. To make this somewhat clearer: since all our hopes and resources are placed in God (this has already been fully proved), so that neither our persons nor our interests can prosper without his blessing, we must constantly submit ourselves and our all to him. Then whatever we deliberate, speak, or do, should be deliberated, spoken, and done under his hand and will; in fine, under the hope of his assistance. God has pronounced a curse upon all who, confiding in themselves or others, form plans and resolutions, who, without regarding his will, or invoking his aid, either plan or attempt to execute (James 4:14; Isaiah 30:1; 31:1). And since, as has already been observed, he receives the honour which is due when he is acknowledged to be the author of all good, it follows that, in deriving all good from his hand, we ought continually to express our thankfulness, and that we have no right to use the benefits which proceed from his liberality, if we do not assiduously proclaim his praise, and give him thanks, these being the ends for which they are given. When Paul declares that every creature of God "is sanctified by the word of God and prayers" (1 Tim. 4:5), he intimates that without the word and prayers none of them are holy and pure, *word* being used metonymically for *faith*. Hence David, on experiencing the loving-kindness of the Lord, elegantly declares, "He hath put a new song in my mouth" (Ps. 40:3); intimating, that our silence is malignant when we leave his blessings unpraised, seeing every blessing he bestows is a new ground of thanksgiving. Thus Isaiah, proclaiming the singular mercies of God, says, "Sing unto the Lord a new song (Is. 42:10)." In the same sense David says in another passage, "O Lord, open thou my lips; and my mouth shall show forth thy praise" (Ps. 51:15). In like manner, Hezekiah and Jonah declare that they will regard it as the end of their deliverance "to celebrate the goodness of God with songs in his temple" (Is. 38:20; Jonah 2:10). David lays down a general rule for all believers in these words, "What shall I render unto the Lord for all his benefits toward me? I will take the cup of salvation, and call upon the name of the Lord" (Ps. 116:12, 13). This rule the Church follows in another psalm, "Save us, O Lord our God, and gather us from among the heathen, to give thanks unto thy holy name, and to triumph in thy praise" (Ps. 106:47). Again, "He will regard the prayer of the destitute, and not despise

their prayer. This shall be written for the generation to come: and the people which shall be created shall praise the Lord." "To declare the name of the Lord in Zion, and his praise in Jerusalem" (Ps. 102:18, 21). Nay, whenever believers beseech the Lord to do anything *for his own name's sake*, as they declare themselves unworthy of obtaining it in their own name, so they oblige themselves to give thanks, and promise to make the right use of his lovingkindness by being the heralds of it. Thus Hosea, speaking of the future redemption of the Church, says, "Take away all iniquity, and receive us graciously; so will we render the calves of our lips" (Hos. 14:2). Not only do our tongues proclaim the kindness of God, but they naturally inspire us with love to him. "I love the Lord, because he hath heard my voice and my supplications" (Ps. 116:1). In another passage, speaking of the help which he had experienced, he says, "I will love thee, O Lord, my strength" (Ps. 18:1). No praise will ever please God that does not flow from this feeling of love. Nay, we must attend to the declaration of Paul, that all wishes are vicious and perverse which are not accompanied with thanksgiving. His words are, "In everything by prayer and supplication with thanksgiving let your requests be made known unto God" (Phil. 4:6). Because many, under the influence of moroseness, weariness, impatience, bitter grief and fear, use murmuring in their prayers, he enjoins us so to regulate our feelings as cheerfully to bless God even before obtaining what we ask. But if this connection ought always to subsist in full vigor between things that are almost contrary, the more sacred is the tie which binds us to celebrate the praises of God whenever he grants our requests. And as we have already shown that our prayers, which otherwise would be polluted) are sanctified by the intercession of Christ, so the Apostle, by enjoining us "to offer the sacrifice of praise to God continually" by Christ (Heb. 13:15), reminds us, that without the intervention of his priesthood our lips are not pure enough to celebrate the name of God. Hence we infer that a monstrous delusion prevails among Papists, the great majority of whom wonder when Christ is called an intercessor. The reason why Paul enjoins, "Pray without ceasing; in every thing give thanks" (1 Thess. 5:17, 18), is, because he would have us with the utmost assiduity, at all times, in every place, in all things, and under all circumstances, direct our prayers to God, to expect all the things which we desire from him, and when obtained ascribe them to him; thus furnishing perpetual grounds for prayer and praise.

29. This assiduity in prayer, though it specially refers to the peculiar private prayers of individuals, extends also in some measure to the public prayers of the Church. These, it may be said, cannot be continual, and ought not to be made, except in the manner which, for the sake of order, has been established by public consent. This I admit, and hence certain hours are fixed beforehand, hours which, though indifferent in regard to God, are necessary for the use of man, that the general convenience may be consulted, and all things be done in the Church, as Paul enjoins, "decently and in order" (1 Cor. 14:40). But there is nothing in this to prevent each church from being now and then stirred up to a more frequent use of prayer and being more zealously affected under the impulse of some greater necessity. Of perseverance in prayer, which is much akin to assiduity, we shall speak towards the close of the chapter (sec. 51, 52). This assiduity, moreover, is very different from the βαττολογίαν, *vain speaking*, which our Saviour has prohibited (Mt. 6:7). For he does not there forbid us to pray long or frequently, or with great fervor, but warns us against supposing that we can extort anything from God by importuning him with garrulous loquacity, as if he were to be persuaded after the manner of men. We know that hypocrites, because they consider not that they have to do with God, offer up their prayers as pompously as if it were part of a triumphal show. The Pharisee, who thanked God that he was not as other men, no doubt proclaimed his praises before men, as if he had wished to gain a reputation for sanctity by his prayers. Hence that *vain speaking*, which for a similar reason prevails so much in the Papacy in the present day, some vainly spinning out the time by a reiteration of the same frivolous prayers, and others employing a long series of verbiage for vulgar display. This childish garrulity being a mockery of God, it is not strange that it is prohibited in the Church, in order that every feeling there expressed may be sincere, proceeding from the inmost heart. Akin to this abuse is another which our Saviour also condemns, namely, when hypocrites for the sake of ostentation court the presence of many witnesses, and would sooner pray in the market-place than pray without applause. The true object of prayer being, as we have already said (sec. 4, 5), to carry our thoughts directly to God, whether to celebrate his praise or implore his aid, we can easily see that its primary seat is in the mind and heart, or rather that prayer itself is properly an effusion and manifestation of internal feeling before Him who is the searcher of hearts. Hence (as has been said), when our divine Master was pleased to lay down the best rule for prayer, his injunction was, "Enter

into thy closet, and when thou hast shut thy door, pray to thy Father which is in secret, and thy Father which seeth in secret shall reward thee openly" (Mt. 6:6). Dissuading us from the example of hypocrites, who sought the applause of men by an ambitious ostentation in prayer, he adds the better course—enter thy chamber, shut thy door, and there pray. By these words (as I understand them) he taught us to seek a place of retirement which might enable us to turn all our thoughts inwards and enter deeply into our hearts, promising that God would hold converse with the feelings of our mind, of which the body ought to be the temple. He meant not to deny that it may be expedient to pray in other places also, but he shows that prayer is somewhat of a secret nature, having its chief seat in the mind, and requiring a tranquillity far removed from the turmoil of ordinary cares. And hence it was not without cause that our Lord himself, when he would engage more earnestly in prayer, withdrew into a retired spot beyond the bustle of the world, thus reminding us by his example that we are not to neglect those helps which enable the mind, in itself too much disposed to wander, to become sincerely intent on prayer. Meanwhile, as he abstained not from prayer when the occasion required it, though he were in the midst of a crowd, so must we, whenever there is need, lift up "pure hands" (1 Tim. 2:8) at all places. And hence we must hold that he who declines to pray in the public meeting of the saints, knows not what it is to pray apart, in retirement, or at home. On the other hand, he who neglects to pray alone and in private, however sedulously he frequents public meetings, there gives his prayers to the wind, because he defers more to the opinion of man than to the secret judgment of God. Still, lest the public prayers of the Church should be held in contempt, the Lord anciently bestowed upon them the most honourable appellation, especially when he called the temple the "*house of prayer*" (Isa. 56:7). For by this expression he both showed that the duty of prayer is a principal part of his worship, and that to enable believers to engage in it with one consent his temple is set up before them as a kind of banner. A noble promise was also added, "Praise waiteth for thee, O God, in Sion: and unto thee shall the vow be performed" (Ps. 65:1). By these words the Psalmist reminds us that the prayers of the Church are never in vain; because God always furnishes his people with materials for a song of joy. But although the shadows of the law have ceased, yet because God was pleased by this ordinance to foster the unity of the faith among us also, there can be no doubt that the same promise belongs to us—a promise which Christ sanctioned with his own lips, and which Paul declares to be perpetually in force.

30. As God in his word enjoins common prayer, so public temples are the places destined for the performance of them, and hence those who refuse to join with the people of God in this observance have no ground for the pretext, that they enter their chamber in order that they may obey the command of the Lord. For he who promises to grant whatsoever two or three assembled in his name shall ask (Mt. 18:20), declares, that he by no means despises the prayers which are publicly offered up, provided there be no ostentation, or catching at human applause, and provided there be a true and sincere affection in the secret recesses of the heart. If this is the legitimate use of churches (and it certainly is), we must, on the other hand, beware of imitating the practice which commenced some centuries ago, of imagining that churches are the proper dwellings of God, where he is more ready to listen to us, or of attaching to them some kind of secret sanctity, which makes prayer there more holy. For seeing we are the true temples of God, we must pray in ourselves if we would invoke God in his holy temple. Let us leave such gross ideas to the Jews or the heathen, knowing that we have a command to pray without distinction of place, "in spirit and in truth" (John 4:23). It is true that by the order of God the temple was anciently dedicated for the offering of prayers and sacrifices, but this was at a time when the truth (which being now fully manifested, we are not permitted to confine to any material temple) lay hid under the figure of shadows. Even the temple was not represented to the Jews as confining the presence of God within its walls, but was meant to train them to contemplate the image of the true temple. Accordingly, a severe rebuke is administered both by Isaiah and Stephen, to those who thought that God could in any way dwell in temples made with hands (Isa. 66:2; Acts 7:48).

31. Hence it is perfectly clear that neither words nor singing (if used in prayer) are of the least consequence, or avail one iota with God, unless they proceed from deep feeling in the heart. Nay, rather they provoke his anger against us, if they come from the lips and throat only, since this is to abuse his sacred name, and hold his majesty in derision. This we infer from the words of Isaiah, which, though their meaning is of wider extent, go to rebuke this vice also: "Forasmuch as this people draw near me with their mouth, and with their lips do honour me, but have removed their heart far from me, and their fear toward me is taught by the precept of men: therefore, behold, I will proceed to do a marvellous work among

this people, even a marvellous work and a wonder: for the wisdom of their wise men shall perish, and the understanding of their prudent men shall be hid" (Isa. 29:13). Still we do not condemn words or singing, but rather greatly commend them, provided the feeling of the mind goes along with them. For in this way the thought of God is kept alive on our minds, which, from their fickle and versatile nature, soon relax, and are distracted by various objects, unless various means are used to support them. Besides, since the glory of God ought in a manner to be displayed in each part of our body, the special service to which the tongue should be devoted is that of singing and speaking, inasmuch as it has been expressly created to declare and proclaim the praise of God. This employment of the tongue is chiefly in the public services which are performed in the meeting of the saints. In this way the God whom we serve in one spirit and one faith, we glorify together as it were with one voice and one mouth; and that openly, so that each may in turn receive the confession of his brother's faith, and be invited and incited to imitate it.

32. It is certain that the use of singing in churches (which I may mention in passing) is not only very ancient, but was also used by the Apostles, as we may gather from the words of Paul, "I will sing with the spirit, and I will sing with the understanding also" (1 Cor. 14:15). In like manner he says to the Colossians, "Teaching and admonishing one another in psalms, and hymns, and spiritual songs, singing with grace in your hearts to the Lord" (Col. 3:16). In the former passage, he enjoins us to sing with the voice and the heart; in the latter, he commends spiritual Songs, by which the pious mutually edify each other. That it was not an universal practice, however, is attested by Augustine (Confess. Lib. 9 cap. 7), who states that the church of Milan first began to use singing in the time of Ambrose, when the orthodox faith being persecuted by Justina, the mother of Valentinian, the vigils of the people were more frequent than usual; and that the practice was afterwards followed by the other Western churches. He had said a little before that the custom came from the East. He also intimates (Retract. Lib. 2) that it was received in Africa in his own time. His words are, "Hilarius, a man of tribunitial rank, assailed with the bitterest invectives he could use the custom which then began to exist at Carthage, of singing hymns from the book of Psalms at the altar, either before the oblation, or when it was distributed to the people; I answered him, at the request of my brethren." And certainly if singing is tempered to a gravity befitting the presence of God and angels, it both gives dignity and grace to sacred actions, and has a very powerful tendency to stir up the mind to true zeal and ardor in prayer. We must, however, carefully beware, lest our ears be more intent on the music than our minds on the spiritual meaning of the words. Augustine confesses (Confess. Lib. 10 cap. 33) that the fear of this danger sometimes made him wish for the introduction of a practice observed by Athanasius, who ordered the reader to use only a gentle inflection of the voice, more akin to recitation than singing. But on again considering how many advantages were derived from singing, he inclined to the other side. If this moderation is used, there cannot be a doubt that the practice is most sacred and salutary. On the other hand, songs composed merely to tickle and delight the ear are unbecoming the majesty of the Church, and cannot but be most displeasing to God.

33. It is also plain that the public prayers are not to be couched in Greek among the Latins, nor in Latin among the French or English (as hitherto has been every where practised), but in the vulgar tongue, so that all present may understand them, since they ought to be used for the edification of the whole Church, which cannot be in the least degree benefited by a sound not understood. Those who are not moved by any reason of humanity or charity, ought at least to be somewhat moved by the authority of Paul, whose words are by no means ambiguous: "When thou shalt bless with the spirit, how shall he that occupieth the room of the unlearned say, Amen, at thy giving of thanks, seeing he understandeth not what thou sayest? For thou verily givest thanks, but the other is not edified" (1 Cor. 14:16, 17). How then can one sufficiently admire the unbridled license of the Papists, who, while the Apostle publicly protests against it, hesitate not to bawl out the most verbose prayers in a foreign tongue, prayers of which they themselves sometimes do not understand one syllable, and which they have no wish that others should understand? Different is the course which Paul prescribes, "What is it then? I will pray with the spirit, and I will pray with the understanding also; I will sing with the spirit, and I will sing with the understanding also:" meaning by the *spirit* the special gift of tongues, which some who had received it abused when they dissevered it from the mind, that is, the understanding. The principle we must always hold is, that in all prayer, public and private, the tongue without the mind must be displeasing to God. Moreover, the mind must be so incited, as in ardor of thought far to surpass what the tongue is able to express. Lastly, the tongue is not even necessary to private prayer, unless in

so far as the internal feeling is insufficient for incitement, or the vehemence of the incitement carries the utterance of the tongue along with it. For although the best prayers are sometimes without utterance, yet when the feeling of the mind is overpowering, the tongue spontaneously breaks forth into utterance, and our other members into gesture. Hence that dubious muttering of Hannah (1 Sam. 1:13), something similar to which is experienced by all the saints when concise and abrupt expressions escape from them. The bodily gestures usually observed in prayer, such as kneeling and uncovering of the head (Calv. in Acts 20:36), are exercises by which we attempt to rise to higher veneration of God.

34. We must now attend not only to a surer method, but also form of prayer, that, namely, which our heavenly Father has delivered to us by his beloved Son, and in which we may recognize his boundless goodness and condescension (Mt. 6:9; Luke 11:2). Besides admonishing and exhorting us to seek him in our every necessity (as children are wont to betake themselves to the protection of their parents when oppressed with any anxiety), seeing that we were not fully aware how great our poverty was, or what was right or for our interest to ask, he has provided for this ignorance; that wherein our capacity failed he has sufficiently supplied. For he has given us a form in which is set before us as in a picture every thing which it is lawful to wish, every thing which is conducive to our interest, every thing which it is necessary to demand. From his goodness in this respect we derive the great comfort of knowing, that as we ask almost in his words, we ask nothing that is absurd, or foreign, or unseasonable; nothing, in short, that is not agreeable to him. Plato, seeing the ignorance of men in presenting their desires to God, desires which if granted would often be most injurious to them, declares the best form of prayer to be that which an ancient poet has furnished: "O king Jupiter, give what is best, whether we wish it or wish it not; but avert from us what is evil even though we ask it" (Plato, Alcibiad. 2) This heathen shows his wisdom in discerning how dangerous it is to ask of God what our own passion dictates; while, at the same time, he reminds us of our unhappy condition in not being able to open our lips before God without dangers unless his Spirit instruct us how to pray aright (Rom. 8:26). The higher value, therefore, ought we to set on the privilege, when the only begotten Son of God puts words into our lips, and thus relieves our minds of all hesitation.

35. This form or rule of prayer is composed of *six petitions*. For I am prevented from agreeing with those who divide it into *seven* by the adversative mode of diction used by the Evangelist, who appears to have intended to unite the two members together; as if he had said, Do not allow us to be overcome by temptation, but rather bring assistance to our frailty, and deliver us that we may not fall. Ancient writers also agree with us, that what is added by Matthew as a seventh head is to be considered as explanatory of the sixth petition. But though in every part of the prayer the first place is assigned to the glory of God, still this is more especially the object of the three first petitions, in which we are to look to the glory of God alone, without any reference to what is called our own advantage. The three remaining petitions are devoted to our interest, and properly relate to things which it is useful for us to ask. When we ask that the name of God may be hallowed, as God wishes to prove whether we love and serve him freely, or from the hope of reward, we are not to think at all of our own interest; we must set his glory before our eyes, and keep them intent upon it alone. In the other similar petitions, this is the only manner in which we ought to be affected. It is true, that in this way our own interest is greatly promoted, because, when the name of God is hallowed in the way we ask, our own sanctification also is thereby promoted. But in regard to this advantage, we must, as I have said, shut our eyes, and be in a manner blind, so as not even to see it; and hence were all hope of our private advantage cut off, we still should never cease to wish and pray for this hallowing, and every thing else which pertains to the glory of God. We have examples in Moses and Paul, who did not count it grievous to turn away their eyes and minds from themselves, and with intense and fervent zeal long for death, if by their loss the kingdom and glory of God might be promoted (Exod. 32:32; Rom. 9:3). On the other hand, when we ask for daily bread, although we desire what is advantageous for ourselves, we ought also especially to seek the glory of God, so much so that we would not ask at all unless it were to turn to his glory. Let us now proceed to an exposition of the Prayer.

OUR FATHER WHICH ART IN HEAVEN.

36. The first thing suggested at the very outset is, as we have already said (sec. 17–19), that all our prayers to God ought only to be presented in the name of Christ, as there is no other name which can recommend them. In calling God our Father, we certainly plead the name of Christ. For with what confidence could any man call God his Father? Who would have the presumption to

arrogate to himself the honour of a son of God were we not gratuitously adopted as his sons in Christ? He being the true Son, has been given to us as a brother, so that that which he possesses as his own by nature becomes ours by adoption, if we embrace this great mercy with firm faith. As John says, "As many as received him, to them gave he power to become the sons of God, even to them that believe in his name" (John 1:12). Hence he both calls himself our Father, and is pleased to be so called by us, by this delightful name relieving us of all distrust, since no where can a stronger affection be found than in a father. Hence, too, he could not have given us a stronger testimony of his boundless love than in calling us his sons. But his love towards us is so much the greater and more excellent than that of earthly parents, the farther he surpasses all men in goodness and mercy (Isaiah 63:16). Earthly parents, laying aside all paternal affection, might abandon their offspring; he will never abandon us (Ps. 27:10), seeing he cannot deny himself. For we have his promise, "If ye then, being evil, know how to give good gifts unto your children, how much more shall your Father which is in heaven give good things to them that ask him?" (Mt. 7:11). In like manner in the prophet, "Can a woman forget her sucking child, that she should not have compassion on the son of her womb? Yea, they may forget, yet will not I forget thee" (Isaiah 49:15). But if we are his sons, then as a son cannot betake himself to the protection of a stranger and a foreigner without at the same time complaining of his father's cruelty or poverty, so we cannot ask assistance from any other quarter than from him, unless we would upbraid him with poverty, or want of means, or cruelty and excessive austerity.

37. Nor let us allege that we are justly rendered timid by a consciousness of sin, by which our Father, though mild and merciful, is daily offended. For if among men a son cannot have a better advocate to plead his cause with his father, and cannot employ a better intercessor to regain his lost favour, than if he come himself suppliant and downcast, acknowledging his fault, to implore the mercy of his father, whose paternal feelings cannot but be moved by such entreaties, what will that "Father of all mercies, and God of all comfort," do? (2 Cor. 1:3). Will he not rather listen to the tears and groans of his children, when supplicating for themselves (especially seeing he invites and exhorts us to do so), than to any advocacy of others to whom the timid have recourse, not without some semblance of despair, because they are distrustful of their father's mildness and clemency? The exuberance of his paternal kindness he sets before us in the parable (Luke 15:20; see Calv. Comm). when the father with open arms receives the son who had gone away from him, wasted his substance in riotous living, and in all ways grievously sinned against him. He waits not till pardon is asked in words, but, anticipating the request, recognizes him afar off, runs to meet him, consoles him, and restores him to favour. By setting before us this admirable example of mildness in a man, he designed to show in how much greater abundance we may expect it from him who is not only a Father, but the best and most merciful of all fathers, however ungrateful, rebellious, and wicked sons we may be, provided only we throw ourselves upon his mercy. And the better to assure us that he is such a Father if we are Christians, he has been pleased to be called not only a Father, but our Father, as if we were pleading with him after this manner, O Father, who art possessed of so much affection for thy children, and art so ready to forgive, we thy children approach thee and present our requests, fully persuaded that thou hast no other feelings towards us than those of a father, though we are unworthy of such a parent. But as our narrow hearts are incapable of comprehending such boundless favour, Christ is not only the earnest and pledge of our adoption, but also gives us the Spirit as a witness of this adoption, that through him we may freely cry aloud, Abba, Father. Whenever, therefore, we are restrained by any feeling of hesitation, let us remember to ask of him that he may correct our timidity, and placing us under the magnanimous guidance of the Spirit, enable us to pray boldly.

38. The instruction given us, however, is not that every individual in particular is to call him Father, but rather that we are all in common to call him Our Father. By this we are reminded how strong the feeling of brotherly love between us ought to be, since we are all alike, by the same mercy and free kindness, the children of such a Father. For if He from whom we all obtain whatever is good is our common Father (Mt. 23:9), every thing which has been distributed to us we should be prepared to communicate to each other, as far as occasion demands. But if we are thus desirous as we ought, to stretch out our hands and give assistance to each other, there is nothing by which we can more benefit our brethren than by committing them to the care and protection of the best of parents, since if He is propitious and favourable nothing more can be desired. And, indeed, we owe this also to our Father. For as he who truly and from the heart loves the father of a family, extends the same love and good-will to all his household, so the zeal and affection which we feel for our heavenly Parent it becomes us to extend towards

his people, his family, and, in fine, his heritage, which he has honoured so highly as to give them the appellation of the "fulness" of his only begotten Son (Eph. 1:23). Let the Christian, then, so regulate his prayers as to make them common, and embrace all who are his brethren in Christ; not only those whom at present he sees and knows to be such, but all men who are alive upon the earth. What God has determined with regard to them is beyond our knowledge, but to wish and hope the best concerning them is both pious and humane. Still it becomes us to regard with special affection those who are of the household of faith, and whom the Apostle has in express terms recommended to our care in every thing (Gal. 6:10). In short, all our prayers ought to bear reference to that community which our Lord has established in his kingdom and family.

39. This, however, does not prevent us from praying specially for ourselves, and certain others, provided our mind is not withdrawn from the view of this community, does not deviate from it, but constantly refers to it. For prayers, though couched in special terms, keeping that object still in view, cease not to be common. All this may easily be understood by analogy. There is a general command from God to relieve the necessities of all the poor, and yet this command is obeyed by those who with that view give succour to all whom they see or know to be in distress, although they pass by many whose wants are not less urgent, either because they cannot know or are unable to give supply to all. In this way there is nothing repugnant to the will of God in those who, giving heed to this common society of the Church, yet offer up particular prayers, in which, with a public mind, though in special terms, they commend to God themselves or others, with whose necessity he has been pleased to make them more familiarly acquainted. It is true that prayer and the giving of our substance are not in all respects alike. We can only bestow the kindness of our liberality on those of whose wants we are aware, whereas in prayer we can assist the greatest strangers, how wide soever the space which may separate them from us. This is done by that general form of prayer which, including all the sons of God, includes them also. To this we may refer the exhortation which Paul gave to the believers of his age, to lift up "holy hands without wrath and doubting" (1 Tim. 2:8). By reminding them that dissension is a bar to prayer, he shows it to be his wish that they should with one accord present their prayers in common.

40. The next words are, WHICH ART IN HEAVEN. From this we are not to infer that he is enclosed and confined within the circumference of heaven, as by a kind of boundaries. Hence Solomon confesses, "The heaven of heavens cannot contain thee" (1 Kings 8:27); and he himself says by the Prophet, "The heaven is my throne, and the earth is my footstool" (Isa. 66:1); thereby intimating, that his presence, not confined to any region, is diffused over all space. But as our gross minds are unable to conceive of his ineffable glory, it is designated to us by *heaven*, nothing which our eyes can behold being so full of splendor and majesty. While, then, we are accustomed to regard every object as confined to the place where our senses discern it, no place can be assigned to God; and hence, if we would seek him, we must rise higher than all corporeal or mental discernment. Again, this form of expression reminds us that he is far beyond the reach of change or corruption, that he holds the whole universe in his grasp, and rules it by his power. The effect of the expressions therefore, is the same as if it had been said, that he is of infinite majesty, incomprehensible essence, boundless power, and eternal duration. When we thus speak of God, our thoughts must be raised to their highest pitch; we must not ascribe to him any thing of a terrestrial or carnal nature, must not measure him by our little standards, or suppose his will to be like ours. At the same time, we must put our confidence in him, understanding that heaven and earth are governed by his providence and power. In short, under the name of Father is set before us that God, who hath appeared to us in his own image, that we may invoke him with sure faith; the familiar name of Father being given not only to inspire confidence, but also to curb our minds, and prevent them from going astray after doubtful or fictitious gods. We thus ascend from the only begotten Son to the supreme Father of angels and of the Church. Then when his throne is fixed in heaven, we are reminded that he governs the world, and, therefore, that it is not in vain to approach him whose present care we actually experience. "He that cometh to God," says the Apostle, "must believe that he is, and that he is a rewarder of them that diligently seek him" (Heb. 11:6). Here Christ makes both claims for his Father, *first*, that we place our faith in him; and, *secondly*, that we feel assured that our salvation is not neglected by him, inasmuch as he condescends to extend his providence to us. By these elementary principles Paul prepares us to pray aright; for before enjoining us to make our requests known unto God, he premises in this way, "The Lord is at hand. Be careful for nothing" (Phil. 4:5, 6). Whence it appears that doubt and perplexity hang over the prayers of those in whose minds the

belief is not firmly seated, that "the eyes of the Lord are upon the righteous" (Ps. 34:15).

41. The first petition is, HALLOWED BE THY NAME. The necessity of presenting it bespeaks our great disgrace. For what can be more unbecoming than that our ingratitude and malice should impair, our audacity and petulance should as much as in them lies destroy, the glory of God? But though all the ungodly should burst with sacrilegious rage, the holiness of God's name still shines forth. Justly does the Psalmist exclaim, "According to thy name, O God, so is thy praise unto the ends of the earth" (Ps. 48:10). For wherever God hath made himself known, his perfections must be displayed, his power, goodness, wisdom, justice, mercy, and truth, which fill us with admiration, and incite us to show forth his praise. Therefore, as the name of God is not duly hallowed on the earth, and we are otherwise unable to assert it, it is at least our duty to make it the subject of our prayers. The sum of the whole is, It must be our desire that God may receive the honour which is his due: that men may never think or speak of him without the greatest reverence. The opposite of this reverence is profanity, which has always been too common in the world, and is very prevalent in the present day. Hence the necessity of the petition, which, if piety had any proper existence among us, would be superfluous. But if the name of God is duly hallowed only when separated from all other names it alone is glorified, we are in the petition enjoined to ask not only that God would vindicate his sacred name from all contempt and insult, but also that he would compel the whole human race to reverence it. Then since God manifests himself to us partly by his word, and partly by his works, he is not sanctified unless in regard to both of these we ascribe to him what is due, and thus embrace whatever has proceeded from him, giving no less praise to his justice than to his mercy. On the manifold diversity of his works he has inscribed the marks of his glory, and these ought to call forth from every tongue an ascription of praise. Thus Scripture will obtain its due authority with us, and no event will hinder us from celebrating the praises of God, in regard to every part of his government. On the other hand, the petition implies a wish that all impiety which pollutes this sacred name may perish and be extinguished, that every thing which obscures or impairs his glory, all detraction and insult, may cease; that all blasphemy being suppressed, the divine majesty may be more and more signally displayed.

42. The second petition is, THY KINGDOM COME. This contains nothing new, and yet there is good reason for distinguishing it from the first. For if we consider our lethargy in the greatest of all matters, we shall see how necessary it is that what ought to be in itself perfectly known should be inculcated at greater length. Therefore, after the injunction to pray that God would reduce to order, and at length completely efface every stain which is thrown on his sacred name, another petition, containing almost the same wish, is added—viz. Thy kingdom come. Although a definition of this kingdom has already been given, I now briefly repeat that God reigns when men, in denial of themselves and contempt of the world and this earthly life, devote themselves to righteousness and aspire to heaven (see Calvin, Harm. Mt. 6) Thus this kingdom consists of two parts; the first is, when God by the agency of his Spirit corrects all the depraved lusts of the flesh, which in bands war against Him; and the second, when he brings all our thoughts into obedience to his authority. This petition, therefore, is duly presented only by those who begin with themselves; in other words, who pray that they may be purified from all the corruptions which disturb the tranquillity and impair the purity of God's kingdom. Then as the word of God is like his royal sceptre, we are here enjoined to pray that he would subdue all minds and hearts to voluntary obedience. This is done when by the secret inspiration of his Spirit he displays the efficacy of his word, and raises it to the place of honour which it deserves. We must next descend to the wicked, who perversely and with desperate madness resist his authority. God, therefore, sets up his kingdom, by humbling the whole world, though in different ways, taming the wantonness of some, and breaking the ungovernable pride of others. We should desire this to be done every day, in order that God may gather churches to himself from all quarters of the world, may extend and increase their numbers, enrich them with his gifts, establish due order among them; on the other hand, beat down all the enemies of pure doctrine and religion, dissipate their counsels, defeat their attempts. Hence it appears that there is good ground for the precept which enjoins daily progress, for human affairs are never so prosperous as when the impurities of vice are purged away, and integrity flourishes in full vigor. The completion, however, is deferred to the final advent of Christ, when, as Paul declares, "God will be all in all" (1 Cor. 15:28). This prayer, therefore, ought to withdraw us from the corruptions of the world which separate us from God, and prevent his kingdom from flourishing within us; secondly, it ought to inflame us with an ardent desire for the mortification of the flesh; and, lastly, it

ought to train us to the endurance of the cross; since this is the way in which God would have his kingdom to be advanced. It ought not to grieve us that the outward man decays provided the inner man is renewed. For such is the nature of the kingdom of God, that while we submit to his righteousness he makes us partakers of his glory. This is the case when continually adding to his light and truth, by which the lies and the darkness of Satan and his kingdom are dissipated, extinguished, and destroyed, he protects his people, guides them aright by the agency of his Spirit, and confirms them in perseverance; while, on the other hand, he frustrates the impious conspiracies of his enemies, dissipates their wiles and frauds, prevents their malice and curbs their petulance, until at length he consume Antichrist "with the spirit of his mouth," and destroy all impiety "with the brightness of his coming" (2 Thess. 2:8, Calv. Com).

43. The third petition is, THY WILL BE DONE ON EARTH AS IT IS IN HEAVEN. Though this depends on his kingdom, and cannot be disjoined from it, yet a separate place is not improperly given to it on account of our ignorance, which does not at once or easily apprehend what is meant by God reigning in the world. This, therefore, may not improperly be taken as the explanation, that God will be King in the world when all shall subject themselves to his will. We are not here treating of that secret will by which he governs all things, and destines them to their end (see chap. 24, s. 17). For although devils and men rise in tumult against him, he is able by his incomprehensible counsel not only to turn aside their violence, but make it subservient to the execution of his decrees. What we here speak of is another will of God, namely, that of which voluntary obedience is the counterpart; and, therefore, heaven is expressly contrasted with earth, because, as is said in The Psalms, the angels "do his commandments, hearkening unto the voice of his word" (Ps. 103:20). We are, therefore, enjoined to pray that as everything done in heaven is at the command of God, and the angels are calmly disposed to do all that is right, so the earth may be brought under his authority, all rebellion and depravity having been extinguished. In presenting this request we renounce the desires of the flesh, because he who does not entirely resign his affections to God, does as much as in him lies to oppose the divine will, since everything which proceeds from us is vicious. Again, by this prayer we are taught to deny ourselves, that God may rule us according to his pleasure; and not only so, but also having annihilated our own may create new thoughts and new minds so that we shall have no desire save that of entire agreement with his will; in short, wish nothing of ourselves, but have our hearts governed by his Spirit, under whose inward teaching we may learn to love those things which please and hate those things which displease him. Hence also we must desire that he would nullify and suppress all affections which are repugnant to his will. Such are the three first heads of the prayer, in presenting which we should have the glory of God only in view, taking no account of ourselves, and paying no respect to our own advantage, which, though it is thereby greatly promoted, is not here to be the subject of request. And though all the events prayed for must happen in their own time, without being either thought of, wished, or asked by us, it is still our duty to wish and ask for them. And it is of no slight importance to do so, that we may testify and profess that we are the servants and children of God, desirous by every means in our power to promote the honour due to him as our Lord and Father, and truly and thoroughly devoted to his service. Hence if men, in praying that the name of God may be hallowed, that his kingdom may come, and his will be done, are not influenced by this zeal for the promotion of his glory, they are not to be accounted among the servants and children of God; and as all these things will take place against their will, so they will turn out to their confusion and destruction.

44. Now comes the second part of the prayer, in which we descend to our own interests, not, indeed, that we are to lose sight of the glory of God (to which, as Paul declares, we must have respect even in meat and drink, 1 Cor. 10:31), and ask only what is expedient for ourselves; but the distinction, as we have already observed, is this: God claiming the three first petitions as specially his own, carries us entirely to himself, that in this way he may prove our piety. Next he permits us to look to our own advantage, but still on the condition, that when we ask anything for ourselves it must be in order that all the benefits which he confers may show forth his glory, there being nothing more incumbent on us than to live and die to him. By the first petition of the second part, GIVE US THIS DAY OUR DAILY BREAD, we pray in general that God would give us all things which the body requires in this sublunary state, not only food and clothing, but everything which he knows will assist us to eat our bread in peace. In this way we briefly cast our care upon him, and commit ourselves to his providence, that he may feed, foster, and preserve us. For our heavenly Father disdains not to take our body under his charge and protection, that he may exercise our faith in those minute

matters, while we look to him for everything, even to a morsel of bread and a drop of water. For since, owing to some strange inequality, we feel more concern for the body than for the soul, many who can trust the latter to God still continue anxious about the former, still hesitate as to what they are to eat, as to how they are to be clothed, and are in trepidation whenever their hands are not filled with corn, and wine, and oil, so much more value do we set on this shadowy, fleeting life, than on a blessed immortality. But those who, trusting to God, have once cast away that anxiety about the flesh, immediately look to him for greater gifts, even salvation and eternal life. It is no slight exercise of faith, therefore, to hope in God for things which would otherwise give us so much concern; nor have we made little progress when we get quit of this unbelief, which cleaves, as it were, to our very bones. The speculations of some concerning supersubstantial bread seem to be very little accordant with our Savior's meaning; for our prayer would be defective were we not to ascribe to God the nourishment even of this fading life. The reason which they give is heathenish—viz. that it is inconsistent with the character of sons of God, who ought to be spiritual, not only to occupy their mind with earthly cares, but to suppose God also occupied with them. As if his blessing and paternal favour were not eminently displayed in giving us food, or as if there were nothing in the declaration that godliness hath "the promise of the life that now is, and of that which is to come" (1 Tim. 4:8). But although the forgiveness of sins is of far more importance than the nourishment of the body, yet Christ has set down the inferior in the prior place, in order that he might gradually raise us to the other two petitions, which properly belong to the heavenly life,—in this providing for our sluggishness. We are enjoined to ask *our bread*, that we may be contented with the measure which our heavenly Father is pleased to dispense, and not strive to make gain by illicit arts. Meanwhile, we must hold that the title by which it is ours is donation, because, as Moses says (Lev. 26:20, Deut. 8:17), neither our industry, nor labour, nor hands, acquire any thing for us, unless the blessing of God be present; nay, not even would abundance of bread be of the least avail were it not divinely converted into nourishment. And hence this liberality of God is not less necessary to the rich than the poor, because, though their cellars and barns were full, they would be parched and pine with want did they not enjoy his favour along with their bread. The terms *this day*, or, as it is in another Evangelist, *daily*, and also the epithet *daily*, lay a restraint on our immoderate desire of fleeting good—a desire which we are extremely apt to indulge to excess, and from which other evils ensue: for when our supply is in richer abundance we ambitiously squander it in pleasure, luxury, ostentation, or other kinds of extravagance. Wherefore, we are only enjoined to ask as much as our necessity requires, and as it were for each day, confiding that our heavenly Father, who gives us the supply of to-day, will not fail us on the morrow. How great soever our abundance may be, however well filled our cellars and granaries, we must still always ask for daily bread, for we must feel assured that all substance is nothing, unless in so far as the Lord, by pouring out his blessing, make it fruitful during its whole progress; for even that which is in our hand is not ours except in so far as he every hour portions it out, and permits us to use it. As nothing is more difficult to human pride than the admission of this truth, the Lord declares that he gave a special proof for all ages, when he fed his people with manna in the desert (Deut. 8:3), that he might remind us that "man shall not live by bread alone, but by every word that proceedeth out of the mouth of God" (Mt. 4:4). It is thus intimated, that by his power alone our life and strength are sustained, though he ministers supply to us by bodily instruments. In like manner, whenever it so pleases, he gives us a proof of an opposite description, by breaking the strength, or, as he himself calls it, the *staff* of bread (Lev. 26:26), and leaving us even while eating to pine with hunger, and while drinking to be parched with thirst. Those who, not contented with daily bread, indulge an unrestrained insatiable cupidity, or those who are full of their own abundance, and trust in their own riches, only mock God by offering up this prayer. For the former ask what they would be unwilling to obtain, nay, what they most of all abominate, namely, daily bread only, and as much as in them lies disguise their avarice from God, whereas true prayer should pour out the whole soul and every inward feeling before him. The latter, again, ask what they do not at all expect to obtain, namely, what they imagine that they in themselves already possess. In its being called *ours*, God, as we have already said, gives a striking display of his kindness, making that to be ours to which we have no just claim. Nor must we reject the view to which I have already adverted—viz. that this name is given to what is obtained by just and honest labour, as contrasted with what is obtained by fraud and rapine, nothing being our own which we obtain with injury to others. When we ask God to *give us*, the meaning is, that the thing asked is simply and freely the gift of God, whatever be the quarter from which it comes to us, even when it seems to have been specially prepared by our own art and industry, and procured by our hands, since it is to his blessing alone that all our labors owe their success.

45. The next petition is, FORGIVE ITS OUR DEBTS. In this and the following petition our Saviour has briefly comprehended whatever is conducive to the heavenly life, as these two members contain the spiritual covenant which God made for the salvation of his Church, "I will put my law in their inward parts, and write it on their hearts." "I will pardon all their iniquities" (Jer. 31:33; 33:8). Here our Saviour begins with the forgiveness of sins, and then adds the subsequent blessing—viz. that God would protect us by the power, and support us by the aid of his Spirit, so that we may stand invincible against all temptations. To sins he gives the name of *debts*, because we owe the punishment due to them, a debt which we could not possibly pay were we not discharged by this remission, the result of his free mercy, when he freely expunges the debt, accepting nothing in return; but of his own mercy receiving satisfaction in Christ, who gave himself a ransom for us (Rom. 3:24). Hence, those who expect to satisfy God by merits of their own or of others, or to compensate and purchase forgiveness by means of satisfactions, have no share in this free pardon, and while they address God in this petition, do nothing more than subscribe their own accusation, and seal their condemnation by their own testimony. For they confess that they are debtors, unless they are discharged by means of forgiveness. This forgiveness, however, they do not receive, but rather reject, when they obtrude their merits and satisfactions upon God, since by so doing they do not implore his mercy, but appeal to his justice. Let those, again, who dream of a perfection which makes it unnecessary to seek pardon, find their disciples among those whose itching ears incline them to imposture (see Calv. on Dan. 9:20); only let them understand that those whom they thus acquire have been carried away from Christ, since he, by instructing all to confess their guilt, receives none but sinners, not that he may soothe, and so encourage them in their sins, but because he knows that believers are never so divested of the sins of the flesh as not to remain subject to the justice of God. It is, indeed, to be wished, it ought even to be our strenuous endeavour, to perform all the parts of our duty, so as truly to congratulate ourselves before God as being pure from every stain; but as God is pleased to renew his image in us by degrees, so that to some extent there is always a residue of corruption in our flesh, we ought by no means to neglect the remedy. But if Christ, according to the authority given him by his Father, enjoins us, during the whole course of our lives, to implore pardon, who can tolerate those new teachers who, by the phantom of perfect innocence, endeavour to dazzle the simple, and make them believe that they can render themselves completely free from guilt? This, as John declares, is nothing else than to make God a liar (1 John 1:10). In like manner, those foolish men mutilate the covenant in which we have seen that our salvation is contained by concealing one head of it, and so destroying it entirely; being guilty not only of profanity in that they separate things which ought to be indissolubly connected; but also of wickedness and cruelty in overwhelming wretched souls with despair—of treachery also to themselves and their followers, in that they encourage themselves in a carelessness diametrically opposed to the mercy of God. It is excessively childish to object, that when they long for the advent of the kingdom of God, they at the same time pray for the abolition of sin. In the former division of the prayer absolute perfection is set before us; but in the latter our own weakness. Thus the two fitly correspond to each other—we strive for the goal, and at the same time neglect not the remedies which our necessities require. In the next part of the petition we pray to be forgiven, "*as we forgive our debtors;*" that is, as we spare and pardon all by whom we are in any way offended, either in deed by unjust, or in word by contumelious treatment. Not that we can forgive the guilt of a fault or offense; this belongs to God only; but we can forgive to this extent: we can voluntarily divest our minds of wrath, hatred, and revenge, and efface the remembrance of injuries by a voluntary oblivion. Wherefore, we are not to ask the forgiveness of our sins from God, unless we forgive the offenses of all who are or have been injurious to us. If we retain any hatred in our minds, if we meditate revenge, and devise the means of hurting; nay, if we do not return to a good understanding with our enemies, perform every kind of friendly office, and endeavour to effect a reconciliation with them, we by this petition beseech God not to grant us forgiveness. For we ask him to do to us as we do to others. This is the same as asking him not to do unless we do also. What, then, do such persons obtain by this petition but a heavier judgment? Lastly, it is to be observed that the condition of being forgiven as we forgive our debtors, is not added because by forgiving others we deserve forgiveness, as if the cause of forgiveness were expressed; but by the use of this expression the Lord has been pleased partly to solace the weakness of our faith, using it as a sign to assure us that our sins are as certainly forgiven as we are certainly

conscious of having forgiven others, when our mind is completely purged from all envy, hatred, and malice; and partly using as a badge by which he excludes from the number of his children all who, prone to revenge and reluctant to forgive, obstinately keep up their enmity, cherishing against others that indignation which they deprecate from themselves; so that they should not venture to invoke him as a Father. In the Gospel of Luke, we have this distinctly stated in the words of Christ.

46. The sixth petition corresponds (as we have observed) to the promise of *writing the law upon our hearts*; but because we do not obey God without a continual warfare, without sharp and arduous contests, we here pray that he would furnish us with armour, and defend us by his protection, that we may be able to obtain the victory. By this we are reminded that we not only have need of the gift of the Spirit inwardly to soften our hearts, and turn and direct them to the obedience of God, but also of his assistance, to render us invincible by all the wiles and violent assaults of Satan. The forms of temptation are many and various. The depraved conceptions of our minds provoking us to transgress the law—conceptions which our concupiscence suggests or the devil excites, are temptations; and things which in their own nature are not evil, become temptations by the wiles of the devil, when they are presented to our eyes in such a way that the view of them makes us withdraw or decline from God. These temptations are both on the right hand and on the left. On the right, when riches, power, and honours, which by their glare, and the semblance of good which they present, generally dazzle the eyes of men, and so entice by their blandishments, that, caught by their snares, and intoxicated by their sweetness, they forget their God: on the left, when offended by the hardship and bitterness of poverty, disgrace, contempt, afflictions, and other things of that description, they despond, cast away their confidence and hope, and are at length totally estranged from God. In regard to both kinds of temptation, which either enkindled in us by concupiscence) or presented by the craft of Satan's war against us, we pray God the Father not to allow us to be overcome, but rather to raise and support us by his hand, that strengthened by his mighty power we may stand firm against all the assaults of our malignant enemy, whatever be the thoughts which he sends into our minds; next we pray that whatever of either description is allotted us, we may turn to good, that is, may neither be inflated with prosperity, nor cast down by adversity. Here, however, we do not ask to be altogether exempted from temptation, which is very necessary to excite, stimulate, and urge us on, that we may not become too lethargic. It was not without reason that David wished to be tried, nor is it without cause that the Lord daily tries his elect, chastising them by disgrace, poverty, tribulation, and other kinds of cross. But the temptations of God and Satan are very different: Satan tempts, that he may destroy, condemn, confound, throw headlong; God, that by proving his people he may make trial of their sincerity, and by exercising their strength confirm it; may mortify, tame, and cauterize their flesh, which, if not curbed in this manner, would wanton and exult above measure. Besides, Satan attacks those who are unarmed and unprepared, that he may destroy them unawares; whereas whatever God sends, he "will with the temptation also make a way to escape, that ye may be able to bear it." Whether by the term evil we understand the devil or sin, is not of the least consequence. Satan is indeed the very enemy who lays snares for our life, but it is by sin that he is armed for our destruction. Our petition, therefore, is, that we may not be overcome or overwhelmed with temptation, but in the strength of the Lord may stand firm against all the powers by which we are assailed; in other words, may not fall under temptation: that being thus taken under his charge and protection, we may remain invincible by sin, death, the gates of hell, and the whole power of the devil; in other words, be delivered from evil. Here it is carefully to be observed, that we have no strength to contend with such a combatant as the devil, or to sustain the violence of his assault. Were it otherwise, it would be mockery of God to ask of him what we already possess in ourselves. Assuredly those who in self-confidence prepare for such a fight, do not understand how bold and well-equipped the enemy is with whom they have to do. Now we ask to be delivered from his power, as from the mouth of some furious raging lion, who would instantly tear us with his teeth and claws, and swallow us up, did not the Lord rescue us from the midst of death; at the same time knowing that if the Lord is present and will fight for us while we stand by, through him "we shall do valiantly" (Ps. 60:12). Let others if they will confide in the powers and resources of their free will which they think they possess; enough for us that we stand and are strong in the power of God alone. But the prayer comprehends more than at first sight it seems to do. For if the Spirit of God is our strength in waging the contest with Satan, we cannot gain the victory unless we are filled with him, and thereby freed from all infirmity of the flesh. Therefore, when we pray to be delivered from sin and Satan, we at

the same time desire to be enriched with new supplies of divine grace, until completely replenished with them, we triumph over every evil. To some it seems rude and harsh to ask God not to lead us into temptation, since, as James declares (James 1:13), it is contrary to his nature to do so. This difficulty has already been partly solved by the fact that our concupiscence is the cause, and therefore properly bears the blame of all the temptations by which we are overcome. All that James means is, that it is vain and unjust to ascribe to God vices which our own consciousness compels us to impute to ourselves. But this is no reason why God may not when he sees it meet bring us into bondage to Satan, give us up to a reprobate mind and shameful lusts, and so by a just, indeed, but often hidden judgment, lead us into temptation. Though the cause is often concealed from men, it is well known to him. Hence we may see that the expression is not improper, if we are persuaded that it is not without cause he so often threatens to give sure signs of his vengeance, by blinding the reprobate, and hardening their hearts.

47. These three petitions, in which we specially commend ourselves and all that we have to God, clearly show what we formerly observed (sec. 38, 39), that the prayers of Christians should be public, and have respect to the public edification of the Church and the advancement of believers in spiritual communion. For no one requests that anything should be given to him as an individual, but we all ask in common for daily bread and the forgiveness of sins, not to be led into temptation, but delivered from evil. Moreover, there is subjoined the reason for our great boldness in asking and confidence of obtaining (sec. 11, 36). Although this does not exist in the Latin copies, yet as it accords so well with the whole, we cannot think of omitting it. The words are, THINE IS THE KINGDOM, AND THE POWER, AND THE GLORY, FOR EVER. Here is the calm and firm assurance of our faith. For were our prayers to be commended to God by our own worth, who would venture even to whisper before him? Now, however wretched we may be, however unworthy, however devoid of commendation, we shall never want a reason for prayer, nor a ground of confidence, since the kingdom, power, and glory, can never be wrested from our Father. The last word is AMEN, by which is expressed the eagerness of our desire to obtain the things which we ask, while our hope is confirmed, that all things have already been obtained and will assuredly be granted to us, seeing they have been promised by God, who cannot deceive. This accords with the form of expression to which we have already adverted: "Grant, O Lord, for thy name's sake, not on account of us or of our righteousness." By this the saints not only express the end of their prayers, but confess that they are unworthy of obtaining did not God find the cause in himself and were not their confidence founded entirely on his nature.

48. All things that we ought, indeed all that we are able, to ask of God, are contained in this formula, and as it were rule, of prayer delivered by Christ, our divine Master, whom the Father has appointed to be our teacher, and to whom alone he would have us to listen (Mt. 17:5). For he ever was the eternal wisdom of the Father, and being made man, was manifested as the Wonderful, the Counsellor (Isa. 11:2). Accordingly, this prayer is complete in all its parts, so complete, that whatever is extraneous and foreign to it, whatever cannot be referred to it, is impious and unworthy of the approbation of God. For he has here summarily prescribed what is worthy of him, what is acceptable to him, and what is necessary for us; in short, whatever he is pleased to grant. Those, therefore, who presume to go further and ask something more from God, first seek to add of their own to the wisdom of God (this it is insane blasphemy to do); secondly, refusing to confine themselves within the will of God, and despising it, they wander as their cupidity directs; lastly, they will never obtain anything, seeing they pray without faith. For there cannot be a doubt that all such prayers are made without faith, because at variance with the word of God, on which if faith do not always lean it cannot possibly stand. Those who, disregarding the Master's rule, indulge their own wishes, not only have not the word of God, but as much as in them lies oppose it. Hence Tertullian (De Fuga in Persequutione) has not less truly than elegantly termed it *Lawful Prayer*, tacitly intimating that all other prayers are lawless and illicit.

49. By this, however, we would not have it understood that we are so restricted to this form of prayer as to make it unlawful to change a word or syllable of it. For in Scripture we meet with many prayers differing greatly from it in word, yet written by the same Spirit, and capable of being used by us with the greatest advantage. Many prayers also are continually suggested to believers by the same Spirit, though in expression they bear no great resemblance to it. All we mean to say is, that no man should wish, expect, or ask anything which is not summarily comprehended in this prayer. Though the words may be very different, there must be no difference in the sense. In this way, all prayers, both those which are contained in the Scripture, and those which come forth from pious breasts, must be referred to it, certainly none

can ever equal it, far less surpass it in perfection. It omits nothing which we can conceive in praise of God, nothing which we can imagine advantageous to man, and the whole is so exact that all hope of improving it may well be renounced. In short, let us remember that we have here the doctrine of heavenly wisdom. God has taught what he willed; he willed what was necessary.

50. But although it has been said above (sec. 7, 27, &c.), that we ought always to raise our minds upwards towards God, and pray without ceasing, yet such is our weakness, which requires to be supported, such our torpor, which requires to be stimulated, that it is requisite for us to appoint special hours for this exercise, hours which are not to pass away without prayer, and during which the whole affections of our minds are to be completely occupied; namely, when we rise in the morning, before we commence our daily work, when we sit down to food, when by the blessing of God we have taken it, and when we retire to rest. This, however, must not be a superstitious observance of hours, by which, as it were, performing a task to God, we think we are discharged as to other hours; it should rather be considered as a discipline by which our weakness is exercised, and ever and anon stimulated. In particular, it must be our anxious care, whenever we are ourselves pressed, or see others pressed by any strait, instantly to have recourse to him not only with quickened pace, but with quickened minds; and again, we must not in any prosperity of ourselves or others omit to testify our recognition of his hand by praise and thanksgiving. Lastly, we must in all our prayers carefully avoid wishing to confine God to certain circumstances, or prescribe to him the time, place, or mode of action. In like manner, we are taught by this prayer not to fix any law or impose any condition upon him, but leave it entirely to him to adopt whatever course of procedure seems to him best, in respect of method, time, and place. For before we offer up any petition for ourselves, we ask that his will may be done, and by so doing place our will in subordination to his, just as if we had laid a curb upon it, that, instead of presuming to give law to God, it may regard him as the ruler and disposer of all its wishes.

51. If, with minds thus framed to obedience, we allow ourselves to be governed by the laws of Divine Providence, we shall easily learn to persevere in prayer, and suspending our own desires wait patiently for the Lord, certain, however little the appearance of it may be, that he is always present with us, and will in his own time show how very far he was from turning a deaf ear to prayers, though to the eyes of men they may seem to be disregarded. This will be a very present consolation, if at any time God does not grant an immediate answer to our prayers, preventing us from fainting or giving way to despondency, as those are wont to do who, in invoking God, are so borne away by their own fervor, that unless he yield on their first importunity and give present help, they immediately imagine that he is angry and offended with them and abandoning all hope of success cease from prayer. On the contrary, deferring our hope with well tempered equanimity, let us insist with that perseverance which is so strongly recommended to us in Scripture. We may often see in The Psalms how David and other believers, after they are almost weary of praying, and seem to have been beating the air by addressing a God who would not hear, yet cease not to pray because due authority is not given to the word of God, unless the faith placed in it is superior to all events. Again, let us not tempt God, and by wearying him with our importunity provoke his anger against us. Many have a practice of formally bargaining with God on certain conditions, and, as if he were the servant of their lust, binding him to certain stipulations; with which if he do not immediately comply, they are indignant and fretful, murmur, complain, and make a noise. Thus offended, he often in his anger grants to such persons what in mercy he kindly denies to others. Of this we have a proof in the children of Israel, for whom it had been better not to have been heard by the Lord, than to swallow his indignation with their flesh (Num. 11:18, 33).

52. But if our sense is not able till after long expectation to perceive what the result of prayer is, or experience any benefit from it, still our faith will assure us of that which cannot be perceived by sense—viz. that we have obtained what was fit for us, the Lord having so often and so surely engaged to take an interest in all our troubles from the moment they have been deposited in his bosom. In this way we shall possess abundance in poverty, and comfort in affliction. For though all things fail, God will never abandon us, and he cannot frustrate the expectation and patience of his people. He alone will suffice for all, since in himself he comprehends all good, and will at last reveal it to us on the day of judgment, when his kingdom shall be plainly manifested. We may add, that although God complies with our request, he does not always give an answer in the very terms of our prayers but while apparently holding us in suspense, yet in an unknown way, shows that our prayers have not been in vain. This is the meaning of the words of John, "If we

know that he hear us, whatsoever we ask, we know that we have the petitions that we desired of him" (1 John 5:15). It might seem that there is here a great superfluity of words, but the declaration is most useful, namely, that God, even when he does not comply with our requests, yet listens and is favourable to our prayers, so that our hope founded on his word is never disappointed. But believers have always need of being supported by this patience, as they could not stand long if they did not lean upon it. For the trials by which the Lord proves and exercises us are severe, nay, he often drives us to extremes, and when driven allows us long to stick fast in the mire before he gives us any taste of his sweetness. As Hannah says, "The Lord killeth, and maketh alive; he bringeth down to the grave, and bringeth up" (1 Sam. 2:6). What could they here do but become dispirited and rush on despair, were they not, when afflicted, desolate, and half dead, comforted with the thought that they are regarded by God, and that there will be an end to their present evils. But however secure their hopes may stand, they in the meantime cease not to pray, since prayer unaccompanied by perseverance leads to no result.

CHAPTER 21

OF THE ETERNAL ELECTION, BY WHICH GOD HAS PREDESTINATED SOME TO SALVATION, AND OTHERS TO DESTRUCTION.

The divisions of this chapter are,—I. The necessity and utility of the doctrine of eternal Election explained. Excessive curiosity restrained, sec. 1, 2. II. Explanation to those who through false modesty shun the doctrine of Predestination, sec. 3, 4. III. The orthodox doctrine expounded.
Sections:

1. The doctrine of Election and Predestination. It is useful, necessary, and most sweet. Ignorance of it impairs the glory of God, plucks up humility by the roots, begets and fosters pride. The doctrine establishes the certainty of salvation, peace of conscience, and the true origin of the Church. Answer to two classes of men: 1. The curious.

2. A sentiment of Augustine confirmed by an admonition of our Savior and a passage of Solomon.

3. An answer to a second class—viz. those who are unwilling that the doctrine should be adverted to. An objection founded on a passage of Solomon, solved by the words of Moses.

4. A second objection—viz. That this doctrine is a stumbling-block to the profane. Answer 1. The same may be said of many other heads of doctrine. 2. The truth of God will always defend itself. Third objection—viz. That this doctrine is dangerous even to believers. Answer 1. The same objection made to Augustine. 2. We must not despise anything that God has revealed. Arrogance and blasphemy of such objections.

5. Certain cavils against the doctrine. 1. Prescience regarded as the cause of predestination. Prescience and predestination explained. Not prescience, but the good pleasure of God the cause of predestination. This apparent from the gratuitous election of the posterity of Abraham and the rejection of all others.

6. Even of the posterity of Abraham some elected and others rejected by special grace.

7. The Apostle shows that the same thing has been done in regard to individuals under the Christian dispensation.

1. The covenant of life is not preached equally to all, and among those to whom it is preached, does not always meet with the same reception. This diversity displays the unsearchable depth of the divine judgment, and is without doubt subordinate to God's purpose of eternal election. But if it is plainly owing to the mere pleasure of God that salvation is spontaneously offered to some, while others have no access to it, great and difficult questions immediately arise, questions which are inexplicable, when just views are not entertained concerning election and predestination. To many this seems a perplexing subject, because they deem it most incongruous that of the great body of mankind some should be predestinated to salvation, and others to destruction. How ceaselessly they entangle themselves will appear as we proceed. We may add, that in the very obscurity which deters them, we may see not only the utility of this doctrine, but also its most pleasant fruits. We shall never feel persuaded as we ought that our salvation flows from the free mercy of God as its fountain, until we are made acquainted with his eternal election, the grace of God being illustrated by the contrast—viz. that he does not adopt all promiscuously to the hope of salvation, but gives to some what he denies to others. It is plain how greatly ignorance of this principle detracts from the glory of God, and impairs true humility. But though thus necessary to be known, Paul declares

that it cannot be known unless God, throwing works entirely out of view, elect those whom he has predestined. His words are, "Even so then at this present time also, there is a remnant according to the election of grace. And if by grace, then it is no more of works: otherwise grace is no more grace. But if it be of works, then it is no more grace: otherwise work is no more work" (Rom. 11:6). If to make it appear that our salvation flows entirely from the good mercy of God, we must be carried back to the origin of election, then those who would extinguish it, wickedly do as much as in them lies to obscure what they ought most loudly to extol, and pluck up humility by the very roots. Paul clearly declares that it is only when the salvation of a remnant is ascribed to gratuitous election, we arrive at the knowledge that God saves whom he wills of his mere good pleasure, and does not pay a debt, a debt which never can be due. Those who preclude access, and would not have any one to obtain a taste of this doctrine, are equally unjust to God and men, there being no other means of humbling us as we ought, or making us feel how much we are bound to him. Nor, indeed, have we elsewhere any sure ground of confidence. This we say on the authority of Christ, who, to deliver us from all fear, and render us invincible amid our many dangers, snares and mortal conflicts, promises safety to all that the Father has taken under his protection (John 10:26). From this we infer, that all who know not that they are the peculiar people of God, must be wretched from perpetual trepidation, and that those therefore, who, by overlooking the three advantages which we have noted, would destroy the very foundation of our safety, consult ill for themselves and for all the faithful. What? Do we not here find the very origin of the Church, which, as Bernard rightly teaches (Serm. in Cantic). could not be found or recognized among the creatures, because it lies hid (in both cases wondrously) within the lap of blessed predestination, and the mass of wretched condemnation?

But before I enter on the subject, I have some remarks to address to two classes of men. The subject of predestination, which in itself is attended with considerable difficulty is rendered very perplexed and hence perilous by human curiosity, which cannot be restrained from wandering into forbidden paths and climbing to the clouds determined if it can that none of the secret things of God shall remain unexplored. When we see many, some of them in other respects not bad men, every where rushing into this audacity and wickedness, it is necessary to remind them of the course of duty in this matter. First, then, when they inquire into predestination, let them remember that they are penetrating into the recesses of the divine wisdom, where he who rushes forward securely and confidently, instead of satisfying his curiosity will enter in inextricable labyrinth. For it is not right that man should with impunity pry into things which the Lord has been pleased to conceal within himself, and scan that sublime eternal wisdom which it is his pleasure that we should not apprehend but adore, that therein also his perfections may appear. Those secrets of his will, which he has seen it meet to manifest, are revealed in his word—revealed in so far as he knew to be conducive to our interest and welfare.

2. "We have come into the way of faith," says Augustine: "let us constantly adhere to it. It leads to the chambers of the king, in which are hidden all the treasures of wisdom and knowledge. For our Lord Jesus Christ did not speak invidiously to his great and most select disciples when he said, 'I have yet many things to say unto you, but ye cannot bear them now,' (John 16:12). We must walk, advance, increase, that our hearts may be able to comprehend those things which they cannot now comprehend. But if the last day shall find us making progress, we shall there learn what here we could not" (August. Hom. in Joann). If we give due weight to the consideration, that the word of the Lord is the only way which can conduct us to the investigation of whatever it is lawful for us to hold with regard to him—is the only light which can enable us to discern what we ought to see with regard to him, it will curb and restrain all presumption. For it will show us that the moment we go beyond the bounds of the word we are out of the course, in darkness, and must every now and then stumble, go astray, and fall. Let it, therefore, be our first principle that to desire any other knowledge of predestination than that which is expounded by the word of God, is no less infatuated than to walk where there is no path, or to seek light in darkness. Let us not be ashamed to be ignorant in a matter in which ignorance is learning. Rather let us willingly abstain from the search after knowledge, to which it is both foolish as well as perilous, and even fatal to aspire. If an unrestrained imagination urges us, our proper course is to oppose it with these words, "It is not good to eat much honey: so for men to search their own glory is not glory" (Prov. 25:27). There is good reason to dread a presumption which can only plunge us headlong into ruin.

3. There are others who, when they would cure this disease, recommend that the subject of predestination should scarcely if ever be mentioned, and tell us to shun every question concerning it as we would a rock.

Although their moderation is justly commendable in thinking that such mysteries should be treated with moderation, yet because they keep too far within the proper measure, they have little influence over the human mind, which does not readily allow itself to be curbed. Therefore, in order to keep the legitimate course in this matter, we must return to the word of God, in which we are furnished with the right rule of understanding. For Scripture is the school of the Holy Spirit, in which as nothing useful and necessary to be known has been omitted, so nothing is taught but what it is of importance to know. Every thing, therefore delivered in Scripture on the subject of predestination, we must beware of keeping from the faithful, lest we seem either maliciously to deprive them of the blessing of God, or to accuse and scoff at the Spirit, as having divulged what ought on any account to be suppressed. Let us, I say, allow the Christian to unlock his mind and ears to all the words of God which are addressed to him, provided he do it with this moderation—viz. that whenever the Lord shuts his sacred mouth, he also desists from inquiry. The best rule of sobriety is, not only in learning to follow wherever God leads, but also when he makes an end of teaching, to cease also from wishing to be wise. The danger which they dread is not so great that we ought on account of it to turn away our minds from the oracles of God. There is a celebrated saying of Solomon, "It is the glory of God to conceal a thing" (Prov. 25:2). But since both piety and common sense dictate that this is not to be understood of every thing, we must look for a distinction, lest under the pretence of modesty and sobriety we be satisfied with a brutish ignorance. This is clearly expressed by Moses in a few words, "The secret things belong unto the Lord our God: but those things which are revealed belong unto us, and to our children for ever" (Deut. 29:29). We see how he exhorts the people to study the doctrine of the law in accordance with a heavenly decree, because God has been pleased to promulgate it, while he at the same time confines them within these boundaries, for the simple reason that it is not lawful for men to pry into the secret things of God.

4. I admit that profane men lay hold of the subject of predestination to carp, or cavil, or snarl, or scoff. But if their petulance frightens us, it will be necessary to conceal all the principal articles of faith, because they and their fellows leave scarcely one of them unassailed with blasphemy. A rebellious spirit will display itself no less insolently when it hears that there are three persons in the divine essence, than when it hears that God when he created man foresaw every thing that was to happen to him. Nor will they abstain from their jeers when told that little more than five thousand years have elapsed since the creation of the world. For they will ask, Why did the power of God slumber so long in idleness? In short, nothing can be stated that they will not assail with derision. To quell their blasphemies, must we say nothing concerning the divinity of the Son and Spirit? Must the creation of the world be passed over in silence? No! The truth of God is too powerful, both here and everywhere, to dread the slanders of the ungodly, as Augustine powerfully maintains in his treatise, De Bono Perseverantiae (cap. 14–20). For we see that the false apostles were unable, by defaming and accusing the true doctrine of Paul, to make him ashamed of it. There is nothing in the allegation that the whole subject is fraught with danger to pious minds, as tending to destroy exhortation, shake faith, disturb and dispirit the heart. Augustine disguises not that on these grounds he was often charged with preaching the doctrine of predestination too freely, but, as it was easy for him to do, he abundantly refutes the charge. As a great variety of absurd objections are here stated, we have thought it best to dispose of each of them in its proper place (see chap. 23). Only I wish it to be received as a general rule, that the secret things of God are not to be scrutinized, and that those which he has revealed are not to be overlooked, lest we may, on the one hand, be chargeable with curiosity, and, on the other, with ingratitude. For it has been shrewdly observed by Augustine (de Genesi ad Literam, Lib. 5), that we can safely follow Scripture, which walks softly, as with a mother's step, in accommodation to our weakness. Those, however, who are so cautious and timid, that they would bury all mention of predestination in order that it may not trouble weak minds, with what color, pray, will they cloak their arrogance, when they indirectly charge God with a want of due consideration, in not having foreseen a danger for which they imagine that they prudently provide? Whoever, therefore, throws obloquy on the doctrine of predestination, openly brings a charge against God, as having inconsiderately allowed something to escape from him which is injurious to the Church.

5. The predestination by which God adopts some to the hope of life, and adjudges others to eternal death, no man who would be thought pious ventures simply to deny; but it is greatly caviled at, especially by those who make prescience its cause. We, indeed, ascribe both prescience and predestination to God; but we say, that it is absurd to make the latter subordinate to the former (see

chap. 22 sec. 1). When we attribute prescience to God, we mean that all things always were, and ever continue, under his eye; that to his knowledge there is no past or future, but all things are present, and indeed so present, that it is not merely the idea of them that is before him (as those objects are which we retain in our memory), but that he truly sees and contemplates them as actually under his immediate inspection. This prescience extends to the whole circuit of the world, and to all creatures. By predestination we mean the eternal decree of God, by which he determined with himself whatever he wished to happen with regard to every man. All are not created on equal terms, but some are preordained to eternal life, others to eternal damnation; and, accordingly, as each has been created for one or other of these ends, we say that he has been predestinated to life or to death. This God has testified, not only in the case of single individuals; he has also given a specimen of it in the whole posterity of Abraham, to make it plain that the future condition of each nation lives entirely at his disposal: "When the Most High divided to the nations their inheritance, when he separated the sons of Adam, he set the bounds of the people according to the number of the children of Israel. For the Lord's portion is his people; Jacob is the lot of his inheritance" (Deut. 32:8, 9). The separation is before the eyes of all; in the person of Abraham, as in a withered stock, one people is specially chosen, while the others are rejected; but the cause does not appear, except that Moses, to deprive posterity of any handle for glorying, tells them that their superiority was owing entirely to the free love of God. The cause which he assigns for their deliverance is, "Because he loved thy fathers, therefore he chose their seed after them" (Deut. 4:37); or more explicitly in another chapter, "The Lord did not set his love upon you, nor choose you, because you were more in number than any people: for ye were the fewest of all people: but because the Lord loved you" (Deut. 7:7, 8). He repeatedly makes the same intimations, "Behold, the heaven, and the heaven of heavens is the Lord's thy God, the earth also, with all that therein is. Only the Lord had a delight in thy fathers to love them, and he chose their seed after them" (Deut. 10:14, 15). Again, in another passage, holiness is enjoined upon them, because they have been chosen to be a peculiar people; while in another, love is declared to be the cause of their protection (Deut. 23:5). This, too, believers with one voice proclaim, "He shall choose our inheritance for us, the excellency of Jacob, whom he loved" (Ps. 47:4). The endowments with which God had adorned them, they all ascribe to gratuitous love, not only because they knew that they had not obtained them by any merit, but that not even was the holy patriarch endued with a virtue that could procure such distinguished honor for himself and his posterity. And the more completely to crush all pride, he upbraids them with having merited nothing of the kind, seeing they were a rebellious and stiff-necked people (Deut. 9:6). Often, also, do the prophets remind the Jews of this election by way of disparagement and opprobrium, because they had shamefully revolted from it. Be this as it may, let those who would ascribe the election of God to human worth or merit come forward. When they see that one nation is preferred to all others, when they hear that it was no feeling of respect that induced God to show more favor to a small and ignoble body, nay, even to the wicked and rebellious, will they plead against him for having chosen to give such a manifestation of mercy? But neither will their obstreperous words hinder his work, nor will their invectives, like stones thrown against heaven, strike or hurt his righteousness; nay, rather they will fall back on their own heads. To this principle of a free covenant, moreover, the Israelites are recalled whenever thanks are to be returned to God, or their hopes of the future to be animated. "The Lord he is God," says the Psalmist; "it is he that has made us, and not we ourselves: we are his people, and the sheep of his pasture" (Ps. 100:3; 95:7). The negation which is added, "not we ourselves," is not superfluous, to teach us that God is not only the author of all the good qualities in which men excel, but that they originate in himself, there being nothing in them worthy of so much honor. In the following words also they are enjoined to rest satisfied with the mere good pleasure of God: "O ye seed of Abraham, his servant; ye children of Jacob, his chosen" (Ps. 105:6). And after an enumeration of the continual mercies of God as fruits of election, the conclusion is, that he acted thus kindly because he remembered his covenant. With this doctrine accords the song of the whole Church, "They got not the land in possession by their own sword, neither did their own arm save them; but thy right hand, and thine arm, and the light of thy countenance, because thou hadst a favor unto them" (Ps. 44:3). It is to be observed, that when the land is mentioned, it is a visible symbol of the secret election in which adoption is comprehended. To like gratitude David elsewhere exhorts the people, "Blessed is the nation whose God is the Lord, and the people whom he has chosen for his own inheritance" (Ps. 33:12). Samuel thus animates their hopes, "The Lord will not forsake his people for his great name's sake: because it has pleased the Lord to make you his people" (1 Sam. 12:22). And when David's faith is assailed, how does he arm himself for the battle? "Blessed is the man whom thou choosest, and causes to approach unto thee, that he may dwell in thy courts" (Ps. 65:4). But as the hidden election of God was confirmed both by a first and second election, and by other intermediate mercies, Isaiah thus applies the terms "The Lord will have mercy on Jacob, and will yet choose Israel" (Isa. 14:1). Referring to a future period, the gathering together of the dispersion, who seemed to have been abandoned, he says, that it will be a sign of a firm and stable election, notwithstanding of the apparent abandonment. When it is elsewhere said, "I have chosen thee, and not cast thee away" (Isa. 41:9), the continual course of his great liberality is ascribed to paternal kindness. This is stated more explicitly in Zechariah by the angel, the Lord "shall choose Jerusalem again," as if the severity of his chastisements had amounted to reprobation, or the captivity had been an interruption of election, which, however, remains inviolable, though the signs of it do not always appear.

6. We must add a second step of a more limited nature, or one in which the grace of God was displayed in a more special form, when of the same family of Abraham God rejected some, and by keeping others within his Church showed that he retained them among his sons. At first Ishmael had obtained the same rank with his brother Isaac, because the spiritual covenant was equally sealed in him by the symbol of circumcision. He is first cut off, then Esau, at last an innumerable multitude, almost the whole of Israel. In Isaac was the seed called. The same calling held good in the case of Jacob. God gave a similar example in the rejection of Saul. This is also celebrated in the psalm, "Moreover he refused the tabernacle of Joseph, and chose not the tribe of Ephraim: but chose the tribe of Judah" (Ps. 78:67, 68). This the sacred history sometimes repeats that the secret grace of God may be more admirably displayed in that change. I admit that it was by their own fault Ishmael, Esau, and others, fell from their adoption; for the condition annexed was, that they should faithfully keep the covenant of God, whereas they perfidiously violated it. The singular kindness of God consisted in this, that he had been pleased to prefer them to other nations; as it is said in the psalm, "He has not dealt so with any nation: and as for his judgments, they have not known them" (Ps. 147:20). But I had good reason for saying that two steps are here to be observed; for in the election of the whole nation, God had already shown that in the exercise of his mere liberality he was under no law but was free, so that he was by no means to be restricted to an equal division of grace, its very inequality proving it to be gratuitous. Accordingly, Malachi enlarges on the ingratitude of Israel, in that being not only selected from the whole human race, but set peculiarly apart from a sacred household; they perfidiously and impiously spurn God their beneficent parent. "Was not Esau Jacob's brother? saith the Lord: yet I loved Jacob, and I hated Esau" (Mal. 1:2, 3). For God takes it for granted, that as both were the sons of a holy father, and successors of the covenant, in short, branches from a sacred root, the sons of Jacob were under no ordinary obligation for having been admitted to that dignity; but when by the rejection of Esau the first born, their progenitor though inferior in birth was made heir, he charges them with double ingratitude, in not being restrained by a double tie.

7. Although it is now sufficiently plain that God by his secret counsel chooses whom he will while he rejects others, his gratuitous election has only been partially explained until we come to the case of single individuals, to whom God not only offers salvation, but so assigns it, that the certainty of the result remains not dubious or suspended. These are considered as belonging to that one seed of which Paul makes mention (Rom. 9:8; Gal. 3:16, &c). For although adoption was deposited in the hand of Abraham, yet as many of his posterity were cut off as rotten members, in order that election may stand and be effectual, it is necessary to ascend to the head in whom the heavenly Father has connected his elect with each other, and bound them to himself by an indissoluble tie. Thus in the adoption of the family of Abraham, God gave them a liberal display of favor which he has denied to others; but in the members of Christ there is a far more excellent display of grace, because those ingrafted into him as their head never fail to obtain salvation. Hence Paul skillfully argues from the passage of Malachi which I quoted (Rom. 9:13; Mal. 1:2), that when God, after making a covenant of eternal life, invites any people to himself, a special mode of election is in part understood, so that he does not with promiscuous grace effectually elect all of them. The words, "Jacob have I loved," refer to the whole progeny of the patriarch, which the prophet there opposes to the posterity of Esau. But there is nothing in this repugnant to the fact, that in the person of one man is set before us a specimen of election, which cannot fail of accomplishing its object. It is not without cause Paul observes, that these are called *a remnant* (Rom. 9:27; 11:5); because experience shows that of the general body

many fall away and are lost, so that often a small portion only remains. The reason why the general election of the people is not always firmly ratified, readily presents itself—viz. that on those with whom God makes the covenant, he does not immediately bestow the Spirit of regeneration, by whose power they persevere in the covenant even to the end. The external invitation, without the internal efficacy of grace which would have the effect of retaining them, holds a kind of middle place between the rejection of the human race and the election of a small number of believers. The whole people of Israel are called the Lord's inheritance, and yet there were many foreigners among them. Still, because the covenant which God had made to be their Father and Redeemer was not altogether null, he has respect to that free favor rather than to the perfidious defection of many; even by them his truth was not abolished, since by preserving some residue to himself, it appeared that his calling was without repentance. When God ever and anon gathered his Church from among the sons of Abraham rather than from profane nations, he had respect to his covenant, which, when violated by the great body, he restricted to a few, that it might not entirely fail. In short, that common adoption of the seed of Abraham was a kind of visible image of a greater benefit which God deigned to bestow on some out of many. This is the reason why Paul so carefully distinguishes between the sons of Abraham according to the flesh and the spiritual sons who are called after the example of Isaac. Not that simply to be a son of Abraham was a vain or useless privilege (this could not be said without insult to the covenant), but that the immutable counsel of God, by which he predestinated to himself whomsoever he would, was alone effectual for their salvation. But until the proper view is made clear by the production of passages of Scripture, I advise my readers not to prejudge the question. We say, then, that Scripture clearly proves this much, that God by his eternal and immutable counsel determined once for all those whom it was his pleasure one day to admit to salvation, and those whom, on the other hand, it was his pleasure to doom to destruction. We maintain that this counsel, as regards the elect, is founded on his free mercy, without any respect to human worth, while those whom he dooms to destruction are excluded from access to life by a just and blameless, but at the same time incomprehensible judgment. In regard to the elect, we regard calling as the evidence of election, and justification as another symbol of its manifestation, until it is fully accomplished by the attainment of glory. But as the Lord seals his elect by calling and justification, so by excluding the reprobate either from the knowledge of his name or the sanctification of his Spirit, he by these marks in a manner discloses the judgment which awaits them. I will here omit many of the fictions which foolish men have devised to overthrow predestination. There is no need of refuting objections which the moment they are produced abundantly betray their hollowness. I will dwell only on those points which either form the subject of dispute among the learned, or may occasion any difficulty to the simple, or may be employed by impiety as specious pretexts for assailing the justice of God.

CHAPTER 22

THIS DOCTRINE CONFIRMED BY PROOFS FROM SCRIPTURE.

The divisions of this chapter are,—I. A confirmation of the orthodox doctrine in opposition to two classes of individuals. This confirmation founded on a careful exposition of our Savior's words, and passages in the writings of Paul, sec. 1–7. II. A refutation of some objections taken from ancient writers, Thomas Aquinas, and more modern writers, sec. 8–10. III. Of reprobation, which is founded entirely on the righteous will of God, sec. 11.

Sections:

1. Some imagine that God elects or reprobates according to a foreknowledge of merit. Others make it a charge against God that he elects some and passes by others. Both refuted, 1. By invincible arguments; 2. By the testimony of Augustine.

2. Who are elected, when, in whom, to what, for what reason.

3. The reason is the good pleasure of God, which so reigns in election that no works, either past or future, are taken into consideration. This proved by notable declarations of one Savior and passages of Paul.

4. Proved by a striking discussion in the Epistle to the Romans. Its scope and method explained. The advocates of foreknowledge refuted by the Apostle, when he maintains that election is special and wholly of grace.

5. Evasion refuted. A summary and analysis of the Apostle's discussion.

6. An exception, with three answers to it. The efficacy of gratuitous election extends only to believers, who are said to be elected according to foreknowledge. This foreknowledge or prescience is not speculative but active.

7. This proved from the words of Christ. Conclusion of the answer, and solution of the objection with regard to Judas.

8. An objection taken from the ancient fathers. Answer from Augustine, from Ambrose, as quoted by Augustine, and an invincible argument by an Apostle. Summary of this argument.

9. Objection from Thomas Aquinas. Answer.

10. Objection of more modern writers. Answers. Passages in which there is a semblance of contradiction reconciled. Why many called and few chosen. An objection founded on mutual consent between the word and faith. Solution confirmed by the words of Paul, Augustine, and Bernard. A clear declaration by our Savior.

11. The view to be taken of reprobation. It is founded on the righteous will of God.

1. Many controvert all the positions which we have laid down, especially the gratuitous election of believers, which, however, cannot be overthrown. For they commonly imagine that God distinguishes between men according to the merits which he foresees that each individual is to have, giving the adoption of sons to those whom he foreknows will not be unworthy of his grace, and dooming those to destruction whose dispositions he perceives will be prone to mischief and wickedness. Thus by interposing foreknowledge as a veil, they not only obscure election, but pretend to give it a different origin. Nor is this the commonly received opinion of the vulgar merely, for it has in all ages had great supporters (see sec. 8). This I candidly confess, lest any one should expect greatly to prejudice our cause by opposing it with their names. The truth of God is here too certain to be shaken, too clear to be overborne by human authority. Others who are neither versed in Scripture, nor entitled to any weight, assail sound doctrine with a petulance and improbity which it is impossible to tolerate. Because God of his mere good pleasure electing some passes by others, they raise a plea against him. But if the fact is certain, what can they gain by quarreling with God? We teach nothing but what experience proves to be true—viz. that God has always been at liberty to bestow his grace on whom he would. Not to ask in what respect the posterity of Abraham excelled others if it be not in a worth, the cause of which has no existence out of God, let them tell why men are better than oxen or asses. God might have made them dogs when he formed them in his own image. Will they allow the lower animals to expostulate with God, as if the inferiority of their condition were unjust? It is certainly not more equitable that men should enjoy the privilege which they have not acquired by any merit, than that he should variously distribute favors as seems to him meet. If they pass to the case of individuals where inequality is more offensive to them, they ought at least, in regard to the example of our Savior, to be restrained by feelings of awe from talking so confidently of this sublime mystery. He is conceived a mortal man of the seed of David; what, I would ask them, are the virtues by which he deserved to become in the very womb, the head of angels the only begotten Son of God, the image and glory of the Father, the light, righteousness, and salvation of the world? It is wisely observed by Augustine, that in the very head of the Church we have a bright mirror of free election, lest it should give any trouble to us the members—viz. that he did not become the Son of God by living righteously, but was freely presented with this great honor, that he might afterwards make others partakers of his gifts. Should any one here ask, why others are not what he was, or why we are all at so great a distance from him, why we are all corrupt while he is purity, he would not only betray his madness, but his effrontery also. But if they are bent on depriving God of the free right of electing and reprobating, let them at the same time take away what has been given to Christ. It will now be proper to attend to what Scripture declares concerning each. When Paul declares that we were chosen in Christ before the foundation of the world (Eph. 1:4), he certainly shows that no regard is had to our own worth; for it is just as if he had said, Since in the whole seed of Adam our heavenly Father found nothing worthy of his election, he turned his eye upon his own Anointed, that he might select as members of his body those whom he was to assume into the fellowship of life. Let believers, then, give full effect to this reason—viz. that we were in Christ adopted unto the heavenly inheritance, because in ourselves we were incapable of such excellence. This he elsewhere observes in another passage, in which he exhorts the Colossians to give thanks that they had been made meet to be partakers of the inheritance of the saints (Col. 1:12). If election precedes that divine grace by which we are made fit to obtain immortal life, what can God find in us to induce him to elect us? What I mean is still more clearly explained in another passage: God, says he, "has chosen us in him before the foundation of the world, that we might be holy and without blame before him in love: having predestinated us unto the adoption of children by Jesus Christ to himself, according to the good plea-

sure of his will" (Eph. 1:4, 5). Here he opposes the good pleasure of God to our merits of every description.

Holiness of life springs from election, and is the object of it. That the proof may be more complete, it is of importance to attend to the separate clauses of that passage. When they are connected together they leave no doubt. From giving them the name of elect, it is clear that he is addressing believers, as indeed he shortly after declares. It is, therefore, a complete perversion of the name to confine it to the age in which the gospel was published. By saying they were elected before the foundation of the world, he takes away all reference to worth. For what ground of distinction was there between persons who as yet existed not, and persons who were afterwards like them to exist in Adam? But if they were elected in Christ, it follows not only that each was elected on some extrinsic ground, but that some were placed on a different footing from others, since we see that all are not members of Christ. In the additional statement that they were elected that they might be holy, the apostle openly refutes the error of those who deduce election from prescience, since he declares that whatever virtue appears in men is the result of election. Then, if a higher cause is asked, Paul answers that God so predestined, and predestined according to the good pleasure of his will. By these words, he overturns all the grounds of election which men imagine to exist in themselves. For he shows that whatever favors God bestows in reference to the spiritual life flow from this one fountain, because God chose whom he would, and before they were born had the grace which he designed to bestow upon them set apart for their use.

3. Wherever this good pleasure of God reigns, no good works are taken into account. The Apostle, indeed, does not follow out the antithesis, but it is to be understood, as he himself explains it in another passage, "Who has called us with a holy calling, not according to our works, but according to his own purpose and grace, which was given us in Christ Jesus before the world began" (2 Tim. 1:9). We have already shown that the additional words, "that we might be holy," remove every doubt. If you say that he foresaw they would be holy, and therefore elected them, you invert the order of Paul. You may, therefore, safely infer, If he elected us that we might be holy, he did not elect us because he foresaw that we would be holy. The two things are evidently inconsistent—viz. that the pious owe it to election that they are holy, and yet attain to election by means of works. There is no force in the cavil to which they are ever recurring, that the Lord does not bestow election in recompense of preceding, but bestows it in consideration of future merits. For when it is said that believers were elected that they might be holy, it is at the same time intimated that the holiness which was to be in them has its origin in election. And how can it be consistently said, that things derived from election are the cause of election? The very thing which the Apostle had said, he seems afterwards to confirm by adding, "According to his good pleasure which he has purposed in himself" (Eph. 1:9); for the expression that God "purposed in himself," is the same as if it had been said, that in forming his decree he considered nothing external to himself; and, accordingly, it is immediately subjoined, that the whole object contemplated in our election is, that "we should be to the praise of his glory." Assuredly divine grace would not deserve all the praise of election, were not election gratuitous; and it would not be gratuitous did God in electing any individual pay regard to his future works. Hence, what Christ said to his disciples is found to be universally applicable to all believers, "Ye have not chosen me, but I have chosen you" (John 15:16). Here he not only excludes past merits, but declares that they had nothing in themselves for which they could be chosen except in so far as his mercy anticipated. And how are we to understand the words of Paul, "Who has first given to him, and it shall be recompensed unto him again?" (Rom. 11:35). His meaning obviously is, that men are altogether indebted to the preventing goodness of God, there being nothing in them, either past or future, to conciliate his favor.

4. In the Epistle to the Romans (Rom. 9:6), in which he again treats this subject more reconditely and at greater length, he declares that "they are not all Israel which are of Israel;" for though all were blessed in respect of hereditary rights yet all did not equally obtain the succession. The whole discussion was occasioned by the pride and vainglorying of the Jews, who, by claiming the name of the Church for themselves, would have made the faith of the Gospel dependent on their pleasure; just as in the present day the Papists would fain under this pretext substitute themselves in place of God. Paul, while he concedes that in respect of the covenant they were the holy offspring of Abraham, yet contends that the greater part of them were strangers to it, and that not only because they were degenerate, and so had become bastards instead of sons, but because the principal point to be considered was the special election of God, by which alone his adoption was ratified. If the piety of some established them in the hope of salvation, and the revolt of others was the sole cause of their being rejected, it would have been foolish and

absurd in Paul to carry his readers back to a secret election. But if the will of God (no cause of which external to him either appears or is to be looked for) distinguishes some from others, so that all the sons of Israel are not true Israelites, it is vain for any one to seek the origin of his condition in himself. He afterwards prosecutes the subject at greater length, by contrasting the cases of Jacob and Esau. Both being sons of Abraham, both having been at the same time in the womb of their mother, there was something very strange in the change by which the honor of the birthright was transferred to Jacob, and yet Paul declares that the change was an attestation to the election of the one and the reprobation of the other.

The question considered is the origin and cause of election. The advocates of foreknowledge insist that it is to be found in the virtues and vices of men. For they take the short and easy method of asserting, that God showed in the person of Jacob, that he elects those who are worthy of his grace; and in the person of Esau, that he rejects those whom he foresees to be unworthy. Such is their confident assertion; but what does Paul say? "For the children being not yet born, neither having done any good or evil, that the purpose of God according to election might stand, not of works, but of him that calleth; it was said unto her, [Rebecca,] The elder shall serve the younger. As it is written, Jacob have I loved, but Esau have I hated" (Rom. 9:11–13). If foreknowledge had anything to do with this distinction of the brothers, the mention of time would have been out of place. Granting that Jacob was elected for a worth to be obtained by future virtues, to what end did Paul say that he was not yet born? Nor would there have been any occasion for adding, that as yet he had done no good, because the answer was always ready, that nothing is hid from God, and that therefore the piety of Jacob was present before him. If works procure favor, a value ought to have been put upon them before Jacob was born, just as if he had been of full age. But in explaining the difficulty, the Apostle goes on to show, that the adoption of Jacob proceeded not on works but on the calling of God. In works he makes no mention of past or future, but distinctly opposes them to the calling of God, intimating, that when place is given to the one the other is overthrown; as if he had said, The only thing to be considered is what pleased God, not what men furnished of themselves. Lastly, it is certain that all the causes which men are wont to devise as external to the secret counsel of God, are excluded by the use of the terms *purpose* and *election*.

5. Why should men attempt to darken these statements by assigning some place in election to past or future works? This is altogether to evade what the Apostle contends for—viz. that the distinction between the brothers is not founded on any ground of works, but on the mere calling of God, inasmuch as it was fixed before the children were born. Had there been any solidity in this subtlety, it would not have escaped the notice of the Apostle, but being perfectly aware that God foresaw no good in man, save that which he had already previously determined to bestow by means of his election, he does not employ a preposterous arrangement which would make good works antecedent to their cause. We learn from the Apostle's words, that the salvation of believers is founded entirely on the decree of divine election, that the privilege is procured not by works but free calling. We have also a specimen of the thing itself set before us. Esau and Jacob are brothers, begotten of the same parents, within the same womb, not yet born. In them all things are equal, and yet the judgment of God with regard to them is different. He adopts the one and rejects the other. The only right of precedence was that of primogeniture; but that is disregarded, and the younger is preferred to the elder. Nay, in the case of others, God seems to have disregarded primogeniture for the express purpose of excluding the flesh from all ground of boasting. Rejecting Ishmael he gives his favor to Isaac, postponing Manasseh he honors Ephraim.

6. Should any one object that these minute and inferior favors do not enable us to decide with regard to the future life, that it is not to be supposed that he who received the honor of primogeniture was thereby adopted to the inheritance of heaven; (many objectors do not even spare Paul, but accuse him of having in the quotation of these passages wrested Scripture from its proper meaning); I answer as before, that the Apostle has not erred through inconsideration, or spontaneously misapplied the passages of Scripture; but he saw (what these men cannot be brought to consider) that God purposed under an earthly sign to declare the spiritual election of Jacob, which otherwise lay hidden at his inaccessible tribunal. For unless we refer the primogeniture bestowed upon him to the future world, the form of blessing would be altogether vain and ridiculous, inasmuch as he gained nothing by it but a multitude of toils and annoyances, exile, sharp sorrows, and bitter cares. Therefore, when Paul knew beyond a doubt that by the external, God manifested the spiritual and unfading blessings, which he had prepared for his servant in his kingdom, he hesitated not in proving the latter to draw an argument from the

former. For we must remember that the land of Canaan was given in pledge of the heavenly inheritance; and that therefore there cannot be a doubt that Jacob was like the angels ingrafted into the body of Christ, that he might be a partaker of the same life. Jacob, therefore, is chosen, while Esau is rejected; the predestination of God makes a distinction where none existed in respect of merit. If you ask the reason the Apostle gives it, "For he saith to Moses, I will have mercy on whom I will have mercy, and I will have compassion on whom I will have compassion" (Rom. 9:15). And what pray, does this mean? It is just a clear declaration by the Lord that he finds nothing in men themselves to induce him to show kindness, that it is owing entirely to his own mercy, and, accordingly, that their salvation is his own work. Since God places your salvation in himself alone, why should you descend to yourself? Since he assigns you his own mercy alone, why will you recur to your own merits? Since he confines your thoughts to his own mercy why do you turn partly to the view of your own works?

We must therefore come to that smaller number whom Paul elsewhere describes as foreknown of God (Rom. 11:2); not foreknown, as these men imagine, by idle, inactive contemplations but in the sense which it often bears. For surely when Peter says that Christ was "delivered by the determinate counsel and foreknowledge of God" (Acts 2:23), he does not represent God as contemplating merely, but as actually accomplishing our salvation. Thus also Peter, in saying that the believers to whom he writes are elect "according to the foreknowledge of God" (1 Pet. 1:2), properly expresses that secret predestination by which God has sealed those whom he has been pleased to adopt as sons. In using the term *purpose* as synonymous with a term which uniformly denotes what is called a fixed determination, he undoubtedly shows that God, in being the author of our salvation, does not go beyond himself. In this sense he says in the same chapters that Christ as "a lamb" "was foreordained before the creation of the world" (1 Pet. 1:19, 20). What could have been more frigid or absurd than to have represented God as looking from the height of heaven to see whence the salvation of the human race was to come? By a people foreknown, Peter means the same thing as Paul does by a remnant selected from a multitude falsely assuming the name of God. In another passage, to suppress the vain boasting of those who, while only covered with a mask, claim for themselves in the view of the world a first place among the godly, Paul says, "The Lord knoweth them that are his" (2 Tim. 2:19). In short, by that term he designates two classes of people, the one consisting of the whole race of Abraham, the other a people separated from that race, and though hidden from human view, yet open to the eye of God. And there is no doubt that he took the passage from Moses, who declares that God would be merciful to whomsoever he pleased (although he was speaking of an elect people whose condition was apparently equal); just as if he had said, that in a common adoption was included a special grace which he bestows on some as a holier treasure, and that there is nothing in the common covenant to prevent this number from being exempted from the common order. God being pleased in this matter to act as a free dispenser and disposer, distinctly declares, that the only ground on which he will show mercy to one rather than to another is his sovereign pleasure; for when mercy is bestowed on him who asks it, though he indeed does not suffer a refusal, he, however, either anticipates or partly acquires a favour, the whole merit of which God claims for himself.

7. Now, let the supreme Judge and Master decide on the whole case. Seeing such obduracy in his hearers, that his words fell upon the multitude almost without fruit, he to remove this stumbling-block exclaims, "All that the Father giveth me shall come to me." "And this is the Father's will which has sent me, that of all which he has given me I should lose nothing" (John 6:37, 39). Observe that the donation of the Father is the first step in our delivery into the charge and protection of Christ. Some one, perhaps, will here turn round and object, that those only peculiarly belong to the Father who make a voluntary surrender by faith. But the only thing which Christ maintains is that though the defections of vast multitudes should shake the world, yet the counsel of God would stand firm, more stable than heaven itself, that his election would never fail. The elect are said to have belonged to the Father before he bestowed them on his only begotten Son. It is asked if they were his by nature? Nay, they were aliens, but he makes them his by delivering them. The words of Christ are too clear to be rendered obscure by any of the mists of caviling. "No man can come to me except the Father which has sent me draw him." "Every man, therefore, that has heard and learned of the Father comes unto me" (John 6:44, 45). Did all promiscuously bend the knee to Christ, election would be common; whereas now in the small number of believers a manifest diversity appears. Accordingly our Savior, shortly after declaring that the disciples who were given to him were the common property of the Father, adds, "I pray not for the world, but for them which thou hast given

me; for they are thine" (John 17:9). Hence it is that the whole world no longer belongs to its Creator, except in so far as grace rescues from malediction, divine wrath, and eternal death, some, not many, who would otherwise perish, while he leaves the world to the destruction to which it is doomed. Meanwhile, though Christ interpose as a Mediator, yet he claims the right of electing in common with the Father, "I speak not of you all: I know whom I have chosen" (John 13:18). If it is asked whence he has chosen them, he answers in another passages "Out of the world;" which he excludes from his prayers when he commits his disciples to the Father (John 15:19). We must, indeed hold, when he affirms that he knows whom he has chosen, first, that some individuals of the human race are denoted; and, secondly, that they are not distinguished by the quality of their virtues, but by a heavenly decree. Hence it follows, that since Christ makes himself the author of election, none excel by their own strength or industry. In elsewhere numbering Judas among the elect, though he was a devil (John 6:70), he refers only to the apostolical office, which though a bright manifestation of divine favor (as Paul so often acknowledges it to be in his own person), does not, however, contain within itself the hope of eternal salvation. Judas, therefore, when he discharged the office of Apostle perfidiously, might have been worse than a devil; but not one of those whom Christ has once ingrafted into his body will he ever permit to perish, for in securing their salvation, he will perform what he has promised; that is, exert a divine power greater than all (John 10:28). For when he says, "Those that thou gavest me I have kept, and none of them is lost but the son of perdition" (John 17:12), the expression, though there is a catachresis in it, is not at all ambiguous. The sum is, that God by gratuitous adoption forms those whom he wishes to have for sons; but that the intrinsic cause is in himself, because he is contented with his secret pleasure.

8. But Ambrose, Origin, and Jerome, were of opinion, that God dispenses his grace among men according to the use which he foresees that each will make of it. It may be added, that Augustine also was for some time of this opinion; but after he had made greater progress in the knowledge of Scripture, he not only retracted it as evidently false, but powerfully confuted it (August. Retract. Lib. 1, c. 13). Nay, even after the retractation, glancing at the Pelagians who still persisted in that error, he says, "Who does not wonder that the Apostle failed to make this most acute observation? For after stating a most startling proposition concerning those who were not yet born, and afterwards putting the question to himself by way of objection, 'What then? Is there unrighteousness with God?' he had an opportunity of answering, that God foresaw the merits of both, he does not say so, but has recourse to the justice and mercy of God" (August. Epist. 106, ad Sixtum). And in another passage, after excluding all merit before election, he says, "Here, certainly, there is no place for the vain argument of those who defend the foreknowledge of God against the grace of God, and accordingly maintain that we were elected before the foundation of the world, because God foreknow that we would be good, not that he himself would make us good. This is not the language of him who says, 'Ye have not chosen me, but I have chosen you,' (John 15:16). For had he chosen us because he foreknow that we would be good, he would at the same time also have foreknown that we were to choose him" (August. in Joann. 8, see also what follows to the same effect). Let the testimony of Augustine prevail with those who willingly acquiesce in the authority of the Fathers: although Augustine allows not that he differs from the others, but shows by clear evidence that the difference which the Pelagians invidiously objected to him is unfounded. For he quotes from Ambrose (Lib. de Prædest. Sanct. cap. 19), "Christ calls whom he pities." Again, "Had he pleased he could have made them devout instead of undevout; but God calls whom he deigns to call, and makes religious whom he will." Were we disposed to frame an entire volume out of Augustine, it were easy to show the reader that I have no occasion to use any other words than his: but I am unwilling to burden him with a prolix statement. But assuming that the fathers did not speak thus, let us attend to the thing itself. A difficult question had been raised—viz. Did God do justly in bestowing his grace on certain individuals? Paul might have disencumbered himself of this question at once by saying, that God had respect to works. Why does he not do so? Why does he rather continue to use a language which leaves him exposed to the same difficulty? Why, but just because it would not have been right to say it? There was no obliviousness on the part of the Holy Spirit, who was speaking by his mouth. He, therefore, answers without ambiguity, that God favors his elect, because he is pleased to do so, and shows mercy because he is pleased to do so. For the words, "I will be gracious to whom I will be gracious, and show mercy on whom I will show mercy" (Exod. 33:19), are the same in effect as if it had been said, God is moved to mercy by no other reason than that he is pleased to show mercy. Augustine's declaration, therefore, remains

true. The grace of God does not find, but makes persons fit to be chosen.

9. Nor let us be detained by the subtlety of Thomas, that the foreknowledge of merit is the cause of predestination, not, indeed, in respect of the predestinating act, but that on our part it may in some sense be so called, namely, in respect of a particular estimate of predestination; as when it is said, that God predestinates man to glory according to his merit, inasmuch as he decreed to bestow upon him the grace by which he merits glory. For while the Lord would have us to see nothing more in election than his mere goodness, for any one to desire to see more is preposterous affectation. But were we to make a trial of subtlety, it would not be difficult to refute the sophistry of Thomas. He maintains that the elect are in a manner predestinated to glory on account of their merits, because God predestines to give them the grace by which they merit glory. What if I should, on the contrary, object that predestination to grace is subservient to election unto life, and follows as its handmaid; that grace is predestined to those to whom the possession of glory was previously assigned the Lord being pleased to bring his sons by election to justification? For it will hence follow that the predestination to glory is the cause of the predestination to grace, and not the converse. But let us have done with these disputes as superfluous among those who think that there is enough of wisdom for them in the word of God. For it has been truly said by an old ecclesiastical writer, Those who ascribe the election of God to merits, are wise above what they ought to be (Ambrose. de Vocat. Gentium, lib. 1, c. 2).

10. Some object that God would be inconsistent with himself, in inviting all without distinction while he elects only a few. Thus, according to them, the universality of the promise destroys the distinction of special grace. Some moderate men speak in this way, not so much for the purpose of suppressing the truth, as to get quit of puzzling questions, and curb excessive curiosity. The intention is laudable, but the design is by no means to be approved, dissimulation being at no time excusable. In those Again who display their petulance, we see only a vile cavil or a disgraceful error. The mode in which Scripture reconciles the two things—viz. that by external preaching all are called to faith and repentance, and that yet the Spirit of faith and repentance is not given to all, I have already explained, and will again shortly repeat. But the point which they assume I deny as false in two respects: for he who threatens that when it shall rain on one city there will be drought in another (Amos 4:7); and declares in another passage, that there will be a famine of the word (Amos 8:11), does not lay himself under a fixed obligation to call all equally. And he who, forbidding Paul to preach in Asian and leading him away from Bithynia, carries him over to Macedonia (Acts 16:6), shows that it belongs to him to distribute the treasure in what way he pleases. But it is by Isaiah he more clearly demonstrates how he destines the promises of salvation specially to the elect (Isa. 8:16); for he declares that his disciples would consist of them only, and not indiscriminately of the whole human race. Whence it is evident that the doctrine of salvation, which is said to be set apart for the sons of the Church only, is abused when it is represented as effectually available to all. For the present let it suffice to observe, that though the word of the gospel is addressed generally to all, yet the gift of faith is rare. Isaiah assigns the cause when he says that the arm of the Lord is not revealed to all (Isa. 53:1). Had he said, that the gospel is malignantly and perversely condemned, because many obstinately refuse to hear, there might perhaps be some color for this universal call. It is not the purpose of the Prophet, however, to extenuate the guilt of men, when he states the source of their blindness to be, that God deigns not to reveal his arm to them; he only reminds us that since faith is a special gift, it is in vain that external doctrine sounds in the ear. But I would fain know from those doctors whether it is mere preaching or faith that makes men sons of God. Certainly when it is said, "As many as received him, to them gave he power to become the sons of God, even to them that believe on his name" (John 1:12), a confused mass is not set before us, but a special order is assigned to believers, who are "born not of blood, nor of the will of the flesh, nor of the will of man, but of God."

But it is said, there is a mutual agreement between faith and the word. That must be wherever there is faith. But it is no new thing for the seed to fall among thorns or in stony places; not only because the majority appear in fact to be rebellious against God, but because all are not gifted with eyes and ears. How, then, can it consistently be said, that God calls while he knows that the called will not come? Let Augustine answer for me: "Would you dispute with me? Wonder with me, and exclaim, O the depth! Let us both agree in dread, lest we perish in error" (August. de Verb. Apost. Serm. 11). Moreover, if election is, as Paul declares, the parent of faith, I retort the argument, and maintain that faith is not general, since election is special. For it is easily inferred from the series of causes and effects, when Paul says, that the Father "has blessed us with all spiritual blessings in heavenly places in Christ, according as he has chosen us in him before the foundation of the world" (Eph. 1:3, 4), that these riches are not common to all, because God has chosen only whom he would. And the reason why in another passage he commends the faith of the elect is, to prevent any one from supposing that he acquires faith of his own nature; since to God alone belongs the glory of freely illuminating those whom he had previously chosen (Tit. 1:1). For it is well said by Bernard, "His friend hear apart when he says to them, Fear not, little flock: to you it is given to know the mysteries of the kingdom. Who are these? Those whom he foreknew and predestinated to be conformed to the image of his Son. He has made known his great and secret counsel. The Lord knoweth them that are his, but that which was known to God was manifested to men; nor, indeed, does he deign to give a participation in this great mystery to any but those whom he foreknew and predestinated to be his own" (Bernard. ad Thomas Præpos. Benerlae. Epist. 107). Shortly after he concludes, "The mercy of the Lord is from everlasting to everlasting upon them that fear him; from everlasting through predestination, to everlasting through glorification: the one knows no beginning, the other no end." But why cite Bernard as a witness, when we hear from the lips of our Master, "Not that any man has seen the Father, save he which is of God"? (John 6:46). By these words he intimates that all who are not regenerated by God are amazed at the brightness of his countenance. And, indeed, faith is aptly conjoined with election, provided it hold the second place. This order is clearly expressed by our Savior in these words, "This is the Father's will which has sent me, that of all which he has given me I should lose nothing;" "And this is the will of him that sent me, that every one which sees the Son, and believes on him, may have everlasting life" (John 6:39, 40). If he would have all to be saved, he would appoint his Son their guardian, and would ingraft them all into his body by the sacred bond of faith. It is now clear that faith is a singular pledge of paternal love, treasured up for the sons whom he has adopted. Hence Christ elsewhere says, that the sheep follow the shepherd because they know his voice, but that they will not follow a stranger, because they know not the voice of strangers (John 10:4). But whence that distinction, unless that their ears have been divinely bored? For no man makes himself a sheep, but is formed by heavenly grace. And why does the Lord declare that our salvation will always be sure and certain, but just because it is guarded by the invincible power of God? (John 10:29). Accordingly, he concludes that unbelievers are not of his sheep (John 10:16). The reason is, because they are not of the number of those who, as the Lord promised by Isaiah, were to be his disciples. Moreover, as the passages which I have quoted imply perseverance, they are also attestations to the inflexible constancy of election.

11. We come now to the reprobate, to whom the Apostle at the same time refers (Rom. 9:13). For as Jacob, who as yet had merited nothing by good works, is assumed into favor; so Esau, while as yet unpolluted by any crime, is hated. If we turn our view to works, we do injustice to the Apostle, as if he had failed to see the very thing which is clear to us. Moreover, there is complete proof of his not having seen it, since he expressly insists that when as yet they had done neither good nor evil, the one was elected, the other rejected, in order to prove that the foundation of divine predestination is not in works. Then after starting the objection, Is God unjust? instead of employing what would have been the surest and plainest defense of his justice—viz. that God had recompensed Esau according to his wickedness, he is contented with a different solution—viz. that the reprobate are expressly raised up, in order that the glory of God may thereby be displayed. At last, he concludes that God has mercy on whom he will have mercy, and whom he will he hardeneth (Rom. 9:18). You see how he refers both to the mere pleasure of God. Therefore, if we cannot assign any reason for his bestowing mercy on his people, but just that it so pleases him, neither can we have any reason for his reprobating others but his will. When God is said to visit in mercy or harden whom he will, men are reminded that they are not to seek for any cause beyond his will.

CHAPTER 23

REFUTATION OF THE CALUMNIES BY WHICH THIS DOCTRINE IS ALWAYS UNJUSTLY ASSAILED.

This chapter consists of four parts, which refute the principal objections to this doctrine, and the various pleas and exceptions founded on these objections. These are preceded by a refutation of those who hold election but deny reprobation, sec. 1. Then follows, I. A refutation of the first objection to the doctrine of reprobation and election, sec. 2–5. II. An answer to the second objection,

sec. 6–9. III. A refutation of the third objection. IV. A refutation of the fourth objection; to which is added a useful and necessary caution, sec. 12–14.

Sections:

1. Error of those who deny reprobation. 1. Election opposed to reprobation. 2. Those who deny reprobation presumptuously plead with God, whose counsels even angels adore. 3. They murmur against God when disclosing his counsels by the Apostle. Exception and answer. Passage of Augustine.

2. First objection—viz. that God is unjustly offended with those whom he dooms to destruction without their own desert. First answer, from the consideration of the divine will. The nature of this will, and how to be considered.

3. Second answer. God owes nothing to man. His hatred against those who are corrupted by sin is most just. The reprobate convinced in their own consciences of the just judgment of God.

4. Exception—viz. that the reprobate seem to have been preordained to sin. Answer. Passage of the Apostle vindicated from calumny.

5. Answer, confirmed by the authority of Augustine. Illustration. Passage of Augustine.

6. Objection, that God ought not to impute the sins rendered necessary by his predestination. First answer, by ancient writers. This not valid. Second answer also defective. Third answer, proposed by Valla, well founded.

7. Objection, that God did not decree that Adam should perish by his fall, refuted by a variety of reasons. A noble passage of Augustine.

8. Objection, that the wicked perish by the permission, not by the will of God. Answer. A pious exhortation.

9. Objection and answer.

10. Objection, that, according to the doctrine of predestination, God is a respecter of persons. Answer.

11. Objection, that sinners are to be punished equally, or the justice of God is unequal. Answer. Confirmed by passages of Augustine.

12. Objection, that the doctrine of predestination produces overweening confidence and impiety. Different answers.

13. Another objection, depending on the former. Answer. The doctrine of predestination to be preached, not passed over in silence.

14. How it is to be preached and delivered to the people. Summary of the orthodox doctrine of predestination, from Augustine.

1. The human mind, when it hears this doctrine, cannot restrain its petulance, but boils and rages as if aroused by the sound of a trumpet. Many professing a desire to defend the Deity from an invidious charge admit the doctrine of election, but deny that any one is reprobated (Bernard. in Die Ascensionis, Serm. 2). This they do ignorantly and childishly since there could be no election without its opposite reprobation. God is said to set apart those whom he adopts for salvation. It were most absurd to say, that he admits others fortuitously, or that they by their industry acquire what election alone confers on a few. Those, therefore, whom God passes by he reprobates, and that for no other cause but because he is pleased to exclude them from the inheritance which he predestines to his children. Nor is it possible to tolerate the petulance of men, in refusing to be restrained by the word of God, in regard to his incomprehensible counsel, which even angels adore. We have already been told that hardening is not less under the immediate hand of God than mercy. Paul does not, after the example of those whom I have mentioned, labour anxiously to defend God, by calling in the aid of falsehood; he only reminds us that it is unlawful for the creature to quarrel with its Creator. Then how will those who refuse to admit that any are reprobated by God explain the following words of Christ? "Every plant which my heavenly Father has not planted shall be rooted up" (Mt. 15:13). They are plainly told that all whom the heavenly Father has not been pleased to plant as sacred trees in his garden, are doomed and devoted to destruction. If they deny that this is a sign of reprobation, there is nothing, however clear, that, can be proved to them. But if they will still murmur, let us in the soberness of faith rest contented with the admonition of Paul, that it can be no ground of complaint that God, "willing to show his wrath, and to make his power known, endured with much long-suffering the vessels of wrath fitted for destruction: and that he might make known the riches of his glory on the vessels of mercy, which he had afore prepared unto glory" (Rom. 9:22, 23). Let my readers observe that Paul, to cut off all handle for murmuring and detraction, attributes supreme sovereignty to the wrath and power of God; for it were unjust that those profound judgments, which transcend all our powers of discernment, should be subjected to our calculation. It is frivolous in our opponents to reply, that God does not altogether reject those whom in levity he tolerates, but

remains in suspense with regard to them, if per adventure they may repent; as if Paul were representing God as patiently waiting for the conversion of those whom he describes as fitted for destruction. For Augustine, rightly expounding this passage, says that where power is united to endurance, God does not permit, but rules (August. Cont. Julian., Lib. 5, c. 5). They add also, that it is not without cause the vessels of wrath are said to be fitted for destruction, and that God is said to have prepared the vessels of mercy, because in this way the praise of salvation is claimed for God, whereas the blame of perdition is thrown upon those who of their own accord bring it upon themselves. But were I to concede that by the different forms of expression Paul softens the harshness of the former clause, it by no means follows, that he transfers the preparation for destruction to any other cause than the secret counsel of God. This, indeed, is asserted in the preceding context, where God is said to have raised up Pharaoh, and to harden whom he will. Hence it follows, that the hidden counsel of God is the cause of hardening. I at least hold with Augustine that when God makes sheep out of wolves, he forms them again by the powerful influence of grace, that their hardness may thus be subdued, and that he does not convert the obstinate, because he does not exert that more powerful grace, a grace which he has at command, if he were disposed to use it (August. de Prædest. Sanct., Lib. 1, c. 2).

2. These observations would be amply sufficient for the pious and modest, and such as remember that they are men. But because many are the species of blasphemy which these virulent dogs utter against God, we shall, as far as the case admits, give an answer to each. Foolish men raise many grounds of quarrel with God, as if they held him subject to their accusations. First, they ask why God is offended with his creatures who have not provoked him by any previous offense; for to devote to destruction whomsoever he pleases, more resembles the caprice of a tyrant than the legal sentence of a judge; and, therefore, there is reason to expostulate with God, if at his mere pleasure men are, without any desert of their own, predestinated to eternal death. If at any time thoughts of this kind come into the minds of the pious, they will be sufficiently armed to repress them, by considering how sinful it is to insist on knowing the causes of the divine will, since it is itself, and justly ought to be, the cause of all that exists. For if his will has any cause, there must be something antecedent to it, and to which it is annexed; this it were impious to imagine. The will of God is the supreme rule of righteousness, so that everything which he wills must be held to be righteous by the mere fact of his willing it. Therefore, when it is asked why the Lord did so, we must answer, Because he pleased. But if you proceed farther to ask why he pleased, you ask for something greater and more sublime than the will of God, and nothing such can be found. Let human temerity then be quiet, and cease to inquire after what exists not, lest perhaps it fails to find what does exist. This, I say, will be sufficient to restrain any one who would reverently contemplate the secret things of God. Against the audacity of the wicked, who hesitate not openly to blaspheme, God will sufficiently defend himself by his own righteousness, without our assistance, when depriving their consciences of all means of evasion, he shall hold them under conviction, and make them feel their guilt. We, however, give no countenance to the fiction of absolute power, which, as it is heathenish, so it ought justly to be held in detestation by us. We do not imagine God to be lawless. He is a law to himself; because, as Plato says, men laboring under the influence of concupiscence need law; but the will of God is not only free from all vice, but is the supreme standard of perfection, the law of all laws. But we deny that he is bound to give an account of his procedure; and we moreover deny that we are fit of our own ability to give judgment in such a case. Wherefore, when we are tempted to go farther than we ought, let this consideration deter us, Thou shalt be "justified when thou speakest, and be clear when thou judges" (Ps. 51:4).

3. God may thus quell his enemies by silence. But lest we should allow them with impunity to hold his sacred name in derision, he supplies us with weapons against them from his word. Accordingly, when we are accosted in such terms as these, Why did God from the first predestine some to death, when, as they were not yet in existence, they could not have merited sentence of death? let us by way of reply ask in our turn, What do you imagine that God owes to man, if he is pleased to estimate him by his own nature? As we are all vitiated by sin, we cannot but be hateful to God, and that not from tyrannical cruelty, but the strictest justice. But if all whom the Lord predestines to death are naturally liable to sentence of death, of what injustice, pray, do they complain? Should all the sons of Adam come to dispute and contend with their Creator, because by his eternal providence they were before their birth doomed to perpetual destruction, when God comes to reckon with them, what will they be able to mutter against this defense? If all are taken from a corrupt mass, it is not strange that all are subject to condemnation. Let them not, therefore, charge God with

injustice, if by his eternal judgment they are doomed to a death to which they themselves feel that whether they will or not they are drawn spontaneously by their own nature. Hence it appears how perverse is this affectation of murmuring, when of set purpose they suppress the cause of condemnation which they are compelled to recognize in themselves, that they may lay the blame upon God. But though I should confess a hundred times that God is the author (and it is most certain that he is), they do not, however, thereby efface their own guilt, which, engraven on their own consciences, is ever and anon presenting itself to their view.

4. They again object, Were not men predestinated by the ordination of God to that corruption which is now held forth as the cause of condemnation? If so, when they perish in their corruptions they do nothing else than suffer punishment for that calamity, into which, by the predestination of God, Adam fell, and dragged all his posterity headlong with him. Is not he, therefore, unjust in thus cruelly mocking his creatures? I admit that by the will of God all the sons of Adam fell into that state of wretchedness in which they are now involved; and this is just what I said at the first, that we must always return to the mere pleasure of the divine will, the cause of which is hidden in himself. But it does not forthwith follow that God lies open to this charge. For we will answer with Paul in these words, "Nay but, O man, who art thou that replies against God? Shall the thing formed say to him that formed it, Why hast thou made me thus? Has not the potter power over the clay, of the same lump to make one vessel unto honor, and another unto dishonor?" (Rom. 9:20, 21). They will deny that the justice of God is thus truly defended, and will allege that we seek an evasion, such as those are wont to employ who have no good excuse. For what more seems to be said here than just that the power of God is such as cannot be hindered, so that he can do whatsoever he pleases? But it is far otherwise. For what stronger reason can be given than when we are ordered to reflect who God is? How could he who is the Judge of the world commit any unrighteousness? If it properly belongs to the nature of God to do judgment, he must naturally love justice and abhor injustice. Wherefore, the Apostle did not, as if he had been caught in a difficulty, have recourse to evasion; he only intimated that the procedure of divine justice is too high to be scanned by human measure, or comprehended by the feebleness of human intellect. The Apostle, indeed, confesses that in the divine judgments there is a depth in which all the minds of men must be engulfed if they attempt to penetrate into it. But he also shows how unbecoming it is to reduce the works of God to such a law as that we can presume to condemn them the moment they accord not with our reason. There is a well-known saying of Solomon (which, however, few properly understand), "The great God that formed all things both rewardeth the fool and rewardeth transgressors" (Prov. 26:10). For he is speaking of the greatness of God, whose pleasure it is to inflict punishment on fools and transgressors though he is not pleased to bestow his Spirit upon them. It is a monstrous infatuation in men to seek to subject that which has no bounds to the little measure of their reason. Paul gives the name of *elect* to the angels who maintained their integrity. If their steadfastness was owing to the good pleasure of God, the revolt of the others proves that they were abandoned. Of this no other cause can be adduced than reprobation, which is hidden in the secret counsel of God.

5. Now, should some Manes or Cœlestinus come forward to arraign Divine Providence (see sec. 8), I say with Paul, that no account of it can be given, because by its magnitude it far surpasses our understanding. Is there any thing strange or absurd in this? Would we have the power of God so limited as to be unable to do more than our mind can comprehend? I say with Augustine, that the Lord has created those who, as he certainly foreknew, were to go to destruction, and he did so because he so willed. Why he willed it is not ours to ask, as we cannot comprehend, nor can it become us even to raise a controversy as to the justice of the divine will. Whenever we speak of it, we are speaking of the supreme standard of justice. (See August. Ep. 106). But when justice clearly appears, why should we raise any question of injustice? Let us not, therefore, be ashamed to stop their mouths after the example of Paul. Whenever they presume to carp, let us begin to repeat: Who are ye, miserable men, that bring an accusation against God, and bring it because he does not adapt the greatness of his works to your meagre capacity? As if every thing must be perverse that is hidden from the flesh. The immensity of the divine judgments is known to you by clear experience. You know that they are called "a great deep" (Ps. 36:6). Now, look at the narrowness of your own minds and say whether it can comprehend the decrees of God. Why then should you, by infatuated inquisitiveness, plunge yourselves into an abyss which reason itself tells you will prove your destruction? Why are you not deterred, in some degree at least, by what the Book of Job, as well as the Prophetical books declare concerning the incomprehensible wisdom and dreadful

power of God? If your mind is troubled, decline not to embrace the counsel of Augustine, "You a man expect an answer from me: I also am a man. Wherefore, let us both listen to him who says, 'O man, who art thou?' Believing ignorance is better than presumptuous knowledge. Seek merits; you will find nought but punishment. O the height! Peter denies, a thief believes. O the height! Do you ask the reason? I will tremble at the height. Reason you, I will wonder; dispute you, I will believe. I see the height; I cannot sound the depth. Paul found rest, because he found wonder. He calls the judgments of God 'unsearchable;' and have you come to search them? He says that his ways are 'past finding out,' and do you seek to find them out?" (August. de Verb. Apost. Serm. 20). We shall gain nothing by proceeding farther. For neither will the Lord satisfy the petulance of these men, nor does he need any other defense than that which he used by his Spirit, who spoke by the mouth of Paul. We unlearn the art of speaking well when we cease to speak with God.

6. Impiety starts another objection, which, however, seeks not so much to criminate God as to excuse the sinner; though he who is condemned by God as a sinner cannot ultimately be acquitted without impugning the judge. This, then is the scoffing language which profane tongues employ. Why should God blame men for things the necessity of which he has imposed by his own predestination? What could they do? Could they struggle with his decrees? It were in vain for them to do it, since they could not possibly succeed. It is not just, therefore, to punish them for things the principal cause of which is in the predestination of God. Here I will abstain from a defense to which ecclesiastical writers usually recur, that there is nothing in the prescience of God to prevent him from regarding; man as a sinner, since the evils which he foresees are man's, not his. This would not stop the caviler, who would still insist that God might, if he had pleased, have prevented the evils which he foresaw, and not having done so, must with determinate counsel have created man for the very purpose of so acting on the earth. But if by the providence of God man was created on the condition of afterwards doing whatever he does, then that which he cannot escape, and which he is constrained by the will of God to do, cannot be charged upon him as a crime. Let us, therefore, see what is the proper method of solving the difficulty. First, all must admit what Solomon says, "The Lord has made all things for himself; yea, even the wicked for the day of evil" (Prov. 16:4). Now, since the arrangement of all things is in the hand of God, since to him belongs the disposal of life and death, he arranges all things by his sovereign counsel, in such a way that individuals are born, who are doomed from the womb to certain death, and are to glorify him by their destruction. If any one alleges that no necessity is laid upon them by the providence of God, but rather that they are created by him in that condition, because he foresaw their future depravity, he says something, but does not say enough. Ancient writers, indeed, occasionally employ this solution, though with some degree of hesitation. The Schoolmen, again, rest in it as if it could not be gainsaid. I, for my part, am willing to admit, that mere prescience lays no necessity on the creatures; though some do not assent to this, but hold that it is itself the cause of things. But Valla, though otherwise not greatly skilled in sacred matters, seems to me to have taken a shrewder and more acute view, when he shows that the dispute is superfluous since life and death are acts of the divine will rather than of prescience. If God merely foresaw human events, and did not also arrange and dispose of them at his pleasure, there might be room for agitating the question, how far his foreknowledge amounts to necessity; but since he foresees the things which are to happen, simply because he has decreed that they are so to happen, it is vain to debate about prescience, while it is clear that all events take place by his sovereign appointment.

7. They deny that it is ever said in distinct terms, God decreed that Adam should perish by his revolt. As if the same God, who is declared in Scripture to do whatsoever he pleases, could have made the noblest of his creatures without any special purpose. They say that, in accordance with free-will, he was to be the architect of his own fortune, that God had decreed nothing but to treat him according to his desert. If this frigid fiction is received, where will be the omnipotence of God, by which, according to his secret counsel on which every thing depends, he rules over all? But whether they will allow it or not, predestination is manifest in Adam's posterity. It was not owing to nature that they all lost salvation by the fault of one parent. Why should they refuse to admit with regard to one man that which against their will they admit with regard to the whole human race? Why should they in caviling lose their labour? Scripture proclaims that all were, in the person of one, made liable to eternal death. As this cannot be ascribed to nature, it is plain that it is owing to the wonderful counsel of God. It is very absurd in these worthy defenders of the justice of God to strain at a gnat and swallow a camel. I again ask how it is that the fall of Adam involves so many nations with their infant children in eternal death without remedy unless

that it so seemed meet to God? Here the most loquacious tongues must be dumb. The decree, I admit, is, dreadful; and yet it is impossible to deny that God foreknew what the end of man was to be before he made him, and foreknew, because he had so ordained by his decree. Should any one here inveigh against the prescience of God, he does it rashly and unadvisedly. For why, pray, should it be made a charge against the heavenly Judge, that he was not ignorant of what was to happen? Thus, if there is any just or plausible complaint, it must be directed against predestination. Nor ought it to seem absurd when I say, that God not only foresaw the fall of the first man, and in him the ruin of his posterity; but also at his own pleasure arranged it. For as it belongs to his wisdom to foreknow all future events, so it belongs to his power to rule and govern them by his hand. This question, like others, is skillfully explained by Augustine: "Let us confess with the greatest benefit, what we believe with the greatest truth, that the God and Lord of all things who made all things very good, both foreknow that evil was to arise out of good, and knew that it belonged to his most omnipotent goodness to bring good out of evil, rather than not permit evil to be, and so ordained the life of angels and men as to show in it, first, what free-will could do; and, secondly, what the benefit of his grace and his righteous judgment could do" (August. Enchir. ad Laurent).

8. Here they recur to the distinction between will and permission, the object being to prove that the wicked perish only by the permission, but not by the will of God. But why do we say that he permits, but just because he wills? Nor, indeed, is there any probability in the thing itself—viz. that man brought death upon himself merely by the permission, and not by the ordination of God; as if God had not determined what he wished the condition of the chief of his creatures to be. I will not hesitate, therefore, simply to confess with Augustine that the will of God is necessity, and that every thing is necessary which he has willed; just as those things will certainly happen which he has foreseen (August. de Gen. ad Lit., Lib. 6, cap. 15). Now, if in excuse of themselves and the ungodly, either the Pelagians, or Manichees, or Anabaptists, or Epicureans (for it is with these four sects we have to discuss this matter), should object the necessity by which they are constrained, in consequence of the divine predestination, they do nothing that is relevant to the cause. For if predestination is nothing else than a dispensation of divine justice, secret indeed, but unblamable, because it is certain that those predestinated to that condition were not unworthy of it, it is equally certain, that the destruction consequent upon predestination is also most just. Moreover, though their perdition depends on the predestination of God, the cause and matter of it is in themselves. The first man fell because the Lord deemed it meet that he should: why he deemed it meet, we know not. It is certain, however, that it was just, because he saw that his own glory would thereby be displayed. When you hear the glory of God mentioned, understand that his justice is included. For that which deserves praise must be just. Man therefore falls, divine providence so ordaining, but he falls by his own fault. The Lord had a little before declared that all the things which he had made were very good (Gen. 1:31). Whence then the depravity of man, which made him revolt from God? Lest it should be supposed that it was from his creation, God had expressly approved what proceeded from himself. Therefore man's own wickedness corrupted the pure nature which he had received from God, and his ruin brought with it the destruction of all his posterity. Wherefore, let us in the corruption of human nature contemplate the evident cause of condemnation (a cause which comes more closely home to us), rather than inquire into a cause hidden and almost incomprehensible in the predestination of God. Nor let us decline to submit our judgment to the boundless wisdom of God, so far as to confess its insufficiency to comprehend many of his secrets. Ignorance of things which we are not able, or which it is not lawful to know, is learning, while the desire to know them is a species of madness.

9. Someone, perhaps, will say, that I have not yet stated enough to refute this blasphemous excuse. I confess that it is impossible to prevent impiety from murmuring and objecting; but I think I have said enough not only to remove the ground, but also the pretext for throwing blame upon God. The reprobate would excuse their sins by alleging that they are unable to escape the necessity of sinning, especially because a necessity of this nature is laid upon them by the ordination of God. We deny that they can thus be validly excused, since the ordination of God, by which they complain that they are doomed to destruction, is consistent with equity,—an equity, indeed, unknown to us, but most certain. Hence we conclude, that every evil which they bear is inflicted by the most just judgment of God. Next we have shown that they act preposterously when, in seeking the origin of their condemnation, they turn their view to the hidden recesses of the divine counsel, and wink at the corruption of nature, which is the true source. They cannot impute this corruption to God, because he bears testimony to the

goodness of his creation. For though, by the eternal providence of God, man was formed for the calamity under which he lies, he took the matter of it from himself, not from God, since the only cause of his destruction was his degenerating from the purity of his creation into a state of vice and impurity.

10. There is a third absurdity by which the adversaries of predestination defame it. As we ascribe it entirely to the counsel of the divine will, that those whom God adopts as the heirs of his kingdom are exempted from universal destruction, they infer that he is an acceptor of persons; but this Scripture uniformly denies: and, therefore Scripture is either at variance with itself, or respect is had to merit in election. First, the sense in which Scripture declares that God is not an acceptor of persons, is different from that which they suppose: since the term *person* means not *man*, but those things which when conspicuous in a man, either procure favor, grace, and dignity, or, on the contrary, produce hatred, contempt, and disgrace. Among, these are, on the one hand, riches, wealth, power, rank, office, country, beauty, &c.; and, on the other hand, poverty, want, mean birth, sordidness, contempt, and the like. Thus Peter and Paul say, that the Lord is no acceptor of persons, because he makes no distinction between the Jew and the Greek; does not make the mere circumstance of country the ground for rejecting, one or embracing the other (Acts 10:34; Rom. 2:10, Gal. 3:28). Thus James also uses the same words, when he would declare that God has no respect to riches in his judgment (James 2:5). Paul also says in another passage, that in judging God has no respect to slavery or freedom (Eph. 6:9; Col. 3:25). There is nothing inconsistent with this when we say, that God, according to the good pleasure of his will, without any regard to merit, elects those whom he chooses for sons, while he rejects and reprobates others. For fuller satisfaction the matter may be thus explained (see August. Epist. 115, et ad Bonif., Lib. 2, cap. 7). It is asked, how it happens that of two, between whom there is no difference of merit, God in his election adopts the one, and passes by the other? I, in my turn, ask, Is there any thing in him who is adopted to incline God towards him? If it must be confessed that there is nothing, it will follow, that God looks not to the man, but is influenced entirely by his own goodness to do him good. Therefore, when God elects one and rejects another, it is owing not to any respect to the individual, but entirely to his own mercy which is free to display and exert itself when and where he pleases. For we have elsewhere seen, that in order to humble the pride of the flesh, "not many wise men after the flesh, not many mighty, not many noble, are called" (1 Cor. 1:26); so far is God in the exercise of his favor from showing any respect to persons.

11. Wherefore, it is false and most wicked to charge God with dispensing justice unequally, because in this predestination he does not observe the same course towards all. If (say they) he finds all guilty, let him punish all alike: if he finds them innocent, let him relieve all from the severity of judgment. But they plead with God as if he were either interdicted from showing mercy, or were obliged, if he show mercy, entirely to renounce judgment. What is it that they demand? That if all are guilty all shall receive the same punishment. We admit that the guilt is common, but we say, that God in mercy succors some. Let him (they say) succor all. We object, that it is right for him to show by punishing that he is a just judge. When they cannot tolerate this, what else are they attempting than to deprive God of the power of showing mercy; or, at least, to allow it to him only on the condition of altogether renouncing judgment? Here the words of Augustine most admirably apply: "Since in the first man the whole human race fell under condemnation, those vessels which are made of it unto honor, are not vessels of self-righteousness, but of divine mercy. When other vessels are made unto dishonor, it must be imputed not to injustice, but to judgment" (August. Epist. 106, De Prædest. et Gratia; De Bone Persever., cap. 12). Since God inflicts due punishment on those whom he reprobates, and bestows unmerited favor on those whom he calls, he is free from every accusation; just as it belongs to the creditor to forgive the debt to one, and exact it of another. The Lord therefore may show favor to whom he will, because he is merciful; not show it to all, because he is a just judge. In giving to some what they do not merit, he shows his free favor; in not giving to all, he declares what all deserve. For when Paul says, "God has concluded them all in unbelief, that he might have mercy upon all," it ought also to be added, that he is debtor to none; for "who has first given to him and it shall be recompensed unto him again?" (Rom. 11:32, 33).

12. Another argument which they employ to overthrow predestination is that if it stand, all care and study of well doing must cease. For what man can hear (say they) that life and death are fixed by an eternal and immutable decree of God, without immediately concluding that it is of no consequence how he acts, since no work of his can either hinder or further the predestination of God? Thus all will rush on, and like

desperate men plunge headlong wherever lust inclines. And it is true that this is not altogether a fiction; for there are multitudes of a swinish nature who defile the doctrine of predestination by their profane blasphemies, and employ them as a cloak to evade all admonition and censure. "God knows what he has determined to do with regard to us: if he has decreed our salvation, he will bring us to it in his own time; if he has doomed us to death, it is vain for us to fight against it." But Scripture, while it enjoins us to think of this high mystery with much greater reverence and religion, gives very different instruction to the pious, and justly condemns the accursed license of the ungodly. For it does not remind us of predestination to increase our audacity, and tempt us to pry with impious presumption into the inscrutable counsels of God, but rather to humble and abase us, that we may tremble at his judgment, and learn to look up to his mercy. This is the mark at which believers will aim. The grunt of these filthy swine is duly silenced by Paul. They say that they feel secure in vices because, if they are of the number of the elect, their vices will be no obstacle to the ultimate attainment of life. But Paul reminds us that the end for which we are elected is, "that we should be holy, and without blame before him" (Eph. 1:4). If the end of election is holiness of life, it ought to arouse and stimulate us strenuously to aspire to it, instead of serving as a pretext for sloth. How wide the difference between the two things, between ceasing from well-doing because election is sufficient for salvation, and its being the very end of election, that we should devote ourselves to the study of good works. Have done, then, with blasphemies which wickedly invert the whole order of election. When they extend their blasphemies farther, and say that he who is reprobated by God will lose his pains if he studies to approve himself to him by innocence and probity of life, they are convicted of the most impudent falsehood. For whence can any such study arise but from election? As all who are of the number of the reprobate are vessels formed unto dishonor, so they cease not by their perpetual crimes to provoke the anger of God against them, and give evident signs of the judgment which God has already passed upon them; so far is it from being true that they vainly contend against it.

13. Another impudent and malicious calumny against this doctrine is, that it destroys all exhortations to a pious life. The great odium to which Augustine was at one time subjected on this head he wiped away in his treatise De Correptione et Gratia, to Valentinus, a perusal of which will easily satisfy the pious and docile. Here, however, I may touch on a few points, which will, I hope, be sufficient for those who are honest and not contentious. We have already seen how plainly and audibly Paul preaches the doctrine of free election: is he, therefore, cold in admonishing and exhorting? Let those good zealots compare his vehemence with theirs and they will find that they are ice, while he is all fervor. And surely every doubt on this subject should be removed by the principles which he lays down, that God has not called us to uncleanness; that every one should possess his vessel in honor; that we are the workmanship of God, "created in Christ Jesus unto good works, which God has before ordained that we should walk in them" (1 Thess. 4:4, 7; Eph. 2:10). In one word, those who have any tolerable acquaintance with the writings of Paul will understand, without a long demonstration, how well he reconciles the two things which those men pretend to be contradictory to each other. Christ commands us to believe in him, and yet there is nothing false or contrary to this command in the statement which he afterwards makes: "No man can come unto me, except it were given him of my Father" (John 6:65). Let preaching then have its free course, that it may lead men to faith, and dispose them to persevere with uninterrupted progress. Nor, at the same time, let there be any obstacle to the knowledge of predestination, so that those who obey may not plume themselves on anything of their own, but glory only in the Lord. It is not without cause our Savior says, "Who has ears to hear, let him hear" (Mt. 13:9). Therefore, while we exhort and preach, those who have ears willingly obey: in those again, who have no ears is fulfilled what is written: "Hear ye indeed, but understand not" (Isaiah 6:9). "But why (says Augustine) have some ears, and others not? Who has known the mind of the Lord? Are we, therefore, to deny what is plain because we cannot comprehend what is hid?" This is a faithful quotation from Augustine; but because his words will perhaps have more authority than mine, let us adduce the following passage from his treatise, De Bone Persever., cap. 15.

"Should some on hearing this turn to indolence and sloth, and leaving off all exertion, rush headlong into lust, are we, therefore to suppose that what has been said of the foreknowledge of God is not true? If God foreknew that they would be good, will they not be good, however great their present wickedness? and if God foreknow that they would be wicked, will they not be wicked, how great soever the goodness now seen in them? For reasons of this description, must the truth which has been stated on the subject of divine foreknowledge be denied or not mentioned? and more especially when, if it is not stated, other errors will arise?" In the sixteenth chapter he says, "The reason for not mentioning the truth is one thing, the necessity for telling the truth is another. It were tedious to inquire into all the reasons for silence. One, however, is, lest those who understand not become worse, while we are desirous to make those who understand better informed. Now such persons, when we say anything of this kind, do not indeed become better informed, but neither do they become worse. But when the truth is of such a nature, that he who cannot comprehend it becomes worse by our telling it, and he who can comprehend it becomes worse by our not telling it, what think ye ought we to do? Are we not to tell the truth, that he who can comprehend may comprehend, rather than not tell it, and thereby not only prevent both from comprehending, but also make the more intelligent of the two to become worse, whereas if he heard and comprehended others might learn through him? And we are unwilling to say what, on the testimony of Scripture, it is lawful to say. For we fear lest, when we speak, he who cannot comprehend may be offended; but we have no fear lest while we are silent, he who can comprehend the truth be involved in falsehood." In chapter twentieth, glancing again at the same view, he more clearly confirms it. "Wherefore, if the apostles and teachers of the Church who came after them did both; if they discoursed piously of the eternal election of God, and at the same time kept believers under the discipline of a pious life, how can those men of our day, when shut up by the invincible force of truth, think they are right in saying, that what is said of predestination, though it is true, must not be preached to the people? Nay, it ought indeed to be preached, that whoso has ears to hear may hear. And who has ears if he has not received them from him who has promised to give them? Certainly, let him who receives not, reject. Let him who receives, take and drink, drink and live. For as piety is to be preached, that God may be duly worshipped; so predestination also is to be preached, that he who has ears to hear may, in regard to divine grace, glory not in himself, but in God."

14. And yet as that holy man had a singular desire to edify, he so regulates his method of teaching as carefully, and as far as in him lay, to avoid giving offense. For he reminds us, that those things which are truly should also be fitly spoken. Were any one to address the people thus: If you do not believe, the reason is, because God has already doomed you to destruction: he would not only encourage sloth, but also give countenance to wickedness. Were any one to give utterance to the sentiment in the future tense, and say, that those who hear will not believe because they are reprobates, it were imprecation rather than doctrine. Wherefore, Augustine not undeservedly orders such, as senseless teachers or minister and ill-omened prophets, to retire from the Church. He, indeed, elsewhere truly contends that "a man profits by correction only when He who causes those whom He pleases to profit without correction, pities and assists. But why is it thus with some, and differently with others? Far be it from us to say that it belongs to the clay and not to the potter to decide." He afterwards says, "When men by correction either come or return to the way of righteousness, who is it that works salvation in their hearts but he who gives the increase, whoever it be that plants and waters? When he is pleased to save, there is no free-will in man to resist. Wherefore, it cannot be doubted that the will of God (who has done whatever he has pleased in heaven and in earth, and who has even done things which are to be) cannot be resisted by the human will, or prevented from doing what he pleases, since with the very wills of men he does so." Again, "When he would bring men to himself, does he bind them with corporeal fetters? He acts inwardly, inwardly holds, inwardly moves their hearts, and draws them by the will, which he has wrought in them." What he immediately adds must not be omitted: "because we know not who belongs to the number of the predestinated, or does not belong, our desire ought to be that all may be saved; and hence every person we meet, we will desire to be with us a partaker of peace. But our peace will rest upon the sons of peace. Wherefore, on our part, let correction be used as a harsh yet salutary medicine for all, that they may neither perish, nor destroy others. To God it will belong to make it available to those whom he has foreknown and predestinated."

CHAPTER 24

ELECTION CONFIRMED BY THE CALLING OF GOD. THE REPROBATE BRING UPON THEMSELVES THE RIGHTEOUS DESTRUCTION TO WHICH THEY ARE DOOMED.

The title of this chapter shows that it consists of two parts,—I. The case of the Elect, from sec. 1–11. II. The case of the Reprobate, from sec. 12–17.

Sections:

1. The election of God is secret, but is manifested by effectual calling. The nature of this effectual calling. How election and effectual calling are founded on the free mercy of God. A cavil of certain expositors refuted by the words of Augustine. An exception disposed of.

2. Calling proved to be free, 1. By its nature and the mode in which it is dispensed. 2. By the word of God. 3. By the calling of Abraham, the father of the faithful. 4. By the testimony of John. 5. By the example of those who have been called.

3. The pure doctrine of the calling of the elect misunderstood, 1. By those who attribute too much to the human will. 2. By those who make election dependent on faith. This error amply refuted.

4. In this and the five following sections the certainty of election vindicated from the assaults of Satan. The leading arguments are: 1. Effectual calling. 2. Christ apprehended by faith. 3. The protection of Christ, the guardian of the elect. We must not attempt to penetrate to the hidden recesses of the divine wisdom, in order to learn what is decreed with regard to us at the judgment-seat. We must begin and end with the call of God. This confirmed by an apposite saying of Bernard.

5. Christ the foundation of this calling and election. He who does not lean on him alone cannot be certain of his election. He is the faithful interpreter of the eternal counsel in regard to our salvation.

6. Another security of our election is the protection of Christ our Shepherd. How it is manifested to us. Objection 1. As to the future state. 2. As to perseverance. Both objections refuted.

7. Objection, that those who seem elected sometimes fall away. Answer. A passage of Paul dissuading us from security explained. The kind of fear required in the elect.

8. Explanation of the saying, that many are called, but few chosen. A twofold call.

9. Explanation of the passage, that none is lost but the son of perdition. Refutation of an objection to the certainty of election.

10. Explanation of the passages urged against the certainty of election. Examples by which some attempt to prove that the seed of election is sown in the hearts of the elect from their very birth. Answer. 1. One or two examples do not make the rule. 2. This view opposed to Scripture. 3. Is expressly opposed by an apostle.

11. An explanation and confirmation of the third answer.

12. Second part of the chapter, which treats of the reprobate. Some of them God deprives of the opportunity of hearing his word. Others he blinds and stupefies the more by the preaching of it.

13. Of this no other account can be given than that the reprobate are vessels fitted for destruction. This confirmed by the case of the elect; of Pharaoh and of the Jewish people both before and after the manifestation of Christ.

14. Question, Why does God blind the reprobate? Two answers. These confirmed by different passages of Scripture. Objection of the reprobate. Answer.

15. Objection to this doctrine of the righteous rejection of the reprobate. The first founded on a passage in Ezekiel. The passage explained.

16. A second objection founded on a passage in Paul. The apostle's meaning explained. A third objection and fourth objection answered.

17. A fifth objection—viz. that there seems to be a twofold will in God. Answer. Other objections and answers. Conclusion.

1. But that the subject may be more fully illustrated, we must treat both of the calling of the elect, and of the blinding and hardening of the ungodly. The former I have already in some measure discussed (chap. 22, sec. 10, 11), when refuting the error of those who think that the general terms in which the promises are made place the whole human race on a level. The special election which otherwise would remain hidden in God, he at length manifests by his calling. "For whom he did foreknow, he also did predestinate to be conformed to the image of his Son." Moreover, "whom he did predestinate, them he also called; and whom he called, them he also justified," that he may one day glorify (Rom. 8:29, 30). Though the Lord, by electing his people, adopted them as his sons, we, however, see that they do not come into possession of this great good until they are called; but when called, the enjoyment of their election is in some measure communicated to them. For which reason the Spirit which they receive is termed by Paul both the "Spirit of adoption," and the "seal" and "earnest" of the future inheritance; because by his testimony he confirms and seals the certainty of future adoption on their hearts. For although the preaching of the gospel springs from the fountain of election, yet being common to them with the reprobate, it would not be in itself a solid proof. God, however, teaches his elect effectually when he brings them to faith, as we formerly quoted from the words of

our Savior, "Not that any man has seen the Father, save he which is of God, he has seen the Father" (John 6:46). Again, "I have manifested thy name unto the men which thou gavest me out of the world" (John 17:6). He says in another passage, "No man can come to me, except the Father which has sent me draw him" (John 6:44). This passage Augustine ably expounds in these words: "If (as Truth says) every one who has learned comes, then every one who does not come has not learned. It does not therefore follow that he who can come does come, unless he have willed and done it; but every one who has learned of the Father, not only can come, but also comes; the antecedence of possibility the affection of will, and the effect of action being now present" (August. de Grat. Chr. Cont. Pelag., Lib. 1, c. 14, 31). In another passage, he says still more clearly, "What means, Every one that has heard and learned of the Father comes unto me, but just that there is no one who hears and learns of the Father that does not come to me? For if every one who has heard and learned, comes; assuredly every one who does not come, has neither heard nor learned of the Father: for if he had heard and learned, he would come. Far removed from carnal sense is this school in which the Father is heard and teaches us to come to the Son" (August. de Prædes. Sanct. c. 8). Shortly after, he says, "This grace, which is secretly imparted to the hearts of men, is not received by any hard heart; for the reason for which it is given is, that the hardness of the heart may first be taken away. Hence, when the Father is heard within, he takes away the stony heart, and gives a heart of flesh. Thus he makes them sons of promise and vessels of mercy, which he has prepared for glory. Why then does he not teach all to come to Christ, but just because all whom he teaches he teaches in mercy, while those whom he teaches not he teaches not in judgment? for he pities whom he will, and hardens whom he will." Those, therefore, whom God has chosen he adopts as sons, while he becomes to them a Father. By calling, moreover, he admits them to his family, and unites them to himself, that they may be one with him. When calling is thus added to election, the Scripture plainly intimates that nothing is to be looked for in it but the free mercy of God. For if we ask whom it is he calls, and for what reason, he answers, it is those whom he had chosen. When we come to election, mercy alone everywhere appears; and, accordingly, in this the saying of Paul is truly realized, "So then, it is not of him that willeth, nor of him that runneth, but of God that showeth mercy" (Rom. 9:16); and that not as is commonly understood by those who share the result between the grace of God and the will and agency of man. For their exposition is, that the desire and endeavor of sinners are of no avail by themselves, unless accompanied by the grace of God, but that when aided by his blessing, they also do their part in procuring salvation. This cavil I prefer refuting in the words of Augustine rather than my own: "If all that the apostle meant is, that it is not alone of him that willeth, or of him that runneth, unless the Lord be present in mercy, we may retort and hold the converse, that it is not of mercy alone, unless willing and running be present" (August. Enchir. ad Laurent., c. 31). But if this is manifestly impious, let us have no doubt that the apostle attributes all to the mercy of the Lord, and leaves nothing to our wills or exertions. Such were the sentiments of that holy man. I set not the value of a straw on the subtlety to which they have recourse—viz. that Paul would not have spoken thus had there not been some will and effort on our part. For he considered not what might be in man; but seeing that certain persons ascribed a part of salvation to the industry of man, he simply condemned their error in the former clause, and then claimed the whole substance of salvation for the divine mercy. And what else do the prophets than perpetually proclaim the free calling of God?

2. Moreover, this is clearly demonstrated by the nature and dispensation of calling, which consists not merely of the preaching of the word, but also of the illumination of the Spirit. Who those are to whom God offers his word is explained by the prophet, "I am sought of them that asked not for me: I am found of them that sought me not: I said, Behold me, behold me, unto a nation that was not called by my name" (Isaiah 65:1). And lest the Jews should think that that mercy applied only to the Gentiles, he calls to their remembrance whence it was he took their father Abraham when he condescended to be his friend (Isaiah 41:8); namely, from the midst of idolatry, in which he was plunged with all his people. When he first shines with the light of his word on the undeserving, he gives a sufficiently clear proof of his free goodness. Here, therefore, boundless goodness is displayed, but not so as to bring all to salvation, since a heavier judgment awaits the reprobate for rejecting the evidence of his love. God also, to display his own glory, withholds from them the effectual agency of his Spirit. Therefore, this inward calling is an infallible pledge of salvation. Hence the words of John, "Hereby we know that he abideth in us by the Spirit which he has given us" (1 John 3:24). And lest the flesh should glory, in at least responding to him, when he calls and spontaneously offers himself, he

affirms that there would be no ears to hear, no eyes to see, did not he give them. And he acts not according to the gratitude of each, but according to his election. Of this you have a striking example in Luke, when the Jews and Gentiles in common heard the discourse of Paul and Barnabas. Though they were all instructed in the same word, it is said, that "as many as were ordained to eternal life believed" (Acts 13:48). How can we deny that calling is gratuitous, when election alone reigns in it even to its conclusion?

3. Two errors are here to be avoided. Some make man a fellow-worker with God in such a sense, that man's suffrage ratifies election, so that, according to them, the will of man is superior to the counsel of God. As if Scripture taught that only the power of being able to believe is given us, and not rather faith itself. Others, although they do not so much impair the grace of the Holy Spirit, yet, induced by what means I know not, make election dependent on faith, as if it were doubtful and ineffectual till confirmed by faith. There can be no doubt, indeed, that in regard to us it is so confirmed. Moreover, we have already seen, that the secret counsel of God, which lay concealed, is thus brought to light, by this nothing more being understood than that that which was unknown is proved, and as it were sealed. But it is false to say that election is then only effectual after we have embraced the gospel, and that it thence derives its vigor. It is true that we must there look for its certainty, because, if we attempt to penetrate to the secret ordination of God, we shall be engulfed in that profound abyss. But when the Lord has manifested it to us, we must ascend higher in order that the effect may not bury the cause. For what can be more absurd and unbecoming, than while Scripture teaches that we are illuminated as God has chosen us, our eyes should be so dazzled with the brightness of this light, as to refuse to attend to election? Meanwhile, I deny not that, in order to be assured of our salvation, we must begin with the word, and that our confidence ought to go no farther than the word when we invoke God the Father. For some to obtain more certainty of the counsel of God (which is nigh us in our mouth, and in our heart, Deut. 30:14), absurdly desire to fly above the clouds. We must, therefore, curb that temerity by the soberness of faith, and be satisfied to have God as the witness of his hidden grace in the external word; provided always that the channel in which the water flows, and out of which we may freely drink, does not prevent us from paying due honor to the fountain.

4. Therefore as those are in error who make the power of election dependent on the faith by which we perceive that we are elected, so we shall follow the best order, if, in seeking the certainty of our election, we cleave to those posterior signs which are sure attestations to it. Among the temptations with which Satan assaults believers, none is greater or more perilous, than when disquieting them with doubts as to their election, he at the same time stimulates them with a depraved desire of inquiring after it out of the proper way. (See Luther in Genes. cap. 26). By inquiring out of the proper way, I mean when puny man endeavors to penetrate to the hidden recesses of the divine wisdom, and goes back even to the remotest eternity, in order that he may understand what final determination God has made with regard to him. In this way he plunges headlong into an immense abyss, involves himself in numberless inextricable snares, and buries himself in the thickest darkness. For it is right that the stupidity of the human mind should be punished with fearful destruction, whenever it attempts to rise in its own strength to the height of divine wisdom. And this temptation is the more fatal, that it is the temptation to which of all others almost all of us are most prone. For there is scarcely a mind in which the thought does not sometimes rise, Whence your salvation but from the election of God? But what proof have you of your election? When once this thought has taken possession of any individual, it keeps him perpetually miserable, subjects him to dire torment, or throws him into a state of complete stupor. I cannot wish a stronger proof of the depraved ideas, which men of this description form of predestination, than experience itself furnishes, since the mind cannot be infected by a more pestilential error than that which disturbs the conscience, and deprives it of peace and tranquillity in regard to God. Therefore, as we dread shipwreck, we must avoid this rock, which is fatal to every one who strikes upon it. And though the discussion of predestination is regarded as a perilous sea, yet in sailing over it the navigation is calm and safe, nay pleasant, provided we do not voluntarily court danger. For as a fatal abyss engulfs those who, to be assured of their election, pry into the eternal counsel of God without the word, yet those who investigate it rightly, and in the order in which it is exhibited in the word, reap from it rich fruits of consolation.

Let our method of inquiry then be, to begin with the calling of God and to end with it. Although there is nothing in this to prevent believers from feeling that the blessings which they daily receive from the hand of God originate in that secret adoption, as they themselves express it in Isaiah, "Thou hast done wonderful things; thy counsels of old are faithfulness and truth" (Isa. 25:1). For with this as a pledge, God is pleased to assure us of as much of his counsel as can be lawfully known. But lest any should think that testimony weak, let us consider what clearness and certainty it gives us. On this subject there is an apposite passage in Bernard. After speaking of the reprobate, he says, "The purpose of God stands, the sentence of peace on those that fear him also stands, a sentence concealing their bad and recompensing their good qualities; so that, in a wondrous manner, not only their good but their bad qualities work together for good. Who will lay any thing to the charge of God's elect? It is completely sufficient for my justification to have him propitious against whom only I have sinned. Every thing which he has decreed not to impute to me, is as if it had never been." A little after he says, "O the place of true rest, a place which I consider not unworthy of the name of inner-chamber, where God is seen, not as if disturbed with anger, or distracted by care, but where his will is proved to be good, and acceptable, and perfect. That vision does not terrify but soothe, does not excite restless curiosity but calms it, does not fatigue but tranquilizes the senses. Here is true rest. A tranquil God tranquilizes all things; and to see him at rest, is to be at rest" (Bernard, super Cantic. Serm. 14).

5. First, if we seek for the paternal mercy and favor of God, we must turn our eyes to Christ, in whom alone the Father is well pleased (Mt. 3:17). When we seek for salvation, life, and a blessed immortality, to him also must we retake ourselves, since he alone is the fountain of life and the anchor of salvation, and the heir of the kingdom of heaven. Then what is the end of election, but just that, being adopted as sons by the heavenly Father, we may by his favor obtain salvation and immortality? How much soever you may speculate and discuss you will perceive that in its ultimate object it goes no farther. Hence, those whom God has adopted as sons, he is said to have elected, not in themselves, but in Christ Jesus (Eph. 1:4); because he could love them only in him, and only as being previously made partakers with him, honor them with the inheritance of his kingdom. But if we are elected in him, we cannot find the certainty of our election in ourselves; and not even in God the Father, if we look at him apart from the Son. Christ, then, is the mirror in which we ought, and in which, without deception, we may contemplate our election. For since it is into his body that the Father has decreed to ingraft those whom from eternity he wished to be his, that he may regard as sons all whom he acknowledges to be his members, if we are in communion with Christ, we have proof sufficiently clear and strong that we are written in the Book of Life. Moreover, he admitted us to sure communion with himself, when, by the preaching of the gospel, he declared that he was given us by the Father, to be ours with all his blessings (Rom. 8:32). We are said to be clothed with him, to be one with him, that we may live, because he himself lives. The doctrine is often repeated, "God so loved the world, that he gave his only begotten Son, that whosoever believeth in him should not perish, but have everlasting life" (John 3:16). He who believes in him is said to have passed from death unto life (John 5:24). In this sense he calls himself the *bread of life*, of which if a man eat, he shall never die (John 6:35). He, I say, was our witness, that all by whom he is received in faith will be regarded by our heavenly Father as sons. If we long for more than to be regarded as sons of God and heirs, we must ascend above Christ. But if this is our final goal, how infatuated is it to seek out of him what we have already obtained in him, and can only find in him? Besides, as he is the Eternal Wisdom, the Immutable Truth, the Determinate Counsel of the Father, there is no room for fear that any thing which he tells us will vary in the minutest degree from that will of the Father after which we inquire. Nay, rather he faithfully discloses it to us as it was from the beginning, and always will be. The practical influence of this doctrine ought also to be exhibited in our prayers. For though a belief of our election animates us to involve God, yet when we frame our prayers, it were preposterous to obtrude it upon God, or to stipulate in this way, "O Lord, if I am elected, hear me." He would have us to rest satisfied with his promises, and not to inquire elsewhere whether or not he is disposed to hear us. We shall thus be disentangled from many snares, if we know how to make a right use of what is rightly written; but let us not inconsiderately wrest it to purposes different from that to which it ought to be confined.

6. Another confirmation tending to establish our confidence is, that our election is connected with our calling. For those whom Christ enlightens with the knowledge of his name, and admits into the bosom of his Church, he is said to take under his guardianship and protection. All whom he thus receives are said to be committed and entrusted to him by the Father, that they may be kept unto life eternal. What would we have? Christ proclaims aloud that all whom the Father is pleased to save he has delivered into his protection (John 6:37–39, 17:6, 12). Therefore, if we would know whether God

cares for our salvation, let us ask whether he has committed us to Christ, whom he has appointed to be the only Savior of all his people. Then, if we doubt whether we are received into the protection of Christ, he obviates the doubt when he spontaneously offers himself as our Shepherd, and declares that we are of the number of his sheep if we hear his voice (John 10:3, 16). Let us, therefore, embrace Christ, who is kindly offered to us, and comes forth to meet us: he will number us among his flock, and keep us within his fold. But anxiety arises as to our future state. For as Paul teaches, that those are called who were previously elected, so our Savior shows that many are called, but few chosen (Mt. 22:14). Nay, even Paul himself dissuades us from security, when he says, "Let him that thinketh he standeth take heed lest he fall" (1 Cor. 10:12). And again, "Well, because of unbelief they were broken off, and thou standest by faith. Be not high-minded, but fear: for if God spared not the natural branches, take heed lest he also spare not thee" (Rom. 11:20, 21). In fine, we are sufficiently taught by experience itself, that calling and faith are of little value without perseverance, which, however, is not the gift of all. But Christ has freed us from anxiety on this head; for the following promises undoubtedly have respect to the future: "All that the Father giveth me shall come to me, and him that comes to me I will in no wise cast out." Again, "This is the will of him that sent me, that of all which he has given me I should lose nothing; but should raise it up at the last day" (John 6:37, 39). Again "My sheep hear my voice, and I know them, and they follow me: and I give unto them eternal life, and they shall never perish, neither shall any man pluck them out of my hand. My Father which gave them me is greater than all: and no man is able to pluck them out of my Father's hand" (John 10:27, 28). Again, when he declares, "Every plant which my heavenly Father has not planted shall be rooted up" (Mt. 15:13), he intimates conversely that those who have their root in God can never be deprived of their salvation. Agreeable to this are the words of John, "If they had been of us, they would no doubt have continued with us" (1 John 2:19). Hence, also, the magnificent triumph of Paul over life and death, things present, and things to come (Rom. 8:38). This must be founded on the gift of perseverance. There is no doubt that he employs the sentiment as applicable to all the elect. Paul elsewhere says, "Being confident of this very thing, that he who has begun a good work in you will perform it until the day of Jesus Christ" (Phil. 1:6). David, also, when his faith threatened to fail, leant on this support, "Forsake not the works of thy hands." Moreover, it cannot be doubted, that since Christ prays for all the elect, he asks the same thing for them as he asked for Peter—viz. that their faith fail not (Luke 22:32). Hence we infer, that there is no danger of their falling away, since the Son of God, who asks that their piety may prove constant, never meets with a refusal. What then did our Savior intend to teach us by this prayer, but just to confide, that whenever we are his our eternal salvation is secure?

7. But it daily happens that those who seemed to belong to Christ revolt from him and fall away: Nay, in the very passage where he declares that none of those whom the Father has given to him have perished, he excepts the son of perdition. This, indeed, is true; but it is equally true that such persons never adhered to Christ with that heartfelt confidence by which I say that the certainty of our election is established: "They went out from us," says John, "but they were not of us; for if they had been of us, they would, no doubt, have continued with us" (1 John 2:19). I deny not that they have signs of calling similar to those given to the elect; but I do not at all admit that they have that sure confirmation of election which I desire believers to seek from the word of the gospel. Wherefore, let not examples of this kind move us away from tranquil confidence in the promise of the Lord, when he declares that all by whom he is received in true faith have been given him by the Father, and that none of them, while he is their Guardian and Shepherd, will perish (John 3:16; 6:39). Of Judas we shall shortly speak (sec. 9). Paul does not dissuade Christians from security simply, but from careless, carnal security, which is accompanied with pride, arrogance, and contempt of others, which extinguishes humility and reverence for God, and produces a forgetfulness of grace received (Rom. 11:20). For he is addressing the Gentiles, and showing them that they ought not to exult proudly and cruelly over the Jews, in consequence of whose rejection they had been substituted in their stead. He also enjoins fear, not a fear under which they may waver in alarm, but a fear which, teaching us to receive the grace of God in humility, does not impair our confidence in it, as has elsewhere been said. We may add, that he is not speaking to individuals, but to sects in general (see 1 Cor. 10:12). The Church having been divided into two parties, and rivalship producing dissension, Paul reminds the Gentiles that their having been substituted in the place of a peculiar and holy people was a reason for modesty and fear. For there were many vain-glorious persons among them, whose empty boasting it was expedient to repress.

But we have elsewhere seen, that our hope extends into the future, even beyond death, and that nothing is more contrary to its nature than to be in doubt as to our future destiny.

8. The expression of our Savior, "Many are called, but few are chosen" (Mt. 22:14), is also very improperly interpreted (see Book 3, chap. 2, sec. 11, 12). There will be no ambiguity in it, if we attend to what our former remarks ought to have made clear—viz. that there are two species of calling: for there is an universal call, by which God, through the external preaching of the word, invites all men alike, even those for whom he designs the call to be a savor of death, and the ground of a severer condemnation. Besides this there is a special call which, for the most part, God bestows on believers only, when by the internal illumination of the Spirit he causes the word preached to take deep root in their hearts. Sometimes, however, he communicates it also to those whom he enlightens only for a time, and whom afterwards, in just punishment for their ingratitude, he abandons and smites with greater blindness. Now, our Lord seeing that the gospel was published far and wide, was despised by multitudes, and justly valued by few, describes God under the character of a King, who, preparing a great feast, sends his servants all around to invite a great multitude, but can only obtain the presence of a very few, because almost all allege causes of excuse; at length, in consequence of their refusal, he is obliged to send his servants out into the highways to invite every one they meet. It is perfectly clear, that thus far the parable is to be understood of external calling. He afterwards adds, that God acts the part of a kind entertainer, who goes round his table and affably receives his guests; but still if he finds any one not adorned with the nuptial garment, he will by no means allow him to insult the festivity by his sordid dress. I admit that this branch of the parable is to be understood of those who, by a profession of faith, enter the Church, but are not at all invested with the sanctification of Christ. Such disgraces to his Church, such cankers God will not always tolerate, but will cast them forth as their turpitude deserves. Few, then, out of the great number of called are chosen; the calling, however, not being of that kind which enables believers to judge of their election. The former call is common to the wicked, the latter brings with it the spirit of regeneration, which is the earnest and seal of the future inheritance by which our hearts are sealed unto the day of the Lord (Eph. 1:13, 14). In one word, while hypocrites pretend to piety, just as if they were true worshipers of God, Christ declares that they will ultimately be ejected from the place which they improperly occupy, as it is said in the psalm, "Lord, who shall abide in thy tabernacle? who shall dwell in thy holy hill? He that walketh uprightly, and worketh righteousness, and speaketh the truth in his heart" (Psalm 15:1, 2). Again in another passage, "This is the generation of them that seek him, that seek thy face, O Jacob" (Psalm 24:6). And thus the Spirit exhorts believers to patience, and not to murmur because Ishmaelites are mingled with them in the Church since the mask will at length be torn off, and they will be ejected with disgrace.

9. The same account is to be given of the passage lately quoted, in which Christ says, that none is lost but the son of perdition (John 17:12). The expression is not strictly proper; but it is by no means obscure: for Judas was not numbered among the sheep of Christ, because he was one truly, but because he held a place among them. Then, in another passage, where the Lord says, that he was elected with the apostles, reference is made only to the office, "Have I not chosen you twelve," says he, "and one of you is a devil?" (John 6:70). That is, he had chosen him to the office of apostle. But when he speaks of election to salvation, he altogether excludes him from the number of the elect, "I speak not of you all: I know whom I have chosen" (John 13:18). Should any one confound the term *election* in the two passages, he will miserably entangle himself; whereas if he distinguish between them, nothing can be plainer. Gregory, therefore, is most grievously and perniciously in error; when he says that we are conscious only of our calling, but are uncertain of our election; and hence he exhorts all to fear and trembling, giving this as the reason, that though we know what we are to-day, yet we know not what we are to be (Gregor. Hom. 38). But in that passage he clearly shows how he stumbled on that stone. By suspending election on the merit of works, he had too good a reason for dispiriting the minds of his readers, while, at the same time, as he did not lead them away from themselves to confidence in the divine goodness, he was unable to confirm them. Hence believers may in some measure perceive the truth of what we said at the outset—viz. predestination duly considered does not shake faith, but rather affords the best confirmation of it. I deny not, however, that the Spirit sometimes accommodates his language to our feeble capacity; as when he says, "They shall not be in the assembly of my people, neither shall they be written in the writing of the house of Israel" (Ezek. 13:9). As if God were beginning to write the names of those whom he counts among his people in the Book of Life; whereas we know, even on

the testimony of Christ, that the names of the children of God were written in the Book of Life from the beginning (Luke 10:20). The words simply indicate the abandonment of those who seemed to have a chief place among the elect, as is said in the psalm, "Let them be blotted out of the Book of the Living, and not be written with the righteous" (Psalm 69:28).

10. For the elect are brought by calling into the fold of Christ, not from the very womb, nor all at the same time, but according as God sees it meet to dispense his grace. Before they are gathered to the supreme Shepherd they wander dispersed in a common desert, and in no respect differ from others, except that by the special mercy of God they are kept from rushing to final destruction. Therefore, if you look to themselves, you will see the offspring of Adam giving token of the common corruption of the mass. That they proceed not to extreme and desperate impiety is not owing to any innate goodness in them, but because the eye of God watches for their safety, and his hand is stretched over them. Those who dream of some seed of election implanted in their hearts from their birth, by the agency of which they are ever inclined to piety and the fear of God, are not supported by the authority of Scripture, but refuted by experience. They, indeed, produce a few examples to prove that the elect before they were enlightened were not aliens from religion; for instance, that Paul led an unblemished life during his Pharisaism, that Cornelius was accepted for his prayers and alms, and so forth (Phil. 3:5; Acts 10:2). The case of Paul we admit, but we hold that they are in error as to Cornelius; for it appears that he was already enlightened and regenerated, so that all which he wanted was a clear revelation of the Gospel. But what are they to extract from these few examples? Is it that all the elect were always endued with the spirit of piety? Just as well might any one, after pointing to the integrity of Aristides, Socrates, Xenocrates, Scipio, Curios, Camillus, and others (see Book 2, c. 4, sec. 4), infer that all who are left in the blindness of idolatry are studious of virtue and holiness. Nay, even Scripture is plainly opposed to them in more passages than one. The description which Paul gives of the state of the Ephesians before regeneration shows not one grain of this seed. His words are, "You has he quickened, who were dead in trespasses and sins; wherein in time past ye walked according to the course of this world, according to the prince of the power of the air, the spirit that now worketh in the children of disobedience: among whom also we all had our conversation in times past in the lusts of our flesh, fulfilling the desires of the flesh and of the mind; and were by nature the children of wrath, even as others" (Eph. 2:1–3). And again, "At that time ye were without Christ," "having no hope, and without God in the world" (Eph. 2:12). Again, "Ye were sometimes darkness, but now are ye light in the Lord: walk as children of light" (Eph. 5:8). But perhaps they will insist that in this last passage reference is made to that ignorance of the true God, in which they deny not that the elect lived before they were called. Though this is grossly inconsistent with the Apostle's inference, that they were no longer to lie or steal (Eph. 4:28). What answer will they give to other passages; such as that in which, after declaring to the Corinthians that "neither fornicators, nor idolaters, nor adulterers, nor effeminate, nor abusers of themselves with mankind, nor thieves, nor covetous, nor drunkards, nor revilers, nor extortioners, shall inherit the kingdom of God," he immediately adds, "Such were some of you: but ye are washed, but ye are sanctified, but ye are justified in the name of the Lord Jesus, and by the Spirit of our God"? (1 Cor. 6:9–11). Again he says to the Romans, "As ye have yielded your members servants to uncleanness and to iniquity unto iniquity; even so now yield your members servants to righteousness unto holiness. For when ye were the servants of sin, ye were free from righteousness. What fruit had ye then in those things whereof ye are now ashamed?" (Rom. 6:19–21).

11. Say, then, what seed of election germinated in those who, contaminated in various ways during their whole lives, indulged as with desperate wickedness in every kind of abomination? Had Paul meant to express this view, he ought to have shown how much they then owed to the kindness of God, by which they had been preserved from falling into such pollution. Thus, too, Peter ought to have exhorted his countrymen to gratitude for a perpetual seed of election. On the contrary, his admonition is, "The time past of our life may suffice us to have wrought the will of the Gentiles" (1 Pet. 4:3). What if we come to examples? Was there any germ of righteousness in Rahab the harlot before she believed? (Josh. 2:4); in Manasseh when Jerusalem was dyed and almost deluged with the blood of the prophets? (2 Kings 23:16); in the thief who only with his last breath thought of repentance? (Luke 23:42). Have done, then, with those arguments which curious men of themselves rashly devise without any authority from Scripture. But let us hold fast what Scripture states—viz. that "All we like sheep have gone astray, we have turned every one to his own way" (Isa. 53:6); that is to perdition. In this gulf of perdition God leaves

those whom he has determined one day to deliver until his own time arrive; he only preserves them from plunging into irremediable blasphemy.

12. As the Lord by the efficacy of his calling accomplishes towards his elect the salvation to which he had by his eternal counsel destined them, so he has judgments against the reprobate, by which he executes his counsel concerning them. Those, therefore, whom he has created for dishonor during life and destruction at death, that they may be vessels of wrath and examples of severity, in bringing to their doom, he at one time deprives of the means of hearing his word, at another by the preaching of it blinds and stupefies them the more. The examples of the former case are innumerable, but let us select one of the most remarkable of all. Before the advent of Christ, about four thousand years passed away, during which he hid the light of saving doctrine from all nations. If any one answer, that he did not put them in possession of the great blessing, because he judged them unworthy, then their posterity will be in no respect more worthy. Of this in addition to experience, Malachi is a sufficient witness; for while charging them with mixed unbelief and blasphemy, he yet declares that the Redeemer will come. Why then is he given to the latter rather than to the former? They will in vain torment themselves in seeking for a deeper cause than the secret and inscrutable counsel of God. And there is no occasion to fear lest some disciple of Porphyry with impunity arraign the justice of God, while we say nothing in its defense. For while we maintain that none perish without deserving it, and that it is owing to the free goodness of God that some are delivered, enough has been said for the display of his glory; there is not the least occasion for our caviling. The supreme Disposer then makes way for his own predestination, when depriving those whom he has reprobated of the communication of his light, he leaves them in blindness. Every day furnishes instances of the latter case, and many of them are set before us in Scripture. Among a hundred to whom the same discourse is delivered, twenty, perhaps, receive it with the prompt obedience of faith; the others set no value upon it, or deride, or spurn, or abominate it. If it is said that this diversity is owing to the malice and perversity of the latter, the answer is not satisfactory: for the same wickedness would possess the minds of the former, did not God in his goodness correct it. And hence we will always be entangled until we call in the aid of Paul's question, "Who maketh thee to differ?" (1 Cor. 4:7), intimating that some excel others, not by their own virtue, but by the mere favour of God.

13. Why, then, while bestowing grace on the one, does he pass by the other? In regard to the former, Luke gives the reason, Because they "were ordained to eternal life" (Acts 13:48). What, then, shall we think of the latter, but that they are vessels of wrath unto dishonor? Wherefore, let us not decline to say with Augustine, "God could change the will of the wicked into good, because he is omnipotent. Clearly he could. Why, then, does he not do it? Because he is unwilling. Why he is unwilling remains with himself" (August. de Genes. ad Lit. Lib. 2). We should not attempt to be wise above what is meet, and it is much better to take Augustine's explanation, than to quibble with Chrysostom, "that he draws him who is willing, and stretching forth his hand" (Chrysost. Hom. de Convers. Pauli), lest the difference should seem to lie in the judgment of God, and not in the mere will of man. So far is it, indeed, from being placed in the mere will of man, that we may add, that even the pious, and those who fear God, need this special inspiration of the Spirit. Lydia, a seller of purple, feared God, and yet it was necessary that her heart should be opened, that she might attend to the doctrine of Paul, and profit in it (Acts 16:14). This was not said of one woman only but to teach us that all progress in piety is the secret work of the Spirit. Nor can it be questioned, that God sends his word to many whose blindness he is pleased to aggravate. For why does he order so many messages to be taken to Pharaoh? Was it because he hoped that he might be softened by the repetition? Nay, before he began he both knew and had foretold the result: "The Lord said unto Moses, When thou goest to return into Egypt see that thou do all those wonders before Pharaoh, which I have put in thine hand: but I will harden his heart, that he will not let the people go" (Exod. 4:21). So when he raises up Ezekiel, he forewarns him, "I send thee to the children of Israel, to a rebellious nation that has rebelled against me." "Be not afraid of their words." "Thou dwellest in the midst of a rebellious house, which has eyes to see, and see not; they have ears to hear, and hear not" (Ezek. 2:3, 6; 12:2). Thus he foretells to Jeremiah that the effect of his doctrine would be, "to root out, and pull down, and to destroy" (Jer. 1:10). But the prophecy of Isaiah presses still more closely; for he is thus commissioned by the Lord, "Go and tell this people, Hear ye indeed, but understand not, and see ye indeed but perceive not. Make the heart of this people fat, and make their ears heavy, and shut their eyes; lest they see with their eyes, and hear with their ears, and understand with their heart, and convert and be healed" (Isa. 6:9, 10). Here he directs

his voice to them, but it is that they may turn a deafer ear; he kindles a light, but it is that they may become more blind; he produces a doctrine, but it is that they may be more stupid; he employs a remedy, but it is that they may not be cured. And John, referring to this prophecy, declares that the Jews could not believe the doctrine of Christ, because this curse from God lay upon them. It is also incontrovertible, that to those whom God is not pleased to illumine, he delivers his doctrine wrapt up in enigmas, so that they may not profit by it, but be given over to greater blindness. Hence our Savior declares that the parables in which he had spoken to the multitude he expounded to the Apostles only, "because it is given unto you to know the mysteries of the kingdom of heaven, but to them it is not given" (Mt. 13:11). What, you will ask, does our Lord mean, by teaching those by whom he is careful not to be understood? Consider where the fault lies, and then cease to ask. How obscure soever the word may be, there is always sufficient light in it to convince the consciences of the ungodly.

14. It now remains to see why the Lord acts in the manner in which it is plain that he does. If the answer be given, that it is because men deserve this by their impiety, wickedness, and ingratitude, it is indeed well and truly said; but still, because it does not yet appear what the cause of the difference is, why some are turned to obedience, and others remain obdurate we must, in discussing it, pass to the passage from Moses, on which Paul has commented, namely, "Even for this same purpose have I raised thee up, that I might show my power in thee, and that my name might be declared throughout all the earth" (Rom. 9:17). The refusal of the reprobate to obey the word of God when manifested to them, will be properly ascribed to the malice and depravity of their hearts, provided it be at the same time added that they were adjudged to this depravity, because they were raised up by the just but inscrutable judgment of God, to show forth his glory by their condemnation. In like manner, when it is said of the sons of Eli, that they would not listen to salutary admonitions "because the Lord would slay them" (1 Sam. 2:25), it is not denied that their stubbornness was the result of their own iniquity; but it is at the same time stated why they were left to their stubbornness, when the Lord might have softened their hearts: namely, because his immutable decree had once for all doomed them to destruction. Hence the words of John, "Though he had done so many miracles before them, yet they believed not on him; that the saying of Esaias the prophet might be fulfilled which he spake, Lord, who has believed our report?" (John 12:37, 38); for though he does not exculpate their perverseness, he is satisfied with the reason that the grace of God is insipid to men, until the Holy Spirit gives it its savor. And Christ, in quoting the prophecy of Isaiah, "They shall be all taught of God" (John 6:45), designs only to show that the Jews were reprobates and aliens from the Church, because they would not be taught: and gives no other reason than that the promise of God does not belong to them. Confirmatory of this are the words of Paul, "Christ crucified" was "unto the Jews a stumbling block, and unto the Greeks foolishness; but unto them which are called, both Jews and Greeks, Christ the power of God, and the wisdom of God" (1 Cor. 1:23). For after mentioning the usual result wherever the gospel is preached, that it exasperates some, and is despised by others, he says, that it is precious to them only who are called. A little before he had given them the name of believers, but he was unwilling to refuse the proper rank to divine grace, which precedes faith; or rather, he added the second term by way of correction, that those who had embraced the gospel might ascribe the merit of their faith to the calling of God. Thus, also, he shortly after shows that they were elected by God. When the wicked hear these things, they complain that God abuses his inordinate power; to make cruel sport with the miseries of his creatures. But let us, who know that all men are liable on so many grounds to the judgment of God, that they cannot answer for one in a thousand of their transgressions (Job 9:3), confess that the reprobate suffer nothing which is not accordant with the most perfect justice. When unable clearly to ascertain the reason, let us not decline to be somewhat in ignorance in regard to the depths of the divine wisdom.

15. But since an objection is often founded on a few passages of Scripture, in which God seems to deny that the wicked perish through his ordination, except in so far as they spontaneously bring death upon themselves in opposition to his warning, let us briefly explain these passages, and demonstrate that they are not adverse to the above view. One of the passages adduced is, "have I any pleasure at all that the wicked should die? saith the Lord God; and not that he should return from his ways and live?" (Ezek. 18:23). If we are to extend this to the whole human race, why are not the very many whose minds might be more easily bent to obey urged to repentance, rather than those who by his invitations become daily more and more hardened? Our Lord declares that the preaching of the gospel and miracles would have produced more fruit among the people of Nineveh and

Sodom than in Judea (Mt. 13:23). How comes it, then, that if God would have all to be saved he does not open a door of repentance for the wretched, who would more readily have received grace? Hence we may see that the passage is violently wrested, if the will of God, which the prophet mentions, is opposed to his eternal counsel, by which he separated the elect from the reprobate. Now, if the genuine meaning of the prophet is inquired into, it will be found that he only means to give the hope of pardon to them who repent. The sum is, that God is undoubtedly ready to pardon whenever the sinner turns. Therefore, he does not will his death, in so far as he wills repentance. But experience shows that this will, for the repentance of those whom he invites to himself, is not such as to make him touch all their hearts. Still, it cannot be said that he acts deceitfully; for though the external word only renders, those who hear it, and do not obey it, inexcusable, it is still truly regarded as an evidence of the grace by which he reconciles men to himself. Let us therefore hold the doctrine of the prophet, that God has no pleasure in the death of the sinner; that the godly may feel confident that whenever they repent God is ready to pardon them; and that the wicked may feel that their guilt is doubled, when they respond not to the great mercy and condescension of God. The mercy of God, therefore will ever be ready to meet the penitent; but all the prophets, and apostles, and Ezekiel himself, clearly tell us who they are to whom repentance is given.

16. The second passage adduced is that in which Paul says that "God will have all men to be saved" (1 Tim. 2:4). Though the reason here differs from the former, they have somewhat in common. I answer, first, That the mode in which God thus wills is plain from the context; for Paul connects two things, a will to be saved, and to come to the knowledge of the truth. If by this they will have it to be fixed by the eternal counsel of God that they are to receive the doctrine of salvation, what is meant by Moses in these words, "What nation is there so great, who has God so nigh unto them?" (Deut. 4:7). How comes it that many nations are deprived of that light of the Gospel which others enjoy? How comes it that the pure knowledge of the doctrine of godliness has never reached some, and others have scarcely tasted some obscure rudiments of it? It will now be easy to extract the purport of Paul's statement. He had commanded Timothy that prayers should be regularly offered up in the church for kings and princes; but as it seemed somewhat absurd that prayer should be offered up for a class of men who were almost hopeless (all of them being not only aliens from the body of Christ, but doing their utmost to overthrow his kingdom), he adds, that it was acceptable to God, who will have all men to be saved. By this he assuredly means nothing more than that the way of salvation was not shut against any order of men; that, on the contrary, he had manifested his mercy in such a way, that he would have none debarred from it. Other passages do not declare what God has, in his secret judgment, determined with regard to all, but declare that pardon is prepared for all sinners who only turn to seek after it. For if they persist in urging the words, "God has concluded all in unbelief, that he might have mercy upon all" (Rom. 11:32), I will, on the contrary, urge what is elsewhere written, "Our God is in the heavens: he has done whatsoever he has pleased" (Ps. 115:3). we must, therefore, expound the passage so as to reconcile it with another, I "will be gracious to whom I will be gracious, and will show mercy on whom I will show mercy" (Exod. 33:19). He who selects those whom he is to visit in mercy does not impart it to all. But since it clearly appears that he is there speaking not of individuals, but of orders of men, let us have done with a longer discussion. At the same time, we ought to observe, that Paul does not assert what God does always, everywhere, and in all circumstances, but leaves it free to him to make kings and magistrates partakers of heavenly doctrine, though in their blindness they rage against it. A stronger objection seems to be founded on the passage in Peter; the Lord is "not willing that any should perish, but that all should come to repentance" (2 Pet. 3:9). But the solution of the difficulty is to be found in the second branch of the sentence, for his will that they should come to repentance cannot be used in any other sense than that which is uniformly employed. Conversion is undoubtedly in the hand of God, whether he designs to convert all can be learned from himself, when he promises that he will give some a heart of flesh, and leave to others a heart of stone (Ezek. 36:26). It is true, that if he were not disposed to receive those who implore his mercy, it could not have been said, "Turn ye unto me, saith the Lord of Hosts, and I will turn unto you, saith the Lord of Hosts" (Zech. 1:3); but I hold that no man approaches God unless previously influenced from above. And if repentance were placed at the will of man, Paul would not say, "If God per adventure will give them repentance" (2 Tim. 2:25). Nay, did not God at the very time when he is verbally exhorting all to repentance, influence the elect by the secret movement of his Spirit, Jeremiah would not say, "Turn thou me, and I shall be turned; for thou art the Lord my God. Surely after that I was turned, I repented" (Jer. 31:18).

17. But if it is so (you will say), little faith can be put in the Gospel promises, which, in testifying concerning the will of God, declare that he wills what is contrary to his inviolable decree. Not at all; for however universal the promises of salvation may be, there is no discrepancy between them and the predestination of the reprobate, provided we attend to their effect. We know that the promises are effectual only when we receive them in faith, but, on the contrary, when faith is made void, the promise is of no effect. If this is the nature of the promises, let us now see whether there be any inconsistency between the two things—viz. that God, by an eternal decree, fixed the number of those whom he is pleased to embrace in love, and on whom he is pleased to display his wrath, and that he offers salvation indiscriminately to all. I hold that they are perfectly consistent, for all that is meant by the promise is, just that his mercy is offered to all who desire and implore it, and this none do, save those whom he has enlightened. Moreover, he enlightens those whom he has predestinated to salvation. Thus the truth of the promises remains firm and unshaken, so that it cannot be said there is any disagreement between the eternal election of God and the testimony of his grace which he offers to believers. But why does he mention all men? Namely that the consciences of the righteous may rest the more secure when they understand that there is no difference between sinners, provided they have faith, and that the ungodly may not be able to allege that they have not an asylum to which they may retake themselves from the bondage of sin, while they ungratefully reject the offer which is made to them. Therefore, since by the Gospel the mercy of God is offered to both, it is faith, in other words, the illumination of God, which distinguishes between the righteous and the wicked, the former feeling the efficacy of the Gospel, the latter obtaining no benefit from it. Illumination itself has eternal election for its rule.

Another passage quoted is the lamentation of our Savior, "O Jerusalem Jerusalem, how often would I have gathered thy children together, even as a hen gathereth her chickens under her wings, and ye would not!" (Mt. 23:37); but it gives them no support. I admit that here Christ speaks not only in the character of man, but upbraids them with having, in every age, rejected his grace. But this will of God, of which we speak, must be defined. For it is well known what exertions the Lord made to retain that people, and how perversely from the highest to the lowest they followed their own wayward desires, and refused to be gathered together. But it does not follow that by the wickedness of men the counsel of God was frustrated. They object that nothing is less accordant with the nature of God than that he should have a double will. This I concede, provided they are sound interpreters. But why do they not attend to the many passages in which God clothes himself with human affections, and descends beneath his proper majesty? He says, "I have spread out my hands all the day unto a rebellious people" (Isa. 65:1), exerting himself early and late to bring them back. Were they to apply these qualities without regarding the figure, many unnecessary disputes would arise which are quashed by the simple solution, that what is human is here transferred to God. Indeed, the solution which we have given elsewhere (see Book 1, c. 18, sec. 3; and Book 3, c. 20, sec. 43) is amply sufficient—viz. that though to our apprehension the will of God is manifold, yet he does not in himself will opposites, but, according to his manifold wisdom (so Paul styles it, Eph. 3:10), transcends our senses, until such time as it shall be given us to know how he mysteriously wills what now seems to be adverse to his will. They also amuse themselves with the cavil, that since God is the Father of all, it is unjust to discard any one before he has by his misconduct merited such a punishment. As if the kindness of God did not extend even to dogs and swine. But if we confine our view to the human race, let them tell why God selected one people for himself and became their father, and why, from that one people, he plucked only a small number as if they were the flower. But those who thus charge God are so blinded by their love of evil speaking, that they consider not that as God "maketh his sun to rise on the evil and on the good" (Mt. 5:45), so the inheritance is treasured up for a few to whom it shall one day be said, "Come, ye blessed of my Father, inherit the kingdom," &c. (Mt. 25:34). They object, moreover, that God does not hate any of the things which he has made. This I concede, but it does not affect the doctrine which I maintain, that the reprobate are hateful to God, and that with perfect justice, since those destitute of his Spirit cannot produce any thing that does not deserve cursing. They add, that there is no distinction of Jew and Gentile, and that, therefore, the grace of God is held forth to all indiscriminately: true, provided they admit (as Paul declares) that God calls as well Jews as Gentiles, according to his good pleasure, without being astricted to any. This disposes of their gloss upon another passage, "God has concluded all in unbelief, that he might have mercy upon all" (Rom. 11:32); in other words, he wills that all who are saved should ascribe their salvation to his mercy, although the blessing of salvation is not common to all.

Finally, after all that has been adduced on this side and on that, let it be our conclusion to feel overawed with Paul at the great depth, and if petulant tongues will still murmur, let us not be ashamed to join in his exclamation, "Nay, but, O man, who art thou that replies against God?" (Rom. 9:20). Truly does Augustine maintain that it is perverse to measure divine by the standard of human justice (De Prædest. et Gra. c. 2).

CHAPTER 25

OF THE LAST RESURRECTION.

There are four principal heads in this chapter,—I. The utility, necessity, truth, and irrefragable evidence of the orthodox doctrine of a final resurrection—a doctrine unknown to philosophers, sec. 1–4. II. Refutation of the objections to this doctrine by Atheists, Sadducees, Chiliasts, and other fanatics, sec. 5–7. III. The nature of the final resurrection explained, sec. 8, 9. IV. Of the eternal felicity of the elect, and the everlasting misery of the reprobate.

Sections:

1. For invincible perseverance in our calling, it is necessary to be animated with the blessed hope of our Savior's final advent.

2. The perfect happiness reserved for the elect at the final resurrection unknown to philosophers.

3. The truth and necessity of this doctrine of a final resurrection. To confirm our belief in it we have, 1. The example of Christ; and, 2. The omnipotence of God. There is an inseparable connection between us and our risen Savior. The bodies of the elect must be conformed to the body of their Head. It is now in heaven. Therefore, our bodies also must rise, and, reanimated by their souls, reign with Christ in heaven. The resurrection of Christ a pledge of ours.

4. As God is omnipotent, he can raise the dead. Resurrection explained by a natural process. The vision of dry bones.

5. Second part of the chapter, refuting objections to the doctrine of resurrection. 1. Atheists. 2. Sadducees. 3. Chiliasts. Their evasion. Various answers. 4. Universalists. Answer.

6. Objections continued. 5. Some speculators who imagine that death destroys the whole man. Refutation. The condition and abode of souls from death till the last day. What meant by the bosom of Abraham.

7. Refutation of some weak men and Manichees, pretending that new bodies are to be given. Refutation confirmed by various arguments and passages of Scripture.

8. Refutation of the fiction of new bodies continued.

9. Shall the wicked rise again? Answer in the affirmative. Why the wicked shall rise again. Why resurrection promised to the elect only.

10. The last part of the chapter, treating of eternal felicity; 1 Its excellence transcends our capacity. Rules to be observed. The glory of all the saints will not be equal.

11. Without rewarding questions which merely puzzle, an answer given to some which are not without use.

12. As the happiness of the elect, so the misery of the reprobate, will be without measure, and without end.

1. Although Christ, the Sun of righteousness, shining upon us through the gospel, has, as Paul declares, after conquering death, given us the light of life; and hence on believing we are said to have passed from "death unto life," being no longer strangers and pilgrims, but fellow citizens with the saints, and of the household of God, who has made us sit with his only begotten Son in heavenly places, so that nothing is wanting to our complete felicity; yet, lest we should feel it grievous to be exercised under a hard warfare, as if the victory obtained by Christ had produced no fruit, we must attend to what is elsewhere taught concerning the nature of hope. For since we hope for what we see not, and faith, as is said in another passage, is "the evidence of things not seen" so long as we are imprisoned in the body we are absent from the Lord. For which reason Paul says, "Ye are dead, and your life is hid with Christ in God. When Christ, who is our life, shall appear, then shall ye also appear with him in glory." Our present condition, therefore, requires us to "live soberly, righteously, and godly;" "looking for that blessed hope, and the glorious appearing of the great God and our Savior Jesus Christ." Here there is need of no ordinary patience, lest, worn out with fatigue, we either turn backwards or abandon our post. Wherefore, all that has hitherto been said of our salvation calls upon us to raise our minds towards heaven, that, as Peter exhorts, though we now see not Christ, "yet believing," we may "rejoice with joy unspeakable and full of glory," receiving the end of our faith, even the salvation of our souls. For this reason Paul says, that the faith and charity of the saints have respect to the faith and hope which is laid up for them in heaven (Col. 1:5). When we thus keep our eyes fixed

upon Christ in heaven, and nothing on earth prevents us from directing them to the promised blessedness, there is a true fulfillment of the saying, "where your treasure is, there will your heart be also" (Mt. 6:21). Hence the reason why faith is so rare in the world; nothing being more difficult for our sluggishness than to surmount innumerable obstacles in striving for the prize of our high calling. To the immense load of miseries which almost overwhelm us, are added the jeers of profane men, who assail us for our simplicity, when spontaneously renouncing the allurements of the present life we seem, in seeking a happiness which lies hid from us, to catch at a fleeting shadow. In short, we are beset above and below, behind and before, with violent temptations, which our minds would be altogether unable to withstand, were they not set free from earthly objects and devoted to the heavenly life, though apparently remote from us. Wherefore, he alone has made solid progress in the Gospel who has acquired the habit of meditating continually on a blessed resurrection.

2. In ancient times philosophers discoursed, and even debated with each other, concerning the chief good: none, however, except Plato acknowledged that it consisted in union with God. He could not, however, form even an imperfect idea of its true nature; nor is this strange, as he had learned nothing of the sacred bond of that union. We even in this our earthly pilgrimage know wherein our perfect and only felicity consists,—a felicity which, while we long for it, daily inflames our hearts more and more, until we attain to full fruition. Therefore I said, that none participate in the benefits of Christ save those who raise their minds to the resurrection. This, accordingly, is the mark which Paul sets before believers, and at which he says they are to aim, forgetting every thing until they reach its (Phil. 3:8). The more strenuously, therefore, must we contend for it, lest if the world engross us we be severely punished for our sloth. Accordingly, he in another passage distinguishes believers by this mark, that their conversation is in heaven, from whence they look for the Savior (Phil. 3:20). And that they may not faint in their course, he associates all the other creatures with them. As shapeless ruins are everywhere seen, he says, that all things in heaven and earth struggle for renovation. For since Adam by his fall destroyed the proper order of nature, the creatures groan under the servitude to which they have been subjected through his sin; not that they are at all endued with sense, but that they naturally long for the state of perfection from which they have fallen. Paul therefore describes them as groaning and travailing in pain (Rom. 8:19); so that we who have received the first-fruits of the Spirit may be ashamed to grovel in our corruption, instead of at least imitating the inanimate elements which are bearing the punishment of another's sin. And in order that he may stimulate us the more powerfully, he terms the final advent of Christ our *redemption*. It is true, indeed, that all the parts of our redemption are already accomplished; but as Christ was once offered for sins (Heb. 9:28), so he shall again appear without sin unto salvation. Whatever, then, be the afflictions by which we are pressed, let this redemption sustain us until its final accomplishment.

3. The very importance of the subject ought to increase our ardor. Paul justly contends, that if Christ rise not the whole gospel is delusive and vain (1 Cor. 15:13–17); for our condition would be more miserable than that of other mortals, because we are exposed to much hatred and insult, and incur danger every hour; nay, are like sheep destined for slaughter; and hence the authority of the gospel would fail, not in one part merely, but in its very essence, including both our adoption and the accomplishment of our salvation. Let us, therefore, give heed to a matter of all others the most serious, so that no length of time may produce weariness. I have deferred the brief consideration to be given of it to this place, that my readers may learn, when they have received Christ, the author of perfect salvation, to rise higher, and know that he is clothed with heavenly immortality and glory in order that the whole body may be rendered conformable to the Head. For thus the Holy Spirit is ever setting before us in his person an example of the resurrection. It is difficult to believe that after our bodies have been consumed with rottenness, they will rise again at their appointed time. And hence, while many of the philosophers maintained the immortality of the soul, few of them assented to the resurrection of the body. Although in this they were inexcusable, we are thereby reminded that the subject is too difficult for human apprehension to reach it. To enable faith to surmount the great difficulty, Scripture furnishes two auxiliary proofs, the one the likeness of Christ's resurrection, and the other the omnipotence of God. Therefore, whenever the subject of the resurrection is considered, let us think of the case of our Savior, who, having completed his mortal course in our nature which he had assumed, obtained immortality, and is now the pledge of our future resurrection. For in the miseries by which we are beset, we always bear "about in the body the dying of the Lord Jesus, that the life also of Jesus might be made manifest in our mortal flesh" (2

Cor. 4:10). It is not lawful, it is not even possible, to separate him from us, without dividing him. Hence Paul's argument, "If there be no resurrection of the dead, then is Christ not risen" (1 Cor. 15:13); for he assumes it as an acknowledged principle, that when Christ was subjected to death, and by rising gained a victory over death, it was not on his own account, but in the Head was begun what must necessarily be fulfilled in all the members, according to the degree and order of each. For it would not be proper to be made equal to him in all respects. It is said in the psalm, "Neither wilt thou suffer thine Holy One to see corruption" (Ps. 16:10). Although a portion of this confidence appertain to us according to the measure bestowed on us, yet the full effect appeared only in Christ, who, free from all corruption, resumed a spotless body. Then, that there may be no doubt as to our fellowship with Christ in a blessed resurrection, and that we may be contented with this pledge, Paul distinctly affirms that he sits in the heavens, and will come as a judge on the last day for the express purpose of changing our vile body, "that it may be fashioned like unto his glorious body" (Phil. 3:21). For he elsewhere says that God did not raise up his Son from death to give an isolated specimen of his mighty power, but that the Spirit exerts the same efficacy in regard to them that believe; and accordingly he says, that the Spirit when he dwells in us is life, because the end for which he was given is to quicken our mortal body (Rom. 8:10, 11; Col. 3:4). I briefly glance at subjects which might be treated more copiously, and deserve to be adorned more splendidly, and yet in the little I have said I trust pious readers will find sufficient materials for building up their faith. Christ rose again that he might have us as partakers with him of future life. He was raised up by the Father, inasmuch as he was the Head of the Church, from which he cannot possibly be dissevered. He was raised up by the power of the Spirit, who also in us performs the office of quickening. In fine, he was raised up to be the resurrection and the life. But as we have said, that in this mirror we behold a living image of the resurrection, so it furnishes a sure evidence to support our minds, provided we faint not, nor grow weary at the long delay, because it is not ours to measure the periods of time at our own pleasure; but to rest patiently till God in his own time renew his kingdom. To this Paul refers when he says, "But every man in his own order: Christ the first-fruits; afterward they that are Christ's at his coming" (1 Cor. 15:23).

But lest any question should be raised as to the resurrection of Christ on which ours is founded, we see how often and in what various ways he has borne testimony to it. Scoffing men will deride the narrative which is given by the Evangelist as a childish fable. For what importance will they attach to a message which timid women bring, and the disciples almost dead with fear, afterwards confirm? Why does not Christ rather place the illustrious trophies of his victory in the midst of the temple and the forum? Why does he not come forth, and in the presence of Pilate strike terror? Why does he not show himself alive again to the priests and all Jerusalem? Profane men will scarcely admit that the witnesses whom he selects are well qualified. I answer, that though at the commencement their infirmity was contemptible, yet the whole was directed by the admirable providence of God, so that partly from love to Christ and religious zeal, partly from incredulity, those who were lately overcome with fear now hurry to the sepulchre, not only that they might be eye-witnesses of the fact, but that they might hear angels announce what they actually saw. How can we question the veracity of those who regarded what the women told them as a fable, until they saw the reality? It is not strange that the whole people and also the governor, after they were furnished with sufficient evidence for conviction, were not allowed to see Christ or the other signs (Mt. 27:66; 28:11). The sepulchre is sealed, sentinels keep watch, on the third day the body is not found. The soldiers are bribed to spread the report that his disciples had stolen the body. As if they had had the means of deforming a band of soldiers, or been supplied with weapons, or been trained so as to make such a daring attempt. But if the soldiers had not courage enough to repel them, why did they not follow and apprehend some of them by the aid of the populace? Pilate, therefore, in fact, put his signet to the resurrection of Christ, and the guards who were placed at the sepulchre by their silence or falsehood also became heralds of his resurrection. Meanwhile, the voice of angels was heard, "He is not here, but is risen" (Luke 24:6). The celestial splendor plainly shows that they were not men but angels. Afterwards, if any doubt still remained, Christ himself removed it. The disciples saw him frequently; they even touched his hands and his feet, and their unbelief is of no little avail in confirming our faith. He discoursed to them of the mysteries of the kingdom of God, and at length, while they beheld, ascended to heaven. This spectacle was exhibited not to eleven apostles only, but was seen by more than five hundred brethren at once (1 Cor. 15:6). Then by sending the Holy Spirit he gave a proof not only of life but also of supreme power, as he had foretold, "It is expedient for you that I go away: for if I go not away, the Comforter will not come unto you" (John 16:7). Paul was not thrown down on the way by the power of a dead man, but felt that he whom he was opposing was possessed of sovereign authority. To Stephen he appeared for another purpose—viz. that he might overcome the fear of death by the certainty of life. To refuse assent to these numerous and authentic proofs is not diffidence, but depraved and therefore infatuated obstinacy.

4. We have said that in proving the resurrection our thoughts must be directed to the immense power of God. This Paul briefly teaches, when he says that the Lord Jesus Christ "shall change our vile body, that it may be fashioned like unto his glorious body, according to the working of that mighty power whereby he is able even to subdue all things unto himself" (Phil. 3:21). Wherefore, nothing can be more incongruous than to look here at what can be done naturally when the subject presented to us is an inestimable miracle, which by its magnitude absorbs our senses. Paul, however, by producing a proof from nature, confutes the senselessness of those who deny the resurrection. "Thou fool, that which thou sowest is not quickened except it die," &c. (1 Cor. 15:36). He says that in seed there is a species of resurrection, because the crop is produced from corruption. Nor would the thing be so difficult of belief were we as attentive as we ought to be to the wonders which meet our eye in every quarter of the world. But let us remember that none is truly persuaded of the future resurrection save he who, carried away with admiration gives God the glory.

Elated with this conviction, Isaiah exclaims, "Thy dead men shall live, together with my dead body shall they arise. Awake and sing, ye that dwell in dust" (Isaiah 26:19). In desperate circumstances he rises to God, the author of life, in whose hand are "the issues from death" (Psalm 68:20). Job also, when liker a dead body than a living being, trusting to the power of God, hesitates not as if in full vigor to rise to that day: "I know that my Redeemer liveth, and that he will stand at the latter day upon the earth;" (that is, that he will there exert his power): "and though after my skin worms destroy this body, yet in my flesh shall I see God; whom I shall see for myself, and mine eyes shall behold, and not another" (Job 19:25–27). For though some have recourse to a more subtle interpretation, by which they wrest these passages, as if they were not to be understood of the resurrection, they only confirm what they are desirous to overthrow; for holy men, in seeking consolation in their misfortunes, have recourse for alleviation merely to the similitude of a resurrection. This is better learned from a passage in Ezekiel. When the Jews scouted the promise of return, and objected that the probability of it was not greater than that of the dead coming forth from the tomb, there is presented to the prophet in vision a field covered with dry bones, which at the command of God recover sinews and flesh. Though under that figure he encourages the people to hope for return, yet the ground of hope is taken from the resurrection, as it is the special type of all the deliverances which believers experience in this world. Thus Christ declares that the voice of the Gospel gives life; but because the Jews did not receive it, he immediately adds, "Marvel not at this; for the hour is coming in which all that are in the grave shall hear his voice, and shall come forth" (John 5:28, 29). Wherefore, amid all our conflicts let us exult after the example of Paul, that he who has promised us future life "is able to keep that" which "is committed unto him," and thus glory that there is laid up for us "a crown of righteousness, which the Lord, the righteous judge, shall give" (2 Tim. 1:12; 4:8). Thus all the hardships which we may endure will be a demonstration of our future life, "seeing it is a righteous thing with God to recompense tribulation to them that trouble you; and to you who are troubled rest with us, when the Lord Jesus shall be revealed from heaven with his mighty angels, in flaming fire" (2 Thess. 1:6–8). But we must attend to what he shortly after adds—viz. that he "shall come to be glorified in his saints, and to be admired in all them that believe," by receiving the Gospel.

5. Although the minds of men ought to be perpetually occupied with this pursuit, yet, as if they actually resolved to banish all remembrance of the resurrection, they have called death the end of all things, the extinction of man. For Solomon certainly expresses the commonly received opinion when he says "A living dog is better than a dead lion" (Eccl. 9:4). And again, "Who knoweth the spirit of man that goes upward, and the spirit of the beast that goes downward to the earth?" In all ages a brutish stupor has prevailed, and, accordingly, it has made its way into the very Church; for the Sadducees had the hardihood openly to profess that there was no resurrection, nay, that the soul was mortal (Mark 12:18; Luke 20:27). But that this gross ignorance might be no excuse, unbelievers have always by natural instinct had an image of the resurrection before their eyes. For why the sacred and inviolable custom of burying, but that it might be the earnest of a new life? Nor can it be said that it had its origin in error, for the solemnity of sepulture always prevailed among the holy patriarchs, and God was pleased that the same cus-

tom should continue among the Gentiles, in order that the image of the resurrection thus presented might shake off their torpor. But although that ceremony was without profit, yet it is useful to us if we prudently consider its end; because it is no feeble refutation of infidelity that all men agreed in professing what none of them believed. But not only did Satan stupefy the senses of mankind, so that with their bodies they buried the remembrance of the resurrection; but he also managed by various fictions so to corrupt this branch of doctrine that it at length was lost. Not to mention that even in the days of Paul he began to assail it (1 Cor. 15), shortly after the Chiliasts arose, who limited the reign of Christ to a thousand years. This fiction is too puerile to need or to deserve refutation. Nor do they receive any countenance from the Apocalypse, from which it is known that they extracted a gloss for their error (Rev. 20:4), since the thousand years there mentioned refer not to the eternal blessedness of the Church, but only to the various troubles which await the Church militant in this world. The whole Scripture proclaims that there will be no end either to the happiness of the elect, or the punishment of the reprobate. Moreover, in regard to all things which lie beyond our sight, and far transcend the reach of our intellect, belief must either be founded on the sure oracles of God, or altogether renounced. Those who assign only a thousand years to the children of God to enjoy the inheritance of future life, observe not how great an insult they offer to Christ and his kingdom. If they are not to be clothed with immortality, then Christ himself, into whose glory they shall be transformed, has not been received into immortal glory; if their blessedness is to have an end, the kingdom of Christ, on whose solid structure it rests, is temporary. In short, they are either most ignorant of all divine things or they maliciously aim at subverting the whole grace of God and power of Christ, which cannot have their full effects unless sin is obliterated, death swallowed up, and eternal life fully renewed. How stupid and frivolous their fear that too much severity will be ascribed to God, if the reprobate are doomed to eternal punishment, even the blind may see. The Lord, forsooth, will be unjust if he exclude from his kingdom those who, by their ingratitude shall have rendered themselves unworthy of it. But their sins are temporary (see Bernard, Epist. 254). I admit it; but then the majesty of God, and also the justice which they have violated by their sins, are eternal. Justly, therefore, the memory of their iniquity does not perish. But in this way the punishment will exceed the measure of the fault. It is intolerable blasphemy to hold the majesty of God in so little estimation, as not to regard the contempt of it as of greater consequence than the destruction of a single soul. But let us have done with these triflers, that we may not seem (contrary to what we first observed) to think their dreams deserving of refutation.

6. Besides these, other two dreams have been invented by men who indulge a wicked curiosity. Some, under the idea that the whole man perishes, have thought that the soul will rise again with the body; while others, admitting that spirits are immortal, hold that they will be clothed with new bodies, and thus deny the resurrection of the flesh. Having already adverted to the former point when speaking of the creation of man, it will be sufficient again to remind the reader how groveling an error it is to convert a spirit, formed after the image of God, into an evanescent breath, which animates the body only during this fading life, and to reduce the temple of the Holy Spirit to nothing; in short, to rob of the badge of immortality that part of ourselves in which the divinity is most Refulgent and the marks of immortality conspicuous, so as to make the condition of the body better and more excellent than that of the soul. Very different is the course taken by Scripture, which compares the body to a tabernacle, from which it describes us as migrating when we die, because it estimates us by that part which distinguishes us from the lower animals. Thus Peter, in reference to his approaching death, says, "Knowing that shortly I must put off this my tabernacle" (2 Pet. 1:14). Paul, again, speaking of believers, after saying, "If our earthly house of this tabernacle were dissolved, we have a building of God," adds, "Whilst we are at home in the body, we are absent from the Lord" (2 Cor. 5:1, 6). Did not the soul survive the body, how could it be present with the Lord on being separated from the body? But an Apostle removes all doubt when he says that we go "to the spirits of just men made perfect" (Heb. 12:23); by these words meaning, that we are associated with the holy patriarchs, who, even when dead, cultivate the same piety, so that we cannot be the members of Christ unless we unite with them. And did not the soul, when unclothed from the body, retain its essence, and be capable of beatific glory, our Savior would not have said to the thief, "Today shalt thou be with me in paradise" (Luke 23:43). Trusting to these clear proofs, let us doubt not, after the example of our Savior, to commend our spirits to God when we come to die, or after the example of Stephen, to commit ourselves to the protection of Christ, who, with good reason, is called "The Shepherd and Bishop" of our souls (Acts 7:59; 1 Pet. 2:25).

Moreover, to pry curiously into their intermediate state is neither lawful nor expedient (see Calv. Psychopannychia). Many greatly torment themselves with discussing what place they occupy, and whether or not they already enjoy celestial glory. It is foolish and rash to inquire into hidden things, farther than God permits us to know. Scripture, after telling that Christ is present with them, and receives them into paradise (John 12:32), and that they are comforted, while the souls of the reprobate suffer the torments which they have merited goes no farther. What teacher or doctor will reveal to us what God has concealed? As to the place of abode, the question is not less futile and inept, since we know that the dimension of the soul is not the same as that of the body. When the abode of blessed spirits is designated as the *bosom of Abraham*, it is plain that, on quitting this pilgrimage, they are received by the common father of the faithful, who imparts to them the fruit of his faith. Still, since Scripture uniformly enjoins us to look with expectation to the advent of Christ, and delays the crown of glory till that period, let us be contented with the limits divinely prescribed to us—viz. that the souls of the righteous, after their warfare is ended, obtain blessed rest where in joy they wait for the fruition of promised glory, and that thus the final result is suspended till Christ the Redeemer appear. There can be no doubt that the reprobate have the same doom as that which Jude assigns to the devils, they are "reserved in everlasting chains under darkness unto the judgment of the great day" (Jude ver. 6).

7. Equally monstrous is the error of those who imagine that the soul, instead of resuming the body with which it is now clothed, will obtain a new and different body. Nothing can be more futile than the reason given by the Manichees—viz. that it were incongruous for impure flesh to rise again: as if there were no impurity in the soul; and yet this does not exclude it from the hope of heavenly life. It is just as if they were to say, that what is infected by the taint of sin cannot be divinely purified; for I now say nothing to the delirious dream that flesh is naturally impure as having been created by the devil. I only maintain, that nothing in us at present, which is unworthy of heaven, is any obstacle to the resurrection. But, first, Paul enjoins believers to purify themselves from "all filthiness of the flesh and spirit" (2 Cor. 7:1 the judgment which is to follow, that every one shall "receive the things done in his body, according to that he has done, whether it be good or bad" (2 Cor. 5:10). With this accords what he says to the Corinthians, "That the life also of Jesus might be made manifest in our body" (2 Cor. 4:10). For which reason he elsewhere says, "I pray God your whole spirit and soul and body be preserved blameless unto the coming of our Lord Jesus Christ" (1 Thess. 5:23). He says "body" as well as "spirit and soul," and no wonder; for it were most absurd that bodies which God has dedicated to himself as temples should fall into corruption without hope of resurrection. What? are they not also the members of Christ? Does he not pray that God would sanctify every part of them, and enjoin them to celebrate his name with their tongues, lift up pure hands, and offer sacrifices? That part of man, therefore, which the heavenly Judge so highly honors, what madness is it for any mortal man to reduce to dust without hope of revival? In like manner, when Paul exhorts, "glorify God in your body, and in your spirit, which are God's," he certainly does not allow that that which he claims for God as sacred is to be adjudged to eternal corruption. Nor, indeed, on any subject does Scripture furnish clearer explanation than on the resurrection of our flesh. "This corruptible (says Paul) must put on incorruption, and this mortal must put on immortality" (1 Cor. 15:53). If God formed new bodies, where would be this change of quality? If it were said that we must be renewed, the ambiguity of the expression might, perhaps, afford room for cavil; but here pointing with the finger to the bodies with which we are clothed, and promising that they shall be incorruptible, he very plainly affirms that no new bodies are to be fabricated. "Nay," as Tertullian says, "he could not have spoken more expressly, if he had held his skin in his hands" (Tertull. de Resurrect. Carnis). Nor can any cavil enable them to evade the force of another passage, in which saying that Christ will be the Judge of the world, he quotes from Isaiah, "As I live, saith the Lord, every knee shall bow to me" (Rom. 14:11; Isa. 45:23); since he openly declares that those whom he was addressing will have to give an account of their lives. This could not be true if new bodies were to be sisted to the tribunal. Moreover, there is no ambiguity in the words of Daniel, "Many of them that sleep in the dust of the earth shall awake, some to everlasting life, and some to shame and everlasting contempt" (Dan. 12:2); since he does not bring new matter from the four elements to compose men, but calls forth the dead from their graves. And the reason which dictates this is plain. For if death, which originated in the fall of man, is adventitious, the renewal produced by Christ must be in the same body which began to be mortal. And, certainly, since the Athenians mocked Paul for asserting the resurrection (Acts 17:32), we may infer what his preaching was: their derision is of no small force to confirm our faith. The saying of our Savior also is worthy of obser-

vation, "Fear not them which kill the body, but are not able to kill the soul: but rather fear him which is able to destroy both soul and body in hell" (Mt. 10:28). Here there would be no ground for fear; were not the body which we now have liable to punishment. Nor is another saying of our Savior less obscure, "The hour is coming, in the which all that are in the graves shall hear his voice, and shall come forth; they that have done good, unto the resurrection of life; and they that have done evil, unto the resurrection of damnation" (John 5:28, 29). Shall we say that the soul rests in the grave, that it may there hear the voice of Christ, and not rather that the body shall at his command resume the vigor which it had lost? Moreover, if we are to receive new bodies, where will be the conformity of the Head and the members? Christ rose again. Was it by forming for himself a new body? Nay, he had foretold, "Destroy this temple, and in three days I will raise it up" (John 2:19). The mortal body which he had formerly carried he again received; for it would not have availed us much if a new body had been substituted, and that which had been offered in expiatory sacrifice been destroyed. We must, therefore, attend to that connection which the Apostle celebrates, that we rise because Christ rose (1 Cor. 15:12); nothing being less probable than that the flesh in which we bear about the dying of Christ, shall have no share in the resurrection of Christ. This was even manifested by a striking example, when, at the resurrection of Christ, many bodies of the saints came forth from their graves. For it cannot be denied that this was a prelude, or rather earnest, of the final resurrection for which we hope, such as already existed in Enoch and Elijah, whom Tertullian calls *candidates for resurrection*, because, exempted from corruption, both in body and soul, they were received into the custody of God.

8. I am ashamed to waste so many words on so clear a matter; but my readers will kindly submit to the annoyance, in order that perverse and presumptuous minds may not be able to avail themselves of any flaw to deceive the simple. The volatile spirits with whom I now dispute adduce the fiction of their own brain, that in the resurrection there will be a creation of new bodies. Their only reason for thinking so is, that it seems to them incredible that a dead body, long wasted by corruption, should return to its former state. Therefore, mere unbelief is the parent of their opinion. The Spirit of God, on the contrary, uniformly exhorts us in Scripture to hope for the resurrection of our flesh. For this reason Baptism is, according to Paul, a seal of our future resurrection; and in like manner the holy Supper invites us confidently to expect it, when with our mouths we receive the symbols of spiritual grace. And certainly the whole exhortation of Paul, "Yield ye your members as instruments of righteousness unto God" (Rom. 6:13), would be frigid, did he not add, as he does in another passage, "He that raised up Christ from the dead shall also quicken your mortal bodies" (Rom. 8:11). For what would it avail to apply feet, hands, eyes, and tongues, to the service of God, did not these afterwards participate in the benefit and reward? This Paul expressly confirms when he says, "The body is not for fornication, but for the Lord; and the Lord for the body. And God has both raised up the Lord, and will also raise up us by his own power" (1 Cor. 6:13, 14). The words which follow are still clearer, "Know ye not that your bodies are the members of Christ?" "Know ye not that your body is the temple of the Holy Ghost?" (1 Cor. 6:15, 19). Meanwhile, we see how he connects the resurrection with chastity and holiness, as he shortly after includes our bodies in the purchase of redemption. It would be inconsistent with reason, that the body, in which Paul bore the marks of his Savior, and in which he magnificently extolled him (Gal. 6:17), should lose the reward of the crown. Hence he glories thus, "Our conversation is in heaven; from whence also we look for the Saviour, the Lord Jesus Christ: Who shall change our vile body, that it may be fashioned like unto his glorious body" (Phil. 3:20, 21). As it is true, "That we must through much tribulation enter into the kingdom of God" (Acts 14:22); so it were unreasonable that this entrance should be denied to the bodies which God exercises under the banner of the cross and adorns with the palm of victory.

Accordingly, the saints never entertained any doubt that they would one day be the companions of Christ, who transfers to his own person all the afflictions by which we are tried, that he may show their quickening power. Nay, under the law, God trained the holy patriarch in this belief, by means of an external ceremony. For to what end was the rite of burial, as we have already seen, unless to teach that new life was prepared for the bodies thus deposited? Hence, also, the spices and other symbols of immortality, by which under the law the obscurity of the doctrine was illustrated in the same way as by sacrifices. That custom was not the offspring of superstition, since we see that the Spirit is not less careful in narrating burials than in stating the principal mysteries of the faith. Christ commends these last offices as of no trivial importance (Mt. 16:10), and that, certainly, for no other reason than just that they raise our eyes from the view of the tombs which corrupts and destroys all things, to the prospect of renovation. Besides, that careful observance of the ceremony for which the patriarchs are praised, sufficiently proves that they found in it a special and valuable help to their faith. Nor would Abraham have been so anxious about the burial of his wife (Gen. 23:4, 19), had not the religious views and something superior to any worldly advantage, been present to his mind; in other words, by adorning her dead body with the insignia of the resurrection, he confirmed his own faith, and that of his family. A clearer proof of this appears in the example of Jacob, who, to testify to his posterity that even death did not destroy the hope of the promised land, orders his bones to be carried thither. Had he been to be clothed with a new body would it not have been ridiculous in him to give commands concerning a dust which was to be reduced to nothing? Wherefore, if Scripture has any authority with us, we cannot desire a clearer or stronger proof of any doctrine. Even tyros understand this to be the meaning of the words, *resurrection*, and *raising up*. A thing which is created for the first time cannot be said to rise again; nor could our Savior have said, "This is the Father's will which has sent me, that of all which he has given me I should lose nothing, but should raise it up again at the last day" (John 6:39). The same is implied in the word *sleeping*, which is applicable only to the body. Hence, too, the name of cemetery, applied to burying-grounds.

It remains to make a passing remark on the mode of resurrection. I speak thus because Paul, by styling it a mystery, exhorts us to soberness, in order that he may curb a licentious indulgence in free and subtle speculation. First, we must hold, as has already been observed, that the body in which we shall rise will be the same as at present in respect of substance, but that the quality will be different; just as the body of Christ which was raised up was the same as that which had been offered in sacrifice, and yet excelled in other qualities, as if it had been altogether different. This Paul declares by familiar examples (1 Cor. 15:39). For as the flesh of man and of beasts is the same in substance, but not in quality: as all the stars are made of the same matter, but have different degrees of brightness: so he shows, that though we shall retain the substance of the body, there will be a change, by which its condition will become much more excellent. The corruptible body, therefore, in order that we may be raised, will not perish or vanish away, but, divested of corruption, will be clothed with incorruption. Since God has all the elements at his disposal, no difficulty can prevent him from commanding the earth, the fire, and the water, to give up what they seem to have destroyed. This, also, though not without figure, Isaiah testifies, "Behold, the Lore comes out of his place to punish the inhabitants of the earth for their iniquity: the earth also shall disclose her blood, and shall no more cover her slain" (Isa. 26:21). But a distinction must be made between those who died long ago, and those who on that day shall be found alive. For as Paul declares, "We shall not all sleep, but we shall all be changed" (1 Cor. 15:51); that is, it will not be necessary that a period should elapse between death and the beginning of the second life, for in a moment of time, in the twinkling of an eye, the trumpet shall sound, raising up the dead incorruptible, and, by a sudden change, fitting those who are alive for the same glory. So, in another passage, he comforts believers who were to undergo death, telling them that those who are then alive shall not take precedence of the dead, because those who have fallen asleep in Christ shall rise first (1 Thess. 4:15). Should any one urge the Apostle's declaration, "It is appointed unto all men once to die" (Heb. 9:27), the solution is easy, that when the natural state is changed there is an appearance of death, which is fitly so denominated, and, therefore, there is no inconsistency in the two things—viz. that all when divested of their mortal body shall be renewed by death; and yet that where the change is sudden, there will be no necessary separation between the soul and the body.

9. But a more difficult question here arises, How can the resurrection, which is a special benefit of Christ, be common to the ungodly, who are lying under the curse of God? We know that in Adam all died. Christ has come to be the resurrection and the life (John 11:25). is it to revive the whole human race indiscriminately? But what more incongruous than that the ungodly in their obstinate blindness should obtain what the pious worshipers of God receive by faith only? It is certain, therefore, that there will be one resurrection to judgment, and another to life, and that Christ will come to separate the kids from the goats (Mt. 25:32). I observe, that this ought not to seem very strange, seeing something resembling it occurs every day. We know that in Adam we were deprived of the inheritance of the whole world, and that the same reason which excludes us from eating of the tree of life excludes us also from common food. How comes it, then, that God not only makes his sun to rise on the evil and on the good, but that, in regard to the uses of the present life, his inestimable liberality is constantly flowing forth in rich abundance? Hence we certainly perceive, that things

which are proper to Christ and his members, abound to the wicked also; not that their possession is legitimate, but that they may thus be rendered more inexcusable. Thus the wicked often experience the beneficence of God, not in ordinary measures, but such as sometimes throw all the blessings of the godly into the shade, though they eventually lead to greater damnation. Should it be objected, that the resurrection is not properly compared to fading and earthly blessings, I again answer, that when the devils were first alienated from God, the fountain of life, they deserved to be utterly destroyed; yet, by the admirable counsel of God, an intermediate state was prepared, where without life they might live in death. It ought not to seem in any respect more absurd that there is to be an adventitious resurrection of the ungodly which will drag them against their will before the tribunal of Christ, whom they now refuse to receive as their master and teacher. To be consumed by death would be a light punishment were they not, in order to the punishment of their rebellion, to be sisted before the Judge whom they have provoked to a vengeance without measure and without end. But although we are to hold, as already observed and as is contained in the celebrated confession of Paul to Felix, "That there shall be a resurrection of the dead, both of the just and unjust" (Acts 24:15); yet Scripture more frequently sets forth the resurrection as intended, along with celestial glory, for the children of God only: because, properly speaking, Christ comes not for the destruction, but for the salvation of the world: and, therefore, in the Creed the life of blessedness only is mentioned.

10. But since the prophecy that death shall be swallowed up in victory (Hosea 13:14), will then only be completed, let us always remember that the end of the resurrection is eternal happiness, of whose excellence scarcely the minutest part can be described by all that human tongues can say. For though we are truly told that the kingdom of God will be full of light, and gladness, and felicity, and glory, yet the things meant by these words remain most remote from sense, and as it were involved in enigma, until the day arrive on which he will manifest his glory to us face to face (1 Cor. 15:54). "Now" says John, "are we the sons of God; and it does not yet appear what we shall be: but we know that, when he shall appear, we shall be like him; for we shall see him as he is" (1 John 3:2). Hence, as the prophets were unable to give a verbal description of that spiritual blessedness, they usually delineated it by corporeal objects. On the other hand, because the fervor of desire must be kindled in us by some taste of its sweetness, let us specially dwell upon this thought, If God contains in himself as an inexhaustible fountain all fulness of blessing, those who aspire to the supreme good and perfect happiness must not long for any thing beyond him. This we are taught in several passages, "Fear not, Abraham; I am thy shield, and thy exceeding great reward" (Gen. 15:1). With this accords David's sentiment, "The Lord is the portion of mine inheritance, and of my cup: thou maintainest my lot. The lines are fallen unto me in pleasant places" (Ps. 16:5, 6). Again, "I shall be satisfied when I awake with thy likeness" (Ps. 17:15). Peter declares that the purpose for which believers are called is, that they may be "partakers of the divine nature" (2 Pet. 1:4). How so? Because "he shall come to be glorified in his saints and to be admired in all them that believe" (2 Thess. 1:10). If our Lord will share his glory, power, and righteousness, with the elect, nay, will give himself to be enjoyed by them; and what is better still, will, in a manner, become one with them, let us remember that every kind of happiness is herein included. But when we have made great progress in thus meditating, let us understand that if the conceptions of our minds be contrasted with the sublimity of the mystery, we are still halting at the very entrance. The more necessary is it for us to cultivate sobriety in this matter, lest unmindful of our feeble capacity we presume to take too lofty a flight, and be overwhelmed by the brightness of the celestial glory. We feel how much we are stimulated by an excessive desire of knowing more than is given us to know, and hence frivolous and noxious questions are ever and anon springing forth: by frivolous, I mean questions from which no advantage can be extracted. But there is a second class which is worse than frivolous; because those who indulge in them involve themselves in hurtful speculations. Hence I call them noxious. The doctrine of Scripture on the subject ought not to be made the ground of any controversy, and it is that as God, in the varied distribution of gifts to his saints in this world, gives them unequal degrees of light, so when he shall crown his gifts, their degrees of glory in heaven will also be unequal. When Paul says, "Ye are our glory and our joy" (1 Thess. 2:20), his words do not apply indiscriminately to all; nor do those of our Savior to his apostles, "Ye also shall sit on twelve thrones judging the twelve tribes of Israel" (Mt. 19:28). But Paul, who knew that as God enriches the saints with spiritual gifts in this world, he will in like manner adorn them with glory in heaven, hesitates not to say, that a special crown is laid up for him in proportion to his labors. Our Savior, also, to commend the dignity of the office which he had conferred on the apostles, reminds

them that the fruit of it is laid up in heaven. This, too, Daniel says, "They that be wise shall shine as the brightness of the firmament; and they that turn many to righteousness as the stars for ever and ever" (Dan. 12:3). Any one who attentively considers the Scriptures will see not only that they promise eternal life to believers, but a special reward to each. Hence the expression of Paul, "The Lord grant unto him that he may find mercy of the Lord in that day" (2 Tim. 1:18; 4:14). This is confirmed by our Savior's promise, that they "shall receive an hundredfold and shall inherit everlasting life" (Mt. 19:29). In short, as Christ, by the manifold variety of his gifts, begins the glory of his body in this world, and gradually increases it, so he will complete it in heaven.

11. While all the godly with one consent will admit this, because it is sufficiently attested by the word of God, they will, on the other hand, avoid perplexing questions which they feel to be a hindrance in their way, and thus keep within the prescribed limits. In regard to myself, I not only individually refrain from a superfluous investigation of useless matters, but also think myself bound to take care that I do not encourage the levity of others by answering them. Men puffed up with vain science are often inquiring how great the difference will be between prophets and apostles, and again, between apostles and martyrs; by how many degrees virgins will surpass those who are married; in short, they leave not a corner of heaven untouched by their speculations. Next it occurs to them to inquire to what end the world is to be repaired, since the children of God will not be in want of any part of this great and incomparable abundance, but will be like the angels, whose abstinence from food is a symbol of eternal blessedness. I answer, that independent of use, there will be so much pleasantness in the very sight, so much delight in the very knowledge, that this happiness will far surpass all the means of enjoyment which are now afforded. Let us suppose ourselves placed in the richest quarter of the globe, where no kind of pleasure is wanting, who is there that is not ever and anon hindered and excluded by disease from enjoying the gifts of God? who does not oftentimes interrupt the course of enjoyment by intemperance? Hence it follows, that fruition, pure and free from all defect, though it be of no use to a corruptible life, is the summit of happiness. Others go further, and ask whether dross and other impurities in metals will have no existence at the restitution, and are inconsistent with it. Though I should go so far as concede this to them, yet I expect with Paul a reparation of those defects which first began with sin, and on account of which the whole creation groaneth and travaileth with pain (Rom. 8:22). Others go a step further, and ask, What better condition can await the human race, since the blessing of offspring shall then have an end? The solution of this difficulty also is easy. When Scripture so highly extols the blessing of offspring, it refers to the progress by which God is constantly urging nature forward to its goal; in perfection itself we know that the case is different. But as such alluring speculations instantly captivate the unwary, who are afterwards led farther into the labyrinth, until at length, every one becoming pleased with his own views there is no limit to disputation, the best and shortest course for us will be to rest contented with seeing through a glass darkly until we shall see face to face. Few out of the vast multitude of mankind feel concerned how they are to get to heaven; all would fain know before the time what is done in heaven. Almost all, while slow and sluggish in entering upon the contest, are already depicting to themselves imaginary triumphs.

12. Moreover, as language cannot describe the severity of the divine vengeance on the reprobate, their pains and torments are figured to us by corporeal things, such as darkness, wailing and gnashing of teeth, inextinguishable fire, the ever-gnawing worm (Mt. 8:12; 22:13; Mark 9:43; Isa. 66:24). It is certain that by such modes of expression the Holy Spirit designed to impress all our senses with dread, as when it is said, "Tophet is ordained of old; yea, for the king it is prepared: he has made it deep and large; the pile thereof is fire and much wood; the breath of the Lord, like a stream of brimstone, does kindle it" (Isa. 30:33). As we thus require to be assisted to conceive the miserable doom of the reprobate, so the consideration on which we ought chiefly to dwell is the fearful consequence of being estranged from all fellowship with God, and not only so, but of feeling that his majesty is adverse to us, while we cannot possibly escape from it. For, first, his indignation is like a raging fire, by whose touch all things are devoured and annihilated. Next, all the creatures are the instruments of his judgment, so that those to whom the Lord will thus publicly manifest his anger will feel that heaven, and earth, and sea, all beings, animate and inanimate, are, as it were, inflamed with dire indignation against them, and armed for their destruction. Wherefore, the Apostle made no trivial declaration, when he said that unbelievers shall be "punished with everlasting destruction from the presence of the Lord, and from the glory of his power" (2 Thess. 1:9). And whenever the prophets strike terror by means of corporeal figures, although

in respect of our dull understanding there is no extravagance in their language, yet they give preludes of the future judgment in the sun and the moon, and the whole fabric of the world. Hence unhappy consciences find no rest, but are vexed and driven about by a dire whirlwind, feeling as if torn by an angry God, pierced through with deadly darts, terrified by his thunderbolts and crushed by the weight of his hand; so that it were easier to plunge into abysses and whirlpools than endure these terrors for a moment. How fearful, then, must it be to be thus beset throughout eternity! On this subject there is a memorable passage in the ninetieth Psalm: Although God by a mere look scatters all mortals, and brings them to nought, yet as his worshippers are more timid in this world, he urges them the more, that he may stimulate then, while burdened with the cross to press onward until he himself shall be all in all.

END OF BOOK THREE.

BOOK FOURTH: OF THE HOLY CATHOLIC CHURCH

ARGUMENT.

In the former Books an exposition has been given of the three parts of the Apostles' Creed concerning God the Creator, the Redeemer, and the Sanctifier. It now remains to treat, in this last Book, of the Church and the Communion of Saints, or of the external means or helps by which God invites us to fellowship with Christ, and keeps us in it.

The twenty Chapters of which it consists may be conveniently reduced to three particular heads—viz. I. Of the Church. II. Of the Sacraments. III. Of Civil Government.

The first head occupies the first thirteen chapters; but these may all be reduced to four—viz. I. Of the marks of the Church, or the means by which the Church may be discerned, since it is necessary to cultivate unity with the Church. This is considered in Chapters 1 and 2—II. Of the rule or government of the Church. The order of government, Chap. 3. The form in use in the primitive Church, Chap. 4. The form at present existing in the Papacy, Chap. 5. The primacy of the Pope, Chap. 6. The gradual rise of his usurpation, Chap. 7—III. Of the power of the Church. The power in relation to doctrine as possessed either by individuals, Chap. 8; or universally as in Councils, Chap. 9. The power of enacting laws, Chap. 10. The extent of ecclesiastical jurisdiction, Chap. 11—IV. Of the discipline of the Church. The chief use of discipline, Chap. 12. The abuse of it, Chap. 13.

The second general head, Of the Sacraments, comprehends three particulars,—I. Of the Sacraments in general, Chap. 14—II. Of the two Sacraments in particular. Of Baptism, Chap. 15. Of Pædobaptism, Chap. 16. Of the Lord's Supper, Chap. 17. Of profaning the Lord's Supper, Chap. 18. Of the five Sacraments falsely so called, Chap. 19.

The third general head, Of Civil Government. This considered first generally, and then under the separate heads of Magistrates, Laws, and People.

CHAPTER I

OF THE TRUE CHURCH. DUTY OF CULTIVATING UNITY WITH HER, AS THE MOTHER OF ALL THE GODLY.

The three divisions of this chapter are,—I. The article of the Creed concerning the Holy Catholic Church and the Communion of Saints briefly expounded. The grounds on which the Church claims our reverence, sec. 1–6. II. Of the marks of the Church, sec. 7–9. III. The necessity of cleaving to the Holy Catholic Church and the Communion of Saints. Refutation of the errors of the Novatians, Anabaptists, and other schismatics, in regard to this matter, sec. 10–29.

Sections:

1. The church now to be considered. With her God has deposited whatever is necessary to faith and good order. A summary of what is contained in this Book. Why it begins with the Church.

2. In what sense the article of the Creed concerning the Church is to be understood. Why we should say, "I believe the Church," not "I believe in the Church." The purport of this article. Why the Church is called Catholic or Universal.

3. What meant by the Communion of Saints. Whether it is inconsistent with various gifts in the saints, or with civil order. Uses of this article concerning the Church and the Communion of Saints. Must the Church be visible in order to our maintaining unity with her?

4. The name of Mother given to the Church shows how necessary it is to know her. No salvation out of the Church.

5. The Church is our mother, inasmuch as God has

committed to her the kind office of bringing us up in the faith until we attain full age. This method of education not to be despised. Useful to us in two ways. This utility destroyed by those who despise the pastors and teachers of the Church. The petulance of such despisers repressed by reason and Scripture. For this education of the Church her children enjoined to meet in the sanctuary. The abuse of churches both before and since the advent of Christ. Their proper use.

6. Her ministry effectual, but not without the Spirit of God. Passages in proof of this.

7. Second part of the Chapter. Concerning the marks of the Church. In what respect the Church is invisible. In what respect she is visible.

8. God alone knoweth them that are his. Still he has given marks to discern his children.

9. These marks are the ministry of the word, and administration of the sacraments instituted by Christ. The same rule not to be followed in judging of individuals and of churches.

10. We must on no account forsake the Church distinguished by such marks. Those who act otherwise are apostates, deserters of the truth and of the household of God, deniers of God and Christ, violators of the mystical marriage.

11. These marks to be the more carefully observed, because Satan strives to efface them, or to make us revolt from the Church. The twofold error of despising the true, and submitting to a false Church.

12. Though the common profession should contain some corruption, this is not a sufficient reason for forsaking the visible Church. Some of these corruptions specified. Caution necessary. The duty of the members.

13. The immoral lives of certain professors no ground for abandoning the Church. Error on this head of the ancient and modern Cathari. Their first objection. Answer to it from three of our Saviour's parables.

14. Second objection. Answer from a consideration of the state of the Corinthian Church, and the Churches of Galatia.

15. Third objection and answer.

16. The origin of these objections. A description of Schismatics. Their portraiture by Augustine. A pious counsel respecting these scandals, and a safe remedy against them.

17. Fourth objection and answer. Answer confirmed by the divine promises.

18. Another confirmation from the example of Christ and of the faithful servants of God. The appearance of the Church in the days of the prophets.

19. Appearance of the Church in the days of Christ and the apostles, and their immediate followers.

20. Fifth objection. Answer to the ancient and modern Cathari, and to the Novatians, concerning the forgiveness of sins

21. Answer to the fifth objection continued. By the forgiveness of sins believers are enabled to remain perpetually in the Church.

22. The keys of the Church given for the express purpose of securing this benefit. A summary of the answer to the fifth objection.

23. Sixth objection, formerly advanced by the Novatians, and renewed by the Anabaptists. This error confuted by the Lord's Prayer.

24. A second answer, founded on some examples under the Old Testament.

25. A third answer, confirmed by passages from Jeremiah, Ezekiel, and Solomon. A fourth answer, derived from sacrifices.

26. A fifth answer, from the New Testament. Some special examples.

27. General examples. A celebrated passage. The arrangement of the Creed.

28 Objection, that voluntary transgression excludes from the Church.

29. Last objection of the Novatians, founded on the solemn renewal of repentance required by the Church for more heinous offences. Answer.

1. In the last Book, it has been shown, that by the faith of the gospel Christ becomes ours, and we are made partakers of the salvation and eternal blessedness procured by him. But as our ignorance and sloth (I may add, the vanity of our mind) stand in need of external helps, by which faith may be begotten in us, and may increase and make progress until its consummation, God, in accommodation to our infirmity, has added such helps, and secured the effectual preaching of the gospel, by depositing this treasure with the Church. He has appointed pastors and teachers, by whose lips he might edify his people (Eph. 4:11); he has invested them with authority, and, in short, omitted nothing that might conduce to holy consent in the faith, and to right order. In particular, he has instituted sacraments, which we feel by experience to be most useful helps in fostering and confirming our faith. For seeing we are shut up in the prison of the body, and have not yet attained to the rank of angels, God, in

accommodation to our capacity, has in his admirable providence provided a method by which, though widely separated, we might still draw near to him. Wherefore, due order requires that we first treat of the Church, of its Government, Orders, and Power; next, of the Sacraments; and, lastly, of Civil Government;—at the same time guarding pious readers against the corruptions of the Papacy, by which Satan has adulterated all that God had appointed for our salvation. I will begin with the Church, into whose bosom God is pleased to collect his children, not only that by her aid and ministry they may be nourished so long as they are babes and children, but may also be guided by her maternal care until they grow up to manhood, and, finally, attain to the perfection of faith. What God has thus joined, let not man put asunder (Mark 10:9): to those to whom he is a Father, the Church must also be a mother. This was true not merely under the Law, but even now after the advent of Christ; since Paul declares that we are the children of a new, even a heavenly Jerusalem (Gal. 4:26).

2. When in the Creed we profess to believe the Church, reference is made not only to the visible Church of which we are now treating, but also to all the elect of God, including in the number even those who have departed this life. And, accordingly, the word used is "believe," because oftentimes no difference can be observed between the children of God and the profane, between his proper flock and the untamed herd. The particle *in* is often interpolated, but without any probable ground. I confess, indeed, that it is the more usual form, and is not unsupported by antiquity, since the Nicene Creed, as quoted in Ecclesiastical History, adds the preposition. At the same time, we may perceive from early writers, that the expression received without controversy in ancient times was to believe "the Church," and not "in the Church." This is not only the expression used by Augustine, and that ancient writer, whoever he may have been, whose treatise, *De Symboli Expositione*, is extant under the name of Cyprian, but they distinctly remark that the addition of the preposition would make the expression improper, and they give good grounds for so thinking. We declare that we believe in God, both because our mind reclines upon him as true, and our confidence is fully satisfied in him. This cannot be said of the Church, just as it cannot be said of the forgiveness of sins, or the resurrection of the body. Wherefore, although I am unwilling to dispute about words, yet I would rather keep to the proper form, as better fitted to express the thing that is meant, than affect terms by which the meaning is causelessly obscured. The object of the expression is to teach us, that though the devil leaves no stone unturned in order to destroy the grace of Christ, and the enemies of God rush with insane violence in the same direction, it cannot be extinguished,—the blood of Christ cannot be rendered barren, and prevented from producing fruit. Hence, regard must be had both to the secret election and to the internal calling of God, because he alone "knoweth them that are his" (2 Tim. 2:19); and as Paul expresses it, holds them as it were enclosed under his seal, although, at the same time, they wear his insignia, and are thus distinguished from the reprobate. But as they are a small and despised number, concealed in an immense crowd, like a few grains of wheat buried among a heap of chaff, to God alone must be left the knowledge of his Church, of which his secret election forms the foundation. Nor is it enough to embrace the number of the elect in thought and intention merely. By the unity of the Church we must understand a unity into which we feel persuaded that we are truly ingrafted. For unless we are united with all the other members under Christ our head, no hope of the future inheritance awaits us. Hence the Church is called Catholic or Universal (August. Ep. 48), for two or three cannot be invented without dividing Christ; and this is impossible. All the elect of God are so joined together in Christ, that as they depend on one head, so they are as it were compacted into one body, being knit together like its different members; made truly one by living together under the same Spirit of God in one faith, hope, and charity, called not only to the same inheritance of eternal life, but to participation in one God and Christ. For although the sad devastation which everywhere meets our view may proclaim that no Church remains, let us know that the death of Christ produces fruit, and that God wondrously preserves his Church, while placing it as it were in concealment. Thus it was said to Elijah, "Yet I have left me seven thousand in Israel" (1 Kings 19:18).

3. Moreover, this article of the Creed relates in some measure to the external Church, that every one of us must maintain brotherly concord with all the children of God, give due authority to the Church, and, in short, conduct ourselves as sheep of the flock. And hence the additional expression, the "communion of saints;" for this clause, though usually omitted by ancient writers, must not be overlooked, as it admirably expresses the quality of the Church; just as if it had been said, that saints are united in the fellowship of Christ on this condition, that all the blessings which God bestows upon them are mutually communicated to each other. This, however, is not

incompatible with a diversity of graces, for we know that the gifts of the Spirit are variously distributed; nor is it incompatible with civil order, by which each is permitted privately to possess his own means, it being necessary for the preservation of peace among men that distinct rights of property should exist among them. Still a community is asserted, such as Luke describes when he says, "The multitude of them that believed were of one heart and of one soul" (Acts 4:32); and Paul, when he reminds the Ephesians, "There is one body, and one Spirit, even as ye are called in one hope of your calling" (Eph. 4:4). For if they are truly persuaded that God is the common Father of them all, and Christ their common head, they cannot but be united together in brotherly love, and mutually impart their blessings to each other. Then it is of the highest importance for us to know what benefit thence redounds to us. For when we believe the Church, it is in order that we may be firmly persuaded that we are its members. In this way our salvation rests on a foundation so firm and sure, that though the whole fabric of the world were to give way, it could not be destroyed. First, it stands with the election of God, and cannot change or fail, any more than his eternal providence. Next, it is in a manner united with the stability of Christ, who will no more allow his faithful followers to be dissevered from him, than he would allow his own members to be torn to pieces. We may add, that so long as we continue in the bosom of the Church, we are sure that the truth will remain with us. Lastly, we feel that we have an interest in such promises as these, "In Mount Zion and in Jerusalem shall be deliverance" (Joel 2:32; Obad. 17); "God is in the midst of her, she shall not be moved" (Ps. 46:5). So available is communion with the Church to keep us in the fellowship of God. In the very term communion there is great consolation; because, while we are assured that everything which God bestows on his members belongs to us, all the blessings conferred upon them confirm our hope. But in order to embrace the unity of the Church in this manner, it is not necessary, as I have observed, to see it with our eyes, or feel it with our hands. Nay, rather from its being placed in faith, we are reminded that our thoughts are to dwell upon it, as much when it escapes our perception as when it openly appears. Nor is our faith the worse for apprehending what is unknown, since we are not enjoined here to distinguish between the elect and the reprobate (this belongs not to us, but to God only), but to feel firmly assured in our minds, that all those who, by the mercy of God the Father, through the efficacy of the Holy Spirit, have become partakers with Christ, are set apart as the proper and peculiar possession of God, and that as we are of the number, we are also partakers of this great grace.

4. But as it is now our purpose to discourse of the visible Church, let us learn, from her single title of Mother, how useful, nay, how necessary the knowledge of her is, since there is no other means of entering into life unless she conceive us in the womb and give us birth, unless she nourish us at her breasts, and, in short, keep us under her charge and government, until, divested of mortal flesh, we become like the angels (Mt. 22:30). For our weakness does not permit us to leave the school until we have spent our whole lives as scholars. Moreover, beyond the pale of the Church no forgiveness of sins, no salvation, can be hoped for, as Isaiah and Joel testify (Isa. 37:32; Joel 2:32). To their testimony Ezekiel subscribes, when he declares, "They shall not be in the assembly of my people, neither shall they be written in the writing of the house of Israel" (Ezek. 13:9); as, on the other hand, those who turn to the cultivation of true piety are said to inscribe their names among the citizens of Jerusalem. For which reason it is said in the psalm, "Remember me, O Lord, with the favour that thou bearest unto thy people: O visit me with thy salvation; that I may see the good of thy chosen, that I may rejoice in the gladness of thy nation, that I may glory with thine inheritance" (Ps. 106:4, 5). By these words the paternal favour of God and the special evidence of spiritual life are confined to his peculiar people, and hence the abandonment of the Church is always fatal.

5. But let us proceed to a full exposition of this view. Paul says that our Saviour "ascended far above all heavens, that he might fill all things. And he gave some, apostles; and some, prophets; and some, evangelists; and some, pastors and teachers; for the perfecting of the saints, for the work of the ministry, for the edifying of the body of Christ: till we all come in the unity of the faith, and of the knowledge of the Son of God, unto a perfect man, unto the measure of the stature of the fulness of Christ" (Eph. 4:10–13). We see that God, who might perfect his people in a moment, chooses not to bring them to manhood in any other way than by the education of the Church. We see the mode of doing it expressed; the preaching of celestial doctrine is committed to pastors. We see that all without exception are brought into the same order, that they may with meek and docile spirit allow themselves to be governed by teachers appointed for this purpose. Isaiah had long before given this as the characteristic of the kingdom of Christ, "My Spirit that is upon thee, and my words which I have put in thy mouth, shall not depart

out of thy mouth, nor out of the mouth of thy seed, nor out of the mouth of thy seed's seed, saith the Lord, from henceforth and for ever" (Isa. 59:21). Hence it follows, that all who reject the spiritual food of the soul divinely offered to them by the hands of the Church, deserve to perish of hunger and famine. God inspires us with faith, but it is by the instrumentality of his gospel, as Paul reminds us, "Faith cometh by hearing" (Rom. 10:17). God reserves to himself the power of maintaining it, but it is by the preaching of the gospel, as Paul also declares, that he brings it forth and unfolds it. With this view, it pleased him in ancient times that sacred meetings should be held in the sanctuary, that consent in faith might be nourished by doctrine proceeding from the lips of the priest. Those magnificent titles, as when the temple is called God's rest, his sanctuary, his habitation, and when he is said to dwell between the cherubims (Ps 32:13, 14; 80:1), are used for no other purpose than to procure respect, love, reverence, and dignity to the ministry of heavenly doctrine, to which otherwise the appearance of an insignificant human being might be in no slight degree derogatory. Therefore, to teach us that the treasure offered to us in earthen vessels is of inestimable value (2 Cor. 4:7), God himself appears and, as the author of this ordinance, requires his presence to be recognised in his own institution. Accordingly, after forbidding his people to give heed to familiar spirits, wizards, and other superstitions (Lev. 19:30, 31), he adds, that he will give what ought to be sufficient for all—namely, that he will never leave them without prophets. For, as he did not commit his ancient people to angels, but raised up teachers on the earth to perform a truly angelical office, so he is pleased to instruct us in the present day by human means. But as anciently he did not confine himself to the law merely, but added priests as interpreters, from whose lips the people might inquire after his true meaning, so in the present day he would not only have us to be attentive to reading, but has appointed masters to give us their assistance. In this there is a twofold advantage. For, on the one hand, he by an admirable test proves our obedience when we listen to his ministers just as we would to himself; while, on the other hand, he consults our weakness in being pleased to address us after the manner of men by means of interpreters, that he may thus allure us to himself, instead of driving us away by his thunder. How well this familiar mode of teaching is suited to us all the godly are aware, from the dread with which the divine majesty justly inspires them.

Those who think that the authority of the doctrine is impaired by the insignificance of the men who are called to teach, betray their ingratitude; for among the many noble endowments with which God has adorned the human race, one of the most remarkable is, that he deigns to consecrate the mouths and tongues of men to his service, making his own voice to be heard in them. Wherefore, let us not on our part decline obediently to embrace the doctrine of salvation, delivered by his command and mouth; because, although the power of God is not confined to external means, he has, however, confined us to his ordinary method of teaching, which method, when fanatics refuse to observe, they entangle themselves in many fatal snares. Pride, or fastidiousness, or emulation, induces many to persuade themselves that they can profit sufficiently by reading and meditating in private, and thus to despise public meetings, and deem preaching superfluous. But since as much as in them lies they loose or burst the sacred bond of unity, none of them escapes the just punishment of this impious divorce, but become fascinated with pestiferous errors, and the foulest delusions. Wherefore, in order that the pure simplicity of the faith may flourish among us, let us not decline to use this exercise of piety, which God by his institution of it has shown to be necessary, and which he so highly recommends. None, even among the most petulant of men, would venture to say, that we are to shut our ears against God, but in all ages prophets and pious teachers have had a difficult contest to maintain with the ungodly, whose perverseness cannot submit to the yoke of being taught by the lips and ministry of men. This is just the same as if they were to destroy the impress of God as exhibited to us in doctrine. For no other reason were believers anciently enjoined to seek the face of God in the sanctuary (Ps. 105:4) (an injunction so often repeated in the Law), than because the doctrine of the Law, and the exhortations of the prophets, were to them a living image of God. Thus Paul declares, that in his preaching the glory of God shone in the face of Jesus Christ (2 Cor. 4:6). The more detestable are the apostates who delight in producing schisms in churches, just as if they wished to drive the sheep from the fold, and throw them into the jaws of wolves. Let us hold, agreeably to the passage we quoted from Paul, that the Church can only be edified by external preaching, and that there is no other bond by which the saints can be kept together than by uniting with one consent to observe the order which God has appointed in his Church for learning and making progress. For this end, especially, as I have observed, believers were anciently enjoined under the Law to flock together to the sanctuary; for when Moses speaks of the habitation of God, he at the same time calls it the place of the name of God, the place where he will record his name (Exod. 20:24); thus plainly teaching that no use could be made of it without the doctrine of godliness. And there can be no doubt that, for the same reason, David complains with great bitterness of soul, that by the tyrannical cruelty of his enemies he was prevented from entering the tabernacle (Ps. 84). To many the complaint seems childish, as if no great loss were sustained, not much pleasure lost, by exclusion from the temple, provided other amusements were enjoyed. David, however, laments this one deprivation, as filling him with anxiety and sadness, tormenting, and almost destroying him. This he does because there is nothing on which believers set a higher value than on this aid, by which God gradually raises his people to heaven. For it is to be observed, that he always exhibited himself to the holy patriarchs in the mirror of his doctrine in such a way as to make their knowledge spiritual. Whence the temple is not only styled his face, but also, for the purpose of removing all superstition, is termed his footstool (Ps. 132:7; 99:5). Herein is the unity of the faith happily realised, when all, from the highest to the lowest, aspire to the head. All the temples which the Gentiles built to God with a different intention were a mere profanation of his worship,—a profanation into which the Jews also fell, though not with equal grossness. With this Stephen upbraids them in the words of Isaiah when he says, "Howbeit the Most High dwelleth not in temples made with hands; as saith the Prophet, Heaven is my throne," &c. (Acts 7:48). For God only consecrates temples to their legitimate use by his word. And when we rashly attempt anything without his order, immediately setting out from a bad principle, we introduce adventitious fictions, by which evil is propagated without measure. It was inconsiderate in Xerxes when, by the advice of the magians, he burnt or pulled down all the temples of Greece, because he thought it absurd that God, to whom all things ought to be free and open, should be enclosed by walls and roofs, as if it were not in the power of God in a manner to descend to us, that he may be near to us, and yet neither change his place nor affect us by earthly means, but rather, by a kind of vehicles, raise us aloft to his own heavenly glory, which, with its immensity, fills all things, and in height is above the heavens.

6. Moreover, as at this time there is a great dispute as to the efficacy of the ministry, some extravagantly overrating its dignity, and others erroneously maintaining, that what is peculiar to the Spirit of God is transferred to mortal man, when we suppose that ministers and teachers penetrate to the mind and heart, so as to correct the blindness of the one, and the hardness of the other; it is necessary to place this controversy on its proper footing. The arguments on both sides will be disposed of without trouble, by distinctly attending to the passages in which God, the author of preaching, connects his Spirit with it, and then promises a beneficial result; or, on the other hand, to the passages in which God, separating himself from external means, claims for himself alone both the commencement and the whole course of faith. The office of the second Elias was, as Malachi declares, to "turn the heart of the fathers to the children, and the heart of the children to their fathers" (Mal. 4:6). Christ declares that he sent the Apostles to produce fruit from his labours (John 15:16). What this fruit is Peter briefly defines, when he says that we are begotten again of incorruptible seed (1 Pet. 1:23). Hence Paul glories, that by means of the Gospel he had begotten the Corinthians, who were the seals of his apostleship (1 Cor. 4:15); moreover, that his was not a ministry of the letter, which only sounded in the ear, but that the effectual agency of the Spirit was given to him, in order that his doctrine might not be in vain (1 Cor. 9:2; 2 Cor. 3:6). In this sense he elsewhere declares that his Gospel was not in word, but in power (1 Thess. 1:5). He also affirms that the Galatians received the Spirit by the hearing of faith (Gal. 3:2). In short, in several passages he not only makes himself a fellow-worker with God, but attributes to himself the province of bestowing salvation (1 Cor. 3:9). All these things he certainly never uttered with the view of attributing to himself one iota apart from God, as he elsewhere briefly explains. "For this cause also thank we God without ceasing, because, when ye received the word of God which ye heard of us, ye received it not as the word of men, but (as it is in truth) the word of God, which effectually worketh also in you that believe" (1 Thess. 2:13). Again, in another place, "He that wrought effectually in Peter to the apostleship of the circumcision, the same was mighty in me toward the Gentiles" (Gal. 2:8). And that he allows no more to ministers is obvious from other passages. "So then neither is he that planteth anything, neither he that watereth; but God that giveth the increase" (1 Cor. 3:7). Again, "I laboured more abundantly than they all: yet not I, but the grace of God which was with me" (1 Cor. 15:10). And it is indeed necessary to keep these sentences in view, since God, in ascribing to himself the illumination of the mind and renewal of the heart, reminds us that it is sacrilege for man to claim any part of either to

himself. Still every one who listens with docility to the ministers whom God appoints, will know by the beneficial result, that for good reason God is pleased with this method of teaching, and for good reason has laid believers under this modest yoke.

7. The judgment which ought to be formed concerning the visible Church which comes under our observation, must, I think, be sufficiently clear from what has been said. I have observed that the Scriptures speak of the Church in two ways. Sometimes when they speak of the Church they mean the Church as it really is before God—the Church into which none are admitted but those who by the gift of adoption are sons of God, and by the sanctification of the Spirit true members of Christ. In this case it not only comprehends the saints who dwell on the earth, but all the elect who have existed from the beginning of the world. Often, too, by the name of Church is designated the whole body of mankind scattered throughout the world, who profess to worship one God and Christ, who by baptism are initiated into the faith; by partaking of the Lord's Supper profess unity in true doctrine and charity, agree in holding the word of the Lord, and observe the ministry which Christ has appointed for the preaching of it. In this Church there is a very large mixture of hypocrites, who have nothing of Christ but the name and outward appearance: of ambitious, avaricious, envious, evil-speaking men, some also of impurer lives, who are tolerated for a time, either because their guilt cannot be legally established, or because due strictness of discipline is not always observed. Hence, as it is necessary to believe the invisible Church, which is manifest to the eye of God only, so we are also enjoined to regard this Church which is so called with reference to man, and to cultivate its communion.

8. Accordingly, inasmuch as it was of importance to us to recognise it, the Lord has distinguished it by certain marks, and as it were symbols. It is, indeed, the special prerogative of God to know those who are his, as Paul declares in the passage already quoted (2 Tim. 2:19). And doubtless it has been so provided as a check on human rashness, the experience of every day reminding us how far his secret judgments surpass our apprehension. For even those who seemed most abandoned, and who had been completely despaired of, are by his goodness recalled to life, while those who seemed most stable often fall. Hence, as Augustine says, "In regard to the secret predestination of God, there are very many sheep without, and very many wolves within" (August. Hom. in Joan. 45). For he knows, and has his mark on those who know neither him nor themselves. Of those again who openly bear his badge, his eyes alone see who of them are unfeignedly holy, and will persevere even to the end, which alone is the completion of salvation. On the other hand, foreseeing that it was in some degree expedient for us to know who are to be regarded by us as his sons, he has in this matter accommodated himself to our capacity. But as here full certainty was not necessary, he has in its place substituted the judgment of charity, by which we acknowledge all as members of the Church who by confession of faith, regularity of conduct, and participation in the sacraments, unite with us in acknowledging the same God and Christ. The knowledge of his body, inasmuch as he knew it to be more necessary for our salvation, he has made known to us by surer marks.

9. Hence the form of the Church appears and stands forth conspicuous to our view. Wherever we see the word of God sincerely preached and heard, wherever we see the sacraments administered according to the institution of Christ, there we cannot have any doubt that the Church of God has some existence, since his promise cannot fail, "Where two or three are gathered together in my name, there am I in the midst of them" (Mt. 18:20). But that we may have a clear summary of this subject, we must proceed by the following steps:—The Church universal is the multitude collected out of all nations, who, though dispersed and far distant from each other, agree in one truth of divine doctrine, and are bound together by the tie of a common religion. In this way it comprehends single churches, which exist in different towns and villages, according to the wants of human society, so that each of them justly obtains the name and authority of the Church; and also comprehends single individuals, who by a religious profession are accounted to belong to such churches, although they are in fact aliens from the Church, but have not been cut off by a public decision. There is, however, a slight difference in the mode of judging of individuals and of churches. For it may happen in practice that those whom we deem not altogether worthy of the fellowship of believers, we yet ought to treat as brethren, and regard as believers, on account of the common consent of the Church in tolerating and bearing with them in the body of Christ. Such persons we do not approve by our suffrage as members of the Church, but we leave them the place which they hold among the people of God, until they are legitimately deprived of it. With regard to the general body we must feel differently; if they have the ministry of the word, and honour the administration of the sacraments, they are undoubtedly

entitled to be ranked with the Church, because it is certain that these things are not without a beneficial result. Thus we both maintain the Church universal in its unity, which malignant minds have always been eager to dissever, and deny not due authority to lawful assemblies distributed as circumstances require.

10. We have said that the symbols by which the Church is discerned are the preaching of the word and the observance of the sacraments, for these cannot anywhere exist without producing fruit and prospering by the blessing of God. I say not that wherever the word is preached fruit immediately appears; but that in every place where it is received, and has a fixed abode, it uniformly displays its efficacy. Be this as it may, when the preaching of the gospel is reverently heard, and the sacraments are not neglected, there for the time the face of the Church appears without deception or ambiguity and no man may with impunity spurn her authority, or reject her admonitions, or resist her counsels, or make sport of her censures, far less revolt from her, and violate her unity (see Chap. 2 sec. 1, 10, and Chap. 8 sec. 12). For such is the value which the Lord sets on the communion of his Church, that all who contumaciously alienate themselves from any Christian society, in which the true ministry of his word and sacraments is maintained, he regards as deserters of religion. So highly does he recommend her authority, that when it is violated he considers that his own authority is impaired. For there is no small weight in the designation given to her, "the house of God," "the pillar and ground of the truth" (1 Tim. 3:15). By these words Paul intimates, that to prevent the truth from perishing in the world. the Church is its faithful guardian, because God has been pleased to preserve the pure preaching of his word by her instrumentality, and to exhibit himself to us as a parent while he feeds us with spiritual nourishment, and provides whatever is conducive to our salvation. Moreover, no mean praise is conferred on the Church when she is said to have been chosen and set apart by Christ as his spouse, "not having spot or wrinkle, or any such thing" (Eph. 5:27), as "his body, the fulness of him that filleth all in all" (Eph. 1:23). Whence it follows, that revolt from the Church is denial of God and Christ. Wherefore there is the more necessity to beware of a dissent so iniquitous; for seeing by it we aim as far as in us lies at the destruction of God's truth, we deserve to be crushed by the full thunder of his anger. No crime can be imagined more atrocious than that of sacrilegiously and perfidiously violating the sacred marriage which the only begotten Son of God has condescended to contract with us.

11. Wherefore let these marks be carefully impressed upon our minds, and let us estimate them as in the sight of the Lord. There is nothing on which Satan is more intent than to destroy and efface one or both of them—at one time to delete and abolish these marks, and thereby destroy the true and genuine distinction of the Church; at another, to bring them into contempt, and so hurry us into open revolt from the Church. To his wiles it was owing that for several ages the pure preaching of the word disappeared, and now, with the same dishonest aim, he labours to overthrow the ministry, which, however, Christ has so ordered in his Church, that if it is removed the whole edifice must fall. How perilous, then, nay, how fatal the temptation, when we even entertain a thought of separating ourselves from that assembly in which are beheld the signs and badges which the Lord has deemed sufficient to characterise his Church! We see how great caution should be employed in both respects. That we may not be imposed upon by the name of Church, every congregation which claims the name must be brought to that test as to a Lydian stone. If it holds the order instituted by the Lord in word and sacraments there will be no deception; we may safely pay it the honour due to a church: on the other hand, if it exhibit itself without word and sacraments, we must in this case be no less careful to avoid the imposture than we were to shun pride and presumption in the other.

12. When we say that the pure ministry of the word and pure celebration of the sacraments is a fit pledge and earnest, so that we may safely recognise a church in every society in which both exist, our meaning is, that we are never to discard it so long as these remain, though it may otherwise teem with numerous faults. Nay, even in the administration of word and sacraments defects may creep in which ought not to alienate us from its communion. For all the heads of true doctrine are not in the same position. Some are so necessary to be known, that all must hold them to be fixed and undoubted as the proper essentials of religion: for instance, that God is one, that Christ is God, and the Son of God, that our salvation depends on the mercy of God, and the like. Others, again, which are the subject of controversy among the churches, do not destroy the unity of the faith; for why should it be regarded as a ground of dissension between churches, if one, without any spirit of contention or perverseness in dogmatising, hold that the soul on quitting the body flies to heaven, and another, without venturing to speak positively as to the abode, holds it for certain that it lives with the Lord? The words of the Apostle are,

"Let us therefore, as many as be perfect, be thus minded: and if in anything ye be otherwise minded, God shall reveal even this unto you" (Phil. 3:15). Does he not sufficiently intimate that a difference of opinion as to these matters which are not absolutely necessary, ought not to be a ground of dissension among Christians? The best thing, indeed, is to be perfectly agreed, but seeing there is no man who is not involved in some mist of ignorance, we must either have no church at all, or pardon delusion in those things of which one may be ignorant, without violating the substance of religion and forfeiting salvation. Here, however, I have no wish to patronise even the minutest errors, as if I thought it right to foster them by flattery or connivance; what I say is, that we are not on account of every minute difference to abandon a church, provided it retain sound and unimpaired that doctrine in which the safety of piety consists, and keep the use of the sacraments instituted by the Lord. Meanwhile, if we strive to reform what is offensive, we act in the discharge of duty. To this effect are the words of Paul, "If anything be revealed to another that sitteth by, let the first hold his peace" (1 Cor. 14:30). From this it is evident that to each member of the Church, according to his measure of grace, the study of public edification has been assigned, provided it be done decently and in order. In other words, we must neither renounce the communion of the Church, nor, continuing in it, disturb peace and discipline when duly arranged.

13. Our indulgence ought to extend much farther in tolerating imperfection of conduct. Here there is great danger of falling, and Satan employs all his machinations to ensnare us. For there always have been persons who, imbued with a false persuasion of absolute holiness, as if they had already become a kind of aërial spirits, spurn the society of all in whom they see that something human still remains. Such of old were the Cathari and the Donatists, who were similarly infatuated. Such in the present day are some of the Anabaptists, who would be thought to have made superior progress. Others, again, sin in this respect, not so much from that insane pride as from inconsiderate zeal. Seeing that among those to whom the gospel is preached, the fruit produced is not in accordance with the doctrine, they forthwith conclude that there no church exists. The offence is indeed well founded, and it is one to which in this most unhappy age we give far too much occasion. It is impossible to excuse our accursed sluggishness, which the Lord will not leave unpunished, as he is already beginning sharply to chastise us. Woe then to us who, by our dissolute licence of wickedness, cause weak consciences to be wounded! Still those of whom we have spoken sin in their turn, by not knowing how to set bounds to their offence. For where the Lord requires mercy they omit it, and give themselves up to immoderate severity. Thinking there is no church where there is not complete purity and integrity of conduct, they, through hatred of wickedness, withdraw from a genuine church, while they think they are shunning the company of the ungodly. They allege that the Church of God is holy. But that they may at the same time understand that it contains a mixture of good and bad, let them hear from the lips of our Saviour that parable in which he compares the Church to a net in which all kinds of fishes are taken, but not separated until they are brought ashore. Let them hear it compared to a field which, planted with good seed, is by the fraud of an enemy mingled with tares, and is not freed of them until the harvest is brought into the barn. Let them hear, in fine, that it is a thrashing-floor in which the collected wheat lies concealed under the chaff, until, cleansed by the fanners and the sieve, it is at length laid up in the granary. If the Lord declares that the Church will labour under the defect of being burdened with a multitude of wicked until the day of judgment, it is in vain to look for a church altogether free from blemish (Mt. 13).

14. They exclaim that it is impossible to tolerate the vice which everywhere stalks abroad like a pestilence. What if the apostle's sentiment applies here also? Among the Corinthians it was not a few that erred, but almost the whole body had become tainted; there was not one species of sin merely, but a multitude, and those not trivial errors, but some of them execrable crimes. There was not only corruption in manners, but also in doctrine. What course was taken by the holy apostle, in other words, by the organ of the heavenly Spirit, by whose testimony the Church stands and falls? Does he seek separation from them? Does he discard them from the kingdom of Christ? Does he strike them with the thunder of a final anathema? He not only does none of these things, but he acknowledges and heralds them as a Church of Christ, and a society of saints. If the Church remains among the Corinthians, where envyings, divisions, and contentions rage; where quarrels, lawsuits, and avarice prevail; where a crime, which even the Gentiles would execrate, is openly approved; where the name of Paul, whom they ought to have honoured as a father, is petulantly assailed; where some hold the resurrection of the dead in derision, though with it the whole gospel must fall; where the gifts of God are made subservient to ambition, not

to charity; where many things are done neither decently nor in order: If there the Church still remains, simply because the ministration of word and sacrament is not rejected, who will presume to deny the title of church to those to whom a tenth part of these crimes cannot be imputed? How, I ask, would those who act so morosely against present churches have acted to the Galatians, who had done all but abandon the gospel (Gal. 1:6), and yet among them the same apostle found churches?

15. They also object, that Paul sharply rebukes the Corinthians for permitting an heinous offender in their communion, and then lays down a general sentence, by which he declares it unlawful even to eat bread with a man of impure life (1 Cor. 5:11, 12). Here they exclaim, If it is not lawful to eat ordinary bread, how can it be lawful to eat the Lord's bread? I admit, that it is a great disgrace if dogs and swine are admitted among the children of God; much more, if the sacred body of Christ is prostituted to them. And, indeed, when churches are well regulated, they will not bear the wicked in their bosom, nor will they admit the worthy and unworthy indiscriminately to that sacred feast. But because pastors are not always sedulously vigilant, are sometimes also more indulgent than they ought, or are prevented from acting so strictly as they could wish; the consequence is, that even the openly wicked are not always excluded from the fellowship of the saints. This I admit to be a vice, and I have no wish to extenuate it, seeing that Paul sharply rebukes it in the Corinthians. But although the Church fail in her duty, it does not therefore follow that every private individual is to decide the question of separation for himself. I deny not that it is the duty of a pious man to withdraw from all private intercourse with the wicked, and not entangle himself with them by any voluntary tie; but it is one thing to shun the society of the wicked, and another to renounce the communion of the Church through hatred of them. Those who think it sacrilege to partake the Lord's bread with the wicked, are in this more rigid than Paul. For when he exhorts us to pure and holy communion, he does not require that we should examine others, or that every one should examine the whole church, but that each should examine himself (1 Cor. 11:28, 29). If it were unlawful to communicate with the unworthy, Paul would certainly have ordered us to take heed that there were no individual in the whole body by whose impurity we might be defiled, but now that he only requires each to examine himself, he shows that it does no harm to us though some who are unworthy present themselves along with us. To the same effect he afterwards adds, "He that eateth and drinketh unworthily, eateth and drinketh damnation to himself." He says not *to others*, but *to himself*. And justly; for the right of admitting or excluding ought not to be left to the decision of individuals. Cognisance of this point, which cannot be exercised without due order, as shall afterwards be more fully shown, belongs to the whole church. It would therefore be unjust to hold any private individual as polluted by the unworthiness of another, whom he neither can nor ought to keep back from communion.

16. Still, however, even the good are sometimes affected by this inconsiderate zeal for righteousness, though we shall find that this excessive moroseness is more the result of pride and a false idea of sanctity, than genuine sanctity itself, and true zeal for it. Accordingly, those who are the most forward, and, as it were, leaders in producing revolt from the Church, have, for the most part, no other motive than to display their own superiority by despising all other men. Well and wisely, therefore, does Augustine say, "Seeing that pious reason and the mode of ecclesiastical discipline ought specially to regard the unity of the Spirit in the bond of peace, which the Apostle enjoins us to keep, by bearing with one another (for if we keep it not, the application of medicine is not only superfluous, but pernicious, and therefore proves to be no medicine); those bad sons who, not from hatred of other men's iniquities, but zeal for their own contentions, attempt altogether to draw away, or at least to divide, weak brethren ensnared by the glare of their name, while swollen with pride, stuffed with petulance, insidiously calumnious, and turbulently seditious, use the cloak of a rigorous severity, that they may not seem devoid of the light of truth, and pervert to sacrilegious schism, and purposes of excision, those things which are enjoined in the Holy Scriptures (due regard being had to sincere love, and the unity of peace), to correct a brother's faults by the appliance of a moderate cure" (August. Cont. Parmen. cap. 1). To the pious and placid his advice is, mercifully to correct what they can, and to bear patiently with what they cannot correct, in love lamenting and mourning until God either reform or correct, or at the harvest root up the tares, and scatter the chaff (Ibid. cap. 2). Let all the godly study to provide themselves with these weapons, lest, while they deem themselves strenuous and ardent defenders of righteousness, they revolt from the kingdom of heaven, which is the only kingdom of righteousness. For as God has been pleased that the communion of his Church shall be maintained in this external society, any one who, from hatred of the ungodly, violates the bond of this society,

enters on a downward course, in which he incurs great danger of cutting himself off from the communion of saints. Let them reflect, that in a numerous body there are several who may escape their notice, and yet are truly righteous and innocent in the eyes of the Lord. Let them reflect, that of those who seem diseased, there are many who are far from taking pleasure or flattering themselves in their faults, and who, ever and anon aroused by a serious fear of the Lord, aspire to greater integrity. Let them reflect, that they have no right to pass judgment on a man for one act, since the holiest sometimes make the most grievous fall. Let them reflect, that in the ministry of the word and participation of the sacraments, the power to collect the Church is too great to be deprived of all its efficacy, by the fault of some ungodly men. Lastly, let them reflect, that in estimating the Church, divine is of more force than human judgment.

17. Since they also argue that there is good reason for the Church being called holy, it is necessary to consider what the holiness is in which it excels, lest by refusing to acknowledge any church, save one that is completely perfect, we leave no church at all. It is true, indeed, as Paul says, that Christ "loved the church, and gave himself for it, that he might sanctify and cleanse it with the washing of water by the word, that he might present it to himself a glorious church, not having spot, or wrinkle, or any such thing; but that it should be holy and without blemish" (Eph. 5:25–27). Nevertheless, it is true, that the Lord is daily smoothing its wrinkles, and wiping away its spots. Hence it follows, that its holiness is not yet perfect. Such, then, is the holiness of the Church: it makes daily progress, but is not yet perfect; it daily advances, but as yet has not reached the goal, as will elsewhere be more fully explained. Therefore, when the Prophets foretel, "Then shall Jerusalem be holy, and there shall no strangers pass through her any more;"—"It shall be called, The way of holiness; the unclean shall not pass over it" (Joel 3:17; Isa. 35:8), let us not understand it as if no blemish remained in the members of the Church: but only that with their whole heart they aspire after holiness and perfect purity: and hence, that purity which they have not yet fully attained is, by the kindness of God, attributed to them. And though the indications of such a kind of holiness existing among men are too rare, we must understand, that at no period since the world began has the Lord been without his Church, nor ever shall be till the final consummation of all things. For although, at the very outset, the whole human race was vitiated and corrupted by the sin of Adam, yet of this kind of polluted mass he always sanctifies some vessels to honour, that no age may be left without experience of his mercy. This he has declared by sure promises, such as the following: "I have made a covenant with my chosen, I have sworn unto David my servant, Thy seed will I establish for ever, and build up thy throne to all generations" (Ps. 89:3, 4). "The Lord hath chosen Zion; he hath desired it for his habitation. This is my rest for ever; here will I dwell" (Ps. 132:13, 14). "Thus saith the Lord, which giveth the sun for a light by day, and the ordinances of the moon and of the stars for a light by night, which divideth the sea when the waves thereof roar; The Lord of hosts is his name: If those ordinances depart from before me, saith the Lord, then the seed of Israel also shall cease from being a nation before me for ever" (Jer. 31:35, 36).

18. On this head, Christ himself, his apostles, and almost all the prophets, have furnished us with examples. Fearful are the descriptions in which Isaiah, Jeremiah, Joel, Habakkuk, and others, deplore the diseases of the Church of Jerusalem. In the people, the rulers, and the priests, corruption prevailed to such a degree, that Isaiah hesitates not to liken Jerusalem to Sodom and Gomorrah (Isa. 1:10). Religion was partly despised, partly adulterated, while in regard to morals, we everywhere meet with accounts of theft, robbery, perfidy, murder, and similar crimes. The prophets, however, did not therefore either form new churches for themselves, or erect new altars on which they might have separate sacrifices, but whatever their countrymen might be, reflecting that the Lord had deposited his word with them, and instituted the ceremonies by which he was then worshipped, they stretched out pure hands to him, though amid the company of the ungodly. Certainly, had they thought that they thereby contracted any pollution, they would have died a hundred deaths sooner than suffered themselves to be dragged thither. Nothing, therefore, prevented them from separating themselves, but a desire of preserving unity. But if the holy prophets felt no obligation to withdraw from the Church on account of the very numerous and heinous crimes, not of one or two individuals, but almost of the whole people, we arrogate too much to ourselves, if we presume forthwith to withdraw from the communion of the Church, because the lives of all accord not with our judgment, or even with the Christian profession.

19. Then what kind of age was that of Christ and the apostles? Yet neither could the desperate impiety of the Pharisees, nor the dissolute licentiousness of manners which everywhere prevailed, prevent them from using

the same sacred rites with the people, and meeting in one common temple for the public exercises of religion. And why so, but just because they knew that those who joined in these sacred rites with a pure conscience were not at all polluted by the society of the wicked? If any one is little moved by prophets and apostles, let him at least defer to the authority of Christ. Well, therefore, does Cyprian say, "Although tares or unclean vessels are seen in the Church, that is no reason why we ourselves should withdraw from the Church; we must only labour that we may be able to be wheat; we must give our endeavour, and strive as far as we can, to be vessels of gold or silver. But to break the earthen vessels belongs to the Lord alone, to whom a rod of iron has been given: let no one arrogate to himself what is peculiar to the Son alone, and think himself sufficient to winnow the floor and cleanse the chaff, and separate all the tares by human judgment. What depraved zeal thus assumes to itself is proud obstinacy and sacrilegious presumption" (Cyprian, Lib. 3 Ep. 5). Let both points, therefore, be regarded as fixed; *first*, that there is no excuse for him who spontaneously abandons the external communion of a church in which the word of God is preached and the sacraments are administered; *secondly*, that notwithstanding of the faults of a few or of many, there is nothing to prevent us from there duly professing our faith in the ordinances instituted by God, because a pious conscience is not injured by the unworthiness of another, whether he be a pastor or a private individual; and sacred rites are not less pure and salutary to a man who is holy and upright, from being at the same time handled by the impure.

20. Their moroseness and pride proceed even to greater lengths. Refusing to acknowledge any church that is not pure from the minutest blemish, they take offence at sound teachers for exhorting believers to make progress, and so teaching them to groan during their whole lives under the burden of sin, and flee for pardon. For they preten that in this way believers are led away from perfection. I admit that we are not to labour feebly or coldly in urging perfection, far less to desist from urging it; but I hold that it is a device of the devil to fill our minds with a confident belief of it while we are still in our course. Accordingly, in the Creed forgiveness of sins is appropriately subjoined to belief as to the Church, because none obtain forgiveness but those who are citizens, and of the household of the Church, as we read in the Prophet (Is. 33:24). The first place, therefore, should be given to the building of the heavenly Jerusalem, in which God afterwards is pleased to wipe away the iniquity of all who betake themselves to it. I say, however, that the Church must first be built; not that there can be any church without forgiveness of sins, but because the Lord has not promised his mercy save in the communion of saints. Therefore, our first entrance into the Church and the kingdom of God is by forgiveness of sins, without which we have no covenant nor union with God. For thus he speaks by the Prophet, "In that day will I make a covenant for them with the beasts of the field, and with the fowls of heaven, and with the creeping things of the ground: and I will break the bow, and the sword, and the battle, out of the earth, and will make them to lie down safely. And I will betroth thee unto me for ever; yea, I will betroth thee unto me in righteousness, and in judgment, and in loving-kindness, and in mercies" (Hos. 2:18, 19). We see in what way the Lord reconciles us to himself by his mercy. So in another passage, where he foretells that the people whom he had scattered in anger will again be gathered together, "I will cleanse them from all their iniquity, whereby they have sinned against me" (Jer. 33:8). Wherefore, our initiation into the fellowship of the Church is, by the symbol of ablution, to teach us that we have no admission into the family of God, unless by his goodness our impurities are previously washed away.

21. Nor by remission of sins does the Lord only once for all elect and admit us into the Church, but by the same means he preserves and defends us in it. For what would it avail us to receive a pardon of which we were afterwards to have no use? That the mercy of the Lord would be vain and delusive if only granted once, all the godly can bear witness; for there is none who is not conscious, during his whole life, of many infirmities which stand in need of divine mercy. And truly it is not without cause that the Lord promises this gift specially to his own household, nor in vain that he orders the same message of reconciliation to be daily delivered to them. Wherefore, as during our whole lives we carry about with us the remains of sin, we could not continue in the Church one single moment were we not sustained by the uninterrupted grace of God in forgiving our sins. On the other hand, the Lord has called his people to eternal salvation, and therefore they ought to consider that pardon for their sins is always ready. Hence let us surely hold that if we are admitted and ingrafted into the body of the Church, the forgiveness of sins has been bestowed, and is daily bestowed on us, in divine liberality, through the intervention of Christ's merits, and the sanctification of the Spirit.

22. To impart this blessing to us, the keys have been

given to the Church (Mt. 16:19; 18:18). For when Christ gave the command to the apostles, and conferred the power of forgiving sins, he not merely intended that they should loose the sins of those who should be converted from impiety to the faith of Christ; but, moreover, that they should perpetually perform this office among believers. This Paul teaches, when he says that the embassy of reconciliation has been committed to the ministers of the Church, that they may ever and anon in the name of Christ exhort the people to be reconciled to God (2 Cor. 5:20). Therefore, in the communion of saints our sins are constantly forgiven by the ministry of the Church, when presbyters or bishops, to whom the office has been committed, confirm pious consciences, in the hope of pardon and forgiveness by the promises of the gospel, and that as well in public as in private, as the case requires. For there are many who, from their infirmity, stand in need of special pacification, and Paul declares that he testified of the grace of Christ not only in the public assembly, but from house to house, reminding each individually of the doctrine of salvation (Acts 20:20, 21). Three things are here to be observed. First, Whatever be the holiness which the children of God possess, it is always under the condition, that so long as they dwell in a mortal body, they cannot stand before God without forgiveness of sins. Secondly, This benefit is so peculiar to the Church, that we cannot enjoy it unless we continue in the communion of the Church. Thirdly, It is dispensed to us by the ministers and pastors of the Church, either in the preaching of the Gospel or the administration of the Sacraments, and herein is especially manifested the power of the keys, which the Lord has bestowed on the company of the faithful. Accordingly, let each of us consider it to be his duty to seek forgiveness of sins only where the Lord has placed it. Of the public reconciliation which relates to discipline, we shall speak at the proper place.

23. But since those frantic spirits of whom I have spoken attempt to rob the Church of this the only anchor of salvation, consciences must be more firmly strengthened against this pestilential opinion. The Novatians, in ancient times, agitated the Churches with this dogma, but in our day, not unlike the Novatians are some of the Anabaptists, who have fallen into the same delirious dreams. For they pretend that in baptism, the people of God are regenerated to a pure and angelical life, which is not polluted by any carnal defilements. But if a man sin after baptism, they leave him nothing except the inexorable judgment of God. In short, to the sinner who has lapsed after receiving grace they give no hope of pardon, because they admit no other forgiveness of sins save that by which we are first regenerated. But although no falsehood is more clearly refuted by Scripture, yet as these men find means of imposition (as Novatus also of old had very many followers), let us briefly show how much they rave, to the destruction both of themselves and others. In the first place, since by the command of our Lord the saints daily repeat this prayer, "Forgive us our debts" (Mt. 6:12), they confess that they are debtors. Nor do they ask in vain; for the Lord has only enjoined them to ask what he will give. Nay, while he has declared that the whole prayer will be heard by his Father, he has sealed this absolution with a peculiar promise. What more do we wish? The Lord requires of his saints confession of sins during their whole lives, and that without ceasing, and promises pardon. How presumptuous, then, to exempt them from sin, or when they have stumbled, to exclude them altogether from grace? Then whom does he enjoin us to pardon seventy and seven times? Is it not our brethren? (Mt. 18:22). And why has he so enjoined but that we may imitate his clemency? He therefore pardons not once or twice only, but as often as, under a sense of our faults, we feel alarmed, and sighing call upon him.

24. And to begin almost with the very first commencement of the Church: the Patriarchs had been circumcised, admitted to a participation in the covenant, and doubtless instructed by their father's care in righteousness and integrity, when they conspired to commit fratricide. The crime was one which the most abandoned robbers would have abominated. At length, softened by the remonstrances of Judah, they sold him; this also was intolerable cruelty. Simeon and Levi took a nefarious revenge on the sons of Sychem, one, too, condemned by the judgment of their father. Reuben, with execrable lust, defiled his father's bed. Judah, when seeking to commit whoredom, sinned against the law of nature with his daughter-in-law. But so far are they from being expunged from the chosen people, that they are rather raised to be its heads. What, moreover, of David? when on the throne of righteousness, with what iniquity did he make way for blind lust, by the shedding of innocent blood? He had already been regenerated, and, as one of the regenerated, received distinguished approbation from the Lord. But he perpetrated a crime at which even the Gentiles would have been horrified, and yet obtained pardon. And not to dwell on special examples, all the promises of divine mercy extant in the Law and the Prophets are so many proofs that the Lord is ready to forgive the offences of his people. For why does Moses promise a future period,

when the people who had fallen into rebellion should return to the Lord? "Then the Lord thy God will turn thy captivity, and have compassion upon thee, and will return and gather thee from all the nations whither the Lord thy God hath scattered thee" (Deut. 30:3).

25. But I am unwilling to begin an enumeration which never could be finished. The prophetical books are filled with similar promises, offering mercy to a people covered with innumerable transgressions. What crime is more heinous than rebellion? It is styled divorce between God and the Church, and yet, by his goodness, it is surmounted. They say, "If a man put away his wife, and she go from him, and become another man's, shall he return unto her again? shall not that land be greatly polluted? But thou hast played the harlot with many lovers; yet return again unto me, saith the Lord." "Return, thou backsliding Israel, saith the Lord; and I will not cause mine anger to fall upon you; for I am merciful, saith the Lord, and I will not keep anger for ever" (Jer. 3:1, 12). And surely he could not have a different feeling who declares, "I have no pleasure in the death of him that dieth;" "Wherefore turn yourselves, and live ye" (Ezek. 18:23, 32). Accordingly, when Solomon dedicated the temple, one of the uses for which it was destined was, that prayers offered up for the pardon of sins might there be heard. "If they sin against thee (for there is no man that sinneth not), and thou be angry with them, and deliver them to the enemy, so that they carry them away captive unto the land of the enemy, far or near; yet if they shall bethink themselves in the land whither they were carried captives, and repent, and make supplication unto thee in the land of them that carried them captives, saying, We have sinned, and have done perversely, we have committed wickedness; and so return unto thee with all their heart, and with all their soul, in the land of their enemies which led them away captive, and pray unto thee towards their land, which thou gavest unto their fathers, the city which thou hast chosen, and the house which I have built for thy name: then hear thou their prayer and their supplication in heaven thy dwelling-place, and maintain their cause, and forgive thy people that have sinned against thee, and all their transgressions wherein they have transgressed against thee" (1 Kings 8:46–50). Nor in vain in the Law did God ordain a daily sacrifice for sins. Had he not foreseen that his people were constantly to labour under the disease of sin, he never would have appointed these remedies.

26. Did the advent of Christ, by which the fulness of grace was displayed, deprive believers of this privilege of supplicating for the pardon of their sins? If they offended against the Lord, were they not to obtain any mercy? What were it but to say that Christ came not for the salvation, but for the destruction of his people, if the divine indulgence in pardoning sin, which was constantly provided for the saints under the Old Testament, is now declared to have been taken away? But if we give credit to the Scriptures, when distinctly proclaiming that in Christ alone the grace and loving-kindness of the Lord have fully appeared, the riches of his mercy been poured out, reconciliation between God and man accomplished (Tit. 2:11; 3:4; 2 Tim. 1:9, 10), let us not doubt that the clemency of our heavenly Father, instead of being cut off or curtailed, is in much greater exuberance. Nor are proofs of this wanting. Peter, who had heard our Saviour declare that he who did not confess his name before men would be denied before the angels of God, denied him thrice in one night, and not without execration; yet he is not denied pardon (Mark 8:38). Those who lived disorderly among the Thessalonians, though chastised, are still invited to repentance (2 Thess. 3:6). Not even is Simon Magus thrown into despair. He is rather told to hope, since Peter invites him to have recourse to prayer (Acts 8:22).

27. What shall we say to the fact, that occasionally whole churches have been implicated in the grossest sins, and yet Paul, instead of giving them over to destruction, rather mercifully extricated them? The defection of the Galatians was no trivial fault; the Corinthians were still less excusable, the iniquities prevailing among them being more numerous and not less heinous, yet neither are excluded from the mercy of the Lord. Nay, the very persons who had sinned above others in uncleanness and fornication are expressly invited to repentance. The covenant of the Lord remains, and ever will remain, inviolable, that covenant which he solemnly ratified with Christ the true Solomon, and his members, in these words: "If his children forsake my law, and walk not in my judgments; if they break my statutes, and keep not my commandments; then will I visit their transgression with the rod, and their iniquity with stripes. Nevertheless, my loving-kindness will I not utterly take from him" (Ps. 89:30–33). In short, by the very arrangement of the Creed, we are reminded that forgiveness of sins always resides in the Church of Christ, for after the Church is as it were constituted, forgiveness of sins is subjoined.

28. Some persons who have somewhat more discernment, seeing that the dogma of Novatus is so clearly refuted in Scripture, do not make every fault unpardonable, but that voluntary transgression of the Law into which a man falls knowingly and willingly. Those who

speak thus allow pardon to those sins only that have been committed through ignorance. But since the Lord has in the Law ordered some sacrifices to be offered in expiation of the voluntary sins of believers, and others to redeem sins of ignorance (Lev. 4), how perverse is it to concede no expiation to a voluntary sin? I hold nothing to be more plain, than that the one sacrifice of Christ avails to remit the voluntary sins of believers, the Lord having attested this by carnal sacrifices as emblems. Then how is David, who was so well instructed in the Law, to be excused by ignorance? Did David, who was daily punishing it in others, not know how heinous a crime murder and adultery was? Did the patriarchs deem fratricide a lawful act? Had the Corinthians made so little proficiency as to imagine that God was pleased with lasciviousness, impurity, whoredom, hatred, and strife? Was Peter, after being so carefully warned, ignorant how heinous it was to forswear his Master? Therefore, let us not by our malice shut the door against the divine mercy, when so benignly manifested.

29. I am not unaware, that by the sins which are daily forgiven to believers, ancient writers have understood the lighter errors which creep in through the infirmity of the flesh, while they thought that the formal repentance which was then exacted for more heinous crimes was no more to be repeated than Baptism. This opinion is not to be viewed as if they wished to plunge those into despair who had fallen from their first repentance, or to extenuate those errors as if they were of no account before God. For they knew that the saints often stumble through unbelief, that superfluous oaths occasionally escape them, that they sometimes boil with anger, nay, break out into open invectives, and labour, besides, under other evils, which are in no slight degree offensive to the Lord; but they so called them to distinguish them from public crimes, which came under the cognisance of the Church, and produced much scandal. The great difficulty they had in pardoning those who had done something that called for ecclesiastical animadversion, was not because they thought it difficult to obtain pardon from the Lord, but by this severity they wished to deter others from rushing precipitately into crimes, which, by their demerit, would alienate them from the communion of the Church. Still the word of the Lord, which here ought to be our only rule, certainly prescribes greater moderation, since it teaches that the rigour of discipline must not be stretched so far as to overwhelm with grief the individual for whose benefit it should specially be designed (2 Cor. 2:7), as we have above discoursed at greater length.

CHAPTER 2

COMPARISON BETWEEN THE FALSE CHURCH AND THE TRUE.

The divisions of the chapter are,—I. Description of a spurious Church, resembling the Papacy vaunting of personal succession, of which a refutation is subjoined. sec. 1–4. II. An answer, in name of the orthodox Churches, to the Popish accusations of heresy and schism. A description of the Churches existing at present under the Papacy.

Sections:

1. Recapitulation of the matters treated in the previous chapter. Substance of the present chapter—viz. Where lying and falsehood prevail, no Church exists. There is falsehood wherever the pure doctrine of Christ is not in vigour.

2. This falsehood prevails under the Papacy. Hence the Papacy is not a Church. Still the Papists extol their own Church, and charge those who dissent from it with heresy and schism. They attempt to defend their vaunting by the name of personal succession. A succession which abandons the truth of Christ proved to be of no importance.

3. This proof confirmed, 1. By examples and passages of Scripture; 2. By reason and the authority of Augustine.

4. Whatever the Papists may pretend, there is no Church where the word of God appears not.

5. The objection of personal succession, and the charge of heresy and schism, refuted, both from Scripture and Augustine.

6. The same thing confirmed by the authority of Cyprian. The anathemas of the Papists of no consequence.

7. The churches of the Papists in the same situation as those of the Israelites, which revolted to superstition and idolatry under Jeroboam.

8. The character of those Israelitish churches.

9. Hence the Papists act unjustly when they would compel us to communion with their Church. Their two demands. Answer to the first. Sum of the question. Why we cannot take part in the external worship of the Papists.

10. Second demand of the Papists answered.

11. Although the Papacy cannot properly be called a Church, still, against the will of Antichrist himself,

there is some vestige of a Church in the Papacy, as Baptism and some other remnants.

12. The name of Church not conceded to the Papacy, though under its domination there have been some kind of churches. Herein is a fulfilment of Paul's prophecy, that Antichrist would sit in the temple of God. Deplorable condition of such churches. Summary of the chapter.

1. How much the ministry of the word and sacraments should weigh with us, and how far reverence for it should extend, so as to be a perpetual badge for distinguishing the Church, has been explained; for we have shown, first, that wherever it exists entire and unimpaired, no errors of conduct, no defects should prevent us from giving the name of Church; and, secondly, that trivial errors in this ministry ought not to make us regard it as illegitimate. Moreover, we have shown that the errors to which such pardon is due, are those by which the fundamental doctrine of religion is not injured, and by which those articles of religion, in which all believers should agree, are not suppressed, while, in regard to the sacraments, the defects are such as neither destroy nor impair the legitimate institution of their Author. But as soon as falsehood has forced its way into the citadel of religion, as soon as the sum of necessary doctrine is inverted, and the use of the sacraments is destroyed, the death of the Church undoubtedly ensues, just as the life of man is destroyed when his throat is pierced, or his vitals mortally wounded. This is clearly evinced by the words of Paul when he says, that the Church is "built upon the foundation of the apostles and prophets, Jesus Christ himself being the chief cornerstone" (Eph. 2:20). If the Church is founded on the doctrine of the apostles and prophets, by which believers are enjoined to place their salvation in Christ alone, then if that doctrine is destroyed, how can the Church continue to stand? The Church must necessarily fall whenever that sum of religion which alone can sustain it has given way. Again, if the true Church is "the pillar and ground of the truth" (1 Tim. 3:15), it is certain that there is no Church where lying and falsehood have usurped the ascendancy.

2. Since this is the state of matters under the Papacy, we can understand how much of the Church there survives. There, instead of the ministry of the word, prevails a perverted government, compounded of lies, a government which partly extinguishes, partly suppresses, the pure light. In place of the Lord's Supper, the foulest sacrilege has entered, the worship of God is deformed by a varied mass of intolerable superstitions; doctrine (without which Christianity exists not) is wholly buried and exploded, the public assemblies are schools of idolatry and impiety. Wherefore, in declining fatal participation in such wickedness, we run no risk of being dissevered from the Church of Christ. The communion of the Church was not instituted to be a chain to bind us in idolatry, impiety, ignorance of God, and other kinds of evil, but rather to retain us in the fear of God and obedience of the truth. They, indeed, vaunt loudly of their Church, as if there was not another in the world; and then, as if the matter were ended, they make out that all are schismatics who withdraw from obedience to that Church which they thus depict, that all are heretics who presume to whisper against its doctrine (see sec 5). But by what arguments do they prove their possession of the true Church? They appeal to ancient records which formerly existed in Italy, France, and Spain, pretending to derive their origin from those holy men who, by sound doctrine, founded and raised up churches, confirmed the doctrine, and reared the edifice of the Church with their blood; they pretend that the Church thus consecrated by spiritual gifts and the blood of martyrs was preserved from destruction by a perpetual succession of bishops. They dwell on the importance which Irenæus, Tertullian, Origen, Augustine, and others, attached to this succession (see sec. 3). How frivolous and plainly ludicrous these allegations are, I will enable any, who will for a little consider the matter with me, to understand without any difficulty. I would also exhort our opponents to give their serious attention, if I had any hope of being able to benefit them by instruction; but since they have laid aside all regard to truth, and make it their only aim to prosecute their own ends in whatever way they can, I will only make a few observations by which good men and lovers of truth may disentangle themselves from their quibbles. First, I ask them why they do not quote Africa, and Egypt, and all Asia, just because in all those regions there was a cessation of that sacred succession, by the aid of which they vaunt of having continued churches. They therefore fall back on the assertion, that they have the true Church, because ever since it began to exist it was never destitute of bishops, because they succeeded each other in an unbroken series. But what if I bring Greece before them? Therefore, I again ask them, Why they say that the Church perished among the Greeks, among whom there never was any interruption in the succession of bishops—a succession, in their opinion, the only guardian and preserver of the Church? They make the Greeks schismatics. Why? because, by revolting from

the Apostolic See, they lost their privilege. What? Do not those who revolt from Christ much more deserve to lose it? It follows, therefore, that the pretence of succession is vain, if posterity do not retain the truth of Christ, which was handed down to them by their fathers, safe and uncorrupted, and continue in it.

3. In the present day, therefore, the presence of the Romanists is just the same as that which appears to have been formerly used by the Jews, when the Prophets of the Lord charged them with blindness, impiety, and idolatry. For as the Jews proudly vaunted of their temple, ceremonies, and priesthood, by which, with strong reason, as they supposed, they measured the Church, so, instead of the Church, we are presented by the Romanists with certain external masks, which often are far from being connected with the Church, and without which the Church can perfectly exist. Wherefore, we need no other argument to refute them than that with which Jeremiah opposed the foolish confidence of the Jews—namely, "Trust ye not in lying words, saying, The temple of the Lord, The temple of the Lord, The temple of the Lord are these" (Jer. 7:4). The Lord recognises nothing as his own, save when his word is heard and religiously observed. Thus, though the glory of God sat in the sanctuary between the cherubim (Ezek. 10:4), and he had promised that he would there have his stated abode, still when the priests corrupted his worship by depraved superstitions, he transferred it elsewhere, and left the place without any sanctity. If that temple which seemed consecrated for the perpetual habitation of God, could be abandoned by God and become profane, the Romanists have no ground to pretend that God is so bound to persons or places, and fixed to external observances, that he must remain with those who have only the name and semblance of a Church. This is the question which Paul discusses in the Epistle to the Romans, from the ninth to the twelfth chapter. Weak consciences were greatly disturbed, when those who seemed to be the people of God not only rejected, but even persecuted the doctrine of the Gospel. Therefore, after expounding doctrine, he removes this difficulty, denying that those Jews, the enemies of the truth, were the Church, though they wanted nothing which might otherwise have been desired to the external form of the Church. The ground of his denial is, that they did not embrace Christ. In the Epistle to the Galatians, when comparing Ishmael with Isaac, he says still more expressly, that many hold a place in the Church to whom the inheritance does not belong, because they were not the offspring of a free parent. From this he proceeds to draw a contrast between two Jerusalems, because as the Law was given on Mount Sinai, but the Gospel proceeded from Jerusalem, so many who were born and brought up in servitude confidently boast that they are the sons of God and of the Church; nay, while they are themselves degenerate, proudly despise the genuine sons of God. Let us also, in like manner, when we hear that it was once declared from heaven, "Cast out the bondmaid and her son," trust to this inviolable decree, and boldly despise their unmeaning boasts. For if they plume themselves on external profession, Ishmael also was circumcised: if they found on antiquity, he was the first-born: and yet we see that he was rejected. If the reason is asked, Paul assigns it (Rom. 9:6), that those only are accounted sons who are born of the pure and legitimate seed of doctrine. On this ground God declares that he was not astricted to impious priests, though he had made a covenant with their father Levi, to be their angel, or interpreter (Mal. 2:4); nay, he retorts the false boast by which they were wont to rise against the Prophets—namely, that the dignity of the priesthood was to be held in singular estimation. This he himself willingly admits: and he disputes with them, on the ground that he is ready to fulfil the covenant, while they, by not fulfilling it on their part, deserve to be rejected. Here, then, is the value of succession when not conjoined with imitation and corresponding conduct: posterity, as soon as they are convicted of having revolted from their origin, are deprived of all honour; unless, indeed, we are prepared to say, that because Caiaphas succeeded many pious priests (nay, the series from Aaron to him was continuous), that accursed assembly deserved the name of Church. Even in earthly governments, no one would bear to see the tyranny of Caligula, Nero, Heliogabalus, and the like, described as the true condition of a republic, because they succeeded such men as Brutus, Scipio, and Camillus. That in the government of the Church especially, nothing is more absurd than to disregard doctrine, and place succession in persons. Nor, indeed, was anything farther from the intention of the holy teachers, whom they falsely obtrude upon us, than to maintain distinctly that churches exist, as by hereditary right, wherever bishops have been uniformly succeeded by bishops. But while it was without controversy that no change had been made in doctrine from the beginning down to their day, they assumed it to be a sufficient refutation of all their errors, that they were opposed to the doctrine maintained constantly, and with unanimous consent, even by the apostles themselves. They have, therefore, no longer any ground for

proceeding to make a gloss of the name of the Church, which we regard with due reverence; but when we come to definition, not only (to use the common expression) does the water adhere to them, but they stick in their own mire, because they substitute a vile prostitute for the sacred spouse of Christ. That the substitution may not deceive us, let us, among other admonitions, attend to the following from Augustine. Speaking of the Church, he says, "She herself is sometimes obscured, and, as it were, beclouded by a multitude of scandals; sometimes, in a time of tranquillity, she appears quiet and free; sometimes she is covered and tossed by the billows of tribulation and trial."—(August. ad Vincent. Epist. 48). As instances, he mentions that the strongest pillars of the Church often bravely endured exile for the faith, or lay hid throughout the world.

4. In this way the Romanists assail us in the present day, and terrify the unskilful with the name of Church, while they are the deadly adversaries of Christ. Therefore, although they exhibit a temple, a priesthood, and other similar masks, the empty glare by which they dazzle the eyes of the simple should not move us in the least to admit that there is a Church where the word of God appears not. The Lord furnished us with an unfailing test when he said, "Every one that is of the truth heareth my voice" (John 18:37). Again, "I am the good shepherd, and know my sheep, and am known of mine." "My sheep hear my voice, and I know them, and they follow me." A little before he had said, when the shepherd "putteth forth his own sheep, he goeth before them, and the sheep follow him; for they know his voice. And a stranger will they not follow, but will flee from him: for they know not the voice of strangers" (John 10:14, 4, 5). Why then do we, of our own accord, form so infatuated an estimate of the Church, since Christ has designated it by a sign in which is nothing in the least degree equivocal, a sign which is everywhere seen, the existence of which infallibly proves the existence of the Church, while its absence proves the absence of everything that properly bears the name of Church? Paul declares that the Church is not founded either upon the judgments of men or the priesthood, but upon the doctrine of the Apostles and Prophets (Eph. 2:20). Nay, Jerusalem is to be distinguished from Babylon, the Church of Christ from a conspiracy of Satan, by the discriminating test which our Saviour has applied to them, "He that is of God, heareth God's words: ye therefore hear them not, because ye are not of God" (John 8:47). In short, since the Church is the kingdom of Christ, and he reigns only by his word, can there be any doubt as to the falsehood of those statements by which the kingdom of Christ is represented without his sceptre, in other words, without his sacred word?

5. As to their charge of heresy and schism, because we preach a different doctrine, and submit not to their laws, and meet apart from them for Prayer, Baptism, the administration of the Supper, and other sacred rites, it is indeed a very serious accusation, but one which needs not a long and laboured defence. The name of heretics and schismatics is applied to those who, by dissenting from the Church, destroy its communion. This communion is held together by two chains—viz. consent in sound doctrine and brotherly charity. Hence the distinction which Augustine makes between heretics and schismatics is, that the former corrupt the purity of the faith by false dogmas, whereas the latter sometimes, even while holding the same faith, break the bond of union (August. Lib. Quæst. in Evang. Mt.). But the thing to be observed is, that this union of charity so depends on unity of faith, as to have in it its beginning, its end, in fine, its only rule. Let us therefore remember, that whenever ecclesiastical unity is commended to us, the thing required is, that while our minds consent in Christ, our wills also be united together by mutual good-will in Christ. Accordingly Paul, when he exhorts us to it, takes for his fundamental principle that there is "one God, one faith, one baptism" (Eph. 4:5). Nay, when he tells us to be "of one accord, of one mind," he immediately adds, "Let this mind be in you which was also in Christ Jesus" (Phil. 2:2, 5); intimating, that where the word of the Lord is not, it is not a union of believers, but a faction of the ungodly.

6. Cyprian, also, following Paul, derives the fountain of ecclesiastical concord from the one bishopric of Christ, and afterwards adds, "There is one Church, which by increase from fecundity is more widely extended to a multitude, just as there are many rays of the sun, but one light, and many branches of a tree, but one trunk upheld by the tenacious root. When many streams flow from one fountain, though there seems wide spreading numerosity from the overflowing copiousness of the supply, yet unity remains in the origin. Pluck a ray from the body of the sun, and the unity sustains no division. Break a branch from a tree, and the branch will not germinate. Cut off a stream from a fountain, that which is thus cut off dries up. So the Church, pervaded by the light of the Lord, extends over the whole globe, and yet the light which is everywhere diffused is one" (Cyprian, de Simplicit. Prælat.). Words could not more elegantly express the inseparable connection which all the members of

Christ have with each other. We see how he constantly calls us back to the head. Accordingly, he declares that when heresies and schisms arise, it is because men return not to the origin of the truth, because they seek not the head, because they keep not the doctrine of the heavenly Master. Let them now go and clamour against us as heretics for having withdrawn from their Church, since the only cause of our estrangement is, that they cannot tolerate a pure profession of the truth. I say nothing of their having expelled us by anathemas and curses. The fact is more than sufficient to excuse us, unless they would also make schismatics of the apostles, with whom we have a common cause. Christ, I say, forewarned his apostles, "they shall put you out of the synagogues" (John 16:2). The synagogues of which he speaks were then held to be lawful churches. Seeing then it is certain that we were cast out, and we are prepared to show that this was done for the name of Christ, the cause should first be ascertained before any decision is given either for or against us. This, however, if they choose, I am willing to leave to them; to me it is enough that we behoved to withdraw from them in order to draw near to Christ.

7. The place which we ought to assign to all the churches on which the tyranny of the Romish idol has seized will better appear if we compare them with the ancient Israelitish Church, as delineated by the prophets. So long as the Jews and Israelites persisted in the laws of the covenant, a true Church existed among them; in other words, they by the kindness of God obtained the benefits of a Church. True doctrine was contained in the law, and the ministry of it was committed to the prophets and priests. They were initiated in religion by the sign of circumcision, and by the other sacraments trained and confirmed in the faith. There can be no doubt that the titles with which the Lord honoured his Church were applicable to their society. After they forsook the law of the Lord, and degenerated into idolatry and superstition, they partly lost the privilege. For who can presume to deny the title of the Church to those with whom the Lord deposited the preaching of his word and the observance of his mysteries? On the other hand, who may presume to give the name of Church, without reservation, to that assembly by which the word of God is openly and with impunity trampled under foot—where his ministry, its chief support, and the very soul of the Church, is destroyed?

8. What then? (some one will say); was there not a particle of the Church left to the Jews from the date of their revolt to idolatry? The answer is easy. First, I say that in the defection itself there were several gradations; for we cannot hold that the lapses by which both Judah and Israel turned aside from the pure worship of God were the same. Jeroboam, when he fabricated the calves against the express prohibition of God, and dedicated an unlawful place for worship, corrupted religion entirely. The Jews became degenerate in manners and superstitious opinions before they made any improper change in the external form of religion. For although they had adopted many perverse ceremonies under Rehoboam, yet, as the doctrine of the law and the priesthood, and the rites which God had instituted, continued at Jerusalem, the pious still had the Church in a tolerable state. In regard to the Israelites, matters which, up to the time of Ahab, had certainly not been reformed, then became worse. Those who succeeded him, until the overthrow of the kingdom, were partly like him, and partly (when they wished to be somewhat better) followed the example of Jeroboam, while all, without exception, were wicked and idolatrous. In Judea different changes now and then took place, some kings corrupting the worship of God by false and superstitious inventions, and others attempting to reform it, until, at length, the priests themselves polluted the temple of God by profane and abominable rites.

9. Now then let the Papists, in order to extenuate their vices as much as possible, deny, if they can, that the state of religion is as much vitiated and corrupted with them as it was in the kingdom of Israel under Jeroboam. They have a grosser idolatry, and in doctrine are not one whit more pure; rather, perhaps, they are even still more impure. God, nay, even those possessed of a moderate degree of judgment, will bear me witness, and the thing itself is too manifest to require me to enlarge upon it. When they would force us to the communion of their Church, they make two demands upon us—first, that we join in their prayers, their sacrifices, and all their ceremonies; and, secondly, that whatever honour, power, and jurisdiction, Christ has given to his Church, the same we must attribute to theirs. In regard to the first, I admit that all the prophets who were at Jerusalem, when matters there were very corrupt, neither sacrificed apart nor held separate meetings for prayer. For they had the command of God, which enjoined them to meet in the temple of Solomon, and they knew that the Levitical priests, whom the Lord had appointed over sacred matters, and who were not yet discarded, how unworthy soever they might be of that honour, were still entitled to hold it (Exod. 24:9). But the principal point in the whole question is, that they were not compelled to any super-

stitious worship, nay, they undertook nothing but what had been instituted by God. But in these men, I mean the Papists, where is the resemblance? Scarcely can we hold any meeting with them without polluting ourselves with open idolatry. Their principal bond of communion is undoubtedly in the Mass, which we abominate as the greatest sacrilege. Whether this is justly or rashly done will be elsewhere seen (see chap. 18; see also Book 2, chap. 15, sec. 6). It is now sufficient to show that our case is different from that of the prophets, who, when they were present at the sacred rites of the ungodly, were not obliged to witness or use any ceremonies but those which were instituted by God. But if we would have an example in all respects similar, let us take one from the kingdom of Israel. Under the ordinance of Jeroboam, circumcision remained, sacrifices were offered, the law was deemed holy, and the God whom they had received from their fathers was worshipped; but in consequence of invented and forbidden modes of worship, everything which was done there God disapproved and condemned. Show me one prophet or pious man who once worshipped or offered sacrifice in Bethel. They knew that they could not do it without defiling themselves with some kind of sacrilege. We hold, therefore, that the communion of the Church ought not to be carried so far by the godly as to lay them under a necessity of following it when it has degenerated to profane and polluted rites.

10. With regard to the second point, our objections are still stronger. For when the Church is considered in that particular point of view as the Church, whose judgment we are bound to revere, whose authority acknowledge, whose admonitions obey, whose censures dread, whose communion religiously cultivate in every respect, we cannot concede that they have a Church, without obliging ourselves to subjection and obedience. Still we are willing to concede what the Prophets conceded to the Jews and Israelites of their day, when with them matters were in a similar, or even in a better condition. For we see how they uniformly exclaim against their meetings as profane conventicles, to which it is not more lawful for them to assent than to abjure God (Isa. 1:14). And certainly if those were churches, it follows, that Elijah, Micaiah, and others in Israel, Isaiah, Jeremiah, Hosea, and those of like character in Judah, whom the prophets, priests, and people of their day, hated and execrated more than the uncircumcised, were aliens from the Church of God. If those were churches, then the Church was no longer the pillar of the truth, but the stay of falsehood, not the tabernacle of the living God, but a receptacle of idols. They were, therefore, under the necessity of refusing consent to their meetings, since consent was nothing else than impious conspiracy against God. For this same reason, should any one acknowledge those meetings of the present day, which are contaminated by idolatry, superstition, and impious doctrine, as churches, full communion with which a Christian must maintain so far as to agree with them even in doctrine, he will greatly err. For if they are churches, the power of the keys belongs to them, whereas the keys are inseparably connected with the word which they have put to flight. Again, if they are churches, they can claim the promise of Christ, "Whatsoever ye bind," &c.; whereas, on the contrary, they discard from their communion all who sincerely profess themselves the servants of Christ. Therefore, either the promise of Christ is vain, or in this respect, at least, they are not churches. In fine, instead of the ministry of the word, they have schools of impiety, and sinks of all kinds of error. Therefore, in this point of view, they either are not churches, or no badge will remain by which the lawful meetings of the faithful can be distinguished from the meetings of Turks.

11. Still, as in ancient times, there remained among the Jews certain special privileges of a Church, so in the present day we deny not to the Papists those vestiges of a Church which the Lord has allowed to remain among them amid the dissipation. When the Lord had once made his covenant with the Jews, it was preserved not so much by them as by its own strength, supported by which it withstood their impiety. Such, then, is the certainty and constancy of the divine goodness, that the covenant of the Lord continued there and his faith could not be obliterated by their perfidy; nor could circumcision be so profaned by their impure hands as not still to be a true sign and sacrament of his covenant. Hence the children who were born to them the Lord called his own (Ezek. 16:20), though, unless by special blessing, they in no respect belonged to him. So having deposited his covenant in Gaul, Italy, Germany, Spain, and England, when these countries were oppressed by the tyranny of Antichrist, He, in order that his covenant might remain inviolable, first preserved baptism there as an evidence of the covenant;—baptism, which, consecrated by his lips, retains its power in spite of human depravity; secondly, He provided by his providence that there should be other remains also to prevent the Church from utterly perishing. But as in pulling down buildings the foundations and ruins are often permitted to remain, so he did not suffer Antichrist either to subvert his Church from its foundation, or to level it with the ground (though,

to punish the ingratitude of men who had despised his word, he allowed a fearful shaking and dismembering to take place), but was pleased that amid the devastation the edifice should remain, though half in ruins.

12. Therefore, while we are unwilling simply to concede the name of Church to the Papists, we do not deny that there are churches among them. The question we raise only relates to the true and legitimate constitution of the Church, implying communion in sacred rites, which are the signs of profession, and especially in doctrine. Daniel and Paul foretold that Antichrist would sit in the temple of God (Dan. 9:27; 2 Thess. 2:4); we regard the Roman Pontiff as the leader and standard-bearer of that wicked and abominable kingdom. By placing his seat in the temple of God, it is intimated that his kingdom would not be such as to destroy the name either of Christ or of his Church. Hence, then, it is obvious that we do not at all deny that churches remain under his tyranny; churches, however, which by sacrilegious impiety he has profaned, by cruel domination has oppressed, by evil and deadly doctrines like poisoned potions has corrupted and almost slain; churches where Christ lies half-buried, the gospel is suppressed, piety is put to flight, and the worship of God almost abolished; where, in short, all things are in such disorder as to present the appearance of Babylon rather than the holy city of God. In one word, I call them churches, inasmuch as the Lord there wondrously preserves some remains of his people, though miserably torn and scattered, and inasmuch as some symbols of the Church still remain—symbols especially whose efficacy neither the craft of the devil nor human depravity can destroy. But as, on the other hand, those marks to which we ought especially to have respect in this discussion are effaced, I say that the whole body, as well as every single assembly, want the form of a legitimate Church.

CHAPTER 3

OF THE TEACHERS AND MINISTERS OF THE CHURCH. THEIR ELECTION AND OFFICE.

The three heads of this chapter are,—I. A few preliminary remarks on Church order, on the end, utility, necessity, and dignity of the Christian ministry, sec. 1–3. II. A separate consideration of the persons performing Ecclesiastical functions, sec. 4–10. III. Of the Ordination or calling of the ministers of the Church, sec. 10–16.

Sections:

1. Summary of the chapter. Reasons why God, in governing the Church, uses the ministry of men. 1. To declare his condescension. 2. To train us to humility and obedience. 3. To bind us to each other in mutual charity. These reasons confirmed by Scripture.

2. This ministry of men most useful to the whole Church. Its advantages enumerated.

3. The honourable terms in which the ministry is spoken of. Its necessity established by numerous examples.

4. Second part of the chapter, treating of Ecclesiastical office-bearers in particular. Some of them, as Apostles, Prophets, and Evangelists, temporary. Others, as Pastors and Teachers, perpetual and indispensable.

5. Considering the office of Evangelist and Apostle as one, we have Pastors corresponding with Apostles, and Teachers with Prophets. Why the name of Apostles specially conferred on the twelve.

6. As to the Apostles so also to Pastors the preaching of the Word and the administration of the sacraments has been committed. How the Word should be preached.

7. Regularly every Pastor should have a separate church assigned to him. This, however, admits of modification, when duly and regularly made by public authority.

8. Bishops, Presbyters, Pastors, and Ministers, are used by the Apostles as one and the same. Some functions, as being temporary, are omitted. Two—namely, those of Elders and Deacons—as pertaining to the ministry of the Word, are retained.

9. Distinction between Deacons. Some employed in distributing alms, others in taking care of the poor.

10. Third part of the chapter, treating of the Ordination or calling of the ministers of the Church.

11. A twofold calling—viz. an external and an internal. Mode in which both are to be viewed.

12. 1. Who are to be appointed ministers? 2. Mode of appointment.

13. 3. By whom the appointment is to be made. Why the Apostles were elected by Christ alone. Of the calling and election of St Paul.

14. Ordinary Pastors are designated by other Pastors. Why certain of the Apostles also were designated by men.

15. The election of Pastors does not belong to one individual. Other Pastors should preside, and the people consent and approve.

16. Form in which the ministers of the Church are

to be ordained. No express precept but one. Laying on of hands.

1. We are now to speak of the order in which the Lord has been pleased that his Church should be governed. For though it is right that he alone should rule and reign in the Church, that he should preside and be conspicuous in it, and that its government should be exercised and administered solely by his word; yet as he does not dwell among us in visible presence, so as to declare his will to us by his own lips, he in this (as we have said) uses the ministry of men, by making them, as it were, his substitutes, not by transferring his right and honour to them, but only doing his own work by their lips, just as an artificer uses a tool for any purpose. What I have previously expounded (chap. 1 sec. 5) I am again forced to repeat. God might have acted, in this respect, by himself, without any aid or instrument, or might even have done it by angels; but there are several reasons why he rather chooses to employ men. First, in this way he declares his condescension towards us, employing men to perform the function of his ambassadors in the world, to be the interpreters of his secret will; in short, to represent his own person. Thus he shows by experience that it is not to no purpose he calls us his temples, since by man's mouth he gives responses to men as from a sanctuary. Secondly, it forms a most excellent and useful training to humility, when he accustoms us to obey his word though preached by men like ourselves, or, it may be, our inferiors in worth. Did he himself speak from heaven, it were no wonder if his sacred oracles were received by all ears and minds reverently and without delay. For who would not dread his present power? who would not fall prostrate at the first view of his great majesty? who would not be overpowered by that immeasurable splendour? But when a feeble man, sprung from the dust, speaks in the name of God, we give the best proof of our piety and obedience, by listening with docility to his servant, though not in any respect our superior. Accordingly, he hides the treasure of his heavenly wisdom in frail earthen vessels (2 Cor. 4:7), that he may have a more certain proof of the estimation in which it is held by us. Moreover, nothing was fitter to cherish mutual charity than to bind men together by this tie, appointing one of them as a pastor to teach the others who are enjoined to be disciples, and receive the common doctrine from a single mouth. For did every man suffice for himself, and stand in no need of another's aid (such is the pride of the human intellect), each would despise all others, and be in his turn despised. The Lord, therefore, has astricted his Church to what he foresaw would be the strongest bond of unity when he deposited the doctrine of eternal life and salvation with men, that by their hands he might communicate it to others. To this Paul had respect when he wrote to the Ephesians, "There is one body, and one Spirit, even as ye are called in one hope of your calling; one Lord, one faith, one baptism, one God and Father of all, who is above all, and through all, and in you all. But unto every one of us is given grace according to the measure of the gift of Christ. Wherefore he saith, When he ascended up on high, he led captivity captive, and gave gifts unto men. (Now that he ascended, what is it but that he also descended first into the lower parts of the earth? He that descended is the same also that ascended up far above all heavens, that he might fill all things.) And he gave some, apostles; and some, prophets; and some, evangelists; and some, pastors and teachers; for the perfecting of the saints, for the work of the ministry, for the edifying of the body of Christ: till we all come in the unity of the faith, and of the knowledge of the Son of God, unto a perfect man, unto the measure of the stature of the fulness of Christ: that we henceforth be no more children, tossed to and fro, and carried about with every wind of doctrine, by the sleight of men, and cunning craftiness, whereby they lie in wait to deceive; but speaking the truth in love, may grow up into him in all things, which is the head, even Christ: from whom the whole body fitly joined together and compacted by that which every joint supplieth, according to the effectual working in the measure of every part, maketh increase of the body unto the edifying of itself in love" (Eph 4:4–16).

2. By these words he shows that the ministry of men, which God employs in governing the Church, is a principal bond by which believers are kept together in one body. He also intimates, that the Church cannot be kept safe, unless supported by those guards to which the Lord has been pleased to commit its safety. Christ "ascended up far above all heavens, that he might fill all things" (Eph. 4:10). The mode of filling is this: By the ministers to whom he has committed this office, and given grace to discharge it, he dispenses and distributes his gifts to the Church, and thus exhibits himself as in a manner actually present by exerting the energy of his Spirit in this his institution, so as to prevent it from being vain or fruitless. In this way, the renewal of the saints is accomplished, and the body of Christ is edified; in this way we grow up in all things unto Him who is the Head, and unite with one another; in this way we are all brought into the unity of Christ, provided prophecy flourishes among us, pro-

vided we receive his apostles, and despise not the doctrine which is administered to us. Whoever, therefore, studies to abolish this order and kind of government of which we speak, or disparages it as of minor importance, plots the devastation, or rather the ruin and destruction, of the Church. For neither are the light and heat of the sun, nor meat and drink, so necessary to sustain and cherish the present life, as is the apostolical and pastoral office to preserve a Church in the earth.

3. Accordingly, I have observed above, that God has repeatedly commended its dignity by the titles which he has bestowed upon it, in order that we might hold it in the highest estimation, as among the most excellent of our blessings. He declares, that in raising up teachers, he confers a special benefit on men, when he bids his prophet exclaim, "How beautiful upon the mountains are the feet of him that bringeth good tidings, that publisheth peace" (Isa. 52:7); when he calls the apostles the light of the world and the salt of the earth (Mt. 5:13, 14). Nor could the office be more highly eulogised than when he said, "He that heareth you heareth me; and he that despiseth you despiseth me" (Luke 10:16). But the most striking passage of all is that in the Second Epistle to the Corinthians, where Paul treats as it were professedly of this question. He contends, that there is nothing in the Church more noble and glorious than the ministry of the Gospel, seeing it is the administration of the Spirit of righteousness and eternal life. These and similar passages should have the effect of preventing that method of governing and maintaining the Church by ministers, a method which the Lord has ratified for ever, from seeming worthless in our eyes, and at length becoming obsolete by contempt. How very necessary it is, he has declared not only by words but also by examples. When he was pleased to shed the light of his truth in greater effulgence on Cornelius, he sent an angel from heaven to despatch Peter to him (Acts 10:3). When he was pleased to call Paul to the knowledge of himself, and ingraft him into the Church, he does not address him with his own voice, but sends him to a man from whom he may both obtain the doctrine of salvation and the sanctification of baptism (Acts 9:6–20). If it was not by mere accident that the angel, who is the interpreter of God, abstains from declaring the will of God, and orders a man to be called to declare it; that Christ, the only Master of believers, commits Paul to the teaching of a man, that Paul whom he had determined to carry into the third heaven, and honour with a wondrous revelation of things that could not be spoken (2 Cor. 12:2), who will presume to despise or disregard as superfluous that ministry, whose utility God has been pleased to attest by such evidence?

4. Those who preside over the government of the Church, according to the institution of Christ, are named by Paul, first, *Apostles*; secondly, *Prophets*; thirdly, *Evangelists*; fourthly, *Pastors*; and, lastly, *Teachers* (Eph. 4:11). Of these, only the two last have an ordinary office in the Church. The Lord raised up the other three at the beginning of his kingdom, and still occasionally raises them up when the necessity of the times requires. The nature of the apostolic function is clear from the command, "Go ye into all the world, and preach the Gospel to every creature" (Mark 16:15). No fixed limits are given them, but the whole world is assigned to be reduced under the obedience of Christ, that by spreading the Gospel as widely as they could, they might everywhere erect his kingdom. Accordingly, Paul, when he would approve his apostleship, does not say that he had acquired some one city for Christ, but had propagated the Gospel far and wide—had not built on another man's foundation, but planted churches where the name of his Lord was unheard. The apostles, therefore, were sent forth to bring back the world from its revolt to the true obedience of God, and everywhere establish his kingdom by the preaching of the Gospel; or, if you choose, they were like the first architects of the Church, to lay its foundations throughout the world. By *Prophets*, he means not all interpreters of the divine will, but those who excelled by special revelation; none such now exist, or they are less manifest. By *Evangelists*, I mean those who, while inferior in rank to the apostles, were next them in office, and even acted as their substitutes. Such were Luke, Timothy, Titus, and the like; perhaps, also, the seventy disciples whom our Saviour appointed in the second place to the apostles (Luke 10:1). According to this interpretation, which appears to me consonant both to the words and the meaning of Paul, those three functions were not instituted in the Church to be perpetual, but only to endure so long as churches were to be formed where none previously existed, or at least where churches were to be transferred from Moses to Christ; although I deny not, that afterward God occasionally raised up Apostles, or at least Evangelists, in their stead, as has been done in our time. For such were needed to bring back the Church from the revolt of Antichrist. The office I nevertheless call extraordinary, because it has no place in churches duly constituted. Next come *Pastors* and *Teachers*, with whom the Church never can dispense, and between whom, I think, there is this difference, that teachers preside not over discipline, or the administration

of the sacraments, or admonitions, or exhortations, but the interpretation of Scripture only, in order that pure and sound doctrine may be maintained among believers. But all these are embraced in the pastoral office.

5. We now understand what offices in the government of the Church were temporary, and what offices were instituted to be of perpetual duration. But if we class evangelists with apostles, we shall have two like offices in a manner corresponding to each other. For the same resemblance which our teachers have to the ancient prophets pastors have to the apostles. The prophetical office was more excellent in respect of the special gift of revelation which accompanied it, but the office of teachers was almost of the same nature, and had altogether the same end. In like manner, the twelve, whom the Lord chose to publish the new preaching of the Gospel to the world (Luke 6:13), excelled others in rank and dignity. For although, from the nature of the case, and etymology of the word, all ecclesiastical officers may be properly called apostles, because they are all sent by the Lord and are his messengers, yet as it was of great importance that a sure attestation should be given to the mission of those who delivered a new and extraordinary message, it was right that the twelve (to the number of whom Paul was afterwards added) should be distinguished from others by a peculiar title. The same name, indeed, is given by Paul to Andronicus and Junia, who, he says, were "of note among the apostles" (Rom. 16:7); but when he would speak properly, he confines the term to that primary order. And this is the common use of Scripture. Still pastors (except that each has the government of a particular church assigned to him) have the same function as apostles. The nature of this function let us now see still more clearly.

6. When our Lord sent forth the apostles, he gave them a commission (as has been lately said) to preach the Gospel, and baptise those who believed for the remission of sins. He had previously commanded that they should distribute the sacred symbols of his body and blood after his example (Mt. 28:19; Luke 22:19). Such is the sacred, inviolable, and perpetual law, enjoined on those who succeed to the place of the apostles,—they receive a commission to preach the Gospel and administer the sacraments. Whence we infer that those who neglect both of these falsely pretend to the office of apostles. But what shall we say of pastors? Paul speaks not of himself only but of all pastors, when he says, "Let a man so account of us, as of the ministers of Christ, and stewards of the mysteries of God" (I Cor. 4:1). Again, in another passage, he describes a bishop as one "holding fast the faithful word as he hath been taught, that he may be able by sound doctrine both to exhort and convince the gainsayers" (Tit. 1:9). From these and similar passages which everywhere occur, we may infer that the two principal parts of the office of pastors are to preach the Gospel and administer the sacraments. But the method of teaching consists not merely in public addresses, it extends also to private admonitions. Thus Paul takes the Ephesians to witness, "I kept back nothing that was profitable to you, but have showed you, and have taught you publicly, and from house to house, testifying both to the Jews, and also to the Greeks, repentance toward God, and faith toward our Lord Jesus Christ." A little after he says, "Remember, that, for the space of three years, I ceased not to warn every one night and day with tears" (Acts 20:20, 31). Our present purpose, however, is not to enumerate the separate qualities of a good pastor, but only to indicate what those profess who call themselves pastors—viz. that in presiding over the Church they have not an indolent dignity, but must train the people to true piety by the doctrine of Christ, administer the sacred mysteries, preserve and exercise right discipline. To those who are set as watchmen in the Church the Lord declares, "When I say unto the wicked, Thou shalt surely die; and thou givest him not warning, nor speakest to warn the wicked from his wicked way, to save his life; the same wicked man shall die in his iniquity; but his blood will I require at thine hand" (Ezek. 3:18). What Paul says of himself is applicable to all pastors: "For though I preach the Gospel, I have nothing to glory of: for necessity is laid upon me; yea, woe is unto me if I preach not the Gospel" (1 Cor. 4:16). In short, what the apostles did to the whole world, every pastor should do to the flock over which he is appointed.

7. While we assign a church to each pastor, we deny not that he who is fixed to one church may assist other churches, whether any disturbance has occurred which requires his presence, or his advice is asked on some doubtful matter. But because that policy is necessary to maintain the peace of the Church, each has his proper duty assigned, lest all should become disorderly, run up and down without any certain vocation, flock together promiscuously to one spot, and capriciously leave the churches vacant, being more solicitous for their own convenience than for the edification of the Church. This arrangement ought, as far as possible, to be commonly observed, that every one, content with his own limits, may not encroach on another's province. Nor is this a human invention. It is an ordinance of God. For we read

that Paul and Barnabas appointed presbyters over each of the churches of Lystra, Antioch, and Iconium (Acts 14:23); and Paul himself enjoins Titus to ordain presbyters in every town (Tit. 1:5). In like manner, he mentions the bishops of the Philippians, and Archippus, the bishop of the Colossians (Phil. 1:1; Col. 4:17). And in the Acts we have his celebrated address to the presbyters of the Church of Ephesus (Acts 20:28). Let every one, then, who undertakes the government and care of one church, know that he is bound by this law of divine vocation, not that he is astricted to the soil (as lawyers speak), that is, enslaved, and, as it were, fixed, as to be unable to move a foot if public utility so require, and the thing is done duly and in order; but he who has been called to one place ought not to think of removing, nor seek to be set free when he deems it for his own advantage. Again, if it is expedient for any one to be transferred to another place, he ought not to attempt it of his own private motive, but to wait for public authority.

8. In giving the name of bishops, presbyters, and pastors, indiscriminately to those who govern churches, I have done it on the authority of Scripture, which uses the words as synonymous. To all who discharge the ministry of the word it gives the name of bishops. Thus Paul, after enjoining Titus to ordain elders in every city, immediately adds, "A bishop must be blameless," &c. (Tit. 1:5, 7). So in another place he salutes several bishops in one church (Phil. 1:1). And in the Acts, the elders of Ephesus, whom he is said to have called together, he, in the course of his address, designates as bishops (Acts 20:17). Here it is to be observed, that we have hitherto enumerated those offices only which consist in the ministry of the word; nor does Paul make mention of any others in the passage which we have quoted from the fourth chapter of the Epistle to the Ephesians. But in the Epistle to the Romans, and the First Epistle to the Corinthians, he enumerates other offices, as powers, gifts of healing, interpretation, government, care of the poor (Rom. 12:7; 1 Cor. 12:28). As to those which were temporary, I say nothing, for it is not worth while to dwell upon them. But there are two of perpetual duration—viz. government and care of the poor. By these governors I understand seniors selected from the people to unite with the bishops in pronouncing censures and exercising discipline. For this is the only meaning which can be given to the passage, "He that ruleth with diligence" (Rom. 12:8). From the beginning, therefore, each church had its senate, composed of pious, grave, and venerable men, in whom was lodged the power of correcting faults. Of this power we shall afterwards speak. Moreover, experience shows that this arrangement was not confined to one age, and therefore we are to regard the office of government as necessary for all ages.

9. The care of the poor was committed to deacons, of whom two classes are mentioned by Paul in the Epistle to the Romans, "He that giveth, let him do it with simplicity;" "he that showeth mercy, with cheerfulness" (Rom. 12:8). As it is certain that he is here speaking of public offices of the Church, there must have been two distinct classes. If I mistake not, he in the former clause designates deacons, who administered alms; in the latter, those who had devoted themselves to the care of the poor and the sick. Such were the widows of whom he makes mention in the Epistle to Timothy (1 Tim. 5:10). For there was no public office which women could discharge save that of devoting themselves to the service of the poor. If we admit this (and it certainly ought to be admitted), there will be two classes of deacons, the one serving the Church by administering the affairs of the poor; the other, by taking care of the poor themselves. For although the term διακονία has a more extensive meaning, Scripture specially gives the name of deacons to those whom the Church appoints to dispense alms, and take care of the poor, constituting them as it were stewards of the public treasury of the poor. Their origin, institution, and office, is described by Luke (Acts 6:3). When a murmuring arose among the Greeks, because in the administration of the poor their widows were neglected, the apostles, excusing themselves that they were unable to discharge both offices, to preach the word and serve tables, requested the multitude to elect seven men of good report, to whom the office might be committed. Such deacons as the Apostolic Church had, it becomes us to have after her example.

10. Now seeing that in the sacred assembly all things ought to be done decently and in order (1 Cor. 14:40), there is nothing in which this ought to be more carefully observed than in settling government, irregularity in any respect being nowhere more perilous. Wherefore, lest restless and turbulent men should presumptuously push themselves forward to teach or rule (an event which actually was to happen), it was expressly provided that no one should assume a public office in the Church without a call (Heb. 5:4; Jer. 17:16). Therefore, if any one would be deemed a true minister of the Church, he must *first* be duly called; and, *secondly*, he must answer to his calling; that is, undertake and execute the office assigned to him. This may often be observed in Paul, who, when

he would approve his apostleship, almost always alleges a call, together with his fidelity in discharging the office. If so great a minister of Christ dares not arrogate to himself authority to be heard in the Church, unless as having been appointed to it by the command of his Lord, and faithfully performing what has been intrusted to him, how great the effrontery for any man, devoid of one or both of them, to demand for himself such honour. But as we have already touched on the necessity of executing the office, let us now treat only of the call.

11. The subject is comprehended under four heads—viz. *who* are to be appointed ministers, *in what way, by whom*, and *with what rite or initiatory ceremony*. I am speaking of the external and formal call which relates to the public order of the Church, while I say nothing of that secret call of which every minister is conscious before God, but has not the Church as a witness of it; I mean, the good testimony of our heart, that we undertake the offered office neither from ambition nor avarice, nor any other selfish feeling, but a sincere fear of God and desire to edify the Church. This, as I have said, is indeed necessary for every one of us, if we would approve our ministry to God. Still, however, a man may have been duly called by the Church, though he may have accepted with a bad conscience, provided his wickedness is not manifest. It is usual also to say, that private men are called to the ministry when they seem fit and apt to discharge it; that is, because learning, conjoined with piety and the other endowments of a good pastor, is a kind of preparation for the office. For those whom the Lord has destined for this great office he previously provides with the armour which is requisite for the discharge of it, that they may not come empty and unprepared. Hence Paul, in the First Epistle to the Corinthians, when treating of the offices, first enumerates the gifts in which those who performed the offices ought to excel. But as this is the first of the four heads which I mentioned, let us now proceed to it.

12. What persons should be elected bishops is treated at length by Paul in two passages (Tit. 1:7; 1 Tim. 3:1). The substance is, that none are to be chosen save those who are of sound doctrine and holy lives, and not notorious for any defect which might destroy their authority and bring disgrace on the ministry. The description of deacons and elders is entirely similar (see chapter 4 sec. 10–13). We must always take care that they are not unfit for or unequal to the burden imposed upon them; in other words, that they are provided with the means which will be necessary to fulfil their office. Thus our Saviour, when about to send his apostles, provided them with the arms and instruments which were indispensably requisite. And Paul, after portraying the character of a good and genuine bishop, admonishes Timothy not to contaminate himself by choosing an improper person for the office. The expression, *in what way*, I use not in reference to the rite of choosing, but only to the religious fear which is to be observed in election. Hence the fastings and prayers which Luke narrates that the faithful employed when they elected presbyters (Acts 14:23). For, understanding that the business was the most serious in which they could engage, they did not venture to act without the greatest reverence and solicitude. But above all, they were earnest in prayer, imploring from God the spirit of wisdom and discernment.

13. The third division which we have adopted is, *by whom* ministers are to be chosen. A certain rule on this head cannot be obtained from the appointment of the apostles, which was somewhat different from the common call of others. As theirs was an extraordinary ministry, in order to render it conspicuous by some more distinguished mark, those who were to discharge it behoved to be called and appointed by the mouth of the Lord himself. It was not, therefore, by any human election, but at the sole command of God and Christ, that they prepared themselves for the work. Hence, when the apostles were desirous to substitute another in the place of Judas, they did not venture to nominate any one certainly, but brought forward two, that the Lord might declare by lot which of them he wished to succeed (Acts 1:23). In this way we ought to understand Paul's declaration, that he was made an apostle, "not of men, neither by man, but by Jesus Christ, and God the Father" (Gal. 1:1). The former—viz. *not of men*—he had in common with all the pious ministers of the word, for no one could duly perform the office unless called by God. The other was proper and peculiar to him. And while he glories in it, he boasts that he had not only what pertains to a true and lawful pastor, but he also brings forward the insignia of his apostleship. For when there were some among the Galatians who, seeking to disparage his authority, represented him as some ordinary disciple, substituted in place of the primary apostles, he, in order to maintain unimpaired the dignity of his ministry, against which he knew that these attempts were made, felt it necessary to show that he was in no respect inferior to the other apostles. Accordingly, he affirms that he was not chosen by the judgment of men, like some ordinary bishop, but by the mouth and manifest oracle of the Lord himself.

14. But no sober person will deny that the regular mode

of lawful calling is, that bishops should be designated by men, since there are numerous passages of Scripture to this effect. Nor, as has been said, is there anything contrary to this in Paul's protestation, that he was not sent either of man, or by man, seeing he is not there speaking of the ordinary election of ministers, but claiming for himself what was peculiar to the apostles: although the Lord in thus selecting Paul by special privilege, subjected him in the meantime to the discipline of an ecclesiastical call: for Luke relates, "As they ministered to the Lord, and fasted, the Holy Ghost said, Separate me Barnabas and Saul for the work whereunto I have called them" (Acts 13:2). Why this separation and laying on of hands after the Holy Spirit had attested their election, unless that ecclesiastical discipline might be preserved in appointing ministers by men? God could not give a more illustrious proof of his approbation of this order, than by causing Paul to be set apart by the Church after he had previously declared that he had appointed him to be the Apostle of the Gentiles. The same thing we may see in the election of Matthias. As the apostolic office was of such importance that they did not venture to appoint any one to it of their own judgment, they bring forward two, on one of whom the lot might fall, that thus the election might have a sure testimony from heaven, and, at the same time, the policy of the Church might not be disregarded.

15. The next question is, Whether a minister should be chosen *by the whole Church*, or only by *colleagues* and *elders*, who have the charge of discipline; or whether they may be appointed by the authority of one individual? Those who attribute this right to one individual quote the words of Paul to Titus "For this cause left I thee in Crete, that thou shouldest set in order the things that are wanting, and ordain elders in every city" (Tit. 1:5); and also to Timothy, "Lay hands suddenly on no man" (1 Tim. 5:22). But they are mistaken if they suppose that Timothy so reigned at Ephesus, and Titus in Crete, as to dispose of all things at their own pleasure. They only presided by previously giving good and salutary counsels to the people, not by doing alone whatever pleased them, while all others were excluded. Lest this should seem to be a fiction of mine, I will make it plain by a similar example. Luke relates that Barnabas and Paul ordained elders throughout the churches, but he at the same time marks the plan or mode when he says that it was done by suffrage. The words are, Χειροτονήσαντες πρεσβυτέρους κατ᾽ ἐκκλησίαν (Acts 14:23). They therefore selected (*creabant*) two; but the whole body, as was the custom of the Greeks in elections, declared by a show of hands which of the two they wished to have. Thus it is not uncommon for Roman historians to say, that the consul who held the comitia elected the new magistrates, for no other reason but because he received the suffrages, and presided over the people at the election. Certainly it is not credible that Paul conceded more to Timothy and Titus than he assumed to himself. Now we see that his custom was to appoint bishops by the suffrages of the people. We must therefore interpret the above passages, so as not to infringe on the common right and liberty of the Church. Rightly, therefore, does Cyprian contend for it as of divine authority, that the priest be chosen in presence of the people, before the eyes of all, and be approved as worthy and fit by public judgment and testimony, (Cyprian, Lib. 1 Ep. 3). Indeed, we see that by the command of the Lord, the practice in electing the Levitical priests was to bring them forward in view of the people before consecration. Nor is Matthias enrolled among the number of the apostles, nor are the seven deacons elected in any other way, than at the sight and approval of the people (Acts 6:2). "Those examples," says Cyprian, "show that the ordination of a priest behoved not to take place, unless under the consciousness of the people assisting, so that ordination was just and legitimate which was vouched by the testimony of all." We see, then, that ministers are legitimately called according to the word of God, when those who may have seemed fit are elected on the consent and approbation of the people. Other pastors, however, ought to preside over the election, lest any error should be committed by the general body either through levity, or bad passion, or tumult.

16. It remains to consider the form of ordination, to which we have assigned the last place in the call (see chap. 4, sec. 14, 15). It is certain, that when the apostles appointed any one to the ministry, they used no other ceremony than the laying on of hands. This form was derived, I think, from the custom of the Jews, who, by the laying on of hands, in a manner presented to God whatever they wished to be blessed and consecrated. Thus Jacob, when about to bless Ephraim and Manasseh, placed his hands upon their heads (Gen. 48:14). The same thing was done by our Lord, when he prayed over the little children (Mt. 19:15). With the same intent (as I imagine), the Jews, according to the injunction of the law, laid hands upon their sacrifices. Wherefore, the apostles, by the laying on of hands, intimated that they made an offering to God of him whom they admitted to the ministry; though they also did the same thing over those on whom they conferred the visible gifts of the Spirit (Acts

8:17; 19:6). However this be, it was the regular form, whenever they called any one to the sacred ministry. In this way they consecrated pastors and teachers; in this way they consecrated deacons. But though there is no fixed precept concerning the laying on of hands, yet as we see that it was uniformly observed by the apostles, this careful observance ought to be regarded by us in the light of a precept (see chap. 14, sec. 20; chap. 19, sec. 31). And it is certainly useful, that by such a symbol the dignity of the ministry should be commended to the people, and he who is ordained, reminded that he is no longer his own, but is bound in service to God and the Church. Besides, it will not prove an empty sign, if it be restored to its genuine origin. For if the Spirit of God has not instituted anything in the Church in vain, this ceremony of his appointment we shall feel not to be useless, provided it be not superstitiously abused. Lastly, it is to observed, that it was not the whole people, but only pastors, who laid hands on ministers, though it is uncertain whether or not several always laid their hands: it is certain, that in the case of the deacons, it was done by Paul and Barnabas, and some few others (Acts 6:6; 13:3). But in another place, Paul mentions that he himself, without any others, laid hands on Timothy. "Wherefore, I put thee in remembrance, that thou stir up the gift of God which is in thee, by the putting on of my hands" (2 Tim. 1:6). For what is said in the First Epistle, of the *laying on of the hands of the presbytery*, I do not understand as if Paul were speaking of the college of Elders. By the expression, I understand the ordination itself; as if he had said, Act so, that the gift which you received by the laying on of hands, when I made you a presbyter, may not be in vain.

CHAPTER 4

OF THE STATE OF THE
PRIMITIVE CHURCH, AND THE MODE
OF GOVERNMENT IN USE
BEFORE THE PAPACY.

The divisions of this chapter are,—I. The mode of government in the primitive Church, sec 1–10. II. The formal ordination of Bishops and Ministers in the primitive Church, sec. 10–15.

Sections:

1. The method of government in the primitive Church. Not in every respect conformable to the rule of the word of God. Three distinct orders of Ministers.

2. First, the Bishop, for the sake of preserving order, presided over the Presbyters or Pastors. The office of Bishop. Presbyter and Bishop the same. The institution of this order ancient.

3. The office of Bishop and Presbyters. Strictly preserved in the primitive Church.

4. Of Archbishops and Patriarchs. Very seldom used. For what end instituted. Hierarchy an improper name, and not used in Scripture.

5. Deacons, the second order of Ministers in the primitive Church. Their proper office. The Bishop their inspector. Subdeacons, their assistants. Archdeacons, their presidents. The reading of the Gospel, an adventitious office conferred in honour on the Deacons.

6. Mode in which the goods of the Church were anciently dispensed. 1. The support of the poor. 2. Due provision for the ministers of the Church.

7. The administration at first free and voluntary. The revenues of the Church afterwards classed under four heads.

8. A third part of the revenues devoted to the fabric of churches. To this, however, when necessary, the claim of the poor was preferred. Sayings, testimonies, and examples to this effect, from Cyril, Acatius, Jerome, Exuperius, Ambrose.

9. The Clerici, among whom were the Doorkeepers and Acolytes, were the names given to exercises used as a kind of training for tyros.

10. Second part of the chapter, treating of the calling of Ministers. Some error introduced in course of time in respect to celibacy from excessive strictness. In regard to the ordination of Ministers, full regard not always paid to the consent of the people. Why the people less anxious to maintain their right. Ordinations took place at stated times.

11. In the ordination of Bishops the liberty of the people maintained.

12. Certain limits afterwards introduced to restrain the inconsiderate licence of the multitude.

13. This mode of election long prevailed. Testimony of Gregory. Nothing repugnant to this in the decretals of Gratian.

14. The form of ordination in the ancient Church.

15. This form gradually changed.

1. Hitherto we have discoursed of the order of church government as delivered to us in the pure word of God, and of ministerial offices as instituted by Christ (chap. 1 sec. 5, 6; chap. 3). Now that the whole subject may

be more clearly and familiarly explained, and also better fixed in our minds, it will be useful to attend to the form of the early church, as this will give us a kind of visible representation of the divine institution. For although the bishops of those times published many canons, in which they seemed to express more than is expressed by the sacred volume, yet they were so cautious in framing all their economy on the word of God, the only standard, that it is easy to see that they scarcely in any respect departed from it. Even if something may be wanting in these enactments, still, as they were sincerely desirous to preserve the divine institution, and have not strayed far from it, it will be of great benefit here briefly to explain what their observance was. As we have stated that three classes of ministers are set before us in Scripture, so the early Church distributed all its ministers into three orders. For from the order of presbyters, part were selected as pastors and teachers, while to the remainder was committed the censure of manners and discipline. To the deacons belonged the care of the poor and the dispensing of alms. Readers and Acolytes were not the names of certain offices; but those whom they called clergy, they accustomed from their youth to serve the Church by certain exercises, that they might the better understand for what they were destined, and afterwards come better prepared for their duty, as I will shortly show at greater length. Accordingly, Jerome, in setting forth five orders in the Church, enumerates Bishops, Presbyters, Deacons, Believers, Catechumens: to the other Clergy and Monks he gives no proper place (Hieron. in Jes. c. 9).

2. All, therefore, to whom the office of teaching was committed, they called presbyters, and in each city these presbyters selected one of their number to whom they gave the special title of bishop, lest, as usually happens, from equality dissension should arise. The bishop, however, was not so superior in honour and dignity as to have dominion over his colleagues, but as it belongs to a president in an assembly to bring matters before them, collect their opinions, take precedence of others in consulting, advising, exhorting, guide the whole procedure by his authority, and execute what is decreed by common consent, a bishop held the same office in a meeting of presbyters. And the ancients themselves confess that this practice was introduced by human arrangement, according to the exigency of the times. Thus Jerome, on the Epistle to Titus, cap. 1, says, "A bishop is the same as a presbyter. And before dissensions were introduced into religion by the instigation of the devil, and it was said among the people, I am of Paul, and I of Cephas, churches were governed by a common council of presbyters. Afterwards, that the seeds of dissension might be plucked up, the whole charge was devolved upon mendatory rescripts, preventions, and the like. But they all conduct one. Therefore, as presbyters know that by the custom of the Church they are subject to him who presides, so let bishops know that they are greater than presbyters more by custom than in consequence of our Lord's appointment, and ought to rule the Church for the common good." In another place he shows how ancient the custom was (Hieron. Epist. ad Evang.). For he says that at Alexandria, from Mark the Evangelist, as far down as Heraclas and Dionysius, presbyters always placed one, selected from themselves, in a higher rank, and gave him the name of bishop. Each city, therefore, had a college of presbyters, consisting of pastors and teachers. For they all performed to the people that office of teaching, exhorting, and correcting, which Paul enjoins on bishops (Tit. 1:9); and that they might leave a seed behind them, they made it their business to train the younger men who had devoted themselves to the sacred warfare. To each city was assigned a certain district which took presbyters from it, and was considered as it were incorporated into that church. Each presbyter, as I have said, merely to preserve order and peace, was under one bishop, who, though he excelled others in dignity, was subject to the meeting of the brethren. But if the district which was under his bishopric was too large for him to be able to discharge all the duties of bishop, presbyters were distributed over it in certain places to act as his substitutes in minor matters. These were called *Chorepiscopi* (rural bishops), because they represented the bishops throughout the province.

3. But, in regard to the office of which we now treat, the bishop as well as the presbyters behoved to employ themselves in the administration of word and sacraments. For, at Alexandria only (as Arius had there troubled the Church), it was enacted, that no presbyter should deliver an address to the people, as Socrates says, Tripartit. Hist. Lib. 9. Jerome does not conceal his dissatisfaction with the enactment (Hieron. Epist. ad Evagr.). It certainly would have been deemed monstrous for one to give himself out as a bishop, and yet not show himself a true bishop by his conduct. Such, then, was the strictness of those times, that all ministers were obliged to fulfil the office as the Lord requires of them. Nor do I refer to the practice of one age only, since not even in the time of Gregory, when the Church had almost fallen (certainly had greatly degenerated from ancient purity), would any bishop have been tolerated who abstained from preach-

ing. In some part of his twenty-fourth Epistle he says, "The priest dies when no sound is heard from him: for he calls forth the wrath of the unseen Judge against him if he walks without the sound of preaching." Elsewhere he says, "When Paul testifies that he is pure from the blood of all men (Acts 20:26), by his words, we, who are called priests, are charged, are arraigned, are shown to be guilty, since to those sins which we have of our own we add the deaths of other men, for we commit murder as often as lukewarm and silent we see them daily going to destruction" (Gregor. Hom. in Ezek. 11:26). He calls himself and others silent when less assiduous in their work than they ought to be. Since he does not spare even those who did their duty partially, what think you would he do in the case of those who entirely neglected it? For a long time, therefore, it was regarded in the Church as the first duty of a bishop to feed the people by the word of God, or to edify the Church, in public and private, with sound doctrine.

4. As to the fact, that each province had an archbishop among the bishops (see chap. 7 sec. 15), and, moreover, that, in the Council of Nice, patriarchs were appointed to be superior to archbishops, in order and dignity, this was designed for the preservation of discipline, although, in treating of the subject here, it ought not to be omitted, that the practice was very rare. The chief reason for which these orders were instituted was, that if anything occurred in any church which could not well be explicated by a few, it might be referred to a provincial synod. If the magnitude or difficulty of the case demanded a larger discussion, patriarchs were employed along with synods, and from them there was no appeal except to a General Council. To the government thus constituted some gave the name of Hierarchy—a name, in my opinion, improper, certainly one not used by Scripture. For the Holy Spirit designed to provide that no one should dream of primacy or domination in regard to the government of the Church. But if, disregarding the term, we look to the thing, we shall find that the ancient bishops had no wish to frame a form of church government different from that which God has prescribed in his word.

5. Nor was the case of deacons then different from what it had been under the apostles (chap. 3 sec. 6). For they received the daily offerings of the faithful, and the annual revenues of the Church, that they might apply them to their true uses; in other words, partly in maintaining ministers, and partly in supporting the poor; at the sight of the bishop, however, to whom they every year gave an account of their stewardship. For, although the canons uniformly make the bishop the dispenser of all the goods of the Church, this is not to be understood as if he by himself undertook that charge, but because it belonged to him to prescribe to the deacon who were to be admitted to the public alimony of the Church, and point out to what persons, and in what portions, the residue was to be distributed, and because he was entitled to see whether the deacon faithfully performed his office. Thus, in the canons which they ascribe to the apostles, it is said, "We command that the bishop have the affairs of the Church under his control. For if the souls of men, which are more precious, have been intrusted to him, much more is he entitled to have the charge of money matters, so that under his control all may be dispensed to the poor by the presbyters and deacons, that the ministration may be made reverently and with due care." And in the Council of Antioch, it was decreed (cap. 35), that bishops, who inter-meddled with the effects of the Church, without the knowledge of the presbyters and deacons, should be restrained. But there is no occasion to discuss this point farther, since it is evident, from many of the letters of Gregory, that even at that time, when the ecclesiastical ordinances were otherwise much vitiated, it was still the practice for the deacons to be, under the bishops, the stewards of the poor. It is probable that at the first subdeacons were attached to the deacons, to assist them in the management of the poor; but the distinction was gradually lost. Archdeacons began to be appointed when the extent of the revenues demanded a new and more exact method of administration, though Jerome mentions that it already existed in his day. To them belonged the amount of revenues, possessions, and furniture, and the charge of the daily offerings. Hence Gregory declares to the Archdeacon Solitanus, that the blame rested with him, if any of the goods of the Church perished through his fraud or negligence. The reading of the word to the people, and exhortation to prayer, was assigned to them, and they were permitted, moreover, to give the cup in the sacred Supper; but this was done for the purpose of honouring their office, that they might perform it with greater reverence, when they were reminded by such symbols that what they discharged was not some profane stewardship, but a spiritual function dedicated to God.

6. Hence, also, we may judge what was the use, and of what nature was the distribution of ecclesiastical goods. You may everywhere find, both from the decrees of synods, and from ancient writers, that whatever the Church possessed, either in lands or in money, was the patrimony of the poor. Accordingly, the saying is ever and anon

sounded in the ears of bishops and deacons, Remember that you are not handling your own property, but that destined for the necessities of the poor; if you dishonestly conceal or dilapidate it, you will be guilty of blood. Hence they are admonished to distribute them to those to whom they are due, with the greatest fear and reverence, as in the sight of God, without respect of persons. Hence, also, in Chrysostom, Ambrose, Augustine, and other like bishops, those grave obtestations in which they assert their integrity before the people. But since it is just in itself, and was sanctioned by a divine law, that those who devote their labour to the Church shall be supported at the public expense of the Church, and some presbyters in that age having consecrated their patrimony to God, had become voluntarily poor, the distribution was so made that aliment was afforded to ministers, and the poor were not neglected. Meanwhile, it was provided that the ministers themselves, who ought to be an example of frugality to others, should not have so much as might be abused for luxury or delicacy; but only what might be needful to support their wants: "For those clergy, who can be supported by their own patrimony," says Jerome, "commit sacrilege if they accept what belongs to the poor, and by such abuse eat and drink judgment to themselves."

7. At first the administration was free and voluntary, when bishops and deacons were faithful of their own accord, and when integrity of conscience and purity of life supplied the place of laws. Afterwards, when, from the cupidity and depraved desires of some, bad examples arose, canons were framed, to correct these evils, and divided the revenues of the Church into four parts, assigning one to the clergy, another to the poor, another to the repair of churches and other edifices, a fourth to the poor, whether strangers or natives. For though other canons attribute this last part to the bishop, it differs in no respect from the division which I have mentioned. For they do not mean that it is his property, which he may devour alone or squander in any way he pleases, but that it may enable him to use the hospitality which Paul requires in that order (1 Tim. 3:2). This is the interpretation of Gelasius and Gregory. For the only reason which Gelasius gives why the bishop should claim anything to himself is, that he may be able to bestow it on captives and strangers. Gregory speaks still more clearly: "It is the custom of the Apostolic See," says he, "to give command to the bishop who has been ordained, to divide all the revenues into four portions—namely, one to the bishop and his household for hospitality and maintenance, another to the clergy, a third to the poor, a fourth to the repair of churches." The bishop, therefore, could not lawfully take for his own use more than was sufficient for moderate and frugal food and clothing. When any one began to wanton either in luxury or ostentation and show, he was immediately reprimanded by his colleagues, and if he obeyed not, was deprived of his honours.

8. Moreover, the sum expended on the adorning of churches was at first very trifling, and even afterwards, when the Church had become somewhat more wealthy, they in that matter observed mediocrity. Still, whatever money was then collected was reserved for the poor, when any greater necessity occurred. Thus Cyril, when a famine prevailed in the province of Jerusalem, and the want could not otherwise be supplied, took the vessels and robes and sold them for the support of the poor. In like manner, Acatius, Bishop of Amida, when a great multitude of the Persians were almost destroyed by famine, having assembled the clergy, and delivered this noble address, "Our God has no need either of chalices or salvers, for he neither eats nor drinks" (Tripart. Hist. Lib. 5 and Lib. 11 c. 16) melted down the plate, that he might be able to furnish food and obtain the means of ransoming the miserable. Jerome also, while inveighing against the excessive splendour of churches, relates that Exuperius, Bishop of Tholouse, in his day, though he carried the body of the Lord in a wicker basket, and his blood in a glass, nevertheless suffered no poor man to be hungry (Hieron. ad Nepotian). What I lately said of Acatius, Ambrose relates of himself. For when the Arians assailed him for having broken down the sacred vessels for the ransom of captives, he made this most admirable excuse: "He who sent the apostles without gold has also gathered churches without gold. The Church has gold not to keep but to distribute, and give support in necessity. What need is there of keeping what is of no benefit? Are we ignorant how much gold and silver the Assyrians carried off from the temple of the Lord? Is it not better for a priest to melt them for the support of the poor, if other means are wanting, than for a sacrilegious enemy to carry them away? Would not the Lord say, Why have you suffered so many poor to die of hunger, and you certainly had gold wherewith to minister to their support? Why have so many captives been carried away and not redeemed? Why have so many been slain by the enemy? It had been better to preserve living than metallic vessels. These charges you will not be able to answer: for what could you say? I feared lest the temple of God should want ornament. He would answer, Sacraments require not gold, and things which are not bought with gold please not by gold. The

ornament of the Sacraments is the ransom of captives" (Ambros. de Offic. Lib. 2 c. 28). In a word, we see the exact truth of what he elsewhere says—viz. that whatever the Church then possessed was the revenue of the needy. Again, A bishop has nothing but what belongs to the poor (Ambros. Lib. 5 Ep. 31, 33).

9. We have now reviewed the ministerial offices of the ancient Church. For others, of which ecclesiastical writers make mention, were rather exercises and preparations than distinct offices. These holy men, that they might leave a nursery of the Church behind them, received young men, who, with the consent and authority of their parents, devoted themselves to the spiritual warfare under their guardianship and training, and so formed them from their tender years, that they might not enter on the discharge of the office as ignorant novices. All who received this training were designated by the general name of *Clerks*. I could wish that some more appropriate name had been given them, for this appellation had its origin in error, or at least improper feeling, since the whole church is by Peter denominated κληρος (*clerus*), that is, the inheritance of the Lord (1 Pet. 5:3). It was in itself, however, a most sacred and salutary institution, that those who wished to devote themselves and their labour to the Church should be brought up under the charge of the bishop; so that no one should minister in the Church unless he had been previously well trained, unless he had in early life imbibed sound doctrine, unless by stricter discipline he had formed habits of gravity and severer morals, been withdrawn from ordinary business, and accustomed to spiritual cares and studies. For as tyros in the military art are trained by mock fights for true and serious warfare, so there was a rudimental training by which they were exercised in clerical duty before they were actually appointed to office. First, then, they intrusted them with the opening and shutting of the church, and called them Ostiarii. Next, they gave the name of Acolytes to those who assisted the bishop in domestic services, and constantly attended him, first, as a mark of respect; and, secondly, that no suspicion might arise. Moreover, that they might gradually become known to the people, and recommend themselves to them, and at the same time might learn to stand the gaze of all, and speak before all, that they might not, when appointed presbyters, be overcome with shame when they came forward to teach, the office of reading in the desk was given them. In this way they were gradually advanced, that they might prove their carefulness in separate exercises, until they were appointed subdeacons. All I mean by this is, that these were rather the rudimentary exercises of tyros than functions which were accounted among the true ministries of the Church.

10. In regard to what we have set down as the first and second heads in the calling of ministers—viz. the persons to be elected and the religious care to be therein exercised—the ancient Church followed the injunction of Paul, and the examples of the apostles. For they were accustomed to meet for the election of pastors with the greatest reverence, and with earnest prayer to God. Moreover, they had a form of examination by which they tested the life and doctrine of those who were to be elected by the standard of Paul (1 Tim. 3:2); only here they sometimes erred from excessive strictness, by exacting more of a bishop than Paul requires, and especially, in process of time, by exacting celibacy: but in other respects their practice corresponded with Paul's description. In regard to our third head, however—viz. Who were entitled to appoint ministers?—they did not always observe the same rule. Anciently none were admitted to the number of the clergy without the consent of the whole people: and hence Cyprian makes a laboured apology for having appointed Aurelius a reader without consulting the Church, because, although done contrary to custom, it was not done without reason. He thus premises: "In ordaining clergy, dearest brethren, we are wont previously to consult you, and weigh the manners and merits of each by the common advice" (Cyprian. Lib. 2 Ep. 5). But as in these minor exercises there was no great danger, inasmuch as they were appointed to a long probation and unimportant function, the consent of the people ceased to be asked. Afterwards, in other orders also, with the exception of the bishopric, the people usually left the choice and decision to the bishop and presbyters, who thus determined who were fit and worthy, unless, perhaps, when new presbyters were appointed to parishes, for then the express consent of the inhabitants of the place behoved to be given. Nor is it strange that in this matter the people were not very anxious to maintain their right, for no subdeacon was appointed who had not given a long proof of his conduct in the clerical office, agreeably to the strictness of discipline then in use. After he had approved himself in that degree, he was appointed deacon, and thereafter, if he conducted himself faithfully, he attained to the honour of a presbyter. Thus none were promoted whose conduct had not, in truth, been tested for many years under the eye of the people. There were also many canons for punishing their faults, so that the Church, if she did not neglect the

remedies, was not burdened with bad presbyters or deacons. In the case of presbyters, indeed, the consent of the citizens was always required, as is attested by the canon (Primus Distinct. 67), which is attributed to Anacletus. In fine, all ordinations took place at stated periods of the year, that none might creep in stealthily without the consent of the faithful, or be promoted with too much facility without witnesses.

11. In electing bishops, the people long retained their right of preventing any one from being intruded who was not acceptable to all. Accordingly, it was forbidden by the Council of Antioch to induct any one on the unwilling. This also Leo I. carefully confirms. Hence these passages: "Let him be elected whom the clergy and people or the majority demand." Again. "Let him who is to preside over all be elected by all" (Leo, Ep. 90, cap. 2). He, therefore, who is appointed while unknown and unexamined, must of necessity be violently intruded. Again, "Let him be elected who is chosen by the clergy, and called by the people, and let him be consecrated by the provincials with the judgment of the metropolitan." So careful were the holy fathers that this liberty of the people should on no account be diminished, that when a general council, assembled at Constantinople, were ordaining Nectarius, they declined to do it without the approbation of the whole clergy and people, as their letter to the Roman synod testified. Accordingly, when any bishop nominated his successor, the act was not ratified without consulting the whole people. Of this you have not only an example, but the form, in Augustine, in the nomination of Eradius (August. Ep. 110). And Theodoret, after relating that Peter was the successor nominated by Athanasius, immediately adds, that the sacerdotal order ratified it, that the magistracy, chief men, and whole people, by their acclamation approved.

12. It was, indeed, decreed (and I admit on the best grounds) by the Council of Laodicea (Can. 18) that the election should not be left to crowds. For it scarcely ever happens that so many heads, with one consent, settle any affair well. It generally holds true, "*Incertum scindi studia in contraria vulgus;*"—"Opposing wishes rend the fickle crowd." For, first, the clergy alone selected, and presented him whom they had selected to the magistrate, or senate, and chief men. These, after deliberation, put their signature to the election, if it seemed proper, if not, they chose another whom they more highly approved. The matter was then laid before the multitude, who, although not bound by those previous proceedings, were less able to act tumultuously. Or, if the matter began with the multitude, it was only that it might be known whom they were most desirous to have; the wishes of the people being heard, the clergy at length elected. Thus, it was neither lawful for the clergy to appoint whom they chose, nor were they, however, under the necessity of yielding to the foolish desires of the people. Leo sets down this order, when he says, "The wishes of the citizens, the testimonies of the people, the choice of the honourable, the election of the clergy, are to be waited for" (Leo, Ep. 87). Again, "Let the testimony of the honourable, the subscription of the clergy, the consent of the magistracy and people, be obtained; otherwise (says he) it must on no account be done." Nor is anything more intended by the decree of the Council of Laodicea, than that the clergy and rulers were not to allow themselves to be carried away by the rash multitude, but rather by their prudence and gravity to repress their foolish desires whenever there was occasion.

13. This mode of election was still in force in the time of Gregory, and probably continued to a much later period. Many of his letters which are extant clearly prove this, for whenever a new bishop is to be elected, his custom is to write to the clergy, magistrates, and people; sometimes also to the governor, according to the nature of the government. But if, on account of the unsettled state of the Church, he gives the oversight of the election to a neighbouring bishop, he always requires a formal decision confirmed by the subscriptions of all. Nay, when one Constantius was elected Bishop of Milan, and in consequence of the incursions of the Barbarians many of the Milanese had fled to Genoa, he thought that the election would not be lawful unless they too were called together and gave their assent (Gregor. Lib. 2 Ep. 69). Nay, five hundred years have not elapsed since Pope Nicholas fixed the election of the Roman Pontiff in this way, first, that the cardinals should precede; next, that they should join to themselves the other clergy; and, lastly, that the election should be ratified by the consent of the people. And in the end he recites the decree of Leo, which I lately quoted, and orders it to be enforced in future. But should the malice of the wicked so prevail that the clergy are obliged to quit the city, in order to make a pure election, he, however, orders that some of the people shall, at the same time, be present. The suffrage of the Emperor, as far as we can understand, was required only in two churches, those of Rome and Constantinople, these being the two seats of empire. For when Ambrose was sent by Valentinianus to Milan with authority to superintend the election of a new bishop, it was an extraordinary proceeding, in consequence of the violent factions which raged among

the citizens. But at Rome the authority of the Emperor in the election of the bishop was so great, that Gregory says he was appointed to the government of the Church by his order (Gregor. Lib. 1 Ep. 5), though he had been called by the people in regular form. The custom, however, was, that when the magistrates, clergy, and people, nominated any one, he was forthwith presented to the Emperor, who either by approving ratified, or by disapproving annulled the election. There is nothing contrary to this practice in the decretals which are collected by Gratian. where all that is said is, that it was on no account to be tolerated, that canonical election should be abolished, and a king should at pleasure appoint a bishop, and that one thus promoted by violent authority was not to be consecrated by the metropolitans. For it is one thing to deprive the Church of her right, and transfer it entirely to the caprice of a single individual; it is another thing to assign to a king or emperor the honour of confirming a legitimate election by his authority.

14. It now remains to treat of the form by which the ministers of the ancient Church were initiated to their office after election. This was termed by the Latins, Ordination or consecration, and by the Greeks χειροτονία, sometimes also χειροθεσία, though χειροτονία properly denotes that mode of election by which suffrages are declared by a show of hands. There is extant a decree of the Council of Nice, to the effect that the metropolitans, with all the bishops of the province, were to meet to ordain him who was chosen. But if, from distance, or sickness, or any other necessary cause, part were prevented, three at least should meet, and those who were absent signify their consent by letter. And this canon, after it had fallen into desuetude, was afterwards renewed by several councils. All, or at least all who had not an excuse, were enjoined to be present, in order that a stricter examination might be had of the life and doctrine of him who was to be ordained; for the thing was not done without examination. And it appears, from the words of Cyprian, that, in old time, they were not wont to be called after the election, but to be present at the election, and with the view of their acting as moderators, that no disorder might be committed by the crowd. For after saying that the people had the power either of choosing worthy or refusing unworthy priests, he immediately adds, "For which reason, we must carefully observe and hold by the divine and apostolic tradition (which is observed by us also, and almost by all the provinces), that for the due performance of ordinations all the nearest bishops of the province should meet with the people over whom the person is proposed to be ordained, and the bishop should be elected in presence of the people. But as they were sometimes too slowly assembled, and there was a risk that some might abuse the delay for purposes of intrigue, it was thought that it would be sufficient if they came after the designation was made, and on due investigation consecrated him who had been approved.

15. While this was done everywhere without exception, a different custom gradually gained ground—namely, that those who were elected should go to the metropolitan to obtain ordination. This was owing more to ambition, and the corruption of the ancient custom, than to any good reason. And not long after, the authority of the Romish See being now increased, another still worse custom was introduced, of applying to it for the consecration of the bishops of almost all Italy. This we may observe from the letters of Gregory (Lib. 2 Ep. 69, 76). The ancient right was preserved by a few cities only which had not yielded so easily; for instance, Milan. Perhaps metropolitan sees only retained their privilege. For, in order to consecrate an archbishop, it was the practice for all the provincial bishops to meet in the metropolitan city. The form used was the laying on of hands (chap. 19 sec. 28, 31). I do not read that any other ceremonies were used, except that, in the public meeting, the bishops had some dress to distinguish them from the other presbyters. Presbyters, also, and deacons, were ordained by the laying on of hands; but each bishop, with the college of presbyters, ordained his own presbyters. But though they all did the same act, yet because the bishop presided, and the ordination was performed as it were under his auspices, it was said to be his. Hence ancient writers often say that a presbyter does not differ in any respect from a bishop except in not having the power of ordaining.

CHAPTER 5

THE ANCIENT FORM OF GOVERNMENT UTTERLY CORRUPTED BY THE TYRANNY OF THE PAPACY.

This chapter consists of two parts,—I. Who are called to the ministry under the Papacy, their character, and the ground of their appointment, sec. 1–7. II. How far they fulfil their office, sec. 8–19.

Sections:

1. Who and what kind of persons are uniformly appointed bishops in the Papacy. 1. No inquiry into

doctrine. 2. In regard to character, the unlearned and dissolute, boys, or men of wicked lives, chosen.

2. The right of the people taken away, though maintained by Leo, Cyprian, and Councils. It follows that there is no Canonical election in the Papacy. Two objections answered. Papal elections, what. Kind of persons elected.

3. A fuller explanation of the answer to the second objection, unfolding the errors of people, bishops, and princes.

4. No election of presbyters and deacons in the Papacy. 1. Because they are ordained for a different end. 2. Contrary to the command of Scripture and the Council of Chalcedon, no station is assigned them. 3. Both the name and thing adulterated by a thousand frauds.

5. Refutation of those corruptions. Proper end of ordination. Of trial, and other necessary things. For these, wicked and sanguinary men have substituted vain show and deplorable blindness.

6. Second corruption relating to the assignation of benefices which they call collation. Manifold abuses here exposed. Why the offices of priests are in the Papacy called benefices.

7. One individual appointed over five or six churches. This most shameful corruption severely condemned by many Councils.

8. Second part of the chapter—viz. how the office is discharged. Monks who have no place among Presbyters. Objection answered.

9. Presbyters divided into beneficiaries and mercenaries. The beneficiaries are bishops, parsons, canons, chaplains, abbots, priors. The mercenaries condemned by the word of God.

10. The name of beneficiaries given to idle priests who perform no office in the church. Objection answered. What kind of persons the canons should be. Another objection answered. The beneficiaries not true presbyters.

11. The bishops and rectors of parishes, by deserting their churches, glory only in an empty name.

12. The seeds of this evil in the age of Gregory, who inveighs against mercenaries. More sharply rebuked by Bernard.

13. The supreme Popish administration described. Ridiculous allegation of those so-called ministers of the Church. Answer.

14. Their shameful morals. Scarcely one who would not have been excommunicated or deposed by the ancient canons.

15. No true diaconate existing in the Papacy, though they have still the shadow of it. Corruption of the practice of the primitive Church in regard to deacons.

16. Ecclesiastical property, which was formerly administered by true deacons, plundered by bishops and canons, in defraud of the poor.

17. Blasphemous defence of these robbers. Answer. Kings doing homage to Christ. Theodosius. A saying of Ambrose.

18. Another defence with regard to the adorning of churches. Answer.

19. Concluding answer, showing that the diaconate is completely subverted by the Papacy.

1. It may now be proper to bring under the eye of the reader the order of church government observed by the Roman See and all its satellites, and the whole of that hierarchy, which they have perpetually in their mouths, and compare it with the description we have given of the primitive and early Church, that the contrast may make it manifest what kind of church those have who plume themselves on the very title, as sufficient to outweigh, or rather overwhelm us. It will be best to begin with the call, that we may see who are called to the ministry, with what character, and on what grounds. Thereafter we will consider how far they faithfully fulfil their office. We shall give the first place to the bishops; would that they could claim the honour of holding the first rank in this discussion! But the subject does not allow me even to touch it lightly, without exposing their disgrace. Still, let me remember in what kind of writing I am engaged, and not allow my discourse, which ought to be framed for simple teaching, to wander beyond its proper limits. But let any of them, who have not laid aside all modesty, tell me what kind of bishops are uniformly elected in the present day. Any examination of doctrine is too old fashioned, but if any respect is had to doctrine, they make choice of some lawyer who knows better how to plead in the forum than to preach in the church. This much is certain, that for a hundred years, scarcely one in a hundred has been elected who had any acquaintance with sacred doctrine. I do not spare former ages because they were much better, but because the question now relates only to the present Church. If morals be inquired into, we shall find few or almost none whom the ancient canons would not have judged unworthy. If one was not a drunkard, he was a fornicator; if one was free from this vice, he was either a gambler or sportsman, or a loose liver in some respect. For there are lighter faults which,

according to the ancient canons, exclude from the episcopal office. But the most absurd thing of all is, that even boys scarcely ten years of age are, by the permission of the Pope, made bishops. Such is the effrontery and stupidity to which they have arrived, that they have no dread even of that last and monstrous iniquity, which is altogether abhorrent even from natural feeling. Hence it appears what kind of elections these must have been, when such supine negligence existed.

2. Then in election, the whole right has been taken from the people. Vows, assents, subscriptions, and all things of this sort, have disappeared; the whole power has been given to the canons alone. First, they confer the episcopal office on whomsoever they please; by-and-by they bring him forth into the view of the people, but it is to be adored, not examined. But Leo protests that no reason permits this, and declares it to be a violent imposition (Leo, Ep. 90, cap. 2). Cyprian, after declaring it to be of divine authority, that election should not take place without the consent of the people, shows that a different procedure is at variance with the word of God. Numerous decrees of councils most strictly forbid it to be otherwise done, and if done, order it to be null. If this is true, there is not throughout the whole Papacy in the present day any canonical election in accordance either with divine or ecclesiastical law. Now, were there no other evil in this, what excuse can they give for having robbed the Church of her right? But the corruption of the times required (they say), that since hatred and party-spirit prevailed with the people and magistrates in the election of bishops more than right and sound judgment, the determination should be confined to a few. Allow that this was the last remedy in desperate circumstances. When the cure was seen to be more hurtful than the disease, why was not a remedy provided for this new evil? But it is said that the course which the Canons must follow is strictly prescribed. But can we doubt, that even in old times the people, on meeting to elect a bishop, were aware that they were bound by the most sacred laws, when they saw a rule prescribed by the word of God? That one sentence in which God describes the true character of a bishop ought justly to be of more weight than ten thousand canons. Nevertheless, carried away by the worst of feelings, they had no regard to law or equity. So in the present day, though most excellent laws have been made, they remain buried in writing. Meanwhile, the general and approved practice is (and it is carried on as it were systematically), that drunkards, fornicators, gamblers, are everywhere promoted to this honour; nay, this is little: bishoprics are the rewards of adulterers and panders: for when they are given to hunters and hawkers, things may be considered at the best. To excuse such unworthy procedure in any way, were to be wicked over much. The people had a most excellent canon prescribed to them by the word of God—viz. that a bishop must be blameless, apt to teach, not a brawler, &c. (1 Tim. 3:2). Why, then, was the province of electing transferred from the people to these men? Just because among the tumults and factions of the people the word of God was not heard. And, on the other hand, why is it not in the present day transferred from these men, who not only violate all laws, but having cast off shame, libidinously, avariciously, and ambitiously, mix and confound things human and divine?

3. But it is not true to say that the thing was devised as a remedy. We read, that in old times tumults often arose in cities at the election of bishops; yet no one ever ventured to think of depriving the citizens of their right: for they had other methods by which they could either prevent the fault, or correct it when committed. I will state the matter as it truly is. When the people began to be negligent in making their choice, and left the business, as less suited to them, to the presbyters, these abused the opportunity to usurp a domination, which they afterwards established by putting forth new canons. Ordination is now nothing else than a mere mockery. For the kind of examination of which they make a display is so empty and trifling, that it even entirely wants the semblance. Therefore. when sovereigns, by paction with the Roman Pontiffs, obtained for themselves the right of nominating bishops, the Church sustained no new injury, because the canons were merely deprived of an election which they had seized without any right, or acquired by stealth. Nothing, indeed, can be more disgraceful, than that bishops should be sent from courts to take possession of churches, and pious princes would do well to desist from such corruption. For there is an impious spoliation of the Church whenever any people have a bishop intruded whom they have not asked, or at least freely approved. But that disorderly practice, which long existed in churches, gave occasion to sovereigns to assume to themselves the presentation of bishops. They wished the benefice to belong to themselves, rather than to those who had no better right to it, and who equally abused it.

4. Such is the famous call, on account of which bishops boast that they are the successors of the apostles. They say, moreover, that they alone can competently appoint presbyters. But herein they most shamefully

corrupt the ancient institution, that they by their ordination appoint not presbyters to guide and feed the people, but priests to sacrifice. In like manner, when they consecrate deacons, they pay no regard to their true and proper office, but only ordain to certain ceremonies concerning the cup and patent. But in the Council of Chalcedon it was, on the contrary, decreed that there should be no absolute ordinations, that is, ordinations without assigning to the ordained a place where they were to exercise their office. This decree is most useful for two reasons—first, That churches may not be burdened with superfluous expense, nor idle men receive what ought to be distributed to the poor; and, secondly, That those who are ordained may consider that they are not promoted merely to an honorary office, but intrusted with a duty which they are solemnly bound to discharge. But the Roman authorities (who think that nothing is to be cared for in religion but their belly) consider the first title to be a revenue adequate to their support, whether it be from their own patrimony or from the priesthood. Accordingly, when they ordain presbyters or deacons, without any anxiety as to where they ought to minister, they confer the order, provided those ordained are sufficiently rich to support themselves. But what man can admit that the title which the decree of the council requires is an annual revenue for sustenance? Again, when more recent canons made bishops liable in the support of those whom they had ordained without a fit title, that they might thus repress too great facility, a method was devised of eluding the penalty. For he who is ordained promises that whatever be the title named he will be contented with it. In this way he is precluded from an action for aliment. I say nothing of the thousand frauds which are here committed, as when some falsely claim the empty titles of benefices, from which they cannot obtain a sixpence of revenue, and others by secret stipulation obtain a temporary appointment, which they promise that they will immediately restore, but sometimes do not. There are still more mysteries of the same kind.

5. But although these grosser abuses were removed, is it not at all times absurd to appoint a presbyter without assigning him a locality? For when they ordain it is only to sacrifice. But the legitimate ordination of a presbyter is to the government of the Church, while deacons are called to the charge of alms. It is true, many pompous ceremonies are used to disguise the act, that mere show may excite veneration in the simple; but what effect can these semblances have upon men of sound minds, when beneath them there is nothing solid or true? They used ceremonies either borrowed from Judaism or devised by themselves; from these it were better if they would abstain. Of the trial (for it is unnecessary to say anything of the shadow which they retain), of the consent of the people, of other necessary things, there is no mention. By shadow, I mean those ridiculous gesticulations framed in inept and frigid imitation of antiquity. The bishops have their vicars, who, previous to ordination, inquire into doctrine. But what is the inquiry? Is it whether they are able to read their Missals, or whether they can decline some common noun which occurs in the lesson, or conjugate a verb, or give the meaning of some one word? For it is not necessary to give the sense of a single sentence. And yet even those who are deficient in these puerile elements are not repelled, provided they bring the recommendation of money or influence. Of the same nature is the question which is thrice put in an unintelligible voice, when the persons who are to be ordained are brought to the altar—viz. Are they worthy of the honour? One (who never saw them, but has his part in the play, that no form may be wanting) answers, They are worthy. What can you accuse in these venerable fathers save that, by indulging in such sacrilegious sport, they shamelessly laugh at God and man? But as they have long been in possession of the thing, they think they have now a legal title to it. For any one who ventures to open his lips against these palpable and flagrant iniquities is hurried off to a capital trial, like one who had in old time divulged the mysteries of Ceres. Would they act thus if they had any belief in a God?

6. Then in the collation of benefices (which was formerly conjoined with ordination, but is now altogether separate), how much better do they conduct themselves? But they have many reasons to give, for it is not bishops alone who confer the office of priests (and even in their case, where they are called Collators, they have not always the full right), but others have the presentation, while they only retain the honorary title of collations. To these are added nominations from schools, resignations, either simple or by way of exchange, commendatory rescripts, preventions, and the like. But they all conduct themselves in such a way that one cannot upbraid another. I maintain that, in the Papacy in the present day, scarcely one benefice in a hundred is conferred without simony, as the ancients have defined it (Calv. in Art. 8:21). I say not that all purchase for a certain sum; but show me one in twenty who does not attain to the priesthood by some sinister method. Some owe their promotion to kindred

or affinity, others to the influence of their parents, while others procure favour by obsequiousness. In short, the end for which the offices are conferred is, that provision may be made not for churches, but for those who receive them. Accordingly, they call them benefices, by which name they sufficiently declare, that they look on them in no other light than as the largesses by which princes either court the favour or reward the services of their soldiers. I say nothing of the fact, that these rewards are conferred on barbers, cooks, grooms, and dross of that sort. At present, indeed, there are no cases in law courts which make a greater noise than those concerning sacerdotal offices, so that you may regard them as nothing else than game set before dogs to be hunted. Is it tolerable even to hear the name of pastors given to those who have forced their way into the possession of a church as into an enemy's country? who have evicted it by forensic brawls? who have bought it for a price? who have laboured for it by sordid sycophancy? who, while scarcely lisping boys, have obtained it like heritage from uncles and relatives? Sometimes even bastards obtain it from their fathers.

7. Was the licentiousness of the people, however corrupt and lawless, ever carried to such a height? But a more monstrous thing still is, that one man (I say not what kind of man, but certainly one who cannot govern himself) is appointed to the charge of five or six churches. In the courts of princes in the present day, you may see youths who are thrice abbots, twice bishops, once archbishops. Everywhere are Canons loaded with five, six, or seven cures, of not one of which they take the least charge, except to draw the income. I will not object that the word of God cries aloud against this: it has long ceased to have the least weight with them. I will not object that many councils denounce the severest punishment against this dishonest practice; these, too, when it suits them, they boldly contemn. But I say that it is monstrous wickedness, altogether opposed to God, to nature, and to ecclesiastical government, that one thief should lie brooding over several churches, that the name of pastor should be given to one who, even if he were willing, could not be present among his flock, and yet (such is their impudence) they cloak these abominations with the name of church, that they may exempt them from all blame. Nay, if you please, in these iniquities is contained that sacred succession to which, as they boast, it is owing that the Church does not perish.

8. Let us now see, as the second mark for estimating a legitimate pastor, how faithfully they discharge their office. Of the priests who are there elected, some are called monks, others seculars. The former herd was unknown to the early Church; even to hold such a place in the Church is so repugnant to the monastic profession, that in old times, when persons were elected out of monasteries to clerical offices, they ceased to be monks. And, accordingly, Gregory, though in his time there were many abuses, did not suffer the offices to be thus confounded (Gregor. Lib. 3 Ep. 11). For he insists that those who have been appointed abbots shall resign the clerical office, because no one can be properly at the same time a monk and a clerk, the one being an obstacle to the other. Now, were I to ask how he can well fulfil his office who is declared by the canons to be unfit, what answer, pray, will they give? They will quote those abortive decrees of Innocent and Boniface, by which monks are admitted to the honour and power of the priesthood, though they remain in their monasteries. But is it at all reasonable that any unlearned ass, as soon as he has seized upon the Roman See, may by one little word overturn all antiquity? But of this matter afterwards. Let it now suffice, that in the purer times of the Church it was regarded as a great absurdity for a monk to hold the office of priest. For Jerome declares that he does not the office of priest while he is living among monks, and ranks himself as one of the people to be governed by the priests. But to concede this to them, what duty do they perform? Some of the mendicants preach, while all the other monks chant or mutter masses in their cells; as if either our Saviour had wished, or the nature of the office permits, presbyters to be made for such a purpose. When Scripture plainly testifies that it is the duty of a presbyter to rule his own church (Acts 20:28), is it not impious profanation to transfer it to another purpose, nay, altogether to change the sacred institution of God? For when they are ordained, they are expressly forbidden to do what God enjoins on all presbyters. For this is their cant, Let a monk, contented with his cell, neither presume to administer the sacraments, nor hold any other public office. Let them deny, if they can, that it is open mockery of God when any one is appointed a presbyter in order to abstain from his proper and genuine office, and when he who has the name is not able to have the thing.

9. I come to the seculars, some of whom are (as they speak) beneficiaries; that is, have offices by which they are maintained, while others let out their services, day by day, to chant or say masses, and live in a manner on a stipend thus collected. Benefices either have a cure of souls, as bishoprics and parochial charges, or they are the stipends

of delicate men, who gain a livelihood by chanting; as prebends, canonries, parsonships, deaneries, chaplainships, and the like; although, things being now turned upside down, the offices of abbot and prior are not only conferred on secular presbyters, but on boys also by privilege, that is, by common and usual custom. In regard to the mercenaries who seek their food from day to day, what else could they do than they actually do, in other words, prostitute themselves in an illiberal and disgraceful manner for gain, especially from the vast multitude of them with which the world now teems? Hence, as they dare not beg openly, or think that in this way they would gain little, they go about like hungry dogs, and by a kind of barking importunity extort from the unwilling what they may deposit in their hungry stomachs. Were I here to attempt to describe how disgraceful it is to the Church, that the honour and office of a presbyter should come to this, I should never have done. My readers, therefore, must not expect from me a discourse which can fully represent this flagitious indignity. I briefly say, that if it is the office of a presbyter (and this both the word of God prescribes (1 Cor. 4:1) and the ancient canons enjoin) to feed the Church, and administer the spiritual kingdom of Christ, all those priests who have no work or stipend, save in the traffic of masses, not only fail in their office, but have no lawful office to discharge. No place is given them to teach, they have no people to govern. In short, nothing is left them but an altar on which to sacrifice Christ; this is to sacrifice not to God but to demons, as we shall afterwards show (see chap.18 sec. 3, 9, 14).

10. I am not here touching on extraneous faults, but only on the intestine evil which lies at the root of the very institution. I will add a sentence which will sound strange in their ears, but which, as it is true, it is right to express, that canons, deans, chaplains, provosts, and all who are maintained in idle offices of priesthood, are to be viewed in the same light. For what service can they perform to the Church? The preaching of the word, the care of discipline, and the administration of the Sacraments, they have shaken off as burdens too grievous to be borne. What then remains on which they can plume themselves as being true presbyters? Merely chanting and pompous ceremonies. But what is this to the point? If they allege custom, use, or the long prescription, I, on the contrary, appeal to the definition by which our Saviour has described true presbyters, and shown the qualities of those who are to be regarded as presbyters. But if they cannot endure the hard law of submitting to the rule of Christ, let them at least allow the cause to be decided by the authority of the primitive Church. Their condition will not be one whit improved when decided according to the ancient canons. Those who have degenerated into Canons ought to be presbyters, as they formerly were, to rule the Church in common with the bishop, and be, as it were, his colleagues in the pastoral office. What they call deaneries of the chapter have no concern with the true government of the Church, much less chaplainships and other similar worthless names. In what light then are they all to be regarded? Assuredly, both the word of Christ and the practice of the primitive Church exclude them from the honour of presbyters. They maintain, however, that they are presbyters; but we must unmask them, and we shall find that their whole profession is most alien from the office of presbyters, as that office is described to us by the apostles, and was discharged in the primitive Church. All such offices, therefore, by whatever titles they are distinguished, as they are novelties, and certainly not supported either by the institution of God or the ancient practice of the Church, ought to have no place in a description of that spiritual government which the Church received, and was consecrated by the mouth of the Lord himself. Or (if they would have me express it in ruder and coarser terms), since chaplains, canons, deans, provosts, and such like lazy-bellies, do not even, with one finger, touch a particle of the office, which is necessarily required in presbyters, they must not be permitted falsely to usurp the honour, and thereby violate the holy institution of Christ.

11. There still remain bishops and rectors of parishes; and I wish that they would contend for the maintenance of their office. I would willingly grant that they have a pious and excellent office if they would discharge it; but when they desert the churches committed to them, and throwing the care upon others, would still be considered pastors, they just act as if the office of pastor were to do nothing. If any usurer, who never stirs from the city, were to give himself out as a ploughman or vine-dresser; or a soldier, who has constantly been in the field or the camp, and has never seen books or the forum, to pass for a lawyer, who could tolerate the absurdity? Much more absurdly do those act who would be called and deemed lawful pastors of the Church, and are unwilling so to be. How few are those who in appearance even take the superintendence of their church? Many spend their lives in devouring the revenues of churches which they never visit even for the purpose of inspection. Some once a-year go themselves or send a steward, that nothing may be lost in the letting of them. When the corruption first crept in,

those who wished to enjoy this kind of vacation pleaded privilege, but it is now a rare case for any one to reside in his church. They look upon them merely in the light of farms, over which they appoint their vicars as grieves or husbandmen. But it is repugnant to common sense to regard him as a shepherd who has never seen a sheep of his flock.

12. It appears that in the time of Gregory some of the seeds of this corruption existed, the rulers of churches having begun to be more negligent in teaching; for he thus bitterly complains: "The world is full of priests, and yet labourers in the harvest are rare, for we indeed undertake the office of the priesthood, but we perform not the work of the office" (Gregor. Hom. 17). Again, "As they have no bowels of love, they would be thought lords, but do not at all acknowledge themselves to be fathers. They change a post of humility into the elevation of ascendancy." Again, "But we, O pastors! what are we doing, we who obtain the hire but are not labourers? We have fallen off to extraneous business; we undertake one thing, we perform another; we leave the ministry of the word, and, to our punishment, as I see, are called bishops, holding the honour of the name, not the power." Since he uses such bitterness of expression against those who were only less diligent or sedulous in their office, what, pray, would he have said if he had seen that very few bishops, if any at all, and scarcely one in a hundred of the other clergy, mounted the pulpit once in their whole lifetime? For to such a degree of infatuation have men come, that it is thought beneath the episcopal dignity to preach a sermon to the people. In the time of Bernard things had become still worse. Accordingly, we see how bitterly he inveighs against the whole order, and yet there is reason to believe that matters were then in a much better state than now.

13. Whoever will duly examine and weigh the whole form of ecclesiastical government as now existing in the Papacy, will find that there is no kind of spoliation in which robbers act more licentiously, without law or measure. Certainly all things are so unlike, nay, so opposed to the institution of Christ, have so degenerated from the ancient customs and practices of the Church, are so repugnant to nature and reason, that a greater injury cannot be done to Christ than to use his name in defending this disorderly rule. We (say they) are the pillars of the Church, the priests of religion, the vicegerents of Christ, the heads of the faithful, because the apostolic authority has come to us by succession. As if they were speaking to stocks, they perpetually plume themselves on these absurdities.

Whenever they make such boasts, I, in my turn, will ask, What have they in common with the apostles? We are not now treating of some hereditary honour which can come to men while they are asleep, but of the office of preaching, which they so greatly shun. In like manner, when we maintain that their kingdom is the tyranny of Antichrist, they immediately object that their venerable hierarchy has often been extolled by great and holy men, as if the holy fathers, when they commended the ecclesiastical hierarchy or spiritual government handed down to them by the apostles, ever dreamed of that shapeless and dreary chaos where bishoprics are held for the most part by ignorant asses, who do not even know the first and ordinary rudiments of the faith, or occasionally by boys who have just left their nurse; or if any are more learned (this, however, is a rare case), they regard the episcopal office as nothing else than a title of magnificence and splendour; where the rectors of churches no more think of feeding the flock than a cobbler does of ploughing, where all things are so confounded by a confusion worse than that of Babel, that no genuine trace of paternal government is any longer to be seen.

14. But if we descend to conduct, where is that light of the world which Christ requires, where the salt of the earth, where that sanctity which might operate as a perpetual censorship? In the present day, there is no order of men more notorious for luxury, effeminacy, delicacy, and all kinds of licentiousness; in no order are more apt or skilful teachers of imposture, fraud, treachery, and perfidy; nowhere is there more skill or audacity in mischief, to say nothing of ostentation, pride, rapacity, and cruelty. In bearing these the world is so disgusted, that there is no fear lest I seem to exaggerate. One thing I say, which even they themselves will not be able to deny: Among bishops there is scarcely an individual, and among the parochial clergy not one in a hundred, who, if sentence were passed on his conduct according to the ancient canons, would not deserve to be excommunicated, or at least deposed from his office. I seem to say what is almost incredible, so completely has that ancient discipline which enjoined strict censure of the morals of the clergy become obsolete; but such the fact really is. Let those who serve under the banner and auspices of the Romish See now go and boast of their sacerdotal order. It is certain that that which they have is neither from Christ, nor his apostles, nor the fathers, nor the early Church.

15. Let the deacons now come forward and show their most sacred distribution of ecclesiastical goods (see chap. 19 sec. 32). Although their deacons are not at all elected

for that purpose, for the only injunction which they lay upon them is to minister at the altar, to read the Gospel, or chant and perform I know not what frivolous acts. Nothing is said of alms, nothing of the care of the poor, nothing at all of the function which they formerly performed. I am speaking of the institution itself; for if we look to what they do, theirs, in fact, is no office, but only a step to the priesthood. In one thing, those who hold the place of deacons in the mass exhibit an empty image of antiquity, for they receive the offerings previous to consecration. Now, the ancient practice was, that before the communion of the Supper the faithful mutually kissed each other, and offered alms at the altar; thus declaring their love, first by symbol, and afterwards by an act of beneficence. The deacon, who was steward of the poor, received what was given that he might distribute it. Now, of these alms no more comes to the poor than if they were cast into the sea. They, therefore, delude the Church by that lying deaconship. Assuredly in this they have nothing resembling the apostolical institution or the ancient practice. The very distribution of goods they have transferred elsewhere, and have so settled it that nothing can be imagined more disorderly. For as robbers, after murdering their victims, divide the plunder, so these men, after extinguishing the light of God's word, as if they had murdered the Church, have imagined that whatever had been dedicated to pious uses was set down for prey and plunder. Accordingly, they have made a division, each seizing for himself as much as he could.

16. All those ancient methods which we have explained are not only disturbed but altogether disguised and expunged. The chief part of the plunder has gone to bishops and city presbyters, who, having thus enriched themselves, have been converted into canons. That the partition was a mere scramble is apparent from this, that even to this day they are litigating as to the proportions. Be this as it may, the decision has provided that out of all the goods of the Church not one penny shall go to the poor, to whom at least the half belonged. The canons expressly assign a fourth part to them, while the other fourth they destine to the bishops, that they may expend it in hospitality and other offices of kindness. I say nothing as to what the clergy ought to do with their portion, or the use to which they ought to apply it, for it has been clearly shown that what is set apart for churches, buildings, and other expenditure, ought in necessity to be given to the poor. If they had one spark of the fear of God in their heart, could they, I ask, bear the consciousness that all their food and clothing is the produce of theft, nay, of sacrilege? But as they are little moved by the judgment of God, they should at least reflect that those whom they would persuade that the orders of their Church are so beautiful and well arranged as they are wont to boast, are men endued with sense and reason. Let them briefly answer whether the diaconate is a licence to rob and steal. If they deny this, they will be forced to confess that no diaconate remains among them, since the whole administration of their ecclesiastical resources has been openly converted into sacrilegious depredation.

17. But here they use a very fair gloss, for they say that the dignity of the Church is not unbecomingly maintained by this magnificence. And certain of their sect are so impudent as to dare openly to boast that thus only are fulfilled the prophecies, in which the ancient prophets describe the splendour of Christ's kingdom, where the sacerdotal order is exhibited in royal attire, that it was not without cause that God made the following promises to his Church: "All kings shall fall down before him: all nations shall serve him" (Ps. 72:11). "Awake, awake; put on thy strength, O Sion; put on thy beautiful garments, O Jerusalem, the holy city" (Isa. 52:1). "All they from Sheba shall come; they shall bring gold and incense, and they shall show forth the praises of the Lord. All the flocks of Kedar shall be gathered together unto thee" (Isa. 60:6, 7). I fear I should seem childish were I to dwell long in refuting this dishonesty. I am unwilling, therefore, to use words unnecessarily; I ask, however, were any Jew to misapply these passages, what answer would they give? They would rebuke his stupidity in making a carnal and worldly application of things spiritually said of Christ's spiritual kingdom. For we know that under the image of earthly objects the prophets have delineated to us the heavenly glory which ought to shine in the Church. For in those blessings with these words literally express, the Church never less abounded than under the apostles; and yet all admit that the power of Christ's kingdom was then most flourishing. What, then, is the meaning of the above passages? That everything which is precious, sublime, and illustrious, ought to be made subject to the Lord. As to its being said expressly of kings, that they will submit to Christ, that they will throw their diadems at his feet, that they will dedicate their resources to the Church, when was this more truly and fully manifested than when Theodosius, having thrown aside the purple and left the insignia of empire, like one of the people humbled himself before God and the Church in solemn repentance? than when he and other like pious princes made it their study and their care to preserve pure doctrine

in the Church, to cherish and protect sound teachers? But that priests did not then luxuriate in superfluous wealth is sufficiently declared by this one sentence of the Council of Aquileia, over which Ambrose presided, *"Poverty in the priests of the Lord is glorious."* It is certain that the bishops then had some means by which they might have rendered the glory of the Church conspicuous, if they had deemed them the true ornaments of the Church. But knowing that nothing was more adverse to the duty of pastors than to plume themselves on the delicacies of the table, on splendid clothes, numerous attendants, and magnificent places, they cultivated and followed the humility and modesty, nay, the very poverty, which Christ has consecrated among his servants.

18. But not to be tedious, let us again briefly sum up and show how far that distribution, or rather squandering, of ecclesiastical goods which now exists differs from the true diaconate, which both the word of God recommends and the ancient Church observed (Book 1 chap. 11. sec. 7, 13; Book 3 chap. 20 sec. 30; *supra*, chap. 4 sec. 8). I say, that what is employed on the adorning of churches is improperly laid out, if not accompanied with that moderation which the very nature of sacred things prescribes, and which the apostles and other holy fathers prescribed, both by precept and example. But is anything like this seen in churches in the present day? Whatever accords, I do not say with that ancient frugality, but with decent mediocrity, is rejected. Nought pleases but what savours of luxury and the corruption of the times. Meanwhile, so far are they from taking due care of living temples, that they would allow thousands of the poor to perish sooner than break down the smallest cup or platter to relieve their necessity. That I may not decide too severely at my own hand, I would only ask the pious reader to consider what Exuperius, the Bishop of Thoulouse, whom we have mentioned, what Acatius, or Ambrose, or any one like minded, if they were to rise from the dead, would say? Certainly, while the necessities of the poor are so great, they would not approve of their funds being carried away from them as superfluous; not to mention that, even were there no poor, the uses to which they are applied are noxious in many respects and useful in none. But I appeal not to men. These goods have been dedicated to Christ, and ought to be distributed at his pleasure. In vain, however, will they make that to be expenditure for Christ which they have squandered contrary to his commands, though, to confess the truth, the ordinary revenue of the Church is not much curtailed by these expenses. No bishoprics are so opulent, no abbacies so productive, in short, no benefices so numerous and ample, as to suffice for the gluttony of priests. But while they would spare themselves, they induce the people by superstition to employ what ought to have been distributed to the poor in building temples, erecting statues, buying plate, and providing costly garments. Thus the daily alms are swallowed up in this abyss.

19. Of the revenue which they derive from lands and property, what else can I say than what I have already said, and is manifest before the eyes of all? We see with what kind of fidelity the greatest portion is administered by those who are called bishops and abbots. What madness is it to seek ecclesiastical order here? Is it becoming in those whose life ought to have been a singular example of frugality, modesty, continence, and humility, to rival princes in the number of their attendants, the splendour of their dwellings, the delicacies of dressing and feasting? Can anything be more contrary to the duty of those whom the eternal and inviolable edict of God forbids to long for filthy lucre, and orders to be contented with simple food, not only to lay hands on villages and castles, but also invade the largest provinces, and even seize on empire itself? If they despise the word of God, what answer will they give to the ancient canons of councils, which decree that the bishop shall have a little dwelling not far from the church, a frugal table and furniture? (Conc. Carth. cap. 14, 15). What answer will they give to the declaration of the Council of Aquileia, in which poverty in the priests of the Lord is pronounced glorious? For, the injunction which Jerome gives to Nepotian, to make the poor and strangers acquainted with his table, and have Christ with them as a guest, they would, perhaps, repudiate as too austere. What he immediately adds it would shame them to acknowledge—viz. that the glory of a bishop is to provide for the sustenance of the poor, that the disgrace of all priests is to study their own riches. This they cannot admit without covering themselves with disgrace. But it is unnecessary here to press them so hard, since all we wished was to demonstrate that the legitimate order of deacons has long ago been abolished, and that they can no longer plume themselves on this order in commendation of their Church. This, I think, has been completely established.

CHAPTER 6

OF THE PRIMACY OF THE ROMISH SEE.

The divisions of this chapter are,—I. Question stated, and an argument for the primacy of the Roman

Pontiff drawn from the Old Testament refuted, sec. 1, 2. II. Reply to various arguments in support of the Papacy founded on the words, "Thou art Peter," &c., sec. 3–17.

Sections:

1. Brief recapitulation. Why the subject of primacy not yet mentioned. Represented by Papists as the bond of ecclesiastical unity. Setting out with this axiom, they begin to debate about their hierarchy.

2. Question stated. An attempted proof from the office of High Priest among the Jews. Two answers.

3. Arguments for primacy from the New Testament. Two answers.

4. Another answer. The keys given to the other apostles as well as to Peter. Other two arguments answered by passages of Cyprian and Augustine.

5. Another argument answered.

6. Answer to the argument that the Church is founded on Peter, from its being said, "Upon this rock I will build my Church."

7. Answer confirmed by passages of Scripture.

8. Even allowing Peter's superiority in some respect, this is no proof of the primacy of the Roman Pontiff. Other arguments answered.

9. Distinction between civil and ecclesiastical government. Christ alone the Head of the Church. Argument that there is still a ministerial head answered.

10. Paul, in giving a representation of the Church, makes no mention of this ministerial head.

11. Even though Peter were ministerial head, it does not follow that the Pope is so also. Argument founded on Paul's having lived and died at Rome.

12. On the hypothesis of the Papists, the primacy belongs to the Church of Antioch.

13. Absurdity of the Popish hypothesis.

14. Peter was not the Bishop of Rome.

15. Same subject continued.

16. Argument that the unity of the Church cannot be maintained without a supreme head on earth. Answer, stating three reasons why great respect was paid in early times to the See of Rome.

17. Opinion of early times on the subject of the unity of the Church. No primacy attributed to the Church of Rome. Christ alone regarded as the Head of the Universal Church.

1. Hitherto we have reviewed those ecclesiastical orders which existed in the government of the primitive Church; but afterwards corrupted by time, and thereafter more and more vitiated, now only retain the name in the Papal Church, and are, in fact, nothing but mere masks, so that the contrast will enable the pious reader to judge what kind of Church that is, for revolting from which we are charged with schism. But, on the head and crown of the whole matter, I mean the primacy of the Roman See, from which they undertake to prove that the Catholic Church is to be found only with them, we have not yet touched, because it did not take its origin either in the institution of Christ, or the practice of the early Church, as did those other parts, in regard to which we have shown, that though they were ancient in their origin, they in process of time altogether degenerated, nay, assumed an entirely new form. And yet they endeavour to persuade the world that the chief and only bond of ecclesiastical unity is to adhere to the Roman See, and continue in subjection to it. I say, the prop on which they chiefly lean, when they would deprive us of the Church, and arrogate it to themselves, is, that they retain the head on which the unity of the Church depends, and without which it must necessarily be rent and go to pieces. For they regard the Church as a kind of mutilated trunk if it be not subject to the Romish See as its head. Accordingly, when they debate about their hierarchy they always set out with the axiom: The Roman Pontiff (as the vicar of Christ, who is the Head of the Church) presides in his stead over the universal Church, and the Church is not rightly constituted unless that See hold the primacy over all others. The nature of this claim must, therefore, be considered, that we may not omit anything which pertains to the proper government of the Church.

2. The question, then, may be thus stated, Is it necessary for the true order of the hierarchy (as they term it), or of ecclesiastical order, that one See should surpass the others in dignity and power, so as to be the head of the whole body? We subject the Church to unjust laws if we lay this necessity upon her without sanction from the word of God. Therefore, if our opponents would prove what they maintain, it behoves them first of all to show that this economy was instituted by Christ. For this purpose, they refer to the office of high priest under the law, and the supreme jurisdiction which God appointed at Jerusalem. But the solution is easy, and it is manifold if one does not satisfy them. First, no reason obliges us to extend what was useful in one nation to the whole world; nay, the cases of one nation and of the whole world are widely different. Because the Jews were hemmed in on every side by idolaters, God fixed the

seat of his worship in the central region of the earth, that they might not be distracted by a variety of religions; there he appointed one priest to whom they might all look up, that they might be the better kept in unity. But now when the true religion has been diffused over the whole globe, who sees not that it is altogether absurd to give the government of East and West to one individual? It is just as if one were to contend that the whole world ought to be governed by one prefect, because one district has not several prefects. But there is still another reason why that institution ought not to be drawn into a precedent. Every one knows that the high priest was a type of Christ; now, the priesthood being transferred, that right must also be transferred. To whom, then, was it transferred? certainly not to the Pope, as he dares impudently to boast when he arrogates this title to himself, but to Christ, who, as he alone holds the office without vicar or successor, does not resign the honour to any other. For this priesthood consists not in doctrine only, but in the propitiation which Christ made by his death, and the intercession which he now makes with the Father (Heb. 7:11).

3. That example, therefore, which is seen to have been temporary, they have no right to bind upon us as by a perpetual law. In the New Testament there is nothing which they can produce in confirmation of their opinion, but its having been said to one, "Thou art Peter, and upon this rock I will build my Church" (Mt. 16:18). Again, "Simon, son of Jonas, lovest thou me?" "Feed my lambs" (John 21:15). But to give strength to these proofs, they must, in the first place, show, that to him who is ordered to feed the flock of Christ power is given over all churches, and that to bind and loose is nothing else than to preside over the whole world. But as Peter had received a command from the Lord, so he exhorts all other presbyters to feed the Church (1 Pet. 5:2). Hence we are entitled to infer, that, by that expression of Christ, nothing more was given to Peter than to the others, or that the right which Peter had received he communicated equally to others. But not to argue to no purpose, we elsewhere have, from the lips of Christ himself, a clear exposition of what it is to bind and loose. It is just to retain and remit sins (John 10:23). The mode of loosing and binding is explained throughout Scripture: but especially in that passage in which Paul declares that the ministers of the Gospel are commissioned to reconcile men to God, and at the same time to exercise discipline over those who reject the benefit (2 Cor. 5:18; 10:16).

4. How unbecomingly they wrest the passages of binding and loosing I have elsewhere glanced at, and will in a short time more fully explain. It may now be worth while merely to see what they can extract from our Saviour's celebrated answer to Peter. He promised him the keys of the kingdom of heaven, and said, that whatever things he bound on earth should be bound in heaven (Mt. 16:19). The moment we are agreed as to the meaning of the keys, and the mode of binding, all dispute will cease. For the Pope will willingly omit that office assigned to the apostles, which, full of labour and toil, would interfere with his luxuries without giving any gain. Since heaven is opened to us by the doctrine of the Gospel, it is by an elegant metaphor distinguished by the name of *keys*. Again, the only mode in which men are bound and loosed is, in the latter case, when they are reconciled to God by faith, and in the former, more strictly bound by unbelief. Were this all that the Pope arrogated to himself, I believe there would be none to envy him or stir the question. But because this laborious and very far from lucrative succession is by no means pleasing to the Pope, the dispute immediately arises as to what it was that Christ promised to Peter. From the very nature of the case, I infer that nothing more is denoted than the dignity which cannot be separated from the burden of the apostolic office. For, admitting the definition which I have given (and it cannot without effrontery be rejected), nothing is here given to Peter that was not common to him with his colleagues. On any other view, not only would injustice be done to their persons, but the very majesty of the doctrine would be impaired. They object; but what, pray, is gained by striking against this stone? The utmost they can make out is, that as the preaching of the same gospel was enjoined on all the apostles, so the power of binding and loosing was bestowed upon them in common. Christ (they say) constituted Peter prince of the whole Church when he promised to give him the keys. But what he then promised to one he elsewhere delivers, and as it were hands over, to all the rest. If the same right, which was promised to one, is bestowed upon all, in what respect is that one superior to his colleagues? He excels (they say) in this, that he receives both in common, and by himself, what is given to the others in common only. What if I should answer with Cyprian, and Augustine, that Christ did not do this to prefer one to the other, but in order to commend the unity of his Church? For Cyprian thus speaks: "In the person of one man he gave the keys to all, that he might denote the unity of all; the rest, therefore, were the same that Peter was, being admitted to an equal participation of honour and power, but a beginning is made from unity that the Church of Christ may be shown

to be one" (Cyprian, de Simplic. Prælat.). Augustine's words are, "Had not the mystery of the Church been in Peter, our Lord would not have said to him, I will give thee the keys. For if this was said to Peter, the Church has them not; but if the Church has them, then when Peter received the keys he represented the whole Church" (August. Hom. in Joann. 50). Again, "All were asked, but Peter alone answers, Thou art the Christ; and it is said to him, I will give thee the keys; as if he alone had received the power of loosing and binding; whereas he both spoke for all, and received in common with all, being, as it were, the representative of unity. One received for all, because there is unity in all" (Hom. 124).

5. But we nowhere read of its being said to any other, "Thou art Peter, and upon this rock I will build my Church"! (Mt. 16:18); as if Christ then affirmed anything else of Peter, than Paul and Peter himself affirm of all Christians (Eph. 2:20; 1 Peter 2:5). The former describes Christ as the chief corner-stone, on whom are built all who grow up into a holy temple in the Lord; the latter describes us as living stones who are founded on that elect and precious stone, and being so joined and compacted, are united to our God, and to each other. Peter (they say) is above others, because the name was specially given to him. I willingly concede to Peter the honour of being placed among the first in the building of the Church, or (if they prefer it) of being the first among the faithful; but I will not allow them to infer from this that he has a primacy over others. For what kind of inference is this? Peter surpasses others in fervid zeal, in doctrine, in magnanimity; therefore, he has power over them: as if we might not with greater plausibility infer, that Andrew is prior to Peter in order, because he preceded him in time, and brought him to Christ (John 1:40, 42); but this I omit. Let Peter have the preeminence, still there is a great difference between the honour of rank and the possession of power. We see that the Apostles usually left it to Peter to address the meeting, and in some measure take precedence in relating, exhorting, admonishing, but we nowhere read anything at all of power.

6. Though we are not yet come to that part of the discussion, I would merely observe at present, how futilely those argue who, out of the mere name of Peter, would rear up a governing power over the whole Church. For the ancient quibble which they at first used to give a colour—viz. The Church is founded upon Peter, because it is said, "On this rock," &c.—is undeserving of notice, not to say of refutation. Some of the Fathers so expounded! But when the whole of Scripture is repugnant to the exposition, why is their authority brought forward in opposition to God? nay, why do we contend about the meaning of these words, as if it were obscure or ambiguous, when nothing can be more clear and certain? Peter had confessed in his own name, and that of his brethren, that Christ was the Son of God (Mt. 16:16). On this rock Christ builds his Church, because it is the only foundation; as Paul says, "Other foundation than this can no man lay" (1 Cor. 3:11). Therefore, I do not here repudiate the authority of the Fathers, because I am destitute of passages from them to prove what I say, were I disposed to quote them; but as I have observed, I am unwilling to annoy my readers by debating so clear a matter, especially since the subject has long ago been fully handled and expounded by our writers.

7. And yet, in truth, none can solve this question better than Scripture, if we compare all the passages in which it shows what office and power Peter held among the apostles, how he acted among them, how he was received by them (Acts 15:7). Run over all these passages, and the utmost you will find is, that Peter was one of twelve, their equal and colleague, not their master. He indeed brings the matter before the council when anything is to be done, and advises as to what is necessary, but he, at the same time, listens to the others, not only conceding to them an opportunity of expressing their sentiments, but allowing them to decide; and when they have decided, he follows and obeys. When he writes to pastors, he does not command authoritatively as a superior, but makes them his colleagues, and courteously advises as equals are wont to do (1 Pet. 5:1). When he is accused of having gone in to the Gentiles, though the accusation is unfounded, he replies to it, and clears himself (Acts 11:3). Being ordered by his colleagues to go with John into Samaria, he declines not (Acts 8:14). The apostles, by sending him, declare that they by no means regard him as a superior, while he, by obeying and undertaking the embassy committed to him, confesses that he is associated with them, and has no authority over them. But if none of these facts existed, the one Epistle to the Galatians would easily remove all doubt, there being almost two chapters in which the whole for which Paul contends is, that in regard to the honour of the apostleship, he is the equal of Peter (Gal. 1:18; 2:8). Hence he states, that he went to Peter, not to acknowledge subjection, but only to make their agreement in doctrine manifest to all; that Peter himself asked no acknowledgment of the kind, but gave him the right hand of fellowship, that they might be common labourers in the vineyard; that not less grace

was bestowed on him among the Gentiles than on Peter among the Jews: in fine, that Peter, when he was not acting with strict fidelity, was rebuked by him, and submitted to the rebuke (Gal. 2:11). All these things make it manifest, either that there was an equality between Paul and Peter, or, at least, that Peter had no more authority over the rest than they had over him. This point, as I have said, Paul handles professedly, in order that no one might give a preference over him, in respect of apostleship, to Peter or John, who were colleagues, not masters.

8. But were I to concede to them what they ask with regard to Peter—viz. that he was the chief of the apostles, and surpassed the others in dignity—there is no ground for making a universal rule out of a special example, or wresting a single fact into a perpetual enactment, seeing that the two things are widely different. One was chief among the apostles, just because they were few in number. If one man presided over twelve, will it follow that one ought to preside over a hundred thousand? That twelve had one among them to direct all is nothing strange. Nature admits, the human mind requires, that in every meeting, though all are equal in power, there should be one as a kind of moderator to whom the others should look up. There is no senate without a consul, no bench of judges without a president or chancellor, no college without a provost, no company without a master. Thus there would be no absurdity were we to confess that the apostles had conferred such a primacy on Peter. But an arrangement which is effectual among a few must not be forthwith transferred to the whole world, which no one man is able to govern. But (say they) it is observed that not less in nature as a whole, than in each of its parts, there is one supreme head. Proof of this it pleases them to derive from cranes and bees, which always place themselves under the guidance of one, not of several. I admit the examples which they produce; but do bees flock together from all parts of the world to choose one queen? Each queen is contented with her own hive. So among cranes, each flock has its own king. What can they prove from this, except that each church ought to have its bishop? They refer us to the examples of states, quoting from Homer, Οὐκ ἀγαθὸν πολυκοιρανίη, "a many-headed rule is not good;" and other "passages to the same effect from heathen writers in commendation of monarchy. The answer is easy. Monarchy is not lauded by Homer's Ulysses, or by others, as if one individual ought to govern the whole world; but they mean to intimate that one kingdom does not admit of two kings, and that empire, as one expresses it (Lucan. Lib. 1), cannot bear a partner.

9. Be it, however, as they will have it (though the thing is most absurd; be it), that it were good and useful for the whole world to be under one monarchy, I will not, therefore, admit that the same thing should take effect in the government of the Church. Her only Head is Christ, under whose government we are all united to each other, according to that order and form of polity which he himself has prescribed. Wherefore they offer an egregious insult to Christ, when under this pretext they would have one man to preside over the whole Church, seeing the Church can never be without a head, "even Christ, from whom the whole body fitly joined together, and compacted by that which every joint supplieth, according to the effectual working in the measure of every part, maketh increase of the body" (Eph. 4:15, 16). See how all men, without exception, are placed in the body, while the honour and name of Head is left to Christ alone. See how to each member is assigned a certain measure, a finite and limited function, while both the perfection of grace and the supreme power of government reside only in Christ. I am not unaware of the cavilling objection which they are wont to urge—viz. that Christ is properly called the only Head, because he alone reigns by his own authority and in his own name; but that there is nothing in this to prevent what they call another *ministerial* head from being under him, and acting as his substitute. But this cavil cannot avail them, until they previously show that this office was ordained by Christ. For the apostle teaches, that the whole subministration is diffused through the members, while the power flows from one celestial Head; or, if they will have it more plainly, since Scripture testifies that Christ is Head, and claims this honour for himself alone, it ought not to be transferred to any other than him whom Christ himself has made his vicegerent. But not only is there no passage to this effect, but it can be amply refuted by many passages.

10. Paul sometimes depicts a living image of the Church, but makes no mention of a single head. On the contrary, we may infer from his description, that it is foreign to the institution of Christ. Christ, by his ascension, took away his visible presence from us, and yet he ascended that he might fill all things: now, therefore, he is present in the Church, and always will be. When Paul would show the mode in which he exhibits himself, he calls our attention to the ministerial offices which he employs: "Unto every one of us is given grace according to the measure of the gift of Christ;" "And he gave some, apostles; and some, prophets; and some, evangelists; and some, pastors and teachers." Why does he not

say, that one presided over all to act as his substitute? The passage particularly required this, and it ought not on any account to have been omitted if it had been true. Christ, he says, is present with us. How? By the ministry of men whom he appointed over the government of the Church. Why not rather by a ministerial head whom he appointed his substitute? He speaks of unity, but it is in God and in the faith of Christ. He attributes nothing to men but a common ministry, and a special mode to each. Why, when thus commending unity, does he not, after saying, "one body, one Spirit, even as ye are called in one hope of your calling, one Lord, one faith, one baptism" (Eph. 4:4), immediately add, one Supreme Pontiff to keep the Church in unity? Nothing could have been said more aptly if the case had really been so. Let that passage be diligently pondered, and there will be no doubt that Paul there meant to give a complete representation of that sacred and ecclesiastical government to which posterity have given the name of hierarchy. Not only does he not place a monarchy among ministers, but even intimates that there is none. There can also be no doubt, that he meant to express the mode of connection by which believers unite with Christ the Head. There he not only makes no mention of a ministerial head, but attributes a particular operation to each of the members, according to the measure of grace distributed to each. Nor is there any ground for subtle philosophical comparisons between the celestial and the earthly hierarchy. For it is not safe to be wise above measure with regard to the former, and in constituting the latter, the only type which it behoves us to follow is that which our Lord himself has delineated in his own word.

11. I will now make them another concession, which they will never obtain from men of sound mind—viz. that the primacy of the Church was fixed in Peter, with the view of remaining for ever by perpetual succession. Still how will they prove that his See was so fixed at Rome, that whosoever becomes Bishop of that city is to preside over the whole world? By what authority do they annex this dignity to a particular place, when it was given without any mention of place? Peter, they say, lived and died at Rome. What did Christ himself do? Did he not discharge his episcopate while he lived, and complete the office of the priesthood by dying at Jerusalem? The Prince of pastors, the chief Shepherd, the Head of the Church, could not procure honour for a place, and Peter, so far his inferior, could! Is not this worse than childish trifling? Christ conferred the honour of primacy on Peter. Peter had his See at Rome, therefore he fixed the seat of the primacy there. In this way the Israelites of old must have placed the seat of the primacy in the wilderness, where Moses, the chief teacher and prince of prophets, discharged his ministry and died.

12. Let us see, however, how admirably they reason. Peter, they say, had the first place among the apostles; therefore, the church in which he sat ought to have the privilege. But where did he first sit? At Antioch, they say. Therefore, the church of Antioch justly claims the primacy. They acknowledge that she was once the first, but that Peter, by removing from it, transferred the honour which he had brought with him to Rome. For there is extant, under the name of Pope Marcellus, a letter to the presbyters of Antioch, in which he says, "The See of Peter, at the outset, was with you, and was afterwards, by the order of the Lord, translated hither." Thus the church of Antioch, which was once the first, yielded to the See of Rome. But by what oracle did that good man learn that the Lord had so ordered? For if the question is to be determined in regular form, they must say whether they hold the privilege to be personal, or real, or mixed. One of the three it must be. If they say personal, then it has nothing to do with place; if real, then when once given to a place it is not lost by the death or departure of the person. It remains that they must hold it to be mixed; then the mere consideration of place is not sufficient unless the person also correspond. Let them choose which they will, I will forthwith infer, and easily prove, that Rome has no ground to arrogate the primacy.

13. However, be it so. Let the primacy have been (as they vainly allege) transferred from Antioch to Rome. Why did not Antioch retain the second place? For if Rome has the first, simply because Peter had his See there at the end of his life, to which place should the second be given sooner than to that where he first had his See? How comes it, then, that Alexandria takes precedence of Antioch? How can the church of a disciple be superior to the See of Peter? If honour is due to a church according to the dignity of its founder, what shall we say of other churches? Paul names three individuals who seemed to be pillars—viz. James, Peter, and John (Gal. 2:9). If, in honour of Peter, the first place is given to the Roman See, do not the churches of Ephesus and Jerusalem, where John and James were fixed, deserve the second and third places? But in ancient times Jerusalem held the last place among the Patriarchates, and Ephesus was not able to secure even the lowest corner. Other churches too have passed away, churches which Paul founded, and over which the apostles presided. The See of Mark, who was

only one of the disciples, has obtained honour. Let them either confess that arrangement was preposterous, or let them concede that it is not always true that each church is entitled to the degree of honour which its founder possessed.

14. But I do not see that any credit is due to their allegation of Peter's occupation of the Roman See. Certainly it is, that the statement of Eusebius, that he presided over it for twenty-five years, is easily refuted. For it appears from the first and second chapters of Galatians, that he was at Jerusalem about twenty years after the death of Christ, and afterwards came to Antioch. How long he remained here is uncertain; Gregory counts seven, and Eusebius twenty-five years. But from our Saviour's death to the end of Nero's reign (under which they state that he was put to death), will be found only thirty-seven years. For our Lord suffered in the eighteenth year of the reign of Tiberius. If you cut off the twenty years, during which, as Paul testifies, Peter dwelt at Jerusalem, there will remain at most seventeen years; and these must be divided between his two episcopates. If he dwelt long at Antioch, his See at Rome must have been of short duration. This we may demonstrate still more clearly. Paul wrote to the Romans while he was on his journey to Jerusalem, where he was apprehended and conveyed to Rome (Rom. 15:15, 16). It is therefore probable that this letter was written four years before his arrival at Rome. Still there is no mention of Peter, as there certainly would have been if he had been ruling that church. Nay, in the end of the Epistle, where he enumerates a long list of individuals whom he orders to be saluted, and in which it may be supposed he includes all who were known to him, he says nothing at all of Peter. To men of sound judgment, there is no need here of a long and subtle demonstration; the nature of the case itself, and the whole subject of the Epistle, proclaim that he ought not to have passed over Peter if he had been at Rome.

15. Paul is afterwards conveyed as a prisoner to Rome. Luke relates that he was received by the brethren, but says nothing of Peter. From Rome he writes to many churches. He even sends salutations from certain individuals, but does not by a single word intimate that Peter was then there. Who, pray, will believe that he would have said nothing of him if he had been present? Nay, in the Epistle to the Philippians, after saying that he had no one who cared for the work of the Lord so faithfully as Timothy, he complains, that "all seek their own" (Phil. 2:21). And to Timothy he makes the more grievous complaint, that no man was present at his first defence, that all men forsook him (2 Tim. 4:16). Where then was Peter? If they say that he was at Rome, how disgraceful the charge which Paul brings against him of being a deserter of the Gospel! For he is speaking of believers, since he adds, "The Lord lay it not to their charge." At what time, therefore, and how long, did Peter hold that See? The uniform opinion of authors is, that he governed that church until his death. But these authors are not agreed as to who was his successor. Some say Linus, others Clement. And they relate many absurd fables concerning a discussion between him and Simon Magus. Nor does Augustine, when treating of superstition, disguise the fact, that owing to an opinion rashly entertained, it had become customary at Rome to fast on the day on which Peter carried away the palm from Simon Magus (August. ad Januar. Ep. 2). In short, the affairs of that period are so involved from the variety of opinions, that credit is not to be given rashly to anything we read concerning it. And yet, from this agreement of authors, I do not dispute that he died there, but that he was bishop, particularly for a long period, I cannot believe. I do not, however, attach much importance to the point, since Paul testifies, that the apostleship of Peter pertained especially to the Jews, but his own specially to us. Therefore, in order that that compact which they made between themselves, nay, that the arrangement of the Holy Spirit may be firmly established among us, we ought to pay more regard to the apostleship of Paul than to that of Peter, since the Holy Spirit, in allotting them different provinces, destined Peter for the Jews and Paul for us. Let the Romanists, therefore, seek their primacy somewhere else than in the word of God, which gives not the least foundation for it.

16. Let us now come to the Primitive Church, that it may also appear that our opponents plume themselves on its support, not less falsely and unadvisedly than on the testimony of the word of God. When they lay it down as an axiom, that the unity of the Church cannot be maintained unless there be one supreme head on earth whom all the members should obey; and that, accordingly, our Lord gave the primacy to Peter, and thereafter, by right of succession, to the See of Rome, there to remain even to the end, they assert that this has always been observed from the beginning. But since they improperly wrest many passages, I would first premise, that I deny not that the early Christians uniformly give high honour to the Roman Church, and speak of it with reverence. This, I think, is owing chiefly to three causes. The opinion which had prevailed (I know not how), that that Church was founded and constituted by the ministry of Peter,

had great effect in procuring influence and authority. Hence, in the East, it was, as a mark of honour, designated the Apostolic See. Secondly, as the seat of empire was there, and it was for this reason to be presumed, that the most distinguished for learning, prudence, skill, and experience, were there more than elsewhere, account was justly taken of the circumstance, lest the celebrity of the city, and the much more excellent gifts of God also, might seem to be despised. To these was added a third cause, that when the churches of the East, of Greece and of Africa, were kept in a constant turmoil by differences of opinion, the Church of Rome was calmer and less troubled. To this it was owing, that pious and holy bishops, when driven from their sees, often betook themselves to Rome as an asylum or haven. For as the people of the West are of a less acute and versatile turn of mind than those of Asia or Africa, so they are less desirous of innovations. It therefore added very great authority to the Roman Church, that in those dubious times it was not so much unsettled as others, and adhered more firmly to the doctrine once delivered, as shall immediately be better explained. For these three causes, I say, she was held in no ordinary estimation, and received many distinguished testimonies from ancient writers.

17. But since on this our opponents would rear up a primacy and supreme authority over other churches, they, as I have said, greatly err. That this may better appear, I will first briefly show what the views of early writers are as to this unity which they so strongly urge. Jerome, in writing to Nepotian, after enumerating many examples of unity, descends at length to the ecclesiastical hierarchy. He says, "Every bishop of a church, every archpresbyter, every archdeacon, and the whole ecclesiastical order, depends on its own rulers." Here a Roman presbyter speaks and commends unity in ecclesiastical order. Why does he not mention that all the churches are bound together by one Head as a common bond? There was nothing more appropriate to the point in hand, and it cannot be said that he omitted it through forgetfulness; there was nothing he would more willingly have mentioned had the fact permitted. He therefore undoubtedly owns, that the true method of unity is that which Cyprian admirably describes in these words: "The episcopate is one, part of which is held entire by each bishop, and the Church is one, which, by the increase of fecundity, extends more widely in numbers. As there are many rays of the sun and one light, many branches of a tree and one trunk, upheld by its tenacious root, and as very many streams flow from one fountain, and though numbers seem diffused by the largeness of the overflowing supply, yet unity is preserved entire in the source, so the Church, pervaded with the light of the Lord, sends her rays over the whole globe, and yet is one light, which is everywhere diffused without separating the unity of the body, extends her branches over the whole globe, and sends forth flowing streams; still the head is one, and the source one" (Cyprian, de Simplie. Prælat.). Afterwards he says, "The spouse of Christ cannot be an adulteress: she knows one house, and with chaste modesty keeps the sanctity of one bed." See how he makes the bishopric of Christ alone universal, as comprehending under it the whole Church: See how he says that part of it is held entire by all who discharge the episcopal office under this head. Where is the primacy of the Roman See, if the entire bishopric resides in Christ alone, and a part of it is held entire by each? My object in these remarks is, to show the reader, in passing, that that axiom of the unity of an earthly kind in the hierarchy, which the Romanists assume as confessed and indubitable, was altogether unknown to the ancient Church.

CHAPTER 7

OF THE BEGINNING AND RISE OF THE ROMISH PAPACY, TILL IT ATTAINED A HEIGHT BY WHICH THE LIBERTY OF THE CHURCH WAS DESTROYED, AND ALL TRUE RULE OVERTHROWN.

There are five heads in this chapter. I. The Patriarchate given and confirmed to the Bishop of Rome, first by the Council of Nice, and afterwards by that of Chalcedon though by no means approved of by other bishops, was the commencement of the Papacy, sec. 1–4. II. The Church at Rome, by taking pious exiles under its protection, and also thereby protecting wicked men who fled to her, helped forward the mystery of iniquity, although at that time neither the ordination of bishops, nor admonitions and censures, nor the right of convening Councils, nor the right of receiving appeals, belonged to the Roman Bishop, whose profane meddling with these things was condemned by Gregory, sec. 5–13. III. After the Council of Turin, disputes arose as to the authority of Metropolitans. Disgraceful strife between the Patriarchs of Rome and Constantinople. The vile assassin Phocas put an end to these brawls at the instigation of Boniface, sec. 14–18. IV. To the dishonest arts of Boniface succeeded fouler frauds devised in more modern times, and expressly condemned by Gregory and Bernard. sec. 19–21. V. The Papacy at length appeared complete in all its parts, the seat of Antichrist. Its impiety, execrable tyranny, and wickedness, portrayed, sec. 23–30.

Sections:

1. First part of the chapter, in which the commencement of the Papacy is assigned to the Council of Nice. In subsequent Councils other bishops presided. No attempt then made to claim the first place.

2. Though the Roman Bishop presided in the Council of Chalcedon, this was owing to special circumstances. The same right not given to his successors in other Councils.

3. The ancient Fathers did not give the title of Primate to the Roman Bishop.

4. Gregory was vehement in opposition to the title when claimed by the Bishop of Constantinople, and did not claim it for himself.

5. Second part of the chapter, explaining the ambitious attempts of the Roman See to obtain the primacy. Their reception of pious exiles. Hearing the appeals and complaints of heretics. Their ambition in this respect offensive to the African Church.

6. The power of the Roman Bishops in ordaining bishops, appointing councils, deciding controversies, &c., confined to their own Patriarchate.

7. If they censured other bishops, they themselves were censured in their turn.

8. They had no right of calling provincial councils except within their own boundaries. The calling of a universal council belonged solely to the Emperor.

9. Appeal to the Roman See not acknowledged by other bishops. Stoutly resisted by the Bishops of France and Africa. The impudence and falsehood of the Roman Pontiff detected.

10. Proof from history that the Roman had no jurisdiction over other churches.

11. The decretal epistles of no avail in support of this usurped jurisdiction.

12. The authority of the Roman Bishop extended in the time of Gregory. Still it only consisted in aiding other bishops with their own consent, or at the command of the Emperor.

13. Even the extent of jurisdiction, thus voluntarily conferred, objected to by Gregory as interfering with better duties.

14. Third part of the chapter, showing the increase of the power of the Papacy in defining the limits of Metropolitans. This gave rise to the decree of the Council of Turin. This decree haughtily annulled by Innocent.

15. Hence the great struggle for precedency between the Sees of Rome and Constantinople. The pride and ambition of the Roman Bishops unfolded.

16. Many attempts of the Bishop of Constantinople to deprive the Bishop of Rome of the primacy.

17. Phocas murders the Emperor, and gives Rome the primacy.

18. The Papal tyranny shortly after established. Bitter complaints by Bernard.

19. Fourth part of the chapter. Altered appearance of the Roman See since the days of Gregory.

20. The present demands of the Romanists not formerly conceded. Fictions of Gregory IX. and Martin.

21. Without mentioning the opposition of Cyprian, of councils, and historical facts, the claims now made were condemned by Gregory himself.

22. The abuses of which Gregory and Bernard complained now increased and sanctioned.

23. The fifth and last part of the chapter, containing the chief answer to the claims of the Papacy—viz. that the Pope is not a bishop in the house of God. This answer confirmed by an enumeration of the essential parts of the episcopal office.

24. A second confirmation by appeal to the institution of Christ. A third confirmation e contrario—viz. That in doctrine and morals the Roman Pontiff is altogether different from a true bishop. Conclusion, that Rome is not the Apostolic See, but the Papacy.

25. Proof from Daniel and Paul that the Pope is Antichrist.

26. Rome could not now claim the primacy, even though she had formerly been the first See, especially considering the base trafficking in which she has engaged.

27. Personal character of Popes. Irreligious opinions held by some of them.

28. John XXII. heretical in regard to the immortality of the soul. His name, therefore, ought to be expunged from the catalogue of Popes, or rather, there is no foundation for the claim of perpetuity of faith in the Roman See.

29. Some Roman Pontiffs atheists, or sworn enemies of religion. Their immoral lives. Practice of the Cardinals and Romish clergy.

30. Cardinals were formerly merely presbyters of the Roman Church, and far inferior to bishops. As they now are, they have no true and legitimate office in the Church. Conclusion.

1. In regard to the antiquity of the primacy of the Roman See, there is nothing in favour of its establishment more ancient than the decree of the Council of Nice, by which the first place among the Patriarchs is assigned to the Bishop of Rome, and he is enjoined to take care of the suburban churches. While the council, in dividing between him and the other Patriarchs, assigns the proper limits of each, it certainly does not appoint him head of all, but only one of the chief. Vitus and Vincentius attended on the part of Julius, who then governed the Roman Church, and to them the fourth place was given. I ask, if Julius was acknowledged the head of the Church, would his legates have been consigned to the fourth place? Would Athanasius have presided in the council where a representative of the hierarchal order should have been most conspicuous? In the Council of Ephesus, it appears that Celestinus (who was then Roman Pontiff) used a cunning device to secure the dignity of his See. For when he sent his deputies, he made Cyril of Alexandria, who otherwise would have presided, his substitute. Why that commission, but just that his name might stand connected with the first See? His legates sit in an inferior place, are asked their opinion along with others, and subscribe in their order, while, at the same time, his name is coupled with that of the Patriarch of Alexandria. What shall I say of the second Council of Ephesus, where, while the deputies of Leo were present, the Alexandrian Patriarch Dioscorus presided as in his own right? They will object that this was not an orthodox council, since by it the venerable Flavianus was condemned, Eutyches acquitted, and his heresy approved. Yet when the council was met, and the bishops distributed the places among themselves, the deputies of the Roman Church sat among the others just as in a sacred and lawful Council. Still they contend not for the first place, but yield it to another: this they never would have done if they had thought it their own by right. For the Roman bishops were never ashamed to stir up the greatest strife in contending for honours, and for this cause alone, to trouble and harass the Church with many pernicious contests; but because Leo saw that it would be too extravagant to ask the first place for his legates, he omitted to do it.

2. Next came the Council of Chalcedon, in which, by concession of the Emperor, the legates of the Roman Church occupied the first place. But Leo himself confesses that this was an extraordinary privilege; for when he asks it of the Emperor Marcian and Pulcheria Augusta, he does not maintain that it is due to him, but only pretends that the Eastern bishops who presided in the Council of Ephesus had thrown all into confusion, and made a bad use of their power. Therefore, seeing there was need of a grave moderator, and it was not probable that those who had once been so fickle and tumultuous would be fit for this purpose, he requests that, because of the fault and unfitness of others, the office of governing should be transferred to him. That which is asked as a special privilege, and out of the usual order, certainly is not due by a common law. When it is only pretended that there is need of a new president, because the former ones had behaved themselves improperly, it is plain that the thing asked was not previously done, and ought not to be made perpetual, being done only in respect of a present danger. The Roman Pontiff, therefore, holds the first place in the Council of Chalcedon, not because it is due to his See, but because the council is in want of a grave and fit moderator, while those who ought to have presided exclude themselves by their intemperance and passion. This statement the successor of Leo approved by his procedure. For when he sent his legates to the fifth Council, that of Constantinople, which was held long after, he did not quarrel for the first seat, but readily allowed Mennas, the patriarch of Constantinople, to preside. In like manner, in the Council of Carthage, at which Augustine was present, we perceive that not the legates of the Roman See, but Aurelius, the archbishop of the place, presided, although there was then a question as to the authority of the Roman Pontiff. Nay, even in Italy itself, a universal council was held (that of Aquileia), at which the Roman Bishop was not present. Ambrose, who was then in high favour with the Emperor, presided, and no mention is made of the Roman Pontiff. Therefore, owing to the dignity of Ambrose, the See of Milan was then more illustrious than that of Rome.

3. In regard to the mere title of primate and other titles of pride, of which that pontiff now makes a wondrous boast, it is not difficult to understand how and in what way they crept in. Cyprian often makes mention of Cornelius (Cyprian. Lib. 2 Ep. 2; Lib. 4 Ep. 6), nor does he distinguish him by any other name than that of brother, or fellow bishop, or colleague. When he writes to Stephen, the successor of Cornelius, he not only makes him the equal of himself and others, but addresses him in harsh terms, charging him at one time with presumption, at another with ignorance. After Cyprian, we have the judgment of the whole African Church on the subject. For the Council of Carthage enjoined that none should be called chief of the priests, or first bishop, but only bishop of the first See. But any one who will examine

the more ancient records will find that the Roman Pontiff was then contented with the common appellation of brother. Certainly, as long as the true and pure form of the Church continued, all these names of pride on which the Roman See afterwards began to plume itself, were altogether unheard of; none knew what was meant by the supreme Pontiff, and the only head of the Church on earth. Had the Roman Bishop presumed to assume any such title, there were right-hearted men who would immediately have repressed his folly. Jerome, seeing he was a Roman presbyter, was not slow to proclaim the dignity of his church, in as far as fact and the circumstances of the times permitted, and yet we see how he brings it under due subordination. "If authority is asked, the world is greater than a city. Why produce to me the custom of one city? Why vindicate a small number with whom superciliousness has originated against the laws of the Church? Wherever the bishop be, whether at Rome, or Eugubium, or Constantinople, or Rhegium, the merit is the same, and the priesthood the same. The power of riches, or the humbleness of poverty, do not make a bishop superior or inferior" (Hieron. Ep. ad Evagr.).

4. The controversy concerning the title of universal bishop arose at length in the time of Gregory, and was occasioned by the ambition of John of Constantinople. For he wished to make himself universal, a thing which no other had ever attempted. In that controversy, Gregory does not allege that he is deprived of a right which belonged to him, but he strongly insists that the appellation is profane, nay, blasphemous, nay the forerunner of Antichrist. "The whole Church falls from its state, if he who is called universal falls" (Greg. Lib. 4 Ep. 76). Again, "It is very difficult to bear patiently that one who is our brother and fellow bishop should alone be called bishop, while all others are despised. But in this pride of his, what else is intimated but that the days of Antichrist are already near? For he is imitating him, who, despising the company of angels, attempted to ascend the pinnacle of greatness" (Lib. 4 Ep. 76). He elsewhere says to Eulogius of Alexandria and Anastasius of Antioch: "None of my predecessors ever desired to use this profane term: for if one patriarch is called universal, it is derogatory to the name of patriarch in others. But far be it from any Christian mind to wish to arrogate to itself that which would in any degree, however slight, impair the honour of his brethren" (Lib. 4 Ep. 80). "To consent to that impious term is nothing else than to lose the faith" (Lib. 4 Ep. 83). "What we owe to the preservation of the unity of the faith is one thing, what we owe to the suppression of pride is another. I speak with confidence, for every one that calls himself, or desires to be called, universal priest, is by his pride a forerunner of Antichrist, because he acts proudly in preferring himself to others" (Lib. 7 Ep. 154). Thus, again, in a letter to Anastasius of Antioch, "I said, that he could not have peace with us unless he corrected the presumption of a superstitious and haughty term which the first apostate invented; and (to say nothing of the injury to your honour) if one bishop is called universal, the whole Church goes to ruin when that universal bishop falls" (Lib. 4 Ep. 188). But when he writes, that this honour was offered to Leo in the Council of Chalcedon (Lib. 4 Ep. 76, 80; Lib. 7 Ep. 76), he says what has no semblance of truth; nothing of the kind is found among the acts of that council. And Leo himself, who, in many letters, impugns the decree which was then made in honour of the See of Constantinople, undoubtedly would not have omitted this argument, which was the most plausible of all, if it was true that he himself repudiated what was given to him. One who, in other respects, was rather too desirous of honour, would not have omitted what would have been to his praise. Gregory, therefore, is incorrect in saying, that that title was conferred on the Roman See by the Council of Chalcedon; not to mention how ridiculous it is for him to say, that it proceeded from that sacred council, and yet to term it wicked, profane, nefarious, proud, and blasphemous, nay, devised by the devil, and promulgated by the herald of Antichrist. And yet he adds, that his predecessor refused it, lest by that which was given to one individually, all priests should be deprived of their due honour. In another place, he says, "None ever wished to be called by such a name; none arrogated this rash name to himself, lest, by seizing on the honour of supremacy in the office of the Pontificate, he might seem to deny it to all his brethren" (Gregor. Lib. 4 Ep. 82).

5. I come now to jurisdiction, which the Roman Pontiff asserts as an incontrovertible proposition that he possesses over all churches. I am aware of the great disputes which anciently existed on this subject: for there never was a time when the Roman See did not aim at authority over other churches. And here it will not be out of place to investigate the means by which she gradually attained to some influence. I am not now referring to that unlimited power which she seized at a comparatively recent period. The consideration of that we shall defer to its own place. But it is worth while here briefly to show in what way, and by what means, she formerly raised herself, so as to arrogate some authority over other churches.

When the churches of the East were troubled and rent by the factions of the Arians, under the Emperors Constantius and Constans, sons of Constantine the Great; and Athanasius, the principal defender of the orthodox faith, had been driven from his see, the calamity obliged him to come to Rome, in order that by the authority of this see he might both repress the rage of his enemies, and confirm the orthodox under their distress. He was honourably received by Julius, who was then bishop, and engaged those of the West to undertake the defence of his cause. Therefore, when the orthodox stood greatly in need of external aid, and perceived that their chief protection lay in the Roman See, they willingly bestowed upon it all the authority they could. But the utmost extent of this was, that its communion was held in high estimation, and it was deemed ignominious to be excommunicated by it. Dishonest bad men afterwards added much to its authority, for when they wished to escape lawful tribunals, they betook themselves to Rome as an asylum. Accordingly, if any presbyter was condemned by his bishop, or if any bishop was condemned by the synod of his province, he appealed to Rome. These appeals the Roman bishops received more eagerly than they ought, because it seemed a species of extraordinary power to interpose in matters with which their connection was so very remote. Thus, when Eutyches was condemned by Flavianus, Bishop of Constantinople, he complained to Leo that the sentence was unjust. He, nothing loth, no less presumptuously than abruptly, undertook the patronage of a bad cause, and inveighed bitterly against Flavianus, as having condemned an innocent man without due investigation: and thus the effect of Leo's ambition was, that for some time the impiety of Eutyches was confirmed. It is certain that in Africa the same thing repeatedly occurred, for whenever any miscreant had been condemned by his ordinary judge, he fled to Rome, and brought many calumnious charges against his own people. The Roman See was always ready to interpose. This dishonesty obliged the African bishops to decree that no one should carry an appeal beyond sea under pain of excommunication.

6. Be this as it may, let us consider what right or authority the Roman See then possessed. Ecclesiastical power may be reduced to four heads—viz. ordination of bishops, calling of councils, hearing of appeals (or jurisdiction), inflicting monitory chastisements or censures. All ancient councils enjoin that bishops shall be ordained by their own Metropolitans; they nowhere enjoin an application to the Roman Bishop, except in his own patriarchate. Gradually, however, it became customary for all Italian bishops to go to Rome for consecration, with the exception of the Metropolitans, who did not allow themselves to be thus brought into subjection; but when any Metropolitan was to be ordained, the Roman Bishop sent one of his presbyters merely to be present, but not to preside. An example of this kind is extant in Gregory (Lib. 2 Ep. 68, 70), in the consecration of Constantius of Milan, after the death of Laurence. I do not, however, think that this was a very ancient custom. At first, as a mark of respect and good-will, they sent deputies to one another to witness the ordination, and attest their communion. What was thus voluntary afterwards began to be regarded as necessary. However this be, it is certain that anciently the Roman Bishop had no power of ordaining except within the bounds of his own patriarchate, that is, as a canon of the Council of Nice expresses it, in suburban churches. To ordination was added the sending of a *synodical epistle*, but this implied no authority. The patriarchs were accustomed, immediately after consecration, to attest their faith by a formal writing, in which they declared that they assented to sacred and orthodox councils. Thus, by rendering an account of their faith, they mutually approved of each other. If the Roman Bishop had received this confession from others, and not given it, he would therein have been acknowledged superior; but when it behoved to give as well as to receive, and to be subject to the common law, this was a sign of equality, not of lordship. Of this we have an example in a letter of Gregory to Anastasius and Cyriac of Constantinople, and in another letter to all the patriarchs together (Gregor. Lib. 1 Ep. 24, 25; Lib. 6 Ep. 169).

7. Next come *admonitions* or *censures*. These the Roman Bishops anciently employed towards others, and in their turn received. Irenæus sharply rebuked Victor for rashly troubling the Church with a pernicious schism, for a matter of no moment. He submitted without objecting. Holy bishops were then wont to use the freedom as brethren, of admonishing and rebuking the Roman Prelate when he happened to err. He in his turn, when the case required, reminded others of their duty, and reprimanded them for their faults. For Cyprian, when he exhorts Stephen to admonish the bishops of France, does not found on his larger power, but on the common right which priests have in regard to each other (Cyprian. Lib. 3 Ep. 13). I ask if Stephen had then presided over France, would not Cyprian have said, "Check them, for they are yours"? but his language is very different. "The brotherly fellowship which binds us together requires that we should mutually admonish each other" (Cyprian. ad Pomp. Cont. Epist. Steph.) And we see also with what

severity of expression, a man otherwise of a mild temper, inveighs against Stephen himself, when he thinks him chargeable with insolence. Therefore, it does not yet appear in this respect that the Roman Bishop possessed any jurisdiction over those who did not belong to his province.

8. In regard to calling of councils, it was the duty of every Metropolitan to assemble a provincial synod at stated times. Here the Roman Bishop had no jurisdiction, while the Emperor alone could summon a general council. Had any of the bishops attempted this, not only would those out of the province not have obeyed the call, but a tumult would instantly have arisen. Therefore the Emperor gave intimation to all alike to attend. Socrates, indeed, relates that Julius expostulated with the Eastern bishops for not having called him to the Council of Antioch, seeing it was forbidden by the canons that anything should be decided without the knowledge of the Roman Bishop (Tripart. Hist. Lib. 4). But who does not perceive that this is to be understood of those decrees which bind the whole Church? At the same time, it is not strange if, in deference both to the antiquity and largeness of the city, and the dignity of the see, no universal decree concerning religion should be made in the absence of the Bishop of Rome, provided he did not refuse to be present. But what has this to do with the dominion of the whole Church? For we deny not that he was one of the principal bishops, though we are unwilling to admit what the Romanists now contend for—viz. that he had power over all.

9. The fourth remaining species of power is that of hearing *appeals*. It is evident that the supreme power belongs to him to whose tribunal appeals are made. Many had repeatedly appealed to the Roman Pontiff. He also had endeavoured to bring causes under his cognisance, but he had always been derided whenever he went beyond his own boundaries. I say nothing of the East and of Greece, but it is certain, that the bishops of France stoutly resisted when he seemed to assume authority over them. In Africa, the subject was long disputed, for in the Council of Milevita, at which Augustine was present, when those who carried appeals beyond seas were excommunicated, the Roman Pontiff attempted to obtain an alteration of the decree, and sent legates to show that the privilege of hearing appeals was given him by the Council of Nice. The legates produced acts of the council drawn from the armoury of their church. The African bishops resisted, and maintained, that credit was not to be given to the Bishop of Rome in his own cause; accordingly, they said that they would send to Constantinople, and other cities of Greece, where less suspicious copies might be had. It was found that nothing like what the Romanists had pretended was contained in the acts, and thus the decree which abrogated the supreme jurisdiction of the Roman Pontiff was confirmed. In this matter was manifested the egregious effrontery of the Roman Pontiff. For when he had fraudulently substituted the Council of Sardis for that of Nice, he was disgracefully detected in a palpable falsehood; but still greater and more impudent was the iniquity of those who added a fictitious letter to the Council, in which some Bishop of Carthage condemns the arrogance of Aurelius his predecessor, in promising to withdraw himself from obedience to the Apostolic See, and making a surrender of himself and his church, suppliantly prays for pardon. These are the noble records of antiquity on which the majesty of the Roman See is founded, while, under the pretext of antiquity, they deal in falsehoods so puerile, that even a blind man might feel them. "Aurelius (says he), elated by diabolical audacity and contumacy, was rebellious against Christ and St Peter, and, accordingly, deserved to be anathematised." What does Augustine say? and what the many Fathers who were present at the Council of Milevita? But what need is there to give a lengthened refutation of that absurd writing, which not even Romanists, if they have any modesty left them, can look at without a deep feeling of shame? Thus Gratian, whether through malice or ignorance, I know not, after quoting the decree, That those are to be deprived of communion who carry appeals beyond seas, subjoins the exception, Unless, perhaps, they have appealed to the Roman See (Grat. 2, Quæst. 4, cap. Placuit.). What can you make of creatures like these, who are so devoid of common sense that they set down as an exception from the law the very thing on account of which, as everybody sees, the law was made? For the Council, in condemning transmarine appeals, simply prohibits an appeal to Rome. Yet this worthy expounder excepts Rome from the common law.

10. But (to end the question at once) the kind of jurisdiction which belonged to the Roman Bishop one narrative will make manifest. Donatus of Casa Nigra had accused Cecilianus the Bishop of Carthage. Cecilianus was condemned without a hearing: for, having ascertained that the bishops had entered into a conspiracy against him, he refused to appear. The case was brought before the Emperor Constantine. who, wishing the matter to be ended by an ecclesiastical decision; gave the cognisance of it to Melciades, the Roman Bishop,

appointing as his colleagues some bishops from Italy, France, and Spain. If it formed part of the ordinary jurisdiction of the Roman See to hear appeals in ecclesiastical causes, why did he allow others to be conjoined with him at the Emperor's discretion? nay, why does he undertake to decide more from the command of the Emperor than his own office? But let us hear what afterwards happened (see August. Ep. 162, *et alibi*). Cecilianus prevails. Donatus of Casa Nigra is thrown in his calumnious action and appeals. Constantine devolves the decision of the appeal on the Bishop of Arles, who sits as judge, to give sentence after the Roman Pontiff. If the Roman See has supreme power not subject to appeal, why does Melciades allow himself to be so greatly insulted as to have the Bishop of Arles preferred to him? And who is the Emperor that does this? Constantine, who they boast not only made it his constant study, but employed all the resources of the empire to enlarge the dignity of that see. We see, therefore, how far in every way the Roman Pontiff was from that supreme dominion, which he asserts to have been given him by Christ over all churches, and which he falsely alleges that he possessed in all ages, with the consent of the whole world.

11. I know how many epistles there are, how many rescripts and edicts in which there is nothing which the pontiffs do not ascribe and confidently arrogate to themselves. But all men of the least intellect and learning know, that the greater part of them are in themselves so absurd, that it is easy at the first sight to detect the forge from which they have come. Does any man of sense and soberness think that Anacletus is the author of that famous interpretation which is given in Gratian, under the name of Anacletus—viz. that Cephas is head? (Dist. 22, cap. Sacrosancta.) Numerous follies of the same kind which Gratian has heaped together without judgment, the Romanists of the present day employ against us in defence of their see. The smoke, by which, in the former days of ignorance, they imposed upon the ignorant, they would still vend in the present light. I am unwilling to take much trouble in refuting things which, by their extreme absurdity, plainly refute themselves. I admit the existence of genuine epistles by ancient Pontiffs, in which they pronounce magnificent eulogiums on the extent of their see. Such are some of the epistles of Leo. For as he possessed learning and eloquence, so he was excessively desirous of glory and dominion; but the true question is, whether or not, when he thus extolled himself, the churches gave credit to his testimony? It appears that many were offended with his ambition, and also resisted his cupidity.

He in one place appoints the Bishop of Thessalonica his vicar throughout Greece and other neighbouring regions (Leo, Ep. 85), and elsewhere gives the same office to the Bishop of Arles or some other throughout France (Ep. 83). In like manner, he appointed Hormisdas, Bishop of Hispala, his vicar throughout Spain, but he uniformly makes this reservation, that in giving such commissions, the ancient privileges of the Metropolitans were to remain safe and entire. These appointments, therefore, were made on the condition, that no bishop should be impeded in his ordinary jurisdiction, no Metropolitan in taking cognisance of appeals, no provincial council in constituting churches. But what else was this than to decline all jurisdiction, and to interpose for the purpose of settling discord only, in so far as the law and nature of ecclesiastical communion admit?

12. In the time of Gregory, that ancient rule was greatly changed. For when the empire was convulsed and torn, when France and Spain were suffering from the many disasters which they ever and anon received, when Illyricum was laid waste, Italy harassed, and Africa almost destroyed by uninterrupted calamities, in order that, during these civil convulsions, the integrity of the faith might remain, or at least not entirely perish, the bishops in all quarters attached themselves more to the Roman Pontiff. In this way, not only the dignity, but also the power of the see, exceedingly increased, although I attach no great importance to the means by which this was accomplished. It is certain, that it was then greater than in former ages. And yet it was very different from the unbridled dominion of one ruling others as he pleased. Still the reverence paid to the Roman See was such, that by its authority it could guide and repress those whom their own colleagues were unable to keep to their duty; for Gregory is careful ever and anon to testify that he was not less faithful in preserving the rights of others, than in insisting that his own should be preserved. "I do not," says he, "under the stimulus of ambition, derogate from any man's right, but desire to honour my brethren in all things" (Gregor. Lib. 2 Ep. 68). There is no sentence in his writings in which he boasts more proudly of the extent of his primacy than the following: "I know not what bishop is not subject to the Roman See, when he is discovered in a fault" (Leo. Lib. 2, Epist. 68). However, he immediately adds, "Where faults do not call for interference, all are equal according to the rule of humility." He claims for himself the right of correcting those who have sinned; if all do their duty,

he puts himself on a footing of equality. He, indeed, claimed this right, and those who chose assented to it, while those who were not pleased with it were at liberty to object with impunity; and it is known that the greater part did so. We may add, that he is then speaking of the primate of Byzantium, who, when condemned by a provincial synod, repudiated the whole judgment. His colleagues had informed the Emperor of his contumacy, and the Emperor had given the cognisance of the matter to Gregory. We see, therefore, that he does not interfere in any way with the ordinary jurisdiction, and that, in acting as a subsidiary to others, he acts entirely by the Emperor's command.

13. At this time, therefore, the whole power of the Roman Bishop consisted in opposing stubborn and ungovernable spirits, where some extraordinary remedy was required, and this in order to assist other bishops, not to interfere with them. Therefore, he assumes no more power over others than he elsewhere gives others over himself, when he confesses that he is ready to be corrected by all, amended by all (Lib. 2 Ep. 37). So, in another place, though he orders the Bishop of Aquileia to come to Rome to plead his cause in a controversy as to doctrine which had arisen between himself and others, he thus orders not of his own authority, but in obedience to the Emperor's command. Nor does he declare that he himself will be sole judge, but promises to call a synod, by which the whole business may be determined. But although the moderation was still such, that the power of the Roman See had certain limits which it was not permitted to overstep, and the Roman Bishop himself was not more above than under others, it appears how much Gregory was dissatisfied with this state of matters. For he ever and anon complains, that he, under the colour of the episcopate, was brought back to the world, and was more involved in earthly cares than when living as a laic; that he, in that honourable office, was oppressed by the tumult of secular affairs. Elsewhere he says, "So many burdensome occupations depress me, that my mind cannot at all rise to things above. I am shaken by the many billows of causes, and after they are quieted, am afflicted by the tempests of a tumultuous life, so that I may truly say I am come into the depths of the sea, and the flood has overwhelmed me." From this I infer what he would have said if he had fallen on the present times. If he did not fulfil, he at least did the duty of a pastor. He declined the administration of civil power, and acknowledged himself subject, like others, to the Emperor. He did not interfere with the management of other churches, unless forced by necessity. And yet he thinks himself in a labyrinth, because he cannot devote himself entirely to the duty of a bishop.

14. At that time, as has already been said, the Bishop of Constantinople was disputing with the Bishop of Rome for the primacy. For after the seat of empire was fixed at Constantinople, the majesty of the empire seemed to demand that that church should have the next place of honour to that of Rome. And certainly, at the outset, nothing had tended more to give the primacy to Rome, than that it was then the capital of the empire. In Gratian, (Dist. 80), there is a rescript under the name of Pope Lucinus, to the effect that the only way in which the cities where Metropolitans and Primates ought to preside were distinguished, was by means of the civil government which had previously existed. There is a similar rescript under the name of Pope Clement, in which he says, that patriarchs were appointed in those cities which had previously had the first flamens. Although this is absurd, it was borrowed from what was true. For it is certain, that in order to make as little change as possible, provinces were distributed according to the state of matters then existing, and Primates and Metropolitans were placed in those cities which surpassed others in honours and power. Accordingly, it was decreed in the Council of Turin, that the cities of every province which were first in the civil government should be the first sees of bishops. But if it should happen that the honour of civil government was transferred from one city to another, then the right of the metropolis should be at the same time transferred thither. But Innocent, the Roman Pontiff, seeing that the ancient dignity of the city had been decaying ever since the seat of empire had been transferred to Constantinople, and fearing for his see, enacted a contrary law, in which he denies the necessity of changing metropolitan churches as imperial metropolitan cities were changed. But the authority of a synod is justly to be preferred to the opinion of one individual, and Innocent himself should be suspected in his own cause. However this be, he by his caveat shows the original rule to have been, that Metropolitans should be distributed according to the order of the empire.

15. Agreeably to this ancient custom, the first Council of Constantinople decreed that the bishop of that city should take precedence after the Roman Pontiff, because it was a new Rome. But long after, when a similar decree was made at Chalcedon, Leo keenly protested (Socrat. Hist. Trop. Lib. 9 cap. 13). And not only did he permit himself to set at nought what six hundred bishops or more had decreed, but he even assailed them with bitter

reproaches, because they had derogated from other sees in the honour which they had presumed to confer on the Church of Constantinople (in Decr. 22, Distinct. cap. Constantinop.). What, pray, could have incited the man to trouble the world for so small an affair but mere ambition? He says, that what the Council of Nice had once sanctioned ought to have been inviolable; as if the Christian faith was in any danger if one church was preferred to another; or as if separate Patriarchates had been established on any other grounds than that of policy. But we know that policy varies with times, nay, demands various changes. It is therefore futile in Leo to pretend that the See of Constantinople ought not to receive the honour which was given to that of Alexandria, by the authority of the Council of Nice. For it is the dictate of common sense, that the decree was one of those which might be abrogated, in respect of a change of times. What shall we say to the fact, that none of the Eastern churches, though chiefly interested, objected? Proterius, who had been appointed at Alexandria instead of Dioscorus, was certainly present; other patriarchs whose honour was impaired were present. It belonged to them to interfere, not to Leo, whose station remained entire. While all of them are silent, many assent, and the Roman Bishop alone resists, it is easy to judge what it is that moves him; just because he foresaw what happened not long after, that when the glory of ancient Rome declined, Constantinople, not contented with the second place, would dispute the primacy with her. And yet his clamour was not so successful as to prevent the decree of the council from being ratified. Accordingly, his successors seeing themselves defeated, quietly desisted from that petulance, and allowed the Bishop of Constantinople to be regarded as the second Patriarch.

16. But shortly after, John, who, in the time of Gregory, presided over the church of Constantinople, went so far as to say that he was universal Patriarch. Here Gregory, that he might not be wanting to his See in a most excellent cause, constantly opposed. And certainly it was impossible to tolerate the pride and madness of John, who wished to make the limits of his bishopric equal to the limits of the empire. This, which Gregory denies to another, he claims not for himself, but abominates the title by whomsoever used, as wicked, impious, and nefarious. Nay, he is offended with Eulogius, Bishop of Alexandria, who had honoured him with this title, "See (says he, Lib. 8 Ep. 30) in the address of the letter which you have directed to me, though I prohibited you, you have taken care to write a word of proud signification by calling me Universal Pope. What I ask is, that your holiness do not go farther, because, whatever is given to another more than reason demands is withdrawn from you. I do not regard that as honour by which I see that the honour of my brethren is diminished. For my honour is the universal honour of the Church, and entire prerogative of my brethren. If your holiness calls me universal Pope, it denies itself to be this whole which it acknowledges me to be." The cause of Gregory was indeed good and honourable; but John, aided by the favour of the Emperor Maurice, could not be dissuaded from his purpose. Cyriac also, his successor, never allowed himself to be spoken to on the subject.

17. At length Phocas, who had slain Maurice, and usurped his place (more friendly to the Romans, for what reason I know not, or rather because he had been crowned king there without opposition), conceded to Boniface III. what Gregory by no means demanded— viz. that Rome should be the head of all the churches. In this way the controversy was ended. And yet this kindness of the Emperor to the Romans would not have been of very much avail had not other circumstances occurred. For shortly after Greece and all Asia were cut off from his communion, while all the reverence which he received from France was obedience only in so far as she pleased. She was brought into subjection for the first time when Pepin got possession of the throne. For Zachary, the Roman Pontiff, having aided him in his perfidy and robbery when he expelled the lawful sovereign, and seized upon the kingdom, which lay exposed as a kind of prey, was rewarded by having the jurisdiction of the Roman See established over the churches of France. In the same way as robbers are wont to divide and share the common spoil, those two worthies arranged that Pepin should have the worldly and civil power by spoiling the true prince, while Zachary should become the head of all the bishops, and have the spiritual power. This, though weak at the first (as usually happens with new power), was afterwards confirmed by the authority of Charlemagne for a very similar cause. For he too was under obligation to the Roman Pontiff, to whose zeal he was indebted for the honour of empire. Though there is reason to believe that the churches had previously been greatly altered, it is certain that the ancient form of the Church was then only completely effaced in Gaul and Germany. There are still extant among the archives of the Parliament of Paris short commentaries on those times, which, in treating of ecclesiastical affairs, make mention of the compacts both of Pepin and Charlemagne with the Roman Pontiff.

Hence we may infer that the ancient state of matters was then changed.

18. From that time, while everywhere matters were becoming daily worse, the tyranny of the Roman Bishop was established, and ever and anon increased, and this partly by the ignorance, partly by the sluggishness, of the bishops. For while he was arrogating everything to himself, and proceeding more and more to exalt himself without measure, contrary to law and right, the bishops did not exert themselves so zealously as they ought in curbing his pretensions. And though they had not been deficient in spirit, they were devoid of true doctrine and experience, so that they were by no means fit for so important an effort. Accordingly, we see how great and monstrous was the profanation of all sacred things, and the dissipation of the whole ecclesiastical order at Rome, in the age of Bernard. He complains (Lib. 1 de Consider. ad Eugen.) that the ambitious, avaricious, demoniacal, sacrilegious, fornicators, incestuous, and similar miscreants, flocked from all quarters of the world to Rome, that by apostolic authority they might acquire or retain ecclesiastical honours: that fraud, circumvention, and violence, prevailed. The mode of judging causes then in use he describes as execrable, as disgraceful, not only to the Church, but the bar. He exclaims that the Church is filled with the ambitious: that not one is more afraid to perpetrate crimes than robbers in their den when they share the spoils of the traveller. "Few (say he) look to the mouth of the legislator, but all to his hands. Not without cause, however: for their hands do the whole business of the Pope. What kind of thing is it when those are bought by the spoils of the Church, who say to you, Well done, well done? The life of the poor is sown in the highways of the rich: silver glitters in the mire: they run together from all sides: it is not the poorer that takes it up, but the stronger, or, perhaps, he who runs fastest. That custom, however, or rather that death, comes not of you: I wish it would end in you. While these things are going on, you, a pastor, come forth robed in much costly clothing. If I might presume to say it, this is more the pasture of demons than of sheep. Peter, forsooth, acted thus; Paul sported thus. Your court has been more accustomed to receive good men than to make them. The bad do not gain much there, but the good degenerate." Then when he describes the abuses of appeals, no pious man can read them without being horrified. At length, speaking of the unbridled cupidity of the Roman See in usurping jurisdiction, he thus concludes (Lib. 3 de Concil.), "I express the murmur and common complaint of the churches. Their cry is, that they are maimed and dismembered. There are none, or very few, who do not lament or fear that plague. Do you ask what plague? Abbots are encroached upon by bishops, bishops by archbishops, &c. It is strange if this can be excused. By thus acting, you prove that you have the fulness of power, but not the fulness of righteousness. You do this because you are able; but whether you also ought to do it is the question. You are appointed to preserve, not to envy, the honour and rank of each." I have thought it proper to quote these few passages out of many, partly that my readers may see how grievously the Church had then fallen, partly, too, that they may see with what grief and lamentation all pious men beheld this calamity.

19. But though we were to concede to the Roman Pontiff of the present day the eminence and extent of jurisdiction which his see had in the middle ages, as in the time of Leo and Gregory, what would this be to the existing Papacy? I am not now speaking of worldly dominion, or of civil power, which will afterwards be explained in their own place (chap. 11 sec. 8–14); but what resemblance is there between the spiritual government of which they boast and the state of those times? The only definition which they give of the Pope is, that he is the supreme head of the Church on earth, and the universal bishop of the whole globe. The Pontiffs themselves, when they speak of their authority, declare with great superciliousness, that the power of commanding belongs to them,—that the necessity of obedience remains with others,—that all their decrees are to be regarded as confirmed by the divine voice of Peter,—that provincial synods, from not having the presence of the Pope, are deficient in authority,—that they can ordain the clergy of any church,—and can summon to their See any who have been ordained elsewhere. Innumerable things of this kind are contained in the farrago of Gratian, which I do not mention, that I may not be tedious to my readers. The whole comes to this, that to the Roman Pontiff belongs the supreme cognisance of all ecclesiastical causes, whether in determining and defining doctrines, or in enacting laws, or in appointing discipline, or in giving sentences. It were also tedious and superfluous to review the privileges which they assume to themselves in what they call reservations. But the most intolerable of all things is their leaving no judicial authority in the world to restrain and curb them when they licentiously abuse their immense power. "No man (say they) is entitled to alter the judgment of this See, on account of the primacy of the Roman Church." Again, "The judge shall not be judged either by the emperor, or

by kings, or by the clergy, or by the people." It is surely imperious enough for one man to appoint himself the judge of all, while he will not submit to the judgment of any. But what if he tyrannises over the people of God? if he dissipates and lays waste the kingdom of Christ? if he troubles the whole Church? if he convert the pastoral office into robbery? Nay, though he should be the most abandoned of all, he insists that none can call him to account. The language of Pontiffs is, "God has been pleased to terminate the causes of other men by men, but the Prelate of this See he has reserved unquestioned for his own judgment." Again, "The deeds of subjects are judged by us; ours by God only."

20. And in order that edicts of this kind might have more weight, they falsely substituted the names of ancient Pontiffs, as if matters had been so constituted from the beginning, while it is absolutely certain that whatever attributes more to the Pontiff than we have stated to have been given to him by ancient councils, is new and of recent fabrication. Nay, they have carried their effrontery so far as to publish a rescript under the name of Anastasius, the Patriarch of Constantinople, in which he testifies that it was appointed by ancient regulations, that nothing should be done in the remotest provinces without being previously referred to the Roman See. Besides its extreme folly, who can believe it credible that such an eulogium on the Roman See proceeded from an opponent and rival of its honour and dignity? But doubtless it was necessary that those Antichrists should proceed to such a degree of madness and blindness, that their iniquity might be manifest to all men of sound mind who will only open their eyes. The decretal epistles collected by Gregory IX., also the Clementines and Extravagants of Martin, breathe still more plainly, and in more bombastic terms bespeak this boundless ferocity and tyranny, as it were, of barbarian kings. But these are the oracles out of which the Romanists would have their Papacy to be judged. Hence have sprung those famous axioms which have the force of oracles throughout the Papacy in the present day—viz. that the Pope cannot err; that the Pope is superior to councils; that the Pope is the universal bishop of all churches, and the chief Head of the Church on earth. I say nothing of the still greater absurdities which are babbled by the foolish canonists in their schools, absurdities, however, which Roman theologians not only assent to, but even applaud in flattery of their idol.

21. I will not treat with them on the strictest terms. In opposition to their great insolence, some would quote the language which Cyprian used to the bishops in the council over which he presided: "None of us styles himself bishop of bishops, or forces his colleagues to the necessity of obeying by the tyranny of terror." Some might object what was long after decreed at Carthage, "Let no one be called the prince of priests or first bishop;" and might gather many proofs from history, and canons from councils, and many passages from ancient writers, which bring the Roman Pontiff into due order. But these I omit, that I may not seem to press too hard upon them. However, let these worthy defenders of the Roman See tell me with what face they can defend the title of universal bishop, while they see it so often anathematised by Gregory. If effect is to be given to his testimony, then they, by making their Pontiff universal, declare him to be Antichrist. The name of *head* was not more approved. For Gregory thus speaks: "Peter was the chief member in the body, John, Andrew, and James, the heads of particular communities. All, however, are under one head members of the Church: nay, the saints before the law, the saints under the law, the saints under grace, all perfecting the body of the Lord, are constituted members: none of them ever wished to be styled universal" (Gregor. Lib. 4 Ep. 83). When the Pontiff arrogates to himself the power of ordering, he little accords with what Gregory elsewhere says. For Eulogius, Bishop of Alexandria, having said that he had received an order from him, he replies in this manner: "This word *order* I beg you to take out of my hearing, for I know who I am, and who you are: in station you are my brethren, in character my fathers. I therefore did not order, but took care to suggest what seemed useful" (Gregor. Lib. 7 Ep. 80). When the Pope extends his jurisdiction without limit, he does great and atrocious injustice not only to other bishops, but to each single church, tearing and dismembering them, that he may build his see upon their ruins. When he exempts himself from all tribunals, and wishes to reign in the manner of a tyrant, holding his own caprice to be his only law, the thing is too insulting, and too foreign to ecclesiastical rule, to be on any account submitted to. It is altogether abhorrent, not only from pious feeling, but also from common sense.

22. But that I may not be forced to discuss and follow out each point singly, I again appeal to those who, in the present day, would be thought the best and most faithful defenders of the Roman See, whether they are not ashamed to defend the existing state of the Papacy, which is clearly a hundred times more corrupt than in the days of Gregory and Bernard, though even then these holy men were so much displeased with it. Gregory everywhere complains (Lib. 1 Ep. 5; *item*, Ep. 7, 25, &c.) that

he was distracted above measure by foreign occupations: that under colour of the episcopate he was taken back to the world, being subject to more worldly cares than he remembered to have ever had when a laic; that he was so oppressed by the trouble of secular affairs, as to be unable to raise his mind to things above; that he was so tossed by the many billows of causes, and afflicted by the tempests of a tumultuous life, that he might well say, "I am come into the depths of the sea." It is certain, that amid these worldly occupations, he could teach the people in sermons, admonish in private, and correct those who required it; order the Church, give counsel to his colleagues, and exhort them to their duty. Moreover, some time was left for writing, and yet he deplores it as his calamity, that he was plunged into the very deepest sea. If the administration at that time was a sea, what shall we say of the present Papacy? For what resemblance is there between the periods? Now there are no sermons, no care for discipline, no zeal for churches, no spiritual function; nothing, in short, but the world. And yet this labyrinth is lauded as if nothing could be found better ordered and arranged. What complaints also does Bernard pour forth, what groans does he utter, when he beholds the vices of his own age? What then would he have done on beholding this iron, or, if possible, worse than iron, age of ours? How dishonest, therefore, not only obstinately to defend as sacred and divine what all the saints have always with one mouth disapproved, but to abuse their testimony in favour of the Papacy, which, it is evident, was altogether unknown to them? Although I admit, in respect to the time of Bernard, that all things were so corrupt as to make it not unlike our own. But it betrays a want of all sense of shame to seek any excuse from that middle period—namely, from that of Leo, Gregory, and the like—for it is just as if one were to vindicate the monarchy of the Cæsars by lauding the ancient state of the Roman empire; in other words, were to borrow the praises of liberty in order to eulogise tyranny.

23. Lastly, Although all these things were granted, an entirely new question arises, when we deny that there is at Rome a Church in which privileges of this nature can reside; when we deny that there is a bishop to sustain the dignity of these privileges. Assume, therefore, that all these things are true (though we have already extorted the contrary from them), that Peter was by the words of Christ constituted head of the universal Church, and that the honour thus conferred upon him he deposited in the Roman See, that this was sanctioned by the authority of the ancient Church, and confirmed by long use; that supreme power was always with one consent devolved by all on the Roman Pontiff, that while he was the judge of all causes and all men, he was subject to the judgment of none. Let even more be conceded to them if they will, I answer, in one word, that none of these things avail if there be not a Church and a Bishop at Rome. They must of necessity concede to me that she is not a mother of churches who is not herself a church, that he cannot be the chief of bishops who is not himself a bishop. Would they then have the Apostolic See at Rome? Let them give me a true and lawful apostleship. Would they have a supreme pontiff, let them give me a bishop. But how? Where will they show me any semblance of a church? They, no doubt, talk of one, and have it ever in their mouths. But surely the Church is recognised by certain marks, and bishopric is the name of an office. I am not now speaking of the people but of the government, which ought perpetually to be conspicuous in the Church. Where, then, is a ministry such as the institution of Christ requires? Let us remember what was formerly said of the duty of presbyters and bishops. If we bring the office of cardinals to that test, we will acknowledge that they are nothing less than presbyters. But I should like to know what one quality of a bishop the Pope himself has? The first point in the office of a bishop is to instruct the people in the word of God; the second and next to it is to administer the sacraments; the third is to admonish and exhort, to correct those who are in fault, and restrain the people by holy discipline. Which of these things does he do? Nay, which of these things does he pretend to do? Let them say, then, on what ground they will have him to be regarded as a bishop, who does not even in semblance touch any part of the duty with his little finger.

24. It is not with a bishop as with a king; the latter, though he does not execute the proper duty of a king, nevertheless retains the title and the honour; but in deciding on a bishop respect is had to the command of Christ, to which effect ought always to be given in the Church. Let the Romanists then untie this knot. I deny that their pontiff is the prince of bishops, seeing he is no bishop. This allegation of mine they must prove to be false if they would succeed in theirs. What then do I maintain? That he has nothing proper to a bishop, but is in all things the opposite of a bishop. But with what shall I here begin? With doctrine or with morals? What shall I say, or what shall I pass in silence, or where shall I end? This I maintain: while in the present day the world is so inundated with perverse and impious doctrines, so

full of all kinds of superstition, so blinded by error and sunk in idolatry, there is not one of them which has not emanated from the Papacy, or at least been confirmed by it. Nor is there any other reason why the pontiffs are so enraged against the reviving doctrine of the Gospel, why they stretch every nerve to oppress it, and urge all kings and princes to cruelty, than just that they see their whole dominion tottering and falling to pieces the moment the Gospel of Christ prevails. Leo was cruel and Clement sanguinary, Paul is truculent. But in assailing the truth, it is not so much natural temper that impels them as the conviction that they have no other method of maintaining their power. Therefore, seeing they cannot be safe unless they put Christ to flight, they labour in this cause as if they were fighting for their altars and hearths, for their own lives and those of their adherents. What then? Shall we recognise the Apostolic See where we see nothing but horrible apostasy? Shall he be the vicar of Christ who, by his furious efforts in persecuting the Gospel, plainly declares himself to be Antichrist? Shall he be the successor of Peter who goes about with fire and sword demolishing everything that Peter built? Shall he be the Head of the Church who, after dissevering the Church from Christ, her only true Head, tears and lacerates her members? Rome, indeed, was once the mother of all the churches, but since she began to be the seat of Antichrist she ceased to be what she was.

25. To some we seem slanderous and petulant, when we call the Roman Pontiff Antichrist. But those who think so perceive not that they are bringing a charge of intemperance against Paul, after whom we speak, nay, in whose very words we speak. But lest any one object that Paul's words have a different meaning, and are wrested by us against the Roman Pontiff, I will briefly show that they can only be understood of the Papacy. Paul says that Antichrist would sit in the temple of God (2 Thess. 2:4). In another passage, the Spirit, portraying him in the person of Antiochus, says that his reign would be with great swelling words of vanity (Dan. 7:25). Hence we infer that his tyranny is more over souls than bodies, a tyranny set up in opposition to the spiritual kingdom of Christ. Then his nature is such, that he abolishes not the name either of Christ or the Church, but rather uses the name of Christ as a pretext, and lurks under the name of Church as under a mask. But though all the heresies and schisms which have existed from the beginning belong to the kingdom of Antichrist, yet when Paul foretells that defection will come, he by the description intimates that that seat of abomination will be erected, when a kind of universal defection comes upon the Church, though many members of the Church scattered up and down should continue in the true unity of the faith. But when he adds, that in his own time, the mystery of iniquity, which was afterwards to be openly manifested, had begun to work in secret, we thereby understand that this calamity was neither to be introduced by one man, nor to terminate in one man (see Calv. in 2 Thess. 2:3; Dan. 7:9). Moreover, when the mark by which he distinguishes Antichrist is, that he would rob God of his honour and take it to himself, he gives the leading feature which we ought to follow in searching out Antichrist; especially when pride of this description proceeds to the open devastation of the Church. Seeing then it is certain that the Roman Pontiff has impudently transferred to himself the most peculiar properties of God and Christ, there cannot be a doubt that he is the leader and standard-bearer of an impious and abominable kingdom.

26. Let the Romanists now go and oppose us with antiquity; as if, amid such a complete change in every respect, the honour of the See can continue where there is no See. Eusebius says that God, to make way for his vengeance, transferred the Church which was at Jerusalem to Pella (Euseb. Lib. 3 cap. 5). What we are told was once done may have been done repeatedly. Hence it is too absurd and ridiculous so to fix the honour of the primacy to a particular spot, so that he who is in fact the most inveterate enemy of Christ, the chief adversary of the Gospel, the greatest devastator and waster of the Church, the most cruel slayer and murderer of the saints, should be, nevertheless, regarded as the vicegerent of Christ, the successor of Peter, the first priest of the Church, merely because he occupies what was formerly the first of all sees. I do not say how great the difference is between the chancery of the Pope and well-regulated order in the Church; although this one fact might well set the question at rest. For no man of sound mind will include the episcopate in lead and bulls, much less in that administration of captions and circumscriptions, in which the spiritual government of the Pope is supposed to consist. It has therefore been elegantly said, that that vaunted Roman Church was long ago converted into a temporal court, the only thing which is now seen at Rome. I am not here speaking of the vices of individuals, but demonstrating that the Papacy itself is diametrically opposed to the ecclesiastical system.

27. But if we come to individuals, it is well known what kind of vicars of Christ we shall find. No doubt, Julius and Leo, and Clement and Paul, will be pillars of the Christian faith, the first interpreters of religion,

though they knew nothing more of Christ than they had learned in the school of Lucian. But why give the names of three or four pontiffs? as if there were any doubt as to the kind of religion professed by pontiffs, with their College of Cardinals, and professors, in the present day. The first head of the secret theology which is in vogue among them is, that there is no God. Another, that whatever things have been written and are taught concerning Christ are lies and imposture. A third, that the doctrine of a future life and final resurrection is a mere fable. All do not think, few speak thus; I confess it. Yet it is long since this began to be the ordinary religion of pontiffs; and though the thing is notorious to all who know Rome, Roman theologians cease not to boast that by special privilege our Saviour has provided that the Pope cannot err, because it was said to Peter, "I have prayed for thee that thy faith fail not"(Luke 22:32). What, pray, do they gain by their effrontery, but to let the whole world understand that they have reached the extreme of wickedness, so as neither to fear God nor regard man?

28. But let us suppose that the iniquity of these pontiffs whom I have mentioned is not known, as they have not published it either in sermons or writings, but betrayed it only at table or in their chamber, or at least within the walls of their court. But if they would have the privilege which they claim to be confirmed, they must expunge from their list of pontiffs John XXII., who publicly maintained that the soul is mortal, and perishes with the body till the day of resurrection. And to show you that the whole See with its chief props then utterly fell, none of the Cardinals opposed his madness, only the Faculty of Paris urged the king to insist on a recantation. The king interdicted his subjects from communion with him, unless he would immediately recant, and published his interdict in the usual way by a herald. Thus necessitated, he abjured his error. This example relieves me from the necessity of disputing further with my opponents, when they say that the Roman See and its pontiffs cannot err in the faith, from its being said to Peter, "I have prayed for thee that thy faith fail not." Certainly by this shameful lapse he fell from the faith, and became a noted proof to posterity, that all are not Peters who succeed Peter in the episcopate; although the thing is too childish in itself to need an answer: for if they insist on applying everything that was said to Peter to the successors of Peter, it will follow, that they are all Satans, because our Lord once said to Peter, "Get thee behind me, Satan, thou art an offence unto me." It is as easy for us to retort the latter saying as for them to adduce the former.

29. But I have no pleasure in this absurd mode of disputation, and therefore return to the point from which I digressed. To fix down Christ and the Holy Spirit and the Church to a particular spot, so that every one who presides in it, should he be a devil, must still be deemed vicegerent of Christ, and the head of the Church, because that spot was formerly the See of Peter, is not only impious and insulting to Christ, but absurd and contrary to common sense. For a long period, the Roman Pontiffs have either been altogether devoid of religion, or been its greatest enemies. The see which they occupy, therefore, no more makes them the vicars of Christ, than it makes an idol to become God, when it is placed in the temple of God (2 Thess. 2:4). Then, if manners be inquired into, let the Popes answer for themselves, what there is in them that can make them be recognised for bishops. First, the mode of life at Rome, while they not only connive and are silent, but also tacitly approve, is altogether unworthy of bishops, whose duty it is to curb the licence of the people by the strictness of discipline. But I will not be so rigid with them as to charge them with the faults of others. But when they with their household, with almost the whole College of Cardinals, and the whole body of their clergy, are so devoted to wickedness, obscenity, uncleanness, iniquity, and crime of every description, that they resemble monsters more than men, they herein betray that they are nothing less than bishops. They need not fear that I will make a farther disclosure of their turpitude. For it is painful to wade through such filthy mire, and I must spare modest ears. But I think I have amply demonstrated what I proposed—viz. that though Rome was formerly the first of churches, she deserves not in the present day to be regarded as one of her minutest members.

30. In regard to those whom they call Cardinals, I know not how it happened that they rose so suddenly to such a height. In the age of Gregory, the name was applied to bishops only (Gregor. Lib. 2 Ep. 15, 77, 79; Ep. 6, 25). For whenever he makes mention of cardinals, he assigns them not only to the Roman Church, but to every other church, so that, in short, *a Cardinal priest* is nothing else than a bishop. I do not find the name among the writers of a former age. I see, however, that they were inferior to bishops, whom they now far surpass. There is a well-known passage in Augustine: "Although, in regard to terms of honour which custom has fixed in the Church, the office of bishop is greater than that of presbyter, yet in many things, Augustine is inferior to Jerome" (August. ad Hieron. Ep. 19). Here, certainly, he is not distinguishing

a presbyter of the Roman Church from other presbyters, but placing all of them alike after bishops. And so strictly was this observed, that at the Council of Carthage, when two legates of the Roman See were present, one a bishop, and the other a presbyter, the latter was put in the lowest place. But not to dwell too much on ancient times, we have account of a Council held at Rome, under Gregory, at which the presbyters sit in the lowest place, and subscribe by themselves, while deacons do not subscribe at all. And, indeed, they had no office at that time, unless to be present under the bishop, and assist him in the administration of word and sacraments. So much is their lot now changed, that they have become associates of kings and Cæsars. And there can be no doubt that they have grown gradually with their head, until they reached their present pinnacle of dignity. This much it seemed proper to say in passing, that my readers may understand how very widely the Roman See, as it now exists, differs from the ancient See, under which it endeavours to cloak and defend itself. But whatever they were formerly, as they have no true and legitimate office in the Church, they only retain a colour and empty mask; nay, as they are in all respects the opposite of true ministers, the thing which Gregory so often writes must, of necessity, have befallen them. His words are, "Weeping, I say, groaning, I declare it; when the sacerdotal order has fallen within, it cannot long stand without" (Gregor. Lib. 4 Ep. 55, 56; Lib. 5 Ep. 7). Nay, rather what Malachi says of such persons must be fulfilled in them: "Ye are departed out of the way; ye have caused many to stumble at the law; ye have corrupted the covenant of Levi, saith the Lord of hosts. Therefore have I also made you contemptible and base before all the people" (Mal. 2:8, 9). I now leave all the pious to judge what the supreme pinnacle of the Roman hierarchy must be, to which the Papists, with nefarious effrontery, hesitate not to subject the word of God itself, that word which should be venerable and holy in earth and heaven, to men and angels.

CHAPTER 8

OF THE POWER OF THE CHURCH IN ARTICLES OF FAITH. THE UNBRIDLED LICENCE OF THE PAPAL CHURCH IN DESTROYING PURITY OF DOCTRINE.

This chapter is divided into two parts,—I. The limits within which the Church ought to confine herself in matters of this kind, sec. 1–9. II. The Roman Church convicted of having transgressed these limits, sec. 10–16.

Sections:

1. The marks and government of the Church having been considered in the seven previous chapters, the power of the Church is now considered under three heads—viz. Doctrine, Legislation, Jurisdiction.

2. The authority and power given to Church-officers not given to themselves, but their office. This shown in the case of Moses and the Levitical priesthood.

3. The same thing shown in the case of the Prophets.

4. Same thing shown in the case of the Apostles, and of Christ himself.

5. The Church astricted to the written Word of God. Christ the only teacher of the Church. From his lips ministers must derive whatever they teach for the salvation of others. Various modes of divine teaching. 1. Personal revelations.

6. Second mode of teaching—viz. by the Law and the Prophets. The Prophets were in regard to doctrine, the expounders of the Law. To these were added Historical Narratives and the Psalms.

7. Last mode of teaching by our Saviour himself manifested in the flesh. Different names given to this dispensation, to show that we are not to dream of anything more perfect than the written word.

8. Nothing can be lawfully taught in the Church, that is not contained in the writings of the Prophets and Apostles, as dictated by the Spirit of Christ.

9. Neither the Apostles, nor apostolic men. nor the whole Church, allowed to overstep these limits. This confirmed by passages of Peter and Paul. Argument a fortiori.

10. The Roman tyrants have taught a different doctrine—viz. that Councils cannot err, and, therefore, may coin new dogmas.

11. Answer to the Papistical arguments for the authority of the Church. Argument, that the Church is to be led into all truth. Answer. This promise made not only to the whole Church, but to every individual believer.

12. Answers continued.

13. Answers continued.

14. Argument, that the Church should supply the deficiency of the written word by traditions. Answer.

15. Argument founded on Mt. 18:17. Answer.

16. Objections founded on Infant Baptism, and the Canon of the Council of Nice, as to the consubstantiality of the Son. Answer.

1. We come now to the third division—viz. the *Power of the Church*, as existing either in individual bishops, or in councils, whether provincial or general. I speak only of the spiritual power which is proper to the Church, and which consists either in doctrine, or jurisdiction, or in enacting laws. In regard to doctrine, there are two divisions—viz. the authority of delivering dogmas, and the interpretation of them. Before we begin to treat of each in particular, I wish to remind the pious reader, that whatever is taught respecting the power of the Church, ought to have reference to the end for which Paul declares (2 Cor. 10:8; 13:10) that it was given—namely, for edification, and not for destruction, those who use it lawfully deeming themselves to be nothing more than servants of Christ, and, at the same time, servants of the people in Christ. Moreover, the only mode by which ministers can edify the Church is, by studying to maintain the authority of Christ, which cannot be unimpaired, unless that which he received of the Father is left to him—viz. to be the only Master of the Church. For it was not said of any other but of himself alone, "Hear him" (Mt. 17:5). Ecclesiastical power, therefore, is not to be mischievously adorned, but it is to be confined within certain limits, so as not to be drawn hither and thither at the caprice of men. For this purpose, it will be of great use to observe how it is described by Prophets and Apostles. For if we concede unreservedly to men all the power which they think proper to assume, it is easy to see how soon it will degenerate into a tyranny which is altogether alien from the Church of Christ.

2. Therefore, it is here necessary to remember, that whatever authority and dignity the Holy Spirit in Scripture confers on priests, or prophets, or apostles, or successors of Apostles, is wholly given not to men themselves, but to the ministry to which they are appointed; or, to speak more plainly, to the word, to the ministry of which they are appointed. For were we to go over the whole in order, we should find that they were not invested with authority to teach or give responses, save in the name and word of the Lord. For whenever they are called to office, they are enjoined not to bring anything of their own, but to speak by the mouth of the Lord. Nor does he bring them forward to be heard by the people, before he has instructed them what they are to speak, lest they should speak anything but his own word. Moses, the prince of all the prophets, was to be heard in preference to others (Exod. 3:4; Deut. 17:9); but he is previously furnished with his orders, that he may not be able to speak at all except from the Lord. Accordingly, when the people embraced his doctrine, they are said to have believed the Lord, and his servant Moses (Exod. 14:31). It was also provided under the severest sanctions, that the authority of the priests should not be despised (Exod. 17:9). But the Lord, at the same time, shows in what terms they were to be heard, when he says that he made his covenant with Levi, that the law of truth might be in his mouth (Mal. 2:4–6). A little after he adds, "The priest's lips should keep knowledge, and they should seek the law at his mouth; for he is the messenger of the Lord of hosts." Therefore, if the priest would be heard, let him show himself to be the messenger of God; that is, let him faithfully deliver the commands which he has received from his Maker. When the mode of hearing, then, is treated of, it is expressly said, "According to the sentence of the law which they shall teach thee" (Deut. 17:11).

3. The nature of the power conferred upon the prophets in general is elegantly described by Ezekiel: "Son of man, I have made thee a watchman unto the house of Israel: therefore hear the word at my mouth, and give them warning from me" (Ezek. 3:17). Is not he who is ordered to hear at the mouth of the Lord prohibited from devising anything of himself? And what is meant by giving a warning from the Lord, but just to speak so as to be able confidently to declare that the word which he delivers is not his own but the Lord's? The same thing is expressed by Jeremiah in different terms, "The prophet that hath a dream, let him tell a dream; and he that hath my word, let him speak my word faithfully" (Jer. 23:28). Surely God here declares the law to all, and it is a law which does not allow any one to teach more than he has been ordered. He afterwards gives the name of chaff to whatever has not proceeded from himself alone. Accordingly, none of the prophets opened his mouth unless preceded by the word of the Lord. Hence we so often meet with the expressions, "The word of the Lord, The burden of the Lord, Thus saith the Lord, The mouth of the Lord hath spoken it." And justly, for Isaiah exclaims that his lips are unclean (Isa. 6:5); and Jeremiah confesses that he knows not how to speak because he is a child (Jer. 1:6). Could anything proceed from the unclean lips of the one, and the childish lips of the other, if they spoke their own language, but what was unclean or childish? But their lips were holy and pure when they began to be organs of the Holy Spirit. The prophets, after being thus strictly bound not to deliver anything but what they received, are invested with great power and illustrious titles. For when the Lord declares, "See, I have this day set thee over the nations, and over the kingdoms, to root out, and to pull down, and to destroy, and to throw down, to build, and

to plant," he at the same time gives the reason, "Behold, I have put my words in thy mouth" (Jer. 1:9, 10).

4. Now, if you look to the apostles, they are commended by many distinguished titles, as the Light of the world, and the Salt of the earth, to be heard in Christ's stead, whatever they bound or loosed on earth being bound or loosed in heaven (Mt. 5:13, 14; Luke 10:16; John 20:23). But they declare in their own name what the authority was which their office conferred on them— viz. if they are apostles they must not speak their own pleasure, but faithfully deliver the commands of him by whom they are sent. The words in which Christ defined their embassy are sufficiently clear, "Go ye, therefore, and teach all nations, teaching them to observe all things whatsoever I have commanded you" (Mt. 28:19, 20). Nay, that none might be permitted to decline this law, he received it and imposed it on himself. "My doctrine is not mine, but his that sent me" (John 7:16). He who always was the only and eternal counsellor of the Father, who by the Father was constituted Lord and Master of all, yet because he performed the ministry of teaching, prescribed to all ministers by his example the rule which they ought to follow in teaching. The power of the Church, therefore, is not infinite, but is subject to the word of the Lord, and, as it were, included in it.

5. But though the rule which always existed in the Church from the beginning, and ought to exist in the present day, is, that the servants of God are only to teach what they have learned from himself, yet, according to the variety of times, they have had different methods of learning. The mode which now exists differs very much from that of former times. First, if it is true, as Christ says, "Neither knoweth any man the Father save the Son, and he to whomsoever the Son will reveal him" (Mt. 11:27), then those who wish to attain to the knowledge of God behoved always to be directed by that eternal wisdom. For how could they have comprehended the mysteries of God in their mind, or declared them to others, unless by the teaching of him, to whom alone the secrets of the Father are known? The only way, therefore, by which in ancient times holy men knew God, was by beholding him in the Son as in a mirror. When I say this, I mean that God never manifested himself to men by any other means than by his Son, that is, his own only wisdom, light, and truth. From this fountain Adam, Noah, Abraham, Isaac, Jacob, and others, drew all the heavenly doctrine which they possessed. From the same fountain all the prophets also drew all the heavenly oracles which they published. For this wisdom did not always display itself in one manner. With the patriarchs he employed secret revelations, but, at the same time, in order to confirm these, had recourse to signs so as to make it impossible for them to doubt that it was God that spake to them. What the patriarchs received they handed down to posterity, for God had, in depositing it with them, bound them thus to propagate it, while their children and descendants knew by the inward teaching of God, that what they heard was of heaven and not of earth.

6. But when God determined to give a more illustrious form to the Church, he was pleased to commit and consign his word to writing, that the priests might there seek what they were to teach the people, and every doctrine delivered be brought to it as a test (Mal. 2:7). Accordingly, after the promulgation of the Law, when the priests are enjoined to teach from the mouth of the Lord, the meaning is, that they are not to teach anything extraneous or alien to that kind of doctrine which God had summed up in the Law, while it was unlawful for them to add to it or take from it. Next followed the prophets, by whom God published the new oracles which were added to the Law, not so new, however, but that they flowed from the Law, and had respect to it. For in so far as regards doctrine, they were only interpreters of the Law, adding nothing to it but predictions of future events. With this exception, all that they delivered was pure exposition of the Law. But as the Lord was pleased that doctrine should exist in a clearer and more ample form, the better to satisfy weak consciences, he commanded the prophecies also to be committed to writing, and to be held part of his word. To these at the same time were added historical details, which are also the composition of prophets, but dictated by the Holy Spirit; I include the Psalms among the Prophecies, the quality which we attribute to the latter belonging also to the former. The whole body, therefore, composed of the Law, the Prophets, the Psalms, and Histories, formed the word of the Lord to his ancient people, and by it as a standard, priests and teachers, before the advent of Christ, were bound to test their doctrine, nor was it lawful for them to turn aside either to the right hand or the left, because their whole office was confined to this—to give responses to the people from the mouth of God. This is gathered from a celebrated passage of Malachi, in which it is enjoined to remember the Law, and give heed to it until the preaching of the Gospel (Mal. 4:4). For he thus restrains men from all adventitious doctrines, and does not allow them to deviate in the least from the path which Moses had faithfully pointed out. And the reason why David so magnificently

extols the Law, and pronounces so many encomiums on it (Ps. 19, 119), was, that the Jews might not long after any extraneous aid, all perfection being included in it.

7. But when at length the Wisdom of God was manifested in the flesh, he fully unfolded to us all that the human mind can comprehend, or ought to think of the heavenly Father. Now, therefore, since Christ, the Sun of Righteousness, has arisen, we have the perfect refulgence of divine truth, like the brightness of noon-day, whereas the light was previously dim. It was no ordinary blessing which the apostle intended to publish when he wrote: "God, who at sundry times and in divers manners, spake in time past unto the fathers by the prophets, hath in these last days spoken unto us by his Son" (Heb. 1:1, 2); for he intimates, nay, openly declares, that God will not henceforth, as formerly, speak by this one and by that one, that he will not add prophecy to prophecy, or revelation to revelation, but has so completed all the parts of teaching in the Son, that it is to be regarded as his last and eternal testimony. For which reason, the whole period of the new dispensation, from the time when Christ appeared to us with the preaching of his Gospel, until the day of judgment, is designated by the *last hour, the last times, the last days*, that, contented with the perfection of Christ's doctrine, we may learn to frame no new doctrine for ourselves, or admit any one devised by others. With good cause, therefore, the Father appointed the Son our teacher, with special prerogative, commanding that he and no human being should be heard. When he said, "Hear him" (Mt. 17:5), he commended his office to us, in few words, indeed, but words of more weight and energy than is commonly supposed, for it is just as if he had withdrawn us from all doctrines of man, and confined us to him alone, ordering us to seek the whole doctrine of salvation from him alone, to depend on him alone, and cleave to him alone; in short (as the words express), to listen only to his voice. And, indeed, what can now be expected or desired from man, when the very Word of life has appeared before us, and familiarly explained himself? Nay, every mouth should be stopped when once he has spoken, in whom, according to the pleasure of our heavenly Father, "are hid all the treasures of wisdom and knowledge" (Col. 2:3), and spoken as became the Wisdom of God (which is in no part defective) and the Messiah (from whom the revelation of all things was expected) (John 4:25); in other words, has so spoken as to leave nothing to be spoken by others after him.

8. Let this then be a sure axiom—that there is no word of God to which place should be given in the Church save that which is contained, first, in the Law and the Prophets; and, secondly, in the writings of the Apostles, and that the only due method of teaching in the Church is according to the prescription and rule of his word. Hence also we infer that nothing else was permitted to the apostles than was formerly permitted to the prophets—namely, to expound the ancient Scriptures, and show that the things there delivered are fulfilled in Christ: this, however, they could not do unless from the Lord; that is, unless the Spirit of Christ went before, and in a manner dictated words to them. For Christ thus defined the terms of their embassy, when he commanded them to go and teach, not what they themselves had at random fabricated, but whatsoever he had commanded (Mt. 28:20). And nothing can be plainer than his words in another passage, "Be not ye called Rabbi: for one is your Master, even Christ" (Mt. 23:8–10). To impress this more deeply in their minds, he in the same place repeats it twice. And because from ignorance they were unable to comprehend the things which they had heard and learned from the lips of their Master, the Spirit of truth is promised to guide them unto all truth (John 14:26; 16:13). The restriction should be carefully attended to. The office which he assigns to the Holy Spirit is to bring to remembrance what his own lips had previously taught.

9. Accordingly, Peter, who was perfectly instructed by his Master as to the extent of what was permitted to him, leaves nothing more to himself or others than to dispense the doctrine delivered by God. "If any man speak, let him speak as the oracles of God" (1 Peter 4:11); that is, not hesitatingly, as those are wont whose convictions are imperfect, but with the full confidence which becomes a servant of God, provided with a sure message. What else is this than to banish all the inventions of the human mind (whatever be the head which may have devised them), that the pure word of God may be taught and learned in the Church of the faithful,—than to discard the decrees, or rather fictions of men (whatever be their rank), that the decrees of God alone may remain steadfast? These are "the weapons of our warfare," which "are not carnal, but mighty through God to the pulling down of strongholds; casting down imaginations, and every high thing that exalteth itself against the knowledge of God, and bringing into captivity every thought to the obedience of Christ" (2 Cor. 10:4, 5). Here is the supreme power with which pastors of the Church, by whatever name they are called, should be invested— namely, to dare all boldly for the word of God, compelling all the virtue,

glory, wisdom, and rank of the world to yield and obey its majesty; to command all from the highest to the lowest, trusting to its power to build up the house of Christ and overthrow the house of Satan; to feed the sheep and chase away the wolves; to instruct and exhort the docile, to accuse, rebuke, and subdue the rebellious and petulant, to bind and loose; in fine, if need be, to fire and fulminate, but all in the word of God. Although, as I have observed, there is this difference between the apostles and their successors, they were sure and authentic amanuenses of the Holy Spirit; and, therefore, their writings are to be regarded as the oracles of God, whereas others have no other office than to teach what is delivered and sealed in the holy Scriptures. We conclude, therefore, that it does not now belong to faithful ministers to coin some new doctrine, but simply to adhere to the doctrine to which all, without exception, are made subject. When I say this, I mean to show not only what each individual, but what the whole Church, is bound to do. In regard to individuals, Paul certainly had been appointed an apostle to the Corinthians, and yet he declares that he has no dominion over their faith (2 Cor. 1:24). Who will now presume to arrogate a dominion to which the apostle declares that he himself was not competent? But if he had acknowledged such licence in teaching, that every pastor could justly demand implicit faith in whatever he delivered, he never would have laid it down as a rule to the Corinthians, that while two or three prophets spoke, the others should judge, and that, if anything was revealed to one sitting by, the first should be silent (1 Cor. 14:29, 30). Thus he spared none, but subjected the authority of all to the censure of the word of God. But it will be said, that with regard to the whole Church the case is different. I answer, that in another place Paul meets the objection also when he says, that faith cometh by hearing, and hearing by the word of God (Rom. 10:17). In other words, if faith depends upon the word of God alone, if it regards and reclines on it alone, what place is left for any word of man? He who knows what faith is can never hesitate here, for it must possess a strength sufficient to stand intrepid and invincible against Satan, the machinations of hell, and the whole world. This strength can be found only in the word of God. Then the reason to which we ought here to have regard is universal: God deprives man of the power of producing any new doctrine, in order that he alone may be our master in spiritual teaching, as he alone is true, and can neither lie nor deceive. This reason applies not less to the whole Church than to every individual believer.

10. But if this power of the church which is here described be contrasted with that which spiritual tyrants, falsely styling themselves bishops and religious prelates, have now for several ages exercised among the people of God, there will be no more agreement than that of Christ with Belial. It is not my intention here to unfold the manner, the unworthy manner, in which they have used their tyranny; I will only state the doctrine which they maintain in the present day, first, in writing, and then, by fire and sword. Taking it for granted, that a universal council is a true representation of the Church, they set out with this principle, and, at the same time, lay it down as incontrovertible, that such councils are under the immediate guidance of the Holy Spirit, and therefore cannot err. But as they rule councils, nay, constitute them, they in fact claim for themselves whatever they maintain to be due to councils. Therefore, they will have our faith to stand and fall at their pleasure, so that whatever they have determined on either side must be firmly seated in our minds; what they approve must be approved by us without any doubt; what they condemn we also must hold to be justly condemned. Meanwhile, at their own caprice, and in contempt of the word of God, they coin doctrines to which they in this way demand our assent, declaring that no man can be a Christian unless he assent to all their dogmas, affirmative as well as negative, if not with explicit, yet with implicit faith, because it belongs to the Church to frame new articles of faith.

11. First, let us hear by what arguments they prove that this authority was given to the Church, and then we shall see how far their allegations concerning the Church avail them. The Church, they say, has the noble promise that she will never be deserted by Christ her spouse, but be guided by his Spirit into all truth. But of the promises which they are wont to allege, many were given not less to private believers than to the whole Church. For although the Lord spake to the twelve apostles, when he said, "Lo! I am with you alway, even unto the end of the world" (Mt. 28:20); and again, "I will pray the Father, and he shall give you another Comforter, that he may abide with you for ever: even the Spirit of truth" (John 14:16, 17), he made these promises not only to the twelve, but to each of them separately, nay, in like manner, to other disciples whom he already had received, or was afterwards to receive. When they interpret these promises, which are replete with consolation, in such a way as if they were not given to any particular Christian but to the whole Church together, what else is it but to deprive Christians of the confidence which they ought thence to have derived, to

animate them in their course? I deny not that the whole body of the faithful is furnished with a manifold variety of gifts, and endued with a far larger and richer treasure of heavenly wisdom than each Christian apart; nor do I mean that this was said of believers in general, as implying that all possess the spirit of wisdom and knowledge in an equal degree: but we are not to give permission to the adversaries of Christ to defend a bad cause, by wresting Scripture from its proper meaning. Omitting this, however, I simply hold what is true—viz. that the Lord is always present with his people, and guides them by his Spirit. He is the Spirit, not of error, ignorance, falsehood, or darkness, but of sure revelation, wisdom, truth, and light, from whom they can, without deception, learn the things which have been given to them (1 Cor. 2:12); in other words, "what is the hope of their calling, and what the riches of the glory of their inheritance in the saints" (Eph. 1:18). But while believers, even those of them who are endued with more excellent graces, obtain in the present life only the first-fruits, and, as it were, a foretaste of the Spirit, nothing better remains to them than, under a consciousness of their weakness, to confine themselves anxiously within the limits of the word of God, lest, in following their own sense too far, they forthwith stray from the right path, being left without that Spirit, by whose teaching alone truth is discerned from falsehood. For all confess with Paul, that "they have not yet reached the goal" (Phil. 3:12). Accordingly, they rather aim at daily progress than glory in perfection.

12. But it will be objected, that whatever is attributed in part to any of the saints, belongs in complete fulness to the Church. Although there is some semblance of truth in this, I deny that it is true. God, indeed, measures out the gifts of his Spirit to each of the members, so that nothing necessary to the whole body is wanting, since the gifts are bestowed for the common advantage. The riches of the Church, however, are always of such a nature, that much is wanting to that supreme perfection of which our opponents boast. Still the Church is not left destitute in any part, but always has as much as is sufficient, for the Lord knows what her necessities require. But to keep her in humility and pious modesty, he bestows no more on her than he knows to be expedient. I am aware, it is usual here to object, that Christ hath cleansed the Church "with the washing of water by the word: that he might present it to himself a glorious Church, not having spot or wrinkle" (Eph. 5:26, 27), and that it is therefore called the "pillar and ground of the truth" (1 Tim. 3:15). But the former passage rather shows what Christ daily performs in it, than what he has already perfected. For if he daily sanctifies all his people, purifies, refines them, and wipes away their stains, it is certain that they have still some spots and wrinkles, and that their sanctification is in some measure defective. How vain and fabulous is it to suppose that the Church, all whose members are somewhat spotted and impure, is completely holy and spotless in every part? It is true, therefore, that the Church is sanctified by Christ, but here the commencement of her sanctification only is seen; the end and entire completion will be effected when Christ, the Holy of holies, shall truly and completely fill her with his holiness. It is true also, that her stains and wrinkles have been effaced, but so that the process is continued every day, until Christ at his advent will entirely remove every remaining defect. For unless we admit this, we shall be constrained to hold with the Pelagians, that the righteousness of believers is perfected in this life: like the Cathari and Donatists we shall tolerate no infirmity in the Church. The other passage, as we have elsewhere seen (chap. 1 sec. 10), has a very different meaning from what they put upon it. For when Paul instructed Timothy, and trained him to the office of a true bishop, he says, he did it in order that he might learn how to behave himself in the Church of God. And to make him devote himself to the work with greater seriousness and zeal, he adds, that the Church is the pillar and ground of the truth. And what else do these words mean, than just that the truth of God is preserved in the Church, and preserved by the instrumentality of preaching; as he elsewhere says, that Christ "gave some, apostles; and some, prophets; and some, evangelists; and some, pastors and teachers;" "that we henceforth be no more children, tossed to and fro, and carried about with every wind of doctrine, by the sleight of men, and cunning craftiness, whereby they lie in wait to deceive; but, speaking the truth in love, may grow up into him in all things, who is the head, even Christ"? (Eph. 4:11, 14, 15) The reason, therefore, why the truth, instead of being extinguished in the world, remains unimpaired, is, because he has the Church as a faithful guardian, by whose aid and ministry it is maintained. But if this guardianship consists in the ministry of the Prophets and Apostles, it follows, that the whole depends upon this—viz. that the word of the Lord is faithfully preserved and maintained in purity.

13. And that my readers may the better understand the hinge on which the question chiefly turns, I will briefly explain what our opponents demand, and what we resist. When they deny that the Church can err, their end and meaning are to this effect: Since the Church is

governed by the Spirit of God, she can walk safely without the word; in whatever direction she moves, she cannot think or speak anything but the truth, and hence, if she determines anything without or beside the word of God, it must be regarded in no other light than if it were a divine oracle. If we grant the first point—viz. that the Church cannot err in things necessary to salvation—our meaning is, that she cannot err, because she has altogether discarded her own wisdom, and submits to the teaching of the Holy Spirit through the word of God. Here then is the difference. They place the authority of the Church without the word of God; we annex it to the word, and allow it not to be separated from it. And is it strange if the spouse and pupil of Christ is so subject to her lord and master as to hang carefully and constantly on his lips? In every well-ordered house the wife obeys the command of her husband, in every well-regulated school the doctrine of the master only is listened to. Wherefore, let not the Church be wise in herself, nor think any thing of herself, but let her consider her wisdom terminated when he ceases to speak. In this way she will distrust all the inventions of her own reason; and when she leans on the word of God, will not waver in diffidence or hesitation but rest in full assurance and unwavering constancy. Trusting to the liberal promises which she has received, she will have the means of nobly maintaining her faith, never doubting that the Holy Spirit is always present with her to be the perfect guide of her path. At the same time, she will remember the use which God wishes to be derived from his Spirit. "When he, the Spirit of truth, is come, he will guide you into all truth" (John 16:13). How? "He shall bring to your remembrance all things whatsoever I have said unto you." He declares, therefore, that nothing more is to be expected of his Spirit than to enlighten our minds to perceive the truth of his doctrine. Hence Chrysostom most shrewdly observes, "Many boast of the Holy Spirit, but with those who speak their own it is a false pretence. As Christ declared that he spoke not of himself (John 12:50; 14:10), because he spoke according to the Law and the Prophets; so, if anything contrary to the Gospel is obtruded under the name of the Holy Spirit, let us not believe it. For as Christ is the fulfilment of the Law and the Prophets, so is the Spirit the fulfilment of the Gospel" (Chrysost. Serm. de Sancto et Adorando Spiritu.) Thus far Chrysostom. We may now easily infer how erroneously our opponents act in vaunting of the Holy Spirit, for no other end than to give the credit of his name to strange doctrines, extraneous to the word of God, whereas he himself desires to be inseparably connected with the word of God; and Christ declares the same thing of him, when he promises him to the Church. And so indeed it is. The soberness which our Lord once prescribed to his Church, he wishes to be perpetually observed. He forbade that anything should be added to his word, and that anything should be taken from it. This is the inviolable decree of God and the Holy Spirit, a decree which our opponents endeavour to annul when they pretend that the Church is guided by the Spirit without the word.

14. Here again they mutter that the Church behoved to add something to the writings of the apostles, or that the apostles themselves behoved orally to supply what they had less clearly taught, since Christ said to them, "I have yet many things to say unto you, but ye cannot bear them now" (John 16:12), and that these are the points which have been received, without writing, merely by use and custom. But what effrontery is this? The disciples, I admit, were ignorant and almost indocile when our Lord thus addressed them, but were they still in this condition when they committed his doctrine to writing, so as afterwards to be under the necessity of supplying orally that which, through ignorance, they had omitted to write? If they were guided by the Spirit of truth unto all truth when they published their writings, what prevented them from embracing a full knowledge of the Gospel, and consigning it therein? But let us grant them what they ask, provided they point out the things which behoved to be revealed without writing. Should they presume to attempt this, I will address them in the words of Augustine, "When the Lord is silent, who of us may say, this is, or that is? or if we should presume to say it, how do we prove it?" (August. in Joann. 96) But why do I contend superfluously? Every child knows that in the writings of the apostles, which these men represent as mutilated and incomplete, is contained the result of that revelation which the Lord then promised to them.

15. What, say they, did not Christ declare that nothing which the Church teaches and decrees can be gainsayed, when he enjoined that every one who presumes to contradict should be regarded as a heathen man and a publican? (Mt. 18:17.) First, there is here no mention of doctrine, but her authority to censure, for correction is asserted, in order that none who had been admonished or reprimanded might oppose her judgment. But to say nothing of this, it is very strange that those men are so lost to all sense of shame, that they hesitate not to plume themselves on this declaration. For what, pray, will they make of it, but just that the consent of the Church, a consent never given but to the word of

God, is not to be despised? The Church is to be heard, say they. Who denies this? since she decides nothing but according to the word of God. If they demand more than this, let them know that the words of Christ give them no countenance. I ought not to seem contentious when I so vehemently insist that we cannot concede to the Church any new doctrine; in other words, allow her to teach and oracularly deliver more than the Lord has revealed in his word. Men of sense see how great the danger is if so much authority is once conceded to men. They see also how wide a door is opened for the jeers and cavils of the ungodly, if we admit that Christians are to receive the opinions of men as if they were oracles. We may add, that our Saviour, speaking according to the circumstances of his times, gave the name of Church to the Sanhedrim, that the disciples might learn afterwards to revere the sacred meetings of the Church. Hence it would follow, that single cities and districts would have equal liberty in coining dogmas.

16. The examples which they bring do not avail them. They say that pædobaptism proceeds not so much on a plain command of Scripture, as on a decree of the Church. It would be a miserable asylum if, in defence of pædobaptism, we were obliged to betake ourselves to the bare authority of the Church; but it will be made plain enough elsewhere (chap. 16) that it is far otherwise. In like manner, when they object that we nowhere find in the Scriptures what was declared in the Council of Nice—viz. that the Son is consubstantial with the Father (see August. Ep. 178)—they do a grievous injustice to the Fathers, as if they had rashly condemned Arius for not swearing to their words, though professing the whole of that doctrine which is contained in the writings of the Apostles and Prophets. I admit that the expression does not exist in Scripture, but seeing it is there so often declared that there is one God, and Christ is so often called true and eternal God, one with the Father, what do the Nicene Fathers do when they affirm that he is of one essence, than simply declare the genuine meaning of Scripture? Theodoret relates that Constantine, in opening their meeting, spoke as follows: "In the discussion of divine matters, the doctrine of the Holy Spirit stands recorded. The Gospels and apostolical writings, with the oracles of the prophets, fully show us the meaning of the Deity. Therefore, laying aside discord, let us take the exposition of questions from the words of the Spirit" (Theodoret. Hist. Eccles. Lib. 1 c. 5). There was none who opposed this sound advice; none who objected that the Church could add something of her own, that the Spirit did not reveal all things to the apostles, or at least that they did not deliver them to posterity, and so forth. If the point on which our opponents insist is true, Constantine, first, was in error in robbing the Church of her power; and, secondly, when none of the bishops rose to vindicate it, their silence was a kind of perfidy, and made them traitors to Ecclesiastical law. But since Theodoret relates that they readily embraced what the Emperor said, it is evident that this new dogma was then wholly unknown.

CHAPTER 9

OF COUNCILS AND THEIR AUTHORITY.

Since Papists regard their Councils as expressing the sentiment and consent of the Church, particularly as regards the authority of declaring dogmas and the exposition of them, it was necessary to treat of Councils before proceeding to consider that part of ecclesiastical power which relates to doctrine. I. First, the authority of Councils in delivering dogmas is discussed, and it is shown that the Spirit of God is not so bound to the Pastors of the Church as opponents suppose. Their objections refuted, sec. 1–7. II. The errors, contradictions, and weaknesses, of certain Councils exposed. A refutation of the subterfuge, that those set over us are to be obeyed without distinction, sec. 8–12. III. Of the authority of Councils as regards the interpretation of Scripture, sec. 13, 14.

Sections:
1. The true nature of Councils.
2. Whence the authority of Councils is derived. What meant by assembling in the name of Christ.
3. Objection, that no truth remains in the Church if it be not in Pastors and Councils. Answer, showing by passages from the Old Testament that Pastors were often devoid of the spirit of knowledge and truth.
4. Passages from the New Testament showing that our times were to be subject to the same evil. This confirmed by the example of almost all ages.
5. All not Pastors who pretend to be so.
6. Objection, that General Councils represent the Church. Answer, showing the absurdity of this objection from passages in the Old Testament.
7. Passages to the same effect from the New Testament.
8. Councils have authority only in so far as accordant

with Scripture. Testimony of Augustine. Councils of Nice, Constantinople, and Ephesus, Subsequent Councils more impure, and to be received with limitation.

9. Contradictory decisions of Councils. Those agreeing with divine truth to be received. Those at variance with it to be rejected. This confirmed by the example of the Council of Constantinople and the Council of Nice; also of the Council of Chalcedon, and second Council of Ephesus.

10. Errors of purer Councils. Four causes of these errors. An example from the Council of Nice.

11. Another example from the Council of Chalcedon. The same errors in Provincial Councils.

12. Evasion of the Papists. Three answers. Conclusion of the discussion as to the power of the Church in relation to doctrine.

13. Last part of the chapter. Power of the Church in interpreting Scripture. From what source interpretation is to be derived. Means of preserving unity in the Church.

14. Impudent attempt of the Papists to establish their tyranny refuted. Things at variance with Scripture sanctioned by their Councils. Instance in the prohibition of marriage and communion in both kinds.

1. Were I now to concede all that they ask concerning the Church, it would not greatly aid them in their object. For everything that is said of the Church they immediately transfer to councils, which, in their opinion, represent the Church. Nay, when they contend so doggedly for the power of the Church, their only object is to devolve the whole which they extort on the Roman Pontiff and his conclave. Before I begin to discuss this question, two points must be briefly premised. First, though I mean to be more rigid in discussing this subject, it is not because I set less value than I ought on ancient councils. I venerate them from my heart, and would have all to hold them in due honour. But there must be some limitation, there must be nothing derogatory to Christ. Moreover, it is the right of Christ to preside over all councils, and not share the honour with any man. Now, I hold that he presides only when he governs the whole assembly by his word and Spirit. Secondly, in attributing less to councils than my opponents demand, it is not because I have any fear that councils are favourable to their cause and adverse to ours. For as we are amply provided by the word of the Lord with the means of proving our doctrine and overthrowing the whole Papacy, and thus have no great need of other aid, so, if the case required it, ancient councils furnish us in a great measure with what might be sufficient for both purposes.

2. Let us now proceed to the subject itself. If we consult Scripture on the authority of councils, there is no promise more remarkable than that which is contained in these words of our Saviour, "Where two or three are gathered together in my name, there am I in the midst of them." But this is just as applicable to any particular meeting as to a universal council. And yet the important part of the question does not lie here, but in the condition which is added—viz. that Christ will be in the midst of a council, provided it be assembled in his name. Wherefore, though our opponents should name councils of thousands of bishops it will little avail them; nor will they induce us to believe that they are, as they maintain, guided by the Holy Spirit, until they make it credible that they assemble in the name of Christ: since it is as possible for wicked and dishonest to conspire against Christ, as for good and honest bishops to meet together in his name. Of this we have a clear proof in very many of the decrees which have proceeded from councils. But this will be afterwards seen. At present I only reply in one word, that our Saviour's promise is made to those only who assemble in his name. How, then, is such an assembly to be defined? I deny that those assemble in the name of Christ who, disregarding his command by which he forbids anything to be added to the word of God or taken from it, determine everything at their own pleasure, who, not contented with the oracles of Scripture, that is, with the only rule of perfect wisdom, devise some novelty out of their own head (Deut. 4:2; Rev. 22:18). Certainly, since our Saviour has not promised to be present with all councils of whatever description, but has given a peculiar mark for distinguishing true and lawful councils from others, we ought not by any means to lose sight of the distinction. The covenant which God anciently made with the Levitical priests was to teach at his mouth (Mal. 2:7). This he always required of the prophets, and we see also that it was the law given to the apostles. On those who violate this covenant God bestows neither the honour of the priesthood nor any authority. Let my opponents solve this difficulty if they would subject my faith to the decrees of man, without authority from the word of God.

3. Their idea that the truth cannot remain in the Church unless it exist among pastors, and that the Church herself cannot exist unless displayed in general councils, is very far from holding true if the prophets have left us a correct description of their own times. In the time of Isaiah there was a Church at Jerusalem which the Lord had not yet

abandoned. But of pastors he thus speaks: "His watchmen are blind; they are all ignorant, they are all dumb dogs, they cannot bark; sleeping, lying down, loving to slumber. Yea, they are greedy dogs which never have enough, and they are shepherds that cannot understand: they all look to their own way" (Isa. 56:10, 11). In the same way Hosea says, "The watchman of Ephraim was with my God: but the prophet is a snare of a fowler in all his ways, and hatred in the house of his God" (Hosea 9:8). Here, by ironically connecting them with God, he shows that the pretext of the priesthood was vain. There was also a Church in the time of Jeremiah. Let us hear what he says of pastors: "From the prophet even unto the priest, every one dealeth falsely." Again, "The prophets prophesy lies in my name: I sent them not, neither have I commanded them, neither spake unto them" (Jer. 6:13; 14:14). And not to be prolix with quotations, read the whole of his thirty-third and fortieth chapters. Then, on the other hand, Ezekiel inveighs against them in no milder terms. "There is a conspiracy of her prophets in the midst thereof, like a roaring lion ravening the prey; they have devoured souls." "Her priests have violated my law, and profaned mine holy things" (Ezek. 22:25, 26). There is more to the same purpose. Similar complaints abound throughout the prophets; nothing is of more frequent recurrence.

4. But perhaps, though this great evil prevailed among the Jews, our age is exempt from it. Would that it were so; but the Holy Spirit declared that it would be otherwise. For Peter's words are clear, "But there were false prophets among the people, even as there shall be false teachers among you, who privily will bring in damnable heresies" (2 Peter 2:1). See how he predicts impending danger, not from ordinary believers, but from those who should plume themselves on the name of pastors and teachers. Besides, how often did Christ and his apostles foretell that the greatest dangers with which the Church was threatened would come from pastors? (Mt. 24:11, 24). Nay, Paul openly declares, that Antichrist would have his seat in the temple of God (2 Thess. 2:4); thereby intimating, that the fearful calamity of which he was speaking would come only from those who should have their seat in the Church as pastors. And in another passage he shows that the introduction of this great evil was almost at hand. For in addressing the Elders of Ephesus, he says, "I know this, that after my departing shall grievous wolves enter in among you, not sparing the flock. Also of your own selves shall men arise, speaking perverse things, to draw away disciples after them" (Acts 20:29, 30). How great corruption might a long series of years introduce among pastors, when they could degenerate so much within so short a time? And not to fill my pages with details, we are reminded by the examples of almost every age, that the truth is not always cherished in the bosoms of pastors, and that the safety of the Church depends not on their state. It was becoming that those appointed to preserve the peace and safety of the Church should be its presidents and guardians; but it is one thing to perform what you owe, and another to owe what you do not perform.

5. Let no man, however, understand me as if I were desirous in everything rashly and unreservedly to overthrow the authority of pastors. All I advise is, to exercise discrimination, and not suppose, as a matter of course, that all who call themselves pastors are so in reality. But the Pope, with the whole crew of his bishops, for no other reason but because they are called pastors, shake off obedience to the word of God, invert all things, and turn them hither and thither at their pleasure; meanwhile, they insist that they cannot be destitute of the light of truth, that the Spirit of God perpetually resides in them, that the Church subsists in them, and dies with them, as if the Lord did not still inflict his judgments, and in the present day punish the world for its wickedness, in the same way in which he punished the ingratitude of the ancient people—namely, by smiting pastors with astonishment and blindness (Zech. 12:4). These stupid men understand not that they are just chiming in with those of ancient times who warred with the word of God. For the enemies of Jeremiah thus set themselves against the truth, "Come, and let us devise devices against Jeremiah; for the law shall not perish from the priest, nor counsel from the wise, nor the word from the prophet" (Jer. 18:18).

6. Hence it is easy to reply to their allegation concerning general councils. It cannot be denied, that the Jews had a true Church under the prophets. But had a general council then been composed of the priests, what kind of appearance would the Church have had? We hear the Lord denouncing not against one or two of them, but the whole order: "The priests shall be astonished, and the prophets shall wonder" (Jer. 4:9). Again, "The law shall perish from the priest, and counsel from the ancients" (Ezek. 7:26). Again, "Therefore night shall be unto you, that ye shall not have a vision; and it shall be dark unto you, that ye shall not divine; and the sun shall go down over the prophets, and the day shall be dark over them," &c. (Micah 3:6). Now, had all men of this description been collected together, what spirit would have presided over their meeting? Of this we have a notable instance in

the council which Ahab convened (1 Kings 22:6, 22). Four hundred prophets were present. But because they had met with no other intention than to flatter the impious king, Satan is sent by the Lord to be a lying spirit in all their mouths. The truth is there unanimously condemned. Micaiah is judged a heretic, is smitten, and cast into prison. So was it done to Jeremiah, and so to the other prophets.

7. But there is one memorable example which may suffice for all. In the council which the priests and Pharisees assembled at Jerusalem against Christ (John 11:47), what is wanting, in so far as external appearance is concerned? Had there been no Church then at Jerusalem, Christ would never have joined in the sacrifices and other ceremonies. A solemn meeting is held; the high priest presides; the whole sacerdotal order take their seats, and yet Christ is condemned, and his doctrine is put to flight. This atrocity proves that the Church was not at all included in that council. But there is no danger that anything of the kind will happen with us. Who has told us so? Too much security in a matter of so great importance lies open to the charge of sluggishness. Nay, when the Spirit, by the mouth of Paul, foretells, in distinct terms, that a defection will take place, a defection which cannot come until pastors first forsake God (2 Thess. 2:3), why do we spontaneously walk blindfold to our own destruction? Wherefore, we cannot on any account admit that the Church consists in a meeting of pastors, as to whom the Lord has nowhere promised that they would always be good, but has sometimes foretold that they would be wicked. When he warns us of danger, it is to make us use greater caution.

8. What, then, you will say, is there no authority in the definitions of councils? Yes, indeed; for I do not contend that all councils are to be condemned, and all their acts rescinded, or, as it is said, made one complete erasure. But you are bringing them all (it will be said) under subordination, and so leaving every one at liberty to receive or reject the decrees of councils as he pleases. By no means; but whenever the decree of a council is produced, the first thing I would wish to be done is, to examine at what time it was held, on what occasion, with what intention, and who were present at it; next I would bring the subject discussed to the standard of Scripture. And this I would do in such a way that the decision of the council should have its weight, and be regarded in the light of a prior judgment, yet not so as to prevent the application of the test which I have mentioned. I wish all had observed the method which Augustine prescribes in his Third Book against Maximinus, when he wished to silence the cavils of this heretic against the decrees of councils, "I ought not to oppose the Council of Nice to you, nor ought you to oppose that of Ariminum to me, as prejudging the question. I am not bound by the authority of the latter, nor you by that of the former. Let thing contend with thing, cause with cause, reason with reason, on the authority of Scripture, an authority not peculiar to either, but common to all." In this way, councils would be duly respected, and yet the highest place would be given to Scripture, everything being brought to it as a test. Thus those ancient Councils of Nice, Constantinople, the first of Ephesus, Chalcedon, and the like, which were held for refuting errors, we willingly embrace, and reverence as sacred, in so far as relates to doctrines of faith, for they contain nothing but the pure and genuine interpretation of Scripture, which the holy Fathers with spiritual prudence adopted to crush the enemies of religion who had then arisen. In some later councils, also, we see displayed a true zeal for religion, and moreover unequivocal marks of genius, learning, and prudence. But as matters usually become worse and worse, it is easy to see in more modern councils how much the Church gradually degenerated from the purity of that golden age. I doubt not, however, that even in those more corrupt ages, councils had their bishops of better character. But it happened with them as the Roman senators of old complained in regard to their decrees. Opinions being numbered, not weighed, the better were obliged to give way to the greater number. They certainly put forth many impious sentiments. There is no need here to collect instances, both because it would be tedious, and because it has been done by others so carefully, as not to leave much to be added.

9. Moreover, why should I review the contests of council with council? Nor is there any ground for whispering to me, that when councils are at variance, one or other of them is not a lawful council. For how shall we ascertain this? Just, if I mistake not, by judging from Scripture that the decrees are not orthodox. For this alone is the sure law of discrimination. It is now about nine hundred years since the Council of Constantinople, convened under the Emperor Leo, determined that the images set up in temples were to be thrown down and broken to pieces. Shortly after, the Council of Nice, which was assembled by Irene, through dislike of the former, decreed that images were to be restored. Which of the two councils shall we acknowledge to be lawful? The latter has usually prevailed, and secured a place for images in churches. But Augustine maintains that this could not be done without the greatest danger of

idolatry. Epiphanius, at a later period, speaks much more harshly (Epist. ad Joann. Hierosolym. et Lib. 3 contra Hæres.). For he says, it is an unspeakable abomination to see images in a Christian temple. Could those who speak thus approve of that council if they were alive in the present day? But if historians speak true, and we believe their acts, not only images themselves, but the worship of them, were there sanctioned. Now it is plain that this decree emanated from Satan. Do they not show, by corrupting and wresting Scripture, that they held it in derision? This I have made sufficiently clear in a former part of the work (see Book I. chap. 11 sec. 14). Be this as it may, we shall never be able to distinguish between contradictory and dissenting councils, which have been many, unless we weigh them all in that balance for men and angels, I mean, the word of God. Thus we embrace the Council of Chalcedon, and repudiate the second of Ephesus, because the latter sanctioned the impiety of Eutyches, and the former condemned it. The judgment of these holy men was founded on the Scriptures, and while we follow it, we desire that the word of God, which illuminated them, may now also illuminate us. Let the Romanists now go and boast after their manner, that the Holy Spirit is fixed and tied to their councils.

10. Even in their ancient and purer councils there is something to be desiderated, either because the otherwise learned and prudent men who attended, being distracted by the business in hand, did not attend to many things beside; or because, occupied with grave and more serious measures, they winked at some of lesser moment; or simply because, as men, they were deceived through ignorance, or were sometimes carried headlong by some feeling in excess. Of this last case (which seems the most difficult of all to avoid) we have a striking example in the Council of Nice, which has been unanimously received, as it deserves, with the utmost veneration. For when the primary article of our faith was there in peril, and Arius, its enemy, was present, ready to engage any one in combat, and it was of the utmost moment that those who had come to attack Arius should be agreed, they nevertheless, feeling secure amid all these dangers, nay, as it were, forgetting their gravity, modesty, and politeness, laying aside the discussion which was before them (as if they had met for the express purpose of gratifying Arius), began to give way to intestine dissensions, and turn the pen, which should have been employed against Arius, against each other. Foul accusations were heard, libels flew up and down, and they never would have ceased from their contention until they had stabbed each other with mutual wounds, had not the Emperor Constantine interfered, and declaring that the investigation of their lives was a matter above his cognisance, repressed their intemperance by flattery rather than censure. In how many respects is it probable that councils, held subsequently to this, have erred? Nor does the fact stand in need of a long demonstration; any one who reads their acts will observe many infirmities, not to use a stronger term.

11. Even Leo, the Roman Pontiff, hesitates not to charge the Council of Chalcedon, which he admits to be orthodox in its doctrines, with ambition and inconsiderate rashness. He denies not that it was lawful, but openly maintains that it might have erred. Some may think me foolish in labouring to point out errors of this description, since my opponents admit that councils may err in things not necessary to salvation. My labour, however, is not superfluous. For although compelled, they admit this in word, yet by obtruding upon us the determination of all councils, in all matters without distinction, as the oracles of the Holy Spirit, they exact more than they had at the outset assumed. By thus acting what do they maintain but just that councils cannot err, of if they err, it is unlawful for us to perceive the truth, or refuse assent to their errors? At the same time, all I mean to infer from what I have said is, that though councils, otherwise pious and holy, were governed by the Holy Spirit, he yet allowed them to share the lot of humanity, lest we should confide too much in men. This is a much better view than that of Gregory Nanzianzen, who says (Ep. 55), that he never saw any council end well. In asserting that all, without exception, ended ill, he leaves them little authority. There is no necessity for making separate mention of provincial councils, since it is easy to estimate, from the case of general councils, how much authority they ought to have in framing articles of faith, and deciding what kind of doctrine is to be received.

12. But our Romanists, when, in defending their cause, they see all rational grounds slip from beneath them, betake themselves to a last miserable subterfuge. Although they should be dull in intellect and counsel, and most depraved in heart and will, still the word of the Lord remains, which commands us to obey those who have the rule over us (Heb. 13:17). Is it indeed so? What if I should deny that those who act thus have the rule over us? They ought not to claim for themselves more than Joshua had, who was both a prophet of the Lord and an excellent pastor. Let us then hear in what terms the Lord

introduced him to his office. "This book of the law shall not depart out of thy mouth; but thou shalt meditate therein day and night, that thou mayest observe to do according to all that is written therein: for then shalt thou make thy way prosperous, and thou shalt have good success" (Josh. 1:7, 8). Our spiritual rulers, therefore, will be those who turn not from the law of the Lord to the right hand or the left. But if the doctrine of all pastors is to be received without hesitation, why are we so often and so anxiously admonished by the Lord not to give heed to false prophets? "Thus saith the Lord of Hosts, Hearken not unto the words of the prophets that prophesy unto you; they make you vain: they speak a vision of their own heart, and not out of the mouth of the Lord" (Jer. 23:16). Again, "Beware of false prophets, which come to you in sheep's clothing but inwardly they are ravening wolves" (Mt. 7:15). In vain also would John exhort us to try the spirits whether they be of God (1 John 4:1). From this judgment not even angels are exempted (Gal. 1:8); far less Satan with his lies. And what is meant by the expression, "If the blind lead the blind, both shall fall into the ditch"? (Mt. 15:14) Does it not sufficiently declare that there is a great difference among the pastors who are to be heard, that all are not to be heard indiscriminately? Wherefore they have no ground for deterring us by their name, in order to draw us into a participation of their blindness, since we see, on the contrary, that the Lord has used special care to guard us from allowing ourselves to be led away by the errors of others, whatever be the mask under which they may lurk. For if the answer of our Saviour is true, blind guides, whether high priests, prelates, or pontiffs, can do nothing more than hurry us over the same precipice with themselves. Wherefore, let no names of councils, pastors, and bishops (which may be used on false pretences as well as truly), hinder us from giving heed to the evidence both of words and facts, and bringing all spirits to the test of the divine word, that we may prove whether they are of God.

13. Having proved that no power was given to the Church to set up any new doctrine, let us now treat of the power attributed to them in the interpretation of Scripture. We readily admit, that when any doctrine is brought under discussion, there is not a better or surer remedy than for a council of true bishops to meet and discuss the controverted point. There will be much more weight in a decision of this kind, to which the pastors of churches have agreed in common after invoking the Spirit of Christ, than if each, adopting it for himself, should deliver it to his people, or a few individuals should meet in private and decide. Secondly, When bishops have assembled in one place, they deliberate more conveniently in common, fixing both the doctrine and the form of teaching it, lest diversity give offence. Thirdly, Paul prescribes this method of determining doctrine. For when he gives the power of deciding to a single church, he shows what the course of procedure should be in more important cases—namely, that the churches together are to take common cognisance. And the very feeling of piety tells us, that if any one trouble the Church with some novelty in doctrine, and the matter be carried so far that there is danger of a greater dissension, the churches should first meet, examine the question, and at length, after due discussion, decide according to Scripture, which may both put an end to doubt in the people, and stop the mouths of wicked and restless men, so as to prevent the matter from proceeding farther. Thus when Arius arose, the Council of Nice was convened, and by its authority both crushed the wicked attempts of this impious man, and restored peace to the churches which he had vexed, and asserted the eternal divinity of Christ in opposition to his sacrilegious dogma. Thereafter, when Eunomius and Macedonius raised new disturbances, their madness was met with a similar remedy by the Council of Constantinople; the impiety of Nestorius was defeated by the Council of Ephesus. In short, this was from the first the usual method of preserving unity in the Church whenever Satan commenced his machinations. But let us remember, that all ages and places are not favoured with an Athanasius, a Basil, a Cyril, and like vindicators of sound doctrine, whom the Lord then raised up. Nay, let us consider what happened in the second Council of Ephesus when the Eutychian heresy prevailed. Flavianus, of holy memory, with some pious men, was driven into exile, and many similar crimes were committed, because, instead of the Spirit of the Lord, Dioscorus, a factious man, of a very bad disposition, presided. But the Church was not there. I admit it; for I always hold that the truth does not perish in the Church though it be oppressed by one council, but is wondrously preserved by the Lord to rise again, and prove victorious in his own time. I deny, however, that every interpretation of Scripture is true and certain which has received the votes of a council.

14. But the Romanists have another end in view when they say that the power of interpreting Scripture belongs to councils, and that without challenge. For they employ it as a pretext for giving the name of an interpretation

of Scripture to everything which is determined in councils. Of purgatory, the intercession of saints, and auricular confession, and the like, not one syllable can be found in Scripture. But as all these have been sanctioned by the authority of the Church, or, to speak more correctly, have been received by opinion and practice, every one of them is to be held as an interpretation of Scripture. And not only so, but whatever a council has determined against Scripture is to have the name of an interpretation. Christ bids all drink of the cup which he holds forth in the Supper. The Council of Constance prohibited the giving of it to the people, and determined that the priest alone should drink. Though this is diametrically opposed to the institution of Christ (Mt. 26:26), they will have it to be regarded as his interpretation. Paul terms the prohibition of marriage a doctrine of devils (1 Tim. 4:1, 3); and the Spirit elsewhere declares that "marriage is honourable in all" (Heb. 13:4). Having afterwards interdicted their priests from marriage, they insist on this as a true and genuine interpretation of Scripture, though nothing can be imagined more alien to it. Should any one venture to open his lips in opposition, he will be judged a heretic, since the determination of the Church is without challenge, and it is unlawful to have any doubt as to the accuracy of her interpretation. Why should I assail such effrontery? to point to it is to condemn it. Their dogma with regard to the power of approving Scripture I intentionally omit. For to subject the oracles of God in this way to the censure of men, and hold that they are sanctioned because they please men, is a blasphemy which deserves not to be mentioned. Besides, I have already touched upon it (Book 1 chap. 7; 8 sec. 9). I will ask them one question, however. If the authority of Scripture is founded on the approbation of the Church, will they quote the decree of a council to that effect? I believe they cannot. Why, then, did Arius allow himself to be vanquished at the Council of Nice by passages adduced from the Gospel of John? According to these, he was at liberty to repudiate them, as they had not previously been approved by any general council. They allege an old catalogue, which they call the Canon, and say that it originated in a decision of the Church. But I again ask, In what council was that Canon published? Here they must be dumb. Besides, I wish to know what they believe that Canon to be. For I see that the ancients are little agreed with regard to it. If effect is to be given to what Jerome says (Præf. in Lib. Solom.), the Maccabees, Tobit, Ecclesiasticus, and the like, must take their place in the Apocrypha: but this they will not tolerate on any account.

CHAPTER 10

OF THE POWER OF MAKING LAWS. THE CRUELTY OF THE POPE AND HIS ADHERENTS, IN THIS RESPECT, IN TYRANNICALLY OPPRESSING AND DESTROYING SOULS.

This chapter treats,—I. Of human constitutions in general. Of the distinction between Civil and Ecclesiastical Laws. Of conscience, why and in what sense ministers cannot impose laws on the conscience, sec. 1–8. II. Of traditions or Popish constitutions relating to ceremonies and discipline. The many vices inherent in them, sec. 9–17. Arguments in favour of those traditions refuted, sec. 17–26. III. Of Ecclesiastical constitutions that are good and lawful, sec. 27–32.

Sections:

1. The power of the Church in enacting laws. This made a source of human traditions. Impiety of these traditions.

2. Many of the Papistical traditions not only difficult, but impossible to be observed.

3. That the question may be more conveniently explained, nature of conscience must be defined.

4. Definition of conscience explained. Examples in illustration of the definition.

5. Paul's doctrine of submission to magistrates for conscience sake, gives no countenance to the Popish doctrine of the obligation of traditions.

6. The question stated. A brief mode of deciding it.

7. A perfect rule of life in the Law. God our only Lawgiver.

8. The traditions of the Papacy contradictory to the Word of God.

9. Ceremonial traditions of the Papists. Their impiety. Substituted for the true worship of God.

10. Through these ceremonies the commandment of God made void.

11. Some of these ceremonies useless and childish. Their endless variety. Introduce Judaism.

12. Absurdity of these ceremonies borrowed from Judaism and Paganism.

13. Their intolerable number condemned by Augustine.

14. Injury thus done to the Church. They cannot be excused.

15. Mislead the superstitious. Used as a kind of show and for incantation. Prostituted to gain.

16. All such traditions liable to similar objections.

17. Arguments in favour of traditions answered.

18. Answer continued.

19. Illustration taken from the simple administration of the Lord's Supper, under the Apostles, and the complicated ceremonies of the Papists.

20. Another illustration from the use of Holy Water.

21. An argument in favour of traditions founded on the decision of the Apostles and elders at Jerusalem. This decision explained.

22. Some things in the Papacy may be admitted for a time for the sake of weak brethren.

23. Observance of the Popish traditions inconsistent with Christian liberty, torturing to the conscience, and insulting to God.

24. All human inventions in religion displeasing to God. Reason. Confirmed by an example.

25. An argument founded on the examples of Samuel and Manoah. Answer.

26. Argument that Christ wished such burdens to be borne. Answer.

27. Third part of the chapter, treating of lawful Ecclesiastical arrangements. Their foundation in the general axiom, that all things be done decently and in order. Two extremes to be avoided.

28. All Ecclesiastical arrangements to be thus tested. What Paul means by things done decently and in order.

29. Nothing decent in the Popish ceremonies. Description of true decency. Examples of Christian decency and order.

30. No arrangement decent and orderly, unless founded on the authority of God, and derived from Scripture. Charity the best guide in these matters.

31. Constitutions thus framed not to be neglected or despised.

32. Cautions to be observed in regard to such constitutions.

1. We come now to the second part of power, which, according to them, consists in the enacting of laws, from which source innumerable traditions have arisen, to be as many deadly snares to miserable souls. For they have not been more scrupulous than the Scribes and Pharisees in laying burdens on the shoulders of others, which they would not touch with their finger (Mt 23:4; Luke 11:16). I have elsewhere shown (Book 3 chap. 4 sec. 4–7) how cruel murder they commit by their doctrine of auricular confession. The same violence is not apparent in other laws, but those which seem most tolerable press tyrannically on the conscience. I say nothing as to the mode in which they adulterate the worship of God, and rob God himself, who is the only Lawgiver, of his right. The power we have now to consider is, whether it be lawful for the Church to bind laws upon the conscience? In this discussion, civil order is not touched; but the only point considered is, how God may be duly worshipped according to the rule which he has prescribed, and how our spiritual liberty, with reference to God, may remain unimpaired. In ordinary language, the name of human traditions is given to all decrees concerning the worship of God, which men have issued without the authority of his word. We contend against these, not against the sacred and useful constitutions of the Church, which tend to preserve discipline, or decency, or peace. Our aim is to curb the unlimited and barbarous empire usurped over souls by those who would be thought pastors of the Church, but who are in fact its most cruel murderers. They say that the laws which they enact are spiritual, pertaining to the soul, and they affirm that they are necessary to eternal life. But thus the kingdom of Christ, as I lately observed, is invaded; thus the liberty, which he has given to the consciences of believers, is completely oppressed and overthrown. I say nothing as to the great impiety with which, to sanction the observance of their laws, they declare that from it they seek forgiveness of sins, righteousness and salvation, while they make the whole sum of religion and piety to consist in it. What I contend for is, that necessity ought not to be laid on consciences in matters in which Christ has made them free; and unless freed, cannot, as we have previously shown (Book 3 chap. 19), have peace with God. They must acknowledge Christ their deliverer, as their only king, and be ruled by the only law of liberty—namely, the sacred word of the Gospel—if they would retain the grace which they have once received in Christ: they must be subject to no bondage, be bound by no chains.

2. These Solons, indeed, imagine that their constitutions are laws of liberty, a pleasant yoke, a light burden: but who sees not that this is mere falsehood. They themselves, indeed, feel not the burden of their laws. Having cast off the fear of God, they securely and assiduously disregard their own laws as well as those which are divine. Those, however, who feel any interest in their salvation, are far from thinking themselves free so long as they are entangled in these snares. We see how great caution Paul employed in this matter, not venturing to impose a fetter

in any one thing, and with good reason: he certainly foresaw how great a wound would be inflicted on the conscience if these things should be made necessary which the Lord had left free. On the contrary, it is scarcely possible to count the constitutions which these men have most grievously enforced, under the penalty of eternal death, and which they exact with the greatest rigour, as necessary to salvation. And while very many of them are most difficult of observance, the whole taken together are impossible; so great is the mass. How, then, possibly can those, on whom this mountain of difficulty lies, avoid being perplexed with extreme anxiety, and filled with terror? My intention here then is, to impugn constitutions of this description; constitutions enacted for the purpose of binding the conscience inwardly before God, and imposing religious duties, as if they enjoined things necessary to salvation.

3. Many are greatly puzzled with this question, from not distinguishing, with sufficient care, between what is called the external forum and the forum of conscience (Book 3 chap. 19 sec 15). Moreover, the difficulty is increased by the terms in which Paul enjoins obedience to magistrates, "not only for wrath, but also for conscience sake" (Rom. 13:5); and from which it would follow, that civil laws also bind the conscience. But if this were so, nothing that we have said of spiritual government, in the last chapter, and are to say in this, would stand. To solve this difficulty, we must first understand what is meant by conscience. The definition must be derived from the etymology of the term. As when men, with the mind and intellect, apprehend the knowledge of things, they are thereby said to know, and hence the name of science or knowledge is used; so, when they have, in addition to this, a sense of the divine judgment, as a witness not permitting them to hide their sins, but bringing them as criminals before the tribunal of the judge, that sense is called conscience. For it occupies a kind of middle place between God and man, not suffering man to suppress what he knows in himself, but following him out until it bring him to conviction. This is what Paul means, when he says that conscience bears witness, "our thoughts the meanwhile accusing or else excusing each other" (Rom. 2:15). Simple knowledge, therefore, might exist in a man, as it were, shut up, and therefore the sense which sits men before the judgment-seat of God has been placed over him as a sentinel, to observe and spy out all his secrets, that nothing may remain buried in darkness. Hence the old proverb, Conscience is a thousand witnesses. For this reason, Peter also uses the "answer of a good conscience towards God" (1 Pet. 3:21); for tranquillity of mind, when, persuaded of the grace of Christ, we with boldness present ourselves before God. And the author of the Epistle to the Hebrews says, that we have "no more conscience of sins," that we are freed or acquitted, so that sin no longer accuses us (Heb. 10:2).

4. Wherefore, as works have respect to men, so conscience bears reference to God; and hence a good conscience is nothing but inward integrity of heart. In this sense, Paul says, that "the end of the commandment is charity out of a pure heart, and of a good conscience, and of faith unfeigned" (1 Tim. 1:5). He afterwards, in the same chapter, shows how widely it differs from intellect, saying, the, "some having put away" a good conscience, "concerning faith have made shipwreck." For by these words he intimates, that it is a living inclination to worship God, a sincere desire to live piously and holily. Sometimes, indeed, it is extended to men also, as when Paul declares, "Herein do I exercise myself, to have always a conscience void of offence toward God, and toward men" (Acts 24:16). But this is said, because the benefits of a good conscience flow forth and reach even to men. Properly speaking, however, it respects God alone, as I have already said. Hence a law may be said to bind the conscience when it simply binds a man without referring to men, or taking them into account. For example, God enjoins us not only to keep our mind chaste and pure from all lust, but prohibits every kind of obscenity in word, and all external lasciviousness. This law my conscience is bound to observe, though there were not another man in the world. Thus he who behaves intemperately not only sins by setting a bad example to his brethren, but stands convicted in his conscience before God. Another rule holds in the case of things which are in themselves indifferent. For we ought to abstain when they give offence, but conscience is free. Thus Paul says of meat consecrated to idols, "If any man say unto you, This is offered in sacrifice unto idols, eat not for his sake that showed it, and for conscience sake;" "conscience, I say, not thine own, but of the other" (1 Cor. 10:28, 29). A believer would sin, if, after being warned, he should still eat such kind of meat. But however necessary abstinence may be in respect of a brother, as prescribed by the Lord, conscience ceases not to retain its liberty. We see how the law, while binding the external work, leaves the conscience free.

5. Let us now return to human laws. If they are imposed for the purpose of forming a religious obligation, as if the observance of them was in itself necessary,

we say that the restraint thus laid on the conscience is unlawful. Our consciences have not to do with men but with God only. Hence the common distinction between the earthly forum and the forum of conscience. When the whole world was enveloped in the thickest darkness of ignorance, it was still held (like a small ray of light which remained unextinguished) that conscience was superior to all human judgments. Although this, which was acknowledged in word, was afterwards violated in fact, yet God was pleased that there should even then exist an attestation to liberty, exempting the conscience from the tyranny of man. But we have not yet explained the difficulty which arises from the words of Paul. For if we must obey princes not only from fear of punishment but for conscience sake, it seems to follow, that the laws of princes have dominion over the conscience. If this is true, the same thing must be affirmed of ecclesiastical laws. I answer, that the first thing to be done here is to distinguish between the genus and the species. For though individual laws do not reach the conscience, yet we are bound by the general command of God, which enjoins us to submit to magistrates. And this is the point on which Paul's discussion turns—viz. that magistrates are to be honoured, because they are ordained of God (Rom. 13:1). Meanwhile, he does not at all teach that the laws enacted by them reach to the internal government of the soul, since he everywhere proclaims that the worship of God, and the spiritual rule of living righteously, are superior to all the decrees of men. Another thing also worthy of observation, and depending on what has been already said, is, that human laws, whether enacted by magistrates or by the Church, are necessary to be observed (I speak of such as are just and good), but do not therefore in themselves bind the conscience, because the whole necessity of observing them respects the general end, and consists not in the things commanded. Very different, however, is the case of those which prescribe a new form of worshipping God, and introduce necessity into things that are free.

6. Such, however, are what in the present day are called ecclesiastical constitutions by the Papacy, and are brought forward as part of the true and necessary worship of God. But as they are without number, so they form innumerable fetters to bind and ensnare the soul. Though, in expounding the law, we have adverted to this subject (Book 3 chap. 4 sec. 6), yet as this is more properly the place for a full discussion of it, I will now study to give a summary of it as carefully as I can. I shall, however, omit the branch relating to the tyranny with which false bishops arrogate to themselves the right of teaching whatever they please, having already considered it as far as seemed necessary, but shall treat at length of the power which they claim of enacting laws. The pretext, then, on which our false bishops burden the conscience with new laws is, that the Lord has constituted them spiritual legislators, and given them the government of the Church. Hence they maintain that everything which they order and prescribe must, of necessity, be observed by the Christian people, that he who violates their commands is guilty of a twofold disobedience, being a rebel both against God and the Church. Assuredly, if they were true bishops, I would give them some authority in this matter, not so much as they demand, but so much as is requisite for duly arranging the polity of the Church; but since they are anything but what they would be thought, they cannot possibly assume anything to themselves, however little, without being in excess. But as this also has been elsewhere shown, let us grant for the present, that whatever power true bishops possess justly belongs to them, still I deny that they have been set over believers as legislators to prescribe a rule of life at their own hands, or bind the people committed to them to their decrees. When I say this, I mean that they are not at all entitled to insist that whatever they devise without authority from the word of God shall be observed by the Church as matter of necessity. Since such power was unknown to the apostles, and was so often denied to the ministers of the Church by our Lord himself, I wonder how any have dared to usurp, and dare in the present day to defend it, without any precedent from the apostles, and against the manifest prohibition of God.

7. Everything relating to a perfect rule of life the Lord has so comprehended in his law, that he has left nothing for men to add to the summary there given. His object in doing this was, first, that since all rectitude of conduct consists in regulating all our actions by his will as a standard, he alone should be regarded as the master and guide of our life; and, secondly, that he might show that there is nothing which he more requires of us than obedience. For this reason James says, "He that speaketh evil of his brother, and judgeth his brother, speaketh evil of the law, and judgeth the law:" "There is one lawgiver, who is able to save and to destroy" (James 4:11, 12). We hear how God claims it as his own peculiar privilege to rule us by his laws. This had been said before by Isaiah, though somewhat obscurely, "The Lord is our judge, the Lord is our lawgiver, the Lord is our king; he will save us" (Isa. 33:22). Both passages show that the power of life and death belongs to him who has power over the soul.

Nay, James clearly expresses this. This power no man may assume to himself. God, therefore, to whom the power of saving and destroying belongs, must be acknowledged as the only King of souls, or, as the words of Isaiah express it, he is our king and judge, and lawgiver and saviour. So Peter, when he reminds pastors of their duty, exhorts them to feed the flock without lording it over the heritage (1 Pet. 5:2); meaning by heritage the body of believers. If we duly consider that it is unlawful to transfer to man what God declares to belong only to himself, we shall see that this completely cuts off all the power claimed by those who would take it upon them to order anything in the Church without authority from the word of God.

8. Moreover, since the whole question depends on this, that God being the only lawgiver, it is unlawful for men to assume that honour to themselves, it will be proper to keep in mind the two reasons for which God claims this solely for himself. The one reason is, that his will is to us the perfect rule of all righteousness and holiness, and that thus in the knowledge of it we have a perfect rule of life. The other reason is, that when the right and proper method of worshipping him is in question, he whom we ought to obey, and on whose will we ought to depend, alone has authority over our souls. When these two reasons are attended to, it will be easy to decide what human constitutions are contrary to the word of the Lord. Of this description are all those which are devised as part of the true worship of God, and the observance of which is bound upon the conscience, as of necessary obligation. Let us remember then to weigh all human laws in this balance, if we would have a sure test which will not allow us to go astray. The former reason is urged by Paul in the Epistle to the Colossians against the false apostles who attempted to lay new burdens on the churches. The second reason he more frequently employs in the Epistle to the Galatians in a similar case. In the Epistle to the Colossians, then, he maintains that the doctrine of the true worship of God is not to be sought from men, because the Lord has faithfully and fully taught us in what way he is to be worshipped. To demonstrate this, he says in the first chapter, that in the gospel is contained all wisdom, that the man of God may be made perfect in Christ. In the beginning of the second chapter, he says that all the treasures of wisdom and knowledge are hidden in Christ, and from this he concludes that believers should beware of being led away from the flock of Christ by vain philosophy, according to the constitutions of men (Col. 2:10). In the end of the chapter, he still more decisively condemns all ἐθελοθρησκείας that is, fictitious modes of worship which men themselves devise or receive from others, and all precepts whatsoever which they presume to deliver at their own hand concerning the worship of God. We hold, therefore, that all constitutions are impious in the observance of which the worship of God is pretended to be placed. The passages in the Galatians in which he insists that fetters are not to be bound on the conscience (which ought to be ruled by God alone), are sufficiently plain, especially chapter 5. Let it, therefore, suffice to refer to them.

9. But that the whole matter may be made plainer by examples, it will be proper, before we proceed, to apply the doctrine to our own times. The constitutions which they call ecclesiastical, and by which the Pope, with his adherents, burdens the Church, we hold to be pernicious and impious, while our opponents defend them as sacred and salutary. Now there are two kinds of them, some relating to ceremonies and rites, and others more especially to discipline. Have we, then, any just cause for impugning both? Assuredly a juster cause than we could wish. First, do not their authors themselves distinctly declare that the very essence of the worship of God (so to speak) is contained in them? For what end do they bring forward their ceremonies but just that God may be worshipped by them? Nor is this done merely by error in the ignorant multitude, but with the approbation of those who hold the place of teachers. I am not now adverting to the gross abominations by which they have plotted the adulteration of all godliness, but they would not deem it to be so atrocious a crime to err in any minute tradition, did they not make the worship of God subordinate to their fictions. Since Paul then declares it to be intolerable that the legitimate worship of God should be subjected to the will of men, wherein do we err when we are unable to tolerate this in the present day? especially when we are enjoined to worship God according to the elements of this world—a thing which Paul declares to be adverse to Christ (Col 2:20). On the other hand, the mode in which they lay consciences under the strict necessity of observing whatever they enjoin, is not unknown. When we protest against this, we make common cause with Paul, who will on no account allow the consciences of believers to be brought under human bondage.

10. Moreover, the worst of all is, that when once religion begins to be composed of such vain fictions, the perversion is immediately succeeded by the abominable depravity with which our Lord upbraids the Pharisees of making the commandment of God void through their traditions (Mt. 15:3). I am unwilling to dispute with our

present legislators in my own words;—let them gain the victory if they can clear themselves from this accusation of Christ. But how can they do so, seeing they regard it as immeasurably more wicked to allow the year to pass without auricular confession, than to have spent it in the greatest iniquity: to have infected their tongue with a slight tasting of flesh on Friday, than to have daily polluted the whole body with whoredom: to have put their hand to honest labour on a day consecrated to some one or other of their saintlings, than to have constantly employed all their members in the greatest crimes: for a priest to be united to one in lawful wedlock, than to be engaged in a thousand adulteries: to have failed in performing a votive pilgrimage, than to have broken faith in every promise: not to have expended profusely on the monstrous, superfluous, and useless luxury of churches, than to have denied the poor in their greatest necessities: to have passed an idol without honour, than to have treated the whole human race with contumely: not to have muttered long unmeaning sentences at certain times, than never to have framed one proper prayer? What is meant by making the word of God void by tradition, if this is not done when recommending the ordinances of God only frigidly and perfunctorily, they nevertheless studiously and anxiously urge strict obedience to their own ordinances, as if the whole power of piety was contained in them;—when vindicating the transgression of the divine Law with trivial satisfactions, they visit the minutest violation of one of their decrees with no lighter punishment than imprisonment, exile, fire, or sword?—When neither severe nor inexorable against the despisers of God, they persecute to extremity, with implacable hatred, those who despise themselves, and so train all those whose simplicity they hold in thraldom, that they would sooner see the whole law of God subverted than one iota of what they call the precepts of the Church infringed. First, there is a grievous delinquency in this, that one contemns, judges, and casts off his neighbour for trivial matters,—matters which, if the judgment of God is to decide, are free. But now, as if this were a small evil, those frivolous elements of this world (as Paul terms them in his Epistle to the Galatians, Gal. 4:9) are deemed of more value than the heavenly oracles of God. He who is all but acquitted for adultery is judged in meat; and he to whom whoredom is permitted is forbidden to marry. This, forsooth, is all that is gained by that prevaricating obedience, which only turns away from God to the same extent that it inclines to men.

11. There are other two grave vices which we disapprove in these constitutions. First, They prescribe observances which are in a great measure useless, and are sometimes absurd; secondly, by the vast multitude of them, pious consciences are oppressed, and being carried back to a kind of Judaism, so cling to shadows that they cannot come to Christ. My allegation that they are useless and absurd will, I know, scarcely be credited by carnal wisdom, to which they are so pleasing, that the Church seems to be altogether defaced when they are taken away. But this is just what Paul says, that they "have indeed a show of wisdom in will-worship, and humility, and neglecting of the body" (Col. 2:23); a most salutary admonition, of which we ought never to lose sight. Human traditions, he says, deceive by an appearance of wisdom. Whence this show? Just that being framed by men, the human mind recognises in them that which is its own, and embraces it when recognised more willingly than anything, however good, which is less suitable to its vanity. Secondly, That they seem to be a fit training to humility, while they keep the minds of men grovelling on the ground under their yoke; hence they have another recommendation. Lastly, Because they seem to have a tendency to curb the will of the flesh, and to subdue it by the rigour of abstinence, they seem to be wisely devised. But what does Paul say to all this? Does he pluck off those masks lest the simple should be deluded by a false pretext? Deeming it sufficient for their refutation to say that they were devices of men, he passes all these things without refutation, as things of no value. Nay, because he knew that all fictitious worship is condemned in the Church, and is the more suspected by believers, the more pleasing it is to the human mind—because he knew that this false show of outward humility differs so widely from true humility that it can be easily discerned; —finally, because he knew that this tutelage is valued at no more than bodily exercise, he wished the very things which commended human traditions to the ignorant to be regarded by believers as the refutation of them.

12. Thus, in the present day, not only the unlearned vulgar, but every one in proportion as he is inflated by worldly wisdom, is wonderfully captivated by the glare of ceremonies, while hypocrites and silly women think that nothing can be imagined better or more beautiful. But those who thoroughly examine them, and weigh them more truly according to the rule of godliness, in regard to the value of all such ceremonies, know, first, that they are trifles of no utility; secondly, that they are impostures which delude the eyes of the spectators with empty show. I am speaking of those ceremonies which the Roman masters will have to be great mysteries, while we know by

experience that they are mere mockery. Nor is it strange that their authors have gone the length of deluding themselves and others by mere frivolities, because they have taken their model partly from the dreams of the Gentiles, partly, like apes, have rashly imitated the ancient rites of the Mosaic Law, with which we have nothing more to do than with the sacrifices of animals and other similar things. Assuredly, were there no other proof, no sane man would expect any good from such an ill-assorted farrago. And the case itself plainly demonstrates that very many ceremonies have no other use than to stupify the people rather than teach them. In like manner, to those new canons which pervert discipline rather than preserve it, hypocrites attach much importance; but a closer examination will show that they are nothing but the shadowy and evanescent phantom of discipline.

13. To come to the second fault, who sees not that ceremonies, by being heaped one upon another, have grown to such a multitude, that it is impossible to tolerate them in the Christian Church? Hence it is, that in ceremonies a strange mixture of Judaism is apparent, while other observances prove a deadly snare to pious minds. Augustine complained that in his time, while the precepts of God were neglected, prejudice everywhere prevailed to such an extent, that he who touched the ground barefoot during his octave was censured more severely than he who buried his wits in wine. He complained that the Church, which God in mercy wished to be free, was so oppressed that the condition of the Jews was more tolerable (August. Ep. 119). Had that holy man fallen on our day, in what terms would he have deplored the bondage now existing? For the number is tenfold greater, and each iota is exacted a hundred times more rigidly than then. This is the usual course; when once those perverse legislators have usurped authority, they make no end of their commands and prohibitions until they reach the extreme of harshness. This Paul elegantly intimated by these words,—"If ye be dead with Christ from the rudiments of the world, why, as though living in the world, are ye subject to ordinances? Touch not, taste not, handle not" (Col. 2:20, 21). For while the word ἅπτεσθαι signifies both to eat and to touch, it is doubtless taken in the former sense, that there may not be a superfluous repetition. Here, therefore, he most admirably describes the progress of false apostles. The way in which superstition begins is this: they forbid not only to eat, but even to chew gently; after they have obtained this, they forbid even to taste. This also being yielded to them, they deem it unlawful to touch even with the finger.

14. We justly condemn this tyranny in human constitutions, in consequence of which miserable consciences are strangely tormented by innumerable edicts, and the excessive exaction of them. Of the canons relating to discipline, we have spoken elsewhere (*supra*, sec. 12; also chapter 12). What shall I say of ceremonies, the effect of which has been, that we have almost buried Christ, and returned to Jewish figures? "Our Lord Christ (says Augustine, Ep. 118) bound together the society of his new people by sacraments, very few in number, most excellent in signification, most easy of observance." How widely different this simplicity is from the multitude and variety of rites in which we see the Church entangled in the present day, cannot well be told. I am aware of the artifice by which some acute men excuse this perverseness. They say that there are numbers among us equally rude as any among the Israelitish people, and that for their sakes has been introduced this tutelage, which though the stronger may do without, they, however, ought not to neglect, seeing that it is useful to weak brethren. I answer, that we are not unaware of what is due to the weakness of brethren, but, on the other hand, we object that the method of consulting for the weak is not to bury them under a great mass of ceremonies. It was not without cause that God distinguished between us and his ancient people, by training them like children by means of signs and figures, and training us more simply, without so much external show. Paul's words are, "The heir, as long as he is a child,"—"is under tutors and governors" (Gal. 4:1, 2). This was the state of the Jews under the law. But we are like adults who, being freed from tutory and curatory, have no need of puerile rudiments. God certainly foresaw what kind of people he was to have in his Church, and in what way they were to be governed. Now, he distinguished between us and the Jews in the way which has been described. Therefore, it is a foolish method of consulting for the ignorant to set up the Judaism which Christ has abrogated. This dissimilitude between the ancient and his new people Christ expressed when he said to the woman of Samaria, "The hour cometh, and now is, when the true worshippers shall worship the Father in spirit and in truth" (John 4:23). This, no doubt, had always been done; but the new worshippers differ from the old in this, that while under Moses the spiritual worship of God was shadowed, and, as it were, entangled by many ceremonies, these have been abolished, and worship is now more simple. Those, accordingly, who confound this distinction, subvert the order instituted and sanctioned by Christ. Therefore you will ask, Are no

ceremonies to be given to the more ignorant, as a help to their ignorance? I do not say so; for I think that help of this description is very useful to them. All I contend for is the employment of such a measure as may illustrate, not obscure Christ. Hence a few ceremonies have been divinely appointed, and these by no means laborious, in order that they may evince a present Christ. To the Jews a greater number were given, that they might be images of an absent Christ. In saying he was absent, I mean not in power, but in the mode of expression. Therefore, to secure due moderation, it is necessary to retain that fewness in number, facility in observance, and significancy of meaning which consists in clearness. Of what use is it to say that this is not done? The fact is obvious to every eye.

15. I here say nothing of the pernicious opinions with which the minds of men are imbued, as that these are sacrifices by which propitiation is made to God, by which sins are expiated, by which righteousness and salvation are procured. It will be maintained that things good in themselves are not vitiated by errors of this description, since in acts expressly enjoined by God similar errors may be committed. There is nothing, however, more unbecoming than the fact, that works devised by the will of man are held in such estimation as to be thought worthy of eternal life. The works commanded by God receive a reward, because the Lawgiver himself accepts of them as marks of obedience. They do not, therefore, take their value from their own dignity or their own merit, but because God sets this high value on our obedience toward him. I am here speaking of that perfection of works which is commanded by God, but is not performed by men. The works of the law are accepted merely by the free kindness of God, because the obedience is infirm and defective. But as we are not here considering how far works avail without Christ, let us omit that question. I again repeat, as properly belonging to the present subject, that whatever commendation works have, they have it in respect of obedience, which alone God regards, as he testifies by the prophet, "I spake not unto your fathers, nor commanded them in the day that I brought them out of the land of Egypt, concerning burnt-offerings or sacrifices: but this thing commanded I them, saying, Obey my voice " (Jer. 7:22). Of fictitious works he elsewhere speaks, "Wherefore do you spend your money for that which is not bread"? (Isa. 55:2; 29:13). Again, "In vain do they worship me, teaching for doctrines the commandments of men" (Mt. 15:9). They cannot, therefore, excuse themselves from the charge of allowing wretched people to seek in these external frivolities a righteousness which they may present to God, and by which they may stand before the celestial tribunal. Besides, is it not a fault deservedly stigmatised, that they exhibit unmeaning ceremonies as a kind of stage-play or magical incantation? For it is certain that all ceremonies are corrupt and noxious which do not direct men to Christ. But the ceremonies in use in the Papacy are separated from doctrine, so that they confine men to signs altogether devoid of meaning. Lastly (as the belly is an ingenious contriver), it is clear, that many of their ceremonies have been invented by greedy priests as lures for catching money. But whatever be their origin, they are all so prostituted to filthy lucre, that a great part of them must be rescinded if we would prevent a profane and sacrilegious traffic from being carried on in the Church.

16. Although I seem not to be delivering the general doctrine concerning human constitutions, but adapting my discourse wholly to our own age, yet nothing has been said which may not be useful to all ages. For whenever men begin the superstitious practice of worshipping God with their own fictions, all the laws enacted for this purpose forthwith degenerate into those gross abuses. For the curse which God denounces—viz. to strike those who worship him with the doctrines of men with stupor and blindness—is not confined to any one age, but applies to all ages. The uniform result of this blindness is, that there is no kind of absurdity escaped by those who, despising the many admonitions of God, spontaneously entangle themselves in these deadly fetters. But if, without any regard to circumstances, you would simply know the character belonging at all times to those human traditions which ought to be repudiated by the Church, and condemned by all the godly, the definition which we formerly gave is clear and certain—viz. That they include all the laws enacted by men, without authority from the word of God, for the purpose either of prescribing the mode of divine worship, or laying a religious obligation on the conscience, as enjoining things necessary to salvation. If to one or both of these are added the other evils of obscuring the clearness of the Gospel by their multitude, of giving no edification, of being useless and frivolous occupations rather than true exercises of piety, of being set up for sordid ends and filthy lucre, of being difficult of observance, and contaminated by pernicious superstitions, we shall have the means of detecting the quantity of mischief which they occasion.

17. I understand what their answer will be—viz. that these traditions are not from themselves, but from God. For to prevent the Church from erring, it is guided by the

Holy Spirit, whose authority resides in them. This being conceded, it at the same time follows, that their traditions are revelations by the Holy Spirit, and cannot be disregarded without impiety and contempt of God. And that they may not seem to have attempted anything without high authority, they will have it to be believed that a great part of their observances is derived from the apostles. For they contend, that in one instance they have a sufficient proof of what the apostles did in other cases. The instance is, when the apostles assembled in council, announced to all the Gentiles as the opinion of the council, that they should "abstain from pollution of idols, and from fornication, and from things strangled, and from blood" (Acts 15:20, 29). We have already explained, how, in order to extol themselves, they falsely assume the name of Church (Chap. 8 sec. 10–13). If, in regard to the present cause, we remove all masks and glosses (a thing, indeed, which ought to be our first care, and also is our highest interest), and consider what kind of Church Christ wishes to have, that we may form and adapt ourselves to it as a standard, it will readily appear that it is not a property of the Church to disregard the limits of the word of God, and wanton and luxuriate in enacting new laws. Does not the law which was once given to the Church endure for ever? "What things soever I command you, observe to do it: thou shalt not add thereto, nor diminish from it" (Deut. 12:32). And in another place, "Add thou not unto his words, lest he reprove thee, and thou be found a liar" (Prov. 30:6). Since they cannot deny that this was said to the Church, what else do they proclaim but their contumacy, when, notwithstanding of such prohibitions, they profess to add to the doctrine of God, and dare to intermingle their own with it? Far be it from us to assent to the falsehood by which they offer such insult to the Church. Let us understand that the name of Church is falsely pretended wherever men contend for that rash human licence which cannot confine itself within the boundaries prescribed by the word of God, but petulantly breaks out, and has recourse to its own inventions. In the above passage there is nothing involved, nothing obscure, nothing ambiguous; the whole Church is forbidden to add to, or take from the word of God, in relation to his worship and salutary precepts. But that was said merely of the Law, which was succeeded by the Prophets and the whole Gospel dispensation! This I admit, but I at the same time add, that these are fulfilments of the Law, rather than additions or diminutions. Now, if the Lord does not permit anything to be added to, or taken from the ministry of Moses, though wrapt up, if I may so speak, in many folds of obscurity, until he furnish a clearer doctrine by his servants the Prophets, and at last by his beloved Son, why should we not suppose that we are much more strictly prohibited from making any addition to the Law, the Prophets, the Psalms, and the Gospel? The Lord cannot forget himself, and it is long since he declared that nothing is so offensive to him as to be worshipped by human inventions. Hence those celebrated declarations of the Prophets, which ought continually to ring in our ears, "I spake not unto your fathers, nor commanded them in the day that I brought them out of the land of Egypt, concerning burnt-offerings or sacrifices; but this thing commanded I them, saying, Obey my voice, and I will be your God, and ye shall be my people: and walk ye in all the ways that I have commanded you" (Jer. 7:22, 23). "I earnestly protested unto your fathers, in the day that I brought them out of the land of Egypt, even unto this day, rising early and protesting, saying, Obey my voice" (Jer. 11:7). There are other passages of the same kind, but the most noted of all is, "Hath the Lord as great delight in burnt-offerings and sacrifices, as in obeying the voice of the Lord? Behold, to obey is better than sacrifice, and to hearken than the fat of rams. For rebellion is as the sin of witchcraft, and stubbornness is as iniquity and idolatry" (1 Sam. 15: 22, 23). It is easy, therefore, to prove, that whenever human inventions in this respect are defended by the authority of the Church, they cannot be vindicated from the charge of impiety, and that the name of Church is falsely assumed.

18. For this reason we freely inveigh against that tyranny of human traditions which is haughtily obtruded upon us in the name of the Church. Nor do we hold the Church in derision (as our adversaries, for the purpose of producing obloquy, unjustly accuse us), but we attribute to her the praise of obedience, than which there is none which she acknowledges to be greater. They themselves rather are emphatically injurious to the Church, in representing her as contumacious to her Lord, when they pretend that she goes farther than the word of God allows, to say nothing of their combined impudence and malice, in continually vociferating about the power of the Church, while they meanwhile disguise both the command which the Lord has given her, and the obedience which she owes to the command. But if our wish is as it ought to be, to agree with the Church, it is of more consequence to consider and remember the injunction which the Lord has given both to us and to the Church, to obey him with one consent. For there can be no doubt that we shall best agree with the Church when we show ourselves obedi-

ent to the Lord in all things. But to ascribe the origin of the traditions by which the Church has hitherto been oppressed to the apostles is mere imposition, since the whole substance of the doctrine of the apostles is, that conscience must not be burdened with new observances, nor the worship of God contaminated by our inventions. Then, if any credit is to be given to ancient histories and records, what they attribute to the apostles was not only unknown to them, but was never heard by them. Nor let them pretend that most of their decrees, though not delivered in writing, were received by use and practice, being things which they could not understand while Christ was in the world, but which they learned after his ascension, by the revelation of the Holy Spirit. The meaning of that passage has been explained elsewhere (Chap. 8 sec. 14). In regard to the present question, they make themselves truly ridiculous, seeing it is manifest that all those mysteries which so long were undiscovered by the apostles, are partly Jewish or Gentile observances, the former of which had anciently been promulgated among the Jews, and the latter among all the Gentiles, partly absurd gesticulations and empty ceremonies, which stupid priests, who have neither sense nor letters, can duly perform; nay, which children and mountebanks perform so appropriately, that it seems impossible to have fitter priests for such sacrifices. If there were no records, men of sense would judge from the very nature of the case, that such a mass of rites and observances did not rush into the Church all at once, but crept in gradually. For though the venerable bishops, who were nearest in time to the apostles, introduced some things pertaining to order and discipline, those who came after them, and those after them again, had not enough of consideration, while they had too much curiosity and cupidity, he who came last always vying in foolish emulation with his predecessors, so as not to be surpassed in the invention of novelties. And because there was a danger that these inventions, from which they anticipated praise from posterity, might soon become obsolete, they were much more rigorous in insisting on the observance of them. This false zeal has produced a great part of the rites which these men represent as apostolical. This history attests.

19. And not to become prolix, by giving a catalogue of all, we shall be contented with one example. Under the apostles there was great simplicity in administering the Lord's Supper. Their immediate successors made some additions to the dignity of the ordinance, which are not to be disapproved. Afterwards came foolish imitators, who, by ever and anon patching various fragments together, have left us those sacerdotal vestments which we see in the mass, those altar ornaments, those gesticulations, and whole farrago of useless observances. But they object, that in old time the persuasion was, that those things which were done with the consent of the whole Church proceeded from the apostles. Of this they quote Augustine as a witness. I will give the explanation in the very words of Augustine. "Those things which are observed over the whole world we may understand to have been appointed either by the apostles themselves, or by general councils, whose authority in the Church is most beneficial, as the annual solemn celebration of our Lord's passion, resurrection, and ascension to heaven, and of the descent of the Holy Spirit, and any other occurrence observed by the whole Church wherever it exists" (August. Ep. 118). In giving so few examples, who sees not that he meant to refer the observances then in use to authors deserving of faith and reverence;—observances few and sober, by which it was expedient that the order of the Church should be maintained? How widely does this differ from the view of our Roman masters, who insist that there is no paltry ceremony among them which is not apostolical?

20. Not to be tedious, I will give only one example. Should any one ask them where they get their holy water, they will at once answer,—from the apostles. As if I did not know who the Roman bishop is, to whom history ascribes the invention, and who, if he had admitted the apostles to his council, assuredly never would have adulterated baptism by a foreign and unseasonable symbol; although it does not seem probable to me that the origin of that consecration is so ancient as is there recorded. For when Augustine says (Ep. 118) that certain churches in his day rejected the formal imitation of Christ in the washing of feet, lest that rite should seem to pertain to baptism, he intimates that there was then no kind of washing which had any resemblance to baptism. Be this as it may, I will never admit that the apostolic spirit gave rise to that daily sign by which baptism, while brought back to remembrance, is in a manner repeated. I attach no importance to the fact, that Augustine elsewhere ascribes other things to the apostles. For as he has nothing better than conjecture, it is not sufficient for forming a judgment concerning a matter of so much moment. Lastly, though we should grant that the things which he mentions are derived from the apostolic age, there is a great difference between instituting some exercise of piety, which believers may use with a free conscience, or may abstain from if they think the observance not to be useful, and enacting a law which brings the conscience

into bondage. Now, indeed, whoever is the author from whom they are derived, since we see the great abuses to which they have led, there is nothing to prevent us from abrogating them without any imputation on him, since he never recommended them in such a way as to lay us under a fixed and immovable obligation to observe them.

21. It gives them no great help, in defending their tyranny, to pretend the example of the apostles. The apostles and elders of the primitive Church, according to them, sanctioned a decree without any authority from Christ, by which they commanded all the Gentiles to abstain from meat offered to idols, from things strangled, and from blood (Acts 15:20). If this was lawful for them, why should not their successors be allowed to imitate the example as often as occasion requires? Would that they would always imitate them both in this and in other matters! For I am ready to prove, on valid grounds, that here nothing new has been instituted or decreed by the apostles. For when Peter declares in that council, that God is tempted if a yoke is laid on the necks of the disciples, he overthrows his own argument if he afterwards allows a yoke to be imposed on them. But it is imposed if the apostles, on their own authority, prohibit the Gentiles from touching meat offered to idols, things strangled, and blood. The difficulty still remains, that they seem nevertheless to prohibit them. But this will easily be removed by attending more closely to the meaning of their decree. The first thing in order, and the chief thing in importance, is, that the Gentiles were to retain their liberty, which was not to be disturbed, and that they were not to be annoyed with the observances of the Law. As yet, the decree is all in our favour. The reservation which immediately follows is not a new law enacted by the apostles, but a divine and eternal command of God against the violation of charity, which does not detract one iota from that liberty. It only reminds the Gentiles how they are to accommodate themselves to their brother, and to not abuse their liberty for an occasion of offence. Let the second head, therefore, be, that the Gentiles are to use an innoxious liberty, giving no offence to the brethren. Still, however, they prescribe some certain thing—viz. they show and point out, as was expedient at the time, what those things are by which they may give offence to their brethren, that they may avoid them; but they add no novelty of their own to the eternal law of God, which forbids the offence of brethren.

22. As in the case where faithful pastors, presiding over churches not yet well constituted, should intimate to their flocks not to eat flesh on Friday until the weak among whom they live become strong, or to work on a holiday, or any other similar things, although, when superstition is laid aside, these matters are in themselves indifferent, still, where offence is given to the brethren, they cannot be done without sin; so there are times when believers cannot set this example before weak brethren without most grievously wounding their consciences. Who but a slanderer would say that a new law is enacted by those who, it is evident, only guard against scandals which their Master has distinctly forbidden? But nothing more than this can be said of the apostles, who had no other end in view, in removing grounds of offence, than to enforce the divine Law, which prohibits offence; as if they had said, The Lord hath commanded you not to hurt a weak brother; but meats offered to idols, things strangled, and blood, ye cannot eat, without offending weak brethren; we, therefore, require you, in the word of the Lord, not to eat with offence. And to prove that the apostles had respect to this, the best witness is Paul, who writes as follows, undoubtedly according to the sentiments of the council: "As concerning, therefore, the eating of those things which are offered in sacrifice unto idols, we know that an idol is nothing in the world, and that there is none other God but one."—"Howbeit, there is not in every man that knowledge: for some with conscience of the idol unto this hour eat it as a thing offered unto an idol; and their conscience being weak is defiled."—"But take heed lest by any means this liberty of yours become a stumbling-block to them that are weak" (1 Cor. 8:4–9). Any one who duly considers these things will not be imposed upon by the gloss which these men employ when, as a cloak to their tyranny, they pretend that the apostles had begun by their decree to infringe the liberty of the Church. But that they may be unable to escape without confessing the accuracy of this explanation, let them tell me by what authority they have dared to abrogate this very decree. It was, it seems, because there was no longer any danger of those offences and dissensions which the apostles wished to obviate, and they knew that the law was to be judged by its end. Seeing, therefore, the law was passed with a view to charity, there is nothing prescribed in it except in so far as required by charity. In confessing that the transgression of this law is nothing but a violation of charity, do they not at the same time acknowledge that it was not some adventitious supplement to the law of God, but a genuine and simple adaptation of it to the times and manners for which it was destined?

23. But though such laws are hundreds of times unjust

and injurious to us, still they contend that they are to be heard without exception; for the thing asked of us is not to consent to errors, but only to submit to the strict commands of those set over us,—commands which we are not at liberty to decline (1 Pet. 2:18). But here also the Lord comes to the succour of his word, and frees us from this bondage by asserting the liberty which he has purchased for us by his sacred blood, and the benefit of which he has more than once attested by his word. For the thing required of us is not (as they maliciously pretend) to endure some grievous oppression in our body, but to be tortured in our consciences, and brought into bondage: in other words, robbed of the benefits of Christ's blood. Let us omit this, however, as if it were irrelevant to the point. Do we think it a small matter that the Lord is deprived of his kingdom which he so strictly claims for himself? Now, he is deprived of it as often as he is worshipped with laws of human invention, since his will is to be sole legislator of his worship. And lest any one should consider this as of small moment, let us hear how the Lord himself estimates it. "Forasmuch as this people draw near me with their mouth, and with their lips do honour me, but have removed their heart far from me, and their fear toward me is taught by the precept of men: therefore, behold, I will proceed to do a marvellous work among the people, even a marvellous work and a wonder; for the wisdom of their wise men shall perish, and the understanding of their prudent men shall be hid" (Isaiah 29:13–14). And in another place, "But in vain do they worship me, teaching for doctrines the commandments of men" (Mt. 15:9). And, indeed, when the children of Israel polluted themselves with manifold idolatries, the cause of the whole evil is ascribed to that impure mixture caused by their disregarding the commandments of God, and framing new modes of worship. Accordingly, sacred history relates that the new inhabitants who had been brought by the king of Assyria from Babylon to inhabit Samaria were torn and destroyed by wild beasts, because they knew not the judgment or statutes of the God of that land (2 Kings 17:24–34). Though they had done nothing wrong in ceremonies, still their empty show could not have been approved by God. Meanwhile he ceased not to punish them for the violation of his worship by the introduction of fictions alien from his word. Hence it is afterwards said that, terrified by the punishment, they adopted the rites prescribed in the Law; but as they did not yet worship God purely, it is twice repeated that they feared him and feared not. Hence we infer that part of the reverence due to him consists in worshipping him simply in the way which he commands, without mingling any inventions of our own. And, accordingly, pious princes are repeatedly praised (2 Kings 22:1, &c.) for acting according to all his precepts, and not declining either to the right hand or the left. I go further: although there be no open manifestation of impiety in fictitious worship, it is strictly condemned by the Spirit, inasmuch as it is a departure from the command of God. The altar of Ahaz, a model of which had been brought from Damascus (2 Kings 16:10), might have seemed to give additional ornament to the temple, seeing it was his intention there to offer sacrifices to God only, and to do it more splendidly than at the first ancient altar: yet we see how the Spirit detests the audacious attempt, for no other reasons but because human inventions are in the worship of God impure corruptions. And the more clearly the will of God has been manifested to us, the less excusable is our petulance in attempting anything. Accordingly, the guilt of Manasses is aggravated by the circumstance of having erected a new altar at Jerusalem, of which the Lord said, "In Jerusalem will I put my name" (2 Kings 22:3, 4), because the authority of God was thereby professedly rejected.

24. Many wonder why God threatens so sternly that he will bring astonishment on the people who worship him with the commandments of men, and declares that it is in vain to worship him with the commandments of men. But if they would consider what it is in the matter of religion, that is, of heavenly wisdom, to depend on God alone, they would, at the same time, see that it is not on slight grounds the Lord abominates perverse service of this description, which is offered him at the caprice of the human will. For although there is some show of humility in the obedience of those who obey such laws in worshipping God, yet they are by no means humble, since they prescribe to him the very laws which they observe. This is the reason why Paul would have us so carefully to beware of being deceived by the traditions of men, and what is called ἐθελοθρησκεία, that is, voluntary worship, worship devised by men without sanction from God. Thus it is, indeed: we must be fools in regard to our own wisdom and all the wisdom of men, in order that we may allow him alone to be wise. This course is by no means observed by those who seek to approve themselves to him by paltry observances of man's devising, and, as it were, against his will obtrude upon him a prevaricating obedience which is yielded to men. This is the course which has been pursued for several ages, and within our own recollection, and is still pursued in the present day in those places in

which the power of the creature is more than that of the Creator, where religion (if religion it deserves to be called) is polluted with more numerous, and more absurd superstitions, than ever Paganism was. For what could human sense produce but things carnal and fatuous, and savouring of their authors?

25. When the patrons of superstition cloak them, by pretending that Samuel sacrificed in Ramath, and though he did so contrary to the Law, yet pleased God (1 Sam 7:17), it is easy to answer, that he did not set up any second altar in opposition to the only true one; but, as the place for the Ark of the Covenant had not been fixed, he sacrificed in the town where he dwelt, as being the most convenient. It certainly never was the intention of the holy prophet to make any innovation in sacred things, in regard to which the Lord had so strictly forbidden addition or diminution. The case of Manoah I consider to have been extraordinary and special. He, though a private man, offered sacrifice to God, and did it not without approbation, because he did it not from a rash movement of his own mind, but by divine inspiration (Judges 13:19). How much God abominates all the devices of men in his worship, we have a striking proof in the case of one not inferior to Manoah—viz. Gideon, whose ephod brought ruin not only on himself and his family, but on the whole people (Judges 8:27). In short, every adventitious invention, by which men desire to worship God, is nothing else than a pollution of true holiness.

26. Why then, they ask, did Christ say that the intolerable burdens, imposed by Scribes and Pharisees, were to be borne? (Mt. 23:3) Nay, rather, why did he say in another place that we were to beware of the leaven of the Pharisees? (Mt. 16:6) meaning by leaven, as the Evangelist Matthew explains it, whatever of human doctrine is mingled with the pure word of God. What can be plainer than that we are enjoined to shun and beware of their whole doctrine? From this it is most certain, that in the other passage our Lord never meant that the consciences of his people were to be harassed by the mere traditions of the Pharisees. And the words themselves, unless when wrested, have no such meaning. Our Lord, indeed, beginning to inveigh against the manners of the Pharisees, first instructs his hearers simply, that though they saw nothing to follow in the lives of the Pharisees, they should not, however, cease to do what they verbally taught when they sat in the seat of Moses, that is, to expound the Law. All he meant, therefore, was to guard the common people against being led by the bad example of their teachers to despise doctrine. But as some are not at all moved by reason, and always require authority, I will quote a passage from Augustine, in which the very same thing is expressed. "The Lord's sheepfold has persons set over it, of whom some are faithful, others hirelings. Those who are faithful are true shepherds; learn, however, that hirelings also are necessary. For many in the Church, pursuing temporal advantages, preach Christ, and the voice of Christ is heard by them, and the sheep follow not a hireling, but the shepherd by means of a hireling. Learn that hirelings were pointed out by the Lord himself. The Scribes and Pharisees, says he, sit in Moses' seat; what they tell you, do, but what they do, do ye not. What is this but to say, Hear the voice of the shepherd by means of hirelings? Sitting in the chair, they teach the Law of God, and therefore God teaches by them; but if they choose to teach their own, hear not, do not." Thus far Augustine. (August. in Joann. Tract. 46)

27. But as very many ignorant persons, on hearing that it is impious to bind the conscience, and vain to worship God with human traditions, apply one blot to all the laws by which the order of the Church is established, it will be proper to obviate their error. Here, indeed, the danger of mistake is great: for it is not easy to see at first sight how widely the two things differ. But I will, in a few words, make the matter so clear, that no one will be imposed upon by the resemblance. First, then, let us understand that if in every human society some kind of government is necessary to insure the common peace and maintain concord, if in transacting business some form must always be observed, which public decency, and hence humanity itself, require us not to disregard, this ought especially to be observed in churches, which are best sustained by a constitution in all respects well ordered, and without which concord can have no existence. Wherefore, if we would provide for the safety of the Church, we must always carefully attend to Paul's injunction, that all things be done decently and in order (1 Cor. 14:40). But seeing there is such diversity in the manners of men, such variety in their minds, such repugnance in their judgments and dispositions, no policy is sufficiently firm unless fortified by certain laws, nor can any rite be observed without a fixed form. So far, therefore, are we from condemning the laws which conduce to this, that we hold that the removal of them would unnerve the Church, deface and dissipate it entirely. For Paul's injunction, that all things be done decently and in order, cannot be observed unless order and decency be secured by the addition of ordinances, as a kind of bonds. In these ordinances, however, we must always attend to

the exception, that they must not be thought necessary to salvation, nor lay the conscience under a religious obligation; they must not be compared to the worship of God, nor substituted for piety.

28. We have, therefore, a most excellent and sure mark to distinguish between those impious constitutions (by which, as we have said, true religion is overthrown, and conscience subverted) and the legitimate observances of the Church, if we remember that one of two things, or both together, are always intended—viz. that in the sacred assembly of the faithful, all things may be done decently, and with becoming dignity, and that human society may be maintained in order by certain bonds, as it were, of moderation and humanity. For when a law is understood to have been made for the sake of public decency, there is no room for the superstition into which those fall who measure the worship of God by human inventions. On the other hand, when a law is known to be intended for common use, that false idea of its obligation and necessity, which gives great alarm to the conscience, when traditions are deemed necessary to salvation, is overthrown; since nothing here is sought but the maintenance of charity by a common office. But it may be proper to explain more clearly what is meant by the decency which Paul commends, and also what is comprehended under order. And the object of decency is, partly that by the use of rites, which produce reverence in sacred matters, we may be excited to piety, and partly that the modesty and gravity which ought to be seen in all honourable actions may here especially be conspicuous. In order, the first thing is, that those who preside know the law and rule of right government, while those who are governed be accustomed to obedience and right discipline. The second thing is, that by duly arranging the state of the Church, provision be made for peace and tranquillity.

29. We shall not, therefore, give the name of decency to that which only ministers an empty pleasure: such, for example, as is seen in that theatrical display which the Papists exhibit in their public service, where nothing appears but a mask of useless splendour, and luxury without any fruit. But we give the name of decency to that which, suited to the reverence of sacred mysteries, forms a fit exercise for piety, or at least gives an ornament adapted to the action, and is not without fruit, but reminds believers of the great modesty, seriousness, and reverence, with which sacred things ought to be treated. Moreover, ceremonies, in order to be exercises of piety, must lead us directly to Christ. In like manner, we shall not make order consist in that nugatory pomp which gives nothing but evanescent splendour, but in that arrangement which removes all confusion, barbarism, contumacy, all turbulence and dissension. Of the former class we have examples (1 Cor. 11:5, 21), where Paul says, that profane entertainments must not be intermingled with the sacred Supper of the Lord; that women must not appear in public uncovered. And there are many other things which we have in daily practice, such as praying on our knees, and with our head uncovered, administering the sacraments of the Lord, not sordidly, but with some degree of dignity; employing some degree of solemnity in the burial of our dead, and so forth. In the other class are the hours set apart for public prayer, sermon, and solemn services; during sermon, quiet and silence, fixed places, singing of hymns, days set apart for the celebration of the Lord's Supper, the prohibition of Paul against women teaching in the Church, and such like. To the same list especially may be referred those things which preserve discipline, as catechising, ecclesiastical censures, excommunication, fastings, &c. Thus all ecclesiastical constitutions, which we admit to be sacred and salutary, may be reduced to two heads, the one relating to rites and ceremonies, the other to discipline and peace.

30. But as there is here a danger, on the one hand, lest false bishops should thence derive a pretext for their impious and tyrannical laws, and, on the other, lest some, too apt to take alarm, should, from fear of the above evils, leave no place for laws, however holy, it may here be proper to declare, that I approve of those human constitutions only which are founded on the authority of God, and derived from Scripture, and are therefore altogether divine. Let us take, for example, the bending of the knee which is made in public prayer. It is asked, whether this is a human tradition, which any one is at liberty to repudiate or neglect? I say, that it is human, and that at the same time it is divine. It is of God, inasmuch as it is a part of that decency, the care and observance of which is recommended by the apostle; and it is of men, inasmuch as it specially determines what was indicated in general, rather than expounded. From this one example, we may judge what is to be thought of the whole class—viz. that the whole sum of righteousness, and all the parts of divine worship, and everything necessary to salvation, the Lord has faithfully comprehended, and clearly unfolded, in his sacred oracles, so that in them he alone is the only Master to be heard. But as in external discipline and ceremonies, he has not been pleased to prescribe every

particular that we ought to observe (he foresaw that this depended on the nature of the times, and that one form would not suit all ages), in them we must have recourse to the general rules which he has given, employing them to test whatever the necessity of the Church may require to be enjoined for order and decency. Lastly, as he has not delivered any express command, because things of this nature are not necessary to salvation, and, for the edification of the Church, should be accommodated to the varying circumstances of each age and nation, it will be proper, as the interest of the Church may require, to change and abrogate the old, as well as to introduce new forms. I confess, indeed, that we are not to innovate rashly or incessantly, or for trivial causes. Charity is the best judge of what tends to hurt or to edify: if we allow her to be guide, all things will be safe.

31. Things which have been appointed according to this rule, it is the duty of the Christian people to observe with a free conscience indeed, and without superstition, but also with a pious and ready inclination to obey. They are not to hold them in contempt, nor pass them by with careless indifference, far less openly to violate them in pride and contumacy. You will ask, What liberty of conscience will there be in such cautious observances? Nay, this liberty will admirably appear when we shall hold that these are not fixed and perpetual obligations to which we are astricted, but external rudiments for human infirmity, which, though we do not all need, we, however, all use, because we are bound to cherish mutual charity towards each other. This we may recognise in the examples given above. What? Is religion placed in a woman's bonnet, so that it is unlawful for her to go out with her head uncovered? Is her silence fixed by a decree which cannot be violated without the greatest wickedness? Is there any mystery in bending the knee, or in burying a dead body, which cannot be omitted without a crime? By no means. For should a woman require to make such haste in assisting a neighbour that she has not time to cover her head, she sins not in running out with her head uncovered. And there are some occasions on which it is not less seasonable for her to speak than on others to be silent. Nothing, moreover, forbids him who, from disease, cannot bend his knees, to pray standing. In fine, it is better to bury a dead man quickly, than from want of graveclothes, or the absence of those who should attend the funeral, to wait till it rot away unburied. Nevertheless, in those matters the custom and institutions of the country, in short, humanity and the rules of modesty itself, declare what is to be done or avoided. Here, if any error is committed through imprudence or forgetfulness, no crime is perpetrated; but if this is done from contempt, such contumacy must be disapproved. In like manner, it is of no consequence what the days and hours are, what the nature of the edifices, and what psalms are sung on each day. But it is proper that there should be certain days and stated hours, and a place fit for receiving all, if any regard is had to the preservation of peace. For what a seed-bed of quarrels will confusion in such matters be, if every one is allowed at pleasure to alter what pertains to common order? All will not be satisfied with the same course if matters, placed as it were on debateable ground, are left to the determination of individuals. But if any one here becomes clamorous, and would be wiser than he ought, let him consider how he will approve his moroseness to the Lord. Paul's answer ought to satisfy us, "If any man seem to be contentious, we have no such custom, neither the churches of God."

32. Moreover, we must use the utmost diligence to prevent any error from creeping in which may either taint or sully this pure use. In this we shall succeed, if whatever observances we use are manifestly useful, and very few in number; especially if to this is added the teaching of a faithful pastor, which may prevent access to erroneous opinions. The effect of this procedure is, that in all these matters each retains his freedom, and yet at the same time voluntarily subjects it to a kind of necessity, in so far as the *decency* of which we have spoken or charity demands. Next, that in the observance of these things we may not fall into any superstition, nor rigidly require too much from others, let us not imagine that the worship of God is improved by a multitude of ceremonies: let not church despise church because of a difference in external discipline. Lastly, instead of here laying down any perpetual law for ourselves, let us refer the whole end and use of observances to the edification of the Church, at whose request let us without offence allow not only something to be changed, but even observances which were formerly in use to be inverted. For the present age is a proof that the nature of times allows that certain rites, not otherwise impious or unbecoming, may be abrogated according to circumstances. Such was the ignorance and blindness of former times; with such erroneous ideas and pertinacious zeal did churches formerly cling to ceremonies, that they can scarcely be purified from monstrous superstitions without the removal of many ceremonies which were formerly established, not without cause, and which in themselves are not chargeable with any impiety.

CHAPTER II

OF THE JURISDICTION OF THE CHURCH, AND THE ABUSES OF IT, AS EXEMPLIFIED IN THE PAPACY.

This chapter may be conveniently comprehended under two heads,—I. Ecclesiastical jurisdiction, its necessity, origin, description, and essential parts—viz. the sacred ministry of the word, and discipline of excommunication, of which the aim, use, and abuse are explained, sec. 1–8. II. Refutation of the arguments advanced by Papists in defence of the tyranny of Pontiffs, the right of both swords, imperial pomp and dignity, foreign jurisdiction, and immunity from civil jurisdiction, sec. 9–16.

Sections:

1. The power of the Church in regard to jurisdiction. The necessity, origin, and nature of this jurisdiction. The power of the keys to be considered in two points of view. The first view expounded.

2. Second view expounded. How the Church binds and looses in the way of discipline. Abuse of the keys in the Papacy.

3. The discipline of excommunication of perpetual endurance. Distinction between civil and ecclesiastical power.

4. The perpetual endurance of the discipline of excommunication confirmed. Duly ordered under the Emperors and Christian magistrates.

5. The aim and use of ecclesiastical jurisdiction in the primitive Church. Spiritual power was kept entirely distinct from the power of the sword.

6. Spiritual power was not administered by one individual, but by a lawful consistory. Gradual change. First, the clergy alone interfered in the judicial proceedings of the Church. The bishop afterwards appropriated them to himself.

7. The bishops afterwards transferred the rights thus appropriated to their officials, and converted spiritual jurisdiction into a profane tribunal.

8. Recapitulation. The Papal power confuted. Christ wished to debar the ministers of the word from civil rule and worldly power.

9. Objections of the Papists. 1. By this external splendour the glory of Christ is displayed. 2. It does not interfere with the duties of their calling. Both objections answered.

10. The commencement and gradual progress of the Papistical tyranny. Causes, 1. Curiosity; 2. Ambition; 3. Violence; 4. Hypocrisy; 5. Impiety.

11. Last cause, the mystery of iniquity, and the Satanic fury of Antichrist usurping worldly dominion. The Pope claims both swords.

12. The pretended donation of Constantine. Its futility exposed.

13. When, and by what means, the Roman Pontiffs attained to imperial dignity. Hildebrand its founder.

14. By what acts they seized on Rome and other territories. Disgraceful rapacity.

15. Claim of immunity from civil jurisdiction. Contrast between this pretended immunity and the moderation of the early bishops.

16. What end the early bishops aimed at in steadfastly resisting civil encroachment.

1. It remains to consider the third, and, indeed, when matters are well arranged, the principal part of ecclesiastical power, which, as we have said, consists in jurisdiction. Now, the whole jurisdiction of the Church relates to discipline, of which we are shortly to treat. For as no city or village can exist without a magistrate and government, so the Church of God, as I have already taught, but am again obliged to repeat, needs a kind of spiritual government. This is altogether distinct from civil government, and is so far from impeding or impairing it, that it rather does much to aid and promote it. Therefore, this power of jurisdiction is, in one word, nothing but the order provided for the preservation of spiritual polity. To this end, there were established in the Church from the first, tribunals which might take cognisance of morals, animadvert on vices, and exercise the office of the keys. This order is mentioned by Paul in the First Epistle to the Corinthians under the name of governments (1 Cor. 12:28): in like manner, in the Epistle to the Romans, when he says, "He that ruleth with diligence" (Rom. 12:8). For he is not addressing magistrates, none of whom were then Christians, but those who were joined with pastors in the spiritual government of the Church. In the Epistle to Timothy, also, he mentions two kinds of presbyters, some who labour in the word, and others who do not perform the office of preaching, but rule well (1 Tim. 5:17). By this latter class there is no doubt he means those who were appointed to the inspection of manners, and the whole use of the keys. For the power of which we speak wholly depends on the keys which Christ bestowed on the Church in the eighteenth chapter

of Matthew, where he orders, that those who despise private admonition should be sharply rebuked in public, and if they persist in their contumacy, be expelled from the society of believers. Moreover, those admonitions and corrections cannot be made without investigation, and hence the necessity of some judicial procedure and order. Wherefore, if we would not make void the promise of the keys, and abolish altogether excommunication, solemn admonitions, and everything of that description, we must, of necessity, give some jurisdiction to the Church. Let the reader observe that we are not here treating of the general authority of doctrine, as in Mt. 21 and John 20, but maintaining that the right of the Sanhedrim is transferred to the fold of Christ. Till that time, the power of government had belonged to the Jews. This Christ establishes in his Church, in as far as it was a pure institution, and with a heavy sanction. Thus it behoved to be, since the judgment of a poor and despised Church might otherwise be spurned by rash and haughty men. And lest it occasion any difficulty to the reader, that Christ in the same words makes a considerable difference between the two things, it will here be proper to explain. There are two passages which speak of binding and loosing. The one is Mt. 16, where Christ, after promising that he will give the keys of the kingdom of heaven to Peter, immediately adds, "Whatsoever thou shalt bind on earth shall be bound in heaven; and whatsoever thou shalt loose on earth shall be loosed in heaven" (Mt. 16:19). These words have the very same meaning as those in the Gospel of John, where, being about to send forth the disciples to preach, after breathing on them, he says, "Whose soever sins ye remit, they are remitted unto them; and whose soever sins ye retain, they are retained" (John 20:23). I will give an interpretation, not subtle, not forced, not wrested, but genuine, natural, and obvious. This command concerning remitting and retaining sins, and that promise made to Peter concerning binding and loosing, ought to be referred to nothing but the ministry of the word. When the Lord committed it to the apostles, he, at the same time, provided them with this power of binding and loosing. For what is the sum of the gospel, but just that all being the slaves of sin and death, are loosed and set free by the redemption which is in Christ Jesus, while those who do not receive and acknowledge Christ as a deliverer and redeemer are condemned and doomed to eternal chains? When the Lord delivered this message to his apostles, to be carried by them into all nations, in order to prove that it was his own message, and proceeded from him, he honoured it with this distinguished testimony, and that as an admirable confirmation both to the apostles themselves, and to all those to whom it was to come. It was of importance that the apostles should have a constant and complete assurance of their preaching, which they were not only to exercise with infinite labour, anxiety, molestation, and peril, but ultimately to seal with their blood. That they might know that it was not vain or void, but full of power and efficacy, it was of importance, I say, that amidst all their anxieties, dangers, and difficulties, they might feel persuaded that they were doing the work of God; that though the whole world withstood and opposed them, they might know that God was for them; that not having Christ the author of their doctrine bodily present on the earth, they might understand that he was in heaven to confirm the truth of the doctrine which he had delivered to them. On the other hand, it was necessary that their hearers should be most certainly assured that the doctrine of the gospel was not the word of the apostles, but of God himself; not a voice rising from the earth, but descending from heaven. For such things as the forgiveness of sins, the promise of eternal life, and message of salvation, cannot be in the power of man. Christ therefore testified, that in the preaching of the gospel the apostles only acted ministerially; that it was he who, by their mouths as organs, spoke and promised all; that, therefore, the forgiveness of sins which they announced was the true promise of God; the condemnation which they pronounced, the certain judgment of God. This attestation was given to all ages, and remains firm, rendering all certain and secure, that the word of the gospel, by whomsoever it may be preached, is the very word of God, promulgated at the supreme tribunal, written in the book of life, ratified firm and fixed in heaven. We now understand that the power of the keys is simply the preaching of the gospel in those places, and in so far as men are concerned, it is not so much power as ministry. Properly speaking, Christ did not give this power to men but to his word, of which he made men the ministers.

2. The other passage, in which binding and loosing are mentioned, is in the eighteenth chapter of Matthew, where Christ says, "If he shall neglect to hear them, tell it unto the Church: but if he neglect to hear the Church, let him be unto thee as an heathen man and a publican. Verily I say unto you, Whatsoever ye shall bind on earth shall be bound in heaven; and whatsoever ye shall loose on earth shall be loosed in heaven" (Mt. 18:17, 18). This passage is not altogether similar to the former, but is to be understood somewhat differently. But in saying that they

are different, I do not mean that there is not much affinity between them. First, they are similar in this, that they are both general statements, that there is always the same power of binding and loosing (namely, by the word of God), the same command, the same promise. They differ in this, that the former passage relates specially to the preaching which the ministers of the word perform, the latter relates to the discipline of excommunication which has been committed to the Church. Now, the Church binds him whom she excommunicates, not by plunging him into eternal ruin and despair, but condemning his life and manners, and admonishing him, that, unless he repent, he is condemned. She looses him whom she receives into communion, because she makes him, as it were, a partaker of the unity which she has in Christ Jesus. Let no one, therefore, contumaciously despise the judgment of the Church, or account it a small matter that he is condemned by the suffrages of the faithful. The Lord testifies that such judgment of the faithful is nothing else than the promulgation of his own sentence, and that what they do on earth is ratified in heaven. For they have the word of God by which they condemn the perverse: they have the word by which they take back the penitent into favour. Now, they cannot err nor disagree with the judgment of God, because they judge only according to the law of God, which is not an uncertain or worldly opinion, but the holy will of God, an oracle of heaven. On these two passages, which I think I have briefly, as well as familiarly and truly expounded, these madmen, without any discrimination, as they are borne along by their spirit of giddiness, attempt to found at one time confession, at another excommunication, at another jurisdiction, at another the right of making laws, at another indulgences. The former passage they adduce for the purpose of rearing up the primacy of the Roman See. So well known are the keys to those who have thought proper to fit them with locks and doors, that you would say their whole life had been spent in the mechanic art.

3. Some, in imagining that all these things were temporary, as magistrates were still strangers to our profession of religion, are led astray, by not observing the distinction and dissimilarity between ecclesiastical and civil power. For the Church has not the right of the sword to punish or restrain, has no power to coerce, no prison nor other punishments which the magistrate is wont to inflict. Then the object in view is not to punish the sinner against his will, but to obtain a profession of penitence by voluntary chastisement. The two things, therefore, are widely different, because neither does the Church assume anything to herself which is proper to the magistrate, nor is the magistrate competent to what is done by the Church. This will be made clearer by an example. Does any one get intoxicated? In a well-ordered city his punishment will be imprisonment. Has he committed whoredom? The punishment will be similar, or rather more severe. Thus satisfaction will be given to the laws, the magistrates, and the external tribunal. But the consequence will be, that the offender will give no signs of repentance, but will rather fret and murmur. Will the Church not here interfere? Such persons cannot be admitted to the Lord's Supper without doing injury to Christ and his sacred institution. Reason demands that he who, by a bad example, gives offence to the Church, shall remove the offence which he has caused by a formal declaration of repentance. The reason adduced by those who take a contrary view is frigid. Christ, they say, gave this office to the Church when there were no magistrates to execute it. But it often happens that the magistrate is negligent, nay, sometimes himself requires to be chastised; as was the case with the Emperor Theodosius. Moreover, the same thing may be said regarding the whole ministry of the word. Now, therefore, according to that view, let pastors cease to censure manifest iniquities, let them cease to chide, accuse, and rebuke. For there are Christian magistrates who ought to correct these things by the laws and the sword. But as the magistrate ought to purge the Church of offences by corporal punishment and coercion, so the minister ought, in his turn, to assist the magistrate in diminishing the number of offenders. Thus they ought to combine their efforts, the one being not an impediment but a help to the other.

4. And indeed, on attending more closely to the words of Christ, it will readily appear that the state and order of the Church there described is perpetual, not temporary. For it were incongruous that those who refuse to obey our admonitions should be transferred to the magistrate—a course, however, which would be necessary if he were to succeed to the place of the Church. Why should the promise, "Verily I say unto you, What thing soever ye shall bind on earth," be limited to one, or to a few years? Moreover, Christ has here made no new enactment, but followed the custom always observed in the Church of his ancient people, thereby intimating, that the Church cannot dispense with the spiritual jurisdiction which existed from the beginning. This has been confirmed by the consent of all times. For when emperors and magistrates began to assume the Christian name, spiritual jurisdiction was not forthwith abolished, but was only so

arranged as not in any respect to impair civil jurisdiction, or be confounded with it. And justly. For the magistrate, if he is pious, will have no wish to exempt himself from the common subjection of the children of God, not the least part of which is to subject himself to the Church, judging according to the word of God; so far is it from being his duty to abolish that judgment. For, as Ambrose says, "What more honourable title can an emperor have than to be called a son of the Church? A good emperor is within the Church, not above the Church" (Ambros. ad Valent. Ep. 32). Those, therefore, who to adorn the magistrate strip the Church of this power, not only corrupt the sentiment of Christ by a false interpretation, but pass no light condemnation on the many holy bishops who have existed since the days of the apostles, for having on a false pretext usurped the honour and office of the civil magistrate.

5. But, on the other hand, it will be proper to see what was anciently the true use of ecclesiastical discipline, and how great the abuses which crept in, that we may know what of ancient practice is to be abolished, and what restored, if we would, after overthrowing the kingdom of Antichrist, again set up the true kingdom of Christ. First, the object in view is to prevent the occurrence of scandals, and when they arise, to remove them. In the use two things are to be considered: first, that this spiritual power be altogether distinct from the power of the sword; secondly, that it be not administered at the will of one individual, but by a lawful consistory (1 Cor. 5:4). Both were observed in the purer times of the Church. For holy bishops did not exercise their power by fine, imprisonment, or other civil penalties, but as became them, employed the word of God only. For the severest punishment of the Church, and, as it were, her last thunderbolt, is excommunication, which is not used unless in necessity. This, moreover, requires neither violence nor physical force, but is contented with the might of the word of God. In short, the jurisdiction of the ancient Church was nothing else than (if I may so speak) a practical declaration of what Paul teaches concerning the spiritual power of pastors. "The weapons of our warfare are not carnal, but mighty through God to the pulling down of strongholds; casting down imaginations, and every high thing that exalteth itself against the knowledge of God, and bringing into captivity every thought to the obedience of Christ; and having in a readiness to revenge all disobedience" (2 Cor. 10:4–6). As this is done by the preaching of doctrine, so in order that doctrine may not be held in derision, those who profess to be of the household of faith ought to be judged according to the doctrine which is taught. Now this cannot be done without connecting with the office of the ministry a right of summoning those who are to be privately admonished or sharply rebuked, a right, moreover, of keeping back from the communion of the Lord's Supper, those who cannot be admitted without profaning this high ordinance. Hence, when Paul elsewhere asks, "What have I to do to judge them also that are without?" (1 Cor. 5:12), he makes the members of the Church subject to censures for the correction of their vices, and intimates the existence of tribunals from which no believer is exempted.

6. This power, as we have already stated, did not belong to an individual who could exercise it as he pleased, but belonged to the consistory of elders, which was in the Church what a council is in a city. Cyprian, when mentioning those by whom it was exercised in his time, usually associates the whole clergy with the bishop (Cyprian, Lib. 3 Ep. 14, 19). In another place, he shows that though the clergy presided, the people, at the same time, were not excluded from cognisance: for he thus writes:—"From the commencement of my bishopric, I determined to do nothing without the advice of the clergy, nothing without the consent of the people." But the common and usual method of exercising this jurisdiction was by the council of presbyters, of whom, as I have said, there were two classes. Some were for teaching, others were only censors of manners. This institution gradually degenerated from its primitive form, so that, in the time of Ambrose, the clergy alone had cognisance of ecclesiastical causes. Of this he complains in the following terms:—"The ancient synagogue, and afterwards the Church, had elders, without whose advice nothing was done: this has grown obsolete, by whose fault I know not, unless it be by the sloth, or rather the pride, of teachers, who would have it seem that they only are somewhat" (Ambros. in 1 Tim. 5). We see how indignant this holy man was because the better state was in some degree impaired, and yet the order which then existed was at least tolerable. What, then, had he seen those shapeless ruins which exhibit no trace of the ancient edifice? How would he have lamented? First, contrary to what was right and lawful, the bishop appropriated to himself what was given to the whole Church. For this is just as if the consul had expelled the senate, and usurped the whole empire. For as he is superior in rank to the others, so the authority of the consistory is greater than that of one individual. It was, therefore, a gross iniquity, when one man, transferring the common power to himself, paved the way for tyrannical licence,

robbed the Church of what was its own, suppressed and discarded the consistory ordained by the Spirit of Christ.

7. But as evil always produces evil, the bishops, disdaining this jurisdiction as a thing unworthy of their care, devolved it on others. Hence the appointment of officials to supply their place. I am not now speaking of the character of this class of persons; all I say is, that they differ in no respect from civil judges. And yet they call it spiritual jurisdiction, though all the litigation relates to worldly affairs. Were there no other evil in this, how can they presume to call a litigious forum a church court? But there are admonitions; there is excommunication. This is the way in which God is mocked. Does some poor man owe a sum of money? He is summoned: if he appears, he is found liable; when found liable, if he pays not, he is admonished. After the second admonition, the next step is excommunication. If he appears not, he is admonished to appear; if he delays, he is admonished, and by-and-by excommunicated. I ask, is there any resemblance whatever between this and the institution of Christ, or ancient custom or ecclesiastical procedure? But there, too, vices are censured. Whoredom, lasciviousness, drunkenness, and similar iniquities, they not only tolerate, but by a kind of tacit approbation encourage and confirm, and that not among the people only, but also among the clergy. Out of many they summon a few, either that they may not seem to wink too strongly, or that they may mulct them in money. I say nothing of the plunder, rapine, peculation, and sacrilege, which are there committed. I say nothing of the kind of persons who are for the most part appointed to the office. It is enough, and more than enough, that when the Romanists boast of their spiritual jurisdiction, we are ready to show that nothing is more contrary to the procedure instituted by Christ, that it has no more resemblance to ancient practice than darkness has to light.

8. Although we have not said all that might here be adduced, and even what has been said is only briefly glanced at, enough, I trust, has been said to leave no man in doubt that the spiritual power on which the Pope plumes himself, with all his adherents, is impious contradiction of the word of God, and unjust tyranny against his people. Under the name of spiritual power, I include both their audacity in framing new doctrines, by which they led the miserable people away from the genuine purity of the word of God, the iniquitous traditions by which they ensnared them, and the pseudo-ecclesiastical jurisdiction which they exercise by suffragans and officials. For if we allow Christ to reign amongst us, the whole of that domination cannot but immediately tumble and fall. The right of the sword which they also claim for themselves, not being exercised against consciences, does not fall to be considered in this place. Here, however, it is worth while to observe, that they are always like themselves, there being nothing which they less resemble than that which they would be thought to be—viz. pastors of the Church. I speak not of the vices of particular men, but of the common wickedness, and, consequently, the pestiferous nature of the whole order, which is thought to be mutilated if not distinguished by wealth and haughty titles. If in this matter we seek the authority of Christ, there can be no doubt that he intended to debar the ministers of his word from civil domination and worldly power when he said, "The princes of the Gentiles exercise dominion over them, and they that are great exercise authority upon them. But it shall not be so among you" (Mt. 20:25, 26). For he intimates not only that the office of pastor is distinct from the office of prince, but that the things differ so widely that they cannot be united in the same individual. Moses indeed held both (Exod. 18:16); but, first, this was the effect of a rare miracle; and, secondly, it was temporary, until matters should be better arranged. For when a certain form is prescribed by the Lord, the civil government is left to Moses, and he is ordered to resign the priesthood to his brother. And justly; for it is more than nature can do, for one man to bear both burdens. This has in all ages been carefully observed in the Church. Never did any bishop, so long as any true appearance of a church remained, think of usurping the right of the sword: so that, in the age of Ambrose, it was a common proverb, that emperors longed more for the priesthood than priests for imperial power. For the expression which he afterwards adds was fixed in all minds, Palaces belong to the emperor, churches to the priest.

9. But after a method was devised by which bishops might hold the title, honour, and wealth of their office without burden and solicitude, that they might be left altogether idle, the right of the sword was given them, or rather, they themselves usurped it. With what pretext will they defend this effrontery? Was it the part of bishops to entangle themselves with the cognisance of causes, and the administration of states and provinces, and embrace occupations so very alien to them—of bishops, who require so much time and labour in their own office, that though they devote themselves to it diligently and entirely, without distraction from other avocations, they are scarcely sufficient? But such is their perverseness,

that they hesitate not to boast that in this way the dignity of Christ's kingdom is duly maintained, and they, at the same time, are not withdrawn from their own vocation. In regard to the former allegation, if it is a comely ornament of the sacred office, that those holding it be so elevated as to become formidable to the greatest monarchs, they have ground to expostulate with Christ, who in this respect has grievously curtailed their honour. For what, according to their view, can be more insulting than these words, "The kings of the Gentiles exercise authority over them"? "But ye shall not be so" (Luke 22:25, 26). And yet he imposes no harder law on his servants than he had previously laid on himself. "Who," says he, "made me a judge or divider over you?" (Luke 12:14) We see that he unreservedly refuses the office of judging; and this he would not have done if the thing had been in accordance with his office. To the subordination to which the Lord thus reduced himself, will his servants not submit? The other point I wish they would prove by experience as easily as they allege it. But as it seemed to the apostles not good to leave the word of God and serve tables, so these men are thereby forced to admit, though they are unwilling to be taught, that it is not possible for the same person to be a good bishop and a good prince. For if those who, in respect of the largeness of the gifts with which they were endued, were able for much more numerous and weighty cares than any who have come after them, confessed that they could not serve the ministry of the word and of tables, without giving way under the burden, how are these, who are no men at all when compared with the apostles, possibly to surpass them a hundred times in diligence? The very attempt is most impudent and audacious presumption. Still we see the thing done; with what success is plain. The result could not but be that they have deserted their own functions, and removed to another camp.

10. There can be no doubt that this great progress has been made from slender beginnings. They could not reach so far at one step, but at one time by craft and wily art, secretly raised themselves before any one foresaw what was to happen; at another time, when occasion offered, by means of threats and terror, extorted some increase of power from princes; at another time, when they saw princes disposed to give liberally, they abused their foolish and inconsiderate facility. The godly in ancient times, when any dispute arose, in order to escape the necessity of a lawsuit, left the decision to the bishop, because they had no doubt of his integrity. The ancient bishops were often greatly dissatisfied at being entangled in such matters, as Augustine somewhere declares; but lest the parties should rush to some contentious tribunal, unwillingly submitted to the annoyance. These voluntary decisions, which altogether differed from forensic strife, these men have converted into ordinary jurisdiction. As cities and districts, when for some time pressed with various difficulties, betook themselves to the patronage of the bishops, and threw themselves on their protection, these men have, by a strange artifice, out of patrons made themselves masters. That they have seized a good part by the violence of faction cannot be denied. The princes, again, who spontaneously conferred jurisdiction on bishops, were induced to it by various causes. Though their indulgence had some appearance of piety, they did not by this preposterous liberality consult in the best manner for the interests of the Church, whose ancient and true discipline they thus corrupted, nay, to tell the truth, completely abolished. Those bishops who abuse the goodness of princes to their own advantage, gave more than sufficient proof by this one specimen of their conduct, that they were not at all true bishops. Had they had one spark of the apostolic spirit, they would doubtless have answered in the words of Paul, "The weapons of our warfare are not carnal," but spiritual (2 Cor. 10:4). But hurried away by blind cupidity, they lost themselves, and posterity, and the Church.

11. At length the Roman Pontiff, not content with moderate districts, laid hands first on kingdoms, and thereafter on empire. And that he may on some pretext or other retain possession, secured by mere robbery, he boasts at one time that he holds it by divine right, at another, he pretends a donation from Constantine, at another, some different title. First, I answer with Bernard, "Be it that on some ground or other he can claim it, it is not by apostolic right. For Peter could not give what he had not, but what he had he gave to his successors—viz. care of the churches. But when our Lord and Master says that he was not appointed a judge between two, the servant and disciple ought not to think it unbecoming not to be judge of all" (Bernard. de Considerat. Lib. 2). Bernard is spearing of civil judgments, for he adds, "Your power then is in sins, not in rights of property, since for the former and not the latter you received the keys of the kingdom of heaven. Which of the two seems to you the higher dignity, the forgiving of sins or the dividing of lands? There is no comparison. These low earthly things have for their judges the kings and princes of the earth. Why do you invade the territories of others?" &c. Again, "You are made superior" (he is addressing Pope

Eugenius), "for what? not to domineer, I presume. Let us therefore remember, however highly we think of ourselves, that a ministry is laid upon us, not a dominion given to us. Learn that you have need of a slender rod, not of a sceptre, to do the work of a prophet." Again, "It is plain that the apostles are prohibited to exercise dominion. Go you, therefore, and dare to usurp for yourself, either apostleship with dominion, or dominion with apostleship." Immediately after he says, "The apostolic form is this; dominion is interdicted, ministry is enjoined." Though Bernard speaks thus, and so speaks as to make it manifest to all that he speaks truth, nay, though without a word the thing itself is manifest, the Roman Pontiff was not ashamed at the Council of Arles to decree that the supreme right of both swords belonged to him of divine right.

12. As far as pertains to the donation of Constantine, those who are moderately versant in the history of the time have no need of being told, that the claim is not only fabulous but also absurd. But to say nothing of history, Gregory alone is a fit and most complete witness to this effect. For wherever he speaks of the emperor he calls him His Most Serene Lord, and himself his unworthy servant. Again, in another passage he says, "Let not our Lord in respect of worldly power be too soon offended with priests, but with excellent consideration, on account of him whose servants they are, let him while ruling them also pay them due reverence." We see how in a common subjection he desires to be accounted one of the people. For he there pleads not another's but his own cause. Again, "I trust in Almighty God that he will give long life to pious rulers, and place us under your hand according to his mercy." I have not adduced these things here from any intention thoroughly to discuss the question of Constantine's donation, but only to show my readers by the way, how childishly the Romanists tell lies when they attempt to claim an earthly empire for their Pontiff. The more vile the impudence of Augustine Steuchus, who, in so desperate a cause, presumed to lend his labour and his tongue to the Roman Pontiff. Valla, as was easy for a man of learning and acuteness to do, had completely refuted this fable. And yet, as he was little versant in ecclesiastical affairs, he had not said all that was relevant to the subject. Steuchus breaks in, and scatters his worthless quibbles, trying to bury the clear light. And certainly he pleads the cause of his master not less frigidly than some wit might, under pretence of defending the same view, support that of Valla. But the cause is a worthy one, which the Pope may well hire such patrons to defend; equally worthy are the hired ravers whom the hope of gain may deceive, as was the case with Eugubinus.

13. Should any one ask at what period this fictitious empire began to emerge, five hundred years have not yet elapsed since the Roman Pontiffs were under subjection to the emperors, and no pontiff was elected without the emperor's authority. An occasion of innovating on this order was given to Gregory VII. by Henry IV., a giddy and rash man, of no prudence, great audacity, and a dissolute life. When he had the whole bishoprics of Germany in his court partly for sale, and partly exposed to plunder, Hildebrand, who had been provoked by him, seized the plausible pretext for asserting his claim. As his cause seemed good and pious, it was viewed with great favour, while Henry, on account of the insolence of his government, was generally hated by the princes. At length Hildebrand, who took the name of Gregory VII., an impure and wicked man, betrayed his sinister intentions. On this he was deserted by many who had joined him in his conspiracy. He gained this much, however, that his successors were not only able to shake off the yoke with impunity, but also to bring the emperors into subjection to them. Moreover, many of the subsequent emperors were liker Henry than Julius Cæsar. These it was not difficult to overcome while they sat at home sluggish and secure, instead of vigorously exerting themselves, as was most necessary, by all legitimate means to repress the cupidity of the pontiffs. We see what colour there is for the grand donation of Constantine, by which the Pope pretends that the western empire was given to him.

14. Meanwhile the pontiff ceased not, either by fraud, or by perfidy, or by arms, to invade the dominions of others. Rome itself, which was then free, they, about a hundred and thirty years ago, reduced under their power. At length they obtained the dominion which they now possess, and to retain or increase which, now for two hundred years (they had begun before they usurped the dominion of the city) they have so troubled the Christian world that they have almost destroyed it. Formerly, when in the time of Gregory, the guardians of ecclesiastical property seized upon lands which they considered to belong to the Church, and, after the manner of the exchequer, affixed their seals in attestation of their claim, Gregory having assembled a council of bishops, and bitterly inveighed against that profane custom, asked whether they would not anathematise the churchman who, of his own accord, attempted to seize some possession by the inscription of a title, and in like manner, the bishop who should order it to be done, or not punish it when done

without his order. All pronounced the anathema. If it is a crime deserving of anathema for a churchman to claim a property by the inscription of a title—then, now that for two hundred years, the pontiffs meditate nothing but war and bloodshed, the destruction of armies, the plunder of cities, the destruction or overthrow of nations, and the devastation of kingdoms, only that they may obtain possession of the property of others—what anathemas can sufficiently punish such conduct? Surely it is perfectly obvious that the very last thing they aim at is the glory of Christ. For were they spontaneously to resign every portion of secular power which they possess, no peril to the glory of God, no peril to sound doctrine, no peril to the safety of the Church ensues; but they are borne blind and headlong by a lust for power, thinking that nothing can be safe unless they rule, as the prophet says, "with force and with cruelty" (Ezek. 34:4).

15. To jurisdiction is annexed the immunity claimed by the Romish clergy. They deem it unworthy of them to answer before a civil judge in personal causes; and consider both the liberty and dignity of the Church to consist in exemption from ordinary tribunals and laws. But the ancient bishops, who otherwise were most resolute in asserting the rights of the Church, did not think it any injury to themselves and their order to act as subjects. Pious emperors also, as often as there was occasion, summoned clergy to their tribunals, and met with no opposition. For Constantine, in a letter to the Nicomedians, thus speaks:—"Should any of the bishops unadvisedly excite tumult, his audacity shall be restrained by the minister of God, that is, by my executive" (Theodoret. Lib. 1 c. 20). Valentinian says, "Good bishops throw no obloquy on the power of the emperor, but sincerely keep the commandments of God, the great King, and obey our laws" (Theodoret. Lib. 4 c. 8). This was unquestionably the view then entertained by all. Ecclesiastical causes, indeed, were brought before the episcopal court; as when a clergyman had offended, but not against the laws, he was only charged by the Canons; and instead of being cited before the civil court, had the bishop for his judge in that particular case. In like manner, when a question of faith was agitated, or one which properly pertained to the Church, cognisance was left to the Church. In this sense the words of Ambrose are to be understood: "Your father, of august memory, not only replied verbally, but enacted by law, that, in a question of faith, the judge should be one who was neither unequal from office, nor incompetent from the nature of his jurisdiction" (Ambros. Ep. 32). Again, "If we attend to the Scriptures, or to ancient examples, who can deny that in a question of faith, a question of faith, I say, bishops are wont to judge Christian emperors, not emperors to judge bishops?" Again, "I would have come before your consistory, O emperor, would either the bishops or the people have allowed me to come: they say that a question of faith should be discussed in the Church before the people." He maintains, indeed, that a spiritual cause, that is, one pertaining to religion, is not to be brought before the civil court, where worldly disputes are agitated. His firmness in this respect is justly praised by all. And yet, though he has a good cause, he goes so far as to say, that if it comes to force and violence, he will yield. "I will not desert the post committed to me, but, if forced, I will not resist: prayers and tears are our weapons" (Ambros. Hom. de Basilic. Traden.). Let us observe the singular moderation of this holy man, his combination of prudence, magnanimity, and boldness. Justina, the mother of the emperor, unable to bring him over to the Arian party, sought to drive him from the government of the Church. And this would have been the result had he, when summoned, gone to the palace to plead his cause. He maintains, therefore, that the emperor is not fit to decide such a controversy. This both the necessity of the times, and the very nature of the thing, demanded. He thought it were better for him to die than consent to transmit such an example to posterity; and yet if violence is offered, he thinks not of resisting. For he says, it is not the part of a bishop to defend the faith and rights of the Church by arms. But in all other causes he declares himself ready to do whatever the emperor commands. "If he asks tribute, we deny it not: the lands of the Church pay tribute. If he asks lands, he has the power of evicting them; none of us interposes." Gregory speaks in the same manner. "I am not ignorant of the mind of my most serene lord: he is not wont to interfere in sacerdotal causes, lest he may in some degree burden himself with our sins." He does not exclude the emperor generally from judging priests, but says that there are certain causes which he ought to leave to the ecclesiastical tribunal.

16. And hence all that these holy men sought by this exception was, to prevent irreligious princes from impeding the Church in the discharge of her duty, by their tyrannical caprice and violence. They did not disapprove when princes interposed their authority in ecclesiastical affairs, provided this was done to preserve, not to disturb, the order of the Church, to establish, not to destroy discipline. For, seeing the Church has not, and ought not to wish to have, the power of compulsion (I speak of civil coer-

cion), it is the part of pious kings and princes to maintain religion by laws, edicts, and sentences. In this way, when the emperor Maurice had commanded certain bishops to receive their neighbouring colleagues, who had been expelled by the Barbarians, Gregory confirms the order, and exhorts them to obey. He himself, when admonished by the same emperor to return to a good understanding with John, Bishop of Constantinople, endeavours to show that he is not to be blamed; but so far from boasting of immunity from the secular forum, rather promises to comply as far as conscience would permit: he at the same time says, that Maurice had acted as became a religious prince, in giving these commands to priests.

CHAPTER 12

OF THE DISCIPLINE OF THE CHURCH, AND ITS PRINCIPAL USE IN CENSURES AND EXCOMMUNICATION.

This chapter consists of two parts:—I. The first part of ecclesiastical discipline, which respects the people, and is called common, consists of two parts, the former depending on the power of the keys, which is considered, sec. 1–14; the latter consisting in the appointment of times for fasting and prayer, sec. 14–21. II. The second part of ecclesiastical discipline relating to the clergy, sec. 22–28.

Sections:

1. Of the power of the keys, or the common discipline of the Church. Necessity and very great utility of this discipline.

2. Its various degrees. 1. Private admonition. 2. Rebukes before witnesses. 3. Excommunication.

3. Different degrees of delinquency. Modes of procedure in both kinds of chastisement.

4. Delicts to be distinguished from flagitious wickedness. The last to be more severely punished.

5. Ends of this discipline. 1. That the wicked may not, by being admitted to the Lord's Table, put insult on Christ. 2. That they may not corrupt others. 3. That they themselves may repent.

6. In what way sins public as well as secret are to be corrected. Trivial and grave offences.

7. No person, not even the sovereign, exempted from this discipline. By whom and in what way it ought to be exercised.

8. In what spirit discipline is to be exercised. In what respect some of the ancient Christians exercised it too rigorously. This done more from custom than in accordance with their own sentiments. This shown from Cyprian, Chrysostom, and Augustine.

9. Moderation to be used, not only by the whole Church, but by each individual member.

10. Our Saviour's words concerning binding and loosing wrested if otherwise understood. Difference between anathema and excommunication. Anathema rarely if ever to be used.

11. Excessive rigour to be avoided, as well by private individuals as by pastors.

12. In this respect the Donatists erred most grievously, as do also the Anabaptists in the present day. Portraiture by Augustine.

13. Moderation especially to be used when not a few individuals, but the great body of the people, have gone astray.

14. A second part of common discipline relating to fastings, prayer, and other holy exercises. These used by believers under both dispensations. To what purposes applied. Of Fasting.

15. Three ends of fasting. The first refers more especially to private fasting. Second and third ends.

16. Public fasting and prayer appointed by pastors on any great emergency.

17. Examples of this under the Law.

18. Fasting consists chiefly in three things—viz. time, the quality, and sparing use of food.

19. To prevent superstition, three things to be inculcated. 1. The heart to be rent, not the garments. 2. Fasting not to be regarded as a meritorious work or kind of divine worship. 3. Abstinence must not be immoderately extolled.

20. Owing to an excess of this kind the observance of Lent was established. This superstitious observance refuted by three arguments. It was indeed used by the ancients, but on different grounds.

21. Laws afterwards made to regulate the choice of food. Various abuses even in the time of Jerome. Practically there is no common ecclesiastical discipline in the Papacy.

22. The second part of discipline having reference to the clergy. What its nature, and how strict it formerly was. How miserably neglected in the present day. An example which may suit the Papists.

23. Of the celibacy of priests, in which Papists place the whole force of ecclesiastical discipline. This impious tyranny refuted from Scripture. An objection of the Papists disposed of.

24. An argument for the celibacy of priests answered.

25. Another argument answered.

26. Another argument answered.

27. An argument drawn from the commendation of virginity as superior to marriage. Answer.

28. The subject of celibacy concluded. This error not favoured by all ancient writers.

1. The discipline of the Church, the consideration of which has been deferred till now, must be briefly explained, that we may be able to pass to other matters. Now discipline depends in a very great measure on the power of the keys and on spiritual jurisdiction. That this may be more easily understood, let us divide the Church into two principal classes—viz. clergy and people. The term clergy I use in the common acceptation for those who perform a public ministry in the Church. We shall speak first of the common discipline to which all ought to be subject, and then proceed to the clergy, who have besides that common discipline one peculiar to themselves. But as some, from hatred of discipline, are averse to the very name, for their sake we observe,—If no society, nay, no house with even a moderate family, can be kept in a right state without discipline, much more necessary is it in the Church, whose state ought to be the best ordered possible. Hence as the saving doctrine of Christ is the life of the Church, so discipline is, as it were, its sinews; for to it, it is owing that the members of the body adhere together, each in its own place. Wherefore, all who either wish that discipline were abolished, or who impede the restoration of it, whether they do this of design or through thoughtlessness, certainly aim at the complete devastation of the Church. For what will be the result if every one is allowed to do as he pleases? But this must happen if to the preaching of the gospel are not added private admonition, correction, and similar methods of maintaining doctrine, and not allowing it to become lethargic. Discipline, therefore, is a kind of curb to restrain and tame those who war against the doctrine of Christ, or it is a kind of stimulus by which the indifferent are aroused; sometimes, also, it is a kind of fatherly rod, by which those who have made some more grievous lapse are chastised in mercy with the meekness of the spirit of Christ. Since, then, we already see some beginnings of a fearful devastation in the Church from the total want of care and method in managing the people, necessity itself cries aloud that there is need of a remedy. Now the only remedy is this which Christ enjoins, and the pious have always had in use.

2. The first foundation of discipline is to provide for private admonition; that is, if any one does not do his duty spontaneously, or behaves insolently, or lives not quite honestly, or commits something worthy of blame, he must allow himself to be admonished; and every one must study to admonish his brother when the case requires. Here especially is there occasion for the vigilance of pastors and presbyters, whose duty is not only to preach to the people, but to exhort and admonish from house to house, whenever their hearers have not profited sufficiently by general teaching; as Paul shows, when he relates that he taught "publicly, and from house to house," and testifies that he is "pure from the blood of all men," because he had not shunned to declare "all the counsel of God" (Acts 20:20, 26, 27) Then does doctrine obtain force and authority, not only when the minister publicly expounds to all what they owe to Christ, but has the right and means of exacting this from those whom he may observe to be sluggish or disobedient to his doctrine. Should any one either perversely reject such admonitions, or by persisting in his faults, show that he contemns them, the injunction of Christ is, that after he has been a second time admonished before witnesses, he is to be summoned to the bar of the Church, which is the consistory of elders, and there admonished more sharply, as by public authority, that if he reverence the Church he may submit and obey (Mt. 18:15, 17). If even in this way he is not subdued, but persists in his iniquity, he is then, as a despiser of the Church, to be debarred from the society of believers.

3. Put as our Saviour is not there speaking of secret faults merely, we must attend to the distinction that some sins are private, others public or openly manifest. Of the former, Christ says to every private individual, "go and tell him his fault between thee and him alone" (Mt. 18:15). Of open sins Paul says to Timothy, "Those that sin rebuke before all, that others also may fear" (1 Tim. 5:20). Our Saviour had previously used the words, "If thy brother shall trespass against thee" This clause, unless you would be captious, you cannot understand otherwise than, If this happens *in a manner known to yourself,* others not being privy to it. The injunction which Paul gave to Timothy to rebuke those openly who sin openly, he himself followed with Peter (Gal. 2:14). For when Peter sinned so as to give public offence, he did not admonish him apart, but brought him forward in face of the Church. The legitimate course, therefore, will be to proceed in correcting secret faults by the steps mentioned by Christ, and in open sins, accompanied with public scandal, to proceed at once to solemn correction by the Church.

4. Another distinction to be attended to is, that some sins are mere delinquencies, others crimes and flagrant iniquities. In correcting the latter, it is necessary to employ not only admonition or rebuke, but a sharper remedy, as Paul shows when he not only verbally rebukes the incestuous Corinthian, but punishes him with excommunication, as soon as he was informed of his crime (1 Cor. 5:4). Now then we begin better to perceive how the spiritual jurisdiction of the Church, which animadverts on sins according to the word of the Lord, is at once the best help to sound doctrine, the best foundation of order, and the best bond of unity. Therefore, when the Church banishes from its fellowship open adulterers, fornicators, thieves, robbers, the seditious, the perjured, false witnesses, and others of that description; likewise the contumacious, who, when duly admonished for lighter faults, hold God and his tribunal in derision, instead of arrogating to itself anything that is unreasonable, it exercises a jurisdiction which it has received from the Lord. Moreover, lest any one should despise the judgment of the Church, or count it a small matter to be condemned by the suffrages of the faithful, the Lord has declared that it is nothing else than the promulgation of his own sentence, and that that which they do on earth is ratified in heaven. For they act by the word of the Lord in condemning the perverse, and by the word of the Lord in taking the penitent back into favour (John 20:23). Those, I say, who trust that churches can long stand without this bond of discipline are mistaken, unless, indeed, we can with impunity dispense with a help which the Lord foresaw would be necessary. And, indeed, the greatness of the necessity will be better perceived by its manifold uses.

5. There are three ends to which the Church has respect in thus correcting and excommunicating. The first is, that God may not be insulted by the name of Christians being given to those who lead shameful and flagitious lives, as if his holy Church were a combination of the wicked and abandoned. For seeing that the Church is the body of Christ, she cannot be defiled by such fetid and putrid members, without bringing some disgrace on her Head. Therefore that there may be nothing in the Church to bring disgrace on his sacred name, those whose turpitude might throw infamy on the name must be expelled from his family. And here, also, regard must be had to the Lord's Supper, which might he profaned by a promiscuous admission. For it is most true, that he who is intrusted with the dispensation of it, if he knowingly and willingly admits any unworthy person whom he ought and is able to repel, is as guilty of sacrilege as if he had cast the Lord's body to dogs. Wherefore, Chrysostom bitterly inveighs against priests, who, from fear of the great, dare not keep any one back. "Blood (says he, Hom. 83, in Mt.) will be required at your hands. If you fear man, he will mock you, but if you fear God, you will be respected also by men. Let us not tremble at fasces, purple, or diadems; our power here is greater. Assuredly I will sooner give up my body to death, and allow my blood to be shed, than be a partaker of that pollution." Therefore, lest this most sacred mystery should be exposed to ignominy, great selection is required in dispensing it, and this cannot be except by the jurisdiction of the Church. A second end of discipline is, that the good may not, as usually happens, be corrupted by constant communication with the wicked. For such is our proneness to go astray, that nothing is easier than to seduce us from the right course by bad example. To this use of discipline the apostle referred when he commanded the Corinthians to discard the incestuous man from their society. "A little leaven leaveneth the whole lump" (1 Cor. 5:6) And so much danger did he foresee here, that he prohibited them from keeping company with such persons. "If any man that is called a brother be a fornicator, or covetous, or an idolater, or a railer, or a drunkard, or an extortioner; with such an one, no not to eat" (1 Cor. 5:11). A third end of discipline is, that the sinner may be ashamed, and begin to repent of his turpitude. Hence it is for their interest also that their iniquity should be chastised, that whereas they would have become more obstinate by indulgence, they may be aroused by the rod. This the apostle intimates when he thus writes —"If any man obey not our word by this epistle, note that man, and have no company with him, that he may be ashamed" (2 Thess. 3:14). Again, when he says that he had delivered the Corinthian to Satan, "that the spirit may be saved in the day of the Lord Jesus" (1 Cor. 5:5); that is, as I interpret it, he gave him over to temporal condemnation, that he might be made safe for eternity. And he says that he gave him over to Satan because the devil is without the Church, as Christ is in the Church. Some interpret this of a certain infliction on the flesh, but this interpretation seems to me most improbable. (August. de Verb. Apostol. Serm. 68)

6. These being the ends proposed, it remains to see in what way the Church is to execute this part of discipline, which consists in jurisdiction. And, first, let us remember the division above laid down, that some sins are public, others private or secret. Public are those which are done not before one or two witnesses, but openly, and to the

offence of the whole Church. By secret, I mean not such as are altogether concealed from men, such as those of hypocrites (for these fall not under the judgment of the Church), but those of an intermediate description, which are not without witnesses, and yet are not public. The former class requires not the different steps which Christ enumerates; but whenever anything of the kind occurs, the Church ought to do her duty by summoning the offender, and correcting him according to his fault. In the second class, the matter comes not before the Church, unless there is contumacy, according to the rule of Christ. In taking cognisance of offences, it is necessary to attend to the distinction between delinquencies and flagrant iniquities. In lighter offences there is not so much occasion for severity, but verbal chastisement is sufficient, and that gentle and fatherly, so as not to exasperate or confound the offender, but to bring him back to himself, so that he may rather rejoice than be grieved at the correction. Flagrant iniquities require a sharper remedy. It is not sufficient verbally to rebuke him who, by some open act of evil example, has grievously offended the Church; but he ought for a time to be denied the communion of the Supper, until he gives proof of repentance. Paul does not merely administer a verbal rebuke to the Corinthian, but discards him from the Church, and reprimands the Corinthians for having borne with him so long (1 Cor. 5:5). This was the method observed by the ancient and purer Church, when legitimate government was in vigour. When any one was guilty of some flagrant iniquity, and thereby caused scandal, he was first ordered to abstain from participation in the sacred Supper, and thereafter to humble himself before God, and testify his penitence before the Church. There were, moreover, solemn rites, which, as indications of repentance, were wont to be prescribed to those who had lapsed. When the penitent had thus made satisfaction to the Church, he was received into favour by the laying on of hands. This admission often receives the name of *peace* from Cyprian, who briefly describes the form. "They act as penitents for a certain time, next they come to confession, and receive the right of communion by the laying on of hands of the bishop and clergy." Although the bishop with the clergy thus superintended the restoration of the penitent, the consent of the people was at the same time required, as he elsewhere explains.

7. So far was any one from being exempted from this discipline, that even princes submitted to it in common with their subjects; and justly, since it is the discipline of Christ, to whom all sceptres and diadems should be subject. Thus Theodosius, when excommunicated by Ambrose, because of the slaughter perpetrated at Thessalonica, laid aside all the royal insignia with which he was surrounded, and publicly in the Church bewailed the sin into which he had been betrayed by the fraud of others, with groans and tears imploring pardon. Great kings should not think it a disgrace to them to prostrate themselves suppliantly before Christ, the King of kings; nor ought they to be displeased at being judged by the Church. For seeing they seldom hear anything in their courts but mere flattery, the more necessary is it that the Lord should correct them by the mouth of his priests. Nay, they ought rather to wish the priests not to spare them, in order that the Lord may spare. I here say nothing as to those by whom the jurisdiction ought to be exercised, because it has been said elsewhere (Chap. 11 sec. 5, 6). I only add, that the legitimate course to be taken in excommunication, as shown by Paul, is not for the elders alone to act apart from others, but with the knowledge and approbation of the Church, so that the body of the people, without regulating the procedure, may, as witnesses and guardians, observe it, and prevent the few from doing anything capriciously. Throughout the whole procedure, in addition to invocation of the name of God, there should be a gravity bespeaking the presence of Christ, and leaving no room to doubt that he is presiding over his own tribunal.

8. It ought not, however, to be omitted, that the Church, in exercising severity, ought to accompany it with the spirit of meekness. For, as Paul enjoins, we must always take care that he on whom discipline is exercised be not "swallowed up with overmuch sorrow" (2 Cor. 2:7): for in this way, instead of cure there would be destruction. The rule of moderation will be best obtained from the end contemplated. For the object of excommunication being to bring the sinner to repentance and remove bad examples, in order that the name of Christ may not be evil spoken of, nor others tempted to the same evil courses: if we consider this, we shall easily understand how far severity should be carried, and at what point it ought to cease. Therefore, when the sinner gives the Church evidence of his repentance, and by this evidence does what in him lies to obliterate the offence, he ought not on any account to be urged farther. If he is urged, the rigour now exceeds due measure. In this respect it is impossible to excuse the excessive austerity of the ancients, which was altogether at variance with the injunction of our Lord, and strangely perilous. For when they enjoined a formal repentance, and excluded from communion for three, or four, or

seven years, or for life, what could the result be, but either great hypocrisy or very great despair? In like manner, when any one who had again lapsed was not admitted to a second repentance, but ejected from the Church, to the end of his life (August. Ep. 54), this was neither useful nor agreeable to reason. Whosoever, therefore, looks at the matter with sound judgment, will here regret a want of prudence. Here, however, I rather disapprove of the public custom, than blame those who complied with it. Some of them certainly disapproved of it, but submitted to what they were unable to correct. Cyprian, indeed, declares that it was not with his own will he was thus rigorous. "Our patience, facility, and humanity (he says, Lib. 1 Ep. 3), are ready to all who come. I wish all to be brought back into the Church: I wish all our fellow-soldiers to be contained within the camp of Christ and the mansions of God the Father. I forgive all; I disguise much; from an earnest desire of collecting the brotherhood, I do not minutely scrutinise all the faults which have been committed against God. I myself often err, by forgiving offences more than I ought. Those returning in repentance, and those confessing their sins with simple and humble satisfaction, I embrace with prompt and full delight." Chrysostom, who is somewhat more severe, still speaks thus: "If God is so kind, why should his priest wish to appear austere?" We know, moreover, how indulgently Augustine treated the Donatists; not hesitating to admit any who returned from schism to their bishopric, as soon as they declared their repentance. But, as a contrary method had prevailed, they were compelled to follow it, and give up their own judgment.

9. But as the whole body of the Church are required to act thus mildly, and not to carry their rigour against those who have lapsed to an extreme, but rather to act charitably towards them, according to the precept of Paul, so every private individual ought proportionately to accommodate himself to this clemency and humanity. Such as have, therefore, been expelled from the Church, it belongs not to us to expunge from the number of the elect, or to despair of, as if they were already lost. We may lawfully judge them aliens from the Church, and so aliens from Christ, but only during the time of their excommunication. If then, also, they give greater evidence of petulance than of humility, still let us commit them to the judgment of the Lord, hoping better of them in future than we see at present, and not ceasing to pray to God for them. And (to sum up in one word) let us not consign to destruction their person, which is in the hand, and subject to the decision, of the Lord alone; but let us merely estimate the character of each man's acts according to the law of the Lord. In following this rule, we abide by the divine judgment rather than give any judgment of our own. Let us not arrogate to ourselves greater liberty in judging, if we would not limit the power of God, and give the law to his mercy. Whenever it seems good to Him, the worst are changed into the best; aliens are ingrafted, and strangers are adopted into the Church. This the Lord does, that he may disappoint the thoughts of men, and confound their rashness; a rashness which, if not curbed, would usurp a power of judging to which it has no title.

10. For when our Saviour promises that what his servants bound on earth should be bound in heaven (Mt. 18:18), he confines the power of binding to the censure of the Church, which does not consign those who are excommunicated to perpetual ruin and damnation, but assures them, when they hear their life and manners condemned, that perpetual damnation will follow if they do not repent. Excommunication differs from anathema in this, that the latter completely excluding pardon, dooms and devotes the individual to eternal destruction, whereas the former rather rebukes and animadverts upon his manners; and although it also punishes, it is to bring him to salvation, by forewarning him of his future doom. If it succeeds, reconciliation and restoration to communion are ready to be given. Moreover, anathema is rarely if ever to be used. Hence, though ecclesiastical discipline does not allow us to be on familiar and intimate terms with excommunicated persons, still we ought to strive by all possible means to bring them to a better mind, and recover them to the fellowship and unity of the Church: as the apostle also says, "Yet count him not as an enemy, but admonish him as a brother" (2 Thess. 3:15). If this humanity be not observed in private as well as public, the danger is, that our discipline shall degenerate into destruction.

11. Another special requisite to moderation of discipline is, as Augustine discourses against the Donatists, that private individuals must not, when they see vices less carefully corrected by the Council of Elders, immediately separate themselves from the Church; nor must pastors themselves, when unable to reform all things which need correction to the extent which they could wish, cast up their ministry, or by unwonted severity throw the whole Church into confusion. What Augustine says is perfectly true: "Whoever corrects what he can, by rebuking it, or without violating the bond of peace, excludes what he cannot correct, or unjustly condemns while he patiently

tolerates what he is unable to exclude without violating the bond of peace, is free and exempted from the curse" (August. contra Parmen. Lib. 2 c. 4). He elsewhere gives the reason. "Every pious reason and mode of ecclesiastical discipline ought always to have regard to the unity of the Spirit in the bond of peace. This the apostle commands us to keep by bearing mutually with each other. If it is not kept, the medicine of discipline begins to be not only superfluous, but even pernicious, and therefore ceases to be medicine" (Ibid. Lib. 3 c. 1). "He who diligently considers these things, neither in the preservation of unity neglects strictness of discipline, nor by intemperate correction bursts the bond of society" (Ibid. cap. 2). He confesses, indeed, that pastors ought not only to exert themselves in removing every defect from the Church, but that every individual ought to his utmost to do so; nor does he disguise the fact, that he who neglects to admonish, accuse, and correct the bad, although he neither favours them, nor sins with them, is guilty before the Lord; and if he conducts himself so that though he can exclude them from partaking of the Supper, he does it not, then the sin is no longer that of other men, but his own. Only he would have that prudence used which our Lord also requires, "lest while ye gather up the tares, ye root up also the wheat with them" (Mt. 13:29). Hence he infers from Cyprian, "Let a man then mercifully correct what he can; what he cannot correct, let him bear patiently, and in love bewail and lament."

12. This he says on account of the moroseness of the Donatists, who, when they saw faults in the Church which the bishops indeed rebuked verbally, but did not punish with excommunication (because they did not think that anything would be gained in this way), bitterly inveighed against the bishops as traitors to discipline, and by an impious schism separated themselves from the flock of Christ. Similar, in the present day, is the conduct of the Anabaptists, who, acknowledging no assembly of Christ unless conspicuous in all respects for angelic perfection, under pretence of zeal overthrow everything which tends to edification. "Such (says Augustin. contra Parmen. Lib. 3 c. 4), not from hatred of other men's iniquity, but zeal for their own disputes, ensnaring the weak by the credit of their name, attempt to draw them entirely away, or at least to separate them; swollen with pride, raving with petulance, insidious in calumny, turbulent in sedition. That it may not be seen how void they are of the light of truth, they cover themselves with the shadow of a stern severity: the correction of a brother's fault, which in Scripture is enjoined to be done with moderation, without impairing the sincerity of love or breaking the bond of peace, they pervert to sacrilegious schism and purposes of excision. Thus Satan transforms himself into an angel of light (2 Cor. 11:14) when, under pretext of a just severity, he persuades to savage cruelty, desiring nothing more than to violate and burst the bond of unity and peace; because, when it is maintained, all his power of mischief is feeble, his wily traps are broken, and his schemes of subversion vanish."

13. One thing Augustine specially commends—viz. that if the contagion of sin has seized the multitude, mercy must accompany living discipline. "For counsels of separation are vain, sacrilegious, and pernicious, because impious and proud, and do more to disturb the weak good than to correct the wicked proud" (August. Ep. 64). This which he enjoins on others he himself faithfully practiced. For, writing to Aurelius, Bishop of Carthage, he complains that drunkenness, which is so severely condemned in Scripture, prevails in Africa with impunity, and advises a council of bishops to be called for the purpose of providing a remedy. He immediately adds, "In my opinion, such things are not removed by rough, harsh, and imperious measures, but more by teaching than commanding, more by admonishing than threatening. For thus ought we to act with a multitude of offenders. Severity is to be exercised against the sins of a few" (August. Ep. 64). He does not mean, however, that the bishops were to wink or be silent because they are unable to punish public offences severely, as he himself afterwards explains. But he wishes to temper the mode of correction, so as to give soundness to the body rather than cause destruction. And, accordingly, he thus concludes: "Wherefore, we must on no account neglect the injunction of the apostle, to separate from the wicked, when it can be done without the risk of violating peace, because he did not wish it to be done otherwise (1 Cor. 5:13); we must also endeavour, by bearing with each other, to keep the unity of the Spirit in the bond of peace" (Eph. 4:2).

14. The remaining part of discipline, which is not, strictly speaking, included in the power of the keys, is when pastors, according to the necessity of the times, exhort the people either to fasting and solemn prayer, or to other exercises of humiliation, repentance, and faith, the time, mode, and form of these not being prescribed by the Word of God, but left to the judgment of the Church. As the observance of this part of discipline is useful, so it was always used in the Church, even from the days of the apostles. Indeed, the apostles themselves were not its first authors, but borrowed the example from the

Law and Prophets. For we there see, that as often as any weighty matter occurred the people were assembled, and supplication and fasting appointed. In this, therefore, the apostles followed a course which was not new to the people of God, and which they foresaw would be useful. A similar account is to be given of the other exercises by which the people may either be aroused to duty, or kept in duty and obedience. We everywhere meet with examples in Sacred History, and it is unnecessary to collect them. In general, we must hold that whenever any religious controversy arises, which either a council or ecclesiastical tribunal behoves to decide; whenever a minister is to be chosen; whenever, in short, any matter of difficulty and great importance is under consideration: on the other hand, when manifestations of the divine anger appear, as pestilence, war, and famine, the sacred and salutary custom of all ages has been for pastors to exhort the people to public fasting and extraordinary prayer. Should any one refuse to admit the passages which are adduced from the Old Testament, as being less applicable to the Christian Church, it is clear that the apostles also acted thus; although, in regard to prayer, I scarcely think any one will be found to stir the question. Let us, therefore, make some observations on fasting, since very many, not understanding what utility there can be in it, judge it not to be very necessary, while others reject it altogether as superfluous. Where its use is not well known it is easy to fall into superstition.

15. A holy and lawful fast has three ends in view. We use it either to mortify and subdue the flesh, that it may not wanton, or to prepare the better for prayer and holy meditation; or to give evidence of humbling ourselves before God, when we would confess our guilt before him. The first end is not very often regarded in public fasting, because all have not the same bodily constitution, nor the same state of health, and hence it is more applicable to private fasting. The second end is common to both, for this preparation for prayer is requisite for the whole Church, as well as for each individual member. The same thing may be said of the third. For it sometimes happens that God smites a nation with war or pestilence, or some kind of calamity. In this common chastisement it behoves the whole people to plead guilty, and confess their guilt. Should the hand of the Lord strike any one in private, then the same thing is to be done by himself alone, or by his family. The thing, indeed, is properly a feeling of the mind. But when the mind is effected as it ought, it cannot but give vent to itself in external manifestation, especially when it tends to the common edification, that all, by openly confessing their sin, may render praise to the divine justice, and by their example mutually encourage each other.

16. Hence fasting, as it is a sign of humiliation, has a more frequent use in public than among private individuals, although as we have said, it is common to both. In regard, then, to the discipline of which we now treat, whenever supplication is to be made to God on any important occasion, it is befitting to appoint a period for fasting and prayer. Thus when the Christians of Antioch laid hands on Barnabas and Paul, that they might the better recommend their ministry, which was of so great importance, they joined fasting and prayer (Acts 13:3). Thus these two apostles afterwards, when they appointed ministers to churches, were wont to use prayer and fasting (Acts 14:23). In general, the only object which they had in fasting was to render themselves more alert and disencumbered for prayer. We certainly experience that after a full meal the mind does not so rise toward God as to be borne along by an earnest and fervent longing for prayer, and perseverance in prayer. In this sense is to be understood the saying of Luke concerning Anna, that she "served God with fastings and prayers, night and day" (Luke 2:37). For he does not place the worship of God in fasting, but intimates that in this way the holy woman trained herself to assiduity in prayer. Such was the fast of Nehemiah, when with more intense zeal he prayed to God for the deliverance of his people (Neh. 1:4). For this reason Paul says, that married believers do well to abstain for a season (1 Cor. 7:5), that they may have greater freedom for prayer and fasting, when by joining prayer to fasting, by way of help, he reminds us it is of no importance in itself, save in so far as it refers to this end. Again, when in the same place he enjoins spouses to render due benevolence to each other, it is clear that he is not referring to daily prayer, but prayers which require more than ordinary attention.

17. On the other hand, when pestilence begins to stalk abroad, or famine or war, or when any other disaster seems to impend over a province and people (Esther 4:16), then also it is the duty of pastors to exhort the Church to fasting, that she may suppliantly deprecate the Lord's anger. For when he makes danger appear, he declares that he is prepared and in a manner armed for vengeance. In like manner, therefore, as persons accused were anciently wont, in order to excite the commiseration of the judge, to humble themselves suppliantly with long beard, dishevelled hair, and coarse garments, so when we are charged before the divine tribunal, to deprecate

his severity in humble raiment is equally for his glory and the public edification, and useful and salutary to ourselves. And that this was common among the Israelites we may infer from the words of Joel. For when he says, "Blow the trumpet in Zion, sanctify a fast, call a solemn assembly," &c. (Joel 2:15), he speaks as of things received by common custom. A little before he had said that the people were to be tried for their wickedness, and that the day of judgment was at hand, and he had summoned them as criminals to plead their cause: then he exclaims that they should hasten to sackcloth and ashes, to weeping and fasting; that is, humble themselves before God with external manifestations. The sackcloth and ashes, indeed, were perhaps more suitable for those times, but the assembly, and weeping and fasting, and the like, undoubtedly belong, in an equal degree, to our age, whenever the condition of our affairs so requires. For seeing it is a holy exercise both for men to humble themselves, and confess their humility, why should we in similar necessity use this less than did those of old? We read not only that the Israelitish Church, formed and constituted by the word of God, fasted in token of sadness, but the Ninevites also, whose only teaching had been the preaching of Jonah. Why, therefore, should not we do the same? But it is an external ceremony, which, like other ceremonies, terminated in Christ. Nay, in the present day it is an admirable help to believers, as it always was, and a useful admonition to arouse them, lest by too great security and sloth they provoke the Lord more and more when they are chastened by his rod. Accordingly, when our Saviour excuses his apostles for not fasting, he does not say that fasting was abrogated, but reserves it for calamitous times, and conjoins it with mourning. "The days will come when the bridegroom shall be taken from them" (Mt. 9:35; Luke 5:34).

18. But that there maybe no error in the name, let us define what fasting is; for we do not understand by it simply a restrained and sparing use of food, but something else. The life of the pious should be tempered with frugality and sobriety, so as to exhibit, as much as may be, a kind of fasting during the whole course of life. But there is another temporary fast, when we retrench somewhat from our accustomed mode of living, either for one day or a certain period, and prescribe to ourselves a stricter and severer restraint in the use of that ordinary food. This consists in three things—viz. the time, the quality of food, and the sparing use of it. By the time I mean, that while fasting we are to perform those actions for the sake of which the fast is instituted. For example, when a man fasts because of solemn prayer, he should engage in it without having taken food. The quality consists in putting all luxury aside, and, being contented with common and meaner food, so as not to excite our palate by dainties. In regard to quantity, we must eat more lightly and sparingly, only for necessity and not for pleasure.

19. But the first thing always to be avoided is, the encroachment of superstition, as formerly happened, to the great injury of the Church. It would have been much better to have had no fasting at all, than have it carefully observed, but at the same time corrupted by false and pernicious opinions, into which the world is ever and anon falling, unless pastors obviate them by the greatest fidelity and prudence. The first thing is constantly to urge the injunction of Joel, "Rend your heart, and not your garments" (Joel 2:13); that is, to remind the people that fasting in itself is not of great value in the sight of God, unless accompanied with internal affection of the heart, true dissatisfaction with sin and with one's self, true humiliation, and true grief, from the fear of God; nay, that fasting is useful for no other reason than because it is added to these as an inferior help. There is nothing which God more abominates than when men endeavour to cloak themselves by substituting signs and external appearance for integrity of heart. Accordingly, Isaiah inveighs most bitterly against the hypocrisy of the Jews, in thinking that they had satisfied God when they had merely fasted, whatever might be the impiety and impure thoughts which they cherished in their hearts. "Is it such a fast that I have chosen?" (Isa. 58:5) See also what follows. The fast of hypocrites is, therefore, not only useless and superfluous fatigue, but the greatest abomination. Another evil akin to this, and greatly to be avoided, is, to regard fasting as a meritorious work and species of divine worship. For seeing it is a thing which is in itself indifferent, and has no importance except on account of those ends to which it ought to have respect, it is a most pernicious superstition to confound it with the works enjoined by God, and which are necessary in themselves without reference to anything else. Such was anciently the dream of the Manichees, in refuting whom Augustine clearly shows, that fasting is to be estimated entirely by those ends which I have mentioned, and cannot be approved by God, unless in so far as it refers to them. Another error, not indeed so impious, but perilous, is to exact it with greater strictness and severity as one of the principal duties, and extol it with such extravagant encomiums as to make men imagine that they have done something admirable when they have fasted. In this respect I dare not entirely excuse ancient writers from hav-

ing sown some seeds of superstition, and given occasion to the tyranny which afterwards arose. We sometimes meet with sound and prudent sentiments on fasting, but we also ever and anon meet with extravagant praises, lauding it as one of the cardinal virtues.

20. Then the superstitious observance of Lent had everywhere prevailed: for both the vulgar imagined that they thereby perform some excellent service to God, and pastors commended it as a holy imitation of Christ; though it is plain that Christ did not fast to set an example to others, but, by thus commencing the preaching of the gospel, meant to prove that his doctrine was not of men, but had come from heaven. And it is strange how men of acute judgment could fall into this gross delusion, which so many clear reasons refute: for Christ did not fast repeatedly (which he must have done had he meant to lay down a law for an anniversary fast), but once only, when preparing for the promulgation of the gospel. Nor does he fast after the manner of men, as he would have done had he meant to invite men to imitation; he rather gives an example, by which he may raise all to admire rather than study to imitate him. In short, the nature of his fast is not different from that which Moses observed when he received the law at the hand of the Lord (Exod. 24:18; 34:28). For, seeing that that miracle was performed in Moses to establish the law, it behoved not to be omitted in Christ, lest the gospel should seem inferior to the law. But from that day, it never occurred to any one, under pretence of imitating Moses, to set up a similar form of fast among the Israelites. Nor did any of the holy prophets and fathers follow it, though they had inclination and zeal enough for all pious exercises; for though it is said of Elijah that he passed forty days without meat and drink (1 Kings 19:8), this was merely in order that the people might recognise that he was raised up to maintain the law, from which almost the whole of Israel had revolted. It was therefore merely false zeal, replete with superstition, which set up a fast under the title and pretext of imitating Christ; although there was then a strange diversity in the mode of the fast, as is related by Cassiodorus in the ninth book of the History of Socrates: "The Romans," says he, "had only three weeks, but their fast was continuous, except on the Lord's day and the Sabbath. The Greeks and Illyrians had, some six, others seven, but the fast was at intervals. Nor did they differ less in the kind of food: some used only bread and water, others added vegetables; others had no objection to fish and fowls; others made no difference in their food." Augustine also makes mention of this difference in his latter epistle to Januarius.

21. Worse times followed. To the absurd zeal of the vulgar were added rudeness and ignorance in the bishops, lust of power, and tyrannical rigour. Impious laws were passed, binding the conscience in deadly chains. The eating of flesh was forbidden, as if a man were contaminated by it. Sacrilegious opinions were added, one after another, until all became an abyss of error. And that no kind of depravity might be omitted, they began, under a most absurd pretence of abstinence, to make a mock of God; for in the most exquisite delicacies they seek the praise of fasting: no dainties now suffice; never was there greater abundance or variety or savouriness of food. In this splendid display they think that they serve God. I do not mention that at no time do those who would be thought the holiest of them wallow more foully. In short, the highest worship of God is to abstain from flesh, and, with this reservation, to indulge in delicacies of every kind. On the other hand, it is the greatest impiety, impiety scarcely to be expiated by death, for any one to taste the smallest portion of bacon or rancid flesh with his bread. Jerome, writing to Nepotian, relates, that even in his day there were some who mocked God with such follies: those who would not even put oil in their food caused the greatest delicacies to be procured from every quarter; nay, that they might do violence to nature, abstained from drinking water, and caused sweet and costly potions to be made for them, which they drank, not out of a cup, but a shell. What was then the fault of a few is now common among all the rich: they do not fast for any other purpose than to feast more richly and luxuriously. But I am unwilling to waste many words on a subject as to which there can be no doubt. All I say is, that, as well in fasts as in all other parts of discipline, the Papists are so far from having anything right, anything sincere, anything duly framed and ordered, that they have no occasion to plume themselves as if anything was left them that is worthy of praise.

22. We come now to the second part of discipline, which relates specially to the clergy. It is contained in the canons, which the ancient bishops framed for themselves and their order: for instance, let no clergyman spend his time in hunting, in gaming, or in feasting; let none engage in usury or in trade; let none be present at lascivious dances, and the like. Penalties also were added to give a sanction to the authority of the canons, that none might violate them with impunity. With this view, each bishop was intrusted with the superintendence of his own clergy, that he might govern them according to the canons, and keep them to their duty. For this purpose, certain annual visitations and synods were

appointed, that if any one was negligent in his office he might be admonished; if any one sinned, he might be punished according to his fault. The bishops also had their provincial synods once, anciently twice, a-year, by which they were tried, if they had done anything contrary to their duty. For if any bishop had been too harsh or violent with his clergy, there was an appeal to the synod, though only one individual complained. The severest punishment was deposition from office, and exclusion, for a time, from communion. But as this was the uniform arrangement, no synod rose without fixing the time and place of the next meeting. To call a universal council belonged to the emperor alone, as all the ancient summonings testify. As long as this strictness was in force, the clergy demanded no more in word from the people than they performed in act and by example; nay, they were more strict against themselves than the vulgar; and, indeed, it is becoming that the people should be ruled by a kindlier, and, if I may so speak, laxer discipline; that the clergy should be stricter in their censures, and less indulgent to themselves than to others. How this whole procedure became obsolete it is needless to relate, since, in the present day, nothing can be imagined more lawless and dissolute than this order, whose licentiousness is so extreme that the whole world is crying out. I admit that, in order not to seem to have lost all sight of antiquity, they, by certain shadows, deceive the eyes of the simple; but these no more resemble ancient customs than the mimicry of an ape resembles what men do by reason and counsel. There is a memorable passage in Xenophon, in which he mentions, that when the Persians had shamefully degenerated from the customs of their ancestors, and had fallen away from an austere mode of life to luxury and effeminacy, they still, to hide the disgrace, were sedulously observant of ancient rites (Cyrop. Lib. 8). For while, in the time of Cyrus, sobriety and temperance so flourished that no Persian required to wipe his nose, and it was even deemed disgraceful to do so, it remained with their posterity, as a point of religion, not to remove the mucus from the nostril, though they were allowed to nourish within, even to putridity, those fetid humours which they had contracted by gluttony. In like manner, according to the ancient custom, it was unlawful to use cups at table; but it was quite tolerable to swallow wine so as to make it necessary to be carried off drunk. It was enjoined to use only one meal a-day: this these good successors did not abrogate, but they continued their surfeit from mid-day to midnight. To finish the day's march, fasting, as the law enjoined it, was the uniform custom; but in order to avoid lassitude, the allowed and usual custom was to limit the march to two hours. As often as the degenerate Papists obtrude their rules that they may show their resemblance to the holy fathers, this example will serve to expose their ridiculous imitation. Indeed, no painter could paint them more to the life.

23. In one thing they are more than rigid and inexorable—in not permitting priests to marry. It is of no consequence to mention with what impunity whoredom prevails among them, and how, trusting to their vile celibacy, they have become callous to all kinds of iniquity. The prohibition, however, clearly shows how pestiferous all traditions are, since this one has not only deprived the Church of fit and honest pastors, but has introduced a fearful sink of iniquity, and plunged many souls into the gulf of despair. Certainly, when marriage was interdicted to priests, it was done with impious tyranny, not only contrary to the word of God, but contrary to all justice. First, men had no title whatever to forbid what God had left free; secondly, it is too clear to make it necessary to give any lengthened proof that God has expressly provided in his Word that this liberty shall not be infringed. I omit Paul's injunction, in numerous passages, that a bishop be the husband of one wife; but what could be stronger than his declaration, that in the latter days there would be impious men "forbidding to marry"? (1 Tim. 4:3) Such persons he calls not only impostors, but devils. We have therefore a prophecy, a sacred oracle of the Holy Spirit, intended to warn the Church from the outset against perils, and declaring that the prohibition of marriage is a doctrine of devils. They think that they get finely off when they wrest this passage, and apply it to Montanus, the Tatians, the Encratites, and other ancient heretics. These (they say) alone condemned marriage; we by no means condemn it, but only deny it to the ecclesiastical order, in whom we think it not befitting. As if, even granting that this prophecy was primarily fulfilled in those heretics, it is not applicable also to themselves; or, as if one could listen to the childish quibble that they do not forbid marriage, because they do not forbid it to all. This is just as if a tyrant were to contend that a law is not unjust because its injustice presses only on a part of the state.

24. They object that there ought to be some distinguishing mark between the clergy and the people; as if the Lord had not provided the ornaments in which priests ought to excel. Thus they charge the apostle with having disturbed the ecclesiastical order, and destroyed its ornament, when, in drawing the picture of a perfect bishop,

he presumed to set down marriage among the other endowments which he required of them. I am aware of the mode in which they expound this—viz. that no one was to be appointed a bishop who had a second wife. This interpretation, I admit, is not new; but its unsoundness is plain from the immediate context, which prescribes the kind of wives whom bishops and deacons ought to have. Paul enumerates marriage among the qualities of a bishop; those men declare that, in the ecclesiastical order, marriage is an intolerable vice; and, indeed, not content with this general vituperation, they term it, in their canons, the uncleanness and pollution of the flesh (Siric. ad Episc. Hispaniar.). Let every one consider with himself from what forge these things have come. Christ deigns so to honour marriage as to make it an image of his sacred union with the Church. What greater eulogy could be pronounced on the dignity of marriage? How, then, dare they have the effrontery to give the name of unclean and polluted to that which furnishes a bright representation of the spiritual grace of Christ?

25. Though their prohibition is thus clearly repugnant to the word of God, they, however, find something in the Scriptures to defend it. The Levitical priests, as often as their ministerial course returned, behoved to keep apart from their wives, that they might be pure and immaculate in handling sacred things; and it were therefore very indecorous that our sacred things, which are more noble, and are ministered every day, should be handled by those who are married: as if the evangelical ministry were of the same character as the Levitical priesthood. These, as types, represented Christ, who, as Mediator between God and men, was, by his own spotless purity, to reconcile us to the Father. But as sinners could not in every respect exhibit a type of his holiness, that they might, however, shadow it forth by certain lineaments, they were enjoined to purify themselves beyond the manner of men when they approached the sanctuary, inasmuch as they then properly prefigured Christ appearing in the tabernacle, an image of the heavenly tribunal, as pacificators, to reconcile men to God. As ecclesiastical pastors do not sustain this character in the present day, the comparison is made in vain. Wherefore the apostle declares distinctly, without reservation, "Marriage is honourable in all, and the bed undefiled; but whoremongers and adulterers God will judge" (Heb. 13:4). And the apostles showed, by their own example, that marriage is not unbefitting the holiness of any function, however excellent; for Paul declares, that they not only retained their wives, but led them about with them (1 Cor. 9:5).

26. Then how great the effrontery when, in holding forth this ornament of chastity as a matter of necessity, they throw the greatest obloquy on the primitive Church, which, while it abounded in admirable divine erudition, excelled more in holiness. For if they pay no regard to the apostles (they are sometimes wont strenuously to contemn them), what, I ask, will they make of all the ancient fathers, who, it is certain, not only tolerated marriage in the episcopal order, but also approved it? They, forsooth, encouraged a foul profanation of sacred things when the mysteries of the Lord were thus irregularly performed by them. In the Council of Nice, indeed, there was some question of proclaiming celibacy: as there are never wanting little men of superstitious minds, who are always devising some novelty as a means of gaining admiration for themselves. What was resolved? The opinion of Paphnutius was adopted, who pronounced legitimate conjugal intercourse to be chastity (Hist. Trip. Lib. 2 c. 14). The marriage of priests, therefore, continued sacred, and was neither regarded as a disgrace, nor thought to cast any stain on their ministry.

27. In the times which succeeded, a too superstitious admiration of celibacy prevailed. Hence, ever and anon, unmeasured encomiums were pronounced on virginity, so that it became the vulgar belief that scarcely any virtue was to be compared to it. And although marriage was not condemned as impurity, yet its dignity was lessened, and its sanctity obscured; so that he who did not refrain from it was deemed not to have a mind strong enough to aspire to perfection. Hence those canons which enacted, first, that those who had attained the priesthood should not contract marriage; and, secondly, that none should be admitted to that order but the unmarried, or those who, with the consent of their wives, renounced the marriage-bed. These enactments, as they seemed to procure reverence for the priesthood, were, I admit, received even in ancient times with great applause. But if my opponents plead antiquity, my first answer is, that both under the apostles, and for several ages after, bishops were at liberty to have wives: that the apostles themselves, and other pastors of primitive authority who succeeded them, had no difficulty in using this liberty, and that the example of the primitive Church ought justly to have more weight than allow us to think that what was then received and used with commendation is either illicit or unbecoming. My second answer is, that the age, which, from an immoderate affection for virginity, began to be less favourable to marriage, did not bind a law of celibacy on the priests, as if the thing were necessary in itself, but gave a preference

to the unmarried over the married. My last answer is, that they did not exact this so rigidly as to make continence necessary and compulsory on those who were unfit for it. For while the strictest laws were made against fornication, it was only enacted with regard to those who contracted marriage that they should be superseded in their office.

28. Therefore, as often as the defenders of this new tyranny appeal to antiquity in defence of their celibacy, so often should we call upon them to restore the ancient chastity of their priests, to put away adulterers and whoremongers, not to allow those whom they deny an honourable and chaste use of marriage, to rush with impunity into every kind of lust, to bring back that obsolete discipline by which all licentiousness is restrained, and free the Church from the flagitious turpitude by which it has long been deformed. When they have conceded this, they will next require to be reminded not to represent as necessary that which, being in itself free, depends on the utility of the Church. I do not, however, speak thus as if I thought that on any condition whatever effect should be given to those canons which lay a bond of celibacy on the ecclesiastical order, but that the better-hearted may understand the effrontery of our enemies in employing the name of antiquity to defame the holy marriage of priests. In regard to the Fathers, whose writings are extant, none of them, when they spoke their own mind, with the exception of Jerome, thus malignantly detracted from the honour of marriage. We will be contented with a single passage from Chrysostom, because he being a special admirer of virginity, cannot be thought to be more lavish than others in praise of matrimony. Chrysostom thus speaks: "The first degree of chastity is pure virginity; the second, faithful marriage. Therefore, a chaste love of matrimony is the second species of virginity" (Chrysost. Hom. de Invent. Crucis.).

CHAPTER 13

OF VOWS. THE MISERABLE ENTANGLEMENTS CAUSED BY VOWING RASHLY.

This chapter consists of two parts,—I. Of vows in general, sec. 1–8. II. Of monastic vows, and specially of the vow of celibacy, sec. 8–21.

Sections:

1. Some general principles with regard to the nature of vows. Superstitious errors not only of the heathen, but of Christians, in regard to vows.

2. Three points to be considered with regard to vows. First, to whom the vow is made—viz. to God. Nothing to be vowed to him but what he himself requires.

3. Second, Who we are that vow. We must measure our strength, and have regard to our calling. Fearful errors of the Popish clergy by not attending to this. Their vow of celibacy.

4. Third point to be attended to—viz. the intention with which the vow is made. Four ends in vowing. Two of them refer to the past, and two to the future. Examples and use of the former class.

5. End of vows which refer to the future.

6. The doctrine of vows in general. Common vow of Christians in Baptism, &c. This vow sacred and salutary. Particular vows how to be tested.

7. Great prevalence of superstition with regard to vows.

8. Vows of monks. Contrast between ancient and modern monasticism.

9. Portraiture of the ancient monks by Augustine.

10. Degeneracy of modern monks. 1. Inconsiderate rigour. 2. Idleness. 3. False boast of perfection.

11. This idea of monastic perfection refuted.

12. Arguments for monastic perfection. First argument answered.

13. Second argument answered.

14. Absurdity of representing the monastic profession as a second baptism.

15. Corrupt manners of monks.

16. Some defects in ancient monasticism.

17. General refutation of monastic vows.

18. Refutation continued.

19. Refutation continued.

20. Do such vows of celibacy bind the conscience? This question answered.

21. Those who abandon the monastic profession for an honest living, unjustly accused of breaking their faith.

1. It is indeed deplorable that the Church, whose freedom was purchased by the inestimable price of Christ's blood, should have been thus oppressed by a cruel tyranny, and almost buried under a huge mass of traditions; but, at the same time, the private infatuation of each individual shows, that not without just cause has so much power been given from above to Satan and his ministers. It was not enough to neglect the command of Christ, and bear any burdens which false teachers might please to impose, but each individual behoved to have

his own peculiar burdens, and thus sink deeper by digging his own cavern. This has been the result when men set about devising vows, by which a stronger and closer obligation might be added to common ties. Having already shown that the worship of God was vitiated by the audacity of those who, under the name of pastors, domineered in the Church, when they ensnared miserable souls by their iniquitous laws, it will not be out of place here to advert to a kindred evil, to make it appear that the world, in accordance with its depraved disposition, has always thrown every possible obstacle in the way of the helps by which it ought to have been brought to God. Moreover, that the very grievous mischief introduced by such vows may be more apparent, let the reader attend to the principles formerly laid down. First, we showed (Book 2 chap. 8 sec. 5) that everything requisite for the ordering of a pious and holy life is comprehended in the law. Secondly, we showed that the Lord, the better to dissuade us from devising new works, included the whole of righteousness in simple obedience to his will. If these positions are true, it is easy to see that all fictitious worship, which we ourselves devise for the purpose of serving God, is not in the least degree acceptable to him, how pleasing soever it may be to us. And, unquestionably, in many passages the Lord not only openly rejects, but grievously abhors such worship. Hence arises a doubt with regard to vows which are made without any express authority from the word of God; in what light are they to be viewed? can they be duly made by Christian men, and to what extent are they binding? What is called a promise among men is a vow when made to God. Now, we promise to men either things which we think will be acceptable to them, or things which we in duty owe them. Much more careful, therefore, ought we to be in vows which are directed to God, with whom we ought to act with the greatest seriousness. Here superstition has in all ages strangely prevailed; men at once, without judgment and without choice, vowing to God whatever came into their minds, or even rose to their lips. Hence the foolish vows, nay, monstrous absurdities, by which the heathen insolently sported with their gods. Would that Christians had not imitated them in this their audacity! Nothing, indeed, could be less becoming; but it is obvious that for some ages nothing has been more usual than this misconduct—the whole body of the people everywhere despising the Law of God, and burning with an insane zeal of vowing according to any dreaming notion which they had formed. I have no wish to exaggerate invidiously, or particularise the many grievous sins which have here been committed; but it seemed right to advert to it in passing, that it may the better appear, that when we treat of vows we are not by any means discussing a superfluous question.

2. If we would avoid error in deciding what vows are legitimate, and what preposterous, three things must be attended to—viz. who he is to whom the vow is made; who we are that make it; and, lastly, with what intention we make it. In regard in the first, we should consider that we have to do with God, whom our obedience so delights, that he abominates all will-worship, how specious and splendid soever it be in the eyes of men (Col. 2:23). If all will-worship, which we devise without authority, is abomination to God, it follows that no worship can be acceptable to him save that which is approved by his word. Therefore, we must not arrogate such licence to ourselves as to presume to vow anything to God without evidence of the estimation in which he holds it. For the doctrine of Paul, that whatsoever is not of faith is sin (Rom. 14:23), while it extends to all actions of every kind, certainly applies with peculiar force in the case where the thought is immediately turned towards God. Nay, if in the minutest matters (Paul was then speaking of the distinction of meats) we err or fall, where the sure light of faith shines not before us, how much more modesty ought we to use when we attempt a matter of the greatest weight? For in nothing ought we to be more serious than in the duties of religion. In vows, then, our first precaution must be, never to proceed to make any vow without having previously determined in our conscience to attempt nothing rashly. And we shall be safe from the danger of rashness when we have God going before, and, as it were, dictating from his word what is good, and what is useless.

3. In the second point which we have mentioned as requiring consideration is implied, that we measure our strength, that we attend to our vocation so as not to neglect the blessing of liberty which God has conferred upon us. For he who vows what is not within his means, or is at variance with his calling, is rash, while he who contemns the beneficence of God in making him lord of all things, is ungrateful. When I speak thus, I mean not that anything is so placed in our hand, that, leaning on our own strength, we may promise it to God. For in the Council of Arausica (cap. 11) it was most truly decreed, that nothing is duly vowed to God save what we have received from his hand, since all things which are offered to him are merely his gifts. But seeing that some things are given to us by the goodness of God, and others withheld by his justice, every man should have respect to the

measure of grace bestowed on him, as Paul enjoins (Rom. 12:3; 1 Cor. 12:11). All then I mean here is, that your vows should be adapted to the measure which God by his gifts prescribes to you, lest by attempting more than he permits, you arrogate too much to yourself, and fall headlong. For example, when the assassins, of whom mention is made in the Acts, vowed "that they would neither eat nor drink till they had killed Paul" (Acts 23:12), though it had not been an impious conspiracy, it would still have been intolerably presumptuous, as subjecting the life and death of a man to their own power. Thus Jephthah suffered for his folly, when with precipitate fervour he made a rash vow (Judges 11:30). Of this class, the first place of insane audacity belongs to celibacy. Priests, monks, and nuns, forgetful of their infirmity, are confident of their fitness for celibacy. But by what oracle have they been instructed, that the chastity which they vow to the end of life, they will be able through life to maintain? They hear the voice of God concerning the universal condition of mankind, "It is not good that the man should be alone" (Gen. 2:18). They understand, and I wish they did not feel that the sin remaining in us is armed with the sharpest stings. How can they presume to shake off the common feelings of their nature for a whole lifetime, seeing the gift of continence is often granted for a certain time as occasion requires? In such perverse conduct they must not expect God to be their helper; let them rather remember the words, "Ye shall not tempt the Lord your God" (Deut. 6:16). But it is to tempt the Lord to strive against the nature implanted by him, and to spurn his present gifts as if they did not appertain to us. This they not only do, but marriage, which God did not think it unbecoming his majesty to institute, which he pronounced honourable in all, which Christ our Lord sanctified by his presence, and which he deigned to honour with his first miracle, they presume to stigmatise as pollution, so extravagant are the terms in which they eulogise every kind of celibacy; as if in their own life they did not furnish a clear proof that celibacy is one thing and chastity another. This life, however, they most impudently style angelical, thereby offering no slight insult to the angels of God, to whom they compare whoremongers and adulterers, and something much worse and fouler still. And, indeed, there is here very little occasion for argument, since they are abundantly refuted by fact. For we plainly see the fearful punishments with which the Lord avenges this arrogance and contempt of his gifts from overweening confidence. More hidden crimes I spare through shame; what is known of them is too much. Beyond all controversy, we ought not to vow anything which will hinder us in fulfilling our vocation; as if the father of a family were to vow to leave his wife and children, and undertake other burdens; or one who is fit for a public office should, when elected to it, vow to live private. But the meaning of what we have said as to not despising our liberty may occasion some difficulty if not explained. Wherefore, understand it briefly thus: Since God has given us dominion over all things, and so subjected them to us that we may use them for our convenience, we cannot hope that our service will be acceptable to God if we bring ourselves into bondage to external things, which ought to be subservient to us. I say this, because some aspire to the praise of humility, for entangling themselves in a variety of observances from which God for good reason wished us to be entirely free. Hence, if we would escape this danger, let us always remember that we are by no means to withdraw from the economy which God has appointed in the Christian Church.

4. I come now to my third position—viz that if you would approve your vow to God, the mind in which you undertake it is of great moment. For seeing that God looks not to the outward appearance but to the heart, the consequence is, that according to the purpose which the mind has in view, the same thing may at one time please and be acceptable to him, and at another be most displeasing. If you vow abstinence from wine, as if there were any holiness in so doing, you are superstitious; but if you have some end in view which is not perverse, no one can disapprove. Now, as far as I can see, there are four ends to which our vows may be properly directed; two of these, for the sake of order, I refer to the past, and two to the future. To the past belong vows by which we either testify our gratitude toward God for favours received, or in order to deprecate his wrath, inflict punishment on ourselves for faults committed. The former, let us if you please call acts of thanksgiving; the latter, acts of repentance. Of the former class, we have an example in the tithes which Jacob vowed (Gen. 28:20), if the Lord would conduct him safely home from exile; and also in the ancient peace-offerings which pious kings and commanders, when about to engage in a just war, vowed that they would give if they were victorious, or, at least, if the Lord would deliver them when pressed by some greater difficulty. Thus are to be understood all the passages in the Psalms which speak of vows (Ps. 22:26; 56:13; 116:14, 18). Similar vows may also be used by us in the present day, whenever the Lord has rescued us from some disaster or dangerous disease, or other peril. For it is not

abhorrent from the office of a pious man thus to consecrate a votive offering to God as a formal symbol of acknowledgment that he may not seem ungrateful for his kindness. The nature of the second class it will be sufficient to illustrate merely by one familiar example. Should any one, from gluttonous indulgence, have fallen into some iniquity, there is nothing to prevent him, with the view of chastising his intemperance, from renouncing all luxuries for a certain time, and in doing so, from employing a vow for the purpose of binding himself more firmly. And yet I do not lay down this as an invariable law to all who have similarly offended; I merely show what may be lawfully done by those who think that such a vow will be useful to them. Thus while I hold it lawful so to vow, I at the same time leave it free.

5. The vows which have reference to the future tend partly, as we have said, to render us more cautious, and partly to act as a kind of stimulus to the discharge of duty. A man sees that he is so prone to a certain vice, that in a thing which is otherwise not bad he cannot restrain himself from forthwith falling into evil: he will not act absurdly in cutting off the use of that thing for some time by a vow. If, for instance, one should perceive that this or that bodily ornament brings him into peril, and yet allured by cupidity he eagerly longs for it, what can he do better than by throwing a curb upon himself, that is, imposing the necessity of abstinence, free himself from all doubt? In like manner, should one be oblivious or sluggish in the necessary duties of piety, why should he not, by forming a vow, both awaken his memory and shake off his sloth? In both, I confess, there is a kind of tutelage, but inasmuch as they are helps to infirmity, they are used not without advantage by the ignorant and imperfect. Hence we hold that vows which have respect to one of these ends, especially in external things, are lawful, provided they are supported by the approbation of God, are suitable to our calling, and are limited to the measure of grace bestowed upon us.

6. It is not now difficult to infer what view on the whole ought to be taken of vows. There is one vow common to all believers, which taken in baptism we confirm, and as it were sanction, by our Catechism, and partaking of the Lord's Supper. For the sacraments are a kind of mutual contracts by which the Lord conveys his mercy to us, and by it eternal life, while we in our turn promise him obedience. The formula, or at least substance, of the vow is, That renouncing Satan we bind ourselves to the service of God, to obey his holy commands, and no longer follow the depraved desires of our flesh. It cannot be doubted that this vow, which is sanctioned by Scripture, nay, is exacted from all the children of God, is holy and salutary. There is nothing against this in the fact, that no man in this life yields that perfect obedience to the law which God requires of us. This stipulation being included in the covenant of grace, comprehending forgiveness of sins and the spirit of holiness, the promise which we there make is combined both with entreaty for pardon and petition for assistance. It is necessary, in judging of particular vows, to keep the three former rules in remembrance: from them any one will easily estimate the character of each single vow. Do not suppose, however, that I so commend the vows which I maintain to be holy that I would have them made every day. For though I dare not give any precept as to time or number, yet if any one will take my advice, he will not undertake any but what are sober and temporary. If you are ever and anon launching out into numerous vows, the whole solemnity will be lost by the frequency, and you will readily fall into superstition. If you bind yourself by a perpetual vow, you will have great trouble and annoyance in getting free, or, worn out by length of time, you will at length make bold to break it.

7. It is now easy to see under how much superstition the world has laboured in this respect for several ages. One vowed that he would be abstemious, as if abstinence from wine were in itself an acceptable service to God. Another bound himself to fast, another to abstain from flesh on certain days, which he had vainly imagined to be more holy than other days. Things much more boyish were vowed though not by boys. For it was accounted great wisdom to undertake votive pilgrimages to holy places, and sometimes to perform the journey on foot, or with the body half naked, that the greater merit might be acquired by the greater fatigue. These and similar things, for which the world has long bustled with incredible zeal, if tried by the rules which we formerly laid down, will be discovered to be not only empty and nugatory, but full of manifest impiety. Be the judgment of the flesh what it may, there is nothing which God more abhors than fictitious worship. To these are added pernicious and damnable notions, hypocrites, after performing such frivolities, thinking that they have acquired no ordinary righteousness, placing the substance of piety in external observances, and despising all others who appear less careful in regard to them.

8. It is of no use to enumerate all the separate forms. But as monastic vows are held in great veneration, because they seem to be approved by the public judgment of the

Church, I will say a few words concerning them. And, first, lest any one defend the monachism of the present day on the ground of the long prescription, it is to be observed, that the ancient mode of living in monasteries was very different. The persons who retired to them were those who wished to train themselves to the greatest austerity and patience. The discipline practiced by the monks then resembled that which the Lacedemonians are said to have used under the laws of Lycurgus, and was even much more rigorous. They slept on the ground, their drink was water, their food bread, herbs, and roots, their chief luxuries oil and pulse. From more delicate food and care of the body they abstained. These things might seem hyperbolical were they not vouched by experienced eye witnesses, as Gregory Nazianzen, Basil, and Chrysostom. By such rudimentary training they prepared themselves for greater offices. For of the fact that monastic colleges were then a kind of seminaries of the ecclesiastical order, both those whom we lately named are very competent witnesses (they were all brought up in monasteries, and thence called to the episcopal office), as well as several other great and excellent men of their age. Augustine also shows that in his time the monasteries were wont to furnish the Church with clergy. For he thus addresses the monks of the island of Caprae: "We exhort you, brethren in the Lord, to keep your purpose, and persevere to the end; and if at any time our mother Church requires your labour, you will neither undertake it with eager elation, nor reject it from the blandishment of sloth, but with meek hearts obey God. You will not prefer your own ease to the necessities of the Church. Had no good men been willing to minister to her when in travail, it would have been impossible for you to be born" (August. Ep. 82). He is speaking of the ministry by which believers are spiritually born again. In like manner, he says to Aurelius (Ep. 76), "It is both an occasion of lapse to them, and a most unbecoming injury to the clerical order, if the deserters of monasteries are elected to the clerical warfare, since from those who remain in the monastery our custom is to appoint to the clerical office only the better and more approved. Unless, perhaps, as the vulgar say, A bad chorister is a good symphonist, so, in like manner, it will be jestingly said of us, A bad monk is a good clergyman. There will be too much cause for grief if we stir up monks to such ruinous pride, and deem the clergy deserving of so grave an affront, seeing that sometimes a good monk scarcely makes a good clerk; he may have sufficient continence, but be deficient in necessary learning." From these passages, it appears that pious men were wont to prepare for the government of the Church by monastic discipline, that thus they might be more apt and better trained to undertake the important office: not that all attained to this object, or even aimed at it, since the great majority of monks were illiterate men. Those who were fit were selected.

9. Augustine, in two passages in particular, gives a portraiture of the form of ancient monasticism. The one is in his book, *De Moribus Ecclesiæ Catholicæ (On the Manners of the Catholic Church)*, where he maintains the holiness of that profession against the calumnies of the Manichees; the other in a treatise, entitled, *De Opere Monachorum (On the Work of Monks)*, where he inveighs against certain degenerate monks who had begun to corrupt that institution. I will here give a summary of what he there delivers, and, as far as I can, in his own words: "Despising the allurements of this world, and congregated in common for a most chaste and most holy life, they pass their lives together, spending their time in prayer, reading, and discourse, not swollen with pride, not turbulent through petulance, not livid with envy. No one possesses anything of his own: no one is burdensome to any man. They labour with their hands in things by which the body may be fed, and the mind not withdrawn from God. The fruit of their labour they hand over to those whom they call deans. Those deans, disposing of the whole with great care, render an account to one whom they call father. These fathers, who are not only of the purest morals, but most distinguished for divine learning, and noble in all things, without any pride, consult those whom they call their sons, though the former have full authority to command, and the latter a great inclination to obey. At the close of the day they assemble each from his cell, and without having broken their fast, to hear their father, and to the number of three thousand at least (he is speaking of Egypt and the East) they assemble under each father. Then the body is refreshed, so far as suffices for safety and health, every one curbing his concupiscence so as not to be profuse in the scanty and very mean diet which is provided. Thus they not only abstain from flesh and wine for the purpose of subduing lust, but from those things which provoke the appetite of the stomach and gullet more readily, from seeming to some, as it were, more refined. In this way the desire of exquisite dainties, in which there is no flesh, is wont to be absurdly and shamefully defended. Any surplus, after necessary food (and the surplus is very great from the labour of their hands and the frugality of their meals), is carefully distributed to the needy, the more carefully that it was not procured

by those who distribute. For they never act with the view of having abundance for themselves, but always act with the view of allowing no superfluity to remain with them" (August. De Mor. Eccl. Cath. c. 31). Afterwards describing their austerity, of which he had himself seen instances both at Milan and elsewhere, he says, "Meanwhile, no one is urged to austerities which he is unable to bear: no one is obliged to do what he declines, nor condemned by the others, whom he acknowledges himself too weak to imitate. For they remember how greatly charity is commended: they remember that to the pure all things are pure (Tit. 1:15). Wherefore, all their vigilance is employed, not in rejecting kinds of food as polluted, but in subduing concupiscence, and maintaining brotherly love. They remember, 'Meats for the belly, and the belly for meats,' &c. (1 Cor. 6:13). Many, however strong, abstain because of the weak. In many this is not the cause of action; they take pleasure in sustaining themselves on the meanest and least expensive food. Hence the very persons who in health restrain themselves, decline not in sickness to use what their health requires. Many do not drink wine, and yet do not think themselves polluted by it, for they most humanely cause it to be given to the more sickly, and to those whose health requires it; and some who foolishly refuse, they fraternally admonish, lest by vain superstition they sooner become more weak than more holy. Thus they sedulously practice piety, while they know that bodily exercise is only for a short time. Charity especially is observed: their food is adapted to charity, their speech to charity, their dress to charity, their looks to charity. They go together, and breathe only charity: they deem it as unlawful to offend charity as to offend God; if any one opposes it, he is cast out and shunned; if any one offends it, he is not permitted to remain one day" (August. De Moribus Eccl. Cath. c. 33). Since this holy man appears in these words to have exhibited the monastic life of ancient times as in a picture, I have thought it right to insert them here, though somewhat long, because I perceive that I would be considerably longer if I collected them from different writers, however compendious I might study to be.

10. Here, however, I had no intention to discuss the whole subject. I only wished to show, by the way, what kind of monks the early Church had, and what the monastic profession then was, that from the contrast sound readers might judge how great the effrontery is of those who allege antiquity in support of present monkism. Augustine, while tracing out a holy and legitimate monasticism, would keep away all rigorous exaction of those things which the word of the Lord has left free. But in the present day nothing is more rigorously exacted. For they deem it an inexpiable crime if any one deviates in the least degree from the prescribed form in colour or species of dress, in the kind of food, or in other frivolous and frigid ceremonies. Augustine strenuously contends that it is not lawful for monks to live in idleness on other men's means. (August. De Oper. Monach.) He denies that any such example was to be found in his day in a well-regulated monastery. Our monks place the principal part of their holiness in idleness. For if you take away their idleness, where will that contemplative life by which they glory that they excel all others, and make a near approach to the angels? Augustine, in fine, requires a monasticism which may be nothing else than a training and assistant to the offices of piety which are recommended to all Christians. What? When he makes charity its chief and almost its only rule, do we think he praises that combination by which a few men, bound to each other, are separated from the whole body of the Church? Nay, he wishes them to set an example to others of preserving the unity of the Church. So different is the nature of present monachism in both respects, that it would be difficult to find anything so dissimilar, not to say contrary. For our monks, not satisfied with that piety, on the study of which alone Christ enjoins his followers to be intent, imagine some new kind of piety, by aspiring to which they are more perfect than all other men.

11. If they deny this, I should like to know why they honour their own order only with the title of perfection, and deny it to all other divine callings. I am not unaware of the sophistical solution that their order is not so called because it contains perfection in itself, but because it is the best of all for acquiring perfection. When they would extol themselves to the people; when they would lay a snare for rash and ignorant youth; when they would assert their privileges and exalt their own dignity to the disparagement of others, they boast that they are in a state of perfection. When they are too closely pressed to be able to defend this vain arrogance, they betake themselves to the subterfuge that they have not yet obtained perfection, but that they are in a state in which they aspire to it more than others; meanwhile, the people continue to admire as if the monastic life alone were angelic, perfect, and purified from every vice. Under this pretence they ply a most gainful traffic, while their moderation lies buried in a few volumes. Who sees not that this is intolerable trifling? But let us treat with them as if they ascribed nothing more to their profession than to call it a state for

acquiring perfection. Surely by giving it this name, they distinguish it by a special mark from other modes of life. And who will allow such honour to be transferred to an institution of which not one syllable is said in approbation, while all the other callings of God are deemed unworthy of the same, though not only commanded by his sacred lips, but adorned with distinguished titles? And how great the insult offered to God, when some device of man is preferred to all the modes of life which he has ordered, and by his testimony approved?

12. But let them say I calumniated them when I declared that they were not contented with the rule prescribed by God. Still, though I were silent, they more than sufficiently accuse themselves; for they plainly declare that they undertake a greater burden than Christ has imposed on his followers, since they promise that they will keep evangelical counsels regarding the love of enemies, the suppression of vindictive feelings, and abstinence from swearing, counsels to which Christians are not commonly astricted. In this what antiquity can they pretend? None of the ancients ever thought of such a thing: all with one voice proclaim that not one syllable proceeded from Christ which it is not necessary to obey. And the very things which these worthy expounders pretend that Christ only counselled they uniformly declare, without any doubt, that he expressly enjoined. But as we have shown above, that this is a most pestilential error, let it suffice here to have briefly observed that monasticism, as it now exists, founded on an idea which all pious men ought to execrate—namely, the pretence that there is some more perfect rule of life than that common rule which God has delivered to the whole Church. Whatever is built on this foundation cannot but be abominable.

13. But they produce another argument for their perfection, and deem it invincible. Our Lord said to the young man who put a question to him concerning the perfection of righteousness, "If thou wilt be perfect, go and sell that thou hast, and give to the poor" (Mt. 19:21). Whether they do so, I do not now dispute. Let us grant for the present that they do. They boast, then, that they have become perfect by abandoning their all. If the sum off perfection consists in this, what is the meaning of Paul's doctrine, that though a man should give all his goods to feed the poor, and have not charity, he is nothing? (1 Cor. 13:3). What kind of perfection is that which, if charity be wanting, is with the individual himself reduced to nothing? Here they must of necessity answer that it is indeed the highest, but is not the only work of perfection. But here again Paul interposes; and hesitates not to declare that charity, without any renunciation of that sort, is the "bond of perfectness" (Col. 3:14). If it is certain that there is no disagreement between the scholar and the master, and the latter clearly denies that the perfection of a man consists in renouncing all his goods, and on the other hand asserts that perfection may exist without it, we must see in what sense we should understand the words of Christ, "If thou wilt be perfect, go and sell that thou hast." Now, there will not be the least obscurity in the meaning if we consider (this ought to be attended to in all our Saviour's discourses) to whom the words are addressed (Luke 10:25). A young man asks by what works he shall enter into eternal life. Christ, as he was asked concerning works, refers him to the law. And justly; for, considered in itself, it is the way of eternal life, and its inefficacy to give eternal life is owing to our depravity. By this answer Christ declared that he did not deliver any other rule of life than that which had formerly been delivered in the law of the Lord. Thus he both bore testimony to the divine law, that it was a doctrine of perfect righteousness, and at the same time met the calumnious charge of seeming, by some new rule of life, to incite the people to revolt from the law. The young man, who was not ill-disposed, but was puffed up with vain confidence, answers that he had observed all the precepts of the law from his youth. It is absolutely certain that he was immeasurably distant from the goal which he boasted of having reached. Had his boast been true, he would have wanted nothing of absolute perfection. For it has been demonstrated above, that the law contains in it a perfect righteousness. This is even obvious from the fact, that the observance of it is called the way to eternal life. To show him how little progress he had made in that righteousness which he too boldly answered that he had fulfilled, it was right to bring before him his besetting sin. Now, while he abounded in riches, he had his heart set upon them. Therefore, because he did not feel this secret wound, it is probed by Christ—"Go," says he, "and sell that thou hast." Had he been as good a keeper of the law as he supposed, he would not have gone away sorrowful on hearing these words. For he who loves God with his whole heart, not only regards everything which wars with his love as dross, but hates it as destruction (Phil. 3:8). Therefore, when Christ orders a rich miser to leave all that he has, it is the same as if he had ordered the ambitious to renounce all his honours, the voluptuous all his luxuries, the unchaste all the instruments of his lust. Thus consciences, which are not reached by any general admonition, are to be recalled to a particular feeling of

their particular sin. In vain, therefore, do they wrest that special case to a general interpretation, as if Christ had decided that the perfection of man consists in the abandonment of his goods, since he intended nothing more by the expression than to bring a youth who was out of measure satisfied with himself to feel his sore, and so understand that he was still at a great distance from that perfect obedience of the law which he falsely ascribed to himself. I admit that this passage was ill understood by some of the Fathers; and hence arose an affectation of voluntary poverty, those only being thought blest who abandoned all earthly goods, and in a state of destitution devoted themselves to Christ. But I am confident that, after my exposition, no good and reasonable man will have any dubiety here as to the mind of Christ.

14. Still there was nothing with the Fathers less intended than to establish that kind of perfection which was afterwards fabricated by cowled monks, in order to rear up a species of double Christianity. For as yet the sacrilegious dogma was not broached which compares the profession of monasticism to baptism, nay, plainly asserts that it is the form of a second baptism. Who can doubt that the Fathers with their whole hearts abhorred such blasphemy? Then what need is there to demonstrate, by words, that the last quality which Augustine mentions as belonging to the ancient monks—viz. that they in all things accommodated themselves to charity—is most alien from this new profession? The thing itself declares that all who retire into monasteries withdraw from the Church. For how? Do they not separate themselves from the legitimate society of the faithful, by acquiring for themselves a special ministry and private administration of the sacraments? What is meant by destroying the communion of the Church if this is not? And to follow out the comparison with which I began, and at once close the point, what resemblance have they in this respect to the ancient monks? These, though they dwelt separately from others, had not a separate Church; they partook of the sacraments with others, they attended public meetings, and were then a part of the people. But what have those men done in erecting a private altar for themselves but broken the bond of unity? For they have excommunicated themselves from the whole body of the Church, and contemned the ordinary ministry by which the Lord has been pleased that peace and charity should be preserved among his followers. Wherefore I hold that as many monasteries as there are in the present day, so many conventicles are there of schismatics, who have disturbed ecclesiastical order, and been cut off from the legitimate society of the faithful. And that there might be no doubt as to their separation, they have given themselves the various names of factions. They have not been ashamed to glory in that which Paul so execrates, that he is unable to express his detestation too strongly. Unless, indeed, we suppose that Christ was not divided by the Corinthians, when one teacher set himself above another (1 Cor. 1:12, 13; 3:4); and that now no injury is done to Christ when, instead of Christians, we hear some called Benedictines, others Franciscans, others Dominicans, and so called, that while they affect to be distinguished from the common body of Christians, they proudly substitute these names for a religious profession.

15. The differences which I have hitherto pointed out between the ancient monks and those of our age are not in manners, but in profession. Hence let my readers remember that I have spoken of monachism rather than of monks; and marked, not the vices which cleave to a few, but vices which are inseparable from the very mode of life. In regard to manners, of what use is it to particularise and show how great the difference? This much is certain, that there is no order of men more polluted by all kinds of vicious turpitude; nowhere do faction, hatred, party-spirit, and intrigue, more prevail. In a few monasteries, indeed, they live chastely, if we are to call it chastity, where lust is so far repressed as not to be openly infamous; still you will scarcely find one in ten which is not rather a brothel than a sacred abode of chastity. But how frugally they live? Just like swine wallowing in their sties. But lest they complain that I deal too unmercifully with them, I go no farther; although any one who knows the case will admit, that in the few things which I have said, I have not spoken in the spirit of an accuser. Augustine though he testifies, that the monks excelled so much in chastity, yet complains that there were many vagabonds, who, by wicked arts and impostures, extracted money from the more simple, plying a shameful traffic, by carrying about the relics of martyrs, and vending any dead man's bones for relics, bringing ignominy on their order by many similar iniquities. As he declares that he had seen none better than those who had profited in monasteries; so he laments that he had seen none worse than those who had backslidden in monasteries. What would he say were he, in the present day, to see now almost all monasteries overflowing, and in a manner bursting, with numerous deplorable vices? I say nothing but what is notorious to all; and yet this charge does not apply to all without a single exception; for, as the rule and discipline of holy living was never so well framed in monasteries as

that there were not always some drones very unlike the others; so I hold that, in the present day, monks have not so completely degenerated from that holy antiquity as not to have some good men among them; but these few lie scattered up and down among a huge multitude of wicked and dishonest men, and are not only despised, but even petulantly assailed, sometimes even treated cruelly by the others, who, according to the Milesian proverb, think they ought to have no good man among them.

16. By this contrast between ancient and modern monasticism, I trust I have gained my object, which was to show that our cowled monks falsely pretend the example of the primitive Church in defence of their profession; since they differ no less from the monks of that period than apes do from men. Meanwhile I disguise not that even in that ancient form which Augustine commends, there was something which little pleases me. I admit that they were not superstitious in the external exercises of a more rigorous discipline, but I say that they were not without a degree of affectation and false zeal. It was a fine thing to cast away their substance, and free themselves from all worldly cares; but God sets more value on the pious management of a household, when the head of it, discarding all avarice, ambition, and other lusts of the flesh, makes it his purpose to serve God in some particular vocation. It is fine to philosophise in seclusion, far away from the intercourse of society; but it ill accords with Christian meekness for any one, as if in hatred of the human race, to fly to the wilderness and to solitude, and at the same time desert the duties which the Lord has especially commanded. Were we to grant that there was nothing worse in that profession, there is certainly no small evil in its having introduced a useless and perilous example into the Church.

17. Now, then, let us see the nature of the vows by which the monks of the present day are initiated into this famous order. First, as their intention is to institute a new and fictitious worship with a view to gain favour with God, I conclude from what has been said above, that everything which they vow is abomination to God. Secondly, I hold that as they frame their own mode of life at pleasure, without any regard to the calling of God, or to his approbation, the attempt is rash and unlawful; because their conscience has no ground on which it can support itself before God; and "whatsoever is not of faith is sin" (Rom. 14:23). Moreover, I maintain that in astricting themselves to many perverse and impious modes of worship, such as are exhibited in modern monasticism, they consecrate themselves not to God but to the devil.

For why should the prophets have been permitted to say that the Israelites sacrificed their sons to devils and not to God (Deut. 32:17;Ps. 106:37), merely because they had corrupted the true worship of God by profane ceremonies; and we not be permitted to say the same thing of monks who, along with the cowl, cover themselves with the net of a thousand impious superstitions? Then what is their species of vows? They offer God a promise of perpetual virginity, as if they had previously made a compact with him to free them from the necessity of marriage. They cannot allege that they make this vow trusting entirely to the grace of God; for, seeing he declares this to be a special gift not given to all (Mt. 19:11), no man has a right to assume that the gift will be his. Let those who have it use it; and if at any time they feel the infirmity of the flesh, let them have recourse to the aid of him by whose power alone they can resist. If this avails not, let them not despise the remedy which is offered to them. If the faculty of continence is denied, the voice of God distinctly calls upon them to marry. By continence I mean not merely that by which the body is kept pure from fornication, but that by which the mind keeps its chastity untainted. For Paul enjoins caution not only against external lasciviousness, but also burning of mind (1 Cor. 7:9). It has been the practice (they say) from the remotest period, for those who wished to devote themselves entirely to God, to bind themselves by a vow of continence. I confess that the custom is ancient, but I do not admit that the age when it commenced was so free from every defect that all that was then done is to be regarded as a rule. Moreover, the inexorable rigour of holding that after the vow is conceived there is no room for repentance, crept in gradually. This is clear from Cyprian. "If virgins have dedicated themselves to Christian faith, let them live modestly and chastely, without pretence. Thus strong and stable, let them wait for the reward of virginity. But if they will not, or cannot persevere, it is better to marry, than by their faults to fall into the fire." In the present day, with what invectives would they not lacerate any one who should seek to temper the vow of continence by such an equitable course? Those, therefore, have wandered far from the ancient custom who not only use no moderation, and grant no pardon when any one proves unequal to the performance of his vow, but shamelessly declare that it is a more heinous sin to cure the intemperance of the flesh by marriage, than to defile body and soul by whoredom.

18. But they still insist and attempt to show that this vow was used in the days of the apostles, because Paul

says that widows who marry after having once undertaken a public office, "cast off their first faith" (1 Tim. 5:12). I by no means deny that widows who dedicated themselves and their labours to the Church, at the same time came under an obligation of perpetual celibacy, not because they regarded it in the light of a religious duty, as afterwards began to be the case, but because they could not perform their functions unless they had their time at their own command, and were free from the nuptial tie. But if, after giving their pledge, they began to look to a new marriage, what else was this but to shake off the calling of God? It is not strange, therefore, when Paul says that by such desires they grow wanton against Christ. In further explanation he afterwards adds, that by not performing their promises to the Church, they violate and nullify their first faith given in baptism; one of the things contained in this first faith being, that every one should correspond to his calling. Unless you choose rather to interpret that, having lost their modesty, they afterwards cast off all care of decency, prostituting themselves to all kinds of lasciviousness and pertness, leading licentious and dissolute lives, than which nothing can less become Christian women. I am much pleased with this exposition. Our answer then is, that those widows who were admitted to a public ministry came under an obligation of perpetual celibacy, and hence we easily understand how, when they married, they threw off all modesty, and became more insolent than became Christian women that in this way they not only sinned by violating the faith given to the Church, but revolted from the common rule of pious women. But, first, I deny that they had any other reason for professing celibacy than just because marriage was altogether inconsistent with the function which they undertook. Hence they bound themselves to celibacy only in so far as the nature of their function required. Secondly, I do not admit that they were bound to celibacy in such a sense that it was not better for them to marry than to suffer by the incitements of the flesh, and fall into uncleanness. Thirdly, I hold that what Paul enjoined was in the common case free from danger, because he orders the selection to be made from those who, contented with one marriage, had already given proof of continence. Our only reason for disapproving of the vow of celibacy is, because it is improperly regarded as an act of worship, and is rashly undertaken by persons who have not the power of keeping it.

19. But what ground can there be for applying this passage to nuns? For deaconesses were appointed, not to soothe God by chantings or unintelligible murmurs, and spend the rest of their time in idleness; but to perform a public ministry of the Church toward the poor, and to labour with all zeal, assiduity, and diligence, in offices of charity. They did not vow celibacy, that they might thereafter exhibit abstinence from marriage as a kind of worship rendered to God, but only that they might be freer from encumbrance in executing their office. In fine, they did not vow on attaining adolescence, or in the bloom of life, and so afterwards learn, by too late experience, over what a precipice they had plunged themselves, but after they were thought to have surmounted all danger, they took a vow not less safe than holy. But not to press the two former points, I say that it was unlawful to allow women to take a vow of continence before their sixtieth year, since the apostle admits such only, and enjoins the younger to marry and beget children. Therefore, it is impossible, on any ground, to excuse the deduction, first of twelve, then of twenty, and, lastly, of thirty years. Still less possible is it to tolerate the case of miserable girls, who, before they have reached an age at which they can know themselves, or have any experience of their character, are not only induced by fraud, but compelled by force and threats, to entangle themselves in these accursed snares. I will not enter at length into a refutation of the other two vows. This only I say, that besides involving (as matters stand in the present day) not a few superstitions, they seem to be purposely framed in such a manner, as to make those who take them mock God and men. But lest we should seem, with too malignant feeling, to attack every particular point, we will be contented with the general refutation which has been given above.

20. The nature of the vows which are legitimate and acceptable to God, I think I have sufficiently explained. Yet, because some ill-informed and timid consciences, even when a vow displeases, and is condemned, nevertheless hesitate as to the obligation, and are grievously tormented, shuddering at the thought of violating a pledge given to God, and, on the other hand, fearing to sin more by keeping it,—we must here come to their aid, and enable them to escape from this difficulty. And to take away all scruple at once, I say that all vows not legitimate, and not duly conceived, as they are of no account with God, should be regarded by us as null. (See Calv. ad Concil. Trident.) For if, in human contracts, those promises only are binding in which he with whom we contract wishes to have us bound, it is absurd to say that we are bound to perform things which God does not at all require of us, especially since our works can only be right when they please God, and have the testimony of our consciences that they do

please him. For it always remains fixed, that "whatsoever is not of faith is sin" (Rom. 14:23). By this Paul means, that any work undertaken in doubt is vicious, because at the root of all good works lies faith, which assures us that they are acceptable to God. Therefore, if Christian men may not attempt anything without this assurance, why, if they have undertaken anything rashly through ignorance, may they not afterwards be freed, and desist from their error? Since vows rashly undertaken are of this description, they not only oblige not, but must necessarily be rescinded. What, then, when they are not only of no estimation in the sight of God, but are even an abomination, as has already been demonstrated? It is needless farther to discuss a point which does not require it. To appease pious consciences, and free them from all doubt, this one argument seems to me sufficient—viz. that all works whatsoever which flow not from a pure fountain, and are not directed to a proper end, are repudiated by God, and so repudiated, that he no less forbids us to continue than to begin them. Hence it follows, that vows dictated by error and superstition are of no weight with God, and ought to be abandoned by us.

21. He who understands this solution is furnished with the means of repelling the calumnies of the wicked against those who withdraw from monasticism to some honest kind of livelihood. They are grievously charged with having perjured themselves, and broken their faith, because they have broken the bond (vulgarly supposed to be indissoluble) by which they had bound themselves to God and the Church. But I say, first, there is no bond when that which man confirms God abrogates; and, secondly, even granting that they were bound when they remained entangled in ignorance and error, now, since they have been enlightened by the knowledge of the truth, I hold that they are, at the same time, free by the grace of Christ. For if such is the efficacy of the cross of Christ, that it frees us from the curse of the divine law by which we were held bound, how much more must it rescue us from extraneous chains, which are nothing but the wily nets of Satan? There can be no doubt, therefore, that all on whom Christ shines with the light of his Gospel, he frees from all the snares in which they had entangled themselves through superstition. At the same time, they have another defence if they were unfit for celibacy. For if an impossible vow is certain destruction to the soul, which God wills to be saved and not destroyed, it follows that it ought by no means to be adhered to. Now, how impossible the vow of continence is to those who have not received it by special gift, we have shown, and experience, even were I silent, declares: while the great obscenity with which almost all monasteries teem is a thing not unknown. If any seem more decent and modest than others, they are not, however, chaste. The sin of unchastity urges, and lurks within. Thus it is that God, by fearful examples, punishes the audacity of men, when, unmindful of their infirmity, they, against nature, affect that which has been denied to them, and despising the remedies which the Lord has placed in their hands, are confident in their ability to overcome the disease of incontinence by contumacious obstinacy. For what other name can we give it, when a man, admonished of his need of marriage, and of the remedy with which the Lord has thereby furnished, not only despises it, but binds himself by an oath to despise it?

CHAPTER 14

OF THE SACRAMENTS.

This chapter consists of two principal parts,—I. Of sacraments in general. The sum of the doctrine stated, sec. 1–6. Two classes of opponents to be guarded against—viz. those who undervalue the power of the sacraments, sec. 7–13; and those who attribute too much to the sacraments, sec. 14–17. II. Of the sacraments in particular, both of the Old and the New Testament. Their scope and meaning. Refutation of those who have either too high or too low ideas of the sacraments.

Sections:

1. Of the sacraments in general. A sacrament defined.
2. Meaning of the word sacrament.
3. Definition explained. Why God seals his promises to us by sacraments.
4. The word which ought to accompany the element, that the sacrament may be complete.
5. Error of those who attempt to separate the word, or promise of God, from the element.
6. Why sacraments are called Signs of the Covenant.
7. They are such signs, though the wicked should receive them, but are signs of grace only to believers.
8. Objections to this view answered.
9. No secret virtue in the sacraments. Their whole efficacy depends on the inward operation of the Spirit.
10. Objections answered. Illustrated by a simile.
11. Of the increase of faith by the preaching of the word.

12. In what way, and how far, the sacraments are confirmations of our faith.

13. Some regard the sacraments as mere signs. This view refuted.

14. Some again attribute too much to the sacraments. Refutation.

15. Refutation confirmed by a passage from Augustine.

16. Previous views more fully explained.

17. The matter of the sacrament always present when the sacrament is duly administered.

18. Extensive meaning of the term sacrament.

19. The ordinary sacraments in the Church. How necessary they are.

20. The sacraments of the Old and of the New Testament. The end of both the same —viz. to lead us to Christ.

21. This apparent in the sacraments of the Old Testament.

22. Apparent also in the sacraments of the New Testament.

23. Impious doctrine of the Schoolmen as to the difference between the Old and the New Testaments.

24. Scholastic objection answered.

25. Another objection answered.

26. Sacraments of the New Testament sometimes excessively extolled by early Theologians. Their meaning explained.

1. Akin to the preaching of the gospel, we have another help to our faith in the sacraments, in regard to which, it greatly concerns us that some sure doctrine should be delivered, informing us both of the end for which they were instituted, and of their present use. First, we must attend to what a sacrament is. It seems to me, then, a simple and appropriate definition to say, that it is an external sign, by which the Lord seals on our consciences his promises of good-will toward us, in order to sustain the weakness of our faith, and we in our turn testify our piety towards him, both before himself, and before angels as well as men. We may also define more briefly by calling it a testimony of the divine favour toward us, confirmed by an external sign, with a corresponding attestation of our faith towards Him. You may make your choice of these definitions, which in meaning differ not from that of Augustine, which defines a sacrament to be a visible sign of a sacred thing, or a visible form of an invisible grace, but does not contain a better or surer explanation. As its brevity makes it somewhat obscure, and thereby misleads the more illiterate, I wished to remove all doubt, and make the definition fuller by stating it at greater length.

2. The reason why the ancients used the term in this sense is not obscure. The old interpreter, whenever he wished to render the Greek term μυστήριον into Latin, especially when it was used with reference to divine things, used the word *sacramentum*. Thus, in Ephesians, "Having made known unto us the mystery (*sacramentum*) of his will;" and again, "If ye have heard of the dispensation of the grace of God, which is given me to you-wards, how that by revelation he made known unto me the mystery" (*sacramentum*) (Eph. 1:9; 3:2). In the Colossians, "Even the mystery which hath been hid from ages and from generations, but is now made manifest to his saints, to whom God would make known what is the riches of the glory of this mystery" (*sacramentum*) (Col. 1:26). Also in the First Epistle to Timothy, "Without controversy, great is the mystery (*sacramentum*) of godliness: God was manifest in the flesh" (1 Tim. 3:16). He was unwilling to use the word *arcanum* (secret), lest the word should seem beneath the magnitude of the thing meant. When the thing, therefore, was sacred and secret, he used the term *sacramentum*. In this sense it frequently occurs in ecclesiastical writers. And it is well known, that what the Latins call *sacramenta*, the Greeks call μυστήρια (mysteries). The sameness of meaning removes all dispute. Hence it is that the term was applied to those signs which gave an august representation of things spiritual and sublime. This is also observed by Augustine, "It were tedious to discourse of the variety of signs; those which relate to divine things are called sacraments" (August. Ep. 5. ad Marcell.).

3. From the definition which we have given, we perceive that there never is a sacrament without an antecedent promise, the sacrament being added as a kind of appendix, with the view of confirming and sealing the promise, and giving a better attestation, or rather, in a manner, confirming it. In this way God provides first for our ignorance and sluggishness, and, secondly, for our infirmity; and yet, properly speaking, it does not so much confirm his word as establish us in the faith of it. For the truth of God is in itself sufficiently stable and certain, and cannot receive a better confirmation from any other quarter than from itself. But as our faith is slender and weak, so if it be not propped up on every side, and supported by all kinds of means, it is forthwith shaken and tossed to and fro, wavers, and even falls. And here, indeed, our merciful Lord, with boundless condescension, so accommodates

himself to our capacity, that seeing how from our animal nature we are always creeping on the ground, and cleaving to the flesh, having no thought of what is spiritual, and not even forming an idea of it, he declines not by means of these earthly elements to lead us to himself, and even in the flesh to exhibit a mirror of spiritual blessings. For, as Chrysostom says (Hom. 60, ad Popul.). "Were we incorporeal, he would give us these things in a naked and incorporeal form. Now because our souls are implanted in bodies, he delivers spiritual things under things visible. Not that the qualities which are set before us in the sacraments are inherent in the nature of the things, but God gives them this signification."

4. This is commonly expressed by saying that a sacrament consists of the word and the external sign. By the word we ought to understand not one which, muttered without meaning and without faith, by its sound merely, as by a magical incantation, has the effect of consecrating the element, but one which, preached, makes us understand what the visible sign means. The thing, therefore, which was frequently done, under the tyranny of the Pope, was not free from great profanation of the mystery, for they deemed it sufficient if the priest muttered the formula of consecration, while the people, without understanding, looked stupidly on. Nay, this was done for the express purpose of preventing any instruction from thereby reaching the people: for all was said in Latin to illiterate hearers. Superstition afterwards was carried to such a height, that the consecration was thought not to be duly performed except in a low grumble, which few could hear. Very different is the doctrine of Augustine concerning the sacramental word. "Let the word be added to the element, and it will become a sacrament. For whence can there be so much virtue in water as to touch the body and cleanse the heart, unless by the agency of the word, and this not because it is said, but because it is believed? For even in the word the transient sound is one thing, the permanent power another. This is the word of faith which we preach says the Apostle" (Rom. 10:8). Hence, in the Acts of the Apostles, we have the expression, "Purify their hearts by faith" (Acts 15:9). And the Apostle Peter says, "The like figure whereunto even baptism doth now save us (not the putting away of the filth of the flesh, but the answer of a good conscience)" (1 Pet. 3:21). "This is the word of faith which we preach: by which word doubtless baptism also, in order that it may be able to cleanse, is consecrated" (August. Hom. in Joann. 13). You see how he requires preaching to the production of faith. And we need not labour to prove this, since there is not the least room for doubt as to what Christ did, and commanded us to do, as to what the apostles followed, and a purer Church observed. Nay, it is known that, from the very beginning of the world, whenever God offered any sign to the holy Patriarchs, it was inseparably attached to doctrine, without which our senses would gaze bewildered on an unmeaning object. Therefore, when we hear mention made of the sacramental word, let us understand the promise which, proclaimed aloud by the minister, leads the people by the hand to that to which the sign tends and directs us.

5. Nor are those to be listened to who oppose this view with a more subtle than solid dilemma. They argue thus: We either know that the word of God which precedes the sacrament is the true will of God, or we do not know it. If we know it, we learn nothing new from the sacrament which succeeds. If we do not know it, we cannot learn it from the sacrament, whose whole efficacy depends on the word. Our brief reply is: The seals which are affixed to diplomas, and other public deeds, are nothing considered in themselves, and would be affixed to no purpose if nothing was written on the parchment, and yet this does not prevent them from sealing and confirming when they are appended to writings. It cannot be alleged that this comparison is a recent fiction of our own, since Paul himself used it, terming *circumcision a seal*(Rom. 4:11), where he expressly maintains that the circumcision of Abraham was not for justification, but was an attestation to the covenant, by the faith of which he had been previously justified. And how, pray, can any one be greatly offended when we teach that the promise is sealed by the sacrament, since it is plain, from the promises themselves, that one promise confirms another? The clearer any evidence is, the fitter is it to support our faith. But sacraments bring with them the clearest promises, and, when compared with the word, have this peculiarity, that they represent promises to the life, as if painted in a picture. Nor ought we to be moved by an objection founded on the distinction between sacraments and the seals of documents—viz. that since both consist of the carnal elements of this world, the former cannot be sufficient or adequate to seal the promises of God, which are spiritual and eternal, though the latter may be employed to seal the edicts of princes concerning fleeting and fading things. But the believer, when the sacraments are presented to his eye, does not stop short at the carnal spectacle, but by the steps of analogy which I have indicated, rises with pious consideration to the sublime mysteries which lie hidden in the sacraments.

6. As the Lord calls his promises covenants (Gen.

6:18; 9:9; 17:2), and sacraments signs of the covenants, so something similar may be inferred from human covenants. What could the slaughter of a hog effect, unless words were interposed or rather preceded? Swine are often killed without any interior or occult mystery. What could be gained by pledging the right hand, since hands are not unfrequently joined in giving battle? But when words have preceded, then by such symbols of covenant sanction is given to laws, though previously conceived, digested, and enacted by words. Sacraments, therefore, are exercises which confirm our faith in the word of God; and because we are carnal, they are exhibited under carnal objects, that thus they may train us in accommodation to our sluggish capacity, just as nurses lead children by the hand. And hence Augustine calls a sacrament a *visible word* (August. in Joann. Hom. 89), because it represents the promises of God as in a picture, and places them in our view in a graphic bodily form (August. cont. Faust. Lib. 19). We might refer to other similitudes, by which sacraments are more plainly designated, as when they are called the pillars of our faith. For just as a building stands and leans on its foundation, and yet is rendered more stable when supported by pillars, so faith leans on the word of God as its proper foundation, and yet when sacraments are added leans more firmly, as if resting on pillars. Or we may call them mirrors, in which we may contemplate the riches of the grace which God bestows upon us. For then, as has been said, he manifests himself to us in as far as our dulness can enable us to recognise him, and testifies his love and kindness to us more expressly than by word.

7. It is irrational to contend that sacraments are not manifestations of divine grace toward us, because they are held forth to the ungodly also, who, however, so far from experiencing God to be more propitious to them, only incur greater condemnation. By the same reasoning, the gospel will be no manifestation of the grace of God, because it is spurned by many who hear it; nor will Christ himself be a manifestation of grace, because of the many by whom he was seen and known, very few received him. Something similar may be seen in public enactments. A great part of the body of the people deride and evade the authenticating seal, though they know it was employed by their sovereign to confirm his will; others trample it under foot, as a matter by no means appertaining to them; while others even execrate it: so that, seeing the condition of the two things to be alike, the appropriateness of the comparison which I made above ought to be more readily allowed. It is certain, therefore, that the Lord offers us his mercy, and a pledge of his grace, both in his sacred word and in the sacraments; but it is not apprehended save by those who receive the word and sacraments with firm faith: in like manner as Christ, though offered and held forth for salvation to all, is not, however, acknowledged and received by all. Augustine, when intending to intimate this, said that the efficacy of the word is produced in the sacrament, *not because it is spoken, but because it is believed.* Hence Paul, addressing believers, includes communion with Christ, in the sacraments, as when he says, "As many of you as have been baptized into Christ have put on Christ" (Gal. 3:27). Again, "For by one Spirit we are all baptized into one body" (1 Cor. 12:13). But when he speaks of a preposterous use of the sacraments, he attributes nothing more to them than to frigid, empty figures; thereby intimating, that however the ungodly and hypocrites may, by their perverseness, either suppress, or obscure, or impede the effect of divine grace in the sacraments, that does not prevent them, where and whenever God is so pleased, from giving a true evidence of communion with Christ, or prevent them from exhibiting, and the Spirit of God from performing, the very thing which they promise. We conclude, therefore, that the sacraments are truly termed evidences of divine grace, and, as it were, seals of the good-will which he entertains toward us. They, by sealing it to us, sustain, nourish, confirm, and increase our faith. The objections usually urged against this view are frivolous and weak. They say that our faith, if it is good, cannot be made better; for there is no faith save that which leans unshakingly, firmly, and undividedly, on the mercy of God. It had been better for the objectors to pray, with the apostles, "Lord, increase our faith" (Luke 17:5), than confidently to maintain a perfection of faith which none of the sons of men ever attained, none ever shall attain, in this life. Let them explain what kind of faith his was who said, "Lord, I believe; help thou mine unbelief" (Mark 9:24). That faith, though only commenced, was good, and might, by the removal of the unbelief, be made better. But there is no better argument to refute them than their own consciousness. For if they confess themselves sinners (this, whether they will or not, they cannot deny), then they must of necessity impute this very quality to the imperfection of their faith.

8. But Philip, they say, replied to the eunuch who asked to be baptized, "If thou believest with all thine heart thou mayest" (Acts 8:37). What room is there for a confirmation of baptism when faith fills the whole heart? I, in my turn, ask them, Do they not feel that a good part of their

heart is void of faith—do they not perceive new additions to it every day? There was one who boasted that he grew old while learning. Thrice miserable, then, are we Christians if we grow old without making progress, we whose faith ought to advance through every period of life until it grow up into a perfect man (Eph. 4:13). In this passage, therefore, to believe *with the whole heart*, is not to believe Christ perfectly, but only to embrace him sincerely with heart and soul; not to be filled with him, but with ardent affection to hunger and thirst, and sigh after him. It is usual in Scripture to say that a thing is done with the whole heart, when it is done sincerely and cordially. Of this description are the following passages:—"With my whole heart have I sought thee" (Ps. 119:10); "I will confess unto thee with my whole heart," &c. In like manner, when the fraudulent and deceitful are rebuked, it is said "with flattering lips, and with a double heart, do they speak" (Ps. 12:2). The objectors next add—"If faith is increased by means of the sacraments, the Holy Spirit is given in vain, seeing it is his office to begin, sustain, and consummate our faith." I admit, indeed, that faith is the proper and entire work of the Holy Spirit, enlightened by whom we recognise God and the treasures of his grace, and without whose illumination our mind is so blind that it can see nothing, so stupid that it has no relish for spiritual things. But for the one Divine blessing which they proclaim we count three. For, first, the Lord teaches and trains us by his word; next, he confirms us by his sacraments; lastly, he illumines our mind by the light of his Holy Spirit, and opens up an entrance into our hearts for his word and sacraments, which would otherwise only strike our ears, and fall upon our sight, but by no means affect us inwardly.

9. Wherefore, with regard to the increase and confirmation of faith, I would remind the reader (though I think I have already expressed it in unambiguous terms), that in assigning this office to the sacraments, it is not as if I thought that there is a kind of secret efficacy perpetually inherent in them, by which they can of themselves promote or strengthen faith, but because our Lord has instituted them for the express purpose of helping to establish and increase our faith. The sacraments duly perform their office only when accompanied by the Spirit, the internal Master, whose energy alone penetrates the heart, stirs up the affections, and procures access for the sacraments into our souls. If he is wanting, the sacraments can avail us no more than the sun shining on the eyeballs of the blind, or sounds uttered in the ears of the deaf. Wherefore, in distributing between the Spirit and the sacraments, I ascribe the whole energy to him, and leave only a ministry to them; this ministry, without the agency of the Spirit, is empty and frivolous, but when he acts within, and exerts his power, it is replete with energy. It is now clear in what way, according to this view, a pious mind is confirmed in faith by means of the sacraments—viz. in the same way in which the light of the sun is seen by the eye, and the sound of the voice heard by the ear; the former of which would not be at all affected by the light unless it had a pupil on which the light might fall; nor the latter reached by any sound, however loud, were it not naturally adapted for hearing. But if it is true, as has been explained, that in the eye it is the power of vision which enables it to see the light, and in the ear the power of hearing which enables it to perceive the voice, and that in our hearts it is the work of the Holy Spirit to commence, maintain, cherish, and establish faith, then it follows, both that the sacraments do not avail one iota without the energy of the Holy Spirit; and that yet in hearts previously taught by that preceptor, there is nothing to prevent the sacraments from strengthening and increasing faith. There is only this difference, that the faculty of seeing and hearing is naturally implanted in the eye and ear; whereas, Christ acts in our minds above the measure of nature by special grace.

10. In this way, also, we dispose of certain objections by which some anxious minds are annoyed. If we ascribe either an increase or confirmation of faith to creatures, injustice is done to the Spirit of God, who alone ought to be regarded as its author. But we do not rob him of the merit of confirming and increasing faith; nay, rather, we maintain that that which confirms and increases faith, is nothing else than the preparing of our minds by his internal illumination to receive that confirmation which is set forth by the sacraments. But if the subject is still obscure, it will be made plain by the following similitude: Were you to begin to persuade a person by word to do something, you would think of all the arguments by which he may be brought over to your view, and in a manner compelled to serve your purpose. But nothing is gained if the individual himself possess not a clear and acute judgment, by which he may be able to weigh the value of your arguments; if, moreover, he is not of a docile disposition, and ready to listen to doctrine; if, in fine, he has no such idea of your faith and prudence as in a manner to prejudice him in your favour, and secure his assent. For there are many obstinate spirits who are not to be bent by any arguments; and where faith is suspected, or authority contemned, little progress is made even with

the docile. On the other hand, when opposite feelings exist, the result will be, that the person whose interests you are consulting will acquiesce in the very counsels which he would otherwise have derided. The same work is performed in us by the Spirit. That the word may not fall upon our ear, or the sacraments be presented to our eye in vain, he shows that it is God who there speaks to us, softens our obdurate hearts, and frames them to the obedience which is due to his word; in short, transmits those external words and sacraments from the ear to the soul. Both word and sacraments, therefore, confirm our faith, bringing under view the kind intentions of our heavenly Father, in the knowledge of which the whole assurance of our faith depends, and by which its strength is increased; and the Spirit also confirms our faith when, by engraving that assurance on our minds, he renders it effectual. Meanwhile, it is easy for the Father of lights, in like manner as he illumines the bodily eye by the rays of the sun, to illumine our minds by the sacraments, as by a kind of intermediate brightness.

11. This property our Lord showed to belong to the external word, when, in the parable, he compared it to seed (Mt. 13:4; Luke 8:15). For as the seed, when it falls on a deserted and neglected part of the field, can do nothing but die, but when thrown into ground properly laboured and cultivated, will yield a hundred-fold; so the word of God, when addressed to any stubborn spirit, will remain without fruit, as if thrown upon the barren waste, but when it meets with a soul which the hand of the heavenly Spirit has subdued, will be most fruitful. But if the case of the seed and of the word is the same, and from the seed corn can grow and increase, and attain to maturity, why may not faith also take its beginning, increase, and completion from the word? Both things are admirably explained by Paul in different passages. For when he would remind the Corinthians how God had given effect to his labours, he boasts that he possessed the ministry of the Spirit (1 Cor. 2:4); just as if his preaching were inseparably connected with the power of the Holy Spirit, in inwardly enlightening the mind, and stimulating it. But in another passage, when he would remind them what the power of the word is in itself, when preached by man, he compares ministers to husbandmen, who, after they have expended labour and industry in cultivating the ground, have nothing more that they can do. For what would ploughing, and sowing, and watering avail, unless that which was sown should, by the kindness of Heaven, vegetate? Wherefore he concludes, that he that planteth, and he that watereth is nothing, but that the whole is to be ascribed to God, who alone gives the increase. The apostles, therefore, exert the power of the Spirit in their preaching, inasmuch as God uses them as instruments which he has ordained for the unfolding of his spiritual grace. Still, however, we must not lose sight of the distinction, but remember what man is able of himself to do, and what is peculiar to God.

12. The sacraments are confirmations of our faith in such a sense, that the Lord, sometimes, when he sees meet to withdraw our assurance of the things which he had promised in the sacraments, takes away the sacraments themselves. When he deprives Adam of the gift of immortality, and expels him from the garden, "lest he put forth his hand and take also of the tree of life, and live for ever" (Gen. 3:22). What is this we hear? Could that fruit have restored Adam to the immortality from which he had already fallen? By no means. It is just as if he had said, Lest he indulge in vain confidence, if allowed to retain the symbol of my promise, let that be withdrawn which might give him some hope of immortality. On this ground, when the apostle urges the Ephesians to remember, that they "were without Christ, being aliens from the commonwealth of Israel, and strangers from the covenants of promise, having no hope, and without God in the world" (Eph. 2:12), he says that they were not partakers of circumcision. He thus intimates metonymically, that all were excluded from the promise who had not received the badge of the promise. To the other objection—viz. that when so much power is attributed to creatures, the glory of God is bestowed upon them, and thereby impaired—it is obvious to reply, that we attribute no power to the creatures. All we say is, that God uses the means and instruments which he sees to be expedient, in order that all things may be subservient to his glory, he being the Lord and disposer of all. Therefore, as by bread and other aliment he feeds our bodies, as by the sun he illumines, and by fire gives warmth to the world, and yet bread, sun, and fire are nothing, save inasmuch as they are instruments under which he dispenses his blessings to us; so in like manner he spiritually nourishes our faith by means of the sacraments, whose only office is to make his promises visible to our eye, or rather, to be pledges of his promises. And as it is our duty in regard to the other creatures which the divine liberality and kindness has destined for our use, and by whose instrumentality he bestows the gifts of his goodness upon us, to put no confidence in them, nor to admire and extol them as the causes of our mercies; so neither ought our confidence to be fixed on the sacraments, nor ought the glory of God

to be transferred to them, but passing beyond them all, our faith and confession should rise to Him who is the Author of the sacraments and of all things.

13. There is nothing in the argument which some found on the very term *sacrament*. This term, they say, while it has many significations in approved authors, has only one which is applicable to signs—namely, when it is used for the formal oath which the soldier gives to his commander on entering the service. For as by that military oath recruits bind themselves to be faithful to their commander, and make a profession of military service; so by our signs we acknowledge Christ to be our commander, and declare that we serve under his standard. They add similitudes, in order to make the matter more clear. As the toga distinguished the Romans from the Greeks, who wore the pallium; and as the different orders of Romans were distinguished from each other by their peculiar insignia; *e. g.*, the senatorial from the equestrian by purple, and crescent shoes, and the equestrian from the plebeian by a ring, so we wear our symbols to distinguish us from the profane. But it is sufficiently clear from what has been said above, that the ancients, in giving the name of sacraments to signs, had not at all attended to the use of the term by Latin writers, but had, for the sake of convenience, given it this new signification, as a means of simply expressing sacred signs. But were we to argue more subtilely, we might say that they seem to have given the term this signification in a manner analogous to that in which they employ the term faith in the sense in which it is now used. For while faith is truth in performing promises, they have used it for the certainty or firm persuasion which is had of the truth. In this way, while a sacrament is the act of the soldier when he vows obedience to his commander, they made it the act by which the commander admits soldiers to the ranks. For in the sacraments the Lord promises that he will be our God, and we that we will be his people. But we omit such subtleties, since I think I have shown by arguments abundantly plain, that all which ancient writers intended was to intimate, that sacraments are the signs of sacred and spiritual things. The similitudes which are drawn from external objects (chap. 15 sec. 1), we indeed admit; but we approve not, that that which is a secondary thing in sacraments is by them made the first, and indeed the only thing. The first thing is, that they may contribute to our faith in God; the secondary, that they may attest our confession before men. These similitudes are applicable to the secondary reason. Let it therefore remain a fixed point, that mysteries would be frigid (as has been seen) were they not helps to our faith, and adjuncts annexed to doctrine for the same end and purpose.

14. On the other hand, it is to be observed, that as these objectors impair the force, and altogether overthrow the use of the sacraments, so there are others who ascribe to the sacraments a kind of secret virtue, which is nowhere said to have been implanted in them by God. By this error the more simple and unwary are perilously deceived, while they are taught to seek the gifts of God where they cannot possibly be found, and are insensibly withdrawn from God, so as to embrace instead of his truth mere vanity. For the schools of the Sophists have taught with general consent that the sacraments of the new law, in other words, those now in use in the Christian Church, justify, and confer grace, provided only that we do not interpose the obstacle of mortal sin. It is impossible to describe how fatal and pestilential this sentiment is, and the more so, that for many ages it has, to the great loss of the Church, prevailed over a considerable part of the world. It is plainly of the devil: for, first, in promising a righteousness without faith, it drives souls headlong on destruction; secondly, in deriving a cause of righteousness from the sacraments, it entangles miserable minds, already of their own accord too much inclined to the earth, in a superstitious idea, which makes them acquiesce in the spectacle of a corporeal object rather than in God himself. I wish we had not such experience of both evils as to make it altogether unnecessary to give a lengthened proof of them. For what is a sacrament received without faith, but most certain destruction to the Church? For, seeing that nothing is to be expected beyond the promise, and the promise no less denounces wrath to the unbeliever than offers grace to the believer, it is an error to suppose that anything more is conferred by the sacraments than is offered by the word of God, and obtained by true faith. From this another thing follows—viz. that assurance of salvation does not depend on participation in the sacraments, as if justification consisted in it. This, which is treasured up in Christ alone, we know to be communicated, not less by the preaching of the Gospel than by the seal of the sacrament, and may be completely enjoyed without this seal. So true is it, as Augustine declares, that there may be invisible sanctification without a visible sign, and, on the other hand, a visible sign without true sanctification (August. de Quæst. Vet. Test. Lib. 3). For, as he elsewhere says, "Men put on Christ, sometimes to the extent of partaking in the sacrament, and sometimes to the extent of holiness of life" (August. de Bapt. Cont. Donat. cap. 24). The former

may be common to the good and the bad, the latter is peculiar to the good.

15. Hence the distinction, if properly understood, repeatedly made by Augustine between the *sacrament* and the *matter of the sacrament*. For he does not mean merely that the figure and truth are therein contained, but that they do not so cohere as not to be separable, and that in this connection it is always necessary to distinguish the thing from the sign, so as not to transfer to the one what belongs to the other. Augustine speaks of the separation when he says that in the elect alone the sacraments accomplish what they represent (Augustin. de Bapt. Parvul.). Again, when speaking of the Jews, he says, "Though the sacraments were common to all, the grace was not common: yet grace is the virtue of the sacraments. Thus, too, the laver of regeneration is now common to all, but the grace by which the members of Christ are regenerated with their head is not common to all" (August. in Ps. 78). Again, in another place, speaking of the Lord's Supper, he says, "We also this day receive visible food; but the sacrament is one thing, the virtue of the sacrament another. Why is it that many partake of the altar and die, and die by partaking? For even the cup of the Lord was poison to Judas, not because he received what was evil, but being wicked he wickedly received what was good" (August. in Joann. Hom. 26). A little after, he says, "The sacrament of this thing, that is, of the unity of the body and blood of Christ, is in some places prepared every day, in others at certain intervals at the Lord's table, which is partaken by some unto life, by others unto destruction. But the thing itself, of which there is a sacrament, is life to all, and destruction to none who partake of it." Some time before he had said, "He who may have eaten shall not die, but he must be one who attains to the virtue of the sacrament, not to the visible sacrament; who eats inwardly, not outwardly; who eats with the heart, and not with the teeth." Here you are uniformly told that a sacrament is so separated from the reality by the unworthiness of the partaker, that nothing remains but an empty and useless figure. Now, in order that you may have not a sign devoid of truth, but the thing with the sign, the Word which is included in it must be apprehended by faith. Thus, in so far as by means of the sacraments you will profit in the communion of Christ, will you derive advantage from them.

16. If this is obscure from brevity, I will explain it more at length. I say that Christ is the matter, or, if you rather choose it, the substance of all the sacraments, since in him they have their whole solidity, and out of him promise nothing. Hence the less toleration is due to the error of Peter Lombard, who distinctly makes them causes of the righteousness and salvation of which they are parts (Sent. Lib. 4 Dist. 1). Bidding adieu to all other causes of righteousness which the wit of man devises, our duty is to hold by this only. In so far, therefore, as we are assisted by their instrumentality in cherishing, confirming, and increasing the true knowledge of Christ, so as both to possess him more fully, and enjoy him in all his richness, so far are they effectual in regard to us. This is the case when that which is there offered is received by us in true faith. Therefore, you will ask, Do the wicked, by their ingratitude, make the ordinance of God fruitless and void? I answer, that what I have said is not to be understood as if the power and truth of the sacrament depended on the condition or pleasure of him who receives it. That which God instituted continues firm, and retains its nature, however men may vary; but since it is one thing to offer, and another to receive, there is nothing to prevent a symbol, consecrated by the word of the Lord, from being truly what it is said to be, and preserving its power, though it may at the same time confer no benefit on the wicked and ungodly. This question is well solved by Augustine in a few words: "If you receive carnally, it ceases not to be spiritual, but it is not spiritual to you" (August. Hom. in Joann. 26). But as Augustine shows in the above passages that a sacrament is a thing of no value if separated from its truth; so also, when the two are conjoined, he reminds us that it is necessary to distinguish, in order that we may not cleave too much to the external sign. "As it is servile weakness to follow the latter, and take the signs for the thing signified, so to interpret the signs as of no use is an extravagant error" (August. de Doct. Christ. Lib. 3 c. 9). He mentions two faults which are here to be avoided; the one when we receive the signs as if they had been given in vain, and by malignantly destroying or impairing their secret meanings, prevent them from yielding any fruit—the other, when by not raising our minds beyond the visible sign, we attribute to it blessings which are conferred upon us by Christ alone, and that by means of the Holy Spirit, who makes us to be partakers of Christ, external signs assisting if they invite us to Christ; whereas, when wrested to any other purpose, their whole utility is overthrown.

17. Wherefore, let it be a fixed point, that the office of the sacraments differs not from the word of God; and this is to hold forth and offer Christ to us, and, in him, the treasures of heavenly grace. They confer nothing, and avail nothing, if not received in faith, just as wine and

oil, or any other liquor, however large the quantity which you pour out, will run away and perish unless there be an open vessel to receive it. When the vessel is not open, though it may be sprinkled all over, it will nevertheless remain entirely empty. We must be aware of being led into a kindred error by the terms, somewhat too extravagant, which ancient Christian writers have employed in extolling the dignity of the sacraments. We must not suppose that there is some latent virtue inherent in the sacraments by which they, in themselves, confer the gifts of the Holy Spirit upon us, in the same way in which wine is drunk out of a cup, since the only office divinely assigned them is to attest and ratify the benevolence of the Lord towards us; and they avail no farther than accompanied by the Holy Spirit to open our minds and hearts, and make us capable of receiving this testimony, in which various distinguished graces are clearly manifested. For the sacraments, as we lately observed (chap. 13 sec. 6; and 14 sec. 6, 7), are to us what messengers of good news are to men, or earnests in ratifying pactions. They do not of themselves bestow any grace, but they announce and manifest it, and, like earnests and badges, give a ratification of the gifts which the divine liberality has bestowed upon us. The Holy Spirit, whom the sacraments do not bring promiscuously to all, but whom the Lord specially confers on his people, brings the gifts of God along with him, makes way for the sacraments, and causes them to bear fruit. But though we deny not that God, by the immediate agency of his Spirit, countenances his own ordinance, preventing the administration of the sacraments which he has instituted from being fruitless and vain, still we maintain that the internal grace of the Spirit, as it is distinct from the external ministration, ought to be viewed and considered separately. God, therefore, truly performs whatever he promises and figures by signs; nor are the signs without effect, for they prove that he is their true and faithful author. The only question here is, whether the Lord works by proper and intrinsic virtue (as it is called), or resigns his office to external symbols? We maintain, that whatever organs he employs detract nothing from his primary operation. In this doctrine of the sacraments, their dignity is highly extolled, their use plainly shown, their utility sufficiently proclaimed, and moderation in all things duly maintained; so that nothing is attributed to them which ought not to be attributed, and nothing denied them which they ought to possess. Meanwhile, we get rid of that fiction by which the cause of justification and the power of the Holy Spirit are included in elements as vessels and vehicles, and the special power which was overlooked is distinctly explained. Here, also, we ought to observe, that what the minister figures and attests by outward action, God performs inwardly, lest that which God claims for himself alone should be ascribed to mortal man. This Augustine is careful to observe: "How does both God and Moses sanctify? Not Moses for God, but Moses by visible sacraments through his ministry, God by invisible grace through the Holy Spirit. Herein is the whole fruit of visible sacraments; for what do these visible sacraments avail without that sanctification of invisible grace?"

18. The term sacrament, in the view we have hitherto taken of it, includes, generally, all the signs which God ever commanded men to use, that he might make them sure and confident of the truth of his promises. These he was pleased sometimes to place in natural objects—sometimes to exhibit in miracles. Of the former class we have an example, in his giving the tree of life to Adam and Eve, as an earnest of immortality, that they might feel confident of the promise as often as they ate of the fruit. Another example was, when he gave the bow in the cloud to Noah and his posterity, as a memorial that he would not again destroy the earth by a flood. These were to Adam and Noah as sacraments: not that the tree could give Adam and Eve the immortality which it could not give to itself; or the bow (which is only a reflection of the solar rays on the opposite clouds) could have the effect of confining the waters; but they had a mark engraven on them by the word of God, to be proofs and seals of his covenant. The tree was previously a tree, and the bow a bow; but when they were inscribed with the word of God, a new form was given to them: they began to be what they previously were not. Lest any one suppose that these things were said in vain, the bow is even in the present day a witness to us of the covenant which God made with Noah (Calv. in Gen. 9:6). As often as we look upon it, we read this promise from God, that the earth will never be destroyed by a flood. Wherefore, if any philosophaster, to deride the simplicity of our faith, shall contend that the variety of colours arises naturally from the rays reflected by the opposite cloud, let us admit the fact; but, at the same time, deride his stupidity in not recognising God as the Lord and governor of nature, who, at his pleasure, makes all the elements subservient to his glory. If he had impressed memorials of this description on the sun, the stars, the earth, and stones, they would all have been to us as sacraments. For why is the shapeless and the coined silver not of the same value, seeing they are the same metal? Just because the former has noth-

ing but its own nature, whereas the latter, impressed with the public stamp, becomes money, and receives a new value. And shall the Lord not be able to stamp his creatures with his word, that things which were formerly bare elements may become sacraments? Examples of the second class were given when he showed light to Abraham in the smoking furnace (Gen. 15:17), when he covered the fleece with dew while the ground was dry; and, on the other hand, when the dew covered the ground while the fleece was untouched, to assure Gideon of victory (Judges 6:37); also, when he made the shadow go back ten degrees on the dial, to assure Hezekiah of his recovery (2 Kings 20:9; Isa. 38:7). These things, which were done to assist and establish their faith, were also sacraments.

19. But my present purpose is to discourse especially of those sacraments which the Lord has been pleased to institute as ordinary sacraments in his Church, to bring up his worshippers and servants in one faith, and the confession of one faith. For, to use the words of Augustine, "In no name of religion, true or false, can men be assembled, unless united by some common use of visible signs or sacraments" (August. cont. Faustum, Lib. 9 c. 11). Our most merciful Father, foreseeing this necessity, from the very first appointed certain exercises of piety to his servants; these, Satan, by afterwards transferring to impious and superstitious worship, in many ways corrupted and depraved. Hence those initiations of the Gentiles into their mysteries, and other degenerate rites. Yet, although they were full of error and superstition, they were, at the same time, an indication that men could not be without such external signs of religion. But, as they were neither founded on the word of God, nor bore reference to that truth which ought to be held forth by all signs, they are unworthy of being named when mention is made of the sacred symbols which were instituted by God, and have not been perverted from their end—viz. to be helps to true piety. And they consist not of simple signs, like the rainbow and the tree of life, but of ceremonies, or (if you prefer it) the signs here employed are ceremonies. But since, as has been said above, they are testimonies of grace and salvation from the Lord, so, in regard to us, they are marks of profession by which we openly swear by the name of God, binding ourselves to be faithful to him. Hence Chrysostom somewhere shrewdly gives them the name of pactions, by which God enters into covenant with us, and we become bound to holiness and purity of life, because a mutual stipulation is here interposed between God and us. For as God there promises to cover and efface any guilt and penalty which we may have incurred by transgression, and reconciles us to himself in his only begotten Son, so we, in our turn, oblige ourselves by this profession to the study of piety and righteousness. And hence it may be justly said, that such sacraments are ceremonies, by which God is pleased to train his people, first, to excite, cherish, and strengthen faith within; and, secondly, to testify our religion to men.

20. Now these have been different at different times, according to the dispensation which the Lord has seen meet to employ in manifesting himself to men. Circumcision was enjoined on Abraham and his posterity, and to it were afterwards added purifications and sacrifices, and other rites of the Mosaic Law. These were the sacraments of the Jews even until the advent of Christ. After these were abrogated, the two sacraments of Baptism and the Lord's Supper, which the Christian Church now employs, were instituted. I speak of those which were instituted for the use of the whole Church. For the laying on of hands, by which the ministers of the Church are initiated into their office, though I have no objection to its being called a sacrament, I do not number among ordinary sacraments. The place to be assigned to the other commonly reputed sacraments we shall see by-and-by. Still the ancient sacraments had the same end in view as our own—viz. to direct and almost lead us by the hand to Christ, or rather, were like images to represent him and hold him forth to our knowledge. But as we have already shown that sacraments are a kind of seals of the promises of God, so let us hold it as a most certain truth, that no divine promise has ever been offered to man except in Christ, and that hence when they remind us of any divine promise, they must of necessity exhibit Christ. Hence that heavenly pattern of the tabernacle and legal worship which was shown to Moses in the mount. There is only this difference, that while the former shadowed forth a promised Christ while he was still expected, the latter bear testimony to him as already come and manifested.

21. When these things are explained singly and separately, they will be much clearer. Circumcision was a sign by which the Jews were reminded that whatever comes of the seed of man—in other words, the whole nature of man—is corrupt, and requires to be cut off; moreover, it was a proof and memorial to confirm them in the promise made to Abraham, of a seed in whom all the nations of the earth should be blessed, and from whom they themselves were to look for a blessing. That saving seed, as we are taught by Paul (Gal. 5:16), was Christ, in whom alone they trusted to recover what they had lost in Adam. Wherefore circumcision was to them what Paul

says it was to Abraham—viz. a sign of the righteousness of faith (Rom. 9:11):—viz. a seal by which they were more certainly assured that their faith in waiting for the Lord would be accepted by God for righteousness. But we shall have a better opportunity elsewhere (chap. 16 sec. 3, 4) of following out the comparison between circumcision and baptism. Their washings and purifications placed under their eye the uncleanness, defilement, and pollution with which they were naturally contaminated, and promised another laver in which all their impurities might be wiped and washed away. This laver was Christ, washed by whose blood we bring his purity into the sight of God, that he may cover all our defilements. The sacrifices convicted them of their unrighteousness, and at the same time taught that there was a necessity for paying some satisfaction to the justice of God; and that, therefore, there must be some high priest, some mediator between God and man, to satisfy God by the shedding of blood, and the immolation of a victim which might suffice for the remission of sins. The high priest was Christ: he shed his own blood, he was himself the victim: for in obedience to the Father, he offered himself to death, and by this obedience abolished the disobedience by which man had provoked the indignation of God (Phil. 2:8; Rom. 5:19).

22. In regard to our sacraments, they present Christ the more clearly to us, the more familiarly he has been manifested to man. ever since he was exhibited by the Father, truly as he had been promised. For Baptism testifies that we are washed and purified; the Supper of the Eucharist that we are redeemed. Ablution is figured by water, satisfaction by blood. Both are found in Christ, who, as John says, "came by water and blood;" that is, to purify and redeem. Of this the Spirit of God also is a witness. Nay, there are three witnesses in one, water, Spirit, and blood. In the water and blood we have an evidence of purification and redemption, but the Spirit is the primary witness who gives us a full assurance of this testimony. This sublime mystery was illustriously displayed on the cross of Christ, when water and blood flowed from his sacred side (John 19:34); which, for this reason, Augustine justly termed the fountain of our sacraments (August. Hom. in Joann. 26). Of these we shall shortly treat at greater length. There is no doubt that, it you compare time with time, the grace of the Spirit is now more abundantly displayed. For this forms part of the glory of the kingdom of Christ, as we gather from several passages, and especially from the seventh chapter of John. In this sense are we to understand the words of Paul, that the law was "a shadow of good things to come, but the body is of Christ" (Col. 2:17). His purpose is not to declare the inefficacy of those manifestations of grace in which God was pleased to prove his truth to the patriarchs, just as he proves it to us in the present day in Baptism and the Lord's Supper, but to contrast the two, and show the great value of what is given to us, that no one may think it strange that by the advent of Christ the ceremonies of the law have been abolished.

23. The Scholastic dogma (to glance at it in passing), by which the difference between the sacraments of the old and the new dispensation is made so great, that the former did nothing but shadow forth the grace of God, while the latter actually confer that it, must be altogether exploded. Since the apostle speaks in no higher terms of the one than of the other, when he says that the fathers ate of the same spiritual food, and explains that that food was Christ (1 Cor. 10:3), who will presume to regard as an empty sign that which gave a manifestation to the Jews of true communion with Christ? And the state of the case which the apostle is there treating militates strongly for our view. For to guard against confiding in a frigid knowledge of Christ, an empty title of Christianity and external observances, and thereby daring to contemn the judgment of God, he exhibits signal examples of divine severity in the Jews, to make us aware that if we indulge in the same vices, the same punishments which they suffered are impending over us. Now, to make the comparison appropriate, it was necessary to show that there is no inequality between us and them in those blessings in which he forbade us to glory. Therefore, he first makes them equal to us in the sacraments, and leaves us not one iota of privilege which could give us hopes of impunity. Nor can we justly attribute more to our baptism than he elsewhere attributes to circumcision, when he terms it a seal of the righteousness of faith (Rom. 4:11). Whatever, therefore, is now exhibited to us in the sacraments, the Jews formerly received in theirs—viz. Christ, with his spiritual riches. The same efficacy which ours possess they experienced in theirs—viz. that they were seals of the divine favour toward them in regard to the hope of eternal salvation. Had the objectors been sound expounders of the Epistle to the Hebrews, they would not have been so deluded, but reading therein that sins were not expiated by legal ceremonies, nay, that the ancient shadows were of no importance to justification, they overlooked the contrast which is there drawn, and fastening on the single point, that the law in itself was of no avail to the worshipper, thought that they were mere figures, devoid

of truth. The purpose of the apostle is to show that there is nothing in the ceremonial law until we arrive at Christ, on whom alone the whole efficacy depends.

24. But they will found on what Paul says of the circumcision of the letter, and object that it is in no esteem with God; that it confers nothing, is empty; that passages such as these seem to set it far beneath our baptism. But by no means. For the very same thing might justly be said of baptism. Indeed, it is said; first by Paul himself, when he shows that God regards not the external ablution by which we are initiated into religion, unless the mind is purified inwardly, and maintains its purity to the end; and, secondly, by Peter, when he declares that the reality of baptism consists not in external ablution, but in the testimony of a good conscience. But it seems that in another passage he speaks with the greatest contempt of circumcision made with hands, when he contrasts it with the circumcision made by Christ. I answer, that not even in that passage is there anything derogatory to its dignity. Paul is there disputing against those who insisted upon it as necessary, after it had been abrogated. He therefore admonishes believers to lay aside ancient shadows, and cleave to truth. These teachers, he says, insist that your bodies shall be circumcised. But you have been spiritually circumcised both in soul and body. You have, therefore, a manifestation of the reality, and this is far better than the shadow. Still any one might have answered, that the figure was not to be despised because they had the reality, since among the fathers also was exemplified that putting off of the old man of which he was speaking, and yet to them external circumcision was not superfluous. This objection he anticipates, when he immediately adds, that the Colossians were buried together with Christ by baptism, thereby intimating that baptism is now to Christians what circumcision was to those of ancient times; and that the latter, therefore, could not be imposed on Christians without injury to the former.

25. But there is more difficulty in explaining the passage which follows, and which I lately quote—viz. that all the Jewish ceremonies were shadows of things to come, but the body is of Christ (Col. 2:17). The most difficult point of all, however, is that which is discussed in several chapters of the Epistle to the Hebrews—namely, that the blood of beasts did not reach to the conscience; that the law was a shadow of good things to come, but not the very image of the things (Heb. 10:1); that worshippers under the Mosaic ceremonies obtained no degree of perfection, and so forth. I repeat what I have already hinted, that Paul does not represent the ceremonies as shadowy because they had nothing solid in them, but because their completion was in a manner suspended until the manifestation of Christ. Again, I hold that the words are to be understood not of their efficiency, but rather of the mode of significancy. For until Christ was manifested in the flesh, all signs shadowed him as absent, however he might inwardly exert the presence of his power, and consequently of his person on believers. But the most important observation is, that in all these passages Paul does not speak simply but by way of reply. He was contending with false apostles, who maintained that piety consisted in mere ceremonies, without any respect to Christ; for their refutation it was sufficient merely to consider what effect ceremonies have in themselves. This, too, was the scope of the author of the Epistle to the Hebrews. Let us remember, therefore, that he is here treating of ceremonies not taken in their true and native signification, but when wrested to a false and vicious interpretation, not of the legitimate use, but of the superstitious abuse of them. What wonder, then, if ceremonies, when separated from Christ, are devoid of all virtue? All signs become null when the thing signified is taken away. Thus Christ, when addressing those who thought that manna was nothing more than food for the body, accommodates his language to their gross opinion, and says, that he furnished a better food, one which fed souls for immortality. But if you require a clearer solution, the substance comes to this: First, the whole apparatus of ceremonies under the Mosaic law, unless directed to Christ, is evanescent and null. Secondly, these ceremonies had such respect to Christ, that they had their fulfilment only when Christ was manifested in the flesh. Lastly, at his advent they behoved to disappear, just as the shadow vanishes in the clear light of the sun. But I now touch more briefly on the point, because I defer the future consideration of it till I come to the place where I intend to compare baptism with circumcision.

26. Those wretched sophists are perhaps deceived by the extravagant eulogiums on our signs which occur in ancient writers: for instance, the following passage of Augustine: "The sacraments of the old law only promised a Saviour, whereas ours give salvation" (August. Proem. in Ps. 73). Not perceiving that these and similar figures of speech are hyperbolical, they too have promulgated their hyperbolical dogmas, but in a sense altogether alien from that of ancient writers. For Augustine means nothing more than in another place where he says, "The sacraments of the Mosaic law foretold Christ, ours announce him" (Quæst. sup. Numer. c. 33). And again,

"Those were promises of things to be fulfilled, these indications of the fulfilment" (Contra Faustum, Lib. 19 c. 14); as if he had said, Those figured him when he was still expected, ours, now that he has arrived, exhibit him as present. Moreover, with regard to the mode of signifying, he says, as he also elsewhere indicates, "The Law and the Prophets had sacraments foretelling a thing future, the sacraments of our time attest that what they foretold as to come has come" (Cont. Liter. Petil. Lib. 2 c. 37). His sentiments concerning the reality and efficacy, he explains in several passages, as when he says, "The sacraments of the Jews were different in the signs, alike in the things signified; different in the visible appearance, alike in spiritual power" (Hom. in Joann. 26). Again, "In different signs there was the same faith: it was thus in different signs as in different words, because the words change the sound according to times, and yet words are nothing else than signs. The fathers drank of the same spiritual drink, but not of the same corporeal drink. See then, how, while faith remains, signs vary. There the rock was Christ; to us that is Christ which is placed on the altar. They as a great sacrament drank of the water flowing from the rock: believers know what we drink. If you look at the visible appearance there was a difference; if at the intelligible signification, they drank of the same spiritual drink." Again, "In this mystery their food and drink are the same as ours; the same in meaning, not in form, for the same Christ was figured to them in the rock; to us he has been manifested in the flesh" (in Ps. 77). Though we grant that in this respect also there is some difference. Both testify that the paternal kindness of God, and the graces of the Spirit, are offered us in Christ, but ours more clearly and splendidly. In both there is an exhibition of Christ, but in ours it is more full and complete, in accordance with that distinction between the Old and New Testaments of which we have discoursed above. And this is the meaning of Augustine (whom we quote more frequently, as being the best and most faithful witness of all antiquity), where he says that after Christ was revealed, sacraments were instituted, fewer in number, but of more august significance and more excellent power (De Doct. Christ. Lib. 3; et Ep. ad Janur.). It is here proper to remind the reader, that all the trifling talk of the sophists concerning the *opus operatum*, is not only false. but repugnant to the very nature of sacraments, which God appointed in order that believers, who are void and in want of all good. might bring nothing of their own, but simply beg. Hence it follows, that in receiving them they do nothing which deserves praise, and that in this action (which in respect of them is merely passive) no work can be ascribed to them.

CHAPTER 15

OF BAPTISM.

There are two parts of this chapter,—I. Dissertation on the two ends of Baptism, sec. 1–13. II. The second part may be reduced to four heads. Of the use of Baptism, sec. 14, 15. Of the worthiness or unworthiness of the minister, sec. 16–18. Of the corruptions by which this sacrament was polluted, sec. 19. To whom reference is had in the dispensation, sec. 20–22.

Sections:

1. Baptism defined. Its primary object. This consists of three things. 1. To attest the forgiveness of sins.

2. Passages of Scripture proving the forgiveness of sins.

3. Forgiveness not only of past but also of future sins. This no encouragement to license in sin.

4 Refutation of those who share forgiveness between Baptism and Repentance.

5 Second thing in Baptism—viz. to teach that we are ingrafted into Christ for mortification and newness of life.

6. Third thing in Baptism—viz. to teach us that we are united to Christ so as to be partakers of all his blessings. Second and third things conspicuous in the baptism both of John and the apostles.

7. Identity of the baptism of John and the apostles.

8. An objection to this refuted.

9. The benefits of baptism typified to the Israelites by the passage of the Red Sea and the pillar of cloud.

10. Objection of those who imagine that there is some kind of perfect renovation after baptism. Original depravity remains after baptism. Its existence in infants. The elect after baptism are righteous in this life only by imputation.

11. Original corruption trying to the pious during the whole course of their lives. They do not, on this account, seek a licence for sin. They rather walk more cautiously and safely in the ways of the Lord.

12. The trouble occasioned by corruption, shown by the example and testimony of the Apostle Paul.

13. Another end of baptism is to serve as our confession to men.

14. Second part of the chapter. Of baptism as a confirmation of our faith.

15. This illustrated by the examples of Cornelius and Paul. Of the use of baptism as a confession of faith.

16. Baptism not affected by the worthiness or unworthiness of the minister. Hence no necessity to rebaptise those who were baptised under the Papacy.

17. Nothing in the argument that those so baptised remained some years blind and unbelieving. The promise of God remains firm. God, in inviting the Jews to repentance, does not enjoin them to be again circumcised.

18. No ground to allege that Paul rebaptised certain of John's disciples. The baptism of John. What it is to be baptised in the name of Christ.

19. The corruptions introduced into baptism. The form of pure Christian baptism. Immersion or sprinkling should be left free.

20. To whom the dispensation of baptism belongs. Not to private individuals or women, but to the ministers of the Church. Origin of the baptism of private individuals and women. An argument in favour of it refuted.

21. Exploded also by Tertullian and Epiphanius.

22. Objection founded on the case of Zipporah. Answer. Children dying before baptism not excluded from heaven, provided the want of it was not caused by negligence or contempt.

1. Baptism is the initiatory sign by which we are admitted to the fellowship of the Church, that being ingrafted into Christ we may be accounted children of God. Moreover, the end for which God has given it (this I have shown to be common to all mysteries) is, first, that it may be conducive to our faith in him; and, secondly, that it may serve the purpose of a confession among men. The nature of both institutions we shall explain in order. Baptism contributes to our faith three things, which require to be treated separately. The first object, therefore, for which it is appointed by the Lord, is to be a sign and evidence of our purification, or (better to explain my meaning) it is a kind of sealed instrument by which he assures us that all our sins are so deleted, covered, and effaced, that they will never come into his sight, never be mentioned, never imputed. For it is his will that all who have believed, be baptised for the remission of sins. Hence those who have thought that baptism is nothing else than the badge and mark by which we profess our religion before men, in the same way as soldiers attest their profession by bearing the insignia of their commander, having not attended to what was the principal thing in baptism; and this is, that we are to receive it in connection with the promise, "He that believeth and is baptised shall be saved" (Mark 16:16).

2. In this sense is to be understood the statement of Paul, that "Christ loved the Church, and gave himself for it, that he might sanctify and cleanse it with the washing of water by the word" (Eph. 5:25, 26); and again, "not by works of righteousness which we have done, but according to his mercy he saved us, by the washing of regeneration and renewing of the Holy Ghost" (Titus 3:5). Peter also says that "baptism also doth now save us" (1 Peter 3:21). For he did not mean to intimate that our ablution and salvation are perfected by water, or that water possesses in itself the virtue of purifying, regenerating, and renewing; nor does he mean that it is the cause of salvation, but only that the knowledge and certainty of such gifts are perceived in this sacrament. This the words themselves evidently show. For Paul connects together the word of life and baptism of water, as if he had said, by the gospel the message of our ablution and sanctification is announced; by baptism this message is sealed. And Peter immediately subjoins, that that baptism is "not the putting away of the filth of the flesh, but the answer of a good conscience toward God, which is of faith." Nay, the only purification which baptism promises is by means of the sprinkling of the blood of Christ, who is figured by water from the resemblance to cleansing and washing. Who, then, can say that we are cleansed by that water which certainly attests that the blood of Christ is our true and only laver? So that we cannot have a better argument to refute the hallucination of those who ascribe the whole to the virtue of water than we derive from the very meaning of baptism, which leads us away as well from the visible element which is presented to our eye, as from all other means, that it may fix our minds on Christ alone.

3. Nor is it to be supposed that baptism is bestowed only with reference to the past, so that, in regard to new lapses into which we fall after baptism, we must seek new remedies of expiation in other so-called sacraments, just as if the power of baptism had become obsolete. To this error, in ancient times, it was owing that some refused to be initiated by baptism until their life was in extreme danger, and they were drawing their last breath, that they might thus obtain pardon for all the past. Against this preposterous precaution ancient bishops frequently inveigh in their writings. We ought to consider that at whatever time we are baptised, we are washed and purified once for the whole of life. Wherefore, as often as we fall, we must recall the remembrance

of our baptism, and thus fortify our minds, so as to feel certain and secure of the remission of sins. For though, when once administered, it seems to have passed, it is not abolished by subsequent sins. For the purity of Christ was therein offered to us, always is in force, and is not destroyed by any stain: it wipes and washes away all our defilements. Nor must we hence assume a licence of sinning for the future (there is certainly nothing in it to countenance such audacity), but this doctrine is intended only for those who, when they have sinned, groan under their sins burdened and oppressed, that they may have wherewith to support and console themselves, and not rush headlong into despair. Thus Paul says that Christ was made a propitiation for us for the remission of sins that are past (Rom. 3:25). By this he denies not that constant and perpetual forgiveness of sins is thereby obtained even till death: he only intimates that it is designed by the Father for those poor sinners who, wounded by remorse of conscience, sigh for the physician. To these the mercy of God is offered. Those who, from hopes of impunity, seek a licence for sin, only provoke the wrath and justice of God.

4. I know it is a common belief that forgiveness, which at our first regeneration we receive by baptism alone, is after baptism procured by means of penitence and the keys (see chap. 19 sec. 17). But those who entertain this fiction err from not considering that the power of the keys, of which they speak, so depends on baptism, that it ought not on any account to be separated from it. The sinner receives forgiveness by the ministry of the Church; in other words, not without the preaching of the gospel. And of what nature is this preaching? That we are washed from our sins by the blood of Christ. And what is the sign and evidence of that washing if it be not baptism? We see, then, that that forgiveness has reference to baptism. This error had its origin in the fictitious sacrament of penance, on which I have already touched. What remains will be said at the proper place. There is no wonder if men who, from the grossness of their minds, are excessively attached to external things, have here also betrayed the defect,— if not contented with the pure institution of God, they have introduced new helps devised by themselves, as if baptism were not itself a sacrament of penance. But if repentance is recommended during the whole of life, the power of baptism ought to have the same extent. Wherefore, there can be no doubt that all the godly may, during the whole course of their lives, whenever they are vexed by a consciousness of their sins, recall the remembrance of their baptism, that they may thereby assure themselves of that sole and perpetual ablution which we have in the blood of Christ.

5. Another benefit of baptism is, that it shows us our mortification in Christ and new life in him. "Know ye not," says the apostle, "that as many of us as were baptised into Jesus Christ, were baptised into his death? Therefore we are buried with him by baptism into death," that we "should walk in newness of life" (Rom. 6:3, 4). By these words, he not only exhorts us to imitation of Christ, as if he had said, that we are admonished by baptism, in like manner as Christ died, to die to our lusts, and as he rose, to rise to righteousness; but he traces the matter much higher, that Christ by baptism has made us partakers of his death, ingrafting us into it. And as the twig derives substance and nourishment from the root to which it is attached, so those who receive baptism with true faith truly feel the efficacy of Christ's death in the mortification of their flesh, and the efficacy of his resurrection in the quickening of the Spirit. On this he founds his exhortation, that if we are Christians we should be dead unto sin, and alive unto righteousness. He elsewhere uses the same argument—viz. that we are circumcised, and put off the old man, after we are buried in Christ by baptism (Col. 2:12). And in this sense, in the passage which we formerly quoted, he calls it "the washing of regeneration, and renewing of the Holy Ghost" (Tit. 3:5). We are promised, first, the free pardon of sins and imputation of righteousness; and, secondly, the grace of the Holy Spirit, to form us again to newness of life.

6. The last advantage which our faith receives from baptism is its assuring us not only that we are ingrafted into the death and life of Christ, but so united to Christ himself as to be partakers of all his blessings. For he consecrated and sanctified baptism in his own body, that he might have it in common with us as the firmest bond of union and fellowship which he deigned to form with us; and hence Paul proves us to be the sons of God, from the fact that we put on Christ in baptism (Gal. 3:27). Thus we see the fulfilment of our baptism in Christ, whom for this reason we call the proper object of baptism. Hence it is not strange that the apostles are said to have baptised in the name of Christ, though they were enjoined to baptise in the name of the Father and Spirit also (Acts 8:16; 19:5; Mt. 28:19). For all the divine gifts held forth in baptism are found in Christ alone. And yet he who baptises into Christ cannot but at the same time invoke the name of the Father and the Spirit. For we are cleansed by his blood, just because our gracious Father, of his incomparable mercy, willing to receive us into favour, appointed

him Mediator to effect our reconciliation with himself. Regeneration we obtain from his death and resurrection only, when sanctified by his Spirit we are imbued with a new and spiritual nature. Wherefore we obtain, and in a manner distinctly perceive, in the Father the cause, in the Son the matter, and in the Spirit the effect of our purification and regeneration. Thus first John baptised, and thus afterwards the apostles by the baptism of repentance for the remission of sins, understanding by the term *repentance*, regeneration, and by the *remission* of sins, ablution.

7. This makes it perfectly certain that the ministry of John was the very same as that which was afterwards delegated to the apostles. For the different hands by which baptism is administered do not make it a different baptism, but sameness of doctrine proves it to be the same. John and the apostles agreed in one doctrine. Both baptised unto repentance, both for remission of sins, both in the name of Christ, from whom repentance and remission of sins proceed. John pointed to him as the Lamb of God who taketh away the sins of the world (John 1:29), thus describing him as the victim accepted of the Father, the propitiation of righteousness, and the author of salvation. What could the apostles add to this confession? Wherefore, let no one be perplexed because ancient writers labour to distinguish the one from the other. Their views ought not to be in such esteem with us as to shake the certainty of Scripture. For who would listen to Chrysostom denying that remission of sins was included in the baptism of John (Hom. in Mt. 1:14), rather than to Luke asserting, on the contrary, that John preached "the baptism of repentance for the remission of sins?" (Luke 3:3). Nor can we admit Augustine's subtlety, that by the baptism of John sins were forgiven in hope, but by the baptism of Christ are forgiven in reality. For seeing the Evangelist clearly declares that John in his baptism promised the remission of sins, why detract from this eulogium when no necessity compels it? Should any one ask what difference the word of God makes, he will find it to be nothing more than that John baptised in the name of him who was to come, the apostles in the name of him who was already manifested (Luke 3:16; Acts 19:4).

8. This fact, that the gifts of the Spirit were more liberally poured out after the resurrection of Christ, does not go to establish a diversity of baptisms. For baptism, administered by the apostles while he was still on the earth, was called his baptism, and yet the Spirit was not poured out in larger abundance on it than on the baptism of John. Nay, not even after the ascension did the Samaritans receive the Spirit above the ordinary measure of former believers, till Peter and John were sent to lay hands on them (Acts 8:14–17). I imagine that the thing which imposed on ancient writers, and made them say that the one baptism was only a preparative to the other, was, because they read that those who had received the baptism of John were again baptised by Paul (Acts 19:3–5; Mt. 3:11). How greatly they are mistaken in this will be most clearly explained in its own place. Why, then, did John say that he baptised with water, but there was one coming who would baptise with the Holy Ghost and with fire? This may be explained in a few words. He did not mean to distinguish the one baptism from the other, but he contrasted his own person with the person of Christ, saying, that while he was a minister of water, Christ was the giver of the Holy Spirit, and would declare this virtue by a visible miracle on the day on which he would send the Holy Spirit on the apostles, under the form of tongues of fire. What greater boast could the apostles make, and what greater those who baptise in the present day? For they are only ministers of the external sign, whereas Christ is the Author of internal grace, as those same ancient writers uniformly teach, and, in particular, Augustine, who, in his refutation of the Donatists, founds chiefly on this axiom, Whoever it is that baptises, Christ alone presides.

9. The things which we have said, both of mortification and ablution, were adumbrated among the people of Israel, who, for that reason, are described by the apostle as having been baptised in the cloud and in the sea (1 Cor. 10:2). Mortification was figured when the Lord, vindicating them from the hand of Pharaoh and from cruel bondage, paved a way for them through the Red Sea, and drowned Pharaoh himself and their Egyptian foes, who were pressing close behind, and threatening them with destruction. For in this way also he promises us in baptism, and shows by a given sign that we are led by his might, and delivered from the captivity of Egypt, that is, from the bondage of sin, that our Pharaoh is drowned; in other words, the devil, although he ceases not to try and harass us. But as that Egyptian was not plunged into the depth of the sea, but cast out upon the shore, still alarmed the Israelites by the terror of his look, though he could not hurt them, so our enemy still threatens, shows his arms and is felt, but cannot conquer. The cloud was a symbol of purification (Num. 9:18). For as the Lord then covered them by an opposite cloud, and kept them cool, that they might not faint or pine away under the burning rays of the sun; so in baptism we perceive that we

are covered and protected by the blood of Christ, lest the wrath of God, which is truly an intolerable flame, should lie upon us. Although the mystery was then obscure, and known to few, yet as there is no other method of obtaining salvation than in those two graces, God was pleased that the ancient fathers, whom he had adopted as heirs, should be furnished with both badges.

10. It is now clear how false the doctrine is which some long ago taught, and others still persist in, that by baptism we are exempted and set free from original sin, and from the corruption which was propagated by Adam to all his posterity, and that we are restored to the same righteousness and purity of nature which Adam would have had if he had maintained the integrity in which he was created. This class of teachers never understand what is meant by original sin, original righteousness, or the grace of baptism. Now, it has been previously shown (Book 2 chap. 1 sec. 8), that original sin is the depravity and corruption of our nature, which first makes us liable to the wrath of God, and then produces in us works which Scripture terms *the works of the flesh* (Gal. 5:19). The two things, therefore, must be distinctly observed—viz. that we are vitiated and perverted in all parts of our nature, and then, on account of this corruption, are justly held to be condemned and convicted before God, to whom nothing is acceptable but purity, innocence, and righteousness. And hence, even infants bring their condemnation with them from their mother's womb; for although they have not yet brought forth the fruits of their unrighteousness, they have its seed included in them. Nay, their whole nature is, as it were, a seed of sin, and, therefore, cannot but be odious and abominable to God. Believers become assured by baptism, that this condemnation is entirely withdrawn from them, since (as has been said) the Lord by this sign promises that a full and entire remission has been made, both of the guilt which was imputed to us, and the penalty incurred by the guilt. They also apprehend righteousness, but such righteousness as the people of God can obtain in this life—viz. by imputation only, God, in his mercy, regarding them as righteous and innocent.

11. Another point is, that this corruption never ceases in us, but constantly produces new fruits—viz. those works of the flesh which we previously described, just as a burning furnace perpetually sends forth flame and sparks, or a fountain is ever pouring out water. For concupiscence never wholly dies or is extinguished in men, until, freed by death from the body of death, they have altogether laid aside their own nature (Book 3 chap. 3 sec. 10–13). Baptism, indeed, tells us that our Pharaoh is drowned and sin mortified; not so, however, as no longer to exist, or give no trouble, but only so as not to have dominion. For as long as we live shut up in this prison of the body, the remains of sin dwell in us, but if we faithfully hold the promise which God has given us in baptism, they will neither rule nor reign. But let no man deceive himself, let no man look complacently on his disease, when he hears that sin always dwells in us. When we say so, it is not in order that those who are otherwise too prone to sin may sleep securely in their sins, but only that those who are tried and stung by the flesh may not faint and despond. Let them rather reflect that they are still on the way, and think that they have made great progress when they feel that their concupiscence is somewhat diminished from day to day, until they shall have reached the point at which they aim—viz. the final death of the flesh; a death which shall be completed at the termination of this mortal life. Meanwhile, let them cease not to contend strenuously, and animate themselves to further progress, and press on to complete victory. Their efforts should be stimulated by the consideration, that after a lengthened struggle much still remains to be done. We ought to hold that we are baptised for the mortification of our flesh, which is begun in baptism, is prosecuted every day, and will be finished when we depart from this life to go to the Lord.

12. Here we say nothing more than the apostle Paul expounds most clearly in the sixth and seventh chapters of the Epistle to the Romans. He had discoursed of free justification, but as some wicked men thence inferred that they were to live as they listed, because their acceptance with God was not procured by the merit of works, he adds, that all who are clothed with the righteousness of Christ are at the same time regenerated by the Spirit, and that we have an earnest of this regeneration in baptism. Hence he exhorts believers not to allow sin to reign in their members. And because he knew that there is always some infirmity in believers, lest they should be cast down on this account, he adds, for their consolation, that they are not under the law. Again, as there may seem a danger that Christians might grow presumptuous because they were not under the yoke of the law, he shows what the nature of the abrogation is, and at the same time what the use of the law is. This question he had already postponed a second time. The substance is, that we are freed from the rigour of the law in order that we may adhere to Christ, and that the office of the law is to convince us of our depravity, and make us confess our impotence and wretchedness. Moreover, as this malignity of nature is not

so easily apparent in a profane man who, without fear of God, indulges his passions, he gives an example in the regenerate man, in other words, in himself. He therefore says that he had a constant struggle with the remains of his flesh, and was kept in miserable bondage, so as to be unable to devote himself entirely to the obedience of the divine law. Hence he is forced to groan and exclaim, "O wretched man that I am! who shall deliver me from the body of this death?" (Rom. 7:24). But if the children of God are kept captive in prison as long as they live, they must necessarily feel very anxious at the thought of their danger, unless their fears are allayed. For this single purpose, then, he subjoins the consolation, that there is "now no condemnation to them which are in Christ Jesus" (Rom. 8:1). Hence he teaches that those whom the Lord has once admitted into favour, and ingrafted into communion with Christ, and received into the fellowship of the Church by baptism, are freed from guilt and condemnation while they persevere in the faith of Christ, though they may be beset by sin and thus bear sin about with them. If this is the simple and genuine interpretation of Paul's meaning, we cannot think that there is anything strange in the doctrine which he here delivers.

13. Baptism serves as our confession before men, inasmuch as it is a mark by which we openly declare that we wish to be ranked among the people of God, by which we testify that we concur with all Christians in the worship of one God, and in one religion; by which, in short, we publicly assert our faith, so that not only do our hearts breathe, but our tongues also, and all the members of our body, in every way they can, proclaim the praise of God. In this way, as is meet, everything we have is made subservient to the glory of God, which ought everywhere to be displayed, and others are stimulated by our example to the same course. To this Paul referred when he asked the Corinthians whether or not they had been baptised in the name of Christ (1 Cor. 1:13); intimating, that by the very circumstance of having been baptised in his name, they had devoted themselves to him, had sworn and bound themselves in allegiance to him before men, so that they could no longer confess any other than Christ alone, unless they would abjure the confession which they had made in baptism.

14. Now that the end to which the Lord had regard in the institution of baptism has been explained, it is easy to judge in what way we ought to use and receive it. For inasmuch as it is appointed to elevate, nourish, and confirm our faith, we are to receive it as from the hand of its author, being firmly persuaded that it is himself who speaks to us by means of the sign; that it is himself who washes and purifies us, and effaces the remembrance of our faults; that it is himself who makes us the partakers of his death, destroys the kingdom of Satan, subdues the power of concupiscence, nay, makes us one with himself, that being clothed with him we may be accounted the children of God. These things, I say, we ought to feel as truly and certainly in our mind as we see our body washed, immersed, and surrounded with water. For this analogy or similitude furnishes the surest rule in the sacraments—viz. that in corporeal things we are to see spiritual, just as if they were actually exhibited to our eye, since the Lord has been pleased to represent them by such figures; not that such graces are included and bound in the sacrament, so as to be conferred by its efficacy, but only that by this badge the Lord declares to us that he is pleased to bestow all these things upon us. Nor does he merely feed our eyes with bare show; he leads us to the actual object, and effectually performs what he figures.

15. We have a proof of this in Cornelius the centurion, who, after he had been previously endued with the graces of the Holy Spirit, was baptised for the remission of sins, not seeking a fuller forgiveness from baptism, but a surer exercise of faith; nay, an argument for assurance from a pledge. It will, perhaps, be objected, Why did Ananias say to Paul that he washed away his sins by baptism (Acts 22:16), if sins are not washed away by the power of baptism? I answer, we are said to receive, procure, and obtain, whatever according to the perception of our faith is exhibited to us by the Lord, whether he then attests it for the first time, or gives additional confirmation to what he had previously attested. All then that Ananias meant to say was, Be baptised, Paul, that you may be assured that your sins are forgiven you. In baptism, the Lord promises forgiveness of sins: receive it, and be secure. I have no intention, however, to detract from the power of baptism. I would only add to the sign the substance and reality, inasmuch as God works by external means. But from this sacrament, as from all others, we gain nothing, unless in so far as we receive in faith. If faith is wanting, it will be an evidence of our ingratitude, by which we are proved guilty before God, for not believing the promise there given. In so far as it is a sign of our confession, we ought thereby to testify that we confide in the mercy of God, and are pure, through the forgiveness of sins which Christ Jesus has procured for us; that we have entered into the Church of God, that with one consent of faith and love we may live in concord with all believers. This last was Paul's meaning,

when he said that "by one Spirit are we all baptised into one body" (1 Cor. 12:13).

16. Moreover, if we have rightly determined that a sacrament is not to be estimated by the hand of him by whom it is administered, but is to be received as from the hand of God himself, from whom it undoubtedly proceeded, we may hence infer that its dignity neither gains nor loses by the administrator. And, just as among men, when a letter has been sent, if the hand and seal is recognised, it is not of the least consequence who or what the messenger was; so it ought to be sufficient for us to recognise the hand and seal of our Lord in his sacraments, let the administrator be who he may. This confutes the error of the Donatists, who measured the efficacy and worth of the sacrament by the dignity of the minister. Such in the present day are our Catabaptists, who deny that we are duly baptised, because we were baptised in the Papacy by wicked men and idolaters; hence they furiously insist on anabaptism. Against these absurdities we shall be sufficiently fortified if we reflect that by baptism we were initiated not into the name of any man, but into the name of the Father, and the Son, and the Holy Spirit; and, therefore, that baptism is not of man, but of God, by whomsoever it may have been administered. Be it that those who baptised us were most ignorant of God and all piety, or were despisers, still they did not baptise us into a fellowship with their ignorance or sacrilege, but into the faith of Jesus Christ, because the name which they invoked was not their own but God's, nor did they baptise into any other name. But if baptism was of God, it certainly included in it the promise of forgiveness of sin, mortification of the flesh, quickening of the Spirit, and communion with Christ. Thus it did not harm the Jews that they were circumcised by impure and apostate priests. It did not nullify the symbol so as to make it necessary to repeat it. It was enough to return to its genuine origin. The objection that baptism ought to be celebrated in the assembly of the godly, does not prove that it loses its whole efficacy because it is partly defective. When we show what ought to be done to keep baptism pure and free from every taint, we do not abolish the institution of God though idolaters may corrupt it. Circumcision was anciently vitiated by many superstitions, and yet ceased not to be regarded as a symbol of grace; nor did Josiah and Hezekiah, when they assembled out of all Israel those who had revolted from God, call them to be circumcised anew.

17. Then, again, when they ask us what faith for several years followed our baptism, that they may thereby prove that our baptism was in vain, since it is not sanctified unless the word of the promise is received with faith, our answer is, that being blind and unbelieving, we for a long time did not hold the promise which was given us in baptism, but that still the promise, as it was of God, always remained fixed, and firm, and true. Although all men should be false and perfidious, yet God ceases not to be true (Rom. 3:3, 4); though all were lost, Christ remains safe. We acknowledge, therefore, that at that time baptism profited us nothing, since in us the offered promise, without which baptism is nothing, lay neglected. Now, when by the grace of God we begin to repent, we accuse our blindness and hardness of heart in having been so long ungrateful for his great goodness. But we do not believe that the promise itself has vanished, we rather reflect thus: God in baptism promises the remission of sins, and will undoubtedly perform what he has promised to all believers. That promise was offered to us in baptism, let us therefore embrace it in faith. In regard to us, indeed, it was long buried on account of unbelief; now, therefore, let us with faith receive it. Wherefore, when the Lord invites the Jewish people to repentance, he gives no injunction concerning another circumcision, though (as we have said) they were circumcised by a wicked and sacrilegious hand, and had long lived in the same impiety. All he urges is conversion of heart. For how much soever the covenant might have been violated by them, the symbol of the covenant always remained, according to the appointment of the Lord, firm and inviolable. Solely, therefore, on the condition of repentance, were they restored to the covenant which God had once made with them in circumcision, though this which they had received at the hand of a covenant-breaking priest, they had themselves as much as in them lay polluted and extinguished.

18. But they seem to think the weapon which they brandish irresistible, when they allege that Paul rebaptised those who had been baptised with the baptism of John (Acts 19:3, 5). For if, by our confession, the baptism of John was the same as ours, then, in like manner as those who had been improperly trained, when they learned the true faith, were rebaptised into it, ought that baptism which was without true doctrine to be accounted as nothing, and hence we ought to be baptised anew into the true religion with which we are now, for the first time, imbued? It seems to some that it was a foolish imitator of John, who, by a former baptism, had initiated them into vain superstition. This, it is thought, may be conjectured from the fact, that they acknowledge their entire

ignorance of the Holy Spirit, an ignorance in which John never would have left his disciples. But it is not probable that the Jews, even though they had not been baptised at all, would have been destitute of all knowledge of the Spirit, who is celebrated in so many passages of Scripture. Their answer, therefore, that they knew not whether there was a Spirit, must be understood as if they had said, that they had not yet heard whether or not the gifts of the Spirit, as to which Paul questioned them, were given to the disciples of Christ. I grant that John's was a true baptism, and one and the same with the baptism of Christ. But I deny that they were rebaptised (see Calv. Instruct. adv. Anabapt.). What then is meant by the words, "They were baptised in the name of the Lord Jesus"? Some interpret that they were only instructed in sound doctrine by Paul; but I would rather interpret more simply, that the baptism of the Holy Spirit, in other words, the visible gifts of the Holy Spirit, were given by the laying on of hands. These are sometimes designated under the name of baptism. Thus, on the day of Pentecost, the apostles are said to have remembered the words of the Lord concerning the baptism of the Spirit and of fire. And Peter relates that the same words occurred to him when he saw these gifts poured out on Cornelius and his family and kindred. There is nothing repugnant to this interpretation in its being afterwards added, "When Paul had laid his hands upon them, the Holy Ghost came on them" (Acts 19:6). For Luke does not narrate two different things, but follows the form of narrative common to the Hebrews, who first give the substance, and then explain more fully. This any one may perceive from the mere context. For he says, "When they heard this they were baptised in the name of the Lord Jesus. And when Paul laid his hands upon them, the Holy Ghost came on them." In this last sentence is described what the nature of the baptism was. But if ignorance vitiates a former, and requires to be corrected by a second baptism, the apostles should first of all have been rebaptised, since for more than three full years after their baptism they had scarcely received any slender portion of purer doctrine. Then so numerous being the acts of ignorance which by the mercy of God are daily corrected in us, what rivers would suffice for so many repeated baptisms?

19. The force, dignity, utility, and end of the sacrament must now, if I mistake not, be sufficiently clear. In regard to the external symbol, I wish the genuine institution of Christ had been maintained as fit to repress the audacity of men. As if to be baptised with water, according to the precept of Christ, had been a contemptible thing, a benediction, or rather incantation, was devised to pollute the true consecration of water. There was afterwards added the taper and chrism, while exorcism was thought to open the door for baptism. Though I am not unaware how ancient the origin of this adventitious farrago is, still it is lawful for me and all the godly to reject whatever men have presumed to add to the institution of Christ. When Satan saw that by the foolish credulity of the world his impostures were received almost without objection at the commencement of the gospel, he proceeded to grosser mockery: hence spittle and other follies, to the open disgrace of baptism, were introduced with unbridled licence. From our experience of them, let us learn that there is nothing holier, or better, or safer, than to be contented with the authority of Christ alone. How much better, therefore, is it to lay aside all theatrical pomp, which dazzles the eyes of the simple, and dulls their minds, and when any one is to be baptised to bring him forward and present him to God, the whole Church looking on as witnesses, and praying over him; to recite the Confession of Faith, in which the catechumen has been instructed, explain the promises which are given in baptism, then baptise in the name of the Father, and the Son, and the Holy Spirit, and conclude with prayer and thanksgiving. In this way, nothing which is appropriate would be omitted, and the one ceremony, which proceeded from its divine Author, would shine forth most brightly, not being buried or polluted by extraneous observances. Whether the person baptised is to be wholly immersed, and that whether once or thrice, or whether he is only to be sprinkled with water, is not of the least consequence: churches should be at liberty to adopt either, according to the diversity of climates, although it is evident that the term *baptise* means to immerse, and that this was the form used by the primitive Church.

20. It is here also pertinent to observe, that it is improper for private individuals to take upon themselves the administration of baptism; for it, as well as the dispensation of the Supper, is part of the ministerial office. For Christ did not give command to any men or women whatever to baptise, but to those whom he had appointed apostles. And when, in the administration of the Supper, he ordered his disciples to do what they had seen him do (he having done the part of a legitimate dispenser), he doubtless meant that in this they should imitate his example. The practice which has been in use for many ages, and even almost from the very commencement of the Church, for laics to baptise, in danger of death, when a minister could not be present in time, cannot, it appears

to me, be defended on sufficient grounds. Even the early Christians who observed or tolerated this practice were not clear whether it were rightly done. This doubt is expressed by Augustine when he says, "Although a laic have given baptism when compelled by necessity, I know not whether any one can piously say that it ought to be repeated. For if it is done without any necessity compelling it, it is usurpation of another's office; but if necessity urges, it is either no fault, or a venial one" (August. Cont. Epist. Parmen. Lib. 2 c. 13). With regard to women, it was decreed, without exception, in the Council of Carthage (cap. 100), that they were not to presume to baptise at all. But there is a danger that he who is sick may be deprived of the gift of regeneration if he decease without baptism! By no means. Our children, before they are born, God declares that he adopts for his own when he promises that he will be a God to us, and to our seed after us. In this promise their salvation is included. None will dare to offer such an insult to God as to deny that he is able to give effect to his promise. How much evil has been caused by the dogma, ill expounded, that baptism is necessary to salvation, few perceive, and therefore think caution the less necessary. For when the opinion prevails that all are lost who happen not to be dipped in water, our condition becomes worse than that of God's ancient people, as if his grace were more restrained than under the Law. In that case, Christ will be thought to have come not to fulfil, but to abolish the promises, since the promise, which was then effectual in itself to confer salvation before the eighth day, would not now be effectual without the help of a sign.

21. What the custom was before Augustine's day is gathered, first, from Tertullian, who says, that a woman is not permitted to speak in the Church, nor yet to teach, or baptise, or offer, that she may not claim to herself any office of the man, not to say of the priest (Tertull. Cont. Hæres. Lib. 1). Of the same thing we have a sufficient witness in Epiphanius, when he upbraids Marcian with giving permission to women to baptise. I am not unaware of the answer given by those who take an opposite view—viz. that common use is very different from an extraordinary remedy used under the pressure of extreme necessity—but since he declares it mockery to allow women to baptise, and makes no exception, it is sufficiently plain that the corruption is condemned as inexcusable on any pretext. In his Third Book, also, when he says that it was not even permitted to the holy mother of Christ, he makes no reservation.

22. The example of Zipporah (Exod. 4:25) is irrelevantly quoted. Because the angel of God was appeased after she took a stone and circumcised her son, it is erroneously inferred that her act was approved by God. Were it so, we must say that God was pleased with a worship which Gentiles brought from Assyria, and set up in Samaria. But other valid reasons prove, that what a foolish woman did is ignorantly drawn into a precedent. Were I to say that there was something special in the case, making it unfit for a precedent—and especially as we nowhere read that the command to circumcise was specially given to priests, the cases of baptism and circumcision are different—I should give a sufficient refutation. For the words of Christ are plain: "Go ye, therefore, and teach all nations, baptising them" (Mt. 28:19). Since he appointed the same persons to be preachers of the Gospel, and dispensers of baptism—and in the Church, "no man taketh this honour unto himself," as the apostle declares (Heb. 5:4), "but he that is called of God, as was Aaron"—any one who baptises without a lawful call usurps another's office. Paul declares, that whatever we attempt with a dubious conscience, even in the minutest matters, as in meat and drink, is sin (Rom. 14:23). Therefore, in baptism by women, the sin is the greater, when it is plain that the rule delivered by Christ is violated, seeing we know it to be unlawful to put asunder what God has joined. But all this I pass; only I would have my readers to observe, that the last thing intended by Zipporah was to perform a service to God. Seeing her son in danger, she frets and murmurs, and, not without indignation, throws down the foreskin on the ground; thus upbraiding her husband, and taking offence at God. In short, it is plain that her whole procedure is dictated by passion: she complains both against her husband and against God, because she is forced to spill the blood of her son. We may add, that however well she might have conducted herself in all other respects, yet her presumption is inexcusable in this, in circumcising her son while her husband is present, and that husband not a mere private individual, but Moses, the chief prophet of God, than whom no greater ever arose in Israel. This was no more allowable in her, than it would be for women in the present day under the eye of a bishop. But this controversy will at once be disposed of when we maintain, that children who happen to depart this life before an opportunity of immersing them in water, are not excluded from the kingdom of heaven. Now, it has been seen, that unless we admit this position, great injury is done to the covenant of God, as if in itself

it were weak, whereas its effect depends not either on baptism, or on any accessaries. The sacrament is afterwards added as a kind of seal, not to give efficacy to the promise, as if in itself invalid, but merely to confirm it to us. Hence it follows, that the children of believers are not baptised, in order that though formerly aliens from the Church, they may then, for the first time, become children of God, but rather are received into the Church by a formal sign, because, in virtue of the promise, they previously belonged to the body of Christ. Hence if, in omitting the sign, their is neither sloth, nor contempt, nor negligence, we are safe from all danger. By far the better course, therefore, is to pay such respect to the ordinance of God as not to seek the sacraments in any other quarter than where the Lord has deposited them. When we cannot receive them from the Church, the grace of God is not so inseparably annexed to them that we cannot obtain it by faith, according to his word.

CHAPTER 16

PÆDOBAPTISM. ITS ACCORDANCE WITH THE INSTITUTION OF CHRIST, AND THE NATURE OF THE SIGN.

Divisions of this chapter,—I. Confirmation of the orthodox doctrine of Pædobaptism, sec. 1–9. II. Refutation of the arguments which the Anabaptists urge against Pædobaptism, sec. 10–30. III. Special objections of Servetus refuted, sec. 31, 32.

Sections:

1. Pædobaptism. The consideration of the question necessary and useful. Pædobaptism of divine origin.

2. This demonstrated from a consideration of the promises. These explain the nature and validity of Pædobaptism.

3. Promises annexed to the symbol of water cannot be better seen than in the institution of circumcision.

4. The promise and thing figured in circumcision and baptism one and the same. The only difference in the external ceremony.

5. Hence the baptism of the children of Christian parents as competent as the circumcision of Jewish children. An objection founded on a stated day for circumcision refuted.

6. An argument for Pædobaptism founded on the covenant which God made with Abraham. An objection disposed of. The grace of God not diminished by the advent of Christ.

7. Argument founded on Christ's invitation to children. Objection answered.

8. Objection, that no infants were baptised by the apostles. Answer. Objection, that pædobaptism is a novelty. Answer.

9. Twofold use and benefit of pædobaptism. In respect, 1. Of parents. 2. Of children baptised.

10 Second part of the chapter, stating the arguments of Anabaptists. Alleged dissimilitude between baptism and circumcision. First answer.

11. Second answer. The covenant in baptism and circumcision not different.

12. Third answer.

13. Infants, both Jewish and Christian, comprehended in the covenant.

14. Objection considered.

15. The Jews being comprehended in the covenant, no substantial difference between baptism and circumcision.

16. Another argument of the Anabaptists considered.

17. Argument that children are not fit to understand baptism, and therefore should not be baptised.

18. Answer continued.

19. Answer continued.

20. Answer continued.

21. Answer continued.

22. Argument, that baptism being appointed for the remission of sins, infants, not having sinned, ought not to be baptised. Answer.

23. Argument against pædobaptism, founded on the practice of the apostles. Answer.

24. Answer continued.

25. Argument founded on a saying of our Lord to Nicodemus. Answer.

26. Error of those who adjudge all who die unbaptised to eternal destruction.

27. Argument against pædobaptism, founded on the precept and example of our Saviour, in requiring instruction to precede baptism. Answer.

28. Answer continued.

29. Answer continued.

30. Argument, that there is no stronger reason for giving baptism to children than for giving them the Lord's Supper. Answer.

31. Last part of the chapter, refuting the arguments of Servetus.

32. Why Satan so violently assails pædobaptism.

1. But since, in this age, certain frenzied spirits have raised, and even now continue to raise, great disturbance in the Church on account of pædobaptism, I cannot avoid here, by way of appendix, adding something to restrain their fury. Should any one think me more prolix than the subject is worth, let him reflect that, in a matter of the greatest moment, so much is due to the peace and purity of the Church, that we should not fastidiously object to whatever may be conducive to both. I may add, that I will study so to arrange this discussion, that it will tend, in no small degree, still farther to illustrate the subject of baptism. The argument by which pædobaptism is assailed is, no doubt, specious—viz. that it is not founded on the institution of God, but was introduced merely by human presumption and depraved curiosity, and afterwards, by a foolish facility, rashly received in practice; whereas a sacrament has not a thread to hang upon, if it rest not on the sure foundation of the word of God. But what if, when the matter is properly attended to, it should be found that a calumny is falsely and unjustly brought against the holy ordinance of the Lord? First, then, let us inquire into its origin. Should it appear to have been devised merely by human rashness, let us abandon it, and regulate the true observance of baptism entirely by the will of the Lord; but should it be proved to be by no means destitute of his sure authority, let us beware of discarding the sacred institutions of God, and thereby insulting their Author.

2. In the first place, then, it is a well-known doctrine, and one as to which all the pious are agreed,—that the right consideration of signs does not lie merely in the outward ceremonies, but depends chiefly on the promise and the spiritual mysteries, to typify which the ceremonies themselves are appointed. He, therefore, who would thoroughly understand the effect of baptism—its object and true character—must not stop short at the element and corporeal object but look forward to the divine promises which are therein offered to us, and rise to the internal secrets which are therein represented. He who understands these has reached the solid truth, and, so to speak, the whole substance of baptism, and will thence perceive the nature and use of outward sprinkling. On the other hand, he who passes them by in contempt, and keeps his thoughts entirely fixed on the visible ceremony, will neither understand the force, nor the proper nature of baptism, nor comprehend what is meant, or what end is gained by the use of water. This is confirmed by passages of Scripture too numerous and too clear to make it necessary here to discuss them more at length. It remains, therefore, to inquire into the nature and efficacy of baptism, as evinced by the promises therein given. Scripture shows, *first*, that it points to that cleansing from sin which we obtain by the blood of Christ; and, *secondly*, to the mortification of the flesh which consists in participation in his death, by which believers are regenerated to newness of life, and thereby to the fellowship of Christ. To these general heads may be referred all that the Scriptures teach concerning baptism, with this addition, that it is also a symbol to testify our religion to men.

3. Now, since prior to the institution of baptism, the people of God had circumcision in its stead, let us see how far these two signs differ, and how far they resemble each other. In this way it will appear what analogy there is between them. When the Lord enjoins Abraham to observe circumcision (Gen. 17:10), he premises that he would be a God unto him and to his seed, adding, that in himself was a perfect sufficiency of all things, and that Abraham might reckon on his hand as a fountain of every blessing. These words include the promise of eternal life, as our Saviour interprets when he employs it to prove the immortality and resurrection of believers: "God," says he, "is not the God of the dead, but of the living" (Mt. 22:32). Hence, too, Paul, when showing to the Ephesians how great the destruction was from which the Lord had delivered them, seeing that they had not been admitted to the covenant of circumcision, infers that at that time they were aliens from the covenant of promise, without God, and without hope (Eph. 2:12), all these being comprehended in the covenant. Now, the first access to God, the first entrance to immortal life, is the remission of sins. Hence it follows, that this corresponds to the promise of our cleansing in baptism. The Lord afterwards covenants with Abraham, that he is to walk before him in sincerity and innocence of heart: this applies to mortification or regeneration. And lest any should doubt whether circumcision were the sign of mortification, Moses explains more clearly elsewhere when he exhorts the people of Israel to circumcise the foreskin of their heart, because the Lord had chosen them for his own people, out of all the nations of the earth. As the Lord, in choosing the posterity of Abraham for his people, commands them to be circumcised, so Moses declares that they are to be circumcised in heart, thus explaining what is typified by that carnal circumcision. Then, lest any one should attempt this in his own strength, he shows that it is the work of divine grace. All this is so often inculcated by the prophets, that there is no occasion here to collect the passages which everywhere occur. We have, therefore, a spiritual promise

given to the fathers in circumcision, similar to that which is given to us in baptism, since it figured to them both the forgiveness of sins and the mortification of the flesh. Besides, as we have shown that Christ, in whom both of these reside, is the foundation of baptism, so must he also be the foundation of circumcision. For he is promised to Abraham, and in him all nations are blessed. To seal this grace, the sign of circumcision is added.

4. There is now no difficulty in seeing wherein the two signs agree, and wherein they differ. The promise, in which we have shown that the power of the signs consists, is one in both—viz. the promise of the paternal favour of God, of forgiveness of sins, and eternal life. And the thing figured is one and the same—viz. regeneration. The foundation on which the completion of these things depends is one in both. Wherefore, there is no difference in the internal meaning, from which the whole power and peculiar nature of the sacrament is to be estimated. The only difference which remains is in the external ceremony, which is the least part of it, the chief part consisting in the promise and the thing signified. Hence we may conclude, that everything applicable to circumcision applies also to baptism, excepting always the difference in the visible ceremony. To this analogy and comparison we are led by that rule of the apostle, in which he enjoins us to bring every interpretation of Scripture to the analogy of faith (Rom. 12:3, 6). And certainly in this matter the truth may almost be felt. For just as circumcision, which was a kind of badge to the Jews, assuring them that they were adopted as the people and family of God, was their first entrance into the Church, while they, in their turn, professed their allegiance to God, so now we are initiated by baptism, so as to be enrolled among his people, and at the same time swear unto his name. Hence it is incontrovertible, that baptism has been substituted for circumcision, and performs the same office.

5. Now, if we are to investigate whether or not baptism is justly given to infants, will we not say that the man trifles, or rather is delirious, who would stop short at the element of water, and the external observance, and not allow his mind to rise to the spiritual mystery? If reason is listened to, it will undoubtedly appear that baptism is properly administered to infants as a thing due to them. The Lord did not anciently bestow circumcision upon them without making them partakers of all the things signified by circumcision. He would have deluded his people with mere imposture, had he quieted them with fallacious symbols: the very idea is shocking. He distinctly declares, that the circumcision of the infant will be instead of a seal of the promise of the covenant. But if the covenant remains firm and fixed, it is no less applicable to the children of Christians in the present day, than to the children of the Jews under the Old Testament. Now, if they are partakers of the thing signified, how can they be denied the sign? If they obtain the reality, how can they be refused the figure? The external sign is so united in the sacrament with the word, that it cannot be separated from it: but if they can be separated, to which of the two shall we attach the greater value? Surely, when we see that the sign is subservient to the word, we shall say that it is subordinate, and assign it the inferior place. Since, then, the word of baptism is destined for infants, why should we deny them the sign, which is an appendage of the word? This one reason, could no other be furnished, would be amply sufficient to refute all gainsayers. The objection, that there was a fixed day for circumcision, is a mere quibble. We admit that we are not now, like the Jews, tied down to certain days; but when the Lord declares, that though he prescribes no day, yet he is pleased that infants shall be formally admitted to his covenant, what more do we ask?

6. Scripture gives us a still clearer knowledge of the truth. For it is most evident that the covenant, which the Lord once made with Abraham, is not less applicable to Christians now than it was anciently to the Jewish people, and therefore that word has no less reference to Christians than to Jews. Unless, indeed, we imagine that Christ, by his advent, diminished, or curtailed the grace of the Father—an idea not free from execrable blasphemy. Wherefore, both the children of the Jews, because, when made heirs of that covenant, they were separated from the heathen, were called a holy seed, and for the same reason the children of Christians, or those who have only one believing parent, are called holy, and, by the testimony of the apostle, differ from the impure seed of idolaters. Then, since the Lord, immediately after the covenant was made with Abraham, ordered it to be sealed in infants by an outward sacrament, how can it be said that Christians are not to attest it in the present day, and seal it in their children? Let it not be objected, that the only symbol by which the Lord ordered his covenant to be confirmed was that of circumcision, which was long ago abrogated. It is easy to answer, that, in accordance with the form of the old dispensation, he appointed circumcision to confirm his covenant, but that it being abrogated, the same reason for confirmation still continues, a reason which we have in common with the Jews. Hence it is always necessary carefully to consider what

is common to both, and wherein they differed from us. The covenant is common, and the reason for confirming it is common. The mode of confirming it is so far different, that they had circumcision, instead of which we now have baptism. Otherwise, if the testimony by which the Jews were assured of the salvation of their seed is taken from us, the consequence will be, that, by the advent of Christ, the grace of God, which was formerly given to the Jews, is more obscure and less perfectly attested to us. If this cannot be said without extreme insult to Christ, by whom the infinite goodness of the Father has been more brightly and benignly than ever shed upon the earth, and declared to men, it must be confessed that it cannot be more confined, and less clearly manifested, than under the obscure shadows of the law.

7. Hence our Lord Jesus Christ, to give an example from which the world might learn that he had come to enlarge rather than to limit the grace of the Father, kindly takes the little children in his arms, and rebukes his disciples for attempting to prevent them from, coming (Mt. 19:13), because they were keeping those to whom the kingdom of heaven belonged away from him, through whom alone there is access to heaven. But it will be asked, What resemblance is there between baptism and our Saviour embracing little children? He is not said to have baptised, but to have received, embraced, and blessed them; and, therefore, if we would imitate his example, we must give infants the benefit of our prayers, not baptise them. But let us attend to the act of our Saviour a little more carefully than these men do. For we must not lightly overlook the fact, that our Saviour, in ordering little children to be brought to him, adds the reason, " of such is the kingdom of heaven." And he afterwards testifies his good-will by act, when he embraces them, and with prayer and benediction commends them to his Father. If it is right that children should be brought to Christ, why should they not be admitted to baptism, the symbol of our communion and fellowship with Christ? If the kingdom of heaven is theirs, why should they be denied the sign by which access, as it were, is opened to the Church, that being admitted into it they may be enrolled among the heirs of the heavenly kingdom? How unjust were we to drive away those whom Christ invites to himself, to spoil those whom he adorns with his gifts, to exclude those whom he spontaneously admits. But if we insist on discussing the difference between our Saviour's act and baptism, in how much higher esteem shall we hold baptism (by which we testify that infants are included in the divine covenant), than the taking up, embracing, laying hands on children, and praying over them, acts by which Christ, when present, declares both that they are his, and are sanctified by him. By the other cavils by which the objectors endeavour to evade this passage, they only betray their ignorance: they quibble that, because our Saviour says "Suffer little children to come," they must have been several years old, and fit to come. But they are called by the Evangelists βπέφη καὶ παιδιά, terms which denote infants still at their mothers' breasts. The term "come" is used simply for "approach." See the quibbles to which men are obliged to have recourse when they have hardened themselves against the truth! There is nothing more solid in their allegation, that the kingdom of heaven is not assigned to children, but to those like children, since the expression is, "of such," not "of themselves." If this is admitted, what will be the reason which our Saviour employs to show that they are not strangers to him from nonage? When he orders that little children shall be allowed to come to him, nothing is plainer than that mere infancy is meant. Lest this should seem absurd, he adds, "Of such is the kingdom of heaven." But if infants must necessarily be comprehended, the expression, "of such," clearly shows that infants themselves, and those like them, are intended.

8. Every one must now see that pædobaptism, which receives such strong support from Scripture, is by no means of human invention. Nor is there anything plausible in the objection, that we nowhere read of even one infant having been baptised by the hands of the apostles. For although this is not expressly narrated by the Evangelists, yet as they are not expressly excluded when mention is made of any baptised family (Acts 16:15, 32), what man of sense will argue from this that they were not baptised? If such kinds of argument were good, it would be necessary, in like manner, to interdict women from the Lord's Supper, since we do not read that they were ever admitted to it in the days of the apostles. But here we are contented with the rule of faith. For when we reflect on the nature of the ordinance of the Lord's Supper, we easily judge who the persons are to whom the use of it is to be communicated. The same we observe in the case of baptism. For, attending to the end for which it was instituted, we clearly perceive that it is not less applicable to children than to those of more advanced years, and that, therefore, they cannot be deprived of it without manifest fraud to the will of its divine Author. The assertion which they disseminate among the common people, that a long series of years elapsed after the resurrection of Christ, during which pædobaptism was unknown, is a shameful

falsehood, since there is no writer, however ancient, who does not trace its origin to the days of the apostles.

9. It remains briefly to indicate what benefit redounds from the observance, both to believers who bring their children to the church to be baptised, and to the infants themselves, to whom the sacred water is applied, that no one may despise the ordinance as useless or superfluous: though any one who would think of ridiculing baptism under this pretence, would also ridicule the divine ordinance of circumcision: for what can they adduce to impugn the one, that may not be retorted against the other? Thus the Lord punishes the arrogance of those who forthwith condemn whatever their carnal sense cannot comprehend. But God furnishes us with other weapons to repress their stupidity. His holy institution, from which we feel that our faith derives admirable consolation, deserves not to be called superfluous. For the divine symbol communicated to the child, as with the impress of a seal, confirms the promise given to the godly parent, and declares that the Lord will be a God not to him only, but to his seed; not merely visiting him with his grace and goodness, but his posterity also to the thousandth generation. When the infinite goodness of God is thus displayed, it, in the first place, furnishes most ample materials for proclaiming his glory, and fills pious breasts with no ordinary joy, urging them more strongly to love their affectionate Parent, when they see that, on their account, he extends his care to their posterity. I am not moved by the objection, that the promise ought to be sufficient to confirm the salvation of our children. It has seemed otherwise to God, who, seeing our weakness, has herein been pleased to condescend to it. Let those, then, who embrace the promise of mercy to their children, consider it as their duty to offer them to the Church, to be sealed with the symbol of mercy, and animate themselves to surer confidence, on seeing with the bodily eye the covenant of the Lord engraven on the bodies of their children. On the other hand, children derive some benefit from their baptism, when, being ingrafted into the body of the Church, they are made an object of greater interest to the other members. Then when they have grown up, they are thereby strongly urged to an earnest desire of serving God, who has received them as sons by the formal symbol of adoption, before, from nonage, they were able to recognise him as their Father. In fine, we ought to stand greatly in awe of the denunciation, that God will take vengeance on every one who despises to impress the symbol of the covenant on his child (Gen. 17:15), such contempt being a rejection, and, as it were, abjuration of the offered grace.

10. Let us now discuss the arguments by which some furious madmen cease not to assail this holy ordinance of God. And, first, feeling themselves pressed beyond measure by the resemblance between baptism and circumcision, they contend that there is a wide difference between the two signs, that the one has nothing in common with the other. They maintain that the things meant are different, that the covenant is altogether different, and that the persons included under the name of children are different. When they first proceed to the proof, they pretend that circumcision was a figure of mortification, not of baptism. This we willingly concede to them, for it admirably supports our view, in support of which the only proof we use is, that baptism and circumcision are signs of mortification. Hence we conclude that the one was substituted for the other, baptism representing to us the very thing which circumcision signified to the Jews. In asserting a difference of covenant, with what barbarian audacity do they corrupt and destroy Scripture? and that not in one passage only, but so as not to leave any passage safe and entire. The Jews they depict as so carnal as to resemble brutes more than men, representing the covenant which was made with them as reaching no farther than a temporary life, and the promises which were given to them as dwindling down into present and corporeal blessings. If this dogma is received, what remains but that the Jewish nation was overloaded for a time with divine kindness (just as swine are gorged in their sty), that they might at last perish eternally? Whenever we quote circumcision and the promises annexed to it, they answer, that circumcision was a literal sign, and that its promises were carnal.

11. Certainly, if circumcision was a literal sign, the same view must be taken of baptism, since, in the second chapter to the Colossians, the apostle makes the one to be not a whit more spiritual than the other. For he says that in Christ we "are circumcised with the circumcision made without hands, in putting off the body of the sins of the flesh, by the circumcision of Christ." In explanation of his sentiment he immediately adds, that we are "buried with him in baptism." What do these words mean, but just that the truth and completion of baptism is the truth and completion of circumcision, since they represent one thing? For his object is to show that baptism is the same thing to Christians that circumcision formerly was to the Jews. Now, since we have already clearly shown that the promises of both signs, and the mysteries which are represented by them, agree, we shall not dwell on the point longer at present. I would only remind believers to reflect,

without anything being said by me, whether that is to be regarded as an earthly and literal sign, which has nothing heavenly or spiritual under it. But lest they should blind the simple with their smoke, we shall, in passing, dispose of one objection by which they cloak this most impudent falsehood. It is absolutely certain that the original promises comprehending the covenant which God made with the Israelites under the old dispensation were spiritual, and had reference to eternal life, and were, of course, in like manner spiritually received by the fathers, that they might thence entertain a sure hope of immortality, and aspire to it with their whole soul. Meanwhile, we are far from denying that he testified his kindness to them by carnal and earthly blessings; though we hold that by these the hope of spiritual promises was confirmed. In this manner, when he promised eternal blessedness to his servant Abraham, he, in order to place a manifest indication of favour before his eye, added the promise of possession of the land of Canaan. In the same way we should understand all the terrestrial promises which were given to the Jewish nation, the spiritual promise, as the head to which the others bore reference, always holding the first place. Having handled this subject fully when treating of the difference between the old and the new dispensations, I now only glance at it.

12. Under the appellation of *children* the difference they observe is this, that the children of Abraham, under the old dispensation, were those who derived their origin from his seed, but that the appellation is now given to those who imitate his faith, and therefore that carnal infancy, which was ingrafted into the fellowship of the covenant by circumcision, typified the spiritual children of the new covenant, who are regenerated by the word of God to immortal life. In these words we indeed discover a small spark of truth, but these giddy spirits err grievously in this, that laying hold of whatever comes first to their hand, when they ought to proceed farther, and compare many things together, they obstinately fasten upon one single word. Hence it cannot but happen that they are every now and then deluded, because they do not exert themselves to obtain a full knowledge of any subject. We certainly admit that the carnal seed of Abraham for a time held the place of the spiritual seed, which is ingrafted into him by faith (Gal. 4:28; Rom. 4:12). For we are called his sons, though we have no natural relationship with him. But if they mean, as they not obscurely show, that the spiritual promise was never made to the carnal seed of Abraham, they are greatly mistaken. We must, therefore, take a better aim, one to which we are directed by the infallible guidance of Scripture. The Lord therefore promises to Abraham that he shall have a seed in whom all the nations of the earth will be blessed, and at the same time assures him that he will be a God both to him and his seed. All who in faith receive Christ as the author of the blessing are the heirs of this promise, and accordingly are called the children of Abraham.

13. Although, after the resurrection of Christ, the boundaries of the kingdom began to be extended far and wide into all nations indiscriminately, so that, according to the declaration of Christ, believers were collected from all quarters to sit down with Abraham, Isaac, and Jacob, in the kingdom of heaven (Mt. 8:11), still, for many ages before, the Jews had enjoyed this great mercy. And as he had selected them (while passing by all other nations) to be for a time the depositaries of his favour, he designated them as his peculiar purchased people (Exod. 19:5). In attestation of this kindness, he appointed circumcision, by which symbol the Jews were taught that God watched over their safety, and they were thereby raised to the hope of eternal life. For what can ever be wanting to him whom God has once taken under his protection? Wherefore the apostle, to prove that the Gentiles, as well as the Jews, were the children of Abraham, speaks in this way: "Faith was reckoned to Abraham for righteousness. How was it then reckoned? when he was in circumcision, or in uncircumcision? Not in circumcision, but in uncircumcision. And he received the sign of circumcision, a seal of the righteousness of the faith which he had yet being uncircumcised; that he might be the father of all them that believe, though they be not circumcised: that righteousness might be imputed to them also: and the father of circumcision to them who are not of the circumcision only, but who also walk in the steps of that faith of our father Abraham, which he had yet being uncircumcised" (Rom. 4:9–12). Do we not see that both are made equal in dignity? For, to the time appointed by the divine decree, he was the father of circumcision. But when, as the apostle elsewhere writes (Eph. 2:14), the wall of partition which separated the Gentiles from the Jews was broken down, to them, also, access was given to the kingdom of God, and he became their father, and that without the sign of circumcision, its place being supplied by baptism. In saying expressly that Abraham was not the father of those who were of the circumcision only, his object was to repress the superciliousness of some who, laying aside all regard to godliness, plumed themselves on mere ceremonies. In like manner, we may, in the present day, refute the vanity of those who, in baptism, seek nothing but water.

14. But in opposition to this is produced a passage from the Epistle to the Romans, in which the apostle says, that those who are of the flesh are not the children of Abraham, but that those only who are the children of promise are considered as the seed (Rom. 9:7). For he seems to insinuate, that carnal relationship to Abraham, which we think of some consequence, is nothing. But we must attend carefully to the subject which the apostle is there treating. His object being to show to the Jews that the goodness of God was not restricted to the seed of Abraham, nay, that of itself it contributes nothing, produces, in proof of the fact, the cases of Ishmael and Esau. These being rejected, just as if they had been strangers, although, according to the flesh, they were the genuine offspring of Abraham, the blessing resides in Isaac and Jacob. This proves what he afterwards affirms—viz. that salvation depends on the mercy which God bestows on whomsoever he pleases, but that the Jews have no ground to glory or plume themselves on the name of the covenant, unless they keep the law of the covenant, that is, obey the word. On the other hand, after casting down their vain confidence in their origin, because he was aware that the covenant which had been made with the posterity of Abraham could not properly prove fruitless, he declares, that due honour should still be paid to carnal relationship to Abraham, in consequence of which, the Jews were the primary and native heirs of the gospel, unless in so far as they were, for their ingratitude, rejected as unworthy, and yet rejected so as not to leave their nation utterly destitute of the heavenly blessing. For this reason, though they were contumacious breakers of the covenant, he styles them holy (such respect does he pay to the holy generation which God had honoured with his sacred covenant), while we, in comparison of them, are termed posthumous, or abortive children of Abraham, and that not by nature, but by adoption, just as if a twig were broken from its own tree, and ingrafted on another stock. Therefore, that they might not be defrauded of their privilege, it was necessary that the gospel should first be preached to them. For they are, as it were, the first-born in the family of God. The honour due, on this account, must therefore be paid them, until they have rejected the offer, and, by their ingratitude, caused it to be transferred to the Gentiles. Nor, however great the contumacy with which they persist in warring against the gospel, are we therefore despise them. We must consider, that in respect of the promise, the blessing of God still resides among them; and, as the apostle testifies, will never entirely depart from them, seeing that "the gifts and calling of God are without repentance" (Rom. 11:29).

15. Such is the value of the promise given to the posterity of Abraham,—such the balance in which it is to be weighed. Hence, though we have no doubt that in distinguishing the children of God from bastards and foreigners, that the election of God reigns freely, we, at the same time, perceive that he was pleased specially to embrace the seed of Abraham with his mercy, and, for the better attestation of it, to seal it by circumcision. The case of the Christian Church is entirely of the same description; for as Paul there declares that the Jews are sanctified by their parents, so he elsewhere says that the children of Christians derive sanctification from their parents. Hence it is inferred, that those who are chargeable with impurity are justly separated from others. Now, who can have any doubt as to the falsehood of their subsequent averment—viz. that the infants who were formerly circumcised only typified the spiritual infancy which is produced by the regeneration of the word of God? When the apostle says, that "Jesus Christ was a minister of the circumcision for the truth of God, to confirm the promises made unto the fathers" (Rom. 15:8), he does not philosophise subtilely, as if he had said, Since the covenant made with Abraham has respect unto his seed, Christ, in order to perform and discharge the promise made by the Father, came for the salvation of the Jewish nation. Do you see how he considers that, after the resurrection of Christ, the promise is to be fulfilled to the seed of Abraham, not allegorically, but literally, as the words express? To the same effect is the declaration of Peter to the Jews: "The promise is unto you and to your children" (Acts 2:39); and in the next chapter, he calls them *the children of the covenant*, that is, heirs. Not widely different from this is the other passage of the apostle, above quoted, in which he regards and describes circumcision performed on infants as an attestation to the communion which they have with Christ. And, indeed, if we listen to the absurdities of those men, what will become of the promise by which the Lord, in the second commandment of his law, engages to be gracious to the seed of his servants for a thousand generations? Shall we here have recourse to allegory? This were the merest quibble. Shall we say that it has been abrogated? In this way, we should do away with the law which Christ came not to destroy, but to fulfil, inasmuch as it turns to our everlasting good. Therefore, let it be without controversy, that God is so good and liberal to his people, that he is pleased, as a mark of his favour, to extend their privileges to the children born to them.

16. The distinctions which these men attempt to draw between baptism and circumcision are not only ridiculous, and void of all semblance of reason, but at variance with each other. For, when they affirm that baptism refers to the first day of spiritual contest, and circumcision to the eighth day, mortification being already accomplished, they immediately forget the distinction, and change their song, representing circumcision as typifying the mortification of the flesh, and baptism as a burial, which is given to none but those who are already dead. What are these giddy contradictions but frenzied dreams? According to the former view, baptism ought to precede circumcision; according to the latter, it should come after it. It is not the first time we have seen the minds of men wander to and fro when they substitute their dreams for the infallible word of God. We hold, therefore, that their former distinction is a mere imagination. Were we disposed to make an allegory of the eighth day, theirs would not be the proper mode of it. It were much better with the early Christians to refer the number eight to the resurrection, which took place on the eighth day, and on which we know that newness of life depends, or to the whole course of the present life, during which, mortification ought to be in progress, only terminating when life itself terminates; although it would seem that God intended to provide for the tenderness of infancy by deferring circumcision to the eighth day, as the wound would have been more dangerous if inflicted immediately after birth. How much more rational is the declaration of Scripture, that we, when already dead, are buried by baptism (Rom. 6:4); since it distinctly states, that we are buried into death that we may thoroughly die, and thenceforth aim at that mortification? Equally ingenious is their cavil, that women should not be baptised if baptism is to be made conformable to circumcision. For if it is most certain that the sanctification of the seed of Israel was attested by the sign of circumcision, it cannot be doubted that it was appointed alike for the sanctification of males and females. But though the right could only be performed on males, yet the females were, through them, partners and associates in circumcision. Wherefore, disregarding all such quibbling distinctions, let us fix on the very complete resemblance between baptism and circumcision, as seen in the internal office, the promise, the use, and the effect.

17. They seem to think they produce their strongest reason for denying baptism to children, when they allege, that they are as yet unfit, from nonage, to understand the mystery which is there sealed—viz. spiritual regeneration, which is not applicable to earliest infancy. Hence they infer, that children are only to be regarded as sons of Adam until they have attained an age fit for the reception of the second birth. But all this is directly opposed to the truth of God. For if they are to be accounted sons of Adam, they are left in death, since, in Adam, we can do nothing but die. On the contrary, Christ bids them be brought to him. Why so? Because he is life. Therefore, that he may quicken them, he makes them partners with himself; whereas these men would drive them away from Christ, and adjudge them to death. For if they pretend that infants do not perish when they are accounted the sons of Adam, the error is more than sufficiently confuted by the testimony of Scripture (1 Cor. 15:22). For seeing it declares that in Adam all die, it follows, that no hope of life remains unless in Christ. Therefore, that we may become heirs of life, we must communicate with him. Again, seeing it is elsewhere written that we are all by nature the children of wrath (Eph. 2:3), and conceived in sin (Ps. 51:5), of which condemnation is the inseparable attendant, we must part with our own nature before we have any access to the kingdom of God. And what can be clearer than the expression, "Flesh and blood cannot inherit the kingdom of God"? (1 Cor. 15:50.) Therefore, let everything that is our own be abolished (this cannot be without regeneration), and then we shall perceive this possession of the kingdom. In fine, if Christ speaks truly when he declares that he is life, we must necessarily be ingrafted into him by whom we are delivered from the bondage of death. But how, they ask, are infants regenerated, when not possessing a knowledge of either good or evil? We answer, that the work of God, though beyond the reach of our capacity, is not therefore null. Moreover, infants who are to be saved (and that some are saved at this age is certain) must, without question, be previously regenerated by the Lord. For if they bring innate corruption with them from their mother's womb, they must be purified before they can be admitted into the kingdom of God, into which shall not enter anything that defileth (Rev. 21:27). If they are born sinners, as David and Paul affirm, they must either remain unaccepted and hated by God, or be justified. And why do we ask more, when the Judge himself publicly declares, that "except a man be born again, he cannot see the kingdom of God"? (John 3:3.) But to silence this class of objectors, God gave, in the case of John the Baptist, whom he sanctified from his mother's womb (Luke 1:15), a proof of what he might do in others. They gain nothing by the quibble to which they here resort—viz. that this was only once done, and

therefore it does not forthwith follow that the Lord always acts thus with infants. That is not the mode in which we reason. Our only object is to show, that they unjustly and malignantly confine the power of God within limits, within which it cannot be confined. As little weight is due to another subterfuge. They allege that, by the usual phraseology of Scripture, "from the womb," has the same meaning as "from childhood." But it is easy to see that the angel had a different meaning when he announced to Zacharias that the child not yet born would be filled with the Holy Spirit. Instead of attempting to give a law to God, let us hold that he sanctifies whom he pleases, in the way in which he sanctified John, seeing that his power is not impaired.

18. And, indeed, Christ was sanctified from earliest infancy, that he might sanctify his elect in himself at any age, without distinction. For as he, in order to wipe away the guilt of disobedience which had been committed in our flesh, assumed that very flesh, that in it he might, on our account, and in our stead, perform a perfect obedience, so he was conceived by the Holy Spirit, that, completely pervaded with his holiness in the flesh which he had assumed, he might transfuse it into us. If in Christ we have a perfect pattern of all the graces which God bestows on all his children, in this instance we have a proof that the age of infancy is not incapable of receiving sanctification. This, at least, we set down as incontrovertible, that none of the elect is called away from the present life without being previously sanctified and regenerated by the Spirit of God. As to their objection that, in Scripture, the Spirit acknowledges no sanctification save that from incorruptible seed, that is, the word of God, they erroneously interpret Peter's words, in which he comprehends only believers who had been taught by the preaching of the gospel (1 Pet. 1:23). We confess, indeed, that the word of the Lord is the only seed of spiritual regeneration; but we deny the inference that, therefore, the power of God cannot regenerate infants. This is as possible and easy for him, as it is wondrous and incomprehensible to us. It were dangerous to deny that the Lord is able to furnish them with the knowledge of himself in any way he pleases.

19. But *faith*, they say, *cometh by hearing*, the use of which infants have not yet obtained, nor can they be fit to know God, being, as Moses declares, without the knowledge of good and evil (Deut. 1:39). But they observe not that where the apostle makes hearing the beginning of faith, he is only describing the usual economy and dispensation which the Lord is wont to employ in calling his people, and not laying down an invariable rule, for which no other method can be substituted. Many he certainly has called and endued with the true knowledge of himself, by internal means, by the illumination of the Spirit, without the intervention of preaching. But since they deem it very absurd to attribute any knowledge of God to infants, whom Moses makes void of the knowledge of good and evil, let them tell me where the danger lies if they are said now to receive some part of that grace, of which they are to have the full measure shortly after. For if fulness of life consists in the perfect knowledge of God, since some of those whom death hurries away in the first moments of infancy pass into life eternal, they are certainly admitted to behold the immediate presence of God. Those, therefore, whom the Lord is to illumine with the full brightness of his light, why may he not, if he so pleases, irradiate at present with some small beam, especially if he does not remove their ignorance, before he delivers them from the prison of the flesh? I would not rashly affirm that they are endued with the same faith which we experience in ourselves, or have any knowledge at all resembling faith (this I would rather leave undecided); but I would somewhat curb the stolid arrogance of those men who, as with inflated cheeks, affirm or deny whatever suits them.

20. In order to gain a stronger footing here, they add, that baptism is a sacrament of penitence and faith, and as neither of these is applicable to tender infancy, we must beware of rendering its meaning empty and vain, by admitting infants to the communion of baptism. But these darts are directed more against God then against us; since the fact that circumcision was a sign of repentance is completely established by many passages of Scripture (Jer. 4:4). Thus Paul terms it a seal of the righteousness of faith (Rom. 4:11). Let God, then, be demanded why he ordered circumcision to be performed on the bodies of infants? For baptism and circumcision being here in the same case, they cannot give anything to the latter without conceding it to the former. If they recur to their usual evasion, that, by the age of infancy, spiritual infants were then figured, we have already closed this means of escape against them. We say, then, that since God imparted circumcision, the sign of repentance and faith, to infants, it should not seem absurd that they are now made partakers of baptism, unless men choose to clamour against an institution of God. But as in all his acts, so here also, enough of wisdom and righteousness shines forth to repress the slanders of the ungodly. For although infants, at the moment when they were cir-

cumcised, did not comprehend what the sign meant, still they were truly circumcised for the mortification of their corrupt and polluted nature—a mortification at which they afterwards aspired when adults. In fine, the objection is easily disposed of by the tact, that children are baptised for future repentance and faith. Though these are not yet formed in them, yet the seed of both lies hid in them by the secret operation of the Spirit. This answer at once overthrows all the objections which are twisted against us out of the meaning of baptism; for instance, the title by which Paul distinguishes it when he terms it the "washing of regeneration and renewing" (Tit. 3:5). Hence they argue, that it is not to be given to any but to those who are capable of such feelings. But we, on the other hand, may object, that neither ought circumcision, which is designated regeneration, to be conferred on any but the regenerate. In this way, we shall condemn a divine institution. Thus, as we have already hinted, all the arguments which tend to shake circumcision are of no force in assailing baptism. Nor can they escape by saying, that everything which rests on the authority of God is absolutely fixed, though there should be no reason for it, but that this reverence is not due to pædobaptism, nor other similar things which are not recommended to us by the express word of God. They always remain caught in this dilemma. The command of God to circumcise infants was either legitimate and exempt from cavil, or deserved reprehension. If there was nothing incompetent or absurd in it, no absurdity can be shown in the observance of pædobaptism.

21. The charge of absurdity with which they attempt to stigmatise it, we thus dispose of. If those on whom the Lord has bestowed his election, after receiving the sign of regeneration, depart this life before they become adults, he, by the incomprehensible energy of his Spirit, renews them in the way which he alone sees to be expedient. Should they reach an age when they can be instructed in the meaning of baptism, they will thereby be animated to greater zeal for renovation, the badge of which they will learn that they received in earliest infancy, in order that they might aspire to it during their whole lives. To the same effect are the two passages in which Paul teaches, that we are buried with Christ by baptism (Rom. 6:4; Col. 2:12). For by this he means not that he who is to be initiated by baptism must have previously been buried with Christ; he simply declares the doctrine which is taught by baptism, and that to those already baptised: so that the most senseless cannot maintain from this passage that it ought to precede baptism. In this way, Moses and the prophets reminded the people of the thing meant by circumcision, which however infants received. To the same effect, Paul says to the Galatians, "As many of you as have been baptised into Christ have put on Christ" (Gal. 3:27). Why so? That they might thereafter live to Christ, to whom previously they had not lived. And though, in adults, the receiving of the sign ought to follow the understanding of its meaning, yet, as will shortly be explained, a different rule must be followed with children. No other conclusion can be drawn from a passage in Peter, on which they strongly found. He says, that baptism is "not the putting away of the filth of the flesh, but the answer of a good conscience toward God by the resurrection of Jesus Christ" (1 Pet. 3:21). From this they contend that nothing is left for pædobaptism, which becomes mere empty smoke, as being altogether at variance with the meaning of baptism. But the delusion which misleads them is, that they would always have the thing to precede the sign in the order of time. For the truth of circumcision consisted in the same answer of a good conscience; but if the truth must necessarily have preceded, infants would never have been circumcised by the command of God. But he himself, showing that the answer of a good conscience forms the truth of circumcision, and, at the same time, commanding infants to be circumcised, plainly intimates that, in their case, circumcision had reference to the future. Wherefore, nothing more of present effect is to be required in pædobaptism, than to confirm and sanction the covenant which the Lord has made with them. The other part of the meaning of the sacrament will follow at the time which God himself has provided.

22. Every one must, I think, clearly perceive, that all arguments of this stamp are mere perversions of Scripture. The other remaining arguments akin to these we shall cursorily examine. They object, that baptism is given for the remission of sins. When this is conceded, it strongly supports our view; for, seeing we are born sinners, we stand in need of forgiveness and pardon from the very womb. Moreover, since God does not preclude this age from the hope of mercy, but rather gives assurance of it, why should we deprive it of the sign, which is much inferior to the reality? The arrow, therefore, which they aim at us, we throw back upon themselves. Infants receive forgiveness of sins; therefore, they are not to be deprived of the sign. They adduce the passage from the Ephesians, that Christ gave himself for the Church, "that he might sanctify and cleanse it with the washing of water by the word" (Eph. 5:26). Nothing could be quoted more

appropriate than this to overthrow their error: it furnishes us with an easy proof. If, by baptism, Christ intends to attest the ablution by which he cleanses his Church, it would seem not equitable to deny this attestation to infants, who are justly deemed part of the Church, seeing they are called heirs of the heavenly kingdom. For Paul comprehends the whole Church when he says that it was cleansed by the washing of water. In like manner, from his expression in another place, that by baptism we are ingrafted into the body of Christ (1 Cor. 7:13), we infer, that infants, whom he enumerates among his members, are to be baptised, in order that they may not be dissevered from his body. See the violent onset which they make with all their engines on the bulwarks of our faith.

23. They now come down to the custom and practice of the apostolic age, alleging that there is no instance of any one having been admitted to baptism without a previous profession of faith and repentance. For when Peter is asked by his hearers, who were pricked in their heart, "What shall we do?" his advise is, "Repent and be baptised, every one of you, in the name of Jesus Christ, for the remission of sins" (Acts 2:37, 38). In like manner, when Philip was asked by the eunuch to baptise him, he answered, "If thou believest with all thine heart, thou mayest." Hence they think they can make out that baptism cannot be lawfully given to any one without previous faith and repentance. If we yield to this argument, the former passage, in which there is no mention of faith, will prove that repentance alone is sufficient, and the latter, which makes no requirement of repentance, that there is need only of faith. They will object, I presume, that the one passage helps the other, and that both, therefore, are to be connected. I, in my turn, maintain that these two must be compared with other passages which contribute somewhat to the solution of this difficulty. There are many passages of Scripture whose meaning depends on their peculiar position. Of this we have an example in the present instance. Those to whom these things are said by Peter and Philip are of an age fit to aim at repentance, and receive faith. We strenuously insist that such men are not to be baptised unless their conversion and faith are discerned, at least in as far as human judgment can ascertain it. But it is perfectly clear that infants must be placed in a different class. For when any one formerly joined the religious communion of Israel, he behoved to be taught the covenant, and instructed in the law of the Lord, before he received circumcision, because he was of a different nation; in other words, an alien from the people of Israel, with whom the covenant, which circumcision sanctioned, had been made.

24. Thus the Lord, when he chose Abraham for himself, did not commence with circumcision, in the meanwhile concealing what he meant by that sign, but first announced that he intended to make a covenant with him, and, after his faith in the promise, made him partaker of the sacrament. Why does the sacrament come after faith in Abraham, and precede all intelligence in his son Isaac? It is right that he who, in adult age, is admitted to the fellowship of a covenant by one from whom he had hitherto been alienated, should previously learn its conditions; but it is not so with the infant born to him. He, according to the terms of the promise, is included in the promise by hereditary right from his mother's womb. Or, to state the matter more briefly and more clearly, If the children of believers, without the help of understanding, are partakers of the covenant, there is no reason why they should be denied the sign, because they are unable to swear to its stipulations. This undoubtedly is the reason why the Lord sometimes declares that the children born to the Israelites are begotten and born to him (Ezek. 16:20; 23:37). For he undoubtedly gives the place of sons to the children of those to whose seed he has promised that he will be a Father. But the child descended from unbelieving parents is deemed an alien to the covenant until he is united to God by faith. Hence, it is not strange that the sign is withheld when the thing signified would be vain and fallacious. In that view, Paul says that the Gentiles, so long as they were plunged in idolatry, were strangers to the covenant (Eph. 2:11). The whole matter may, if I mistake not, be thus briefly and clearly expounded: Those who, in adult age, embrace the faith of Christ, having hitherto been aliens from the covenant, are not to receive the sign of baptism without previous faith and repentance. These alone can give them access to the fellowship of the covenant, whereas children, deriving their origin from Christians, as they are immediately on their birth received by God as heirs of the covenant, are also to be admitted to baptism. To this we must refer the narrative of the Evangelist, that those who were baptised by John confessed their sins (Mt. 3:6). This example, we hold, ought to be observed in the present day. Were a Turk to offer himself for baptism, we would not at once perform the rite without receiving a confession which was satisfactory to the Church.

25. Another passage which they adduce is from the third chapter of John, where our Saviour's words seem to them to imply that a present regeneration is required

in baptism, "Except a man be born of water, and of the Spirit, he cannot enter into the kingdom of God" (John 3:5). See, they say, how baptism is termed regeneration by the lips of our Lord himself, and on what pretext, therefore, with what consistency is baptism given to those who, it is perfectly obvious, are not at all capable of regeneration? First, they are in error in imagining that there is any mention of baptism in this passage, merely because the word water is used. Nicodemus, after our Saviour had explained to him the corruption of nature, and the necessity of being born again, kept dreaming of a corporeal birth, and hence our Saviour intimates the mode in which God regenerates us—viz. by water and the Spirit; in other words, by the Spirit, who, in irrigating and cleansing the souls of believers, operates in the manner of water. By "water and the Spirit," therefore, I simply understand the Spirit, which is water. Nor is the expression new. It perfectly accords with that which is used in the third chapter of Matthew, "He that cometh after me is mightier than I;" "he shall baptise you with the Holy Ghost, and with fire" (Mt. 3:11). Therefore, as to baptise with the Holy Spirit, and with fire, is to confer the Holy Spirit, who, in regeneration, has the office and nature of fire, so to be born again of water, and of the Spirit, is nothing else than to receive that power of the Spirit, which has the same effect on the soul that water has on the body. I know that a different interpretation is given, but I have no doubt that this is the genuine meaning, because our Saviour's only purpose was to teach, that all who aspire to the kingdom of heaven must lay aside their own disposition. And yet were we disposed to imitate these men in their mode of cavilling, we might easily, after conceding what they wish, reply to them, that baptism is prior to faith and repentance, since, in this passage, our Saviour mentions it before the Spirit. This certainly must be understood of spiritual gifts, and if they follow baptism, I have gained all I contend for. But, cavilling aside, the simple interpretation to be adopted is that which I have given—viz. that no man, until renewed by living water, that is, by the Spirit, can enter the kingdom of God.

26. This, moreover, plainly explodes the fiction of those who consign all the unbaptised to eternal death. Let us suppose, then, that, as they insist, baptism is administered to adults only. What will they make of a youth who, after being embued duly and properly with the rudiments of piety, while waiting for the day of baptism, is unexpectedly carried off by sudden death? The promise of our Lord is clear, "He that heareth my word, and believeth on him that sent me, hath everlasting life, and shall not come into condemnation, but is passed from death unto life" (John 5:24). We nowhere read of his having condemned him who was not yet baptised. I would not be understood as insinuating that baptism may be contemned with impunity. So far from excusing this contempt, I hold that it violates the covenant of the Lord. The passage only serves to show, that we must not deem baptism so necessary as to suppose that every one who has lost the opportunity of obtaining it has forthwith perished. By assenting to their fiction, we should condemn all, without exception, whom any accident may have prevented from procuring baptism, how much soever they may have been endued with the faith by which Christ himself is possessed. Moreover, baptism being, as they hold, necessary to salvation, they, in denying it to infants, consign them all to eternal death. Let them now consider what kind of agreement they have with the words of Christ, who says, that "of such is the kingdom of heaven" (Mt. 19:14). And though we were to concede everything to them, in regard to the meaning of this passage, they will extract nothing from it, until they have previously overthrown the doctrine which we have already established concerning the regeneration of infants.

27. But they boast of having their strongest bulwark in the very institution of baptism, which they find in the last chapter of Matthew, where Christ, sending his disciples into all the world, commands them to teach and then baptise. Then, in the last chapter of Mark, it is added, "He that believeth, and is baptised, shall be saved" (Mark 16:16). What more (say they) do we ask, since the words of Christ distinctly declare, that teaching must precede baptism, and assign to baptism the place next to faith? Of this arrangement our Lord himself gave an example, in choosing not to be baptised till his thirtieth year. In how many ways do they here entangle themselves, and betray their ignorance! They err more than childishly in this, that they derive the first institution of baptism from this passage, whereas Christ had, from the commencement of his ministry, ordered it to be administered by the apostles. There is no ground, therefore, for contending that the law and rule of baptism is to be sought from these two passages. as containing the first institution. But to indulge them in their error, how nerveless is this mode of arguing? Were I disposed to evasion, I have not only a place of escape, but a wide field to expatiate in. For when they cling so desperately to the order of the words, insisting that because it is said, "Go, preach and baptise," and

again, "Whosoever believes and is baptised," they must preach before baptising, and believe before being baptised, why may not we in our turn object, that they must baptise before teaching the observance of those things which Christ commanded, because it is said, "Baptise, teaching whatsoever I have commanded you"? The same thing we observed in the other passage in which Christ speaks of the regeneration of water and of the Spirit. For if we interpret as they insist, then baptism must take precedence of spiritual regeneration, because it is first mentioned. Christ teaches that we are to be born again, not of the Spirit and of water, but of water and of the Spirit.

28. This unassailable argument, in which they confide so much, seems already to be considerably shaken; but as we have sufficient protection in the simplicity of truth, I am unwilling to evade the point by paltry subtleties. Let them, therefore, have a solid answer. The command here given by Christ relates principally to the preaching of the gospel: to it baptism is added as a kind of appendage. Then he merely speaks of baptism in so far as the dispensation of it is subordinate to the function of teaching. For Christ sends his disciples to publish the gospel to all nations of the world, that by the doctrine of salvation they may gather men, who were previously lost, into his kingdom. But who or what are those men? It is certain that mention is made only of those who are fit to receive his doctrine. He subjoins, that such, after being taught, were to be baptised, adding the promise, Whosoever believeth and is baptised, shall be saved. Is there one syllable about infants in the whole discourse? What, then, is the form of argument with which they assail us? Those who are of adult age are to be instructed and brought to the faith before being baptised, and therefore it is unlawful to make baptism common to infants. They cannot, at the very utmost, prove any other thing out of this passage, than that the gospel must be preached to those who are capable of hearing it before they are baptised; for of such only the passage speaks. From this let them, if they can, throw an obstacle in the way of baptising infants.

29. But I will make their fallacies palpable even to the blind, by a very plain similitude. Should any one insist that infants are to be deprived of food, on the presence that the apostle permits none to eat but those who labour (2 Thess. 3:10), would he not deserve to be scouted by all? Why so? Because that which was said of a certain class of men, and a certain age, he wrests and applies to all indifferently. The dexterity of these men in the present instance is not greater. That which every one sees to be intended for adult age merely, they apply to infants, subjecting them to a rule which was laid down only for those of riper years. With regard to the example of our Saviour, it gives no countenance to their case. He was not baptised before his thirtieth year. This is indeed true, but the reason is obvious; because he then determined to lay the solid foundation of baptism by his preaching, or rather to confirm the foundation which John had previously laid. Therefore, when he was pleased with his doctrine to institute baptism, that he might give the greater authority to his institution, he sanctified it in his own person, and that at the most befitting time, namely, the commencement of his ministry. In fine, they can prove nothing more than that baptism received its origin and commencement with the preaching of the gospel. But if they are pleased to fix upon the thirtieth year, why do they not observe it, but admit any one to baptism according to the view which they may have formed of his proficiency? Nay, even Servetus, one of their masters, although he pertinaciously insisted on this period, had begun to act the prophet in his twenty-first year; as if any man could be tolerated in arrogating to himself the office of a teacher in the Church before he was a member of the Church.

30. At length they object, that there is not greater reason for admitting infants to baptism than to the Lord's Supper, to which, however, they are never admitted: as if Scripture did not in every way draw a wide distinction between them. In the early Church indeed, the Lord's Supper was frequently given to infants, as appears from Cyprian and Augustine (August. ad Bonif. Lib. 1); but the practice justly became obsolete. For if we attend to the peculiar nature of baptism, it is a kind of entrance, and as it were initiation into the Church, by which we are ranked among the people of God, a sign of our spiritual regeneration, by which we are again born to be children of God; whereas, on the contrary, the Supper is intended for those of riper years, who, having passed the tender period of infancy, are fit to bear solid food. This distinction is very clearly pointed out in Scripture. For there, as far as regards baptism, the Lord makes no selection of age, whereas he does not admit all to partake of the Supper, but confines it to those who are fit to discern the body and blood of the Lord, to examine their own conscience, to show forth the Lord's death, and understand its power. Can we wish anything clearer than what the apostle says, when he thus exhorts, "Let a man examine himself, and so let him eat of that bread, and drink of that cup"? (1 Cor. 11:28.) Examination, therefore, must precede, and this it were vain to expect from infants. Again, "He that eateth and drinketh unworthily, eateth and drinketh

damnation to himself, not discerning the Lord's body." If they cannot partake worthily without being able duly to discern the sanctity of the Lord's body, why should we stretch out poison to our young children instead of vivifying food? Then what is our Lord's injunction? "Do this in remembrance of me." And what the inference which the apostle draws from this? "As often as ye eat this bread, and drink this cup, ye do show the Lord's death till he come." How, pray, can we require infants to commemorate any event of which they have no understanding; how require them "to show forth the Lord's death," of the nature and benefit of which they have no idea? Nothing of the kind is prescribed by baptism. Wherefore, there is the greatest difference between the two signs. This also we observe in similar signs under the old dispensation. Circumcision, which, as is well known, corresponds to our baptism, was intended for infants, but the passover, for which the Supper is substituted, did not admit all kinds of guests promiscuously, but was duly eaten only by those who were of an age sufficient to ask the meaning of it (Exod. 12:26). Had these men the least particle of soundness in their brain, would they be thus blind as to a matter so very clear and obvious?

31. Though I am unwilling to annoy the reader with the series of conceits which Servetus, not the least among the Anabaptists, nay, the great honour of this crew, when girding himself for battle, deemed, when he adduced them, to be specious arguments, it will be worth while briefly to dispose of them. He pretends that as the symbols of Christ are perfect, they require persons who are perfect, or at least capable of perfection. But the answer is plain. The perfection of baptism, which extends even to death, is improperly restricted to one moment of time; moreover, perfection, in which baptism invites us to make continual progress during life, is foolishly exacted by him all at once. He objects, that the symbols of Christ were appointed for remembrance, that every one may remember that he was buried together with Christ. I answer, that what he coined out of his own brain does not need refutation, nay, that which he transfers to baptism properly belongs to the Supper, as appears from Paul's words, "Let a man examine himself," words similar to which are nowhere used with reference to baptism. Whence we infer, that those who from nonage are incapable of examination are duly baptised. His third point is, That all who believe not in the Son remain in death, the wrath of God abideth on them (John 3:36); and, therefore, infants who are unable to believe lie under condemnation. I answer, that Christ does not there speak of the general guilt in which all the posterity of Adam are involved, but only threatens the despisers of the gospel, who proudly and contumaciously spurn the grace which is offered to them. But this has nothing to do with infants. At the same time, I meet him with the opposite argument. Every one whom Christ blesses is exempted from the curse of Adam, and the wrath of God. Therefore, seeing it is certain that infants are blessed by him, it follows that they are freed from death. He next falsely quotes a passage which is nowhere found, Whosoever is born of the Spirit, hears the voice of the Spirit. Though we should grant that such a passage occurs in Scripture, all he can extract from it is, that believers, according as the Spirit works in them, are framed to obedience. But that which is said of a certain number, it is illogical to apply to all alike. His fourth objection is, As that which precedes is animal (1 Cor. 15:46), we must wait the full time for baptism, which is spiritual. But while I admit that all the posterity of Adam, born of the flesh, bear their condemnation with them from the womb, I hold that this is no obstacle to the immediate application of the divine remedy. Servetus cannot show that by divine appointment, several years must elapse before the new spiritual life begins. Paul's testimony is, that though lost by nature, the children of believers are holy by supernatural grace. He afterwards brings forward the allegory that David, when going up into mount Zion, took with him neither the blind nor the lame, but vigorous soldiers (2 Sam. 5:8). But what if I meet this with the parable in which God invites to the heavenly feast the lame and the blind? In what way will Servetus disentangle this knot? I ask, moreover, whether the lame and the maimed had not previously served with David? But it is superfluous to dwell longer on this argument, which, as the reader will learn from the sacred history, is founded on mere misquotation. He adds another allegory— viz. that the apostles were fishers of men, not of children. I ask, then, What does our Saviour mean when he says that in the net are caught all kinds of fishes? (Mt. 9:19; 13:47.) But as I have no pleasure in sporting with allegory, I answer, that when the office of teaching was committed to the apostles, they were not prohibited from baptising infants. Moreover, I should like to know why, when the Evangelist uses the term ἀνθρώπους (which comprehends the whole human race without exception), he denies that infants are included. His seventh argument is, Since spiritual things accord with spiritual (1 Cor 2:13), infants, not being spiritual, are unfit for baptism. It is plain how perversely he wrests this passage of Paul. It relates to doctrine. The Corinthians,

pluming themselves excessively on a vain acuteness, Paul rebukes their folly, because they still require to be imbued with the first rudiments of heavenly doctrine. Who can infer from this that baptism is to be denied to infants, whom, when begotten of the flesh, the Lord consecrates to himself by gratuitous adoption? His objection, that if they are new men, they must be fed with spiritual food, is easily obviated. By baptism they are admitted into the fold of Christ, and the symbol of adoption is sufficient for them, until they grow up and become fit to bear solid food. We must, therefore, wait for the time of examination, which God distinctly demands in the sacred Supper. His next objection is, that Christ invites all his people to the sacred Supper. But as it is plain that he admits those only who are prepared to celebrate the commemoration of his death, it follows that infants, whom he honoured with his embrace, remain in a distinct and peculiar position until they grow up, and yet are not aliens. When he objects, that it is strange why the infant does not partake of the Supper, I answer, that souls are fed by other food than the external eating of the Supper, and that accordingly Christ is the food of infants, though they partake not of the symbol. The case is different with baptism, by which the door of the Church is thrown open to them. He again objects, that a good householder distributes meat to his household in due season (Mt. 24:45). This I willingly admit; but how will he define the time of baptism, so as to prove that it is not seasonably given to infants? He, moreover, adduces Christ's command to the apostles to make haste, because the fields are already white to the harvest (John 4:35). Our Saviour only means that the apostles, seeing the present fruit of their labour, should bestir themselves with more alacrity to teach. Who will infer from this, that harvest only is the fit time for baptism? His eleventh argument is, That in the primitive Church, Christians and disciples were the same; but we have already seen that he argues unskilfully from the part to the whole. The name of disciples is given to men of full age, who had already been taught, and had assumed the name of Christ, just as the Jews behoved to be disciples under the law of Moses. Still none could rightly infer from this that infants, whom the Lord declared to be of his household, were strangers. Moreover, he alleges that all Christians are brethren, and that infants cannot belong to this class, so long as we exclude them from the Supper. But I return to my position, first, that none are heirs of the kingdom of heaven but those who are the members of Christ; and, secondly, that the embracing of Christ was the true badge of adoption, in which infants are joined in common with adults, and that temporary abstinence from the Supper does not prevent them from belonging to the body of the Church. The thief on the cross, when converted, became the brother of believers, though he never partook of the Lord's Supper. Servetus afterwards adds, that no man becomes our brother unless by the Spirit of adoption, who is only conferred by the hearing of faith. I answer, that he always falls back into the same paralogism, because he preposterously applies to infants what is said only of adults. Paul there teaches that the ordinary way in which God calls his elect, and brings them to the faith, is by raising up faithful teachers, and thus stretching out his hand to them by their ministry and labours. Who will presume from this to give the law to God, and say that he may not ingraft infants into Christ by some other secret method? He objects, that Cornelius was baptised after receiving the Holy Spirit; but how absurdly he would convert a single example into a general rule, is apparent from the case of the Eunuch and the Samaritans, in regard to whom the Lord observed a different order, baptism preceding the gifts of the Holy Spirit. The fifteenth argument is more than absurd. He says that we become gods by regeneration, but that they are gods to whom the word of God is sent (John 10:35; 2 Pet. 1:4), a thing not possible to infant children. The attributing of deity to believers is one of his ravings, which this is not the proper place to discuss; but it betrays the utmost effrontery to wrest the passage in the psalm (Ps. 82:6) to a meaning so alien to it. Christ says, that kings and magistrates are called gods by the prophet, because they perform an office divinely appointed them. This dexterous interpreter transfers what is addressed by special command to certain individuals to the doctrine of the Gospel, so as to exterminate infants from the Church. Again, he objects, that infants cannot be regarded as new men, because they are not begotten by the word. But what I have said again and again I now repeat, that, for regenerating us, doctrine is an incorruptible seed, if indeed we are fit to perceive it; but when, from nonage, we are incapable of being taught, God takes his own methods of regenerating. He afterwards returns to his allegories, and says, that under the law, the sheep and the goat were not offered in sacrifice the moment they were dropt (Exod. 12:5). Were I disposed to deal in figures, I might obviously reply, first, that all the first-born, on opening the matrix, were sacred to the Lord (Exod. 13:12); and, secondly, that a lamb of a year old was to be sacrificed: whence it follows, that it was not necessary to wait for mature age, the young and tender offspring having been selected by God for sacrifice. He contends, moreover, that none could come to Christ but those who were previously prepared by John; as if John's ministry had not been temporary. But, to omit this, assuredly there was no such preparation in the children whom Christ took up in his arms and blessed. Wherefore, let us have done with his false principle. He at length calls in the assistance of Trismegistus and the Sybils, to prove that sacred ablutions are fit only for adults. See how honourably he thinks of Christian baptism, when he tests it by the profane rites of the Gentiles, and will not have it administered except in the way pleasing to Trismegistus. We defer more to the authority of God, who has seen it meet to consecrate infants to himself, and initiate them by a sacred symbol, the significancy of which they are unable from nonage to understand. We do not think it lawful to borrow from the expiations of the Gentiles, in order to change, in our baptism, that eternal and inviolable law which God enacted in circumcision. His last argument is, If infants, without understanding, may be baptised, baptism may be mimicked and jestingly administered by boys in sport. Here let him plead the matter with God, by whose command circumcision was common to infants before they received understanding. Was it, then, a fit matter for ridicule or boyish sport, to overthrow the sacred institution of God? But no wonder that these reprobate spirits, as if they were under the influence of frenzy, introduce the grossest absurdities in defence of their errors, because God, by this spirit of giddiness, justly avenges their pride and obstinacy. I trust I have made it apparent how feebly Servetus has supported his friends the Anabaptists.

32. No sound man, I presume, can now doubt how rashly the Church is disturbed by those who excite quarrels and disturbances because of pædobaptism. For it is of importance to observe what Satan means by all this craft—viz. to rob us of the singular blessing of confidence and spiritual joy, which is hence to be derived, and in so far to detract from the glory of the divine goodness. For how sweet is it to pious minds to be assured not only by word, but even by ocular demonstration, that they are so much in favour with their heavenly Father, that he interests himself in their prosperity! Here we may see how he acts towards us as a most provident parent, not ceasing to care for us even after our death, but consulting and providing for our children. Ought not our whole heart to be stirred up within us, as David's was (Ps. 48:11), to bless his name for such a manifestation of goodness? Doubtless the design of Satan in assaulting pædobaptism with all his forces is to keep out of view, and gradually efface, that attestation of divine grace which the promise itself presents to our eyes. In this way, not only would men be impiously ungrateful for the mercy of God, but be less careful in training their children to piety. For it is no slight stimulus to us to bring them up in the fear of God, and the observance of his law, when we reflect, that from their birth they have been considered and acknowledged by him as his children. Wherefore, if we would not maliciously obscure the kindness of God, let us present to him our infants, to whom he has assigned a place among his friends and family, that is, the members of the Church.

CHAPTER 17

OF THE LORD'S SUPPER, AND THE BENEFITS CONFERRED BY IT.

This chapter is divided into two principal heads.—I. The first part shows what it is that God exhibits in the Holy Supper, sec. 1–4; and then in what way and how far it becomes ours, sec. 5–11. II. The second part is chiefly occupied with a refutation of the errors which superstition has introduced in regard to the Lord's Supper. And, first, Transubstantiation is refuted, sec. 12–15. Next, Consubstantiation and Ubiquity, sec. 16–19. Thirdly, It is shown that the institution itself is opposed to those hyperbolical doctors, sec. 20–25. Fourth, The orthodox view is confirmed by other arguments derived from Scripture, sec. 26–27. Fifth, The authority of the Fathers is shown to support the same view. Sixth, The presence for which opponents contend is overthrown, and another presence established, sec. 29–32. Seventh, What the nature of our communion ought to be, sec. 33, 34. Eighth, The adoration introduced by opponents refuted. For what end the Lord's Supper was instituted, sec. 35–39. Lastly, The examination of communicants is considered, sec. 40–42. Of the external rites to be observed. Of frequent communion in both kinds. Objections refuted, sec. 43–50.

Sections:

1. Why the Holy Supper was instituted by Christ. The knowledge of the sacrament, how necessary. The signs used. Why there are no others appointed.

2. The manifold uses and advantages of this sacrament to the pious.

3. The Lord's Supper exhibits the great blessings of redemption, and even Christ himself. This even evident from the words of the institution. The thing specially to be considered in them. Congruity of the signs and the things signified.

4. The chief parts of this sacrament.

5. How Christ, the Bread of Life, is to be received by us. Two faults to be avoided. The receiving of it must bear reference both to faith and the effect of faith. What meant by eating Christ. In what sense Christ the bread of life.

6. This mode of eating confirmed by the authority of Augustine and Chrysostom.

7. It is not sufficient, while omitting all mention of flesh and blood, to recognise this communion merely as spiritual. It is impossible fully to comprehend it in the present life.

8. In explanation of it, it may be observed,—I. There is no life at all save in Christ. II. Christ has life in a twofold sense; first, in himself, as he is God; and, secondly, by transfusing it into the flesh which he assumed, that he might thereby communicate life to us.

9. This confirmed from Cyril, and by a familiar example. How the flesh of Christ gives life, and what the nature of our communion with Christ.

10. No distance of place can impede it. In the Supper it is not presented as an empty symbol, but, as the apostle testifies, we receive the reality. Objection, that the expression is figurative. Answer. A sure rule with regard to the sacraments.

11. Conclusion of the first part of the chapter. The sacrament of the Supper consists of two parts—viz. corporeal signs, and spiritual truth. These comprehend the meaning, matter, and effect. Christ truly exhibited to us by symbols.

12. Second part of the chapter, reduced to nine heads. The transubstantiation of the Papists considered and refuted. Its origin and absurdity. Why it should be exploded.

13. Transubstantiation as feigned by the Schoolmen. Refutation. The many superstitions introduced by their error.

14. The fiction of transubstantiation why invented contrary to Scripture, and the consent of antiquity. The term of transubstantiation never used in the early Church. Objection. Answer.

15. The error of transubstantiation favoured by the consecration, which was a kind of magical incantation. The bread is not a sacrament to itself, but to those who receive it. The changing of the rod of Moses into a serpent gives no countenance to Popish transubstantiation. No resemblance between it and the words of institution in the Supper. Objection. Answer.

16. Refutation of consubstantiation; whence the idea of ubiquity.

17. This ubiquity confounds the natures of Christ. Subtleties answered.

18. Absurdities connected with consubstantiation. Candid exposition of the orthodox view.

19. The nature of the true presence of Christ in the Supper. The true and substantial communion of the body and blood of the Lord. This orthodox view assailed by turbulent spirits.

20. This view vindicated from their calumnies. The words of the institution explained in opposition to the glosses of transubstantiators and consubstantiators. Their subterfuges and absurd blasphemies.

21. Why the name of the thing signified is given to the sacramental symbols. This illustrated by passages of Scripture; also by a passage of Augustine.

22. Refutation of an objection founded on the words, This is. Objection answered.

23. Other objections answered.

24. Other objections answered. No question here as to the omnipotence of God.

25. Other objections answered.

26. The orthodox view further confirmed. I. By a consideration of the reality of Christ's body. II. From our Saviour's declaration that he would always be in the world. This confirmed by the exposition of Augustine.

27. Refutation of the sophisms of the Ubiquitists. The evasion of visible and invisible presence refuted.

28. The authority of Fathers not in favour of these errors as to Christ's presence. Augustine opposed to them.

29. Refutation of the invisible presence maintained by opponents. Refutation from Tertullian, from a saying of Christ after his resurrection, from the definition of a true body, and from different passages of Scripture.

30. Ubiquity refuted by various arguments.

31. The imaginary presence of Transubstantiators, Consubstantiators, and Ubiquitists, contrasted with the orthodox doctrine.

32. The nature of our Saviour's true presence explained. The mode of it incomprehensible.

33. Our communion in the blood and flesh of Christ. Spiritual not oral, and yet real. Erroneous view of the Schoolmen.

34. This view not favoured by Augustine. How the

wicked eat the body of Christ. Cyril's sentiments as to the eating of the body of Christ.

35. Absurdity of the adoration of sacramental symbols.

36. This adoration condemned. I. By Christ himself. II. By the Council of Nice. III. By ancient custom. IV. By Scripture. This adoration is mere idolatry.

37. This adoration inconsistent with the nature and institution of the sacrament. Ends for which the sacrament was instituted.

38. Ends for which the sacrament was instituted.

39. True nature of the sacrament, contrasted with the Popish observance of it.

40. Nature of an unworthy approach to the Lord's table. The great danger of it. The proper remedy in serious self-examination.

41. The spurious examination introduced by the Papists. Refutation.

42. The nature of Christian examination.

43. External rites in the administration of the Supper. Many of them indifferent.

44. Duty of frequent communion. This proved by the practice of the Church in its purer state, and by the canons of the early bishops.

45. Frequent communion in the time of Augustine. The neglect of it censured by Chrysostom.

46. The Popish injunction to communicate once a-year an execrable invention.

47. Communion in one kind proved to be an invention of Satan.

48. Subterfuges of the Papists refuted.

49. The practice of the early Church further considered.

50. Conclusion.

1. After God has once received us into his family, it is not that he may regard us in the light of servants, but of sons, performing the part of a kind and anxious parent, and providing for our maintenance during the whole course of our lives. And, not contented with this, he has been pleased by a pledge to assure us of his continued liberality. To this end, he has given another sacrament to his Church by the hand of his only-begotten Son—viz. a spiritual feast, at which Christ testifies that he himself is living bread (John 6:51), on which our souls feed, for a true and blessed immortality. Now, as the knowledge of this great mystery is most necessary, and, in proportion to its importance, demands an accurate exposition, and Satan, in order to deprive the Church of this inestimable treasure, long ago introduced, first, mists, and then darkness, to obscure its light, and stirred up strife and contention to alienate the minds of the simple from a relish for this sacred food, and in our age, also, has tried the same artifice, I will proceed, after giving a simple summary adapted to the capacity of the ignorant, to explain those difficulties by which Satan has tried to ensnare the world. First, then, the signs are bread and wine, which represent the invisible food which we receive from the body and blood of Christ. For as God, regenerating us in baptism, ingrafts us into the fellowship of his Church, and makes us his by adoption, so we have said that he performs the office of a provident parent, in continually supplying the food by which he may sustain and preserve us in the life to which he has begotten us by his word. Moreover, Christ is the only food of our soul, and, therefore, our heavenly Father invites us to him, that, refreshed by communion with him, we may ever and anon gather new vigour until we reach the heavenly immortality. But as this mystery of the secret union of Christ with believers is incomprehensible by nature, he exhibits its figure and image in visible signs adapted to our capacity, nay, by giving, as it were, earnests and badges, he makes it as certain to us as if it were seen by the eye; the familiarity of the similitude giving it access to minds however dull, and showing that souls are fed by Christ just as the corporeal life is sustained by bread and wine. We now, therefore, understand the end which this mystical benediction has in view—viz. to assure us that the body of Christ was once sacrificed for us, so that we may now eat it, and, eating, feel within ourselves the efficacy of that one sacrifice,—that his blood was once shed for us so as to be our perpetual drink. This is the force of the promise which is added, "Take, eat; this is my body, which is broken for you" (Mt. 26:26, &c.). The body which was once offered for our salvation we are enjoined to take and eat, that, while we see ourselves made partakers of it, we may safely conclude that the virtue of that death will be efficacious in us. Hence he terms the cup the covenant in his blood. For the covenant which he once sanctioned by his blood he in a manner renews, or rather continues, in so far as regards the confirmation of our faith, as often as he stretches forth his sacred blood as drink to us.

2. Pious souls can derive great confidence and delight from this sacrament, as being a testimony that they form one body with Christ, so that everything which is his they may call their own. Hence it follows, that we can confidently assure ourselves, that eternal life, of which he himself is the heir, is ours, and that the kingdom of heaven,

into which he has entered, can no more be taken from us than from him; on the other hand, that we cannot be condemned for our sins, from the guilt of which he absolves us, seeing he has been pleased that these should be imputed to himself as if they were his own. This is the wondrous exchange made by his boundless goodness. Having become with us the Son of Man, he has made us with himself sons of God. By his own descent to the earth he has prepared our ascent to heaven. Having received our mortality, he has bestowed on us his immortality. Having undertaken our weakness, he has made us strong in his strength. Having submitted to our poverty, he has transferred to us his riches. Having taken upon himself the burden of unrighteousness with which we were oppressed, he has clothed us with his righteousness.

3. To all these things we have a complete attestation in this sacrament, enabling us certainly to conclude that they are as truly exhibited to us as if Christ were placed in bodily presence before our view, or handled by our hands. For these are words which can never lie nor deceive—Take, eat, drink. This is my body, which is broken for you: this is my blood, which is shed for the remission of sins. In bidding us take, he intimates that it is ours: in bidding us eat, he intimates that it becomes one substance with us: in affirming of his body that it was broken, and of his blood that it was shed for us, he shows that both were not so much his own as ours, because he took and laid down both, not for his own advantage, but for our salvation. And we ought carefully to observe, that the chief, and almost the whole energy of the sacrament, consists in these words, It is broken for you: it is shed for you. It would not be of much importance to us that the body and blood of the Lord are now distributed, had they not once been set forth for our redemption and salvation. Wherefore they are represented under bread and wine, that we may learn that they are not only ours, but intended to nourish our spiritual life; that is, as we formerly observed, by the corporeal things which are produced in the sacrament, we are by a kind of analogy conducted to spiritual things. Thus when bread is given as a symbol of the body of Christ, we must immediately think of this similitude. As bread nourishes, sustains, and protects our bodily life, so the body of Christ is the only food to invigorate and keep alive the soul. When we behold wine set forth as a symbol of blood, we must think that such use as wine serves to the body, the same is spiritually bestowed by the blood of Christ; and the use is to foster, refresh, strengthen, and exhilarate. For if we duly consider what profit we have gained by the breaking of his sacred body, and the shedding of his blood, we shall clearly perceive that these properties of bread and wine, agreeably to this analogy, most appropriately represent it when they are communicated to us.

4. Therefore, it is not the principal part of a sacrament simply to hold forth the body of Christ to us without any higher consideration, but rather to seal and confirm that promise by which he testifies that his flesh is meat indeed, and his blood drink indeed, nourishing us unto life eternal, and by which he affirms that he is the bread of life, of which, whosoever shall eat, shall live for ever—I say, to seal and confirm that promise, and in order to do so, it sends us to the cross of Christ, where that promise was performed and fulfilled in all its parts. For we do not eat Christ duly and savingly unless as crucified, while with lively apprehension we perceive the efficacy of his death. When he called himself the bread of life, he did not take that appellation from the sacrament, as some perversely interpret; but such as he was given to us by the Father, such he exhibited himself when becoming partaker of our human mortality, he made us partakers of his divine immortality; when offering himself in sacrifice, he took our curse upon himself, that he might cover us with his blessing, when by his death he devoured and swallowed up death, when in his resurrection he raised our corruptible flesh, which he had put on, to glory and incorruption.

5. It only remains that the whole become ours by application. This is done by means of the gospel, and more clearly by the sacred Supper, where Christ offers himself to us with all his blessings, and we receive him in faith. The sacrament, therefore, does not make Christ become for the first time the bread of life; but, while it calls to remembrance that Christ was made the bread of life that we may constantly eat him, it gives us a taste and relish for that bread, and makes us feel its efficacy. For it assures us, first, that whatever Christ did or suffered was done to give us life; and, secondly, that this quickening is eternal; by it we are ceaselessly nourished, sustained, and preserved in life. For as Christ would not have not been the bread of life to us if he had not been born, if he had not died and risen again; so he could not now be the bread of life, were not the efficacy and fruit of his nativity, death, and resurrection, eternal. All this Christ has elegantly expressed in these words, "The bread that I will give is my flesh, which I will give for the life of the world" (John 6:51); doubtless intimating, that his body will be as bread in regard to the spiritual life of the soul, because it was to be delivered to death for our salvation,

and that he extends it to us for food when he makes us partakers of it by faith. Wherefore he once gave himself that he might become bread, when he gave himself to be crucified for the redemption of the world; and he gives himself daily, when in the word of the gospel he offers himself to be partaken by us, inasmuch as he was crucified, when he seals that offer by the sacred mystery of the Supper, and when he accomplishes inwardly what he externally designates. Moreover, two faults are here to be avoided. We must neither, by setting too little value on the signs, dissever them from their meanings to which they are in some degree annexed, nor by immoderately extolling them, seem somewhat to obscure the mysteries themselves. That Christ is the bread of life by which believers are nourished unto eternal life, no man is so utterly devoid of religion as not to acknowledge. But all are not agreed as to the mode of partaking of him. For there are some who define the eating of the flesh of Christ, and the drinking of his blood, to be, in one word, nothing more than believing in Christ himself. But Christ seems to me to have intended to teach something more express and more sublime in that noble discourse, in which he recommends the eating of his flesh—viz. that we are quickened by the true partaking of him, which he designated by the terms eating and drinking, lest any one should suppose that the life which we obtain from him is obtained by simple knowledge. For as it is not the sight but the eating of bread that gives nourishment to the body, so the soul must partake of Christ truly and thoroughly, that by his energy it may grow up into spiritual life. Meanwhile, we admit that this is nothing else than the eating of faith, and that no other eating can be imagined. But there is this difference between their mode of speaking and mine. According to them, to eat is merely to believe; while I maintain that the flesh of Christ is eaten by believing, because it is made ours by faith, and that that eating is the effect and fruit of faith; or, if you will have it more clearly, according to them, eating is faith, whereas it rather seems to me to be a consequence of faith. The difference is little in words, but not little in reality. For, although the apostle teaches that Christ dwells in our hearts by faith (Eph. 3:17), no one will interpret that dwelling to be faith All see that it explains the admirable effect of faith, because to it, it is owing that believers have Christ dwelling in them. In this way, the Lord was pleased, by calling himself the bread of life, not only to teach that our salvation is treasured up in the faith of his death and resurrection, but also, by virtue of true communication with him, his life passes into us and becomes ours, just as bread when taken for food gives vigour to the body.

6. When Augustine, whom they claim as their patron, wrote, that we eat by believing, all he meant was to indicate that that eating is of faith, and not of the mouth. This I deny not; but I at the same time add, that by faith we embrace Christ, not as appearing at a distance, but as uniting himself to us, he being our head, and we his members. I do not absolutely disapprove of that mode of speaking; I only deny that it is a full interpretation, if they mean to define what it is to eat the flesh of Christ. I see that Augustine repeatedly used this form of expression, as when he said (De Doct. Christ. Lib. 3), " Unless ye eat the flesh of the Son of Man" is a figurative expression enjoining us to have communion with our Lord's passion, and sweetly and usefully to treasure in our memory that his flesh was crucified and wounded for us. Also when he says, "These three thousand men who were converted at the preaching of Peter (Acts 2:41), by believing, drank the blood which they had cruelly shed." But in very many other passages he admirably commends faith for this, that by means of it our souls are not less refreshed by the communion of the blood of Christ, than our bodies with the bread which they eat. The very same thing is said by Chrysostom, "Christ makes us his body, not by faith only, but in reality." He does not mean that we obtain this blessing from any other quarter than from faith: he only intends to prevent any one from thinking of mere imagination when he hears the name of faith. I say nothing of those who hold that the Supper is merely a mark of external profession, because I think I sufficiently refuted their error when I treated of the sacraments in general (Chap. 14 sec. 13). Only let my readers observe, that when the cup is called the covenant in blood (Luke 22:20), the promise which tends to confirm faith is expressed. Hence it follows, that unless we have respect to God, and embrace what he offers, we do not make a right use of the sacred Supper.

7. I am not satisfied with the view of those who, while acknowledging that we have some kind of communion with Christ, only make us partakers of the Spirit, omitting all mention of flesh and blood. As if it were said to no purpose at all, that his flesh is meat indeed, and his blood is drink indeed; that we have no life unless we eat that flesh and drink that blood; and so forth. Therefore, if it is evident that full communion with Christ goes beyond their description, which is too confined, I will attempt briefly to show how far it extends, before proceeding to speak of the contrary vice of excess. For I shall have a

longer discussion with these hyperbolical doctors, who, according to their gross ideas, fabricate an absurd mode of eating and drinking, and transfigure Christ, after divesting him of his flesh, into a phantom: if, indeed, it be lawful to put this great mystery into words, a mystery which I feel, and therefore freely confess that I am unable to comprehend with my mind, so far am I from wishing any one to measure its sublimity by my feeble capacity. Nay, I rather exhort my readers not to confine their apprehension within those too narrow limits, but to attempt to rise much higher than I can guide them. For whenever this subject is considered, after I have done my utmost, I feel that I have spoken far beneath its dignity. And though the mind is more powerful in thought than the tongue in expression, it too is overcome and overwhelmed by the magnitude of the subject. All then that remains is to break forth in admiration of the mystery, which it is plain that the mind is inadequate to comprehend, or the tongue to express. I will, however, give a summary of my view as I best can, not doubting its truth, and therefore trusting that it will not be disapproved by pious breasts.

8. First of all, we are taught by the Scriptures that Christ was from the beginning the living Word of the Father, the fountain and origin of life, from which all things should always receive life. Hence John at one time calls him the Word of life, and at another says, that in him was life; intimating, that he, even then pervading all creatures, instilled into them the power of breathing and living. He afterwards adds, that the life was at length manifested, when the Son of God, assuming our nature, exhibited himself in bodily form to be seen and handled. For although he previously diffused his virtue into the creatures, yet as man, because alienated from God by sin, had lost the communication of life, and saw death on every side impending over him, he behoved, in order to regain the hope of immortality, to be restored to the communion of that Word. How little confidence can it give you, to know that the Word of God, from which you are at the greatest distance, contains within himself the fulness of life, whereas in yourself, in whatever direction you turn, you see nothing but death? But ever since that fountain of life began to dwell in our nature, he no longer lies hid at a distance from us, but exhibits himself openly for our participation. Nay, the very flesh in which he resides he makes vivifying to us, that by partaking of it we may feed for immortality. "I," says he, "am that bread of life;" "I am the living bread which came down from heaven;" "And the bread that I will give is my flesh, which I will give for the life of the world" (John 6:48, 51). By these words he declares, not only that he is life, inasmuch as he is the eternal Word of God who came down to us from heaven, but, by coming down, gave vigour to the flesh which he assumed, that a communication of life to us might thence emanate. Hence, too, he adds, that his flesh is meat indeed, and that his blood is drink indeed: by this food believers are reared to eternal life. The pious, therefore, have admirable comfort in this, that they now find life in their own flesh. For they not only reach it by easy access, but have it spontaneously set forth before them. Let them only throw open the door of their hearts that they may take it into their embrace, and they will obtain it.

9. The flesh of Christ, however, has not such power in itself as to make us live, seeing that by its own first condition it was subject to mortality, and even now, when endued with immortality, lives not by itself. Still it is properly said to be life-giving, as it is pervaded with the fulness of life for the purpose of transmitting it to us. In this sense I understand our Saviour's words as Cyril interprets them, "As the Father hath life in himself, so hath he given to the Son to have life in himself" (John 5:26). For there properly he is speaking not of the properties which he possessed with the Father from the beginning, but of those with which he was invested in the flesh in which he appeared. Accordingly, he shows that in his humanity also fulness of life resides, so that every one who communicates in his flesh and blood, at the same time enjoys the participation of life. The nature of this may be explained by a familiar example. As water is at one time drunk out of the fountain, at another drawn, at another led away by conduits to irrigate the fields, and yet does not flow forth of itself for all these uses, but is taken from its source, which, with perennial flow, ever and anon sends forth a new and sufficient supply; so the flesh of Christ is like a rich and inexhaustible fountain, which transfuses into us the life flowing forth from the Godhead into itself. Now, who sees not that the communion of the flesh and blood of Christ is necessary to all who aspire to the heavenly life? Hence those passages of the apostle: The Church is the "body" of Christ; his "fulness." He is "the head," "from whence the whole body fitly joined together, and compacted by that which every joint supplieth," "maketh increase of the body" (Eph. 1:23; 4:15,16). Our bodies are the "members of Christ" (1 Cor. 6:15). We perceive that all these things cannot possibly take place unless he adheres to us wholly in body and spirit. But the very close connection which unites us to his flesh, he illus-

trated with still more splendid epithets, when he said that we "are members of his body, of his flesh, and of his bones" (Eph. 5:30). At length, to testify that the matter is too high for utterance, he concludes with exclaiming, "This is a great mystery" (Eph. 5:32). It were, therefore, extreme infatuation not to acknowledge the communion of believers with the body and blood of the Lord, a communion which the apostle declares to be so great, that he chooses rather to marvel at it than to explain it.

10. The sum is, that the flesh and blood of Christ feed our souls just as bread and wine maintain and support our corporeal life. For there would be no aptitude in the sign, did not our souls find their nourishment in Christ. This could not be, did not Christ truly form one with us, and refresh us by the eating of his flesh, and the drinking of his blood. But though it seems an incredible thing that the flesh of Christ, while at such a distance from us in respect of place, should be food to us, let us remember how far the secret virtue of the Holy Spirit surpasses all our conceptions, and how foolish it is to wish to measure its immensity by our feeble capacity. Therefore, what our mind does not comprehend let faith conceive—viz. that the Spirit truly unites things separated by space. That sacred communion of flesh and blood by which Christ transfuses his life into us, just as if it penetrated our bones and marrow, he testifies and seals in the Supper, and that not by presenting a vain or empty sign, but by there exerting an efficacy of the Spirit by which he fulfils what he promises. And truly the thing there signified he exhibits and offers to all who sit down at that spiritual feast, although it is beneficially received by believers only who receive this great benefit with true faith and heartfelt gratitude. For this reason the apostle said, "The cup of blessing which we bless, is it not the communion of the blood of Christ? The bread which we break, is it not the communion of the body of Christ"? (1 Cor. 10:16.) There is no ground to object that the expression is figurative, and gives the sign the name of the thing signified. I admit, indeed, that the breaking of bread is a symbol, not the reality. But this being admitted, we duly infer from the exhibition of the symbol that the thing itself is exhibited. For unless we would charge God with deceit, we will never presume to say that he holds forth an empty symbol. Therefore, if by the breaking of bread the Lord truly represents the partaking of his body, there ought to be no doubt whatever that he truly exhibits and performs it. The rule which the pious ought always to observe is, whenever they see the symbols instituted by the Lord, to think and feel surely persuaded that the truth of the thing signified is also present. For why does the Lord put the symbol of his body into your hands, but just to assure you that you truly partake of him? If this is true let us feel as much assured that the visible sign is given us in seal of an invisible gift as that his body itself is given to us.

11. I hold then (as has always been received in the Church, and is still taught by those who feel aright), that the sacred mystery of the Supper consists of two things—the corporeal signs, which, presented to the eye, represent invisible things in a manner adapted to our weak capacity, and the spiritual truth, which is at once figured and exhibited by the signs. When attempting familiarly to explain its nature, I am accustomed to set down three things—the thing meant, the matter which depends on it, and the virtue or efficacy consequent upon both. The thing meant consists in the promises which are in a manner included in the sign. By the matter, or substance, I mean Christ, with his death and resurrection. By the effect, I understand redemption, justification, sanctification, eternal life, and all other benefits which Christ bestows upon us. Moreover, though all these things have respect to faith, I leave no room for the cavil, that when I say Christ is conceived by faith, I mean that he is only conceived by the intellect and imagination. He is offered by the promises, not that we may stop short at the sight or mere knowledge of him, but that we may enjoy true communion with him. And, indeed, I see not how any one can expect to have redemption and righteousness in the cross of Christ, and life in his death, without trusting first of all to true communion with Christ himself. Those blessings could not reach us, did not Christ previously make himself ours. I say then, that in the mystery of the Supper, by the symbols of bread and wine, Christ, his body and his blood, are truly exhibited to us, that in them he fulfilled all obedience, in order to procure righteousness for us— first that we might become one body with him; and, secondly, that being made partakers of his substance, we might feel the result of this fact in the participation of all his blessings.

12. I now come to the hyperbolical mixtures which superstition has introduced. Here Satan has employed all his wiles, withdrawing the minds of men from heaven, and imbuing them with the perverse error that Christ is annexed to the element of bread. And, first, we are not to dream of such a presence of Christ in the sacrament as the artificers of the Romish court have imagined, as if the body of Christ, locally present, were to be taken into the hand, and chewed by the teeth, and swallowed by the throat. This was the form of Palinode, which Pope

Nicholas dictated to Berengarius, in token of his repentance, a form expressed in terms so monstrous, that the author of the Gloss exclaims, that there is danger, if the reader is not particularly cautious, that he will be led by it into a worse heresy than was that of Berengarius (Distinct. 2 c. Ego Berengarius). Peter Lombard, though he labours much to excuse the absurdity, rathers inclines to a different opinion. As we cannot at all doubt that it is bounded according to the invariable rule in the human body, and is contained in heaven, where it was once received, and will remain till it return to judgment, so we deem it altogether unlawful to bring it back under these corruptible elements, or to imagine it everywhere present. And, indeed, there is no need of this, in order to our partaking of it, since the Lord by his Spirit bestows upon us the blessing of being one with him in soul, body, and spirit. The bond of that connection, therefore, is the Spirit of Christ, who unites us to him, and is a kind of channel by which everything that Christ has and is, is derived to us. For if we see that the sun, in sending forth its rays upon the earth, to generate, cherish, and invigorate its offspring, in a manner transfuses its substance into it, why should the radiance of the Spirit be less in conveying to us the communion of his flesh and blood? Wherefore the Scripture, when it speaks of our participation with Christ, refers its whole efficacy to the Spirit. Instead of many, one passage will suffice. Paul, in the Epistle to the Romans (Rom. 8:9–11), shows that the only way in which Christ dwells in us is by his Spirit. By this, however, he does not take away that communion of flesh and blood of which we now speak, but shows that it is owing to the Spirit alone that we possess Christ wholly, and have him abiding in us.

13. The Schoolmen, horrified at this barbarous impiety, speak more modestly, though they do nothing more than amuse themselves with more subtle delusions. They admit that Christ is not contained in the sacrament circumscriptively, or in a bodily manner, but they afterwards devise a method which they themselves do not understand, and cannot explain to others. It, however, comes to this, that Christ may be sought in what they call the species of bread. What? When they say that the substance of bread is converted into Christ, do they not attach him to the white colour, which is all they leave of it? But they say, that though contained in the sacrament, he still remains in heaven, and has no other presence there than that of abode. But, whatever be the terms in which they attempt to make a gloss, the sum of all is, that that which was formerly bread, by consecration becomes Christ: so that Christ thereafter lies hid under the colour of bread. This they are not ashamed distinctly to express. For Lombard's words are, "The body of Christ, which is visible in itself, lurks and lies covered after the act of consecration under the species of bread" (Lombard. Sent. Lib. 4 Dist. 12). Thus the figure of the bread is nothing but a mask which conceals the view of the flesh from our eye. But there is no need of many conjectures to detect the snare which they intended to lay by these words, since the thing itself speaks clearly. It is easy to see how great is the superstition under which not only the vulgar but the leaders also, have laboured for many ages, and still labour, in Popish Churches. Little solicitous as to true faith (by which alone we attain to the fellowship of Christ, and become one with him), provided they have his carnal presence, which they have fabricated without authority from the word, they think he is sufficiently present. Hence we see, that all which they have gained by their ingenious subtlety is to make bread to be regarded as God.

14. Hence proceeded that fictitious transubstantiation for which they fight more fiercely in the present day than for all the other articles of their faith. For the first architects of local presence could not explain, how the body of Christ could be mixed with the substance of bread, without forthwith meeting with many absurdities. Hence it was necessary to have recourse to the fiction, that there is a conversion of the bread into body, not that properly instead of bread it becomes body, but that Christ, in order to conceal himself under the figure, reduces the substance to nothing. It is strange that they have fallen into such a degree of ignorance, nay, of stupor, as to produce this monstrous fiction not only against Scripture, but also against the consent of the ancient Church. I admit, indeed, that some of the ancients occasionally used the term *conversion*, not that they meant to do away with the substance in the external signs, but to teach that the bread devoted to the sacrament was widely different from ordinary bread, and was now something else. All clearly and uniformly teach that the sacred Supper consists of two parts, an earthly and a heavenly. The earthly they without dispute interpret to be bread and wine. Certainly, whatever they may pretend, it is plain that antiquity, which they often dare to oppose to the clear word of God, gives no countenance to that dogma. It is not so long since it was devised; indeed, it was unknown not only to the better ages, in which a purer doctrine still flourished, but after that purity was considerably impaired. There is no early Christian writer who does not admit in distinct terms that the sacred

symbols of the Supper are bread and wine, although, as has been said, they sometimes distinguish them by various epithets, in order to recommend the dignity of the mystery. For when they say that a secret conversion takes place at consecration, so that it is now something else than bread and wine, their meaning, as I already observed, is, not that these are annihilated, but that they are to be considered in a different light from common food, which is only intended to feed the body, whereas in the former the spiritual food and drink of the mind are exhibited. This we deny not. But, say our opponents, if there is conversion, one thing must become another. If they mean that something becomes different from what it was before, I assent. If they will wrest it in support of their fiction, let them tell me of what kind of change they are sensible in baptism. For here, also, the Fathers make out a wonderful conversion, when they say that out of the corruptible element is made the spiritual laver of the soul, and yet no one denies that it still remains water. But say they, there is no such expression in Baptism as that in the Supper, *This is my body;* as if we were treating of these words, which have a meaning sufficiently clear, and not rather of that term *conversion*, which ought not to mean more in the Supper than in Baptism. Have done, then, with those quibbles upon words, which betray nothing but their silliness. The meaning would have no congruity, unless the truth which is there figured had a living image in the external sign. Christ wished to testify by an external symbol that his flesh was food. If he exhibited merely an empty show of bread, and not true bread, where is the analogy or similitude to conduct us from the visible thing to the invisible? For, in order to make all things consistent, the meaning cannot extend to more than this, that we are fed by the species of Christ's flesh; just as, in the case of baptism, if the figure of water deceived the eye, it would not be to us a sure pledge of our ablution; nay, the fallacious spectacle would rather throw us into doubt. The nature of the sacrament is therefore overthrown, if in the mode of signifying the earthly sign corresponds not to the heavenly reality; and, accordingly, the truth of the mystery is lost if true bread does not represent the true body of Christ. I again repeat, since the Supper is nothing but a conspicuous attestation to the promise which is contained in the sixth chapter of John—viz. that Christ is the bread of life, who came down from heaven, that visible bread must intervene, in order that that spiritual bread may be figured, unless we would destroy all the benefits with which God here favours us for the purpose of sustaining our infirmity. Then on what ground could Paul infer that we are all one bread, and one body in partaking together of that one bread, if only the semblance of bread, and not the natural reality, remained?

15. They could not have been so shamefully deluded by the impostures of Satan had they not been fascinated by the erroneous idea, that the body of Christ included under the bread is transmitted by the bodily mouth into the belly. The cause of this brutish imagination was, that consecration had the same effect with them as magical incantation. They overlooked the principle, that bread is a sacrament to none but those to whom the word is addressed, just as the water of baptism is not changed in itself, but begins to be to us what it formerly was not, as soon as the promise is annexed. This will better appear from the example of a similar sacrament. The water gushing from the rock in the desert was to the Israelites a badge and sign of the same thing that is figured to us in the Supper by wine. For Paul declares that they drank the same spiritual drink (1 Cor. 10:4). But the water was common to the herds and flocks of the people. Hence it is easy to infer, that in the earthly elements, when employed for a spiritual use, no other conversion takes place than in respect of men, inasmuch as they are to them seals of promises. Moreover, since it is the purpose of God, as I have repeatedly inculcated, to raise us up to himself by fit vehicles, those who indeed call us to Christ, but to Christ lurking invisibly under bread, impiously, by their perverseness, defeat this object. For it is impossible for the mind of man to disentangle itself from the immensity of space, and ascend to Christ even above the heavens. What nature denied them, they attempted to gain by a noxious remedy. Remaining on the earth, they felt no need of a celestial proximity to Christ. Such was the necessity which impelled them to transfigure the body of Christ. In the age of Bernard, though a harsher mode of speech had prevailed, transubstantiation was not yet recognised. And in all previous ages, the similitude in the mouths of all was, that a spiritual reality was conjoined with bread and wine in this sacrament. As to the terms, they think they answer acutely, though they adduce nothing relevant to the case in hand. The rod of Moses (they say), when turned into a serpent, though it acquires the name of a serpent, still retains its former name, and is called a rod; and thus, according to them, it is equally probable that though the bread passes into a new substance, it is still called by catachresis, and not inaptly, what it still appears to the eye to be. But what resemblance, real or apparent, do they find between an illustrious miracle and their fictitious illusion, of which

no eye on the earth is witness? The magi by their impostures had persuaded the Egyptians, that they had a divine power above the ordinary course of nature to change created beings. Moses comes forth, and after exposing their fallacies, shows that the invincible power of God is on his side, since his rod swallows up all the other rods. But as that conversion was visible to the eye, we have already observed, that it has no reference to the case in hand. Shortly after the rod visibly resumed its form. It may be added, that we know not whether this was an extemporary conversion of substance. For we must attend to the illusion to the rods of the magicians, which the prophet did not choose to term serpents, lest he might seem to insinuate a conversion which had no existence, because those impostors had done nothing more than blind the eyes of the spectators. But what resemblance is there between that expression and the following? "The bread which we break;"—"As often as ye eat this bread;"—"They communicated in the breaking of bread;" and so forth. It is certain that the eye only was deceived by the incantation of the magicians. The matter is more doubtful with regard to Moses, by whose hand it was not more difficult for God to make a serpent out of a rod, and again to make a rod out of a serpent, than to clothe angels with corporeal bodies, and a little after unclothe them. If the case of the sacrament were at all akin to this, there might be some colour for their explanation. Let it, therefore, remain fixed that there is no true and fit promise in the Supper, that the flesh of Christ is truly meat, unless there is a correspondence in the true substance of the external symbol. But as one error gives rise to another, a passage in Jeremiah has been so absurdly wrested, to prove transubstantiation, that it is painful to refer to it. The prophet complains that wood was placed in his bread, intimating that by the cruelty of his enemies his bread was infected with bitterness, as David by a similar figure complains, "They gave me also gall for my meat: and in my thirst they gave me vinegar to drink" (Psalm 69:21). These men would allegorise the expression to mean, that the body of Christ was nailed to the wood of the cross. But some of the Fathers thought so! As if we ought not rather to pardon their ignorance and bury the disgrace, than to add impudence, and bring them into hostile conflict with the genuine meaning of the prophet.

16. Some, who see that the analogy between the sign and the thing signified cannot be destroyed without destroying the truth of the sacrament, admit that the bread of the Supper is truly the substance of an earthly and corruptible element, and cannot suffer any change in itself, but must have the body of Christ included under it. If they would explain this to mean, that when the bread is held forth in the sacrament, an exhibition of the body is annexed, because the truth is inseparable from its sign, I would not greatly object. But because fixing the body itself in the bread, they attach to it an ubiquity contrary to its nature, and by adding *under* the bread, will have it that it lies hid under it, I must employ a short time in exposing their craft, and dragging them forth from their concealments. Here, however, it is not my intention professedly to discuss the whole case; I mean only to lay the foundations of a discussion which will afterwards follow in its own place. They insist, then, that the body of Christ is invisible and immense, so that it may be hid under bread, because they think that there is no other way by which they can communicate with him than by his descending into the bread, though they do not comprehend the mode of descent by which he raises us up to himself. They employ all the colours they possibly can, but after they have said all, it is sufficiently apparent that they insist on the local presence of Christ. How so? Because they cannot conceive any other participation of flesh and blood than that which consists either in local conjunction and contact, or in some gross method of enclosing.

17. Some, in order obstinately to maintain the error which they have once rashly adopted, hesitate not to assert that the dimensions of Christ's flesh are not more circumscribed than those of heaven and earth. His birth as an infant, his growth, his extension on the cross, his confinement in the sepulchre, were effected, they say, by a kind of dispensation, that he might perform the offices of being born, of dying, and of other human acts: his being seen with his wonted bodily appearance after the resurrection, his ascension into heaven, his appearance, after his ascension, to Stephen and Paul, were the effect of the same dispensation, that it might be made apparent to the eye of man that he was constituted King in heaven. What is this but to call forth Marcion from his grave? For there cannot be a doubt that the body of Christ, if so constituted, was a phantasm, or was phantastical. Some employ a rather more subtle evasion, That the body which is given in the sacrament is glorious and immortal, and that, therefore, there is no absurdity in its being contained under the sacrament in various places, or in no place, and in no form. But, I ask, what did Christ give to his disciples the day before he suffered? Do not the words say that he gave the mortal body, which was to be delivered shortly after? But, say they, he had previously

manifested his glory to the three disciples on the mount (Mt. 17:2). This is true; but his purpose was to give them for the time a taste of immortality. Still they cannot find there a twofold body, but only the one which he had assumed, arrayed in new glory. When he distributed his body in the first Supper, the hour was at hand in which he was "stricken, smitten of God, and afflicted" (Isa. 53:4). So far was he from intending at that time to exhibit the glory of his resurrection. And here what a door is opened to Marcion, if the body of Christ was seen humble and mortal in one place, glorious and immortal in another! And yet, if their opinion is well-founded, the same thing happens every day, because they are forced to admit that the body of Christ, which is in itself visible, lurks invisibly under the symbol of bread. And yet those who send forth such monstrous dogmas, so far from being ashamed at the disgrace, assail us with virulent invectives for not subscribing to them.

18. But assuming that the body and blood of Christ are attached to the bread and wine, then the one must necessarily be dissevered from the other. For as the bread is given separately from the cup, so the body, united to the bread, must be separated from the blood, included in the cup. For since they affirm that the body is in the bread, and the blood is in the cup, while the bread and wine are, in regard to space, at some distance from each other, they cannot, by any quibble, evade the conclusion that the body must be separated from the blood. Their usual pretence—viz. that the blood is in the body, and the body again in the blood, by what they call concomitance, is more than frivolous, since the symbols in which they are included are thus distinguished. But if we are carried to heaven with our eyes and minds, that we may there behold Christ in the glory of his kingdom, as the symbols invite us to him in his integrity, so, under the symbol of bread, we must feed on his body, and, under the symbol of wine, drink separately of his blood, and thereby have the full enjoyment of him. For though he withdrew his flesh from us, and with his body ascended to heaven, he, however, sits at the right hand of the Father; that is, he reigns in power and majesty, and the glory of the Father. This kingdom is not limited by any intervals of space, nor circumscribed by any dimensions. Christ can exert his energy wherever he pleases, in earth and heaven, can manifest his presence by the exercise of his power, can always be present with his people, breathing into them his own life, can live in them, sustain, confirm, and invigorate them, and preserve them safe, just as if he were with them in the body; in fine, can feed them with his own body, communion with which he transfuses into them. After this manner, the body and blood of Christ are exhibited to us in the sacrament.

19. The presence of Christ in the Supper we must hold to be such as neither affixes him to the element of bread, nor encloses him in bread, nor circumscribes him in any way (this would obviously detract from his celestial glory); and it must, moreover, be such as neither divests him of his just dimensions, nor dissevers him by differences of place, nor assigns to him a body of boundless dimensions, diffused through heaven and earth. All these things are clearly repugnant to his true human nature. Let us never allow ourselves to lose sight of the two restrictions. First, Let there be nothing derogatory to the heavenly glory of Christ. This happens whenever he is brought under the corruptible elements of this world, or is affixed to any earthly creatures. Secondly, Let no property be assigned to his body inconsistent with his human nature. This is done when it is either said to be infinite, or made to occupy a variety of places at the same time. But when these absurdities are discarded, I willingly admit anything which helps to express the true and substantial communication of the body and blood of the Lord, as exhibited to believers under the sacred symbols of the Supper, understanding that they are received not by the imagination or intellect merely, but are enjoyed in reality as the food of eternal life. For the odium with which this view is regarded by the world, and the unjust prejudice incurred by its defence, there is no cause, unless it be in the fearful fascinations of Satan. What we teach on the subject is in perfect accordance with Scripture, contains nothing absurd, obscure, or ambiguous, is not unfavourable to true piety and solid edification; in short, has nothing in it to offend, save that, for some ages, while the ignorance and barbarism of sophists reigned in the Church, the clear light and open truth were unbecomingly suppressed. And yet as Satan, by means of turbulent spirits, is still, in the present day, exerting himself to the utmost to bring dishonour on this doctrine by all kinds of calumny and reproach, it is right to assert and defend it with the greatest care.

20. Before we proceed farther, we must consider the ordinance itself, as instituted by Christ, because the most plausible objection of our opponents is, that we abandon his words. To free ourselves from the obloquy with which they thus load us, the fittest course will be to begin with an interpretation of the words. Three Evangelists and Paul relate that our Saviour took bread, and after giving thanks, brake it, and gave it to his disciples, saying, Take,

eat: this is my body which is given or broken for you. Of the cup, Matthew and Mark say, "This is my blood of the new testament, which is shed for many for the remission of sins" (Mt. 26:26; Mark 14:22). Luke and Paul say, "This cup is the new testament in my blood" (Luke 22:20; 1 Cor. 11:25). The advocates of transubstantiation insist, that by the pronoun, *this*, is denoted the appearance of bread, because the whole complexion of our Saviour's address is an act of consecration, and there is no substance which can be demonstrated. But if they adhere so religiously to the words, inasmuch as that which our Saviour gave to his disciples he declared to be his body, there is nothing more alien from the strict meaning of the words than the fiction, that what was bread is now body. What Christ takes into his hands, and gives to the apostles, he declares to be his body; but he had taken bread, and, therefore, who sees not that what is given is still bread? Hence, nothing can be more absurd than to transfer what is affirmed of bread to the species of bread. Others, in interpreting the particle *is*, as equivalent to being transubstantiated, have recourse to a gloss which is forced and violently wrested. They have no ground, therefore, for pretending that they are moved by a reverence for the words. The use of the term *is*, for being converted into something else, is unknown to every tongue and nation. With regard to those who leave the bread in the Supper, and affirm that it is the body of Christ, there is great diversity among them. Those who speak more modestly, though they insist upon the letter, This is my body, afterwards abandon this strictness, and observe that it is equivalent to saying that the body of Christ is with the bread, in the bread, and under the bread. To the reality which they affirm, we have already adverted, and will by-and-by, at greater length. I am not only considering the words by which they say they are prevented from admitting that the bread is called body, because it is a sign of the body. But if they shun everything like metaphor, why do they leap from the simple demonstration of Christ to modes of expression which are widely different? For there is a great difference between saying that the bread is the body, and that the body is with the bread. But seeing it impossible to maintain the simple proposition that the bread is the body, they endeavoured to evade the difficulty by concealing themselves under those forms of expression. Others, who are bolder, hesitate not to assert that, strictly speaking, the bread is body, and in this way prove that they are truly of the letter. If it is objected that the bread, therefore, is Christ, and, being Christ, is God,—they will deny it, because the words of Christ do not expressly say so. But they gain nothing by their denial, since all agree that the whole Christ is offered to us in the Supper. It is intolerable blasphemy to affirm, without figure, of a fading and corruptible element, that it is Christ. I now ask them, if they hold the two propositions to be identical, Christ is the Son of God, and Bread is the body of Christ? If they concede that they are different (and this, whether they will or not, they will be forced to do), let them tell wherein is the difference. All which they can adduce is, I presume, that the bread is called body in a sacramental manner. Hence it follows, that the words of Christ are not subject to the common rule, and ought not to be tested grammatically. I ask all these rigid and obstinate exactors of the letter, whether, when Luke and Paul call the cup *the testament in blood*, they do not express the same thing as in the previous clause, when they call bread the body? There certainly was the same solemnity in the one part of the mystery as in the other, and, as brevity is obscure, the longer sentence better elucidates the meaning. As often, therefore, as they contend, from the one expression, that the bread is body, I will adduce an apt interpretation from the longer expression, That it is a testament in the body. What? Can we seek for surer or more faithful expounders than Luke and Paul? I have no intention, however, to detract, in any respect, from the communication of the body of Christ, which I have acknowledged. I only meant to expose the foolish perverseness with which they carry on a war of words. The bread I understand, on the authority of Luke and Paul, to be the body of Christ, because it is a covenant in the body. If they impugn this, their quarrel is not with me, but with the Spirit of God. However often they may repeat, that reverence for the words of Christ will not allow them to give a figurative interpretation to what is spoken plainly, the pretext cannot justify them in thus rejecting all the contrary arguments which we adduce. Meanwhile, as I have already observed, it is proper to attend to the force of what is meant by a testament in the body and blood of Christ. The covenant, ratified by the sacrifice of death, would not avail us without the addition of that secret communication, by which we are made one with Christ.

21. It remains, therefore, to hold, that on account of the affinity which the things signified have with their signs, the name of the thing itself is given to the sign figuratively, indeed, but very appropriately. I say nothing of allegories and parables, lest it should be alleged that I am seeking subterfuges, and slipping out of the present question. I say that the expression which is uniformly used

in Scripture, when the sacred mysteries are treated of, is metonymical. For you cannot otherwise understand the expressions, that circumcision is a "covenant"—that the lamb is the Lord's "passover"—that the sacrifices of the law are expiations—that the rock from which the water flowed in the desert was Christ,—unless you interpret them metonymically." Nor is the name merely transferred from the superior to the inferior, but, on the contrary, the name of the visible sign is given to the thing signified, as when God is said to have appeared to Moses in the bush; the ark of the covenant is called God, and the face of God, and the dove is called the Holy Spirit. For although the sign differs essentially from the thing signified, the latter being spiritual and heavenly, the former corporeal and visible,—yet, as it not only figures the thing which it is employed to represent as a naked and empty badge, but also truly exhibits it, why should not its name be justly applied to the thing? But if symbols humanly devised, which are rather the images of absent than the marks of present things, and of which they are very often most fallacious types, are sometimes honoured with their names,—with much greater reason do the institutions of God borrow the names of things, of which they always bear a sure, and by no means fallacious signification, and have the reality annexed to them. So great, then, is the similarity, and so close the connection between the two, that it is easy to pass from the one to the other. Let our opponents, therefore, cease to indulge their mirth in calling us Tropists, when we explain the sacramental mode of expression according to the common use of Scripture. For, while the sacraments agree in many things, there is also, in this metonymy, a certain community in all respects between them. As, therefore, the apostle says that the rock from which spiritual water flowed forth to the Israelites was Christ (1 Cor. 10:4), and was thus a visible symbol under which, that spiritual drink was truly perceived, though not by the eye, so the body of Christ is now called bread, inasmuch as it is a symbol under which our Lord offers us the true eating of his body. Lest any one should despise this as a novel invention, the view which Augustine took and expressed was the same: "Had not the sacraments a certain resemblance to the things of which they are sacraments, they would not be sacraments at all. And from this resemblance, they generally have the names of the things themselves. This, as the sacrament of the body of Christ, is, after a certain manner, the body of Christ, and the sacrament of Christ is the blood of Christ; so the sacrament of faith is faith" (August. Ep. 23, ad Bonifac.). He has many similar passages, which it would be superfluous to collect, as that one may suffice. I need only remind my readers, that the same doctrine is taught by that holy man in his Epistle to Evodius. Where Augustine teaches that nothing is more common than metonymy in mysteries, it is a frivolous quibble to object that there is no mention of the Supper. Were this objection sustained, it would follow, that we are not entitled to argue from the genus to the species; *e. g.*, Every animal is endued with motion; and, therefore, the horse and the ox are endued with motion. Indeed, longer discussion is rendered unnecessary by the words of the Saint himself, where he says, that when Christ gave the symbol of his body, he did not hesitate to call it his body (August. Cont. Adimantum, cap. 12). He elsewhere says, "Wonderful was the patience of Christ in admitting Judas to the feast, in which he committed and delivered to the disciples the symbol of his body and blood" (August. in. Ps. 3).

22. Should any morose person, shutting his eyes to everything else, insist upon the expression, *This is*, as distinguishing this mystery from all others, the answer is easy. They say that the substantive verb is so emphatic, as to leave no room for interpretation. Though I should admit this, I answer, that the substantive verb occurs in the words of Paul (1 Cor. 10:16), where he calls the bread the *communion* of the body of Christ. But communion is something different from the body itself. Nay, when the sacraments are treated of, the same word occurs: "My covenant shall be in your flesh for an everlasting covenant" (Gen. 17:13). "This is the ordinance of the passover" (Exod. 12:43). To say no more, when Paul declares that the rock was Christ (1 Cor. 10:4), why should the substantive verb, in that passage, be deemed less emphatic than in the discourse of Christ? When John says, "The Holy Ghost was not yet given, because that Jesus was not yet glorified" (John 7:39), I should like to know what is the force of the substantive verb? If the rule of our opponents is rigidly observed, the eternal essence of the Spirit will be destroyed, as if he had only begun to be after the ascension of Christ. Let them tell me, in fine, what is meant by the declaration of Paul, that baptism is "the washing of regeneration, and renewing of the Holy Ghost" (Tit. 3:5); though it is certain that to many it was of no use. But they cannot be more effectually refuted than by the expression of Paul, that the Church is Christ. For, after introducing the similitude of the human body, he adds, "So also is Christ" (1 Cor. 7:12), when he means not the only-begotten Son of God in himself, but in his members. I think I have now gained this much, that all

men of sense and integrity will be disgusted with the calumnies of our enemies, when they give out that we discredit the words of Christ; though we embrace them not less obediently than they do, and ponder them with greater reverence. Nay, their supine security proves that they do not greatly care what Christ meant, provided it furnishes them with a shield to defend their obstinacy, while our careful investigation should be an evidence of the authority which we yield to Christ. They invidiously pretend that human reason will not allow us to believe what Christ uttered with his sacred mouth; but how naughtily they endeavour to fix this odium upon us, I have already, in a great measure, shown, and will still show more clearly. Nothing, therefore, prevents us from believing Christ speaking, and from acquiescing in everything to which he intimates his assent. The only question here is, whether it be unlawful to inquire into the genuine meaning?

23. Those worthy masters, to show that they are of the letter, forbid us to deviate, in the least, from the letter. On the contrary, when Scripture calls God a man of war, as I see that the expression would be too harsh if not interpreted, I have no doubt that the similitude is taken from man. And, indeed, the only pretext which enabled the Anthropomorphites to annoy the orthodox Fathers was by fastening on the expressions, "The eyes of God see;" "It ascended to his ears;" "His hand is stretched out;" "The earth is his footstool;" and exclaimed, that God was deprived of the body which Scripture assigns to him. Were this rule admitted, complete barbarism would bury the whole light of faith. What monstrous absurdities shall fanatical men not be able to extract, if they are allowed to urge every knotty point in support of their dogmas? Their objection, that it is not probable that when Christ was providing special comfort for the apostles in adversity, he spoke enigmatically or obscurely,—supports our view. For, had it not occurred to the apostles that the bread was called the body figuratively, as being a symbol of the body, the extraordinary nature of the thing would doubtless have filled them with perplexity. For, at this very period, John relates, that the slightest difficulties perplexed them (John 14:5, 8; 16:17). They debate, among themselves, how Christ is to go to the Father, and not understanding that the things which were said referred to the heavenly Father, raise a question as to how he is to go out of the world until they shall see him? How, then, could they have been so ready to believe what is repugnant to all reason—viz. that Christ was seated at table under their eye, and yet was contained invisible under the bread? As they attest their consent by eating this bread without hesitation, it is plain that they understood the words of Christ in the same sense as we do, considering what ought not to seem unusual when mysteries are spoken of, that the name of the thing signified was transferred to the sign. There was therefore to the disciples, as there is to us, clear and sure consolation, not involved in any enigma; and the only reason why certain persons reject our interpretation is, because they are blinded by a delusion of the devil to introduce the darkness of enigma, instead of the obvious interpretation of an appropriate figure. Besides, if we insist strictly on the words, our Saviour will be made to affirm erroneously something of the bread different from the cup. He calls the bread body, and the wine blood. There must either be a confusion in terms, or there must be a division separating the body from the blood. Nay, "This is my body," may be as truly affirmed of the cup as of the bread; and it may in turn be affirmed that the bread is the blood. If they answer, that we must look to the end or use for which symbols were instituted, I admit it: but still they will not disencumber themselves of the absurdity which their error drags along with it—viz. that the bread is blood, and the wine is body. Then I know not what they mean when they concede that bread and body are different things, and yet maintain that the one is predicated of the other, properly and without figure, as if one were to say that a garment is different from a man, and yet is properly called a man. Still, as if the victory depended on obstinacy and invective, they say that Christ is charged with falsehood, when it is attempted to interpret his words. It will now be easy for the reader to understand the injustice which is done to us by those carpers at syllables, when they possess the simple with the idea that we bring discredit on the words of Christ; words which, as we have shown, are madly perverted and confounded by them, but are faithfully and accurately expounded by us.

24. This infamous falsehood cannot be completely wiped away without disposing of another charge. They give out that we are so wedded to human reason, that we attribute nothing more to the power of God than the order of nature admits, and common sense dictates. From these wicked calumnies, I appeal to the doctrine which I have delivered,—a doctrine which makes it sufficiently clear that I by no means measure this mystery by the capacity of human reason, or subject it to the laws of nature. I ask, whether it is from physics we have learned that Christ feeds our souls from heaven with his flesh, just as our bodies are nourished by bread and wine? How

has flesh this virtue of giving life to our souls? All will say, that it is not done naturally. Not more agreeable is it to human reason to hold that the flesh of Christ penetrates to us, so as to be our food. In short, every one who may have tasted our doctrine, will be carried away with admiration of the secret power of God. But these worthy zealots fabricate for themselves a miracle, and think that without it God himself and his power vanish away. I would again admonish the reader carefully to consider the nature of our doctrine, whether it depends on common apprehension, or whether, after having surmounted the world on the wings of faith, it rises to heaven. We say that Christ descends to us, as well by the external symbol as by his Spirit, that he may truly quicken our souls by the substance of his flesh and blood. He who feels not that in these few words are many miracles, is more than stupid; since nothing is more contrary to nature than to derive the spiritual and heavenly life of the soul from flesh, which received its origin from the earth, and was subjected to death, nothing more incredible than that things separated by the whole space between heaven and earth should, notwithstanding of the long distance, not only be connected, but united, so that souls receive aliment from the flesh of Christ. Let preposterous men, then, cease to assail us with the vile calumny, that we malignantly restrict the boundless power of God. They either foolishly err, or wickedly lie. The question here is not, What could God do? but, What has he been pleased to do? We affirm that he has done what pleased him, and it pleased him that Christ should be in all respects like his brethren, "yet without sin" (Heb. 4:15). What is our flesh? Is it not that which consists of certain dimensions? is confined within a certain place? is touched and seen? And why, say they, may not God make the same flesh occupy several different places, so as not to be confined to any particular place, and so as to have neither measure nor species? Fool! why do you require the power of God to make a thing to be at the same time flesh and not flesh? It is just as if you were to insist on his making light to be at the same time light and darkness. He wills light to be light, darkness to be darkness, flesh to be flesh. True, when he so chooses, he will convert darkness into light, and light into darkness: but when you insist that there shall be no difference between light and darkness, what do you but pervert the order of the divine wisdom? Flesh must therefore be flesh, and spirit spirit; each under the law and condition on which God has created them. Now, the condition of flesh is, that it should have one certain place, its own dimensions, its own form. On that condition, Christ assumed the flesh, to which, as Augustine declares (Ep. ad Dardan.), he gave incorruption and glory, but without destroying its nature and reality.

25. They object that they have the word by which the will of God has been openly manifested; that is if we permit them to banish from the Church the gift of interpretation, which should throw light upon the word. I admit that they have the word, but just as the Anthropomorphites of old had it, when they made God corporeal; just as Marcion and the Manichees had it when they made the body of Christ celestial or phantastical. They quoted the passages, "The first man is of the earth, earthy; the second man is the Lord from heaven" (1 Cor. 15:47): Christ "made himself of no reputation, and took upon him the form of a servant, and was made in the likeness of men" (Phil. 2:7). But these vain boasters think that there is no power of God unless they fabricate a monster in their own brains, by which the whole order of nature is subverted. This rather is to circumscribe the power of God, to attempt to try, by our fictions, what he can do. From this word, they have assumed that the body of Christ is visible in heaven, and yet lurks invisible on the earth under innumerable bits of bread. They will say that this is rendered necessary, in order that the body of Christ may be given in the Supper. In other words, because they have been pleased to extract a carnal eating from the words of Christ, carried away by their own prejudice, they have found it necessary to coin this subtlety, which is wholly repugnant to Scripture. That we detract, in any respect, from the power of God, is so far from being true, that our doctrine is the loudest in extolling it. But as they continue to charge us with robbing God of his honour, in rejecting what, according to common apprehension, it is difficult to believe, though it had been promised by the mouth of Christ; I answer, as I lately did, that in the mysteries of faith we do not consult common apprehension, but, with the placid docility and spirit of meekness which James recommends (James 1:21), receive the doctrine which has come from heaven. Wherein they perniciously err, I am confident that we follow a proper moderation. On hearing the words of Christ, this is my body, they imagine a miracle most remote from his intention; and when, from this fiction, the grossest absurdities arise, having already, by their precipitate haste, entangled themselves with snares, they plunge themselves into the abyss of the divine omnipotence, that, in this way, they may extinguish the light of truth. Hence the supercilious moroseness. We have no wish to know how Christ is hid under the bread: we are satisfied with his own words,

"This is my body." We again study, with no less obedience than care, to obtain a sound understanding of this passage, as of the whole of Scripture. We do not, with preposterous fervour, rashly, and without choice, lay hold on whatever first presents itself to our minds; but, after careful meditation, embrace the meaning which the Spirit of God suggests. Trusting to him, we look down, as from a height, on whatever opposition may be offered by earthly wisdom. Nay, we hold our minds captive, not allowing one word of murmur, and humble them, that they may not presume to gainsay. In this way, we have arrived at that exposition of the words of Christ, which all who are moderately versant in Scripture know to be perpetually used with regard to the sacraments. Still, in a matter of difficulty, we deem it not unlawful to inquire, after the example of the blessed Virgin, "How shall this be?" (Luke 1:34).

26. But as nothing will be more effectual to confirm the faith of the pious than to show them that the doctrine which we have laid down is taken from the pure word of God, and rests on its authority, I will make this plain with as much brevity as I can. The body with which Christ rose is declared, not by Aristotle, but by the Holy Spirit, to be finite, and to be contained in heaven until the last day. I am not unaware how confidently our opponents evade the passages which are quoted to this effect. Whenever Christ says that he will leave the world and go away (John 14:2, 28), they reply, that that departure was nothing more than a change of mortal state. Were this so, Christ would not substitute the Holy Spirit, to supply, as they express it, the defect of his absence, since he does not succeed in place of him, nor, on the other hand, does Christ himself descend from the heavenly glory to assume the condition of a mortal life. Certainly the advent of the Spirit and the ascension of Christ are set against each other, and hence it necessarily follows that Christ dwells with us according to the flesh, in the same way as that in which he sends his Spirit. Moreover, he distinctly says that he would not always be in the world with his disciples (Mt. 26:11). This saying, also, they think they admirably dispose of, as if it were a denial by Christ that he would always be poor and mean, or liable to the necessities of a fading life. But this is plainly repugnant to the context, since reference is made not to poverty and want, or the wretched condition of an earthly life, but to worship and honour. The disciples were displeased with the anointing by Mary, because they thought it a superfluous and useless expenditure, akin to luxury, and would therefore have preferred that the price which they thought wasted should have been expended on the poor. Christ answers, that he will not be always with them to receive such honour. No different exposition is given by Augustine, whose words are by no means ambiguous. When Christ says, "Me ye have not always," he spoke of his bodily presence. In regard to his majesty, in regard to his providence, in regard to his ineffable and invisible grace, is fulfilled what he said: "Lo, I am with you alway, even unto the end of the world" (Mt. 28:20); but in regard to the flesh which the Word assumed—in regard to that which was born of the Virgin—in regard to that which was apprehended by the Jews, nailed to the tree, suspended on the cross, wrapt in linen clothes, laid in the tomb, and manifested in the resurrection,—"Me ye have not always." Why? Since he conversed with his disciples in bodily presence for forty days, and, going out with them, ascended, while they saw but followed not. He is not here, for he sits there, at the right hand of the Father. And yet he is here: for the presence of his majesty is not withdrawn. Otherwise, as regards the presence of his majesty, we have Christ always; while, in regard to his bodily presence, it was rightly said, "Me ye have not always." In respect of bodily presence, the Church had him for a few days: now she holds him by faith, but sees him not with the eye (August. Tract. in Joann. 50). Here (that I may briefly note this) he makes him present with us in three ways—in majesty, providence, and ineffable grace; under which I comprehend that wondrous communion of his body and blood, provided we understand that it is effected by the power of the Holy Spirit, and not by that fictitious enclosing of his body under the element, since our Lord declared that he had flesh and bones which could be handled and seen. *Going away*, and *ascending*, intimate, not that he had the appearance of one going away and ascending, but that he truly did what the words express. Some one will ask, Are we then to assign a certain region of heaven to Christ? I answer with Augustine, that this is a curious and superfluous question, provided we believe that he is in heaven.

27. What? Does not the very name of ascension, so often repeated, intimate removal from one place to another? This they deny, because by height, according to them, the majesty of empire only is denoted. But what was the very mode of ascending? Was he not carried up while the disciples looked on? Do not the Evangelists clearly relate that he was carried into heaven? These acute Sophists reply, that a cloud intervened, and took him out of their sight, to teach the disciples that he would not afterwards be visible in the world. As if he ought not rather to have vanished in a moment, to make them

believe in his invisible presence, or the cloud to have gathered around him before he moved a step. When he is carried aloft into the air, and the interposing cloud shows that he is no more to be sought on earth, we safely infer that his dwelling now is in the heavens, as Paul also asserts, bidding us look for him from thence (Phil. 3:20). For this reason, the angels remind the disciples that it is vain to keep gazing up into heaven, because Jesus, who was taken up, would come in like manner as they had seen him ascend. Here the adversaries of sound doctrine escape, as they think, by the ingenious quibble, that he will come in visible form, though he never departed from the earth, but remained invisible among his people. As if the angels had insinuated a two-fold presence, and not simply made the disciples eye-witnesses of the ascent, that no doubt might remain. It was just as if they had said, By ascending to heaven, while you looked on, he has asserted his heavenly power: it remains for you to wait patiently until he again arrive to judge the world. He has not entered into heaven to occupy it alone, but to gather you and all the pious along with him.

28. Since the advocates of this spurious dogma are not ashamed to honour it with the suffrages of the ancients, and especially of Augustine, how perverse they are in the attempt I will briefly explain. Pious and learned men have collected the passages, and therefore I am unwilling to plead a concluded cause: any one who wishes may consult their writings. I will not even collect from Augustine what might be pertinent to the matter, but will be contented to show briefly, that without all controversy he is wholly ours. The pretence of our opponents, when they would wrest him from us, that throughout his works the flesh and blood of Christ are said to be dispensed in the Supper—namely, the victim once offered on the cross, is frivolous, seeing he, at the same time, calls it either the eucharist or sacrament of the body. But it is unnecessary to go far to find the sense in which he uses the terms *flesh* and *blood*, since he himself explains, saying (Ep. 23, ad Bonif.) that the sacraments receive names from their similarity to the things which they designate; and that, therefore, the sacrament of the body is after a certain manner the body. With this agrees another well-know passage, "The Lord hesitated not to say, This is my body, when he gave the sign" (Cont. Adimant. Manich. cap. 12). They again object that Augustine says distinctly that the body of Christ falls upon the earth, and enters the mouth. But this is in the same sense in which he affirms that it is consumed, for he conjoins both at the same time. There is nothing repugnant to this in his saying that the bread is consumed after the mystery is performed: for he had said a little before, "As these things are known to men, when they are done by men they may receive honour as being religious, but not as being wonderful" (De Trinit. Lib. 3 c. 10). His meaning is not different in the passage which our opponents too rashly appropriate to themselves—viz. that Christ in a manner carried himself in his own hands, when he held out the mystical bread to his disciples. For by interposing the expression, *in a manner*, he declares that he was not really or truly included under the bread. Nor is it strange, since he elsewhere plainly contends, that bodies could not be without particular localities, and being nowhere, would have no existence. It is a paltry cavil that he is not there treating of the Supper, in which God exerts a special power. The question had been raised as to the flesh of Christ, and the holy man professedly replying, says, "Christ gave immortality to his flesh, but did not destroy its nature. In regard to this form, we are not to suppose that it is everywhere diffused: for we must beware not to rear up the divinity of the man, so as to take away the reality of the body. It does not follow that that which is in God is everywhere as God" (Ep. ad Dardan.). He immediately subjoins the reason, "One person is God and man, and both one Christ, everywhere, inasmuch as he is God, and in heaven, inasmuch as he is man." How careless would it have been not to except the mystery of the Supper, a matter so grave and serious, if it was in any respect adverse to the doctrine which he was handling? And yet, if any one will attentively read what follows shortly after, he will find that under that general doctrine the Supper also is comprehended, that Christ, the only-begotten Son of God, and also Son of man, is everywhere wholly present as God, in the temple of God, that is, in the Church, as an inhabiting God, and in some place in heaven, because of the dimensions of his real body. We see how, in order to unite Christ with the Church, he does not bring his body out of heaven. This he certainly would have done had the body of Christ not been truly our food, unless when included under the bread. Elsewhere, explaining how believers now possess Christ, he says, "You have him by the sign of the cross, by the sacrament of baptism, by the meat and drink of the altar" (Tract. in Joann. 50). How rightly he enumerates a superstitious rite, among the symbols of Christ's presence, I dispute not; but in comparing the presence of the flesh to the sign of the cross, he sufficiently shows that he has no idea of a twofold body of Christ, one lurking concealed under the bread, and another sitting visible in heaven. If there is any need of explanation, it is immedi-

ately added, "In respect of the presence of his majesty, we have Christ always: in respect of the presence of his flesh, it is rightly said, 'Me ye have not always.'" They object that he also adds, "In respect of ineffable and invisible grace is fulfilled what was said by him, 'I am with you always, even to the end of the world.'" But this is nothing in their favour. For it is at length restricted to his majesty, which is always opposed to body, while the flesh is expressly distinguished from grace and virtue. The same antithesis elsewhere occurs, when he says that "Christ left the disciples in bodily presence, that he might be with them in spiritual presence." Here it is clear that the essence of the flesh is distinguished from the virtue of the Spirit, which conjoins us with Christ, when, in respect of space, we are at a great distance from him. He repeatedly uses the same mode of expression, as when he says, "He is to come to the quick and the dead in bodily presence, according to the rule of faith and sound doctrine: for in spiritual presence he was to come to them, and to be with the whole Church in the world until its consummation. Therefore, this discourse is directed to believers, whom he had begun already to save by corporeal presence, and whom he was to leave in coporeal absence, that by spiritual presence he might preserve them with the Father." By corporeal to understand visible is mere trifling, since he both opposes his body to his divine power, and by adding, that he might "preserve them with the Father," clearly expresses that he sends his grace to us from heaven by means of the Spirit.

29. Since they put so much confidence in his hiding-place of invisible presence, let us see how well they conceal themselves in it. First, they cannot produce a syllable from Scripture to prove that Christ is invisible; but they take for granted what no sound man will admit, that the body of Christ cannot be given in the Supper, unless covered with the mask of bread. This is the very point in dispute; so far is it from occupying the place of the first principle. And while they thus prate, they are forced to give Christ a twofold body, because, according to them, it is visible in itself in heaven, but in the Supper is invisible, by a special mode of dispensation. The beautiful consistency of this may easily be judged, both from other passages of Scripture, and from the testimony of Peter. Peter says that the heavens must receive, or contain Christ, till he come again (Acts 3:21). These men teach that he is in every place, but without form. They say that it is unfair to subject a glorious body to the ordinary laws of nature. But this answer draws along with it the delirious dream of Servetus, which all pious minds justly abhor, that his body was absorbed by his divinity. I do not say that this is their opinion; but if it is considered one of the properties of a glorified body to fill all things in an invisible manner, it is plain that the corporeal substance is abolished, and no distinction is left between his Godhead and his human nature. Again, if the body of Christ is so multiform and diversified, that it appears in one place, and in another is invisible, where is there anything of the nature of body with its proper dimensions, and where is its unity? Far more correct is Tertullian, who contends that the body of Christ was natural and real, because its figure is set before us in the mystery of the Supper, as a pledge and assurance of spiritual life (Tertull. Cont. Marc. Lib. 4). And certainly Christ said of his glorified body, "Handle me, and see; for a spirit hath not flesh and bones, as ye see me have" (Luke 24:39). Here, by the lips of Christ himself, the reality of his flesh is proved, by its admitting of being seen and handled. Take these away, and it will cease to be flesh. They always betake themselves to their lurking-place of dispensation, which they have fabricated. But it is our duty so to embrace what Christ absolutely declares, as to give it an unreserved assent. He proves that he is not a phantom, because he is visible in his flesh. Take away what he claims as proper to the nature of his body, and must not a new definition of body be devised? Then, however they may turn themselves about, they will not find any place for their fictitious dispensation in that passage, in which Paul says, that "our conversation is in heaven; from whence we look for the Saviour, the Lord Jesus Christ: who shall change our vile body, that it may be fashioned like unto his glorious body" (Phil. 3:20, 21). We are not to hope for conformity to Christ in these qualities which they ascribe to him as a body, without bounds, and invisible. They will not find any one so stupid as to be persuaded of this great absurdity. Let them not, therefore, set it down as one of the properties of Christ's glorious body, that it is, at the same time, in many places, and in no place. In short, let them either openly deny the resurrection of his flesh, or admit that Christ, when invested with celestial glory, did not lay aside his flesh, but is to make us, in our flesh, his associates, and partakers of the same glory, since we are to have a common resurrection with him. For what does Scripture throughout deliver more clearly than that, as Christ assumed our flesh when he was born of the Virgin, and suffered in our true flesh when he made satisfaction for us, so on rising again he resumed the same true flesh, and carried it with him to

heaven? The hope of our resurrection, and ascension to heaven, is, that Christ rose again and ascended, and, as Tertullian says (De Resurrect. Carnis), "Carried an earnest of our resurrection along with him into heaven." Morever, how weak and fragile would this hope be, had not this very flesh of ours in Christ been truly raised up, and entered into the kingdom of heaven. But the essential properties of a body are to be confined by space, to have dimension and form. Have done, then, with that foolish fiction, which affixes the minds of men, as well as Christ, to bread. For to what end this occult presence under the bread, save that those who wish to have Christ conjoined with them may stop short at the symbol? But our Lord himself wished us to withdraw not only our eyes, but all our senses, from the earth, forbidding the woman to touch him until he had ascended to the Father (John 20:17). When he sees Mary, with pious reverential zeal, hastening to kiss his feet, there could be no reason for his disapproving and forbidding her to touch him before he had ascended to heaven, unless he wished to he sought nowhere else. The objection, that he afterwards appeared to Stephen, is easily answered. It was not necessary for our Saviour to change his place, as he could give the eyes of his servant a power of vision which could penetrate to heaven. The same account is to be given of the case of Paul. The objection, that Christ came forth from the closed sepulchre, and came in to his disciples while the doors were shut (Mt. 28:6; John 20:19), gives no better support to their error. For as the water, just as if it had been a solid pavement, furnished a path to our Saviour when he walked on it (Mt. 14.), so it is not strange that the hard stone yielded to his step; although it is more probable that the stone was removed at his command, and forthwith, after giving him a passage, returned to its place. To enter while the doors were shut, was not so much to penetrate through solid matter, as to make a passage for himself by divine power, and stand in the midst of his disciples in a most miraculous manner. They gain nothing by quoting the passage from Luke, in which it is said, that Christ suddenly vanished from the eyes of the disciples, with whom he had journed to Emmaus (Luke 24:31). In withdrawing from their sight, he did not become invisible: he only disappeared. Thus Luke declares that, on the journeying with them, he did not assume a new form, but that " their eyes were holden." But these men not only transform Christ that he may live on the earth, but pretend that there is another elsewhere of a different description. In short, by thus trifling, they, not in direct terms indeed, but by a circumlocution, make a spirit of the flesh of Christ; and, not contented with this, give him properties altogether opposite. Hence it necessarily follows that he must be twofold.

30. Granting what they absurdly talk of the invisible presence, it will still be necessary to prove the immensity, without which it is vain to attempt to include Christ under the bread. Unless the body of Christ can be everywhere without any boundaries of space, it is impossible to believe that he is hid in the Supper under the bread. Hence, they have been under the necessity of introducing the monstrous dogma of ubiquity. But it has been demonstrated by strong and clear passages of Scripture, first, that it is bounded by the dimensions of the human body; and, secondly, that its ascension into heaven made it plain that it is not in all places, but on passing to a new one, leaves the one formerly occupied. The promise to which they appeal, "I am with you always, even to the end of the world," is not to be applied to the body. First, then, a perpetual connection with Christ could not exist, unless he dwells in us corporeally, independently of the use of the Supper; and, therefore, they have no good ground for disputing so bitterly concerning the words of Christ, in order to include him under the bread in the Supper. Secondly, the context proves that Christ is not speaking at all of his flesh, but promising the disciples his invincible aid to guard and sustain them against all the assaults of Satan and the world. For, in appointing them to a difficult office, he confirms them by the assurance of his presence, that they might neither hesitate to undertake it, nor be timorous in the discharge of it; as if he had said, that his invincible protection would not fail them. Unless we would throw everything into confusion, must it not be necessary to distinguish the mode of presence? And, indeed, some, to their great disgrace, choose rather to betray their ignorance than give up one iota of their error. I speak not of Papists, whose doctrine is more tolerable, or at least more modest; but some are so hurried away by contention as to say, that on account of the union of natures in Christ, wherever his divinity is, there his flesh, which cannot be separated from it, is also; as if that union formed a kind of medium of the two natures, making him to be neither God nor man. So held Eutyches, and after him Servetus. But it is clearly gathered from Scripture that the one person of Christ is composed of two natures, but so that each has its peculiar properties unimpaired. That Eutyches was justly condemned, they will not have the hardihood to deny. It is strange that they attend not to the cause of condemnation—viz.

that destroying the distinction between the natures, and insisting only on the unity of person, he converted God into man and man into God. What madness, then, is it to confound heaven with earth, sooner than not withdraw the body of Christ from its heavenly sanctuary? In regard to the passages which they adduce, "No man has ascended up to heaven, but he that came down from heaven, even the Son of man which is in heaven" (John 3:13); "The only-begotten Son, who is in the bosom of the Father, he hath declared him" (John 1:18), they betray the same stupidity, scouting the communion of properties (*idiomatum*, κοινωνίαν), which not without reason was formerly invented by holy Fathers. Certainly when Paul says of the princes of this world that they "crucified the Lord of glory" (1 Cor. 2:8), he means not that he suffered anything in his divinity, but that Christ, who was rejected and despised, and suffered in the flesh, was likewise God and the Lord of glory. In this way, both the Son of man was in heaven because he was also Christ; and he who, according to the flesh, dwelt as the Son of man on earth, was also God in heaven. For this reason, he is said to have descended from heaven in respect of his divinity, not that his divinity quitted heaven to conceal itself in the prison of the body, but because, although he filled all things, it yet resided in the humanity of Christ coporeally, that is, naturally, and in an ineffable manner. There is a trite distinction in the schools which I hesitate not to quote. Although the whole Christ is everywhere, yet everything which is in him is not everywhere. I wish the Schoolmen had duly weighed the force of this sentence, as it would have obviated their absurd fiction of the corporeal presence of Christ. Therefore, while our whole Mediator is everywhere, he is always present with his people, and in the Supper exhibits his presence in a special manner; yet so, that while he is wholly present, not everything which is in him is present, because, as has been said, in his flesh he will remain in heaven till he come to judgment.

31. They are greatly mistaken in imagining that there is no presence of the flesh of Christ in the Supper, unless it be placed in the bread. They thus leave nothing for the secret operation of the Spirit, which unites Christ himself to us. Christ does not seem to them to be present unless he descends to us, as if we did not equally gain his presence when he raises us to himself. The only question, therefore, is as to the mode, they placing Christ in the bread, while we deem it unlawful to draw him down from heaven. Which of the two is more correct, let the reader judge. Only have done with the calumny that Christ is withdrawn from his Supper if he lurk not under the covering of bread. For seeing this mystery is heavenly, there is no necessity to bring Christ on the earth that he may be connected with us.

32. Now, should any one ask me as to the mode, I will not be ashamed to confess that it is too high a mystery either for my mind to comprehend or my words to express; and to speak more plainly, I rather feel than understand it. The truth of God, therefore, in which I can safely rest, I here embrace without controversy. He declares that his flesh is the meat, his blood the drink, of my soul; I give my soul to him to be fed with such food. In his sacred Supper he bids me take, eat, and drink his body and blood under the symbols of bread and wine. I have no doubt that he will truly give and I receive. Only, I reject the absurdities which appear to be unworthy of the heavenly majesty of Christ, and are inconsistent with the reality of his human nature. Since they must also be repugnant to the word of God, which teaches both that Christ was received into the glory of the heavenly kingdom, so as to be exalted above all the circumstances of the world (Luke 24:26), and no less carefully ascribes to him the properties belonging to a true human nature. This ought not to seem incredible or contradictory to reason (Iren. Lib. 4 cap. 34); because, as the whole kingdom of Christ is spiritual, so whatever he does in his Church is not to be tested by the wisdom of this world; or, to use the words of Augustine, "this mystery is performed by man like the others, but in a divine manner, and on earth, but in a heavenly manner." Such, I say, is the corporeal presence which the nature of the sacrament requires, and which we say is here displayed in such power and efficacy, that it not only gives our minds undoubted assurance of eternal life, but also secures the immortality of our flesh, since it is now quickened by his immortal flesh, and in a manner shines in his immortality. Those who are carried beyond this with their hyperboles, do nothing more by their extravagances than obscure the plain and simple truth. If any one is not yet satisfied, I would have him here to consider with himself that we are speaking of the sacrament, every part of which ought to have reference to faith. Now by participation of the body, as we have explained, we nourish faith not less richly and abundantly than do those who drag Christ himself from heaven. Still I am free to confess that that mixture or transfusion of the flesh of Christ with our soul, which they teach, I repudiate, because it is enough for us that Christ, out of the substance of his flesh, breathes life into our souls, nay, diffuses his own life into us, though the real flesh of Christ

does not enter us. I may add, that there can be no doubt that the analogy of faith by which Paul enjoins us to test every interpretation of Scripture, is clearly with us in this matter. Let those who oppose a truth so clear, consider to what standard of faith they conform themselves: "Ever spirit that confesseth not that Jesus Christ is come in the flesh is not of God" (1 John 4:3); 2 John ver. 7). These men, though they disguise the fact, or perceive it not, rob him of his flesh.

33. The same view must be taken of communion, which, according to them, has no existence unless they swallow the flesh of Christ under the bread. But no slight insult is offered to the Spirit if we refuse to believe that it is by his incomprehensible agency that we communicate in the body and blood of Christ. Nay, if the nature of the mystery, as delivered to us, and known to the ancient Church for four hundred years, had been considered as it deserves, there was more than enough to satisfy us; the door would have been shut against many disgraceful errors. These have kindled up fearful dissensions, by which the Church, both anciently and in our own times, has been miserably vexed; curious men insisting on an extravagant mode of presence to which Scripture gives no countenance. And for a matter thus foolishly and rashly devised they keep up a turmoil, as if the including of Christ under the bread were, so to speak, the beginning and end of piety. It was of primary importance to know how the body of Christ once delivered to us becomes ours, and how we become partakers of his shed blood, because this is to possess the whole of Christ crucified, so as to enjoy all his blessings. But overlooking these points, in which there was so much importance, nay, neglecting and almost suppressing them, they occupy themselves only with this one perplexing question, How is the body of Christ hidden under the bread, or under the appearance of bread? They falsely pretend that all which we teach concerning spiritual eating is opposed to true and what they call real eating, since we have respect only to the mode of eating. This, according to them, is carnal, since they include Christ under the bread, but according to us is spiritual, inasmuch as the sacred agency of the Spirit is the bond of our union with Christ. Not better founded is the other objection, that we attend only to the fruit or effect which believers receive from eating the flesh of Christ. We formerly said, that Christ himself is the matter of the Supper, and that the effect follows from this, that by the sacrifice of his death our sins are expiated, by his blood we are washed, and by his resurrection we are raised to the hope of life in heaven. But a foolish imagination, of which Lombard was the author, perverts their minds, while they think that the sacrament is the eating of the flesh of Christ. His words are, "The sacrament and not the thing are the forms of bread and wine; the sacrament and the thing are the flesh and blood of Christ; the thing and not the sacrament is his mystical flesh" (Lombard, Lib. 4 Dist. 8). Again a little after, "The thing signified and contained is the proper flesh of Christ; the thing signified and not contained is his mystical body." To his distinction between the flesh of Christ and the power of nourishing which it possesses, I assent; but his maintaining it to be a sacrament, and a sacrament contained under the bread, is an error not to be tolerated. Hence has arisen that false interpretation of sacramental eating, because it was imagined that even the wicked and profane, however much alienated from Christ, eat his body. But the very flesh of Christ in the mystery of the Supper is no less a spiritual matter than eternal salvation. Whence we infer, that all who are devoid of the Spirit of Christ can no more eat the flesh of Christ than drink wine that has no savour. Certainly Christ is shamefully lacerated, when his body, as lifeless and without any vigour, is prostituted to unbelievers. This is clearly repugnant to his words, "He that eateth my flesh, and drinketh my blood, dwelleth in me, and I in him" (John 6:56). They object that he is not there speaking of sacramental eating; this I admit, provided they will not ever and anon stumble on this stone, that his flesh itself is eaten without any benefit. I should like to know how they confine it after they have eaten. Here, in my opinion, they will find no outlet. But they object, that the ingratitude of man cannot in any respect detract from, or interfere with, faith in the promises of God. I admit and hold that the power of the sacrament remains entire, however the wicked may labour with all their might to annihilate it. Still, it is one thing to be offered, another to be received. Christ gives this spiritual food and holds forth this spiritual drink to all. Some eat eagerly, others superciliously reject it. Will their rejection cause the meat and drink to lose their nature? They will say that this similitude supports their opinion—viz. that the flesh of Christ, though it be without taste, is still flesh. But I deny that it can be eaten without the taste of faith, or (if it is more agreeable to speak with Augustine), I deny that men carry away more from the sacrament than they collect in the vessel of faith. Thus nothing is detracted from the sacrament, nay, its reality and efficacy remain unimpaired, although the wicked, after externally partaking of it, go away empty. If, again, they object, that it derogates from the expression, "This is my body," if the

wicked receive corruptible bread and nothing besides, it is easy to answer, that God wills not that his truth should be recognised in the mere reception, but in the constancy of his goodness, while he is prepared to perform, nay, liberally offers to the unworthy what they reject. The integrity of the sacrament, an integrity which the whole world cannot violate, lies here, that the flesh and blood of Christ are not less truly given to the unworthy than to the elect believers of God; and yet it is true, that just as the rain falling on the hard rock runs away because it cannot penetrate, so the wicked by their hardness repel the grace of God, and prevent it from reaching them. We may add, that it is no more possible to receive Christ without faith, than it is for seed to germinate in the fire. They ask how Christ can have come for the condemnation of some, unless they unworthily receive him; but this is absurd, since we nowhere read that they bring death upon themselves by receiving Christ unworthily, but by rejecting him. They are not aided by the parable in which Christ says, that the seed which fell among thorns sprung up, but was afterwards choked (Mt. 13:7), because he is there speaking of the effect of a temporary faith, a faith which those who place Judas in this respect on a footing with Peter, do not think necessary to the eating of the flesh and the drinking of the blood of Christ. Nay, their error is refuted by the same parable, when Christ says that some seed fell upon the wayside, and some on stony ground, and yet neither took root. Hence it follows that the hardness of believers is an obstacle which prevents Christ from reaching them. All who would have our salvation to be promoted by this sacrament, will find nothing more appropriate than to conduct believers to the fountain, that they may draw life from the Son of God. The dignity is amply enough commended when we hold, that it is a help by which we may be ingrafted into the body of Christ, or, already ingrafted, may be more and more united to him, until the union is completed in heaven. They object, that Paul could not have made them guilty of the body and blood of the Lord if they had not partaken of them (1 Cor. 11:7); I answer, that they were not condemned for having eaten. but only for having profaned the ordinance by trampling under foot the pledge, which they ought to have reverently received, the pledge of sacred union with God.

34. Moreover, as among ancient writers, Augustine especially maintaine this head of doctrine, that the grace figured by the sacraments is not impaired or made void by the infidelity or malice of men, it will be useful to prove clearly from his words, how ignorantly and erroneously those who cast forth the body of Christ to be eaten by dogs, wrest them to their present purpose. Sacramental eating, according to them, is that by which the wicked receive the body and blood of Christ without the agency of the Spirit, or any gracious effect. Augustine, on the contrary, prudently pondering the expression. "Whoso eateth my flesh, and drinketh my blood, hath eternal life" (John 6:54), says: "That is the virtue of the sacrament, and not merely the visible sacrament: the sacrament of him who eats inwardly, not of him who eats outwardly, or merely with the teeth" (Hom. in Joann. 26). Hence he at length concludes, that the sacrament of this thing, that is, of the unity of the body and blood of Christ in the Lord's Supper, is set before some for life, before others for destruction: while the matter itself, of which it is the sacrament, is to all for life, to none for destruction, whoever may have been the partaker. Lest any one should here cavil that by *thing* is not meant body, but the grace of the Spirit, which may be separated from it, he dissipates these mists by the antithetical epithets, Visible and Invisible. For the body of Christ cannot be included under the former. Hence it follows, that unbelievers communicate only in the visible symbol; and the better to remove all doubt, after saying that this bread requires an appetite in the inner man, he adds (Hom. in Joann. 59), "Moses, and Aaron, and Phinehas, and many others who ate manna, pleased God. Why? Because the visible food they understood spiritually, hungered for spiritually, tasted spiritually, and feasted on spiritually. We, too, in the present day, have received visible food: but the sacrament is one thing, the virtue of the sacrament is another." A little after, he says: "And hence, he who remains not in Christ, and in whom Christ remains not, without doubt neither spiritually eats his flesh, nor drinks his blood, though with his teeth he may carnally and visibly press the symbol of his body and blood." Again, we are told that the visible sign is opposed to spiritual eating. This refutes the error that the invisible body of Christ is sacramentally eaten in reality, although not spiritually. We are told, also, that nothing is given to the impure and profane beyond the visible taking of the sign. Hence his celebrated saying, that the other disciples ate *bread which was the Lord,* whereas Judas ate *the bread of the Lord* (Hom. in Joann. 62). By this, he clearly excludes unbelievers from participation in his body and blood. He has no other meaning when he says, "Why do you wonder that the bread of Christ was given to Judas, though he consigned him to the devil, when you see, on the contrary, that a messenger of the devil was given to Paul to perfect him in Christ?"

(August. de Bapt. Cont. Donat. Lib. 5). He indeed says elsewhere, that the bread of the Supper was the body of Christ to those to whom Paul said, "He that eateth and drinketh unworthily, eateth and drinketh damnation to himself; and that it does not follow that they received nothing because they received unworthily." But in what sense he says this, he explains more fully in another passage (De Civit. Dei, Lib. 21 c. 25). For undertaking professedly to explain how the wicked and profane, who, with the mouth, profess the faith of Christ, but in act deny him, eat the body of Christ; and, indeed, refuting the opinion of some who thought that they ate not only sacramentally, but really, he says: "Neither can they be said to eat the body of Christ, because they are not to be accounted among the members of Christ. For, not to mention other reasons, they cannot be at the same time the members of Christ and the members of a harlot. In fine, when Christ himself says, 'He that eateth my flesh, and drinketh my blood, dwelleth in me, and I in him' (John 6:56), he shows what it is to eat the body of Christ, not sacramentally, but in reality. It is to abide in Christ, that Christ may abide in him. For it is just as if he had said, Let not him who abides not in me, and in whom I abide not, say or think that he eats my body or drinks my blood." Let the reader attend to the antithesis between eating sacramentally and eating really, and there will be no doubt. The same thing he confirms not less clearly in these words: "Prepare not the jaws, but the heart; for which alone the Supper is appointed. We believe in Christ when we receive him in faith: in receiving, we know what we think: we receive a small portion, but our heart is filled: it is not therefore that which is seen, but that which is believed, that feeds (August. Cont. Faust. Lib. 8 c. 16). Here, also, he restricts what the wicked take to be the visible sign, and shows that the only way of receiving Christ is by faith. So, also, in another passage, declaring distinctly that the good and the bad communicate by signs, he excludes the latter from the true eating of the flesh of Christ. For had they received the reality, he would not have been altogether silent as to a matter which was pertinent to the case. In another passage, speaking of eating, and the fruit of it, he thus concludes: "Then will the body and blood of Christ be life to each, if that which is visibly taken in the sacrament is in reality spiritually eaten, spiritually drunk" (De Verb. Apost. Serm. 2) Let those, therefore, who make unbelievers partakers of the flesh and blood of Christ, if they would agree with Augustine, set before us the visible body of Christ, since, according to him, the whole truth is spiritual. And certainly his words imply that sacramental eating, when unbelief excludes the entrance of the reality, is only equivalent to visible or external eating. But if the body of Christ may be truly and yet not spiritually eaten, what could he mean when he elsewhere says: "Ye are not to eat this body which you see, nor to drink the blood which will be shed by those who are to crucify me? I have committed a certain sacrament to you: it is the spiritual meaning which will give you life" (August. in Ps. 98). He certainly meant not to deny that the body offered in the Supper is the same as that which Christ offered in sacrifice; but he adverted to the mode of eating—viz. that the body, though received into the celestial glory, breathes life into us by the secret energy of the Spirit. I admit, indeed, that he often uses the expression, "that the body of Christ is eaten by unbelievers;" but he explains himself by adding, "in the sacrament." And he elsewhere speaks of a spiritual eating, in which our teeth do not chew grace (Hom. in Joann. 27). And, lest my opponents should say that I am trying to overwhelm them with the mass of my quotations, I would ask how they get over this one sentence: "In the elect alone, the sacraments effect what they figure." Certainly they will not venture to deny, that by the bread in the Supper, the body of Christ is figured. Hence it follows, that the reprobate are not allowed to partake of it. That Cyril did not think differently is clear from these words: "As one in pouring melted wax on melted wax mixes the whole together, so it is necessary, when one receives the body and blood of the Lord, to be conjoined with him, that Christ may be found in him, and he in Christ." From these words, I think it plain that there is no true and real eating by those who only eat the body of Christ sacramentally, seeing the body cannot be separated from its virtue, and that the promises of God do not fail, though, while he ceases not to rain from heaven, rocks and stones are not penetrated by the moisture.

35. This consideration will easily dissuade us from that carnal adoration which some men have, with perverse temerity, introduced into the sacrament, reasoning thus with themselves: If it is body, then it is also soul and divinity which go along with the body, and cannot be separated from it; and, therefore, Christ must there be adored. First, if we deny their pretended concomitance, what will they do? For, as they chiefly insist on the absurdity of separating the body of Christ from his soul and divinity, what sane and sober man can persuade himself that the body of Christ is Christ? They think that they completely establish this by their syllogisms. But since

Christ speaks separately of his body and blood, without describing the mode of his presence, how can they in a doubtful matter arrive at the certainty which they wish? What then? Should their consciences be at any time exercised with some more grievous apprehension, will they forthwith set them free, and dissolve the apprehensions by their syllogisms? In other words, when they see that no certainty is to be obtained from the word of God, in which alone our minds can rest, and without which they go astray the very first moment when they begin to reason, when they see themselves opposed by the doctrine and practice of the apostles, and that they are supported by no authority but their own, how will they feel? To such feelings other sharp stings will be added. What? Was it a matter of little moment to worship God under this form without any express injunction? In a matter relating to the true worship of God, were we thus lightly to act without one word of Scripture? Had all their thoughts been kept in due subjection to the word of God, they certainly would have listened to what he himself has said, "Take, eat, and drink," and obeyed the command by which he enjoins us to receive the sacrament, not worship it. Those who receive, without adoration, as commanded by God, are secure that they deviate not from the command. In commencing any work, nothing is better than this security. They have the example of the apostles, of whom we read not that they prostrated themselves and worshipped, but that they sat down, took and ate. They have the practice of the apostolic Church, where, as Luke relates, believers communicated not in adoration, but in the breaking of bread (Acts 2:42). They have the doctrine of the apostles as taught to the Corinthian Church by Paul, who declares that what he delivered he had received of the Lord (1 Cor. 11:23).

36. The object of these remarks is to lead pious readers to reflect how dangerous it is in matters of such difficulty to wander from the simple word of God to the dreams of our own brain. What has been said above should free us from all scruple in this matter. That the pious soul may duly apprehend Christ in the sacrament, it must rise to heaven. But if the office of the sacrament is to aid the infirmity of the human mind, assisting it in rising upwards, so as to perceive the height of spiritual mysteries, those who stop short at the external sign stray from the right path of seeking Christ. What then? Can we deny that the worship is superstitious when men prostrate themselves before bread that they may therein worship Christ? The Council of Nice undoubtedly intended to meet this evil when it forbade us to give humble heed to the visible signs. And for no other reason was it formerly the custom, previous to consecration, to call aloud upon the people to raise their hearts, *sursum corda*. Scripture itself, also, besides carefully narrating the ascension of Christ, by which he withdrew his bodily presence from our eye and company, that it might make us abandon all carnal thoughts of him, whenever it makes mention of him, enjoins us to raise our minds upwards and seek him in heaven, seated at the right hand of the Father (Col. 3:2). According to this rule, we should rather have adored him spiritually in the heavenly glory, than devised that perilous species of adoration replete with gross and carnal ideas of God. Those, therefore, who devised the adoration of the sacrament, not only dreamed it of themselves, without any authority from Scripture, where no mention of it can be shown (it would not have been omitted, had it been agreeable to God); but, disregarding Scripture, forsook the living God, and fabricated a god for themselves, after the lust of their own hearts. For what is idolatry if it is not to worship the gifts instead of the giver? Here the sin is twofold. The honour robbed from God is transferred to the creature, and God, moreover, is dishonoured by the pollution and profanation of his own goodness, while his holy sacrament is converted into an execrable idol. Let us, on the contrary, that we may not fall into the same pit, wholly confine our eyes, ears, hearts, minds, and tongues, to the sacred doctrine of God. For this is the school of the Holy Spirit, that best of masters, in which such progress is made, that while nothing is to be acquired anywhere else, we must willingly be ignorant of whatever is not there taught.

37. Then, as superstition, when once it has passed the proper bounds, has no end to its errors, men went much farther; for they devised rites altogether alien from the institution of the Supper, and to such a degree that they paid divine honours to the sign. They say that their veneration is paid to Christ. First, if this were done in the Supper, I would say that that adoration only is legitimate which stops not at the sign, but rises to Christ sitting in heaven. Now, under what pretext do they say that they honour Christ in that bread, when they have no promise of this nature? They consecrate the host, as they call it, and carry it about in solemn show, and formally exhibit it to be admired, reverenced, and invoked. I ask by what virtue they think it duly consecrated? They will quote the words, "This is my body." I, on the contrary, will object, that it was at the same time said, "Take, eat." Nor will I count the other passage as nothing; for I hold that since the promise is annexed to the command, the former is so

included under the latter, that it cannot possibly be separated from it. This will be made clearer by an example. God gave a command when he said, "Call upon me," and added a promise, "I will deliver thee" (Psal. 50:15). Should any one invoke Peter or Paul, and found on this promise, will not all exclaim that he does it in error? And what else, pray, do those do who, disregarding the command to eat, fasten on the mutilated promise, "This is my body," that they may pervert it to rites alien from the institution of Christ? Let us remember, therefore, that this promise has been given to those who observe the command connected with it, and that those who transfer the sacrament to another end have no countenance from the word of God. We formerly showed how the mystery of the sacred Supper contributes to our faith in God. But since the Lord not only reminds us of this great gift of his goodness, as we formerly explained, but passes it, as it were, from hand to hand, and urges us to recognise it, he, at the same time, admonishes us not to be ungrateful for the kindness thus bestowed, but rather to proclaim it with such praise as is meet, and celebrate it with thanksgiving. Accordingly, when he delivered the institution of the sacrament to the apostles, he taught them to do it in remembrance of him, which Paul interprets, "to show forth his death" (1 Cor. 11:26). And this is, that all should publicly and with one mouth confess that all our confidence of life and salvation is placed in our Lord's death, that we ourselves may glorify him by our confession, and by our example excite others also to give him glory. Here, again, we see what the aim of the sacrament is—namely, to keep us in remembrance of Christ's death. When we are ordered to show forth the Lord's death till he come again, all that is meant is, that we should, with confession of the mouth, proclaim what our faith has recognised in the sacrament—viz. that the death of Christ is our life. This is the second use of the sacrament, and relates to outward confession.

38. Thirdly, The Lord intended it to be a kind of exhortation, than which no other could urge or animate us more strongly, both to purity and holiness of life, and also to charity, peace, and concord. For the Lord there communicates his body so that he may become altogether one with us, and we with him. Moreover, since he has only one body of which he makes us all to be partakers, we must necessarily, by this participation, all become one body. This unity is represented by the bread which is exhibited in the sacrament. As it is composed of many grains, so mingled together, that one cannot be distinguished from another; so ought our minds to be so cordially united, as not to allow of any dissension or division. This I prefer giving in the words of Paul: "The cup of blessing which we bless, is it not the communion of the blood of Christ? The bread which we break, is it not the communion of the body of Christ? For we being many, are one bread and one body, for we are all partakers of that one bread" (1 Cor. 10:15, 16). We shall have profited admirably in the sacrament, if the thought shall have been impressed and engraven on our minds, that none of our brethren is hurt, despised, rejected, injured, or in any way offended, without our, at the same time, hurting, despising, and injuring Christ; that we cannot have dissension with our brethren, without at the same time dissenting from Christ; that we cannot love Christ without loving our brethren; that the same care we take of our own body we ought to take of that of our brethren, who are members of our body; that as no part of our body suffers pain without extending to the other parts, so every evil which our brother suffers ought to excite our compassion. Wherefore Augustine not inappropriately often terms this sacrament *the bond of charity*. What stronger stimulus could be employed to excite mutual charity, than when Christ, presenting himself to us, not only invites us by his example to give and devote ourselves mutually to each other, but inasmuch as he makes himself common to all, also makes us all to be one in him.

39. This most admirably confirms what I elsewhere said—viz. that there cannot be a right administration of the Supper without the word. Any utility which we derive from the Supper requires the word. Whether we are to be confirmed in faith, or exercised in confession, or aroused to duty, there is need of preaching. Nothing, therefore, can be more preposterous than to convert the Supper into a dumb action. This is done under the tyranny of the Pope, the whole effect of consecration being made to depend on the intention of the priest, as if it in no way concerned the people, to whom especially the mystery ought to have been explained. This error has originated from not observing that those promises by which consecration is effected are intended, not for the elements themselves, but for those who receive them. Christ does not address the bread and tell it to become his body, but bids his disciples eat, and promises them the communion of his body and blood. And, according to the arrangement which Paul makes, the promises are to be offered to believers along with the bread and the cup. Thus, indeed, it is. We are not to imagine some magical incantation, and think it sufficient to mutter the words, as if they were

heard by the elements; but we are to regard those words as a living sermon, which is to edify the hearers, penetrate their minds, being impressed and seated in their hearts, and exert its efficacy in the fulfilment of that which it promises. For these reasons, it is clear that the setting apart of the sacrament, as some insist, that an extraordinary distribution of it may be made to the sick, is useless. They will either receive it without hearing the words of the institution read, or the minister will conjoin the true explanation of the mystery with the sign. In the silent dispensation, there is abuse and defect. If the promises are narrated, and the mystery is expounded, that those who are to receive may receive with advantage, it cannot be doubted that this is the true consecration. What then becomes of that other consecration, the effect of which reaches even to the sick? But those who do so have the example of the early Church. I confess it; but in so important a matter, where error is so dangerous, nothing is safer than to follow the truth.

40. Moreover, as we see that this sacred bread of the Lord's Supper is spiritual food, is sweet and savoury, not less than salutary, to the pious worshippers of God, on tasting which they feel that Christ is their life, are disposed to give thanks, and exhorted to mutual love; so, on the other hand, it is converted into the most noxious poison to all whom it does not nourish and confirm in the faith, nor urge to thanksgiving and charity. For, just as corporeal food, when received into a stomach subject to morbid humours, becomes itself vitiated and corrupted, and rather hurts than nourishes, so this spiritual food also, if given to a soul polluted with malice and wickedness, plunges it into greater ruin, not indeed by any defect in the food, but because to the "defiled and unbelieving is nothing pure" (Titus 1:15), however much it may be sanctified by the blessing of the Lord. For, as Paul says, "Whosoever shall eat this bread, and drink this cup of the Lord, unworthily, shall be guilty of the body and blood of the Lord;" "eateth and drinketh damnation to himself, not discerning the Lord's body" (1 Cor. 11:27, 29). For men of this description, who without any spark of faith, without any zeal for charity, rush forward like swine to seize the Lord's Supper, do not at all discern the Lord's body. For, inasmuch as they do not believe that body to be their life, they put every possible affront upon it, stripping it of all its dignity, and profane and contaminate it by so receiving; inasmuch as while alienated and estranged from their brethren, they dare to mingle the sacred symbol of Christ's body with their dissensions. No thanks to them if the body of Christ is not rent and torn to pieces. Wherefore they are justly held guilty of the body and blood of the Lord, which, with sacrilegious impiety, they so vilely pollute. By this unworthy eating, they bring judgment on themselves. For while they have no faith in Christ, yet, by receiving the sacrament, they profess to place their salvation only in him, and abjure all other confidence. Wherefore they themselves are their own accusers; they bear witness against themselves; they seal their own condemnation. Next being divided and separated by hatred and ill-will from their brethren, that is, from the members of Christ, they have no part in Christ, and yet they declare that the only safety is to communicate with Christ, and be united to him. For this reason Paul commands a man to examine himself before he eats of that bread, and drinks of that cup (1 Cor. 11:28). By this, as I understand, he means that each individual should descend into himself, and consider, first, whether, with inward confidence of heart, he leans on the salvation obtained by Christ, and with confession of the mouth, acknowledges it; and, secondly, whether with zeal for purity and holiness he aspires to imitate Christ; whether, after his example, he is prepared to give himself to his brethren, and to hold himself in common with those with whom he has Christ in common; whether, as he himself is regarded by Christ, he in his turn regards all his brethren as members of his body, or, like his members, desires to cherish, defend, and assist them, not that the duties of faith and charity can now be perfected in us, but because it behoves us to contend and seek, with all our heart, daily to increase our faith.

41. In seeking to prepare for eating worthily, men have often dreadfully harassed and tortured miserable consciences, and yet have in no degree attained the end. They have said that those *eat worthily* who are in a state of grace. *Being in a state of grace,* they have interpreted to be pure and free from all sin. By this definition, all the men that ever have been, and are upon the earth, were debarred from the use of this sacrament. For if we are to seek our worthiness from ourselves, it is all over with us; only despair and fatal ruin await us. Though we struggle to the utmost, we will not only make no progress, but then be most unworthy after we have laboured most to make ourselves worthy. To cure this ulcer, they have devised a mode of procuring worthiness—viz. after having, as far as we can, made an examination, and taken an account of all our actions, to expiate our unworthiness by contrition, confession, and satisfaction. Of the nature of this expiation we have spoken at the proper place (Book 3 chap. 4 sec. 2, 17, 27). As far as regards our

present object, I say that such things give poor and evanescent comfort to alarmed and downcast consciences, struck with terror at their sins. For if the Lord, by his prohibition, admits none to partake of his Supper but the righteous and innocent, every man would require to be cautious before feeling secure of that righteousness of his own which he is told that God requires. But how are we to be assured that those who have done what in them lay have discharged their duty to God? Even were we assured of this, who would venture to assure himself that he had done what in him lay? Thus there being no certain security for our worthiness, access to the Supper would always be excluded by the fearful interdict, "He that eateth and drinketh unworthily, eateth and drinketh damnation to himself."

42. It is now easy to judge what is the nature, and who is the author, of that doctrine which prevails in the Papacy, and which, by its inhuman austerity, deprives and robs wretched sinners, oppressed with sorrow and trembling, of the consolation of this sacrament, a sacrament in which all that is delightful in the gospel was set before them. Certainly the devil could have no shorter method of destroying men than by thus infatuating them, and so excluding them from the taste and savour of this food with which their most merciful Father in heaven had been pleased to feed them. Therefore, lest we should rush over such a precipice, let us remember that this sacred feast is medicine to the sick, comfort to the sinner, and bounty to the poor; while to the healthy, the righteous, and the rich, if any such could be found, it would be of no value. For while Christ is therein given us for food, we perceive that without him we fail, pine, and waste away, just as hunger destroys the vigour of the body. Next, as he is given for life, we perceive that without him we are certainly dead. Wherefore, the best and only worthiness which we can bring to God, is to offer him our own vileness, and, if I may so speak, unworthiness, that his mercy may make us worthy; to despond in ourselves, that we may be consoled in him; to humble ourselves, that we may be elevated by him; to accuse ourselves, that we may be justified by him; to aspire, moreover, to the unity which he recommends in the Supper; and, as he makes us all one in himself, to desire to have all one soul, one heart, one tongue. If we ponder and meditate on these things, we may be shaken, but will never be overwhelmed by such considerations as these, how shall we, who are devoid of all good, polluted by the defilements of sin, and half dead, worthily eat the body of the Lord? We shall rather consider that we, who are poor, are coming to a benevolent giver, sick to a physician, sinful to the author of righteousness, in fine, dead to him who gives life; that worthiness which is commanded by God, consists especially in faith, which places all things in Christ, nothing in ourselves, and in charity, charity which, though imperfect, it may be sufficient to offer to God, that he may increase it, since it cannot be fully rendered. Some, concurring with us in holding that worthiness consists in faith and charity, have widely erred in regard to the measure of worthiness, demanding a perfection of faith to which nothing can be added, and a charity equivalent to that which Christ manifested towards us. And in this way, just as the other class, they debar all men from access to this sacred feast. For, were their view well founded, every one who receives must receive unworthily, since all, without exception, are guilty, and chargeable with imperfection. And certainly it were too stupid, not to say idiotical, to require to the receiving of the sacrament a perfection which would render the sacrament vain and superfluous, because it was not instituted for the perfect, but for the infirm and weak, to stir up, excite, stimulate, exercise the feeling of faith and charity, and at the same time correct the deficiency of both.

43. In regard to the external form of the ordinance, whether or not believers are to take into their hands and divide among themselves, or each is to eat what is given to him: whether they are to return the cup to the deacon or hand it to their neighbour; whether the bread is to be leavened or unleavened, and the wine to be red or white, is of no consequence. These things are indifferent, and left free to the Church, though it is certain that it was the custom of the ancient Church for all to receive into their hand. And Christ said, "Take this, and divide it among yourselves" (Luke 22:17). History relates that leavened and ordinary bread was used before the time of Alexander the Bishop of Rome, who was the first that was delighted with unleavened bread: for what reason I see not, unless it was to draw the wondering eyes of the populace by the novelty of the spectacle, more than to train them in sound religion. I appeal to all who have the least zeal for piety, whether they do not evidently perceive both how much more brightly the glory of God is here displayed, and how much more abundant spiritual consolation is felt by believers than in these rigid and histrionic follies, which have no other use than to impose on the gazing populace. They call it restraining the people by religion, when, stupid and infatuated, they are drawn hither and thither by superstition. Should any one choose to defend such inventions by antiquity, I am not unaware how

ancient is the use of chrism and exorcism in baptism, and how, not long after the age of the apostles, the Supper was tainted with adulteration; such, indeed, is the forwardness of human confidence, which cannot restrain itself, but is always sporting and wantoning in the mysteries of God. But let us remember that God sets so much value on obedience to his word, that, by it, he would have us to judge his angels and the whole world. All this mass of ceremonies being abandoned, the sacrament might be celebrated in the most becoming manner, if it were dispensed to the Church very frequently, at least once a-week. The commencement should be with public prayer; next, a sermon should be delivered: then the minister, having placed bread and wine on the table, should read the institution of the Supper. He should next explain the promises which are therein given; and, at the same time, keep back from communion all those who are debarred by the prohibition of the Lord. He should afterwards pray that the Lord, with the kindness with which he has bestowed this sacred food upon us, would also form and instruct us to receive it with faith and gratitude; and, as we are of ourselves unworthy, would make us worthy of the feast by his mercy. Here, either a psalm should be sung, or something read, while the faithful, in order, communicate at the sacred feast, the minister breaking the bread, and giving it to the people. The Supper being ended, an exhortation should be given to sincere faith, and confession of faith, to charity, and lives becoming Christians. Lastly, thanks should be offered, and the praises of God should be sung. This being done, the Church should be dismissed in peace.

44. What we have hitherto said of the sacrament, abundantly shows that it was not instituted to be received once a-year and that perfunctorily (as is now commonly the custom); but that all Christians might have it in frequent use, and frequently call to mind the sufferings of Christ, thereby sustaining and confirming their faith: stirring themselves up to sing the praises of God, and proclaim his goodness; cherishing and testifying towards each other that mutual charity, the bond of which they see in the unity of the body of Christ. As often as we communicate in the symbol of our Saviour's body, as if a pledge were given and received, we mutually bind ourselves to all the offices of love, that none of us may do anything to offend his brother, or omit anything by which he can assist him when necessity demands, and opportunity occurs. That such was the practice of the Apostolic Church, we are informed by Luke in the Acts, when he says, that "they continued stedfastly in the apostles' doctrine and fellowship, and in breaking of bread, and in prayers" (Acts 2:42). Thus we ought always to provide that no meeting of the Church is held without the word, prayer, the dispensation of the Supper, and alms. We may gather from Paul that this was the order observed by the Corinthians, and it is certain that this was the practice many ages after. Hence, by the ancient canons, which are attributed to Anacletus and Calixtus, after the consecration was made, all were to communicate who did not wish to be without the pale of the Church. And in those ancient canons, which bear the name of Apostolical, it is said that those who continue not to the end, and partake not of the sacred communion, are to be corrected, as causing disquiet to the Church. In the Council of Antioch it was decreed, that those who enter the Church, hear the Scriptures, and abstain from communion, are to be removed from the Church until they amend their fault. And although, in the first Council of Tholouse, this was mitigated, or at least stated in milder terms, yet there also it was decreed, that those who after hearing the sermon, never communicated, were to be admonished, and if they still abstained after admonition, were to be excluded.

45. By these enactments, holy men wished to retain and ensure the use of frequent communion, as handed down by the apostles themselves; and which, while it was most salutary to believers, they saw gradually falling into desuetude by the negligence of the people. Of his own age, Augustine testifies: "The sacrament of the unity of our Lord's body is, in some places, provided daily, and in others at certain intervals, at the Lord's table; and at that table some partake to life, and others to destruction" (August. Tract. 26, in Joann. 6). And in the first Epistle to Januarius he says: "Some communicate daily in the body and blood of the Lord; others receive it on certain days: in some places, not a day intervenes on which it is not offered: in others, it is offered only on the Sabbath and the Lord's day: in others, on the Lord's day only." But since, as we have said, the people were sometimes remiss, holy men urged them with severe rebukes, that they might not seem to connive at their sluggishness. Of this we have an example in Chrysostom, on the Epistle to the Ephesians (Hom. 26). "It was not said to him who dishonoured the feast, Why have you not taken your seat? 'But how camest thou in?' (Mt. 22:12). Whoever partakes not of the sacred rites is wicked and impudent in being present: should any one who was invited to a feast come in, wash his hands, take his seat, and seem to prepare to eat, and thereafter taste nothing, would he not,

I ask, insult both the feast and the entertainer? So you, standing among those who prepare themselves by prayer to take the sacred food, profess to be one of the number by the mere fact of your not going away, and yet you do not partake,—would it not have been better not to have made your appearance? I am unworthy, you say. Then neither were you worthy of the communion of prayer, which is the preparation for taking the sacred mystery."

46. Most assuredly, the custom which prescribes communion once a-year is an invention of the devil, by what instrumentality soever it may have been introduced. They say that Zephyrinus was the author of the decree, though it is not possible to believe that it was the same as we now have it. It may be, that as times then were, he did not, by his ordinance, consult ill for the Church. For there cannot be a doubt that at that time the sacred Supper was dispensed to the faithful at every meeting; nor can it be doubted that a great part of them communicated. But as it scarcely ever happened that all could communicate at the same time, and it was necessary that those who were mingled with the profane and idolaters, should testify their faith by some external symbol, this holy man, with a view to order and government, had appointed that day, that on it the whole of Christendom might give a confession of their faith by partaking of the Lord's Supper. The ordinance of Zephyrinus, which was otherwise good, posterity perverted, when they made a fixed law of one communion in the year. The consequence is, that almost all, when they have once communicated, as if they were discharged as to all the rest of the year, sleep on secure. It ought to have been far otherwise. Each week, at least, the table of the Lord ought to have been spread for the company of Christians, and the promises declared on which we might then spiritually feed. No one, indeed, ought to be forced, but all ought to be exhorted and stimulated; the torpor of the sluggish, also, ought to be rebuked, that all, like persons famishing, should come to the feast. It was not without cause, therefore, I complained, at the outset, that this practice had been introduced by the wile of the devil; a practice which, in prescribing one day in the year, makes the whole year one of sloth. We see, indeed, that this perverse abuse had already crept in in the time of Chrysostom; but we, also, at the same time, see how much it displeased him. For he complains in bitter terms, in the passage which I lately quoted, that there is so great an inequality in this matter, that they did not approach often, at other times of the year, even when prepared, but only at Easter, though unprepared. Then he exclaims: "O custom! O presumption! In vain, then, is the daily oblation made: in vain do we stand at the altar. There is none who partakes along with us." So far is he from having approved the practice by interposing his authority to it.

47. From the same forge proceeded another constitution, which snatched or robbed a half of the Supper from the greater part of the people of God—namely, the symbol of blood, which, interdicted to laics and profane (such are the titles which they give to God's heritage), became the peculiar possession of a few shaven and anointed individuals. The edict of the eternal God is, that all are to drink. This an upstart dares to antiquate and abrogate by a new and contrary law, proclaiming that all are not to drink. And that such legislators may not seem to fight against their God without any ground, they make a pretext of the dangers which might happen if the sacred cup were given indiscriminately to all: as if these had not been observed and provided for by the eternal wisdom of God. Then they reason acutely, forsooth, that the one is sufficient for the two. For if the body is, as they say, the whole Christ, who cannot be separated from his body, then the blood includes the body by concomitance. Here we see how far our sense accords with God, when to any extent whatever it begins to rage and wanton with loosened reins. The Lord, pointing to the bread, says, "This is my body." Then pointing to the cup, he calls it his blood. The audacity of human reason objects and says, The bread is the blood, the wine is the body, as if the Lord had without reason distinguished his body from his blood, both by words and signs; and it had ever been heard that the body of Christ or the blood is called God and man. Certainly, if he had meant to designate himself wholly, he might have said, It is I, according to the Scriptural mode of expression, and not, "This is my body," "This is my blood." But wishing to succour the weakness of our faith, he placed the cup apart from the bread, to show that he suffices not less for drink than for food. Now, if one part be taken away, we can only find the half of the elements in what remains. Therefore, though it were true, as they pretend, that the blood is in the bread, and, on the other hand, the body in the cup, by concomitance, yet they deprive the pious of that confirmation of faith which Christ delivered as necessary. Bidding adieu, therefore, to their subtleties, let us retain the advantage which, by the ordinance of Christ, is obtained by a double pledge.

48. I am aware, indeed, how the ministers of Satan, whose usual practice is to hold the Scriptures in derision, here cavil. First, they allege that from a simple fact we are not to draw a rule which is to be perpetually obligatory on the Church. But they state an untruth when they

call it a simple fact. For Christ not only gave the cup, but appointed that the apostles should do so in future. For his words contain the command, "Drink ye all of it." And Paul relates, that it was so done, and recommends it as a fixed institution. Another subterfuge is, that the apostles alone were admitted by Christ to partake of this sacred Supper, because he had already selected and chosen them to the priesthood. I wish they would answer the five following questions, which they cannot evade, and which easily refute them and their lies. First, By what oracle was this solution so much at variance with the word of God revealed to them? Scripture mentions twelve who sat down with Jesus, but it does not so derogate from the dignity of Christ as to call them priests. Of this appellation we shall afterwards speak in its own place. Although he then gave to twelve, he commanded them to "do this;" in other words, to distribute thus among themselves. Secondly, Why during that purer age, from the days of the apostles downward for a thousand years, did all, without exception, partake of both symbols? Did the primitive Church not know who the guests were whom Christ would have admitted to his Supper? It were the most shameless impudence to carp and quibble here. We have extant ecclesiastical histories, we have the writings of the Fathers, which furnish clear proofs of this fact. "The flesh," says Tertullian, "feeds on the body and blood of Christ, that the soul may be satiated by God" (Tertull. de Resurr. Carnis.). "How," says Ambrose to Theodosius, "will you receive the sacred body of the Lord with such hands? how will you have the boldness to put the cup of precious blood to your lips?" Jerome speaks of "the priests who perform the Eucharist and distribute the Lord's blood to the people" (Hieron. in Malach. cap. 2). Chrysostom says, "Not as under the ancient law the priest ate a part and the people a part, but one body and one cup is set before all. All the things which belong to the Eucharist are common to the priest and the people" (Chrysost. in Cor. cap. 8, Hom. 18). The same thing is attested by Augustine in numerous passages.

49. But why dispute about a fact which is perfectly notorious? Look at all Greek and Latin writers. Passages of the same kind everywhere occur. Nor did this practice fall into desuetude so long as there was one particle of integrity in the Church. Gregory, whom you may with justice call the last Bishop of Rome, says that it was observed in his age. "What the blood of the Lamb is you have learned, not by hearing, but by drinking it. His blood is poured into the mouths of the faithful." Nay, four hundred years after his death, when all things had degenerated, the practice still remained. Nor was it regarded as the custom merely, but as an inviolable law. Reverence for the divine institution was then maintained, and they had no doubt of its being sacrilege to separate what the Lord had joined. For Gelasius thus speaks: "We find that some taking only the portion of the sacred body, abstain from the cup. Undoubtedly let those persons, as they seem entangled by some strange superstition, either receive the whole sacrament, or be debarred from the whole. For the division of this mystery is not made without great sacrilege" (De Consec. Dist. 2). Reasons were given by Cyprian, which surely ought to weigh with Christian minds. "How," says he, "do we teach or incite them to shed their blood in confessing Christ, if we deny his blood to those who are to serve; or how do we make them fit for the cup of martyrdom, if we do not previously admit them by right of communion in the Church, to drink the cup of the Lord?" (Cyprian, Serm. 5, de Lapsis). The attempt of the Canonists to restrict the decree of Gelasius to priests is a cavil too puerile to deserve refutation.

50. Thirdly, Why did our Saviour say of the bread simply, "Take, eat," and of the cup, "drink ye all of it;" as if he had purposely intended to provide against the wile of Satan? Fourthly, If, as they will have it, the Lord honoured priests only with his Supper, what man would ever have dared to call strangers, whom the Lord had excluded, to partake of it, and to partake of a gift which he had not in his power, without any command from him who alone could give it? Nay, what presumption do they show in the present day in distributing the symbol of Christ's body to the common people, if they have no command or example from the Lord? Fifthly, Did Paul lie when he said to the Corinthians, "I have received of the Lord that which also I delivered unto you?" (1 Cor. 11:23). The thing delivered, he afterwards declares to be, that all should communicate promiscuously in both symbols. But if Paul received of the Lord that all were to be admitted without distinction, let those who drive away almost the whole people of God see from whom they have received, since they cannot now pretend to have their authority from God, with whom there is not "yea and nay" (2 Cor. 1:19, 20). And yet these abominations they dare to cloak with the name of the Church, and defend under this pretence, as if those Antichrists were the Church who so licentiously trample under foot, waste, and abrogate the doctrine and institutions of Christ, or as if the Apostolic Church, in which religion flourished in full vigour, were not the Church.

CHAPTER 18

OF THE POPISH MASS. HOW IT NOT ONLY PROFANES, BUT ANNIHILATES THE LORD'S SUPPER.

The principal heads of this chapter are,—I. The abomination of the Mass, sec. 1. Its manifold impiety included under five heads, sec. 2–7. Its origin described. sec. 8, 9. II. Of the name of sacrifice which the ancients gave to the holy Supper, sec. 10–12. An apposite discussion on sacrifice, refuting the arguments of the Papists for the sacrifice of the Mass, sec. 13–18. III. A summary of the doctrine of the Christian Church respecting sacraments, paving the way for the subsequent discussion of the five sacraments, falsely so called, sec. 19, 20.

Sections:

1. The chief of all the abominations set up in opposition to the Lord's Supper is the Papal Mass. A description of it.

2. Its impiety is five-fold. 1. Its intolerable blasphemy in substituting priests to him the only Priest. Objections of the Papists answered.

3. Impiety of the Mass continued. 2. It overthrows the cross of Christ by setting up an altar. Objections answered.

4. Other objections answered.

5. Impiety of the Mass continued. 3. It banishes the remembrance of Christ's death. It crucifies Christ afresh. Objections answered.

6. Impiety of the Mass continued. 4. It robs us of the benefit of Christ's death.

7. Impiety of the Mass continued. 5. It abolishes the Lord's Supper. In the Supper the Father offers Christ to us; in the Mass, priestlings offer Christ to the Father. The Supper is a sacrament common to all Christians; the Mass confined to one priest.

8. The origin of the Mass. Private masses an impious profanation of the Supper.

9. This abomination unknown to the purer Church. It has no foundation in the word of God.

10. Second part of the chapter. Some of the ancients call the Supper a sacrifice, but not propitiatory, as the Papists do the Mass. This proved by passages from Augustine.

11. Some of the ancients seem to have declined too much to the shadows of the law.

12. Great distinction to be made between the Mosaic sacrifices and the Lord's Supper, which is called a eucharistic sacrifice. Same rule in this discussion.

13. The terms sacrifice and priest. Different kinds of sacrifices. 1. Propitiatory. 2. Eucharistic. None propitiatory but the death of Christ.

14. The Lord's Supper not properly called a propitiatory sacrifice, still less can the Popish Mass be so called. Those who mutter over the mass cannot be called priests.

15. Their vanity proved even by Plato.

16. To the eucharistic class of sacrifice belong all offices of piety and charity. This species of sacrifice has no connection with the appeasing of God.

17. Prayer, thanksgiving, and other exercises of piety, called sacrifices. In this sense the Lord's Supper called the eucharist. In the same sense all believers are priests.

18. Conclusion. Names given to the Mass.

19. Last part of the chapter, recapitulating the views which ought to be held concerning baptism and the Lord's Supper. Why the Lord's Supper is, and Baptism is not, repeated.

20. Christians should be contented with these two sacraments. They are abolished by the sacraments decreed by men.

1. By these and similar inventions, Satan has attempted to adulterate and envelop the sacred Supper of Christ as with thick darkness, that its purity might not be preserved in the Church. But the head of this horrid abomination was, when he raised a sign by which it was not only obscured and perverted, but altogether obliterated and abolished, vanished away and disappeared from the memory of man—namely, when, with most pestilential error, he blinded almost the whole world into the belief that the Mass was a sacrifice and oblation for obtaining the remission of sins. I say nothing as to the way in which the sounder Schoolmen at first received this dogma. I leave them with their puzzling subtleties, which, however they may be defended by cavilling, are to be repudiated by all good men, because, all they do is to envelop the brightness of the Supper in great darkness. Bidding adieu to them, therefore, let my readers understand that I am here combating that opinion with which the Roman Antichrist and his prophets have imbued the whole world— viz. that the mass is a work by which the priest who offers Christ, and the others who in the oblation receive him, gain merit with God, or that it is an expiatory victim by which they regain the favour of God. And this is not merely the common opinion of the vulgar, but

the very act has been so arranged as to be a kind of propitiation, by which satisfaction is made to God for the living and the dead. This is also expressed by the words employed, and the same thing may be inferred from daily practice. I am aware how deeply this plague has struck its roots; under what a semblance of good it conceals its true character, bearing the name of Christ before it, and making many believe that under the single name of Mass is comprehended the whole sum of faith. But when it shall have been most clearly proved by the word of God, that this mass, however glossed and splendid, offers the greatest insult to Christ, suppresses and buries his cross, consigns his death to oblivion, takes away the benefit which it was designed to convey, enervates and dissipates the sacrament, by which the remembrance of his death was retained, will its roots be so deep that this most powerful axe, the word of God, will not cut it down and destroy it? Will any semblance be so specious that this light will not expose the lurking evil?

2. Let us show, therefore, as was proposed in the first place, that in the mass intolerable blasphemy and insult are offered to Christ. For he was not appointed Priest and Pontiff by the Father for a time merely, as priests were appointed under the Old Testament. Since their life was mortal, their priesthood could not be immortal, and hence there was need of successors, who might ever and anon be substituted in the room of the dead. But Christ being immortal, had not the least occasion to have a vicar substituted for him. Wherefore he was appointed by his Father a priest for ever, after the order of Melchizedek, that he might eternally exercise a permanent priesthood. This mystery had been typified long before in Melchizedek, whom Scripture, after once introducing as the priest of the living God, never afterwards mentions, as if he had had no end of life. In this way Christ is said to be a priest after his order. But those who sacrifice daily must necessarily give the charge of their oblations to priests, whom they surrogate as the vicars and successors of Christ. By this surrogation they not only rob Christ of his honour, and take from him the prerogative of an eternal priesthood, but attempt to remove him from the right hand of his Father, where he cannot sit immortal without being an eternal priest. Nor let them allege that their priestlings are not substituted for Christ, as if he were dead, but are only substitutes in that eternal priesthood, which therefore ceases not to exist. The words of the apostle are too stringent to leave them any means of evasion—viz. "They truly were many priests, because they were not suffered to continue by reason of death: but this man, because he continueth ever, hath an unchangeable priesthood" (Heb. 7:23, 24). Yet such is their dishonesty, that to defend their impiety they arm themselves with the example of Melchizedek. As he is said to have "brought forth (*obtulisse*) bread and wine" (Gen. 14:18), they infer that it was a prelude to their mass, as if there was any resemblance between him and Christ in the offering of bread and wine. This is too silly and frivolous to need refutation. Melchizedek gave bread and wine to Abraham and his companions, that he might refresh them when worn out with the march and the battle. What has this to do with sacrifice? The humanity of the holy king is praised by Moses: these men absurdly coin a mystery of which there is no mention. They, however, put another gloss upon their error, because it is immediately added, he was "priest of the most high God." I answer, that they erroneously wrest to bread and wine what the apostle refers to blessing. "This Melchizedek, king of Salem, priest of the most high God, who met Abraham," "and blessed him." Hence the same apostle (and a better interpreter cannot be desired) infers his excellence. "Without all contradiction, the less is blessed of the better." But if the oblation of Melchizedek was a figure of the sacrifice of the mass, I ask, would the apostle, who goes into the minutest details, have forgotten a matter so grave and serious? Now, however they quibble, it is in vain for them to attempt to destroy the argument which is adduced by the apostle himself—viz. that the right and honour of the priesthood has ceased among mortal men, because Christ, who is immortal, is the one perpetual priest.

3. Another iniquity chargeable on the mass is, that it sinks and buries the cross and passion of Christ. This much, indeed, is most certain,—the cross of Christ is overthrown the moment an altar is erected. For if, on the cross, he offered himself in sacrifice that he might sanctify us for ever, and purchase eternal redemption for us, undoubtedly the power and efficacy of his sacrifice continues without end. Otherwise, we should not think more honourably of Christ than of the oxen and calves which were sacrificed under the law, the offering of which is proved to have been weak and inefficacious because often repeated. Wherefore, it must be admitted, either that the sacrifice which Christ offered on the cross wanted the power of eternal cleansing, or that he performed this once for ever by his one sacrifice. Accordingly, the apostle says, "Now once in the end of the world hath he appeared to put away sin by the sacrifice of himself." Again: "By the which act we are sanctified through the offering of the body of Jesus Christ once for

all." Again: "For by one offering he hath perfected for ever them that are sanctified." To this he subjoins the celebrated passage: "Now, where remission of these is, there is no more offering for sin." The same thing Christ intimated by his latest voice, when, on giving up the ghost, he exclaimed, "It is finished." We are accustomed to observe the last words of the dying as oracular. Christ, when dying, declares, that by his one sacrifice is perfected and fulfilled whatever was necessary to our salvation. To such a sacrifice, whose perfection he so clearly declared, shall we, as if it were imperfect, presume daily to append innumerable sacrifices? Since the sacred word of God not only affirms, but proclaims and protests, that this sacrifice was once accomplished, and remains eternally in force, do not those who demand another, charge it with imperfection and weakness? But to what tends the mass which has been established, that a hundred thousand sacrifices may be performed every day, but just to bury and suppress the passion of our Lord, in which he offered himself to his Father as the only victim? Who but a blind man does not see that it was Satanic audacity to oppose a truth so clear and transparent? I am not unaware of the impostures by which the father of lies is wont to cloak his fraud—viz. that the sacrifices are not different or various, but that the one sacrifice is repeated. Such smoke is easily dispersed. The apostle, during his whole discourse, contends not only that there are no other sacrifices, but that that one was once offered, and is no more to be repeated. The more subtle try to make their escape by a still narrower loophole—viz. that it is not repetition, but application. But there is no more difficulty in confuting this sophism also. For Christ did not offer himself once, in the view that his sacrifice should be daily ratified by new oblations, but that by the preaching of the gospel and the dispensation of the sacred Supper, the benefit of it should be communicated to us. Thus Paul says, that "Christ, our passover, is sacrificed for us," and bids us "keep the feast" (1 Cor. 5:7, 8). The method, I say, in which the cross of Christ is duly applied to us is when the enjoyment is communicated to us, and we receive it with true faith.

4. But it is worth while to hear on what other foundation besides they rear up their sacrifice of the mass. To this end they drag in the prophecy of Malachi, in which the Lord promises that "in every place incense shall be offered unto my name, and a pure offering" (Mal. 1:11). As if it were new or unusual for the prophets, when they speak of the calling of the Gentiles, to designate the spiritual worship of God to which they call them, by the external rites of the law, more familiarly to intimate to the men of their age that they were to be called into the true fellowship of religion, just as in general they are wont to describe the truth which has been exhibited by the gospel by the types of their own age. Thus they use going up to Jerusalem for conversion to the Lord, the bringing of all kinds of gifts for the adoration of God—dreams and visions for the more ample knowledge with which believers were to be endued in the kingdom of Christ. The passage they quote from Malachi resembles one in Isaiah, in which the prophet speaks of three altars to be erected in Assyria, Egypt, and Judea. First, I ask, whether or not they grant that this prophecy is fulfilled in the kingdom of Christ? Secondly, Where are those altars, or when were they ever erected? Thirdly, Do they suppose that a single temple is destined for a single kingdom, as was that of Jerusalem? If they ponder these things, they will confess, I think, that the prophet, under types adapted to his age, prophesied concerning the propagation of the spiritual worship of God over the whole world. This is the answer which we give them; but, as obvious examples everywhere occur in the Scripture, I am not anxious to give a longer enumeration; although they are miserably deluded in this also, that they acknowledge no sacrifice but that of the mass, whereas in truth believers now sacrifice to God and offer him a pure offering, of which we shall speak by-and-by.

5. I now come to the third part of the mass, in regard to which, we are to explain how it obliterates the true and only death of Christ, and drives it from the memory of men. For as among men, the confirmation of a testament depends upon the death of the testator, so also the testament by which he has bequeathed to us remission of sins and eternal righteousness, our Lord has confirmed by his death. Those who dare to make any change or innovation on this testament deny his death, and hold it as of no moment. Now, what is the mass but a new and altogether different testament? What? Does not each mass promise a new forgiveness of sins, a new purchase of righteousness, so that now there are as many testaments as there are masses? Therefore, let Christ come again, and, by another death, make this new testament; or rather, by innumerable deaths, ratify the innumerable testaments of the mass. Said I not true, then, at the outset, that the only true death of Christ is obliterated by the mass? For what is the direct aim of the mass but just to put Christ again to death, if that were possible? For, as the apostle says, "Where a testament is, there must also of necessity be the death of the testator" (Heb. 9:16). The novelty of the mass bears, on the face of it, to be a testament

of Christ, and therefore demands his death. Besides, it is necessary that the victim which is offered be slain and immolated. If Christ is sacrificed at each mass, he must be cruelly slain every moment in a thousand places. This is not my argument, but the apostle's: "Nor yet that he should offer himself often;" "for then must he often have suffered since the foundation of the world" (Heb. 9:25, 26). I admit that they are ready with an answer, by which they even charge us with calumny; for they say that we object to them what they never thought, and could not even think. We know that the life and death of Christ are not at all in their hand. Whether they mean to slay him, we regard not: our intention is only to show the absurdity consequent on their impious and accursed dogma. This I demonstrate from the mouth of the apostle. Though they insist a hundred times that this sacrifice is bloodless (ἀναίμακτον), I will reply, that it depends not on the will of man to change the nature of sacrifice, for in this way the sacred and inviolable institution of God would fall. Hence it follows, that the principle of the apostle stands firm, "without shedding of blood is no remission" (Heb. 9:22).

6. The fourth property of the mass which we are to consider is, that it robs us of the benefit which redounded to us from the death of Christ, while it prevents us from recognising it and thinking of it. For who can think that he has been redeemed by the death of Christ when he sees a new redemption in the mass? Who can feel confident that his sins have been remitted when he sees a new remission? It will not do to say that the only ground on which we obtain forgiveness of sins in the mass is, because it has been already purchased by the death of Christ. For this is just equivalent to saying that we are redeemed by Christ on the condition that we redeem ourselves. For the doctrine which is disseminated by the ministers of Satan, and which, in the present day, they defend by clamour, fire, and sword, is, that when we offer Christ to the Father in the mass, we, by this work of oblation, obtain remission of sins, and become partakers of the sufferings of Christ. What is now left for the sufferings of Christ, but to be an example of redemption, that we may thereby learn to be our own redeemers? Christ himself, when he seals our assurance of pardon in the Supper, does not bid his disciples stop short at that act, but sends them to the sacrifice of his death; intimating, that the Supper is the memento, or, as it is commonly expressed, the memorial from which they may learn that the expiatory victim by which God was to be appeased was to be offered only once. For it is not sufficient to hold that Christ is the only victim, without adding that his is the only immolation, in order that our faith may be fixed to his cross.

7. I come now to the crowning point—viz. that the sacred Supper, on which the Lord left the memorial of his passion formed and engraved, was taken away, hidden, and destroyed, when the mass was erected. While the supper itself is a gift of God, which was to be received with thanksgiving, the sacrifice of the mass pretends to give a price to God to be received as satisfaction. As widely as giving differs from receiving, does sacrifice differ from the sacrament of the Supper. But herein does the wretched ingratitude of man appear,— that when the liberality of the divine goodness ought to have been recognised, and thanks returned, he makes God to be his debtor. The sacrament promised, that by the death of Christ we were not only restored to life once, but constantly quickened, because all the parts of our salvation were then completed. The sacrifice of the mass uses a very different language—viz. that Christ must be sacrificed daily, in order that he may lend something to us. The Supper was to be dispensed at the public meeting of the Church, to remind us of the communion by which we are all united in Christ Jesus. This communion the sacrifice of the mass dissolves, and tears asunder. For after the heresy prevailed, that there behoved to be priests to sacrifice for the people, as if the Supper had been handed over to them, it ceased to be communicated to the assembly of the faithful according to the command of the Lord. Entrance has been given to private masses, which more resemble a kind of excommunication than that communion ordained by the Lord, when the priestling, about to devour his victim apart, separates himself from the whole body of the faithful. That there may be no mistake, I call it a private mass whenever there is no partaking of the Lord's Supper among believers, though, at the same time, a great multitude of persons may be present.

8. The origin of the name of Mass I have never been able certainly to ascertain. It seems probable that it was derived from the offerings which were collected. Hence the ancients usually speak of it in the plural number. But without raising any controversy as to the name, I hold that private masses are diametrically opposed to the institution of Christ, and are, therefore, an impious profanation of the sacred Supper. For what did the Lord enjoin? Was it not to take and divide amongst ourselves? What does Paul teach as to the observance of this command? Is it not that the breaking of bread is the communion of body and blood? (1 Cor. 10:16). Therefore, when one person takes without distributing, where is the

resemblance? But that one acts in the name of the whole Church. By what command? Is it not openly to mock God when one privately seizes for himself what ought to have been distributed among a number? But as the words, both of our Saviour and of Paul, are sufficiently clear, we must briefly conclude, that wherever there is no breaking of bread for the communion of the faithful, there is no Supper of the Lord, but a false and preposterous imitation of the Supper. But false imitation is adulteration. Moreover, the adulteration of this high ordinance is not without impiety. In private masses, therefore, there is an impious abuse: and as in religion, one fault ever and anon begets another, after that custom of offering without communion once crept in, they began gradually to make innumerable masses in all the separate corners of the churches, and to draw the people hither and thither, when they ought to have formed one meeting, and thus recognised the mystery of their unity. Let them now go and deny their idolatry when they exhibit the bread in their masses, that it may be adored for Christ. In vain do they talk of those promises of the presence of Christ, which, however they may be understood, were certainly not given that impure and profane men might form the body of Christ as often as they please, and for whatever abuse they please; but that believers, while, with religious observance, they follow the command of Christ in celebrating the Supper, might enjoy the true participation of it.

9. We may add, that this perverse course was unknown to the purer Church. For however the more impudent among our opponents may attempt to gloss the matter, it is absolutely certain that all antiquity is opposed to them, as has been above demonstrated in other instances, and may be more surely known by the diligent reading of the Fathers. But before I conclude, I ask our missal doctors, seeing they know that obedience is better than sacrifice, and God commands us to listen to his voice rather than to offer sacrifice (1 Sam. 15:22),—how they can believe this method of sacrificing to be pleasing to God, since it is certain that he does not command it, and they cannot support it by one syllable of Scripture? Besides, when they hear the apostle declaring that "no man taketh this honour to himself, but he that is called of God, as was Aaron," so also Christ glorified not himself to be made an high priest, but he that said unto him, "Thou art my Son: this day have I begotten thee" (Heb. 5:4, 5). They must either prove God to be the author and founder of their priesthood, or confess that there is no honour from God in an office, into which, without being called, they have rushed with wicked temerity. They cannot produce one iota of Scripture in support of their priesthood. And must not the sacrifices be vain, since they cannot be offered without a priest?

10. Should any one here obtrude concise sentences of the ancients, and contend, or their authority, that the sacrifice which is performed in the Supper is to be understood differently from what we have explained it, let this be our brief reply,—that if the question relates to the approval of the fiction of sacrifice, as imagined by Papists in the mass, there is nothing in the Fathers to countenance the sacrilege. They indeed use the term sacrifice, but they, at the same time, explain that they mean nothing more than the commemoration of that one true sacrifice which Christ, our only sacrifice (as they themselves everywhere proclaim), performed on the cross. "The Hebrews," says Augustine (Cont. Faust. Lib. 20 c. 18), "in the victims of beasts which they offered to God, celebrated the prediction of the future victim which Christ offered: Christians now celebrate the commemoration of a finished sacrifice by the sacred oblation and participation of the body of Christ." Here he certainly teaches the same doctrine which is delivered at greater length in the Treatise on Faith, addressed to Peter the deacon, whoever may have been the author. The words are, "Hold most firmly, and have no doubt at all, that the Only-Begotten became incarnate for us, that he offered himself for us, an offering and sacrifice to God for a sweet-smelling savour; to whom, with the Father and the Holy Spirit, in the time of the Old Testament, animals were sacrificed, and to whom now, with the Father and the Holy Spirit (with whom there is one Godhead), the holy Church, throughout the whole world, ceases not to offer the sacrifice of bread and wine. For, in those carnal victims, there was a typifying of the flesh of Christ, which he himself was to offer for our sins, and of the blood which he was to shed for the forgiveness of sins. But in that sacrifice there is thanksgiving and commemoration of the flesh of Christ which he offered for us, and of the blood which he shed for us." Hence Augustine himself, in several passages (Ep. 120, ad Honorat. Cont. Advers. Legis.), explains, that it is nothing else than a sacrifice of praise. In short, you will find in his writings, *passim*, that the only reason for which the Lord's Supper is called a sacrifice is, because it is a commemoration, an image, a testimonial of that singular, true, and only sacrifice by which Christ expiated our guilt. For there is a memorable passage (De Trinitate, Lib. 4 c. 24), where, after discoursing of the only sacrifice, he thus concludes: "Since, in a sacrifice, four things are

considered—viz. to whom it is offered, by whom, what and for whom, the same one true Mediator, reconciling us to God by the sacrifice of peace, remains one with him to whom he offered, made himself one with those for whom he offered, is himself the one who offered, and the one thing which he offered." Chrysostom speaks to the same effect. They so strongly claim the honour of the priesthood for Christ alone, that Augustine declares it would be equivalent to Antichrist for any one to make a bishop to be an intercessor between God and man (August. Cont. Parmen. Lib. 2 c. 8).

11. And yet we deny not that in the Supper the sacrifice of Christ is so vividly exhibited as almost to set the spectacle of the cross before our eyes, just as the apostle says to the Galatians, that Jesus Christ had been evidently set forth before their eyes, when the preaching of the cross was delivered to them (Gal. 3:1). But because I see that those ancient writers have wrested this commemoration to a different purpose than was accordant to the divine institution (the Supper somehow seemed to them to present the appearance of a repeated, or at least renewed, immolation), nothing can be safer for the pious than to rest satisfied with the pure and simple ordinance of God, whose Supper it is said to be, just because his authority alone ought to appear in it. Seeing that they retained a pious and orthodox view of the whole ordinance—and I cannot discover that they wished to derogate in the least from the one sacrifice of the Lord—I cannot charge them with any impiety, and yet I think they cannot be excused from having erred somewhat in the mode of action. They imitated the Jewish mode of sacrificing more closely than either Christ had ordained, or the nature of the gospel allowed. The only thing, therefore, for which they may be justly censured is, that preposterous analogy, that not contented with the simple and genuine institution of Christ, they declined too much to the shadows of the law.

12. Any who will diligently consider, will perceive that the word of the Lord makes this distinction between the Mosaic sacrifices and our eucharist—that while the former represented to the Jewish people the same efficacy of the death of Christ which is now exhibited to us in the Supper, yet the form of representation was different. There the Levitical priests were ordered to typify the sacrifice which Christ was to accomplish; a victim was placed to act as a substitute for Christ himself; an altar was erected on which it was to be sacrificed; the whole, in short, was so conducted as to bring under the eye an image of the sacrifice which was to be offered to God in expiation. But now that the sacrifice has been performed, the Lord has prescribed a different method to us—viz. to transmit the benefit of the sacrifice offered to him by his Son to his believing people. The Lord, therefore, has given us a table at which we may feast, not an altar on which a victim may be offered; he has not consecrated priests to sacrifice, but ministers to distribute a sacred feast. The more sublime and holy this mystery is, the more religiously and reverently ought it to be treated. Nothing, therefore, is safer than to banish all the boldness of human sense, and adhere solely to what Scripture delivers. And certainly, if we reflect that it is the Supper of the Lord and not of men, why do we allow ourselves to be turned aside one nail's-breadth from Scripture, by any authority of man or length of prescription? Accordingly, the apostle, in desiring completely to remove the vices which had crept into the Church of Corinth, as the most expeditious method, recalls them to the institution itself, showing that thence a perpetual rule ought to be derived.

13. Lest any quarrelsome person should raise a dispute with us as to the terms *sacrifice* and *priest*, I will briefly explain what in the whole of this discussion we mean by sacrifice, and what by priest. Some, on what rational ground I see not, extend the term *sacrifice* to all sacred ceremonies and religious acts. We know that by the uniform use of Scripture, the name of sacrifice is given to what the Greeks call at one time θυσια, at another προσφορὰ, at another τελετνὴ. This, in its general acceptation, includes everything whatever that is offered to God. Wherefore, we ought to distinguish, but so that the distinction may derive its analogy from the sacrifices of the Mosaic Law, under whose shadows the Lord was pleased to represent to his people the whole reality of sacrifices. Though these were various in form, they may all be referred to two classes. For either an oblation for sin was made by a certain species of satisfaction, by which the penalty was redeemed before God, or it was a symbol and attestation of religion and divine worship, at one time in the way of supplication to demand the favour of God; at another, by way of thanksgiving, to testify gratitude to God for benefits received; at another, as a simple exercise of piety, to renew the sanction of the covenant, to which latter branch, burnt-offerings, and libations, oblations, first-fruits, and peace offerings, referred. Hence let us also distribute them into two classes. The other class, with the view of explaining, let us call λατπευτικὸν, and σεβαστιχὸν, as consisting of the veneration and worship which believers both owe and render to God; or, if you prefer it, let us call it ευχαριστικὸν, since it is exhibited to God by none but those who, enriched with his boundless

benefits, offer themselves and all their actions to him in return. The other class let us call *propitiatory* or *expiatory*. A sacrifice of expiation is one whose object is to appease the wrath of God, to satisfy his justice, and thereby wipe and wash away the sins, by which the sinner being cleansed and restored to purity, may return to favour with God. Hence the name which was given in the Law to the victims which were offered in expiation of sin (Exod. 29:36); not that they were adequate to regain the favour of God, and wipe away guilt, but because they typified the true sacrifice of this nature, which was at length performed in reality by Christ alone; by him alone, because no other could, and once, because the efficacy and power of the one sacrifice performed by Christ is eternal, as he declared by his voice, when he said, "It is finished;" that is, that everything necessary to regain the favour of the Father, to procure forgiveness of sins, righteousness, and salvation, that all this was performed and consummated by his one oblation, and that hence nothing was wanting. No place was left for another sacrifice.

14. Wherefore, I conclude, that it is an abominable insult and intolerable blasphemy, as well against Christ as the sacrifice, which, by his death, he performed for us on the cross, for any one to think of repeating the oblation, of purchasing the forgiveness of sins, of propitiating God, and obtaining justification. But what else is done in the mass than to make us partakers of the sufferings of Christ by means of a new oblation? And that there might be no limit to their extravagance, they have deemed it little to say, that it properly becomes a common sacrifice for the whole Church, without adding, that it is at their pleasure to apply it specially to this one or that, as they choose; or rather, to any one who is willing to purchase their merchandise from them for a price paid. Moreover, as they could not come up to the estimate of Judas, still, that they might in some way refer to their author, they make the resemblance to consist in the number. He sold for thirty pieces of silver: they, according to the French method of computation, sell for thirty pieces of brass. He did it once: they as often as a purchaser is met with. We deny that they are priests in this sense—namely, that by such oblations they intercede with God for the people, that by propitiating God they make expiation for sins. Christ is the only Pontiff and Priest of the New Testament: to him all priestly offices were transferred, and in him they closed and terminated. Even had Scripture made no mention of the eternal priesthood of Christ, yet, as God, after abolishing those ancient sacrifices, appointed no new priest, the argument of the apostle remains invincible, "No man taketh this honour unto himself, but he that is called of God, as was Aaron" (Heb. 5:4). How, then, can those sacrilegious men, who by their own account are murderers of Christ, dare to call themselves the priests of the living God?

15. There is a most elegant passage in the second book of Plato's Republic. Speaking of ancient expiations, and deriding the foolish confidence of wicked and iniquitous men, who thought that by them, as a kind of veils, they concealed their crimes from the gods; and, as if they had made a paction with the gods, indulged themselves more securely, he seems accurately to describe the use of the expiation of the mass, as it exists in the world in the present day. All know that it is unlawful to defraud and circumvent another. To do injustice to widows, to pillage pupils, to molest the poor, to seize the goods of others by wicked arts, to get possession of any man's succession by fraud and perjury, to oppress by violence and tyrannical terror, all admit to be impious. How then do so many, as if assured of impunity, dare to do all those things? Undoubtedly, if we duly consider, we will find that the only thing which gives them so much courage is, that by the sacrifice of the mass as a price paid, they trust that they will satisfy God, or at least will easily find a means of transacting with him. Plato next proceeds to deride the gross stupidity of those who think by such expiations to redeem the punishments which they must otherwise suffer after death. And what is meant by anniversaries and the greater part of masses in the present day, but just that those who through life have been the most cruel tyrants, or most rapacious plunderers, or adepts in all kinds of wickedness, may, as if redeemed at this price, escape the fire of purgatory?

16. Under the other kind of sacrifice, which we have called eucharistic, are included all the offices of charity, by which, while we embrace our brethren, we honour the Lord himself in his members; in fine, all our prayers, praises, thanksgivings, and every act of worship which we perform to God. All these depend on the greater sacrifice with which we dedicate ourselves, soul and body, to be a holy temple to the Lord. For it is not enough that our external acts be framed to obedience, but we must dedicate and consecrate first ourselves, and, secondly, all that we have, so that all which is in us may be subservient to his glory, and be stirred up to magnify it. This kind of sacrifice has nothing to do with appeasing God, with obtaining remission of sins, with procuring justification, but is wholly employed in magnifying and extolling God, since it cannot be grateful and acceptable to God

unless at the hand of those who, having received forgiveness of sins, have already been reconciled and freed from guilt. This is so necessary to the Church, that it cannot be dispensed with. Therefore, it will endure for ever, so long as the people of God shall endure, as we have already seen above from the prophet. For in this sense we may understand the prophecy, "From the rising of the sun, even unto the going down of the same, my name shall be great among the Gentiles; and in every place incense shall be offered unto my name, and a pure offering: for my name shall be great among the heathen, said the Lord of hosts" (Malachi 1:11); so far are we from doing away with this sacrifice. Thus Paul beseeches us by the mercies of God, to present our bodies "a living sacrifice, holy, acceptable unto God," our "reasonable service" (Rom. 12:1). Here he speaks very significantly when he adds, that this service is reasonable, for he refers to the spiritual mode of worshipping God, and tacitly opposes it to the carnal sacrifices of the Mosaic Law. Thus to do good and communicate are called sacrifices with which God is well pleased (Heb. 13:16). Thus the kindness of the Philippians in relieving Paul's want is called "an odour of a sweet smell, a sacrifice acceptable, well pleasing to God" (Phil. 4:18); and thus all the good works of believers are called spiritual sacrifices.

17. And why do I enumerate? This form of expression is constantly occurring in Scripture. Nay, even while the people of God were kept under the external tutelage of the law, the prophets clearly expressed that under these carnal sacrifices there was a reality which is common both to the Jewish people and the Christian Church. For this reason David prayed, "Let my prayer ascend forth before thee as incense" (Ps. 141:2). And Hosea gives the name of "calves of the lips" (Hos. 14:3) to thanksgivings, which David elsewhere calls "sacrifices of praise;" the apostle, imitating him, speaks of offering "the sacrifice of praise," which he explains to mean, "the fruit of our lips, giving thanks to his name" (Heb. 13:15). This kind of sacrifice is indispensable in the Lord's Supper, in which, while we show forth his death, and give him thanks, we offer nothing but the sacrifice of praise. From this office of sacrificing, all Christians are called "a royal priesthood," because by Christ we offer that sacrifice of praise of which the apostle speaks, the fruit of our lips, giving thanks to his name (1 Pet. 2:9; Heb. 13:15). We do not appear with our gifts in the presence of God without an intercessor. Christ is our Mediator, by whose intervention we offer ourselves and our all to the Father; he is our High Priest, who, having entered into the upper sanctuary, opens up an access for us; he is the altar on which we lay our gifts, that whatever we do attempt, we may attempt in him; he it is, I say, who "hath made us kings and priests unto God and his Father" (Rev. 1:6).

18. What remains but for the blind to see, the deaf to hear, children even to perceive this abomination of the mass, which, held forth in a golden cup, has so intoxicated all the kings and nations of the earth, from the highest to the lowest; so struck them with stupor and giddiness, that, duller than the lower animals, they have placed the vessel of their salvation in this fatal vortex. Certainly Satan never employed a more powerful engine to assail and storm the kingdom of Christ. This is the Helen for whom the enemies of the truth in the present day fight with so much rage, fury, and atrocity; and truly the Helen with whom they commit spiritual whoredom, the most execrable of all. I am not here laying my little finger on those gross abuses by which they might pretend that the purity of their sacred mass is profaned; on the base traffic which they ply; the sordid gain which they make; the rapacity with which they satiate their avarice. I only indicate, and that in few and simple terms, how very sacred the sanctity of the mass is, how well it has for several ages deserved to be admired and held in veneration! It were a greater work to illustrate these great mysteries as they deserve, and I am unwilling to meddle with their obscene impurities, which are daily before the eyes and faces of all, that it may be understood that the mass, taken in the most choice form in which it can be exhibited, without any appendages, teems from head to foot with all kinds of impiety, blasphemy, idolatry, and sacrilege.

19. My readers have here a compendious view of all that I have thought it of importance to know concerning these two sacraments, which have been delivered to the Christian Church, to be used from the beginning of the new dispensation to the end of the world, Baptism being a kind of entrance into the Church, an initiation into the faith, and the Lord's Supper the constant aliment by which Christ spiritually feeds his family of believers. Wherefore, as there is but one God, one faith, one Christ, one Church, which is his body, so Baptism is one, and is not repeated. But the Supper is ever and anon dispensed, to intimate, that those who are once allured into the Church are constantly fed by Christ. Besides these two, no other has been instituted by God, and no other ought to be recognised by the assembly of the faithful. That sacraments are not to be instituted and set up by the will of men, is easily understood by him who remembers what has been above with sufficient

plainness expounded —viz. that the sacraments have been appointed by God to instruct us in his promise, and testify his goodwill towards us; and who, moreover, considers, that the Lord has no counsellor (Isa. 40:13; Rom. 11:34); who can give us any certainty as to his will, or assure us how he is disposed towards us, what he is disposed to give, and what to deny? From this it follows, that no one can set forth a sign which is to be a testimonial of his will, and of some promise. He alone can give the sign, and bear witness to himself. I will express it more briefly, perhaps in homelier, but also in clearer terms,—There never can be a sacrament without a promise of salvation. All men collected into one cannot, of themselves, give us any promise of salvation, and, therefore, they cannot, of themselves, give out and set up a sacrament.

20. With these two, therefore, let the Christian Church be contented, and not only not admit or acknowledge any third at present, but not even desire or expect it even until the end of the world. For though to the Jews were given, besides his ordinary sacraments, others differing somewhat according to the nature of the times (as the manna, the water gushing from the rock, the brazen serpent, and the like), by this variety they were reminded not to stop short at such figures, the state of which could not be durable, but to expect from God something better, to endure without decay and without end. Our case is very different. To us Christ has been revealed. In him are hidden all the treasures of wisdom and knowledge (Col. 2:3), in such richness and abundance, that to ask or hope for any new addition to these treasures is truly to offend God and provoke him against us. It behoves us to hunger after Christ only, to seek him, look to him, learn of him, and learn again, until the arrival of the great day on which the Lord will fully manifest the glory of his kingdom, and exhibit himself as he is to our admiring eye (1 John 3:2). And, for this reason, this age of ours is designated in Scripture by the last hour, the last days, the last times, that no one may deceive himself with the vain expectation of some new doctrine or revelation. Our heavenly Father, who "at sundry times, and in divers manners, spake in time past unto the fathers by the prophets, hath in these last days spoken unto us" by his beloved Son, who alone can manifest, and, in fact, has fully manifested, the Father, in so far as is of importance to us, while we now see him through a mirror. Now, since men have been denied the power of making new sacraments in the Church of God, it were to be wished, that in those which are of God, there should be the least possible admixture of human invention. For just as when water is infused, the wine is diluted, and when leaven is put in, the whole mass is leavened, so the purity of the ordinances of God is impaired, whenever man makes any addition of his own. And yet we see how far the sacraments as at present used have degenerated from their genuine purity. There is everywhere more than enough of pomp, ceremony, and gesticulation, while no account is taken, or mention made, of the word of God, without which, even the sacraments themselves are not sacraments. Nay, in such a crowd, the very ceremonies ordained by God cannot raise their head, but lie as it were oppressed. In Baptism, as we have elsewhere justly complained, how little is seen of that which alone ought to shine and be conspicuous there, I mean Baptism itself? The Supper was altogether buried when it was turned into the Mass. The utmost is, that it is seen once a year, but in a garbled, mutilated, and lacerated form.

CHAPTER 19

OF THE FIVE SACRAMENTS, FALSELY SO CALLED. THEIR SPURIOUSNESS PROVED, AND THEIR TRUE CHARACTER EXPLAINED.

There are two divisions of this chapter,—I. A general discussion of these five sacraments, sec. 1–3. II. A special consideration of each. 1. Of Confirmation, sec. 4–13. 2. Of Penance, sec. 14–17. 3. Of Extreme Unction, sec. 18–21. 4. Of Order, in which the seven so-called sacraments have originated, sec. 22–23. 5. Of Marriage, sec. 34–37.

Sections:

1. Connection of the present discussion with that concerning Baptism and the Lord's Supper. Impiety of the popish teachers in attributing more to human rites than to the ordinances of God.

2. Men cannot institute sacraments. Necessary to keep up a distinction between sacraments and other ceremonies.

3. Seven sacraments not to be found in ecclesiastical writers. Augustine, who may represent all the others, acknowledged two sacraments only.

4. Nature of confirmation in ancient times. The laying on of hands.

5. This kind of confirmation afterwards introduced. It is falsely called a sacrament.

6. Popish argument for confirmation answered.

7. Argument confirmed by the example of Christ. Absurdity and impiety of Papists in calling their oil the oil of salvation.

8. Papistical argument, that Baptism cannot be complete without Confirmation. Answered.

9. Argument, that without confirmation we cannot be fully Christians. Answer.

10. Argument, that the Unction in confirmation is more excellent than Baptism. Answer.

11. Answer continued. Argument, that confirmation has greater virtue.

12. Argument from the practice of antiquity. Augustine's view of confirmation.

13. The ancient confirmation very praiseworthy. Should be restored in churches in the present day.

14. Of Penitence. Confused and absurd language of the Popish doctors. Imposition of hands in ancient times. This made by the Papists a kind of foundation of the sacrament of Penance.

15. Disagreement among Papists themselves, as to the grounds on which penance is regarded as a sacrament.

16. More plausibility in calling the absolution of the priest, than in calling penance a sacrament.

17. Penance not truly a sacrament. Baptism the sacrament of penitence.

18. Extreme Unction described. No foundation for it in the words of James.

19. No better ground for making this unction a sacrament, than any of the other symbols mentioned in Scripture.

20. Insult offered by this unction to the Holy Spirit. It cannot be a sacrament, as it was not instituted by Christ, and has no promise annexed to it.

21. No correspondence between the unction enjoined by James and the anointing of the Papists.

22. Of ecclesiastical orders. Two points for discussion. Absurdities here introduced. Whether ecclesiastical order is a sacrament. Papists not agreed as to holy orders.

23. Insult to Christ in attempting to make him their colleague.

24. The greater part of these orders empty names implying no certain office. Popish exorcists.

25. Absurdity of the tonsure.

26. The Judaizing nature of the tonsure. Why Paul shaved his head in consequence of a vow.

27. Origin of this clerical tonsure as given by Augustine. Absurd ceremonies in consecrating Doorkeepers, Readers, Exorcists, and Acolytes.

28. Of the higher class of orders called Holy Orders. Insult offered to Christ when ministers are regarded as priests. Holy orders have nothing of the nature of a sacrament.

29. Absurd imitation of our Saviour in breathing on his apostles.

30. Absurdity of the anointing employed.

31. Imposition of hands. Absurdity of, in Papistical ordination.

32. Ordination of deacons. Absurd forms of Papists.

33. Of sub-deacons.

34. Marriage not a sacrament.

35. Nothing in Scripture to countenance the idea that marriage is a sacrament.

36. Origin of the notion that marriage is a sacrament.

37. Practical abuses from this erroneous idea of marriage. Conclusion.

1. The above discourse concerning the sacraments might have the effect, among the docile and sober-minded, of preventing them from indulging their curiosity, or from embracing, without authority from the word, any other sacraments than those two, which they know to have been instituted by the Lord. But since the idea of seven sacraments, almost common in the mouths of all, and circulated in all schools and sermons, by mere antiquity, has struck its roots. and is even now seated in the minds of men, I thought it might be worth while to give a separate and closer consideration of the other five, which are vulgarly classed with the true and genuine sacraments of the Lord, and, after wiping away every gloss, to hold them up to the view of the simple, that they may see what their true nature is, and how falsely they have hitherto been regarded as sacraments. Here, at the outset, I would declare to all the pious, that I engage not in this dispute about a word for love of wrangling, but am induced, by weighty causes, to impugn the abuse of it. I am not unaware that Christians are the masters of words, as they are of all things, and that, therefore, they may at pleasure adapt words to things, provided a pious meaning is retained, though there should be some impropriety in the mode of expression. All this I concede, though it were better to make words subordinate to things than things to words. But in the name of sacrament, the case is different. For those who set down seven sacraments, at the same time give this definition to all—viz. that they are visible forms of invisible grace; and at the same time, make them all vehicles of the Holy Spirit, instruments for conferring righteousness, causes of procuring grace.

Accordingly, the Master of Sentences himself denies that the sacraments of the Mosaic Law are properly called by this name, because they exhibited not what they figured. Is it tolerable, I ask, that the symbols which the Lord has consecrated with his own lips, which he has distinguished by excellent promises, should be regarded as no sacraments, and that, meanwhile, this honour should be transferred to those rites which men have either devised of themselves, or at least observe without any express command from God? Therefore, let them either change the definition, or refrain from this use of the word, which may afterwards give rise to false and absurd opinions. Extreme unction, they say, is a figure and cause of invisible grace, because it is a sacrament. If we cannot possibly admit the inference, we must certainly meet them on the subject of the name, that we may not receive it on terms which may furnish occasion for such an error. On the other hand, when they prove it to be a sacrament, they add the reason, because it consists of the external sign and the word. If we find neither command nor promise, what else can we do than protest against it?

2. It now appears that we are not quarreling about a word, but raising a not unnecessary discussion as to the reality. Accordingly, we most strenuously maintain what we formerly confirmed by invincible argument, that the power of instituting a sacrament belongs to God alone, since a sacrament ought, by the sure promise of God, to raise up and comfort the consciences of believers, which could never receive this assurance from men. A sacrament ought to be a testimony of the good-will of God toward us. Of this no man or angel can be witness, since God has no counsellor (Isa. 40:13; Rom. 11:34). He himself alone, with legitimate authority, testifies of himself to us by his word. A sacrament is a seal of attestation or promise of God. Now, it could not be sealed by corporeal things, or the elements of this world, unless they were confirmed and set apart for this purpose by the will of God. Man, therefore, cannot institute a sacrament, because it is not in the power of man to make such divine mysteries lurk under things so abject. The word of God must precede to make a sacrament to be a sacrament, as Augustine most admirably shows (Hom. in Joann. 80). Moreover, it is useful to keep up some distinction between sacraments and other ceremonies, if we would not fall into many absurdities. The apostles prayed on their bended knees; therefore our knees may not be bent without a sacrament (Acts 9:20; 20:36). The disciples are said to have prayed toward the east; thus looking at the east is a sacrament. Paul would have men in every place to lift up pure hands (1 Tim. 2:8); and it is repeatedly stated that the saints prayed with uplifted hands, let the outstretching, therefore, of hands also become a sacrament; in short, let all the gestures of saints pass into sacraments, though I should not greatly object to this, provided it was not connected with those greater inconveniences.

3. If they would press us with the authority of the ancient Church, I say that they are using a gloss. This number seven is nowhere found in the ecclesiastical writers, nor is it well ascertained at what time it crept in. I confess, indeed, that they sometimes use freedom with the term *sacrament*, but what do they mean by it? all ceremonies, external writs, and exercises of piety. But when they speak of those signs which ought to be testimonies of the divine favour toward us, they are contented with those two, Baptism and the Eucharist. Lest any one suppose that this is falsely alleged by me, I will here give a few passages from Augustine. "First, I wish you to hold that the principle point in this discussion is, that our Lord Jesus Christ (as he himself says in the gospel) has placed us under a yoke which is easy, and a burden which is light. Hence he has knit together the society of his new people by sacraments, very few in number, most easy of observance, and most excellent in meaning; such is baptism consecrated by the name of the Trinity: such is the communion of the body and blood of the Lord, and any other, if recommended in the canonical Scriptures" (August. ad. Januar. Ep. 118). Again, "After the resurrection of our Lord, our Lord himself, and apostolic discipline, appointed, instead of many, a few signs, and these most easy of performance, most august in meaning, most chaste in practice; such is baptism and the celebration of the body and blood of the Lord" (August. De. Doct. Christ. Lib. 3 cap. 9). Why does he here make no mention of the sacred number, I mean seven? Is it probable that he would have omitted it if it had then been established in the Church, especially seeing he is otherwise more curious in observing numbers than might be necessary? Nay, when he makes mention of Baptism and the Supper, and is silent as to others, does he not sufficiently intimate that these two ordinances excel in special dignity, and that other ceremonies sink down to an inferior place? Wherefore, I say, that those sacramentary doctors are not only unsupported by the word of God, but also by the consent of the early Church, however much they may plume themselves on the pretence that they have this consent. But let us now come to particulars.

OF CONFIRMATION.

4. It was anciently customary for the children of Christians, after they had grown up, to appear before the bishop to fulfil that duty which was required of such adults as presented themselves for baptism. These sat among the catechumens until they were duly instructed in the mysteries of the faith, and could make a confession of it before bishop and people. The infants, therefore, who had been initiated by baptism, not having then given a confession of faith to the Church, were again, toward the end of their boyhood, or on adolescence, brought forward by their parents, and were examined by the bishop in terms of the Catechism which was then in common use. In order that this act, which otherwise justly required to be grave and holy, might have more reverence and dignity, the ceremony of laying on of hands was also used. Thus the boy, on his faith being approved, was dismissed with a solemn blessing. Ancient writers often make mention of this custom. Pope Leo says (Ep. 39), "If any one returns from heretics, let him not be baptised again, but let that which was there wanting to him—viz. the virtue of the Spirit, be conferred by the laying on of the hands of the bishop." Our opponents will here exclaim, that the name of sacrament is justly given to that by which the Holy Spirit is conferred. But Leo elsewhere explains what he means by these words (Ep. 77); "Let not him who was baptised by heretics be rebaptised, but be confirmed by the laying on of hands with the invocation of the Holy Spirit, because he received only the form of baptism without sanctification." Jerome also mentions it (Contra Luciferian). Now though I deny not that Jerome is somewhat under delusion when he says that the observance is apostolical, he is, however, very far from the follies of these men. And he softens the expression when he adds, that this benediction is given to bishops only, more in honour of the priesthood than from any necessity of law. This laying on of hands, which is done simply by way of benediction, I commend, and would like to see restored to its pure use in the present day.

5. A later age having almost obliterated the reality, introduced a kind of fictitious confirmation as a divine sacrament. They feigned that the virtue of confirmation consisted in conferring the Holy Spirit, for increase of grace, on him who had been prepared in baptism for righteousness, and in confirming for contest those who in baptism were regenerated to life. This confirmation is performed by unction, and the following form of words: "I sign thee with the sign of the holy cross, and confirm thee with the chrism of salvation, in the name of the Father, and of the Son, and of the Holy Spirit." All fair and venerable. But where is the word of God which promises the presence of the Holy Spirit here? Not one iota can they allege. How will they assure us that their chrism is a vehicle of the Holy Spirit? We see oil, that is, a thick and greasy liquid, but nothing more. "Let the word be added to the element," says Augustine, "and it will become a sacrament." Let them, I say, produce this word if they would have us to see anything more in the oil than oil. But if they would show themselves to be ministers of the sacraments as they ought, there would be no room for further dispute. The first duty of a minister is not to do anything without a command. Come, then, and let them produce some command for this ministry, and I will not add a word. If they have no command they cannot excuse their sacrilegious audacity. For this reason our Saviour interogated the Pharisees as to the baptism of John, "Was it from heaven, or of men?" (Mt. 21:25). If they had answered, Of men, he held them confessed that it was frivolous and vain; if Of heaven, they were forced to acknowledge the doctrine of John. Accordingly, not to be too contumelious to John, they did not venture to say that it was of men. Therefore, if confirmation is of men, it is proved to be frivolous and vain; if they would persuade us that it is of heaven, let them prove it.

6. They indeed defend themselves by the example of the apostles, who, they presume, did nothing rashly. In this they are right, nor would they be blamed by us if they showed themselves to be imitators of the apostles. But what did the apostles do? Luke narrates (Acts 8:15, 17), that the apostles who were at Jerusalem, when they heard that Samaria had received the word of God, sent thither Peter and John, that Peter and John prayed for the Samaritans, that they might receive the Holy Spirit, who had not yet come upon any of them, they having only been baptised in the name of Jesus; that after prayer they laid their hands upon them, and that by this laying on of hands the Samaritans received the Holy Spirit. Luke repeatedly mentions this laying on of hands. I hear what the apostles did, that is, they faithfully executed their ministry. It pleased the Lord that those visible and admirable gifts of the Holy Spirit, which he then poured out upon his people, should be administered and distributed by his apostles by the laying on of hands. I think that there was no deeper mystery under this laying on of hands, but I interpret that this kind of ceremony was used by them to intimate, by the outward act, that

they commended to God, and, as it were, offered him on whom they laid hands. Did this ministry, which the apostles then performed, still remain in the Church, it would also behove us to observe the laying on of hands: but since that gift has ceased to be conferred, to what end is the laying on of hands? Assuredly the Holy Spirit is still present with the people of God; without his guidance and direction the Church of God cannot subsist. For we have a promise of perpetual duration, by which Christ invites the thirsty to come to him, that they may drink living water (John 7:37). But those miraculous powers and manifest operations, which were distributed by the laying on of hands, have ceased. They were only for a time. For it was right that the new preaching of the gospel, the new kingdom of Christ, should be signalised and magnified by unwonted and unheard-of miracles. When the Lord ceased from these, he did not forthwith abandon his Church, but intimated that the magnificence of his kingdom, and the dignity of his word, had been sufficiently manifested. In what respect then can these stage-players say that they imitate the apostles? The object of the laying on of hands was, that the evident power of the Holy Spirit might be immediately exerted. This they effect not. Why then do they claim to themselves the laying on of hands, which is indeed said to have been used by the apostles, but altogether to a different end?

7. The same account is to be given were any one to insist that the breathing of our Lord upon his disciples (John 20:22) is a sacrament by which the Holy Spirit is conferred. But the Lord did this once for all, and did not also wish us to do it. In the same way, also, the apostles laid their hands, agreeably to that time at which it pleased the Lord that the visible gifts of the Spirit should be dispensed in answer to their prayers; not that posterity might, as those apes do, mimic the empty and useless sign without the reality. But if they prove that they imitate the apostles in the laying on of hands (though in this they have no resemblance to the apostles, except it be in manifesting some absurd false zeal), where did they get their oil which they call the oil of salvation? Who taught them to seek salvation in oil? Who taught them to attribute to it the power of strengthening? Was it Paul, who draws us far away from the elements of this world, and condemns nothing more than clinging to such observances? This I boldly declare, not of myself, but from the Lord: Those who call oil the oil of salvation abjure the salvation which is in Christ, deny Christ, and have no part in the kingdom of God. Oil for the belly, and the belly for oil, but the Lord will destroy both. For all these weak elements, which perish even in the using, have nothing to do with the kingdom of God, which is spiritual, and will never perish. What, then, some one will say, do you apply the same rule to the water by which we are baptised, and the bread and wine under which the Lord's Supper is exhibited? I answer, that in the sacraments of divine appointment, two things are to be considered: the substance of the corporeal thing which is set before us, and the form which has been impressed upon it by the word of God, and in which its whole force lies. In as far, then, as the bread, wine, and water, which are presented to our view in the sacraments, retain their substance, Paul's declaration applies, "meats for the belly, and the belly for meats: but God shall destroy both it and them" (1 Cor. 6:13). For they pass and vanish away with the fashion of this world. But in as far as they are sanctified by the word of God to be sacraments, they do not confine us to the flesh, but teach truly and spiritually.

8. But let us make a still closer inspection, and see how many monsters this greasy oil fosters and nourishes. Those anointers say that the Holy Spirit is given in baptism for righteousness, and in confirmation, for increase of grace, that in baptism we are regenerated for life, and in confirmation, equipped for contest. And, accordingly, they are not ashamed to deny that baptism can be duly completed without confirmation. How nefarious! Are we not, then, buried with Christ by baptism, and made partakers of his death, that we may also be partners of his resurrection? This fellowship with the life and death of Christ, Paul interprets to mean the mortification of our flesh, and the quickening of the Spirit, our old man being crucified in order that we may walk in newness of life (Rom 6:6). What is it to be equipped for contest, if this is not? But if they deemed it as nothing to trample on the word of God, why did they not at least reverence the Church, to which they would be thought to be in everything so obedient? What heavier charge can be brought against their doctrine than the decree of the Council of Melita? "Let him who says that baptism is given for the remission of sins only, and not in aid of future grace, be anathema." When Luke, in the passage which we have quoted, says, that the Samaritans were only "baptised in the name of the Lord Jesus" (Acts 8:16), but had not received the Holy Spirit, he does not say absolutely that those who believed in Christ with the heart, and confessed him with the mouth, were not endued with any gift of the Spirit. He means that receiving of the Spirit by which miraculous power and visible graces were received. Thus the apostles are said to have received the Spirit on the day of Pentecost

(Acts 2:4), whereas Christ had long before said to them, "It is not ye that speak, but the Spirit of your Father which speaketh in you" (Mt. 10:20). Ye who are of God see the malignant and pestiferous wile of Satan. What was truly given in baptism, is falsely said to be given in the confirmation of it, that he may stealthily lead away the unwary from baptism. Who can now doubt that this doctrine, which dissevers the proper promises of baptism from baptism, and transfers them elsewhere, is a doctrine of Satan? We have discovered on what foundation this famous unction rests. The word of God says, that as many as have been baptised into Christ, have put on Christ with his gifts (Gal. 3:27). The word of the anointers says that they received no promise in baptism to equip them for contest (De Consecr. Dist. 5, cap. Spir. Sanct). The former is the word of truth, the latter must be the word of falsehood. I can define this baptism more truly than they themselves have hitherto defined it— viz. that it is a noted insult to baptism, the use of which it obscures—nay, abolishes: that it is a false suggestion of the devil, which draws us away from the truth of God; or, if you prefer it, that it is oil polluted with a lie of the devil, deceiving the minds of the simple by shrouding them, as it were, in darkness.

9. They add, moreover, that all believers ought, after baptism, to receive the Holy Spirit by the laying on of hands, that they may become complete Christians, inasmuch as there never can be a Christian who has not been *chrismed* by episcopal confirmation. These are their exact words. I thought that everything pertaining to Christianity was prescribed and contained in Scripture. Now I see that the true form of religion must be sought and learned elsewhere than in Scripture. Divine wisdom, heavenly truth, the whole doctrine of Christ, only begins the Christian; it is the oil that perfects him. By this sentence are condemned all the apostles and the many martyrs who, it is absolutely certain, were never chrismed, the oil not yet being made, besmeared with which, they might fulfil all the parts of Christianity, or rather become Christians, which, as yet, they were not. Though I were silent, they abundantly refute themselves. How small the proportion of the people whom they anoint after baptism! Why, then, do they allow among their flock so many half Christians, whose imperfection they might easily remedy? Why, with such supine negligence, do they allow them to omit what cannot be omitted without grave offence? Why do they not more rigidly insist on a matter so necessary, that, without it, salvation cannot be obtained unless, perhaps, when the act has been anticipated by sudden death? When they allow it to be thus licentiously despised, they tacitly confess that it is not of the importance which they pretend.

10. Lastly, they conclude that this sacred unction is to be held in greater veneration than baptism, because the former is specially administered by the higher order of priests, whereas the latter is dispensed in common by all priests whatever (Distinct. 5, De his vero). What can you here say, but that they are plainly mad in thus pluming themselves on their own inventions, while, in comparison with these, they carelessly contemn the sacred ordinances of God? Sacrilegious mouth! dare you oppose oil merely polluted with your fetid breath, and charmed by your muttered words, to the sacrament of Christ, and compare it with water sanctified by the word of God? But even this was not enough for your improbity: you must also prefer it. Such are the responses of the holy see, such the oracles of the apostolic tripod. But some of them have begun to moderate this madness, which, even in their own opinion, was carried too far (Lombard. Sent. Lib. 4 Dist. 7, c. 2). It is to be held in greater veneration, they say, not perhaps because of the greater virtue and utility which it confers, but because it is given by more dignified persons, and in a more dignified part of the body, the forehead; or because it gives a greater increase of virtue, though baptism is more effectual for forgiveness. But do they not, by their first reason, prove themselves to be Donatists, who estimate the value of the sacrament by the dignity of the minister? Grant, however, that confirmation may be called more dignified from the dignity of the bishop's hand, still should any one ask how this great perrogative was conferred on the bishops, what reason can they give but their own caprice? The right was used only by the apostles, who alone dispensed the Holy Spirit. Are bishops alone apostles? Are they apostles at all? However, let us grant this also; why do they not, on the same grounds, maintain that the sacrament of blood in the Lord's Supper is to be touched only by bishops? Their reason for refusing it to laics is, that it was given by our Lord to the apostles only. If to the apostles only, why not infer then to bishops only? But in that place, they make the apostles simple Presbyters, whereas here another vertigo seizes them, and they suddenly elect them bishops. Lastly, Ananias was not an apostle, and yet Paul was sent to him to receive his sight, to be baptised and filled with the Holy Spirit (Acts 9:17). I will add, though cumulatively, if, by divine right, this office was peculiar to bishops, why have they dared to transfer it to plebeian Presbyters, as we read in one of the Epistles of Gregory? (Dist. 95, cap. Pervenis)

11. How frivolous, inept, and stolid the other reason, that their confirmation is worthier than the baptism of God, because in confirmation it is the forehead that is besmeared with oil, and in baptism the cranium. As if baptism were performed with oil, and not with water! I take all the pious to witness, whether it be not the one aim of these miscreants to adulterate the purity of the sacraments by their leaven. I have said elsewhere, that what is of God in the sacraments, can scarcely be got a glimpse of among the crowd of human inventions. If any did not then give me credit for the fact, let them now give it to their own teachers. Here, passing over water, and making it of no estimation, they set a great value on oil alone in baptism. We maintain, against them, that in baptism also the forehead is sprinkled with water, in comparison with which, we do not value your oil one straw, whether in baptism or in confirmation. But if any one alleges that oil is sold for more, I answer, that by this accession of value any good which might otherwise be in it is vitiated, so far is it from being lawful fraudulently to vend this most vile imposture. They betray their impiety by the third reason, when they pretend that a greater increase of virtue is conferred in confirmation than in baptism. By the laying on of hands the apostles dispensed the visible gifts of the Spirit. In what respect does the oil of these men prove its fecundity? But have done with these guides, who cover one sacrilege with many acts of sacrilege. It is a Gordian knot, which it is better to cut than to lose so much labour in untying.

12. When they see that the word of God, and everything like plausible argument, fail them, they pretend, as usual, that the observance is of the highest antiquity, and is confirmed by the consent of many ages. Even were this true, they gain nothing by it. A sacrament is not of earth, but of heaven; not of men, but of God only. They must prove God to be the author of their confirmation, if they would have it to be regarded as a sacrament. But why obtrude antiquity, seeing that ancient writers, whenever they would speak precisely, nowhere mention more than two sacraments? Were the bulwark of our faith to be sought from men, we have an impregnable citadel in this, that the fictitious sacraments of these men were never recognised as sacraments by ancient writers. They speak of the laying on of hands, but do they call it a sacrament? Augustine distinctly affirms that it is nothing but prayer (De Bapt. cont. Donat. Lib. 3 cap. 16). Let them not here yelp out one of their vile distinctions, that the laying on of hands to which Augustine referred was not the confirmatory, but the curative or reconciliatory. His book is extant and in men's hands; if I wrest it to any meaning different from that which Augustine himself wrote it, they are welcome not only to load me with reproaches after their wonted manner, but to spit upon me. He is speaking of those who returned from schism to the unity of the Church. He says that they have no need of a repetition of baptism, for the laying on of hands is sufficient, that the Lord may bestow the Holy Spirit upon them by the bond of peace. But as it might seem absurd to repeat laying on of hands more than baptism, he shows the difference: "What," he asks, "is the laying on of hands but prayer over the man?" That this is his meaning is apparent from another passage, where he says, "Because of the bond of charity, which is the greatest gift of the Holy Spirit, without which all the other holy qualities which a man may possess are ineffectual for salvation, the hand is laid on reformed heretics" (Lib. 5 cap. 23).

13. I wish we could retain the custom, which, as I have observed, existed in the early Church, before this abortive mask of a sacrament appeared. It would not be such a confirmation as they pretend, one which cannot even be named without injury to baptism, but catechising by which those in boyhood, or immediately beyond it, would give an account of their faith in the face of the Church. And the best method of catechising would be, if a form were drawn up for this purpose, containing, and briefly explaining, the substance of almost all the heads of our religion, in which the whole body of the faithful ought to concur without controversy. A boy of ten years of age would present himself to the Church, to make a profession of faith, would be questioned on each head, and give answers to each. If he was ignorant of any point, or did not well understand it, he would be taught. Thus, while the whole Church looked on and witnessed, he would profess the one true sincere faith with which the body of the faithful, with one accord, worship one God. Were this discipline in force in the present day, it would undoubtedly whet the sluggishness of certain parents, who carelessly neglect the instruction of their children, as if it did not at all belong to them, but who could not then omit it without public disgrace; there would be greater agreement in faith among the Christian people, and not so much ignorance and rudeness; some persons would not be so readily carried away by new and strange dogmas; in fine, it would furnish all with a methodical arrangement of Christian doctrine.

OF PENITENCE.

14. The next place they give to Penitence, of which they discourse so confusedly and unmethodically, that

consciences cannot derive anything certain or solid from their doctrine. In another place (Book 3 chap. 3 and 4), we have explained at length, first, what the Scriptures teach concerning repentance, and, secondly, what these men teach concerning it. All we have now to advert to is the grounds of that opinion of it as a sacrament which has long prevailed in schools and churches. First, however, I will speak briefly of the rite of the early Church, which those men have used as a pretext for establishing their fiction. By the order observed in public repentance, those who had performed the satisfactions imposed upon them were reconciled by the formal laying on of hands. This was the symbol of absolution by which the sinner himself regained his confidence of pardon before God, and the Church was admonished to lay aside the remembrance of the offence, and kindly receive him into favour. This Cyprian often terms *to give peace*. In order that the act might have more weight and estimation with the people, it was appointed that the authority of the bishop should always be interposed. Hence the decree of the second Council of Carthage, "No presbyter may publicly at mass reconcile a penitent;" and another, of the Council of Arausica, "Let those who are departing this life, at the time of penitence, be admitted to communion without the reconciliatory laying on of hands; if they recover from the disease, let them stand in the order of penitents, and after they have fulfilled their time, receive the reconciliatory laying on of hands from the bishop." Again, in the third Council of Carthage, "A presbyter may not reconcile a penitent without the authority of the bishop." The object of all these enactments was to prevent the strictness, which they wished to be observed in that matter, from being lost by excessive laxity. Accordingly, they wished cognisance to be taken by the bishop, who, it was probable, would be more circumspect in examining. Although Cyprian somewhere says that not the bishop only laid hands, but also the whole clergy. For he thus speaks, "They do penitence for a proper time; next they come to communion, and receive the right of communion by the laying on of the hands of the bishop and clergy" (Lib. 3 Ep 14). Afterwards, in process of time, the matter came to this, that they used the ceremony in private absolutions also without public penitence. Hence the distinction in Gratian (Decret. 26, Quæst. 6) between public and private reconciliation. I consider that ancient observance of which Cyprian speaks to have been holy and salutary to the Church, and I could wish it restored in the present day. The more modern form, though I dare not disapprove, or at least strongly condemn, I deem to be less necessary. Be this as it may, we see that the laying on of hands in penitence was a ceremony ordained by men, not by God, and is to be ranked among indifferent things, and external exercises, which indeed are not to be despised, but occupy an inferior place to those which have been recommended to us by the word of the Lord.

15. The Romanists and Schoolmen, whose wont it is to corrupt all things by erroneous interpretation, anxiously labour to find a sacrament here, and it cannot seem wonderful, for they seek a thing where it is not. At best, they leave the matter involved, undecided, uncertain, confused, and confounded by the variety of opinions. Accordingly, they say (Sent. Lib. 4 Dist. 22, cap. 3), either that external penitence is a sacrament, and, if so, ought to be regarded as a sign of internal penitence; *i. e.*, contrition of heart, which will be the matter of the sacrament, or that both together make a sacrament, not two, but one complete; but that the external is the sacrament merely, the internal, the matter, and the sacrament, whereas the forgiveness of sins is the matter only, and not the sacrament. Let those who remember the definition of a sacrament, which we have given above, test by it that which they say is a sacrament, and it will be found that it is not an external ceremony appointed by God for the confirmation of our faith. But if they allege that my definition is not a law which they are necessarily bound to obey, let them hear Augustine, whom they pretend to regard as a saint. "Visible sacraments were instituted for the sake of carnal men, that by the ladder of sacraments they may be conveyed from those things which are seen by the eye, to those which are perceived by the understanding" (August. Quæst. Vet. Test. Lib. 3). Do they themselves see, or can they show to others, anything like this in that which they call the sacrament of penance? In another passage, he says, "It is called a sacrament, because in it one thing is seen, another thing is understood. What is seen has bodily appearance, what is understood has spiritual fruit" (Serm. de Bapt. Infant). These things in no way apply to the sacrament of penance, as they feign it; there, there is no bodily form to represent spiritual fruit.

16. And (to despatch these beasts in their own arena) if any sacrament is sought here, would it not have been much more plausible to maintain that the absolution of the priest is a sacrament, than penitence either external or internal? For it might obviously have been said that it is a ceremony to confirm our faith in the forgiveness of sins, and that it has the promise of the keys, as they describe them: "Whatsoever ye shall bind or loose on earth, shall be bound or loosed in heaven." But some one will object

that to most of those who are absolved by priests nothing of the kind is given by the absolution, whereas, according to their dogma, the sacraments of the new dispensation ought to effect what they figure. This is ridiculous. As in the eucharist, they make out a twofold eating—a sacramental, which is common to the good and bad alike, and a spiritual, which is proper only to the good; why should they not also pretend that absolution is given in two ways? And yet I have never been able to understand what they meant by their dogma. How much it is at variance with the truth of God, we showed when we formally discussed that subject. Here I only wish to show that no scruple should prevent them from giving the name of a sacrament to the absolution of the priest. For they might have answered by the mouth of Augustine, that there is a sanctification without a visible sacrament, and a visible sacrament without internal sanctification. Again, that in the elect alone sacraments effect what they figure. Again, that some put on Christ so far as the receiving of the sacrament, and others so far as sanctification; that the former is done equally by the good and the bad, the latter by the good only. Surely they were more deluded than children, and blind in the full light of the sun when they toiled with so much difficulty, and perceived not a matter so plain and obvious to every man.

17. Lest they become elated, however, whatever be the part in which they place the sacrament, I deny that it can justly be regarded as a sacrament; first, because there exists not to this effect any special promise of God, which is the only ground of a sacrament; and, secondly, because whatever ceremony is here used is a mere invention of man; whereas, as has already been shown, the ceremonies of sacraments can only be appointed by God. Their fiction of the sacrament of penance, therefore, was falsehood and imposture. This fictitious sacrament they adorned with the befitting eulogium, that it was the second plank in the case of shipwreck, because if any one had, by sin, injured the garment of innocence received in baptism, he might repair it by penitence. This was a saying of Jerome. Let it be whose it may, as it is plainly impious, it cannot be excused if understood in this sense; as if baptism were effaced by sin, and were not rather to be recalled to the mind of the sinner whenever he thinks of the forgiveness of sins, that he may thereby recollect himself, regain courage, and be confirmed in the belief that he shall obtain the forgiveness of sins which was promised him in baptism. What Jerome said harshly and improperly—viz. that baptism, which is fallen from by those who deserve to be excommunicated from the Church, is repaired by penitence, these worthy expositors wrest to their own impiety. You will speak most correctly, therefore, if you call baptism the sacrament of penitence, seeing it is given to those who aim at repentance to confirm their faith and seal their confidence. But lest you should think this our invention, it appears, that besides being conformable to the words of Scripture, it was generally regarded in the early Church as an indubitable axiom. For in the short Treatise on Faith addressed to Peter, and bearing the name of Augustine, it is called, *The sacrament of faith and repentance.* But why have recourse to doubtful writings, as if anything can be required more distinct than the statement of the Evangelist, that John preached "the baptism of repentance for the remission of sins"? (Mark 1:4; Luke 3:3).

OF EXTREME UNCTION, SO CALLED.

18. The third fictitious sacrament is Extreme Unction, which is performed only by a priest, and, as they express it, *in extremis*, with oil consecrated by the bishop, and with this form of words, "By this holy unction, and his most tender mercy, may God forgive you whatever sin you have committed, by the eye, the ear, the smell, the touch, the taste" (see Calv. Epist. de Fugiend. Illicit. Sac.). They pretend that there are two virtues in it—the forgiveness of sins, and relief of bodily disease, if so expedient; if not expedient, the salvation of the soul. For they say, that the institution was set down by James, whose words are, "Is any sick among you? let him send for the elders of the Church; and let them pray over him, anointing him with oil in the name of the Lord; and the prayer of faith shall save the sick, and the Lord shall raise him up: and if he have committed sins, they shall be forgiven him" (James 5:14). The same account is here to be given of this unction as we lately gave of the laying on of hands; in other words, it is mere hypocritical stage-play, by which, without reason or result, they would resemble the apostles. Mark relates that the apostles, on their first mission, agreeably to the command which they had received of the Lord, raised the dead, cast out devils, cleansed lepers, healed the sick, and, in healing, used oil. He says, they "anointed with oil many that were sick, and healed them" (Mark 6:13). To this James referred when he ordered the presbyters of the Church to be called to anoint the sick. That no deeper mystery lay under this ceremony will easily be perceived by those who consider how great liberty both our Lord and his apostles used in those external things. Our Lord, when about to give sight to the blind man, spat on the ground, and made clay of the spittle;

some he cured by a touch, others by a word. In like manner the apostles cured some diseases by word only, others by touch, others by anointing. But it is probable that neither this anointing nor any of the other things were used at random. I admit this; not, however, that they were instruments of the cure, but only symbols to remind the ignorant whence this great virtue proceeded, and prevent them from ascribing the praise to the apostles. To designate the Holy Spirit and his gifts by oil is trite and common (Ps. 45:8). But the gift of hearing disappeared with the other miraculous powers which the Lord was pleased to give for a time, that it might render the new preaching of the gospel for ever wonderful. Therefore, even were we to grant that anointing was a sacrament of those powers which were then administered by the hands of the apostles, it pertains not to us, to whom no such powers have been committed.

19. And what better reason have they for making a sacrament of this unction, than of any of the other symbols which are mentioned in Scripture? Why do they not dedicate some pool of Siloam, into which, at certain seasons the sick may plunge themselves? That, they say, were done in vain. Certainly not more in vain than unction. Why do they not lay themselves on the dead, seeing that Paul, in raising up the dead youth, lay upon him? Why is not clay made of dust and spittle a sacrament? The other cases were special, but this is commanded by James. In other words, James spake agreeably to the time when the Church still enjoyed this blessing from God. They affirm, indeed, that there is still the same virtue in their unction, but we experience differently. Let no man now wonder that they have with so much confidence deluded souls which they knew to be stupid and blind, because deprived of the word of God, that is, of his light and life, seeing they blush not to attempt to deceive the bodily perceptions of those who are alive, and have all their senses about them. They make themselves ridiculous, therefore, by pretending that they are endued with the gift of healing. The Lord, doubtless, is present with his people in all ages, and cures their sicknesses as often as there is need, not less than formerly; and yet he does not exert those manifest powers, nor dispense miracles by the hands of apostles, because that gift was temporary, and owing, in some measure, to the ingratitude of men, immediately ceased.

20. Wherefore, as the apostles, not without cause, openly declared, by the symbol of oil, that the gift of healing committed to them was not their own, but the power of the Holy Spirit; so, on the other hand, these men insult the Holy Spirit by making his power consist in a filthy oil of no efficacy. It is just as if one were to say that all oil is the power of the Holy Spirit, because it is called by that name in Scripture, and that every dove is the Holy Spirit, because he appeared in that form. Let them see to this: it is sufficient for us that we perceive, with absolute certainty, that their unction is no sacrament, as it is neither a ceremony appointed by God, nor has any promise. For when we require, in a sacrament, these two things, that it be a ceremony appointed by God, and have a promise from God, we at the same time demand that that ceremony be delivered to us, and that that promise have reference to us. No man contends that circumcision is now a sacrament of the Christian Church, although it was both an ordinance of God, and had his promise annexed to it, because it was neither commanded to us, nor was the promise annexed to it given us on the same condition. The promise of which they vaunt so much in unction, as we have clearly demonstrated, and they themselves show by experience, has not been given to us. The ceremony behoved to be used only by those who had been endued with the gift of healing, not by those murderers, who do more by slaying and butchering than by curing.

21. Even were it granted that this precept of unction, which has nothing to do with the present age, were perfectly adapted to it, they will not even thus have advanced much in support of their unction, with which they have hitherto besmeared us. James would have all the sick to be anointed: these men besmear, with their oil, not the sick, but half-dead carcasses, when life is quivering on the lips, or, as they say, *in extremis*. If they have a present cure in their sacrament, with which they can either alleviate the bitterness of disease, or at least give some solace to the soul, they are cruel in never curing in time. James would have the sick man to be anointed by the elders of the Church. They admit no anointer but a priestling. When they interpret the elders of James to be priests, and allege that the plural number is used for honour, the thing is absurd; as if the Church had at that time abounded with swarms of priests, so that they could set out in long procession, bearing a dish of sacred oil. James, in ordering simply that the sick be anointed, seems to me to mean no other anointing than that of common oil, nor is any other mentioned in the narrative of Mark. These men deign not to use any oil but that which has been consecrated by a bishop, that is warmed with much breath, charmed by much muttering, and saluted nine times on bended knee, Thrice Hail, holy oil! thrice Hail, holy

chrism! thrice Hail, holy balsam! From whom did they derive these exorcisms? James says, that when the sick man shall have been anointed with oil, and prayer shall have been made over him, if he have committed sins, they shall be forgiven him—viz. that his guilt being forgiven, he shall obtain a mitigation of the punishment, not meaning that sins are effaced by oil, but that the prayers by which believers commended their afflicted brother to God would not be in vain. These men are impiously false in saying that sins are forgiven by their sacred, that is, abominable unction. See how little they gain, even when they are allowed to abuse the passage of James as they list. And to save us the trouble of a laborious proof, their own annals relieve us from all difficulty; for they relate that Pope Innocent, who presided over the church of Rome in the age of Augustine, ordained, that not elders only, but all Christians, should use oil in anointing, in their own necessity, or in that of their friends. Our authority for this is Sigebert, in his Chronicles.

OF ECCLESIASTICAL ORDERS.

22. The fourth place in their catalogue is held by the sacrament of Orders, one so prolific, as to beget of itself seven lesser sacraments. It is very ridiculous that, after affirming that there are seven sacraments, when they begin to count, they make out thirteen. It cannot be alleged that they are one sacrament, because they all tend to one priesthood, and are a kind of steps to the same thing. For while it is certain that the ceremonies in each are different, and they themselves say that the graces are different, no man can doubt that if their dogmas are admitted, they ought to be called seven sacraments. And why debate it as a doubtful matter, when they themselves plainly and distinctly declare that they are seven? First, then, we shall glance at them in passing, and show to how many absurdities they introduce us when they would recommend their orders to us as sacraments; and, secondly, we shall see whether the ceremony which churches use in ordaining ministers ought at all to be called a sacrament. They make seven ecclesiastical orders, or degrees, which they distinguish by the title of a sacrament. These are Doorkeepers, Readers, Exorcists, Acolytes, Subdeacons, Deacons, and Priests. And they say that they are seven, because of the seven kinds of graces of the Holy Spirit with which those who are promoted to them ought to be endued. This grace is increased and more liberally accumulated on promotion. The mere number has been consecrated by a perversion of Scripture, because they think they read in Isaiah that there are seven gifts of the Holy Spirit, whereas truly not more than six are mentioned by Isaiah, who, however, meant not to include all in that passage. For, in other passages are mentioned the spirit of life, of sanctification, of the adoption of sons, as well as there, the spirit of wisdom and understanding, the spirit of counsel and might, the spirit of knowledge, and of the fear of the Lord. Although others who are more acute make not seven orders, but nine, in imitation, as they say, of the Church triumphant. But among these, also, there is a contest; because some insist that the clerical tonsure is the first order of all, and the episcopate the last; while others, excluding the tonsure, class the office of archbishop among the orders. Isiodorus distinguishes differently, for he makes Psalmists and Readers different. To the former, he gives the charge of chanting; to the latter, that of reading the Scriptures for the instruction of the common people. And this distinction is observed by the canons. In this great variety, what would they have us to follow or to avoid? Shall we say that there are seven orders? So the master of the school teaches, but the most illuminated doctors determine otherwise. On the other hand, they are at variance among themselves. Besides, the most sacred canons call us in a different direction. Such, indeed, is the concord of men when they discuss divine things apart from the word of God.

23. But the crowning folly of all is, that in each of these they make Christ their colleague. First, they say he performed the office of Doorkeeper when, with a whip of small cords, he drove the buyers and sellers from the temple. He intimates that he is a Doorkeeper when he says, "I am the door." He assumed the office of Reader, when he read Isaiah in the synagogue. He performed the office of Exorcist when, touching the tongue and ears of the deaf and dumb man with spittle, he restored his hearing. He declared that he was an Acolyte by the words, "He that followeth me shall not walk in darkness." He performed the office of Subdeacon, when, girding himself with a towel, he washed the feet of his disciples. He acted the part of a Deacon, when he distributed his body and blood in the Supper. He performed the part of a Priest, when, on the cross, he offered himself in sacrifice to the Father. As these things cannot be heard without laughter, I wonder how they could have been written without laughter, if, indeed, they were men who wrote them. But their most noteworthy subtlety is that in which they speculate on the name of Acolyte, calling him Ceroferarius—a magical term, I presume, one certainly unknown to all nations and tongues; ἀκόλουθος, in Greek, meaning simply *attendant*. Were I to stop and seriously refute these

things, I might myself justly be laughed at, so frivolous are they and ludicrous.

24. Still, lest they should be able to impose on silly women, their vanity must be exposed in passing. With great pomp and solemnity they elect their readers, psalmists, doorkeepers, acolytes, to perform those services which they give in charge, either to boys, or at least to those whom they call laics. Who, for the most part, lights the tapers, who pours wine and water from the pitcher, but a boy or some mean person among laics, who gains his bread by so doing? Do not the same persons chant? Do they not open and shut the doors of Churches? Who ever saw, in their churches, either an acolyte or doorkeeper performing his office? Nay, when he who as a boy performed the office of acolyte, is admitted to the order of acolyte, he ceases to be the very thing he begins to be called, so that they seem professedly to wish to cast away the office when they assume the title. See why they hold it necessary to be consecrated by sacraments, and to receive the Holy Spirit! It is just to do nothing. If they pretend that this is the defect of the times, because they neglect and abandon their offices, let them, at the same time, confess that there is not in the Church, in the present day, any use or benefit of these sacred orders which they wondrously extol, and that their whole Church is full of anathema, since the tapers and flagons, which none are worthy to touch but those who have been consecrated acolytes, she allows to be handled by boys and profane persons; since her chants, which ought to be heard only from consecrated lips, she delegates to children. And to what end, pray, do they consecrate exorcists? I hear that the Jews had their exorcists, but I see they were so called from the exorcisms which they practised (Acts 19:13). Who ever heard of those fictitious exorcists having given one specimen of their profession? It is pretended that power has been given them to lay their hands on energumens, catechumens, and demoniacs, but they cannot persuade demons that they are endued with such power, not only because demons do not submit to their orders, but even command themselves. Scarcely will you find one in ten who is not possessed by a wicked spirit. All, then, which they babble about their paltry orders is a compound of ignorant and stupid falsehoods. Of the ancient acolytes, doorkeepers, and readers, we have spoken when explaining the government of the Church. All that we here proposed was to combat that novel invention of a sevenfold sacrament in ecclesiastical orders of which we nowhere read except among silly raving Sorbonnists and Canonists.

25. Let us now attend to the ceremonies which they employ. And first, all whom they enroll among their militia they initiate into the clerical status by a common symbol. They shave them on the top of the head, that the crown may denote regal honour, because clergy ought to be kings in governing themselves and others. Peter thus speaks of them: "Ye are a chosen generation, a royal priesthood, a holy nation, a peculiar people" (1 Pet. 2:9). But it was sacrilege in them to arrogate to themselves alone what is given to the whole Church, and proudly to glory in a title of which they had robbed the faithful. Peter addresses the whole Church: these men wrest it to a few shaven crowns, as if it had been said to them alone, Be ye holy: as if they alone had been purchased by the blood of Christ: as if they alone had been made by Christ kings and priests unto God. Then they assign other reasons (Sent. Lib. 4 Dist. 24). The top of the head is bared, that their mind may be shown to be free, with unveiled face, to behold the glory of God; or that they may be taught to cut off the vices of the eye and the lip. Or the shaving of the head is the laying aside of temporal things, while the circumference of the crown is the remnants of good which are retained for support. Everything is in figure, because forsooth, the veil of the temple is not yet rent. Accordingly, persuaded that they have excellently performed their part because they have figured such things by their crown, they perform none of them in reality. How long will they delude us with such masks and impostures? The clergy, by shaving off some hair, intimate (Sent. loco cit.) that they have cast away abundance of temporal good—that they contemplate the glory of God—that they have mortified concupiscence of the ear and the eye: but no class of men is more rapacious, more stupid, more libidinous. Why do they not rather exhibit true sanctity, than give a hypocritical semblance of it in false and lying signs?

26. Moreover, when they say that the clerical crown has its origin and nature from the Nazarenes, what else do they say than that their mysteries are derived from Jewish ceremonies, or rather are mere Judaism? When they add that Priscilla, Aquila, and Paul himself, after they had taken a vow, shaved their head that they might be purified, they betray their gross ignorance. For we nowhere read this of Priscilla, while, with regard to Aquila, it is uncertain, since that tonsure may refer equally well to Paul as to Aquila (Acts 18:18). But not to leave them in possession of what they ask—viz. that they have an example in Paul, it is to be observed, to the more simple, that Paul never shaved his head for any sanctification, but

only in subservience to the weakness of brethren. Vows of this kind I am accustomed to call vows of charity, not of piety; in other words, vows not undertaken for divine worship, but only in deference to the infirmity of the weak, as he himself says, that to the Jews he became a Jew (1 Cor. 9:20). This, therefore, he did, and that once and for a short time, that he might accommodate himself for a little to the Jews. When these men would, for no end, imitate the purifications of the Nazarenes (Num. 6:18), what else do they than set up a new, while they improperly affect to rival the ancient Judaism? In the same spirit the Decretal Epistle was composed, which enjoins the clergy, after the apostle, not to nourish their hair, but to shave it all round (Cap. Prohibitur, Dist. 24); as if the apostle, in showing what is comely for all men, had been solicitous for the spherical tonsure of the clergy. Hence, let my readers consider what kind of force or dignity there can be in the subsequent mysteries, to which this is the introduction.

27. Whence the clerical tonsure had its origin, is abundantly clear from Augustine alone (De Opera. Monach. et Retract). While in that age none wore long hair but the effeminate, and those who affected an unmanly beauty and elegance, it was thought to be of bad example to allow the clergy to do so. They were therefore enjoined either to cut or shave their hair, that they might not have the appearance of effeminate indulgence. And so common was the practice, that some monks, to appear more sanctimonious than others by a notable difference in dress, let their locks hang loose. But when hair returned to use, and some nations, which had always worn long hair, as France, Germany, and England, embraced Christianity, it is probable that the clergy everywhere shaved the head, that they might not seem to affect ornament. At length, in a more corrupt age, when all ancient customs were either changed, or had degenerated into superstition, seeing no reason for the clerical tonsure (they had retained nothing but a foolish imitation), they betook themselves to mystery, and now superstitiously obtrude it upon us in support of their sacrament. The Doorkeepers, on consecration, receive the keys of the Church, by which it is understood that the custody of it is committed to them; the Readers receive the Holy Bible; the Exorcists, forms of exorcism which they use over the possessed and catechumens; the Acolytes, tapers and the flagon. Such are the ceremonies which, it would seem, possess so much secret virtue, that they cannot only be signs and badges, but even causes of invisible grace. For this, according to their definition, they demand, when they would have them to be classed among sacraments. But to despatch the matter in a few words, I say that it is absurd for schools and canons to make sacraments of those minor orders, since, even by the confession of those who do so, they were unknown to the primitive Church, and were devised many ages after. But sacraments as containing a divine promise ought not to be appointed, either by angels or men, but by God only, to whom alone it belongs to give the promise.

28. There remain the three orders which they call major. Of these, what they call the subdeaconate was transferred to this class, after the crowd of minor began to be prolific. But as they think they have authority for these from the word of God, they honour them specially with the name of Holy Orders. Let us see how they wrest the ordinances of God to their own ends. We begin with the order of presbyter or priest. To these two names they give one meaning, understanding by them, those to whom, as they say, it pertains to offer the sacrifice of Christ's body and blood on the altar, to frame prayers, and bless the gifts of God. Hence, at ordination, they receive the patena with the host, as symbols of the power conferred upon them of offering sacrifices to appease God, and their hands are anointed, this symbol being intended to teach that they have received the power of consecrating. But of the ceremonies afterwards. Of the thing itself, I say that it is so far from having, as they pretend, one particle of support from the word of God, that they could not more wickedly corrupt the order which he has appointed. And first, it ought to be held as confessed (this we maintained when treating of the Papal Mass), that all are injurious to Christ who call themselves priests in the sense of offering expiatory victims. He was constituted and consecrated Priest by the Father, with an oath, after the order of Melchisedek, without end and without successor (Psalm 110:4; Heb. 5:6; 7:3). He once offered a victim of eternal expiation and reconciliation, and now also having entered the sanctuary of heaven, he intercedes for us. In him we all are priests, but to offer praise and thanksgiving, in fine, ourselves, and all that is ours, to God. It was peculiar to him alone to appease God and expiate sins by his oblation. When these men usurp it to themselves, what follows, but that they have an impious and sacrilegious priesthood? It is certainly wicked over much to dare to distinguish it with the title of sacrament. In regard to the true office of presbyter, which was recommended to us by the lips of Christ, I willingly give it that place. For in it there is a ceremony which, first, is taken from the Scriptures; and, secondly, is declared by Paul to be not

empty or superfluous, but to be a faithful symbol of spiritual grace (1 Tim. 4:14). My reason for not giving a place to the third is, because it is not ordinary or common to all believers, but is a special rite for a certain function. But while this honour is attributed to the Christian ministry, Popish priests may not plume themselves upon it. Christ ordered dispensers of his gospel and his sacred mysteries to be ordained, not sacrificers to be inaugurated, and his command was to preach the gospel and feed the flock, not to immolate victims. He promised the gift of the Holy Spirit, not to make expiation for sins, but duly to undertake and maintain the government of the Church (Matt. 28:19; Mark 16:15; John 21:15).

29. With the reality the ceremonies perfectly agree. When our Lord commissioned the apostles to preach the gospel, he breathed upon them (John 20:22). By this symbol he represented the gift of the Holy Spirit which he bestowed upon them. This breathing these worthy men have retained; and, as they were bringing the Holy Spirit from their throat, mutter over their priestlings, "Receive the Holy Spirit." Accordingly, they omit nothing which they do not preposterously mimic. I say not in the manner of players (who have art and meaning in their gestures), but like apes who imitate at random without selection. We observe, say they, the example of the Lord. But the Lord did many things which he did not intend to be examples to us. Our Lord said to his disciples, "Receive the Holy Spirit" (John 20:22). He said also to Lazarus, "Lazarus, come forth" (John 11:43). He said to the paralytic, "Rise, take up thy bed, and walk" (John 5:8). Why do they not say the same to all the dead and paralytic? He gave a specimen of his divine power when, in breathing on the apostles, he filled them with the gift of the Holy Spirit. If they attempt to do the same, they rival God, and do all but challenge him to the contest. But they are very far from producing the effect, and only mock Christ by that absurd gesture. Such, indeed, is the effrontery of some, that they dare to assert that the Holy Spirit is conferred by them; but what truth there is in this, we learn from experience, which cries aloud that all who are consecrated priests, of horses become asses, and of fools, madmen. And yet it is not here that I am contending against them; I am only condemning the ceremony itself, which ought not to be drawn into a precedent, since it was used as the special symbol of a miracle, so far is it from furnishing them with an example for imitation.

30. But from whom, pray, did they receive their unction? They answer, that they received it from the sons of Aaron, from whom also their order derived its origin (Sent. Lib. 4 Dist. 14, cap. 3, et in Canon. Dist. 21, cap. 1). Thus they constantly choose to defend themselves by perverse examples, rather than confess that any of their rash practices is of their own devising. Meanwhile, they observe not that in professing to be the successors of the sons of Aaron, they are injurious to the priesthood of Christ, which alone was adumbrated and typified by all ancient priesthoods. In him, therefore, they were all concluded and completed, in him they ceased, as we have repeatedly said, and as the Epistle to the Hebrews, unaided by any gloss, declares. But if they are so much delighted with Mosaic ceremonies, why do they not hurry oxen, calves, and lambs, to their sacrifices? They have, indeed, a great part of the ancient tabernacle, and of the whole Jewish worship. The only thing wanted to their religion is, that they do not sacrifice oxen and calves. Who sees not that this practice of unction is much more pernicious than circumcision, especially when to it is added superstition and a Pharisaical opinion of the merit of the work? The Jews placed their confidence of justification in circumcision, these men look for spiritual gifts in unction. Therefore, in desiring to be rivals of the Levites, they become apostates from Christ, and discard themselves from the pastoral office.

31. It is, if you please, the sacred oil which impresses an indelible character. As if oil could not be washed away by sand and salt, or if it sticks the closer, with soap. But that character is spiritual. What has oil to do with the soul? Have they forgotten what they quote from Augustine, that if the word be withdrawn from the water, there will be nothing but water, but that it is owing to the word that it is a sacrament? What word can they show in their oil? Is it because Moses was commanded to anoint the sons of Aaron? (Exod. 30:30). But he there receives command concerning the tunic, the ephod, the breastplate, the mitre, the crown of holiness with which Aaron was to be adorned; and concerning the tunics, belts, and mitres which his sons were to wear. He receives command about sacrificing the calf, burning its fat, about cutting and burning rams, about sanctifying ear-rings and vestments with the blood of one of the rams, and innumerable other observances. Having passed over all these, I wonder why the unction of oil alone pleases them. If they delight in being sprinkled, why are they sprinkled with oil rather than with blood? They are attempting, forsooth, an ingenious device; they are trying, by a kind of patchwork, to make one religion out of Christianity, Judaism, and Paganism. Their unction, therefore, is without savour; it

wants salt, that is, the word of God. There remains the laying on of hands, which, though I admit it to be a sacrament in true and legitimate ordination, I do deny to have any such place in this fable, where they neither obey the command of Christ, nor look to the end to which the promise ought to lead us. If they would not have the sign denied them, they must adapt it to the reality to which it is dedicated.

32. As to the order of the diaconate, I would raise no dispute, if the office which existed under the apostles, and a purer Church, were restored to its integrity. But what resemblance to it do we see in their fictitious deacons? I speak not of the men, lest they should complain that I am unjustly judging their doctrine by the vices of those who profess it; but I contend that those whom their doctrine declares to us, derive no countenance from those deacons whom the apostolic Church appointed. They say that it belongs to their deacons to assist the priests, and minister at all the things which are done in the sacraments, as in baptism, in chrism, the patena, and chalice, to bring the offerings and lay them on the altar, to prepare and dress the table of the Lord, to carry the cross, announce and read out the gospel and epistle to the people (Sent. Lib. 4 Dist. 24, cap. 8; Item, Cap. Perlectis, Dist. 25). Is there here one word about the true office of deacon? Let us now attend to the appointment. The bishop alone lays hands on the deacon who is ordained; he places the prayer-book and stole upon his left shoulder, that he may understand that he has received the easy yoke of the Lord, in order that he may subject to the fear of the Lord every thing pertaining to the left side: he gives him a text of the gospel, to remind him that he is its herald. What have these things to do with deacons? But they act just as if one were to say he was ordaining apostles, when he was only appointing persons to kindle the incense, clean the images, sweep the churches, set traps for mice, and put out dogs. Who can allow this class of men to be called apostles, and to be compared with the very apostles of Christ? After this, let them not pretend that those whom they appoint to mere stage-play are deacons. Nay, they even declare, by the very name, what the nature of the office is. For they call them Levites, and wish to trace their nature and origin to the sons of Levi. As far as I am concerned, they are welcome, provided they do not afterwards deck themselves in borrowed feathers.

33. What use is there in speaking of subdeacons? For, whereas in fact they anciently had the charge of the poor, they attribute to them some kind of nugatory function, as carrying the chalice and patena, the pitcher with water, and the napkin to the altar, pouring out water for the hands, &c. Then, by the offerings which they are said to receive and bring in, they mean those which they swallow up, as if they had been destined to anathema. There is an admirable correspondence between the office and the mode of inducting to it—viz. receiving from the bishop the patena and chalice, and from the archdeacon the pitcher with water, the manual and trumpery of this kind. They call upon us to admit that the Holy Spirit is included in these frivolities. What pious man can be induced to grant this? But to have done at once, we may conclude the same of this as of the others, and there is no need to repeat at length what has been explained above. To the modest and docile (it is such I have undertaken to instruct), it will be enough that there is no sacrament of God, unless where a ceremony is shown annexed to a promise, or rather where a promise is seen in a ceremony. Here there is not one syllable of a certain promise, and it is vain, therefore, to seek for a ceremony to confirm the promise. On the other hand, we read of no ceremony appointed by God in regard to those usages which they employ, and, therefore, there can be no sacrament.

OF MARRIAGE.

34. The last of all is marriage, which, while all admit it to be an institution of God, no man ever saw to be a sacrament, until the time of Gregory. And would it ever have occurred to the mind of any sober man? It is a good and holy ordinance of God. And agriculture, architecture, shoemaking, and shaving, are lawful ordinances of God; but they are not sacraments. For in a sacrament, the thing required is not only that it be a work of God, but that it be an external ceremony appointed by God to confirm a promise. That there is nothing of the kind in marriage, even children can judge. But it is a sign, they say, of a sacred thing, that is, of the spiritual union of Christ with the Church. If by the term sign they understand a symbol set before us by God to assure us of our faith, they wander widely from the mark. If they mean merely a sign because it has been employed as a similitude, I will show how acutely they reason. Paul says, "One star differeth from another star in glory. So also is the resurrection of the dead" (1 Cor. 15:41, 42). Here is one sacrament. Christ says, "The kingdom of heaven is like to a grain of mustard-seed" (Mt. 13:31). Here is another sacrament. Again, "The kingdom of heaven is like unto leaven" (Mt. 13:33). Here is a third sacrament. Isaiah says, "He shall feed his flock like a shepherd" (Isaiah 40:11). Here is a fourth sacrament. In another pas-

sage he says, "The Lord shall go forth as a mighty man" (Isaiah 42:13). Here is a fifth sacrament. And where will be the end or limit? Everything in this way will be a sacrament. All the parables and similitudes in Scripture will be so many sacraments. Nay, even theft will be a sacrament, seeing it is written, "The day of the Lord so cometh as a thief in the night" (1 Thess. 5:2). Who can tolerate the ignorant garrulity of these sophists? I admit, indeed, that whenever we see a vine, the best thing is to call to mind what our Saviour says, "I am the true vine, and my father is the husbandman." "I am the vine, ye are the branches" (John 15:1, 5). And whenever we meet a shepherd with his flock, it is good also to remember, "I am the good shepherd, and know my sheep, and am known of mine" (John 10:14). But any man who would class such similitudes with sacraments should be sent to bedlam.

35. They adduce the words of Paul, by which they say that the name of a sacrament is given to marriage, "He that loveth his wife loveth himself. For no man ever yet hated his own flesh; but nourisheth and cherisheth it, even as the Lord the Church: for we are members of his body, of his flesh, and of his bones. For this cause shall a man leave his father and mother, and shall be joined unto his wife, and they two shall be one flesh. This is a great mystery: but I speak concerning Christ and the Church" (Eph. 5:28, 32). To treat Scripture thus is to confound heaven and earth. Paul, in order to show husbands how they ought to love their wives, sets Christ before them as an example. As he shed his bowels of affection for the Church, which he has espoused to himself, so he would have every one to feel affected toward his wife. Then he adds, "He that loveth his wife loveth himself," "even as the Lord the Church." Moreover, to show how Christ loved the Church as himself, nay, how he made himself one with his spouse the Church, he applies to her what Moses relates that Adam said of himself. For after Eve was brought into his presence, knowing that she had been formed out of his side, he exclaimed, "This is now bone of my bones, and flesh of my flesh" (Gen. 2:23). That all this was spiritually fulfilled in Christ, and in us, Paul declares, when he says, that we are members of his body, of his flesh, and of his bones, and so one flesh with him. At length he breaks out into the exclamation, "This is a great mystery;" and lest any one should be misled by the ambiguity, he says, that he is not speaking of the connection between husband and wife, but of the spiritual marriage of Christ and the Church. And truly it is a great mystery that Christ allowed a rib to be taken from himself, of which we might be formed; that is, that when he was strong, he was pleased to become weak, that we might be strengthened by his strength, and should no longer live ourselves, but he live in us (Gal. 2:20).

36. The thing which misled them was the term *sacrament*. But, was it right that the whole Church should be punished for the ignorance of these men? Paul called it a mystery. When the Latin interpreter might have abandoned this mode of expression as uncommon to Latin ears, or converted it into "secret," he preferred calling it *sacramentum*, but in no other sense than the Greek term μυστηπιον was used by Paul. Let them go now and clamour against skill in languages, their ignorance of which leads them most shamefully astray in a matter easy and obvious to every one. But why do they so strongly urge the term sacrament in this one passage, and in others pass it by with neglect? For both in the First Epistle to Timothy (1 Tim. 3:9, 16), and also in the Epistle to the Ephesians, it is used by the Vulgate interpreter, and in every instance, for mystery. Let us, however, pardon them this lapsus, though liars ought to have good memories. Marriage being thus recommended by the title of a sacrament, can it be anything but vertiginous levity afterwards to call it uncleanness, and pollution, and carnal defilement? How absurd is it to debar priests from a sacrament! If they say that they debar not from a sacrament but from carnal connection, they will not thus escape me. They say that this connection is part of the sacrament, and thereby figures the union which we have with Christ in conformity of nature, inasmuch as it is by this connection that husband and wife become one flesh; although some have here found two sacraments, the one of God and the soul, in bridegroom and bride, another of Christ and the Church, in husband and wife. Be this as it may, this connection is a sacrament from which no Christian can lawfully be debarred, unless, indeed, the sacraments of Christians accord so ill that they cannot stand together. There is also another absurdity in these dogmas. They affirm that in a sacrament the gift of the Holy Spirit is conferred; this connection they hold to be a sacrament, and yet they deny that in it the Holy Spirit is ever present.

37. And, that they might not delude the Church in this matter merely, what a long series of errors, lies, frauds, and iniquities have they appended to one error? So that you may say they sought nothing but a hiding-place for abominations when they converted marriage into a sacrament. When once they obtained this, they appropriated to themselves the cognisance of conjugal causes: as the thing was spiritual, it was not to be intermeddled with by profane judges. Then they enacted laws by which they

confirmed their tyranny,—laws partly impious toward God, partly fraught with injustice toward men; such as, that marriages contracted between minors, without the consent of their parents, should be valid; that no lawful marriages can be contracted between relations within the seventh degree, and that such marriages, if contracted, should be dissolved. Moreover, they frame degrees of kindred contrary to the laws of all nations, and even the polity of Moses, and enact that a husband who has repudiated an adulteress may not marry again—that spiritual kindred cannot be joined in marriage—that marriage cannot be celebrated from Septuagesimo to the Octaves of Easter, three weeks before the nativity of John, nor from Advent to Epiphany, and innumerable others, which it were too tedious to mention. We must now get out of their mire, in which our discourse has stuck longer than our inclination. Methinks, however, that much has been gained if I have, in some measure, deprived these asses of their lion's skin.

CHAPTER 20

OF CIVIL GOVERNMENT.

This chapter consists of two principal heads,—I. General discourse on the necessity, dignity, and use of Civil Government, in opposition to the frantic proceedings of the Anabaptists, sec. 1–3. II. A special exposition of the three leading parts of which Civil Government consists, sec. 4–32.

The first part treats of the function of Magistrates, whose authority and calling is proved, sec. 4–7. Next, the three Forms of civil government are added, sec. 8. Thirdly, Consideration of the office of the civil magistrate in respect of piety and righteousness. Here, of rewards and punishments—viz. punishing the guilty, protecting the innocent, repressing the seditious, managing the affairs of peace and war, sec. 9–13. The second part treats of Laws, their utility, necessity, form, authority, constitution, and scope, sec. 14–16. The last part relates to the People, and explains the use of laws, courts, and magistrates, to the common society of Christians, sec. 17–21. Deference which private individuals owe to magistrates, and how far obedience ought to be carried, sec. 22–32.

Sections:
1. Last part of the whole work, relating to the institution of Civil Government. The consideration of it necessary. 1. To refute the Anabaptists. 2. To refute the flatterers of princes. 3. To excite our gratitude to God. Civil government not opposed to Christian liberty. Civil government to be distinguished from the spiritual kingdom of Christ.

2. Objections of the Anabaptists. 1. That civil government is unworthy of a Christian man. 2. That it is diametrically repugnant to the Christian profession. Answer.

3. The answer confirmed. Discourse reduced to three heads, 1. Of Laws. 2. Of Magistrates. 3. Of the People.

4. The office of Magistrates approved by God. 1. They are called Gods. 2. They are ordained by the wisdom of God. Examples of pious Magistrates.

5. Civil government appointed by God for Jews, not Christians. This objection answered.

6. Divine appointment of Magistrates. Effect which this ought to have on Magistrates themselves.

7. This consideration should repress the fury of the Anabaptists.

8. Three forms of civil government, Monarchy, Aristocracy, Democracy. Impossible absolutely to say which is best.

9. Of the duty of Magistrates. Their first care the preservation of the Christian religion and true piety. This proved.

10. Objections of Anabaptists to this view. These answered.

11. Lawfulness of War.

12 Objection, that the lawfulness of war is not taught in Scripture. Answer.

13. Right of exacting tribute and raising revenues.

14. Of Laws, their necessity and utility. Distinction between the Moral, Ceremonial, and Judicial Law of Moses.

15. Sum and scope of the Moral Law. Of the Ceremonial and Judicial Law. Conclusion.

16. All Laws should be just. Civil Law of Moses; how far in force, and how far abrogated.

17. Of the People, and of the use of laws as respects individuals.

18. How far litigation lawful.

19. Refutation of the Anabaptists, who condemn all judicial proceedings.

20. Objection, that Christ forbids us to resist evil. Answer.

21. Objection, that Paul condemns law-suits absolutely. Answer.

22. Of the respect and obedience due to Magistrates.

23. Same subject continued.
24. How far submission due to tyrants.
25. Same continued.
26. Proof from Scripture.
27. Proof continued.
28. Objections answered.
29. Considerations to curb impatience under tyranny.
30. Considerations considered.
31. General submission due by private individuals.
32. Obedience due only in so far as compatible with the word of God.

1. Having shown above that there is a twofold government in man, and having fully considered the one which, placed in the soul or inward man, relates to eternal life, we are here called to say something of the other, which pertains only to civil institutions and the external regulation of manners. For although this subject seems from its nature to be unconnected with the spiritual doctrine of faith, which I have undertaken to treat, it will appear as we proceed, that I have properly connected them, nay, that I am under the necessity of doing so, especially while, on the one hand, frantic and barbarous men are furiously endeavouring to overturn the order established by God, and, on the other, the flatterers of princes, extolling their power without measure, hesitate not to oppose it to the government of God. Unless we meet both extremes, the purity of the faith will perish. We may add, that it in no small degree concerns us to know how kindly God has here consulted for the human race, that pious zeal may the more strongly urge us to testify our gratitude. And first, before entering on the subject itself, it is necessary to attend to the distinction which we formerly laid down (Book 3 Chap. 19 sec. 16, et supra, Chap. 10), lest, as often happens to many, we imprudently confound these two things, the nature of which is altogether different. For some, on hearing that liberty is promised in the gospel, a liberty which acknowledges no king and no magistrate among men, but looks to Christ alone, think that they can receive no benefit from their liberty so long as they see any power placed over them. Accordingly, they think that nothing will be safe until the whole world is changed into a new form, when there will be neither courts, nor laws, nor magistrates, nor anything of the kind to interfere, as they suppose, with their liberty. But he who knows to distinguish between the body and the soul, between the present fleeting life and that which is future and eternal, will have no difficulty in understanding that the spiritual kingdom of Christ and civil government are things very widely separated. Seeing, therefore, it is a Jewish vanity to seek and include the kingdom of Christ under the elements of this world, let us, considering, as Scripture clearly teaches, that the blessings which we derive from Christ are spiritual, remember to confine the liberty which is promised and offered to us in him within its proper limits. For why is it that the very same apostle who bids us "stand fast in the liberty wherewith Christ hath made us free, and be not again entangled with the yoke of bondage" (Gal. 5:1), in another passage forbids slaves to be solicitous about their state (1 Cor. 7:21), unless it be that spiritual liberty is perfectly compatible with civil servitude? In this sense the following passages are to be understood: "There is neither Jew nor Greek, there is neither bond nor free, there is neither male nor female" (Gal. 3:28). Again, "There is neither Greek nor Jew, circumcision nor uncircumcision, barbarian, Scythian, bond nor free: but Christ is all and in all" (Col. 3:11). It is thus intimated, that it matters not what your condition is among men, nor under what laws you live, since in them the kingdom of Christ does not at all consist.

2. Still the distinction does not go so far as to justify us in supposing that the whole scheme of civil government is matter of pollution, with which Christian men have nothing to do. Fanatics, indeed, delighting in unbridled license, insist and vociferate that, after we are dead by Christ to the elements of this world, and being translated into the kingdom of God sit among the celestials, it is unworthy of us, and far beneath our dignity, to be occupied with those profane and impure cares which relate to matters alien from a Christian man. To what end, they say, are laws without courts and tribunals? But what has a Christian man to do with courts? Nay, if it is unlawful to kill, what have we to do with laws and courts? But as we lately taught that that kind of government is distinct from the spiritual and internal kingdom of Christ, so we ought to know that they are not adverse to each other. The former, in some measure, begins the heavenly kingdom in us, even now upon earth, and in this mortal and evanescent life commences immortal and incorruptible blessedness, while to the latter it is assigned, so long as we live among men, to foster and maintain the external worship of God, to defend sound doctrine and the condition of the Church, to adapt our conduct to human society, to form our manners to civil justice, to conciliate us to each other, to cherish common peace and tranquillity. All these I confess to be superfluous, if the kingdom of God, as it now exists within us, extinguishes

the present life. But if it is the will of God that while we aspire to true piety we are pilgrims upon the earth, and if such pilgrimage stands in need of such aids, those who take them away from man rob him of his humanity. As to their allegation that there ought to be such perfection in the Church of God that her guidance should suffice for law, they stupidly imagine her to be such as she never can be found in the community of men. For while the insolence of the wicked is so great, and their iniquity so stubborn, that it can scarcely be curbed by any severity of laws, what do we expect would be done by those whom force can scarcely repress from doing ill, were they to see perfect impunity for their wickedness?

3. But we shall have a fitter opportunity of speaking of the use of civil government. All we wish to be understood at present is, that it is perfect barbarism to think of exterminating it, its use among men being not less than that of bread and water, light and air, while its dignity is much more excellent. Its object is not merely, like those things, to enable men to breathe, eat, drink, and be warmed (though it certainly includes all these, while it enables them to live together); this, I say, is not its only object, but it is, that no idolatry, no blasphemy against the name of God, no calumnies against his truth, nor other offences to religion, break out and be disseminated among the people; that the public quiet be not disturbed, that every man's property be kept secure, that men may carry on innocent commerce with each other, that honesty and modesty be cultivated; in short, that a public form of religion may exist among Christians, and humanity among men. Let no one be surprised that I now attribute the task of constituting religion aright to human polity, though I seem above to have placed it beyond the will of man, since I no more than formerly allow men at pleasure to enact laws concerning religion and the worship of God, when I approve of civil order which is directed to this end—viz. to prevent the true religion, which is contained in the law of God, from being with impunity openly violated and polluted by public blasphemy. But the reader, by the help of a perspicuous arrangement, will better understand what view is to be taken of the whole order of civil government, if we treat of each of its parts separately. Now these are three: The Magistrate, who is president and guardian of the laws; the Laws, according to which he governs; and the People, who are governed by the laws, and obey the magistrate. Let us consider, then, first, What is the function of the magistrate? Is it a lawful calling approved by God? What is the nature of his duty? What the extent of his power? Secondly, What are the laws by which Christian polity is to be regulated? And, lastly, What is the use of laws as regards the people? And, What obedience is due to the magistrate?

4. With regard to the function of magistrates, the Lord has not only declared that he approves and is pleased with it, but, moreover, has strongly recommended it to us by the very honourable titles which he has conferred upon it. To mention a, few. When those who bear the office of magistrate are called gods, let no one suppose that there is little weight in that appellation. It is thereby intimated that they have a commission from God, that they are invested with divine authority, and, in fact, represent the person of God, as whose substitutes they in a manner act. This is not a quibble of mine, but is the interpretation of Christ. "If Scripture," says he, "called them Gods, to whom the word of God came." What is this but that the business was committed to them by God, to serve him in their office, and (as Moses and Jehoshaphat said to the judges whom they were appointing over each of the cities of Judah) to exercise judgment, not for man, but for God? To the same effect Wisdom affirms, by the mouth of Solomon, "By me kings reign, and princes decree justice. By me princes rule, and nobles, even all the judges of the earth" (Prov. 8:15, 16). For it is just as if it had been said, that it is not owing to human perverseness that supreme power on earth is lodged in kings and other governors, but by Divine Providence, and the holy decree of Him to whom it has seemed good so to govern the affairs of men, since he is present, and also presides in enacting laws and exercising judicial equity. This Paul also plainly teaches when he enumerates offices of rule among the gifts of God, which, distributed variously, according to the measure of grace, ought to be employed by the servants of Christ for the edification of the Church (Rom. 12:8). In that place, however, he is properly speaking of the senate of grave men who were appointed in the primitive Church to take charge of public discipline. This office, in the Epistle to the Corinthians, he calls κυβερνήσεις, *governments* (1 Cor. 12:28). Still, as we see that civil power has the same end in view, there can be no doubt that he is recommending every kind of just government. He speaks much more clearly when he comes to a proper discussion of the subject. For he says that "there is no power but of God: the powers that be are ordained of God;" that rulers are the ministers of God, "not a terror to good works, but to the evil" (Rom. 13:1, 3). To this we may add the examples of saints, some of whom held the offices of kings, as David, Josiah, and Hezekiah; others of governors, as Joseph and Daniel; others of civil magistrates among a

free people, as Moses, Joshua, and the Judges. Their functions were expressly approved by the Lord. Wherefore no man can doubt that civil authority is, in the sight of God, not only sacred and lawful, but the most sacred, and by far the most honourable, of all stations in mortal life.

5. Those who are desirous to introduce anarchy object that, though anciently kings and judges presided over a rude people, yet that, in the present day, that servile mode of governing does not at all accord with the perfection which Christ brought with his gospel. Herein they betray not only their ignorance, but their devilish pride, arrogating to themselves a perfection of which not even a hundredth part is seen in them. But be they what they may, the refutation is easy. For when David says, "Be wise now therefore, O ye kings: be instructed, ye judges of the earth;" "Kiss the Son, lest he be angry" (Psalm 2:10, 12), he does not order them to lay aside their authority and return to private life, but to make the power with which they are invested subject to Christ, that he may rule over all. In like manner, when Isaiah predicts of the Church, "Kings shall be thy nursing-fathers, and their queens thy nursing-mothers" (Isaiah 49:23), he does not bid them abdicate their authority; he rather gives them the honourable appellation of patrons of the pious worshippers of God; for the prophecy refers to the advent of Christ. I intentionally omit very many passages which occur throughout Scripture, and especially in the Psalms, in which the due authority of all rulers is asserted. The most celebrated passage of all is that in which Paul, admonishing Timothy, that prayers are to be offered up in the public assembly for kings, subjoins the reason, "that we may lead a quiet and peaceable life in all godliness and honesty" (1 Tim. 2:2). In these words, he recommends the condition of the Church to their protection and guardianship.

6. This consideration ought to be constantly present to the minds of magistrates, since it is fitted to furnish a strong stimulus to the discharge of duty, and also afford singular consolation, smoothing the difficulties of their office, which are certainly numerous and weighty. What zeal for integrity, prudence, meekness, continence, and innocence, ought to sway those who know that they have been appointed ministers of the divine justice! How will they dare to admit iniquity to their tribunal, when they are told that it is the throne of the living God? How will they venture to pronounce an unjust sentence with that mouth which they understand to be an ordained organ of divine truth? With what conscience will they subscribe impious decrees with that hand which they know has been appointed to write the acts of God? In a word, if they remember that they are the vicegerents of God, it behoves them to watch with all care, diligence, and industry, that they may in themselves exhibit a kind of image of the Divine Providence, guardianship, goodness, benevolence, and justice. And let them constantly keep the additional thought in view, that if a curse is pronounced on him that "doeth the work of the Lord deceitfully," a much heavier curse must lie on him who deals deceitfully in a righteous calling. Therefore, when Moses and Jehoshaphat would urge their judges to the discharge of duty, they had nothing by which they could more powerfully stimulate their minds than the consideration to which we have already referred,— "Take heed what ye do: for ye judge not for man, but for the Lord, who is with you in the judgment. Wherefore now let the fear of the Lord be upon you; take heed and do it: for there is no iniquity with the Lord our God, nor respect of persons, nor taking of gifts" (2 Chron. 19:6, 7, compared with Deut. 1:16, &c.). And in another passage it is said, "God standeth in the congregation of the mighty; he judgeth among the gods" (Psalm 82:1; Isaiah 3:14), that they may be animated to duty when they hear that they are the ambassadors of God, to whom they must one day render an account of the province committed to them. This admonition ought justly to have the greatest effect upon them; for if they sin in any respect, not only is injury done to the men whom they wickedly torment, but they also insult God himself, whose sacred tribunals they pollute. On the other hand, they have an admirable source of comfort when they reflect that they are not engaged in profane occupations, unbefitting a servant of God, but in a most sacred office, inasmuch as they are the ambassadors of God.

7. In regard to those who are not debarred by all these passages of Scripture from presuming to inveigh against this sacred ministry, as if it were a thing abhorrent from religion and Christian piety, what else do they than assail God himself, who cannot but be insulted when his servants are disgraced? These men not only speak evil of dignities, but would not even have God to reign over them (1 Sam. 7:7). For if this was truly said of the people of Israel, when they declined the authority of Samuel, how can it be less truly said in the present day of those who allow themselves to break loose against all the authority established by God? But it seems that when our Lord said to his disciples, "The kings of the gentiles exercise lordship over them; and they that exercise authority upon

them are called benefactors. But ye shall not be so: but he that is greatest among you, let him be as the younger; and he that is chief; as he that doth serve" (Luke 22:25, 26); he by these words prohibited all Christians from becoming kings or governors. Dexterous expounders! A dispute had arisen among the disciples as to which of them should be greatest. To suppress this vain ambition, our Lord taught them that their ministry was not like the power of earthly sovereigns, among whom one greatly surpasses another. What, I ask, is there in this comparison disparaging to royal dignity? nay, what does it prove at all unless that the royal office is not the apostolic ministry? Besides, though among magisterial offices themselves there are different forms, there is no difference in this respect, that they are all to be received by us as ordinances of God. For Paul includes all together when he says that "there is no power but of God," and that which was by no means the most pleasing of all, was honoured with the highest testimonial—I mean the power of one. This, as carrying with it the public servitude of all (except the one to whose despotic will all is subject), was anciently disrelished by heroic and more excellent natures. But Scripture, to obviate these unjust judgments, affirms expressly that it is by divine wisdom that "kings reign," and gives special command "to honour the king" (1 Peter 2:17).

8. And certainly it were a very idle occupation for private men to discuss what would be the best form of polity in the place where they live, seeing these deliberations cannot have any influence in determining any public matter. Then the thing itself could not be defined absolutely without rashness, since the nature of the discussion depends on circumstances. And if you compare the different states with each other, without regard to circumstances, it is not easy to determine which of these has the advantage in point of utility, so equal are the terms on which they meet. Monarchy is prone to tyranny. In an aristocracy, again, the tendency is not less to the faction of a few, while in popular ascendancy there is the strongest tendency to sedition. When these three forms of government, of which philosophers treat, are considered in themselves, I, for my part, am far from denying that the form which greatly surpasses the others is aristocracy, either pure or modified by popular government, not indeed in itself, but because it very rarely happens that kings so rule themselves as never to dissent from what is just and right, or are possessed of so much acuteness and prudence as always to see correctly. Owing, therefore, to the vices or defects of men, it is safer and more tolerable when several bear rule, that they may thus mutually assist, instruct, and admonish each other, and should any one be disposed to go too far, the others are censors and masters to curb his excess. This has already been proved by experience, and confirmed also by the authority of the Lord himself, when he established an aristocracy bordering on popular government among the Israelites, keeping them under that as the best form, until he exhibited an image of the Messiah in David. And as I willingly admit that there is no kind of government happier than where liberty is framed with becoming moderation, and duly constituted so as to be durable, so I deem those very happy who are permitted to enjoy that form, and I admit that they do nothing at variance with their duty when they strenuously and constantly labour to preserve and maintain it. Nay, even magistrates ought to do their utmost to prevent the liberty, of which they have been appointed guardians, from being impaired, far less violated. If in this they are sluggish or little careful, they are perfidious traitors to their office and their country. But should those to whom the Lord has assigned one form of government, take it upon them anxiously to long for a change, the wish would not only be foolish and superfluous, but very pernicious. If you fix your eyes not on one state merely, but look around the world, or at least direct your view to regions widely separated from each other, you will perceive that Divine Providence has not, without good cause, arranged that different countries should be governed by different forms of polity. For as only elements of unequal temperature adhere together, so in different regions a similar inequality in the form of government is best. All this, however, is said unnecessarily to those to whom the will of God is a sufficient reason. For if it has pleased him to appoint kings over kingdoms, and senates or burgomasters over free states, whatever be the form which he has appointed in the places in which we live, our duty is to obey and submit.

9. The duty of magistrates, its nature, as described by the word of God, and the things in which it consists, I will here indicate in passing. That it extends to both tables of the law, did Scripture not teach, we might learn from profane writers; for no man has discoursed of the duty of magistrates, the enacting of laws, and the common weal, without beginning with religion and divine worship. Thus all have confessed that no polity can be successfully established unless piety be its first care, and that those laws are absurd which disregard the rights of God, and consult only for men. Seeing then that among philosophers religion holds the first place, and that the same thing has always been observed with the universal

consent of nations, Christian princes and magistrates may be ashamed of their heartlessness if they make it not their care. We have already shown that this office is specially assigned them by God, and indeed it is right that they exert themselves in asserting and defending the honour of him whose vicegerents they are, and by whose favour they rule. Hence in Scripture holy kings are especially praised for restoring the worship of God when corrupted or overthrown, or for taking care that religion flourished under them in purity and safety. On the other hand, the sacred history sets down anarchy among the vices, when it states that there was no king in Israel, and, therefore, every one did as he pleased (Judges 21:25). This rebukes the folly of those who would neglect the care of divine things, and devote themselves merely to the administration of justice among men; as if God had appointed rulers in his own name to decide earthly controversies, and omitted what was of far greater moment, his own pure worship as prescribed by his law. Such views are adopted by turbulent men, who, in their eagerness to make all kinds of innovations with impunity, would fain get rid of all the vindicators of violated piety. In regard to the second table of the law, Jeremiah addresses rulers, "Thus saith the Lord, Execute ye judgment and righteousness, and deliver the spoiled out of the hand of the oppressor: and do no wrong, do no violence to the stranger, the fatherless, nor the widow, neither shed innocent blood" (Jer. 22:3). To the same effect is the exhortation in the Psalm, "Defend the poor and fatherless; do justice to the afflicted and needy. Deliver the poor and needy; rid them out of the hand of the wicked" (Psalm 82:3, 4). Moses also declared to the princes whom he had substituted for himself, "Hear the causes between your brethren, and judge righteously between every man and his brother, and the stranger that is with him. Ye shall not respect persons in judgment; but ye shall hear the small as well as the great: ye shall not be afraid of the face of man, for the judgment is God's" (Deut. 1:16). I say nothing as to such passages as these, "He shall not multiply horses to himself, nor cause the people to return to Egypt;" "neither shall he multiply wives to himself; neither shall he greatly multiply to himself silver and gold;" "he shall write him a copy of this law in a book;" "and it shall be with him, and he shall read therein all the days of his life, that he may learn to fear the Lord his God;" "that his heart be not lifted up above his brethren" (Deut. 17:16–20). In here explaining the duties of magistrates, my exposition is intended not so much for the instruction of magistrates themselves, as to teach others why there are magistrates, and to what end they have been appointed by God. We say, therefore, that they are the ordained guardians and vindicators of public innocence, modesty, honour, and tranquillity, so that it should be their only study to provide for the common peace and safety. Of these things David declares that he will set an example when he shall have ascended the throne. "A froward heart shall depart from me: I will not know a wicked person. Whoso privily slandereth his neighbour, him will I cut off: him that hath an high look and a proud heart will not I suffer. Mine eyes shall be upon the faithful of the land, that they may dwell with me: he that walketh in a perfect way, he shall serve me" (Psalm 101:4–6). But as rulers cannot do this unless they protect the good against the injuries of the bad, and give aid and protection to the oppressed, they are armed with power to curb manifest evil-doers and criminals, by whose misconduct the public tranquillity is disturbed or harassed. For we have full experience of the truth of Solon's saying, that all public matters depend on reward and punishment; that where these are wanting, the whole discipline of states totters and falls to pieces. For in the minds of many the love of equity and justice grows cold, if due honour be not paid to virtue, and the licentiousness of the wicked cannot be restrained, without strict discipline and the infliction of punishment. The two things are comprehended by the prophet when he enjoins kings and other rulers to execute "judgment and righteousness" (Jer. 21:12; 22:3). It is righteousness (justice) to take charge of the innocent, to defend and avenge them, and set them free: it is judgment to withstand the audacity of the wicked, to repress their violence, and punish their faults.

10. But here a difficult, and, as it seems, a perplexing question arises. If all Christians are forbidden to kill, and the prophet predicts concerning the holy mountain of the Lord, that is, the Church, "They shall not hurt or destroy," how can magistrates be at once pious and yet shedders of blood? But if we understand that the magistrate, in inflicting punishment, acts not of himself, but executes the very judgments of God, we shall be disencumbered of every doubt. The law of the Lord forbids to kill; but, that murder may not go unpunished, the Lawgiver himself puts the sword into the hands of his ministers, that they may employ it against all murderers. It belongs not to the pious to afflict and hurt; but to avenge the afflictions of the pious, at the command of God, is neither to afflict nor hurt. I wish it could always be present to our mind, that nothing is done here by the rashness of man, but all in obedience to the authority

of God. When it is the guide, we never stray from the right path, unless, indeed, divine justice is to be placed under restraint, and not allowed to take punishment on crimes. But if we dare not give the law to it, why should we bring a charge against its ministers? "He beareth not the sword in vain," says Paul, "for he is the minister of God, a revenger to execute wrath on him that doeth evil" (Rom. 13:4). Wherefore, if princes and other rulers know that nothing will be more acceptable to God than their obedience, let them give themselves to this service if they are desirous to improve their piety, justice, and integrity to God. This was the feeling of Moses when, recognising himself as destined to deliver his people by the power of the Lord, he laid violent hands on the Egyptian, and afterwards took vengeance on the people for sacrilege, by slaying three thousand of them in one day. This was the feeling of David also, when, towards the end of his life, he ordered his son Solomon to put Joab and Shimei to death. Hence, also, in an enumeration of the virtues of a king, one is to cut off the wicked from the earth, and banish all workers of iniquity from the city of God. To the same effect is the praise which is bestowed on Solomon, "Thou lovest righteousness, and hatest wickedness." How is it that the meek and gentle temper of Moses becomes so exasperated, that, besmeared and reeking with the blood of his brethren, he runs through the camp making new slaughter? How is it that David, who, during his whole life, showed so much mildness, almost at his last breath, leaves with his son the bloody testament, not to allow the grey hairs of Joab and Shimei to go to the grave in peace? Both, by their sternness, sanctified the hands which they would have polluted by showing mercy, inasmuch as they executed the vengeance committed to them by God. Solomon says, "It is an abomination to kings to commit wickedness; for the throne is established by righteousness." Again, "A king that sitteth in the throne of judgment, scattereth away all evil with his eyes." Again, "A wise king scattereth the wicked, and bringeth the wheel over them." Again, "Take away the dross from the silver, and there shall come forth a vessel for the finer. Take away the wicked men from before the king, and his throne shall be established in righteousness." Again, "He that justifieth the wicked, and he that condemneth the just, even they both are an abomination to the Lord." Again, "An evil man seeketh only rebellion, therefore an evil messenger shall be sent against him." Again, "He that saith unto the wicked, Thou art righteous; him shall the people curse, nations shall abhor him." Now, if it is true justice in them to pursue the guilty and impious with drawn sword, to sheath the sword, and keep their hands pure from blood, while nefarious men wade through murder and slaughter, so far from redounding to the praise of their goodness and justice, would be to incur the guilt of the greatest impiety; provided always they eschew reckless and cruel asperity, and that tribunal which may be justly termed a rock on which the accused must founder. For I am not one of those who would either favour an unseasonable severity, or think that any tribunal could be accounted just that is not presided over by mercy, that best and surest counsellor of kings, and, as Solomon declares, "upholder of the throne" (Prov. 20:28). This, as was truly said by one of old, should be the primary endowment of princes. The magistrate must guard against both extremes; he must neither, by excessive severity, rather wound than cure, nor by a superstitious affectation of clemency, fall into the most cruel inhumanity, by giving way to soft and dissolute indulgence to the destruction of many. It was well said by one under the empire of Nerva, It is indeed a bad thing to live under a prince with whom nothing is lawful, but a much worse to live under one with whom all things are lawful.

11. As it is sometimes necessary for kings and states to take up arms in order to execute public vengeance, the reason assigned furnishes us with the means of estimating how far the wars which are thus undertaken are lawful. For if power has been given them to maintain the tranquillity of their subjects, repress the seditious movements of the turbulent, assist those who are violently oppressed, and animadvert on crimes, can they use it more opportunely than in repressing the fury of him who disturbs both the ease of individuals and the common tranquillity of all; who excites seditious tumult, and perpetrates acts of violent oppression and gross wrongs? If it becomes them to be the guardians and maintainers of the laws, they must repress the attempts of all alike by whose criminal conduct the discipline of the laws is impaired. Nay, if they justly punish those robbers whose injuries have been afflicted only on a few, will they allow the whole country to be robbed and devastated with impunity? Since it makes no difference whether it is by a king or by the lowest of the people that a hostile and devastating inroad is made into a district over which they have no authority, all alike are to be regarded and punished as robbers. Natural equity and duty, therefore, demand that princes be armed not only to repress private crimes by judicial inflictions, but to defend the subjects committed to their guardianship whenever they are hostilely assailed.

Such even the Holy Spirit, in many passages of Scripture, declares to be lawful.

12. But if it is objected, that in the New Testament there is no passage or example teaching that war is lawful for Christians, I answer, first, that the reason for carrying on war, which anciently existed, still exists in the present day, and that, on the other hand, there is no ground for debarring magistrates from the defence of those under them; and, secondly, that in the Apostolical writings we are not to look for a distinct exposition of those matters, their object being not to form a civil polity, but to establish the spiritual kingdom of Christ; lastly, that there also it is indicated, in passing, that our Saviour, by his advent, made no change in this respect. For (to use the words of Augustine) "if Christian discipline condemned all wars, when the soldiers ask counsel as to the way of salvation, they would have been told to cast away their arms, and withdraw altogether from military service. Whereas it was said (Luke 3:14), Concuss no one, do injury to no one, be contented with your pay. Those whom he orders to be contented with their pay he certainly does not forbid to serve" (August. Ep. 5 ad Marcell.) But all magistrates must here be particularly cautious not to give way, in the slightest degree, to their passions. Or rather, whether punishments are to be inflicted, they must not be borne headlong by anger, nor hurried away by hatred, nor burn with implacable severity; they must, as Augustine says (De Civit. Dei. Lib. 5 cap. 24), "even pity a common nature in him in whom they punish an individual fault;" or whether they have to take up arms against an enemy, that is, an armed robber, they must not readily catch at the opportunity, nay, they must not take it when offered, unless compelled by the strongest necessity. For if we are to do far more than that heathen demanded, who wished war to appear as desired peace, assuredly all other means must be tried before having recourse to arms. In fine, in both cases, they must not allow themselves to be carried away by any private feeling, but be guided solely by regard for the public. Acting otherwise, they wickedly abuse their power which was given them, not for their own advantage, but for the good and service of others. On this right of war depends the right of garrisons, leagues, and other civil munitions. By garrisons, I mean those which are stationed in states for defence of the frontiers; by leagues, the alliances which are made by neighbouring princes, on the ground that if any disturbance arise within their territories, they will mutually assist each other, and combine their forces to repel the common enemies of the human race; under civil munitions, I include everything pertaining to the military art.

13. Lastly, we think it proper to add, that taxes and imposts are the legitimate revenues of princes, which they are chiefly to employ in sustaining the public burdens of their office. These, however, they may use for the maintenance of their domestic state, which is in a manner combined with the dignity of the authority which they exercise. Thus we see that David, Hezekiah, Josiah, Jehoshaphat, and other holy kings, Joseph also, and Daniel, in proportion to the office which they sustained, without offending piety, expended liberally of the public funds; and we read in Ezekiel, that a very large extent of territory was assigned to kings (Ezek. 48:21). In that passage, indeed, he is depicting the spiritual kingdom of Christ, but still he borrows his representation from lawful dominion among men. Princes, however, must remember, in their turn, that their revenues are not so much private chests as treasuries of the whole people (this Paul testifies, Rom. 13:6), which they cannot, without manifest injustice, squander or dilapidate; or rather, that they are almost the blood of the people, which it were the harshest inhumanity not to spare. They should also consider that their levies and contributions, and other kinds of taxes, are merely subsidies of the public necessity, and that it is tyrannical rapacity to harass the poor people with them without cause. These things do not stimulate princes to profusion and luxurious expenditure (there is certainly no need to inflame the passions, when they are already, of their own accord, inflamed more than enough), but seeing it is of the greatest consequence that, whatever they venture to do, they should do with a pure conscience, it is necessary to teach them how far they can lawfully go, lest, by impious confidence, they incur the divine displeasure. Nor is this doctrine superfluous to private individuals, that they may not rashly and petulantly stigmatise the expenditure of princes, though it should exceed the ordinary limits.

14. In states, the thing next in importance to the magistrates is laws, the strongest sinews of government, or, as Cicero calls them after Plato, the soul, without which, the office of the magistrate cannot exist; just as, on the other hand, laws have no vigour without the magistrate. Hence nothing could be said more truly than that the law is a dumb magistrate, the magistrate a living law. As I have undertaken to describe the laws by which Christian polity is to be governed, there is no reason to expect from me a long discussion on the best kind of laws. The subject is of vast extent, and belongs not to this place. I will only briefly observe, in passing, what the laws are which may

be piously used with reference to God, and duly administered among men. This I would rather have passed in silence, were I not aware that many dangerous errors are here committed. For there are some who deny that any commonwealth is rightly framed which neglects the law of Moses, and is ruled by the common law of nations. How perilous and seditious these views are, let others see: for me it is enough to demonstrate that they are stupid and false. We must attend to the well known division which distributes the whole law of God, as promulgated by Moses, into the moral, the ceremonial, and the judicial law, and we must attend to each of these parts, in order to understand how far they do, or do not, pertain to us. Meanwhile, let no one be moved by the thought that the judicial and ceremonial laws relate to morals. For the ancients who adopted this division, though they were not unaware that the two latter classes had to do with morals, did not give them the name of moral, because they might be changed and abrogated without affecting morals. They give this name specially to the first class, without which, true holiness of life and an immutable rule of conduct cannot exist.

15. The moral law, then (to begin with it), being contained under two heads, the one of which simply enjoins us to worship God with pure faith and piety, the other to embrace men with sincere affection, is the true and eternal rule of righteousness prescribed to the men of all nations and of all times, who would frame their life agreeably to the will of God. For his eternal and immutable will is, that we are all to worship him and mutually love one another. The ceremonial law of the Jews was a tutelage by which the Lord was pleased to exercise, as it were, the childhood of that people, until the fulness of the time should come when he was fully to manifest his wisdom to the world, and exhibit the reality of those things which were then adumbrated by figures (Gal. 3:24; 4:4). The judicial law, given them as a kind of polity, delivered certain forms of equity and justice, by which they might live together innocently and quietly. And as that exercise in ceremonies properly pertained to the doctrine of piety, inasmuch as it kept the Jewish Church in the worship and religion of God, yet was still distinguishable from piety itself, so the judicial form, though it looked only to the best method of preserving that charity which is enjoined by the eternal law of God, was still something distinct from the precept of love itself. Therefore, as ceremonies might be abrogated without at all interfering with piety, so, also, when these judicial arrangements are removed, the duties and precepts of charity can still remain perpetual. But if it is true that each nation has been left at liberty to enact the laws which it judges to be beneficial, still these are always to be tested by the rule of charity, so that while they vary in form, they must proceed on the same principle. Those barbarous and savage laws, for instance, which conferred honour on thieves, allowed the promiscuous intercourse of the sexes, and other things even fouler and more absurd, I do not think entitled to be considered as laws, since they are not only altogether abhorrent to justice, but to humanity and civilised life.

16. What I have said will become plain if we attend, as we ought, to two things connected with all laws—viz. the enactment of the law, and the equity on which the enactment is founded and rests. Equity, as it is natural, cannot be the same in all, and therefore ought to be proposed by all laws, according to the nature of the thing enacted. As constitutions have some circumstances on which they partly depend, there is nothing to prevent their diversity, provided they all alike aim at equity as their end. Now, as it is evident that the law of God which we call moral, is nothing else than the testimony of natural law, and of that conscience which God has engraven on the minds of men, the whole of this equity of which we now speak is prescribed in it. Hence it alone ought to be the aim, the rule, and the end of all laws. Wherever laws are formed after this rule, directed to this aim, and restricted to this end, there is no reason why they should be disapproved by us, however much they may differ from the Jewish law, or from each other (August. de Civit. Dei, Lib. 19 c. 17). The law of God forbids to steal. The punishment appointed for theft in the civil polity of the Jews may be seen in Exodus 22. Very ancient laws of other nations punished theft by exacting the double of what was stolen, while subsequent laws made a distinction between theft manifest and not manifest. Other laws went the length of punishing with exile, or with branding, while others made the punishment capital. Among the Jews, the punishment of the false witness was to "do unto him as he had thought to have done with his brother" (Deut. 19:19). In some countries, the punishment is infamy, in others hanging, in others crucifixion. All laws alike avenge murder with blood, but the kinds of death are different. In some countries, adultery was punished more severely, in others more leniently. Yet we see that amidst this diversity they all tend to the same end. For they all with one mouth declare against those crimes which are condemned by the eternal law of God—viz. murder, theft, adultery, and false witness; though they agree not as to the mode of punishment. This is not necessary, nor even expedient.

There may be a country which, if murder were not visited with fearful punishments, would instantly become a prey to robbery and slaughter. There may be an age requiring that the severity of punishments should be increased. If the state is in troubled condition, those things from which disturbances usually arise must be corrected by new edicts. In time of war, civilisation would disappear amid the noise of arms, were not men overawed by an unwonted severity of punishment. In sterility, in pestilence, were not stricter discipline employed, all things would grow worse. One nation might be more prone to a particular vice, were it not most severely repressed. How malignant were it, and invidious of the public good, to be offended at this diversity, which is admirably adapted to retain the observance of the divine law. The allegation, that insult is offered to the law of God enacted by Moses, where it is abrogated, and other new laws are preferred to it, is most absurd. Others are not preferred when they are more approved, not absolutely, but from regard to time and place, and the condition of the people, or when those things are abrogated which were never enacted for us. The Lord did not deliver it by the hand of Moses to be promulgated in all countries, and to be everywhere enforced; but having taken the Jewish nation under his special care, patronage, and guardianship, he was pleased to be specially its legislator, and as became a wise legislator, he had special regard to it in enacting laws.

17. It now remains to see, as was proposed in the last place, what use the common society of Christians derive from laws, judicial proceedings, and magistrates. With this is connected another question —viz. What difference ought private individuals to pay to magistrates, and how far ought obedience to proceed? To very many it seems that among Christians the office of magistrate is superfluous, because they cannot piously implore his aid, inasmuch as they are forbidden to take revenge, cite before a judge, or go to law. But when Paul, on the contrary, clearly declares that he is the minister of God to us for good (Rom. 13:4), we thereby understand that he was so ordained of God, that, being defended by his hand and aid against the dishonesty and injustice of wicked men, we may live quiet and secure. But if he would have been appointed over us in vain, unless we were to use his aid, it is plain that it cannot be wrong to appeal to it and implore it. Here, indeed, I have to do with two classes of men. For there are very many who boil with such a rage for litigation, that they never can be quiet with themselves unless they are fighting with others. Law-suits they prosecute with the bitterness of deadly hatred, and with an insane eagerness to hurt and revenge, and they persist in them with implacable obstinacy, even to the ruin of their adversary. Meanwhile, that they may be thought to do nothing but what is legal, they use this pretext of judicial proceedings as a defence of their perverse conduct. But if it is lawful for brother to litigate with brother, it does not follow that it is lawful to hate him, and obstinately pursue him with a furious desire to do him harm.

18. Let such persons then understand that judicial proceedings are lawful to him who makes a right use of them; and the right use, both for the pursuer and for the defender, is for the latter to sist himself on the day appointed, and, without bitterness, urge what he can in his defence, but only with the desire of justly maintaining his right; and for the pursuer, when undeservedly attacked in his life or fortunes, to throw himself upon the protection of the magistrate, state his complaint, and demand what is just and good; while, far from any wish to hurt or take vengeance—far from bitterness or hatred —far from the ardour of strife, he is rather disposed to yield and suffer somewhat than to cherish hostile feelings towards his opponent. On the contrary, when minds are filled with malevolence, corrupted by envy, burning with anger, breathing revenge, or, in fine, so inflamed by the heat of the contest, that they, in some measure, lay aside charity, the whole pleading, even of the justest cause, cannot but be impious. For it ought to be an axiom among all Christians, that no plea, however equitable, can be rightly conducted by any one who does not feel as kindly towards his opponent as if the matter in dispute were amicably transacted and arranged. Some one, perhaps, may here break in and say, that such moderation in judicial proceedings is so far from being seen, that an instance of it would be a kind of prodigy. I confess that in these times it is rare to meet with an example of an honest litigant; but the thing itself, untainted by the accession of evil, ceases not to be good and pure. When we hear that the assistance of the magistrate is a sacred gift from God, we ought the more carefully to beware of polluting it by our fault.

19. Let those who distinctly condemn all judicial distinction know, that they repudiate the holy ordinance of God, and one of those gifts which to the pure are pure, unless, indeed, they would charge Paul with a crime, because he repelled the calumnies of his accusers, exposing their craft and wickedness, and, at the tribunal, claimed for himself the privilege of a Roman citizen, appealing, when necessary, from the governor to Cæsar's judgment-seat. There is nothing contrary to this in the

prohibition, which binds all Christians to refrain from revenge, a feeling which we drive far away from all Christian tribunals. For whether the action be of a civil nature, he only takes the right course who, with innocuous simplicity, commits his cause to the judge as the public protector, without any thought of returning evil for evil (which is the feeling of revenge); or whether the action is of a graver nature, directed against a capital offence, the accuser required is not one who comes into court, carried away by some feeling of revenge or resentment from some private injury, but one whose only object is to prevent the attempts of some bad men to injure the commonweal. But if you take away the vindictive mind, you offend in no respect against that command which forbids Christians to indulge revenge. But they are not only forbidden to thirst for revenge, they are also enjoined to wait for the hand of the Lord, who promises that he will be the avenger of the oppressed and afflicted. But those who call upon the magistrate to give assistance to themselves or others, anticipate the vengeance of the heavenly Judge. By no means, for we are to consider that the vengeance of the magistrate is the vengeance not of man, but of God, which, as Paul says, he exercises by the ministry of man for our good (Rom. 13:8).

20. No more are we at variance with the words of Christ, who forbids us to resist evil, and adds, "Whosoever shall smite thee on thy right cheek, turn to him the other also. And if any man will sue thee at the law, and take away thy coat, let him have thy cloak also" (Mt. 5:39, 40). He would have the minds of his followers to be so abhorrent to everything like retaliation, that they would sooner allow the injury to be doubled than desire to repay it. From this patience we do not dissuade them. For verily Christians were to be a class of men born to endure affronts and injuries, and be exposed to the iniquity, imposture, and derision of abandoned men, and not only so, but were to be tolerant of all these evils; that is, so composed in the whole frame of their minds, that, on receiving one offence, they were to prepare themselves for another, promising themselves nothing during the whole of life but the endurance of a perpetual cross. Meanwhile, they must do good to those who injure them, and pray for those who curse them, and (this is their only victory) strive to overcome evil with good (Rom. 12:20, 21). Thus affected, they will not seek eye for eye, and tooth for tooth (as the Pharisees taught their disciples to long for vengeance), but (as we are instructed by Christ), they will allow their body to be mutilated, and their goods to be maliciously taken from them, prepared to remit and spontaneously pardon those injuries the moment they have been inflicted. This equity and moderation, however, will not prevent them, with entire friendship for their enemies, from using the aid of the magistrate for the preservation of their goods, or, from zeal for the public interest, to call for the punishment of the wicked and pestilential man, whom they know nothing will reform but death. All these precepts are truly expounded by Augustine, as tending to prepare the just and pious man patiently to sustain the malice of those whom he desires to become good, that he may thus increase the number of the good, not add himself to the number of the bad by imitating their wickedness. Moreover, it pertains more to the preparation of the heart which is within, than to the work which is done openly, that patience and good-will may be retained within the secret of the heart, and that may be done openly which we see may do good to those to whom we ought to wish well (August. Ep. 5 ad. Marcell.).

21. The usual objection, that law-suits are universally condemned by Paul (1 Cor. 6:6), is false. It may easily be understood from his words, that a rage for litigation prevailed in the Church of Corinth to such a degree, that they exposed the gospel of Christ, and the whole religion which they professed, to the calumnies and cavils of the ungodly. Paul rebukes them, first for traducing the gospel to unbelievers by the intemperance of their dissensions; and, secondly, for so striving with each other while they were brethren. For so far were they from bearing injury from another, that they greedily coveted each other's effects, and voluntarily provoked and injured them. He inveighs, therefore, against that madness for litigation, and not absolutely against all kinds of disputes. He declares it to be altogether a vice or infirmity, that they do not submit to the loss of their effects, rather than strive, even to contention, in preserving them; in other words, seeing they were so easily moved by every kind of loss, and on every occasion, however slight, ran off to the forum and to law-suits, he says, that in this way they showed that they were of too irritable a temper, and not prepared for patience. Christians should always feel disposed rather to give up part of their right than to go into court, out of which they can scarcely come without a troubled mind, a mind inflamed with hatred of their brother. But when one sees that his property, the want of which he would grievously feel, he is able, without any loss of charity, to defend, if he should do so, he offends in no respect against that passage of Paul. In short, as we said at first, every man's best adviser is charity. Everything in which we engage without charity, and all the disputes

which carry us beyond it, are unquestionably unjust and impious.

22. The first duty of subjects towards their rulers, is to entertain the most honourable views of their office, recognising it as a delegated jurisdiction from God, and on that account receiving and reverencing them as the ministers and ambassadors of God. For you will find some who show themselves very obedient to magistrates, and would be unwilling that there should be no magistrates to obey, because they know this is expedient for the public good, and yet the opinion which those persons have of magistrates is, that they are a kind of necessary evils. But Peter requires something more of us when he says, "Honour the king" (1 Pet. 2:17); and Solomon, when he says, "My son, fear thou the Lord and the king" (Prov. 24:21). For, under the term honour, the former includes a sincere and candid esteem, and the latter, by joining the king with God, shows that he is invested with a kind of sacred veneration and dignity. We have also the remarkable injunction of Paul, "Be subject not only for wrath, but also for conscience sake" (Rom. 13:5). By this he means, that subjects, in submitting to princes and governors, are not to be influenced merely by fear (just as those submit to an armed enemy who see vengeance ready to be executed if they resist), but because the obedience which they yield is rendered to God himself, inasmuch as their power is from God. I speak not of the men as if the mask of dignity could cloak folly, or cowardice, or cruelty, or wicked or flagitious manners, and thus acquire for vice the praise of virtue; but I say that the station itself is deserving of honour and reverence, and that those who rule should, in respect of their office, be held by us in esteem and veneration.

23. From this, a second consequence is, that we must with ready minds prove our obedience to them, whether in complying with edicts, or in paying tribute, or in undertaking public offices and burdens, which relate to the common defence, or in executing any other orders. "Let every soul," says Paul, "be subject unto the higher powers." "Whosoever, therefore, resisteth the power, resisteth the ordinance of God" (Rom. 13:1, 2). Writing to Titus, he says, "Put them in mind to be subject to principalities and powers, to obey magistrates, to be ready to every good work" (Tit. 3:1). Peter also says, "Submit yourselves to every human creature" (or rather, as I understand it, "ordinance of man"), "for the Lord's sake: whether it be to the king, as supreme; or unto governors, as unto them that are sent by him for the punishment of evil-doers, and for the praise of them that do well" (1 Pet. 2:13). Moreover, to testify that they do not feign subjection, but are sincerely and cordially subject, Paul adds, that they are to commend the safety and prosperity of those under whom they live to God. "I exhort, therefore," says he, "that, first of all, supplications, prayers, intercessions, and giving of thanks, be made for all men; for kings, and for all that are in authority: that we may lead a quiet and peaceable life in all godliness and honesty" (1 Tim. 2:1, 2). Let no man here deceive himself, since we cannot resist the magistrate without resisting God. For, although an unarmed magistrate may seem to be despised with impunity, yet God is armed, and will signally avenge this contempt. Under this obedience, I comprehend the restraint which private men ought to impose on themselves in public, not interfering with public business, or rashly encroaching on the province of the magistrate, or attempting anything at all of a public nature. If it is proper that anything in a public ordinance should be corrected, let them not act tumultuously, or put their hands to a work where they ought to feel that their hands are tied, but let them leave it to the cognisance of the magistrate, whose hand alone here is free. My meaning is, let them not dare to do it without being ordered. For when the command of the magistrate is given, they too are invested with public authority. For as, according to the common saying, the eyes and ears of the prince are his counsellors, so one may not improperly say that those who, by his command, have the charge of managing affairs, are his hands.

24. But as we have hitherto described the magistrate who truly is what he is called—viz. the father of his country, and (as the Poet speaks) the pastor of the people, the guardian of peace, the president of justice, the vindicator of innocence, he is justly to be deemed a madman who disapproves of such authority. And since in almost all ages we see that some princes, careless about all their duties on which they ought to have been intent, live, without solicitude, in luxurious sloth; others, bent on their own interest, venally prostitute all rights, privileges, judgments, and enactments; others pillage poor people of their money, and afterwards squander it in insane largesses; others act as mere robbers, pillaging houses, violating matrons, and slaying the innocent; many cannot be persuaded to recognise such persons for princes, whose command, as far as lawful, they are bound to obey. For while in this unworthy conduct, and among atrocities so alien, not only from the duty of the magistrate, but also of the man, they behold no appearance of the image of God, which ought to be conspicuous in the magistrate, while they see not a vestige of that minister of God, who

was appointed to be a praise to the good and a terror to the bad, they cannot recognise the ruler whose dignity and authority Scripture recommends to us. And, undoubtedly, the natural feeling of the human mind has always been not less to assail tyrants with hatred and execration, than to look up to just kings with love and veneration.

25. But if we have respect to the word of God, it will lead us farther, and make us subject not only to the authority of those princes who honestly and faithfully perform their duty toward us, but all princes, by whatever means they have so become, although there is nothing they less perform than the duty of princes. For though the Lord declares that a ruler to maintain our safety is the highest gift of his beneficence, and prescribes to rulers themselves their proper sphere, he at the same time declares, that of whatever description they may be, they derive their power from none but him. Those, indeed, who rule for the public good, are true examples and specimens of his beneficence, while those who domineer unjustly and tyrannically are raised up by him to punish the people for their iniquity. Still all alike possess that sacred majesty with which he has invested lawful power. I will not proceed further without subjoining some distinct passages to this effect. We need not labour to prove that an impious king is a mark of the Lord's anger, since I presume no one will deny it, and that this is not less true of a king than of a robber who plunders your goods, an adulterer who defiles your bed, and an assassin who aims at your life, since all such calamities are classed by Scripture among the curses of God. But let us insist at greater length in proving what does not so easily fall in with the views of men, that even an individual of the worst character, one most unworthy of all honour, if invested with public authority, receives that illustrious divine power which the Lord has by his word devolved on the ministers of his justice and judgment, and that, accordingly, in so far as public obedience is concerned, he is to be held in the same honour and reverence as the best of kings.

26. And, first, I would have the reader carefully to attend to that Divine Providence which, not without cause, is so often set before us in Scripture, and that special act of distributing kingdoms, and setting up as kings whomsoever he pleases. In Daniel it is said, "He changeth the times and the seasons: he removeth kings, and setteth up kings" (Dan. 2:21, 37). Again, "That the living may know that the Most High ruleth in the kingdom of men, and giveth it to whomsoever he will" (Dan. 4:17, 25). Similar sentiments occur throughout Scripture, but they abound particularly in the prophetical books. What kind of king Nebuchadnezzar, he who stormed Jerusalem, was, is well known. He was an active invader and devastator of other countries. Yet the Lord declares in Ezekiel that he had given him the land of Egypt as his hire for the devastation which he had committed. Daniel also said to him, "Thou, O king, art a king of kings: for the God of heaven hath given thee a kingdom, power, and strength, and glory. And wheresoever the children of men dwell, the beasts of the field and the fowls of the heaven hath he given into thine hand, and hath made thee ruler over them all" (Dan. 2:37, 38). Again, he says to his son Belshazzar, "The most high God gave Nebuchadnezzar thy father a kingdom, and majesty, and glory, and honour: and for the majesty that he gave him, all people, nations, and languages, trembled and feared before him" (Dan. 5:18, 19). When we hear that the king was appointed by God, let us, at the same time, call to mind those heavenly edicts as to honouring and fearing the king, and we shall have no doubt that we are to view the most iniquitous tyrant as occupying the place with which the Lord has honoured him. When Samuel declared to the people of Israel what they would suffer from their kings, he said, "This will be the manner of the king that shall reign over you: He will take your sons, and appoint them for himself, for his chariots, and to be his horsemen; and some shall run before his chariots. And he will appoint him captains over thousands, and captains over fifties; and will set them to ear his ground, and to reap his harvest, and to make his instruments of war, and instruments of his chariots. And he will take your daughters to be confectioneries, and to be cooks, and to be bakers. And he will take your fields, and your vineyards, and your oliveyards, even the best of them, and give them to his servants. And he will take the tenth of your seed, and of your vineyards, and give to his officers, and to his servants. And he will take your men-servants, and your maid-servants, and your goodliest young men, and your asses, and put them to his work. He will take the tenth of your sheep: and ye shall be his servants" (1 Sam. 8:11–17). Certainly these things could not be done legally by kings, whom the law trained most admirably to all kinds of restraint; but it was called justice in regard to the people, because they were bound to obey, and could not lawfully resist: as if Samuel had said, To such a degree will kings indulge in tyranny, which it will not be for you to restrain. The only thing remaining for you will be to receive their commands, and be obedient to their words.

27. But the most remarkable and memorable passage

is in Jeremiah. Though it is rather long, I am not indisposed to quote it, because it most clearly settles this whole question. "I have made the earth, the man and the beast that are upon the ground, by my great power, and by my outstretched arm, and have given it unto whom it seemed meet unto me. And now have I given all these lands into the hand of Nebuchadnezzar the king of Babylon, my servant: and the beasts of the field have I given him also to serve him. And all nations shall serve him, and his son, and his son's son, until the very time of his land come: and then many nations and great kings shall serve themselves of him. And it shall come to pass, that the nation and kingdom which will not serve the same Nebuchadnezzar the king of Babylon, and that will not put their neck under the yoke of the king of Babylon, that nation will I punish, saith the Lord, with the sword, and with famine, and with pestilence, until I have consumed them by his hand" (Jer. 27:5–8). Therefore "bring your necks under the yoke of the king of Babylon, and serve him and his people, and live" (v. 12). We see how great obedience the Lord was pleased to demand for this dire and ferocious tyrant, for no other reason than just that he held the kingdom. In other words, the divine decree had placed him on the throne of the kingdom, and admitted him to regal majesty, which could not be lawfully violated. If we constantly keep before our eyes and minds the fact, that even the most iniquitous kings are appointed by the same decree which establishes all regal authority, we will never entertain the seditious thought, that a king is to be treated according to his deserts, and that we are not bound to act the part of good subjects to him who does not in his turn act the part of a king to us.

28. It is vain to object, that that command was specially given to the Israelites. For we must attend to the ground on which the Lord places it—"I have given the kingdom to Nebuchadnezzar; therefore serve him and live." Let us doubt not that on whomsoever the kingdom has been conferred, him we are bound to serve. Whenever God raises any one to royal honour, he declares it to be his pleasure that he should reign. To this effect we have general declarations in Scripture. Solomon says—"For the transgression of a land, many are the princes thereof" (Prov. 28:2). Job says—"He looseth the bond of kings, and girdeth their loins with a girdle" (Job. 12:18). This being confessed, nothing remains for us but to serve and live. There is in Jeremiah another command in which the Lord thus orders his people—"Seek the peace of the city whither I have caused you to be carried away captives, and pray unto the Lord for it: for in the peace thereof shall ye have peace" (Jer. 29:7). Here the Israelites, plundered of all their property, torn from their homes, driven into exile, thrown into miserable bondage, are ordered to pray for the prosperity of the victor, not as we are elsewhere ordered to pray for our persecutors, but that his kingdom may be preserved in safety and tranquillity, that they too may live prosperously under him. Thus David, when already king elect by the ordination of God, and anointed with his holy oil, though causelessly and unjustly assailed by Saul, holds the life of one who was seeking his life to be sacred, because the Lord had invested him with royal honour. "The Lord forbid that I should do this thing unto my master, the Lord's anointed, to stretch forth mine hand against him, seeing he is the anointed of the Lord." "Mine eyes spare thee; and I said, I will not put forth mine hand against my lord; for he is the Lord's anointed" (1 Sam. 24:6, 11). Again,—"Who can stretch forth his hand against the Lord's anointed, and be guiltless"? "As the Lord liveth the Lord shall smite him, or his day shall come to die, or he shall descend into battle, and perish. The Lord forbid that I should stretch forth mine hand against the Lord's anointed" (l Sam. 24:9–11).

29. This feeling of reverence, and even of piety, we owe to the utmost to all our rulers, be their characters what they may. This I repeat the oftener, that we may learn not to consider the individuals themselves, but hold it to be enough that by the will of the Lord they sustain a character on which he has impressed and engraven inviolable majesty. But rulers, you will say, owe mutual duties to those under them. This I have already confessed. But if from this you conclude that obedience is to be returned to none but just governors, you reason absurdly. Husbands are bound by mutual duties to their wives, and parents to their children. Should husbands and parents neglect their duty; should the latter be harsh and severe to the children whom they are enjoined not to provoke to anger, and by their severity harass them beyond measure; should the former treat with the greatest contumely the wives whom they are enjoined to love and to spare as the weaker vessels; would children be less bound in duty to their parents, and wives to their husbands? They are made subject to the froward and undutiful. Nay, since the duty of all is not to look behind them, that is, not to inquire into the duties of one another, but to submit each to his own duty, this ought especially to be exemplified in the case of those who are placed under the power of others. Wherefore, if we are cruelly tormented by a savage, if we are rapaciously pillaged by an avaricious or luxurious, if we are neglected by a sluggish, if, in short, we

are persecuted for righteousness' sake by an impious and sacrilegious prince, let us first call up the remembrance of our faults, which doubtless the Lord is chastising by such scourges. In this way humility will curb our impatience. And let us reflect that it belongs not to us to cure these evils, that all that remains for us is to implore the help of the Lord, in whose hands are the hearts of kings, and inclinations of kingdoms. "God standeth in the congregation of the mighty; he judgeth among the gods." Before his face shall fall and be crushed all kings and judges of the earth, who have not kissed his anointed, who have enacted unjust laws to oppress the poor in judgment, and do violence to the cause of the humble, to make widows a prey, and plunder the fatherless.

30. Herein is the goodness, power, and providence of God wondrously displayed. At one time he raises up manifest avengers from among his own servants, and gives them his command to punish accursed tyranny, and deliver his people from calamity when they are unjustly oppressed; at another time he employs, for this purpose, the fury of men who have other thoughts and other aims. Thus he rescued his people Israel from the tyranny of Pharaoh by Moses; from the violence of Chusa, king of Syria, by Othniel; and from other bondage by other kings or judges. Thus he tamed the pride of Tyre by the Egyptians; the insolence of the Egyptians by the Assyrians; the ferocity of the Assyrians by the Chaldeans; the confidence of Babylon by the Medes and Persians,—Cyrus having previously subdued the Medes, while the ingratitude of the kings of Judah and Israel, and their impious contumacy after all his kindness, he subdued and punished,—at one time by the Assyrians, at another by the Babylonians. All these things, however, were not done in the same way. The former class of deliverers being brought forward by the lawful call of God to perform such deeds, when they took up arms against kings, did not at all violate that majesty with which kings are invested by divine appointment, but armed from heaven, they, by a greater power, curbed a less, just as kings may lawfully punish their own satraps. The latter class, though they were directed by the hand of God, as seemed to him good, and did his work without knowing it, had nought but evil in their thoughts.

31. But whatever may be thought of the acts of the men themselves, the Lord by their means equally executed his own work, when he broke the bloody sceptres of insolent kings, and overthrew their intolerable dominations. Let princes hear and be afraid; but let us at the same time guard most carefully against spurning or violating the venerable and majestic authority of rulers, an authority which God has sanctioned by the surest edicts, although those invested with it should be most unworthy of it, and, as far as in them lies, pollute it by their iniquity. Although the Lord takes vengeance on unbridled domination, let us not therefore suppose that that vengeance is committed to us, to whom no command has been given but to obey and suffer. I speak only of private men. For when popular magistrates have been appointed to curb the tyranny of kings (as the Ephori, who were opposed to kings among the Spartans, or Tribunes of the people to consuls among the Romans, or Demarchs to the senate among the Athenians; and perhaps there is something similar to this in the power exercised in each kingdom by the three orders, when they hold their primary diets). So far am I from forbidding these officially to check the undue license of kings, that if they connive at kings when they tyrannise and insult over the humbler of the people, I affirm that their dissimulation is not free from nefarious perfidy, because they fradulently betray the liberty of the people, while knowing that, by the ordinance of God, they are its appointed guardians.

32. But in that obedience which we hold to be due to the commands of rulers, we must always make the exception, nay, must be particularly careful that it is not incompatible with obedience to Him to whose will the wishes of all kings should be subject, to whose decrees their commands must yield, to whose majesty their sceptres must bow. And, indeed, how preposterous were it, in pleasing men, to incur the offence of Him for whose sake you obey men! The Lord, therefore, is King of kings. When he opens his sacred mouth, he alone is to be heard, instead of all and above all. We are subject to the men who rule over us, but subject only in the Lord. If they command anything against Him let us not pay the least regard to it, nor be moved by all the dignity which they possess as magistrates—a dignity to which no injury is done when it is subordinated to the special and truly supreme power of God. On this ground Daniel denies that he had sinned in any respect against the king when he refused to obey his impious decree (Dan. 6:22), because the king had exceeded his limits, and not only been injurious to men, but, by raising his horn against God, had virtually abrogated his own power. On the other hand, the Israelites are condemned for having too readily obeyed the impious edict of the king. For, when Jeroboam made the golden calf, they forsook the temple of God, and, in submissiveness to him, revolted to new superstitions (1 Kings 12:28). With the same facility pos-

terity had bowed before the decrees of their kings. For this they are severely upbraided by the Prophet (Hosea 5:11). So far is the praise of modesty from being due to that pretence by which flattering courtiers cloak themselves, and deceive the simple, when they deny the lawfulness of declining anything imposed by their kings, as if the Lord had resigned his own rights to mortals by appointing them to rule over their fellows, or as if earthly power were diminished when it is subjected to its author, before whom even the principalities of heaven tremble as suppliants. I know the imminent peril to which subjects expose themselves by this firmness, kings being most indignant when they are contemned. As Solomon says, "The wrath of a king is as messengers of death" (Prov. 16:14). But since Peter, one of heaven's heralds, has published the edict, "We ought to obey God rather than men" (Acts 5:29), let us console ourselves with the thought, that we are rendering the obedience which the Lord requires, when we endure anything rather than turn aside from piety. And that our courage may not fail, Paul stimulates us by the additional consideration (1 Cor. 7:23), that we were redeemed by Christ at the great price which our redemption cost him, in order that we might not yield a slavish obedience to the depraved wishes of men, far less do homage to their impiety.

END OF THE INSTITUTES.

ONE HUNDRED APHORISMS

CONTAINING, WITHIN A NARROW COMPASS, THE SUBSTANCE AND ORDER OF THE FOUR BOOKS OF THE INSTITUTES OF THE CHRISTIAN RELIGION.

BOOK 1

1. The true wisdom of man consists in the knowledge of God the Creator and Redeemer.

2. This knowledge is naturally implanted in us, and the end of it ought to be the worship of God rightly performed, or reverence for the Deity accompanied by fear and love.

3. But this seed is corrupted by ignorance, whence arises superstitious worship; and by wickedness, whence arise slavish dread and hatred of the Deity.

4. It is also from another source that it is derived namely, from the structure of the whole world, and from the Holy Scriptures.

5. This structure teaches us what is the goodness, power, justice, and wisdom of God in creating all things in heaven and earth, and in preserving them by ordinary and extraordinary government, by which his Providence is more clearly made known. It teaches also what are our wants, that we may learn to place our confidence in the goodness, power, and wisdom of God, to obey his commandments, to flee to him in adversity, and to offer thanksgiving to him for the gifts which we enjoy.

6. By the Holy Scriptures, also, God the Creator is known. We ought to consider what these Scriptures are; that they are true, and have proceeded from the Spirit of God; which is proved by the testimony of the Holy Spirit, by the efficacy and antiquity of the Scriptures, by the certainty of the Prophecies, by the miraculous preservation of the Law, by the calling and writings of the Apostles, by the consent of the Church, and by the steadfastness of the martyrs, whence it is evident that all the principles of piety are overthrown by those fanatics who, laying aside the Scripture, fly to revelations.

7. Next, what they teach; or, what is the nature of God in himself, and in the creation and government of all things.

8. The nature of God in himself is infinite, invisible, eternal, almighty; whence it follows that they are mistaken who ascribe to God a visible form. In his one essence there are three persons, the Father, the Son, and the Holy Spirit.

9. In the creation of all things there are chiefly considered, 1. Heavenly and spiritual substances, that is, angels,

of which some are good and the protectors of the godly, while others are bad, not by creation, but by corruption; 2. Earthly substances, and particularly man, whose perfection is displayed in soul and in body.

10. In the government of all things the nature of God is manifested. Now his government is, in one respect, universal, by which he directs all the creatures according to the properties which he bestowed on each when he created them.

11. In another respect, it is special; which appears in regard to contingent events, so that if any person is visited either by adversity or by any prosperous result, he ought to ascribe it wholly to God; and with respect to those things which act according to a fixed law of nature, though their peculiar properties were naturally bestowed on them, still they exert their power only so far as they are directed by the immediate hand of God.

12. It is viewed also with respect to time past and future. *Past*, that we may learn that all things happen by the appointment of God, who acts either by means, or without means, or contrary to means; so that everything which happens yields good to the godly and evil to the wicked. *Future*, to which belong human deliberations, and which shows that we ought to employ lawful means; since that Providence on which we rely furnishes its own means.

13. Lastly, by attending to the advantage which the godly derive from it. For we know certainly, 1. That God takes care of the whole human race, but especially of his Church. 2. That God governs all things by his will, and regulates them by his wisdom. 3. That he has most abundant power of doing good; for in his hand are heaven and earth, all creatures are subject to his sway, the godly rest on his protection, and the power of hell is restrained by his authority. That nothing happens by chance, though the causes may be concealed, but by the will of God; by his secret will which we are unable to explore, but adore with reverence, and by his will which is conveyed to us in the Law and in the Gospel.

BOOK 2

14. The knowledge of God the Redeemer is obtained from the fall of man, and from the material cause of redemption.

15. In the fall of man, we must consider what he ought to be, and what he may be.

16. For he was created after the image of God; that is, he was made a partaker of the divine Wisdom, Righteousness, and Holiness, and, being thus perfect in soul and in body, was bound to render to God a perfect obedience to his commandments.

17. The immediate causes of the fall were—Satan, the Serpent, Eve, the forbidden fruit; the remote causes were—unbelief, ambition, ingratitude, obstinacy. Hence followed the obliteration of the image of God in man, who became unbelieving, unrighteous, liable to death.

18. We must now see what he may be, in respect both of soul and of body. The understanding of the soul in divine things, that is, in the knowledge and true worship of God, is blinder than a mole; good works it can neither contrive nor perform. In human affairs, as in the liberal and mechanical arts, it is exceedingly blind and variable. Now the will, so far as regards divine things, chooses only what is evil. So far as regards lower and human affairs, it is uncertain, wandering, and not wholly at its own disposal.

19. The body follows the depraved appetites of the soul, is liable to many infirmities, and at length to death.

20. Hence it follows that redemption for ruined man must be sought through Christ the Mediator; because the first adoption of a chosen people, the preservation of the Church, her deliverance from dangers, her recovery after dispersions, and the hope of the godly, always depended on the grace of the Mediator. Accordingly, the law was given, that it might keep their minds in suspense till the coming of Christ; which is evident from the history of a gracious covenant frequently repeated, from ceremonies, sacrifices, and washings, from the end of adoption, and from the law of the priesthood.

21. The material cause of redemption is Christ, in whom we must consider three things; 1. How he is exhibited to men; 2. How he is received; 3. How men are retained in his fellowship.

22. Christ is exhibited to men by the Law and by the Gospel.

23. The Law is threefold: Ceremonial, Judicial, Moral. The use of the Ceremonial Law is repealed, its effect is perpetual. The Judicial or Political Law was peculiar to the Jews, and has been set aside, while that universal justice which is described in the Moral Law remains. The latter, or Moral Law, the object of which is to cherish and maintain godliness and righteousness, is perpetual, and is incumbent on all.

24. The use of the Moral Law is threefold. The first use shows our weakness, unrighteousness, and condemnation; not that we may despair, but that we may flee to Christ. The second is, that those who are not moved by promises, may be urged by the terror of threatenings. The third is, that we may know what is the will of God; that

we may consider it in order to obedience; that our minds may be strengthened for that purpose; and that we may be kept from falling.

25. The sum of the Law is contained in the Preface, and in the two Tables. In the Preface we observe, 1. The power of God, to constrain the people by the necessity of obedience; 2. A promise of grace, by which he declares himself to be the God of the Church; 3. A kind act, on the ground of which he charges the Jews with ingratitude, if they do not requite his goodness.

26. The first Table, which relates to the worship of God, consists of four commandments.

27. The design of the First Commandment is, that God alone may be exalted in his people. To God alone, therefore, we owe adoration, trust, invocation, thanksgiving.

28. The design of the Second Commandment is, that God will not have his worship profaned by superstitious rites. It consists of two parts. The former restrains our licentious daring, that we may not subject God to our senses, or represent him under any visible shape. The latter forbids us to worship any images on religious grounds, and, therefore, proclaims his power, which he cannot suffer to be despised,—his jealousy, for he cannot bear a partner,—his vengeance on children's children,—his mercy to those who adore his majesty.

29. The Third Commandment enjoins three things: 1. That whatever our mind conceives, or our tongue utters, may have a regard to the majesty of God; 2. That we may not rashly abuse his holy word and adorable mysteries for the purposes of ambition or avarice; 3. That we may not throw obloquy on his works, but may speak of them with commendatians of his Wisdom, Long-suffering, Power, Goodness, Justice. With these is contrasted a threefold profanation of the name of God, by perjury, unnecessary oaths, and idolatrous rites; that is, when we substitute in the place of God saints, or creatures animate or inanimate.

30. The design of the Fourth Commandment is, that, being dead to our own affections and works, we may meditate on the kingdom of God. Now there are three things here to be considered: 1. A spiritual rest, when believers abstain from their own works, that God may work in them; 2. That there may be a stated day for calling on the name of God, for hearing his word, and for performing religious rites; 3. That servants may have some remission from labour.

31. The Second Table, which relates to the duties of charity towards our neighbour, contains the last Six Commandments. The design of the Fifth Commandment is, that, since God takes pleasure in the observance of his own ordinance, the degrees of dignity appointed by him must be held inviolable. We are therefore forbidden to take anything from the dignity of those who are above us, by contempt, obstinacy, or ingratitude; and we are commanded to pay them reverence, obedience, and gratitude.

32. The design of the Sixth Commandment is, that, since God has bound mankind by a kind of unity, the safety of all ought to be considered by each person; whence it follows that we are forbidden to do violence to private individuals, and are commanded to exercise benevolence.

33. The design of the Seventh Commandment is, that, because God loves purity, we ought to put away from us all uncleanness. He therefore forbids adultery in mind, word, and deed.

34. The design of the Eighth Commandment is, that, since injustice is an abomination to God, he requires us to render to every man what is his own. Now men steal, either by violence, or by malicious imposture, or by craft, or by sycophancy, &c.

35. The design of the Ninth Commandment is, that, since God, who is truth, abhors falsehood, he forbids calumnies and false accusations, by which the name of our neighbour is injured,—and lies, by which any one suffers loss in his fortunes. On the other hand, he requires every one of us to defend the name and property of our neighbour by asserting the truth.

36. The design of the Tenth Commandment is, that, since God would have the whole soul pervaded by love, every desire averse to charity must be banished from our minds; and therefore every feeling which tends to the injury of another is forbidden.

37. We have said that Christ is revealed to us by the Gospel. And, first, the agreement between the Gospel, or the New Testament, and the Old Testament is demonstrated: 1. Because the godly, under both dispensations, have had the same hope of immortality; 2. They have had the same covenant, founded not on the works of men, but on the mercy of God; 3. They have had the same Mediator between God and men—Christ.

38. Next, five points of difference between the two dispensations are pointed out. 1. Under the Law the heavenly inheritance was held out to them under earthly blessings; but under the Gospel our minds are led directly to meditate upon it. 2. The Old Testament, by means of figures, presented the image only, while the reality was absent; but the New Testament exhibits the present truth. 3. The former, in respect of the Law, was the ministry

of condemnation and death; the latter, of righteousness and life. 4. The former is connected with bondage, which begets fear in the mind; the latter is connected with freedom, which produces confidence. 5. The word had been confined to the single nation of the Jews; but now it is preached to all nations.

39. The sum of evangelical doctrine is, to teach, 1. What Christ is; 2. Why he was sent; 3. In what manner he accomplished the work of redemption.

40. Christ is God and man: *God*, that he may bestow on his people righteousness, sanctification, and redemption; *Man*, because he had to pay the debt of man.

41. He was sent to perform the office, 1. Of a Prophet, by preaching the truth, by fulfilling the prophecies, by teaching and doing the will of his Father; 2. Of a King, by governing the whole Church and every member of it, and by defending his people from every kind of adversaries; 3. Of a Priest, by offering his body as a sacrifice for sins, by reconciling God to us though his obedience, and by perpetual intercession for his people to the Father.

42. He performed the office of a Redeemer by dying for our sins, by rising again for our justification, by opening heaven to us through his ascension, by sitting at the right hand of the Father whence he will come to judge the quick and the dead; and, therefore, he procured for us the grace of God and salvation.

BOOK 3

43. We receive Christ the Redeemer by the power of the Holy Spirit, who unites us to Christ; and, therefore, he is called the Spirit of sanctification and adoption, the earnest and seal of our salvation, water, oil, a fountain, fire, the hand of God.

44. Faith is the hand of the soul, which receives, through the same efficacy of the Holy Spirit, Christ offered to us in the Gospel.

45. The general office of faith is, to assent to the truth of God, whenever, whatever, and in what manner soever he speaks; but its peculiar office is, to behold the will of God in Christ, his mercy, the promises of grace, for the full conviction of which the Holy Spirit enlightens our minds and strengthens our hearts.

46. Faith, therefore, is a steady and certain knowledge of the divine kindness towards us, which is founded on a gracious promise through Christ, and is revealed to our minds and sealed on our hearts by the Holy Spirit.

47. The effects of faith are four: 1. Repentance; 2. A Christian life; 3. Justification; 4. Prayer.

48. True repentance consists of two parts: 1. Mortification, which proceeds from the acknowledgment of sin, and a real perception of the divine displeasure; 2. Quickening, the fruits of which are—piety towards God, charity towards our neighbour, the hope of eternal life, holiness of life. With this true repentance is contrasted false repentance, the parts of which are, Contrition, Confession, and Satisfaction. The two former may be referred to true repentance, provided that there be contrition of heart on account of the acknowledgment of sin, and that it be not separated from the hope of forgiveness through Christ; and provided that the confession be either *private* to God alone, or made to the pastors of the Church willingly and for the purpose of consolation, not for the enumeration of offences, and for introducing a torture of the conscience; or *public*, which is made to the whole Church, or to one or many persons in presence of the whole Church. What was formerly called Ecclesiastical Satisfaction, that is, what was made for the edification of the Church on account of repentance and public confession of sins, was introduced as due to God by the Sophists; whence sprung the supplements of Indulgences in this world, and the fire of Purgatory after death. But that Contrition of the Sophists, and auricular Confession (as they call it), and the Satisfaction of actual performance, are opposed to the free forgiveness of sins.

49. The two parts of a Christian life are laid down: 1. The love of righteousness; that we may be holy, because God is holy, and because we are united to him, and are reckoned among his people; 2. That a rule may be prescribed to us, which does not permit us to wander in the course of righteousness, and that we may be conformed to Christ. A model of this is laid down to us, which we ought to copy in our whole life. Next are mentioned the blessings of God, which it will argue extreme ingratitude if we do not requite.

50. The sum of the Christian life is denial of ourselves.

51. The ends of this self-denial are four. 1. That we may devote ourselves to God as a living sacrifice. 2. That we may not seek our own things, but those which belong to God and to our neighbour. 3. That we may patiently bear the cross, the fruits of which are—acknowledgment of our weakness, the trial of our patience, correction of faults, more earnest prayer, more cheerful meditation on eternal life. 4. That we may know in what manner we ought to use the present life and its aids, for necessity and delight. Necessity demands that we possess all things as though we possessed them not; that we bear poverty with mildness, and abundance with moderation; that we know how to endure patiently fulness, and hunger, and want;

that we pay regard to our neighbour, because we must give account of our stewardship; and that all things correspond to our calling. The delight of praising the kindness of God ought to be with us a stronger argument.

52. In considering Justification, which is the third effect of faith, the first thing that occurs is an explanation of the word. He is said to be justified who, in the judgment of God, is deemed righteous. He is justified by works, whose life is pure and blameless before God; and no such person ever existed except Christ. They are justified by faith who, shut out from the righteousness of works, receive the righteousness of Christ. Such are the elect of God.

53. Hence follows the strongest consolation; for instead of a severe Judge, we have a most merciful Father. Justified in Christ, and having peace, trusting to his power, we aim at holiness.

54. Next follows Christian liberty, consisting of three parts. 1. That the consciences of believers may rise above the Law, and may forget the whole righteousness of the Law. 2. That the conscience, free from the yoke of the Law, may cheerfully obey the will of God. 3. That they may not be bound by any religious scruples before God about things indifferent. But here we must avoid two precipices. 1. That we do not abuse the gifts of God. 2. That we avoid giving and taking offence.

55. The fourth effect of faith is Prayer; in which are considered its fruits, laws, faults, and petitions.

56. The fruit of prayer is fivefold. 1. When we are accustomed to flee to God, our heart is inflamed with a stronger desire to seek, love, and adore him. 2. Our heart is not a prey to any wicked desire, of which we would be ashamed to make God our witness. 3. We receive his benefits with thanksgiving. 4. Having obtained a gift, we more earnestly meditate on the goodness of God. 5. Experience confirms to us the Goodness, Providence, and Truth of God.

57. The laws are Four. 1. That we should have our heart framed as becomes those who enter into converse with God; and therefore the lifting up of the hands, the raising of the heart, and perseverance, are recommended. 2. That we should feel our wants. 3. That we should divest ourselves of every thought of our own glory, giving the whole glory to God. 4. That while we are prostrated amidst overwhelming evils, we should be animated by the sure hope of succeeding, since we rely on the command and promise of God.

58. They err who call on the Saints that are placed beyond this life. 1. Because Scripture teaches that prayer ought to be offered to God alone, who alone knows what is necessary for us. He chooses to be present, because he has promised. He can do so, for he is Almighty. 2. Because he requires that he be addressed in faith, which rests on his word and promise. 3. Because faith is corrupted as soon as it departs from this rule. But in calling on the saints there is no word, no promise; and therefore there is no faith; nor can the saints themselves either hear or assist.

59. The summary of prayer, which has been delivered to us by Christ the Lord, is contained in a Preface and two Tables.

60. In the Preface, the Goodness of God is conspicuous, for he is called *our Father*. It follows that we are his children, and that to seek supplies from any other quarter would be to charge God either with poverty or with cruelty; that sins ought not to hinder us from humbly imploring mercy; and that a feeling of brotherly love ought to exist amongst us. The power of God is likewise conspicuous in this Preface, for he is *in Heaven*. Hence we infer that God is present everywhere, and that when we seek him, we ought to rise above perceptions of the body and the soul; that he is far beyond all risk of change or corruption; that he holds the whole universe in his grasp, and governs it by his power.

61. The First Table is entirely devoted to the glory of God, and contains Three petitions. 1. That the *name* of God, that is, his power, goodness, wisdom, justice, and truth, *may be hallowed*; that is, that men may neither speak nor think of God but with the deepest veneration. 2. That God may correct, by the agency of his Spirit, all the depraved lusts of the flesh; may bring all our thoughts into obedience to his authority; may protect his children; and may defeat the attempts of the wicked. The use of this petition is threefold. (1). It withdraws us from the corruptions of the world. (2). It inflames us with the desire of mortifying the flesh. (3). It animates us to endure the cross. 3. The Third petition relates not to the secret will of God, but to that which is made known by the Scriptures, and to which voluntary obedience is the counterpart.

62. The Second Table contains the Three remaining petitions, which relate to ourselves and our neighbours. 1. It asks everything which the body needs in this sublunary state; for we commit ourselves to the care and providence of God, that he may feed, foster, and preserve us. 2. We ask those things which contribute to the spiritual life, namely, the *forgiveness of sins*, which implies satisfaction, and to which is added a condition, that when we

have been offended by deed or by word, we nevertheless forgive them their offences against us. 3. We ask *deliverance from temptations*, or, that we may be furnished with armour and defended by the Divine protection, that we may be able to obtain the victory. *Temptations* differ in their *cause*, for God, Satan, the world, and the flesh *tempt*; in their *matter*, for we are tempted, on the right hand, in respect of riches, honours, beauty, &c., and on the left hand, in respect of poverty, contempt, and afflictions: and in their *end*, for God tempts the godly for good, but Satan, the flesh, and the world, tempt them for evil.

63. Those Four effects of faith bring us to the certainty of election, and of the final resurrection.

64. The causes of election are these. The *efficient* cause is—the free mercy of God, which we ought to acknowledge with humility and thanksgiving. The *material* cause is—Christ, the well-beloved Son. The *final* cause is—that, being assured of our salvation, because we are God's people, we may glorify him both in this life and in the life which is to come, to all eternity. The effects are, in respect either of many persons, or of a single individual; and that by electing some, and justly reprobating others. The elect are called by the preaching of the word and the illumination of the Holy Spirit, are justified, and sanctified, that they may at length be glorified.

65. The final resurrection will take place. 1. Because on any other supposition we cannot be perfectly glorified. 2. Because Christ rose in our flesh. 3. Because God is Almighty.

BOOK 4

66. God keeps us united in the fellowship of Christ by means of Ecclesiastical and Civil government.

67. In Ecclesiastical government Three things are considered. 1. What is the Church? 2. How is it governed? 3. What is its power?

68. The Church is regarded in two points of view; as Invisible and Universal, which is the communion of saints; and as Visible and Particular. The Church is discerned by the pure preaching of the word, and by the lawful administration of the sacraments.

69. As to the government of the Church, there are Five points of inquiry. 1. Who rule? 2. What are they? 3. What is their calling? 4. What is their office? 5. What was the condition of the ancient Church?

70. They that rule are not Angels, but Men. In this respect, God declares his condescension towards us: we have a most excellent training to humility and obedience, and it is singularly fitted to bind us to mutual charity.

71. These are Prophets, Apostles, Evangelists, whose office was temporary; Pastors and Teachers, whose office is of perpetual duration.

72. Their calling is twofold; *internal* and *external*. The *internal* is from the Spirit of God. In the *external* there are Four things to be considered. 1. What sort of persons ought to be chosen? Men of sound doctrine and holy lives. 2. In what manner? With fasting and prayer. 3. By whom? Immediately, by God, as Prophets and Apostles. Mediately, with the direction of the word, by Bishops, by Elders, and by the people. 4. With what rite of ordination? By the laying on of hands, the use of which is threefold. 1. That the dignity of the ministry may be commended. 2. That he who is called may know that he is devoted to God. 3. That he may believe that the Holy Spirit will not desert this holy ministry.

73. The duty of Pastors in the Church is, to preach the Word, to administer the Sacraments, to exercise Discipline.

74. The condition of the ancient Church was distributed into Presbyters, Elders, Deacons, who dispensed the funds of the Church to the Bishops, the Clergy, the poor, and for repairing churches.

75. The power of the Church is viewed in relation to Doctrine, Legislation, and Jurisdiction.

76. Doctrine respects the articles of faith, none of which must be laid down without the authority of the word of God, but all must be directed to the glory of God and the edification of the Church. It respects also the application of the articles, which must agree with the analogy of faith.

77. Ecclesiastical laws, in precepts necessary to be observed, must be in accordance with the written word of God. In things indifferent, regard must be had to places, persons, times, with a due attention to order and decorum. Those constitutions ought to be avoided which have been laid down by pretended pastors instead of the pure worship of God, which bind the consciences by rigid necessity, which make void a commandment of God, which are useless and trifling, which oppress the consciences by their number, which lead to theatrical display, which are considered to be propitiatory sacrifices, and which are turned to the purposes of gain.

78. Jurisdiction is twofold. 1. That which belongs to the Clergy, which was treated of under the head of Provincial and General Synods. 2. That which is common to

the Clergy and the people, the design of which is twofold, that scandals may be prevented, and that scandal which has arisen may be removed. The exercise of it consists in private and public admonitions, and likewise in excommunication, the object of which is threefold. 1. That the Church may not be blamed; 2. That the good may not be corrupted by intercourse with the bad; 3. That they who are excommunicated may be ashamed, and may begin to repent.

79. With regard to Times, Fasts are appointed, and Vows are made. The design of Fasts is, that the flesh may be mortified, that we may be better prepared for prayer, and that they may be evidences of humility and obedience. They consist of Three things, the time, the quality, and the quantity of food. But here we must beware lest we rend our garments only, and not our hearts, as hypocrites do, lest those actions be regarded as a meritorious performance, and lest they be too rigorously demanded as necessary to salvation.

80. In Vows we must consider; 1. To whom the vow is made—namely, to God. Hence it follows that nothing must be attempted but what is approved by his word, which teaches us what is pleasing and what is displeasing to God. 2. Who it is that vows—namely, a man. We must, therefore, beware lest we disregard our liberty, or promise what is beyond our strength or inconsistent with our calling. 3. What is vowed. Here regard must be had to time; to the *past*, such as a vow of thanksgiving and repentance; to the *future*, that we may afterwards be more cautious, and may be stimulated by them to the performance of duty. Hence it is evident what opinion we ought to form respecting Popish vows.

81. In explaining the Sacraments, there are Three things to be considered. 1. What a sacrament is—namely, an external sign, by which God seals on our consciences the promises of his good-will towards us, in order to sustain the weakness of our faith. We in our turn testify our piety towards him. 2. What things are necessary;—namely, the Sign, the Thing signified, the Promise, and the general Participation. 3. What is the number of them—namely, Baptism and the Lord's Supper.

82. The Sign in Baptism is water; the Thing Signified is the blood of Christ; the Promise is eternal life; the Communicants or Partakers are, adults, after making a confession of their faith, and likewise infants; for Baptism came in the place of Circumcision, and in both the mystery, promise, use, and efficacy, are the same. Forgiveness of sins also belongs to infants, and therefore it is likewise a sign of this forgiveness.

83. The end of Baptism is twofold. 1. To promote our faith towards God. For it is a sign of our washing by the blood of Christ, and of the mortification of our flesh, and the renewal of our souls in Christ. Besides, being united to Christ, we believe that we shall be partakers of all his blessings, and that we shall never fall under condemnation. 2. To serve as our confession before our neighbour; for it is a mark that we choose to be regarded as the people of God, and we testify that we profess the Christian religion, and that our desire is, that all the members of our body may proclaim the praise of God.

84. The Lord's Supper is a spiritual feast, by which we are preserved in that life into which God hath begotten us by his word.

85. The design of the Lord's Supper is threefold. 1. To aid in confirming our faith towards God. 2. To serve as a confession before men. 3. To be an exhortation to charity.

86. We must beware lest, by undervaluing the signs, we separate them too much from their mysteries, with which they are in some measure connected; and lest, on the other hand, by immoderately extolling them, we appear to obscure the mysteries themselves.

87. The parts are two. 1. The *spiritual truth* in which the meaning is beheld, consists in the promises; the *matter*, or substance, is Christ dead and risen; and the *effect* is our redemption and justification. 2. The visible signs are, bread and wine.

88. With the Lord's Supper is contrasted the Popish Mass. 1. It offers insult and blasphemy to Christ. 2. It buries the cross of Christ. 3. It obliterates his death. 4. It robs us of the benefits which we obtain in Christ. 5. It destroys the Sacraments in which the memorial of his death was left.

89. The Sacraments, falsely so called, are enumerated, which are, Confirmation, Penitence, Extreme Unction, Orders [which gave rise to the (seven) less and the (three) greater], and Marriage.

90. Next comes Civil government, which belongs to the external regulation of manners.

91. Under this head are considered Magistrates, Laws, and the People.

92. The Magistrate is God's vicegerent, the father of his country, the guardian of the laws, the administrator of justice, the defender of the Church.

93. By these names he is excited to the performance of duty. 1. That he may walk in holiness before God, and before men may maintain uprightness, prudence, temperance, harmlessness, and righteousness. 2. That by

wonderful consolation it may smooth the difficulties of his office.

94. The kinds of Magistracy or Civil Government are, Monarchy, Aristocracy, Democracy.

95. As to Laws, we must see what is their constitution in regard to God and to men: and what is their equity in regard to times, places, and nations.

96. The People owe to the Magistrate, 1. Reverence heartily rendered to him as God's ambassador. 2. Obedience, or compliance with edicts, or paying taxes, or undertaking public offices and burdens. 3. That love which will lead us to pray to God for his prosperity.

97. We are enjoined to obey not only good magistrates, but all who possess authority, though they may exercise tyranny; for it was not without the authority of God that they were appointed to be princes.

98. When tyrants reign, let us first remember our faults, which are chastised by such scourges; and, therefore, humility will restrain our impatience. Besides, it is not in our power to remedy these evils, and all that remains for us is to implore the assistance of the Lord, in whose hand are the hearts of men and the revolutions of kingdoms.

99. In Two ways God restrains the fury of tyrants; either by raising up from among their own subjects open avengers, who rid the people of their tyranny, or by employing for that purpose the rage of men whose thoughts and contrivances are totally different, thus overturning one tyranny by means of another.

100. The obedience enjoined on subjects does not prevent the interference of any popular Magistrates whose office it is to restrain tyrants and to protect the liberty of the people. Our obedience to Magistrates ought to be such, that the obedience which we owe to the King of kings shall remain entire and unimpaired.

The Obedience of a Christian Man and How Christian Rulers Ought to Govern

In which also (if you mark diligently) you shall find eyes to perceive the crafty conveyance of all jugglers.

Set forth by William Tyndale 1528. October 2.

Ed. Thomas Russell, A.M. London

TO THE READER

WILLIAM TYNDALE, OTHERWISE CALLED HITCHINS: TO THE READER.

Grace, peace, and increase of knowledge in our Lord Jesus Christ, be with you, reader, and with all that call on the name of the Lord unfeignedly and with a pure conscience. Amen.

Let it not make you despair, nor yet discourage you, O reader, that it is forbidden you, upon pain of life and goods, or that it is breaking the king's peace, or treason to his highness, to read the word of your soul's health. But much rather, be bold in the Lord, and comfort your soul: forasmuch as you are sure, and have an evident token through such persecution, that it is the true word of God, which is ever hated by the world. Nor was his word ever without persecution, (as you see in all the stories of the Bible, both in the New Testament and also in the Old), nor can it be, no more than the sun can be without light. And contrariwise, you may be just as sure that the pope's doctrine is not of God, which (as you see) is so agreeable to the world, and is so received by the world. Or rather, the pope's doctrine receives the world and the pleasures of the world. It seeks nothing but the possessions of the world, and the authority in the world, and to bear rule in the world. It persecutes the word of God, and with all wiliness, it drives people from it. With false and sophistical reasons, it makes them afraid of it. Indeed, it curses and excommunicates them, and brings them to believe they are damned if they look at it. That is but doctrine to deceive men. It moves the blind powers of the world to slay with fire, water, and sword, all who cleave to God's word. For the world loves what is the pope's, and it hates what is chosen out of the world to serve God in the Spirit. As Christ says to his disciples, John 15:19, "If you were of the world, the world would love its own; but I have chosen you out of the world, and therefore the world hates you."

Another comfort you have is that, just as the weak powers of the world defend the doctrine of the world, so the mighty power of God defends the doctrine of God. You will evidently perceive it, if you call to mind the wonderful deeds which God has ever wrought for his word in extreme necessity, since the world began, beyond all man's reason. These are written, (as Paul says, Romans 15:4) "for our learning, (and not for our deceiving), that we through patience and comfort of the Scripture might have hope." The nature of God's word is to fight against hypocrites. It began at Abel, and it has ever since continued, and shall continue, I do not doubt, until the last day. Hypocrites always have the world on their side, as you see in the time of Christ. They had the elders, that is, the rulers of the Jews on their side. They had Pilate and the emperor's power on their side. They also had Herod on their side. Moreover they brought all their worldly wisdom to bear, and all that they could thin, or imagine to serve their purpose. First, to frighten the people with, they excommunicated all that believed in him, and put them out of the temple, as you see in John 9:34. Secondly, they found the means to have him condemned by the emperor's power, and made it treason to Caesar to believe in him. Thirdly, they sought to have him hanged as a thief or a murderer, which, after their fleshly-wisdom, was a cause above all causes that no man should believe in him. For the Jews take it for a sure token of everlasting damnation, if a man is hanged. For it is written in their law, Deut 21:22–23 "Cursed is everyone that hangs on a tree." Moses also in the same place commands, if any man is hanged, to take him down the same day and bury him, for fear of polluting or defiling the country; that is, lest they bring the wrath and curse of God upon them. Therefore, the wicked Jews themselves, with so venomous a hatred, persecuted the doctrine of Christ. They did all they could to shame him, though they would have had Christ continue to hang on the cross and rot there, (as he should have done by the emperor's law), yet for fear of defiling their Sabbath, and bringing the wrath and curse of God upon them, they begged Pilate to take him down, John 19, which went against themselves.

Finally, when they had done all they could, and all that they thought was sufficient, and when Christ was in the heart of the earth, and so many bills and pole-axes were around him to keep him down, and when it was past man's help, then God helped. When man could not bring him back again, God's truth fetched him again. The oath that God had sworn to Abraham, to David, and to other holy fathers and prophets, raised him up again, to bless and save all that believe in him. Thus the wisdom of the hypocrites became foolishness. Look, this was written for your learning and comfort.

How awfully were the children of Israel locked in Egypt! In what tribulation, suffering, and adversity they were in! Also the land that was promised to them was far off, and full of great cities, walled with high walls up to the sky, and inhabited with great giants. Yet God's truth brought them out of Egypt, and planted them in the land of the giants. This was also written for our learning. For there is no power against God's, nor any wisdom against God's wisdom. He is stronger and wiser than all his enemies. What did it help Pharaoh to drown the male children? So little (I fear not) shall it at the last help the pope and his bishops, to burn our male children who manfully confess that Jesus Christ is the Lord, and that there is no other name given to men to be saved by, as Peter testifies in Acts 4:12.

Who dried up the Red sea? Who slew Goliath? Who did all those wonderful deeds which you read about in the Bible? Who delivered the Israelites evermore from thraldom and bondage, as soon as they repented and turned to God? Faith truly, and God's truth, and trust in the promises which he had made. Read the 11 Th chapter to the Hebrews for your consolation.

When the children of Israel were ready to despair, because of the greatness and the multitude of the giants, Moses ever comforted them, saying, Remember what your Lord God has done for you in Egypt, his awful plagues, his miracles, his wonders, his mighty hand, his stretched out arm, and what he has done for you up to now. He shall destroy them; he shall take their hearts from them, and make them fear and flee before you. He shall storm them, and stir up a tempest among them, and scatter them, and bring them to nothing. He has sworn; he is true; he will fulfill the promises that he has made to Abraham, Isaac, and Jacob. This is written for our learning: for truly he is a true God; and he is our God as well as theirs; and his promises are with us, as well as with them; and he is present with us, as well as he was with them. If we ask, we shall obtain; if we knock, he will open; if we seek, we shall find; if we thirst, his truth shall fulfill our desires. Christ is with us until the world's end. Let his little flock be bold therefore. For if God is on our side, what does it matter who is against us, be they bishops, cardinals, popes, or whatever names they may have?

Mark this also, if God sends you to the sea, and promises to go with you, and to bring you safe to land, he will raise up a tempest against you, to prove whether you will abide by his word, and so that you may feel your faith, and perceive his goodness. For if it was always fair weather, and you were never brought into such jeopardy, from where his mercy alone could deliver you, then your faith would be but a presumption, and you should be ever unthankful to God, and merciless to your neighbor.

If God promises riches, the way to them is poverty. Whom he loves, he chastens: whom he exalts, he casts down: whom he saves, he first damns. He brings no man to heaven, except he sends him to hell first. If he promises life, he slays first: when he builds, he first tears all down. He is no patcher; he cannot build on another man's foundation. He will not work until all is past remedy, and brought to such a case, that men may see how his hand, his power, his mercy, his goodness and truth, has wrought it all together. He will let no man partake with him of his praise and glory. His works are wonderful, and contrary to man's works. Who but God delivered his own Son, his only Son, his dear Son, to death, and did that for his enemies' sake, to win his enemy, and to overcome him with love, so that he might see love, and love again, and of love, to do likewise to other men, and overcome them with well doing?

Joseph saw the sun and the moon and the eleven stars worshipping him. Nevertheless, before that came to pass, God laid him where he could neither see sun nor moon, nor any star of the sky, and that was so for many years; and also undeserved. It was done to nurture him, to humble him, to make him meek, and to teach him God's ways, and to make him apt and fit for the place and honor he came to; so that he might perceive and feel that it came from God, and that he might be strong in the spirit to minister it in a godly fashion.

He promised the children of Israel a land with rivers of milk and honey; but he brought them for the space of forty years into a land where not only rivers of milk and honey were absent, but where not so much as a drop of water was to be had. He did it to nurture them, and teach them, as a father does his son, and to do them good at the end; and so that they might be strong in their spirit and souls, to use his gifts and benefits in a godly fashion, and after his will. He promised David a kingdom, and immediately stirred up King Saul against him to persecute him; to hunt him as men hunt hares with greyhounds, and to ferret him out of every hole, and he did that for the space of many years. He did it to tame him, to make him meek, to kill his lusts; to make him feel other men's diseases; to make him merciful; to make him understand that he was made king to minister to and to win his brothers. He did it so that David would not think that his subjects were made to minister to his own lusts, or that it was lawful for him to take away from them their life and goods at his pleasure.

Oh that our kings were so nurtured now-a-days! Our holy bishops teach in a far different manner, saying, Your grace shall take your pleasure; indeed, take what pleasure you are inclined to; spare nothing; we shall dispense with you; we have the power, we are God's vicars. Leave us alone with the realm; we will make it painful for you, and see that nothing is well with you. Your grace will but defend the faith only.

Let us, therefore, look diligently to what we are called (Christians), so that we do not deceive ourselves. We are not called to dispute, as the pope's disciples do; but to die with Christ, so that we may live with him; and to suffer with him, so that we may reign with him. We are called to a kingdom that must be won with suffering only, just as a sick man wins his health. God is the one that does all things for us, and fights for us; and we do but suffer only. Christ says, "As my Father sent me, so I send you;" John 20:21. And, "If they persecute me, then shall they persecute you." (John 15:20) Christ says, "I send you forth as sheep among wolves." (Mat 10:16) The sheep do not fight; but the shepherd fights for them, and cares for them. "Be harmless as doves, therefore," says Christ, "and wise as serpents." The doves imagine no defense, nor seek to avenge themselves. The serpent's wisdom is to keep his head, and those parts in which his life rests. Christ is our head, and God's word is what our life rests in. Therefore, cleave fast to Christ, and to those promises which God has made us for his sake. This is our wisdom. "Beware of men," he says; "for they shall deliver you up to their councils, and scourge you; and you shall be brought before rulers and kings for my sake. The brother shall betray, or deliver, his brother to death, and the father will betray the son; and the children shall rise against father and mother, and put them to death." Hear what Christ further says: "The disciple is not greater than his master; nor is the servant greater, or better, than his lord. If they have called the good man of the house "Beelzebub," then how much more will they call his household servants so!" In Luke 14:28–30, Christ says, "Which of you, disposed to build a tower, does not sit down first and count the cost, whether he has sufficient to finish it? Lest when he has laid the foundation, and then is not able to finish, all that behold it will begin to mock him, saying, This man began to build, and was not able to make an end of it. So likewise none of you, who does not forsake all that he has, can be my disciple." Whoever, therefore, does not consider this beforehand, 'I must jeopardize life, goods, honor, worship, and all that there is, for Christ's sake,' deceives himself. He makes a mockery of himself to the godless hypocrites and infidels. "No man can serve two masters, God and mammon;" that is to say, wicked riches also, Mat 6:24. You must love Christ above all things, but you do not do that if you are not ready to forsake all for his sake. If you have forsaken all for his sake, then are you sure that you love him. Tribulation is our right baptism;

and it is signified by plunging into the water. "We that are baptized in the name of Christ," says Paul, "are baptized to die with him."

The Spirit through tribulation purges us, and kills our fleshly wit, our worldly understanding, and our belly-wisdom; and he fills us full of the wisdom of God. Tribulation is a blessing that comes from God, as witnesses Christ: "Blessed are they that suffer persecution for righteousness' sake; for theirs is the kingdom of heaven." Is this not a comforting word? Who would not rather choose and desire to be blessed with Christ in a little tribulation, than to be cursed perpetually, along with the world, for a little pleasure?

Prosperity is a right curse, and a thing that God gives to his enemies. "Woe to you rich;" says Christ, Luke 6:25–26, "look, you have your consolation: woe to you that are full, for you shall hunger: woe to you that laugh, for you shall weep: woe to you when men praise you, for so did their fathers do to the false prophets." Indeed, and so have our fathers done to the false hypocrites. The hypocrites, with worldly preaching, have not only gotten the praise, but even the possessions and the dominion and the rule of the whole world.

Tribulation for righteousness is not only a blessing, but also a gift that God gives to none but his special friends. The apostles rejoiced that they were counted worthy to suffer rebuke for Christ's sake. And Paul, in 2 Tim 3:12, says to Timothy, "All that will live godly in Christ Jesus must suffer persecution:" and in Phil 1:29 he says, "To you it is given, not only to believe in Christ, but also to suffer for his sake." Here you see that it is God's gift to suffer for Christ's sake. Peter in 1 Pet 4:14 says, "Happy are you if you suffer for the name of Christ; for the glorious Spirit of God rests in you." Is it not a happy thing, to be sure that you are sealed with God's Spirit to everlasting life? Truly, you are sure of it, if you suffer patiently for his sake. By suffering you are sure; but by persecuting you can never be sure. For Paul, in Rom 5:3, says, "Tribulation makes us joyful;" that is, it makes us feel the goodness of God, and his help, and the working of his Spirit. And, in 2 Cor 12:9, the Lord said to Paul, "My grace is sufficient for you; for my strength is made perfect through weakness." Look, Christ is never strong in us till we are weak. As our strength abates, so grows the strength of Christ in us. When we are completely emptied of our own strength, then we are full of Christ's strength. Look, however much of our own strength remains in us, so much is lacking of the strength of Christ. "Therefore," says Paul, in the second epistle to the Corinthians, "very gladly will I rejoice in my weakness, that the strength of Christ may dwell in me. Therefore I take pleasure," says Paul, "in infirmities, in rebukes, in need, in persecutions, and in anguish for Christ's sake; for when I am weak, then am I strong." Meaning, that the weakness of the flesh is the strength of the Spirit. And by flesh understand wit, wisdom, and all that is in a man before the Spirit of God comes; and whatever does not spring from the Spirit of God, and from God's word. The Scripture is full of similar testimonies.

Behold, God sets before us a blessing and also a curse. It is a blessing, truly, and a glorious and everlasting blessing, if we suffer tribulation and adversity with our Lord and Savior Christ. And it is an everlasting curse if, for a little pleasure's sake, we withdraw ourselves from the chastising and nurture of God, with which he teaches all his sons, and fashions them after his godly will, and makes them perfect (as he did Christ). By chastising, he makes them apt and fit vessels to receive his grace and his Spirit, so that they might perceive and feel the exceeding mercy which we have in Christ, and the innumerable blessings and unspeakable inheritance, to which we are called and chosen, and sealed in our Savior Jesus Christ, to whom be praise forever. Amen.

Finally, those whom God chooses to reign everlastingly with Christ, he seals with his mighty Spirit, and pours strength into his heart, to suffer afflictions with Christ for bearing witness to the truth. This is the difference between the children of God and of salvation, and the children of the devil and of damnation. The children of God have power in their hearts to suffer for God's word; it is their life and salvation, their hope and trust, and whereby they live in the soul and spirit before God. And the children of the devil, in time of adversity, fly from Christ, whom they followed feignedly for their hearts were not sealed with his holy and mighty Spirit; they get themselves to the standard of their father the devil, and take his wages, which are the pleasures of this world. They are the earnest of everlasting damnation. Hebrews 12:5–7 well confirms this, saying, "My son, do not despise not chastising of the Lord, nor faint when you are rebuked by him: for those whom the Lord loves, he chastises; indeed, he scourges every son whom he receives." Look, persecution and adversity for the truth's sake is God's scourge, and God's rod, and it pertains to all his children indifferently. For when he said that he scourges every son, he makes no exceptions. Moreover, says the text: "If you endure chastising, God offers himself to you as to sons. What son is it that the Father does not chastise? If you are not under correction, of which all partake, then you are bastards, and not sons."

We must, then, be baptized in tribulations, and go through the Red sea, and a great and fearful wilderness, and a land of cruel giants, into our natural country. Indeed, it is plain that there is no other way into the kingdom of life than through persecution, suffering pain, and death, following the example of Christ. Therefore, let us arm our souls with the comfort of the Scriptures: how God is ever ready at hand to help us in our time of need; and how such tyrants and persecutors are but God's scourge, and his rod to chastise us. The father has always, in time of correction, held the rod fast in his hand, so that the rod does nothing but as the father moves it. Even so, God has all tyrants in his hand, and he does not let them do whatever they would, but only as much as he appoints them to do, and as far as it is necessary for us. As when a child submits himself to his father's correction and nurture, and altogether humbles himself to the will of his father, then the rod is taken away—even so, when we have come to the knowledge of the right way, and have forsaken our own will, and offer ourselves completely to the will of God, to walk whichever way he will have us, then he turns away the tyrants. Or else, if they try to persecute us any further, he puts them out of the way, according to the comfortable examples we have in the Scripture.

Moreover, let us arm our souls with the promises both of help and assistance, and also of the glorious reward that follows. "Great is your reward in heaven," says Christ, Matthew 5:12; and, "He that acknowledges me before men, him will I knowledge before my Father that is in heaven;" and, "Call on me in time of tribulation, and I will deliver you," Psalm 50:15; and, "Behold the eyes of the Lord are over those that fear him, and over those that trust in his mercy, to deliver their souls from death, and to feed them in time of hunger." In Psalm 34:15, 18–20 David says: "The Lord is near those that are troubled in their hearts, and the meek in spirit he will save. The tribulations of the righteous are many, and the Lord will deliver them out of them all. The Lord keeps all the bones of them, so that not one of them shall be bruised. The Lord shall redeem the souls of his servants." The psalms are full of similar consolations. Would to God when you read them, you understood them! And, Mat 10:19–20, "When they deliver you, take no thought what you shall say; it shall be given to you the same hour what you shall say: for it is not you that speaks, but the Spirit of your Father which speaks in you." "The very hairs of your head are numbered," says Christ, Mat 10:30. If God cares for our hairs, he much more cares for our souls, which he has sealed with his Holy Spirit. Therefore says Peter, "Cast all your care upon him; for he cares for you." (1 Peter 5:7) Paul, in 1 Cor 10:13, says: "God is true; he will not allow you to be tempted above your might." And Psalm 55:22, "Cast your care upon the Lord."

Let your care be to prepare yourself with all your strength, to walk whichever way he will have you; and to believe that he will go with you, and assist you, and strengthen you against all tyrants, and deliver you out of all tribulation. But by which way or means he will do it, commit that to him and to his godly pleasure and wisdom; cast that care upon him. Though it seems unlikely or impossible to natural reason, yet believe steadfastly that he will do it: and then he shall (according to his old use) change the course of the world, even in the twinkling of an eye, and come suddenly upon our giants like a thief in the night, and surround them in their wiles and worldly wisdom. "When they cry, Peace and all is safe, then shall their sorrows begin, as the pangs of a woman that travails with child." Then he shall destroy them, and deliver you, to the glorious praise of his mercy and truth. Amen.

And pertaining to those who despise God's word, considering it a fantasy or a dream; and to those also that for fear of a little persecution fall from it, set this before your eyes: God, since the beginning of the world, before a general plague, always sent his true prophets and the preachers of his word, to warn the people; and he gave them time to repent. But the great part of them hardened their hearts, and persecuted the word that was sent to save them. Then God destroyed them utterly, and took them completely from the earth. You see what followed the preaching of Noah in the old world; and what followed the preaching of Lot among the Sodomites; and the preaching of Moses and Aaron among the Egyptians; and all of that happened suddenly, against all possibility of man's wit. Moreover, as often as the children of Israel fell from God to the worshipping of images, he sent his prophets to them; but they persecuted the prophets and grew hard-hearted. Then he sent them into captivity in all the places of the world. Last of all, he sent his own Son to them; and they waxed more hard-hearted than ever before. See what a fearful example of his wrath and cruel vengeance he has made of them to all the world, now almost fifteen hundred years later.

Gildas preached to the old Britons also (who dwelled where our nation does now). He rebuked them for their wickedness, and prophesied both to the spiritual (as they will be called) and to the laymen also, what vengeance would follow unless they repented. But they grew hardhearted; and so God sent his plagues and pestilences among them; and he sent their enemies in upon them on every side; and he destroyed them utterly.

Mark also how Christ threatens those who forsake him, for whatever cause it is—whether for fear or shame, or for the loss of honor, friends, life, or goods. "Whoever denies me before men, I

will deny him before my Father that is in heaven. He that loves father or mother more than me, is not worthy of me." He says all this in Mat 10:33, 37. And in Mark 8:38 he says: "Whoever is ashamed of me, or my words, among this adulterous and sinful generation, the Son of Man shall be ashamed of him when he comes in the glory of his Father with his holy angels." Luke 9:62 also: "None that lays his hand to the plough, and looks back, is fit for the kingdom of heaven."

Nevertheless, if any man has resisted ignorantly, as Paul did, let him look at the truth which Paul wrote after he came to knowledge. Also, if any man, completely against his heart (but overcome with the weakness of the flesh), and for fear of persecution, has denied Christ, as Peter did, or has surrendered his Bible or put it away secretly, then let him (if he repents), come again and take better hold, and not despair, or take it as a sign that God has forsaken him. For God often takes his strength even from his elect, when they either trust in their own strength, or they neglect to call to him for his strength. He does that to teach them, and to make them feel that in that fire of tribulation, for his word's sake, nothing can endure and abide, except his work and that strength which he promised us. He would have us pray to him night and day for this strength, with all due attention.

The Scripture ought to be in the English tongue. The following may help you perceive how the Scripture ought to be translated into the native tongue, and why the reasons for the contrary are but sophistry and false wiles to frighten you away from the light, so that you will follow them blindfolded, and be their captive to honor their ceremonies, and to offer to their belly:

First, God gave the children of Israel a law by the hand of Moses in their native tongue; and all the prophets wrote in their native tongue, and all the psalms were in their native tongue. And there Christ was figured, and described in ceremonies, riddles, and parables, and in dark prophecies. Why may we not have the Old Testament along with the new, which is the light of the old, and in which is openly declared before the eyes, what was darkly prophesied in the Old? I can imagine no cause, truly, except that it is to keep us from seeing the work of antichrist and the juggling of hypocrites. What cause should there be that we, who walk in the broad day, should not see as well as those who walked in the night; or that we should not see as well at noon, as they did in twilight? Did Christ come to make the world more blind? By this means Christ is made the darkness of the world, and not the light as he himself says he is.

Moreover Moses says, Deut 6:7–9, "Hear, Israel; let these words which I command you this day stick fast in your heart, and whet them on your children, and talk of them as you sit in your house, and as you walk by the way, and when you lie down, and when you rise up; and bind them for a token to your hand, and let them be a remembrance between your eyes, and write them on the posts and gates of your house." This was commanded generally to all men. How does it happen that God's word pertains less to us than to them? Indeed, how does it happen that our "Moseses" forbid us, and command us to do the contrary; and threaten us if we do; and will not allow us once to speak about God's word? How can we whet God's word (that is, put it into practice; use and exercise it) upon our children and household, when we are forcefully kept from it and do not know it? How can we (as Peter commands) give a reason for our hope when we do not know what God has promised, or what to hope? Moses also commands in the same chapter, if the son asks what the testimonies, laws, and observances of the Lord mean, then the father is to teach him. If our children ask what our ceremonies mean (which are more than the Jews' were), no father can tell his son. In the eleventh chapter, he repeats it all again, for fear of forgetting.

They will say perhaps, that the Scripture requires a pure and quiet mind. Therefore the layman, because he is encumbered with worldly business, cannot understand them. If that is the cause, then it is plain that our prelates do not understand the Scriptures themselves: for no layman is so entangled with worldly business as they are. The great things of the world are ministered by them; nor do the lay-people do anything great, unless it is assigned to them. 'If the Scripture were in the native tongue,' they might say, 'then the lay-people would understand it, every man in his own way.' What end does the curate serve, but to teach him the right way? Is this not why the holy days were made, so that the people may come and learn? I say, are you not then abominable schoolmasters, in taking such great wages, if you will not teach? If you would teach, how could you do it so well, and with so great a profit, as when the lay-people have the Scripture before them in their native tongue? For then they would see, by the order of the text, whether you juggle them or not. And then they would believe it, because it is the Scripture of God, now matter how abominable your living may be. But now, because your living and your preaching are so contrary, and because they grope out your open and manifest lies in every sermon, and smell your insatiable covetousness, they do not believe you when you preach the truth. But, alas! The curates themselves (for the most part) no more know what the New or Old Testaments mean than the Turks do. Nor do they know any more than what they read at mass, matins, and evensong, which they still do not understand. Nor do they care, except to mumble as much each day as the magpie and popinjay speak—which do not know what to fill their bellies with. They will not let the layman have the word of God in his native tongue, and yet they let the priests have it—when a great part of them do not understand Latin at all. They only sing, say, and patter all day with their lips, what their heart does not understand.

Christ commands us to search the Scriptures, John 5:39. Though miracles bare record to his doctrine, yet he desired no faith be given either to his doctrine, or to his miracles, without the record of the Scripture. When Paul preached, Acts 17:11, the Bereans searched the Scriptures daily, to see whether they were as he cited them. Why should I not likewise see whether it is the Scripture that you cite? Indeed, why should I not see the Scripture, and the circumstances, and what goes before and after, so that I may know whether your interpretation is the right sense; or whether you juggle and stretch the Scripture forcefully to your carnal and fleshly purpose? Are you about to teach me, or deceive me?

Christ says that false prophets shall come in his name, and say that they themselves are Christ; that is, they shall so preach Christ that men must believe in them, in their holiness, and in the things of their imagination, without God's word. Indeed, that Against-Christ or Antichrist which will come, is nothing but a false prophet, who juggles the Scripture and beguiles the people with false interpretations—just as all the false prophets, scribes, and Pharisees did in the Old Testament. How shall I know whether you are that Against-Christ, or false prophets, seeing that you will not let me see how you cite the Scriptures? Christ says, "By their deeds you shall know them." Now when we look at your deeds, we see that you are all sworn together, and have separated yourselves from the lay-people, and have a separate kingdom among yourselves, and separate laws of your own making. With these you forcefully bind the lay-people, who never consented to their making. A thousand things forbid you, whom Christ made free from the law, to dispense them again for money. Nor is there any exception to this, except for a lack of money. You have a secret council by yourselves. You know all other men's secrets and counsels, and yet no man knows yours. You seek only honor, riches, promotion, authority, and to reign over all, and you will obey no man. If the father gives nothing out of courtesy, you will compel the son to give it forcefully, whether he will or not, by the craft of your own laws. These deeds are against Christ.

When a whole parish of us hire a schoolmaster to teach our children, what reason is there that we should be compelled to pay this schoolmaster his wages, and yet that he should have license to go wherever he will, even to dwell in another country, and to leave our children untaught? Does not the pope do just that? Have we not given our tithes of courtesy to someone to teach us God's word; and does not the pope come and compel us to forcefully pay those who never teach us? Does he not make one parson who never comes to us? Indeed, one shall have five or six, or as many as he can get, and never knows where one of them stands. Another is made vicar, to whom he gives a dispensation to go wherever he will, and to sit in as a parish priest, who can only minister a sort of silent ceremony. And, because he has the most labor and the least profit, he polls on his part; and he sets here a masspenny, there a trental, yonder dirige-money, and for his bead-roll, with a confession-penny, and such. Thus we are never taught, yet nevertheless we are compelled to pay for it; indeed, we are compelled to hire many costly schoolmasters. These deeds are truly against Christ. Shall we therefore judge you by your deeds, as Christ commands? So are you false prophets, and the disciples of Antichrist, or Against-Christ.

The sermons which you read in the Acts of the Apostles, and all that the apostles preached, were no doubt preached in the native tongue. Why then might they not be written in the native tongue? Just as, if one of us preaches a good sermon, why may it not be written down? Saint Jerome translated the Bible into his native tongue: why may we not also translate it? They will say it cannot be translated into our tongue, because the tongue is too rude. It is not so rude as them being liars. For the Greek tongue agrees more with the English tongue than with the Latin. And the properties of the Hebrew tongue agree a thousand times more with the English tongue than with Latin. The manner of speaking is the same; so that in a thousand places you need only translate it into English, word for word. But you must seek a workaround in the Latin, and yet still have much work to translate it favorably, so that it has the same grace and sweetness, the same sense and pure understanding, as it has in the Hebrew. It may be translated into the English a thousand times better than into the Latin. Indeed, and unless my memory fails me, and I have forgotten what I read when I was a child, you will find in the English chronicle, how King Adelstone had the holy Scripture translated into the tongue that was then used in England, and how the prelates exhorted him to do it.

Moreover, one of you always preaches contrary to another; and when two of you meet, the one disputes and brawls with the other as if they were two scolds. One holds to this doctor, and another to that; one follows Duns, another St. Thomas, another Bonaventure, Alexander de Hales, Raymond, Lyre, Brygot, Dorbel, Holcot, Gorram, Trumbett, Hugo de Sancto Victore, De Monte Regio, De Nova Villa, De Media Villa, and such beyond number. So that if you had but one book from every author, you could not pile them up in any warehouse in London, and every author is contrary to another. There is such a great diversity of spirits, how shall I know who lies, and who says the truth? By what shall I try and judge them? Truly, by God's word, which alone is true. But how shall I do that when you will not let me see the Scripture?

No, they say, the Scripture is so hard, that you could never understand it except by the doctors. That is, I must measure the yardstick by the cloth. Here are twenty cloths of diverse lengths and of various breadths: how shall I be sure of the length of the yardstick by them? I suppose, rather, I must be first sure of the length of the yardstick, and thereby measure and judge the cloths. If I must first believe the doctor, then the doctor is true first, and the truth of the Scripture depends of his truth; and so the truth of God springs from the truth of man. Thus Antichrist turns the roots of the trees upward. What is the cause that we damn some of Origen's works, and allow others? How do we know that some is heresy and some is not? By the Scripture, I believe. How do we know that St. Augustine (which is the best, or one of the best, that ever wrote about the Scripture) wrote many things that are amiss at the beginning, as many other doctors do? Truly, by the Scriptures—as he himself well-perceived afterward, when he looked more diligently at them, and revoked many things. He wrote of many things which he did not understand when he was newly converted, before he had thoroughly seen the Scriptures; and when he followed the opinions of Plato, and the common persuasions of man's wisdom that were then famous.

They will say yet more shamefully, that no man can understand the Scriptures without *philautia*, that is to say, philosophy. A man must be first well-versed in Aristotle, before he can understand the Scripture, they say. Aristotle's doctrine is, that the world was without beginning, and it shall be without end; and that the first man never was, and the last shall never be; and that God does everything out of necessity. He does not care what we do, nor will he ask for any accounts of what we do. Without this doctrine, how could we understand the Scripture that says God created the world out of nothing; and God works all things of his free will, and for a secret purpose; and that we shall all rise again; and that God will have an accounting of all that we have done in this life! Aristotle says, Give a man a law, and he has power of himself to do or to fulfill the law, and he becomes righteous by working righteously. But Paul, and all the Scripture says, that the law reveals sin only, and it does not help. Nor does any man have power to fulfill the law, till the Spirit of God is given to him through faith in Christ. Is it not madness, then, to say that we could not understand the Scripture without Aristotle? Aristotle's righteousness, and all his virtues, spring from man's free will. A Turk, and every infidel and idolater, may be righteous and virtuous with that righteousness, and those virtues. Moreover, Aristotle's felicity and blessedness rests in avoiding all tribulations; it rests in riches, health, honor, worship, friends, and authority. This felicity pleases our clergy well. Now, without these, and a thousand similar points, you could not understand Scripture, which says that righteousness comes by Christ, and not of man's will; and virtues are the fruits and the gift of God's Spirit; and Christ blesses us in tribulations, persecution, and adversity! How, I say, you could understand the Scripture without philosophy, is that Paul, in the second chapter to the Colossians, warned them to 'beware lest any man should spoil them' (that is to say, rob them of their faith in Christ) 'through philosophy and deceitful vanities, and through the traditions of men, and the ordinances according to the world, and not according to Christ?' By this means, then, you would have no man teach another; but every man takes the Scripture, and learns by himself. No, truly, I say not. Nevertheless, seeing that you will not teach, if any man thirsts for the truth, and reads the Scripture by himself, desiring God to open the door of knowledge to him, then God for his truth's sake will and must teach him.

My meaning is that, just as a master teaches his apprentice to know all the points of the yardstick; first, how many inches, then how many feet, and the half-yard, the quarter, and the nail; and then he teaches him to measure other things by it—even so I would have you teach the people God's law, and what obedience God requires of us to father and mother, master, lord, king, and all superiors, and with what friendly love he commands one to love another, Teach them to know that natural venom and birth-poison, which moves the very hearts of us to rebel against the ordinances and the will of God. Prove that no man is righteous in the sight of God, but that we are all damned by the law. And then, when you have made them meek, and frightened them with the law, teach them the testament and promises which God has made to us in Christ, and how much he loves us in Christ. Teach them the principles and the ground of the faith, and what the sacraments signify. Then the Spirit will work with your preaching, and make them feel it. So it would come to pass, that as we know by natural wit what follows from a true principle of natural reason, even so, by the principles of the faith, and by the plain Scriptures, and by the circumstances of the text, we should judge all men's exposition, and all men's doctrine, and receive the best, and refuse the worst. I would have you teach them also the properties and manner of speaking of the Scripture, and how to expound proverbs and similitudes. And then, if they go abroad and walk by the fields and meadows of all kinds of doctors and philosophers, they could catch no harm. They would be able to discern the poison from the honey, and bring home nothing but what is wholesome.

But now you do the complete opposite. You drive them from God's word, and you will let no man come to it until he has been two years a master of arts. First, they nosel them in sophistry, and in *bene fundatum*. And there they corrupt their judgments with apparent arguments, and with reporting to them texts of logic, of natural philautia, of metaphysic, and moral philosophy, from all kinds of Aristotle's books, and from all manner of doctors they never saw. Moreover, one holds this, another that; one is a Real, another is a Nominal. What wonderful dreams they have of their predicaments, universals, second intentions, quiddities, hoecceities, and relatives; and whether species fundata in chimera are vera species; and whether this proposition is true, *Non ens est aliquid*; whether ens is *oequivocum*, or *univocum*. Ens is a voice only, say some. Ens is univocum, says another, and it descends into ens creatum, and into ens increatum, per modos intrinsecos. When they have in this way brawled eight, ten, twelve or more years, and after that their judgments are utterly corrupt, then they begin their divinity—but not at the Scripture.

Rather every man takes a different doctor. The one being contrary to the other, these doctors are as sundry and as diverse, as there are diverse fashions and odd shapes; none like another among our sects of religion. Every religion, every university, and almost every man, has a different divinity.

Now whatever opinions every man finds with his doctor, that is his gospel, and that is only true with him; and that he holds all his life long: and every man, to maintain his doctor, corrupts the Scripture, and fashions it after his own imagination, as a potter does his clay. From what text you prove hell, another will prove purgatory; another limbo patrum; and another the assumption of our lady: and another shall prove from the same text that an ape has a tail. And from what text the gray friar proves that our lady was without original sin, from the same text the black friar will prove that she was conceived in original sin. And they do all this with apparent reasons, with false similitudes and likenesses, and with arguments and persuasions of man's wisdom. Now there is no other division or heresy in the world except man's wisdom, and when man's foolish wisdom interprets the Scripture. Man's wisdom scatters, divides, and makes sects. While the wisdom of one says that a white coat is best to serve God in, another says it is black, another gray, and another blue. And while one says that God will hear your prayer in this place, another says it is in that place. While one says this place is holier, another says that place is holier; and this religion is holier than that; and this saint is greater with God than that; and an hundred thousand things like it. Man's wisdom is plain idolatry. Nor is there any other idolatry than to imagine about God after man's wisdom. God is not man's imagination; but only that which he says of himself. God is nothing but his law and his promises; that is to say, that which he bids you to do, and that which he bids you to believe and hope. God is but his word, as Christ says, John 8:58 "I am, what I say to you;" that is to say, That which I preach I am; my words are spirit and life. God is only what he testifies of himself; and to imagine any other thing of God than that, is damnable idolatry. Therefore says Psalm 119:2, "Happy are those who keep the testimonies of the Lord, who seek Him;" that is to say, seek what God testifies and witnesses to us. But how shall I do that, when you will not let me have his testimonies, or witnesses, in a tongue which I understand? Will you resist God? Will you forbid him to give his Spirit to the layman as well as to you? Has he not made the English tongue? Why do you forbid him to speak in the English tongue then, as well as in the Latin?

Finally, it is evident, and clearer than the sun, that threatening and forbidding lay people to read the Scripture is not for the love of your souls (which they care for as the fox cares for the geese). Consider that they permit you to read Robin Hood, and Bevis of Hampton, Hercules, Hector and Troilus, with a thousand histories and fables of love and wantonness, and of ribaldry, as filthy as the heart can think, to corrupt the minds of youth with, completely contrary to the doctrine of Christ and of his apostles. For Paul says, "See that fornication, and all uncleanness, or covetousness, are not once named among you, as it becomes saints; nor filthiness, nor foolish talking or jesting, which are not attractive. For this you know: that no whoremonger, or unclean person, or covetous person, which is the worshipper of images, has any inheritance in the kingdom of Christ and of God." And after, he says, "Through such things the wrath of God comes upon the children of unbelief." Now seeing that they permit you to freely read those things which corrupt your minds and rob you of the kingdom of God and Christ, and bring the wrath of God upon you, how is forbidding Scripture done for the love of your souls?

A thousand reasons more might be made, as you may see in Paraclesis Erasmi, and in his preface to the Paraphrase of Matthew, to which they should be compelled to hold their peace, or to give embarrassing answers. But I hope that these are sufficient for those who thirst after the truth. God for his mercy and truth shall well open them more, indeed, and other secrets of his godly wisdom, if they are diligent to cry to him—may God grant such grace. Amen.

THE PROLOGUE TO THE BOOK.

Because our holy prelates and spiritually religious, who ought to defend God's word, speak evil of it instead, and shame it all they can, and rail on it; and bear their captives in hand, so that it causes insurrection and teaches the people to disobey their heads and governors, and moves them to rise against their princes, and to make everything common, and to make havoc of other men's goods: therefore have I made this little treatise that follows, containing all obedience that is of God. Whoever reads it will easily perceive not only their contrary teachings—that they lie—but also the very cause of such blasphemy, and what stirs them to so furiously rage and to belie the truth.

However, it is nothing new to the word of God to be railed upon. Nor is this the first time that hypocrites have ascribed to God's word the vengeance of which they themselves were ever the cause. For the hypocrites, with their false doctrine and idolatry, have evermore led the wrath and vengeance of God upon the people, so sorely, that God could no longer forbear or defer his punishment. Yet God, who is always merciful, before he would take vengeance, has always sent his true prophets and true preachers to warn the people so that they might repent. But the people for the most part, and namely the heads and rulers, through the comfort and persuading of the hypocrites, have waxed ever more hard-hearted than before; they have persecuted the word of God and his prophets. Then God, who is also righteous, has always poured his plagues upon them without delay. The hypocrites ascribe these plagues to God's word, saying, 'See what mischief has come upon us since this new learning came up, and this new sect, and this new doctrine.' You see this in Jeremiah 44:18, where the people cried to go back to their old idolatry, saying, "Since we left it, we have been in need, and have been consumed with war and hunger." But the prophet answered them that their idolatry went to the heart of God, so that he could no longer allow the maliciousness of their own imaginations or inventions; and that the cause of all such mischiefs was because they would not hear the voice of the Lord, and walk in his law, ordinances, and testimonies. The scribes and the Pharisees also laid to Christ's charge, in Luke 23:2–5, that he moved the people to sedition. They said to Pilate, "We have found this fellow perverting the people, and forbidding them to pay tribute to Caesar, and he says that he is Christ, a king." And again in the same chapter, "He moves the people," they said, "teaching throughout Jewry, and he began at Galilee even to this place." They laid the same thing to the apostles' charge, as you may see in the Acts. St. Cyprian also, and St. Augustine, and many others, wrote works in defense of the word of God against such blasphemies. So you see how it is nothing new, but an old and customary thing with hypocrites, to blame God's word and true preachers for all the mischief which their lying doctrine is the very cause of.

Nevertheless indeed, after the preaching of God's word, because it is not truly received, God sends great trouble into the world. He does this partly to avenge himself of the tyrants and persecutors of his word, and partly to destroy those worldly people who make of God's word nothing but a cloak for their fleshly liberty. They are not all good that follow the gospel. Christ (Mat 13:47) likens the kingdom of heaven to a net cast into the sea, that catches fishes both good and bad. The kingdom of heaven is the preaching of the gospel, to which come both good and bad. But the good are few. Christ therefore calls them a "little flock," Luke 12:32. For they are ever few that come to the gospel from a true intent, seeking nothing in it but the glory and praise of God, and offering themselves freely and willingly to receive adversity with Christ for the gospel's sake, and to bear witness to the truth, so that all men may hear it. The great number come, and ever came, and followed even Christ himself, for a worldly purpose. You may well see this in John 6, where almost five thousand followed Christ, and they would also have made him a king, because he had fed them well. He rebuked them, saying, "You do not seek me because you saw the miracles, but because you ate the bread and were filled;" he drove them away from him with hard preaching.

Even so, now as ever, most seek liberty. They are glad when they hear that the insatiable covetousness of the clergy is rebuked; when they hear their falsehood and wiles spoken about; when tyranny and oppression are preached against; when they hear how kings and all officers should rule in a Christian and brotherly way, and seek nothing else than to save the wealth of their subjects. But then they hear that the clergy have no authority from God to pill and poll as they do, and to raise taxes and gatherings to maintain their fantasies, and to make war for some unknown reason. Therefore, because the heads will not rule in this way, the people will no longer obey. Instead, they resist and rise up against their evil heads; one wicked man destroys another. Yet, God's word is not the cause of this, nor yet the preachers. For Christ himself taught all obedience, how it is not lawful to resist wrong; it is for the officer appointed to that duty. A man must love his enemy, and pray for those who persecute him, and bless those who curse him. All vengeance must be remitted to God. A man must forgive if he would be forgiven by God; yet the people for the most part did not receive it. They were ever ready to rise and to fight. For whenever the scribes and Pharisees went to take Christ, they were afraid of the people. "Not on the holy day," they said, Matthew 26:5, "lest an uproar arise among the people." Matthew 21:46, "They would have taken him but they feared the people." And Luke 20:40–44, Christ asked the Pharisees a question to which they dared not answer, for the people might stone them. Last of all, the very disciples and apostles of Christ, after hearing for so long of Christ's doctrine, were still ready to fight for Christ, completely against Christ's teaching. Matthew 26:51–52, Peter drew his sword, but he was rebuked; and Luke 9:54, James and John would have had fire rain down from heaven to consume the Samaritans, and to avenge the injury of Christ, but they were likewise rebuked. If Christ's disciples were carnal for so long, is it any wonder that we are not all perfect the first day? Indeed, this is what we are taught (even babes!): to kill a Turk, to slay a Jew, to burn a heretic, to fight for the liberties and rights of the church (as they call it). Indeed, we are brought to believe that if we shed even the blood of a Christian, or if a son sheds the blood of his father, for the defense not only of the pope's godhead, but also for whatever cause it may be (indeed, even if it is for no cause), just because his holiness commands it—that we deserve as much as Christ deserved for us, when he died on the cross. Or if we are slain in the pope's battle, that our souls go—no, fly—to heaven, and they are there before our blood is cold. Inasmuch, I say, as we have sucked such bloody imaginations into the bottom of our hearts, even with our mother's milk, and have been hardened in it for so long, is it any wonder that if, while we are still young in Christ, we think it would be lawful to fight for the true word of God? Yes, a man might be thoroughly persuaded that it is not lawful to resist his king, even if the king were to wrongfully take away his life and goods; yet might he think that it is lawful to resist the hypocrites, and to rise up, not against his king but with his king, to deliver his king out of the bondage and captivity in which the hypocrites hold him with their wiles and falsehood, so that no man may be allowed to come to his king, to tell him the truth.

See this, that it is the bloody doctrine of the pope

which causes disobedience, rebellion and insurrection. For he teaches to fight and to defend his traditions, and whatever he dreams, with fire, water, and sword; and to disobey father, mother, master, lord, king, and emperor. Indeed, he teaches to invade whatever land or nation that will not receive and admit his godhead. Where the peaceable doctrine of Christ teaches to obey and to suffer for the word of God, and to remit the vengeance and the defense of the word to God, who is mighty and able to defend it; and who, as soon as the word is openly preached, and testified, or witnessed to the world, and when he has given them a season to repent, is ready at once to take vengeance upon his enemies, He shoots arrows with heads dipped in deadly poison at them; and pours his plagues from heaven down upon them; and sends the murrain and pestilence among them; and sinks their cities; and makes the earth swallow them; and encompasses them in their wiles; and takes them in their own traps and snares, and casts them into the pits which they dug for others; and makes them dazed in the head; and utterly destroys them with their own subtle counsel.

Prepare your mind therefore for this little treatise; read it discreetly; and judge it objectively. When I cite any Scripture, look at the text to see whether I interpret it rightly. You will easily perceive it by the circumstance and process of the texts if you make Christ the foundation and the ground, and build it all on him, and refer it all to him. You will also find that the exposition agrees with the common articles of faith and open Scriptures. And may God the Father of mercy, who for his truth's sake raised our Savior Christ up again to justify us, give you his Spirit to judge what is righteous in his eyes; and give you strength to abide by it, and to maintain it with all patience and long-suffering, for the example and edifying of his congregation, and for the glory of his name. Amen.

THE OBEDIENCE OF ALL DEGREES PROVED BY GOD'S WORD.

OBEDIENCE OF CHILDREN TO THEIR ELDERS.

God, who works all in all things, for a secret judgment and purpose, and for his godly pleasure, provided an hour that your father and mother should come together, to make you through them. He was present with you in your mother's womb, and fashioned you and breathed life into you; and, for the great love he had for you, provided milk in your mother's breasts for you when you were born; he also moved your father and mother, and all others, to love you, pity you, and care for you.

And just as he made you through them, so has he cast you under the power and authority of them, to obey and serve them in his stead, saying, "Honor your father and mother." Exodus 20:12. This is not to be understood only as bowing the knee, and taking off your hat, but that you love them with all your heart; and fear and dread them, and wait on their commandments; and seek their worship, pleasure, will, and profit in all things; and give your life for them, counting them worthy of all honor; remembering that you are their good and possession, and that you owe them yourself, and all you are able to do—indeed, more than you are able.

Understand also, that whatever you do unto them, whether good or bad, you do unto God. When you please them, you please God; when you displease them, you displease God; when they are angry with you, God is angry with you. Nor is it possible for you to come to God's favor again, though all the angels of heaven pray for you, until you have submitted yourself to your father and mother again.

If you obey, though it is but carnally, either for fear, for vain glory, or profit, your blessing will be long life on the earth. For he says, "Honour your father and mother, that you may live long upon the earth." (Exo 20:12) Contrariwise, if you disobey them, your life shall be shortened on the earth. For it follows, Exodus 21:15, "He that strikes his father or mother shall be put to death for it. And he that curses," that is to say, rails or dishonors his father or mother with offensive words, "shall be slain for it." And, "If any man has a stubborn and disobedient son, who does not listen to the voice of his father and the voice of his mother, though they have disciplined him, and he disregards them—then let his father and mother take him, and bring him to the seniors or elders of the city, and to the gate of that place: and let them say to the seniors of that city, 'Our son is stubborn and disobedient: he will not hearken to our voice: he is a rioter and a drunkard.' Then let all the men of the city stone him to death with stones: so shall you put away wickedness from among you, and all Israel shall hear and shall fear." (Deut 21:18–21)

Though the temporal officers (to their own damnation) are negligent in punishing such disobedience, (as the spiritual officers are to teach it), and wink at it, or look at it through the fingers, yet they shall not escape unpunished. For the vengeance of God shall accompany them (as you may see in Deut 28:15 ff) with all misfortune and evil luck; and shall not depart from them until they are murdered, drowned, or hanged; or until, by one mischance or another, they are utterly brought to nothing. Indeed, the world often hangs many a man for what they never deserved. But God hangs them because they would not obey, or hearken to their elders—as the consciences of many will find when they come to the gallows. There they can preach and teach others what they themselves would not learn in season.

The marriage also of the children pertains to their elders, as you may see in 1 Corinthians 7 and throughout the Scripture, from the authority of the commandment, "Child, obey your father and mother." The heathen and gentiles have always kept this, and keep it to this day, to the great shame and rebuke of us Christians. The weddings of our virgins (it is shameful to speak of) are more like breeding dogs than marrying a reasonable creature. Do we not daily see three or four men seeking matrimony with one woman before the commissary or official, of which not one has the consent of her father and mother? And yet the one with the most money has the best right, and will have her, despite all her friends and in defiance of God's ordinances.

Moreover, when she is given by the judge to the one party, and is married, even then the contrary party often sues before a higher judge, or another that succeeds him. And then for money, he divorces her again. In this way, the covetousness and ambition of our prelates shamefully mocks the laws of God. I will pass over with silence how many years they prolong the sentence with cavils and subtlety, if they are well-monied on both sides. If a damsel promises to marry two men, how shameful is the counsel the prelates will give the second one; and then the religious ones of Satan will separate inseparable matrimony. For after you are lawfully married at the commandment of father and mother, and with the consent of all your friends, yet if you are willing to be disguised like one of them, and swear obedience to their traditions, you may disobey father and mother, break the oath which you swore to God before his holy congregation, and withdraw your love and charity, the highest of God's commandments. You may withdraw that duty and service which you owe your wife, which Christ cannot dispense with. For Christ is not against God, but with God; and he did not come to break God's ordinances, but to fulfill them. That is, he came to overcome you with kindness; and to make you do, out of love, the thing which the law compels you to do. For only love, and serving your neighbor, will fulfill the law in the sight of God. To be a monk or a friar, you may thus forsake your wife before you have lain with her; but not to be a secular priest. And yet, after you are professed, the pope will dispense with your marriage for money, both for your coat and all your obedience; and he will make a secular priest of you. Likewise, it is simony to sell a benefice, as they call it; but to resign on a pension, and then redeem it, is not simony at all. O crafty jugglers and mockers of the word of God!

OBEDIENCE OF WIVES TO THEIR HUSBANDS.

After Eve was deceived by the serpent, God said to her, Genesis 3:16, "Your lust or appetite shall pertain to your husband; and he shall rule you, or reign over you." God, who created the woman, knows what is in that weak vessel (as Peter calls her), and has therefore put her under the obedience of her husband, to rule her lusts and wanton appetites. 1 Peter 3:1 exhorts wives to "be in subjection to their husbands," following the example of the holy women of old who trusted in God, "just as Sara obeyed Abraham and called him lord." Sara, before she was married, was Abraham's sister, and equal with him; but, as soon as she was married, she was in subjection, and became (without comparison) inferior—for this is the nature of wedlock, by the ordinance of God. It would be much better if our wives followed the example of the holy women of old in obeying their husbands, rather than to worship them with a Paternoster, an Ave and a Credo, or to set candles before their images. Paul, in Ephesians 5:22–24, says, "Women, submit yourselves to your own husbands as to the Lord. For the husband is the wife's head, even as Christ is the head of the congregation. Therefore, as the congregation is in subjection to Christ, likewise let wives be in subjection to their husbands in all things."

"Let the woman, therefore, fear her husband," as Paul says in the same place. For her husband is, to her, in the place of God; so she obeys him, and waits on his commandments; and his commandments are God's commandments. If she therefore grudges against him, or resists him, she grudges against God, and resists God.

OBEDIENCE OF SERVANTS TO THEIR MASTERS.

"Servants, obey your carnal masters with fear and trembling, in singleness of your hearts, as unto Christ; not with service in the eye-sight as men-pleasers, but as the servants of Christ, doing the will of God from the heart, with good will, as though you served the Lord, and not men." (Colossians 3:22–23) And, 1 Peter 2:18–21, "Servants, obey your masters with all fear, not only if they are good and courteous, but also if they are unjust. For it comes of grace, if a man, for conscience' sake towards God, endures grief and suffering wrongfully. For what praise is there if you take it patiently when you are beaten for your faults? But if you behave well, and yet you suffer wrong and take it patiently, then there is favor with God. To this, truly, you were called. For Christ also suffered for our sakes, leaving us an example to follow his steps."

Therefore, whatever kind of servant you are, during the period of your contract, your master is in the place of God to you; and through him God feeds you, clothes you, rules you, and teaches you. His commandments are God's commandments; and you ought to obey him as to God, and in all things seek his pleasure and profit. For you are his good and possession, as are his ox and horse. Whoever desires to take you from your master, without his love and license, is condemned by God, who says, "See that you do not covet your neighbour's servants." (Exodus 20:10)

Paul the apostle sent Onesimus home to his master, as you read in Paul's epistle to Philemon. Philemon, like his servant, was converted by Paul, and was indebted to Paul, and to the word that Paul preached, not only for his servant but also for himself. Though Paul was in need, and lacked someone to minister to him in the bonds which he suffered for the gospel's sake, yet Paul would not retain the servant needed to further the gospel, without the consent of the master. O how sorely the doctrine of Christ and his apostles differs from the doctrine of the pope and his apostles! For if any man will obey neither father nor mother, neither lord nor master, neither king nor prince, that man needs only to take the mark of the beast, that is, to shave himself as a monk, friar, or priest, and then he is immediately free and exempted from all service and obedience due to man. Someone who will obey no man (as they will not) is most acceptable to them. The more disobedient you are to God's ordinances, the more apt and fit you are for theirs. Professing, vowing, and swearing obedience to their ordinances, is nothing other than defying, denying, and foreswearing obedience to the ordinances of God.

OBEDIENCE TO KINGS, PRINCES, AND RULERS.

"Let every soul submit himself to the authority of the higher powers. There is no power except from God: the powers that be are ordained by God. Whoever therefore resists that power, resists the ordinance of God. Those who resist will receive damnation for themselves. For rulers are not to be feared for good works, but for evil. Do you want to be without fear of that power? Then do well, and so you shall be praised by him; for he is the minister of God for your good. But if you do evil, then fear: for he does not bear a sword for nothing; for he is the minister of God to take vengeance on those who do evil. Therefore you must obey; not for fear of vengeance only, but also because of conscience. It is for this reason that you pay tribute: for they are God's ministers serving for that purpose. Give to every man therefore his duty: tribute to whom tribute belongs; custom to whom custom is due; fear to whom fear belongs; honour to whom honour pertains. Owe nothing to any man; but to love one another: for he that loves another fulfills the law. For these commandments, you shall not commit adultery, you shall not kill, you shall not steal, you shall not bear false witness, you shall not covet, and if there are any other commandments, they are all comprehended in this saying, 'Love your neighbor as yourself.' Love does no harm to a neighbor: therefore love is the fulfillment of the law."A father is both lord and judge over his children, forbidding one brother to avenge himself on another; if any cause of strife is between them, he will have it brought to himself or his assigns, to be judged and corrected. So God forbids all men to avenge themselves, and takes the authority and office of avenging to himself; saying, "Vengeance is mine, and I will reward," Deut 32:35. Paul repeats this text in Romans 12:19; for it is impossible for a man to be a righteous, equitable, and indifferent judge in his own cause—lusts and appetites so blind us. Moreover, when you avenge yourself, you do not make peace; rather, you stir up more debate.

God has therefore given laws to all nations, and in all lands he has put kings, governors, and rulers in his place, to rule the world through them. He has commanded that all causes be brought before them, as you read in Exodus 22:9–11, "In all causes (he says) of injury or wrong, whether it be over an ox, ass, sheep, or vesture, or anything lost which another challenges, let the cause of both parties be brought to the gods; the one whom the gods condemn, shall pay double to his neighbor." Note that judges are called gods in the Scriptures, because they are in God's place, and they execute the commandments of God. In another place in the same chapter (22:28), Moses charges them, saying: "See that you do not rail at the gods, nor speak evil of the ruler of your people." Whoever therefore resists them, resists God, for they are in the place of God; and those who resist shall receive damnation.

Such obedience to father and mother, master, husband, emperor, king, lords and rulers, requires a God of all nations, indeed, even of the Turks and infidels. The blessing and reward of those that keep them is the life of this world; as you read, "Keep my ordinances and laws; which if a man keeps them, he shall live by them." (Lev 18:5) Paul repeats this text in Romans 10:5, proving thereby that the righteousness of the law is but worldly, and the reward for it is the life of this world; but the curse of those who break the law is the loss of this life; as you see by the punishment appointed for them.

Whoever keeps the law (whether for fear, vainglory, or profit), though no man rewards him, yet God will bless him abundantly, and send him worldly prosperity; you read in Deuteronomy 28 what good blessings accompany the keeping of the law. We see that the Turks far exceed us Christian men in worldly prosperity, for justly keeping their temporal laws. Likewise, even if no man punishes law-breakers, God will send his curses upon them till they are utterly brought to nothing, as you read most terribly in the same passage.

Nor may the inferior person avenge himself on the superior, or violently resist him, for whatever wrong it may be. If he does, he is condemned in doing the deed; it is as if he took for himself what belongs to God alone, who says, "Vengeance is mine, and I will reward." Deut 32:35. And Christ says, Matthew 26:52, "All that take the sword shall perish by the sword." Do you take a sword to avenge yourself? If so, then you give God no opportunity to avenge you; instead, you rob him of his most high honor, by not letting him be judge over you.

If any man might have avenged himself on his superior, David could most righteously have done so on king Saul, who so wrongly persecuted David, for no other cause than God had anointed him king, and promised him the kingdom. Yet when God delivered Saul into the hands of David, so that he might have done what he would with him, as you see in 1 Sam 24, Saul came into the camp where David was and David came to him secretly, and cut off a piece of his garment. As soon as he did it, his heart struck him, because he had done so much to his lord. When his men encouraged him to slay Saul, David answered, "The Lord forbid that I should lay my hand on him;" nor did he allow his men to hurt Saul. When Saul left, David followed him, and showed him the piece of his garment, and said, "Why do you believe the words of men who say David goes about to do you harm? Look and see that there is neither evil nor wickedness in my hand, and that I have not trespassed against you, and yet you lie in wait for my life. May God judge between you and me, and avenge me on you; but my hand is not upon you. As the old proverb says (said David), 'Out of the wicked shall wickedness proceed, but my hand is not upon you,'" meaning that God ever punishes one wicked man by another. Again David said, "May God be judge, and decide between you and me, and behold and plead my cause, and deliver me from your hand." In the 26th chapter of the same book, when Saul persecuted David again, David came to Saul by night, as he and all his men slept, and took his spear and a cup of water from his head. Then Abishai, David's servant, said "God has delivered your enemy into your hand this day: let me now therefore nail him to the ground with my spear, and give him but one strike and no more." David forbade him, saying, "Do not kill him; for who may lay hands on the Lord's anointed, and not be guilty? The Lord lives," or by the Lord's life, "he does not die unless the Lord strikes him, or his day to die has come, or else he goes into battle and perishes there." Why did David not slay Saul, seeing that he was so wicked, not only in persecuting David, but in disobeying God's commandments, and having wrongfully slain eighty-five of God's priests? Truly, it was not lawful. If he did it, then he must have sinned against God; for God made the king in every realm judge over all, and there is no judge over him. The one who judges the king judges God; and the one that lays hands on the king, lays hand on God; and the one who resists the king, resists God and he damns God's law and ordinance. If the subjects sin, then they must be brought to the king's judgment. If the king sins, then he must be reserved for the judgment, wrath, and vengeance of God. As it is to resist the king, so is it to resist his officer, who is set or sent to execute the king's commandment.

In the first chapter of the second book of Samuel, David commanded the young man to be slain, who brought him the crown and bracelet of Saul, and who, to please David, said that he himself had slain Saul. In the fourth chapter of the same book, David commanded that those two be slain who brought him the head of Ishbosheth, Saul's son; and yet, by their act, the whole kingdom returned to David, according to the promise of God.

In Luke 13:1–3, when they showed Christ the blood of the Galileans, which Pilate mingled with their own sacrifice, Christ answered, "Do you suppose that these Galileans were sinners above all other Galileans, because they suffered such punishment? I tell you, no; but unless you repent, you will likewise perish." This was told to Christ, no doubt, with the same intent they had when they asked him, "Is it lawful to give tribute to Caesar or not?" (Matthew 22:17).

They thought it was not a sin to resist a heathen prince; and few of us would think, if we were under the Turk, that it would be a sin to rise up against him, and rid ourselves of his dominion. In thinking so, it is clear that our bishops have sorely robbed us of the true doctrine of Christ. But Christ condemned their deeds, and also the secret thoughts of all others who consented to it, saying: "Unless you repent, you will likewise perish." As Christ would say, I know that you are, within your hearts, like those who were outward in their deeds, and you are under the same damnation. Unless you repent quickly, you will break out at last into like deeds, and likewise perish; as it came to pass afterward.

Hereby you see that the king is in this world without law; and may at his lust do right or wrong, and shall give an account only to God.

Another conclusion is this, that no person, or any degree of person, is exempt from this ordinance of God. Nor can the profession of monks and friars, or anything that the pope or bishops can lay out for themselves, exempt them from the sword of the emperor or kings, if they break the laws. For it is written, "Let every soul submit himself to the authority of the higher powers." Here no man is excepted; all souls must obey. The higher powers are the temporal kings and princes to whom God has given the sword to punish whoever sins. God has not given them swords to punish one, and let another go free, or let sin go unpunished. Moreover, with what face did the clergy, which ought to be the light and an example of good living to all others, dare to sin unpunished, or to be excepted from tribute, toll, or custom, or not bear the pain of their brothers in the maintenance of kings and others, whom God ordained to punish sin? "There is no power but of God." By power, understand the authority of kings and princes. "The powers that be are ordained by God. Whoever therefore resists power, resists God:" indeed, even though he is pope, bishop, monk, or friar. "Those who resist will receive damnation." Why? For God's word is against them, which will have all men under the power of the temporal sword: for "rulers are not to be feared for good works, but for evil." Here you see that those who resist the powers, or seek to be exempt from their authority, have evil consciences. They seek the liberty to sin unpunished, and to be free from bearing pain with their brothers. "Do you want to be without fear of the power? Then do well, and you shall have praise from him," that is to say, from the ruler. The clergy ought to rid themselves from fear of the temporal sword with good living; not with craft, or by blinding the kings, and bringing God's vengeance upon them, or by purchasing a license to sin unpunished.

"For he is the minister of God for your good:" to defend you from a thousand inconveniences, from thieves, murderers, and those who would defile your wife, your daughter, and take from you all that you have, indeed, life and all, if you resisted. Furthermore, though he is the great tyrant in the world, yet to you he is a great benefit of God, and a thing for which you ought to thank God highly. For it is better to have something, than to be completely stripped of all. It is better to pay a tenth than to lose all. It is better to suffer one tyrant than many, and to suffer wrong from one man than from every man. Indeed, it is better to have a tyrant for your king than a shadow: a passive king that does nothing himself, but allows others to do with him what they will, and to lead him wherever they want. For a tyrant, though he does wrong to the good, yet he punishes the evil, and makes all men obey; nor does he allow any man to poll but himself. A king that is soft as silk and effeminate, that is to say, who is turned into the nature of a woman, — with his own lusts, which are like the longing of a woman with child, so that he cannot resist them, and is under the wily tyranny of those who ever rule him — a soft king is much more grievous to the realm than an outright tyrant. Read the chronicles, and you will find it always so. "But if you do evil, then fear; for he does not bear a sword for nothing: for he is the minister of God, to take vengeance on those who do evil." If the office of princes, given to them by God, are to take vengeance on evil-doers, then by this text and by God's word, every prince is damned who gives liberty or license to the clergy to sin unpunished; and not only to sin unpunished themselves, but to open sanctuaries for sinners, privileged places, churchyards, and even St. John's hold. Indeed, if they come short of all these, they may quote a neck-verse to save all kinds of trespassers from the fear of the sword—the vengeance of God—put in the hands of princes to take vengeance on all such evil-doers. GOD requires the law to be kept by all men, let them keep it for whatever purpose they will. Will they not keep the law? So vouchsafes he not that they enjoy this temporal life. Now are there three natures of men: one is altogether brutish; in no way do they receive the law in their hearts, but instead they rise against princes and rulers whenever they are able to make their party good. These are signified by those who worshipped the golden calf: for Moses broke the tables of the law, before he came at them.

The second are not so brutish; they receive the law; and the law comes to them; but they do not look Moses in the face: for his countenance is too bright for them; that is, they do not understand that the law is spiritual, and it requires the heart. They look at the pleasure, profit, and promotion that follow keeping the law, and with regard to the reward, they keep the law outwardly with their works, but not in their heart. For if they could obtain the same honor, glory, promotion and dignity, and avoid all inconveniences if they broke the law, then they would just as readily break the law, and follow their lusts. The third are spiritual; they look Moses openly in the face. They are, as Paul says, Romans 2:14, "a law to themselves;" they have the law written in their hearts by the Spirit of God. These need neither king nor officers to drive them, nor any man to offer them a reward in order to keep the law; for they do it naturally. The first work only from the fear of the sword: the second work for the reward: the third work for love, freely. They look at the exceeding mercy, love, and kindness, which God showed them in Christ, and therefore they love in return, and work freely. Heaven they take as the free gift of God, through Christ's deservings; and they hope without any doubt that God, according to his promise, will also defend them in this world, and do all things for them, out of his goodness and for Christ's sake, and not for any goodness that is in them. They consent to the law, that it is holy and just; and that all men ought to do whatever God commands, for no other reason than God commands it. And their great sorrow is that there is no strength in their members to do what their heart desires to do, and is thirsty to do. This last sort keep the law of their own accord, and they do that in the heart; they have professed perpetual war against the lusts and appetites of the flesh, till they are utterly subdued: yet it is not through their own strength—rather, knowing and acknowledging their weakness, they ever cry to God for strength, who has promised assistance to all that call upon him. These follow God and they are led by his Spirit. The other two are led by their lusts and appetites. Lusts and appetites are diverse and many in each man; indeed, one lust is contrary to another, and the greater lust carries a man away with it. We are also changed from one lust to another. We are disposed to one when we are children; to another when we are young men; and to another when we are old. We are disposed to one in the evening, and to another in the morning. Indeed, sometimes it alters six times in an hour. How does all this play out? Because the will of man follows the affection, and it is subject to the affection; as the affection errs, so does the will; as the affection is in captivity, so is the will; nor is it possible for the will to be free, where the affection is in bondage.

So that you may perceive and feel the thing in your heart, and not be a vain sophister, disputing about words without perceiving their meaning, mark this: the root of all evil, the great damnation and most terrible wrath and vengeance of God that we are in, is natural blindness. We are all out of the right way; every man is in his own ways: one judges this to be best, and another that to be best. Now worldly affection is nothing but craft and subtlety, to obtain what we falsely judge to be best. As I err in my affection, so I err in my will. When I judge something to be evil which indeed is good, then I hate what is good. And when I suppose that what is evil indeed, is good, then I love evil. It is as if I am persuaded that my best friend is my enemy; and then I hate my best friend. And if I am brought to believe that my worst enemy is my friend, then I love my worst enemy. Now when we say that every man has free will to do what he lusts after, then I say, truly, men do what they lust after. Notwithstanding, to follow our lusts is not freedom; rather, it is captivity and bondage. If God opens any man's wits, to make him feel in his heart that lusts and appetites are damnable, and God gives him the power to hate and resist those appetites; then he is free, even with the freedom with which Christ makes us free. And he then has the power to do the will of God.

You may hereby perceive, that all that is done in the world before the Spirit of God comes, and gives us light, is damnable sin; and the more glorious, the more damnable; so that what the world counts most glorious is more damnable in the sight of God, than that which the whore, thief, and murderer do. Using the blind reasons of worldly wisdom you may change the minds of youth, and make them give themselves to what you will, either for fear, for praise, or for profit; and yet it but changes them from one vice to another—just as the persuasions of her friends made Lucretia chaste. Lucrece believed if she was a good housewife and chaste, that she should be most glorious, and that all the world would give her honor, and praise her. She sought her own glory in her chastity, and not God's. When she had lost her chastity, then she counted herself most abominable in the sight of all men. The pain and thought which she had, was not that she had displeased God, but that she had lost her honor; and so she slew herself. Look how great her pain and sorrow was for the loss of her chastity, and how great her glory and rejoicing were in it, and how she so much despised those who were otherwise, and did not pity them. God more abhors this sort of pride than the vice of any whore. The moral virtues of Aristotle, Plato, and Socrates are like it, and all the doctrine of the philosophers—the very gods of our school-men.

It is the same way for most of our most holy religions. For with a similar imagination, they do things which those of Bedlam may see are but madness. Look at the miracles which God did by the saints. They were to move the unbelieving to the faith, and to confirm the truth of his promises in Christ, whereby all who believe are made saints—as you see in the last chapter of Mark. "They preached," he says, "everywhere, the Lord working with them, and confirming their preaching with miracles that followed." In Acts chapter four, the disciples prayed that God would stretch forth his hands, to do miracles and wonders in the name of Jesus. And Paul in 1 Corinthians 14 says, that the miracle of speaking with diverse tongues is but a sign for unbelievers, and not for those who believe. But these others turn such miracles to another purpose, saying in their blind hearts, 'See what miracles God showed for this saint; he must be truly great with God!' — and at once they turn themselves from God's word, and put their trust and confidence in the saint and in his merits; they make a god of the saint. From their blind imagination they make a testament, or a bond, between the saint and them—but the testament of Christ's blood has been clean forgotten. They look at the saints' garments and lives, or rather lies which men lay on the saints, and imagine in their hearts, saying, 'This saint, for wearing such a garment, and for such deeds, has become so glorious in heaven, that if I do likewise, then I will also become glorious.' They do not see the faith and trust which the saints had in Christ; nor the word of God which the saints preached; nor the intent of the saints: how the saints did such things to tame their bodies, and to be an example to the world, and to teach that those things which the world most wonders at and magnifies, are to be despised. They do not see that some lands are so hot that a man can neither drink wine nor eat flesh in them; nor do they consider the complexion of the saints; and they do not see a thousand similar things. So when they have brutalized their bodies, and brought them to such a condition that hardly any restorative can regain their health again, yet they would rather die than eat flesh. Why? For they think, 'I have for twenty, thirty, or forty years eaten no flesh; and so I have no doubt that by now I have earned as high a place as the best of them—should I now lose that? No, I would rather die!' They are like Lucretia, who had similar thoughts—she would rather have been slain than to lose her glory (if he had not been too strong for her). They ascribe heaven to their imaginations and to their mad inventions; they do not receive it from the liberality of God, by the merits and deservings of Christ.

One who is now renewed in Christ, keeps the law without any written law, or any compulsion by a ruler or officer, but only by the leading of the Spirit. However, the natural man is enticed and moved to keep the law carnally, for carnal reasons and worldly persuasions, such as for glory, honor, riches, and dignity. But the last remedy of all, when all others fail, is fear. Beat one, and the rest will abstain for fear—just as Moses continually put Israel in remembrance, saying, 'Kill, stone, burn; so shall you put evil away from you, and all Israel shall hear and fear,' and do so no more. If fear does not help, then God will that they are taken out of this life.

Kings were ordained then, as I said before, and the sword was put in their hands, to take vengeance on evildoers, so that others might fear. Kings were not ordained to fight one against another, or to rise up against the emperor to defend the false authority of the pope, that very antichrist. But it seems only bishops can minister the temporal sword. Their office is the preaching of God's word, laid apart—but they will neither do that, nor allow any other man to do it. Instead, they slay with the temporal sword, which they have gotten out of the hand of all princes, those who would. The preaching of God's word is hateful and contrary to them. Why? For it is impossible to preach Christ, unless you preach against antichrist. That is to say, with their false doctrine and violent sword, they quench the true doctrine of Christ with force. Just as you cannot heal any disease unless you begin at the root; even so you cannot preach against mischief, unless you begin with the bishops. Kings are but shadows—vain names and idle things. They have nothing to do in the world, until our holy father needs their help.

The pope, contrary to all conscience, and against the doctrine of Christ who says, "My kingdom is not of this world" (John 18:36), has usurped the right of the emperor. By the policy of the bishops of Almany, and by corrupting the electors, or choosers of the emperor, with money, it happens that no one is ever chosen emperor who is not able to make his party good with the pope. To stop the emperor, so that he will not come to Rome, he brings the French king up to Milan; and on the other side he brings the Venetians. If the Venetians come too near, the bishops of France must bring in the French king. And the Socheners are called, sent for to come and succor. And for their labor, he gives a rose to some, and a cap of maintenance to another. One is called Most Christian King; another, Defender of the Faith; another, the Eldest Son of the Most Holy Seat. He emblazons the coat of arms of others; and puts in the holy cross, the crown of thorn, or the nails, and so forth. If the French king goes too far, and creeps up either to Bononia or Naples; then our English bishops must bring in our king. The craft of the bishops is to entitle one king with another's realm. He is called king of Denmark and of England; and this one is the king of England and of France. To blind the lords and the commoners, the king must assert his right. Then the land must be taxed and every man must pay; the treasure is borne out of the realm, and the land is beggared. How many thousands of men's lives it has cost! And how many hundreds of thousands of pounds have been carried out of the realm in our memory! Besides that, how abominable an example of gathering there was! Truly, no tyrant since the world began ever did such a thing. Indeed, it was never before heard of or thought about among the Jews, Saracens, Turks, or heathen, since God created the sun to shine. That a beast should break into the temple of God, that is to say, into the heart and consciences of men, and compel every man to swear what he was worth, and to lend what would never be paid back. How many thousands forswore themselves! How many thousands set themselves above their ability, partly for fear lest they be forsworn, and partly to save their credence! When the pope has his purpose, then peace is made, though no man knows how; and our worst enemy is now our best friend.

Now because the emperor is able to obtain his right, French, English, Venetians and all must be upon him. O great whore of Babylon, how she abuses the princes of the world! How drunk she has made them with her wine! How shameful are the licenses she gives them, to use necromancy, to hold whores, to divorce themselves, to break the faith and break promises that one makes with another; that the confessors shall deliver to the king the confession of whomever he will, and even exempts them from the law of God—which Christ himself cannot do!

AGAINST THE POPE'S FALSE POWER.
Christ says to Peter, "Put your sword into its sheath; for all that lay their hand upon the sword shall perish with the sword." (Mat 26:52) That is, whoever without the commandment of the temporal officer, to whom God has given the sword, lays a hand on the sword to take vengeance, deserves death in doing the deed. God put not only Peter under the temporal sword, but also Christ himself; as it appears in the fourth chapter to the Galatians. And Christ says, Mat 3:15, "Thus it becomes us to fulfill all righteousness," that is to say, all ordinances of God. If the head is then under the temporal sword, how can the members be excepted? If Peter sinned in defending Christ against the temporal sword, (whose authority and ministers the elders abused against Christ then, as ours do now), who can excuse our prelates of sin, who obey neither king nor emperor? Indeed, who can excuse from sin either the kings that give these exemptions, or the bishops that receive them, contrary to God's ordinances and Christ's doctrine?

In Matthew 17:24–27, both Christ and Peter pay tribute. The meaning of Christ's question to Peter is that, 'if princes take tribute only from strangers and not from their children, then truly I ought to be free, who am the Son of God. They are my servants and ministers, and they have their authority from me.' Yet because they did not know that, and because Christ did not come to use that authority, but for our sakes to be our servant, and to bear our burden, and to obey all ordinances both right and wrong, and to teach us—therefore he said to St. Peter, "Pay for you and me, lest we offend them." Moreover, though Christ and Peter (because they were poor) might have escaped payment, yet he would not escape it for fear of offending others and hurting their consciences. For he might well have given occasion to the tribute-gatherers to misjudge both him and his doctrine. Indeed, the Jews might happily have been offended by it, and then have thought it unlawful for them to pay tribute to heathen princes and idolaters, seeing that Christ, so great a prophet, did not pay. Indeed, what other thing causes the commoners to so little regard their princes, as seeing them both despised and disobeyed by the clergy? But our prelates, who care nothing for offending consciences, and care less for God's ordinances, will pay nothing, except when princes must fight in our most holy father's quarrel, and against Christ. Then they are the first. There also are none so poor then, that they do not have something to give.

Mark here, how our school doctors are past all shame, (as Rochester is in his sermon against Martin Luther), who disputes about this text of Matthew saying that, because Peter paid tribute, he is greater than the other apostles, and has more authority and power than they do, and was head of them all. This is contrary to so many clear texts, where Christ rebukes them, saying, that it is a heathenish thing to climb above another, or desire to be greater. To be great in the kingdom of heaven is to be a servant; and he that most humbles himself, and becomes a servant to others, (following the example of Christ, I mean, and his apostles, and not of the pope and his apostles, our cardinals and bishops), that person is great in the kingdom. If Peter became great by paying tribute, then how is it that these clergy pay none at all? But paying tribute is a sign of subjection, truly. The reason why Christ paid, was because he had a household; and Peter paid for the same reason: he had a house, a ship and nets, as you read in the gospel. But let us go back to Paul. "Therefore you must obey, not for fear of vengeance only, but also because of conscience." That is, you are so wicked (as now for many years our pope and prelates everywhere are), though you need not obey the temporal sword for fear of vengeance, yet you must obey because of conscience. First, because of your own conscience. For though you are able to resist, you will never have a good conscience as long as God's word, law, and ordinance are against you. Secondarily, for your neighbor's conscience. For though, through craft and violence you might escape, and obtain liberty or privilege to be free from all manner of duties, yet you should neither sue for nor seek any such thing. Nor should you admit or accept it if it were proffered, lest your freedom make your weaker brother grudge and rebel. He sees you discharged, and he himself is more laden, and so your portion is laid on his shoulders. Do you not see, that if a man favors one son more than another, or one servant more than another, how all the rest will grudge, and how love, peace, and unity is broken? What Christianly love do you have toward your neighbor, when you can find it in your heart to go up and down by him all day long, discharged, and see him over-charged, indeed, to fall under his burden, and yet you will not once reach out your hand to help him? What good conscience can there be among our clergy, to gather so great a treasure together, and with hypocrisy about their false learning to rob almost every man of house and lands; and yet not be content with it, but with all craft and wiliness to purchase such great liberties and exemptions from all manner of bearing with their brothers, seeking in Christ nothing but lucre?

I pass over with silence how they teach princes in every land to load new exactions and tyranny on their subjects, more and more daily, nor do I say for what purpose they do it. God, I trust, will shortly disclose their juggling, and bring their falsehood to light; and place a medicine on them to make their scabs break out. Nevertheless, I say that they have robbed all realms, not only of God's word, but also of all wealth and prosperity. They have driven peace out of all the lands, and withdrawn themselves from all obedience to princes, and separated themselves from the laymen, counting them viler than dogs; and they have set up that great idol, the whore of Babylon, the antichrist of Rome whom they call pope; and they have conspired against all commonwealths and have made them a several kingdom in which it is lawful to work all kinds of abominations unpunished. They have spies in every parish, and in every great man's house, and in every tavern and alehouse. And through confessions they know all secrets, so that no man may open his mouth to rebuke what they do, without shortly being made a heretic. One of them is in every council; indeed, the majority and the chief rulers of the councils are comprised of them: but no outsider is a member of their council.

"Even for this reason you pay tribute", that is, to your neighbor for conscience' sake, and for the cause that follows: "For they are God's ministers, serving for the same purpose." Because God will so have it, we must obey. We do not look (if we have Christ's Spirit in us) to what is good, profitable, glorious and honorable for us; nor on our own will, but on God's will only. "Give to every man therefore his duty; tribute to whom tribute belongs; custom to whom custom is due; fear to whom fear belongs; honour to whom honour pertains."So that you might feel the working of the Spirit of God in you, and lest the beauty of the deed deceive you, and make you think that the law of God, which is spiritual, is satisfied and fulfilled by the outward and bodily deed, this follows: "Owe nothing to any man, but to love one another: for he that loves another fulfills the law. For these commandments—you shall not commit adultery, you shall not kill, you shall not steal, you shall not bear false witness, you shall not desire, and so forth, and if any other commandments—are all comprehended or contained in this saying, 'Love your neighbor.' Therefore love is the fulfillment of the law." Here you have sufficient evidence against all the sophisters, holiness-workers, and justifiers, in the world, who so magnify their deeds. The law is spiritual, and it requires the heart. It is never fulfilled by the deed in the sight of God. With the deed you fulfill the law before the world, and live by it; that is, you enjoy this present life, and avoid the wrath and vengeance, the death and punishment, which the law threatens against those who break it. But before God you keep the law only if you love. Now what will make us love? Truly, faith will do that. If you behold how much God loves you in Christ, and what vengeance he has delivered you from for his sake, and what kingdom he has made you an heir of, then you will see cause enough to love your enemy without respect to any reward, either in this life or in the life to come—but only because God would have it so, and Christ has deserved it. Yet you should feel in your heart that all your deeds to come are already abundantly recompensed in Christ.

You will say perhaps, If love fulfills the law, then it justifies. I say that that what a man fulfills the law with declares him justified; but what gives him that with which to fulfill the law, justifies him. By justifying, understand the forgiveness of sins and the favor of God. Now the text says, Romans 10:4, "The end of the law," or the cause for which the law was made, "is Christ, to justify all that believe." That is, the law is given to identify sin, to kill the conscience, to damn our deeds, to bring us to repentance, and to drive us to Christ. In him, God has promised his favor, and forgiveness of sin, to all who repent and consent to the law, that it is good. If you believe the promises, then God's truth justifies you, that is, it forgives you, and receives you into favor for Christ's sake. In surety of this, and to certify your heart, he seals you with the Spirit, Eph 1:13 and 4:30, and (2 Cor 5:5) Paul says, "Who gave us his Spirit in earnest." Now the Spirit is given to us through Christ. Nevertheless the Spirit, and his fruits with which the heart is purified, such as faith, hope, love, patience, long-suffering, and obedience, could never be seen without outward experience. For if you were not brought into affliction sometimes, from which only God could deliver you, you would never see your faith. Indeed, unless you fought sometimes against desperation, hell, death, sin, and the powers of this world, for your faith's sake, you should never know true faith from a dream. Unless your brother now and then offended you, you could not know whether your love was godly. For a Turk is not angry till he is hurt and offended. But if you love those who do you evil, then your love of God is evident. Likewise, if your rulers were always kind, you would not know whether your obedience was pure or not. But and if you can patiently obey evil rulers in everything that is not to the dishonor of God, and when you do not hurt your neighbors, then you are sure that God's Spirit works in you, and that your faith is no dream, nor is it any false imagination.

Therefore Paul counsels, "Recompense evil to no man. And on your part, have peace with all men. Dearly beloved, do not avenge yourselves, but give way to the wrath of God: for it is written, Vengeance is mine, and I will reward, says the Lord. Therefore, if your enemy hungers, feed him; if he thirsts, give him drink: for in so doing, you shall heap coals of fire on his head," that is, you shall kindle love in him. "Do not be overcome by evil;" (Romans 12) that is, do not let another man's wickedness make you wicked also. "But overcome evil with good;" that is, with softness, kindness, and all patience win him; even as God with kindness won you.

The law was given in thunder, lightning, fire, smoke, and the noise of a trumpet and a terrible sight; so that the people quaked for fear, and stood far off, saying to Moses, "You speak to us, and we will hear: do not let the Lord speak to us, lest we die." No ear, if it is awakened and understands the meaning, is able to abide the voice of the law, unless the promises of mercy are nearby. Thunder, unless the rain of mercy is joined with it, destroys all, and does not build. The law is a witness against us, and testifies that God abhors the sins that are in us, and abhors us for our sins' sake.

In a similar way, when God gave the people of Israel a king, it thundered and rained, so that the people feared so sorely, that they cried to Samuel to pray for them so that they should not die. As the law is a terrible thing, even so is the king: for he is ordained to take vengeance, and he has a sword in his hand, and not peacocks' feathers. Fear him, therefore, and look at him as you would look at a sharp sword that hung over your head by a hair.

Heads and governors are ordained by God, and are even the gift of God, whether they are good or bad. Whatever is done to us by them, God does, whether good or bad. If they are evil, why are they evil? Truly, for our wickedness' sake they are evil; because if they were good, we would not receive that goodness by the hand of God, and be thankful, submitting ourselves to his laws and ordinances; but we would have abused the goodness of God for our sensual and beastly lusts. Therefore God makes his scourge of them, and turns them into wild beasts, contrary to the nature of their names and offices, even into lions, bears, foxes, and unclean swine, to avenge himself on our unnatural and blind unkindness, and on our rebellious disobedience.

In Psalm 107:33–34 you read, "He destroyed the rivers, and dried up the springs of water, and turned the fruitful land into barrenness, for the wickedness of the inhabitants in it." When the children of Israel had forgotten God in Egypt, God moved the hearts of the

Egyptians to hate them, and to subdue them with craft and wiliness, Psalm 105:24–25:1 In Deuteronomy 3:26, Moses repeats this, saying, "God was angry with me for your sakes." So that the wrath of God fell on Moses for the wickedness of the people. In 2 Sam. 24:2–4, 15,2 God was angry with the people, and moved David to number them; Joab and the other lords wondered why he wanted them numbered, because they feared some evil would follow. They tried to dissuade the king; yet it did not help. God hardened David's heart in his purpose, in order to have an occasion to slay the wicked people.

Evil rulers then are a sign that God is angry; and angry with us. Is it not out of great wrath and vengeance, that a father and mother would hate their children, even their flesh and blood? Or that a husband would be unkind to his wife, or a master to the servant that waits on him for his profit? Or that lords and kings would be tyrants to their subjects and tenants who pay them tribute, toll, custom, and rent, and who labor and toil to ensure their honor, and maintain them in their estate? The prelates and shepherds of our souls, were to feed Christ's flock with Christ's doctrine, and walk before them, living according to that doctrine. They were to give their lives for them as an example and for their edification, to strengthen their weak faiths. Is this not a fearful judgment of God, and a cruel wrath, that they are now so sorely changed, that if they smell that one of their flock (as they now call them, and no longer Christ's) just once longs for or desires the true knowledge of Christ, they will slay him, burning him with fire most cruelly? What is the cause of this, that they also teach false doctrine, and confirm it with lies? Truly, it is the hand of God to avenge the wickedness of those who have no love or passion for the truth of God when it is preached, but rejoice in unrighteousness. You may see this in 2 Thess 2:9–11, where Paul speaks of the coming of antichrist, "Whose coming shall be," he says, "by the working of Satan, with all miracles, signs and wonders, which are but lies, and in all deceivable unrighteousness among those who perish, because they did not receive any love towards the truth to have been saved. Therefore God shall send them strong delusion, to believe lies." Mark how God, to avenge his truth, sends false doctrine and false miracles to the unthankful, to confirm them, and to harden their hearts in their false way. Afterward it shall not be possible for them to admit the truth: as you see in Exodus 7 and Exodus 8, how God allowed false miracles to be shown in the sight of Pharaoh, to harden his heart so that he should not believe the truth; his sorcerers turned their rods into serpents, and turned water into blood, and made frogs by their enchantment: so he thought that Moses did all his miracles by the same craft, and not by the power of God, and therefore he abode in unbelief, and perished in resisting God.

Let us receive all things from God, whether it is good or bad. Let us humble ourselves under his mighty hand, and submit ourselves to his nurture and chastising, and not withdraw ourselves from his correction. Read Hebrews 12 for your comfort. Let us not take the staff by the end, or seek to avenge ourselves on his rod, which is what the evil rulers do. The child will not be without a rod as long as he seeks to avenge himself on the rod, for he has an evil heart; he does not think that the correction is right, or that he deserved it. Nor does he repent; instead he rejoices in his wickedness. Indeed, as long as he is this way, the rod shall be made sharper and sharper. If he acknowledges his fault and takes the correction meekly, and even kisses the rod, and amends himself with the instruction and nurture of his father and mother, then the rod will be taken away and burnt.

So, if we resist evil rulers, seeking to set ourselves at liberty, we shall, no doubt, bring ourselves into more evil bondage, and wrap ourselves in much more misery and wretchedness. For if the heads overcome, then they lay more weight on their backs, and make their yoke sorer, and tie them shorter. If they overcome their evil rulers, then they make way for a more cruel nation, or for some tyrant of their own nation, which has no right to the crown. If we submit ourselves to the chastising of God, and meekly acknowledge our sins for which we are scourged, and kiss the rod, and amend our living, then will God take the rod away. That is, he will give the rulers a better heart. Or if they continue their malice and persecute you for well-doing, and because you put your trust in God, God will deliver you out of their tyranny for his truth's sake. It is the same God now that was in the old time, who delivered the fathers and the prophets, the apostles and other holy saints. And whatever he swore to them he has sworn to us. As he delivered them out of all temptation, suffering, and adversity, because they consented and submitted themselves to his will, and trusted in his goodness and truth, even so he will do to us, if we do likewise.

Whenever the children of Israel fell from the way which God commanded them to walk in, he gave them up to one tyrant or another. As soon as they came to the knowledge of themselves, and repented, crying for mercy, and leaning toward the truth of his promises, he sent one to deliver them, as the histories of the Bible make mention.

A Christian man, in respect to God, is but a passive thing; a thing that suffers only and can do nothing; just as the sick, in respect to the surgeon or physician, suffers only. The surgeon lances and cuts out the dead flesh, searches the wounds, thrusts in tents, sears, burns, sews or stitches, and applies caustics to draw out the corruption; and last of all, he applies healing plasters, and makes it whole. The physician likewise gives purgations and drinks to drive out the disease, and then with restoratives, he brings health. Now if the sick resist the razor, the searching iron, and so forth, does he not resist his own health, and becomes the cause of his own death? So likewise it is with us if we resist evil rulers, which are the rod and scourge with which God chastises us; they are the instruments with which God searches our wounds; and the bitter drinks that drive out the sin and to make it apparent, and the caustics to draw out by the roots the core of the pocks of the soul that frets inwardly. A Christian man, therefore, receives all things by the hand of God, both good and bad, both sweet and sour, both wealth and woe. If any person does me good, whether it is father, mother, and so forth, I receive that from God, and I give thanks to God: for he gave the means for it, and he gave a commandment, and moved his heart so to do. I also receive adversity from the hand of God as a wholesome medicine, though it is somewhat bitter. Temptation and adversity both kill sin, and also express it.

For even though a Christian man knows everything necessary to live, yet the flesh is so weak that he can never take up his cross himself, to kill and mortify the flesh. He must have someone else lay his cross on his back. In many, also, sin lies hidden within, and it festers; it rots inwardly and is not seen, so that they think they are good and perfect, and keep the law. As the young man in Matthew 19 said, he observed all the law from childhood; and yet he lied falsely in his heart, as the text following well declares. When all is at peace, and no man troubles us, we think that we are patient and that we love our neighbors as ourselves; but let our neighbor hurt us, in word or deed, and then find we that it is otherwise. We fume, and rage, and set up the bristles, and bend ourselves to take vengeance. If we loved with godly love, for Christ's kindness' sake, we should desire no vengeance; but instead we would pity him, and desire God to forgive and amend him, knowing well that no flesh can do otherwise than sin, unless God preserves him. You will say, What good does such persecution and tyranny have for the righteous? First, it makes them feel God's Spirit working in them, and that their faith is unfeigned. Secondarily, I say that no man is so great a sinner, if he repents and believes, that he cannot be righteous in Christ, and included in the promises. Yet if you look at the flesh, and to the law, there is no man so perfect that he is not found to be a sinner; nor is any man so pure that he does not have something yet to be purged. This shall suffice at this time as concerning obedience.

Because God excludes no rank from his mercy, whoever repents and believes his promises, (of whatever rank he may be), that person shall partake of his grace. Therefore, as I have described the obedience of those who are under power and rule, even so, with God's help, I will (as it is my duty) declare how the rulers, whom God shall graciously call to the knowledge of the truth, ought to rule.

OFFICE OF A FATHER, AND HOW HE SHOULD RULE.

"Fathers, do not move your children to wrath, but bring them up in the nurture and information of the Lord." (Ephesians 6) and "Fathers, do not berate your children, lest they be of desperate mind;" (Colossians 3).

That is, lest you discourage them. For where the fathers and mothers are wayward, hasty and churlish, ever brawling and chiding, there the children are shortly discouraged and heartless, and apt for nothing; nor can they do anything rightly. "Bring them up in the nurture and information of the Lord." Teach them to know Christ, and set God's ordinance before them, saying, 'Son, or daughter, God has created you and made you, through us your father and mother; and at his commandment we have so long kindly brought you up this way, and kept you from all perils. He has commanded you also to obey us, saying, Child, obey your father and mother. If you meekly obey, so shall you grow both in the favor of God and man, and in the knowledge of our Lord Christ. If you will not obey us at his commandment, then we are charged to correct you; indeed, if you do not repent and amend yourself, God will slay you by his officers, or punish you everlastingly.' Do not nurture them in a worldly way, and with worldly wisdom, saying, 'You will come to honor, dignity, promotion, and riches; you will be better than such and such; you will have three or four benefices, and be a great doctor or a bishop, and have so many men waiting on you, and do nothing but hawk and hunt, and live at your pleasure; you will not need to sweat, labor, or take any pains for your living,' and so forth. This fills them full of pride, disdain, and ambition, and corrupting their minds with worldly persuasions. Let the fathers and mothers mark how they themselves were disposed at all ages; and help their children by the experience of their own infirmities, and keep them from such occasions. Let them teach their children to ask their fathers and mothers for marriages. And let their elders provide marriages for them in season; teaching them also to know that she is not his wife whom the son takes, nor is he her husband which the daughter takes, if it is without the consent and good-will of their elders, or of those who have authority over them. If their friends will not marry them, then they are to blame if they marry on their own. Do not let the fathers and mothers always take extremes in their authority with their children; but at times suffer with them, and bear their weaknesses, as Christ does ours. Seek Christ in your children, in your wives, servants, and subjects. Father, mother, son, daughter, master, servant, king, and subject, are names in the worldly regiment. In Christ we are all one thing; none is better than another, all are brothers; and all must seek Christ and our brother's profit in Christ. He that has the knowledge of Christ, whether he is the lord or king, is bound to submit himself, and to serve his brothers, and give himself for them, to win them to Christ.

OFFICE OF A HUSBAND, AND HOW HE OUGHT TO RULE.

"Husbands, love your wives as Christ loved the congregation, and gave himself for it, to sanctify it and cleanse it. Men ought to love their wives as their own bodies. For this cause a man shall leave father and mother, and shall continue with his wife, and both shall be made one flesh. See that every one of you loves his wife even as his own body." (Ephesians 5) Paul says all this, and he also says, "Husbands, love your wives, and do not be bitter towards them."

Peter says in 1 Peter 3:7, "Men, dwell with your wives according to knowledge" (i.e., according to the doctrine of Christ), "giving reverence to the wife, as to the weaker vessel" (i.e., help her to bear her infirmities); "and as to those who are also heirs of the grace of life, so that your prayers will not be hindered." In many things God has made the men stronger than the women; not to rage against them and be tyrants to them, but only to help them bear their weakness. Be courteous to them, therefore, and win them to Christ; overcome them with kindness, so that from love they may obey the ordinance that God has made between man and wife.

OFFICE OF A MASTER, AND HOW HE OUGHT TO RULE.

Paul (Eph 6:9) says: "Masters, do the same things to them" (that is, be masters following the example and doctrine of Christ, as Paul taught the servants before to obey their masters as they would Christ), "putting away threatening," that is, give them fair words, and exhort them kindly to do their duty; indeed, nurture them as your own sons with the Lord's nurture, so that they may see in Christ a cause why they ought to lovingly obey. And "also remember (he says) that your master is in heaven; and there is no respect of persons with him." That is, he is unbiased and impartial: a servant is as great in his sight as a master. And in Colossians 4:1 he says: "You masters, do to your servants what is just and equal, remembering that you also have a master in heaven." Give your servants kind words, food, raiment, and learning. Do not be bitter towards them, or rail on them; give them no cruel looks: but deal with them according to the example and doctrine of Christ. And when they labor hard, cherish them in return. When you correct them, let it be by God's word; and do it with such good manner, that they may see how you do it only to amend them, and to bring them into the way which God bids us to walk in, and not to avenge yourselves, or wreak your malice on them. If sometimes through hastiness you exceed proper measure in punishing, then recompense it another way, and pardon them another time.

DUTY OF LANDLORDS.

Let Christian landlords be content with their rent and old charges; not raising the rent or fines, or bringing up new charges to oppress their tenants; nor letting two or three tenantries to one man. Let them not remove their commons, nor make parks nor pastures out of whole parishes. For God gave the earth to man to inhabit; and not to sheep and wild deer. Be like fathers to your tenants: indeed, be to them as Christ was to us, and show them all love and kindness. Whatever business is among them, do not be partial, favoring one more than another. Consider the shall leave father and mother, and shall continue with his wife, and both shall be made one flesh. See that every one of you loves his wife even as his own body." (Ephesians 5) Paul says all this, and he also says, "Husbands, love your wives, and do not be bitter towards them."

Peter says in 1 Peter 3:7, "Men, dwell with your wives according to knowledge" (i.e., according to the doctrine of Christ), "giving reverence to the wife, as to the weaker vessel" (i.e., help her to bear her infirmities); "and as to those who are also heirs of the grace of life, so that your prayers will not be hindered." In many things God has made the men stronger than the women; not to rage against them and be tyrants to them, but only to help them bear their weakness. Be courteous to them, therefore, and win them to Christ; overcome them with kindness, so that from love they may obey the ordinance that God has made between man and wife.

OFFICE OF A MASTER, AND HOW HE OUGHT TO RULE.

Paul (Eph 6:9) says: "Masters, do the same things to them" (that is, be masters following the example and doctrine of Christ, as Paul taught the servants before to obey their masters as they would Christ), "putting away threatening," that is, give them fair words, and exhort them kindly to do their duty; indeed, nurture them as your own sons with the Lord's nurture, so that they may see in Christ a cause why they ought to lovingly obey. And "also remember (he says) that your master is in heaven; and there is no respect of persons with him." That is, he is unbiased and impartial: a servant is as great in his sight as a master. And in Colossians 4:1 he says: "You masters, do to your servants what is just and equal, remembering that you also have a master in heaven." Give your servants kind words, food, raiment, and learning. Do not be bitter towards them, or rail on them; give them no cruel looks: but deal with them according to the example and doctrine of Christ. And when they labor hard, cherish them in return. When you correct them, let it be by God's word; and do it with such good manner, that they may see how you do it only to amend them, and to bring them into the way which God bids us to walk in, and not to avenge yourselves, or wreak your malice on them. If sometimes through hastiness you exceed proper measure in punishing, then recompense it another way, and pardon them another time.

DUTY OF LANDLORDS.

Let Christian landlords be content with their rent and old charges; not raising the rent or fines, or bringing up new charges to oppress their tenants; nor letting two or three tenantries to one man. Let them not remove their commons, nor make parks nor pastures out of whole parishes. For God gave the earth to man to inhabit; and not to sheep and wild deer. Be like fathers to your tenants: indeed, be to them as Christ was to us, and show them all love and kindness. Whatever business is among them, do not be partial, favoring one more than another. Consider the complaints, quarrels, and strife that exist among them as the diseases of sick people; and as a merciful physician, heal them with wisdom and good counsel. Be compassionate and tenderhearted toward them, and do not let one of your tenants tear out another's throat. Rather, judge their causes indifferently, and compel them to make their ditches, hedges, gates, and ways. For you were made landlords for such causes; and for such causes men paid rent at the beginning. For if there were no such order, then one would slay another, and all would go to waste. If your tenant labors and toils all year to pay you your rent, and after he has bestowed all his labor, his neighbors' cattle devour his fruits, then how tedious and bitter his life would be! See therefore that you do your duties again; and allow no man to do them wrong, except the king only. If he does them wrong, then they must abide God's judgment.

DUTY OF KINGS, JUDGES, AND OFFICERS.

If kings would be Christian in deed and not only name, then let them give themselves altogether to the wealth of their realms, following the example of Christ. Let them remember that the people are God's, and not theirs—indeed, they are Christ's inheritance and possession, bought with his blood. The most despised person in his realm is still the king's brother, a fellow-member with him, and equal with him in the kingdom of God and of Christ. Let him therefore not think himself too good to render service to his people, or seek anything other in them than a father seeks in his children, indeed, than Christ sought in us. The king, in the temporal regiment, stands in the place of God, and represents God himself, and is better than his subjects, without compare. Yet let him put that off, and become a brother, doing and leaving undone all things with regard to the commonwealth, so that all men may see that he seeks nothing but the profit of his subjects. When a cause that requires execution is brought before him, let him take the person of God on himself. Like God, let him favor no creature, but hear all indifferently, whether it is a stranger or one of his own realm, the small as well as the great. Let him judge righteously, "for the judgment is the Lord's." In time of judgment he is not a minister in the kingdom of Christ; he preaches no gospel, except the sharp law of vengeance. Let him take the holy judges of the Old Testament for his example, namely Moses, who was merciless in executing the law. Otherwise Moses is more than a mother to them, never avenging his own wrongs, but suffering all things; bearing every man's weakness, teaching, warning, exhorting, and ever caring for them. He so tenderly loved them, that he desired God either to forgive them, or to damn him with them.

Let the judges also privately, when they have put off

the person of a judge, exhort with good counsel, and warn the people, and help them so that they do not come under God's judgment. But in the causes that are brought to them, when they sit in God's stead, let them judge and condemn the trespasser under lawful witnesses. Let them not bind the consciences of men, in the manner of antichrist's disciples, and compel them either to disavow themselves by the almighty God and by the holy gospel of his merciful promises, or else testify against themselves. Our prelates learned this abomination from Caiphas, Matthew 26, saying to Christ, "I adjure or charge you in the name of the living God, to tell us whether you are Christ, the Son of God." Let what is known only to God, and of which no proof can be made or lawful witness brought, abide until the coming of the Lord, who will reveal all secrets. If any malice issues from this, let them judge that only. God has given them no further authority.

Moses (Deut 16:18–20) warns judges to keep themselves upright, and to respect no man's person; that is, that they do not prefer the high before the low, the great before the small, the rich before poor; his acquaintance, friend, kinsman, countryman, or one of his own nation, before a stranger, a friend or an alien—indeed, or one of their own faith before an infidel. Rather, they should look at the cause only, to judge it indifferently. For the position that they are in, and the law that they execute, are God's. Because God has made all, and is God of all, and all are his sons, even so he is judge over all, and he will have all judged by his law indifferently, and all will have the right of his law, and he will avenge the wrong done to the Turk or Saracen. For although they are not under the everlasting testament of God in Christ (as few of us which are called Christian are), and are not greater than those to whom God has sent his promises, and although God has not poured his Spirit into their hearts to believe them, nor through faith has he graven a hunger in their hearts to fulfill the law of love—yet they are under the testament of the Natural Law, which is the law of every land, made for the commonwealth there, made for peace and unity, so that one may live with another. And if the infidels keep these laws, they have promises of worldly things. Whoever, therefore, hinders even an infidel from the right of that law, sins against God, and God will be avenged of him. Moreover, Moses warns the judges that they must receive no gifts, rewards, or bribes. For those two points—favoring of one person more than another, and receiving rewards—pervert all right and equity. They are the unique pestilence of all judges.

He warns (Deut 17:15–20) that their kings not have too many wives, lest their hearts turn away; and that they always read in the law of God, to learn to fear him, lest their hearts be lifted above their brothers. These two points—women and pride, and despising their subjects who are indeed their own brothers—are the common pestilence of all princes. Read the stories, and see.

The sheriffs, bailiffs, constables, and similar officers, may let no man that hurts his neighbor escape, but must bring them before the judges—unless in the meantime they come to agree with their neighbors, and make amends.

Let kings defend their subjects from the wrongs of other nations, but do not pick quarrels for every trifle. Nor let our most holy father any longer make them so drunk with vain names, with caps of maintenance, and similar baubles, as if it were puppetry for children, to beggar their realms, and to murder their people, for defending our holy father's tyranny. If a lawful peace that stands with God's word is made between prince and prince, and the name of God is taken to record, and the body of our Savior is broken between them upon the bond which they have made—then our holy father cannot dispense with that peace or bond, nor loose it with all the keys he has. No, truly, Christ cannot break it. For he did not come to break the law, but to fulfill it.

If any man has broken the law or a good ordinance, and he repents and comes to the right way again, then Christ has power to forgive him. But he cannot give license to break the law; much less can his disciples and vicars, as they call themselves, do it. The keys which they so greatly boast of are not carnal things, but spiritual; and they are nothing else than knowledge of the law, and of the promises or gospel. If any man, for lack of spiritual feeling, desires the authority of men, then let him read the old doctors. If any man desires the authority of Scripture, Christ says, "Woe to you lawyers, for you have taken away the key of knowledge: you do not enter in yourselves, and those that would come in, you forbid." (Luke 11:52)

That is, they blinded the Scripture (whose knowledge, like a key, lets us into God) with glosses and traditions. You find likewise in Matthew 23:13. As Peter answered in the name of all, so Christ promised him the keys in the person of all. (Matthew 16:15–19) And in John 20:22–23 he paid them, saying, "Receive the Holy Ghost: whoever's sins you remit, they are remitted" or forgiven; "and whoever's sins you retain, they are retained" or held. By preaching the promises, they loose as many as repent and believe. And for that John says, "Receive the Holy

Ghost." Luke, in his last chapter, says, "Then he opened their minds, that they might understand the Scriptures, and said to them, Thus it is written, and thus it was necessary for Christ to suffer, and to rise again the third day; and that repentance and remission of sins should be preached in his name among all nations." Men repent at the preaching of the law; and they believe at the preaching of the promises, and they are saved. Peter in the second chapter of the Acts practiced his keys; and by preaching the law he brought the people into the knowledge of themselves, and he bound their consciences, so that "they were pricked in their hearts, and said to Peter and to the other apostles, What shall we do?" Then they brought forth the key of the sweet promises, saying, "Repent, and be baptized every one of you in the name of Jesus Christ, for the remission of sins, and you shall receive the gift of the Holy Ghost. For the promise was made to you, and to your children, and to all who are afar, even as many as the Lord shall call." The Book of Acts is full of similar examples, and Peter's epistles, and Paul's epistles, and all the Scripture. Nor does our holy father have any other authority from Christ, or by reason of his predecessor Peter, than to preach God's word. Just as Christ compares the understanding of Scripture to a key, so he compares it to a net, and to leaven, and to many other things for certain properties they contain. I marvel, therefore, that they do not boast of their net and their leaven, as well as their keys; for they are all one thing. But just as Christ bids us to beware of the leaven of the Pharisees, so we must beware their counterfeited keys, and their false net—which are their traditions and ceremonies, their hypocrisy and false doctrine, with which they catch, not souls for Christ, but authority and riches for themselves.

Let Christian kings therefore uphold their faith and truth, and all lawful promises and bonds, not only with one another, but even with the Turk, or whatever infidel it is. For so it is right before God, as the Scriptures and examples of the Bible testify. Whoever vows an unlawful vow, or promises an unlawful promise, or swears an unlawful oath, sins against God and therefore ought to break that vow. He does not need to sue Rome for a license, for he has God's word, and not just a license, but also a commandment to break it. Therefore those who are sworn to be true to their cardinals and bishops, that is to say, who are sworn to be false to God, the king, and the realm, may break their oaths lawfully, without grudge of conscience; and they may do so by the authority of God's word. In making these vows they sinned; but in repenting and breaking them, they please God highly, and they receive forgiveness in Christ. Let kings assume their duty for their subjects, and what is necessary to the defense of the realm. Let them rule their realms themselves, with the help of laymen that are sage, wise, learned, and expert. Is it not a shame above all shames, and a monstrous thing, that no man may be found able to govern a worldly kingdom, except bishops and prelates who have forsaken the world, and are taken out of the world, and appointed to preach the kingdom of God? Christ says that his "kingdom is not of this world." John 18:36. And in Luke 12:14, to the young man who desired him to bid his brother to give him part of the inheritance, Jesus answered, "Who made me a judge or a divider among you?" "No man that lays his hand to the plough, and looks back, is apt for the kingdom of heaven." (Luke 9:62) "No man can serve two masters, but he must despise the one." (Matthew 6:24)

To preach God's word is too much for half a man: and to minister a temporal kingdom is also too much for half a man. Either other requires a whole man. One therefore cannot do both well. The one who avenges himself on every trifle is not fit to preach the patience of Christ, how a man ought to forgive and to suffer all things. The one who is overwhelmed with all manner of riches, and only seeks more daily, is not fit to preach poverty. The one who will obey no man is not fit to preach how we ought to obey all men. Peter says, "It is not fitting that we should leave the word of God, and serve tables." (Acts 6:2)

Paul says in 1 Cor 9:16, "Woe is me if I do not preach." This is truly a terrible saying for popes, cardinals, and bishops! If he had said, 'Woe to me if I do not fight and move princes to war, or if I do not increase St. Peter's patrimony,' as they call it, then it would have been an easier saying for them.

Christ forbids his disciples and often, not only to climb above lords, kings, and emperors in worldly rule, but he also forbids them to exalt themselves one above another in the kingdom of God. But it is in vain, for the pope would not hear it, even though he had commanded it ten thousand times. God's word alone should rule; and not bishops' decrees, or the pope's pleasure. They ought to preach that purely and spiritually, and fashion their lives after it, and set an example for all of godly living and long-suffering in order to draw all to Christ. They should not expound the Scriptures carnally and with worldly wisdom, saying, 'God spoke this to Peter, and I am his successor; therefore this authority is mine alone'—and then bring in the tyranny of their fleshly wisdom, *In proesentia majoris cessat potestas minoris*; that is, in the presence of the greater, the lesser has no power. There is no brotherhood where such a philosophy is taught. To teach such philosophy, and to so abuse the Scriptures, and to mock with God's word, is after the manner of the bishop of Rochester's divinity. For he, in his 'Sermon of the condemnation of Martin Luther,' proves by a shadow of the Old Testament, that is, by Moses and Aaron, that our most holy father the pope (who is Satan and antichrist), is Christ's vicar and head of Christ's congregation. Moses, he says, signifies Christ; and Aaron signifies the pope. And yet the epistle to the Hebrews proves that the high priest of the old law signifies Christ; his single offering and going in once a year into the inner temple, signify the offering with which Christ offered himself, and Christ's going in to the Father, and that he is an everlasting mediator or intercessor for us. Nevertheless, Rochester proves the contrary by a shadow; by a shadow, truly: for they walk in shadows without any shame. They will not come to the light, but enforce to stop and quench it with all craft and falsehood, lest their abominable juggling should be seen. If any man looks in the light of the New Testament, he will clearly see that the shadow may not be understood so. Understand therefore, that one thing in the Scripture represents diverse things. A serpent figures Christ in one place, and the devil in another; and a lion does likewise. Christ by leaven signifies God's word in one place; and in another signifies the traditions of the Pharisees, which soured and altered God's word for their advantage. Now Moses truly in the same place represents Christ; and Aaron, who was not yet high priest, did not represent only Peter or his successor, as my lord of Rochester would have it, (for Peter was too little to bear Christ's message to all the world), but he signifies every disciple of Christ, and every true preacher of God's word. For Moses put in Aaron's mouth what he should say; and Aaron was Moses' prophet, and did not speak his own message, as the pope and bishops do; rather, he spoke only what Moses received from God and delivered to him (Exo 4:13–16; 7:1–2). So every preacher ought to preach God's word purely, neither adding nor diminishing. A true messenger must be true to his message, and say neither more nor less than he is commanded. Aaron, when he is high priest, and offers and purges the people of their worldly sin which they fell into by touching unclean things, and in eating forbidden meats (just as we sin in handling the chalice and the altar stone, and are purged with the bishop's blessing), represents Christ, who purges us from all sin in the sight of God, as the epistle to the Hebrews mentions. When Moses had gone up into the mount, and Aaron was left behind and made the golden calf there, Aaron represents all false preachers, and namely our most holy father the pope; in the same manner as the golden calf, the pope makes us believe in a bull—the bishop of Rochester full-well cites that passage for support in his sermon.

If the pope is signified by Aaron, and Christ is signified by Moses, then why is the pope not as well content with Christ's law and doctrine, as Aaron was with Moses'? What is the reason that our bishops preach the pope, and not Christ—seeing that the apostles did not preach Peter, but Christ? Paul says of himself and his fellow apostles, "We do not preach ourselves, but Christ Jesus the Lord, and we preach ourselves as your servants for Jesus' sake:" (2 Cor 4:5) and, "Let no man rejoice in men, for all things are yours, whether it is Paul, or Apollos, or Peter; whether it is the world, or life, or death; whether they are present things, or things to come; all are yours, and you are Christ's, and Christ is God's." He leaves out, you are Peter's, or you are the pope's. And in the chapter following he says, "Let men thus esteem us, even as ministers of Christ," etc. And (2 Cor 11:2–5) Paul was jealous over his Corinthians, because they fell from Christ to whom he had married them, and they cleaved to the authority of men; for even then false prophets sought authority in the name of the high apostles: "I am (he says) jealous over you with godly jealousy: for I coupled you to one man, to make you a chaste virgin to Christ; but I fear lest, just as the serpent deceived Eve through his subtlety, even so your minds should be corrupted from the singleness that is in Christ." And it follows: "If he that comes to you preached another Jesus, or if you receive another Spirit or another gospel, then might you have been well content:" that is, you might have well suffered him to have authority above me: "but I suppose," he says, "that I was not behind the high apostles;" meaning in preaching Jesus and his gospel, and in ministering the Spirit. And so, in 2 Corinthians 11 he proves, by the doctrine of Christ, that he is greater than the high apostles, for Christ says, to be great in the kingdom of God is to serve and sacrifice for another. Paul argues this rule for himself, saying, "If they are the ministers of Christ, I am more; in labors more abundant, in stripes above measure, in prison more plenteously, in danger of death often," and so forth. If Paul preached Christ more than Peter, and suffered more for his congregation, then he is greater than Peter, by the testimony of Christ. And in 2 Cor 12:11–13 he says, "In nothing was I inferior to the high apostles: though

I am nothing, yet the tokens of an apostle were worked among you with all patience, with signs, and wonders, and mighty deeds." So he proved his authority, not with a bull from Peter, sealed with cold lead, nor with shadows of the Old Testament falsely expounded.

Moreover the apostles were sent immediately from Christ; and from Christ they received their authority, as Paul boasts himself everywhere. "Christ," he says, "sent me to preach the gospel." 1 Cor 1:17. And, "I received of the Lord that which I delivered to you." 1 Cor 11:23. And Galatians 1:11–12, "I certify to you, brothers, that the gospel which was preached by me was not after the manner of men, (that is, carnal or fleshly), nor did I receive it from man, nor was it taught me, but I received it by the revelation of Jesus Christ." And Galatians 2:8, "He that was mighty in Peter in the apostleship over the circumcision, was mighty in me among the gentiles." And in 1 Timothy 1:11–12, you read likewise. And in John 20:21–23, Christ sent them forth indifferently, and gave them the same power: "As my Father sent me," he says, "so send I you;" that is, to preach and to suffer as I have done; and not to conquer empires and kingdoms, and to subdue all temporal power under you with disguised hypocrisy. He gave them the Holy Ghost, to bind and loose indifferently, as you see; and afterward he sent forth Paul with the same authority, as you see in the Acts. And in the last of Matthew he says: "All power is given me in heaven and in earth; go therefore, and teach all nations, baptizing them in the name of the Father, and of the Son, and of the Holy Ghost; teaching them to observe whatever I commanded you." The authority that Christ gave them was to preach; yet not what they would imagine, but what he had commanded. "Lo," he says, "I am with you always, even to the end of the world." He did not say, "I go my way, and lo, here is Peter in my stead;" but he sent every man to a various country, wherever the Spirit carried them, and went with them himself. And as he worked with Peter where he went, so he worked with the others where they went—just as Paul boasts of himself to the Galatians. Seeing now that we have Christ's doctrine, and Christ's holy promises, and seeing that Christ is ever present with us himself, how may Christ not reign immediately over us, as well as the pope who never comes to us? Seeing also that the office of an apostle is only to preach, then how can the pope rightly assert any authority, where he does not preach? How is it also that Rochester will not let us be called one congregation by reason of one God, one Christ, one Spirit, one gospel, one faith, one hope, and one baptism, as well as because of one pope?

If any natural beast, striving with his worldly wisdom, claims that one is greater than another, just because in a congregation one is sent by another, as we see in the Acts 17:10, 14—I answer that Peter sent no man, but was sent himself; and John was sent, and Paul, Silas, and Barnabas were sent. Sending in such a manner is not worldly, as princes send ambassadors; no, nor as friars send their limiters to gather their brotherhoods who must obey, whether they want to or not. Here (in Scripture) all things are done freely and willingly. And the Holy Ghost brings them together, which makes their wills free, and ready to give themselves for their neighbor's profit. Those who come, offer themselves and all they have, or can do, to serve the Lord and their brothers. Every man, as he is found apt and fit to serve his neighbor, so is he sent or put in office. They are sent by the Holy Ghost, with the consent of their brothers, and with their own consent also. And God's word rules in that congregation; every man conforms his will to that word; and Christ, who is always present, is the head. But as our bishops do not hear Christ's voice, so they do not see him present, and therefore they make themselves a god on the earth, of the kind, I suppose, of Aaron's calf: for the pope brings forth no other fruit except bulls.

Since also Christ is as great as Peter, why is his seat not as great as Peter's? Had the head of the empire been at Jerusalem, there would have been no mention made of Peter. It is truly, as Paul says in the 11 Th chapter of the second epistle to the Corinthians, "The false apostles are deceitful workers, and fashion themselves like the apostles of Christ." (2 Cor 11:13); that is, the shaven nation preaches Christ falsely; indeed, under the name of Christ they preach themselves, and reign in Christ's stead. They have also taken away the key of knowledge, and wrapped the people in ignorance, and taught them to believe in themselves, in their traditions and false ceremonies—so that Christ is but a vain name. And after they put Christ out of his place, they got to the emperor and kings, and so long ministered their business till they also put them out of their places, and got their authorities from them, and also reigned in their stead—so that the emperor and kings are but vain names and shadows, just as Christ is, having nothing left to do in the world. Thus they reign instead of God and man, and they have all power under them, and do whatever they are inclined to do. Let us see another point of our great clerk. A little after the beginning of his sermon, he intends to prove what is clearer than the sun, but it serves no more for his purpose than *Ite missa est* serves to prove that our lady was born without original sin. He alleges that Martin Luther says this, "If we affirm that any one epistle of Paul or any one place in his epistles does not pertain to the universal church, (that is, to the whole congregation of those that believe in Christ), we take away all St. Paul's authority." Upon which Rochester says: "If it is thus with the words of St. Paul, then it is much rather true of the gospels of Christ and every place in them." O malicious blindness! First, note his blindness. He understands by this word "gospel" no more than the four evangelists, Matthew, Mark, Luke, and John; and he does not think that the Acts of apostles, and the epistles of Peter, Paul, and John, and others, are also the gospel. Paul calls his preaching the gospel. The gospel is one, everywhere in Scripture, though it is preached diversely. And it signifies glad tidings. That is, the gospel is an open preaching of Christ, and the holy testament, and the gracious promises that God has made in Christ's blood to all that repent and believe. Now, there is more gospel in one epistle of Paul—that is to say, Christ is more clearly preached and more promises are repeated in one epistle of Paul—than in the three first evangelists, Matthew, Mark, and Luke.

Consider also the clerk's maliciousness—how wickedly and how craftily he takes away the authority of Paul! 'It is much rather true of the gospels, and of every place in them, than of Paul.' If what the four evangelists wrote is truer than what Paul wrote, then it is not one gospel that they preached, nor one Spirit that taught them. If it is one gospel and one Spirit, how is one truer than the other? Paul proves his authority to the Galatians and to the Corinthians, (1) because he received his gospel by revelation from Christ, and not from man; and (2) because when he communed with Peter and the high apostles about his gospel and preaching, they could improve nothing, nor teach him anything; and also (3) because just as many were converted, and just as great miracles were shown by his preaching as by the preaching of the high apostles—therefore Paul will be of no less authority than Peter and the other high apostles, nor will his gospel be of less reputation than theirs.

Finally, so that you may know Rochester forever, and all the remnant by him, what they are within the skin; mark how he plays bo-peep with the Scripture. He cites for support the beginning of the tenth chapter to the Hebrews, *Umbram habens lex futurorum benorum*, "the law has but a shadow of things to come;" and he immediately expounds the phrase clean contrary to the following chapter, and to the whole epistle. He makes Aaron a figure of the pope, whom the epistle makes a figure of Christ.

He cites half a text of Paul, "In the latter days some shall depart from the faith, giving heed to spirits of error and devilish doctrine." (1 Tim 4:1) But it follows in the text: "Giving attendance, or heed, to the devilish doctrine of those who speak falsely through hypocrisy, and have their consciences marked with a hot iron, forbidding to marry, and commanding to abstain from meats, which God has created to be received with thanksgiving." Who ever did these two things, except the pope, Rochester's god? Making sin in the creatures, which God has created for man's use, to be received with thanks. "The kingdom of heaven is not meat and drink," says Paul, "but righteousness, peace, and joy in the Holy Ghost. For whoever serves Christ in these things, pleases God, and is allowed by men." If Rochester, therefore, did not have a conscience seared with the hot iron of malice, so that he cannot consent to the will of God and the glory of Christ, he would not have cited the text; which is contrary to none but themselves.

He cites another text of Paul, in the second chapter of his second epistle to the Thessalonians, *Erit discessio primum*: that is, Rochester says, before the coming of antichrist there will be a notable departing from the faith. And, Paul says, "The Lord does not come, unless there is a departing first." Paul's meaning is that the last day does not come so shortly, but that antichrist shall come first and destroy the faith, and sit in the temple of God, and make all men worship him, and believe in him (as the pope does); and then God's word shall come to light again (as it does at this time), and destroy him, and reveal his juggling—then Christ comes for judgment. What do you say about this crafty conveyer? Do you suppose that someone would spare to cite and twist other doctors pestilently, who does not fear to juggle the holy Scripture of God, attributing to antichrist what Paul speaks about Christ? No, you may be sure of it. But in this very manner they pervert the whole Scripture and all doctors; twisting them to their abominable purpose, clean contrary to the meaning of the text, and to the circumstances that go before and after. This devilish falsehood, lest the laymen be able to perceive it, is the very reason why they will not allow the Scripture to be had in the English tongue; nor will they allow any work to be done that would bring the people to the knowledge of the truth.

For the pope's authority, he cites St. Cyprian, St. Augustine, Ambrose, Jerome, and Origen, none of whom ever knew of any authority that one bishop should have above another. And he cites St. Gregory, who would receive no such authority above his brothers when it was offered to him. Just as it is the way to call Tully chief of orators for his singular eloquence, and Aristotle chief of philosophers, and Virgil chief of poets, for their singular learning, and not for any authority that they had over others—so it was the way to call Peter chief of the apostles for his singular activity and boldness, and not that he should be lord over his brothers, for this was contrary to his own doctrine. Yet compare that chief apostle to Paul, and he is found a great way inferior. This is not to say that I would have any man make a god of Paul, contrary to his own learning. Notwithstanding, this way of speaking is left to us from our elders—that when we say "the apostle says so," we understand it to mean Paul, for his excellence above the other apostles. I would have Rochester tell you how Jerome, Augustine, Bede, Origen, and other doctors expound this text: "Upon this rock I will build my congregation:" and how they interpret the keys also. To that end, Pasce, pasce, pasce, which Rochester leaves without any English, does not signify poll, sheer, and shave. Upon this text, behold the faithful Exposition of Bede. Note also how craftily he would enfeoff the apostles of Christ with their wicked traditions and false ceremonies, which they themselves have feigned, citing Paul in 2 Thes 2. I answer that Paul taught by mouth those things which he wrote in his epistles. And his traditions were the gospel of Christ, and honest manners and living, and of such a good order as becomes the doctrine of Christ. It included such things as that a woman obey her husband, have her head covered, keep silence, and go womanly and Christianly apparelled; that children and servants be in subjection: and that the young obey their elders; that no man eat unless he labors and works; and that men make an earnest thing of God's word and of his holy sacraments; and to watch, fast, and pray, and such things as the Scripture commands—which if someone were to break them, he would be no Christian man. But we may well complain, and cry to God for help, that it is not lawful for the pope's tyranny to teach the people what prayer is, what fasting is, and how it serves. There were also certain customs always, which were not commanded upon pain of hell, or everlasting damnation—such as to watch all night, and to kiss one another—which, as soon as the people abused these, then they broke them. For this reason, the bishops might break many things now in the same way. Paul also, in many things which God had made free, gave pure and faithful counsel, without tangling any man's conscience, and without all manner of commanding under pain of cursing, pain of excommunication, pain of heresy, pain of burning, pain of deadly sin, pain of hell, and pain of damnation. As you may see in 1 Corinthians 7, where he counsels the unmarried, the widows, and virgins, that it is good to remain so, if they have the gift of chastity. This is not to win heaven thereby (for neither circumcision neither uncircumcision is anything at all, but keeping the commandments is everything). But he counsels them so that they might be without trouble, and might also wait better on God's word, and more freely serve their brothers. And he says, as a faithful servant, that he had no authority from the Lord to give them any commandment. But the assertion that the apostles gave us any blind ceremonies, for which we should not know the reason, I deny and defy any such thing. It is clean contrary to the teaching of Paul everywhere.

For Paul commands that no man should speak in the church, that is, in the congregation, except in a tongue that all men understand, unless there is an interpreter nearby. He commands us to labor for knowledge, understanding, and feeling; and to beware of superstition, and of the persuasions of worldly wisdom, philosophy, and beware of hypocrisy and ceremonies, and of all manner of disguising, and to walk in the plain and open truth. "You were once darkness," he says, "but now are you light in the Lord; walk therefore as the children of light." Ephesians 5:8. How Paul also wishes them an increase of grace in every epistle! How he cries to God to augment their knowledge so that they should no longer be children, wavering with every wind of doctrine; but that God would grant to make them full men in Christ, and in the understanding of the mysteries or secrets of Christ, so that it would not be possible for any man to deceive them with any enticing reasons of worldly wisdom, or to beguile them with blind ceremonies, or to lead them out of the way with superstition of disguised hypocrisy! The spiritual officers are ordained to bring them to such full knowledge (Ephesians 4:11–14). Rochester loves shadows and darkness. What he lays on believers is far from what Christ's apostles should give them: the traditions of blind ceremonies, without significance, and for which no man should know the reason. May God stop his blasphemous mouth!

Consider also, how studiously Rochester cites Origen, both for his pope, and also to establish his blind ceremonies. Yet this same Origen is condemned as the greatest of all heretics. 'He is an ancient doctor,' Rochester says, indeed one 'to whom great faith is to be given in this point.' Indeed, truly, Aristotle and Plato, and even Robin Hood himself, are to be believed in such a point which so greatly maintains our holy father's authority, and all his disguisings.

Last of all: Just as when a crafty thief is spotted and chased, cries out to the other people, 'Stop the thief! Stop the thief!'—and just as someone will be the first throw in another man's teeth what he fears would be laid to his own charge—even so Rochester lays to Martin Luther's charge the slaying and murdering of Christian men. This is because Rochester and his brothers will not believe in his doctrine. They have not ceased from this slaying and murdering for these certain hundred years, and have done it with such malice, that when their opponents are dead, they still rage against them, burning their bodies, which they themselves likely killed beforehand secretly. All the world knows that Martin Luther slays no man, but kills only with the spiritual sword—the word of God—putting to death such cankered consciences as Rochester has. Luther does not persecute, but suffers persecution. Yet Rochester, with a goodly argument, proves that he would slay if he could! And mark, I pray you, what an orator he is, and how vehemently he persuades it! Martin Luther has burned the pope's decretals; a manifest sign, he says, that he would have burned the pope's holiness as well if he had him! I make a similar argument, which I suppose to be rather true: Rochester and his holy brothers have burnt Christ's testament; it is an evident sign, truly, that they would have burnt Christ himself as well, if they had him!

Truly I had almost left out the most important point of all. Rochester, is both abominable and shameless indeed, and stark mad with pure malice, and so addled in the brains with spite that he cannot overcome the truth that he does not see, or rather he does not care what he says. In the end of his first destruction, as I would say, or instruction, as he calls it, intending to prove that we are justified through holy works, cites half a text of Paul, in the fifth chapter to the Galatians, (as it is his manner to juggle and convey craftily), *Fides per dilectionem operans*. Which he translates into English this way: "Faith, which is wrought by love;" he makes a verb passive from a verb deponent. Rochester would have love go before, and then faith springs out of love. Thus antichrist turns the roots of the tree upward! I must first love a bitter medicine, (following Rochester's doctrine), and then believe that it is wholesome. When by natural reason, I first hate a bitter medicine, until I am brought to belief by the physician, that the medicine is wholesome, and that the bitterness will heal me. And then afterward I will love it, from that belief. Does the child love the father first, and then believe that he is his son or heir? Or rather, because he knows that he is his son or heir, and beloved, therefore he loves in return? John says, in the third of his first epistle, "See what love the Father has showed us, that we should be called his sons." Because we are sons, therefore we love. Now, by faith we are sons, as John says in the first chapter of his gospel: "He gave them power to be the sons of God, in that they believed on his name." And Paul says, in the third chapter of his epistle to the Galatians, "We are all the sons of God by the faith which is in Jesus Christ." And John, in the same chapter of his epistle, says, "By this we perceive love, that he gave his life for us." We could see no love, nor have any cause to love him in return, unless we believed that he died for us, and that we were saved through his death. And in the subsequent chapter, John says, "In this is love; not that we loved God, but that he loved us, and sent his Son to make agreement for our sins." So God did not send his Son for any love that we had towards him; rather, from the love that he had towards us, he sent his Son, that we might so love, and love in return. Paul likewise, in Romans 8, after he has declared the infinite love of God toward us, in that he did not spare his own Son, but gave him for us, cries out, saying, "Who shall separate us from the love of God? Shall persecution, shall a sword? etc." No, he says; "I am sure that no creature shall separate us from the love of God that is in Christ Jesus our Lord." It is as if to say, "We see so great a love in God toward us in Christ's death, that though all misfortune should fall on us, we cannot but love in return." Now how do we know that God loves us? Truly, by faith. So therefore, though Rochester is a faithless beast, yet natural reason ought to have taught him that love springs out of faith and knowledge; and not faith and knowledge out of love. But let us see the text. Paul says thus: "In Christ Jesus neither circumcision is worth anything, nor uncircumcision, but faith which works through love;" or "which through love is strong, or mighty, in working;" and not "which is wrought by love," as this juggler says. Faith that loves God's commandments, justifies a man. If you believe God's promises in Christ, and love his commandments, then you are safe. If you love the commandment, then you are sure that your faith is unfeigned, and that God's Spirit is in you.

How faith justifies us before God in the heart; and how love springs from faith, and compels us to work—and how our works justify us before the world, and testify what we are, and certify that our faith is unfeigned, and that the right Spirit of God is in us—see in my book about the Justifying of Faith; and there you shall see all these things abundantly. Also see there about the controversy between Paul and James. Nevertheless, when Rochester says if faith alone justified us, then both the devils and also sinners that remain in sin would be saved, his argument is not worth a straw. For neither the devils, nor yet sinners, that continue in sin purposely and out of delectation, have any such faith as Paul speaks of. For Paul's faith is to believe God's promises. "Faith," he says, Romans 10, "comes by hearing, and hearing comes by the word of God." "And how shall they hear without a preacher, and how shall they preach unless they are sent? As it is written," he says, "How beautiful are the feet that bring glad tidings of peace, and bring glad tidings of good things!" Now when God has sent any messengers to the devils, to preach peace to them, or any good thing? The devil has no promise; he is therefore excluded from Paul's faith. The devil believes that Christ died, but not that he died for his sins. Nor does anyone, who consents in their heart to continue in sin, believe that Christ died for him. For to believe that Christ died for us is to see our horrible damnation, and how we were appointed to eternal pains, and to feel, and to be sure, that we are delivered from that through Christ—in this, we have the power to hate our sins, and to love God's commandments. All those who repent and have their hearts loosed from captivity and bondage to sin, and are therefore justified through faith in Christ. Wicked sinners have no faith, but have only imaginations and opinions about Christ—just as our schoolmen have faith in their principles, about which they so quickly brawl with one another. It is quite another thing to believe that the king is rich, and that he is rich toward me, and that my portion is in this—and that he will not spare a penny of his riches at my need. When I believe that the king is rich, I am not moved. But when I believe that he is rich for me, and that he will never fail me at my need, then I love; and from that love I am ready to work to the utmost of my power.

But let us return at last to our purpose. What is the cause that laymen cannot now rule as well as they did in times past, and as the Turks still do? Truly, because that antichrist with the mist of his juggling has beguiled our eyes, and has cast a superstitious fear upon the world of Christian men. He has taught them to dread not God and his word, but himself and his word; not God's law and the ordinances, princes and officers which God has set to rule the world, but his own law and the ordinances, traditions and ceremonies, and disguised disciples, which he has set everywhere to deceive the world—and to expel the light of God's word, so that his darkness may have room. For we see by daily experience, of certain a hundred years long, that the one who fears neither God nor his word, nor regards father, mother, master, or Christ himself—the one who might rebel against God's ordinances, and rises against the king's, and resists the king's officers, dare not once lay hands on one of the pope's anointed. No, not even if he were to slay his father before his face, or do violence to his brother, or defile his sister, wife, or mother. We give the same honor to his traditions and ceremonies. What devotion do we have when we are blessed (as they call it) with the chalice, or when the bishop lifts up his holy hand over us? Who dares to handle the chalice, touch the altar-stone, or put his hand in the font, or his finger into the holy oil? What reverence we give to holy water, holy fire, holy bread, holy salt, hallowed bells, holy wax, holy boughs, holy candles, and holy ashes! And last of all, we commit our souls to the holy candle at our last departing. Indeed, what lay-person would dare be so bold as to unloose the knot of the cloth which the bishop, or his chaplain standing by, knits about children's necks at confirmation? You may ask, 'Do not such things bring the Holy Ghost, and put away sin, and drive away spirits?' I say that a steadfast faith, or belief in Christ and in the promises that God has sworn to give us for his sake, brings the Holy Ghost, as all the Scriptures mention, and as Paul says, "Have you received the Holy Ghost through faith, or believing? Faith is the rock upon which Christ builds his congregation, against which, says Christ, the gates of hell shall not prevail. As soon as you believe in Christ, the Holy Ghost comes, sin falls away, and devils fly. When we throw holy water at the devil, or ring the bells, he flees as men do from young children, and mocks us, to bring us away from the true faith that is in God's word, and bring us to a superstitious and a false belief of our own imagination. If you had faith and threw an unhallowed stone at his head, he would earnestly flee, and without mocking; indeed, though you threw nothing at all, he would not still abide.

If at the beginning, miracles were shown through such ceremonies, it was to move the infidels to believe the word of God. You read how the apostles anointed the sick with oil, and healed them; and Paul sent his handkerchief or apron to the sick, and healed them too. Yet it was not the ceremony that did the miracle, but the faith of the preacher and the truth of God, which had promised to confirm and establish his gospel with such miracles. Therefore, as soon as the gift of miracles ceased, the ceremony ought to have ceased also; or else if they need to have a ceremony to signify some promise or benefit of God (which I do not praise, but would have God's word preached every Sunday; this is the intent for which Sundays and holy days were ordained), then let them tell the people what it means; and not set up a bald and a naked ceremony without signification, to make the people believe in it, and to quench the faith that ought to be given to the word of God.

Also, what does it help that the priest, when he goes to mass, disguises himself with a great part of the passion of Christ, and plays out the rest in silence, with signs and proffers, with nodding, becking and mowing, jackanapes as it were, when neither he nor any other man knows what he means? Not at all, truly. Rather, it hurts, and exceedingly so, in that it not only destroys the faith, and quenches the love that should be given for the commandments, but it also makes the people unthankful. It leads them into such superstition that they think that they have done more than enough for God. Indeed, they think it is deserving above measure if they are present once a day at such mumming. And it makes the infidels mock and abhor us, in that they see nothing but such apes' play among us, for which no man can give a reason.

All this comes to pass to fulfill the prophecy which Christ prophesied: that there shall come in his name, those who will say that they themselves are Christ. This is what the pope and our holy orders of religion truly do. For under the name of Christ, they preach themselves— their own word and their own traditions—and teach the people to believe in them. The pope gives pardons of his full power, of the treasure of the church, and of the merits of saints. The friars likewise make their benefactors (which they only call their brothers and sisters) partakers of their masses, fasting, watchings, prayings, and woolward goings. Indeed, when a novice of the Observants is professed, the father asks him, 'Will you keep the rules of holy St. Francis?' And he says, yes. 'Will you so indeed?' the father asks. The other answers, 'Indeed, truly, father.' Then the father says, 'and I promise you everlasting life in return.' O blasphemy! If eternal life is due to the pilled traditions of lousy friars, what has become of the testament that God made to us in Christ's blood? Christ says, 'That there shall come pseudo-Christi;' For a consideration, I have translated this "false Christs," keeping the Greek word. Yet it signifies in English 'false anointed,' and it ought to be translated so. "There shall come," says Christ, "false anointed, and false prophets, and they shall do miracles and wonders so greatly that, if it were possible, the very elect, or chosen, should be brought out of the way." Compare the pope's doctrine to the word of God, and you will find that there has been, and still is, a great departure from the way; and that evil men and deceivers (as Paul prophesied in 2 Timothy 3) have prevailed, and waxed worse and worse, beguiling others, just as they are beguiled themselves. You tremble and quake, saying, 'Shall God let us go so badly out of the right way?' I answer, it is Christ who warns us. He knew all that would follow, so he prophesied beforehand; and he is a true prophet and his prophecies must be fulfilled.

God anointed his son Jesus with the Holy Ghost, and therefore he called him Christ; which is to say, anointed. Outwardly he did not disguise him, but made him like other men. He sent him into the world to bless us, and to offer himself for us as a sacrifice of a sweet savor, to kill the stench of our sins, so that God would smell them no more, nor think about them anymore. He sent him to make full and sufficient satisfaction, or amends, for all those who repent, believing the truth of God, and submitting themselves to his ordinances for their sins that they do, have done, and will do. For through fragility we sin ever so often. Yet as soon as we repent and come into the right way again, and to the testament which God has made in Christ's blood, our sins vanish away as smoke in the wind, and as darkness at the coming of light—or as you throw a little blood, or milk into the sea. Whoever tries to make satisfaction for his sins toward God, saying in his heart, 'This much have I sinned, this much I will do in repayment; or I will live this way to make amends with God; or I will do this to get to heaven—that person is an infidel—faithless and damned in his deed-doing. He has lost his part in Christ's blood, because he is disobedient to God's testament. He sets up another testament from his own imagination, which he would compel God to obey. If we love God, we have a commandment to love our neighbor also, as John says in his epistle. And if we have offended him, we are to make amends with him; or if we have no way to do that, then we are to ask forgiveness from him, and to do and suffer all things for his sake to win him to God, and to nourish peace and unity. But toward God, Christ is an everlasting satisfaction, and he is ever sufficient.

When he had fulfilled his course, Christ anointed his apostles and disciples with the same Spirit, and sent them forth, without any disguise, like other men, to preach the atonement and peace which Christ had made between God and man. The apostles likewise disguised no man, but chose men anointed with the same Spirit: one to preach the word of God, whom we call a bishop or a priest, after the Greek tongue; in English, it is an overseer or elder. You may read how he was anointed, "A bishop or an overseer must be faultless, the husband of one wife." (1 Tim 3:2)

Many Jews, and also Gentiles, that were converted to the faith, had diverse wives at that time, yet they were not compelled to put any of them away. But Paul, to set an example, would not have them as preachers, because in Christ we return again to the first ordinance of God, that one man and one woman should go together. "He must be sober, of honest behavior, honestly apparelled, harborous," that is, ready to lodge strangers; "apt to teach, not a drunkard, not a fighter, not given to filthy lucre; but gentle, abhorring fighting, abhorring covetousness, and one who rules his own household honestly, having children under obedience with all honesty. For if a man cannot rule his own house, how can he care for the congregation of God? He may not be young in the faith," or, as we would say, a novice, "lest he swell and fall into the judgment of the evil speaker;" that is, he may not be unlearned in the secrets of the faith, for such men are at once stubborn and headstrong, and do not set a little by themselves. But, alas! We have over twenty thousand who know no more Scripture than is written in their portesses; and among them, one is considered exceedingly well-learned if he can turn that to his service. "He must be well reported by outsiders, lest he fall into rebuke, and into the snare of the evil speaker;" that is, lest the infidels, who do not yet believe, should be hurt by him, and driven from the faith, if a man that was defamed were made head or overseer of the congregation. He must have a wife for two causes: one, so it may be known by it, who is fit for the position. One is not apt for so chargeable an office, if he never had a household to rule. Another cause is that chastity is so rare a gift; and unchastity is exceedingly perilous for that degree. This is because the people look as much at the living as the preaching, and they are hurt at once if his living disagrees with his preaching, or if he falls from the faith and does not believe the word.

This overseer, because he was taken from his own business and labor, to preach God's word to the parish, has the right, by the authority of his office, to challenge the parish to give him an honest living, as you may see in the evangelists, and also in Paul. For who has a servant, and will not give him meat, drink, and raiment, and the all things necessary? How they would pay him, whether it would be in money, or assign him so much rent, or in tithes, as the guise now is in many countries, was at their liberty.

Likewise, in every congregation they chose another following the same example, and anointed him, as it is in the same chapter of Paul (1 Tim 3), and in Acts 6. Following the Greek word, we call him a deacon; that is to say in English, a servant or a minister. His office was to help and assist the priest, and to gather up his duty, and to gather for the poor of the parish, who were destitute of friends and could not work. Common beggars were not then allowed to run from door to door. On the saints' days, namely those who suffered death for the word's sake, men came together into the church and the priest preached to them, and exhorted them to cleave fast to the word, and to be strong in the faith, and to fight against the powers of the world, with suffering for their faith's sake, after the example of the saints. And he taught them not to believe in the saints, and to trust in their merits, and to make gods of them; but he took the saints for an example only, and prayed God to give them like faith and trust in his word, and like strength and power to suffer therefore, and to give them so sure a hope of the life to come as you may see in the collects of St. Lawrence and of St. Stephen in our lady matins. And in such days, as we now offer, so they gave every man his portion according to his ability, and as God put it in his heart, to maintain the priest, deacon, and other common ministers, and the poor, and to find learned men to teach, and so forth. And all this was put in the hands of the deacon; as you may see in the life of St. Lawrence, and in the histories. And for such purposes, men gave their lands afterwards, to ease the parishes; and made hospitals, and also places to teach their children and to bring them up, and to nurture them in God's word. These lands our monks now devour.

ANTICHRIST.

Antichrist in another manner has sent forth his disciples, those "false anointed," of which Christ warned us beforehand, so they would come and show miracles and wonders, even to bring the very elect out of the way, if it were possible. He anoints them in the manner of the Jews; and shaves them and shears them in the way of the heathen priests who serve idols. He sends them forth not only with false oil, but with false names also. For compare their names to their deeds, and you will find them false. He sends them forth, as Paul prophesied of them, with lying signs and wonders. What sign is the anointing? That they are full of the Holy Ghost. Compare them to the signs of the Holy Ghost which Paul reckons, and you will find it a false sign.

"A bishop must be faultless, the husband of one wife." No, says the pope, the husband of no wife, but the holder of as many whores as he desires. God commands all degrees to marry, if they burn with lust and cannot live chaste. The pope says, if you burn, take a dispensation for a concubine, and put her away when you are old; or else, as our lawyers say, *Si non caste, tamen caute*; that is, If you do not live chaste, then see that you carry on cleanly, and play the knave secretly.

"Harborous" indeed: harborous to whores and bawds. For a poor man would as soon break his neck as to break his fast with them, but he will break it from the scraps and with the dogs, when dinner is done.

"Apt to teach," and, as Peter says, "always ready to give an answer to every man that asks you a reason for the hope that you have, and do that with meekness." Which thing is signified by the boots which the doctors of divinity are created in, because they should always be ready to go through thick and thin to preach God's word; and by the bishop's two-horned mitre, which represents the absolute and perfect knowledge that they ought to have in the New Testament and the Old. Are these not false signs? For they only beat the air, and do not teach. 'Indeed,' says the pope, 'If they will not be ruled, then cite them to appear; and ask them sharply, what they hold about the pope's power, his pardons, his bulls, purgatory, ceremonies, confession, and similar creations of our most holy father's. If they miss in any point, they make heretics of them, and burn them. If they are of my anointed, and bear my mark, disgrace them (I would say, disgraduate them), and following the example of noble Antiochus (2 Maccabees 7:24) they pare their crowns and fingers, and torment them craftily; pain will make them deny the truth.' 'But now,' say our bishops, 'because the truth has come too far abroad, and the lay-people begin to smell our wiles, it is best to oppress them with craft secretly, and tame them in prison. Indeed, let us find the means to put them in the king's prison, and make treason of such doctrine. Indeed, we must stir up some war, one way or another, to bring the people into another way of thinking. If they are gentlemen, abjure them secretly.'

Curse them four times a year. Make them afraid of everything; namely, to touch my anointed. Make them fear the sentence of the church, suspensions, excommunications, and curses. Whether they are right or wrong, bear them in hand, for my anointed are still to be feared. Preach me and my authority, and how terrible a thing my curse is, and how black it makes their souls. On the holidays, which were ordained to preach God's word, set up long ceremonies, long matins, long masses, and long evensongs, and all in Latin, so that they do not understand; and roll them in darkness, so that you may lead them where you will. And lest such things be too tedious, sing some, say some, pipe some, ring the bells, and lull them and rock them asleep.' And yet Paul (1 Cor 14) forbids speaking in the church or congregation, except in the tongue that all can understand. For the layman is not edified or taught by it. How shall the layman say Amen (says Paul) to your blessing or thanksgiving, when he does not know what you say? He does not know whether you bless or curse. What then does the pope say? 'What do I care for Paul? I command as a virtue of obedience, that the gospel be read in Latin. Do not let them pray except in Latin, no, not even their Paternoster.

If any are sick, go and speak a gospel to them, all in Latin. Indeed, preach the gospel in Latin to the corn and fruits of the field during procession week; make the people believe the crop will grow all the better.' Truly, you may as well preach it to swine as to men, if you preach it in a tongue they do not understand. How will I prepare myself for God's commandments? How will I be thankful to Christ for his kindness? How will I believe the truth and promises which God has sworn, while you tell them to me in a tongue I do not understand? What then does my lord of Canterbury say to a priest that would have had the New Testament distributed in English? "What," he says, "would you have lay-people come to know what we do?"

"No fighter;" I suppose this is signified by the cross that is borne before the high prelates, and borne before those in processions. Is that also not a false sign? What realm can be in peace with such turmoilers? What little parish is it, that they will not pick one quarrel or another with them, either for some surplice, chrisom, or mortuary, either for one trifle or other, and cite them to the Arches? They are traitors to all creatures, and have a secret conspiracy between themselves. The craft they have is to make many small kingdoms, and to nourish old titles or quarrels, so that they may move them to war at their pleasure, at any time. And if many lands by any chance fall to one man, they are ever ready to throw a bone in the way, so that he will never be able to obtain it, as we now see with the emperor. Why? For as long as the kings are small, if God would open the eyes of any to set a reformation in his realm, then the pope would interdict his land, and send in other princes to conquer it.

"Not given to filthy lucre, but abhorring covetousness;" and, as Peter says, "Taking oversight of them, not as though you were compelled to it, but willingly; not out of a desire for filthy lucre, but of a good mind; not as though you were lords over the parishes." 'Over the parishes,' he quotes! O Peter, Peter, you were too long a fisherman; you were never brought up at the Arches, nor were you Master of the Rolls, nor yet Chancellor of England. They are not content to reign over king and emperor, and the whole earth; but they also challenge authority in heaven and in hell! It is not enough for them to reign over all that are alive, but have created a purgatory to also reign over the dead, and to have one more kingdom than God himself has. "But that you be an example to the flock," says Peter; "and when the chief Shepherd appears, you shall receive an incorruptible crown of glory." This "abhorring of covetousness" is signified, I suppose, by them shaving and shearing their hair, to show they have no superfluity. But is not this also a false sign? Truly, to them it serves as a remembrance to shear and shave, and to heap benefice upon benefice, promotion upon promotion, dignity upon dignity, bishopric upon bishopric, with pluralities, unions, and *tot quots*.

First, by the authority of the gospel, those who preach the word of God in every parish, and other necessary ministers, have the right to ask for an honest living like one of the brothers; and they ought to be content with that. Bishops and priests who do not preach, or who preach anything other than God's word, are none of Christ's, nor are they of his anointing. Rather, they are servants of the beast whose mark they bear, and whose word they preach, and whose law they maintain clean against God's law. And with their false sophistry, they give the beast greater power than God ever gave to his Son Christ.

But as insatiable beasts, they are not unmindful of why they were shaven and shorn, because they will stand at no man's grace, nor be in any man's danger. They have gotten into their own hands, first the tithe or tenth of all the realm, and then I suppose within a little while, altogether a third of all the temporal lands.

Mark well how many parsonages or vicarages there are in the realm, which have at least a plowland apiece. Then note the lands of the bishops, abbots, priors, nuns, and knights of St. John's, of cathedral churches, colleges, chauntries, and free-chapels. For though the house falls into decay, and the ordinance of the founder has been lost, yet they will not lose the lands. What comes in once, may never go out again. They make a free-chapel of it, so that the one who enjoys it will do nothing for it. Besides all this, how many chaplains do gentlemen fund at their own cost, in their houses? How many sing for souls, by testaments? Then there is the proving of testaments, and the apprizing of goods, which is the bishop of Canterbury's prerogative—is there not much of this throughout the realm in a year? Four offering days and privy tithes. There is no servant who does not pay something from his wages. None will receive the body of Christ at Easter, no matter how poor a beggar, or however young a lad or maid may be, unless they pay something for it; then mortuaries for forgotten tithes (as they say). And yet what parson or vicar will forget to have a pigeon-house to peck up something both at sowing-time and harvest, when corn is ripe? They will forget nothing. No man wants to die in debt; or if any man does, he will pay it when he is dead. They will lose nothing. Why do they do it? It is God's, not theirs. 'It is St. Hubert's rents, St. Alban's lands, St. Edmond's right, St. Peter's patrimony,' they say, 'and none of ours.' Item: if a man dies in another man's parish, besides having to pay at home a mortuary for forgotten tithes, he must pay the best that he has there also; whether it is a horse of twenty pounds, or however goods he has; either a chain of gold of an hundred marks, or five hundred pounds, if it so happens. It is much, truly, for so little pains-taking in confession, and in ministering the sacraments. Then bead-rolls. Item: chrysome, churchings, banns, weddings, an offering at weddings, an offering at burials, offering to images, offering of wax and lights, which come to their advantage; besides the superstitious waste of wax in torches and tapers throughout the land. Then brotherhoods and pardoners.

What? Do they also gain by confessions? Indeed, and many enjoin penance to give a certain [sum] for so many masses said, and they desire to provide a chaplain themselves; soul-masses, dirges, month-minds, year-minds, All-souls-day, and trentals. The mother church, and the high altar, must have something in every testament. Offerings at priests' first masses. Item: no man is professed, however religious it may be, unless he brings something. The hallowing (or rather conjuring) of churches, chapels, altars, super-altars, chalice, vestments, and bells. Then book, bell, candlestick, organs, chalice, vestments, copes, altar-cloths, surplices, towels, basins, ewers, ship, censer, and all manner of ornament, must be found for them freely; they will not give a mite for it. Last of all, what swarms of begging friars there are! The parson shears, the vicar shaves, the parish priest polls, the friar scrapes, and the pardoner pares; all we lack is a butcher to pull off the skin.

What do they gain by their spiritual law (as they call it) in a year, at the Arches and in every diocese? What do the commissaries and officials gain in a year with their summoners and apparitors, by pandering? Will you not find enough curates who, to flatter the commissaries and officials with something to acquit themselves, will reveal to them the confessions of the richest of their parishes, whom they cite privately, and lay charges against secretly? If their parishioner desire to know their accusers, 'No,' they say, 'the matter is known well enough, and to more than you are aware of. Come, lay your hand on the book; if you deny it, we will bring proofs; we will handle you and make an example of you.' Oh, how terrible they are! 'Come,' they say, 'and swear that you will be obedient to our injunctions.' And by that craft they wring others' purses, and make them drop, as long as there is a penny left in them. In three or four years in those offices, they will get enough to pay for a bishop's bull. What else are these, but horse-leeches, maggots, cankers, and caterpillars? They devour all that is green. They are the wolves which Paul prophesied would come, and would not spare the flock; Christ said they would come in lamb's skins, and urged us to beware of them, and judge them by their works.

As I sufficiently proved before, a Christian man must suffer all things, however great a wrong, as long as it is not against God's commandment. Nor is it lawful for him to take any burden off his back by his own authority, till God pulls it off—who laid it on us for our deserts. Yet if they were Christians, kings everywhere ought to defend their realms from such oppression. But this is seldom seen and truly, it is a hard thing, though not impossible. For, alas! They are captives before they are ever kings, indeed, almost before they are born. No man is allowed around them except flatterers, and those who are sworn to be true to our most holy fathers first, the bishops; that is to say, false to God and man.

If any of the nobles of the realm are true to the king, and so bold as to dare counsel him what would be to his honor and for the wealth of the realm, they would wait a season for him, as men say; they would provide a spiritual father for him. God bring their wickedness to light! There is no mischief of which they are not the root, nor bloodshed that is not through their cause, either by their counsel, or because they do not preach true obedience, and do not teach the people to fear God. If any faithful servant is in the court, he will have twenty spies waiting for him; he will be thrown out of the court, or, as the saying goes, he will be 'conveyed to Calais,' and made a captain or an ambassador; he will be kept far enough from the king's presence. I say, the kings ought to remember that they stand in God's stead, and they are ordained by God, not for themselves, but for the wealth of their subjects. Let them remember that their subjects are their brothers, their flesh and blood, members of their own body, and of themselves in Christ. Therefore they ought to pity them, and rid them of such vile tyranny which increases more and more daily. And though the kings, by the falsehood of the bishops and abbots, are sworn to defend church liberties, they should not keep their oaths, but break them. That is because they are wrong and clean against God's ordinance. They are nothing but cruel oppression, contrary to brotherly love and charity. Moreover, the spiritual officer ought not to punish any sin. Rather, if any sin breaks out, the king is ordained to punish it, and they are not. They are ordained only to preach, and to exhort others to fear God and not to sin.

Let the kings put down such tyranny, and turn some of the proceeds towards the commonwealth. If a tenth of such tyranny were given to the king yearly, and laid up in the shire-towns for the needs of the realm, what would it grow to in a few years? Moreover, one king and one law is God's ordinance in every realm. Therefore the king ought not to allow them to have a separate law for themselves, nor to bind his subjects to it. 'It is not fitting,' they will say, 'that a spiritual man should be judged by a worldly or temporal man.' O abomination! See how they divide and separate themselves: if a layman is of the world, somehow he is not of God! If he believes in Christ, then he is a member of Christ, Christ's brother, Christ's flesh, Christ's blood, Christ's spouse, co-heir with Christ, and he has Christ's Spirit in earnest, and he is also spiritual. If they would rob us of the Spirit of God, why should they fear to rob us of worldly goods? Because you are put in office to preach God's word, are you therefore no longer one of the brothers? Is the mayor of London no longer one of the city, because he is the chief officer? Is the king no longer of the realm, because he is head of it? The king is in the place of God, and his law is God's law, which is nothing but the law of nature and natural equity which God engraved in the hearts of men. Yet antichrist is too good to be judged by the law of God. He must have a new law, of his own making. It would be fitting, truly, if they went to no law at all. No longer would they need the law, if they would study to preach God's word truly, and be content with what is sufficient, and be like one of their brothers.

If any question arose about the faith of the Scripture, let them judge that by the manifest and open Scriptures; and do not exclude the laymen. For there are many laymen who are as wise as the officers. Or else, when the officer dies, how could we put another in his place? Will you teach for twenty, thirty, forty, or fifty years in such a way that no man will have knowledge or judgment in God's word except you? Is it not a shame that we Christians come so often to church in vain: when someone eighty years of age knows no more than someone born yesterday?

Moreover, when the spiritual officers have excommunicated a man, or condemned an opinion as heresy, do not let the king or temporal officers punish and slay them by the commandment of these men. But let them look at God's word, and compare their judgment to the Scripture, and see whether it is right or not. Do not believe at the first chop, whatever these clergy say, especially in things that pertain to their own authorities and power; for no man is a right judge in his own cause. Why does Christ command the Scripture to be preached to all creatures, unless it requires all men to know them? Christ himself refers to the Scriptures in John 5:38–39:1 And in Matthew 11:5, to the question from John the Baptist's disciples, he answered, "The blind see, the lepers are cleansed, the dead arise again," etc. meaning that 'If I do the works which were prophesied that Christ would do when he comes, then why do you doubt whether I am him or not?' It is as if to say, "Ask the Scripture, whether I am Christ or not, and not myself." How does it happen, then, that our prelates will not come to the light as well, so that we may see whether their works are wrought in God, or not? Why do they fear to let the laymen see what they do? Why do they hold all their examinations in darkness? Why do they not examine their causes of heresy openly, as laymen do with their felons and murderers? Is this not why Christ and his apostles warned us so diligently of Antichrist, and of false prophets that would come? Was it that we should slumber or carelessly sleep? Or was it rather that we should look in the light of the Scripture with all diligence, to spy these men when they come, and not allow ourselves to be deceived and led out of the way by them? John bids us to judge the spirits. How shall we judge them except by the Scriptures? How will you know whether the prophet is true or false, or whether he speaks God's word, or from his own head, if you will not see the Scriptures? Why did David say, in the second psalm, "Be instructed, you that judge the earth, lest the Lord be angry with you, and you perish from the right way?" This is a terrible warning, truly. Indeed, look at the stories well, and you will find very few kings, since the beginning of the world, that have not perished from the right way, because they would not be instructed.

The emperor and kings now-a-days are nothing but hangmen to the pope and bishops, to kill whomever they condemn, without any fuss—as Pilate was to the scribes, Pharisees, and high bishops: to hang Christ. For just as those prelates answered Pilate (when he asked what he had done), "If he were not an evil-doer, we would not have brought him to you;" as if to say, 'We are too holy to do anything amiss, and so you may believe us well enough.' Yes, and "his blood be on our heads," they said; kill him cruelly, and we will bear the charge, our souls for yours. "We also have a law by which he ought to die, for he calls himself God's son:" — in the same way, our prelates say, 'He ought to die by our laws, for he speaks against the church.' And, 'Your grace is sworn to defend the liberties and ordinances of the church, and to maintain our most holy father's authority; our souls for yours, you shall do a meritorious deed in this.' Nevertheless, as Pilate did not escape the judgment of God, even so is it to be feared lest our temporal powers will not escape it. "Therefore, be instructed, you that judge the earth, lest the Lord be angry with you, and you perish from the right way."

Who slew the prophets? Who slew Christ? Who slew his apostles? Who slew the martyrs, and all the righteous that ever were slain? The kings and the temporal sword slew them at the request of false prophets. They deserved to murder, and to have their portion with the hypocrites, because they would not be instructed, and see the truth themselves. Why did the prophets suffer? Because they rebuked the hypocrites who beguiled the world, specifically princes and rulers, and taught them to put their trust in things of vanity, and not in God's word. And they taught them to do deeds of mercy which were profitable to no man, but only to the false prophets themselves. They made merchandise of God's word. Why did they slay Christ? For rebuking the hypocrites, because he said, "Woe to you scribes and Pharisees, hypocrites, for you shut up the kingdom of heaven before men" (Mat 23:13) that is, as it is written, "You have taken away the key of knowledge." (Luk 11:52)

The law of God, which is the key with which men bind, and the promises, which are the keys with which men loose, our hypocrites have also taken away. They will allow no man to know God's word, but burn it instead, and make it heresy. Indeed, and because the people begin to smell their falsehood, they make it treason to the king, and the breaking of the king's peace, to have so much as their Paternoster in English. Instead of God's law, they bind with their own law; and instead of God's promises, they loose and justify with pardons and ceremonies, which they themselves have imagined for their own profit. They preach, 'It would be better for you to eat flesh on Good Friday, than to hate your neighbor.' But let any man eat flesh except on a Saturday, or break any other tradition of theirs, and he will be bound and not loosed till he has paid the uttermost farthing, either with the most vile shame, or the most cruel death. But hate your neighbor as much as you will, and you will receive no rebuke from them. Indeed, rob him, murder him, and then come to them and be welcomed. They have a sanctuary for you, to save you—yes, and they will provide a neck-verse, if you can just read a little Latin, however badly, so that you are ready to receive the beast's mark. They do not care for understanding. It is enough if you can roll up a pair of matins, or an even-song, and mumble a few ceremonies. And because they are rebuked in this way, they rage. "Be instructed, therefore, you that judge the world, lest God be angry with you, and you perish from the right way."

"Woe to you, scribes and Pharisees, hypocrites!" says Christ, Mat 23:14: "for you devour widows' houses under a pretense of long prayer." Our hypocrites not only rob the widows, but knight, squire, lord, duke, king, and emperor, and even the whole world, under the same pretense. They teach the people to trust in their prayers, and not in Christ, for whose sake God has forgiven all the sin of the whole world to as many as repent and believe. They frighten them with purgatory, and they promise to pray perpetually, lest the lands should ever be returned to the rightful heirs. What have you bought by robbing your heirs, or by giving the hypocrites what you rob from other men? Perpetual prayer? Indeed, perpetual pain—for they have appointed no time of deliverance for you, their prayers are so 'mighty.' The pope, for money, can empty purgatory whenever he wants. And it is truly purgatory, for it purges and makes a clean riddance of things. Yes, it is hell; for it devours all things. His 'Fatherhood' sends them to heaven with *Scala coeli*; that is, with a ladder to scale the walls. For they will not let them come in by the door, who is Christ. They have stopped up that door, so you must buy ladders from them. For some they pray daily, those who gave them perpetuities, and even make saints of them, receiving offerings in their names, and teaching others to pray to them. None of those who take it upon themselves to save others with their prayers, trust to be saved by it themselves; instead, they hire others to pray for them.

Moses testified before God, that he did not take so much as an ass from any of the people; nor did he trouble any of them. Samuel, in 1 Kings 12, asked all Israel whether he had taken any man's ox or ass, or had troubled any man, or had taken a gift or reward from any man? And all the people testified, 'No.' Yet these two men taught the people, and also prayed for them, as much as our prelates do. Peter, in 1 Peter 5:2, exhorts the elders to take oversight of Christ's flock, not for filthy lucre, but from a good will, even for love. Paul, in Acts 20:17–35, calls for the priests (or elders) to witness, that he had taught repentance and faith, and all the counsel of God; and yet he had desired no man's gold, silver, or clothing, but fed himself with the labor of his hands. And yet these two men taught and prayed for the people as much as our prelates do, with whom the common saying goes, 'No penny, no Paternoster:' As these prelates do not teach, but only beat the air, so they do not know what prayer means.

Moreover, the law of love, which Christ left among us, is to give and not to receive. What prayer is it then, that robs the whole world in this way, contrary to that great commandment, which is the end of all commandments, and in which all others are contained? If men continue to buy prayer four or five hundred years more, as they have done, there will not be a foot of ground left in Christendom, nor any worldly thing, which those who would be called 'spiritual' only, would not possess. And thus everything would be called 'spiritual.'

"Woe to you lawyers! For you load men down with burdens which they are not able to bear, and you yourselves do not touch the packs with one of your fingers," says Christ, Luke 11:46, Our lawyers, truly, have loaded us down a thousand times more. What spiritual kindred they have made in baptism, to let matrimony be possible! Besides that, they have added certain degrees to the natural law for the same purpose. What an unbearable burden of chastity they violently thrust on other men's backs, and how easily they bear it themselves! How sore a burden, how cruel a hangman, how grievous a torment, indeed, and how painful a hell, this ear-confession is to men's consciences! For the people are brought to believe that without it, they cannot be saved—to such an extent that some will fast certain days in the year, and pray certain superstitious prayers all their lives, so that they may not die without confession. When in peril of death, if the priest is not nearby, shipmen confess themselves to the mast. If any priests are present, then every man ran to his ear. But they do not fly to God's promises, for they do not know them. If any man has a deadly wound, he cries immediately for a priest. If a man dies without confession, many take it as a sign of damnation. Many, by reason of that false belief, die in desperation. Many, for shame, keep back of their confession twenty or thirty years, and think all the while that they are damned. I knew a poor woman with child, who so longed for flesh, and being overcome by her passion, ate flesh on a Friday. She dared not confess this for eighteen years; she thought all that while that she had been damned; and yet she did not sin at all. Is this not a sore burden, that so weighs down the soul to the bottom of hell? What should I say? A large book would not be sufficient to repeat the snares which they have laid to rob men both of their goods, and also of the trust which they should have in God's word. "The scribes and Pharisees do all their works to be seen by men. They make their phylacteries broad, and make long borders on their garments, and love to sit uppermost at feasts, and to have the best seats in the synagogues;" that is, in the congregations or councils, "and to be called Rabbi;" that is to say, masters, says Christ, Matthew 23:5–7. Behold the deeds of our clergy, and how many thousand fashions there are to be known by among them. Just as none is like another, so none loves another, for every one of them supposes that all the others poll too fast, and make too many captives. Yet they are all agreed to resist Christ, lest they all be compelled to deliver up their prisoners to him. Behold the monsters, how they are disguised with mitres, crosiers, and hats, with crosses, pillars, and pole-axes, and with three crowns!

What names do they have? My lord prior, my lord abbot, my lord bishop, my lord archbishop, cardinal, and legate; if it please your fatherhood; if it please your lordship; if it please your grace; if it please your holiness; and innumerable titles like these. Behold how esteemed they are, and how high they have crept above all—not only into worldly seats, but into the seat of God, and into the hearts of men, where they sit above God himself. For they, and whatever they make up out of their own heads, is more to be feared and dreaded than God and his commandments. We put more trust in them and in their deservings than in Christ and his merits. We give more faith to their promises than to the promises which God has sworn in Christ's blood.

The hypocrites say to the kings and lords, 'These heretics would have us put down first, and then you, to make us all common.' No, you hypocrites and right heretics, approved by open Scripture, the kings and lords are already down; and down so low, that they cannot go lower. You tread them under your feet, and lead them captive. You have made them your bond-servants to wait on your filthy lusts, and to avenge your malice on every man, contrary to the right of God's word. You have not only robbed them of their land, authority, honor, and the due obedience which you owe them, but you have robbed them of their wits also. Not only are they without understanding in God's word, but even in worldly matters that pertain to their offices, they are no more than children. You bear them in hand to have them do what you will. You have made them like those who dance naked in nets, believing they are invisible. We would have them raised up again, and restored to the place and authority which God has given them, and of which you robbed them. We only speak about your inward falsehood with the light of God's word, so that your hypocrisy might be seen. "Be instructed, therefore, you that judge the world, lest God be angry with you, and you perish from the right way." "Woe to you, scribes and Pharisees, hypocrites! For you clean the outside of the cup and platter, but within they are full of bribery and excess," says Christ, Mat 23:25. Are what our hypocrites eat and drink, and all their riotous excess, anything other than robbery, or what they falsely obtained with their lying doctrine? "Be instructed, therefore, you that judge the world," and compel them to make restitution again.

"You blind guides," says Christ, "You strain out a gnat and swallow a camel." Mat 23:24. Do not our blind guides also stumble at a straw, and leap over a block—restricting consciences at trifles, and at matters of no weight at all? If anyone happens to swallow his spittle; or swallows any of the water he washes his mouth with before he goes to mass; or if he touches the sacrament with his nose; or if the ass forgets to breathe on him, or happens to handle the sacrament with any of his fingers that are not anointed; or if he says 'Alleluia' instead of '*Laus tibi, Domine*;' or '*Ite, missa est*' instead of '*Benedicamus Domino*;' or if he pours too much wine in the chalice; or if he reads the gospel without light; or does not make his crosses correctly—then how he trembles! How he fears! What a horrible sin has been committed! 'I cry to God for mercy,' he says, 'and to you, my spiritual father.' But to hold a whore, or another man's wife, or to buy a benefice, or to set one realm at variance with another, and to cause twenty thousand men to die on a single day, is only a trifle and a pastime with them!

The Jews boasted about Abraham; and Christ said to them, John 8:39, "If you were Abraham's children, you would do the deeds of Abraham." Our hypocrites boast of the authority of Peter, and Paul, and the other apostles, and yet they do clean contrary to the deeds and doctrine of Peter, and Paul, and the other apostles. Those men obeyed all worldly authority and power, usurping none for themselves; and they taught all others to fear kings and rulers, and to obey them in all things that are not contrary to the commandment of God; and not to resist them, even if they took away life and goods wrongfully; but to patiently wait for God's vengeance. Our clergy never did this, or taught it. They did not teach to fear God in his commandments, but to fear them in their traditions, and to such an extent that even evil people, who do not fear to resist a good king and to rise up against him, dare not lay hands on any of them, not even for defiling a wife, daughter, or mother. When all other men lose life and lands, these men always remain secure and in safety, and always win something. For whoever conquers other men's lands unrightfully, always gives them a portion. To these men, all things are lawful. In all councils and parliaments, they are the chief. Without them, no king may be crowned, and not until he is sworn to uphold their liberties. They know all secrets, even the thoughts of men's hearts. All things are ministered by them. No king or realm may, through their falsehood, live in peace. They do not teach to believe in Christ, but in themselves, and their disguised hypocrisy. And they compel all men to buy redemption and forgiveness of sins from them. They eat the people's sin, and they grow fat from it. The more wicked the people are, the more prosperous their commonwealth. If kings and great men do something amiss, they must build abbeys and colleges; men of means build chantreys; the poor find trentals, and brotherhoods, and begging friars. Men disinherit their own heirs, to endow these clergy. All kings are compelled to submit themselves to them. Read the story of King John, and of other kings. The clergy will have their causes avenged, though whole realms should perish for it. Take their disguises from them, so they are not spiritual. Compare what they have taught us to the Scripture; so much are we without faith.

Christ says, "How can you believe, who receive glory from one another?" (John 5:45) If those who seek to be glorious can have no faith, then our prelates are faithless, truly. And in John 7:18, Jesus says: "He that speaks of himself, seeks his own glory." If to seek glory and honor is a sure sign that a man speaks about himself, and gives his own message and not his master's, then the doctrine of our prelates is from themselves, and not from God. "Be instructed, therefore, you that judge the earth, lest God be angry with you, and you perish from the right way."

Be instructed, lest the hypocrites bring the wrath of God upon your heads, and compel you to shed innocent blood; as they have compelled your predecessors to slay the prophets, to kill Christ and his apostles, and all the righteous that have been slain since. God's word pertains to all men; just as it pertains to all servants to know their master's will and pleasure; and to all subjects to know the laws of their prince. Do not let the hypocrites do all things secretly. What reason is it that my enemy should put me in prison at his pleasure, and there starve me, and handle me as he desires; and judge me himself, and do that secretly; and condemn me by a law of his own making, and then deliver me to Pilate to murder me? Let God's word try every man's doctrine, and whomever God's word proves unclean, let him be taken for a leper. One Scripture will help to declare another. And the circumstances, that is to say, the passages that go before and after, will give light to the text in the middle. And the open and plain Scriptures will ever improve the false and wrong exposition of the darker sentences. Let the temporal power, to whom God has given the sword to take vengeance, look before they leap, and see what they do. Let the causes be disputed before them, and let him that is accused have opportunity to answer for himself. The powers to whom God has committed the sword, will give accounts for every drop of blood that is shed on the earth. Their ignorance will not excuse them then, nor will the sayings of the hypocrites help them. 'My soul for yours, your grace will do a meritorious deed;' 'your grace ought not to hear them;' 'it is an old heresy condemned by the church.' If he would punish it, then the king ought to look in the Scripture, and see whether it was truly condemned or not. If the king, or his officer for him, would slay me, then the king or his officer ought to judge me. The king cannot, except to his own damnation, lend his sword to kill those whom he does not judge by his own laws. Let the accused stand on one side, and the accuser on the other; and let the king's judge sit and judge the cause, if the king would kill, and not be a murderer before God.

From this you may see, not only that our persecution is for the same cause that Christ's was, and that we say nothing that Christ did not say, but also that all our persecution is only for rebuking hypocrisy. That is to say, for rebuking man's self-righteousness, and holy deeds, by which man has imagined to please God, and to be saved by them, without God's word, and apart from the testament that God has made in Christ. Christ rebuked the Pharisees because they taught the people to believe in their traditions and holiness, and believe in offerings that were to their own advantage. They taught the widows and those with dead friends, to believe in their prayers; and that through their prayers the dead would be saved. By that means, they robbed them both of their goods, and of the testament and promises that God made, to all who repented in the Christ to come. If Christ had not rebuked them, he might have been uncrucified to this day. If St. Paul also had not preached against circumcision, that it did not justify; and that vows, offerings, and ceremonies did not justify; and that righteousness and forgiveness of sins did not come by any deserving of our deeds, but by faith, or believing the promises of God, and by the deserving and merits of Christ only—then he might have lived to this hour. Likewise, if we did not preach against pride, covetousness, lechery, extortion, usury, simony, and against the evil living of both the spiritual and temporal rulers, and against enclosing parks, raising rents and fines, and carrying wool out of the realm—then we too might endure long enough. But if you touch the scab of hypocrisy, or pope-holiness, and go around speaking about their false doctrine by which they reign as gods in the hearts and consciences of men, and by which they rob men not only of their lands, goods, and authority, but also the testament of God, and the salvation that is in Christ—then you will not be helped by God's word, and not even if you could do miracles. For this offense, you are not only a heretic, and have the devil within you, but you are also a breaker of the king's peace, and a traitor. But let us return to our lying signs again.

What signifies that the prelates are so bloody, and clothed in red? It is that they are ready every hour to permit martyrdom for the testimony of God's word. Is that not also a false sign? It is when no man dares, because of them, to open his mouth even once to ask a question about God's word, because the prelates are ready to burn him for it.

What do the pole-axes signify that are carried before high legates a latere? Whatever false sign they make of them, I do not care. But of this I am sure: that just as the old hypocrites, when they had slain Christ, set pole-axes to keep him in his sepulcher so he would not rise again, even so our hypocrites have buried the testament that God made for us in Christ's blood; and all they study is how to keep it down so it will not rise again; these pole-axes are the sign of it.

Is that shepherd's hook, the bishop's cross, not a false sign? Is that white rochet that the bishops and canons wear, so like a nun's and so effeminate, not a false sign? What else are their sandals, gloves, mitres, and the whole pomp of their disguise, than the false signs in which Paul prophesied they would come? And just as Christ warned us to beware of wolves in lamb's skins, and told us to look at their fruits and deeds rather than wonder at their disguises, if you run throughout all our holy religions, you will find that likewise, they are all clothed in falsehood.

OF THE SACRAMENTS.

Since we have come to signs, we will speak a word or two about the signs which God has ordained; that is to say, the sacraments which Christ left among us for our comfort, so that we may walk in light and in truth, and feel the power of God. For "he that walks in the day does not stumble;" by contrast, he that walks in the night stumbles, John 11:9–10. And "they that walk in darkness do not know where they go." This word sacrament means a holy sign, and it always represents some promise of God. In the Old Testament, God ordained that the rainbow would represent and signify to all men an oath that God swore to Noah and to all men after him, that he would no more drown the world through water.

SACRAMENT OF THE BODY AND BLOOD OF CHRIST.

So the sacrament of the body and blood of Christ has a promise annexed to it, which the priest should declare in the English tongue. "This is my body, that is broken for you." "This is my blood, that is shed for many, for the forgiveness of sins." "This do in remembrance of me," says Christ, Luke 22:19 and 1 Cor 11:24. If when you see the sacrament, or eat his body, or drink his blood, you have this promise fast in your heart, that his body was slain and his blood shed for your sins, and you believe it, so you are saved and justified thereby. If not, it will not help you, though you hear a thousand masses a day, or though you do nothing else all your life than eat his body or drink his blood. It will help you no more than, being dead thirsty, you behold a bush at a tavern door, not knowing that the bush is a sign that there is wine within to be sold.

BAPTISM.

Baptism also has God's word and promise, which the priest ought to teach the people, and christen them in the English tongue; and not play the popinjay—with Credo you say Volo you say Baptismum—for there ought to be no mumming in such a matter. Rather, before he baptizes, the priest should ask, 'Do you believe in God the Father Almighty, and in his Son Jesus Christ, and in the Holy Ghost, and that the congregation of Christ is holy?' And they say, 'Yes.' Then the priest, upon this profession of faith, baptizes the child in the name of the Father, and of the Son, and of the Holy Ghost, for the forgiveness of sins, as Peter says in Acts 2:38.

Washing without the word does not help: but through the word, washing purifies and cleanses us. You read in Ephesians 5:26 how Christ cleanses the congregation in the fountain of water through the word; the word is the promise that God has made. Now, just as a preacher, in preaching the word of God, saves the hearers who believe, so does the washing—it "preaches" and represents to us the promise that God has made to us in Christ. The washing preaches to us that we are cleansed with Christ's bloodshedding—it was an offering and satisfaction for the sin of all who repent and believe, consenting and submitting themselves to the will of God. Plunging into the water signifies that we die and are buried with Christ, concerning the old life of sin which is in Adam. And pulling out again signifies that we rise again with Christ in a new life, full of the Holy Ghost, who will teach and guide us, and work the will of God in us, as you see in Romans 6.

OF WEDLOCK.

Matrimony, or wedlock, is a state or degree ordained by God, and an office in which the husband serves the wife, and the wife serves the husband. It was ordained for a remedy, and to increase the world; and for the man to help the woman, and the woman to help the man, with all love and kindness—and not to signify any promise that ever I heard or read of in the Scripture. Therefore it ought not to be called a sacrament. It has a promise that we do not sin in that state, if a man receive his wife as a gift given to him from God, and the wife receives her husband likewise. In the same way, all kinds of meats and drinks have a promise that we do not sin, if we use them measurably and with thanksgiving. If they call matrimony a sacrament because the Scripture uses the similitude of matrimony to express the marriage, or wedlock, that exists between us and Christ, then I will call mustard-seed, leaven, a net, keys, bread, water, and a thousand other things sacraments, because Christ and the prophets and all the Scripture use them to express the kingdom of heaven and God's word. They praise wedlock with their mouth, and say, 'It is a holy thing,' as it is truly—but they would rather be sanctified with a whore, than to come within the sanctuary [of marriage].

OF ORDER.

Subdeacon, deacon, priest, bishop, cardinal, patriarch, and pope, are names of offices and service, or should be, and not sacraments. There is no promise coupled with them. If they minister their offices truly, it is a sign that Christ's Spirit is in them; if not, it is a sign that the devil is in them. Are these all sacraments, or which one of them? Or what thing in them is that holy sign or sacrament? The shaving, or the anointing? Also, what is the promise that is signified by it? Which word imprints in them that character, or that spiritual seal [of a sacrament]? O dreamers and natural beasts who are without the seal of the Spirit of God; but instead are sealed with the mark of the beast, and with cankered consciences!

There is a word called in Latin *sacerdos*, in Greek *hiereus*, in Hebrew *cohan*, that is, a minister, an officer, a sacrificer or priest—as Aaron was a priest, and sacrificed for the people, and was a mediator between God and them. In English it should have had some other name than priest. But Antichrist has deceived us with unknown and strange terms to bring us into confusion and superstitious blindness. Christ is a priest of that kind forever; and all we are priests through him, and no longer need any such priest on earth to be a mediator for us to God. For Christ has brought us all into the inner temple, within the veil or forehanging, and to the mercy-seat of God. He has coupled us to God, where we offer, every man for himself, the desires and petitions of his heart; and we sacrifice and kill the lusts and appetites of our flesh with prayer, fasting, and all manner of godly living.

There is another word in Greek, called presbyter, in Latin senior, in English an elder; and this is nothing but an officer to teach, and not to be a mediator between God and us. This needs no anointing of man. Those in the Old Testament were anointed with oil, to signify the anointing of Christ, and our anointing with the Holy Ghost through Christ. No man is made a priest in this way, but only one that is chosen; just as in a time of necessity, every person may christen, so every man may teach his wife and household, and the wife her children. So in time of need, if I see my brother sin, I may rebuke him, between him and me, and damn his deed by the law of God; and I may also comfort those who are in despair, with the promises of God; and save them if they believe.

By "priest" then, in the New Testament, we understand simply that an elder is to teach the younger, to bring them to the full knowledge and understanding of Christ; and to minister the sacraments which Christ ordained (which is simply to preach Christ's promises). And we understand that those who give all their study to quench the light of truth, and to hold the people in darkness, are the disciples of Satan and messengers of antichrist, whatever names they may have, or whatever they may call themselves. And as concerning our clergy (as they will be called) who make themselves holier than the lay-people, and take such great lands and goods, and ask for them, and who promise pardons and forgiveness of sins, or absolution, without preaching of Christ's promises—this is falsehood, and the working of antichrist. As I have said, they are the ravenous wolves which Paul prophesied would come after his departing, Act 20:29 not sparing the flock. Their doctrine is that merchandise of which Peter speaks, saying: "Through covetousness, with feigned words, they will make merchandise of you." (2 Pet 2:3)

And the reasons with which they prove their doctrine are, as Paul says, "Superfluous disputings, arguings or brawlings of men with corrupt minds, and destitute of truth, who think that lucre is godliness." (1 Tim 6:5) But Christ says (Mat 7:16), "By their fruits you will know them;" that is, by their filthy covetousness, and shameless ambition, and drunken desire for honor, contrary to the example and doctrine of Christ and his apostles. Christ said to Peter in John 21:16, "Feed my sheep:" and not, 'Shear your flock.' And Peter says (1 Pet 5:3), "Not being lords over the flock." But these clergy shear, and they have become lords. Paul says (2 Cor 1:24), "Not that we are lords over your faith:" but these will be lords; and they would compel us to believe whatever they lust for, without any witness of Scripture; indeed, clean contrary to the Scripture where the clear text rebukes it. Paul says, "It is better to give, than to receive" (acts 20:35) But these clergy do nothing but lay snares to catch and receive whatever comes by, like the gaping mouth of hell. And 2 Cor 12:14, "I do not seek yours, but you." Yet these me do not seek you for Christ, but yours for themselves; and therefore, lest their deeds be rebuked, they will not come to the light.

Nevertheless the truth is that we are all equally beloved in Christ, and God has sworn to all indifferently. Therefore, according to how every man believes God's promises, longs for them, and is diligent to pray to God to fulfill them, so his prayer is heard. And the prayer of a cobbler is as good as the prayer of a cardinal, and that of a butcher as good as that of a bishop; and the blessing of a baker who knows the truth is as good as the blessing of our most holy father the pope. And by blessing, do not understand the wagging of the pope's or bishop's hand over your head, but prayer; as when we say, 'God make you a good man,' 'May Christ put his Spirit in you,' or 'May God give you grace and power to walk in the truth, and to follow his commandments,' etc. This is how Rebecca's friends blessed her when she departed (Gen 24:60) saying, "You are our sister: grow to a thousand thousands, and your seed possess the gates of their enemies." And this is how Isaac blessed Jacob, (Gen 27:28) saying, "God give you of the dew of heaven, and the fatness of the earth, abundance of corn, wine and oil," etc. And again, (Gen 28:3–4) "Almighty God bless you, and make you grow, and multiply you, that you may be a great multitude of people, and give to you and to your seed after you the blessings of Abraham; that you may possess the land in which you are a stranger, which he promised to your grandfather," and such blessings as those.

Last of all, they have one singular doubt. They do not know what makes the priest: the anointing, or the laying on of hands, or a particular ceremony, or specific words? They brawl and scold about this, ready to tear out another's throat. One says this, and another that—but they cannot agree. Neither can any of them give so strong a reason that another cannot improve. For they are all out of the right way, and without the Spirit of God, to judge such spiritual things. Even so, to this I answer that when Christ called twelve up into the mountain, and chose them, then immediately, without any anointing or ceremony, they were his apostles. That is, they were ministers chosen to be sent to preach his testament to the whole world. And after the resurrection, when he opened their minds, and gave them wits to understand the secrets of his testament, and how to bind and loose, and what he would have them to do in all things—then he sent them forth with a commandment to preach, and to bind the unbelieving that continue in sin, and to loose the believing that repent. And that commandment, or charge, made them bishops, priests, popes, and everything else. If they say that Christ made them priests at his Maundy (or last supper), when he said, "Do this in remembrance of me," I answer that, the apostles did not then know what he meant—yet I will not strive nor say anything against it. Nevertheless the commandment and the charge which he gave them, made them priests.

And (Acts 1:26), when Matthias was chosen by lot, it is not to be doubted that the apostles, in their usual manner, prayed for him, that God would give him grace to minister his office truly; and that they put their hands on him, and exhorted him, and gave him charge to be diligent and faithful; and then he was as great as the best of them. And (Acts 6:3–6), when the disciples that believed had chosen seven deacons to minister to the widows, the apostles prayed and put their hands on them, and admitted them without more ado. Laying on hands did not follow the manner of the silent blessing of our holy bishops, with two fingers. Rather, they spoke to them, and told them their duty, and gave them a charge, and warned them to be faithful in the Lord's business—just as we choose temporal officers, and read their duty to them, and they promise to be faithful ministers, and then they are admitted. Nor is there any other manner or ceremony at all required in making our spiritual officers than to choose an able person, and then to repeat to him his duty, and give him his charge, and so put him in his position. As for that other solemn doubt (as they call it), whether Judas was a priest or not, I do not care what he was then. But I am sure of this, that now he is not only priest, but also bishop, cardinal, and pope!

OF PENANCE.

Penance is a word of the clergy's own forging, to deceive us with, as with many other things. In the [Latin] Scripture we find *poenitentia*, "repentance:" *agite poenitentiam*, "do repent;" *poeniteat vos*, "let it repent you." In Greek, it is *metanoyte*, "repent," or "let it repent you." But they have made penance out of repentance to blind the people, and to make them think that they must take pains, and do some holy deeds, in order to make satisfaction for their sins—namely those things which the clergy enjoin them to do.

As you may see in the chronicles, when great kings and tyrants, by the violence of the sword, conquered other kings' lands, and slew all before them—when these kings came to their senses, and their conscience was struck by their wicked deeds, then these bishops coupled them, not to Christ, but to the pope. They preached the pope to them, and made these kings submit themselves and their realms to the holy father the pope. And they made these kings do penance, as they call it. That is, they made them obey such injunctions as the pope and bishops would command them to do: to build abbeys; to endow the clergy with a livelihood; to pray for the clergy forever; and to give the clergy exemptions, privilege, and license to do whatever they lusted after, unpunished. Emperor Henry IV submits to pope Gregory VII

Repentance goes before faith, and it prepares the way to Christ, and to the promises. For Christ only comes to those who see their sins in the law, and repent. Repentance, that is to say, this mourning and sorrow of the heart, lasts all our lives, for we find ourselves, all our lives, too weak for God's law; and therefore we sorrow and mourn, longing for strength. Repentance is not a sacrament, just as faith, hope, love, and knowledge of a man's sins, are not to be called sacraments. For they are spiritual and invisible. Now a sacrament must be an outward sign that may be seen, to signify, represent, and put a man in remembrance of some spiritual promise which cannot be seen except by faith alone. Repentance, and all the good deeds which accompany it to slay the lusts of the flesh, are signified by baptism. For Paul says, Rom 6:3, as it is repeated above: "Do you not remember," he says, "that all we who are baptized in the name of Christ Jesus, are baptized to die with him?" We are buried with him in baptism to die; that is, to kill the lusts and rebellion which remain in the flesh. And after that he says, "You are dead, as concerning sin, but alive to God through Christ Jesus our Lord." If you look at the profession of our hearts, and the Spirit and forgiveness which we have received through Christ's merits, we are fully dead. But if you look at the rebellion of the flesh, we only begin to die, and to be baptized, that is, to drown and quench the lusts; and we are fully baptized at the last minute of death. As concerning the working of the Spirit, we begin to live, and grow every day more and more, both in knowledge and also in godly living, according to how our lusts abate—just as a child receives its entire soul on the first day of life, and yet grows daily in the operations and workings of it. Charlemagne holding both sword and cross

OF CONFESSION.

Confession is diverse, and inseparably follows true faith. It is confessing and acknowledging with the mouth, what we put our trust and confidence in. As when we say our Credo, we confess that we trust in God the Father Almighty, and in his truth and promises; and in his Son Jesus, our Lord, and in his merits and deservings; and in the Holy Ghost, and in his power, assistance and guiding. This confession is necessary for all men that will be saved. For Christ says, Mat 10:33, "Whoever denies me before men, I will deny him before my Father that is in heaven."

And of this confession, says the holy apostle Paul, Rom 10:10, "the belief of the heart justifies; and to acknowledge with the mouth makes a man safe." This is a wonderful text for our philosophers, or rather sophisters, our worldly-wise enemies of the wisdom of God, our deep and profound wells without water, our clouds without moisture of rain—that is to say, natural souls without the Spirit of God and without feeling of godly things. To justify, and to make safe, are both one thing. And to confess with the mouth is a good work, and the fruit of a true faith, as all other works are.

If you repent and believe the promises, then God's truth justifies you; that is, God forgives you your sins, and seals you with his holy Spirit, and makes you heir of everlasting life through Christ's deservings. Now if you have true faith, so that you see the exceeding and infinite love and mercy which God has showed you freely in Christ, then you must love in return. And love cannot but compel you to work, and to boldly confess and acknowledge your Lord Christ, and the trust which you have in his word. And this knowledge makes you safe; that is, it declares that you are safe already. It certifies your heart, and makes you feel that your faith is right, and that God's Spirit is in you, as all other good works will do. For if, when it comes to the point, you had no desire to work, nor power to confess, then how could you presume to think that God's Spirit was in you?

There is another confession which goes before faith, and accompanies repentance. For whoever repents, acknowledges his sins in his heart. And whoever acknowledge his sins, receives forgiveness, as John says (1 Joh 1:9), "If we knowledge our sins, he is faithful and just to forgive us our sins, and to cleanse us from all unrighteousness;" that is, because he has promised, he must do it for his truth's sake. This confession is necessary all our lives, as is repentance. And what you understand of repentance, so understand of this confession; for it is likewise included in the sacrament of baptism. For we always repent, and always acknowledge or confess our sins to God, and yet we do not despair; for we remember that we are washed in Christ's blood, which our baptism represents and signifies to us.

Confession in the ear is truly a work of Satan—the falsest ever wrought; and which has most devoured the faith. It began among the Greeks, but it was not then used (as it is now) to account for all of a man's sins in the priest's ear. Rather, it was to ask counsel about doubts men had, as you may see in St. Jerome, and other authors. Nor did they go to priests only, which were very few at that time—only to those who preached the word of God; for this advantage in having so many priests saying masses was not yet found; but they went indifferently to where they saw a good and a learned man. And because of a little knavery, which a deacon at Constantinople played through confession with one of the chief wives of the city, it was abandoned. But we, antichrist's possession, the more knavery that we see growing by this practice daily, the more we establish it. A Christian man is a spiritual thing; and he has God's word in his heart, and God's Spirit to certify all things to him. He is not bound to come to any man's ear.

And as for the reasons for this practice, which the clergy make up, these are all but persuasions of man's wisdom. First, as pertaining to the keys and manner of binding and loosing, it was repeated enough above and in other places. You may also see how the apostles used them in the Acts; and, in Paul's epistles, how the Spirit came at the preaching of faith, and certified to their hearts that they were justified through believing the promises.

When a man feels that his heart consents to the law of God, and feels meek, patient, courteous, and, merciful to his neighbor, altered and fashioned like Christ; why should he doubt that God has forgiven him, and chosen him, and put his Spirit in him, though he never crooned his sin into the priest's ear?

They give one blind reason for it, saying, 'How will the priest unbind, loose, and forgive the sin which he does not know?' How did the apostles? These men forsake the Scripture, and run to their blind reasons, stretching Scripture for a carnal purpose. When I have said in your ear all that I have done my life, in order, with all the circumstances in the most shameful manner, what more can you do than preach the promises to me, saying, 'If you repent and believe, God's truth will save you for Christ's sake?' You do not see my heart; you do not know whether I repent or not; nor whether I consent to the law that it is holy, righteous, and good. Moreover, whether I believe the promises or not is also unknown to you. If you preach the law and the promises (as the apostles did), those whom God has chosen should repent, and believe, and be saved, now as well as then. Yet antichrist must know all secrets—to establish his kingdom, and work his mysteries.

They also bring up the story of the ten lepers, Luke 17:12–19. Here mark their falsehood, and learn to recognize them forever. The fourteenth Sunday after the feast of the Trinity, the beginning of the seventh lesson, is this gospel; and the eighth and the ninth lessons, along with the rest of the seventh, is the exposition of Bede on this passage. Bede says, "Of all that Christ healed, of whatever disease, he sent none to the priest but the lepers;" and he interprets "lepers" as followers of false doctrine. Spiritual officers and the learned men of the congregation, Bede says, ought to examine and correct their learning with God's word, and warn the congregation to beware those who follow false doctrine. If such wayward men are afterward healed by the grace of Christ, then they ought to come before the congregation, and there openly confess their true faith. But all other vices (Bede says), God heals within, in the conscience. Though clergy read this at their matins, yet at high mass, if they have any sermon at all, they lie—saying things clean contrary to this open truth. Nor are they ashamed of it at all. Why? Because they walk in complete darkness.

OF CONTRITION.

Contrition and repentance are both one thing; they are simply a sorrowful and mourning heart. And because God has promised mercy to a contrite heart, that is, to a sorrowful and repenting heart, the clergy have twisted God's word in order to establish their wicked tradition, and have feigned that new word, attrition. They say, 'You cannot know whether your sorrow or repentance is contrition or attrition, unless you are confessed. When you are confessed, then it is true contrition.' O foxy Pharisee! That is your leaven of which Christ so diligently warned us to beware, Mat 16:6. And it is the prophecy of Peter, "Through covetousness, with feigned words, they will make merchandise of you." 2 Pet 2:3. With such glosses they corrupt God's word, to sit over the consciences of the people, to lead them captive, and to make a prey of them—buying and selling sins to satisfy their insatiable covetousness. Nevertheless, the truth is that, when any man has trespassed against God, if he repents and acknowledges his trespass, God promises him forgiveness without ear-confession.

If someone has offended his neighbor, and he repents and acknowledges his fault, asking forgiveness, and his neighbor forgives him, then God also forgives him by his holy promise, (Mat 18:35). Likewise, someone who sins publicly, if he repents and turns when he is openly rebuked, then if the congregation forgives him, God forgives him. And so whoever repents when he is rebuked, if he acknowledges his fault, he is forgiven.

Also, the one who doubts, or has his conscience tangled, ought to share his mind with a faithful brother who is learned, and that brother will give him faithful counsel to help him with it. I ought to confess to someone I trespass against. But I am not bound to confess myself to you, O antichrist, whom I have not offended.

Those under the old law had no confession in the ear. Nor did the apostles and those who followed hundreds of years after, know of any such whispering. How then was their attrition turned into contrition? Indeed, why are we, whom Christ came to loose, more bound than the Jews? Indeed, why are we more bound without Scripture? For Christ did not come to make us more bound; but to loose us, and to make a thousand things not sin which were sin before—and yet have now become sin again. He left no other law with us than the law of love. He did not loose us from Moses to bind us to antichrist's ear. God has not tied Christ to antichrist's car, nor has he poured all his mercy in there. For there is no record in the Old Testament that antichrist's ear should be *Propitiatorium*, that is, God's mercy-stool; or that God should creep into so narrow a hole so that he could be found nowhere else. Nor did God write his laws, or yet his holy promises, in antichrist's ear. Rather, he has engraved them with his holy Spirit in the hearts of those who believe, so that they might have them always ready at hand to be saved by them.

SATISFACTION.

As pertaining to satisfaction, understand this, that the one who loves God has a commandment to "love his neighbor also." (1 Joh 4:20) If you have offended your neighbor, you must make amends or satisfaction, or at least, if you are notable, ask his forgiveness. And if he would have the mercy of God, he is bound to forgive you. If he will not, yet God forgives you, if you thus submit yourself. But to God, Christ is a perpetual and an everlasting satisfaction, forevermore.

As often as you fall through frailty, repent and come back, and you are safe and welcome—as you may see by the example of the riotous son, Luke 15:1 If you have leaped out of sanctuary, come in again. If you have fallen from the way of truth, come back to it, and you are safe: if you have gone astray, come to the fold again, and the shepherd, Christ, shall save you. Indeed, the angels of heaven will rejoice at your coming, so far is it that any man would beat you or chide you for it. If any Pharisee envies you, resents you, or rails against you, your Father will answer for you, as you see in the fore-mentioned example or parable. Whoever therefore has gone out of the way, by whatever chance it may happen, let him come to his baptism again, and to its profession, and he shall be safe.

For though the washing of baptism is past, yet its power, that is to say, the word of God which baptism preaches, lasts and speaks forever. Just as Paul is past and gone, nevertheless the word that Paul preached is everlasting, and it ever saves as many as come to it with a repenting heart and a steadfast faith.

By this you can see that when the clergy make penance out of repentance, and call it a sacrament, and divide it into contrition, confession, and satisfaction, they speak from their own heads, and lie falsely.

ABSOLUTION.

Their absolution also justifies no man from sin. "For with the heart men believe, to be justified with it," Paul says (Rom 10:9). That is, through faith and believing the promises are we justified, as I have sufficiently proved in other places with the Scripture. "Faith" (says Paul in the same place) "comes by hearing," that is to say, by hearing the preacher who is sent from God, and who preaches God's promises. Now, when you absolve in Latin, the unlearned does not hear, or, "How," says Paul, 1 Cor 14:16, "when you bless in an unknown tongue, will the unlearned say Amen to your thanksgiving? For he does not know what you say." So likewise the lay-person does not know whether you loose or bind, or whether you bless or curse. It is the same way if the lay-person understands Latin, or even if the priest absolves in English. For in his absolution, the priest does not repeat any promise of God; instead, he speaks his own words, saying, 'By the authority of Peter and Paul, I absolve or loose you from all your sins.' You say this, and you are only a lying man; and never more truly than now.

You say, 'I forgive you your sins;' yet the Scripture, Joh 1:29, says that only Christ forgives, and "takes away the sins of the world." And Paul and Peter, and all the apostles, preach that all is forgiven in Christ, and for Christ's sake. Only God's word looses, and you in preaching that word also loose, or else sins are not loosed.

Whoever has ears, let him hear, and let him that has eyes, see. If any man loves to be blind, his blindness is on his own head, and not on mine.

They allege for themselves the words of Christ to Peter, Mat 16:19, "Whatever you bind on earth, it will be bound; and whatever you loose," and so forth. 'Look, they say, whatever we bind, and whatever we loose—nothing is excepted here.' And they use another text of Christ, in the last chapter of Matthew: "All power is given to me," says Christ, "in heaven and in earth: go therefore and preach," etc. Preaching leaves the pope out; it says, 'Look, all power is given to me in heaven and in earth;' and thereupon the pope takes upon himself temporal power above king and emperor, and he makes laws and binds them to it. And he takes similar power over God's laws, and dispenses with them at his pleasure, making no sin of what God makes sin, and makes sin where God makes none. Indeed, he clean wipes out God's laws, and makes laws at his pleasure. And whatever he lusts after is lawful for him. He binds where God looses, and looses where God binds. He blesses where God curses, and curses where God blesses. He takes authority also to bind and loose in purgatory. I allow that he may do that, for it is a creature of his own making. He also binds the angels: for we read of popes that have commanded the angels to fetch various persons out of purgatory. Be that as it may, I am not yet certified to say whether they obeyed or not.

Understand, therefore, that to bind and to loose is to preach the law of God and the gospel, or the promises. As you may see in the third chapter of the second epistle to the Corinthians, Paul calls the preaching of the law, the ministration of death and damnation, and the preaching of the promises the ministering of the Spirit and of righteousness. For when the law is preached, all men are found sinners, and therefore they are damned. And when the gospel and glad tidings are preached, then all who repent and believe, are found righteous in Christ, And this is how all the old doctors expound it. Saint Jerome says of this phrase 'whatever you bind,' that the bishops and priests, for lack of understanding, take a little presumption of the Pharisees upon themselves, and think that they have authority to bind innocents, and to loose the wicked; which is what our pope and bishops do. For they say the curse is to be feared, whether right or wrong. Though you have not deserved it, yet if the pope curses you, then you are said to be in peril of your soul—as they lie about it. Indeed, no matter how wrongfully cursed a man may be, they say he must be willing to buy absolution. But Saint Jerome says, 'As the priest of the old law made the lepers clean or unclean, so the priest of the new law binds and unbinds.' But in fact the priest of the old law made no man a leper, nor did he cleanse any man, but only God; and the priest judged only by Moses' law, as to who was clean and unclean, when they were brought to him.

So here we have the law of God to judge what sin is and what it is not, and who is bound and who is not. Moreover, if any man has sinned, if he repents and believes the promise, we are sure by God's word that he is loosed and forgiven in Christ. The priests do not have any other authority to preach than this. Christ's apostles had no other authority themselves, as it appears throughout the New Testament. Therefore it is manifest that these clergy have none.

St. Paul says, 1 Cor 15:27 "When we say all things are under Christ, he is to be excepted that put all things under him." God the Father is not under Christ, but above Christ, and Christ's head. Christ says, John 12:49–50, "I have not spoken of my own head, but my Father, who sent me, commanded what I should say and what I should speak. Whatever I speak therefore, even as my Father told me, so I speak."

If Christ had a law for what he should do, then how

can it happen that the pope runs at large, lawless? Though all power was given to Christ in heaven and in earth, he still had no power over his Father, nor to reign temporally over temporal princes. Instead, he had a commandment to obey them. How then does the pope have such temporal authority over king and emperor? How does he have authority above God's laws, and to command the angels, the saints, and even God himself?

Christ's authority, which he gave to his disciples, was to preach the law, and to bring sinners to repentance, and then to preach the promises to them which the Father had made to all men for Christ's sake. And he sent his apostles to preach only the same. When a king sends out his judges and gives them his authority, saying, 'What you do, that will I do; I give you my full power,' he does not mean, by that full power, that they should destroy any town or city they please, or oppress any man, or do whatever they are inclined, or that they should reign over the lords and dukes of his realm, and even over himself. Rather, he gives them a law, and the authority to bind and loose as far as that law stretches and mentions—that is, to punish the evil ones who do wrong, and to avenge the poor who suffer wrong. As far as the law stretches, the king will defend his judges against all men. And just as temporal judges bind and loose temporally, so the priests bind and loose spiritually, and in no other ways. Even so, by falsehood and subtlety, the pope reigns under Christ, just as his cardinals and bishops reign under kings: lawless.

The pope (they say) absolves or looses a *poena et culpa*; that is, from the fault or trespass, and from the pain due to the trespass. They say that if a man repents, God forgives the offense only, and not the pain as well. He turns the everlasting pain into a temporal pain, and he appoints seven years in purgatory for every deadly sin. But the pope, for money, will forgive both, and thus he has more power than God, and he is more merciful than God. 'I do this,' says the pope, 'of my full power, and of the treasure of the church; of the deservings of martyrs and confessors, and of the merits of Christ.'

First, the merits of the saints did not save them, but they were saved by Christ's merits only.

Secondarily, God has promised Christ's merits to all who repent; so that whoever repents, is immediately heir of all Christ's merits, and beloved of God just as Christ is. How then did this foul monster come to be lord over Christ's merits, so that he has power to sell what God gives freely? O dreamers! Indeed, O devils, and O venomous scorpions, what poison you have in your tails! O pestilent leaven, that so turns the sweet bread of Christ's doctrine into the bitterness of gall!

The friars run in the same spirit, and teach, saying, 'Do good deeds, and redeem the pains that await you in purgatory; indeed, give us something to do good works for you.' And thus sin has become the most profitable merchandise in the world. O the cruel wrath of God upon us, because we do not love the truth!

For this is the damnation and judgment of God, to send a false prophet to one who will not hear the truth. "I know you," says Christ, (John 5:42–43) "that you do not have the love of God in you. I have come in my Father's name, and you do not receive me; if another comes in his own name, you will you receive him." Thus God avenges himself on the malicious hearts which have no love for his truth.

They have either wiped out all the promises of God, or they have thus leavened them with open lies to establish their confession. And to keep us from the knowledge of the truth, they do all things in Latin. They pray in Latin, they christen in Latin, they bless in Latin, they give absolution in Latin; they only curse in the English tongue. In this they take greater authority upon themselves than ever God gave them. For in their curses (as they call them) with book, bell, and candle, they command God and Christ, and the angels, and all the saints, to curse them: 'Curse them God (they say), Father, Son, and Holy Ghost; curse them Virgin Mary,' etc. O you abominable! Who gave you authority to command God to curse? God commands you to bless, and you command him to curse! "Bless them that persecute you: bless, but do not curse," says St. Paul, Rom 12:14. What tyranny will these clergy not use over men, these men who presume and take upon themselves to be lords over God, and to command him? If God curses any man, who will bless and make him better? No man can amend himself unless God pours his Spirit into him. Do we not have a commandment to love our neighbor as ourselves? How can I love him, and curse him also? James says, "It is not possible for blessing and cursing to both come out of one mouth." Christ commands, Mat 5:44, "Love your enemies. Bless those that curse you. Do good to those that hate you. Pray for those that do you wrong and persecute you; so that you may be the children of your heavenly Father."

In the marches of Wales, it is the custom that if any man has an ox or a cow stolen, he comes to the curate, and desires him to curse the thief; and he commands every man in the parish to give him God's curse and his own: 'He has God's curse and mine,' says every man in the parish. O merciful God! What is blasphemy if not this, and the shaming of the doctrine of Christ?

Understand therefore, that the power of excommunication is this: if any man sins openly, and does not amend when he is warned, then he ought to be openly rebuked before the whole parish. And the priest ought to prove by the Scripture, that all such persons have no part with Christ. For Christ serves only for those who love the law of God, and consent that it is good, holy, and righteous; and who repent, sorrowing and mourning for the power and strength to fulfill his law. And the whole parish ought to be warned to avoid the company of all such persons, and consider them heathen. This is not done so that he should perish; but to save him, to make him ashamed, and to kill the lusts of the flesh, so that the spirit might come to the knowledge of truth. We ought to pity him, and to have compassion on him, and with all diligence to pray to God for him, to give him grace to repent and to come to the right way again; and not use such tyranny over God and man, commanding God to curse him. And if he repents, then with all mercy we ought to receive him again. This you may see in Mat 18, 1 Cor 5, and 2 Cor 2:5–11.

CONFIRMATION.

If Confirmation has a promise, then it justifies as far as the promise extends. If it has no promise, then it is not from God, as the bishops are not. The apostles and ministers of God preach God's word; and God's signs or sacraments signify God's word, and they put us in remembrance of the promises which God has made to us in Christ. By contrast, antichrist's bishops do not preach; and their sacraments do not speak; but like the disguised bishop's mum, so their superstitious sacraments are silent. After the bishops abandoned preaching, they feigned this silent ceremony of confirmation, to have something, at least, by which they might reign over their dioceses. They also reserved to themselves the christening of bells, and the conjuring or "hallowing" of churches and churchyards, and of altars and super-altars, and the hallowing of chalices, and so forth—whatever is of honor or profit to them. This confirmation, and the other conjurations also, they have now committed to their suffragans; because they themselves have no leisure to minister such things, because of their lusts and pleasures, and the abundance of all things, and because of the burden they have involving the king's matters and the business of the realm. One keeps the privy seal; another the great seal; the third is confessor, (that is to say, a privy traitor and a secret Judas); this one is president of the prince's council; that one is an ambassador; another a member of the king's secret council. Woe to the realms where they belong to the council. Truly, they are as profitable to the realms with their counsel, as wolves are to the sheep, or as foxes are to the geese.

They will say that the Holy Ghost is given through such ceremonies. If God had promised it, so it would be; but Paul says, (Gal 3:2) that the Spirit is received through the preaching of the faith. And (Acts 10:44) while Peter preached the faith, the Holy Ghost fell on Cornelius and on his household. What then shall we say to what they will lay against us, in the eighth chapter of the Acts of the apostles, where Peter and John put their hands on the Samaritans, and the Holy Ghost came? I say, that "by putting," or "with putting, "or "as they put their hands on them," the Holy Ghost came. Nevertheless, putting on hands neither helped nor hindered. For the text says, "They prayed for them that they might receive the Holy Ghost." God had made the apostles a promise, that with such miracles he would confirm their preaching, and move others to the faith. (Mark 16:17–20) The apostles, therefore, believed and prayed that God would fulfill his promise; and God, for his truth's sake, did so. So was it the prayer of faith that brought the Holy Ghost? You may see this in the last chapter of James. "If any man is sick," says James, "call the elders of the congregation, and let them pray over him, anointing him with oil in the name of the Lord, and the prayer of faith shall heal the sick." Where a promise is made, there is bold faith to pray, and God is true to give her her petition. Putting on hands is an indifferent thing. For the Holy Ghost came by the preaching of the faith, and miracles were done at the prayer of faith as well, without putting on hands, as you see in many places. Putting on hands was the way of that nation, just as it was to rend their clothes, and to put on sackcloth, and to sprinkle themselves with ashes and earth when they heard of or saw anything sorrowful. It was Paul's way to stretch out his hand when he preached; and it is our manner to hold up our hands when we pray. Some kiss their thumbnail, and put it to their eyes, and we put our hands on children's heads when we bless them, saying, 'Christ bless you, my son, and God make you a good man.' These gestures neither help nor hinder. You may well see this in Acts 13:2–3, where the Holy Ghost commanded the church to separate Paul and Barnabas to go and preach. Then the others fasted and prayed, and put their hands on their heads, and sent them out. So they did not receive the Holy Ghost by putting on hands. But the others, as they put their hands on Paul and Barnabas' heads, prayed for them: that God would go with them, and strengthen them; and encouraged them also, bidding them to be strong in God; and they warned them to be faithful and diligent in the work of God, and so forth.

ANOINTING WITH OIL

Last of all comes anointing with oil. It is without a promise, and therefore it is without the Spirit, and without profit; rather, it is altogether unfruitful and superstitious. The sacraments, as the clergy have conceived them, are all without a promise, and therefore they do not help. For "whatever is not of faith is sin." (Rom 14:23). Now without a promise there can be no faith. The sacraments which Christ himself ordained, did have promises, and so they would save us if we knew them, and believed them, and they were not ministered in the Latin tongue. So they have become as unfruitful as their other rituals. Indeed, the clergy make us believe that the work itself, without the promise, saves us—this is a doctrine they learned from Aristotle. And thus we have become a hundred times worse than the wicked Jews who believed that it was the work of the sacrifice that justified them. Paul fights against this in every epistle, proving that nothing helps except the promises which God has sworn in Christ. Ask the people what they understand by their baptism or washing? You will see that they believe the mere plunging into water is what saves them. They know nothing of the promises, nor what is signified by baptism. Baptism is called volowing in many places of England, because the priest says, 'Volo [I wish it] say you.' 'The child was well-volowed' (they say); 'yes, and our vicar is as fair a volower as any a priest within twenty miles.' Behold how narrowly the people look at the ceremony. If anything is left out, or if the child is not entirely dipped in the water, or if, because the child is sick, the priest dares not plunge him into the water, but pours water on his head, how they tremble! How they quake! 'What do you say, sir John, (the priest asks) is this child christened enough? Does it have its full christendom?' They truly believe that the child is not christened. Indeed, I have known priests that have gone to the orders again, supposing that they were not priests, just because the bishop left one of his ceremonies undone. What they call confirmation, the people call bishoping. They think that if the bishop butters the child on the forehead, that it is safe. They think that the work is what makes safe, and likewise they suppose about anointing with oil. Now this is false doctrine, truly. For James says, in the first chapter of his epistle: "Of his good will he birthed us with the word of life;" 8 that is, with the word of promise in which we are made God's sons, and heirs of the goodness of God, before any good works. For we cannot work God's will until we are his sons, and know his will, and have his Spirit to teach us. And St. Paul says, in the fifth chapter of his epistle to the Ephesians: "Christ cleansed the congregation in the fountain of water through the word." And Peter says, in the first of his first epistle: "You are born anew, not of mortal seed, but of immortal seed, by the word of God, which lives and lasts forever." Paul in every epistle warns us that we should put no trust in works, and to beware of persuasions or arguments of man's wisdom, of superstition, of ceremonies, of pope-holiness, and of all kinds of disguising. He exhorts us to cleave fast to the naked and pure word of God. The promise of God is the anchor that saves us in all temptations. If all the world is against us, God's word is stronger than the world. If the world kills us, that will make us alive again. If it is possible for the world to throw us into hell, from there God's word shall yet bring us back.

By this you see that it is not the work, but the promise that justifies us through faith. Now where there is no promise, there can be no faith, and therefore no justifying, no matter how glorious the works may be. They preach the sacrament of Christ's body in this way: you must believe that it is no longer bread, but the very body of Christ, flesh, blood and bone, even as he went about here on earth, except for his coat. For that is still here; I do not know in how many places. I pray you, what does all this help? There is no promise here. The devils know that Christ died on a Friday, and the Jews also. How are they helped by it? We have a promise that Christ, and his body, and his blood, and all that he did, and suffered, is a sacrifice, a ransom, and a full satisfaction for our sins; and that God for his sake will think no more about them, if we have the power to repent and believe it.

Holy-work men think that God rejoices in the deed itself, without any further respect. They also think that God, as a cruel tyrant, rejoices and takes pleasure in our pain, without any further respect. And therefore many of them martyr themselves without cause, following the example of Baal's priests who cut themselves to please their god, and just as the old heathen pagans sacrificed their children in the fire to their gods. The monks of the Charterhouse think that eating fish in itself pleases God, and they do not relate the eating to the chastening of the body. For when they have slain their bodies with cold phlegm, from fish-eating, they will still eat no flesh, and slay themselves before their time. We too, when we offer our sons or daughters, and compel or persuade them to vow and profess chastity, think that the pain, and the rage and burning which they suffer in abstaining from marriage, pleases God; and so we do not relate our chastity to our neighbor's profit. For we see thousands fall to innumerable diseases by it, and die before their days. Indeed, though we see them break the commandments of God daily, and also being impatient, they work abominations against nature, too shameful to be spoken of—yet we will we not let them marry, but compel them to continue in it, by force. This is what our divines teach, as it appears by their arguments. The one who endures the most pain, they say, is the greatest; and so forth.

The people are thoroughly brought to believe that the deed in itself, without any further respect, saves them: if they are so long at church; or say so many paternosters; and read so much in a tongue they do not understand; or go so long on a pilgrimage; and endure so much pain; or fast such a superstitious fast; or observe such a superstitious observance, neither profitable to themselves nor to their neighbors. But these things must be done with good intentions, the clergy say, to please God with. Indeed, they think that the kiss of peace is a meritorious deed, when loving their neighbor, and forgiving him, (which is the thing signified by it), they do not study to do, nor do they have the power to do it, nor do they think they are bound to do it if they are offended by their neighbor. So sorely have our false prophets led the people out of their wits, and wrapped them in darkness, and rocked them asleep in blindness and ignorance. Now all such doctrine is false doctrine, and all such faith is false faith. For the deed does not please, but only as far as it is applied to our neighbor's profit, or to the taming of our bodies in order to keep the commandment.

Now the body must be tamed only, and not killed. And that should be done with the remedies God has ordained. You must not reject the natural remedy which God has ordained, and bring yourself into such a state that you break God's commandment, or kill yourself, or burn night and day without rest, so that you cannot once think a godly thought. Nor is it lawful to abandon your neighbor, and withdraw yourself from serving him, just to get yourself into a den and live idly, profitable to no man, but robbing all men first of your faith, and then of your goods and land and all you have—along with making men believe in the hypocrisy of these superstitious prayers and pope-holy deeds. The prayer of faith, and the deeds of faith that spring from love, are accepted before God. The prayer is good according to the proportion of faith; and the deed is good according to the measure of love.

Now he that bids in the world, as monks call it, has more faith than the cloisterer; for he depends on God in all things. He must trust God to send him good speed, good luck, favor, help, a good master, a good neighbor, a good servant, a good wife, a good chapman-merchant to send his merchandise safely to land, and a thousand similar provisions. He also loves more; this is apparent in that he always does service to his neighbor. We are equally bound to pray for one another, and to pray is a thing that we may always do, whatever we have in hand; and no man may hire another to do that. Christ's blood has hired us already. Thus God delights in the deed as far as we do it, either to serve our neighbor (as I have said), or to tame the flesh, so that we may fulfill the commandment from the bottom of the heart. And as for enduring our pain, God does not rejoice in it like a tyrant; but he pities us, and as it were, he mourns with us, and is always ready and at hand to help us if we call, just as a merciful father and a kind mother would be. Nevertheless, God allows us to fall into many temptations and much adversity: indeed, he himself lays the cross of tribulation on our backs—not that he rejoices in our sorrow, but he does it to drive sin out of the flesh, for none can be cured otherwise. The physician and surgeon do many things which are painful to the sick, not that they rejoice in the pains of these poor wretches, but they do it to persecute and drive out the diseases which cannot otherwise be healed.

When people believe therefore, that if they do so much work, or suffer so much pain, or go so far on a pilgrimage, that they are safe, that is a false faith. For a Christian man is not saved by works, but by faith in the promises before all good works. Although the works (when we work God's commandment with a good will, and not works of our own imagination) declare that we are safe, and they declare that the Spirit of him that has made us safe is in us. Indeed, just as God purges and justifies the heart through the preaching of faith, even so he purges and justifies the members through the working of deeds, making us perfect both in body and soul, after the likeness of Christ.

Nor does a Christian man need to run here or there to Rome, Jerusalem, St. James, or any other pilgrimage far or near, to be saved by it, or to purchase forgiveness of his sins. For a Christian man's health and salvation is within him, even in his mouth. Romans 10:8, "The word is near you, even in your mouth and in your heart; that is, the word of faith which we preach," says Paul. If we believe the promises with our hearts, and confess them with our mouths, we are safe. This is our health within us. "But how shall they believe what they do not hear? And how shall they hear without a preacher?" says Paul (Romans 10:14). For looking at the promises of God, all our preachers are silent; or if they preach them, they so sauce and leaven them, that no stomach can stand them, or find any savor in them. For they paint us such a picture of ear-confession that it is impossible to keep it, and more impossible to have it stand with the promises and testament of God. They enjoin the people to do penance, as they call it—to fast, go on pilgrimages, and give so much to make satisfaction for sins. They preach their masses, their merits, their pardons, their ceremonies, and thus put the promise clean out of men's possession. The word of health and salvation "is near you, in your mouth and your heart," says Paul. No, they say, your salvation is in our faithful ear. This is their hold on men: by ear-confession they know all secrets; thereby they mock all men and all men's wives; they beguile knight and squire, lord and king, and betray all realms. The bishops, along with the pope, have a certain conspiring and secret treason against the whole world; by confession, they know what kings and emperors think. If anything is against the clergy, they do ever so much evil, then they move their captives to war and to fight, and give them pardons to slay whomever they would have taken out of their way. By falsehood, they have taken from all kings and emperors their rights and duties, which the clergy now claim as their freedoms, liberties, and privileges. They have perverted the ordinances that God left in the world, and have made every king swear to defend the clergy's falsehood against them. So that now, if any man preaches God's word in truth, and shows the freedom and liberty of the soul which we have in Christ, or if he intends to restore kings to their duties and rights again, and to the position and authority which they have from God, and from shadows to make them into kings in deed, and to put the world in his order again—then the kings will offer their swords and authority to these hypocrites, to slay such a person, so drunk are they with the wine of the whore. The text that follows in Paul they will happily lay to my charge, and others. "How will they preach unless they are sent?" asks Paul (Rom 10:15). These men will say, 'We are the pope, cardinals, and bishops: all authority is ours. The Scripture pertains to us, and it is our possession. And we have a law that whoever presumes to preach without the authority of the bishops, is excommunicated in doing so.' They will ask, 'Therefore, from where do you have your authority?' The old Pharisees likewise had the Scripture in captivity; and they asked Christ, "By what authority do you do these things?" It was as if to say, 'We are Pharisees, and you are not of our order, nor do you have authority from us.' Christ asked them another question—and I will ask it of our hypocrites. 'Who sent you? God? No, he that is sent from God speaks God's word.' Now you do not speak God's word, or anything except your own laws, which are made clean contrary to God's word. Christ's apostles preached Christ, and not themselves. He that is of the truth, preaches the truth. Now you preach nothing but lies, and therefore you are of the devil, the father of all lies, and you are sent by him. As for my authority, or who sent me, my works report me to be the Christ. If God's word bears record that I speak the truth, then why should any man doubt that God, the Father of truth and of light, has sent me—just as the father of lies and of darkness has sent you; and that the Spirit of truth and of light is with me, just as the spirit of lies and of darkness is with you?' They will respond, 'By this means you would have every man be a preacher.' No, truly. For God will not have that, and therefore I will not have it—no more than I would have every man of London be the mayor, or every man of the realm be its king. God is not the author of dissension and strife, but of unity and peace, and of good order. I would have it, therefore, that where a congregation is gathered together in Christ, one be chosen following the rule of Paul, that only he preach and no one else openly; but every man should teach his household following the same doctrine. If the preacher preaches falsely, and God moves someone's heart to rebuke and reprove the false teacher with the clear and manifest Scripture, then it will be lawful for him to do so; he is no doubt a true prophet sent by God. For the Scripture is God's, and theirs who believe it—not false prophets.

A sacrament then, is the same as a holy sign. And the sacraments which Christ ordained, preach God's word to us. Therefore they justify and minister the Spirit to those who believe. Paul, through preaching the gospel, was a minister of righteousness, and of the Spirit, to all who believed his preaching. Silent ceremonies are not sacraments, but superstition. Christ's sacraments preach the faith of Christ, just as his apostles did, and thereby they justify. Antichrist's silent ceremonies do not preach the faith that is in Christ, just as antichrist's apostles (our bishops and cardinals) do not. But as antichrist's bishops are ordained to kill whoever preaches the true faith of Christ, so are his ceremonies ordained to quench the faith which Christ's sacraments preach. By this you may know the difference between Christ's signs or sacraments, and antichrist's signs or ceremonies: Christ's signs speak, and antichrist's are silent.

By this you see what is to be thought about all other ceremonies, such as hallowed water, bread, salt, boughs, bells, wax, ashes, and so forth; and all the other disguisings and apes'-play; and all kinds of conjurations, such as conjuring churches and church-yards, altar-stones, and the like. Where there is no promise of God, there can be no faith, nor justifying, nor forgiveness of sins. For it is more than madness to look for anything from God beyond what he has promised. However far he has promised, that is how far he is bound to those who believe, and no farther. Therefore, it is plain idolatry to have faith or trust in anything where God has not promised; it is worshipping your own imagination instead of God.

Let us see the pith of a ceremony or two, to judge the rest by. In conjuring holy water, they pray that whoever is sprinkled with it may receive health in body and soul. They do likewise in making holy bread and so forth in the conjurations of other ceremonies. Now we see by daily experience that half their prayer is unheard, for no man receives bodily health by it. It is no more likely that they receive soul-health by it, and indeed, we confirm that by experience. For no man, by sprinkling himself with holy water, or by eating holy bread, is more merciful than before, or forgives wrong more readily, or becomes one with his enemy, or is more patient, and less covetous, and so forth; all of which are sure tokens of soul-health.

They also preach that wagging the bishop's hand over us blesses us, and puts away our sins. Are these works not against Christ? How can they do more shame to Christ's blood? For if the wagging of the bishop's hand over me is so precious a thing in the sight of God that I am thereby blessed, how then am I fully "blessed with all spiritual blessing in Christ?" as Paul says, Eph 1:3. Or if my sins are fully taken away in Christ, how do any remain to be taken away by such fantasies? The apostles knew no ways to put away sin, or to bless us, except by preaching Christ. Paul says, Gal 2:21, "If righteousness comes by the law, then Christ died in vain." So I make this argument: If blessing comes by the wagging of the bishop's hand, then Christ died in vain, and his death does not bless us. And a little before (Gal 2:17) Paul says, "If while we seek to be justified by Christ, we are yet found sinners" (so that we must be justified by the law or ceremonies), "is Christ not then a minister of sin?" So I make this argument: If while we seek to be blessed in Christ we are yet unblessed, and must be blessed by the wagging of the bishop's hand, then what do we have from Christ but curse? You may say: When we come first to the faith, then Christ forgives us and blesses us; but the sins which we commit afterward are forgiven through such things. I answer that, if any man truly repents and comes to the faith, and puts his trust in Christ, then as often as he sins from frailty, at the sigh of the heart his sin is put away in Christ's blood. For Christ's blood ever purges and ever blesses. For John says, "I write this to you, so that you will not sin. And if any man sins" (meaning from frailty, and so repents) "yet we have an Advocate with the Father, Jesus Christ who is righteous, and he is the one who obtains grace for our sins." (1 Joh 2:1) And it is written (Heb 7:24–25), "But this man" (meaning Christ), "because he lasts or abides forever, has an everlasting priesthood. Therefore he is also able to ever save those who come to God through him, seeing that he ever lives to make intercession for us." The bishops therefore ought to bless us by preaching Christ, and not deceive us and bring the curse of God upon us by wagging their hands over us. To preach is their only duty, and not to offer their feet to be kissed. We also sense, by experience, that after the blessing of the pope, bishop, or cardinal, our souls are not otherwise disposed than before.

Let this be sufficient concerning the sacraments and ceremonies, with this protestation: that if anyone can say it better, or improve this with God's word, then no man will be more content with it than I. For I seek nothing but the truth, and to walk in the light. I therefore submit this work, and all other that I have made or will make (if God wills that I make more) to the judgments, not of those who furiously burn all truth, but of those who are ready to correct with God's word if anything is said amiss, and to further God's word.

I will speak a word or two with them, following worldly wisdom, and make an end of this matter. If the sacraments justify, as they say (and I understand justifying as the forgiveness of sins), then they do wrong to the sacraments through confession—robbing them greatly of their effect and of the cause for which they were ordained. For no man may receive the body of Christ, no man may marry, no man may be oiled or anointed with oil as they call it, no man may receive orders, unless he is first confessed. Now, when sins are forgiven by confession beforehand, there is nothing left for the sacraments to do. They will answer that, at a minimum, they increase grace. And not only do the sacraments do this, but also hearing mass, matins and even-song, and receiving holy water, holy bread, and of the bishop's blessing, and so forth—grace increases by all these ceremonies, they say.

By grace I understand the favor of God, and also the gifts and working of his Spirit in us—such as love, kindness, patience, obedience, mercifulness, despising worldly things, peace, harmony, and such things.

After you have heard so many masses, matins, and evensongs; and after you have received holy bread, holy water, and the blessing of the bishop, cardinal, or pope—then, if you are kinder to your neighbor; if you love your neighbor better than before; if you are more obedient to your superiors; if you are more merciful; if you are readier to forgive wrongs done to you; if you despise the world more; if you thirst after spiritual things more; or if after taking his orders, a priest is less covetous than before; or if after a wife's many and frequent pilgrimages, she is more chaste and obedient to her husband; and if she is kinder to her maids and other servants—then such ceremonies increase grace; and if not, they are a lie.

And gentlemen, knights, lords, kings, and emperors, after they have said the daily service so often with their chaplains, if they know more of Christ than before; if they have more skill to Christianly rule their tenants, subjects, and realms than before; if they can be content with their duties—then such ceremonies increase grace; and if not, they are a lie.

Whether it is so or not, I refer to my experience. If they have any other interpretations of justifying or grace, then I ask them to teach them to me, for I would gladly learn them. Now let us return to our purpose again.

OF MIRACLES AND WORSHIPPING SAINTS.

Antichrist will not only come with lying signs, and disguised with falsehood, but also with lying miracles and wonders, says Paul (2 Thes 2:9). All true miracles of God, (as I showed above) will move us to hear God's word, and establish our faith in it, and confirm the truth of God's promises, so that we might believe them without all doubting. For God's word through faith brings the Spirit into our hearts and also life, as Christ says (John 6:63), "The words which I speak are spirit and life." The word also purges and cleanses us, as Christ says (John 15:3), "You are clean by means of the word." Paul says (1 Tim 2:5–6), "There is one God, one Mediator" (that is, one advocate, intercessor, or at-one-maker) "between God and man, the man Christ Jesus, who gave himself a ransom for all men." Peter says of Christ (Acts 4:12), "Nor is there health in any other—nor any other name given to men by which we must be saved." So now Christ is our peace, our redemption (or ransom) for our sins, our righteousness, satisfaction—and "all the promises of God are yes and Amen in him," 2 Cor 1:20. And we, because of the great and infinite love which God has towards us in Christ, love him in return, and also love his laws, and love one another. And the deeds we do from then on, we do not do to make satisfaction, or to obtain heaven—but to succor our neighbor, to tame the flesh so that we may grow perfect and strong men in Christ, to be thankful to God in return for his mercy, and to glorify his name.

By contrast, the miracles of antichrist are done to pull you away from the word of God, and from believing his promises, and from Christ; they are intended to make you put your trust in a man, or in a ceremony not found in God's word. As soon as God's word is believed, and the faith is spread abroad, then the miracles of God cease. But the miracles of antichrist, because they are wrought by the devil to quench the faith, grow more and more daily. They will not cease until the world's end; and so they remain among those who do not believe God's word and promises. Do you see how God has loosed and sent forth all the devils in the old world among the heathen (or gentiles)? And how the devils wrought miracles, and spoke to the heathen in every image? Even so, the devil using one craft or another will work falsehood among those who do not believe God's word, until the world's end. For the judgment and damnation of someone who has no desire to hear the truth, is to hear lies instead, and to be established and grounded in them through false miracles. He that will not see is worthy to be blind; and he that bids the Spirit of God to leave him, is worthy to be without him.

Paul, Peter, and all true apostles preached Christ alone. The miracles only confirmed and established their preaching, and those everlasting promises and eternal testament that God had made between man and him in Christ's blood—and the miracles testified also that they were true servants of Christ. Paul did not preach himself; he did not teach any man to trust in him or in his holiness, or in Peter or in any ceremony, but only in the promises which God has sworn: indeed, he mightily resists all such false doctrine, to the Corinthians, Galatians, Ephesians, and everywhere. If this is true (as it is true and nothing is more true), that if Paul had preached himself, or taught any man to believe in his holiness or prayer, or in anything except the promises that God has made and sworn to give us for Christ's sake, then he would have been a false prophet. Would I not also be a false prophet if I taught you to trust in Paul, or in his holiness or prayer, or in anything except in God's word, as Paul did? If Paul were here and loved me, (as he loved those of his time to whom he was sent, and to whom he was a servant to preach Christ), what good could he do for me or wish me, except to preach Christ, and to pray to God for me, to open my heart, to give me his Spirit, and to bring me to the full knowledge of Christ? Once I have come into port or haven, I am as safe as Paul, and a fellow with Paul, a joint heir with Paul of all the promises of God—and God's truth hears my prayer as well as Paul's. I also now could not help but love Paul, and wish him good, and pray for him, that God would strengthen him in all his temptations, and give him victory, just as he would do for me. Nevertheless, there are many weak and young consciences always in the congregation, whom those that have the office preaching ought to teach, and not deceive them.

What prayers do our clergy pray for us, which stop us and exclude us from Christ, and seek all the means possible to keep us from a knowledge of Christ? They compel us to hire friars, monks, nuns, canons, and priests, and to buy their abominable merits, and to hire the saints that are dead to pray for us. They have turned the saints into hirelings also, because the saints' offerings are to their profit. What do all those papists pray? That we might come to the knowledge of Christ, as the apostles did? No, truly. For it is plain that all those who use force to keep us from Christ, do not pray that we might come to the knowledge of Christ. And as for past saints (whose prayer was, when they were alive, that we might be grounded, established and strengthened in Christ alone), if it were from God that we should worship them in this way, contrary to their own doctrine, then I dare be bold to affirm that, by means of their prayers, we would have been brought long ago to the knowledge of God and Christ again—even though these beasts had done their worst to oppose it. Let us therefore set our hearts at rest in Christ and in God's promises, for so I think it best; and let us take past saints only as an example, and let us do as they both taught and did.

Let us set God's promises before our eyes, and desire him for his mercy, and to have him fulfill them for Christ's sake. And he is as true as ever he was, and will do it as well as he ever did; for the promises are made to us as well as to them.

Moreover, the end of God's miracles is good; but the end of these miracles is evil. For the offerings, which are the reason for the miracles, only minister and maintain vice, sin, and all abomination, and they are given to those who have too much; so that it is for this abundance that they foam out their own shame, and corrupt the whole world with the stench of their filthiness.

To that end, "whatever is not of faith is sin." And "Faith comes by hearing God's word." When now you fast or do anything in the worship of any saint, believing you come to the favor of God or to be saved by it—if you have God's word, then it is true faith, and it shall save you. But if you do not have God's word, then it is a false faith, superstition, and idolatry, and damnable sin.

Also in the collects of the saints, we ask God to save us through the merits or deservings of the saints. Yet these saints were not themselves saved by their own deservings. We say, *per Christum Dominum nostrum*; that is, 'for Christ our Lord's sake.' We say, 'Save us, good Lord, through the saints' merits for Christ's sake.' How can he save us through the saints' merits for Christ's sake, and yet still have it be for his deserving merits and love? Take an example. A gentleman says to me, 'I will do for you to the utmost of my power, because of the love which I owe to your father. Though you have never done me any pleasure, yet I love your father well. Your father is my friend, and deserves that I do all I can for you, etc.' Here is a testament and a promise made to me in the love of my father only. But if I come to this same gentleman in the name of one of his own servants, whom I never saw, and never spoke with, and never had any acquaintance with at all, and say, 'Sir, I ask you to be a good master to me in such a cause. I do not deserve that you should do so; nevertheless I ask that you do it for that servant's sake. Indeed, I ask you, because of the love you owe my father, to do it for me, for that servant's sake:' If I this was the way I made my petition, would men not think that I had lately come out of St. Patrick's purgatory, and left my wits behind? Yet this is what we do! For the testament and promises are all made to us in Christ. And yet we desire God to fulfill his promises for the saints' sake—indeed, that for Christ's sake, he will do it for the saints' sake.

The papists also have martyrs who never preached God's word, or died for it; rather, they died for privileges and liberties which they falsely purchased, contrary to God's ordinances. Indeed, such saints, even though they are dead, now rob us as fast as they ever did; nor are they any less covetous now than when they were alive. I do not doubt that they will make a saint of my lord cardinal after our death, we who know his juggling and crafty conveyance. They will enshrine him gloriously for mightily defending the right of the holy church, unless we are diligent to leave a commemoration of that Nimrod behind us. The reasons with which they prove their doctrine are but fleshly, and as Paul calls them, "enticing words of man's wisdom;" that is, they are sophistry, and brawling arguments of men with corrupt minds and who are destitute of the truth, whose God is their belly. Whoever does not offer to this idol is a heretic, and worthy to be burnt. They say, 'The saint was great with God when he was alive, as it appears from the miracles which God showed for him; he must therefore be great now.' This reason appears wise; but it is foolishness with God. For the miracle was not shown so that you would put your trust in the saint, but in the word which the saint preached. This word, if you believe, would save you, as God has promised and sworn, and it would also make you as great with God, as it did the saint.

'If a man has a matter to discuss with a great man, or a king, he must first go to one of his lowly servants, and then higher and higher till he comes to the king.' This enticing argument is but a blind reason of man's wit. It is not alike in the kingdom of the world, and in the kingdom of God and Christ. With kings, for the most part, we have no acquaintance or promise. They are also most commonly merciless. Moreover, if they promise, they are still men, as inconstant as other people, and as untrue. But with God, if we have belief, we are accounted, and have an open way to him by the door Christ, which is never shut, except through unbelief. Nor is there a porter to keep any man out. "By him," says Paul, Eph 2:18–19, that is to say, by Christ, "we have an open way to the Father. So now you are no longer strangers and foreigners," he says, "but citizens with the saints, and of the household of God." God has also made us promises, and he has sworn—indeed, he has made a testament or a covenant—and bound himself, and sealed his obligation with Christ's blood, and confirmed it with miracles. He is also merciful and kind, and complains that we will not come to him. He is mighty and able to perform what he promises. He is true, and can only be true, just as he can only be God. Therefore is it not alike with the king and God.

'We are sinners,' the papists say, 'God will not hear us.' Behold how they flee from God as from a merciless tyrant. A man flees soonest to the one he considers most merciful to him. But these teachers dare not come to God. Why? For they are the children of Cain. If the saints love whom God hates, then God and his saints are divided. When you pray to the saints, how would they know it, unless God—the one whom you consider merciless—tells them? If God is so cruel, and so hates you, then it is not likely he will tell the saints that you are praying to them.

When they say, 'We are sinners.' I answer that Christ is no sinner, except as a satisfaction and an offering for sin. Take Christ from the saints, and what are they? What is Paul without Christ? Is he anything but a blasphemer, a persecutor, a murderer, and a shedder of Christian blood? But as soon as he came to Christ, he was no longer a sinner, but a minister of righteousness: he did not go to Rome to take penance upon himself, but he went and preached to his brothers the same mercy which he had received freely, without doing penance, or hiring saints, monks or friars. Moreover, if it is God's word that says you should put your trust in the saints' merits or prayers, then be bold, for God's word shall defend you, and save you. But if it is just your own reason, then fear. For God commands by Moses, Deut 12:32, saying, "What I command you, observe and do it, and add nothing to it, nor take anything from it;" yes, and Moses warns us in a hundred places to be circumspect, that we do only what God commands, and what seems good and righteous in his sight, and not in our own sight. For nothing brings the wrath of God so soon and so sorely on a man, as the idolatry of his own imagination.

Last of all, these arguments are contrary to the arguments of Christ and of his apostles. Christ argues in Luke 11:11–13, saying: "If the son asks the father for bread, will he give him a stone? Or if he asks him for a fish, will he give him a serpent?" and so forth. "If you then," he says, "who are evil, can give good gifts to your children, how much more shall your heavenly Father give a good Spirit to those who ask him!" And a little before, in the same chapter, he says: "If a man came however inconveniently to his neighbor to borrow bread, even when his neighbor is in his bed-chamber, with the door shut, and all his servants with him; nevertheless, if he continues knocking and praying, his neighbor will rise and give him as much as he needs, though not out of love, but to be rid of him, so that he may have rest." As if to say, 'What would God do if a man prays him, seeing that prayer overcomes an evil man?' "Ask," therefore, Jesus says, "and it shall be given you; seek, and you shall find; knock, and it shall be opened to you." And in Luke 18, he puts forth the parable, or similitude, of the wicked judge who was overcome with the importunate prayer of the widow. He concludes, saying: "Hear what the wicked judge did. And will God not avenge his elect who cry out to him night and day? Whether, therefore, we complain of the intolerable oppression and persecution that we suffer, or of the flesh that encumbers and resists the Spirit, God is merciful to hear us and to help us. Do you not also see how Christ cures many, and casts devils out of many, though not spoken to? How will he not help if he is desired and spoken to? When the old Pharisees (whose nature it was to drive sinners from Christ) asked Christ why he ate with publicans and sinners? Christ answered that, "the healthy do not need the physician, but the sick;" that is, he came to have conversation with sinners to heal them. He was a gift given to sinners, and a treasure to pay their debts. And Christ sent the complaining and disdaining Pharisees to the text of the prophet Hosea saying: "Go and learn what this means, I desire (or require) mercy, and not sacrifice." As if to say, 'You Pharisees love sacrifice and offering to feed the god of your bellies with; but God commands you to be merciful.' Sinners are ever captives, and a prey to the Pharisees and hypocrites, to offer them to their bellies, and have them buy merits, pardons, and forgiveness of sins from them. Therefore these papists frighten them away from Christ with arguments from their belly-wisdom; for those who receive forgiveness freely from Christ, will buy no forgiveness from them. "I came," says Christ, "to call, not the righteous, but sinners to repentance." The Pharisees are righteous, and therefore they have no part with Christ, nor do they need it; for they are gods themselves, and saviors. But sinners who repent, pertain to Christ. If we repent, Christ has made satisfaction for us already. "God so loved the world that he gave his only Son, that none who believe on him should perish, but should have everlasting life. For God did not send his Son into the world to condemn the world, but so that the world might be saved through him. He that believes on him shall not be damned; but he that does not believe is damned already." (John 3:16–18)

Paul, Rom 5:1, says, "Because we are justified through faith, we are at peace with God through our Lord Jesus Christ:" that is, because God, who cannot lie, has promised and sworn to be merciful to us, and to forgive us for Christ's sake, we believe, and are at peace in our consciences. We do not run here and there for pardon; we do not trust in this friar or that monk, nor in anything except the word of God. It is like a child whose father threatens him for his fault; the child will never rest till he hears the word of mercy and forgiveness from his father's mouth again. But as soon as he hears his father say, 'Go your way; do me no more wrong; I forgive you this fault,'—then his heart is at rest; then he is at peace; then he runs to no man to make intercession for him. If a false merchant came to him, saying, 'What will you give me if I obtain the pardon of your father for you?'— he will not allow himself to be beguiled. No, he will not buy from a wily fox, what his father has already given him freely.

It follows then that, "God sets out his love that he has for us;" (that is, he makes it apparent, so that men may perceive his love if they are not stock blind) "considering," says Paul, "that while we were yet sinners, Christ died for us. Much more now" (he says), "seeing that we are justified by his blood, shall we be preserved from wrath through him: for if when we were enemies, we were reconciled to God by the death of his Son; much more, seeing that we are reconciled, we shall be preserved by his life." It is as if saying, 'If God loved us when we did not know him, then he loves us much more now that we do know him. If he were merciful to us while we hated his law, then how much more merciful will he be now that we love his law, and desire the strength to fulfill it!' And in Rom 5:8 he argues: "If God did not spare his own Son, but gave him for us all, how shall he not with him give us all things also?"

Christ prayed, John 17:20, not for the apostles only, but also for as many as would believe through their preaching, and he was heard. Whatever we ask in his name, the Father gives us. Christ is also as merciful as the saints. Why do we not go straight to him? Truly, because we do not feel the mercy of God, nor believe his truth. 'God will, at least,' they say, 'hear us sooner for the saints' sake.' Then he must love the saints better than Christ and his own truth. He hears us for the saints' sake?? If so, then he does not hear us for his mercy: for merits and mercy cannot stand together.

Finally: If you put any trust in your own deeds, or in the deeds of any other man, even of a saint, then you diminish the truth, mercy, and goodness of God. For if God looks to your works, or to the works of any other man, or to the goodness of the saint, then he does not do all things of pure mercy and of his goodness, and for the truth's sake which he has sworn in Christ. Now Paul says, it is "not for the righteous deeds we did, but by his mercy he saved us." (Titus 3:5)

Our blind disputers will say, 'If our good deeds do not justify us; if God does not look at our good deeds or regard them, and does not love us better for them, then why do we need to do good deeds?' I answer that, God does look at our good deeds and does loves them; yet he does not love us for their sakes. God loves us first in Christ, out of his goodness and mercy, and he pours his Spirit into us, and gives us power to do good deeds. And because he loves us, he forgives us our evil deeds, which we do from frailty, not purposefully, or on occasion. Our good deeds testify only that we are justified and beloved. For unless we were beloved, and had God's Spirit, we could neither do or yet consent to any good deed. Antichrist turns the roots of the trees upward. He makes the goodness of God the branches, and our goodness the roots. We must be first good, according to antichrist's doctrine, and move God, and compel him to be good in return for our goodness' sake. Thus God's goodness must spring out of our goodness. No, truly, God's goodness is the root of all goodness; and our goodness, if we have any, springs out of his goodness.

OF PRAYER.

In my book, the Justifying of Faith, I have written abundantly about prayer and good deeds, and of the order of love, or charity. Nevertheless, so that you may see the worth of the prayers and good works of our monks and friars, and of other spiritual people, I will say a word or two, and make an end of it. Paul says, "All of you are the sons of God through faith in Jesus Christ; for all you that are baptized have put Christ on you;" (Gal 3:27–28) that is, you have become Christ himself. "There is no Jew," he says, "no Greek, no bond or free, no man or woman, but you are all one thing in Christ Jesus." In Christ there is neither French nor English; but the Frenchman is the Englishman's own self, and the Englishman is the Frenchman's own self. In Christ there is neither father nor son, neither master nor servant, neither husband nor wife, neither king nor subject: but the father is the son's self, and the son the father's own self; and the king is the subject's own self, and the subject is the king's own self; and so forth. I am you yourself, and you are me myself, and there can be no nearer of kin. We are all the sons of God, all Christ's servants bought with his blood; and every man is Christ's own self to others. And Col 3:10–11, "You have put on the new man, which is renewed in the knowledge of God, after the image of him that made him (that is to say, Christ) "where there is" (he says) "neither Greek nor Jew, circumcision nor uncircumcision, barbarous or Scythian, bond or free; but Christ is all in all things." I do not love you now because you are my father, and have done so much for me; or my mother, and you have borne me and suckled me (for so do Jews and Saracens), but because of the great love that Christ has showed me. I serve you, not because you are my master, or my king, or for hope of reward, or from fear of pain, but for the love of Christ. For the children of faith are under no law (as you see in the epistles to the Romans, Galatians, and 1 Timothy), but are free. The Spirit of Christ has written the lively law of love in their hearts which drives them to work of their own accord, freely and willingly, only for the sake of the great love which they see in Christ; and therefore need they no law to compel them. Christ is all in all things to those who believe, and he is the cause of all love. Paul says, "Servants, obey your carnal or fleshly masters with fear and trembling, in singleness of heart, as if to Christ—not with eye-service, as men-pleasers, but as the servants of Christ, doing the will of God from the heart, as though you served the Lord, and not men. And remember, that whatever good thing any man does, he shall receive it back from the Lord, whether he is bond or free." (Eph 6:8)

Thus Christ is all in all things, and the cause of all, to a Christian man. And Christ says, "As you have done it unto the least of these my brothers, you have done it to me. And as you have not done it unto one of the least of these, you have not done it to me." (Mat 25:40, 45) Here you see that we are Christ's brothers, and even Christ himself; and whatever we do one to another, we do it to Christ. If we are in Christ, we work for no worldly purpose, but from love. As Paul says, 2 Cor 5:14, "The love of Christ compels us:" (as if to say, 'We do not work for a fleshly purpose') "for we know no man according to the flesh anymore; no, though we once knew Christ according to the flesh, now we do so no more." We are other-minded than when Peter drew his sword to fight for Christ. We are now ready to suffer with Christ, and to lose life and all for our enemies, to bring them to Christ. If we are in Christ, we are like-minded with Christ who knew nothing according to the flesh, or following the will of the flesh. In Mat 12:46–50, when someone said to Jesus, "Look, your mother and your brothers stand outside, desiring to speak with you." He answered, "Who is my mother, and who are my brothers?" And he stretched his hand over his disciples saying, "See, my mother and my brothers. For whoever does the will of my Father which is in heaven, the same is my brother, my sister, and my mother." He did not know his mother in that she bore him, but in that she did the will of his Father in heaven. So now, just as God the Father's will and commandment is all to Christ, even so, Christ is all to a Christian man.

Christ is the cause why I love you, why I am ready to do the utmost of my power for you, and why I pray for you. And as long as the cause abides, so long will the effect last—just as it is always day so long as the sun shines. Therefore do the worst you can to me: take away my goods; take away my good name; yet as long as Christ remains in my heart, that is how long I will love you, and not a whit less; and for so long you will be as dear to me as my own soul, and for so long I am ready to do you good for your evil; and so long I will pray for you with all my heart. For Christ desires it of me, and he has deserved it of me. Your un-kindness compared to his kindness is nothing at all. Indeed, it is swallowed up as a little smoke by a mighty wind, and it is no more seen or thought about. Moreover, that evil which you did to me, I did not receive from your hand, but from the hand of God, as God's scourge to teach me patience, and to nurture me. And therefore I have no cause to be angry with you, no more than the child has cause to be angry with his father's rod; or a sick man has with a sour or bitter medicine that heals him; or a prisoner has with his fetters, or the one lawfully punished has with the officer that punishes him.

Thus Christ is all, and the whole cause why I love you. And to "all," nothing can be added. Therefore a little money cannot make me love you better, or make me more bound to pray for you, or make God's commandment greater. Last of all, if I am in Christ, then "the love of Christ compels me." And therefore I am ready to give you mine, and not take yours from you. If I am able, I will serve you freely. If not, then if you minister to me in return, I receive it from the hand of God who ministers it to me by you. For God cares for his own, and he ministers all things to them, and moves Turks and Saracens, and all manner of infidels, to do them good. You see this in the lives of Abraham, Isaac, and Jacob, and how God went with Joseph into Egypt, and got him favor in the prison, and in every other place. Joseph received this favor from the hand of God, and he gave thanks to God. Thus God and Christ are all in all; I receive good and bad from God. I love those who are good, because they are in Christ; and I love those who are evil, to bring them to Christ. When any man does good, I rejoice that God is honored; and when any man does evil, I sorrow because God is dishonored. Finally, because God has created all, and Christ has bought all with his blood, therefore all ought to seek God and Christ in all, or else nothing. But to the contrary, to monks, friars, and others of our holy clergy, the belly is all in all, and it is the cause of all love. As you make an offering to their belly, so you are father, mother, sister, and brother to them. Do you not offer? So they do not know you; you are not father, mother, sister, brother, nor any kin at all to them. 'She is a sister of ours, he is a brother of ours,' they say; 'he is truly a good man, for he does so much for our religion. She is a mother to our convent; we are greatly bound to pray for them. And as for such and such,' they say, 'we do not know whether they are good or bad, or whether they are fish or flesh, for they do nothing for us. We are more bound to pray for our benefactors,' they say, 'and for those who give to us, than for those who give us nothing.' For to those who give little, the clergy are bound little, and love them little. And for those who give much, they are bound much, and they love them much. And for those who give nothing, they are bound by nothing, and they do not love them at all. And just as they love you when you give, so they hate you when you take away from them; they all run under a stool, and curse you as black as pitch. So cloister-love is belly-love; cloister-prayer is belly-prayer; and cloister-brotherhood is belly-brotherhood. Moreover, love that springs from Christ does not seek herself, but forgets herself (1 Cor 13:5), and gives herself for her neighbor's profit, just as Christ sought our profit and not his own. He did not seek the favor of God for himself, but for us. Indeed, he took the wrath and vengeance of God from us to himself, and bore it on his own back to bring us into favor. A Christian man likewise gives to his brothers, and does not rob them as the friars and monks do. Rather, as Paul commands, Eph 4:28, he labors with his hands at some good work to have something with which to help the needy. The clergy do not give, but only receive. They do not labor, but live idly from the sweat of the poor. There is none who is so poor a widow, who has nothing for herself and her children, nor any money to give, that the friar will not snatch a cheese or something from her. 'They preach,' you papists say, 'and labor in the word.' First, I say they are not called to do that, and therefore they ought not to labor in the word. For that is the curate's office. 'The curate cannot do it,' you say. Then what does this thief do there?? Secondarily, a true preacher preaches Christ's testament only; and he makes Christ the cause and reward of all our deeds; and he teaches every man to bear his cross willingly for Christ's sake. But these papists are enemies to the cross of Christ, and they preach their belly, which is their god (Phil. 3:19). They think that lucre is the serving of God, 1 Tim 6:5. That is, they think that only those who make offerings to the papists' bellies are Christian; and when you have filled their bellies, then they will spew out prayers for you, to be your reward, and yet they do not know what "prayer" means. Prayer is the longing for God's promises—as they do not preach these promises, so they do not long for them, nor do they wish them for any man. Their longing is to fill their paunch, whom they serve, and not Christ; and so through sweet preaching and flattering words, they deceive the hearts of the simple and unlearned.

Finally, as Christ is the whole cause why we do all

things for our neighbor, even so he is the cause why God does all things for us, why he receives us into his holy testament, and makes us heirs of all his promises, and pours his Spirit into us, and makes us his sons, and fashions us like Christ, and makes us such as he would have us be. The assurance that we are beloved sons and heirs with Christ, and have God's Spirit in us, is the consent of our hearts to the law of God. This law is all perfection, and the mark at which we all ought to shoot. He that hits the mark, so that he fulfills the law with all his heart, soul, and might, and with full love and desire, without any hindrance or resistance, is pure gold. He does not need to be put in the fire any longer: he is straight and right, and no longer needs to be shaven. He is full-fashioned like Christ, and he can have no more added to him.

Nevertheless there is none so perfect in this life, that does not find hindrance and resistance by reason of original sin, or birth-poison, that remains in him, as you may see in the lives of all the saints throughout all the Scripture. As Paul describes, Rom 7:18–23, "The will is present, but I find no means to perform what is good. I do not do that good thing which I would: but I do that evil which I would not. I find by the law, that, when I would do good, evil is present with me. I delight in the law, as concerning the inner man; but I find another law in my members, rebelling against the law of my mind, and subduing me to the law of sin." This law of sin is nothing but a corrupt and poisoned nature, which breaks out into evil lusts, and from evil lusts into wicked deeds; it must be purged with the true purgatory of the cross of Christ. That is, you must hate it with all your heart, and desire God to take it from you. And then, whatever cross God puts on your back, bear it patiently, whether it is poverty, sickness, or persecution, or whatever it may be, and take it as the right purgatory, and think that God has nailed you fast to it, to purge you by it. For he that does not love the law and hate his sin, and has not professed in his heart to fight against it, and does not mourn to God to take it away and to purge him of it, that person has no part with Christ.

If you love the law, and find that you still have sin hanging on you, of which you sorrow to be delivered and purged—as for example, you have a covetous mind, and mistrust God, and therefore are moved to beguile your neighbor, and are merciless to him, not caring whether he sinks or swims, just so you may gain by him, or get from him what he has—then get to the Observant, who is so purged from that sin, that he would not touch a penny. And with that wile, the subtle fox makes the goose come flying into his hole, ready prepared for his mouth, without his labor or sweat. Buy his merits, which he has in store. Do not give your money into his holy hands, but offer it to someone he has hired, either with part of his prayers or part of his prey, to take sin on himself and to handle his money for him. In the same way, if any person that is under obedience to God's ordinance (whether it be son, daughter, servant, wife or subject) consents to the ordinance, and yet finds he has contrary inclinations, then let him go to those who have professed an obedience to ordinances of their own making, and buy part of their merits. If your wife gives you nine words for three, go to the Charterhouse, and buy some of their silence for her. And so, if abstaining from handling money on the part of the Observant heals your heart from desiring money; and if the obedience of those who obey nothing but their own ordinances heals your disobedience to God's ordinance; and if the silence of the Charterhouse monk tames your wife's tongue; then you may believe that their prayers will deliver your soul from the pains of that terrible and fearful purgatory which they have feigned in order to empty your purse.

The clergy increases daily. More prelates, more priests, more monks, friars, canons, nuns, and more heretics (I would say heremites), with similar speed. Set before you the increase of the disciples of St. Francis in so few years. Reckon how many thousands, indeed, how many twenty thousands—not only disciples, but whole cloisters of them—have sprung out of hell in so little time. The pattering of prayers increases daily. Their "service," as they call it, waxes longer and longer, and the labor of their lips grows greater—new saints, new service, new feasts, and new holidays. What do all these take away? Sin? No; for we see the contrary by experience, that sin grows as they grow. But they take away first God's word, with faith, hope, peace, unity, love and concord; then they take house and land, rent and fee, tower and town, goods and cattle, and the very meat out of men's mouths. All these clergy live by purgatory. When others weep for their friends, they sing merrily; when others lose their friends, they get friends. The pope, with all his pardons, is grounded on purgatory. Priests, monks, canons, friars, along with all other swarms of hypocrites, only empty purgatory to fill hell. Every mass, they claim, delivers one soul out of purgatory. If that were true, indeed, if ten masses were enough for one soul, then just the parish priests and curates of every parish would be sufficient to scour purgatory, and all the other costly workmen might well be let go.

THE FOUR SENSES OF THE SCRIPTURE.

They divide the Scripture into four senses, the literal, tropological, allegorical, and anagogical. The literal sense has become nothing at all: for the pope has taken it clean away, and has made it his possession. He has partly locked it up with the false and counterfeited keys of his traditions, ceremonies, and feigned lies; and he partly drives men from it with the violence of the sword: for no man dare abide by the literal sense of the text, except under protest: 'If it shall please the pope.' The tropological sense pertains to good manners (they say), and teaches what we ought to do. The allegory is appropriate to faith; and the anagogical to hope, and to things above. Tropological and anagogical are terms of their own feigning, and they are altogether unnecessary. For they are both but allegories; and this word allegory comprehends them both, and is sufficient. For tropological is but an allegory of manners; anagogical is an allegory of hope. And allegory is the same as saying strange speaking, or borrowed speech—as when we say of a wanton child, 'This sheep has maggots in his tail, and he must be anointed with birchen salve;' I borrow this speech from the shepherds. You shall understand, therefore, that the Scripture has but one sense, which is the literal sense. And that literal sense is the root and ground of all, the anchor that never fails, which if you cling to it, you can never err or go out of the way. And if you leave the literal sense, you cannot but go out of the way. Nevertheless, the Scripture uses proverbs, similitudes, riddles, or allegories, as all other speeches do; but what the proverb, similitude, riddle, or allegory signifies, is always the literal sense, which you must seek out diligently. In English we borrow words and sentences from one thing, and apply them to another, and give them new meanings. We say, 'Let the sea swell and rise as high as he will, yet God has appointed how far he shall go'—meaning that the tyrants shall not do what they would, but only what God has appointed them to do. 'Look before you leap:' whose literal sense is, 'Do nothing suddenly, or without advisement.' 'Do not cut the bough that you stand on:' whose literal sense is, 'Do not oppress the commoners;' and is borrowed from hewers. When a thing does not go quickly, we borrow speech, and say, 'The bishop has blessed it;' because nothing goes quickly that they meddle with. If the porridge is burned, or the meat is over-roasted, we say, 'The bishop has put his foot in the pot,' or, 'The bishop has played the cook;' because the bishops burn whomever they desire, and whoever displeases them. 'He is a pontifical fellow;' that is, he is proud and stately. 'He is popish;' that is, he is superstitious and faithless. 'It is a pastime for a prelate.' 'It is a pleasure for a pope.' 'He would be free, and yet will not have his head shaven.' 'He would have no man strike him, and yet he does not have the pope's mark.' And of someone who is betrayed, and does not know how, we say, 'He has been at confession.' 'She is master parson's sister's daughter;' 'He is the bishop's sister's son;' 'He has a cardinal to his uncle;' 'She is a spiritual whore;' 'It is the gentlewoman of the parsonage;' 'He gave me a *Kyrie eleyson*. And of a wife who answers her husband six words for one, we say, 'She is a sister of the Charterhouse:' as if to say, 'She thinks that she is not bound to keep silence; their silence shall be a satisfaction for her.' And of someone who will not be saved by Christ's merits, but only by the works of his own imagination, we say, 'It is a holy-work-man.' Thus we borrow and feign new speech in every tongue. All fables, prophecies, and riddles, are allegories; such as Aesop's Fables, and Merlin's Prophecies; and yet the interpretations of them are the literal sense.

So in like manner, the Scripture borrows words and sentences from all manner of things, and makes proverbs and similitudes, or allegories. As Christ says, Luke 4:23, "Physician, heal yourself;" whose interpretation is, 'Do at home, what you do in strange places;' and that is the literal sense. So when I say, 'Christ is a lamb;' I do not mean a lamb that bears wool, but a meek and a patient lamb, which is beaten for other men's faults. When I say, 'Christ is a vine,' it is not that he bears grapes, but out of his root the branches that believe suck the Spirit of life, and mercy, and grace, and power to be the sons of God, and to do his will. The similitudes of the gospel are allegories, borrowed from worldly matters, to express spiritual things. The Apocalypse or Revelations of John, are allegories whose literal sense is hard to find in many places.

Beyond all this, when we have found the literal sense of the Scripture by the process of the text, or by a like text in another place, then we go, and just as the Scripture borrows similitudes from worldly things, even so we borrow similitudes or allegories from the Scripture, and apply them to our purposes. These allegories are not the sense of the Scripture, but free things beside the Scripture, and altogether in the liberty of the Spirit to use. I may not at all turn these allegories into wild adventures; but I must keep myself within the compass of the faith, and ever apply my allegory to Christ, and to the faith.

Take an example: you have the story of Peter—how he struck off Malchus' ear and how Christ healed it again. There in the plain text you have great learning, great fruit, and great edifying, which I will pass over because of tediousness. Then, when I preach about the law and the gospel, and I borrow this example, I express the nature of the law and of the gospel. I paint it for you before your eyes and make of Peter and his sword, the law; and of Christ, the gospel, saying,

> Just as Peter's sword cuts off the ear, so does the law: the law damns, the law kills, and it mangles the conscience. There is no ear so righteous that it can abide hearing the law. There is no deed so good that the law does not damn it. But Christ, that is to say, the gospel, which is the promises and testament that God has made in Christ, heals the ear and conscience which the law has hurt. The gospel is life, mercy, and forgiveness freely given, and it is altogether a healing plaster. Just as Peter only hurts and wounds where was no wound before, even so that's what the law does. For when we think that we are holy and righteous, and full of good deeds, then if the law is preached rightly, our righteousness and good deeds vanish away, like smoke in the wind, and we are left damnable sinners only. And just as you see that Christ did not heal till Peter had wounded, and just as a healing plaster does not help till the corrosive has irritated the wound; even so the gospel does not help, except when the law has wounded the conscience, and brought the sinner into the knowledge of his sin.

This allegory proves nothing, nor can it do anything. For it is not the Scripture, but an example or likeness borrowed from the Scripture to declare a text, or to declare a conclusion of the Scripture more expressly, and to root it and engrave it in the heart. For a similitude or example, imprints a thing much deeper in the wits of a man than plain speaking does; and it leaves behind him, as it were, a sting to prick him forward, and to awake him with. Moreover, if I could not prove with a clear text what the allegory expresses, then the allegory would be a thing to jest at, and of no greater value than a tale of Robin Hood. The first part of this allegory is proved by Paul in Romans 4:15, where he says, "The law causes wrath;" and in Romans 7:9, "When the law or commandment came, sin revived, and I became dead;" and in 2 Corinthians 3:6–7, the law is called "the minister of death and damnation," etc. Concerning the second part of the allegory, Paul says to the Romans in 5:1, "Since we are justified by faith, we are at peace with God." And in 2 Corinthians 3:8–9, the gospel is called "the ministration of justifying and of the Spirit." And, Gal 3:2, 5, "The Spirit comes by the preaching of the faith," etc. Thus the literal sense proves the allegory, and bears it as the foundation bears the house. And because allegories prove nothing, therefore they are to be used soberly and seldom, and only where the text offers you an allegory.

And in this manner (as I did above) Paul borrows a similitude, figure, or allegory from Genesis, to express the nature of the law and of the gospel. By Agar and her son, he declares the property of the law, and of her bond-children who will be justified by deeds; by Sarah and her son, he declares the property of the gospel, and of her free children who are justified by faith. He shows how the children of the law, who believe in their works, persecute the children of the gospel, who believe in the mercy and truth of God and in the testament of his Son Jesus our Lord. Likewise we borrow likenesses or allegories from the Scripture, as of Pharaoh and Herod, and of the scribes and Pharisees, to express our miserable captivity and persecution under antichrist the pope. The great cause of this captivity, and the decay of the faith, and this blindness in which we now find ourselves, sprang first from allegories, for Origen and the doctors of his time drew all of the Scripture into allegories. Those who came after followed his example for so long, that at last they forgot the order and process of the text, supposing that the Scripture served only to feign their allegories upon— and did so to such an extent that twenty doctors expound one text twenty ways, like children who descant on a plain song. Then our sophisters came with their anagogical and chopological sense, and with an anti-theme half an inch thick, out of which some of them draw a thread nine days long. Indeed, you find enough who preach Christ, and prove whatever point of the faith you want, but do it as well from a fable of Ovid or any other poet, as they will from St. John's gospel or Paul's epistles. Indeed, they have come to such blindness, that they not only say that the literal sense does not profit, but that it is hurtful, noisome, and kills the soul. They prove this damnable doctrine by a text from Paul, 2 Cor 3:6, where he says, "The letter kills, but the spirit gives life." 'Look,' they say, 'the literal sense kills, and the spiritual sense gives life. We must therefore seek out some chopological sense.'

Here learn what sophistry is, and how blind they are, so that you may abhor them and spew them out of your stomach for ever. Paul by 'the letter' means Moses' law, which the process of the text which follows declares brighter than the sun. But it is not their guise to look at the order of any text, but as they find it in their doctors, so they allege it, and so they understand it. Paul makes a comparison between the law and the gospel. He calls the law the letter, because the law was graven in two tables of cold stone with letters. For the law does nothing but kill, and damns the consciences, as long as there is no desire in the heart to do what the law commands. By contrast, he calls the gospel the administration of the Spirit, and of righteousness or justifying. For when Christ is preached, and the promises which God has made in Christ are believed, the Spirit enters the heart, and looses the heart, and gives the desire to do the law, and so it makes the law a lively thing in the heart. Now as soon as the heart desires to do the law, then we are righteous before God, and our sins are forgiven. Nevertheless, the law of the letter engraved in stone, and not in their hearts, was so glorious, and Moses' face shone so bright, that the children of Israel could not behold his face for its brightness. The law was also given in thunder and lightning and terrible signs; so that they came to Moses out of fear, and desired him to speak to them, and let God speak no more: "Lest we die (they said) if we hear him anymore," as you may see in Exodus 20:19. For this reason, Paul makes his comparison, saying: "If the ministration of death through the letters figured in stones was glorious, so that the children of Israel could not behold the face of Moses for the glory of his countenance, then why would the administration of the Spirit not be glorious?" And again: "If the administration of damnation is glorious, much more shall the administration of righteousness exceed it in glory." That is, if the law which kills sinners, and does not help them, is glorious, then the gospel which pardons sinners, and gives them the power to be the sons of God, and to overcome sin, is much more glorious.

And the text that precedes this passage is just as clear. For the holy apostle Paul says: "You Corinthians are our epistle, which is understood and read by all men, in that you are known as the epistle of Christ ministered by us, and written, not with ink" (as Moses' law was), "but with the Spirit of the living God; not in tables of stone" (as the ten commandments were), "but in the fleshy tables of the heart:" as if to say, 'We do not write a dead law with ink and on parchment, nor do we engrave what damned you in tables of stone; but we preach to you what brings the Spirit of life into your breasts; this Spirit writes and engraves the law of love in your hearts, and gives you the desire to do the will of God.' And furthermore, he says, "Our ability comes from God, who has made us able to minister the New Testament, not of the letter" (that is to say, not of the law), "but of the Spirit. For the letter" (that is to say, the law) "kills; but the Spirit gives life." That is to say, the Spirit of God, which enters your hearts when you believe the glad tidings that are preached to you in Christ, quickens your hearts, and gives you life and desire, and makes you do from love and your own accord, without compulsion, what the law compelled you to do, and damned you because you could not do it with love and desire, and naturally. Thus you see that the letter does not signify the literal sense, and the spirit does not signify the spiritual sense. And in Romans 2:27, Paul uses this term *Litera* for the law; and in Romans 7, he makes it so plain, that if the great wrath of God had not blinded these papists, they would never have stumbled at it.

God is a Spirit, and all his words are spiritual, His literal sense is spiritual, and all his words are spiritual. When you read (Mat 1:21) "She shall bear a son, and you shall call his name Jesus; for he shall save his people from their sins:" this literal sense is spiritual, and everlasting life to as many as believe it. And the literal sense of these words, (Mat 5:7) "Blessed are the merciful, for they shall have mercy;" these words are spiritual and life, by which those who are merciful may rightfully, by the truth and promise of God, challenge for mercy. It is like these words, Mat 6:15, "If you forgive other men their sins, your heavenly Father shall forgive you yours." And so it is with all the promises of God.

Finally, all God's words are spiritual, if you have the eyes of God to see the right meaning of the text, and what the Scripture pertains to, and the final end and cause of it. All Scripture contains the promises and testament of God in Christ, and the stories pertaining to that testament are to strengthen your faith; or else the law and the stories pertaining to it are to frighten you from doing evil. There is no story or tale in Scripture, however simple or vile to the world, that you will not find spirit and life in it, and edification in the literal sense. For it is God's Scripture, written for your learning and comfort. There is no cloth or rag there that does not have precious relics wrapped in it of faith, hope, patience and long suffering, and of the truth of God, and also of his righteousness.

Set the story of Reuben before you, who defiled his father's bed. Mark what a cross God allowed to fall on the neck of his elect Jacob. Consider first his shame among the heathen, when he and his household were the only portion of the world within the testament of God. I refer to our prelates, who swear by their honor, whether it was a cross or not. Do you not see how our wicked builders rage, because they see their buildings burn, now that they are tried by the fire of God's word? And how they stir up the whole world to quench the word of God for fear of losing their honor? Then do you see what a chore Jacob had to pacify his children? Look what turmoil he had at the defiling of his daughter Dinah. And you may be sure that the brothers there were no more furious for the defiling of their sister, than the sons were here for the defiling of their mother. Mark what followed Reuben, recorded to frighten others, so that they do not shame their fathers and mothers. Reuben was cursed, and lost the kingdom, and also the priestdom. His tribe or generation was evermore few in number, as it appears in the stories of the Bible.

The adultery of David with Bathsheba is an example, not to move us to evil—but if while we follow the way of righteousness, any chance should drive us aside, that we would not despair. For if we did not see such infirmities in God's elect, then we who are so weak and fall so often, would utterly despair, and think that God had clean forsaken us. It is therefore a sure and an undoubted conclusion, whether we are holy or unholy, we are all sinners. But the difference is that God's sinners do not consent to their sin. They consent to the law that is both holy and righteous, and mourn to have their sin taken away. But the devil's sinners consent to their sin, and would have the law and hell taken away, and are enemies to the righteousness of God.

Likewise in the simple tale of Noah, when he was drunk, and lay uncovered in his tent, you have great edifying in the literal sense. You see what became of the cursed children of wicked Ham, who saw his father's nakedness, and jested about it to his brothers. You also see what blessing fell on Shem and Japhet, who went backward and covered their father's nakedness, and did not see him. And thirdly, you see what infirmity accompanies God's elect, however holy they may be, whose infirmity is yet not imputed to them, for the faith and trust they have in God covers all their sins.

Notwithstanding, this text offers us an apt and attractive allegory or similitude to describe our wicked Ham, antichrist the pope, who for many hundreds of years has done all the shame that the heart can think of to the word of promise, or to the word of faith, as Paul calls it, Romans 10:8; and to the gospel and testament of Christ, with which we are begotten; as you see in 1 Peter 1:3, and James 1:18. The cursed children of Ham grew into giants so mighty and great that the children of Israel seemed but grasshoppers in respect to them; In the same way, the cursed sons of our Ham—the pope, his cardinals, bishops, abbots, monks, and friars—have become mighty giants, above all power and authority, so that the children of faith, in respect to them, are much less than grasshoppers. They heap mountain upon mountain, and will themselves to heaven by their own strength, by a way of their own making, and not by the way Christ. Nevertheless, God utterly destroyed those giants of old, for the wickedness and abominations which they had wrought—part of them by the children of Lot, and part of them by the children of Esau, and seven nations of them by the children of Israel. So no doubt God shall destroy these "giants" for similar abominations, and he will do that shortly. For their kingdom is but the kingdom of lies and falsehood which must perish at the coming of the truth of God's word, just as the night vanishes away at the presence of day. The children of Israel did not slay those giants, but the power of God did—God's truth and promises—as you may see in Deuteronomy. So it is not we who shall destroy these giants, as you may see by Paul, speaking of our Ham, the antichrist, "Whom the Lord shall destroy," he says, "with the spirit of his mouth," that is, by the words of truth, "and by the brightness of his coming," that is, by the preaching of his gospel. (2 Thes 2:8)

And as I have said about allegories, so it is true of worldly similitudes, which we make either when we preach, or when we expound the Scripture. The similitudes prove nothing, but are made to express more plainly what is contained in the Scripture, and to lead you into the spiritual understanding of the text. The similitude of matrimony is taken to express the marriage between Christ and our souls, and the exceeding mercy we have there, which all the Scriptures mention. And there is the similitude of the members of the body, how every one of them cares for others, is taken to make you feel what it means to love your neighbor as yourself. Therefore the preacher who uses a bare similitude to prove what is contained in no text of Scripture, nor follows a text, you should count as a deceiver, a leader who is out of the way, and a false prophet. Beware his philosophy and the persuasions of man's wisdom. As Paul says: "My words and my preaching were not with enticing words and persuasions of man's wisdom, but in showing the Spirit and power." That is, he did not preach dreams, confirming them with similitudes, but he preached God's word, confirming it with miracles and with the working of the Spirit, which made them feel everything in their hearts. He did it, "that your faith," he said, "would not stand in the wisdom of man; but in the power of God." For the reasons and similitudes of man's wisdom do not make faith, but only wavering and uncertain opinions. One draws me this way with his argument, and another that way; and by the principle with which you prove black, another proves white. And so I am ever uncertain, as when you tell me of something done in a far land, and another tells me the contrary; I do not know what to believe. But faith is wrought by the power of God. That is, when God's word is preached, the Spirit enters your heart and makes your soul feel it. He makes you so sure of it, that neither adversity, nor persecution, nor death, neither hell, nor the powers of hell, nor yet all the pains of hell could prevail against you, or move you from the sure rock of God's word, so you would not believe what God has sworn.

And Peter says, "We did not follow deceivable fables when we opened to you the power and coming of our Lord Jesus Christ; but with our own eyes we saw his majesty." And again, "We have" (he says) "a more sure word of prophecy to which, if you take heed, as to a light shining in a dark place, you do well." The word of prophecy was the Old Testament, which bears record to Christ in every place. Outside this record, the apostles made neither similitudes nor arguments by worldly wit. From this you see that all the allegories, similitudes, persuasions and arguments which the papists bring, outside Scripture, to prove praying to saints, purgatory, and ear-confession; and that God will hear your prayer more in one place than in another; and that it is more meritorious to eat fish than flesh; and that to disguise yourself, and put on this or that kind of coat, is more acceptable than to go as God has made you; and that widowhood is better than matrimony, and virginity than widowhood; and to prove the assumption of our lady, and that she was born without original sin (indeed with a kiss, say some)—are but false doctrines.

Take an example, how they prove that widowhood and virginity exceed matrimony. They bring this worldly similitude: 'the one who takes the most pain for a man deserves the most, and a man is most bound to him; so likewise it must be with God,' and so forth. 'Now the widow and virgin take more pain in resisting their lusts than the married wife; therefore their state is holier.' First, I say that in their own sophistry, a similitude is the worst and feeblest argument that can be made, and it proves the least, and it deceives the soonest. Though one son does more service for his father than another, yet the father is free to and may rightly reward them all alike. For if I had a thousand brothers, and did more than all of them, yet I am not doing my duty. The fathers and mothers also care the most for the least and weakest, and for those who can do the least. Indeed, they care most for the worst, and would spend not only their goods, but their blood, to bring them to the right way. So it is with the kingdom of Christ, as you may well see in the similitude of the riotous son (Luke 15:11 ff). Moreover Paul says, (1 Cor 7:9) "It is better to marry than to burn." For the person that burns cannot quietly serve God, since his mind is drawn away, and the thoughts of his heart are occupied with awful and monstrous imaginations. He cannot see, hear, or read, for his wits are rapt, and he is clean out of himself.

And again, he says, "circumcision is nothing, and uncircumcision is nothing; but keeping the commandments" is all. See where you can best keep the commandments; get yourself there, and abide there—whether you are a widow, wife, or maid—and then you have all with God. If we have infirmities that draw us away from the laws of God, let us cure them with the remedies that God has made. If you burn, then marry: for God has promised you no chastity, as long as you may use the remedy that he has ordained; no more than he has promised to slake your hunger without meat. Now, to ask from God more than he has promised, comes from a false faith, and it is plain idolatry. And to desire a miracle where there is natural remedy, is tempting God. As for taking pains, understand it this way: he that takes pains to keep the commandments of God, is sure thereby that he loves God, and that he has God's Spirit in him. And the more pain a man takes (I mean patiently and without grudging), the more he loves God, and the more perfect he is, and nearer to that health which the souls of all Christian men long for; and he is more purged from the infirmity and sin that remain in the flesh. But to look for any other reward or promotion in heaven, or in the life to come, than what God has promised for Christ's sake, and which Christ has deserved for us with his own pains-taking, is abominable in the sight of God. For only Christ has purchased the reward, and our pains-taking to keep the commandments only purges the sin that remains in the flesh. It certifies to us that we are chosen and sealed with God's Spirit to the reward that Christ has purchased for us.

Once I was at the creating of doctors of divinity, where the opponent brought the same reason to prove that the widow had more merit than the virgin—she had greater pain because she had once proved the pleasures of matrimony. *Ego nego, domine doctor*, said the respondent: 'for though the virgin has not yet proved it, she imagines that the pleasure is greater than it is indeed, and therefore it is she who is more moved, and has greater temptation and greater pain.' Are they not the disputers that Paul speaks of in the first epistle to Timothy? "They are not content with the wholesome words of our Lord Jesus Christ, and the doctrine of godliness; and therefore they know nothing, but waste their brains about questions and strife over words, from which spring envy, strife, and the railing of men with corrupt minds, destitute of the truth." As pertaining to our lady's body, where it is, or where the body of Elijah, or John the evangelist, and many others are, is not for us to know. Of one thing we are sure, that they are where God has laid them. If they are in heaven, we gain no more in Christ by it; if they are not there, we gain no less. Our duty is to prepare ourselves for the commandments, and to be thankful for what is opened to us, and not to search the unsearchable secrets of God. We can know nothing more of God's secrets than he opens to us. If God shuts, who shall open? How then can natural reason come by the knowledge of that which God has hidden for himself? Yet let us see one of their reasons with which they prove it. The chief reason is this: Every man does more for his mother, they say, than for others. In the same way, Christ must do more for his mother. Therefore she has this preeminence, so that her body is in heaven. And yet Christ, in the 12th chapter of Matthew, does not know her as his mother, but only as far as she has kept his Father's commandments. And Paul, in 2 Cor 5:16, does not know Christ himself in fleshly form, or for a worldly purpose. Last of all, God is free, and is no further bound than he binds himself. If he has made her any promise, he is bound; if not, then is he not. Finally, if you set the mentioned Matthew chapter before you, where Christ would not know his mother, and the 2nd of John where he rebuked her, and the 2nd of Luke where she lost him, and how negligent she was to leave him behind her at Jerusalem unawares, and to go a day's journey before she sought him, then you might resolve many of the reasons which the papists give in this matter, and for the claim that she was without original sin. Read also Erasmus' Annotations for those passages.

As for me, I commit all such matters to those idle bellies, who have nothing else to do than push such questions. I give them free liberty to hold to whatever they are inclined, as long as it does not hurt the faith, whether it is so or not. Yet, with Paul, I exhort all who want to please God, and obtain the salvation that is in Christ, to give no heed to unnecessary and quarrelsome disputes; and to labor for the knowledge of those things without which they cannot be saved. Remember that the sun was given to us to guide us in our way, and it works physically. Now if you ignore the natural use of the sun, and look directly at it to see how bright it is, then with such curiosity, the sun will blind you. So too the Scripture was given to us to guide us in our way, and it works spiritually. The way is Christ; and the promises in him are our salvation, if we long for them. Now if we ignore that right use of Scripture, and turn ourselves to vain questions, to search out the unsearchable secrets of God, then no doubt the Scripture will blind us, as it has blinded our schoolmen and our subtle disputers.

Those who prove with allegories, similitudes, and worldly reasons, what is nowhere mentioned in the Scripture, are false prophets. Likewise, count them false prophets who expound the Scriptures, stretching them for a worldly purpose, contrary to the example, living, and practice of Christ and his apostles, and of all the holy prophets. For Peter says (2 Peter 1:20), "No prophecy in the Scripture has any private interpretation. For the Scripture did not come by the will of man; but the holy men of God spoke as they were moved by the Holy Ghost." No place of the Scripture may have a private exposition—that is, it may not be expounded following the will of man, or the will of the flesh, or stretched for a worldly purpose contrary to its clear texts, and to the general articles of the faith, and the whole course of the Scripture, and contrary to the life and practice of Christ and the apostles and holy prophets. For just as prophecies did not come by the will of man, so they may not be stretched or expounded according to the will of man. But as they came by the Holy Ghost, so must they be expounded and understood by the Holy Ghost. The Scripture is what God uses to draw us to himself, and not what leads us away from him. The Scriptures spring out of God, and flow into Christ, and were given to lead us to Christ. You must therefore go along by the Scripture as by a line, until you come to Christ, who is the way's end and resting-place. If any man, therefore, uses the Scripture to draw you away from Christ, and to nosel you in anything except in Christ, that person is a false prophet. And so that you may perceive what Peter means, it follows in the text mentioned, "There were false prophets among the people" (whose prophecies were belly-wisdom), "as there will be false teachers among you, who will secretly bring in damnable sects" (as you see we are now divided into monstrous sects or orders of religion), "even denying the Lord who bought them." For every one of them takes it on himself to sell you for money what God in Christ promises you freely. "And many shall follow their damnable ways, by whom the way of truth shall be spoken evil of:" as you see how the way of truth has become heresy, seditious, or the cause of insurrection, and the breaking of the king's peace, and treason to his highness. "And through covetousness, with feigned words, they shall make merchandise of you." Covetousness is the conclusion of it. For covetousness and ambition, that is to say, lucre and the desire for honor, is the final end for all false prophets and all false teachers. Look at the pope's false doctrine. What is its end, and what do they seek by it? What purpose does purgatory serve, but to purge your purse, and to poll you, and rob both you and your heirs of house and lands, and of all you have, so that they may live in honor? Do not pardons serve the same purpose? What does praying to the saints pertain to, except to offer to their bellies? What does confession serve, except to sit over your conscience and make you fear and tremble at whatever they dream up, so that you worship them as gods? In all their traditions, ceremonies, and conjurations, they do not serve the Lord, but their bellies.

As for their false expounding of the Scripture, stretching it to suit their damnable covetousness and filthy ambition, contrary to the example of Christ and the apostles and the holy prophets, take an example: When Peter says to Christ, (Mat 16:16–18) "You are the Son of the living God;" and Christ answered, "You are Peter, and upon this rock I will build my congregation;" they interpret the "rock" as Peter. Then comes the pope, and he would be Peter's successor, whether Peter wills it or not; indeed, whether God wills it or not; and even though all of the Scripture says, 'No,' to any such succession. And yet the pope says, 'Look, I am the rock, the foundation, and the head of Christ's church.' Now, all the Scripture says that the rock is Christ, the faith, and God's word. As Christ says, (Mat 7:24) "He that hears my words, and does them, is like a man that builds on a rock." For the house that is built on God's word will stand, though heaven should fall. And John 15:5: "Christ is the vine, and we are the branches:" so Christ is the rock, the stock, and the foundation on which we are built. And Paul (1 Cor 3:10–11) calls Christ our foundation; and all others, whether Peter or Paul, he calls our servants to preach Christ, and to build us on Christ. If therefore the pope is Peter's successor, then his duty is to preach Christ only; he has no other authority. And (2 Cor 11:2) Paul marries us to Christ, and drives us from all trust and confidence in man. And (Eph 2:19–21) Paul says, "You are built on the foundation of the apostles and prophets;" that is, on the word which they preached; "Christ being," he says, "the head corner-stone, in whom every building coupled together grows up into a holy temple in the Lord; in whom also you are built together and made a habitation for God in the Spirit." And Peter (1 Pet 2:5), builds us on Christ; contrary to the pope, who builds us on himself. Hell-gates shall not prevail against it; that is to say, against the congregation that is built upon Christ's faith, and upon God's word. Now if the pope were the rock, then hell-gates could not prevail against him—for the house could not stand if the rock and foundation on which it is built perished. But we see the contrary in our popes. For hell-gates have prevailed against them many hundreds of years, and have swallowed them up—if God's word is true, and the stories that are written about them; indeed, if what we see with our eyes is true. "I will give you the keys of heaven," says Christ, and not, "I give." And John 20:17, 21–23, after the resurrection he paid it, and gave the keys to them all, indifferently.

"Whatever you bind on earth, it shall be bound in heaven; and whatever you loose on earth, it shall be loosed in heaven." The pope makes what he will of this text; and he expounds it contrary to all the Scripture, contrary to Christ's practice and that of the apostles and all the prophets. Now the Scripture gives testimony of Christ, and it always expounds itself by another clear text. If the pope then cannot bring for his exposition the practice of Christ, or of the apostles and prophets, or a clear text, then his exposition is false doctrine. Christ expounds himself, saying: "If your brother sins against you, rebuke him between him and you alone. If he hears you, you have won your brother: but if he does not hear you, then take one or two with you," and so forth (Mat 18:15–18), as it stands in the text. He concludes, saying to them all: "Whatever you bind in earth, it shall be bound in heaven; and whatever you loose on earth, it shall be loosed in heaven," where binding is but to rebuke those who sin; and loosing is to forgive those who repent. And, "Whose sins you forgive, they are forgiven; and whose sins you hold, they are held." And Paul binds (1 Cor 5:11–13); and looses (2 Cor 2:10), in the same manner.

Also, this binding and loosing is one power: as he binds, so he looses; indeed, he binds first before he can loose. For who can loose what is not bound? Now whatever Peter binds, or his successor (as he wants to be called but is not; indeed, he is the very successor of Satan), is not to be understood in such a way that Peter, or the pope, has power to command a man to be in deadly sin, or to be damned, or to go to hell, saying, 'Be in deadly sin; be damned; go to hell; go to purgatory.' For that exposition of the text is contrary to the everlasting testament that God has made to us in Christ. He sent his Son Christ to loose us from sin, and damnation, and hell; and he sent his disciples to testify of that to the world, (Acts 1:8). Paul also has no power to destroy, but to edify. 2 Cor 10:13. How can Christ give his disciples power against himself, and against his everlasting testament? Can he send them to preach salvation, and give them power to damn whom they please? What mercy and profit do we have in Christ's death, and in his gospel, if the pope, who surpasses all men in wickedness, has power to send whomever he will to hell, and to damn whom he pleases? We would have no cause to call him Jesus, that is to say, Savior; but might rightly call him destroyer. Therefore, then, this binding is to be understood as Christ interprets it in the places mentioned above, and as the apostles practiced it; and it means only to rebuke men of their sins by preaching the law. A man must first sin against God's law, before the pope can bind him. Indeed, a man must first sin against God's law, before he needs to fear the pope's curse. For cursing and binding are both one; and nothing more than rebuking a man for his sins by God's law. It follows also, then, that loosing is a similar thing; and it is nothing but forgiving those who repent of sin, through preaching the promises which God has made in Christ. In him alone we have complete forgiveness of sins, as Christ interprets it, and as the apostles and prophets practiced it. So it is a false power that the pope takes on himself to loose God's laws—such as giving a man license to put away his wife to whom God has bound him, and to bind them to chastity, whom God commands to marry—that is, those who burn and cannot live chastely. It is also a false power to bind what God's word makes free, making sin of the creations that God has made for man's use.

The pope, who so quickly looses and purges in purgatory, cannot, with all the loosings and purgations that he has, either loose or purge the appetites, lust, and rebellion that are in us against the law of God. And yet purging them is rightly "purgatory." If he cannot purge those who are alive, how can he purge those who are dead? The apostles know no other way to purge except through preaching God's word, which only is the only word that purges the heart, as you may see in John 15:3. "You are pure," says Christ, "through the word." Now the pope does not preach to those whom they pretend to lie in purgatory, any more than he preaches to us who are alive. How then does he purge them? The pope is kin to Robin Goodfellow, who sweeps the house, washes the dishes, and purges all by night; but when day comes, there is nothing found clean.

Some man will say, the pope does not bind them; they bind themselves. I answer that the one who binds himself to the pope is a fool, who would rather have his life and soul ruled by the pope's will than by the will of God, and by the pope's word than by the word of God. And he that would rather be bond than free is not wise. And he that will not abide in the freedom in which Christ has set us, is also mad. And he that makes deadly sin where none exists, and seeks causes for hatred between him and God, is not in his right wits. Furthermore, no man can bind himself further than he has power over himself. He that is under the power of another man cannot bind himself without permission, such as a son, daughter, wife, servant, and subject. Nor can you give God what is not in your power to give. You cannot give chastity further than God lends it to you. If you cannot live chastely, then you are bound to marry or be damned. Last of all, the purpose for which you bind yourself must be seen. If you do it to obtain what Christ has purchased for you freely, you are an infidel and have no part with Christ. If you would see more about this matter, look in Deuteronomy, and there you will find it treated at large.

Take another example of their false expounding of the Scripture. Christ says, "The scribes and Pharisees sit on Moses' seat: whatever they bid you to observe, observe and do it; but do not follow their works." 'Look,' say our sophisters or hypocrites, 'however abominably we live, yet our authority is never less. Do as we teach therefore,' they say, 'and not as we do.' And yet Christ says they sit on Moses' seat; that is, as long they teach Moses, do as they teach. For the Law of Moses is the law of God. But Christ rebuked them for their own traditions and false doctrine, and he disobeyed them, and taught others to beware of their leaven. So if our Pharisees sit on Christ's seat and preach him, we ought to hear them; but when they sit on their own seat, we ought to beware of their pestilent doctrine as well as their abominable living.

Likewise where they find mention made of a sword, they turn it into the pope's power. The disciples said to Christ, Luke 22:38, "Look, here are two swords." And Christ answered, "Two is enough." Look, the papists say, the pope has two swords, the spiritual sword and the temporal sword. And therefore is it lawful for him to fight and make war.

Christ, a little before he went to his passion, asked his disciples (Luk 22:35–38), "When I sent you out without any provision, did you lack anything? And they said, no. And he answered, But now let him that has a wallet take it with him, and one that has a scrip do likewise; and let him that never had a sword, sell his coat and buy one:" as if to say, 'It shall go differently now than before. Then you went out in faith at my word, and my Father's promises; and it fed you and made provision for you, and it was your sword, shield, and defender; but now it shall go as you read in Zechariah 13:7:"I will strike the shepherd, and the sheep of the flock will be scattered." Now my Father shall leave me in the hands of the wicked; and you also shall be forsaken and destitute of faith, and shall trust in yourselves, and in your own provision, and in your own defense.' Christ gave no commandment; but only prophesied what would happen: and because they did not understand him, they answered, "Here are two swords." And Christ (to make an end of such babbling) answered, "Two is enough." For if he had commanded every man to buy a sword, how would two have been enough? Also, if two were enough, and pertained only to the pope, then why are they each commanded to buy a sword? By the "sword," therefore, Christ prophesied that they would be left to their own defense. And two swords were enough; indeed, one would have been enough: for if every one of them had ten swords, they still would have fled before midnight.

In the same chapter of Luke, not twelve lines from the foresaid text, the disciples, even at the last supper, asked who would be the greatest. And Christ rebuked them, and said it was a heathenish thing to ask; there should be no such thing among them, but the greatest would be the least, and to be great was to do service as Christ did. But this text, because it is brighter than the sun, they can make no sophistry out of it, and therefore they will not hear it or let others know it.

You now partly see the falsehood of our prelates, and how all their study is to deceive us and keep us in darkness, to sit as gods in our consciences, and handle us at their pleasure, and to lead us where they desire. Therefore I say to you, get to God's word, and test all doctrine by it, and receive nothing against it: not any exposition that is contrary to the clear texts, nor any that are contrary to the general articles of the faith, nor contrary to the life and practice of Christ and his apostles. And when they cry, 'Fathers, fathers,' remember that it was the fathers that blinded and robbed the whole world, and brought us into this captivity, in which these papists forcefully keep us still. Furthermore, as those of olden times are fathers to us, so shall these foul monsters be fathers to those who come after us; and the hypocrites that follow us will cry about these men and their doings, 'Fathers, fathers,' just as these papists cry 'Fathers, fathers,' about those who are past. And just as we feel about our fathers, so did those who are past feel about their fathers. [They would have us think] there were no other fathers in the world than the ones we have both seen and felt these many hundreds of years, the ones their own decrees bear record of, and their stories and chronicles well testify to. If God's word appeared anywhere, they all agreed against it. When they had put that to sleep, then they strove with one another about their own traditions. One pope condemned another's decrees, and sometimes there were two, indeed, three popes at once. One bishop went to court against another, and one cursed another for their own fantasies, and about things they had falsely gotten. Their great saints are those who most defended the "liberties" of the church (as they call it), which they falsely obtained by blinding kings. Nor did the world have any rest for many hundreds of years, to reform friars and monks, and to cease the schisms among our clergy. And as for the holy doctors, such as Augustine, Jerome, Cyprian, Chrysostomus, and Bede, these papists will not hear them. If the early fathers wrote anything negligently (because they were mere men), then these papists draw out something clean contrary to their meaning, and they triumph over it. Those doctors knew of no authority that one bishop should have above another, nor did they once think or dream that any such thing would ever be, nor any such whispering, pardons, or the scouring of purgatory as these papists have invented.

And when they cry, 'Miracles, miracles,' remember that God has made an everlasting testament with us in Christ's blood, against which we may receive no miracles—no, not the preaching of Paul himself if he came again (by his own teaching to the Galatians), not even the preaching of the angels of heaven. Therefore either these are not miracles and they have feigned them (such as the miracle that St. Peter hallowed Westminster); or else if there are miracles that confirm doctrine contrary to God's word, then they are done by the devil (such as the maid of Ipswich and of Kent). They prove us, whether we will cleave fast to God's word, and they deceive those who have no love for the truth of God's word, nor any desire to walk in his laws.

They seek to deceive with, and arm themselves against [God's word and laws] with arguments and persuasions of fleshly wisdom, with worldly similitudes, with shadows, with false allegories, with false expositions of the

Scripture, contrary to the life and practice of Christ and the apostles, with lies and false miracles, with false names, silent ceremonies, with the disguise of hypocrisy, with the authorities of the fathers, and last of all with the violence of the temporal sword. Therefore, you do the contrary: arm yourself in defense against these, as Paul teaches in the last chapter of the Ephesians: "Gird yourself with the sword of the Spirit, which is God's word, and take up the shield of faith," which is not to believe a tale of Robin Hood, or Gesta Romanorum, or the Chronicles, but to believe God's word that lasts ever.

And when the pope with his falsehood challenges temporal authority above king and emperor, set before you the 26th chapter of St. Matthew, where Christ commands Peter to put up his sword. And set before you Paul, 2 Cor 10:4, where he says, "The weapons of our war are not carnal things, but mighty in God to bring all understanding in captivity under the obedience of Christ;" that is, the weapons are God's word and doctrine, not swords of iron and steel. And set before you the doctrine of Christ and of his apostles, and their practice.

And when the pope asserts authority over his fellow bishops and over all the congregation of Christ by succession of Peter, set before you the first chapter of the Acts where Peter, for all his authority, would himself put no man in place of Judas. Rather, all the apostles chose two men indifferently and cast lots, desiring God to temper them, that the lot might fall on the ablest. In Acts 8:14, the apostles sent Peter [to see what had happened in Samaria]; and in the 11th chapter they called him to give an account of what he did [with regard to the Gentiles]. And when the pope's law commands that, although the pope lives ever so wickedly, and draws with him, through his evil example, innumerable thousands into hell, yet see to it that no man presumes to rebuke him—for he is head over all, and no man is head over him—then set before you where Paul rebukes Peter openly See how both to the Corinthians and the Galatians, he would have no superior but God's word, and whoever could teach better by God's word. And when he reported his preaching and his doings to the high apostles, they could improve nothing; therefore he was equal with the best of them. And when the friars say they do more than their duty when they preach, and more than they are bound to do ('We are bound to our service,' they say, 'and that is our duty; but to preach is more than we are bound to') set before you how Christ's blood-shedding has bound us to love one another with all our might, and to do the utmost of our power for one another. Paul says, "Woe to me, if I do not preach." (1 Cor 9:16) Indeed, woe to him that has the means to help his neighbor, and to make him better, and does not. If they think it is more than their duty to preach Christ to you, then they think it is more than their duty to pray that you would come to the knowledge of Christ. And therefore it is no marvel that they take such great labors—yes, and so many wages as well—to keep you still in darkness.

And when they cry furiously, 'Hold the heretics to the wall, and if they will not recant, burn them without any more ado; do not reason with them, it is an article condemned by the fathers;' then set before you this saying of Peter, 1 Pet 3:15: "To all that ask you, be ready to give an answer of the hope that is in you, and do that with meekness." The fathers of the Jews and the bishops, who had as great authority over them as ours have over us, condemned Christ and his doctrine. If it is enough to say the fathers have condemned it, then the Jews are to be excused; indeed, they are still in the right way, and we are in the false. But if the Jews are bound to look in the Scripture, and to see whether their fathers have done right or wrong, then we are likewise bound to look in the Scripture, whether our fathers have done right or wrong, and we ought to believe nothing without a reason from the Scripture, and authority from God's word.

And in this way defend yourself against all manner of wickedness from our sprites; always be armed with God's word, and with a strong and a steadfast faithfulness to it. Without God's word, do nothing. And to his word, add nothing; nor remove anything from it, as Moses everywhere teaches. Serve God in the spirit, and serve your neighbor with all outward service. Serve God as he has appointed you, and not just with your good intentions and good zeal. Remember, Saul was cast away from God forever for his good intentions. God requires obedience to his word; and he abhors all good intentions and good zeal which are outside God's word—for they are nothing but plain idolatry, and the worshipping of false gods.

And remember that Christ is the end of all things. He alone is our resting-place, and he is our peace. For just as there is no salvation in any other name, so is there no peace in any other name. You shall never have rest in your soul, nor shall the worm of conscience ever cease to gnaw your heart, till you come to Christ; till you hear the glad tidings, how God for his sake has forgiven you all freely. If you trust in your works, there is no rest. You will think, 'I have not done enough. Have I done it with as great a love as I should have? Was I as glad in doing, as I would have been to receive help in my need? Have I left this or that undone?' and such things. If you trust in confession, then you will think, 'Have I told all? Have I told all the circumstances? Did I repent enough? Did I have as great a sorrow in my repentance for my sins, as I had pleasure in doing them?' Likewise in our holy pardons and pilgrimages you get no rest. For you see that the very "gods" themselves, who sell their pardons so good and cheap, or sometimes freely for glory's sake, do not trust in them themselves. They build colleges and make perpetuities to be prayed for forever; and they fill the lips of their beadmen, or chaplains, with so many masses and dirges, and give so long a service, that I have known of some who asked the devil to take their founders' souls, for the impatience and weariness of so painful a labor.

As pertaining to good deeds, therefore, do the best you can, and desire God to give you the strength to do better daily; but put your trust in Christ, and in the pardon and promises that God has made you for his sake; and on that rock build your house, and dwell there. For only there will you be safe from all storms and tempests, and from all the wily assaults of our wicked spirits, who study with all falsehood to undermine us. And the God of all mercy give you grace to do so, to whom be glory forever! Amen.

A COMPENDIOUS SUMMARY.

I have described to you the obedience of children, servants, wives, and subjects. These four orders are of God's making, and the rules for them are God's word. He that keeps them shall be blessed, indeed, is blessed already; and he that breaks them shall be cursed. If any person of impatience, or of a stubborn and rebellious mind, withdraws himself from any of these, and gets himself to any other order, do not let him think that by doing so he will avoid the vengeance of God for obeying the rules and traditions of man's imagination. If you trim your hair in the worship of your father, and yet break his commandments, should you escape? Or if you paint your master's image on a wall, and stick a candle in front of it, should that make satisfaction for breaking his commandments? Or if you wear a blue coat in the worship of the king, and yet break his laws, should you be acquitted? Let a man's wife make herself a sister of the Charterhouse, and answer her husband when he asks her to hold her peace, saying, 'My brothers keep silence for me'—see if she will escape with that. You may be sure that God is more jealous over his commandments than man is over his own, or than any man is over his wife.

Because we are blind, God has appointed in the Scripture how we should serve and please him. As pertaining to his own person, he is abundantly pleased when we believe his promises and his holy testament, which he has made to us in Christ; and for the mercy which he showed us there, love his commandments. All bodily service must be done to man in God's stead. We must give obedience, honor, toll, tribute, custom, and rent to whom they belong. Then if you have anything more to bestow, give to the poor, who are left here in Christ's stead, so that we may show mercy to them. If we keep the commandments of love, then we are sure that we fulfill the law in the sight of God, and that our blessing shall be everlasting life. Now when we obey evil princes who oppress and persecute us, and do so patiently and without grudging, and are kind and merciful to those who are merciless to us and do the worst they can to us—and thus take all fortune patiently, and kiss whatever cross God lays on our backs—then we are sure that we keep the commandments of love.

I declared that God has taken all vengeance into his own hands, and he will avenge all unrighteousness himself—either by the powers or officers which are appointed for that purpose, or else, if they are negligent in their duties, he will send his curses upon the transgressors, and destroy them with his secret judgments. I showed also, that whoever avenges himself is damned in doing the deed, and he falls into the hands of the temporal sword. This is because he takes the office of God upon himself, and robs God of his most high honor, in that he will not patiently await God's judgment. I showed you about the authority of princes, how they are in God's stead, and how they may not be resisted; however much evil they do, they must be reserved to the wrath of God. Nevertheless, if they command us to do evil, then we must then disobey, and say, 'We are otherwise commanded by God;' but do not rise against them. 'They will kill us then,' you say. To this I say that a Christian is called to suffer even bitter death for his hope's sake, and because he will do no evil. I showed also that the kings and rulers (however evil they may be) are still a great gift of the goodness of God; they defend us from a thousand things we do not see.

I proved also that all men without exception are under the temporal sword, whatever names they may give themselves. Because the priest is chosen out of the laymen to teach this obedience, is that a lawful cause for him to disobey? Because he preaches that the layman should not steal, is it therefore lawful for him to steal unpunished? Because you teach me that I may not kill, or if I do, the king must kill me in return, is it therefore lawful for you to kill, and yet go free? Is it not rather fitting that you, who are my guide to teach me the right way, should walk in the right way before me? The priests of the old law, along with their high bishop Aaron, and all his successors, even though they were anointed by God's commandment, and appointed to serve God in his temple, and were exempt from all offices and from ministering in worldly matters, they were nevertheless under the temporal sword if they broke the laws. Christ says to Peter, "All who take up the sword shall perish by the sword." Here there is no exception. Paul says, "All souls must obey." Here there is no exception. Paul himself is not exempt here. God says, "Whoever sheds man's blood, by man shall his blood be shed again." Here there is no exception.

Moreover, Christ became poor to make other men rich; and he was bound to make others free. He also left the law of love with his disciples. Now love does not seek her own profit, but her neighbor's; love does not seek her own freedom, but becomes a surety and bond to make her neighbor free. Therefore, the clergy are damned by all the laws of God, from which, through falsehood and disguised hypocrisy, they have sought so great a profit, so great riches, so great authority, and so great liberties. They have so beggared the lay-people, and so brought them into subjection and bondage, and so despised them, that they have set up franchises in all the towns and villages for whoever robs, murders, or slays them, even for traitors to the king's person.

I proved also that no king has power to grant these papists such liberty; but they are as well damned for giving it, as these papists are for falsely purchasing it. For just as God gives the father power over his children, even so he gives him a commandment to execute it, and not to allow his children to do wickedly and go unpunished; otherwise it is to his own damnation, as you may see by Eli, the high priest, etc. And just as the master has authority over his servants, even so he has a commandment to govern them. And just as the husband is head over his wife, even so he has a commandment to rule her appetites; and he is damned if he allows her to be a whore and a mis-liver, or submits himself to her, and makes her his head. And in the same way that God makes the king head over his realm, he gives the king a commandment to execute the laws upon all men indifferently. For the law is God's, and not the king's. The king is only a servant to execute the law of God, and not to rule according to his own imagination.

I showed also that the law and the king are to be feared, as things that were given in fire, thunder, lightning, and terrible signs. I showed the cause why rulers are evil, and by what means we might obtain better rulers. I showed also how wholesome those bitter medicines, evil princes, are to righteous Christian men.

I declared how those whom God has made governors in the world, ought to rule, if they are Christians. They ought to remember that they are heads and arms to defend the body, to minister peace, health, and wealth, and even to save the body—and that they have received their offices from God, to minister and to do service to their brothers. King, subject, master, servant, are names in the world, but not in Christ. In Christ we are all one, and even brothers. No man is his own; but we are all Christ's servants, bought with Christ's blood. Therefore no man ought to seek himself, or his own profit, but Christ and his will. In Christ no man rules as a king to his subjects, or as a master to his servants; but he serves as one hand serves another, and as the hands serve the feet, and the feet serve the hands, as you see 1 Corinthians 12: We also serve, not as servants to masters, but as those who are bought with Christ's blood serve Christ himself. Here we are all servants to Christ. For whatever we do one to another in Christ's name, we do as to Christ, and we shall receive the reward of that from Christ. The king considers his commoners as Christ himself; and therefore he serves them willingly, seeking no more from them than is sufficient to maintain peace and unity, and to defend the realm. And they obey in return willingly and lovingly, as unto Christ. And every man seeks his reward from Christ.

I warned the judges that they should not take an example of how to minister their offices from our clergy, who are bought and sold to do the will of Satan; but from the Scripture, from where they have their authority. Let what is secret remain secret till God opens it, who is the judge of secrets. For it is more than a cruel thing to break apart a man's heart, and compel him to put either soul or body in jeopardy, or else to shame himself. If Peter, that great pillar, abandoned his master for fear of death, ought we not to spare weak consciences?

I declared how the king ought to rid his realm of the wily tyranny of the hypocrites, and to bring the hypocrites under his laws—indeed, how he ought to be instructed, and to hear, and to look at the causes himself for which he will punish; and not to believe the hypocrites, nor to give them his sword to kill whomever they will.

The king ought to count what he has spent in the pope's quarrels since he was king. The first voyage cost over fourteen hundred thousand pounds. Reckon since what has been spent by sea and land between us and the Frenchmen and the Scots, and then in triumphs, and in embassies, and what has been sent out of the realm secretly, and all to maintain our holy father. I have no doubt that it will surmount the sum of forty or fifty hundred thousand pounds—for we had no cause to spend one penny, except for our holy father. The king therefore ought to make them pay this money, every farthing, and fetch it out of their mitres, crosses, shrines, and all manner of church treasures, and pay it back to his commoners. And not only what the cardinal and his bishops compelled the commoners to lend, and made them swear with such an example of tyranny as was never thought of before—but also all that he has gathered from them: or else by the consent of the commoners to keep it in store for the defense of the realm. Indeed, the king ought to look in the Chronicles, at what the popes have done to kings in times past, and make them restore that also. And he ought to take away from these papists their lands which they have gotten with their false prayers, and restore it to the rightful heirs again—or with advice and consent, turn these lands toward maintaining the poor, and bringing up youth virtuously, and maintaining necessary officers and ministers to defend the commonwealth.

If he will not do it, then the commoners ought to take it patiently, and take it as God's scourge; and think that God has blinded the king for their own sins' sake; and commit their cause to God. And then God shall make a scourge for them, and drive them out of his temple, after his awful judgment.

On the other side, I have also uttered the wickedness of the clergy, the falsehood of the bishops, and the juggling of the pope, and how they have disguised themselves, borrowing some of their pomp from the Jews, and some from the gentiles; and with subtle wiles they have turned the obedience that should be given to God's ordinance, to themselves. I uttered how they have set aside God's testament and God's truth, and set up their own traditions and lies in their place; and they have taught the people to believe in these; and thereby they sit in their consciences as God. By that means, they have robbed the world of lands and goods, of peace and unity, and of all temporal authority, and they have brought the people into the ignorance of God, and have heaped the wrath of God upon all the realms, and namely upon the kings—whom they have robbed not only of worldly things, but even of their natural wits. They make others believe that they are the most Christian, when they live the most abominably, and will allow no man in their realms who believes in Christ. And they make others believe that they are "defenders of the faith," when they burn the gospel and the promises of God, out of which all faith springs.

I showed how they ministered Christ, king, and emperor out of their rightful places; and how they have made them a several kingdom, which they got at first by deceiving princes; and now they pervert the whole Scripture to prove that they have such authority from God. And the greatest cause of this present persecution, is to keep the laymen from seeing how falsely they cite the passages of the Scripture.

They have feigned confession for the same purpose, to establish their kingdom with. They know all secrets thereby. The bishop knows the confession of those he desires throughout his diocese. Indeed, his chancellor commands the spiritual father to deliver it in writing. The pope, his cardinals and bishops, know the confessions of the emperor, kings, and all lords—and by this confession they know all their captives. If any believe in Christ, by confession they know him. Confess yourself wherever you will, whether at Sion, Charterhouse, or at the Observants, your confession is known well enough. And if you believe in Christ, you are waited for. Awful are the things that are wrought thereby. The wife is feared and compelled to utter not only her own secrets, but also the secrets of her husband; and the servant is compelled to utter the secrets of his master. Besides that, through confession they quench faith in all the promises of God, and they take away the effect and virtue of all the sacraments of Christ.

They have also corrupted the saints' lives with lies and feigned miracles, and they have put many things outside the sentence or great curse, such as raising rents and fines, and hiring men out of their houses, and whatever wickedness they do themselves. And they have put a great part of the stories and Chronicles out of the way, lest their falsehood should be seen. For there is no mischief or disorder, whether in the temporal regiment, or in the spiritual, of which they are not the chief causes, and even the very fountain and springs of it, or as we say, the well-head. So that it is impossible to preach against any mischief, unless you begin preaching to them; or to begin any reformation in the world, unless you reform them first. Now they are as hardened and tough as Pharaoh, and will not bow to any right way or order. And therefore they persecute God's word and the preachers of it. And on the other side, they lie in wait for all princes, and stir up all the mischief in the world, and send them to war, and occupy their minds with it, or with other lavish living, lest they have leisure to hear the word of God, and to set their realms in order.

All things are ministered by these papists, and all kings are ruled by them. Indeed, they sit in every king's conscience before he is king, and they persuade every king of whatever they desire. They make them believe what they will, and do what they will. Nor can any king or realm have rest for their own business. Behold King Henry V, whom they sent out for the same purpose they sent out our current king. See how the realm is inhabited. Ask where the goodly towns and their walls are, and what has become of the people who used to be in them; and what has become of the royal blood of the realm? Turn your eyes wherever you will, and you shall see nothing prosperous except their subtle polling. With that, it is like flowing water; and indeed I expect it will shortly be a full sea. In all their doings, though they pretend outwardly the honor of God or of a commonwealth, their intent and secret counsel is only to bring everything under their own power, and to remove whoever lets them, or is too mighty for them. As when they send the princes to Jerusalem to conquer the holy land, and to fight against the Turks. Whatever they pretend outwardly, their secret intent is that, while the princes there conquer more bishoprics for them, they will conquer the princes' lands with their false hypocrisy, and bring everything under themselves. You may easily perceive this by the fact that they will not let us know the faith of Christ. And once they are on high, then they become tyrants above all tyrants, whether they are Turks or Saracens. How do they minister the proving of wills? What are the causes for wedlock? Or what happens if any man dies intestate? If a poor man dies, and leaves his wife and half a dozen young children, and they have but one cow between them, the papists will mercilessly take it for a mortuary fee, whatever may become of the wife and children. Indeed, let anything be done against their pleasure, and these papists will interdict the whole realm, sparing no one.

Read the Chronicles of England, (from which they excluded a great part of their wickedness), and you will find that they have always been both rebellious and disobedient to the kings, and also churlish and unthankful; so that when the entire realm gave the king something to maintain him in his right, these papists would not give a mite. Consider the story of King John, where I have no doubt they put the best and fairest description for themselves, and the worst for King John—for I suppose they wrote the chronicles themselves. Compare the doings of their "holy church" (as they always call it) to the learning of Christ and of his apostles. Did not the legate of Rome relieve all the lords of the realm from their due obedience which they owed to the king by the ordinance of God? Would the legate not have cursed the king with his solemn pomp, because the king would have done what God commands every king to do, and for which God has put the sword in every king's hand? Namely, King John would have punished a wicked clerk who had coined false money. Laymen who had not done half so great a fault must die, but the clerk must escape free by the legate's order! Did the pope not also send to the king of France, remission of his sins, to go and conquer King John's realm? So now remission of sins does not come by faith in the testament that God has made in Christ's blood, but by fighting and murdering for the pope's pleasure. Last of all, was not king John willing to deliver his crown to the legate, and to yield up his realm to the pope, for which we pay Peter-pence? They might also be called the "polling-pence of false prophets" well enough. They do not care by what mischief they attain their purpose. War and conquering of lands is their harvest. The more wicked the people are, the more they hold the hypocrites in reverence, the more they fear them, and the more they believe in them. And those who conquer other men's lands, when they die, make these papists their heirs, to pray for them forever. Let there come one more conquest in the realm, and you shall see them get yet as much more as they now have (if they can suppress God's word so that their juggling does not come to light). Indeed, you will see them take the realm entirely into their hands, and crown one of themselves its king. Truly, I see no other likelihood, but that the land will shortly be conquered. The stars of the Scripture promise us no other fortune, since with the wicked Jews, we deny Christ and will not have him reign over us; but we will still be children of darkness under antichrist, and antichrist's possession—burning the gospel of Christ, and defending a faith that may not stand with his holy testament.

If any man sheds blood in the church, it shall be interdicted till he has paid for the hallowing. If he is not able, the parish must pay, or else it will always stand interdicted. The papists will be avenged on those who never offended them. Paul full well prophesied of them, in the 2nd epistle to Timothy; chapter 3. Someone will say, 'Would you have men fight in the church unpunished?' No, but let the king ordain a punishment for them, as he does for those who fight in his palace; and do not let all the parish be troubled for one man's fault. And as for their hallowing, it is the juggling of antichrist. A Christian man is the temple of God and of the Holy Ghost, and he is hallowed in Christ's blood. A Christian man is holy in himself, by reason of the Spirit who dwells in him; and the place where he is, is holy because of him, whether he is in the field or town. A Christian husband sanctifies an unchristian wife, and a Christian wife sanctifies an unchristian husband, says Paul to the Corinthians (concerning matrimony). If now, while we seek to be hallowed in Christ, we are found to be unholy, and must be hallowed by the ground, place, or walls about us, then Christ died in vain. Nevertheless, antichrist must have the means to sit in men's consciences, and to make them fear where is no fear, and to rob them of their faith, and to make them trust in what cannot help them, and to seek holiness from what is not holy in itself.

After the old king of France was brought down out of Italy, mark what pageants have been played, and are still playing, to separate us from the emperor, lest by our help or aid he might be able to recover his right from the pope, and to couple us to the Frenchmen, whose might the pope continually abuses to keep the emperor from Italy. What does it prevail any king to marry his daughter or his son to another, or to make any peace or good ordinance for the wealth of his realm? For it will last no longer than it is profitable to the papists. Their treason is so secret that the world cannot perceive it. They dissimulate those things for which they are only cause, and they simulate discord among themselves when they are most agreed. One will hold this view, and another will argue the contrary, but the outcome will be what best maintains their falsehood, no matter how God's word contradicts it. What have they wrought in our days, indeed, and what do they still work to the perpetual dishonor of the king, and to the rebuke of the realm, and to the shame of the nation, in whatever realms they go!

I uttered to you partly the malicious blindness of the bishop of Rochester, his juggling, his conveying, his foxy wiliness, his bo-peep, his wresting, renting, and shameful abusing of the Scripture; his oratory and alleging of heretics, and how he would make the apostles authors of blind ceremonies without significance, contrary to their own doctrine; and I have set him as an example to judge all others by. Whatever you are that read this, I exhort you in Christ to compare his sermon, and what I have written, and the Scripture, and then judge. There you will find out about our holy father's authority, and what it is to be great, and how to know the great.

Then follows the cause why laymen cannot rule over temporal offices, which is the falsehood of the bishops. There you will find out about miracles and ceremonies without significance; of false anointing, and lying signs, and false names; and how the clergy are disguised in falsehood; and how they roll the people in darkness, and do all things in the Latin tongue; and of their petty pillage. Their polling is like a soaking consumption, in which a man complains of feebleness and faintness, and does not know where his disease comes from. It is like a pock that corrodes inwardly, and consumes the very marrow of the bones. There you see the cause why it is impossible for kings to come to the knowledge of the truth. For the sprites lay in wait for them, and serve their appetites at all points; and through confession they buy and sell and betray both the kings and all their true friends, and lay baits for them, and never leave them till they have blinded them with their sophistry, and have brought them into their nets. And then, when the king is captive, they compel all the rest by the violence of his sword. For if any man will not obey them, whether right or wrong, they cite him, suspend him, and curse or excommunicate him. If then he does not obey, they deliver him to Pilate, that is, to the temporal officers, to destroy him. Last of all, there you find the very cause of all persecution, which is preaching against hypocrisy.

Then we come to the sacraments, where you see that the work of the sacrament is nothing; but it is only faith in the promise, which the sacrament signifies, that justifies us. There a priest is but a servant, to teach only; and whatever he takes upon himself more than to preach and to minister the sacraments of Christ (which is also preaching) is falsehood.

Then comes how they juggle through silent ceremonies, and how they make merchandise with feigned words—penance, *a poena eta culpa*, satisfaction, attrition, character, purgatory-pick-purse—and how through confession they make the sacraments and all the promises of no effect or value. There see you that absolving is merely preaching the promises; and cursing or excommunicating, is preaching the law. And there you see about their power, and their keys, false miracles, and praying to saints. There see you that ceremonies did no miracles, but only faith—even as Moses' rod did no miracles, but it was Moses' faith in the promises of God. You see also that to have faith, where God has made no promise, is idolatry. And there you may also see how the pope exalts himself above God, and commands God to obey his tyranny. Last of all, you have there that no man ought to preach unless he is called. Then follows the belly-brotherhood of monks and friars. For Christ has deserved nothing with them: for his sake you get no favor. You must offer to their bellies, and then they will pray bitterly for you. There see you that

Christ is the only cause, indeed, all the cause, why God does anything for us, and hears our complaint. And there you have doctrine for how to know, and to be sure, that you are elect and have God's Spirit in you. And there you have learning to test the doctrine of our spirits.

Then follow the four senses of the Scripture, of which three are no senses at all; and the fourth, that is the literal sense, is the very sense that the pope has taken to himself. It may have no other meaning than as it pleases his fatherhood, and we must abide his interpretation, we are told. And as his bellies think, so we must think—even though it is impossible to gather any such meaning from the Scripture. Then you have the use of allegories, and how they are nothing but examples borrowed from the Scripture to express a text, or an open conclusion of the Scripture, and then, as it were, to paint it before your eyes, so that you may feel the meaning and the power of the Scripture in your heart. Then comes the use of worldly similitudes, and how those who bring a worldly similitude for any other purpose than to express more plainly what is contained in an clear text, are false prophets. And so are those who stretch the Scripture in a way that is contrary to the clear verses, and contrary to the example, life, and practices of Christ, the apostles, and of the holy prophets. And then, finally, you have been shown something of our holy father's power, and of his keys, and of his binding and excommunicating, and of his cursing and blessing, with examples of everything.

THE END OF THE OBEDIENCE OF A CHRISTIAN MAN.

Sermons on Several Occasions

John Wesley

Published in four volumes, in the year, 1771

And to which reference is made in the trust-deeds of the Methodist Chapels, as constituting, with Mr. Wesley's notes on the New Testament, the standard doctrines of the Methodist connexion.

INCLUDED ONLY PARTIALLY WITHIN THIS WORK.

SERMON I: SALVATION BY FAITH.

"By grace are ye saved through faith." Eph. 2:8.

1. All the blessings which God hath bestowed upon man are of his mere grace, bounty, or favour; his free, undeserved favour; favour altogether undeserved; man having no claim to the least of his mercies. It was free grace that "formed man of the dust of the ground, and breathed into him a living soul," and stamped on that soul the image of God, and "put all things under his feet." The same free grace continues to us, at this day, life, and breath, and all things. For there is nothing we are, or have, or do, which can deserve the least thing at God's hand. "All our works, Thou, O God, hast wrought in us." These, therefore, are so many more instances of free mercy: and whatever righteousness may be found in man, this is also the gift of God.

2. Wherewithal then shall a sinful man atone for any the least of his sins? With his own works? No. Were they ever so many or holy, they are not his own, but God's. But indeed they are all unholy and sinful themselves, so that every one of them needs a fresh atonement. Only corrupt fruit grows on a corrupt tree. And his heart is altogether corrupt and abominable; being "come short of the glory of God," the glorious righteousness at first impressed on his soul, after the image of his great Creator. Therefore, having nothing, neither righteousness nor works, to plead, his mouth is utterly stopped before God.

3. If then sinful men find favour with God, it is "grace upon grace!" If God vouchsafe still to pour fresh blessings upon us, yea, the greatest of all blessings, salvation; what can we say to these things, but, "Thanks be unto God for his unspeakable gift!" And thus it is. herein "God commendeth his love toward us, in that, while we were yet sinners, Christ died" to save us "By grace" then "are ye saved through faith." Grace is the source, faith the condition, of salvation.

Now, that we fall not short of the grace of God, it concerns us carefully to inquire, —

I. What faith it is through which we are saved.
II. What is the salvation which is through faith.
III. How we may answer some objections.

I. What faith it is through which we are saved.

1. And, first, it is not barely the faith of a heathen.

Now, God requireth of a heathen to believe, "that God is; that he is a rewarder of them that diligently seek him;" and that he is to be sought by glorifying him as God, by giving him thanks for all things, and by a careful practice of moral virtue, of justice, mercy, and truth, toward their fellow creatures. A Greek or Roman, therefore, yea, a Scythian or Indian, was without excuse if he did not believe thus much: the being and attributes of God, a future state of reward and punishment, and the obligatory nature of moral virtue. For this is barely the faith of a heathen.

2. Nor, secondly, is it the faith of a devil, though this goes much farther than that of a heathen. For the devil believes, not only that there is a wise and powerful God, gracious to reward, and just to punish; but also, that Jesus is the Son of God, the Christ, the Saviour of the world. So we find him declaring, in express terms, "I know Thee who Thou art; the Holy One of God" (Luke 4:34). Nor can we doubt but that unhappy spirit believes all those words which came out of the mouth of the Holy One, yea, and whatsoever else was written by those holy men of old, of two of whom he was compelled to give that glorious testimony, "These men are the servants of the most high God, who show unto you the way of salvation." Thus much, then, the great enemy of God and man believes, and trembles in believing,—that God was made manifest in the flesh; that he will "tread all enemies under his feet;" and that "all Scripture was given by inspiration of God." Thus far goeth the faith of a devil.

3. Thirdly. The faith through which we are saved, in that sense of the word which will hereafter be explained, is not barely that which the Apostles themselves had while Christ was yet upon earth; though they so believed on him as to "leave all and follow him;" although they had then power to work miracles, to "heal all manner of sickness, and all manner of disease;" yea, they had then "power and authority over all devils;" and, which is beyond all this, were sent by their Master to "preach the kingdom of God."

4. What faith is it then through which we are saved? It may be answered, first, in general, it is a faith in Christ: Christ, and God through Christ, are the proper objects of it. herein, therefore, it is sufficiently, absolutely distinguished from the faith either of ancient or modern heathens. And from the faith of a devil it is fully distinguished by this: it is not barely a speculative, rational thing, a cold, lifeless assent, a train of ideas in the head; but also a disposition of the heart. For thus saith the Scripture, "With the heart man believeth unto righteousness;" and, "If thou shalt confess with thy mouth the Lord Jesus, and shalt believe in thy heart that God hath raised him from the dead, thou shalt be saved."

5. And herein does it differ from that faith which the Apostles themselves had while our Lord was on earth, that it acknowledges the necessity and merit of his death, and the power of his resurrection. It acknowledges his death as the only sufficient means of redeeming man from death eternal, and his resurrection as the restoration of us all to life and immortality; inasmuch as he "was delivered for our sins, and rose again for our justification." Christian faith is then, not only an assent to the whole gospel of Christ, but also a full reliance on the blood of Christ; a trust in the merits of his life, death, and resurrection; a recumbency upon him as our atonement and our life, as given for us, and living in us; and, in consequence hereof, a closing with him, and cleaving to him, as our "wisdom, righteousness, sanctification, and redemption," or, in one word, our salvation.

II. What salvation it is, which is through this faith, is the Second thing to be considered.

1. And, First, whatsoever else it imply, it is a present salvation. It is something attainable, yea, actually attained, on earth, by those who are partakers of this faith. For thus saith the Apostle to the believers at Ephesus, and in them to the believers of all ages, not, *Ye shall be*(though that also is true), but, "*Ye are saved through faith.*"

2. *Ye are saved* (to comprise all in one word) from sin. This is the salvation which is through faith. This is that great salvation foretold by the angel, before God brought his First-begotten into the world: "Thou shalt call his name Jesus; for he shall save his people from their sins." And neither here, nor in other parts of holy writ, is there any limitation or restriction. All his people, or, as it is elsewhere expressed, "all that believe in him," he will save from all their sins; from original and actual, past and present sin, "of the flesh and of the spirit." Through faith that is in him, they are saved both from the guilt and from the power of it.

3. First. From the guilt of all past sin: for, whereas all the world is guilty before God, insomuch that should he "be extreme to mark what is done amiss, there is none that could abide it;" and whereas, "by the law is" only "the knowledge of sin," but no deliverance from it, so that, "by" fulfilling "the deeds of the law, no flesh can be justified in his sight": now, "the righteousness of God, which is by faith of Jesus Christ, is manifested unto all that believe." Now, "they are justified freely by his grace, through the redemption that is in Jesus Christ." "Him God hath set forth to be a propitiation through faith in his blood, to declare his righteousness for (or by) the remission of the sins that are past." Now hath Christ taken away "the curse of the law, being made a curse for us." he hath "blotted out the handwriting that was against us, taking it out of the way, nailing it to his cross." "There is therefore no condemnation now to them which" believe "in Christ Jesus."

4. And being saved from guilt, they are saved from fear. Not indeed from a filial fear of offending; but from all servile fear; from that fear which hath torment; from fear of punishment; from fear of the wrath of God, whom they now no longer regard as a severe Master, but as an indulgent Father. "They have not received again the spirit of bondage, but the Spirit of adoption, whereby they cry, Abba, Father: the Spirit itself also bearing witness with their spirits, that they are the children of God." They are also saved from the fear, though not from the possibility, of falling away from the grace of God, and coming short of the great and precious promises. Thus have they "peace with God through our Lord Jesus Christ. They rejoice in hope of the glory of God. And the love of God is shed abroad in their hearts, through the Holy Ghost, which is given unto them." And hereby they are persuaded (though perhaps not at all times, nor with the same fullness of persuasion), that "neither death, nor life, nor things present, nor things to come, nor height, nor depth, nor any other creature, shall be able to separate them from the love of God, which is in Christ Jesus our Lord."

5. Again: through this faith they are saved from the power of sin, as well as from the guilt of it. So the Apostle declares, "Ye know that he was manifested to take away our sins; and in him is no sin. Whosoever abideth in him sinneth not" (1 John 3:5ff.). Again, "Little children, let no man deceive you. he that committeth sin is of the devil. Whosoever believeth is born of God. And whosoever is born of God doth not commit sin; for his seed remaineth in him: and he cannot sin, because he is born of God." Once more: "We know that whosoever is born of God sinneth not; but he that is begotten of God keepeth himself, and that wicked one toucheth him not" (1 John 5:18).

6. he that is, by faith, born of God sinneth not (1.) by any habitual sin; for all habitual sin is sin reigning: But sin cannot reign in any that believeth. Nor (2.) by any wilful sin: for his will, while he abideth in the faith, is utterly set against all sin, and abhorreth it as deadly poison. Nor (3.) By any sinful desire; for he continually desireth the holy and perfect will of God. and any tendency to an unholy desire, he by the grace of God, stifleth in the birth. Nor (4.) Doth he sin by infirmities, whether in act, word, or thought; for his infirmities have no concurrence of his will; and without this they are not properly sins. Thus, "he that is born of God doth not commit sin": and though he cannot say he hath not sinned, yet now "he sinneth not."

7. This then is the salvation which is through faith, even in the present world: a salvation from sin, and the consequences of sin, both often expressed in the word *justification*; which, taken in the largest sense, implies a deliverance from guilt and punishment, by the atonement of Christ actually applied to the soul of the sinner now believing on him, and a deliverance from the power of sin, through Christ *formed in his heart*. So that he who is thus justified, or saved by faith, is indeed *born again*. he is *born again of the Spirit* unto a new life, which "is hid with Christ in God." And as a new-born babe he gladly receives the *adolon*, "*sincere* milk of the word, and grows thereby;" going on in the might of the Lord his God, from faith to faith, from grace to grace, until at length, he come unto "a perfect man, unto the measure of the stature of the fullness of Christ."

III. The first usual objection to this is,

1. That to preach salvation or justification, by faith only, is to preach against holiness and good works. To which a short answer might be given: "It would be so, if we spake, as some do, of a faith which was separate from these; but we speak of a faith which is not so, but productive of all good works, and all holiness."

2. But it may be of use to consider it more at large; especially since it is no new objection, but as old as St. Paul's time. For even then it was asked, "Do we not make void the law through faith?" We answer, First, all who preach not faith do manifestly make void the law; either directly and grossly, by limitations and comments that eat out all the spirit of the text; or indirectly, by not pointing out the only means whereby it is possible to perform it. Whereas, Secondly, "we establish the law," both by showing its full extent and spiritual meaning; and by calling all to that living way, whereby "the righteousness of the law may be fulfilled in them." These, while they trust in the blood of Christ alone, use all the ordinances which he hath appointed, do all the "good works which he had before prepared that they should walk therein," and enjoy and manifest all holy and heavenly tempers, even the same mind that was in Christ Jesus.

3. But does not preaching this faith lead men into pride? We answer, Accidentally it may: therefore ought every believer to be earnestly cautioned, in the words of the great Apostle "Because of unbelief," the first branches "were broken off: and thou standest by faith. Be not highminded, but fear. If God spared not the natural branches, take heed lest he spare not thee. Behold therefore the goodness and severity of God! On them which fell,

severity; but towards thee, goodness, if thou continue in his goodness; otherwise thou also shalt be cut off." And while he continues therein, he will remember those words of St. Paul, foreseeing and answering this very objection (Rom. 3:27), "Where is boasting then? It is excluded. By what law? of works? Nay: but by the law of faith." If a man were justified by his works, he would have whereof to glory. But there is no glorying for him "that worketh not, but believeth on him that justifieth the ungodly" (Rom. 4:5). To the same effect are the words both preceding and following the text (Eph. 2:4ff.): "God, who is rich in mercy, even when we were dead in sins, hath quickened us together with Christ (by grace ye are saved), that he might show the exceeding riches of his grace in his kindness toward us through Christ Jesus. For by grace are ye saved through faith; and that not of yourselves." Of yourselves cometh neither your faith nor your salvation: "it is the gift of God;" the free, undeserved gift; the faith through which ye are saved, as well as the salvation which he of his own good pleasure, his mere favour, annexes thereto. That ye believe, is one instance of his grace; that believing ye are saved, another. "Not of works, lest any man should boast." For all our works, all our righteousness, which were before our believing, merited nothing of God but condemnation; so far were they from deserving faith, which therefore, whenever given, is not of works. Neither is salvation of the works we do when we believe, for it is then God that worketh in us: and, therefore, that he giveth us a reward for what he himself worketh, only commendeth the riches of his mercy, but leaveth us nothing whereof to glory.

4. "However, may not the speaking thus of the mercy of God, as saving or justifying freely by faith only, encourage men in sin?" Indeed, it may and will: Many will "continue in sin that grace may abound:" But their blood is upon their own head. The goodness of God ought to lead them to repentance; and so it will those who are sincere of heart. When they know there is yet forgiveness with him, they will cry aloud that he would blot out their sins also, through faith which is in Jesus. And if they earnestly cry, and faint not, it they seek him in all the means he hath appointed; if they refuse to be comforted till he come; "he will come, and will not tarry." And he can do much work in a short time. Many are the examples, in the Acts of the Apostles, of God's working this faith in men's hearts, even like lightning falling from heaven. So in the same hour that Paul and Silas began to preach, the jailer repented, believed, and was baptized; as were three thousand, by St. Peter, on the day of Pentecost, who all repented and believed at his first preaching And, blessed be God, there are now many living proofs that he is still "mighty to save."

5. Yet to the same truth, placed in another view, a quite contrary objection is made: "If a man cannot be saved by all that he can do, this will drive men to despair." True, to despair of being saved by their own works, their own merits, or righteousness. And so it ought; for none can trust in the merits of Christ, till he has utterly renounced his own. he that "goeth about to stablish his own righteousness" cannot receive the righteousness of God. The righteousness which is of faith cannot be given him while he trusteth in that which is of the law.

6. But this, it is said, is an uncomfortable doctrine. The devil spoke like himself, that is, without either truth or shame, when he dared to suggest to men that it is such. It is the only comfortable one, it is "very full of comfort," to all self-destroyed, self-condemned sinners. That "whosoever believeth on him shall not be ashamed that the same Lord over all is rich unto all that call upon him": here is comfort, high as heaven, stronger than death! What! Mercy for all? For Zacchaeus, a public robber? For Mary Magdalene, a common harlot? Methinks I hear one say "Then I, even I, may hope for mercy!" And so thou mayest, thou afflicted one, whom none hath comforted! God will not cast out thy prayer. Nay, perhaps he may say the next hour, "Be of good cheer, thy sins are forgiven thee;" so forgiven, that they shall reign over thee no more; yea, and that "the Holy Spirit shall bear witness with thy spirit that thou art a child of God." O glad tidings! tidings of great joy, which are sent unto all people! "Ho, every one that thirsteth, come ye to the waters: Come ye, and buy, without money and without price." Whatsoever your sins be, "though red like crimson," though more than the hairs of your head, "return ye unto the Lord, and he will have mercy upon you, and to our God, for he will abundantly pardon."

7. When no more objections occur, then we are simply told that salvation by faith only ought not to be preached as the first doctrine, or, at least, not to be preached at all. But what saith the Holy Ghost? "Other foundation can no man lay than that which is laid, even Jesus Christ." So then, that "whosoever believeth on him shall be saved," is, and must be, the foundation of all our preaching; that is, must be preached first. "Well, but not to all." To whom, then are we not to preach it? Whom shall we except? The poor? Nay; they have a peculiar right to have the gospel preached unto them. The unlearned? No. God hath revealed these things unto unlearned and ignorant

men from the beginning. The young? By no means. "Suffer these," in any wise, "to come unto Christ, and forbid them not." The sinners? Least of all. "He came not to call the righteous, but sinners to repentance." Why then, if any, we are to except the rich, the learned, the reputable, the moral men. And, it is true, they too often except themselves from hearing; yet we must speak the words of our Lord. For thus the tenor of our commission runs, "Go and preach the gospel to every creature." If any man wrest it, or any part of it, to his destruction, he must bear his own burden. But still, "as the Lord liveth, whatsoever the Lord saith unto us, that we will speak."

8. At this time, more especially, will we speak, that "by grace are ye saved through faith": because, never was the maintaining this doctrine more seasonable than it is at this day. Nothing but this can effectually prevent the increase of the Romish delusion among us. It is endless to attack, one by one, all the errors of that Church. But salvation by faith strikes at the root, and all fall at once where this is established. It was this doctrine, which our Church justly calls *the strong rock and foundation of the Christian religion*, that first drove Popery out of these kingdoms; and it is this alone can keep it out. Nothing but this can give a check to that immorality which hath "overspread the land as a flood." Can you empty the great deep, drop by drop? Then you may reform us by dissuasives from particular vices. But let the "righteousness which is of God by faith be brought in, and so shall its proud waves be stayed. Nothing but this can stop the mouths of those who "glory in their shame, and openly deny the Lord that bought them." They can talk as sublimely of the law, as he that hath it written by God in his heart To hear them speak on this head might incline one to think they were not far from the kingdom of God: but take them out of the law into the gospel; begin with the righteousness of faith; with Christ, "the end of the law to every one that believeth;" and those who but now appeared almost, if not altogether, Christians, stand confessed the sons of perdition; as far from life and salvation (God be merciful unto them!) as the depth of hell from the height of heaven.

9. For this reason the adversary so rages whenever "salvation by faith" is declared to the world: for this reason did he stir up earth and hell, to destroy those who first preached it. And for the same reason, knowing that faith alone could overturn the foundations of his kingdom, did he call forth all his forces, and employ all his arts of lies and calumny, to affright Martin Luther from reviving it. Nor can we wonder thereat; for, as that man of God observes, "How would it enrage a proud, strong man armed, to be stopped and set at nought by a little child coming against him with a reed in his hand!" especially when he knew that little child would surely overthrow him, and tread him under foot. Even so, Lord Jesus! Thus hath Thy strength been ever "made perfect in weakness!" Go forth then, thou little child that believest in him, and his "right hand shall teach thee terrible things!" Though thou art helpless and weak as an infant of days, the strong man shall not be able to stand before thee. Thou shalt prevail over him, and subdue him, and overthrow him and trample him under thy feet. Thou shalt march on, under the great Captain of thy salvation, "conquering and to conquer," until all thine enemies are destroyed, and "death is swallowed up in victory."

Now, thanks be to God, which giveth us the victory through our Lord Jesus Christ; to whom, with the Father and the Holy Ghost, be blessing, and glory, and wisdom, and thanksgiving, and honour, and power, and might, for ever and ever. Amen.

SERMON 2: THE ALMOST CHRISTIAN.

**"Almost thou persuadest me to be a Christian."
Acts 26:28.**

And many there are who go thus far: ever since the Christian religion was in the world, there have been many in every age and nation who were almost persuaded to be Christians. But seeing it avails nothing before God to go *only thus far*, it highly imports us to consider,

First. What is implied in being *almost*,

Secondly. What in being *altogether, a Christian*.

I. (I.) 1. Now, in the being *almost a Christian* is implied, First, heathen honesty. No one, I suppose, will make any question of this: especially, since by heathen honesty here, I mean, not that which is recommended in the writings of their philosophers only, but such as the common heathens expected one of another, and many of them actually practised. By the rules of this they were taught that they ought not to be unjust; not to take away their neighbour's goods, either by robbery or theft; not to oppress the poor, neither to use extortion toward any; not to cheat or overreach either the poor or rich, in whatsoever commerce they had with them; to defraud no man of his right; and, if it were possible, to owe no man anything.

2. Again: the common heathens allowed, that some regard was to be paid to truth, as well as to justice. And,

accordingly, they not only held him in abomination who was forsworn, who called God to witness to a lie; but him also who was known to be a slanderer of his neighbour, who falsely accused any man. And indeed, little better did they esteem wilful liars of any sort, accounting them the disgrace of human kind, and the pests of society.

3. Yet again: there was a sort of love and assistance which they expected one from another. They expected whatever assistance any one could give another, without prejudice to himself. And this they extended not only to those little offices of humanity which are performed without any expense or labour, but likewise to the feeding the hungry, if they had food to spare; the clothing the naked with their own superfluous raiment; and, in general. the giving, to any that needed, such things as they needed not themselves. Thus far, in the lowest account of it, heathen honesty went; the first thing implied in the being *almost a Christian*.

(II.) 4. A second thing implied in the being *almost a Christian*, is, the having a form of godliness; of that godliness which is prescribed in the gospel of Christ; the having the *outside of a real Christian*. Accordingly, the almost Christian does nothing which the gospel forbids. he taketh not the name of God in vain; he blesseth, and curseth not; he sweareth not at all, but his communication is, yea, yea; nay, nay. he profanes not the day of the Lord, nor suffers it to be profaned, even by the stranger that is within his gates. he not only avoids all actual adultery, fornication, and uncleanness, but every word or look that either directly or indirectly tends thereto; nay, and all idle words, abstaining both from detraction, backbiting, talebearing, evil speaking, and from "all foolish talking and jesting"—*eutrapelia*, a kind of virtue in the heathen moralist's account;—briefly, from all conversation that is not "good to the use of edifying," and that, consequently, "grieves the Holy Spirit of God, whereby we are sealed to the day of redemption."

5. He abstains from "wine wherein is excess"; from revellings and gluttony. He avoids, as much as in him lies, all strife and contention, continually endeavouring to live peaceably with all men. And, if he suffer wrong, he avengeth not himself, neither returns evil for evil. he is no railer, no brawler, no scoffer, either at the faults or infirmities of his neighbour. he does not willingly wrong, hurt, or grieve any man; but in all things act and speaks by that plain rule, "Whatsoever thou wouldest not he should do unto thee, that do not thou to another."

6. And in doing good, he does not confine himself to cheap and easy offices of kindness, but labours and suffers for the profit of many, that by all means he may help some. In spite of toil or pain, "whatsoever his hand findeth to do, he doeth it with his might;" whether it be for his friends, or for his enemies; for the evil, or for the good. For being "not slothful" in this, or in any "business," as he "hath opportunity" he doeth "good," all manner of good, "to all men;" and to their souls as well as their bodies. he reproves the wicked, instructs the ignorant, confirms the wavering, quickens the good, and comforts the afflicted. he labours to awaken those that sleep; to lead those whom God hath already awakened to the "Fountain opened for sin and for uncleanness," that they may wash therein and be clean; and to stir up those who are saved through faith, to adorn the gospel of Christ in all things.

7. he that hath the form of godliness uses also the means of grace; yea, all of them, and at all opportunities. he constantly frequents the house of God; and that, not as the manner of some is, who come into the presence of the Most High, either loaded with gold and costly apparel, or in all the gaudy vanity of dress, and either by their unseasonable civilities to each other, or the impertinent gaiety of their behaviour, disclaim all pretensions to the form as well as to the power of godliness. Would to God there were none even among ourselves who fall under the same condemnation! who come into this house, it may be, gazing about, or with all the signs of the most listless, careless indifference, though sometimes they may *seem* to use a prayer to God for his blessing on what they are entering upon; who, during that awful service, are either asleep, or reclined in the most convenient posture for it; or, as though they supposed God was asleep, talking with one another, or looking round, as utterly void of employment. Neither let these be accused of the form of godliness. No; he who has even this, behaves with seriousness and attention, in every part of that solemn service. More especially, when he approaches the table of the Lord, it is not with a light or careless behaviour, but with an air, gesture, and deportment which speaks nothing else but "God be merciful to me a sinner!"

8. To this, if we add the constant use of family prayer, by those who are masters of families, and the setting times apart for private addresses to God, with a daily seriousness of behaviour; he who uniformly practises this outward religion, has the form of godliness. There needs but one thing more in order to his being *almost a Christian*, and that is, sincerity.

(III.) 9. By sincerity I mean, a real, inward principle of religion, from whence these outward actions flow. And, indeed if we have not this, we have not heathen honesty; no, not so much of it as will answer the demand of a heathen Epicurean poet. Even this poor wretch, in his sober intervals, is able to testify,

Oderunt peccare boni, virtutis amore;
Oderunt peccare mali, formidine poenae.
[Good men avoid sin from the love of virtue;
Wicked men avoid sin from a fear of punishment.]

So that, if a man only abstains from doing evil in order to avoid punishment, Non pasces in cruce corvos, [Thou shalt not be hanged.], saith the Pagan; there, "thou hast thy reward." But even he will not allow such a harmless man as this to be so much as a *good heathen*. If, then, any man, from the same motive, viz., to avoid punishment, to avoid the loss of his friends, or his gain, or his reputation, should not only abstain from doing evil, but also do ever so much good; yea, and use all the means of grace; yet we could not with any propriety say, this man is even *almost a Christian*. If he has no better principle in his heart, he is only a hypocrite altogether.

10. Sincerity, therefore, is necessarily implied in the being *almost a Christian*; a real design to serve God, a hearty desire to do his will. It is necessarily implied, that a man have a sincere view of pleasing God in all things; in all his conversation; in all his actions; in all he does or leaves undone. This design, if any man be *almost a Christian*, runs through the whole tenor of his life. This is the moving principle, both in his doing good, his abstaining from evil, and his using the ordinances of God.

11. But here it will probably be inquired, "Is it possible that any man living should go so far as this, and, nevertheless, be *only almost a Christian*"? What more than this, can be implied in the being *a Christian altogether*? I answer, First, that it is possible to go thus far, and yet be but *almost a Christian*, I learn, not only from the oracles of God, but also from the sure testimony of experience.

12. Brethren, great is "my boldness towards you in this behalf." And "forgive me this wrong," if I declare my own folly upon the house-top, for yours and the gospel's sake. —Suffer me, then, to speak freely of myself, even as of another man. I am content to be abased, so ye may be exalted, and to be yet more vile for the glory of my Lord.

13. I did go thus far for many years, as many of this place can testify; using diligence to eschew all evil, and to have a conscience void of offence; redeeming the time; buying up every opportunity of doing all good to all men; constantly and carefully using all the public and all the private means of grace; endeavouring after a steady seriousness of behaviour, at all times, and in all places; and, God is my record, before whom I stand, doing all this in sincerity; having a real design to serve God; a hearty desire to do his will in all things; to please him who had called me to "fight the good fight," and to "lay hold of eternal life." Yet my own conscience beareth me witness in the Holy Ghost, that all this time I was but *almost a Christian.*

II. If it be inquired, "What more than this is implied in the being *altogether a Christian?*" I answer,

(I.) 1. First. The love of God. For thus saith his word, "Thou shalt love the Lord thy God with all thy heart, and with all thy soul, and with all thy mind, and with all thy strength." Such a love is this, as engrosses the whole heart, as rakes up all the affections, as fills the entire capacity of the soul and employs the utmost extent of all its faculties. he that thus loves the Lord his God, his spirit continually "rejoiceth in God his Saviour." his delight is in the Lord, his Lord and his All, to whom "in everything he giveth thanks. All his desire is unto God, and to the remembrance of his name." his heart is ever crying out, "Whom have I in heaven but Thee? and there is none upon earth that I desire beside Thee." Indeed, what can he desire beside God? Not the world, or the things of the world: for he is "crucified to the world, and the world crucified to him." he is crucified to "the desire of the flesh, the desire of the eye, and the pride of life." Yea, he is dead to pride of every kind: for "love is not puffed up" but "he that dwelling in love, dwelleth in God, and God in him," is less than nothing in his own eyes.

(II.) 2. The Second thing implied in the being *altogether a Christian* is, the love of our neighbour. For thus said our Lord in the following words, "Thou shalt love thy neighbour as thyself." If any man ask, "Who is my neighbour?" we reply, Every man in the world; every child of his who is the Father of the spirits of all flesh. Nor may we in any wise except our enemies or the enemies of God and their own souls. But every Christian loveth these also as himself, yea, "as Christ loved us." he that would more fully understand what manner of love this is, may consider St. Paul's description of it. It is "long-suffering and kind." It "envieth not." It is not rash or hasty in judging. It "is not puffed up;" but maketh him that loves, the least, the servant of all. Love "doth not behave itself unseemly," but becometh "all things to all men." She "seeketh not her own;" but only the good of others, that they may be saved. "Love is not provoked." It casteth out wrath, which he who hath is wanting in love. "It thinketh no evil. It rejoiceth not in iniquity, but rejoiceth in the truth. It covereth all things, believeth all things, hopeth all things, endureth all things."

(III.) 3. There is yet one thing more that may be separately considered, though it cannot actually be separate from the preceding, which is implied in the being *altogether a Christian*; and that is the ground of all, even faith. Very excellent things are spoken of this throughout the oracles of God. "Every one," saith the beloved disciple, "that believeth is born of God." "To as many as received him, gave he power to become the sons of God. even to them that believe on his name." And "this is the victory that overcometh the world, even our faith." Yea, our Lord himself declares, "He that believeth in the Son hath everlasting life; and cometh not into condemnation, but is passed from death unto life."

4. But here let no man deceive his own soul. "It is diligently to be noted, the faith which bringeth not forth repentance, and love, and all good works, is not that right living faith, but a dead and devilish one. For, even the devils believe that Christ was born of a virgin: that he wrought all kinds of miracles, declaring himself very God: that, for our sakes, he suffered a most painful death, to redeem us from death everlasting; that he rose again the third day: that he ascended into heaven, and sitteth at the right hand of the Father and at the end of the world shall come again to judge both the quick and dead. These articles of our faith the devils believe, and so they believe all that is written in the Old and New Testament. And yet for all this faith, they be but devils. They remain still in their damnable estate lacking the very true Christian faith." [Homily on the Salvation of Man.]

5. "The right and true Christian faith is" (to go on the words of our own Church), "not only to believe that Holy Scripture and the Articles of our Faith are true, but also to have a sure trust and confidence to be saved from everlasting damnation by Christ. It is a sure trust and confidence which a man hath in God, that, by the merits of Christ, his sins are forgiven, and he reconciled to the favour of God; whereof doth follow a loving heart, to obey his commandments."

6. Now, whosoever has this faith, which "purifies the heart" (by the power of God, who dwelleth therein) from "pride, anger, desire, from all unrighteousness" from "all filthiness of flesh and spirit;" which fills it with love stronger than death, both to God and to all mankind; love that doeth the works of God, glorying to spend and to be spent for all men, and that endureth with joy, not only the reproach of Christ, the being mocked, despised, and hated of all men, but whatsoever the wisdom of God permits the malice of men or devils to inflict,—whosoever has this faith thus working by love is not almost only, but altogether, a Christian.

7. But who are the living witnesses of these things? I beseech you, brethren, as in the presence of that God before whom "hell and destruction are without a covering—how much more the hearts of the children of men?"—that each of you would ask his own heart, "Am I of that number? Do I so far practise justice, mercy, and truth, as even the rules of heathen honesty require? If so, have I the very *outside* of a Christian? the form of godliness? Do I abstain from evil,—from whatsoever is forbidden in the written Word of God? Do I, whatever good my hand findeth to do, do it with my might? Do I seriously use all the ordinances of God at all opportunities? And is all this done with a sincere design and desire to please God in all things?"

8. Are not many of you conscious, that you never came thus far; that you have not been even *almost a Christian*; that you have not come up to the standard of heathen honesty; at least, not to the form of Christian godliness?—much less hath God seen sincerity in you, a real design of pleasing him in all things. You never so much as intended to devote all your words and works. your business, studies, diversions, to his glory. You never even designed or desired, that whatsoever you did should be done "in the name of the Lord Jesus," and as such should be "a spiritual sacrifice, acceptable to God through Christ."

9. But, supposing you had, do good designs and good desires make a Christian? By no means, unless they are brought to good effect. "Hell is paved," saith one, "with good intentions." The great question of all, then, still remains. Is the love of God shed abroad in your heart? Can you cry out, "My God, and my All"? Do you desire nothing but him? Are you happy in God? Is he your glory, your delight, your crown of rejoicing? And is this commandment written in your heart, "That he who loveth God love his brother also"? Do you then love your neighbour as yourself? Do you love every man, even your enemies, even the enemies of God, as your own soul? as Christ loved you? Yea, dost thou believe that Christ loved thee, and gave himself for thee? Hast thou faith in his blood? Believest thou the Lamb of God hath taken away thy sins, and cast them as a stone into the depth of the sea? that he hath blotted out the handwriting that was

against thee, taking it out of the way, nailing it to his cross? Hast thou indeed redemption through his blood, even the remission of thy sins? And doth his Spirit bear witness with thy spirit, that thou art a child of God?

10. The God and Father of our Lord Jesus Christ, who now standeth in the midst of us, knoweth, that if any man die without this faith and this love, good it were for him that he had never been born. Awake, then, thou that sleepest, and call upon thy God: call in the day when he may be found. Let him not rest, till he make his "goodness to pass before thee;" till he proclaim unto thee the name of the Lord, "The Lord, the Lord God, merciful and gracious, long-suffering, and abundant in goodness and truth, keeping mercy for thousands, forgiving iniquity, and transgression, and sin." Let no man persuade thee, by vain words, to rest short of this prize of thy high calling. But cry unto him day and night, who, "while we were without strength, died for the ungodly," until thou knowest in whom thou hast believed, and canst say, "My Lord, and my God!" Remember, "always to pray, and not to faint," till thou also canst lift up thy hand unto heaven, and declare to him that liveth for ever and ever, "Lord, Thou knowest all things, Thou knowest that I love Thee."

11. May we all thus experience what it is to be, not almost only; but altogether Christians; being justified freely by his grace, through the redemption that is in Jesus; knowing we have peace with God through Jesus Christ; rejoicing in hope of the glory of God; and having the love of God shed abroad in our hearts, by the Holy Ghost given unto us!

SERMON 3: AWAKE, THOU THAT SLEEPEST.

"Awake, thou that sleepest, and arise from the dead, and Christ shall give thee light." Eph. 5:14.

In discoursing on these words, I shall, with the help of God, —

First. Describe the sleepers, to whom they are spoken:

Secondly. Enforce the exhortation, "Awake, thou that sleepest, and arise from the dead:" And,

Thirdly. Explain the promise made to such as do awake and arise: "Christ shall give thee light."

I. 1. And first, as to the sleepers here spoken to. By sleep is signified the natural state of man; that deep sleep of the soul, into which the sin of Adam hath cast all who spring from his loins: That supineness, indolence, and stupidity, that insensibility of his real condition, wherein every man comes Into the world, and continues till the voice of God awakes him.

2. Now, "they that sleep, sleep in the night." The state of nature is a state of utter darkness; a state wherein "darkness covers the earth, and gross darkness the people." The poor unawakened sinner, how much knowledge soever he may have as to other things, has no knowledge of himself: in this respect "he knoweth nothing yet as he ought to know." He knows not that he is a fallen spirit, whose only business in the present world, is to recover from his fall, to regain that image of God wherein he was created. he sees *no necessity* for the *one thing needful*, even that inward universal change, that "birth from above," figured out by baptism, which is the beginning of that total renovation. that sanctification of spirit, soul, and body, "without which no man shall see the Lord."

3. Full of all diseases as he is, he fancies himself in perfect health. Fast bound in misery and iron, he dreams that he is at liberty. he says, "Peace! Peace!" while the devil, as "a strong, man armed," is in full possession of his soul. he sleeps on still and takes his rest, though hell is moved from beneath to meet him; though the pit from whence there is no return hath opened its mouth to swallow him up. A fire is kindled around him, yet he knoweth it not; yea, it burns him, yet he lays it not to heart.

4. By one who sleeps, we are, therefore, to understand (and would to God we might all understand it!) a sinner satisfied in his sins; contented to remain in his fallen state, to live and die without the image of God; one who is ignorant both of his disease, and of the only remedy for it; one who never was warned, or never regarded the warning voice of God, "to flee from the wrath to come;" one that never yet saw he was in danger of hell-fire, or cried out in the earnestness of his soul, "What must I do to be saved?"

5. If this sleeper be not outwardly vicious, his sleep is usually the deepest of all: whether he be of the Laodicean spirit, "neither cold nor hot," but a quiet, rational, inoffensive, good-natured professor of the religion of his fathers; or whether he be zealous and orthodox, and, "after the most straitest sect of our religion," live "a Pharisee;" that is, according to the scriptural account, one that justifies himself; one that labours to establish his own righteousness, as the ground of his acceptance with God.

6. This is he, who, "having a form of godliness, denies the power thereof;" yea, and probably reviles it, wheresoever it is found, as mere extravagance and delusion. Meanwhile, the wretched self-deceiver thanks God, that

he is "not as other men are; adulterers, unjust, extortioners": no, he doeth no wrong to any man. he "fasts twice in a week," uses all the means of grace, is constant at church and sacrament, yea, and "gives tithes of all that he has;" does all the good that he can "touching the righteousness of the law," he is "blameless": he wants nothing of godliness, but the power; nothing of religion, but the spirit; nothing of Christianity, but the truth and the life.

7. But know ye not, that, however highly esteemed among men such a Christian as this may be, he is an abomination in the sight of God, and an heir of every woe which the Son of God, yesterday, to-day, and for ever, denounces against "scribes and Pharisees, hypocrites"? he hath "made clean the outside of the cup and the platter," but within is full of all filthiness. "An evil disease cleaveth still unto him, so that his inward parts are very wickedness." Our Lord fitly compares him to a "painted sepulchre," which "appears beautiful without;" but, nevertheless, is "full of dead men's bones, and of all uncleanness." The bones indeed are no longer dry; the sinews and flesh are come upon them, and the skin covers them above: but there is no breath in them, no Spirit of the living God. And, "if any man have not the Spirit of Christ, he is none of his." "Ye are Christ's, if so be that the Spirit of God dwell in you": but, if not, God knoweth that ye abide in death, even until now.

8. This is another character of the sleeper here spoken to. he abides in death, though he knows it not. he is dead unto God, "dead in trespasses and sins." For, "to be carnally minded is death" Even as it is written, "By one man sin entered into the world, and death by sin; and so death passed upon all men;" not only temporal death, but likewise spiritual and eternal. "In that day that thou eatest," said God to Adam, "thou shalt surely die;" not bodily (unless as he then became mortal), but spiritually: thou shalt lose the life of thy soul; thou shalt die to God: shalt be separated from him, thy essential life and happiness.

9. Thus first was dissolved the vital union of our soul with God; insomuch that "in the midst of" natural "life, we are" now in spiritual "death." And herein we remain till the Second Adam becomes a quickening Spirit to us; till he raises the dead, the dead in sin, in pleasure, riches or honours. But, before any dead soul can live, he "hears" (hearkens to) "the voice of the Son of God": he is made sensible of his lost estate, and receives the sentence of death in himself. he knows himself to be "dead while he liveth;" dead to God, and all the things of God; having no more power to perform the actions of a living Christian, than a dead body to perform the functions of a living man.

10. And most certain it is, that one dead in sin has not "senses exercised to discern spiritual good and evil." "Having eyes, he sees not; he hath ears, and hears not." he doth not "taste and see that the Lord is gracious." he "hath not seen God at any time," nor "heard his voice," nor "handled the word of life." In vain is the name of Jesus "like ointment poured forth, and all his garments smell of myrrh, aloes, and cassia." The soul that sleepeth in death hath no perception of any objects of this kind. his heart is "past feeling," and understandeth none of these things.

11. And hence, having no spiritual senses, no inlets of spiritual knowledge, the natural man receiveth not the things of the Spirit of God; nay, he is so far from receiving them, that whatsoever is spiritually discerned is mere foolishness unto him. he is not content with being utterly ignorant of spiritual things, but he denies the very existence of them. And spiritual sensation itself is to him the foolishness of folly. "How," saith he, "can these things be? How can any man *know* that he is alive to God?" Even as you know that your body is now alive. Faith is the life of the soul; and if ye have this life abiding in you, ye want no marks to evidence it *to yourself,* but elegchos pneumatos, that divine consciousness, that *witness* of God, which is more and greater than ten thousand human witnesses.

12. If he doth not now bear witness with thy spirit, that thou art a child of God, O that he might convince thee, thou poor unawakened sinner, by his demonstration and power, that thou art a child of the devil! O that, as I prophesy, there might now be "a noise and a shaking;" and may "the bones come together, bone to his bone!" Then "come from the four winds, O Breath! and breathe on these slain, that they may live!" And do not ye harden your hearts, and resist the Holy Ghost, who even now is come to convince you of sin, "because you believe not on the name of the only begotten Son of God."

II. 1. Wherefore, "awake, thou that sleepest, and arise from the dead." God calleth thee now by my mouth; and bids thee know thyself, thou fallen spirit, thy true state and only concern below. "What meanest thou, O sleeper? Arise! Call upon thy God, if so be thy God will think upon thee, that thou perish not." A mighty tempest is stirred up round about thee, and thou art sinking into the depths of perdition, the gulf of God's judgements. If thou wouldest escape them, cast thyself into them. "Judge thyself, and thou shalt not be judged of the Lord."

2. Awake, awake! Stand up this moment, lest thou "drink at the Lord's hand the cup of his fury." Stir up thyself to lay hold on the Lord, the Lord thy Righteousness, mighty to save! "Shake thyself from the dust." At least, let the earthquake of God's threatenings shake thee. Awake, and cry out with the trembling jailer, "What must I do to be saved?" And never rest till thou believest on the Lord Jesus, with a faith which is his gift, by the operation of his Spirit.

3. If I speak to any one of you, more than to another, it is to thee, who thinkest thyself unconcerned in this exhortation. "I have a message from God unto thee." In his name, I warn thee "to flee from the wrath to come." Thou unholy soul, see thy picture in condemned Peter, lying in the dark dungeon, between the soldiers, bound with two chains, the keepers before the door keeping the prison. The night is far spent, the morning is at hand, when thou art to be brought forth to execution. And in these dreadful circumstances, thou art fast asleep; thou art fast asleep in the devil's arms, on the brink of the pit, in the jaws of everlasting destruction!

4. O may the Angel of the Lord come upon thee, and the light shine into thy prison! And mayest thou feel the stroke of an Almighty Hand, raising thee, with, "Arise up quickly, gird thyself, and bind on thy sandals, cast thy garment about thee, and follow Me."

5. Awake, thou everlasting spirit, out of thy dream of worldly happiness! Did not God create thee for himself? Then thou canst not rest till thou restest in him. Return, thou wanderer! Fly back to thy ark, This is not thy home. Think not of building tabernacles here. Thou art but a stranger, a sojourner upon earth; a creature of a day, but just launching out into an unchangeable state. Make haste. Eternity is at hand. Eternity depends on this moment. An eternity of happiness, or an eternity of misery!

6. In what state is thy soul? Was God, while I am yet speaking, to require it of thee, art thou ready to meet death and judgement? Canst thou stand in his sight, who is of "purer eyes than to behold iniquity"? Art thou "meet to be partaker of the inheritance of the saints in light"? Hast thou "fought a good fight, and kept the faith"? Hast thou secured the one thing needful? Hast thou recovered the image of God, even righteousness and true holiness? Hast thou put off the old man, and put on the new? Art thou clothed upon with Christ?

7. Hast thou oil in thy lamp? grace in thy heart? Dost thou "love the Lord thy God with all thy heart, and with all thy mind and with all thy soul, and with all thy strength"? Is that mind in thee, which was also in Christ Jesus? Art thou a Christian indeed, that is, a new creature? Are old things passed away, and all things become new?

8. Art thou a "partaker of the divine nature"? Knowest thou not, that "Christ is in thee, except thou be reprobate"? Knowest thou, that God "dwelleth in thee, and thou in God, by his Spirit, which he hath given thee"? Knowest thou not that "thy body is a temple of the Holy Ghost, which thou hast of God"? Hast thou the witness in thyself? the earnest of thine inheritance? Hast thou "received the Holy Ghost"? Or dost thou start at the question, not knowing "whether there be any Holy Ghost"?

9. If it offends thee, be thou assured, that thou neither art a Christian, nor desirest to be one. Nay, thy very prayer is turned into sin; and thou hast solemnly mocked God this very day, by praying for the inspiration of his Holy Spirit, when thou didst not believe there was any such thing to be received.

10. Yet, on the authority of God's Word, and our own Church, I must repeat the question, "Hast thou received the Holy Ghost?" If thou hast not, thou art not yet a Christian. For a Christian is a man that is "anointed with the Holy Ghost and with power." Thou art not yet made a partaker of pure religion and undefiled. Dost thou know what religion is? —that it is a participation of the divine nature; the life of God in the soul of man; Christ formed in the heart; "Christ in thee, the hope of glory;" happiness and holiness; heaven begun upon earth; "a kingdom of God within thee; not meat and drink," no outward thing; "but righteousness, and peace, and joy in the Holy Ghost;" an everlasting kingdom brought into thy soul; a "peace of God that passeth all understanding;" a "joy unspeakable, and full of glory"?

11. Knowest thou, that "in Jesus Christ, neither circumcision availeth anything, nor uncircumcision; but faith that worketh by love;" but a new creation? Seest thou the necessity of that inward change, that spiritual birth, that life from the dead, that holiness? And art thou throughly convinced, that without it no man shall see the Lord? Art thou labouring after it? —"giving all diligence to make thy calling and election sure," "working out thy salvation with fear and trembling," "agonizing to enter in at the strait gate"? Art thou in earnest about thy soul? And canst thou tell the Searcher of hearts, "Thou, O God, art the thing that I long for! Lord, Thou knowest all things; Thou knowest that I *would* love Thee!"

12. Thou hopest to be saved; but what reason hast thou to give of the hope that is in thee? Is it because

thou hast done no harm? or, because thou hast done much good? or, because thou art not like other men; but wise, or learned, or honest, and morally good; esteemed of men, and of a fair reputation? Alas! all this will never bring thee to God. It is in his account lighter than vanity. Dost thou know Jesus Christ, whom he hath sent? Hath he taught thee, that "by grace we are saved through faith; and that not of ourselves: it is the gift of God: not of works, lest any man should boast"? Hast thou received the faithful saying as the whole foundation of thy hope, "that Jesus Christ came into the world to save sinners"? Hast thou learned what that meaneth, "I came not to call the righteous, but sinners to repentance? I am not sent, but unto the lost sheep"? Art thou (he that heareth, let him understand!) lost, dead, *damned already?* Dost thou know thy deserts? Dost thou feel thy wants? Art thou "poor in spirit"? mourning for God, and refusing to be comforted? Is the prodigal "come to himself," and well content to be therefore thought beside himself" by those who are still feeding upon the husks which he hath left? Art thou willing to live godly in Christ Jesus? And dost thou therefore suffer persecution? Do men say all manner of evil against thee falsely, for the Son of Man's sake?

13. O that in all these questions ye may hear the voice that wakes the dead; and feel that hammer of the Word, which breaketh the rocks in pieces! "If ye will hear his voice to-day, while it is called to-day, harden not your hearts." Now, "awake, thou that sleepest" in spiritual death, that thou sleep not in death eternal! Feel thy lost estate, and "arise from the dead." Leave thine old companions in sin and death. Follow thou Jesus, and let the dead bury their dead. "Save thyself from this untoward generation." "Come out from among them, and be thou separate, and touch not the unclean thing, and the Lord shall receive thee." "Christ shall give thee light."

III. 1. This promise, I come, lastly, to explain. And how encouraging a consideration is this, that whosoever thou art, who obeyest his call, thou canst not seek his face in vain! If thou even now "awakest, and arisest from the dead," he hath bound himself to "give thee light." "The Lord shall give thee grace and glory;" the light of his grace here, and the light of his glory when thou receivest the crown that fadeth not away. "Thy light shall break forth as the morning, and thy darkness be as the noon-day." "God, who commanded the light to shine out of darkness, shall shine in thy heart; to give the knowledge of the glory of God in the face of Jesus Christ." On them that fear the Lord shall "the Sun of Righteousness arise with healing in his wings." And in that day it shall be said unto thee, "Arise, shine; for thy light is come, and the glory of the Lord is risen upon thee." For Christ shall reveal himself in thee: and he is the true Light.

2. God is light, and will give himself to every awakened sinner that waiteth for him; and thou shalt then be a temple of the living God, and Christ shall "dwell in thy heart by faith;" and, "being rooted and grounded in love, thou shalt be able to comprehend with all saints, what is the breadth, and length, and depth, and height of that love of Christ which passeth knowledge."

3. Ye see your calling, brethren. We are called to be "an habitation of God through his Spirit;" and, through his Spirit dwelling in us, to be saints here, and partakers of the inheritance of the saints in light. So exceeding great are the promises which are given unto us, actually given unto us who believe! For by faith "we receive, not the spirit of the world, but the Spirit which is of God" —the sum of all the promises— "that we may know the things that are freely given to us of God."

4. The Spirit of Christ is that great gift of God, which at sundry times, and in divers manners, he hath promised to man, and hath fully bestowed since the time that Christ was glorified. Those promises, before made to the fathers, he hath thus fulfilled: "I will put My spirit within you, and cause you to walk in My statutes" (Ezek. 36:27). "I will pour water upon him that is thirsty, and floods upon the dry ground; I will pour My Spirit upon thy seed, and My blessing upon thine offspring (Isa. 44:3).

5. Ye may all be living witnesses of these things; of remission of sins, and the gift of the Holy Ghost. "If thou canst believe, all things are possible to him that believeth." "Who among you is there that feareth the Lord, and" yet walketh on "in darkness, and hath no light?" I ask thee, in the name of Jesus, Believest thou that his arm is not shortened at all? that he is still mighty to save? that he is the same yesterday, to-day, and for ever? that he hath now power on earth to forgive sins? "Son, be of good cheer; thy sins are forgiven." God, for Christ's sake, hath forgiven thee. Receive this, "not as the word of man; but as it is indeed, the word of God;" and thou art justified freely through faith. Thou shalt be sanctified also through faith which is in Jesus, and shalt set to thy seal, even thine, that "God hath given unto us eternal life, and this life is in his Son."

6. Men and brethren, let me freely speak unto you, and suffer ye the word of exhortation, even from one the least

esteemed in the Church. Your conscience beareth you witness in the Holy Ghost, that these things are so, if so be ye have tasted that the Lord is gracious. "This is eternal life, to know the only true God, and Jesus Christ, whom he hath sent." This experimental knowledge, and this alone, is true Christianity. he is a Christian who hath received the Spirit of Christ. he is not a Christian who hath not received him. Neither is it possible to have received him, and not know it. "For, at that day" (when he cometh, saith our Lord), "ye shall know that I am in My Father, and you in Me, and I in you." This is that "Spirit of Truth, whom the world cannot receive, because it seeth him not, neither knoweth him: but ye know him; for he dwelleth with you, and shall be in you" (John 14:17).

7. The world cannot receive him, but utterly reject the Promise of the Father, contradicting and blaspheming. But every spirit which confesseth not this is not of God. Yea, "this is that spirit of Antichrist, whereof ye have heard that it should come into the world; and even now it is in the world." he is Antichrist whosoever denies the inspiration of the Holy Ghost, or that the indwelling Spirit of God is the common privilege of all believers, the blessing of the gospel, the unspeakable gift, the universal promise, the criterion of a real Christian.

8. It nothing helps them to say, "We do not deny the *assistance* of God's Spirit; but only this *inspiration*, this *receiving the Holy Ghost*: and being *sensible* of it. It is only this *feeling of the* Spirit, this being *moved* by the Spirit, or *filled* with it, which we deny to have any place in sound religion." But, in *only denying this,* you deny the whole Scriptures; the whole truth, and promise, and testimony of God.

9. Our own excellent Church knows nothing of this devilish distinction; but speaks plainly of "feeling the Spirit of Christ" [Article 17]; of being "moved by the Holy Ghost" [Office of consecrating Priests] and knowing and "feeling there is no other name than that of Jesus," [Visitation of the Sick] whereby we can receive" life and salvation. She teaches us all to pray for the "inspiration of the Holy Spirit" [Collect before Holy Communion]; yea, that we may be "filled with the Holy Ghost" [Order of Confirmation]. Nay, and every Presbyter of hers professes to receive the Holy Ghost by the imposition of hands. Therefore, to deny any of these, is, in effect, to renounce the Church of England, as well as the whole Christian revelation.

10. But "the wisdom of God" was always "foolishness with men." No marvel, then, that the great mystery of the gospel should be now also "hid from the wise and prudent," as well as in the days of old; that it should be almost universally denied, ridiculed, and exploded, as mere frenzy; and that all who dare avow it still are branded with the names of madmen and enthusiasts! This is "that falling away" which was to come—that general apostasy of all orders and degrees of men, which we even now find to have overspread the earth. "Run to and fro in the streets of Jerusalem, and see if ye can find a man," a man that loveth the Lord his God with all his heart, and serveth him with all his strength. How does our own land mourn (that we look no farther) under the overflowings of ungodliness! What villanies of every kind are committed day by day; yea, too often with impunity, by those who sin with a high hand, and glory in their shame! Who can reckon up the oaths, curses, profaneness blasphemies; the lying, slandering, evil-speaking; the Sabbath-breaking, gluttony, drunkenness, revenge; the whoredoms, adulteries, and various uncleanness; the frauds, injustice, oppression, extortion, which overspread our land as a flood?

11. And even among those who have kept themselves pure from those grosser abominations; how much anger and pride how much sloth and idleness, how much softness and effeminacy how much luxury and self-indulgence, how much covetousness and ambition, how much thirst of praise, how much love of the world, how much fear of man, is to be found! Meanwhile, how little of true religion! For, where is he that loveth either God or his neighbour, as he hath given us commandment? On the one hand, are those who have not so much as the form of godliness; on the other, those who have the form only: there stands the *open,* there the *painted,* sepulchre. So that in very deed, whosoever were earnestly to behold any public gathering together of the people (I fear those in our churches are not to be excepted) might easily perceive, "that the one part were Sadducees, and the other Pharisees": the one having almost as little concern about religion, as if there were "no resurrection, neither angel nor spirit;" and the other making it a mere lifeless form, a dull round of external performances, without either true faith, or the love of God, or joy in the Holy Ghost!

12. Would to God I could except *us* of this place! "Brethren, my heart's desire, and prayer to God, for you is, that ye may be saved" from this overflowing of ungodliness; and that here may its proud waves be stayed! But is it so indeed? God knoweth, yea, and our

own consciences, it is not. Ye have not kept yourselves pure. Corrupt are we also and abominable; and few are there that understand any more; few that worship God in spirit and in truth. We, too, are "a generation that set not our hearts aright, and whose spirit cleaveth not steadfastly unto God." he hath appointed us indeed to be "the salt of the earth: but if the salt hath lost its savour, it is thenceforth good for nothing; but to be cast out, and to be trodden underfoot of men."

13. And "shall I not visit for these things, saith the Lord? Shall not My soul be avenged on such a nation as this?" Yea, we know not how soon he may say to the sword, "Sword, go through this land!" he hath given us long space to repent. he lets us alone this year also: but he warns and awakens us by thunder. his judgements are abroad in the earth; and we have all reason to expect the heaviest of all, even that he "should come unto us quickly, and remove our candlestick out of its place, except we repent and do the first works;" unless we return to the principles of the Reformation, the truth and simplicity of the gospel. Perhaps we are now resisting the last effort of divine grace to save us. Perhaps we have well-nigh "filled up the measure of our iniquities," by rejecting the counsel of God against ourselves, and casting out his messengers.

14. O God, "in the midst of wrath, remember mercy!" Be glorified in our reformation, not in our destruction! Let us "hear the rod, and him that appointed it!" Now that Thy "judgements are abroad in the earth," let the inhabitants of the world "learn righteousness!"

15. My brethren, it is high time for us to awake out of sleep before the "great trumpet of the Lord be blown," and our land become a field of blood. O may we speedily see the things that make for our peace, before they are hid from our eyes! "Turn Thou us, O good Lord, and let Thine anger cease from us. O Lord, look down from heaven, behold and visit this vine;" and cause us to know "the time of our visitation." "Help us, O God of our salvation, for the glory of Thy name! O deliver us, and be merciful to our sins, for Thy name's sake! And so we will not go back from Thee. O let us live, and we shall call upon Thy name. Turn us again, O Lord God of Hosts! Show the light of Thy countenance, and we shall be whole."

"Now unto him that is able to do exceeding abundantly above all that we can ask or think, according to the power that worketh in us, unto him be glory in the church by Christ Jesus throughout all ages; world without end. —Amen!"

SERMON 4: SCRIPTURAL CHRISTIANITY.

"Whosoever heareth the sound of the trumpet, and taketh not warning; if the sword come, and take him away, his blood shall be upon his own head." Ezek. 33:4.

"And they were all filled with the Holy Ghost." Acts 4:31.

1. The same expression occurs in the second chapter, where we read, "When the day of Pentecost was fully come, they were all" (the Apostles, with the women, and the mother of Jesus, and his brethren) "with one accord in one place. And suddenly there came a sound from heaven as of a rushing mighty wind. And there appeared unto them cloven tongues like as of fire, and it sat upon each of them. And they were all filled with the Holy Ghost:" one immediate effect whereof was, they "began to speak with other tongues;" insomuch that both the Parthians, Medes, Elamites, and the other strangers who "came together, when this was noised abroad, heard them speak, in their several tongues, the wonderful works of God" (Acts 2:1–6).

2. In this chapter we read, that when the Apostles and brethren had been praying, and praising God, "the place was shaken where they were assembled together, and they were all filled with the Holy Ghost." Not that we find any visible appearance here, such as had been in the former instance: nor are we informed that the *extraordinary gifts* of the Holy Ghost were then given to all or any of them; such as the gifts of "healing, of working" other "miracles, of prophecy, of discerning spirits, the speaking with divers kinds of tongues, and the interpretation of tongues (1 Cor. 12:9, 10).

3. Whether these gifts of the Holy Ghost were designed to remain in the church throughout all ages, and whether or no they will be restored at the nearer approach of the "restitution of all things," are questions which it is not needful to decide. But it is needful to observe this, that, even in the infancy of the church, God divided them with a sparing hand. Were all even then prophets? Were all workers of miracles? Had all the gifts of healing? Did all speak with tongues? No, in no wise. Perhaps not one in a thousand. Probably none but the teachers in the church, and only some of them (1 Cor. 12:28–30). It was therefore, for a more excellent purpose than this, that "they were all filled with the Holy Ghost."

4. It was, to give them (what none can deny to be essential to all Christians in all ages) the mind which was in Christ, those holy fruits of the Spirit, which whosoever hath not, is none of his; to fill them with "love, joy, peace, long-suffering, gentleness, goodness" (Gal. 5:22–24); to endue them with faith (perhaps it might be rendered, *fidelity*), with meekness and temperance; to enable them to crucify the flesh, with its affections and lusts, its passions and desires; and in consequence of that inward change, to fulfil all outward righteousness; to "walk as Christ also walked," in "the work of faith, in the patience of hope, the labour of love" (1 Thess. 1:3).

5. Without busying ourselves, then, in curious, needless inquiries, touching those *extraordinary gifts* of the Spirit, let us take a nearer view of these his *ordinary* fruits, which we are assured will remain throughout all ages; — of that great work of God among the children of men, which we are used to express by one word, "Christianity;" not as it implies a set of opinions, a system of doctrines, but as it refers to men's hearts and lives. And this Christianity it may be useful to consider under three distinct views:

I. As beginning to exist in individuals:

II. As spreading from one to another:

III. As covering the earth.

I design to close these considerations with a plain, practical application.

I. 1. And, first, let us consider Christianity in its rise, as beginning to exist in individuals.

Suppose, then, one of those who heard the Apostle Peter preaching repentance and remission of sins, was pricked to the heart, was convinced of sin, repented, and then believed in Jesus. By this faith of the operation of God, which was the very substance, or subsistence, of things hoped for (Heb. 11:1,) the demonstrative evidence of invisible things, he instantly received the Spirit of adoption, whereby he now cried, "Abba, Father" (Rom. 8:15). Now first it was that he could call Jesus Lord, by the Holy Ghost (1 Cor. 12:3), the Spirit itself bearing witness with his spirit, that he was a child of God (Rom. 8:16). Now it was that he could truly say, "I live not, but Christ liveth in me; and the life which I now live in the flesh, I live by faith in the Son of God, who loved me, and gave himself for me" (Gal. 2:20).

2. This, then, was the very essence of his faith, a divine elegchos (*evidence* or *conviction*) of the love of God the Father, through the Son of his love, to him a sinner, now accepted in the Beloved. And, being justified by faith, he had peace with God (Rom. 5:1), yea, the peace of God ruling in his heart; a peace, which passing all understanding (panta noun, all barely rational conception), kept his heart and mind from all doubt and fear, through the knowledge of him in whom he had believed. he could not, therefore, "be afraid of any evil tidings;" for his "heart stood fast, believing in the Lord." he feared not what man could do unto him, knowing the very hairs of his head were all numbered. he feared not all the powers of darkness, whom God was daily bruising under his feet. Least of all was he afraid to die; nay, he desired to "depart, and to be with Christ" (Phil. 1:23); who, "through death, had destroyed him that had the power of death, even the devil; and delivered them who, through fear of death, were all their life-time," till then, "subject to bondage" (Heb. 2:15).

3. his soul, therefore, magnified the Lord, and his spirit rejoiced in God his Saviour. "He rejoiced in him with joy unspeakable," who had reconciled him to God, even the Father; "in whom he had redemption through his blood, the forgiveness of sins." he rejoiced in that witness of God's Spirit with his spirit, that he was a child of God; and more abundantly, "in hope of the glory of God;" in hope of the glorious image of God, and full renewal of his soul in righteousness and true holiness, and in hope of that crown of glory, that "inheritance, incorruptible, undefiled, and that fadeth not away."

4. "The love of God was also shed abroad in his heart by the Holy Ghost which was given unto him" (Rom. 5:5). "Because he was a son God had sent forth the Spirit of his Son into his heart, crying Abba, Father!" (Gal. 4:6). And that filial love of God was continually increased by the witness he had in himself (1 John 5:10) of God's pardoning love to him; by "beholding what manner of love it was which the Father had bestowed upon him, that he should be called a child of God" (1 John 3:1). So that God was the. desire of his eyes, and the joy of his heart; his portion in time and in eternity.

5. he that thus *loved* God could not but love his brother also; and "not in word only, but in deed and in truth." "If God," said he, "so loved us, we ought also to love one another" (1 John 4:11); yea, every soul of man, as "the mercy of God is over all his works" (Ps. 145:9). Agreeably hereto, the affection of this lover of God embraced all mankind for his sake; not excepting those whom he had never seen in the flesh, or those of whom he knew nothing more than that they were "the offspring of God," for whose souls his Son had died; not excepting the "evil" and "unthankful," and least of all his enemies, those who hated, or persecuted, or despitefully used him

for his Master's sake. These had a peculiar place, both in his heart and in his prayers. he loved them "even as Christ loved us."

6. And "love is not puffed up" (1 Cor. 13:4). It abases to the dust every soul wherein it dwells. Accordingly, he was lowly of heart, little, mean, and vile in his own eyes. he neither sought nor received the praise of men, but that which cometh of God only. he was meek and long-suffering, gentle to all, and easy to be entreated. Faithfulness and truth never forsook him: they were "bound about his neck, and wrote on the table of his heart." By the same spirit he was enabled to be temperate in all things, refraining his soul even as a weaned child. he was "crucified to the world, and the world crucified to him;" superior to "the desire of the flesh, the desire of the eye, and the pride of life." By the same almighty love was he saved, both from passion and pride; from lust and vanity; from ambition and covetousness; and from every temper which was not in Christ.

7. It may be easily believed, he who had this love in his heart would work no evil to his neighbour. It was impossible for him, knowingly and designedly, to do harm to any man. he was at the greatest distance from cruelty and wrong, from any unjust or unkind action. With the same care did he "set a watch before his mouth, and keep the door of his lips," lest he should offend in tongue, either against justice, or against mercy or truth. he put away all lying, falsehood; and fraud; neither was guile found in his mouth. he spake evil of no man; nor did an unkind word ever come out of his lips.

8. And as he was deeply sensible of the truth of that word "Without me ye can do nothing," and, consequently, of the need he had to be watered of God every moment; so he continued daily in all the ordinances of God, the stated channels of his grace to man: "in the Apostles' doctrine," or teaching, receiving that food of the soul with all readiness of heart; in "the breaking of bread," which he found to be the communion of the body of Christ; and "in the prayers" and praises offered up by the great congregation. And thus, he daily grew in grace, increasing in strength, in the knowledge and love of God.

9. But it did not satisfy him, barely to abstain from doing evil. his soul was athirst to do good. The language of his heart continually was, "'My Father worketh hitherto, and I work.' My Lord went about doing good; and shall not I tread in his steps?" As he had opportunity therefore, if he could do no good of a higher kind, he fed the hungry, clothed the naked, helped the fatherless or stranger, visited and assisted them that were sick or in prison. he gave all his goods to feed the poor. he rejoiced to labour or to suffer for them; and whereinsoever he might profit another, there especially to "deny himself." he counted nothing too dear to part with for them, as well remembering the word of his Lord, "Inasmuch as ye have done it unto one of the least of these My brethren, ye have done it unto Me" (Matt. 25:40).

10. Such was Christianity in its rise. Such was a Christian in ancient days. Such was every one of those who, when they heard the threatenings of the chief priests and elders, "lifted up their voice to God with one accord, and were all filled with the Holy Ghost. The multitude of them that believed were of one heart and of one soul:" So did the love of him in whom they had believed constrain them to love one another! "Neither said any of them that aught of the things which he possessed was his own but they had all things common:" So fully were they crucified to the world, and the world crucified to them! "And they continued steadfastly with one accord in the Apostles" doctrine, and in the breaking of bread, and in prayers" (Acts 2:42). "And great grace was upon them all; neither was there any among them that lacked: for as many as were possessors of lands or houses sold them, and brought the prices of the things that were sold, and laid them down at the Apostles' feet: And distribution was made unto every man according as he had need." (Acts 4:31–35.)

II. 1. Let us take a view, in the Second place, of this Christianity, as spreading from one to another, and so gradually making its way into the world: For such was the will of God concerning it, who did not "light a candle to put it under a bushel, but that it might give light to all that were in the house." And this our Lord had declared to his first disciples, "Ye are the salt of the earth," "the light of the world;" at the same time that he gave that general command, "Let your light so shine before men, that they may see your good works, and glorify your Father which is in heaven." (Matt. 5:13–16).

2. And, indeed, supposing a few of these lovers of mankind to see "the whole world lying in wickedness," can we believe they would be unconcerned at the sight, at the misery of those for whom their Lord died? Would not their bowels yearn over them, and their hearts melt away for very trouble? Could they then stand idle all the day long, even were there no command from him whom they loved? Rather, would they not labour by all possible means, to pluck some of these brands out of the burning? Undoubtedly they would: they would spare no pains to

bring back whomsoever they could of those poor "sheep that had gone astray, to the great Shepherd and Bishop of their souls" (1 Pet. 2:25).

3. So the Christians of old did. They laboured, having opportunity, "to do good unto all men" (Gal. 6:10), warning them to flee from the wrath to come; now, now to escape the damnation of hell. They declared, "The times of ignorance God winked at; but now he calleth all men everywhere to repent." (Acts 17:30) They cried aloud, Turn ye, turn ye, from your evil ways: "so iniquity shall not be your ruin" (Ezek. 18:30). They "reasoned" with them of "temperance, and righteousness," or justice—of the virtues opposite to their reigning sins; "and of judgement to come,"—of the wrath of God which would surely be executed on evildoers in that day when he should judge the world (Acts 24:25).

4. They endeavoured herein to speak to every man severally as he had need. To the careless, to those who lay unconcerned in darkness and in the shadow of death, they thundered, "Awake thou that sleepest; arise from the dead, and Christ shall give thee light." But to those who were already awakened out of sleep, and groaning under a sense of the wrath of God, their language was, "We have an Advocate with the Father; he is the propitiation for our sins." Meantime, those who had believed, they provoked to love and to good works; to patient continuance in well-doing; and to abound more and more in that holiness without which no man can see the Lord. (Heb 12:14)

5. And their labour was not in vain in the Lord. his word ran and was glorified. It grew mightily and prevailed. But so much the more did offences prevail also. The world in general were offended, "because they testified of it, that the works thereof were evil" (John 7:7). The men of pleasure were offended, not only because these men were made, as it were, to reprove their thoughts ("He professeth," said they, "to have the knowledge of God; he calleth himself the child of the Lord, his life is not like other men's; his ways are of another fashion; he abstaineth from our ways, as from filthiness; he maketh his boast, that God is his Father" Wis. 2:13–16;) but much more, because so many of their companions were taken away, and would no more run with them to "the same excess of riot." (1 Pet. 4:4.) The men of reputation were offended, because, as the gospel spread, they declined in the esteem of the people; and because many no longer dared to give them flattering titles, or to pay man the homage due to God only. The men of trade called one another together, and said, "Sirs, ye know that by this craft we have our wealth: but ye see and hear that these men have persuaded and turned away much people; so that this our craft is in danger to be set at nought" (Acts 19:25ff.). Above all, the men of religion, so called, the men of *outside* religion, "the saints of the world," were offended, and ready at every opportunity to cry out, "Men of Israel, help! We have found these men pestilent fellows, movers of sedition throughout the world" (Acts 24:5). "These are the men that teach all men everywhere against the people, and against this place" (Acts 21:28).

6. Thus it was that the heavens grew black with clouds, and the storm gathered amain. For the more Christianity spread, the more hurt was done, in the account of those who received it not; and the number increased of those who were more and more enraged at these "men who thus turned the world upside down;" (Acts 17:6;) insomuch that more and more cried out, "Away with such fellows from the earth; it is not fit that they should live;" yea, and sincerely believed, that whosoever should kill them would do God service.

7. Meanwhile they did not fail to cast out their name as evil; (Luke 6:22;) so that this "sect was everywhere spoken against." (Acts 27:22.) Men said all manner of evil of them, even as had been done of the prophets that were before them (Matt. 5:12). And whatsoever any would affirm, others would believe; so that offences grew as the stars of heaven for multitude. And hence arose, at the time fore-ordained of the Father, persecution in all its forms. Some, for a season, suffered only shame and reproach; some, "the spoiling of their goods;" "some had trial of mocking and scourging; some of bonds and imprisonment;" and others "resisted unto blood" (Heb. 10:34; 11:36ff.)

8. Now it was that the pillars of hell were shaken, and the kingdom of God spread more and more. Sinners were everywhere "turned from darkness to light, and from the power of Satan unto God." he gave his children "such a mouth, and such wisdom, as all their adversaries could not resist;" and their lives were of equal force with their words. But above all, their sufferings spake to all the world. They "approved themselves the servants of God, in afflictions, in necessities, in distresses, in stripes, in imprisonments, in tumults, in labours; in perils in the sea, in perils in the wilderness, in weariness and painfulness, in hunger and thirst, in cold and nakedness" (2 Cor. 6:4ff.). And when, having fought the good fight, they were led as sheep to the slaughter, and offered up on the sacrifice and service of their faith, then the blood of each found a voice, and the heathen owned, "He being dead, yet speaketh."

9. Thus did Christianity spread itself in the earth. But how soon did the tares appear with the wheat, and the *mystery of iniquity* work, as well as the *mystery of godliness!* How soon did Satan find a seat, even *in the temple of God*, "till the woman fled into the wilderness," and "the faithful were again minished from the children of men!" here we tread a beaten path: the still unceasing corruptions of the succeeding generations have been largely described, from time to time, by those witnesses God raised up, to show that he had "built his church upon a rock, and the gates of hell should not" wholly "prevail against her." (Matt. 16:18.)

III. 1. But shall we not see greater things than these? Yea, greater than have been yet from the beginning of the world. Can Satan cause the truth of God to fail, or his promises to be of none effect? If not, the time will come when Christianity will prevail over all, and cover the earth. Let us stand a little, and survey (the Third thing which was proposed) this strange sight, a *Christian World*. Of this the Prophets of old inquired and searched diligently (1 Pet. 1:10, 11ff.:) of this the Spirit which was in them testified: "It shall come to pass in the last days, that the mountain of the Lord's house shall be established in the top of the mountains, and shall be exalted above the hills; and all nations shall flow unto it. And they shall beat their swords into ploughshares, and their spears into pruninghooks. Nation shall not lift up sword against nation; neither shall they learn war any more." (Isa. 2:1–4.) "In that day there shall be a Root of Jesse, which shall stand for an Ensign of the people. To it shall the Gentiles seek: and his rest shall be glorious. And it shall come to pass in that day, that the Lord shall set his hand again to recover the remnant of his people; and he shall set up an Ensign for the nations, and shall assemble the outcasts of Israel, and gather together the dispersed of Judah, from the four corners of the earth." (Isa. 11:10–12.) "The wolf shall then dwell with the lamb, and the leopard shall lie down with the kid; and the calf and the young lion and the fatling together; and a little child shall lead them. They shall not hurt nor destroy, saith the Lord, in all my holy mountain. For the earth shall be full of the knowledge of the Lord, as the waters cover the sea" (Isa. 11:6–9).

2. To the same effect are the words of the great Apostle, which it is evident have never yet been fulfilled. "Hath God cast away his people? God forbid." "But through their fall salvation is come to the Gentiles." "And if the diminishing of them be the riches of the Gentiles, how much more their fullness?" "For I would not, brethren, that ye should be ignorant of this mystery; that blindness in part is happened to Israel, until the fullness of the Gentiles be come in: And so all Israel shall be saved." (Rom. 11:1, 11, 25, 26.)

3. Suppose now the fullness of time to be come, and the prophecies to be accomplished. What a prospect is this! All is peace, "quietness, and assurance for ever." here is no din of arms, no "confused noise," no "garments rolled in blood." "Destructions are come to a perpetual end." Wars are ceased from the earth. Neither are there any intestine jars remaining; no brother rising up against brother; no country or city divided against itself, and tearing out its own bowels. Civil discord is at an end for evermore, and none is left either to destroy or hurt his neighbour. here is no oppression to "make" even "the wise man mad;" no extortion to "grind the face of the poor;" no robbery or wrong; no rapine or injustice; for all are "content with such things as they possess." Thus "righteousness and peace have kissed each other;" (Ps. 85:10;) they have "taken root and filled the land;" "righteousness flourishing out of the earth;" and "peace looking down from heaven."

4. And with righteousness or justice, mercy is also found. The earth is no longer full of cruel habitations. The Lord hath destroyed both the blood-thirsty and malicious, the envious and revengeful man. Were there any provocation, there is none that now knoweth to return evil for evil; but indeed there is none that doeth evil, no, not one; for all are harmless as doves. And being filled with peace and joy in believing, and united in one body, by one Spirit, they all love as brethren, they are all of one heart and of one soul. "Neither saith any of them, that aught of the things which he possesseth is his own." There is none among them that lacketh: for every man loveth his neighbour as himself. And all walk by one rule: "Whatever ye would that men should do unto you, even so do unto them."

5. It follows, that no unkind word can ever be heard among them, no strife of tongues, no contention of any kind, no railing or evil-speaking, but every one "opens his mouth with wisdom, and in his tongue there is the law of kindness." Equally incapable are they of fraud or guile: their love is without dissimulation: Their words are always the just expression of their thoughts, opening a window into their breast, that whosoever desires may look into their hearts, and see that only love and God are there.

6. Thus, where the Lord Omnipotent taketh to himself his mighty power and reigneth, doth he "subdue all things to himself," cause every heart to overflow with

love, and fill every mouth with praise. "Happy are the people that are in such a case: yea, blessed are the people who have the Lord for their God" (Psalm 144:15.) "Arise, shine;" (saith the Lord;) "for thy light is come, and the glory of the Lord is risen upon thee." "Thou hast known that I the Lord am thy Saviour and thy Redeemer, the mighty God of Jacob. I have made thy officers peace, and thy exactors righteousness. Violence shall no more be heard in thy land, wasting nor destruction within thy borders; but thou shalt call thy walls Salvation and thy gates Praise." "Thy people are all righteous; they shall inherit the land for ever; the branch of my planting, the work of my hands, that I may be glorified." "The sun shall be no more thy light by day; neither for brightness shall the moon give light unto thee: but the Lord shall be unto thee an everlasting light, and thy God thy glory" (Isa. 60:1, 16–19).

IV. Having thus briefly considered Christianity, as beginning, as going on, and as covering the earth, it remains only that I should close the whole with a plain, practical application.

1. And, first, I would ask, Where does this Christianity now exist? Where, I pray, do the Christians live? Which is the country, the inhabitants whereof are all thus filled with the Holy Ghost? —are all of one heart and of one soul? cannot suffer one among them to lack anything, but continually give to every man as he hath need; who, one and all, have the love of God filling their hearts, and constraining them to love their neighbour as themselves; who have all "put on bowels of mercy, humbleness of mind, gentleness, long-suffering?" who offend not in any kind, either by word or deed, against justice, mercy, or truth; but in every point do unto all men; as they would these should do unto them? With what propriety can we term any a Christian country, which does not answer this description? Why then, let us confess we have never yet seen a Christian country upon earth.

2. I beseech you, brethren, by the mercies of God, if ye do account me a madman or a fool, yet, *as a fool bear with me*. It is utterly needful that some one should use great plainness of speech towards you. It is more especially needful at *this* time; for who knoweth but it is the *last*? Who knoweth how soon the righteous Judge may say, "I will no more be entreated for this people?" "Though Noah, Daniel, and Job were in this land, they should but deliver their own souls." And who will use this plainness, if I do not? Therefore I, even I, will speak. And I adjure you, by the living God, that ye steel not your breasts against receiving a blessing at *my* hands. Do not say in your hearts, Non persuadebis, etiamsi persuaseris;" [Your persuasions shall not prevail with us, even though they should really convince us.—EDIT.] or, in other words, "Lord, thou shalt not *send by whom thou wilt send*; let me rather perish in my blood, than be saved by this man!"

3. Brethren, "I am persuaded better things of you, though I thus speak." Let me ask you then, in tender love, and in the spirit of meekness, Is this city a Christian city? Is Christianity, scriptural Christianity, found here? Are we, considered as a community of men, so "filled with the Holy Ghost," as to enjoy in our hearts, and show forth in our lives, the genuine fruits of that Spirit? Are all the Magistrates, all heads and Governors of Colleges and Halls, and their respective Societies (not to speak of the inhabitants of the town), "of one heart "and one soul?" Is "the love of God shed abroad in our hearts?" Are our tempers the same that were in him? And are our lives agreeable thereto? Are we "holy as he who hath called us is holy in all manner of conversation?"

4. I entreat you to observe, that here are no peculiar notions now under consideration; that the question moved is not concerning *doubtful opinions* of one kind or another, but concerning the undoubted, fundamental branches (if there be any such) of our common Christianity. And for the decision thereof, I appeal to your own conscience, guided by the Word of God. he therefore that is not condemned by his own heart, let him go free.

5. In the fear, then, and in the presence of the great God, before whom both you and I shall shortly appear, I pray you that are in authority over us, whom I reverence for your office sake, to consider (and not after the manner of dissemblers with God), are you "filled with the Holy Ghost?" Are you lively portraitures of him whom ye are appointed to represent among men? "I have said, Ye are gods," ye magistrates and rulers; ye are by office so nearly allied to the God of heaven! In your several stations and degrees, ye are to show forth unto us "the Lord our Governor." Are all the thoughts of your hearts, all your tempers and desires, suitable to your high calling? Are all your words like unto those which come out of the mouth of God? Is there in all your actions dignity and love? —a greatness which words cannot express, which can flow only from a heart "full of God;" and yet consistent with the character of "man that is a worm, and the son of man that is a worm?"

6. Ye venerable men, who are more especially called to form the tender minds of youth, to dispel thence the shades of ignorance and error, and train them up to be wise unto salvation, are you "filled with the Holy Ghost?"

with all those "fruits of the Spirit," which your important office so indispensably requires? Is your heart whole with God? full of love and zeal to set up his kingdom on earth? Do you continually remind those under your care, that the one rational end of all our studies, is to know, love and serve "the only true God, and Jesus Christ whom he hath sent?" Do you inculcate upon them day by day, that love alone never faileth (whereas, whether there be tongues, they shall fail, or philosophical knowledge, it shall vanish away); and that without love, all learning is but splendid ignorance, pompous folly, vexation of spirit? Has all you teach an actual tendency to the love of God, and of all mankind for his sake? Have you an eye to this end in whatever you prescribe, touching the kind, the manner, and the measure of their studies; desiring and labouring that, wherever the lot of these young soldiers of Christ is cast, they may be so many burning and shining lights, adorning the gospel of Christ in all things? And permit me to ask, Do you put forth all your strength in the vast work you have undertaken? Do you labour herein with all your might? exerting every faculty of your soul, using every talent which God hath lent you, and that to the uttermost of your power?

7. Let it not be said, that I speak here, as if all under your care were intended to be clergymen. Not so: I only speak as if they were all intended to be Christians. But what example is set them by us who enjoy the beneficence of our forefathers? —by Fellows, Students, Scholars; more especially those who are of some rank and eminence? Do ye, brethren, abound in the fruits of the Spirit, in lowliness of mind, in self-denial and mortification, in seriousness and composure of spirit, in patience, meekness, sobriety, temperance; and in unwearied, restless endeavours to do good in every kind unto all men, to relieve their outward wants, and to bring their souls to the true knowledge and love of God? Is this the general character of Fellows of Colleges? I fear it is not. Rather, have not pride and haughtiness of spirit, impatience and peevishness, sloth and indolence, gluttony and sensuality, and even a proverbial uselessness, been objected to us, perhaps not always by our enemies, nor wholly without ground? O that God would roll away this reproach from us, that the very memory of it might perish for ever!

8. Many of us are more immediately consecrated to God, called to minister in holy things. Are we then patterns to the rest, "in word, in conversation, in charity, in spirit, in faith, in purity" (1 Tim. 4:12)? Is there written on our forehead and on our heart, "Holiness to the Lord?" From what motives did we enter upon this office? Was it indeed with a single eye "to serve God, trusting that we were inwardly moved by the Holy Ghost to take upon us this ministration, for the promoting of his glory, and the edifying of his people?" And have we "clearly determined, by God's grace, to give ourselves wholly to this office?" Do we forsake and set aside, as much as in us lies, all worldly cares and studies? Do we apply ourselves wholly to this one thing, and draw all our cares and studies this way? Are we apt to teach? Are we taught of God, that we may be able to teach others also? Do we know God? Do we know Jesus Christ? Hath "God revealed his Son in us?" And hath he "made us able ministers of the new covenant?" Where then are the "seals of our apostleship?" Who, that were dead in trespasses and sins, have been quickened by our word? Have we a burning zeal to save souls from death, so that for their sake we often forget even to eat our bread? Do we speak plain, "by manifestation of the truth commending ourselves to every man's conscience in the sight of God" (2 Cor. 4:2)? Are we dead to the world, and the things of the world, "laying up all our treasure in heaven?" Do we lord over God's heritage? Or are we the least, the servants of all? When we bear the reproach of Christ, does it sit heavy upon us? Or do we rejoice therein? When we are smitten on the one cheek, do we resent it? Are we impatient of affronts? Or do we turn the other also; not resisting the evil, but overcoming evil with good? Have we a bitter zeal, inciting us to strive sharply and passionately with them that are out of the way? Or is our zeal the flame of love, so as to direct all our words with sweetness, lowliness, and meekness of wisdom?

9. Once more: what shall we say concerning the youth of this place? Have you either the form or the power of Christian godliness? Are you humble, teachable, advisable; or stubborn, self-willed, heady, and highminded? Are you obedient to your superiors as to parents? Or do you despise those to whom you owe the tenderest reverence? Are you diligent in your easy business, pursuing your studies with all your strength? Do you redeem the time, crowding as much work into every day as it can contain? Rather, are ye not conscious to yourselves, that you waste away day after day, either in reading what has no tendency to Christianity, or in gaming, or in—you know not what? Are you better managers of your fortune than of your time? Do you, out of principle, take care to owe no man anything? Do you "remember the Sabbath day, to keep it holy;" to spend it in the more immediate worship of God? When you are in his house, do you consider that God is there? Do you behave "as seeing him

that is invisible?" Do you know how to possess your bodies in sanctification and honour?" Are not drunkenness and uncleanness found among you? Yea, are there not of you who "glory in their shame?" Do not many of you "take the name of God in vain," perhaps habitually, without either remorse or fear? Yea, are there not a multitude of you that are forsworn? I fear, a swiftly-increasing multitude. Be not surprised, brethren. Before God and this congregation, I own myself to have been of the number, solemnly swearing to observe all those customs, which I then knew nothing of; and those statutes, which I did not so much as read over, either then, or for some years after. What is perjury, if this is not? But if it be, O what a weight of sin, yea, sin of no common dye, lieth upon us! And doth not the Most High regard it?

10. May it not be one of the consequences of this, that so many of you are a generation of triflers; triflers with God, with one another, and with your own souls? For, how few of you spend, from one week to another, a single hour in private prayer! How few have any thought of God in the general tenor of your conversation! Who of you is in any degree acquainted with the work of his Spirit, his supernatural work in the souls of men? Can you bear, unless now and then in a church, any talk of the Holy Ghost? Would you not take it for granted, if one began such a conversation, that it was either hypocrisy or enthusiasm? In the name of the Lord God Almighty, I ask, what religion are you of? Even the talk of Christianity, ye cannot, will not bear. O my brethren, what a Christian city is this! "It is time for Thee, Lord, to lay to Thine hand!"

11. For, indeed, what probability, what possibility, rather (speaking after the manner of men), is there that Christianity, scriptural Christianity, should be again the religion of this place? that all orders of men among us should speak and live as men "filled with the Holy Ghost?" By whom should this Christianity be restored? By those of you that are in authority? Are you convinced then that this is scriptural Christianity? Are you desirous it should be restored? And do ye not count your fortune, liberty, life, dear unto yourselves, so ye may be instrumental in the restoring of it? But suppose ye have this desire, who hath any power proportioned to the effect? Perhaps some of you have made a few faint attempts, but with how small success! Shall Christianity then be restored by young, unknown, inconsiderable men? I know not whether ye yourselves could suffer it. Would not some of you cry out, "Young man, in so doing thou reproachest us?" But there is no danger of your being put to the proof; so hath iniquity overspread us like a flood. Whom then shall God send? —the famine, the pestilence (the last messengers of God to a guilty land), or the sword, "the armies of the" Romish "aliens," to reform us into our first love? Nay, "rather let us fall into thy hand, O Lord, and let us not fall into the hand of man." Lord, save, or we perish! Take us out of the mire, that we sink not! O help us against these enemies! for vain is the help of man. Unto thee all things are possible. According to the greatness of thy power, preserve thou those that are appointed to die; and preserve us in the manner that seemeth to thee good; not as we will, but as thou wilt!

SERMON 5: JUSTIFICATION BY FAITH.

> "To him that worketh not, but believeth on him that justifieth the ungodly, his faith is counted for righteousness." Romans 4:5.

1. How a sinner may be justified before God, the Lord and Judge of all, is a question of no common importance to every child of man. It contains the foundation of all our hope, inasmuch as while we are at enmity with God, there can be no true peace, no solid joy, either in time or in eternity. What peace can there be, while our own heart condemns us; and much more, He that is "greater than our heart, and knoweth all things?" What solid joy, either in this world or that to come, while "the wrath of God abideth on us?"

2. And yet how little hath this important question been understood! What confused notions have many had concerning it! Indeed, not only confused, but often utterly false; contrary to the truth, as light to darkness; notions absolutely inconsistent with the oracles of God, and with the whole analogy of faith. And hence, erring concerning the very foundation, they could not possibly build thereon; at least, not "gold, silver, or precious stones," which would endure when tried as by fire; but only "hay and stubble," neither acceptable to God, nor profitable to man.

3. In order to justice, in far as in me lies, to the vast importance of the subject, to save those that seek the truth in sincerity from "vain jangling and strife of words," to clear the confusedness of thought into which so many have already been led thereby, and to give them true and just conceptions of this great mystery of godliness, I shall endeavour to show,

First. What is the general ground of this whole doctrine of justification.

Secondly. What justification is.

Thirdly. Who they are that are justified. And,

Fourthly. On what terms they are justified. I. I am, First, to show, what is the general ground of this whole doctrine of justification.

1. In the image of God was man made, holy as he that created him is holy; merciful as the Author of all is merciful; perfect as his Father in heaven is perfect. As God is love, so man, dwelling in love, dwelt in God, and God in him. God made him to be an "image of his own eternity," an incorruptible picture of the God of glory. He was accordingly pure, as God is pure, from every spot of sin. He knew not evil in any kind or degree, but was inwardly and outwardly sinless and undefiled. He "loved the Lord his God with all his heart, and with all his mind, and soul, and strength."

2. To man thus upright and perfect, God gave a perfect law, to which he required full and perfect obedience. He required full obedience in every point, and this to be performed without any intermission, from the moment man became a living soul, till the time of his trial should be ended. No allowance was made for any falling short: As, indeed, there was no need of any; man being altogether equal to the task assigned, and thoroughly furnished for every good word and work.

3. To the entire law of love which was written in his heart, (against which, perhaps, he could not sin directly,) it seemed good to the sovereign wisdom of God to superadd one positive law: "Thou shalt not eat of the fruit of the tree that groweth in the midst of the garden;" annexing that penalty thereto, "In the day that thou eatest thereof, thou shalt surely die."

4. Such, then, was the state of man in Paradise. By the free, unmerited love of God, he was holy and happy: He knew, loved, enjoyed God, which is, in substance, life everlasting. And in this life of love, he was to continue for ever, if he continued to obey God in all things; but, if he disobeyed him in any, he was to forfeit all. "In that day," said God, "thou shalt surely die."

5. Man did disobey God. He "ate of the tree, of which God commanded him, saying, Thou shalt not eat of it." And in that day he was condemned by the righteous judgment of God. Then also the sentence whereof he was warned before, began to take place upon him. For the moment he tasted that fruit, he died. His soul died, was separated from God; separate from whom the soul has no more life than the body has when separate from the soul. His body, likewise, became corruptible and mortal; so that death then took hold on this also. And being already dead in spirit, dead to God, dead in sin, he hastened on to death everlasting; to the destruction both of body and soul, in the fire never to be quenched

6. Thus "by one man sin entered into the world, and death by sin. And so death passed upon all men," as being contained in him who was the common father and representative of us all. Thus, "through the offence of one," all are dead, dead to God, dead in sin, dwelling in a corruptible, mortal body, shortly to be dissolved, and under the sentence of death eternal. For as, "by one man's disobedience," all "were made sinners;" so, by that offence of one, "judgment came upon all men to condemnation." (Romans v. 12)

7. In this state we were, even all mankind, when "God so loved the world, that he gave his only-begotten Son, to the end we might not perish, but have everlasting life." In the fullness of time he was made Man, another common Head of mankind, a second general Parent and Representative of the whole human race. And as such it was that "he bore our griefs," "the Lord laying upon him the iniquities of us all." Then was he "wounded for our transgressions, and bruised for our iniquities." "He made his soul an offering for sin:" He poured out his blood for the transgressors: He "bare our sins in his own body on the tree," that by his stripes we might be healed: And by that one oblation of himself, once offered, he hath redeemed me and all mankind; having thereby "made a full, perfect, and sufficient sacrifice and satisfaction for the sins of the whole world."

8. In consideration of this, that the Son of God hath "tasted death for every man," God hath now "reconciled the world to himself, not imputing to them their" former "trespasses." And thus, "as by the offence of one judgment came upon all men to condemnation, even so by the righteousness of one the free gift came upon all men unto justification." So that, for the sake of his well-beloved Son, of what he hath done and suffered for us, God now vouchsafes, on one only condition, (which himself also enables us to perform,) both to remit the punishment due to our sins, to reinstate us in his favour, and to restore our dead souls to spiritual life, as the earnest of life eternal.

9. This, therefore, is the general ground of the whole doctrine of justification. By the sin of the first Adam, who was not only the father, but likewise the representative, of us all, we all fell short of the favour of God; we all became children of wrath; or, as the Apostle expresses it, "judgment came upon all men to condemnation." Even so, by the sacrifice for sin made by the Second Adam, as the

Representative of us all, God is so far reconciled to all the world, that he hath given them a new covenant; the plain condition whereof being once fulfilled, "there is no more condemnation" for us, but "we are justified freely by his grace, through the redemption that is in Jesus Christ."

II. 1. But what is it to be "justified?" What is "justification?" This was the Second thing which I proposed to show. And it is evident, from what has been already observed, that it is not the being made actually just and righteous. This is "sanctification;" which is, indeed, in some degree, the immediate fruit of justification, but, nevertheless, is a distinct gift of God, and of a totally different nature. The one implies what God does for us through his Son; the other, what he works in us by his Spirit. So that, although some rare instances may be found, wherein the term "justified" or "justification" is used in so wide a sense as to include "sanctification" also; yet, in general use, they are sufficiently distinguished from each other, both by St. Paul and the other inspired writers.

2. Neither is that far-fetched conceit, that justification is the clearing us from accusation, particularly that of Satan, easily provable from any clear text of holy writ. In the whole scriptural account of this matter, as above laid down, neither that accuser nor his accusation appears to be at all taken in. It can not indeed be denied, that he is the "accuser" of men, emphatically so called. But it does in nowise appear, that the great Apostle hath any reference to this, more or less, in all he hath written touching justification, either to the Romans or the Galatians.

3. It is also far easier to take for granted, than to prove from any clear scripture testimony, that justification is the clearing us from the accusation brought against us by the law: At least if this forced, unnatural way of speaking mean either more or less than this, that, whereas we have transgressed the law of God, and thereby deserved the damnation of hell, God does not inflict on those who are justified the punishment which they had deserved.

4. Least of all does justification imply, that God is deceived in those whom he justifies; that he thinks them to be what, in fact, they are not; that he accounts them to be otherwise than they are. It does by no means imply, that God judges concerning us contrary to the real nature of things; that he esteems us better than we really are, or believes us righteous when we are unrighteous. Surely no. The judgment of the all-wise God is always according to truth. Neither can it ever consist with his unerring wisdom, to think that I am innocent, to judge that I am righteous or holy, because another is so. He can no more,

in this manner, confound me with Christ, than with David or Abraham. Let any man to whom God hath given understanding, weigh this without prejudice; and he cannot but perceive, that such a notion of justification is neither reconcilable to reason nor Scripture.

5. The plain scriptural notion of justification is pardon, the forgiveness of sins. It is that act of God the Father, hereby, for the sake of the propitiation made by the blood of his Son, he "showeth forth his righteousness (or mercy) by the remission of the sins that are past." This is the easy, natural account of it given by St. Paul, throughout this whole epistle. So he explains it himself, more particularly in this and in the following chapter. Thus, in the next verses but one to the text, "Blessed are they," saith he, "whose iniquities are forgiven, and whose sins are covered: Blessed is the man to whom the Lord will not impute sin." To him that is justified or forgiven, God "will not impute sin" to his condemnation. He will not condemn him on that account, either in this world or in that which is to come. His sins, all his past sins, in thought, word, and deed, are covered, are blotted out, shall not be remembered or mentioned against him, any more than if they had not been. God will not inflict on that sinner what he deserved to suffer, because the Son of his love hath suffered for him. And from the time we are "accepted through the Beloved," "reconciled to God through his blood," he loves, and blesses, and watches over us for good, even as if we had never sinned.

Indeed the Apostle in one place seems to extend the meaning of the word much farther, where he says, "Not the hearers of the law, but the doers of the law, shall be justified." Here he appears to refer our justification to the sentence of the great day. And so our Lord himself unquestionably doth, when he says, "By thy words thou shalt be justified;" proving hereby, that "for every idle word men shall speak, they shall give an account in the day of judgment." But perhaps we can hardly produce another instance of St. Paul's using the word in that distant sense. In the general tenor of his writings, it is evident he doth not; and least of all in the text before us, which undeniably speaks, not of those who have already "finished their course," but of those who are now just "setting out," just beginning to "run the race which is set before them."

III. 1. But this is the third thing which was to be considered, namely, Who are they that are justified? And the Apostle tells us expressly, the ungodly: "He (that is, God) justifieth the ungodly;" the ungodly of every kind and degree; and none but the ungodly. As "they that are righteous need no repentance," so they need no forgiveness. It is only sinners that have any occasion for pardon: It is sin alone which admits of being forgiven. Forgiveness, therefore, has an immediate reference to sin, and, in this respect, to nothing else. It is our "unrighteousness" to which the pardoning God is "merciful:" It is our "iniquity" which he "remembereth no more."

2. This seems not to be at all considered by those who so vehemently contend that a man must be sanctified, that is, holy, before he can be justified; especially by such of them as affirm, that universal holiness or obedience must precede justification. (Unless they mean that justification at the last day, which is wholly out of the present question.) So far from it, that the very supposition is not only flatly impossible, (for where there is no love of God, there is no holiness, and there is no love of God but from a sense of his loving us,) but also grossly, intrinsically absurd, contradictory to itself. For it is not a saint but a sinner that is forgiven, and under the notion of a sinner. God justifieth not the godly, but the ungodly; not those that are holy already, but the unholy. Upon what condition he doeth this, will be considered quickly: but whatever it is, it cannot be holiness. To assert this, is to say the Lamb of God takes away only those sins which were taken away before.

3. Does then the good Shepherd seek and save only those that are found already? No: He seeks and saves that which is lost. He pardons those who need his pardoning mercy. He saves from the guilt of sin, (and, at the same time, from the power,) sinners of every kind, of every degree: men who, till then, were altogether ungodly; in whom the love of the Father was not; and, consequently, in whom dwelt no good thing, no good or truly Christian temper, —but all such as were evil and abominable, —pride, anger, love of the world, —the genuine fruits of that "carnal mind" which is "enmity against God."

4. These who are sick, the burden of whose sins is intolerable, are they that need a Physician; these who are guilty, who groan under the wrath of God, are they that need a pardon. These who are "condemned already," not only by God, but also by their own conscience, as by a thousand witnesses, of all their ungodliness, both in thought, and word, and work, cry aloud for Him that "justifieth the ungodly," through the redemption that is in Jesus; —the ungodly, and "him that worketh not;" that worketh not, before he is justified, anything that is good, that is truly virtuous or holy, but only evil continually. For his heart is necessarily, essentially evil, till the love of God is shed abroad therein. And while the tree is corrupt, so are the fruits; "for an evil tree cannot bring forth good fruit."

5. If it be objected, "Nay, but a man, before he is justified, may feed the hungry, or clothe the naked; and these are good works;" the answer is easy: He may do these, even before he is justified; and these are, in one sense, "good works;" they are "good and profitable to men." But it does not follow, that they are, strictly speaking, good in themselves, or good in the sight of God. All truly "good works" (to use the words of our Church) "follow after justification;" and they are therefore good and "acceptable to God in Christ," because they "spring out of a true and living faith." By a parity of reason, all "works done before justification are not good," in the Christian sense, "forasmuch as they spring not of faith in Jesus Christ;" (though from some kind of faith in God they may spring;) "yea, rather, for that they are not done as God hath willed and commanded them to be done, we doubt not" (how strange soever it may appear to some) "but they have the nature of sin."

6. Perhaps those who doubt of this have not duly considered the weighty reason which is here assigned, why no works done before justification can be truly and properly good. The argument plainly runs thus: —

No works are good, which are not done as God hath willed and commanded them to be done.

But no works done before justification are done as God hath willed and commanded them to be done:

Therefore, no works done before justification are good.

The first proposition is self-evident; and the second, that no works done before justification are done as God hath willed and commanded them to be done, will appear equally plain and undeniable, if we only consider, God hath willed and commanded that "all our works" should "be done in charity;" (en agape) in love, in that love to God which produces love to all mankind. But none of our works can be done in this love, while the love of the Father (of God as our Father) is not in us; and this love can not be in us till we receive the Spirit of Adoption, crying in , our hearts, Abba, Father. If, therefore, God doth not justify the ungodly, and him that (in this sense) worketh not, then hath Christ died in vain; then, notwithstanding his death, can no flesh living be justified.

IV. 1. But on what terms, then, is he justified who is altogether "ungodly," and till that time "worketh not?" on one alone; which is faith: he "believeth is him that justifieth the ungodly." And "he that believeth is not condemned;" yea, he is "passed from death unto life." "For the righteousness (or mercy) of God is by faith of Jesus Christ unto all and upon all them that believe: Whom God hath set forth for a propitiation, through faith in his blood; that he might be just, and" (consistently with his justice) "the Justifier of him which believeth in Jesus:" "Therefore we conclude that a man is justified by faith without the deeds of the law;" without previous obedience to the moral law, which, indeed, he could not, till now, perform. That it is the moral law, and that alone, which is here intended, appears evidently from the words that follow: "Do we then make void the law through faith? God forbid: Yea, we establish the law. What law do we establish by faith? Not the ritual law: Not the ceremonial law of Moses. In nowise; but the great, unchangeable law of love, the holy love of God and of our neighbour."

2. Faith in general is a divine, supernatural "elegchos," "evidence" or "conviction," "of things not seen," not discoverable by our bodily senses, as being either past, future, or spiritual. Justifying faith implies, not only a divine evidence or conviction that "God was in Christ, reconciling the world unto himself;" but a sure trust and confidence that Christ died for "my" sins, that he loved "me," and gave himself for "me." And at what time soever a sinner thus believes, be it in early childhood, in the strength of his years, or when he is old and hoary-haired, God justifieth that ungodly one: God, for the sake of his Son, pardoneth and absolveth him, who had in him, till then, no good thing. Repentance, indeed, God had given him before; but that repentance was neither more nor less than a deep sense of the want of all good, and the presence of all evil. And whatever good he hath, or doeth, from that hour when he first believes in God through Christ, faith does not "find," but "bring." This is the fruit of faith. First the tree is good, and then the fruit is good also.

3. I cannot describe the nature of this faith better than in the words of our own Church: "The only instrument of salvation" (whereof justification is one branch) "is faith; that is, a sure trust and confidence that God both hath and will forgive our sins, that he hath accepted us again into His favour, for the merits of Christ's death and passion. —But here we must take heed that we do not halt with God, through an inconstant, wavering faith: Peter, coming to Christ upon the water, because he fainted in faith, was in danger of drowning; so we, if we begin to waver or doubt, it is to be feared that we shall sink as Peter did, not into the water, but into the bottomless pit of hell fire." ("Second Sermon on the Passion")

"Therefore, have a sure and constant faith, not only that the death of Christ is available for all the world, but that he hath made a full and sufficient sacrifice for "thee," a perfect cleansing of "thy" sins, so that thou mayest say, with the Apostle, he loved "thee," and gave himself for "thee." For this is to make Christ "thine own," and to apply his merits unto "thyself." ("Sermon on the Sacrament, First Part")

4. By affirming that this faith is the term or "condition of justification," I mean, First, that there is no justification without it. "He that believeth not is condemned already;" and so long as he believeth not, that condemnation cannot be removed, but "the wrath of God abideth on him." As "there is no other name given under heaven," than that of Jesus of Nazareth, no other merit whereby a condemned sinner can ever be saved from the guilt of sin; so there is no other way of obtaining a share in his merit, than "by faith in his name." So that as long as we are without this faith, we are "strangers to the covenant of promise," we are "aliens from the commonwealth of Israel, and without God in the world." Whatsoever virtues (so called) a man may have, —I speak of those unto whom the gospel is preached; for "what have I to do to judge them that are without?" —whatsoever good works (so accounted) he may do, it profiteth not; he is still a "child of wrath," still under the curse, till he believes in Jesus.

5. Faith, therefore, is the "necessary" condition of justification; yea, and the "only necessary" condition thereof. This is the Second point carefully to be observed; that, the very moment God giveth faith (for "it is the gift of God") to the "ungodly" that "worketh not," that "faith is counted to him for righteousness." He hath no righteousness at all, antecedent to this, not so much as negative righteousness, or innocence. But "faith is imputed to him for righteousness," the very moment that he believeth. Not that God (as was observed before) thinketh him to be what he is not. But as "he made Christ to be sin for us," that is, treated him as a sinner, punishing him for our sins; so he counteth us righteous, from the time we believe in him: That is, he doth not punish us for our sins; yea, treats us as though we are guiltless and righteous.

6. Surely the difficulty of assenting to this proposition, that "faith is the "only condition" of justification," must arise from not understanding it. We mean thereby thus

much, that it is the only thing without which none is justified; the only thing that is immediately, indispensably, absolutely requisite in order to pardon. As, on the one hand, though a man should have every thing else without faith, yet he cannot be justified; so, on the other, though he be supposed to want everything else, yet if he hath faith, he cannot but be justified. For suppose a sinner of any kind or degree, in a full sense of his total ungodliness, of his utter inability to think, speak, or do good, and his absolute meetness for hell-fire; suppose, I say, this sinner, helpless and hopeless, casts himself wholly on the mercy of God in Christ, (which indeed he cannot do but by the grace of God,) who can doubt but he is forgiven in that moment? Who will affirm that any more is "indispensably required" before that sinner can be justified?

Now, if there ever was one such instance from the beginning of the world, (and have there not been, and are there not, ten thousand times ten thousand?) it plainly follows, that faith is, in the above sense, the sole condition of justification.

7. It does not become poor, guilty, sinful worms, who receive whatsoever blessings they enjoy, (from the least drop of water that cools our tongue, to the immense riches of glory in eternity,) of grace, of mere favour, and not of debt, to ask of God the reasons of his conduct. It is not meet for us to call Him in question "who giveth account to none of his ways;" to demand, "Why didst thou make faith the condition, the only condition, of justification? Wherefore didst thou decree, "He that believeth," and he only, "shall be saved?" This is the very point on which St. Paul so strongly insists in the ninth chapter of this Epistle, viz., That the terms of pardon and acceptance must depend, not on us, but "on him that calleth us;" that there is no "unrighteousness with God," in fixing his own terms, not according to ours, but his own good pleasure; who may justly say, "I will have mercy on whom I will have mercy;" namely, on him who believeth in Jesus. "So then it is not of him that willeth, nor of him that runneth," to choose the condition on which he shall find acceptance; "but of God that showeth mercy;" that accepteth none at all, but of his own free love, his unmerited goodness. "Therefore hath he mercy on whom he will have mercy," viz., on those who believe on the Son of his love; "and whom he will," that is, those who believe not, "he hardeneth," leaves at last to the hardness of their hearts.

8. One reason, however, we may humbly conceive, of God's fixing this condition of justification, "If thou believest in the Lord Jesus Christ, thou shalt be saved," was to "hide pride from man." Pride had already destroyed the very angels of God, had cast down "a third part of the stars of heaven." It was likewise in great measure owing to this, when the tempter said, "Ye shall be as gods," that Adam fell from his own steadfastness, and brought sin and death into the world. It was therefore an instance of wisdom worthy of God, to appoint such a condition of reconciliation for him and all his posterity as might effectually humble, might abase them to the dust. And such is faith. It is peculiarly fitted for this end: For he that cometh unto God by this faith, must fix his eye singly on his own wickedness, on his guilt and helplessness, without having the least regard to any supposed good in himself, to any virtue or righteousness whatsoever. He must come as a "mere sinner," inwardly and outwardly, self-destroyed and self-condemned, bringing nothing to God but ungodliness only, pleading nothing of his own but sin and misery. Thus it is, and thus alone, when his "mouth is stopped," and he stands utterly "guilty before" God, that he can "look unto Jesus," as the whole and sole "Propitiation for his sins." Thus only can he be "found in him," and receive the "righteousness which is of God by faith."

9. Thou ungodly one, who hearest or readest these words! thou vile, helpless, miserable sinner! I charge thee before God, the Judge of all, go straight unto him, with all thy ungodliness. Take heed thou destroy not thy own soul by pleading thy righteousness, more or less. Go as altogether ungodly, guilty, lost, destroyed, deserving and dropping into hell; and thou shalt then find favour in his sight, and know that he justifieth the ungodly. As such thou shalt be brought unto the "blood of sprinkling," as an undone, helpless, damned sinner. Thus "look unto Jesus!" There is "the Lamb of God," who "taketh away thy sins!" Plead thou no works, no righteousness of thine own! no humility, contrition, sincerity! In nowise. That were, in very deed, to deny the Lord that bought thee. No: Plead thou, singly, the blood of the covenant, the ransom paid for thy proud, stubborn, sinful soul. Who art thou, that now seest and feelest both thine inward and outward ungodliness? Thou art the man! I want thee for my Lord! I challenge "thee" for a child of God by faith! The Lord hath need of thee. Thou who feelest thou art just fit for hell, art just fit to advance his glory; the glory of his free grace, justifying the ungodly and him that worketh not. O come quickly! Believe in the Lord Jesus; and thou, even thou, art reconciled to God.

SERMON 6: THE RIGHTEOUSNESS OF FAITH.

"Moses describeth the righteousness which is of the law, That the man which doeth those things shall live by them. But the righteousness which is of faith speaketh on this wise, Say not in thine heart, Who shall ascend into heaven? (that is, to bring Christ down from above:) Or, Who shall descend into the deep? (that is, to bring up Christ again from the dead.) But what saith it? The word is nigh thee, even in thy mouth, and in thy heart: That is, the word of faith, which we preach." Rom. 10:5–8.

1. The Apostle does not here oppose the covenant given by Moses, to the covenant given by Christ. If we ever imagined this, it was for want of observing, that the latter as well as the former part of these words were spoken by Moses himself to the people of Israel, and that concerning the covenant which then was. (Deut. 30:11, 12, 14.) But it is the covenant of grace, which God, through Christ, hath established with men in all ages, (as well before and under the Jewish dispensation, as since God was manifest in the flesh,) which St. Paul here opposes to the covenant of works, made with Adam while in Paradise, but commonly supposed to be the only covenant which God had made with man, particularly by those Jews of whom the Apostle writes.

2. Of these it was that he so affectionately speaks in the begin-fling of this chapter: "My heart's desire and prayer to God for Israel is, that they may be saved. For I bear them record, that they have a zeal for God, but not according to knowledge. For they being ignorant of God's righteousness," (of the justification that flows from his mere grace and mercy, freely forgiving our sins through the Son of his love, through the redemption which is in Jesus,) "and seeking to establish their own righteousness," (their own holiness, antecedent to faith in "him that justifieth the ungodly," as the ground of their pardon and acceptance,) "have not submitted themselves unto the righteousness of God," and consequently seek death in the error of their life.

3. They were ignorant that "Christ is the end of the law for righteousness to every one that believeth;" — that, by the oblation of himself once offered, he had put an end to the first law or covenant, (which, indeed, was not given by God to Moses, but to Adam in his state of innocence,) the strict tenor whereof, without any abatement, was, "Do this, and live;" and, at the same time, purchased for us that better covenant," Believe, and live;" believe, and thou shalt be saved; now saved, both from the guilt and power of sin, and, of consequence, from the wages of it.

4. And how many are equally ignorant now, even among those who are called by the name of Christ! How many who have now a "zeal for God," yet have it not "according to knowledge;" but are still seeking "to establish their own righteousness," as the ground of their pardon and acceptance; and therefore, vehemently refuse to "submit themselves unto the righteousness of God!" Surely my heart's desire, and prayer to God for you, brethren, is, that ye may be saved. And, in order to remove this grand stumbling-block out of your way, I will endeavour to show, First, what the righteousness *is*, which is of the law; and what "the righteousness which is of faith;" Secondly, the folly of trusting in the righteousness of the law, and the wisdom of submitting to that which is of faith.

I. 1. And, First, "the righteousness which is of the law saith, The man which doeth these things shall live by them." Constantly and perfectly observe all these things to do them, and then thou shalt live for ever. This law, or covenant, (usually called the Covenant of Works,) given by God to man in Paradise, required an obedience perfect in all its parts, entire and wanting nothing, as the condition of his eternal continuance in the holiness and happiness wherein he was created.

2. It required that man should fulfil all righteousness, inward and outward, negative and positive: That he should not only abstain from every idle word, and avoid every evil work, but should keep every affection, every desire, every thought, in obedience to the will of God: That he should continue holy, as he which had created him was holy, both in heart, and in all manner of conversation: That he should be pure in heart, even as God is pure; perfect as his Father in heaven was perfect: That he should love the Lord his God with all his heart, with all his soul, with all his mind, and with all his strength; that he should love every soul which God had made, even as God had loved him: That by this universal benevolence, he should dwell in God, (who is love,) and God in him: That he should serve the Lord his God with all his strength, and in all things singly aim at his glory.

3. These were the things which the righteousness of the law required, that he who did them might live thereby. But it farther required, that this entire obedience to God,

this inward and outward holiness, this conformity both of heart and life to his will, should be perfect in *degree*. No abatement, no allowance could possibly be made, for falling short in any degree, as to any jot or tittle, either of the outward or the inward law. If every commandment, relating to outward things, was obeyed, yet that was not sufficient unless every one was obeyed with all the strength, in the highest measure, and most perfect manner. Nor did it answer the demand of this covenant, to love God with every power and faculty, unless he were loved with the full capacity of each, with the whole possibility of the soul.

4. One thing more was indispensably required by the righteousness of the law, namely, that this universal obedience, this perfect holiness both of heart and life, should be perfectly uninterrupted also, should continue without any intermission, from the moment wherein God created man, and breathed into his nostrils the breath of life, until the days of his trial should be ended, and he should be confirmed in life everlasting.

5. The righteousness, then, which is of the law, speaketh on this wise: "Thou, O man of God, stand fast in love, in the image of God wherein thou art made. If thou wilt remain in life, keep the commandments, which are now written in thy heart. Love the Lord thy God with all thy heart. Love, as thyself, every soul that he hath made. Desire nothing but God. Aim at God in every thought, in every word and work. Swerve not, in one motion of body or soul, from him, thy mark, and the prize of thy high calling; and let all that is in thee praise his holy name, every power and faculty of thy soul, in every kind, in every degree, and at every moment of thine existence. 'This do, and thou shalt live:' Thy light shall shine, thy love shall flame more and more, till thou art received up into the house of God in the heavens, to reign with him for ever and ever."

6. "But the righteousness which is of faith speaketh on this wise: Say not in thine heart, Who shall ascend into heaven? that is, to bring down Christ from above;" (as though it were some impossible task which God required thee previously to perform in order to thine acceptance;) "or, Who shall descend into the deep? that is, to bring up Christ from the dead;" (as though that were still remaining to be done, for the sake of which thou wert to be accepted;) "but what saith it? The word," according to the tenor of which thou mayest now be accepted as an heir of life eternal, "is nigh thee, even in thy mouth, and in thy heart; that is, the word of faith which we preach;" — the new covenant which God hath now established with sinful man, through Christ Jesus.

7. By "the righteousness which is of faith" is meant, that condition of justification, (and, in consequence, of present and final salvation, if we endure therein unto the end,) which was given by God to *fallen man*, through the merits and mediation of his only-begotten Son. This was in part revealed to Adam, soon after his fall; being contained in the original promise, made to him and his seed, concerning the Seed of the Woman, who should "bruise the serpent's head." (Gen. 3:15.) It was a little more clearly revealed to Abraham, by the angel of God from heaven, saying, "By myself have I sworn, saith the Lord, that in thy seed shall all the nations of the world be blessed." (Gen. 12:15, 18.) It was yet more fully made known to Moses, to David, and to the Prophets that followed; and, through them, to many of the people of God in their respective generations. But still the bulk even of these were ignorant of it; and very few understood it clearly. Still "life and immortality" were not so "brought to light" to the Jews of old, as they are now unto us "by the gospel."

8. Now, this covenant saith not to sinful man, "Perform unsinning obedience, and live." If this were the term, he would have no more benefit by all which Christ hath done and suffered for him, than if he was required, in order to life, to "ascend into heaven, and bring down Christ from above;" or to "descend into the deep," into the invisible world, and "bring up Christ from the dead." It doth not require any impossibility to be done: (Although to mere man, what it requires would be impossible; but not to man assisted by the Spirit of God:) This were only to mock human weakness. Indeed, strictly speaking, the covenant of *grace* doth not require us to *do* anything at all, as absolutely and indispensably necessary in order to our justification; but only, to *believe* in Him who, for the sake of his Son, and the propitiation which he hath made, "justifieth the ungodly that worketh not," and imputes his faith to him for righteousness. Even so Abraham "believed in the Lord, and he counted it to him for righteousness." (Gen. 15:6.) "And he received the sign of circumcision, a seal of the righteousness of faith, — that he might be the father of all them that believe, — that righteousness might be imputed unto them also." (Rom. 4:11.) "Now it was not written for his sake alone, that it," *i.e.,* faith, "was imputed to him; but for us also, to whom it shall be imputed," to whom faith shall be imputed for righteousness, shall stand in the stead of perfect obedience, in order to our acceptance with God, "if we believe

on him who raised up Jesus our Lord from the dead; who was delivered" to death "for our offences, and was raised again for our justification:" (Rom. 4:23–25:) For the assurance of the remission of our sins, and of a second life to come, to them that believe.

9. What saith then the covenant of forgiveness, of unmerited love, of pardoning mercy? "Believe in the Lord Jesus Christ, and thou shalt be saved." In the day thou believest, thou shalt surely live. Thou shalt be restored to the favour of God; and in his pleasure is life. Thou shalt be saved from the curse, and from the wrath of God. Thou shalt be quickened, from the death of sin into the life of righteousness. And if thou endure to the end, believing in Jesus, thou shalt never taste the second death; but, having suffered with thy Lord, shalt also live and reign with him for ever and ever.

10. Now, "this word is nigh thee." This condition of life is plain, easy, always at hand. "It is in thy mouth, and in thy heart," through the operation of the Spirit of God. The moment "thou believest in thine heart" in him whom God "hath raised from the dead," and "confessest with thy mouth the Lord Jesus," as *thy* Lord and *thy* God, "thou shalt be saved" from condemnation, from the guilt and punishment of thy former sins, and shalt have power to serve God in true holiness all the remaining days of thy life.

11. What is the difference then between the "righteousness which is of the law," and the "righteousness which is of faith ? — between the first covenant, or the covenant of works, and the second, the covenant of grace? The essential, unchangeable difference is this: The one supposes him to whom it is given to be already holy and happy, created in the image and enjoying the favour of God; and prescribes the condition whereon he may continue therein, in love and joy, life and immortality: The other supposes him to whom it is given to be now unholy and unhappy, fallen short of the glorious image of God, having the wrath of God abiding on him, and hastening, through sin, whereby his soul is dead, to bodily death, and death everlasting; and to man in this state it prescribes the condition whereon he may regain the pearl he has lost, may recover the favour and image of God, may retrieve the life of God in his soul, and be restored to the knowledge and the love of God, which is the beginning of life eternal.

12. Again: The covenant of works, in order to man's *continuance* in the favour of God, in his knowledge and love, in holiness and happiness, required of perfect man a *perfect* and uninterrupted *obedience* to every point of the law of God. Whereas, the covenant of grace, in order to man's *recovery* of the favour and the life of God, requires only *faith;* living faith in Him who, through God, justifies him that obeyed not.

13. Yet, again: The covenant of works required of Adam and all his children, to pay the price themselves, in consideration of which they were to receive all the future blessings of God. But, in the covenant of grace, seeing we have nothing to pay, God "frankly forgives us all:" Provided only, that we believe in Him who hath paid the price for us; who hath given himself a "Propitiation for our sins, for the sins of the whole world."

14. Thus the first covenant required what is now *afar off* from all the children of men; namely, unsinning obedience, which is far from those who are "conceived and born in sin." Whereas, the second requires what is nigh at hand; as though it should say, "Thou art sin! God is love! Thou by sin art fallen short of the glory of God; yet there is mercy with him. Bring then all thy sins to the pardoning God, and they shall vanish away as a cloud. If thou wert not ungodly, there would be no room for him to justify thee as ungodly. But now draw near, in full assurance of faith. He speaketh, and it is done. Fear not, only believe; for even the just God justifieth all that believe in Jesus."

II. 1. These things considered, it would be easy to show, as I proposed to do in the Second place, the folly of trusting in the "righteousness which is of the law," and the wisdom of submitting to "the righteousness which is of faith."

The folly of those who still trust in the "righteousness which is of the law," the terms of which are, "Do this, and live," may abundantly appear from hence: They set out wrong; their very first step is a fundamental mistake: For, before they can ever think of claiming any blessing on the terms of this covenant, they must suppose themselves to be in his state with whom this covenant was made. But how vain a supposition is this; since it was made with Adam in a state of innocence! How weak, therefore, must that whole building be, which stands on such a foundation! And how foolish are they who thus build on the sand! who seem never to have considered, that the covenant of works was not given to man when he was "dead in trespasses and sins," but when he was alive to God, when he knew no sin, but was holy as God is holy; who forget, that it was never designed for the *recovery* of the favour and life of God once lost, but only for the *continuance* and increase thereof, till it should be complete in life everlasting.

2. Neither do they consider, who are thus seeking to establish their "own righteousness, which is of the law," what manner of obedience or righteousness that is which the law indispensably requires. It must be perfect and entire in every point, or it answers not the demand of the law. But which of you is able to perform such obedience; or, consequently, to live thereby? Who among you fulfils every jot and tittle even of the outward commandments of God? doing nothing, great or small, which God forbids? leaving nothing undone which he enjoins? speaking no *idle word?* having your conversation always "meet to minister grace to the hearers?" and, "whether you eat or drink, or whatever you do, doing all to the glory of God?" And how much less are you able to fulfil all the inward commandments of God! those which require that every temper and motion of your soul should be holiness unto the Lord! Are you able to "love God with all your heart?" to love all mankind as your own soul? to "pray without ceasing? in every thing to give thanks?" to have God always before you? and to keep every affection, desire, and thought, in obedience to his law?

3. You should farther consider, that the righteousness of the law requires, not only the obeying every command of God, negative and positive, internal and external, but likewise in the perfect degree. In every instance whatever, the voice of the law is, "Thou shalt serve the Lord thy God with all thy strength." It allows no abatement of any kind: It excuses no defect: It condemns every coming short of the full measure of obedience, and immediately pronounces a curse on the offender: It regards only the invariable rules of justice, and saith, "I know not to show mercy."

4. Who then can appear before such a Judge, who is "extreme to mark what is done amiss?" How weak are they who desire to be tried at the bar where "no flesh living can be justified!" — none of the offspring of Adam. For, suppose we did now keep every commandment with all our strength; yet one single breach which ever was, utterly destroys our whole claim to life. If we have ever offended in any one point, this righteousness is at an end. For the law condemns all who do not perform uninterrupted as well as perfect obedience. So that, according to the sentence of this, for him who hath once sinned, in any degree, "there remaineth only a fearful looking for of fiery indignation, which shall devour the adversaries" of God.

5. Is it not then the very foolishness of folly, for fallen man to seek life by this righteousness? for man, who was "shapen in wickedness, and in sin did his mother conceive him?" man, who is, by nature, all "earthly, sensual, devilish;" altogether corrupt and abominable;" in whom, till he find grace, "dwelleth no good thing;" nay, who cannot of himself think one good thought; who is indeed all sin, a mere lump of ungodliness, and who commits sin in every breath he draws; whose actual transgressions, in word and deed, are more in number than the hairs of his head? What stupidity, what senselessness must it be for such an unclean, guilty, helpless worm as this, to dream of seeking acceptance by his own righteousness, of living by "the righteousness which is of the law!"

6. Now, whatsoever considerations prove the folly of trusting in the "righteousness which is of the law," prove equally the wisdom of submitting to the "righteousness which is of God by faith." This were easy to be shown with regard to each of the preceding considerations. But, to wave this, the wisdom of the first step hereto, the disclaiming our own righteousness, plainly appears from hence, that it is acting according to truth, to the real nature of things. For, what is it more, than to acknowledge, with our heart as well as lips, the true state wherein we are? to acknowledge that we bring with us into the world a corrupt, sinful nature; more corrupt, indeed, than we can easily conceive, or find words to express? that hereby we are prone to all that is evil, and averse from all that is good; that we are full of pride, self will, unruly passions, foolish desires, vile and inordinate affections; lovers of the world, lovers of pleasure more than lovers of God? that our lives have been no better than our hearts, but many ways ungodly and unholy; insomuch that our actual sins, both in word and deed, have been as the stars of heaven for multitude; that, on all these accounts, we are displeasing to Him who is of purer eyes than to behold iniquity, and deserve nothing from him but indignation and wrath and death, the due wages of sin? that we cannot, by any of our righteousness, (for indeed we have none at all,) nor by any of our works, (for they are as the tree upon which they grow,) appease the wrath of God, or avert the punishment we have justly deserved; yea, that, if left to ourselves, we shall only wax worse and worse, sink deeper and deeper into sin, offend God more and more, both with our evil works, and with the evil tempers of our carnal mind, till we fill up the measure of our iniquities, and bring upon ourselves swift destruction? And is not this the very state wherein by nature we are? To acknowledge this, then, both with our heart and lips, that is, to disclaim our own righteousness, "the righteousness which is of the law," is to act accord-

ing to the real nature of things, and, consequently, is an instance of true wisdom.

7. The wisdom of submitting to "the righteousness of faith" appears farther, from this consideration, that it is the righteousness of God: I mean here, it is that method of reconciliation with God which hath been chosen and established by God himself, not only as he is the God of wisdom, but as he is the sovereign Lord of heaven and earth, and of every creature which he hath made. Now, as it is not meet for man to say unto God, "What doest thou?" — as none who is not utterly void of understanding, will contend with One that is mightier than he, with Him whose kingdom ruleth over all; so it is true wisdom, it is a mark of sound understanding, to acquiesce in whatever he hath chosen; to say in this, as in all things, "It is the Lord: Let him do what seemeth him good."

8. It may be farther considered, that it was of mere grace, of free love, of undeserved mercy, that God hath vouchsafed to sinful man any way of reconciliation with himself, that we were not cut away from his hand, and utterly blotted out of his remembrance. Therefore, whatever method he is pleased to appoint, of his tender mercy, of his unmerited goodness, whereby his enemies, who have so deeply revolted from him, so long and obstinately rebelled against him, may still find favour in his sight, it is doubtless our wisdom to accept it with all thankfulness.

9. To mention but one consideration more. It is wisdom to aim at the best end by the best means. Now the best end which any creature can pursue is, happiness in God. And the best end a fallen creature can pursue is, the recovery of the favour and image of God. But the best, indeed the only, means under heaven given to a man, whereby he may regain the favour of God, which is better than life itself, or the image of God, which is the true life of the soul, is the submitting to the "righteousness which is of faith," the believing in the only-begotten Son of God.

III. 1. Whosoever therefore thou art, who desirest to be forgiven and reconciled to the favour of God, do not say in thy heart, "I must *first do this;* I must *first* conquer every sin; break off every evil word and work, and do all good to all men; or, I must *first* go to church, receive the Lord's Supper, hear more sermons, and say more prayers." Alas, my brother! Thou art clean gone out of the way. Thou art still "ignorant of the righteousness of God," and art "seeking to establish thy own righteousness," as the ground of thy reconciliation. Knowest thou not, that thou canst do nothing but sin, till thou art reconciled to God? Wherefore, then, dost thou say," I must do this and this *first,* and then I shall believe?" Nay, but *first believe!* Believe in the Lord Jesus Christ, the Propitiation for thy sins. Let this good foundation first be laid, and then thou shalt do all things well.

2. Neither say in thy heart, "I cannot be accepted yet, because I am not *good enough.*" Who is *good enough* — who ever was — to merit acceptance at God's hands? Was ever any child of Adam *good enough* for this? or will any till the consummation of all things? And as for thee, thou art not good at all: There dwelleth in thee no good thing. And thou never wilt be, till thou believe in Jesus. Rather, thou wilt find thyself worse and worse. But is there any need of being worse, in order to be accepted? Art thou not *bad enough* already? Indeed thou art, and that God knoweth. And thou thyself canst not deny it. Then delay not. All things are now ready. "Arise, and wash away thy sins." The fountain is open. Now is the time to wash thee white in the blood of the Lamb. Now he shall "purge" thee as "with hyssop," and thou shalt "be clean:" He shall "wash" thee, and thou shalt "be whiter than snow."

3. Do not say, "But I am not *contrite enough:* I am not *sensible enough* of my sins." I know it. I would to God thou wert more *sensible* of them, more *contrite* a thousand fold than thou art. But do not stay for this. It may be, God will make thee so, not before thou believest, but by believing. It may be, thou wilt not weep much till thou lovest much because thou hast had much forgiven. In the mean time, look unto Jesus. Behold, how he loveth thee! What could he have done more for thee which he hath not done?

> O Lamb of God, was ever pain,
> Was ever love like thine?
> Look steadily upon him, till he looks on thee,
> and breaks thy hard heart. Then shall thy "head"
> be "waters," and thy "eyes fountains of tears."

4. Nor yet do thou say, "I must *do* something more *before* I come to Christ." I grant, supposing thy Lord should delay his coming, it were meet and right to wait for his appearing, in doing, so far as thou hast power, whatsoever he hath commanded thee. But there is no necessity for making such a supposition. How knowest thou that he will delay? Perhaps he will appear, as the dayspring from on high, before the morning light. O do not set him a time! Expect him every hour. Now he is nigh! even at the door!

5. And to what end wouldest thou wait for *more sincerity, before* thy sins are blotted out? to make thee more

worthy of the grace of God? Alas, thou art still "establishing thy own righteousness." He will have mercy, not because thou art worthy of it, but because his compassions fail not; not because thou art righteous, but because Jesus Christ hath atoned for thy sins.

Again, if there be anything good in *sincerity*, why dost thou expect it *before* thou hast faith? — seeing faith itself is the only root of whatever is really good and holy.

Above all, how long wilt thou forget, that whatsoever thou doest, or whatsoever thou hast, before thy sins are forgiven thee, it avails nothing with God toward the procuring of thy forgiveness? yea, and that it must all be cast behind thy back, trampled under foot, made no account of, or thou wilt never find favour in God's sight; because, until then, thou canst not ask it, as a mere sinner, guilty, lost, undone, having nothing to plead, nothing to offer to God, but only the merits of his well-beloved Son, "who loved *thee*, and gave himself for *thee!*"

6. To conclude. Whosoever thou art, O man, who hast the sentence of death in thyself, who feelest thyself a condemned sinner, and hast the wrath of God abiding on thee: Unto thee saith the Lord, not, "Do this," — perfectly obey all my commands, — "and live;" but, "Believe in the Lord Jesus Christ, and thou shalt be saved." "The word of faith is nigh unto thee:" Now, at this instant, in the present moment, and in thy present state, sinner as thou art, just as thou art, believe the gospel; and "I will be merciful unto *thy* unrighteousness, and *thy* iniquities will I remember no more."

SERMON 7: THE WAY TO THE KINGDOM.

"The kingdom of God is at hand: repent ye, and believe the gospel." Mark 1:15

These words naturally lead us to consider, First, the nature of true religion, here termed by our Lord, "the kingdom of God," which, saith he, "is at hand;" and, Secondly, the way thereto, which he points out in those words, "Repent ye, and believe the gospel."

I. 1. We are, First, to consider the nature of true religion, here termed by our Lord, "the kingdom of God." The same expression the great Apostle uses in his Epistle to the Romans, where he likewise explains his Lord's words, saying, "The kingdom of God is not meat and drink; but righteousness, and peace, and joy in the Holy Ghost." (Rom. 14:17.)

2. "The kingdom of God," or true religion, "is not meat and drink." It is well known that not only the unconverted Jews, but great numbers of those who had received the faith of Christ, were, notwithstanding "zealous of the law," (Acts 21:20,) even the ceremonial law of Moses. Whatsoever, therefore, they found written therein, either concerning meat and drink offerings, or the distinction between clean and unclean meats, they not only observed themselves, but vehemently pressed the same even on those "among the Gentiles" (or heathens) "who were turned to God;" yea, to such a degree, that some of them taught, wheresoever they came among them, "Except ye be circumcised, and keep the law," (the whole ritual law,) "ye cannot be saved." (Acts 15:1, 24.)

3. In opposition to these, the Apostle declares, both here and in many other places, that true religion does not consist in *meat* and *drink*, or in any ritual observances; nor, indeed in any outward thing whatever; in anything exterior to the heart; the whole substance thereof lying in "righteousness, peace, and joy in the Holy Ghost."

4. Not in any *outward thing;* such as *forms,* or *ceremonies,* even of the most excellent kind. Supposing these to be ever so decent and significant, ever so expressive of inward things: supposing them ever so helpful, not only to the vulgar, whose thought reaches little farther than their sight; but even to men of understanding, men of strong capacities, as doubtless they may sometimes be: Yea, supposing them, as in the case of the Jews, to be appointed by God himself; yet even during the period of time wherein that appointment remains in force, true religion does not principally consist therein; nay, strictly speaking, not at all. How much more must this hold concerning such rites and forms as are only of human appointment! The religion of Christ rises infinitely higher, and lies immensely deeper, than all these. These are good in their place; just so far as they are in fact subservient to true religion. And it were superstition to object against them, while they are applied only as occasional helps to human weakness. But let no man carry them farther. Let no man dream that they have any intrinsic worth; or that religion cannot subsist without them. This were to make them an abomination to the Lord.

5. The nature of religion is so far from consisting in these, in forms of worship, or rites and ceremonies, that it does not properly consist in any outward actions, of what kind so ever. It is true, a man cannot have any religion who is guilty of vicious, immoral actions; or who does to others what he would not they should do to him, if he

were in the same circumstance. And it is also true, that he can have no real religion who "knows to do good, and doth it not." Yet may a man both abstain from outward evil, and do good, and still have no religion. Yea, two persons may do the same outward work; suppose, feeding the hungry, or clothing the naked; and, in the meantime, one of these may be truly religious, and the other have no religion at all: For the one may act from the love of God, and the other from the love of praise. So manifest it is, that although true religion naturally leads to every good word and work, yet the real nature thereof lies deeper still, even in "the hidden man of the heart."

6. I say of *the heart*. For neither does religion consist Orthodoxy, or right opinions; which, although they are not properly outward things, are not in the heart, but the understanding. A man may be orthodox in every point; he may not only espouse right opinions, but zealously defend them against all opposers; he may think justly concerning the incarnation of our Lord, concerning the ever-blessed Trinity, and every other doctrine contained in the oracles of God; he may assent to all the three creeds, — that called the Apostles', the Nicene, and the Athanasian; and yet it is possible he may have no religion at all, no more than a Jew, Turk, or pagan. He may be almost as orthodox — as the devil, (though, indeed, not altogether; for every man errs in something; whereas we can't well conceive him to hold any erroneous opinion,) and may, all the while be as great a stranger as he to the religion of the heart.

7. This alone is religion, truly so called: This alone is in the sight of God of great price. The Apostle sums it all up in three particulars, "righteousness, and peace, and joy in the Holy Ghost." And, First, *righteousness*. We cannot be at a loss concerning this, if we remember the words of our Lord, describing the two grand branches thereof, on which "hang all the law and the prophets;" "Thou shalt love the Lord thy God with all thy heart, and with all thy mind, and with all thy soul, and with all thy strength: This is the first and great commandment;" (Mark 12:30;) the first and great branch of Christian righteousness. Thou shalt delight thyself in the Lord thy God; thou shalt seek and find all happiness in him. He shall be "thy shield, and thy exceeding great reward," in time and in eternity. All thy bones shall say, "Whom have I in heaven but thee? And there is none upon earth that I desire beside thee!" Thou shalt hear and fulfil His word who saith, "My son, give me thy heart." And, having given him thy heart, thy inmost soul, to reign there without a rival, thou mayest well cry out, in the fullness of thy heart, "I will love thee, O Lord, my strength. The Lord is my strong rock, and my defence; my Saviour, my God, and my might, in whom I will trust; my buckler, the horn also of my salvation, and my refuge."

8. And the second commandment is like unto this; the Second great branch of Christian righteousness is closely and inseparably connected therewith; even, "Thou shalt love thy neighbour as thyself." *Thou shalt love,* — thou shalt embrace with the most tender good-will, the most earnest and cordial affection, the most inflamed desires of preventing or removing all evil, and of procuring for him every possible good, — *Thy neighbour;* — that is, not only thy friend, thy kinsman, or thy acquaintance; not only the virtuous, the friendly, him that loves thee, that prevents or returns thy kindness; but every child of man, every human creature, every soul which God hath made; not excepting him whom thou never hast seen in the flesh, whom thou knowest not, either by face or name; not excepting him whom thou knowest to be evil and unthankful, him that still despitefully uses and persecutes thee: Him thou shalt love *as thyself;* with the same invariable thirst after his happiness in every kind; the same unwearied care to screen him from whatever might grieve or hurt either his soul or body.

9. Now is not this love "the fulfilling of the law?" the sum of all Christian righteousness? — of all inward righteousness; for it necessarily implies "bowels of mercies, humbleness of mind," (seeing "love is not puffed up,") "gentleness, meekness, long-suffering:" (for love "is not provoked;" but "believeth, hopeth, endureth all things:") And of all outward righteousness; for "love worketh no evil to his neighbour," either by word or deed. It cannot willingly hurt or grieve any one. And it is zealous of good works. Every lover of mankind, as he hath opportunity, "doth good unto all men," being (without partiality and without hypocrisy) "full of mercy and good fruits."

10. But true religion, or a heart right toward God and man, implies happiness as well as holiness. For it is not only "righteousness," but also "peace and joy in the Holy Ghost." What peace? "The peace of God," which God only can give, and the world cannot take away; the peace which "passeth all under-standing," all barely rational conception; being a supernatural sensation, a divine taste, of "the powers of the world to come;" such as the natural man knoweth not, how wise soever in the things of this world; nor, indeed, can he know it, in his present state, "because it is spiritually discerned." It is a peace that

banishes all doubt, all painful uncertainty; the Spirit of God bearing witness with the spirit of a Christian, that he is "a child of God." And it banishes fear, all such fear as hath torment; the fear of the wrath of God; the fear of hell; the fear of the devil; and, in particular, the fear of death: he that hath the peace of God, desiring, if it were the will of God, "to depart, and to be with Christ."

11. With this peace of God, wherever it is fixed in the soul, there is also "joy in the Holy Ghost;" joy wrought in the heart by the Holy Ghost, by the ever-blessed Spirit of God. He it is that worketh in us that calm, humble rejoicing in God, through Christ Jesus, "by whom we have now received the atonement," katallagen, the reconciliation with God; and that enables us boldly to confirm the truth of the royal Psalmists declaration, Blessed is the man (or rather, *happy*) whose unrighteousness is forgiven, and whose sin is covered. he it is that inspires the Christian soul with that even, solid joy, which arises from the testimony of the Spirit that he is a child of God; and that gives him to rejoice with joy unspeakable, in hope of the glory of God; hope both of the glorious image of God, which is in part and shall be fully "revealed in him;" and of that crown of glory which fadeth not away, reserved in heaven for him.

12. This holiness and happiness, joined in one, are sometimes styled, in the inspired writings, "the kingdom of God," (as by our Lord in the text,) and sometimes, "the kingdom of heaven." It is termed "the kingdom of God," because it is the immediate fruit of Gods reigning in the soul. So soon as ever he takes unto himself his mighty power, and sets up his throne in our hearts, they are instantly filled with this "righteousness, and peace, and joy in the holy Ghost." It is called "the kingdom of heaven" because it is (in a degree) heaven opened in the soul. For whosoever they are that experience this, they can aver before angels and men,

everlasting life is won,
Glory is on earth begun,

according to the constant tenor of Scripture, which everywhere bears record, God "hath given unto us eternal life, and this life is in his Son. he that hath the Son" (reigning in his heart) "hath life," even life everlasting. (1 John 5:11, 12.) For "this is life eternal, to know thee, the only true God, and Jesus Christ, whom thou hast sent." (John 17:3.) And they, to whom this is given, may confidently address God, though they were in the midst of a fiery furnace,

Thee, Lord, safe shielded by thy power,
Thee, Son of God, Jehovah, we adore;
In form of man descending to appear:
To thee be ceaseless hallelujahs given,
Praise, as in heaven thy throne, we offer here;
For where thy presence is displayed, is heaven.

13. And this "kingdom of God," or of heaven, "is at hand." As these words were originally spoken, they implied that "the time" was then fulfilled, God being "made manifest in the flesh," when he would set up his kingdom among men, and reign in the hearts of his people. And is not the time now fulfilled? For, "Lo! (saith he,) I am with you always," you who preach remission of sins in my name, "even unto the end of the world." (Matt. 28:20.) Wheresoever, therefore, the gospel of Christ is preached, this his "kingdom is nigh at hand." It is not far from every one of you. Ye may this hour enter thereinto, if so be ye hearken to his voice, "Repent ye, and believe the gospel."

II. 1. This is the way: walk ye in it. And, First, "repent;" that is, know yourselves. This is the first repentance, previous to faith; even conviction, or self-knowledge. Awake, then, thou that sleepest. Know thyself to be a sinner, and what manner of sinner thou art. Know that corruption of thy inmost nature, whereby thou art very far gone from original righteousness, whereby "the flesh lusteth" always "contrary to the Spirit," through that "carnal mind" which "is enmity against God," which "is not subject to the law of God, neither indeed can be." Know that thou art corrupted in every power, in every faculty of thy soul; that thou art totally corrupted in every one of these, all the foundations being out of course. The eyes of thine understanding are darkened, so that they cannot discern God, or the things of God. The clouds of ignorance and error rest upon thee, and cover thee with the shadow of death. Thou knowest nothing yet as thou oughtest to know, neither God, nor the world, nor thyself. Thy will is no longer the will of God, but is utterly perverse and distorted, averse from all good, from all which God loves, and prone to all evil, to every abomination which God hateth. Thy affections are alienated from God, and scattered abroad over all the earth. All thy passions, both thy desires and aversions, thy joys and sorrows, thy hopes and fears, are out of frame, are either undue in their degree, or placed on undue objects. So that there is no soundness in thy soul; but "from the crown of the head, to the sole of the foot," (to use the strong expression of the Prophet,) there are only "wounds, and bruises, and putrefying sores."

2. Such is the inbred corruption of thy heart, of thy very inmost nature. And what manner of branches canst thou expect to grow from such an evil root? Hence springs unbelief; ever departing from the living God; saying, "Who is the Lord, that I should serve him? Tush! Thou, God, carest not for it." Hence independence; affecting to be like the Most High. Hence pride, in all its forms; teaching thee to say, "I am rich, and increased in goods, and have need of nothing." From this evil fountain flow forth the bitter streams of vanity, thirst of praise, ambition, covetousness, the lust of the flesh, the lust of the eye, and the pride of life. From this arise anger, hatred, malice, revenge, envy, jealousy, evil surmisings: From this, all the foolish and hurtful lusts that now "pierce thee through with many sorrows," and if not timely prevented, will at length drown thy soul in everlasting perdition.

3. And what fruits can grow on such branches as these? only such as are bitter and evil continually. of pride cometh contention, vain boasting, seeking and receiving praise of men, and so robbing God of that glory which he cannot give unto another. of the lust of the flesh, come gluttony or drunkenness, luxury or sensuality, fornication, uncleanness; variously defiling that body which was designed for a temple of the Holy Ghost: of unbelief, every evil word and work. But the time would fail, shouldst thou reckon up all; all the idle words thou hast spoken, provoking the Most High, grieving the Holy One of Israel; all the evil works thou hast done, either wholly evil in themselves, or, at least, not done to the glory of God. For thy actual sins are more than thou art able to express, more than the hairs of thy head. Who can number the sands of the sea, or the drops of rain, or thy iniquities?

4. And knowest thou not that "the wages of sin is death?" death, not only temporal, but eternal. "The soul that sinneth, it shall die;" for the mouth of the Lord hath spoken it." It shall die the second death. This is the sentence, to "be punished" with never-ending death, "with everlasting destruction from the presence of the Lord, and from the glory of his power." Knowest thou not that every sinner, enochos estai eis ten geennan tou pyros, not properly, "is in danger of hell-fire" is far too weak; but rather, "is under the sentence of hell-fire;" doomed already, just dragging to execution. Thou art guilty of everlasting death. It is the just reward of thy inward and outward wickedness. It is just that the sentence should now take place. Dost thou see, dost thou feel this? Art thou thoroughly convinced that thou deservest God's wrath, and everlasting damnation? Would God do thee no wrong, if he now commanded the earth to open, and swallow thee up? if thou wert now to go down quick into the pit, into the fire that never shall be quenched? If God hath given thee truly to repent, thou hast a deep sense that these things are so; and that it is of his mere mercy thou art not consumed, swept away from the face of the earth.

5. And what wilt thou do to appease the wrath of God, to atone for all thy sins, and to escape the punishment thou hast so justly deserved? Alas, thou canst do nothing; nothing that will in anywise make amends to God for one evil work, or word, or thought. If thou couldst now do all things well, if from this very hour, till thy soul should return to God thou couldst perform perfect, uninterrupted obedience, even this would not atone for what is past. The not increasing thy debt would not discharge it. It would still remain as great as ever. Yea, the present and future obedience of all the men upon earth, and all the angels in heaven, would never make satisfaction to the justice of God for one single sin. How vain, then, was the thought of atoning for thy own sins, by anything thou couldest do! It costeth far more to redeem one soul, than all mankind is able to pay. So that were there no other help for a guilty sinner, without doubt he must have perished everlastingly.

6. But suppose perfect obedience, for the time to come, could atone for the sins that are past, this would profit thee nothing; for thou art not able to perform it; no, not in any one point. Begin now: Make the trial. Shake off that outward sin that so easily besetteth thee. Thou canst not. How then wilt thou change thy life from all evil to all good? Indeed, it is impossible to be done, unless first thy heart be changed. For, so long as the tree remains evil, it cannot bring forth good fruit. But art thou able to change thy own heart, from all sin to all holiness? to quicken a soul that is dead in sin, — dead to God and alive only to the world? No more than thou art able to quicken a dead body, to raise to life him that lieth in the grave. Yea, thou art not able to quicken thy soul in any degree, no more than to give any degree of life to the dead body. Thou canst do nothing, more or less, in this matter; thou art utterly without strength. To be deeply sensible of this, how helpless thou art, as well as how guilty and how sinful, — this is that "repentance not to be repented of," which is the forerunner of the kingdom of God.

7. If to this lively conviction of thy inward and outward sins, of thy utter guiltiness and helplessness, there be added suitable affections, —sorrow of heart, for having despised thy own mercies, — remorse, and self-condemnation, having thy mouth stopped, — shame

to lift up thine eyes to heaven, — fear of the wrath of God abiding on thee, of his curse hanging over thy head, and of the fiery indignation ready to devour those who forget God, and obey not our Lord Jesus Christ, — earnest desire to escape from that indignation, to cease from evil, and learn to do well; — then I say unto thee, in the name of the Lord, "Thou art not far from the kingdom of God." One step more and thou shalt enter in. Thou dost "repent." Now, "believe the gospel."

8. *The gospel,* (that is, good tidings, good news for guilty, helpless sinners,) in the largest sense of the word, means, the whole revelation made to men by Jesus Christ; and sometimes the whole account of what our Lord did and suffered while he tabernacled among men. The substance of all is, "Jesus Christ came into the world to save sinners;" or, "God so loved the world that he gave his only-begotten Son, to the end we might not perish, but have everlasting life;" or, "He was bruised for our transgressions, he was wounded for our iniquities; the chastisement of our peace was upon him; and with his stripes we are healed."

9. *Believe* this, and the kingdom of God is thine. By faith thou attainest the promise. "He pardoneth and absolveth all that truly repent, and unfeignedly believe his holy gospel." As soon as ever God hath spoken to thy heart, "Be of good cheer, thy sins are forgiven thee," his kingdom comes: Thou hast "righteousness, and peace, and joy in the Holy Ghost."

10. Only beware thou do not deceive thy own soul with regard to the nature of this faith. It is not, as some have fondly conceived, a bare assent to the truth of the Bible, of the articles of our creed, or of all that is contained in the Old and New Testament. The devils believe this, as well as I or thou! And yet they are devils still. But it is, over and above this, a sure trust in the mercy of God, through Christ Jesus. It is a confidence in a pardoning God. It is a divine evidence or conviction that "God was in Christ, reconciling the world to himself, not imputing to them their" former "trespasses;" and, in particular, that the Son of God hath loved *me,* and given himself for *me;* and that I, even I, am now reconciled to God by the blood of the cross.

11. Dost thou thus believe? Then the peace of God is in thy heart, and sorrow and sighing flee away. Thou art no longer in doubt of the love of God; it is clear as the noon-day sun. Thou criest out, "My song shall be always of the loving-kindness of the Lord: With my mouth will I ever be telling of thy truth, from one generation to another." Thou art no longer afraid of hell, or death, or him that had once the power of death, the devil; no, nor painfully afraid of God himself; only thou hast a tender, filial fear of offending him. Dost thou believe? Then thy "soul doth magnify the Lord," and thy "spirit rejoiceth in God thy Saviour." Thou rejoicest in that thou hast "redemption through his blood, even the forgiveness of sins." Thou rejoicest in that "Spirit of adoption," which crieth in thy heart, "Abba, Father!" Thou rejoicest in a "hope full of immortality;" in reaching forth unto the "mark of the prize of thy high calling;" in an earnest expectation of all the good things which God hath prepared for them that love him.

12. Dost thou now believe? Then "the love of God is" now "shed abroad in thy heart." Thou lovest him, because he first loved us. And because thou lovest God, thou lovest thy brother also. And being filled with "love, peace, joy," thou art also filled with "long-suffering, gentleness, fidelity, goodness, meekness, temperance," and all the other fruits of the same Spirit; in a word, with whatever dispositions are holy, are heavenly or divine. For while thou "beholdest with open," uncovered "face" (the veil now being taken away) "the glory of the Lord," his glorious love, and the glorious image wherein thou wast created, thou art "changed into the same image, from glory to glory, by the Spirit of the Lord."

13. This repentance, this faith, this peace, joy, love, this change from glory to glory, is what the wisdom of the world has voted to be madness, mere enthusiasm, utter distraction. But thou, O man of God, regard them not; be thou moved by none of these things. Thou knowest in whom thou hast believed. See that no man take thy crown. Whereunto thou hast already attained, hold fast, and follow, till thou attain all the great and precious promises. And thou who hast not yet known him, let not vain men make thee ashamed of the gospel of Christ. Be thou in nothing terrified by those who speak evil of the things which they know not. God will soon turn thy heaviness into joy. O let not thy hands hang down! Yet a little longer, and he will take away thy fears, and give thee the spirit of a sound mind. He is nigh "that justifieth: Who is he that condemneth? It is Christ that died, yea rather, that rose again, who is even now at the right hand of God, making intercession" for thee.

"Now cast thyself on the Lamb of God, with all thy sins, how many soever they be; and "an entrance shall" now "be ministered unto thee, into the kingdom of our Lord and Saviour Jesus Christ!"

SERMON 8: THE FIRST FRUITS OF THE SPIRIT.

"There is therefore now no condemnation to them which are in Christ Jesus, who walk not after the flesh, but after the Spirit." Rom. 8:1.

1. By "them which are in Christ Jesus," St. Paul evidently means, those who truly believe in him; those who, "being justified by faith, have peace with God through our Lord Jesus Christ." They who thus believe do no longer "walk after the flesh," no longer follow the motions of corrupt nature, but "after the Spirit"; both their thoughts, words, and works are under the direction of the blessed Spirit of God.

2. "There is therefore now no condemnation to" these. There is no condemnation to them from God; for he hath *justified* them "freely by his grace, through the redemption that is in Jesus." he hath forgiven all their iniquities, and blotted out all their sins. And there is no condemnation to them from within; for they "have received, not the spirit of the world, but the Spirit which is of God; that they might know the things which are freely given to them of God" (1 Cor. 2:12); which Spirit "beareth witness with their spirits, that they are the children of God." And to this is added the testimony of their conscience, "that in simplicity and godly sincerity, not with fleshly wisdom, but by the grace of God, they have had their conversation in the world" (2 Cor. 1:12).

3. But because this scripture has been so frequently misunderstood, and that in so dangerous a manner; because such multitudes of "unlearned and unstable men" (*hoi amatheis kai asteriktoi*, men untaught of God, and consequently unestablished in the truth which is after godliness) have wrested it to their own destruction; I propose to show, as clearly as I can, first who those are which are in Christ Jesus, and walk not after the flesh, but after the Spirit: and, secondly, how there is no condemnation to these. I shall conclude with some practical inferences.

I. 1. First, I am to show, who those are that "are in Christ Jesus." And are they not those who believe in his name? those who are "found in him, not having their own righteousness, but the righteousness which is of God by faith?" these, "who have redemption through his blood," are properly said to be *in him*; for they dwell in Christ, and Christ in them. They are joined unto the Lord in one Spirit. They are ingrafted into him as branches into the vine. They are united, as members to their head, in a manner which words cannot express, nor could it before enter into their hearts to conceive.

2. Now "whosoever abideth in him, sinneth not"; "walketh not after the flesh." The flesh, in the usual language of St. Paul, signifies corrupt nature. In this sense he uses the word, writing to the Galatians, "The works of the flesh are manifest" (Gal. 5:19); and a little before, "Walk in the Spirit, and ye shall not fulfil the lust" (or desire) "of the flesh" (v. 16). To prove which, namely, that those who "walk by the Spirit, "do not "fulfil the lusts of the flesh," he immediately adds, "For the flesh lusteth against the Spirit, and the Spirit lusteth against the flesh (for these are contrary to each other); that ye may not do the things which ye would." So the words are literally translated; *hina me ha an thelete, tauta poiete*, not, "So that ye cannot do the things that ye would"; as if the flesh overcame the Spirit: a translation which hath not only nothing to do with the original text of the Apostle, but likewise makes his whole argument nothing worth; yea, asserts just the reverse of what he is proving.

3. They who are of Christ, who abide in him, "have crucified the flesh with its affections and lusts." They abstain from all those works of the flesh; from "adultery and fornication"; from "uncleanness and lasciviousness"; from "idolatry, witchcraft, hatred, variance" from "emulations, wrath, strife, sedition, heresies, envyings, murders, drunkenness, revellings"; from every design, and word, and work, to which the corruption of nature leads. Although they feel the root of bitterness in themselves, yet are they endued with power from on high to trample it continually under foot, so that it cannot "spring up to trouble them"; insomuch that every fresh assault which they undergo, only gives them fresh occasion of praise, of crying out, "Thanks be unto God, who giveth us the victory through Jesus Christ our Lord."

4. They now "walk after the Spirit," both in their hearts and lives. They are taught of him to love God and their neighbour, with a love which is as "a well of water, springing up into everlasting life." And by him they are led into every holy desire, into every divine and heavenly temper, till every thought which arises in their heart is holiness unto the Lord.

5. They who "walk after the Spirit," are also led by him into all holiness of conversation. Their "speech is always in grace, seasoned with salt"; with the love and fear of God. "No corrupt communication comes out of their mouth; but only that which is good," that which is "to the use of edifying," which is "meet to minister grace to

the hearers." And herein likewise do they exercise themselves day and night, to do only the things which please God; in all their outward behaviour to follow him "who left us an example that we might tread in his steps"; in all their intercourse with their neighbour, to walk in justice, mercy, and truth; and "whatsoever they do," in every circumstances of life, to "do all to the glory of God."

6. These are they who indeed "walk after the Spirit." Being filled with faith and with the holy Ghost, they possess in their hearts, and show forth in their lives, in the whole course of their words and actions, the genuine fruits of the Spirit of God, namely, "love, joy, peace, long-suffering, gentleness, goodness, fidelity, meekness, temperance," and whatsoever else is lovely or praiseworthy. "They adorn in all things the gospel of God our Saviour"; and give full proof to all mankind, that they are indeed actuated by the same Spirit "which raised up Jesus from the dead."

II. 1. I proposed to show, in the second place, how "there is no condemnation to them which are" thus "in Christ Jesus," and thus "walk not after the flesh, but after the Spirit."

And, first, to believers in Christ, walking thus, "there is no condemnation" on account of their past sins. God condemneth them not for any of these; they are as though they had never been; they are cast "as a stone into the depth of the sea," and he remembereth them no more. God, having "set forth his Son to be a propitiation "for them, "through faith in his blood," hath declared unto them "his righteousness for the remission of the sins that are past." he layeth therefore none of these to their charge; their memorial is perished with them.

2. And there is no condemnation in their own breast; no sense of guilt, or dread of the wrath of God. They "have the witness in themselves:" they are conscious of their interest in the blood of sprinkling. "They have not received again the spirit of bondage unto fear," unto doubt and racking uncertainty; but they "have received the Spirit of adoption," crying in their heart, "Abba, Father." Thus, being "justified by faith," they have the peace of God ruling in their hearts; flowing from a continual sense of his pardoning mercy, and "the answer of a good conscience toward God."

3. If it be said, "But sometimes a believer in Christ may lose his sight of the mercy of God; sometimes such darkness may fall upon him that he no longer sees him that is invisible, no longer feels that witness in himself of his part in the atoning blood; and then he is inwardly condemned, he hath again "the sentence of death in himself": I answer, supposing it so to be, supposing him not to see the mercy of God, then he is not a believer: For faith implies light, the light of God shining upon the soul. So far, therefore, as any one loses this light, he, for the time, loses his faith. And, no doubt, a true believer in Christ may lose the light of faith; and so far as this is lost, he may, for a time, fall again into condemnation. But this is not the case of them who now "are in Christ Jesus," who now believe in his name. For so long as they believe, and walk after the Spirit, neither God condemns them, nor their own heart.

4. They are not condemned, secondly, for any present sins, for now transgressing the commandments of God. For they do not transgress them: they do not "walk after the flesh, but after the Spirit." This is the continual proof of their "love of God, that they keep his commandments"; even as St. John bears witness. "Whosoever is born of God doth not commit sin. For his seed remaineth in him, and he cannot sin, because he is born of God:" he cannot, so long as that seed of God, that loving, holy faith remaineth in him. So long as "he keepeth himself" herein, "that wicked one toucheth him not." Now it is evident, he is not condemned for the sins which he doth not commit at all. They, therefore, who are thus "led by the Spirit, are not under the law" (Gal. 5:18): not under the curse or condemnation of it; for it condemns none but those who break it. Thus, that law of God, "Thou shalt not steal," condemns none but those who do steal. Thus, "Remember the Sabbath-day to keep it holy," condemns those only who do not keep it holy. But against the fruits of the Spirit "there is no law" (5:23); as the Apostle more largely declares in those memorable words of his former epistle to Timothy: "We know that the law is good, if a man use it lawfully; knowing this," (if, while he uses the law of God, in order either to convince or direct, he know and remember this),hoti dikaio nomos ou keitai, (not, "that the law is not made for a righteous man," but) "that the law does not lie against a righteous man:" it has no force against him, no power to condemn him; "but against the lawless and disobedient, against the ungodly and sinners, against the unholy and profane; according to the glorious gospel of the blessed God." (1 Tim. 1:8, 9, 11).

5. They are not condemned, thirdly, for inward sin, even though it does now remain. That the corruption of nature does still remain, even in those who are the children of God by faith; that they have in them the seeds of pride and vanity, of anger, lust, and evil desire, yea, sin of every kind; is too plain to be denied, being matter of daily

experience. And on this account it is, that St. Paul, speaking to those whom he had just before witnessed to be "in Christ Jesus," (1 Cor. 1:2, 9), to have been "called of God into the fellowship" (or participation) "of his Son Jesus Christ"; yet declares, "Brethren, I could not speak unto you as unto spiritual, but as unto carnal, even as unto babes in Christ" (1 Cor. 3:1): "babes in Christ"; so we see they were "in Christ"; they were believers in a low degree. And yet how much of sin remained in them! of that "carnal mind, which is not subject to the law of God!"

6. And yet, for all this, they are not condemned. Although they feel the flesh, the evil nature, in them; although they are more sensible, day by day, that their "heart is deceitful and desperately wicked"; yet, so long as they do not yield thereto; so long as they give no place to the devil; so long as they maintain a continual war with all sin, with pride, anger, desire, so that the flesh hath not dominion over them, but they still "walk after the Spirit"; "there is no condemnation to them which are in Christ Jesus." God is well pleased with their sincere, though imperfect. obedience; and they "have confidence toward God," knowing they are his, "by the Spirit which he hath given" them. (1 John 3:24).

7. Nay, fourthly, although they are continually convinced of sin cleaving to all they do; although they are conscious of not fulfilling the perfect law, either in their thoughts, or words, or works; although they know they do not love the Lord their God with all their heart, and mind, and soul, and strength; although they feel more or less of pride, or self-will, stealing in, and mixing with their best duties; although even in their more immediate intercourse with God, when they assemble themselves with the great congregation, and when they pour out their souls in secret to him who seeth all the thoughts and intents of the heart, they are continually ashamed of their wandering thoughts, or of the deadness and dulness of their affections; yet there is no condemnation to them still, either from God or from their own heart. The consideration of these manifold defects only gives them a deeper sense, that they have always need of that blood of sprinkling which speaks for them in the ears of God, and that Advocate with the Father "who ever liveth to make intercession for them." So far are these from driving them away from him in whom they have believed, that they rather drive them the closer to him whom they feel the want of every moment. And, at the same time, the deeper sense they have of this want, the more earnest desire do they feel, and the more diligent they are, as they "have received the Lord Jesus, so to walk in him."

8. They are not condemned, fifthly, for sins of infirmity, as they are usually called. Perhaps it were advisable rather to call them *infirmities*: that we may not seem to give any countenance to sin, or to extenuate it in any degree, by thus coupling it with infirmity. But (if we must retain so ambiguous and dangerous an expression), by sins of infirmity I would mean, such involuntary failings as the saying a thing we believe true, though, in fact, it prove to be false; or, the hurting our neighbour without knowing or designing it, perhaps when we designed to do him good. Though these are deviations from the holy, and acceptable, and perfect will of God, yet they are not properly sins, nor do they bring any guilt on the conscience of "them which are in Christ Jesus." They separate not between God and them, neither intercept the light of his countenance; as being no ways inconsistent with their general character of "walking not after the flesh, but after the Spirit."

9. Lastly. "There is no condemnation "to them for anything whatever which it is not in their power to help; whether it be of an inward or outward nature, and whether it be doing something or leaving something undone. For instance, the Lord's Supper is to be administered; but you do not partake thereof. Why do you not? You are confined by sickness; therefore, you cannot help omitting it; and for the same reason you are not condemned. There is no guilt, because there is no choice. As there "is a willing mind, it is accepted according to that a man hath, not according to that he hath not."

10. A believer, indeed, may sometimes be *grieved*: because he cannot do what his soul longs for. He may cry out, when he is detained from worshipping God in the great congregation, "Like as the hart panteth after the water-brooks, so panteth my soul after thee, O God. My soul is athirst for God, yea, even for the living God: When shall I come to appear in the presence of God?" he may earnestly desire (only still saying in his heart, "Not as I will, but as thou wilt") to "go again with the multitude, and bring them forth into the house of God." But still, if he cannot go, he feels no condemnation, no guilt, no sense of God's displeasure; but can cheerfully yield up those desires with, "O my soul, put thy trust in God! for I will yet give him thanks, who is the help of my countenance and my God."

11. It is more difficult to determine concerning those which are usually styled sins of surprise: as when one who commonly in patience possesses his soul, on a sudden and violent temptation, speaks or acts in a manner not consistent with the royal law, "Thou shalt love thy

neighbour as thyself." Perhaps it is not easy to fix a general rule concerning transgressions of this nature. We cannot say, either that men are, or that they are not, condemned for sins of surprise in general: but it seems, whenever a believer is by surprise overtaken in a fault, there is more or less condemnation, as there is more or less concurrence of his will. In proportion as a sinful desire, or word, or action is more or less voluntary, so we may conceive God is more or less displeased, and there is more or less guilt upon the soul.

12. But if so, then there may be some sins of surprise which bring much guilt and condemnation. For, in some instances, our being surprised is owing to some wilful and culpable neglect; or, to a sleepiness of soul which might have been prevented, or shaken off before the temptation came. A man may be previously warned either of God or man, that trials and dangers are at hand; and yet may say in his heart, "A little more slumber, a little more folding of the hands to rest." Now, if such an one afterwards fall, though unawares, into the snare which he might have avoided, —that he fell unawares, is no excuse; he might have foreseen and have shunned the danger. The falling, even by surprise, in such an instance as this, is, in effect, a wilful sin; and, as such, must expose the sinner to condemnation, both from God and his own conscience.

13. On the other hand, there may be sudden assaults, either from the world, or the god of this world, and frequently from our own evil hearts, which we did not, and hardly could, foresee. And by these even a believer, while weak in faith, may possibly be borne down, suppose into a degree of anger, or thinking evil of another, with scarce any concurrence of his will. Now in such a case, the jealous God would undoubtedly show him that he had done foolishly. He would be convinced of having swerved from the perfect law, from the mind which was in Christ, and consequently, *grieved* with a godly sorrow, and lovingly *ashamed* before God. Yet need he not come into condemnation. God layeth not folly to his charge, but hath compassion upon him, "even as a father pitieth his own children." And his heart condemneth him not: in the midst of that sorrow and shame he can still say, "I will trust and not be afraid; for the Lord Jehovah is my strength and my song; he also is become my salvation."

III. 1. It remains only to draw some practical inferences from the preceding considerations. And, first, if there be "no condemnation to them which are in Christ Jesus," and "walk not after the flesh , but after the Spirit," on account of their past sin; then why art thou fearful, O thou of little faith? Though thy sins were once more in number than the sand, what is that to thee, now thou art in Christ Jesus? "Who shall lay anything to the charge of God's elect? It is God that justifieth: Who is he that condemneth?" all the sins thou hast committed from thy youth up, until the hour when thou wast "accepted in the Beloved," are driven away as chaff, are gone, are lost, swallowed up, remembered no more. Thou art now "born of the Spirit:" wilt thou be troubled or afraid of what is done before thou wert born? Away with thy fears! thou art not called to fear, but to the "spirit of love and of a sound mind." know thy calling! rejoice in God thy Saviour, and give thanks to God thy Father through him!

2. Wilt thou say, "But I have again committed sin, since I had redemption through his blood? And therefore it is, that "I abhor myself, and repent in dust and ashes." It is meet thou shouldest abhor thyself; and it is God who hath wrought thee to this self-same thing. But, dost thou now believe? hath he again enabled thee to say, "I know that my Redeemer liveth"; "and the life which I now live, I live by faith in the Son of God?" Then that faith again cancels all that is past, and there is no condemnation to thee. At whatsoever time thou truly believest in the name of the Son of God, all thy sins, antecedent to that hour, vanish away as the morning dew. Now then, "stand thou fast in the liberty wherewith Christ hath made thee free." he hath once more made thee free from the power of sin, as well as from the guilt and punishment of it. O "be not entangled again with the yoke of bondage!" —neither the vile, devilish bondage of sin, of evil desires, evil tempers, or words, or works, the most grievous yoke on this side hell; nor the bondage of slavish, tormenting fear, of guilt and self-condemnation.

3. But secondly, do all they which abide "in Christ Jesus, walk not after the flesh, but after the Spirit?" Then we cannot but infer, that whosoever now committeth sin, hath no part or lot in this matter. He is even now condemned by his own heart. But, "if our heart condemn us," if our own conscience beareth witness that we are guilty, undoubtedly God doth; for "He is greater than our heart, and knoweth all things" so that we cannot deceive him, if we can ourselves. And think not to say, "I was justified once; my sins were once forgiven me:" I know not that; neither will I dispute whether they were or no. Perhaps, at this distance of time, it is next to impossible to know, with any tolerable degree of certainty, whether

that was a true, genuine work of God, or whether thou didst only deceive thy own soul. But this I know, with the utmost degree of certainty, "he that committeth sin is of the devil." Therefore, thou art of thy father the devil. It cannot be denied: for the works of thy father thou doest. O flatter not thyself with vain hopes! Say not to thy soul, "Peace peace!" For there is no peace. Cry aloud! Cry unto God out of the deep; if haply he may hear thy voice. Come unto him as at first, as wretched and poor, as sinful, miserable, blind and naked! And beware thou suffer thy soul to take no rest, till his pardoning love be again revealed; till he "heal thy backslidings," and fill thee again with the "faith that worketh by love."

4. Thirdly. Is there no condemnation to them which "walk after the Spirit," by reason of *inward sin* still remaining, so long as they do not give way thereto; nor by reason of *sin cleaving* to all they do? Then fret not thyself because of ungodliness, though it still remain in thy heart. Repine not, because thou still comest short of the glorious image of God; nor yet because pride, self-will, or unbelief, cleave to all thy words and works. And be not afraid to know all this evil of thy heart, to know thyself as also thou art known. Yea, desire of God, that thou mayest not think of thyself more highly than thou oughtest to think. Let thy continual prayer be,

> Show me, as my soul can bear,
> The depth of inbred sin;
> All the unbelief declare,
> The pride that lurks within.

But when he heareth thy prayer, and unveils thy heart; when he shows thee throughly what spirit thou art of; then beware that thy faith fail thee not, that thou suffer not thy shield to be torn from thee. Be abased. Be humbled in the dust. See thyself nothing, less than nothing, and vanity. But still, "Let not thy heart be troubled, neither let it be afraid." Still hold fast, "I, even I, have an Advocate with the Father, Jesus Christ the righteous." "And as the heavens are higher than the earth, so is his love higher than even my sins." Therefore, God is merciful to thee a sinner! such a sinner as thou art! God is love; and Christ hath died! Therefore, the Father himself loveth thee! Thou art his child! Therefore he will withhold from thee no manner of thing that is good. Is it good, that the whole body of sin, which is now crucified in thee, should be destroyed? It shall be done! Thou shalt be "cleansed from all filthiness, both of flesh and spirit."

Is it good, that nothing should remain in thy heart but the pure love of God alone? Be of good cheer! "Thou shalt love the Lord thy God, with all thy heart, and mind, and soul, and strength." "Faithful is he that hath promised, who also will do it." It is thy part, patiently to continue in the work of faith, and in the labour of love; and in cheerful peace, in humble confidence, with calm and resigned and yet earnest expectation, to wait till the zeal of the Lord of hosts shall perform this.

5. Fourthly. If they that "are in Christ," and "walk after the Spirit," are not condemned for *sins of infirmity*: as neither for *involuntary failings*, nor for anything whatever which they are not able to help; then beware, O thou that hast faith in his blood, that Satan herein gain no advantage over thee. Thou art still foolish and weak, blind and ignorant; more weak than any words can express; more foolish than it call yet enter into thy heart to conceive; knowing nothing yet as thou oughtest to know. Yet let not all thy weakness and folly, or any fruit thereof, which thou art not yet able to avoid, shake thy faith, thy filial trust in God, or disturb thy peace or joy in the Lord. The rule which some give, as to wilful sins, and which, in that case, may perhaps be dangerous, is undoubtedly wise and safe if it be applied only to the case of weakness and infirmities. Art thou fallen, O man of God? yet, do not lie there, fretting thyself and bemoaning thy weakness; but meekly say, "Lord, I shall fall every moment, unless thou uphold me with thy hand." And then arise! Leap and walk! Go on thy way! "run with patience the race that is set before Thee."

6. Lastly. Since a believer need not come into condemnation, even though he be *surprised* into what his soul abhors; (suppose his being surprised is not owing to any carelessness or wilful neglect of his own); if thou who believest art thus overtaken in a fault, then grieve unto the Lord; it shall be a precious balm. Pour out thy heart before him, and show him of thy trouble, and pray with all thy might to him who is "touched with the feeling of thy infirmities, "that he would establish, and strengthen and settle thy soul, and suffer thee to fall no more. But still he condemneth thee not. Wherefore shouldest thou fear? Thou hast no need of any "fear that hath torment." Thou shalt love him that loveth thee, and it sufficeth: more love will bring more strength. And, as soon as thou lovest him with all thy heart, thou shalt be perfect and entire, lacking nothing." Wait in peace for that hour, when the God of peace shall sanctify thee wholly, so that thy whole spirit and soul and body may be preserved blameless unto the coming of our Lord Jesus Christ!"

SERMON 9: THE SPIRIT OF BONDAGE AND OF ADOPTION.

> "Ye have not received the spirit of bondage again unto fear; but ye have received the Spirit of adoption, whereby we cry Abba, Father."
> Romans 8:15.

1. St. Paul here speaks to those who are the children of God by faith. "Ye," saith he, who are indeed his children, have drank into his Spirit; "ye have not received the spirit of bondage again unto fear;" "but, because ye are sons, God hath sent forth the Spirit of his Son into your hearts." "Ye have received the Spirit of adoption, whereby we cry, Abba, Father."

2. The spirit of bondage and fear is widely distant from this loving Spirit of adoption: Those who are influenced only by slavish fear, cannot be termed "the sons of God;" yet some of them may be styled his servants, and are "not far from the kingdom of heaven."

3. But it is to be feared, the bulk of mankind, yea, of what is called the Christian world, have not attained even this; but are still afar off, "neither is God in all their thoughts." A few names may be found of those who love God; a few more there are that fear him; but the greater part have neither the fear of God before their eyes, nor the love of God in their hearts.

4. Perhaps most of you, who, by the mercy of God, now partake of a better spirit, may remember the time when ye were as they, when ye were under the same condemnation. But at first ye knew it not, though ye were wallowing daily in your sins and in your blood; till, in due time, ye "received the spirit of fear;" (*ye received*, for this also is the gift of God;) and afterwards, fear vanished away, and the Spirit of love filled your hearts.

5. One who is in the first state of mind, without fear of love, is in Scripture termed a "natural man:" One who is under the spirit of bondage and fear, is sometimes said to be "under the law:" (Although that expression more frequently signifies one who is under the Jewish dispensation, or who thinks himself obliged to observe all the rites and ceremonies of the Jewish law:) But one who has exchanged the spirit of fear for the Spirit of love, is properly said to be "under grace."

Now, because it highly imports us to know what spirit we are of, I shall endeavour to point out distinctly, First, the state of a "natural man:" Secondly, that of one who is "under the law:" And Thirdly, of one who is "under grace."

I. 1. And, First, the state of a *natural man*. This the Scripture represents as a state of sleep: The voice of God to him is, "Awake thou that sleepest." For his soul is in a deep sleep: His spiritual senses are not awake; They discern neither spiritual good nor evil. The eyes of his understanding are closed; They are sealed together, and see not. Clouds and darkness continually rest upon them; for he lies in the valley of the shadow of death. Hence having no inlets for the knowledge of spiritual things, all the avenues of his soul being shut up, he is in gross, stupid ignorance of whatever he is most concerned to know. He is utterly ignorant of God, knowing nothing concerning him as he ought to know. He is totally a stranger to the law of God, as to its true, inward, spiritual meaning. He has no conception of that evangelical holiness, without which no man shall see the Lord; nor of the happiness which they only find whose "life is hid with Christ in God."

2. And for this very reason, because he is fast asleep, he is, in some sense, at rest. Because he is blind, he is also secure; He saith, "Tush, there shall no harm happen unto me." The darkness which covers him on every side, keeps him in a kind of peace; so far as peace can consist with the works of the devil, and with an earthly, devilish mind. He *sees* not that he stands on the edge of the pit, therefore he *fears* it not. He cannot *tremble* at the danger he does not *know*. He has not understanding enough to fear. Why is it that he is in no dread of God? Because he is totally ignorant of him: If not saying in his heart, "There is no God;" or, that "he sitteth on the circle of the heavens, and humbleth" not "himself to behold the things which are done on earth:" yet satisfying himself as well to all Epicurean intents and purposes, by saying, "God is merciful;" confounding and swallowing up all at once in that unwieldy idea of mercy, all his holiness and essential hatred of sin; all his justice, wisdom, and truth. He is in no dread of the vengeance denounced against those who obey not the blessed law of God, because he understands it not. He imagines the main point is to *do thus*, to be *outwardly* blameless; and sees not that it extends to every temper, desire, thought, motion of the heart. Or he fancies that the obligation hereto is ceased; that Christ came to "destroy the Law and the Prophets;" to save his people *in*, not *from* their sins; to bring them to heaven without holiness: — Notwithstanding his own words, "Not one jot or tittle of the law shall pass away, till all things are fulfilled;" and "Not every one that saith unto me, Lord, Lord! shall enter into the kingdom of heaven; but he that doeth the will of my Father which is in heaven."

3. He is secure, because he is utterly ignorant of him-

self. Hence he talks of "repenting by and by;" he does not indeed exactly know when, but some time or other before he dies; taking it for granted, that this is quite in his own power. For what should hinder his doing it, if he will? if he does but once set a resolution, no fear but he will make it good!

4. But this ignorance never so strongly glares, as in those who are termed, *men of learning*. If a natural man be one of these, he can talk at large of his rational faculties, of the freedom of his will, and the absolute necessity of such freedom, in order to constitute man a moral agent. He reads, and argues, and proves to a demonstration, that every man may do as he will; may dispose his own heart to evil or good, as it seems best in his own eyes. Thus the god of this world spreads a double veil of blindness over his heart, lest, by any means, "the light of the glorious gospel of Christ should shine" upon it.

5. From the same ignorance of himself and God, there may sometimes arise, in the natural man, a kind of *joy*, in congratulating himself upon his own wisdom and goodness: And what the world calls joy, he may often possess. He may have pleasure in various kinds; either in gratifying the desires of the flesh, or the desire of the eye, or the pride of life; particularly if he has large possessions; if he enjoy an affluent fortune; then he may "clothe" himself "in purple and fine linen, and fare sumptuously every day." And so long as he thus doeth well unto himself, men will doubtless speak good of him. They will say, "He is a happy man." For, indeed, this is the sum of worldly happiness; to dress, and visit, and talk, and eat, and drink, and rise up to play.

6. It is not surprising, if one in such circumstances as these, dosed with the opiates of flattery and sin, should imagine, among his other waking dreams, that he walks in great *liberty*. How easily may he persuade himself, that he is at liberty from all *vulgar errors*, and from the *prejudice* of education; judging exactly right, and keeping clear of all extremes. "I am free," may he say, "from all the *enthusiasm* of weak and narrow souls; from *superstition*, the disease of fools and cowards, always righteous over much; and from *bigotry*, continually incident to those who have not a free and generous way of thinking." And too sure it is, that he is altogether free from the "wisdom which cometh from above," from holiness, from the religion of the heart, from the whole mind which was in Christ.

7. For all this time he is the servant of sin. He commits sin, more or less, day by day. Yet he is not troubled: He "is in no bondage," as some speak; he feels no condemnation. He contents himself (even though he should profess to believe that the Christian Revelation is of God) with, "Man is frail. We are all weak. Every man has his infirmity." Perhaps he quotes Scripture: "Why, does not Solomon say, — The righteous man falls into sin seven times a day! — And, doubtless, they are all hypocrites or enthusiasts who pretend to be better than their neighbours." If, at any time, a serious thought fix upon him, he stifles it as soon as possible, with, "Why should I fear, since God is merciful, and Christ died for sinners?" Thus, he remains a willing servant of sin, content with the bondage of corruption; inwardly and outwardly unholy, and satisfied therewith; not only not conquering sin, but not striving to conquer, particularly that sin which doth so easily beset him.

8. Such is the state of every *natural man*; whether he be a gross, scandalous transgressor, or a more reputable and decent sinner, having the form, though not the power of godliness. But how can such an one be *convinced of sin*? How is he brought to repent? To be *under the law*? To receive the *spirit of bondage unto fear*? This is the point which in next to be considered.

II. 1. By some awful providence, or by his word applied with the demonstration of his Spirit, God touches the heart of him that lay asleep in darkness and in the shadow of death. He is terribly shaken out of his sleep, and awakes into a consciousness of his danger. Perhaps in a moment, perhaps by degrees, the eyes of his understanding are opened, and now first (the veil being in part removed) discern the real state he is in. Horrid light breaks in upon his soul; such light, as may be conceived to gleam from the bottomless pit, from the lowest deep, from a lake of fire burning with brimstone. He at last sees the loving, the merciful God is also "a consuming fire;" that he is a just God and a terrible, rendering to every man according to his words, entering into judgment with the ungodly for every idle word, yea, and for the imaginations of the heart. He now clearly perceives, that the great and holy God is "of purer eyes than to behold iniquity;" that he is an avenger of every one who rebelleth against him, and repayeth the wicked to his face; and that "it is a fearful thing to fall into the hands of the living God."

2. The inward, spiritual meaning of the law of God now begins to glare upon him. He perceives "the commandment is exceeding broad," and there is "nothing hid from the light thereof." He is convinced, that every part of it relates, not barely to outward sin or obedience, but to what passes in the secret recesses of the soul, which no eye but God's can penetrate. If he now hears, "Thou

shalt not kill," God speaks in thunder, "He that hateth his brother is a murderer;" "he that saith unto his brother, Thou fool, is obnoxious to hell-fire." If the law say, "Thou shalt not commit adultery," the voice of the Lord sounds in his ears, "He that looketh on a woman to lust after he hath committed adultery with her already in his heart." And thus, in every point, he feels the word of God "quick and powerful, sharper than a two-edged sword." It "pierces even to the dividing asunder of his soul and spirit, his joints and marrow." And so much the more, because he is conscious to himself of having neglected so great salvation; of having "trodden under foot the son of God," who would have saved him from his sins, and "counted the blood of the covenant an unholy," a common, unsanctifying thing.

3. And as he knows, "all things are naked and open unto the eyes of him with whom we have to do," so he sees himself naked, stripped of all the fig-leaves which he had sewed together, of all his poor pretenses to religion or virtue, and his wretched excuses for sinning against God. He now sets himself like the ancient sacrifices, cleft in sunder, as it were, from the neck downward, so that all within him stands confessed. His heart is bare, and he sees it is all sin, "deceitful above all things, desperately wicked;" that it is altogether corrupt and abominable, more than it is possible for tongue to express; that there dwelleth therein no good thing, but unrighteousness and ungodliness only; every motion thereof, every temper and thought, being only evil continually.

4. And he not only sees, but feels in himself, by an emotion of soul which he cannot describe, that for the sins of his heart were his life without blame, (which yet it is not, and cannot be; seeing "an evil tree cannot bring forth good fruit,") he deserves to be cast into the fire that never shall be quenched. He feels that "the wages," the just reward "of sin," of his sin above all, "is death;" even the second death; the death which dieth not; the destruction of body and soul in hell.

5. Here ends his pleasing dream, his delusive rest, his false peace, his vain security. His joy now vanishes as a cloud; pleasures, once loved, delight no more. They pall upon the taste: He loathes the nauseous sweet; he is weary to bear them. The shadows of happiness flee away, and sink into oblivion: So that he is stripped of all, and wanders to and fro, seeking rest, but finding none.

6. The fumes of those opiates being now dispelled, he feels the anguish of a wounded spirit. He finds that sin let loose upon the soul (whether it be pride, anger, or evil desire, whether self-will, malice, envy, revenge, or any other) is perfect misery: He feels sorrow of heart for the blessings he has lost, and the curse which is come upon him: remorse for having thus destroyed himself, and despised his own mercies; fear, from a lively sense of the wrath of God, and of the consequences of his wrath, of the punishment which he has justly deserved, and which he sees hanging over his head; — fear of death, as being to him the gate of hell, the entrance of death eternal; — fear of the devil, the executioner of the wrath and righteous vengeance of God; — fear of men, who, if they were able to kill his body, would thereby plunge both body and soul into hell; fear, sometimes arising to such a height, that the poor, sinful, guilty soul, is terrified with everything, with nothing, with shades, with a leaf shaken of the wind. Yea, sometimes it may even border upon distraction, making a man "drunken though not with wine," suspending the exercise of the memory, of the understanding, of all the natural faculties. Sometimes it may approach to the very brink of despair; so that he who trembles at the name of death, may yet be ready to plunge into it every moment, to "choose strangling rather than life." Well may such a man roar, like him of old, for the very disquietness of his heart. Well may he cry out, "The spirit of a man may sustain his infirmities; but a wounded spirit who can bear?"

7. Now he truly desires to break loose from sin, and begins to struggle with it. But though he strive with all his might, he cannot conquer: Sin is mightier than he. He would fain escape; but he is so fast in prison, that he cannot get forth. He resolved against sin, but yet sins on: He sees the snare, and abhors, and runs into it. So much does his boasted reason avail, — only to enhance his guilt, and increase his misery! Such is the freedom of his will; free only to evil; free to "drink in iniquity like water;" to wander farther and farther from the living God, and do more "despite to the Spirit of grace!"

8. The more he strive, wishes, labours to be free, the more does he feel his chains, the grievous chains of sin, wherewith Satan binds and "leads him captive at his will;" his servant he is, though he repine ever so much; though he rebel, he cannot prevail. He is still in bondage and fear, by reason of sin: Generally, of some outward sin, to which he is peculiarly disposed, either, by nature, custom, or outward circumstance; but always, of some inward sin, some evil temper or unholy affection. And the more he frets against it, the more it prevails; he may bite but cannot break his chain. Thus he toils without end, repent-

ing and sinning, and repenting and sinning again, till at length the poor, sinful, helpless wretch is even at his wit's end and can barely groan, "O wretched man that I am! who shall deliver me from the body of this death?"

9. This whole struggle of one who is "under the law," under the "spirit of fear and bondage," is beautifully described by the Apostle in the foregoing chapter, speaking in the person of an awakened man. "I," saith he, "was alive without the law once:" (Verse 9:) I had much life, wisdom, strength, and virtue; so I thought: "But, when the commandment came, sin revived, and I died:" When the commandment, in its spiritual meaning, came to my heart, with the power of God, my inbred sin was stirred up, fretted, inflamed, and all my virtue died away. "And the commandment, which was ordained to life, I found to be unto death. For sin taking occasion by the commandment, deceived me, and by it slew me:" (Verses 10, 11:) It came upon me unaware; slew all my hopes; and plainly showed, in the midst of life I was in death. "Wherefore the law is holy, and the commandment holy, and just, and good:" (Verse 12:) I no longer lay the blame on this, but on the corruption of my own heart. I acknowledge that "the law is spiritual; but I am carnal, sold under sin:" (Verse 14:) I now see both the spiritual nature of the law; and my own carnal, devilish heart "sold under sin," totally enslaved: (Like slave bought with money, who were absolutely at their master's disposal:) "For that which I do, I allow not; for what I would, I do not, but what I hate, that I do:" (Verse 15:) Such is the bondage under which I groan; such the tyranny of my hard master. "To will is present with me, but how to perform that which is good I find not. For the good that I would, I do not; but the evil which I would not, that I do:" (Verses 18, 19:) "I find a law," an inward constraining power, "that when I would do good, evil is present with me. For I delight in "or consent to "the law of God, after the inward man:" (Verses 21, 22:) In my "mind:" (So the Apostle explains himself in the words that immediately follow; and so, o eso anthropos, *the inward man*, is understood in all other Greek writers:) But I see another law in my members, another constraining power, warring against the law of my mind, or inward man, and bringing me into captivity to the law or power "of sin:" (Verse 23:) Dragging me, as it were, at my conquerors chariot-wheels, into the very thing which my soul abhors. "o wretched man that I am! who shall deliver me from the body of this death?" (Verse 24.) Who shall deliver me from this help-less, dying life, from this bondage of sin and misery? Till this is done, "I myself" (or rather, *that I*, autos ego, that man I am now personating) "with the mind," or inward man, "serve the law of God;" my mind, my conscience is on God's side; "but with my flesh," with my body, "the law of sin," (verse 25,) being hurried away by a force I cannot resist.

10. How lively a portraiture is this of one "under the law;" one who feels the burden he cannot shake off; who pants after liberty, power, and love, but is in fear and bondage still! until the time that God answers the wretched man, crying out, "Who shall deliver me" from this bondage of sin, from this body of death? — "The grace of God, through Jesus Christ thy Lord."

III. 1. Them it is that this miserable bondage ends, and he is no more "under the law, but under grace." This state we are, Thirdly, to consider; the state of one who has found *grace* or favour in the sight of God, even the Father, and who has the *grace* or power of the Holy Ghost, reigning in his heart; who has received, in the language of the Apostle, the "Spirit of adoption, whereby" he now cries, "Abba, Father!"

2. "He cried unto the Lord in his trouble, and God delivers him out of his distress." His eyes are opened in quite another manner than before, even to see a loving, gracious God. While he is calling, "I beseech thee, show me thy glory!" — he hears a voice in the inmost soul, "I will make all my goodness pass before thee, and I will proclaim the name of the Lord: I will be gracious to whom I will be gracious, and I will show mercy to whom I will show mercy." And, it is not long before "the Lord" descends in the cloud, and proclaims the name of the Lord." Then he sees, but not with eyes of flesh and blood, "The Lord, the Lord God, merciful and gracious, long-suffering, and abundant in goodness and truth; keeping mercy for thousands, and forgiving iniquities, and transgressions and sin."

3. Heavenly, healing light now breaks in upon his soul. He "looks on him whom he had pierced;" and "God, who out of darkness commanded light to shine, shineth in his heart." He sees the light of the glorious love of God, in the face of Jesus Christ. He hath a divine "evidence of things not seen" by sense, even of the "deep things of God;" more particularly of the love of God, of his pardoning love to him that believes in Jesus. Overpowered with the sight, his whole soul cried out, "My Lord and my God;" For he sees all his iniquities laid on Him, who "bare them in his own body on the tree;" he beholds the

Lamb of God taking away his sins. How clearly now does he discern, that "God was in Christ, reconciling the world unto himself; making him sin for us, who knew no sin, that we might be made the righteousness of God through him;" — and that he himself is reconciled to God, by that blood of the covenant!

4. Here end both the guilt and power of sin. He can now say, "I am crucified with Christ: Nevertheless I live; yet not I but Christ liveth in me: And the life which I now live in the flesh," (even in this mortal body,) "I live by faith in the Son of God, who loved me, and gave himself for me." Here end remorse, and sorrow of heart, and the anguish of a wounded spirit. "God turneth his heaviness into joy." He made sore, and now his hands bind up. Here ends also that bondage unto fear; for "his heart standeth fast, believing in the Lord." He cannot fear any longer the wrath of God; for he knows it is now turned away from him, and looks upon Him no more as an angry Judge, but as a loving Father. He cannot fear the devil, knowing he has "no power, except it be given him from above." He fears not hell; being an heir of the kingdom of heaven: Consequently, he has no fear of death; by reason whereof he was in time past, for so many years, "subject to bondage." Rather, knowing that "if the earthly house of this tabernacle be dissolved, he hath a building of God, a house not made with hands, eternal in the heavens; he groaneth earnestly, desiring to be clothed upon with that house which is from heaven." He groans to shake off this house of earth, that "mortality" may be "swallowed up of life;" knowing that God "hath wrought him for the self-same thing; who hath also given him the earnest of his Spirit."

5. And "where the Spirit of the Lord is, there is liberty;" liberty, not only from guilt and fear, but from sin, from that heaviest of all yokes, that basest of all bondage. His labour is not now in vain. The snare is broken, and he is delivered. He not only strives, but likewise prevails; he not only fights, but conquers also. "Henceforth he does not serve sin." (Chap. 6:6) He is "dead unto sin, and alive unto God;" "sin doth not now reign," even "in his mortal body," nor doth he "obey it in the desires thereof." He does not "yield his members as instruments of unrighteousness unto sin, but as instruments of righteousness unto God." For "being now made free from sin, he is become the servant of righteousness."

6. Thus, "having peace with God, through our Lord Jesus Christ," "rejoicing in hope of the glory of God," and having power over all sin, over every evil desire, and temper, and word, and work, he is a living witness of the "glorious liberty of the sons of God;" all of whom, being partakers of like precious faith, bear record with one voice, "We have received the Spirit of adoption, whereby we cry, Abba, Father!"

7. It is this spirit which continually, "worketh in them, both to will and to do of his good pleasure." It is he that sheds the love of God abroad in their hearts, and the love of all mankind; thereby purifying their hearts from the love of world, from the lust of the flesh, the lust of the eye, and the pride of life. It is by him they are delivered from anger and pride, from all vile and inordinate affections. In consequence, they are delivered from evil words and works, from all unholiness of conversation; doing no evil to any child of man, and being zealous of all good works.

8. To sum up all: the *natural* man neither fears nor loves God; one *under the law*, fears, — one *under grace*, loves him. The first has no light in the things of God, but walks in utter darkness; the second sees the painful light of hell; the third, the joyous light of heaven. He that sleeps in death, has a false peace; he that is awakened, has no peace at all; he that believes, has true peace, — the peace of God filling and ruling his heart. The Heathen, baptized or unbaptized, hath a fancied liberty, which is indeed licentiousness; the Jew, or one under the Jewish dispensation, is in heavy, grievous bondage; the Christian enjoys the true glorious liberty of the sons of God. An unawakened child of the devil sins willingly, one that is awakened sins unwillingly; a child of God "sinneth not," but "keepeth himself, and the wicked one toucheth him not." To conclude: the natural man neither conquers nor fights; the man under the law fights with sin, but cannot conquer; the man under grace fights and conquers, yea, is "more than conqueror, through him that loveth him."

IV. 1. From this plain account of the three-fold state of man, the *natural*, the *legal*, and the *evangelical*, it appears that it is not sufficient to divide mankind into sincere and insincere. A man may be sincere in any of these states; not only when he has the "Spirit of adoption," but while he has the "spirit of bondage unto fear;" yea, while he has neither this fear, nor love. For undoubtedly there may be sincere Heathens, as well as sincere Jews, or Christians. This circumstance, them does by no means prove, that, a man is in a state of acceptance with God.

"Examine yourselves, therefore," not only whether ye are sincere, but "whether ye be in the faith." Examine narrowly, (for it imports you much,) what is the ruling principle in your soul! Is it the love of God? Is it the fear of God? Or is it neither one nor the other? Is it not rather the love of the world? the love of pleasure, or gain? of ease, or reputation? If so, you are not come so far as a Jew. You are but a Heathen still. Have you heaven in your heart? Have you the Spirit of adoption, ever crying, Abba, Father? Or do you cry unto God, as "out of the belly of hell," overwhelmed with sorrow and fear? Or are you a stranger to this whole affair, and cannot imagine what I mean? Heathen, pull off the mask! Thou hast never put on Christ! Stand barefaced! Look up to heaven; and own before Him that liveth for ever and ever, thou hast no part, either among the sons of servants of God!

Whosoever thou art: Dost thou commit sin, or dost thou not? If thou dost, is it willingly, or unwillingly? In either case, God hath told thee whose thou art: "He that committeth sin is of the devil." If thou committest it willingly, thou art his faithful servant: He will not fail to reward thy labour. If unwillingly, still thou art his servant. God deliver thee out of his hands!

Art thou daily fighting against all sin? And daily more than conqueror? I acknowledge thee for a child of God. O stand fast in thy glorious liberty! Art thou fighting, but not conquering? striving for the mastery, but not able to attain? Then thou art not yet a believer in Christ; but follow on, and thou shalt know the Lord. Art thou not fighting at all, but leading an easy, indolent, fashionable life! O how hast thou dared to name the name of Christ, only to make it a reproach among the Heathen? Awake, thou sleeper! Call upon thy God before the deep swallow thee up!

2. Perhaps one reason why so many think of themselves more highly than they ought to think, why they do not discern what state they are in, is because these several states of soul are often mingled together, and in some measure meet in one and the same person. Thus experience shows, that the legal state, or state of fear, is frequently mixed with the natural; for few men are so fast asleep in sin, but they are sometimes more or less awakened. As the Spirit of God does not "wait for the call of man," so, at some times he *will* be heard. He puts them in fear, so that, for a season at least, the Heathen "know themselves to be but men." They feel the burden of sin, and earnestly desire to flee from the wrath to come. But not long: They seldom suffer the arrows of conviction to go deep into their souls; but quickly stifle the grace of God, and return to their wallowing in the mire.

In like manner, the evangelical state, or state of love, is frequently mixed with the legal. For few of those who have the spirit of bondage and fear, remain always without hope. The wise and gracious God rarely suffers this; "for he remembereth that we are but dust;" and he willeth not that "the flesh should fail before him, or the spirit which he hath made." Therefore, at such times as he seeth good, he gives a dawning of light unto them that sit in darkness. He cause a part of his goodness to pass before them, and shows he is a "God that heareth the prayer." They see the promise, which is by faith in Christ Jesus, though it be yet afar off; and hereby they are encouraged to "run with patience the race which is set before them."

3. Another reason why many deceive themselves, is, because they do not consider how far a man may go, and yet be in a natural, or, at best, a legal state. A man may be of a compassionate and a benevolent temper; he may be affable, courteous, generous, friendly; he may have some degree of meekness, patience, temperance, and of many other moral virtues. He may feel many desires of shaking off all vice, and of attaining higher degrees of virtue. He may abstain from much evil; perhaps from all that is grossly contrary to justice, mercy, or truth. He may do much good, may feed the hungry, clothe the naked, relieve the widow and fatherless. He may attend public worship, use prayer in private, read many books of devotion; and yet, for all this, he may be a mere natural man, knowing neither himself nor God; equally a stranger to the spirit of fear and to that of love; having neither repented, nor believed the gospel.

But suppose there were added to all this a deep conviction of sin, with much fear of the wrath of God; vehement desires to cast off every sin, and to fulfill all righteousness; frequent rejoicing in hope, and touches of love often glancing upon the soul; yet neither do these prove a man to be *under grace*; to have true, living, Christian faith, unless the Spirit of adoption abide in his heart, unless he can continually cry, "Abba, Father!"

4. Beware, then, thou who art called by the name of Christ, that thou come not short of the mark of thy high calling. Beware thou rest, not, either in a natural state with too many that are accounted *good Christians*; or in a legal state, wherein those who are highly esteemed of men are generally content to live and die. Nay, but God hath prepared better things for thee, if thou follow on till thou attain. Thou art not called to fear and tremble like devils; but to rejoice and love, like the angels of God. "Thou shalt love the lord thy God will all thy heart, and

with all thy soul, and with all thy mind, and with all thy strength." Thou shalt "rejoice evermore;" thou shalt "pray without ceasing:" thou shalt "in everything give thanks." Thou shalt do the will of God on earth as it is done in heaven. O prove thou "what is that good, and acceptable, and perfect will of God!" Now present thyself "a living sacrifice, holy, acceptable to God." "Whereunto thou hast already attained, hold fast," by "reaching forth unto those things which are before:" until "the God of peace make thee perfect in every good work, working in thee that which is well-pleasing in his sight through Jesus Christ: To whom be glory for ever and ever! Amen!"